THE YEARBOOK OF WORLD SOCCER

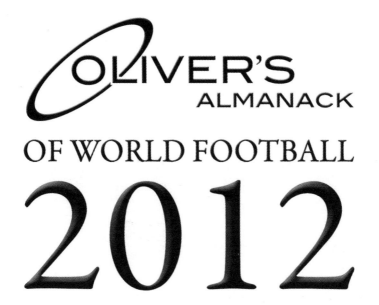

OLIVER'S ALMANACK

OF WORLD FOOTBALL

2012

GUY OLIVER

HARPASTUM PUBLISHING

OLIVERSALMANACK.COM

Copyright © 2012 Guy Oliver

The right of Guy Oliver to be identified as the Author of
the Work has been asserted by him in accordance with the
Copyright, Designs and Patents Act 1988.

First published in 2012
by HARPASTUM PUBLISHING LIMITED

1

Front cover photographs: (left) Brazil's Neymar celebrates winning the Copa Libertadores with Santos -
Action Images; (centre left) FIFA Women's World Player of the Year Homare Sawa of Japan lifts the FIFA
Women's World Cup after beating the USA on penalties in the 2011 final - *Action Images*;
(centre right) Barcelona's Lionel Messi with the 2011 FIFA Ballon d'Or - *Action Images*; (right) The Zambian
team celebrate their victory in the final of the 2012 CAF Africa Cup of Nations - *Action Images*

Spine photograph: Barcelona players with the European Cup after beating Manchester United in the 2011
UEFA Champions League Final at Wembley - *Action Images*

Back cover photographs: (left) Mexico celebrate victory over the USA in the 2011 CONCACAF Gold Cup
Final - *Action Images*; (centre left) Kristine Lilly, the world's most capped player with 352 appearances for the
USA, finally calls it a day 24 years after making her debut - *Action Images*; (centre right) Uruguay lift the
Copa America after beating Paraguay 3-0 in the 2011 final in Buenos Aires - *Action Images*; (right) Zlatan
Ibrahimovic in action for Milan. By winning the 2011 Serie A title with Milan, Ibrahimovic collected his
eighth consecutive championship medal and his ninth in ten seasons - *Action Images*

A CIP catalogue record for this title is available from the British Library

ISBN 978-0-9564909-2-6

Design and layout: Guy Oliver
Cover design: Helen Williams

Printed and bound in India at Nutech Print Services

The data within the Almanack of World Football has been obtained from a variety of sources, official
and unofficial. The Author cannot vouch for the accuracy of the data in all cases.

HARPASTUM PUBLISHING LIMITED
Vatcher's Farm, Thorney Hill
Christchurch, Dorset
United Kingdom, BH23 8DF

CONTENTS

PART ONE – FIFA AND WORLD FOOTBALL

PART TWO – THE NATIONS OF THE WORLD

CONTENTS

PART THREE – THE
CONTINENTAL CONFEDERATIONS

ASIA

AFRICA

CENTRAL AMERICA, NORTH AMERICA & THE CARIBBEAN

SOUTH AMERICA

OCEANIA

EUROPE

ALPHABETICAL LISTING OF THE NATIONS OF THE WORLD

COUNTRY		PAGE	COUNTRY		PAGE
Kuwait	KUW	477	Rwanda	RWA	658
Kyrgyzstan	KGZ	459	Samoa	SAM	661
Laos	LAO	480	San Marino	SMR	697
Latvia	LVA	502	São Tomé e Príncipe	STP	711
Lebanon	LIB	491	Saudi Arabia	KSA	474
Lesotho	LES	489	Scotland	SCO	663
Liberia	LBR	482	Senegal	SEN	679
Libya	LBY	484	Serbia	SRB	704
Liechtenstein	LIE	494	Seychelles	SEY	682
Lithuania	LTU	496	Sierra Leone	SLE	691
Luxembourg	LUX	499	Singapore	SIN	685
Macau	MAC	505	Slovakia	SVK	719
Macedonia FYR	MKD	527	Slovenia	SVN	723
Madagascar	MAD	507	Solomon Islands	SOL	700
Malawi	MWI	551	Somalia	SOM	702
Malaysia	MAS	513	South Africa	RSA	648
Maldives	MDV	520	(South Korea) Korea Republic	KOR	461
Mali	MLI	530	Spain	ESP	281
Malta	MLT	533	Sri Lanka	SRI	708
Mauritania	MTN	549	St Kitts and Nevis	SKN	688
Mauritius	MRI	544	St Lucia	LCA	487
Mexico	MEX	523	St Vincent and the Grenadines	VIN	814
Moldova	MDA	517	Sudan	SDN	676
Mongolia	MNG	539	Surinam	SUR	717
Montenegro	MNE	536	Swaziland	SWZ	731
Montserrat	MSR	547	Sweden	SWE	727
Morocco	MAR	510	Switzerland	SUI	713
Mozambique	MOZ	541	Syria	SYR	734
Myanmar (Burma)	MYA	554	Tahiti (French Polynesia)	TAH	737
Namibia	NAM	556	(Taiwan) Chinese Taipei	TPE	759
Nepal	NEP	579	Tajikistan	TJK	750
Netherlands (Holland)	NED	565	Tanzania	TAN	740
New Caledonia	NCL	562	Thailand	THA	746
New Zealand	NZL	594	Timor-Leste (East Timor)	TLS	755
Nicaragua	NCA	559	Togo	TOG	757
Niger	NIG	584	Tonga	TGA	744
Nigeria	NGA	581	Trinidad and Tobago	TRI	761
Northern Ireland	NIR	586	Tunisia	TUN	764
(North Korea) Korea DPR	PRK	636	Turkey	TUR	768
Norway	NOR	590	Turkmenistan	TKM	752
Oman	OMA	597	Turks and Caicos Islands	TCA	742
Pakistan	PAK	600	Uganda	UGA	775
Palestine	PLE	614	Ukraine	UKR	778
Panama	PAN	603	United Arab Emirates	UAE	772
Papua New Guinea	PNG	616	United States of America	USA	786
Paraguay	PAR	606	Uruguay	URU	782
Peru	PER	609	US Virgin Islands	VIR	816
Philippines	PHI	612	Uzbekistan	UZB	800
Poland	POL	618	Vanuatu	VAN	803
Portugal	POR	622	Venezuela	VEN	805
Puerto Rico	PUR	638	Vietnam	VIE	811
Qatar	QAT	640	Wales	WAL	818
Republic of Ireland	IRL	397	Yemen	YEM	822
Romania	ROU	644	Zambia	ZAM	825
Russia	RUS	653	Zimbabwe	ZIM	828

A NOTE FOR THE 2012 EDITION

For the fifth edition of Oliver's Almanack of World Football we broke away from the traditional August publication date for Eurocentric football yearbooks and switched our editorial coverage to the calendar year. That remains the case for this the seventh edition and for future editions - with one minor alteration. Feedback from readers has indicated that they would prefer to see details of a tournament kept together in one edition of the book - even if the tournament is played over the course of more than a year. Therefore, it is now our intention to include a tournament based on the year in which it finishes. By way of an example, our detailed coverage of the UEFA Euro 2012 tournament - both qualifiers and finals - will appear in next year's Oliver's Almanack which will cover the year of football in 2012.

ACKNOWLEDGEMENTS

Once again my heartfelt gratitude goes out to the many people who contribute their knowledge and expertise to the growing body of football related matter on the internet both professional and amateur - there are just too many to list. We try and obtain information from official sources where possible but sometimes the non-official outlets are just more accurate and up to date. One exception is FIFA.com and I am proud to produce Oliver's Almanack in association with them once again. My thanks to Matt Stone and his team there as well as to Stephanie Fulton and the Content Management Services Team at FIFA for their help and input over the year. My thanks once again to Michael Church and Mark Gleeson for their input with regard to Asia and Africa respectively as well as to Steven Torres at CONCACAF for his generous contribution. A quick word for Tom Chittick - your patience and forbearance is greatly appreciated. Finally thanks to Helen Williams, Marion and Oliver Greenleaves, Michael Oliver and the rest of my family for your multi-faceted contributions. I couldn't do it without you. As ever, this is for Sharyn, Ally and Archie with love.

Guy Oliver, The New Forest, March 2011

HOW TO USE OLIVER'S ALMANACK

Oliver's Almanack of World Football contains many traditional techniques used across the world to present information, most of which will be familiar to the seasoned football fan. This guide serves a tool for those who are, perhaps, less familiar. We have tried to be as international in our language as possible - hence, for example, our referring to Red Star Belgrade as Crvena Zvezda Beograd except in written reviews. This may not be to everyone's taste but to see Bayern München and FC København written is becoming much more commonplace. Another tricky area is accents and we have taken the decision to remove them from players names but to keep them for the names of teams and stadia. Inconsistent maybe, but Peñarol just doesn't look right as Penarol. Many players by contrast don't use accents on their names and where do you draw the line with some of the more obscure languages of the world. A word about our football field match graphics... Again, they should be self explanatory. Each player is located on the pitch in his position at the start of the match. The two following examples from the Brazil - Côte d'Ivoire World Cup match show that Kaka played in the number 10 shirt, was booked in the 85th and 88th minutes and sent-off in the 88th minute. The other box shows that Salomon Kalou was substituted by Kader Keita after 68 minutes and that Keita was then booked in the 75th minute.

THE LEAGUE TABLE

② ↓

BRAZIL 2009

③ → SERIE A   ⑤ ↗ ↓ ↘

	Pl	W	D	L	F	A	Pts	Flamengo	Internacional	São Paulo	Cruzeiro	Palmeiras
① → **Flamengo**	38	19	10	9	58	44	**67**		4-0	2-1	1-2	1-2
Internacional	38	19	8	11	65	44	**65**	0-0		2-2	2-3	2-0
São Paulo FC	38	18	11	9	57	42	**65**	2-2	1-0		3-0	0-0
Cruzeiro	38	18	8	12	58	53	**62**	2-0	1-1	1-2		1-2	← ④
Palmeiras	38	17	11	10	58	45	**62**	0-2	2-1	0-0	3-1	

① The club in bold at the top of the league ladder are the league champions. If the club is not in bold it means that there was a further stage to be played. The relegated teams are also listed in bold at the foot of the table.

② This refers to the season in which the league campaign was played. In this instance the Brazilian championship was played through the course of 2009. Other leagues overlap the end of the year - 2008–09 for instance.

③ The league in Brazil is known as Serie A. Sponsors names are also included where applicable whilst (2) after the name means that the league is at the second level. (3) would mean the third level and so on.

④ The scoreline of 1-2 indicated in the box refers to the match between Cruzeiro at home against Palmeiras who were the visiting team. The first number (1) refers to the number of goals the home team Cruzeiro scored, the second (2) to the goals scored by Palmeiras, the away team. So in this instance Cruzeiro lost 1-2 at home to Palmeiras.

⑤ These columns refer to the number of games played during the season (Pl), games won (W), games drawn (D), games lost (L), goals scored (F), goals conceded (A) and the number of points obtained (Pts) during the course of the season by the team listed in each row. Different languages use the annotations listed in the table below.

English	Pl	W	D	L	F	A	Pts
French	J	G	N	P	Bp	Bc	Pts
German	Sp	G	U	V	Tore		Pkte
Italian	G	V	N	P	RF	RS	Pt
Portuguese	J	V	E	D	Gp	Gc	Pt
Spanish	J	G	E	P	Gf	Gc	Pts

CUP BRACKETS

① ↓

SAA SUPA 8 CUP 2008

First Round		Semi–finals			Final		
Kaiser Chiefs *	4						
Santos	0	Kaiser Chiefs	2	0			
Ajax Cape Town	3	Swallows	0	1			
Swallows *	4				Kaiser Chiefs	0	4p
SuperSport Utd	2				Sundowns	0	3p
Orlando Pirates*	1	SuperSport Utd	1	3			
Free State Stars	0	Sundowns	2	2			
Sundowns *	1						

② → (Kaiser Chiefs/Santos first round)
③ → (SuperSport Utd / Sundowns semi-final)
④ → (Kaiser Chiefs / Sundowns final)

① The name of the Cup tournament and the year in which it was played. In this case the tournament is South Africa's SAA Supa 8 Cup that was played in 2008.

② This shows that Kaiser Chiefs played Santos at home - indicated by the asterisk - in the first round winning 4-0. The brackets are constructed so that the Cup winners always feature as the top bracket in each round with the beaten finalists as the bottom bracket. The winners of each tie are indicated in bold.

③ This bracket shows that Sundowns played SuperSport United in the semi-final over two legs. The asterisk indicates that Sundowns played the first leg at home and won 2-1. In the second leg, played away from home, Sundowns lost 2-3. When a tie finishes level on aggregate, as this tie did, away goals are used to determine the winners unless stated. With two goals scored away from home as opposed to the one goal scored away from home by SuperSport United, Sundowns qualified for the final.

④ This bracket indicates that the final of the 2008 Supa 8 Cup was between Kaiser Chiefs and Sundowns. The match finished 0-0 but Chiefs won the Cup after winning the penalty shoot-out 4-3.

COUNTRY INFORMATION

Most of the items on the front page for each country should be self explanatory. The FIFA Big Count 2006 was a survey conducted by FIFA in 2006 of all of the member associations and followed a similar survey carried out in 2000. The information for the box at the bottom of each page is sourced from the CIA Factbook whilst the population figures for cities and towns are sourced from the World Gazetteer.

① The local football association box contains the following information - the name of the association and its abbreviation, address, phone, fax, email, website - along with the year the FA was formed (FA), the year it joined its continental confederation (CON) and the year it joined FIFA. The names beside 'P' are the president of the FA and the secretary-general 'GS'.

FEDERATA SHQIPTARE E FUTBOLIT (FSHF)

Rruga Labinoti,
Pallati perballe Shkolles, "Gjuhet e Huaja" Tirana
☎ +355 43 46 605
+355 43 46 609
fshf@fshf.org.al
www.fshf.org
FA 1930 CON 1954 FIFA 1932
P Armand Duka
GS Eduard Prodani

① ↑

② The information in the country information box is self explanatory. The name of the country is given in its local form first and then in the English form. The figures in brackets are the world rankings of the country according to the CIA Factbook in the category listed. Therefore Albania's population of 3,639,453 (a 2009 estimate) is the 129th largest (out of 228) in the world.

REPUBLIKA E SHQIPERISE • REPUBLIC OF ALBANIA

Capital	Tirana	Population	3 639 453 (129)	% in cities	47%
GDP per capita	$6000 (132)	Area km²	28 748 km² (144)	GMT + / -	+1
Neighbours (km)	Greece 282, Macedonia 151, Montenegro 172, Kosovo 112 • Coast 362				

② →

MATCH BOXES

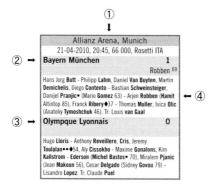

① This match was played at the Allianz Arena in Munich on the 21st April, 2010. Kick-off was at 20:45 in the evening and there were 66,000 fans in the stadium. The match referee was Italy's Rosetti.

② Bayern Munich were the home side and scored one goal. The goalscorer was Arjen Robben in the 69th minute. Had the goal been scored from a penalty the time indicator would have read 69p. A + after the minute of the goal indicates that it was scored in injury-time. Thus 93+ means a goal was scored in the third minute of stoppage time. 93 on the other hand would mean that the goal was scored in the 93rd minute - ie the third minute of extra-time.

③ Olympique Lyonnais were the away team. They did not score and lost the match 0-1.

④ This box indicates the line-up of the Bayern Munich team. Each team is divided by three hyphens into Goalkeepers - Defenders - Midfielders - Forwards where it is possible to gather this information. For the major tournaments we have also listed the players from right to left across the field. Thus in this UEFA Champions League semi-final Philipp Lahm played at right back with Van Buyten and Demichelis in the central defensive positions and Diego Contento at left back. If a player has • after his name it indicates that he was booked. If a player has ♦37 as in the case of Frank Ribery, it means he was sent off in the 37th minute. Jeremy Toulalan on the other hand has ••♦54 after his name indicating that he was sent off in the 54th minute after receiving two yellow cards.

The exact composition of match boxes varies from tournament to tournament - in some tournaments players are listed with shirt numbers for example - but the principles remain the same.

CLUB BY CLUB GUIDES

In the club by club guides - to the leagues in Argentina, Australia, Brazil, England, France, Germany, Italy, Japan, Korea Republic, Netherlands, Portugal, Scotland, Spain and the USA - simple annotations are used to describe matches. A competition is given an identifier which is unique to that particular country and is listed at the start of the guide to each country. So in Italy for instance, SA refers to Serie A. The Coppa Italia is referred to IC with ICr1 referring to a first round match, ICqf to a quarter-final, ICsf a semi-final and ICf to the final. A UEFA Champions League match played in group A, for example would be referred to as CLgA. Matches that are shaded are home matches for the club concerned whilst no shading indicates that the match was either played away from home or on a neutral ground. The figures for the player appearances and goals consist of three elements - matches started+appearances as a substitute/goals scored - for league matches only.

PART ONE

FIFA AND WORLD FOOTBALL

FIFA

Fédération Internationale de Football Association

2011 may have been a post FIFA World Cup year, but there was much to celebrate in international competition, none more so than the extraordinary success of the Japanese women's team in winning the FIFA Women's World Cup 2011 in Germany. Against the background of the earthquake and tsunami, which had devastated the country in March, Japan wrote the good news story of the year by beating the hosts and favourites Germany in the quarter-final and then the USA on penalties in the final. Played out before huge crowds, the tournament marked a significant breakthrough for the women's game and the establishment of a new centre of power in the Far East as the Japanese broke the European and North American stranglehold on winning the tournament. 2011 also saw the qualifying tournament for the 2014 FIFA World Cup in Brazil get underway and by the end of the year the hopes and dreams of 65 nations were over for another four years with qualifying in Asia, Oceania, the Americas and Africa in full flow. Amongst the bigger nations to have fallen early on were former finalists China PR, Korea DPR, Kuwait and the United Arab Emirates. FIFA also staged two other national team tournaments in 2011 - the FIFA U-20 World Cup in Colombia

THE FIFA BIG COUNT OF 2006

	Male	Female			Total
Number of players	238 557 000	25 995 000	Referees and assistant referees		843 000
Professionals	113 000		Admin, coaches, technical, medical		4 214 000
Amateurs 18+	15 481 000		Number of clubs		301 000
Youth under 18	21 547 000		Number of teams		1 752 000
Unregistered	226 702 000		Clubs with women's teams		26 000
Total players	262 986 904		Players as % of population		4.13%

and the FIFA U-17 World Cup in Mexico. Brazil's youngsters emerged victorious in the U-20 event after beating Portugal 3-2 in the final in Bogota. It was only their second triumph since the mid-1990s - during which time rivals Argentina have emerged victorious in five tournaments - and the Brazilians now stand just one behind the Argentine record of six titles. Brazil's U-17 team fared less well in Mexico, losing their semi-final against Uruguay, and it was hosts Mexico who were crowned U-17 world champions after beating the Uruguayans 2-0 in the final in Mexico City's Aztec Stadium. There was a fitting end to the year when the FIFA Club World Cup returned to Japan after a two-year absence. It gave the locals the chance to see two of the most iconic names in club football play each other in the final, with Barcelona beating Santos 4-0 to further enhance their growing reputation as one of the greatest teams of all-time. Lionel Messi scored twice and there was little surprise when he won the FIFA Ballon d'Or in January 2012 - his third in a row, something that only Michel Platini has managed to do before. There can be little doubt that Messi must now be regarded as one of the greatest footballers ever to have played the game.

Fédération Internationale de Football Association (FIFA)
FIFA-Strasse 20, PO Box, 8044 Zurich, Switzerland
Tel +41 43 222 7777   Fax +41 43 222 7878
contact@fifa.org
www.fifa.com
President: Joseph S. Blatter
Secretary General: Jérôme Valcke
Deputy Secretary General: Markus Kattner

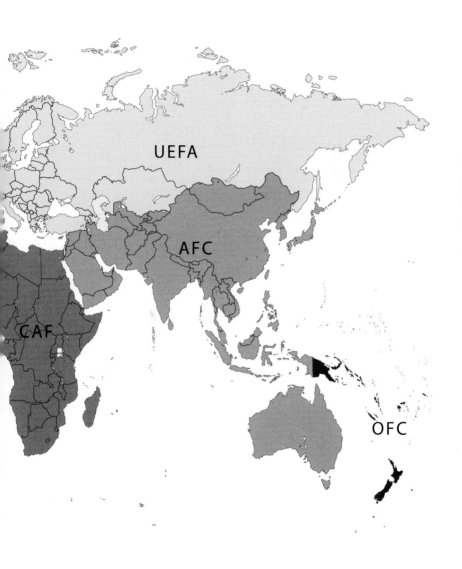

FIFA EXECUTIVE COMMITTEE

President: Joseph S. Blatter SUI   Senior Vice-President: Julio H. Grondona ARG   Vice-President: Issa Hayatou CMR
Vice-President: Angel Maria Villar Llona ESP   Vice-President: Michel Platini FRA   Vice-President: David Chung PNG
Vice-President: HRH Prince Ali Bin Al Hussein JOR   Vice-President: Jim Boyce NIR

ORDINARY MEMBERS OF THE EXECUTIVE COMMITTEE

Michel D'Hooghe BEL	Ricardo Terra Teixeira BRA	Senes Erzik TUR
Worawi Makudi THA	Chuck Blazer USA	Nicolas Leoz PAR
Marios Lefkaritis CYP	Jacques Anouma CIV	Rafael Salguero GUA
Hany Abo Rida EGY	Vitaliy Mutko RUS	Mohamed Raouraoua ALG
V. Manilal Fernando SRI	Theo Zwanziger GER	Zhang Jilong CHN

Secretary General: Jérôme Valcke

FIFA COMMITTEES, JUDICIAL BODIES AND GOVERNANCE BODIES

	Chairman		Chairman
Appeal Committee	Larry Mussenden BER	Medical Committee	Michel D'Hooghe BEL
Disciplinary Committee	Marcel Mathier SUI	Players' Status Committee	Theo Zwanziger GER
Ethics Committee	Claudio Sulser SUI	Referees Committee	Angel María Villar Llona ESP
Associations Committee	Senes Erzik TUR	Stadium and Security Committee	V. Manilal Fernando SRI
Audit Committee	TBC	Strategic Committee	Joseph S. Blatter SUI
Beach Soccer Committee	Ricardo Terra Teixeira BRA	Task Force Ethics Committee	Claudio Sulser SUI
Bureau 2014 FIFA World Cup Brazil	Nicolas Leoz PAR	Task Force Football 2014	Franz Beckenbauer GER
Committee for Club Football	Jacques Anouma CIV	Task Force Revision of Statutes	Theo Zwanziger GER
Fair Play and Social Responsibility	HRH Ali Bin Al Hussein JOR	Task Force Transparency & Compliance	Frank van Hattum NZL
Development Committee	Issa Hayatou CMR	Independent Governance Committee	Mark Pieth SUI
Emergency Committee	Joseph S. Blatter SUI	Organising Committee for...	Chairman
Football Committee	Michel Platini FRA	the FIFA World Cup	Nicolas Leoz PAR
Futsal Committee	V. Manilal Fernando SRI	the FIFA Confederations Cup	Vitaly Mutko RUS
Legal Committee	Angel María Villar Llona ESP	the Olympic Football Tournaments	Zhang Jilong CHN
Marketing & TV Committee	Marios Lefkaritis CYP	the FIFA U-20 World Cup	Jim Boyce NIR
Media Committee	Mohamed Raouraoua ALG	the FIFA U-17 World Cup	Rafael Salguero GUA
Dispute Resolution Chamber	Geoff Thompson ENG	Women's Football and FIFA Women's World Cup	Worawi Makudi THA
FIFA Development Officers	11 members	the U-20 Women's World Cup	David Chung PNG
FIFA Medical Assessment and Research Centre	Michel D'Hooghe BEL	the U-17 Women's World Cup	Hany Abo Rida EGY
		the FIFA Club World Cup	Chuck Blazer USA

FIFA NATIONAL TEAM TOURNAMENTS

FIFA WORLD CUP

Year	Host country	Winners	Score	Runners-up	Venue
1930	Uruguay	Uruguay	4-2	Argentina	Centenario, Montevideo
1934	Italy	Italy	2-1	Czechoslovakia	PNF, Rome
1938	France	Italy	4-2	Hungary	Colombes, Paris
1950	Brazil	Uruguay	2-1	Brazil	Maracana, Rio de Janeiro
1954	Switzerland	Germany FR	3-2	Hungary	Wankdorf, Berne
1958	Sweden	Brazil	5-2	Sweden	Råsunda, Stockholm
1962	Chile	Brazil	3-1	Czechoslovakia	Estadio Nacional, Santiago
1966	England	England	4-2	Germany FR	Wembley, London
1970	Mexico	Brazil	4-1	Italy	Azteca, Mexico City
1974	Germany FR	Germany FR	2-1	Netherlands	Olympiastadion, Munich
1978	Argentina	Argentina	3-1	Netherlands	Monumental, Buenos Aires
1982	Spain	Italy	3-1	Germany FR	Bernabeu, Madrid
1986	Mexico	Argentina	3-2	Germany FR	Azteca, Mexico City
1990	Italy	Germany FR	1-0	Argentina	Olimpico, Rome
1994	USA	Brazil	0-0 3-2p	Italy	Rose Bowl, Pasadena
1998	France	France	3-0	Brazil	Stade de France, Paris
2002	Korea Rep/Japan	Brazil	2-0	Germany	International Stadium, Yokohama
2006	Germany	Italy	1-1 5-3p	France	Olympiastadion, Berlin
2010	South Africa	Spain	1-0	Netherlands	Soccer City, Johannesburg
2014	Brazil				Maracana, Rio de Janeiro

FIFA WORLD CUP MEDALS TABLE

Country	G	S	B	F	SF
Brazil	5	2	2	7	7
Italy	4	2	1	6	7
Germany	3	4	4	7	11
Argentina	2	2		4	3
Uruguay	2			2	4
France	1	1	2	2	5
England	1			1	2
Spain	1			1	1
Netherlands		3		3	2
Czechoslovakia		2		2	2
Hungary		2		2	2
Sweden		1	2	1	3
Poland			2		1
Austria			1		2
Portugal			1		2
Yugoslavia			1		2
Chile			1		1
Croatia			1		1
Turkey			1		1
USA			1		1
Belgium					1
Bulgaria					1
Korea Republic					1
Soviet Union					1
	19	19	20	38	64

This table represents the Gold (winners), Silver (runners-up) and Bronze (3rd place) wins of nations in the FIFA World Cup, along with the number of appearances in the final and semi-finals

FIFA CONFEDERATIONS CUP

Year	Host country	Winners	Score	Runners-up	Venue
1992	Saudi Arabia †	Argentina	3-1	Saudi Arabia	King Fahd, Riyadh
1995	Saudi Arabia †	Denmark	2-0	Argentina	King Fahd, Riyadh
1997	Saudi Arabia	Brazil	6-0	Australia	King Fahd, Riyadh
1999	Mexico	Mexico	4-3	Brazil	Azteca, Mexico City
2001	Korea/Japan	France	1-0	Japan	International Stadium, Yokohama
2003	France	France	1-0	Cameroon	Stade de France, Paris
2005	Germany	Brazil	4-1	Argentina	Waldstadion, Frankfurt
2009	South Africa	Brazil	3-2	USA	Ellis Park, Johannesburg

† Intercontinental Champions Cup

MEN'S OLYMPIC FOOTBALL TOURNAMENT

Year	Host city	Winners	Score	Runners-up	Venue
1896	Athens ‡	No tournament took place			
1900	Paris ‡	Great Britain	4-0	France	Vélodrome Municipal, Paris
1904	St Louis ‡	Canada	4-0	USA	Francis Field, St Louis
1906	Athens ‡	Denmark	9-0	Greece	Podilatodromino, Athens
1908	London	England (as GBR)	2-0	Denmark	White City, London
1912	Stockholm	England (as GBR)	4-2	Denmark	Stockholms Stadion, Stockholm
1916	Berlin	Games cancelled			
1920	Antwerp	Belgium	2-0	Czechoslovakia	Olympisch Stadion, Antwerp
1924	Paris	Uruguay	3-0	Switzerland	Colombes, Paris
1928	Amsterdam	Uruguay	1-1 2-1	Argentina	Olympisch Stadion, Amsterdam
1932	Los Angeles	No football tournament played			
1936	Berlin	Italy	2-1	Austria	Olympiastadion, Berlin
1940	Tokyo/Helsinki	Games cancelled			
1944	London	Games cancelled			

MEN'S OLYMPIC FOOTBALL TOURNAMENT (CONT'D)

Year	Host city	Winners	Score	Runners-up	Venue
1948	London	Sweden	3-1	Yugoslavia	Wembley, London
1952	Helsinki	Hungary	2-0	Yugoslavia	Olympiastadion, Helsinki
1956	Melbourne	Soviet Union	1-0	Yugoslavia	Melbourne Cricket Ground
1960	Rome	Yugoslavia	3-1	Denmark	Flaminio, Rome
1964	Tokyo	Hungary	2-1	Czechoslovakia	National Stadium, Tokyo
1968	Mexico City	Hungary	4-1	Bulgaria	Azteca, Mexico City
1972	Munich	Poland	2-1	Hungary	Olympiastadion, Munich
1976	Montreal	German DR	3-1	Poland	Olympic Stadium, Montreal
1980	Moscow	Czechoslovakia	1-0	German DR	Centralny, Moscow
1984	Los Angeles	France	2-0	Brazil	Rose Bowl, Pasadena
1988	Seoul	Soviet Union	2-1	Brazil	Olympic Stadium, Seoul
1992	Barcelona	Spain	3-2	Poland	Camp Nou, Barcelona
1996	Atlanta	Nigeria	3-2	Argentina	Sanford Stadium, Athens
2000	Sydney	Cameroon	2-2 5-3p	Spain	Olympic Stadium, Sydney
2004	Athens	Argentina	1-0	Paraguay	Olympic Stadium, Athens
2008	Beijing	Argentina	1-0	Nigeria	Bird's Nest, Beijing

‡ Unofficial tournament • In 1920 Czechoslovakia were disqualified. Spain won the silver medal after a play-off

FIFA CLUB TOURNAMENTS

FIFA CLUB WORLD CUP

Year	Host country	Winners		Score		Runners-up	Venue
2000	Brazil	Corinthians	BRA	0-0 4-3p	BRA	Vasco da Gama	Maracana, Rio de Janeiro
2005	Japan	São Paulo FC	BRA	1-0	ENG	Liverpool	International, Yokohama
2006	Japan	Internacional	BRA	1-0	ESP	Barcelona	International, Yokohama
2007	Japan	Milan	ITA	4-2	ARG	Boca Juniors	International, Yokohama
2008	Japan	Manchester United	ENG	1-0	ECU	LDU Quito	International, Yokohama
2009	UAE	Barcelona	ESP	2-1	ARG	Estudiantes LP	Zayed SC, Abu Dhabi
2010	UAE	Internazionale	ITA	3-0	COD	TP Mazembe	Zayed SC, Abu Dhabi
2011	Japan	Barcelona	ESP	4-0	BRA	Santos	International, Yokohama

FIFA YOUTH TOURNAMENTS

FIFA U-20 WORLD CUP

Year	Host Country	Winners	Score	Runners-up	Final Venue
1977	Tunisia	Soviet Union	2-2 9-8p	Mexico	El Menzah, Tunis
1979	Japan	Argentina	3-1	Soviet Union	National Stadium, Tokyo
1981	Australia	Germany FR	4-0	Qatar	Sydney Cricket Ground
1983	Mexico	Brazil	1-0	Argentina	Azteca, Mexico City
1985	Soviet Union	Brazil	1-0	Spain	Centralny, Moscow
1987	Chile	Yugoslavia	1-1 5-4p	Germany FR	Estadio Nacional, Santiago
1989	Saudi Arabia	Portugal	2-0	Nigeria	King Fahd, Riyadh
1991	Portugal	Portugal	0-0 4-2p	Brazil	Da Luz, Lisbon
1993	Australia	Brazil	2-1	Ghana	Sydney Football Stadium, Sydney
1995	Qatar	Argentina	2-0	Brazil	Khalifa, Doha
1997	Malaysia	Argentina	2-1	Uruguay	Shahalam Stadium, Shah Alam
1999	Nigeria	Spain	4-0	Japan	Surulere, Lagos
2001	Argentina	Argentina	3-0	Ghana	Jose Amalfitani, Buenos Aires
2003	UAE	Brazil	1-0	Spain	Zayed Sports City, Abu Dhabi
2005	Netherlands	Argentina	2-1	Nigeria	Galgenwaard, Utrecht
2007	Canada	Argentina	2-1	Czech Republic	National Soccer Stadium, Toronto
2009	Egypt	Ghana	0-0 4-3p	Brazil	International, Cairo
2011	Colombia	Brazil	3-2	Portugal	El Campin, Bogota

FIFA U-17 WORLD CUP

Year	Host Country	Winners	Score	Runners-up	Final Venue
1985	China PR	Nigeria	2-0	Germany FR	Workers' Stadium, Beijing
1987	Canada	Soviet Union	1-1 3-1p	Nigeria	Varsity Stadium, Toronto
1989	Scotland	Saudi Arabia	2-2 5-4p	Scotland	Hampden Park, Glasgow
1991	Italy	Ghana	1-0	Spain	Comunale, Florence
1993	Japan	Nigeria	2-1	Ghana	National Stadium, Tokyo
1995	Ecuador	Ghana	3-2	Brazil	Monumental, Guayaquil
1997	Egypt	Brazil	2-1	Ghana	National Stadium, Cairo
1999	New Zealand	Brazil	0-0 8-7p	Australia	North Harbour, Auckland
2001	Trinidad & Tobago	France	3-0	Nigeria	Hasely Crawford, Port of Spain
2003	Finland	Brazil	1-0	Spain	Töölö, Helsinki
2005	Peru	Mexico	3-0	Brazil	Estadio Nacional, Lima
2007	Korea Republic	Nigeria	0-0 3-0p	Spain	World Cup Stadium, Seoul
2009	Nigeria	Switzerland	1-0	Nigeria	National Stadium, Abuja
2011	Mexico	Mexico	2-0	Uruguay	Azteca, Mexico City

First three tournaments played as a U-16 event

FIFA WOMEN'S TOURNAMENTS

FIFA WOMEN'S WORLD CUP

Year	Host Country	Winners	Score	Runners-up	Venue
1991	China PR	USA	2-1	Norway	Tianhe, Guangzhou
1995	Sweden	Norway	2-0	Germany	Råsunda, Stockholm
1999	USA	USA	0-0 5-4p	China PR	Rose Bowl, Pasadena
2003	USA	Germany	2-1	Sweden	Home Depot Centre, Carson
2007	China PR	Germany	2-0	Brazil	Hongkou, Shanghai
2011	Germany	Japan	2-2 3-1p	USA	Commerzbank, Frankfurt/Main

FIFA WOMEN'S WORLD CUP MEDALS TABLE

	Country	G	S	B	F	SF
1	USA	2	1	3	3	6
2	Germany	2	1		3	4
3	Norway	1	1		2	4
4	Japan	1			1	1
	Brazil		1	1	1	2
6	Sweden		1	2	1	3
7	China PR		1		1	2
	Canada					1
	France					1
		6	6	6	12	24

This table represents the Gold (winners), Silver (runners-up) and
Bronze (3rd place) wins of nations in the FIFA Women's World Cup,
along with the number of appearances in the final and semi-finals

WOMEN'S OLYMPIC FOOTBALL TOURNAMENT

Year	Host City	Winners	Score	Runners-up	Venue
1996	Atlanta	USA	2-1	China PR	Sanford Stadium, Athens
2000	Sydney	Norway	3-2	USA	Sydney Football Stadium, Sydney
2004	Athens	USA	2-1	Brazil	Karaiskaki, Piraeus
2008	Beijing	USA	1-0	Brazil	Worker's Stadium, Beijing

FIFA U-17 WOMEN'S WORLD CUP

Year	Host Country	Winners	Score	Runners-up	Final Venue
2008	New Zealand	Korea DPR	2-1	USA	North Harbour, Auckland
2010	Trinidad & Tobago	Korea Republic	3-3 5-4p	Japan	Hasely Crawford, Port of Spain

FIFA U-20 WOMEN'S WORLD CUP

Year	Host Country	Winners	Score	Runners-up	Final Venue
2002	Canada	USA	1-0	Canada	Commonwealth, Edmonton
2004	Thailand	Germany	2-0	China PR	Rajamangala National, Bangkok
2006	Russia	Korea DPR	5-0	China PR	Lokomotiv, Moscow
2008	Chile	USA	2-1	Korea DPR	Municipal, La Florida, Santiago
2010	Germany	Germany	2-0	Nigeria	Schüco Arena, Bielefeld

First two tournaments played as a U-19 event

FIFA BALLON D'OR 2011

FIFA BALLON D'OR 2011

Rank	Player	Club	Nat	Total %
1	Lionel Messi	Barcelona	ARG	47.88
2	Cristiano Ronaldo	Real Madrid	POR	21.60
3	Xavi Hernandez	Barcelona	ESP	9.23
4	Andres Iniesta	Barcelona	ESP	6.01
5	Wayne Rooney	Manchester United	ENG	2.31
6	Luis Suarez	Liverpool	URU	1.48
7	Diego Forlan	Internazionale	URU	1.43
8	Samuel Eto'o	Anzhi Makhachkala	CMR	1.34
9	Iker Casillas	Real Madrid	ESP	1.29
10	Neymar	Santos	BRA	1.12
11	Mesut Ozil	Real Madrid	GER	0.76
12	Wesley Sneijder	Internazionale	NED	0.72
13	Thomas Muller	Bayern München	GER	0.64
14	David Villa	Barcelona	ESP	0.53
15	Bastian Schweinsteiger	Bayern München	GER	0.50
16	Xabi Alonso	Real Madrid	ESP	0.48
17	Sergio Aguero	Manchester City	ARG	0.48
18	Eric Abidal	Barcelona	FRA	0.36
19	Dani Alves	Barcelona	BRA	0.34
20	Karim Benzema	Real Madrid	FRA	0.34
21	Cesc Fabregas	Barcelona	ESP	0.29
22	Nani	Manchester United	POR	0.26
23	Gerard Pique	Barcelona	ESP	0.22

FIFA WOMEN'S WORLD PLAYER OF THE YEAR 2011

Rank	Player	Club	Nat	Total %
1	Homare Sawa	INAC Kobe Leonessa	JPN	28.51
2	Marta	Western New York Flash	BRA	17.28
3	Abby Wambach	magicJack	USA	13.26
4	Aya Miyama	Okayama Yunogo Belle	JPN	12.18
5	Hope Solo	magicJack	USA	7.83
6	Lotta Schelin	Olympique Lyonnais	SWE	4.85
7	Kerstin Garefrekes	FFC Frankfurt	GER	4.73
8	Alex Morgan	Western New York Flash	USA	4.34
9	Louisa Necib	Olympique Lyonnais	FRA	3.21
10	Sonia Bompastor	Olympique Lyonnais	FRA	2.99

FIFA WORLD COACH OF THE YEAR FOR MEN'S FOOTBALL 2011

Rank	Coach	Team	Nat	Total %
1	Josep Guardiola	Barcelona	ESP	41.92
2	Sir Alex Ferguson	Manchester United	SCO	15.61
3	Jose Mourinho	Real Madrid	POR	12.43
4	Vicente Del Bosque	Spain	ESP	9.12
5	Oscar Tabarez	Uruguay	URU	7.47
6	Joachim Low	Germany	GER	4.40
7	Andre Villas-Boas	FC Porto/Chelsea	POR	4.16
8	Arsene Wenger	Arsenal	FRA	1.91
9	Jurgen Klopp	Borussia Dortmund	GER	1.54
10	Rudi Garcia	Lille OSC	FRA	0.89

FIFA WORLD COACH OF THE YEAR FOR WOMEN'S FOOTBALL 2011

Rank	Coach	Team	Nat	Total %
1	Norio Sasaki	Japan	JPN	45.57
2	Pia Sundhage	USA	SWE	15.83
3	Brubo Bini	France	FRA	10.28
4	Maren Meinert	Germany U-20	GER	7.42
5	Patrice Lair	Olympique Lyonnais	FRA	5.80
6	Thomas Dennerby	Sweden	SWE	4.31
7	Hope Powell	England	ENG	3.01
8	Jorge Vilda	Spain U-17	ESP	2.85
9	Leonardo Cuellar	Mexico	MEX	2.38
10	Tom Sermanni	Australia	SCO	2.02

The Ballon d'Or was awarded by *France Football* magazine from 1956 until 2009. Until 1994 it was open only to Europeans. From 1995 until 2006 it was open to any player signed to a European club but in the final three years it was open to any player in the world. In 2010, the Ballon d'Or and FIFA's World Player of the Year award combined to form the FIFA Ballon d'Or.

BALLON D'OR WINNERS

1956	Stanley Matthews	Blackpool	ENG	1974	Johan Cruyff	Barcelona	NED	1992	Marco van Basten	Milan	NED
1957	Alfredo Di Stefano	Real Madrid	ESP	1975	Oleg Blokhin	Dynamo Kyiv	URS	1993	Roberto Baggio	Juventus	ITA
1958	Raymond Kopa	Real Madrid	FRA	1976	Franz Beckenbauer	Bay. München	GER	1994	Hristo Stoichkov	Barcelona	BUL
1959	Alfredo Di Stefano	Real Madrid	ESP	1977	Alan Simonsen	B. M'gladbach	DEN	1995	George Weah	Milan	LBR
1960	Luis Suarez	Barcelona	ESP	1978	Kevin Keegan	Hamburger SV	ENG	1996	Matthias Sammer	Bor. Dortmund	GER
1961	Omar Sivori	Juventus	ITA	1979	Kevin Keegan	Hamburger SV	ENG	1997	Ronaldo	Internazionale	BRA
1962	Josef Masopust	Dukla Praha	CZE	1980	K-H Rummenigge	Bay. München	GER	1998	Zinedine Zidane	Juventus	FRA
1963	Lev Yashin	Dyn. Moskva	URS	1981	K-H Rummenigge	Bay. München	GER	1999	Rivaldo	Barcelona	BRA
1964	Denis Law	Man United	SCO	1982	Paolo Rossi	Juventus	ITA	2000	Luis Figo	Real Madrid	POR
1965	Eusebio	Benfica	POR	1983	Michel Platini	Juventus	FRA	2001	Michael Owen	Liverpool	ENG
1966	Bobby Charlton	Man United	ENG	1984	Michel Platini	Juventus	FRA	2002	Ronaldo	Real Madrid	BRA
1967	Florian Albert	Ferencvaros	HUN	1985	Michel Platini	Juventus	FRA	2003	Pavel Nedved	Juventus	CZE
1968	George Best	Man United	NIR	1986	Igor Belanov	Dynamo Kyiv	URS	2004	Andriy Shevchenko	Milan	UKR
1969	Gianni Rivera	Milan	ITA	1987	Ruud Gullit	Milan	NED	2005	Ronaldinho	Barcelona	BRA
1970	Gerd Müller	Bay. München	GER	1988	Marco van Basten	Milan	NED	2006	Fabio Cannavaro	Real Madrid	ITA
1971	Johan Cruyff	Ajax	NED	1989	Marco van Basten	Milan	NED	2007	Kaká	Milan	BRA
1972	Franz Beckenbauer	Bay. München	GER	1990	Lothar Matthäus	Internazionale	GER	2008	Cristiano Ronaldo	Man United	POR
1973	Johan Cruyff	Barcelona	NED	1991	Jean-Pierre Papin	Oly. Marseille	FRA	2009	Lionel Messi	Barcelona	ARG

FIFA BALLON D'OR WINNERS

	1st	2nd	3rd
1991	Lothar Matthäus	Jean-Pierre Papin	Gary Lineker
1992	Marco van Basten	Hristo Stoichkov	Thomas Hassler
1993	Roberto Baggio	Romario	Dennis Bergkamp
1994	Romario	Hristo Stoichkov	Roberto Baggio
1995	George Weah	Paolo Maldini	Jürgen Klinsmann
1996	Ronaldo	George Weah	Alan Shearer
1997	Ronaldo	Roberto Carlos	Bergkamp/Zidane
1998	Zinedine Zidane	Ronaldo	Davor Suker
1999	Rivaldo	David Beckham	Gabriel Batistuta
2000	Zinedine Zidane	Luis Figo	Rivaldo
2001	Luis Figo	David Beckham	Raul
2002	Ronaldo	Oliver Kahn	Zinedine Zidane
2003	Zinedine Zidane	Thierry Henry	Ronaldo
2004	Ronaldinho	Thierry Henry	Andriy Shevchenko
2005	Ronaldinho	Frank Lampard	Samuel Eto'o
2006	Fabio Cannavaro	Zinedine Zidane	Ronaldinho
2007	Kaka	Lionel Messi	Cristiano Ronaldo
2008	Cristiano Ronaldo	Lionel Messi	Fernando Torres
2009	Lionel Messi	Cristiano Ronaldo	Xavi
2010	Lionel Messi	Andres Iniesta	Xavi
2011	Lionel Messi	Cristiano Ronaldo	Xavi

Known as the FIFA World Player of the Year 1991-2009

FIFA WOMEN'S WORLD PLAYER WINNERS

	1st	2nd	3rd
	Mia Hamm	Sun Wen	Tiffeny Milbrett
	Mia Hamm	Birgit Prinz	Sun Wen
	Birgit Prinz	Mia Hamm	Hanna Ljungberg
	Birgit Prinz	Mia Hamm	Marta
	Birgit Prinz	Marta	Shannon Boxx
	Marta	Kristine Lilly	Renate Lingor
	Marta	Birgit Prinz	Cristiane
	Marta	Birgit Prinz	Cristiane
	Marta	Birgit Prinz	Kelly Smith
	Marta	Birgit Prinz	Fatmire Bajramaj
	Homare Sawa	Marta	Abby Wambach

FIFA WOMEN'S WORLD CUP GERMANY 2011

FIFA WOMEN'S WORLD CUP GERMANY 2011

First round groups		Quarter-finals		Semi-finals		Final	
	Pts						
Germany	9						
France	6	**Japan**	1				
Nigeria	3	Germany	0				
Canada	0						
				Japan	3		
	Pts			Sweden	1		
England	7						
Japan	6	Australia	1				
Mexico	2	**Sweden**	3				
New Zealand	1						
						Japan	
	Pts					USA	
Sweden	9						
USA	6	**France**	1 4p				
Korea DPR	1	England	1 3p				
Colombia	1						
				France	1		
	Pts			**USA**	3		
Brazil	9						
Australia	6	Brazil	2 3p			**3rd Place Play-off**	
Norway	3	**USA**	2 5p			**Sweden**	2
Equatorial Guinea	0					France	1

Top scorers: **5** - Homare Sawa JPN • **4** - Marta BRA & Abby Wambach USA • **3** - Lisa Dahlkvist SWE • **2** - 16 players with 2 goals
adidas Golden Ball: Homare Sawa JPN
adidas Golden Boot: Homare Sawa JPN
adidas Golden Glove: Hope Solo USA
FIFA Fair Play Award: Japan
Hyundai Best Young Player: Caitlin Foord AUS

	GROUP A	PL	W	D	L	F	A	PTS	FRA	NGA	CAN
1	**Germany**	3	3	0	0	7	3	9	4-2	1-0	2-1
2	**France**	3	2	0	1	7	4	6		1-0	4-0
3	Nigeria	3	1	0	2	1	2	3			1-0
4	Canada	3	0	0	3	1	7	0			

Olympiastadion, Berlin. 26-06-2011, 18:00, 73 680, Melksham AUS

Germany   **2**

Kerstin Garefrekes [10], Celia Okoyino Da Mbabi [42]

Nadine **Angerer** - Saskia **Bartusiak**, Babett **Peter**, Annike **Krahn•**, Linda **Bresonik** - Simone **Laudehr•**, Melanie **Behringer** (Fatmire **Bajramaj** 71), Celia **Okoyino da Mbabi** (Inka **Grings** 65), Kim **Kulig**, Kerstin **Garefrekes** - Birgit **Prinz**(c) (Alexandra **Popp** 56). Tr: Silvia **Neid**

Canada   **1**

Christine Sinclair [82]

Erin **McLeod** - Emily **Zurrer**, Rhian **Wilkinson**, Candace **Chapman**, Marie-Eve **Nault** (Robyn **Gayle** 46) - Kaylyn **Kyle** (Kelly **Parker** 46), Diana **Matheson**, Sophie **Schmidt** - Christine **Sinclair**(c), Melissa **Tancredi** (Brittany **Timko** 80), Jonelle **Filigno**. Tr: Carolina **Morace**

Rhein-Neckar Arena, Sinsheim. 26-06-2011, 15:00, 25 475, Seitz USA

Nigeria   **0**

Precious **Dede**(c) - Onome **Ebi**, Helen **Ukaonu**, Osinachi **Ohale**, Faith **Ikidi** (Josephine **Chukwunonye** 34) - Perpertua **Nkwocha**, Rita **Chikwelu**, Glory **Iroka**, Ebere **Orji** (Uchechi **Sunday** 78) - Stella **Mbachu**, Desire **Oparanozie** (Sarah **Michael** 66). Tr: Ngozi **Uche**

France   **1**

Marie-Laure Delie [56]

Berangere **Sapowicz** - Wendie **Renard** (Laure **Lepailleur** 69), Laura **Georges**, Ophelie **Meilleroux**, Sonia **Bompastor** - Sandrine **Soubeyrand**(c) (Eugenie **Le Sommer** 46), Camille **Abily**, Louisa **Necib**, Elise **Bussaglia** - Gaetane **Thiney** (Elodie **Thomis** 57), Marie-Laure **Delie**. Tr: Bruno **Bini**

Frankfurt/Main. 30-06-2011, 20:45, 48 817, Cha Sung Mi KOR

Germany	1
	Simone Laudehr [54]

Nadine Angerer - Saskia Bartusiak, Babett Peter, Annike Krahn, Linda Bresonik - Simone Laudehr, Melanie Behringer (Alexandra Popp 31), Celia Okoyino da Mbabi (Fatmire Bajramaj 87), Kim Kulig•, Kerstin Garefrekes - Birgit Prinz(c) (Inka Grings 53). Tr: Silvia Neid

Nigeria	0

Precious Dede(c) - Onome Ebi, Helen Ukaonu, Osinachi Ohale•, Faith Ikidi - Perpertua Nkwocha, Rita Chikwelu, Ebere Orji (Amenze Aighewi 63) - Stella Mbachu (Francisca Ordega 85), Desire Oparanozie, Sarah Michael (Uchechi Sunday 70). Tr: Ngozi Uche

---

Bochum. 30-06-2011, 18:00, 16 591, Fukano JPN

Canada	0

Erin McLeod - Emily Zurrer, Rhian Wilkinson, Candace Chapman, Brittany Timko (Chelsea Stewart 77) - Kaylyn Kyle (Desiree Scott 60), Diana Matheson•, Sophie Schmidt - Christine Sinclair(c), Christina Julien (Melissa Tancredi 60), Jonelle Filigno. Tr: Carolina Morace

France	4
	Gaetane Thiney 2 [24 60], Camile Abily [66], Elodie Thomis [83]

Berangere Sapowicz - Laura Georges, Sonia Bompastor•, Laure Lepailleur, Sabrina Viguier - Sandrine Soubeyrand(c), Camille Abily (Eugenie Le Sommer 82), Louisa Necib, Elise Bussaglia - Gaetane Thiney (Laure Boulleau 79), Marie-Laure Delie (Elodie Thomis 74). Tr: Bruno Bini

---

Mönchengladbach. 5-07-2011, 20:45, 45 867, Heikkinen FIN

France	2
	Marie-Laure Delie [56], Laura Georges [72]

Berangere Sapowicz◆65 - Wendie Renard•, Laura Georges•, Laure Lepailleur, Laure Bolleau - Sandrine Soubeyrand(c), Louisa Necib (Camille Abily 46), Eugenie Le Sommer (Celine Deville 68), Elise Bussaglia - Gaetane Thiney, Elodie Thomis (Marie-Laure Delie 46). Tr: Bruno Bini

Germany	4
	Kerstin Garfrekes [25], Inka Grings 2 [32 68p], Celia Okoyino Da Mbabi [89]

Nadine Angerer - Bianca Schmidt, Saskia Bartusiak, Babett Peter, Annike Krahn (Alexandra Popp 78) - Lena Goeßling•, Simone Laudehr (Ariane Hingst 46), Celia Okoyino da Mbabi, Fatmire Bajramaj•, Kerstin Garefrekes(c) - Inka Grings. Tr: Silvia Neid

---

Dresden. 5-07-2011, 20:45, 13 638, Vulivuli FIJ

Canada	0

Karina LeBlanc - Emily Zurrer, Rhian Wilkinson, Candace Chapman, Marie-Eve Nault - Kaylyn Kyle (Desiree Scott 78), Diana Matheson, Sophie Schmidt - Christine Sinclair(c), Melissa Tancredi (Jodi-Ann Robinson 84), Jonelle Filigno (Christina Julien 56). Tr: Carolina Morace

Nigeria	1
	Perpetua Nkwocha [73]

Precious Dede(c) - Onome Ebi•, Helen Ukaonu, Osinachi Ohale, Faith Ikidi - Perpertua Nkwocha, Rita Chikwelu, Glory Iroka, Ebere Orji (Ogonna Chukwudi 54) - Stella Mbachu (Francisca Ordega 72), Desire Oparanozie (Uchechi Sunday 84). Tr: Ngozi Uche

---

	GROUP B	PL	W	D	L	F	A	PTS		JPN	MEX	NZL
1	England	3	2	1	0	5	2	7		2-0	1-1	2-1
2	Japan	3	2	0	1	6	3	6			4-0	2-1
3	Mexico	3	0	2	1	3	7	2				2-2
4	New Zealand	3	0	1	2	4	6	1				

Bochum. 27-06-2011, 15:00, 12 538, Heikkinen FIN

Japan	2
	Yuki Nagasato [6], Aya Miyama [68]

Ayumi Kaihori - Yukari Kinga, Azusa Iwashimizu, Saki Kumagai, Aya Sameshima - Shinobu Ohno (Mana Iwabuchi 55), Mizuho Sakaguchi, Homare Sawa(c), Aya Miyama - Kozue Ando (Asuna Tanaka 92+) Yuki Nagasato (Karina Maruyama 76). Tr: Norio Sasaki

New Zealand	1
	Amber Hearn [12]

Jenny Bindon - Ria Percival (Annalie Longo 76), Anna Green, Abby Erceg, Rebecca Smith(c)•, Ali Riley - Katie Bowen• (Hayley Moorwood 46), Katie Hoyle, Betsy Hassett - Amber Hearn•, Sarah Gregorius (Hannah Wilkinson 62). Tr: John Herdman

---

Wolfsburg. 27-06-2011, 18:00, 18 702, Reyes PER

Mexico	1
	Monica Ocampo [33]

Cecilia Santiago - Marlene Sandoval, Alina Garciamendez•, Luz Saucedo, Natalie Vinti - Teresa Worbis, Dinora Garza (Teresa Noyola 85), Nayeli Rangel - Maribel Dominguez(c) (Juana Lopez 76), Monica Ocampo, Sandra Mayor. Tr: Leonardo Cuellar

England	1
	Fara Williams [21]

Karen Bardsley - Alex Scott, Rachel Unitt, Faye White(c) (Sophie Bradley 83), Casey Stoney• - Jill Scott, Fara Williams - Rachel Yankey, Kelly Smith, Karen Carney (Ellen White 72), Eniola Aluko. Tr: Hope Powell

---

Leverkusen. 1-07-2011, 15:00, 22 291, Pedersen NOR

Japan	4
	Homare Sawa 3 [13 39 80], Shinobu Ohno [15]

Ayumi Kaihori - Yukari Kinga, Azusa Iwashimizu, Saki Kumagai, Aya Sameshima - Shinobu Ohno (Nahomi Kawasumi 69), Mizuho Sakaguchi, Homare Sawa(c) (Rumi Utsugi 83), Aya Miyama - Kozue Ando (Mana Iwabuchi 69), Yuki Nagasato. Tr: Norio Sasaki

Mexico	0

Cecilia Santiago - Alina Garciamendez, Luz Saucedo, Natalie Garcia, Natalie Vinti - Dinora Garza, Nayeli Rangel (Liliana Mercado 46) - Maribel Dominguez(c) (Kenti Robles 62), Monica Ocampo, Veronica Perez (Teresa Noyola 79), Sandra Mayor. Tr: Leonardo Cuellar

---

Dresden. 1-07-2011, 18:15, 19 110, Neguel CMR

New Zealand	1
	Sarah Gregorius [18]

Jenny Bindon - Ria Percival (Rosie White 71), Anna Green, Abby Erceg, Rebecca Smith•(c), Ali Riley - Katie Bowen (Hayley Moorwood 46), Katie Hoyle, Betsy Hassett - Amber Hearn, Sarah Gregorius (Hannah Wilkinson 90). Tr: John Herdman

England	2
	Jill Scott [63], Jessica Clarke [81]

Karen Bardsley - Alex Scott, Rachel Unitt, Faye White(c) (Sophie Bradley 86), Casey Stoney - Jill Scott, Fara Williams - Rachel Yankey (Jessica Clarke 65), Kelly Smith, Ellen White, Eniola Aluko (Karen Carney 46). Tr: Hope Powell

Augsburg. 5-07-2011, 18:15, 20 777, Chenard CAN

England	2
	Ellen White [15], Rachel Yankey [66]

Karen **Bardsley** - Alex **Scott**, Rachel **Unitt**, Sophie **Bradley**, Casey **Stoney**(c) - Jill **Scott**, Anita **Asante** - Jessica **Clarke** (Rachel **Yankey** 46), Kelly **Smith** (Eniola **Aluko** 62), Ellen **White** (Laura **Bassett** 90), Karen **Carney**. Tr: Hope **Powell**

Japan	0

Ayumi **Kaihori** - Yukari **Kinga**, Azusa **Iwashimizu**, Saki **Kumagai**, Aya **Sameshima** - Shinobu **Ohno** (Nahomi **Kawasumi** 82), Mizuho **Sakaguchi** (Mana **Iwabuchi** 75), Homare **Sawa**(c), Aya **Miyama** - Kozue **Ando** (Karina **Maruyama** 56), Yuki **Nagasato**. Tr: Norio **Sasaki**

Sinsheim. 5-07-2011, 18:15, 20 451, Palmqvist SWE

New Zealand	2
	Stephany Mayor [2], Maribel Dominguez [29]

Jenny **Bindon** - Anna **Green**, Abby **Erceg**, Rebecca **Smith**(c), Ali **Riley** - Hayley **Moorwood** (Kirsty **Yallop** 60), Katie **Hoyle**, Betsy **Hassett** (Ria **Percival** 79) - Amber **Hearn**, Sarah **Gregorius**, Rosie **White•** (Hannah **Wilkinson** 55). Tr: John **Herdman**

Mexico	2
	Rebecca Smith [90], Hannah Wilkinson [94]+

Cecilia **Santiago** - Kenti **Robles** (Luz **Saucedo** 81), Alina **Garciamendez**, Natalie **Garcia**, Natalie **Vinti** - Nayeli **Rangel** (Dinora **Garza** 46), Teresa **Worbis** - Maribel **Dominguez•**(c), Monica **Ocampo**, Veronica **Perez**, Sandra **Mayor** (Veronica **Corral** 70). Tr: Leonardo **Cuellar**

	GROUP C	PL	W	D	L	F	A	PTS	USA	PRK	COL
1	Sweden	3	3	0	0	4	1	9	2-1	1-0	1-0
2	USA	3	2	0	1	6	2	6		2-0	3-0
3	Korea DPR	3	0	1	2	0	3	1			0-0
4	Colombia	3	0	1	2	0	4	1			

Dresden. 28-06-2011, 18:15, 21 859, Steinhaus GER

USA	2
	Lauren Cheney [54], Rachel Buehler [76]

Hope **Solo** - Ali **Krieger**, Rachel **Buehler**, Christie **Rampone**(c), Amy **LePeilbet** - Heather **O'Reilly** (Megan **Rapinoe** 79), Carli **Lloyd**, Shannon **Boxx**, Amy **Rodriguez** (Alex **Morgan** 75) - Lauren **Cheney**, Abby **Wambach**. Tr: Pia **Sundhage**

Korea DPR	0

Hong **Myong Hui** - Song **Jong Sun**, Ri **Un Hyang**, Ho **Un Byol** (Kwon Song Hwa 81), Jong **Pok Sim** - Kim **Su Gyong**, Jo **Yun Mi**(c), Ri **Ye Gyong**, Jon **Myong Hwa** (Kim **Un Ju** 68) - Yun **Hyon Hi** (Paek Sol Hui 48), Ra **Un Sim**. Tr: Kim **Kwang Min**

Leverkusen. 28-06-2011, 15:00, 21 106, Chennard CAN

Colombia	0

Sandra **Sepulveda** - Natalia **Gaitan**(c), Nataly **Arias**, Kelis **Peduzine**, Andrea **Peralta** (Ingrid **Vidal** 79) - Daniela **Montoya** (Yulieth **Dominguez** 66), Yoreli **Rincon**, Diana **Ospina**, Carmen **Rodallega** - Catalina **Usme** (Katerin **Castro** 59), Lady **Andrade**. Tr: Ricardo **Ocampo**

Sweden	1
	Jessica Landstrom [57]

Hedvig **Lindahl** - Charlotte **Rohlin**, Annica **Svensson**, Sara **Thunebro**, Sara **Larsson** - Caroline **Seger•**(c) (Nilla **Fischer** 69), Therese **Sjogran**, Lisa **Dahlkvist** - Linda **Forsberg** (Sofia **Jakobsson** 54), Lotta **Schelin**, Jessica **Landstrom** (Madelaine **Edlund** 81). Tr: Thomas **Dennerby**

Sinsheim. 2-07-2011, 18:00, 25 475, Damkova CZE

USA	3
	Heather O'Reilly [12], Megan Rapinoe [50], Carli Lloyd [57]

Hope **Solo** - Ali **Krieger**, Rachel **Buehler**, Christie **Rampone**(c), Amy **LePeilbet** (Stephanie **Cox** 56) - Heather **O'Reilly** (Tobin **Heath** 62), Carli **Lloyd**, Lori **Lindsey**, Amy **Rodriguez** (Megan **Rapinoe** 46) - Lauren **Cheney**, Abby **Wambach•**. Tr: Pia **Sundhage**

Colombia	0

Sandra **Sepulveda** - Natalia **Gaitan**(c), Nataly **Arias**, Kelis **Peduzine**, Fatima **Montano** - Liana **Salazar** (Yoreli **Rincon** 55), Yulieth **Dominguez**, Diana **Ospina**, Carmen **Rodallega** - Catalina **Usme** (Orianica **Velasquez** 53), Katerin **Castro**. Tr: Ricardo **Ocampo**

Augsburg. 2-07-2011, 14:00, 23 768, Alvarez ARG

Korea DPR	0

Hong **Myong Hui** - Song **Jong Sun**, Ri **Un Hyang**, Ho **Un Byol**, Jong **Pok Sim** - Kim **Su Gyong** (Kim **Un Ju** 67), Jo **Yun Mi**(c), Ri **Ye Gyong** (Kim **Chung Sim** 82), Jon **Myong Hwa** - Yun **Hyon Hi** (Choe **Mi Gyong** 79), Ra **Un Sim**. Tr: Kim **Kwang Min**

Sweden	1
	Lisa Dahlkvist [64]

Hedvig **Lindahl** - Charlotte **Rohlin**, Annica **Svensson**, Sara **Thunebro**, Sara **Larsson** - Caroline **Seger•**(c) (Nilla **Fischer** 86), Lisa **Dahlkvist** - Linda **Forsberg**, Lotta **Schelin**, Jessica **Landstrom** (Josefine **Oqvist** 76). Tr: Thomas **Dennerby**

Wolfsburg. 6-07-2011, 20:45, 23 468, Fukano JPN

Sweden	2
	Lisa Dahlkvist [16p], Nilla Fischer [35]

Hedvig **Lindahl** - Charlotte **Rohlin**, Annica **Svensson**, Sara **Thunebro**, Sara **Larsson** - Therese **Sjogran** (Antonia **Goransson** 65), Nilla **Fischer•**(c) (Linda **Sembrant** 88), Lisa **Dahlkvist** (Marie **Hammarstrom** 77) - Linda **Forsberg**, Lotta **Schelin**, Josefine **Oqvist**. Tr: Thomas **Dennerby**

USA	1
	Abby Wambach [67]

Hope **Solo** - Ali **Krieger**, Rachel **Buehler**, Christie **Rampone**(c), Amy **LePeilbet•** (Stephanie **Cox** 59) - Megan **Rapinoe** (Kelley **O'Hara** 73), Carli **Lloyd**, Shannon **Boxx**, Amy **Rodriguez** (Alex **Morgan** 46) - Lauren **Cheney**, Abby **Wambach**. Tr: Pia **Sundhage**

Bochum. 6-07-2011, 20:45, 7805, Pedersen NOR

Korea DPR	0

Hong **Myong Hui** - Paek **Sol Hui**, Ri **Un Hyang**, Ho **Un Byol**, Yu **Jong Hui** - Kim **Su Gyong** (Kim **Chung Sim** 48), Jo **Yun Mi**(c), Ri **Ye Gyong**, Jon **Myong Hwa**, Kim **Un Ju**, Ra **Un Sim** (Yun **Hyon Hi** 56) (Choe Mi Gyong 76). Tr: Kim **Kwang Min**

Colombia	0

Sandra **Sepulveda** - Natalia **Gaitan**(c), Nataly **Arias**, Kelis **Peduzine**, Fatima **Montano** - Daniela **Montoya** (Liana **Salazar** 89), Yulieth **Dominguez**, Diana **Ospina**, Carmen **Rodallega** - Orianica **Velasquez**, Katerin **Castro** (Ingrid **Vidal** 88). Tr: Ricardo **Ocampo**

GROUP D	PL	W	D	L	F	A	PTS		AUS	NOR	EQG
1 Brazil	3	3	0	0	7	0	9		1-0	3-0	3-0
2 Australia	3	2	0	1	5	4	6			2-1	3-2
3 Norway	3	1	0	2	2	5	3				1-0
4 Equatorial Guinea	3	0	0	3	2	7	0				

Mönchengladbach. 29-06-2011, 18:15, 27 258, Palmqvist SWE

Brazil 1
Rosana 54

Andreia - Daiane, Aline(c), Erika, Maurine, Rosana - Ester, Formiga (Francielle 84), Fabiana - Marta, Cristiane. Tr: Kleiton Lima

Australia 0

Melissa Barbieri(c) - Kim Carroll, Elise Kellond-Knight, Servet Uzunlar - Heather Garriock, Emily van Egmond (Sally Shipard 61), Tameka Butt (Clare Polkinghorne 86), Collette McCallum - Lisa De Vanna, Caitlin Foord, Kyah Simon (Samantha Kerr 79). Tr: Tom Sermanni

Augsburg. 29-06-2011, 15:00, 12 928, Alvarado MEX

Norway 1
Emilie Haavi 84

Ingrid Hjelmseth - Nora Holstad Berge, Maren Mjelde•, Marita Skammelsrud Lund, Trine Ronning, Hedda Gardsjord - Ingvild Stensland(c), Emilie Haavi - Isabell Herlovsen (Cecilie Pedersen 62), Madeleine Giske (Lene Mykjaland 46) (Leni Larsen Kaurin 70), Elise Thorsnes•. Tr: Eli Landsem

Equatorial Guinea 0

Miriam - Bruna, Dulcia, Carolina - Ana Cristina, Vania, Dorine, Anonman(c), Jumaria (Chinasa 52), Christelle (Laetitia 46) - Diala (Adriana 65). Tr: Marcelo Frigerio

Wolfsburg. 3-07-2011, 18:15, 26 067, Seitz USA

Brazil 3
Marta 2 22 48, Rosana 46

Andreia - Daiane• (Renata Costa 85), Aline(c), Erika, Maurine, Rosana - Ester (Grazielle 89), Formiga, Fabiana (Francielle 76) - Marta, Cristiane. Tr: Kleiton Lima

Norway 0

Ingrid Hjelmseth - Nora Holstad Berge, Maren Mjelde, Marita Skammelsrud Lund, Trine Ronning, Guro Knutsen Mienna - Ingvild Stensland(c) (Gry Tofte Ims 67), Emilie Haavi (Cecilie Pedersen 52) - Isabell Herlovsen, Leni Larsen Kaurin (Elise Thorsnes 46), Madeleine Giske. Tr: Eli Landsem

Bochum. 3-07-2011, 14:00, 15 640, Gaal HUN

Australia 3
Leena Khamis 8, Emily Van Egmond 48, Lisa De Vanna 51

Melissa Barbieri - Kim Carroll, Elise Kellond-Knight, Servet Uzunlar - Heather Garriock, Emily van Egmond, Collette McCallum(c) (Clare Polkinghorne 78), Sally Shipard (Lisa De Vanna• 46), Lauren Colthorpe - Leena Khamis, Samantha Kerr (Teigen Allen 69). Tr: Tom Sermanni

Equatorial Guinea 2
Anonman 2 21 83

Miriam - Bruna (Laetitia 83), Dulcia, Carolina - Ana Cristina•, Vania, Dorine, Anonman•(c), Jumaria (Sinforosa 66), Chinasa (Adriana 57) - Diala. Tr: Marcelo Frigerio

Frankfurt/Main. 6-07-2011, 18:00, 35 859, Steinhaus GER

Equatorial Guinea 0

Miriam - Bruna•, Laetitia, Dulcia•, Carolina - Ana Cristina (Sinforosa 71), Vania, Dorine, Anonman(c), Jumaria - Diala• (Adriana 86). Tr: Marcelo Frigerio

Brazil 3
Erika 49, Cristiane 2 54 93+

Andreia - Aline(c), Renata Costa•, Erika, Maurine, Rosana (Francielle• 70) - Ester, Formiga (Beatriz 90), Fabiana (Thais Guedes 82) - Marta, Cristiane. Tr: Kleiton Lima

Leverkusen. 6-07-2011, 18:00, 18 474, Alvarez ARG

Australia 2
Kyah Simon 2 57 87

Melissa Barbieri(c) - Kim Carroll•, Elise Kellond-Knight, Servet Uzunlar - Heather Garriock•, Clare Polkinghorne, Collette McCallum - Lisa De Vanna, Caitlin Foord (Ellyse Perry 89), Kyah Simon, Samantha Kerr (Laura Alleway 80). Tr: Tom Sermanni

Norway 1
Elise Thorsnes 56

Ingrid Hjelmseth (Erika Skarbo 46) - Maren Mjelde, Hedda Gardsjord•, Trine Ronning, Guro Knutsen Mienna - Ingvild Stensland(c), Gry Tofte Ims (Isabell Herlovsen 81), Lene Mykjaland, Emilie Haavi (Kristine Hegland 46) - Elise Thorsnes, Cecilie Pedersen. Tr: Eli Landsem

QUARTER-FINAL PENALTIES FRA v ENG 5-4

FRA		ENG	
✗1	Abily		
		Smith	✓
✓	Bussaglia		
		Carney	✓
✓	Thiney		
		Stoney	✓
✓	Bompastor		
		Rafferty	✗2
✓	Le Sommer		
		White	✗2

QUARTER-FINAL PENALTIES USA v BRA 5-3

USA		BRA	
✓	Boxx		
		Cristiane	✓
✓	Lloyd		
		Marta	✓
✓	Wambach		
		Daiane	✗1
✓	Rapinoe		
		Francielle	✓
✓	Krieger		

1 = saved • 2 = missed

QUARTER-FINALS

Wolfsburg. 9-07-2011, 20:45, 26 067, Alvarado MEX	
Germany	**0**

Nadine **Angerer** - Saskia **Bartusiak**, Babett **Peter•**, Annike **Krahn**, Linda **Bresonik** (Lena **Goeßling** 65) - Melanie **Behringer**, Simone **Laudehr**, Celia **Okoyino da Mbabi**, Kerstin **Garefrekes**(c), Kim **Kulig** (Bianca **Schmidt** 8) - Inka **Grings** (Alexandra **Popp** 102). Tr: Silvia **Neid**

Japan	**1**
	Karina **Maruyama** [108]

Ayumi **Kaihori** - Yukari **Kinga**, Azusa **Iwashimizu•**, Saki **Kumagai•**, Aya **Sameshima** - Shinobu **Ohno** (Mana **Iwabuchi** 66) (Rumi **Utsugi** 116), Mizuho **Sakaguchi•**, Homare **Sawa•**(c), Aya **Miyama** - Kozue **Ando**, Yuki **Nagasato** (Karina **Maruyama** 46). Tr: Norio **Sasaki**

Leverkusen. 9-07-2011, 18:00, 26 395, Palmqvist SWE	
England	**1 3p**
	Jill **Scott** [59]

Karen **Bardsley•** - Alex **Scott** (Claire **Rafferty** 81), Rachel **Unitt** (Steph **Houghton** 81), Faye **White**(c), Casey **Stoney** - Jill **Scott•**, Fara **Williams•** - Rachel **Yankey** (Anita **Asante** 84), Kelly **Smith**, Ellen **White•**, Karen **Carney**. Tr: Hope **Powell**

France	**1 4p**
	Elise **Bussaglia** [88]

Celine **Deville** - Laura **Georges**, Sonia **Bompastor**, Laure **Lepailleur**, Sabrina **Viguier** - Sandrine **Soubeyrand**(c) (Elodie **Thomis** 67), Camille **Abily**, Louisa **Necib** (Sandrine **Bretigny** 79) (Eugenie **Le Sommer** 106), Elise **Bussaglia** - Gaetane **Thiney**, Marie-Laure **Delie**. Tr: Bruno **Bini**

Augsburg. 10-07-2011, 13:00, 24 605, Reyes PER	
Sweden	**3**
	Therese Sjogran [11], Lisa Dahlkvist [16], Lotta Schelin [52]

Hedvig **Lindahl** - Charlotte **Rohlin**, Annica **Svensson** (Lina **Nilsson** 92+), Sara **Thunebro**, Sara **Larsson** - Therese **Sjogran•**, Caroline **Seger**(c), Lisa **Dahlkvist** - Linda **Forsberg** (Nilla **Fischer•** 67), Lotta **Schelin**, Josefine **Oqvist** (Madelaine **Edlund** 83). Tr: Thomas **Dennerby**

Australia	**1**
	Ellyse Perry [40]

Melissa **Barbieri**(c) - Kim **Carroll**, Ellyse **Perry** (Tameka **Butt** 59), Elise **Kellond-Knight**, Servet **Uzunlar** - Heather **Garriock•**, Emily **Van Egmond** (Clare **Polkinghorne** 58), Collette **McCallum** (Sally **Shipard** 79) - Lisa **De Vanna**, Caitlin **Foord**, Kyah **Simon•**. Tr: Tom **Sermanni**

Dresden. 10-07-2011, 17:30, 25 598, Melksham AUS	
Brazil	**2 3p**
	Marta 2 [68p] [92]

Andreia - Daiane, Aline•(c), Erika•, Maurine•, Rosana (Francielle 85) - Ester, Formiga (Renata Costa 113), Fabiana - Marta•, Cristiane. Tr: Kleiton Lima

USA	**2 5p**
	Daiane OG [2], Abby Wambach [122+]

Hope **Solo•** - Ali **Krieger**, Rachel **Buehler♦65**, Christie **Rampone**(c), Amy **LePeilbet** - Heather **O'Reilly** (Tobin **Heath** 108), Carli **Lloyd•**, Shannon **Boxx•**, Amy **Rodriguez** (Alex **Morgan** 72) - Lauren **Cheney** (Megan **Rapinoe•** 55), Abby **Wambach**. Tr: Pia **Sundhage**

SEMI-FINALS

Frankfurt/Main. 13-07-2011, 20:45, 45 434, Chenard CAN	
Japan	**3**
	Nahomi Kawasumi 2 [19] [64], Homare Sawa [60]

Ayumi **Kaihori** - Yukari **Kinga**, Azusa **Iwashimizu**, Saki **Kumagai**, Aya **Sameshima** - Shinobu **Ohno** (Megumi **Takase** 86), Mizuho **Sakaguchi**, Homare **Sawa**(c), Aya **Miyama** (Megumi **Kamionobe** 89) - Kozue **Ando**, Nahomi **Kawasumi** (Yuki **Nagasato** 74). Tr: Norio **Sasaki**

Sweden	**1**
	Josefine Oqvist [10]

Hedvig **Lindahl** - Charlotte **Rohlin**(c), Annica **Svensson•**, Sara **Thunebro**, Sara **Larsson** - Therese **Sjogran**, Marie **Hammarstrom** (Jessica **Landstrom** 69), Lisa **Dahlkvist** - Linda **Forsberg** (Sofia **Jakobsson** 65), Lotta **Schelin**, Josefine **Oqvist** (Antonia **Goransson** 75). Tr: Thomas **Dennerby**

Mönchengladbach. 13-07-2011, 18:00, 25 676, Heikkinen FIN	
France	**1**
	Sonia Bompastor [55]

Berangere **Sapowicz** - Laura **Georges**, Sonia **Bompasteur**, Ophelie **Meilleroux**, Laure **Lepailleur** - Sandrine **Soubeyrand**(c) (Elodie **Thomis•** 78), Camille **Abily**, Louisa **Necib**, Elise **Bussaglia** - Gaetane **Thiney**, Marie-Laure **Delie** (Eugenie **Le Sommer** 46). Tr: Bruno **Bini**

USA	**3**
	Lauren Cheney [9], Abby Wambach [79], Alex Morgan [82]

Hope **Solo** - Ali **Krieger**, Becky **Sauerbrunn**, Christie **Rampone**(c), Amy **LePeilbet** - Heather **O'Reilly** (Tobin **Heath** 87), Carli **Lloyd** (Megan **Rapinoe** 65), Shannon **Boxx**, Amy **Rodriguez** (Alex **Morgan** 56) - Lauren **Cheney**, Abby **Wambach**. Tr: Pia **Sundhage**

THIRD PLACE PLAY-OFF

Sinsheim. 16-07-2011, 17:30, 25 475, Seitz USA	
Sweden	**2**
	Lotta Schelin [29], Marie Hammarstrom [82]

Hedvig **Lindahl** - Charlotte **Rohlin**, Annica **Svensson**, Sara **Thunebro**, Sara **Larsson** - Therese **Sjogran**, Nilla **Fischer**(c) (Linda **Sembrant** 73), Lisa **Dahlkvist** - Linda **Forsberg** (Marie **Hammarstrom** 62), Lotta **Schelin**, Josefine **Oqvist♦68**. Tr: Thomas **Dennerby**

France	**1**
	Elodie Thomas [56]

Berangere **Sapowicz** (Celine **Deville** 32) - Wendie **Renard**, Laura **Georges**, Corine **Franco** (Caroline **Pizzala** 84), Sonia **Bompastor** - Sandrine **Soubeyrand**(c), Camille **Abily**, Louisa **Necib** (Elodie **Thomis** 32), Eugenie **Le Sommer**, Elise **Bussaglia** - Gaetane **Thiney**. Tr: Bruno **Bini**

FIFA Women's World Cup Final 2011	Frankfurt/Main	Sunday 17-07-2011
Kick-off: 20:45	Partly Cloudy　　16°	Attendance: 48817

JAPAN　　2　2　　USA

Aya Miyama [81], Homare Sawa [117]　　**3 P S O 1**　　Alex Morgan [69], Abby Wambach [104]

JAPAN
Navy blue shirts with white trimmings, Navy blue shorts, Navy blue socks
Tr: Norio Sasaki

Ayumi Kaihori †

Yukari Kinga　Azusa Iwashimizu [121+]　Saki Kumagai　Aya Sameshima

Mizuho Sakaguchi　　Homare Sawa (c)

[66] Shinobu Ohno
[119] Karina Maruyama
Mana Iwabuchi

Aya Miyama [97]

[66] Kozu Ando
Yuki Nagasato　　Nahomi Kawasumi

Abby Wambach

[46] Lauren Cheney
Alex Morgan

[114] Megan Rapinoe　Shannon Boxx　Carli Lloyd　Heather O'Reilly
Tobin Heath

Amy LePeilbet　Christie Rampone (c)　Rachel Buehler　Ali Kreiger

Hope Solo

Tr: Pia Sundhage SWE
White shirts with blue trimmings, White shorts, White socks

USA

MATCH STATS

JPN		USA
14	Shots	27
6	Shots on goal	5
11	Fouls committed	10
4	Corner kicks	8
2	Caught offside	3
53%	Possession	47%

MATCH OFFICIALS
REFEREE
Bibiana Steinhaus GER
ASSISTANTS
Marina Wozniak GER
Katrin Rafalski GER
4TH OFFICIAL
Jenny Palmqvist SWE

(C) Captain
† Player of the Match

PENALTIES

JPN			USA	
		Boxx	✗	1
✓	Miyama			
		Lloyd	✗	2
✗ 1	Nagasato.Y			
		Heath	✗	1
✓	Sakaguchi			
		Wambach	✓	
✓	Kumagai			

1 Saved, 2 Missed

We were quite rigid at times and we didn't always play our game. Our defence was very focused and organised, very much like the game against Germany. We didn't really get into the game 100 per cent like we would have liked to. There simply wasn't enough space to play passes. Considering the current situation in Japan I would like to take this opportunity to thank everyone for their support, and in particular for the support we received from Germany.
Norio Sasaki

We gave the crowd a good game today. It will be a final to remember and credit to both teams. I am very happy with how we played in the first half. Playing in the final at the highest level, you have to take your chances, and we weren't sharp enough with the two goals conceded. There is something to be said about the way Japan play. They are comfortable with the ball even when they are behind and that kind of thing is good for women's football.
Pia Sundhage

FIFA U-17 WORLD CUP
MEXICO 2011

FIFA U-17 WORLD CUP MEXICO 2011

First round groups		Round of 16		Quarter-finals		Semi-finals		Final	
Group A	Pts								
Mexico	9	Mexico	2						
Congo	4	Panama	0						
Korea DPR	2			Mexico	2				
Netherlands	1			France	1				
Group B	Pts	Côte d'Ivoire	2						
Japan	7	France	3						
France	5					Mexico	3		
Argentina	3					Germany	2		
Jamaica	1	England	1 4p						
Group C	Pts	Argentina	1 2p						
England	7			England	2				
Uruguay	6			Germany	3				
Canada	2	USA	0						
Rwanda	1	Germany	4						
								Mexico	2
Group D	Pts							Uruguay	0
Uzbekistan	6	Brazil	2						
USA	4	Ecuador	0						
New Zealand	4			Brazil	3				
Czech Republic	3			Japan	2				
Group E	Pts	New Zealand	0						
Germany	9	Japan	6						
Ecuador	6					Brazil	0		
Panama	3					Uruguay	3		
Burkina Faso	0	Uzbekistan	4						
Group F	Pts	Australia	0						
Brazil	7			Uzbekistan	0				
Côte d'Ivoire	4			Uruguay	2			3rd place play-off	
Australia	4	Congo	1					Germany	4
Denmark	1	Uruguay	2					Brazil	3

Top scorers: **9** - Souleymane Coulibaly CIV • **6** - Samed Yesil GER • **5** - Adryan; Ademilson BRA & Yassine Benzia FRA
adidas Golden Ball: Julio Gomez MEX
adidas Golden Boot: Souleymane Coulibaly CIV
adidas Golden Glove: Jonathan Cubero URU
FIFA Fair Play Award: Japan

GROUP A	PL	W	D	L	F	A	PTS	CGO	PRK	NED
1 Mexico	3	3	0	0	8	4	9	2-1	3-1	3-2
2 Congo	3	1	1	1	3	3	4		1-1	1-0
3 Korea DPR	3	0	2	1	3	5	2			1-1
4 Netherlands	3	0	1	2	3	5	1			

Estadio Morelos, Morelia
18-06-2011, 18:00, 34 312, Perea PAN

Congo 1

Justalain Kounkou [53]

Chill Ngakosso - Cisse **Bassoumba**, Stevy **Samba**, Ramaric **Etou**, Gloire **Mayanith**• (c), Charvely **Mabiala**, Ange **Sitou**, Hardy **Binguila**, Justalain **Kounkou** (Amour **Loussoukou** 78), Bel **Epako** (Kader **Bidimbou** 65), Mavis **Tchibota** (Gildas **Mpassi** 76). Tr: Eddie **Hudanski**

Netherlands 0

Boy de **Jong** - Daan **Disveld**• (c), Terence **Kongolo**, Karim **Rekik**, Jetro **Willems**, Kyle **Ebecilio**, Yassine **Ayoub** (Nathan **Ake** 72), Tonny **Trindade de Vilhena**, Anass **Achahbar**, Memphis **Depay** (Thom **Haye** 82), Danzell **Gravenberch** (Gyliano **van Velzen** 60). Tr: Albert **Stuivenberg**

Estadio Morelos, Morelia
18-06-2011, 15:00, 34 312, Studer SUI

Mexico 3

Carlos Fierro [37], Jong Kwang Sok OG [68], Giovani Casillas [86]

Richard **Sanchez** - Francisco **Flores**, Carlos **Guzman**, Antonio **Briseno** (c), Jorge **Caballero** (Felipe **Sifuentes** 87), Julio **Gomez** (Jose **Tostado** 74), Kevin **Escamilla**, Jorge **Espericueta**, Arturo **Gonzalez** (Giovani **Casillas** 61), Carlos **Fierro**, Marco **Bueno**. Tr: Raul **Gutierrez**

Korea DPR 1

Jo Kwang [3]

Cha Jong **Hun**◆54 - Jong Kwang **Sok**, **Choe** Chol **Ryong**, **Jong** Il **Hyok**, **Kim** Chol **Bom**, **Kang** Nam **Gwon** (c) (**Kwon** Chung **Hyok** 66), **Ju** Jong **Chol**, **Pak** Myong **Song** (**An** Kang **Chol** 57), **Choe** Myong **Song**•, **Jang** Ok **Chol**, **Jo** Kwang (**O** Jin **Song** 53). Tr: **An** Ye **Gun**

Estadio Morelos, Morelia
21-06-2011, 15:00, 7500, Alioum CMR

Korea DPR 1

Kang Nam Gwon [48]

An Kang **Chol** - **Jong** Kwang **Sok**•, **Choe** Chol **Ryong**, **Jong** Il **Hyok**, **Kim** Chol **Bom**, **Kang** Nam **Gwon** • (c), **Ju** Jong **Chol**, **Pak** Myong **Song** (**Kwon** Chung **Hyok** 78), **Choe** Myong **Song**, **Jang** Ok **Chol** (**O** Jin **Song** 82), **So** Jong **Hyok** (**Jo** Kwang 50). Tr: **An** Ye **Gun**

Netherlands 1

Danzell Gravenberch [75]

Boy de **Jong** - Daan **Disveld** (Nathan **Ake** 90), Terence **Kongolo**, Karim **Rekik**, Jetro **Willems**, Kyle **Ebecilio**, Yassine **Ayoub** (Adnan **Bajic** 60), Tonny **Trindade de Vilhena**, Anass **Achahbar**, Memphis **Depay** (Jordi **Bitter** 70), Danzell **Gravenberch**. Tr: Albert **Stuivenberg**

Estadio Morelos, Morelia
21-06-2011, 18:00, 25 710, Chapron FRA

Mexico 2

Jorge Espericueta [40], Julio Gomez [85]

Richard **Sanchez** - Francisco **Flores** (Jose **Tostado** 80), Carlos **Guzman**•, Antonio **Briseno** (c), Jorge **Caballero**, Julio **Gomez**, Kevin **Escamilla** (Giovani **Casillas** 72), Jorge **Espericueta**, Arturo **Gonzalez** (Marcelo **Gracia** 46), Carlos **Fierro**, Marco **Bueno**•. Tr: Raul **Gutierrez**

Congo 1

Bel Epako [73]

Chill **Ngakosso** - Cisse **Bassoumba**◆52, Stevy **Samba**, Ramaric **Etou**•, Gloire **Mayanith**•(c), Charvely **Mabiala**, Tierry **Kouyikou** (Gildas **Mpassi** 71◆78), Ange **Sitou** (Kader **Bidimbou**• 81), Hardy **Binguila**•, Bel **Epako**, Mavis **Tchibota** (Melvan **Lekandza** 55). Tr: Eddie **Hudanski**

Estadio Morelos, Morelia
24-06-2011, 18:00, 14 206, Kralovec CZE

Korea DPR 1

Ju Jong Chol [14]

Cha Jong **Hun** - Jong Kwang **Sok**, **Choe** Chol **Ryong**, **Jong** Il **Hyok**•, **Kim** Chol **Bom**, **Kang** Nam **Gwon** (c), **Ju** Jong **Chol**, **Pak** Myong **Song** (**Kwon** Chung **Hyok**• 76), **Choe** Myong **Song**, **Jang** Ok **Chol**• (**Jo** Kwang 64), **So** Jong **Hyok** (**O** Jin **Song** 60). Tr: **An** Ye **Gun**

Congo 1

Christ Nkounkou [75]

Chill **Ngakosso** - Stevy **Samba**, Melvan **Lekandza** (Tierry **Kouyikou**• 37), Ramaric **Etou**, Charvely **Mabiala**, Ange **Sitou**•, Hardy **Binguila**, Justalain **Kounkou**, Christ **Nkounkou** (Amour **Loussoukou** 81), Bel **Epako** (c), Mavis **Tchibota** (Elvia **Ipamy** 74). Tr: Eddie **Hudanski**

Universitario, Monterrey
24-06-2011, 18:00, 29 000, Carrillo PER

Mexico 3

Giovani Casillas [29], Carlos Fierro [43], Arturo Gonzalez [94+]

Richard **Sanchez** - Francisco **Flores**, Carlos **Guzman**, Antonio **Briseno**• (c), Jorge **Caballero**, Julio **Gomez**, Jorge **Espericueta**, Enrique **Flores** (Jose **Tostado** 63), Giovani **Casillas** (Arturo **Gonzalez** 69), Carlos **Fierro**, Marco **Bueno** (Daniel **Hernandez** 58). Tr: Raul **Gutierrez**

Netherlands 2

Memphis Depay [47], Kyle Ebecilio [63]

Boy de **Jong** - Terence **Kongolo**, Karim **Rekik**•, Jetro **Willems**, Menno **Koch**•, Kyle **Ebecilio**•, Yassine **Ayoub** (Nathan **Ake** 46), Tonny **Trindade de Vilhena**, Anass **Achahbar**, Memphis **Depay** (Thom **Haye** 84), Danzell **Gravenberch** (Jordi **Bitter** 32). Tr: Albert **Stuivenberg**

GROUP B	PL	W	D	L	F	A	PTS	FRA	ARG	JAM
1 Japan	3	2	1	0	5	2	7	1-1	3-1	1-0
2 France	3	1	2	0	5	2	5		3-0	1-1
3 Argentina	3	1	0	2	3	7	3			2-1
4 Jamaica	3	0	1	2	2	4	1			

Universitario, Monterrey
18-06-2011, 18:00, 16 200, Garcia MEX

France 3

Yassine Benzia 2 [35] [45], Sebastien Haller [38]

Lionel **Mpasi Nzau** - Jordan **Ikoko**, Benjamin **Mendy**•, Raphael **Calvet** (c), Kurt **Zouma**, Adrien **Tameze**, Soualiho **Meite**, Abdallah **Yaisien** (Timoue **Bakayoko** 86), Lenny **Nangis**, Sebastien **Haller** (Jordan **Nkusu** 77), Yassine **Benzia** (Jordan **Vercleyen** 77). Tr: Patrick **Gonfalone**

Argentina 0

Nicolas **Sequeira** - Edgardo **Baez** (c), Marcos **Pinto**, Enzo **Beloso**, Maximiliano **Padilla**, Gaspar **Iniguez**, Brian **Ferreira** (Martin **Benitez** 65), Pablo **Carreras**, Agustin **Allione** (Jonathan **Silva** 55), Lucas **Ocampos**, Lucas **Pugh** (Matias **Montero** 46). Tr: Oscar **Garre**

Universitario, Monterrey
18-06-2011, 15:00, 8000, Alioum CMR

Japan 1

Masaya Matsumoto [61]

Kosuke **Nakamura** - Takuya **Iwanami** (c), Naomichi **Ueda**, Sei **Muroya**, Fumiya **Hayakawa**, Reo **Mochizuki**, Hideki **Ishige**, Hideyuki **Nozawa**, Hiroki **Akino** (Kazuki **Fukai** 71), Ryuga **Suzuki** (Musashi **Suzuki** 46), Shoya **Nakajima**• (Masaya **Matsumoto** 56). Tr: Hirofumi **Yoshitake**

Jamaica 0

Nico **Campbell** - Oshane **Jenkins**, Kemo **Wallace**, Alvas **Powell**•, Romario **Williams**, Zhelano **Barnes**, Omar **Holness** (c) (Anthony **Walker** 57), Andre **Lewis**, Shawn-Claud **Lawson** (Cardel **Benbow** 63), Jason **Wright**, Jevani **Brown** (Patrick **Palmer** 46). Tr: Wendell **Downswell**

Universitario, Monterrey
21-06-2011, 15:00, 4827, Carrillo PER

Japan 1

Hideki Ishige [49p]

Kosuke **Nakamura** - Naoki **Kawaguchi**, Takuya **Iwanami** (c), Naomichi **Ueda**, Sei **Muroya**•, Fumiya **Hayakawa**, Kazuki **Fukai**, Reo **Mochizuki**•, Hideki **Ishige**, Takuya **Kida** (Takumi **Minamino** 46), Musashi **Suzuki** (Masaya **Matsumoto** 74). Tr: Hirofumi **Yoshitake**

France 1

Abdallah Yaisien [24]

Lionel **Mpasi Nzau** - Raphael **Calvet** (c), Kurt **Zouma**, Antoine **Conte** (Jordan **Ikoko** 70), Aymeric **Laporte**, Adrien **Tameze**, Adam **Nkusu**• (Yassine **Benzia**• 63), Abdallah **Yaisien**, Tiemoue **Bakayoko**, Lenny **Nangis**, Sebastien **Haller** (Soualiho **Meite** 46). Tr: Patrick **Gonfalone**

Universitario, Monterrey
21-06-2011, 18:00, 9150, Kralovec CZE

Jamaica 1
Zhelano Barnes [89]

Nico Campbell - Oshane Jenkins•, Kemo Wallace•, Alvas Powell•, Romario Williams, Patrick Palmer, Zhelano Barnes•, Omar Holness (c), Andre Lewis (Cardel Benbow 66), Melvin Blair (Romario Jones 46), Jason Wright (Anthony Walker 69). Tr: Wendell Downswell

Argentina 2
Jonathan Silva [23], Lucas Pugh [63]

Nicolas Sequeira - Edgardo Baez (c), Enzo Beloso, Maximiliano Padilla, Alexis Zarate, Jonathan Silva•, Gaspar Iniguez•, Matias Montero, Lucas Ocampos (Pablo Carreras 91+), Lucas Vera Piris (Martin Benitez 66), Lucas Pugh (Jorge Valdez 78). Tr: Oscar Garre

---

Estadio Morelos, Morelia
24-06-2011, 15:00, 10 200, Alioum CMR

Japan 3
Daisuke Takagi [4], Naomichi Ueda [20], Hiroki Akino [74]

Ayumi Niekawa - Naoki Kawaguchi, Naomichi Ueda, Fumiya Hayakawa, Jumpei Arai (c), Daisuke Takagi (Musashi Suzuki 66), Kazuki Fukai• (Ryuga Suzuki 86), Takuya Kida, Hideyuki Nozawa (Masaya Matsumoto 46), Hiroki Akino, Takumi Minamino. Tr: Hirofumi Yoshitake

Argentina 1
Brian Ferreira [87]

Nicolas Sequeira - Edgardo Baez (c), Enzo Beloso•, Maximiliano Padilla, Alexis Zarate• (Marcos Pinto 59), Jonathan Silva•, Gaspar Iniguez, Matias Montero◆68, Lucas Ocampos, Lucas Vera Piris (Brian Ferreira 46), Lucas Pugh (Agustin Allione 72). Tr: Oscar Garre

---

Universitario, Monterrey
24-06-2011, 15:00, 7566, Martins ANG

Jamaica 1
Andre Lewis [9]

Richard Trench - Oshane Jenkins (Jason Wint 55◆79), Kemo Wallace, Quante Smith•, Romario Williams•, Zhelano Barnes, Romario Jones, Omar Holness (c), Andre Lewis, Jason Wright (Cardel Benbow 59), Anthony Walker (Troy Moo Penn 68). Tr: Wendell Downswell

France 1
Yassine Benzia [58]

Quentin Beunardeau - Jordan Ikoko, Benjamin Mendy•, Raphael Calvet• (c), Aymeric Laporte, Pierre Bourdin (Abdallah Yaisien 56), Soualiho Meite (Adrien Tameze 48), Kharl Madianga, Jordan Vercleyen, Gaetan Laborde (Lenny Nangis 73), Yassine Benzia. Tr: Patrick Gonfalone

---

	GROUP C	PL	W	D	L	F	A	PTS	URU	CAN	RWA
1	England	3	2	1	0	6	2	7	2-0	2-2	2-0
2	Uruguay	3	2	0	1	4	2	6		3-0	1-0
3	Canada	3	0	2	1	2	5	2			0-0
4	Rwanda	3	0	1	2	0	3	1			

Hidalgo, Pachuca
19-06-2011, 15:00, 12 640, Hauata TAH

Rwanda 0

Marcel Nzarora - Michel Rusheshangoga•, Emery Bayisenge (c), Jean Marie Rusingizandekwe, Robert Ndatimana, Andrew Buteera, Heritier Turatsinze, Eric Nsabimana, Mwesigye Tibingana (Ibrahim Itangishaka 62), Bonfils Kabanda, Justin Mico (Sulaiman Kakira 85). Tr: Richard Tardy

England 2
Hallam Hope [68], Raheem Sterling [86]

Jordan Pickford - Jordan Cousins, Bradley Smith (Matthew Regan 73), Nathaniel Chalobah (c), Samuel Magri, John Lundstram, Raheem Sterling, Nicholas Powell, Jake Caskey (Max Clayton 77), Hallam Hope (Adam Morgan 85), Blair Turgott. Tr: John Peacock

---

Hidalgo, Pachuca
19-06-2011, 18:00, 12 699, Nikolaev RUS

Uruguay 3
Juan Cruz Mascia [52], Guillermo Mendez [85p], Elbio Alvarez [93+]

Jonathan Cubero - Emiliano Velazquez (c) (Heber Ratti 46), Gaston Silva, Gianni Rodriguez, Alejandro Furia, Leonardo Pais, Elbio Alvarez, Jim Varela (Santiago Carrera 74), Rodrigo Aguirre, Juan Cruz Mascia, Juan San Martin (Guillermo Mendez 64). Tr: Fabian Coito

Canada 0

Maxime Crepeau (Quillan Roberts 89) - Adam Polakiewicz•, Daniel Stanese, Parker Seymour, Luca Gasparotto, Samuel Piette (Matteo Pasquotti 76), Bryce Alderson (c), Yassin Essa (Omari Morris 67), Michael Petrasso, Sadi Jalali, Keven Aleman. Tr: Sean Fleming

---

Hidalgo, Pachuca
22-06-2011, 15:00, 12 999, Moen NOR

Uruguay 1
Leonardo Pais [95+]

Jonathan Cubero - Gaston Silva (c), Santiago Carrera, Gianni Rodriguez, Alejandro Furia, Leonardo Pais, Elbio Alvarez (Sergio Cortelezzi 77), Jim Varela, Rodrigo Aguirre (Maximiliano Moreira 63), Juan Cruz Mascia•, Juan San Martin. Tr: Fabian Coito

Rwanda 0

Marcel Nzarora - Michel Rusheshangoga•, Emery Bayisenge• (c), Faustin Usengimana (Heritier Turatsinze 22), Jean Marie Rusingizandekwe, Robert Ndatimana, Andrew Buteera• (Alfred Mugabo 74), Eric Nsabimana, Mwesigye Tibingana, Bonfils Kabanda, Justin Mico. Tr: Richard Tardy

---

Hidalgo, Pachuca
22-06-2011, 18:00, 17 882, Ponce ECU

Canada 2
Sadi Jalali [50], Quillan Roberts [87]

Quillan Roberts - Adam Polakiewicz, Daniel Stanese, Parker Seymour, Luca Gasparotto, Samuel Piette (Sergio Camargo 85), Bryce Alderson (c) (Matteo Pasquotti 86), Yassin Essa, Michael Petrasso (Christopher Nanco 72), Sadi Jalali, Keven Aleman. Tr: Sean Fleming

England 2
Adam Morgan [46], Blair Turgott [77]

Jordan Pickford - Jordan Cousins, Nathaniel Chalobah (c), Samuel Magri, Matthew Regan, John Lundstram (Blair Turgott 70), Raheem Sterling, Nicholas Powell (Max Clayton 59), Jake Caskey, Adam Morgan, Nathan Redmond (Jack Dunn 81). Tr: John Peacock

---

Nuevo Estadio Corona, Torreon
25-06-2011, 15:00, 11 410, Albadwawi UAE

Uruguay 0

Jonathan Cubero - Emiliano Velazquez (c), Gaston Silva, Gianni Rodriguez, Alejandro Furia, Heber Ratti, Leonardo Pais (Maximiliano Moreira 63), Guillermo Mendez (Rodrigo Aguirre 76), Sebastian Canobra, Sergio Cortelezzi, Juan San Martin (Elbio Alvarez 46). Tr: Fabian Coito

England 2
Nathaniel Chalobah [45], Max Clayton [58]

Jordan Pickford - Jordan Cousins, Bradley Smith•, Nathaniel Chalobah (c), Samuel Magri, Adam Jackson• 53), Nicholas Powell (Jack Dunn 71), Jake Caskey• (George Evans 53), Hallam Hope•, Max Clayton, Alex Henshall, Blair Turgott. Tr: John Peacock

---

Hidalgo, Pachuca
25-06-2011, 15:00, 5803, Chapron FRA

Canada 0

Quillan Roberts - Adam Polakiewicz, Ismail Benomar, Parker Seymour, Luca Gasparotto, Samuel Piette, Bryce Alderson (c) (Sergio Camargo 82), Yassin Essa, Michael Petrasso (Christopher Nanco 59), Sadi Jalali (Jay Chapman 70), Keven Aleman•. Tr: Sean Fleming

Rwanda 0

Marcel Nzarora - Eugene Habyarimana, Emery Bayisenge• (c), Jean Marie Rusingizandekwe, Robert Ndatimana, Andrew Buteera, Heritier Turatsinze, Eric Nsabimana, Mwesigye Tibingana (Janvier Benedata 83), Bonfils Kabanda (Alfred Mugabo 77), Justin Mico (Farouk Ruhinda 68). Tr: Richard Tardy

GROUP D	PL	W	D	L	F	A	PTS	USA	NZL	CZE
1 Uzbekistan	3	2	0	1	5	6	6	2-1	1-4	2-1
2 USA	3	1	1	1	4	2	4		0-0	3-0
3 New Zealand	3	1	1	1	4	2	4			0-1
4 Czech Republic	3	1	0	2	2	5	3			

Nuevo Estadio Corona, Torreon
19-06-2011, 15:00, 7561, Martins ANG

Uzbekistan 1

Timur Khakimov [39]

Ganisher **Kholmurodov**• - Mirzamurod Jurabaev, Ravshanjon **Haydarov**, Asiljon **Mansurov**, Javlon **Mirabdullaev** (c), Azizbek **Muratov**, Sardor **Sabirkhodjaev** (Muhsinjon **Ubaydullaev** 82), Kholmurod **Kholmurodov** (Davlatbek **Yarbekov** 57), Bobir **Davlatov**, Timur **Khakimov** (Nodirhon **Kamolov** 83), Zabikhillo **Urinboev**. Tr: Aleksey **Evstafeev**

New Zealand 4

Stephen Carmichael 3 [10 36 53], Jordan Vale [87]

Scott **Basalaj** - Harshae **Raniga**, Reece **Lambert**, Luke **Adams** (c), Bill **Tuiloma** (Kip **Colvey** 77), Jordan **Vale**, Rhys **Jordan**•, Tim **Payne**, Cameron **Howieson** (Calvin **Opperman**• 74), Jesse **Edge**, Stephen **Carmichael** (James **Debenham** 67). Tr: Aaron **McFarland**

Nuevo Estadio Corona, Torreon
22-06-2011, 18:00, 10 105, Garcia MEX

Czech Republic 1

Lukas Julis [28]

Lukas **Zima** - Ondrej **Karafiat**, Lubos **Adamec**•, Michael **Luftner**, Jan **Sterba**• (c), Ales **Cermak** (Michal **Travnik** 95+), Jindrich **Kadula**•, Nikolas **Salasovic**, Marek **Strada** (Petr **Nerad** 82), Lukas **Julis**, Daniel **Cerny** (Patrik **Svoboda** 59). Tr: Josef **Csaplar**

New Zealand 0

Scott **Basalaj** - Harshae **Raniga**, Reece **Lambert**, Luke **Adams** (c), Bill **Tuiloma**, Jordan **Vale** (Ryan **Howlett** 81), Rhys **Jordan**, Tim **Payne**, Cameron **Howieson**• (James **Debenham** 77), Jesse **Edge** (Harley **Tahau** 84), Stephen **Carmichael**. Tr: Aaron **McFarland**

Nuevo Estadio Corona, Torreon
19-06-2011, 18:00, 15 083, Abal ARG

USA 3

Alejandro Guido [5], Esteban Rodriguez [51], Alfred Koroma [89]

Kendall **McIntosh** - Zachary **Carroll**, Joseph **Amon**, Mobi **Fehr**, Kellyn **Acosta**, Matthew **Dunn**, Esteban **Rodriguez**, Alejandro **Guido** (Tarik **Salkicic**• 74), Marc **Pelosi** (c), Mario **Rodriguez** (Alfred **Koroma** 87), Paul **Arriola** (Nico **Melo** 90). Tr: Wilmer **Cabrera**

Czech Republic 0

Lukas **Zima** - Ondrej **Karafiat**, Jan **Filip**, Michael **Luftner**, Lubos **Adamec** (c), Ales **Cermak** 54), Ales **Cermak**, Nikolas **Salasovic** (Michal **Travnik** 71), Dominik **Masek** (Jindrich **Kadula** 60), Lukas **Julis**, Patrik **Svoboda**. Tr: Josef **Csaplar**

Hidalgo, Pachuca
25-06-2011, 18:00, 8556, Nijhuis NED

USA 0

Kendall **McIntosh** - Zachary **Carroll**, Joseph **Amon**, Mobi **Fehr**, Kellyn **Acosta**, Matthew **Dunn**, Esteban **Rodriguez**, Alejandro **Guido**, Marc **Pelosi**(c)•••68, Alfred **Koroma**, Mario **Rodriguez** (Alessandro **Mion** 87). Tr: Wilmer **Cabrera**

New Zealand 0

Scott **Basalaj** - Harshae **Raniga**, Reece **Lambert**, Luke **Adams** (c), Bill **Tuiloma**, Jordan **Vale**•, Rhys **Jordan**, Tim **Payne**, Cameron **Howieson**• (James **Debenham** 54), Jesse **Edge** (Cameron **Martin** 87), Stephen **Carmichael**. Tr: Aaron **McFarland**

Nuevo Estadio Corona, Torreon
22-06-2011, 15:00, 4133, Nikolaev RUS

USA 1

Alfred Koroma [47]

Kendall **McIntosh** - Zachary **Carroll**•, Joseph **Amon**• (Nathan **Smith** 46), Mobi **Fehr**•, Kellyn **Acosta**, Matthew **Dunn**, Esteban **Rodriguez** (Alfred **Koroma** 46), Alejandro **Guido** (Nico **Melo** 82), Marc **Pelosi** (c), Mario **Rodriguez**, Paul **Arriola**. Tr: Wilmer **Cabrera**

Uzbekistan 2

Bobir Davlatov [13], Abbosbek Makhstaliev [54p]

Ganisher **Kholmurodov** - Sardor **Rakhmanov**, Ravshanjon **Haydarov** (Mirzamurod **Jurabaev** 90), Asiljon **Mansurov**, Javlon **Mirabdullaev** (c), Abbosbek **Makhstaliev**, Azizbek **Muratov**, Sardor **Sabirkhodjaev**, Kholmurod **Kholmurodov** (Davlatbek **Yarbekov** 60), Bobir **Davlatov**, Timur **Khakimov**• (Muhsinjon **Ubaydullaev** 82). Tr: Aleksey **Evstafeev**

Nuevo Estadio Corona, Torreon
25-06-2011, 18:00, 14 673, Bogle JAM

Czech Republic 1

Lukas Julis [23p]

Lukas **Zima** - Ondrej **Karafiat**, Lubos **Adamec**, Michael **Luftner**, Dominik **Spavelko**• (Petr **Nerad** 56), Jindrich **Kadula**, Nikolas **Salasovic** (c), Marek **Strada** (Ales **Cermak** 46), Michal **Travnik** (Ales **Cermak** 46), Lukas **Julis**, Daniel **Cerny** (Patrik **Svoboda** 66). Tr: Josef **Csaplar**

Uzbekistan 2

Timur Khakimov [44], Abbosbek Makhstaliev [73]

Ganisher **Kholmurodov** - Sardor **Rakhmanov**, Asiljon **Mansurov**, Javlon **Mirabdullaev**• (c), Abbosbek **Makhstaliev**, Azizbek **Muratov** (Zabikhillo **Urinboev** 84), Sardor **Sabirkhodjaev**, Kholmurod **Kholmurodov** (Davlatbek **Yarbekov** 71), Bobir **Davlatov**, Muhsinjon **Ubaydullaev**, Timur **Khakimov** (Jasurbek **Khakimov** 92+). Tr: Aleksey **Evstafeev**

GROUP E	PL	W	D	L	F	A	PTS	ECU	PAN	BFA
1 Germany	3	3	0	0	11	1	9	6-1	2-0	3-0
2 Ecuador	3	2	0	1	5	7	6		2-1	2-0
3 Panama	3	1	0	2	2	4	3			1-0
4 Burkina Faso	3	0	0	3	0	6	0			

Corregidora, Queretaro
20-06-2011, 15:00, 23 500, Bonilla SLV

Germany 6

Samed Yesil 2 [31 69], Climo Rocker [54], Levant Aycicek [61], Marvin Ducksch [85], Okan Aydin [90]

Odisseas **Vlachodimos** - Mitchell **Weiser**, Cimo **Rocker**, Koray **Gunter**, Nico **Perrey**, Robin **Yalcin**, Emre **Can** (c), Levent **Aycicek** (Sven **Mende** 66), Mirco **Born** (Kaan **Ayhan** 40), Samed **Yesil**• (Marvin **Ducksch** 73), Okan **Aydin**. Tr: Steffen **Freund**

Ecuador 1

Carlos Gruezo [51]

Walter **Chavez** - Jordan **Jaime**, Ridder **Alcivar** (c), Luis **Canga**, Cristian **Ramirez**, Junior **Sornoza**, Eddy **Corozo**, Jose **Cevallos** (Dennys **Hurtado** 66), Jonny **Uchuari**, Luis **Batioja** (Esteban **Troya** 64), Carlos **Gruezo**. Tr: Javier **Rodriguez**

Corregidora, Queretaro
20-06-2011, 18:00, 25 167, Nijhuis NED

Burkina Faso 0

Seni **Ouedraogo** - Ismael **Bande**•, Sounkalo **Sanou** (c), Abdou **Kabre**, Issouf **Paro**, Aziz **Kabore**•, Faical **Ouedraogo**, Abdoul **Kabre**, Ibrahim **Ilie** (Sounkalo **Sanou**• 46), Faical **Ouedraogo** (c) (Ben **Zerbo** 67♦82), Romaric **Pitroipa**, Yaya **Dambo**••♦27, Zoniou **Sana**. Tr: Rui **Pereira**

Panama 1

Jorman Aguilar [22]

Ivan **Picart** - Jordy **Melendez**, Roberto **Chen** (c), Francisco **Narbon**, Alexander **Goot**•, Dario **Wright**, Bryan **Santamaria** (Aldair **Paredes** 75), Alexander **Gonzalez**, Omar **Browne**, Jorman **Aguilar** (Jose **Maughn** 91+), Alfredo **Stephens** (Romario **Piggott** 95+). Tr: Jorge **Dely Valdes**

Corregidora, Queretaro
23-06-2011, 15:00, 14 603, Delgadillo MEX

Burkina Faso 0

Seni **Ouedraogo** - Ismailia **Zoungrana** (Ismael **Bande** 67), Romaric **Banaba**, Abdou **Kabre**, Issouf **Paro**•, Aziz **Kabore**•, Ibrahim **Ilie**• (Sounkalo **Sanou**• 46), Faical **Ouedraogo** (c) (Ben **Zerbo** 67♦82), Romaric **Pitroipa**, Yaya **Dambo**••♦27, Zoniou **Sana**. Tr: Rui **Pereira**

Germany 1

Koray Gunter [4], Levant Aycicek [26p], Mitchell Weiser [64]

Odisseas **Vlachodimos** - Mitchell **Weiser** (Fabian **Schnellhardt** 77), Cimo **Rocker**, Koray **Gunter**•, Nico **Perrey**, Kaan **Ayhan**, Emre **Can** (c), Levent **Aycicek** (Rani **Khedira**• 68), Sven **Mende**, Samed **Yesil**, Okan **Aydin** (Marvin **Ducksch** 62). Tr: Steffen **Freund**

Corregidora, Queretaro
23-06-2011, 18:00, 18 650, Shukralla BHR

Panama   **1**
Jorman Aguilar [33]

Ivan Picart - Jordy Melendez, Roberto Chen (c), Francisco Narbon, Alonzo Goot, Dario Wright, Bryan Santamaria• (Aldair Paredes 57), Alexander Gonzalez, Omar Browne♦51, Jorman Aguilar (Romario Piggott 78), Alfredo Stephens (Juan Cedeno 67). Tr: Jorge Dely Valdes

Ecuador   **2**
Jordan Jaime [61], Jose Cevallos [82]

Walter Chavez - Jordan Jaime, Marlon Mejia, Ridder Alcivar• (c), Cristian Ramirez, Junior Sornoza (Joel Valencia 79), Jose Cevallos, Jonny Uchuari, Luis Batioja (Kevin Barzola 76), Esteban Troya (Kevin Mercado 51), Carlos Gruezo. Tr: Javier Rodriguez

---

Estadio Omnilife, Guadalajara
26-06-2011, 15:00, 15 165, Nikolaev RUS

Burkina Faso   **0**

Seni Ouedraogo - Ismael Bande, Romaric Banaba, Sounkalo Sanou (c), Issouf Paro, Ibrahim Ili•, Faical Ouedraogo, Rashade Sido (Hassim Traore 76), Abdoul Sanou (Seydou Belem 68), Romaric Pitroipa, Zaniou Sana (Ousmane Nana 59). Tr: Rui Pereira

Ecuador   **2**
Jose Cevallos [74], Kevin Mercado [76]

Darwin Cuero - Jordan Jaime, Marlon Mejia, Ridder Alcivar (c), Cristian Ramirez, Junior Sornoza (Gabriel Cortez 91+), Jose Cevallos, Kevin Mercado, Jonny Uchuari, Luis Batioja (Joel Valencia 46), Carlos Gruezo. Tr: Javier Rodriguez

---

Corregidora, Queretaro
26-06-2011, 15:00, 28 500, Hauata TAH

Panama   **0**

Ivan Picart - Joseph Vargas (Jordy Melendez 46), Jose Maughn, Roberto Chen (c), Alonzo Goot, Juan Cedeno (Dario Wright 68), Darwin Pinzon (Edson Samms 82), Bryan Santamaria, Alexander Gonzalez•, Jorman Aguilar, Alfredo Stephens•. Tr: Jorge Dely Valdes

Germany   **2**
Okan Aydin [10], Mitchell Weiser [39]

Odisseas Vlachodimos - Mitchell Weiser, Cimo Rocker, Koray Gunter (Noah Korczowski 46), Nico Perrey, Kaan Ayhan, Emre Can (c), Levent Aycicek, Sven Mende (Koray Kacinoglu 85), Samed Yesil (Nils Quaschner 68), Okan Aydin♦66. Tr: Steffen Freund

---

GROUP F	PL	W	D	L	F	A	PTS	CIV	AUS	DEN
1 Brazil	3	2	1	0	7	3	7	3-3	1-0	3-0
2 Côte d'Ivoire	3	1	1	1	8	7	4		1-2	4-2
3 Australia	3	1	1	1	3	3	4			1-1
4 Denmark	3	0	1	2	3	8	1			

Estadio Omnilife, Guadalajara
20-06-2011, 15:00, 18 845, Albadwawi UAE

Brazil   **3**
Ademilson 2 [32] [78], Wallace [57]

Charles - Wallace, Marquinhos• (c), Matheus, Emerson, Guilherme (Nathan 67), Marlon Bica, Lucas Piazon (Misael• 80), Hernani (Bruno Sabia 86), Ademilson, Adryan. Tr: Emerson Avila

Denmark   **0**

Oliver Korch - Mads Aaquist•, Frederik Holst• (c), Nicolai Johannesen, Riza Durmisi, Patrick Olsen, Christian Norgaard (Lucas Andersen 59), Vigen Christensen, Kenneth Zohore (Yurary Poulsen• 74), Viktor Fischer (Rochester Sorensen 78), Danny Amankwaa. Tr: Thomas Frank

---

Estadio Omnilife, Guadalajara
20-06-2011, 18:00, 20 728, Bogle JAM

Australia   **2**
Jesse Makarounas [51], Dylan Tombides [77]

Paul Izzo - Jake Monaco (Riley Woodcock 46), Connor Chapman (c), Tom King, Corey Brown, Yianni Perkatis• (Milos Degenek 67), Mitch Cooper, Jacob Melling, Hernan Espindola (Teeboy Kamara 65), Dylan Tombides, Jesse Makarounas. Tr: Jan Versleijen

Côte d'Ivoire   **1**
Souleymane Coulibaly [18]

Yored Konate - Mory Kone, Jean Thome (c), Mehoue Traore, Jean-Eudes Aholou (Guy Bedi 78), Daniel Soungole, Victorien Angban, Lionel Lago (Jean Kouassi 78), Drissa Diarrassouba, Ibrahim Coulibaly, Souleymane Coulibaly. Tr: Alain Gouamene

---

Estadio Omnilife, Guadalajara
23-06-2011, 15:00, 21 159, Studer SUI

Australia   **0**

Paul Izzo - Connor Chapman (c), Tom King, Corey Brown, Riley Woodcock, Yianni Perkatis♦36 (Milos Degenek 66), Mitch Cooper, Jacob Melling•, Hernan Espindola (Mitchell Oxborrow 66), Dylan Tombides, Jesse Makarounas (Stefan Mauk 83). Tr: Jan Versleijen

Brazil   **1**
Adryan [76]

Charles - Wallace, Marquinhos (c), Matheus•, Emerson, Guilherme (Nathan• 60), Marlon Bica, Lucas Piazon•, Hernani (Misael 60), Ademilson (Wellington 89), Adryan. Tr: Emerson Avila

---

Estadio Omnilife, Guadalajara
23-06-2011, 18:00, 22 126, Bonilla SLV

Côte d'Ivoire   **4**
Souleymane Coulibaly 4 [23] [37] [41p] [69]

Yored Konate - Mory Kone, Ibrahima Bah, Jean Thome (c), Jean-Eudes Aholou, Daniel Soungole, Victorien Angban, Lionel Lago (Jean Kouassi 58), Drissa Diarrassouba (Guy Bedi 82), Ibrahim Coulibaly, Souleymane Coulibaly• (Mehoue Traore 90). Tr: Alain Gouamene

Denmark   **2**
Kenneth Zohore [9], Viktor Fischer [32]

Oliver Korch• - Mads Aaquist, Frederik Holst (c), Nicolai Johannesen, Riza Durmisi•, Patrick Olsen• (Patrick Jensen 74), Vigen Christensen•, Lucas Andersen (Yurary Poulsen 61), Kenneth Zohore, Viktor Fischer, Danny Amankwaa (Christian Norgaard 61). Tr: Thomas Frank

---

Corregidora, Queretaro
26-06-2011, 18:00, 24 943, Garcia MEX

Côte d'Ivoire   **3**
Souleymane Coulibaly 3 [11] [33] [58]

Yored Konate - Mory Kone•, Ibrahima Bah, Jean Thome (c), Jean-Eudes Aholou, Daniel Soungole, Jean Kouassi• (Guy Bedi 70), Victorien Angban•, Drissa Diarrassouba, Ibrahim Coulibaly, Souleymane Coulibaly (Banvo Anderson 87). Tr: Alain Gouamene

Brazil   **3**
Lucas Piazon [8], Ademilson [14], Adryan [93+]

Charles - Matheus, Claudio Winck, Josue•, Jonathan, Marlon Bica• (Leo 69), Lucas Piazon, Hernani (Wallace 78), Ademilson, Adryan•, Nathan (Wellington 69). Tr: Emerson Avila

---

Estadio Omnilife, Guadalajara
27-06-2011, 10:00, 2000, Abal ARG

Australia   **1**
Luke Remington [89]

Paul Izzo• - Connor Chapman (c), Tom King, Corey Brown, Riley Woodcock, Mitch Cooper, Stefan Mauk (Luke Remington 46), Jacob Melling, Hernan Espindola (Jesse Makarounas 66), Dylan Tombides (Teeboy Kamara 89). Tr: Jan Versleijen

Denmark   **1**
Rochester Sorensen [35]

Oliver Korch - Frederik Holst (c), Nicolai Johannesen, Patrick Jensen, Jacob Barrett, Patrick Olsen (Pierre Hojbjerg 70), Vigen Christensen (Kristian Lindberg 70), Rochester Sorensen (Christian Norgaard 60), Kenneth Zohore, Viktor Fischer, Yurary Poulsen. Tr: Thomas Frank

ROUND OF 16

Hidalgo, Pachuca
30-06-2011, 18:00, 15 415, Moen NOR

Mexico   **2**

Carlos Fierro [2], Marco Bueno [89]

Richard **Sanchez** - Francisco **Flores**, Carlos **Guzman•**, Antonio **Briseno** (c), Jorge **Caballero**, Julio **Gomez**, Kevin **Escamilla•** (Jose **Tostado** 56), Jorge **Espericueta**, Arturo **Gonzalez** (Giovani **Casillas** 66), Carlos **Fierro**, Daniel **Hernandez** (Marco **Bueno** 49). Tr: Raul **Gutierrez**

Panama   **0**

Ivan **Picart** - Jordy **Melendez•**, Roberto **Chen** (c), Francisco **Narbon**, Dario **Wright** (Edson **Samms** 86), Juan **Cedeno**, Darwin **Pinzon** (Aldair **Paredes** 76), Bryan **Santamaria** (Jose **Maughn** 90), Alexander **Gonzalez**, Jorman **Aguilar**, Alfredo **Stephens**. Tr: Jorge **Dely Valdes**

Corregidora, Queretaro
30-06-2011, 18:00, 18 192, Bonilla SLV

France   **3**

Yassine Benzia 2 [37p 74], Lenny Nangis [65]

Lionel **Mpasi Nzau•** - Jordan **Ikoko**, Raphael **Calvet** (c), Kurt **Zouma**, Pierre **Bourdin** (Aymeric **Laporte** 76), Adrien **Tameze** (Tiemoue **Bakayoko** 83), Abdallah **Yaisien**, Kharl **Madianga**, Lenny **Nangis••♦86**, Sebastien **Haller** (Jordan **Vercleyen** 63), Yassine **Benzia**. Tr: Patrick **Gonfalone**

Côte d'Ivoire   **2**

Souleymane Coulibaly [3], Drissa Diarrassouba [25]

Yored **Konate** - Mory **Kone**, Ibrahima **Bah**, Jean **Thome** (c), Jean-Eudes **Aholou** (Banvo **Anderson** 86), Daniel **Soungole•**, Jean **Kouassi** (Guy **Bedi** 53), Victorien **Angban•** (Wilfried **Gnahore** 70), Drissa **Diarrassouba**, Ibrahim **Coulibaly**, Souleymane **Coulibaly**. Tr: Alain **Gouamene**

Hidalgo, Pachuca
30-06-2011, 15:00, 6807, Shukralla BHR

England   **1 4p**

Raheem Stirling [40]

Jordan **Pickford** - Jordan **Cousins**, Bradley **Smith**, Nathaniel **Chalobah** (c), Samuel **Magri**, Raheem **Sterling•** (Adam **Morgan** 81), Nicholas **Powell** (John **Lundstram** 65), Jake **Caskey**, Hallam **Hope**, Max **Clayton**, Blair **Turgott•** (Nathan **Redmond** 71). Tr: John **Peacock**

Argentina   **1 2p**

Maximiliano Padilla [12]

Bruno **Galvan** - Edgardo **Baez** (c), Marcos **Pinto••♦90**, Enzo **Beloso**, Maximiliano **Padilla**, Alexis **Zarate**, Gaspar **Iniguez•**, Brian **Ferreira•** (Lucas **Pugh** 83), Pablo **Carreras**, Agustin **Allione•**, Lucas **Ocampos**. Tr: Oscar **Garre**

Corregidora, Queretaro
30-06-2011, 15:00, 16 191, Ponce ECU

Germany   **4**

Koray Guenter [20], Mitchell Weisner [40], Samed Yesil [43], Marvin Ducksch [50]

Odisseas **Vlachodimos** - Mitchell **Weiser** (Mirco **Born** 79), Cimo **Rocker**, Koray **Gunter**, Nico **Perrey**, Robin **Yalcin**, Kaan **Ayhan**, Emre **Can** (c), Levent **Aycicek** (Fabian **Schnellhardt** 58), Samed **Yesil** (Rani **Khedira** 69), Marvin **Ducksch**. Tr: Steffen **Freund**

USA   **0**

Kendall **McIntosh** - Zachary **Carroll**, Joseph **Amon** (Nathan **Smith** 46), Mobi **Fehr**, Kellyn **Acosta**, Matthew **Dunn**, Esteban **Rodriguez**, Alejandro **Guido**, Alfred **Koroma**, Mario **Rodriguez** (Jack **McBean** 57), Paul **Arriola** (Nico **Melo** 54). Tr: Wilmer **Cabrera**

Estadio Omnilife, Guadalajara
29-06-2011, 15:00, 19 335, Kralovec CZE

Brazil   **2**

Ademilson [16], Leo [87]

Charles - **Wallace** (Claudio **Winck** 42), **Morquinhos** (c), **Matheus**, **Emerson**, **Misael**, **Marlon Bica•**, **Lucas Piazon•** (Hernani 85), **Ademilson**, **Adryan**, **Nathan•** (Leo 61). Tr: Emerson **Avila**

Ecuador   **0**

Darwin **Cuero** - Jordan **Jaime**, Marlon **Mejia**, Ridder **Alcivar** (c), Cristian **Ramirez•**, Junior **Sornoza** (Dennys **Hurtado** 74), Jose **Cevallos•**, Jonny **Uchuari**, Luis **Batioja** (Kevin **Mercado** 55), Carlos **Gruezo**, Joel **Valencia•** (Kevin **Barzola** 88). Tr: Javier **Rodriguez**

Universitario, Monterrey
29-06-2011, 18:00, 7930, Studer SUI

Japan   **6**

Hideki Ishige 2 [20 22], Fumiya Hayakawa 2 [32 80], Kip Colvey OG [42], Takumi Minamino [56]

Kosuke **Nakamura** (Shunta **Awaka** 85) - Naoki **Kawaguchi**, Takuya **Iwanami** (c), Naomichi **Ueda**, Sei **Muroya**, Fumiya **Hayakawa**, Reo **Mochizuki** (Takumi **Minamino** 44), Hideki **Ishige**, Takuya **Kida**, Hiroki **Akino**, Masaya **Matsumoto** (Musashi **Suzuki** 57). Tr: Hirofumi **Yoshitake**

New Zealand   **0**

Scott **Basalaj** - Reece **Lambert**, Luke **Adams•** (c), Bill **Tuiloma**, Jordan **Vale** (Ken **Yamamoto** 46), Kip **Colvey**, Rhys **Jordan** (Harley **Tahau** 46), Tim **Payne**, Jesse **Edge**, Stephen **Carmichael•**, Cameron **Martin**, Dylan **Stanfield** (Jesse **Edge** 74). Tr: Aaron **McFarland**

Nuevo Estadio Corona, Torreon
29-06-2011, 15:00, 8340, Carrillo PER

Uzbekistan   **4**

Abbosbek Makhstaliev [11], Timur Khakimov [40], Chapman OG [66], Davlatbek Yarbekov [89]

Ganisher **Kholmurodov** - Sardor **Rakhmanov**, Asiljon **Mansurov**, Javlon **Mirabdullaev** (c), Abbosbek **Makhstaliev** (Jasurbek **Khakimov** 84), Azizbek **Muratov**, Sardor **Sabirkhodjaev**, Kholmurod **Kholmurodov**, Bobir **Davlatov** (Davlatbek **Yarbekov•** 22), Muhsinjon **Ubaydullaev**, Timur **Khakimov** (Dior **Usmankhodjaev** 89). Tr: Aleksey **Evstafeev**

Australia   **0**

Paul **Izzo** - Jake **Monaco**, Connor **Chapman** (c), Tom **King**, Corey **Brown•**, Riley **Woodcock•** (Anthony **Proia** 55), Mitch **Cooper** (Mitchell **Oxborrow** 80), Luke **Remington** (Teeboy **Kamara** 55••♦90), Jacob **Melling**, Hernan **Espindola**, Dylan **Tombides♦59**. Tr: Jan **Versleijen**

Estadio Morelos, Morelia
29-06-2011, 18:00, 12 350, Bogle JAM

Congo   **1**

Hardy Binguila [53]

Chill **Ngakosso** - Cisse **Bassoumba**, Stevy **Samba**, Ramaric **Etou**, Gloire **Mayanith•** (c), Charvely **Mabiala**, Hardy **Binguila**, Justalain **Kounkou•** (Ange **Sitou** 71), Gildas **Mpassi•** (Mavis **Tchibota** 77), Christ **Nkounkou** (Kader **Bidimbou** 86), Bel **Epako**. Tr: Eddie **Hudanski**

Uruguay   **2**

Maximiliano Moreira [65], Gaston Silva [86]

Jonathan **Cubero** - Emiliano **Velazquez** (c), Gaston **Silva**, Maximiliano **Moreira•** (Sebastian **Canobra** 87), Gianni **Rodriguez**, Alejandro **Furia**, Leonardo **Pais**, Elbio **Alvarez**, Jim **Varela•**, Rodrigo **Aguirre•**, Santiago **Charamoni** (Guillermo **Mendez** 46). Tr: Fabian **Coito**

ROUND OF 16 PENALTIES
ENG v ARG (4-2)

	ENG		ARG
✓	Magri		
		Ocampos	✓
✓	Morgan		
		Pugh	✓
✗2	Clayton		
		Iniguez	✗1
✓	Caskey		
		Allione	✗1
✓	Chalobah		

1 = saved • 2 = missed

QUARTER-FINALS

Hidalgo, Pachuca
4-07-2011, 18:00, 21 960, Albadawai UAE

France   **1**

Jordan Ikoko [17]

Lionel **Mpasi Nzau** - Jordan **Ikoko**, Benjamin **Mendy•**, Raphael **Calvet** (c), Kurt **Zouma**, Adrien **Tameze**, Abdallah **Yaisien** (Sebastien **Haller** 12) (Coualiho **Meite** 57), Kharl **Madianga**, Jordan **Vercleyen**, Gaetan **Laborde•** (Aymeric **Laporte•** 73), Yassine **Benzia**. Tr: Patrick **Gonfalone**

Mexico   **2**

Kevin Escamilla [14], Carlos Fierro [50]

Richard **Sanchez** - Francisco **Flores•**, Antonio **Briseno** (c), Jorge **Caballero**, Julio **Gomez**, Luis **Solorio**, Kevin **Escamilla** (Jose **Tostado** 87), Jorge **Espericueta**, Giovani **Casillas** (Arturo **Gonzalez** 62), Carlos **Fierro•**, Marco **Bueno** (Marcelo **Gracia** 32). Tr: Raul **Gutierrez**

Estadio Morelos, Morelia
4-07-2011, 15:00, 16 020, Kralovec CZE

Germany   **3**

Samed Yesil 2 [7 53], Kaan Ayhan [24]

Odisseas **Vlachodimos•** - Mitchell **Weiser** (Rani **Khedira** 78), Cimo **Rocker**, Nico **Perrey•**, Robin **Yalcin**, Kaan **Ayhan** (Fabian **Schnellhardt** 86), Noah **Korczowski•**, Emre **Can** (c), Levent **Aycicek** (Sven **Mende** 45), Samed **Yesil**, Marvin **Ducksch**. Tr: Steffen **Freund**

England   **2**

Samuel Magri [67p], Hallam Hope [83]

Jordan **Pickford** - Jordan **Cousins**, Bradley **Smith•**, Nathaniel **Chalobah** (c), Samuel **Magri**, John **Lundstram•** (Jack **Dunn** 68), Raheem **Sterling**, Jake **Caskey** (Nathan **Redmond** 79), Hallam **Hope**, Max **Clayton**, Alex **Henshall** (Nicholas **Powell** 46). Tr: John **Peacock**

Corregidora, Queretaro
3-07-2011, 18:00, 30 123, Garcia MEX

Japan 2
Shoya Nakajima [77], Fumiya Hayakawa [88]

Kosuke **Nakamura** - Naoki **Kawaguchi**, Takuya
Iwanami (c), Naomichi **Ueda**, Sei **Muroya**, Fumiya
Hayakawa, Kazuki **Fukai**, Hideki **Ishige**, Takuya **Kida**
(Shoya **Nakajima** 65), Hiroki **Akino** (Masaya
Matsumoto 46), Takumi **Minamino** (Daisuke
Takagi 75). Tr: Hirofumi **Yoshitake**

Brazil 3
Leo [16], Ademilson [48], Adryan [60]

Charles - **Wallace**, **Marquinhos** (c), **Matheus**,
Emerson, **Misael**, **Guilherme** (Hernani 80), **Marlon**
Bica, **Ademilson**, **Adryan•**, **Leo** (Wellington 69).
Tr: Emerson **Avila**

Universitario, Monterrey
3-07-2011, 15:00, 11 015, Alioum CMR

Uruguay 2
Santiago Charamoni [29], Rodrigo Aguirre [64]

Jonathan **Cubero** - Emiliano **Velazquez** (c)
(Sebastian **Canobra** 20), Gaston **Silva**, Maximiliano
Moreira, Gianni **Rodriguez•**, Alejandro **Furia**,
Leonardo **Pais**, Elbio **Alvarez** (Guillermo **Mendez** 73),
Jim **Varela•**, Rodrigo **Aguirre**, Santiago **Charamoni•**
(Heber **Ratti** 62). Tr: Fabian **Coito**

Uzbekistan 0

Ganisher **Kholmurodov** - Sardor **Rakhmanov**,
Asiljon **Mansurov**, Javlon **Mirabdullaev** (c), Abbosbek
Makhstaliev, Azizbek **Muratov** (Davlatbek **Yarbekov**
62), Sardor **Sabirkhodjaev**, Kholmurod **Kholmurodov**
(Jasurbek **Khakimov** 65), Bobir **Davlatov** (Mirzamurod
Jurabaev 76), Muhsinjon **Ubaydullaev**, Timur
Khakimov. Tr: Aleksey **Evstafeev**

SEMI-FINALS

Nuevo Estadio Corona, Torreon
7-07-2011, 18:00, 26 086, Ponce ECU

Germany 2
Samed Yesil [10], Emre Can [60]

Odisseas **Vlachodimos** - Mitchell **Weiser** (Marvin
Ducksch 88), Cimo **Rocker**, Nico **Perrey**, Robin
Yalcin, Kaan **Ayhan**, Noah **Korczowski**, Emre **Can** (c)
(Rani **Khedira** 74), Levent **Aycicek** (Sven **Mende** 64),
Samed **Yesil**, Okan **Aydin**. Tr: Steffen **Freund**

Mexico 3
Julio Gomez 2 [3 90], Jorge Espericueta [76]

Richard **Sanchez** - Francisco **Flores•**, Carlos
Guzman, Antonio **Briseno** (c), Jorge **Caballero**, Julio
Gomez, Kevin **Escamilla** (Jose **Tostado** 66), Jorge
Espericueta, Arturo **Gonzalez** (Giovani **Casillas** 63),
Carlos **Fierro**, Marco **Bueno** (Marcelo **Gracia** 66).
Tr: Raul **Gutierrez**

Estadio Omnilife, Guadalajara
7-07-2011, 15:00, 29 315, Nikolaev RUS

Uruguay 3
Elbio Alvarez [20p], Juan San Martin [72],
Guillermo Mendez [95+]

Jonathan **Cubero•** - Gaston **Rodriguez**, Emiliano
Velazquez (c), Gaston **Silva**, Maximiliano **Moreira**
(Sebastian **Canobra** 81), Alejandro **Furia**, Heber **Ratti**,
Leonardo **Pais**, Elbio **Alvarez•** (Guillermo **Mendez•**
68), Rodrigo **Aguirre**, Santiago **Charamoni** (Juan **San**
Martin 46). Tr: Fabian **Coito**

Brazil 0

Charles - **Wallace**, **Marquinhos** (c), **Matheus•**,
Emerson, **Misael** (Nathan 46), **Guilherme**
(Wellington 73), **Marlon Bica**, Lucas **Piazon**,
Ademilson, **Leo•** (Hernani 77). Tr: Emerson **Avila**

3RD PLACE PLAY-OFF

Azteca, Mexico City
10-07-2011, 15:00, 94 379, Garcia MEX

Brazil 3
Wellington [22], Adryan 2 [29p 33]

Charles - **Wallace**, **Marquinhos** (c), **Matheus•**,
Emerson, **Misael** (Hernani 76), **Marlon Bica**, Lucas
Piazon, **Wellington•** (Nathan 56), **Ademilson**
(Guilherme 71), **Adryan**. Tr: Emerson **Avila**

Germany 4
Okan Aydin 2 [20 63], Koray Gunter [45],
Levent Aycicek [55]

Odisseas **Vlachodimos•** - Mitchell **Weiser** (Fabian
Schnellhardt 82), Cimo **Rocker**, Nico **Perrey**, Robin
Yalcin (c), Kaan **Ayhan** (Koray **Gunter•** 36), Noah
Korczowski, Levent **Aycicek** (Emre **Can** 95+), Rani
Khedira, Samed **Yesil**, Okan **Aydin**. Tr: Steffen **Freund**

FINAL

Azteca, Mexico City
10-07-2011, 18:00, 98 943, Moen NOR

Mexico 2
Antonio Briseno [31], Giovani Casillas [92+]

Richard **Sanchez** - Francisco **Flores**, Carlos **Guzman**,
Antonio **Briseno** (c), Jorge **Caballero**, Jose **Tostado**
(Julio **Gomez** 63), Kevin **Escamilla**, Jorge **Espericueta**,
Arturo **Gonzalez**, Carlos **Fierro** (Giovani **Casillas** 85),
Marco **Bueno** (Marcelo **Gracia** 75). Tr: Raul **Gutierrez**

Uruguay 0

Jonathan **Cubero•** - Emiliano **Velazquez** (c), Gaston
Silva•, Maximiliano **Moreira** (Sebastian **Canobra** 69),
Gianni **Rodriguez**, Alejandro **Furia**, Leonardo **Pais**,
Elbio **Alvarez**, Guillermo **Mendez•** (Santiago
Charamoni 79), Jim **Varela**, Rodrigo **Aguirre** (Juan
San Martin 26). Tr: Fabian **Coito**

FIFA U-20 WORLD CUP COLOMBIA 2011

FIFA U-20 WORLD CUP COLOMBIA 2011

First round groups		Round of 16		Quarter-finals		Semi-finals		Final	
Group A	Pts								
Colombia	9	Brazil	3						
France	6	Saudi Arabia	0						
Korea Republic	3			Brazil	2 4p				
Mali	0			Spain	2 2p				
Group B	Pts	Korea Republic	0 6p						
Portugal	7	Spain	0 7p						
Cameroon	4					Brazil	2		
New Zealand	2					Mexico	0		
Uruguay	2	Colombia	3						
Group C	Pts	Costa Rica	2						
Spain	9			Colombia	1				
Ecuador	4			Mexico	3				
Costa Rica	3	Cameroon	1 0p						
Australia	1	Mexico	1 3p						
								Brazil	3
Group D	Pts							Portugal	2
Nigeria	9	France	1						
Saudi Arabia	6	Ecuador	0						
Guatemala	3			France	3				
Croatia	0			Nigeria	2				
Group E	Pts	England	0						
Brazil	7	Nigeria	1						
Egypt	7					France	0		
Panama	1					Portugal	2		
Austria	1	Argentina	2						
Group F	Pts	Egypt	1						
Argentina	7			Argentina	0 4p				
Mexico	4			Portugal	0 5p			3rd place play-off	
England	3	Guatemala	0					Mexico	3
Korea DPR	1	Portugal	1					France	1

Top scorers: **5** - Henrique BRA; Alvaro Vazquez ESP & Alexandre Lacazette FRA • **4** - Nelson Oliveira POR & Luis Muriel COL • **3** - 13 players
adidas Golden Ball: Henrique BRA
adidas Golden Boot: Henrique BRA
adidas Golden Glove: Mika POR
FIFA Fair Play Award: Nigeria

GROUP A	PL	W	D	L	F	A	PTS		FRA	KOR	MLI
1 Colombia	3	3	0	0	7	1	9		4-1	1-0	2-0
2 France	3	2	0	1	6	5	6			3-1	2-0
3 Korea Republic	3	1	0	2	3	4	3				2-0
4 Mali	3	0	0	3	0	6	0				

El Campin, Bogotá
30-07-2011, 18:00, 36 111, Clattenburg ENG

Mali 0

Cheick Abdul Cadry Sy - Amara Konate•, Boubacar Sylla, Mohamed Konate, Mohamed Traore•, Kalifa Traore, Amara Malle (Adama Toure 68), Soumaila Sidibe (Moussa Guindo 78), Ibrahim Kalil Diakite (Seydou Diallo 68), Cheick Fanta Mady Diarra, Kalifa Coulibaly. Tr: Sekou Diallo

Korea Republic 2
Kim Kyung Jung 50, Jang Hyun Soo 80p

Yang Han Been - Rim Chang Woo (Kim Jin Su 67), Hwang Do Yeon (Min Sang Gi 46), Jang Hyun Soo•, Choi Sung Guen, Baek Sung Dong, Kim Kyung Jung•, Lee Ki Je, Kim Young Uk, Lee Yong Jae (Jung Seung Yong 90), Yun Il Lok. Tr: Lee Kwang Jong

El Campin, Bogotá
30-07-2011, 21:00, 36 111, O'Leary NZL

Colombia 4
James Rodriguez 30p, Luis Muriel 2 48 66, Santiago Arias 64

Cristian Bonilla - Pedro Franco (c), Santiago Arias (Juan Diaz 71), Hector Quinones, Jeison Murillo, Didier Moreno, Michael Ortega, Juan Cabezas, Luis Muriel (Duvan Zapata 87), James Rodriguez (Javier Calle 78), Jose Valencia. Tr: Eduardo Lara

France 1
Gilles Sunu 21

Jonathan Ligali - Kalidou Koulibaly•, Maxime Colin, Sebastien Faure, Gueida Fofana (c), Francis Coquelin, Gael Kakuta (Clement Grenier 68), Gilles Sunu, Antoine Griezmann (Yannis Tafer 83), Cedric Bakambu (Alexandre Lacazette 46). Tr: Francis Smerecki

El Campin, Bogotá
2-08-2011, 17:00, 36 103, Seneme BRA

France 3
Gilles Sunnu 27, Gueida Fofana 81, Alexandre Lacazette 91+

Jonathan Ligali - Loic Nego•, Kalidou Koulibaly•, Timothee Kolodziejczak, Sebastien Faure, Gueida Fofana (c), Francis Coquelin, Gael Kakuta (Clement Grenier 76), Gilles Sunu, Antoine Griezmann (Lionel Carole 83), Cedric Bakambu (Alexandre Lacazette 62). Tr: Francis Smerecki

Korea Republic 1
Kim Young Uk 59

Yang Han Been - Rim Chang Woo, Kim Jin Su•, Jang Hyun Soo, Choi Sung Guen, Baek Sung Dong, Kim Kyung Jung (Lee Jong Ho 83), Lee Ki Je, Kim Young Uk, Jung Seung Yong (Nam Seung Woo 81), Yun Il Lok (Lee Yong Jae 88). Tr: Lee Kwang Jong

El Campin, Bogotá
2-08-2011, 20:00, 36 103, Vad HUN

Colombia 2
Jose Valencia 23, James Rodriguez 91+

Cristian Bonilla - Pedro Franco (c), Santiago Arias•, Hector Quinones, Jeison Murillo•, Didier Moreno, Michael Ortega (Jerson Condelo 71), Juan Cabezas•, Luis Muriel (Javier Calle 85), James Rodriguez, Jose Valencia (Fabian Castillo 61). Tr: Eduardo Lara

Mali 0

Cheick Abdul Cadry Sy - Amara Konate, Boubacar Sylla, Moussa Coulibaly, Mohamed Konate, Kalifa Traore••♦89, Adama Toure•, Soumaila Sidibe (Moussa Guindo• 78), Ibrahim Kader Coulibaly• (Ibrahim Kalil Diakite 59), Cheick Fanta Mady Diarra•, Kalifa Coulibaly (Ibrahima Diallo 64). Tr: Sekou Diallo

Pascual Guerrero, Cali
5-08-2011, 20:00, 31 395, Arias PAR

France 2
Cedric Bakambu 70, Alexandre Lacazette 77

Jonathan Ligali - Loic Nego, Kalidou Koulibaly•, Timothee Kolodziejczak (Thomas Fontaine 80), Sebastien Faure, Gueida Fofana (c), Francis Coquelin, Gael Kakuta (Clement Grenier 46), Gilles Sunu•, Antoine Griezmann (Alexandre Lacazette 64), Cedric Bakambu. Tr: Francis Smerecki

Mali 0

Cheick Abdul Cadry Sy - Amara Konate (Moussa Guindo 62), Boubacar Sylla, Moussa Coulibaly, Mohamed Konate••♦69, Amara Malle (Seydou Diallo 83), Adama Toure, Soumaila Sidibe•, Ibrahim Kader Coulibaly, Cheick Fanta Mady Diarra, Ibrahima Diallo (Kalifa Coulibaly 66). Tr: Sekou Diallo

El Campin, Bogotá
5-08-2011, 20:00, 36 082, Stromb'sson SWE

Colombia 1
Luis Muriel 37

Cristian Bonilla - Pedro Franco• (c), Hector Quinones, Juan Diaz, Jeison Murillo, Didier Moreno, Michael Ortega (Javier Calle 63), Juan Cabezas (Jonny Mosquera 72), Luis Muriel, James Rodriguez (Yerson Candelo 69), Jose Valencia. Tr: Eduardo Lara

Korea Republic 0

No Dong Geon - Rim Chang Woo (Kim Jin Su 52), Min Sang Ki, Jang Hyun Soo, Choi Sung Guen• (Yun Il Lok 79), Baek Sung Dong, Kim Kyung Jung, Lee Ki Je•, Kim Young Uk, Lee Yong Jae•, Jung Seung Yong (Moon Sang Yun 71). Tr: Lee Kwang Jong

GROUP B	PL	W	D	L	F	A	PTS		CMR	NZL	URU
1 Portugal	3	2	1	0	2	0	7		1-0	1-0	0-0
2 Cameroon	3	1	1	1	2	2	4			1-1	1-0
3 New Zealand	3	0	2	1	2	3	2				1-1
4 Uruguay	3	0	2	1	1	2	2				

Pascual Guerrero, Cali
30-07-2011, 17:00, 35 262, Collum SCO

Cameroon 1
Christ Mbondi 33

Jean Efala - Eric Nyatchou, Ambroise Oyongo, Banana Yaya, Serge Tchaha, Ghislain Mvom, Clarence Bitang (Emmanuel Mbongo 68), Franck Kom, Yazid Atouba, Franck Ohandza, Christ Mbondi•. Tr: Martin Ndtoungou

New Zealand 1
Serge Tchana OG 40

Stefan Marinovic• - Nick Branch, Anthony Hobbs, James Musa, Luke Rowe, Adam Thomas, Ryan Cain (Sean Lovemore 66), Andrew Milne (Tim Payne 48), Colin Murphy, Andrew Bevin, Dakota Lucas (Ethan Galbraith 90). Tr: Chris Milicich

Pascual Guerrero, Cali
30-07-2011, 20:00, 35 262, Abdou QAT

Portugal 0

Mika - Nuno Reis, Roderick, Cedric, Luis Martins, Pele (Julio Alves 84), Sana• (Tiago Ferreira 87), Danilo, Sergio Oliveira••♦80, Nelson Oliveira, Rafael Lopes (Alex 75). Tr: Ilidio Vale

Uruguay 0

Salvador Ichazo - Diego Polenta (c), Guillermo de los Santos, Leandro Cabrera, Ramon Arias, Angel Cayetano, Cesar Teixeira, Nicolas Prieto (Federico Rodriguez 85), Camilo Mayada (Maximiliano Olivera 81), Ignacio Lores (Pablo Cepellini 60), Matias Vecino. Tr: Juan Verzeri

Pascual Guerrero, Cali
2-08-2011, 17:00, 28 884, Cakir TUR

Uruguay 1
Adrian Luna 74

Salvador Ichazo - Diego Polenta (c), Guillermo de los Santos, Leandro Cabrera, Maximiliano Olivera• (Ignacio Lores 66), Angel Cayetano, Adrian Luna, Pablo Cepellini, Cesar Teixeira (Diego Rolan 86), Camilo Mayada, Matias Vecino. Tr: Juan Verzeri

New Zealand 1
Andrew Bevin 57

Stefan Marinovic - Nick Branch• (c), Anthony Hobbs, James Musa, Luke Rowe, Adam Thomas, Ryan Cain (Andrew Milne• 84), Colin Murphy, Marco Rojas (Cameron Lindsay 75), Andrew Bevin, Dakota Lucas• (Sean Lovemore 73). Tr: Chris Milicich

Pascual Guerrero, Cali
2-08-2011, 20:00, 28 884, Arias PAR

Portugal 1

Nelson Oliveira [19]

Mika - Nuno Reis (c), Roderick, Cedric, Luis Martins• (Mario Rui 46), Pele, Julio Alves (Ricardo Dias 69), Alex•, Danilo, Nelson Oliveira, Caetano• (Amido Balde 83). Tr: Ilidio Vale

Cameroon 0

Jean Efala (c) - Eric Nyatchou, Ambroise Oyongo, Banana Yaya, Serge Tchaha•, Ghislain Mvom♦71, Emmanuel Mbongo (Maxime Mengue 75), Clarence Bitang (Yazid Atouba 47), Franck Kom•, Franck Ohandza, Christ Mbondi (Yannick Makota 63). Tr: Martin Ndtoungou

Pascual Guerrero, Cali
5-08-2011, 17:00, 31 395, Kim Dong Jin KOR

Portugal 1

Mario Rui [31]

Mika - Nuno Reis (c), Roderick (Tiago Ferreira 46), Cedric, Mario Rui•, Pele, Julio Alves, Alex, Danilo (Sergio Oliveira 72), Nelson Oliveira, Caetano (Ricardo Dias 83). Tr: Ilidio Vale

New Zealand 0

Stefan Marinovic - Nick Branch (c), Anthony Hobbs, James Musa, Luke Rowe, Adam Thomas, Cameron Lindsay (Ethan Galbraith 56), Colin Murphy, Marco Rojas (Ryan Cain 77), Andrew Bevin, Dakota Lucas. Tr: Chris Milicich

El Campin, Bogotá
5-08-2011, 17:00, 36 082, Geiger USA

Uruguay 0

Salvador Ichazo - Diego Polenta• (c), Guillermo de los Santos, Leandro Cabrera•, Ramon Arias, Angel Cayetano (Ignacio Lores 76), Adrian Luna, Pablo Cepellini•, Nicolas Prieto, Camilo Mayada (Cesar Texeira 46), Federico Rodriguez (Matias Vecino 46). Tr: Juan Verzeri

Cameroon 1

Emmanuel Mbongo [28]

Jean Efala (c) - Ambroise Oyongo•, Banana Yaya, Idriss Nguessi, Maxime Mengue, Emmanuel Mbongo (Clarence Bitang 84), Franck Kom•, Yazid Atouba (Eric Nyatchou 46), Herve Mbega (Yann Songo'o 63), Franck Ohandza, Christ Mbondi. Tr: Martin Ndtoungou

GROUP C	PL	W	D	L	F	A	PTS		ECU	CRC	AUS
1 Spain	3	3	0	0	11	2	9		2-0	4-1	5-1
2 Ecuador	3	1	1	1	4	3	4			3-0	1-1
3 Costa Rica	3	1	0	2	4	9	3				3-2
4 Australia	3	0	1	2	4	9	1				

Palogrande, Manizales
31-07-2011, 15:00, 17 075, Ubriaco URU

Costa Rica 1

John Ruiz [65]

Mauricio Vargas - Jordan Smith•, Ariel Contreras, Joseph Mora, Juan Golobio, Diego Calvo (John Ruiz 59), Ariel Soto (c), Yeltsin Tejeda, Mynor Escoe• (Joshua Diaz 82), Joel Campbell, Bryan Vega (Deyver Vega 81). Tr: Ronald Gonzalez

Spain 4

Rodrigo 2 [14 48], Koke [81], Isco [94+p]

Aitor - Hugo Mallo, Antonio Luna•, Marc Bartra (c), Jorge Pulido•, Isco, Koke, Sergi Roberto (Ezequiel 57), Oriol Romeu•, Rodrigo (Alvaro Vazquez 79), Daniel Pacheco• (Recio 71). Tr: Julen Lopetegui

Palogrande, Manizales
31-07-2011, 18:00, 17 075, Haimoudi ALG

Australia 1

Tommy Oar [89]

Mark Birighitti - Dylan McGowan, Trent Sainsbury, Marc Warren, Rhyan Grant, Ben Kantarovski• (c) (Terry Antonis 59), Mustafa Amini (Bernie Ibini Isei 54), Kofi Danning, Kerem Bulut, Tommy Oar, Dimitri Petratos. Tr: Jan Versleijen

Ecuador 1

Juan Govea [24]

John Jaramillo - Mario Pineda, John Narvaez•, Dennis Quinonez (c), Edder Fuertes, Fernando Gaibor, Juan Govea (Juan Cazares 82), Christian Ona, Marlon de Jesus (Dixon Arroyo 86), Marcos Caicedo (Danny Luna 78), Edson Montano. Tr: Sixto Vizuete

Palogrande, Manizales
3-08-2011, 17:00, 10 130, O'Leary NZL

Ecuador 0

John Jaramillo - Mario Pineda, John Narvaez, Dennis Quinonez (c), Edder Fuertes, Fernando Gaibor (Dixon Arroyo 90), Juan Govea (Christian Cruz 80), Christian Ona••♦65, Marlon de Jesus, Marcos Caicedo (Juan Cazares 81), Edson Montano. Tr: Sixto Vizuete

Spain 2

Sergio Canales [67], Alvaro Vzzquez [85]

Fernando Pacheco - Hugo Mallo, Marc Bartra (c), Carles Planas, Jordi Amat•, Isco (Recio 83), Koke, Oriol Romeu• (Alvaro Vazquez 71), Daniel Pacheco (Sergio Canales 56), Christian Tello. Tr: Julen Lopetegui

Palogrande, Manizales
3-08-2011, 20:00, 10 130, Schoerg'hofer AUT

Australia 2

Tommy Oar [26], Francisco Calvo OG [64]

Mark Birighitti - Trent Sainsbury, Marc Warren, Rhyan Grant Ben Kantarovski• (c) (Sam Gallagher 72), Terry Antonis, Brendan Hamill, Kofi Danning (Bernie Ibini Isei 59), Kerem Bulut•, Tommy Oar, Dimitri Petratos (Mustafa Amini 59). Tr: Jan Versleijen

Costa Rica 3

Joel Campbell 2 [22 27], John Ruiz [72]

Mauricio Vargas - Jordan Smith, Ariel Contreras, Joseph Mora, Juan Golobio (Pablo Martinez 74), Francisco Calvo, Yeltsin Tejeda, John Ruiz, Mynor Escoe, Joel Campbell (Vianney Blanco 89), Bryan Vega (Diego Calvo 62). Tr: Ronald Gonzalez

Hernan Ramirez Villegas, Pereira
6-08-2011, 17:00, 13 714, Cakir TUR

Ecuador 3

Edson Montano [2], Marlon De Jesus 2 [13 69]

John Jaramillo - Mario Pineda, John Narvaez, Brayan de la Torre (Juan Cazares 64) Dennis Quinonez (c), Edder Fuertes, Fernando Gaibor (Yeison Ordonez 81), Dixon Arroyo, Marlon de Jesus, Marcos Caicedo, Edson Montano (Juan Govea 72). Tr: Sixto Vizuete

Costa Rica 0

Mauricio Vargas - Jordan Smith, Keyner Brown (Diego Calvo 68), Ariel Contreras, Joseph Mora, Juan Golobio (Rafael Chavez 56), Francisco Calvo, Yeltsin Tejeda•, John Ruiz•, Joel Campbell, Bryan Vega (Deyver Vega 62). Tr: Ronald Gonzalez

Palogrande, Manizales
6-08-2011, 17:00, 14 722, Seneme BRA

Australia 1

Kerem Bulut [27]

Mark Birighitti - Trent Sainsbury• (Dylan McGowan• 46), Marc Warren, Rhyan Grant, Terry Antonis, Mustafa Amini, Brendan Hamill, Kofi Danning, Kerem Bulut, Tommy Oar, Bernie Ibini Isei (Dimitri Petratos 46). Tr: Jan Versleijen

Spain 5

Sergi Roberto [1], Alvaro Vazquez 3 [6 13 18], Sergio Canales [31p]

Fernando Pacheco (Alex 46) - Hugo Mallo (Ezequiel 62), Antonio Luna, Marc Bartra (c) (Carles Planas 46), Jorge Pulido, Kiko, Recio, Sergio Canales, Sergi Roberto, Daniel Pacheco, Alvaro Vazquez. Tr: Julen Lopetegui

GROUP D	PL	W	D	L	F	A	PTS		KSA	GUA	CRO
1 Nigeria	3	3	0	0	12	2	9		2-0	5-0	5-2
2 Saudi Arabia	3	2	0	1	8	2	6			6-0	2-0
3 Guatemala	3	1	0	2	1	11	3				1-0
4 Croatia	3	0	0	3	2	8	0				

Centenario, Armenia
31-07-2011, 15:00, 11 116, Schoerg'hofer AUT
Nigeria   **5**
Edafe Egbedi 2 ⁸ ³⁹, Abdul Ajagun ⁴⁷,
Olarenwaju Kayode ⁵³, Ahmed Musa ⁷⁶
Dami **Paul** - Terna **Suswam**, Kenneth **Omeruo**, Ganiu **Ogungbe•**, Emmanuel **Anyanwu**, Philemon **Daniel**, Ramon **Azeez** (c) (Sani **Tahir** 90), Ahmed **Musa**, Olarenwaju **Kayode**, Abdul **Ajagun**, Edafe **Egbedi** (Sani **Emmanuel** 90). Tr: John **Obuh**
Guatemala   **0**

Jose **Garcia** - Jose **Andrade** (Jose **Lemus•** 46), Willian **Ramirez**, Elias **Vasquez•** (c), Sixto **Betancourt**, Jose **del Aguila•**, Marvin **Ceballos**, Jose **Castillo** (Marco **Rivas** 55), Henry **Lopez**, Abner **Bonilla** (Walter **Arriola** 46), Gerson **Lima**. Tr: Ever **Almeida**

Centenario, Armenia
31-07-2011, 18:00, 11 116, Doue CIV
Croatia   **0**

Matej **Delac** - Renato **Kelic**, Tomislav **Glumac•**, Franko **Andrijasevic** (Anton **Maglica** 72), Zvonko **Pamic•**, Arijan **Ademi**, Filip **Ozobic** (Roberto **Puncec** 46), Mario **Ticnovic**, Antonio **Jakolis** (Dejan **Glavica** 46), Andrej **Kramaric**, Ivan **Lendric**. Tr: Ivan **Grnja**
Saudi Arabia   **2**
Yasir Alfahmi ⁵⁴, Fhad Almuwallad ⁶⁹
Abdullah **Alsdairy** - Saleh **Al Qumayzi**, Salem **Al Dawsari**, Mohammed **Al Fatil**, Abdullah **Al Hafith**, Yasir **Al Shahrani**, Ibrahim **Al Ibrahim**, Maan **Khodary**, Abdullah **Otayf** (Fahed **Al Johani** 88), Yasir **Al Fahmi** (Fhad **Al Muwallad** 67), Yahya **Dagriri** (Mustafa **Al Bassas** 85). Tr: Khalid **Al Koroni**

Centenario, Armenia
3-08-2011, 17:00, 8861, Collum SCO
Saudi Arabia   **6**
Yahya Dagriri ¹⁷, Yasir Alfahmi ²⁷, Mohammed Alfatil ⁵⁸, Yasir Alshahrani ⁶⁶, Ibrahim Alibrahim ⁸³, Salem Aldawsari ⁸⁹
Abdullah **Alsdairy** - Saleh **Al Qumayzi** (Ali **Al Zubaidi** 62), Salem **Al Dawsari•**, Mohammed **Al Fatil**, Abdullah **Al Hafith**, Yasir **Al Shahrani**, Ibrahim **Al Ibrahim•**, Maan **Khodary** (Fhad **Al Muwallad** 46), Abdullah **Otayf**, Yasir **Al Fahmi** (Abdulelah **Al Nasser** 65), Yahya **Dagriri**. Tr: Khalid **Al Koroni**
Guatemala   **0**

Roberto **Padilla** - Willian **Ramirez•**, Elias **Vasquez**(c), Sixto **Betancourt**, Walter **Arriola**, Jose **del Aguila**, Marvin **Ceballos** (Henry **Lopez** 46), Marco **Rivas** (Kevin **Norales** 46), Gabriel **Navas**, Cristian **Lima** (Jose **Castillo** 28), Gerson **Lima**. Tr: Ever **Almeida**

Centenario, Armenia
3-08-2011, 20:00, 8861, Ubriaco URU
Croatia   **2**
Ivan Lendric ⁴², Andrej Kramaric ⁶⁶
Matej **Delac** - Renato **Kelic•**, Tomislav **Glumac**, Roberto **Puncec**, Dejan **Glavica** (Frano **Mlinar** 65), Zvonko **Pamic•**, Arijan **Ademi** (Franko **Andrijasevic** 74), Mario **Ticnovic•**, Ivan **Blazevic** (Filip **Ozobic** 81), Andrej **Kramaric**, Ivan **Lendric**. Tr: Ivan **Grnja**
Nigeria   **5**
Olarenwaju Kayode ²⁵, Terna Suswan ³⁰, Ahmed Musa ⁶², Uche Nwofor 2 ⁶⁹ ⁷³
Dami **Paul** - Terna **Suswam**, Kenneth **Omeruo**, Ganiu **Ogungbe** (Sani **Tahir** 90), Emmanuel **Anyanwu**, Philemon **Daniel**, Ramon **Azeez** (c), Ahmed **Musa**, Olarenwaju **Kayode** (Chimezie **Mbah** 90), Abdul **Ajagun**, Edafe **Egbedi** (Uche **Nwofor** 67). Tr: John **Obuh** (Uche **Nwofor** 67)

Hernan Ramirez Villegas, Pereira
6-08-2011, 20:00, 13 714, Buitrago COL
Saudi Arabia   **0**

Abdullah **Alsdairy** - Salem **Al Dawsari** (Mohammed **Majrashi** 85), Mohammed **Al Fatil**, Abdullah **Al Hafith•**, Ali **Al Zubaidi**, Yasir **Al Shahrani**, Ibrahim **Al Ibrahim**, Maan **Khodary•**, Abdullah **Otayf**, Yasir **Al Fahmi** (Fahed **Al Johani** 46), Yahya **Dagriri** (Fhad **Al Muwallad** 46). Tr: Khalid **Al Koroni**
Nigeria   **2**
Ahmed Musa ⁴⁵, Olarenwaju Kayode ⁸⁵
Dami **Paul** - Terna **Suswam**, Kenneth **Omeruo**, Chimeze **Mbah**, Emmanuel **Anyanwu**, Philemon **Daniel**, Ramon **Azeez** (c), Omoh **Ojabu** (Olarenwaju **Kayode** 64), Ahmed **Musa**, Abdul **Ajagun** (Sani **Tahir** 88), Uche **Nwofor**. Tr: John **Obuh**

Centenario, Armenia
6-08-2011, 20:00, 4209, Abdou QAT
Croatia   **0**

Matej **Delac** - Renato **Kelic** (Anton **Maglica** 46), Tomislav **Glumac**, Marko **Leskovic•**, Roberto **Puncec**, Arijan **Ademi**, Filip **Ozobic** (Franko **Andrijasevic** 73), Mario **Ticnovic•**, Antonio **Jakolis**, Frano **Mlinar** (Dejan **Glavica** 85), Ivan **Lendric**. Tr: Ivan **Grnja**
Guatemala   **1**
Marvin Ceballos ⁸¹
Roberto **Padilla** - Jose **Andrade**, Manuel **Moreno**, Elias **Vasquez** (c), Jose **Lemus**, Jose **del Aguila**, Marvin **Ceballos•** (Cristian **Lima** 86), Jose **Castillo** Marco **Rivas•**, Kevin **Norales** (Abner **Bonilla** 46), Gerson **Lima** (Gabriel **Navas•** 73). Tr: Ever **Almeida**

GROUP E	PL	W	D	L	F	A	PTS		EGY	PAN	AUT
1 Brazil	3	2	1	0	8	1	7		1-1	4-0	3-0
2 Egypt	3	2	1	0	6	1	7			1-0	4-0
3 Panama	3	0	1	2	0	5	1				0-0
4 Austria	3	0	1	2	0	7	1				

Metropolitano, Barranquilla
29-07-2011, 21:00, 45 170, Cakir TUR
Brazil   **1**
Danilo ¹²
Gabriel - **Danilo•**, Bruno **Uvini** (c), Juan **Jesus•**, Gabriel **Silva**, Fernando, **Casemiro** (Dudu 70), Philippe **Coutinho**, Oscar, Alan **Patrick** (Negueba 46), **Willian** (Henrique 80). Tr: Ney **Franco**
Egypt   **1**
Omar Gaber ²⁶
Ahmed **El Shenawy** (c) (Mohamed **Awwad** 89) - Mohamed **Abdel Fatah**, Ahmed **Hegazi•**, Ahmed **Sobhy**, Mohamed **Hamdy•**, Mohamed **Salah** (Ahmed **Nabil** 95+), Ahmed **Tawfik**, Mohamed **Ibrahim** (Saleh **Gomaa** 71), Mohamed **El Neny•**, Omar **Gaber•**, Aly **Fathy**. Tr: El Sayed **Diaa**

Olimpico, Cartagena
29-07-2011, 17:30, 17:30, 13 198, Arias PAR
Austria   **0**

Samuel **Radlinger** - Emir **Dilaver**, Michael **Schimpelsberger** (c), Lukas **Rath**, Tobias **Kainz**, Robert **Gucher**, Daniel **Offenbacher** (Marco **Meilinger** 69), Patrick **Farkas**, Daniel **Schutz** (Christian **Klem** 46), Andreas **Weimann**, Robert **Zulj** (Georg **Teigl•** 59). Tr: Andreas **Heraf**
Panama   **0**

Luis **Mejia** (c) - Edward **Benitez**, Harold **Cummings**, Josue **Flores**, Francisco **Vence**, Jairo **Jimenez** (Algish **Dixon** 46), Paul **Cordero** (Jose **Gomez** 65), Eric **Davis**, Manuel **Vargas**, Cecilio **Waterman**, Jose **Alvarez** (Gabriel **Avila** 73). Tr: Alfredo **Poyatos**

Metropolitano, Barranquilla
1-08-2011, 17:00, 11 101, Kim Dong Jin KOR
Egypt   **1**
Ahmed Hegazi ⁶⁷
Ahmed **El Shenawy** (c) - Mohamed **Abdel Fatah**, Ahmed **Hegazi**, Ahmed **Sobhy** (Ahmed **Nabil** 72), Mohamed **Hamdy** (Saleh **Gomaa** 79), Mohamed **Salah**, Ahmed **Tawfik•**, Mohamed **Ibrahim** (Ayman **Ashraf** 87), Mohamed **El Neny**, Omar **Gaber**, Aly **Fathy**. Tr: El Sayed **Diaa**
Panama   **0**

Luis **Mejia** (c) - Edward **Benitez**, Harold **Cummings**, Josue **Flores**, Francisco **Vence**, Eric **Davis** (Paul **Cordero** 79), Roderick **Miller**, Algish **Dixon** (Jose **Alvarez** 52), Manuel **Vargas** (Alan **Hernandez** 63), Josimar **Gomez**, Cecilio **Waterman**. Tr: Alfredo **Poyatos**

Metropolitano, Barranquilla	Metropolitano, Barranquilla	Olimpico, Cartagena
1-08-2011, 20:00, 11 101, Geiger USA	4-08-2011, 20:00, 16 513, Clattenburg ENG	4-08-2011, 20:00, 16 042, Lopez GUA
Brazil 3	**Brazil** 4	**Egypt** 4
Henrique [37], Philippe Coutinho [52p], Willian [63]	Henrique [40], Philippe Coutinho 2 [45] [52], Dudu [89]	Mohamed Sobhi [31], Mohamed Ibrahim 3 [60] [62] [82]

Brazil 3 — Gabriel - Danilo, Bruno Uvini (c), Juan Jesus•, Alex Sandro (Gabriel Silva 13), Fernando, Casemiro, Philippe Coutinho, Oscar, Willian (Dudu 73), Henrique (Negueba 65). Tr: Ney Franco

Austria 0 — Samuel Radlinger - Richard Windbichler•, Emir Dilaver, Michael Schimpelsberger (c), Lukas Rath, Tobias Kainz, Robert Gucher (Radovan Mitrovic 46), Marcel Ziegl (Georg Teigl 57), Patrick Farkas, Christian Klem, Andreas Weimann (Robert Zulj 68). Tr: Andreas Heraf

Brazil 4 — Gabriel - Danilo, Bruno Uvini (c), Romario Leiria, Gabriel Silva, Fernando• (Dudu 18), Casemiro, Philippe Coutinho (Negueba 78), Oscar, Willian (Galhardo 39), Henrique. Tr: Ney Franco

Panama 0 — Luis Mejia (c) - Edward Benitez, Harold Cummings, Francisco Vence, Paul Cordero (Jose Gomez• 59), Eric Davis, Roderick Miller•, Manuel Vargas (Josue Flores 71), Cecilio Waterman, Alan Hernandez (Gabriel Avila 56), Jose Alvarez. Tr: Alfredo Poyatos

Egypt 4 — Mohamed Sobhi [31], Mohamed Ibrahim 3 [60] [62] [82] - Ahmed El Shenawy (c) - Ayman Ashraf, Mohamed Abdel Fatah, Ahmed Hegazi (Mahmoud Ezzat 75), Ahmed Sobhy, Ahmed Hassan (Ahmed Tawfik 59), Mohamed Salah, Mohamed Ibrahim, Mohamed El Neny, Mohamed Sobhi, Aly Fathy (Hussein Sayed 63). Tr: El Sayed Diaa

Austria 0 — Samuel Radlinger - Emir Dilaver, Lukas Rotpuller•, Michael Schimpelsberger• (c), Lukas Rath, Tobias Kainz (Robert Gucher 46), Patrick Farkas, Christian Klem, Daniel Schutz• (Marco Meilinger 63), Andreas Weimann• (Daniel Offenbacher 46), Robert Zulj. Tr: Andreas Heraf

	GROUP F	PL	W	D	L	F	A	PTS	MEX	ENG	PRK
1	**Argentina**	3	2	1	0	4	0	7	1-0	0-0	3-0
2	**Mexico**	3	1	1	1	3	1	4		0-0	3-0
3	**England**	3	0	3	0	0	0	3			0-0
4	Korea DPR	3	0	1	2	0	6	1			

Atanasio Girardot, Medellin	Atanasio Girardot, Medellin	Atanasio Girardot, Medellin
29-07-2011, 14:30, 25 995, Seneme BRA	29-07-2011, 17:30, 25 995, Vad HUN	1-08-2011, 17:00, 40 704, Stromb'sson SWE
England 0	**Argentina** 1	**Mexico** 3

England 0 — Jack Butland - Blair Adams•, Nathan Baker, Reece Brown, Adam Smith, Reece Wabara, Billy Knott (Dean Parrett 74), Jason Lowe (c), Matthew Phillips, Saido Berahino, Callum McManaman (Joshua Morris 59). Tr: Brian Eastick

Korea DPR 0 — Om Jin Song - Jang Song Hyok (c), Ri Hyong Mu, Ri Yong Chol, Kang Il Nam, Ri Hyon Song (Ri Il Jin 84), Ri Hyong Jin• (Han Song Hyok 65), Pak Song Chol, Mun Hyok, Jong Il Gwan (Jang Kuk Chol 71), Kim Ju Song. Tr: Jo Tong Sop

Argentina 1 — Erik Lamela [70] - Esteban Andrada - German Pezzella (c), Nicolas Tagliafico, Hugo Nervo, Adrian Martinez (Rodrigo Battaglia 94+), Leandro Gonzalez Pirez, Matias Laba• (Juan Iturbe 46), Roberto Pereyra, Erik Lamela, Alan Ruiz, Facundo Ferreyra (Agustin Vuletich• 71). Tr: Walter Perazzo

Mexico 0 — Carlos Lopez - Kristian Alvarez, Nestor Araujo, Cesar Ibanez•, Diego Reyes, Diego de Buen• (Erick Torres 78), Saul Villalobos (Carlos Orrantia 46), Jorge Enriquez (c), Taufic Guarch, Ulises Davila, Alan Pulido (Edson Rivera 64). Tr: Juan Carlos Chavez

Mexico 3 — Ri Yong Chol OG [45], Taufic Guarch [54], Diego De Buen [94+] - Carlos Lopez - Kristian Alvarez, Nestor Araujo, Cesar Ibanez, Diego Reyes, Diego de Buen, Carlos Orrantia (Lugiani Gallardo 81), Jorge Enriquez (c), Taufic Guarch (Edson Rivera 72), Ulises Davila, Alan Pulido (Erick Torres 46). Tr: Juan Carlos Chavez

Korea DPR 0 — Om Jin Song - Jang Song Hyok• (c), Ri Hyong Mu, Ri Yong Chol• (Ri Il Jin 59), Kang Il Nam, Ri Hyon Song, Ri Hyong Jin (Han Song Chol 56), Pak Song Chol, Mun Hyok (Kang Won Myong 83), Jong Il Gwan, Kim Ju Song. Tr: Jo Tong Sop

Atanasio Girardot, Medellin	Olimpico, Cartagena	Atanasio Girardot, Medellin
1-08-2011, 20:00, 40 704, Lopez GUA	4-08-2011, 17:00, 16 042, Haimoudi ALG	4-08-2011, 17:00, 14 647, Doue CIV
Argentina 0	**Mexico** 0	**Argentina** 3

Argentina 0 — Esteban Andrada - German Pezzella (c), Nicolas Tagliafico, Hugo Nervo, Adrian Martinez, Leandro Gonzalez Pirez, Roberto Pereyra•, Erik Lamela, Alan Ruiz• (Carlos Luque 77), Facundo Ferreyra (Matias Laba 59), Juan Iturbe. Tr: Walter Perazzo

England 0 — Jack Butland - Blair Adams, Nathan Baker (James Wallace 31), Reece Brown, Adam Smith, Reece Wabara, Billy Knott, Jason Lowe (c), Matthew Phillips, Saido Berahino (James Hurst• 82), Callum McManaman (Michael Ngoo 72). Tr: Brian Eastick

Mexico 0 — Jose Rodriguez - Kristian Alvarez• (Hector Acosta 46), Nestor Araujo, Cesar Ibanez, Diego Reyes, Diego de Buen, Carlos Orrantia (Saul Villalobos 60), Jorge Enriquez (c), Taufic Guarch (David Izazola 46), Erick Torres, Ulises Davila. Tr: Juan Carlos Chavez

England 0 — Jack Butland - Nathan Baker, Reece Brown, Ben Gordon•, Adam Smith, Reece Wabara•, Billy Knott (Dean Parrett 46), Jason Lowe (c), Matthew Phillips, Saido Berahino (Michael Ngoo 64), Callum McManaman (James Wallace 90). Tr: Brian Eastick

Argentina 3 — Facundo Ferreyra [36], Lucas Villafanez [84], Adrian Cirigliano [96+] - Esteban Andrada - German Pezzella (c) (Leonel Galeano 32), Nicolas Tagliafico, Adrian Martinez•, Leandro Gonzalez Pirez, Matias Laba, Roberto Pereyra• (Adrian Cirigliano 82), Rodrigo Battaglia, Carlos Luque, Facundo Ferreyra (Lucas Villafanez 80), Juan Iturbe•. Tr: Walter Perazzo

Korea DPR 0 — Om Jin Song - Jang Song Hyok• (c), Ri Hyong Mu, Kang Il Nam, Ri Il Jin, Ri Hyon Song (Pak Song Chol 40••♦95+), Kang Won Myong, Han Song Hyok (Kim Ju Song 66), Mun Hyok (Ri Yong Chol 83), Jong Il Gwan•, Jang Kuk Chol•. Tr: Jo Tong Sop

ROUND OF 16

Metropolitano, Barranquilla
10-08-2011, 20:00, 37 448, Vad HUN

Brazil	3

Henrique [46], Gabriel Silva [69], Dudu [86]

Gabriel - Danilo, Bruno Uvini (c), Juan Jesus, Gabriel Silva•, Galhardo, Fernando, Casemiro (Willian 46), Philippe Coutinho (Negueba 78), Oscar, Henrique (Dudu 62). Tr: Ney Franco

Saudi Arabia	0

Abdullah Alsdairy - Mohammed Al Fatil (Abdullah Al Hafith 75), Ali Al Zubaidi, Yasir Al Shahrani, Motaz Hawsawi, Ibrahim Al Ibrahim, Maan Khodary, Abdullah Otayf (Salem Al Dawsari 67), Yasir Al Fahmi, Yahya Dagriri, Fhad Al Muwallad (Abdulelah Al Nasser 80). Tr: Khalid Al Koroni

---

Palogrande, Manizales
10-08-2011, 17:00, 23 618, Geiger USA

Spain	0 7p

Fernando Pacheco - Hugo Mallo, Antonio Luna, Marc Bartra (c), Jordi Amat, Sergio Canales (Alvaro Vasquez 58), Koke, Oriol Romeu•, Rodrigo (Recio 90), Daniel Pacheco (Isco 50), Cristian Tello. Tr: Julen Lopetegui

Korea Republic	0 6p

No Dong Geon - Kim Jin Su, Min Sang Ki, Jang Hyun Soo, Choi Sung Guen• (Nam Seung Woo 98), Baek Sung Dong, Lee Ki Je•, Kim Young Uk, Moon Sang Yun (Jung Seung Yong 77), Lee Yong Jae, Yun Il Lok (Kim Kyung Jung 59). Tr: Lee Kwang Jong

---

El Campin, Bogotá
9-08-2011, 20:00, 36 084, Clattenburg ENG

Colombia	3

Luis Muriel [56], Pedro Franco [79], James Rodrigues [93+p]

Cristian Bonilla - Pedro Franco (c), Santiago Arias, Hector Quinones (Javier Calle 46), Jeison Murillo•, Didier Moreno• (Duvan Zapata 67), Michael Ortega, Juan Cabezas, Luis Muriel, James Rodriguez, Jose Valencia (Sebastian Perez 60). Tr: Eduardo Lara

Costa Rica	2

John Ruiz [63], Mynor Escoe [65]

Aaron Cruz• - Jordan Smith, Ariel Contreras•, Joseph Mora, Rafael Chavez (Deyver Vega 59), Juan Golobio•, Ariel Soto, Pablo Martinez (Diego Calvo 87), John Ruiz• (Bryan Vega 82), Mynor Escoe•, Joel Campbell•. Tr: Ronald Gonzalez

---

Hernan Ramirez Villegas, Pereira
9-08-2011, 20:00, 21 744, Seneme BRA

Cameroon	1 0p

Franck Ohandza [79]

Jean Efala (c) - Eric Nyatchou, Ambroise Oyongo, Banana Yaya, Idriss Nguessi, Maxime Mengue, Emmanuel Mbongo (Jushua Mbuluba 90), Yazid Atouba (Serge Tchaha• 57), Herve Mbega (Clarence Bitang 77), Franck Ohandza, Christ Mbondi. Tr: Martin Ndtoungou

Mexico	1 3p

Carlos Orrantia [81]

Jose Rodriguez - Kristian Alvarez• (Hector Acosta 74), Nestor Araujo, Cesar Ibanez, Diego Reyes, Diego de Buen (Marvin Pinon 66), Carlos Orrantia, Jorge Enriquez (c), Taufic Guarch (Erick Torres 46), Ulises Davila, Alan Pulido•. Tr: Juan Carlos Chavez

---

Olimpico, Cartagena
10-08-2011, 20:00, 15 958 Kim Dong Jin KOR

France	1

Antoine Griezmann [75]

Jonathan Ligali - Loic Nego, Thomas Fontaine, Timothee Kolodziejczak, Sebastien Faure, Clement Grenier•, Gueida Fofana (c), Francis Coquelin, Gilles Sunu (Enzo Reale 88), Antoine Griezmann (Gael Kakuta 76), Cedric Bakambu (Alexandre Lacazette 50). Tr: Francis Smerecki

Ecuador	0

John Jaramillo - Mario Pineida, John Narvaez, Brayan de la Torre (Juan Cazares 46), Dennis Quinonez (c), Edder Fuertes•, Fernando Gaibor, Dixon Arroyo, Marlon de Jesus, Marcos Caicedo, Edson Montano. Tr: Sixto Vizuete

---

**ROUND OF 16
PENALTIES
CMR v MEX**

	MEX		CMR
✓	Torres		
		Ohandza	✗ 1
✓	Davila		
		Nguessi	✗ 2
✓	Pinon		
		Mbondi	✗ 2

1 = saved • 2 = missed

Centenario, Armenia
10-08-2011, 17:00, 18 291, Arias PAR

Nigeria	1

Edafe Egbedi [52]

Dami Paul - Terna Suswam, Kenneth Omeruo, Ganiu Ogungbe, Emmanuel Anyanwu•, Philemon Daniel (Uche Nwofor 62), Ramon Azeez (c), Ahmed Musa, Olarenwaju Kayode (Sani Tahir 81), Abdul Ajagun, Edafe Egbedi. Tr: John Obuh

England	0

Jack Butland - Nathan Baker•, Reece Brown•, Ben Gordon, Adam Smith•, Reece Wabara (James Wallace• 22), Billy Knott, Jason Lowe (c), Matthew Phillips, Callum McManaman (Joshua Morris 77), Michael Ngoo (Saido Berahino 60). Tr: Brian Eastick

---

Atanasio Girardot, Medellin
9-08-2011, 17:00, 40 147, Stromb'gsson SWE

Argentina	2

Erik Lamela 2 [42p 64p]

Esteban Andrada - Nicolas Tagliafico•, Hugo Nervo•, Leonel Galeano, Adrian Martinez•, Leandro Gonzalez Pirez, Matias Laba, Erick Lamela (Alan Ruiz 83), Rodrigo Battaglia• (Adrian Cirigliano 75), Carlos Luque•, Facundo Ferreyra (Juan Iturbe 60). Tr: Walter Perazzo

Egypt	1

Mohamed Salah [70p]

Ahmed El Shenawy (c) - Mohamed Abdel Fatah•, Ahmed Hegazie•, Ahmed Sobhy, Mohamed Hamdy, Mohamed Salah, Ahmed Tawfik (Ahmed Hassan 59), Mohamed Ibrahim• (Saleh Gomaa 65) (Ayman Ashraf 78), Mohamed El Neny•, Omer Gaber•, Aly Fathy. Tr: El Sayed Diaa

---

Pascual Guerrero, Cali
9-08-2011, 17:00, 34 264, Haimoudi ALG

Portugal	1

Nelson Oliveira [7p]

Mika - Tiago Ferreira, Nuno Reis (c), Cedric•, Mario Rui•, Alex• (Rafael Lopes 86), Danilo, Sergio Oliveira, Ricardo Dias (Pele 46), Nelson Oliveira, Caetano (Roderick 90). Tr: Ilidio Vale

Guatemala	0

Roberto Padilla - Jose Andrade, Manuel Moreno, Willian Ramirez, Elias Vasquez (c), Jose Lemus (Jose Melgar 24), Jose del Aguila, Marvin Ceballos, Jose Castillo, Cristian Lima (Kevin Norales 56), Gabriel Lima (Gabriel Navas 37). Tr: Ever Almeida

---

QUARTER-FINALS

Hernan Ramirez Villegas, Pereira
14-08-2011, 18:00, 29 318, Lopez GUA

Brazil	2 4p

Willian [35], Dudu [100]

Gabriel - Danilo, Bruno Uvini (c), Juan Jesus, Gabriel Silva•, Fernando, Casemiro, Philippe Coutinho (Dudu 78), Oscar (Allan 98), Willian• (Negueba 63), Henrique•. Tr: Ney Franco

Spain	2 2p

Rodrigo [57], Alvaro Velazquez [102]

Fernando Pacheco - Hugo Mallo, Marc Bartra (c), Carles Planas, Jordi Amat, Sergio Canales (Daniel Pacheco 91), Isco• - Koke, Oriol Romeu, Rodrigo (Alvaro Vasquez• 83), Cristian Tello (Sergi Roberto 46). Tr: Julen Lopetegui

---

**QUARTER-FINAL
PENALTIES
BRA v ESP (4-2)**

	ESP		BRA
✗ 1	Jordi Amat		
		Casemiro	✓
✓	Sergi Roberto		
		Danilo	✓
✓	Marc Bartra		
		Henrique	✓
✗ 1	Alvaro Vazquez		
		Dudu	✓

1 = saved • 2 = missed

El Campin, Bogotá
13-08-2011, 20:00, 35 969, Cakir TUR

Mexico	3

Erick Torres [38p], Edson Rivera 2 [69 88]

Jose Rodriguez• - Hector Acosta (Jorge Valencia 71), Nestor Araujo, Cesar Ibanez, Diego Reyes, Diego de Buen, Carlos Orrantia, Jorge Enriquez (c), Erick Torres (Marvin Pinon 87), Ulises Davila•, Alan Pulido (Edson Rivera 36). Tr: Juan Carlos Chavez

Colombia	1

Duvan Zapata [60]

Cristian Bonilla - Luciano Ospina, Pedro Franco (c), Santiago Arias, Hector Quinones, Didier Moreno, Michael Ortega• (Javier Calle 76), Juan Cabezas (Fabian Castillo 72), Luis Muriel, James Rodriguez, Duvan Zapata (Jose Valencia 84). Tr: Eduardo Lara

Pascual Guerrero, Cali
14-08-2011, 15:00, 33 007, Ubriaco URU

France 3
Alexandre Lacazette 2 50 104, Gueida Fofana 102
Jonathan **Ligali**• - Loic **Nego**, Kalidou **Koulibaly**,
Timothee **Kolodziejczak**, Sebastien **Faure**, Clement
Grenier (Florian Lejeune 106), Gueida **Fofana** (c),
Francis **Coquelin**, Gilles **Sunu** (Alexandre **Lacazette**•
33), Antoine **Griezmann**, Cedric **Bakambu**• (Gael
Kakuta 78). Tr: Francis **Smerecki**

Nigeria 2
Maduabuchi Ejike 2 93+ 111
Dami **Paul** - Terna **Suswam**, Kenneth **Omeruo**, Ganiu
Ogungbe, Emmanuel **Anyanwu**, Philemon **Daniel**
(Sani **Emmanuel** 84), Ramon **Azeez** (c), Ahmed
Musa• (Maduabuchi **Elike** 92), Olarenwaju **Kayode**
(Uche **Nwofor** 57), Abdul **Ajagun**, Edafe **Egbedi**. Tr:
John **Obuh**

Olimpico, Cartagena
13-08-2011, 17:00, 15 946, O'Leary NZL

Portugal 0 5p

Mika - **Roderick**, Nuno **Reis** (c), **Cedric**, Luis **Martins**
(Tiago **Ferreira** 122+), **Pele**, Julio **Alves** (**Sana**• 69),
Danilo, Sergio **Oliveira**•, Nelson **Oliveira**•, **Caetano**
(Rafael **Lopes** 94). Tr: Ilidio **Vale**

Argentina 0 4p

Esteban **Andrada** - Nicolas **Tagliafico**, Hugo **Nervo**
(c), Leonel **Galeano**, Leandro **Gonzalez Pirez**•,
Matias **Laba**, Roberto **Pereyra** (Agustin **Vuletich** 98),
Erick **Lamela**, Rodrigo **Battaglia**•, Carlos **Luque**•
(Alan **Ruiz** 81), Facundo **Ferreyra** (Juan Iturbe 60).
Tr: Walter **Perazzo**

SEMI-FINALS

Hernan Ramirez Villegas, Pereira
17-08-2011, 20:00, 29 812, Clattenburg ENG

Brazil 2
Henrique 2 80 84

Gabriel - **Danilo**, Bruno **Uvini** (c), Juan **Jesus**•,
Gabriel Silva• (**Allan** 69), **Fernando**, **Casemiro**,
Philippe **Coutinho** (**Dudu** 69), **Oscar**, **Willian**
(**Negueba** 55), **Henrique**. Tr: Ney **Franc**

Mexico 0

Jose **Rodriguez** - Hector **Acosta** (Alan **Pulido** 85),
Nestor **Araujo**•, Cesar **Ibanez**•, Diego **Reyes**, Diego
de **Buen** (Marvin **Pinon** 56), Carlos **Orrantia**, Jorge
Enriquez• (c), Taufic **Guarch** (Edson **Rivera**• 46),
Erick **Torres**•, Ulises **Davila**. Tr: Juan Carlos **Chavez**

Atanasio Girardot, Medellin
17-08-2011, 17:00, 40 598, Cakir TUR

France 0

Jonathan **Ligali** - Loic **Nego**•, Thomas **Fontaine**•,
Kalidou **Koulibaly**•, Timothee **Kolodziejczak** (Florian
Lejeune• 73), Clement **Grenier**, Gueida **Fofana** (c),
Francis **Coquelin**, Gilles **Sunu** (Gael **Kakuta** 61),
Antoine **Griezmann**, Cedric **Bakambu** (Alexandre
Lacazette 53). Tr: Francis **Smerecki**

Portugal 2
Danilo 9, Nelson Oliveira 40p

Mika - **Roderick**, Nuno **Reis** (c), **Cedric**, Mario **Rui**,
Pele, Julio **Alves**, **Alex** (Luis **Martins** 69), **Danilo**,
Sergio **Oliveira** (Tiago **Ferreira** 89), Nelson **Oliveira**
(Rafael **Lopes** 74). Tr: Ilidio **Vale**

3RD PLACE PLAY-OFF

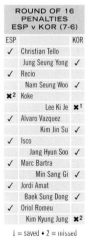

ROUND OF 16
PENALTIES
ESP v KOR (7-6)

	ESP	KOR
✓	Christian Tello	
	Jung Seung Yong	✓
✓	Recio	
	Nam Seung Woo	✓
✗2	Koke	
	Lee Ki Je	✗1
✓	Alvaro Vazquez	
	Kim Jin Su	✓
✓	Isco	
	Jang Hyun Soo	✓
✓	Marc Bartra	
	Min Sang Gi	✓
✓	Jordi Amat	
	Baek Sung Dong	✓
✓	Oriol Romeu	
	Kim Kyung Jung	✗2

1 = saved • 2 = missed

El Campin, Bogotá
20-08-2011, 17:00, 36 058, Arias PAR

Mexico 3
Ulises Davila 12, Jorge Enriquez 49,
Edson Rivera 71
Jose **Rodriguez** - Kristian **Alvarez**, Nestor **Araujo**
(David **Izazola** 46), Cesar **Ibanez**, Diego **Reyes**, Diego
de **Buen** (Marvin **Pinon** 79), Carlos **Orrantia**, Jorge
Enriquez (c), Erick **Torres** (Jorge **Valencia** 46), Ulises
Davila, Edson **Rivera**. Tr: Juan Carlos **Chavez**

France 1
Alexandre Lacazette 8
Jonathan **Ligali** - Thomas **Fontaine**, Kalidou
Koulibaly, Timothee **Kolodziejczak**, Maxim **Colin**,
Clement **Grenier** (Enzo **Reale** 76), Gueida **Fofana**•
(c), Francis **Coquelin**, Gilles **Sunu** (Cedric **Bakambu**
76), Antoine **Griezmann** (Gael **Kakuta** 72), Alexandre
Lacazette•. Tr: Francis **Smerecki**

FINAL

El Campin, Bogotá
20-08-2011, 20:00, 36 058, Geiger USA

Brazil 3
Oscar 3 5 78 111

Gabriel - **Danilo**, Bruno **Uvini** (c), Juan **Jesus**•,
Gabriel Silva (**Allan** 46), **Fernando**, **Casemiro**,
Philippe **Coutinho** (**Dudu** 62), **Oscar**, **Willian**
(**Negueba** 46), **Henrique**•. Tr: Ney **Franc**

Portugal 2
Alex 9, Nelson Oliveira 59

Mika - **Roderick**•, Nuno **Reis** (c), **Cedric** (Julio
Alves• 57), Mario **Rui**, **Pele**•, **Sana**• (Ricardo
Dias 100), **Alex** (**Caetano** 82), **Danilo**, Sergio
Oliveira•, Nelson **Oliveira**•. Tr: Ilidio **Vale**

QUARTER-FINAL
PENALTIES
POR v ARG (5-4)

	POR	ARG
✓	Nuno Reis	
	Lamela	✓
✗1	Danilo	
	Iturbe	✓
✗1	Roderick	
	Nervo	✓
✓	Rafael Lopez	
	Gonzalez Piriz	✗2
✓	Nelson Oliveira	
	Ruiz	✗1
✓	Tiago Ferreira	
	Vuletich	✓
✓	Sergio Oliveira	
	Tagliafico	✗1

1 = saved • 2 = missed

FIFA CLUB WORLD CUP JAPAN 2011

FIFA CLUB WORLD CUP JAPAN 2011

Quarter-finals			Semi-finals		Final	
Barcelona	ESP	Bye				
			Barcelona	4		
			Al Sadd	0		
Espérance Tunis	TUN	1				
Al Sadd	QAT	2				
					Barcelona	4
					Santos	0
Kashiwa Reysol	JPN	1 4p				
Monterrey	MEX	1 3p				
			Kashiwa Reysol	1		
			Santos	3		
Santos	BRA	Bye				

Preliminary round			Fifth place play-off		Third place play-off		
Kashiwa Reysol	JPN	2	**Monterrey**	3	**Al Sadd**	0	5p
Auckland City	NZL	0	Espérance Tunis	2	Kashiwa Reysol	0	3p

PRELIMINARY ROUNDS

Preliminary Round
Toyota Stadium, Toyota
8-12-2011, 19:45, 18 754, Rizzoli ITA

Kashiwa Reysol **2**
Junya Tanaka [37], Masato Kudo [40]

Takanori Sugeno - Hiroki Sakai (Koki Mizuno 67), Tatsuya Masushima, Naoya Kondo•, Wataru Hashimoto - Leandro Domingues, Akimi Barada (Ryoichi Kurisawa 82), Hidekazu Otani, Jorge Wagner - Masato Kudo, Junya Tanaka (Hideaki Kitajima 85). Tr: Nelsinho

Auckland City **0**

Jacob Spoonley - James Pritchett, Ivan Vicelich, Angel Berlanga, Ian Hogg - Andreu - Alex Feneridis (Luis Corrales 49), David Mulligan, Albert Riera (Daniel Koprivic 69), Manel Exposito - Adam Dickinson (Emiliano Tade 68). Tr: Ramon Tribulietx

---

Quarter-final
Toyota Stadium, Toyota
11-12-2011, 16:00, 21 251, Osses CHI

Espérance Tunis **1**
Ousama Darragi [60]

Moez Ben Cherifa - Idrissa Coulibaly (Harrison Afful 46), Walid Hichri•, Banana Yaya, Khalil Chemmam - Mejdi Traoui, Khaled Mouelhi• - Wajdi Bouazzi, Oussama Darragi (Khaled Ayari 75), Youssef Msakni - Yannick N'Djeng. Tr: Nabil Maaloul

Al Sadd **2**
Khalfan Ibrahim [33], Abdulla Koni [49]

Mohammed Saqr - Ibrahim Majid, Mohammed Kasola•, Lee Jung Soo, Nadir Belhadj - Abdulla Koni• - Talal Al Bloushi, Khalfan Ibrahim (Yusef Ali 75), Wesam Rizik (Taher Zakaria 72) - Mamadou Niang (Hasan Al Haidos 90), Abdulkader Keita, Tr: Jorge Fossati

---

Quarter-final
Toyota Stadium, Toyota
11-12-2011, 19:30, 27 525, O'Leary NZL

Kashiwa Reysol **1 4p**
Leandro Domingues [53]

Takanori Sugeno - Hiroki Sakai, Tatsuya Masushima, Naoya Kondo, Wataru Hashimoto• - Leandro Domingues•, Ryoichi Kurisawa•, Hidekazu Otani, Jorge Wagner - Masato Kudo (Ryohei Hayashi 107), Junya Tanaka. Tr: Nelsinho

Monterrey **1 3p**
Humberto Suazo [58]

Jonathan Orozco - Ricardo Osorio, Hiram Mier, Jose Basanta•, Darvin Chavez• (Walter Ayovi 91) - Sergio Santana (Aldo de Nigris 97), Luis Perez, Jesus Zavala, Neri Cardozo (Sergio Perez 100) - Humberto Suazo, Cesar Delgado. Tr: Victor Vucetich

SEMI-FINALS

Semi-final
International Stadium, Yokohama
15-12-2011, 19:30, 66 298, Aguilar SLV

Barcelona **4**
Adriano 2 [25 43], Seydou Keita [64], Maxwell [81]

Victor Valdes - Carles Puyol, Javier Mascherano, Eric Abidal (Maxwell 66) - Adriano, Thiago, Seydou Keita, Andres Iniesta, Pedro - Lionel Messi, David Villa (Alexis Sanchez 39) (Isaac Cuenca 70). Tr: Josep Guardiola

Al Sadd **0**

Mohammed Saqr - Mohammed Kasola•, Abdulla Koni, Lee Jung Soo, Ibrahim Majid•, Nadir Belhadj - Abdulkader Keita (Hasan Al Haidos 85), Talal Al Bloushi (Abdulrab Al Yazidi 65), Wesam Rizik, Khalfan Ibrahim - Mamadou Niang (Yusef Ali 77). Tr: Jorge Fossati

---

Semi-final
Toyota Stadium, Toyota
14-12-2011, 19:30, 29 173, Rizzoli ITA

Kashiwa Reysol **1**
Hiroki Sakai [54]

Takanori Sugeno - Hiroki Sakai, Tatsuya Masushima, Naoya Kondo, Wataru Hashimoto (Akihiro Hyodo 79) - Leandro Domingues•, Ryoichi Kurisawa•, Hidekazu Otani, Jorge Wagner - Masato Kudo (Hideaki Kitajima 46), Junya Tanaka (Masakatsu Sawa 65). Tr: Nelsinho

Santos **3**
Neymar [19], Borges [24], Danilo [63]

Rafael - Danilo (Bruno Aguiar 90), Edu Dracena, Bruno Rodrigo, Durval - Elano (Alan Kardec 59), Henrique•, Arouca - Borges (Ibson 80), Ganso, Neymar. Tr: Muricy Ramalho

PLAY-OFFS

Fifth place play-off
Toyota Stadium, Toyota
14-12-2011, 16:30, 13 639, Irmatov UZB

Monterrey **3**
Hiram Mier [39], Aldo De Nigris [44], Jesus Zavala [44]

Jonathan Orozco - Sergio Perez•, Hiram Mier, Jose Basanta•, Darvin Chavez - Sergio Santana (Severo Meza 87), Luis Perez (Hector Morales 29), Jesus Zavala, Walter Ayovi, Neri Cardozo - Aldo De Nigris. Tr: Victor Vucetich

Espérance Tunis **2**
Yannick N'Djeng [31], Khaled Mouelhi [76p]

Moez Ben Cherifa - Idrissa Coulibaly•, Walid Hichri, Banana Yaya, Khalil Chemmam (Khaled Ayari 54) - Harrison Afful, Mejdi Traoui, Khaled Mouelhi, Wajdi Bouazzi (Oussama Darragi 77) - Youssef Msakni, Yannick N'Djeng. Tr: Nabil Maaloul

---

Third place play-off
International Stadium, Yokohama
18-12-2011, 16:30, 60 527, Doue CIV

Kashiwa Reysol **0 3p**

Takanori Sugeno - Hiroki Sakai, Tatsuya Masushima, Naoya Kondo, Wataru Hashimoto - Koki Mizuno, Akimi Barada, Hidekazu Otani, Jorge Wagner - Hideaki Kitajima (Ryohei Hayashi 81), Junya Tanaka (Masakatsu Sawa 75). Tr: Nelsinho

Al Sadd **0 5p**

Mohammed Saqr - Abdulla Koni, Lee Jung Soo, Ibrahim Majid - Mesaad Al Hamad (Taher Zakaria 90), Abdulrab Al Yazidi (Hasan Al Haidos 83), Wesam Rizik, Nadir Belhadj - Abdulkader Keita, Khalfan Ibrahim (Ali Hasan Yahya 73) - Mamadou Niang. Tr: Jorge Fossati

FIFA Club World Cup Final	International Stadium Yokohama	Sunday 18-12-2011
Kick-off: 19:30		Attendance: 68 166

BARCELONA   4   0   SANTOS

Lionel Messi 2 [17] [82], **Xavi** [24], **Cesc Fabregas** [45]

BARCELONA

Red and blue striped shirts, Blue shorts, Blue socks

Tr: Josep Guardiola ESP

Victor Valdes

Dani Alves   Gerard Pique [39]   Carles Puyol(c) [85]   Eric Abidal
  [56] Javier Mascherano [71]   Andreu Fontas

Sergio Busquets

Xavi   Andres Iniesta

Cesc Fabregas

Lionel Messi   [79] Thiago Pedro

Neymar   [79] Borges / Alan Kardec

[83] Ganso [73] / Ibson

Leo   Henrique   Arouca   [31] Danilo / Elano

Durval   Edu Dracena(c) [74]   Bruno Rodrigo

Rafael Cabral

Tr: Muricy Ramalho

White shirts, White shorts, White socks

SANTOS

MATCH STATS

Barcelona		Santos
16	Shots	8
9	Shots on goal	3
13	Fouls committed	13
4	Corner kicks	2
6	Caught offside	0
71%	Possession	29%

MATCH OFFICIALS

REFEREE
Ravshan Irmatov UZB

ASSISTANTS
Abdukhamidullo Rasulov UZB
Bakhadyr Kochkarov UZB

4TH OFFICIAL
Yuichi Nishimura JPN

I'm delighted with the team's performance and especially with the standard of our play in the first half. Winning the UEFA Champions League was no mean achievement and this is the perfect way to round the whole process off. We managed to isolate Neymar and stop him linking up with Ganso. The secret of our success is simple. We study our opponents closely, use space well, keep control of the ball and move it around very quickly.

Josep Guardiola

I don't think there's any team out there today that can beat Barcelona, though maybe someone will find the secret in the future. They've changed the whole concept of attacking by playing without a genuine striker. Messi showed once again tonight that he's the number one but I think Neymar's time will come. We shouldn't start doubting ourselves just because we've lost to Barcelona. There's no shame in that.

Muricy Ramalho

PART TWO

THE
NATIONS OF
THE WORLD

AFG – AFGHANISTAN

FIFA/COCA-COLA WORLD RANKING

'93	'94	'95	'96	'97	'98	'99	'00	'01	'02	'03	'04	'05	'06	'07	'08	'09	'10	'11	'12
-	-	-	-	-	-	-	-	-	-	196	200	189	180	191	183	193	195	177	

	Jan	Feb	Mar	Apr	May	Jun	Jul	Aug	Sep	Oct	Nov	Dec		High	Low	Av
2011	195	195	195	173	164	166	179	181	183	184	178	177		164	204	190

Afghanistan's position on the periphery of Asian football came to an end as the once-beleaguered national team overcame the odds to reach the final of the South Asian Football Federation Championship in late 2011. Yousef Kargar's team lost out to hosts India in the final in New Delhi, but the defeat could do little to dampen the enthusiasm surrounding one of the finest stories in the continental game since Iraq's victory at the AFC Asian Cup in 2007. The Afghan squad featured a blend of locally-based amateurs and members of the country's diaspora, many playing in the lower leagues in Germany. They began the year with back-to-back wins over Bhutan in the qualifying rounds of the AFC Challenge Cup, kick-started by a hat-trick from Sediq Walizada in the first leg, although they were then knocked out in the second qualifying round by Korea DPR and Nepal. Palestine ended their interest in the 2014 FIFA World Cup qualifiers but it was at the SAFF Championship that Afghanistan underlined their progress. A draw with India in the opening game was followed by wins over Sri Lanka and Bhutan - by a record 8-1 scoreline - earning Afghanistan a place in the last four, where a Belal Arezou goal saw off Nepal. The final saw them lose 4-0 to hosts India, but a second place finish showed the potential that exists in Afghanistan.

FIFA WORLD CUP RECORD
1930-2002 DNE   2006-2014 DNQ

AFGHANISTAN FOOTBALL FEDERATION (AFF)

PO Box 128, Kabul

☎ +93 75 2023770
📠 +93 75 2023770
✉ aff.kabul@gmail.com
🖥 www.aff.com
FA 1933 CON 1954 FIFA 1948
P Keramuddin Karim
GS Mustafa Bakhshi

FIFA BIG COUNT 2006

Total players	526 781
% of population	1.70%
Male	526 441
Female	340
Amateurs 18+	4928
Youth under 18	13 188
Unregistered	4000
Professionals	0
Referees	100
Admin & coaches	45
Number of clubs	224
Number of teams	500

MAJOR CITIES/TOWNS

		Population
1	Kabul	2 413 032
2	Herat	395 877
3	Kandahar	358 845
4	Mazar-e-Sharif	277 302
5	Jalabad	143 525
6	Kunduz	113 746
7	Balkh	89 782
8	Baglan	76 968
9	Meymaneh	58 801
10	Gurian	52 573
11	Ghazni	50 535
12	Khanabad	49 701
13	Taluqan	44 658
14	Pagman	44 072
15	Sibargan	39 412
16	Charikar	38 850
17	Aqcah	38 734
18	Pil-e Humri	378 374
19	Tash Gozar	29 875

AFGHANESTAN • AFGHANISTAN

Capital	Kabul	Population	28 396 000 (43)	% in cities	24%
GDP per capita	$700 (219)	Area km²	652 230 km² (41)	GMT +/-	+4.5

Neighbours (km) China 76, Iran 936, Pakistan 2430, Tajikistan 1206, Turkmenistan 744, Uzbekistan 137

RECENT INTERNATIONALS PLAYED BY AFGHANISTAN

2005	Opponents	Score		Venue	Comp	Scorers	Att	Referee
9-11	Tajikistan	L	0-4	Dushanbe	Fr			
7-12	Maldives	L	1-9	Karachi	SAFr1	Sayed Maqsood [39]		
9-12	Pakistan	L	0-1	Karachi	SAFr1			
11-12	Sri Lanka	W	2-1	Karachi	SAFr1	Hafizullah Qadami [35], Abdul Maroof Gullistani [41]		
2006								
1-04	India	L	0-2	Chittagong	CCr1		2 500	Al Ghatrifi OMA
3-04	Chinese Taipei	D	2-2	Chittagong	CCr1	Hafizullah Qadami 2 [20 23]	2 500	Lee Gi Young KOR
5-04	Philippines	D	1-1	Chittagong	CCr1	Sayed Maqsood [26]	3 000	Mujghef JOR
2007								
8-10	Syria	L	0-3	Damascus	WCq		3 000	Al Ghamdi KSA
26-10	Syria	L	1-2	Dushanbe	WCq	Obaidullah Karimi [15]	2 000	Irmatov UZB
2008								
5-05	Bangladesh	D	0-0	Bishkek	CCq		3 000	Al Senan UAE
7-05	Kyrgyzstan	W	1-0	Bishkek	CCq	Ata Yamrali [38]	7 000	Shaharul MAS
4-06	Sri Lanka	D	2-2	Colombo	SAFr1	Harez-Arian Habib 2 [7 49]		
6-06	Bangladesh	D	2-2	Colombo	SAFr1	Ata Yamrali [7], Mustafa Hadid [24]		
8-06	Bhutan	L	1-3	Colombo	SAFr1	Harez-Arian Habib [87]		
30-07	India	L	0-1	Hyderabad	CCr1		300	Iemoto JPN
1-08	Turkmenistan	L	0-5	Hyderabad	CCr1		350	Shamsuzzaman BAN
3-08	Tajikistan	L	0-4	Hyderabad	CCr1		150	Vo Minh Tri VIE
17-10	Nepal	D	2-2	Petaling Jaya	Fr	Hashmatullah Barekzai 2 [62 72]		
20-10	Malaysia	L	0-6	Petaling Jaya	Fr			
2009								
5-12	India †	L	0-1	Dhaka	SAFr1			
7-12	Maldives	L	1-3	Dhaka	SAFr1	Hashmatullah Barekzai [30]		
9-12	Nepal	L	0-3	Dhaka	SAFr1			
2010								
17-11	Tajikistan	L	0-1	Dushanbe	Fr			
2011								
23-03	Bhutan	W	3-0	Gurgaon	CCq	Sediq Walizada 3 [2 36 80]	200	Mahapab THA
25-03	Bhutan	W	2-0	Gurgaon	CCq	Wahid Nadeem [61], Israfeel Kohistani [65]	2 000	Mombeni IRN
7-04	Nepal	L	0-1	Kathmandu	CCq		9 100	Abdul Baki OMA
9-04	Sri Lanka	W	1-0	Kathmandu	CCq	Mustafa Hadid [82]	1 800	Adday IRQ
11-04	Korea DPR	L	0-2	Kathmandu	CCq		1 000	Abdul Baki OMA
29-06	Palestine	L	0-2	Tursunzade	WCq		5 000	Al Ghafari JOR
3-07	Palestine	D	1-1	Al Ram	WCq	Mohammad Arezou [63]	9 000	Al Dosari QAT
3-12	India	D	1-1	New Delhi	SAFr1	Mohammad Arezou [5]		Noor Mohamed MAS
5-12	Sri Lanka	W	3-1	New Delhi	SAFr1	Sanjar Ahmadi 2 [22 36], Ata Yamrali [78]		Faizullin KGZ
7-12	Bhutan	W	8-1	New Delhi	SAFr1	Ata Yamrali [4], Zohib Amiri [10], Mohammad Arezou 4 [15 18 45 83], Mohammad Mashriqi [60], Djelaludin Sharityar [48]		Gamini SRI
9-12	Nepal	W	1-0	New Delhi	SAFsf	Mohammad Arezou [101]		Tufaylieh SYR
11-12	India	L	0-4	New Delhi	SAFf		20 000	Singh SIN

SAF = South Asian Football Federation Cup • AC = Asian Cup • CC = AFC Challenge Cup • WC = FIFA World Cup
q = qualifier • r1 = first round group • † Not a full international

AFGHANISTAN NATIONAL TEAM HISTORICAL RECORDS

Caps **31** - Israfeel Kohistani 2005-

Goals **7** - Mohammad Balal Arezou 2011-

Coaches Holger Obermann GER 2003 • Mir Ali Akbarzada 2003 • Ali Askar Lali 2003-05 • Klaus Stark 2005-08 • Mohammad Yousef Kargar 2008-09 • Mohammad Farid 2009 • Mohammad Yousef Kargar 2010-

AIA – ANGUILLA

FIFA/COCA-COLA WORLD RANKING

'93	'94	'95	'96	'97	'98	'99	'00	'01	'02	'03	'04	'05	'06	'07	'08	'09	'10	'11	'12
-	-	-	-	190	197	202	197	194	196	198	197	198	196	198	201	203	203	201	

2011													High	Low	Av
Jan	Feb	Mar	Apr	May	Jun	Jul	Aug	Sep	Oct	Nov	Dec				
203	203	202	202	202	197	199	200	198	197	197	201		189	205	197

Anguilla's 2014 FIFA World Cup qualifying campaign came to a swift and predictable end after two defeats in a preliminary round tie against the Dominican Republic. Unable to stage a match at home, both games were held in the Dominican Republic at the Estadio Panamericano. In 2010 their opponents had inflicted a record 17-0 thrashing on the British Virgin Islands but thankfully the Anguillans were able to avoid a repeat performance, restricting the Dominican Republic to just two in the first leg. The two had met in the 2006 FIFA World Cup qualifiers and, as then, Anguilla lost the tie 6-0 on aggregate - a 4-0 defeat in the second leg meaning that after four World Cup qualifying campaigns Anguilla are still looking for a first victory in the eight games they have played. Only one of those eight games has been played at home and until the island can stage more matches in the future, that record is unlikely to improve. Club football in Anguilla continues to develop with the 2010-11 season dominated by Kicks United from The Valley. They won their second title in five years, finishing four points ahead of defending champions Roaring Lions. The two also met in the Cup final with Kicks United completing the double, the fourth year in a row that the league champions have also walked away with the cup.

FIFA WORLD CUP RECORD
1930-1998 DNE 2002-2014 DNQ

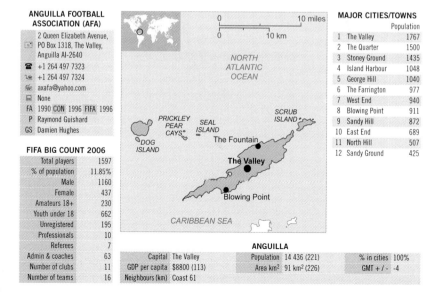

ANGUILLA FOOTBALL ASSOCIATION (AFA)

- 2 Queen Elizabeth Avenue, PO Box 1318, The Valley, Anguilla AI-2640
- ☎ +1 264 497 7323
- 📠 +1 264 497 7324
- ✉ axafa@yahoo.com
- 🖥 None
- FA 1990 CON 1996 FIFA 1996
- P Raymond Guishard
- GS Damien Hughes

FIFA BIG COUNT 2006

Total players	1597
% of population	11.85%
Male	1160
Female	437
Amateurs 18+	230
Youth under 18	662
Unregistered	195
Professionals	10
Referees	7
Admin & coaches	63
Number of clubs	11
Number of teams	16

MAJOR CITIES/TOWNS

		Population
1	The Valley	1767
2	The Quarter	1500
3	Stoney Ground	1435
4	Island Harbour	1048
5	George Hill	1040
6	The Farrington	977
7	West End	940
8	Blowing Point	911
9	Sandy Hill	872
10	East End	689
11	North Hill	507
12	Sandy Ground	425

ANGUILLA

Capital	The Valley	Population	14 436 (221)	% in cities	100%
GDP per capita	$8800 (113)	Area km²	91 km² (226)	GMT +/-	-4
Neighbours (km)	Coast 61				

RECENT INTERNATIONALS PLAYED BY ANGUILLA

2004	Opponents		Score	Venue	Comp	Scorers	Att	Referee
19-03	Dominican Republic	D	0-0	Santo Domingo	WCq		400	Mattus CRC
21-03	Dominican Republic	L	0-6	Santo Domingo	WCq		850	Porras CRC
2005								
No international matches played in 2005								
2006								
20-09	Antigua and Barbuda	L	3-5	St John's	CCq	Gaekwad St Hillaire [13], Kapil Assent [51], Richard O'Connor [90]	300	Wijngaarde SUR
22-09	St Kitts and Nevis	L	1-6	St John's	CCq	Richard O'Connor [22]	500	Phillips GRN
24-09	Barbados	L	1-7	St John's	CCq	Girdon Connor [48]	2 800	Wijngaarde SUR
2007								
No international matches played in 2007								
2008								
6-02	El Salvador	L	0-12	San Salvador	WCq		15 000	Jauregui ANT
26-03	El Salvador	L	0-4	Washington DC	WCq		22 670	Bedeau GRN
17-09	St Vincent/Grenadines	L	1-3	Fort de France	CCq	Troy Jeffers OG [38]	100	Fanus LCA
19-09	Martinique †	L	1-3	Fort de France	CCq	Kapil Battice [83]	500	George LCA
2009								
No international matches played in 2009								
2010								
18-09	British Virgin Islands	L	1-2	Saint Martin	Fr			
2-10	Puerto Rico	L	1-3	Bayamon	CCq	Walwyn Benjamin [54p]	2 050	Thomas JAM
4-10	Cayman Islands	L	1-4	Bayamon	CCq	Javille Brooks [32]	500	Davis TRI
6-10	Saint Martin †	W	2-1	Bayamon	CCq	Javille Brooks [19], Terrence Rogers [38]	500	Davis TRI
2011								
19-06	US Virgin Islands	D	0-0	The Valley	Fr		550	Burton AIA
8-07	Dominican Republic	L	0-2	San Cristobal	WCq		1 000	Brizan TRI
10-07	Dominican Republic	L	0-4	San Cristobal	WCq		1 500	Brea CUB

Fr = Friendly match • WC = FIFA World Cup • CC = Digicel Caribbean Cup • q = qualifier • † Not a full international

CCCAFA CUP 2011

RWP Annexe, The Valley,

Kicks United	Roaring Lions

ALB – ALBANIA

FIFA/COCA-COLA WORLD RANKING

'93	'94	'95	'96	'97	'98	'99	'00	'01	'02	'03	'04	'05	'06	'07	'08	'09	'10	'11	'12
92	100	91	116	116	106	83	72	96	93	89	86	82	87	80	81	96	65	74	

	2011															
Jan	Feb	Mar	Apr	May	Jun	Jul	Aug	Sep	Oct	Nov	Dec		High	Low	Av
64	66	73	50	50	59	59	57	71	71	75	74		50	124	89

For only the second time in the history of the league in Albania a club from the capital Tirana failed to finish in the top three. The first occasion had been way back in 1933, just four years after the creation of the championship. Skenderbeu Korce had won their first title that year and, remarkably, 2011 saw them win their second - 78 years later. Having just missed out on relegation in 2010 their success was largely down to wealthy owner Agim Seqo who gave the club the resources to put together a competitive team. KF Tirana were the best placed club from the capital - in fifth place while 2010 champions Dinamo suffered the ignominy of having to take part in a relegation play-off, only keeping their top-flight status after beating Beselidhja. Spare a thought, however, for the capital's third club Partizani. With 15 league titles and 15 cup triumphs to their name, they were relegated to the obscurity of the third division. At national team level, 2011 ended in huge disappointment, especially given the promise shown in 2010. Defeat at the hands of Luxembourg during the Euro 2012 qualifiers was the low point and it led to the exit of Croatian coach Josip Kuze at the end of the campaign. He was replaced for the 2014 FIFA World Cup qualifiers by the Italian Giovanni de Biasi who was appointed in December 2011.

UEFA EUROPEAN CHAMPIONSHIP RECORD
1960 DNE 1964-1972 DNQ 1976-1980 DNE 1984-2012 DNQ

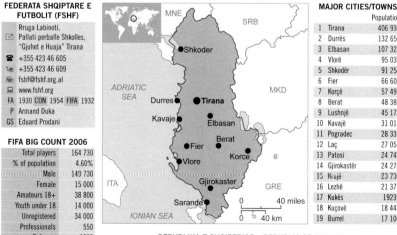

FEDERATA SHQIPTARE E FUTBOLIT (FSHF)

	Rruga Labinoti,
✉	Pallati perballe Shkolles,
	"Gjuhet e Huaja" Tirana
☎	+355 423 46 605
📠	+355 423 46 609
@	fshf@fshf.org.al
🖥	www.fshf.org
FA	1930 CON 1954 FIFA 1932
P	Armand Duka
GS	Eduard Prodani

FIFA BIG COUNT 2006

Total players	164 730
% of population	4.60%
Male	149 730
Female	15 000
Amateurs 18+	38 800
Youth under 18	14 000
Unregistered	34 000
Professionals	550
Referees	1200
Admin & coaches	5000
Number of clubs	440
Number of teams	574

MAJOR CITIES/TOWNS

		Population
1	Tirana	406 936
2	Durrës	132 655
3	Elbasan	107 323
4	Vlorë	95 033
5	Shkodër	91 257
6	Fier	66 600
7	Korçë	57 494
8	Berat	48 385
9	Lushnjë	45 171
10	Kavajë	31 014
11	Pogradec	28 333
12	Laç	27 055
13	Patosi	24 749
14	Gjirokastër	24 278
15	Kruje	23 704
16	Lezhë	21 371
17	Kukës	19239
18	Kuçovë	18 448
19	Burrel	17 100

REPUBLIKA E SHQIPERISE • REPUBLIC OF ALBANIA

Capital	Tirana	Population	3 639 453 (129)	% in cities	47%
GDP per capita	$6000 (132)	Area km²	28 748 km² (144)	GMT + / -	+1
Neighbours (km)	Greece 282, Macedonia 151, Montenegro 172, Kosovo 112 • Coast 362				

RECENT INTERNATIONALS PLAYED BY ALBANIA

2008 Opponents	Score		Venue	Comp	Scorers	Att	Referee
27-05 Poland	L	0-1	Reutlingen	Fr		2 200	Kircher GER
20-08 Liechtenstein	W	2-0	Tirana	Fr	Hyka [1], Kapllani [18]	1 500	Vlk SVK
6-09 Sweden	D	0-0	Tirana	WCq		13 522	Undiano ESP
10-09 Malta	W	3-0	Tirana	WCq	Bogdani [45], Duro [84], Dallku [90]	7 400	Schoergenhofer AUT
11-10 Hungary	L	0-2	Budapest	WCq		18 000	Circhetta SUI
15-10 Portugal	D	0-0	Braga	WCq		29 500	Kircher GER
19-11 Azerbaijan	D	1-1	Baku	Fr	Skela [12]	10 000	Silagava GEO
2009							
11-02 Malta	D	0-0	Ta'Qali	WCq		2041	Deaconu ROU
28-03 Hungary	L	0-1	Tirana	WCq		12 000	Kuipers NED
1-04 Denmark	L	0-3	Copenhagen	WCq		24 320	Skomina SVN
6-06 Portugal	L	1-2	Tirana	WCq	Bogdani [29]	13 320	Meyer GER
10-06 Georgia	D	1-1	Tirana	Fr	Agolli [58]	2 000	Stavrev MKD
12-08 Cyprus	W	6-1	Tirana	Fr	Skela 2 [25p 44p], Bogdani [65], OG [67], Agolli [71], Vila [75]		Yildrim TUR
9-09 Denmark	D	1-1	Tirana	WCq	Bogdani [51]	8 000	Cakir TUR
14-10 Sweden	L	1-4	Stockholm	WCq	Salihi [57]	25 342	Ivanov.N RUS
14-11 Estonia	D	0-0	Tallinn	Fr		2 110	Kancleris LTU
2010							
3-03 Northern Ireland	W	1-0	Tirana	Fr	Skela [25]	7 500	Pilav BIH
25-05 Montenegro	W	1-0	Podgorica	Fr	Salihi [79]	7 000	Strahonja CRO
2-06 Andorra	W	1-0	Tirana	Fr	Salihi [44]	3 000	Meckarovski MKD
11-08 Uzbekistan	W	1-0	Durres	Fr	Salihi [14]	8 000	Radovanovic MNE
3-09 Romania	D	1-1	Piatra-Neamt	ECq	Muzaka [87]	13 000	Schorgenhofer AUT
7-09 Luxembourg	W	1-0	Shkoder	ECq	Salihi [37]	11 800	Trutz SVK
8-10 Bosnia-Herzegovina	D	1-1	Tirana	ECq	Duro [45]	11 300	Jakobsson ISL
12-10 Belarus	L	0-2	Minsk	ECq		7 000	Rasmussen DEN
17-11 Macedonia FYR	D	0-0	Korce	Fr		12 000	Gocek TUR
2011							
9-02 Slovenia	L	1-2	Tirana	Fr	Bulku [62]		Koukoulakis GRE
26-03 Belarus	W	1-0	Tirana	ECq	Salihi [62]	13 826	Strombergsson SWE
7-06 Bosnia-Herzegovina	L	0-2	Zenica	ECq		9 000	Blom NED
20-06 Argentina	L	0-4	Buenos Aires	Fr		21 000	Larrionda URU
10-08 Montenegro	W	3-2	Tirana	Fr	Bogdani [33], Hyka [64], Salihi [69]	5 500	Genov BUL
2-09 France	L	1-2	Tirana	ECq	Bogdani [46]	15 600	Nikolaev RUS
6-09 Luxembourg	L	1-2	Luxembourg	ECq	Bogdani [64]	2 132	Kari FIN
7-10 France	L	0-3	Paris	ECq		65 239	Koukoulakis GRE
11-10 Romania	D	1-1	Tirana	ECq	Salihi [24]	3 000	Mazeika LTU
11-11 Azerbaijan	L	0-1	Tirana	Fr		1 200	Mazzoleni ITA
15-11 Macedonia FYR	D	0-0	Prilep	Fr		4 500	Vincic SVN

Fr = Friendly match • EC = UEFA EURO 2012 • WC = FIFA World Cup • q = qualifier

ALBANIA NATIONAL TEAM HISTORICAL RECORDS

Caps
79 - Altin Lala 1998- • 77 - Klodian Duro 2000- • 75 - Ervin Skela 2000- • 73 - Foto Strakosha 1990-2004 • 68 - Igli Tare 1997-2007 • 67 - Alban Bushi 1995-2007 • 66 - Altin Haxhi 1995-2009 • 65 - Erjon Bogdani 1996- • 63 - Altin Rraklli 1992-2005 • 59 - Rudi Vata 1990-2000

Goals
15 - Erjon Bogdani 1996- • 14 - Alban Bushi 1995-2007 • 13 - Ervin Skela 2000- • 11 - Altin Rraklli 1992-2005 • 10 - Sokol Kushta 1987-96, Igli Tare 1997-2007 • 9 - Hamdi Salihi 2006- • 8 - Adrian Aliaj 2002-06 • 6 - Loro Borici 1946-58, Edmond Kapllani 2004-08, Bledar Kola 1994-2001 & Klodian Duro 2000-

Past Coaches
Ljubisa Brocic YUG 1946 • Adem Karapici 1947 • Sllave Llambi 1948-50 • Miklos Vadas HUN 1953 • Zyber Konci 1963-65 • Loro Borici 1965-72 • Myslym Alla 1972-73 • Ilia Shuke 1973 • Zyber Konci 1980 • Loro Borici 1981 • Shyqyri Rreli 1982-85 • Agron Sulaj 1985-88 • Shyqyri Rreli 1988-90 • Agron Sulaj 1990 • Bejkush Birce 1990-94 • Neptun Bajko 1994-96 • Astrit Hafizi 1996-99 • Medin Zhega 2000-01 • Sulejman Demollari 2001-02 • Giuseppe Dossena ITA 2002 • Hans-Peter Briegel GER 2002-06 • Otto Baric CRO 2006-07 • Slavko Kovacic 2007 • Arie Haan NED 2008-09 • Josip Kuze CRO 2009-11 • Gianni De Biasi ITA 2011

ALBANIA 2010-11
KATEGORIA SUPERIORE

Team	Pl	W	D	L	F	A	Pts
Skënderbeu Korçë †	33	23	4	6	52	23	73
Flamurtari Vlorë §3 ‡	33	22	3	8	62	27	66
Vllaznia Shkodër ‡	33	17	8	8	41	27	59
Laçi	33	14	5	14	44	44	47
KF Tirana ‡	33	11	11	11	42	31	44
Bylis Ballshi	33	13	4	16	44	48	43
Teuta Durrës	33	11	9	13	38	40	42
Kastrioti Krujë	33	11	9	13	40	47	42
Shkumbini Peqin	33	12	6	15	43	54	42
Dinamo Tiranë	33	10	9	14	46	50	39
Besa Kavajë	33	10	9	14	35	47	39
KF Elbasani	33	4	3	26	30	79	12

Results grid (home results; Skënderbeu, Flamurtari, Vllaznia, Laçi, KF Tirana, Bylis, Teuta, Kastrioti, Shkumbini, Dinamo, Besa, Elbasani):

	Skë	Fla	Vll	Laç	Tir	Byl	Teu	Kas	Shk	Din	Bes	Elb
Skënderbeu		1-0	2-0 3-0	2-1 2-0	2-1	2-0 3-1	2-0 1-0	5-1	1-0 2-0	3-2	4-0	1-0 1-0
Flamurtari	4-0 1-0		2-0	1-0 2-1	2-1 1-0	1-0	3-0 1-0	4-2	3-1 6-2	1-0 3-0	4-0	8-0
Vllaznia	2-1	1-3 3-0		2-1	0-0 1-0	3-2	0-0	1-0 1-1	0-0	0-4 3-1	2-1 2-0	3-0 3-1
Laçi	0-1	0-1 1-1	0-1 1-3		1-1	3-1	1-0 2-0	3-1	2-0	0-0 1-0	1-0 3-2	1-0 3-1
KF Tirana	0-0	0-1	2-1 0-2	2-0 4-0		2-1 0-2	2-0	1-2 4-0	0-0	1-0 1-1	0-0	3-1 6-1
Bylis	1-1	1-0	1-0 0-0	2-0 1-2	1-0		1-1	3-0 1-0	1-0	3-2	2-0	3-1 1-2
Teuta	2-0	2-1	1-1	0-3	0-0 0-3	2-0		0-0 6-0	1-1	1-0 3-1	1-2	1-2 4-2 2-1
Kastrioti	1-0	0-0 0-2	1-2	0-0	3-1	0-0	2-0		2-1 2-1	3-1	2-0 1-2	4-3 2-1 3-1
Shkumbini	3-1	3-1	2-1	1-0	1-0	2-1	2-5	1-3		4-2 1-1	2-2 2-1	1-0 2-2 3-2
Dinamo	1-3 2-3	0-1	0-0	3-3	1-2	0-0	2-1	1-1 1-2	0-0		1-0 4-1	2-1 2-1 3-1
Besa	0-2 0-0	0-0	0-1	1-2	2-1	3-2 2-1	2-1	0-0	0-0 3-2	2-1		1-1 1-0 2-0
KF Elbasani	1-0	1-2	0-4	2-3	1-1	3-2	0-2	2-0	2-4	1-1 2-1	1-2 1-2	1-3 1-1 0-1

21/08/2010 - 16/05/2011 • † Qualified for the UEFA Champions League • ‡ Qualified for the Europa League • § = points deducted • Matches in bold awarded • Relegation play-offs: **Shkumbini** 1-0 Adriatiku • Besëlidhja 1-4 **Dinamo** • Top scorers: **19** - Daniel Xhafa, Flamurtari • **14** - Pero Pejic CRO, Tirana • **13** - Brunild Pepa, Teuta; Emiljano Vila, Dinamo; Alfredo Sosa ARG, Skënderbeu & Vilfor Hysa, Laçi

ALBANIA 2010-11
KATEGORIA E PARE (2)

Team	Pl	W	D	L	F	A	Pts
Pogradeci	30	22	2	6	56	27	68
Tomori Berat	30	20	3	7	50	24	63
Kamza	30	17	9	4	42	20	60
Apolonia Fier	30	18	6	6	50	31	60
Besëlidhja Lezhë	30	16	9	5	40	17	57
Adriatiku Mamurrasi	30	13	4	13	29	29	43
KS Lushnja	30	12	3	15	35	25	39
Gramozi Ersekë	30	12	3	15	34	45	39
Ada Velipojë	30	11	4	15	40	42	37
Burreli	30	10	6	14	29	36	36
Vlora	30	10	4	16	36	47	34
Luftëtari Gjirokastër	30	9	7	13	20	34	34
Gramshi	30	8	7	15	23	33	31
Tërbuni Pukë	30	8	7	15	27	42	31
Bilisht Sport	30	8	3	19	31	64	27
Partizani Tiranë	30	4	5	20	16	42	17

11/09/2010 - 15/05/2011

MEDALS TABLE

		Overall			League			Cup	
		G	S	B	G	S	B	G	S
1	KF Tirana	37	21	12	24	13	12	13	8
2	Partizani Tiranë	30	27	8	15	19	8	15	8
3	Dinamo Tiranë	31	15	11	18	9	11	13	6
4	Vllaznia Shkodër	15	18	15	9	11	15	6	7
5	Teuta Durrës	4	11	5	1	5	5	3	6
6	SK Elbasani	4	2	1	2	1	1	2	1
7	Flamurtari Vlorë	4	15	3	1	7	3	3	8
8	Besa Kavajë	2	8	10		2	10	2	6
9	Skënderbeu Korçë	2	6	2	2	3	2		3
10	Apollonia Fier	1						1	
11	Lushnja		3						3
12	Tomori Berat		2			1			1
13	Albpetrol Patosi		1			1			
	Luftëtari Gjirokastër			1			1		
15	Bylis Ballshi			1					1

KUPA E SHQIPERISE 2010-11

Round of 16			Quarter-finals			Semi-finals			Final		
KF Tirana *	3	1									
Ada Velipojë	0	2	KF Tirana	1	5						
Flamurtari Vlorë *	0	0	Bylis Ballshi *	2	1						
Bylis Ballshi	0	1				KF Tirana *	1	1			
Skënderbeu Korçë *	0	2				Besa Kavajë	0	1			
Teuta Durrës	0	0	Skënderbeu Korçë *	1	2						
KS Lushnja	0	0	Besa Kavajë	3	2						
Besa Kavajë *	0	1									
Vllaznia Shkodër *	1	4							KF Tirana	1	4p
KF Elbasani	0	0	Vllaznia Shkodër *	2	4				Dinamo Tiranë	1	3p
Gramozi Ersekë	2	0	Laçi	0	2						
Laçi *	2	4				Vllaznia Shkodër *	2	0			
Shkumbini Peqin *	3	2				Dinamo Tiranë	1	1			
Kastrioti Krujë	1	2	Shkumbini Peqin *	2 1	8p						
Kamza	2	0	Dinamo Tiranë	1 2	9p						
Dinamo Tiranë *	3	2									

* Home team in the first leg • ‡ Qualified for the Europa League

CUP FINAL
Niko Dovana, Durres
22-05-2011, Att: 3000, Ref: Jemini
Scorers - Pejic 52 for Tirana; Brkic 19 for Dinamo

Cup Final line-ups: **Tirana** - Ilion Lika - Ivan Gvozdenovic, Andi Lila, Tefik Osmani••◆105, Erjon Dushku - Mladen Zizovic (Elvis Sina 90), Erindo Karabeci (Gentian Muca• 46), Gilman Lika (Bekim Bala 54), Jahmir Hyka - Sabien Lilaj, Pero Pejic•. Tr: Miso Krsticevic
Dinamo - Alban Hoxha - Nertil Ferraj, Milovan Milovic, Renato Mallota (Asjon Daja 90), Lucas Malacarne, Nurudeen Orelesi• - Igli Allmuca, Emiljano Vila, Jordan Opoku - Nestor Martinena•, Mladen Brkic (Roland Peqini 90••◆117). Tr: Artan Mergjyshi

ALG – ALGERIA

FIFA/COCA-COLA WORLD RANKING

'93	'94	'95	'96	'97	'98	'99	'00	'01	'02	'03	'04	'05	'06	'07	'08	'09	'10	'11	'12
35	57	48	49	59	71	86	82	75	68	62	73	80	80	79	64	26	35	30	

2011												High	Low	Av
Jan	Feb	Mar	Apr	May	Jun	Jul	Aug	Sep	Oct	Nov	Dec			
36	55	55	40	41	51	52	46	46	35	30	30	26	103	62

After a semi-final appearance at the 2010 CAF Africa Cup of Nations finals in Angola and participation at the FIFA World Cup finals in South Africa, the promise of an end to Algeria's long slump looked on the cards. 2011 proved to be a disappointment, however, with failure to qualify for the Nations Cup in Gabon and Equatorial Guinea along with Algerian clubs' continued inability to make any impact in African continental competition. The Nations Cup failure led to the resignation of Abdelhak Benchikha, replaced as national team coach by Vahid Halilhodzic who agreed a three-year contract starting in July 2011. He is tasked with qualification to the 2014 FIFA World Cup where Algeria have been grouped with Benin, Mali and Rwanda. In club football there was a surprise first league title for ASO Chlef, a club based in a provincial town some 200km west from the capital Algiers. Founded in 1947, Chlef have only recently begun to make their mark in Algerian football. Their only other honour came in 2005 when they won the cup but under coach Meziane Ighil finally broke their duck in the league finishing 13 points clear of JSM Béjaïa. JS Kabylie may be Algeria's most successful club, but their Cup Final win over USM El Harrach was surprisingly their first since 1994 and came thanks to a early Fares Hamiti goal in a 1-0 win.

CAF AFRICA CUP OF NATIONS RECORD

1957-1965 DNE **1968** r1 1970-1978 DNQ **1980** 2 F **1982** 4 SF **1984** 3 SF **1986** r1 **1988** 3 SF **1990** 1 Winners (Hosts) **1992** r1 **1994** Disqualified **1996** 5 QF **1998** r1 **2000** 6 QF **2002** r1 **2004** 8 QF 2006-2008 DNQ **2010** 4 SF **2012** DNQ

FEDERATION ALGERIENNE DE FOOTBALL (FAF)

Chemin Ahmed Ouaked,
Boite Postale
Dely Ibrahim 39, Alger

☎ +213 21 366800
📠 +213 21 360318
✉ faffoot@yahoo.fr
🖥 www.faf.dz
FA 1962 CON 1964 FIFA 1963
P Mohamed Raouraoua
GS Nadir Bouzenad

FIFA BIG COUNT 2006

Total players	1 790 200
% of population	5.44%
Male	1 719 100
Female	71 100
Amateurs 18+	138 800
Youth under 18	64 800
Unregistered	248 300
Professionals	300
Referees	1700
Admin & coaches	22 800
Number of clubs	2090
Number of teams	2560

MAJOR CITIES/TOWNS

		Population
1	Algiers	2 203 698
2	Oran	679 877
3	Constantine	462 779
4	Batna	297 835
5	Djelfa	261 026
6	Setif	233 913
7	Biskra	211 890
8	Annaba	205 597
9	Tibissah	197 636
10	Sidi bel Abbès	197 603
11	Tiyaret	194 392
12	El Bouni	193 422
13	Bordj B Arreridj	179 969
14	Ouargla	174 122
15	Chlef	171 815
16	Béjaïa	171 673
17	Blida	170 773
36	Tlemcen	122 329
39	Tizi-Ouzou	116 318

AL JAZA'IR • PEOPLE'S DEMOCRATIC REPUBLIC OF ALGERIA

Capital Algiers	Population 34 178 188 (36)	% in cities 65%
GDP per capita $6900 (126)	Area km² 2 381 741 km² (11)	GMT +/- +1
Neighbours (km) Libya 982, Mali 1376, Mauritania 463, Morocco 1559, Niger 956, Tunisia 965 • Coast 998		

RECENT INTERNATIONALS PLAYED BY ALGERIA

2009	Opponents	Score	Venue	Comp	Scorers	Att	Referee
11-02	Benin	W 2-1	Blida	Fr	Ghezzal 35, Ghilas 45		
28-03	Rwanda	D 0-0	Kigali	WCq		22 000	Codjia BEN
7-06	Egypt	W 3-1	Blida	WCq	Matmour 60, Ghezzal 64, Djebbour 77	26 500	Bennett RSA
20-06	Zambia	W 2-0	Chililabombwe	WCq	Bougherra 21, Saifi 66	9 000	Evehe CMR
12-08	Uruguay	W 1-0	Algiers	Fr	Djebbour 79	20 000	Harzi TUN
6-09	Zambia	W 1-0	Blida	WCq	Saifi 59	30 000	Seechurn MRI
11-10	Rwanda	W 3-1	Blida	WCq	Ghezzal 22, Belhadj 45, Ziani 95+p	22 000	Keita GUI
14-11	Egypt	L 0-2	Cairo	WCq		75 000	Damon RSA
18-11	Egypt	W 1-0	Omdurman	WCpo	Yahia 40	35 000	Maillet SEY
2010							
11-01	Malawi	L 0-3	Luanda	CNr1		1 000	Diatta SEN
14-01	Mali	W 1-0	Luanda	CNr1	Halliche 43	4 000	Ssegonga UGA
18-01	Angola	D 0-0	Luanda	CNr1		40 000	Damon RSA
24-01	Côte d'Ivoire	W 3-2	Cabinda	CNqf	Matmour 39, Bougherra 92+, Bouazza 92	10 000	Maillet SEY
28-01	Egypt	L 0-4	Benguela	CNsf		30 000	Codjia BEN
30-01	Nigeria	L 0-1	Benguela	CN3p		12 000	Diatta SEN
3-03	Algeria	L 0-3	Algiers	Fr		65 000	Diatta SEN
28-05	Republic of Ireland	L 0-3	Dublin	Fr		16 800	Braamhaar NED
5-06	UAE	W 1-0	Fürth	Fr	Ziani 51p	12 500	Grafe GER
13-06	Slovenia	L 0-1	Polokwane	WCr1		30 325	Batres GUA
18-06	England	D 0-0	Cape Town	WCr1		64 100	Irmatov UZB
23-06	USA	L 0-1	Pretoria	WCr1		35 827	De Bleeckere BEL
11-08	Gabon	L 1-2	Algiers	Fr	Djebbour 85	55 000	Rouaissi MAR
3-09	Tanzania	D 1-1	Blida	CNq	Guedioura 44	30 000	Djaoupe TOG
8-10	Central African Rep	L 0-2	Bangui	CNq		25 000	Carvalho ANG
17-11	Luxembourg	D 0-0	Luxembourg	Fr		7 033	Sippel GER
2011							
27-03	Morocco	W 1-0	Annaba	CNq	Yebda 7	60 000	Seechurn MRI
4-06	Morocco	L 0-4	Marrakech	CNq			Doue CIV
3-09	Tanzania	D 1-1	Dar es Salaam	CNq	Bouazza 52		Djaoupe TOG
9-10	Central African Rep	W 2-0	Blida	CNq	Yebda 2, Kadir 30		Fall SEN
12-11	Tunisia	W 1-0	Algiers	Fr		25 000	Laachiri MAR

Fr = Friendly match • CN = CAF African Cup of Nations • WC = FIFA World Cup • q = qualifier • r1 = first round group • qf = quarter-final

ALGERIA NATIONAL TEAM HISTORICAL RECORDS

Caps
89 - Lakhdar Belloumi 1978-89 • 86 - Rabah Madjer 1978-92 • 81 - Billel Dziri 1992-2005 • 80 - Djamel Menad 1980-95 • 79 - Abdelhafid Tasfaout 1991-2002 • 77 - Mahieddine Meftah 1989-2002 • 75 - Mahmoud Guendouz 1977-86 • 69 - Salah Assad 1977-89 • 68 - Fodil Megharia 1984-92 • 67 - Yazid Mansouri 2001-

Goals
35 - Abdelhafid Tasfaout 1990-2002 • 34 - Lakhdar Belloumi 1978-92 • 29 - Rabah Madjer 1978-92 • 24 - Djamel Menad 1982-95 • 22 - Tedj Bensaoula 1979-86 • 18 - Rafik Saifi 1999- • 13 - Salah Assad 1978-88 • 12 - Hacene Lalmas 1964-74 • 10 - Ali Mecabih 1995-2003 • 9 - Billel Dziri 1993-2002

Past Coaches
Kader Firoud 1963 • Smail Khabatou 1963-64 • Abderrahmane Ibrir 1964-65 • Smail Khabatou 1965-66 • Lucien Leduc FRA 1966-69 • Said Amara 1969 • Hamid Zouba & Abdelaziz Ben Tifour 1969-70 • Hamid Zouba 1970-71 • Rachid Mekloufi 1971-72 • Mohamed El Kenz & Abdulhamid Sellal 1972-73 • Said Amara 1973 • Valentin Makkri ROU 1974-75 • Rachid Mekloufi 1975-79 • Mahieddine Khalef 1979 • Mahieddine Khalef & Zdravko Rajkov YUG 1979-80 • Zdravko Rajkov YUG 1980-81 • Evgeni Rogov URS, Mohamed Maouche & Rabah Saadane 1981-82 • Mahieddine Khalef 1982 • Hamid Zouba 1982-84 • Mahieddine Khalef 1984 • Rabah Saadane 1984-86 • Evgeni Rogov 1986-88 • Kamel Lemoui 1988-89 • Abdelhamid Kermali & Ali Fergani 1989-92 • Meziane Ighil 1992-93 • Rabah Madjer 1993-95 • Ali Fergani & Mourad Abdelouahab 1995-96 • Hamid Zouba & Abdelhamid Kermali 1996-97 • Abderrahmane Mehdaoui 1997-98 • Meziane Ighil & Marcel Pigulea ROU 1998-99 • Boualem Charef & Rabah Saadane 1999 • Nacer Sandjak 1999-2000 • Abdelghani Djaadaoui 2000-01 • Hamid Zouba & Abdelhamid Kermali 2001 • Rabah Madjer 2001-02 • Hamid Zouba 2002-03 • Rachid Bouaratta 2003 • George Leekens BEL 2003 • Rabah Saadane 2003-04 • Robert Waseige BEL 2004 • Ali Fergani & Lakhdar Belloumi 2004-05 • Meziane Ighil 2005-06 • Jean-Michel Cavalli FRA 2006-07 • Rabah Saadane 2007-10 • Abdelhak Benchikha 2010-11 • Vahid Halilhodzic BIH 2011-

ALGERIA 2010–11

CHAMPIONNAT NATIONAL DIVISION 1

	Pl	W	D	L	F	A	Pts	ASO	JSMB	ESS	USMH	CRB	MCS	MCO	ASK	USMA	MCA	JSK	WAT	MCEE	USMAn	CABBA	USMB
ASO Chlef †	30	19	6	5	51	20	63		2-0	1-0	2-0	2-1	0-0	2-1	2-0	3-2	1-0	3-0	3-1	5-0	4-0	1-0	2-0
JSM Béjaïa †	30	14	8	8	47	32	50	4-1		2-0	0-2	1-1	4-0	1-0	0-0	3-2	1-1	4-2	0-1	5-2	1-0	3-0	1-0
ES Sétif ‡	30	12	11	7	43	31	47	2-2	1-2		2-0	2-0	3-1	0-0	1-1	2-0	2-2	2-0	3-1	1-0	2-1	3-0	2-2
USM El Harrach	30	12	10	8	36	31	46	1-3	3-3	2-1		1-0	2-1	3-3	1-1	0-0	1-0	1-0	1-0	1-1	3-0	2-0	2-0
CR Bélouizdad	30	12	9	9	33	26	45	2-1	0-1	0-0	0-1		1-0	2-1	1-1	0-0	2-1	7-1	1-0	3-1	2-0	2-0	1-0
MC Saïda	30	11	9	10	33	35	42	1-1	0-0	1-1	1-1	2-1		1-0	3-0	1-1	2-1	1-0	5-2	1-0	1-0	1-0	3-2
MC Oran	30	11	8	11	26	27	41	1-0	2-1	1-0	2-2	1-2	1-0		1-0	1-0	1-1	0-0	2-0	1-1	1-0	1-0	1-1
AS Khroub	30	10	9	11	30	36	39	0-3	4-2	3-3	1-0	0-0	2-1	1-2		0-0	2-3	1-0	2-1	0-0	3-1	2-0	1-0
USM Alger	30	9	11	10	32	28	38	0-0	2-3	1-2	0-0	0-0	2-2	2-0	1-0		1-2	3-1	0-0	2-0	3-0	2-1	3-1
MC Alger	30	8	13	9	30	28	37	0-1	0-0	1-1	2-0	1-1	0-0	0-1	0-0	0-0		1-1	1-0	3-1	2-2	3-1	1-0
JS Kabylie ‡	30	10	7	13	26	37	37	0-0	1-0	1-1	1-0	1-1	0-0	1-0	3-2	1-0	0-0		3-0	3-2	1-0	1-0	0-1
WA Tlemcen	30	10	7	13	35	36	37	1-0	1-1	1-1	2-2	4-0	1-2	2-1	2-0	0-2	1-2	2-1		2-0	2-0	5-1	0-0
MC El Eulma	30	9	9	12	32	40	36	2-4	0-2	0-1	3-0	0-0	5-2	1-0	2-1	1-1	1-0	2-0	0-0		2-0	2-0	1-0
USM Annaba	30	10	6	14	23	34	36	0-0	1-0	2-0	2-1	1-0	1-0	2-0	3-0	1-0	2-1	2-1	1-1	0-0		0-0	1-1
CA Bordj Bou Arréridj	30	8	5	17	21	46	29	1-0	2-2	3-1	0-3	2-1	2-0	1-0	0-1	2-1	1-1	0-2	0-1	1-1	1-0		0-0
USM Blida	30	7	8	15	16	30	29	0-2	1-0	0-3	0-0	0-1	1-0	0-0	0-1	0-1	1-0	1-0	1-0	1-1	1-1	1-0	1-2

24/09/2010 - 8/07/2011 • † Qualified for the CAF Champions League • ‡ Qualified for the CAF Confederation Cup
Top scorers: **18** - El Arbi Hillel Soudani, ASO Chlef • **14** - Yannick N'Djeng CMR, JSM Bejaïa • **11** - Hamza Boulemdaïs, MC El Eulma; Salim Boumechra, USM El Harrach; Noureddine Daham, USM Alger & Mohamed Messaoud, ASO Chlef

MEDALS TABLE

		Overall			League			Cup			Africa		
		G	S	B	G	S	B	G	S	B	G	S	B
1	JS Kabylie	JSK	25	14	6	14	10	4	5	4		6		2
2	MC Alger	MCA	14	2	4	7	2	4	6			1		
3	USM Alger	USMA	12	13	3	5	4	1	7	9				2
4	CR Belouizdad	CRB	12	5	3	6	3	2	6	2				1
5	ES Sétif	ESS	12	4	6	4	3	5	7			1	1	1
6	MC Oran	MCO	8	12	4	4	9	3	4	2			1	1
7	USM El Harrach	USMH	3	3		1	2		2	1				
8	NA Hussein Dey	NAHD	2	8	5	1	4	4	1	3		1	1	
9	WA Tlemcem	WAT	2	3	3				3	2	3			
10	ASO Chlef	ASO	2	2	3	1	1	3	1	1				
11	USM Annaba	USMAn	2			1								

ALGERIA 2010–11

CHAMPIONNAT NATIONAL DIVISION 2

	Pl	W	D	L	F	A	Pts	CSC	NAHD	CAB	USMBA	Olympique	RCK	ASMO	MSPB	SAM	ESM	USB	MOC	ABM	PAC	JSMS	CRT
CS Constantine	30	14	14	2	35	15	56		1-1	0-0	0-0	2-0	1-0	1-0	2-0	3-0	1-0	1-1	0-0	1-0	1-1	2-0	4-1
NA Hussein Dey	30	14	10	6	37	19	52	1-1		1-1	2-2	1-0	0-0	2-1	2-0	3-1	0-0	1-0	1-1	1-1	2-0	4-1	1-0
CA Batna	30	14	9	7	32	24	51	1-0	1-0		2-2	0-0	1-0	1-0	1-1	1-2	1-0	2-1	1-0	0-0	2-0	2-1	1-0
USM Bel Abbès	30	13	8	9	38	32	47	0-1	1-0	1-1		3-1	3-0	1-1	1-0	2-1	2-1	3-0	4-0	1-0	1-0	2-1	2-2
Olympique Médéa	30	11	10	9	40	35	43	5-5	1-0	1-1	1-0		1-0	2-1	1-1	1-1	3-0	4-1	1-0	3-1	2-1	0-0	2-0
RC Kouba	30	12	7	11	37	33	43	1-1	1-0	1-0	2-1	1-1		1-2	0-0	4-0	3-1	3-0	3-2	6-0	1-0	2-1	4-1
ASM Oran	30	11	9	10	39	33	42	1-1	1-1	0-0	1-0	1-1	0-0		0-1	4-5	2-1	4-1	0-0	3-1	3-0	2-0	4-1
MSP Batna	30	11	8	11	36	33	41	0-0	0-4	2-2	0-1	1-1	3-1	1-2		4-1	0-1	1-0	2-3	2-0	3-2	1-1	6-1
SA Mohamadia	30	12	5	13	41	51	41	0-0	0-4	2-2	0-1	1-3	3-1	1-2	2-1		2-2	1-2	1-0	2-1	1-0	1-0	2-0
ES Mostaganem	30	11	5	14	32	37	38	0-1	0-1	2-0	3-2	2-4	3-0	0-1	1-4			1-0	2-0	2-0	2-1	0-0	1-0
US Biskra	30	10	7	13	32	37	37	1-1	1-2	2-1	2-0	2-0	2-0	0-0	2-0	1-0	0-1		3-1	0-0	0-0	2-0	2-1
MO Constantine	30	8	12	10	39	40	36	0-0	0-2	3-1	2-1	1-1	2-2	4-0	2-2	4-1	4-2	2-1		1-1	0-0	1-1	2-0
AB Mérouana	30	8	10	12	36	44	34	1-1	0-2	2-1	3-3	1-0	4-1	1-2	2-2	3-1	2-1	4-1	1-1		0-0	1-0	3-1
Paradou AC	30	8	9	13	32	33	33	0-0	0-1	3-2	3-3	1-0	0-0	0-1	0-1	1-1	1-1	1-0	2-1	1-1		2-2	1-0
JSM Skikda	30	8	8	14	25	37	32	1-2	1-0	1-3	2-2	2-0	1-0	0-0	1-0	0-1	0-0	2-0	0-1	0-2	2-1		1-0
CR Témouchent	30	6	5	19	31	61	23	3-1	1-1	3-2	0-1	3-2	1-0	0-1	2-0	2-4	1-0	1-1	3-1	1-1	2-6	4-1	

24/09/2010 - 17/06/2011

Round of 32

JS Kabylie	1	
ES Mostaganem *	0	
AC Arbaâ	0	
MC El Eulma *	2	
NTS Tadamoun Souf	1	
ARB Ghriss *	0	
IRB Robah *	1	7p
CR Bélouizdad	1	8p
MC Alger	0	4p
MC Mekhadma *	0	2p
USM Blida	0	
JSM Béjaïa *	2	
USM Aïn Beïda *	0	4p
US Biskra	0	3p
ASM Oran *	0	
MC Oran	1	
ES Sétif *	2	
NA Hussein Dey	1	
Paradou AC	0	4p
CA Batna *	0	5p
CRB Hennaya *	1	4p
ES Berrouaghia	1	2p
	0	4p
AB Mérouana *	0	5p
MC Saïda *	1	
USM Bel Abbès	0	
CA Bordj Bou Arréridj	0	
ASO Chlef *	1	
MO Béjaïa *	1	
US Tebessa	0	
NARB Réghaïa	1	
USM El Harrach *	2	

Round of 16

JS Kabylie *	2	
MC El Eulma	1	
NTS Tadamoun Souf	0	
CR Bélouizdad *	3	
MC Alger	0	5p
JSM Béjaïa *	0	4p
USM Aïn Beïda *	1	
MC Oran	3	
ES Sétif *	2	
CA Batna	0	
CRB Hennaya	1	
AB Mérouana *	2	
MC Saïda *	1	
ASO Chlef	0	
MO Béjaïa *	0	
USM El Harrach	1	

Quarter-finals

JS Kabylie *	4
CR Bélouizdad	2
MC Alger *	0 4p
MC Oran	0 5p
ES Sétif	1
AB Mérouana *	0
MC Saïda	0
USM El Harrach *	1

Semi-finals

JS Kabylie *	2
MC Oran	1
ES Sétif	2
USM El Harrach *	3

Final

JS Kabylie ‡	1
USM El Harrach	0

CUP FINAL

Stade 5 Juillet, Algiers
1-05-2011, Att: 60 000, Ref: Abid Charef
Scorer - Fares Hamiti [12]
JSK - Malik Asselah - Belkacem Remache,
Sofiane Khelil•, Ali Rial, Chemseddine
Nessakh• (Nassim Oussalah 64) - Sofiane
Younes•, Hocine El Orfi, Lyes Saidi, Saad
Tedjar (Mokhtar Lemhane• 78) - Sid Ali Yahia
Cherif• (Lamara Douicher 85), Fares Hamiti.
Tr: Rachid Belhout
USMH - Azzedine Doukha - Abdelmalek
Djeghbala•, Adlen Griche (c) (Fares
Benabderrahmane 46), Abdelghani Demou,
Mohamed Legraa (Amine Touahri 46) - Ali Sami
Yachir (Chaouki Chache 67), Messaoud Gharbi,
Karim Hendou, Brahim Ledraa - Mohamed
Boualem, Salim Boumechra. Tr: Boualem
Charef

* Home team • ‡ Qualified for the CAF Confederation Cup

AND – ANDORRA

FIFA/COCA-COLA WORLD RANKING

'93	'94	'95	'96	'97	'98	'99	'00	'01	'02	'03	'04	'05	'06	'07	'08	'09	'10	'11	'12
-	-	-	187	185	171	145	145	140	137	147	138	125	164	175	194	202	202	206	

2011												High	Low	Av
Jan	Feb	Mar	Apr	May	Jun	Jul	Aug	Sep	Oct	Nov	Dec	High	Low	Av
202	202	202	202	202	203	203	203	203	203	204	206	125	206	164

Thirty-five games and counting... that's how long it has been since Andorra last came away with anything from an international match, a losing sequence stretching back to the start of 2007. It is a disasterous run that has seen the national team tumble down the rankings from a high of 125 in 2005 to rock bottom by the end of 2011 - a position they shared with San Marino and Montserrat. The qualifiers for Euro 2012 yielded just one goal over the ten matches, down from the four scored in the 2010 World Cup qualifying campaign, although on the plus-side the number of goals conceded was down to 'just' 25. It was Andorra's fourth qualifying campaign in the European Championship and they have yet to pick up a single point in the 40 games played since first taking part in 1998. In club football, Santa Coloma won their third championship in four seasons, successfully defending the title won the previous season. Both they and Sant Julia lost just once during the campaign but there was consolation for Sant Julia when they won the cup for the second year running. Santa Coloma and Sant Julia have now between them won every trophy on offer for the past four seasons with Rangers' two championship seasons in 2006 and 2007 the only break on the monopoly of the two clubs since 2003.

UEFA EUROPEAN CHAMPIONSHIP RECORD
1960-1996 DNE 2000-2012 DNQ

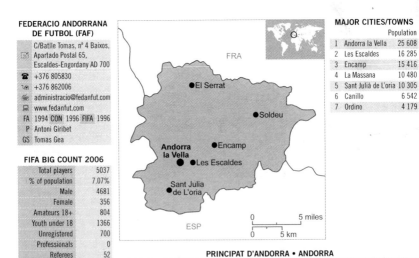

**FEDERACIO ANDORRANA
DE FUTBOL (FAF)**

C/Batlle Tomas, nº 4 Baixos,
Apartado Postal 65,
Escaldes-Engordany AD 700
☎ +376 805830
📠 +376 862006
📧 administracio@fedanfut.com
🖥 www.fedanfut.com
FA 1994 CON 1996 FIFA 1996
P Antoni Giribet
GS Tomas Gea

FIFA BIG COUNT 2006

Total players	5037
% of population	7.07%
Male	4681
Female	356
Amateurs 18+	804
Youth under 18	1366
Unregistered	700
Professionals	0
Referees	52
Admin & coaches	116
Number of clubs	26
Number of teams	34

FRA

●El Serrat

●Soldeu

**Andorra
la Vella**   ●Encamp
● ●Les Escaldes

Sant Julia
●de L'oria

ESP

0   5 miles
0   5 km

MAJOR CITIES/TOWNS
		Population
1	Andorra la Vella	25 608
2	Les Escaldes	16 285
3	Encamp	15 416
4	La Massana	10 480
5	Sant Julià de L'oria	10 305
6	Canillo	6 542
7	Ordino	4 179

PRINCIPAT D'ANDORRA • ANDORRA

Capital	Andorra La Vella	Population	83 888 (199)	% in cities	89%
GDP per capita	$42 500 (15)	Area km^2	468 km^2 (195)	GMT +/-	+1
Neighbours (km)	France 56, Spain 63				

RECENT INTERNATIONALS PLAYED BY ANDORRA

2006	Opponents	Score		Venue	Comp	Scorers	Att	Referee
16-08	Belarus	L	0-3	Minsk	Fr			
2-09	England	L	0-5	Manchester	ECq		56 290	Brugger AUT
6-09	Israel	L	1-4	Nijmegan	ECq	Fernández [84]	400	Zrnic BIH
7-10	Croatia	L	0-7	Zagreb	ECq		17 618	Zammit MLT
11-10	FYR Macedonia	L	0-3	Andorra la Vella	ECq		300	Silagava GEO
2007								
7-02	Armenia	D	0-0	Andorra la Vella	Fr			
28-03	England	L	0-3	Barcelona	ECq		12 800	Duarte Paixao POR
2-06	Russia	L	0-4	St Petersburg	ECq		21 520	Skjerven NOR
6-06	Israel	L	0-2	Andorra la Vella	ECq		680	Stokes IRL
22-08	Estonia	L	1-2	Tallinn	ECq	Silva [82]	7 500	McCourt NIR
12-09	Croatia	L	0-6	Andorra la Vella	ECq		925	Thual FRA
17-10	FYR Macedonia	L	0-3	Skopje	ECq		17 500	Malzinskas LTU
17-11	Estonia	L	0-2	Andorra la Vella	ECq		700	Collum SCO
21-11	Russia	L	0-1	Andorra la Vella	ECq		780	Hauge NOR
2008								
26-03	Latvia	L	0-3	Andorra la Vella	Fr			Perez ESP
4-06	Azerbaijan	L	1-2	Andorra la Vella	Fr	Lima.I [71]		Gomes POR
20-08	Kazakhstan	L	0 3	Almaty	WCq		7 700	Banari MDA
6-09	England	L	0-2	Barcelona	WCq		10 300	Cakir TUR
10-09	Belarus	L	1-3	Andorra la Vella	WCq	Pujol [67p]	600	Evans WAL
15-10	Croatia	L	0-4	Zagreb	WCq		14 441	Vad HUN
2009								
11-02	Lithuania	L	1-3	Albufeira	Fr	Lima.I [78p]		Xistra POR
1-04	Croatia	L	0-2	Andorra la Vella	WCq		1 100	Trattou CYP
6-06	Belarus	L	1-5	Grodno	WCq	Lima.I [93+p]	8 500	Kranjc SVN
10-06	England	L	0-6	London	WCq		57 897	Nijhuis NED
5-09	Ukraine	L	0-5	Kyiv	WCq		14 870	Sipailo LVA
9-09	Kazakhstan	L	1-3	Andorra la Vella	WCq	Sonejee [70]	510	Toussaint LUX
14-10	Ukraine	L	0-6	Andorra la Vella	WCq		820	Thomson SCO
2010								
29-05	Iceland	L	0-4	Reykjavik	Fr		2 567	Reinert FRO
2-06	Albania	L	0-1	Tirana	Fr		3 000	Meckarovski MKD
11-08	Cyprus	L	0-1	Larnaca	Fr		1 700	Spathas GRE
3-09	Russia	L	0-2	Andorra la Vella	ECq		1 100	Borg MLT
7-09	Republic of Ireland	L	1-3	Dublin	ECq	Martinez [45]	40 283	Trattou CYP
8-10	FYR Macedonia	L	0-2	Andorra La Vella	ECq		550	Mazeika LTU
12-10	Armenia	L	0-4	Yerevan	ECq		12 000	Mikulski POL
2011								
9-02	Moldova	L	1-2	Lagos	Fr	Josep Ayala [52]		Lopes POR
26-03	Slovakia	L	0-1	Andorra La Vella	ECq		850	Masiah ISR
4-06	Slovakia	L	0-1	Bratislava	ECq		4 300	Jemini ALB
2-09	Armenia	L	0-3	Andorra la Vella	ECq		750	Kostadinov BUL
6-09	FYR Macedonia	L	0-1	Skopje	ECq		5 000	Whitby WAL
7-10	Republic of Ireland	L	0-2	Andorra la Vella	ECq		860	Kovarik CZE
11-10	Russia	L	0-6	Moscow	ECq		38 790	Hacmon ISR

Fr = Friendly match • EC = UEFA EURO 2008/2012 • WC = FIFA World Cup • q = qualifier

ANDORRA NATIONAL TEAM HISTORICAL RECORDS

App
85 - Oscar Sonejee 1997- • **78** - Koldo 1998-2009 • **75** - Manolo Jimenez 1998- • **71** - Josep Txema 1997- • **67** - Ildefons Lima 1997-
• **65** - Justo Ruiz 1996-2008 & Jordi Escura 1998-

G
7 - Ildefons Lima 1997- • **3** - Oscar Sonejee 1997-, Fernando Silva 2002-, Jesus Julian Lucendo 1996-2003

Tr
Isidrea Codina 1996 • Manuel Miloie 1997-99, David Rodrigo 1999-2010 • Koldo Alvarez 2010-

ANDORRA 2010–11

LLIGA ANDORRANA PRIMERA DIVISIO

	Pl	W	D	L	F	A	Pts	Santa Coloma	Sant Julià	Lusitans	UE Santa Coloma	Principat	Inter Escaldes	Encamp	Benfica
Santa Coloma †	20	14	5	1	71	11	47		0-0 1-0	3-0 3-2	2-1 1-0	3-0	3-0	6-0	12-1
Sant Julià ‡	20	12	7	1	47	9	43	0-0 1-1		0-0 1-1	2-0 3-1	4-1	4-0	3-0	6-0
Lusitans ‡	20	11	5	4	43	20	38	2-1 1-1	1-1 1-1		3-2 3-0	2-0	1-0	5-0	3-0
UE Santa Coloma ‡	20	10	0	10	54	27	30	1-2 0-1	1-3 0-2	1-0 2-1		4-1	8-0	4-2	4-0
Principat	20	8	4	8	49	34	28	2-2	0-3	0-2	0-4		4-12-2	5-1 8-0	5-0 4-1
Inter Escaldes	20	6	3	11	28	54	21	0-10	0-2	1-5	0-5	1-2 0-0		2-1 1-2	2-1 1-1
Encamp	20	4	1	15	24	79	13	0-9	0-8	2-7	1-6	4-1 0-1	1-2 1-3		1-1 4-1
Casa del Benfica	20	1	3	16	15	97	6	0-10	1-3	1-3	0-10	0-0 0-13	1-7 0-5	4-1 2-3	

19/09/2010 - 20/03/2011 • † Qualified for the UEFA Champions League • ‡ Qualified for the Europa League
Relegation play-off: FC Encamp 1-3 0-2 **UE Engordany**
Top scorers: **16** - Victor Bernat, UE Santa Coloma • **15** - Nortberto Urbani, Santa Coloma • **13** - Juan Raya, Lusitans

ANDORRA 2010–11 SEGONA DIVISIO (2)

	Pl	W	D	L	F	A	Pts
Lusitans B	24	19	2	3	80	22	59
Ranger's ‡	24	18	2	4	74	24	56
Engordany	24	14	2	8	58	37	44
Extremenya	24	12	2	10	72	43	38
Santa Coloma B	18	11	1	6	42	40	34
Athlètic Escaldes	18	5	2	11	32	54	17
Penya Encarnada	18	4	1	13	27	50	13
La Massana	18	3	4	11	25	55	13
Principat B	18	4	1	13	24	66	13
Jenlai	18	3	1	14	25	68	10

12/09/2011 - 10/04/2011 • ‡ Qualified for play-off
(Lusitans B ineligible for promotion)

MEDALS TABLE

		Overall			League			Cup	
		G	S	B	G	S	B	G	S
1	Santa Coloma	14	8	4	6	5	4	8	3
2	Principat	9	1	1	3	1	1	6	
3	Sant Julià	4	12	3	2	6	3	2	6
4	Encamp	2	2	3	2	1	3		1
5	Ranger's	2	2	2	2	1	2		1
6	Constelacio	2			1				1
7	Lusitans	1	2	1				1 1	2
8	UE Santa Coloma	2			1				1
9	Inter Escaldes	1	2					2	1
10	Veterans	1			1				

COPA CONSTITUCIO 2010–11

Round of 16
- Sant Julià — Bye
- Principat 1 / Ranger's 3
- Encamp 6 / Engordany 1
- Santa Coloma — Bye
- Lusitans — Bye
- Athlètic Escaldes 1 / Inter Escaldes 6
- Casa del Benfica 2 / Extremenya 1
- UE Santa Coloma — Bye

Quarter-finals
- Sant Julià 3 8
- Ranger's * 0 1
- Encamp * 0 0
- Santa Coloma 9 10
- Lusitans 6 2
- Inter Escaldes * 0 1
- Casa del Benfica * 0 0
- UE Santa Coloma 7 4

Semi-finals
- Sant Julià 3 2 4p
- Santa Coloma * 2 3 1p
- Lusitans 1 1
- UE Santa Coloma * 2 2

Final
- Sant Julià ‡ 3
- UE Santa Coloma 1

CUP FINAL
Comunal d'Aixovall
8-05-2011
Scorers - Varela [49], Salvat [94], Iguacel [102] for Sant Julia; Anton [51] for UE Santa Coloma

* Home team in the first leg • ‡ Qualified for the Europa League

Cup Final line-ups: **Sant Julia** - Perianes - Wagner, Ruiz, Varela, Peppe, Edjang (Matamala 106, Jacques, Munoz, Riera (Iguacel 46), Salvat, Sebas Gomes (Trejo 80). Tr: Daniel Tremonti
UE Santa Coloma - Rivas - Rubio, Nieto (Rui Goncalves 105), Alex Martinez, Roca (Vall 110), Aloy (Guida 73), Anton, Rodriguez, Alves, Lopez, Bernat. Tr: Luis Miguel Aloy

ANG – ANGOLA

FIFA/COCA-COLA WORLD RANKING

'93	'94	'95	'96	'97	'98	'99	'00	'01	'02	'03	'04	'05	'06	'07	'08	'09	'10	'11	'12
102	106	80	70	58	50	52	55	55	76	83	72	61	55	73	70	95	88		

2011												High	Low	Av
Jan	Feb	Mar	Apr	May	Jun	Jul	Aug	Sep	Oct	Nov	Dec			
88	107	104	107	105	102	100	96	84	86	84	83	45	124	73

Angola were surprise finalists at the African Nations Championships in Sudan at the start of the year, riding their luck to reach the final of a tournament created for national teams comprising home-based players only. Lito Vidigal had become the fourth coach of the Angolan side in the space of 12 months when he succeeded Zeca Amaral in January 2011 and a month later the youthful coach had taken his group of players from the GiraBola to the final in Khartoum. Angola won only a single game, against Rwanda, finishing second in their opening round group behind Tunisia. They beat Cameroon and Sudan on penalties in the knockout rounds to qualify for the final where they lost 3-0 to Tunisia. They had further good fortune in October when they squeezed into the 2012 CAF Africa Cup of Nations finals in Equatorial Guinea and Gabon, but it was there that they ran out of steam. Group leaders Uganda had failed to win their final home match to Kenya, allowing the 'Palancas Negras' to grab top place with an away win over Guinea Bissau. Sacked national coach Zeca Amaral went to work at Recreativo Libolo, and restored his reputation as they won a first-ever GiraBola title. It came after a dogged contest with Kabuscorp, another side without previous success who helped break down the long-standing monopoly of a handful of Luanda-based clubs.

CAF AFRICA CUP OF NATIONS RECORD

1957-1982 DNE **1984** DNQ **1986** DNE **1988-1994** DNQ **1996** 13 r1 **1998** 13 r1 **2000-2004** DNQ
2006 9 r1 **2008** 6 QF **2010** 6 QF (Hosts) **2012** 11 r1

FEDERACAO ANGOLANA DE FUTEBOL (FAF)

Senado de Camara,
Compl. da Cidadela
Desportiva, Luanda - 3449,
☎ +244 222 264948
📠
📧 sgeral@fafutebol.ebonet.net
🖥 www.fafutebol-angola.og.ao
FA 1979 CON 1996 FIFA 1980
P Pedro Neto
GS Jose Manuel Cardoso

FIFA BIG COUNT 2006

Total players	664 690
% of population	5.48%
Male	634 090
Female	30 600
Amateurs 18+	5240
Youth under 18	10 800
Unregistered	36 250
Professionals	0
Referees	259
Admin & coaches	1800
Number of clubs	100
Number of teams	500

MAJOR CITIES/TOWNS

		Population
1	Luanda	2 583 981
2	Cabinda	377 931
3	Huambo	333 387
4	Lubango	250 921
5	Kuito	180 764
6	Malanje	156 829
7	Lobito	145 652
8	Benguela	131 281
9	Uige	116 751
10	Namibe	89 442
11	Luena	84 619
12	Saurimo	78 417
13	Soyo	75 224
14	Sumbe	50 458
15	N'Dalatando	45 295
16	Caála	41 181
17	Cubal	41 142
18	Dundo	40 055
19	Negage	37 622

REPUBLICA DE ANGOLA • REPUBLIC OF ANGOLA

Capital Luanda	Population 12 799 293 (69)	% in cities 57%
GDP per capita $8800 (112)	Area km² 1 246 700 km² (23)	GMT +/- +1
Neighbours (km) Congo DR 2511, Congo 201, Namibia 1376, Zambia 1110 • Coast 1600		

RECENT INTERNATIONALS PLAYED BY ANGOLA

2008 Opponents	Score	Venue	Comp	Scorers	Att	Referee
23-01 South Africa	D 1-1	Tamale	CNr1	Manucho 30		Coulibaly MLI
27-01 Senegal	W 3-1	Tamale	CNr1	Manucho 2 50 67, Flavio 78		Haimoudi ALG
31-01 Tunisia	D 0-0	Tamale	CNr1			Codjia BEN
4-02 Egypt	L 1-2	Kumasi	CNqf	Manucho 27		Nichimura JPN
1-06 Benin	W 3-0	Luanda	WCq	Flavio 62, Job 81, Mendonca 86	6 000	Damon RSA
8-06 Niger	W 2-1	Niamey	WCq	Flavio 30, Yamba Asha 71	23 000	Jedidi TUN
14-06 Uganda	L 1-3	Kampala	WCq	Mantorras 91+	20 000	Mailett SEY
23-06 Uganda	D 0-0	Luanda	WCq		16 000	Mana NGA
20-08 Tunisia	D 1-1	Monastir	Fr	Santana 90		
7-09 Benin	L 2-3	Cotonou	WCq	Flavio 12, Loco 84	30 000	Benouza ALG
12-10 Niger	W 3-1	Luanda	WCq	Daouda OG 53, Gilberto 66, Ze Kalanga 70	3 200	Gasingwa RWA
19-11 Venezuela	D 0-0	Barinas	Fr		15 000	Argote VEN
2009						
11-02 Mali	L 0-4	Bois-Guillaume	Fr			
25-03 Cape Verde Islands	L 0-1	Olhao	Fr			
31-03 Morocco	L 0-2	Lisbon	Fr			
4-04 Namibia	D 0-0	Dundo	Fr			
14-06 Guinea	D 0-0	Amadora	Fr			
12-08 Togo	W 2-0	Lisbon	Fr	Flavio 55, Mateus 73	700	Proença POR
5-09 Senegal	D 1-1	Portimao	Fr	Mangane OG 66	300	Paixao POR
9-09 Cape Verde Islands	D 1-1	Faro	Fr	Gilberto 23p		
10-10 Malta	W 2-1	Vila Real	Fr	Djalma 37, Andre Makanga 64		Almeida POR
14-10 Cameroon	D 0-0	Olhao	Fr			
14-11 Congo	D 1-1	Luanda	Fr	Flavio 2		
18-11 Ghana	D 0-0	Luanda	Fr			
30-12 Estonia	L 0-1	Vila Real	Fr		200	Almeida POR
2010						
3-01 Gambia	D 1-1	Vila Real	Fr	Manucho 29		
10-01 Mali	D 4-4	Luanda	CNr1	Flávio 2 36 42, Gilberto 67p, Manucho 74p	45 000	Abd El Fatah EGY
14-01 Malawi	W 2-0	Luanda	CNr1	Flávio 49, Manucho 55	48 500	Doue CIV
18-01 Algeria	D 0-0	Luanda	CNr1		40 000	Damon RSA
24-01 Ghana	L 0-1	Luanda	CNqf		50 000	Benouza ALG
13-05 Mexico	L 0-1	Houston	Fr		70 099	Toledo USA
11-08 Uruguay	L 0-2	Lisbon	Fr		1 000	Hugo Miguel POR
4-09 Uganda	L 0-3	Kampala	CNq			Osman EGY
9-10 Guinea-Bissau	W 1-0	Luanda	CNq	Gilberto 22p		Coulibaly MLI
12-10 UAE	W 2-0	Abu Dhabi	Fr	Rasca 23, Vado 89		
2011						
2-01 Iran	L 0-1	Al Rayyan	Fr		BCD	
4-01 Saudi Arabia	D 0-0	Dammam	Fr			
26-03 Kenya	L 1-2	Nairobi	CNq	Manucho 18		
5-06 Kenya	W 1-0	Luanda	CNq	Manucho 69		Maillet SEY
10-08 Liberia	D 0-0	Monrovia	Fr			
27-08 Congo DR	L 1-2	Dundo	Fr	Joao Martins 13		
4-09 Uganda	W 2-0	Luanda	CNq	Manucho 57, Flavio 73		El Ahrach MAR
8-10 Guinea-Bissau	W 2-0	Bissau	CNq	Manucho 8, Mateus 70		
14-12 Cameroon	D 1-1	Cabinda	Fr	Love 21		
18-12 Zambia	W 1-0	Dundo	Fr	Love 59		
22-12 Namibia	D 0-0	Lubango	Fr			
2012						
11-01 Nigeria	D 0-0	Abuja	Fr			
14-01 Sierra Leone	W 3-1	Cabinda	Fr	Manucho 15, Galiano 39, Flavio 76		
22-01 Burkina Faso	W 2-1	Malabo	CNr1	Mateus 47, Manucho 68	17 000	Seechurn MRI
26-01 Sudan	D 2-2	Malabo	CNr1	Manucho 2 4 50p	2 500	Lemghaifry MTN
30-01 Côte d'Ivoire	L 0-2	Malabo	CNr1		1 500	Jedidi TUN

Fr = Friendly match • CN = CAF African Cup of Nations • WC = FIFA World Cup • q = qualifier • r1 = first round group • qf = quarter-final

ANGOLA 2011

CAMPEONATO NACIONAL XXXIII GIRABOLA 1° DIVISAO

	Pl	W	D	L	F	A	Pts	Líbolo	Kabuscorp	Petro Atlético	Caála	InterClube	1° Agosto	Sagrada	Onze Bravos	ASA	Académica S	Santos	Progresso	Benfica	Cabinda	1° Maio	Académica L
Recreativo Líbolo †	30	17	6	7	49	26	57		3-1	1-2	1-0	1-2	0-0	1-0	3-1	2-1	2-0	2-0	4-0	3-0	3-3	3-1	2-0
Kabuscorp Palanca	30	17	5	8	47	30	56	2-1		2-2	3-2	1-1	2-1	1-1	2-0	1-0	2-1	1-2	0-1	3-0	1-1	2-0	2-1
Petro Atlético	30	13	12	5	46	28	51	0-1	2-3		1-1	2-0	2-0	2-1	7-0	1-0	1-0	2-0	1-1	2-0	0-2	1-1	3-0
Recreativo Caála	30	14	6	10	37	34	48	1-0	2-1	1-2		1-0	2-1	0-0	3-1	1-2	1-1	1-0	2-1	2-1	1-0	3-0	1-0
InterClube ‡	30	11	15	4	31	17	48	0-0	1-0	0-0	1-1		1-1	1-0	1-1	2-0	0-0	3-1	2-1	0-1	1-0	2-1	1-0
Primeiro de Agosto	30	10	15	5	37	28	45	1-1	1-3	2-1	3-0	0-0		2-0	2-2	1-0	1-0	2-2	2-1	1-1	3-0	0-0	1-1
Sagrada Esperança	30	10	11	9	26	25	41	1-1	1-0	2-2	2-0	0-0	1-3		1-0	2-0	2-0	1-1	0-1	0-1	1-0	3-0	2-1
Onze Bravos Maqui	30	9	11	10	36	41	38	1-2	0-1	1-1	2-2	0-0	1-1	0-0		1-0	1-2	2-1	1-0	2-1	3-1	3-0	1-0
Atlético Aviação	30	9	10	11	28	29	37	2-3	1-2	0-0	5-0	0-0	0-0	2-2	1-1		1-1	1-0	1-0	0-2	2-1	2-1	1-0
Académica Soyo	30	9	10	11	26	28	37	1-1	1-0	0-1	2-1	1-1	0-1	0-1	1-0	1-1		1-0	0-0	0-0	1-0	0-0	2-1
Santos	30	8	12	10	34	40	36	3-1	1-2	2-2	1-3	1-1	1-0	1-1	3-2	1-1	3-5		1-1	0-0	1-1	1-1	1-0
Progresso Sambizanga	30	9	9	12	28	37	36	2-1	0-1	0-0	1-0	0-5	1-3	0-1	1-1	0-0	2-1	1-1		2-0	1-0	1-1	2-3
Benfica Luanda	30	9	8	13	33	36	35	0-1	0-1	2-2	0-2	2-1	1-1	2-0	2-2	1-0	1-1	0-1	1-3		1-1	0-1	5-1
FC Cabinda	30	7	12	11	25	30	33	1-0	0-2	1-1	2-1	0-0	1-1	1-1	1-1	0-1	1-0	0-0	1-0	1-4		1-1	2-0
Primeiro de Maio	30	7	9	14	30	42	30	0-2	1-5	3-0	1-0	1-1	1-2	0-0	1-3	1-2	2-0	1-2	1-2	1-0	0-0		3-0
Académica Lobito	30	2	7	21	19	62	13	0-2	1-1	1-3	0-0	0-3	1-1	1-0	0-2	1-1	1-0	2-2	2-2	1-4	0-2	1-5	

11/03/2011 - 6/11/2011 • † Qualified for CAF Champions League • ‡ Qualified for CAF Confederation Cup

MEDALS TABLE

		Overall G	S	B	League G	S	B	Cup G	S	Africa G	S	B	City
1	Petro Atlético	23	6	6	15	3	6	8	2		1		Luanda
2	Primeiro de Agosto	14	9	4	9	3	4	5	5		1		Luanda
3	Atlético Sport Aviação	6	7	2	3	5	1	3	2			1	Luanda
4	Primeiro de Maio	5	8		2	5		3	2		1		Benguela
5	InterClube	5	7	4	2	1	4	3	5		1		Luanda
6	Sagrada Esperança	3	5		1	3		2	2				Dundo
7	Ferroviário Huíla	2	1	1			1	2	1				Lubango
8	Atlético Petróleas Namibe	2						2					Namibe
9	Recreativo Líbolo	1	2	1	1	1	1		1				Calulo
10	Progresso Sambiganza	1						1					Luanda
	Santos	1						1					Viana
12	Petro Huambo	2	3		1	3							Huambo
13	SL Benfica Luanda	2	1			1		2					Luanda
	Independente	2	1			1		2					Tombwa
15	Nacional Benguela	1	1		1	1							Benguela

TACA NACIONAL 2011

Round of 16		Quarter-finals		Semi-finals		Final	
InterClube	2						
Onze Bravos Maqui *	0	InterClube	2				
Atlético Aviação	1	Santos *	0				
Santos *	2			InterClube	1		
Domant Bengo *	2			Benfica Luanda *	0		
Sporting Cabinda	1	Domant Bengo *	0				
Recreativo Líbolo	2 5p	Benfica Luanda	2				
Benfica Luanda *	2 6p					InterClube ‡	1 4p
Primeiro de Maio *	2					Primeiro de Agosto	1 2p
Es. Norberto Castro	0	Primeiro de Maio *	2				
Progresso Sambizanga	1	Recreativo Caála	0				
Recreativo Caála *	2			Primeiro de Maio	1		
Kabuscorp Palanca *	2			Primeiro de Agosto *	2		
Sagrada Esperança	0	Kabuscorp Palanca	1 3p				
17 de Maio Benguela*	0	Primeiro de Agosto *	1 4p				
Primeiro de Agosto	3						

CUP FINAL

Cidadela, Luanda, 11-11-2010
Att: 10 000, Ref: Helder Martins
Scorers - Alex [78] for InterClube; Amaro [40] for 1° Agosto

* Home team • ‡ Qualified for CAF Confederation Cup

ARG – ARGENTINA

FIFA/COCA-COLA WORLD RANKING

'93	'94	'95	'96	'97	'98	'99	'00	'01	'02	'03	'04	'05	'06	'07	'08	'09	'10	'11	'12
8	10	7	22	17	5	6	3	2	5	5	3	4	3	1	6	8	5	10	

	2011														
	Jan	Feb	Mar	Apr	May	Jun	Jul	Aug	Sep	Oct	Nov	Dec	High	Low	Av
	5	5	4	5	5	10	10	9	10	10	10	10	1	24	6

Argentina's recent miserable record in the Copa America continued in 2011 but there was double the disappointment at the quarter-final exit given the tournament was staged on home soil. The last time Argentina won the trophy was in 1993 but you have to go back to 1959 when they last won it in front of their own fans. The quarter-final defeat at the hands of Uruguay saw the end of Sergio Batista's short reign as coach and the major challenge for the new incumbent - former Estudiantes coach Alex Sabella - will be to get the best out of the sensational Lionel Messi whose performances for Barcelona throughout 2011 continued to dazzle. A World Cup win with Argentina in 2014 in Brazil would surely elevate him to the same status as Pele and Maradona. At club level the year was dominated by the relegation of River Plate - for the first time in the history of the club - and by the title won by Boca Juniors in December. River Plate's demise was shocking in that the system whereby relegation is decided over three years was introduced to protect the big clubs. Boca's triumph was notable for the fact that they went through the 19-game Apertura without losing, part of a 29-game unbeaten streak from April to the end of the year.

COPA AMERICA RECORD

1916 2 1917 2 1919 2 1920 2 **1921** Winners 1922 4 1923 2 1924 2 **1925** Winners 1926 2 **1927** Winners **1929** Winners 1935 2 **1937** Winners 1939 DNE **1941** Winners 1942 2 **1945** Winners **1946** Winners **1947** Winners 1949-1953 DNE **1955** Winners 1956 3 **1957** Winners **1959** Winners 1959 2 1963 3 1967 2 1975 5 r1 1979 8 r1 1983 6 r1 1987 4 SF 1989 3 r2 **1991** Winners **1993** Winners 1995 5 QF 1997 6 QF 1999 7 QF 2001 DNE 2004 2 F 2007 2 F 2011 7 QF

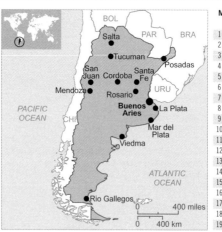

ASOCIACIÓN DEL FÚTBOL ARGENTINO (AFA)

Viamonte 1366/76, Buenos Aires - 1053

☎ +54 11 43719400
📠 +54 11 43754410
✉ gerencia@afa.org.ar
🖥 www.afa.org.ar

FA	1893	CON	1916	FIFA	1912
P   Julio Grondona
GS Miguel Silva

FIFA BIG COUNT 2006

Total players	2 658 811
% of population	6.66%
Male	2 349 811
Female	30 900
Amateurs 18+	88 090
Youth under 18	231 196
Unregistered	1 225 000
Professionals	3 530
Referees	3340
Admin & coaches	33 821
Number of clubs	3348
Number of teams	23 623

MAJOR CITIES/TOWNS

		Population
1	Buenos Aires	12 197 347
2	Córdoba	1 531 510
3	Rosario	1 235 558
4	Mendoza	929 045
5	Tucumán	830 370
6	La Plata	736 954
7	Mar del Plata	589 291
8	Salta	551 284
9	Santa Fé	506 360
10	San Juan	486 553
11	Resistencia	402 921
12	Santiago dE	370 074
13	Corrientes	360 299
14	Posadas	339 003
15	Jujuy	332 900
16	Bahía Blanca	292 636
17	Paraná	279 923
18	Neuquén	261 426
19	Formosa	239 770

REPUBLICA ARGENTINA • ARGENTINE REPUBLIC

Capital Buenos Aires	Population 40 913 584 (31)	% in cities 92%
GDP per capita $14 200 (80)	Area km² 2 780 400 km² (8)	GMT + / - -3

Neighbours (km) Bolivia 832, Brazil 1261, Chile 5308, Paraguay 1880, Uruguay 580 • Coast 4989

RECENT INTERNATIONAL MATCHES PLAYED BY ARGENTINA

2010	Opponents	Score	Venue	Comp	Scorers	Att	Referee
26-01	Costa Rica	W 3-2	San Juan	Fr	Sosa 12, Burdisso 38, Jara 79	19 000	Amarilla PAR
10-02	Jamaica	W 2-1	Mar del Plata	Fr	Palermo 77, Canuto 93+	20 000	Rivera PER
3-03	Germany	W 1-0	Munich	Fr	Higuain 45	65 152	Atkinson ENG
5-05	Haiti	W 4-0	Cutral Co	Fr	Bertoglio 2 33 56, Palermo 42, Blanco 50	16 500	Osses CHI
24-05	Canada	W 5-0	Buenos Aires	Fr	Maxi Rodriguez 2 15 31, Di Maria 36, Tevez 62, Aguero 74	60 000	Rivera PER
12-06	Nigeria	W 1-0	Johannesburg	WCr1	Heinze 6	55 686	Stark GER
17-06	Korea Republic	W 4-1	Johannesburg	WCr1	Park Chu Young OG 17, Higuain 3 33 76 80	82 174	De Bleeckere BEL
22-06	Greece	W 2-0	Polokwane	WCr1	Demichelis 77, Palermo 89	38 891	Irmatov UZB
27-06	Mexico	W 3-1	Johannesburg	WCr2	Tevez 2 26 52, Higuain 33	84 377	Rosetti ITA
3-07	Germany	L 0-4	Cape Town	WCqf		64 100	Irmatov UZB
11-08	Republic of Ireland	W 1-0	Dublin	Fr	Di Maria 20	49 500	Rasmussen DEN
7-09	Spain	W 4-1	Buenos Aires	Fr	Messi 10, Higuain 13, Tevez 34, Aguero 90	53 000	Ruiz COL
8-10	Japan	L 0-1	Saitama	Fr		57 735	Gil POL
17-11	Brazil	W 1-0	Doha	Fr	Messi 92+	40 000	Balideh QAT
2011							
9-02	Portugal	W 2-1	Geneva	Fr	Di Maria 14, Messi 90p	30 000	Busacca SUI
16-03	Venezuela	W 4-1	San Juan	Fr	Chavez 20, Mouche 2 35 53, Aued 75	25 000	Puga CHI
26-03	USA	D 1-1	New York	Fr	Cambiasso 42	78 936	Garcia MEX
29-03	Costa Rica	D 0-0	San Jose	Fr		35 000	Rodriguez.M MEX
20-04	Ecuador	D 2-2	Mar Del Plata	Fr	Yacob 31, Hauche 34	9 000	Silvera URU
25-05	Paraguay	W 4-2	Resistencia	Fr	Hauche 2 12 45, Fernandez 37, Perez 74	24 000	Silvera URU
1-06	Nigeria	L 1-4	Abuja	Fr	Boselli 98+p	30 000	Chaibou NIG
5-06	Poland	L 1-2	Warsaw	Fr	Ruben 47	12 000	Grafe GER
20-06	Albania	W 4-0	Buenos Aires	Fr	Lavezzi 6, Messi 43, Aguero 75, Tevez 90	21 000	Larrionda URU
1-07	Bolivia	D 1-1	La Plata	CAr1	Aguero 76	52 700	Silvera URU
7-07	Colombia	D 0-0	Cordoba	CAr1		47 000	Fagundes BRA
11-07	Costa Rica	W 3-0	Cordoba	CAr1	Aguero 2 45 52, Di Maria 63	57 000	Rivera PER
16-07	Uruguay	D 1-1	Santa Fe	CAqf	Higuain 18. L 4-5p	47 000	Amarilla PAR
2-09	Venezuela	W 1-0	Calcutta	Fr	Otamendi 70	90 000	Rowan IND
6-09	Nigeria	W 3-1	Dhaka	Fr	Higuain 24, Di Maria 26, OG 65	36 000	Shamsuzzaman BAN
14-09	Brazil	D 0-0	Cordoba	Fr		50 000	Osses CHI
28-09	Brazil	L 0-2	Belem	Fr		43 038	Larrionda URU
7-10	Chile	W 4-1	Buenos Aires	WCq	Higuain 3 7 52 63, Messi 25	26 161	Roldan COL
11-10	Venezuela	L 0-1	Puerto La Cruz	WCq		35 600	Silvera URU
11-11	Bolivia	D 1-1	Buenos Aires	WCq	Lavezzi 60	27 592	Vera ECU
15-11	Colombia	W 2-1	Barranquilla	WCq	Messi 60, Aguero 83	49 600	Fagundes BRA

Fr = Friendly match • CA = Copa América • WC = FIFA World Cup
q = qualifier • r1 = 1st round group stage • r2 = first knockout round • qf = quarter-final • sf = semi-final • f = final

ARGENTINA NATIONAL TEAM HISTORICAL RECORDS

Caps
145 - Javier Zanetti 1994- • **115** - Roberto Ayala 1994-2007 • **106** - Diego Simeone 1988-2002 • **97** - Oscar Ruggeri 1983-94 • **91** - Diego Maradona 1977-94 • **87** - Ariel Ortega 1993-2010 • **78** - Gabriel Batistuta 1991-2002 & Javier Mascherano 2003- • **76** - Juan Pablo Sorin 1995-2006 • **73** - Americo Gallego 1975 82 & Juan Sebastian Veron 1996- • **70** - Gabriel Heinze 2003- & Daniel Passarella 1976-86

Goals
56 - Gabriel Batistuta 1991-2002 • **35** - Hernan Crespo 1995-2007 • **34** - Diego Maradona 1977-94 • **24** - Luis Artime 1961-67 • **22** - Leopoldo Luque 1975-81 & Daniel Passarella 1976-86 • **21** - Jose Sanfilippo 1956-62 & Herminio Masantonio 1935-42 • **20** - Mario Kempes 1973-82 • **19** - Lionel Messi 2005- , Norberto Mendez 1945-56, Jose Manuel Moreno 1936-50 & Rene Pontoni 1942-47

Past Coaches
Angel Vazquez 1924-25 • Jose Lago Millan 1927-28 • Francisco Olazar 1928-29 • Francisco Olazar & Juan Jose Tramutola 1929-30 • Felipe Pascucci 1934 • Manuel Seoane 1934-37 • Angel Roca 1937-39 • Guillermo Stabile 1939-60 • Victorio Spinetto 1960-61 • Jose D'Amico 1961 • Juan Carlos Lorenzo 1962-63 • Alejandro Galan 1963 • Horacio Torres 1963-64 • Jose Maria Minella 1964-68 • Renato Cesarini 1968 • Humberto Maschio 1968-69 • Adolfo Pedernera 1969 • Juan Jose Pizzuti 1969-72 • Enrique Sivori 1972-74 • Vladislao Cap & Jose Varacka 1974 • Cesar Luis Menotti 1974-83 • Carlos Bilardo 1983-90 • Alfio Basile 1990-94 • Daniel Passarella 1994-98 • Marcelo Bielsa 1998-2004 • Jose Pekerman 2004-06 • Alfio Basile 2006-08 • Diego Maradona 2008-10 • Sergio Batista 2010-11 • Alejandro Sabella 2011-

ARGENTINA 2010-11
PRIMERA A APERTURA

	Pl	W	D	L	F	A	Pts
Estudiantes LP †	19	14	3	2	32	8	45
Vélez Sarsfield	19	13	4	2	33	9	43
Arsenal	19	9	5	5	22	19	32
River Plate	19	8	7	4	21	18	31
Godoy Cruz	19	7	8	4	32	25	29
Racing Club	19	8	5	6	25	18	29
Lanús	19	8	4	7	20	25	28
All Boys	19	7	5	7	24	23	26
Newell's Old Boys	19	6	8	5	13	12	26
Colón Santa Fe	19	7	5	7	21	29	26
Boca Juniors	19	7	4	8	20	20	25
Tigre	19	7	4	8	24	24	25
Argentinos Juniors	19	6	6	7	22	21	24
San Lorenzo	19	6	6	7	18	20	24
Banfield	19	4	8	7	20	19	20
Quilmes	19	4	7	8	14	23	19
Olimpo	19	5	3	11	18	26	18
Huracán	19	4	4	11	16	33	16
Gimnasia La Plata	19	3	6	10	13	23	15
Independiente	19	2	8	9	13	26	14

6/08/2010 - 6/02/2011 • † Qualified for Copa Libertadores
Top scorers: 11 - Santiago Silva URU, Velez & Denis Stracqualursi, Tigre • 10 - Juan Manuel Martinez, Velez • 8 - Mauro Matos, All Boys; Martin Palermo, Boca & David Ramirez, Godoy • 7 - Mauro Obolo, Arsenal

ARGENTINA 2010-11
PRIMERA A CLAUSURA

	Pl	W	D	L	F	A	Pts
Vélez Sarsfield †	19	12	3	4	36	17	39
Lanús	19	10	5	4	28	15	35
Godoy Cruz	19	10	4	5	33	28	34
Argentinos Juniors	19	7	9	3	16	11	30
Olimpo	19	8	6	5	28	23	30
Independiente	19	7	8	4	30	20	29
Boca Juniors	19	7	7	5	24	22	28
Banfield	19	7	6	6	24	24	27
River Plate	19	6	8	5	15	15	26
Arsenal	19	6	7	6	25	22	25
Tigre	19	6	7	6	25	26	25
All Boys	19	7	4	8	14	19	25
Estudiantes LP	19	6	6	7	18	19	24
San Lorenzo	19	5	8	6	19	17	23
Racing Club	19	7	2	10	25	26	23
Colón Santa Fe	19	6	3	10	20	27	21
Quilmes	19	5	5	9	24	27	20
Gimnasia LP	19	3	9	7	19	25	18
Newell's Old Boys	19	4	4	11	16	32	16
Huracán	19	3	5	11	18	42	14

11/02/2011 - 19/06/2011 • † Qualified for Copa Libertadores
Top scorers: 11 - Javier Campora, Huracan & Teofilo Gutierrez COL, Racing • 10 - Denis Stracqualursi, Tigre • 9 - Esteban Fuertes, Colon & Mauro Obolo, Arsenal • 8 - Ravid Ramirez, Velez; Silvio Romero, Lanus & Diego Valeri, Lanus

ARGENTINA 2010-11
PRIMERA A APERTURA & CLAUSURA RESULTS AND RELEGATION TABLE

	08-09	09-10	10-11	Pts	Pl	RA	Vélez Sarsfield	Lanús	Estudiantes LP	Banfield	Godoy Cruz	Argentinos Jun	Newell's Old Boys	San Lorenzo	Boca Juniors	Colón Santa Fe	All Boys	Racing Club	Independiente	Arsenal	Tigre	Olimpo	River Plate	Gimnasia LP	Huracán	Quilmes
Vélez Sarsfield † ‡	66	61	82	209	114	1.833		1-0	0-0	2-0	2-0	2-0	2-0	2-0	1-0	6-0	1-2	2-1	1-0	3-0	2-1	3-0	2-1	2-0	2-0	2-3
Lanús ‡	75	60	63	198	114	1.737	3-2		0-0	0-0	1-4	0-1	1-1	2-0	2-0	1-2	1-0	4-1	0-0	3-1	2-0	1-1	1-4	0-0	3-0	2-1
Estudiantes LP † ‡	57	71	69	197	114	1.728	0-4	3-0		0-1	0-1	3-1	2-1	0-0	1-0	0-2	3-0	2-0	0-2	2-0	2-2	2-0	1-1	2-0	2-0	2-0
Banfield	46	73	47	166	114	1.456	2-3	2-1	0-0		1-1	0-2	0-0	1-1	0-0	1-1	3-1	1-2	4-0	1-1	2-0	1-1	2-1	2-2	0-0	2-2	3-4
Godoy Cruz † ‡	49	53	63	165	114	1.447	0-4	2-0	1-2	2-1		1-0	0-0	0-2	1-1	2-3	1-0	1-1	4-1	1-4	1-2	1-0	2-2	2-2	3-1	2-0
Argentinos Juniors † ‡	38	73	54	165	114	1.447	1-1	1-2	0-0	1-0	0-0		1-2	1-0	0-2	3-0	1-0	2-1	0-0	1-0	1-0	1-1	0-0	1-1	1-2	0-0
Newell's Old Boys	52	69	42	163	114	1.43	2-0	2-1	0-1	0-1	1-3	0-2		0-0	1-0	1-0	1-0	0-2	1-1	2-2	0-0	1-1	0-3	3-3	1-1
San Lorenzo	63	52	48	162	114	1.421	1-0	1-0	1-2	1-2	1-2	2-0	0-0		1-0	1-2	3-1	1-2	1-1	1-2	2-0	0-1	1-0	0-1	1-3	0-0	0-2
Boca Juniors	61	47	53	161	114	1.412	2-1	1-2	2-1	1-1	1-4	0-2	1-0	1-2		3-1	0-0	1-2	1-1	2-1	3-3	0-2	2-0	1-1	2-0	1-0
Colón Santa Fe	57	55	47	159	114	1.395	1-1	0-1	1-1	0-1	1-3	1-2	1-0	2-0	0-1		1-1	0-4	1-1	0-1	1-0	0-2	1-2	1-3	3-0	2-0
All Boys	0	0	51	51	38	1.342	1-2	0-0	2-1	2-1	2-2	0-0	2-0	0-3	2-0	0-2		0-1	3-1	1-0	3-3	1-0	1-0	1-0	3-1	1-0
Racing Club	52	46	52	150	114	1.316	0-2	4-0	0-1	1-3	2-3	2-3	1-0	2-1	1-2	1-0		2-0	2-2	1-2	4-3	0-1	2-0	3-0	1-1
Independiente † ‡	39	68	43	150	114	1.316	2-2	1-2	1-2	1-1	3-0	1-4	0-1	1-0	0-3	1-2	2-1	1-0		1-2	0-1	1-1	0-1	1-0	5-1	0-0
Arsenal ‡	46	46	57	149	114	1.307	0-0	1-2	1-0	1-0	1-3	1-0	0-0	2-1	2-2	2-1	0-0	1-2	3-0		2-0	2-0	1-1	1-1	2-0	2-2
Tigre	62	32	50	144	114	1.263	2-1	0-3	2-1	1-2	2-2	1-1	1-0	1-0	1-2	3-0	0-1	0-0	0-0	1-2		3-2	0-0	2-0	3-1	3-0
Olimpo	0	0	48	48	38	1.263	1-2	1-0	2-2	1-3	3-1	1-1	1-0	1-1	3-2	1-0	1-0	1-2	1-1	2-2		0-0	1-0	4-0	0-1
River Plate ‡ ‡	41	43	57	141	114	1.237	1-2	1-2	0-4	1-0	1-2	0-0	2-1	1-1	1-0	1-0	2-1	1-3	2-1	0-1	0-0		0-0	2-0	1-1
Gimnasia LP ‡ ‡	55	37	33	125	114	1.096	0-0	0-2	0-2	2-0	1-3	2-4	1-2	0-0	2-2	0-0	3-1	0-0	1-2	2-3	2-1	1-3	0-0		3-0	1-0
Huracán	58	37	30	125	114	1.096	0-2	1-2	0-3	2-2	1-1	1-1	1-3	3-0	0-3	1-2	1-1	0-0	1-0	1-1	3-2	1-2	0-1	2-0		2-1
Quilmes	0	0	39	39	38	1.026	0-2	1-1	0-1	0-2	2-1	2-2	3-1	1-0	2-2	1-1	2-1	2-0	1-0	0-1	1-2	0-1	0-1	2-2	1-2	

† Qualified for the Copa Libertadores • ‡ Qualified for the Copa Sudamericana • Apertura results are in the shaded boxes • RA = Relegation average based on the average number of points per game over the past three seasons • ‡‡ play-off against Primera B Nacional team
Pre relegation play-off (tied on points): Huracán 0-2 Gimnasia LP. Huracán relegated to Primera B. Gimnasia proceed to the relegation play-offs
Relegation play-offs: **Belgrano Cordoba** 2-0 1-1 River Plate • **San Martin San Juan** 1-0 1-1 Gimnasia LP. River Plate and Gimnasia LP relegated

ARGENTINA 2010-11

PRIMERA B NACIONAL (2)

Team	Pl	W	D	L	F	A	Pts	At. Rafaela	Unión	San Martín SJ	Belgrano	Gimnasia J	Almirante B	Aldosivi	Boca Unidos	At. Tucumán	Instituto	Dep. Merlo	Rosario Cent	Patronato	Ferro Carril	San Martín T	Chacarita Jun	Defensa y J	Independiente	Tiro Federal	CAI
Atlético Rafaela	38	23	8	7	65	26	77	—	1-2	4-1	2-1	6-0	1-1	2-0	3-0	0-0	4-0	2-0	0-1	1-0	3-0	2-1	2-0	2-1	2-2	1-1	5-1
Unión Santa Fé	38	22	3	13	49	38	69	0-1	—	1-2	0-3	1-2	1-0	0-3	3-0	1-0	1-0	0-1	1-0	2-1	0-2	1-2	2-0	2-3	1-2	3-0	2-1
San Martín San Juan †	38	18	10	10	46	32	64	1-0	3-1	—	0-0	2-1	2-1	1-2	1-0	1-2	0-0	3-0	4-0	3-1	0-0	0-1	1-0	1-0	1-0	0-2	2-2
Belgrano Córdoba †	38	15	14	9	53	37	59	0-0	3-2	1-1	—	1-1	1-2	1-0	2-1	2-0	2-2	1-0	1-1	2-1	1-1	4-0	1-1	2-0	3-0	2-3	0-0
Gimnasia y Esg Jujuy	38	13	15	10	40	41	54	2-2	0-2	2-1	1-1	—	2-1	2-2	1-0	2-1	3-3	0-0	3-3	1-0	0-0	1-1	0-0	0-0	1-0	2-1	4-2
Almirante Brown	38	13	13	12	32	28	52	0-1	2-0	0-0	1-2	0-0	—	1-0	3-1	0-0	1-0	1-0	1-0	1-2	1-1	1-0	0-1	2-0	2-2	2-0	1-0
Aldosivi	38	14	10	14	45	47	52	1-0	2-1	2-0	2-1	0-0	1-0	—	2-0	0-3	0-0	1-0	0-5	4-1	5-1	0-1	2-0	2-0	1-1	1-1	0-1
Boca Unidos	38	13	13	12	43	46	52	0-1	2-1	1-1	3-3	0-0	1-1	0-0	—	2-0	1-3	1-0	2-0	0-0	3-2	2-0	0-0	2-2	1-0	1-0	1-1
Atlético Tucumán	38	14	9	15	44	41	51	0-2	0-1	1-2	2-0	0-3	3-0	2-1	1-1	—	1-2	2-1	4-2	2-0	0-0	1-0	0-1	1-0	2-1	0-0	4-1
Instituto Córdoba	38	11	18	9	38	35	51	0-0	0-1	1-0	0-0	2-0	1-1	4-0	0-0	0-1	—	1-2	3-3	0-0	1-2	0-0	0-2	0-1	0-1	1-1	1-1
Deportivo Merlo	38	13	12	13	32	37	51	1-0	1-1	0-3	0-2	2-0	0-2	0-2	2-2	3-2	0-1	—	1-0	1-1	2-1	1-1	0-0	1-1	0-0	3-2	0-0
Rosario Central	38	14	8	16	44	44	50	0-1	0-1	1-1	2-1	0-1	0-1	1-0	2-1	0-0	1-0	1-0	—	3-0	0-0	1-2	0-0	2-0	1-0	1-1	1-0
Patronato	38	14	8	16	41	43	50	0-1	0-2	0-2	2-0	1-0	0-1	3-0	3-1	2-1	0-0	0-1	2-2	—	0-0	0-0	3-1	0-2	2-2	4-1	1-0
Ferro Carril Oeste	38	11	14	13	38	47	47	2-0	0-2	1-0	1-1	1-0	0-0	3-1	0-2	2-1	1-1	0-2	1-0	0-2	—	1-0	3-0	0-0	1-0	1-3	2-2
San Martín Tucumán ‡	38	11	12	15	33	41	45	0-3	1-1	2-1	0-1	1-0	2-1	1-0	2-0	1-1	1-1	2-3	2-0	2-1	1-1	—	0-0	0-2	1-2	2-0	0-1
Chacarita Juniors	38	10	14	14	24	36	44	1-2	1-0	0-1	0-0	0-1	1-1	1-1	1-1	1-0	2-0	0-1	3-0	3-1	1-0	1-0	—	0-0	0-0	0-0	0-1
Defensa y Justicia	38	10	13	15	37	42	43	0-1	0-1	2-0	2-3	1-3	0-0	0-1	1-1	2-0	0-2	2-1	1-1	1-1	0-0	3-1	0-1	—	2-2	5-1	2-1
Independiente R'via ‡	38	9	13	16	44	49	40	3-1	1-2	0-1	0-2	0-1	1-0	2-3	3-1	1-1	1-1	0-1	0-1	3-0	1-1	1-1	0-2	3-1	—	2-0	0-0
Tiro Federal	38	8	13	17	37	56	37	2-4	0-2	1-1	0-2	1-0	1-1	3-1	1-2	2-4	0-0	1-1	1-2	1-0	4-1	0-2	1-1	0-0	1-2	—	1-1
CAI	38	6	16	16	38	57	34	0-0	1-2	0-1	1-1	1-0	0-0	2-2	1-3	1-1	0-1	3-1	0-2	0-3	1-0	1-3	2-2	3-3	1-2	1-1	—

7/08/2010 - 18/06/2011 • † Promotion play-off (see Primera A)
‡ Relegation play-off: **Sportivo Desamparados** 1-0 1-1 San Martín Tucuman • Defensores de Belgrano 0-0 2-2 **Independiente Rivadavia**

ARGENTINA 2010-11 — PRIMERA DIVISION B METROPOLITANA (3)

Team	Pl	W	D	L	F	A	Pts
Atlanta	42	26	8	8	68	37	86
Estudiantes BA †	42	21	10	11	53	42	73
Defensores de Belgrano †	42	19	14	9	48	28	71
Nueva Chicago †	42	19	14	9	43	35	71
Brown Adrogué †	42	19	13	10	54	36	70
Deportivo Armenio †	42	17	14	11	43	31	65
Barracas Central †	42	15	19	8	50	29	64
Deportivo Morón †	42	14	19	9	44	37	61
Villa San Carlos †	42	18	6	18	45	43	60
Comunicaciones	42	17	9	16	41	41	60
Almagro	42	16	10	16	52	51	58
Acassuso	42	13	17	12	46	43	56
Flandria	42	13	15	14	37	31	54
Colegiales	42	13	14	15	34	36	53
Platense	42	11	20	11	30	33	53
Sportivo Italiano	42	11	14	17	27	40	47
Tristán Suárez	42	11	13	18	40	54	46
Temperley	42	12	8	22	38	57	44
San Telmo	42	10	12	20	35	52	42
Sarmiento Junín	42	8	13	21	27	51	37
Deportivo Español	42	7	14	21	26	55	35
Los Andes ‡	42	6	16	20	40	59	34

24/07/2010 - 4/05/2011
† Promotion play-offs (See Primera B Nacional for final)
Deportivo Español relegated on three season average
‡ Relegation play-off • Central Córdoba 0-1 0-1 Los Andes

PROMOTION PLAY-OFFS
Quarter-finals: N.Chicago 3-3 Barracas • Defensores 1-0
Morón • Brown 1-1 D. Armenio • Estudiantes 1-3 San Carlos
Semi-finals: N.Chicago 2-1 Brown • Defensores 2-0 San Carlos
Final: Defensores de Belgrano 1-2 1-0 Nueva Chicago

ARGENTINA 2010-11 — PRIMERA DIVISION C METROPOLITANA (4)

Team	Pl	W	D	L	F	A	Pts
General Lamadrid	38	22	9	7	57	34	75
Argentino Merlo †	38	20	11	7	49	33	71
Talleres R de Escalada †	38	19	12	7	58	40	69
Central Córdoba †	38	17	13	8	51	28	64
Deportivo Laferrere †	38	17	13	8	51	33	64
Liniers †	38	18	10	10	53	43	64
UAI-Urquiza †	38	14	16	8	51	35	58
Excursionistas †	38	14	14	10	33	27	56
Berazategui †	38	13	16	9	42	39	55
Justo Jose de Urquiza	38	13	11	14	37	41	50
Luján	38	12	13	13	26	37	49
Defensores Unidos	38	13	9	16	44	54	48
Villa Dálmine	38	11	13	14	48	47	46
San Miguel	38	8	16	14	32	40	40
Defensores Cambaceres	38	9	11	18	23	35	38
El Porvenir	38	8	13	17	35	56	37
F.C. Midland	38	6	17	15	25	38	35
Leandro N. Alem	38	6	14	18	32	48	32
Sacachispas ‡	38	7	11	20	27	47	32
Fénix	38	6	12	20	27	46	30

31/07/2010 - 13/05/2011
† Promotion play-offs (See Primera B Metropolitana for final)
Fénix relegated on three season average • ‡ relegation play-off
• Sacachispas 0-2 San Miguel • Atlas 0-1 1-0 Sacachispas

PLAY-OFFS
Quarter-finals: UAI Urquiza 2-1 0-1 Central Córdoba • Liniers
1-3 0-1 Laferrere • Excursionistas 3-1 0-1 Talleres •
Berazategui 3-5 1-1 Argentino Merlo
Semi-finals: Laferrere 1-2 1-2 Central Córdoba •
Excursionistas 1-2 0-0 Argentino Merlo
Final: Central Córdoba 2-0 0-0 Argentino Merlo

ARGENTINA 2010–11
PRIMERA DIVISION D
METROPOLITANA (5)

	Pl	W	D	L	F	A	Pts
Sportivo Dock Sud	34	21	9	4	58	23	72
Atlas †	34	20	6	8	53	22	66
San Martín Burzaco †	34	17	7	10	53	39	58
Deportivo Riestra †	34	16	9	9	39	33	57
Centro Español †	34	15	10	9	41	38	55
Argentino Quilmes †	34	16	6	12	50	43	54
Ituzaingó †	34	14	9	11	48	38	51
Claypole †	34	14	8	12	46	41	50
Juventud Unida †	34	13	11	10	33	29	50
Atlético Lugano	34	13	9	12	35	40	48
Argentino Rosario	34	13	7	14	48	35	46
Cañuelas	34	8	16	10	21	31	40
Central Ballester	34	10	9	15	32	43	39
Deportivo Paraguayo	34	11	5	18	34	43	38
Sp. Barracas Bolívar	34	7	12	15	26	31	33
Victoriano Arenas	34	9	6	19	28	51	33
Yupanqui	34	6	9	19	27	59	27
Puerto Nuevo	34	4	10	20	23	56	22

7/08/2010 - 14/05/2011
† Promotion play-offs (See Primera C Metropolitana for final)
Puerto Novo relegated on three season average

PLAY-OFFS
Quarter-finals: Juventud 1-3 2-3 **Atlas** • **Claypole** 2-0 0-1 San
Martin Burzaco • **Ituzaingo** 2-0 2-3 Dep. Riestra • Argentino
Quilmes 2-1 0-3 **Centro Español**
Semi-finals: Claypole 0-0 0-0 **Atlas** •
Ituzaingo 2-1 0-1 **Central Español**
Final: Centro Español 1-1 0-1 **Atlas**

ARGENTINA 2010–11
TORNEO ARGENTINA A (3)
SECOND STAGE

	Pl	W	D	L	F	A	Pts
Guillermo Brown	8	6	1	1	16	5	19
Central Norte	8	5	1	2	14	10	16
Libertad Sunchales	8	3	2	3	13	12	11
Unión Mar del Plata	8	3	2	3	12	11	11
Sportivo Belgrano	8	3	2	3	8	10	11
Unión Sunchales	8	2	4	2	12	11	10
Desamparados	8	2	3	3	7	10	9
Talleres Córdoba	8	2	2	4	10	13	8
Huracán Tres Arroyos	8	1	1	6	6	16	4

26/03/2011 - 14/05/2011 • Guillermo Brown promoted to
Primera B Nacional. The other teams enter the third stage

THIRD STAGE PLAY-OFFS
Huracán Tres Arroyos 0-1 0-1 **Central Norte**
Talleres Córdoba 0-2 2-1 **Libertad Sunchales**
Desamparados 3-2 1-1 Unión Mar del Plata
Unión Sunchales 0-0 1-5 **Sportivo Belgrano**
Winners qualify for the fourth stage

ARGENTINA 2010–11
TORNEO ARGENTINA A (3)
FOURTH STAGE

Quarter-finals: Racing Córdoba 1-2 2-1 **Central Norte** •
Deportivo Maipú 2-0 0-4 **Libertad Sunchales** • Douglas Haig
3-2 1-2 **Desamparados** • Crucero del Norte 0-0 0-0 **Sp Belgrano**
Semi-finals: **Desamparados** 0-1 0 1-0 Central Norte •
Sportivo Belgrano 0-1 3-0 Libertad Sunchales
Final: **Desamparados** 1-0 0-0 Sportivo Belgrano

ARGENTINA 2010–11
TORNEO ARGENTINA A (3)
FIRST STAGE

Group A	Pl	W	D	L	F	A	Pts
Guillermo Brown †	28	15	12	1	53	22	57
Unión Mar del Plata †	28	12	9	7	40	30	45
Huracán Tres Arroyos †	28	10	7	11	31	34	37
Cipolletti	28	8	10	10	40	43	34
Douglas Haig	28	7	12	9	30	30	33
Rivadavia Lincoln	28	9	6	13	23	33	33
Santamarina	28	7	10	11	23	36	31
Villa Mitre	28	5	12	11	28	40	27

Group B	Pl	W	D	L	F	A	Pts
Talleres Córdoba †	28	15	3	10	49	35	48
Sportivo Belgrano †	28	15	3	10	42	33	48
Desamparados †	28	10	11	7	31	22	41
Juventud Unida Univ.	28	9	11	8	26	27	38
Racing Córdoba	28	8	14	6	26	27	38
Alumni Villa María	28	5	13	10	33	41	28
Estudiantes Río Cuarto	28	6	10	12	32	42	28
Deportivo Maipú	28	5	13	10	23	35	28

Group C	Pl	W	D	L	F	A	Pts
Central Norte †	28	12	9	7	37	22	45
Unión Sunchales †	28	12	9	7	38	25	45
Libertad Sunchales †	28	10	11	7	30	27	41
Juventud Antoniana	28	11	7	10	30	31	40
Gimnasia Concepción	28	11	7	10	30	33	40
Crucero del Norte	28	10	6	12	25	30	36
Central Córdoba Santiago	28	8	9	11	35	46	33
9 de Julio Rafaela	28	5	8	15	31	42	23

21/08/2010 - 20/03/2011 • † Qualified for the second stage
The rest take part in the Revalida

ARGENTINA 2010–11
TORNEO ARGENTINA A (3)
REVALIDA

Group A	Pl	W	D	L	F	A	Pts
Douglas Haig †	8	5	3	0	12	5	18
Cipolletti	8	2	4	2	6	5	10
Rivadavia Lincoln	8	2	3	3	5	8	9
Villa Mitre	8	2	2	4	11	13	8
Santamarina	8	1	4	3	6	9	7

Group B	Pl	W	D	L	F	A	Pts
Deportivo Maipú †	8	6	1	1	13	6	19
Racing Córdoba †	8	5	1	2	13	8	16
Estudiantes Río Cuarto	8	2	3	3	10	11	9
Alumni Villa María	8	3	0	5	11	17	9
Juventud Unida Univ.	8	1	1	6	9	14	4

Group C	Pl	W	D	L	F	A	Pts
Crucero del Norte †	8	4	1	3	13	8	13
Juventud Antoniana	8	4	1	3	11	8	13
Central Córdoba Santiago	8	3	2	3	14	12	11
Gimnasia Concepción	8	3	2	3	12	15	11
9 de Julio Rafaela	8	2	2	4	11	18	8

27/03/2011 - 22/05/2011 • † Qualified for the fourth stage

Guillermo Brown promoted to Primera B Nacional as Torneo
Argentina A champions • Desamparados qualified to meet San
Martín Tucuman (see Primera B Nacional)
Fourth stage played from 28/05/2011 - 19/06/2011

MEDALS TABLE

#	Team	Overall			League			Amateur			Pro			National			Metro			AP/CL			South Am		
		G	S	B	G	S	B	G	S	B	G	S	B	G	S	B	G	S	B	G	S	B	G	S	B
1	Boca Juniors	39	25	21	30	21	17	6	3	5	10	8	5	3			2	2	3	9	8	4	9	4	4
2	River Plate	37	34	29	34	30	14	1	5	4	14	11	5	3	7		4	2		12	5	5	3	4	15
3	Independiente	26	17	14	16	16	9	2	2	3	6	8	6	3	1		3	2		2	3		10	1	5
4	Racing Club	18	9	14	16	8	12	9	1	1	6	3	7			1		2		1	2	3	2	1	2
5	San Lorenzo	15	13	22	13	13	16	3	2	2	3	7	5	2	1	3	2	1	2	3	2	4	2		6
6	Velez Sarsfield	10	8	13	8	8	9		1			1	1	1	1	2		2	1	7	3	5	2		4
7	Alumni	10	2		10	2		10	2																
8	Estudiantes La Plata	9	9	11	5	7	9	1	3	2			3	1	2		2	1	2	1	1	2	4	2	2
9	Huracán	5	6	8	5	6	7	4	2	3			3				1	2	1		2				1
10	Rosario Central	5	5	5	4	4	2				1			3	2			1			1	2	1	1	3
11	Newell's Old Boys	5	5	3	5	3	3				2	2	1				1		1	2	1	1		2	
12	Lomas Athletic	5	2	3	5	2	3	5	2	3															
13	Argentinos Juniors	4	2	4	3	2	1			1				1	1		1	1		1			1		3
14	Belgrano Athletic	3	3	3	3	3	3	3	3	3															
15	Lanús	2	5	5	1	4	5					1								1	3	4	1	1	
16	Ferro Carril Oeste	2	3	1	2	3	1							2	1			2	1						
17	CA Porteño	2	2		2	2		2	2																
18	Quilmes	2	1	3	2	1	3	1		3					1		1								
19	Estudiantil Porteño	2			2			2																	
20	Gimnasia y Esgrima LP	1	6	4	1	6	3	1	1				1								5	2			1
21	Banfield	1	4	4	1	4	4		2	2		1								1	1	2			
22	Talleres Córdoba	1	1	2		1	2								1				1			1	1		
23	Lomas Academy	1	1		1	1		1	1																
24	Chacarita Juniors	1	1		1	1											1	1							
	Sportivo Barracas	1		1	1		1	1		1															
	Sportivo Doc Sud	1		1	1		1	1		1															
27	Arsenal Sarandi	1																					1		
	St Andrews	1			1			1																	
	Old Caledonians	1			1			1																	
30	San Isidro		3	3		3	3		3	3															
31	Estudiantes BA		2	2		2	2		2	2															
32	Flores AC		2	1		2	1		2	1															
33	Lobos AC		2			2			2																
	Nueva Chicago		2			2			2																
	Tigre		2			2															2				
36	Platense		1	4		1	4		1	3			1												
37	Colón Santa Fe		1	3		1	2														1	2			1
38	Unión Santa Fe		1	1		1	1								1				1						
	Barracas AC		1	1		1	1		1	1															
	Godoy Cruz		1	1		1	1														1	1			
41	Almagro		1			1			1																
	Barracas Central		1			1			1																
	Colegiales		1			1			1																
	Del Plata		1			1			1																
	Gimnasia y Esgrima BA		1			1			1																
	Lanus AC		1			1			1																
	Racing Cordoba		1			1									1										
	Rosario AC		1			1			1																
	Sportivo Palermo		1			1			1																
	Temperley		1			1			1																
51	Deportivo Español			3			3						2									1			
52	Atlanta			2			2									1									
	Argentino Quilmes			2			2			2															
	Quilmes Rowers			2			2			2															
55	Belgrano A			1			1			1															
	El Porvenir			1			1			1															
	Defensores Belgrano			1			1			1															
	Old Boys			1			1			1															
	Rosario Railway			1			1			1															
	Sporting Almagro			1			1			1															
	Sportivo Buenos Aires			1			1			1															

Amateur = Amateur Championship 1891-1934 • Pro = Professional Championship 1931-66 & 1986-91 • National = National Championship 1967-85 • Metro = Metropoltian Championship 1967-84 • AP/CL = Apertura and Clausura tournaments 1991- • League column is a combination of all

CLUB BY CLUB GUIDE TO 2011 IN ARGENTINA

ARGENTINA 2010–11
PRIMERA A CLAUSURA

	Pl	W	D	L	F	A	Pts
Vélez Sarsfield	19	12	3	4	36	17	39
Lanús	19	10	5	4	28	15	35
Godoy Cruz	19	10	4	5	33	28	34
Argentinos Juniors	19	7	9	3	16	11	30
Olimpo	19	8	6	5	28	23	30
Independiente	19	7	8	4	30	20	29
Boca Juniors	19	7	5	5	24	22	28
Banfield	19	7	6	6	24	24	27
River Plate	19	6	8	5	15	15	26
Arsenal	19	6	7	6	25	22	25
Tigre	19	6	7	6	25	26	25
All Boys	19	7	4	8	14	19	25
Estudiantes LP	19	6	6	7	18	19	24
San Lorenzo	19	5	8	6	19	17	23
Racing Club	19	7	2	10	25	26	23
Colón Santa Fe	19	6	3	10	20	27	21
Quilmes	19	5	5	9	24	27	20
Gimnasia LP	19	3	9	7	19	25	18
Newell's Old Boys	19	4	4	11	16	32	16
Huracán	19	3	5	11	18	42	14

11/02/2011 - 19/06/2011

ARGENTINA 2011–12
PRIMERA A APERTURA

	Pl	W	D	L	F	A	Pts
Boca Juniors	19	12	7	0	25	6	43
Racing Club	19	7	10	2	16	8	31
Vélez Sarsfield	19	9	4	6	22	17	31
Belgrano Córdoba	19	8	7	4	21	16	31
Colón Santa Fe	19	8	7	4	19	15	31
Lanús	19	7	8	4	20	14	29
Tigre	19	7	6	6	22	19	27
Independiente	19	7	6	6	18	17	27
San Martín San Juan	19	6	8	5	17	14	26
Atlético Rafaela	19	8	2	9	22	26	26
Unión Santa Fé	19	6	7	6	14	18	25
Godoy Cruz	19	6	6	7	28	24	24
Arsenal	19	6	6	7	21	20	24
Argentinos Juniors	19	5	7	7	18	24	22
All Boys	19	4	9	6	15	23	21
Estudiantes LP	18	5	5	8	22	23	20
San Lorenzo	19	5	4	10	14	18	19
Newell's Old Boys	19	1	13	5	13	18	16
Olimpo	19	2	10	7	15	25	16
Banfield	18	3	2	13	12	27	11

5/08/2011 - 13/12/2011

ALL BOYS 2011

Feb	13 Racing	L	0-1	Ca		20 000
	20 Vélez	W	2-1	Ca	Grazzini 2 [24] [57]	22 000
	27 Boca Jun	D	0-0	Ca		42 000
Mar	4 S. Lorenzo	L	0-3	Ca		14 500
	12 Olimpo	L	0-1	Ca		14 000
	19 Colón	L	0-2	Ca		12 000
	26 Estudiantes	L	0-3	Ca		15 000
	2 Lanús	D	0-0	Ca		12 000
	10 Tigre	W	1-0	Ca	Barrientos [9]	15 000
Apr	16 Huracán	W	3-1	Ca	Fabiani 2 [14] [20], Gigliotti [52p]	13 000
	23 Indep'iente	D	2-2	Ca	Ereros [78], Gigliotti [82]	28 000
	30 Arg Juniors	D	0-0	Ca		15 000
	8 River Plate	W	2-0	Ca	Gigliotti [37], Rodriguez [90]	45 000
May	14 Arsenal	W	1-0	Ca	Gigliotti [53]	10 000
	20 Newells OB	L	0-1	Ca		30 000
	28 Quilmes	W	1-0	Ca	Torassa [89]	15 000
Jun	4 Banfield	L	1-3	Ca	Matos [4p]	13 000
	11 Gimnasia	W	1-0	Ca	Gigliotti [39]	13 000
	19 Godoy Cruz	L	0-1	Ca		14 000

12th   Att: 124 500 • Av: 13 833

Aug	6 Belgrano	D	1-1	Ap	Matos [55]	15 000
	17 Colón	D	1-1	Ap	Matos [74]	25 000
	21 At. Rafaela	L	1-2	Ap	Matos [1]	8 000
	27 Vélez	W	1-0	Ap	Perea [69]	16 000
	3 Racing	D	0-0	Ap		18 000
Sep	10 Godoy Cruz	L	1-6	Ap	Dominguez [22]	7 000
	17 Banfield	L	0-1	Ap		12 000
	20 Arsenal	W	2-1	Ap	Ferreyra 2 [19] [35p]	4 500
	25 Tigre	D	1-1	Ap	Matos [45]	16 000
Oct	2 Olimpo	L	1-2	Ap	Matos [45]	12 000
	15 Unión	D	1-1	Ap	Sanchez [8]	18 000
	24 Newells OB	D	1-1	Ap	Rodriguez [33]	13 000
Nov	4 Indep'iente	D	2-2	Ap	Matos 2 [18] [61]	12 000
	12 S.Lorenzo	W	1-0	Ap	OG [39]	17 000
	19 San Martin	D	0-0	Ap		8 000
	26 Lanús	D	0-0	Ap		12 000
Dec	2 Estudiantes	L	0-3	Ap		16 000
	6 Arg Juniors	W	1-0	Ap	Zapata [13]	8 000
	11 Boca Jun	L	0-1	Ap		35 000

15th   Att: 110 000 • Av: 12 222 • Islas Malvinas 21 000

ALL BOYS LEAGUE APPEARANCES/GOALS 2011
Goalkeepers Nicolas Cambiasso **19** 19
Defenders Mariano Brau **3+1/0** • Carlos Casteglione **13/0**
Maximiliano Coronel 3+3/0 • Eduardo Dominguez **17/0** 17/1
Carlos Madeo **2/0** • Francisco Martinez 2+2/0 • Armando Panceri **5+3/0**
Facundo Quiroga 19 • Matias Rudler **1/0** 6+1/0 • Carlos Soto **16/0** 16/0
Cristian Varela **3+2/0** • Cristian Vella **18/0** 13/0
Midfield Hugo Barrientos **15/1** 8/0 • Sebastien Grazzini **6+6/2**
Victor David Lopez **2/0** • Emanuel Perea **5+4/0** 6+3/1
Patricio Perez 0+6/0 • Matias Perez Garcia 14+1/0
Lucas Rimoldi **1+4/0** • Juan Pablo Rodriguez URU **15/1** 15+3/1
Fernando Sanchez **18/0** - 19/1 • Dario Stefanatto 10+1/0
Martin Zapata 8+8/1 • Ariel Zarate **8+3/0**
Forwards Hugo Bargas 0+4/0 • Gustavo Bartelt **0+1/0**
Sebastian Ereros **1+9/1** • Cristian Fabbiani **4+2/2**
Juan Ferreyra 1+10/2 • Emanuel Gigliotti **12+3/5**
Mauro Matos **17/1** 18/7 • Ariel Ortega **6+6/0** • Henry Rui 0+1/0
Matias Saad **0+1/0** • Carlos Salom 2+7/0
Agustin Torassa **2+9/1** 13+2/0
Coach Jose Santos Romero

The 2011 guide to club football in Argentina covers the two league tournaments staged during the course of 2011 although the Argentine season technically runs from August to May. The tables from those two campaigns are listed above for ease of reference • Ca = Clausura • Ap = Apertura • CL = Copa Libertadores • CS = Copa Sudamericana • RSA = Recopa Sudamericana. For further details see the key on page 13. Appearances and goals for the 2010-11 Clausura are marked in bold • Appearances and goals for the 2011-12 Apertura are in normal type

ARGENTINOS JUNIORS 2011

Mon	Date	Opponent	Res	Score	Comp	Scorers	Att
Feb	9	Fluminense	D	2-2	CLg3	Niell 2 [44 70]	15 939
	14	Huracan	D	1-1	Ca	Blandi [89]	10 000
	19	Indep'iente	D	0-0	Ca		13 000
	24	América	W	3-1	CLg3	Salcedo 2 [45p 73], Sanchez Prette [93+]	4 373
	27	Velez	D	1-1	Ca	Niell [68]	14 000
Mar	2	Nacional	W	1-0	CLg3	Niell [21]	8 991
	6	River Plate	D	0-0	Ca		45 000
	12	Arsenal	W	1-0	Ca	Salcedo [78]	8 000
	15	Nacional	L	0-1	CLg3		6 834
	20	Newells OB	W	2-0	Ca	Rius [5], Bogado [80]	31 000
	25	Quilmes	D	0-0	Ca		7 000
	1	Banfield	W	2-0	Ca	Niell [32], Bogado [79]	9 000
	6	América	L	1-2	CLg3	Niell [48]	19 451
Apr	10	Gimnasia	D	1-1	Ca	Rius [29]	10 000
	16	Godoy Cruz	L	0-1	Ca		10 000
	20	Fluminense	L	2-4	CLg3	Salcedo [25p], Oberman [54]	5 706
	24	Racing	D	2-1	Ca	Salcedo [58], Prosperi [77]	10 000
	30	All Boys	D	0-0	Ca		15 000
	8	Boca Jun	L	0-2	Ca		25 000
May	14	S. Lorenzo	W	2-1	Ca	Hernandez [7], Basualdo [45]	14 000
	21	Olimpo	L	0-1	Ca		13 000
	28	Colon	W	2-1	Ca	Blandi [21], Niell [65]	13 000
	6	Estudiantes	D	0-0	Ca		8 000
Jun	12	Lanus	W	1-0	Ca	Blandi [58]	27 000
	18	Tigre	D	1-1	Ca	Blandi [22]	10 000

4th | Att: 118 000 • Av: 11 800 (+5.4%)

Mon	Date	Opponent	Res	Score	Comp	Scorers	Att
Aug	5	Unión	D	1-1	Ap	Salcedo [47]	20000
	16	Newells OB	D	1-1	Ap	OG [29]	8 000
	20	S. Lorenzo	L	1-3	Ap	Morales [69]	20 000
	28	Indep'iente	D	0-0	Ap		16 000
Sep	1	Vélez	D	0-0	CSr2		
	4	San Martin	D	0-0	Ap		10 000
	8	Vélez	L	0-4	CSr2		
	12	Lanús	L	0-4	Ap		10 000
	18	Estudiantes	L	3-4	Ap	Salcedo [3], Barzola [31], Barrera [85]	18 000
	22	Tigre	L	0-1	Ap		8 000
	25	Boca Jun	D	0-0	Ap		15 000
Oct	1	Belgrano	W	2-1	Ap	Morales [4], Brum [57]	36 000
	16	Colón	D	0-0	Ap		2 500
	25	At. Rafaela	L	1-3	Ap	Oberman [75]	13 000
	29	Vélez	W	3-1	Ap	Salcedo 2 [45 72], OG [55]	14 000
	6	Racing	L	0-1	Ap		25 000
Nov	19	Godoy Cruz	W	1-0	Ap	Oberman [37]	6 000
	27	Banfield	D	2-2	Ap	Bordagaray [26], Salcedo [90]	8 000
	3	Arsenal	W	2-1	Ap	Salcedo 2 [30 90]	8 000
Dec	6	All Boys	L	0-1	Ap		8 000
	11	Olimpo	W	1-0	Ap	Naguel [63]	6 000

14th | Att: 94 500 • Av: 9 450 • Diego Armando Maradona 24 800

ARSENAL 2011

Mon	Date	Opponent	Res	Score	Comp	Scorers	Att
Feb	14	Lanus	L	1-3	Ca	Caffa [84]	15 000
	21	Tigre	W	2-2	Ca	Lopez [5], Ortiz [86]	3 000
	28	Huracan	D	1-1	Ca	Obolo [64]	9 000
	7	Indep'iente	W	3-0	Ca	Caffa 4, Krupoviesa 34p, Leguizamon [80]	15 000
Mar	12	Arg Juniors	L	0-1	Ca		8 000
	19	River Plate	D	1-1	Ca	Obolo [16]	20 000
	27	Velez	L	0-3	Ca		20 000
	2	Newells OB	D	2-2	Ca	Leguizamon [26], Obolo [30]	28 000
	9	Quilmes	D	2-2	Ca	Lopez [72], Leguizamon [90]	7 000
Apr	18	Banfield	L	0-1	Ca		13 000
	24	Gimnasia	D	1-1	Ca	Obolo [33]	5 000
	30	Godoy Cruz	W	4-1	Ca	Lopez [11], Gonzalez [22], Obolo 2 [62 71]	7 000
	7	Racing	L	1-2	Ca	Alustiza [84]	16 000
May	14	All Boys	L	0-1	Ca		10 000
	22	Boca Jun	D	2-2	Ca	Obolo [23], Lopez [61]	18 000
	28	S. Lorenzo	D	1-1	Ca	Gonzalez [18]	15 000
Jun	3	Olimpo	W	2-0	Ca	Obolo [38], Lopez [43]	2 500
	11	Colon	W	1-0	Ca	Blanco [45]	13 000
	19	Estudiantes	W	1-0	Ca	Obolo [74]	2 000

10th | Att: 88 500 • Av: 9 833

Mon	Date	Opponent	Res	Score	Comp	Scorers	Att
Aug	6	Colón	L	1-2	Ap	Burdisso [36]	6 000
	15	At. Rafaela	W	3-1	Ap	Obolo [13], Leguizamon 2 [18 33]	11 000
	19	Vélez	L	0-1	Ap		6 000
	26	Racing	D	0-0	Ap		28 000
	30	Estudiantes	W	2-0	CSr2	Lopez [50], Trombetta [75]	
	3	Godoy Cruz	L	1-2	Ap	Obolo [90]	4 000
Sep	6	Estudiantes	L	0-1	CSr2		
	11	Banfield	W	1-0	Ap	Zelaya [6]	10 000
	17	Tigre	D	2-2	Ap	Zelaya [33], Trombetta [85]	10 000
	20	All Boys	L	1-2	Ap	Lopez [90]	4 500
	24	Olimpo	D	2-2	Ap	Lopez [39], Zelaya [48]	8 000
	29	Olimpia	D	0-0	CSr3		
Oct	4	Unión	W	2-1	Ap	Tombetta [20], Obolo [82]	3 000
	14	Newells OB	D	0-0	Ap		35 000
	19	Olimpia	W	3-2	CSr3	Trombetta [16], Zelaya [20], Blanco [84]	
	25	S. Lorenzo	W	1-0	Ap	Gonzalez [75]	5 000
	30	Indep'iente	D	0-0	Ap		13 000
Nov	3	U de Chile	L	1-2	CSqf	Obolo [47]	
	8	San Martin	W	2-0	Ap	Zelaya [4], Caffa [52]	3 000
	18	U de Chile	L	0-3	CSqf		
	22	Lanús	W	1-0	Ap	Burdisso [20]	10 000
	27	Estudiantes	L	1-2	Ap	Obolo [20]	5 000
Dec	3	Arg Juniors	L	1-2	Ap	Gonzalez [18]	8 000
	7	Boca Jun	D	2-2	Ap	Burdisso [47], Obolo [54]	15 000
	11	Belgrano	L	0-1	Ap		15 000

13th | Att: 47 000 • Av: 3 194 • El Viaducto 16 300

ARGENTINOS LEAGUE APPEARANCES/GOALS 2011

Goalkeepers Nereo Fernandez 7+1 • Nicolas Navarro 13
Luis Ojeda 6 12
Midfield Pablo Barzola 13+2/1 • Nicolas Batista 3+2/0
Nicolas Berardo 11+2/0 12+1/0 • Sergio Escudero 7+1/0
Santiago Gentiletti 18/0 • Jefferson Hurtado ECU 5+1/0
Federico Pistone 2+2/0 3/0 • Gonzalo Prosperi 18/1 19/0
Lucas Rodriguez 0+1/0 • Juan Sabia 19/0 13/0
Miguel Torren 6+1/0 13/0
Midfield German Basualdo 8+2/1 11+1/0 • Mauro Bogado 4+6/2
Fabian Bordagaray 5+1/1 • Roberto Brum URU 12+1/1
Rodrigo Diaz Ponce 0+1/0 0+1/0 • Emilio Hernandez CHI 8+1/1 7+2/0
Gaspar Iniguez 3 i 2/0 • Matias Laba 11+3/0 11+1/0
Juan Mercier 15/0 • Santiago Naguel 0+3/1
Gustavo Oberman 14+2/0 17/2 • Dario Ocampo 0+2/0
Juan Ramirez 0+3/0 3+6/0 • Ciro Rius 12+4/2 6+5/0
Andres Romero 1+4/0 0+4/0 • Cristian Sanchez Prette 1+4/0
Forwards Leandro Barrera 0+4/1 • Nicolas Blandi 6+4/4
Pablo Hernandez 3+2/0 13+4/0• Juan Morales 9+5/2
Franco Niell 14+1/3 • Gabriel Perez Tarifa 0+5/0
Hernan Salazar 0+1/0 0+2/0 • Santiago Salcedo PAR 12+2/2 12+1/7
Gonzalo Vargas URU 0+5/0
Coach Pedro Troglio • Nestor Gorosito (20/09/2011)

ARSENAL LEAGUE APPEARANCES/GOALS 2011

Goalkeepers Christian Campestrini 18 18 • Catriel Orcellet 1 1+1
Matias Perez 0+1
Defenders Pablo Aguilar PAR 14/0 • Cristian Alvarez 3+2/0
Ignacio Boggino 5/0 • Guillermo Burdisso 16/3 • Victor Cuesta 2/0
Danilo Gerlo 8+1/0 • Juan Krupoviesa 7/1 • Lisandro Lopez 19/5 16/2
Hugo Nervo 16/0 12+1/0 • Cristian Trombetta 6+6/2
Midfield Marcos Aguirre 6+2/0 13+3/0 • Dario Benedetto 0+1/0
Juan Caffa 16+2/2 7+2/1 • Julian Cardozo 1+1/0
Gonzalo Choy URU 0+3/0 • Juan Cobo 2+3/0
Gaston Esmerado 8+3/0 14+2/0 • Andres Franzoia 2+9/0
Adrian Gonzalez 10+5/2 9+6/2 • Ivan Marcone 16/0 18/0
Leonardo Morales • Jorge Ortiz 18/1 14+1/0
Damian Perez 12/0 15+1/0 • Sergio Sena 2+2/0 0+2/0
Forwards Matias Alustiza 2+6/1 • Gustavo Blanco 7+1/1 2+5/0
Luciano Leguizamon 7+5/3 5+8/2 • Franco Mendoza 0+5/0
Claudio Mosca 1+7/0 2+1/0 • Ivan Obolo 19/9 18+1/5
Diego Torres 12+4/0 • Emilio Zelaya 11+5/4
Coach Gustavo Alfaro

ATLETICO RAFAELA 2011

Aug	5 Banfield	W 2-0	Ap	Gandin 2 9p 12	14 000
	15 Arsenal	L 1-3	Ap	Castro 75p	11 000
	21 All Boys	W 2-1	Ap	Gonzalez 75, Gaitan 85	8 000
	27 Olimpo	W 3-1	Ap	Castro 39, Gandin 68, Serrano 77	13 000
Sep	4 Union	W 1-0	Ap	OG 18	21 000
	9 Newells OB	D 0-0	Ap		15 000
	18 S.Lorenzo	W 3-1	Ap	Gandin 69, Gonzalez 90, Castro 90	23 000
	21 Indep'iente	L 1-3	Ap	Castro 63	14 500
	25 San Martin	L 1-2	Ap	Gandin 10	7 000
Oct	1 Lanus	W 2-1	Ap	Fontanini 51, Gonzalez 54	12 000
	16 Estudiantes	L 0-3	Ap		5 000
	25 Arg Juniors	W 3-1	Ap	Gandin 5p, Gonzalez 19, Camiello 33	13 000
	30 Boca Jun	L 1-3	Ap	Castro 88	40 000
Nov	4 Belgrano	D 0-0	Ap		13 000
	20 Colón	L 0-1	Ap		25 000
	25 Tigre	L 0-3	Ap		18 000
Dec	4 Velez	W 2-0	Ap	Castro 1, Carrera 87	13 000
	7 Racing	L 0-1	Ap		25 000
	13 Godoy Cruz	L 0-2	Ap		11 000

10th — Att: 115 500 • Av: 12 833 • Nuevo Monumental 16 000

RAFAELA LEAGUE APPEARANCES/GOALS 2011

Goalkeepers Jorge Carranza 0+1 • Guillermo Sara 19
Defenders Oscar Carniello 18/1 • Francisco Dutari 3/0
Julian Fernandez 9/0 • Fabricio Fontanini 16/1 • Hugo Iriarte 4+5/0
Martin Zbrun 18
Midfield German Caceres 5+5/0 • Sebastian Carrera 3+7/1
Nicolas Castro 19/6 • Jhersson Cordoba COL 2+4/0
Rodrigo Depetris 0+1/0 • Matias Fissore 16+1/0 • Walter Gaitan 1+8/1
Ivan Juarez 14/0 • Luis Lagrutta 0+3/0 • Alexis Niz 6+1/0
Walter Serrano 18/1
Forwards Nicolas Capellino 0+3/0 • Lucio Filomeno 3+1/0
Dario Gandin 17/6 • Federico Gonzalez 13+1/4 • Jonathan Lopez 1+4/0
Matias Zbrun 4+3/0
Coach Carlos Trullet

BELGRANO CORDOBA 2011

Aug	6 All Boys	D 1-1	Ap	Pereyra 47	15 000
	17 Olimpo	D 1-1	Ap	Vazquez 56	16 000
	23 Union	D 0-0	Ap		18 000
	28 Newells OB	L 2-3	Ap	Turus 9, Maldonado 14	37 000
Sep	3 S.Lorenzo	W 1-0	Ap	Mansanelli 39	25 000
	11 Indep'iente	W 2-0	Ap	Pereyra 2 37 46	40 000
	17 San Martin	W 1-0	Ap	Perez 82	10 000
	21 Lanus	D 0-0	Ap		35 000
	26 Estudiantes	W 3-2	Ap	Farre 10, Mansanelli 45, Graba 75	9 000
Oct	1 Arg Juniors	L 1-2	Ap	Almerares 65	36 000
	16 Boc Jun	D 0-0	Ap		45 000
	26 Tigre	W 1-0	Ap	Mancuello 5	7 000
	30 Colon	L 0-1	Ap		30 000
Nov	4 At.Rafaela	D 0-0	Ap		13 000
	20 Velez	L 1-3	Ap	Vazquez 70	27 000
	26 Racing	W 3-2	Ap	Pereyra 2 29 42, Turus 36	18 000
Dec	4 Godoy Cruz	D 1-1	Ap	Mansanelli 57	15 000
	8 Banfield	W 2-0	Ap	Pereyra 2 11 24	9 000
	11 Arsenal	W 1-0	Ap	Vazquez 13	15 000

4th — Att: 251 000 • Av: 27 888 • Olimpico Chateau Carreras 46 083

BELGRANO LEAGUE APPEARANCES/GOALS 2011

Goalkeepers Juan Olave 19
Defenders Pier Barrios 1+3/0 • Fernando Gonzalez 0+1/0
Hernan Grana 4+9/1 • Daniel Lembo URU 17/0 • Claudio Perez 17/1
Juan Quiroga 14/0 • Gaston Turus 19/2
Midfield Gaston Alvarez 0+1/0 • Giuliano Bardin 1+3/0
Guillermo Farre 17/1 • Esteban Gonzalez 10+3/0 • Luciano Lollo 4+1/0
Juan Maldonado 2+6/1 • Federico Mancuello 9+3/1
Cesar Mansanelli 19/3 • Lucas Parodi 2+4/0 • Lisandro Pereyra 19/7
Ribair Rodriguez URU 11+3/0 • Franco Vazquez 17+1/3
Forwards Federico Almerares ITA 1+11/1 • Tobias Figueroa 0+1/0
Andres Silvera 6+3/0
Coach Ricardo Zielinski

BANFIELD 2011

Feb	12 Olimpo	L 1-2	Ca	Victor Lopez 48	8 000
	19 Colon	D 1-1	Ca	Achucarro 6	8 000
	27 Estudiantes	W 1-0	Ca	Achucarro 60	17 000
Mar	6 Lanus	W 2-1	Ca	Bologna 12p, Achucarro 90	25 000
	12 Tigre	W 2-1	Ca	Ruso 24, Ferreyra 90	17 000
	22 Huracan	D 2-2	Ca	Gomez 21, Ruso 23	12 000
	27 Indep'iente	D 1-1	Ca	Ruso 43	18 000
	2 Arg Juniors	L 0-2	Ca		9 000
	10 River Plate	L 0-1	Ca		45 000
Apr	19 Arsenal	W 1-0	Ca	Ferreyra 63	13 000
	23 Newells OB	W 1-0	Ca	Achucarro 58	32 000
	30 Quilmes	L 3-4	Ca	Quinteros 24, Ferreyra 51, Barbaro 61	10 000
	10 Velez	L 0-2	Ca		20 000
May	14 Gimnasia	L 0-2	Ca		13 000
	21 Godoy Cruz	D 1-1	Ca	Sigali 59	14 000
	29 Racing	W 3-1	Ca	Ferreyra 19, OG 29, Bustos 90	23 000
Jun	4 All Boys	W 3-1	Ca	Ferreyra 7, Bustamente 84, Mendez 90	13 000
	13 Boca Jun	D 1-1	Ca	Ferreyra 83	50 000
	19 S. Lorenzo	D 1-1	Ca	Toledo 32	12 000

8th — Att: 116 000 • Av: 12 888 (-26.8%)

Aug	5 At.Rafaela	L 0-2	Ap		14 000
	15 Velez	L 0-3	Ap		12 000
	22 Racing	L 0-1	Ap		15 000
	26 Godoy Cruz	L 0-1	Ap		7 000
	2 Tigre	L 0-1	Ap		12 000
	11 Arsenal	L 0-1	Ap		10 000
Sep	17 All Boys	W 1-0	Ap	Eluchans 69	12 000
	21 Olimpo	D 1-1	Ap	Rolle 26	7 500
	26 Union	L 0-1	Ap		19 000
	3 Newells OB	W 2-0	Ap	Ferreyra 2 53 72	9 000
	15 S.Lorenzo	L 0-1	Ap		18 000
Oct	25 Indep'iente	W 3-0	Ap	Ferreyra 2 54 58, Acevedo 90	15 000
	31 San Martin	L 1-2	Ap	Gomez 87	10 000
	6 Lanus	L 1-2	Ap	OG 7	20 000
Nov	21 Estudiantes	L 1-2	Ap	Lopez 9	12 000
	27 Arg Juniors	D 2-2	Ap	Gomez 56, Ferreyra 88	8 000
Dec	4 Boca Jun	L 0-3	Ap		50 000
	8 Belgrano	L 0-2	Ap		9 000
	12 Colon	L 1-4	Ap	Ferreyra 90	18 000

20th — Att: 107 000 • Av: 11 888 • Florencia Sola 34 901

BANFIELD LEAGUE APPEARANCES/GOALS 2011

Goalkeepers Enrique Bologna 19/1 • Cristian Lucchetti 19
Defenders Julio Barraza 9/0 • Gonzalo Bettini 1/0 • Ariel Broggi 1+1/0
Marcelo Bustamente 16/1 13+1/0 • Alejandro Delfino 4+7/0
Mauro Dos Santos 16/0 6/0 • Santiago Ladino 0+2/0 9+5/0
Victor Lopez 16/1 17/0 • Adrian Reta 1/0 • Favio Segovia 1/0
Nicolas Tagliafico 6+3/0 15/0 • Gustavo Toledo 10/1 6+1/0
Midfield Walter Acevedo 11+2/1 • Alejandro Barbaro 3+4/1 2+12/0
Maximiliano Bustos 13+2/1 • Ezequiel Carboni 13/0
Marcelo Carrusca 9/0 • Diego De Souza URU 13+2/0 3+3/0
Juan Eluchans 16/1 • Jonatan Gomez 16+2/1 12+3/2
Gabriel Mendez 0+9/1 • Maximiliano Laso 2+5/1 • Diego Molina 1/0
Rodrigo Pepe 0+2/0 • Marcelo Quinteros 11+5/1 14+2/0
Julian Rojas COL 1/0 4+3/0 • Sebastian Romero 4+4/0
Javier Rosada 7+5/0 • Ruso 8/3
Forwards Jorge Achucarro PAR 16+2/5 7+7/0 • Nicolas Bauchet 0+2/0
Andres Chavez 0+1/0 0+2/0 • Facundo Ferreyra 11+5/6 16/6
Rodrigo Lopez URU 6+3/1 • Emiliano Terzaghi 1/0 1+2/0
Cipriano Treppo 0+1/0
Coach Sebastian Mendez • Ricardo La Volpe (28/08/2011) • Jorge da Silva (23/12/2011)

BOCA JUNIORS 2011

Feb	13	Godoy Cruz	L 1-4	Ca	Erviti [53]	42 000
	20	Racing	W 1-0	Ca	Mouche [47]	35 000
	27	All Boys	D 0-0	Ca		42 000
Mar	7	Velez	L 0-1	Ca		35 000
	12	S. Lorenzo	L 0-1	Ca		37 000
	20	Olimpo	L 0-2	Ca		38 000
	27	Colon	W 1-0	Ca	Riquelme [60]	28 000
Apr	3	Estudiantes	W 2-1	Ca	Riquelme [15], Viatri [89]	50 000
	10	Lanus	L 0-2	Ca		30 000
	17	Tigre	D 3-3	Ca	Colazo [43], Riquelme [45], Rodriguez [78]	35 000
	24	Huracan	W 3-0	Ca	Chavez [19], Colazo [46], Palermo [83]	26 000
May	3	Indep'iente	D 1-1	Ca	Palermo [20]	38 000
	8	Arg Juniors	W 2-0	Ca	Palermo [4], Riquelme [21]	25 000
	15	River Plate	W 2-0	Ca	OG [28], Palermo [31]	40 000
	23	Arsenal	D 2-2	Ca	Viatri [53], Mouche [82]	18 000
	29	Newells OB	W 1-0	Ca	Palermo [50]	28 000
Jun	5	Quilmes	D 2-2	Ca	Palermo [63], Chavez [66]	28 000
	13	Banfield	D 1-1	Ca	Colazo [47]	50 000
	18	Gimnasia	D 2-2	Ca	Cellay 2 [33 90]	32 000

7th — Att: 363 000 • Av: 40 333

Aug	7	Olimpo	D 0-0	Ap		23 000
	16	Union	W 4-0	Ap	Viatri 2 [1 80], Riquelme [85], Colazo [86]	40 000
	21	Newells OB	W 1-0	Ap	Mouche [89]	37 000
	28	S.Lorenzo	D 1-1	Ap	Cvitanich [50]	45 000
Sep	4	Indep'iente	W 1-0	Ap	Schiavi [50]	28 000
	11	San Martin	W 1-0	Ap	Erviti [75]	35 000
	18	Lanus	W 2-1	Ap	Viatri [9], Erviti [65]	30 000
	22	Estudiantes	W 1-0	Ap	Rodriguez [17]	37 000
	25	Arg Juniors	D 0-0	Ap		15 000
Oct	2	Tigre	W 1-0	Ap	OG [13]	50 000
	16	Belgrano	D 0-0	Ap		45 000
	25	Colon	W 2-0	Ap	Blandi 2 [14 63]	32 000
	30	At.Rafaela	W 3-1	Ap	Blandi 2 [6 16], Chavez [86]	40 000
Nov	6	Velez	D 0-0	Ap		25 000
	20	Racing	D 0-0	Ap		40 000
	27	Godoy Cruz	W 2-1	Ap	Cvitanich [9], Schiavi [36p]	38 000
Dec	4	Banfield	W 3-0	Ap	Cvitanich 2 [10 44], Rivero [47]	50 000
	7	Arsenal	D 2-2	Ap	Erviti [40], Chavez [71]	15 000
	11	All Boys	W 1-0	Ap	Cvitanich [79]	35 000

1st — Att: 417 000 • Av: 41 700 • La Bombonera 49 000

COLON SANTA FE 2011

Feb	13	Quilmes	W 2-0	Ca	Fuertes 2 [52 71]	23 000
	19	Banfield	D 1-1	Ca	Fuertes [45]	8 000
	25	Gimnasia	L 1-3	Ca	Graciani [8]	20 000
Mar	6	Godoy Cruz	W 3-2	Ca	Acosta [24], Fuertes 2 [40 87]	8 000
	13	Racing	L 0-4	Ca		28 000
	19	All Boys	W 2-0	Ca	Higuain [21], Fabianesi [77]	12 000
	27	Boca Jun	L 0-1	Ca		28 000
Apr	3	S. Lorenzo	W 2-1	Ca	Acosta 2 [19 36]	20 000
	9	Olimpo	L 0-2	Ca		20 000
	17	Velez	D 1-1	Ca	Fabianesi [65]	18 000
	23	Estudiantes	W 2-0	Ca	Fuertes [40], Diaz [90]	22 000
	2	Lanus	L 0-1	Ca		17 000
	7	Tigre	L 0-3	Ca		16 000
May	15	Huracan	W 3-0	Ca	Diaz 2 [9 40], Fuertes [28]	13 000
	22	Indep'iente	L 1-3	Ca	Fuertes [63]	18 000
	28	Arg Juniors	L 1-2	Ca	Fabianesi [72]	13 000
Jun	6	River Plate	D 1-1	Ca	Fuertes [57]	45 000
	11	Arsenal	L 0-1	Ca		13 000
	19	Newells OB	L 0-1	Ca		20 000

16th — Att: 193 000 • Av: 19 300

Aug	6	Arsenal	W 2-1	Ap	Costa [74], Fuertes [77]	6 000
	17	All Boys	D 1-1	Ap	OG [15]	25 000
	22	Olimpo	W 1-0	Ap	Fabianesi [49]	12 000
	28	Union	L 0-2	Ap		33 000
Sep	2	Newell's OB	D 0-0	Ap		32 000
	10	S.Lorenzo	W 3-1	Ap	Fuertes 2 [22 49], Higuain [87]	22 000
	16	Indep'iente	W 1-0	Ap	Higuain [16]	16 000
	20	San Martin	D 0-0	Ap		28 000
Oct	26	Lanus	D 1-1	Ap	Pellegrino [76]	17 000
	3	Estudiantes	D 1-1	Ap	Higuain [59]	28 000
	16	Arg Juniors	D 0-0	Ap		2 500
	26	Boca Jun	L 0-2	Ap		32 000
Nov	30	Belgrano	W 1-0	Ap	Fuertes [80p]	30 000
	5	Tigre	L 1-2	Ap	Fabianesi [75]	14 000
	20	At.Rafaela	W 1-0	Ap	Fuertes [71]	25 000
	27	Velez	D 1-1	Ap	Chevanton [46]	18 000
Dec	3	Racing	L 0-2	Ap		20 000
	8	Godoy Cruz	W 1-0	Ap	Higuain [46]	6 000
	12	Banfield	W 4-1	Ap	Higuain [5], Chevanton 2 [45 70], Graciani [52]	18 000

5th — Att: 231 000 • Av: 25 666 • Cementario d.L Elefantes 33 458

BOCA LEAGUE APPEARANCES/GOALS 2011

Goalkeepers Javier Garcia 6 • Cristian Lucchetti 13 • Agustin Orion 19
Defenders Jose Calvo 5/0 • Matias Caruzzo 18/0 3+2/0
Christian Cellay 8/2 • Juan Insaurralde 18/0 16/0
Luciano Monzon 13+1/0 • Clemente Rodriguez 15/1 19/1
Facundo Roncaglia 19/0 • Enzo Ruiz 1+2/0 • Gaston Sauro 1/0
Rolando Schiavi 19/2 • Orlando Gaona PAR 0+1/0
Franco Sosa 2/0
Midfield Sebastian Battaglia 5/0 0+1/0
Cristian Chavez 14+4/2 10+6/2 • Nicolas Colazo 14+3/3 0+12/1
Cristian Erbes 1+1/0 3+3/0 • Walter Erviti 11+5/1 19/3
Leandro Graciani 0+2/0 • Jonathan Mazzola 0+1/0
Esteban Orfano 0+2/0 • Leandro Paredes 0+2/0
Roman Riquelme 11/4 14+2/5 • Diego Rivero 4+6/0 16/1
Juan Sanchez Mino 0+1/0 0+4/0 • Leandro Somoza 16/0 17/0
Forwards Sergio Araujo 0+1/0 1+4/0 • Nicolas Blandi 3+5/4
Dario Cvitanich 12+1/5 • Orlando Gaona PAR 0+1/0
Pablo Mouche 16+2/2 12+6/1 • Ricardo Noir 0+8/0
Martin Palermo 19/6 • Tanque Silva URU • Lucas Viatri 0+13/2 11/3
Coach Julio Falcioni (18/12/2010)

COLON LEAGUE APPEARANCES/GOALS 2011

Goalkeepers Marcos Diaz 4+1 • Diego Pozo 19 15
Defenders Mauricio Arias 0+1/0 • Julio Barraza 7/0
Maximiliano Caire 2/0 0+1/0 • Salustiano Candia PAR 13+1/0 17+1/0
Ariel Garce 15/0 1+2/0 • Marcelo Goux 7/0
Gabriel Graciani 5+4/1 4+2/1 • Pablo Lima URU 3+2/0
Humberto Mendoza COL 3+3/0 • Maximiliano Pellegrino 15+1/1
Ismael Quilez 12+5/0 0+5/0 • Juan Quiroga 14+1/0
Ronald Raldes BOL 10/0 17+1/0 • Bruno Urribarri 18/0
Midfield Lucas Acosta 6+6/3 • Adrian Bastia 11+3/0
Mauro Bollono 2 i 3/0 • Tomas Costa 16/1 • Damian Diaz 18/3
Marcos Fernandez 0+1/0 • Ricardo Gomez 0+1/0
Federico Higuain 5+5/1 14+2/5 • Cristian Ledesma 12+2/0 1/0
Ivan Moreno y Fabianesi 18/3 15+2/2 • Lucas Mugni 0+4/0 0+2/0
Sebastian Prediger 18/0 17/0 • Santiago Soto 0+1/0
Forwards Lucas Alario 0+3/0 • German Cano 3+2/0
Ernesto Chevanton 3+4/3 • Facundo Curuchet 0+4/0
Esteban Fuertes 17/9 16/5 • Leandro Gonzalez 7+7/0
Joaquin Larrivey 0+4/0 • German Lessman 5+3/0 1+3/0
Carlos Luque 5+4/0 7+4/0
Coach Fernando Gamboa • Mario Sciaqua (11/04/2011)

ESTUDIANTES LA PLATA 2011

Feb	11	Newell's OB	W	2-1	Ca	Fernandez 13, Mercado 23	19 000
	17	Cruzeiro	L	0-5	CLg7		10 955
	20	Quilmes	W	1-0	Ca	Mercado 45	18 000
	23	Tolima	W	1-0	CLg7	Barrientos 44	29 034
	27	Banfield	L	0-1	Ca		17 000
Mar	5	Gimnasia	W	2-0	Ca	Fernandez 52, Perez 84p	35 000
	10	Guarani	W	2-1	CLg7	Barrientos 50, Gonzalez 53	1 078
	13	Godoy Cruz	L	0-1	Ca		25 000
	17	Guarani	W	5-1	CLg7	Lopez 3 1 18 58, Gonzalez 2 24 81	13 318
	20	Racing	W	1-0	Ca	Lopez 84	40 000
	26	All Boys	W	3-0	Ca	OG 18, Vella 23, Gonzalez 53	15 000
	30	Tolima	D	1-1	CLg7	Fernandez 23	7 797
Apr	3	Boca Jun	L	1-2	Ca	Lopez 7	50 000
	8	S. Lorenzo	D	0-0	Ca		16 000
	14	Cruzeiro	L	0-3	CLg7		14 828
	17	Olimpo	D	2-2	Ca	OG 55, Fernandez 59	15 000
	23	Colon	L	0-2	Ca		22 000
	27	C. Porteno	D	0-0	CLr2		15 815
May	1	Velez	L	0-4	Ca		26 000
	6	C. Porteno	D	0-0	CLr2	L 3-5p	20 408
	8	Lanus	L	0-0	Ca		16 000
	15	Tigre	D	2-2	Ca	Fernandez 45p, Perez 58	12 000
	29	Indep'iente	L	0-2	Ca		12 000
Jun	2	Huracan	W	3-0	Ca	Pereyra 6, Lopez 29, Sarulyte 41	BCD
	6	Arg Juniors	D	0-0	Ca		8 000
	12	River Plate	D	1-1	Ca	Sarulyte 54	18 000
	19	Arsenal	L	0-1	Ca		2 000

13th   Att: 182 000 • Av: 18 200

Aug	7	Newell's OB	D	0-0	Ap		34 000
	15	S. Lorenzo	L	0-2	Ap		27 000
	21	Indep'iente	L	0-1	Ap		20 000
	26	San Martin	D	2-2	Ap	Fernandez 8, Boselli 20	18 000
	31	Arsenal	L	0-2	CSr2		
Sep	4	Lanus	L	1-2	Ap	Gonzalez 29	15 000
	7	Arsenal	W	1-0	CSr2	Sanchez 63	
	10	Tigre	L	1-3	Ap	OG 61	18 000
	18	Arg Juniors	W	4-3	Ap	Mercado 2 36 86, Carrillo 42, Fernandez 45	18 000
Oct	23	Boca Jun	L	0-1	Ap		37 000
	26	Belgrano	L	2-3	Ap	Veron 71p, Zapata 89	9 000
	3	Colon	D	1-1	Ap	Brana 45	28 000
	16	At.Rafaela	W	3-0	Ap	Fernandez 2 23 73, Boselli 60	5 000
	25	Velez	L	0-1	Ap		17 000
	31	Racing	D	0-0	Ap		18 000
Nov	5	Godoy Cruz	L	1-3	Ap	OG 45	8 000
	21	Banfield	W	2-1	Ap	Boselli 69, Mercado 81	12 000
	27	Arsenal	W	2-1	Ap	Fernandez 56, Veron 81	5 000
Dec	2	All Boys	W	3-0	Ap	Gonzalez 30, Fernandez 32, Boselli 62	16 000
	6	Olimpo	D	0-0	Ap		9 000
	11	Union	W	2-0	Ap	Boselli 45, Cellay 78	25 000

16th   Att: 157 000 • Av: 15 700 • Centenario 30 200

ESTUDIANTES LEAGUE APPEARANCES/GOALS 2011
Goalkeepers Damian Albil 13 • Agustin Orion 18+1
Agustin Silva 2+2 • Cesar Taborda 1 • Justo Villar PAR 4
Defenders Nelson Benitez 5/0 • Christian Cellay 12/1
Leandro Desabato 17/0 18/0 • Juan Dominguez COL 8+1/0
Federico Fernandez 16/0 • Dylan Ghissi 0+1/0
Raul Iberbia 15/0 7+1/0 • Gabriel Mercado 16+1/2 17/3
German Re 9/0 17 • Facundo Roncaglia 12+3/0
Matias Sarulyte 3+1/2 4/0
Midfield Carlos Auzqui 0+2/0 • Diego Auzqui 2+2/0 0+1/0
Pablo Barrientos 5+8/0 • Leandro Benitez 11+3/0 6+6/0
Rodrigo Brana 11/0 13/1 • Carlos Carbonero COL 4+6/0
Facundo Coria 8/0 • Jose Fernandez 1+4/0 • Diego Galvan 2+5/0
Mariano Gonzalez 12+5/2 • Leonardo Jara 3/0 0+1/0
Sergio Modon 2+1/0 • Maximiliano Nunez 1+5/0 • Gabriel Penalba 1/0
Enzo Perez 15+1/2 • Matias Sanchez 8+4/0 9+3/0
Dario Stefanatto 1+4/0 • Juan Sebastian Veron 9/0 11/2
Forwards Mauro Boselli 15/5 • Guido Carrillo 3+1/0 4+4/1
Gaston Fernandez 7+3/4 15+3/5• Mauro Fernandez 5+8/1
Leandro Gonzalez 8+8/1 • Rodrigo Lopez URU 9+4/3 • Juan Pereyra 3+4/1
Duvan Zapata COL 0+3/0
Coach Eduardo Berizzo (7/02/2011) • Luis Suarez (30/05/2011) •
Miguel Russo (21/06/2011) • Juan Azconzabal (9/11/2011)

GIMNASIA LA PLATA 2011

Feb	12	S. Lorenzo	D	1-1	Ca	Neira 72p	30 000
	18	Olimpo	L	1-3	Ca	Cordoba 65	17 000
	25	Colon	W	3-1	Ca	Neira 2 6 25, Castro 90	20 000
	5	Estudiantes	L	0-2	Ca		35 000
Mar	12	Lanus	D	0-0	Ca		10 000
	21	Tigre	W	2-1	Ca	Neira 2 37 74	16 000
	26	Huracan	L	0-2	Ca		24 000
	1	Indep'iente	L	1-2	Ca	Masuero 19	19 000
	10	Arg Juniors	D	1-1	Ca	Vizcarra 25	10 000
Apr	7	River Plate	D	0-0	Ca		30 000
	24	Arsenal	D	1-1	Ca	Schelotto 67	5 000
	29	Newells OB	L	1-2	Ca	Schelotto 33	15 000
	7	Quilmes	D	2-2	Ca	Castro 33, Graf 65	17 000
May	14	Banfield	W	2-0	Ca	Graf 37, Capurro 55	13 000
	22	Velez	L	0-2	Ca		20 000
	31	Godoy Cruz	D	2-2	Ca	Capurro 31, Castro 90	14 000
	5	Racing	D	0-0	Ca		20 000
Jun	11	All Boys	L	0-1	Ca		13 000
	18	Boca Jun	D	2-2	Ca	Graf 9, Schelotto 13p	32 000

18th   Att: 197 000 • Av: 21 888 • El Bosque 24 544

Gimnasia were relegated at the end of the 2010-11 Clausura

GIMNASIA LEAGUE APPEARANCES/GOALS 2011
Goalkeepers Fernando Monetti 12+1 • Gaston Sessa 7
Defenders Ariel Aguero 8+2/0 • Oliver Benitez 7/0 • Pablo Fontanello 9/0
Hugo Iriarte 3/0 • Lisandro Magallan 4/0 • Abel Masuero 15/1
Cristian Piarrou 1/0 • Boris Rieloff CHI 8+2/0 • Leandro Sapetti 11/0
Midfield Luciano Aued 12/0 • Guillermo Barros Schelotto 16+1/3
Alejandro Capurro 10+2/2 • Milton Casco 11+3/0 • Lucas Castro 9+5/3
Hernan Encina 9+3/0 • Cesar Gonzalez VEN 8+3/0
Emiliano Mendez 0+3/0 • Dardo Miloc 2/0
Fabian Rinaudo 18/0 • Alan Ruiz 1+5/0
Forwards Jorge Cordoba 3+9/1 • Agustin Curima 0+1/0
Claudio Graf 8+1/3 • Juan Neira 11+4/5 • German Pacheco 1+4/0
Antonio Rojano 1+1/0 • Joaquin Romea 2/0 • Jose Vizcarra 2+3/1
Coach Angel Cappa • Hernan Ortiz (2/05/2011)

HURACAN 2011

Feb	15	Arg Juniors	D	1-1	Ca	Campora 3p	10 000
	20	River Plate	L	0-2	Ca		37 000
	28	Arsenal	D	1-1	Ca	Campora 52	9 000
	5	Newells OB	W	3-3	Ca	Maidana 28, OG 41, Quintana 45	30 000
Mar	14	Quilmes	W	2-1	Ca	Zarate 39, Campora 67	17 000
	22	Banfield	D	2-2	Ca	Zarate 37, Campora 85	12 000
	26	Gimnasia	W	2-0	Ca	Battaglia 8, Campora 18	24 000
	3	Godoy Cruz	L	1-3	Ca	Campora 6	6 000
	9	Racing	D	0-0	Ca		23 000
Apr	16	All Boys	L	1-3	Ca	Campora 21	13 000
	24	Boca Jun	L	0-3	Ca		26 000
	30	S. Lorenzo	L	0-3	Ca		24 000
	7	Olimpo	L	1-2	Ca	Campora 50	10 000
May	15	Colon	L	0-3	Ca		13 000
	30	Lanus	L	0-3	Ca		15 000
	2	Estudiantes	L	0-3	Ca		BCD
Jun	5	Tigre	W	3-2	Ca	Machin 37, Campora 2 39 50	BCD
	12	Velez	L	0-2	Ca		BCD
	18	Indep'iente	L	1-5	Ca	Campora 79p	16 000

20th   Att: 119 000 • Av: 11 900 • Tomás Adolfo Ducó 48 314

Huracan were relegated at the end of the 2010-11 Clausura

HURACAN LEAGUE APPEARANCES/GOALS 2011
Goalkeepers Lucas Calvino 1+1 • Gaston Monzon 18
Defenders David Alcides Angeloff 2+2/0 • Kevin Cura 6+1/0 • Ezequiel
Filipetto 3+1/0 • Jonathan Herenu 1/0 • Rodrigo Lemos 15+1/0
Emiliano Lopez 0+1/0 • Luciano Ospina 5+2/0 • Agustin Pena 3+2/0
Carlos Quintana 6/1 • Facundo Quiroga 15/0 • Leonardo Villan 6+1/0
Midfield Rodrigo Battaglia 16+2/1 • Marcos Britez Ojeda 15/0
Franco Chivilo 0+1/0 • Gaston Machin 16+1/1 • Cristian
Maidana 13+1/1 • Angel Morales 4+3/0 • Luciano Nieto 3+3/0
Andres Nunez 3+3/0 • Matias Quiroga 10+3/0 • Guillermo Roffes 0+2/0
Dario Soplan 10+5/0 • Mariano Torres 2+5/0
Forwards Julian Bottaro 0+4/0 • Javier Campora 19/11 • Claudio
Guerra 2+6/0 • Emiliano Lencina 0+3/0 • Rolando Zarate 15+1/2
Coach Miguel Brindisi • Roberto Pompei (24/02/2011)

GODOY CRUZ 2011

							Att
Feb	13 Boca Jun	W	4-1	Ca	Ramirez 2 14 38, Torres 51, Sanchez.C 90		42 000
	18 LDU Quito	W	2-1	CLg8	Sanchez.C 16, Sanchez.N 59		19 524
	22 S. Lorenzo	L	0-2	Ca			22 000
	25 Olimpo	D	3-3	Ca	Navarro 52, Nunez 2 55 66		14 000
	1 Penarol	L	1-3	CLg8	Ramirez 30		12 946
	6 Colon	L	2-3	Ca	Faccoili 26, Villar 68		8 000
Mar	11 Indep'iente	W	3-1	CLg8	OG 28, Rojas 32, Ramirez 56		10 625
	13 Estudiantes	W	1-0	Ca	Damonte 61		25 000
	19 Lanus	W	2-0	Ca	Olmedo 37, OG 68		7 000
	23 Indep'iente	D	1-1	CLg8	Ramirez 33		11 819
	27 Tigre	D	2-2	Ca	Donda 28, Navarro 45		13 000
	1 Penarol	L	1-2	CLg8	OG 57		43 179
	3 Huracan	W	3-1	Ca	Navarro 2 4 15, Salinas 39p		6 000
Apr	9 Indep'iente	L	0-3	Ca			17 000
	12 LDU Quito	L	0-2	CLg8			15 516
	17 Arg Juniors	W	1-0	Ca	Villar 2		10 000
	23 River Plate	W	2-1	Ca	Garcia 50, Donda 85		45 000
	30 Arsenal	L	1-4	Ca	Navarro 26		7 000
May	7 Newells OB	W	3-1	Ca	Sigali 17, Donda 36, Sanchez.C 90		30 000
	14 Quilmes	W	2-0	Ca	Ramirez 13, Villar 30		8 000
	21 Banfield	L	0-1	Ca	Sigali 59		14 000
	31 Gimnasia	D	2-2	Ca	Ramirez 17, Donda 54		14 000
	7 Velez	L	0-2	Ca			22 000
Jun	14 Racing	W	3-2	Ca	Donda 2 45 90p, Ramirez 55		17 000
	19 All Boys	W	1-0	Ca	Sanchez.N 52		14 000

3rd   Att: 96 000 • Av: 10 666

							Att
Aug	6 Velez	D	1-1	Ap	Ramirez 35		12 000
	17 Racing	L	0-3	Ap			25 000
	21 Tigre	L	1-2	Ap	Villar 70		15 000
	26 Banfield	W	1-0	Ap	Ramirez 55		7 000
	1 Lanus	D	2-2	CSr2	Rojas 26, Navarro 34		
	3 Arsenal	W	2-1	Ap	Navarro 53, Ramirez 90		4 000
	8 Lanus	D	0-0	CSr2			
Sep	10 All Boys	W	6-1	Ap	Ramirez 2 28, OG 44, Caruso 54, Villar 59, Curbelo 87		7 000
	16 Olimpo	D	2-2	Ap	Sanchez.N 44, Caruso 76		13 000
	22 Union	D	1-1	Ap	Cabrera 89		5 000
	27 Newells OB	D	1-1	Ap	Castillon 59		37 000
	30 Univ'sitario	D	1-1	CSr3	Cabrera 89		
Oct	3 S.Lorenzo	W	2-0	Ap	Sigali 39, Ramirez 60		12 000
	15 Indep'iente	L	1-2	Ap	Ramirez 63		10 000
	21 Univ'sitario	D	1-1	CSr3	Damonte 45, L 2-3p		
	26 San Martin	D	2-2	Ap	Ramirez 2 48 82		18 000
	30 Lanus	L	1-2	Ap	OG 48		7 000
Nov	5 Estudiantes	W	3-1	Ap	Rojas 5, Ramirez 16, Cooper 77		8 000
	19 Arg Juniors	L	0-1	Ap			6 000
	27 Boca Jun	W	1-0	Ap	Rojas 86		38 000
Dec	4 Belgrano	D	1-1	Ap	Ramirez 58		15 000
	7 Colon	L	0-1	Ap			6 000
	13 At.Rafaela	W	2-0	Ap	Rojas 41, Ramirez 73		11 000

12th   Att: 113 000 • Av: 12 555 • Malvinas Argentinas 45 268

INDEPENDIENTE 2011

							Att
Ja	26 Dep Quito	W	2-0	CLr1	Defederico 49, Rodriguez 70		16 844
	2 Dep Quito	L	0-1	CLr1			12 029
Feb	12 Velez	D	2-2	Ca	Parra 7, Battion 36		22 000
	19 Arg Juniors	D	0-0	Ca			13 000
	24 Penarol	W	3-0	CLg8	Parra 46, Pellerano 70, Silvera 85		21 354
	27 River Plate	L	0-1	Ca			30 000
	4 LDU Quito	L	0-3	CLg8			13 768
	7 Arsenal	L	0-3	Ca			15 000
	11 Godoy Cruz	L	1-3	CLg8	Parra 15		10 625
Mar	15 Newells OB	W	4-0	Ca	Cabrera 2 4 12, Silvera 25, Castillo 80		30 000
	19 Quilmes	D	1-1	Ca	Parra 24		15 000
	23 Godoy Cruz	D	1-1	CLg8	Defederico 1		11 819
	27 Banfield	D	1-1	Ca	Tuzzio 8		18 000
	1 Gimnasia	W	2-1	Ca	Silvera 56, Pellerano 90		19 000
	6 LDU Quito	D	1-1	CLg8	Nunuz 23p		13 270
	9 Godoy Cruz	W	3-0	Ca	Perez.I 55, Fredes 66, Nunez 86		17 000
Apr	12 Penarol	W	1-0	CLg8	Parra 33		51 989
	16 Racing	L	0-2	Ca			45 000
	23 All Boys	D	2-2	Ca	Parra 41, Battion 56		28 000
	3 Boca Jun	D	1-1	Ca	Villafanez 77		38 000
	9 San Lorenzo	D	1-1	Ca	Parra 33		24 000
May	15 Olimpo	W	2-1	Ca	Parra 49, Rodriguez 88		15 000
	22 Colon	W	3-1	Ca	Parra 20, Rodriguez 23, Silvera 86		18 000
	29 Estudiantes	W	2-0	Ca	Galeano 45, Villafanez 76		12 000
	7 Lanus	L	1-2	Ca	Velazquez 80		18 000
Jun	12 Tigre	D	0-0	Ca			15 000
	18 Huracan	W	5-1	Ca	Parra 1C, Silvera 32, Rodriguez 2 51 71, Nunez 90		16 000

6th   Att: 221 000 • Av: 24 555

							Att
Aug	16 Lanus	L	0-1	Ap			10 000
	21 Estudiantes	W	1-0	Ap	Perez.M 47		20 000
	29 Arg Juniors	D	0-0	Ap			16 000
	4 Boc Juniors	L	0-1	Ap			28 000
	8 San Martin	W	2-1	Ap	Pellerano 21, OG 41		14 000
	11 Belgrano	L	0-2	Ap			40 000
Sep	16 Colon	L	0-1	Ap			16 000
	21 At Rafaela	W	3-1	Ap	Nunez 21, Nieva 22, Ferreyra 47		14 500
	25 Velez	L	0-1	Ap			20 000
	28 LDU Quito	L	0-2	CSr2			
	2 Racing	D	1-1	Ap	Parra 27		40 000
Oct	13 LDU Quito	W	1-0	CSr2	Nunez 24		
	15 Godoy Cruz	W	2-1	Ap	Nunez 49, Perez.M 90		10 000
	24 Banfield	L	0-3	Ap			15 000
	29 Arsenal	D	0-0	Ap			13 000
	4 All Boys	D	2-2	Ap	Defederico 9, Perez.I 53		12 000
Nov	19 Olimpo	W	3-0	Ap	Tuzzio 35, Perez.I 49, Parra 78		15 000
	28 Union	D	0-0	Ap			21 000
	4 Newells OB	D	1-1	Ap	Benitez 52		20 000
Dec	8 San Lorenzo	W	1-0	Ap	Benitez 68		32 000
	13 Tigre	W	2-1	Ap	Parra 57, Fredes 66		25 000

8th   Att: 181 000 • Av: 18 100 • Libertadores de América 46 000

GODOY CRUZ LEAGUE APPEARANCES/GOALS 2011

Goalkeepers Nelson Ibanez 1 2 • Sebastian Torrico 18 17
Defenders Lucas Ceballos 4/0 7+3/0 • Jorge Curbelo URU 9+4/1
Emir Faccioli 7/1 • Zelmar Garcia 7+1/1 7+2/0 • Roberto Russo 17/0 7/0
Nicolas Sanchez 17/1 18/1 • Leonardo Sigali 14/2 16/1
German Voboril 8/0 12/0
Midfield Emanuel Aguilera 2+1/0 2+1/0 • Gonzalo Cabrera 7+6/0
Armando Cooper 4+6/2 • Israel Damonte 16/1 11+3/0
Mariano Donda 11+7/6 1/0 • Juan Carlos Falcon 7+6/0 4+2/0
Gabriel Oscar Moyano 0+1/0 • Nicolas Olmedo 10+1/1 14/0
Ariel Rojas 10+5/0 18+1/3 • Carlos Sanchez URU 15+2/2
Sorgio Sanchez 0+1/0 0+1/0 • Adrian Torres 3+1/1 1/0
Diego Villar 14+1/3 16+1/2
Forwards Leandro Caruso 6+5/2 • Facundo Castillon 6+6/1
Juan Garro 0+1/0 0+1/0 • Pablo Miranda 4+5/0 3+1/0
Alvaro Navarro URU 7+8/5 4+9/1 • Fabricio Nunez URU 3+5/2
Ruben Ramirez 11+3/5 16+1/12 • Franklin Salas ECU 1+1/0
Rodrigo Salinas 3+5/1
Coach Jorge Da Silva URU • Nery Pumpido (23/12/2011)

INDEPENDIENTE LEAGUE APPEARANCES/GOALS 2011

Goalkeepers Fabian Assmann 4+1 12 • Adrian Gabbarini 1 3 • Hilario
Navarro 13 4 • Diego Rodriguez 1
Defenders Adrian Argacha 5/0 • Cristian Baez 4/0 1/0
Leonel Galeano 10+1/1 1+3/0 • Lucas Mareque 9+3/0
Carlos Matheu 12/0 1+1/0 • Gabriel Milito 19/0 • Eduardo Tuzzio 15/1 16/1
Gabriel Valles 0+2/0 • Julian Velazquez 13/0 15/0
Maximiliano Velazquez 12/1 14+1/0 • Ivan Velez 14+1/0 5/0
Midfield Roberto Battion 5+9/2 3+1/0 • Walter Busse 0+3/0 0+5/0
Nicolas Cabrera 8+3/2 3+4/0 • Nicolas Delmonte 2+1/0
Osmar Ferreyra 11+6/1 • Hernan Fredes 16+1/1 5+3/1
Fernando Godoy 0+3/0 13+2/0 • Leandro Gracian 4+3/0
Federico Mancuello 1+0/0 • Nicolas Martinez 1/0
Cristian Pellerano 14+2/1 14+1/1 • Ivan Perez 2+1/1 6+4/2
Patricio Rodriguez 12+4/4 2+2/0
Forwards Martin Benitez 2+3/2 • Juan Castillo 1+1/1
Diego Churin 1+1/0 • Gino Clara 0+1/0
Matias Defederico 4+1/0 11+3/1 • Brian Nieva 3+2/1
Leonel Nunez 1+8/2 9+4/2 • Facundo Parra 15+3/7 17+1/3
Marco Perez COL 7+5/2 • Francisco Pizzini 0+1/0
Andres Silvera 13+2/4 • Lucas Villafanez 4+3/2 2/0
Coach Antonio Mohamed • Ramon Diaz (12/09/2011)

LANUS 2011

	Date	Opponent	Res	Score	Comp	Scorers	Att
Feb	14	Arsenal	W	3-1	Ca	Valeri 56, Regueiro 90, Romero 90	15 000
	19	Newells OB	L	1-2	Ca	Valeri 69	32 000
	21	Quilmes	W	2-1	Ca	Valeri 2 8 37	12 000
Mar	6	Banfield	L	1-2	Ca	Regueiro 90	25 000
	12	Gimnasia	D	0-0	Ca		10 000
	19	Godoy Cruz	L	0-2	Ca		7 000
	26	Racing	W	4-1	Ca	Regueiro 59, Carranza 69, Izquierdoz 84, Pizarro 90	20 000
Apr	2	All Boys	D	0-0	Ca		12 000
	10	Boca Jun	W	2-0	Ca	Valeri 80, Hoyos 86	30 000
	16	S. Lorenzo	D	1-1	Ca	Goltz 68	21 000
	26	Olimpo	D	1-1	Ca	Romero 77	8 000
May	2	Colon	W	1-0	Ca	Diaz 57	17 000
	8	Estudiantes	D	0-0	Ca		16 000
	16	Velez	W	3-2	Ca	Hoyos 15, Valeri 40, Romero 52	15 000
	21	Tigre	W	3-0	Ca	Romero 3 16 50 56	10 000
	30	Huracan	W	3-0	Ca	Valeri 12, Romero 33, Pizarro 43	15 000
Jun	7	Indep'iente	W	2-1	Ca	Valeri 12, Camoranesi 75	18 000
		Arg Juniors	L	0-1	Ca		27 000
	18	River Plate	W	2-1	Ca	Romero 30, Diaz 90	50 000

2nd Att: 168 000 • Av: 16 800

	Date	Opponent	Res	Score	Comp	Scorers	Att
Aug	7	S.Lorenzo	W	1-0	Ap	Regueiro 30	26 000
	16	Indep'iente	W	1-0	Ap	Pavone 90	10 000
	20	San Martin	D	0-0	Ap		13 000
	27	Tigre	D	0-0	Ap		10 000
	1	Godoy Cruz	D	2-2	CSr2	Gonzalez 19, Neira 90	
	4	Estudiantes	W	2-1	Ap	Regueiro 14, Romero 30	15 000
	8	Godoy Cruz	D	0-0	CSr2		
Sep	12	Arg Juniors	W	4-0	Ap	Regueiro 21, Pavone 21, Gonzalez 21, Valeri 88p	10 000
	18	Boc Juniors	L	1-2	Ap	OG 46	30 000
	21	Belgrano	D	0-0	Ap		35 000
	26	Colon	D	1-1	Ap	Pereyra 2	17 000
	1	At.Rafaela	L	1-2	Ap	Regueiro 20	12 000
Oct	17	Velez	L	1-2	Ap	Valeri 35p	10 000
	27	Racing	D	1-1	Ap	Valeri 19p	20 000
	30	Godoy Cruz	W	2-1	Ap	Goltz 25, Regueiro 81	7 000
Nov	6	Banfield	W	2-1	Ap	Pavone 26, Izquierdoz 38	20 000
	22	Arsenal	L	0-1	Ap		10 000
	26	All Boys	D	0-0	Ap		12 000
Dec	3	Olimpo	D	0-0	Ap		6 500
	7	Union	W	1-0	Ap	Fritzler 16	18 000
	12	Newells OB	D	2-2	Ap	Romero 20, Regueiro 53	10 000

6th Att: 125 500 • Av: 12 550 • La Fortaleza 46 519

NEWELL'S OLD BOYS 2011

	Date	Opponent	Res	Score	Comp	Scorers	Att
Feb	11	Estudiantes	L	1-2	Ca	Cobelli 90	19 000
	19	Lanus	W	2-1	Ca	Bieler 46, Cobelli 89	32 000
	1	Tigre	L	0-1	Ca		10 000
Mar	5	Huracan	D	3-3	Ca	Bieler 5, Fideleff 24, Sperdutti 57	30 000
	15	Indep'iente	L	0-4	Ca		30 000
	20	Arg Juniors	L	0-2	Ca		31 000
	26	River Plate	L	1-2	Ca	Sperdutti 41	45 000
	2	Arsenal	D	2-2	Ca	Cobelli 46, Almiron 54	28 000
	11	Velez	L	0-2	Ca		20 000
Apr	16	Quilmes	L	1-3	Ca	Sperdutti 26	13 000
	23	Banfield	L	0-1	Ca		32 000
	29	Gimnasia	W	2-1	Ca	Schiavi 76, Bieler 82	15 000
	7	Godoy Cruz	L	1-3	Ca	Velazquez 89	30 000
May	15	Racing	L	0-3	Ca		25 000
	20	All Boys	W	1-0	Ca	Schiavi 28	30 000
	29	Boca Jun	L	0-1	Ca		28 000
	11	Olimpo	D	1-1	Ca	Fideleff 66	11 000
Jun	15	S. Lorenzo	D	0-0	Ca		25 000
	19	Colon	W	1-0	Ca	Sperdutti 88	20 000

19th Att: 258 000 • Av: 28 666

	Date	Opponent	Res	Score	Comp	Scorers	Att
	7	Estudiantes	D	0-0	Ap		34 000
Aug	17	Arg Juniors	D	1-1	Ap	Sperdutti 41	8 000
	21	Boc Juniors	L	0-1	Ap		37 000
	28	Belgrano	W	3-2	Ap	Aquino 43, Noir 2 67 70	37 000
	2	Colon	D	0-0	Ap		32 000
	9	At.Rafaela	D	0-0	Ap		15 000
Sep	18	Velez	D	1-1	Ap	Valencia 88	35 000
	22	Racing	L	0-1	Ap		28 000
	27	Godoy Cruz	D	1-1	Ap	Aquino 37	37 000
	3	Banfield	L	0-2	Ap		9 000
Oct	14	Arsenal	D	0-0	Ap		35 000
	24	All Boys	D	1-1	Ap	Munoz 45	13 000
	29	Olimpo	D	2-2	Ap	Vergini 47, Urruti 60	29 000
Nov	6	Union	L	1-2	Ap	Tonso 77	19 000
	18	Tigre	L	0-1	Ap		22 000
	26	S.Lorenzo	D	0-0	Ap		26 000
	4	Indep'iente	D	1-1	Ap	Perez 17	20 000
Dec	8	San Martin	D	0-0	Ap		20 000
	12	Lanus	D	2-2	Ap	Mateo 40, Perez 44	10 000

18th Att: 307 000 • Av: 30 700 • El Coloso del Parque 38 095

LANUS LEAGUE APPEARANCES/GOALS 2011

Goalkeepers Mauricio Caranta 11 1 • Agustin Marchesin 8+2 18
Defenders Carlos Araujo 10/0 14/0 • Luciano Balbi 15/0 18/0
Diego Braghieri 8+1/0 • Rodrigo Erramuspe 3+1/0
Paolo Goltz 18/1 14/1 • Santiago Hoyos 14+1/2
Carlos Izquierdoz 13+2/1 17/1 • Maximiliano Lugo 3+1/0
Midfield Fernando Barrientos 1+1/0
Mauro Camoranesi ITA 14+3/1 10+1/0 • Cesar Carranza 6+7/1 5+3/0
Javier Carrasco 0+1/0 • Matias Fritzler 18/1
Diego Gonzalez 2+9/0 3+4/1 • Eduardo Ledesma PAR 9+4/0 11+1/0
Lucas Manicelli 0+1/0 • Agustin Pelletieri 18/0
Mauricio Pereyra URU 10+7/1 • Guido Pizarro 15+2/2 9+8/0
Mario Regueiro URU 13+3/3 18/6 • Diego Valeri 18/8 13+1/3
Forwards Gonzalo Castillejos 5+7/0 • Leandro Diaz 4+4/2 4+6/0
Diego Lagos 0+3/0 • Juan Neira 1+7/0 • Mariano Pavone 5+8/3
Silvio Romero 10+6/8 11+7/2
Coach Gabriel Schurrer

NEWELL'S LEAGUE APPEARANCES/GOALS 2011

Goalkeepers Sebastian Peratta 19 19
Defenders Marcos Benitez 1/0 • Gabriel Cichero VEN 7+1/0
Carlos Del Giorno 1/0 • Cristian Diaz 10+2/0 14/0
Ignacio Fideleff 7/2 4/0 • Fabricio Fuentes 5+1/0
Gaston Guruceaga 1/0 • Christian Lema 10/0 • Alexis Machuca 3/0 7/0
Augusto Mainguyague 0+1/0 • Hernan Pellerano 16/0
Rolando Schiavi 17/2 • Johnatan Valle 1/0 0+1/0
Luciano Vella 9+2/0 • Santiago Vergini 15/1
Midfield Lucas Bernardi 10+3/0 17+1/0
Nestor Camacho PAR 6+6/0 2+4/0 • Pablo Dolci 4+2/0
Marcelo Estigarribia PAR 12+1/0 • Lorenzo Faravelli 0+10/0 0+1/0
Guillermo Ferracutti 3/0 8+4/0 • Victor Figueroa 9+5/0
Gabriel Hachen 0+2/0 • Diego Mateo 17/0 18/1 • Fabian Munoz 3/1
Marcos Perez 0+1/0 • Pablo Perez 12+5/2 • Marcos Riveros 1+2/0
Mauricio Sperdutti 17/4 13+2/1 • Martin Tonso 7+5/5 5+1/1
Leonel Vangioni 7+1/0 12/0 • Leandro Velazquez 0+4/1
Raul Villalba 10/0 5+3/0
Forwards Sergio Almiron 2+9/1 • Victor Aquino 7+6/2
Claudio Bieler 12+1/3 • Juan Cobelli 1+5/3 • Federico Falcone 5/0 4/0
Ricardo Noir 11+5/2 • Luis Rodriguez 1+1/0 • Daniel Salvatierra 1+1/0
Maximiliano Urruti 2/0 5+2/1 • Carmelo Valencia COL 2+6/1
Maximiliano Velasco 1+2/0
Coach Roberto Sensini • Javier Torrente (18/04/2011) • Diego Cagna 29/09/2011) • Gerardo Martino (26/12/2011)

OLIMPO 2011

	Date	Opponent	Res	Score		Scorers	Att
Feb	12	Banfield	W	2-1	Ca	Vega 64, Salom 90	8 000
	18	Gimnasia	W	3-1	Ca	Dominguez 48, Maggiolo 71, Rolle 76	17 000
Mar	25	Godoy Cruz	D	3-3	Ca	Maggiolo 17, Bareiro 2 33 90	14 000
	6	Racing	L	3-4	Ca	Maggiolo 2 50 56, Arce 58	35 000
	12	All Boys	W	1-0	Ca	Maggiolo 61	14 000
	20	Boca Jun	W	2-0	Ca	Rolle 40, Furch 89	38 000
	26	S. Lorenzo	L	0-1	Ca		14 000
Apr	2	Velez	L	1-2	Ca	Rolle 39p	15 000
	9	Colon	W	2-0	Ca	Bareiro 16, Litre 67	20 000
	17	Estudiantes	D	2-2	Ca	Galvan 30p, Bareiro 64	15 000
	26	Lanus	D	1-1	Ca	Cobo 89	8 000
May	2	Tigre	D	2-2	Ca	Galvan 6, Bareiro 57	11 000
	7	Huracan	W	2-1	Ca	Galvan 49, Bareiro 90	10 000
	15	Indep'iente	L	1-2	Ca	Furch 90	15 000
	21	Arg Juniors	W	1-0	Ca	Aguirre 85	13 000
	30	River Plate	D	0-0	Ca		18 000
Jun	4	Arsenal	L	0-2	Ca		2 500
	11	Newells OB	D	1-1	Ca	Rolle 50p	11 000
	18	Quilmes	W	1-0	Ca	Rolle 8	25 000

5th — Att: 133 000 • Av: 13 300

	Date	Opponent	Res	Score		Scorers	Att
Aug	7	Boca Jun	D	0-0	Ap		23 000
	17	Belgrano	D	1-1	Ap	Rolle 8	16 000
	22	Colon	L	0-1	Ap		12 000
	27	At.Rafaela	L	1-3	Ap	Bareiro 90	13 000
Sep	5	Velez	W	2-1	Ap	Rolle 11, Bareiro 70	13 000
	11	Racing	L	0-1	Ap		35 000
	16	Godoy Cruz	D	2-2	Ap	Furch 2 61 66	13 000
	21	Banfield	D	1-1	Ap	Rolle 26	7 500
	24	Arsenal	D	2-2	Ap	Rolle 2 73 76	8 000
Oct	2	All Boys	W	2-1	Ap	Furch 45, Franzoia 45	12 000
	14	Tigre	D	1-1	Ap	Aquino 73	12 000
	24	Union	L	0-1	Ap		8 000
	29	Newells OB	D	2-2	Ap	Rolle 63, Lucero 88	29 000
Nov	5	S.Lorenzo	D	1-1	Ap	Furch 74	10 000
	19	Indep'iente	L	0-3	Ap		15 000
	27	San Martin	L	0-3	Ap		8 000
Dec	3	Lanus	D	0-0	Ap		6 500
	6	Estudiantes	D	0-0	Ap		9 000
	11	Arg Juniors	L	0-1	Ap		6 000

19th — Att: 116 000 • Av: 11 600 • Roberto Carminatti 20 000

RACING CLUB 2011

	Date	Opponent	Res	Score		Scorers	Att
Feb	13	All Boys	W	1-0	Ca	Hauche 74	20 000
	20	Boca Jun	L	0-1	Ca		35 000
	26	S. Lorenzo	W	2-1	Ca	Gutierrez 2 44 53	30 000
Mar	6	Olimpo	W	4-3	Ca	Luguercio 2 10 11, Licht 17, Gutierrez 47	35 000
	13	Colon	W	4-0	Ca	Luguercio 15, Gutierrez 2 42 72, Hauche 85	28 000
	20	Estudiantes	L	0-1	Ca		40 000
	26	Lanus	L	1-4	Ca	Toranzo 28	20 000
Apr	3	Tigre	L	1-2	Ca	Yacob 77	25 000
	9	Huracan	D	0-0	Ca		23 000
	16	Indep'iente	W	2-0	Ca	Hauche 44, Gutierrez 86	45 000
	25	Arg Juniors	L	1-2	Ca	Gutierrez 18	10 000
	30	River Plate	L	0-1	Ca		30 000
May	8	Arsenal	W	2-1	Ca	Viola 80, Toranzo 82	16 000
	15	Newells OB	W	3-0	Ca	Gutierrez 2 15 86, Aveldano 35	25 000
	22	Quilmes	L	0-2	Ca		18 000
	29	Banfield	L	1-3	Ca	OG 72	23 000
Jun	5	Gimnasia	D	0-0	Ca		20 000
	14	Godoy Cruz	L	2-3	Ca	Gutierrez 2 1 28	17 000
	19	Velez	L	1-2	Ca	Hauche 10	45 000

15th — Att: 275 000 • Av: 30 555

	Date	Opponent	Res	Score		Scorers	Att
Aug	8	Tigre	D	1-1	Ap	Guterrez 26	20 000
	18	Godoy Cruz	W	3-0	Ap	Gutierrez 2 11 76, Castro 70	25 000
	22	Banfield	W	1-0	Ap	Cahais 8	15 000
	27	Arsenal	D	0-0	Ap		28 000
Sep	3	All Boys	D	0-0	Ap		18 000
	11	Olimpo	W	1-0	Ap	Gutierrez 19p	35 000
	19	Union	D	1-1	Ap	Moreno 11	22 000
	22	Newells OB	W	1-0	Ap	Gutierrez 7	28 000
	25	S.Lorenzo	D	0-0	Ap		35 000
Oct	2	Indep'iente	D	1-1	Ap	Hauche 1	40 000
	16	San Martin	D	0-0	Ap		19 000
	27	Lanus	D	1-1	Ap	Hauche 59	20 000
	31	Estudiantes	D	0-0	Ap		18 000
Nov	6	Arg Juniors	W	1-0	Ap	Moreno 54	25 000
	20	Boca Jun	D	0-0	Ap		40 000
	26	Belgrano	L	2-3	Ap	Moreno 36, Viola 68	18 000
Dec	3	Colon	W	2-0	Ap	Yacob 30, Viola 56	20 000
	6	At.Rafaela	W	1-0	Ap	Gutierrez 50p	25 000
	13	Velez	L	0-1	Ap		20 000

2nd — Att: 244 000 • Av: 27 111 • El Cilindro 51 389

OLIMPO LEAGUE APPEARANCES/GOALS 2011

Goalkeepers Matias Ibanez 0+1 3 • Laureano Tombolini 19 16
Defenders Arturo Aquino PAR 9+1/1 • Nicolas Bianchi Arce 16/1
Eduardo Casais 15+1/0 11/0 • Gabriel Diaz 0+1/0 2/0
Federico Dominguez 17/1 • Emir Faccioli 12/0 • Pablo Jerez 4+2/0
Federico Mancinelli 2/0 • Julio Mosset 16/0 • Ezequiel Parnisari 3/0
Walter Sanchez 1+2/0 • Juan Tejera URU 8+1/0 11/0
Cristian Villanueva 1+2/0 13/0 • Oswaldo Vizcarrondo VEN 14/0
Midfield Martin Aguirre 6+6/1 • Roberto Brum URU 10+1/0
Juan Cobo 16/1 • Andres Franzoia 8+5/1 • Diego Galvan 11/3
Sebastian Longo 4+4/0 • Adrian Lucero 8+8/1 • Juan Mauri 1+1/0 7/0
Damian Musto 6+2/0 • Martin Perez Guedes 3+2/0 • Marcelo Ricci 4/0
Leonel Rios 5+4/0 • Martin Rolle 17+2/5 18+1/6
Emiliano Romero 1+9/0 • Javier Rosada 13/0
Juan Schefer 0+6/0 4+2/0 • David Vega 5/1 14+1/0
Forwards Nestor Bareiro PAR 16/6 12+3/2 • Facundo Castillon 3+4/0
Julio Furch 3+8/2 9+5/4 • Marcos Litre 0+3/1 0+5/0
Ezequiel Maggiolo 17+1/5 • Nicolas Pavlovich 5+6/0
Carlos Salom 0+8/1
Coach Omar De Felippe • Hector Rivoira (2/12/2011)

RACING LEAGUE APPEARANCES/GOALS 2011

Goalkeepers Jorge De Olivera 9 • Roberto Fernandez PAR 10
Sebastian Saja 18
Defenders Lucas Aveldano 7+3/1 2+2/0
Marcos Caceres PAR 14/0 4+2/0 • Matias Cahais 16/0 18/1
Gonzalo Garcia 2+1/0 • Lucas Licht 16/1 18/0
Braian Lluy 0+5/0 0+2/0 • Matias Martinez 17/0 17/0
Ivan Pillud 19/0 16/0 • Nicolas Sainz 1+3/0 2/0
Midfield Luciano Aued 5+1/0 • Lucas Castro 11+2/1
Gonzalo Espinoza CHI 2+3/0 • Luis Farina 1+5/0
Giovanni Moreno COL 1/0 14+1/3 • Agustin Pelletieri 17/0
Raul Poclaba 3/0 • Juan Cruz Respuela 2+3/0 • Brian Sarmiento 0+4/0
Patricio Toranzo 14/2 12+4/0 • Luciano Vietto 0+1/0
Claudio Yacob 13/1 15/1 • Bruno Zuculini 1+6/0 1/0
Franco Zuculini 11+3/0
Forwards Gaston Cellerino 0+2/0 • Ignacio Colombini 0+2/0
Teofilo Gutierrez COL 15+1/11 15/6 • Gabriel Hauche 19/4 15+3/2
Pablo Luguercio 17+1/3 5+10/0 • Valentin Viola 1+8/1 2+13/2
Coach Miguel Russo • Diego Simeone (21/06/2011) •
Alfio Basile (26/12/2011)

QUILMES 2011

					Scorers	Att
Feb	12	Colon	L	0-2	Ca		23 000
	20	Estudiantes	L	0-1	Ca		18 000
	26	Lanus	L	1-2	Ca	Garnier [35]	12 000
Mar	6	Tigre	L	1-2	Ca	Caneo [23]	8 000
	14	Huracan	L	1-2	Ca	Cauteruccio [79]	17 000
	19	Indep'iente	D	1-1	Ca	Morales [68]	15 000
	25	Arg Juniors	D	0-0	Ca		7 000
Apr	3	River Plate	L	0-1	Ca		22 000
	9	Arsenal	D	2-2	Ca	Vazquez [26], Garnier [82]	7 000
	15	Newells OB	W	3-1	Ca	Romeo 2 [23][85], Cauteruccio [62]	13 000
	23	Velez	W	3-2	Ca	Caneo [65], Vazquez 2 [81][82]	25 000
	29	Banfield	W	4-3	Ca	Romeo [23], Caneo [31p], Vazquez [76], Cauteruccio [84]	10 000
May	7	Gimnasia	D	2-2	Ca	Vazquez [2], Kalinski [78]	17 000
	13	Godoy Cruz	L	0-2	Ca		8 000
	22	Racing	W	2-0	Ca	Cauteruccio [55], Caneo [75]	18 000
	28	All Boys	L	0-1	Ca		15 000
Jun	5	Boca Jun	D	2-2	Ca	OG [27], Gerlo [43]	28 000
	11	S. Lorenzo	W	2-0	Ca	Cerro [12], Cauteruccio [88]	21 000
	18	Olimpo	L	0-1	Ca		25 000

17th   Att: 164 000 • Av: 18 222 • Centenario 30 200

Quilmes were relegated at the end of the 2010-11 Clausura

QUILMES LEAGUE APPEARANCES/GOALS 2011

Goalkeepers Hernan Galindez 9 • Emanuel Tripodi 10
Defenders Ariel Broggi 4+1/0 • Claudio Corvalan 14/0 • Fabricio Fontanini 15+1/0 • Danilo Gerlo 17/1 • Facundo Martin Gomez 0+1/0 • Hernan Grana 9+4/0 • Damian Leyes 7+1/0 • Sebastian Martinez URU 10/0 • Martin Quiles 2/0
Midfield Miguel Caneo 16+2/4 • Francisco Cerro 12+2/1 • Leandro Coronel 1+1/0 • Pablo Garnier 17/2 • Arnaldo Gonzalez 1+2/0 • Sergio Hipperdinger 0+1/0 • Enzo Kalinski 17/1 • Gervasio Nunez 5+3/0 • Santiago Raymonda 3+8/0 • Gustavo Varela URU 9+9/5 • Juan Morales 6+4/1
Forwards Martin Cauteruccio URU 9+9/5 • Juan Morales 6+4/1 • Bernardo Romeo 7+2/3 • Diego Torres 12+4/0 • Pablo Vazquez 3+6/5
Coach Leonardo Madelon • Ricardo Caruso (8/03/2011)

RIVER PLATE 2011

						Scorers	Att
Feb	13	Tigre	D	0-0	Ca		22 000
	20	Huracan	W	2-0	Ca	Lamela [51], Ferrari [59]	37 000
	27	Indep'iente	W	1-0	Ca	Pavone [88]	30 000
Mar	6	Arg Juniors	D	0-0	Ca		45 000
	13	Velez	L	1-2	Ca	Pavone [48p]	50 000
	19	Arsenal	D	1-1	Ca	Maidana [13]	20 000
	26	Newells OB	W	2-1	Ca	Caruso 2 [35][72]	45 000
Apr	3	Quilmes	W	1-0	Ca	Ferrari [13]	22 000
	9	Banfield	W	1-0	Ca	Pavone [69]	45 000
	17	Gimnasia	D	0-0	Ca		30 000
	23	Godoy Cruz	L	1-2	Ca	Maidana [38]	45 000
	30	Racing	W	1-0	Ca	Pavone [34p]	30 000
May	8	All Boys	L	0-2	Ca		45 000
	15	Boca Jun	L	0-2	Ca		40 000
	22	S. Lorenzo	D	1-1	Ca	Caruso [29]	45 000
	29	Olimpo	D	0-0	Ca		18 000
Jun	5	Colon	L	1-3	Ca	Caruso [82]	45 000
	12	Estudiantes	D	1-1	Ca	Ferrari [48]	18 000
	18	Lanus	L	1-2	Ca	Lamela [49]	50 000
	23	Belgrano	L	0-2	Capo		20 000
	26	Belgrano	D	1-1	Capo	Pavone [5]	50 000

9th   Att: 452 000 • Av: 45 000 • Monumental 57 921

River Plate were relegated at the end of the 2010-11 Clausura

RIVER PLATE LEAGUE APPEARANCES/GOALS 2011

Goalkeepers Juan Carrizo 14 • Leandro Chichizola 5
Defenders Carlos Arano 1+2/0 • Juan Diaz URU 16+1/0 • Paulo Ferrari 18/3 • Alexis Ferrero 19/0 • Leandro Gonzalez Pirez 2+3/0 • Jonatan Maidana 16/2 • Adalberto Roman PAR 18/0
Midfield Walter Acevedo 14/0 • Facundo Affranchino 0+1/0 • Matias Almeyda 18/0 • Josepmir Ballon PER 2/0 • Adrian Cirigliano 1+5/0 • Mauro Diaz 0+1/0 • Erik Lamela 19/2 • Manuel Lanzini 9+5/0 • Roberto Pereyra 7+5/0
Forwards Fabian Bordagaray 0+6/0 • Diego Buonanotte 5+6/0 • Leandro Caruso 7+6/4 • Rogelio Funes Mori USA 3+4/0 • Hugo Pavone 15+2/4
Coach Juan Jose Lopez

SAN LORENZO 2011

						Scorers	Att
Feb	12	Gimnasia	D	1-1	Ca	Mensequez [17]	30 000
	22	Godoy Cruz	W	2-0	Ca	Mensequez [51], Benitez [90]	22 000
	26	Racing	L	1-2	Ca	Bottinelli [11]	30 000
Mar	4	All Boys	W	3-0	Ca	Mensequez [69], Velazquez [88], Salgueiro [90]	14 500
	12	Boca Jun	W	1-0	Ca	Torres [66]	37 000
	26	Olimpo	W	1-0	Ca	Salgueiro [73]	14 000
Apr	3	Colon	L	1-2	Ca	Carmona [90]	20 000
	8	Estudiantes	D	0-0	Ca		16 000
	16	Lanus	D	1-1	Ca	Mensequez [52]	21 000
	20	Velez	L	0-2	Ca		0
	24	Tigre	L	0-1	Ca		18 000
	30	Huracan	W	3-0	Ca	Ortigoza [54p], Salgueiro [61], Velazquez [68]	24 000
May	9	Indep'iente	D	1-1	Ca	Salgueiro [49]	24 000
	14	Arg Juniors	L	1-2	Ca	Romagnoli [20]	14 000
	22	River Plate	D	1-1	Ca	Ferrari [74]	45 000
	28	Arsenal	L	1-1	Ca	Salgueiro [48]	15 000
Jun	11	Quilmes	L	0-2	Ca		21 000
	15	Newells OB	D	0-0	Ca		25 000
	19	Banfield	D	1-1	Ca	OG [89]	12 000

14th   Att: 212 000 • Av: 23 555

						Scorers	Att
Aug	7	Lanus	L	0-1	Ap		26 000
	15	Estudiant	W	2-0	Ap	Gigliotti [60], Mendez [62]	27 000
	20	Arg Juniors	W	3-1	Ap	Gigliotti [25], Romeo [79], Tellechea [90]	20 000
	28	Boca Jun	D	1-1	Ap	Mendez [30]	45 000
Sep	3	Belgrano	L	0-1	Ap		25 000
	9	Colon	L	1-3	Ap	Gigliotti [67]	22 000
	17	At Rafaela	L	1-3	Ap	Gonzalez [89]	23 000
	21	Velez	W	2-1	Ap	Kalinski [49], Salgueiro [90]	19 000
	25	Racing	D	0-0	Ap		35 000
Oct	3	Godoy Cruz	L	0-2	Ap		12 000
	14	Banfield	W	1-0	Ap	Salgueiro [71]	18 000
	25	Arsenal	L	0-1	Ap		5 000
Nov	4	Olimpo	D	1-1	Ap	Kalinski [3]	10 000
	12	All Boys	L	0-1	Ap		17 000
	20	Union	L	0-1	Ap		22 000
	26	Newells OB	D	0-0	Ap		26 000
Dec	5	Tigre	W	1-0	Ap	Arce [1]	21 000
	8	Indep'iente	L	0-1	Ap		32 000
	12	San Martin	L	0-1	Ap		16 000

17th   Att: 239 000 • Av: 23 900 • Nuevo Gasómetro 43 494

SAN LORENZO LEAGUE APPEARANCES/GOALS 2011

Goalkeepers Damian Albil 1 • Nereo Champagne 7 • Pablo Migliore 18 12
Defenders Nicolas Bianchi Arce 11+1/1 18/0 • Jonathan Bottinelli 17/1 18/0 • Gonzalo Bozzoni ESP 0+2/0 • Jonathan Ferrari 10+2/1 1+2/0 • Diego Herner 4+2/0 • Sebastian Luna 8+3/0 5/0 • Adrian Martinez 6/0 • Fernando Meza 5/0 • Jose Palomino 6+1/0 11+1/0 • Diego Placente 3+2/0 • Jose San Roman 1/0 • Cristian Tula 16/0 13/0
Midfield Pablo Alvarado 2+1/0 0+1/0 • Gonzalo Bazan 13/0 • Giancarlo Carmona PER 14+1/1 1+1/0 • Leandro Chaparro 1/0 • Matias Gimenez 5+5/0 • Sebastian Gonzalez 1+3/0 3+5/1 • Fernando Gutierrez 8+2/0 • Enzo Kalinski 18/2 • Gabriel Mendez 8+7/2 • Leandro Navarro 0+2/0 • Nestor Ortigoza 16/1 15+1/0 • Jonathan Pacheco 0+1/0 3+2/0 • Guillermo Pereyra 9+3/0 • Julio Ramirez 1+2/0 3+3/0 • Salvador Reynoso 3+2/0 • Leandro Romagnoli 9+4/1 7+6/0 • Sebastian Rusculleda 1+3/0 • Emiliano Tellechea URU 4+4/1 • Aureliano Torres PAR 14/1 • Juan Torres 5+6/0
Forwards Nahuel Benitez 0+1/1 1+1/0 • Cristian Chavez 1/0 • Emanuel Gigliotti 17+1/3 • Cesar Lamanna 0+1/0 • Juan Mensequez 13+3/4 1+4/0 • Fabricio Pedrozo 1+2/0 • Bernardo Romeo 3+8/1 • Juan Salgueiro URU 19/5 12+3/2 • Pablo Velazquez PAR 13+4/2
Coach Ramon Diaz • Miguel Tojo (24/05/2011) • Omar Asad (20/06/2011) • Leonardo Madelon (22/11/2011)

SAN MARTIN SAN JUAN 2011

Month	Date	Opponent				Scorers	Att
Aug	16	Tigre	W	2-1	Ap	Robervai 40, Landa 84	12 000
	20	Lanus	D	0-0	Ap		13 000
	26	Estudiantes	D	2-2	Ap	Mas 45, Nunez 66	18 000
	4	Arg Juniors	D	0-0	Ap		10 000
	7	Indep'iente	L	1-2	Ap	Garcia 53	14 000
Sep	11	Boca Jun	L	0-1	Ap		35 000
	16	Belgrano	L	0-1	Ap		10 000
	20	Colon	D	0-0	Ap		28 000
	24	At.Rafaela	W	2-1	Ap	Landa 54, Saavedra 84	7 000
	1	Velez	L	0-1	Ap		16 000
Oct	15	Racing	D	0-0	Ap		19 000
	26	Godoy Cruz	D	2-2	Ap	Penco 44, Saavedra 52	18 000
	31	Banfield	W	2-1	Ap	Caprari 11, Penco 38p	10 000
Nov	7	Arsenal	L	0-2	Ap		3 000
	18	All Boys	L	0-2	Ap		8 000
	26	Olimpo	W	3-0	Ap	Caprari 2 18 77, Bogado 34p	8 000
Dec	3	Union	W	2-0	Ap	Penco 44, Bogado 58	9 000
	8	Newells OB	D	0-0	Ap		20 000
	13	S.Lorenzo	W	1-0	Ap	Penco 2	16 000

9th Att: 114 000 • Av: 11 400 • Ingeniero Hilario Sanchez 19 000

TIGRE 2011

Month	Date	Opponent				Scorers	Att
Feb	14	River Plate	D	0-0	Ca		22 000
	21	Arsenal	L	0-2	Ca		3 000
	1	Newells OB	W	1-0	Ca	Stracqualursi 8	10 000
	6	Quilmes	W	2-1	Ca	Stracqualursi 52, Echeverria 71	8 000
Mar	12	Banfield	L	1-2	Ca	Morales 56	17 000
	21	Gimnasia	L	1-2	Ca	Morales 26	16 000
	27	Godoy Cruz	D	2-2	Ca	Stracqualursi 2 62 90	13 000
	3	Racing	W	2-1	Ca	Pernia 24, Stracqualursi 51	25 000
Apr	10	All Boys	L	0-1	Ca		15 000
	17	Boca Jun	D	3-3	Ca	Stracqualursi 3 22 35 69p	35 000
	24	S. Lorenzo	W	1-0	Ca	OG 5	18 000
	2	Olimpo	D	2-2	Ca	Martinez 2 34 50	11 000
May	7	Colon	W	3-0	Ca	Morales 2 31 60, Stracqualursi 57	16 000
	15	Estudiantes	D	2-2	Ca	Leone 49, Echeverria 74	12 000
	21	Lanus	L	0-3	Ca		10 000
	29	Velez	W	2-1	Ca	Stracqualursi 25p, Diaz 65	20 000
Jun	5	Huracan	L	2-3	Ca	Echeverria 43, Gonzalez 64	0
	12	Indep'iente	D	0-0	Ca		15 000
	18	Arg Juniors	D	1-1	Ca	Martinez 29	10 000

11th Att: 156 000 • Av: 15 600

Month	Date	Opponent				Scorers	Att
	7	Racing	D	1-1	Ap	Leone 75	20 000
Aug	16	San Martin	L	1-2	Ap	Pio 90	12 000
	21	Godoy Cruz	W	2-1	Ap	Maggiolo 2 23 63	15 000
	27	Lanus	D	0-0	Ap		10 000
Sep	2	Banfield	W	1-0	Ap	Echeverria 32	12 000
	10	Estudiantes	W	3-1	Ap	Luna 5, Morales 22p, Martinez 25	18 000
	17	Arsenal	D	2-2	Ap	Morales 53p, Echeverria 60	12 000
	22	Arg Juniors	W	1-0	Ap	Luna 55	8 000
	25	All Boys	D	1-1	Ap	Martinez 85	16 000
Oct	2	Boca Jun	L	0-1	Ap		50 000
	14	Olimpo	D	1-1	Ap	Carrasco 79	12 000
	26	Belgrano	L	0-1	Ap		7 000
	31	Union	D	1-1	Ap	Carrasaco 68	18 000
Nov	5	Colon	W	2-1	Ap	Luna 35, Carrasco 73	14 000
	18	Newells OB	W	1-0	Ap	Casteglione 37	22 000
	25	At.Rafaela	W	3-0	Ap	Luna 16, Castano 66, Morales 77p	18 000
Dec	5	S.Lorenzo	L	0-1	Ap		21 000
	8	Velez	L	1-3	Ap	Morales 44	10 000
	12	Indep'iente	L	1-2	Ap	Morales 13	25 000

7th Att: 124 000 • Av: 13 777 • Monumental de Victoria 26 282

SAN MARTIN LEAGUE APPEARANCES/GOALS 2011

Goalkeepers Luciano Pocrnjic 19
Defenders Cristian Alvarez 9+2/0 • Marcos Galarza 17/0
Cristian Grabinski 19/0 • Lucas Landa 19/2 • Juan Mattia 0+1/0
Raul Saavedra 2+10/2 • Diego Sosa 4/0
Midfield Marcos Aguirre 2+1/0 • Mauro Bogado 11+3/2
Maximiliano Bustos 8+2/0 • Pablo Cantero 16/0 • Matias Carabajal 0+1/0
Marcelo Carrusca 5/0 • Emanuel Mas 19/1 • Maximiliano Nunez 6+5/1
Lucas Oviedo 2+2/0 • Federico Poggi 14+1/0 • Martin Wagner 3+3/0
Forwards Nestor Ayala PAR 3+5/0 • Gaston Caprari 8+2/3
Diego Garcia 1+8/1 • Claudio Graf 7+7/0 • Sebastian Penco 11+1/4
Roberval BRA 4+2/1
Coach Daniel Garnero

TIGRE LEAGUE APPEARANCES/GOALS 2011

Goalkeepers Luis Ardente 2+1 • Javier Garcia 19 • Daniel Islas 17
Defenders Juan Blengio 10+1/0 15/0 • Pablo Caceres URU 9+2/0
Carlos Casteglione 16/1 • Mariano Echeverria 18/3 19/2
Christian Lema 1/0 • Maximiliano Montero URU 1/0 • Lucas Orban 2/0
Norberto Paparatto 2+3/0 • Mariano Pernia ESP 9/1
Andres Rodales URU 17/0 4+4/0 • Cristian Trombetta 2+3/0
Renzo Vera 10+1/0
Midfield Ruben Botta 2+11/0 0+4/0 • Javier Carrasco 1+16/3
Diego Castano 9+6/0 18+1/1 • Gaston Diaz 3+4/1 16+2/0
Matias Escobar 0+2/0 • Martin Galmarini 16/0 6+6/0
Esteban Gonzalez 18+1/1 • Ramiro Leone 12+4/1 14+2/1
Roman Martinez 14/3 17/2 • Diego Morales 16+1/4 19/5
Emmanuel Pio 4+10/1 • Fernando Telechea 2+3/0
Forwards Leonel Altobolli 0+3/0 • Diego Ftacla 1+2/0
Martin Gomez 5+6/0 • Leandro Leguizamon 0+2/0 • Carlos Luna 19/4
Ezequiel Maggiolo 16+2/2 • Denis Stracqualursi 17+2/10
Coach Rodolfo Arruabarrena

UNION SANTA FE 2011

	Date	Opponent	Res	Score	Comp	Scorers	Att
Aug	5	Arg Juniors	D	1-1	Ap	Avendano 53	20 000
	15	Boca Jun	L	0-4	Ap		40 000
	22	Belgrano	D	0-0	Ap		18 000
	28	Colon	W	2-0	Ap	Rosales 8, Montero 18	33 000
Sep	4	At Rafaela	L	0-1	Ap		21 000
	11	Velez	W	1-0	Ap	Rosales 88	18 000
	18	Racing	D	1-1	Ap	Bologna 68	22 000
	22	Godoy Cruz	D	1-1	Ap	Erramuspe 63	5 000
	26	Banfield	W	1-0	Ap	Barrales 79	19 000
Oct	3	Arsenal	L	1-2	Ap	Rosales 8p	3 000
	15	All Boys	D	1-1	Ap	Rosales 32p	18 000
	24	Olimpo	W	1-0	Ap	Avendano 59	8 000
	31	Tigre	D	1-1	Ap	Avendano 73	18 000
Nov	6	Newells OB	W	2-1	Ap	Barrales 48, Bologna 88p	19 000
	20	S.Lorenzo	W	1-0	Ap	Rosales 73	22 000
	28	Indep'iente	D	0-0	Ap		21 000
Dec	3	San Martin	L	0-2	Ap		9 000
	6	Lanus	L	0-1	Ap		18 000
	11	Estudiantes	L	0-2	Ap		25 000

11th Att: 194 000 • Av: 19 400 • Estadio 15 de Abril 22 852

UNION LEAGUE APPEARANCES/GOALS 2011
Goalkeepers Enrique Bologna 19/2
Defenders Juan Avendano 16/3 • Juan Pablo Cardenas 12+1/0
Nicolas Correa URU 15+1/0 • Rodrigo Erramuspe 17/1
Renzo Vera 11+1/0 Santiago Zurbriggen 1+1
Midfield Pablo Bruna 13+3/0 • Alexis Fernandez 5/0 • Pablo
Miguez URU 1+2/0 • Fausto Montero 13+3/1 • Emanuel Moreno 2/0
Alejandro Perez 1+4/0 • Ronald Quinteros PER 3+7/0
Paulo Rosales 17+1/5 • Marcelo Sarmiento 12+1/0
Matias Soto Torres 1+4/0 • Jorge Velazquez 17/0
Sebastian Vidal 6+3/0
Forwards Jeronimo Barrales 12+1/2 • Pablo Magnin 1+3/0
Fabricio Nunez URU 5+7/0 • Juan Pereyra 4+7/0
Matias Quiroga 5+6/0
Coach Frank Dario Kudelka

VELEZ LEAGUE APPEARANCES/GOALS 2011
Goalkeepers Marcelo Barovero 19 17 • German Montoya 2+1
Defenders Mariano Bittolo 1/0 3/0 • Gaston Diaz 7+3/0 2+1/0
Sebastian Dominguez 16/0 15/0 • Emanuel Olivera 1/0
Fernando Ortiz 17/1 17/2 • Gino Peruzzi 1+1/0 • Juan Sills 1+1/0 1/0
Fernando Tobio 7+1/0 6+1/0
Midfield Ricardo Alvarez 11+3/3 • Ivan Bella 4+10/0 11+4/2
Francisco Cerro 5+7/0 • Jorge Correa 0+1/0 • Fabian Cubero 10/1 15/0
Leandro Desabato 0+3/0 1+1/0 • Augusto Fernandez 13+4/4 14+3/3
Brian Ferreira 1+4/0 • Federico Freire 1/0 • Maximiliano Moralez 13+2/4
Emiliano Papa 16/1 15+1/0 • David Ramirez 9+4/8 12+2/3
Franco Razzotti 11/0 • Leandro Velazquez 3+6/1
Victor Zapata 13/2 9/0
Forwards Guillermo Franco MEX 1+5/0 8+4/5 • Maximiliano Giusti
1+4/0 Juan Martinez 14+4/3 9/1 • Jonathan Ramirez URU 6+8/1
Ezequiel Rescaldani 0+2/0 3+7/2 • Tanque Silva URU 13/7 2/1
Agustin Vuletich 2+7/1 3+3/0
Coach Ricardo Gareca

VELEZ SARSFIELD 2011

	Date	Opponent	Res	Score	Comp	Scorers	Att
Feb	11	Indep'iente	D	2-2	Ca	Maralez 47, Martinez 78	22 000
	15	Caracas	W	3-0	CLg4	Moralez 44, Ramirez 59, Martinez 83p	7 351
	19	All Boys	L	1-2	Ca	Ramirez 54	22 000
	27	Arg Juniors	D	1-1	Ca	Ramirez 7	14 000
Mar	3	U. Católica	L	3-4	CLg4	Ortiz 20, Fernandez 21, Papa 45	8 954
	6	Boca Jun	W	1-0	Ca	Ortiz 39	35 000
	10	U. Española	L	1-2	CLg4	Ramirez 68	6 209
	13	River	W	2-1	Ca	Silva 2 35 84	50 000
	24	U. Española	W	2-1	CLg4	Papa 23, Silva 68	5 913
	27	Arsenal	W	3-0	Ca	Silva 24p, Alvarez 35, Martinez 63	20 000
Apr	2	Olimpo	W	2-1	Ca	Alvarez 2, Papa 51	15 000
	7	U. Católica	D	0-0	CLg4		11 143
	10	Newells OB	W	2-0	Ca	Silva 8, Fernandez 78	20 000
	14	Caracas	W	3-0	CLg4	Moralez 20, Silva 2 46 54	17 824
	16	Colon	D	1-1	Ca	Zapata 90	18 000
	20	S. Lorenzo	W	2-0	Ca	Silva 75, Fernandez 88	BCD
	23	Quilmes	L	2-3	Ca	Canteros 39, Vuletich 90	25 000
	26	LDU Quito	W	3-0	CLr2	Fernandez 2 7 10, Dominguez 54	7 134
	30	Estudiantes	W	4-0	Ca	Fernandez 36, Moralez 2 41 62p, Ramirez 89	26 000
May	5	LDU Quito	W	2-0	CLr2	Alvarez 45, Bella 80	19 158
	9	Banfield	W	2-0	Ca	Cubero 83, Ramirez 90	20 000
	12	Libertad	W	3-0	CLqf	Moralez 20, Martinez 2 75p 80	9 086
	15	Lanus	L	2-3	Ca	Ramirez 2 4 28	15 000
	1	Libertad	W	4-2	CLqf	Moralez 2 44 66, Franco 86p, Fernandez 87	2 300
	22	Gimnasia	W	2-0	Ca	Silva 26, Moralez 82p	20 000
	26	Peñarol	L	0-1	CLsf		52 904
	29	Tigre	L	1-2	Ca	Alvarez 63	20 000
Jun	2	Peñarol	W	2-1	CLsf	Tobio 45, Silva 66	45 000
	6	Godoy Cruz	W	2-0	Ca	Martinez 64, Ramirez 90	22 000
	12	Huracan	W	2-0	Ca	Silva 51, Ramirez 90p	BCD
	19	Racing	W	2-1	Ca	Zapata 15, Fernandez 19	45 000

1st Att: 229 000 • Av: 22 900

	Date	Opponent	Res	Score	Comp	Scorers	Att
Aug	6	Godoy Cruz	D	1-1	Ap	Bella 67	12 000
	15	Banfield	W	3-0	Ap	Silva 23p, Ortiz 49, Martinez 83	12 000
	19	Arsenal	W	1-0	Ap	Franco 90	6 000
	27	All Boys	L	0-1	Ap		16 000
Sep	1	Arg Juniors	D	0-0	CSr2		
	4	Olimpo	L	1-2	Ap	Franco 40	13 000
	8	Arg Juniors	W	4-0	CSr2	Franco 24, Fernandez 55, Martinez 75p, Canteros 84	
	11	Unión	L	0-1	Ap		18 000
	18	Newells OB	D	1-1	Ap	Fernandez 77	35 000
	21	S. Lorenzo	L	1-2	Ap	Fernandez 37	19 000
	25	Indep'iente	W	1-0	Ap	Ramirez.J 34	20 000
Oct	1	San Martin	W	1-0	Ap	Rescaldani 66	16 000
	5	U Católica	W	2-0	CSr3	Franco 15, Bella 42	
	16	Lanús	W	2-1	Ap	Canteros 42, Ortiz 88	10 000
	20	U.Católica	D	1-1	CSr3	Ortiz 77	
	25	Estudiantes	W	1-0	Ap	Ramirez.D 6	17 000
	29	Arg Juniors	L	1-3	Ap	Franco 63	14 000
	1	Santa Fe	D	1-1	CSqf	Ramirez.D 76	
Nov	6	Boca Jun	D	0-0	Ap		25 000
	10	Santa Fe	W	3-2	CSqf	Franco 2 8 20, Martinez 90p	
	19	Belgrano	W	3-1	Ap	Bella 24, Franco 30, Rescaldani 75	27 000
	24	LDU Quito	L	0-2	CSsf		
	27	Colón	D	1-1	Ap	Velazquez 21	18 000
	29	LDU Quito	L	0-1	CSsf		
Dec	3	At. Rafaela	L	0-2	Ap		13 000
	8	Tigre	W	3-1	Ap	Ramirez.D 30, Fernandez 35, Franco 62	10 000
	12	Racing	W	1-0	Ap	Ramirez.D 55	20 000

3rd Att: 161 000 • Av: 17 888 • José Amalfitani 49 540

ARM – ARMENIA

FIFA/COCA-COLA WORLD RANKING

'93	'94	'95	'96	'97	'98	'99	'00	'01	'02	'03	'04	'05	'06	'07	'08	'09	'10	'11	'12
-	141	113	106	105	100	85	90	95	107	113	119	108	123	93	113	100	60	46	

						2011									
Jan	Feb	Mar	Apr	May	Jun	Jul	Aug	Sep	Oct	Nov	Dec		High	Low	Av
60	62	65	62	62	70	70	71	44	46	46	46		44	159	102

Armenia went into their final Euro 2012 qualifier against the Republic of Ireland in Dublin knowing that a win would take them through to the play-offs. It didn't happen but the rise in fortunes of the national team is one of the success stories of European football over recent years. Particular care has been paid to the youth setup and with young players like Henrikh Mkhitaryan - a double winner in Ukraine with Shakhtar Donetsk - they won five of their ten matches in the qualifiers to finish third. Central to the recent rise in fortunes has been coach Vardan Minasyan, who doubles up his responsibilities as coach of Pyunik Yerevan. With the club having won ten consecutive titles there was little to indicate any shift in fortunes before the 2011 season started, but they were beaten to the title by Ulysses Yerevan, a team founded only in 2000. Under coach Sevada Arzumanyan, Ulysses have built solid foundations on and off the pitch and whilst the senior team was winning the title for the first time, the club's reserve team, which plays under the name Shengavit Yerevan, won the second division title. There was only ever going to be one winner when the Armenian Cup Final paired Mika Ashtarak and Shirak Gyumri - Mika maintaining their 100% success rate in the final with a record sixth win while Shirak have now been in four finals with nothing to show for it.

UEFA EUROPEAN CHAMPIONSHIP RECORD
1960-1992 DNE (Played as part of the Soviet Union) **1996-2012** DNQ

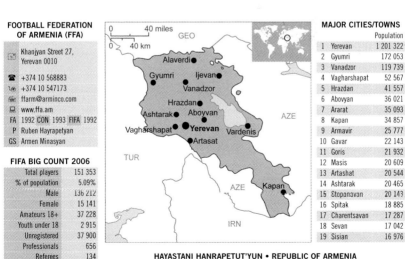

FOOTBALL FEDERATION OF ARMENIA (FFA)

Khanjyan Street 27, Yerevan 0010

☎ +374 10 568883
📠 +374 10 547173
✉ ffarm@arminco.com
🖥 www.ffa.am
FA 1992 CON 1993 FIFA 1992
P Ruben Hayrapetyan
GS Armen Minasyan

FIFA BIG COUNT 2006

Total players	151 353
% of population	5.09%
Male	136 212
Female	15 141
Amateurs 18+	37 228
Youth under 18	2 915
Unregistered	37 900
Professionals	656
Referees	134
Admin & coaches	4 810
Number of clubs	80
Number of teams	178

MAJOR CITIES/TOWNS

		Population
1	Yerevan	1 201 322
2	Gyumri	172 053
3	Vanadzor	119 739
4	Vagharshapat	52 567
5	Hrazdan	41 557
6	Abovyan	36 021
7	Ararat	35 093
8	Kapan	34 857
9	Armavir	25 777
10	Gavar	22 143
11	Goris	21 932
12	Masis	20 609
13	Artashat	20 544
14	Ashtarak	20 465
15	Stepanavan	20 143
16	Spitak	18 885
17	Charentsavan	17 287
18	Sevan	17 042
19	Sisian	16 976

HAYASTANI HANRAPETUT'YUN • REPUBLIC OF ARMENIA

Capital	Yerevan	Population	2 967 004 (137)	% in cities	64%
GDP per capita	$6300 (128)	Area km²	29 743 km² (142)	GMT +/-	+4
Neighbours (km)	Azerbaijan 787, Georgia 164, Iran 35, Turkey 268				

RECENT INTERNATIONALS PLAYED BY ARMENIA

2008	Opponents	Score		Venue	Comp	Scorers	Att	Referee
2-02	Malta	W	1-0	Ta'Qali	Fr	Ara Hakopyan [69]		Porisson ISL
4-02	Belarus	W	2-1	Ta'Qali	Fr	Arakelyan [18], Ara Hakopyan [76]		Zammit MLT
6-02	Iceland	L	0-2	Ta'Qali	Fr			Attard MLT
26-03	Kazakhstan	W	1-0	Pernis	Fr	Manucharyan [62]		Vink NED
28-05	Moldova	D	2-2	Tiraspol	Fr	Pizzelli [25], Pachajyan [54]		Ishchenko UKR
1-06	Greece	D	0-0	Offenbach/Main	Fr		8 032	Rafati GER
6-09	Turkey	L	0-2	Yerevan	WCq		30 000	Ovrebo NOR
10-09	Spain	L	0-4	Albacete	WCq		16 996	Asumaa FIN
11-10	Belgium	L	0-2	Brussels	WCq		20 949	Rasmussen DEN
15-10	Bosnia-Herzegovina	L	1-4	Zenica	WCq	Minasyan [85]	13 000	Kenan ISR
2009								
11-02	Latvia	D	0-0	Limassol	Fr		150	
28-03	Estonia	D	2-2	Yerevan	WCq	Mkhitaryan [33], Ghazaryan [87]	3 000	Wilmes LUX
1-04	Estonia	L	0-1	Tallinn	WCq		5 200	Zimmermann SUI
12-08	Moldova	L	1-4	Yerevan	Fr	Arakelyan [75]	1 000	Silagava GEO
5-09	Bosnia-Herzegovina	L	0-2	Yerevan	WCq		1 800	Braamhaar NED
9-09	Belgium	W	2-1	Yerevan	WCq	Goharyan [23], Hovsepyan [50]	2 300	Stavrev MKD
10-10	Spain	L	1-2	Yerevan	WCq	Arzumanyan [58]	10 500	Jech CZE
14-10	Turkey	L	0-2	Bursa	WCq		16 200	Hansson SWE
2010								
3-03	Belarus	L	1-3	Antalya	Fr	Pachajyan [59]	BCD	
25-05	Uzbekistan	W	3-1	Yerevan	Fr	Mkhitaryan [7], Manucharyan 2 [18p 27]	20 000	Kvaratskhelia GEO
11-08	Iran	L	1-3	Yerevan	Fr	Mkrtchyan [37]	3 000	Kvaratskhelia GEO
3-09	Republic of Ireland	L	0-1	Yerevan	ECq		8 600	Szabo HUN
7-09	Macedonia FYR	D	2-2	Skopje	ECq	Movsisyan [41], Manucharyan [91+]	9 000	Berntsen NOR
8-10	Slovakia	W	3-1	Yerevan	ECq	Movsisyan [23], Ghazaryan [50], Mkhitaryan [89]	8 500	Orsato ITA
12-10	Andorra	W	4-0	Yerevan	ECq	Ghazaryan [4], Mkhitaryan [16], Movsisyan [33], Pizzelli [33]	12 000	Undiano ESP
2011								
9-02	Georgia	L	1-2	Limassol	Fr	Manucharyan [60p]		Giannis CYP
26-03	Russia	D	0-0	Yerevan	ECq		14 800	Thomson SCO
4-06	Russia	L	1-3	St Petersburg	ECq	Pizzelli [25]	18 000	Lannoy FRA
10-08	Lithuania	L	0-3	Kaunas	Fr			Sipailo LVA
2-09	Andorra	W	3-0	Andora La Vella	ECq	Pizzelli [35], Ghazaryan [75], Mkhitaryan [91+p]	750	Kostadinov BUL
6-09	Slovakia	W	4-0	Zilina	ECq	Movsisyan [57], Mkhitaryan [70], Ghazaryan [80], Sarkisov [91+]	7 238	Borski POL
7-10	Macedonia FYR	W	4-1	Yerevan	ECq	Pizzelli [28], Mkhitaryan [34], Ghazaryan [69], Sarkisov [91+]	14 403	Schorgenhofer AUT
11-10	Republic of Ireland	L	1-2	Dublin	ECq	Mkhitaryan [62]	45 200	Iturralde ESP

Fr = Friendly match • EC = UEFA EURO 2008/2012 • WC = FIFA World Cup • q = qualifier

ARMENIA NATIONAL TEAM HISTORICAL RECORDS

Caps
125 - Sargis Hovsepyan 1992- • **69** - Arthur Petrosyan 1992-2005 & Roman Berezovsky 1996- • **62** - Harutyun Vardanyan 1994-2004 • **56** - Hamlet Mkhitaryan 1994-2008 • **54** - Romik Khachatryan 1997-2008 • **53** - Arthur Voskanyan 1999 & Armen Shahgeldyan 1992-2007 • **50** - Artavazd Karamyan 2000-10 • **49** - Robert Arzumanyan 2005- • **48** - Karen Dokhoyan 1999-2008 & Arman Karamyan 2000-

Goals
11 - Arthur Petrosyan 1992-2005 • **8** - Henrikh Mkhitaryan 2007- • **7** - Ara Hakobyan 1998-2008 • **6** - Edgar Manucharyan 2000- ; Gevorg Ghazaryan 2007- & Armen Shahgeldyan 1992-2007 • **5** - Marcos Pizzelli 2008- & Arman Karamyan 2000- • **4** - Robert Arzumanyan 2005- ; Yura Movsisyan 2010- & Tigran Yesayan 1996-99

Past Coaches
Eduard Markarov 1992-1994 • Samvel Darbinyan 1995-1996 • Khoren Hovhannisyan 1996-1997 • Souren Barseghyan 1998-1999 • Varuzhan Sukiasyan 2000-2001 • Andranik Adamyan 2002 • Oscar Lopez ARG 2002 • Andranik Adamyan 2003 • Mihai Stoichita ROU 2003-2004 • Bernard Casoni FRA 2004-2005 • Henk Wisman NED 2005-2006 • Ian Porterfield SCO 2006-2007 • Vardan Minasyan & Tom Jones ENG 2007 • Jan Poulsen DEN 2008-2009 • Vardan Minasyan 2009-

ARMENIA 2011

PREMIER LEAGUE

	Pl	W	D	L	F	A	Pts	Ulysses	Gandzasar	Pyunik	Banants	Mika	Impuls	Shirak	Ararat
Ulysses Yerevan †	28	15	8	5	38	22	53		0-0 0-0	1-0 1-1	1-0 1-0	1-2 0-3	0-1 2-1	1-0 2-2	3-0 5-0
Gandzasar Kapan ‡	28	12	10	6	31	18	46	0-0 0-1		1-3 1-2	2-0 0-1	1-0 2-2	0-0 1-0	1-0 4-0	5-0 2-0
Pyunik Yerevan ‡	28	12	10	6	33	28	46	3-1 0-0	1-1 1-1		1-1 0-3	0-1 1-2	2-2 2-2	1-0 1-0	1-0 1-0
Banants Yerevan	28	12	8	8	42	30	44	1-3 2-1	0-1 0-0	3-4 3-0		2-2 3-1	2-1 3-2	2-2 3-1	2-1 1-0
Mika Ashtarak ‡	28	12	8	8	36	25	44	2-3 0-1	0-1 1-0	0-1 0-0	0-0 0-0		3-2 2-1	0-0 4-1	2-1 2-0
Impuls Dilijan	28	10	7	11	37	36	37	0-1 1-1	2-2 1-1	0-1 1-1	1-0 3-1	1-0 0-2		2-1 2-1	2-0 2-1
Shirak Gyumri	28	6	7	15	27	42	25	1-3 0-2	0-2 1-0	2-0 0-0	1-1 0-2	1-0 1-1	2-1 2-3		1-1 1-0
Ararat Yerevan	28	2	4	22	14	57	10	1-1 1-2	0-1 0-1	1-4 0-1	1-1 0-5	0-3 1-1	2-1 0-2	2-1 1-3	

5/03/2011 - 5/11/2011 • † Qualified for the UEFA Champions League • ‡ Qualified for the Europa League • No team relegated
Top scorers: **16** - Bruno Correa BRA, Banants • **11** - Narek Beglaryan, Mika • **10** - Andranik Barikyan, Shirak • **8** - Zaven Badoyan, Impuls; Giorgi Krasovski GEO, Ulysses & Edgar Manucharyan, Pyunik • **7** - Artem Adamyan, Ulysses & Norayr Gyozalyan, Impuls

ARMENIA 2011 SECOND DIVISION

	Pl	W	D	L	F	A	Pts
Shengavit Yerevan	24	17	2	5	53	24	53
Mika-2 Ashtarak	24	13	7	4	51	19	46
Pyunik-2 Yerevan	24	12	3	9	44	30	39
Shirak-2 Gyumri	24	10	7	7	29	25	37
Gandzasar-2 Kapan	24	11	3	10	48	42	36
Impuls-2 Dilijan	24	10	5	9	38	40	35
Banants-2 Yerevan	24	10	4	10	35	35	34
Pyunik-3 Yerevan	24	6	1	17	27	61	19
Ararat-2 Yerevan	24	2	2	20	15	64	8

5/04/2011 - 10/10/2011 • No team promoted

MEDALS TABLE

		Overall			League			Cup	
		G	S	B	G	S	B	G	S
1	Pyunik Yerevan	16	4	1	13	1	1	5	3
2	Ararat Yerevan	6	6	1	1	4	1	5	2
3	Mika Ashtarak	6	3	2		3	2	6	
4	Shirak Gyumri	3	9	2	3	5	2		4
5	Tsement Yerevan	3	1		1	1		2	
6	Banants Yerevan	2	9	3		4	3	2	5
7	FK Yerevan	1	1	3	1		3	1	
8	Ulysses Yerevan	1	2		1	2			
9	Araks Ararat	1			1				
10	Zvartnots Yerevan		3			1			2
11	Kotayk Abovyan		2	2		2			2
12	Gandzasar Kapan	1	1		1	1			
13	Kilikia Yerevan	1						1	
	Homenmen Yerevan		1			1			
	Spartak Yerevan		1			1			

ARMENIAN CLUBS IN THE SOVIET UNION

		G	S	B	G	S	B	G	S
8	Ararat Yerevan	3	4		1	2		2	2

FFA CUP 2011

1st Round			Semi-finals			Final		
Mika *	3	2						
Impuls	0	2	Mika *	3	1			
Gandzasar	0	1	Banants	3	0			
Banants *	3	0				Mika ‡	4	
Ulysses *	1	1				Shirak	1	
Ararat	0	0	Ulysses	1	0			
Pyunik	1	0	Shirak *	0	2			
Shirak	1	1						

* Home team in the first leg • ‡ Qualified for the Europa League

CUP FINAL 2011

Hanrapetakan, Yerevan, 11-05-2011, 16:00
Att: 6000, Ref: David Fernandez ESP

Mika Ashtarak	4	Alex Henrique 16, Narek Beglaryan 2 35 68, Dong Fangzhuo 91+
Shirak Gyumri	1	Andranik Barikyan 42

Mika - Gevork Kasparov - Gevork Poghosyan• (Dong Fangzhuo 65), Alex Henrique, Alexander Tadevosyan, Hrayr Mkoyan, Aghvan Mkrtchyan, Pedro Lopez (Andranik Shahgeldyan 82), Ferreira Edney, Andranik Voskanyan (Armen Petrosyan 57), Narek Beglaryan, Aram Voskanyan (Constantin Mandricenco 46). Tr: Armen Shahgeldyan
Shirak - Igor Logvinov - Armen Ghazaryan (Karen Khachatryan 46), Gevorg Hovhannisyan, Tiago Lopes (Hovhannes Grigoryan 22), Armen Tigranyan, Karen Aleksanyan, Tigran Davtyan, Artak Oseyan (Hrachya Mnatsakanyan 85), David Hakobyan, Andranik Barikyan•, Mkrtich Nalbandyan. Tr: Felix Khojoyan

ARU – ARUBA

FIFA/COCA-COLA WORLD RANKING

'93	'94	'95	'96	'97	'98	'99	'00	'01	'02	'03	'04	'05	'06	'07	'08	'09	'10	'11	'12
165	173	171	181	177	180	191	184	185	189	195	198	200	198	201	193	198	199	199	164

2011												High	Low	Av
Jan	Feb	Mar	Apr	May	Jun	Jul	Aug	Sep	Oct	Nov	Dec			
199	199	199	198	199	200	168	170	170	172	172	164	164	202	186

Aruba missed out on the first group stage of the 2014 FIFA World Cup qualifiers in the worst possible manner - by losing a penalty shoot-out. Having been drawn against St Lucia in a preliminary knock-out round, Aruba made an excellent start by beating their opponents 4-2 at home in Oranjestad. Aruba does not have a great World Cup qualifying record - 1998 was the first tournament that the national team entered and a single victory over Puerto Rico in 2000 was all they had to show for their efforts before the victory over St Lucia - so it was disappointing for football fans in the country to see their team go down 4-2 in the return in Castries. That meant a penalty shoot-out and with the first nine having been scored Jelano Cruden missed and Aruba were out. In club football, Racing Club Aruba brought to an end any hopes that Britannia may have had of completing a third consecutive double. At the start of 2011 Britannia had beaten Bubali 4-1 to win the Copa Betico Croes for the fourth time in a row but they missed out on qualifying for a fourth consecutive championship final after losing 2-1 to Racing in the final round. Instead Racing took on Nacional, a tie they won over the three legs but which was overshadowed by the death of their 23-year-old player Eduardo Mayora Ponse who drowned whilst diving before the third match.

FIFA WORLD CUP RECORD
1930-1994 DNE **1998-2014** DNQ

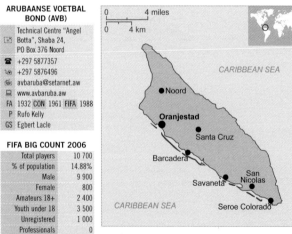

**ARUBAANSE VOETBAL
BOND (AVB)**

Technical Centre "Angel
Botta", Shaba 24,
PO Box 376 Noord
☎ +297 5877357
📠 +297 5876496
✉ avbaruba@setarnet.aw
🖥 www.avbaruba.aw
FA 1932 CON 1961 FIFA 1988
P Rufo Kelly
GS Egbert Lacle

FIFA BIG COUNT 2006

Total players	10 700
% of population	14.88%
Male	9 900
Female	800
Amateurs 18+	2 400
Youth under 18	3 500
Unregistered	1 000
Professionals	0
Referees	26
Admin & coaches	100
Number of clubs	60
Number of teams	140

MAJOR CITIES/TOWNS

		Population
1	Oranjestad	33 575
2	San Nicolas	18 395
3	Noord	16 944
4	Santa Cruz	12 326
5	Savaneta	9 996
6	Paradera	9 037

ARUBA

Capital	Oranjestad	Population	103 065 (193)	% in cities	47%
GDP per capita	$21 800 (57)	Area km²	180 km² (217)	GMT +/-	-5
Neighbours (km)	Coast 68				

RECENT INTERNATIONALS PLAYED BY ARUBA

2011	Opponents	Score	Venue	Comp	Scorers	Att	Referee
8-07	St Lucia	W 4-2	Oranjestad	WCq	Erik Santos [13], Maurice Escalona [48], Frederick Gomez [76], David Abdul [85]	300	Foster CAY
12-07	St Lucia	L 2-4	Castries	WCq	Frederick Gomez [44], Rensy Barradas [76]. L 4-5p	500	Lancaster GUY
2-12	Suriname	D 0-0	Paramaribo	Fr	W 5-3p	150	Jauregui CUW
4-12	Bonaire †	D 2-2	Paramaribo	Fr	Jean-Luc Bergen [52], Frederick Gomez [76]. L 3-4p	50	Wijngaarde SUR

Fr = Friendly match • CC = Digicel Caribbean Cup • WCq = FIFA World Cup • q = qualifier • † Not an official international

ARUBA NATIONAL TEAM HISTORICAL RECORDS

Coach Rene Notten NED 1995 • Marco Rasmijn 2000 • Marcelo Munoz ARG 2004 • Azing Griever NED 2004-06 • Marcelo Munoz ARG 2008-10 • Epi Albertus 2010-

ARUBA 2010-11

DIVISION DI HONOR FIRST STAGE

	Pl	W	D	L	F	A	Pts	RCA	Britannia	Nacional	La Fama	Bubali	Estrella	Caravel	Riverplate	Juventud	Sporting
Racing Club Aruba †	18	13	4	1	44	13	43		3-4	1-1	5-0	3-3	3-0	3-2	0-0	6-0	2-1
Britannia †	18	13	2	3	57	19	41	0-1		2-2	1-0	4-3	0-1	2-1	8-2	2-1	12-1
Nacional †	18	10	5	3	31	19	35	0-1	0-3		2-1	1-1	2-0	1-1	1-0	2-1	1-0
La Fama †	18	11	1	6	29	23	34	1-2	2-1	3-1		2-2	0-1	1-0	1-0	1-0	3-1
Bubali	17	8	6	3	47	22	30	1-1	0-1	1-1	1-2		2-1	4-0	3-1	5-5	3-0
Estrella	18	7	2	9	28	28	23	0-2	1-1	0-1	3-0	0-4		2-4	2-1	3-2	1-0
Independiente Caravel	18	4	4	10	19	40	16	0-3	0-4	1-3	1-5	0-6	1-1		0-0	2-1	0-1
Riverplate	18	3	4	11	15	34	13	0-3	0-2	0-3	0-2	0-2	3-2	0-1		0-0	3-0
Juventud T'ki Leendert	18	3	3	12	31	53	12	0-2	1-6	2-4	1-2	0-6	2-1	3-5	2-2		5-3
Sporting	17	1	1	15	12	62	4	0-3	0-4	1-5	1-3	n/p	0-9	0-0	2-3	1-5	

17/09/2010 - 18/04/2011 • † Qualified for the championship play-off

DIVISION DI HONOR CHAMPIONSHIP PLAY-OFF

	Pl	W	D	L	F	A	Pts	RCA	Na	Br	LF
Racing Club Aruba †	6	4	1	1	9	4	13		0-1	1-0	0-0
Nacional †	6	2	1	3	8	6	7	2-0		0-2	1-1
Britannia	6	1	3	2	5	6	6	1-2	1-1		1-2
La Fama	6	1	3	2	5	11	6	1-5	1-1	0-3	

10/05/2011 - 5/06/2011 • † Qualified for the final and the CFU Championship

MEDALS TABLE

		All	Lge	Cp	Town
		G	G	G	
1	Dakota	16	15	1	Oranjestad
2	Estrella	12	12		Santa Cruz
	Racing Club	12	12		Oranjestad
4	Britannia	7	3	4	Paradera
5	Nacional	4	4		Noord
6	Riverplate	2	2		Oranjestad
7	Bubali	1	1		Noord
	Estudiantes	1		1	Oranjestad
	San Luis	1	1		Savaneta
	Sportboys	1		1	Santa Cruz

FINAL

1st leg. 8-06-2011. Scorer - Ronald Gomez
2nd leg. 11-06-2011. Scorer - Roderick Lampe
Play-off. 20-06-2011. Scorer - Erik Santos
Racing 1-0 0-1 1-0 Nacional

COPA BETICO CROES 2010-11

First Round		Quarter-finals		Semi-finals		Final	
Britannia	Bye						
		Britannia	6				
Brazil Juniors	2	San Nicolas	0				
San Nicolas	6			Britannia	3		
Dakota	2			Juventud T Leendert	1		
Riverplate	1	Dakota	1				
Estrella	2	Juventud T Leendert	2			Britannia	4
Juventud T Leendert	4					Bubali	1
La Fama	5						
San Luis	0	La Fama	4				
		Racing Club Aruba	2				
Racing Club Aruba	Bye			La Fama	2		
Nacional	Bye			Bubali	3		
		Nacional	1				
		Bubali	2				
Bubali	Bye	3rd place: La Fama 5-2 Juventud TL					

CUP FINAL

Frans Figaroa, Oranjestad
25-01-2011

ASA – AMERICAN SAMOA

FIFA/COCA-COLA WORLD RANKING

'93	'94	'95	'96	'97	'98	'99	'00	'01	'02	'03	'04	'05	'06	'07	'08	'09	'10	'11	'12
-	-	-	-	-	193	199	203	201	201	202	204	205	198	201	201	203	203	186	

2011												High	Low	Av
Jan	Feb	Mar	Apr	May	Jun	Jul	Aug	Sep	Oct	Nov	Dec	High	Low	Av
203	203	202	202	202	203	203	203	203	203	204	186	186	205	201

The national team of American Samoa wrote one of the most unlikely stories of the year in 2011 when they managed to beat Tonga 2-1 in a 2014 FIFA World Cup qualifier - their first ever win in an international match. It propelled the team into the international limelight as their exploits were shown on news bulletins the world over. Goalscorers Ramon Ott and Shalom Luani were feted as heroes and after drawing their next match in the group against the Cook Islands there was the very real prospect of qualifying for the main group stage of the Oceania qualifiers for Brazil. In their final match, against group hosts Samoa, the American Samoans hung on until the 89th minute before conceding the goal that meant they finished second in the group and missed out on what would have surely been the most extraordinary story of the year. There had been little hint of what was to come in the World Cup qualifiers when two months previously American Samoa had come away from the football tournament of the Pacific Games empty handed, finishing bottom of their group without having scored a goal and having let in 26. Prior to their historic win, the national team had played 32 matches - of which two were unofficial - scoring just 12 goals and conceding a spectacular 243.

FIFA WORLD CUP RECORD
1930-1998 DNE **2002-2014** DNQ

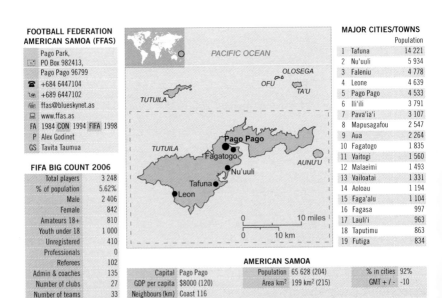

FOOTBALL FEDERATION AMERICAN SAMOA (FFAS)

Pago Park,
PO Box 982413,
Pago Pago 96799
☎ +684 6447104
📠 +689 6447102
📧 ffas@blueskynet.as
🖥 www.ffas.as
FA 1984 CON 1994 FIFA 1998
P Alex Godinet
GS Tavita Taumua

FIFA BIG COUNT 2006

Total players	3 248
% of population	5.62%
Male	2 406
Female	842
Amateurs 18+	810
Youth under 18	1 000
Unregistered	410
Professionals	0
Referees	102
Admin & coaches	135
Number of clubs	27
Number of teams	33

MAJOR CITIES/TOWNS

		Population
1	Tafuna	14 221
2	Nu'uuli	5 934
3	Faleniu	4 778
4	Leone	4 639
5	Pago Pago	4 533
6	Ili'ili	3 791
7	Pava'ia'i	3 107
8	Mapusagafou	2 547
9	Aua	2 264
10	Fagatogo	1 835
11	Vaitogi	1 560
12	Malaeimi	1 493
13	Vailoatai	1 331
14	Aoloau	1 194
15	Faga'alu	1 104
16	Fagasa	997
17	Lauli'i	963
18	Taputimu	863
19	Futiga	834

AMERICAN SAMOA

Capital	Pago Pago	
GDP per capita	$8000 (120)	
Neighbours (km)	Coast 116	
Population	65 628 (204)	
Area km²	199 km² (215)	
% in cities	92%
GMT + / -	-10

INTERNATIONALS PLAYED BY AMERICAN SAMOA

1994	Opponents	Score		Venue	Comp	Scorers	Att	Referee
24-11	Samoa	L	1-3	Apia	ONCq			
25-11	Tahiti	L	1-2	Apia	ONCq			
28-11	Tonga	L	1-2	Apia	ONCq			
1995-1997								
No international matches played between 1995 & 1997								
1998								
2-09	Tonga	L	0-3	Rarotonga	ONCq			
3-09	Cook Islands	L	3-4	Rarotonga	ONCq			
7-09	Tahiti	L	0-12	Rarotonga	ONCq			
8-09	Samoa	L	0-4	Rarotonga	ONCq			
1999								
No international matches played in 1999								
2000								
8-06	Tahiti	L	0-18	Papeete	ONCq			
12-06	Cook Islands	L	0-3	Papeete	ONCq			
14-06	Samoa	L	1-6	Papeete	ONCq			
16-06	Tonga	L	1-2	Papeete	ONCq			
2001								
7-04	Fiji	L	0-13	Coffs Harbour	WCq			
9-04	Samoa	L	0-8	Coffs Harbour	WCq			
11-04	Australia	L	0-31	Coffs Harbour	WCq			
14-04	Tonga	L	0-5	Coffs Harbour	WCq			
2002								
9-03	New Caledonia †	L	0-10	Apia	ONCq			
12-03	Tonga	L	2-7	Apia	ONCq	Duane Atualevao [15], Savaliga Afu [70]		
14-03	Samoa	L	0-5	Apia	ONCq			
18-03	Papua New Guinea	L	0-7	Apia	ONCq			
2003								
No international matches played in 2003								
2004								
10-05	Samoa	L	0-4	Apia	WCq		500	Afu SOL
12-05	Vanuatu	L	1-9	Apia	WCq	Natia Natia [39]	400	Fox NZL
15-05	Fiji	L	0-11	Apia	WCq		300	Fox NZL
17-05	Papua New Guinea	L	0-10	Apia	WCq		150	Afu SOL
2005-2006								
No international matches played in 2005 or 2006								
2007								
25-08	Solomon Islands	L	1-12	Apia	WCq	Ramin Ott [55p]	300	Sosongan PNG
27-08	Samoa	L	0-7	Apia	WCq		2 800	Minan PNG
29-08	Vanuatu	L	0-15	Apia	WCq		200	Hester NZL
1-09	Tonga	L	0-4	Apia	WCq		200	Minan PNG
2008-2010								
No international matches played between 2008 & 2010								
2011								
27-08	Tuvalu †	L	0-4	Noumea	PGr1			Jacques TAH
30-08	Solomon Islands	L	0-4	Noumea	PGr1			Jacques TAH
1-09	Guam	L	0-2	Noumea	PGr1			George VAN
3-09	New Caledonia	L	0-8	Noumea	PGr1			Varman FIJ
5-09	Vanuatu	L	0-4	Noumea	PGr1			Achari FIJ
22-11	Tonga	W	2-1	Apia	WCq	Ramin Ott [43], Shalom Luani [74]	150	Achari FIJ
24-11	Cook Islands	D	1-1	Apia	WCq	Shalom Luani [24]	300	George VAN
26-11	Samoa	L	0-1	Apia	WCq		800	O'Leary NZL

WC = FIFA World Cup • ON = OFC Nations Cup • PG = Pacific Games • q = qualifier • † Unofficial match as opponents were not members of FIFA

AMERICAN SAMOA NATIONAL TEAM HISTORICAL RECORDS

Coach: Anthony Langkilde 2001 • Tunoa Lui 2001-02 • Ian Crook ENG 2004 • Nathan Mease 2007 • David Brand ENG 2007-10 • Iofi Lalogafuafua 2011 • Thomas Rongen NED 2011

ATG – ANTIGUA AND BARBUDA

FIFA/COCA-COLA WORLD RANKING

'93	'94	'95	'96	'97	'98	'99	'00	'01	'02	'03	'04	'05	'06	'07	'08	'09	'10	'11	'12
117	136	137	145	159	137	147	144	157	155	170	153	154	132	151	128	130	106	87	

					2011								High	Low	Av
Jan	Feb	Mar	Apr	May	Jun	Jul	Aug	Sep	Oct	Nov	Dec			
103	104	101	100	100	111	106	106	101	90	83	87	83	170	139

The national team of Antigua and Barbuda is steadily building a strong reputation amongst the smaller Caribbean islands and having impressed in 2010 with qualification for the finals of the Caribbean Cup, they did even better in 2011. By the end of the year they were one of just 12 of the 35 CONCACAF nations left in the 2014 FIFA World Cup qualifiers and had scored more goals on the road to Brazil than any nation anywhere else in the world. After receiving a bye to the first group stage, the Antiguans demolished Curacao 5-2 in their opening match before beating the US Virgin Islands 8-1 away from home. That was just one goal short of a record score for the team but following a key 1-0 win away to Curacao, they did set a new record in the return against the USVI - a 10-0 thrashing before an ecstatic home crowd in St John's. That left two deciding games against group favourites Haiti but a 1-0 win at home in the first saw Antigua through to the next round. 2012 is likely to be more of a challenge, however, having been drawn in the same group as the USA, Jamaica and Guatemala. Club football continues to thrive at home with Parham winning their first championship since 2003. 2010 champions Bassa had been due to take part in the 2011 CFU club championship but pulled out of their tie with Guyana's Alpha United.

FIFA WORLD CUP RECORD
1930-1970 DNE 1974 DNQ 1978-1982 DNE 1986-2010 DNQ

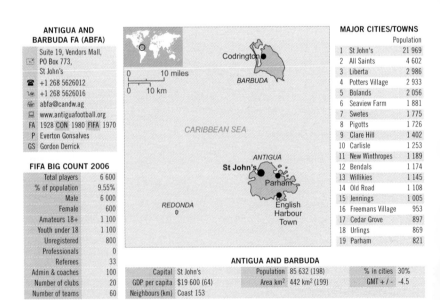

ANTIGUA AND BARBUDA FA (ABFA)

Suite 19, Vendors Mall,
PO Box 773,
St John's

☎ +1 268 5626012
📠 +1 268 5626016
✉ abfa@candw.ag
🖥 www.antiguafootball.org
FA 1928 CON 1980 FIFA 1970
P Everton Gonsalves
GS Gordon Derrick

FIFA BIG COUNT 2006

Total players	6 600
% of population	9.55%
Male	6 000
Female	600
Amateurs 18+	1 100
Youth under 18	1 100
Unregistered	800
Professionals	0
Referees	33
Admin & coaches	100
Number of clubs	20
Number of teams	60

MAJOR CITIES/TOWNS

		Population
1	St John's	21 969
2	All Saints	4 602
3	Liberta	2 986
4	Potters Village	2 933
5	Bolands	2 056
6	Seaview Farm	1 881
7	Swetes	1 775
8	Pigotts	1 726
9	Clare Hill	1 402
10	Carlisle	1 253
11	New Winthropes	1 189
12	Bendals	1 174
13	Willikies	1 145
14	Old Road	1 108
15	Jennings	1 005
16	Freemans Village	953
17	Cedar Grove	897
18	Urlings	869
19	Parham	821

ANTIGUA AND BARBUDA

Capital	St John's	Population	85 632 (198)	% in cities 30%
GDP per capita	$19 600 (64)	Area km²	442 km² (199)	GMT +/- -4.5
Neighbours (km)	Coast 153		

RECENT INTERNATIONALS PLAYED BY ANTIGUA AND BARBUDA

2010	Opponents	Score	Venue	Comp	Scorers	Att	Referee
23-09	St Lucia	W 5-0	St John's	Fr	Randolph Burton 2 [17 55], Peter Byers 2 [45 67], Jamie Thomas 75	500	Willett ATG
10-11	Suriname	W 2-1	St John's	CCq	Randolph Burton [18], Justin Cochrane [64]	2 000	Morrison JAM
12-11	Dominica	D 0-0	St John's	CCq		400	Purser JAM
14-11	Cuba	D 0-0	St John's	CCq		500	Campbell JAM
27-11	Jamaica	L 1-3	Riviere-Pilote	CCr1	Gayson Gregory [49]	3 000	Wijngaarde SUR
29-11	Guyana	W 1-0	Riviere-Pilote	CCr1	Gayson Gregory [69]	3 000	Wijngaarde SUR
1-12	Guadeloupe †	L 0-1	Riviere-Pilote	CCr1		3 000	Lopez GUA
2011							
27-05	Grenada	D 2-2	St George's	Fr	Randolph Burton [51], Kimoi Alexander [73]	3 500	Bedeau GRN
26-08	St Vincent/Grenadines	W 1-0	St John's	Fr	Kerry Skepple [11]	2 000	Willett ATG
28-08	St Vincent/Grenadines	D 2-2	St John's	Fr	George Dublin [45], Jamie Thomas [89]	2 500	Charles ATG
2-09	Curacao	W 5-2	St John's	WCq	Marc Joseph [42], Quinton Griffith [45], Tamarley Thomas [54], Peter Byers 2 [75 80]	2 000	Santos PUR
6-09	US Virgin Islands	W 8-1	Fredericksted	WCq	Ranja Christian [18], Peter Byers 3 [38p 51 57], Justin Cochrane [47], George Dublin [54], Randolph Burton 2 [68 74]	250	Lancaster GUY
7-10	Curacao	W 1-0	Willemstad	WCq	Tamarley Thomas [73]	2 563	Reyna GUA
11-10	US Virgin Islands	W 10-0	St John's	WCq	Tamarley Thomas 3 [7 41 78], Peter Byers 3 [24 31 40], Randolph Burton 2 [55 65], Jamie Thomas [86], Keiran Murtagh [92+]	1 500	Matthew SKN
11-11	Haiti	W 1-0	St John's	WCq	Kerry Skepple [81]	8 000	Pineda HON
15-11	Haiti	L 1-2	Port-au-Prince	WCq	Tamarley Thomas [10]	3 000	Toledo USA

Fr = Friendly match • CC = Digicel Caribbean Cup • WC = FIFA World Cup • q = qualifier • † Not an official FIFA international

ANTIGUA AND BARBUDA NATIONAL TEAM HISTORICAL RECORDS

Coach: Rolston Williams 2004 • Vernon Edwards 2004-05 • Derrick Edwards 2005-08 • Rowan Benjamin 2008-11 • Tom Curtis ENG 2011-

MEDALS TABLE

		Overall G	Lge G	Cup G
1	Empire	13	13	
2	Bassa	7	5	2
3	Sap	4	2	2
	Lion Hill	4	4	
	Parham (incl J & J)	4	4	
6	English Harbour	3	3	
7	Villa Lions	2	2	
	Liberta	2	2	
9	Five Islands	1	1	
	Golden Stars	1	1	
	Freemansville	1		1

ANTIGUA AND BARBUDA 2010-11

DIGICEL, HADEED AND OBSERVER GROUP PREMIER DIVISION

	Pl	W	D	L	F	A	Pts	Parham	Hoppers	Old Road	Empire	Bassa	Sea View	All Saints	Sap	Villa Lions	Smitty
Parham	18	12	2	4	49	17	**38**		1-0	4-0	6-0	3-3	0-1	0-2	5-1	0-0	3-1
Hoppers	18	11	2	5	33	25	**35**	0-1		3-1	2-0	2-1	1-1	1-0	5-2	2-1	4-0
Old Road	18	9	5	4	30	18	**32**	2-1	4-1		0-0	1-2	1-1	3-0	0-1	2-0	0-0
Empire	18	7	3	8	31	34	**24**	1-5	6-1	0-3		4-0	1-2	3-1	1-2	0-2	2-1
Bassa	18	5	8	5	32	30	**23**	1-4	3-3	1-1	3-3		2-3	1-3	3-0	0-0	0-0
Sea View Farm	18	5	8	5	21	22	**23**	2-4	0-1	0-1	1-3	2-2		0-0	2-1	2-0	1-1
All Saints United	18	6	4	8	33	33	**22**	3-1	2-3	1-2	3-4	0-3	1-1		2-2	4-0	4-1
Sap	18	6	4	8	25	39	**22**	0-5	1-0	1-3	2-0	1-1	1-1	3-1		0-3	2-2
Villa Lions	18	5	5	8	19	22	**20**	0-2	0-1	1-1	0-0	1-3	1-1	2-3	3-0		2-1
Smitty	18	1	5	12	16	49	**8**	1-5	1-3	1-5	0-3	0-4	1-0	3-3	2-5	0-3	

19/09/2010 - 20/02/2011 • Promotion/relegation play-offs: Potters 0-0 SAP; Swetes 1-2 Potters; SAP 9-0 Swetes. SAP remain in Premier Division. Willikies and Bullets ptomoted automatically

AUS – AUSTRALIA

FIFA/COCA-COLA WORLD RANKING

'93	'94	'95	'96	'97	'98	'99	'00	'01	'02	'03	'04	'05	'06	'07	'08	'09	'10	'11	'12
49	58	51	50	35	39	89	73	48	50	82	58	48	39	48	28	21	26	23	

2011														
Jan	Feb	Mar	Apr	May	Jun	Jul	Aug	Sep	Oct	Nov	Dec	High	Low	Av
26	21	20	20	20	22	22	22	19	20	22	23	14	92	47

Brisbane Roar powered to a first national title in 2011, winning the A-League in sensational style. Coached by Ange Postecoglou, Roar lost just once all season and finished the campaign on an 28-game unbeaten run but it was the manner of their victory in the Grand Final that really caught the imagination of the public. Trailing 2-0 with just three minutes of extra-time remaining, Roar somehow managed to conjure up two goals through Henrique and Erik Paartalu to take the final to penalties, which they then won. The exciting climax to the season did, however, mask some worrying concerns over the financial health of the league - notably the collapse of Townsville-based North Queensland Fury - with the failure to win the hosting rights for the 2022 World Cup adding to the sense of gloom in Australian football as a successful bid was seen as a crucial platform for raising the profile of the game. On the pitch the Socceroos continue to make their presence felt in Asian football and after finishing as runners-up at the 2011 AFC Asian Cup at the start of the year they then got their qualifying campaign for the 2014 FIFA World Cup off to a comfortable start. Holger Osieck's men qualified for the second group stage by winning their first round group stage, a 3-1 win away to Saudi Arabia ensuring they took control of the group early on.

FIFA WORLD CUP RECORD
1930-1962 DNE **1966-1970** DNQ **1974** 14 r1 **1978-2002** DNQ **2006** 16 r2 **2010** 21 r1

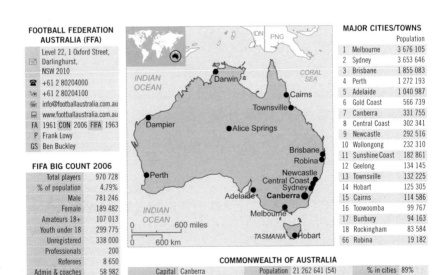

FOOTBALL FEDERATION AUSTRALIA (FFA)

Level 22, 1 Oxford Street,
Darlinghurst,
NSW 2010
☎ +61 2 80204000
📠 +61 2 80204100
✉ info@footballaustralia.com.au
🖥 www.footballaustralia.com.au
FA 1961 CON 2006 FIFA 1963
P Frank Lowy
GS Ben Buckley

FIFA BIG COUNT 2006

Total players	970 728
% of population	4.79%
Male	781 246
Female	189 482
Amateurs 18+	107 013
Youth under 18	299 775
Unregistered	338 000
Professionals	200
Referees	8 650
Admin & coaches	58 982
Number of clubs	2 316
Number of teams	20 018

MAJOR CITIES/TOWNS

		Population
1	Melbourne	3 676 105
2	Sydney	3 653 646
3	Brisbane	1 855 083
4	Perth	1 272 193
5	Adelaide	1 040 987
6	Gold Coast	566 739
7	Canberra	331 755
8	Central Coast	302 341
9	Newcastle	292 516
10	Wollongong	232 310
11	Sunshine Coast	182 861
12	Geelong	134 145
13	Townsville	132 225
14	Hobart	125 305
15	Cairns	114 586
16	Toowoomba	99 767
17	Bunbury	94 163
18	Rockingham	83 584
66	Robina	19 182

COMMONWEALTH OF AUSTRALIA

Capital	Canberra	Population	21 262 641 (54)	% in cities	89%
GDP per capita	$38 100 (25)	Area km²	7 741 220 km² (6)	GMT +/-	+10
Neighbours (km)	Coast 25 760				

RECENT INTERNATIONALS PLAYED BY AUSTRALIA

2009	Opponents	Score		Venue	Comp	Scorers	Att	Referee
12-08	Republic of Ireland	W	3-0	Limerick	Fr	Cahill 2 [38 44], Carney [90]	19 000	Perez ESP
5-09	Korea Republic	L	1-3	Seoul	Fr	Kisnorbo [33]	40 215	Mohd Salleh MAS
10-10	Netherlands	D	0-0	Sydney	Fr		40 537	Minoru JPN
14-10	Oman	W	1-0	Melbourne	ACq	Cahill [73]	20 595	Maasaki JPN
14-11	Oman	W	2-1	Muscat	ACq	Wilkshire [43], Emerton [83]	12 000	Sun Baojie CHN
2010								
6-01	Kuwait	D	2-2	Kuwait City	ACq	Wilkshire [3], Heffernan [5]	20 000	Irmatov UZB
3-03	Indonesia	W	1-0	Brisbane	ACq	Milligan [42]	20 422	Ogiya JPN
24-05	New Zealand	W	2-1	Melbourne	Fr	Vidosic [57], Holman [90]	55 659	Salazar USA
1-06	Denmark	W	1-0	Roodepoort	Fr	Kennedy [71]	5 000	Bennet RSA
5-06	USA	L	1-3	Roodepoort	Fr	Cahill [19]	6 000	Ebrahim RSA
13-06	Germany	L	0-4	Durban	WCr1		62 660	Rodriguez MEX
19-06	Ghana	D	1-1	Rustenburg	WCr1	Holman [11]	34 812	Rosetti ITA
23-06	Serbia	W	2-1	Nelspruit	WCr1	Cahill [69], Holman [73]	37 836	Larrionda URU
11-08	Slovenia	L	0-2	Ljubljana	Fr		16 135	Tagliavento ITA
3-09	Switzerland	D	0-0	St Gall	Fr		14 660	Einwaller AUT
7-09	Poland	W	2-1	Krakow	Fr	Holman [15], Wilkshire [26p]	17 000	Bebek CRO
9-10	Paraguay	W	1-0	Sydney	Fr	Carney [53]	25 210	Nishimura JPN
17-11	Egypt	L	0-3	Cairo	Fr			Genov BUL
2011								
5-01	UAE	D	0-0	Al Ain	Fr		13 300	Shaban KUW
10-01	India	W	4-0	Doha	ACr1	Cahill 2 [12 65], Kewell [25], Holman [45]	9 783	Albadwawi UAE
14-01	Korea Republic	D	1-1	Doha	ACr1	Jedinak [62]	15 526	Abdou QAT
18-01	Bahrain	W	1-0	Doha	ACr1	Jedinak [37]	3 919	Nishimura JPN
22-01	Iraq	W	1-0	Doha	ACqf	Kewell [118]	7 889	Abdou QAT
25-01	Uzbekistan	W	6-0	Doha	ACsf	Kewell [5], Ognenovski [35], Carney [65], Emerton [73], Valeri [82], Kruse [83]	24 826	Albadwawi UAE
29-01	Japan	L	0-1	Doha	ACf		37 174	Irmatov UZB
29-03	Germany	W	2-1	Monchengladbach	Fr	Carney [61], Wilkshire [64p]	30 152	Lannoy FRA
5-06	New Zealand	W	3-0	Adelaide	Fr	Kennedy 2 [10 59], Troisi [90p]	21 281	Tojo JPN
7-06	Serbia	D	0-0	Melbourne	Fr		28 149	Tojo JPN
10-08	Wales	W	2-1	Cardiff	Fr	Cahill [43], Kruse [60]	6 378	Tohver EST
2-09	Thailand	W	2-1	Brisbane	WCq	Kennedy [58], Brosque [86]	24 540	Balideh QAT
6-09	Saudi Arabia	W	3-1	Dammam	WCq	Kennedy 2 [40 56], Wilkshire [77p]	15 000	Nishimura JPN
7-10	Malaysia	W	5-0	Canberra	Fr	Wilkshire [3], Kennedy 2 [33 45], Brosque 2 [39 69]	10 041	Lee Min Hu KOR
11-10	Oman	W	3-0	Sydney	WCq	Holman [8], Kennedy [65], Jedinak [85]	24 732	Kovalenko UZB
11-11	Oman	L	0-1	Muscat	WCq		4 500	Abdulnabi BHR
15-11	Thailand	W	1-0	Bangkok	WCq	Holman [77]	19 400	Mozaffari IRN

Fr = Friendly match • AC = AFC Asian Cup • WC = FIFA World Cup
q = qualifier • r1 = first round group • qf = quarter-final • sf = semi-final • f = final

AUSTRALIA NATIONAL TEAM HISTORICAL RECORDS

Caps

94 - Mark Schwarzer 1993- • 91 - Brett Emerton 1998- • 87 - Alex Tobin 1988-98 • 84 - Paul Wade 1986-96 • 79 - Lucas Neill 1996- • 76 - Tony Vidmar 1991-2006 • 68 - Scott Chipperfield 1998- • 65 - Luke Wilkshire 2005- • 64 - Peter Wilson 1970-79 • 61 - Attila Abonyi 1967-77 • 60 - John Kosmina 1976-88 & Stan Lazaridis 1993-2006

Goals

29 - Damian Mori 1992-2002 • 27 - John Aloisi 1997-2008 • 25 - John Kosmina 1976-88 & Attila Abonyi 1967-77 • 24 - Tim Cahill 2004- • 21 - Archie Thompson 2001- • 20 - David Zdrilic 1997-2005 • 19 - Graham Arnold 1985-97 • 18 - Ray Baartz 1967-74 & Brett Emerton 1998- • 17 - Gary Cole 1978-82 & Aurelio Vidmar 1991-2001

Past Coaches

Tiko Jelisavcic YUG 1965 • Jozef Venglos CZE 1965-67 • Joe Vlatsis YUG 1967-69 • Rale Rasic YUG 1970-74 • Brian Green ENG 1976 • Jim Shoulder ENG 1976-78 • Rudi Gutendorf GER 1979-81 • Les Scheinflug 1981-83 • Frank Arok YUG 1983-89 • Eddie Thomson SCO 1990-96 • Raul Blanco 1996 • Terry Venables ENG 1997-98 • Raul Blanco 1998-99 • Frank Farina 1999-2005 • Guus Hiddink NED 2005-06 • Graham Arnold 2006-07 • Pim Verbeek NED 2007-10 • Holger Osieck GER 2010-

AUSTRALIA 2010-11

HYUNDAI A-LEAGUE

	Pl	W	D	L	F	A	Pts	Brisbane	Mariners	Adelaide	Gold Coast	Victory	Wellington	Newcastle	Heart	Sydney	Perth	Fury
Brisbane Roar †	30	18	11	1	58	26	**65**		2-0	1-1 4-0	2-2 4-0	2-1	1-0 2-0	1-1	4-0 2-1	**1-0**	3-2 1-1	1-1
Central Coast Mariners†	30	16	9	5	50	31	**57**	1-5 3-3		1-1 2-0	2-3	2-0 1-2	1-0	1-0	4-0 2-2	5-0	3-2 1-0	
Adelaide United ‡	30	15	5	10	51	36	**50**	0-1	1-2		2-1	2-1	3-0 0-1 0-0	2-1 3-2 1-2	2-0	2-0 2-0	2-0 8-1	
Gold Coast United ‡	30	12	10	8	40	32	**46**	0-0	0-0 1-3 0-0-0-0			0-1	3-1 2-0 1-0 5-1	3-0	3-1	0-0	. 1-2 4-0	
Melbourne Victory ‡	30	11	10	9	45	39	**43**	3-0 3-3	2-2 2-1 1-4 0-1 2-0				0-0	2-1 2-0	2-2	3-0	0-2 2-0	2-2
Wellington Phoenix ‡	30	12	5	13	39	41	**41**	1-4	2-0 0-3	2-1	3-3	2-2 2-0		4-0 1-0 2-2 2-0	2-1	4-0	2-1 3-1	
Newcastle Jets	30	9	8	13	29	33	**35**	0-0 1-1 1-1 0-2	3-1	2-0	0-0	1-0			1-1 0-2 1-2 1-1-2-0 4-0		1-0	1-0
Melbourne Heart	30	8	11	11	32	42	**35**	1-2	0-1 1-1	0-2	0-0 1-1 2-1 1-3	2-1	0-2	.		0-0 2-2	2-2	1-0 2-0
Sydney FC	30	8	10	12	35	40	**34**	1-1 0-1	1-1	1-3 1-2 1-1-2-0	3-3 1-1 3-1	1-0	1-0	0-1			2-0	1-1
Perth Glory	30	5	8	17	27	54	**23**	1-2	1-1 1-2	4-2	0-1 1-2	3-1	2-1 0-1	1-0	0-0 1-1 0-3 0-2			3-3
North Queensland Fury	30	4	7	19	28	60	**19**	0-2 1-2	0-1	2-3	1-2	0-0 0-3	1-1	0-2 1-2	2-3	2-1 1-0 2-1	1-1	

5/08/2010 - 13/02/2011 • † Qualified for the Major Semi-final • ‡ Qualified for the play-off first round • Top scorers: **16** - Sergio van Dijk NED, Adelaide United • **12** - Kosta Barbarouses, Brisbane Roar • **11** - Matt Simon, Central Coast; Jean Carlos Solorzano CRC, Brisbane Roar; Robbie Kruse, Melbourne Victory & Adam Kwasnik, Central Coast • Brisbane Roar and Central Coast Mariners qualified for the 2012 AFC Champions League

A-LEAGUE FINALS SERIES

First Round					
Gold Coast United	1				
Melbourne Victory	0	**Minor Semi-final**			
		Gold Coast United	3		
		Adelaide United	2		
Wellington Phoenix	0				
Adelaide United	1				

Major Semi-final		
Brisbane Roar	2	2
Central Coast Mariners	0	2

Grand Final		
Brisbane Roar	2	4p
Central Coast Mariners	2	2p

Preliminary Final		
Gold Coast United	1	2
Central Coast Mariners	2	2

18/02/2010 - 13/03/2011 • The loser of the Major Semi-final meets the winner of the Minor Semi-final in the Preliminary Final • The winners of the Major Semi-final and the Preliminary Final meet in the Grand Final

GRAND FINAL 2011

Suncorp Stadium, Brisbane, 13-03-2011, 16:00, Att: 50 168, Ref: Breeze

Brisbane Roar	2 4p	Henrique [117], Paartalu [120]
Central Coast Mariners	2 2p	Kwasnik [96], Bozanic [103]

Brisbane - Michael Theoklitos - Ivan Franjic, Matt Smith, Milan Susak (Rocky Visconte 102), Shane Stefanutto - Erik Paartalu - Mitch Nichols (Massimo Murdocca 82), Matt McKay (c) - Kosta Barbarouses (Henrique 71), Jean Carlos Solorzano, Thomas Broich. Tr: Ange Postecoglou
Central Coast - Matthew Ryan - Pedj Bojic, Alex Wilkinson (c), Patrick Zwaanswijk, Joshua Rose - Rostyn Griffiths - Michael McGlinchey, Oliver Bozanic - Mustafa Amini - Matt Simon, Adam Kwasnik. Tr: Graham Arnold

GRAND FINAL PENALTY SHOOT-OUT

Central Coast		Brisbane	
✓	Hutchinson		
		Franjic	✓
✓	Wilkinson		
		Paartalu	✓
✗[1]	McBreen		
		McKay	✓
✗[1]	Bojic		
		Henrique	✓

1 = saved

MEDALS TABLE

		Overall			A-Lge			Asia			City/Town
		G	S	B	G	S	B	G	S	B	
1	Melbourne Victory	2	1		2	1					Melbourne
2	Sydney FC	2			2						Sydney
3	Brisbane Roar	1			1						Brisbane
	Newcastle Jets	1			1						Newcastle
5	Adelaide United		3			2			1		Adelaide
	Central Coast Mariners		3			3					Gosford
7	Gold Coast United										Gold Coast
	Melbourne Heart										Melbourne
	Perth Glory										Perth
	Wellington Phoenix										Wellington
		6	7		6	6			1		

MEDALS TABLE PRE A-LEAGUE

		Overall			League			Cup		CL	ST	
		G	S	B	G	S	B	G	S	G	G	City
1	Sydney City	7	4	1	4	3	1	3	1		5	Sydney
2	South Melbourne	7	3	2	4	2	2	2	1	1	7	Melbourne
3	Adelaide City	7	3		3	2		3	1	1	12	Adelaide
4	Marconi Stallions	5	6		4	3		1	3			Sydney
5	Sydney Olympic	4	6		2	4		2	2			Sydney
6	APIA Leichhardt Tigers	4	3		1			3	3		4	Sydney
7	Melbourne Knights	3	4		2	3		1	1		1	Melbourne
8	Wollongong City Wolves	3	1		2	1				1		Wollongong
9	Heidelberg United	2	6	1	2	1		2	4		1	Melbourne
10	Perth Glory	2	2		2	2						Perth
11	Parramatta Eagles	2	1					2	1			Sydney
	Brisbane City	2	1					1	2			Brisbane
13	Sydney United	1	4		3			1	1			Sydney

League = League championship 1977-2004 • Cup = Cup tournament 1962-77 • CL = OFC Champions Cup • ST = State Championship pre 1977

CLUB BY CLUB GUIDE TO THE 2010–11 SEASON IN AUSTRALIA

ADELAIDE UNITED 2010–11

Mon	Date	Opponent	Res	Score	Comp	Scorers	Att
Aug	6	Newcastle	D	0-0	AL		8 479
Aug	15	Cent. Coast	D	1-1	AL	Fyfe 45	8 447
Aug	20	Mel. Heart	W	3-2	AL	Leckie 3, Ramsay 2 53 88	**7 370**
Aug	28	NQ Fury	W	3-2	AL	Flores 22, Studman 50, Mullen 57	6 130
Sep	4	Sydney	W	3-1	AL	Van Dijk 2 9 53, Leckie 37	7 558
Sep	11	Newcastle	W	2-1	AL	Leckie 23, Flores 66	9 571
Sep	18	Brisbane	D	1-1	AL	Leckie 28	7 080
Sep	24	Perth	W	2-0	AL	Van Dijk 2 70 73	13 310
Oct	4	Sydney	W	2-1	AL	OG 56, Ramsay 90	7 071
Oct	17	Gold Coast	D	0-0	AL		2 389
Oct	22	Wellington	W	3-0	AL	Van Dijk 70, Flores 72, Dodd 76	11 206
Oct	29	Melbourne V	L	1-2	AL	Fyfe 1	16 269
Nov	6	Brisbane	L	0-4	AL		13 248
Nov	10	Perth	W	2-0	AL	Fyfe 64, Van Dijk 90	10 023
Nov	13	Newcastle	L	1-3	AL	Fyfe 78	8 278
Nov	19	Mel. Heart	W	2-0	AL	Cornthwaite 5, Flores 73	6 538
Nov	26	Gold Coast	W	2-1	AL	Reid 10, Dodd 48	12 005
Dec	5	Wellington	L	1-2	AL	Van Dijk 14	14 108
Dec	10	NQ Fury	W	2-0	AL	Flores 5, Van Dijk 16	8 786
Dec	17	Mel. Heart	L	1-2	AL	Van Dijk 45	10 011
Dec	22	Perth	L	2-4	AL	Keenan 22, Van Dijk 51	7 193
Dec	26	Cent. Coast	L	0-2	AL		6 249
Dec	29	Sydney	W	2-0	AL	Van Dijk 35, OG 58	16 429
Jan	2	Brisbane	L	0-1	AL		14 420
Jan	9	Melbourne V	W	4-1	AL	Flores 12, Van Dijk 2 12 78, Barbiero 74	18 558
Jan	21	NQ Fury	W	8-1	AL	Flores 3 4 37 89, Dodd 28, Ramsay 42, Van Dijk 3 47 67 89	10 986
Jan	29	Cent. Coast	L	1-2	AL	Dodd 90	12 109
Feb	2	Gold Coast	D	0-0	AL		2 138
Feb	5	Wellington	L	0-1	AL		7 498
Feb	11	Melbourne V	W	2-1	AL	Reid 6, Dodd 78	21 083
Feb	18	Wellington	W	1-0	ALrl	Dodd 70	10 825
Feb	27	Cent. Coast	L	2-3	ALms	Van Dijk 56p, Leckie 70	15 028

3rd Att: 199 139 • Av: 11 714 (+8.8%) • Hindmarsh 17 000 (68%)

BRISBANE ROAR 2010–11

Mon	Date	Opponent	Res	Score	Comp	Scorers	Att
Aug	8	Gold Coast	D	0-0	AL		6 394
Aug	21	Sydney	W	1-0	AL	McKay 53	10 339
Aug	27	Wellington	W	1-0	AL	Barbarouses 73	7 339
Sep	5	Newcastle	D	0-0	AL		7 066
Sep	12	Melbourne V	L	0-3	AL		13 792
Sep	18	Adelaide	D	1-1	AL	Broich 35	7 080
Sep	25	Mel. Heart	W	4-0	AL	Barbarouses 24, Paartalu 38, Reinaldo 47p, Nichols 76	6 342
Oct	3	Perth	W	2-1	AL	Reinaldo 1, Visconte 90	9 758
Oct	16	Newcastle	D	1-1	AL	Reinaldo 77	10 191
Oct	20	Cent. Coast	W	2-0	AL	Broich 21, Franjic 61	5 051
Oct	23	Melbourne V	W	2-1	AL	Nichols 26, Solorzano 77	9 425
Oct	30	Sydney	D	1-1	AL	DeVere 7	10 744
Nov	3	Wellington	W	4-1	AL	Barbarouses 4, Broich 44, Murdocca 76, Nichols 90	5 529
Nov	4	Adelaide	W	4-0	AL	Reinaldo 43, Smith 55, Barbarouses 2 62 66	13 248
Nov	14	Mel. Heart	W	2-1	AL	Barbarouses 65, Solorzano 88	7 034
Nov	17	Newcastle	D	1-1	AL	Solorzano 79	7 829
Nov	20	NQ Fury	D	1-1	AL	Franjic 85	10 126
Nov	24	Perth	W	3-2	AL	Solorzano 2 41 76p, Smith 57	6 836
Nov	28	Cent. Coast	W	5-1	AL	Solorzano 2 8 10, Nichols 24, Reinaldo 87, OG 89	5 858
Dec	3	Melbourne V	D	3-3	AL	OG 30, Solorzano 45, McKay 90	11 886
Dec	12	Sydney	W	1-0	AL	Barbarouses 41	7 554
Dec	18	NQ Fury	W	2-0	AL	Barbarouses 2 6 75	4 412
Dec	26	Gold Coast	D	2-2	AL	Barbarouses 30, Solorzano 66p	13 065
Jan	2	Adelaide	W	1-0	AL	Solorzano 69	14 420
Jan	7	Perth	D	1-1	AL	Nichols 63	11 574
Jan	12	Cent. Coast	D	3-3	AL	Paartalu 23, Broich 65, Meyer 79	7 312
Jan	18	Wellington	W	2-0	AL	Meyer 2 84 88	**3 522**
Jan	29	Mel. Heart	W	2-1	AL	Solorzano 5, Meyer 62	4 213
Feb	8	NQ Fury	W	2-1	AL	Nichols 14, Henrique 58	1 033
Feb	12	Gold Coast	W	4-0	AL	Barbarouses 3, Paartalu 42, Henrique 65, Broich 85	20 831
Feb	19	Cent. Coast	D	0-0	ALsf	Barbarouses 52, McKay 72	10 166
Feb	26	Cent. Coast	D	2-2	ALsf	Broich 63, Henrique 90	25 168
Ma	13	Cent. Coast	D	2-2	ALf	W 4-2p.Henrique 117, Paartalu 2	**50 168**

1st Att: 214 518 • Av: 12 618 (+45.8%) • Suncorp 52 500 (24%)

ADELAIDE LEAGUE APPEARANCES/GOALS 2010-11
Goalkeepers Mark Birighitti 3 • Eugene Galekovic 27
Defenders Dario Bodrusic CRO 2/0 • Nigel Boogaard 9+1/0
Cassio BRA 28/0 • Robert Cornthwaite 17+7/1 • Iain Fyfe 28/4
Joe Keenan ENG 10+7/1 • Daniel Mullen 9+4/1 • Bradley Norton 0+2/0
Midfield Fabian Barbiero 10+6/1 • Travis Dodd 13+7/5 • Marcos
Flores ARG 27/9 • Adam Hughes 28+1/0 • Mathew Leckie 11+2/4
Osama Malik 0+1/0 • Matthew Mullen 0+1/0 • Lucas Pantelis 18+8/0
Iain Ramsay 14+16/4 • Paul Reid 25+4/2 • Shin In Seob KOR 2+6/0
Francisco Usucar URU 6/0 • Cameron Watson 16+10/0
Forwards Francesco Monterosso 0+2/0 • Andwele Slory NED 1+2/0
Sergio van Dijk NED 28/16
Coach Rini Coolen NED (5-07-2010)

BRISBANE LEAGUE APPEARANCES/GOALS 2010-11
Goalkeepers Andrew Redmayne 0+1 • Michael Theoklitos 33
Defenders Luke DeVere 20/1 • Ivan Franjic 21 ı 2/2
Matt Mundy 5+10/0 • Matt Smith 33/2 • Shane Stefanutto 22+1/0
Milan Susak 2+4/0
Midfield Luke Brattan 0+6/0 • Thomas Broich GER 32/6
Chris Bush 0+1/0 • Matt McKay 27/3 • James Meyer 2+2/4
Massimo Murdocca 18+9/1 • Mitch Nichols 21+11/6
Erik Paartalu 33/4 • Rocky Visconte 1+14/1
Forwards Kosta Barbarouses NZL 29+4/12 • Henrique BRA 7+7/4
Reinaldo BRA 13+5/5 • Jean Carlos Solorzano CRC 15+10/11
Coach Ange Postecoglou

CENTRAL COAST MARINERS 2010–11

Month	Date	Opponent	Res	Score	Comp	Scorers	Att
Aug	5	Mel. Heart	W	1-0	AL	Wilkinson 16	11 050
Aug	15	Adelaide	D	1-1	AL	Simon 86	8 447
Aug	22	Wellington	L	0-2	AL		9 553
Aug	28	Sydney	D	1-1	AL	Perez 73p	10 147
Sep	3	Melbourne V	W	2-0	AL	Griffiths 21, McBreen 50	6 829
Sep	10	Mel. Heart	W	1-0	AL	McBreen 20	6 326
Sep	19	Gold Coast	D	0-0	AL		2 037
Oct	2	NQ Fury	W	3-2	AL	Simon 47, Perez 57, Zwaanswijk 47	6 656
Oct	20	Brisbane	L	0-2	AL		5 051
Oct	30	Perth	W	5-0	AL	Griffiths 37, Simon 60, Kwasnik 78, Lewis 86, OG 90	10 746
Nov	5	NQ Fury	W	1-0	AL	Zwaanswijk 35	3 625
Nov	13	Wellington	W	3-0	AL	Rose 2 17 80, Kwasnik 86	5 778
Nov	18	Melbourne V	D	2-2	AL	McBreen 29, OG 78	9 674
Nov	21	Gold Coast	L	2-3	AL	Simon 42, Kwasnik 71	9 732
Nov	24	Newcastle	D	1-1	AL	Simon 49	7 730
Nov	28	Brisbane	L	1-5	AL	Kwasnik 50	5 858
Dec	4	Sydney	W	4-0	AL	Kwasnik 2 1 23, Simon 5, OG 46	7 160
Dec	12	Perth	D	1-1	AL	Zwaanswijk 87	6 536
Dec	22	NQ Fury	W	1-0	AL	Kwasnik 28	5 979
Dec	26	Adelaide	W	2-0	AL	Simon 50, OG 78	6 249
Dec	31	Melbourne V	L	1-2	AL	OG 48	12 409
Jan	9	Wellington	W	1-0	AL	McGlinchey 41	6 844
Jan	12	Brisbane	D	3-3	AL	Kwasnik 37, Simon 47, Perez 74p	7 312
Jan	16	Newcastle	W	2-0	AL	Simon 14, Hutchinson 87	13 463
Jan	19	Perth	W	2-1	AL	McBreen 22, Simon 23	6 828
Jan	23	Sydney	D	2-2	AL	Perez 49, Simon 57	10 546
Jan	29	Adelaide	W	2-1	AL	Perez 11, Rose 30	12 109
Feb	4	Mel. Heart	D	1-1	AL	McBreen 50	3 667
Feb	9	Gold Coast	W	3-1	AL	Ibini-Isei 13, Amini 40, Duke 68	2 037
Feb	13	Newcastle	W	1-0	AL	Perez 89	9 975
Feb	19	Brisbane	L	0-2	ALsf		10 166
Feb	26	Brisbane	D	2-2	ALsf	OG 39, Bozanic 40	25 168
Mar	5	Gold Coast	W	1-0	ALpf	Kwasnik 75	7 539
Mar	13	Brisbane	D	2-2	ALf	L 2-4p. Kwasnik 96, Bozanic 103	50 168
2nd		Att: 138 773 • Av: 8163 (+9.8%) • Bluetongue 20 119 (40%)					

GOLD COAST UNITED 2010–11

Month	Date	Opponent	Res	Score	Comp	Scorers	Att
Aug	8	Brisbane	D	0-0	AL		6 394
Aug	13	Wellington	D	3-3	AL	Smeltz 2 36 74, Culina 86	8 398
Aug	29	Melbourne V	L	0-1	AL		3 624
Sep	12	Perth	W	1-0	AL	Culina 23	10 450
Sep	19	Cent. Coast	D	0-0	AL		2 037
Sep	22	Newcastle	W	1-0	AL	Curtis 90	2 091
Sep	26	Sydney	D	1-1	AL	Djite 45	9 977
Oct	1	Wellington	W	3-1	AL	Djite 2 5 69, Brown 81	2 943
Oct	8	Adelaide	D	0-0	AL		2 389
Oct	23	Mel. Heart	D	0-0	AL		6 150
Oct	31	NQ Fury	W	2-1	AL	Traore 11, Djulbic 84	7 195
Nov	6	Melbourne V	W	1-0	AL	OG 55	15 534
Nov	12	Sydney	W	3-1	AL	Porter 2 14 54, Culina 44	2 536
Nov	21	Cent. Coast	W	3-2	AL	Djulbic 45, Pantelidis 69, Barisic 69	9 732
Nov	26	Adelaide	L	1-2	AL	Van den Brink 45	12 005
Dec	1	NQ Fury	L	1-2	AL	Robson 10	1 714
Dec	5	Mel. Heart	W	3-0	AL	Van den Brink 40, Culina 2 58 78	**1 658**
Dec	11	Wellington	W	2-0	AL	Van den Brink 21, Brown 66	1 716
Dec	15	Newcastle	L	0-2	AL		8 046
Dec	26	Brisbane	D	2-2	AL	Djulbic 13, Robson 55	13 065
Jan	3	Perth	D	0-0	AL		2 931
Jan	8	Sydney	L	0-2	AL		6 135
Jan	14	NQ Fury	W	4-0	AL	Djite 2 22 43, Smeltz 52, Harold 83	2 514
Jan	19	Mel. Heart	D	1-1	AL	Djite 40	5 187
Jan	22	Newcastle	W	5-1	AL	Traore 9, Djite 3 36 80 87, Smeltz 83	**14 783**
Jan	30	Melbourne V	L	0-2	AL		8 287
Feb	2	Adelaide	D	0-0	AL		2 138
Feb	6	Perth	W	2-1	AL	Smeltz 2 33p 55p	6 617
Feb	9	Cent. Coast	L	1-3	AL	Smeltz 83	2 037
Feb	12	Brisbane	L	0-4	AL		20 831
Feb	20	Melbourne V	W	1-0	ALrl	Djulbic 90	3 281
Feb	27	Adelaide	W	3-2	ALms	Smeltz 2 38 79p, Djite 71	15 028
Ma	5	Cent. Coast	D	0-1	ALpf		7 539
4th		Att: 54 786 • Av: 3424 (-35.4%) • Robina 27 400 (12%)					

MARINERS LEAGUE APPEARANCES/GOALS 2010-11

Goalkeepers Matthew Ryan 31 • Jess Vanstrattan 3
Defenders Pedj Bojic 26+1/0 • Chris Doig SCO 3+10/0 Joshua Rose 31/3 • Trent Sainsbury 7+2/0 • Alex Wilkinson 34/1 Patrick Zwaanswijk NED 33/3
Midfield Mustafa Amini 11+12/1 • Oliver Bozanic 33/2 • Rostyn Griffiths 27+3/2 • John Hutchinson MLT 15+11/1 • Michael McGlinchey 34/1 • Patricio Perez ARG 15+3/6 • Bradley Porter 3+3/0
Forwards Michael Baird 0+3/0 • Mitchell Duke 0+1/1 • Bernie Ibini-Isei 2+2/1 • Adam Kwasnik 13+15/10 • Matthew Lewis 0+8/1 Daniel McBreen 23+8/5 • Nik Mrdja 0+6/0 • Matt Simon 30+1/11
Coach Graham Arnold (10/02/2010)

GOLD COAST LEAGUE APPEARANCES/GOALS 2010-11

Goalkeepers Scott Higgins 2 • Glen Moss NZL 30 • Jerrad Tyson 1
Defenders Anderson BRA 20+2/0 • Zachary Anderson 0+2/0 John Curtis ENG 12+7/1 • Dino Djulbic 32/4 • Steven Pantelidis 20+9/1 Kristian Rees 19+7/0 • Michael Thwaite 28/0
Midfield Joshua Brillante 2/0 • James Brown 9+3/2 • Zenon Caravella 25+3/0 • Jason Culina 18/5 • Steve Fitzsimmons 7+8/0 Ben Halloran 2+3/0 • Kim Sung Kil 1/0 • Steve Lustica 0+2/0 Peter Perchtold GER 10/0 • Robson BRA 13+6/2
Forwards Andrew Barisic 2+9/1 • Chris Broadfoot 0+5/0 • Bruce Djite 23/10 • Chris Harold 2+8/1 • Gol Gol Mebrahtu 4+4/0 • Tahj Minniecon 11+7/0 • Joel Porter 8+8/2 • Shane Smeltz NZL 12/9
Coach Miron Bleiberg ISR

KEY
AL = A-League • CL = AFC Champions League
See page 13 for further explanations

MELBOURNE HEART 2010–11

Month	Date	Opponent	Res	Score	Comp	Scorers	Att
Aug	5	Cent. Coast	L	0-1	AL		11 050
	13	Newcastle	D	1-1	AL	OG 79	8 735
	20	Adelaide	L	2-3	AL	Worm 43, Babalj 74	7 370
	29	Perth	D	2-2	AL	Sibon 5p, Kalmar 37	5 878
Sep	4	NQ Fury	W	1-0	AL	Kalmar 11	4 184
	10	Cent. Coast	L	0-1	AL		6 326
	19	Wellington	W	2-1	AL	Aloisi 50, Alex Terra 66	5 698
	25	Brisbane	L	0-4	AL		6 342
Oct	8	Melbourne V	W	2-1	AL	Aloisi 11, Alex Terra 56	**25 897**
	17	Wellington	D	2-2	AL	Aloisis 13p, Thompson 36	5 211
	23	Gold Coast	D	0-0	AL		6 150
	31	Newcastle	W	2-0	AL	Kalmar 53, Sibon 90p	3 114
Nov	3	Perth	D	0-0	AL		5 745
	10	NQ Fury	W	3-2	AL	Babalj 50, Sibon 59, Zahra 64	2 866
	14	Brisbane	L	1-2	AL	Sibon 11	7 034
	19	Adelaide	L	0-2	AL		6 538
	24	Wellington	L	0-2	AL		4 700
	27	Sydney	D	0-0	AL		5 128
Dec	5	Gold Coast	L	0-3	AL		1 658
	8	Newcastle	L	2-2	AL		**2 754**
	11	Melbourne V	L	1-3	AL	Sibon 18	23 059
	17	Adelaide	W	2-1	AL	Colosimo 88, Aloisi 90	10 011
	23	Sydney	W	1-0	AL	Zahra 86	6 639
Jan	2	NQ Fury	W	2-0	AL	Aloisi 59, Sibon 83	6 482
	5	Perth	D	1-1	AL	Alex Terra 70	7 962
	19	Gold Coast	D	1-1	AL	Alex Terra 16	5 187
	22	Melbourne V	D	2-2	AL	Aloisi 2 45 52	32 321
	29	Brisbane	L	1-2	AL	Sibon 75	4 213
Feb	4	Cent. Coast	D	1-1	AL	Thompson 49	3 667
	12	Sydney	D	2-2	AL	Worm 41, Aloisi 62	6 019

8th Att: 124 725 • Av: 8315 • AAMI Park 30 050 (27%)

HEART LEAGUE APPEARANCES/GOALS 2010-11
Goalkeepers Clint Bolton 30
Defenders Michael Beauchamp 19+4/0 • Simon Colosimo 22+4/1
Brendan Hamill 5+7/0 • Dean Heffernan 9+4/0
Michael Marrone 29/0 • Matt Thompson 29/0
Midfield Aziz Behich 23+4/0 • Nick Kalmar 17+12/3
Kristian Sarkies 2+3/0 • Josip Skoko 21+1/0 • Wayne Srhoj 25+1/0
Kliment Taseski 0+4/0 • Adrian Zahra 17+2/2
Forwards Alex Terra BRA 14+6/4 • John Aloisi 17+3/8
Eli Babalj 1+12/2 • Jason Hoffman 3+9/0 • Kamal Ibrahim 1+2/0
Gerald Sibon NED 24+3/7 • Rutger Worm NED 22+4/2
Coach Johnny van't Schip NED (12/10/2009)

NEWCASTLE JETS 2010–11

Month	Date	Opponent	Res	Score	Comp	Scorers	Att
Aug	6	Adelaide	D	0-0	AL		8 479
	13	Mel. Heart	D	1-1	AL	Brockie 60	8 735
	21	Perth	L	0-1	AL		12 031
Sep	5	Brisbane	D	0-0	AL		7 066
	11	Adelaide	L	1-2	AL	Rooney 90	9 571
	17	Perth	W	2-0	AL	Bridges 10, Haliti 89	6 977
	22	Gold Coast	L	0-1	AL		2 091
	25	MelbourneV	D	0-0	AL		8 652
Oct	16	Brisbane	D	0-0	AL		10 191
	31	Mel. Heart	L	0-2	AL	OG.18	**3 114**
Nov	7	Sydney	L	0-1	AL		8 512
	13	Adelaide	W	3-1	AL	Topor-Stanley 4, Jesic 2 13 52	8 278
	17	Brisbane	D	1-1	AL	Kantarovski 54	7 829
	20	Wellington	W	1-0	AL	Jesic 56	12 147
	24	Cent. Coast	D	1-1	AL	Petrovski 90	7 730
Dec	4	NQ Fury	W	2-0	AL	Topor-Stanley 78, Petrovski 90	3 573
	8	Mel. Heart	W	2-0	AL	Jeffers 12, Jesic 19	2 754
	15	Gold Coast	W	2-0	AL	Abbas 77, Petrovski 82	8 046
	18	Wellington	L	0-4	AL		6 053
	27	MelbourneV	L	1-2	AL	Zadkovich 54	16 378
Jan	3	Sydney	L	1-2	AL	Haliti 66	12 118
	8	NQ Fury	W	3-1	AL	Zadkovich 12, Haliti 15, Griffiths 69	4 315
	11	NQ Fury	W	1-0	AL	Jesic 12	8 218
	16	Cent. Coast	L	0-2	AL		**13 463**
	22	Gold Coast	L	1-5	AL	Zhang Shuo 75	14 783
	30	Wellington	L	0-1	AL		10 917
Feb	2	MelbourneV	L	0-2	AL		11 296
	6	Sydney	D	1-1	AL	Petrovski 84	6 780
	10	Perth	W	4-0	AL	Haliti 13, Brockie 54, Petrovski 2 68p 69	7 286
	13	Cent. Coast	L	0-1	AL		9 975

7th Att: 126 439 • Av: 8429 (+32.9%) • EnergyAustralia 26 100 (32%)

MELBOURNE VICTORY 2010–11

Month	Date	Opponent	Res	Score	Comp	Scorers	Att
Aug	7	Sydney	D	3-3	AL	Broxham 66, Dugandzic 68, Celeski 73	12 106
	14	Perth	L	0-2	AL		20 358
	22	NQ Fury	D	2-2	AL	Muscat 2 30p 75p	13 318
	29	Gold Coast	W	1-0	AL	Kruse 20	3 624
Sep	3	Cent. Coast	L	0-2	AL		6 829
	12	Brisbane	W	3-0	AL	Pondeljak 51, Ricardinho 56, Brebner 71	13 792
	15	Wellington	D	0-0	AL		11 513
	18	NQ Fury	D	0-0	AL		4 922
	25	Newcastle	D	0-0	AL		8 652
Oct	8	Mel. Heart	L	1-2	AL	Kruse 37	25 897
	16	Sydney	W	3-0	AL	Vargas 20, Hernandez 49, Kruse 89	17 299
	23	Brisbane	L	1-2	AL	Kruse 48	9 425
	29	Adelaide	W	2-1	AL	Kruse 22, Hernandez 68	16 269
Nov	6	Gold Coast	L	0-1	AL		15 534
	14	Perth	L	1-3	AL	Dugandzic 79	6 217
	18	Cent. Coast	D	2-2	AL	Vargas 62, Hernandez 64	9 674
	27	Wellington	D	2-2	AL	Thompson 20, Kruse 40	6 475
Dec	3	Brisbane	D	3-3	AL	Kruse 2 63 77, Thompson 70	11 886
	11	Mel. Heart	W	3-1	AL	Kruse 2 12 28, Leijer 54	23 059
	18	Perth	W	2-0	AL	Thompson 45, Vargas 63	12 164
	27	Newcastle	W	2-1	AL	Hernandez 20, Ricardinho 90	16 378
	31	Cent. Coast	W	2-1	AL	Ferreira 85, Brebner 88	12 409
Jan	5	Wellington	L	0-2	AL		9 496
	9	Adelaide	L	1-4	AL	Dugandzic 90	18 558
	15	Sydney	D	1-1	AL	Allsopp 51	11 387
	22	Mel. Heart	D	2-2	AL	Allsopp 11, Hernandez 32	**32 321**
	26	NQ Fury	W	3-0	AL	Allsopp 27, Dugandzic 2 69 73	4 093
	30	Gold Coast	W	2-0	AL	Allsopp 2 28 56	**8 287**
Feb	2	Newcastle	W	2-0	AL	Pondeljak 57, Kruse 70	11 296
	11	Adelaide	L	1-2	AL	Thompson 65	21 083
	20	Gold Coast	L	0-1	ALr1		3 281
Mar	1	Gamba	L	1-5	CLgE	Muscat 21p	12 949
	15	Jeju Utd	L	1-2	CLgE	Allsopp 37	4 825
Apr	5	Tianjin	D	1-2	CLgE	Muscat 52	25 456
	20	Tianjin	W	2-1	CLgE	Hernandez 44, Muscat 45p	5 693
May	4	Gamba	D	1-1	CLgE	Leijer 12	7 437
	11	Jeju Utd	D	1-1	CLgE	Ferreira 61	1 519

8th Att: 228 647 • Av: 15 243 (-31.1%) • Etihad 53 355 (28%)

VICTORY LEAGUE APPEARANCES/GOALS 2010-11
Goalkeepers Michael Petkovic 31
Defenders Evan Berger 7+4/0 • Diogo Ferreira 10+11/1
Matthew Foschini 0+6/0 • Petar Franjic 5/0 • Matthew Kemp 8/0
Adrian Leijer 28/1 • Kevin Muscat 21/2 • Luke Pilkington 0+2/0
Surat Sukha THA 16+2/0 • Rodrigo Vargas 29+1/3
Midfield Marvin Angulo CRC 16+11/0 • Grant Brebner SCO 24+1/2
Leigh Broxham 16+6/1 • Billy Celeski 20+5/1
Mate Dugandzic 16+11/5 • Carlos Hernandez CRC 28+2/5
Geoff Kellaway ENG 1+8/0 • Tom Pondeljak 21+7/2 • Nick Ward 1/0
Forwards Danny Allsopp 8+1/5 • Robbie Kruse 19/11
Ricardinho BRA 11+8/2 • Archie Thompson 6+3/4
Coach Ernie Merrick SCO • Mehmet Durakovic (12/03/2011)

NEWCASTLE LEAGUE APPEARANCES/GOALS 2010-11
Goalkeepers Ben Kennedy 26 • Matthew Nash 4+1
Defenders Tarek Elrich 26+1/0 • Sam Gallaway 5/0
Ruben Milicevic 18+1/0 • Taylor Regan 10/0 • Mario Simic 3+1/0
Nikolai Topor-Stanley 28/2
Midfield Ali Abbas IRQ 18+6/1 • Jeremy Brockie NZL 11+3/2
Marcello Fiorentini ITA 8+8/0 • Labinot Haliti 13+13/4
Ben Kantarovski 14+1/1 • Kaz Patafta 1+3/0 • Jacob Pepper 1+5/0
James Virgili 2+6/0 • Kasey Wehrman 22+1/0
Jobe Wheelhouse 14+4/0 • Ruben Zadkovich 21/2
Forwards Michael Bridges ENG 7/1 • Ryan Griffiths 8/1
Francis Jeffers ENG 9/1 • Marko Jesic 26+1/5 • Tomislav Misura 1/0
Brodie Mooy 2+1/0 • Saso Petrovski 0+16/6 • Sean Rooney 3+5/1
Zhang Shuo CHN 4+4/1
Coach Branko Culina

NORTH QUEENSLAND FURY 2010–11

Aug	6	Perth	D	3-3	AL	Payne[35], Williams[64], Grossman[90]	16 019
	14	Sydney	W	2-1	AL	Grossman[64], Daal[83]	5 177
	22	Melbourne V	D	2-2	AL	Ssepuya[15], Payne[82p]	13 318
	28	Adelaide	L	2-3	AL	Cernak[8], Williams[88]	6 130
Sep	4	Mel. Heart	L	0-1	AL		4 184
	18	Melbourne V	D	0-0	AL		4 922
	24	Wellington	L	1-2	AL	Hughes[67]	7 212
	29	Sydney	D	1-1	AL	Williams[76]	6 978
Oct	2	Cent. Coast	L	2-3	AL	Storey[12], Hughes[78]	6 656
	15	Perth	W	2-1	AL	Payne[16], Williams[72]	4 011
	31	Gold Coast	L	1-2	AL	Hughes[45]	7 195
Nov	5	Cent. Coast	L	0-1	AL		3 625
	10	Mel. Heart	L	2-3	AL	Daal[12], Ufuk Talay[85p]	2 866
	20	Brisbane	D	1-1	AL	Edds[9]	10 126
	28	Perth	D	1-1	AL	Hughes[80]	4 466
Dec	1	Gold Coast	W	2-1	AL	Williams[28], Ufuk Talay[68]	1 714
	4	Newcastle	L	0-1	AL		3 573
	10	Adelaide	L	0-2	AL		8 786
	15	Sydney	W	1-0	AL	Ufuk Talay[70]	2 761
	18	Brisbane	L	0-2	AL		4 412
	22	Cent. Coast	L	0-1	AL		5 979
	27	Wellington	D	1-1	AL	Payne[12]	5 107
Jan	2	Mel. Heart	L	0-2	AL		6 482
	8	Newcastle	L	1-3	AL	Hughes[90p]	4 315
	11	Newcastle	L	0-1	AL		8 218
	14	Gold Coast	L	0-4	AL		2 514
	21	Adelaide	L	1-8	AL	Nikas[72]	10 986
	26	Melbourne V	L	0-3	AL		4 093
Feb	8	Brisbane	L	1-2	AL	Grossman[65]	1 033
	13	Wellington	L	1-3	AL	Studman[66]	12 718

11th Att: 63 686 • Av: 4246 (-36.9%) • Willows 27 000 (15%)

PERTH GLORY 2010–11

Aug	6	NQ Fury	D	3-3	AL	Jelic[5], Neville[73], Sterjovski[79]	**16 019**
	14	Melbourne V	W	2-0	AL	Harnwell[23], Sterjovski[49]	20 358
	21	Newcastle	W	1-0	AL	Jelic[45]	12 031
	29	Mel. Heart	D	2-2	AL	OG[19], Fowler[90p]	5 878
Sep	5	Wellington	W	2-1	AL	Sterjovski[5], Fowler[61]	10 834
	12	Gold Coast	L	0-1	AL		10 450
	17	Newcastle	L	0-2	AL		6 977
	24	Adelaide	L	0-2	AL		13 310
Oct	3	Brisbane	L	1-2	AL	Neville[6]	9 758
	15	NQ Fury	L	1-2	AL	Baird[22]	4 011
	24	Sydney	L	0-3	AL		8 870
	30	Cent. Coast	L	0-5	AL		10 746
Nov	3	Mel. Heart	D	0-0	AL		5 745
	7	Wellington	L	0-1	AL		6 676
	10	Adelaide	L	0-2	AL		10 023
	14	Melbourne V	W	3-1	AL	Fowler 3 [13 54 61]	6 217
	21	Sydney	L	0-2	AL		6 654
	24	Brisbane	L	2-3	AL	Fowler[66p], Pellegrino[83]	6 836
	28	NQ Fury	D	1-1	AL	Fowler[23]	4 466
Dec	12	Cent. Coast	D	1-1	AL	Mitchell[4]	6 536
	18	Melbourne V	L	0-2	AL		12 164
	22	Adelaide	W	4-2	AL	Coyne[6], Sterjovski[35], Fowler 2 [65 77p]	7 193
Jan	3	Gold Coast	D	0-0	AL		2 931
	7	Brisbane	D	1-1	AL	Sterjovski[31]	11 574
	15	Mel. Heart	D	1-1	AL	Howarth[34]	7 962
	19	Cent. Coast	L	1-2	AL	Howarth[38]	6 828
	23	Wellington	L	0-4	AL		5 115
	29	Sydney	L	0-2	AL		**5 536**
Feb	6	Gold Coast	L	1-2	AL	Taggart[75]	6 617
	10	Newcastle	L	0-4	AL		7 286

10th Att: 127 272 • Av: 8485 (-7.9%) • Members Equity 18 450 (45%)

NQ FURY LEAGUE APPEARANCES/GOALS 2010-11
Goalkeepers Justin Pasfield 26 • Sebastian Usai 4
Defenders Eric Akoto TOG 14+1/0 • Jack Hingert 14+6/0 • Mark Hughes ENG 30/5 • Andre Kilian GER 18+1/0 • Brad McDonald 18+7/0
Lorenzo Sipi 1+4/0 • Simon Storey 24+1/1 • Brett Studman 5+4/1
Midfield Isaka Cernak 12+2/1 • Gareth Edds 25+1/1
Chris Grossman 16+6/3 • Osama Malik 15+2/0
Panagiotis Nikas 15+3/1 • Jason Spagnuolo 5+13/0
Ramazan Tavsancioglu 8+4/0 • Ufuk Talay 17+5/3
Forwards Adam Casey 5+4/0 • Dyron Daal ANT 8+8/2
Chris Payne 15+6/4 • Alex Read 2/0 • Eugene Ssepuya UGA 7+6/1
David Williams 28/5
Coach Frantisek Straka (7/06/2010)

PERTH GLORY LEAGUE APPEARANCES/GOALS 2010-11
Goalkeepers Tando Velaphi 28 • Alex Velaphi 2
Defenders Jamie Coyne 23/1 • Brent Griffiths 5+4/0
Jamie Harnwell 18+3/1 • Josh Mitchell 15+3/1 • Scott Neville 26/2
Ryan Pearson 1+2/0 • Joshua Risdon 6/0 • Naum Sekulovski 19+1/0
Andy Todd 12+3/0
Midfield Jacob Burns 24/0 • Cameron Edwards 0+1/0
Howard Fondyke 6+8/0 • Todd Howarth 23+5/2 • Andrija Jukic 1+1/0
Steven McGarry SCO 26+2/0 • Adriano Pellegrino 23+5/1
Forwards Tommy Amphlett 6+9/0 • Michael Baird 10+3/1
Robbie Fowler ENG 25+3/9 • Branko Jelic SRB 6+9/2
Victor Sikora NED 0+1/0 • Anthony Skorich 3+10/0
Mile Sterjovski 20+3/5 • Adam Taggart 2+4/1
Coach David Mitchell • Ian Ferguson SCO (12/10/2010)

SYDNEY FC 2010-11

Mon	Date	Opponent		Score	Comp	Scorers	Att
Aug	7	Melbourne V	D	3-3	AL	Brosque 36, McFlynn 53, Cole 84	12 106
Aug	14	NQ Fury	L	1-2	AL	Jamieson 82	5 177
Aug	21	Brisbane	L	0-1	AL		10 339
Aug	28	Cent. Coast	D	1-1	AL	Grant 47	10 147
Sep	4	Adelaide	L	1-3	AL	Keller 58	7 558
Sep	11	Wellington	L	1-2	AL	Cazarine 67	8 453
Sep	26	Gold Coast	D	1-1	AL	Cazarine 20	9 977
Sep	29	NQ Fury	D	1-1	AL	Cole 37	6 978
Oct	4	Adelaide	L	1-2	AL	Brosque 40p	7 071
Oct	16	Melbourne V	L	0-3	AL		17 299
Oct	24	Perth	W	3-0	AL	Cazarine 2 25 82, Brosque 53	8 870
Oct	30	Brisbane	D	1-1	AL	Brosque 34	10 746
Nov	7	Newcastle	W	1-0	AL	Cazarine 76	8 512
Nov	12	Gold Coast	L	1-3	AL	Cazarine 58	2 536
Nov	21	Perth	W	2-0	AL	Cole 75, Brosque 80	6 654
Nov	27	Mel. Heart	D	0-0	AL		5 128
Dec	1	Wellington	W	3-1	AL	Gan 14, Bridge 73, Brosque 76	4 012
Dec	4	Cent. Coast	L	0-4	AL		7 160
Dec	12	Brisbane	L	0-1	AL		7 554
Dec	15	NQ Fury	L	0-1	AL		2 761
Dec	23	Mel. Heart	L	0-1	AL		6 639
Dec	29	Adelaide	L	0-2	AL		16 429
Jan	3	Newcastle	W	2-1	AL	Moriyasu 36, Cazarine 45	12 118
Jan	8	Gold Coast	W	2-0	AL	Petratos 32, Makela 90	6 135
Jan	15	Melbourne V	D	1-1	AL	Makela 90	11 387
Jan	23	Cent. Coast	D	2-2	AL	Petratos 2 17 27	10 546
Jan	29	Perth	W	2-0	AL	Carle 9, Cazarine 53	5 536
Feb	6	Newcastle	D	1-1	AL	Cazarine 77	6 780
Feb	9	Wellington	W	2-0	AL	OG 54, Gan 69	4 732
Feb	12	Mel. Heart	D	2-2	AL	Carle 2 35p 88	6 019
Mar	2	Suwon	D	0-0	CLgH		7 095
Mar	6	Shanghai	D	1-1	CLgH	Carle 12	7 007
Apr	13	Kashima	L	0-3	CLgH		7 320
Apr	19	Shanghai	W	3-2	CLgH	Cazarine 2 45 59, Bridge 90	10 215
May	3	Suwon	L	1-3	CLgH	Cazarine 51	9 495
May	10	Kashima	L	1-2	CLgH	Jurman 26	3 164

9th Att: 120 208 • Av: 8014 (-41.5%) • Sydney Football Stadium 45 000

WELLINGTON PHOENIX 2010-11

Mon	Date	Opponent		Score	Comp	Scorers	Att
Aug	13	Gold Coast	D	3-3	AL	Ifill 6, Greenacre 2 37 55	8 398
Aug	22	Cent. Coast	W	2-0	AL	Bertos 10, Ifill 61	9 553
Aug	27	Brisbane	L	0-1	AL		7 339
Sep	5	Perth	L	1-2	AL	Sigmund 72	10 834
Sep	11	Sydney	W	2-1	AL	Ifill 50p, Ward 72	8 453
Sep	15	Melbourne V	D	0-0	AL		11 513
Sep	19	Mel. Heart	L	1-2	AL	Brown 75	5 698
Sep	24	NQ Fury	W	2-1	AL	Greenacre 3, Bertos 12	7 212
Oct	1	Gold Coast	L	1-3	AL	Ifill 9p	2 943
Oct	17	Mel. Heart	D	2-2	AL	Greenacre 6, Bertos 59	5 211
Oct	22	Adelaide	L	0-3	AL		11 206
Nov	3	Brisbane	L	1-4	AL	Brown 37	5 529
Nov	7	Perth	W	1-0	AL	Brown 1	6 676
Nov	13	Cent. Coast	L	0-3	AL		5 778
Nov	20	Newcastle	L	0-1	AL		12 147
Dec	24	Mel. Heart	W	2-0	AL	Ifill 2 62 73	4 700
Dec	27	Melbourne V	D	2-2	AL	Brown 17, Ifill 84	6 475
Dec	1	Sydney	L	1-3	AL	Macallister 83	4 012
Dec	5	Adelaide	W	2-1	AL	Brown 46, Sigmund 90	14 108
Dec	11	Gold Coast	L	0-2	AL		1 716
Dec	18	Newcastle	W	4-0	AL	Brown 18, Rojas 31, Greenacre 41, Macallister 88	6 053
Dec	27	NQ Fury	D	1-1	AL	Macallister 76	5 107
Jan	5	Melbourne V	W	2-0	AL	Macallister 67, Rojas 71	9 496
Jan	9	Cent. Coast	L	0-1	AL		6 844
Jan	23	Perth	W	4-0	AL	Ward 10, Macallister 48, Lia 59, Greenacre 90	5 115
Jan	26	Brisbane	L	0-2	AL		3 522
Jan	30	Newcastle	W	1-0	AL	Macallister 20	10 917
Feb	5	Adelaide	W	1-0	AL	Greenacre 34	7 498
Feb	9	Sydney	L	0-2	AL		4 732
Feb	13	NQ Fury	W	3-1	AL	Greenacre 7, Macallister 11, Vukovic 90p	12 718
Feb	18	Adelaide	L	0-1	ALr1		10 825

6th Att: 119 716 • Av: 7981 (-30.9%) • Westpac 34 500 (23%)

SYDNEY LEAGUE APPEARANCES/GOALS 2010-11
Goalkeepers Ivan Necevski 12+1 • Liam Reddy 18
Defenders Byun Sung Hwan KOR 24+2/0 • Shannon Cole 21+9/3
Hayden Foxe 14+2/0 • Anthony Golec 0+1/0 • Rhyan Grant 10+1/1
Scott Jamieson 22+4/1 • Matthew Jurman 8/0
Stephan Keller SUI 27+1/1 • Sebastian Ryall 16+12/0
Midfield Terry Antonis 2+3/0 • Nick Carle 15+2/3 • Brendan Gan 4+6/2
Terry McFlynn NIR 27/1 • Hirofumi Moriyasu JPN 23+5/1
Stuart Musialik 22+3/0
Forwards Mark Bridge 17+1/1 • Alex Brosque 13+2/6
Bruno Cazarine BRA 20+2/9 • Kofi Danning 3+9/0
Juho Makela FIN 2+6/2 • Dimitri Petratos 10+6/3
Coach Vitezslav Lavicka CZE

WELLINGTON LEAGUE APPEARANCES/GOALS 2010-11
Goalkeepers Mark Paston NZL 15 • Danny Vukovic AUS 16+1/1
Defenders Andrew Durante AUS 27+1/0 • Tony Lochhead NZL 16/0
James Musa NZL 2+1/0 • Manny Muscat MLT 28/0
Jade North AUS 19/0 • Ben Sigmund NZL 28/2
Midfield Leo Bertos NZL 18+4/3 • Tim Brown NZL 30/6
Oscar Roberto Cornejo ARG 0+5/0 • Daniel BRA 9+20/0
Simon Elliott NZL 4/0 • Troy Hearfield AUS 22+5/0
Vince Lia AUS 23+1/1 • Marco Rojas NZL 10+7/2 • Nick Ward AUS 17+7/2
Forwards Chris Greenacre ENG 21+10/8 • Paul Ifill BRB 20+1/7
Sean Lovemore NZL 0+1/0 • Dylan Macallister AUS 15+7/7
Mirjan Pavlovic AUS 1+9/0
Coach Ricki Herbert NZL

AUT – AUSTRIA

FIFA/COCA-COLA WORLD RANKING

'93	'94	'95	'96	'97	'98	'99	'00	'01	'02	'03	'04	'05	'06	'07	'08	'09	'10	'11	'12
36	49	39	34	25	22	28	44	56	65	67	83	69	65	94	92	61	46	70	

2011												High	Low	Av
Jan	Feb	Mar	Apr	May	Jun	Jul	Aug	Sep	Oct	Nov	Dec			
46	45	61	73	74	65	66	68	77	72	71	70	17	105	55

After a very promising start to the Euro 2012 qualifiers, Austria's campaign fell apart in 2011 with four consecutive defeats, all against their main group rivals. That left the team above only Azerbaijan and Kazakhstan in the final standings, the decline in fortunes prompting the resignation of coach Dietmar Constantini in September. Willibald Ruttensteiner oversaw the final two qualifiers before Switzerland's Marcell Koller was brought in to take Austria through the 2014 FIFA World Cup qualifiers, a decision that was not greeted with universal enthusiasm. The Euro 2012 failure meant that the Austrians maintained their record of never having made it through the qualifying groups of the European Championship - they qualified in 2008 as co-hosts - and the odds don't look great in the World Cup qualifiers with Germany once again in their group. At home there were surprise winners of both the league and cup with Sturm Graz winning an exciting race in the Bundesliga and SV Ried beating Austria Lustenau in the Cup Final - a repeat of the 1998 season when Sturm had won the league for the first time and Ried the cup for the first time. 2011 saw long-serving Sturm coach Franco Foda celebrate 10 years in the job having also been a player with the club in their 1998 and 1999 title winning teams.

UEFA EUROPEAN CHAMPIONSHIP RECORD
1960 QF **1964** r1 **1968-2004** DNQ **2008** r1 (co-hosts) **2012** DNQ

OSTERREICHISCHER FUSSBALL-BUND (OFB)

Ernst Happel Stadion,
✉ Sektor A/F, Postfach 340,
Meiereistrasse 7, Wien 1021
☎ +43 1 727180
✆ +43 1 7281632
✉ office@oefb.at
🖥 www.oefb.at
FA 1904 CON 1954 FIFA 1907
P Leo Windtner
GS Alfred Ludwig

FIFA BIG COUNT 2006

Total players	967 281
% of population	11.81%
Male	912 580
Female	54 701
Amateurs 18+	370 828
Youth under 18	221 547
Unregistered	260 000
Professionals	906
Referees	2 302
Admin & coaches	390 500
Number of clubs	2 211
Number of teams	9 685

MAJOR CITIES/TOWNS

		Population
1	Vienna	1 690 103
2	Graz	253 554
3	Linz	189 612
4	Salzburg	150 112
5	Innsbruck	119 092
6	Klagenfurt	92 895
7	Wels	58 939
8	Villach	58 822
9	Sankt Pölten	51 908
10	Dornbirn	44 954
11	Wiener Neustadt	40 557
12	Steyr	38 780
13	Feldkirch	30 545
14	Bregenz	27 107
15	Baden	25 456
16	Klosterneuburg	25 388
17	Wolfsberg	25 356
18	Leoben	24 879
19	Krems	24 229

REPUBLIK OESTERREICH • REPUBLIC OF AUSTRIA

Capital	Wien (Vienna)	Population 8 210 281 (92)	% in cities 67%
GDP per capita	$40 200 (20)	Area km² 83 871 km² (113)	GMT +/- +1
Neighbours (km)	Czech Republic 362, Germany 784, Hungary 366, Italy 430, Liechtenstein 35, Slovakia 91, Slovenia 330, Switzerland 164		

RECENT INTERNATIONALS PLAYED BY AUSTRIA

2008	Opponents	Score		Venue	Comp	Scorers	Att	Referee
8-06	Croatia	L	0-1	Vienna	ECrl		51 428	Vink NED
12-06	Poland	D	1-1	Vienna	ECrl	Vastic 93+	51 428	Webb ENG
16-06	Germany	L	0-1	Vienna	ECrl		51 428	Mejuto Gonzalez ESP
20-08	Italy	D	2-2	Nice	Fr	Pogatetz 15, Janko 39	14 000	Coue FRA
6-09	France	W	3-1	Vienna	WCq	Janko 8, Aufhauser 41, Ivanschitz 72p	48 000	Larsen DEN
10-09	Lithuania	L	0-2	Marijampole	WCq		4 500	Tagliavento ITA
11-10	Faroe Islands	D	1-1	Torshavn	WCq	Stranzl 49	1 890	Ceferin SVN
15-10	Serbia	L	1-3	Vienna	WCq	Janko 80	47 998	Riley ENG
19-11	Turkey	L	2-4	Vienna	Fr	Holzl 2 28 53	23 100	Grafe GER
2009								
11-02	Sweden	L	0-2	Graz	Fr		11 800	Kassai HUN
1-04	Romania	W	2-1	Klagenfurt	WCq	Hoffer 2 26 44	23 000	Thomas SCO
6-06	Serbia	L	0-1	Belgrade	WCq		41 000	Vink NED
12-08	Cameroon	L	0-2	Klagenfurt	Fr		28 800	Olsiak SVK
5-09	Faroe Islands	W	3-1	Graz	WCq	Maierhofer 1, Janko 2 15 58p	12 300	Borg MLT
9-09	Romania	D	1-1	Bucharest	WCq	Schiemer 83	7 505	Atkinson ENG
10-10	Lithuania	W	2-1	Innsbruck	WCq	Janko 16, Wallner 80p	14 200	Gumienny BEL
14-10	France	L	1-3	Paris	WCq	Janko 49	78 099	Proença POR
18-11	Spain	L	1-5	Vienna	Fr	Jantscher 8	32 000	Meyer GER
2010								
3-03	Denmark	W	2-1	Vienna	Fr	Schiemer 11, Wallner 37	13 500	Kralovec CZE
19-05	Croatia	L	0-1	Klagenfurt	Fr		20 000	Blom NED
11-08	Switzerland	L	0-1	Klagenfurt	Fr		18 000	Rubinos ESP
7-09	Kazakhstan	W	2-0	Salzburg	ECq	Linz 91+, Hoffer 92+	22 500	Strahonja CRO
8-10	Azerbaijan	W	3-0	Vienna	ECq	Prodl 3, Arnautovic 2 53 92+	26 500	Vollquartz DEN
12-10	Belgium	D	4-4	Brussels	ECq	Schiemer 2 14 62, Arnautovic 29, Harnik 93+	24 231	Dean ENG
17-11	Greece	L	1-2	Vienna	Fr	Fuchs 67	16 200	Kever SUI
2011								
9-02	Netherlands	L	1-3	Eindhoven	Fr	Arnautovic 84p	35 000	Brych GER
25-03	Belgium	L	0-2	Vienna	ECq		44 300	Bezborodov RUS
29-03	Turkey	L	0-2	Istanbul	ECq		40 420	Kralovec CZE
3-06	Germany	L	1-2	Vienna	ECq	OG 50	47 500	Busacca SUI
7-06	Latvia	W	3-1	Graz	Fr	Dibon 75, Harnik 2 81 94+p	8 500	Evans WAL
10-08	Slovakia	L	1-2	Klagenfurt	Fr	Hoffer 62	13 000	Ceferin SVN
2-09	Germany	L	2-6	Gelsenkirchen	ECq	Arnautovic 42, Harnik 51	53 313	Tagliavento ITA
6-09	Turkey	D	0-0	Vienna	ECq		47 500	Undiano ESP
7-10	Azerbaijan	W	4-1	Baku	ECq	Ivanschitz 34, Janko 2 52 62, Junuzovic 91+	6 000	Studer SUI
11-10	Kazakhstan	D	0-0	Astana	ECq		11 000	Kaasik EST
15-11	Ukraine	L	1-2	Lviv	Fr	OG 71	31 879	Moen NOR

Fr = Friendly match • EC = UEFA EURO 2008/2012 • WC = FIFA World Cup • q = qualifier • rl = first round group

AUSTRIA NATIONAL TEAM HISTORICAL RECORDS

Caps

103 - Andreas Herzog 1988-2003 • 95 - Anton Polster 1982-2000 • 93 - Gerhard Hanappi 1948-62 • 86 - Karl Koller 1952-65 • 84 - Friedrich Koncilia 1970-85 & Bruno Pezzey 1975-90 • 83 - Herbert Prohaska 1974-89 • 69 - Hans Krankl 1973-85 • 68 - Heribert Weber 1976-89 • 65 - Peter Stoger 1988-99 • 64 - Walter Schachner 1976-94 • 63 - Andreas Ogris 1986-97, Anton Pfeffer 1988-99 & Peter Schottel

Goals

44 - Anton Polster 1982-2000 • 34 - Hans Krankl 1973-85 • 29 - Hans Horvath 1924-34 • 28 - Eric Hof 1957-69 • 27 - Anton Schall 1927-34 • 26 - Matthias Sindelar 1926-37 & Andreas Herzog 1988-2003 • 24 - Karl Zischek 1931-45 • 23 - Walter Schachner 1976-94 • 22 - Theodor Wagner 1946-57 • 19 - Karl Decker 1945-52 • 18 - Erich Probst 1951-60, Ferdinand Swatosch 1914-25 & Jan Studnicka 1902-18

Past Coaches

Hugo Meisl 1912-1914 • Heinrich Retschury 1914-19 • Hugo Meisl 1919-37 • Heinrich Retschury 1937 • Karl Zankl 1945 • Edi Bauer 1945-48 • Eduard Fruhwirth 1948 • Walter Nausch 1948-54 (1954 World Cup) • Hans Kaulich 1954-55 • Josef Molzer 1955 • Karl Geyer 1955-56 • Josef Argauer & Josef Molzer 1956-58 (1958 World Cup) • Alfred Frey, Franz Putzendopler, Egon Selzer & Josef Molzer 1958 • Karl Decker 1958-64 • Josef Walter & Bela Guttmann HUN 1964 • Eduard Fruhwirth 1964-67 • Erwin Alge & Hans Pesser 1967-68 • Leopold Stasny CZE 1968-75 • Branko Elsner YUG 1975 • Helmut Senekowitsch 1976-78 (1978 World Cup) • Karl Stotz 1978-81 • Georg Schmidt & Felix Latzke 1982 (1982 World Cup) • Erich Hof 1982-84 • Branko Elsner YUG 1985-87 • Josef Hickersberger 1988-90 (1990 World Cup) • Alfred Riedl 1990-91 • Dietmar Constantini 1991 • Ernst Happel 1992 • Dietmar Constantini 1992 • Herbert Prohaska 1993-99 (1998 World Cup) • Otto Bari 1999-2001 • Hans Krankl 2002-05 • Willibald Ruttensteiner, Andreas Herzog & Slavko Kovacic 2005 • Josef Hickersberger 2006-08 (Euro 2008) • Karel Bruckner CZE 2008-09 • Dietmar Constantini 2009-11 • Willibald Ruttensteiner 2011 • Marcel Koller SUI 2011-

AUSTRIA 2010-11

TIPP 3 BUNDESLIGA POWERED BY T-MOBILE

	Pl	W	D	L	F	A	Pts	Sturm Graz	Salzburg	FK Austria	Ried	Rapid	Wacker	W Neustadt	Kapfenberg	Mattersburg	LASK
SK Sturm Graz †	36	19	9	8	66	33	66		0-0 0-3	0-2 1-1	0-1 1-0	0-2 3-3	2-0 2-1	4-2 1-0	2-0 2-0	2-0 4-0	5-0 1-1
FC RB Salzburg ‡	36	17	12	7	53	31	63	2-0 2-1		1-1 1-1	4-0 2-3	4-2 4-0	0-2 4-2	1-0 2-0	0-0 0-1		
FK Austria Wien ‡	36	17	10	9	65	37	61	2-3 2-2	0-0 2-4		0-1 0-0	1-0 0-1	0-3 1-0	1-1 4-0	5-1 2-0	2-0 0-1	4-1 5-0
SV Ried ‡	36	16	10	10	51	38	58	0-3 0-0	1-2 2-2	2-1 1-1		3-1 2-1	1-0 2-2	2-0 1-0	1-0 2-0	1-3 1-1	1-0 2-0
SK Rapid Wien	36	14	11	11	52	42	53	3-1 0-2	2-1 1-2	0-1 **0-3**	3-0 2-0		1-1 3-3	1-2 4-1	3-2 2-0	2-0 0-0	5-0 0-0
FC Wacker Innsbruck	36	13	11	12	43	42	50	2-2 1-0	0-1 1-1	0-1 0-3	1-0 1-1	4-0 0-3		0-0 1-0	1-3 1-1	1-2 1-2	0-2 0-0
SCM Wiener Neustadt	36	14	8	14	44	52	50	0-3 1-2	1-0 1-0	0-0 4-2	0-5 0-2	1-1 2-0	1-0 2-2		3-0 1-1	1-0 2-1	5-0 0-0
SV Kapfenberg	36	9	11	16	42	61	38	0-4 0-5	0-0 0-1	1-1 3-3	3-3 2-1	0-0 1-2	4-0 0-1	2-0 1-0		3-1 2-1	4-1 2-2
SV Mattersburg	36	7	10	19	29	56	31	1-1 1-1	1-0 0-1	0-3 1-2	1-4 2-2	2-2 1-0	0-2 2-1	0-3 1-1	0-1 1-1		3-3 1-1
LASK Linz	36	3	10	23	22	74	19	0-4 0-1	2-1 1-3	4-0 4-0	3-1 1-0	1-0 2-0	0-0 1-2	1-3 0-2	3-4 0-1	2-3 0-1	0-1 0-1

17/07/2010 - 25/05/2011 • † Qualified for the UEFA Champions League • ‡ Qualified for the Europa League • Match in bold awarded

Top scorers: **21** - Roland Linz, FK Austria • **19** - Roman Kienast, Sturm Graz • **18** - Roman Wallner, RB Salzburg & Hamdi Salihi ALB, Rapid • **14** - Deni Alar, Kapfenburg & Patrick Berger, Mattersburg • **11** - Johannes Aigner, Wiener Neustadt • **10** - Marcel Schreter, Wacker Innsbruck

AUSTRIA 2010-11

ADEG ERSTE LIGA (2)

	Pl	W	D	L	F	A	Pts	Admira	R'dorf Altach	Austria L'nau	St Andrä	Sankt Pölten	Grödig	Lustenau 07	Hartberg	First Vienna	Gratkorn
FCT Admira	36	23	6	7	85	45	75		3-2 1-1	2-0 5-3	2-0 0-1	3-2 5-1	3-0 1-1	1-1 3-0	5-1 3-1	4-1 1-3	3-0 7-3
SC Rheindorf Altach	36	22	8	6	76	37	74	3-3 4-0		2-0 2-1	3-1 3-3	2-1 3-0	4-0 3-0	2-1 2-2	4-0 1-2	2-1 0-1	0-1 3-1
SC Austria Lustenau	36	16	6	14	55	51	54	2-1 0-1	2-0 2-1		0-1 3-0	4-0 0-3	2-1 2-1	1-2 1-0	1-0 2-2	3-1 3-2	2-1 2-1
WAC St Andrä	36	15	7	14	56	50	52	1-2 5-0	3-1 0-0	0-0 4-2		1-3 3-1	4-2 2-1	1-3 1-2	2-0 0-0	2-0 1-0	4-1 3-0
SKN Sankt Pölten	36	13	12	11	55	55	51	1-4 1-0	0-0 1-0	1-0 1-1	0-6 2		1-1 1-2	1-0 1-0	1-3 3-0	3-2 1-1	3-1 0-0
SV Grödig	36	12	10	14	51	60	46	1-1 3-1	0-2 0-1	3-2 2-2	4-0 2-1	1-1 2-2		0-6 2-1	3-2 3-0	4-1 3-2	1-4 0-0
FC Lustenau 07	36	11	9	16	51	60	42	0-3 0-1	3-3 2-4	0-3 1-2	2-2 0-0	3-1 3-1	1-1 2-0		2-2 1-3	0-4 0-1	1-0 1-3
TSV Hartberg	36	10	9	17	44	60	39	1-2 1-2	0-2 1-2	2-1 1-1	0-2 2-0	2-2 0-0	2-0 1-1	1-2 1-1		3-1 2-0	1-2 2-0
First Vienna FC	36	9	7	20	47	67	34	1-3 0-0	1-2 1-1	0-2 3-0	1-0 0-4	3-4 2-0	3-2 0-0	4-1 1-1	0-1 1-4		1-1 3-1
FC Gratkorn	36	9	6	21	47	82	33	0-3 0-6	0-5 0-2	2-2 2-1	3-2 3-2	1-5 2-2	0-2 1-3	0-2 3-4	3-1 3-1	4-0 1-1	

12/07/2010 - 24/05/2011

Top scorer: **19** - Benjamin Sulimani, Admira

MEDALS TABLE

		Overall			League			Cup		Europe			
		G	S	B	G	S	B	G	S	G	S	B	
1	FK Austria Wien	52	28	18	23	18	14	27	9	2	1	4	
2	SK Rapid Wien	47	39	22	32	23	20	14	12	1	4	2	
3	FC Wacker Innsbruck	17	11	7	10	5	6	7	6		1		
4	Admira Wien	13	6	6	8	5	5	5		1	1		1905-71
5	First Vienna FC	10	12	13	6	6	11	3	6	1		2	
6	SK Sturm Graz	7	9	4	3	5	4	4	4				
7	FC RB Salzburg	6	11	1	6	6	1	4		1			
8	Grazer AK	5	4	6	1	2	6	4	2				
9	Wiener Sport-Club	4	14	5	3	7	5	1	7				
10	Wiener AC	4	5	6	1	1	6	3	3	1			
11	Wacker Wien	2	8	3	1	7	3	1	1				1908-71
12	Linzer ASK	2	5	4	1	1	4	1	4				
13	Wiener AF	2	2	3	1	2	3	1					1912-35
14	SV Ried	2	1		1			2					
15	FC Linz	1	4	1	1	2	1	2					1949-97
16	Floridsdorfer AC	1	3	1	1	3	1						1901-39
17	FC Kärnten	1	1					1	1				
	Hakoah Wien	1	1		1	1							
19	Kremser SC	1						1					
	SV Stockerau	1						1					
21	VfB Admira Wacker	6	3		1	3		5					

European medals include those won in the Mitropa Cup 1927-1939

OFB SAMSUNG CUP 2010–11

Second Round

Team	Score
SV Ried	4
FC Waidhofen/Ybbs *	0
1.SC Sollenau *	24
LASK Linz	
SK Vorwärts Steyr *	3
WAC St Andrä	2
SV-ESV Parndorf 1919 *	1
SK Sturm Graz	2
SV Mattersburg	2
FC Dornbirn 1913 *	1
FC RB Salzburg	1
FC Blau-Weiß Linz *	3
TSV Hartberg	6
SV Seekirchen 1945 *	2
FK Austria Wien II *	1 4p
SK Rapid Wien	1 5p
SV Kapfenberg *	3
FC Gratkorn	1
SV Union Gleinstätten *	2
FC Lustenau 07	4
SC Rheindorf Altach	2
SKU Amstetten *	0
ASK Voitsberg *	0
First Vienna FC	1
FK Austria Wien	3
SV Kapfenberg II *	0
SV Gaflenz *	1
FC Wacker Innsbruck	5
SV Grödig	3
FC Kufstein *	0
FC Höchst *	0
SC Austria Lustenau	3

Round of 16

Team	Score
SV Ried	1
LASK Linz *	0
SK Vorwärts Steyr *	0
SK Sturm Graz	1
SV Mattersburg	1
FC Blau-Weiß Linz *	0
TSV Hartberg	0
SK Rapid Wien *	3
SV Kapfenberg *	2
FC Lustenau 07	0
SC Rheindorf Altach	1
First Vienna FC *	2
FK Austria Wien *	2
FC Wacker Innsbruck	1
SV Grödig	0 4p
SC Austria Lustenau *	0 5p

Quarter-finals

Team	Score
SV Ried *	2
SK Sturm Graz	1
SV Mattersburg	0
SK Rapid Wien *	2
SV Kapfenberg	2
First Vienna FC *	0
FK Austria Wien *	0
SC Austria Lustenau	4

Semi-finals

Team	Score
SV Ried *	2
SK Rapid Wien	1
SV Kapfenberg *	1
SC Austria Lustenau	2

Final

Team	Score
SV Ried ‡	2
SC Austria Lustenau	0

CUP FINAL

Ernst-Happel-Stadion, Vienna, 29-05-2011, 16:30, Att. 14 500. Ref. Krassnitzer

Scorer - Hammerer 2 42 68

Ried - Thomas Gebauer - Martin Stocklasa, Oliver Glasner, Jan Marc Riegler (Mark Prettenthaler 63) - Ewald Brenner, Florian Mader, Thomas Schrammel - Stefan Lexa●, Ivan Carril (Anel Hadzic 82), Daniel Royer - Markus Hammerer (Nacho 86). Tr: Paul Gludovatz

Austria Lustenau - Alexander Kofler - Benedikt Zech, Christoph Stuckler, Jurgen Kampel●, Teodoro Soares - Harald Durre●, Mario Leitgeb (Dominik Rotter 71) - Danijel Micic, Felix Roth, Sascha Boller (Manuel Honeck 88) - Dursun Karatay (Gerald Krajic● 70). Tr: Edmund Stohr

* Home team ● ‡ Qualified for the Europa League

AZE – AZERBAIJAN

FIFA/COCA-COLA WORLD RANKING

'93	'94	'95	'96	'97	'98	'99	'00	'01	'02	'03	'04	'05	'06	'07	'08	'09	'10	'11	'12
-	147	141	125	123	99	97	115	113	113	119	113	114	125	115	134	114	98	112	

	2011														
	Jan	Feb	Mar	Apr	May	Jun	Jul	Aug	Sep	Oct	Nov	Dec	High	Low	Av
	97	99	100	108	108	112	111	112	97	117	113	112	90	170	118

Although Baku may be regarded as a long shot in the race to host the 2020 Olympic Games, the fact that the Azerbaijani capital has even entered a bid speaks volumes for the sporting ambitions of this small but oil-rich Caspian Sea nation. A first step on the way to greater international recognition for the development of sport in the country will be the 2012 FIFA Women's U-17 World Cup, which Azerbaijan will host in September 2012. Both Baku and Lenkoran will be the host cities for the tournament and between them they scooped both honours available in club football in 2011. Khazar Lenkoran kept up their excellent recent record in the Azeri Cup, beating Inter Baku on penalties in the final to win the trophy for the third time in five years. In the league there was a return to form of Neftchi Baku, the most successful club in the country during the Soviet era and in the first decade after independence but without a trophy since 2005. As is the norm in Azeri football, Neftchi relied heavily on foreign imports, notably Belgian striker Emile Mpenza. The national team didn't have a great Euro 2012 qualifying campaign, finishing above only Kazakhstan in what was a difficult group, and the federation decided it was in the long-term interests of the team to persist with Berti Vogts as coach for the 2014 FIFA World Cup qualifiers.

UEFA EUROPEAN CHAMPIONSHIP RECORD
1960-1992 DNE (part of the Soviet Union) **1996-2012** DNQ

ASSOCIATION OF FOOTBALL FEDERATIONS OF AZERBAIJAN (AFFA)

✉ 2208 Nobel prospekti, Baku AZ-1025
☎ +994 12 4908721
📠 +994 12 4908722
✉ info@affa.az
🖥 www.affa.az
FA 1992 CON 1994 FIFA 1994
P Rovnag Abdullayev
GS Elkhan Mammadov

FIFA BIG COUNT 2006

Total players	306 370
% of population	3.85%
Male	267 900
Female	38 470
Amateurs 18+	3 150
Youth under 18	14 120
Unregistered	82 700
Professionals	400
Referees	100
Admin & coaches	12 900
Number of clubs	80
Number of teams	320

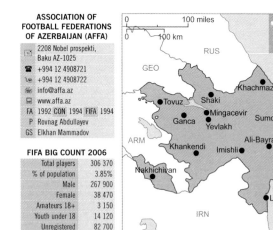

MAJOR CITIES/TOWNS

		Population
1	Baku	1 194 524
2	Gäncä	323 760
3	Sumqayit	282 280
4	Mingäcevir	100 778
5	Qaraçuxur	78 730
6	Ali Bayramli	76 648
7	Naxçivan	75 972
8	Bakikhanov	71 836
9	Shäki	65 616
10	Yevlakh	57 449
11	Xankändi	55 282
12	Lenkoran	50 534
13	Räsulzadä	48 716
14	Biläcäri	45 678
15	Mastaga	42 635
16	Agdam	42 587
17	Barda	40 741
22	Shamkir	38 331
70	Tovuz	13 612

AZARBAYCAN RESPUBLIKASI • REPUBLIC OF AZERBAIJAN

Capital Baku	Population 8 238 672 (91)	% in cities 52%
GDP per capita $9 500 (107)	Area km² 86 600 km² (112)	GMT +/- +5
Neighbours (km) Armenia 787, Georgia 322, Iran 611, Russia 284, Turkey 9 • Coast 713 (Caspian Sea)		

RECENT INTERNATIONALS PLAYED BY AZERBAIJAN

2008	Opponents	Score		Venue	Comp	Scorers	Att	Referee
6-09	Wales	L	0-1	Cardiff	WCq		17 106	Stavrev MKD
10-09	Liechtenstein	D	0-0	Baku	WCq		25 000	Georgiev BUL
11-10	Finland	L	0-1	Helsinki	WCq		22 124	Collum SCO
15-10	Bahrain	W	2-1	Manama	Fr	Zeynal Zeynalov [45], Elvin Mammadov [65]		Al Mirdas KSA
19-11	Albania	D	1-1	Baku	Fr	Branimir Subasic [4]	10 000	Silagava GEO
2009								
1-02	Uzbekistan	D	1-1	Dubai	Fr	Fabio Ramin [63p]		Albadwawi UAE
11-02	Kuwait	D	1-1	Kuwait City	Fr	Vagif Javadov [1]		Al Mirdas KSA
28-03	Russia	L	0-2	Moscow	WCq		62 000	Gumienny BEL
2-06	Turkey	L	0-2	Kayseri	Fr			Vlk SVK
6-06	Wales	L	0-1	Baku	WCq		25 000	Strombersson SWE
9-06	Spain	L	0-6	Baku	Fr		20 000	Ischenko UKR
12-08	Germany	L	0-2	Baku	WCq		22 500	Kelly IRL
5-09	Finland	L	1-2	Lenkoran	WCq	Elvin Mammadov [49]	12 000	Trifonos CYP
9-09	Germany	L	0-4	Hanover	WCq		35 369	Kakos GRE
10-10	Liechtenstein	W	2-0	Vaduz	WCq	Vagif Javadov [55], Elvin Mammadov [82]	1 635	Radovanovic MNE
14-10	Russia	D	1-1	Baku	WCq	Vagif Javadov [53]	17 000	Webb ENG
15-11	Iraq	L	0-1	Al Ain	Fr			
18-11	Czech Republic	W	2-0	Al Ain	Fr	Vagif Javadov [24], Samir Abasov [89]		Al Marzouqi UAE
2010								
25-02	Jordan	W	2-0	Amman	Fr	Fabio Ramin [1], Afran Ismaylov [31]		Shaaban EGY
3-03	Luxembourg	W	2-1	Luxembourg	Fr	Farid Guliyev [28], Elvin Mammadov [37]	874	Kari FIN
26-05	Moldova	D	1-1	Seekirchen	Fr	Elvin Mammadov [21]	200	Lechner AUT
29-05	FYR Macedonia	L	1-3	Villach	Fr	Elvin Mammadov [89]	100	Drabek AUT
2-06	Honduras	D	0-0	Zell Am See	Fr		500	Brandner AUT
11-08	Kuwait	D	1-1	Baku	Fr	Elvin Mammadov [42]	9 000	Karasev RUS
7-09	Germany	L	1-6	Cologne	ECq	Vagif Javadov [57]	43 751	Strombergsson SWE
8-10	Austria	L	0-3	Vienna	ECq		26 500	Vollquartz DEN
12-10	Turkey	W	1-0	Baku	ECq	Rashad F. Sadygov [38]	29 500	Deaconu ROU
17-11	Montenegro	L	0-2	Podgorica	Fr		3 000	Stavrev MKD
2011								
9-02	Hungary	L	0-2	Dubai	Fr		500	Al Zarooni UAE
29-03	Belgium	L	1-4	Brussels	ECq	Ruslan Abishov [16]	34 985	Stalhammar SWE
3-06	Kazakhstan	L	1-2	Astana	ECq	Vuqar Nadirov [63]	10 000	Norris SCO
7-06	Germany	L	1-3	Baku	ECq	Murad Huseynov [89]	29 858	Koukoulakis GRE
10-08	Macedonia FYR	L	0-1	Baku	Fr			Kulbakov BLR
2-09	Belgium	D	1-1	Baku	ECq	Rauf Aliyev [86]	9 300	Probert ENG
6-09	Kazakhstan	W	3-2	Baku	ECq	Rauf Aliyev [53], Mahir Shukurov [62], Vagif Javadov [67]	9 112	Hermansen DEN
7-10	Austria	L	1-4	Baku	ECq	Vuqar Nadirov [74]	6 000	Studer SUI
11-10	Turkey	L	0-1	Istanbul	ECq		32 174	Rasmussen DEN
11-11	Albania	W	1-0	Tirana	Fr	Rauf Aliyev [22]	1 200	Mazzoleni ITA

Fr = Friendly match • EC = UEFA EURO 2012 • WCq = FIFA World Cup • q = qualifier

AZERBAIJAN NATIONAL TEAM HISTORICAL RECORDS

Caps
79 - Aslan Kerimov 1994-2007 • 77 - Rashad F. Sadygov 2001- • 73 - Tarlan Akhmedov 1992-2005 • 72 - Makhmud Gurbanov 1994-2008 • 68 - Gurban Gurbanov 1992-2005 • 65 - Emin Aghaev 1994-2005 • 54 - Mahir Sukurov 2004- • 49 - Emin Guliyev 2000-08 • 46 - Kamal Guliyev 2000-05 • 45 - Vyacheslav Lichkin 1995-2001 • 44 - Emin Imamaliev 2000-07 & Samir Abbasov 2004-

Goals
12 - Gurban Gurbanov 1992-2005 • 7 - Elvin Mammadov 2008- & Vagif Javadov 2006- • 6 - Branimir Subasic 2007-09 & Zaur Tagizade 1997-2005 • 5 - Farrukh Ismayilov 1998-2006, Vidadi Rzayev 1992-2001 & Nazim Suleymanov 1992-98

Past Coaches
Alakbar Mammadov 1992-1993 • Kazbek Tuayev 1993-1994 • Agaselim Mirjavadov 1994-1995 • Kazbek Tuayev 1995-1997 • Vagif Sadygov 1997-1998 • Ahmad Alaskarov 1998-2000 • Igor Ponomaryov 2000-2001 • Vagif Sadygov 2002 • Asgar Abdullayev 2003-2004 • Carlos Alberto Torres BRA 2004-2005 • Vagif Sadygov 2005 • Shahin Diniyev 2005-2007 • Gjoko Hadzievski MKD 2007-2008 • Berti Vogts GER 2008-

AZERBAIJAN 2010–11

UNIBANK PREMYER LIGA (1)

	Pl	W	D	L	F	A	Pts	Neftchi	Khazar	Karabakh	Inter Baku	FK Baku	Gabala	Mugan	Ganca	Turan	Simurq	MOIK
Neftchi Baku †	32	19	10	3	53	17	67		0-0 1-1	1-2 0-1	0-2 1-1	1-0 0-0	2-2 0-0	0-0	1-0	6-2	2-0	4-0	1-0
Khazar Lenkoran ‡	32	16	12	4	38	18	60	1-0 1-1		1-2 1-1	2-1 3-0	0-0 1-1	1-1 2-0	1-0	2-0	1-0	2-0	1-0	3-0
Karabakh Agdam ‡	32	17	7	8	44	22	58	0-1 3-0	0-1 0-0		0-0 1-0	1-0 1-0	1-0 2-0	2-2	3-0	2-0	3-0	5-1	3-2	3-0
AZAL Baku ‡	32	13	10	9	36	28	49	0-0 1-3	0-1 1-0	2-0 3-1		5-0 1-0	0-0 1-0	2-2	2-0	0-0	1-0	2-1	2-0
Inter Baku	32	13	10	9	29	24	49	0-2 1-1	1-3 1-1	1-0 0-0	2-1 1-0	0	1-0 1-1	0-0	1-0	1-0	3-0	2-0	1-0
FK Baku	32	10	10	12	33	32	40	0-2 0-1	1-1 0-0	1-0 0-0	0-0 2-3	2-1 1-2 0-1		2-1	1-1	1-1	3-1	0-1	2-1
FK Gabala	32	13	12	7	31	18	51	0-2	1-0	2-1	0-0	0-1	0-1		2-0 2-1	0-0 1-1	1-0 1-0	4-0 3-0	0-0 0-0
Mugan Salyan -R	32	13	8	11	29	31	47	0-3	0-0	0-0	3-1	1-0	1-0	1-0 1-2		1-1 2-1 0-0	2-1 1-0	3-0 1-0 1-0
FK Ganca	32	8	12	12	33	37	36	0-4	4-1	0-1	1-1	1-0	1-3	0-0 0-3 0-1 1-		1-1 1-0 1-1	0-1 1-0 1-0
Turan Tovuz	32	7	6	19	24	47	27	2-2	1-2	0-1	1-2	0-3	0-1	0-1 0-2 1-1	0-1 2-1 1-0		1-1 2-1 2-0 1-0
Simurq Zaqatala	32	4	7	21	20	52	19	0-3	0-2	0-1	0-1	0-1	1-1	0-2 0-0 0-1 1-1	3-0 0-4 3-2 2-0 1		1-1 1-2
MOIK Baku	32	4	6	22	14	55	18	0-2	0-1	0-1	0-0	1-1	0-4	0-4 3-1 1-3	2-0 0-0 5-0	2-0 2-4	1-0 2-1 0	

7/08/2010 - 19/05/2011 • † Qualified for the UEFA Champions League • ‡ Qualified for the Europa League
Top scorers: **18** - Giorgi Adamia GEO, Karabakh • **15** - Bakhodir Nasimov UZB, Neftchi • **11** - Flavinho BRA, Neftchi

AZERBAIJAN 2010–11 BIRINCI DASTA (2)

	Pl	W	D	L	F	A	Pts
FC Absheron	26	23	3	0	75	6	72
Ravan Baku	26	19	3	4	54	14	60
Bakili Baku	26	16	4	6	37	24	52
Neftchi ISM Baku	26	15	5	6	47	24	50
MTK-Araz Imishli	26	15	3	8	49	34	48
Shahdag Khusar	26	13	8	5	45	22	47
FC Sumgayit	26	13	5	8	34	26	44
Karvan Yevlakh	26	6	8	12	26	40	26
FK Shamkir	26	5	7	14	15	36	22
ANSAD-Petrol Neftçala	26	5	6	15	28	48	21
Geyazan Gazakh	26	5	4	17	22	50	19
Energetik Mingacevir	26	4	6	16	17	50	18
FC Shusha	26	3	8	15	20	41	17
Adliyya Baku	26	3	4	19	13	67	13

4/09/2010 - 15/05/2011 • FC Absheron folded in July 2011.
Their place in the Premyer Liga was taken by FC Sumgayit

MEDALS TABLE

		Overall			League			Cup	
		G	S	B	G	S	B	G	S
1	Neftchi Baku	11	3	4	6	2	4	5	1
2	FK Ganca	7	1	2	3	1	2	4	
3	Karabakh Agdam	4	6	3	1	3	3	3	3
4	Khazar Lenkoran	4	4		1	2		3	2
5	FK Baku	4	1	1	2	1	1	2	
6	Inter Baku	2	5		2	1			4
7	FK Shamkir	2	4	1	2	1	1		3
8	Turan Tovuz	1	1	1	1	1	1		
9	Inshaatchi Baku	1						1	
	Shafa Baku	1							1
11	Karvan Yevlakh		2	1		1	1		1
	Khazri Buznova		2	1		1	1		1
13	Khazar Sumgayit		2			2			
	Kur-Nur Mingäcevir		2						2
15	Dinamo Baku		1	1		1	1		
16	Inshaatchi Sabirabad		1						1
	MTK-Araz Imishli		1						1
	AZAL Baku (ex Olimpik)		1			1			
19	Simurq Zaqatala			1					1

AZERBAIJAN KUBOKU 2010–11

First Round		Quarter–finals		Semi–finals		Final	
Khazar Lenkoran *	3						
MTK-Araz Imishli	1	**Khazar Lenkoran**	4 1				
FK Ganca *	1	Neftchi Baku *	3 1				
Neftchi Baku	3			**Khazar Lenkoran** *	1 1		
FK Gabala *	2			FK Baku	0 2		
Neftchi ISM Baku	0	FK Gabala *	0 0				
Mugan Salyan	1 3p	**FK Baku**	0 1				
FK Baku *	1 5p					**Khazar Lenkoran** ‡	1 4p
AZAL Baku	2					Inter Baku	1 2p
Ravan Baku *	0	**AZAL Baku** *	2 1				
Karabakh Agdam *	0 3p	Turan Tovuz	0 1				

CUP FINAL

Turan Tovuz	0 4p	AZAL Baku	0 0

Turan Tovuz	0 4p
FC Absheron	1 4p	AZAL Baku	0 0
Simurq Zaqatala *	1 1p	FC Absheron *	0 0	Inter Baku *	0 1
Susa *	1	**Inter Baku**	0 1
Inter Baku	4

CUP FINAL

Tofik Bakramov, Baku
24-05-2011, 24 000
Scorers - Winston Parks [91] for
Khazar; Girts Karlsons [100] for Inter

* Home team in the first leg • ‡ Qualified for the Europa League

Preliminary Round: Karvan 1-1 3-4p **MTK Araz** • Bakili 0-1 **Neftchi ISM** • ANSAD-Petrol 0-2 **Susa** • Semkir 1-3 **Ravan** • Sahdag 0-3 **Ganca** • **Absheron** 4-0 MOIK

BAH – BAHAMAS

FIFA/COCA-COLA WORLD RANKING

'93	'94	'95	'96	'97	'98	'99	'00	'01	'02	'03	'04	'05	'06	'07	'08	'09	'10	'11	'12
167	-	-	-	-	-	189	178	184	187	193	192	193	146	174	170	180	194		

2011												High	Low	Av
Jan	Feb	Mar	Apr	May	Jun	Jul	Aug	Sep	Oct	Nov	Dec	High	Low	Av
194	194	193	196	196	197	152	151	152	154	153	154	138	197	179

The Bahamas national team kicked off its 2014 FIFA World Cup qualifying campaign in convincing fashion with a 10-0 aggregate victory over minnows Turks and Caicos in the preliminary round but then withdrew from the tournament in August just before the first group stage got underway. The Bahamas had been scheduled to host matches at the new Chinese-built 23,000 capacity stadium in Nassau but it hadn't been completed in time. It was a big disappointment for the team, especially striker Lesley St Fleur who was unable to add to his five goals scored in the 6-0 victory over the Turks and Caicos Islands in the second leg of the preliminary round. At club level Bears kicked off the season by beating fierce rivals Lyford Cay 3-2 in the Charity Shield and once again they dominated the season but unlike the previous year they didn't have it all their own way. They lost their first match of the league campaign and it wasn't until the final match that they clinched the title in a winner-takes-all game against Lyford Cay. A draw would have seen them home and dry but they did better than that, winning a nine-goal thriller 6-3. Two weeks later Bears beat Dynamos 4-2 in the Cup Final to complete the treble but they were denied a successive quadruple having earlier lost 2-1 to Cavalier in the President's Cup Final.

FIFA WORLD CUP RECORD
1930-1998 DNE **2002-2010** DNQ

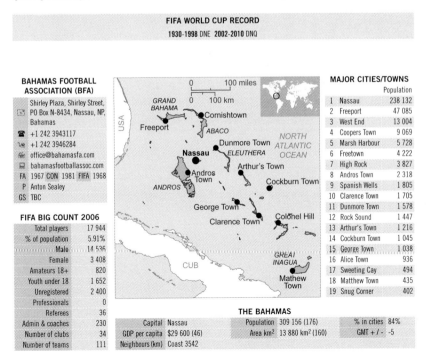

BAHAMAS FOOTBALL ASSOCIATION (BFA)

Shirley Plaza, Shirley Street, PO Box N-8434, Nassau, NP, Bahamas

☎ +1 242 3943117
📠 +1 242 3946284
✉ office@bahamasfa.com
🖥 bahamasfootballassoc.com
FA 1967 CON 1981 FIFA 1968
P Anton Sealey
GS TBC

FIFA BIG COUNT 2006

Total players	17 944
% of population	5.91%
Male	14 536
Female	3 408
Amateurs 18+	820
Youth under 18	1 652
Unregistered	2 400
Professionals	0
Referees	36
Admin & coaches	230
Number of clubs	34
Number of teams	111

MAJOR CITIES/TOWNS

		Population
1	Nassau	238 132
2	Freeport	47 085
3	West End	13 004
4	Coopers Town	9 069
5	Marsh Harbour	5 728
6	Freetown	4 222
7	High Rock	3 827
8	Andros Town	2 318
9	Spanish Wells	1 805
10	Clarence Town	1 705
11	Dunmore Town	1 578
12	Rock Sound	1 447
13	Arthur's Town	1 216
14	Cockburn Town	1 045
15	George Town	1 038
16	Alice Town	936
17	Sweeting Cay	494
18	Matthew Town	435
19	Snug Corner	402

THE BAHAMAS

Capital	Nassau	Population	309 156 (176)	% in cities 84%
GDP per capita	$29 600 (46)	Area km²	13 880 km² (160)	GMT +/- -5
Neighbours (km)	Coast 3542			

RECENT INTERNATIONAL MATCHES PLAYED BY BAHAMAS

2006	Opponents	Score			Venue	Comp	Scorers	Att	Referee
2-09	Cayman Islands	W	3-1		Havana	CCq	OG [5], Moseley [36], Thompson [86]	200	Stewart JAM
4-09	Cuba	L	0-6		Havana	CCq		100	Prendergast JAM
6-09	Turks & Caicos Isl	W	3-2		Havana	CCq	Nassies [59], Hall [63], Jean [87]	120	Campbell JAM
19-11	Barbados	L	1-2		Bridgetown	CCq	Jean [76p]	4 500	Jauregui ANT
21-11	Bermuda	L	0-4		Bridgetown	CCq		3 500	Angela URU
23-11	St Vincent/Grenadines	L	2-3		Bridgetown	CCq	Christie [55], Moseley [65]	4 000	Angela URU
2007									
No international matches played in 2007									
2008									
26-03	British Virgin Islands	D	1-1		Nassau	WCq	St Fleur [47]	450	Moreno PAN
30-03	British Virgin Islands	D	2-2		Nassau	WCq	Bethel [41], Mitchell [57]	940	Suazo DOM
15-06	Jamaica	L	0-7		Kingston	WCq		20 000	Navarro CAN
18-06	Jamaica	L	0-6		Greenfield-Tr'wny	WCq		10 500	Archundia MEX
2009									
No international matches played in 2009									
2010									
No international matches played in 2010									
2011									
2-07	Turks and Caicos Isl	W	4-0		Providenciales	WCq	Nesley Jean 2 [32 61], Cameron Hepple [36p], Jackner Louis [92+]	1 021	Cruz CRC
9-07	Turks and Caicos Isl	W	6-0		Nassau	WCq	Gibson OG [4], Lesley St Fleur 5 [17 64 73 84 90]	1 600	Santos PUR

Fr = Friendly match • CC = Digicel Caribbean Cup • WC = FIFA World Cup • q = qualifier

BAHAMAS 2011

BFA SENIOR LEAGUE

	Pl	W	D	L	F	A	Pts	Bears	Lyford Cay	Dynamos	United	Cavalier	Baha Jun	COB
Bears	12	10	0	2	49	14	30		3-2	1-2	1-0	4-2	10-0	7-1
Lyford Cay	12	8	2	2	45	20	26	3-6		3-0	2-1	3-2	7-2	7-0
Dynamos	12	7	2	3	27	21	23	0-6	1-1		0-0	2-0	4-1	3-1
United	12	5	2	5	24	17	17	1-0	3-4	2-1		0-0	2-0	3-4
Cavalier	12	4	2	6	24	23	14	0-4	0-0	2-4	4-1		1-2	6-1
Baha Juniors	12	3	0	9	16	49	9	2-5	1-4	1-4	0-6	1-5		4-0
College of Bahamas	12	1	0	11	15	56	3	1-2	1-9	3-6	1-5	1-2	1-2	

23/01/2011 - 15/05/2011 • All matches played at Roscoe Davies Soccer Field • Top scorers: 16 - Nesley Jean, Bears & Lesly St Fleur, Bears

BFA KNOCK-OUT CUP 2011

Quarter-finals		Semi-finals		Final	
Bears	Bye				
		Bears	4		
Cavalier	2	Lyford Cay	2		
Lyford Cay	4			Bears	4
Baha Juniors	2 4p			Dynamos	2
COB	2 2p	Baha Juniors	1		
United	0	Dynamos	4	29-05-2011	
Dynamos	6				

MEDALS TABLE

		Overall	Lge	Cup
		G	G	G
1	Bears	12	7	5
2	Cavalier	6	4	2
3	Britam United	4	4	
4	Caledonia Celtic	3	2	1
5	Abacom United	1	1	
	Freeport	1	1	
	JJ Johnson	1		1

BAN – BANGLADESH

FIFA/COCA-COLA WORLD RANKING

'93	'94	'95	'96	'97	'98	'99	'00	'01	'02	'03	'04	'05	'06	'07	'08	'09	'10	'11	'12
116	130	138	136	141	157	130	151	146	159	151	167	160	144	168	174	149	159	157	

					2011								High	Low	Av
Jan	Feb	Mar	Apr	May	Jun	Jul	Aug	Sep	Oct	Nov	Dec		High	Low	Av
158	157	174	166	163	163	147	139	138	141	142	157		110	183	149

Sheikh Jamal promised to ruffle a few feathers when the club was reorganised in 2010 and, following-on from their appearance in the final of the 2010 Federation Cup, they crowned their first season in the Bangladesh League by winning the title, although it turned out to be a tight race with Muktijoddha finishing just one point behind. Sheikh Jamal had raided rivals Mohammedan and defending champions Abahani at the start of the season for players and it paid off for coach Pakeer Ali, who could call on the bulk of the national team during the campaign as well as a strong contingent of five players from Nigeria and Cameroon. In January 2012, they completed the double after beating BJMC 3-1 in the final of the 2011 Federation Cup. Macedonian coach Nikola Ilievski stepped down from his position at the helm of the national team citing health problems following his side's disappointing performance at the South Asian Football Federation Championship in India in December. Ilievski had taken over in the middle of the year after the national side had missed out on a place in the finals of the AFC Challenge Cup following losses to Palestine and the Philippines. He guided the team to the second phase of qualifying for the FIFA World Cup finals, defeating Pakistan on aggregate in the opening round only to see his side eliminated by Lebanon.

FIFA WORLD CUP RECORD
1930-1982 DNE 1986-2010 DNQ

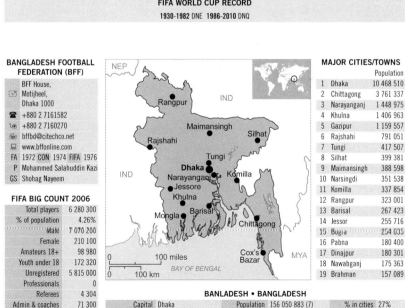

BANGLADESH FOOTBALL FEDERATION (BFF)

BFF House,
Motijheel,
Dhaka 1000
☎ +880 2 7161582
📠 +880 2 7160270
✉ bffbd@citechco.net
🖥 www.bffonline.com
FA 1972 CON 1974 FIFA 1976
P Mohammed Salahuddin Kazi
GS Shohag Nayeem

FIFA BIG COUNT 2006

Total players	6 280 300
% of population	4.26%
Male	7 070 200
Female	210 100
Amateurs 18+	98 980
Youth under 18	172 320
Unregistered	5 815 000
Professionals	0
Referees	4 304
Admin & coaches	71 300
Number of clubs	4 100
Number of teams	8 200

MAJOR CITIES/TOWNS

		Population
1	Dhaka	10 468 510
2	Chittagong	3 761 337
3	Narayanganj	1 448 975
4	Khulna	1 406 963
5	Gazipur	1 159 557
6	Rajshahi	791 051
7	Tungi	417 507
8	Silhat	399 381
9	Maimansingh	388 598
10	Narsingdi	351 538
11	Komilla	337 854
12	Rangpur	323 001
13	Barisal	267 423
14	Jessor	255 716
15	Bugra	254 035
16	Pabna	180 400
17	Dinajpur	180 301
18	Nawabganj	175 363
19	Brahman	157 089

BANLADESH • BANGLADESH

Capital	Dhaka	Population	156 050 883 (7)	% in cities	27%
GDP per capita	$1500 (196)	Area km²	143 998 km² (94)	GMT +/-	+6
Neighbours (km)	Myanmar 193, India 4053 • Coast 580				

RECENT INTERNATIONAL MATCHES PLAYED BY BANGLADESH

2006	Opponents	Score		Venue	Comp	Scorers	Att	Referee
16-08	Qatar	L	1-4	Chittagong	ACq	Mohamad Arman [23]	7 000	Al Yarimi YEM
6-09	Qatar	L	0-3	Doha	ACq		500	Najm LIB
11-10	Uzbekistan	L	0-4	Dhaka	ACq		120	Tan Hai CHN
15-11	Hong Kong	L	0-2	Hong Kong	ACq		1 273	Kim Dong Jin KOR
2007								
18-08	Syria	L	0-2	New Delhi	Fr			
20-08	India	L	0-1	New Delhi	Fr			
22-08	Cambodia	D	1-1	New Delhi	Fr	Abdul Hossain [30]		
24-08	Kyrgyzstan	L	0-3	New Delhi	Fr			
8-10	Tajikistan	D	1-1	Dhaka	WCq	Zumratul Hossain Mithu [50]	700	Al Hilali OMA
28-10	Tajikistan	L	0-5	Dushanbe	WCq		10 000	Chynybekov KGZ
2008								
5-05	Afghanistan	D	0-0	Bishkek	CCq		3 000	Al Senan UAE
9-05	Kyrgyzstan	L	1-2	Bishkek	CCq		5 000	Al Enezi KUW
4-06	Bhutan	D	1-1	Colombo	SAFr1	Arup Baidya [26]		
6-06	Afghanistan	D	2-2	Colombo	SAFr1	Hasan Ameli [52], Mamunul Islam Mamun [76]		
8-06	Sri Lanka	L	0-1	Colombo	SAFr1			
18-10	Myanmar	L	0-1	Kuala Lumpur	Fr			
11-11	Myanmar	D	0-0	Yangon	Fr			
13-11	Indonesia	L	0-2	Yangon	Fr			
2009								
26-04	Cambodia	W	1-0	Dhaka	CCq	Anamul Hoque [73]	8 060	Yazdi IRN
28-04	Myanmar	L	1-2	Dhaka	CCq	Anamul Hoque [12]	14 000	Matsuo JPN
30-04	Macau	W	3-0	Dhaka	CCq	Mamunul Islam Mamun [38], Zahid Hossain 2 [68 71]	8 700	Mashentsev KGZ
4-12	Bhutan	W	4-1	Dhaka	SAFr1	Das [11], Anamul Hoque 2 [22 51], Ameli [72]		
6-12	Pakistan	D	0-0	Dhaka	SAFr1			
8-12	Sri Lanka	W	2-1	Dhaka	SAFr1	Anamul Hoque 2 [8 64]		
11-12	India †	L	0-1	Dhaka	SAFsf			
2010								
16-02	Tajikistan	W	2-1	Colombo	CCr1	Anamul Hoque [67], Atiqur Meshu [74]	1 000	Matsuo JPN
18-02	Myanmar	L	1-2	Colombo	CCr1	Mohammed Hossain [49]	500	Al Yarimi YEM
20-02	Sri Lanka	L	0-3	Colombo	CCr1		600	Mahapab THA
2011								
21-03	Palestine	L	0-2	Yangon	CCq		1 000	
23-03	Myanmar	W	2-0	Yangon	CCq	Ahmed Shakil [10], Abdulbaten Mojumder [88]	3 000	
25-03	Philippines	L	0-3	Yangon	CCq		200	Kim Jong Hyeok KOR
29-06	Pakistan	W	3-0	Dhaka	WCq	Jahid Hasan [1], Zahid Hossain [22], Karim Razaul [56]	5 326	Abu Loum JOR
3-07	Pakistan	D	0-0	Lahore	WCq		3 500	Abdulnabi BHR
23-07	Lebanon	L	0-4	Beirut	WCq		2 000	Auda IRQ
28-07	Lebanon	W	2-0	Dhaka	WCq	Mithun Chowdhury [52], Jahid Hassan [87]	11 000	Aonrak THA
2-12	Pakistan	D	0-0	New Delhi	SAFr1			Faizullin KGZ
4-12	Nepal	L	0-1	New Delhi	SAFr1			Kumar IND
6-12	Maldives	L	1-3	New Delhi	SAFr1	Alam Shahed [29]		Tufaylieh SYR

SAF = South Asian Football Federation Cup • AC = AFC Asian Cup • CC = AFC Challenge Cup • WCq = FIFA World Cup
q = qualifier • r1 = first round group • sf = semi-final • f = final

BANGLADESH NATIONAL TEAM HISTORICAL RECORDS

Past Coaches Hamzah Hussain Wahid 1992 • Kazi Salahuddin 1993 • Oldrich Svab SUI • Man Yang Kang KOR 1994 • Otto Pfister GER 1994-97 • Samir Shakir IRQ 1998-99 • Mark Harrison ENG 2000 • Aurel Ticleanu ROU 2002 • Gyorgy Kottan AUT 2002-03 • Andres Cruciani ARG 2005-07 • Syed Nayeemuddin IND 2007 • Sayeed Hassan Kanan 2007-08 • Abu Yusuf Mohammad Bilal 2008 • Shafiq Islam Malik 2008 • Dido BRA 2009 • Rizwan Ali Jahed 2009 • Zoran Djordjevic SRB 2010 • Saiful Bari Titu 2010 • Robert Rupcic CRO 2010-11 • Gjore Jovanovski 2011 • Nikola Olievski 2011

BANGLADESH 2010-11

CITYCELL BANGLADESH LEAGUE

	Pl	W	D	L	F	A	Pts	Sheikh Jamal	Muktijoddha S	Sheikh Russell	Abahani Dhaka	Brothers Union	Mohammedan	Arambagh	Rahmatganj	Feni	Farashganj	Mohammedan C	Abahani C
Sheikh Jamal †	22	15	6	1	42	12	51		2-0	0-0	3-1	2-2	1-0	0-1	5-2	1-0	2-1	4-0	6-0
Muktijoddha Sangsad	22	15	5	2	52	15	50	1-1		0-1	1-1	2-0	1-0	3-0	5-1	2-1	1-1	6-0	3-2
Sheikh Russell	22	13	5	4	35	16	44	0-1	0-3		0-2	4-0	0-1	3-1	1-0	3-0	1-0	2-1	5-0
Abahani Dhaka	22	13	5	4	30	15	44	0-0	0-0	0-1		1-0	1-0	2-1	4-1	3-1	0-1	2-0	1-0
Brothers Union	22	8	6	8	31	30	30	1-2	1-4	2-2	0-1		3-1	0-0	5-2	2-0	1-1	1-1	3-1
Mohammedan	22	8	6	8	26	26	30	1-3	2-2	0-1	0-0	0-2		4-1	3-1	3-2	1-1	2-1	1-0
Arambagh	22	7	6	9	26	27	27	0-2	0-1	1-1	1-2	2-3	0-0		1-2	1-1	0-0	3-2	4-0
Rahmatganj	22	7	3	12	29	48	24	1-2	1-5	2-2	1-0	1-2	2-0	0-4		1-1	2-2	2-1	1-0
Feni	22	4	9	9	22	30	21	0-0	0-2	1-2	1-1	0-0	2-2	0-0	2-1		2-1	1-2	1-0
Farashganj	22	4	7	11	17	32	19	0-2	0-5	0-2	2-4	2-1	0-1	0-2	0-1	2-2		0-0	1-0
Mohammedan Ch'gong	22	4	5	13	18	41	17	0-2	1-2	0-3	1-2	1-0	2-2	0-1	2-1	0-3	2-1		0-0
Abahani Chittagong	22	0	5	17	9	45	5	1-1	0-3	1-1	0-2	0-2	0-2	1-2	1-3	1-1	0-1	1-1	

27/12/2010 - 27/06/2011 • † Qualified for the AFC President's Cup

MEDALS TABLE

		Overall		Nat		Fed Cup		Dhaka	
		G	S	G	B	G	S	G	City
1	Mohammedan SC	31	9	2	5	10	4	19	Dhaka
2	Abahani Ltd	23	9	4	2	8	7	11	Dhaka
3	Dhaka Wanderers	7	1				1	7	Dhaka
4	Muktijoddha SKC	6	4	1	1	3	3	2	Dhaka
5	Brothers Union	6	2	1		3	2	2	Dhaka
6	Bangladesh IDC	4						4	Dhaka
7	Victoria SC	3						3	Dhaka
8	Sheikh Jamal Dhanmondi Club	2	1	1		1	1		Dhaka
9	Azad	1						1	Dhaka
10	Bangladesh Jute Mill Corp.	1	1				1	1	Dhaka
11	Bengal Government Press	1						1	Dhaka
12	East Pakistan Gymkhana	1						1	Dhaka
13	Fakirerpool Young Men's Club	1						1	Dhaka
	Arambagh KS		1				1		Dhaka

FEDERATION CUP 2011

First Round Groups

Group A	Pl	W	D	L	F	A	Pts	Mu	CC	Mo
BJMC	3	2	1	0	9	2	7	3-2	6-0	0-0
Muktijoddha	3	2	0	1	15	4	6		10-0	3-1
Cox City FC	3	1	0	2	1	16	3			1-0
Mohammedan	3	0	1	2	1	4	1			

Group B	Pl	W	D	L	F	A	Pts	Ar	Fe	Po
Abahani Dhaka	3	2	0	1	9	3	6	2-1	1-2	6-0
Arambagh	3	1	1	1	3	2	4		0-0	2-0
Feni	3	1	1	1	2	2	4			0-1
BD Police	3	1	0	2	1	8	3			

Group C	Pl	W	D	L	F	A	Pts	SJ	Vi	AB
Sheikh Russell	3	3	0	0	7	1	9	2-1	2-0	3-0
Sheikh Jamal	3	2	0	1	3	2	6		1-0	1-0
Victoria SC	3	0	1	2	1	4	1			1-1
Agrani Bank	3	0	1	2	1	5	1			

Group D	Pl	W	D	L	F	A	Pts	Ra	BU	Wa
Farashganj	3	2	1	0	3	0	7	0-0	1-0	2-0
Rahmatganj	3	1	2	0	6	3	5		3-3	3-0
Brothers Union	3	0	2	1	3	4	2			0-0
Wari Club	3	0	1	2	0	5	1			

Quarter-finals

Sheikh Jamal 2 4p
Abahani Dhaka 2 3p

Arambagh 2
Sheikh Russell 4

Muktijoddha 1 5p
Farashganj 1 3p

Rahmatganj 1
BJMC 3

Semi-finals

Sheikh Jamal 2
Sheikh Russell 0

Muktijoddha 0
BJMC 2

Final

Sheikh Jamal 3
BJMC 1

CUP FINAL

Bangabandhu, Dhaka
24-01-2012
Scorers - Mintu Shiekh [55], Kester [59], Sobuj [90] for Sheikh Jamal; Ikanga [73] for BJMC

BDI – BURUNDI

FIFA/COCA-COLA WORLD RANKING

'93	'94	'95	'96	'97	'98	'99	'00	'01	'02	'03	'04	'05	'06	'07	'08	'09	'10	'11	'12
101	126	146	137	152	141	133	126	139	135	145	152	147	117	109	136	126	128	140	

					2011									
Jan	Feb	Mar	Apr	May	Jun	Jul	Aug	Sep	Oct	Nov	Dec	High	Low	Av
140	144	144	148	149	139	143	145	141	141	145	140	96	160	135

Burundi were surprisingly eliminated from the 2014 FIFA World Cup qualifiers after being beaten 3-2 on aggregate by minnows Lesotho. After losing by only one goal away in the first leg in Maseru, they were expected to overcome their opponents in the return but were held to a 2-2 draw. This followed on from a third-place finish in their 2012 CAF Africa Cup of Nations qualifying group while their year ended with defeat by Sudan in the quarter-finals of the East and Central African Senior Challenge Cup in Tanzania. It was a busy year for coach Adel Amrouche and his 'Intamba Mu Ragauba' side with 13 matches, but they only won three. Captain Valery Nahayo saw a big money move to Gent in Belgium from South African club Kaizer Chiefs, adding to the small number of players from east African country playing professionally in Europe. At home, league honours were won by Atlético Olympique, comfortably ahead of Lydia Ludic Burundi Academic although between them they lost just one match all season with Olympique remaining undefeated throughout the whole 22-match campaign. Neither lost in October's President's Cup, with LLB Academic beating the champions on post-match penalties for their first-ever silverware. LLB are a Spanish development foundation active across the African continent.

CAF AFRICA CUP OF NATIONS RECORD
1957-1974 DNE **1976** DNQ **1978-1992** DNQ **1994** DNQ **1996-1998** DNE **2000-2012** DNQ

FEDERATION DE FOOTBALL DU BURUNDI (FFB)

Avenue Muyinga, Boite postale 3426, Bujumbura, Burundi

☎ +257 79 928762
📠 +257 22 242892
✉ lydiansekera@yahoo.fr
🖥

FA 1948 CON 1972 FIFA 1972
P Lydia Nsekera
GS Jeremie Manirakiza

FIFA BIG COUNT 2006

Total players	352 334
% of population	4.36%
Male	335 284
Female	17 050
Amateurs 18+	5 612
Youth under 18	6 289
Unregistered	17 400
Professionals	3
Referees	412
Admin & coaches	9 220
Number of clubs	165
Number of teams	189

MAJOR CITIES/TOWNS

		Population
1	Bujumbura	367 544
2	Muyinga	95 840
3	Ruyigi	44 854
4	Makamba	25 231
5	Gitega	24 794
6	Rutana	24 150
7	Ngozi	23 779
8	Bururi	21 862
9	Muramvya	21 287
10	Kayanza	20 647
11	Cibitoke	17 142
12	Bubanza	14 945
13	Karuzi	12 729
14	Cankuzo	7 498
15	Kirundo	7 034
16	Rumonge	6 727
17	Mwaro	5 270

REPUBLIKA Y'U BURUNDI • REPUBLIC OF BURUNDI

Capital	Bujumbura	Population	8 988 091 (89)	% in cities	10%
GDP per capita	$400 (227)	Area km²	27 830 km² (146)	GMT +/-	+2
Neighbours (km)	Congo DR 233, Rwanda 290, Tanzania 451				

RECENT INTERNATIONAL MATCHES PLAYED BY BURUNDI

2010	Opponents	Score		Venue	Comp	Scorers	Att	Referee
5-09	Benin	D	1-1	Cotonou	CNq	Didier Kavumbagu [86]		Bennett RSA
9-10	Côte d'Ivoire	L	0-1	Bujumbura	CNq			El Raay LBY
28-11	Somalia	W	2-0	Dar Es Salaam	CCr1	Claude Nahimana [18], Jean-Paul Habarugira [72]		
30-11	Zambia	D	0-0	Dar Es Salaam	CCr1			
4-12	Tanzania	L	0-2	Dar Es Salaam	CCr1			
2011								
5-01	Uganda	L	1-3	Cairo	Fr	Jean-Paul Habarugira [38]		
8-01	Tanzania	D	1-1	Cairo	Fr	Tambwe Amissi [49]		
11-01	Egypt	L	0-3	Ismailia	Fr			
26-03	Rwanda	L	1-3	Kigali	CNq	Faty Papy [37]		
5-06	Rwanda	W	3-1	Bujumbura	CNq	Saidi Ntibazonkiza 2 [29 53], Didier Kavumbagu [84]		
4-09	Benin	D	1-1	Bujumbura	CNq	Faty Papy [92+]		
9-10	Côte d'Ivoire	L	1-2	Abidjan	CNq	Claude Nahimana [77]		
11-11	Lesotho	L	0-1	Maseru	WCq		5 000	Shikongo NAM
15-11	Lesotho	D	2-2	Bujumbura	WCq	Cedric Amissi [29], Yamin Ndikumana [88p]	7 200	Raphael MWI
25-11	Somalia	W	4-1	Dar es Salaam	CCr1	Floribert Ndayisaba [30], Faty Papy [45], Cedric Amissi [54], Fuadi Ndayisenga [86]		
27-11	Zanzibar †	D	0-0	Dar es Salaam	CCr1			
1-12	Uganda	W	1-0	Dar es Salaam	CCr1	Cedric Amissi [40]		
5-12	Sudan	L	0-2	Dar es Salaam	CCqf			

Fr = Friendly match • CN = CAF African Cup of Nations qualifier • CC = CECAFA Cup • WCq = FIFA World Cup • † Not a full international

BURUNDI 2010–11

LIGUE A

	Pl	W	D	L	F	A	Pts	Atlético	Académic	Vital'O	Inter Star	Royal	Union	Tchité	Espoir	Muzinga	Flamengo	Prince Louis	Maniema
Atlético Olympique †	22	18	4	0	45	6	58		1-1	1-0	1-0	4-0	3-0	1-0	1-0	5-0	0-0	2-0	7-0
LLB Académic ‡	22	14	7	1	50	15	49	0-0		0-0	2-0	1-0	3-2	0-1	1-1	3-2	2-0	2-1	6-2
Vital'O	22	14	4	4	42	12	46	0-1	0-0		0-0	4-1	2-0	1-2	6-0	2-0	2-0	1-2	3-0
Inter Star	22	13	4	5	36	20	43	1-2	1-3	0-1		3-3	2-2	3-0	3-0	3-2	2-0	1-0	4-0
Royal FC Muramvya	22	9	3	10	30	36	30	0-1	1-2	1-2	1-3		1-0	3-1	1-1	0-1	0-0	**2-0**	3-1
Union Sporting	22	7	6	9	32	36	27	1-3	1-1	0-2	0-1	5-1		2-1	1-0	4-0	1-1	3-3	0-2
Académie Tchité	22	7	4	11	16	27	25	1-1	0-4	2-4	0-1	**0-2**	0-0		0-0	0-1	2-0	1-0	2-1
Espoir Gatumba	22	5	8	9	20	31	23	0-2	1-1	0-0	1-1	1-2	2-3	1-0		3-1	1-0	0-0	**2-0**
Muzinga	22	7	2	13	25	41	23	1-2	0-2	1-4	0-1	0-1	5-0	1-0	0-0		1-2	3-2	3-2
Flamengo de Ngagara	22	5	7	10	21	32	22	0-2	0-7	0-2	1-3	2-1	0-0	0-1	3-0	1-1		1-1	3-0
Prince Louis	22	5	4	13	30	34	19	1-2	1-3	1-2	1-2	3-4	**0-2**	0-1	4-0	4-0	2-2		2-0
Maniema Fantastique	22	1	1	20	15	72	4	0-3	0-6	0-4	0-1	1-2	3-5	1-1	1-6	0-2	1-5	0-2	

29/10/2010 - 18/09/2011 • † Qualified for the CAF Champions League • ‡ Qualified for the CAF Confederation Cup • Matches in bold awarded

COUPE DU PRESIDENT DE LA REPUBLIQUE 2011

First Round		Quarter-finals		Semi-finals		Final		
LLB Académic	1							
Union Sporting	0	**LLB Académic**	1					
Olympic Muremera	0 2p	Aigle Noir	0					
Aigle Noir	0 4p			**LLB Académic**	2			
Flambeau de l"Est	1 4p			Wazee	1			
Royal FC Muramvya	1 3p	Flambeau de l"Est	2 2p					
Inter Star	0	**Wazee**	2 4p					
Wazee	1					**LLB Académic**	0	6p
Vital'O	5					Atlético Olympique	0	5p
Delta Star	1	**Vital'O**	2					
Mugina	1	Maniema Fantastique	0	**Vital'O**	0	CUP FINAL		
Maniema Fantastique	2			**Atlético Olympique**	1			
Muzinga	3							
Boundès	0	Muzinga	0			1-10-2011		
Nile Olympique	0	**Atlético Olympique**	4					
Atlético Olympique	4							

BEL – BELGIUM

FIFA/COCA-COLA WORLD RANKING

'93	'94	'95	'96	'97	'98	'99	'00	'01	'02	'03	'04	'05	'06	'07	'08	'09	'10	'11	'12
25	24	24	42	41	35	33	27	20	17	16	45	55	53	49	54	66	57	41	

2011												High	Low	Av
Jan	Feb	Mar	Apr	May	Jun	Jul	Aug	Sep	Oct	Nov	Dec	High	Low	Av
58	58	62	37	37	35	37	37	34	37	41	41	16	71	37

Over the 40 games played by the top clubs in the Belgian league, Genk had comfortably the best record but thanks to the bizarre points system now used they almost had the title snatched away from them. With Anderlecht - winners of the first stage - out of the running, it turned into a duel between Genk and Standard Liege with the two meeting on the final day of the season. Standard needed a win in Genk's Cristal Arena to clinch their third title in four years and they were on course with just 12 minutes to go until Kennedy Nwanganga scored the equaliser to give Frank Vercauteren's Genk their first title since 2002 and their third since the merger in 1988 of Winterslag and Waterschei which saw the creation of the club. Four days later there was consolation for Standard who beat Westerlo 2-0 in the Cup Final - their first triumph in the competition since 1993 and only their second since the early 1980s. The Belgian national team came unstuck in the Euro 2012 qualifiers, unable to live with the irresistible Germans who won all ten games in the group. It was the failure to beat Turkey in the battle for a play-off spot that caused problems for George Leekens' team and they finished in third place, two points behind the Turks. Leekens agreed to stay on for the World Cup qualifiers as the Belgians look to qualify for their first finals since 2002.

UEFA EUROPEAN CHAMPIONSHIP RECORD

1960 DNE   1964 DNQ   1968 DNQ   **1972** 3 SF   1976 DNQ   **1980** 2 F   **1984** 6 r1   1988-1996 DNQ   **2000** 12 r1 (co-hosts)   2004-2012 DNQ

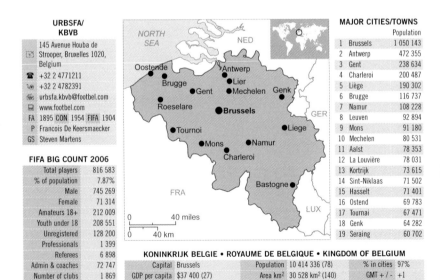

URBSFA/ KBVB

145 Avenue Houba de Strooper, Bruxelles 1020, Belgium

☎ +32 2 4771211
🖷 +32 2 4782391
✉ urbsfa.kbvb@footbel.com
🖳 www.footbel.com
FA 1895 CON 1954 FIFA 1904
P   Francois De Keersmaecker
GS Steven Martens

FIFA BIG COUNT 2006

Total players	816 583
% of population	7.87%
Male	745 269
Female	71 314
Amateurs 18+	212 009
Youth under 18	208 551
Unregistered	128 200
Professionals	1 399
Referees	6 898
Admin & coaches	72 747
Number of clubs	1 869
Number of teams	17 960

MAJOR CITIES/TOWNS

		Population
1	Brussels	1 050 143
2	Antwerp	472 355
3	Gent	238 634
4	Charleroi	200 487
5	Liège	190 302
6	Brugge	116 737
7	Namur	108 228
8	Leuven	92 894
9	Mons	91 180
10	Mechelen	80 531
11	Aalst	78 353
12	La Louvière	78 031
13	Kortrijk	73 615
14	Sint-Niklaas	71 502
15	Hasselt	71 401
16	Ostend	69 783
17	Tournai	67 471
18	Genk	64 282
19	Seraing	60 702

KONINKRIJK BELGIE • ROYAUME DE BELGIQUE • KINGDOM OF BELGIUM

Capital	Brussels	Population	10 414 336 (78)	% in cities	97%
GDP per capita	$37 400 (27)	Area km²	30 528 km² (140)	GMT +/-	+1
Neighbours (km)	France 620, Germany 167, Luxembourg 148, Netherlands 450 • Coast 66				

RECENT INTERNATIONAL MATCHES PLAYED BY BELGIUM

2008	Opponents	Score		Venue	Comp	Scorers	Att	Referee
26-03	Morocco	L	1-4	Brussels	Fr	Witsel [50]	24 000	Nijhuis NED
30-05	Italy	L	1-3	Florence	Fr	Sonck [92+]	12 500	Atkinson ENG
20-08	Germany	L	0-2	Nuremberg	Fr		34 117	Vejlgaard DEN
6-09	Estonia	W	3-2	Liege	WCq	Sonck 2 [39 81], Delfour [75]	17 992	Dean ENG
10-09	Turkey	D	1-1	Istanbul	WCq	Sonck [32]	34 097	Lannoy FRA
11-10	Armenia	W	2-0	Brussels	WCq	Sonck [21], Fellaini [37]	20 949	Ramussen DEN
15-10	Spain	L	1-2	Brussels	WCq	Sonck [7]	45 888	Ovrebo NOR
19-11	Luxembourg	D	1-1	Luxembourg	Fr	Mirallas [21]	4 172	Riley ENG
2009								
11-02	Slovenia	W	2-0	Genk	Fr	Van Buyten 2 [21 86]	13 135	Kever SUI
28-03	Bosnia-Herzegovina	L	2-4	Genk	WCq	Dembele [66], Sonck [85p]	20 041	Ivanov.N RUS
1-04	Bosnia-Herzegovina	L	1-2	Zenica	WCq	Swerts [88]	13 800	Hrinak SVK
29-05	Chile	D	1-1	Chiba	Fr	Roelandts [15]	9 700	Tojo JPN
31-05	Japan	L	0-4	Chiba	Fr		42 520	Styles ENG
12-08	Czech Republic	L	1-3	Teplice	Fr	Vertonghen [12]	13 890	Sippel GER
5-09	Spain	L	0-5	La Coruña	WCq		30 441	Layec FRA
9-09	Armenia	L	1-2	Yerevan	WCq	Van Buyten [92+]	2 300	Stavrev MKD
10-10	Turkey	W	2-0	Brussels	WCq	Mpenza.E 2 [7 84]	30 131	Trefolini ITA
14-10	Estonia	L	0-2	Tallinn	WCq		4 680	Vollquartz DEN
14-11	Hungary	W	3-0	Gent	Fr	Fellaini [39], Vermaelen [55], Mirallas [61p]	8 000	Picirillo FRA
17-11	Qatar	W	2-0	Sedan	Fr	Witsel [20], Sonck [54]	3 000	Buquet FRA
2010								
19-05	Bulgaria	W	2-1	Brussels	Fr	Lepoint [89], Kompany [91+]	15 000	Weiner GER
11-08	Finland	L	0-1	Turku	Fr		7 451	Hamer LUX
3-09	Germany	L	0-1	Brussels	ECq		41 126	Hauge NOR
7-09	Turkey	L	2-3	Istanbul	ECq	Van Buyten 2 [28 69]	43 538	Skomina SVN
8-10	Kazakhstan	W	2-0	Astana	ECq	Ogunjimi 2 [52 70]	8 500	Borski POL
12-10	Austria	D	4-4	Brussels	ECq	Vossen [11], Fellaini [47], Ogunjimi [87], Lombaerts [90]	24 231	Dean ENG
17-11	Russia	W	2-0	Voronezh	Fr	Lukaku 2 [2 73]	31 743	Kaasik EST
2011								
9-02	Finland	D	1-1	Gent	Fr	Witsel [60]	12 000	Zimmerman SUI
25-03	Austria	W	2-0	Vienna	ECq	Witsel 2 [6 50]	44 300	Bezborodov RUS
29-03	Azerbaijan	W	4-1	Brussels	ECq	Vertonghen [12], Simons [32p], Chadli [45], Vossen [74]	34 985	Stalhammar SWE
3-06	Turkey	D	1-1	Brussels	ECq	Ogunjimi [4]	44 185	Rizzoli ITA
10-08	Slovenia	D	0-0	Ljubljana	Fr		12 230	Strahonja CRO
2-09	Azerbaijan	D	1-1	Baku	ECq	Simons [55p]	9 300	Probert ENG
6-09	USA	W	1-0	Brussels	Fr	Lombaerts [55]	21 946	Collum SCO
7-10	Kazakhstan	W	4-1	Brussels	ECq	Simmons [40p], Hazard [43], Kompany [49], Ogunjimi [84]	29 758	Mazic SRB
11-10	Germany	L	1-3	Dusseldorf	ECq	Fellaini [86]	48 483	Moen NOR
11-11	Romania	W	2-1	Liege	Fr	Van Buyten [11], OG [43]	20 000	Ennjimi FRA
15-11	France	D	0-0	Paris	Fr		52 825	Muniz ESP

Fr = Friendly match • EC = UEFA EURO 2012 • WCq = FIFA World Cup • q = qualifier

BELGIUM NATIONAL TEAM HISTORICAL RECORDS

Caps

96 - Jan Ceulemans 1977-91 • **89** - Timmy Simons 2001- • **86** - Eric Gerets 1975-91 & Franky Van der Elst 1984-98 • **84** - Enzo Scifo 1984-99 • **81** - Paul Van Himst 1960-74 • **78** - Bart Goor 1999-2008 • **77** - Georges Grun 1984-95 • **70** - Lorenzo Staelens 1990-2000 & Marc Wilmots 1990-2002 • **68** - Victor Mees 1949-60 • **67** - Georges Heylens 1961-73 • **66** - Daniel Van Buyten 2001- • **64** - Joseph Jurion 1965-67 & Joan Mario Pfaff 1976-87 • **63** - Franky Vercauteren 1977-8 & Marc Degryse 1984-2002 • **63** - Bernard Voorhoof 1928-40

Goals

30 - Bernard Voorhoof 1928-40 & Paul van Himst 1960-74 • **28** - Marc Wilmots 1990-2002 • **27** - Joseph Mermans 1945-56 • **26** - Robert de Veen 1906-13 & Raymond Braine 1925-39 • **24** - Wesley Sonck 2001- • **23** - Marc Degryse 1984-96 & Jan Ceulemans 1976-91 • **21** - Henri 'Rik' Coppens 1949-59 • **20** - Leopold Anoul 1947-54 & Erwin Vandenbergh 1979-91

Past Coaches

William Maxwell SCO 1910-13 • Charles Bunyan ENG 1914 • William Maxwell SCO 1920-28 • Victor Lowenfelt 1928-30 •Hector Goetinck 1930-34 • Jules Turnauer 1935 • Jack Butler ENG 1935-40 • François Demol 1944-46 • Bill Gormlie ENG 1947-53 • Dougall Livingstone SCO 1953-54 • Andre Vandeweyer 1955-57 • Louis Nicolay 1957 • Geza Toldi HUN 1957-58 • Constant Vanden Stock 1958-68 • Raymond Goethals 1968-76 • Guy Thys 1976-89 • Walter Meeuws 1989-90 • Guy Thys 1990-91 • Paul Van Himst 1991-96 • Wilfried Van Moer 1996 • Georges Leekens 1997-99 • Robert Waseige 1999-2002 • Aime Anthuenis 2002-05 • Rene Vandereycken 2006-09 • Franky Vercauteren 2009 • Dick Advocaat NED 2009-10 • Georges Leekens 2010-

BELGIUM 2010–11

JUPILER PRO LEAGUE FIRST ROUND

	Pl	W	D	L	F	A	Pts	Anderlecht	Genk	Gent	Brugge	Lokeren	Standard	Mechelen	Westerlo	Cercle	Kortrijk	Z-Waregem	St-Truiden	Beerschot	Lierse SK	Eupen	Charleroi
RSC Anderlecht †	30	19	8	3	58	20	65		1-1	3-2	2-2	0-0	2-0	5-0	2-0	1-0	3-0	0-0	2-0	4-0	6-0	4-1	4-1
KRC Genk †	30	19	7	4	64	27	64	1-2		1-2	1-0	3-1	4-2	1-0	0-2	3-0	3-2	3-0	1-1	2-1	4-1	5-1	5-0
KAA Gent †	30	17	6	7	59	42	57	1-2	0-4		0-2	2-1	4-1	3-1	4-4	1-0	2-0	5-3	2-0	1-0	4-1	2-1	2-1
Club Brugge †	30	16	5	9	60	35	53	0-2	2-2	3-2		2-1	2-2	1-2	4-3	0-1	4-1	2-0	4-1	1-0	2-0	4-0	5-0
KSC Lokeren †	30	13	11	6	43	36	50	0-3	2-2	3-2	1-0		2-1	3-1	3-1	2-1	1-1	2-1	3-0	1-0	1-1	0-2	1-1
Standard Club Liège †	30	15	4	11	50	38	49	5-1	0-2	2-1	2-2	3-3		3-0	2-1	2-0	1-0	1-1	1-0	1-0	7-0	1-3	2-1
KV Mechelen ‡	30	13	9	8	34	30	48	0-0	2-2	1-1	0-1	2-0	1-0		3-1	2-2	1-0	0-0	0-0	5-1	1-0	2-0	2-0
KVC Westerlo ‡	30	11	8	11	41	40	41	2-0	1-1	0-1	1-2	1-2	1-2	1-1		2-1	2-1	1-1	3-0	1-1	2-0	1-1	2-2
Cercle Brugge ‡	30	11	6	13	33	34	39	1-0	0-1	0-1	3-1	1-1	1-0	0-1	0-1		2-1	1-3	4-2	1-1	3-0	2-1	1-1
KV Kortrijk ‡	30	11	5	14	36	39	38	0-2	1-0	0-1	1-0	0-0	2-1	1-0	1-2	2-1		2-2	2-0	4-0	3-1	3-1	3-0
Zulte-Waregem ‡	30	7	12	11	39	41	33	1-2	0-1	2-2	2-3	1-1	2-0	1-2	2-0	4-0	1-1		1-2	4-3	1-1	0-0	1-1
Sint-Truiden VV ‡	30	8	5	17	20	51	29	0-2	0-2	1-1	2-1	0-2	1-0	0-1	1-2	0-3	1-0	0-3		1-0	1-0	1-1	3-2
Germinal Beerschot ‡	30	5	11	14	24	40	26	0-1	0-1	2-2	2-1	1-1	0-1	1-0	0-0	3-1	3-0	0-0			1-1	0-0	1-0
Lierse SK	30	4	12	14	26	58	24	1-1	1-1	2-2	0-0	2-2	1-4	2-1	2-1	0-1	1-2	0-0	1-2	2-2		1-1	1-0
AS Eupen ‡‡	30	5	8	17	28	50	23	1-1	1-4	0-3	1-4	0-1	0-1	0-1	0-1	0-1	0-3	0-2	6-0	0-1	2-2		1-0
RSC Charleroi ‡‡	30	4	7	19	20	54	19	0-0	1-3	1-3	0-5	1-2	0-2	0-0	0-1	0-3	0-0	2-0	1-0	2-0	0-1	2-0	

30/07/2010 - 20/03/2011 • † Qualified for the Championship round • ‡ Qualified for the Play-off II round • ‡‡ Relegation play-off
Points totals were halved and rounded up for the second round • Top scorers (all rounds): 22 - Ivan Perisic CRO, Club Brugge • 20 - Jelle Vossen, Genk • 18 - Paulo Henrique BRA, Westerlo • 16 - Romelu Lukaku, Anderlecht • 15 - Marvin Ogunjimi, Genk & Ronald Vargas VEN, Club Brugge

JUPILER PRO LEAGUE PLAY-OFFS

Championship

	Pl	W	D	L	F	A	Pts	Ge	St	An	CB	Ge	Lo
KRC Genk †	10	6	1	3	16	12	51		1-1	1-0	3-1	3-0	2-1
Standard CL †	10	8	2	0	18	6	51	2-1		2-1	1-0	1-0	3-0
RSC Anderlecht ‡	10	3	2	5	14	16	44	2-0	1-3		0-0	4-1	3-4
Club Brugge ‡	10	4	4	2	13	6	43	3-0	1-1	3-0		3-0	0-0
KAA Gent	10	0	4	6	9	22	33	2-3	1-3	1-1	1-1		2-2
KSC Lokeren	10	1	3	6	9	17	31	0-2	0-1	1-2	0-1	1-1	

Play-off 2 Group A

	Pl	W	D	L	F	A	Pts	CB	Li	Me	ST
Cercle Brugge ‡‡	6	2	3	1	5	5	9		0-0	3-1	1-0
Lierse SK	6	2	2	2	10	8	8	3-0		1-2	1-1
KV Mechelen	6	2	2	2	9	10	8	0-0	4-3		1-1
Sint-Truiden VV	6	1	3	2	6	7	6	1-1	1-2	2-1	

Play-off 2 Group B

	Pl	W	D	L	F	A	Pts	We	ZW	GB	Ko
KVC Westerlo ‡‡	6	3	3	0	16	6	12		7-1	1-0	3-0
Zulte-Waregem	6	3	1	2	6	10	10	1-1		1-0	2-0
G'minal Beerschot	6	1	3	2	6	6	6	3-3	2-0		0-0
KV Kortrijk	6	0	3	3	2	8	3	1-1	0-1	1-1	

2/04/2011 - 17/05/2011 • † Qualified for the UEFA Champions League •
‡ Qualified for the Europa League • ‡‡ Qualified for Play-off 2 final
Final: **Westerlo** 3-0 2-2 Cercle Brugge . Westerlo had already qualified for the Europa League via the Cup so no play-off against Club Brugge was needed

MEDALS TABLE

		Overall			League			Cup			Europe		
		G	S	B	G	S	B	G	S	B	G	S	B
1	RSC Anderlecht	42	27	10	**30**	20	8	9	3		3	4	2
2	Club Brugge	23	25	15	13	17	13	**10**	6			2	2
3	Standard Liège	16	21	21	10	11	19	6	9			1	2
4	Union St Gilloise	13	8	8	11	8	7	2					1
5	Beerschot VAV	9	8	5	7	7	5	2	1				
6	Racing CB	7	5	3	6	5	3	1					
7	Royal Antwerp	6	14	7	4	12	7	2	1			1	
8	KV Mechelen	6	9	4	4	5	3	1	4		1		1
9	Royal FC Liègeois	6	4	5	5	3	4	1	1				1
10	Lierse SK	6	3	2	4	2	2	2	1				
11	KRC Genk	6	2		3	2		3					
12	Daring CB	5	5	4	5	4	4						
13	Cercle Brugge	5	4	6	3		6	2	4				
14	SK Beveren	4	3	1	2			2	3				1
15	KAA Gent	3	3	6		2	6	3	1				

Relegation play-off: **AS Eupen** 3-2 0-2 4-2 2-2 RSC Charleroi (Played as best of five matches. The team with the least points - RSC Charleroi - were relegated. Eupen started with three bonus points having finished higher in the league.

BELGIUM 2010–11 TWEEDE CLASSE (2)

	Pl	W	D	L	F	A	Pts
Oud-Heverlee Leuven	34	22	7	5	75	38	73
Lommel United ‡	34	20	5	9	73	44	65
RAEC Mons ‡	34	17	8	9	63	38	59
Waasland-Beveren ‡	34	15	11	8	51	35	56
CS Visé	34	14	9	11	52	48	51
Royal Antwerp	34	14	8	12	54	53	50
Verbroedering Dender	34	15	4	15	54	54	49
AFC Tubize	34	13	8	13	46	55	47
KV Oostende	34	13	6	15	41	48	45
KSK Heist	34	12	7	15	57	67	43
FC Brussels	34	12	6	16	50	51	42
Standaard Wetteren	34	10	12	12	42	51	42
Boussu Dour Borinage	34	11	8	15	48	52	41
KVK Tienen	34	11	8	15	35	47	41
KSV Roeselare	34	10	11	13	38	42	41
KV Turnhout	34	10	10	14	48	59	40
Rupel Boom	34	10	7	17	36	56	37
RFC Tournai	34	5	9	20	38	63	24

18/08/2010 - 1/05/2011 • ‡ Qualified for promotion play-off
Top scorer: **25** - Hamdi Harbaoui TUN, OH Leuven

PROMOTION/RELEGATION PLAY-OFFS

	Pl	W	D	L	F	A	Pts	Mo	WB	LU	Eu
RAEC Mons	6	4	1	1	18	7	**13**		2-2	4-0	3-1
W'land-Beveren	6	4	1	1	13	9	**13**	3-2		2-1	4-2
Lommel United	6	3	0	3	12	14	**9**	1-5	2-1		4-1
AS Eupen	6	0	0	6	5	18	**0**	0-2	0-1	1-4	

8/05/2011 - 26/05/2011 • Play-off: **Mons** 2-1 Waasland-Beveren
Mons promoted, Eupen relegated

COUPE DE BELGIQUE/BEKER VAN BELGIE 2010-11

Round of 32

Team	Score
Standard Club Liège *	2
Royal Antwerp	1
KVV Koksijde	0
KRC Genk *	3
KV Kortrijk *	2
Excelsior Virton	1
Racing Waregem	0
KV Mechelen *	7
White Star Woluwe *	2
Zulte-Waregem	1
Standaard Wetteren *	2
KSC Lokeren	4
AS Eupen *	2
KV Turnhout	1
KVK Tienen	1
KAA Gent *	4
Cercle Brugge *	4
KFC Lille	0
RSC Charleroi *	4
Waasland-Beveren	2
Club Brugge *	3
Lommel United	1
Eendracht Aalst	0
Germinal Beerschot *	3
Lierse SK *	4
Rupel Boom	0
Sint-Truiden VV	1
RFC Tournai *	2
RSC Anderlecht	2 4p
URS du Centre *	2 1p
KSV Roeselare	0
KVC Westerlo *	2

Round of 16

Team	Score
Standard Club Liège *	2
KRC Genk	1
KV Kortrijk *	1
KV Mechelen	2
White Star Woluwe *	1
KSC Lokeren	0
AS Eupen	1
KAA Gent *	3
Cercle Brugge *	3
Waasland-Beveren	1
Club Brugge	1
Germinal Beerschot *	2
Lierse SK *	4
RFC Tournai	1
RSC Anderlecht	0
KVC Westerlo *	1

Quarter-finals

Team	Score
Standard Club Liège *	2 4
KV Mechelen	0 1
White Star Woluwe *	0 0
KAA Gent	2 1
Cercle Brugge *	2 1
Germinal Beerschot	0 1
Lierse SK	2 2
KVC Westerlo *	1 3

Semi-finals

Team	Score
Standard Club Liège	0 4
KAA Gent *	1 2
Cercle Brugge	0 3
KVC Westerlo *	0 3

Final

Team	Score
Standard Club Liège	2
KVC Westerlo ‡	0

CUP FINAL

Roi Baudouin, Brussels
21-05-2011, 20.30, Ref: De Bleeckere
Scorers - Mangala 34 Mravac OG 61
Standard - Sinan Bolat - Daniel Opare,
Abdelfettah Boukhriss, Eliaquim Mangala,
Kanu - Reginal Goreux (Mbaye Leye 78), Steven
Defour (c), Axel Witsel, Pape Abdou Camara,
Jelle Van Damme● (Aloys Nong 86) -
Mohammed Tchite (Koen Daerden 90).
Tr: Dominique D'Onofrio
Westerlo - Bart Deelkens - Wouter Corstjens,
Jef Delen (c), Adnan Mravac, Steven De Petter●
- Jens Cools, Christian Bruls, Evariste Ngolok -
Oleksandr Yakovenko (Ellenton Liliu 72), Dieter
Dekelver (Lens Annab 72), Paulo Henrique.
Tr: Jan Ceulemans

* Home team/home team in 1st leg ● ‡ Qualified for the Europa League

BEN – BENIN

FIFA/COCA-COLA WORLD RANKING

'93	'94	'95	'96	'97	'98	'99	'00	'01	'02	'03	'04	'05	'06	'07	'08	'09	'10	'11	'12
130	143	161	143	137	127	140	148	152	146	121	122	113	114	97	101	59	71	124	

	2011														
	Jan	Feb	Mar	Apr	May	Jun	Jul	Aug	Sep	Oct	Nov	Dec	**High**	**Low**	**Av**
	72	83	80	80	80	87	86	83	92	119	124	124	**59**	**165**	**122**

Benin finished bottom of their CAF Africa Cup of Nations qualifying group at the end of a year of turmoil for football in the country. A loss at home in their last game, to Rwanda, meant they ended behind both Burundi and the Rwandans in the standings - teams considered much weaker than the Beninoise - and way off group winners Cote d'Ivoire who swept into the finals with a 100 per cent record in the group. The atmosphere was in stark contrast to two years earlier when they had qualified of their 2010 Nations Cup in Angola. Of the five matches played in 2011 four of them were lost. French coach Jean Marc Nobilo and Denis Goavec both had spells in charge but the turmoil besetting the federation meant that neither stayed for very long. Political machinations at the head of the federation saw president Anjorin Moucharafou arrested after being accused of misappropriation of funds linked to a sponsorship deal. FIFA had to intervene to regularise the running of the game in the country, which had seen the league suspended as the campaign was entering the final stages. Tonnerre were leading at the time and qualified for the CAF Champions League in 2012. A transition league launched towards the end of the year saw the defection of several key clubs as the crisis threatened to continue.

CAF AFRICA CUP OF NATIONS RECORD

1957-1970 DNE   1972 DNQ   1974-1978 DNE   1980 DNQ   1982 DNE   1984-1994 DNQ   1996 DNE   1998-2002 DNQ   **2004** 16 r1   **2006** DNQ
2008 15 r1   **2010** 14 r1   **2012** DNQ

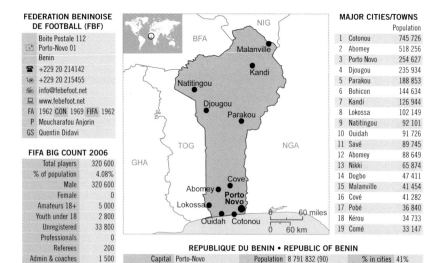

FEDERATION BENINOISE DE FOOTBALL (FBF)

Boite Postale 112	
Porto-Novo 01	
Benin	
☎ +229 20 214142	
📠 +229 20 215455	
📧 info@febefoot.net	
🖥 www.febefoot.net	
FA 1962 CON 1969 FIFA 1962	
P Moucharafou Anjorin	
GS Quentin Didavi	

FIFA BIG COUNT 2006

Total players	320 600
% of population	4.08%
Male	320 600
Female	0
Amateurs 18+	5 000
Youth under 18	2 800
Unregistered	33 800
Professionals	0
Referees	200
Admin & coaches	1 500
Number of clubs	110
Number of teams	440

MAJOR CITIES/TOWNS

		Population
1	Cotonou	745 726
2	Abomey	518 256
3	Porto Novo	254 627
4	Djougou	235 934
5	Parakou	188 853
6	Bohicon	144 634
7	Kandi	126 944
8	Lokossa	102 149
9	Natitingou	92 101
10	Ouidah	91 726
11	Savé	89 745
12	Abomey	88 649
13	Nikki	65 874
14	Dogbo	47 411
15	Malanville	41 454
16	Cové	41 282
17	Pobé	36 840
18	Kérou	34 733
19	Comé	33 147

REPUBLIQUE DU BENIN • REPUBLIC OF BENIN

Capital Porto-Novo	Population 8 791 832 (90)	% in cities 41%
GDP per capita $1500 (198)	Area km² 112 622 km² (101)	GMT + / - +1
Neighbours (km) Burkina Faso 306, Niger 266, Nigeria 773, Togo 644 • Coast 121			

RECENT INTERNATIONAL MATCHES PLAYED BY BENIN

2009	Opponents	Score		Venue	Comp	Scorers	Att	Referee
29-03	Ghana	L	0-1	Kumasi	WCq		39 000	Bennett RSA
7-06	Sudan	W	1-0	Cotonou	WCq	Razak Omotoyossi [22]	26 000	Marange ZIM
21-06	Mali	L	1-3	Bamako	WCq	Seidath Tchomogo [15]	40 000	Abd El Fatah EGY
11-08	Gabon	D	1-1	Dieppe	Fr	Abou Maiga [10]		
6-09	Mali	D	1-1	Cotonou	WCq	Mohamed Aoudou [87]	33 000	Damon RSA
11-10	Ghana	W	1-0	Cotonou	WCq	Mohamed Aoudou [89]	20 000	Lwanja MWI
14-11	Sudan	W	2-1	Omdurman	WCq	Razak Omotoyossi [34p], Djiman Koukou [62]	600	Jedidi TUN
2010								
6-01	Libya	W	1-0	Cotonou	Fr	Stephane Sessegnon [19]		
12-01	Mozambique	D	2-2	Benguela	CNr1	Razak Omotoyossi [14p], Khan OG [20]	15 000	Abdel Rahman SUD
16-01	Nigeria	L	0-1	Benguela	CNr1		8 000	Carvalho ANG
20-01	Egypt	L	0-2	Benguela	CNr1		12 500	Bennett RSA
11-08	Niger	D	0-0	Porto Novo	Fr			
5-09	Burundi	D	1-1	Cotonou	CNq	Mickael Pote [2]		Bennett RSA
9-10	Rwanda	W	3-0	Kigali	CNq	Seidath Tchomogo [68], Razak Omotoyossi [81], Stephane Sessegnon [88]		Haimoudi ALG
2011								
9-02	Libya	L	2-3	Tripoli	Fr			
27-03	Côte d'Ivoire	L	1-2	Accra	CNq	Seidath Tchomogo [13]		Kayindi-Ngobi UGA
5-06	Côte d'Ivoire	L	2-6	Cotonou	CNq	Stephane Sessegnon 2 [55 60p]		Benouza ALG
4-09	Burundi	D	1-1	Bujumbura	CNq	Guy Akpagba [55]		
9-10	Rwanda	L	0-1	Cotonou	CNq			

Fr = Friendly match • CN = CAF African Cup of Nations • WCq = FIFA World Cup • q = qualifier • r1 = first round group

BENIN NATIONAL TEAM HISTORICAL RECORDS

Coach: Cecil Jones Attuquayefio GHA 2003-04 • Herve Revelli FRA 2004 • Edme Codjo 2005-07 • Didier Notheaux FRA 2007 • Reinhard Fabisch GER 2007-08 • Michel Dussuyer FRA 2008-10 • Jean-Marc Nobilo FRA 2011 • Denis Goavec FRA 2011 • Manuel Amoros 2012-

MEDALS TABLE

	Overall	Lge	Cup	Africa			City/Town
	G	G	G	G	S	B	
1 Dragons de l'Ouémé	17	12	5			1	Porto-Novo
2 Mogas 90	12	3	9				Porto-Novo
3 Requins de l'Atlantique	8	3	5				Cotonou
4 Buffles du Borgou	5	2	3				Parakou
5 AS Porto Novo	3	3					Porto-Novo
6 ASPAC	2	1	1				Cotonou
7 Etoile Sportive	2	1	1				Porto-Novo
8 Univ National de Benin	2		2				Porto-Novo

COUPE DE LA FEDERATION

Final. Charles de Gaulle, Porto Novo, 1-05-2011

Dragons de l'Ouémé 2-1 AS Oussou Saka

Scorers - Charles Houngbo 2 [48 60] for Dragons;
Oudei Ekililou [5] for ASOS

BENIN 2010-11

PREMIERE DIVISION	Pl	W	D	L	F	A	Pts	Tonnerre	Soleil	Avrankou	CIFAS	Mogas 90	JA Plateau	USS Kraké	ASPAC	Buffles	Mambas	Dynamo	Dragons	Panthères	Requins
Tonnerre d'Abomey †	16	8	5	3	19	10	29		1-0			1-2	0-0	3-0	1-1		2-1			2-0	1-0
Soleil FC	16	8	3	5	18	15	27	1-2		2-1		1-0		2-1	0-0	2-1			1-0	2-0	
Avrankou Omnisport	16	8	2	6	14	12	26	0-0			1-0	1-0	2-0		2-0			1-0	0-1		
CIFAS	17	7	4	6	20	14	25	1-0	3-1			1-1	2-0	3-0	1-1		2-0	1-0			
Mogas 90	17	7	4	6	23	20	25	2-1		3-1			3-1	1-1			3-1	1-1		3-1	1-0
JA Plateau	16	7	4	5	12	13	25		1-0					1-0	1-0	1-0	1-1	1-0	2-0	2-1	0-2
USS Kraké	17	6	6	5	13	17	24			1-0	1-0	2-1			0-0	3-2	1-0	1-1	1-1		1-0
ASPAC	16	5	8	3	14	10	23			0-0	2-1	2-0		1-0		1-1	3-0			0-0	2-1
Buffles du Borgou	16	4	6	6	12	13	22	0-0		1-0	1-1	2-1	1-0				0-2	0-1	1-0		
Mambas Noirs	16	6	3	7	19	22	21		1-0	3-1	1-2		0-0			1-0		0-2	2-2	4-2	
Dynamo Abomey	17	4	7	6	7	8	19	0-0	0-1	0-1	1-0			0-0	0-0				0-0	0-1	1-0
Dragons de l'Ouémé ‡	16	4	5	7	16	18	17	1-2	1-2		2-1	1-1			2-1	0-0				3-1	0-1
Panthères Djougou	17	4	4	9	14	24	16		2-2	1-2	1-0	2-0		1-1		0-1		0-0			1-0
Requins de l'Atlantique	17	4	3	10	13	18	15	1-3	1-1	0-1	1-1		1-1			0-1	1-2		2-1	2-0	

18/09/2010 - 9/04/2011 • Season unfinished • † Qualified for the CAF Champions League • ‡ Qualified for the CAF Confederation Cup

BER – BERMUDA

FIFA/COCA-COLA WORLD RANKING

'93	'94	'95	'96	'97	'98	'99	'00	'01	'02	'03	'04	'05	'06	'07	'08	'09	'10	'11	'12
84	102	140	167	176	185	163	153	166	172	183	157	161	107	147	124	142	175	107	

2011												High	Low	Av
Jan	Feb	Mar	Apr	May	Jun	Jul	Aug	Sep	Oct	Nov	Dec			
172	167	165	163	162	180	185	185	189	132	109	107	76	189	149

For the second FIFA World Cup qualifying campaign in a row, Bermuda put up a much better than expected performance against higher ranked opposition and in the process jumped 80 places in the FIFA/Coca-Cola World Ranking. Drawn in the first group stage against Trinidad, Guyana and Barbados, Bermuda just missed out on making it through to the next round, finishing just three points behind group winners Guyana. In club football, North Village Rams captured their first championship since 2006 and reinforced their position as the most successful club on the island by also winning the Dudley Eve Cup and the Friendship Trophy. It was a triumph for their coach Shaun Goater with Rams finishing a point ahead of PHC Zebras and also beating them in the semi-finals on the way to both of their cup triumphs. In the final of the Friendship Trophy they beat Devonshire Cougars, a match that came a week after the murder of Randy Robinson, a former player for both teams. Robinson was a victim of the gang-related violence that has shocked this normally peaceful and prosperous country. A month later it claimed another football victim, Cougars's Jason Smith. His murder came on the heels of his team's triumph in the FA Cup Final against Southampton Rangers as Cougars retained the trophy that they had won for the first time in 2010.

FIFA WORLD CUP RECORD

1930-1966 DNE 1970 DNQ 1974-1990 DNE 1994 DNQ 1998 DNE 2002-2010 DNQ

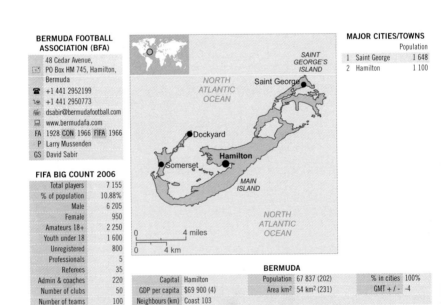

BERMUDA FOOTBALL ASSOCIATION (BFA)

48 Cedar Avenue,
PO Box HM 745, Hamilton, Bermuda
☎ +1 441 2952199
📠 +1 441 2950773
📧 dsabir@bermudafootball.com
🖥 www.bermudafa.com
FA 1928 CON 1966 FIFA 1966
P Larry Mussenden
GS David Sabir

FIFA BIG COUNT 2006

Total players	7 155
% of population	10.88%
Male	6 205
Female	950
Amateurs 18+	2 250
Youth under 18	1 600
Unregistered	800
Professionals	5
Referees	35
Admin & coaches	220
Number of clubs	50
Number of teams	100

MAJOR CITIES/TOWNS

		Population
1	Saint George	1 648
2	Hamilton	1 100

SAINT GEORGE'S ISLAND
NORTH ATLANTIC OCEAN
Saint George
Dockyard
Hamilton
Somerset
MAIN ISLAND
NORTH ATLANTIC OCEAN
0   4 miles
0   4 km

BERMUDA

Capital	Hamilton	Population	67 837 (202)	% in cities	100%
GDP per capita	$69 900 (4)	Area km²	54 km² (231)	GMT + / -	-4
Neighbours (km)	Coast 103				

RECENT INTERNATIONAL MATCHES PLAYED BY BERMUDA

2008	Opponents		Score	Venue	Comp	Scorers	Att	Referee
3-02	Cayman Islands	D	1-1	Hamilton	WCq	Tyrell Burgess [18]	2 000	Navarro CAN
30-03	Cayman Islands	W	3-1	Georgetown	WCq	Devaun DeGraff 2 [19 23], Kwame Steede [53]	3 200	Marrufo USA
6-06	Barbados	W	2-1	Hamilton	Fr	Omar Shakir [41], Damon Ming [86]	2 000	Raynor BER
9-06	Barbados	W	3-0	Hamilton	Fr	Keishen Bean 2 [12 18], John Nusum [45]	2 200	Francis BER
15-06	Trinidad and Tobago	W	2-1	Macoya	WCq	John Nusum 2 [7 38]	4 585	Quesada CRC
22-06	Trinidad and Tobago	L	0-2	Prospect	WCq		5 000	Batres GUA
27-08	Antigua and Barbuda	L	0-4	Grand Cayman	CCq		300	Stennett JAM
30-08	Saint Martin †	W	7-0	Grand Cayman	CCq	Reggie Lambe 4 [23 45 60 85], Damon Ming [26], Antonio Lowe [83], Casey Castle [88]	350	Morisson JAM
31-08	Cayman Islands	D	0-0	Grand Cayman	CCq		350	Hospedales TRI
2009								

No international matches played in 2009

| 2010 | | | | | | | | |

No international matches played in 2010

2011								
2-09	Trinidad and Tobago	L	0-1	Port of Spain	WCq		6 000	Perea PAN
6-09	Guyana	L	1-2	Georgetown	WCq	Khano Smith [90]	3 500	Geiger USA
7-10	Trinidad and Tobago	W	2-1	Prospect	WCq	Antwan Russell [52], Nahki Wells [63]	2 243	Solis CRC
11-10	Guyana	D	1-1	Prospect	WCq	John Nusum [71]	2 573	Angela ARU
11-11	Barbados	W	2-1	Prospect	WCq	Khano Smith [28p], Kwame Steede [49]	1 000	Barrios GUA
14-11	Barbados	W	2-1	Prospect	WCq	Nahki Wells [46], Khano Smith [72p]	1 000	Moreno PAN

Fr = Friendly match • CC = Digicel Caribbean Cup • WC = FIFA World Cup • q = qualifier • † Not a full international

BERMUDA 2010–11

CINGULAR WIRELESS PREMIER DIVISION

	Pl	W	D	L	F	A	Pts	Rams	Zebras	Hornets	Cougars	St G Colts	Rangers	Blazers	Warriors	Eagles	Dev Colts
North Village Rams	18	13	2	3	48	17	41		7-1	1-2	4-2	1-1	2-0	3-0	7-0	3-0	4-2
PHC Zebras	18	13	1	4	37	25	40	2-1		2-1	2-1	1-3	2-0	4-1	2-1	2-0	4-1
Dandy Town Hornets	18	11	3	4	38	26	36	2-1	2-0		0-3	3-1	1-4	2-2	3-0	3-3	1-0
Devonshire Cougars	18	10	3	5	46	23	33	0-1	3-0	3-0		1-3	3-1	1-1	7-1	3-1	2-3
St George's Colts	18	7	5	6	30	21	26	0-1	0-1	1-4	1-1		1-0	1-1	4-0	3-0	4-1
Southampton Rangers	18	7	0	11	24	30	21	0-3	2-3	1-3	1-4	1-0		0-2	4-0	2-1	1-0
Boulevard Blazers	18	5	5	8	27	37	20	1-2	0-4	1-1	1-2	2-1	2-1		2-3	2-3	4-4
St David's Warriors	18	6	0	12	23	49	18	1-3	0-2	1-2	2-4	0-3	2-0	5-1		2-1	2-1
Somerset Eagles	18	4	4	10	30	40	16	3-4	2-2	1-5	1-1	2-2	1-3	0-1	3-1		6-1
Devonshire Colts	18	1	3	14	15	50	6	0-0	0-3	1-3	0-5	1-1	0-3	0-3	0-2	0-2	

3/10/2010 - 27/03/2011 • Top scorers: 13 - Raymond Beach, Hornets & Kwame Steede, Cougars • 12 - Temiko Wilson, Blazers & Ralph Bean, Rams

BERMUDA 2010–11 SECOND DIVISION (2)

	Pl	W	D	L	F	A	Pts
Somerset Trojans	20	16	2	2	62	18	50
Robin Hood	20	16	1	3	60	16	49
X'roads Warriors	20	12	5	3	35	15	41
MR Onions	20	12	1	7	76	33	37
Wolves	20	11	3	6	59	23	36
Hamilton Parish	20	9	2	9	44	26	29
YMSC Bluebirds	20	8	3	9	45	29	27
RAA Wanderers	20	8	2	10	42	37	26
Prospect United	20	4	1	15	25	50	13
Ireland Rangers	20	2	0	18	20	107	6
Paget Lions	20	2	0	18	15	129	6

3/10/2010 - 27/03/2011

MEDALS TABLE

		Overall		Lge		Cup		FT		Mart		DE	
		G	S	G	S	G	S	G	S	G	S	G	S
1	North Village Rams	44	22	8	10	10	2	10	2	8	5	8	3
2	PHC Zebras	38	27	9	5	10	8	10	5	3	6	6	3
3	Somerset Trojans	37	25	9	9	9	3	9	3	7	4	3	6
4	Dandy Town Hornets	19	25	5	8	1	8	4	4	6	2	3	3
5	Devonshire Colts	17	33	3	4	5	10	4	11	2	6	3	2
6	Vasco da Gama	16	9	3	1	5	2	1	3	3	2	4	1
7	Boulevard Blazers	12	8	2	2	5	1	1	1	3	3	1	1
8	Devonshire Cougars	10	15	3	2	2	2	1	5	3	3	1	3
9	Hotels International	7	6	2	2		1		2	2	2		
10	YMSC	6	5	3	1	3	1		2		1		
11	Southampton Rangers	5	11	1		1	5	3	3		3		
12	Wolves	2	2			1				1	1	1	
13	Dock Hill Rangers	1	4	1	1	3							
14	BAA Wanderers	1	1			1	1						
	Casuals SC	1	1	1	1								
	St George's Colts	1	1					1	1				
	Wellington Rovers	1	1			1			1				
18	Somerset Eagles		3			1		2					

FRIENDSHIP TROPHY 2010-11

First Round		Semi-finals		Final	
North Village Rams	7				
St David's Warriors	0	**North Village Rams**	2		
Boulevard Blazers	1	PHC Zebras	1		
PHC Zebras	5			**North Village Rams**	3
St George's Colts	1 2			Devonshire Cougars	1
Southampton Rangers	1 0	St George's Colts	0		
Devonshire Colts	0	**Devonshire Cougars**	1	National Stadium, 10-04-2011
Devonshire Cougars	2				

Scorers - Tyrrell Burgess [30], Ralph Bean 2 [78] [81] for Rams; Kwame Steede [80] for Cougars
Line-ups: **Rams** - J Williams, S DeGraff, R Bean, J Lee (J DeShields, 57), S Fubler, T Manders, K Bean, K Dill, D Tankard, T Burgess (V Tankard, 81), J Boyles (T Watson 75). Tr: Shaun Goater • **Cougars** - R Brangman, D Cox, K Steede, T Steede, C Caisey (M Smith, 88), K Tucker (J Seymour, 80), K Franks, L Simmons (M. Steede, 75), J Butterfield, S Brangman, M Steede. Tr: Kieshon Smith

DUDLEY EVE TROPHY 2010

First Round Group Stage									Semi-finals		Final	
Group A	Pl	W	D	L	F	A	Pts	PHC	BB			
Dandy Town Hornets	2	1	0	1	6	4	**3**	3-4	3-0			
PHC Zebras	2	1	0	1	6	6	**3**		2-3	**North Village Rams**	1	
Boulevard Blazers	2	1	0	1	3	5	**3**			PHC Zebras	0	
												North Village Rams 4 4p
												Devonshire Cougars 4 1p
Group B	Pl	W	D	L	F	A	Pts	DC	SE	Dandy Town Hornets	0 4p	
North Village Rams	2	2	0	0	5	1	**6**	1-0	4-1	**Devonshire Cougars**	0 5p	Wellington Oval, 11-11-2010
Devonshire Cougars	2	0	1	1	2	1	**1**		1-1			Ref: Cann
Somerset Eagles	2	0	1	1	2	5	**1**					

Scorers - Sammy DeGraff [85], Jason Lee [90], Keishan Bean [112], Thomas Watson [120] for Rams; Tumaini Steede [38], Domico Coddington [89], Taurean Manders OG [109], Lejuan Simmons [116] for Cougars • Line-ups: **Rams** - J Williams, K Dill, S Fubler (J Sousa 61), D Tankard, T Manders, T Watson, J Jennings, S DeGraff, K Bean, R Lee, K Bean. Tr: Shaun Goater • **Cougars** - R Brangman, K Franks (J Smith 116), D Cox, J Butterfield, K Tucker, M Steede, T Steede (S Pearman 72), D Coddington, C Caisey, S Brangman, L Simmons. Tr: Kieshon Smith

FA CUP 2010-11

First Round		Quarter–finals		Semi–finals		Final	
Devonshire Cougars	2						
X'roads Warriors	1	**Devonshire Cougars**	1 4				
Hamilton Parish	0	St George's Colts	1 3				
St George's Colts	1			**Devonshire Cougars**	3		
Prospect United	3			PHC Zebras	0		
Boulevard Blazers	1	Prospect United	0				
Devonshire Colts	1	**PHC Zebras**	1				
PHC Zebras	4					**Devonshire Cougars**	4
St David's Warriors	4					Southampton Rangers	1
Ireland Rangers	0	**St David's Warriors**	5				
Robin Hood	1 0	Wolves	3			**CUP FINAL**	
Wolves	1 1			St David's Warriors	2 9p		
Dandy Town Hornets	1 2			**Southampton Rangers**	2 10p	National Stadium, 17-04-2011
North Village Rams	1 1	Dandy Town Hornets	0			Scorers - Tumaini Steede 2 [8] [50],
MR Onions	1	**Southampton Rangers**	1			Jesse Seymour [40], Lejuan
Southampton Rangers	6					Simmons [90] for Cougars; Travis
						Wilkinson [85] for Rangers

Elimination round: Paget Lions 0-2 **Robin Hood** • Somerset Eagles 1-2 **Boulevard Blazers** •
MR Onions 1-0 YMSC • Somerset Trojans 4-5 **Southampton Rangers** • **Devonshire Cougars** 4-2 BAA

Cup Final line-ups: **Cougars** - Ricardo Brangman - Josh Butterfield, Christopher Caisey, Domico Coddington (Lejuan Simmons), Darius Cox, Kijuan Franks, Jesse Seymour, Kwame Steede, M Steede, Tumaini Steede (Kori Goddard), Zico White. Tr: Kieshon Smith • **Southampton** - Sean Perinchief - Jermaine Dill, Travis Wilkinson, Kimon Simmons, Ijahmon Mallory, Michael Williams, Jemar Charles, V Peronchief (Janerio Tucker), Dennis Russell, Calil Simon, Kwame Tucker. Tr: Keith Jennings

BFA – BURKINA FASO

FIFA/COCA-COLA WORLD RANKING

'93	'94	'95	'96	'97	'98	'99	'00	'01	'02	'03	'04	'05	'06	'07	'08	'09	'10	'11	'12
127	97	101	107	106	75	71	69	78	75	78	84	87	61	113	62	49	41	62	

					2011								High	Low	Av
	Jan	Feb	Mar	Apr	May	Jun	Jul	Aug	Sep	Oct	Nov	Dec			
	42	41	40	42	44	37	39	40	41	54	62	62	37	127	78

Burkina Faso won a first-ever continental title with success in the African U-17 Championship in Rwanda at the start of 2011. The young Burkinabe beat hosts Rwanda 2-1 in the final in Kigali to qualify for the FIFA U-17 World Cup in Mexico in mid-year. They scored seven goals in their last two group games against Senegal and Egypt to ensure top place in their group and then beat Congo on post-match penalties in the semi-final. Successful coach Rui Vieira had been put into the post by compatriot Paulo Duarte, the coach of the senior team, who was the subject of much controversy over his selection policy as he attempted to strengthen the national team with players from other countries. The use of Cameroon defender Herve Zengue in the 2012 CAF Africa Cup of Nations qualifiers led to a protest by Namibia, who claimed Zengue did not qualify to play for "Le Etalons'. The case went all the way to the Court of Arbitration for Sport in Switzerland before being resolved in Burkina Faso's favour, but even though they won the case, the Burkinabe did not take the Russian-based player to the Nations Cup in Equatorial Guinea and Gabon. Burkina Faso lost all of their group games, signaling the end of Duarte's four year tenure at the helm of the team. He spent much time criticising his own federation in press interviews at the tournament.

CAF AFRICA CUP OF NATIONS RECORD

1957-1965 DNE **1968** DNQ **1970-1972** DNE **1974** DNQ **1976** DNE **1978** 8 r1 **1980** DNE **1982** DNQ **1984-1988** DNE **1990-1992** DNQ
1994 Withdrew **1996** 15 r1 **1998** 4 SF (Hosts) **2000** 15 r1 **2002** 13 r1 **2004** 14 r1 **2006-2008** DNQ **2010** 13 r1 **2012** 14 r1

FEDERATION BURKINABE DE FOOT-BALL (FBF)

Centre Technique National,
Ouaga 2000, Boite Postale
57, Ouagadougou 01
☎ +226 50 396864
📠 +226 50 396866
📧 febefoo@fasonet.bf
🖥 www.fasofoot.org
FA 1960 CON 1964 FIFA 1964
P Theodore Sawadogo
GS Emmanuel Zombre

FIFA BIG COUNT 2006

Total players	605 100
% of population	4.35%
Male	576 800
Female	28 300
Amateurs 18+	13 000
Youth under 18	10 200
Unregistered	45 900
Professionals	0
Referees	700
Admin & coaches	2 400
Number of clubs	100
Number of teams	850

MAJOR CITIES/TOWNS

		Population
1	Ouagadougou	1 351 245
2	Bobo Dioulasso	471 426
3	Koudougou	85 157
4	Banfora	80 491
5	Ouahigouya	76 392
6	Pouytenga	71 278
7	Kaya	57 295
8	Garango	55 851
9	Fada N'gourma	44 629
10	Tenkodogo	43 447
11	Houndé	39 575
12	Dédougou	39 187
13	Tanghin-D'ouri	37 477
14	Kindi	31 614
15	Léo	28 541
16	Réo	28 401
17	Kongoussi	27 155
18	Gaoua	26 835
19	Gourcy	26 527

BURKINA FASO

Capital	Ouagadougou	Population	15 746 232 (61)	% in cities	20%
GDP per capita	$1200 (208)	Area km²	274 200 km² (74)	GMT +/-	0
Neighbours (km)	Benin 306, Cote d'Ivoire 584, Ghana 549, Mali 1000, Niger 628, Togo 126				

RECENT INTERNATIONAL MATCHES PLAYED BY BURKINA FASO

2007 Opponents	Score	Venue	Comp	Scorers	Att	Referee
3-06 Mozambique	L 1-3	Maputo	CNq	Wilfried Sanou [38]		Raolimanana MAD
9-06 Mali	L 0-1	Ouagadougou	Fr			
16-06 Tanzania	L 0-1	Ouagadougou	CNq			Coulibaly MLI
22-08 Mali	L 2-3	Paris	Fr	Wilfried Sanou, Pierre Coulibaly		
8-09 Senegal	L 1-5	Dakar	CNq	Alain Traore [34]		Haimoudi ALG
2008						
24-05 Cape Verde Islands	L 0-1	Alcochete	Fr			
1-06 Tunisia	W 2-1	Rades	WCq	Yssouf Kone 2 [85 87]	15 000	Ambaya LBY
7-06 Burundi	W 2-0	Ouagadougou	WCq	Moumouni Dagano 2 [23p 44p]		Ndume GAB
14-06 Seychelles	W 3-2	Victoria	WCq	Moumouni Dagano 3 [25 57 78]	1 000	Seechurn MRI
21-06 Seychelles	W 4-1	Ouagadougou	WCq	Charles Kabore [21], Mahamoudou Kere [28], Issouf Ouattara [54], Yssouf Kone [89]	12 500	Lamptey GHA
20-08 Bahrain	L 1-3	Manama	Fr	Dieudonne Minoungou [64]		
6-09 Tunisia	D 0-0	Ouagadougou	WCq		10 000	Katjimune NAM
12-10 Burundi	W 3-1	Bujumbura	WCq	Aristide Bance [15], Moumouni Dagano 2 [60 80]	10 000	Ssegonga UGA
2009						
11-02 Togo	D 1-1	Le Petit-Quevilly	Fr	Jonathan Pitroipa [32]		
28-03 Guinea	W 4-2	Ouagadougou	WCq	Mahamoudou Kere [23], Alain Traore [30], Moumouni Dagano 2 [55p 71]	30 000	Benouza ALG
6-06 Malawi	W 1-0	Blantyre	WCq	Moumouni Dagano [68]	25 000	Bennaceur TUN
20-06 Côte d'Ivoire	L 2-3	Ouagadougou	WCq	Jonathan Pitroipa [27], Aristide Bance [78]	33 056	Damon RSA
12-08 Mali	L 0-3	Le Petit-Quevilly	Fr			
5-09 Côte d'Ivoire	L 0-5	Abidjan	WCq		28 209	Maillet SEY
11-10 Guinea	W 2-1	Accra	WCq	Moumouni Dagano [37], Habib Bamogo [59]	5 000	Ambaya LBY
14-11 Malawi	W 1-0	Ouagadougou	WCq	Moumouni Dagano [47]	20 000	Abd El Fatah EGY
2010						
11-01 Côte d'Ivoire	D 0-0	Cabinda	CNr1		5 000	Bennaceur TUN
19-01 Ghana	L 0-1	Luanda	CNr1		8 000	Maillet SEY
11-08 Congo	W 3-0	Senlis	Fr	Moumouni Dagano [17], Saidou Panandetiguiri [30], Alain Traore [81]		
6-09 Gabon	D 1-1	Cannes	Fr	Alain Traore [87p]		
9-10 Gambia	W 3-1	Ouagadougou	CNq	Moumouni Dagano [16], Benjamin Balima [57], Charles Kabore [69]		Osman EGY
17-11 Guinea	W 2-1	Mantes-La-Ville	Fr	Jonathan Pitroipa [35], Benjamin Balima [84]		
2011						
9-02 Cape Verde Islands	L 0-1	Obidos	Fr			
26-03 Namibia	W 4-0	Ouagadougou	CNq	Alain Traore 3 [25 45 80], OG [73]		Cordier CHA
4-06 Namibia	W 4-1	Windhoek	CNq	Abdou Razak Traore [12], Aristide Bance [57p], Alain Traore [80], Jonathan Pitroipa [92+]		
10-08 South Africa	L 0-3	Johannesburg	Fr			
3-09 Equatorial Guinea	W 1-0	Bobo-Dioulasso	Fr	Alain Traore [61]		
8-10 Gambia	D 1-1	Bakau	CNq	Moumouni Dagano [90]		
11-11 Mali	D 1-1	St Leu La Foret	Fr	Aristide Bance [55]		
15-11 Guinea	D 1-1	Mantes La Jolie	Fr	Moumouni Dagano [10]		
2012						
9-01 Gabon	D 0-0	Bitam	Fr			
22-01 Angola	L 1-2	Malabo	CNr1	Alain Traore [58]	17 000	Benouza ALG
26-01 Côte d'Ivoire	L 0-2	Malabo	CNr1		4 000	Grisha EGY
30-01 Sudan	L 1-2	Bata	CNr1	Issiakka Ouedraogo [95+]	132	Otogo-Castane GAB

Fr = Friendly match • CN = CAF African Cup of Nations • WC = FIFA World Cup • q = qualifier, r1 = first round group

BURKINA FASO NATIONAL TEAM HISTORICAL RECORDS

Coaches   Moussa Namoko 1961-65 • Guy Fabre 1966-71 • Bernard Bayala 1971-73 • Jacques Yameogo 1973-76 • Otto Pfister GER 1976-78 • Daniel Coulibaly 1980-82 • Soumaila Diallo 1984 • Piourhi Webonga 1987-88 • Heinz-Peter Uberjahn 1988-90 • Carlo Barrios BRA 1990-91 • Amokrane Waliken ALG 1991-92 • Idrissa Traore 1992-96 • Calixte Zagre 1996 • Ivan Vutov BUL 1996-97 • Malik Jabir GHA 1997 • Philippe Troussier FRA 1997-98 • Didier Notheaux FRA 1998-99 • Rene Taelman BEL 2000 • Sidiki Diarra 2000-01 • Oscar Fullone ARG 2001-02 • Jacques Yameogo & Pihouri Weboanga 2002 • Jean-Paul Rabier FRA 2002-04 • Ivica Todorov SRB 2004-05 • Bernard Simondi FRA 2005-06 • Idrissa Traore 2006-07 • Didier Notheaux FRA & Sidiki Diarra 2007 • Paulo Duarte POR 2008-

BURKINA FASO 2010-11

PREMIERE DIVISION

	Pl	W	D	L	F	A	Pts	ASFA/Y	USO	SONABEL	USFA	EFO	RCB	BPS	Bobo Sport	Koupèla	Yatenga	Maya	Sourou	USCO	Sanmatinga
ASFA/Yennenga †	26	19	3	4	46	15	60		1-2	1-0	3-0	0-0	4-1	1-0	2-0	1-1	3-1	2-1	4-2	1-0	4-1
US Ouagadougou	26	16	6	4	46	12	54	2-1		1-0	3-0	1-1	3-1	5-1	0-0	0-0	3-0	2-0	5-1	7-0	2-0
AS SONABEL	26	14	6	6	34	13	48	0-2	2-1		0-0	0-1	2-0	1-0	3-0	2-0	1-0	1-1	1-0	7-0	5-0
US Forces Armées	26	14	6	6	29	17	48	2-1	0-2	0-1		1-1	0-0	0-1	0-0	2-0	3-1	1-0	3-1	4-1	1-0
Etoile Filante	26	12	11	3	33	11	47	0-0	0-1	1-0	1-0		1-0	0-0	2-0	0-0	4-0	0-0	1-1	5-0	1-1
Racing Club B-D	26	12	5	9	24	18	41	1-0	0-0	0-1	0-1	1-0		1-0	0-1	2-0	5-0	1-0	1-1	2-1	2-0
Bouloumpokou FC	26	12	5	9	23	20	41	0-1	1-3	2-1	0-1	1-1	1-0		1-0	0-1	0-0	0-0	2-0	2-1	5-1
Bobo Sport	26	9	9	8	17	17	36	0-1	0-0	2-2	0-3	1-2	0-1	0-0		1-0	1-0	0-0	0-0	2-0	
AS Koupèla	26	5	15	6	13	15	30	0-1	1-0	1-1	0-0	0-0	0-0	1-2	0-0		0-0	1-0	1-0	1-1	1-1
US Yatenga	26	5	10	11	17	34	25	0-3	1-0	0-0	0-2	0-1	0-0	1-0	0-3	1-1		0-0	0-0	3-1	1-0
AS Maya B-D	26	5	9	12	11	22	24	0-1	0-0	0-1	0-1	1-5	2-1	0-1	0-0	0-0	1-1		2-1	0-1	1-0
Sourou Sport	26	2	11	13	13	33	17	1-3	1-0	0-1	0-0	0-3	0-1	0-1	0-2	0-0	0-0	0-0		0-0	2-2
US Comoé	26	3	7	16	12	49	16	0-4	0-1	0-0	1-3	1-2	0-1	0-1	1-0	0-0	2-2	0-1	0-2		1-0
Sanmatinga Kaya	26	0	5	21	6	48	5	0-1	0-2	0-1	0-1	0-1	0-2	0-1	0-2	0-3	0-5	0-1	0-0	0-0	

27/11/2010 - 16/07/2011 • † Qualified for the CAF Champions League

MEDALS TABLE

				Overall			Lge	Cup	Africa		
				G	S	B	G	G	G	S	B
1	Etoile Filante	EFO	Ougadougou	33			12	21			
2	ASFA/Yennega (ex Jeanne d'Arc)	ASFA-Y	Ougadougou	14			11	3			
3	Union Sportive des Forces Armées	USFA	Ougadougou	10			7	3			
4	Silures (folded in 1982)		Bobo-Dioulasso	8			7	1			
5	Racing Club de Bobo	RCB	Bobo-Dioulasso	8			3	5			
6	Union Sportive du Foyer de la Regie Abidjan-Niger	USFRAN	Bobo-Dioulasso	8			3	5			
7	Association Sportive des Fonctionnaires de Bobo	ASFB	Bobo-Dioulasso	7			2	5			
8	Union Sportive Ouagadougou	USO	Ougadougou	3			2	1			
9	Rail Club Kadiogo	RCK	Kadiogo	2	2		1	1			2
10	Commune	CFO	Ougadougou	2			1	1			

COUPE NATIONALE DU FASO XXV 2010-11

Round of 16		Quarter–finals		Semi–finals		Final	
Etoile Filante	1						
US Ouagadougou	0	Etoile Filante †	0				
US Forces Armées	0	Santos	1				
Santos	2			Etoile Filante	3		
Bobo Sports	5			US Yatenga	0		
ASSIJ/DAFRA	0	Bobo Sports	1 6p				
Siyosi Junior	0	US Yatenga	1 7p				
US Yatenga	2					Etoile Filante ‡	0 4p
US Comoé	0 3p					AS SONABEL	0 3p
Canon du Sud	0 2p	US Comoé	0 6p				
Racing Club B-D	0	ASFA/Yennenga	0 5p				
ASFA/Yennenga	1			US Comoé	0	CUP FINAL	
Bouloumpokou FC	2			AS SONABEL	1		
Princes	0	Bouloumpokou FC	0			Stade di 4-août, Ouagadougou	
Ramongo	0	AS SONABEL †	1			5-08-2011	
AS SONABEL	1						

‡ Qualified for the CAF Confederation Cup

3rd Place Play-off: US Yatenga beat US Comoé • † matches abandoned. Etoile and SONABEL qualified

BHR – BAHRAIN

FIFA/COCA-COLA WORLD RANKING

'93	'94	'95	'96	'97	'98	'99	'00	'01	'02	'03	'04	'05	'06	'07	'08	'09	'10	'11	'12
78	73	99	118	121	119	136	138	110	105	64	49	52	97	102	80	60	93	101	

					2011								High	Low	Av
	Jan	Feb	Mar	Apr	May	Jun	Jul	Aug	Sep	Oct	Nov	Dec			
	93	93	96	95	97	102	98	101	102	101	102	101	44	139	93

The Hubail brothers A'ala and Mohamed along with Sayed Mohamed Adnan, Abbas Ayaad and Ali Saeed were among 150 athletes arrested as part of the crackdown against anti-government protesters in Bahrain, critically undermining the unity of a national team that had done much to help raise the level of the game in the country over the past decade with two strong FIFA World Cup campaigns and qualification for three consecutive appearances in the finals of the AFC Asian Cup. The discord around the team hampered Bahrain's attempt to finally qualify for the finals of the FIFA World Cup - having been eliminated in the final round of intercontinental playoffs in 2006 and 2010 - with the nation bowing out of Asia's qualifying tournament for Brazil at the penultimate stage as they finished in third place in their group behind Iran and Qatar. Muharraq reclaimed the title in a season that was disrupted by the protests with both Shabab and Malikiya expelled after the political unrest began. The title went right down to the wire with defending champions Al Ahli losing 2-1 to Muharraq on the final day of the season, a second half goal from Fahed Shwitr ending their hopes of leapfrogging their rivals. Later in the year Muharraq won the delayed King's Cup by beating Busaiteen 3-0 in the final to claim the double.

FIFA WORLD CUP RECORD
1930-1974 DNE **1978-1986** DNQ **1990** DNE **1994-2010** DNQ

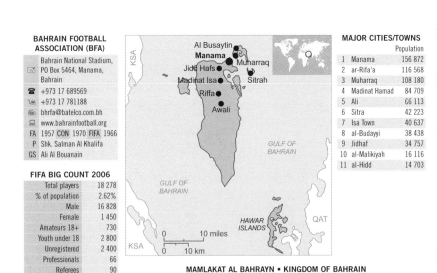

BAHRAIN FOOTBALL ASSOCIATION (BFA)

Bahrain National Stadium,
PO Box 5464, Manama,
Bahrain
☎ +973 17 689569
📠 +973 17 781188
✉ bhrfa@batelco.com.bh
🖥 www.bahrainfootball.org
FA 1957 CON 1970 FIFA 1966
P Shk. Salman Al Khalifa
GS Ali Al Bouanain

FIFA BIG COUNT 2006

Total players	18 278
% of population	2.62%
Male	16 828
Female	1 450
Amateurs 18+	730
Youth under 18	2 800
Unregistered	2 400
Professionals	66
Referees	90
Admin & coaches	620
Number of clubs	48
Number of teams	150

MAJOR CITIES/TOWNS

		Population
1	Manama	156 872
2	ar-Rifa'a	116 568
3	Muharraq	108 180
4	Madinat Hamad	84 709
5	Ali	66 113
6	Sitra	42 223
7	Isa Town	40 637
8	al-Budayyi	38 438
9	Jidhaf	34 757
10	al-Malikiyah	16 116
11	al-Hidd	14 703

MAMLAKAT AL BAHRAYN • KINGDOM OF BAHRAIN

Capital	Manama	Population	727 785 (162)	% in cities	89%
GDP per capita	$37 300 (28)	Area km²	741 km² (190)	GMT +/-	+3
Neighbours (km)	Coast 161				

RECENT INTERNATIONAL MATCHES PLAYED BY BAHRAIN

2009	Opponents	Score	Venue	Comp	Scorers	Att	Referee
26-08	Kenya	W 2-1	Manama	Fr	Husain Ahmed 2 [25 44]		
31-08	Iran	W 4-2	Manama	Fr	Mahmood Abdulrahman [12], Ismaeel Latif [30], Salman Isa [54], Sayed Mohamed [99+p]		
5-09	Saudi Arabia	D 0-0	Manama	WCpo		16 000	Nishimura JPN
9-09	Saudi Arabia	D 2-2	Riyadh	WCpo	Jaycee Okunwanne [42], Ismaeel Latif [93+]	50 000	Irmatov UZB
10-10	New Zealand	D 0-0	Manama	WCpo		37 000	Kassai HUN
6-11	Togo	W 5-1	Manama	Fr	Abdulla Fatadi 2 [39 90], Ismaeel Latif 2 [40 57], Hussain Ali [86p]		
14-11	New Zealand	L 0-1	Wellington	WCpo		36 500	Larrionda URU
18-11	Yemen	W 4-0	Manama	ACq	Ismaeel Latif [20], Abdulla Fatadi [28], Husein Salman [64], OG [75]	1 000	Basma SYR
2010							
6-01	Hong Kong	W 4-0	Manama	ACq	Ismaeel Latif 3 [34 40 43], Abdulla Al Dakeel [79]	1 550	Balideh QAT
20-01	Yemen	L 0-3	Sana'a	ACq		7 000	Torky IRN
25-02	Kuwait	L 1-4	Al Ain City	Fr	Mahmood Abdulrahman [19]		
3-03	Japan	L 0-2	Toyota	ACq		38 042	Abdul Bashir SIN
11-08	China PR	D 1-1	Nanning	Fr	Ismaeel Latif [17]		
3-09	Qatar	D 1-1	Doha	Fr	Faouzi Aaish [21]		
19-09	Jordan	L 0-2	Zarqa	Fr			
24-09	Iran	L 0-3	Amman	WAr1		8 000	Darwish JOR
26-09	Oman	W 2-0	Amman	WAr1	Ismaeel Latif 2 [63 67]	500	
8-10	Kuwait	W 3-1	Kuwait City	Fr	Ismaeel Latif [9], Faouzi Aaish [47], Salman Isa [51]	10 000	
12-10	Uzbekistan	L 2-4	Manama	Fr	Faouzi Aaish [30], Hussein Salman [53]		
10-11	Uganda	D 0-0	Manama	Fr			
14-11	Syria	L 0-2	Manama	Fr			
23-11	Oman	D 1-1	Aden	GCr1	Ebrahim Moshkhas [67]		Al Enezi KUW
26-11	Iraq	L 2-3	Aden	GCr1	Faouzi Aaish [44], Ismaeel Latif [96+p]		Allabany YEM
29-11	UAE	L 1-3	Aden	GCr1	Abdulla Fatadi [35]		Al Marry BHR
28-12	Jordan	W 2-1	Dubai	Fr	Faouzi Aaish [32p], Ismaeel Latif [69]		
31-12	Saudi Arabia	L 0-1	Riffa	Fr			
2011							
4-01	Korea DPR	L 0-1	Riffa	Fr			
10-01	Korea Republic	L 1-2	Doha	ACr1	Faouzi Aaish [86p]	6 669	Al Hilali OMA
14-01	India	W 5-2	Doha	ACr1	Faouzi Aaish [8p], Ismaeel Latif 4 [16 20 35 77]	11 032	Mohd Salleh MAS
18-01	Australia	L 0-1	Doha	ACr1		3 919	Nishimura JPN
14-02	Kuwait	D 0-0	Manama	Fr			
10-08	Oman	D 1-1	Dubai	Fr	Mahmood Abdulrahman [34]		
26-08	Sudan	W 1-0	Manama	Fr	Mahmood Abdulrahman [14]		
2-09	Qatar	D 0-0	Manama	WCq		5 000	Zarouni UAE
6-09	Indonesia	W 2-0	Jakarta	WCq	Sayed Dhiya 45, Ismaeel Latif [70]	85 000	Lee Min Hu KOR
11-10	Iran	L 0-6	Tehran	WCq		82 000	Green AUS
4-11	Kuwait	W 1-0	Kuwait City	Fr	Mahmood Abdulrahman [45]		
11-11	Iran	D 1-1	Manama	WCq	Mohamed Tayeb [45]	18 000	Bashir SIN
15-11	Qatar	D 0-0	Doha	WCq		10 509	Nishimura JPN
6-12	Palestine	L 0-1	Al Muharraq	Fr			
10-12	Qatar	D 2-2	Doha	PGr1	Sami Al Husaini 2 [71 89]		Jiyed MAR
13-12	Iraq	W 3-0	Doha	PGr1	Fahad Hardan [41], Ismaeel Latif 2 [63p 70]		Haimoudi ALG
20-12	Palestine	W 3-1	Doha	PGsf	Mohamed Al Alawi [6], Salman Isa [44], OG [58]		El Haddad LIB
23-12	Jordan	W 1-0	Doha	PGf	Ismaeel Latif [89]		Balideh QAT

Fr = Friendly match • AC = AFC Asian Cup • GC = Gulf Cup • WA = West Asian Championship • WC = FIFA World Cup • PG = Pan Arab Games
q = qualifier • r1 = first round group • qf = quarter-final • sf = semi-final • f = final • 3p = third place play-off • po = play-off

BAHRAIN NATIONAL TEAM HISTORICAL RECORDS

Past Coaches (Since 2003) Wolfgang Sidka GER 2000-03 • Yves Herbet FRA 2003 • Srecko Juricic CRO 2004-05 • Wolfgang Sidka GER 2005 • Luka Peruzovic CRO 2005-06 • Riyadh Al Thawadi BHR 2006 • Hans-Peter Briegel GER 2006-07 • Milan Macala CZE 2007-10 • Josef Hickersberger AUT 2010 • Salman Sharida 2010-11 • Peter Taylor ENG 2011-

BAHRAIN 2010–11

PREMIER LEAGUE

	Pl	W	D	L	F	A	Pts	Muharraq	Riffa	Ahli	Hadd	Manama	Busaiteen	Najma	Hala	Malikiya	Shabab
Muharraq	14	8	4	2	26	14	28		1-1	3-4	5-0	2-1	2-0	3-1	2-1	0-3	5-1
Riffa	14	7	5	2	31	18	26	0-1		3-3	2-1	2-3	1-1	2-0	**3-0**		
Al Ahli	14	7	3	4	30	21	24	1-2	0-1		2-1	3-0	1-2	1-1	3-1		
Al Hadd	14	5	5	4	24	28	20	3-1	1-5	2-1		3-2	3-3	2-2	2-1		
Manama	14	5	4	5	22	22	19	1-1	2-4	0-2	2-2		1-0	1-1	3-0		0-0
Busaiteen	14	2	7	5	18	24	13	0-0	2-2	2-3	0-2	1-1		4-1	1-1		
Al Hala	14	1	7	6	14	28	10	1-1	1-3	1-4	1-1	0-3	2-2			1-0	1-1
Al Najma	14	1	5	8	15	25	8	0-2	2-2	2-2	1-1	1-2	4-0		1-1		0-0
Malikiya	Expelled after six matches								1-2	1-1							3-0
Al Shabab	Expelled after six matches								2-2	0-2			0-2				

14/10/2010 - 29/05/2011

MEDALS TABLE

		All	Lge	KC	FAC	CPC	Asia		
		G	G	G			G	S	B
1	Muharraq	67	32	28	2	5	2		
2	Riffa	21	9	5	3	4			
3	Al Ahli	14	5	8	1				
4	Bahrain Club	7	5	2					
5	Al Hala	4	1	3					
6	East Riffa	3	1	2					
	Al Wahda	3		3					
8	Al Arabi	2	1	1					
	Al Najma	2		2					
10	Al Shabab	1		1					
	Busaiteen	1			1				
	Al Nasr	1	1						

KINGS CUP 2010–11

First Round		Quarter–finals		Semi–finals		Final	
Muharraq	5						
Al Hala	0	**Muharraq**	3				
Al Ittifaq	0	Manama	0				
Manama	8			**Muharraq** ‡	3		
Budaia	3			Al Hadd	0		
Qalali	2	Budaia	1				
Riffa	1	**Al Hadd**	5				
Al Hadd	3					**Muharraq**	3
Al Ahli	1					Busaiteen	0
Malikiya	0	**Al Ahli**	2 4p				
East Riffa	1	Bahrain Club	2 2p				
Bahrain Club	3			Al Ahli	0 3p		
Al Najma	2			**Busaiteen**	0 4p		
Setra	1	Al Najma	0				
Al Ittihad	0	**Busaiteen**	3				
Busaiteen	2						

‡ Muharraq awarded match after Hadd failed to show

CUP FINAL

National Stadium, Manama
29-10-2011
Scorers - Ismael Abdullatif [9], Sayed Dhiya Saeed [38], Diego da Silva [57] for Muharraq

Preliminary Round: Isa Town 0-3 **Al Ahli** • Manama 2-1 Al Shabbab • Al Tadamun 0-5 **Busaiteen**

BHU – BHUTAN

FIFA/COCA-COLA WORLD RANKING

'93	'94	'95	'96	'97	'98	'99	'00	'01	'02	'03	'04	'05	'06	'07	'08	'09	'10	'11	'12
-	-	-	-	-	-	-	201	202	199	187	187	190	192	198	187	196	197	202	

					2011										
Jan	Feb	Mar	Apr	May	Jun	Jul	Aug	Sep	Oct	Nov	Dec		**High**	**Low**	**Av**
197	197	197	196	196	201	201	201	200	199	198	202		187	202	194

After a year's absence from the international scene for the Bhutan national team, there was little to cheer for the Himalayan kingdom throughout a 2011 that yielded a string of defeats. Back-to-back defeats at the hands of Nepal in friendlies in March were followed by swift elimination from the qualifying rounds for the AFC Challenge Cup thanks to a pair of losses against Afghanistan. The disappointing run under new coach Hiroaki Matsuyama continued at the South Asian Football Federation Championship in New Delhi at the end of the year, when Bhutan were beaten by Sri Lanka, hosts India and once again by the Afghans, this time to the tune of an 8-1 thrashing. Matsuyama's contract with the Bhutan Football Federation expired at the end of the year, with the Japanese coach returning to look for work in his homeland. Bhutan football was offered no respite at club level either as Yeedzin, the 2010 champions, endured three defeats in the preliminary group stages of the AFC President's Cup, the continental club tournament featuring sides from the lower tier of the Asian Football Confederation. Losses against Palestine's Jabal Al Mukaber, Yadanarbon of Myanmar and Esteghlal from Tajikistan ended the club's participation in the competition and left them at the bottom of the three-team group without a goal scored.

FIFA WORLD CUP RECORD
1930-2014 DNE

BHUTAN FOOTBALL FEDERATION (BFF)

PO Box 365, Thimphu

☎ +975 2 322350
📠 +975 2 321131
✉ mindubff_05@yahoo.com
🖥
FA 1983 CON 1993 FIFA 2000
P Ugen Dorji
GS Ugyen Wangchhuk

FIFA BIG COUNT 2006

Total players	17 100
% of population	0.75%
Male	17 100
Female	0
Amateurs 18+	600
Youth under 18	600
Unregistered	2 900
Professionals	0
Referees	100
Admin & coaches	100
Number of clubs	10
Number of teams	70

MAJOR CITIES/TOWNS

		Population
1	Thimphu	90 300
2	Phuentsholing	22 467
3	Geylegphug	9 901
4	Wangdue	7 174
5	Samdrup Jongkhar	6 389
6	Samtse	5 272
7	Gedu	4 691
8	Bumthang	4 507
9	Gomtu	4 503
10	Monggar	3 722
11	Chhukha	3 123
12	Trashiyangtse	2 900
13	Trongsa	2 866
14	Deothang	2 838
15	Sarpang	2 819
16	Ha	2 657
17	Tsimalakha	2 583
18	Trashigang	2 513
19	Tshongdue	2 477

DRUK GYALKHAP • KINGDOM OF BHUTAN

Capital Thimphu	Population 691 141 (163)	% in cities 35%
GDP per capita $5200 (138)	Area km² 38 394 km² (136)	GMT + / - +6
Neighbours (km) China 470, India 605		

RECENT INTERNATIONAL MATCHES PLAYED BY BHUTAN

2003 Opponents		Score	Venue	Comp	Scorers	Att	Referee
6-10 Indonesia	L	0-2	Jeddah	ACq			
8-10 Saudi Arabia	L	0-6	Jeddah	ACq			
10-10 Yemen	L	0-8	Jeddah	ACq			
13-10 Indonesia	L	0-2	Jeddah	ACq			
15-10 Saudi Arabia	L	0-4	Jeddah	ACq			
17-10 Yemen	L	0-4	Jeddah	ACq			
2004							
No international matches played in 2004							
2005							
8-12 Bangladesh	L	0-3	Karachi	SAFr1			
10-12 India	L	0-3	Karachi	SAFr1			
12-12 Nepal	L	1-3	Karachi	SAFr1	Pradhan [47]		
2006							
2-04 Nepal	L	0-2	Chittagong	CCr1		3 500	Gosh BAN
4-04 Sri Lanka	L	0-1	Chittagong	CCr1			Saidov UZB
6-04 Brunei Darussalam	D	0-0	Chittagong	CCr1		2 000	Al Ghatrifi OMA
2007							
No international matches played in 2007							
2008							
13-05 Tajikistan	L	1-3	Barotac	CCq	Pasang Tshering [69]	5 000	Ng Chiu Kok HGK
15-05 Brunei Darussalam	D	1-1	Barotac	CCq	Nawang Dendup [12]	4 000	Mahapab THA
17-05 Philippines	L	0-3	Barotac	CCq		7 000	Saleem MDV
4-06 Bangladesh	D	1-1	Colombo	SAFr1	Nima Sanghe [79]		
6-06 Sri Lanka	L	0-2	Colombo	SAFr1			
8-06 Afghanistan	W	3-1	Colombo	SAFr1	Kinlay Dorji [13], Gyeltshen 2 [31 80]		
11-06 India	L	1-2	Male	SAFsf	Kinlay Dorji [18]		
2009							
14-04 Philippines	L	0-1	Male	CCq		200	Lazeem IRQ
16-04 Turkmenistan	L	0-7	Male	CCq		300	Perera SRI
18-04 Maldives	L	0-5	Male	CCq		9 000	Lazeem IRQ
29-11 Nepal	L	1-2	Calcutta	Fr	Pasang Tshering [59p]		
4-12 Bangaldesh	L	1-4	Dhaka	SAFr1	Nawang Dendup [42p]		
6-12 Sri Lanka	L	0-6	Dhaka	SAFr1			
8-12 Pakistan	L	0-7	Dhaka	SAFr1			
2010							
No international matches played in 2010							
2011							
17-03 Nepal	L	0-1	Pokhara	Fr			
19-03 Nepal	L	1-2	Pokhara	Fr	Chencho Gyeltshen [91+]		
23-03 Afghanistan	L	0-3	Gurgaon	CCq		200	Mahapab THA
25-03 Afghanistan	L	0-2	Gurgaon	CCq		2 000	Mombeni IRN
3-12 Sri Lanka	L	0-3	New Delhi	SAFr1			Tufaylieh SYR
5-12 India	L	0-5	New Delhi	SAFr1			Singh SIN
7-12 Afghanistan	L	1-8	New Delhi	SAFr1	Chencho Gyeltshen [22]		Robesh SRI

SAF = South Asian Football Federation Cup • AC = AFC Asian Cup • CC = AFC Challenge Cup • q = qualifier • r1 = first round group

BHUTAN NATIONAL TEAM HISTORICAL RECORDS

Coach — Kang Byung Chan KOR 2000-02 • Yoo Kee Heung KOR 2002 • Aric Schanz NED 2002 • Henk Walk NED 2002-03 • Kharga Basnet 2005-06 • Koji Gyotoku JPN 2008-11 • Hiroaki Matsuyama JPN 2011

BIH – BOSNIA-HERZEGOVINA

FIFA/COCA-COLA WORLD RANKING

'93	'94	'95	'96	'97	'98	'99	'00	'01	'02	'03	'04	'05	'06	'07	'08	'09	'10	'11	'12
-	-	-	152	99	96	75	78	69	87	59	79	65	59	51	61	51	44	20	

					2011									
Jan	Feb	Mar	Apr	May	Jun	Jul	Aug	Sep	Oct	Nov	Dec	High	Low	Av
45	42	56	44	45	39	41	39	22	21	23	20	20	173	72

For the second qualifying tournament running Bosnia-Hercegovina suffered the heartbreak of a play-off defeat at the hands of the Portuguese. Having lost 2-0 on aggregate in the 2010 FIFA World Cup play-offs, the Bosnians managed to draw the first leg at home in the UEFA Euro 2012 play-offs but then came unstuck in Lisbon where they lost 6-2 to a Cristiano Ronaldo-inspired team to miss out on a first appearance at the finals of a major tournament. Bosnia could have ensured automatic qualification if they had beaten France in Paris in their final group game in the qualifiers and they were just 13 minutes away from doing just that before a Sami Nasri equaliser from the penalty spot sent the French through. There is genuine hope, however, that the current golden generation of players including high profile stars such as Manchester City's Edin Dzeko and Roma's Miralem Pjanic, can finally break their duck in a very winnable 2014 FIFA World Cup qualifying group where their main rivals look to be Greece and Slovakia. At home there was a first championship for Borac Banja Luka who finished comfortably ahead of their two Sarajevo rivals FK Sarajevo and Zeljeznicar although for Zelejeznicar there was a cup triumph to celebrate after a 4-0 aggregate victory over Celik Zenica in the final.

UEFA EUROPEAN CHAMPIONSHIP RECORD
1960-1992 DNE (part of Yugoslavia) **1996** DNE **2000-2012** DNQ

FOOTBALL FEDERATION OF BOSNIA–HERZEGOVINA (FFBH/NSBIH)

Ferhadija 30, Sarajevo - 71000
☎ +387 33 276660
📠 +387 33 444332
📧 nsbih@bih.net.ba
🖥 www.nfsbih.ba
FA 1992 CON 1996 FIFA 1996
P Sulejman Colakovic
GS Jasmin Bakovic

FIFA BIG COUNT 2006

Total players	200 240
% of population	4.45%
Male	181 640
Female	18 600
Amateurs 18+	40 370
Youth under 18	26 570
Unregistered	36 200
Professionals	430
Referees	1 720
Admin & coaches	10 100
Number of clubs	763
Number of teams	1 000

MAJOR CITIES/TOWNS

		Population
1	Banja Luka	221 686
2	Sarajevo	192 264
3	Samac	110 246
4	Tuzla	97 038
5	Zenica	93 043
6	Bijeljina	70 528
7	Mostar	70 270
8	Gradiska	42 262
9	Prijedor	41 938
10	Bihac	39 683
11	Brcko	36 483
12	Pale	34 617
13	Teslic	34 556
33	Zepce	12 504
44	Banovici	10 619
58	Modrica	8 763
60	Siroki Brijeg	8 434
117	Posusje	4 137
188	Orasje	3 088

BOSNA I HERCEGOVINA • BOSNIA AND HERZEGOVINA

Capital Sarajevo	Population 4 613 414 (119)	% in cities 47%
GDP per capita $6500 (127)	Area km² 51 197 km² (128)	GMT +/- +1
Neighbours (km) Croatia 932, Montenegro 249, Serbia 357 • Coast 20		

RECENT INTERNATIONAL MATCHES PLAYED BY BOSNIA–HERZEGOVINA

2008 Opponents	Score	Venue	Comp	Scorers	Att	Referee
30-01 Japan	L 0-3	Tokyo	Fr		26 971	Kim Eui Soo KOR
26-03 FYR Macedonia	D 2-2	Zenica	Fr	Damjanovic 2 [17 20]		Svilokos CRO
1-06 Azerbaijan	W 1-0	Zenica	Fr	Nokolic [72]	800	Radovanovic MNE
20-08 Bulgaria	L 1-2	Zenica	Fr	Ibricic [59]	7 000	Stankovic SRB
6-09 Spain	L 0-1	Murcia	WCq		29 152	Thomson SCO
10-09 Estonia	W 7-0	Zenica	WCq	Misimovic 3 [24 30p 56], Muslimovic [59], Dzeko 2 [60 72], Ibricic [88]	12 500	Balaj ROU
11-10 Turkey	L 1-2	Istanbul	WCq	Dzeko [26]	23 628	Kassai HUN
15-10 Armenia	W 4-1	Zenica	WCq	Spahic [31], Dzeko [39], Muslimovic 2 [56 89]	13 000	Kenan ISR
19-11 Slovenia	W 4-3	Maribor	Fr	Ibisevic 2 [2 62], Misimovic [11p], Dzeko [53]	10 000	Kari FIN
2009						
28-03 Belgium	W 4-2	Genk	WCq	Dzeko [7], Jahic [75], Bajramovic [77], Misimovic [81]	20 041	Ivanov.N RUS
1-04 Belgium	W 2-1	Zenica	WCq	Dzeko 2 [12 14]	13 800	Hrinak SVK
1-06 Uzbekistan	D 0-0	Tashkent	Fr		15 000	Kovalenko UZB
9-06 Oman	W 2-1	Cannes	Fr	Dzeko [14], Salihovic [85]		
12-08 Iran	L 2-3	Sarajevo	Fr	Dzeko 2 [52 69]		
5-09 Armenia	W 2-0	Yerevan	WCq	Ibricic [6], Muslimovic [74]	1 800	Braamhaar NED
9-09 Turkey	D 1-1	Zenica	WCq	Salihovic [25]	14 000	Benquerença POR
10-10 Estonia	W 2-0	Tallinn	WCq	Dzeko [30], Ibisevic [64]	6 450	Rizzoli ITA
14-10 Spain	L 2-5	Zenica	WCq	Dzeko [90], Misimovic [92+]	13 500	Plautz AUT
14-11 Portugal	L 0-1	Lisbon	WCpo		60 588	Atkinson ENG
18-11 Portugal	L 0-1	Zenica	WCpo		15 000	Rosetti ITA
2010						
3-03 Ghana	W 2-1	Sarajevo	Fr	Ibisevic [40], Pjanic [65]	10 000	Batinic CRO
29-05 Sweden	L 2-4	Stockholm	Fr	Salihovic [47], Zec [90]	22 589	Grafe GER
3-06 Germany	L 1-3	Frankfurt	Fr	Dzeko [15]	48 000	Rizzoli ITA
10-08 Qatar	D 1-1	Sarajevo	Fr	Ibisevic [9]	18 000	Vuckov CRO
3-09 Luxembourg	W 3-1	Luxembourg	ECq	Ibricic [6], Pjanic [12], Dzeko [16]	7 327	Banari MDA
7-09 France	L 0-2	Sarajevo	ECq		28 000	Brych GER
8-10 Albania	D 1-1	Tirana	ECq	Ibisevic [21]	14 220	Jakobsson ISL
17-11 Slovakia	W 3-2	Bratislava	Fr	Medunjanin [28], Pjanic [50], Dzeko [60]	7 822	Mikulski POL
10-12 Poland	D 2-2	Antalya	Fr	Subasic [23], Misimovic [56p]	100	Ogretmenoglu TUR
2011						
9-02 Mexico	L 0-2	Atlanta	Fr		45 000	Murrufo USA
26-03 Romania	W 2-1	Zenica	ECq	Ibisevic [63], Dzeko [83]	13 000	Teixeira ESP
3-06 Romania	L 0-3	Bucharest	ECq		8 200	Eriksson SWE
7-06 Albania	W 2-0	Zenica	ECq	Medunjanin [67], Maletic [91+]	9 000	Blom NED
10-08 Greece	D 0-0	Sarajevo	Fr		10 000	Dabanovic MNE
2-09 Belarus	W 2-0	Minsk	ECq	Salihovic [22p], Medunjanin [24]	28 500	Kassai HUN
6-09 Belarus	W 1-0	Zenica	ECq	Misimovic [87]	12 000	Atkinson ENG
7-10 Luxembourg	W 5-0	Zenica	ECq	Dzeko [12], Misimovic 2 [15 22p], Pjanic [36], Medunjanin [51]	12 000	Evans WAL
11-10 France	D 1-1	Paris	ECq	Dzeko [40]	78 467	Thomson SCO
11-11 Portugal	D 0-0	Zenica	ECpo		12 352	Webb ENG
15-11 Portugal	L 2-6	Lisbon	ECpo	Misimovic [41p], Spahic [65]	47 728	Stark GER

Fr = Friendly match • EC = UEFA EURO 2012 • WC = FIFA World Cup • q = qualifier • po = play-off

BOSNIA-HERZEGOVINA NATIONAL TEAM HISTORICAL RECORDS

Caps: **64** - Zvjezdan Misimovic 2004- • **55** - Emir Spahic 2003- • **51** - Elvir Bolic 1996-2006 • **47** - Sergej Barbarez 1998-2006 • **45** - Vedin Music 1995-2007 • **44** - Kenan Hasagic 2002- • **43** - Hasan Salihamidzic 1996-2006 • **41** - Edin Dzeko 2007- • **40** - Muhamed Konjic 1995-2004 • **39** - Elvir Baljic 1996-2005 • **38** - Sasa Papac 2002- • **36** - Mirsad Hibic 1997-2004 • **35** - Zlatan Bajramovic 2002-

Goals: **22** - Elvir Bolic 1996-2006 • **20** - Zvjezdan Misimovic 2004- & Edin Dzeko 2007- • **17** - Sergej Barbarez 1998-2006 • **14** - Elvir Baljic 1996-2005 • **11** - Zlatan Muslimovic 2006- • **8** - Vedad Ibisevic 2007- • **6** - Hasan Salihamidzic 1996-2006 & Dzelaludin Muharemovic 1997-2001

Past Coaches: Mirsad Fazlagic 1992-1993 • Fuad Muzurovic 1993-1998 • Dzemaludin Musovic 1998-99 • Faruk Hadzibegic 1999 • Miso Smajlovic 1999-2002 • Blaz Sliskovic 2002-2006 • Fuad Muzurovic 2006-2007 • Meho Kodro 2008 • Miroslav Blazevic 2008-2009 • Safet Susic 2009-

BOSNIA-HERZEGOVINA 2010-11

PREMIJER LIGA

	Pl	W	D	L	F	A	Pts	Borac	Sarajevo	Zeljeznicar	Siroki	Olimpik	Sloboda	Zrinjski	Zvijezda	Rudar	Celik	Slavija	Travnik	Velez	Leotar	Buducnost	Drina
Borac Banja Luka †	30	19	7	4	37	15	64		2-0	1-0	2-3	2-1	2-0	2-0	1-0	0-0	1-0	4-1	2-0	1-1	2-2	2-1	1-0
Sarajevo ‡	30	17	6	7	51	26	57	0-1		0-0	3-0	3-1	3-0	1-0	2-1	5-1	1-0	4-2	1-0	1-0	3-0	2-0	1-1
Zeljeznicar Sarajevo ‡	30	17	4	9	50	25	55	0-1	0-0		0-1	3-0	0-1	3-1	2-0	4-2	2-1	2-0	3-0	3-2	8-0	2-0	2-0
Siroki Brijeg ‡	30	16	2	12	59	45	50	1-2	2-1	4-1		1-3	4-0	4-1	3-0	1-2	2-2	4-1	2-1	4-1	3-1	2-1	5-1
Olimpik Sarajevo	30	14	6	10	35	33	48	0-0	2-1	0-2	1-0		2-2	2-0	1-0	2-0	1-0	0-0	5-3	0-1	1-0	1-1	2-1
Sloboda Tuzla	30	14	4	12	28	29	46	1-0	0-0	2-0	0-1	0-1		0-1	2-1	2-1	2-0	2-1	2-0	1-0	1-1	1-0	3-0
Zrinjski Mostar	30	13	3	14	41	39	42	0-0	4-2	0-1	4-3	1-0	1-0		1-2	1-0	1-0	4-2	3-1	2-0	4-0	0-0	3-0
Zvijezda Gradacac	30	11	9	10	40	38	42	1-0	1-1	0-0	6-1	2-2	0-1	1-1		0-0	1-1	2-1	2-1	0-0	1-0	0-0	2-1
Rudar Prijedor	30	11	8	11	37	41	41	0-1	1-1	3-2	2-1	3-1	3-0	2-0	1-3		1-1	2-2	1-1	2-0	1-1	2-1	1-0
Celik Zenica	30	11	7	12	30	30	40	0-1	2-1	1-1	0-0	0-1	1-0	2-1	4-1	2-1		1-0	2-0	1-0	3-0	2-1	1-0
Slavija Sarajevo	30	11	5	14	44	46	38	0-0	2-1	1-0	1-0	0-0	1-0	3-2	2-0	3-0	5-1		1-1	2-1	4-0	2-3	0-1
Travnik	30	11	4	15	44	43	37	1-2	1-2	2-1	4-0	1-0	2-0	2-1	2-2	2-1	0-0	5-3		5-1	1-0	0-1	6-0
Velez Mostar	30	11	3	16	31	43	36	0-0	1-2	1-3	2-5	3-0	2-0	1-0	1-4	3-0	1-0	2-1	1-0		0-2	2-0	1-0
Leotar Trebinje	30	10	5	15	29	49	35	2-1	0-2	0-1	1-0	0-1	1-3	4-1	3-0	0-0	2-1	2-1	1-0	2-1		1-1	1-0
Buducnost Banovici	30	6	7	17	25	44	25	0-1	1-2	1-2	1-0	2-1	0-0	**0-3**	2-5	1-3	1-1	0-1	3-1	0-1	2-1		1-1
Drina Zvornik	30	7	2	21	18	53	23	0-2	0-5	0-2	0-2	1-3	0-2	1-0	1-2	0-1	1-0	2-1	0-1	2-0	2-1	2-0	

31/07/2010 - 28/05/2011 • † Qualified for the UEFA Champions League • ‡ Qualified for the Europa League • Match in bold awarded
Top scorers: **15** - Nusmir Fajic, Travnik & Ivan Lendric CRO, Zrinjski • **14** - Mirza Dzafic, Rudar • **13** - Damir Tosunovic, Zvijezda

BOSNIA 2010-11
PRVA LIGA NS FBIH (2)

	Pl	W	D	L	F	A	Pts
GOSK Gabela	30	16	8	6	38	21	56
Capljina	30	15	3	12	49	41	48
Iskra Bugojno	30	13	8	9	45	35	47
Krajina Cazin	30	14	5	11	41	31	47
Orasje	30	14	5	11	40	31	47
Jedinstvo Bihac	30	14	4	12	38	39	46
Gorazde	30	14	3	13	50	39	45
Gradina Srebrenik	30	13	5	12	44	39	44
Krajisnik	30	13	5	12	41	40	44
Rudar Kakanj	30	11	10	9	46	44	43
Napredak Sarajevo	30	13	4	13	49	49	43
Omladinac Mionica	30	13	3	14	37	39	42
Bosna Visoko	30	12	5	13	39	44	41
Slaven Zivinice	30	10	4	16	27	42	34
Igman Konjic	30	9	4	17	34	57	31
Radnik Hadzici	30	4	8	18	26	53	20

31/07/2010 - 28/05/2011

BOSNIA 2010-11
PRVA LIGA FS RS (2)

	Pl	W	D	L	F	A	Pts
Kozara Gradiska	26	18	4	4	46	12	58
Radnik Bijeljina	26	13	4	9	38	20	43
Sutjeska Foca	26	12	7	7	37	27	43
Mladost Gacko	26	13	1	12	35	38	40
Podrinje Janja	26	11	6	9	39	27	39
Sloga Doboj	26	10	8	8	35	41	38
Proleter Teslic	26	11	4	11	30	26	37
Sloboda Novi Grad	26	9	9	8	37	33	36
Modrica Maksima	26	10	5	11	32	33	35
Laktasi	26	9	8	9	21	28	35
Sloboda Mrkonjic Grad	26	8	6	12	30	33	30
Drina Visegrad	26	8	5	13	26	36	29
Famos Vojkovici	26	8	4	14	29	42	28
BSK Banja Luka	26	4	5	17	15	54	17

31/07/2010 - 28/05/2011

MEDALS TABLE

	Overall			League			Cup			Europe		
	G	S	B	G	S	B	G	S	B	G	S	B
1 Zeljeznicar Sarajevo	8	6	1	4	3	1	4	3				
2 FK Sarajevo	5	7	3	1	5	3	4	2				
3 Celik Zenica	5	1	1	3			2	1				
4 NK Siroki Brijeg	3	5	1	2	3	1	1	2				
5 Zrinjski Mostar	3	1	1	2	1	1	1					
6 Borac Banja Luka	2	1	1	1			1	1				
7 FK Modrica Maxima	2			1								
8 Slavija Sarajevo	1	2	1	1	1		1	1				
9 Brotnjo Citluk	1	1	1	1	1	1						
10 Leotar Trebinje	1	1		1							1	
11 Bosna Visoko	1	2					2	1				
12 NK Orasje	1						1					
13 Sloboda Tuzla	5	2					2				5	
14 Buducnost Banovici	1			1								
Radniki Lukavac												

BOSNIAN CLUBS IN YUGOSLAV FOOTBALL

	Overall			League			Cup			Europe		
	G	S	B	G	S	B	G	S	B	G	S	B
7 Velez Mostar	2	5	4		3	4	2	2				
9 FK Sarajevo	2	4		2	2			2				
13 Zeljeznicar Sarajevo	1	2	2	1	1	2	1				1	
14 Borac Banja Luka	1	1					1	1				
21 Slavia	1	1		1	1							
21 Sloboda Tuzla	1	1		1								
23 SASK Sarajevo	1			1								

KUP BIH 2010-11

First Round

Zeljeznicar Sarajevo *	2
Rudar Prijedor	0
TOSK Tesanj	0
Borac Banja Luka *	2
Leotar Trebinje *	1
Zvijezda Gradacac	0
Doboj Istok	0
Branitelj Mostar *	7
Sarajevo *	2
Sloga Uskoplje	0
Orasje	0
Sloboda Novi Grad *	1
Omladinac Mionica	1
BSK Banja Luka *	0
Sutjeska Foca	0
Siroki Brijeg *	6
Olimpik Sarajevo *	1
Vitez *	0
Modrica Maksima	1
UNIS Vogosca *	2
Kozara Gradiska *	0
Travnik *	1
Bosna Sarajevo *	0
Sloboda Tuzla	1
Zrinjski Mostar *	3
Buducnost Banovici	1
Drina Zvornik	0 3p
Proleter Teslic *	0 4p
Slavija Sarajevo *	3
Jedinstvo Bihac	1
Velez Mostar	0
Celik Zenica *	2

Round of 16

Zeljeznicar Sarajevo	0	3
Borac Banja Luka *	0	0
Leotar Trebinje *	1	0
Branitelj Mostar	1	1
Sarajevo *	4	3
Sloboda Novi Grad	1	1
Omladinac Mionica *	2	0
Siroki Brijeg	0	4
Olimpik Sarajevo *	5	2
UNIS Vogosca	1	1
Kozara Gradiska *	1	2
Sloboda Tuzla	1	4
Zrinjski Mostar *	2	3
Proleter Teslic *	4	0
Slavija Sarajevo	1	0
Celik Zenica *	1	1

Quarter-finals

Zeljeznicar Sarajevo *	6	3	
Branitelj Mostar	0	0	
Sarajevo *	2	0	
Siroki Brijeg	2	1	
Olimpik Sarajevo *	1	1	6p
Sloboda Tuzla	1	1	5p
Zrinjski Mostar *	2	0	
Celik Zenica	0	3	

Semi-finals

Zeljeznicar Sarajevo *	0	1
Siroki Brijeg	0	1
Olimpik Sarajevo	0	1
Celik Zenica *	1	1

Final

CUP FINAL 1ST LEG

Grbavica, Sarajevo
28-04-2011. Att: 7000. Ref: Goran Paradzik
Scorer - Zeba 1

Zeljeznicar - Ibrahim Sehic - Patrick Gerhardt, Velibor Vasilic, Mirsad Beslija• (Elvir Colic 62), Zajko Zeba, Goran Markovic (Benjamin Colic 80), Milam Culum•, Muamer Svraka•, Edin Visca• (Srdan Savic 83), Lazar Popovic, Srdan Stanic. Tr: Amar Osim

Celik - Luka Bilobrk• - Mehmedalija Covic, Semjon Milosevic•, Elmir Kuduzovic, Zoran Brkovic• Armin Kapetan, Dario Puric (Elvis Sadikovic 89), Kenan Horic• (Eldar Hasanovic 64), Emir Hadzic, Adin Dzafic (Aldin Sisic 82), Eldin Adilovic. Tr: Abdulah Ibrakovic

Zeljeznicar Sarajevo ‡	1	3
Celik Zenica	0	0

CUP FINAL 2ND LEG

Bilino Polje, Zenica
25-05-2011. Att: 11000. Ref: Midhat Arnautovic
Scorers - Savic 12, Zeba 71, Stanic 73

Celik - Luka Bilobrk - Mehmedalija Covic, Semjon Milosevic, Elmir Kuduzovic, Zoran Brkovic, Dario Puric, Aldin Isakovic, Aldin Sisic• (Kenan Horic 76), Emir Hadzic (Kenan Nemeljakovic 79), Adin Dzafic (Eldar Hasanovic 66), Eldin Adilovic. Tr: Abdulah Ibrakovic

Zeljeznicar - Ibrahim Sehic• - Jadranko Bogicevic•, Mirko Radovanovic (Omar Baljic 78), Patrick Gerhardt, Srdan Savic, Benjamin Colic, Mirsad Beslija• (Nermin Zolotic 82), Zajko Zeba, Muamer Svraka, Lazar Popovic (Mirsad Ramic 87), Srdan Stanic. Tr: Amar Osim

Olimpik Sarajevo	0	1
Celik Zenica *	1	1

* Home team/Home team in the 1st leg ‡ Qualified for the Europa League

BLR – BELARUS

FIFA/COCA-COLA WORLD RANKING

'93	'94	'95	'96	'97	'98	'99	'00	'01	'02	'03	'04	'05	'06	'07	'08	'09	'10	'11	'12
137	121	88	90	110	104	95	96	85	74	90	69	61	70	60	84	80	38	64	

2011												High	Low	Av
Jan	Feb	Mar	Apr	May	Jun	Jul	Aug	Sep	Oct	Nov	Dec			
37	36	37	53	53	40	42	41	56	61	65	64	36	142	84

Having started their Euro 2012 qualifying campaign in such positive fashion, notably with the 1-0 victory over France in Paris, a final position of fourth in the group was a crushing disappointment for fans in Belarus and having been drawn in a 2014 FIFA World Cup qualifying group containing both France and defending champions Spain, it will take a superhuman effort for the team to make it to Brazil and qualify for their first finals. The damage was done with successive defeats against Bosnia in September and at the end of the year coach Bernard Stange stood down after over four years in the job, his replacement Georgy Kondtariev moving up from his position with the youth squads. In club football, BATE Borisov once again dominated the year, winning their sixth consecutive championship. Four of those have come under their youthful coach Viktor Goncharenko who once again took BATE to the group stages of the UEFA Champions League. In the 2011-12 competition BATE found themselves in the same group as Barcelona and Milan and although they secured two draws against the Italians they lost all their games against Barcelona and Viktoria Plzen and finished bottom of the group. Earlier in the year BATE had been eliminated from the first knockout round of the 2010-11 Europea League on away goals by PSG.

UEFA EUROPEAN CHAMPIONSHIP RECORD
1960-1992 DNE (Played as part of the Soviet Union) **1996-2012** DNQ

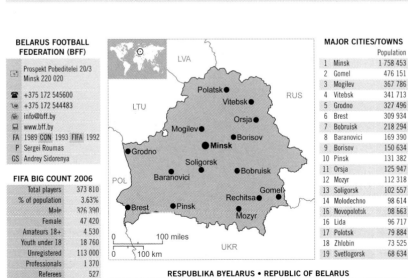

BELARUS FOOTBALL FEDERATION (BFF)

Prospekt Pobeditelei 20/3
Minsk 220 020

☎ +375 172 545600
🖷 +375 172 544483
📧 info@bff.by
🖳 www.bff.by
FA 1989 CON 1993 FIFA 1992
P Sergei Roumas
GS Andrey Sidorenya

FIFA BIG COUNT 2006

Total players	373 810
% of population	3.63%
Male	326 390
Female	47 420
Amateurs 18+	4 530
Youth under 18	18 760
Unregistered	113 000
Professionals	1 370
Referees	527
Admin & coaches	948
Number of clubs	155
Number of teams	270

MAJOR CITIES/TOWNS

		Population
1	Minsk	1 758 453
2	Gomel	476 151
3	Mogilev	367 786
4	Vitebsk	341 713
5	Grodno	327 496
6	Brest	309 934
7	Bobruisk	218 294
8	Baranovici	169 390
9	Borisov	150 634
10	Pinsk	131 382
11	Orsja	125 947
12	Mozyr	112 318
13	Soligorsk	102 557
14	Molodechno	98 614
15	Novopolotok	98 863
16	Lida	96 717
17	Polotsk	79 884
18	Zhlobin	73 525
19	Svetlogorsk	68 634

RESPUBLIKA BYELARUS • REPUBLIC OF BELARUS

Capital Minsk	Population 9 648 533 (86)	% in cities 73%
GDP per capita $11 800 (93)	Area km² 207 600 km² (85)	GMT +/- +2
Neighbours (km) Latvia 171, Lithuania 680, Poland 605, Russia 959, Ukraine 891		

RECENT INTERNATIONAL MATCHES PLAYED BY BELARUS

2008	Opponents	Score		Venue	Comp	Scorers	Att	Referee
2-02	Iceland	W	2-0	Ta'Qali	Fr	Vasilyuk [33], Plaskonny [47]	100	Lautier MLT
4-02	Armenia	L	1-2	Ta'Qali	Fr	Hleb.V [5]	100	Zammit MLT
6-02	Malta	W	1-0	Ta'Qali	Fr	Romaschenko [89]	1 000	Tshagharyan ARM
26-03	Turkey	D	2-2	Minsk	Fr	Kutuzov [35], Hleb.V [64]	12 000	Malzinskas LTU
27-05	Germany	D	2-2	Kaiserslautern	Fr	Bulyga 2 [61 88]	47 258	Ceferin SVN
2-06	Finland	D	1-1	Turku	Fr	Shitov [90]	6 474	Skomina SVN
20-08	Argentina	D	0-0	Minsk	Fr			Sukhina RUS
6-09	Ukraine	L	0-1	Lviv	WCq		24 000	Rizzoli ITA
10-09	Andorra	W	3-1	Andorra La Vella	WCq	Verkhovtsov [37], Rodionov [79], Hleb [90]	600	Evans WAL
15-10	England	L	1-3	Minsk	WCq	Sitko [28]	29 600	Hauge NOR
19-11	Cyprus	L	1-2	Nicosia	Fr	Kovel [55]	300	Kenan ISR
2009								
1-04	Kazakhstan	W	5-1	Almaty	WCq	Hleb.A [48], Kalachev 2 [54 64], Stasevich [57], Rodionov [88]	19 000	Jech CZE
6-06	Andorra	W	5-1	Grodno	WCq	Blizniuk 2 [1 76], Kalachev [44], Kornilenko 2 [50 65]	8 500	Kranjc SVN
10-06	Moldova	D	2-2	Borisov	Fr	Rodionov [4], Bliznyuk [27]	2 000	Mazeika LTU
12-08	Croatia	L	1-3	Minsk	WCq	Verkhovtsov [81]	21 651	Brych GER
5-09	Croatia	L	0-1	Zagreb	WCq		25 628	Plautz AUT
9-09	Ukraine	D	0-0	Minsk	WCq		21 727	Kassai HUN
10-10	Kazakhstan	W	4-0	Brest	WCq	Bordachev [23], Kalachev 2 [69 92+], Kovel [86]	9 530	Ennjimmi FRA
14-10	England	L	0-3	London	WCq		76 897	Batista POR
14-11	Saudi Arabia	D	1-1	Dammam	Fr	Bordachev [20]		
18-11	Montenegro	L	0-1	Podgorica	Fr		5 000	Stavrev MKD
2010								
3-03	Armenia	W	3-1	Antalya	Fr	Putsila [58], Hleb [73], Rodionov [86]	BCD	
27-05	Honduras	D	2-2	Villach	Fr	Putsila 2 [57 60]	400	Eisner AUT
30-05	Korea Republic	W	1-0	Kufstein	Fr	Kislyak [53]	1 000	Brugger AUT
2-06	Sweden	L	0-1	Minsk	Fr		12 000	Nikolaev RUS
11-08	Lithuania	W	2-0	Kaunas	Fr	Hleb.V 2 [49 90]	3 500	Satchi MDA
3-09	France	W	1-0	Paris	ECq	Kislyak [86]	76 395	Collum SCO
7-09	Romania	D	0-0	Minsk	ECq		26 354	Kralovec CZE
8-10	Luxembourg	D	0-0	Luxembourg	ECq		1 857	Stavrev MKD
12-10	Albania	W	2-0	Minsk	ECq	Rodionov [10], Krivets [77]	7 000	Rasmussen DEN
17-11	Oman	W	4-0	Muscat	Fr	Martynovich 2 [5 11], Hleb.V [35], Rodionov [57p]	1 000	Al Amri KSA
2011								
9-02	Kazakhstan	D	1-1	Antalya	Fr	Hleb.V [44p]	1 500	Banari MDA
26-03	Albania	L	0-1	Tirana	ECq		13 826	Strombergsson SWE
29-03	Canada	L	0-1	Antalya	Fr		100	Yildirim TUR
3-06	France	D	1-1	Minsk	ECq	OG [20]	26 500	Fernandez ESP
7-06	Luxembourg	W	2-0	Minsk	ECq	Kornilenko [48p], Putilo [73]	9 500	Salmanov AZE
10-08	Bulgaria	W	1-0	Minsk	Fr	Kislyak [33]	6 500	Dunauskas LTU
2-09	Bosnia-Herzegovina	L	0-2	Minsk	ECq		28 500	Kassai HUN
6-09	Bosnia-Herzegovina	L	0-1	Zenica	ECq		12 000	Atkinson ENG
7-10	Romania	D	2-2	Bucharest	ECq	Kornilenko [45], Dragun [82]	29 486	Kelly IRL
11-10	Poland	L	0-2	Wiesbaden	Fr		5 116	Sippel GER
15-11	Libya	D	1-1	Dubai	Fr	Kornilenko [77]	250	Mohamed UAE

Fr = Friendly match • EC = UEFA EURO 2012 • WC = FIFA World Cup • q = qualifier

BELARUS NATIONAL TEAM HISTORICAL RECORDS

Caps
89 - Aleksandr Kulchiy 1996- • **80** - Sergei Gurenko 1994-2006 • **74** - Sergei Omelyanchuk 2002- • **71** - Sergei Shtanyuk 1995-2007 • **64** - Maksim Romaschenko 1998-2008 • **56** - Valentin Byalkevich 1992-2005 • **55** - Aleksandr Hleb 2001- • **53** - Timofei Kalachev 2004- **52** - Vitaly Kutuzov 2002- ; Sergei Kornilenko 2003- & Andrei Ostrovskiy 1994-2005-

Goals
20 - Maksim Romaschenko 1998-2008 • **13** - Vitaly Kutuzov 2002- • **12** - Vyacheslav Hleb 2004- & Sergei Kornilenko 2003- • **10** - Valentin Byalkevich 1992-2005 & Roman Vasilyuk 2000-08 • **8** - Vitaly Bulyga 2003-08 • **7** - Sergei Gerasimets 1992-99 & Timofei Kalachev 2004-

Past Coaches
Mihail Verhejenka 1992-1994 • Siarhej Barouski 1994-1996 • Mihail Verhejenka 1997-1999 • Siarhej Barouski 1999-2000 • Eduard Malofeev 2000-2003 • Anatoly Baidachny RUS 2003-2005 • Yuri Puntus 2006-2007 • Bernd Stange GER 2007-11 • Georgy Kondratiev 2011-

BELARUS 2011

VYSSHAYA LIGA

	Pl	W	D	L	F	A	Pts	BATE	Shakhter	Gomel	Dinamo M	Belshina	Torpedo	Naftan	Neman	FK Minsk	Dinamo B	Vitebsk	Dnepr
BATE Borisov †	33	18	12	3	53	20	66		2-2	1-1 0-0	1-0 2-2	1-0	1-0 4-2	1-0 2-0	1-1	1-1	2-0	4-1 2-2	5-0 1-2
Shakhter Soligorsk ‡	33	17	10	6	46	24	61	0-2 0-0		1-1 4-0	1-3	0-0	1-0	3-0 1-0	5-0 0-0	1-0	2-0 1-0	1-0	2-2
FC Gomel ‡	33	13	15	5	36	24	54	0-0	0-0		5-1 2-1	3-1	0-0 1-0	0-1 1-0	1-0	2-1 1-0	2-0	2-2 2-0	2-1 1-1
Dinamo Minsk	33	14	7	12	50	43	49	2-0	0-2 3-2	0-0		3-1 0-3	0-1	0-1	0-1	1-2 3-4	1-1	2-2 2-0	2-0 4-1
Belshina Bobruisk	33	12	12	9	41	35	48	0-2 1-1	2-0 0-2	1-0 0-0	2-3		2-2 1-1	0-0	1-1 2-3	2-2	1-1 1-0	2-0	2-2
Torpedo Zhodino	33	9	14	10	37	41	41	0-3	1-0 1-3	1-1	1-0 1-1	0-1		3-2 3-1	2-2	2-2	1-1 1-2	0-3	1-1 1-1
Naftan Novopolotsk	33	10	7	16	35	45	37	0-2	1-1	1-1	1-4 1-3	1-0 1-2	0-2		1-2	0-0 1-3	1-1	1-1 1-1	6-0 1-0
Neman Grodno	33	8	13	12	33	45	37	0-3 0-1	0-1	0-0 2-2	0-2 1-2	2-0	2-2 0-0	4-2 1-0		0-1	2-3	0-1	1-1 1-1
FK Minsk	33	8	11	14	33	40	35	1-0	0-2	0-1 1-1	2-1 0-0	1-2	0-1	0-1 0-0	1-3		3-1 0-0	1-1 1-1	1-3 1-3
Dinamo Brest	33	8	11	14	38	46	35	0-3	1-1 4-0	1-2	0-2	2-0 1-1	1-4 1-3	1-3	0-1	1-1 3-0		2-2	3-0 2-0
FK Vitebsk	33	8	8	17	29	46	32	0-1 0-2	1-1	1-0 1-3	0-1 0-3	1-1	0-2	0-1 0-1	2-3	1-0 1-0	2-1		3-0 0-2
Dnepr Mogilev	33	6	14	13	29	51	32	1-1	0-1 0-4	0-0	0-1	2-2 0-0	3-1	1-2	1-1	0-2 1-0	1-1 0-2	0-0 1-0	

2/04/2011 - 27/11/2011 • † Qualified for the UEFA Champions League • ‡ Qualified for the Europa League

Relegation/promotion play-off: **Partizan Minsk** 2-0 1-2 FK Vitebsk

Top scorers: **13** - Renan Bressan BRA, BATE • **11** - Yahor Zubovich, Belshina; Artsyom Solovey, Torpedo Zhodino & Bruno Furlan BRA, Dinamo Minsk

BELARUS 2011 PERSHAYA LIGA (2)

	Pl	W	D	L	F	A	Pts
Slavija Moazyr	30	22	5	3	53	17	71
Partizan Minsk	30	20	5	5	59	26	65
FC Gorodeya	30	16	7	7	51	31	55
SKVICh Minsk	30	16	6	8	57	27	54
FC Slutsk	30	13	10	7	44	33	49
Vedrich-97 Rechitsa	30	13	7	10	40	34	46
Volna Pinsk	30	13	6	11	52	38	45
Granit Mikashevichi	30	11	10	9	38	35	43
Klechesk Kletsk	30	12	5	13	45	42	41
FC Polatsak	30	9	8	13	36	39	35
FC Smorgon	30	9	7	14	32	45	34
DSK Gomel	30	8	10	12	28	34	34
FK Rudensk	30	9	6	15	25	40	33
Khimik Svetlogorsk	30	10	2	18	32	48	32
Belcard Grodno	30	8	5	17	30	55	29
FC Baranovichi	30	0	3	27	10	90	3

23/04/2011 - 19/11/2011

MEDALS TABLE

		Overall			League			Cup	
		G	S	B	G	S	B	G	S
1	Dinamo Minsk	10	8	2	7	6	2	3	2
2	BATE Borisov	10	7	1	8	4	1	2	3
3	Slavija Mozyr	4	4		2	2		2	2
4	Belshina Bobruisk	4	2	2	1	1	2	3	1
5	FC Gomel	3	2	2	1	1	2	2	1
6	Shakhter Soligorsk	2	5	4	1	2	4	1	3
7	Partizan Minsk (ex MTZ)	2						2	2
8	Dinamo-93 Minsk	1	2	3	1		3	1	1
9	Lokomotiv Vitebsk	1	2	2				2	2
10	Dnepr-Transmash	1	2		1	1		1	
	Neman Grodno	1	2		1			1	1
12	Dinamo Brest	1	1					1	1
13	Naftan Novopolotsk	1						1	
14	Lokomotiv Minsk	1						1	
	Torpedo Mogilev	1						1	
	Torpedo-SKA Minsk	1						1	
	Torpedo Zhodino	1						1	
	Vedrich Rechitsa	1						1	
19	Dnepr Mogilev		1						1
	FK Minsk		1						1

BELARUS CLUBS IN THE SOVIET ERA

		Overall			League			Cup	
14	Dinamo Minsk	1	1	3	1		3		1

KUBOK 2010-11

Round of 16

FC Gomel	5
FK Rudensk *	0
Dinamo Minsk	0
Partizan Minsk *	1
Dinamo Brest	1
BATE Borisov *	0
Volna Pinsk	0
Shakhter Soligorsk *	4
Belshina Bobruisk *	2
Kommunalnik Slonim	1
DSK Gomel	1
FK Minsk *	3
Naftan Novopolotsk *	4
FC Gorodeya	2
FK Vitebsk *	1 4p
Neman Grodno	1 5p

Quarter-finals

FC Gomel	0 3
Partizan Minsk *	0 2
Dinamo Brest	1 1
Shakhter Soligorsk *	2 1
Belshina Bobruisk *	0 2
FK Minsk	1 0
Naftan Novopolotsk	1 0
Neman Grodno *	1 2

Semi-finals

FC Gomel	2 2
Shakhter Soligorsk	1 1
Belshina Bobruisk	0 0
Neman Grodno	1 0

Final

FC Gomel ‡	2
Neman Grodno	0

CUP FINAL

Traktor Stadium, Minsk
29-05-2011, Ref: Tsinkevich
Scorers - Rybak OG 87, Covalenko OG 90 for Gomel

* Home team in the 1st leg • ‡ Qualified for the Europa League

BLZ – BELIZE

FIFA/COCA-COLA WORLD RANKING

'93	'94	'95	'96	'97	'98	'99	'00	'01	'02	'03	'04	'05	'06	'07	'08	'09	'10	'11	'12
-	-	173	182	179	186	190	186	167	158	174	181	180	198	201	173	173	172	141	

2011															
Jan	Feb	Mar	Apr	May	Jun	Jul	Aug	Sep	Oct	Nov	Dec	**High**	**Low**	**Av**	
173	170	166	171	172	154	148	148	134	143	140	141	**134**	**201**	**177**	

The bitter dispute between the Belize Football Federation and the Belize Professional Football League reared its head once again with the BPFL withdrawing from the federation in May. The latest crisis led to the playing of just 16 league matches over the course of the year and the abandonment of the tournament - with the final between Defence Force and FC Belize left unplayed. With the federation involved in another dispute with the National Sports Council, clubs had found it difficult to find suitable venues, with the NSC unwilling to santion matches on any of their grounds. By pulling out of the federation, the clubs suddenly found themselves with nowhere to play and there was no option but to call the league to a close. In June, FIFA had no option but to suspend Belize due to the government interference. Thankfully, the suspension was lifted to allow Belize to take part on the 2014 FIFA World Cup qualifiers where after knocking out Montserrat in the preliminary round, they came a very creditable second behind Guatemala in a four-team second round group - ahead of both St Vincent and Grenada. Unfortunately for Belize only the group winners advanced to the third round and their World Cup adventure, led by 70-year-old Honduran 'Chelato' Herrera, was over but it had propelled Belize to a record high of 134 in the FIFA/Coca-Cola World Ranking.

FIFA WORLD CUP RECORD
1930-1994 DNE 1998-2010 DNQ

FOOTBALL FEDERATION OF BELIZE (FFB)

26 Hummingbird Highway, Belmopan, PO Box 1742, Belize City

☎ +501 822 3410

📠 +501 822 3377

✉ belizefootball@gmail.com

🖥 www.belizefootball.bz

FA 1980 CON 1986 FIFA 1986

P Bertie Chimilio

GS Marguerite Hulse

FIFA BIG COUNT 2006

Total players	17 800
% of population	6.19%
Male	14 800
Female	3 000
Amateurs 18+	1 700
Youth under 18	1 300
Unregistered	3 650
Professionals	150
Referees	45
Admin & coaches	625
Number of clubs	32
Number of teams	140

MAJOR CITIES/TOWNS

		Population
1	Belize City	68 170
2	San Ignacio	19 906
3	Belmopan	19 151
4	Orange Walk	16 530
5	San Pedro	12 535
6	Dangriga	12 431
7	Corozal	9 458
8	Benque Viejo	9 300
9	Punta Gorda	5 469

BELIZE

Capital	Belmopan	Population	307 899 (177)	% in cities 52%
GDP per capita	$8400 (116)	Area km²	22 966 km² (151)	GMT + / - -6
Neighbours (km)	Guatemala 266, Mexico 250 • Coast 386		

RECENT INTERNATIONAL MATCHES PLAYED BY BELIZE

2009	Opponents		Score	Venue	Comp	Scorers	Att	Referee
22-01	Honduras	L	1-2	Tegucigalpa	UCr1	Lisby Castillo [86]	20 000	Moreno PAN
24-01	El Salvador	L	1-4	Tegucigalpa	UCr1	Jerome James [73]	20 000	Quesada CRC
26-01	Nicaragua	D	1-1	Tegucigalpa	UCr1	Bryon Usher [27]	8 000	Moncada HON
2010								
10-09	Trinidad and Tobago	D	0-0	Belmopan	Fr		5 000	Mejia SLV
9-10	Guatemala	L	2-4	San Jose	Fr	Harrison Roches [43], Elroy Kuylen [54]	5 500	Bermudez SLV
2011								
14-01	Panama	L	0-2	Panama City	UCr1		10 000	Pineda HON
16-01	El Salvador	L	2-5	Panama City	UCr1	Elroy Smith [45p], Orlando Jimenez [76]	1 500	Cerdas CRC
18-01	Nicaragua	D	1-1	Panama City	UCr1	Daniel Jimenez [81]	10 000	Brea CUB
15-06	Montserrat	W	5-2	Couva	WCq	Deon McCauley 3 [24 75 83], Harrison Roches [50], Elroy Kuylen [53]	100	Willett ATG
17-07	Montserrat	W	3-1	San Pedro Sula	WCq	Daniel Jimenez [23], Deon McCauley [59], Luis Mendez [61]	150	Reyna GUA
2-09	Grenada	W	3-0	St George's	WCq	Deon McCauley 2 [11 79], Harrison Roches [35]	2 600	Rubalcaba CUB
6-09	Guatemala	L	1-2	Belmopan	WCq	Deon McCauley [77]	3 027	Mejia SLV
7-10	Grenada	L	1-4	Belmopan	WCq	Ryan Simpson [90]	1 200	Jarquin NCA
11-10	Guatemala	L	1-3	Guatemala City	WCq	Deon McCauley [31]	21 107	Penaloza MEX
11-11	St Vincent/Grenadines	D	1-1	Belmopan	WCq	Deon McCauley [22]	300	Skeete BRB
15-11	St Vincent/Grenadines	W	2-0	Kingstown	WCq	Deon McCauley 2 [78 81p]	500	Thomas JAM

UC = UNCAF Cup/Copa Centroamericana • WC = FIFA World Cup • q = qualifier

BELIZE NATIONAL TEAM HISTORICAL RECORDS

Caps 15 - Deon McCauley 2007- • 5 - Dion Fraser 2000-08 • 4 - Harrison Roches 2004- • 3 - Norman Nunez 1995-2005; Vallan Symms 2000- & Bent Burgess 2000-02 • 2 - David MacCauley 1995-96; Aaron Nolberto 1999-2001; Elroy Smith 2004-; Elroy Kuylen 2009- & Daniel Jimenez

Coach Michael Winston 1995-96 • Manuel Bilches 2000 • Leroy Sherrier Lewis CRC 2001 • Eduardo Santana BRA 2003 • Anthony Adderly 2004-06 • Antonio Carlos Vieira BRA • Jose Palmiro Salas GUA 2008 • Ian Mork USA 2008 • Renan Couch 2008-09 • Jose de la Paz Herrera 2010-

BELIZE 2011

BPFL CUP

	Pl	W	D	L	F	A	Pts	Defence	FC Belize	San Felipe	Hankook
Defence Force †	7	4	2	1	18	9	14		4-1	7-2 1-1	1-0 2-1
FC Belize †	7	3	2	2	11	10	11	1-1		2-2 2-0	4-2
San Felipe Barcelona †	7	2	2	3	12	21	8	3-2			3-2
Hankook Verdes Utd †	7	2	0	5	11	12	6		0-1 1-0	5-1	

20/03/2011 - 23/04/2011 • † Qualified for the play-offs

PLAY-OFFS

Semi-finals

Defence Force	3
Hankook Verdes Utd	0

Finals

Defence Force	n/p
FC Belize	

San Felipe Barcelona	2
FC Belize	3

BOL – BOLIVIA

FIFA/COCA-COLA WORLD RANKING

'93	'94	'95	'96	'97	'98	'99	'00	'01	'02	'03	'04	'05	'06	'07	'08	'09	'10	'11	'12
58	44	53	39	24	61	61	65	70	92	99	94	96	101	108	58	56	97	108	

2011														
	Jan	Feb	Mar	Apr	May	Jun	Jul	Aug	Sep	Oct	Nov	Dec	**High**	**Low**	**Av**
	96	99	98	102	102	94	80	85	81	115	106	108	**18**	**115**	**72**

For the third Copa América running Bolivia opened their campaign with a hard-earned draw against the host nation, but once again they failed to build on that early promise and departed after the first round. In the 2011 tournament they were fifteen minutes away from a 1-0 win over Argentina before Sergio Aguero saved the blushes of the hosts but the Bolivians then lost their remaining two matches - against Costa Rica and Colombia - which meant they finished 11th out of the 12 teams. At the end of the year Gustavo Quinteros's side found themselves bottom of the qualifiers for the 2014 FIFA World Cup in Brazil having lost three of their first four matches, their only point coming from what was seemingly the hardest of the games - against Argentina in Buenos Aires. In club football there was a reorganisation in the calendar in order to be in line with the August to May seasons elsewhere in the world. Bolivar won the first title of the year when they finished two points ahead of Real Potosi, leapfrogging their rivals on the final day of the season with a 2-1 victory over La Paz after Potosi could only draw with cross-town rivals Nacional. In the Apertura, played during the second half of the year, The Strongest won the title after beating Universitario 3-1 on aggregate in the final - their first success in 14 campaigns.

COPA AMERICA RECORD

1916-1925 DNE **1926** 5/5 **1927** 4/4 **1929-1942** DNE **1945** 6/7 **1946** 6/6 **1947** 7/8 **1949** 4/8 **1953** 6/7 **1955-1957** DNE **1959** 7/7 **1959** DNE **1963** 1/7 Winners (Hosts) **1967** 6/6 **1975** 8/10 r1 **1979**/10 7 r1 **1983** 8/10 r1 **1987** 7/10 r1 **1989** 9/10 r1 **1991** 9/10 r1 **1993** 10/12 r1 **1995** 8/12 r1 **1997** 2 F (Hosts) **1999** 9/12 r1 **2001** 11/12 r1 **2004** 9/12 r1 **2007** 10/12 r1 **2011** 11/12 r1

FEDERACION BOLIVIANA DE FÚTBOL (FBF)

Av. Libertador Bolivar 1168, Cochabamba

☎ +591 4 4244982
📠 +591 4 4282132
📧 fbfcba@hotmail.com
🖥 www.fbf.com.bo
FA 1925 CON 1926 FIFA 1926
P Carlos Alberto Chavez
GS Jose Pedro Zambrano

FIFA BIG COUNT 2006

Total players	578 800
% of population	6.44%
Male	504 700
Female	74 100
Amateurs 18+	16 400
Youth under 18	33 300
Unregistered	236 600
Professionals	400
Referees	500
Admin & coaches	2 800
Number of clubs	890
Number of teams	1 100

MAJOR CITIES/TOWNS

		Population
1	Santa Cruz	1 614 618
2	El Alto	949 912
3	La Paz	887 512
4	Cochabamba	616 943
5	Sucre	295 455
6	Oruro	232 114
7	Tarija	204 423
8	Potosí	164 600
9	Sacaba	105 105
10	Montero	100 911
11	Trinidad	94 348
12	Riberalta	88 059
13	Yacuiba	87 914
14	Quillacollo	85 224
15	Colcapirhua	47 430
16	Cobija	43 813
17	Guayaramerín	37 612
18	Viacha	35 968
19	Villazón	34 787

BOLIVIA

Capital La Paz; Sucre	Population 9 775 246 (84)	% in cities 66%
GDP per capita $4 500 (148)	Area km² 1 098 581 km² (28)	GMT +/- -4
Neighbours (km) Argentina 832, Brazil 3423, Chile 860, Paraguay 750, Peru 1075		

RECENT INTERNATIONAL MATCHES PLAYED BY BOLIVIA

2008	Opponents	Score		Venue	Comp	Scorers	Att	Referee
6-02	Peru	W	2-1	La Paz	Fr	Pedriel [65], Reyes.L [88]		
26-03	Venezuela	W	1-0	Puerto La Cruz	Fr	Cichero OG [79]	16 000	Buitrago COL
15-06	Chile	L	0-2	La Paz	WCq		27 722	Rivera PER
18-06	Paraguay	W	4-2	La Paz	WCq	Botero 2 [23 70], Garcia.R [25], Martins [76]	8 561	Gaciba BRA
6-08	Guatemala	L	0-3	Washington DC	Fr		18 000	Toledo USA
20-08	Panama	W	1-0	Santa Cruz	Fr	Cabrera [78]		Antequera BOL
6-09	Ecuador	L	1-3	Quito	WCq	Botero [40]	35 000	Pozo CHI
10-09	Brazil	D	0-0	Rio de Janeiro	WCq		31 422	Intriago ECU
11-10	Peru	W	3-0	La Paz	WCq	Botero 2 [3 16], Garcia.R [81]	23 147	Buitrago COL
14-10	Uruguay	D	2-2	La Paz	WCq	Martins 2 [15 41]	21 075	Baldassi ARG
22-10	El Salvador	L	0-2	Washington DC	Fr		20 000	Ward CAN
2009								
11-03	Mexico	L	1-5	Commerce City	Fr	Torrico [68]	20 000	Toledo USA
28-03	Colombia	L	0-2	Bogota	WCq		22 044	Intriago ECU
1-04	Argentina	W	6-1	La Paz	WCq	Martins [12], Botero 3 [34p 55 66], Da Rosa [45], Torrico [87]	30 487	Vazquez URU
6-06	Venezuela	L	0-1	La Paz	WCq		23 427	Vera ECU
10-06	Chile	L	0-4	Santiago	WCq		60 214	Silvera URU
5-09	Paraguay	L	0-1	Asuncion	WCq		25 094	Carrillo PER
9-09	Ecuador	L	1-3	La Paz	WCq	Yecerotte [85]	10 200	Baldassi ARG
11-10	Brazil	W	2-1	La Paz	WCq	Olivares [10], Martins [32]	16 557	Pozo CHI
14-10	Peru	L	0-1	Lima	WCq		4 373	Soto VEN
2010								
24-02	Mexico	L	0-5	San Francisco	Fr		34 244	Vaughn USA
11-08	Colombia	D	1-1	La Paz	Fr	Galindo [64]	4 000	Favale ARG
7-10	Venezuela	L	1-3	Santa Cruz	Fr	Moreno [53]	35 000	Chaibou NIG
2011								
25-03	Panama	L	0-2	Panama City	Fr		4 000	Lopez GUA
28-03	Guatemala	D	1-1	Mazatenango	Fr	Pedriel [72]	6 154	Aguilar SLV
4-06	Paraguay	L	0-2	Santa Cruz	Fr		27 000	Garay PER
7-06	Paraguay	D	0-0	Ciudad del Este	Fr		15 000	Heber BRA
1-07	Argentina	D	1-1	La Plata	CAr1	Rojas [48]	52 700	Silvera URU
7-07	Costa Rica	L	0-2	Jujuy	CAr1		23 000	Vera ECU
10-07	Colombia	L	0-2	Santa Fe	CAr1		12 000	Chacon MEX
10-08	Panama	L	1-3	Santa Cruz	Fr	Arce [7]	10 000	Carrillo PER
2-09	Peru	D	2-2	Lima	Fr	Escobar [6], Cardozo [70]	35 000	Soto VEN
5-09	Peru	D	0-0	La Paz	Fr		16 670	Quintana PAR
7-10	Uruguay	L	2-4	Montevideo	WCq	Cardozo [17], Martins [87p]	25 500	Carrillo PER
11-10	Colombia	L	1-2	La Paz	WCq	Flores [85]	33 155	Amarilla PAR
11-11	Argentina	D	1-1	Buenos Aires	WCq	Martins [55]	27 592	Vera ECU
15-11	Venezuela	L	0-1	San Cristobal	WCq		33 351	Buckley PER

Fr = Friendly match • CA = Copa America • WC = FIFA World Cup • q = qualifier • r1 = first round group

BOLIVIA NATIONAL TEAM HISTORICAL RECORDS

Caps

93 - Luis Hector Cristaldo 1989-2005 & Marco Antonio Sandy 1993-2003 • **89** - Jose Milton Melgar 1980-97 • **88** - Carlos Fernando Borja 1979-97 • **85** - Julio Cesar Baldivieso 1991-2005 & Juan Manuel Pena 1991-2009 • **80** - Miguel Angel Rimba 1989-2000 • **78** - Oscar Sanchez 1994-2006 • **75** - Jaime Moreno 1991-2008 • **71** - Marco Antonio Etcheverry 1989-2003

Goals

20 - Joaquin Botero 1999-2009 • **16** - Victor Agustin Ugarte 1947-63 • **15** - Carlos Aragones 1977-81, Julio Cesar Baldivieso 1991-2005 & Erwin Sanchez 1989-2005 • **13** - Marco Antonio Etcheverry 1989-2003 & Maximo Alcocer 1953-63 • **10** - Miguel Aguilar 1977-83 & Marcelo Martins 2007- • **9** - Jaime Moreno 1991-2008 & William Ramallo 1989-97

Past Coaches

Jorge Luis Valderrama 1927 • Ulises Sauchedo 1930 • Julio Borelli 1938 & 1945 • Diogenes Lara 1946-47 • Felix Deheza 1948-49 • Mario Pretto ITA 1950 • Cesar Vicino 1953 • Vicente Arraya 1959 • Danilo Alvim BRA 1963 • Freddy Valda 1965 • Carlos Trigo 1967 • Freddy Valda 1969 & 1973 • Carlos Trigo 1973 • Freddy Valda 1975 • Wilfredo Camacho 1977 • Ramiro Blacutt 1979-81 • Jose Saldanha BRA 1981 • Wilfredo Camacho 1983 • Carlos Rodrigues ARG 1985 • Osvaldo Veiga ARG 1987 • Jorge Habbegger ARG 1989 • Ramiro Blacutt 1991 • Xabier Azkargorta ESP 1993-94 • Antonio Lopez ESP 1995 • Antoino Lopez ESP 1996-97 • Hector Veira ARG 1999 • Carlos Aragones 2000-01 • Jorge Habbegger ARG 2001 • Carlos Trucco 2001-02 • Vladimir Soria 2002 • Walter Roque 2003 • Dalcio Giovagnoli 2003 • Nelson Acosta CHI 2003-04 • Ramiro Blacutt 2004 • Ovidio Messa 2004-06 • Erwin Sanchez 2006-09 • Eduardo Villegas 2009-10 • Gustavo Quinteros 2010-

BOLIVIA 2011

CAMPEONATO ENTEL

	Pl	W	D	L	F	A	Pts	Bolívar	Real Potosí	O. Petrolero	Strongest	Blooming	San José	Aurora	Universitario	Guabirá	Nacional	Real Mamoré	La Paz FC
Bolívar	22	11	7	4	32	24	40		3-0	1-1	1-0	1-0	3-2	1-1	3-0	3-2	0-0	4-0	2-1
Real Potosí	22	11	5	6	32	22	38	0-0		0-3	1-1	3-1	1-1	2-1	2-0	3-1	3-0	4-0	1-0
Oriente Petrolero	22	11	3	8	46	25	36	6-0	2-2		3-2	1-2	2-1	2-0	0-0	2-3	3-1	3-1	6-0
The Strongest	22	10	5	7	33	26	35	0-0	2-1	1-0		4-0	0-0	1-3	1-2	4-0	1-0	1-0	3-1
Blooming	22	11	2	9	34	28	35	2-0	1-2	0-2	1-1		2-1	3-1	4-1	4-1	1-0	1-0	3-0
San José	22	10	4	8	29	27	34	3-2	2-1	1-0	2-1	2-1		1-0	1-0	5-0	2-1	2-1	0-1
Aurora	22	9	6	7	31	25	33	0-0	1-0	3-2	0-1	0-0	1-1		2-2	2-0	3-1	3-0	3-2
Universitario Sucre	22	9	2	11	28	31	29	0-1	0-1	1-0	2-1	0-2	0-1	3-1		3-1	3-2	2-1	5-1
Guabirá	22	9	2	11	29	43	29	1-1	2-1	0-1	1-0	0-3	3-1	2-0	1-3		1-0	3-0	3-1
Nacional Potosí	22	8	4	10	28	30	28	2-1	0-0	2-1	3-4	3-1	3-0	0-2	2-0	4-1		1-1	2-1
Real Mamoré	22	6	2	14	27	44	20	1-2	1-2	2-5	6-2	2-1	2-0	1-1	1-0	2-3	2-0		3-2
La Paz FC	22	5	2	15	21	45	17	2-3	0-2	2-1	1-1	3-1	1-0	0-3	0-2	0-0	0-1	2-0	

15/01/2011 - 29/05/2011 • † Qualified for the Copa Libertadores • ‡ Qualified for the Copa Sudamericana
Top scorers: **19** - Juan Maraude ARG, Real Mamoré • **12** - Mauricio Saucedo, Oriente Petrolero • **10** - Ze Carlos BRA, Bolívar • **9** - Alcides Pena, Oriente Petrolero & Jair Reynoso COL, Aurora • **8** - Joaquin Botero, San José; Oscar Diaz, Blooming & Christian Ruiz ARG, The Strongest

BOLIVIA 2011–12

CAMPEONATO APERTURA FIRST STAGE

Serie A

	Pl	W	D	L	F	A	Pts	Bolívar	Universitario	Guabirá	San José	Real Potosí	Blooming	Aurora	O. Petrolero	Nacional	Strongest	La Paz FC	Real Mamoré
Bolívar †	12	5	4	3	22	12	19		1-2	6-1	0-0	1-1	2-0				3-1		
Universitario Sucre †	12	5	4	3	17	14	19	1-1		2-1	0-1	1-1	4-3					2-0	
Guabirá †	12	6	1	5	16	23	19	1-0	2-2		1-0	3-2	0-2						2-0
San José †	12	5	3	4	10	7	18	0-0	0-1	2-0		0-2	3-0	2-1					
Real Potosí	12	4	5	3	20	11	17	1-3	1-0	6-0	0-2		5-0			0-0			
Blooming	12	2	4	6	11	22	10	1-0	1-1	1-3	0-0	1-1			1-2				

Serie B

	Pl	W	D	L	F	A	Pts	Bolívar	Universitario	Guabirá	San José	Real Potosí	Blooming	Aurora	O. Petrolero	Nacional	Strongest	La Paz FC	Real Mamoré
Aurora †	12	8	0	4	23	13	24				2-0				0-3	2-0	2-1	2-0	3-1
Oriente Petrolero †	12	7	2	3	26	18	23						1-1	2-1		4-1	1-1	3-1	4-1
Nacional Potosí †	12	4	4	4	23	15	16					0-0		1-2	4-2		2-1	0-0	9-0
The Strongest †	12	4	3	5	34	23	15	3-5						2-1	5-0	2-2		6-2	9-1
La Paz FC	12	4	2	6	16	29	14		2-1					1-5	1-0	0-4	3-3		3-1
Real Mamoré	12	2	0	10	10	41	6			0-2				0-2	1-4	2-0	1-0	2-3	

28/08/2011 - 1/12/2011 • † Qualified for the Apertura play-offs
Top scorers (whole Apertura): **16** - William Ferreira URU, Bolívar • **13** - Pablo Escobar, The Strongest • **12** - Gualberto Mojica, Oriente Petrolero

CAMPEONATO APERTURA PLAY-OFFS

Quarter-finals			Semi-finals			Final		
The Strongest	0	4						
Bolívar *	1	0	The Strongest *	5	0			
Guabirá *	0	1	Oriente Petrolero	3	1			
Oriente Petrolero	0	4				The Strongest *	2	1
San José *	1	2				Universitario Sucre	0	1
Aurora	0	0	San José	0	1			
Nacional Potosí *	2	0	Universitario Sucre *	2	0			
Universitario Sucre	3	1	Third place: **Oriente Petrolero** 1-1 2-1 San José					

* Home team in 1st leg • † Qualified for the Copa Sudamericana

<table>
<tr><td colspan="2">APERTURA FINAL 2011 1ST LEG</td></tr>
</table>

APERTURA FINAL 2011 1ST LEG

Hernando Silas, La Paz
18-12-2011, 16:00, Att: 28 304, Ref: Jorge Mancilla

The Strongest   2   Luis Melgar [45], Enrique Parada [91+]

Universitario   0

The Strongest - Daniel Vaca - Enrique Parada●, Nelvin Soliz (Luis Mendez 73), Jair Torrico, Alejandro Bejarano●, Alejandro Chumacero, Leonel Reyes, Marco Paz, Luis Hernan Melgar (Sebastian Gonzalez● 88), Sacha Lima●, Pablo Escobar (Rodrigo Ramallo 85). Tr: Mauricio Soria
Universitario - Sergio Rios - Marcos Barrera (Marcos Ovejero 75), Jeferson Lopes, Alejandro Morales, Oscar Anez●, Edgar Olivares●, Milton Melgar●, Marcelo Gomez, Luis Liendo, Ronald Gallegos (Boris Alfaro 46), Carlos Castilla (Freddy Chispas 46). Tr: Claudio Chacior

APERTURA FINAL 2011 2ND LEG

Olimpico Patria, Sucre
22-12-2011, 20:00, Att: 26 031, Ref: Nelio Garcia

Universitario   1   Jeferson Lopes [86]

The Strongest   1   Pablo Escobar [4]

Universitario - Sergio Rios - Alejandro Morales, Jeferson Lopes, Marcos Barrera (Edgar Olivares 76), Oscar Anez●, Milton Melgar●, Marcelo Gomez, Luis Liendo●, Ronald Gallegos (Marcos Ovejero 76), Boris Alfaro, Freddy Chispas (Juan Fierro 54). Tr: Claudio Chacior
The Strongest - Daniel Vaca - Delio Ojeda, Luis Mendez, Enrique Parada (Matias Marchesini 90), Nelvin Soliz (Luis Hernan Melgar 83), Jair Torrico●, Alejandro Bejarano (Leonel Reyes 72), Alejandro Chumacero, Marco Paz, Sacha Lima, Pablo Escobar. Tr: Mauricio Soria

MEDALS TABLE

		Overall G	S	B	Pro G	S	Nat G	S	LL G	S	Sth Am G	S	B	City
1	Bolívar	21	11	2	17	8	4	2	12	11	1	2		La Paz
2	Jorge Wilstermann	10	7	1	5	5	5	2	12	3		1		Cochabamba
3	The Strongest	9	8		8	6	1	2	18	10				La Paz
4	Oriente Petrolero	5	13		4	11	1	2	7	3				Santa Cruz
5	Blooming	5	3	1	5	3			1	2		1		Santa Cruz
6	San José	3	2		2	2	1		9	2				Oruro
7	Real Potosí	1	4		1	4								Potosi
	Deportivo Municipal	1	4				1	4	4	3				La Paz
9	Always Ready	1	2				1	2	2	5				La Paz
	Guabirá	1	2			1	1	1	1	1				Montero
11	Aurora	1	1		1	1			3	8				Cochabamba
	Chaco Petrolero	1	1				1	1		1				La Paz
13	Universitario	1	1		1	1								Sucre
	Litoral	1					1		4	1				La Paz
	Universitario	1					1		1	4				La Paz
16	La Paz FC		2			2								La Paz
17	31 de Octubre		1				1		1	2				La Paz
	Deportivo Chaco		1				1		1					La Paz
19	Destroyers								2	1				Santa Cruz
	Real Santa Cruz													Santa Cruz
	Union Central													Tarija

Pro = the Professional League played since 1977 ● Nat = the various national competitions played between 1954 and 1976 ● LL = the local leagues played throughout the country until 1976 ● The totals for the local leagues are not included in the overall totals

BOT – BOTSWANA

FIFA/COCA-COLA WORLD RANKING

'93	'94	'95	'96	'97	'98	'99	'00	'01	'02	'03	'04	'05	'06	'07	'08	'09	'10	'11	'12
140	145	155	161	162	155	165	150	153	136	112	102	101	108	103	117	118	53	95	

					2011								High	Low	Av
Jan	Feb	Mar	Apr	May	Jun	Jul	Aug	Sep	Oct	Nov	Dec		High	Low	Av
54	67	67	69	69	74	71	78	95	89	96	95		53	165	128

Botswana achieved their best-ever feat in March when they qualified for the 2012 CAF Africa Cup of Nations. In so doing they became the first side to book a place at the finals, coming top in a qualifying group that included two former FIFA World Cup finalists. It was an unexpected success for a country usually confined to the fringes of African football. The Zebras found their debut at the finals in Equatorial Guinea and Gabon a traumatic experience, however, going down to a record defeat to Guinea in Franceville. Their 1-6 loss was the biggest at the finals since 1970. There were much better performances in their other two games against Ghana and Mali, but the gap in quality was evident from the outset and it is unsure whether Botswana's qualification signals the arrival of a new force in African football or was something of a one-off. The build-up to the finals was characterised by a power struggle between football association officials and coach Stanley Tshosane, who stood his ground in the face of some divisive interference. In club football, Township Rollers retained the Premier League title, finishing 11 points ahead of Centre Chiefs. There was a first trophy in 17 years for Lobatse-based Extension Gunners who beat Motlakase 3-0 in the Cup Final in front of their own ecstatic fans at the Lobatse Stadium at the end of April.

CAF AFRICA CUP OF NATIONS RECORD
1957-1992 DNE 1994-2010 DNQ **2012** 16 r1

BOTSWANA FOOTBALL ASSOCIATION (BFA)

☒ PO Box 1396, Gaborone

☎ +267 3900279
📠 +267 3900280
📧 bfa@bfa.co.bw
🖥 www.bfa.co.bw
FA 1970 CON 1976 FIFA 1978
P David Fani
GS Duncan Kgame

FIFA BIG COUNT 2006

Total players	98 632
% of population	6.01%
Male	93 712
Female	4 920
Amateurs 18+	10 440
Youth under 18	4 000
Unregistered	12 180
Professionals	12
Referees	208
Admin & coaches	2 370
Number of clubs	63
Number of teams	348

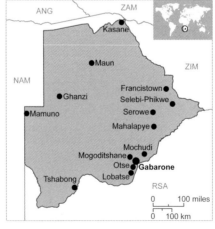

MAJOR CITIES/TOWNS

		Population
1	Gaborone	230 936
2	Francistown	96 292
3	Molepolole	72 122
4	Selibe Phikwe	57 161
5	Mogoditshane	56 251
6	Maun	56 043
7	Serowe	52 324
8	Mahalapye	49 050
9	Kanye	48 362
10	Mochudi	46 715
11	Palapye	35 114
12	Lobatse	31 660
13	Tlokweng	30 384
14	Thamaga	23 296
15	Moshupa	22 243
16	Bobonong	22 175
17	Ramotswa	21 708
18	Letlhakane	21 681
19	Tonota	19 853

REPUBLIC OF BOTSWANA

Capital	Gaborone	Population	1 990 876 (146)	% in cities	60%
GDP per capita	$13 900 (83)	Area km²	581 730 km² (71)	GMT +/-	+2
Neighbours (km)	Namibia 1360, South Africa 1840, Zimbabwe 813				

RECENT INTERNATIONAL MATCHES PLAYED BY BOTSWANA

2008	Opponents	Score		Venue	Comp	Scorers	Att	Referee
16-01	South Africa	L	1-2	Durban	Fr	Moemedi Moatlhaping [54]		
9-02	Swaziland	W	4-1	Mbabane	Fr	Jerome Ramatlhakwane 2 [21 45], Moemedi Moatlhaping [54], Pontsho Moloi [73]		
26-03	Zimbabwe	L	0-1	Gaborone	Fr			
31-05	Madagascar	D	0-0	Gaborone	WCq		11 087	Kaoma ZAM
8-06	Mozambique	W	2-1	Maputo	WCq	Diphetogo Selolwane [30], Boitumelo Mafoko [82]	30 000	Fakudze SWZ
14-06	Côte d'Ivoire	D	1-1	Gaborone	WCq	Diphetogo Selolwane [25]	21 400	Ssegonga UGA
22-06	Côte d'Ivoire	L	0-4	Abidjan	WCq		15 000	Bennaceur TUN
27-07	Mozambique	L	0-2	Secunda	CCqf			Katjimune NAM
20-08	Zimbabwe	L	0-1	Harare	Fr			
30-08	Lesotho	W	1-0	Gaborone	Fr	Praxis Rabemananjara [18]		
7-09	Madagascar	L	0-1	Antananarivo	WCq		20 000	Seechurn MRI
11-10	Mozambique	L	0-1	Gaborone	WCq		2 000	Seck SEN
2009								
21-03	Namibia	D	0-0	Keetmanshoop	Fr			
1-04	Lesotho	D	0-0	Maseru	Fr			
6-06	New Zealand	D	0-0	Gaborone	Fr			
5-07	Iran	D	1-1	Gaborone	Fr	Mokgathi Mokgathi [30]		
30-09	China PR	L	1-4	Hohhot	Fr	Mokgathi Mokgathi [68]		
18-10	Comoros	D	0-0	Bulawayo	CCr1			Rachide MOZ
20-10	Swaziland	W	1-0	Bulawayo	CCr1	Malepa Bolelang [56]		Seechurn MRI
22-10	Seychelles	W	2-0	Bulawayo	CCr1	Pontsho Moloi [6], Malepa Bolelang [39]		Seechurn MRI
26-10	Zimbabwe	L	0-1	Bulawayo	CCqf			Carvalho ANG
2010								
3-03	Mozambique	W	1-0	Maputo	Fr	Michael Mogaladi [6p]		
21-03	Namibia	D	0-0	Windhoek	Fr			
1-07	Tunisia	W	1-0	Tunis	CNq	Jerome Ramatlhkwane [31]		Ditta SEN
9-07	Chad	W	1-0	Gaborone	CNq	Phenyo Mongala [49]		Seechurn MRI
4-08	Zimbabwe	W	2-0	Selibe-Phikwe	Fr	Mokgathi Mokgathi [9], Jerome Ramatlhkwane [14]		
11-08	Malawi	D	1-1	Blantyre	CNq	Jerome Ramatlhkwane [62]		Martins ANG
4-09	Togo	W	2-1	Gaborone	CNq	Joel Mogorosi [6], Jerome Ramatlhkwane [47]		Kagabo RWA
12-10	Equatorial Guinea	W	2-0	Malabo	Fr	Mogogi Gabonamong, Phenyo Mongala		
17-11	Tunisia	W	1-0	Gaborone	CNq	Jerome Ramatlhkwane [45]		
2011								
19-01	Sweden	L	1-2	Cape Town	Fr	Joel Mogorosi [47]		
9-02	Mozambique	D	1-1	Maputo	Fr	Moemedi Moatlhaping [35]		
16-03	Namibia	D	1-1	Maun	Fr	Lemponye Tshireletso [65]		
26-03	Chad	W	1-0	N'Djamena	CNq	Jerome Ramatlhkwane [52]		
25-05	Swaziland	D	0-0	Manzini	Fr			
5-06	Malawi	D	0-0	Lobatse	CNq			Diatta SEN
31-07	Swaziland	W	2-0	Pretoria	Fr	Onalethata Tshekiso [29], Bakang Moeng [88]		
10-08	Kenya	W	1-0	Gaborone	Fr	Moemedi Moatlhaping [87p]		
30-08	Lesotho	L	1-2	Gaborone	Fr			
4-09	Togo	L	0-1	Lome	CNq			Dembele CIV
12-11	Nigeria	D	0-0	Benin City	Fr			
15-11	Niger	D	1-1	Niamey	Fr	Patrick Motsepe [23]		
21-12	Lesotho	W	3-0	Rustenburg	Fr	Jerome Ramatlhkwane 2, Pontsho Moloi		
2012								
7-01	Zimbabwe	D	0-0	Gaborone	Fr			
24-01	Ghana	L	0-1	Franceville	CNr1		5 000	Diatta SEN
28-01	Guinea	L	1-6	Franceville	CNr1	Diphetogo Selolwane [23p]	4 000	El Ahrach MAR
1-02	Mali	L	1-2	Libreville	CNr1	Mogakolodi Ngele [50]	5 500	Bennett RSA

Fr = Friendly match • CN = CAF African Cup of Nations • CC = COSAFA Cup • WC = FIFA World Cup • q = qualifier • r1 = first round group

BOTSWANA 2010–11

PREMIER LEAGUE

Team	Pl	W	D	L	F	A	Pts	Rollers	Chiefs	Greens	Gaborone Utd	BDF	Nico Utd	UF Santos	BMC	Police	TAFIC	Notwane	Gunners	Miscellaneous	Motlakase	TASC	Black Peril
Township Rollers †	30	24	4	2	79	24	76		2-3	2-2	1-1	3-2	3-1	2-0	2-1	3-0	4-0	3-1	2-0	1-0	1-1	1-1	5-1
Centre Chiefs	30	19	8	3	80	24	65	1-2		1-1	3-0	4-0	2-0	1-1	0-0	4-0	4-1	1-1	1-1	6-0	3-0	2-1	8-1
ECCO City Greens	30	16	7	7	54	44	55	0-5	2-3		3-2	1-2	1-3	2-0	1-5	2-1	0-0	2-1	1-1	3-1	2-2	3-2	5-2
Gaborone United	30	14	7	9	47	36	49	0-1	1-1	0-1		2-0	5-0	1-1	2-1	2-2	1-1	1-4	1-2	1-1	2-1	2-0	3-1
Defence Force	30	14	6	10	43	40	48	1-2	1-2	2-2	1-1		1-0	2-1	1-0	1-0	3-1	3-1	0-2	3-1	1-2	1-0	3-2
Nico United	30	14	6	10	53	55	48	1-6	1-2	1-2	2-1	1-1		3-1	3-2	1-1	3-2	1-0	3-1	3-2	2-1	2-2	5-5
Uniao Flamengo Santos	30	14	4	12	53	52	46	2-6	0-4	0-3	1-0	3-0	3-1		0-2	3-1	0-1	2-0	3-2	1-0	3-3	5-0	5-2
Bot. Meat Commission	30	11	9	10	49	40	42	1-2	1-1	1-2	2-3	1-1	1-1	3-4		0-3	2-2	2-2	3-0	1-1	2-0	1-0	2-1
Police	30	11	7	12	36	42	40	2-1	0-4	1-2	0-1	1-0	2-1	2-1	3-1		0-2	1-1	4-0	4-2	0-0	0-1	1-0
TAFIC	30	9	10	11	34	42	37	0-1	1-0	0-4	1-2	1-4	3-0	1-1	1-1	3-0		2-0	3-1	0-0	0-3	0-1	2-1
Notwane FC	30	9	9	12	42	46	36	0-4	1-1	0-1	1-4	1-1	2-2	1-0	0-1	1-0			4-0	3-1	3-2	2-2	1-0
Extension Gunners	30	10	4	16	36	47	34	0-2	2-0	0-2	2-1	1-1	2-2	3-4	0-1	0-1	0-1	0-2		2-0	4-0	0-1	1-0
Miscellaneous Serowe	30	6	8	16	38	60	26	1-3	1-5	2-0	1-2	2-4	2-3	4-1	2-4	0-0	1-1	2-2	1-0		0-3	1-0	3-2
Motlakase	30	5	9	16	37	58	24	0-1	1-4	2-3	1-2	0-1	1-2	1-2	0-2	2-2	1-1	2-2	1-4	1-5		2-2	2-1
TASC	30	5	9	16	27	51	24	0-5	0-3	1-1	0-2	1-2	0-2	1-3	0-0	1-0	3-3	1-2	1-2	1-1	1-1		3-1
Black Peril	30	4	3	23	32	79	15	1-3	1-6	1-0	0-1	1-0	2-3	0-2	2-5	3-3	0-0	1-3	1-3	0-0	0-1	1-0	

21/08/2010 - 22/05/2011 • † Qualified for the CAF Champions League

MEDALS TABLE

		Overall G	Lge G	Cup G	City
1	Township Rollers	17	11	6	Gaborone
2	Gaborone United	12	6	6	Gaborone
3	Botswana Defence Force	10	7	3	Gaborone
4	Mogoditshane Fighters	7	4	3	Mogoditshane
5	Notwane FC	6	3	3	Gaborone
	Extension Gunners	6	3	3	Lobatse
7	Centre Chiefs	3	1	2	Mochudi
	Police XI	2	1	1	Otse
	TASC (Tati Sporting Club)	2		2	Francistown
10	Botswana Meat Commission	1		1	Lobatse
	ECCO City Greens	1	1		Francistown
	Nico United	1		1	Selibe-Pikwe
	TAFIC	1		1	Francistown
	Uniao Flamengo Santos	1		1	Gabane

COCA-COLA CUP 2010–11

Round of 16

- Extension Gunners * 1
- Nico United 0
- Killer Giants * 1
- Notwane FC 3
- Defence Force * 1
- Jwaneng Comets 0
- Kanye Swallows 0
- Centre Chiefs * 9
- UF Santos * 3
- Gaborone United 0
- ECCO City Greens 1
- Township Rollers * 5
- Bot. Meat Commission 2
- TAFIC * 0
- Modipane United 1 5p
- Motlakase * 1 6p

Quarter–finals

- Extension Gunners * 1 6p
- Notwane FC 1 5p
- Defence Force 0
- Centre Chiefs * 1
- UF Santos 1 4p
- Township Rollers * 1 3p
- Bot. Meat Comm'sion * 1 2p
- Motlakase 1 3p

Semi–finals

- Extension Gunners * 1
- Centre Chiefs 0
- UF Santos * 0 2p
- Motlakase 0 4p

Final

- Extension Gunners ‡ 3
- Motlakase 1

CUP FINAL

Lobatse Stadium, 30-04-2011
Scorers - Maano Ditshupo [48], Kgololo Leteane 2 [80][81] for Gunners; Owen Baruti [78] for Motlakase

* Home Team • ‡ Qualified for the CAF Confederation Cup

BRA – BRAZIL

FIFA/COCA-COLA WORLD RANKING

'93	'94	'95	'96	'97	'98	'99	'00	'01	'02	'03	'04	'05	'06	'07	'08	'09	'10	'11	'12
3	1	1	1	1	1	1	1	3	1	1	1	1	1	2	5	2	4		

					2011									
	Jan	Feb	Mar	Apr	May	Jun	Jul	Aug	Sep	Oct	Nov	Dec	High	Low	Av
	4	4	4	3	3	5	4	6	7	5	6	6	1	8	1

Brazil's excellent record at recent Copa America tournaments came to a shuddering halt in 2011 after an abject display in Argentina. Statistically it was their worst-ever performance in the 95-year history of the tournament, an extraordinary fact given that they had won four of the past five competitions. An opening 0-0 draw against Venezuela set the tone for the four games played which saw Brazil win just once - a 4-2 victory against Ecuador which ensured qualification for a quarter-final against Paraguay. Coach Mano Menezes faces a difficult time preparing for the 2014 World Cup, a task that was made much more difficult by an awful performance against the Paraguayans, in what would be his team's last competitive match for two years, as Brazil failed to find the net - even in the penalty shoot-out. There was better news at club level as Santos rekindled the glory days of the Pele era at the club by winning the Copa Libertadores for the first time since 1963, wonderkid Neymar leading the side to a 2-1 aggregate victory over Peñarol in the final. Santos also won the 2011 Paulista but it was Corinthians who emerged as Serie A champions - their first title since 2005 - while Vasco da Gama won their first ever Copa do Brasil, beating Coritiba in the final.

COPA AMERICA RECORD

1916 3/4 1917 3/4 **1919** 1/4 Winners (Hosts) 1920 3/4 1921 2/4 **1922** 1/5 Winners (Hosts) 1923 4/4 1924 DNE 1925 2/3 1926-1935 DNE
1937 2/6 1939-1941 DNE 1942 3/7 1945 2/7 1946 2/6 1947 DNE **1949** 1/8 Winners (Hosts) 1953 2/7 1955 DNE 1956 4/6 1957 2/7
1959 2/7 1959 3/5 1963 4/7 1967 DNE 1975 3/10 SF 1979 3/10 SF 1983 2/10 F 1987 5/10 r1 **1989** 1/10 Winners (Hosts) 1991 2/10 r2
1993 6/12 QF 1995 2/12 F **1997** 1/12 Winners **1999** 1/12 Winners 2001 6/12 QF **2004** 1/12 Winners **2007** 1/12 Winners 2011 8/12 QF

CONFEDERACAO BRASILEIRA DE FUTEBOL (CBF)

Rua Victor Civita 66, Bloco
1 - Edificio 5 - 5 Andar, Barra da Tijuca, Rio de Janeiro
☎ +55 21 35721900
📠 +55 21 35721989
✉ cbf@cbf.com.br
🖥 www.cbf.com.br
FA 1914 CON 1916 FIFA 1923
P Jose Maria Marin
GS Julio Cesar Avelleda

FIFA BIG COUNT 2006

Total players	13 197 733
% of population	7.02%
Male	11 752 783
Female	1 444 950
Amateurs 18+	472 165
Youth under 18	1 347 100
Unregistered	6 080 000
Professionals	16 200
Referees	16 000
Admin & coaches	45 000
Number of clubs	28 970
Number of teams	86 910

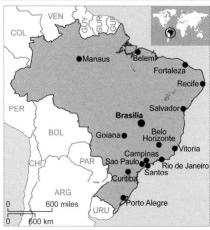

MAJOR CITIES/TOWNS

		Population
1	São Paulo	10 328 094
2	Rio de Janeiro	6 227 355
3	Salvador	2 949 222
4	Fortaleza	2 513 812
5	Belo Horizonte	2 506 025
6	Brasília	2 463 923
7	Curitiba	1 871 087
8	Manaus	1 817 778
9	Belém	1 554 295
10	Recife	1 542 678
11	Porto Alegre	1 421 272
12	Guarulhos	1 325 997
13	Goiânia	1 267 151
14	Campinas	1 111 854
15	Maceió	1 111 536
16	Nova Iguaçu	1 087 086
17	São Luís	1 007 604
18	São Gonçalo	998 325
19	Natal	821 794

REPUBLICA FEDERATIVA DO BRASIL • FEDERATIVE REPUBLIC OF BRAZIL

Capital	Brasilia	Population	198 739 269 (5)	% in cities	86%
GDP per capita	$10 200 (102)	Area km²	8 514 877 km² (5)	GMT + / -	-3
Neighbours (km)		Argentina 1261, Bolivia 3423, Colombia 1644, French Guiana 730, Guyana 1606, Paraguay 1365, Peru 2995, Suriname 593, Uruguay 1068, Venezuela 2200 • Coast 7491			

RECENT INTERNATIONAL MATCHES PLAYED BY BRAZIL

2010	Opponents		Score	Venue	Comp	Scorers	Att	Referee
2-03	Republic of Ireland	W	2-0	London	Fr	OG [44], Robinho [76]	40 082	Dean ENG
2-06	Zimbabwe	W	3-0	Harare	Fr	Michel Bastos [42], Robinho [43], Elano [57]	30 000	Martins ANG
7-06	Tanzania	W	5-1	Dar es Salaam	Fr	Robinho 2 [10 33], Ramires 2 [53 90], Kaka [75]	35 000	Ssegonga UGA
15-06	Korea DPR	W	2-1	Johannesburg	WCr1	Maicon [55], Elano [72]	54 331	Kassai HUN
20-06	Côte d'Ivoire	W	3-1	Johannesburg	WCr1	Luis Fabiano 2 [25 50], Elano [62]	84 445	Lannoy FRA
25-06	Portugal	D	0-0	Durban	WCr1		62 712	Archundia MEX
28-06	Chile	W	3-0	Johannesburg	WCr2	Juan [35], Luis Fabiano [38], Robinho [59]	54 096	Webb ENG
2-07	Netherlands	L	1-2	Port Elizabeth	WCqf	Robinho [10]	40 186	Nishimura JPN
10-08	USA	W	2-0	New Jersey	Fr	Neymar [29], Pato [45]	77 223	Petrescu CAN
7-10	Iran	W	3-0	Abu Dhabi	Fr	Dani Alves [14], Pato [69], Nilmar [90]	49 000	Al Marzouqi UAE
11-10	Ukraine	W	2-0	Derby	Fr	Dani Alves [25], Pato [64]	13 088	Atkinson ENG
17-11	Argentina	L	0-1	Doha	Fr		50 000	Balideh QAT
2011								
9-02	France	L	0-1	Paris	Fr		79 712	Stark GER
27-03	Scotland	W	2-0	London	Fr	Neymar 2 [43 77p]	53 087	Webb ENG
4-06	Netherlands	D	0-0	Goiania	Fr		36 449	Amarilla PAR
7-06	Romania	W	1-0	São Paulo	Fr	Fred [23]	30 059	Pezzotta ARG
3-07	Venezuela	D	0-0	La Plata	CAr1		35 000	Orozco BOL
9-07	Paraguay	D	2-2	Cordoba	CAr1	Jadson [38], Fred [89]	57 000	Roldan COL
13-07	Ecuador	W	4-2	Cordoba	CAr1	Pato 2 [28 61], Neymar 2 [48 71]	39 000	Silvera URU
17-07	Paraguay	D	0-0	La Plata	CAqf	L 0-2p	36 000	Pezzotta ARG
10-08	Germany	L	2-3	Stuttgart	Fr	Robinho [71], Neymar [90]	54 767	Kassai HUN
5-09	Ghana	W	1-0	London	Fr	Leandro Damiao [45]	25 700	Dean ENG
14-09	Argentina	D	0-0	Cordoba	Fr		50 000	Osses CHI
28-09	Argentina	W	2-0	Belem	Fr		43 038	Larrionda URU
7-10	Costa Rica	W	1-0	San Jose	Fr		25 000	Lopez GUA
11-10	Mexico	W	2-1	Torreon	Fr	Ronaldinho [79], Marcelo Vieira [89]	30 000	Mejia SLV
10-11	Gabon	W	2-0	Libreville	Fr	Sandro [11], Hernanes [34]		Hlungwani RSA
14-11	Egypt	W	2-0	Al Rayyan	Fr	Jonas 2 [38 59]	18 000	Al Dosari QAT

Fr = Friendly match • CA = Copa America • CC = FIFA Confederations Cup • WC = FIFA World Cup
q = qualifier • r1 = 1st round group • r2 = second round • qf = quarter-final • sf = semi-final • f = final

BRAZIL NATIONAL TEAM HISTORICAL RECORDS

Caps

142 - Cafu 1990-2006 • 125 - Roberto Carlos 1992-2006 • 105 - Lucio 2000- • 101 - Claudio Taffarel 1988-98 • 98 - Djalma Santos 1952-68 • 97 - Ronaldo 1994-2006 • 94 - Gilmar 1953-69 • 93 - Gilberto Silva 2001- & Ronaldinho 1999- • 92 - Pele 1957-71 & Rivelino 1965-78 • 91 - Dunga 1987-98 & Dida 1995-2006 • 90 - Robinho 2003- • 84 - Ze Roberto 1995-2006 • 82 - Kaka 2002- • 81 - Jairzinho 1964-82 & Aldair 1989-2000 • 80 - Emerson Leao 1970-86 • 79 - Juan 2001- • 75 - Bebeto 1985-98 & Nilton Santos 1949-62

Goals

77 - Pele 1957-71 • 62 - Ronaldo 1994-2006 • 55 - Romario 1987-2005 • 52 - Zico 1976-86 • 39 - Bebeto 1985-98 • 34 - Rivaldo 1993-2003 • 33 - Jairzinho 1964-82 & Ronaldinho 1999- • 32 - Ademir 1945-53 & Tostao 1966-72 • 30 - Zizinho 1942-57 • 29 - Careca 1982-93 • 28 - Luis Fabiano 2003- • 27 - Adriano 2000- & Kaka 2002- • 26 - Rivelino 1965-78 & Robinho 2003- • 22 - Jair 1940-50 & Socrates 1979-86 • 21 - Leonidas 1932-46 • 20 - Didi 1952-62 & Roberto Dinamite 1975-84 • 16 - Baltazar 1950-56 & Pepe 1956-63

Past Coaches

Silvio Lagreca 1914-17 • Haroldo Domingues 1919 • Silvio Lagreca 1920 • Lais 1921-22 • Francisco Abatte 1922 • Almeda Rego 1923 • Joaquim Guimaraes 1925 • Pindaro de Carvalho Rodrigues 1930 • Luis Vinhaes 1931-34 • Carlito Rocha 1934 • Adhemar Pimenta 1936-38 • Carlos Nascimento 1939 • Armando Del Debbio 1940 • Jayme Barcelos 1940 • Adhemar Pimenta 1942 • Flavio Costa 1944-50 • Zeze Moreira 1952 • Aymore Moreira 1953 • Zeze Moreira 1954-55 • Vicente Feola 1955 • Flavio Costa 1955 • Osvaldo Brandao 1955-56 • Tele Duarte 1956 • Flavio Costa 1956 • Osvaldo Brandao 1957 • Silvio Pirillo 1957 • Pedrinho 1957 • Vicente Feola 1958-59 • Gentil Cardoso 1959 • Foguinho 1960 • Vicente Feola 1960 • Aymore Moreira 1961-63 • Vicente Feola 1964-65 • Aymore Ferreira 1965 • Carlos Froner 1966 • Vicente Feola 1966 • Aymore Ferreira 1967-68 • Antonio 1968 • Mario Zagallo 1968 • Aymore Ferreira 1968 • Dorival Yustrich 1968 • Joao Saldanha 1969-70 • Mario Zagallo 1970-74 • Osvaldo Brandao 1975-77 • Claudio Coutinho 1977-79 • Tele Santana 1980-82 • Carlos Alberto Parreira 1983 • Edu 1984 • Evaristo de Macedo 1985 • Tele Santana 1985-86 • Carlos Alberto Silva 1987-88 • Sebastiao Lazaroni 1989-90 • Paulo Roberto Falcao 1990-91 • Ernesto Paulo 1991 • Carlos Alberto Parreira 1991-94 • Mario Zagallo 1994-98 • Vanderlei Luxemburgo 1998-2000 • Candido 2000 • Emerson Leao 2000-01 • Luiz Felipe Scolari 2001-02 • Mario Zagallo 2002 • Carlos Alberto Parreira 2001-06 • Dunga 2006-10 • Mano Menezes 2010-

BRAZIL 2011

SERIE A

	Pl	W	D	L	F	A	Pts	Corinthians	Vasco da Gama	Fluminense	Flamengo	Internacional	São Paulo FC	Figueirense	Coritiba	Botafogo	Santos	Palmeiras	Grêmio	At. Goianiense	Bahia	At. Mineiro	Cruzeiro	At. Paranaense	Ceará	América Mineiro	Avaí
Corinthians †	38	21	8	9	53	36	71		2-1	2-0	2-1	1-0	5-0	0-2	2-1	0-2	1-3	0-0	3-2	3-0	1-0	2-1	0-1	2-1	2-2	2-1	2-1
Vasco da Gama †	38	19	12	7	57	40	69	2-2		1-1	1-1	2-0	0-0	1-1	2-0	2-0	2-0	1-0	4-0	1-1	1-1	2-0	0-3	2-1	3-1	3-0	2-0
Fluminense †	38	20	3	15	60	51	63	1-0	1-2		0-1	2-0	0-2	3-0	3-1	1-2	3-2	1-0	5-4	3-2	0-1	0-2	2-1	3-1	4-0	1-2	3-1
Flamengo †	38	15	16	7	59	47	61	1-1	0-0	3-2		1-0	1-0	0-0	1-0	0-0	1-1	1-1	2-0	1-4	1-3	4-1	5-1	1-2	1-1	2-1	4-0
Internacional †	38	16	12	10	57	43	60	1-1	3-0	1-2	2-2		0-3	4-1	1-1	1-0	3-3	2-1	0-0	1-0	2-1	3-2	1-0	0-1	4-2	4-2	
São Paulo FC ‡	38	16	11	11	57	46	59	0-0	0-2	1-2	1-2	0-0		1-0	0-0	0-2	4-1	1-1	3-1	2-2	3-0	2-1	2-1	2-2	4-0	3-1	2-0
Figueirense ‡	38	15	13	10	46	45	58	0-1	1-1	0-4	2-2	1-1	1-2		0-0	2-0	2-1	0-1	0-0	2-0	2-1	2-1	1-0	2-0	1-1	2-1	2-3
Coritiba ‡	38	16	9	13	57	41	57	1-0	5-1	3-1	2-0	1-1	3-4	3-0		5-0	1-0	1-1	2-0	0-1	0-0	3-0	2-1	1-1	3-1	3-1	1-0
Botafogo ‡	38	16	8	14	52	49	56	0-2	4-0	1-1	1-1	2-2	2-0	1-3	1-0		3-1	2-1	1-1	2-2	3-1	1-0	2-0	4-0	4-2	2-1	
Santos †	38	15	8	15	55	55	53	0-0	2-0	2-1	4-5	1-1	1-1	2-3	2-3	2-0		1-0	0-1	1-1	1-2	1-1	1-0	4-1	1-0	1-0	3-1
Palmeiras ‡	38	11	17	10	43	39	50	2-1	1-1	1-2	0-0	0-3	1-0	1-2	0-2	1-0	3-0		0-0	2-0	1-1	3-2	1-1	1-0	1-0	1-1	5-0
Grêmio ‡	38	13	9	16	50	57	48	1-2	1-1	2-1	4-2	2-1	1-0	1-3	2-0	0-1	1-0	2-2		2-2	2-0	2-2	2-0	4-0	1-3	1-1	2-2
Atlético Goianiense ‡	38	12	12	14	50	45	48	0-1	0-1	0-1	0-0	1-3	0-1	1-3	1-2	0-2	0-0	1-1	1-0		0-1	1-0	2-0	0-3	4-1	5-1	0-1
Bahia ‡	38	11	13	14	43	49	46	0-1	0-2	3-0	3-3	1-1	4-3	3-1	0-0	1-1	1-2	0-2	1-2	2-1		1-1	0-0	1-0	2-1	0-0	3-2
Atlético Mineiro	38	13	6	19	50	60	45	2-3	1-2	1-0	1-1	0-4	0-1	1-2	2-1	4-0	2-1	2-1	0-2	2-2	2-0		1-2	3-0	1-1	0-0	5-0
Cruzeiro	38	11	10	17	48	51	43	0-1	0-3	1-2	0-1	1-0	3-3	2-4	2-1	0-1	1-1	1-1	2-0	3-2	2-1	6-1		1-1	1-0	0-0	5-0
Atlético Paranaense	38	10	11	17	38	55	41	1-1	2-2	1-1	1-1	2-0	1-0	0-0	1-0	2-1	3-2	2-2	0-1	0-2	0-1	2-1		1-0	2-2	0-0	
Ceará	38	10	9	19	47	64	39	0-1	1-3	1-2	0-1	1-1	0-2	1-1	3-2	2-2	2-3	0-1	1-3	0-3	0-2	2-1		4-0	0-3		
América Mineiro	38	8	13	17	51	69	37	2-1	4-1	3-0	2-3	2-4	1-1	0-0	1-3	2-1	1-2	1-2	1-2	2-1	0-0	1-1	2-1	4-1			2-2
Avaí	38	7	10	21	45	75	31	3-2	0-2	0-1	3-2	1-3	1-2	1-1	0-0	3-2	1-2	1-1	1-2	2-2	2-2	1-3	0-0	3-0	1-2	2-2	

21/05/2011 - 4/12/2011 • † Qualified for the Copa Libertadores • ‡ Qualified for the Copa Sudamericana
Top scorers: **23** - Borges, Santos • **22** - Fred, Fluminense • **15** - Deivid, Flamengo • **14** - Leandro Damiao, Internacional; Ronaldinho, Flamengo & William Souza, Avai • **13** - Sebastian Abreu URU, Botafogo; Neymar, Santos & Kempes, América Mineiro • **12** - Liedson POR, Corinthians; Walter Montillo ARG, Cruzeiro; Thiago Neves, Flamengo & Anselmo Atlético GO

BRAZIL 2011

SERIE B

	Pl	W	D	L	F	A	Pts	Portuguesa	Náutico	Ponte Preta	Sport Recife	Vitória	Bragantino	Boa Esporte	Americana	Grêmio	ABC	Goiás	Guarani	Paraná	Criciúma	São Caetano	ASA Arapiraca	Icasa	Vila Nova	Salgueiro	Duque
Portuguesa	38	23	12	3	82	38	81		4-0	2-1	2-3	2-5	0-1	1-0	0-4	2-2	3-3	0-3	3-2	2-1	2-0	5-2	2-0	3-3	0-1	1-0	4-0
Náutico	38	17	13	8	51	41	64	0-0		2-2	2-0	2-0	2-2	3-1	2-2	1-2	1-0	2-1	2-0	1-1	2-1	2-1	1-0	2-2	4-2	1-0	1-1
Ponte Preta	38	17	12	9	63	45	63	0-3	3-3		1-1	0-0	1-3	1-2	0-0	2-0	4-1	2-1	2-0	4-3	3-0	1-0	5-0	4-1	1-1	1-0	2-1
Sport Recife	38	17	10	11	62	44	61	2-3	2-0	3-1		4-0	1-1	4-1	4-0	1-0	2-0	0-1	3-1	3-0	0-0	1-3	3-0	1-0	2-0	3-0	1-1
Vitória	38	17	9	12	61	48	60	0-2	3-2	2-0	2-0		4-1	0-1	5-2	1-2	1-1	3-2	0-1	1-0	3-1	1-2	1-0	1-1	1-0	5-1	5-1
Bragantino	38	16	10	12	65	53	58	1-1	2-1	1-1	3-2	2-2		1-2	2-2	1-1	4-0	0-0	2-1	2-2	1-2	0-1	1-1	1-0	5-3	3-0	
Boa Esporte	38	16	9	13	44	40	57	1-2	2-1	1-1	3-0	1-2	1-2		0-0	2-0	0-0	1-1	2-0	4-1	2-1	0-0	0-0	0-2	0-0		
Americana	38	15	11	12	40	45	56	2-3	0-0	0-2	2-1	0-0	1-1	2-1		1-0	2-1	1-3	1-2	1-0	0-0	1-0	1-1	1-0	2-1	1-0	1-1
Grêmio Prudente	38	15	8	15	48	53	53	1-1	0-0	2-1	2-3	1-0	3-2	2-0	1-3	2-0	1-3	1-0	0-0	0-3	1-0	1-2	1-0	2-1	2-1		
ABC	38	13	14	11	52	53	53	1-1	1-0	1-1	3-0	0-0	0-5	2-0	3-1	2-2		2-0	2-1	1-1	1-2	1-1	1-1	1-2	1-1	3-0	
Goiás	38	16	4	18	51	57	52	1-4	1-2	2-1	2-1	4-1	2-1	2-0	3-1	1-0	1-2		3-0	0-3	1-0	1-0	4-1	0-0	1-1	0-1	4-1
Guarani	38	15	7	16	51	48	52	0-2	3-1	0-3	1-1	0-0	3-2	0-1	2-0	1-3	2-0	1-2		1-1	4-2	1-0	0-1	0-1	0-1	1-7	4-0
Paraná	38	14	10	14	48	44	52	1-1	2-0	0-1	1-2	1-1	1-0	2-0	0-1	1-3	1-0	1-3	0-0		0-2	2-3	1-2	2-0	2-1	1-0	3-1
Criciúma	38	13	12	13	43	43	51	1-1	0-0	1-1	0-2	1-1	0-0	0-1	0-2	2-2	1-1	1-1	1-0	2-2		1-1	5-2	3-1	3-0	2-0	
São Caetano	38	12	15	11	57	51	51	3-3	0-0	1-1	3-3	2-2	0-2	0-2	1-1	1-1	4-0	2-1	1-2	1-1	1-0		2-0	2-2	3-0	3-1	4-2
ASA Arapiraca	38	13	9	16	44	54	48	2-0	1-2	1-2	1-1	1-2	2-1	2-1	2-1	1-1	4-3	1-1	3-2	4-2	3-1	1-0		2-1	1-0	0-1	2-0
Icasa	38	11	14	13	52	55	47	0-2	1-2	1-1	2-3	1-2	0-0	1-2	2-0	1-1	3-4	2-1	1-3	1-0	1-0	0-1	1-1		1-0	1-0	4-2
Vila Nova	38	7	11	20	34	53	32	1-3	0-0	3-1	0-1	0-3	1-2	1-2	1-3	2-2	2-2	2-3	0-0	0-1	2-0	2-0	1-1	1-2		1-0	1-1
Salgueiro	38	8	5	25	32	63	26	1-2	0-2	2-3	0-1	0-2	0-1	0-1	1-4	0-1	2-0	1-4	2-1	2-1	1-1	1-1	3-5	1-1			2-0
Duque de Caxias	38	2	11	25	32	84	17	0-0	0-0	0-2	1-1	2-3	2-6	2-2	0-2	2-3	1-0	2-3	0-2	0-0	1-2	1-3	2-1	1-1	1-1	1-2	

21/05/2011 - 26/11/2011 • Top scorers: **21** - Kieza, Náutico • **20** - Lincom, Bragantino • **19** - Ricardo Jesus, Ponte Preta • **15** - Neto Baiano, Vitória

BRAZIL 2011
SERIE C (3) FINAL ROUNDS

Group A	Pl	W	D	L	F	A	Pts
CRB †	6	3	3	0	7	2	12
América Natal	6	2	3	1	6	4	9
Paysandu	6	2	1	3	5	8	7
Luverdense	6	0	3	3	4	8	3

Group B	Pl	W	D	L	F	A	Pts
Joinville †	6	5	1	0	14	5	16
Ipatinga	6	3	0	3	9	11	9
Chapecoense	6	1	2	3	12	12	5
Brasiliense	6	1	1	4	9	16	4

19/01/2011 - 13/02/2011 • † Qualified for the final
Final: CRB 1-3 0-4 **Joinville. Joinville** win Serie C

BRAZIL 2011
SERIE D (4) FINAL ROUNDS

Quarter-finals		Semi-finals		Final	
Tupi	4 2				
Anapolina	1 2	**Tupi**	3 3		
Mirassol	3 1 3p	Oeste	0 1		
Oeste	1 3 4p			**Tupi**	1 2
Cuiabá	2 4			Santa Cruz	0 0
Independente	0 2	Cuiabá	0 1		
Treze	3 0	**Santa Cruz**	1 2		
Santa Cruz	3 0				

* Home team in the 1st leg

Tupi, Oeste, Cuiabá and Santa Cruz are promoted

BRAZIL STATE CHAMPIONSHIPS 2011

State	Winners	Score	Runners-up	State	Winners	Score	Runners-up
Acre	Rio Branco	1-1 1-0	Plácido de Castro	Paraíba	Treze	1-1 1-1	Campinense
Alagoas	ASA	6-2 4-3	Coruripe	Paraná	Coritiba	‡	Atlético PR
Amapá	Trem	1-0 0-1 5-2p	Santos AP	Pernambuco	Santa Cruz	2-0 0-1	Sport Recife
Amazonas	Peñarol	1-1 1-1 4-3p	Nacional AM	Piauí	4 de Julho	1-0 1-1	Comercial PI
Bahia	Bahia de Feira	2-2 2-1	Vitória	Rio de Janeiro	Flamengo	‡	Fluminense
Ceará	Ceará	‡	Guarani/J	Rio Grande Nor.	ABC	0-1 3-1	Santa Cruz RN
Distrito Federal	Brasiliense	1-1 0-0	Gama	Rio Grande Sul	Internacional	2-3 3-2 5-4p	Grêmio
Espírito Santo	São Mateus	1-1 2-0	Linhares	Rondônia	Espigão	1-0 0-1 6-5p	Ariquemes
Goiás	Atlético GO	1-1 1-1	Goiás	Roraima	Real	‡	São Raimundo
Maranhão	Sampaio Corrêa	‡	Maranhão	Santa Catarina	Chapecoense	0-1 1-0	Criciúma
Mato Grosso	Cuiabá	3-1 1-1	Barra do Garças	São Paulo	Santos	0-0 2-1	Corinthians
Mato Grosso Sul	CENE	3-1 0-2	Aquidauanense	Sergipe	River Plate	3-0 1-1	São Domingos
Minas Gerais	Cruzeiro	1-2 2-0	Atlético MG	Tocantins	Gurupi	2-1 0-1	Interporto
Pará	Independente	2-2 3-3 3-0p	Paysandu				

‡ Won both stages so no final needed • † Played on a league basis

BRAZIL STATE CHAMPIONSHIPS 2011 – RIO DE JANEIRO

TAÇA GUANABARA

Group A	Pl	W	D	L	F	A	Pts
Flamengo †	7	7	0	0	14	4	21
Boavista †	7	4	1	2	15	11	13
Resende	7	4	1	2	9	5	13
Nova Iguçu	7	3	2	2	12	11	11
Vasco da Gama	7	2	1	4	16	9	7
Volta Redonda	7	1	2	4	4	7	5
Americano	7	1	2	4	7	14	5
América	7	1	1	5	6	22	4

Group B	Pl	W	D	L	F	A	Pts
Fluminense †	7	6	0	1	20	9	18
Botafogo †	7	5	2	0	19	7	17
Olaria	7	3	1	3	10	14	10
Bangu	7	2	3	2	7	7	9
Duque de Caxias	7	2	1	4	13	14	7
Macaé	7	1	4	2	11	13	7
Madureira	7	1	2	4	8	13	5
Cabofriense	7	1	1	5	7	18	4

19/01/2011 - 13/02/2011 • † Qualified for the semis

GUANABARA PLAY-OFFS

Semi–finals		Final	
Flamengo	1 3p		
Botafogo	1 1p	**Flamengo**	1
Fluminense	2 2p	Boavista	0
Boavista	2 4p		

Engenhão, Rio, 27-02-2011, Att: 41 708, Ref: Marcelo
de Lima. Scorer - Ronaldinho [72] for Flamengo

TAÇA RIO

Group A	Pl	W	D	L	F	A	Pts
Vasco da Gama †	8	5	2	1	19	10	17
Flamengo †	8	4	4	0	13	7	16
Americano	8	4	2	2	10	14	14
Boavista	8	4	1	3	13	8	13
Volta Redonda	8	3	2	3	11	12	11
Resende	8	2	2	4	12	12	8
Nova Iguçu	8	2	1	5	7	12	7
América	8	1	1	6	7	15	4

Group B	Pl	W	D	L	F	A	Pts
Fluminense †	8	5	2	1	13	6	17
Olaria †	8	4	3	1	11	6	15
Botafogo	8	4	2	2	13	8	14
Madureira	8	3	2	3	16	15	11
Duque de Caxias	8	3	2	3	10	14	11
Macaé	8	2	2	4	11	14	8
Bangu	8	2	1	5	9	15	7
Cabofriense	8	1	1	6	7	14	4

3/03/2011 - 17/04/2011 • † Qualified for the semis

TAÇA RIO PLAY-OFFS

Semi–finals		Final	
Flamengo	1 5p		
Fluminense	1 4p	**Flamengo**	0 3p
Olaria	0	Vasco da Gama	0 1p
Vasco da Gama	1		

Engenhão, Rio, 1-05-2011, Att: 39 029, Ref: Silva

BRAZIL STATE CHAMPIONSHIPS 2011 – RIO DE JANEIRO

CAMPEONATO CARIOCA 2011 RESULTS

	Flamengo	Fluminense	Botafogo	Boavista	Olaria	Vasco	Resende	Americano	Nova Iguçu	Duque de Caxias	Madureira	V. Redonda	Bangu	Macaé	Cabofriense	América
Flamengo		0-0		3-2		1-0	2-0	1-0		3-3	2-0			1-1		
Fluminense			2-3	0-2	6-2	0-0			1-0	3-1					3-1	3-1
Botafogo	0-2			3-1		1-1	4-0			2-1	4-1	4-2			1-1	
Boavista	2-3		0-0		3-1	0-1				3-0			3-1		3-1	1-1
Olaria			2-0			2-2			2-0		1-0		1-0	1-1	2-0	1-0
Vasco da Gama	1-2		2-0		0-1		3-0			4-2		0-0	4-0		2-1	
Resende		1-2		1-2				1-1	1-2		1-1	1-0		5-2		
Americano		1-5		2-3	0-0				1-1		2-1	2-1			2-1	
Nova Iguçu			0-1	3-5		3-2				1-2		1-1		1-1	3-2	2-0
Duque de Caxias	0-2			4-2			2-1	2-2				3-3	0-0		4-1	
Madureira		0-1		2-1		2-4			3-1				0-1		2-1	2-0
Volta Redonda		1-2		0-1	0-0				1-1		3-2			2-1		2-0
Bangu	1-2	0-1	1-1			0-1	1-2		1-0		2-1				2-2	
Macaé			2-1		3-1		0-1			2-2	2-2				3-0	1-1
Cabofriense	0-0	2-4	0-5				2-1	0-1		2-0		1-2				
América	1-3		1-3			0-9	1-4	3-1		1-2			1-3		2-0	

Clubs listed according to overall position • Taça Guanabara results in shaded boxes • Taça Rio results in unshaded boxes
Top scorers: **10** - Fred, Fluminense & Carlos Frontini ARG, Boavista • **9** - Sebastian Abreu URU, Botafogo • **8** - Somalia, Duque & Max, Boavista

BRAZIL STATE CHAMPIONSHIPS 2011 – SÃO PAULO

CAMPEONATO PAULISTA SERIE A1 FIRST ROUND

	Pl	W	D	L	F	A	Pts	São Paulo	Palmeiras	Corinthians	Santos	Ponte Preta	Oeste	Mirassol	Portuguesa	São Caetano	Paulista	Mogi Mirim	Americana	Botafogo	Linense	Bragantino	Ituano	São Bernardo	Grêmio Pr	Noroeste	Santo André
São Paulo FC ‡	19	13	2	4	39	19	41		1-1	2-1	0-1	1-1	1-0											3-2	4-0	2-0	3-0
Palmeiras ‡	19	12	5	2	28	8	41	0-1						3-1		1-0	0-0	3-0	3-0					2-0	2-0		0-0
Corinthians ‡	19	11	5	3	33	12	38				3-1	0-1	3-0		2-0	1-2		2-0	1-0			4-0				4-0	1-1
Santos ‡	19	11	5	3	40	20	38		2-0	0-1				3-0	3-0	3-3	3-0	3-1		2-1						1-1	2-0
Ponte Preta ‡	19	9	5	5	22	16	32		2-1				2-2			0-0	0-0	2-1	0-3	1-1			1-2				1-1
Oeste ‡	19	9	4	6	25	17	31	0-1							0-2	2-1		0-1		3-0	1-1			1-0	1-0	2-0	4-0
Mirassol ‡	19	8	6	5	26	26	30	0-1		2-3			0-3		2-1		3-1			2-0	2-0	3-0				2-2	1-1
Portuguesa ‡	19	8	4	7	24	23	28	2-3	0-2			1-3	1-0	4-1						1-0				0-0	1-0	0-2	0-0
São Caetano	19	7	5	7	22	22	26	0-2	1-1					1-0			2-1	0-1		0-2	2-0	0-1	6-1	1-0			
Paulista	19	7	4	8	23	24	25	3-2	0-0									1-0	0-2	0-1	2-3			2-1	1-1		0-0
Mogi Mirim	19	7	4	8	24	28	25	0-2	0-0										0-1	1-3	1-2	1-1	0-1	3-1		1-1
Americana	19	7	2	10	20	19	23	3-4					0-0		1-1		0-2	0-1				2-1		1-0	2-0		3-1
Botafogo RP	19	5	7	7	22	27	22	2-1	0-0					3-0	1-4		1-1	2-1			0-4	1-1				2-2	1-0
Linense	19	6	3	10	23	31	21	0-2	1-4					1-3	3-2		0-2			2-1			0-2	0-1			2-0
Bragantino	19	5	4	10	21	30	19	1-1	2-1	0-1				1-2			0-1	2-3					2-1	3-0			2-1
Ituano	19	5	3	11	21	33	18	1-4	2-3	2-3	0-0						0-1	3-1	3-3						2-0	2-0
São Bernardo	19	5	3	11	21	36	18			2-2	0-1	0-2	4-1				2-4	0-2		3-1	2-0	2-1					
Grêmio Prudente	19	4	5	10	21	35	17				0-1			2-4		0-2	1-1	3-3		1-2	1-0	1-1				2-4	1-0
Noroeste	19	3	8	8	21	35	17		1-4			1-2				1-0		0-0	4-1	1-5			2-2				2-2
Santo André	19	2	9	8	14	29	15			0-2	1-1	0-2	2-2					1-0	0-4		1-0		1-1		1-1	1-3	

15/01/2010 - 17/04/2011 • ‡ Qualified for the quarter-finals

PAULISTA 2011 FINAL ROUNDS

Quarter-finals		Semi-finals		Final		
Santos *	1					
Ponte Preta	0	Santos	2			
Portuguesa	0	São Paulo *	0			
São Paulo *	2			Santos	0	2
Palmeiras *	2			Corinthians *	0	1
Mirassol	1	Palmeiras *	1 5p			
Oeste	1	Corinthians	1 6p			
Corinthians *	2	* Home team in the 1st leg				

1st leg. Pacaembu, São Paulo, 8-05-2011, Att: 34 547, Ref: Cleber
2nd leg. Vila Belmiro, Santos, 15-05-2011, Att: 14 322, Ref: Oliveira
Scorers - Arouca 16, Neymar 83 for Santos; Morais 86 for Corinthians
Santos are the 2011 São Paulo state champions

COPA DO BRASIL 2011

First Round

Team	Score
Vasco da Gama	6
Comercial MS *	1
Barras *	1 1
ABC	1 2
Bangu *	3 0
Portuguesa	1 1
Trem *	2 0
Náutico	1 6
Bahia	0 5
São Domingos *	0 1
Peñarol *	2 2
Paysandu	3 2
Paulista	0 3
EC São José *	1 0
Rio Branco *	2 1
Atlético Paranaense	1 3
São Paulo FC	3
Treze *	0
Corinthians RN *	1
Santa Cruz	4
Ponte Preta	1
Baré *	0
Vitória ES *	1
Goiás	4
Botafogo	0 1 1p
River Plate *	1 0 4p
Gurupi *	1 0
Paraná	1 3
Ipatinga	1 3
Rio Branco ES *	0 0
Vilhena *	0
Avaí	3
Ceará	2
Cuiabá *	0
Aguia de Marabá *	1 0
Brasiliense	1 2
Atlético Mineiro	3 8
Iape *	2 1
Iraty *	3 0
Grêmio Prudente	1 3
Horizonte	3 3
ASA *	1 3
União Rondonópolis	4 0
Guarani	4 0
Fortaleza	0 4
Fast Clube *	2 1
Murici *	0
Flamengo	3
Palmeiras	2 5
Comercial PI *	1 1
Santa Helena *	1
Uberaba	3
Sampaio Corrêa *	0 2
Sport Recife	0 2
Naviraiense *	1 0
Santo André	2 1
Caxias	5
Ceilândia *	0
Vitória	1 0
Botafogo PB *	3 0
Atlético Goiâniense	2 1
Brusque *	3 0
Ypiranga Erechim *	0 0
Coritiba	1 2

Second Round

Team	Score
Vasco da Gama	0 2
ABC *	0 1
Bangu *	0
Náutico	2
Bahia	0 2
Paysandu *	0 1
Paulista *	0
Atlético Paranaense	2
São Paulo FC	0 2
Santa Cruz *	1 0
Ponte Preta *	0
Goiás	3
Botafogo	2 3
Paraná *	1 0
Ipatinga *	1 1
Avaí	1 4
Ceará	0 2
Brasiliense *	0 1
Atlético Mineiro	1 0
Grêmio Prudente *	2 0
Horizonte *	1 2
Guarani	1 2
Fortaleza *	0
Flamengo	3
Palmeiras	4
Uberaba *	0
Sampaio Corrêa *	3 0
Santo André	2 1
Caxias	1 3
Botafogo PB *	0 1
Atlético Goiâniense *	1 1
Coritiba	2 3

Third Round

Team	Score
Vasco da Gama	3 0
Náutico *	0 0
Bahia *	1 0
Atlético Paranaense	1 5
São Paulo FC	1 1
Goiás *	0 0
Botafogo *	2 1
Avaí	2 1
Ceará *	2 2
Grêmio Prudente	1 1
Horizonte	1 0
Flamengo *	1 3
Palmeiras	2 1
Santo André *	1 0
Caxias	0 0
Coritiba *	4 1

If the away team wins the first leg by two goals in the first or second round no second leg is played

COPA DO BRASIL 2011

Quarter-finals	Semi-finals	Final

Vasco da Gama   2   1
Atlético Paranaense *   2   1

Vasco da Gama *   1   2
Avaí   1   0

São Paulo FC *   1   1
Avaí   0   3

Vasco da Gama * †   1   2
Coritiba   0   3

Ceará   2   2
Flamengo *   1   2

Ceará *   0   0
Coritiba   0   1

COPA DO BRASIL FINAL

São Januário, Rio de Janeiro, 2-06-2011, 21:50, Att: 21 365, Ref: Oliveira

Vasco da Gama   1   Alecsandro [51]
Coritiba   0

Vasco - Fernando Prass (c) - Allan, Anderson Martins, Dede, Marcio Careca - Romulo, Eduardo Costa, Felipe (Felipe Bastos 66), Diego Souza, Bernardo, Alecsandro (Elton 84). Tr: Ricardo Gomes

Palmeiras   0   2
Coritiba *   6   0

Coritiba - Edson Bastos - Jonas, Demerson, Emerson (c), Lucas Mendes - Willian, Leo Gago, Rafinha, Davi (Geraldo 73), Anderson Aquino• (Marcos Paulo 73), Bill (Leonardo 70). Tr: Marcelo Oliveira

Couto Pereira, Curitiba, 8-06-2011, 21:50, Att: 31 516, Ref: Fagundes

Coritiba   3   Bill [29], Davi [44], Willian [66]
Vasco da Gama   2   Alecsandro [12], Eder Luis [57]

Coritiba - Edson Bastos - Jonas, Demerson, Emerson (c), Lucas Mendes (Eltinho 58) - Willian, Leo Gago• (Marcos Aurelio 60), Marcos Paulo (Leonardo• 27), Rafinha - Davi, Bill•. Tr: Marcelo Oliveira

Vasco - Fernando Prass (c)• - Allan, Anderson Martins, Dede, Ramon - Romulo, Eduardo Costa•, Felipe• (Jumar 79), Diego Souza (Bernardo 79) - Eder Luis•, Alecsandro. Tr: Ricardo Gomes

† Qualified for the Copa Libertadores
* Home team in the first leg

MEDALS TABLE

		Overall			Nat			Cup		TRGP	Rio-SP	SL	Sth Am			
#	Club	G	S	B	G	S	B	G	S				G	S	B	City
1	Santos	13	7	4	2	4		**6**	2	1	**5** 1	19 9	4	1	4	Santos
2	São Paulo FC	11	10	8	**6**	5	3		1		1 5 1	21 17	5	4	5	São Paulo
3	Palmeiras	11	9	3	4	2		3	1	2 1	**5** 1 3	22 23	2	5	3	São Paulo
4	Cruzeiro	10	11	5	1	4	1	5	1	1		37	4	5	4	Belo Horizonte
5	Flamengo	10	7	4	**6**		1	2	4		1 3 2	32 25	2	3	3	Rio de Janeiro
6	Grêmio	8	6	6	2	2	1	4	2			36	2	2	5	Porto Alegre
7	Corinthians	8	5	6	5	3	1	3	2		**5** 3 2	26 19			3	São Paulo
8	Internacional	7	10	8	3	5		1	2	2		40	3	1	3	Porto Alegre
9	Vasco da Gama	7	5	3	4	3		1	2	1	3 5 2	22 21	2		2	Rio de Janeiro
10	Atlético Mineiro	3	4	5	1	3				1		40	2	1	4	Belo Horizonte
11	Botafogo	3	4	2	1	2		1	2		4 3 1	18 15	1		2	Rio de Janeiro
12	Fluminense	4	4	1	2		1	1	2	1	2 1 1	30 21		2		Rio de Janeiro
13	EC Bahia	2	2		1			1	2			45				Salvador
14	Sport Recife	2	1		1			1	1			38				Recife
15	Guarani	1	2	1	1	2						1			1	Campinas
	Atlético Paranaense	1	2	1	1	1						22		1	1	Curitiba
17	Coritiba	1	1		1				1			35				Curitiba
18	Criciúma	1						1				8				Criciúma
	Juventude	1						1				1				Caxias do Sul
	Paulista	1						1								Jundiai
	Santo André	1						1				1				Santo Andre
22	São Caetano		3			2						1 1		1		São Caetano
23	Goiãs AC		2	1			1		1			22		1		Goiânia
24	Fortaleza		2						2			39				Fortaleza
	Vitória		2			1			1			26				Salvador
26	Portuguesa		1			1					2 3	3 4				São Paulo
	Bangu		1			1					1	2 6				Rio de Janeiro
	Bragantino		1			1						1				Bragança Paulista
	Brasiliense		1						1			7				Taguatinga
	Ceará SC		1						1			40				Fortaleza
	CSA		1									37			1	Maceió
	Figueirense		1						1			15				Florianópolis
	Nautico		1						1			21				Recife
34	Sampaio Corrêa			1								29			1	São Luis
	São Raimundo			1								7			1	Manaus

Nat = the national championship played since 1971 • Cup = the Copa do Brasil played between 1959-68 and since 1989 • TRGP = Torneio Roberto Gomes Pedrosa played from 1967-70 • Rio-SP = Torneio Rio-São Paulo played in 1933, 1950-66, 1993 & 1997-2002 • SL = the state leagues played throughout the country • The totals for the Torneio Rio-São Paulo and the state leagues are not included in the overall totals as they are not national competitions

CLUB BY CLUB GUIDE TO 2011 IN BRAZIL

The following guide covers the state championships played in Brazil in the first half of the year along with Serie A in the second half of the year
SA = Serie A • CB = Copa do Brasil • CL = Copa Libertadores • CS = Copa Sudamericana • g1 = group 1 etc • r1 = first round etc • qf = quarter-final • sf = semi-final • f = final
State championship abbreviations
CG = Campeonato Goiano (Atlético GO & Goiás) • CM = Campeonato Mineiro (Atlético MG & Cruzeiro) • CP = Campeonato Paranaense (Atlético PR) • CC = Campeonato Catarinense (Avai) • TG & TR = Taça Guanabara & Taça Rio (Botafogo, Flamengo, Fluminense & Vasco) • CC1 = Campeonato Cearense round 1 etc (Ceara) • CP = Campeonato Paulista (Corinthians, Grêmio Prudente, Palmeiras, Santos & São Paulo. Guarani played the 2010 season at the second) • CG = Campeonato Gaúcho (Grêmio & Internacional) • TB = Campeonato Baiano (Vitória)

AMERICA MINEIRO 2011

	Date	Opponent		Score		Scorers	Att
Ja	29	Uberaba	D	1-1	CM	Fabio Junior 36	6 286
	3	Caldense	W	2-0	CM	Luciano 17, Fabio Junior 33	1 355
Feb	13	Ipatinga	W	4-1	CM	Luciano 32, Fabio Junior 3 48 83 89	701
	20	Funorte	W	2-1	CM	Camilo 8, Rodrigo 13	580
	27	Atlético MG	W	2-1	CM	Fabio Junior 2 20 72	17 036
Mar	12	Guarani	W	4-2	CM	Fabio Junior 3 57 61 88, Gabriel Santos 74	1 567
	18	América TO	L	1-3	CM	Fabio Junior 68	693
	27	Cruzeiro	L	2-3	CM	Leandro Ferreira 2 4 53	13 152
	2	Tupi	W	1-0	CM	Camilo 37	1 478
Apr	10	Democrata	W	4-3	CM	Leandro Ferreira 2 35 46, Fabio Junior 49, Irenio 63	652
	17	Villa Nova	D	2-2	CM	Eliandro 20, Fabio Junior 37	1 248
	24	Atlético MG	L	1-3	CMsf	Gabriel Santos 22	2 818
	30	Atlético MG	L	1-2	CMsf	Luciano 60	16 132
May	22	Bahia	W	2-1	SA	Rodriguinho 49, Alessandro 88	1 253
	29	Vasco	L	0-3	SA		2 626
	5	Inter	L	2-4	SA	Rodriguinho 56, Alessandro 84	4 541
Jun	11	Avaí	D	2-2	SA	Alessandro 37, Fabio Junior 55p	3 764
	19	Cruzeiro	L	1-3	SA	Fabio Junior 54	5 027
	29	Flamengo	L	2-3	SA	Alessandro 38, Anderson 45	7 475
	2	Santos	L	0-1	SA		5 912
	8	Palmeiras	D	1-1	SA	Alessandro 66	1 503
	10	Atlético MG	L	0-2	SA		7 379
Jul	17	Ceará	L	0-4	SA		11 179
	23	Figueirense	D	0-0	SA		752
	27	Grêmio	D	1-1	SA	Marcos Rocha 16	15 033
	31	Coritiba	L	1-3	SA	Kempes 56	732
	3	Corinthians	L	1-2	SA	Kempes 14	30 121
	7	Fluminense	W	3-0	SA	Rodriguinho 9, Alessandro 52, Marcos Rocha 77	2 782
Aug	14	Botafogo	L	2-4	SA	Alessandro 2, Rodriguinho 8	13 101
	19	São Paulo	L	1-2	SA	Kempes 88	2 636
	21	Atlético PR	D	2-2	SA	Kempes 28, Andre Dias 73	13 487
	27	Atlético GO	L	1-2	SA	Marcos Rocha 28	1 255
	2	Bahia	D	0-0	SA		9 807
	4	Vasco	W	4-1	SA	Andre Dias 2 19 85, Kempes 43, Marcos Rocha 58	2 644
Sep	7	Inter	L	2-4	SA	Andre Dias 25, Kempes 36	28 896
	10	Avaí	D	2-2	SA	Gilson 8, Andre Dias 27	734
	18	Cruzeiro	D	0-0	SA		8 915
	22	Santos	L	1-2	SA	Kempes 67	18 562
	24	Flamengo	L	1-2	SA	Kempes 29	9 445
	1	Palmeiras	D	1-1	SA	Kempes 45	9 285
	8	Atlético MG	D	0-0	SA		752
Oct	12	Ceará	W	4-1	SA	Fabio Junior 25, Rodriguinho 66, Gilson 79, Leo 90	939
	15	Figueirense	L	1-2	SA	Rodriguinho 37	7 421
	22	Grêmio	D	2-2	SA	Thiago Carleto 11, Anderson 86	829
	30	Coritiba	L	1-3	SA	Kempes 17	10 962
	6	Corinthians	W	2-1	SA	Fabio Junior 33, Amaral 87	37 034
	12	Fluminense	W	2-1	SA	Kempes 39, Alessandro 78	40 232
Nov	16	Botafogo	W	2-1	SA	Kempes 34, Fabio Junior 40	1 507
	19	São Paulo	L	1-3	SA	Alessandro 77	9 057
	27	Atlético PR	W	2-1	SA	Kempes 18, Gilson 85	841
Dc	4	Atlético GO	L	1-5	SA	OG 35	5 787

19th — Att: 91 798 • Av: 4831 • Arena do Jacaré 25 000

AMERICA SERIE A APPEARANCES/GOALS 2010-11

Goalkeepers Flavio 10 • Glaycon 1 • Neneca 27
Defenders Anderson 17+1/2 • Gabriel Santos 19+1/0 • Gilson 26/3 Marcos Rocha 30/4 • Micao 25/0 • Otavio 12+3/0 • Preto 3+1/0 Rodrigo 0+1/0 • Shcalon 5 i 2/0 • Thiago Carleto 11 i 4/1 Willian 17+1/0 • Everton 11/0
Midfield Alessandro 14+9/9 • Amaral 33/1 • Caleb 3/0 • Camilo 0+3/0 China 4+3/0 • Davi Ceara 0+1/0 • Dudu 21+3/0 • Fabricio Souza 3+6/0 • Glauber 7+2/0 • Irenio Soares 3+4/0 • Leandro Ferreira 21+6/0 • Luciano 2+6/0 • Netinho 1+8/0 Rodriguinho 26+10/6 • Ulisses 4+2/0
Forwards Eliandro 3+4/0 • Fabio Junior 22+8/5 • Kempes 23+9/13 Leo 6+8/1 • Andre Dias 8+2/5
Coach Mauro Fernandes • Antonio Lopes (12/07/2011) • Givanildo Oliveira (1/08/2011)

ATLETICO GOIANIENSE 2011

	Date	Opponent		Score		Scorers	Att
	17	S'ta Helena	W	3-2	CG	Marcao 47, Paulo Henrique 60, Diogo Campos 83	2 502
Jan	20	Ap'cidense	W	3-2	CG	Diogo Campos 66, Marcao 2 77 90	1 861
	23	Morrinhos	W	1-0	CG	Keninha 20	2 215
	27	Trindade	W	3-0	CG	Pituca 2 19 82, Josiel 64	833
	29	Goiás	L	0-1	CG		6 514
	2	Goianésia	W	3-0	CG	Felipe 64, Diogo Campos 78, Preto 91+	1 121
	5	Vila Nova	W	2-1	CG	Marcao 15, Gilson 73	11 156
Feb	13	CRAC	W	4-2	CG	Marcao 30, Felipe 60, Josiel 79, Marcio 94+	3 272
	20	Anapolina	L	0-1	CG		7 955
	24	Brusque	L	2-3	CBr1	Felipe 11, Marcao 66	1 866
	27	Morrinhos	W	4-0	CG	Preto 47, Marcao 2 55 78, Felipe 83	1 058
	3	Brusque	W	1-0	CBr1	Felipe 61	5 356
	9	Goianésia	W	3-1	CG	Marcao 34, Gilson 45, Felipe 72	1 567
	13	Goiás	W	2-0	CG	Josiel 5, Diogo Campos 86	11 752
	18	Coritiba	L	1-2	CBr2	Gilson 21	4 452
Mar	20	CRAC	W	2-1	CG	Marcao 26, Juninho 37	1 083
	24	Trindade	W	3-1	CG	Marcao 2p, Victor Ferraz 69, Diogo Campos 89	1 226
	27	Vila Nova	L	0-1	CG		7 152
	31	Coritiba	L	1-3	CBr2	Juninho 70	9 444
	5	Anapolina	L	2-3	CG	Juninho 2 10 62	2 779
	12	Ap'cidense	L	1-3	CG	Jairo 74	2 278
Apr	17	S'ta Helena	L	1-2	CG	Diogo Campos 45	4 030
	26	Anapolina	W	1-0	CGsf	Gilson 25	9 198
	30	Anapolina	W	4-2	CGsf	Marcao 3 14 82 85, Vitor Junior 28	9 253
	8	Goiás	D	1-1	CGf	Marcao 38	18 005
May	15	Goiás	D	1-1	CGf	Adriano Lara 12	21 663
	22	Coritiba	W	1-0	SA	Marcao 73	18 198
	29	Fluminense	L	0-1	SA		5 643
	5	Figueirense	L	0-2	SA		6 913
	12	Ceará	W	2-1	SA	Anselmo 2 26 74, Adriano 39, Bida 60	2 140
Jun	19	Atlético MG	D	2-2	SA	Marcao 31, Vitor Junior 81	15 106
	26	Vasco	L	0-1	SA		11 959
	30	Palmeiras	L	0-2	SA		9 450
	7	Botafogo	D	1-1	SA	Anselmo 15	13 649
	10	Corinthians	L	0-1	SA		19 150
	16	Avaí	L	0-1	SA		2 694
Jul	23	São Paulo	D	2-2	SA	Bida 44, Anselmo 69	23 487
	27	Cruzeiro	W	2-0	SA	Felipe 2 9 90	5 593
	31	Inter	D	0-0	SA		12 163
	5	Atlético PR	L	0-3	SA		3 050
	7	Bahia	L	1-2	SA	Juninho 48	12 147
	13	Santos	W	2-0	SA	Anselmo 69, Diogo Campos 79	11 668
Aug	19	Flamengo	W	1-4	SA	Pituca 13, Juninho 37, Anselmo 51, Diogo Campos 81	7 649
	21	Grêmio	W	1-0	SA	Diogo Campos 90	5 226
	27	América MG	W	1-2	SA	Juninho 2 70 77	1 255
	1	Coritiba	W	3-1	SA	Marcio 34, Agenor 63, Anselmo 90	3 146
	3	Fluminense	L	2-3	SA	Bida 10, Marcio 62	6 473
	8	Figueirense	D	1-1	SA	Agenor 14	2 514
Sep	11	Ceará	D	1-1	SA	Felipe 87	12 371
	17	América MG	W	1-0	SA	Vitor Junior 63	6 186
	23	Vasco	L	0-1	SA	Anselmo 23	14 576
	25	Palmeiras	D	1-1	SA	Thiago Feltri 81	12 422
	2	Botafogo	W	2-0	SA	Felipe 2 1 10	12 264
	9	Corinthians	L	0-3	SA		33 609
Oct	12	Avaí	D	2-2	SA	Anselmo 35, Vitor Junior 41	10 850
	16	São Paulo	W	3-0	SA	Gilson 26, Felipe 59, Anselmo 69	23 906
	23	Cruzeiro	L	2-3	SA	Thiago Feltri 16, Felipe 67	5 595
	30	Inter	L	0-1	SA		6 337
	6	Atlético PR	L	1-2	SA	Anselmo 26	11 200
	13	Bahia	L	0-1	SA		2 931
Nov	17	Santos	D	1-1	SA	Leonardo 37	18 044
	20	Flamengo	D	0-0	SA		37 828
	27	Grêmio	D	2-2	SA	Anselmo 25, Anderson 84	7 493
Dc	4	América MG	W	5-1	SA	Felipe 11, Marcio 15, Gilson 38, Anailson 71, Paulo Henrique 85	5 787

13th — Att: 180 444 • Av: 9497 (+20.3%) • Serra Dourada 50 049

ATLETICO GO SERIE A APPEARANCES/GOALS 2010-11

Goalkeepers Marcio 38/3 • Rafael 0+1 • Roberto 0+2
Defenders Adriano 12+2/1 • Anderson 34/1 • Gerson 0+1/0
Gilson 33/2 • Leonardo 8+6/1 • Paulo Henrique 1+6/1 • Rafael
Cruz 26+3/0 • Thiago Feltri 35/2 • Ernandes 13+9/0
Midfield Agenor 27+2/2 • Anailson 0+2/1 • Bida 33/3 • Elvis 0+2/0
Felipe Brisola 0+5/0 • Maurinho 9+2/0 • Pituca 28+1/1 • Preto 0+2/0
Ramalho 3/0 • Renato Augusto 0+3/0 • Thiaguinho 11+2/0 • Vitor
Junior 24+3/3 • Joilson 6+12/0 • Adriano Pimenta 0+2/0 • Dodo 0+2/0
Forwards Anselmo 34+1/12 • Diogo Campos 0+14/3 • Felipe 18+8/8
Juninho 15+8/4 • Marcao 8+10/2
Coach Rene Simoes • Paulo Cesar Gusmao 3/04/2011) • Helio dos
Anjos (12/08/2011)

ATLETICO MINEIRO (CONTD)

	2	Ceará	D 1-1	SA	Carlos Cesar [12]	14 174
	8	América MG	D 0-0	SA		752
Oct	13	Santos	W 2-1	SA	Rever [6], Magno Alves [58]	12 351
	16	Vasco	L 0-2	SA		15 269
	22	Fluminense	W 2-0	SA	Daniel Carvalho [10], Andre [45]	19 525
	30	Palmeiras	W 2-0	SA	Neto Berola [37], Fillipe Soutto [63]	17 119
Nov	5	Grêmio	W 2-0	SA	Andre [41], Marquinhos [76]	17 387
	12	Figueirense	L 1-2	SA	Werley [38]	10 151
	17	Coritiba	W 2-1	SA	Neto Berola [20], Leonardo Silva [79]	16 872
	20	Corinthians	L 1-2	SA	Leonardo Silva [55]	35 011
	27	Botafogo	W 4-0	SA	Daniel Carvalho [15], Andre 2 [25 77], Leonardo Silva [90]	18 281
Dc	4	Cruzeiro	L 1-6	SA	Rever [61]	18 850

15th Att: 267 635 • Av: 14 086 (+4.7%) • Arena do Jacaré 25 000

ATLETICO MG SERIE A APPEARANCES/GOALS 2010-11

Goalkeepers Giovanni 10 • Lee 0+1 • Renan Ribeiro 28
Defenders Eron 5+1/0 • Guilherme Santos 7+1/0 • Leandro 6/0
Leonardo Silva 32/6 • Lima 6+1/0 • Luiz Eduardo 0+1/0 • Patric 13/0
Rever 30/4 • Roger 2+1/0 • Werley 12+2/1 • Triginho 11+4/0
Carlos Cesar 10+2/1
Midfield Bernard 19+4/0 • Caio 9+1/0 • Dudu Cearense 6+7/3
Fillipe Soutto 25/2 • Gilberto 2+4/0 • Giovanni Augusto 7+3/0
Mancini 10+5/1 • Renan Oliveira 5+6/2 • Richarlyson 26+5/0
Serginho 23+5/0 • Toro 7+2/1 • Wendel 0+1/0 • Wesley 1+7/1
Pierre 19/0
Forwards Daniel Carvalho 21+3/4 • Guilherme 10+4/2
Jonatas Obina 5+5/2 • Magno Alves 23+8/7 • Marquinhos 0+5/0
Neto Berola 10+16/4 • Andre 17+5/7
Coach Dorival Junior • Cuca (8/08/2011)

ATLETICO MINEIRO 2011

Ja	30	Funorte	W 2-1	CM	Magno Alves [55], Diego Tardelli [78]	4 900
	6	Tupi	W 4-1	CM	Neto Berola 2 [46 81], Magno Alves [50 66]	7 271
Feb	12	Cruzeiro	W 4-3	CM	Diego Tardelli 3 [25 27 50], Neto Berola [71]	9 793
	20	Guarani	W 4-2	CM	Ricardinho 2 [25 29], Magno Alves [37], Neto Berola [39]	4 050
	24	Iape	W 3-2	CBr1	Renan Oliveira [6], Diego Tardelli [46], Ricardo Bueno [76]	12 709
	27	América MG	L 1-2	CM	Neto Berola [13]	17 036
	3	Iape	W 8-1	CBr1	Renan Oliveira 1 [21], Ricardinho [9], Jobson 2 [67 86], Neto Berola [77], Toro [79], Diego Tardelli [87]	5 433
Mar	13	Ipatinga	D 2-2	CM	Neto Berola [46], Renan Oliveira [77]	7 617
	20	Villa Nova	W 2-1	CM	Ricardo Bueno [63], OG [89]	9 745
	24	Uberaba	D 1-1	CM	Ricardo Bueno [48]	4 263
	1	Grêmio Pr.	L 1-2	CBr2	Magno Alves [34]	989
	3	Democrata	W 3-1	CM	Magno Alves [10], Rever [35], Neto Berola [78]	2 703
	7	Grêmio Pr.	D 0-0	CBr2		6 968
	10	Caldense	W 2-0	CM	Ricardo Bueno [47], Magno Alves [58]	4 980
Apr	17	América TO	W 7-1	CM	Magno Alves 3 [14 76 88], Mancini [22], Renan Oliveira 2 [36 55], Giovanni Augusto [56]	6 340
	24	América MG	W 3-1	CMsf	Patric [45], Neto Berola [55], Serginho Mineiro [70]	2 818
	30	América MG	W 2-1	CMsf	Magno Alves [64], Serginho Mineiro [67]	16 132
	8	Cruzeiro	W 2-1	CMf	Mancini [4], Patric [37]	17 729
May	15	Cruzeiro	L 0-2	CMf		17 384
	21	Atlético PR	W 3-0	SA	Toro [5], Magno Alves 2 [26 75]	13 597
	28	Avaí	W 3-1	SA	Leonardo Silva 2 [16 66], Rever [46]	4 551
	9	São Paulo	L 0-1	SA		17 397
Jun	12	Bahia	D 1-1	SA	Neto Berola [76]	18 889
	19	Atlético GO	D 2-2	SA	Renan Oliveira [76], Guilherme [85]	15 106
	25	Flamengo	L 1-4	SA	Dudu Cearense [52]	16 870
	1	Inter	L 0-4	SA		7 595
	7	Ceará	L 0-3	SA		10 941
	10	América MG	W 2-0	SA	Jonatas Obina [34], Neto Berola [70]	7 379
Jul	17	Santos	L 1-2	SA	Jonatas Obina [27]	4 717
	24	Vasco	L 1-2	SA	Magno Alves [42]	16 100
	27	Fluminense	W 1-0	SA	Andre [75]	16 100
	31	Palmeiras	L 2-3	SA	Magno Alves [16], Wesley [80]	9 983
	3	Grêmio	D 2-2	SA	Andre [52], Leonardo Silva [88]	10 725
	7	Figueirense	L 1-2	SA	Dudu Cearense [47]	15 689
	10	Botafogo	L 1-2	CSr1	Richarlyson [44]	
Aug	14	Coritiba	L 0-3	SA		16 328
	18	Corinthians	L 2-3	SA	Dudu Cearense [14], Guilherme [27]	11 167
	20	Botafogo	L 1-3	SA	Andre [90]	8 481
	23	Botafogo	L 0-1	CSr1		
	28	Cruzeiro	L 1-2	SA	Felipe Soutto [57]	16 720
	1	Atlético PR	W 1-0	SA	Mancini [70]	11 823
	3	Avaí	W 2-0	SA	OG [28], Daniel Carvalho [80]	9 761
	7	São Paulo	L 1-2	SA	Rever [11]	60 514
Sep	11	Bahia	W 2-0	SA	Magno Alves 2 [45 55]	10 991
	17	Atlético GO	W 1-0	SA		6 186
	22	Flamengo	D 1-1	SA	Daniel Carvalho [50]	13 849
	25	Inter	L 1-2	SA	Renan Oliveira [69]	16 198

ATLETICO PARANAENSE 2011

	16	Arapongas	L 1-2	CP	Paulinho [82]	9 985
	19	Corinthians	W 2-1	CP	OG [78], Madson [80]	1 021
Jan	22	Iraty	W 2-1	CP	Lucas 2 [57 62]	8 848
	27	Operário	L 0-1	CP		5 063
	30	Roma	W 4-2	CP	Paulo Baier 2 [18 70], Madson [50], Lucas [60]	8 223
	3	Cascavel	L 0-2	CP		1 454
	6	Paraná	W 5-1	CP	Paulo Baier 3 [15 20 22], Madson [65], Guerron [81]	11 236
Feb	10	Cianorte	W 4-2	CP	Vitor [44], Madson [48], Nieto [65], Paulo Baier [79]	9 670
	13	Paranavaí	W 3-2	CP	Claiton [5], Paulo Baier [68], Nieto [80]	1 549
	20	Coritiba	L 2-4	CP	Nieto 2 [45 47]	24 704
	24	Rio Branco	L 1-2	CBr1	Lucas [78]	10 000
	27	Rio Branco	W 2-0	CP	Heverton [34], Gabriel Valongo [79]	6 853
	2	Rio Branco	W 3-1	CBr1	Guerron [51], Lucas 2 [66 68]	9 620
	5	Arapongas	W 2-0	CP	Guerron [51], Paulo Baier [93+]	551
	10	Corinthians	D 1-1	CP	Kleberson [61]	8 879
Mar	13	Iraty	W 4-2	CP	Madson [51], Nieto [76], Guerron [79], Paulinho [84]	3 105
	16	Paulista	W 2-0	CBr2	Nieto 2 [25 61]	3 474
	19	Operário	L 0-2	CP		10 007
	24	Roma	W 3-2	CP	Guerron [8], Paulo Baier 2 [66 89]	2 130
	27	Cascavel	W 2-0	CP	Lucas 2 [58 71], Adailton [84]	7 498
	3	Paraná	W 3-2	CP	Madson 2 [58 71], Adailton [90]	5 484
	10	Cianorte	W 1-0	CP	Guerron [20]	1 372
	14	Bahia	D 1-1	CBr3	Guerron [45]	12 574
Apr	16	Paranavaí	W 2-1	CP	Adailton 2 [65 75]	7 424
	21	Bahia	W 5-0	CBr3	Paulo Baier 2 [22 40], Manoel [26], Rafael Santos [34], Adailton [51]	14 037
	24	Coritiba	L 0-3	CP		17 501
	30	Rio Branco	W 3-1	CP	Madson 2 [29 62], Paulinho [84]	555

ATLETICO PARANAENSE (CONTD)

Mo	Day	Opponent	Res	Score	Rnd	Scorers	Att
May	5	Vasco	D	2-2	CBqf	Guerron 51, Paulo Baier 88p	15 969
	12	Vasco	D	1-1	CBqf	Nieto 73	21 206
	21	Atlético MG	L	0-3	SA		13 597
	29	Grêmio	L	0-1	SA		15 841
Jun	4	Palmeiras	L	0-1	SA		10 372
	12	Flamengo	D	1-1	SA	Madson 60	20 022
	19	Figueirense	L	0-2	SA		10 315
	25	Bahia	L	0-2	SA		12 448
	1	Fluminense	L	1-3	SA	Edigar 86	5 114
	6	Inter	L	0-1	SA		12 094
Jul	10	Avaí	D	0-0	SA		10 054
	16	Vasco	L	1-2	SA	Kleberson 10	9 775
	23	Botafogo	W	2-1	SA	Santiago Garcia 2 41 74	12 714
	29	Ceará	L	1-2	SA	Madson 15	13 068
	31	Santos	W	3-2	SA	Cleber Santana 6, Manoel 9, Marcinho 90	20 461
	5	Atlético GO	W	3-0	SA	Fabricio 45, Manoel 73, Kleberson 79	3 050
	7	Corinthians	D	1-1	SA	Cleber Santana 35	25 335
Aug	10	Flamengo	L	0-1	CSr1		
	13	São Paulo	D	2-2	SA	Fransergio 20, Edigar 77	23 657
	17	Cruzeiro	W	2-1	SA	Marcinho 31, Cleber Santana 89	14 977
	21	América MG	D	2-2	SA	Marcinho 1, Edigar 25	13 487
	24	Flamengo	L	0-1	CSr1		
	27	Coritiba	D	1-1	SA	Edison 69	28 249
Sep	1	Atlético MG	L	0-1	SA		11 823
	4	Grêmio	L	0-4	SA		16 245
	8	Palmeiras	D	2-2	SA	Joffre Guerron 35, Marcinho 71	10 798
	11	Flamengo	W	2-1	SA	Heracles 39, Joffre Guerron 46	7 846
	18	Figueirense	D	0-0	SA		14 103
	22	Bahia	L	0-1	SA		14 439
	24	Fluminense	D	1-1	SA	Paulo Baier 63	11 010
Oct	2	Inter	W	2-0	SA	Federico Nieto 57 83	14 431
	9	Avaí	L	0-3	SA		8 531
	13	Vasco	D	2-2	SA	Paulo Baier 16, Joffre Guerron 23	10 813
	16	Botafogo	L	0-2	SA		23 372
	23	Ceará	W	1-0	SA	Paulo Baier 33	12 186
	29	Santos	L	1-4	SA	Joffre Guerron 51	16 679
	6	Atlético GO	W	2-1	SA	Federico Nieto 47 56	11 200
Nov	13	Corinthians	L	1-2	SA	Paulo Baier 48	37 157
	16	São Paulo	W	1-0	SA	Joffre Guerron 11	18 303
	20	Cruzeiro	D	1-1	SA	Marcinho 28	18 139
	27	América MG	L	1-2	SA	Paulo Baier 60	841
Dc	4	Coritiba	W	1-0	SA	Joffre Guerron 73	14 891

17th Att: 274 888 • Av: 14 468 (-10.1%) • Arena da Baixada 28 237

ATLETICO PR SERIE A APPEARANCES/GOALS 2010-11

Goalkeepers Marcio 6 • Renan Rocha 32
Defenders Fabricio 18+2/1 • Heracles 15/1 • Manoel 33/2
Paulinho 19/0 • Rafael Santos 13+1/0 • Romulo 5/0 • Wagner
Diniz 12+3/0 • Edilson 15+3/1 • Gustavo Araujo 13+4/0
Midfield Branquinho 4+13/0 • Cleber Santana 25+5/3 • Deivid 34/0 •
Fransergio 3+6/1 • Renan 9+2/0 • Jenison 0+1/0 • Kleberson 12+6/2 •
Madson 18+4/2 • Marcelo Oliveira 21/0 • Paulo Baier 20+2/5
Paulo Roberto 1/0 • Robston 2+3/0 • Victor Esquerdinha 0+2/0
Wendel 9+10/0 • Marcinho 21+4/5
Forwards Adailton 6+13/0 • Santiago Garcia URU 13+2/2 • Joffre
Guerron ECU 18+4/6 • Federico Nieto ARG 13+6/4 • Pablo 2+2/0
Edigar 4+8/3 • Rodriguinho 2+5/0
Coach Leandro Niehues • Geninho (22/02/2011) • Adilson Batista
(5/04/2011) • Renato Gaucho (4/07/2011) • Antonio Lopes (1/09/2011)

AVAI 2011

Mo	Day	Opponent	Res	Score	Rnd	Scorers	Att
Jan	15	Chap'ense	L	1-2	CC	Rafael Costa 42	3 802
	20	Brusque	L	0-3	CC		1 454
	23	Criciúma	L	0-2	CC		3 583
	27	Imbituba	L	0-1	CC		4 461
	30	Metropol'no	D	0-0	CC		2 448
	3	Joinville	W	2-1	CC	Rafael Coelho 36, Marquinhos 52	4 078
	6	Figueirense	D	2-2	CC	Rafael Coelho 11, William 53	18 307
	9	Marc'o Dias	W	2-1	CC	William 2 28 62	3 545
Feb	12	Concórdia	W	4-3	CC	Marquinhos 19, Estrada 66, William 80, Rafael Coelho 90	1 588
	24	Vilhena	W	3-0	CBr1	Estrada 4, William 2 64 77	1 001
	5	Chap'ense	L	0-2	CC		4 559
	7	Brusque	W	4-2	CC	Cristian 11, Julinho 37, Evando 79, Rafael Coelho 94+	3 765
	13	Criciúma	D	2-2	CC	Marcio Glad 28, Marquinhos 33	4 718
	17	Ipatinga	D	1-1	CBr2	Rafael Coelho 89	1 280
Mar	20	Imbituba	W	4-0	CC	William 2 20 27, Rafael Coelho 46, Marquinhos 55	1 460
	23	Metropol'no	W	3-1	CC	William 14, Maquinhos Gabriel 23, Gustavo 81	4 502
	27	Joinville	L	0-4	CC		5 490
	31	Ipatinga	W	4-1	CBr2	Rafael Coelho 3 13 34 72, Acleisson 65	4 148
Apr	3	Figueirense	L	0-1	CC		12 326
	10	Marc'o Dias	W	2-1	CC	Rafael Coelho 14, Marquinhos Gabriel 94+	1 647
	13	Botafogo	D	2-2	CBr3	William 13, Rafael Coelho 21	5 574
	17	Concórdia	W	4-0	CC	Fabiano 8, Marquinhos Gabriel 45, Mauricio Osmar 68, Peterson 81	4 513
	20	Botafogo	D	1-1	CBr3	William 87	7 209
	24	Figueirense	W	2-0	CCsf	William 14, Estrada 65	15 626
	1	Chap'ense	D	2-2	CCf	William 7, Rafael Coelho 26	10 059
	5	São Paulo	L	0-1	CBqf		20 815
May	13	São Paulo	W	3-1	CBqf	William 16, Bruno Silva 30, Marquinhos Gabriel 47	12 956
	19	Vasco	D	1-1	CBsf	Julinho 80	19 136
	21	Flamengo	L	0-4	SA		5 973
	26	Vasco	L	0-2	CBsf		15 868
	28	Atlético MG	L	1-3	SA	Fabio Santos 8	4 551
Jun	5	Santos	L	1-3	SA	Mauricio 90	4 109
	11	América MG	D	2-2	SA	Julinho 54, Cassio 90	3 764
	19	Palmeiras	L	0-5	SA		12 138
	26	Fluminense	L	0-1	SA		4 139
	29	Grêmio	D	2-2	SA	Gustavo Bastos 4, Rafael Coelho 53	10 346
Jul	6	Bahia	D	2-2	SA	Rafael Coelho 20, G'tavo Bastos 58	4 916
	10	Atlético PR	D	0-0	SA		10 045
	16	Atlético GO	W	0-1	SA	William Souza 12	2 694
	21	Inter	L	1-3	SA	William Souza 45	6 471
	27	Botafogo	L	1-2	SA	Dirceu 7	5 111
	31	Corinthians	W	3-2	SA	William Souza 49, R.Coelho 2 58 81	8 442
Aug	3	Ceará	W	3-0	SA	William Souza 18, Rafael Coelho 81, Cleverson 90	10 864
	7	São Paulo	L	1-2	SA	William Souza 60	11 107
	13	Cruzeiro	L	0-5	SA		6 642
	17	Vasco	L	0-2	SA		5 620
	21	Coritiba	D	0-0	SA		5 620
	28	Figueirense	W	3-2	SA	Lincoln 39, William Souza 2 60 87	17 933
Sep	1	Flamengo	D	3-2	SA	Robson 4, Lincoln 68, Rafael Coelho 71	12 692
	3	Atlético MG	L	0-2	SA		9 761
	7	Santos	L	1-2	SA	William Souza 33	5 630
	10	América MG	D	2-2	SA	William Souza 77, Dirceu 82	734
	18	Palmeiras	D	1-1	SA	Batista 5	8 312
	22	Fluminense	L	1-3	SA	William Souza 8	6 689
	25	Grêmio	L	1-2	SA	Pedr Ken 70	6 542
Oct	1	Bahia	L	2-3	SA	Fernandinho 46, Pedro Ken 53	16 697
	8	Atlético PR	W	3-0	SA	Lincoln 9, Gian 32, Rafael Coelho 45	8 531
	12	Atlético GO	D	2-2	SA	William Souza 2 17 90	10 850
	16	Inter	L	2-4	SA	Robson 8, William Souza 72	20 788
	22	Botafogo	W	3-2	SA	Robson 16, Cleverson 18, Robert 85	7 784
	30	Corinthians	L	1-2	SA	Robson 13	36 700
Nov	6	Ceará	L	1-2	SA	William Souza 60	6 342
	12	São Paulo	L	1-2	SA		11 134
	16	Cruzeiro	D	0-0	SA		2 842
	19	Vasco	L	0-2	SA		19 834
	27	Coritiba	L	0-1	SA		15 680
Dc	4	Figueirense	D	1-1	SA	Diogo Orlando 44	6 109

20th Att: 133 371 • Av: 7020 (-29.4%) • Ressacada 19 000

AVAI SERIE A APPEARANCES/GOALS 2010-11

Goalkeepers Aleksander 5 • Rafael Santos 1 • Moretto 3 • Renan 2
Defenders Cassio 9/1 • Daniel 16+3/0 • George Lucas 4/0 • Gian 12/1 • Gustavo 0+1/0 • Gustavo Bastos 19/2 • Julinho 5/1 • Romano 16+1/0 • Welton Felipe 13+1/0 • Arlan 15+1/0 • Fernandinho 11/1 • Cacapa 6/0 • Para 3+2/0 • Leo Campos 1/0 • Thiago Sales 0+1/0 **Midfield** Acleison 8+4/0 • Batista 12+6/1 • Bruno 31/0 • Cleverson 18+10/2 • Dinelson 1+2/0 • Diogo Orlando 14+6/1 • Dirceu 17/2 • Jonathan Estrada COL 4+7/0 • Fabiano 8+9/0 • Marcinho Guerreiro 4/0 • Mauricio 0+9/1 • Pedro Ken 25+1/2 • Robson 21+8/4 • Lincoln 17/3 • Junior Urso 11/0 • Leandro Lima 3+6/0 • Marcos Paulo 3+4/0 • Caique 2+4/0 **Forwards** Fabio Santos 3+5/1 • Felipe 28/0 • Marquinhos 3+2/0 • Rafael Coelho 15+9/7 • William Souza 28+1/14 • Dieguinho 0+4/0 • Anderson Lessa 0+3/0 • Robert 0+3/1 • Jhonny Dias 0+1/0 **Coach** Vagner Benazzi • Silas (20/02/2011) • Alexandre Gallo (14/06/2011) • Toninho Cecilio (22/08/2011) • Edson Neguinho (14/11/2011)

BAHIA (CONTD)

	2	América MG	D	0-0	SA		9 807
Sep	4	Flamengo	W	3-1	SA	Titi [22], Dodo [33], Souza [45]	9 755
	9	Grêmio	L	1-2	SA	Souza [58]	17 977
	11	Atlético MG	L	0-2	SA		10 991
	18	Fluminense	W	3-0	SA	Souza 2 [28 71], OG [58]	15 356
	22	Atlético PR	W	1-0	SA	Jose Junior [75]	14 439
	25	Corinthians	L	0-1	SA		23 765
Oct	1	Avai	W	3-2	SA	Jose Junior 2 [36 77], Lulinha [81]	16 697
	8	Botafogo	D	2-2	SA	Souza 2 [28 60]	6 765
	13	Cruzeiro	D	0-0	SA		13 904
	16	Coritiba	D	0-0	SA		11 896
	23	Vasco	L	0-2	SA		32 157
	30	Figueirense	L	1-2	SA	Diones [55]	9 387
Nov	5	São Paulo	W	4-3	SA	Souza [46], Lulinha [68], Fahel [74], OG [83]	31 230
	13	Atlético GO	W	1-0	SA	Souza [10]	2 931
	16	Inter	L	0-1	SA		8 541
	20	Palmeiras	L	0-2	SA		32 157
	27	Santos	D	1-1	SA	Souza [8]	12 052
Dc	4	Ceará	W	2-1	SA	Camacho [13], Lulinha [43]	32 157
14th					Att: 434 670 • Av: 22 877 • Pituaçu 32 179	

BAHIA SERIE A APPEARANCES/GOALS 2010-11

Goalkeepers Marcelo Lomba 33 • Omar 1 • Tiago 4+1
Defenders Avine 18+1/1 • Danny Morais 6+4/0 • Diego Jussani 1+1/0 • Dodo 15/1 • Jancarlos 11/0 • Marcos 20+6/0 • Paulo Miranda 31+1/1 • Thiego 5/0 • Titi 32/2 **Midfield** Boquita 0+1/0 • Camacho 9+3/1 • Carlos Alberto 17+3/0 • Diones 17+1/1 • Fahel 34/3 • Helder 12/6 • Jones 9+10/1 • Lulinha 15+14/5 • Magno 3/0 • Maranhao 3+13/0 • Marcone 19/2 • Nikao 0+8/0 • Ricardinho 13+8/0 • Zezinho 0+1/0 • Fabinho 20+2/0 **Forwards** Gabriel 11+7/0 • Jobson 15/6 • Jose Junior 13+14/5 • Rafael 0+4/0 • Souza 21/11 • Reinaldo 10+7/2 **Coach** Rogerio Lourenco • Chiquinho (8/02/2011) • Vagner Benazzi (18/02/2011) • Rene Simoes (14/04/2011) • Joel Santana (4/09/2011)

BAHIA 2011

Jan	16	Serrano	L	1-2	TB	Jael [15]	5 040
	23	Feirense	W	2-0	TB	Camacho [83], Avine [86]	5 159
	27	Ipitanga	D	3-3	TB	Jael [3p], Camacho [25], Maricio [88]	2 247
	30	Fluminense	L	1-2	TB	Camacho [24]	4 433
Feb	6	Vitória	L	0-3	TB		14 836
	9	Camaçari	W	2-0	TB	Souza [36p], Maranhao [73]	3 688
	13	Camaçari	L	2-3	TB	Souza [17], Jones Carioca [49]	936
	17	S.Domingos	D	0-0	CBr1		2 005
	20	Vitória	W	2-0	TB	Marcone [44], Avine [73p]	14 149
	24	S.Domingos	W	5-1	CBr1	Marcos 2 [3 50], Ramon [37], Rafael 2 [52 66]	7 754
	27	Fluminense	W	4-0	TB	Marcos [2], Jones Carioca [39], Rafael [53], Helder [82]	9 593
Mar	2	Ipitanga	W	3-0	TB	Ramon [52], Bruno Paulo [58], Moreno [72p]	6 776
	10	Feirense	D	0-0	TB		5 288
	13	Serrano	W	1-0	TB	Rafael [48]	8 327
	20	V.Conquista	D	2-2	TB	Marcos [50], Ramon [85]	6 610
	25	Alagoinhas	W	1-0	TB	Rafael [49]	5 084
	27	B. de Feira	W	3-0	TB	Jones Carioca [4], Dodo [35], Robert [59]	5 864
	31	Paysandu	D	0-0	CBr2		14 637
Apr	3	B. de Feira	L	0-1	TB		5 750
	7	Paysandu	W	2-1	CBr2	Souza 2 [31p 42]	15 321
	10	Alagoinhas	L	0-1	TB		5 547
	14	Atlético PR	D	1-1	CBr3	Camacho [83]	12 574
	17	V.Conquista	W	4-0	TB	Mauricio [12], Souza 2 [69 76], Rafael [79]	7 442
	21	Atlético PR	L	0-5	CBr3		14 037
	24	Vitória	L	0-1	TBsf		21 458
May	1	Vitória	W	3-2	TBsf	Marcone 2 [2 46], Souza [92+p]	20 534
	22	América MG	L	1-2	SA	Souza [21]	1 253
	29	Flamengo	D	3-3	SA	Lulinha [16], Jobson 2 [37 90]	32 157
Jun	5	Grêmio	L	0-2	SA		15 835
	12	Atlético MG	D	1-1	SA	Souza [51]	18 889
	18	Fluminense	W	1-0	SA	Jobson [90]	6 827
	25	Atlético PR	W	2-0	SA	Marcone [65], Lulinha [87]	12 448
	30	Corinthians	L	0-1	SA		32 157
Jul	6	Avai	D	2-2	SA	Jose Junior [24], Paulo Miranda [26]	4 916
	10	Botafogo	D	1-1	SA	Fahel [78]	32 157
	17	Cruzeiro	L	1-2	SA	Jobson [14]	6 666
	24	Coritiba	D	0-0	SA		21 151
	28	Vasco	D	1-1	SA	Reinaldo [4]	18 873
	31	Figueirense	W	3-1	SA	Reinaldo [42], Avine [72], Jones [90]	16 735
Aug	5	São Paulo	L	0-3	SA		11 262
	7	Atlético GO	W	2-1	SA	Jobson [27], Fahel [73]	12 147
	14	Inter	D	1-1	SA	Jobson [78]	21 239
	19	Palmeiras	D	1-1	SA	Titi [67]	6 266
	21	Santos	L	1-2	SA	Jose Junior [30]	32 157
	28	Ceará	L	0-3	SA		18 923

BOTAFOGO 2011

	20	D de Caxias	W	2-1	TG	Abreu [78p], Caio [82]	19 206
	23	Cabofriense	W	5-0	TG	OG 2 [24 29], Renata Caja [75], Caio [80], Antonio Carlos [89]	3 291
	27	Madureira	W	4-1	TG	Herrera [15], Abreu [43], Alessandro [81], Caio [88]	2 536
	29	Olaria	W	3-1	TG	Renato Caja [1], Abreu 2 [53 59]	5 812
	2	Bangu	D	1-1	TG	Abreu [25]	5 635
Feb	6	Fluminense	W	3-2	TG	Renato Caja [23], Abreu [56], Herrera [63]	16 759
	13	Macaé	D	1-1	TG	Renato Caja [48]	6 229
	20	Flamengo	D	1-1	TGsf	Abreu [48]. L 1-3p	26 854
	23	River Plate	L	0-1	CBr1		10 497
Mar	2	River Plate	W	1-0	CBr1	OG [41]. W 4-1p	3 901
	5	V Redonda	W	4-2	TR	Herrera [4], Caio [19], Rodrigo Mancha [46], Alex [57]	3 219
	9	Nova Iguaçu	W	1-0	TR	Everton [10]	2 984
	12	Americano	W	4-0	TR	Herrera 2 [14 69], Abreu [27], Joao Filipe [50]	4 044
	20	Vasco	L	0-2	TR		31 267
	26	Boavista	D	0-0	TR		2 108
	30	Parana	W	2-1	CBr2	Antonio Carlos [16], Willian [47]	4 490
Apr	3	Resende	D	1-1	TR	Antonio Carlos [75]	4 733
	6	Parana	W	3-0	CBr2	Abreu 2 [29 55], Caio [88p]	6 014
	10	Flamengo	W	2-0	TR		21 422
	13	Avaí	D	2-2	CBr3	Herrera [23], Abreu [44]	5 574
	17	América RJ	W	3-1	TR	Lucas 2 [1 81], Abreu [55]	1 558
	20	Avaí	L	0-1	CBr3	Abreu [72]	7 209
	23	Boavista	L	2-5	TR	Jairo [9], Vitinho [20]	900

BOTAFOGO (CONTD)

	Date	Opponent	Res	Comp	Scorers	Att
May	22	Palmeiras	L 0-1	SA		13 705
	28	Santos	W 1-0	SA	Fabio Ferreira 36	8 662
Jun	4	Ceará	D 2-2	SA	Elkeson 28, Antonio Carlos 72	9 455
	12	Coritiba	W 3-1	SA	Maicosuel 17, Elkeson 38, Alex 90	8 390
	19	Flamengo	D 0-0	SA		15 832
	26	Grêmio	W 2-1	SA	Marcelo Mattos 71, Elkeson 82	13 983
	30	São Paulo	W 0-2	SA	Elkeson 37, Herrera 50	8 361
Jul	7	Atlético GO	D 1-1	SA	Herrera 4	13 649
	10	Bahia	D 1-1	SA	Elkeson 30	32 157
	21	Corinthians	L 0-2	SA		8 128
	23	Atlético PR	L 1-2	SA	Alex 88	12 714
	27	Avaí	W 2-1	SA	Maicosuel 28, Herrera 38	5 111
	30	Cruzeiro	W 1-0	SA	Abreu 56	7 821
Aug	3	Figueirense	L 0-2	SA		8 965
	7	Vasco	W 4-0	SA	Antonio Carlos 10, Abreu 2 28 40, Herrera 90	21 238
	11	Atlético MG	W 2-1	CSr1	Herrera 6, Maicosuel 38	
	14	América MG	W 4-2	SA	Elkeson 31, Antonio Carlos 63, Alex 2 77 79	13 101
	18	Inter	L 0-1	SA		11 080
	20	Atlético MG	W 3-1	SA	Elkeson 17, Felipe Menezes 2 35 55	8 481
	24	Atlético MG	W 1-0	CSr1	Herrera 45	
Sep	27	Fluminense	W 2-1	SA	Elkeson 57, Lucas 64	22 762
	1	Palmeiras	W 3-1	SA	Herrera 3, Gustavo 23, Maicosuel 63	8 352
	4	Ceará	W 4-0	SA	Herrera 2 5 58, Abreu 73, Cidinho 83	36 995
	11	Coritiba	L 0-5	SA		17 142
	18	Flamengo	D 1-1	SA	Abreu 26	20 805
	23	Grêmio	W 1-0	SA	Abreu 67	17 324
	25	São Paulo	D 2-2	SA	Abreu 2 24 39	26 026
	30	Santa Fe	D 1-1	CSr2	Caio 66	
Oct	2	Atlético GO	L 0-2	SA		12 264
	8	Bahia	D 2-2	SA	Alex 55, Caio 60	6 765
	12	Corinthians	W 2-0	SA	Abreu 13, Maicosuel 34	34 593
	16	Atlético PR	W 2-0	SA	Antonio Carlos 17, Abreu 80	23 372
	19	Santos	L 0-2	SA		5 770
	22	Avaí	L 2-3	SA	Abreu 10, Renato 63	7 784
	26	Santa Fe	L 1-4	CSr2	Alexandre Oliveira 86	
	29	Cruzeiro	W 1-0	SA	Abreu 54	12 397
Nov	5	Figueirense	L 0-1	SA		21 104
	13	Vasco	L 0-2	SA		33 778
	16	América MG	L 1-2	SA	Abreu 63	1 507
	20	Inter	L 1-2	SA	Felipe Menezes 76	7 840
	27	Atlético MG	L 0-4	SA		18 281
Dc	4	Fluminense	D 1-1	SA	Felipe Menezes 11	4 790

9th Att: 269 189 • Av: 14 168 (-12.5%) • Engenhão 46 931

BOTAFOGO SERIE A APPEARANCES/GOALS 2010-11
Goalkeepers Jefferson 30 • Renan 8
Defenders Alessandro 21+3/0 • Antonio Carlos 32/4 • Bruno Cortes 28/0 • Fabio Ferreira 35/1 • Joao Filipe 1/0 • Lucas 17+4/1 Marcio Azevedo 7+2/0 • Gustavo 9+2/1
Midfield Araruama 1/0 • Egidio Arevalo URU 1/0 • Bruno 1+4/0 Cidinho 0+15/1 • Elkeson 34+1/8 • Everton 10+7/0 • Leo 3+5/0 Lucas Zen 12+6/0 • Maicosuel 35/4 • Marcelo Mattos 32/1 Renato 28/1 • Somalia 3+2/0 • Thiago Galhardo 2+9/0 Felipe Menezes 9+13/4
Forwards Sebastian Abreu URU 23/13 • Alex 4+9/5 • Caio 3+17/1 German Herrera ARG 27+5/7 • Willian 0+1/0 • Alexandre Oliveira 2+4/0
Coach Joel Santana • Caio Junior (23/03/2011) • Flavio Tenius (17/11/2011)

CEARA 2011

	Date	Opponent	Res	Comp	Scorers	Att
Jan	13	Limoeiro	W 1-0	CC1	Washington 86	10 613
	16	Horizonte	W 2+1	CC1	Luizinho 21, Clodoaldo 40	4 202
	19	Guarani/J	D 1-1	CC1	Washington 87	5 246
	23	Quixadá	W 1-0	CC1	Marcelo Nicacio 57	15 654
	27	Crato	W 1-0	CC1	Iarley 54	1 326
	30	Fortaleza	W 2-1	CC1	Iarley 70, Geraldo 77	29 935
Feb	3	Icasa	W 2-0	CC1	OG 22, Eusebio 30	1 099
	6	Ferroviário	W 3-1	CC1	Junior Pipoca 2 49 68, Sergio Mota 66	14 428
	10	Itapipoca	W 5-1	CC1	Junior Pipoca 30, Boiadeiro 31, Geraldo 52, M. Nicacio 2 87p 91+	1 500
	13	Tiradentes	W 2-0	CC1	Geraldo 11, Junior Pipoca 21	9 656
	20	Guarani/S	D 2-2	CC1	Marcelo Nicacio 63, Washington 80	3 789

CEARA (CONTD)

	Date	Opponent	Res	Comp	Scorers	Att
Feb	24	Cuiabá	W 2-0	CBr1	Iarely 1, Eusebio 79	409
	27	Horizonte	W 4-0	CCsf	Junior Pipoca 30, Iarley 56, Michel 70, Marcelo Nicacio 90	16 460
Mar	3	Fortaleza	W 1-0	CCf	Osvaldo 87	44 766
	10	Limoeiro	W 4-1	CC2	Marcelo Nicacio 2 57 59, Sergio Mota 85, Boiadeiro 90	776
	12	Horizonte	W 4-2	CC2	Michel 19, Geraldo 37, Washington 83, Osvaldo 85	8 736
	17	Brasiliense	D 0-0	CBr2		5 109
	20	Guarani/J	L 0-1	CC2		1 733
	24	Quixadá	W 2-1	CC2	Thiago Humberto 44, Washington 83	1 347
	27	Fortaleza	L 0-1	CC2		23 304
	31	Brasiliense	W 2-1	CBr2	Fabricio 27, Marcelo Nicacio 93+	32 179
Apr	2	Crato	W 4-0	CC2	Th. Humberto 29, Washington 40, Marcelo Nicacio 49, Geovane 91+	3 876
	7	Icasa	W 4-2	CC2	Marcelo Nicacio 2 3 21, Thiago Humberto 33, Geraldo 80	4 084
	10	Ferroviário	W 5-0	CC2	Thiago Humberto 17, Marcelo Nicacio 2 21 45, Iarley 59, Washington 75	4 253
	14	Tiradentes	W 1-0	CC2	Thiago Humberto 10	1 277
	17	Itapipoca	W 1-0	CC2	Marcelo Nicacio 32	5 805
	22	Grêmio Pr	W 2-1	CBr3	Geraldo 56p, Washington 89	7 626
	24	Guarany/S	L 2-3	CC2	Geovane 5, Murilo 44	BCD
	27	Grêmio Pr	W 2-1	CBr3	Iarley 1, Joao Marcos 24	4 282
May	1	Guarany/S	W 1-0	CCsf	Marcelo Nicacio 45	6 096
	6	Flamengo	W 2-1	CBqf	Marcelo Nicacio 43, Geraldo 66	17 127
	8	Guarani/J	W 5-0	CCf	Thiago Humberto 2 15 48, Marcelo Nicacio 2 35 38, Osvaldo 58	11 459
	12	Flamengo	D 2-2	CBqf	Washington 2 35 41	12 936
	19	Coritiba	D 0-0	CBsf		12 101
	21	Vasco	L 1-3	SA	Cleber 66	9 422
	26	Coritiba	L 0-1	CBsf		27 317
	28	Inter	W 1-0	SA	Iarley	15 412
Jun	4	Botafogo	D 2-2	SA	Osvaldo 35, Michel 61	9 455
	12	Atlético GO	L 1-4	SA	Thiago Humberto 23	2 140
	15	São Paulo	L 0-2	SA		13 000
	26	Palmeiras	W 2-0	SA	Washington 8, Th. Humberto 45	13 000
	30	Coritiba	L 1-3	SA	Washington 56	10 799
Jul	7	Atlético MG	W 3-0	SA	Marcelo Nicacio 2, Boiadeiro 78, Osvaldo 83	10 941
	10	Figueirense	D 1-1	SA	Washington 2	8 527
	17	América MG	W 4-0	SA	Fabricio 32, Washington 2 42 70, Felipe Azevedo 82	11 179
	24	Flamengo	D 1-1	SA	Felipe Azevedo 80	6 154
	29	Atlético PR	W 2-1	SA	Marcelo Nicacio 2 82 90	13 068
	31	Fluminense	L 0-4	SA		6 850
Aug	3	Avaí	L 0-3	SA		10 864
	7	Santos	L 0-1	SA		10 105
	10	São Paulo	L 2-1	CSr1	Rudnei 45, Marcelo Nicacio 90	
	14	Corinthians	D 2-2	SA	Osvaldo 29, Rudnei 84	26 762
	17	Grêmio	W 3-0	SA	Eusebio 34, Ma. Nicacio 2 47 71	11 824
	20	Cruzeiro	L 0-1	SA		6 478
		São Paulo	L 0-3	CSr1		
	28	Bahia	W 3-0	SA	Thiago Humberto 16, Felipe Azevedo 80, Edmilson 90	18 923
	31	Vasco	L 1-3	SA	Washington 64	5 428
Sep	4	Inter	D 1-1	SA	Washington 36	11 732
	7	Botafogo	L 0-4	SA		36 995
	11	Atlético GO	D 1-1	SA	Edigo 37	12 371
	17	São Paulo	L 0-4	SA		23 681
	23	Palmeiras	L 0-1	SA		6 621
	25	Coritiba	W 3-2	SA	Roger 2 7 68, Edmilson 39	10 133
Oct	3	Atlético MG	D 1-1	SA	Leandro Chaves 37	14 174
	9	Figueirense	D 1-1	SA	Washington 45	13 617
	12	América MG	L 1-4	SA	Felipe Azevedo 83	939
	15	Flamengo	L 0-1	SA		13 061
	23	Atlético PR	L 0-1	SA		12 186
	29	Fluminense	L 1-2	SA	Felipe Azevedo 7	17 554
Nov	6	Avaí	W 2-1	SA	Thiago Humberto 15, Felipe Azevedo 57	6 342
	13	Santos	L 2-3	SA	Felipe Azevedo 24, Osvaldo 36	15 406
	16	Corinthians	L 0-1	SA		17 532
	19	Grêmio	W 3-1	SA	Felipe Azevedo 3 30 49 58	7 130
	20	Cruzeiro	D 2-2	SA	Osvaldo 20, Daniel Marques 82	17 331
Dc	4	Bahia	L 1-2	SA	Felipe Azevedo 45	32 157

18th Att: 256 413 • Av: 13 495 (-43.1%) • Presidente Vargas 20 600

CEARA SERIE A APPEARANCES/GOALS 2010-11

Goalkeepers Adilson 1 • Diego 14+1 • Fernando Henrique 23
Defenders Anderson Luis 4+1/0 • Boiadeiro 22+4/1 • Cleber 2+1/1
Diego Macedo 2+1/0 • Diego Sacoman 12/0 • Egidio 7+5/1
Erivelton 8/0 • Ernandes 1/0 • Eusebio 17+3/1 • Fabricio 32/1
Murilo 4/0 • Patrick 1+2/0 • Vicente 27/0 • Edmilson 5+6/2
Daniel Marques 10/1 • Thiago Matias 6+1/0
Midfield Careca 3/0 • Diguinho 0+2/0 • Felipe Azevedo 10+19/11
Geraldo 1+4/0 • Heleno 29+2/0 • Joao Marcos 26/0 • Michel 31/1
Rudnei 12+7/1 • Thiago Humberto 25+2/4 • Leandro Chaves 4+5/1
Enrico 2+6/0 • Juca 5/0 • Paulinho 0+2/0
Forwards Iarley 3+3/1 • Marcelo Nicacio 10+11/5 • Osvaldo 34+2/5
Sinho 2+4/0 • Washington 14+14/8 • Roger 8+2/2 • Jose Junior 1+1/1
Preto 0+1/0
Coach Dimas Filgueiras • Vagner Mancini (1/04/2011) • Estevam
Soares (14/09/2011) • Dimas Filgueiras (24/10/2011)

CORINTHIANS (CONTD)

	2 Vasco	D	2-2	SA	Alex [20], Danilo [66]	22 855
	9 Atlético GO	W	3-0	SA	Leandro Castan [8], Willian [37], Alex [42]	33 609
Oct	13 Botafogo	L	0-2	SA		34 593
	16 Cruzeiro	W	1-0	SA	Paulinho [66]	17 004
	23 Inter	D	1-1	SA	Alex [90]	38 072
	30 Avaí	W	2-1	SA	Emerson [61], Liedson [77]	36 700
	6 América MG	L	1-2	SA	Chicao [45p]	37 034
	13 Atlético PR	W	2-1	SA	Paulinho [2], Emerson [5]	37 157
Nov	16 Ceará	W	1-0	SA	Luis Ramirez [81]	17 532
	20 Atlético MG	W	2-1	SA	Liedson [77], Adriano [90]	35 011
	27 Figueirense	W	1-0	SA	Liedson [69]	17 254
Dc	4 Palmeiras	D	0-0	SA		36 708

1st Att: 569 061 • Av: 29 951 (+5.9%) • Pacaembu 37 952

CORINTHIANS SERIE A APPEARANCES/GOALS 2010-11

Goalkeepers Danilo Fernandes 2 • Julio Cesar 33 • Renan 3
Defenders Alessandro 22/0 • Chicao 21+1/4 • Fabio Santos 26+1/0
Leandro Castan 35/1 • Paulo Andre 15+1/0 • Wallace 8+8/0
Weldinho 17+9/0 • Ramon 9/1
Midfield Alex 19+9/6 • Danilo 31+5/3 • Edenilson 4+22/0
Moradei 4+5/0 • Morais 2+9/0 • Paulinho 35/8 • Ralf 33/1
Luis Ramirez PER 1+5/1
Forwards Adriano 0+4/1 • Elias Fernandes 0+4/0
Emerson QAT 15+13/6 • Jorge Henrique 23+8/3
Liedson POR 27+1/12 • Taubate 0+1/0 • Willian 33+3/6
Coach Tite

CORINTHIANS 2011

	16 Portuguesa	W	2-0	CP	Paulinho [11], Roberto Carlos [19]	22 472
	20 Bragantino	D	1-1	CP	Jorge Henrique [37]	13 442
Jan	23 Noroeste	D	1-1	CP	Dentinho [40]	15 443
	27 Dep Tolima	D	0-0	CLpr		
	30 S. Bernardo	D	2-2	CP	Danilo [39], Ramirez [80]	15 159
	3 Dep Tolima	L	0-2	CLpr		
	6 Palmeiras	W	1-0	CP	Alessandro [82]	23 714
	10 Ituano	W	4-0	CP	Ramirez [2], Chicao [21], Liedson 2 [75 91+]	6 594
Feb	13 Paulista	D	0-0	CP		8 770
	17 Mogi Mirim	W	2-0	CP	Liedson 2 [71 86]	7 248
	20 Santos	W	3-1	CP	Fabio Santos 2 [23 60], Liedson [86]	19 448
	26 Grêmio Pr	W	4-0	CP	Fabio Santos [13p], Liedson 2 [21 87], Dentinho [28]	15 783
	5 Linense	W	2-0	CP	OG [35], Liedson [65]	6 234
	10 Ponte Preta	L	0-1	CP		12 126
Mar	13 Mirassol	W	3-2	CP	Willian 2 [47 65], Bruno Cesar [91+]	10 990
	20 Americana	W	1-0	CP	Liedson [9]	16 673
	24 Oeste	W	3-0	CP	Paulinho [35], Liedson [49], Dentinho [73]	8 600
	27 São Paulo	L	1-2	CP	Dentinho [67]	17 633
	3 BotafogoRP	D	0-0	CP		15 446
Apr	10 S. Caetano	L	1-2	CP	Paulinho [80]	17 260
	17 SantoAndré	W	2-0	CP	Paulo Andre [21], Edno [88]	4 352
	23 Oeste	W	2-1	CPqf	Liedson [9], Willian [64]	28 025
	1 Palmeiras	D	1-1	CPsf	Willian [64]. W 6-5p	33 861
	8 Santos	D	0-0	CPf		34 547
May	15 Santos	L	1-2	CPf	Morais [86]	14 322
	22 Grêmio	W	2-1	SA	Chicao [65], Liedson [72]	22 147
	29 Coritiba	W	2-1	SA	Paulinho [4], Danilo [80]	17 096
	5 Flamengo	D	1-1	SA	Willian [18]	42 000
Jun	12 Fluminense	W	2-0	SA	Willian 2 [6 30]	18 400
	26 São Paulo	W	5-0	SA	Danilo [47], Liedson 3 [54 61 79], Jorge Henrique [83]	30 351
	30 Bahia	W	1-0	SA	Chicao [15]	32 157
	7 Vasco	W	2-1	SA	Ralf [22], Paulinho [42]	28 453
	10 Atlético GO	W	1-0	SA	Willian [70]	19 150
Jul	15 Inter	W	1-0	SA	Willian [76]	33 329
	21 Botafogo	W	2-0	SA	Liedson [43], Paulinho [90]	8 128
	24 Cruzeiro	L	0-1	SA		34 462
	31 Avaí	L	2-3	SA	Emerson [31], Jorge Henrique [90]	8 442
	3 América MG	W	2-1	SA	Jorge Henrique [1], Paulinho [67]	30 121
	7 Atlético PR	D	1-1	SA	Alex [47]	25 335
	11 Santos	D	0-0	SA		9 714
	14 Ceará	D	2-2	SA	Paulinho [24], Alex [30]	26 762
Aug	18 Atlético MG	W	3-2	SA	Emerson [49], Alex [53], Liedson [75]	11 167
	20 Figueirense	L	0-2	SA		26 256
	28 Palmeiras	L	1-2	SA	Emerson [18]	36 299
	31 Grêmio	W	3-2	SA	Chicao [18p], Paulinho [65], Ramon [67]	16 588
	4 Coritiba	L	0-1	SA		29 248
	9 Flamengo	W	2-1	SA	Liedson 2 [62 89]	35 392
Sep	11 Fluminense	L	0-1	SA		26 979
	18 Santos	L	1-3	SA	Liedson [12]	34 308
	22 São Paulo	D	0-0	SA		44 950
	25 Bahia	W	1-0	SA	Emerson [57]	23 765

CORITIBA 2011

	16 Opérário PR	W	1-0	CP	Marcos Aurelio [9]	7 025
	20 Paranavaí	W	3-1	CP	Pereira [31], Marcos Aurelio 2 [38 81]	9 712
Jan	23 Paraná	D	1-1	CP	Eltinho [29]	3 495
	27 Cascavel	W	1-0	CP	Davi [57]	9 961
	30 Arapongas	D	1-1	CP	Bill [69]	6 956
	3 Iraty	W	5-0	CP	Rafinha [2], Bill [13], Davi [18], Geraldo [80], Marcos Aurelio [90]	9 919
	6 Rio Branco	W	4-1	CP	Bill 2 [14 69], Pereira [45], Anderson Aquino [81]	3 152
	10 Corinthians	W	2-1	CP	Davi [13], Bill [35]	1 279
Feb	13 Roma	W	3-0	CP	Rafinha [4], Leandro Donizete [38], OG [48]	9 147
	16 Ypiranga	W	1-0	CBr1	Jonas [21]	1 743
	20 Atlético PR	W	4-2	CP	Bill [18], Jonas [23], Davi 2 [25 72]	24 704
	24 Ypiranga	W	2-0	CBr1	Eltinho [76], Rafinha [82]	8 640
	27 Cianorte	W	2-1	CP	Anderson Aquino [30], Tcheco [71]	889
	6 Opérário PR	W	3-2	CP	Marcos Aurelio [24], Davi [37], Bill [77]	8 654
	10 Paranavaí	W	3-0	CP	Emerson 2 [53 67], Davi [59]	1 704
	13 Paraná	W	4-2	CP	Davi [19], Bill [24], Emerson [44], Anderson Aquino [89]	18 457
	18 Atlético GO	W	2-1	CBr2	Marcos Aurelio 2 [37 64]	4 452
Mar	20 Cascavel	W	3-0	CP	Anderson Aquino [9], Rafinha [19], Marcos Aurelio [73]	1 282
	23 Arapongas	W	2-0	CP	Marcos Aurelio 2 [25 62]	358
	26 Iraty	W	4-2	CP	Anderson Aquino 2 [1 11], Davi 2 [50 62]	2 643
	31 Atlético GO	W	3-1	CBr2	Anderson Aquino 2 [9 17], Everton Ribeiro [85]	9 444

CORITIBA (CONTD)

					Scorers	Att
Apr	2 Rio Branco	W	6-2	CP	Pereira 5, Davi 16, Anderson Aquino 2 57 61, Bill 69, Leonardo 83	9 855
	10 Corinthians	W	1-0	CP	Davi 50p	14 007
	15 Caxias	W	4-0	CBr3	Davi 20, Bill 2 42 78, Rafinha 51	12 677
	17 Roma	W	4-1	CP	Everton Ribeiro 3, Bill 52, Emerson 60, Marcos Aurelio 90	2 622
	24 Atlético PR	W	3-0	CP	Bill 2 32 45, Leonardo 87	17 501
	28 Caxias	W	1-0	CBr3	Emerson 72	2 485
	1 Cianorte	W	2-0	CP	Anderson Aquino 40, Pereira 52	12 216
	5 Palmeiras	W	6-0	CBqf	Emerson 11, Davi 21, Leo Gago 43, Bill 56p, Geraldo 91+, Anderson Aquino 93+	28 870
May	12 Palmeiras	L	0-2	CBqf		6 541
	19 Ceará	D	0-0	CBsf		12 101
	22 Atlético GO	L	0-1	SA		
	26 Ceará	W	1-0	CBsf	Anderson Aquino 49	27 317
	29 Corinthians	L	1-2	SA		
	2 Vasco	L	0-1	CBf		23 058
	5 Vasco	W	5-1	SA	Tcheco 3, Anderson Aquino 3 11 15 20, Maranhao 65	16 691
	9 Vasco	W	3-2	CBf	Bill 29, Davi 44, Willian 66	31 516
Jun	12 Botafogo	L	1-3	SA	Bill 1	8 390
	19 Inter	D	1-1	SA	Davi 76	19 693
	26 Cruzeiro	L	1-2	SA	Marco Aurelio 79	
	30 Ceará	W	3-1	SA	Leonardo 32, Everton Costa 36, Leo Gago 56	10 799
Jul	7 Figueirense	W	3-0	SA	Emerson 75, Leo Gago 90, Anderson Aquino 90	17 464
	10 Grêmio	L	0-2	SA		16 988
	16 Fluminense	L	3-4	SA	Ma.Aurelio 15, Pereira 25, Bill 51	18 524
	24 Bahia	D	0-0	SA		21 151
	28 São Paulo	L	3-4	SA	Rafinha 68, Bill 2 75 87	23 185
	31 América MG	W	3-1	SA	Marcos Aurelio 2 5 72, Bill 28	732
Aug	4 Palmeiras	D	1-1	SA	Jeci 9	17 818
	6 Flamengo	L	0-1	SA		28 930
	14 Atlético MG	W	3-0	SA	Bill 32, Rafinha 77, Leonardo 89p	16 328
	18 Santos	W	3-2	SA	Jeci 33, Marcos Aurelio 64, Leo Gago 86	5 143
	21 Avaí	D	0-0	SA		5 620
	27 Atlético PR	D	1-1	SA	Emerson 23	28 249
	1 Atlético GO	L	1-3	SA	Anderson Aquino 86	3 146
	4 Corinthians	W	1-0	SA	Jonas 72	29 248
	9 Vasco	L	0-2	SA		9 397
Sep	11 Botafogo	W	5-0	SA	Emerson 43, Ma.Aurelio 55p, Bill 65, Rafinha 81, Everton Costa 88	17 142
	18 Inter	D	1-1	SA	Emerson 47	20 360
	22 Cruzeiro	W	2-1	SA	Marcos Aurelio 23, Bill 59	17 766
	25 Ceará	L	2-3	SA	Bill 2 18 48	10 133
	2 Figueirense	D	0-0	SA		9 403
	8 Grêmio	W	2-0	SA	Marcos Aurelio 15, Jeci 74	19 951
Oct	13 Fluminense	L	1-3	SA	Marcos Aurelio 45	8 832
	16 Bahia	D	0-0	SA		11 896
	23 São Paulo	D	0-0	SA		14 298
	30 América MG	W	3-1	SA	Rafinha 20, Davi 24, Jeci 85	10 962
	6 Palmeiras	W	2-0	SA	Davi 22, Leonardo 56	7 513
	13 Flamengo	W	2-0	SA	Leonardo 29, Maranhao 36	26 229
Nov	17 Atlético MG	L	1-2	SA	Bill 88	16 872
	20 Santos	W	1-0	SA	Leonardo 60	16 447
	27 Avaí	W	1-0	SA	Jeco 86	15 680
Dc	4 Atlético PR	L	0-1	SA		14 891

8th — Att: 352 270 • Av: 18 541 • Couto Pereira 37 182

CORITIBA SERIE A APPEARANCES/GOALS 2010-11

Goalkeepers Edson Bastos 18 • Vanderlei 20
Defenders Ceara 1/0 • Cleiton 2/0 • Demerson 1/0 • Eltinho 14+3/0 • Emerson 33/4 • Everton Ribeiro 7+7/0 • Jeci 42+1/5 • Jonas 32+1/1 • Lucas Mendes 24/0 • Luccas Claro 6+1/0 • Maranhao 5+8/2 • Pereira 11/1 • Triguinho 0+3/0
Midfield Davi 10+6/3 • Djair 2/0 • Geraldo ANG 1+14/0 • Gil 2+9/0 • Leandro Donizete 17+2/0 • Leo Gago 31/3 • Marcos Paulo 3/0 • Rafinha 28/4 • Tcheco 23+4/1 • Willian 18+6/0 • Willian Leandro 1/0
Forwards Anderson Aquino 7+14/5 • Bill 25+6/11 • Caio 0+3/0 • Everton Costa 14+12/2 • Leonardo 13+10/6 • Marcos Aurelio 27+3/9
Coach Marcelo Oliveira

CRUZEIRO 2011

					Scorers	Att
Ja	30 Caldense	W	3-0	CM	Wellington 65, Diego Renan 68, Dudu 85	4 151
	6 Villa Nova	W	1-0	CM	Andre Dias 87	4 144
	12 Atlético MG	L	3-4	CM	Wellington 19, Henrique 48, Gil 85	9 793
Feb	17 Estudiantes	W	5-0	CLg7	Wallyson 2 1 82, Roger 18, Montillo 2 39 59	
	19 Ipatinga	W	2-0	CM	Thiago Ribeiro 51, Wallyson 55	1 664
	22 Guaraní	W	4-0	CLg7	Wallyson 2 30 64, Farias 86, Thiago Ribeiro 89	
	26 América TO	W	2-1	CM	Wallyson 44, OG 91+	5 000
	2 Tolima	D	0-0	CLg7		
	10 Tupi	D	0-0	CM		4 453
	13 Democrata	W	7-0	CM	Thiago Ribeiro 3 3 20 32, OG 40, Farias 42, Ortigoza 68, A. Dias 80	1 217
Mar	17 Tolima	W	6-1	CLg7	Montillo 3, Wallyson 32, Roger 2 62 71p, Gilberto 88, Thiago Ribeiro 92+	
	19 Funorte	W	3-0	CM	Wellington 38p, Thiago Ribeiro 2 55 93+	3 641
	27 América MG	W	3-2	CM	Thiago Ribeiro 41, Leo 49, Montillo 84	13 152
	31 Guaraní	W	2-0	CLg7	Thiago Ribeiro 17, Ortigoza 92+	
	3 Guaraní MG	W	4-1	CM	Gil 21, Montillo 22, Thiago Ribeiro 34, Wallyson 75	5 098
Apr	14 Estudiantes	W	3-0	CLg7	Thiago Ribeiro 11, Wallyson 45, Gilberto 82	
	17 Uberaba	W	1-0	CM	Montillo 44	3 336
	23 América TO	W	8-1	CMst	Henrique 22, Gilberto 31, Leo 2 55 62, Montillo 3 64 76 79, Wallyson 86	3 389
	28 Once Caldas	W	2-1	CLr2	Wallyson 72, Ortigoza 83	
	1 América TO	W	5-1	CMsf	Edcarlos 2 17 48, Pedro Ken 21, Dudu 72, Farias 89	4 037
	5 Once Caldas	L	0-2	CLr2		
May	8 Atlético MG	L	1-2	CMf	Wallyson 27	17 729
	15 América MG	W	2-0	CMf	Wallyson 75, Gilberto 87	17 384
	22 Figueirense	L	0-1	SA		10 231
	29 Palmeiras	D	1-1	SA	Anselmo Ramon 74	9 080
	4 Fluminense	L	1-2	SA	Anselmo Ramon 66	6 674
	11 Santos	D	1-1	SA	Montillo 55p	7 133
Jun	19 América MG	D	1-1	SA	Fabricio 15	5 027
	26 Coritiba	W	2-1	SA	Montillo 52p 84	5 256
	29 Vasco	W	3-0	SA	Leandro Guerreiro 53, Montillo 89, Roger 90p	7 695
	6 Grêmio	W	2-0	SA	Montillo 26 55	10 625
	9 São Paulo	L	1-2	SA	Wallyson 71	11 965
Jul	17 Bahia	W	2-1	SA	Wallyson 2 4 52	6 666
	24 Corinthians	W	1-0	SA	Wallyson 55	34 462
	27 Atlético GO	L	0-2	SA		5 593
	30 Botafogo	L	0-1	SA		7 821
	4 Flamengo	L	0-1	SA		14 863
	7 Inter	L	2-3	SA	An. Roman 11, Le. Guerreiro 82	16 286
Aug	13 Avaí	W	5-0	SA	Fabrício 27, Anselmo Roman 36, Montillo 44p, Thiago Ribeiro 81, Ortigoza 83	6 642
	17 Atlético PR	L	1-2	SA	Wellington Paulista 35	14 977
	20 Ceará	W	1-0	SA	Montillo 71p	6 478
	28 Atlético MG	W	2-1	SA	Montillo 2 13 88	16 720
	1 Figueirense	L	2-4	SA	Charles 2 38 60	14 738
	4 Palmeiras	D	1-1	SA	Montillo 68	10 345
	8 Fluminense	L	1-2	SA	Montillo 68	9 256
Sep	10 Santos	L	0-1	SA		9 637
	18 América MG	D	0-0	SA		8 915
	22 Coritiba	L	1-2	SA	Bobo 65	17 766
	25 Vasco	L	0-3	SA		6 348
	2 Grêmio	L	0-2	SA		21 058
	5 São Paulo	D	3-3	SA	Keirrison 12, Charles 72, Anselmo Ramon 80	9 944
Oct	12 Bahia	D	0-0	SA		13 904
	16 Corinthians	L	0-1	SA		17 004
	23 Atlético GO	W	3-2	SA	Farias 41, Anselmo Ramon 2 70 75	5 595
	29 Botafogo	L	0-1	SA		12 397
	6 Flamengo	L	1-5	SA	Anselmo Ramon 22	39 842
	13 Inter	W	1-0	SA	Farias 20	16 967
Nov	16 Avaí	D	0-0	SA		2 842
	20 Atlético PR	D	1-1	SA	Charles 44	18 139
	27 Ceará	D	2-2	SA	Anselmo Ramon 22, Ortigoza 50	17 331
Dc	4 Atlético MG	W	6-1	SA	Roger 8, Leandro Guerreiro 28, Anselmo Ramon 33, Fabrico 45, Wellington Paulista 56, Everton 90	18 850

16th — Att: 200 347 • Av: 10 545 (-34.8%) • Arena do Jacaré 25 000

CRUZEIRO SERIE A APPEARANCES/GOALS 2010-11
Goalkeepers Fabio 34 • Rafael 4+1
Defenders Diego Renan 18+1/0 • Gabriel Araujo 3+2/0 • Gil 16/0
Gil Bahia 1+1/0 • Leo 26+1/0 • Naldo 19+3/0 • Pablo 1+2/0
Mauricio Victorino URU 15/0 • Cribari 4+1/0
Midfield Bruninho 0+3/0 • Dudu 0+6/0 • Eber 1+2/0
Everton 16+7/1 • Fabricio 28+1/3 • Gilberto 12+2/0 • Henrique 5/0
Leandro Guerreiro 19+4/3 • Marquinhos Parana 35/0
Walter Montillo ARG 34/12 • Roger 19+9/2 • Vitor 21/0
Charles 14+2/4 • Elber 0+8/0 • Sandro Manoel 1+3/0
Forwards Anselmo Ramon 16+9/10 • Brandao 1+4/0
Ernesto Farias ARG 7+2/2 • Jose Ortigoza PAR 7+17/2 • Reis 1+3/0
Seba 7+1/0 • Thiago Ribeiro 6+1/1 • Wallyson 15/4 • Keirrison 4+4/1
Bobo 3+3/1 • Wellington Paulista 11+3/2
Coach Cuca • Joel Santana (20/06/2011) • Emerson Avila (2/09/2011)
• Vagner Mancini (26/09/2011)

FIGUEIRENSE (CONTD)

1 Cruzeiro	W	4-2	SA	Julio Cesar 2 [29 58], Elias [35], Wellington Nem [50]	14 738
3 São Paulo	L	1-2	SA	Joao Paulo [48]	12 263
8 Atlético GO	D	1-1	SA	Wellington Nem [10]	2 514
11 Vasco	D	1-1	SA	Wellington Nem [4]	12 877
18 Atlético PR	D	0-0	SA		14 103
22 Inter	D	1-1	SA	Ygor [39]	12 342
24 Santos	W	3-2	SA	Julio Cesar 2 [8 84p], Wellington Nem [26]	7 059
2 Coritiba	D	0-0	SA		9 403
9 Ceará	D	1-1	SA	Juninho [43]	13 617
12 Grêmio	W	3-1	SA	Aloisio [33], Elias [36], Wellington Nem [75]	23 151
15 América MG	W	2-1	SA	Julio Cesar 2 [68 80]	7 421
21 Palmeiras	W	2-1	SA	Wellington Nem [15], Julio Cesar [75]	3 897
30 Bahia	W	2-1	SA	Fernandes 2 [56 69]	9 387
5 Botafogo	W	1-0	SA	Julio Cesar [5]	21 104
12 Atlético MG	W	2-1	SA	Wellington Nem [52], Julio Cesar [88]	10 151
17 Flamengo	D	0-0	SA		28 497
20 Fluminense	L	0-4	SA		16 279
27 Corinthians	L	0-1	SA		17 254
4 Avaí	D	1-1	SA	Heber [46]	6 109

7th Att: 219 578 • Av: 11 557 • Orlando Scarpelli 19 908

FIGUEIRENSE SERIE A APPEARANCES/GOALS 2010-11
Goalkeepers Ricardo 2 • Wilson 36
Defenders Edson 26/3 • Edson 8/0 • Helder 3+4/0
Joao Paulo 22+4/1 • Roger Carvalho 20+7/0 • Pablo Barros 3+2/0
Midfield Coutinho 15+12/0 • Fernandes 12+12/2 • Jackson
Sousa 1+6/0 • Joilson 0+1/0 • Jonatas 5+7/0 • Juninho 34/2
Leandro Chaves 0+4/0 • Maicon 29/1 • Wilson Pittoni PAR 6+13/1
Rhayner 5+9/0 • Tulio 29+1/0 • Wellington Nem 23+3/9 • Ygor 33/2
Elias 20+2/4 • Jean Deretti 2/0
Forwards Aloisio 14+7/4 • Bruno 32/0 • Heber 9+7/3
Juninho Frizzi 1/0 • Lenny 0+1/0 • Reinaldo 3+2/0 • Wellington 0+3/1
Julio Cesar 22/11 • Somalia 3+6/1 • William Pottker 0+1/0
Coach Marcio Goiano • Jorginho (1/03/2011)

FIGUEIRENSE 2011

16 Met'politano	D	1-1	CC1	Washington [78]	3 045
20 Joinville	W	4-0	CC1	Renato [5], Heber [21], Wellington Sousa [57], Fernando Gabriel [86]	6 868
23 Brusque	W	5-2	CC1	Tulio [11], Renato [19], Heber [28], Breitner [41], Wellington Sousa [63]	5 936
27 Marc'o Dias	D	1-1	CC1	Reinaldo [60]	2 748
29 Concórdia	W	3-0	CC1	Maicon [47], Heber [74], Fernandes [86]	5 611
2 Chap'ense	D	3-3	CC1	Renato [46], Breitner [65], Joao Paulo [81]	6 526
6 Avaí	D	2-2	CC1	Heber [4], Wellington Sousa [59]	18 307
10 Criciúma	L	0-2	CC1		7 106
13 Imbituba	W	4-1	CC1	Fernandes [25], Heber 2 [50 79], Joao Paulo [64]	5 897
20 Joinville	W	3-1	CCsf	Breitner [6], Fernandes 2 [16 77]	9 897
27 Criciúma	L	0-1	CCf		15 219
4 Met'politano	W	5-1	CC2	Heber 2 [2 73], Maicon 2 [10 76p], Breitner [60]	4 699
10 Joinville	D	1-1	CC2	Breitner [26]	5 758
16 Brusque	D	1-1	CC2	Heber [23]	1 368
20 Marc'o Dias	W	2-0	CC2	Joao Paulo [62], Dudu [92+]	6 595
24 Concórdia	W	2-0	CC2	Reinaldo [9]	2 416
27 Chap'ense	W	2-1	CC2	Pittoni [43], Fernandes [90]	7 595
3 Avaí	W	1-0	CC2	Reinaldo [63]	12 326
10 Criciúma	W	3-2	CC2	Joao Paulo [57], Tulio [60], Pittoni [70]	9 168
17 Imbituba	W	6-0	CC2	Wellington Sousa 4 [5 43 70 89], Juninho Barbosa [85], Heber [88]	582
24 Avaí	L	0-2	CCsf		15 626
22 Joinville	W	1-0	SA	OG [48]	10 231
29 São Paulo	L	0-1	SA		9 931
5 Atlético GO	W	2-0	SA	Heber [69], Edson [74]	6 913
12 Vasco	D	1-1	SA	Aloisio [89]	17 777
19 Atlético PR	W	2-0	SA	Heber [15], Juninho [19]	10 315
26 Inter	L	1-4	SA	Wellington Nem [89]	11 714
30 Santos	W	2-1	SA	Aloisio 2 [5 32]	5 360
7 Coritiba	L	0-3	SA		17 464
10 Ceará	D	1-1	SA	Maicon [63]	8 527
21 Grêmio	D	0-0	SA		12 175
23 América MG	D	0-0	SA		752
28 Palmeiras	L	0-1	SA		13 283
31 Bahia	L	1-3	SA	Wellington Sousa [85]	16 735
3 Botafogo	W	2-0	SA	Edson [17], Julio Cesar [39p]	8 965
7 Atlético MG	W	2-1	SA	Elias [8 45]	15 689
14 Flamengo	D	2-2	SA	Somalia [54], Edson [71]	18 499
17 Fluminense	L	0-3	SA		5 765
20 Corinthians	W	2-0	SA	Wellington Nem [35], Pittoni [90]	26 256
28 Avaí	L	2-3	SA	Ygor [19], Julio Cesar [45]	17 933

FLAMENGO 2011

20 V Redonda	W	2-0	TG	Vander [40], Wanderley [61]	9 088
22 América RJ	W	3-1	TG	Renato Abreu [11], David [32], Deivid [51]	7 832
26 Americano	W	2-0	TG	Wanderley 2 [69 71]	10 000
30 Vasco	W	2-1	TG	Deivid [22], Thiago Neves [44]	15 356
3 Nova Iguaçu	W	1-0	TG	Wanderley [85]	42 108
6 Boavista	W	3-2	TG	Ronaldinho [23p], Deivid [49], Negueba [83]	10 000
13 Resende	W	1-0	TG	Deivid [77]	6 384
17 Murici	W	3-0	CBr1	Ronaldinho [66], Renato Abreu [72], Negueba [90]	15 100
20 Botafogo	D	1-1	TGsf	Ronaldo Angelim [14], W ?-?p	26 854
27 Boavista	W	1-0	TGf	Ronaldinho [72]	41 708
5 Olaria	W	3-2	TR	Thiago Neves 2 [45 70], Ronaldinho [48]	6 779
10 Bangu	W	2-1	TR	Ronaldinho [24p], Diego Mauricio [90]	6 958
13 Fluminense	D	0-0	TR		16 131
17 Fortaleza	W	3-0	CBr2	Renato Abreu [20], Wanderley [60], Diego Mauricio [90]	21 089
20 Cabofriense	D	0-0	TR		2 447
27 Madureira	D	3-3	TR	Leo Moura [42], Deivid [75], Thiago Neves [82]	5 072
2 D de Caxias	W	2-0	TR	Renato Abreu [73], David [90]	11 791
10 Botafogo	W	2-0	TR	Thiago Neves 2 [34 88]	21 422
17 Macaé	D	1-1	TR	Jean [56]	5 330
21 Horizonte	D	1-1	CBr3	Wanderley [17]	9 029
24 Fluminense	D	1-1	TRsf	Thiago Neves [66], W 5-4p	23 915
28 Horizonte	W	3-0	CBr3	Galhardo [8], Deivid [48], Willians [80]	5 058
1 Vasco	D	0-0	TRf	W 3-1p	39 029
6 Ceará	L	1-2	CBqf	Wanderley [75]	17 127
12 Ceará	D	2-2	CBqf	Thiago Neves 2 [19 27]	12 936
21 Avaí	W	4-0	SA	Bottinelli [22], Ronaldinho [62], Th.Neves [69], Diego Mauricio [87]	5 973
29 Bahia	D	3-3	SA	Ronaldinho [29], Bottinelli [55], Egigo [72]	32 157

FLAMENGO (CONTD)

Mon	Date	Opponent	Res	Score	Comp	Scorers	Att
Jun	5	Corinthians	D	1-1	SA	Renato 39	42 000
	12	Atlético PR	D	1-1	SA	Deivid 80	20 022
	19	Botafogo	D	0-0	SA		15 832
	25	Atlético MG	W	4-1	SA	Ronaldinho 66, Th.Neves 76, Deivid 86 90	16 870
	29	América MG	W	3-2	SA	Ronaldinho 2 11 85, Deivid 56	7 475
Jul	7	São Paulo	W	1-0	SA	Bottinelli 71	15 790
	10	Fluminense	W	1-0	SA	Willians 45	18 884
	21	Palmeiras	D	0-0	SA		33 575
	24	Ceará	D	1-1	SA	Renato 32	6 154
	28	Santos	W	5-4	SA	Ronaldinho 3 28 68 81, Thiago Neves 32, Deivid 44	12 968
	30	Grêmio	W	2-0	SA	Thiago Neves 28, Ronaldinho 74	28 793
Aug	4	Cruzeiro	W	1-0	SA	Deivid 45	14 863
	6	Coritiba	W	1-0	SA	Jael 90	28 930
	11	Atlético PR	W	1-0	CSr1	Ronaldinho 83p	
	14	Figueirense	D	2-2	SA	Deivid 2 36 51	18 499
	19	Atlético GO	L	1-4	SA	Jael 83	7 649
	21	Inter	D	2-2	SA	Ronaldinho 25, Jael 60	34 579
	25	Atlético PR	W	1-0	CSr1	Ronaldinho 73	
	28	Vasco	D	0-0	SA		33 206
Sep	1	Avaí	L	2-3	SA	Ronaldinho 2 37 88	12 692
	4	Bahia	L	1-3	SA	Renato 29	9 755
	9	Corinthians	L	1-2	SA	Deivid 29	35 392
	11	Atlético PR	L	1-2	SA	Wellington Souza 83	7 846
	18	Botafogo	D	1-1	SA	Jael 49	20 805
	22	Atlético MG	L	1-0	SA	Ronaldinho 62	13 849
	24	América MG	W	2-1	SA	Deivid 62, Thiago Neves 89	9 445
Oct	2	São Paulo	W	2-1	SA	Thiago Neves 63, Renato 83	63 871
	9	Fluminense	W	3-2	SA	Th.Neves 68, Bottinelli 2 87 90	21 052
	12	Palmeiras	D	1-1	SA	Thiago Neves 56	22 573
	15	Ceará	W	1-0	SA	Deivid 38	19 061
	19	U. de Chile	L	0-4	CSr2		
	23	Santos	D	1-1	SA	Deivid 78	18 257
	26	U. de Chile	L	0-1	CSr2		
	30	Grêmio	L	2-4	SA	Deivid 23, Thiago Neves 35	44 781
Nov	6	Cruzeiro	W	5-1	SA	Deivid 2 35 48, T.Neves 3 54 57 70	39 842
	13	Coritiba	L	0-2	SA		26 229
	17	Figueirense	D	0-0	SA		28 497
	20	Atlético GO	D	0-0	SA		37 828
	27	Inter	W	1-0	SA	Ronaldinho 45	12 911
Dc	4	Vasco	D	1-1	SA	Renato 54	34 064

4th Att: 371 375 • Av: 19 546 (+22.6%) • Engenhão 46 931

FLAMENGO SERIE A APPEARANCES/GOALS 2010-11
Goalkeepers Felipe 35 • Paulo Victor 3
Defenders David 12+4/0 • Jean 0+3/0 • Junior Cesar 33+1/0
Leo Moura 35/0 • Rafael Galhardo 3+2/0 • Rodrigo Alvim 2+1/0
Ronaldo Angelim 14+1/0 • Welinton Souza 32/1 • Alex Silva 17/0
Edigo 3/1 • Gustavo 3/0
Midfield Airton 18/0 • Dario Bottinelli ARG 14+12/5 • Fernando 0+2/0
• Luiz Antonio 7+2/0 • Luiz Philipe 3+10/0 • Claudio
Maldonado CHI 5+3/0 • Renato 36/5 • Ronaldinho 31/14
Thiago Neves 33/12 • Willians 30+1/1
Forwards Deivid 28+5/15 • Diego Mauricio 3+18/1 • Gonzalo
Fierro CHI 2+9/0 • Negueba 2+16/0 • Wanderley 5+1/0 • Jael 4+12/4
Thomas Jaguaribe 4+5/0
Coach Vanderlei Luxemburgo

FLUMINENSE (CONTD)

Mon	Date	Opponent	Res	Score	Comp	Scorers	Att
Mar	3	América	L	0-1	CLg3		
	5	Resende	W	2-1	TR	Aroujo 41, Leandro Euzebio 52	937
	9	América RJ	W	3-1	TR	Conca 33, Rafael Moura 2 54 72	4 153
	13	Flamengo	D	0-0	TR		26 131
	19	Boavista	L	0-2	TR		6 614
	24	América	W	3-2	CLg3	Gum 21, Araujo 80, Deco 87	
	27	Vasco	D	0-0	TR		27 480
Apr	2	V Redonda	W	2-1	TR	Souza 54, Emerson 56	6 137
	7	Nacional	L	0-2	CLg3		
	10	Americano	W	5-1	TR	Conca 34, Araujo 2 36 55, Mariano 50, Marquinho 87	3 094
	17	Nova Iguaçu	W	1-0	TR	Fred 28p	5 922
	21	Arg Juniors	W	4-2	CLg3	Julio Cesar 18, Fred 2 40 89p, Rafael Moura 68	
	24	Flamengo	D	1-1	TRsf	Rafael Moura 22, L 4-5p	23 915
	29	Libertad	W	3-1	CLr2	Rafael Moura 4, Marquinho 73, Conca 75	
May	5	Libertad	L	0-3	CLr2		
	22	São Paulo	L	0-2	SA		5 732
	29	Atlético GO	W	1-0	SA	Leandro Euzebio 12	5 643
Jun	4	Cruzeiro	W	2-1	SA	Rafael Moura 2 45 71	6 674
	12	Corinthians	L	0-2	SA		18 400
	18	Bahia	L	0-1	SA		6 827
	26	Avaí	W	1-0	SA	Dario Conca 35	4 139
Jul	1	Atlético PRL	W	3-1	SA	Mariano 41, Ciro 2 43 59	5 114
	10	Flamengo	L	0-1	SA	Willians 45	18 884
	16	Coritiba	L	1-3	SA	Matheus Carvalho 76	18 524
	24	Palmeiras	W	1-0	SA	Marquinho 74	9 214
	27	Atlético MG	L	0-1	SA		16 100
Aug	31	Ceará	W	4-0	SA	Fred 35, Souza 48, Rafael Sobis 63, Rafael Moura 77	6 850
	5	Inter	W	2-0	SA	Souza 56, Rafael Moura 86p	6 399
	7	América MG	L	0-3	SA		2 782
	14	Grêmio	L	1-2	SA	Fred 24	15 180
	17	Figueirense	W	3-0	SA	Edinho 48, Rafael Moura 2 50 69	5 765
	21	Vasco	D	1-1	SA	Rafael Moura 64	16 991
	25	Santos	L	1-2	SA	Rafael Moura 38	6 855
	27	Botafogo	L	1-2	SA	Fred 55	22 762
Sep	1	São Paulo	W	2-1	SA	M.Lanzini 18, Rafael Sobis 64	7 910
	3	Atlético GO	W	3-2	SA	Rafael Sobis 2 83 87, Rafael Moura 90	6 473
	8	Cruzeiro	W	2-1	SA	Fred 34p, Marquinho 61	9 256
	11	Corinthians	W	1-0	SA	Fred 23	26 979
	18	Bahia	L	0-3	SA		15 356
	22	Avaí	W	3-1	SA	Fred 2 4 35, Martinuccio 79	6 689
	24	Atlético PR	D	1-1	SA	Fred 90p	11 010
Oct	1	Santos	W	3-2	SA	Marquinho 39, Rafael Sobis 71, Marcio Rosario 90	15 256
	9	Flamengo	L	2-3	SA	Rafel Sobis 60, M.Lanzini 79	21 052
	13	Coritiba	W	3-1	SA	Fred 3 25 73 76	8 832
	16	Palmeiras	W	2-1	SA	Fred 2 10 86	3 649
	22	Atlético MG	L	0-2	SA		19 525
Nov	29	Ceará	W	2-1	SA	Rafael Sobis 2 31 64	17 554
	6	Inter	W	2-1	SA	Rafael Moura 17, Rafael Sobis 45	38 142
	12	América MG	L	1-2	SA	Rafael Moura 81	40 232
	16	Grêmio	W	5-4	SA	Fred 4 25 35 78p 81, Rafael Sobis 61	11 395
	20	Figueirense	W	0-4	SA	Fred 3 48 57 86, Marquinho 72	16 279
	27	Vasco	L	1-2	SA	Fred 83	29 476
Dc	4	Botafogo	D	1-1	SA	Fred 4	4 790

3rd Att: 259 078 • Av: 13 636 (-36.3%) • Engenhão 46 931

FLUMINENSE 2011

Mon	Date	Opponent	Res	Score	Comp	Scorers	Att
Jan	20	Bangu	W	1-0	TG	Fred 81	19 206
	23	Olaria	W	6-2	TG	Marquinho 2 11 82, Fred 2 26 42, Rodriguinho 2 45 65	6 140
	27	Macaé	W	3-1	TG	Carlinhos 36, Souza 2 47 54	10 190
	30	Cabofriense	W	4-2	TG	Fred 2 6 79, Andre Luis 65, Willians 83	6 484
Feb	3	D de Caxias	W	3-2	TG	Fred 3 53 73 89	5 973
	6	Botafogo	L	2-3	TG	Rafael Moura 2 30 44	16 759
	10	Arg Juniors	D	2-2	CLg3	Rafael Moura 2 58 74	
	13	Madureira	W	1-0	TG	Rafael Moura 74	3 995
	19	Boavista	D	2-2	TGsf	Marquinho 8, Fred 37. L 2-4p	18 377
	24	Nacional	D	0-0	CLg3		

FLUMINENSE SERIE A APPEARANCES/GOALS 2010-11
Goalkeepers Berna 4 • Diego Cavalieri 34
Defenders Carlinhos 30+1/0 • Digao 7+3/0 • Elivelton 7+2/0
Gum 24/0 • Julio Cesar 5+1/0 • Leandro Euzebio 20/1 • Marcio
Rosario 18+2/1 • Mariano 36/1 • Wallace 1+2/0 • Jefferson 1/0
Midfield Dario Conca ARG 7/1 • Deco POR 15+3/0 • Diguinho 14+3/0
• Diogo 10+3/0 • Edinho 33/1 • Fernando Bob 7+10/0
Marquinho 30+3/4 • Rodrigo Oliveira Lindoso 3+1/0 • Souza 13+10/2
Tarta 1/0 • Edwin Valencia COL 14+5/0 • Manuel Lanzini 13+9/2
Forwards Araujo 0+6/0 • Ciro 9+4/2 • Fred 25/22 • Matheus
Carvalho 0+8/1 • Rafael Moura 14+11/11 • Rodriguinho 3+1/0
Rafael Sobis 18+8/10 • Alejandro Martinuccio 2+12/1
Coach Muricy Ramalho • Ronaldo Torres (15/03/2011) • Enderson
Moreira (31/03/2011) • Abel Braga (8/06/2011)

GREMIO 2011

	Date	Opponent		Score	Comp	Scorers	Att
Jan	15	Lajeadense	D	2-2	CG	Rafael Marques 38, Jonas 44	13 269
	20	Ypiranga	D	1-1	CG	Junior Vicosa 50	7 115
	21	São José	W	2-1	CG	Jonas 2 76 80	7 311
	23	Canoas	W	1-0	CG	Junior Vicosa 40	1 723
	27	Liverpool	D	2-2	CLpr	Andre Lima 6, Douglas 14	
	30	Inter	W	2-1	CG	Bruno Collaco 59, Lins 72	4 010
Feb	3	Liverpool	W	3-1	CLpr	Andre Lima 38, V.Pacheco 2 57 74	
	5	Caxias	W	2-1	CG	Douglas 6, Vilson 23	9 094
	10	São Luis	W	1-0	CG	Maylson 8	2 225
	13	NHamburgo	L	0-2	CG		2 020
	17	O Petrolero	W	3-0	CLg2	Douglas 2 43p 70, Gilson 48	
	20	Ypiranga	W	5-0	CGgf	Andre Lima 2 2 26, Douglas 32, Borges 52, Leandro 90	10 149
	25	At. Junior	L	1-2	CLg2	Borges 5	
	27	Cruzeiro RS	W	4-2	CGsf	Borges 3 35 55 60, Gabriel 92+	13 812
Mar	3	León	W	2-0	CLg2	Andre Lima 42, Borges 55p	
	10	Caxias	D	2-2	CGf	William Magrao 43, Rafael Marques 95+. W 4-1p	21 147
	12	Cruzeiro RS	L	0-2	CG		6 545
	17	León	D	1-1	CLg2	Carlos Alberto 54	
	20	Porto Alegre	W	3-0	CG	Escudero 5, J.Vicosa 27, V.Pacheco 90	2 358
	24	SantaMaria	W	6-0	CG	Douglas 3, Mario Fernandes 24, Junior Vicosa 52, Rafael Marques 66, Leandro 2 76 88	4 291
	27	Pelotas	W	3-1	CG	William Magrao 53, Rodolfo 73, Rafael Marques 89	8 133
	31	Juventude	L	2-3	CG	Andre Lima 55	7 554
Apr	3	Veranópolis	W	2-1	CG	Leandro 57, Borges 83	9 941
	7	At. Junior	W	2-0	CLg2	Lucio 33, Borges 60	
	10	Santa Cruz	D	1-1	CG	Borges 87	1 835
	15	O Petrolero	L	0-3	CLg2		
	17	Ypiranga	D	1-1	CGgf	Douglas 24. W ?-?p	7 330
	23	Cruzeiro RS	W	3-2	CGsf	Leandro 40, Willian Magrao 51, Rafael Marques 74	3 850
	26	U Católica	L	1-2	CLr2	Douglas 59	
May	1	Inter	D	1-1	CGf	Junior Vicosa 86. L 2-4p	25 479
	5	U Católica	L	0-1	CLr2		
	8	Inter	W	3-2	CGf	Junior Vicosa 2 38 86, Leandro 46	29 824
	15	Inter	L	2-3	CGf	Lucio 15, Borges 80. L 4-5p	42 282
	22	Corinthians	L	1-2	SA	Douglas 58p	22 147
	29	Atlético PR	W	1-0	SA	OG 13	15 841
Jun	5	Bahia	W	2-0	SA	Junior Vicosa 2 5 32	15 835
	11	São Paulo	L	1-3	SA	OG 52	14 671
	19	Vasco	D	1-1	SA	Roberson 81	16 322
	26	Botafogo	L	1-2	SA	Rafael Marques 88	13 983
	29	Avaí	D	2-2	SA	Douglas 73p, Rafael Marques 90	10 346
Jul	6	Cruzeiro	L	0-2	SA		10 652
	10	Coritiba	W	2-0	SA	Gilberto Silva 63, Andre Lima 70	16 988
	21	Figueirense	D	0-0	SA		12 175
	27	América MG	D	1-1	SA	Ezequiel Miralles 60	15 033
	30	Flamengo	L	0-2	SA		28 793
Aug	3	Atlético MG	D	2-2	SA	Leandro 50, Rochemback 80p	10 725
	6	Palmeiras	D	0-0	SA		15 762
	14	Fluminense	W	2-1	SA	Marquinhos 2 31 45	15 180
	17	Ceará	L	0-3	SA		11 824
	21	Atlético GO	L	0-1	SA		5 226
	28	Inter	W	2-1	SA	Marquinhos 16, Douglas 78p	26 694
	31	Corinthians	L	2-3	SA	Douglas 40, Andre Lima 71	16 588
Sep	4	Atlético PR	W	4-0	SA	Escudero 19, An.Lima 3 32 59 65p	16 245
	9	Bahia	W	2-1	SA	Brandao 29, Escudero 35	17 977
	11	São Paulo	W	1-0	SA	Douglas 64	30 078
	17	Vasco	L	0-4	SA		16 014
	23	Botafogo	L	0-1	SA		17 324
	25	Avaí	W	2-1	SA	Mario Fernandes 42, Douglas 46	8 727
Oct	2	Cruzeiro	W	2-0	SA	Rafael Marques 4, Escudero 49	21 058
	5	Santos	W	1-0	SA	Brandao 9	26 020
	8	Coritiba	L	0-2	SA		19 951
	12	Figueirense	L	1-3	SA	Edcarlos 58	23 151
	16	Santos	W	1-0	SA	Escudero 19	3 477
	22	América MG	D	2-2	SA	Andre Lima 2 35 52	829
	30	Flamengo	W	4-2	SA	Andre Lima 2 41 50, Douglas 80, Miralles 84	44 781
Nov	5	Atlético MG	L	0-2	SA		17 387
	13	Palmeiras	D	2-2	SA	Brandao 69, Fernando 90	15 062
	16	Fluminense	W	4-5	SA	Rafael Marques 17, Marquinhos 45, Brabdao 74, Adilson 76	11 395
	19	Ceará	L	1-3	SA	Douglas 37	7 130
	27	Atlético GO	D	2-2	SA	Willian Magrao 55, Marquinhos 56	7 493
Dc	4	Inter	L	0-1	SA		35 041

12th   Att: 357 612 • Av: 18 822 (-15.2%) • Olímpico 45 000

GREMIO SERIE A APPEARANCES/GOALS 2010-11

Goalkeepers Marcelo Grohe 6 • Victor 32
Defenders Bruno Collaco 7+5/0 • Edilson 0+1/0 • Gabriel 8+6/0
Mario Fernandes 33/1 • Neuton 8/0 • Rafael Marques 28/4
Rodolfo 1/0 • Saimon 19+2/0 • Vilson 9+3/0 • Julio Cesar 19/0
Edcarlos 9+3/1
Midfield Adilson 13+10/1 • Douglas 33/8 • Damian
Escudero ARG 26+5/4 • Fabio Rochemback 33/1 • Fernando 22/1
Lucio 13+3/0 • Marquinhos 23+8/5 • Mithyue 0+1/0 • Pessalli 0+1/0
Willian Magrao 5+7/1 • Gilberto Silva 18+3/1
Forwards Andre Lima 25+2/9 • Diego 1+5/0 • Junior Vicosa 5/2
Leandro 10+12/1 • Lins 4+3/0 • Ezequiel Miralles ARG 4+15/2
Roberson 0+5/1 • Brandao 6+8/4 • Everaldo 0+1/0 • Yuri 0+1/0
Coach Renato Gaucho • Julio Camargo (2/07/2011) • Celso Roth (4/08/2011)

INTERNACIONAL 2011

	Date	Opponent		Score	Comp	Scorers	Att
Jan	16	Cruzeiro RS	L	0-1	CG		408
	19	Porto Alegre	W	1-0	CG	Ricardo Goulart 57	4 278
	22	Santa Cruz	W	1-0	CG	Ricardo Goulart 84	2 323
	26	SantaMaria	W	4-1	CG	Rodrigo 10, Ricardo Goulart 29, Thiago Humberto 40, Mineiro 92+	843
	30	Grêmio	L	1-2	CG	Augusto Fraga 38	4 010
Feb	3	Juventude	W	3-1	CG	Leandro Damiao 12, D'Alessandro 2 29 82	11 683
	6	Veranópolis	L	1-2	CG	Leandro Damiao 3	257
	13	Pelotas	W	3-2	CG	Leandro Damiao 3 24 52 77	9 544
	17	Emelec	D	1-1	CLg6	Bolatti 79	
	19	Cruzeiro RS	D	1-1	CGgf	Ricardo Goulart 52. L 4-5p	4 384
	24	Jaguares	W	4-0	CLg6	Bolatti 2 20 44, Leandro Damiao 66, Oscar 91+	
Mar	10	Ypiranga	W	4-0	CG	Leandro Damiao 3 14 30 67, Ze Roberto 46	3 766
	13	Caxias	D	3-3	CG	Leandro Damiao 3 20 45 76	9 606
	16	Wilstermann	W	4-1	CLg6	OG 16, Leandro Damiao 19, Ze Roberto 25, Kleber 87	
	19	NHamburgo	D	0-0	CG		9 542
	24	São José	W	1-0	CG	Andre 37	1 646
	26	São Luis	D	0-0	CG		4 407
	31	Wilstermann	W	3-0	CLg6	Oscar 18, D'Alessandro 58, Ze Roberto 72	
Apr	2	Lajeadense	D	1-1	CG	Leandro Damiao 12	3 300
	6	Jaguares	L	0-1	CLg6		
	10	Canoas	W	6-2	CG	Rafael Sobis 2 26 40, D'Alessandro 2 41 43, Cavenaghi 81, Leandro Damiao 85	9 584
	16	Santa Cruz	W	1-0	CGgf	Leandro Damiao 32	16 237
	20	Emelec	W	2-0	CLg6	Rafael Sobis 52, Leandro Damiao 85	
	24	Juventude	W	2-1	CGsf	Bolatti 19, Tinga 77	11 182
	28	Peñarol	D	1-1	CLr2	Leandro Damiao 65	
May	1	Grêmio	D	1-1	CGf	Leandro Damiao 23. W 4-2p	25 479
	4	Peñarol	L	1-2	CLr2	Oscar 1	
	8	Grêmio	L	2-3	CGf	Andre 8, Leandro Damiao 81	29 824
	15	Grêmio	W	3-2	CGf	Leandro Damiao 31, Andre 45, D'Alessandro 74p. W 5-4p	42 282
	22	Santos	D	1-1	SA	Ze Roberto 35	4 532
	28	Ceará	L	0-1	SA		15 412
Jun	5	América MG	W	4-2	SA	Oscar 2 14 22, D'Alessandro 16, Cavenaghi 61	4 541
	6	Palmeiras	D	2-2	SA	OG 50, Leandro Damiao 90	21 952
	19	Coritiba	D	1-1	SA	Glaydson 50	19 693
	26	Figueirense	W	4-1	SA	Bolivar 17, Oscar 20, Leandro Damiao 59, Goulart 80	11 714
Jul	1	Atlético MG	W	4-0	SA	Leandro Damiao 54, Ze Roberto 56, D'Alessandro 76, Oscar 80	7 595
	6	Atlético PR	W	1-0	SA	Oscar 75	12 094
	9	Vasco	L	0-2	SA		6 223
	15	Corinthians	L	0-1	SA		33 329
	17	São Paulo	L	0-3	SA		13 630
	21	Avaí	W	3-1	SA	Andrezinho 66, Leandro Damiao 70, D'Alessandro 90	6 471
	31	Atlético GO	D	0-0	SA		12 163

INTERNACIONAL (CONTD)

	Date	Opponent	Res	Score	Comp	Scorers	Att
	5	Fluminense	L	0-2	SA		6 399
	7	Cruzeiro	W	3-2	SA	D'Alessandro 20, Andrezinho 38, Leandro Damiao 73	16 286
	11	Indep'iente	L	1-2	RSA	Leandro Damiao 37	
Aug	14	Bahia	D	1-1	SA	Leandro Damiao 41	21 239
	18	Botafogo	W	1-0	SA	Leandro Damiao 58	11 080
	21	Flamengo	D	2-2	SA	Indio 50, Leandro Damiao 77	34 579
	25	Indep'iente	W	3-1	RSA	Leandro Damiao 2 21 25, Kleber 83p	
	28	Grêmio	L	1-2	SA	Indio 27	26 694
	1	Santos	D	3-3	SA	Bolivar 15, Leandro Damiao 15, Oscar 71p	17 180
	4	Ceará	D	1-1	SA	Jo 46	11 732
Sep	7	América MG	W	4-2	SA	Moledo 3, Leandro Damiao 8, D'Alessandro 14p, Oscar 35	28 896
	11	Palmeiras	W	3-0	SA	Leandro Damiao 3 25 83 90	9 702
	18	Coritiba	D	1-1	SA	Oscar 1	20 360
	22	Figueirense	D	1-1	SA	Jo 50	12 342
	25	Atlético MG	W	2-1	SA	Bolatti 26, Fabricio 73	16 198
	2	Atlético PR	L	0-2	SA		14 431
	9	Vasco	W	3-0	SA	D'Alessandro 49, Indio 76, Tinga 90	23 797
	12	São Paulo	D	0-0	SA		24 460
Oct	16	Avaí	W	4-2	SA	D'Alessandro 2 52 75, Kleber 80, Nei 83	20 788
	23	Corinthians	D	1-1	SA	Nei 66	38 072
	30	Atlético GO	W	1-0	SA	Kleber 59	6 337
	5	Fluminense	L	1-2	SA	Oscar 36	38 142
	13	Cruzeiro	L	0-1	SA		16 967
Nov	16	Bahia	W	1-0	SA	Gilberto 8	8 541
	20	Botafogo	W	2-1	SA	Leandro Damiao 45, Oscar 73	7 840
	27	Flamengo	L	0-1	SA		12 911
Dc	4	Grêmio	W	1-0	SA	D'Alessandro 61	35 041

5th Att: 395 925 • Av: 20 838 (+9.1%) • Olímpico 45 000

INTER SERIE A APPEARANCES/GOALS 2010-11

Goalkeepers Lauro 1 • Muriel 34 • Renan 3
Defenders Boilvar 25/2 • Fabricio 5+13/1 • Indio 14/3 • Juan 17+1/0 Kleber 31/2 • Nei 34/2 • Rodrigo 3/0 • Rodrigo Moledo 18+1/1 Daniel 2/0
Midfield Andrezinho 18+6/2 • Augusto 0+1/0 • Mario Bolatti ARG 17+3/1 • Andres D'Alessandro ARG 30/9 • Elton 13+4/0 Glaydson 4+6/1 • Pablo Guinazu ARG 30/0 • Oscar 24+2/10 Ricardo Goulart 2+8/1 • Tinga 19+6/1 • Wilson Mathias 3+1/0 Ze Roberto 11+4/2 • Joao Paulo 2+12/0 • Guilherme 7+5/0 Ilsinho 2+9/0 • Sandro Silva 2+3/0 • Ze Mario 3+1/0
Forwards Alex 1+4/0 • Fernando Cavenaghi ARG 1+1/1 Gilberto 5+8/1 • Leandro Damiao 28/14 • Jo 9+7/2 Lucas Rogio 0+2/0
Coach Celso Roth • Falcao (14/04/2011) • Dorival Junior (12/08/2011)

PALMEIRAS 2011

	Date	Opponent	Res	Score	Comp	Scorers	Att
	15	BotafogoRP	D	0-0	CP		7 043
	20	Ituano	W	4-1	CP	Kleber 2 27 60, Dinei 53, Tinga 91+	3 821
Jan	23	Oeste	W	1-0	CP	Patrik 86	4 302
	27	Paulista	W	3-1	CP	Marcos Assuncao 19, Kleber 44, Patrik 56	6 113
	30	Portuguesa	W	2-0	CP	Cicinho 81, Kleber 90	9 304
	3	Mirassol	W	1-0	CP	Patrik 77	7 383
	6	Corinthians	L	0-1	CP		23 714
Feb	12	Americana	W	1-0	CP	Kleber 54	9 891
	20	Mogi Mirim	D	0 0	CP		7 710
	24	Comercial	W	2-1	CBr1	Adriano 31, Kleber 46	13 286
	27	São Paulo	D	1-1	CP	Adriano 84	26 138
	3	Comercial	W	5-1	CBr1	Adriano 4 62 65 78 80, Gabriel Silva 83	3 509
	5	SantoAndré	D	0-0	CP		6 059
	9	Noroeste	W	2-1	CP	Valdivia 82, Vinicius 85	5 024
Mar	12	S. Bernardo	W	2-0	CP	Danilo 23, Patrik 32	7 676
	17	Uberaba	W	4-0	CBr2	Luan 2 12 22, Kleber 2 43 90	8 206
	20	S. Caetano	D	1-1	CP	Kleber 6	9 527
	23	Linense	W	3-0	CP	Patrik 2 39 61, Kleber 43p	3 986
	26	Bragantino	W	3-0	CP	Thiago Heleno 2 2 80, Joao Vitor 87	10 460

PALMEIRAS (CONTD)

	Date	Opponent	Res	Score	Comp	Scorers	Att
	3	Santos	W	1-0	CP	Kleber 79	10 719
	9	Grêmio Pr	W	2-0	CP	Thiago Heleno 30, OG 75	13 557
Apr	14	SantoAndré	W	2-1	CBr3	Kleber 2 22 70	7 039
	17	Ponte Preta	L	1-2	CP	Max Santos 20	9 956
	21	SantoAndré	W	1-0	CBr3	Danilo 77	33 614
	24	Mirassol	L	1-2	CPqf	Valdivia 10, Marcio Araujo 56	16 653
	1	Corinthians	D	1-1	CPsf	Leandro Amaro 52, L 5-6p	33 861
	5	Coritiba	L	0-6	CBqf		28 870
May	12	Coritiba	W	2-0	CBqf	OG 46, Marcos Assuncao 65	6 541
	22	Botafogo	W	1-0	SA	Kleber 65	13 705
	29	Cruzeiro	D	1-1	SA	Luan 60	9 080
	4	Atlético PR	W	1-0	SA	Chico 75	10 372
	12	Inter	D	1-1	SA	Kleber 54, Luan 66	21 952
Jun	19	Avaí	W	5-0	SA	OG 18, Luan 2 22 41, Kleber 43 72p	12 138
	26	Ceará	L	0-2	SA		13 000
	30	Atlético GO	W	2-0	SA	Maikon Leite 46, Marcos Assuncao 34p	9 450
	8	América MG	D	1-1	SA	Mauricio Ramos 76	1 503
	10	Santos	W	3-0	SA	Maikon Leite 21, Mauricio Ramos 29, Patrik 45	16 751
	21	Flamengo	D	0-0	SA		33 575
	24	Fluminense	L	0-1	SA		9 214
	28	Figueirense	W	1-0	SA	Mauricio Ramos 82	13 283
	31	Atlético MG	W	3-2	SA	Marcos Assuncao 15, Luan 62, Patrik 78	9 983
	4	Coritiba	D	1-1	SA	Marcos Assuncao 19	17 818
	6	Grêmio	D	0-0	SA		15 762
	11	Vasco	L	0-2	CSr1		
	14	Vasco	L	0-1	SA		7 830
Aug	19	Bahia	D	1-1	SA	Jorge Valdivia 54	6 266
	21	São Paulo	D	1-1	SA	Henrique 63	16 813
	25	Vasco	W	3-1	CSr1	Luan 13, Kleber 54, Marcos Assuncao 34p	
	28	Corinthians	W	2-1	SA	Luan 36, Fernando 55	36 299
	1	Botafogo	D	1-3	SA	Marcos Assuncao 90	8 352
	4	Cruzeiro	D	1-1	SA	Luan 68	10 345
	8	Atlético PR	D	2-2	SA	Henrique 15, Fernandao 53	10 798
Sep	11	Inter	L	0-3	SA		9 702
	18	Avaí	D	1-1	SA	Chico 41	8 312
	23	Ceará	W	1-0	SA	OG 44	6 621
	25	Atlético GO	D	1-1	SA	Henrique 23	12 422
	1	América MG	D	1-1	SA	Marcos Assuncao 30	9 285
	9	Santos	L	0-1	SA		7 373
	12	Flamengo	D	1-1	SA	Maikon Leite 63	22 573
Oct	16	Fluminense	L	1-2	SA	Jorge Valdivia 73p	3 649
	22	Figueirense	L	1-2	SA	Ricardo Bueno 90	3 897
	30	Atlético MG	L	1-2	SA	Luan 84	17 119
	6	Coritiba	L	0-2	SA		7 513
	13	Grêmio	D	2-2	SA	Cicinho 25, Marcos Assuncao 60	15 062
Nov	16	Vasco	D	1-1	SA	Luan 64	8 153
	20	Bahia	W	2-0	SA	Ricardo Bueno 19, Marcos Assuncao 90	32 157
	27	São Paulo	W	1-0	SA	Marcos Assuncao 55	18 364
Dc	4	Corinthians	D	0-0	SA		36 708

11th Att: 241 830 • Av: 12 728 (+14.8%) • Pacaembu 37 952

PALMEIRAS SERIE A APPEARANCES/GOALS 2010-11

Goalkeepers Deola 19 • Marcos 19
Defenders Cicinho 30/1 • Danilo 4/0 • Gabriel Silva 19/0 Leandro Amaro 9+2/0 • Mauricio Ramos 17/3 • Thiago Heleno 27+2/0 Henrique 20+1/3 • Gerley 11+2/0 • Paulo Henrique 1+1/0
Midfield Chico 16+12/2 • Joao Vitor 5+14/0 • Lincoln 4+2/0 Luan 33+1/9 • Marcio Araujo 34+1/0 • Marcos Assuncao 34/8 Pierre 0+1/0 • Rivaldo 8+3/0 • Tinga 9+9/0 • Jorge Valdivia CHI 15/2 Pedro Carmona 1+2/0
Forwards Adriano 3+3/0 • Dinei 4+9/0 • Kleber 19/4 • Patrik 18+9/2 Vinicius 2+5/0 • Wellington Paulista 5+1/0 • Maikon Leite 13+8/3 Fernandao 11+7/2 • Ricardo Bueno 8+8/2
Coach Luiz Felipe Scolari

SANTOS 2011

Mon	Date	Opponent	Res	Score	Comp	Scorers	Att
	15	Linense	W	4-1	CP	Maikon Leite 2 8 66, Ze Eduardo 33, Keirrison 41	4 875
	19	Mirassol	W	3-0	CP	Maikon Leite 27, Ze Eduardo 2 47 75	11 496
Jan	23	Grêmio Pr	W	4-2	CP	Elano 2 13 23p, Keirrison 54, Maikon Leite 61	6 670
	26	S. Caetano	D	3-3	CP	Elano 2 8 52, Keirrison 48	6 765
	30	São Paulo	W	2-0	CP	Elano 10, Maikon Leite 73	9 334
	2	Ponte Preta	D	2-2	CP	Elano 40, Maikon Leite 85	8 101
	5	Santo André	D	1-1	CP	Rodrigo Possebon 45	8 310
Feb	11	Noroeste	W	2-0	CP	Ze Eduardo 9, Felipe Anderson 70	10 054
	16	Táchira	D	0-0	CLg5		
	20	Corinthians	L	1-3	CP	Elano 40	19 448
	26	S. Bernardo	D	1-1	CP	Elano 44p	8 945
	3	C. Porteño	D	1-1	CLg5	Elano 55p	
	6	Oeste	W	2-0	CP	Ze Eduardo 2 44 70	2 003
	10	Portuguesa	W	3-0	CP	Neymar 2 40 49, Leo 67	7 843
	12	BotafogoRP	W	2-1	CP	Elano 46, Ganso 55	12 134
Mar	17	Colo Colo	L	2-3	CLg5	Elano 5, Neymar 49	
	19	Bragantino	L	1-2	CP	Elano 31p	11 146
	23	Mogi Mirim	W	3-1	CP	Ze Eduardo 6, Keirrison 49, Edu Dracena 74	3 785
	27	Ituano	W	3-2	CP	Tiago Alves 27, Keirrison 34, Jonathan 66	5 301
	3	Palmeiras	L	0-1	CP		10 719
	7	Colo Colo	W	3-2	CLg5	Elano 34, Danilo 36, Neymar 52	
	10	Americana	D	0-0	CP		11 030
	15	C. Porteño	W	2-1	CLg5	Danilo 12, Maikon Leite 48	
Apr	17	Paulista	W	3-0	CP	Keirrison 1, Alan Patrick 2, Maikon Leite 79	4 263
	20	Táchira	W	3-1	CLg5	Neymar 4, Jonathan 13, Danilo 72	
	23	Ponte Preta	W	1-0	CPqf	Neymar 21	12 225
	28	América	W	1-0	CLr2	Ganso 38	
	30	São Paulo	W	2-0	CPsf	Elano 60, Ganso 72	44 675
	4	América	D	0-0	CLr2		
	8	Corinthians	D	0-0	CPf		34 547
	12	O. Caldas	L	0-1	CLqf	Alan Patrick 42	
May	15	Corinthians	W	2-1	CPf	Arouca 16, Neymar 83	14 322
	19	O. Caldas	D	1-1	CLqf	Neymar 12	
	22	Inter	D	1-1	SA	Keirrison 27p	4 532
	26	C. Porteño	W	1-0	CLsf	Edu Dracena 43	
	28	Botafogo	L	0-1	SA		8 662
	2	C. Porteño	D	3-3	CLsf	Ze Eduardo 2, OG 28, Neymar 45	
	5	Avaí	W	3-1	SA	Borges 2 9 53, Rychely 90	4 109
Jun	11	Cruzeiro	D	1-1	SA	Borges 90	7 133
	16	Peñarol	D	0-0	CLf		
	21	Peñarol	W	2-1	CLf	Neymar 47, Danilo 69	
	30	Figueirense	L	1-2	SA	Rychely 6	5 360
	2	América MG	W	1-0	SA	OG 7	5 912
	4	Palmeiras	L	0-3	SA		16 751
Jul	17	Atlético MG	W	3-2	SA	Danilo 25, Borges 42p	4 717
	8	Flamengo	L	4-5	SA	Borges 2 5 16, Neymar 2 26 51	12 968
	31	Atlético PR	L	2-3	SA	Neymar 13, Borges 63	20 461
	4	Vasco	L	0-2	SA		17 118
	7	Ceará	W	1-0	SA	Borges 33	10 105
	11	Corinthians	D	0-0	SA		9 714
Aug	13	Atlético GO	L	0-2	SA		11 668
	18	Coritiba	L	2-3	SA	Borges 2 4 54	5 143
	21	Bahia	W	2-1	SA	Neymar 3p, Alan Kardec 81	32 157
	25	Fluminense	W	2-1	SA	Borges 2 13 41	6 855
	28	São Paulo	D	1-1	SA	Ganso 80	12 498
	1	Inter	D	3-3	SA	Borges 2 75 86, Alan Kardec 80	17 180
	7	Avaí	W	2-1	SA	Borges 70, Felipe Anderson 77	5 630
Sep	10	Cruzeiro	W	1-0	SA	Borges 11	9 637
	18	Corinthians	W	3-1	SA	Henrique 37, Borges 54, OG 80	34 308
	22	América MG	W	2-1	SA	Borges 61, Edu Dracena 79	18 562
	24	Figueirense	L	2-3	SA	Borges 24, Leo 45	7 059
	1	Fluminense	L	2-3	SA	Neymar 32, Wason Renteria 89	13 125
	5	Grêmio	L	0-1	SA		26 020
	9	Palmeiras	W	1-0	SA	Borges 74	7 373
Oct	13	Atlético MG	L	1-2	SA	Borges 49p	12 351
	16	Grêmio	L	0-1	SA		2 477
	19	Botafogo	W	2-0	SA	Neymar 16, Borges 28	5 770
	23	Flamengo	D	1-1	SA	Neymar 48p	18 257
	29	Atlético PR	W	4-1	SA	Neymar 4 3p 54p 56 70	16 679
	6	Vasco	W	2-0	SA	Neymar 3, Borges 71	12 305
	13	Ceará	W	3-2	SA	Bruno Aguiar 2 9 51, Diogo 72	15 406
Nov	17	Atlético GO	D	1-1	SA	Henrique 90	18 044
	20	Coritiba	L	0-1	SA		16 447
	27	Bahia	D	1-1	SA	Neymar 31	12 052

SANTOS (CONTD)

Mon	Date	Opponent	Res	Score	Comp	Scorers	Att
	4	São Paulo	L	1-4	SA	Elano 61	4 948
Dec	14	Kashiwa	W	3-1	CWsf	Neymar 19, Borges 24, Danilo 63	29 173
	18	Barcelona	L	0-4	CWf		68 166

10th   Att: 168 949 • Av: 8 892 (-9.7%) • Vila Belmiro 20 120

SANTOS SERIE A APPEARANCES/GOALS 2010-11

Goalkeepers Aranha 5 • Rafael 32 • Vladimir 1+1

Defenders Alex Sandro 6/0 • Bruno Aguiar 7+10/2
Bruno Rodrigo 16+2/0 • Crystian 2+4/0 • Danilo 23/1 • Durval 31/0
Edu Dracena 27/1 • Leo 20+2/1 • Para 17+3/4 • Rafael Caldeira 1/0
Vinicius 6+1/0 • Walace 0+1/0 • Wesley Santos 1/0 • Eder Lima 4+2/0
Leandro Silva 3+1/0

Midfield Adriano 17+4/0 • Alan Patrick 2/0 • Anderson Carvalho 3+2/0
Arouca 26/0 • Charles 3+1/0 • Elano 12/1 • Ganso 14/1
Rodrigo Possebon ITA 6+2/0 • Roger 3+4/0 • Henrique 22+1/2
Ibson 13+5/0 • Breitner 0+3/0 • Alison 1/0

Forwards Borges 26/23 • Diogo 6+5/1 • Felipe Anderson 7+11/1
Keirrison 2/0 • Maikon Leite 0+1/0 • Neymar 21/13 • Renan Mota 0+1/0
• Rychely 4+3/2 • Tiago Alves 3+5/0 • Ze Eduardo 1/0
Alan Kardec 16+12/2 • Wason Renteria 3+5/1

Coach Adilson Batista • Marcelo Martelotte (28/02/2011) •
Muricy Ramalho (8/04/2011)

SAO PAULO FC 2011

Mon	Date	Opponent	Res	Score	Comp	Scorers	Att
	16	Mogi Mirim	W	2-0	CP	Rogerio Ceni 4p, Marcelinho Paraiba 87	5 166
	20	S. Bernardo	W	3-0	CP	Dagoberto 4, Marlos 41, Fernandinho 76	6 398
Jan	22	Ponte Preta	L	0-1	CP		11 743
	27	Americana	W	4-3	CP	OG 34, Dagoberto 2 48 57, Jean 73	8 705
	30	Santos	L	0-2	CP		9 334
	3	Linense	W	3-2	CP	Rivaldo 56, Marlos 63, Rogerio Ceni 85	14 481
	6	BotafogoRP	L	1-2	CP	Marcelinho Paraiba 92+	6 701
Feb	13	Portuguesa	W	3-2	CP	Fernandinho 29, Rogerio Ceni 39, Rhodolfo 75	10 828
	17	Treze	W	3-0	CBr1	Dagoberto 2 11 26, Fernandinho 48	12 350
	19	Bragantino	W	4-0	CP	Miranda 18, Fernandinho 43, Lucas Silva 62, Willian Jose 76	14 315
	27	Palmeiras	D	1-1	CP	Fernandinho 25	26 138
	5	S. Caetano	W	2-0	CP	Rhodolfo 74, Jean 90	5 744
	11	Ituano	W	2-0	CP	Jean 41, Dagoberto 49	8 373
	13	Santo André	W	3-0	CP	Dagoberto 9, Lucas Silva 59, Casimiro 67	16 840
Mar	20	Grêmio Pr	W	1-0	CP	Henrique 74	10 929
	24	Paulista	L	2-3	CP	Rogerio Ceni 52p, Dagoberto 70	6 437
	27	Corinthians	W	2-1	CP	Dagoberto 41, Rogerio Ceni 53	17 633
	31	Santa Cruz	L	0-1	CBr2		46 681
	3	Mirassol	W	1-0	CP	Lucas Silva 27	5 912
	7	Santa Cruz	W	2-0	CBr2	Rhodolfo 10, Ilsinho 73	21 066
	10	Noroeste	W	4-1	CP	Rogerio Ceni 35p, Marlos 60, Dagoberto 76, Ilsinho 90	7 658
Apr	17	Oeste	D	1-1	CP	Henrique 72	5 550
	21	Goiás	W	1-0	CBr3	Dagoberto 47	28 526
	24	Portuguesa	W	2-0	CPqf	Ilsinho 41, Dagoberto 80	11 134
	28	Goiás	W	1-0	CBr3	Dagoberto 19	34 544
	30	Santos	L	0-2	CPsf		44 675
	5	Avaí	W	1-0	CBqf	OG 48	20 815
	13	Avaí	L	1-3	CBqf	Casimiro 15	12 956
May	22	Fluminense	W	2-0	SA	Dagoberto 34, Lucas 48	5 732
	29	Figueirense	W	1-0	SA	Lucas 90	9 931
	9	Atlético MG	W	1-0	SA	Casimiro 21	11 737
	11	Grêmio	W	3-1	SA	Casemiro 13, Marlos 67, Jean 85	14 671
Jun	19	Ceará	W	2-0	SA	Marlos 35, Lucas 64	13 000
	26	Corinthians	L	0-5	SA		30 351
	30	Botafogo	L	0-2	SA		8 361
	7	Flamengo	L	0-1	SA		15 790
	9	Cruzeiro	W	2-1	SA	Dagoberto 21, Marlos 46	11 965
Jul	17	Inter	W	3-0	SA	Casemiro 20, Fernandinho 40, Carlinhos Paraiba 90	13 630
	23	Atlético GO	D	2-2	SA	Rhodolfo 8, Rivaldo 53	23 487
	28	Coritiba	W	4-3	SA	Carlinhos Paraiba 18, Juan 23, Dagoberto 31, Lucas 55	23 185
	31	Vasco	L	0-2	SA		22 231

SAO PAULO FC (CONT)

Month	Day	Opponent	Res	Venue	Scorers	Att
Aug	5	Bahia	W 3-0	SA	Rogerio Ceni 28p, Dagoberto 44, Lucas 50	11 262
	7	Avaí	W 2-1	SA	Cicero 2 65 69	11 107
	10	Ceará	L 1-2	CSr1	Rivaldo 23	
	13	Atlético PR	D 2-2	SA	Ilsinho 24, Rivaldo 89	23 657
	19	América MG	D 1-1	SA	Marlos 86	2 636
	21	Palmeiras	D 1-1	SA	Dagoberto 42	16 813
	25	Ceará	W 3-0	CSr1	Cicero 56, Lucas 62, Dagoberto 65	
	28	Santos	D 1-1	SA	Lucas 45	12 498
Sep	1	Fluminense	L 1-2	SA	Rogerio Ceni 74p	7 910
	3	Figueirense	W 2-1	SA	Cicero 42, Rivaldo 60	12 263
	7	Atlético MG	W 2-1	SA	Lucas 1, Dagoberto 54	60 514
	11	Grêmio	L 0-1	SA		30 078
	17	Ceará	W 4-0	SA	Juan 42, Ivan Piris 44, Casemiro 65, Rivaldo 70	23 681
	22	Corinthians	D 0-0	SA		44 950
	25	Botafogo	D 2-2	SA	Henrique 65, Rivaldo 90	26 026
Oct	2	Flamengo	L 1-2	SA	Dagoberto 78	63 871
	5	Cruzeiro	D 3-3	SA	Cicero 60, Dagoberto 65, Juan 77	9 944
	12	Inter	D 0-0	SA		24 460
	16	Atlético GO	L 0-3	SA		23 906
	19	Libertad	W 1-0	CSr2	Luis Fabiano 77	
	23	Coritiba	D 0-0	SA		14 298
	26	Libertad	L 0-2	CSr2		
	30	Vasco	D 0-0	SA		17 575
Nov	5	Bahia	L 3-4	SA	Wellington 21, Lucas 47, Cicero 60	31 230
	12	Avaí	W 2-0	SA	Luis Fabiano 2 59 65	11 134
	16	Atlético PR	L 0-1	SA		18 303
	19	América MG	W 3-1	SA	Luis Fabiano 2 25 41, Juan 49	9 057
	27	Palmeiras	L 0-1	SA		18 364
Dc	4	Santos	W 4-1	SA	Luis Fabiano 2 12 80, Cicero 33, Lucas 38	4 948

6th Att: 407 201 • Av: 21 432 (+45.8%) • Morumbi 67 428

SAO PAULO SERIE A APPEARANCES/GOALS 2010-11

Goalkeepers Denis 2+1 • Rogerio Ceni 36/2
Defenders Bruno Uvini 1+5/0 • Juan 31/4 • Luiz Eduardo 9+2/0 Rhodolfo 31/1 • Xandao 22+1/0 • Joao Filipe 18/0 • Ivan Piris 16+1/1
Midfield Carlinhos Paraiba 26+4/2 • Casemiro 17+4/4 • Dener 0+1/0 Henrique 1+6/0 • Ilsinho 2+4/1 • Jean 21+7/1 • Lucas 28/9
Marlos 8+18/4 • Rivaldo 11+19/5 • Rodrigo Caio 4+4/0
Rodrigo Souto 8/0 • Wellington 34/1 • Ze Vitor 1+1/0 • Cicero 22+5/6
Denilson 12+2/0 • Marcelo Canete 0+2/0
Forwards Dagoberto 30/8 • Fernandinho 10+9/1 • Henrique 3+5/1
Luis Fabiano 10/6 • Willian 4+5/0 • Bruno 0+1/0
Coach Paulo Cesar Carpeggiani • Adilson Batista (16/07/2011)

VASCO DA GAMA 2011

Month	Day	Opponent	Res	Venue	Scorers	Att
Jan	19	Resende	L 0-1	TG		8 576
	23	Nova Iguaçu	L 2-3	TG	Romulo 52, Marcel 59p	3 194
	27	Boavista	L 1-3	TG	Marcel 61	10 190
	30	Flamengo	L 1-2	TG	Romulo 75	15 356
Feb	3	V Redonda	D 0-0	TG		2 614
	6	Americano	W 3-0	TG	Marcel 35, Dede 53, Jeferson 79	2 572
	12	América RJ	W 9-0	TG	Fagner 5, Felipe 18, Ramon 2 22 63, Marcel 25, Enrico 2 37 89, Caique 50, Jeferson Silva 69	2 096
	24	Comercial	W 6-1	CBr1	Felipe Bastos 4, Marcel 2 16 24, Jeferson Silva 45, Eder Luis 57, Romulo 66	4 381
Mar	4	Macaé	L 1-3	TR	Elton 52	5 315
	10	D de Caxias	W 4-2	TR	Felipe 10, Anderson Martins 37, Bernardo 16, Dede 78	9 581
	13	Madureira	W 4-2	TR	Bernardo 3 40 67 85, Felipe Bastos 89	4 857
	20	Botafogo	W 2-0	TR	Diego Souza 59, Eder Luis 70	31 267
	27	Fluminense	D 0-0	TR		27 480
	31	ABC	D 0-0	CBr2		11 641
Apr	3	Bangu	W 4-0	TR	Dede 43, Eder Luis 47, Alecsandro 73, Felipe 75	16 330
	7	ABC	W 2-1	CBr2	Alecsandro 53p, Bernardo 78	18 009
	9	Cabofriense	W 2-1	TR	Bernardo 20, Alecsandro 88	17 081
	14	Náutico	W 3-0	CBr3	Dede 31, Alecsandro 51, Bernardo 92+	12 244

VASCO DA GAMA (CONTD)

Month	Day	Opponent	Res	Venue	Scorers	Att
Apr	17	Olaria	D 2-2	TR	Bernardo 63p, Romulo 91+	4 619
	23	Olaria	W 1-0	TRsf	Eder Luis 37	28 675
	28	Náutico	D 0-0	CBr3		5 557
	1	Flamengo	D 0-0	TRf	L 1-3p	39 029
	5	Atlético PR	D 2-2	CBqf		15 969
May	12	Atlético PR	D 1-1	CBqf	Elton 80	21 206
	19	Avaí	D 1-1	CBsf	Diego Souza 93+p	19 136
	21	Ceará	W 3-1	SA	Bernardo 2 77 80, Jeferson 89	9 422
	26	Avaí	D 2-0	CBsf	OG 3, Diego Souza 34	15 868
	29	América MG	W 3-0	SA	Bernardo 9p, Enrico 48, Elton 90	2 626
Jun	2	Coritiba	W 1-0	CBf	Alecsandro 51	23 058
	5	Coritiba	L 1-5	SA	Elton 67	16 691
	11	Coritiba	L 2-3	CBf	Alecsandro 12, Eder Luis 57	31 516
	12	Figueirense	D 1-1	SA	Elton 17	17 777
	19	Grêmio	D 1-1	SA	Bernardo 73	16 322
	26	Atlético GO	W 1-0	SA	Felipe 1	11 959
	29	Cruzeiro	L 0-3	SA		7 695
Jul	2	Corinthians	L 1-2	SA	Juninho 2	28 453
	9	Inter	W 2-0	SA	Eder Luis 25, Dede 83	6 223
	16	Atlético PR	W 2-1	SA	Alecsandro 2 45 71	9 775
	24	Atlético MG	W 2-1	SA	Diego Souza 2 18 90	16 100
	28	Bahia	D 1-1	SA	Elton 90	18 873
	31	São Paulo	W 2-0	SA	Eder Luis 51, Felipe 90	22 231
Aug	4	Santos	W 2-0	SA	Diego Souza 3, Dede 20	17 118
	7	Botafogo	L 0-4	SA		21 238
	12	Palmeiras	W 2-0	CSr1	Diego Souza 43, Elton 79	
	14	Palmeiras	W 1-0	SA	Bernardo 80	7 830
	17	Avaí	W 2-0	SA	Diego Souza 27, Dede 67	6 542
	21	Fluminense	D 1-1	SA	Juninho 36	16 991
	26	Palmeiras	L 1-3	CSr1	Jumar 58	
	28	Flamengo	D 0-0	SA		33 026
	31	Ceará	W 3-1	SA	Elton 2 52 65, Eder Luis 61	5 428
Sep	4	América MG	L 1-4	SA	Juninho 21	2 644
	9	Coritiba	W 2-0	SA	Juninho 16, Romulo 55	9 397
	11	Figueirense	D 1-1	SA	Fagner 16	12 877
	17	Grêmio	W 4-0	SA	Elton 4, Diego Souza 34, Eder Luis 52, Fagner 61	16 014
	23	Atlético GO	D 1-1	SA	Diego Souza 33	14 576
	25	Cruzeiro	W 3-0	SA	Diego Souza 3 38 60 81	6 348
	2	Corinthians	D 2-2	SA	Dede 16, Fagner 45	22 855
Oct	2	Aurora	L 1-3	CSr2	Bernardo 41	
	9	Inter	L 0-3	SA		23 797
	13	Atlético PR	D 2-2	SA	Elton 2 66 82	10 813
	16	Atlético MG	W 2-0	SA	Elton 2, Fagner 19	15 269
	23	Bahia	W 2-0	SA	Felipe 23, Diego Souza 90	32 157
	26	Aurora	W 8-3	CSr2	Bernardo 2 9 78, Alecsandro 2 38 44, Leandro 49, Julinho 69, Douglas 83, Allan 90	
	30	São Paulo	D 0-0	SA		17 575
	2	Univ'sitario	L 0-2	CSqf		
	6	Santos	D 0-2	SA		12 305
Nov	9	Univ'sitario	W 5-2	CSqf	Diego Souza 23p, Elton 48, Dede 2 58 73, Alecsandro 82	
	13	Botafogo	W 2-0	SA	Felipe Bastos 16, Dede 60	33 778
	16	Palmeiras	D 1-1	SA	Dede 4	8 153
	19	Avaí	W 2-0	SA	Felipe 50, Elton 66	19 834
	23	U. de Chile	D 1-1	CSsf	Bernardo 34	
	27	Fluminense	W 2-1	SA	Alecsandro 77, Bernardo 90	29 476
	30	U. de Chile	L 0-2	CSsf		
Dc	4	Flamengo	D 1-1	SA	Diego Souza 30	34 064

2nd Att: 293 698 • Av: 15 458 (+29.2%) • São Januário 20 150

VASCO SERIE A APPEARANCES/GOALS 2010-11

Goalkeepers Alessandro 0+1 • Fernando Prass 38
Defenders Anderson Martins 15/0 • Dede 30/6 • Douglas 2+2/0 • Fagner 35/4 • Fernando 3/0 • Julio Irrazabal PAR 0+1/0 • Jomar 2+1/0 • Marcio Careca 1+1/0 • Max 2+1/0 • Ramon 1+2/0 • Renato Silva 19/0 • Julinho 8+/0 • Vitor Ramos 4+2/0
Midfield Allan 11+7/0 • Bernardo 5+24/6 • Leandro Chaparro ARG 0+4/0 • Diego Rosa 1+9/0 • Diego Souza 30/11 • Eduardo Costa 15+3/0 • Enrico 2+1/1 • Felipe 19+1/4 • Fellipe Bastos 12+5/1 • Jeferson 3+1/1 • Jumar 23+3/0 • Nilton 4+3/0 • Romulo 32/1 • Juninho Pernambucano 19+2/4
Forwards Alecsandro 18+3/3 • Eder Luis 32/4 • Elton 17+11/11 • Leandro 2+15/0 • Misael 0+1/0 • Kim 0+2/0
Coach Ricardo Gomes (31/01/2011) • Cristavo Borges (29/08/2011)

BRB – BARBADOS

FIFA/COCA-COLA WORLD RANKING

'93	'94	'95	'96	'97	'98	'99	'00	'01	'02	'03	'04	'05	'06	'07	'08	'09	'10	'11	'12
114	107	103	110	113	121	113	104	107	99	124	121	115	98	128	122	129	131	165	

	2011													
	Jan	Feb	Mar	Apr	May	Jun	Jul	Aug	Sep	Oct	Nov	Dec	**High** **Low** **Av**	
	130	132	137	132	132	141	145	147	150	148	161	165	**92** **165** **114**	

2011 was a disasterous year for the Barbados national team and it ended with them slumping to their lowest-ever position in the FIFA/Coca-Cola World Ranking. In 11 games played, Barbados won just once - a friendly against St Lucia - and having received a bye to the first group stage of qualifiers for the 2014 FIFA World Cup, the team then lost all six of their matches against Guyana, Bermuda and Trinidad. Identifying players born in the UK of Bajan descent has been a policy of the BFA but the logistics of regular appearances can be a problem, none more so than with Wigan's Emerson Boyce who appeared in just two of the qualifiers - only his third and fourth appearances for Barbados since his debut in 2008. In club football there was a welcome return to the limelight for one of the great names of Bajan football when Weymouth Wales won the 2011 cup - the first trophy for almost a quarter of a century for the most successful club on the island. In the final a Dwayne Stanford goal was enough to beat surprise finalists St Peter's Cosmos and earn Weymouth Wales their eighth win in the history of the tournament. They also managed to break into the top three of the league but the title was won by Youth Milan for only the second time in their history. Defending champions Notre Dame were runners-up but they declined to take part in the 2011 CFU Club Championship.

FIFA WORLD CUP RECORD
1930-1974 DNE 1978 DNQ 1982-1990 DNE 1994-2014 DNQ

BARBADOS FOOTBALL ASSOCIATION (BFA)

	Richmond Welches,
✉	PO Box 1362, Bridgetown, St Michael, BB 11000
☎	+1 246 2281707
📠	+1 246 2286484
✉	bdosfootball@caribsurf.com
🖥	www.barbadossoccer.com
FA	1910 CON 1968 FIFA 1968
P	Ronald Jones
GS	David Hinds

FIFA BIG COUNT 2006

Total players	37 550
% of population	13.41%
Male	33 590
Female	3 960
Amateurs 18+	7 095
Youth under 18	8 505
Unregistered	18 710
Professionals	0
Referees	86
Admin & coaches	1 240
Number of clubs	130
Number of teams	240

MAJOR CITIES/TOWNS

		Population
1	Bridgetown	93 312
2	Speightstown	2 402
3	Bathsheba	1 575
4	Holetown	1 494
5	Oistins	1 444
6	Bulkeley	1 115
7	Crane	1 016
8	Crab Hill	716
9	Blackmans	550
10	Greenland	524
11	Hillaby	509

BARBADOS

Capital	Bridgetown	Population	284 589 (180)	% in cities	40%
GDP per capita	$19 100 (66)	Area km²	430 km² (200)	GMT + / -	-4
Neighbours (km)	Coast 97				

RECENT INTERNATIONAL MATCHES PLAYED BY BARBADOS

2006	Opponents	Score	Venue	Comp	Scorers	Att	Referee
20-09	St Kitts and Nevis	D 1-1	St John's	CCq	Ifill [42]	300	Campbell JAM
22-09	Antigua & Barbuda	W 3-1	St John's	CCq	Williams [44], McCammon [58], Lovell [90]	2 500	Frederick VIR
24-09	Anguilla	W 7-1	St John's	CCq	McCammon 3 [35 44 76], Ifill 3 [40 58 83], Niblett [75]	2 800	Wijngaarde SUR
5-11	Grenada	D 2-2	Black Rock	Fr	Parris [28], Goodridge [67p]		
19-11	Bahamas	W 2-1	Bridgetown	CCq	Forde.N [38], Skinner [44]	4 500	Jauregui ANT
21-11	St Vincent/Grenadines	W 3-0	Bridgetown	CCq	James [16], Forde.N [34], Ifill [60p]	3 500	Jauregui ANT
23-11	Bermuda	D 1-1	Bridgetown	CCq	Ifill [4]	4 000	Jauregui ANT
2007							
12-01	Trinidad and Tobago	D 1-1	Port of Spain	CCr1	Harvey [66]		Moreno PAN
15-01	Haiti	L 0-2	Port of Spain	CCr1			Jauregua ANT
17-01	Martinique	L 2-3	Port of Spain	CCr1	Harvey [27], Soares [42]		Jauregua ANT
25-03	Guatemala	D 0-0	Bridgetown	Fr		2 500	Forde BRB
2008							
13-01	Antigua & Barbuda	W 3-2	Black Rock	Fr	Vaughan [17], Straker [39], Lynch [63]	2 700	Small BRB
6-02	Dominica	D 1-1	Roseau	WCq	Rashida Williams [43]	4 200	Quesada CRC
13-03	St Vincent/Grenadines	W 2-0	Kingstown	Fr	Stanford [38], Norman Forde [87]	1 050	Cambridge VIN
15-03	Grenada	D 1-1	St George's	Fr	Worrell [75]	2 500	Phillip GRN
26-03	Dominica	W 1-0	Bridgetown	WCq	Stanford [80]	4 150	Batres GUA
11-05	Trinidad and Tobago	L 0-3	Macoya	Fr		1 200	Brizan TRI
6-06	Bermuda	L 1-2	Hamilton	Fr	Norman Forde [44]	2 000	Raynor BER
9-06	Bermuda	L 0-3	Hamilton	Fr		2 200	Francis BER
15-06	USA	L 0-8	Carson	WCq		11 500	Rodriguex MEX
22-06	USA	L 0-1	Bridgetown	WCq		2 000	Moreno PAN
26-09	British Virgin Isles	W 2-1	Basseterre	CCq	Rashida Williams [11], Norman Forde [53]	150	Baptiste DMA
28-09	St Kitts and Nevis	W 3-1	Basseterre	CCq	Straker [35], Skeete [45], Rashida Williams [80]	500	Charles DMA
23-10	Surinam	W 3-2	Havana	CCq	Norman Forde 3 [62 65 70]	100	Morrison JAM
25-10	Cuba	D 1-1	Havana	CCq	Doyle [66]	1 000	Campbell JAM
27-10	Netherlands Antilles	W 2-1	Havana	CCq	Norman Forde [6p], Parris [20]	1 000	Morrison JAM
3-12	Jamaica	L 1-2	Kingston	CCr1	Riviere Williams [45]	20 000	Aguilar SLV
5-12	Trinidad and Tobago	L 1-2	Montego Bay	CCr1	Goodridge [17]	2 000	Jauregui ANT
7-12	Grenada	L 2-4	Trelawny	CCr1	Riviere Williams 2 [71 79]	9 000	Aguilar SLV
2009							
8-02	Grenada	W 5-0	Bridgetown	Fr	Jeffrey Williams 2 [35 68], Stanford [43], Harte [44], Chandler [88]	3 000	Forde BRB
2010							
25-09	Dominica	L 0-2	Bridgetown	Fr		625	Taylor BRB
26-09	Dominica	L 1-3	Bridgetown	Fr	Harte [21]	580	Skeete DMA
6-10	St Kitts and Nevis	D 1-1	Kingstown	CCq	Rashida Williams [14]	250	Elskampr SUR
8-10	Montserrat	W 5-0	Kingstown	CCq	Norman Forde 2 [19 83], Riviere Williams [36], Terry Adamson [53], Kadeem Atkins [90]	350	Pinas SUR
10-10	St Vincent/Grenadines	D 0-0	Kingstown	CCq		5 420	Jauregui ANT
2011							
20-05	Guyana	L 0-1	Linden	Fr		300	Lancaster GUY
22-05	Guyana	L 2-3	Georgetown	Fr	Mardona Lavine [1], Riviere Williams [15]	2 500	Young GUY
27-05	St Vincent/Grenadines	D 0-0	Bridgetown	Fr		3 500	Skeete BRB
29-05	Guyana	D 1-1	Bridgetown	Fr	Rashida Williams [24]	2 055	Taylor BRB
21-08	St Lucia	W 4-0	Bridgetown	Fr	Riviere Williams [35], Kadeem Atkins 2 [45 56], Kyle Gibson [90]	3 500	Skeete BRB
2-09	Guyana	L 0-2	Georgetown	WCq		4 500	St Catherine LCA
6-09	Trinidad and Tobago	L 0-2	Bridgetown	WCq		775	Bonilla SLV
7-10	Guyana	L 0-2	Bridgetown	WCq		2 500	Georges HAI
11-10	Trinidad and Tobago	L 0-4	Port of Spain	WCq		3 000	Bogle JAM
11-11	Bermuda	L 1-2	Prospect	WCq	Diquan Adamson [7]	1 000	Barrios GUA
14-11	Bermuda	L 1-2	Prospect	WCq	Sheridan Grosvenor [92+]	1 000	Moreno PAN

Fr = Friendly match • CC = Digicel Caribbean Cup • WC = FIFA World Cup • q = qualifier • r1 = first round group

BARBADOS 2011

DIGICEL PREMIER LEAGUE

	Pl	W	D	L	F	A	Pts	Youth Milan	Notre Dame	Weymouth W	Brittons Hill	Pinelands Utd	Paradise	Gall Hill	Bagatelle	St John's	Ellerton
Youth Milan	18	12	2	4	35	13	38		2-1	2-0	3-0	1-1	2-1	0-1	0-0	1-0	0-1
Notre Dame	18	9	6	3	40	20	33	2-0		2-1	1-3	0-1	2-2	4-2	2-1	5-0	3-1
Weymouth Wales	18	10	3	5	27	17	33	1-1	1-1		0-2	1-1	2-0	1-0	5-2	1-0	2-1
Brittons Hill	18	10	1	7	27	21	31	0-2	1-4	2-0		0-1	1-0	0-0	2-1	1-2	2-3
Pinelands United	18	8	6	4	28	22	30	1-3	1-0	0-0	0-3		0-0	2-1	2-1	2-2	2-0
Paradise	18	8	4	6	35	21	28	0-3	2-2	0-2	2-1	5-2		3-0	0-1	3-1	4-0
Pride of Gall Hill	18	6	3	9	28	30	21	2-3	1-1	0-3	0-2	2-5	0-3		5-0	5-1	5-1
Bagatelle	18	5	3	10	27	32	18	1-0	1-1	0-3	1-3	1-2	2-5	0-0		1-3	1-0
St John's Sonnets	18	4	2	12	20	39	14	1-5	0-2	1-2	1-2	1-0	0-0	1-2	1-2		3-4
Ellerton	18	3	0	15	14	55	9	0-6	0-6	1-2	0-2	0-5	0-5	0-2	1-3	1-2	

12/02/2011 - 2/07/2011 • † Qualified for the CFU Club Championship
Top scorers: **12** - Armando Lashley, Paradise • **11** - Kenroy Skinner, Youth Milan • **10** - Peter Stoute, Pinelands • **9** - Walton Burrowes, Brittons Hill

BARBADOS 2011 DIVISION ONE

	Pl	W	D	L	F	A	Pts
Bar'dos Defence Force	22	15	5	2	52	15	50
Dayrells Road	22	15	4	3	52	17	49
Silver Sands	22	14	3	5	49	20	45
St Peter's Cosmos	22	11	3	8	30	24	36
Empire	22	9	6	7	50	36	33
Univ. West Indies	22	10	2	10	35	44	32
Deacons	22	9	4	9	43	41	31
Clarkes Hill	22	9	3	10	29	34	30
Benfica	22	6	5	11	39	47	23
Maxwell	22	3	8	11	25	45	17
Technico	22	4	4	14	23	61	16
Haynesville	22	2	3	17	20	63	9

16/02/2011 - 6/06/2011

MEDALS TABLE

		Overall	Lge	Cup	Town
		G	G	G	
1	Weymouth Wales	23	15	8	Carrington
2	Notre Dame	15	9	6	Bayville
3	Everton	9	5	4	Dover
4	Paradise	9	4	5	Gall Hill
5	Pride of Gall Hill	6	2	4	Checker Hall
6	Youth Milan	4	2	2	Pinelands
7	Pinelands	4	3	1	Paragon
8	BDF	3	2	1	Brittons Hill
9	Brittons Hill	3	2	1	

FA CUP 2011

Round of 16		Quarter–finals		Semi–finals		Final	
Weymouth Wales	2						
Ellerton	1	**Weymouth Wales**	2				
Fairy Valley	1	Bagatelle	0				
Bagatelle	2			**Weymouth Wales**	3		
L & R United	5			Notre Dame	2		
Checker Hall	0	L & R United	1				
Pride of Gall Hill	0	**Notre Dame**	5				
Notre Dame	4					**Weymouth Wales**	1
Paradise	0 4p					St Peter's Cosmos	0
Brittons Hill	0 3p	**Paradise**	2				
Empire	2	Bar'dos Defence Force	1				
Bar'dos Defence Force	3			Paradise	1		
Crumpton	1			**St Peter's Cosmos**	2		
Benfica	0	Crumpton	1				
Carlton	1	**St Peter's Cosmos**	2				
St Peter's Cosmos	3						

3rd place: Notre Dame 2-1 Paradise

CUP FINAL
National Stadium, Waterford
10-07-2011
Scorer - Dwayne Stanford 36

BRU – BRUNEI DARUSSALAM

FIFA/COCA-COLA WORLD RANKING

'93	'94	'95	'96	'97	'98	'99	'00	'01	'02	'03	'04	'05	'06	'07	'08	'09	'10	'11	'12
151	165	167	170	178	183	185	193	189	194	194	199	199	175	188	181	191	197	202	

						2011								High	Low	Av
Jan	Feb	Mar	Apr	May	Jun	Jul	Aug	Sep	Oct	Nov	Dec		High	Low	Av
197	197	197	199	196	197	198	199	198	197	198	202		140	202	183

The troubled recent history of football in Brunei Darussalam took a step nearer to normalisation when the newly formed National Football Association of Brunei Darussalam was recognised by FIFA and the international suspension on the country lifted. That was major news for the biggest club in the country, DPMM, who were readmitted to Singapore's S.League for the 2012 season. They had been forced to withdraw in 2009 as the FIFA ban prevented Brunei from engaging in any football outside of its own borders. Most of DPMM's players had taken up positions with clubs in the local championship, but in a bizarre twist the ending of the ban actually saw the Brunei Premier League suspended whilst only at the halfway stage. As it was being organised by the rival football association, it no longer had a mandate to continue and was left unfinished. The NFABD was left with the task of re-registering all the clubs in the country before it could contemplate the task of organising a championship of its own for 2012. The one tournament completed in 2011 was the League Cup which was won by Majra, surprise winners over army club ABDB thanks to an extra-time winner in the final. The FIFA ban had a major consequence for the Brunei national team which was unable to enter the 2014 FIFA World Cup qualifiers.

FIFA WORLD CUP RECORD
1930-1982 DNE **1986** DNQ **1990-1998** DNE **2002** DNQ **2006-2014** DNE

NATIONAL FOOTBALL ASSOCIATION OF BRUNEI DARUSSALAM (NAFBD)

NFABD House, Jalan Pusat Persidangan, Bandar Seri Begawan, BB 4313, Brunei

☎ +673 2 380047
📠 +673 2 380057
✉ nfabd@hotmail.com
💻

FA 1959 CON 1970 FIFA 1969
P Dato Abdul Rahman Mohiddin
GS Mohd Noor bin Haji Abdullah

FIFA BIG COUNT 2006

Total players	7 500
% of population	1.98%
Male	7 300
Female	200
Amateurs 18+	300
Professionals	0
Referees	33
Admin & coaches	100
Number of clubs	20
Number of teams	40

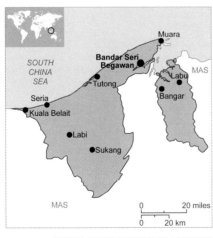

MAJOR CITIES/TOWNS

		Population
1	Bandar S Begawan	33 026
2	Kuala Belait	27 726
3	Seria	27 620
4	Tutong	20 962
5	Bangar	3 501

NEGARA BRUNEI DARUSSALAM • BRUNEI DARUSSALAM

Capital Bandar Seri Begawan	Population 388 190 (175)	% in cities 75%
GDP per capita $53 100 (8)	Area km² 5 765 km² (172)	GMT +/- +8
Neighbours (km) Malaysia 381 • Coast 161		

RECENT INTERNATIONAL MATCHES PLAYED BY BRUNEI DARUSSALAM

2007 Opponents	Score	Venue	Comp	Scorers	Att	Referee
No international matches played in 2007						
2008						
13-05 Philippines	L 0-1	Iloilo City	CCq		3 500	Saleem MDV
15-05 Bhutan	D 1-1	Barotac	CCq	Muhammad Khayrun Bin Salleh 76	4 000	Mahapab THA
17-05 Tajikistan	L 0-4	Iloilo City	CCq		450	Al Badwawi UAE
19-10 Philippines	D 1-1	Phnom Penh	AFFq	Shahraezn Said 17	12 000	
21-10 Timor-Leste	W 4-1	Phnom Penh	AFFq	Shahraezn Said 2 9 26, Azwan Saleh 57, Sallehuddin Damit 76p		
23-10 Laos	L 2-3	Phnom Penh	AFFq	Hardi Bujang 28, Abu Bakar Mahari 84		
25-10 Cambodia	L 1-2	Phnom Penh	AFFq	Hardi Bujang 28,	15 000	
2009						
4-04 Sri Lanka	L 1-5	Colombo	CCq	Kamarul Ariffin Ramlee 82	700	Zhao Liang CHN
6-04 Pakistan	L 0-6	Colombo	CCq		200	Orzuev TJK
8-04 Chinese Taipei	L 0-5	Colombo	CCq		1 000	Al Zahrani KSA
2010						
No international matches played in 2010						
2011						
No international matches played in 2011						

CC = AFC Challenge Cup • AFF = ASEAN Championship • q = qualifier

DST GROUP BRUNEI LEAGUE CUP 2011

Round of 16		Quarter–finals		Semi–finals		Final	
Majra	4p						
Prisons Department	2p	Majra	2				
AM Gunners	2 7p	Indera	0				
Indera	2 8p			Majra	6		
Jerudong	4			DST Group FT	0		
Muara Vella	2	Jerudong	1				
Kilanas	0	DST Group FT	5				
DST Group FT	1					Majra	2
QAF	7					ABDB	1
Lun Bawang	1	QAF	3				
Mengalit	1	Brunei Youth Team	0				
Brunei Youth Team	3			QAF	1		
Wijaya	3			ABDB	3		
BIBD FT	2	Wijaya	0				
LLRC FT	0	ABDB	2				
ABDB	2						

LEAGUE CUP FINAL

Hassanal Bolkiah National Stadium,
Berakas, 6-06-2011
Scorers - Abdul Azim 47, Adi Md
Said 100 for Majra;
Ak Md Fakharrazi 70 for ABDB

BRUNEI DARUSSALAM 2011

DST GROUP BRUNEI PREMIER LEAGUE	Pl	W	D	L	F	A	Pts	ABDB	AM Gunners	Majra	QAF	Indera	Jerudong	Wijaya	Penjara	LLRC FT
ABDB	8	7	1	0	28	6	22		3-2	1-0				6-0	6-1	4-1
AM Gunners	8	5	1	2	27	18	16				4-4	3-4			2-1	5-1
Majra	8	4	2	2	16	10	14		1-2			1-1	3-2	4-1	1-1	
QAF	8	4	2	2	21	16	14	1-1		2-3		3-1	5-3	3-1		
Indera	7	3	2	2	14	13	11	1-3					1-1		3-1	
Jerudong	8	2	2	4	14	20	8	0-4	0-2					2-0		1-1
Wijaya	7	2	0	5	10	21	6	2-5							3-1	
Penjara	8	1	1	6	11	22	4				2-3		2-3			2-1
LLRC FT	8	1	1	6	6	21	4		0-3	1-0				0-3		

7/03/2011 - 15/05/2011 • League suspended and remained unfinished

BUL – BULGARIA

FIFA/COCA-COLA WORLD RANKING

'93	'94	'95	'96	'97	'98	'99	'00	'01	'02	'03	'04	'05	'06	'07	'08	'09	'10	'11	'12
31	16	17	15	36	49	37	53	51	42	34	37	39	43	18	27	30	49	84	

					2011										
	Jan	Feb	Mar	Apr	May	Jun	Jul	Aug	Sep	Oct	Nov	Dec	High	Low	Av
	49	51	47	45	46	46	48	51	55	75	85	84	8	85	35

2011 was another wretched year for the Bulgarian national team which finished in last place in its Euro 2012 qualifying group. That was an embarrassing first for the team which was then compunded by slipping to an all-time low of 85 in the FIFA/Coca-Cola World Ranking - a drop of over 50 places since the end of 2009. Having taken over as coach in October 2010, Lothar Matthaus survived less than year in the job, leaving in September 2011 after the defeats at the hands of England and Switzerland. Luboslav Penev was handed the reigns at the end of the year and he will hope to emulate his uncle Dimitar who led the Bulgarians to the semi-finals of the 1994 World Cup. One moment of note during the year came in the 3-0 defeat to England when Stilian Petrov overtook Borislav Mihaylov to become the all-time record cap winner for Bulgaria. Earlier in the year Lubo Penev had coached Litex Lovech to the Bulgarian championship as they won back-to-back titles - just as they had done at the end of the 1990s. The player of the season was Levski striker Garra Dembele who scored at over a goal a game but he and Levski ended the season trophyless despite a strong finish in the league. The cup was won by rivals CSKA Sofia who beat first-time finalists Slavia Sofia 2-0 to take the trophy for only the second time since the turn of the century.

UEFA EUROPEAN CHAMPIONSHIP RECORD

1960 r1 **1964** r2 **1968-1992** DNQ **1996** 11 r1 **2000** DNQ **2004** 16 r1 **2008-2012** DNQ

BULGARIAN FOOTBALL UNION (BFU)

✉ 26 Tzar Ivan Assen II Str., Sofia - 1124

☎ +359 2 9426253
📠 +359 2 9426200
✉ bfu@bfunion.bg
🖥 www.bfunion.bg
FA 1923 CON 1954 FIFA 1924
P Borislav Mihailov
GS Borislav Popov

FIFA BIG COUNT 2006

Total players	327 033
% of population	4.43%
Male	289 348
Female	37 685
Amateurs 18+	31 324
Youth under 18	17 389
Unregistered	90 400
Professionals	1 060
Referees	1 411
Admin & coaches	1 160
Number of clubs	559
Number of teams	1 301

MAJOR CITIES/TOWNS

		Population
1	Sofia	1 125 101
2	Plovdiv	348 165
3	Varna	325 818
4	Burgas	190 239
5	Ruse	157 671
6	Stara Zagora	143 736
7	Pleven	115 388
8	Sliven	101 632
9	Dobrich	100 867
10	Shumen	85 668
11	Pernik	81 685
12	Yambol	80 225
13	Khaskovo	77 419
14	Pazardzhik	76 967
15	Blagoevgrad	68 686
16	Vratsa	64 889
17	Gabrovo	63 865
18	Veliko Tarnovo	61 788
29	Lovech	39 414

REPUBLIKA BALGARIYA • REPUBLIC OF BULGARIA

Capital Sofia	Population 7 204 687 (98)	% in cities 71%
GDP per capita $12 900 (85)	Area km² 110 879 km² (104)	GMT + / - +2
Neighbours (km) Greece 494, Macedonia 148, Romania 608, Serbia 318, Turkey 240 • Coast 354		

RECENT INTERNATIONAL MATCHES PLAYED BY BULGARIA

2008 Opponents	Score	Venue	Comp	Scorers	Att	Referee
20-08 Bosnia-Hercegovina	W 2-1	Zenica	Fr	Berbatov 2 [26] [57]	7 000	Stankovic SRB
6-09 Montenegro	D 2-2	Podgorica	WCq	Petrov.S [11], Georgiev [92+]	9 000	Oriekhov UKR
11-10 Italy	D 0-0	Sofia	WCq		35 000	Lannoy FRA
15-10 Georgia	D 0-0	Tbilisi	WCq		35 250	Kuipers NED
19-11 Serbia	L 1-6	Belgrade	Fr	Georgiev [20]	6 000	Sippel GER
2009						
11-02 Switzerland	D 1-1	Geneva	Fr	Popov [34]	9 500	Duarte POR
28-03 Republic of Ireland	D 1-1	Dublin	WCq	Kilbane OG [74]	60 002	Bebek CRO
1-04 Cyprus	W 2-0	Sofia	WCq	Popov [8], Makriev [94+]	16 916	Ingvarsson SWE
6-06 Republic of Ireland	D 1-1	Sofia	WCq	Telkiyski [29]	38 000	Larsen DEN
12-08 Latvia	W 1-0	Sofia	Fr	Rangelov [54]	2 000	Pamporidis GRE
5-09 Montenegro	W 4-1	Sofia	WCq	Kishishev [45], Telkiyski [49], Berbatov [83], Domovchiyski [91+]	7 543	Asumaa FIN
9-09 Italy	L 0-2	Turin	WCq		26 122	Meyer GER
10-10 Cyprus	L 1-4	Larnaca	WCq	Berbatov [44]	3 700	Allaerts BEL
14-10 Georgia	W 6-2	Sofia	WCq	Berbatov 3 [6] [23] [35], Petrov.M 2 [14] [44], Angelov [31]	700	Jakobsson ISL
18-11 Malta	W 4-1	Paola	Fr	Bozhinov [5], Berbabtov 2 [76] [83], Georgiev [81]		Nijhuis NED
2010						
3-03 Poland	L 0-2	Warsaw	Fr		6 800	Kever SUI
19-05 Belgium	L 1-2	Brussels	Fr	Popov [31]	15 000	Weiner GER
24-05 South Africa	D 1-1	Johannesburg	Fr	Bojinov [31]	25 000	Fagla TOG
11-08 Russia	L 0-1	St. Petersburg	Fr		8 200	Rizzoli ITA
3-09 England	L 0-4	London	ECq		73 426	Kassai HUN
7-09 Montenegro	L 0-1	Sofia	ECq		9 470	Bezborodov RUS
8-10 Wales	W 1-0	Cardiff	ECq	Popov [48]	14 061	Eriksson SWE
12-10 Saudi Arabia	W 2-0	Istanbul	Fr	Rangelov [39], Domovchiyski [44]	100	Gocek TUR
17-11 Serbia	L 0-1	Sofia	Fr		1 500	Avram ROU
2011						
9-02 Estonia	D 2-2	Antalya	Fr	Popov 2 [40p] [83p]		
26-03 Switzerland	D 0-0	Sofia	ECq		9 600	Collum SCO
29-03 Cyprus	W 1-0	Larnaca	Fr	Petrov [35]		Borg MLT
4-06 Montenegro	D 1-1	Podgorica	ECq	Popov [66]	11 500	Yefet ISR
10-08 Belarus	L 0-1	Minsk	Fr		6 500	Dunauskas LTU
2-09 England	L 0-3	Sofia	ECq		27 230	De Bleeckere BEL
6-09 Switzerland	L 1-3	Basel	ECq	Ivanov.I [9]	16 880	Kralovec CZE
7-10 Ukraine	L 0-3	Kyiv	Fr			Kralovec CZE
11-10 Wales	L 0-1	Sofia	ECq		1 672	Gil POL

Fr = Friendly match • EC = UEFA EURO 2012 • WC = FIFA World Cup • q = qualifier

BULGARIA NATIONAL TEAM HISTORICAL RECORDS

Caps

105 - Stilian Petrov 1998- • **102** - Borislav Mihaylov 1983-98 • **96** - Hristo Bonev 1967-79 • **92** - Krasimir Balakov 1988-2003 • **90** - Dimitar Penev 1965-74 • **89** - Martin Petrov 1999- • **88** - Radostin Kishishev 1996-2009 • **83** - Hristo Stoichkov 1986-99 • **80** - Zlatko Yankov 1989-99 • **79** - Anyo Sadkov 1981-91 • **78** - Dimitar Berbatov 1999- & Nasko Sirakov 1983-96 • **77** - Georgi Dimitrov 1978-87

Goals

48 - Dimitar Berbatov 1999- • **47** - Hristo Bonev 1967-79 • **37** - Hristo Stoichkov 1986-99 • **26** - Emil Kostadinov 1988-98 • **25** - Lyubomir Angelov 1931-40, Ivan Kolev 1950-63 & Petar Jekov 1963-72 • **23** - Nasko Sirakov 1983-96 • **20** - Dimitar Milanov 1948-59 • **19** - Georgi Asparukov 1962-70, Dinko Dermendjiev 1966-77 & Martin Petrov 1999- • **16** - Krasimir Balakov 1988-2003 & Todor Diev 1955-65

Past Coaches

Leopold Nich AUT 1924 • Willibold Scheiscal AUT 1925 • Pavel Grozdanov 1927-30 • Carl Nemes 1930 AUT • Otto Feist GER 1931 • Pavel Grozdanov 1932-33 • Karoly Foggle HUN 1934-35 • Nikola Kalkandzhiev 1935 • Ivan Batandzhiev 1936 • Geno Mateev 1936 • Stanislav Toms CZE 1937-38 • Kostantin Maznikov 1938 • Ivan Radoev 1939 • Franz Koler AUT 1940-41 • Ivan Radoev 1942 • Ivan Batandzhiev 1943 • Todor Konov 1946 • Mihail Manov 1947 • Rezso Somlaly HUN & Ivan Radoev 1947 • Ivan Radoev 1947 • Lubomir Angelov 1948 • Andor Haidu HUN 1948-49 • Ivan Radoev 1950 • Lubomir Angelov 1950 • Andor Haidu HUN 1950 • Lubomir Angelov 1953 • Stoyan Ormandzhiev 1950-53 • Stoyan Ormandzhiev & Krum Milev 1954-60 • Georgi Pachedzhiev 1955-62 • Stoyan Ormandzhiev 1963 • Bella Volentik HUN 1963-64 • Rudolf Vytlacil CZE 1965-66 • Dobromir Tashkov 1966 • Stefan Bozhkov 1967-70 • Vasil Spasov 1970-72 • Hristo Mladenov 1972-74 • Stoyan Ormandzhiev 1974-77 • Cvetan Ilchev 1978-80 • Atanas Purzhelov 1980-82 • Ivan Vutsov 1982-86 • Hristo Mladenov 1986-87 • Boris Angelov 1988-89 • Ivan Vutsov 1989-91 • Krasimir Borisov 1991 • Dimitar Penev 1991-96 • Hristo Bonev 1996-98 • Dimitar Dimitrov 1998-99 • Stoycho Mladenov 2000-01 • Plamen Markov 2002-04 • Hristo Stoichkov 2004-07 • Stanimir Stoilov 2007 • Dimitar Penev 2007 • Plamen Markov 2008 • Stanimir Stoilov 2009-10 • Lothar Matthaus GER 2010-11 • Michail Madanski 2011- • Luboslav Penev 2011

BULGARIA 2010-11
'A' PFG

Team	Pl	W	D	L	F	A	Pts	Litex Lovech	Levski Sofia	CSKA Sofia	Lokomotiv S	Lokomotiv P	Cherno More	Beroe	Chernomorets	Minyor Pernik	Montana	Slavia Sofia	Kaliakra	Pirin	Vidima	Akademik	Sliven
Litex Lovech †	30	23	6	1	56	13	75		2-1	0-0	1-0	1-0	3-1	4-0	0-0	2-1	4-1	2-0	0-0	2-1	4-0	2-0	4-0
Levski Sofia ‡	30	23	3	4	67	24	72	2-0		1-3	3-1	1-2	1-0	2-1	1-0	4-0	3-0	3-0	4-1	2-0	1-0	5-0	
CSKA Sofia ‡	30	18	7	5	53	26	61	1-1	0-1		3-1	1-0	1-0	3-2	1-2	2-0	2-0	1-0	0-0	2-2	1-0	3-1	2-0
Lokomotiv Sofia ‡	30	16	4	10	47	33	52	1-3	0-2	2-2		3-0	1-1	3-0	2-1	0-3	2-0	4-3	4-0	2-0	2-1	2-0	3-0
Lokomotiv Plovdiv	30	14	10	6	54	28	52	2-2	2-3	4-1	0-0		2-0	1-1	2-0	3-0	4-0	1-1	5-0	2-2	3-0	3-0	3-0
Cherno More Varna	30	15	6	9	36	28	51	0-1	2-3	1-0	1-0	1-1		1-0	0-1	3-0	0-0	3-2	2-0	2-1	5-0	1-0	3-0
Beroe Stara Zagora	30	13	7	10	33	34	46	1-1	2-3	0-2	1-0	1-0	0-0		0-0	2-0	2-1	2-1	2-0	0-0	1-1	1-0	1-0
Chernomorets Burgas	30	9	10	11	19	28	37	0-1	2-1	0-4	2-1	1-2	1-2	0-2		0-0	0-1	2-1	0-1	1-0	1-0	0-0	0-0
Minyor Pernik	30	10	6	14	33	45	36	0-3	0-0	2-4	1-3	2-2	1-1	2-0	0-1		1-0	1-2	1-0	1-0	2-1	1-0	4-1
Montana	30	8	8	14	30	46	32	0-2	0-3	1-4	0-1	1-1	4-0	2-1	0-0	3-1		1-0	3-2	3-0	1-1	2-2	2-2
Slavia Sofia	30	9	5	16	34	38	32	0-1	2-2	1-0	0-1	2-1	0-1	1-2	0-1	1-2	3-2		0-1	1-1	2-0	2-0	0-0
Kaliakra Kavarna	30	8	6	16	19	40	30	0-1	0-3	0-3	0-1	1-3	4-0	2-2	1-1	2-1	0-0	0-1		0-0	1-0	0-1	2-1
Pirin Blagoevgrad	30	6	9	15	32	39	27	1-2	2-3	0-1	2-1	1-1	0-1	2-0	1-1	1-1	3-0	0-2	1-0		1-1	6-0	2-1
Vidima-Rakovski	30	6	7	17	26	52	25	0-3	1-2	2-2	1-1	1-1	0-1	1-2	3-0	2-2	0-1	2-1	1-0	2-1		0-1	2-1
Akademik 1947 Sofia	30	5	5	20	16	51	20	0-3	0-3	1-1	2-3	1-2	0-0	1-3	1-1	2-0	1-0	0-4	0-1	1-0	1-2		0-1
Sliven 2000	30	4	7	19	22	52	19	0-1	1-1	1-3	0-2	0-1	1-3	0-1	0-0	0-3	1-1	1-1	0-1	1-0	6-1	3-0	

31/07/2010 - 28/05/2011 • † Qualified for the UEFA Champions League • ‡ Qualified for the Europa League

Top scorers: 26 - Garra Dembele MLI, Levski • 14 - Zdravko Lazarov, Lokomotiv Plovdiv • 13 - Spas Delev, CSKA • 12 - Doka Mudureira BRA, Litex • 11 - Tsvetan Genkov, Lokomotiv Sofia & Hristo Zlatinski, Lokomotiv Plovdiv • 10 - Michel BRA, CSKA; Vladislav Zlatinov, Beroe; Carvalho GNB Lok Plovdiv & Nikolay Bozhov, Slavia

BULGARIA 2010-11
WESTERN 'B' PFG (2)

Team	Pl	W	D	L	F	A	Pts
Botev Vratsa	30	20	2	8	52	28	62
Sportist Svoge †	30	15	7	8	36	15	52
Etar Veliko Tarnovo †	30	13	12	5	33	19	51
Bansko 1951	30	14	6	10	42	35	48
Chavdar Etropole	30	13	5	12	37	34	44
Septemvri Simitli	30	12	7	11	30	31	43
Vihren Sandanski - R	30	13	3	14	37	32	42
Pirin Gotse Delchev	30	10	6	14	27	38	36
Chavdar Byala Slatina	30	9	7	14	27	36	34
Malesh Mikrevo	30	8	8	14	22	37	32
Botev Krivodol	30	4	5	21	25	63	17
Kom Minyor Berkovitsa	Withdrew after 16 games						

31/07/2010 - 28/05/2011 • † Play-off
Etar 1-3 Svetkavitsa

BULGARIA 2010-11
EASTERN 'B' PFG (2)

Team	Pl	W	D	L	F	A	Pts
Ludogorets Razgrad	24	12	8	4	38	16	44
Chernomorets Pomorie†	24	9	9	6	23	19	36
Spartak Plovdiv - R	24	10	6	8	26	17	36
Svetkavitsa Targovishte	24	8	9	7	24	23	33
Nesebar	24	9	5	10	20	22	32
Lyubimets	24	7	9	8	22	26	30
Dorostol Silistra	24	7	7	10	18	22	28
Brestnik Plovdiv - R	24	6	8	10	21	29	26
Dobrudzha Dobrich	24	7	5	12	14	30	26
Chernomorets Balchik	Withdrew after 14 games						
Dunav Ruse	Withdrew after 14 games						
Ravda	Withdrew after 10 games						

31/07/2010 - 28/05/2011 • † Play-off
Promotion play-off: Sportist Svoge 1-2 Chernomorets Pomorie
Vidima-Rakovski 0-3 **Chernomorets Pomorie**
Chernomorets later refused a license. Vidima remain in APFG

MEDALS TABLE

#	Club	Overall G	S	B	League G	S	B	Cup G	S	SAC G	S	Europe G	S	B
1	Levski Sofia	51	40	8	26	31	8	12	5	13	4			
2	CSKA Sofia	50	32	7	31	20	4	10	6	9	6			3
3	Slavia Sofia	14	11	13	7	9	12	1		6	2			1
4	Lokomotiv Sofia	8	8	9	4	6	9	1		3	2			
5	Litex Lovech	8	4	2	4	1	2	4	3					
6	Botev Plovdiv	4	10	11	2	2	11			4	2			4
7	Cherno More Varna	4	8	3	4	6	3	2						
8	Spartak Sofia	3	4					2		2		1	2	
9	Beroe Stara Zagora	2	4	1	1		1	1						4
10	Spartak Plovdiv	2	3		1	1				1	2			
11	AC 23 Sofia	2			1					1				
12	Lokomotiv Plovdiv	1	5	4	1	1	4							4
13	Spartak Varna	1	4	1	1	2	1	1						1

KUPA NA BULGARIYA 2010–11

Second Round

Team	Score
CSKA Sofia	3
Sliven 2000 *	1
Vidima-Rakovski	0 4p
Malesh Mikrevo *	0 5p
Kom Minyor Berkovitsa	2
Botev Krivodol *	0
Montana *	0
Cherno More Varna	1
Levski Sofia	3
Bansko 1951 *	1
Chavdar Etropole *	0
Beroe Stara Zagora	1
Chernomorets Pomorie	1
Topolite *	0
Chernomorets Balchik *	1
Litex Lovech	2
Pirin Blagoevgrad	0 5p
Dorostol Silistra *	0 3p
Sozopol *	0
Kaliakra Kavarna	1
Minyor Pernik *	1 4p
Akademik 1947 Sofia	1 3p
Lokomotiv Sofia *	0 3p
Lokomotiv Plovdiv	0 4p
Chernomorets Burgas	5
Vihren Sandanski *	0
Botev Vratsa	1
Dobrudzha Dobrich *	0
Etar Veliko Tarnovo	0 4p
Chavdar Byala Slatina *	0 2p
Ludogorets Razgrad *	0
Slavia Sofia	2

Round of 16

CSKA Sofia
Malesh Mikrevo *
Kom Minyor Berkovitsa *
Cherno More Varna
Levski Sofia *
Beroe Stara Zagora
Chernomorets Pomorie *
Litex Lovech
Pirin Blagoevgrad *
Kaliakra Kavarna
Minyor Pernik
Lokomotiv Plovdiv *
Chernomorets Burgas
Dobrudzha Dobrich *
Etar Veliko Tarnovo
Slavia Sofia

Quarter-finals

Team	Score
CSKA Sofia *	2
Cherno More Varna	0
Levski Sofia	1 2p
Litex Lovech *	1 4p
Pirin Blagoevgrad	2
Lokomotiv Plovdiv *	1
Chernomorets Burgas *	4 3p
Slavia Sofia	4 5p

Semi-finals

Team	Score
CSKA Sofia *	2
Litex Lovech	1
Pirin Blagoevgrad	1 6p
Slavia Sofia *	1 7p

Final

Team	Score
CSKA Sofia ‡	1
Slavia Sofia	0

CUP FINAL
Vasil Levski, Sofia
25-05-2011, 19:00
Att: 17 500. Ref: Ivaylo Stoyanov
Scorer – Spas Delev [39] for CSKA
CSKA - Ivan Karadzhov - Ivan Bandalovski,
Giuseppe Aquaro, Apostol Popov, Rumen
Trifonov - Todor Yanchev (c), Boris Galchev -
Spas Delev● Marquinhos● (Petar Stoyanov 82),
Gregory Nelson● (Cillian Sheridan 90). Michel
(Aleksandar Tonev 76). Tr: Milen Radukanov
Slavia - Emil Petrov (c) - Filip Filipov, Josias
Basso●●♦89. Dian Moldovanov, Victor Genev -
Tom Mansharov - Jose Junior (Martin Kushev●
78), Pavle Popara (Georgi Hristov 58), Radoslav
Dimitrov - Iliya Iliev (Spas Georgiev 53) -
Nikolay Bozhov. Tr: Emil Velev

'A' PFG teams enter at the second round ● Home team • * Home team • ‡ Qualified for the Europa League

CAM – CAMBODIA

FIFA/COCA-COLA WORLD RANKING

'93	'94	'95	'96	'97	'98	'99	'00	'01	'02	'03	'04	'05	'06	'07	'08	'09	'10	'11	'12
-	-	180	186	170	162	168	169	169	176	178	184	188	174	183	178	175	166	170	

2011													High	Low	Av
Jan	Feb	Mar	Apr	May	Jun	Jul	Aug	Sep	Oct	Nov	Dec		High	Low	Av
165	166	154	169	176	174	174	176	174	176	169	170		154	188	175

Phnom Penh Crown narrowly missed out on becoming the first club from Cambodia to secure a continental title when they lost 3-2 in the final of the 2011 AFC President's Cup to Taiwan's Taipower. The 2010 Cambodian champions, coached by Englishman David Booth, progressed to the final for the first time after wins in Kaohsiung over Kyrgyzstan's Neftchi Kochkorata and Yadanarbon from Myanmar set up the meeting with their Taiwanese hosts. A late goal by Sun Sovannrithy gave Phnom Penh a chance late in the game, but Taipower held on to take the trophy. There was less joy for the Lee Tae Hoon-coached national team, despite earning a place in the second round of the qualifying tournament for the 2012 AFC Challenge Cup thanks to a narrow 5-4 aggregate win over Macau early in the year. Defeats against hosts Maldives as well as Tajikistan ensured Cambodia would not progress to the competition proper. A 4-2 win the first leg of the opening round of qualifying for the FIFA World Cup finals against Laos had the Cambodians hopeful of progressing but a 6-2 extra-time loss in the return in Vientiane saw them eliminated. At home, Phnom Penh Crown successfully defended their league title in 2011 whilst there was a first trophy for cup winners Preah Khan Reach - 2-0 victors over Build Bright United in the final.

FIFA WORLD CUP RECORD
1930-1994 DNE 1998-2002 DNQ 2006 DNE 2010-2014 DNQ

CAMBODIAN FOOTBALL FEDERATION (CFF)

National Football Centre, Road Kabsrov, Sangkat Samrongkrom, Khan Dangkor, Phnom Penh 2327 PPT3

☎ +855 23 364889
📠 +855 23 223537
✉ info@the-ffc.com
🖥 ffcambodia.com
FA 1933 CON 1957 FIFA 1953
P Sokha Sao
GS Sophana Kul

FIFA BIG COUNT 2006

Total players	229 511
% of population	1.65%
Male	229 411
Female	100
Amateurs 18+	1 600
Unregistered	6 000
Professionals	11
Referees	70
Admin & coaches	160
Number of clubs	65
Number of teams	420

MAJOR CITIES/TOWNS

		Population
1	Phnom Penh	1 438 317
2	Bat Dâmbâng	182 574
3	Preah Sihanouk	148 139
4	Siem Reab	131 497
5	Kâmpóng Chhnang	86 876
6	Prey Veaeng	64 659
7	Kâmpóng Cham	61 814
8	Pousat	53 622
9	Phumi Takaev	52 422
10	Ta Khmau	49 443
11	Dong Tong	38 524
12	Phumi Sâmraông	34 494
13	Kâmpóng Spoeu	32 782
14	Stueng Traeng	29 665
15	Sisophon	26 364
16	Phumi Sâmraông	26 201
17	Tbeng Mean Chey	25 286
18	Svay Rieng	25 002
19	Kâmpôt	21 601

PREAHREACHEANACHAKR KAMPUCHEA • KINGDOM OF CAMBODIA

Capital	Phnom Penh	Population	14 494 293 (65)	% in cities	22%
GDP per capita	$2000 (187)	Area km²	181 035 km² (89)	GMT +/-	+7
Neighbours (km)	Laos 541, Thailand 803, Vietnam 1228 • Coast 443				

RECENT INTERNATIONAL MATCHES PLAYED BY CAMBODIA

2009 Opponents	Score		Venue	Comp	Scorers	Att	Referee
26-04 Bangladesh	L	0-1	Dhaka	CCq		8 060	Yazdi IRN
28-04 Macau	W	2-1	Dhaka	CCq	Teab Vathanak [12], Keo Sokngon [66]	6 000	Saleem MDV
30-04 Myanmar	L	0-1	Dhaka	CCq		2 500	Yazdi IRN
2010							
22-10 Laos	D	0-0	Vientiane	AFFq			Abdul Wahab MAS
24-10 Timor-Leste	W	4-2	Vientiane	AFFq	Khim Borey 3 [26 29 40], Nuth Sinoun [75]		Phung VIE
26-10 Philippines	D	0-0	Vientiane	AFFq			Abdul Wahab MAS
2011							
9-02 Macau	W	3-1	Phnom Penh	CCq	Samel Nasa 2 [48 53], Khuon Laboravy [59]	2 000	Win Cho MYA
16-02 Macau	L	2-3	Macau	CCq	Khim Borey [45], Samel Nasa [107]	100	Perera SRI
21-03 Maldives	L	0-4	Male	CCq		8 000	Zhao Liang CHN
23-03 Tajikistan	L	0-3	Male	CCq		550	Patwal IND
25-03 Kyrgyzstan	L	3-4	Male	CCq	Kouch Sokumpheak 2 [39 49], Sok Rithy [89]	1 000	Zhao Liang CHN
29-06 Laos	W	4-2	Phnom Penh	WCq	Khuon Laboravy [52], Samel Nasa 2 [59 89], Kouch Sokumpheak [68]	25 000	Jahanbazi IRN
3-07 Laos	L	2-6	Vientiane	WCq	Chhin Chhoeun [45], Kouch Sokumpheak [75]	9 000	Sato JPN

Fr = Friendly match • AFF = ASEAN Football Federation Championship • CC = AFC Challenge Cup • WC = FIFA World Cup • r1 = first round group

CAMBODIA NATIONAL TEAM HISTORICAL RECORDS

Coach: Scott O'Donnell AUS 2005-08 • Som Saran 2008 • Yoo Kee Heung KOR 2008 • Prak Sovannara 2008-09 • Scott O'Donnell AUS 2009-10 • Lee Tae Hoon KOR 2010-

CAMBODIA 2011

METFONE C–LEAGUE	Pl	W	D	L	F	A	Pts	PP Crown	Naga Corp	Preah Khan	Defence	Build Bright	Kirivon	Police	Chhlam Samuth	Prek Pra Keila	Rithy Sen
Phnom Penh Crown †	18	14	3	1	54	17	45		3-3	2-2	1-0	3-0	2-0	2-0	5-3	1-0	5-0
Naga Corp	18	13	2	3	71	24	41	4-0		2-0	3-1	2-2	2-1	1-2	5-0	2-3	11-1
Preah Khan Reach	18	10	4	4	42	21	34	0-1	1-2		2-2	1-0	2-2	3-0	1-1	1-0	8-0
Defence Ministry	18	9	2	7	32	22	29	0-1	1-4	3-1		0-3	1-0	5-1	2-0	0-0	6-0
Build Bright United	18	9	1	8	38	25	28	1-4	2-1	1-2	2-1		1-2	1-2	2-3	3-0	2-1
Kirivon Sok Sen Chey	18	8	2	8	38	32	26	4-4	2-7	0-2	2-0	0-1		2-3	0-3	3-0	6-1
Police	18	7	2	9	26	35	23	0-5	0-1	1-3	0-1	3-1	2-3		4-1	0-0	1-0
Chhlam Samuth	18	5	1	12	31	52	16	0-2	3-8	0-3	1-5	0-2	1-3	1-3		2-3	5-2
Prek Pra Keila	18	4	3	11	16	42	15	0-4	1-3	4-5	0-1	0-8	0-3	2-1	1-4		1-1
Rithy Sen	18	0	2	16	12	90	2	0-9	1-10	0-5	1-3	0-6	0-5	3-3	1-3	0-1	

2/04/2011 - 4/09/2011 • † Qualified for the AFC President's Cup

HUN SEN CUP 2011

Round of 16		Quarter–finals		Semi–finals		Final	
Preah Khan Reach	3						
Neak Khiev	2	**Preah Khan Reach**	5				
Battambang	1	Prek Pra Keila	1				
Prek Pra Keila	5			**Preah Khan Reach**	4		
Police	3			Naga Corp	0		
Military Police	0	Police	2				
Koh Kong	0	**Naga Corp**	3				
Naga Corp	4					**Preah Khan Reach**	2
Defence Ministry	2					Build Bright United	0
Chhma Khmao	1	**Defence Ministry**	4				
Takeo	1	Kirivon Sok Sen Chey	1				
Kirivon Sok Sen Chey	4			Defence Ministry	1	**CUP FINAL**	
Phnom Penh Crown	5			**Build Bright United**	2	National Olympic, Phnom Penh, 12-03-2011	
Chhlam Samoth	1	Phnom Penh Crown	2 4p			Scorers - Samel Nasa [35], Khuon Laboravy [76]	
Rithy Sen	1	**Build Bright United**	2 5p				
Build Bright United	6			Third place: Naga Corp 1-0 Defence Ministry			

CAN – CANADA

FIFA/COCA-COLA WORLD RANKING

'93	'94	'95	'96	'97	'98	'99	'00	'01	'02	'03	'04	'05	'06	'07	'08	'09	'10	'11	'12
44	63	65	40	66	101	81	63	92	70	87	90	84	82	55	90	56	84	72	

2011													High	Low	Av
Jan	Feb	Mar	Apr	May	Jun	Jul	Aug	Sep	Oct	Nov	Dec		High	Low	Av
84	80	84	75	77	83	105	102	87	83	72	72		40	105	73

A 1-0 win over Guadeloupe in the 2011 CONCACAF Gold Cup group stage was not enough to take the Canadians through to the quarter-finals, missing out as the third place team with the worst record. It was a close run thing, however, as the Canadians were just seconds away from making it through. In their final group game they were leading Panama 1-0 before an injury-time equaliser from Luis Tejada saw the Panamanians qualify instead. There was better news later in the year when Canada made it through the first group stage of qualifying for the 2014 FIFA World Cup. They were rarely troubled by St Lucia, St Kitts or Puerto Rico although the real test lies ahead. With Canada taking a more involved role in club football, the national team can only benefit from the increased exposure of Canadian players in Major League Soccer where Vancouver Whitecaps made their debut in 2011. In 2012 Montreal Impact will become the third Canadian club in the league though like both Toronto and Vancouver they might find the going tough. Vancouver finished 2011 with the worst record in MLS although that didn't deter the crowds, especially at the refurbished BC Place Stadium. Vancouver's intense and passionate rivalry with both Portland and Seattle was one of the major features of the 2011 MLS season.

CONCACAF GOLD CUP RECORD

1991 r1 **1993** r1 **1996** r1 **1998** DNQ **2000** Winners **2002** SF 3p **2003** r1 **2005** r1 **2007** SF **2009** QF **2011** r1

THE CANADIAN SOCCER ASSOCIATION (CSA)

Place Soccer Canada,
237 Metcalfe Street,
Ottawa, Ontario, K2P 1R2
☎ +1 613 2377678
📠 +1 613 2371516
✉ info@soccercan.ca
🖥 www.canadasoccer.com
FA 1912 CON 1978 FIFA 1912
P Dominique Maestracci
GS Peter Montopoli

FIFA BIG COUNT 2006

Total players	2 695 712
% of population	8.14%
Male	1 800 378
Female	895 334
Amateurs 18+	129 725
Youth under 18	715 837
Unregistered	800 000
Professionals	150
Referees	19 624
Admin & coaches	170 000
Number of clubs	7 000
Number of teams	55 000

MAJOR CITIES/TOWNS

		Population
1	Toronto	4 977 164
2	Montreal	3 402 994
3	Vancouver	2 021 735
4	Calgary	1 055 546
5	Edmonton	912 067
6	Ottawa	875 097
7	Quebec	672 755
8	Hamilton	663 099
9	Winnipeg	647 411
10	Kitchener	443 774
11	London	360 894
12	Victoria	313 928
13	St Catharines	313 261
14	Windsor	286 329
15	Ushawa	286 310
16	Halifax	286 141
17	Saskatoon	204 931
18	Barrie	181 252
19	Regina	178 960

CANADA

Capital	Ottawa	Population	33 487 208 (37)	% in cities	80%
GDP per capita	$39 100 (22)	Area km²	9 984 670 km² (2)	GMT + / -	-3.5 to -8
Neighbours (km)	USA 8893 • Coast 202 080				

RECENT INTERNATIONAL MATCHES PLAYED BY CANADA

2009 Opponents	Score	Venue	Comp	Scorers	Att	Referee
30-05 Cyprus	W 1-0	Larnaca	Fr	Jackson [53]	200	Kenan ISR
30-06 Guatemala	W 3-0	Oxnard	Fr	Gerba 2 [4 67p], Bernier [55]	200	Singh USA
3-07 Jamaica	W 1-0	Carson	GCr1	Gerba [75]	27 000	Vaughn USA
7-07 El Salvador	W 1-0	Columbus	GCr1	Gerba [32]	7 059	Garcia MEX
10-07 Costa Rica	D 2-2	Miami	GCr1	Bernier [25], De Jong [28]	17 269	Vaughn USA
18-07 Honduras	L 0-1	Philadelphia	GCqf		31 987	Aguilar SLV
14-11 Macedonia FYR	L 0-3	Strumica	Fr		6 000	Genov BUL
18-11 Poland	L 0-1	Bydgoszcz	Fr		10 400	Christoffersen DEN
2010						
31-01 Jamaica	L 0-1	Kingston	Fr		18 000	Hospedales TRI
24-05 Argentina	L 0-5	Buenos Aires	Fr		60 000	Rivera PER
29-05 Venezuela	D 1-1	Merida	Fr	McCallum [90]	20 000	Buitrago COL
4-09 Peru	L 0-2	Toronto	Fr		10 619	Jurisevic USA
7-09 Honduras	W 2-1	Montreal	Fr	Simpson [29], McKenna [42]	7 525	Geiger USA
8-10 Ukraine	D 2-2	Kyiv	Fr	Jackson [13], Hutchinson [29]	10 000	Mikulski POL
2011						
9-02 Greece	L 0-1	Larissa	Fr		14 800	Moen NOR
29-03 Belarus	W 1-0	Antalya	Fr	Hainault [58]	2 500	Yildirim TUR
1-06 Ecuador	D 2-2	Toronto	Fr	Dunfield [23], Ricketts [90]	14 356	Bogle JAM
7-06 USA	L 0-2	Detroit	GCr1		28 209	Lopez GUA
11-06 Guadeloupe	W 1-0	Tampa	GCr1	De Rosario [50p]	27 731	Taylor BRB
14-06 Panama	D 1-1	Kansas City	GCr1	De Rosario [62p]	20 109	Lopez GUA
2-09 St Lucia	W 4-1	Toronto	WCq	Simpson 2 [6 61], De Rosario [50], Johnson [91+]	11 500	Marrufo USA
6-09 Puerto Rico	W 3-0	Bayamon	WCq	Hume [42], Jackson [84], Ricketts [93+]	4 000	Wijngaarde SUR
7-10 St Lucia	W 7-0	Gros Islet	WCq	Jackson 3 [18 28 40], Occean 2 [34 51], Hume 2 [72 86]	1 005	Vidal PAN
11-10 Puerto Rico	D 0-0	Toronto	WCq		12 178	Lancaster GUY
11-11 St Kitts and Nevis	D 0-0	Basseterre	WCq		4 000	Bonilla SLV
15-11 St Kitts and Nevis	W 4-0	Toronto	WCq	Occean [28], De Rosario [36p], Simpson [45], Ricketts [88]	10 235	Cerdas CRC

Fr = Friendly match • GC = CONCACAF Gold Cup • WC = FIFA World Cup • † Not a full international
q = qualifier • r1 = first round group • qf = quarter-final • sf = semi-final

CANADA NATIONAL TEAM HISTORICAL RECORDS

Caps
84 - Paul Staltieri 1997- • **82** - Randy Samuel 1983-97 • **77** - Mark Watson 1991-2004 • **66** - Lyndon Hooper 1986-97 • **64** - Alex Bunbury 1986-97 • **61** - Nick Dasovic 1992-2004, Colin Miller 1983-97 & Mike Sweeney 1980-93 • **59** - Carlo Corazzin 1994-2004 & Richard Hastings 1998- • **57** - Pat Onstad 1988- & Bruce Wilson 1974-86 • **55** - Dwayne DeRosario 2000-, Craig Forrest 1988-2001 & Dale Mitchell 1980-93 • **53** - Paul Peschisolido 1992-2004 • **52** - Paul Dolan 1984-97 & Frank Yallop 1990-97 • **51** - Dave Norman 1983-94

Goals
19 - John Catliff 1984-94 & Dale Mitchell 1980-93 • **16** - Alex Bunbury 1986-97 • **15** - Dwayne DeRosario 2000- & Ali Gerba 2005- • **12** - Igor Vrablic 1984-86 • **11** - Carlo Corazzin 1994-2004 & Paul Peschisolido 1992-2004 • **10** - Tomasz Radzinski 1995- & Kevin McKenna 2000-

Past Coaches
Don Petrie 1957 • Peter Dinsdale ENG 1968-70 • Frank Pike ENG 1970-73 • Bill McAllister 1973 • Eckhard Krautzun GER 1973-75 • Bill McAllister 1975 • Eckhard Krautzun GER 1975-77 • Barrie Clarke 1978-81 • Tony Waiters ENG 1981-86 • Bob Bearpark ENG 1986-87 • Tony Taylor SCO 1988-89 • Bob Lenarduzzi 1989-90 • Tony Waiters ENG 1990-91 • Bob Lenarduzzi 1992-97 • Bruce Twamley 1998 • Holger Osieck GER 1999-2003 • Colin Miller 2003 • Frank Yallop 2004-06 • Stephen Hart TRI 2006-07 • Dale Mitchell 2007-09 • Stephen Hart TRI 2009-

CANADA 2011
Nutralite Canadian Championship

Semi-finals			Finals		
Toronto FC	3	1			
FC Edmonton	0	0	**Toronto FC** †	1	2
Montreal Impact	0	1	Vancouver Whitecaps	1	1
Vancouver Whitecaps	1	1			

† Qualified for CONCACAF Champions League • See USA for MLS details

CAY – CAYMAN ISLANDS

FIFA/COCA-COLA WORLD RANKING

'93	'94	'95	'96	'97	'98	'99	'00	'01	'02	'03	'04	'05	'06	'07	'08	'09	'10	'11	'12
154	150	131	148	164	153	148	159	165	164	181	176	181	189	192	172	183	157	183	

2011												High	Low	Av
Jan	Feb	Mar	Apr	May	Jun	Jul	Aug	Sep	Oct	Nov	Dec			
156	156	158	157	158	160	172	172	174	185	181	183	127	192	166

The Cayman Islands national team was drawn in one of the most difficult groups as qualifying in the CONCACAF zone for the 2014 FIFA World Cup got underway and it was no disgrace when the team emerged beaten - but not bruised - with just a single point from the six games played. Former finalists El Salvador inflicted the most damage scoring four in both matches but Suriname were restricted to two 1-0 victories, with the sole point coming from a 1-1 draw against the Dominican Republic at home in Georgetown. That the Caymans Islands has such a well-organised football scene can partly be attributed to the wealth of the country but it also shows a real passion for the game within this small Caribbean nation of roughly 50,000 inhabitants. The three annual tournaments - the league, FA Cup and Digicel Cup - are keenly contested and hard fought and in 2011 it was Elite who emerged as league champions ahead of George Town. Based in West Bay, it was the second title won by Elite although for the second year in a row George Town won both of the cup tournaments. A convincing 5-0 victory over second division champions Cayman Athletic saw them clinch the cup double by winning the FA Cup, having earlier in the season beaten Roma 3-1 to win the Digicel Cup.

FIFA WORLD CUP RECORD
1930-1994 DNE 1998-2014 DNQ

CAYMAN ISLANDS FOOTBALL ASSOCIATION (CIFA)

Centre for Excellence	
✉	Poindexter Road, PO Box 178 Grand Cayman KYI-1104
☎	+1 345 9495775
📠	+1 345 9457673
✉	cifa@candw.ky
🖥	www.cifa.ky
FA 1966	CON 1993	FIFA 1992
P	Jeffrey Webb
GS	Bruce Blake

FIFA BIG COUNT 2006

Total players	3 700
% of population	8.14%
Male	3 400
Female	300
Amateurs 18+	700
Youth under 18	600
Unregistered	1 100
Professionals	0
Referees	100
Admin & coaches	200
Number of clubs	10
Number of teams	50

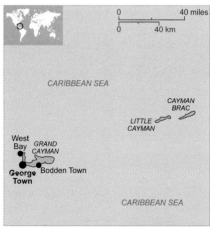

CARIBBEAN SEA

CAYMAN BRAC

LITTLE CAYMAN

West Bay
GRAND CAYMAN
George Town
Bodden Town

CARIBBEAN SEA

MAJOR CITIES/TOWNS

		Population
1	George Town	35 633
2	West Bay	12 620
3	Bodden Town	7 634
4	East End	1 619
5	North Side	1 313

CAYMAN ISLANDS

Capital	George Town	Population	49 035 (207)	% in cities	100%
GDP per capita	$43 800 (13)	Area km²	264 km² (210)	GMT +/-	-5
Neighbours (km)	Coast 160				

RECENT INTERNATIONAL MATCHES PLAYED BY THE CAYMAN ISLANDS

2006	Opponents		Score	Venue		Scorers	Att.	Referee
2-09	Bahamas	L	1-3	Havana	CCq	Leon Whittaker [76]	200	Stewart JAM
4-09	Turks & Caicos Isl	L	0-2	Havana	CCq		100	Stennett JAM
6-09	Cuba	L	0-7	Havana	CCq		120	Stewart JAM
2007								
No international matches played in 2007								
2008								
3-02	Bermuda	D	1-1	Hamilton	WCq	Allean Grant [87]	2 000	Navarro CAN
30-03	Bermuda	L	1-3	Georgetown	WCq	Marshall Forbes [64p]	3 200	Marrufo USA
27-08	Saint Martin †	W	3-0	Grand Cayman	CCq	Calvin Jefford [55], Jairo Sanchez [65], Nikolai Hill [90]	300	Thomas JAM
30-08	Antigua and Barbuda	D	1-1	Grand Cayman	CCq	O'Neil Taylor [67]	350	Hospedales
31-08	Bermuda	D	0-0	Grand Cayman	CCq		350	Hospedales
11-10	Guadeloupe †	L	1-7	Abymes	CCq	Carson Fagan [86]	4 200	McArthur GUY
13-10	Martinique †	L	0-1	Abymes	CCq		1 000	Matthew SKN
15-10	Grenada	L	2-4	Abymes	CCq	Erickson Brown 2 [32 83]	3 358	Willett ATG
9-11	Jamaica	L	0-2	Grand Cayman	Fr		500	Whittaker CAY
2009								
28-06	Jamaica	L	1-4	Grand Cayman	Fr	Rene Carter [40]	500	Holder CAY
2010								
2-10	Saint Martin †	D	1-1	Bayamon	CCq	Paul Brown [18p]	600	Campbell JAM
4-10	Anguilla	W	4-1	Bayamon	CCq	Mark Ebanks 2 [45p 49], Theron Wood [57], Paul Brwn [59]	500	Davis TRI
6-10	Puerto Rico	L	0-2	Bayamon	CCq		3 800	Campbell JAM
2011								
2-09	Suriname	L	0-1	Paramaribo	WCq		1 000	Skeete BRB
6-09	El Salvador	L	1-4	Georgetown	WCq	Mark Ebanks [73p]	2 200	Rodas GUA
7-10	Suriname	L	0-1	Georgetown	WCq		2 100	Jurisevic USA
11-10	El Salvador	L	0-4	San Salvador	WCq		17 570	Cruz CRC
11-11	Dominican Republic	L	0-4	San Cristobal	WCq		1 000	Guerrero NCA
14-11	Dominican Republic	D	1-1	Georgetown	WCq	Mark Ebanks [72]	1 750	Matthew SKN

Fr = Friendly match • CC = Digicel Caribbean Cup • WC = FIFA World Cup • q = qualifier • † Not an official international

CAYMAN ISLANDS 2010–11

CIFA PREMIER LEAGUE

	Pl	W	D	L	F	A	Pts	Elite	George Town	Bodden Town	Scholars	Roma	Future	Tigers	East End Utd
Elite	21	14	4	3	61	33	46		3-2	4-3 2-2	5-3 1-4	2-1 0-1	3-1	3-2	2-0
George Town	21	10	5	6	37	30	35	1-3 2-2		3-3 1-0	2-1 1-0	0-1 1-2	1-1	1-2	1-3 1-1
Bodden Town	21	9	5	7	43	37	32	1-7	1-3		0-4 1-1	1-0	3-0 3-0	6-1	1-1
Scholars International	21	9	3	9	37	27	30	2-2	1-2	1-3		3-0 2-1	2-1 0-1	3-0 0-1	1-1 0-1
Roma	21	10	0	11	32	35	30	2-3	1-4	1-2 3-2	1-2		1-0 0-2	2-3 1-4	3-1
Future	21	7	4	10	31	44	25	0-5 1-0	1-1 3-4	0-0	2-1	0-2		4-4 1-3	4-2 5-3
Tigers	21	8	1	12	40	52	19	0-2 4-8	0-1 0-2	3-2 0-3	0-2	0-2	1-2		4-2
East End United	21	4	4	13	33	56	16	1-1 0-3	1-3	2-4 0-2	1-4	2-4 1-3	5-2	2-1 3-7	

10/10/2010 - 2/05/2011 • Top scorers: 18 - Dwayne Wright, Elite • 17 - Alex Belcher, Elite

CIFA FA CUP 2011

Quarter–finals		Semi–finals		Final	
George T					
Bodden T		**George T**	2		
Academy	1	North Side	1		
North Side	4			**George Town**	5
Tigers	4			Cayman Athletic	0
Academy	2	Tigers	3	Truman Bodden SC	
Roma	2	**Cayman Ath**	5	8-05-2010	
Cayman Ath	4				

CIFA DIGICEL CAYMAN CUP 2011

First Round		Semi–finals		Final	
George T	3				
Elite	2	**George T**	0 17p		
Future	1	Scholars	1 0 6p		
Scholars	2			**George Town**	3
East End	2			Roma	1
Bodden T	1	East End	1 2	TE McField SC,	
Tigers	3	**Roma**	2 2	9-03-2011	
Roma	4				

CGO – CONGO

FIFA/COCA-COLA WORLD RANKING

'93	'94	'95	'96	'97	'98	'99	'00	'01	'02	'03	'04	'05	'06	'07	'08	'09	'10	'11	'12
103	114	119	100	101	112	94	86	94	97	108	117	110	89	91	68	101	121	133	

							2011							High	Low	Av
	Jan	Feb	Mar	Apr	May	Jun	Jul	Aug	Sep	Oct	Nov	Dec		High	Low	Av
	122	119	120	122	121	129	129	132	144	138	131	133		57	144	102

The establishment of a national centre for youth football in Congo continued to deliver results as the country qualified for the FIFA U-17 World Cup in Mexico. Congo finished third at the CAF African U-17 Championship in Rwanda at the start of the year, beaten in the semi-finals only on post-match penalties by eventual winners Burkina Faso before going onto win the bronze medal match 2-1 against Cote d'Ivoire. A total of 19 of the 21 players who went to Mexico came from the CNFF, established in 2005 in co-operation with the French club Auxerre. Frenchman Eddie Hudanski coached the side past the first round in Mexico to the round of 16 where they lost to Uruguay. The national side finished third in their 2012 CAF Africa Cup of Nations qualifying group after losing both home and away to Ghana and Sudan, their only points coming from wins against Swaziland. French coach Jean-Guy Wallemme, formerly at Racing Lens, was appointed in August to take over the side and in November saw them through the early stages of the 2014 FIFA World Cup qualifiers. A 6-1 win over Sao Tome e Principe proved a routine win in the first stage on the road to Brazil. Diables Noirs won the national championship with victory over AC Leopard Dolisie in the league play-off. Three months earlier the result has been reversed in the Cup Final.

CAF AFRICA CUP OF NATIONS RECORD

1957-1965 DNE **1968** 7 r1 1970 DNE **1972** 1 Winners **1974** 4 SF 1976 DNQ **1978** 7 r1 1980-1988 DNQ 1990 DNE **1992** 7 QF
1994-1998 DNQ **2000** 14 r1 2002-2012 DNQ

FEDERATION CONGOLAISE DE FOOTBALL (FECOFOOT)

PO Box 1423, Brazzaville

☎ +242 811563

✉ fecofoot@yahoo.fr

FA 1962 CON 1966 FIFA 1962
P Jean Michel Mbono
GS Badji Mombo Wantete

FIFA BIG COUNT 2006

Total players	200 210
% of population	5.41%
Male	191 600
Female	8 610
Amateurs 18+	5 410
Youth under 18	3 650
Unregistered	35 150
Professionals	0
Referees	504
Admin & coaches	595
Number of clubs	90
Number of teams	320

MAJOR CITIES/TOWNS

		Population
1	Brazzaville	1 158 513
2	Pointe Noire	634 995
3	Loubomo	130 080
4	Nkayi	58 559
5	Gamboma	29 357
6	Kinkala	29 248
7	Ouesso	27 142
8	Madingou	23 342
9	Impfondo	20 729
10	Mossendjo	20 414
11	Sibiti	20 096
12	Loandjili	18 488
13	Owando	15 871
14	Djambala	13 570
15	Ngamaba-Mfilou	11 380
16	Makoua	7 427
17	Matsanga	6 246
18	Ewo	5 859
19	Sembé	4 047

REPUBLIQUE DU CONGO • REPUBLIC OF THE CONGO

Capital Brazzaville	Population 4 012 809 (127)	% in cities 61%
GDP per capita $3900 (154)	Area km² 342 000 km² (63)	GMT +/- +1
Neighbours (km) Angola 201, Cameroon 523, C. African Rep 467, Congo DR 2410, Gabon 1903 • Coast 169		

RECENT INTERNATIONAL MATCHES PLAYED BY CONGO

2006	Opponents		Score	Venue	Comp	Scorers	Att	Referee
5-03	Equatorial Guinea	W	2-1	N'Djamena	CMr1	Likibi [81], Ngoua [94+]		
7-03	Gabon	D	2-2	N'Djamena	CMr1	Lepaye 2 [27 44]		
12-03	Central African Rep	W	4-1	N'Djamena	CMsf	Lepaye [4], Likibi 2 [28 84], Beaulia [47]		
16-03	Gabon	W	1-0	N'Djamena	CMf	Papou [59]		
25-03	Zambia	D	0-0	Brazzaville	CNq			Coulibaly MLI
4-04	Angola	D	0-0	Cabinda	Fr			
28-05	Congo DR	W	2-1	Brazzaville	Fr	Minga [35], De Bouisson [55p]		
2-06	Zambia	L	0-3	Chililabombwe	CNq			Rahman SUD
17-06	South Africa	D	1-1	Pointe-Noire	CNq	Bantsimba [65]		Eyene CMR
9-09	Chad	D	1-1	N'Djamena	CNq	Mayembi [6]		Pare BFA
2008								
1-06	Mali	L	2-4	Bamoko	WCq	Mouithys 2 [5 74]	40 000	Bennaceur TUN
8-06	Sudan	W	1-0	Brazzaville	WCq	Endzanga [70]	25 000	Mana NGA
14-06	Chad	L	1-2	N'Djamena	WCq	Batota [42]	8 000	Doue CIV
22-06	Chad	W	2-0	Brazzaville	WCq	Mouithys [14], Ibara [64]	8 000	Diouf SEN
7-09	Mali	W	1-0	Brazzaville	WCq	Endzanga [87]	16 000	Haimoudi ALG
11-10	Sudan	L	0-2	Omdurman	WCq		27 000	Ambaya LBY
2009								
27-05	Jordan	D	1-1	Amman	Fr	Epako [47]		
31-05	Bahrain	L	1-3	Manama	Fr	Kapolongo [20]		
12-08	Morocco	D	1-1	Rabat	Fr	Moussilou [18]		
13-10	Korea DPR	D	0-0	Le Mans	Fr			
14-11	Angola	D	1-1	Luanda	Fr	Douniama [91+]		
2010								
11-08	Burkina Faso	L	0-3	Senlis	Fr			
4-09	Sudan	L	0-2	Khartoum	CNq			Kaoma ZAM
10-10	Swaziland	W	3-1	Brazzaville	CNq	Mouko [21p], Sembolo 2 [35 74]		Ssegonga UGA
2011								
27-03	Ghana	L	0-3	Brazzaville	CNq			Bennett RSA
3-06	Ghana	L	1-3	Kumasi	CNq	Moussilou [75]		
4-09	Sudan	L	0-1	Brazzaville	CNq			
8-10	Swaziland	W	1-0	Lobamba	CNq	Nkolo [47]		
11-11	Sao Tome e Principe	W	5-0	Sao Tome	WCq	Moussilou [1], Douniama [7], Malonga [27], Oniangue [54], Tchilimbou [69]	3 000	Ngbokaye CTA
15-11	Sao Tome e Principe	D	1-1	Pointe Noire	WCq	Nganga [56]	12 000	Mahamat CHA

Fr = Friendly match • CN = African Cup of Nations • CM = CEMAC Cup • WC = FIFA World Cup
q = qualifier • r1 = first round group • sf = semi-final • 3p = third place play-off

CONGO NATIONAL TEAM HISTORICAL RECORDS

Coach   Noel Tosi FRA 2006-07 • Ivica Todorov SRB 2008-10 • Robert Corfu 2010-11 • Jean-Guy Wallemme 2011-

	MEDALS TABLE	Overall			Lge	Cup		Africa			City/Town
		G	S	B	G	G	S	G	S	B	
1	Etoile du Congo	18	5		13	5	5				Brazzaville
2	CARA Brazzaville	13	3		9	3	3	1			Brazzaville
3	Diables Noirs	12	4		8	4	4				Brazzaville
4	V. Club Mokanda	6	3		3	3	3				Pointe Noire
5	Inter Club	5	3	2	2	3	3			2	Brazzaville
6	Patronage St Anne	3	1		2	1	1				Brazzaville
7	AS Police	3		1	2	1				1	Brazzaville
8	AS Cheminots	3			1	2					Pointe Noire
9	Munisport	3			2	1					Pointe Noire
10	St Michel Ouenzé	2			2						Brazzaville
11	AC Léopard Dolisie	2				2					Dolisie

CONGO 2011

CHAMPIONNAT NATIONALE MTN LIGUE 1 GROUP A BRAZZAVILLE

	Pl	W	D	L	F	A	Pts	Diables Noirs	JS Talangai	Ajax Ouénzé	Etoile	Cuvette	Inter Club	SMO	Kondzo	CARA	ACM	Patronage	AS Police
Diables Noirs †	22	17	3	2	33	7	54		0-0	3-1	1-0	1-0	2-0	2-0	2-0	1-0	1-0	2-0	1-0
JS Talangai †	22	12	4	6	36	25	40	0-2		3-3	0-2	1-2	1-0	4-1	1-0	1-0	2-3	1-0	1-0
Ajax Ouénzé	22	9	10	3	26	19	37	1-0			0-0	2-1	1-1	2-1	1-1	0-0	3-1	2-0	2-1
Etoile du Congo	22	8	9	5	26	18	33	0-2	1-2	1-1		2-1	5-0	1-1	1-0	1-1	0-0	0-0	0-1
Cuvette	22	9	6	7	27	27	33	2-1	1-0	2-1	0-1		1-1	0-1	2-1	1-0	2-1	1-0	1-1
Inter Club	22	7	8	7	23	25	29	1-2	1-2	1-0	2-1	1-1		0-0	0-1	2-1	2-0	2-1	2-0
St Michel Ouenzé	22	7	7	8	27	28	28	0-0	2-5	0-0	2-2	2-3	0-0		0-1	0-2	3-2	0-1	2-1
Kondzo	22	6	7	9	24	25	25	1-2	1-3	1-1	2-2	2-1	1-1	1-2		0-0	2-1	0-1	1-1
CARA Brazzaville	22	5	7	10	13	17	22	1-1	0-1	1-2	0-1	0-0	1-0	0-2	1-1		3-0	1-0	1-0
AC Moranzambé	22	5	7	10	22	31	22	0-1	1-1	0-0	0-2	4-1	1-1	1-1	0-4	2-0		0-0	3-1
Patronage St Anne	22	5	6	11	17	26	21	0-4	3-1	0-1	1-2	0-0	1-1	0-2	2-1	0-0	1-2		1-1
AS Police	22	2	6	14	18	44	12	0-2	1-5	0-1	1-1	4-4	2-4	0-5	0-2	1-0	0-0	2-5	

3/03/2011 - 30/08/2011 • † Qualified for the semi-finals

CONGO 2011

CHAMPIONNAT NATIONALE MTN LIGUE 1 GROUP B POINTE NOIRE

	Pl	W	D	L	F	A	Pts	AC Léopard	V. Club	Munisport	ASP	Olymp Vision	Pigeon Vert	La Mancha	Cheminots	Nico-Nicoyé	Olymp Nkayi	St Pierre	Bougainvillées
AC Léopard Dolisie †	22	18	1	3	68	10	55		0-1	3-1	5-0	5-0	2-0	4-1	2-0	6-0	9-0	5-0	2-1
V. Club Mokanda †	22	14	4	4	37	16	46	1-0		1-0	1-0	1-0	2-0	3-1	1-1	2-3	7-0	2-0	2-1
Munisport	22	13	3	6	36	16	42	1-1	2-1		3-1	3-0	1-2	3-1	0-0	4-1	0-3	2-0	
AS Ponténégrine	22	11	4	7	26	25	37	0-3	0-0	2-1		1-0	1-2	2-0	0-0	0-1	1-0	1-2	4-0
Olympique Vision	22	10	8	8	39	23	34	1-0	0-0	0-2	1-2		1-2	0-0	0-3	3-0	5-0	0-3	8-1
Pigeon Vert	22	10	1	11	28	33	31	1-4	1-0	0-1	1-1	1-0		4-2	0-1	1-0	4-2	0-2	3-0
La Mancha	22	8	5	9	31	36	29	0-5	2-0	1-2	2-3	2-1	2-0		0-0	0-2	2-0	3-0	2-2
AS Cheminots	22	7	7	8	21	25	28	0-1	1-1	0-1	1-0	1-2	1-2	2-2		2-0	1-0	1-1	4-1
Nico-Nicoyé	22	6	6	10	21	29	24	1-2	0-1	0-0	0-0	2-4	1-1	0-1			1-0	1-1	5-0
Olympic Nkayi	22	6	2	14	15	45	20	1-3	0-1	0-2	1-0	1-1	2-0	0-2	2-0	1-1		2-0	1-0
US St Pierre	22	4	5	13	21	47	17	0-3	3-5	0-0	2-1	2-1	0-1	3-1	2-2	0-1	0-1		2-1
JS Bougainvillées	22	3	2	17	20	58	11	0-3	1-4	1-0	2-3	1-3	0-0	1-3	0-1	3-2		1-1	

3/03/2011 - 30/08/2011 • † Qualified for the semi-finals

CONGO 2011
CHAMPIONNAT NATIONALE PLAY-OFFS

Semi-finals

Diables Noirs	1	4
V. Club Mokanda *	1	0
JS Talangai *	2	0
AC Léopard Dolisie	4	1

Finals

Diables Noirs †	2
AC Léopard Dolisie	0

* Home team in 1st leg

† Qualified for The CAF Champions League • Final played 17/09/2011 in Pointe Noire. Scorers - Tchilimbou 40, Vvedette 71 for Diables Noirs

COUPE DU CONGO 2011

Quarter-finals

AC Léopard Dolisie	2
AC Moranzambé	0
Africain Pointe Noire	0
St Michel Ouenzé	0
CARA Brazzaville	2
Olympic Nkayi	0
Olympique Vision	1
Diables Noirs	1

Semi-finals

AC Léopard Dolisie	1	4
St Michel Ouenzé	1	0
CARA Brazzaville	2	0
Diables Noirs	2	1

Final

AC Léopard Dolisie ‡	1
Diables Noirs	0

Alphonse Massamba Débat, Brazzaville, 14-08-2011
Scorer - Cesaire Ngandze 27

‡ Qualified for the CAF Confederation Cup

CHA – CHAD

FIFA/COCA-COLA WORLD RANKING

'93	'94	'95	'96	'97	'98	'99	'00	'01	'02	'03	'04	'05	'06	'07	'08	'09	'10	'11	'12
166	175	180	188	184	178	166	163	176	173	152	168	159	142	141	119	145	141	143	

						2011									
	Jan	Feb	Mar	Apr	May	Jun	Jul	Aug	Sep	Oct	Nov	Dec	**High**	**Low**	**Av**
	140	139	142	148	149	152	158	154	161	152	141	143	118	190	160

Chad played an unwitting role in the 2012 CAFE Africa Cup of Nations qualifying campaign by helping the cause of Tunisia and sinking that of Malawi. Chad finished bottom of Group K without a single win in their eight matches but their 2-2 draw with Malawi in their final match allowed Tunisia to finish second and grab one of the qualifying berths. Malawi had been leading 2-1 in Ndjamena when youthful striker Karl-Max Barthelemy grabbed an equalising goal five minutes into stoppage time. Chad's poor Nations Cup performance was followed in November by elimination from the 2014 FIFA World Cup qualifiers on away goals - despite winning the away leg against Tanzania thanks to a goal by French-based forward Mahatma Ahmad Labor. In September Chad changed coach with the Egyptian Sherif Khalkha replaced by former Chad international Moody Kotta, who returned home from a job with Equatorial Guinea club Sony Elegances. In club football, Tourbillon withdrew after the first leg of their CAFE African Champions League tie against Raja Casablanca after a 10-1 hiding in the first leg in Morocco - a matter of much embarrassment for the Ndjamena club. Tourbillon were succeeded as league champions by first-time winners Foullah Edifice, who were then denied the double after losing the Cup Final to Renaissance.

CAF AFRICA CUP OF NATIONS RECORD
1957-1990 DNE **1992** DNQ **1994** Withdrew **1996-1998** DNE **2000** DNQ **2002** DNE **2004-2008** DNQ **2010** Disqualified **2012** DNQ

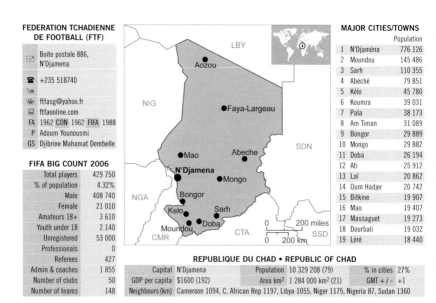

FEDERATION TCHADIENNE DE FOOTBALL (FTF)

Boite postale 886, N'Djamena

☎ +235 518740

📠

📧 ftfasg@yahoo.fr

🖥 ftfaonline.com

FA 1962 CON 1962 FIFA 1988

P Adoum Younousmi

GS Djibrine Mahamat Dembelle

FIFA BIG COUNT 2006

Total players	429 750
% of population	4.32%
Male	408 740
Female	21 010
Amateurs 18+	3 610
Youth under 18	2 140
Unregistered	53 000
Professionals	0
Referees	427
Admin & coaches	1 855
Number of clubs	50
Number of teams	148

MAJOR CITIES/TOWNS

		Population
1	N'Djaména	776 126
2	Moundou	145 486
3	Sarh	110 355
4	Abéché	79 851
5	Kélo	45 780
6	Koumra	39 031
7	Pala	38 173
8	Am Timan	31 089
9	Bongor	29 889
10	Mongo	29 882
11	Doba	26 194
12	Ati	25 912
13	Laï	20 862
14	Oum Hadjer	20 742
15	Bitkine	19 907
16	Mao	19 407
17	Massaguet	19 273
18	Dourbali	19 032
19	Léré	18 440

REPUBLIQUE DU CHAD • REPUBLIC OF CHAD

Capital	N'Djamena	Population	10 329 208 (79)	% in cities	27%
GDP per capita	$1600 (192)	Area km²	1 284 000 km² (21)	GMT + / -	+1

Neighbours (km) Cameroon 1094, C. African Rep 1197, Libya 1055, Niger 1175, Nigeria 87, Sudan 1360

RECENT INTERNATIONAL MATCHES PLAYED BY CHAD

2008	Opponents		Score	Venue	Comp	Scorers	Att	Referee
7-06	Mali	L	1-2	N'Djamena	WCq	Kedigui [37]	15 000	Aguidissou BEN
14-06	Congo	W	2-1	N'Djamena	WCq	Kedigui [44p], Syriakata Hassan [48]	8 000	Doue CIV
22-06	Congo	L	0-2	Brazzaville	WCq		8 000	Diouf SEN
24-08	Libya	L	0-3	Tripoli	Fr			
6-09	Sudan	W	2-1	Cairo	WCq	Mbaiam [29], Syriakata Hassan [81]	4 000	Trabelsi TUN
10-09	Sudan	L	1-3	Cairo	WCq	Djime [34]	10 000	Diatta SEN
11-10	Mali	L	1-2	Bamako	WCq	Misdongarde [64]	40 000	Keita GUI
2009								
No international matches played in 2009								
2010								
19-06	Niger	D	1-1	Niamey	Fr	Barthelemy [39]		
1-07	Togo	D	2-2	N'Djamena	CNq	Djimrangar [20], Mbaiam [28]		Benouza ALG
9-07	Botswana	L	0-1	Gaborone	CNq			Seechurn MRI
11-08	Tunisia	L	1-3	N'Djamena	CNq	N'Douassel [72]		Doue CIV
29-08	Ethiopia	L	0-1	Addis Abeba	Fr			
9-10	Malawi	L	2-6	Blantyre	CNq	N'Douassel [26], Mbaiam [81]		Kirwa KEN
17-11	Togo	D	0-0	Lome	CNq			Coulibaly MLI
2011								
8-02	Equatorial Guinea	L	0-2	Malabo	Fr			
26-03	Botswana	L	0-1	N'Djamena	CNq			
5-06	Tunisia	L	0-5	Sousse	CNq			
8-10	Malawi	D	2-2	N'Djamena	CNq	Labo [65], Barthelemy [94+]		
11-11	Tanzania	L	1-2	N'Djamena	WCq	Labo [16]	10 000	Ogunkolade NGA
15-11	Tanzania	W	1-0	Dar es Salaam	WCq	Labo [47]	42 700	Nampiandraza MAD

Fr = Friendly match • CN = African Cup of Nations • WC = FIFA World Cup • q = qualifier

CHAD 2011

LIGUE DE N'DJAMENA PREMIERE DIVISION		Pl	W	D	L	F	A	Pts	F'llah Edifice	Tourbillon	Renaissance	DGSSIE	Gazelle	ASCOT	Elect-Sport	Postel 2000	Toumai	Geyser
Foullah Edifice †		18	14	1	3	34	11	43		1-0	1-0	2-1	1-0	2-0	0-4	0-0	1-0	6-0
Tourbillon		18	11	2	5	33	15	35	0-3		2-1	2-1	0-1	3-1	2-2	3-1	3-0	5-0
Renaissance ‡		18	9	5	4	26	15	32	0-1	2-0		1-1	0-0	2-3	3-1	2-1	3-1	3-1
AS DGSSIE		18	9	5	4	23	16	32	2-1	1-0	1-1		3-0	0-1	2-1	1-0	0-3	2-2
Gazelle		18	7	5	6	18	16	26	0-1	0-1	**0-2**	0-0		1-0	0-0	1-1	1-0	**0-2**
AS CotonTchad		18	8	2	8	24	23	26	1-0	0-3	1-2	1-2	1-2		2-1	4-1	1-0	2-0
Elect-Sport		18	6	6	6	27	26	24	0-2	0-3	1-1	0-3	2-2	2-0		2-0	2-2	2-0
Postel 2000		18	3	5	10	18	30	14	1-4	0-3	0-1	1-2	1-2	1-1	2-2		0-0	3-1
Toumai		18	3	4	11	13	24	13	0-1	0-0	0-0	0-1	0-1	0-4	2-4	0-1		4-1
Geyser		18	1	3	14	13	53	6	2-7	1-3	0-2	0-0	1-7	1-1	0-1	1-4	0-1	

31/01/2011 - 2/06/2011 • † Qualified for the CAF Champions League • ‡ Qualified for the CAF Confederation Cup • Match in bold awarded

COUPE DE LIGUE DE N'DJAMENA 2011

Quarter-finals		Semi-finals		Final	
Renaissance	b				
AS BNF	1	Renaissance	2		
Gazelle	0	Tourbillon	1		
Tourbillon	1			Renaissance ‡	2
AS CotonTchad	6p			Foullah Edifice	1
Postel 2000	5p	AS CotonTchad	0	Stade Omnisports,
Toumai	14p	Foullah Edifice	1	N'Djamena, 21-07-2011
Foullah Edifice	15p			‡ Qualified for the CAF Confederation Cup

CHI – CHILE

FIFA/COCA-COLA WORLD RANKING

'93	'94	'95	'96	'97	'98	'99	'00	'01	'02	'03	'04	'05	'06	'07	'08	'09	'10	'11	'12
55	47	36	26	16	16	23	19	39	84	80	74	64	41	45	31	15	15	13	

							2011									
Jan	Feb	Mar	Apr	May	Jun	Jul	Aug	Sep	Oct	Nov	Dec		High	Low	Av
15	14	14	14	13	27	11	11	14	16	13	13		6	84	38

Chile remain one of three South American nations, alongside Ecuador and Venezuela, never to have won the Copa America and it was the latter who ended their hopes at the 2011 tournament in Argentina at the quarter-final stage. After topping their first round group ahead of eventual winners Uruguay, Chile went into their quarter-final with the knowledge that both the hosts Argentina and defending champions Brazil had already been knocked out, but they failed to capitalise on what would have been a great opportunity to break their duck with a shock 2-1 defeat at the hands of the Venezuelans. The end of the year did see continental success at club level when the hugely popular Universidad de Chile from the capital Santiago won the Copa Sudamericana. They beat Ecuador's LDU Quito with ease in the final with the sought-after Eduardo Vargas scoring three of his side's four goals over the two legs. He finished with a record haul of 11 goals as Universidad de Chile won a first-ever continental title and only Chile's second overall following Colo Colo's Copa Libertadores triumph of 1991. There was no stopping them at home either as they won both the Apertura and Clausura titles playing with an attacking flair that won them many plaudits.

COPA AMERICA RECORD

1916 4/4 1917 4/4 1919 4/4 1920 4/4 (Hosts) 1921 DNE 1922 5/5 1923 DNE 1924 4/4 1925 DNE 1926 3/5 (Hosts) 1927 DNE 1929 DNE
1935 4/4 1937 5/6 1939 4/5 1941 3/5 (Hosts) 1942 6/7 1945 3/7 (Hosts) 1946 5/6 1947 4/8 1949 5/8 1953 4/7 1955 2/6 (Hosts) 1956 2/6
1957 6/6 1959 4/7 1959 DNE 1963 DNE 1967 3/6 1975 6/10 r1 1979 2/10 F 1983 5/10 r1 1987 2/10 F 1989 5/10 r1 1991 3/10 r2 (Hosts)
1993 10/12 r1 1995 11/12 r1 1997 11/12 r1 1999 4/12 SF 2001 7/12 QF 2004 10/12 r1 2007 8/12 QF 2011 5/12 QF

**FEDERACION DE FUTBOL
DE CHILE (FFCH)**

Av. Quilin No. 5635, Comuna
Peñalolén, Casilla No. 3733,
Santiago de Chile
☎ +56 2 8101800
🖷 +56 2 2843510
🖳 ffch@anfpchile.cl
🖳 www.anfp.cl
FA 1895 CON 1916 FIFA 1913
P Sergio Jadue
GS Nibaldo Jaque

FIFA BIG COUNT 2006

Total players	2 608 337
% of population	16.17%
Male	2 469 837
Female	138 500
Amateurs 18+	138 200
Youth under 18	326 500
Unregistered	2 010 000
Professionals	637
Referees	5 204
Admin & coaches	21 170
Number of clubs	5 715
Number of teams	31 228

MAJOR CITIES/TOWNS

		Population
1	Santiago	5 145 599
2	Puente Alto	745 752
3	Antofagasta	344 919
4	San Bernardo	298 757
5	Viña del Mar	289 147
6	Valparaíso	268 965
7	Temuco	250 454
8	Rancagua	240 286
9	Talca	223 499
10	Iquique	222 618
11	Concepción	215 097
12	Puerto Montt	198 446
13	Arica	192 278
14	La Serena	189 416
15	Coquimbo	188 995
16	Chillán	155 488
17	Quilpué	153 933
18	Talcahuano	153 532
19	Calama	146 334

REPUBLICA DE CHILE • REPUBLIC OF CHILE

Capital Santiago	Population 16 601 707 (60)	% in cities 88%
GDP per capita $14 900 (77)	Area km² 576 102 km² (38)	GMT + / - -4
Neighbours (km) Argentina 5308, Bolivia 860, Peru 171 • Coast 6435		

RECENT INTERNATIONAL MATCHES PLAYED BY CHILE

2010	Opponents	Score	Venue	Comp	Scorers	Att	Referee
20-01	Panama	W 2-1	Coquimbo	Fr	Paredes 2 51 53	15 000	Vazquez URU
31-03	Venezuela	D 0-0	Temuco	Fr		20 000	Silvera URU
5-05	Trinidad and Tobago	W 2-0	Iquique	Fr	Morales 2, Toro 48	10 000	Antequera BOL
16-05	Mexico	L 0-1	Mexico City	Fr		95 000	Geiger USA
26-05	Zambia	W 3-0	Calama	Fr	Sanchez 2 54 85, Valdivia 87	12 000	Favale ARG
30-05	Northern Ireland	W 1-0	Chillan	Fr	Paredes 30	12 000	Prudente URU
30-05	Israel	W 3-0	Concepcion	Fr	Suazo 22, Sanchez 49, Tello 90	25 000	Arias PAR
16-06	Honduras	W 1-0	Nelspruit	WCr1	Beausejour 34	32 664	Maillet SEY
21-06	Switzerland	W 1-0	Port Elizabeth	WCr1	Gonzalez 75	34 872	Al Ghamdi KSA
25-06	Spain	L 1-2	Pretoria	WCr1	Millar 47	41 958	Rodriguez MEX
28-06	Brazil	L 0-3	Johannesburg	WCr2		54 096	Webb ENG
7-09	Ukraine	L 1-2	Kyiv	Fr	Isla 86	10 000	Sevastsyanik BLR
9-10	UAE	W 2-0	Abu Dhabi	Fr	Cereceda 6p, Morales 37	500	Al Ghamdi KSA
12-10	Oman	W 1-0	Muscat	Fr	Morales 21	9 000	Blooshi KUW
17-11	Uruguay	W 2-0	Santiago	Fr	Sanchez 38, Vidal 74	45 017	Torres PAR
2011							
22-01	USA	D 1-1	Carson/LA	Fr	Paredes 53	18 580	Chacon MEX
26-03	Portugal	D 1-1	Leiria	Fr	Fernandez 42	10 694	Blom NED
29-03	Colombia	W 2-0	Den Haag	Fr	Fernandez 7, Beausejour 31	15 000	Vink NED
19-06	Estonia	W 4-0	Santiago	Fr	Fernandez 21, Ponce 42, Suazo 45p, Sanchez 50	20 000	Vazquez URU
23-06	Paraguay	D 0-0	Asuncion	Fr		12 000	Oliveira BRA
4-07	Mexico	W 2-1	Mendoza	CAr1	Paredes 66, Vidal 72	25 000	Soto VEN
8-07	Uruguay	D 1-1	Mendoza	CAr1	Sanchez 64	45 000	Amarilla PAR
12-07	Peru	W 1-0	Mendoza	CAr1	OG 92+	42 000	Fagundes BRA
17-07	Venezuela	L 1-2	San Juan	CAqf	Suazo 69	23 000	Vera ECU
10-08	France	D 1-1	Montpellier	Fr	Cordova 76	30 000	Attwell ENG
2-09	Spain	L 2-3	St Gall	Fr	Isla 11, Vargas 20	14 605	Laperriere SUI
4-09	Mexico	L 0-1	Barcelona	Fr		15 000	Muniz ESP
7-10	Argentina	L 1-4	Buenos Aires	WCq	Fernandez 59	26 161	Roldan COL
11-10	Peru	W 4-2	Santiago	WCq	Ponce 2, Vargas 18, Medel 48, Suazo 63p	39 000	Orosco BOL
11-11	Uruguay	L 0-4	Montevideo	WCq		40 500	Baldassi ARG
15-11	Paraguay	W 2-0	Santiago	WCq	Contreras 28, Campos 86	44 726	Lopes BRA
21-12	Paraguay	W 3-2	La Serena	Fr	Pinto 3 19 62p 74	12 000	Orozco BOL

Fr = Friendly match • CA = Copa America • WC = FIFA World Cup • q = qualifier • r1 = first round group

CHILE NATIONAL TEAM HISTORICAL RECORDS

Caps

84 - Leonel Sanchez 1955-68 • **73** - Nelson Tapia 1994-2005 • **70** - Alberto Fouilloux 1960-72 & Marcelo Salas 1994-2009 • **69** - Ivan Zamorano 1987-2001 & Fabian Estay 1990-2001 • **64** - Pablo Contreras 1999- • **63** - Javier Margas 1990-2000 • **62** - Miguel Ramirez 1991-2003 & Claudio Bravo 2004- • **61** - Clarence Acuna 1995-2004 • **57** - Juan Carlos Letelier 1979-89 • **55** - Pedro Reyes 1994-2001

Goals

37 - Marcelo Salas 1994-2009 • **34** - Ivan Zamorano 1987-2001 • **29** - Carlos Caszely 1969-85 • **23** - Leonel Sanchez 1955-68 • **22** - Jorge Aravena 1983-89 • **21** - Humberto Suazo 2005 • **18** - Juan Carlos Letelier 1979-89 • **17** - Enrique Hormazabal 1950-63 • **14** - Alexis Sanchez 2006- • **12** - Hugo Eduardo Rubio 1983-91; Jaime Ramirez 1954-66; Raul Toro 1936-41 & Alberto Foulloux 1960-72 • **11** - Pedro Araya 1964-71; Julio Crisosto 1971-77 & Matias Fernandez 2005-

Past Coaches

Carlos Fanta 1916 • Julian Bertola URU 1917 • Hector Parra 1918-19 • Juan Carlos Bertone URU 1920-22 • Carlos Acuna 1924 • Jose Rosetti ITA 1926 • Frank Powell ITA 1928 • Gyorgy Orth HUN 1930 • Pedro Mazullo URU 1936-39 • Maximum Garay HUN 1941 • Franz Platko HUN 1941-45 • Luis Tirado 1946-56 • Jose Salerno ARG 1956-57 • Ladislao Pakozdi HUN 1957 • Fernando Riera 1958-62 • Francisco Hormazabal 1962-65 • Luis Alamos 1965-66 • Alejandro Scopelli ARG 1966-67 • Salvador Nocetti 1968-69 • Francisco Hormazabal 1970 • Fernando Riera 1970 • Luis Vera 1971 • Raul Pino 1971-72 • Rudi Gutendorf GER 1972 • Luis Alamos 1973-74 • Pedro Morales 1974-75 • Caupolican Pena 1976-77 • Luis Santibanez 1977-82 • Luis Ibarra 1983 • Isaac Carrasco 1984 • Vicente Cantatore ARG 1984 • Pedro Morales 1985 • Luis Ibarra 1986 • Orlando Aravena 1987 • Manuel Rodriguez 1987 • Orlando Aravena 1988-89 • Arturo Salah 1990-93 • Nelson Acosta 1993 • Mirko Jozic CRO 1994 • Xabier Azkargorta ESP 1995-96 • Nelson Acosta 1996-2000 • Pedro Garcia 2001 • Jorge Garces 2001 • Cesar Vaccia 2002 • Juvenal Olmos 2003-05 • Nelson Acosta 2005-07 • Marcelo Bielsa ARG 2007-11 • Claudio Borghi 2011-

CHILE 2011 — PRIMERA DIVISION APERTURA

	Pl	W	D	L	F	A	Pts
Universidad Católica †	17	11	5	1	34	18	38
Universidad de Chile †	17	10	5	2	39	20	35
Unión Española †	17	9	5	3	33	18	32
Palestino †	17	9	3	5	26	20	30
O'Higgins †	17	8	3	6	29	26	27
Unión La Calera †	17	7	4	6	18	18	25
Unión San Felipe †	17	7	3	7	24	21	24
Colo Colo †	17	7	3	7	28	26	24
Huachipato	17	6	4	7	24	27	22
Deportes La Serena	17	5	6	6	28	28	21
Audax Italiano	17	6	3	8	24	28	21
Deportes Iquique	17	5	6	6	18	22	21
Univ. de Concepción	17	6	2	9	24	26	20
Santiago Wanderers	17	5	4	8	23	31	19
Cobreloa	17	4	6	7	16	22	18
Santiago Morning	17	3	7	7	22	30	16
Cobresal	17	5	1	11	26	41	16
Nublense	17	4	2	11	17	31	14

29/01/2011 - 22/05/2011 • † Qualified for the play-offs
Top scorers (overall): 12 - Matias Urbano ARG, Unión San Felipe • 11 - Gustavo Canales, U de Chile • 9 - Edson Puch, U de Chile & Eduardo Vargas, U de Chile • 8 - Nicolas Canales, Palestino; Sebastian Jaime ARG, Unión Española & Carlos Muniz, Wanderers

APERTURA 2011 PLAY-OFFS

Quarter-finals

Un. de Chile	2	1
U.San Felipe *	1	1
Palestina	1	0
O'Higgins *	1	3
U. La Calera *	1	0
Un. Española	0	0
Colo Colo *	2	1
Un. Católica	4	1

Semi-finals

Un. de Chile	1	7
O'Higgins *	0	1
U. La Calera *	1	1
Un. Católica	2	0

Final

Un. de Chile *	0	4
Un. Católica	2	1

* At home in the first leg

APERTURA 2011 FINAL

1st leg. Estadio Nacional, Santiago, 9-06-2011, Att: 30 248, Ref: Claudio Puga
Universidad de Chile — 0
Universidad Católica — 2   Costa 59, Mirosevic 91+

Un. de Chile - Johnny Herrera• - Matias Rodriguez (Edson Puch 41), Albert Acevedo•, Jose Rojas, Eugenio Mena, Felipe Seymour, Guillermo Marino•, Charles Aranguiz•, Eduardo Vargas, Gustavo Canales (Marcelo Diaz 72), Francisco Castro (Diego Rivarola 54). Tr: Jorge Sampaoli

Católica - Christopher Toselli• - Hans Martinez, Enzo Andia, Alfonso Parot, Juan Eluchans, Jorge Ormeno, Tomas Costa•, Felipe Gutierrez (Francisco Pizarro• 79), Milovan Mirosevic, Fernando Meneses (Gonzalo Sepulveda 87), Lucas Pratto• (Jose Luis Villanueva 91+). Tr: Juan Antonio Pizzi

2nd leg. Estadio Nacional, Santiago, 12-06-2011, Att: 39 685, Ref: Enrique Osses
Universidad Católica — 1   Pratto 23
Universidad de Chile — 4   Canales 3 16p 51p 55, Eluchans OG 25

Católica - Christopher Toselli• - Rodrigo Valenzuela• (Jose Luis Villanueva 86), Enzo Andia, Alfonso Parot•♦66, Juan Eluchans - Jorge Ormeno• (Roberto Gutierrez• 74), Francisco Silva, Tomas Costa••♦36, Milovan Mirosevic•, Fernando Meneses (Felipe Gutierrez 62) - Lucas Pratto. Tr: Juan Antonio Pizzi

U de Chile - Johnny Herrera - Matias Rodriguez (Albert Acevedo• 65), Marcos Gonzalez, Jose Rojas, Eugenio Mena - Charles Aranguiz•, Felipe Seymour, Guillermo Marino (Marcelo Diaz 62) - Eduardo Vargas, Gustavo Canales••♦78, Edson Puch• (Diego Rivarola 76). Tr: Jorge Sampaoli.

CHILE 2011 — PRIMERA DIVISION AGGREGATE TABLE

	Pl	W	D	L	F	A	Pts	U de Chile	Católica	Unión	Colo Colo	Audax	La Calera	Cobreloa	La Serena	Palestino	O'Higgins	Iquique	Cobresal	U Concepción	Huachipato	Wanderers	San Felipe	S'go Morning	Nublense
Universidad de Chile †	34	21	11	2	78	35	74		0-0	2-1	2-1	2-1	3-2	3-1	3-0	0-0	3-0	2-2	3-1	2-0	5-3	4-1	0-2	1-2	3-1
Universidad Católica ††	34	19	9	6	63	36	66	2-2		0-0	4-0	3-1	4-0	2-0	4-1	2-0	4-1	5-2	2-1	2-1	1-1	0-1	2-1	0-3	1-0
Unión Española ††	34	15	10	9	64	41	55	0-1	1-2		1-2	5-2	3-1	4-3	0-0	3-1	3-0	3-0	1-1	4-2	2-1	3-0	1-0	3-1	0-3
Colo Colo	34	16	6	12	55	54	54	2-2	1-1	3-2		3-0	2-0	1-1	4-1	3-1	5-1	1-1	0-3	1-5	1-2	3-1	2-2	3-1	2-1
Audax Italiano	34	14	8	12	53	51	50	1-1	0-0	1-2	2-1		2-1	1-0	2-1	1-3	1-3	3-0	3-2	1-1	1-1	4-0	2-1	5-0	2-0
Unión La Calera	34	14	7	13	38	36	49	0-2	2-1	0-0	3-0	3-1		0-1	2-0	3-2	1-0	2-1	0-0	1-0	1-0	1-0	2-0	2-0	
Cobreloa	34	13	10	11	43	39	49	1-4	2-0	0-0	0-3	3-4	0-1		3-3	1-0	2-3	0-0	1-0	1-1	1-0	1-0	1-2	3-1	1-0
Deportes La Serena	34	13	10	11	54	51	49	1-1	2-2	3-2	4-0	2-3	0-0	2-1		2-3	1-2	0-0	2-1	2-0	1-0	0-3	1-2	0-0	3-1
Palestino	34	13	10	11	45	44	49	1-1	1-2	1-2	0-3	0-0	1-1	0-2	1-1		2-2	1-0	2-1	3-2	1-0	1-1	1-0	2-4	1-0
O'Higgins	34	12	8	14	52	52	44	1-1	2-3	0-0	2-0	0-1	0-2	2-1	1-1	1-2		0-1	3-3	0-4	4-1	3-0	2-1	1-1	
Deportes Iquique	34	10	11	13	48	63	41	2-2	0-2	1-5	1-1	2-0	1-0	2-4	1-1	1-3	3-2		1-1	1-3	3-2	4-1	1-1	4-2	2-1
Cobresal	34	11	6	17	48	70	39	2-5	2-2	2-2	0-2	3-2	3-1	0-3	2-1	2-1	1-0	3-3		4-3	3-2	3-2	2-2	1-4	1-2
Univ. de Concepción	34	10	9	15	44	47	39	1-5	1-2	2-3	3-0	1-0	0-0	0-1	0-0	0-0	0-1	3-1	0-0		1-1	2-2	2-1	2-1	1-0
Huachipato	34	10	9	15	49	57	39	1-3	1-1	2-1	1-2	1-1	1-0	1-0	0-4	0-1	2-1	3-1	1-0			3-1	2-2	1-3	3-1
Santiago Wanderers ‡	34	10	9	15	42	53	39	1-1	2-0	1-1	2-1	2-0	1-1	2-0	0-2	1-1	0-2	2-2	3-0	2-1	2-1		1-2	4-1	0-1
Unión San Felipe ‡	34	9	10	15	40	50	37	0-3	1-2	1-1	2-0	2-2	1-1	1-1	0-1	2-3	3-1	2-1	1-1	1-3	2-1	0-2		3-1	1-2
Santiago Morning	34	9	8	17	51	55	35	0-2	3-2	1-1	0-1	2-2	1-1	1-1	4-1	0-4	2-4	3-1	5-0	0-3	1-1	3-0	1-1		1-3
Nublense	34	10	3	21	39	63	33	1-4	2-0	0-5	2-3	0-0	1-3	2-1	2-3	3-1	2-3	1-2	0-2	2-1	2-4	2-0	1-0	1-0	

Matches in the shaded boxes were played in the Apertura
† Qualified for Copa Libertadores as Apertura/Clausura winners • †† Qualified for Copa Libertadores on season record
‡ Relegation play-offs: **Santiago Wanderers** 1-0 2-2 Deportes Naval • **Unión San Felipe** 0-1 2-0 Everton

CHILE 2011
PRIMERA DIVISION CLAUSURA

	Pl	W	D	L	F	A	Pts
Universidad de Chile †	17	11	6	0	39	15	**39**
Cobreloa †	17	9	4	4	27	17	**31**
Colo Colo †	17	9	3	5	27	28	**30**
Audax Italiano †	17	8	5	4	29	23	**29**
Universidad Católica †	17	8	4	5	29	18	**28**
Deportes La Serena †	17	8	4	5	26	23	**28**
Unión La Calera †	17	7	3	7	20	18	**24**
Unión Española †	17	6	5	6	31	23	**23**
Cobresal	17	6	5	6	22	29	**23**
Santiago Wanderers	17	5	5	7	19	22	**20**
Deportes Iquique	17	5	5	7	30	41	**20**
Santiago Morning	17	6	1	10	29	34	**19**
Nublense	17	6	1	10	22	32	**19**
Univ. de Concepción	17	4	7	6	20	21	**19**
Palestino	17	4	7	6	19	24	**19**
O'Higgins	17	4	5	8	23	26	**17**
Huachipato	17	4	5	8	25	30	**17**
Unión San Felipe	17	2	7	8	16	29	**13**

30/07/2011 - 27/11/2011 • † Qualified for the play-offs
Top scorers (overall): **14** - Esteban Paredes, Colo Colo • **13** - Sebastian Pinto, O'Higgins • **11** - Facundo Pereyra ARG, Audax Italiano • **9** - Nicolas Canales, Palestino, Miguel Cuellar BOL, Cobresal & Diego Barrios PAR, Cobreloa

CLAUSURA 2011 PLAY-OFFS

Quarter–finals		Semi–finals		Final	
Un. de Chile	1 3				
Un. Española*	0 0	**Un. de Chile**	2 1		
Audax Italiano	1 0	Univ. Católica*	1 2		
Univ. Católica*	3 1			**Un. de Chile**	0 3
Colo Colo	6 3			Cobreloa	0 0
La Serena *	2 1	Colo Colo *	2 2		
Un. La Calera*	0 3	**Cobreloa**	3 1		
Cobreloa	1 4	* At home in the first leg			

CLAUSURA 2011 FINAL

1st leg. Municipal, Calama, 26-12-2011, Att: 10 268, Ref: Eduardo Gamboa

Cobreloa 0
Universidad de Chile 0

Cobreloa - Nicolas Peric - Carlos Gomez, Christian Suarez, Sebastian Roco•, Andres Oroz - Sebastian Zuniga, Felipe Rojas (Cristian Rojas• 70), Pedro Vera (Alvaro Lopez 79), Bryan Cortes, Nicolas Trecco, Diego Barrios Suarez (Patricio Schwob 86). Tr: Nelson Acosta

U de Chile - Johnny Herrera - Osvaldo Gonzalez, Marco Gonzalez, Jose Rojas - Matias Rodriguez (Gustavo Lorenzetti 46), Marcelo Diaz, Charles Aranguiz, Eugenio Mena - Paulo Magalhaes, Gustavo Canales• (Gabriel Vargas 68), Francisco Castro• (Felipe Gallegos 81). Tr: Jorge Sampaoli

2nd leg. Estadio Nacional, Santiago, 29-12-2011, Att: 44 870, Ref: Enrique Osses

Universidad de Chile 3 Canales [24], Vargas [28], Rodriguez [35]
Cobreloa 0

U de Chile - Johnny Herrera - Osvaldo Gonzalez, Marcos Gonzalez (Albert Acevedo 46), Jose Rojas - Charles Aranguiz, Marcelo Diaz, Eugenio Mena, Gustavo Lorenzetti (Diego Rivarola 57) - Eduardo Vargas•, Gustavo Canales (Matias Rodriguez 32), Francisco Castro. Tr: Jorge Sampaoli

Cobreloa - Nicolas Peric (Luciano Palos 43) - Carlos Gomez, Christian Suarez•, Sebastian Roco•, Andres Oroz - Pedro Vera•, Felipe Rojas (Boris Gonzalez 55), Bryan Cortes (Sebastian Zuniga 46), Hugo Lusardi - Diego Barrios, Nicolas Trecco. Tr: Nelson Acosta

COPA CHILE 2011

Quarter-finals		Semi-finals		Final	
Universidad Católica *	2 1 4p				
Audax Italiano	0 3 2p	**Universidad Católica**	1 5		
Huachipato	0 2	Univ. de Concepción *	0 4		
Univ. de Concepción *	3 5			**Universidad Católica ***	0 1 4p
Deportes La Serena *	2 1			Magallanes	1 0 2p
Deportes Iquique	1 0	Deportes La Serena *	0 0		
Santiago Morning	1 0	**Magallanes**	1 3		
Magallanes *	0 3	* Home team in the first leg			

COPA CHILE 2011 FINAL 2011

1st leg. San Carlos, Santiago
9-11-2011, Att: 7000, Ref: Eduardo Gamboa

Universidad Católica 0
Magallanes 1 Cardenas [85]

Católica - Christopher Toselli - Hans Martinez•, Roberto Cereceda, Christian Alvarez, Marko Biskupovic - Jorge Ormeno (Kevin Harbottle 83), Francisco Silva•, Fernando Meneses•, Felipe Gutierrez (Matias Mier• 63) - Cesar Carignano, Francisco Pizarro (Daud Gazale 68). Tr: Mario Lepe

Magallanes - Hector Barra - Gonzalo Abascal (Rodrigo Aguilera• 18), Juan Cornejo, Isaias Meneses•, Carlos Cisternas•, Felipe Hernandez, Esteban Bravo, Claudio Latorre, Felipe Reyreno (David Cordova 86), Patricio Salas (Mario Nunez 81), Paulo Cardenas. Tr: Osvaldo Hurtado

COPA CHILE 2011 FINAL

2nd leg. Santa Laura, Santiago
16-11-2011, Att: 9040, Ref: Julio Bascunan

Magallanes 0 2p
Universidad Católica 1 4p Gazale [88]

Magallanes - Hector Barra - Rodrigo Aguilera, Juan Cornejo♦50, Isaias Meneses, Carlos Cisternas, Felipe Hernandez, Esteban Bravo•, Claudio Latorre, Felipe Reyreno (Carlos Opazo 67), Patricio Salas• (Sergio Moreno• 53), Paulo Cardenas. Tr: Osvaldo Hurtado

Católica - Christopher Toselli - Hans Martinez•, Roberto Cereceda•, Christian Alvarez - Jorge Ormeno, Milovan Mirosevic•, Felipe Gutierrez, Matias Mier (Francisco Pizarro 60), Juan Gomez (Fernando Meneses 46), Stefano Magnasco (Pablo Calandria 74), Daud Gazale. Tr: Mario Lepe

CHILE 2011 PRIMERA B (2) APERTURA

North	Pl	W	D	L	F	A	Pts
Coquimbo Unido	6	3	2	1	9	6	11
Everton	6	3	1	2	9	5	10
Antofagasta	6	3	1	2	5	8	10
Deportes Copiapó	6	3	0	3	5	5	9
San Luis	6	2	2	2	6	4	8
Magallanes	6	2	1	3	7	9	7
San Marcos Arica	6	1	1	4	9	13	4

South	Pl	W	D	L	F	A	Pts
Rangers Talca	6	5	0	1	9	3	15
Deportes Concepción	6	4	0	2	8	4	12
Naval Talcahuano	6	3	1	2	7	6	10
Unión Temuco	6	2	1	3	6	6	7
Prov. Curicó Unido	6	2	1	3	6	10	7
Puerto Montt	6	1	2	3	5	8	5
Lota Schwager	6	1	1	4	2	6	4

26/02/2011 - 3/04/2011

CHILE 2011 PRIMERA B (2) CLAUSURA

North	Pl	W	D	L	F	A	Pts
Antofagasta	6	3	2	1	14	5	11
San Marcos Arica	6	3	2	1	9	6	11
Everton	6	3	2	1	6	4	11
Coquimbo Unido	6	3	0	3	8	8	9
Deportes Copiapó	6	1	2	3	4	12	5
Magallanes	6	0	4	2	5	7	4
San Luis	6	0	4	2	5	9	4

South	Pl	W	D	L	F	A	Pts
Naval Talcahuano	6	4	1	1	15	8	13
Puerto Montt	6	4	1	1	8	3	13
Deportes Concepción	6	2	2	2	8	5	8
Unión Temuco	6	2	2	2	8	2	8
Rangers Talca	6	2	1	3	9	9	7
Lota Schwager	6	1	2	3	2	8	5
Prov. Curicó Unido	6	1	1	4	3	8	4

30/07/2011 - 22/09/2011

CHILE 2011 PRIMERA B (2) APERTURA

	Pl	W	D	L	F	A	Pts
Antofagasta	13	9	3	1	21	11	30
Rangers Talca	13	7	3	3	22	18	24
Deportes Concepción	13	5	5	3	19	14	20
Prov. Curicó Unido	13	5	4	4	25	20	19
San Marcos Arica	13	5	4	4	22	17	19
Puerto Montt	13	5	4	4	15	14	19
Unión Temuco	13	5	3	5	19	15	18
Lota Schwager	13	5	3	5	15	15	18
San Luis	13	5	2	6	21	21	17
Naval Talcahuano	13	4	5	4	17	18	17
Coquimbo Unido	13	4	3	6	15	20	15
Magallanes	13	3	5	5	18	23	14
Everton	13	2	5	6	12	22	11
Deportes Copiapó	13	2	1	10	16	29	7

9/04/2011 - 3/07/2011

Antofagasta and *Rangers* promoted

Everton & Deportes Naval qualified for the play-offs (see Primera A)

CHILE 2011 PRIMERA B (2) CLAUSURA

	Pl	W	D	L	F	A	Pts
Everton	13	8	4	1	18	9	28
San Luis	13	8	1	4	13	10	25
Antofagasta	13	7	1	5	22	17	22
Lota Schwager	13	6	4	3	15	10	22
Naval Talcahuano	13	7	1	5	17	17	22
Deportes Concepción	13	6	2	5	22	22	20
Unión Temuco	13	5	3	5	15	16	18
Coquimbo Unido	13	4	4	5	17	18	16
Magallanes	13	4	3	6	17	18	15
Deportes Copiapó	13	3	6	4	15	17	15
San Marcos Arica	13	4	2	7	14	21	14
Rangers Talca	13	4	1	8	17	16	13
Puerto Montt	13	2	5	6	18	23	11
Prov. Curicó Unido	13	2	5	6	13	19	11

11/09/2011 - 20/11/2011

MEDALS TABLE

		Overall			League			Cup		Sth Am			City
		G	S	B	G	S	B	G	S	G	S	B	
1	Colo Colo	40	23	20	29	17	15	10	4	1	2	5	Santiago
2	Universidad de Chile	19	8	17	15	8	13	3		1	4		Santiago
3	Universidad Catolica	14	25	9	10	17	4	4	7	1	5		Santiago
4	Cobreloa	9	13	6	8	8	5	1	3	2	1		Calama
5	Unión Española	8	11	6	6	8	5	2	2	1	1		Santiago
6	Santiago Wanderers	5	5	2	3	3	2	2	2				Valparaíso
7	Everton	5	2		4	2		1					Viña del Mar
8	Audax Italiano	4	10	4	4	8	9		2				Santiago
9	Palestino	4	5	3	2	4	2	2	1		1		Santiago
10	Magallanes	4	5	2	4	4	2		1				Santiago
11	Deportes Iquique	2	1	1			1	2	1				Iquique
12	Union San Felipe	2			1			1					San Felipe
13	Santiago Morning	1	3	1	1	2	1		1				Santiago
14	Cobresal	1	2			2		1					El Salvador
15	Deportes La Serena	1	1	2			2	1	1				La Serena
16	Universidad Concepción	1	1		1			1					Concepción
17	Temuco	1		2	1		2						Temuco
18	Huachipato	1		1	1		1						Talcahuano
19	Luis Cruz Martinez	1						1					Curicó
20	Rangers		3	2		2	2						Talca
21	O'Higgins		2	3			3	2				1	Rancagua
22	Deportes Concepción		2	1			1	1				1	Concepción

CHN – CHINA PR

FIFA/COCA-COLA WORLD RANKING

'93	'94	'95	'96	'97	'98	'99	'00	'01	'02	'03	'04	'05	'06	'07	'08	'09	'10	'11	'12
53	40	66	76	55	37	88	75	54	63	86	54	72	84	81	100	93	87	71	

					2011									
Jan	Feb	Mar	Apr	May	Jun	Jul	Aug	Sep	Oct	Nov	Dec	High	Low	Av
79	75	76	77	75	75	73	69	73	70	72	71	37	108	68

China's woes on the international stage continued as the world's most populous nation once again missed out on a place at the FIFA World Cup finals. In the qualifying tournament for Brazil 2014, China failed to progress to the last round of Asian qualifying for the third straight tournament. Former Real Madrid coach Jose Antonio Camacho took charge of the team just 10 days prior to the start of the group stage - hardly an ideal introduction for him and it showed with their third place finish behind Iraq and Jordan. There may be despair amongst football fans when it comes to the national team, but the mood is improving in club football where big-spending Guangzhou Evergrande completed an impressive two-year period by adding the Chinese Super League title to the second-tier crown they claimed in 2010. Guangzhou spent heavily on a number of the country's leading stars - including Zheng Zhi and Gao Lin - before signing Argentina's Dario Conca in a deal that made the former Cruzeiro midfielder one of the highest-paid players in the world. Other clubs are following suit as the league looks to develop the potential that clearly exists in the country. Tianjin were the other trophy winners after winning the CFA Cup which returned after a five-year absence. Coached by Arie Haan they beat Sandong Luneng 2-1 in the final.

FIFA WORLD CUP RECORD
1930-1954 DNE **1958** DNQ **1962-1978** DNE **1982-1998** DNQ **2002** 31 r1 **2006-2014** DNQ

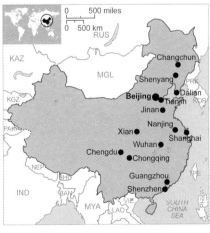

FOOTBALL ASSOCIATION OF THE PEOPLE'S REPUBLIC OF CHINA (CFA)

Building A, Dong Jiu Da Sha, Xi Zhao Si Street, Chongwen District, Beijing 100061
☎ +86 10 59291030
📠 +86 10 59290309
✉ info.footballchina@gmail.com
🖥 www.fa.org.cn
FA 1924 CON 1974 FIFA 1974
P Yuan Weimin
GS Wei Di

FIFA BIG COUNT 2006

Total players	26 166 335
% of population	1.99%
Male	24 266 330
Female	1 900 000
Amateurs 18+	325 992
Youth under 18	382 762
Unregistered	5 045 100
Professionals	2 239
Referees	21 6574
Admin & coaches	107 400
Number of clubs	1 621
Number of teams	11 347

MAJOR CITIES/TOWNS

		Population
1	Shanghai	15 968 867
2	Beijing	7 817 968
3	Chongqing	4 579 725
4	Xian	4 445 222
5	Wuhan	4 303 340
6	Chengdu	3 916 581
7	Tianjin	3 666 320
8	Shenyang	3 543 444
9	Harbin	3 363 096
10	Nanjing	3 320 712
11	Guangzhou	3 103 466
12	Taiyuan	2 786 596
13	Changchun	2 750 684
14	Shijiazhuang	2 319 694
15	Changsha	2 267 008
16	Jinan	2 191 110
17	Dalian	2 158 193
18	Jilin	2 150 510
19	Nanchang	2 092 603

ZHONGHUA RENMIN GONGHEGUO • PEOPLE'S REPUBLIC OF CHINA

Capital	Beijing	Population	1 338 612 968 (1)	% in cities	43%
GDP per capita	$6000 (133)	Area km²	9 596 961 km² (4)	GMT +/-	+8

Neighbours (km): Afghanistan 76, Bhutan 470, Burma 2185, India 3380, Kazakhstan 1533, Korea DPR 1416, Kyrgyzstan 858, Laos 423, Mongolia 4677, Nepal 1236, Pakistan 523, Russia 3645, Tajikistan 414, Vietnam 1281 • Coast 14 500

RECENT INTERNATIONAL MATCHES PLAYED BY CHINA PR

2009 Opponents	Score	Venue	Comp	Scorers	Att	Referee
12-08 Singapore	D 1-1	Singapore	Fr	Yang Hao 27. W 4-3p		
15-08 Malaysia	D 0-0	Kuala Lumpur	Fr			
30-09 Botswana	W 4-1	Hohhot	Fr	Gao Lin 29, Qu Bo 52, Zhao Peng 54, Yu Hai 58		
8-11 Kuwait	D 2-2	Kuwait City	Fr	Zheng Long 55, Han Peng 59		
14-11 Lebanon	W 2-0	Beirut	ACq	Yu Hai 44, Qu Bo 72	2 000	Albadwawi UAE
22-11 Lebanon	W 1-0	Zheijang	ACq	Du Wei 19	21 520	Breeze AUS
30-12 Jordan	D 2-2	Jinan	Fr	Zhang Linpeng 48, Han Peng 56		
2010						
6-01 Syria	D 0-0	Zheijang	ACq		29 570	Toma JPN
17-01 Vietnam	W 2-1	Hanoi	ACq	Xu Yang 35, Zhang Linpeng 43	3 000	Abdul Bashir SIN
6-02 Japan	D 0-0	Tokyo	EAC		25 964	Delovski AUS
10-02 Korea Republic	W 3-0	Tokyo	EAC	Yu Hai 5, Gao Lin 27, Deng Zhuoxiang 60	3 629	Ng Kai Lam HKG
14-02 Hong Kong	W 2-0	Tokyo	EAC	Qu Bo 2 44 74p	16 439	Kim Jong Hyeok KOR
4-06 France	W 1-0	Saint-Pierre (REU)	Fr	Deng Zhuoxiang 68	10 043	Proenca POR
26-06 Tajikistan	W 4-0	Kunming	Fr	Yan Xiangchuang 10, Yu Hanchao 2 47 78, Qu Bo 78		
11-08 Bahrain	D 1-1	Nanning	Fr	Hai Yu 10		
3-09 Iran	L 0-2	Zhengzhou	Fr			
7-09 Paraguay	D 1-1	Nanjing	Fr	Gao Lin 33		
8-10 Syria	W 2-1	Kunming	Fr	Zhao Peng 38, Zhang Linpeng 50		
12-10 Uruguay	L 0-4	Wuhan	Fr		50 000	Lee Dong Jun KOR
17-11 Latvia	W 1-0	Kunming	Fr	Xu Yang 89	7 500	Ko Hyung Jin KOR
18-12 Estonia	W 3-0	Zhuhai	Fr	Du Wei 17, Yu Hai 20, Yang Xu 38	8 500	Ko Hyung Jin KOR
22-12 Macedonia FYR	W 1-0	Guangzhou	Fr	Deng Zhuoxiang 90	8 000	
2011						
8-01 Kuwait	W 2-0	Doha	ACr1	Zhang Linpeng 58, Deng Zhuoxiang 67	7 423	Williams AUS
12-01 Qatar	L 0-2	Doha	ACr1		30 778	Kim Dong Jin KOR
16-01 Uzbekistan	D 2-2	Doha	ACr1	Yu Hai 6, Hao Junmin 56	3 529	Al Hilali OMA
25-03 New Zealand	D 1-1	Wuhan	Fr	OG 3		Toma JPN
26-03 Costa Rica	D 2-2	San Jose	Fr	Gao Lin 2 46 90	35 000	Moreno PAN
29-03 Honduras	W 3-0	Wuhan	Fr	Huang Bowen 18, Yang Xu 2 37 86	10 000	Iemoto JPN
5-06 Uzbekistan	W 1-0	Kunming	Fr	Gao Lin 65	40 000	Ko Hyung Jin KOR
8-06 Korea DPR	W 2-0	Guiyang	Fr	Deng Zhuoxiang 38, Gao Lin 41	27 000	
23-07 Laos	W 7-2	Kunming	WCq	Yang Xu 3 45 54 73, Chen Tao 2 58 88, Hao Junmin 2 81 91+	13 500	Delovski AUS
28-07 Laos	W 6-1	Vientiane	WCq	Qu Bo 24, Yu Hanchao 2 36 87, Deng Zhuoxiang 2 67 82, Yang Xu 93+	13 000	Shamsuzzaman BAN
10-08 Jamaica	W 1-0	Hefei	Fr	Zhao Peng 9	60 000	Lee Min Hu KOR
2-09 Singapore	W 2-1	Kunming	WCq	Zheng Zhi 69, Yu Hai 73	17 000	El Haddad LIB
6-09 Jordan	L 1-2	Amman	WCq	Hao Junmin 57	19 000	Irmatov UZB
6-10 UAE	W 2-1	Shenzhen	Fr	Sun Xiang 5, Gao Lin 15	18 652	Singh SIN
11-10 Iraq	L 0-1	Shenzhen	WCq		25 021	Mozaffari IRN
11-11 Iraq	L 0-1	Doha	WCq		5 000	Green AUS
15-11 Singapore	W 4-0	Singapore	WCq	Yu Hai 41, Li Weifeng 56, Zheng Zheng 2 73 81	5 474	Balideh QAT

Fr = Friendly match • EAC = East Asian Championship • AC = AFC Asian Cup • WC = FIFA World Cup • q = qualifier

CHINA PR NATIONAL TEAM HISTORICAL RECORDS

Caps
112 - Li Weifeng 1998- • **103** - Hao Haidong 1987-2004 • **102** - Fan Zhiyi 1992-2002 • **89** - Li Tie 1997-2007 • **86** - Zhu Bo 1983-93 • **85** Li Ming 1992-2004 & Ma Mingyu 1996-2002 • **78** - Sun Jihai 1996-2008 • **72** - Qu Bo 2001- & Xu Yunlong 2000-08 • **71** - Zhao Junzhe 1998-2008 • **69** - Li Jinyu 1997-2008 • **67** - Li Bing 1992-2001 • **66** - Ou Chuliang 2992-2002 • **65** - Jia Xiuquan 1983-92 • **64** - Du Wei 2001- • **63** - Lin Lefeng 1977-85 • **62** - Zhang Enhua 1995-2002 • **59** - Zheng Zhi 2002- • **58** - Liu Haiguang 1983-90

Goals
37 - Hao Haidong 1992-2004 • **27** - Su Maozhen 1992-2002 • **24** - Li Jinyu 1997-2008 • **21** - Ma Lin 1985-90 • **20** - Liu Haiguang 1983-90 • **19** - Li Bing 1992-2001 & Zhao Dayu 1982-86 • **18** - Qu Bo 2000- • **16** - Fan Zhiyi 1992-2002 & Mai Chao 1986-92

Past Coaches
Li Fenglou 1951-52 • A Joseph HUN 1954-56 • Dai Linjing 1957 • Chen Chengda 1958-62 • Nian Weisi 1963 • Fang Renqiu 1964 • Nian Weisi 1965-73 • Nian Weisi & Ren Bin 1974-76 • Zhang Honggen 1977 • Nian Weisi 1978 • Zhang Honggen 1979 • Nian Weisi 1980 • Su Yongshun 1980-82 • Zhang Honggen 1982 • Zeng Xuelin 1983-85 • Nian Weisi 1985-86 • Gao Fengwen 1986-90 • Xu Genbao 1991-92 • Klaus Schlappner GER 1992-93 • Qi Wusheng 1994-97 • Bobby Houghton ENG 1997-99 • Jin Zhiyang 2000 • Bora Milutinovic SRB 2000-02 • Shen Xiangfu 2002 • Arie Haan NED 2002-04 • Zhu Guanghu 2005-07 • Vladimir Petrovic SRB & Ratomir Dujkovic SRB 2007-08 • Yin Tiesheng 2008-09 • Gao Hongbo 2009-2011 • Jose Camacho ESP 2011-

CHINA PR 2011

CSL (CHINESE SUPER LEAGUE)

	Pl	W	D	L	F	A	Pts	Guangzhou	Beijing	Liaoning	Jiangsu	Shandong	Qingdao	Changchun	Hangzhou	Shaanxi	Tianjin	Shanghai	Dalian	Henan	Nanchang	Chengdu	Shenzhen
Guangzhou Evergrande†	30	20	8	2	67	23	68		2-2	2-1	2-1	2-0	4-0	1-1	3-0	2-0	4-0	3-0	1-0	3-1	5-0	4-0	4-1
Beijing Guoan †	30	14	11	5	49	21	53	1-1		0-0	2-1	1-1	2-0	4-1	1-3	2-3	1-1	3-0	3-0	3-0	1-0	3-1	4-0
Liaoning Whowin †	30	14	8	8	38	23	50	1-1	0-0		2-4	0-1	0-0	1-0	1-0	1-0	2-0	1-0	3-0	1-0	1-0	1-0	6-1
Jiangsu Sainty	30	14	5	11	43	28	47	5-2	0-2	0-1		2-0	3-1	1-0	2-0	1-0	2-2	3-2	4-0	1-1	1-0	1-0	3-0
Shandong Luneng	30	13	8	9	37	31	47	0-0	1-1	2-1	1-0		0-1	1-0	1-2	2-1	1-1	2-0	0-0	1-0	1-0	3-3	2-0
Qingdao Jonoon	30	12	9	9	37	33	45	0-2	1-0	2-0	1-0	2-0		0-1	3-1	0-1	3-0	2-1	2-1	1-1	4-1	0-0	2-0
Changchun Yatai	30	11	12	7	33	31	45	2-1	2-1	0-0	1-0	1-1	0-2		1-1	3-0	3-3	0-0	2-2	0-0	0-2	1-1	2-1
Hangzhou Greentown	30	10	9	11	28	32	39	1-3	0-0	1-0	1-0	1-0	1-0	2-0		0-0	1-2	1-0	0-0	1-2	2-0	1-1	2-1
Shaanxi Renhe	30	10	8	12	34	41	38	1-4	1-1	2-0	0-0	2-1	2-2	1-1	2-1		1-1	1-0	1-3	3-2	1-3	0-1	1-1
Tianjin Teda †	30	8	13	9	37	41	37	0-1	0-1	1-3	2-1	3-1	1-1	1-2	2-2	2-2		1-0	2-2	3-1	3-0	0-1	1-0
Shanghai Shenhua	30	11	4	15	31	41	37	0-2	1-0	1-1	3-2	1-0	3-3	0-2	3-2	2-1	2-1		1-0	1-2	0-1	4-1	2-0
Dalian Shide	30	7	11	12	27	43	32	1-3	0-0	1-0	0-3	0-3	3-2	1-1	1-1	1-0	1-1	1-2		2-1	2-1	2-0	0-0
Henan Construction	30	7	11	12	29	35	32	1-1	1-1	2-1	0-0	1-1	4-1	0-1	0-0	1-0	0-0	1-2	0-1		2-0	2-3	0-0
Nanchang Hengyuan	30	8	5	17	20	41	29	1-1	0-3	1-2	0-1	2-5	0-0	0-1	1-0	2-3	0-0	0-0	1-0	0-0		1-0	1-0
Chengdu Blades	30	5	12	13	27	47	27	2-2	0-3	0-4	0-0	1-2	0-0	2-2	2-0	1-3	1-1	2-0	0-0	0-2	0-1		2-2
Shenzhen Ruby	30	5	8	17	27	53	23	0-1	0-3	1-1	2-1	2-3	1-1	1-2	0-0	0-1	1-2	2-0	4-2	2-1	2-1	2-2	

1/04/2011 - 2/11/2011 • † Qualified for the AFC Champions League

Top scorers: **16** - Muriqui BRA, Guangzhou • **14** - Leandro Netto BRA, Henan • **13** - Cristian Danalache ROU, Jiangsu • **12** - Yu Hanchao, Liaoning & Luis Salmeron ARG, Shanghai • **11** - Joel Griffiths AUS, Beijing; Gao Lin, Guangzhou & Aleksandar Jevtic SRB, Jiangsu • **10** - Walter Martinez HON, Beijing; Martin Kamburov BUL, Dalian; Cleo BRA Guangzhou & Obina BRA, Shandong

MEDALS TABLE

		Overall			League			Cup			Asia			City
		G	S	B	G	S	B	G	S	B	G	S	B	
1	Liaoning Whowin	11	9	6	8	6	5	2	2		1	1	1	Anshan & Fushun
2	Dalian Shide	11	6	6	8		5	3	4		2	1		Dalian
3	Beijing Guoan	10	7	13	6	4	12	4	3				1	Beijing
4	Shandong Luneng	8	6	2	4	3	2	4	3					Ji'nan
5	Shanghai Shenhua	7	13	5	4	11	5	3	2					Shanghai
6	August 1st	6	6	5	5	6	5	1						Liuzhou
7	Tianjin Teda	4	7	4	2	6	4	2	1					Tianjin
8	North East China	2	1		2	1								
9	Guangdong Hongyuan	1	5	1	1	1	1				4			Guiyang
10	Guangzhou Evergrande	1	3	1	1	2	1	1						Guangzhou
11	Shenzhen Ruby	1	1	1	1	1							1	Shenzhen
12	Changchun Yatai	1	1		1	1								Changchun

CHINA PR 2011

CHINA LEAGUE ONE (2)

	Pl	W	D	L	F	A	Pts	Dalian	Guangzhou	Guangdong	Hunan	Shenyang D	Shenyang S	Hubei	Chongqing	Shanghai	Yanbian	Beijing B	Tianjin	Beijing 361°	Guizhou
Dalian Aerbin	26	16	6	4	45	20	54		1-0	2-0	6-2	2-1	2-2	4-0	0-1	2-1	3-1	2-1	2-0	2-0	1-1
Guangzhou R&F	26	13	8	5	36	27	47	1-1		0-2	2-0	1-1	1-1	1-1	2-2	1-0	2-1	0-0	3-2	4-1	1-0
Guangdong S'ray Cave	26	13	7	6	42	29	46	1-1	1-1		3-2	2-3	3-0	3-1	2-2	2-2	1-0	0-1	2-0	0-0	2-1
Hunan Billows	26	12	6	8	39	35	42	1-1	4-0	2-3		2-2	0-0	0-2	2-1	2-1	1-0	0-1	0-0	1-0	3-2
Shenyang Dongjin	26	9	10	7	32	25	37	0-0	0-2	3-0	3-1		1-2	0-0	0-0	1-1	0-1	2-0	1-1	2-1	1-0
Shonyang Shenbei	26	8	10	8	31	31	34	1-0	0-2	0-2	0-3	1-1		1-2	2-0	1-0	3-2	0-1	1-1	1-0	1-1
Hubei Zhongbo	26	8	9	9	26	28	33	1-2	2-1	2-3	1-2	1-2	1-1		1-1	0-0	2-0	4-0	2-1	2-0	0-1
Chongqing Lifan	26	8	9	9	30	35	33	1-4	0-2	1-2	3-2	1-2	0-3	0-0		1-0	2-0	1-1	2-2	1-1	1-1
Shanghai East Asia	26	7	11	8	29	25	32	0-1	1-1	2-1	2-2	2-2	2-1	0-0	0-1		4-0	1-0	2-2	0-0	0-0
Yanbian Baekdu	26	8	6	12	30	36	30	0-1	3-0	2-0	0-2	1-1	3-3	3-0	3-2	0-1		1-0	1-3	1-1	2-0
Beijing Baxy	26	7	9	10	18	28	30	1-0	0-2	0-0	2-3	2-1	0-2	0-0	3-2	0-2	2-2		1-1	0-0	1-0
Tianjin Songjiang	26	5	10	11	23	31	25	2-1	1-2	0-0	0-1	0-2	1-3	0-0	2-2	2-0	1-0	0-0		0-0	1-2
Beijing 361°	26	5	9	12	15	33	24	0-3	0-1	1-4	0-1	1-0	1-1	2-0	0-2	1-4	1-1	2-1	2-1		1-0
Guizhou Toro	26	4	8	14	15	28	20	0-1	2-3	0-3	0-0	1-0	1-0	0-1	0-1	1-1	0-2	0-0	0-1	1-0	

26/03/2011 - 30/10/2011 • Top scorers: **13** - Johnny Woodly CRC, Dalian & Mitchel Brown HON, Hunan • **12** - Wu Lei, Shanghai

CFA CUP 2011

First Round

Team	Score
Tianjin Teda	Bye
Liaoning Whowin *	1
Guangzhou R&F	0
Guangzhou Evergrande	1 10p
Shaanxi Renhe *	1 11p
Yanbian Baekdu	2
Dalian Shide *	1
Tianjin Songjiang	0
Guangdong Sunray Cave *	1
Shanghai Shenhua	Bye
Beijing Guoan *	1
Shanghai East Asia	0
Dalian Aerbin	0
Nanchang Hengyuan *	2
Hangzhou Greentown	Bye
Henan Construction *	1 3p
Chongqing Lifan	1 1p
Shenyang Shenbei	0
Changchun Yatai *	4
Shandong Luneng	Bye

Second Round

Team	Score
Tianjin Teda	Bye
Liaoning Whowin *	0
Shaanxi Renhe	1
Yanbian Baekdu *	1 2p
Guangdong Sunray Cave	1 1p
Shanghai Shenhua	Bye
Beijing Guoan *	6
Nanchang Hengyuan	1
Hangzhou Greentown	Bye
Henan Construction *	2
Changchun Yatai	0
Shandong Luneng	Bye

Quarter-finals

Team	Score
Tianjin Teda *	2
Shaanxi Renhe	0
Yanbian Baekdu	0
Shanghai Shenhua *	1
Beijing Guoan	2
Hangzhou Greentown *	0
Henan Construction	2 3p
Shandong Luneng *	2 4p

Semi-finals

Team	Score
Tianjin Teda *	2
Shanghai Shenhua	0
Beijing Guoan	0 3p
Shandong Luneng *	0 4p

Final

Team	Score
Tianjin Teda †	2
Shandong Luneng	1

CUP FINAL

Olympic Sports Centre, Hefei
19-11-2011, 16:00,
Att: 19 813, Ref: Yudai Yamamoto JPN
Scorers - Wang XinXin 12; Yu Dabao 63 for Tianjin; Han Peng 3 for Shandong
Tianjin - Song Zhenyu● - Cao Yang●, Li Weifeng, Marko Zoric● Bai Yuefeng - Song Chong Gug - Hu Rentian (Wu Weian 92+), Chen Tao, Wang Xinxin (c)● Li Benjian (Nie Tao 97+) - Yu Dabao●. Tr: Arie Haan
Shandong - Yang Cheng - Yuan Weiwei, Fabiano, Ricardo, Zheng Zheng - Wang Tong (Hao Junmin 64), Zhou Haibin, Roda Antar, Wang Yongpo (Mirahmetjan Muzepper 85) - Lu Zheng (Obina 75). Han Peng (c). Tr: Manuel Barbosa

* Home team ● † Qualified for the AFC Champions League

CIV – COTE D'IVOIRE

FIFA/COCA-COLA WORLD RANKING

'93	'94	'95	'96	'97	'98	'99	'00	'01	'02	'03	'04	'05	'06	'07	'08	'09	'10	'11	'12
33	25	20	51	52	44	53	51	44	64	70	40	42	18	37	29	16	21	16	

	2011												High	Low	Av
Jan	Feb	Mar	Apr	May	Jun	Jul	Aug	Sep	Oct	Nov	Dec				
21	26	25	21	21	14	15	15	16	19	16	16		14	75	37

Cote d'Ivoire failed to live up to their billing as pre-tournament favourites at the 2012 CAF Africa Cup of Nations but it could have been a completely different story had Didier Drogba not missed a second half penalty against Zambia in the final in Libreville. Instead the much vaunted Elephants lost on post-match penalties to the Zambians - despite going through the six games they played in the tournament without conceding a goal. It was the second time in the last four tournaments that the Ivorians have lost the final on penalties and the star-studded team was visibly crushed at the end. Cote d'Ivoire had progressed through the tournament with same efficiency they had shown in the qualifying campaign. They were the only side with a 100 percent record in the qualifiers and won all their matches in the group stage at the finals, before beating Equatorial Guinea in the last eight and Mali in the semi-finals. At club level, the start of the 2011 season was delayed due to the political crisis and the fighting that followed the 2010 presidential elections. When it kicked-off in May the single round robin format was replaced by two first-round groups and a six-team final stage. ASEC Mimosas had the best record going into the final phase but that counted for nothing and they finished bottom with the title going to arch-rivals Africa Sports.

CAF AFRICA CUP OF NATIONS RECORD

1957-1963 DNE **1965** 3 r1 **1968** 3 SF **1970** 4 SF 1972 DNQ **1974** 7 r1 1976 DNQ 1978 DNE **1980** 6 r1 1982 DNE **1984** 5 r1 (Hosts) **1986** 3 SF 1988-1990 DNQ **1992** 1 Winners **1994** 3 SF **1996** 11 r1 **1998** 5 QF **2000** 9 r1 **2002** 16 r1 2004 DNQ **2006** 2 F **2008** 4 SF **2010** 5 QF **2012** 2 F

FEDERATION IVOIRIENNE DE FOOTBALL (FIF)

Treichville Avenue 1 - 01
Boîte postale 1202
Abidjan 01 0181462 T
☎ +225 21240027
📠 +225 21259552
📧 fifci@aviso.ci
🖥 www.fif-ci.com
FA 1960 CON 1960 FIFA 1960
P Augustin Diallo
GS Sory Diabate

FIFA BIG COUNT 2006

Total players	801 700
% of population	4.54%
Male	801 700
Female	0
Amateurs 18+	12 100
Youth under 18	11 000
Unregistered	82 500
Professionals	100
Referees	600
Admin & coaches	3 900
Number of clubs	220
Number of teams	1320

MAJOR CITIES/TOWNS

		Population
1	Abidjan	4 011 262
2	Bouaké	641 787
3	Daloa	241 395
4	Yamoussoukro	234 788
5	Korhogo	206 340
6	San-Pédro	163 304
7	Man	160 404
8	Gagnoa	143 830
9	Divo	136 188
10	Anyama	115 325
11	Abengourou	107 433
12	Soubré	101 079
13	Grand Bassam	81 349
14	Dabou	79 815
15	Agboville	76 154
16	Duékoué	70 292
17	Bouaflé	66 302
18	Sinfra	65 169
19	Bondouku	62 564

REPUBLIQUE DE COTE D'IVOIRE • REPUBLIC OF COTE D'IVOIRE

Capital Yamoussoukro	Population 20 617 068 (56)	% in cities 49%
GDP per capita $1700 (191)	Area km² 322 463 km² (68)	GMT + / - 0
Neighbours (km) Burkina Faso 584, Ghana 668, Guinea 610, Liberia 716, Mali 532 • Coast 515			

RECENT INTERNATIONAL MATCHES PLAYED BY COTE D'IVOIRE

2008	Opponents	Score		Venue	Comp	Scorers	Att	Referee
8-06	Madagascar	D	0-0	Antananarivo	WCq			Labrosse SEY
14-06	Botswana	D	1-1	Gaborone	WCq	Meite [65]	21 400	Ssegonga UGA
22-06	Botswana	W	4-0	Abidjan	WCq	Sanogo [16], Zokora [22], Sekou Cisse 2 [46 70]	15 000	Bennaceur TUN
20-08	Guinea	W	2-1	Chantilly	Fr	Bakary Kone [10], Sanogo [45]		
7-09	Mozambique	D	1-1	Maputo	WCq	Kone [48]	35 000	El Achiri MAR
11-10	Madagascar	W	3-0	Abidjan	WCq	Sanogo 2 [41 55], Kalou [65]	24 000	Benouza ALG
19-11	Israel	D	2-2	Tel Aviv	Fr	Strul OG [32], Sanogo [85]	27 167	
2009								
11-02	Turkey	D	1-1	Izmir	Fr	Drogba [92+]		Corpodean ROU
29-03	Malawi	W	5-0	Abidjan	WCq	Romaric [1], Drogba 2 [6p 27], Kalou [59], Bakary Kone [70]	34 000	Haimoudi ALG
7-06	Guinea	W	2-1	Conakry	WCq	Bakary Kone [43], Romaric [70]	14 000	Abd El Fatah EGY
20-06	Burkina Faso	W	3-2	Ouagadougou	WCq	Yaya Toure [14], Tall OG [54], Drogba [70]	33 056	Damon RSA
12-08	Tunisia	D	0-0	Sousse	Fr			
5-09	Burkina Faso	W	5-0	Abidjan	WCq	OG 9, Drogba 2 [48 64], Yaya Toure [54], Keita [68]	28 209	Maillet SEY
10-10	Malawi	D	1-1	Blantyre	WCq	Drogba [67]	25 000	El Achiri MAR
14-11	Guinea	W	3-0	Abidjan	WCq	Gervinho 2 [16 31], Tiene [67]	28 000	Marange ZIM
18-11	Germany	D	2-2	Gelsenkirchen	Fr	Eboue [57], Doumbia [85]	33 015	Kuipers NED
2010								
4-01	Tanzania	W	1-0	Dar es Salaam	Fr	Drogba [37]	60 000	Mbaga TAN
7-01	Rwanda	W	2-0	Dar es Salaam	Fr	Bamba [85], Angoua [90]	5 000	Waziri TAN
11-01	Burkina Faso	D	0-0	Cabinda	CNr1		5 000	Bennaceur TUN
15-01	Ghana	W	3-1	Cabinda	CNr1	Gervinho [23], Tiéné [66], Drogba [90]	23 000	Damon RSA
24-01	Algeria	L	2-3	Cabinda	CNqf	Kalou [4], Keita [89]	10 000	Maillet SEY
3-03	Korea Republic	L	0-2	London	Fr		6 000	Marriner ENG
30-05	Paraguay	D	2-2	Thonon-Les-Bains	Fr	Drogba [53], Bamba [73]	2 000	Bien FRA
4-06	Japan	W	2-0	Sion	Fr	OG [13], Kolo Toure [80]	4 919	Studer SUI
15-06	Portugal	D	0-0	Port Elizabeth	WCr1		34 850	Nishimura JPN
20-06	Brazil	L	1-3	Johannesburg	WCr1	Drogba [79]	84 445	Lannoy FRA
25-06	Korea DPR	W	3-0	Nelspruit	WCr1	Yaya Toure [14], Romaric [20], Kalou [82]	34 763	Undiano ESP
10-08	Italy	W	1-0	London	Fr	Kolo Toure [55]	11 176	Atkinson ENG
4-09	Rwanda	W	3-0	Abidjan	CNq	Yaya Toure [10], Kalou [19], Eboue [39]		Maillet SEY
9-10	Burundi	W	1-0	Bujumbura	CNq	Romaric [34]		El Raay LBY
17-11	Poland	L	1-3	Poznan	Fr	Gervinho [45]	42 000	Toma JPN
2011								
8-02	Mali	W	1-0	Valence	Fr	Ya Konen [2]		
27-03	Benin	W	2-1	Accra	CNq	Drogba 2 [45 75]		Kayindi-Ngobi UGA
5-06	Benin	W	6-2	Cotonou	CNq	Ya Konan [13], Drogba 2 [21 73], Gervinho 2 [30 79], Bony [86]		Benouza ALG
10-08	Israel	W	4-3	Geneva	Fr	Yaya Toure [44], Ya Konan [45], Kone [67], Drogba [81p]	2 000	
3-09	Rwanda	W	5-0	Kigali	CNq	Kalou [33], Bony 2 [42 43], Ya Konan [68], Gervinho [83]		
9-10	Burundi	W	2-1	Abidjan	CNq	Kolo Toure [70], Gervinho [91+]		
12-11	South Africa	D	1-1	Port Elizabeth	Fr	OG [36]		
2012								
13-01	Tunisia	W	2-0	Abu Dhabi	Fr	Kalou [44], Drogba [47p]		Al Junaibi UAE
16-01	Libya	W	1-0	Abu Dhabi	Fr	Kalou [60]		
22-01	Sudan	W	1-0	Malabo	CNr1	Drogba [39]	5 000	Seechurn MRI
26-01	Burkina Faso	W	2-0	Malabo	CNr1	Kalou [16], OG [82]	4 000	Grisha EGY
30-01	Angola	W	2-0	Malabo	CNr1	Eboue [33], Bony [64]	1 500	Jedidi TUN
4-02	Equatorial Guinea	W	3-0	Malabo	CNqf	Drogba 2 [35 69], Yaya Toure [81]	12 500	Maillet SEY
8-02	Mali	W	1-0	Libreville	CNsf	Gervinho [45]	32 000	Bennett RSA
12-02	Zambia	D	0-0	Libreville	CNf	L 7-8p	40 000	Diatta SEN

Fr = Friendly match • CN = African Cup of Nations • WC = FIFA World Cup
q = qualifier • r1 = first round group • qf = quarter-final • sf = semi-final • f = final

COTE D'IVOIRE NATIONAL TEAM HISTORICAL RECORDS

Coach: Henri Michel FRA 2004-06 • Uli Stielike GER 2006-08 • Vahid Halilhodzic BIH 2008-10 • Sven-Goran Eriksson SWE 2010 • Francois Zahoui 2010-

COTE D'IVOIRE 2011

LIGUE 1 MTN — FIRST ROUND GROUPS

Group A	Pl	W	D	L	F	A	Pts	ASEC	SOA	Séwé Sport	Bassam	Issia Wazi	Stade	Adzopé
ASEC Mimosas	12	9	1	2	26	15	28		1-0	1-0	2-1	3-1	3-2	4-1
SO Armée	12	6	3	3	20	15	21	1-3		1-1	1-0	3-3	3-1	4-2
Séwé San Pedro	12	4	6	2	13	9	18	0-2	1-1		0-0	2-0	1-1	2-1
USC Bassam	12	4	5	3	9	6	17	2-0	0-1	1-1		3-1	0-0	0-0
Issia Wazi	12	2	5	5	12	23	11	5-4	0-4	0-3	0-0		0-0	0-0
Stade Abidjan	12	2	4	6	11	14	10	1-1	3-0	0-1	0-1	1-2		1-2
FC Adzopé	12	1	4	7	8	17	7	1-2	0-1	1-1	0-1	0-0	0-1	

Group B	Pl	W	D	L	F	A	Pts	Stella	AFAD	Abengourou	Africa Sports	Denguélé	JCA	Ouragahio
Stella Adjamé	12	8	4	0	16	5	28		1-0	2-1	1-0	2-0	1-0	2-2
AFAD Djékanou	12	6	4	2	13	6	22	1-1		1-1	0-1	1-0	0-0	2-0
ASI Abengourou	12	5	3	4	8	8	18	0-2	0-0		0-1	1-0	0-0	1-0
Africa Sports	12	5	3	4	8	8	18	0-2	0-2	1-0		1-2	0-0	1-1
Denguélé Odienné	12	3	4	5	8	10	13	0-0	0-1	0-1	0-0		0-0	3-1
Jeunesse Abidjan	12	0	7	5	2	8	7	0-1	1-2	0-1	0-2	0-0		0-0
ASC Ouragahio	12	0	5	7	10	20	5	1-1	1-3	1-2	0-1	2-3	1-1	

28/05/2011 - 8/10/2011 • † Qualified for the final round

COTE D'IVOIRE 2011

LIGUE 1 MTN — FINAL ROUND

	Pl	W	D	L	F	A	Pts	Africa Sports	AFAD	Séwé Sport	SOA	Stella	ASEC
Africa Sports †	10	5	4	1	16	8	19		0-0	4-0	1-1	1-0	3-2
AFAD Djékanou †	10	4	3	3	14	13	15	2-1		1-2	0-1	1-1	1-3
Séwé San Pedro ‡	10	4	2	4	10	13	14	0-2	2-4		0-1	3-0	1-1
SO Armée	10	2	5	3	9	10	11	2-2	2-2	0-1		0-1	0-0
Stella Adjamé	10	3	2	5	7	10	11	0-0	1-2	0-1	2-1		2-0
ASEC Mimosas ‡	10	2	4	4	11	13	10	1-2	1-2	0-0	1-1	2-1	

15/10/2011 - 23/11/2011 • † Qualified for the CAF Champions League • ‡ Qualified for the CAF Confederation Cup

COUPE NATIONALE 2011

Quarter-finals		Semi-finals		Final	
ASEC Mimosas	3				
CO Bouaflé	0	ASEC Mimosas	2		
Stella	1	AFAD Djékanou	1		
AFAD Djékanou	3			ASEC Mimosas ‡	1 5p
SO Armée †	4			ASI Abengourou	1 4p
Bouaké FC	1	Ban FC	0		
ASI Abengourou	2	ASI Abengourou	1		

† SOA expelled from the competition • ‡ Qualified for the CAF Confederation Cup
Final: Stade Robert Champroux, Abidjan, 22-10-2011
Scorers - Bakayoko Adama [12] for ASEC; Kone Lakou Alain [34] for Abengourou

MEDALS TABLE

		Overall			Lge	Cup		Africa		
		G	S	B	G	G	S	G	S	B
1	ASEC Mimosas	42	5	6	24	17	4	1	1	6
2	Africa Sports	34	10	2	17	15	7	2	3	2
3	Stade Abidjan	11	7	1	5	5	7	1		1
4	Stella Adjamé	6	6		3	2	5	1	1	
5	Onze Freres	2			2					
6	SC Gagnoa	1	7		1		7			
7	ASC Bouaké	1	2			1	2			
	Jeunesse Abidjan	1	2			1	2			
9	Alliance Bouaké	1	1			1	1			
	Réveil Daloa	1	1			1	1			
	SO Armée	1	1			1	1			
	Issia Wazi	1	1			1	1			
	ASI Abengourou	1	1			1	1			
14	CO Bouaflé	1				1				
	Espoir Man	1				1				
16	Séwé San Pedro		2				2			

CMR – CAMEROON

FIFA/COCA-COLA WORLD RANKING

'93	'94	'95	'96	'97	'98	'99	'00	'01	'02	'03	'04	'05	'06	'07	'08	'09	'10	'11	'12
23	31	37	56	53	41	58	39	38	16	14	23	23	11	24	14	11	37	50	

	2011												High	Low	Av
	Jan	Feb	Mar	Apr	May	Jun	Jul	Aug	Sep	Oct	Nov	Dec			
	38	43	42	48	49	48	50	52	48	47	48	50	11	62	29

A disastrous year for the Indomitable Lions culminated in an embarrassing player strike that caused the postponement of a friendly in Algeria and severe diplomatic embarrassment. Samuel Eto'o and vice-captain Enoh Eyong were handed long bans for their part in the refusal by the national team to play the match, for which more than 40 000 tickets had been sold, in what was a battle of wills with the country's football federation and powerful sports ministry over unpaid bonuses and appearance money. Cameroon had already missed out on qualifying for the 2012 CAF Africa Cup of Nations, finishing second in their group behind Senegal - the first time since 1994 that Cameroon had failed to qualify for the finals. Rifts in the team, which stemmed from the FIFA World Cup finals in South Africa, continued until a reconciliation was sought between captain Eto'o and midfielder Alexandre Song. French coach Denis Lavagne, who has had considerable domestic success with Garoua club Cotonsport, was brought in to replace Javier Clemente, after Cotonsport once again dominated the club scene in 2011 with a league and cup double. By winning the league for the 11th time in just 15 seasons, they overtook the long-established record of 10 championships held by Canon Yaoundé.

CAF AFRICA CUP OF NATIONS RECORD
1957-1965 DNE **1968** DNQ **1970** 5 r1 **1972** 3 SF (Hosts) **1974** 3 SF **1976** 3 r2 **1978-1980** DNQ **1982** 5 r1
1984 1 Winners **1986** 2 F **1988** 1 Winners **1990** 5 r1 **1992** 4 SF **1994** DNQ **1996** 10 r1 **1998** 8 QF **2000** 1 Winners
2002 1 Winners **2004** 6 QF **2006** 6 QF **2008** 2 F **2010** 7 QF **2012** DNQ

FEDERATION CAMEROUNAISE DE FOOTBALL (FECAFOOT)

Avenue du 27 aout 1940,
Tsinga-Yaoundé,
Boite Postale 1116, Yaoundé
☎ +237 22210012
📠 +237 22216662
✉ fecafoot@fecafootonline.com
🖥 www.fecafootonline.com
FA 1959 CON 1963 FIFA 1962
P Mohammed Iya
GS Sidiki Tombi a Roko

FIFA BIG COUNT 2006

Total players	785 515
% of population	4.53%
Male	749 576
Female	35 939
Amateurs 18+	10 975
Youth under 18	10 110
Unregistered	45 470
Professionals	540
Referees	2 260
Admin & coaches	5 516
Number of clubs	220
Number of teams	1 100

MAJOR CITIES/TOWNS

		Population
1	Douala	2 054 147
2	Yaoundé	1 743 482
3	Garoua	546 060
4	Bamenda	515 593
5	Maroua	415 251
6	Bafoussam	365 017
7	Ngaoundéré	298 016
8	Bertoua	281 139
9	Loum	234 471
10	Kumbo	207 438
11	Edéa	197 861
12	Mbouda	175 986
13	Kumba	173 380
14	Foumban	164 272
15	Djang	140 861
16	Nkongsamba	129 168
17	Ebolowa	123 116
18	Limbe	120 249
19	Guider	116 312

REPUBLIQUE DU CAMEROUN • REPUBLIC OF CAMEROON

Capital	Yaoundé	Population	18 879 301 (58)	% in cities	57%
GDP per capita	$2300 (177)	Area km²	475 440 km² (53)	GMT +/-	+1
Neighbours (km)	Central African Republic 797, Chad 1094, Congo 523, Equatorial Guinea 189, Gabon 298, Nigeria 1690 • Coast 402				

RECENT INTERNATIONAL MATCHES PLAYED BY CAMEROON

2008	Opponents	Score		Venue	Comp	Scorers	Att	Referee
4-02	Tunisia	W	3-2	Tamale	CNqf	Mbia 2 [18 92], Geremi [27]		Coulibaly MLI
7-02	Ghana	W	1-0	Accra	CNsf	Nkong [72]		El Arjoun MAR
10-02	Egypt	L	0-1	Accra	CNf			Codjia BEN
31-05	Cape Verde Islands	W	2-0	Yaoundé	WCq	Rigobert Song [8], Eto'o [57p]	20 000	Djaoupe TOG
8-06	Mauritius	W	3-0	Curepipe	WCq	Bikey [11], Eto'o [27], Bebey [87]	2 400	Martins ANG
14-06	Tanzania	D	0-0	Dar es Salaam	WCq		55 000	Codjia BEN
21-06	Tanzania	W	2-1	Yaoundé	WCq	Eto'o 2 [65 89]	25 000	Mendy GAM
6-09	Cape Verde Islands	W	2-1	Praia	WCq	Emana [51], Somen [65]	5 000	Labrosse SEY
11-10	Mauritius	W	5-0	Yaoundé	WCq	Eto'o 2 [26 46p], Meyong Ze 2 [56 72], Makoun [70]	12 000	Lemhambodj MTN
19-11	South Africa	L	2-3	Rustenburg	Fr	Kome [27], Somen [34]	35 000	Mwanza ZAM
2009								
11-02	Guinea	W	3-1	Bondoufle	Fr	Geremi [31], Eto'o 2 [58 87]		
28-03	Togo	L	0-1	Accra	WCq		26 450	Abd El Fatah EGY
7-06	Morocco	D	0-0	Yaoundé	WCq		35 000	Seechurn MRI
12-08	Austria	W	2-0	Klagenfurt	Fr	Webo 2 [28 35]	28 800	Olsiak SVK
5-09	Gabon	W	2-0	Libreville	WCq	Emana [65], Eto'o [67]	10 000	Ndinya KEN
9-09	Gabon	W	2-1	Yaoundé	WCq	Makoun [25], Eto'o [64]	38 000	Bennaceur TUN
10-10	Togo	W	3-0	Yaoundé	WCq	Geremi [29], Makoun [46], Emana [54]	36 401	Kaoma ZAM
14-10	Angola	D	0-0	Olhao	Fr			
14-11	Morocco	W	2-0	Fes	WCq	Webo [19], Eto'o [52]	17 000	Bennett RSA
2010								
9-01	Kenya	W	3-1	Nairobi	Fr	Webo [36], Emana [56], Idrissou [58]	6 000	Amwayi KEN
13-01	Gabon	L	0-1	Lubango	CNr1		15 000	Bennett RSA
17-01	Zambia	W	3-2	Lubango	CNr1	Geremi [68], Eto'o [72], Idrissou [86]	15 000	Al Ghamdi KSA
21-01	Tunisia	D	2-2	Lubango	CNr1	Eto'o [47], N'Guemo [64]	19 000	Doue CIV
25-01	Egypt	L	1-3	Benguela	CNqf	Emana [25]	12 000	Damon RSA
3-03	Italy	D	0-0	Monte Carlo	Fr		10 752	Ennjimi FRA
25-05	Georgia	D	0-0	Linz	Fr		3 500	Brugger AUT
29-05	Slovakia	D	1-1	Klagenfurt	Fr	Enoh [84]	10 000	Lechner AUT
1-06	Portugal	L	1-3	Covilha	Fr	Webo [69]	6 125	Weiner GER
5-06	Serbia	L	3-4	Belgrade	Fr	Webo 2 [5 20], Choupo-Moting [67]	30 000	Trattou CYP
14-06	Japan	L	0-1	Bloemfontein	WCr1		30 620	Benquerenca POR
19-06	Denmark	L	1-2	Pretoria	WCr1	Eto'o [10]	38 074	Larrionda URU
24-06	Netherlands	L	1-2	Cape Town	WCr1	Eto'o [65p]	63 093	Pozo CHI
11-08	Poland	W	3-0	Szczecin	Fr	Eto'o 2 [30 52], Aboubakar [86]	17 000	Asumaa FIN
4-09	Mauritius	W	3-1	Bellevue	CNq	Eto'o 2 [39 47], Choupo-Moting [63p]		Damon RSA
9-10	Congo DR	D	1-1	Garoua	CNq	OG [54]		Maillet SEY
2011								
9-02	Macedonia FYR	W	1-0	Skopje	Fr	Mbuta [75]	3 000	Kaluderovic MNE
26-03	Senegal	L	0-1	Dakar	CNq			Saadallah TUN
4-06	Senegal	D	0-0	Yaounde	CNq			Carvalho ANG
7-06	Russia	D	0-0	Salzburg	Fr		3 000	Einwaller AUT
3-09	Mauritius	W	5-0	Yaounde	CNq	Kweuke [54], Mbuta [65], Eto'o [70p], N'Guemo [85], Choupo-Moting [93+]		Bangoura GUI
7-10	Congo DR	W	3-2	Kinshasa	CNq	Eto'o [18], Mbuta [75], Choupo-Moting [79]		
11-10	Equatorial Guinea	D	1-1	Malabo	Fr	Kweuke [13]	20 000	
11-11	Sudan	W	3-1	Marrakech	Fr	Enoh [32], Angbwa [35], Eto'o [82]		
13-11	Morocco	D	1-1	Marrakech	Fr	Eto'o [73], W 4-2p	20 000	Amalou ALG
14-12	Angola	D	1-1	Cabinda	Fr	Momasso [40]		

Fr = Friendly match • CN = Africa Cup of Nations • WC = FIFA World Cup • q = qualifier

CAMEROON NATIONAL TEAM HISTORICAL RECORDS

Past Coaches Dominique Colonna FRA 1965-70 • Peter Schnittger FRG 1970-73 • Vladimir Beara YUG 1973-75 • Ivan Ridanovic YUG 1975-80 • Branko Zutic YUG 1980-82 • Jean Vincent 1982 • Claude Le Roy 1985-88 • Valeri Nepomniachi RUS 1988-90 • Philippe Redon FRA 1991-92 • Jules Nyongha 1992-93 • Henri Michel FRA 1994 • Jules Nyongha 1994-96 • Henri Depireux BEL 1996-97 • Jean Manga Onguene 1997-98 • Claude Le Roy FRA 1998 • Pierre Lechantre FRA 1998-00 • Jean-Paul Akono 2000-01 • Pierre Lechantre FRA 2001 • Robert Corfu FRA 2001 • Winfried Schafer GER 2001-04 • Artur Jorge POR 2005-06 • Arie Haan NED 2006-07 • Jules Nyongha 2007 • Otto Pfister GER 2007-09 • Thomas Nkono 2009 • Paul Le Guen FRA 2009-10 • Javier Clemente ESP 2010-11 • Denis Lavagne FRA 2011-

CAMEROON 2010-11

MTN ELITE ONE

	Pl	W	D	L	F	A	Pts	Cotonsport	Les Astres	Union Douala	Unisport	YOSA	Tiko United	Sable Batie	Canon	Panthère	Renaissance	Scorpion	Ngaoundéré	Caïman	Lausanne
Cotonsport Garoua †	26	16	8	2	48	17	56		2-0	2-0	2-1	1-1	1-0	2-1	3-2	1-0	5-0	5-2	4-0	2-0	3-0
Les Astres Douala †	26	14	3	9	29	26	45	2-4		1-0	1-0	2-0	1-4	2-1	1-3	2-3	1-0	1-1	2-2	0-1	3-0
Union Douala ‡	26	12	6	8	26	19	42	0-1	0-1		1-0	0-1	2-1	2-0	2-2	0-0	2-2	1-0	1-0	0-0	2-0
Unisport Bafang ‡	26	12	5	9	26	20	41	0-0	2-0	1-0		1-0	3-0	0-1	1-0	2-0	3-0	0-0	1-1	1-1	1-0
Young Sports Academy	26	11	7	8	17	17	40	1-0	0-1	0-1	1-0		1-0	0-0	0-0	0-1	2-0	0-0	1-0	1-0	1-0
Tiko United	26	10	9	7	33	27	39	1-1	1-0	1-0	4-0	2-1		1-1	1-1	3-2	1-1	3-0	0-0	0-0	1-0
Sable Batie	26	8	12	6	22	16	36	0-0	2-0	0-0	0-0	0-0	2-0		1-1	1-1	1-0	1-1	0-1	1-1	3-0
Canon Yaoundé	26	10	6	10	36	30	36	1-1	0-1	1-3	3-1	3-0	2-1	0-1		1-2	0-1	1-0	2-1	3-2	3-0
Panthère Bangangté	26	9	8	9	28	26	35	2-2	0-0	1-2	0-2	1-1	1-1	0-0	1-0		0-0	0-1	3-0	2-0	3-1
Renaissance Ngoumou	26	9	6	11	25	33	33	1-1	0-2	1-0	1-2	1-2	1-2	1-2	1-1	1-0		1-0	1-0	2-1	4-0
Scorpion Bey	26	8	9	9	25	29	33	1-3	0-1	0-0	2-0	1-1	2-2	1-0	1-0	3-2	1-2		2-1	1-0	1-1
Université Ngaoundéré	26	8	8	10	20	24	32	0-0	0-1	0-1	1-0	2-0	2-0	1-0	1-2	1-0	1-1	0-0		1-0	2-0
Caïman Douala	26	6	7	13	24	35	25	1-0	0-2	1-3	1-2	0-1	2-3	1-1	2-1	1-2	2-0	3-1	1-1		2-1
Lausanne Yaoundé	26	0	4	22	9	49	4	0-2	0-1	2-3	0-2	0-1	0-0	0-2	1-3	0-1	1-2	0-1	1-1	1-1	

13/11/2010 - 25/07/2011 • † Qualified for the CAF Champions League • ‡ Qualified for the Confederation Cup

CAMEROON 2010-11 MTN ELITE TWO (2)

	Pl	W	D	L	F	A	Pts
New Star Douala	26	15	5	6	32	19	50
Njala Quan Academy	26	13	9	4	37	18	48
Aigle Royal Dschang	26	13	9	4	31	18	48
APEJES Mfou	26	14	5	7	34	17	47
Fovu Baham	26	12	8	6	25	19	44
Matelots Douala	26	10	10	6	22	21	40
Tonnerre Kalara	26	11	6	9	22	19	39
Douala AC	26	10	7	9	24	23	37
Santos	26	7	9	10	19	24	30
Achille Yaoundé	26	8	6	12	24	26	30
Sahel Maroua	26	7	6	13	16	23	27
Mayo Rey	26	5	9	12	14	26	24
Avenir Bertoua	26	5	6	15	20	33	21
Roumdé Adjia	26	1	7	18	12	46	7

21/11/2010 - 28/07/2011 • § = points deducted

MEDALS TABLE

		Overall			Lge	Cup		Africa			City
		G	S	B	G	G	S	G	S	B	
1	Canon	25	8	4	10	11	5	4	3	4	Yaoundé
2	Cotonsport	16	3	1	11	5	1		2	1	Garoua
3	Union	12	6	1	4	6	6	2		1	Douala
4	Tonnerre Kalara	10	5	1	5	4	3	1	2	1	Yaoundé
5	Oryx	9	1	1	5	3	1	1		1	Douala
6	Racing Club	5	3		4	1	3				Bafoussam
7	Diamant	4	4	1	1	3	4			1	Yaoundé
8	Lion Club	4				4					Yaoundé
9	Caïman	3	3		3		3				Douala
10	Fovu	3	1		1	2	1				Baham
11	Dynamo	3				3					Douala
12	Aigle Royal	2	2		2		2				Nkongsamba
13	Léopards	2	1	1	2		1			1	Douala
14	Olympique	2				2					Mvolyé
	Panthère	2				2					Bagante
16	Sable	1	2		1		2				Batié
	Unisport	1	3		1		3				Bafang
17	Dihep Nkam	1	1			1	1				Yabassi

COUPE DU CAMEROUN 2011

Round of 16			Quarter-finals			Semi-finals			Final		
Cotonsport *	1	2									
Renaissance Ngoumou	1	0	Cotonsport *	4	1						
Njala Quan Academy	1	0	Les Astres Douala	0	1						
Les Astres Douala *	1	1				Cotonsport *	6	2			
Univ. Ngaoundéré *	2	1				AS FAP	0	1			
Aigle Royal Dschang	1	1	Univ. Ngaoundéré *	0	1						
Matelots Douala *	0	0	AS FAP	1	1						
AS FAP	0	1							Cotonsport	0	3p
Sahel Maroua	2	0							Unisport Bafang ‡	0	0p
Nka United *	1	0	Sahel Maroua	1	2						
YOSA *	0	1	AS Etoa Meki *	2	0						
AS Etoa Meki	0	2				Sahel Maroua	1	0			
Avenir Bertoua *	3	0				Unisport Bafang *	3	2			
Jeunesse	0	0	Avenir Bertoua	0	0						
Achille Yaoundé *	1	0	Unisport Bafang *	1	1						
Unisport Bafang	1	0									

CUP FINAL

Ahmadou Ahidjo, Yaoundé
11-12-2011

* Home team in the 1st leg • ‡ Qualified for the Confederation Cup

COD – CONGO DR

FIFA/COCA-COLA WORLD RANKING

'93	'94	'95	'96	'97	'98	'99	'00	'01	'02	'03	'04	'05	'06	'07	'08	'09	'10	'11	'12
71	68	68	66	76	62	59	70	77	65	56	78	77	66	74	91	107	130	125	

						2011							High	Low	Av
Jan	Feb	Mar	Apr	May	Jun	Jul	Aug	Sep	Oct	Nov	Dec				
128	122	123	116	127	124	123	127	129	133	125	125		51	133	81

DR Congo failed for a third successive time to reach the CAF Africa Cup of Nations finals, their campaign condemned to failure before it had effectively even started after a defeat at home to Senegal in the first match in what was a tough group that also contained Cameroon. The Senegal game was the first game back in charge for nomadic French coach Claude Le Roy, who agreed a three-year contract in September after compatriot Robert Nouzaret quit blaming poor organisation for a frustrating year in charge of the side. The national team's failure was overshadowed by the dramatic disqualification of holders TP Mazembe Englebert from the 2011 CAF Champions League, denying them the chance of an unprecedented third successive triumph. The Lubumbashi-based club were found guilty of fielding Janvier Bokungu in the early rounds of the competition. He was ruled ineligible as the Confederation of African Football found he was still contracted to Esperance of Tunisia. It was a cruel blow for Mazembe - the one real success story for football in the Congo in recent years - but they made sure of qualification for the 2012 edition after winning the Super League by a point from Vita Kinshasa. US Tshinkunku, from the city of Kananga, won the Cup for the first time after beating Veti Matadi on penalties in the final.

CAF AFRICA CUP OF NATIONS RECORD

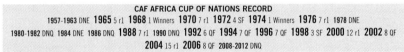

1957-1963 DNE **1965** 5 r1 **1968** 1 Winners **1970** 7 r1 **1972** 4 SF **1974** 1 Winners **1976** 7 r1 **1978** DNE
1980-1982 DNQ **1984** DNE **1986** DNQ **1988** 7 r1 **1990** DNQ **1992** 6 QF **1994** 7 QF **1996** 7 QF **1998** 3 SF **2000** 12 r1 **2002** 8 QF
2004 15 r1 **2006** 8 QF 2008-2012 DNQ

FEDERATION CONGOLAISE DE FOOTBALL-ASSOCIATION (FECOFA)

31 Avenue de la Justice, c/Gombe, Boite postale 1284, Kinshasa 1

☎ +243 81 9049788
📠 +243 81 3013527
✉ fecofa_sg@yahoo.fr
🖥

FA 1919 CON 1973 FIFA 1962
P Constant Omari Selemani
GS Gregoire Badi Elonga

FIFA BIG COUNT 2006

Total players	2 515 600
% of population	4.01%
Male	2 515 600
Female	0
Amateurs 18+	55 600
Youth under 18	22 000
Unregistered	165 000
Professionals	0
Referees	2 900
Admin & coaches	7 700
Number of clubs	770
Number of teams	3 300

MAJOR CITIES/TOWNS

		Population
1	Kinshasa	9 518 988
2	Lubumbashi	1 713 852
3	Mbuji-Mayi	1 546 705
4	Kolwezi	970 520
5	Kisangani	600 011
6	Boma	527 725
7	Likasi	521 341
8	Kananga	514 070
9	Tshikapa	317 830
10	Bukavu	241 690
11	Mwene-Ditu	218 782
12	Uvira	202 240
13	Kikwit	200 880
14	Mbandaka	199 333
15	Matadi	194 903
16	Gandajika	181 987
17	Kalemie	181 496
18	Butembo	180 721
19	Goma	164 348

REPUBLIQUE DEMOCRATIQUE DU CONGO • DEMOCRATIC REPUBLIC OF THE CONGO

Capital	Kinshasa	Population	68 692 542 (18)	% in cities	34%
GDP per capita	$300 (228)	Area km²	2 344 858 km² (12)	GMT +/-	+1
Neighbours (km)	Angola 2511, Burundi 233, Central African Republic 1577, Congo 2410, Rwanda 217, Sudan 628, Tanzania 459, Uganda 765, Zambia 1930 • Coast 37				

RECENT INTERNATIONAL MATCHES PLAYED BY CONGO DR

2009 Opponents	Score	Venue	Comp	Scorers	Att	Referee
9-05 Tanzania	W 2-0	Dar es Salaam	Fr	Kaluyitukadioko 2 [5 49]		
6-06 Namibia	L 0-4	Windhoek	Fr			
12-08 Senegal	L 1-2	Blois	Fr	Makiadi [73]		
14-10 Qatar	D 2-2	Sannois St-Gratien	Fr	Mbayo 2 [35 72p]		
2010						
3-03 Nigeria	L 2-5	Abuja	Fr	Bedi 2 [43 71]	5 000	
21-05 Saudi Arabia	L 0-2	Innsbruck	Fr			
11-08 Egypt	L 3-6	Cairo	Fr	Ilunga [17], Matumona 2 [54 69p]		
5-09 Senegal	L 2-4	Kinshasa	CNq	Mihayo [42], Kabangu [71]		Haimoudi ALG
9-10 Cameroon	D 1-1	Garoua	CNq	Diba [37]		Maillet SEY
17-11 Mali	L 1-3	Evreux	Fr	Ilunga [16]		
2011						
8-01 Kenya	W 1-0	Cairo	Fr	Bongeli [28p]		
11-01 Sudan	W 2-1	Cairo	Fr	Salakiaku [33], Bongeli [93+]		
14-01 Uganda	L 0-1	Cairo	Fr			
17-01 Kenya	W 1-0	Ismailia	Fr	Kasongo [33]		
9-02 Gabon	L 0-2	Mantes La Ville	Fr			
27-03 Mauritius	W 3-0	Kinshasa	CNq	Lua Lua [28p], Matumona [48], Ilunga [61p]		
5-06 Mauritius	W 2-1	Bellevue	CNq	Diba [20], Kabangu [45]		Ngosi MWI
10-08 Gambia	L 0-3	Bakau	Fr			
27-08 Angola	W 2-1	Dundo	Fr	Bakongolia [41], Niemba [62]		
3-09 Senegal	L 0-2	Dakar	CNq			Doue CIV
7-10 Cameroon	L 2-3	Kinshasa	CNq	Kaluyiyuka [11], Kanda [40]		
6-11 Lesotho	W 3-0	Pretoria	Fr	Mputu [30], Kanda [40], Mihayo [82]		
11-11 Swaziland	W 3-1	Lobamba	WCq	Kaluyituka [18], Mputu [22], Bokese [72]	785	Sikazwe ZAM
15-11 Swaziland	W 5-1	Kinshasa	WCq	Mputu 2 [8 49], Kaluyituka 2 [46 61], Diba [66]	24 000	Moukoko CGO

Fr = Friendly match • CN = CAF African Cup of Nations • WC = FIFA World Cup • q = qualifier

CONGO DR 2011

LINAFOOT SUPER LEAGUE

	Pl	W	D	L	F	A	Pts	Mazembe	Vita	St Eloi	RCK	DCMP	Don Bosco	Elima	Malekesa
TP Mazembe †	14	8	6	0	33	6	30		1-1	1-1	4-0	2-0	4-1	5-2	8-0
AS Vita Club	14	8	5	1	22	7	29	0-0		2-0	5-1	1-0	0-0	4-1	**3-0**
St Eloi Lupopo	14	6	4	4	15	11	22	1-1	**0-2**		0-1	1-0	0-1	2-0	2-1
Racing Club	14	7	1	6	14	24	22	0-3	1-2	0-1		1-0	2-1	1-0	**3-0**
DC Motema Pembe	14	5	4	5	14	7	19	0-0	0-0	1-1	2-0		1-0	4-0	**3-0**
CS Don Bosco	14	5	2	7	13	20	17	0-3	2-0	0-2	1-2	1-0		2-0	2-1
TC Elima	14	3	5	6	14	23	14	0-0	1-1	1-1	0-0	0-0	**3-0**		1-3
TS Malekesa	14	1	1	12	10	37	4	0-1	0-1	**0-3**	2-3	**0-3**	2-2	1-2	

9/04/2011 - 23/10/2011 • † Qualified for the CAF Champions League • ‡ Qualified for the CAF Confederation Cup • Matches in bold awarded

COUPE DU CONGO 2011

Semi-finals		Finals	
US Tshinkunku	1		
Sanga Balende	0		
		US Tshinkunku	1 4p
		AS Veti Matadi	1 3p
Bukavu Dawa	0		
AS Veti Matadi	2		

Final. Stades de Jeunes de Katoka, Kananga, 30-08-2011
Scorers - Aliango [2] for UST; Lukako [19] for Veti

MEDALS TABLE

	Overall			Lge	Cup	Africa			
	G	S	B	G	G	G	S	B	City
1 DC Motema Pembe	26		3	12	13	1		3	Kinshasa
2 AS Vita Club	22	1	3	12		1	1	3	Kinshasa
3 TP Mazembe	21	2	2	11	5	5	2	2	Lubumbashi
4 AS Dragons	9	2		4	5		2		Kinshasa
5 St Eloi Lupopo	8		1	6	2			1	Lubumbashi
6 AS Kalamu	4				4				Kinshasa
7 US Bilombe	2			1	1				Bilombe
US Tshinkunku	2			1	1				Kananga

COK – COOK ISLANDS

FIFA/COCA-COLA WORLD RANKING

'93	'94	'95	'96	'97	'98	'99	'00	'01	'02	'03	'04	'05	'06	'07	'08	'09	'10	'11	'12
-	-	-	188	192	173	182	170	179	182	190	190	194	197	200	201	184	188	195

	2011											High	Low	Av
Jan	Feb	Mar	Apr	May	Jun	Jul	Aug	Sep	Oct	Nov	Dec	High	Low	Av
188	188	188	190	190	195	195	197	197	196	196	195	169	202	188

Despite their recent slide down the FIFA/Coca-Cola World Ranking there has been a much more competitive edge to the Cook Islands national team recently, although results didn't go their way in either the football tournament of the 2011 Pacific Games in Noumea, New Caledonia, or in the preliminary round of qualifying in Oceania for the 2014 FIFA World Cup in Brazil. An injury-time goal by Samoa denied the Cook Islands a deserved draw in their opening game of the World Cup qualifiers, Campbell Best having seemingly secured a point with just five minutes to go. A draw with American Samoa - against whom they previously had a 100 per cent record - secured their only point as they finished bottom of the four-team group having also lost to another injury-time goal against Tonga. There were heavy defeats, however in the Pacific Games to Fiji, Tahiti and Papua New Guinea with their solitary 3-0 victory over Kiribati not counting towards the official records as their opponents are not members of FIFA. At home Tupapa and Nikao once again dominated the championship with both clubs winning 10 of their 12 league games. Tupapa's 1-0 victory over Nikao at the start of November proved to be the difference as they finished a point ahead of their rivals to retain the title. Nikao gained some revenge by beating Tupapa in the Cup Final.

FIFA WORLD CUP RECORD
1930-1994 DNE 1998-2014 DNQ

COOK ISLANDS FOOTBALL ASSOCIATION (CIFA)

Matavera Main Road,
PO Box 29, Avarua

☎ +682 28980
📠 +682 28981
✉ cifa@cisoccer.org.ck
🖥 cookislandsfootball.com
FA 1971 CON 1994 FIFA 1994
P Lee Harmon
GS Mii Piri

FIFA BIG COUNT 2006

Total players	2 200
% of population	10.29%
Male	2 200
Female	0
Amateurs 18+	800
Youth under 18	1 000
Unregistered	200
Professionals	0
Referees	100
Admin & coaches	100
Number of clubs	40
Number of teams	120

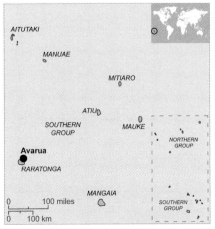

MAJOR CITIES/TOWNS

		Population
1	Avarua	13 273
2	Amuri	329
3	Mangaia	290
4	Atiu	159
5	Omoka	131
6	Mauke	118
7	Mitiaro	78
8	Nassau	49
9	Roto	47
10	Tauhunu	39
11	Rakahanga	32

COOK ISLANDS

Capital	Avarua	Population	11 870 (224)	% in cities 74%
GDP per capita	$9100 (109)	Area km² 236 km² (214)	GMT + / - -10
Neighbours (km)	Coast 120		

RECENT INTERNATIONAL MATCHES PLAYED BY COOK ISLANDS

2004	Opponents	Score		Venue	Comp	Scorers	Att	Referee
5-05	Samoa	D	0-0	Auckland	Fr			
10-05	Tahiti	L	0-2	Honiara	WCq		12 000	Singh FIJ
12-05	Solomon Islands	L	0-5	Honiara	WCq		14 000	Fred VAN
15-05	Tonga	L	1-2	Honiara	WCq	John Pareanga [59]	15 000	Sosongan PNG
17-05	New Caledonia	L	0-8	Honiara	WCq		400	Singh FIJ
2005								
No international matches played in 2005								
2006								
No international matches played in 2006								
2007								
27-08	Fiji	L	0-4	Apia	WCq		400	Fred VAN
29-08	New Caledonia	L	0-3	Apia	WCq		200	Fox NZL
1-09	Tuvalu †	W	4-1	Apia	WCq	Teariki Mateariki 2 [28 69], Tom Le Mouton [88], Kunda Tom [93+]	200	Hester NZL
3-09	Tahiti	L	0-1	Apia	WCq		100	Aimaasu SAM
2008								
No international matches played in 2008								
2009								
11-06	Tonga	D	1-1	Atele	Fr	Joseph Ngauora [29]		
13-06	Tonga	W	2-1	Atele	Fr	Campbell Best [3], Joseph Ngauora [8]	204	Cross NZL
2010								
No international matches played in 2010								
2011								
27-08	Papua New Guinea	L	0-4	Boulari	PGr1			Billon NCL
30-08	Tahiti	L	0-7	Boulari	PGr1			Oiaka SOL
1-09	Kiribati †	W	3-0	Boulari	PGr1	Taylor Saghabi 2 [27 89], John Pareanga [92+]		Billon NCL
3-09	Fiji	L	1-4	Boulari	PGr1	Joseph Ngauora [41]		Ambassa NCL
22-11	Samoa	L	2-3	Apia	WCq	Campbell Best 2 [35 84]	600	O'Leary NZL
24-11	American Samoa	D	1-1	Apia	WCq	OG [62]	300	George VAN
26-11	Tonga	L	1-2	Apia	WCq	Grover Harmon [35]	200	Ambassa NCL

Fr = Friendly match • WC = FIFA World Cup • q = qualifier • † Not an official international

COOK ISLANDS 2011

RAROTONGA LEAGUE ROUND CUP	Pl	W	D	L	F	A	Pts	Tupapa	Nikao	Takuvaine	Arorangi	Titikaveka	Avatiu	Matavera
Tupapa	12	10	2	0	55	6	**32**		1-0	7-0	1-1	3-0	5-1	4-0
Nikao Sokattak	12	10	1	1	40	8	**31**	2-2		2-1	5-2	9-0	5-0	2-0
Takuvaine	12	5	1	6	20	26	**16**	1-4	0-4		6-0	2-3	2-0	1-0
Arorangi	12	4	2	6	13	26	**14**	0-3	0-2	3-1		3-2	1-3	2-1
Titikaveka	12	4	2	6	15	39	**14**	0-9	0-5	2-4	2-0		2-2	1-1
Avatiu	12	2	3	7	12	29	**9**	1-5	1-2	1-1	0-0	1-2		2-1
Matavera	12	1	1	10	7	28	**4**	0-11	1-2	0-1	0-1	0-1	3-0	

17/09/2011 - 29/11/2011

CIFA CUP FINAL 2011
CIFA HQ, Rarotonga, 21-12-2011
Nikao Sokattak 1-0 Tupapa
Scorer - Jonathon Rowe for Nikao

COL – COLOMBIA

FIFA/COCA-COLA WORLD RANKING

'93	'94	'95	'96	'97	'98	'99	'00	'01	'02	'03	'04	'05	'06	'07	'08	'09	'10	'11	'12
21	17	15	4	10	34	25	15	5	37	39	26	24	34	17	49	39	48	36	

	2011												High	Low	Av
	Jan	Feb	Mar	Apr	May	Jun	Jul	Aug	Sep	Oct	Nov	Dec			
	48	50	50	49	50	54	35	35	32	31	36	36	4	54	25

After a great start to their Copa America campaign which saw them win their first round group ahead of hosts Argentina, Colombia were hugely unlucky in their quarter-final against Peru in Cordoba, losing 2-0 after missing a penalty and having hit the woodwork twice. Fredy Guarin looked to have won the match for Colombia deep into injury-time only for Raul Fernandez to tip his shot onto the bar and send the match into extra-time - during which the Peruvians scored two smash and grab goals to secure an unlikely victory. Colombia's plans for the 2014 FIFA World Cup qualifiers were then thrown into chaos when coach Hernan Dario Gomez was forced to resign after an altercation with a woman in bar and his replacement Leonel Alvarez was then sacked after just three games following a home defeat to Argentina. In club football, both championships in 2011 were decided by penalties with Atlético Medellin securing the first against La Equidad, who suffered their third defeat in a final in four years. The second title went to Junior who beat Once Caldas but the major talking point of the year was the relegation of América Cali for the first time in their history. Millonarios were the cup winners, beating Boyaca Chico in the final.

COPA AMERICA RECORD

1916-1942 DNE **1945** 5/7 **1946** DNE **1947** 8/8 **1949** 8/8 **1953-1956** DNE **1957** 5/7 **1959** DNE **1959** DNE **1963** 7/7 **1967** DNE **1975** 2/10 F

1979 5/10 r1 **1983** 7/10 r1 **1987** 3/10 SF **1989** 6/10 r1 **1991** 4/10 r2 **1993** 3/12 SF **1995** 3/12 SF **1997** 8/12 QF **1999** 5/12 QF

2001 1/12 Winners (Hosts) **2004** 4/12 SF **2007** 9/12 r1 **2011** 6/12 QF

FEDERACION COLOMBIANA DE FUTBOL (COLFUTBOL)

Avenida 32,
No. 16-22 Piso 5°,
Apdo Aéreo 17602, Bogotá
☎ +57 1 2889838
📠 +57 1 2889793
✉ info@colfutbol.org
🖥 www.colfutbol.org
FA 1924 CON 1940 FIFA 1936
P Luis Bedoya
GS Celina Sierra

FIFA BIG COUNT 2006

Total players	3 043 229
% of population	6.98%
Male	2 670 029
Female	364 200
Amateurs 18+	89 000
Youth under 18	166 000
Unregistered	1 440 000
Professionals	929
Referees	2 200
Admin & coaches	13 600
Number of clubs	2 750
Number of teams	7 700

MAJOR CITIES/TOWNS

		Population
1	Bogotá	7 240 836
2	Medellin	2 318 002
3	Cali	2 195 218
4	Barranquilla	1 145 015
5	Cartagena	900 111
6	Cúcuta	596 735
7	Soledad	546 854
8	Bucaramanga	519 207
9	Ibagué	494 669
10	Soacha	458 672
11	Santa Marta	429 670
12	Villavicencio	401 559
13	Pereira	387 796
14	Bello	383 740
15	Manizales	363 255
16	Valledupar	332 135
17	Pasto	330 423
18	Buenaventura	315 594
19	Neiva	314 693

REPUBLICA DE COLOMBIA • REPUBLIC OF COLOMBIA;

Capital	Bogotá	Population	45 644 023 (28)	% in cities	74%
GDP per capita	$8800 (114)	Area km²	1 138 914 km² (26)	GMT +/-	-5
Neighbours (km)	Brazil 1644, Ecuador 590, Panama 225, Peru 1800, Venezuela • Coast 3208				

RECENT INTERNATIONAL MATCHES PLAYED BY COLOMBIA

2008	Opponents	Score		Venue	Comp	Scorers	Att	Referee
20-08	Ecuador	L	0-1	New Jersey	Fr		32 439	Prus USA
6-09	Uruguay	L	0-1	Bogota	WCq		35 024	Gaciba BRA
10-09	Chile	L	0-4	Santiago	WCq		47 459	Larrionda URU
11-10	Paraguay	L	0-1	Bogota	WCq		26 000	Lunati ARG
15-10	Brazil	D	0-0	Rio de Janeiro	WCq		54 910	Selman CHI
19-11	Nigeria	W	1-0	Cali	Fr	Radamel Falcao [82]	10 000	Duarte COL
2009								
11-02	Haiti	W	2-0	Pereira	Fr	Marin [14], Torres [60]	20 000	Ruiz COL
28-03	Bolivia	W	2-0	Bogota	WCq	Torres [26], Renteria [88]	22 044	Intriago ECU
31-03	Venezuela	L	0-2	Puerto Ordaz	WCq		35 000	Pozo CHI
6-06	Argentina	L	0-1	Buenos Aires	WCq		55 000	Ortube BOL
10-06	Peru	W	1-0	Medellin	WCq	Radamel Falcao [25]	32 300	Simon BRA
7-08	El Salvador	W	2-1	Houston	Fr	Gutierrez [12], Mendoza [87]	20 418	Marrufo USA
12-08	Venezuela	L	1-2	New Jersey	Fr	Radamel Falcao [38]		Prus USA
5-09	Ecuador	W	2-0	Medellin	WCq	Martinez [82], Gutierrez [94+]	42 000	Pezzotta ARG
9-09	Uruguay	L	1-3	Montevideo	WCq	Martinez [63]	30 000	Torres PAR
30-09	Mexico	W	2-1	Dallas	Fr	Giovanni Moreno [44], Quintero [79]	50 000	Salazar USA
10-10	Chile	L	2-4	Medellin	WCq	Martinez [14], Giovanni Moreno [53]	18 000	Rivera PER
14-10	Paraguay	W	2-0	Asuncion	WCq	Ramos [61], Rodallega [80]	17 503	De Oliveira BRA
2010								
27-05	South Africa	L	1-2	Johannesburg	Fr	Giovanni Moreno [19p]	76 000	Kipngetich KEN
30-05	Nigeria	D	1-1	Milton Keynes	Fr	Valdez [19]	BCD	Atkinson ENG
11-08	Bolivia	D	1-1	La Paz	Fr	Bacca [40]	4 000	Favale ARG
3-09	Venezuela	W	2-0	Puerto La Cruz	Fr	Cuadrado [17], Dayro Moreno [66]	30 000	Moreno PAN
7-09	Mexico	L	0-1	Monterrey	Fr		43 000	Pineda HON
8-10	Ecuador	W	1-0	Harrison	Fr	Radamel Falcao [88]	25 000	Chapin USA
12-10	USA	D	0-0	Chester	Fr		8 823	Garcia MEX
17-11	Peru	D	1-1	Bogota	Fr	Luis Nunez [74]	6 900	Laverni ARG
2011								
9-02	Spain	L	0-1	Madrid	Fr		70 000	Trutz SVK
26-03	Ecuador	W	2-0	Madrid	Fr	Fredy Guarin [24], Radamel Falcao [74]	15 000	Mateu ESP
29-03	Chile	L	0-2	Den Haag	Fr		15 000	Vink NED
2-07	Costa Rica	W	1-0	Jujuy	CAr1	Adrian Ramos [44]	23 500	Osses CHI
6-07	Argentina	D	0-0	Cordoba	CAr1		47 000	Fagundes BRA
10-07	Bolivia	W	2-0	Santa Fe	CAr1	Radamel Falcao 2 [14 28p]	12 000	Chacon MEX
16-07	Peru	L	0-2	Cordoba	CAqf		30 000	Chacon MEX
3-09	Honduras	W	2-0	New York	Fr	Teofilo Gutierrez 2 [25p 72]	15 000	Gonzalez USA
6-09	Jamaica	W	2-0	Fort Lauderdale	Fr	Teofilo Gutierrez [55], Jackson Martinez [90]	8 000	Dellavie USA
11-10	Bolivia	W	2-1	La Paz	WCq	Dorlan Pabon [48], Radamel Falcao [93+]	33 155	Amarilla PAR
11-11	Venezuela	D	1-1	Barranquilla	WCq	Fredy Guarin [11]	43 953	Ponce ECU
15-11	Argentina	L	1-2	Barranquilla	WCq	Dorlan Pabon [44]	49 600	Fagundes BRA

Fr = Friendly match • CA = Copa America • WC = FIFA World Cup • q = qualifier

COLOMBIA NATIONAL TEAM HISTORICAL RECORDS

Caps
111 - Carlos Valderrama 1985-98 • 101 - Leonel Alvarez 1985-97 • 84 - Freddy Rincon 1990-2001 • 78 - Luis Carlos Perea 1987-94 • 73 - Ivan Cordoba 1997-, Mario Yepes 1999- & Oscar Cordoba 1993-2006 • 68 - Arnoldo Iguaran 1979-93 & Rene Higuita 1987-99 • 67 - Alexis Mendoza 1987-97 • 66 - Victor Aristizabal 1993-2003 • 61 - Luis Herrera 1987-96 • 57 - Faustino Asprilla 1993-2001

Goals
25 - Arnoldo Iguaran 1979-93 • 20 - Faustino Asprilla 1993-2001 • 17 - Freddy Rincon 1990-2001 • 15 - Victor Aristizabal 1993-2003 • 14 - Adolfo Valencia 1992-98 • 13 - Ivan Valenciano 1991-2000 & Anthony de Avila 1983-98 • 12 - Willington Ortiz 1973-85 • 11 - Carlos Valderrama 1985-98 • 9 - Juan Pablo Angel 1996-2006, Edixon Perea 2004-08 & Hernan Herrera 1979-85 • 8 - Hugo Rodallega 2005-

Past Coaches
Alfonso Novoa 1938 • Fernando Paternoster ARG 1938 • Roberto Melendez 1945 • Jose Arana Cruz PER 1946 • Lino Taioli ARG 1947 • Pedro Lopez 1957 • Rafael Orlandi ARG 1957 • Adolfo Pedernera ARG 1961-62 • Gabriel Ochoa Uribe 1963 • Efrain Sanchez 1963 • Antonio Julio De la Hoz 1965 • Cesar Lopez Fretes PAR 1966 • Francisco Zuluaga 1968 • Cesar Lopez Fretes PAR 1970 • Toza Veselinovic YUG 1972-73 • Efrain Sanchez 1975 • Blagoje Vidinic YUG 1976-79 • Carlos Bilardo ARG 1980-81 • Efrain Sanchez 1983-84 • Gabriel Ochoa Uribe 1985 • Francisco Maturana 1987-90 • Luis Garcia 1991 • Humberto Ortiz 1992 • Francisco Maturana 1993-94 • Hernan Dario Gomez 1995-98 • Javier Alvarez 1999 • Luis Garcia 2000-01 • Francisco Maturana 2001 • Reynaldo Rueda 2002 • Francisco Maturana 2002-03 • Reynaldo Rueda 2004-06 • Jorge Pinto 2007-08 • Eduardo Lara 2008-09 • Hernan Dario Gomez 2010-

COLOMBIA 2011
PRIMERA A LIGA POSTEBON I

	Pl	W	D	L	F	A	Pts
Once Caldas †	18	11	3	4	32	17	36
Deportes Tolima †	18	10	4	4	35	21	34
At. Nacional Medellín †	18	10	3	5	33	27	33
Envigado †	18	8	8	2	29	21	32
La Equidad Bogotá †	18	8	5	5	22	14	29
Millonarios †	18	8	4	6	31	23	28
Deportivo Cali †	18	8	3	7	21	24	27
Cúcuta Deportivo †	18	6	8	4	22	19	26
Boyacá Chico	18	8	1	9	25	24	25
Deportes Quindío	18	7	4	7	22	29	25
Itagüí Ditaires	18	6	6	6	24	23	24
América Cali	18	7	3	8	23	25	24
Real Cartagena	18	6	5	7	24	25	23
Santa Fe	18	5	6	7	18	22	21
Atlético Junior	18	5	4	9	19	28	19
Atlético Huila	18	4	5	9	25	36	17
Indep. Medellín	18	4	3	11	19	30	15
Deportivo Pereira	18	1	5	12	16	34	8

5/02/2011 – 21/05/2011 • † Qualified for the second stage
Top scorers (overall): **12** - Carlos Renteria, Nacional •
11 - Dorlan Pabon, Nacional & Edison Toloza, Millonarios •
10 - Wason Renteria, Once Caldas • **9** - Wilder Medina, Tolima

LIGA POSTEBON I SECOND STAGE

Quarter-finals — **Semi-finals** — **Final**

At. Nacional 0 2 4p
Dep. Cali * 1 1 1p **At. Nacional ** 3 0
Cúcuta * 1 1 Dep. Tolima 1 1
Dep. Tolima 3 1 **At. Nacional** 1 2 3p
Millonarios * 1 0 5p La Equidad * 2 1 2p
Once Caldas 0 1 4p Millonarios * 2 1
Envigado 0 1 **La Equidad** 2 2
La Equidad 1 1 * Home team in 1st leg

LIGA POSTEBON I FINAL
1st leg. Metropolitano, Bogotá, 12-06-2011, Att: 7800, Ref: Albert Duarte
La Equidad 2 Juan Nunez [44], Edwin Rivas [62]
Atlético Nacional 1 Carlos Renetria [7]
Equidad - German Caffa - Edwin Rivas, Hanyer Mosquera, Hugo Soto, Dager Palacios•, Juan Nunez, Dahwling Leudo•, Marco Canchila, Javier Araujo• (Edward Zea 87), Roberto Polo (Luis Yanez 78), Wilberto Cosme (Darwin Andrade 72). Tr: Alexis Garcia
Nacional - Gaston Pezzuti - Stephen Barrientos, Edgar Zapata, Victor Giraldo, Danny Aguilar, Jairo Patino (Segundo Ibarbo 70), Macnelly Torres•, Jairo Palomino, Sebastian Perez (Stefan Medina 50), Dorlan Pabon, Carlos Renteria (Orlando Berrio 82). Tr: Santiago Escobar
2nd leg. Atanasio Girardot, Medellin, Att: 44 537, Ref: Imer Machado
Atlético Nacional 2 3p Pabon [44], Renteria [80]
La Equidad 1 2p Polo [93+]
Nacional - Gaston Pezzuti - Stephen Barrientos, Edgar Zapata, Victor Giraldo•, Danny Aguilar, Segundo Ibarbo•, Macnelly Torres, Jairo Palomino (Sebastian Perez 85), Jhon Valencia• (Jairo Patino 77), Dorlan Pabon, Carlos Renteria (Orlando Berrio 83). Tr: Santiago Escobar
Equidad - Diego Novoa - Edwin Rivas, Hanyer Mosquera•, Darwin Andrade• (Roberto Polo• 54), Hugo Soto•, Dager Palacios, Juan Nunez (Luis Yanez 83), Dahwling Leudo, Marco Canchila • (Felix Garcia 57), Javier Araujo, Wilberto Cosme. Tr: Alexis Garcia

Atlético Nacional qualified for the Copa Libertadores

FINAL PENALTIES
Equ		Nac
✘	Polo	
	Pabon	✓
✘	Cosme	
	Torres	✘
✓	Mosquera	
	Aguilar	✓
✓	Yanez	
	Patino	✓
✘	Araugo	

COLOMBIA 2011 PRIMERA A REGULAR SEASON RESULTS

DIMAYOR PRIMERA A	América	Cali	Cartagena	Chico	Cúcuta	Envigado	Huila	Itagüí	Junior	La Equidad	Medellín	Millonarios	Nacional	Once Caldas	Pereira	Quindío	Santa Fe	Tolima
América Cali		2-3 0-1	2-1	2-1	3-0	2-1	2-1	2-1	0-1	1-1	1-2	1-1	2-4	2-1	3-2	1-0	2-0	2-3
Deportivo Cali	0-3 2-0		1-0	2-2	1-2	3-2	1-2	1-0	1-0	0-0	0-2	0-0	2-1	1-1	2-1	1-0	0-0	0-2
Real Cartagena	3-0	1-1		0-1	1-1	1-1	2-1	2-0	4-2 1-1	2-1	2-0	3-2	0-0	1-1	2-2	3-0	1-2	2-1
Boyacá Chico	1-1	2-0	3-0		1-1	0-0	3-0	1-2	3-0	1-2 1-0	0-0	1-0	2-1	1-1	1-2	2-1	3-2	1-0
Cúcuta Deportivo	0-0	0-1	3-2	1-0		1-1	1-0	1-1	0-0	0-0	1-2	0-1	0-0	1-1	4-0	2-0 1-1	0-1	2-3
Envigado	1-1	1-0	2-0	2-1	1-1		1-1	2-2 2-0	2-0	0-0	1-0	2-0	1-3	2-1	1-0	1-0	3-1	0-0
Atlético Huila	1-2	1-4	3-0	1-1	1-1	1-0		1-1	2-3	1-1	2-0	2-1	1-3	1-0	1-1	0-1	2-0	4-7 1-0
Itagüí Ditaires	1-0	2-1	3-1	1-1	1-1 1-1 1-1	3-3		3-0	2-1	2-1	2-1	1-0	0-1	1-0	1-0	2-2	2-2
Atlético Junior	1-1	2-0	2-0 0-3	1-2	2-2	1-2	3-0	0-0		3-0	4-3	3-2	1-1	1-2	2-1	4-0	3-3	1-0
La Equidad Bogotá	1-0	1-2	0-0	2-0 0-1	1-1	0-2	1-1	0-2	3-0		5-0	1-2	1-1	1-1	0-2	1-3	1-1	1-1
Indep. Medellín	1-0	3-0	4-1	1-0	2-3	1-2	3-2	0-3	0-0	0-1		3-3	2-3 0-2	3-4	2-2	1-2	1-0	3-1
Millonarios	2-0	3-1	3-0	3-1	1-1	1-0	2-3	2-1	0-0	3-2	1-1		1-2	0-2	0-0	5-0	1-1 2-0	2-1
At. Nacional Medellín	3-1	2-1	0-3	1-1	3-0	2-3	1-2	3-1	4-1	1-2	1-0 1-1	0-2		2-1	2-2	2-2	5-1	3-2
Once Caldas	4-0	2-0	3-2	3-1	5-0	3-2	2-1	2-0	1-2	0-1	1-0	0-1	3-1		2-0 1-1	5-1	2-2	2-2
Deportivo Pereira	1-1	0-0	0-0	0-1	2-1	4-0	0-0	0-2	1-2	0-1	2-2	1-2	0-2	1-0 2-3		3-0	1-1	2-2
Deportes Quindío	2-0	0-1	2-1	2-2	0-1 3-3	3-3	2-1	2-1	1-1	1-1	2-1	3-0	2-1	2-0	4-3		3-1	2-1
Santa Fe	0-1	1-1	1-0	2-0	3-1	2-1	1-0	3-2	2-0	1-0	1-0	0-2 1-0	0-0	1-2	1-0	0-1		3-0
Deportes Tolima	1-4	3-1	1-0	3-2	2-1	1-2	3-1 1-0	0-0	0-0	2-0	2-0	1-0	5-0	1-3	1-0	0-0	1-0	

Apertura 2011 results are shown in the shaded boxes • Local rivals play each other four times in the regular season. In this instance the Liga Postobon I results are listed first • Deportivo Pereira relegated with the worst record over three seasons • América Cali had the second worst record and entered a play-off • Relegation play-off: América Cali 1-1 1-1 3-4p **Patriotas**. América relegated

COLOMBIA 2011
PRIMERA A LIGA POSTEBON II

	Pl	W	D	L	F	A	Pts
Atlético Junior †	18	8	7	3	28	22	31
Itagüí Ditaires †	18	8	6	4	24	18	30
Once Caldas †	18	8	5	5	34	23	29
Millonarios †	18	8	4	6	21	17	28
Santa Fe †	18	8	4	6	22	19	28
Envigado †	18	8	4	6	20	18	28
Boyacá Chico †	18	6	9	3	19	16	27
América Cali †	18	7	4	7	22	24	25
Deportes Quindío	18	7	4	7	23	26	25
Deportivo Pereira	18	5	9	4	23	16	24
Deportivo Cali	18	6	5	7	15	20	23
At. Nacional Medellín	18	5	7	6	24	23	22
Indep. Medellín	18	6	4	8	26	28	22
Atlético Huila	18	6	4	8	20	22	22
Deportes Tolima	18	6	4	8	21	25	22
Real Cartagena	18	5	4	9	21	25	19
La Equidad Bogotá	18	3	7	8	12	22	16
Cúcuta Deportivo	18	2	9	7	17	28	15

27/08/2011 - 27/11/2011 • † Qualified for the second stage
Top scorers (overall): **12** - Carlos Bacca, Junior • **10** - German Cano, Pereira; John Pajoy, Once Caldas & Lionard Pajoy, Itagüí • **9** - Edison Toloza, Millonarios

FINAL PENALTIES

	Jun	OC
Hernandez.G	✓	
Nunez		✓
Valencia	✓	
Pajoy		✗
Cardenas	✓	
Del Valle		✓
Paez	✓	
Beltran		✗

LIGA POSTEBON II SECOND STAGE

Quarter-finals		Semi-finals		Final	
At. Junior	0 2				
Boyacá Chico*	0 2	At. Junior	0 3 5p		
Envigado *	2 1 6p	Millonarios *	3 0 4p		
Millonarios	1 2 7p			At. Junior *	3 1 4p
Santa Fe *	3 1			Once Caldas	2 2 2p
Itagüí Ditaires	2 0	Santa Fe	1 1		
América Cali *	0 0	Once Caldas *	1 2		
Once Caldas	0 2	* Home team in 1st leg			

LIGA POSTEBON II FINAL
1st leg. Metropolitano, Barranquilla, 18-12-2011, Att: 40 200, Ref: Imer Machado
Atlético Junior   3   Bacca 2 [44][57], Hernandez.V [53]
Once Caldas   2   Nunez 2 [19][40]
Junior - Carlos Rodriguez - Andres Gonzalez, Juan Valencia•, Braynner Garcia•, Jaider Romero•, Luis Narvaez (Jose Amaya 21), Giovanni Hernandez, Vladimir Hernandez, Jossymar Gomez (Victor Cortes 50), Luis Ruiz (Sherman Cardenas 77), Carlos Bacca. Tr: Jose Hernandez
Once Caldas - Neco Martinez - Mauricio Casierra, David Alvarez, Alexis Henriquez•, Elkin Calle, Diego Amaya, Jorge Nunez•, Harrison Henao (Pepe Moreno 46) (Oliver Fula 59), Alexander Mejia••♦68, Jhon Pajoy, Jefferson Cuero (Yedinson Palacios 73). Tr: Luis Paez
2nd leg. Palogrande, Manizales, 22-12-2011, Att: 28 678, Ref: Wilmar Roldan
Once Caldas   2   2 Pajoy [45], Beltran [70]
Atlético Junior   1   4p Bacca [59]
Once Caldas - Juan Henao - Mauricio Casierra, Alexis Henriquez, Elkin Calle•, Diego Amaya, Jorge Nunez, Ayron Del Valle•, Harrison Henao (Guillermo Beltran 64), Mario Gonzalez•, Pepe Moreno (Jefferson Cuero 18), Jhon Pajoy. Tr: Luis Paez
Junior - Sebastian Viera - Andres Gonzalez•, Juan Valencia•, Braynner Garcia (Cesar Fawcett• 75), Harold Macias•, Jaider Romero, Giovanni Hernandez, Jose Amaya, Vladimir Hernandez (Sherman Cardenas 83), Luis Ruiz (Luis Paez 70), Carlos Bacca. Tr: Jose Hernandez

Atlético Junior qualified for the Copa Libertadores. Once Caldas also qualified for the Copa Libertadores as the team with the best overall record in the season

COLOMBIA 2011
PRIMERA B LIGA POSTEBON I (2)

	Pl	W	D	L	F	A	Pts
Deportivo Pasto †	18	12	3	3	32	8	39
Rionegro †	18	10	2	6	25	19	32
Pacífico †	18	8	5	5	24	19	29
Academia Bogotá †	18	8	5	5	18	15	29
Patriotas Tunja †	18	8	5	5	22	20	29
Valledupar †	18	8	4	6	16	14	28
Uniautonoma †	18	8	3	7	30	22	27
Corporación Tuluá †	18	8	3	7	21	18	27
Atlético Bucaramanga	18	8	3	7	20	25	27
Fortaleza	18	6	8	4	20	19	26
Bogotá FC	18	7	3	8	20	24	24
Expreso Rojo	18	5	7	6	25	24	22
Depor Jamundí	18	5	6	7	22	28	21
Real Santander	18	5	5	8	24	25	20
Centauros Villavicencio	18	5	3	10	22	25	18
Barranquilla FC	18	4	6	8	13	19	18
Unión Magdalena	18	4	4	10	24	38	16
Alianza Petrolera	18	3	5	10	12	28	14

27/08/2011 - 27/11/2011 • † Qualified for the second stage

COLOMBIA 2011
PRIMERA B LIGA POSTEBON II (2)

	Pl	W	D	L	F	A	Pts
Deportivo Pasto †	18	9	7	2	32	15	34
Centauros Villav'cio †	18	8	7	3	28	25	31
Alianza Petrolera †	18	8	5	5	24	16	29
Bogotá FC †	18	8	5	5	26	21	29
Rionegro †	18	8	4	6	33	23	28
Uniautonoma †	18	8	4	6	33	24	28
Expreso Rojo †	18	7	7	4	21	15	28
Academia Bogotá †	18	7	7	4	27	24	28
Real Santander	18	7	6	5	23	19	27
Fortaleza	18	6	8	4	20	18	26
Atlético Bucaramanga	18	5	8	5	16	18	23
Valledupar	18	7	2	9	22	28	23
Unión Magdalena	18	5	5	8	19	22	20
Corporación Tuluá	18	4	8	6	22	27	20
Patriotas Tunja	18	4	6	8	21	25	18
Pacifico	18	3	6	9	14	28	15
Barranquilla FC	18	3	5	10	12	28	14
Depor Jamundí	18	2	6	10	15	32	12

27/08/2011 - 27/11/2011 • † Qualified for the second stage

LIGA POSTEBON I SECOND STAGE

Quarter-finals		Semi-finals		Final	
Patriotas *	0 2				
Academia	1 0	Patriotas	1 1		
Pasto	0 1 2p	Valledupar *	0 0		
Valledupar *	0 1 3p			Patriotas	0 0 5p
Pacifico	1 2 4p			Cortuluá	0 0 4p
Uniaut'ma *	3 0 1p	Pacifico *	1 0 4p		
Rionegro	0 0	Cortuluá	0 1 5p		
Cortuluá *	1 2			* Home team in 1st leg	

LIGA POSTEBON II SECOND STAGE

Quarter-finals		Semi-finals		Final	
Pasto	1 4				
Uniaut'ma *	1 0	Pasto	1 5		
Bogotá	0 0 4p	Ex. Rojo *	1 1		
Ex. Rojo *	0 0 5p			Pasto	1 1
Rionegro *	3 1			Centauros *	1 0
Alianza	0 1	Rionegro *	1 2 4p		
Academia *	2 2 2p	Centauros	0 3 4p		
Centauros	0 4 4p			* Home team in 1st leg	

Primera B Championship Final: Patriotas 1-0 0-1 0-2p Deportivo Pasto
Deportivo Pasto promoted. Patriotas also promoted after winning a play-off against América Cali

COPA COLOMBIA POSTOBON 2011

Round of 16		Quarter-finals		Semi-finals		Final	
Millonarios	3 1						
Uniautonoma *	2 1	Millonarios	2 2				
Deportivo Cali	0 1	Deportes Tolima *	3 0				
Deportes Tolima *	3 0						
Valledupar *	1 1			Millonarios *	4 0		
Deportivo Pasto	0 0	Valledupar	0 1 2p	Atlético Junior	1 0		
Once Caldas *	1 1 2p	Atlético Junior *	0 1 4p				
Atlético Junior	1 1 4p						
At. Nacional Medellín *	3 1					Millonarios †	1 1
Atlético Huila	2 0	At. Nacional Medellín	1 4			Boyacá Chico *	0 0
Itagüí Ditaires	2 1 2p	Real Santander *	1 2				
Real Santander *	0 3 4p						
Patriotas Tunja	0 2 4p			At. Nacional Medellín	1 1 6p		
Expreso Rojo *	1 1 3p	Patriotas Tunja *	1 1 1p	Boyacá Chico *	1 1 7p		
Santa Fe *	1 0	Boyacá Chico	1 1 3p				
Boyacá Chico	2 1						

CUP FINAL
1st leg. 19-10-2011
2nd leg. 3-11-2010
For details see below

† Qualified for Copa Sudamericana • * Home team in the first leg

1st leg. Independencia, Tunja, 19-10-2011, Ref: Hector Parra. Scorer: Rafael Robayo [83] for Millonarios. Chico - Bonilla - Pino, Galicia, Montano, Mostasilla, Rivas• (Navarro 46), Movil (Arzuaga 72), Ramirez, Chica (Perlaza 81), Gordillo•, Correa. Tr: Gamero • Millonarios - Ramos - Ochoa, Martinez, Cichero, Franco, Robayo, Ortiz, Candelo (Blanco 94+), Mosquera• (Preciado• 75), Toloza, Moreno (Tancredi 81). Tr: Paez

2nd leg. El Campin, Bogotá, 27-10-2011, Ref: Adrian Velez. Scorer: Mayer Candelo [84] for Millonarios. Millonarios - Ramos - Ochoa, Martinez•, Cichero, Franco, Robayo•, Ortiz•, Candelo (Mera 89), Mosquera (Blanco 85), Toloza, Moreno (Tancredi 58). Tr: Paez • Chico - Bonilla - Pino (Perlaza• 23), Galicia•, Montano•, Mostasilla, Rivas••♦73, Movil• (Mena 77), Ramirez•, Navarro (Chica• 63), Gordillo•, Correa. Tr: Gamero

MEDALS TABLE

		Overall			League			Cup		Sth Am			
		G	S	B	G	S	B	G	S	G	S	B	City
1	Millonarios	15	10	13	13	9	8	1		1	1	5	Bogotá
2	América Cali	14	11	12	13	7	5			1	4	7	Cali
3	Atlético Nacional	14	11	10	11	9	5			3	2	5	Medellin
4	Deportivo Cali	9	15	8	8	12	6	1			3	2	Cali
5	Atlético Junior	7	6	3	7	6	2					1	Barranquilla
6	Santa Fe	7	5	5	6	3	4	1			2	1	Bogotá
7	Independiente Medellín	5	7	4	5	7	3					1	Medellin
8	Once Caldas	5	3	1	4	2	1	1		1			Manizales
9	Deportes Tolima	1	5	2	1	5	1					1	Ibagué
10	La Equidad	1	3			3		1					Bogotá
11	Deportes Quindío	1	2	1	1	2	1						Armenia
12	Deportivo Pasto	1	1	?	1	1							Pasto
13	Cúcuta Deportivo	1	1	3	1	1	2					1	Cúcuta
14	Boyacá Chico	1	1		1				1				Tunja
15	Union Magdalena	1			1								Santa Marta
16	Boca Junior		2	2		2	2						Cali
17	Atlético Huila		2			2							Neiva
18	Atlético Bucaramanga		1	3		1	3						Bucaramanga
19	Real Cartagena		1			1							Cartagena
	Itagüí Ditaires			1					1				Itagüí, Medellín
21	Deportivo Pereira			4			4						Pereira

COM – COMOROS

FIFA/COCA-COLA WORLD RANKING

'93	'94	'95	'96	'97	'98	'99	'00	'01	'02	'03	'04	'05	'06	'07	'08	'09	'10	'11	'12
-	-	-	-	-	-	-	-	-	-	-	-	-	207	187	198	176	186	187	

2011													High	Low	Av
Jan	Feb	Mar	Apr	May	Jun	Jul	Aug	Sep	Oct	Nov	Dec				
186	186	187	188	188	164	175	182	178	183	186	187		164	207	187

The Comoros Islands appeared in a full programme of matches in 2011, the busiest year yet for the national team, the Coelacanthes, since obtaining membership of FIFA in 2006. The country attained an all-time high on the FIFA/Coca-Cola World Ranking in July 2011 as they moved to 164th place but they were last in their 2012 CAF Africa Cup of Nations group with a single point from six matches. They also went out early in the African qualifiers for the 2014 FIFA World Cup finals in Brazil, beaten 5-1 on aggregate by Mozambique. But with more international games, the side is becoming increasingly experienced and has extended, for the first time, its player pool to include footballers based in Europe. Captain Nadjim Abdou is from English club Millwall and the 22-year-old midfielder Ali M'Madi plays at French Ligue 1 club Evian. This progress has been undermined, however, by the high financial cost of regular competition which saw the federation decide not to enter the 2013 Africa Cup of Nations qualifiers. At the 2011 Indian Ocean Island Games, failure to win any of their three matches saw the Comoros fall at the group stage. They drew with hosts Seychelles and with the Maldives but lost 2-0 in a decisive game with Mauritius. Coin Nord were the stand-out team of the year in club football, winning both the league and cup.

CAF AFRICA CUP OF NATIONS RECORD
1957-2008 DNE 2010-2012 DNQ

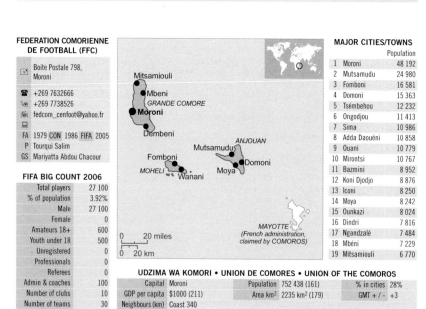

FEDERATION COMORIENNE DE FOOTBALL (FFC)

Boite Postale 798, Moroni

☎ +269 7632666
🖷 +269 7738526
✉ fedcom_cenfoot@yahoo.fr
🖥

FA 1979 CON 1986 FIFA 2005
P Tourqui Salim
GS Mariyatta Abdou Chacour

FIFA BIG COUNT 2006

Total players	27 100
% of population	3.92%
Male	27 100
Female	0
Amateurs 18+	600
Youth under 18	500
Unregistered	0
Professionals	0
Referees	0
Admin & coaches	100
Number of clubs	10
Number of teams	30

MAJOR CITIES/TOWNS
Population

1	Moroni	48 192
2	Mutsamudu	24 980
3	Fomboni	16 581
4	Domoni	15 363
5	Tsémbehou	12 232
6	Ongodjou	11 413
7	Sima	10 986
8	Adda Daouéni	10 858
9	Ouani	10 779
10	Mirontsi	10 767
11	Bazmini	8 952
12	Koni Djodjo	8 876
13	Iconi	8 250
14	Moya	8 242
15	Ounkazi	8 024
16	Dindri	7 816
17	Ngandzalé	7 484
18	Mbéni	7 229
19	Mitsamiouli	6 770

UDZIMA WA KOMORI • UNION DE COMORES • UNION OF THE COMOROS

Capital	Moroni	Population	752 438 (161)	% in cities	28%
GDP per capita	$1000 (211)	Area km²	2235 km² (179)	GMT +/-	+3
Neighbours (km)	Coast 340				

RECENT INTERNATIONAL MATCHES PLAYED BY COMOROS

2003	Opponents	Score	Venue	Comp	Scorers	Att	Referee
30-08	Reunion †	L 0-1	Flacq	IOr1		103	Labrosse SEY
2-09	Reunion †	L 0-4	Flacq	IOr1			
4-09	Mauritius †	L 0-5	Curepipe	IOsf		4 500	Labrosse SEY
6-09	Seychelles †	L 0-2	Curepipe	IO3p			
2004							
No international matches played in 2004							
2005							
No international matches played in 2005							
2006							
14-12	Yemen	L 0-2	Sana'a	ARq			
17-12	Djibouti	W 4-2	Sana'a	ARq	Meknesh Bin Daoud [5], Ahmed Seif 2 [33 75], Mohamed Moni [70]		
2007							
14-08	Madagascar	L 0-3	Antananarivo	Fr			
14-10	Madagascar	L 2-6	Antananarivo	WCq	Daoud Midtadi [6], Ibor Bakar [53p]	7 754	Kaoma ZAM
17-11	Madagascar	L 0-4	Moroni	WCq		1 610	Damon RSA
2008							
20-07	Namibia	L 0-3	Secunda	CCr1			Labrosse SEY
22-07	Malawi	L 0-1	Secunda	CCr1			Marange ZIM
24-07	Lesotho	L 0-1	Secunda	CCr1			Labrosse SEY
2009							
18-10	Botswana	D 0-0	Bulawayo	CCr1			Rachide MOZ
20-10	Seychelles	W 2-1	Bulawayo	CCr1	Ahmed Ali [9], Mouigni Mohamed [64]		Rachide MOZ
22-10	Swaziland	L 0-3	Bulawayo	CCr1			Carvalho ANG
2010							
29-08	Madagascar	L 0-1	Mahajanga	Fr			
5-09	Zambia	L 0-4	Lusaka	CNq			Eyob Russom ERI
9-10	Mozambique	L 0-1	Moroni	CNq			Ibada TAN
2011							
28-03	Libya	L 0-3	Bamaoko	CNq			Diatta SEN
5-06	Libya	D 1-1	Mitsamiouli	CNq	Abdoulaide Mze Mbaba [83]		
4-08	Seychelles	D 0-0	Praslin	IOr1		1 800	Dubec REU
6-08	Maldives	D 2-2	Roche Caiman	IOr1	Mchinda Madihali [9], Athoumane Soulaimane [54]	1 000	Dubec REU
9-08	Mauritius	L 0-2	Praslin	IOr1		300	Rassuhi MYT
4-09	Zambia	L 1-2	Mitsamiouli	CNq	Youssouf M'Changama [32]		
8-10	Mozambique	L 0-3	Maputo	CNq			
11-11	Mozambique	L 0-1	Mitsamiouli	WCq		3 000	Jane LES
15-11	Mozambique	L 1-4	Maputo	WCq	Mohamed Youssouf [72]	10 000	Ruzive ZIM

IO = Indian Ocean Games • CC = COSAFA Castle Cup • AR = Arab Cup • q = qualifier • r1 = first round group
† Not regarded as a full international because Comoros was not yet a member of FIFA

COMOROS 2011

	Pl	W	D	L	F	A	Pts	CN	FC	SNS
Coin Nord †	4	2	1	1	4	2	7		2-0	2-0
Fomboni Club	4	2	0	2	3	3	6	2-0		1-0
Style Nouvel Sima	4	1	1	2	1	3	4	0-0	1-0	

21/11/2011 - 3/12/2011 • † Qualified for the CAF Champions League

COUPE DES COMORES 2011

Semi-finals		Finals	
Coin Nord	3		
Asmina Mbatse	0		
		Coin Nord	1 4p
		Fomboni Club	1 2p
AS Tsembehou	1		
Fomboni Club	2		

Final. Stade Ahmed Matoire, Fomboni, 23-01-2011

CPV – CAPE VERDE ISLANDS

FIFA/COCA-COLA WORLD RANKING

'93	'94	'95	'96	'97	'98	'99	'00	'01	'02	'03	'04	'05	'06	'07	'08	'09	'10	'11	'12
147	161	144	155	171	167	177	156	159	154	143	129	118	78	111	107	97	75	58	

2011												High	Low	Av
Jan	Feb	Mar	Apr	May	Jun	Jul	Aug	Sep	Oct	Nov	Dec			
75	73	73	79	79	81	82	72	91	66	57	58	57	182	133

Cape Verde Islands' growing stature in African football and their flirtation with a first-ever appearance in a major finals was reflected in a record high in the FIFA/Coca-Cola World Ranking. The island archipelago moved to 57th in the world in November after they fell just short of qualifying for the 2012 CAF Africa Cup of Nations finals in Gabon and Equatorial Guinea. They were in contention until the last round of action in their group but lost 3-0 to Mali in Bamako and were pipped to the top spot by their opponents. Coach Luis Antunes, who had taken temporary leave from his job as an air traffic controller, was supposed to go back to his trade at the end of the year but has now agreed to stay on longer. He has continued the policy of tapping into the large Cape Verdian diaspora. The majority of the players in the squad come from Portugal but there are others from the large communities who live in the Netherlands and in France. In club football, CS Mindelense were crowned champions to equal the record number of league successes set previously by Sporting Praia. Mindelense beat Sporting in the final to clinch their eighth title overall and their first since 1998. That meant they could have taken part in CAF Champions League but once again the high cost of travel from the islands meant the opportunity was passed up.

CAF AFRICA CUP OF NATIONS RECORD
1957-1992 DNE 1994 DNQ 1996-1998 DNQ 2000-2012 DNQ

FEDERACAO CABOVERDIANA DE FUTEBOL (FCF)

FCF CX, Case postale 234, Praia
☎ +238 2 600847
🖷 +238 2 611362
📧 fcf@cvtelecom.cv
🖥 www.fcf.cv
FA 1982 CON 1986 FIFA 1986
P Mario Semedo
GS Jose João Rezende

FIFA BIG COUNT 2006

Total players	35 100
% of population	8.34%
Male	33 500
Female	1 600
Amateurs 18+	7 000
Youth under 18	4 500
Unregistered	4 200
Professionals	0
Referees	256
Admin & coaches	500
Number of clubs	82
Number of teams	180

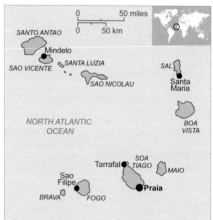

MAJOR CITIES/TOWNS

		Population
1	Praia	128 653
2	Mindelo	76 014
3	Santa Maria	21 195
4	Pedra Badejo	10 237
5	Assomada	8 553
6	São Filipe	8 212
7	Tarrafal	6 974
8	São Miguel	5 888
9	Porto Novo	5 523
10	Ribeira Brava	5 121
11	Ponta do Sol	4 023
12	Vila do Maio	3 264
13	São Domingos	3 220
14	Sal Rei	2 200
15	Pombas	1 799
16	Nova Sintra	1 793
17	Mosteiros	478

REPUBLICA DE CABO VERDE • REPUBLIC OF CAPE VERDE

Capital	Praia	Population	429 474 (171)	% in cities	60%
GDP per capita	$3800 (156)	Area km²	4033 km² (175)	GMT +/-	-1
Neighbours (km)	Coast 965				

RECENT INTERNATIONAL MATCHES PLAYED BY THE CAPE VERDE ISLANDS

2008	Opponents		Score	Venue	Comp	Scorers	Att	Referee
24-05	Burkina Faso	W	1-0	Alcochete	Fr	Toy Adao		
27-05	Luxembourg	D	1-1	Luxembourg	Fr	Valter [83]	2 051	Radovanovic MNE
31-05	Cameroon	L	0-2	Yaoundé	WCq		20 000	Djaoupe TOG
7-06	Tanzania	W	1-0	Praia	WCq	Babanco [73]	6 000	El Achiri MAR
15-06	Mauritius	W	1-0	Curepipe	WCq	Dady [43p]	1 480	Kaoma ZAM
22-06	Mauritius	W	3-1	Praia	WCq	Dady 2 [45 58], Marco Soares [78]	2 850	Coulibaly MLI
6-09	Cameroon	L	1-2	Praia	WCq	Lito [38]	5 000	Labrosse SEY
11-10	Tanzania	L	1-3	Dar es Salaam	WCq	Semedo [35]	10 000	Damon RSA
2009								
25-03	Angola	W	1-0	Olhao	Fr	Dady [33p]		
28-03	Equatorial Guinea	W	5-0	Sal	Fr	Cadu 2 [6 44], Dario [38p], Rodi 2 [45 90]		
4-09	Malta	W	2-0	Ta'Qali	Fr	Heldon Ramos [15p], Adilson Monteiro [40]		
9-09	Angola	D	1-1	Faro	Fr	Dario [35p]		
2010								
24-05	Portugal	D	0-0	Covilha	Fr		6 000	Gomez ESP
11-08	Senegal	L	0-1	Dakar	Fr			
4-09	Mali	W	1-0	Praia	CNq	Varela [44]		Benouza ALG
10-10	Zimbabwe	D	0-0	Harare	CNq			Ndume GAB
16-11	Guinea-Bissau	W	2-1	Lisbon	Fr	Lito [6], Ronny Souto [24]		
2011								
9-02	Burkina Faso	W	1-0	Obidos	Fr	Heldon [63]		
26-03	Liberia	W	4-2	Praia	CNq	Heldon 2 [14 45], Babanco [25], Odair Fortes [53]		Ould Ali MTN
5-06	Liberia	L	0-1	Paynesville	CNq			
3-09	Mali	L	0-3	Bamako	CNq			Diatta SEN
8-10	Zimbabwe	W	2-1	Praia	CNq	Valdo [3], Ryan Mendes [13]		

Fr = Friendly match • CN = CAF African Cup of Nations • WC = FIFA World Cup • q = qualifier

CAPE VERDE ISLANDS NATIONAL TEAM HISTORICAL RECORDS

Coach

Carlos Alinho 2003-06 • Ze Rui 2006 • Ricardo Rocha BRA 2007 • Joao de Deus POR 2008-10 • Lucio Antunes 2010-

CAPE VERDE ISLANDS 2010-11
CAMPEONATO NACIONAL

First Round Group Stage

Group A	Pl	W	D	L	F	A	Pts	SP	Ben	Vul	Ult	SR
CS Mindelense	5	4	1	0	13	1	**13**	1-0	0-0	6-0	4-1	2-0
Sporting da Praia	5	4	0	1	7	2	**12**		1-0	2-1	2-0	2-0
Benfica	5	2	2	1	5	4	**8**			1-1	3-2	1-0
Vulcânicos	4	1	1	2	3	9	**4**				1-0	n/p
FC Ultramarina	5	1	0	4	6	11	**3**					3-1
Sal-Rei SC	4	0	0	4	1	8	**0**					

Semi-finals

CS Mindelense	2	0
Académico do Sal	1	1

Final

C3 Mindelense	1	0
Sporting da Praia	0	0

Group B	Pl	W	D	L	F	A	Pts	AS	AB	OU	Ros
Académica Pt Novo	4	2	2	0	11	4	**8**	2-2	0-0	4-0	5-2
Académica do Sal	4	2	2	0	8	5	**8**		3-1	2-1	1-1
Académica Boavista	4	2	1	1	9	4	**7**			2-1	6-0
Onze Unidos	4	1	0	3	4	9	**3**				2-1
Rosariense	4	0	1	3	4	14	**1**				

Académica Pt Novo	2	0
Sporting da Praia	1	4

1st leg. 1-07-2011

2nd leg. 9-07-2011

13/05/2011 - 9/07/2011

CRC – COSTA RICA

FIFA/COCA-COLA WORLD RANKING

'93	'94	'95	'96	'97	'98	'99	'00	'01	'02	'03	'04	'05	'06	'07	'08	'09	'10	'11	'12
42	65	78	72	51	67	64	60	30	21	17	27	21	68	70	53	44	69	65	

2011															
Jan	Feb	Mar	Apr	May	Jun	Jul	Aug	Sep	Oct	Nov	Dec		High	Low	Av
69	49	53	55	56	55	56	60	57	62	64	65		17	93	49

Costa Rica took part in three tournaments during the course of 2011, all of which confirmed that their reputation as the best team in Central America was under threat from Honduras. A 2-1 defeat at the hands of the Hondurans in the Copa Centroamericana at the start of the year was followed by a quarter-final exit in the CONCACAF Gold Cup in New York by the same opponents, although this time Honduras needed a penalty shoot-out victory to get past their rivals. Overall it was a disappointing performance by Costa Rica who won just one game - a 5-0 victory over Cuba in their opening game. There was more disappointment at the Copa America in Argentina when an experimental team was sent to the tournament and was knocked out in the first round. In club football Alajuelense continued their recent good form in the championship winning both tournaments staged in 2011. In the first they beat surprise team San Carlos in the final, winning both legs 1-0, whilst in December they beat Herediano on penalties in the final for the second time in three tournaments and they are now just two titles shy of the record holders Saprisa. It was Saprissa who flew the flag for Costa Rica in the CONCACAF Champions League but after beating Olimpia from Honduras in the quarter-finals, they then lost to Real Salt Lake in the semi-finals.

FIFA WORLD CUP RECORD
1930-1954 DNE   1958-1986 DNQ   **1990** 13 r2   1994-1998 DNQ   **2002** 19 r1   **2006** 31 r1   **2010** DNQ

FEDERACION COSTARRICENSE DE FUTBOL (FEDEFUTBOL)

Radial Santa Ana Belen,
500 mts Este del cruce de la Panasonic,
San José 670-1000
☎ +506 25891450
📠 +506 25891457
✉ ejecutivo@fedefutbol.com
🖥 www.fedefutbol.org
FA 1921 CON 1962 FIFA 1927
P Eduardo Li
GS Lidia Rojas

FIFA BIG COUNT 2006

Total players	1 084 588
% of population	26.61%
Male	1 050 120
Female	34 468
Amateurs 18+	17 500
Professionals	1 025
Referees	630
Admin & coaches	4 236
Number of clubs	248
Number of teams	1 391

MAJOR CITIES/TOWNS
Population

1	San José	345 447
2	San Francisco	70 200
3	Limón	66 620
4	Liberia	54 852
5	Alajuela	49 930
6	Paraíso	48 400
7	San Isidro	39 833
8	Desamparados	39 767
9	Curridabat	37 263
10	Puntarenas	37 080
11	San Vicente	35 624
12	San José	33 913
13	Purral	32 125
14	Turrialba	31 987
15	Mercedes	31 713
16	San Rafael Abajo	31 251
17	San Rafael	31 023
18	San Miguel	30 834
19	Aguacaliente	30 547

REPUBLICA DE COSTA RICA • REPUBLIC OF COSTA RICA

Capital San José	Population 4 253 877 (123)	% in cities 63%
GDP per capita $11 500 (95)	Area km² 51 100 km² (129)	GMT +/- -6
Neighbours (km) Nicaragua 309, Panama 330 • Coast 1290		

RECENT INTERNATIONAL MATCHES PLAYED BY COSTA RICA

2010	Opponents	Score		Venue	Comp	Scorers	Att	Referee
26-01	Argentina	L	2-3	San Juan	Fr	Michael Barrantes [20], Diego Madrigal [76]	22 000	Amarilla PAR
26-05	France	L	1-2	Lens	Fr	Carlos Hernandez [11]	40 000	Bezborodov RUS
1-06	Switzerland	W	1-0	Sion	Fr	Winston Parks [57]	10 000	Buttimer IRL
5-06	Slovakia	L	0-3	Bratislava	Fr		12 000	Messner AUT
11-08	Paraguay	L	0-2	Asuncion	Fr		22 000	Beligoy ARG
3-09	Panama	D	2-2	Panama City	Fr	Michael Barrantes [7], Alvaro Saborio [52]	23 005	Delgadillo MEX
5-09	Jamaica	L	0-1	Kingston	Fr		15 000	Brizan TRI
8-10	Peru	L	0-2	Lima	Fr		15 000	Ponce ECU
12-10	El Salvador	W	2-1	Quesada	Fr	Jose Sanchez [10], Josue Martinez [87]	4 000	Rodriguez PAN
17-11	Jamaica	D	0-0	Fort Lauderdale	Fr		4 000	Renso USA
2011								
14-01	Honduras	D	1-1	Panama City	UCr1	Victor Nunez [42]	6 000	Garcia MEX
16-01	Guatemala	W	2-0	Panama City	UCr1	Marcos Urena 2 [48 81]	1 500	Moreno PAN
21-01	Panama	D	1-1	Panama City	UCsf	Celso Borges [67], W 4-2p	10 000	Aguilar SLV
23-01	Honduras	L	1-2	Panama City	UCf	Marcos Urena [73]	2 000	Lopez GUA
9-02	Venezuela	D	2-2	Puerto La Cruz	Fr	Bryan Oviedo [7], Marcos Urena [70]	15 000	Gambeta PER
26-03	China PR	D	2-2	San Jose	Fr	Alvaro Saborio [38], Randall Brenes [45]	35 000	Moreno PAN
29-03	Argentina	D	0-0	San Jose	Fr		35 000	Rodriguez.M MEX
5-06	Cuba	W	5-0	Arlington	GCr1	Marco Urena 2 [6 46], Alvaro Saborio [41], Heiner Mora [47], Christian Bolanos [71]	80 108	Moreno PAN
9-06	El Salvador	D	1-1	Charlotte	GCr1	Randall Brenes [95+]	46 012	Marrufo USA
12-06	Mexico	L	1-4	Chicago	GCr1	Marco Urena [69]	62 000	Moreno PAN
18-06	Honduras	D	1-1	New York	GCqf	Dennis Marshall [56], L 2-4p	78 807	Moreno PAN
2-07	Colombia	L	0-1	Jujuy	CAr1		23 500	Osses CHI
7-07	Bolivia	W	2-0	Jujuy	CAr1	Josue Martinez [59], Joel Campbell [78]	23 000	Vera ECU
11-07	Argentina	L	0-3	Cordoba	CAr1		57 000	Rivera PER
10-08	Ecuador	L	0-2	San Jose	Fr		18 000	Aguilar SLV
2-09	USA	W	1-0	Carson	Fr	Rodney Wallace [65]	15 798	Molina HON
6-09	Ecuador	L	0-4	Quito	Fr		6 000	Roldan COL
7-10	Brazil	L	0-1	San Jose	Fr		25 000	Lopez GUA
11-11	Panama	L	0-2	Panama City	Fr		5 000	Garcia MEX
15-11	Spain	D	2-2	San Jose	Fr	Randall Brenes [30], Joel Campbell [41]	25 000	Navarro CAN
11-12	Cuba	D	1-1	Havana	Fr	Kenny Cunningham [90]	10 000	Lopez GUA
22-12	Venezuela	W	2-0	Barquisimeto	Fr	Rodney Wallace [42], Jose Miguel Cubero [54]	33 000	Angela ARU

Fr = Friendly match • UC = UNCAF Cup/Copa Centroamericana • GC = CONCACAF Gold Cup • WC = FIFA World Cup
q = qualifier • r1 = first round group • qf = quarter-finals • † not a full international

COSTA RICA NATIONAL TEAM HISTORICAL RECORDS

Caps
137 - Walter Centeno 1995-2009 • 128 - Luis Marin 1993-2006 • 110 - Mauricio Solis 1993-2006 • 109 - Rolando Fonseca 1992-2008 • 101 - Harold Wallace 1995-2009 • 91 - Ronald Gomez 1993-2008 • 89 - Hernan Medford 1987-2002 • 76 - Erick Lonnis 1992-2002 & Wilmer Lopez 1995-2003 • 75 - Oscar Ramirez 1985-97 • 73 - Jervis Drummond 1995-2008 & Paulo Wanchope 1996-2008

Goals
47 - Rolando Fonseca 1992-2008 • 45 - Paulo Wanchope 1996-2008 • 27 - Juan Ulloa 1955-70 • 24 - Walter Centeno 1995-2009 & Ronald Gomez 1993-2000 • 23 - Jorge Monge 1954-60 & Alvaro Saborio 2002- • 10 - Hernan Medford 1987-2002 • 15 - Rafael Madrigal • 14 - Rodolfo Herrera • 12 - Roy Saenz

Past Coaches
Randolph Galloway ENG 1946-48 • Otto Bumbel BRA 1950-56 • Luis Lucho Tirado CHI 1956-58 • Hugo Tassara Olivares CHI 1958-60 • Eduardo Toba ESP 1960-61 • Alfredo Piedra 1961-62 • Mario Cordero 1962-65 • Eduardo Viso Abella ESP 1965-71 • Humberto Maschio ARG 1971-75 • Jose Etchegoyen URU 1975-80 • Antonio Moyano Reyna ESP 1980-85 • Odir Jacques BRA 1985-87 • Gustavo de Simone URU 1987-89 • Marvin Rodriguez 1989-90 • Bora Milutinovic SRB 1990 • Rolando Villalobos 1991-92 • Hector Nunez URU 1992 • Juan Jose Gamez 1993 • Toribio Rojas 1993-95 • Valdeir Viera BRA 1996 • Horacio Cordero ARG 1997 • Juan Hernandez 1997 • Rolando Villalobos 1998 • Francisco Maturana COL 1999 • Marvin Rodriguez 1999-2000 • Gilson Siqueira Nunes BRA 2000 • Alexandre Guimaraes BRA 2001-02 • Rodrigo Kenton 2002 • Steve Sampson USA 2002-04 • Jorge Luis Pinto COL 2004-05 • Alexandre Guimaraes BRA 2005-06 • Hernan Medford 2006-08 • Rodrigo Kenton 2008-09 • Rene Simoes BRA 2009 • Ronald Gonzalez 2009-10 • Ricardo La Volpe ARG 2010-11 • Ronald Brenes 2011 • Jorge Luis Pinto COL 2011

COSTA RICA 2010-11

PRIMERA DIVISION — TORNEO CLAUSURA VERANO

Group 1	Pl	W	D	L	F	A	Pts	Saprissa	Limon	Cartaginés	P. Zeledón	Puntarenas	B. Mexico	Alajuelense	San Carlos	Herediano	Santos	Brujas	UCR
Deportivo Saprissa †	16	10	3	3	31	14	33		0-3	0-0	1-0	2-0	3-0		3-0	0-2	3-0		
Limon FC †	16	8	5	3	31	18	29	0-2		2-2	4-0	3-1	1-1	1-0				2-1	3-0
CS Cartaginés †	16	7	7	2	25	14	28	1-2	4-1		2-2	2-0	3-0	1-1				1-1	1-0
AD Pérez Zeledón †	16	6	3	7	23	21	21	2-3	1-1	0-1		3-1	3-0		0-1	2-2	3-0		
Puntarenas FC	16	3	2	11	16	27	11	2-2	1-4	0-1	1-2		3-0		0-2	0-1	2-0		
Barrio Mexico	16	2	2	12	11	37	8	0-3	0-3	1-3	1-2	1-0		3-2				0-2	2-4

Group 2	Pl	W	D	L	F	A	Pts	Saprissa	Limon	Cartaginés	P. Zeledón	Puntarenas	B. Mexico	Alajuelense	San Carlos	Herediano	Santos	Brujas	UCR
LD Alajuelense †	16	9	4	3	26	20	31	2-1				1-0	3-2		0-0	1-1	3-2	4-1	2-2
San Carlos †	16	9	3	4	23	16	30		2-0	1-0			2-1	1-2		2-1	1-0	3-0	1-0
CS Herediano †	16	6	8	2	25	19	26		2-2	3-3			1-1	0-1	3-2		2-0	2-1	1-0
Santos †	16	4	4	8	18	24	16		1-1	0-0			2-0	1-2	1-1	1-1		1-2	4-1
Brujas FC	16	4	4	8	22	31	16	0-4				1-3	1-1	3-0	3-3	2-2	1-2		1-2
Universidad Costa Rica	16	3	4	9	18	28	15	2-2				1-0	0-2	1-2	2-1	1-1	1-3	1-2	

9/01/2011 - 15/05/2011 • † Qualified for the play-off quarter-finals
Play-off quarter-finals: **Herediano** 2-0 2-2 Limón • Cartaginés 1-1 1-4 **San Carlos** • Santos 1-2 1-1 **Saprissa** • Pérez Zeledón 1-1 0-1 **Alajuelense**
Play-off semi-finals: Herediano 4-2 0-4 **Alajuelense** • San Carlos 1-2 2-0 Saprissa
Play-off final: San Carlos 0-1 0-1 **Alajuelense**. **LD Alajuelense** are the Verano champions • Barrio Mexico and Universidad Costa Rica relegated

COSTA RICA 2011-12

PRIMERA DIVISION — TORNEO APERTURA INVIERNO

	Pl	W	D	L	F	A	Pts	Herediano	Alajuelense	Saprissa	Cartaginés	Puntarenas	P. Zeledón	Santos	San Carlos	Belén	Limon	Brujas
CS Herediano †	20	11	6	3	39	19	39		4-0	1-1	6-3	3-1	2-1	1-0	5-0	1-1	1-1	1-0
LD Alajuelense †	20	11	4	5	38	23	37	2-2		1-1	4-0	0-1	4-0	0-2	3-1	1-0	0-2	4-2
Deportivo Saprissa †	20	9	8	3	34	21	35	1-0	2-2		3-1	1-1	2-0	1-0	2-1	0-0	0-1	1-0
CS Cartaginés †	20	7	9	4	31	27	30	3-1	2-0	2-1		3-0	2-2	1-1	0-0	3-2	3-0	3-1
Puntarenas FC	20	7	7	6	27	34	28	1-1	1-3	3-3	2-1		3-2	2-2	2-0	3-0	1-0	2-1
AD Pérez Zeledón	20	7	5	8	31	30	26	2-1	1-3	2-2	0-0	7-1		2-1	1-0	0-1	1-1	5-1
Santos	20	6	7	7	26	27	25	0-0	0-3	3-2	1-1	3-0	1-1		2-2	1-1	2-1	1-2
San Carlos	20	5	6	9	22	33	21	0-4	0-3	1-4	1-1	0-0	3-0	3-1		4-0	2-1	2-2
Belén Siglo XXI	20	4	7	9	21	30	19	1-2	1-2	1-1	1-1	1-0	1-3	3-0	1-1		3-1	1-1
Limon FC	20	5	4	11	19	30	19	1-2	0-2	0-2	1-1	3-3	1-0	0-2	0-1	2-1		3-2
Orión FC	20	4	5	11	20	34	17	0-1	1-1	1-4	0-0	0-0	0-1	1-3	1-0	3-1	1-0	

31/07/2011 - 18/12/2011 • † Qualified for the play-off semi-finals • Brujas changed their name to Orión
Play-off semi-finals: Saprissa 0-1 2-2 Alajuelense • Cartagines 1-2 0-1 **Herediano**
Play-off final: **Alajuelense** 1-1 0-0 6-5p Herediano. **LD Alajuelense** are the Invierno champions

MEDALS TABLE

		Overall			League			CON'CAF			City
		G	S	B	G	S	B	G	S	B	
1	Deportivo Saprissa	32	17	8	29	15	1	3	2	7	San José
2	Liga Deportiva Alajuelense	29	23	13	27	20	9	2	3	4	Alajuela
3	CS Herediano	21	15	12	21	15	11			1	Heredia
4	CS La Libertad	6	7	4	6	7	4				San José
5	CS Cartaginés	4	10	7	3	10	7	1			Cartago
6	Orión FC	2	6	7	2	6	7				
7	Municipal Puntarenas	1	3	1	1	3	1				Puntarenas
8	CS Uruguay	1	1		1	1					Coronado
9	Universidad de Costa Rica	1		3	1		3				San José
10	Orión FC	1			1						San José
	AD Carmelita	1			1						Alajuela
	Liberia Mia	1			1						Liberia

CRO – CROATIA

FIFA/COCA-COLA WORLD RANKING

'93	'94	'95	'96	'97	'98	'99	'00	'01	'02	'03	'04	'05	'06	'07	'08	'09	'10	'11	'12
122	62	41	24	19	4	9	18	19	32	20	23	20	15	10	7	10	10	8	

						2011								High	Low	Av
Jan	Feb	Mar	Apr	May	Jun	Jul	Aug	Sep	Oct	Nov	Dec			High	Low	Av
9	9	8	10	10	8	9	10	9	12	8	8			3	125	24

Having lost a critical match to group winners Greece in their penultimate Euro 2012 qualifier, Croatia found themselves in a play-off against Turkey, but once again when it really mattered, they put in a magnificent performance away from home to clinch a place at the European Championship finals. At the end of 2007 they had travelled to England and won 4-1 at Wembley; four years later it was the Turks in Istanbul who were on the receiving end. Early in the second half the Croatians were 3-0 up with the tie effectively won. There were no further goals and with the return drawn 0-0, Croatia qualified for their fourth finals since becoming an independent nation. It was a personal triumph for coach Slaven Bilic, one of only two coaches from the 16 finalists in 2008 still with his national team. In club football, it was another stroll in the park for Dinamo Zagreb who walked away with the league and cup double for the fourth time in five years. It was the sixth league crown in succession for the Zagreb club but the achievement was put in perspective when after qualifying for the group stage of the UEFA Champions League for the first time since the 1990s, they lost all six games played against Real Madrid, Lyon and Ajax with a goal difference of minus 19 - statistically the worst performance in the history of the Champions League group stage.

UEFA EUROPEAN CHAMPIONSHIP RECORD
1960-1992 DNE (part of Yugoslavia) **1996** 7 QF **2000** DNQ **2004** 13 r1 **2008** 5 QF **2012** Qualified

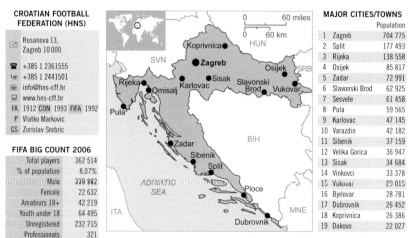

CROATIAN FOOTBALL FEDERATION (HNS)

Rusanova 13,
Zagreb 10 000

☎ +385 1 2361555
✆ +385 1 2441501
✉ info@hns-cff.hr
🖥 www.hns-cff.hr
FA 1912 CON 1993 FIFA 1992
P Vlatko Markovic
GS Zorislav Srebric

FIFA BIG COUNT 2006

Total players	362 514
% of population	8.07%
Male	339 882
Female	22 632
Amateurs 18+	42 219
Youth under 18	64 495
Unregistered	232 715
Professionals	321
Referees	2 380
Admin & coaches	15 108
Number of clubs	1 463
Number of teams	3 353

MAJOR CITIES/TOWNS

		Population
1	Zagreb	704 775
2	Split	177 493
3	Rijeka	138 558
4	Osijek	85 817
5	Zadar	72 991
6	Slavonski Brod	62 925
7	Sesvete	61 458
8	Pula	59 565
9	Karlovac	47 145
10	Varazdin	42 182
11	Sibenik	37 159
12	Velika Gorica	36 947
13	Sisak	34 684
14	Vinkovci	33 378
15	Vukovar	29 015
16	Bjelovar	28 781
17	Dubrovnik	26 452
18	Koprivnica	26 386
19	Dakovo	22 027

REPUBLIKA HRVATSKA • REPUBLIC OF CROATIA

Capital Zagreb	Population 4 489 409 (121)	% in cities 57%
GDP per capita $18 300 (67)	Area km² 56 594 km² (126)	GMT +/- +1
Neighbours (km) Bosnia-Herzegovina 932, Hungary 329, Serbia 241, Montenegro 25, Slovenia 455 • Coast 5835		

RECENT INTERNATIONAL MATCHES PLAYED BY CROATIA

2008	Opponents	Score		Venue	Comp	Scorers	Att	Referee
6-02	Netherlands	L	0-3	Split	Fr		28 000	Fernandez ESP
26-03	Scotland	D	1-1	Glasgow	Fr	Kranjcar [10]	28 821	Hauge NOR
24-05	Moldova	W	1-0	Rijeka	Fr	Kovac.N [30]	7 000	Ceferin SVN
31-05	Hungary	D	1-1	Budapest	Fr	Kovac.N 24	10 000	Ledentu FRA
8-06	Austria	W	1-0	Vienna	ECr1	Modric [4p]	51 428	Vink NED
12-06	Germany	W	2-1	Klagenfurt	ECr1	Srna [24], Olic [62]	30 461	De Bleeckere BEL
16-06	Poland	W	1-0	Klagenfurt	ECr1	Klasnic [53]	30 461	Vassaras GRE
20-06	Turkey	D	1-1	Vienna	ECqf	Klasnic [119]. L 1-3p	51 428	Rosetti ITA
20-08	Slovenia	W	3-2	Maribor	Fr	Rakitic 2 [37 64], Srna [58p]	11 500	Circhetta SUI
6-09	Kazakhstan	W	3-0	Zagreb	WCq	Kovac.N [13], Modric [36], Petric [81]	17 424	Johannesson SWE
10-09	England	L	1-4	Zagreb	WCq	Mandzukic [78]	35 218	Michel SVK
11-10	Ukraine	D	0-0	Kharkov	WCq		38 500	Braamhaar NED
15-10	Andorra	W	4-0	Zagreb	WCq	Rakitic 2 [16 87p], Olic [32], Modric [75]	14 441	Vad HUN
2009								
11-02	Romania	W	2-1	Bucharest	Fr	Rakitic [28], Kranjcar [75]	9 000	Balaj ROU
1-04	Andorra	W	2-0	Andorra La Vella	WCq	Klasnic [15], Eduardo [36]	1 100	Trattou CYP
6-06	Ukraine	D	2-2	Zagreb	WCq	Petric [2], Modric [68]	32 073	Hauge NOR
12-08	Belarus	W	3-1	Minsk	WCq	Olic 2 [22 83], Eduardo [69]	21 651	Brych GER
5-09	Belarus	W	1-0	Zagreb	WCq	Rakitic [24]	25 628	Plautz AUT
9-09	England	L	1-5	London	WCq	Eduardo [71]	87 319	Undiano ESP
8-10	Qatar	W	3-2	Rijeka	Fr	Corluka [7], Klasnic [11], Jelavic [90]	5 000	Balaj ROU
14-10	Kazakhstan	W	2-1	Astana	WCq	Vukojevic [10], Kranjcar [93+]	10 250	Circhetta SUI
14-11	Liechtenstein	W	5-0	Vinkovci	Fr	Bilic 2 [1 48], Srna [10], Eduardo 2 [24 46]	10 000	Fabian HUN
2010								
19-05	Austria	W	1-0	Klagenfurt	Fr	Bilic [86]	20 000	Blom NED
23-05	Wales	W	2-0	Osijek	Fr	Rakitic [45], Gabric [81]	15 000	Vincic SVN
26-05	Estonia	D	0-0	Tallinn	Fr		3 000	Svendsen DEN
11-08	Slovakia	D	1-1	Bratislava	Fr	Jelavic [54]	6 366	Matejek CZE
3-09	Latvia	W	3-0	Riga	ECq	Petric [43], Olic [51], Srna [82]	7 600	Kuipers NED
7-09	Greece	D	0-0	Zagreb	ECq		24 399	Larsen DEN
9-10	Israel	W	2-1	Tel Aviv	ECq	Kranjcar 2 [36p 41]	33 421	Stark GER
12-10	Norway	W	2-1	Zagreb	Fr	Mandzukic [35], Kranjcar [50]	3 000	Skomina SVN
17-11	Malta	W	3-0	Zagreb	ECq	Kranjcar 2 [18 42], Kalinic [81]	9 000	Gomes POR
2011								
9-02	Czech Republic	W	4-2	Pula	Fr	Eduardo [10], Kalinic 2 [13 61], Ilicevic [75]	9 500	Orsato ITA
26-03	Georgia	L	0-1	Tbilisi	ECq		55 000	Tagliavento ITA
29-03	France	D	0-0	Paris	Fr		60 000	Kelly IRL
3-06	Georgia	W	2-1	Split	ECq	Mandzukic [76], Kalinic [78]	28 000	Johannesson SWE
10-08	Republic of Ireland	D	0-0	Dublin	Fr		20 179	Hagen NOR
2-09	Malta	W	3-1	Ta'Qali	ECq	Vukojevic [11], Badelj [32], Lovren [68]	6 150	Chapron FRA
6-09	Israel	W	3-1	Zagreb	ECq	Modric [47], Eduardo 2 [55 57]	13 688	Velasco ESP
7-10	Greece	L	0-2	Piaeus	ECq		27 200	Webb ENG
11-10	Latvia	W	2-0	Rijeka	ECq	Eduardo [66], Mandzukic [72]	8 370	Gautier FRA
11-11	Turkey	W	3-0	Istanbul	ECpo	Olic [2], Mandzukic [32], Corluka [51]	42 863	Brych GER
15-11	Turkey	D	0-0	Zagreb	ECpo		26 371	Proenca POR

Fr = Friendly match • EC = UEFA EURO 2008/12 • WC = FIFA World Cup • q = qualifier • r1 = first round group • qf = quarter-final

CROATIA NATIONAL TEAM HISTORICAL RECORDS

Caps
100 - Dario Simic 1996-2008 • **92** - Josip Simunic 2001- • **89** - Darijo Srna 2002- & Stipe Pletikosa 1999- • **84** - Robert Kovac 1999-2009 • **83** - Niko Kovac 1996-2008 • **81** - Robert Jarni 1990-2002 • **76** - Ivica Olic 2002- • **69** - Davor Suker 1990-2002 • **68** - Niko Kranjcar 2004- • **62** - Aljosa Asanovic 1990-2000 • **61** - Zvonimir Soldo 1994-2002 • **59** - Drazen Ladic 1990-99 & Jerko Leko 2002-

Goals
45 - Davor Suker 1990-2002 • **22** - Eduardo da Silva 2004- • **19** - Darijo Srna 2002- • **15** - Goran Vlaovic 1992-2002; Niko Kranjcar 2004- & Ivica Olic 2002- • **14** - Niko Kovac 1996-2008 • **12** - Zvonimir Boban 1990-99; Ivan Klasnic 2004-; Mladen Petric 2001- & Franjo Wolfl 1940-44 • **10** - Bosko Balaban 2000-07; Alen Boksic 1993-2002 & Robert Prosinecki 1993-2002

Past Coaches
Drazan Jerkovic 1990-91 • Stanko Poklepovic 1992 • Vlatko Markovic 1993 • Miroslav Blazevic 1994-2000 • Mirko Jozic 2000-02 • Otto Baric 2002-04 • Zlatko Kranjcar 2004-06 • Slaven Bilic 2006-

CROATIA 2010–11

PRVA HNL OZUJSKO (1)

Team	Pl	W	D	L	F	A	Pts	Dinamo	Hajduk	Radniki	Cibalia	Inter Zapresic	Karlovac	Slaven	Osijek	Rijeka	Zadar	Varazdin	Sibenik	NK Zagreb	Lokomotiva	Istra	Hrvatski
Dinamo Zagreb †	30	22	6	2	52	12	72		2-0	1-1	2-0	1-0	4-2	0-0	1-0	1-2	1-0	1-1	1-0	1-0	1-0	4-0	4-1
Hajduk Split ‡	30	16	7	7	54	32	55	1-1		3-1	1-2	0-0	2-3	1-0	2-1	1-1	4-1	2-0	2-0	4-1	2-0	6-1	2-1
Radniki Split ‡	30	16	5	9	38	22	53	0-1	1-1		2-1	1-1	0-1	3-0	1-0	2-3	3-2	4-0	1-0	2-0	1-0	2-0	1-0
Cibalia Vinkovci	30	12	8	10	33	24	44	0-1	2-1	0-1		1-0	1-0	1-2	3-0	4-1	0-0	2-0	3-1	2-2	2-1	1-0	3-0
Inter Zapresic	30	12	6	12	31	35	42	0-3	0-5	0-2	2-1		0-0	0-1	1-0	1-1	1-0	2-0	3-2	0-2	5-0	3-1	3-2
NK Karlovac	30	11	8	11	25	27	41	0-1	1-1	1-0	0-0	3-0		1-0	1-0	0-1	1-0	1-0	1-1	2-1	1-2	1-1	2-0
Slaven B. Koprivnica	30	10	10	10	34	30	40	0-2	1-2	1-2	1-1	0-0	4-0		2-1	0-1	2-0	1-0	1-0	1-2	2-2	2-1	3-0
NK Osijek	30	9	12	9	31	29	39	1-3	2-2	1-0	1-0	1-0	0-0	1-1		0-0	3-2	0-0	3-1	0-0	0-0	2-1	0-0
NK Rijeka	30	9	12	9	29	35	39	0-2	0-1	1-0	0-0	0-2	0-0	2-1	1-5		0-2	1-1	1-1	1-1	3-0	2-0	3-0
NK Zadar	30	11	5	14	31	34	38	0-0	0-2	1-0	0-0	1-0	2-0	1-1	1-1	1-0		3-0	1-4	2-1	1-0	2-0	1-0
NK Varazdin ‡	30	9	9	12	32	38	36	1-1	3-0	0-0	2-1	3-0	1-0	1-1	2-4	3-0	2-1		2-2	0-0	0-1	2-1	2-0
NK Sibenik	30	8	11	11	37	38	35	0-2	1-3	3-0	0-0	0-1	2-1	3-3	2-1	1-1	2-0	1-0		0-1	0-0	2-2	2-2
NK Zagreb	30	9	8	13	32	39	35	0-1	2-2	0-2	0-2	2-1	1-2	1-3	0-0	3-1	1-0	2-2	1-1		3-1	0-1	0-1
Lokomotiva Zagreb	30	8	9	13	24	37	33	0-2	0-1	0-0	2-0	2-4	0-0	0-0	0-0	3-2	1-2	0-0	2-0	1-0			3-2
Istra Pula	30	7	7	16	24	44	31	2-1	2-0	0-1	1-0	0-1	1-0	1-0	1-2	0-0	1-0	2-0	1-4	0-2	1-0		2-1
Hrvatski Dragovoljac	30	5	8	17	24	55	23	0-6	2-0	0-4	0-0	0-0	1-0	0-0	1-1	2-2	1-4	3-2	0-1	2-3	1-2	1-1	

23/07/2010 – 21/05/2011 • † Qualified for the UEFA Champions League • ‡ Qualified for the Europa League • Top scorers: 19 - Ivan Krstanovic BIH, NK Zagreb • 14 - Ante Vukusic, Hajduk • 11 - Mehmed Alispahic BIH, Sibenik; Nino Bule, Lokomotiva & Dino Kresinger, Cibalia

CROATIA 2010–11

DRUGA HNL (2)

Team	Pl	W	D	L	F	A	Pts	Gorica	Lucko	Pomorac	Rudes	Imotski	Solin	Medimurje	Dugopolje	Junak	Vinogradar	Sesvete	MV Croatia	HASK	Mosor	Vukovar	Suhopolje
HNK Gorica	30	20	4	6	54	21	64		2-0	2-1	3-1	3-1	4-0	3-1	1-0	2-0	2-0	1-0	3-1	2-2	4-0	3-0	4-0
NK Lucko	30	19	2	9	54	28	59	2-1		2-1	0-1	3-0	2-1	3-1	1-0	3-2	1-0	1-0	2-0	3-1	3-0	4-0	2-1
Pomorac Kostrena	30	16	8	6	50	23	56	2-0	5-2		3-1	2-1	3-0	4-1	2-1	1-0	3-0	2-0	1-0	3-1	3-1	6-0	0-0
Rudes Zagreb	30	15	7	8	52	39	52	1-1	3-1	2-1		1-1	1-0	4-2	3-0	2-2	1-0	2-0	4-0	2-1	0-0	1-2	4-2
NK Imotski	30	14	6	10	35	32	48	1-0	1-0	0-0	1-0		2-1	2-1	0-1	0-0	1-2	3-1	1-0	1-0	1-0	3-1	4-0
NK Solin	30	13	6	11	35	33	45	2-0	1-0	1-1	2-3	2-0		1-0	3-1	0-1	1-0	1-2	1-2	2-0	2-1	5-1	2-0
Medimurje Cakovec	30	12	6	12	53	49	42	0-2	0-2	2-1	3-0	1-1	1-0		1-1	3-1	2-2	3-2	2-1	1-1	3-1	10-0	5-0
NK Dugopolje	30	10	11	9	39	30	41	2-0	1-1	1-1	2-0	2-2	0-0	0-0		2-2	4-0	5-1	0-0	3-0	2-1	3-0	2-0
Junak Sinj	30	10	10	10	40	34	40	0-2	3-1	1-1	2-0	3-0	1-0	1-1	0-1		3-1	1-1	1-1	3-1	1-1	3-1	2-0
Vinogradar Lokosin Dol	30	12	4	14	43	38	40	0-1	0-0	2-0	1-1	4-1	1-1	4-0	3-0	3-1		1-2	2-0	1-0	2-0	4-1	4-1
Croatia Sesvete	30	12	4	14	37	41	40	0-1	1-0	0-0	1-1	1-1	1-2	1-0	1-0	1-0	3-2		3-1	2-1	1-0	4-0	4-0
MV Croatia	30	11	6	13	42	42	39	1-1	1-0	1-0	1-3	1-0	1-1	1-2	2-2	2-1	2-1	1-3		1-1	4-0	5-1	1-0
HASK Zagreb	30	11	5	14	40	42	38	2-1	0-2	0-0	4-1	0-1	2-0	3-1	1-1	2-0	2-0	3-2	3-2		2-0	3-0	1-0
Mosor Zrnovnica	30	9	7	14	32	41	34	1-1	0-2	1-1	2-2	1-0	6-0	1-1	0-0	3-0	1-0	3-2				2-0	3-0
HNK Vukovar '91	30	6	2	22	21	83	20	0-2	1-4	0-1	0-3	0-2	1-1	0-3	1-0	0-2	1-0	**3-0**	2-7	2-0	0-0		3-0
NK Suhopolje	30	5	2	23	22	73	17	0-1	2-0	0-7	0-1	1-4	1-2	3-0	1-3	2-1	1-1	2-3	1-0	0-2	2-1	1-2	

21/08/2010 – 29/05/2011 • Match in bold awarded • Gorica did not obtain a licence for the top level
Top scorers: 19 - Hrvoje Tokic, Mosor/MV Croatia • 15 - Nikola Buckovic, Vinogradar • 14 - Matej Jelic, Lucko & Marko Tadic, Rudes

MEDALS TABLE

	Club	Overall			League			Cup			Europe			City
		G	S	B	G	S	B	G	S	B	G	S	B	
1	Dinamo Zagreb	24	7	2	13	3	2	11	4					Zagreb
2	Hajduk Split	11	15	1	6	11	1	5	4					Split
3	NK Rijeka	2	3	2		2	2	2	1					Rijeka
4	NK Zagreb	1	3	3	1	2	3	1						Zagreb
5	Inter Zapresic	1	1			1		1						Zapresic
6	NK Osijek	1		6					6	1				Osijek
7	NK Varazdin		6	3			3		6					Varazdin
8	Slaven Belupo			2			1			1				Koprivnica

CROATIAN CLUBS IN YUGOSLAV FOOTBALL

	Club	Overall			League			Cup			Europe			
3	Hajduk Split	19	16	11	9	10	10	9	5		1	1	1	
4	Dinamo Zagreb	12	20	8	4	12	6	8	8				2	

HRVATSKOG NOGOMETNOG KUPA 2010-11

First Round

Dinamo Zagreb *	6
Zadrugar *	0
Moslavina	0
NK Karlovac *	5
NK Sibenik	4
Slavija Pleternica *	3
MV Croatia *	1
NK Osijek	2
NK Zagreb	2
Vrbovec *	0
Granicar *	0
Pomorac Kostrena	2
NK Suhopolje *	3
Segesta	1
Opatija *	0
Slaven B. Koprivnica	2
Cibalia Vinkovci	3
Rudes Zagreb *	0
Lokomotiva Zagreb *	1
Inter Zapresic	2
Hajduk Split	10
Rudar 47 *	2
Hrvatski Dragovoljac	1
Istra Pula *	3
NK Rijeka *	4
Nosteria *	2
Konavljanin	1
Medimurje Cakovec *	3
HASK Zagreb	4
Zagora Unesic *	2
BSK Bijelo Brdo *	0
NK Varazdin	2

Round of 16

Dinamo Zagreb	2
NK Karlovac *	0
NK Sibenik	1
NK Osijek *	2
NK Zagreb	1
Pomorac Kostrena *	0
NK Suhopolje	0
Slaven B. Koprivnica *	2
Cibalia Vinkovci	3
Inter Zapresic *	0
Hajduk Split *	0
Istra Pula	1
NK Rijeka *	3
Medimurje Cakovec	1
HASK Zagreb	0
NK Varazdin *	1

Quarter-finals

Dinamo Zagreb *	2	3
NK Osijek	0	1
NK Zagreb *	1	1
Slaven B. Koprivnica	1	5
Cibalia Vinkovci	3	2
Istra Pula *	2	0
NK Rijeka	1	2
NK Varazdin *	2	4

Semi-finals

Dinamo Zagreb *	4	1
Slaven B. Koprivnica	1	0
Cibalia Vinkovci *	1	0
NK Varazdin	0	3

Final

Dinamo Zagreb	5	3
NK Varazdin ‡	1	1

CUP FINAL 1ST LEG

Maksimir, Zagreb

11-05-2011, 20:10, Att: 5000, Ref: Ivan Bebek

Scorers - Sammir [10], Tonel [45], Beciraj 2 [72 79], Badelj [80] for Dinamo; Dino Skvorc [35] for Varteks

Dinamo - Ivan Kelava - Sime Vrsaljko, Tonel, Leandro Cufre, Luis Ibanez - Milan Badelj, Adrian Calello• - Ante Rukavina (Arijan Ademi 81), Sammir (Josip Brezovec 85), Pedro Morales (Ivan Tomecak 65) - Fatos Beqiraj.
Tr: Marijo Tot

Varteks - Denis Krklec - Karlo Simek, Dino Skvorc, Adam Susac, Josip Kvesic - Mario Brlecic, Nikola Safaric - Srebrenko Posavec (Dominik Glavina 75), Filip Skvorc, Josip Golubar - Davor Vugrinec (Dejan Glavica 65).
Tr: Samir Toplak

CUP FINAL 2ND LEG

Andelko Herjavec, Varazdin

25-05-2011, 20:10, 3500, Ref: Domagoj Vuckov

Scorers - Safaric 6 for Varteks; Ibanez 10, Badelj 70, Beciraj 82 for Dinamo

Varazdin - Denis Krklec (Ante Mrmic 73) - Nikola Halcic, Mario Brlecic, Dino Skvorc, Roberto Puncec• Josip Kvesic - Adnan Aganovic, Dejan Glavica (Josip Golubar 61), Nikola Safaric (Sasa Hojski 77) - Dominik Glavina•, Filip Skvorc•. Tr: Samir Toplak

Dinamo - Ivan Kelava - Sime Vrsaljko• (Leonard Mesaric 73), Tonel, Luis Ezequiel Ibanez - Milan Badelj•, Mathias Chago• - Ante Rukavina (Fatos Beqiraj 57), Sammir, Arijan Ademi• Mateo Kovacic (Josip Brezovec 79), Ivan Tomecak. Tr: Marijo Tot

* Home team/home team in the first leg • ‡ Qualified for the UEFA Europa League

CTA – CENTRAL AFRICAN REPUBLIC

FIFA/COCA-COLA WORLD RANKING

'93	'94	'95	'96	'97	'98	'99	'00	'01	'02	'03	'04	'05	'06	'07	'08	'09	'10	'11	'12
157	174	180	183	188	192	175	176	182	179	177	180	183	179	182	199	200	111	129	

					2011									
Jan	Feb	Mar	Apr	May	Jun	Jul	Aug	Sep	Oct	Nov	Dec	High	Low	Av
112	114	112	114	113	91	90	104	111	125	128	129	90	202	177

2011 was a year without precedent for football in the Central African Republic, reaching heights never attained before in their modest history. Although it all came to nothing in the end, the national team were mathematically still in the running for a place at the 2012 CAF Africa Cup of Nations finals right up to the last round of qualifiers in October - a unique situation for 'Les Fauves'. Ultimately their 2-0 loss in Algeria meant Morocco qualified top of the group but by beating Tanzania in mid-year, with a last minute goal by Charlie Dopekoulouyen for a 2-1 home triumph, and then holding Morocco to a 0-0 draw in Bangui in September, football was given an enormous boost in the country. The victory over Tanzania also saw the team reach a record high of 90 in the FIFA/Coca-Cola World Ranking which meant they avoided the preliminary stage of the 2014 FIFA World Cup qualifiers and went straight into a group with Botswana, Ethiopia and South Africa. Veteran French coach Jules Accorsi had begun the confidence-boosting run with a win at home over Algeria, fresh from the FIFA World Cup finals in South Africa, and kept it going through the rest of the campaign. At home DCF8 were crowned league champions for the second time in three years but were denied the double when they lost the Cup Final to Tempête Mocaf.

CAF AFRICA CUP OF NATIONS RECORD

1957-1972 DNE 1974 DNQ 1976-1986 DNE 1988 DNQ 1990-1996 DNE 1998 DNQ 2000 DNE 2002-2004 DNQ 2006-2010 DNE 2012 DNQ

FEDERATION CENTRAFRICAINE DE FOOTBALL (RCA)

Avenue de Martyrs,
Boite Postale 344, Bangui

☎ +236 70169828

✉ fedefoot60@yahoo.fr

FA 1961 CON 1965 FIFA 1963
P Edouard Patrice Ngaissona
GS Elie Delphin Feidangamo

FIFA BIG COUNT 2006

Total players	192 404
% of population	4.47%
Male	183 004
Female	9 400
Amateurs 18+	5 200
Youth under 18	3 200
Unregistered	13 000
Professionals	4
Referees	360
Admin & coaches	3 250
Number of clubs	80
Number of teams	400

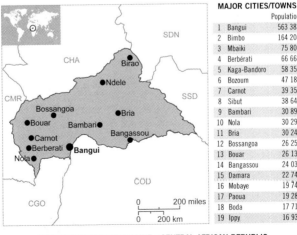

MAJOR CITIES/TOWNS

		Population
1	Bangui	563 383
2	Bimbo	164 208
3	Mbaiki	75 809
4	Berbérati	66 668
5	Kaga-Bandoro	58 353
6	Bozoum	47 187
7	Carnot	39 353
8	Sibut	38 643
9	Bambari	30 894
10	Nola	30 292
11	Bria	30 241
12	Bossangoa	26 259
13	Bouar	26 134
14	Bangassou	24 039
15	Damara	22 749
16	Mobaye	19 742
17	Paoua	19 282
18	Boda	17 719
19	Ippy	16 936

REPUBLIQUE CENTRAFRICAINE • CENTRAL AFRICAN REPUBLIC

Capital Bangui	Population 4 511 488 (120)	% in cities 39%
GDP per capita $700 (221)	Area km² 622 984 km² (44)	GMT +/- +1
Neighbours (km) Cameroon 797, Chad 1197, Congo DR 1577, Congo 467, Sudan 1165		

RECENT INTERNATIONAL MATCHES PLAYED BY THE CENTRAL AFRICAN REPUBLIC

2003	Opponents		Score	Venue	Comp	Scorers	Att	Referee
4-05	Congo	L	1-2	Brazzaville	CNq	Igor Makita [84]		
8-06	Congo	D	0-0	Bangui	CNq			Hissene CHA
22-06	Mozambique	L	0-1	Maputo	CNq		15 000	
6-07	Burkina Faso	L	0-3	Bangui	CNq			
7-12	Cameroon	D	2-2	Brazzaville	CMr1	Armel Oroko [10], Sandjo [30]		Mbera GAB
9-12	Cameroon	W	1-0	Brazzaville	CMr1	Sandjo [85]		Mandioukouta CGO
11-12	Gabon	W	2-0	Brazzaville	CMsf			
13-12	Cameroon	L	2-3	Brazzaville	CMf	Armel Oroko [63], Cyr Destin [74]		Bansimba CGO
2004								
No international matches played in 2004								
2005								
3-02	Gabon	L	0-4	Libreville	CMr1			
5-02	Congo	L	0-1	Libreville	CMr1			
2006								
6-03	Cameroon	L	0-2	Malabo	CMr1			
8-03	Gabon	D	2-2	Malabo	CMr1			
2007								
6-03	Chad	L	2-3	N'Djamena	CMr1	Hilaire Momi [14], Greyanda Fiacre [34]		
8-03	Cameroon	D	0-0	N'Djamena	CMr1			
12-03	Congo	L	1-4	N'Djamena	CMsf	Zinda Romaric [15]		
16-03	Chad	L	0-1	N'Djamena	CM3p			
2008								
No international matches played in 2008								
2009								
No international matches played in 2009								
2010								
4-09	Morocco	D	0-0	Rabat	CNq			Coulibaly MLI
10-10	Algeria	W	2-0	Bangui	CNq	Charlie Dopekoulouyen [81], Hilaire Momi [85]		Carvalho ANG
2011								
26-03	Tanzania	L	1-2	Dar es Salaam	CNq	Vianney Mabide [13]		
29-05	Tunisia	L	0-3	Sousse	Fr			
5-06	Tanzania	W	2-1	Bangui	CNq	Hilaire Momi [38], Charlie Dopekoulouyen [89]		
10-08	Malta	L	1-2	Ta'Qali	Fr	Hilaire Momi [25]		Ozkalfa TUR
4-09	Morocco	D	0-0	Bangui	CNq			
7-09	Equatorial Guinea	L	0-3	Malabo	Fr			
9-10	Algeria	L	0-2	Blida	CNq			

CN = CAF African Cup of Nations • CM = CEMAC Cup
q = qualifier • r1 = first round group • sf = semi-final • 3p = third place play-off • f = final

COUPE BARTHELEMY BOGANDA 2011

Semi-finals		Finals	
Tempête Mocaf	3		
Ouaka	1		
		Tempête Mocaf	2
		DFC8	1
Lobaye	0		
DFC8	4		

COUPE BARTHELEMY BOGANDA FINAL

Complex Sportif Barthelemy Boganda, Bangui, 1-12-2011, Att: 15 000

Tempête Mocaf	2-1	DFC8

Scorers - Romaric Oubangui [15], Stephane Sacre Senouss [100] for Tempête Mocaf; Ledesstin Bongolo [53] for DFC8

CUB – CUBA

FIFA/COCA-COLA WORLD RANKING

'93	'94	'95	'96	'97	'98	'99	'00	'01	'02	'03	'04	'05	'06	'07	'08	'09	'10	'11	'12
159	175	96	68	88	107	77	77	76	71	75	76	75	46	71	79	119	62	115	

						2011										
	Jan	Feb	Mar	Apr	May	Jun	Jul	Aug	Sep	Oct	Nov	Dec		High	Low	Av
	62	65	64	82	81	102	100	99	103	100	92	115		46	175	89

2011 was a far from vintage year for the Cuba national team and given their poor form it was fortunate that they were given a bye through to the second group stage of qualifying for the 2014 FIFA World Cup. Of particular concern was the abject performance of the team in the finals of the 2011 CONCACAF Gold Cup during which they were on the receiving end of three very heavy defeats. Cuba opened their campaign with a 5-0 reverse at the hands of Costa Rica in Arlington, a score that was repeated in the next game against Mexico. Perhaps most embarrassingly of all, however, was their performance in the final group match against El Salvador who beat them 6-1. Visiting the USA, where the Gold Cup is traditionally held, is always a difficult experience for the Cuban authorities and at the tournament Yosniel Mesa defected, as did Yisel Rodriguez and Yezenia Gallardo - members of the women's team - while playing at the CONCACAF Olympic qualifiers in Vancouver at the start of 2012. At home, the Campeonato Nacional was split into two divisions with promotion and relegation between the two but the play-offs to decide the champions were retained and it was Villa Clara who emerged victorious to take their record tally of titles to 11 after beating Guantánamo 3-0 on aggregate in the final.

FIFA WORLD CUP RECORD

1930 DNE 1934 DNQ **1938** 8 QF 1950-1962 DNE 1966 DNQ 1970-1974 DNE 1978-1982 DNQ 1986 DNE 1990 DNQ 1994 DNE 1998-2014 DNQ

ASOCIACION DE FUTBOL DE CUBA (AFC)

Estadio Pedro Marrero,
Escuela Nacional de Futbol,
✉ Mario Lopez Avenida 41, 44
y 46,
Municipio Playa La Habana
☎ +53 7 2076440
📠 +53 7 2043563
📧 futbol@inder.cu
FA 1924 CON 1961 FIFA 1932
P Luis Hernandez
GS Luis Yero

FIFA BIG COUNT 2006

Total players	1 141 825
% of population	10.03%
Male	1 045 900
Female	95 925
Amateurs 18+	27 375
Unregistered	1 012 400
Professionals	100
Referees	225
Admin & coaches	5 030
Number of clubs	338
Number of teams	1 500

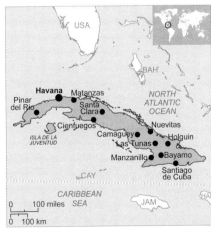

MAJOR CITIES/TOWNS

		Population
1	Havana	2 133 920
2	Santiago de Cuba	443 585
3	Camagüey	309 818
4	Holguín	291 638
5	Guantánamo	221 373
6	Santa Clara	219 713
7	Las Tunas	165 601
8	Bayamo	162 747
9	Cienfuegos	160 060
10	Pinar del Rio	158 392
11	Matanzas	139 765
12	Ciego de Ávila	121 769
13	Sancti Spíritus	113 739
14	Manzanillo	103 209
15	Cárdenas	97 402
16	Palma Soriano	77 471
17	Mayarí	65 425
18	Moa	64 618
19	Nueva Gerona	60 579

REPUBLICA DE CUBA • REPUBLIC OF CUBA

Capital	Havana	Population	11 451 652 (72)	% in cities	76%
GDP per capita	$9500 (108)	Area km²	110 860 km² (105)	GMT +/-	-5
Neighbours (km)	Coast 3735				

RECENT INTERNATIONAL MATCHES PLAYED BY CUBA

2007 Opponents		Score	Venue	Comp	Scorers	Att	Referee
8-06 Mexico	L	1-2	New Jersey	GCr1	Alcantara [22]	20 230	Aguilar SLV
10-06 Panama	D	2-2	New Jersey	GCr1	Jaime Colome [29], Alcantara [78]	68 123	Davis TRI
13-06 Honduras	L	0-5	Houston	GCr1		68 417	Aguilar SLV
2008							
22-02 Guyana	L	1-2	Linden	Fr	Alvarez [12]	1 000	Lancaster GUY
24-02 Guyana	D	0-0	Georgetown	Fr		2 500	James GUY
7-06 St Vincent/Grenadines	W	1-0	Havana	Fr		400	Duran CUB
17-06 Antigua and Barbuda	W	4-3	St John's	WCq	Jaime Colome 2 [10 74], Linares [22], Duarte [85]	4 500	Moreno PAN
22-06 Antigua and Barbuda	W	4-0	Havana	WCq	Linares 2 [9 53], Gonsalves OG [45], Marquez [69]	2 000	Quesada CRC
20-08 Trinidad and Tobago	L	1-3	Havana	WCq	Marquez [88]	4 000	Archundia MEX
6-09 USA	L	0-1	Havana	WCq		12 000	Aguilar SLV
10-09 Guatemala	L	1-4	Guatemala City	WCq	Linares [25]	19 750	Rodriguez MEX
11-10 USA	L	1-6	Washington DC	WCq	Munoz [31]	20 249	Moreno PAN
15-10 Guatemala	W	2-1	Havana	WCq	Jaime Colome [45p], Urgelles [90]	6 000	Campbell JAM
23-10 Netherlands Antilles	W	7-1	Havana	CCq	Duarte 2 [21 45], Marquez [25], Linares 2 [39 86], Jaime Colome [79], Clavelo [82]	1 000	Whittaker CAY
25-10 Barbados	D	1-1	Havana	CCq	Clavelo [68]	1 000	Campbell JAM
27-10 Suriname	W	6-0	Havana	CCq	Cervantes 2 [11 38], Marquez [47], Linares [54], Duarte [64], Dranguet [76]	1 000	Holder CAY
19-11 Trinidad and Tobago	L	0-3	Port of Spain	WCq		18 000	Wijngaarde SUR
4-12 Guadeloupe †	W	2-1	Montego Bay	CCr1	Fernandez [8], Linares [74]	2 500	Brizan TRI
6-12 Antigua and Barbuda	W	3-0	Trelawny	CCr1	Marquez [7], Linares [21], Jaime Colome [35]	1 000	Campbell JAM
8-12 Haiti	L	0-1	Montego Bay	CCr1		1 500	Brizan TRI
11-12 Grenada	D	2-2	Kingston	CCsf	Joel Colome [14], Linares [33]. L 5-6p	10 000	Moreno PAN
14-12 Guadeloupe †	D	0-0	Kingston	CC3p	L 4-5p	9 000	Taylor BRB
2009							
No international matches played in 2009							
2010							
26-10 Panama	W	3-0	Pamama City	Fr	Marquez [44], Coroneaux 2 [45 90]	2 116	Moreno PAN
10-11 Dominica	W	4-2	St John's	CCq	Coroneaux [9], Fernandez [20], Joel Colome [27], Hernandez [35]	500	Lancaster GUY
12-11 Suriname	D	3-3	St John's	CCq	Coroneaux [45], Cervantes [65], Ramos [87]	400	Campbell JAM
14-11 Antigua and Barbuda	D	0-0	St John's	CCq		500	Campbell JAM
26-11 Trinidad and Tobago	W	2-0	Fort-de-France	CCr1	Jaime Colome [23], Linares [79]	5 000	Lancaster GUY
28-11 Martinique †	W	1-0	Fort-de-France	CCr1	Marquez [29]	500	Taylor BRB
30-11 Grenada	D	0-0	Fort-de-France	CCr1		2 000	Bogle JAM
3-12 Guadeloupe †	L	1-2	Fort-de-France	CCsf	Fernandez [35]	2 001	Wijngaarde SUR
5-12 Grenada	W	1-0	Fort-de-France	CC3p	Linares [12]	4 000	Lopez GUA
2011							
24-03 El Salvador	L	0-1	Havana	Fr		3 500	Rodriguez PAN
29-03 Panama	L	0-2	Havana	Fr		6 000	Espana GUA
26-05 Nicaragua	D	1-1	Havana	Fr	Hernandez [90]	3 500	Brea CUB
28-05 Nicaragua	W	2-1	Havana	Fr	Hernandez [10], Lahera [17]	2 950	Rubalcaba CUB
5-06 Costa Rica	L	0-5	Arlington	GCr1		80 108	Moreno PAN
9-06 Mexico	L	0-5	Charlotte	GCr1		46 012	Campbell JAM
12-06 El Salvador	L	1-6	Chicago	GCr1	Marquez [83]	62 000	Brizan TRI
11-12 Costa Rica	D	1-1	Havana	Fr	Cordovez [57p]	10 000	Lopez GUA

Fr = Friendly match • CC = Caribbean Championship • GC = CONCACAF Gold Cup • WC = FIFA World Cup • q = qualifier
r1 = first round group • sf = semi-final • 3p = third place play-off • † Not a full international

CUBA NATIONAL TEAM HISTORICAL RECORDS

Coaches
Jose Tapia 1930-38 • Marcelino Minsal 1947-49 • Frantisek Churda CZE 1963-64 • Karoly Kocza HUN 1966 • Laszlo Mohaczy HUN 1967 • Kim Yong Ha PRK 1970-71 • Sergio Padron 1976 • Tibor Ivanicz 1980-81 • Giovanni Campari ITA 1990-92 • William Bennett 1998 • Miguel Company PER 2000-04 • Armelio Luis 2005 • Reinhold Fanz GER 2006-08 • Raul Gonzalez 2008-

CUBA 2011

CAMPEONATO NACIONAL DE FUTBOL	Pl	W	D	L	F	A	Pts	Camagüey	Villa Clara	Ciudad Habana	Guantánamo	Las Tunas	Ciego de Avila	Cienfuegos	La Habana
Camagüey †	14	6	5	3	18	9	23		1-0	1-0	1-3	2-0	0-1	5-0	4-0
Villa Clara †	14	6	4	4	16	10	22	0-0		0-0	2-1	3-1	2-1	3-0	1-1
Ciudad de La Habana†	14	5	6	3	18	13	21	1-1	2-3		0-0	0-0	4-1	0-0	1-1
Guantánamo †	14	5	6	3	16	13	21	0-0	1-0	1-2		1-1	2-1	3-0	0-0
Las Tunas	14	4	5	5	17	18	17	1-1	1-0	2-3	1-1		1-0	1-2	1-0
Ciego de Avila	14	5	2	7	13	15	17	1-1	1-0	2-0	3-0	2-0		0-0	0-1
Cienfuegos ‡	14	4	4	6	12	21	16	2-0	0-2	0-1	1-1	3-3	2-0		2-0
La Habana	14	3	4	7	9	20	13	0-1	0-0	1-4	1-2	0-4	2-0	2-0	

5/02/2011 - 16/06/2011 • † Qualified for the semi-finals • ‡ Relegation play-off
Relegation play-off: Isla de la Juventud 1-1 1-4 Cienfuegos. Both clubs remain in the same division

CAMPEONATO NACIONAL DE FUTBOL PLAY-OFFS

Semi-finals   **Finals**

Villa Clara   3 3
Ciudad Habana   3 21

	Villa Clara	2 1
	Guantánamo	0 0

Camagüey   2 3   3rd place:
Guantánamo   2 4   **Ciudad Habana** 4-0 Camagüey

CAMPEONATO NACIONAL FINAL
1st leg. 2-07-2011
Villa Clara   2-0   Guantánamo
Scorers - Yenier Márquez [44], Reydenis Duenas [83] for Villa Clara

CAMPEONATO NACIONAL FINAL
2nd leg. 5-07-2011
Guantánamo   0-1   **Villa Clara**
Scorer - Reydenis Duenas [83] for Villa Clara

CUBA 2011

TORNEO DE ASCENSO (2)	Pl	W	D	L	F	A	Pts	Granma	Juventud	Holguín	Santiago	Matanzas	Pinar del Río	Sancti Sp'tus
Granma	12	7	4	1	18	9	25		2-0	3-1	1-1	1-0	2-2	2-0
Isla de la Juventud †	12	7	3	2	14	7	24	1-0		2-1	0-0	1-0	1-0	2-0
Holguín	12	5	5	2	14	8	20	1-1	1-1		1-1	1-0	1-0	1-0
Santiago de Cuba	12	3	8	1	8	5	17	1-1	0-1	0-0		1-0	1-0	0-0
Matanzas	12	3	2	7	10	16	11	0-1	5-2	0-4	0-0		1-1	1-0
Pinar del Río	12	2	3	7	8	13	9	0-1	0-0	0-2	0-2	1-2		1-0
Sancti Spíritus	12	1	3	8	4	18	6	2-3	1-0	0-0	1-1	0-4	0-3	

3/05/2011 - 30/06/2011 • † Qualified for the promotion play-off

MEDALS TABLE						
		Overall	Lge	CON'CAF		City/Town
		G	G	G	S B	
1	Villa Clara	11	11			Santa Clara
2	DC Gallego	8	8			Havana
	Real Iberia	8	8			Havana
4	Pinar del Río	7	7		2	Pinar del Río
5	Ciudad de La Habana	6	6			Havana
	Dep. San Francisco	6	6			San Francisco
7	Granjeros	5	5			Granjeros
	Hispano America	5	5			Havana
9	Industriales	4	4			Havana
	La Habana	4	4			Havana
	Cienfuegos	4	4			Cienfuegos
	Ciego de Avila	4	4			Ciego de Avila

CUW – CURACAO

FIFA/COCA-COLA WORLD RANKING

'93	'94	'95	'96	'97	'98	'99	'00	'01	'02	'03	'04	'05	'06	'07	'08	'09	'10	'11	'12
128	152	125	142	156	156	167	175	183	177	188	163	168	177	183	152	168	151	151	

	2011												High	Low	Av
	Jan	Feb	Mar	Apr	May	Jun	Jul	Aug	Sep	Oct	Nov	Dec			
	150	150	146	152	152	150	157	166	178	171	149	151	98	188	

Curacao celebrated its first full year as an independent member of FIFA for over 60 years after taking over the Netherlands Antilles affiliation to FIFA but with half of the population to call on, it remains to be seen if football will be critically weakened or whether the new identity will inspire a new generation of players. The national team travelled to San Cristobal in the Dominican Republic for a first official appearance as Curacao since March 1948 but the focus for the year was the 2014 FIFA World Cup qualifying campaign that began in September. Drawn in a first round group with Antigua, Haiti and the US Virgin Islands, Curacao got off to a poor start by losing their first three matches although there was a draw in Port-au-Prince and then two comfortable wins over the Virgin Islands to celebrate in the final three. There was huge controversy at the end of the 2010-11 club championship when the Hubentut Fortuna player Anthony Espacia failed a drugs test before the final against Centro Barber. Hubentut went on to win the match on penalties after a 2-2 draw but Centro Barber contested both the result and a third test which proved negative. The dispute rumbled on until three months later when a replay took place. The result, however, was the same with Hubentut winning a third consecutive title thanks to a 1-0 victory on the night.

FIFA WORLD CUP RECORD
1930-1954 DNE 1958-2014 DNQ

FEDERASHON FUTBOL KORSOU (FFK)

Bonamweg 49, PO Box 341, Willemstad, Curaçao
☎ +599 97365040
📠 +599 97365047
✉ navusoccer@interneeds.net
🖥 www.cura.net/ffk
FA 1921 CON 1961 FIFA 1932
P Rignaal Francisca
GS Franklin Mathilda

FIFA BIG COUNT 2006

Total players	4220
% of population	1.90%
Male	3940
Female	280
Amateurs 18+	780
Youth under 18	980
Unregistered	2400
Professionals	0
Referees	42
Admin & coaches	320
Number of clubs	40
Number of teams	75

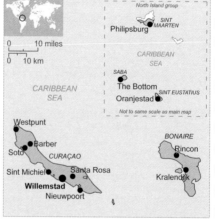

MAJOR CITIES/TOWNS

		Population
1	Willemstad	101 096
2	Princess Quarter	16 081
3	Cul De Sac	10 435
4	Cole Bay	8 006
5	Sint Michiel	5 323
6	Montaña Abou	4 390
7	Tera Cora	3 797
8	Montaña Rey	3 699
9	Souax	3 618
10	Kralendijk	3 265
11	Antriol	3 157
12	Little Bay	2 881
13	Groot Piscadera	2 669
14	Barber	2 511
15	Labadera	2 441
16	Soto	2 059

Bold = Curaçao
Italic = Sint Maarten
Underlined = Bonaire

KORSOU • CURACAO

Capital	Willemstad	Population	142 180 (187)	% in cities	93%
GDP per capita	$15 000 (75)	Area km²	444 km² (199)	GMT +/-	-4
Neighbours (km)	Coast 364 (includes Bonaire, Curacao, Saba, Sint Eustatius & Sint Maarten)				

RECENT INTERNATIONAL MATCHES PLAYED BY CURACAO

2009	Opponents	Score		Venue	Comp	Scorers	Att	Referee
28-10	French Guiana ‡	L	1-4	Paramaribo	Fr	Riangelo Rodriguez [41]	500	Wijngaarde SUR
30-10	Guyana	L	0-1	Paramaribo	Fr		500	Pinas SUR
1-11	Suriname	D	1-1	Paramaribo	Fr	Lisandro Trenidad [28]	2 500	
2010								
13-10	Suriname	L	1-2	Paramaribo	CCq	Lacey Pauletta [81]	800	Willet ATG
15-10	Guyana	L	2-3	Paramaribo	CCq	Hujoybert Delando [74p], Kenneth Kunst [84]	750	Matthew SKN
17-10	St Lucia	D	2-2	Paramaribo	CCq	Lisandro Trenidad [30], Bryan Anastatia [89p]	2 800	Willet ATG
29-10	Aruba	W	3-0	Willemstad	Fr	Everon Espacia, Lisandro Trenidad, Giandro Steba		Dimie ANT
31-10	Suriname	D	2-2	Willemstad	Fr	Everon Espacia, Vilyson Lake. L 5-6p		
2011								
20-08	Dominican Republic	L	0-1	San Cristobal	Fr		250	Vasquez DOM
21-08	Dominican Republic	L	0-1	San Cristobal	Fr		300	Hidalgo DOM
2-09	Antigua and Barbuda	L	2-5	St John's	WCq	Rihairo Meulens [9], Richmar Siberie [74]	2 000	Santos PUR
6-09	Haiti	L	2-4	Willemstad	WCq	Orin De Waard [12], Angelo Zimmerman [43]	5 000	Solis CRC
23-09	Suriname	L	0-2	Paramaribo	Fr		2 000	Botland SUR
25-09	Suriname	D	2-2	Paramaribo	Fr	Mirco Colina 2 [27 66]	2 500	Pierau SUR
7-10	Antigua and Barbuda	L	0-1	Willemstad	WCq		2 563	Reyna GUA
11-10	Haiti	D	2-2	Port-au-Prince	WCq	Richmar Siberie [7], Sendley Bito [14]	7 800	Clarke LCA
11-11	US Virgin Islands	W	3-0	Frederikstad	WCq	Richmar Siberie 2 [8 14], Sendley Bito [26]	210	Navarro CAN
15-11	US Virgin Islands	W	6-1	Willemstad	WCq	Shanon Carmelia 2 [33 78], Richmar Siberie 2 [40 86], Everon Espacia [73], Angelo Cijntje [90]	2 000	Legister JAM
4-12	Suriname	L	0-2	Paramaribo	Fr		50	Angela ARU

Fr = Friendly match • CC = Digicel Caribbean Cup • WC = FIFA World Cup • q = qualifier • ‡ Not a full international

CURACAO 2010-11

SEKSHON PAGA FIRST STAGE

	Pl	W	D	L	F	A	Pts	Dominguito	J Holland	Hubentut	C Barber	Sithoc	VESTA	Victory	SUBT	Undeba	J Colombia
Centro Dominguito †	18	12	3	3	37	16	39		0-1	2-1	2-3	2-1	1-0	4-0	3-1	1-0	4-1
Jong Holland †	18	10	4	4	26	19	34	0-3		3-1	1-0	0-1	1-0	2-1	1-1	2-1	3-1
Hubentut Fortuna †	18	9	6	3	36	22	33	2-2	1-1		1-1	2-2	1-0	4-2	3-1	3-0	2-1
Centro Barber †	18	8	5	5	28	18	29	1-1	2-3	1-2		3-1	0-0	3-1	0-2	1-0	4-1
Sithoc †	18	6	6	6	28	24	24	0-2	0-1	1-1	1-1		1-1	3-1	1-1	3-1	1-1
VESTA †	18	5	8	5	17	19	23	2-1	0-0	1-1	0-0	1-4		0-3	1-1	0-0	2-0
Victory Boys	18	5	4	9	22	35	19	0-3	0-0	1-4	0-3	4-2	1-2		2-1	3-2	2-1
SUBT	18	4	6	8	25	30	18	2-3	2-4	0-3	2-1	2-1	1-3	0-0		1-1	5-0
Undeba	18	2	6	10	14	28	12	1-3	2-1	2-0	0-3	0-2	2-3	0-0	2-2		0-0
Jong Colombia	18	2	6	10	13	35	12	0-0	3-2	1-4	0-1	0-3	1-1	1-1	1-0	0-0	

28/11/2010 - 11/05/2011 • † Qualified for the Kaya 6

PLAY-OFF KAYA 6

	Pl	W	D	L	F	A	Pts	JH	Sit	CB	Ves	CD
Hubentut Fortuna †	5	3	0	2	11	6	9	2-0	3-4	1-2	3-0	2-0
Jong Holland †	5	3	0	2	5	4	9		2-0	0-1	1-0	2-1
Sithoc †	5	2	2	1	8	8	8			0-0	2-1	2-2
Centro Barber †	5	2	2	1	4	4	8				0-2	1-1
VESTA	5	2	0	3	5	7	6					2-1
Centro Dominguito	5	0	2	3	5	9	2					

13/05/2011 - 7/06/2011 • † Qualified for the Kaya 4

PLAY-OFF KAYA 4

	Pl	W	D	L	F	A	Pts	HF	JH	Sit
Centro Barber †	3	2	1	0	6	2	7	2-1	1-1	3-0
Hubentut Fortuna †	3	1	1	1	5	4	6		1-0	3-2
Jong Holland	3	0	2	1	2	3	2			1-1
Sithoc	3	0	1	2	3	7	1			

10/06/2011 - 23/06/2011 • † Qualified for the final

FINAL

Ergilio Hato, Willemstad, 28-09-2011

Hubentut Fortuna 1-0 Centro Barber

A first match, played on 26-06-2011, was declared void after a Hubentut player failed a drugs test. Hubentut had won 9-8 on penalties after a 2-2 draw

CYP – CYPRUS

FIFA/COCA-COLA WORLD RANKING

'93	'94	'95	'96	'97	'98	'99	'00	'01	'02	'03	'04	'05	'06	'07	'08	'09	'10	'11	'12
72	67	73	78	82	78	63	62	79	80	97	108	96	73	66	94	68	90	127	

2011															
Jan	Feb	Mar	Apr	May	Jun	Jul	Aug	Sep	Oct	Nov	Dec		High	Low	Av
89	91	91	89	90	80	80	76	86	120	126	127		43	127	79

Although the Cyprus national team has had its fair share of positive headlines in recent years, the qualifiers for Euro 2012 were seen as a return to the bad old days when the Cypriots were regarded as one of the whipping boys of European football. After a great opening match in which a last minute goal had earned them a 4-4 draw away to Portugal, the remaining seven matches yielded just one further point - a 0-0 draw at home to Iceland. After six and a half years as coach Angelos Anastasiadis was sacked after the defeat in a friendly to Bulgaria, but despite winning his first game in charge in a friendly over Moldova, new coach Nikos Nioplias oversaw a run of five straight defeats - their worst sequence of results for nearly 20 years. The mood was very different in club football, however, as the 2011 champions APOEL stunned the whole of European football by not only qualifying for the 2011-12 UEFA Champions League group stage but by then winning their group ahead of Zenit St Petersburg, Porto and Shakhtar Donetsk in what must rank as one of the greatest achievements in the history of Cypriot football. Earlier in the year APOEL had won the Cypriot championship with some ease - a record 21st triumph for the club - thanks to a cosmopolitan line-up that included four Brazilians and top scorer Esteban Solari from Argentina.

UEFA EUROPEAN CHAMPIONSHIP RECORD
1960-1964 DNE 1968-2012 DNQ

CYPRUS FOOTBALL ASSOCIATION (CFA)

10 Achaion Street,
2413 Engomi, 25071
Nicosia 1306

☎ +357 22 352341
📠 +357 22 590544
✉ info@cfa.com.cy
🖥 www.cfa.com
FA 1934 CON 1962 FIFA 1948
P Costakis Koutsokoumnis
GS Phivos Vakis

FIFA BIG COUNT 2006

Total players	52 403
% of population	6.68%
Male	47 768
Female	4 635
Amateurs 18+	10 091
Youth under 18	6 644
Unregistered	20 200
Professionals	800
Referees	200
Admin & coaches	2 000
Number of clubs	100
Number of teams	328

MAJOR CITIES/TOWNS

		Population
1	Nicosia	215 551
2	Limassol	169 507
3	Nicosia (T)	53 045
4	Larnaca	52 949
5	Paphos	42 296
6	Famagusta (T)	36 481
7	Girne (T)	29 723
8	Aradippou	16 155
9	Morphou (T)	13 324
10	Paralimni	13 052
11	Gönyeli	12 985
12	Geri	9 446
13	Ypsonas	8 715
14	Lefka (T)	8 456
15	Degirmenlik	8 114
16	Dali	7 008
17	Tseri	6 332
18	Lapta (T)	6 315
(T) = in Turkish controlled zone		

KYPRIAKI DIMOKRATIA • REPUBLIC OF CYPRUS

Capital Nicosia	Population 796 740 (159)	% in cities 70%
GDP per capita $21 300 (58)	Area km² 9 251 km² (170)	GMT +/- +2
Neighbours (km) Coast 648		

RECENT INTERNATIONAL MATCHES PLAYED BY CYPRUS

2007	Opponents	Score	Venue	Comp	Scorers	Att	Referee
22-08	San Marino	W 1-0	Serravalle	ECq	Okkas [54]	552	Janku ALB
8-09	Armenia	W 3-1	Larnaca	Fr	Michael [31], Okkas [42], Constantinou [52]		Trattos CYP
12-09	San Marino	W 3-0	Nicosia	ECq	Makridis [15], Aloneftis 2 [41 92+]	1 000	Kulbakov BLR
13-10	Wales	W 3-1	Nicosia	ECq	Okkas 2 [59 68], Charalampidis [79]	2 852	Bertolini SUI
17-10	Republic of Ireland	D 1-1	Dublin	ECq	Okkarides [80]	54 861	Vuorela FIN
17-11	Germany	L 0-4	Hanover	ECq		45 016	Rasmussen DEN
21-11	Czech Republic	L 0-2	Nicosia	ECq		5 866	Paniashvili GEO
2008							
6-02	Ukraine	D 1-1	Nicosia	Fr	Aloneftis [19p]	500	
19-05	Greece	L 0-2	Patras	Fr		16 216	MacDonald SCO
20-08	Switzerland	L 1-4	Geneva	Fr	Makridis [35]	14 500	Ceferin SVN
6-09	Italy	L 1-2	Larnaca	WCq	Aloneftis [28]	6 000	Vink NED
11-10	Georgia	D 1-1	Tbilisi	WCq	Konstantinou.M [67]	40 000	Matejak CZE
15-10	Republic of Ireland	L 0-1	Dublin	WCq		55 833	Tudor ROU
19-11	Belarus	W 2-1	Nicosia	Fr	Christofi [29], Avraam [48]		
2009							
10-02	Serbia	L 0-2	Nicosia	Fr			
11-02	Slovakia	W 3-2	Nicosia	Fr	Maragkos [32p], Nicolaou [74], Okkas [82]	300	
28-03	Georgia	W 2-1	Larnaca	WCq	Konstantinou.M [33], Christofi [56]	1 500	Fautrel FRA
1-04	Bulgaria	L 0-2	Sofia	WCq		16 916	Ingvarsson SWE
30-05	Canada	L 0-1	Larnaca	Fr			
6-06	Montenegro	D 2-2	Larnaca	WCq	Konstantinou.M [14], Michail [45p]	3 000	Velasco ESP
12-08	Albania	L 1-6	Tirana	Fr	Charalampidis		Yildirim TUR
5-09	Republic of Ireland	L 1-2	Nicosia	WCq	Ilia [30]	5 191	Einwaller AUT
9-09	Montenegro	D 1-1	Podgorica	WCq	Okkas [63]	4 000	Zimmermann SUI
10-10	Bulgaria	W 4-1	Larnaca	WCq	Charalampidis 2 [11 20], Konstantinou.M [58], Aloneftis [78]	3 700	Allaerts BEL
14-10	Italy	L 2-3	Parma	WCq	Makridis [12], Michail [48]	15 009	Yefet ISR
2010							
3-03	Iceland	D 0-0	Larnaca	Fr			Yordanov.N BUL
11-08	Andorra	W 1-0	Larnaca	Fr	Konstantinou [4]	1 700	Spathas GRE
3-09	Portugal	D 4-4	Guimaraes	ECq	Aloneftis [3], Konstantinou [11], Okkas [57], Avraam [89]	9 100	Clattenburg ENG
8-10	Norway	L 1-2	Larnaca	ECq	Okkas [58]	7 648	Gumienny BEL
12-10	Denmark	L 0-2	Copenhagen	ECq		15 544	Muniz ESP
16-11	Jordan	D 0-0	Amman	Fr		3 500	Ebrahim BHR
2011							
9-02	Romania	D 1-1	Paralimni	Fr	Konstantinou [84]. L 4-5p	2 500	Shvetov UKR
26-03	Iceland	D 0-0	Nicosia	ECq		2 088	Ceferin SVN
29-03	Bulgaria	L 0-1	Larnaca	Fr			Borg MLT
10-08	Moldova	W 3-2	Nicosia	Fr	Avraam 2 [13 51], Dobrasinovic [89]	2 000	Mazic SRB
2-09	Portugal	L 0-4	Nicosia	ECq		15 444	Rocchi ITA
6-09	Iceland	L 0-1	Reykjkavik	ECq		5 267	Jovanetic SRB
7-10	Denmark	L 1-4	Nicosia	ECq	Avraam [45]	2 408	Strahonja CRO
11-10	Norway	L 1-3	Oslo	ECq	Okkas [42]	13 490	Collum SCO
11-11	Scotland	L 1-2	Larnaca	Fr	Christofi [60]	2 000	Levi ISR

Fr = Friendly match • EC = UEFA EURO 2008/2012 • WC = FIFA World Cup • q = qualifier

CYPRUS NATIONAL TEAM HISTORICAL RECORDS

Caps
106 - Yiannis Okkas 1997- • 82 - Michalis Konstantinou 1998- & Pambos Pittas 1987-99 • 78 - Nicos Panayiotou 1994-2006 •
70 - Giorgos Theodotou 1996-2008 • 68 - Yiannis Yiangoudakis 1980-94 • 67 - Chrysis Michail 2000- • 64 - Kostas Charalambides 2003-
• 63 - Yiasemakis Yiasoumi 1998-2009 • 62 - Marinos Satsias 2000- • 60 - Marios Charalambous 1991-2002

Goals
32 - Michalis Konstantinou 1998- • 27 - Yiannis Okkas 1997- • 11 - Kostas Charalambides 2003- • 10 - Marios Agathokleous 1994-2003
• 9 - Efstathios Aloneftis 2005- • 8 - Andros Sotiriou 1991-99, Phivos Vrahimis 1977-82; Milenko Spoljaric 1997-2001 & Sinisa Gogic 1994-99

Past Coaches
Gyula Zsengeller HUN 1958-59 • Argyrios Gavalas GRE 1960-67 • Pambos Avraamidis 1968-69 • Ray Wood ENG 1969-71 • Sima Milovanov YUG 1972 • Pambos Avraamidis 1972-76 • Panikos Krystallis 1976-77 • Kostas Talianos GRE 1977-82 • Vassil Spasov BUL 1982-84 • Panikos Iakovou 1984-91 • Andreas Michaelides 1991-97 • Panikos Georgiou 1997-99 • Stavros Papadopoulos 1999-2001 • Momcilo Vukotic SRB 2001-04 • Angelos Anastasiadis GRE 2004-11 • Nikos Nioplias GRE 2011 -

CYPRUS 2010-11

MARFIN LAIKI A KATEGORIA (1)

	Pl	W	D	L	F	A	Pts	APOEL	Omonia	Anorthosis	AEK	Apollon	ENP	AEL	Olympiakos	Ethnikos	Alki	Ermis	AEP	Doxa	APOP
APOEL Nicosia †	32	24	2	6	63	22	74		3-0	2-0	2-1	0-1	1-0	3-0	2-1	2-1	2-0	4-1	0-1	1-0 5-1	3-1 6-2
Omonia Nicosia ‡	32	18	9	5	45	19	63	0-1 1-0		1-0	1-0 1-0-2-0 3-0	3-1	0-0	2-0	2-2	1-0	2-0	4-1	1-1	6-0	0-1
Anorthosis Famagusta ‡	32	16	7	9	51	34	55	2-0 1-2-0-0 0-0			2-1 2-0	1-2	3-1	4-0	2-1	1-1	1-2	4-0	1-1	4-1	3-0
AEK Larnaca ‡	32	12	6	14	37	42	42	1-2 0-1 1-2 1-2-3-0 0-1				2-2	0-2	0-0	1-1	1-1	0-2	2-1	2-1	2-0	3-2
Apollon Limassol	32	14	7	11	55	44	49	0-5	2-0	1-2	1-2		1-2	0-2	1-1	1-1	0-2	2-1	2-1	2-0	4-0 2-1
ENP Paralimni	32	12	8	12	33	34	44	1-0	0-1	0-0	0-2 2-1-2-1	1-1-2-3-1-3-1-0		1-2	0-2	3-1	2-1	1-0	4-0	2-1	
AEL Limassol	32	10	11	11	37	45	41	2-2	0-0	1-3	1-2 2-3-1-1-0-0-1-1		3-2-2-1		2-1	1-0	1-2	1-0	3-0	2-0	
Olympiakos Nicosia	32	10	11	11	48	53	41	1-2	0-2	2-2	2-3 2-1-2-2-1-1-1-1-0-2-2-1					3-2	1-1	3-2	2-2	1-0	1-1
Ethnikos Achnas	32	10	9	13	29	37	39	0-1	0-0	0-2	0-1	0-2	2-2	0-0	0-1		2-1-0-3-1-0-0-1-2-1-0-3	3-2	0-0		
Alki Larnaca	32	11	6	15	40	48	39	2-1	0-4	2-3	1-2	2-3	0-3	3-0	0-0 2-2-2-3			0-1-1-0-2-1-3	1-1	0-0	
Ermis Aradippou	32	9	11	12	38	45	38	0-2	0-0	3-0	1-1	2-2	1-0	0-0	2-2 1-1-0-3-1-1-2				2-2-3-3	2-1	1-1
AEP Paphos	32	8	11	13	44	44	35	1-1	1-1	1-2	2-0	1-0	0-1	2-2	1-3 0-1-0-1-1-2-1-1-3-1-1-1					5-0	0-0
Doxa Katokopia	26	5	5	16	25	55	20	0-1	2-3	2-2	1-4	1-1	1-0	0-0	1-2	0-2	3-0	1-0	2-1		4-3
APOP/Kinyras	26	4	7	15	24	47	19	0-5	0-1	3-1	0-0	2-1	0-2	3-4	1-3	1-0	1-2	1-3	1-0	1-1	

28/08/2010 - 14/05/2011 • † Qualified for the UEFA Champions League • ‡ Qualified for the Europa League • Match in bold awarded
Top scorers: 21 - Miljan Mrdakovic SRB, Apollon • 17 - Michalis Konstantinou, Omonia • 16 - Joao Paulo POR, Olympiakos • 13 - Cafu CPV, Anorthosis & Joeano BRA, Ermis • 11 - Ivan Trickovski MKD, APOEL; Esteban Solari ARG, APOEL & Emmanuel Kenmogne CMR, Olympiakos

CYPRUS 2010-11 B KATEGORIA (2)

	Pl	W	D	L	F	A	Pts
Aris Limassol	32	16	9	7	49	25	57
Nea Salamina	32	14	13	5	50	25	55
Anagennisi Dherynia	32	15	9	8	37	27	54
Omonia Aradippou	32	15	6	11	42	41	51
Othellos Athienou	26	10	11	5	28	22	41
Atromitas	26	12	4	10	35	26	40
PAEEK	26	10	6	10	36	36	36
Akritas Chloraka	26	9	7	10	34	38	34
APEP	26	8	9	9	33	34	33
Halkanoras Dhaliou	26	9	6	11	41	44	33
Onisilos Sotiras	26	8	8	10	26	30	32
ASIL	26	6	5	15	20	41	23
Digenis Morfu	26	5	6	15	24	45	21
Adonis Idalion	26	4	7	15	24	45	19

18/09/2010 - 15/05/2011

MEDALS TABLE

		Overall G	S	B	League G	S	B	Cup G	S
1	APOEL Nicosia	40	29	15	21	19	15	19	10
2	Omonia Nicosia	33	21	8	20	15	8	13	6
3	Anorthosis Famagusta	23	16	8	13	10	8	10	6
4	AEL Limassol	12	9	6	6	1	6	6	8
5	Apollon Limassol	9	11	4	3	4	4	6	7
6	EPA Larnaca	7	9	4	2	6	4	5	3
7	Olympiakos Nicosia	4	7	2	3	4	2	1	3
8	Trust AC	4	3					3	1
9	Pezoporikos Larnaca	3	15	14	2	8	14	1	7
10	Chetin Kaya	3	3	3	1	1	3	2	2
11	NEA Salamina	1	2	4			4	1	2
12	AEK Larnaca	1	2		-			1	2
13	APOP/Kinyras	1						1	
14	Union Paralimni (ENP)		5	2		1	2		4
15	Alki Larnaca		5	1		1			5
16	Digenis Morphou		2			1			1
17	Aris Limassol	1	1		1	1			1
18	Ethnikos Achnas	1							1

KYPELLO KYPROY 2010-11

Round of 16

Omonia Nicosia *	6	2
Atromitos Yeroskipou	0	2
AEL Limassol *	0	0
Aris Limassol	1	0
Alki Larnaca	1	4
ENP Paralimni *	0	3
Ermis Aradippou *	0	1
Ethnikos Achnas	1	1
Anorthosis Famagusta*	2	1
APEP	0	0
Doxa Katokopia *	0	1
AEK Larnaca	1	4
Olympiakos Nicosia	0	3
AEP Paphos *	0	1
APOEL Nicosia *	1	0
Apollon Limassol	1	2

Quarter-finals

Omonia Nicosia *	3	3
Aris Limassol	0	1
Alki Larnaca *	0	2
Ethnikos Achnas	3	0
Anorthosis Famagusta	2	1
AEK Larnaca *	1	1
Olympiakos Nicosia *	1	2
Apollon Limassol	1	3

Semi-finals

Omonia Nicosia *	1	1
Ethnikos Achnas	0	1
Anorthosis Famagusta	1	1
Apollon Limassol *	1	2

Final

Omonia Nicosia ‡	1	4p
Apollon Limassol	1	3p

* Home team in the first leg • ‡ Qualified for the Europa League

CUP FINAL
GSZ, Larnaca
18-05-2011, 13 000, Busacca SUI
Scorers - Michalis Konstantinou 12 for Omonia; OG 84 for Apollon

CZE – CZECH REPUBLIC

FIFA/COCA-COLA WORLD RANKING

'93	'94	'95	'96	'97	'98	'99	'00	'01	'02	'03	'04	'05	'06	'07	'08	'09	'10	'11	'12
-	34	14	5	3	8	2	5	14	15	6	4	2	10	6	11	25	30	33	

	2011											High	Low	Av
Jan	Feb	Mar	Apr	May	Jun	Jul	Aug	Sep	Oct	Nov	Dec			
30	30	31	32	32	36	38	42	40	47	33	33	2	67	13

The Czech Republic qualified for the finals of Euro 2012 in Poland and the Ukraine but never with the swagger and authority that has been a mark of the side in recent years. Admittedly they were grouped with world champions Spain but with three defeats and a draw in the eight games played the Czechs only clinched the play-off spot two points ahead of Scotland. They made sure of maintining their ever-present record in the finals with a 3-0 aggregate win over Montenegro but they will do well to repeat the heroics of reaching the final in 1996 and the semi-final in 2004 even though they have been drawn in the most open group in the finals along with Poland, Greece and Russia. At home there was a surprise first league title for Viktoria Plzen as the club celebrated its centenary in some style. In 2010 Viktoria had won their first-ever trophy by winning the cup and they started the new season by winning 11 games in a row under attack-minded coach Pavel Vrba, a run that meant they led the table from start to finish. The town of Plzen, and no doubt the famous beer which takes its name from the town, was then on the itinery for fans of Barcelona and Milan when the club then qualified for the group stage of the UEFA Champions League. There were also first time winners of the Czech Cup - Mlada Boleslav beating Sigma Olomouc in the final.

UEFA EUROPEAN CHAMPIONSHIP RECORD
1960 3 SF **1964** r1 **1968-1972** DNQ **1976** 1 Winners **1980** 3 **1984-1992** DNQ (as Czechoslovakia)
1996 2 F **2000** 10 r1 **2004** 3 SF **2008** 11 r1 **2012** Qualified

FOOTBALL ASSOCIATION OF CZECH REPUBLIC (CMFS)

Diskarska 2431,
PO Box 11,
Praha 16017
☎ +420 2 33029111
📠 +420 2 33353107
✉ facr@fotbal.cz
🖥 www.fotbal.cz
FA 1901 CON 1954 FIFA 1907
P Miroslav Pelta
GS Rudolf Repka

FIFA BIG COUNT 2006

Total players	1 040 357
% of population	10,16%
Male	976 355
Female	64 002
Amateurs 18+	435 605
Youth under 18	208 451
Unregistered	103 100
Professionals	1 558
Referees	4 351
Admin & coaches	8 530
Number of clubs	3 968
Number of teams	15 463

MAJOR CITIES/TOWNS

		Population
1	Prague	1 183 473
2	Brno	364 126
3	Ostrava	311 467
4	Plzen	164 845
5	Olomouc	101 081
6	Liberec	98 035
7	Hradec Králové	94 141
8	Ceske Budejovice	93 791
9	Usti nad Labem	93 680
10	Pardubice	87 164
11	Havirov	84 868
12	Zlin	78 055
13	Kladno	69 544
14	Most	68 416
15	Karvina	62 739
16	Frydek-Mistek	59 780
17	Opava	59 549
18	Decin	52 284
19	Teplice	52 193

CESKA REPUBLIKA • CZECH REPUBLIC

Capital Prague (Praha)	Population 10 211 904 (80)	% in cities 73%	
GDP per capita $25 900 (51)	Area km² 78 867 km² (115)	GMT +/- +1	
Neighbours (km) Austria 362, Germany 815, Poland 615, Slovakia 197			

RECENT INTERNATIONAL MATCHES PLAYED BY THE CZECH REPUBLIC

2008	Opponents	Score		Venue	Comp	Scorers	Att	Referee
7-06	Switzerland	W	1-0	Basel	ECr1	Sverkos [71]	39 730	Rosetti ITA
11-06	Portugal	L	1-3	Geneva	ECr1	Sionko [17]	29 016	Vassaras GRE
15-06	Turkey	L	2-3	Geneva	ECr1	Koller [34], Plasil [62]	29 016	Fröjdfeldt SWE
20-08	England	D	2-2	London	Fr	Baros [22], Jankulovski [48]	69 738	Hauge NOR
10-09	Northern Ireland	D	0-0	Belfast	WCq		12 882	Bebek CRO
11-10	Poland	L	1-2	Chorzow	WCq	Fenin [87]	38 293	Stark GER
15-10	Slovenia	W	1-0	Teplice	WCq	Sionko [62]	15 220	Atkinson ENG
19-11	San Marino	W	3-0	Serravalle	WCq	Kovac [47], Pospech [53], Necid [66]	1 318	Kaasik EST
2009								
11-02	Morocco	D	0-0	Casablanca	Fr		38 000	Alakim TUN
28-03	Slovenia	D	0-0	Maribor	WCq		12 500	Proença POR
1-04	Slovakia	L	1-2	Prague	WCq	Jankulovski [30]	14 956	Undiano ESP
5-06	Malta	W	1-0	Jablonec	Fr	Necid [77]	6 019	Fautrel Fra
12-08	Belgium	W	3-1	Teplice	Fr	Hubnik [27], Baros [42p], Rozehnal [78]	13 890	Sippel GER
5-09	Slovakia	D	2-2	Bratislava	WCq	Pudil [68], Baros [83]	23 800	Ovrebo NOR
9-09	San Marino	W	7-0	Uherske Hradiste	WCq	Baros 4 [28 44 45 66], Sverkos 2 [47 94+], Necid [86]	8 121	Amirkhanyan ARM
10-10	Poland	W	2-0	Prague	WCq	Necid [51], Plasil [72]	14 010	Larsen DEN
14-10	Northern Ireland	D	0-0	Prague	WCq		8 002	Duhamel FRA
15-11	UAE	D	0-0	Al Ain	Fr	L 2-3p	5 000	Dalkam JOR
18-11	Azerbaijan	L	0-2	Al Ain	Fr			Al Marzouqi UAE
2010								
3-03	Scotland	L	0-1	Glasgow	Fr		26 530	Fautrel FRA
22-05	Turkey	L	1-2	Harrison	Fr	Cerny [81]	16 371	Geiger USA
25-05	USA	W	4-2	East Hartford	Fr	Sivok [44], Polak [58], Fenin [77], Necid [90]	36 218	Morales MEX
11-08	Latvia	W	4-1	Liberec	Fr	Bednar [49], Fenin [54], Pospech [74], Necid [77]	7 456	Dankovsky UKR
7-09	Lithuania	L	0-1	Olomouc	ECq		12 038	Yefet ISR
8-10	Scotland	W	1-0	Prague	ECq	Hubnik [69]	14 922	Bebek CRO
12-10	Liechtenstein	W	2-0	Vaduz	ECq	Necid [12], Vaclav Kadlec [29]	2 555	Sukhina RUS
17-11	Denmark	D	0-0	Aarhus	Fr		9 184	Webb ENG
2011								
9-02	Croatia	L	2-4	Pila	Fr	Sivok [20], Rosicky [45]	9 500	Orsato ITA
25-03	Spain	L	1-2	Granada	ECq	Plasil [29]	16 301	Kassai HUN
29-03	Liechtenstein	W	2-0	Ceske Budejovice	ECq	Baros [3], Michal Kadlec [70]	6 600	Hategan ROU
4-06	Peru	D	0-0	Matsumoto	Fr		7 592	Sato JPN
7-06	Japan	D	0-0	Yokohama	Fr		65 856	Atkinson ENG
10-08	Norway	L	0-3	Oslo	Fr		12 734	Black NIR
3-09	Scotland	D	2-2	Glasgow	ECq	Plasil [78], Michal Kadlec [90p]	51 564	Blom NED
6-09	Ukraine	W	4-0	Prague	Fr	Michal Kadlec 2 [3p 12], Rezek [47], Kolar [51]	7 322	Trutz SVK
7-10	Spain	L	0-2	Prague	ECq		18 800	Tagliavento ITA
11-10	Lithuania	W	4-1	Kaunas	ECq	Michal Kadlec 2 [2p 85p], Rezek 2 [16 45]	4 000	Fernandez ESP
11-11	Montenegro	W	2-0	Prague	ECpo	Pilar [63], Sivok [92+]	14 560	Atkinson ENG
15-11	Montenegro	W	1-0	Podgorica	ECpo	Jiracek [81]	10 100	Rizzoli ITA

Fr = Friendly match • EC = UEFA EURO 2008/2012 • WC = FIFA World Cup • q = qualifier • po = play-off • r1 = first round group

CZECH REPUBLIC NATIONAL TEAM HISTORICAL RECORDS

Caps: 118 - Karel Poborsky 1994-2006 • 91 - Jan Koller 1999-2009 & Pavel Nedved 1994-2006 • 88 - Petr Cech 2002- • 86 - Milan Baros 2001- • 85 - Tomas Rosicky 2000- • 81 - Vladimir Smicer 1993-2005 • 78 - Tomas Ujfalusi 2001-09 • 77 - Marek Jankulovski 2000-09 • 74 - Vratislav Lokvenc 1995-2006 • 69 - Tomas Galasek 1995-2008 • 64 (84) - Jiri Nemec 1994-2001 • 63 (87) - Pavel Kuka 1994-2001 Figures in brackets include overall total including matches played for Czechoslovakia

Goals: 55 - Jan Koller 1999-2009 • 39 - Milan Baros 2001- • 27 - Vladimir Smicer 1993-2005 • 22 (29) - Pavel Kuka 1994-2001 • 20 - Tomas Rosicky 2000- • 18 - Patrick Berger 1994-2001 & Pavel Nedved 1994-2006 • 14 - Vratislav Lokvenc 1995-2006

Past Coaches: Vaclav Jezek 1993 • Dusan Uhrin 1994-97 • Jozef Chovanec 1998-2001 • Karel Bruckner 2001-08 • Petr Rada 2008-09 • Frantisek Straka 2009 • Ivan Hasek 2009 • Michal Bilek 2009-

CZECH REPUBLIC 2010-11

I. GAMBRINUS LIGA

	Pl	W	D	L	F	A	Pts	Viktoria	Sparta	Jablonec	Sigma	Mladá	Bohemians	Slovan	Hradec	Slavia	Teplice	Dynamo	Slovácko	Pribram	Banik	Zbrojovka	Usti
Viktoria Plzen †	30	21	6	3	70	28	69		1-0	1-1	2-2	3-1	2-1	1-1	2-1	1-2	2-2	4-2	2-1	3-0	2-1	4-1	7-0
Sparta Praha ‡	30	22	2	6	54	21	68	0-1		1-0	2-0	1-1	2-0	3-2	3-1	2-0	0-2	2-0	2-1	1-0	4-0	2-0	4-1
FK Jablonec ‡	30	17	7	6	65	34	58	1-2	2-1		3-2	1-1	3-1	3-0	7-0	2-2	1-1	5-0	3-0	5-1	3-3	1-0	2-0
Sigma Olomouc	30	14	5	11	47	29	47	2-1	0-1	4-1		0-0	3-1	4-0	2-0	0-0	3-0	5-1	0-2	3-1	2-0	3-0	3-0
Mladá Boleslav ‡	30	13	7	10	49	40	46	4-3	1-2	1-2	2-0		3-2	3-1	1-2	3-1	3-3	1-1	2-3	3-0	1-0	5-0	2-0
Bohemians 1905 Praha	30	12	7	11	33	33	43	1-0	0-1	0-1	2-1	3-1		3-1	1-0	1-1	1-1	2-2	1-0	1-0	1-1	2-1	1-0
Slovan Liberec	30	12	7	11	45	36	43	2-3	1-2	1-1	3-0	4-0	1-0		3-0	0-2	6-2	3-3	1-0	0-0	4-1	3-1	3-0
Hradec Králové	30	11	8	11	26	36	41	0-3	2-1	1-0	1-0	0-0	1-1	1-0		0-0	0-0	2-0	0-0	2-1	2-1	1-0	3-3
Slavia Praha	30	9	13	8	41	36	40	0-1	1-2	0-3	1-1	1-0	3-0	1-3	0-0		4-1	4-0	2-0	3-2	1-1	1-3	2-0
FK Teplice	30	10	9	11	39	46	39	0-1	2-2	1-2	1-0	1-2	0-2	1-0	2-1	2-1		1-1	1-1	1-2	4-0	1-2	2-1
Dy. Ceské Budejovice	30	7	12	11	30	48	33	0-3	1-0	2-1	1-0	1-3	1-1	0-0	0-0	1-1	2-2		0-0	3-0	2-1	1-0	2-0
1.FC Slovácko	30	8	7	15	27	43	31	2-2	0-2	1-1	0-2	1-2	1-3	0-1	2-1	3-0	3-0	2-0		2-0	0-0	0-2	1-1
1.FK Pribram	30	8	7	15	22	36	31	0-3	0-1	1-2	0-0	0-0	0-0	1-0	1-0	1-1	1-1	2-0	0-1		0-0	1-0	3-3
Baník Ostrava	30	7	9	14	31	46	30	0-2	0-2	1-3	1-2	1-0	0-0	0-0	1-0	1-0	0-1	3-2	2-1	0-2		3-0	3-3
Zbrojovka Brno	30	7	3	20	33	55	24	1-1	0-5	3-4	2-0	3-1	1-0	0-1	1-2	2-3	0-1	1-1	7-0	0-1	0-2		1-3
Usti nad Labem	30	4	7	19	22	67	19	0-5	1-3	2-1	0-3	0-2	1-0	0-0	0-2	1-1	0-2	1-1	2-0	0-3	0-4	2-3	

16/07/2010 - 28/05/2011 • † Qualified for the UEFA Champions League • ‡ Qualified for the Europa League
Top scorers: 19 - David Lafata, Jablonec • 18 - Tomas Pekhart, Jablonec/Sparta • 14 - Leonard Kweuke CMR, Sparta • 13 - Daniel Kolar, Viktoria

CZECH REPUBLIC 2010-11

DRUHA LIGA (2)

	Pl	W	D	L	F	A	Pts	Dukla	Viktoria	Jihlava	Karviná	Trinec	Sokolov	Vlasim	Cáslav	Spartak	Sparta	Zlin	Most	Varnsdorf	Znojmo	Kladno	Hlucin
Dukla Praha	30	18	9	3	53	18	63		1-1	3-1	3-1	2-0	1-0	1-0	5-0	1-1	2-0	2-0	2-0	4-0	2-0	3-1	2-0
Viktoria Zizkov	30	16	7	7	44	31	55	2-1		0-0	1-0	1-2	1-0	0-1	0-1	2-0	3-1	1-0	1-1	2-0	2-1	0-2	1-1
Vysocina Jihlava	30	15	8	7	49	29	53	0-0	3-3		2-0	0-0	2-1	1-0	6-1	2-1	5-1	1-1	1-1	1-0	2-0	2-1	3-1
MFK Karviná	30	13	7	10	42	36	46	1-1	1-2	2-1		2-1	0-0	0-0	5-0	2-0	2-1	4-3	4-0	2-0	3-3	0-2	3-1
Trinec	30	12	8	10	32	34	44	1-1	1-4	1-0	0-0		2-2	0-0	2-0	1-0	3-0	2-1	1-2	2-1	0-3	2-0	1-0
Baník Sokolov	30	12	7	11	53	51	43	3-3	2-1	2-1	1-0	2-2		3-1	0-2	5-1	2-2	2-3	0-1	1-3	1-2	4-2	4-2
Graffin Vlasim	30	12	6	12	38	32	42	2-1	0-1	0-1	4-1	0-1	0-1		2-3	2-1	2-2	3-1	2-0	1-0	2-1	2-3	2-0
Zenit Cáslav	30	11	8	11	37	48	41	0-2	1-1	1-1	1-1	4-1	3-0	2-1		1-1	1-1	2-0	0-1	2-0	0-0	3-1	3-2
Spartak Sezimovo Usti	30	11	7	12	42	40	40	1-2	2-0	2-0	0-0	1-0	4-1	0-1	1-1		1-2	3-2	3-1	3-0	1-1	1-1	0-1
Sparta Praha B	30	11	6	13	35	47	39	0-3	2-1	2-0	0-1	1-2	0-1	1-0	4-1	1-1		2-0	1-1	2-0	2-1	1-2	1-0
Tescoma Zlin	30	11	5	14	46	45	38	0-0	0-1	1-4	4-1	1-0	4-0	1-1	1-0	2-0	5-0		4-1	3-2	1-2	2-1	2-2
Banik Most	30	10	7	13	35	46	37	1-1	0-1	1-0	2-1	0-0	0-2	2-3	1-0	2-3	1-1	3-1		1-1	0-1	2-2	3-0
Slovan Varnsdorf	30	10	7	13	33	38	37	0-0	3-3	0-0	2-0	2-0	1-0	0-3	3-1	3-1	2-0	0-1	1-2		2-0	1-3	1-2
1.SC Znojmo	30	10	6	14	30	38	36	0-1	0-1	0-0	1-4	0-1	2-5	3-0	1-1	1-4	2-1	1-0	0-1	0-1		2-0	1-0
SK Kladno	30	8	7	15	42	48	31	0-2	1-3	1-2	0-1	1-1	3-3	1-1	3-0	1-2	0-0	2-0	5-3	1-0	0-1		3-0
FC Hlucin	30	6	3	21	36	66	21	2-1	3-4	2-3	1-3	1-3	3-2	0-5	1-2	1-3	2-3	2-1	1-2	2-0	0-0	3-2	

30/07/2010 - 11/06/2011 • Top scorer: 19 - Dani Chigou CMR, Dukla

CZECH REPUBLIC MEDALS TABLE POST 1993

#	Club	Overall G	S	B	League G	S	B	Cup G	S
1	Sparta Praha	16	8		11	5		5	3
2	Slavia Praha	6	9	2	3	9	2	3	
3	Slovan Liberec	3	2	1	2		1	1	2
4	Baník Ostrava	2	2	3	1		3	1	2
5	Viktoria Zizkov	2	1	2			2	2	1
6	FK Teplice	2	1	1		1	1	2	
7	Viktoria Plzen	2			1				
8	FK Jablonec	1	4	3		1	3	1	3
9	Mladá Boleslav	1	1	1		1	1	1	
10	FC Hradec Králové	1						1	
11	Sigma Olomouc		2	3				1	3
12	1.FK Drnovice	2	1				1	2	
13	1.FC Slovácko	2							2

CLUBS IN CZECHOSLOVAKIAN FOOTBALL 1925–1993

#	Club	Overall G	S	B	League G	S	B	Cup G	S	Europe
1	Sparta Praha	27	21	8	19	16	7	8	5	1
2	Dukla Praha	19	9	5	11	7	3	8	2	2
4	Slavia Praha	9	11	8	9	9	7		2	1
6	Baník Ostrava	6	7	2	3	6	1	3	1	1
10	Bohemians Praha	1	2	12	1	1	11		1	1

CLUBS IN CZECH FOOTBALL 1896–1946

#	Club	Overall G	S	B	League G	S	B	Cup G	S
1	Sparta Praha	25	15		11	3		14	12
2	Slavia Praha	25	13		10	7		15	6
3	Viktoria Zizkov	7	4	3	1	2		7	3

POHAR CMFS 2010–11

Third Round			Round of 16				Quarter-finals			Semi-finals			Final		
Mladá Boleslav	1	4p	Mladá Boleslav	0	3	6p	Mladá Boleslav *	2	2	Mladá Boleslav *	1	3	Mladá Boleslav ‡	1	4p
TJ Kunice *	1	2p	Baník Sokolov *	3	0	5p	Viktoria Plzen	1	1	Hanacka Kromeriz	1	1	Sigma Olomouc	1	3p
Sparta Praha	1	1p													
Baník Sokolov *	1	4p													
Slezsky Opava *	2		Slezsky Opava	0	3										
Slovan Varnsdorf	1		Viktoria Plzen *	3	3										
Graffin Vlasim *	0														
Viktoria Plzen	2														
Zbrojovka Brno	2	4p	Zbrojovka Brno	0	4		Zbrojovka Brno *	1	0						
Sokol Ovcary *	2	2p	MFK Karviná *	2	0		Hanacka Kromeriz	2	1						
Slovan Liberec	1														
MFK Karviná *	2														
FC TVD Slavicin	1	5p	FC TVD Slavicin *	1	0										
MSK Breclav *	1	4p	Hanacka Kromeriz	5	0										
SFK Vrchovina *	2														
Hanacka Kromeriz	3														
Slavia Praha *	3		Slavia Praha	1	3		Slavia Praha	1	1	Slavia Praha * †	0	0			
Usti nad Labem	2		Viktoria Zizkov *	1	0		FK Teplice *	2	0	Sigma Olomouc	3	1			
FK OEZ Letohrad *	1														
Viktoria Zizkov	3														
Dy. Ceské Budejovice	3		Dy. Ceské Budejovice	1	0										
SK Hlavice *	1		FK Teplice *	0	2										
Horácky Trebic *	1														
FK Teplice	2														
FK Jablonec	1	4p	FK Jablonec	2	5		FK Jablonec	0	2						
Dukla Praha *	1	3p	1.HFK Olomouc *	4	0		Sigma Olomouc *	2	1						
Sokol Konice *	0														
1.HFK Olomouc	2														
FC Pisek *	3		FC Pisek *	3	1										
Trinec	1		Sigma Olomouc	3	1										
Spartak Hulin *	1														
Sigma Olomouc	3														

CUP FINAL

Jiraskove ulici, Jihlava
25-05-2011, 20:15
Att: 5430. Ref: Libor Kovarík
Scorers – Ivo Taborsky [73] for Mlada: Tomas Horava [58] for Sigma
Mlada - Miroslav Miller - Jan Kysela•, Adrian Rolko, Petr Johana• - Radek Sirl - Alexandre Mendy•, Ondrej Kudela (Vaclav Prochazka• 8), Lukas Opiela, Ivo Taborsky (Elini Dimoutsos 80) - Marek Kulic (c) (Jakub Reznicek 57), Jan Chramosta. Tr: Ladislav Minar
Sigma - Petr Drobisz - Tomas Janotka, Ales Skerle•, Radim Kucera (c), Michal Veprek - Daniel Rossi, Tomas Horava, Lukas Bajer - Jan Schulmeister• (Jakub Petr 61), Pavel Suites, Jan Navratil (Michal Ordos 67). Tr: Zdenek Psotka

† First match awarded 3-0. Match suspended at 1-1 due to pitch invasion • Home team in the first leg ‡ Qualified for the Europa League

DEN – DENMARK

FIFA/COCA-COLA WORLD RANKING

'93	'94	'95	'96	'97	'98	'99	'00	'01	'02	'03	'04	'05	'06	'07	'08	'09	'10	'11	'12
6	14	9	6	8	19	11	22	18	12	13	14	13	21	31	37	28	28	11	

	2011														
	Jan	Feb	Mar	Apr	May	Jun	Jul	Aug	Sep	Oct	Nov	Dec	**High**	**Low**	**Av**
	28	28	28	28	27	20	21	21	17	10	11	11	**3**	**38**	**17**

Denmark's impressive record in the European Championship continued when they qualified for the 2012 finals in Poland and the Ukraine, the seventh time they have made it to the finals in eight tournaments. A 2-1 win over Portugal at the Parken in the final match of the qualifiers saw them finish top of their group, three points ahead of the Portuguese and Norway in what was a great achievement for coach Morten Olsen. At the helm since 2000, he has been in the job longer than any other serving national team coach and is just one of three coaches at the finals to qualify twice. There was a certain sense of deja-vu in club football in 2011 when for the third year running the top three placings in the Superliga remained the same and there was even a repeat of the 2010 Cup Final with Nordsjælland once again taking the trophy. For league champions FC København, that meant a first hat-trick of titles amongst the eight won in the past 11 years and they did it in some style. Along with a record points total, they broke a number of other records including the most wins, fewest defeats and the earliest date during the season to clinch the title. Coach Stale Solbakken also led the team through the group stage of the UEFA Champions League for the first time although their run ended against Chelsea in the first knockout round.

UEFA EUROPEAN CHAMPIONSHIP RECORD

1960 r1 **1964** 4 SF **1968-1980** DNQ **1984** 3 SF **1988** 7 r1 **1992** 1 Winners **1996** 9 r1
2000 16 r1 **2004** 8 QF **2008** DNQ **2012** Qualified

DANSK BOLDSPIL-UNION (DBU)

DBU Allé 1,
Brøndby 2605

☎ +45 43 262222
📠 +45 43 262245
✉ dbu@dbu.dk
🖥 www.dbu.dk
FA 1889 CON 1954 FIFA 1904
P Allan Hansen
GS Jim Stjerne Hansen

FIFA BIG COUNT 2006

Total players	511 333
% of population	9.38%
Male	420 258
Female	91 075
Amateurs 18+	111 757
Youth under 18	188 724
Unregistered	100 000
Professionals	852
Referees	2 992
Admin & coaches	54 000
Number of clubs	1 615
Number of teams	17 365

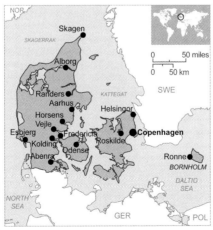

MAJOR CITIES/TOWNS

		Population
1	Copenhagen	1 081 788
2	Aarhus	228 723
3	Odense	159 162
4	Aalborg	100 601
5	Esbjerg	70 872
6	Randers	56 134
7	Kolding	55 147
8	Horsens	53 008
9	Vejle	49 901
10	Roskilde	48 219
11	Silkeborg	45 752
12	Herning	44 968
13	Næstved	42 091
14	Greve Strand	40 725
15	Fredericia	37 087
16	Køge	35 860
17	Viborg	35 517
18	Helsingør	35 149
19	Holstebro	32 161

KONGERIGET DANMARK • KINGDOM OF DENMARK

Capital Copenhagen (København)	Population 5 500 510 (110)	% in cities 87%
GDP per capita $37 200 (30)	Area km² 43 094 km² (133)	GMT +/- +1
Neighbours (km) Germany 68 • Coast 7314		

RECENT INTERNATIONAL MATCHES PLAYED BY DENMARK

2008	Opponents	Score	Venue	Comp	Scorers	Att	Referee
20-08	Spain	L 0-3	Copenhagen	Fr		26 155	Hansson SWE
6-09	Hungary	D 0-0	Budapest	WCq		18 984	Hamer LUX
10-09	Portugal	W 3-2	Lisbon	WCq	Bendtner [83], Christian Poulsen [88], Jensen [92+]	33 000	Webb ENG
11-10	Malta	W 3-0	Copenhagen	WCq	Larsen 2 [10 46], Daniel Agger [29p]	33 124	Paniashvili GEO
19-11	Wales	L 0-1	Brøndby	Fr		10 271	Weiner GER
2009							
11-02	Greece	D 1-1	Piraeus	Fr	Borring [49]		Undiano ESP
28-03	Malta	W 3-0	Ta'Qali	WCq	Larsen 2 [12 23], Nordstrand [89]	6 235	Mikulski POL
1-04	Albania	W 3-0	Copenhagen	WCq	Andreason [31], Larsen [37], Christian Poulsen [80]	24 320	Skomina SVN
6-06	Sweden	W 1-0	Stockholm	WCq	Kahlenberg [22]	33 619	Riley ENG
12-08	Chile	L 1-2	Brøndby	Fr	Schone [63]	8 700	Jakobsen ISL
5-09	Portugal	D 1-1	Copenhagen	WCq	Bendtner [43]	37 998	Busacca SUI
9-09	Albania	D 1-1	Tirana	WCq	Bendtner [40]	8 000	Cakir TUR
10-10	Sweden	W 1-0	Copenhagen	WCq	Jakob Poulsen [78]	37 800	Mejuto ESP
14-10	Hungary	L 0-1	Copenhagen	WCq		36 956	Meyer GER
14-11	Korea Republic	D 0-0	Esbjerg	Fr		15 789	Hansson SWE
18-11	USA	W 3-1	Aarhus	Fr	Absalonsen [47], Rieks [52], Bernburg [55]	15 172	Thomson SCO
2010							
3-03	Austria	L 1-2	Vienna	Fr	Bendtner [17]	13 500	Kralovec CZE
27-05	Senegal	W 2-0	Aalborg	Fr	Christian Poulsen [26], Enevoldsen [90]	14 112	Nijhuis NED
1-06	Australia	L 0-1	Roodepoort	Fr		6 000	Bennett RSA
5-06	South Africa	L 0-1	Atteridgeville	Fr		28 000	Mbaga TAN
14-06	Netherlands	L 0-2	Johannesburg	WCr1		83 465	Lannoy FRA
19-06	Cameroon	W 2-1	Pretoria	WCr1	Bendtner [33], Rommedahl [61]	38 074	Larrionda URU
24-06	Japan	L 1-3	Rustenburg	WCr1	Tomasson [81p]	27 967	Damon RSA
11-08	Germany	D 2-2	Copenhagen	Fr	Rommedahl [74], Junker [87]	19 071	Kelly IRL
7-09	Iceland	W 1-0	Copenhagen	ECq	Kahlenberg [91+]	18 908	McDonald SCO
8-10	Portugal	L 1-3	Porto	ECq	OG [79]	27 117	Braamhaar NED
12-10	Cyprus	W 2-0	Copenhagen	ECq	Morten Rasmussen [48], Lorentzen [81]	15 544	Muniz ESP
17-11	Czech Republic	D 0-0	Aarhus	Fr		9 184	Webb ENG
2011							
9-02	England	L 1-2	Copenhagen	Fr	Agger [8]	21 523	Eriksson SWE
26-03	Norway	D 1-1	Oslo	ECq	Rommedahl [27]	24 828	Rocchi ITA
29-03	Slovakia	W 2-1	Trnava	Fr	OG [3], Krohn-Delhi [72]	4 927	Fernandez ESP
4-06	Iceland	W 2-0	Reykjavik	ECq	Schone [60], Eriksen [75]	7 629	Aydinus TUR
10-08	Scotland	L 1-2	Glasgow	Fr	Eriksen [31]	17 582	Borg MLT
6-09	Norway	W 2-0	Copenhagen	ECq	Bendtner 2 [24 44]	37 167	Lannoy FRA
7-10	Cyprus	W 4-1	Nicosia	ECq	Jacobsen [7], Rommedahl 2 [11 22], Krohn-Dehli [20]	2 408	Strahonja CRO
11-10	Portugal	W 2-1	Copenhagen	ECq	Krohn-Dehli [13], Bendtner [63]	37 012	Rizzoli ITA
11-11	Sweden	W 2-0	Copenhagen	Fr	Bendtner [35], Krohn-Delhi [80]	18 057	Moen NOR
15-11	Finland	W 2-1	Esbjerg	Fr	Agger [57], Bendtner [59]	15 100	Jakobsson ISL

Fr = Friendly match • EC = UEFA EURO 2012 • WC = FIFA World Cup • q = qualifier • r1 = first round group • qf = quarter-final

DENMARK NATIONAL TEAM HISTORICAL RECORDS

Caps
129 - Peter Schmeichel 1987-2001 • **113** - Dennis Rommedahl 2000- • **112** - Jon Dahl Tomasson 1997-2010 • **108** - Thomas Helveg 1994-2008 • **104** - Michael Laudrup 1982-98 • **102** - Morten Olsen 1970-89 & Martin Jorgensen 1998-2011 • **99** - Thomas Sorensen 1999- • **89** - Christian Poulsen 2001- • **87** - John Sivebæk 1982-92 • **86** - Jan Heintze 1988-2002 • **84** - Lars Olsen 1986-96 • **82** - Brian Laudrup 1987-98 • **80** - Jesper Gronkjær 1999- • **77** - Kim Vilfort 1983-96 • **75** - Per Rontved 1970-82

Goals
52 - Poul Nielsen 1910-25 & Jon Dahl Tomasson 1997-2010 • **44** - Pauli Jorgensen 1925-39 • **42** - Ole Madsen 1958-69 • **38** - Preben Elkjær-Larsen 1977-88 • **37** - Michael Laudrup 1982-98 • **29** - Henning Enoksen 1958-66 • **22** - Michael Rohde 1915-31 & Ebbe Sand 1998-2004 • **21** - Brian Laudrup 1987-98, Flemming Povlsen 1987-94 & Dennis Rommedahl 2000- • **20** - Allan Simonsen 1972-86

Past Coaches
Charles Willims ENG 1908-10 • Axel Anderson Byrval 1913-5 & 1917-18 • Arne Sorensen 1956-61 • Poul Petersen 1962-66 • Erik Hansen 1967-69 • John Hansen 1969 • Rudi Strittich AUT 1970-75 • Kurt Nielsen 1976-79 • Sepp Piontek GER 1979-90 • Richard Moller Nielsen 1990-96 • Bo Johansson 1996-2000 • Morten Olsen 2000-

DENMARK 2010-11

SUPERLIGAEN

	Pl	W	D	L	F	A	Pts	København	OB	Brøndby	Midtjylland	Silkeborg	Nordsjælland	SønderjyskE	Lyngby	Horsens	AaB	Randers	Esbjerg
FC København †	33	25	6	2	77	29	81		5-0	2-0 3-1	5-2	2-2 2-0	2-0 2-1	3-0	3-0 3-2	4-0	1-1 2-0	1-0 3-1	3-1
OB Odense ‡	33	16	7	10	55	41	55	2-3 3-0		1-1	2-1 3-2	0-0	0-1 1-2	1-2	3-1 2-0	3-3	6-0	1-1 1-0	3-0 1-0
Brøndby IF ‡	33	13	12	8	52	39	51	1-1	2-2 2-0		1-0 2-2	0-2 2-2	1-1	3-1 2-0	1-1	0-1 0-0	1-2	2-1	1-1 3-0
FC Midtjylland ‡	33	13	10	10	50	42	49	0-3 2-0	1-1	1-0		2-0 2-1	4-0 2-2	2-1	1-2 4-4	1-0	2-1 2-2	1-1 2-2	2-2
Silkeborg IF	33	10	13	10	43	49	43	0-3	3-1 1-1	2-2	1-0		1-0	3-1 1-0	2-2 0-1	1-2 2-1	4-3	1-1 2-2	1-1
FC Nordsjælland ‡	33	10	9	14	38	50	39	1-3	1-4	1-3 1-1	0-0	4-1 3-2		1-2 1-1	2-1	3-0 2-1	0-0 3-3	2-1	1-2
SønderjyskE	33	11	6	16	32	46	39	1-3 3-3	1-3 0-2	0-2	0-2 2-1	1-2	0-2		1-0	2-0 0-3	1-0	1-1	3-0 2-1
Lyngby BK	33	10	8	15	42	52	38	1-2	2-0	3-3 1-2	1-0	1-1	2-0 1-0	1-0 1-0		1-0 0-2 2-4	1-2	3-3	1-2
AC Horsens	33	9	10	14	29	40	37	1-2 1-1	1-0 2-1	2-1	0-2 0-2	1-2	0-0	1-1	2-0		0-0	0-0 0-0 0-3 1-1	
AaB Aalborg	33	8	11	14	38	48	35	0-1	1-2 0-1 0-2 1-2	2-0 0-1 1-2 0-1	2-1	2-3 0-0				4-1	0-2 1-1		
Randers FC	33	6	16	11	41	48	34	0-3	1-2	3-2 0-4	1-1	4-0	0-2 4-0 0-0 0-0 2-1 1-1	1-0	2-3 0-0				2-2
Esbjerg FB	33	7	12	14	36	49	33	1-2 1-1	1-2	1-2	0-3 0-1 2-1 1-1 1-1 2-0	0-1	2-3 0-0	2-1		0-0	2-2 1-3		

17/07/2010 - 29/05/2011 • † Qualified for the UEFA Champions League • ‡ Qualified for the Europa League
Top scorers: **25** - Dame N'Doye SEN, København • **17** - Cesar Santin BRA, København • **14** - Peter Utaka NGA, OB • **12** - Kim Aabech, Lyngby; Hans Henrik Andreasen, OB & Michael Krohn-Dehli, Brøndby • **9** - Mikkel Thygesen, Midtjylland & Jesper Lange, Esbjerg

DENMARK 2010-11
VIASAT SPORT DIVISION (2)

	Pl	W	D	L	F	A	Pts
AGF Aarhus	30	22	6	2	66	25	72
HB Køge	30	19	4	7	58	35	61
Vejle BK	30	14	10	6	49	32	52
Skive IK	30	13	8	9	55	47	47
Brønshøj BK	30	13	7	10	38	38	46
FC Fredericia	30	13	6	11	53	41	45
FC Vestsjælland	30	10	12	8	58	57	42
FC Roskilde	30	11	9	10	45	45	42
Akademisk Boldclub	30	9	10	11	48	49	37
Næstved BK	30	8	9	13	43	44	33
Viborg FF	30	9	6	15	37	43	33
Hobro IK	30	8	9	13	41	55	33
FC Hjørring	30	8	9	13	40	57	33
Kolding FC	30	6	12	12	38	53	30
FC Fyn	30	6	8	16	45	60	26
Hvidovre IF	30	6	5	19	36	69	23

6/08/2010 - 29/05/2011

MEDALS TABLE

		Overall			League			Cup		Europe			
		G	S	B	G	S	B	G	S	G	S	B	City
1	KB København	16	19	8	15	15	8	1	4				Copenhagen
2	Brøndby IF	16	11	6	10	9	5	6	2		1		Copenhagen
3	AGF Aarhus	14	8	11	5	5	11	9	3				Aarhus
4	FC København	13	6	2	9	3	2	4	3				Copenhagen
5	B 93 København	11	5	9	10	5	9	1					Copenhagen
6	Vejle BK	11	4	2	5	3	2	6	1				Vejle
7	Akademisk København	10	14	11	9	11	11	1	3				Copenhagen
8	B 1903 København	9	10	8	7	8	8	2	2				Copenhagen
9	Frem København	8	15	9	6	12	9	2	3				Copenhagen
10	OB Odonco	8	7	5	3	6	5	5	1				Odense
11	Esbjerg FB	7	9	2	5	3	2	2	6				Esbjerg
12	AaB Aalborg	5	8	3	3		3	2	8				Aalborg
13	Lyngby BK	5	5	3	2	3	3	3	2				Lyngby
14	B 1909 Odense	4	1	1	2		1	2	1				Odense
	Hvidovre IF	4	1	1	3	1	1	1					Copenhagen
16	Randers FC	4	1			1		4					Randers
17	Køge BK	2	3		2	1			2				Køge
18	Silkeborg IF	2	1	2	1	1	2	1					Silkeborg
19	FC Nordsjælland	2		1			1	2					Farum

DBU LANDSPOKAL 2010-11

Third Round		Round of 16		Quarter-finals		Semi-finals		Final	
FC Nordsjælland	1	FC Nordsjælland	3						
FC Hjørring*	0			FC Nordsjælland	1				
BK Marienlyst*	0	OB Odense*	2						
OB Odense	2					FC Nordsjælland*	1 0		
FC København	4	FC København*	2						
Viby IF*	1			AC Horsens*	0				
FC Vestsjælland*	2	AC Horsens	4					FC Nordsjælland ‡	3
AC Horsens	6							FC Midtjylland	2
Lyngby BK	2	Lyngby BK	2 5p						
Kastrup BK*	1			Lyngby BK	0				
Brønshøj BK*	0	Hvidovre IF*	2 4p						
Hvidovre IF	1					Randers FC	0 0		
FC Fredericia	2	FC Fredericia*	1						
Hellerup IK*	1			Randers FC*	3				
Nordvest FC*	1	Randers FC	2						
Randers FC	5								
Esbjerg FB*	3	Esbjerg FB*	2						
FC Svendborg*	0			Esbjerg FB	2				
B 93 København*	0	Silkeborg IF	0						
Silkeborg IF	5					Esbjerg FB	2 1 4p		
Viborg FF	1	Viborg FF*	1 4p						
Hobro IK*	0			AaB Aalborg*	0				
Næstved BK*	1	AaB Aalborg	1 5p						
AaB Aalborg	1					FC Midtjylland*	1 2 5p		
AGF Aarhus*	6	AGF Aarhus	1						
Skive IK	3			AGF Aarhus*	0				
Brøndby IF	2	Varde IF*	0						
Varde IF*	4								
HB Køge	3	HB Køge*	0						
Thisted FC*	1			FC Midtjylland	1				
Avedøre IF*	2	FC Midtjylland	4						
FC Midtjylland	3								

CUP FINAL
Parken, Copenhagen
22-05-2011, Att: 14 646, Ref: Claus Bo Larsen
Scorers – Lawan 2 [16][54], Christensen [92+] for Nordsjælland; Thygesen 2 [37][71] for Midtjylland
Nordsjælland - Jesper Hansen - Andreas Bjelland, Bryan Oviedo, Michael Parkhurst, Henrik Kildentoft - Jores Okore, Enoch Adu (Matti Nielsen 53), Andreas Laudrup (Morten Nordstrand 62), Nikolai Stokholm, Tobias Mikkelsen (Søren Christensen 79) - Rawez Lawan. Tr: Morten Wieghorst
Midtjylland - Jonas Lössl - Kasper Hansen, Kristian Nielsen, Kristijan Ipsa, Jesper Kristensen - Mikkel Thygesen, Danny Olsen (Ken Fagerberg 67), Jakob Poulsen, Rilwan Hassan (Jonas Borring 90), Izunna Uzochukwu - Sylvester Igboun. Tr: Glen Riddersholm

* Home team/home team in the first leg • ‡ Qualified for the Europa League

DJI – DJIBOUTI

FIFA/COCA-COLA WORLD RANKING

'93	'94	'95	'96	'97	'98	'99	'00	'01	'02	'03	'04	'05	'06	'07	'08	'09	'10	'11	'12
-	169	177	185	189	191	195	189	193	195	197	201	200	198	173	188	189	191	198	

2011														
Jan	Feb	Mar	Apr	May	Jun	Jul	Aug	Sep	Oct	Nov	Dec	High	Low	Av
192	192	192	192	192	193	194	196	196	195	200	198	169	201	191

After failing to compete in any international games in 2010, Djibouti played six matches in 2011 but still finished the year as Africa's second-lowest ranked country. They were beaten 8-0 on aggregate by Namibia in the preliminary round of the 2014 FIFA World Cup qualifiers, losing 4-0 at home in the first leg and then by the same scoreline away in Windhoek four days later. The country also entered the East and Central African Senior Challenge Cup in Tanzania in December but 'Les Requins' went home after three losses, to Zimbabwe, Tanzania and Rwanda in Group A in Dar-es-Salaam. Tunisian Noureddine Gharsalli was brought in to coach the side after almost a decade of working in the Gulf region, although his appointment was only on a short term basis. After elimination from the FIFA World Cup qualifiers, Djibouti's national team face a long hiatus from competition as it did not enter the 20-13 CAF Africa Cup of Nations. AS Port won the league championship by edging Guelleh Batal by two points. They then completed the league and cup double in mid-year by beating AS Ali Sabieh 2-0 in the final of the Coupe du 27 Juin. The new season kicked off in November 2011 with live television transmission of matches - a new breakthrough for football in the Red Sea state.

CAF AFRICA CUP OF NATIONS RECORD
1957-1998 DNE 2000-2002 DNQ 2004-2008 DNE 2010 DNQ 2012-2013 DNE

FEDERATION DJIBOUTIENNE DE FOOTBALL (FDF)

Centre Technique National, Boite postale 2694, Djibouti

☎ +253 353599
📠 +253 353588
✉ fdf-1979@yahoo.fr
🖥 www.fdf.dj
FA 1979 CON 1986 FIFA 1994
P Fadoul Houssein
GS Ali Kamil Ali

FIFA BIG COUNT 2006

Total players	36 320
% of population	7.47%
Male	34 480
Female	1 840
Amateurs 18+	1 800
Youth under 18	720
Unregistered	2 800
Professionals	0
Referees	75
Admin & coaches	405
Number of clubs	6
Number of teams	84

MAJOR CITIES/TOWNS

		Population
1	Djibouti	610 608
2	Ali Sabieh	22 999
3	Dikhil	16 721
4	Arta	11 635
5	Tadjoura	8 740
6	Obock	7 469
7	Ali Adde	5 419
8	Holhol	3 517
9	Yoboki	3 109
10	We'a	3 000
11	Airoli	2 577
12	Dorra	1 465

REPUBLIQUE DE DJIBOUTI • JUMHURIYAT JIBUTI • REPUBLIC OF DJIBOUTI

Capital Djibouti	Population 516 055 (168)	% in cities 87%
GDP per capita $2700 (170)	Area km² 23 200 km² (150)	GMT +/- +3
Neighbours (km) Eritrea 109, Ethiopia 349, Somalia 58 • Coast 314		

RECENT INTERNATIONAL MATCHES PLAYED BY DJIBOUTI

2009	Opponents	Score		Venue	Comp	Scorers	Att	Referee
2-01	Burundi	L	0-4	Jinja	CCr1			
4-01	Sudan	D	1-1	Jinja	CCr1	Ahmed Hassan Daher [59]		
6-01	Kenya	L	1-5	Jinja	CCr1	Ahmed Hassan Daher [53]		
30-11	Ethiopia	L	0-5	Nairobi	CCr1			
2-12	Kenya	L	0-2	Nairobi	CCr1			
4-12	Zambia	L	0-6	Nairobi	CCr1			
2010								
No international matches played in 2010								
2011								
1-11	Somalia	W	1-0	Djibouti	Fr			
11-11	Namibia	L	0-4	Djibouti	WCq		3 000	Bamlak ETH
15-11	Namibia	L	0-4	Windhoek	WCq		2 145	Chirinda MOZ
27-11	Zimbabwe	L	0-2	Dar es Salaam	CCr1			
29-11	Tanzania	L	0-3	Dar es Salaam	CCr1			
2-12	Rwanda	L	2-5	Dar es Salaam	CCr1	Ahmed Hassan Daoud 2 [25 34]		

CC = CECAFA Cup • AR = Arab Cup • WC = FIFA World Cup • q = qualifier • r1 = First round group

DJIBOUTI 2010–11

DIVISION 1

	Pl	W	D	L	F	A	Pts	Port	Guelleh	ASAS	Tadjourah	SID	ONEAD	Gendarmerie	CDE-Colas	Hôpital	Kartileh
AS Port	18	16	0	2	54	14	48		0-2	3-0	2-1	1-0	5-2	3-0	3-2	2-0	5-1
Guelleh Batal	18	15	1	2	54	11	46	1-2		0-1	4-1	0-0	4-0	1-0	6-1	4-1	8-0
AS Ali Sabieh	18	13	1	4	50	21	40	1-3	1-3		1-0	2-1	0-2	3-2	5-1	5-0	8-1
AS Tadjourah	18	8	3	7	40	27	27	2-1	1-3	0-0		0-3	3-1	0-1	3-1	4-0	3-3
SID	18	7	2	9	24	29	23	0-4	0-1	0-4	2-4		1-0	2-1	2-4	3-1	2-1
ONEAD	18	6	3	9	30	30	21	1-3	1-2	1-2	2-2	2-2		2-1	0-1	5-1	3-2
Gendarmerie	18	6	2	10	24	30	20	0-3	0-2	1-8	2-0	0-2	2-1		1-1	3-0	6-0
CDE-Colas	18	5	4	9	30	39	19	1-3	0-4	1-2	0-3	2-0	2-3	0-0		2-2	3-0
Hôpital	18	4	3	11	20	43	15	0-2	2-3	1-2	1-4	1-0	1-1	1-0	1-1		3-1
Kartileh	18	0	1	17	15	92	1	0-9	0-6	1-5	0-9	1-4	1-3	1-4	1-7	1-4	

4/11/2010 - 20/03/2011

COUPE DU 27 JUIN 2010–11

Eighth-finals		Quarter-finals		Semi-finals		Final	
AS Port	2						
ONEAD	0	AS Port	7				
Obock	4	Hôpital	2				
Hôpital	5			AS Port	7		
EAD	3			ETS Abdi	0		
APEJAS	2	EAD	1				
Cité du Stade	4	ETS Abdi	2				
ETS Abdi	5					AS Port	2
Guelleh Batal	8					AS Ali Sabieh	0
Ambouli	1	Guelleh Batal	5				
SID	3	Gendarmerie	1			CUP FINAL	
Gendarmerie	4			Guelleh Batal	1		
CDE-Colas	4			AS Ali Sabieh	4	17-06-2011	
Hadji-Dideh	2	CDE-Colas	4			Scorers - Jean Bosco [14], Mohamed	
AS Tadjourah	0	AS Ali Sabieh	5			Omar Champika [50] for Port	
AS Ali Sabieh	2						

DMA – DOMINICA

FIFA/COCA-COLA WORLD RANKING

'93	'94	'95	'96	'97	'98	'99	'00	'01	'02	'03	'04	'05	'06	'07	'08	'09	'10	'11	'12
-	-	158	138	139	133	149	152	161	174	185	165	172	181	189	191	197	129	171	

	2011												High	Low	Av
	Jan	Feb	Mar	Apr	May	Jun	Jul	Aug	Sep	Oct	Nov	Dec			
	129	128	130	131	131	133	133	136	149	152	173	171	128	198	163

2010 may have seen plenty for the Dominica national team to celebrate, especially their dramatic jump of nearly 70 places up the FIFA/Coca-Cola World Ranking, but the same can not be said for 2011. Dominica not only lost all five games played but they also failed to score a single goal. Thanks to their form of the previous year, the Dominicans were spared taking part in a preliminary round of 2014 FIFA World Cup qualifying. Instead they were drawn against Nicaragua and Panama in the first group stage but any hope of making an impact in the group was removed when the Bahamas decided to withdraw. Against group favourites Panama, a team that has emerged as one of the strongest in the region, Dominica lost 5-0 at home in Roseau and 3-0 in Panama City, which along with the two - admittedly narrower - defeats against Nicaragua, saw the Dominicans slip down the rankings almost as quickly as they had risen. In club football the 2010 League champions Centre Bath Estate entered the 2011 CFU Club Championship but for the second year running they pulled out, mindful perhaps of their 12-1 thrashing at the hands of Trinidad's W Connection in the 2009 tournament. There was little local football played during 2011 with the kick-off of the Premier League delayed until the start of December.

FIFA WORLD CUP RECORD
1930-1994 DNE   1998-2014 DNQ

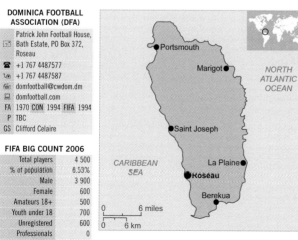

DOMINICA FOOTBALL ASSOCIATION (DFA)

Patrick John Football House, Bath Estate, PO Box 372, Roseau
☎ +1 767 4487577
📠 +1 767 4487587
✉ domfootball@cwdom.dm
🖥 domfootball.com
FA 1970 CON 1994 FIFA 1994
P TBC
GS Clifford Celaire

FIFA BIG COUNT 2006

Total players	4 500
% of population	6.53%
Male	3 900
Female	600
Amateurs 18+	500
Youth under 18	700
Unregistered	600
Professionals	0
Referees	39
Admin & coaches	100
Number of clubs	20
Number of teams	20

Portsmouth

Marigot

NORTH ATLANTIC OCEAN

Saint Joseph

CARIBBEAN SEA

La Plaine

Roseau

Berekua

0   6 miles
0   6 km

MAJOR CITIES/TOWNS

		Population
1	Roseau	13 623
2	Canefield	3 363
3	Portsmouth	3 277
4	Marigot	2 669
5	Salisbury	2 531
6	Atkinson	2 257
7	Berekua	2 061
8	Saint Joseph	1 919
9	Castle Bruce	1 870
10	Wesley	1 625
11	Soufrière	1 518
12	La Plaine	1 250
13	Pointe Michel	1 229
14	Mahaut	1 199
15	Woodford Hill	951
16	Calibishie	913
17	Rosalie	760
18	Petite Savane	742
19	Pont Cassé	702

DOMINICA

Capital	Roseau	Population	72 660 (201)	% in cities	74%
GDP per capita	$10 000 (106)	Area km²	751 km² (188)	GMT +/-	-4
Neighbours (km)	Coast 148				

RECENT INTERNATIONAL MATCHES PLAYED BY DOMINICA

2004	Opponents	Score		Venue	Comp	Scorers	Att	Referee
28-01	British Virgin Islands	W	1-0	Tortola	Fr	Elry Cuffy [34]	200	Matthew SKN
31-01	US Virgin Islands	W	5-0	St Thomas	Fr	OG [12], Shane Marshall [42], George Dangler [68], Vincent Casimir [87], Sherwin George [90]	550	Matthew SKN
1-02	British Virgin Islands	W	2-1	Tortola	Fr	Shane Marshall [44], Kelly Peters [70]	100	Charles DMA
12-03	Barbados	L	1-2	Bridgetown	Fr	Kelly Peters [88]	46	Small BRB
26-03	Bahamas	D	1-1	Nassau	WCq	Vincent Casimir [88]	800	Forde BRB
28-03	Bahamas	W	3-1	Nassau	WCq	Vincent Casimir 2 [39 86], Kelly Peters [85]	900	Pineda HON
19-06	Mexico	L	0-10	San Antonio, USA	WCq		36 451	Callender BRB
27-06	Mexico	L	0-8	Aguascalientes	WCq		17 000	Stott USA
10-11	Martinique †	L	1-5	Fort de France	CCq	Peltier [42]	1 110	Arthur LCA
12-11	Guadeloupe †	L	0-7	Rivière-Pilote	CCq		2 400	Arthur LCA
14-11	French Guyana †	L	0-4	Fort de France	CCq		5 800	Fenus LCA
2005								
30-09	Guyana	L	0-3	Linden	Fr		800	Lancaster GUY
2-10	Guyana	L	0-3	Georgetown	Fr		1 000	Kia SUR
2006								
3-09	Antigua and Barbuda	L	0-1	St John's	Fr		400	Willett ATG
17-09	Barbados	L	0-5	Roseau	Fr		900	Charles DMA
20-09	Martinique †	L	0-4	Abymes	CCq		1 000	Fanus LCA
22-09	Guadeloupe †	L	0-1	Abymes	CCq		1 100	Willett ATG
24-09	Saint Martin †	D	0-0	Abymes	CCq		500	Willett ATG
2007								
No international matches played in 2007								
2008								
6-02	Barbados	D	1-1	Roseau	WCq	Richard Pacquette [21]	4 200	Quesada CRC
26-03	Barbados	L	0-1	Bridgetown	WCq		4 150	Batres GUA
8-08	Guyana	L	0-3	Georgetown	CCq		3 000	Forde BRB
9-08	Surinam	L	1-3	Georgetown	CCq	Prince Austrie [7]	175	Taylor BRB
2009								
5-12	British Virgin Islands	W	4-0	Roseau	Fr	Prince Austrie [8], Kelly Peters [23], Kurlson Benjamin [25], Cheston Benjamin [85]	600	Baptiste DMA
2010								
25-09	Barbados	W	2-0	Bridgetown	Fr	Kurlson Benjamin [24], Mitchell Joseph [38]	625	Taylor BRB
26-09	Barbados	W	3-1	Bridgetown	Fr	Kurlson Benjamin 3 [35 45 74]	580	Skeete DMA
15-10	British Virgin Islands	W	10-0	San Cristobal	CCq	Mitchell Joseph 3 [1 12 13], Chad Bertrand [55], Kurlson Benjamin 5 [47 71 81 84 85], Donald Jervier [87]	200	Santos PUR
17-10	Dominican Republic	W	1-0	San Cristobal	CCq	Elmond Derrick [66]	600	Lebron PUR
10-11	Cuba	L	2-4	St John's	CCq	Kurlson Benjamin 2 [11 87]	500	Lancaster GUY
12-11	Antigua and Barbuda	D	0-0	St John's	CCq		400	Purser JAM
14-11	Suriname	L	0-5	St John's	CCq		500	Lancaster GUY
2011								
2-09	Nicaragua	L	0-2	Roseau	WCq		8 000	Vaughn USA
11-09	St Vincent/Grenadines	L	0-1	Kingstown	Fr		2 500	Cambridge VIN
7-10	Panama	L	0-5	Roseau	WCq		4 000	Wijngaarde SUR
11-11	Nicaragua	L	0-1	Managua	WCq		2 100	Cruz CRC
15-11	Panama	L	0-3	Panama City	WCq		8 000	Vaughn

Fr = Friendly match • CC = Digicel Caribbean Cup • WC = FIFA World Cup • q = qualifier • † Not a full international

DOM – DOMINICAN REPUBLIC

FIFA/COCA-COLA WORLD RANKING

'93	'94	'95	'96	'97	'98	'99	'00	'01	'02	'03	'04	'05	'06	'07	'08	'09	'10	'11	'12
153	164	159	130	144	152	155	157	160	149	171	170	174	136	166	185	190	168	131	

2011													High	Low	Av
Jan	Feb	Mar	Apr	May	Jun	Jul	Aug	Sep	Oct	Nov	Dec				
167	168	166	171	172	172	132	133	139	128	129	131		116	190	159

The Dominican Republic played more matches in 2011 than in any other year in the history of the national team and with six wins and two draws in the ten matches played, it was also one of the most successful. All but two of those games were World Cup qualifiers although by the end of the year their campaign had come to an end. Drawn against Anguilla in a preliminary round tie, the Dominican Republic eased into the first group stage with two comfortable wins where they were drawn with the Cayman Islands, Suriname and group favourites El Salvador. Making it through to the second group stage was always going to be a tall order but by finishing ahead of both the Surinamese and the Cayman Islanders, the team exceeded all expectations. The 3-1 away victory over Suriname in Paramaribo must rank as one of the best results in the history of the team and came courtesy of their star strikers, Puerto Rico based Jonathan Fana, and Erick Ozuno. The Dominican Republic's two defeats came in the crucial matches against El Salvador but both were close games lost only by the odd goal. With the national team centre stage, club football was limited to the Copa Independencia in the first half of the year - won by Barcelona thanks to a 1-0 win over Salcedo - while the 2011 Liga Mayor didn't kick off until early December.

FIFA WORLD CUP RECORD
1930-1974 DNE **1978** DNQ **1982-1990** DNE **1994-2014** DNQ

FEDERACION DOMINICANA DE FUTBOL (FEDOFUTBOL)

	Centro Olimpico, Ensanche Miraflores, Apartado postal 1953, Santo Domingo
☎	+1 809 5426923
📠	+1 809 3812734
✉	fedofutbol.f@codetel.net.do
🖥	www.fedofutbol.org
FA	1953 CON 1964 FIFA 1958
P	Osiris Guzman
GS	Angel Miranda

FIFA BIG COUNT 2006

Total players	501 004
% of population	5.46%
Male	417 804
Female	83 200
Amateurs 18+	35 000
Youth under 18	12 000
Unregistered	106 000
Professionals	4
Referees	1 420
Admin & coaches	190
Number of clubs	250
Number of teams	600

NORTH ATLANTIC OCEAN

CARIBBEAN SEA

0   40 miles
0   40 km

MAJOR CITIES/TOWNS

		Population
1	Santo Domingo	2 491 547
2	Santiago	643 162
3	San Pedro	262 142
4	La Romana	240 235
5	San Cristóbal	183 890
6	Higüey	160 651
7	Puerto Plata	134 206
8	San Francisco	131 000
9	La Vega	110 276
10	Barahona	81 960
11	San Juan	80 560
12	Baní	75 621
13	Bonao	75 464
14	Bajos de Haina	73 199
15	Moca	67 171
16	Azua	64 229
17	Boca Chica	60 169
18	Mao	50 093
19	Villa Altagracia	45 930

REPUBLICA DOMINICANA • DOMINICAN REPUBLIC

Capital	Santo Domingo	Population	9 650 054 (85)	% in cities	69%
GDP per capita	$8200 (119)	Area km²	48 670 km² (131)	GMT +/-	-4
Neighbours (km)	Haiti 360 • Coast 1288				

RECENT INTERNATIONAL MATCHES PLAYED BY THE DOMINICAN REPUBLIC

2004	Opponents	Score		Venue	Comp	Scorers	Att	Referee
19-03	Anguilla	D	0-0	Santo Domingo	WCq		400	Mattus CRC
21-03	Anguilla	W	6-0	Santo Domingo	WCq	Omar Zapata [15], Kervin Severino 2 [38 61p], Juan Contrera 2 [57 90], Luis Vasquez [77]	850	Porras CRC
27-04	Netherlands Antilles	L	1-3	Willemstad	Fr	Omar Zapata [9]	800	Faneijte ANT
13-06	Trinidad and Tobago	L	0-2	Santo Domingo	WCq		2 500	Moreno PAN
20-06	Trinidad and Tobago	L	0-4	Marabella	WCq		5 500	Pinas SUR
2005								
No international matches played in 2005								
2006								
15-09	Haiti	L	1-3	Saint-Marc	Fr	Manuel Perez [22]	600	
17-09	Haiti	L	1-2	Port-au-Prince	Fr	Manuel Perez [30p]	950	Grant HAI
29-09	Bermuda	L	1-3	Charlotte Amalie	CCq	Jonathan Fana [85]	300	Martis ANT
1-10	US Virgin Islands	W	6-1	Charlotte Amalie	CCq	Luis Corporan [14], Jonathan Fana 4 [25 55 82 89], Kerbi Rodriguez [87]	250	Davis TRI
24-11	Guadeloupe	L	0-3	Georgetown	CCq		5 000	Wijngaarde SUR
26-11	Antigua and Barbuda	W	2-0	Georgetown	CCq	Kervin Severino [70p], Darly Batista [81]	5 000	Brizan TRI
28-11	Guyana	L	0-4	Georgetown	CCq		5 000	Brizan TRI
2007								
No international matches played in 2007								
2008								
27-02	Haiti	L	1-2	San Cristobal	Fr		1 300	Minyetty DOM
28-02	Haiti	L	0-2	San Cristobal	Fr		825	Minyetty DOM
26-03	Puerto Rico	L	0-1	Bayamon	WCq		8 000	Morales MEX
8-10	Trinidad and Tobago	L	0-9	Port of Spain	Fr		2 000	
2009								
No international matches played in 2009								
2010								
14-10	British Virgin Islands	W	17-0	San Cristobal	CCq	Darly Batista 5 [4 67 68 72 78], Domingo Peralta 3 [21 43 76], Inoel Navarro 3 [26 47 81], Manuel Reinoso 2 [60 73], Kerwin Severino [63], Erick Obuna 2 [83 90], Gonzalo Frechilla [90]	200	Lebron PUR
17-10	Dominica	L	0-1	San Cristobal	CCq		600	Lebron PUR
2011								
8-07	Anguilla	W	2-0	San Cristobal	WCq	Domingo Peralta [7], Jonathan Fana [42]	1 000	Brizan TRI
10-07	Anguilla	W	4-0	San Cristobal	WCq	Inoel Navarro 2 [18 42], Jhoan Sanchez [27], Jonathan Fana [42]	1 500	Brea CUB
20-08	Curacao	W	1-0	San Cristobal	Fr	Johan Cruz [70]	250	Vasquez DOM
21-08	Curacao	W	1-0	San Cristobal	Fr	Fernando Casanova [28]	300	Hidalgo DOM
2-09	El Salvador	L	2-3	San Salvador	WCq	Johan Cruz [66], Domingo Peralta [89]	25 272	Rodriguez PAN
6-09	Suriname	D	1-1	San Cristobal	WCq	Erick Ozuna [68]	2 300	Castro HON
7-10	El Salvador	L	1-2	San Cristobal	WCq	Erick Ozuna [54]	2 323	Cerdas CRC
11-10	Suriname	W	3-1	Paramaribo	WCq	Jonathan Fana [9], Erick Ozuna 2 [47 76]	1 200	Ward CAN
11-11	Cayman Islands	W	4-0	San Cristobal	WCq	Inoel Navarro [17], Erick Ozuna [38], Kelvin Rodriguez [64], Jack Morillo [79]	1 000	Guerrero NCA
14-11	Cayman Islands	D	1-1	Georgetown	WCq	Cesar Garcia [41]	1 750	Matthew SKN

Fr = Friendly match • CC = Digicel Caribbean Cup • WC = FIFA World Cup • q = qualifier

COPA INDEPENDENCIA 2011

Semi-finals		Finals	
Barcelona	5		
Universidad OyM	1		
		Barcelona	1
		Salcedo	0
Don Bosco	1	5-06-2011	
Salcedo	3	Scorer - Dahiana Joseph [105]	

ECU – ECUADOR

'93	'94	'95	'96	'97	'98	'99	'00	'01	'02	'03	'04	'05	'06	'07	'08	'09	'10	'11	'12
48	55	55	33	28	63	65	54	37	31	37	39	37	30	56	36	37	53	42	

	2011														
	Jan	Feb	Mar	Apr	May	Jun	Jul	Aug	Sep	Oct	Nov	Dec	High	Low	Av
	52	54	49	56	64	68	67	66	69	52	42	42	24	76	45

2011 proved to be a year of two halves for the Ecuador national team which went the first 10 matches without a win but which after August chalked up six wins in the final seven games of the year. Unfortunately the Copa America in Argentina fell within the former as the team once again fell at the first hurdle. Just twice since the league-only format was abandoned in the 1970s have Ecuador made it through to the knock-out stage, the last time being when the tournament was held at altitude in Bolivia in 1997. In contrast, Ecuador have experienced unprecedented success at club level in South America thanks to the exploits of LDU Quito and at the end of 2011 they came within a whisker of winning a third continental title in four years. Having beaten Argentina's Independiente and Velez Sarsfield to reach the Copa Sudamericana final, they were favourites to beat Chile's Universidad de Chile but were beaten 4-0 over two games. At home it was LDU's city rivals Deportivo who dominated, winning the title for the third time in four years. Under coach Carlos Ischia they beat Emelec 1-0 in both legs of the final, a fantastic change in fortunes for a club that had gone from 1968 to 2008 without winning a single championship.

COPA AMERICA RECORD

1916-1937 DNE **1939** 5/5 **1941** 5/5 **1942** 7/7 **1945** 7/7 **1946** DNE **1947** 6/8 (Hosts) **1949** 7/8 **1953** 7/7 **1955** 6/6 **1956** DNE **1957** 7/7 **1959** DNE **1959** 4/5 **1963** 6/7 **1967** DNE **1975** 9/10 r1 **1979** 9/10 r1 **1983** 9/10 r1 **1987** 8/10 r1 **1989** 7/10 r1 **1991** 7/10 r1 **1993** 4/12 SF (Hosts) **1995** 9/12 r1 **1997** 5/12 QF **1999** 11/12 r1 **2001** 9/12 r1 **2004** 12/12 r1 **2007** 11/12 r1 **2011** 10/12 r1

FEDERACION ECUATORIANA DE FUTBOL (FEF)

Avenida las Aguas y Calle, Alianza, PO Box 09-01-7447, Guayaquil 593
☎ +593 42 880610
📠 +593 42 880615
📧 fef@gye.satnet.net
🖥 www.ecuafutbol.org
FA 1925 CON 1930 FIFA 1926
P Luis Chiriboga
GS Francisco Acosta

FIFA BIG COUNT 2006

Total players	1 029 655
% of population	7.60%
Male	918 800
Female	110 855
Amateurs 18+	12 855
Youth under 18	9 800
Unregistered	811 800
Professionals	700
Referees	405
Admin & coaches	4 050
Number of clubs	199
Number of teams	416

MAJOR CITIES/TOWNS

		Population
1	Guayaquil	2 248 800
2	Quito	1 621 817
3	Cuenca	322 955
4	Machala	247 290
5	Santo Domingo	232 207
6	Manta	210 712
7	Portoviejo	195 941
8	Eloy Alfaro	193 293
9	Ambato	180 048
10	Quevedo	140 945
11	Riobamba	139 778
12	Loja	128 578
13	Ibarra	128 288
14	Milagro	126 831
15	Esmeraldas	112 192
16	Babahoyo	90 016
17	La Libertad	87 417
18	El Carmen	80 270
19	Rosa Zárate	62 813

REPUBLICA DEL ECUADOR • REPUBLIC OF ECUADOR

Capital Quito	Population 14 573 101 (64)	% in cities 66%
GDP per capita $7500 (123)	Area km² 283 561 km² (73)	GMT + / - -5
Neighbours (km) Colombia 590, Peru 1420 • Coast 2237		

RECENT INTERNATIONAL MATCHES PLAYED BY ECUADOR

2009	Opponents		Score	Venue	Comp	Scorers	Att	Referee
29-03	Brazil	D	1-1	Quito	WCq	Cristian Noboa [89]	40 000	Chandia CHI
1-04	Paraguay	D	1-1	Quito	WCq	Cristian Noboa [63]	36 853	Roldan COL
27-05	El Salvador	L	1-3	Los Angeles	Fr	Jefferson Montero [9]		
7-06	Peru	W	2-1	Lima	WCq	Jefferson Montero [38], Carlos Tenorio [58]	17 050	Torres PAR
10-06	Argentina	W	2-0	Quito	WCq	Walter Ayovi [72], Pablo Palacios [83]	36 359	Chandia CHI
12-08	Jamaica	D	0-0	New Jersey	Fr			Marrufo USA
5-09	Colombia	L	0-2	Medellin	WCq		42 000	Pezzotta ARG
9-09	Bolivia	W	3-1	La Paz	WCq	Edison Mendez [4], Luis Valancia [46], Cristian Benitez [66]	10 200	Baldassi ARG
10-10	Uruguay	L	1-2	Quito	WCq	Luis Valencia [68]	42 700	Fagundes BRA
14-10	Chile	L	0-1	Santiago	WCq		47 000	Torres PAR
2010								
7-05	Mexico	D	0-0	New York	Fr		77 507	Depiero CAN
16-05	Korea Republic	L	0-2	Seoul	Fr		62 209	Wongkamdee THA
4-09	Mexico	W	2-1	Guadalajara	Fr	Cristian Benitez [i], Jaime Ayovi [58]	43 800	Quesada CRC
7-09	Venezuela	L	0-1	Barquisimento	Fr		37 262	Torres PAN
8-10	Colombia	L	0-1	Harrison	Fr		25 000	Chapin USA
12-10	Poland	D	2-2	Montreal	Fr	Cristian Benitez 2 [31 78]	1 000	Navarro CAN
17-11	Venezuela	W	4-1	Quito	Fr	Cristian Benitez 2 [2 4], Walter Ayovi 2 [45p 46]	9 000	Chaibou NGA
2011								
9-02	Honduras	D	1-1	La Ceiba	Fr	Pablo Palacios [13]. W 5-4p	15 100	Lopez GUA
26-03	Colombia	L	0-2	Madrid	Fr		15 000	Mateu ESP
29-03	Peru	D	0-0	Den Haag	Fr			Braamhaar NED
20-04	Argentina	D	2-2	Mar Del Plata	Fr	Michael Quinonez [27], Segundo Castillo [68p]	9 000	Silvera URU
28-04	Mexico	D	1-1	Seattle	Fr	Michael Arroyo [37]	50 300	Jurisevic USA
1-06	Canada	D	2-2	Toronto	Fr	Cristian Benitez [62], Michael Arroyo [64]	14 356	Bogle JAM
7-06	Greece	D	1-1	New York	Fr	Frickson Erazo [58]	39 656	Geiger USA
3-07	Paraguay	D	0-0	Santa Fe	CAr1		20 000	Pezzotta ARG
9-07	Venezuela	L	0-1	Salta	CAr1		12 000	Quesada CRC
13-07	Brazil	L	2-4	Cordoba	CAr1	Felipe Caicedo 2 [36 58]	39 000	Silvera URU
10-08	Costa Rica	W	2-0	San Jose	Fr	Cristian Suarez [53], Edison Mendez [66]	18 000	Aguilar SLV
2-09	Jamaica	W	5-2	Quito	Fr	Jaime Ayovi [20], Cristian Suarez [38], Cristian Benitez 2 [45 50], Segundo Castillo [64]	6 000	Buitrago COL
6-09	Costa Rica	W	4-0	Quito	Fr	Cristian Suarez [21], Jaime Ayovi [27], Segundo Castillo [59], Cristian Benitez [75]	6 000	Roldan COL
7-10	Venezuela	W	2-0	Quito	WCq	Jaime Ayovi [15], Cristian Benitez [75]	32 278	Osses CHI
11-10	USA	W	1-0	Harrison, New York	Fr	Jaime Ayovi [79]	20 707	Aguilar SLV
11-11	Paraguay	L	1-2	Asuncion	WCq	Joao Rojas [92+]	11 173	Buitrago COL
15-11	Peru	W	2-0	Quito	WCq	Edison Mendez [69], Cristian Benitez [88]	34 481	Larrionda URU

Fr = Friendly match • CA = Copa America • WC = FIFA World Cup • q = qualifier • r1 = first round group

ECUADOR NATIONAL TEAM HISTORICAL RECORDS

Caps — **168** - Ivan Hurtado 1992- • **109** - Alex Aguinaga 1987-2004 • **102** - Ulises de la Cruz 1995- • **100** - Luis Capurro 1985-2003 • **90** - Edison Mendez 2000- & Giovanny Espinoza 2000- • **89** - José Francisco Cevallos 1994- • **86** - Cleber Chala 1994-2004 • **78** - Edwin Tenorio 1998-2007 • **77** - Angel Fernandez 1991-2004

Goals — **31** - Agustin Delgado 1994-2006 • **26** - Eduardo Hurtado 1992-2000 • **23** - Alex Aguinaga 1987-2004 • **16** - Ivan Kaviedes 1998- & Raul Aviles 1987-2003 • **15** - Ariel Graziani 1997-2000, Edison Mendez 2000- & Christian Benitez 2005-

Past Coaches — Enrique Lamas CHI 1938 • Ramon Unamuno 1939 • Juan Parodi ARG 1941-42 • Rodolfo Orlandini ARG 1945 • Ramon Unamuno 1947 • Jose Planas ESP 1949 • Gregorio Esperon ARG 1953 • Jose Maria Diaz Granados 1955 • Eduardo Spandre ARG 1957 • Juan Lopez URU 1959-60 • Fausto Montalvan 1963 • Jose Maria Rodriguez URU 1965 • Fausto Montalvan 1966 • Jose Gomes Nogueira BRA 1969 • Ernesto Guerra 1970 • Jorge Lazo 1972 • Roque Resquin ARG 1973 • Roque Maspoli URU 1975-77 • Hector Morales 1979 • Otto Vieira BRA 1981 • Juan Eduardo Hohberg URU 1981 • Ernesto Guerra 1983 • Antoninho Ferreira BRA 1984-85 • Luis Grimaldi URU 1986-87 • Dusan Draskovic YUG 1988-93 • Carlos Torres Garces 1994 • Carlos Ron 1994 • Francisco Maturana COL 1995-97 • Luis Fernando Suarez COL 1997 • Francisco Maturana COL 1997 • Polo Carrera 1998 • Carlos Sevilla 1999 • Hernan Dario Gomez COL 1999-2004 • Luis Fernando Suarez COL 2004-07 • Sixto Vizuete 2007-10 • Reinaldo Rueda COL 2010-

ECUADOR 2011

SERIE A COPA CREDIFE PRIMERA ETAPA

	Pl	W	D	L	F	A	Pts	Emelec	LDU Quito	Dep Quito	El Nacional	LDU Loja	Dep Cuenca	Olmedo	Barcelona	Manta	Imbabura	José Terán	Espoli
Emelec ‡	22	12	8	2	31	15	44		1-0	0-0	1-1	3-2	0-0	3-1	1-1	2-1	1-0	3-1	2-0
LDU Quito	22	11	7	4	29	13	40	0-1		0-1	2-1	1-1	1-0	1-1	3-0	5-0	2-0	2-1	2-0
Deportivo Quito	22	11	6	5	39	25	39	0-0	0-0		1-1	2-4	3-1	3-1	1-0	2-1	3-2	2-3	3-2
El Nacional	22	9	5	8	31	23	32	2-0	1-2	0-3		0-1	4-2	2-1	0-0	4-1	1-2	1-0	3-0
LDU Loja	22	9	5	8	27	27	32	1-4	1-2	1-0	2-1		0-0	1-0	0-0	3-0	0-2	3-2	0-0
Deportivo Cuenca	22	8	7	7	27	30	31	0-1	0-2	1-1	2-2	1-2		2-1	1-1	3-2	1-1	3-1	2-1
Olmedo	22	8	5	9	27	32	29	2-1	1-0	2-2	0-4	1-0	0-0		4-0	2-1	2-0	2-2	3-0
Barcelona	22	6	9	7	22	23	27	0-0	0-0	0-1	0-1	1-1	0-2	4-0		1-1	1-0	1-1	4-1
Manta	22	7	6	9	20	26	27	1-1	1-1	2-0	1-0	2-0	0-1	0-0	1-0		2-0	2-0	0-1
Imbabura	22	6	5	11	25	33	23	1-1	1-1	3-2	0-1	3-2	1-2	3-1	0-2	0-1		2-2	1-0
Indep. José Terán	22	4	7	11	29	44	19	0-3	1-2	1-6	1-0	1-0	1-2	2-0	2-3	0-0	3-3		1-1
Espoli	22	3	6	13	20	38	15	1-2	0-0	0-3	1-1	1-2	3-1	1-2	2-3	0-0	2-0	3-3	

29/01/2011 - 19/06/2011 • ‡ Qualified for the Championship final

ECUADOR 2011

SERIE A COPA CREDIFE SEGUNDA ETAPA

	Pl	W	D	L	F	A	Pts	Dep Quito	Barcelona	El Nacional	Emelec	LDU Quito	Dep Cuenca	José Terán	Olmedo	Manta	Imbabura	LDU Loja	Espoli
Deportivo Quito ‡	22	13	5	4	34	15	44		1-0	0-1	2-0	1-1	2-1	2-2	1-0	4-0	2-2	3-0	2-0
Barcelona	22	12	4	6	29	21	40	1-0		3-1	2-0	2-3	2-1	1-0	1-0	1-0	3-1	2-0	1-0
El Nacional	22	11	4	7	40	33	37	0-3	2-0		2-1	2-3	1-1	2-2	4-2	0-1	5-1	4-3	2-1
Emelec	22	10	4	8	34	23	34	0-0	1-1	1-1		2-1	0-0	2-0	3-0	1-0	5-0	4-1	4-0
LDU Quito	22	10	4	8	32	23	34	1-0	0-0	2-1	1-0		4-1	1-2	0-0	6-0	1-2	3-0	1-0
Deportivo Cuenca	22	8	8	6	29	23	32	0-1	0-0	1-1	2-0	2-1		3-0	1-1	2-0	2-1	4-0	0-0
Indep. José Terán	22	9	4	9	32	30	31	0-1	0-3	1-2	5-0	2-0	0-1		3-0	3-2	1-1	3-6	1-0
Olmedo	22	7	6	9	22	28	27	2-2	1-2	4-1	0-3	2-0	1-1	1-0		0-1	2-1	1-0	2-1
Manta	22	7	4	11	18	30	25	2-0	2-0	0-1	2-1	0-0	1-0	0-0	2-1		0-1	3-1	0-1
Imbabura	22	7	4	11	26	40	25	1-4	3-1	1-3	2-1	0-1	1-0	0-1	0-0	4-2		0-0	3-0
LDU Loja	22	7	3	12	31	42	24	0-1	3-1	0-3	0-2	3-2	4-2	1-2	1-1	2-0	4-0		1-0
Espoli	22	4	4	14	16	35	16	1-2	2-2	2-1	1-3	1-0	2-3	1-4	0-1	0-0	2-1	1-1	

23/07/2011 - 4/12/2011 • ‡ Qualified for the Championship final • 3rd Place Play-off (overall): **El Nacional** 2-1 1-1 LDU Quito
Top scorers (all stages): **28** - Narciso Mina, José Terán • **21** - Juan Luis Anangoni, El Nacional • **20** - Julio Bevacqua ARG, Deportivo Quito & Fabio Renato BRA, LDU Loja • **16** - Hernan Barcos ARG, LDU Quito • Imbabura & Espoli relegated

CHAMPIONSHIP FINAL 2011 1ST LEG

Olimpico Atahualpa, Quito, 11-12-2011, Att: 21 635, Ref: Jose Carpio

Emelec 0
Deportivo Quito 1   Fidel Martinez 29

Emelec - Wilmer Zumba - Eduardo Morante, Oscar Bagui, Gabriel Achilier•, Enner Valencia (Fernando Gaibor 46), David Quiroz, Pedro Quinonez (Polo Wila 70), Fernando Gimenez, Edison Mendez, Nicolas Vigneri, Marcos Caicedo (Angel Mena 46). Tr: Juan Carrasco
Dep Quito - Marcelo Elizaga• - Isaac Mina, Luis Checa, Jayro Campos•, Pedro Velasco•, Alex Bolanos•, Oswaldo Minda, Luis Saritama (Dixon Arroyo 71), Fidel Martinez, Juan Carlos Paredes (Angel Escobar 62), Julio Bevacqua (Matias Alustiza 55). Tr: Carlos Ischia

CHAMPIONSHIP FINAL 2011 2ND LEG

Olimpico Atahualpa, Quito, 17-12-2011, Att: 32 325, Ref: Intriago

Deportivo Quito 1   Matias Alustiza 88
Emelec 0

Dep Quito - Marcelo Elizaga• - Isaac Mina, Luis Checa•, Jayro Campos, Pedro Velasco, Alex Bolanos, Oswaldo Minda, Luis Saritama, Fidel Martinez (Byron Cano 78), Angel Escobar (Pedro Esterilla 82), Julio Bevacqua (Matias Alustiza 60). Tr: Carlos Ischia
Emelec - Wilmer Zumba - Carlos Quinonez (Jose Quinonez 55), Eduardo Morante♦53, Oscar Bagui, Gabriel Achilier, David Quiroz, Pedro Quinonez, Fernando Gimenez (Enner Valencia 65), Fernando Gaibor, Nicolas Vigneri (Walter Iza 31), Angel Mena. Tr: Juan Carrasco

MEDALS TABLE

		Overall			League			Sth Am			City
		G	S	B	G	S	B	G	S	B	
1	Barcelona	13	13	10	13	11	5		2	5	Guayaquil
2	El Nacional	13	7	8	13	7	5			3	Quito
3	LDU Quito	12	4	10	10	3	6	2	1	4	Quito
4	Emelec	10	12	13	10	11	11		1	2	Guayaquil
5	Deportivo Quito	5	3	4	5	3	4				Quito
6	Deportivo Cuenca	1	5	1	1	5	1				Cuenca
7	Olmedo	1	1	2	1	1	2				Riobamba
8	Everest	1		1	1		1				Guayaquil

EGY – EGYPT

FIFA/COCA-COLA WORLD RANKING

'93	'94	'95	'96	'97	'98	'99	'00	'01	'02	'03	'04	'05	'06	'07	'08	'09	'10	'11	'12
26	22	23	28	32	28	38	33	41	39	32	34	32	27	39	16	24	9	31	

					2011										
Jan	Feb	Mar	Apr	May	Jun	Jul	Aug	Sep	Oct	Nov	Dec		High	Low	Av
10	33	35	36	36	34	34	34	36	29	31	31		9	44	30

The first decade of this century has seen Egypt dominate African football with a golden generation of players for both the national team and leading club side Al Ahly. But with political change sweeping through the Arab world these are difficult times for Egyptian society and football has not been immune from the violence that has accompanied this change. On February 1, 2012, 73 fans were killed during a riot in Port Said at a match between Al Masry and Al Ahly, an incident that left the authorities with no choice but to cancel the rest of the 2011-12 Premier League season. That came on top of the failure to qualify for the 2012 CAF Africa Cup of Nations. Coach Hassan Shehata, who had taken the Pharaohs to three successive Nations Cup triumphs, was the major casualty of the early elimination from the qualifiers, resigning with two games still left to play. 2011 league champions Al Ahly won just a single point in the group phase of the 2011 CAF Champions League while Zamalek were eliminated in the second round and were heavily punished for violent scenes when their fans invaded the pitch and attacked the players of Tunisian opponents Club Africain. It was left to the U-20 side to lift the gloom after they impressed at the FIFA U-20 World Cup in Colombia in August before losing 2-1 to Argentina in the Round of 16.

FIFA WORLD CUP RECORD

1930 DNE **1934** 13 r1 1938-1950 DNE 1954 DNQ 1958-1970 DNE 1974-1986 DNQ **1990** 20 r1 1994- 2010 DNQ

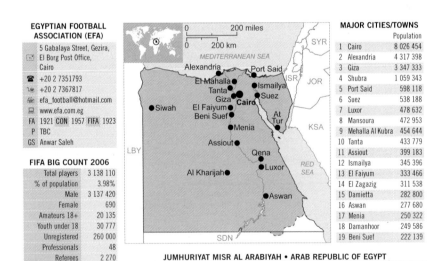

EGYPTIAN FOOTBALL ASSOCIATION (EFA)

5 Gabalaya Street, Gezira, El Borg Post Office, Cairo

☎ +20 2 7351793
📠 +20 2 7367817
✉ efa_football@hotmail.com
🖥 www.efa.com.eg

FA	1921	CON	1957	FIFA 1923

P   TBC
GS Anwar Saleh

FIFA BIG COUNT 2006

Total players	3 138 110
% of population	3.98%
Male	3 137 420
Female	690
Amateurs 18+	20 135
Youth under 18	30 777
Unregistered	260 000
Professionals	48
Referees	2 270
Admin & coaches	16 000
Number of clubs	590
Number of teams	6 495

MAJOR CITIES/TOWNS

		Population
1	Cairo	8 026 454
2	Alexandria	4 317 398
3	Giza	3 347 333
4	Shubra	1 059 343
5	Port Said	598 118
6	Suez	538 188
7	Luxor	478 632
8	Mansoura	472 953
9	Mehalla Al Kubra	454 644
10	Tanta	433 779
11	Assiout	399 183
12	Ismailya	345 396
13	El Faiyum	333 466
14	El Zagazig	311 538
15	Damietta	282 800
16	Aswan	277 680
17	Menia	250 322
18	Damanhoor	249 586
19	Beni Suef	222 139

JUMHURIYAT MISR AL ARABIYAH • ARAB REPUBLIC OF EGYPT

Capital	Cairo	Population	83 082 869 (15)	% in cities	43%
GDP per capita	$5800 (134)	Area km²	1 001 450 km² (30)	GMT +/-	+2
Neighbours (km)	Gaza Strip 11, Israel 266, Libya 1115, Sudan 1273 • Coast 2450				

RECENT INTERNATIONAL MATCHES PLAYED BY EGYPT

2009	Opponents	Score		Venue	Comp	Scorers	Att	Referee
15-06	Brazil	L	3-4	Bloemfontein	CCr1	Zidan 2 [9 55], Shawky [54]	27 851	Webb ENG
18-06	Italy	W	1-0	Johannesburg	CCr1	Homos [40]	52 150	Hansson SWE
21-06	USA	L	0-3	Rustenburg	CCr1		23 140	Hester NZL
5-07	Rwanda	W	3-0	Cairo	WCq	Aboutrika 2 [64 90], Hosny Abd Rabo [74p]	18 000	Imiere NGA
12-08	Guinea	D	3-3	Cairo	Fr	Hosny Abd Rabo 2 [3 31], Abdelmalek [90]		
5-09	Rwanda	W	1-0	Kigali	WCq	Ahmed Hassan [67]	20 000	Lamptey GHA
2-10	Mauritius	W	4-0	Cairo	Fr	Aboutrika 2 [7 83], Ahmed Hassan [17p], Amr Zaki [90p]		
10-10	Zambia	W	1-0	Chililabombwe	WCq	Hosny Abd Rabo [69]	10 000	Djaoupe TOG
5-11	Tanzania	W	5-1	Aswan	Fr	Moteab 2 [8 33], Amr Zaki [19], Barakat [42], Raouf [86]		
14-11	Algeria	W	2-0	Cairo	WCq	Amr Zaki [3], Moteab [95+]	75 000	Damon RSA
18-11	Algeria	L	0-1	Omdurman	WCpo		35 000	Maillet SEY
29-12	Malawi	D	1-1	Cairo	Fr	Hosny Abd Rabo [45p]		
2010								
4-01	Mali	W	1-0	Dubai	Fr	Geddo [65]		
12-01	Nigeria	W	3-1	Benguela	CNr1	Moteab [34], Ahmed Hassan [54], Geddo [87]	18 000	Seechurn MRI
16-01	Mozambique	W	2-0	Benguela	CNr1	Khan OG [47], Geddo [81]	16 000	Djaoupe TOG
20-01	Benin	W	2-0	Benguela	CNr1	Al Muhamadi [7], Moteab [23]	12 500	Bennett RSA
25-01	Cameroon	W	3-1	Benguela	CNqf	Ahmed Hassan 2 [37 103], Geddo [92]	12 000	Damon RSA
28-01	Algeria	W	4-0	Benguela	CNsf	Hosny Abd Rabo [39p], Zidan [65], Abdel Shafy [80], Geddo [92+]	25 000	Codjia BEN
31-01	Ghana	W	1-0	Luanda	CNf	Geddo [85]	50 000	Coulibaly MLI
3-03	England	L	1-3	London	Fr	Zidan [23]	80 602	Torres PAR
11-08	Congo DR	W	6-3	Cairo	Fr	Ahmed Ali Kamal 2 [3 34], Ahmed Fathy [41], Aboutrika [44], Ahmed Hassan [49], Geddo [67]		
5-09	Sierra Leone	D	1-1	Cairo	CNq	Mahmoud Fathallah [61]		Diatta SEN
10-10	Niger	L	0-1	Niamey	CNq			Doue CIV
17-11	Australia	W	3-0	Cairo	Fr	El Zaher [29], Geddo [60], Zidan [90p]		Genov BUL
16-12	Qatar	L	1-2	Doha	Fr	Walid Soliman [72]		
2011								
5-01	Tanzania	W	5-1	Cairo	Fr	Hamdy 2 [5 57], Aboutrika [12], OG [24], Ahmed Ali [78]		
8-01	Uganda	W	1-0	Cairo	Fr	Geddo [93+]		
11-01	Burundi	W	3-0	Ismailia	Fr	Geddo [2], Ahmed Ali [11], Hamdy [80]		
14-01	Kenya	W	5-1	Cairo	Fr	Ahmad Belal 3 [13 69 90], Hamdy [21], Gomaa [25]		
17-01	Uganda	W	3-1	Ismailia	Fr	Hamdy 2 [38 70], Geddo [81]		
26-03	South Africa	L	0-1	Johannesburg	CNq			Coulibaly MLI
5-06	South Africa	D	0-0	Cairo	CNq			Jedidi TUN
3-09	Sierra Leone	L	1-2	Freetown	CNq	Marwan Mohsen [44]		
8-10	Niger	W	3-0	Cairo	CNq	Marwan Mohsen 2 [48 71], Mohamed Salah [56]		
14-11	Brazil	L	0-2	Al Rayyan	Fr		18 000	Al Dossari QAT

Fr = Friendly match • CN = CAF African Cup of Nations • CC = FIFA Confederations Cup • WC = FIFA World Cup

EGYPT NATIONAL TEAM HISTORICAL RECORDS

Caps
179 - Ahmed Hassan 1995- • 169 - Hossam Hassan 1985-2006 • 125 - Ibrahim Hassan 1985-2004 • 124 - Hany Ramzy 1988-2003 • 122 - Essam El Hadary 1997- • 110 - Nader El Sayed 1992-2005 & Abdel Zaher El Sakka 1997- • 106 - Wael Gomaa 2001- • 97 - Ismail Youssef 1985-97 • 93 - Magdi Abdelghani 1980-90

Goals
69 - Hossam Hassan 1985-2006 • 39 - Mahmoud Al Khatib 1974-86 • 34 - Magdi Abdelghani 1980-90 • 32 - Ahmed Hassan 1995- • 31 - Emad Moteab 2005- • 28 - Amr Zaki 2004- • 26 - Mohamed Aboutrika 2004- • 19 - Ahmed Hossam 'Mido' 2001-

Past Coaches
Hussein Ilegazi 1920-24 • James McRea SCO 1934-36 • Tawfik Abdullah 1940 44 • Eric Keen ENG 1947-48 • Edward Jones ENG 1949-52 • Committee 1953-54 • Ljubisa Brociae YUG 1954-55 • Mourad Fahmy 1955-58 • Mohamed El-Guindy & Hanafy Bastan 1958 • Pal Titkos HUN 1959-61 • Mohamed El Guindy & Hanafy Bastan 1962 • Foad Sidqui 1963 • Vendler YUG 1964 • Kovae YUG 1965 • Mohamed Abdou Saleh El-Wahsh & Kamal El Sabagh 1969-70 • Dettmar Cramer GER 1971-74 • Burkhard Pape GER 1975-77 • Dusan Nenkovic YUG 1977-78 • Taha Ismail 1978 • Bundzsak Dezso HUN 1979 • Foad Sidqui 1980 • Abdel Monem El-Hajj 1980 • Hamada El-Sharqawy 1980 • Karl-Heinz Heddergott GER 1980-82 • Mohamed Abdou Saleh El-Wahsh & Ali Osman 1982-85 • Mike Smith WAL 1985-88 • Foad Sidqui 1988 • Mahmoud El Gohary 1988-90 • Dietrich Weise GER 1990-91 • Mahmoud El Gohary 1991-93 • Mohamed Sadiq "Shehta" 1993 • Mircea Radulescu ROU 1993-94 • Taha Ismail 1994 • Nol de Ruiter NED 1994-95 • Mohsen Saleh 1995 • Ruud Krul NED 1995-96 • Farouk Gaafar 1996-97 • Mahmoud El-Gohary 1997-99 • Anwar Salama 1999 • Gerard Gili FRA 1999-2000 • Mahmoud El-Gohary 2000 • Mohsen Saleh 2000-03 • Marco Tardelli ITA 2003-04 • Hassan Shehata 2004-

EGYPT 2010-11

ETISALAT PREMIER LEAGUE

	Pl	W	D	L	F	A	Pts	Ahly	Zamalek	Ismaily	Shorta	ENPPI	Misr	Masry	Haras	Jaish	Petrojet	Gouna	Wadi Degla	Intag Harby	Ittihad	Smouha	Mokawloon
Al Ahly †	30	16	13	1	47	27	61		0-0	2-1	0-0	3-2	2-2	1-1	2-1	1-0	2-0	1-0	1-0	2-2	1-0	2-2	1-1
Zamalek †	30	15	11	4	49	32	56	2-2		3-2	2-0	0-0	0-1	1-0	2-1	0-0	2-0	1-1	1-1	0-0	4-3	3-0	1-0
Ismaily	30	14	7	9	48	33	49	3-1	0-0		4-1	2-1	1-1	0-0	3-2	3-0	1-1	2-1	1-0	5-0	2-0	3-2	0-1
Ittihad Al Shorta	30	12	11	7	31	23	47	1-2	1-3	2-1		0-1	3-0	2-0	1-0	2-0	1-1	1-0	1-0	3-0	0-0	1-1	2-0
ENPPI ‡	30	13	8	9	37	30	47	1-2	3-1	0-0	0-1		1-1	1-0	1-3	1-0	3-1	3-2	2-0	1-1	2-1		
Misr Al Maqasah	30	10	15	5	41	28	45	1-1	3-4	0-0	1-1	1-0		1-1	1-1	1-1	3-1	0-0	6-2	0-0	4-0	2-0	2-0
Al Masry	30	10	13	7	28	22	43	0-0	2-0	2-0	0-0	1-0	1-0		1-0	2-1	0-0	1-1	2-0	1-0	2-2	1-3	0-0
Haras Al Hedod	30	11	6	13	40	39	39	0-3	2-2	2-0	1-0	2-3	0-1	1-0		1-1	3-1	1-1	1-0	1-1	0-2	1-0	1-1
Al Jaish	30	8	12	10	25	31	36	0-1	2-2	1-0	1-0	0-2	0-0	1-1	1-2		1-0	2-1	2-1	0-0	3-1	0-1	2-1
Petrojet	30	9	8	13	31	38	35	0-1	1-2	0-1	0-0	1-1	2-1	0-1	3-0	2-2		1-0	1-1	1-0	1-1	1-0	1-3
Al Gouna	30	8	10	12	26	33	34	1-1	2-1	2-3	0-0	2-1	2-2	2-1	2-0	2-2	1-0		0-2	1-0	0-2	1-0	2-1
Wadi Degla	30	9	6	15	39	49	33	1-2	0-2	2-1	2-3	2-3	1-1	0-4	0-5	2-0	4-2	3-1		0-0	1-0	1-2	4-1
Intag Harby	30	7	12	11	33	44	33	1-2	1-3	1-1	2-3	0-0	2-1	0-0	1-4	0-0	3-2	1-0	1-1		2-1	1-0	1-1
Ittihad Al Sakandary	30	7	9	14	36	51	30	2-2	1-1	1-3	0-0	1-0	1-1	3-1	2-1	0-1	2-3	0-0	0-2	3-6		0-3	3-2
Smouha	30	6	10	14	33	45	28	1-1	1-3	2-4	1-1	0-0	0-1	2-1	2-2	1-1	0-1	0-0	2-2	3-2	2-4		0-2
Mokawloon	30	5	9	16	27	46	24	1-5	2-3	2-1	0-0	1-2	0-2	1-1	0-1	0-0	0-1	0-0	0-3	2-3	1-1	2-1	

5/08/2010 - 11/07/2011 • † Qualified for the CAF Champions League • ‡ Qualified for the CAF Confederation Cup • No relegation
Top scorers: **13** - Ahmed Abd El Zaher, ENPPI & Shikabala, Zamalek • **11** - Ahmed Eid Abdel Malek, Haras • **10** - Ahmed Gaafar, Zamalek

EGYPT 2010-11 — SECOND DIVISION A (2)

Upper Egypt	Pl	W	D	L	F	A	Pts
Telefonad Beni Suef	30	20	8	2	47	17	68
Aswan	30	20	7	3	54	20	67
Assiout Petrol	30	16	10	4	54	29	58
Aluminium N Hammadi	30	14	7	9	40	26	49
Al Fayoum	30	14	7	9	42	32	49
Sohag	30	13	9	8	48	43	48
Sokar Al Hawamdia	30	13	8	9	34	27	47
Al Minya	30	9	13	8	38	30	40
Maragha FC	31	9	7	15	27	43	34
Maghagha FC	29	7	11	11	25	35	32
Markhaz Shabab	30	8	8	14	26	52	32
Sukar Abu Qourqas	30	8	7	15	41	48	31
Nasr Mining	30	6	12	12	29	37	30
Grand Hotel Hurghada	30	8	6	16	30	43	30
Shabab Al Waladeya	30	5	6	19	30	49	21
Al Wosta	30	3	8	19	19	53	17

27/09/2010 - 30/07/2011

EGYPT 2010-11 — SECOND DIVISION B (2)

Cairo	Pl	W	D	L	F	A	Pts
Al Dakhleya	30	22	5	3	68	23	71
Itesalat Al Masry	30	16	9	5	55	34	57
Itesalat	29	15	11	3	30	15	56
Al Tersana	30	15	10	5	54	33	55
Tanta FC	30	12	11	7	66	45	47
Al Nasr Egypt	29	11	12	6	30	22	45
Gasco	29	11	9	9	40	36	42
Montakhab Al Suweis	29	11	7	11	38	38	40
Olympi Al Qanal	30	8	13	9	29	34	37
Al Mareekh	30	9	9	11	36	45	36
Al Rabat we Al Anwar	30	8	10	12	29	37	34
Suez Cement	29	7	10	12	36	39	31
Al Sharkya	30	7	10	13	32	45	31
Al Shams	30	5	9	16	18	35	24
Al Gendi	30	3	9	18	24	58	18
Zefta FC	30	3	4	23	19	65	13

27/09/2010 - 30/07/2011

EGYPT 2010-11 — SECOND DIVISION C (2)

Lower Egypt	Pl	W	D	L	F	A	Pts
Ghazl Al Mehalla	27	21	5	1	60	19	68
Al Mansoura	27	19	4	4	47	22	61
Al Koroum	28	16	6	6	55	25	54
Abou Qair Semadis	28	15	7	6	36	22	52
Samanod	28	11	8	9	34	28	41
Olympic	26	11	7	8	27	22	40
Meyah Al Behairah	27	10	8	9	29	26	38
Maleyet Kafr Al Zayiat	28	10	6	12	26	24	36
Baladeyet Al Mahalla	28	7	14	7	27	25	35
Ala'ab Damanhour	28	10	5	13	34	36	35
Razja'h	27	8	10	9	26	25	34
Shabab Al Hamam	28	8	9	11	20	32	33
Nabrouh	28	6	8	14	26	45	26
Bani Ebeid	28	6	6	16	25	41	24
Matrouh	28	4	10	14	16	30	22
Al Hamoul	28	2	1	25	15	81	7

27/09/2010 - 30/07/2011

MEDALS TABLE

		Overall			League			Cup			Africa			City
		G	S	B	G	S	B	G	S	B	G	S	B	
1	Al Ahly	80	22	5	36	10	2	35	10		10	2	3	Cairo
2	Zamalek	38	42	10	11	30	6	21	11		6	1	4	Cairo
3	Al Tersana	7	8	7	1	4	7	6	4					Cairo
4	Mokawloon	7	3	2	1			3	3		3		1	Cairo
5	Ismaily	6	12	20	3	6	16	2	4		1	2	4	Ismailya
6	Al Ittihad	6	4	3				2	6	4			1	Alexandria
7	Olympic	3	3	1	1			1	2	3				Alexandria
8	ENPPI	2	3	2				1	1		2	2		Cairo
9	Haras Al Hedod	2		1				1		2				Alexandria
10	Al Masry	1	9	7				5	1	9			2	Port Said
11	Ghazl Al Mehalla	1	7	6	1			5		6		1	1	Al Mehalla
12	Suez	1	3	1				1	1	3				Suez
13	Al Teram	1						1						Alexandria
14	Sekka	6						6						Cairo
15	Mansoura		1	2				1	1				1	Mansoura

EGYPT CUP 2011

Second Round

Team	Score
ENPPI	2
Al Rabat we Al Anwar *	1
Kima Aswan	0
Al Ahly *	4
Petrojet	3
Tanta FC *	1
Markhaz Shabab Toh	1
Ittihad Al Shorta *	2
Ismaily	2
Kafr Al Sheikh *	1
Intag Harby	0 4p
Telefonad Beni Suef *	0 5p
Al Jaish	1
Al Seka Al Hadid *	0
Montakhab Al Suweis *	0
Mokawloon	2
Haras Al Hedod	2
Sokar Al Hawamdia *	0
Al Sharkya	2
Smouha *	3
Ittihad *	3
Matrouh	1
Misr Al Maqasah *	0 2p
Al Nasr Egypt	0 3p
Al Gouna	2
Ala'ab Damanhour	1
Al Masry	0
Assiout Petrol *	1
Wadi Degla *	2
Al Fayoum	1
Bani Ebeid	0
Zamalek *	6

Third Round

Team	Score
ENPPI *	1
Al Ahly	0
Petrojet *	1
Ittihad Al Shorta	2
Ismaily *	4
Telefonad Beni Suef	0
Al Jaish	0
Mokawloon *	1
Haras Al Hedod	1
Smouha *	0
Ittihad *	0 2p
Al Nasr Egypt	0 3p
Al Gouna	3 7p
Assiout Petrol *	3 6p
Wadi Degla *	1
Zamalek	4

Quarter-finals

Team	Score
ENPPI *	0 6p
Ittihad Al Shorta	0 5p
Ismaily	1
Mokawloon *	3
Haras Al Hedod *	1
Al Nasr Egypt	0
Al Gouna	2
Zamalek *	3

Semi-finals

Team	Score
ENPPI *	2 8p
Mokawloon	2 7p
Haras Al Hedod	1
Zamalek *	2

Final

Team	Score
ENPPI ‡	2
Zamalek	1

CUP FINAL

Cairo International, 11-10-2011

Scorers - Adel Moustafa [54], Ahmed Abdel Zaher [81] for ENPPI; Amr Zaki [49] for Zamalek

ENPPI - Mohamed Abou Gabal - Osama Ragab, Abdel Zaher El-Saqua (Rami Sabri), Celcio Halelio Abdul 'Mano', Amr Fahim (Hussein Ali), Mohamed Nasef - Mohamed Sobhi, Mohamed Shaaban, Adel Moustafa - Ahmed Abdel Zaher, Ahmed Raouf (Saleh Gomaa). Tr: Hossam Al Badry

Zamalek - Abdel Wahed El-Sayed - Hazem Emam (Omar Gaber), Mahmoud Fathallah, Salah Soliman, Mohamed Abdel Shafi - Ahmed Hassan (Hussein Hamdi), Ibrahim Salah, Ahmed Merghani, Mahmoud Abdel Razek Shikabala - Amr Zaki, Ahmed Gaafar (Alaa Ali). Tr: Hassan Shehata

* Home team • ‡ Qualified for the CAF Confederation Cup

ENG – ENGLAND

FIFA/COCA-COLA WORLD RANKING

'93	'94	'95	'96	'97	'98	'99	'00	'01	'02	'03	'04	'05	'06	'07	'08	'09	'10	'11	'12
11	18	21	12	4	9	12	17	10	7	8	8	9	5	12	8	9	6	5	

	2011											High	Low	Av
Jan	Feb	Mar	Apr	May	Jun	Jul	Aug	Sep	Oct	Nov	Dec			
6	6	6	6	6	4	6	4	8	7	5	5	4	27	10

2011 proved to be a great year for the city of Manchester with United winning an historic and record breaking 19th league title and City winning the FA Cup - their first trophy for 35 years. With Birmingham City winning the League Cup it meant that for the first since time 2001 London clubs ended the season without a trophy. Manchester United's title was grounded on the back of a fantastic home record which saw them win 26 and draw three of the 29 matches played at Old Trafford in all competitions. In a disappointing finale to the season, however, they were outclassed by Barcelona in the UEFA Champions League final, held for the first time at the new Wembley, in a year that marked a quarter of a century in charge for manager Sir Alex Ferguson. Ferguson had had to wait four years for his first trophy but Robert Mancini delivered a trophy at Manchester City in his first full season, an early return for the Abu Dhabi-based owner Sheikh Mansour. The England national team successfully qualified for the Euro 2012 finals in Poland and Ukraine, finishing a comfortable six points ahead of second placed Montenegro and they will set out to try and win a tournament in which they have never progressed beyond the semi-finals and in which they have only once progressed beyond the group stage away from home - in 2004.

UEFA EUROPEAN CHAMPIONSHIP RECORD

1960 DNE 1964 r1 **1968** 3 SF 1972 DNQ 1976 DNQ **1980** 5 r1 1984 r1 **1988** 8 r1 **1992** 7 r1
1996 3 SF (hosts) **2000** 11 r1 **2004** 5 QF 2008 DNQ **2012** Qualified

THE FOOTBALL ASSOCIATION (FA)

Wembley Stadium,
PO Box 1966,
London SW1P 9EQ
☎ +44 844 9808200
📠 +44 844 9808201
✉ communique@thefa.com
🖥 www.TheFA.com
FA 1863 CON 1954 FIFA 1905
P David Bernstein
GS Alex Horne

FIFA BIG COUNT 2006

Total players	4 164 110
% of population	8.47%
Male	3 829 000
Female	335 110
Amateurs 18+	656 800
Youth under 18	820 000
Unregistered	2 415 000
Professionals	6 110
Referees	33 186
Admin & coaches	135 000
Number of clubs	40 000
Number of teams	119 000

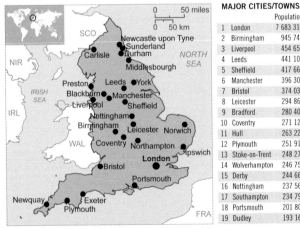

MAJOR CITIES/TOWNS

		Population
1	London	7 683 316
2	Birmingham	945 747
3	Liverpool	454 654
4	Leeds	441 108
5	Sheffield	417 666
6	Manchester	396 309
7	Bristol	374 037
8	Leicester	294 864
9	Bradford	280 407
10	Coventry	271 129
11	Hull	263 227
12	Plymouth	251 916
13	Stoke-on-Trent	248 276
14	Wolverhampton	246 754
15	Derby	244 663
16	Nottingham	237 567
17	Southampton	234 791
18	Portsmouth	201 808
19	Dudley	193 161

ENGLAND (PART OF THE UNITED KINGDOM)

Capital	London	Population	49 138 831 (23)	% in cities	90%
GDP per capita	$43 785 (20)	Area km²	130 439 km² (96)	GMT + / -	0
Neighbours (km)	Scotland 164, Wales 468 • Coast 3200				

RECENT INTERNATIONAL MATCHES PLAYED BY ENGLAND

2008	Opponents	Score		Venue	Comp	Scorers	Att	Referee
20-08	Czech Republic	D	2-2	London	Fr	Brown [45], Cole.J [92+]	69 738	Hauge NOR
6-09	Andorra	W	2-0	Barcelona	WCq	Cole.J 2 [48 55]	10 300	Cakir TUR
10-09	Croatia	W	4-1	Zagreb	WCq	Walcott 3 [26 59 82], Rooney [63]	35 218	Michel SVK
11-10	Kazakhstan	W	5-1	London	WCq	Ferdinand [52], OG [64], Rooney 2 [76 86], Defoe [90]	89 107	Allarts BEL
15-10	Belarus	W	3-1	Minsk	WCq	Gerrard [1], Rooney 2 [50 74]	29 600	Hauge NOR
19-11	Germany	W	2-1	Berlin	Fr	Upson [23], Terry [84]	74 244	Busacca SUI
2009								
11-02	Spain	L	0-2	Seville	Fr		42 102	Lannoy FRA
28-03	Slovakia	W	4-0	London	Fr	Heskey [7], Rooney 2 [70 90], Lampard [82]	85 512	Hamer LUX
1-04	Ukraine	W	2-1	London	WCq	Crouch [29], Terry [85]	87 548	Larsen Den
6-06	Kazakhstan	W	4-0	Almaty	WCq	Barry [40], Heskey [45], Rooney [72], Lampard [77p]	24 000	Jakobsson ISL
10-06	Andorra	W	6-0	London	WCq	Rooney 2 [4 39], Lampard [29], Defoe 2 [73 75], Crouch [80]	57 897	Nijhuis NED
12-08	Netherlands	D	2-2	Amsterdam	Fr	Defoe 2 [49 77]	48 000	Rizzoli ITA
5-09	Slovenia	W	2-1	London	Fr	Lampard [31p], Defoe [63]	67 232	Eriksson SWE
9-09	Croatia	W	5-1	London	WCq	Lampard 2 [7p 59], Gerrard 2 [18 67], Rooney [77]	87 319	Undiano ESP
10-10	Ukraine	L	0-1	Dnepropetrovsk	WCq		31 000	Skomina SVN
14-10	Belarus	W	3-0	London	WCq	Crouch 2 [4 76], Wright-Phillips [60]	76 897	Batista POR
14-11	Brazil	L	0-1	Doha	Fr		50 000	Abdou QAT
2010								
3-03	Egypt	W	3-1	London	Fr	Crouch 2 [56 80], Wright-Phillips [75]	80 602	Torres PAR
24-05	Mexico	W	3-1	London	Fr	King [17], Crouch [34], Johnson [47]	88 638	Toma JPN
30-05	Japan	W	2-1	Graz	Fr	Tanaka.MT OG [72], Nakazawa OG [83]	15 326	Eisner AUT
12-06	USA	D	1-1	Rustenburg	WCr1	Gerrard [4]	38 646	Simon BRA
18-06	Algeria	D	0-0	Cape Town	WCr1		64 100	Irmatov UZB
23-06	Slovenia	W	1-0	Port Elizabeth	WCr1	Defoe [23]	36 893	Stark GER
27-06	Germany	L	1-4	Bloemfontein	WCr2	Upson [37]	40 510	Larrionda URU
11-08	Hungary	W	2-1	London	Fr	Gerrard 2 [69 73]	72 024	Lannoy FRA
3-09	Bulgaria	W	4-0	London	ECq	Defoe 3 [3 61 86], Johnson.A [83]	73 426	Kassai HUN
7-09	Switzerland	W	3-1	Basel	ECq	Rooney [10], Johnson.A [69], Bent [88]	37 500	Rizzoli ITA
12-10	Montenegro	D	0-0	London	ECq		73 451	Grafe GER
17-11	France	L	1-2	London	Fr	Crouch [86]	85 495	Larsen DEN
2011								
9-02	Denmark	W	2-1	Copenhagen	Fr	Bent [10], Young [68]	21 523	Eriksson SWE
26-03	Wales	W	2-0	Cardiff	ECq	Lampard [7p], Bent [15]	68 959	Benquerenca POR
29-03	Ghana	D	1-1	London	Fr	Carroll [43]	80 102	Cakir TUR
4-06	Switzerland	D	2-2	London	ECq	Lampard [37p], Young [51]	84 459	Skomina SUI
2-09	Bulgaria	W	3-0	Sofia	ECq	Cahill [13], Rooney 2 [21 45]	27 230	De Bleeckere BEL
6-09	Wales	W	1-0	London	ECq	Young [35]	77 128	Schorgenhofer AUT
7-10	Montenegro	D	2-2	Podgorica	ECq	Young [11], Bent [31]	11 340	Stark GER
12-11	Spain	W	1-0	London	Fr	Lampard [49]	87 189	De Bleeckere BEL
15-11	Sweden	W	1-0	London	Fr	Barry [22]	48 876	Kralovec CZE

Fr = Friendly • EC = UEFA EURO 2012 • WC = FIFA World Cup • q = qualifier

ENGLAND NATIONAL TEAM HISTORICAL RECORDS

Caps
125 - Peter Shilton 1970-90 • **115** - David Beckham 1996-2009 • **108** - Bobby Moore 1962-73 • **106** - Bobby Charlton 1958-70 • **105** - Billy Wright 1946-59 • **93** - Ashley Cole 2001- • **90** - Frank Lampard 1999- & Bryan Robson 1980-91 • **89** - Michael Owen 1998-2008 & Steven Gerrard 2000- • **86** - Kenny Sansom 1979-88 • **85** - Gary Neville 1995-2007 • **84** - Ray Wilkins 1976-86 • **81** - Rio Ferdinand 1997- • **80** - Gary Lineker 1984-92 • **79** - John Barnes 1983-95 • **78** - Stuart Pearce 1987-99 • **77** - Terry Butcher 1980-90 • **76** - Tom Finney 1946-58 • **75** - David Seaman 1988-2002 • **73** - Gordon Banks 1963-72, Sol Campbell 1996-2007 & Wayne Rooney 2003- • **72** - Alan Ball 1965-75

Goals
49 - Bobby Charlton 1958-70 • **48** - Gary Lineker 1984-92 • **44** - Jimmy Greaves 1959-67 • **40** - Michael Owen 1998-2008 • **30** - Tom Finney 1946-58, Nat Lofthouse 1950-58 & Alan Shearer 1992-2000 • **29** - Vivian Woodward 1903-11 • **28** - Steve Bloomer 1895-1907 • **28** - Wayne Rooney 2003- • **27** - David Platt 1986-96 • **26** - Bryan Robson 1980-91 • **24** - Geoff Hurst 1966-72 • **23** - Stan Mortensen 1947-53 & Frank Lampard 1999- • **22** - Tommy Lawton 1938-48 & Peter Crouch 2005- • **21** - Mick Channon 1972-77 & Kevin Keegan 1972-82 • **20** - Martin Peters 1966-74 • **19** - Steven Gerrard 2000- • **18** - George Camsell 1929-36, Dixie Dean 1927-32, Roger Hunt 1962-69 & Johnny Haynes 1954-62 • **17** - David Beckham 1996-2009 & Tommy Taylor 1953-57 & Tony Woodcock 1978-86 • **15** - Jermain Defoe 2004-

Past Coaches
Walter Winterbottom 1946-63 • Alf Ramsey 1963-74 • Joe Mercer 1974 • Don Revie 1974-77 • Ron Greenwood 1977-82 • Bobby Robson 1982-90 • Graham Taylor 1990-93 • Terry Venables 1994-96 • Glenn Hoddle 1996-99 • Howard Wilkinson 1999 • Kevin Keegan 1999-2000 • Howard Wilkinson 2000 • Peter Taylor 2000 • Sven-Goran Eriksson SWE 2001-06 • Steve McLaren 2006-07 • Fabio Capello ITA 2008-12

ENGLAND 2010–11

BARCLAYS PREMIER LEAGUE

	Pl	W	D	L	F	A	Pts	Man Utd	Chelsea	Man City	Arsenal	Spurs	Liverpool	Everton	Fulham	Aston Villa	Sunderland	West Brom	Newcastle	Stoke City	Bolton W	Blackburn	Wigan Ath	Wolves	B'ham City	Blackpool	West Ham
Manchester United †	38	23	11	4	78	37	80		2-1	2-1	1-0	2-0	3-2	1-0	2-0	3-1	2-0	2-2	3-0	2-1	1-0	7-1	2-0	2-1	5-0	4-2	3-0
Chelsea †	38	21	8	9	69	33	71	2-1		2-0	2-0	2-1	0-1	1-1	1-0	3-0	3-6	0-2	2-2	2-0	1-0	2-0	1-0	2-0	3-1	4-0	3-0
Manchester City †	38	21	8	9	60	33	71	0-0	1-0		0-3	1-0	3-0	1-2	1-1	4-0	5-0	3-0	2-1	3-0	1-0	1-1	1-0	4-3	0-0	1-0	2-1
Arsenal †	38	19	11	8	72	43	68	1-0	3-1	0-0		2-3	1-1	2-1	2-1	1-2	0-0	2-3	0-1	1-0	4-1	0-0	3-0	2-0	2-1	6-0	1-0
Tottenham Hotspur ‡	38	16	14	8	55	46	62	0-0	1-1	0-0	3-3		2-1	1-1	1-0	2-1	1-1	2-2	2-0	3-2	2-1	4-2	0-1	3-1	2-1	1-1	0-0
Liverpool	38	17	7	14	59	44	58	3-1	2-0	3-0	1-1	0-2		2-2	1-0	3-0	2-2	1-0	3-0	2-0	2-1	2-1	1-1	0-1	5-0	1-2	3-0
Everton	38	13	15	10	51	45	54	3-3	1-0	2-1	1-1	2-2	1-2		2-0	2-1	2-2	2-0	1-4	0-1	1-0	1-1	2-0	0-0	1-1	5-3	2-2
Fulham	38	11	16	11	49	43	49	2-2	0-0	1-4	2-2	1-2	2-5	0-0		1-1	0-0	3-0	1-0	2-0	3-0	3-2	2-0	2-1	1-1	3-0	1-3
Aston Villa	38	12	12	14	48	59	48	2-2	0-0	1-0	2-4	1-2	1-0	1-0	2-2		0-1	2-1	1-0	1-1	4-1	1-1	0-1	0-0	3-2	3-0	2-3
Sunderland	38	12	11	15	45	56	47	0-0	2-4	1-0	1-1	1-2	0-2	2-2	0-3	1-0		2-3	1-1	2-0	1-0	3-0	4-2	1-3	2-2	0-2	1-0
West Bromwich Albion	38	12	11	15	56	71	47	1-2	1-3	0-2	2-2	1-1	2-1	1-1	0-2	1-2	1-0		3-1	0-3	1-1	1-3	2-2	1-1	3-1	3-2	3-3
Newcastle United	38	11	13	14	56	57	46	0-0	1-1	1-3	4-4	1-1	3-1	1-2	0-0	6-0	5-1	3-3		1-2	1-1	1-2	2-2	4-1	2-1	0-2	5-0
Stoke City ‡	38	13	7	18	46	48	46	1-2	1-1	1-1	3-1	1-2	2-0	0-0	2-2	1-3	2-1	1-4	1-0		2-0	1-0	0-1	3-0	3-2	0-1	1-1
Bolton Wanderers	38	12	10	16	52	56	46	2-2	0-4	0-2	2-1	4-2	0-1	2-0	0-0	0-3	2-1	2-2	2-0	5-1		2-1	1-1	1-0	2-2	2-2	3-0
Blackburn Rovers	38	11	10	17	46	59	43	1-1	1-2	0-1	1-2	0-1	3-1	1-0	1-1	2-0	0-0	2-0	0-0	0-2	1-0		2-1	3-0	1-1	2-2	1-1
Wigan Athletic	38	9	15	14	40	61	42	0-4	0-6	0-2	2-2	0-0	1-1	1-1	1-1	2-1	1-0	1-1	0-0	1-2	2-1	1-4		3-2	0-2	1-0	4-3
Wolverhampton Wand	38	11	7	20	46	66	40	2-1	1-0	2-1	0-2	3-3	0-3	0-3	1-1	1-2	3-2	3-1	1-1	2-2	3-2	3-1	2-1		1-0	4-0	1-1
Birmingham City ‡	38	8	15	15	37	58	39	1-1	1-0	2-0	3-1	1-0	0-0	0-2	0-2	1-1	2-0	1-3	0-2	1-0	2-1	2-1	0-0	1-1		2-0	2-2
Blackpool	38	10	9	19	55	78	39	2-3	1-3	2-3	1-3	3-1	2-1	2-2	2-2	1-1	1-2	2-1	1-1	4-0	4-3	1-2	1-3	2-1	1-2		1-3
West Ham United	38	7	12	19	43	70	33	2-4	1-3	1-3	0-3	1-0	3-1	1-1	1-1	1-2	0-3	2-2	1-2	3-0	1-3	1-1	3-1	3-1	2-0	0-1	

14/08/2010 - 22/05/2011 • † Qualified for the UEFA Champions League • ‡ Qualified for the Europa League

Top scorers: **20** - Dimitar Berbatov BUL, Manchester United & Carlos Tevez ARG, Manchester City • **18** - Robin van Persie NED, Arsenal • **17** - Darren Bent, Sunderland/Aston Villa • **15** - Peter Odemwingie NGA, West Bromwich Albion

ENGLAND 2010–11

COCA-COLA FOOTBALL LEAGUE CHAMPIONSHIP (2)

	Pl	W	D	L	F	A	Pts	QPR	Norwich	Swansea	Cardiff	Reading	Nottm For	Leeds Utd	Burnley	Millwall	Leicester	Hull City	Midd'boro	Ipswich T	Watford	Bristol City	Portsmouth	Barnsley	Coventry C	Derby Co	C Palace	Doncaster	PNE	Sheff Utd	Scunthorpe
Queens Park Rang's	46	24	16	6	71	32	88		0-0	4-0	2-1	3-1	1-1	1-2	1-0	0-1	0-1	1-3	0-2	0-1	3-2	2-2	0-4	0-2	1-0	0-2	1-3	0-3	1-3	0-3	2-0
Norwich City	46	23	15	8	83	58	84	1-0		2-0	1-1	2-1	1-2	1-1	2-2	1-4	3-0	2-1	0-4	1-2	3-3	1-0	2-2	1-2	2-3	2-1	2-1	1-1	1-1	4-2	6-0
Swansea City ‡	46	24	8	14	69	42	80	0-3	0-0		0-1	1-0	3-2	3-0	1-0	1-1	2-0	1-1	1-0	4-1	1-1	0-1	1-2	1-0	2-1	0-2	1-0	0-3	0-4	0-4	0-2
Cardiff City ‡	46	23	11	12	76	54	80	2-2	3-1	0-1		2-2	0-2	1-1	2-1	1-2	2-1	0-0	2-4	3-0	2-2	2-2	0-4	1-0	0-4	0-1	1-0	4-1	1-2	3-1	2-1
Reading ‡	46	20	17	9	77	51	77	0-1	3-1	3-1	1-1		1-0	0-2	1-2	1-3	1-1	1-5	2-1	0-1	1-4	1-2	0-3	0-0	0-0	2-1	3-0	4-3	2-1	2-3	1-2
Nottingham Forest ‡	46	20	15	11	69	50	75	0-0	1-3	1-2	1-3	4-1		1-2	0-1	3-2	0-1	1-0	1-1	0-1	0-1	2-2	1-5	2-3	0-0	0-2	2-1	5-1	5-2	3-0	0-0
Leeds United	46	19	15	12	81	70	72	2-0	2-2	1-0	4-0	0-4	1-1		1-0	3-1	1-2	2-1	1-0	0-2	2-3	1-3	3-3	3-1	0-1	2-2	1-5	2-4	6-1	0-4	0-4
Burnley	46	18	14	14	65	61	68	0-0	2-1	2-1	1-1	0-4	1-0	2-3		0-3	3-0	4-0	3-1	1-2	3-0	0-0	3-3	2-2	2-2	1-1	0-1	3-1	1-4	3-4	2-0
Millwall	46	18	13	15	62	48	67	2-0	1-1	0-2	3-3	0-0	0-0	3-2	1-0		2-0	4-0	4-0	3-2	1-6	0-0	0-1	2-0	3-1	2-0	3-1	1-0	4-0	1-0	4-0
Leicester City	46	19	10	17	76	71	67	0-2	2-3	2-1	2-1	1-2	1-0	2-2	4-0	4-2		1-1	0-0	4-2	4-2	1-0	1-4	1-2	0-1	4-1	1-5	1-1	0-2	3-1	2-3
Hull City	46	16	17	13	52	51	65	0-0	1-1	2-0	0-2	1-1	0-0	2-0	1-0	0-1	0-1		2-4	1-0	0-0	2-0	1-2	2-0	0-0	2-0	1-3	1-1	0-0	1-0	0-1
Middlesbrough	46	17	11	18	68	68	62	0-3	1-3	4-1	0-3	1-1	1-1	2-2	1-0	1-3	3-2	2-1		3-2	1-2	1-2	1-2	1-3	0-1	1-0	2-0	1-2	3-0	1-0	1-0
Ipswich Town	46	18	8	20	62	68	62	0-3	1-5	1-3	2-0	1-3	0-1	2-1	1-2	0-3	0-1	3-1	3-2		0-3	2-0	0-2	1-3	1-2	0-2	2-2	1-2	3-0	0-2	1-0
Watford	46	16	13	17	77	71	61	0-2	2-2	3-4	4-1	1-1	1-0	1-1	3-0	1-3	1-0	3-1	2-3	1-2		3-3	3-0	1-0	2-2	3-0	1-2	2-2	2-3	3-0	0-2
Bristol City	46	17	9	20	62	65	60	1-1	0-3	0-2	3-0	1-0	2-3	0-2	2-0	0-3	2-0	3-0	0-4	0-1	0-2		2-0	3-3	1-2	2-0	0-1	1-1	0-1	3-0	2-0
Portsmouth	46	15	12	19	53	60	57	1-1	0-0	0-0	2-1	2-1	2-1	2-1	1-6	1-2	3-0	0-0	0-3	2-3	1-1	0-0		3-1	1-1	0-2	3-1	1-1	0-2	3-1	1-0
Barnsley	46	14	14	18	55	66	56	0-1	0-2	1-1	2-0	1-3	2-5	1-2	0-0	2-1	2-1	0-0	0-4	2-1	0-4	2-1	1-0		4-2	0-3	0-2	1-1	1-1	1-2	0-0
Coventry City	46	14	13	19	54	58	55	0-2	1-2	0-1	1-2	0-2	1-3	1-0	2-1	1-0	1-1	0-1	1-2	0-1	1-2	0-1	4-2	0-3		2-1	2-1	2-1	2-0	0-1	1-1
Derby County	46	13	10	23	58	71	49	2-2	1-2	2-1	1-2	1-2	0-1	2-4	0-0	0-2	0-1	3-1	1-1	2-4	1-0	2-2	0-0	2-2	5-0		1-3	3-0	0-1	3-2	1-2
Crystal Palace	46	12	12	22	44	69	48	1-2	0-0	0-3	1-0	3-3	0-3	1-0	0-0	0-1	3-2	0-0	4-1	2-3	2-0	0-4	1-2	1-2	0-2	2-2		1-0	1-0	1-0	1-2
Doncaster Rovers	46	11	15	20	55	81	48	0-1	3-1	1-1	3-0	3-1	1-0	0-1	0-1	2-1	1-3	1-2	1-0	6-1	1-1	1-0	2-0	2-1	1-2	3-0	0-2		1-2	0-3	0-0
Preston North End	46	10	12	24	54	79	42	1-1	0-1	2-1	0-1	1-2	1-2	0-0	1-0	1-2	1-3	1-0	3-1	0-4	1-0	1-4	1-0	1-2	2-4	3-0	2-1	1-2		1-2	3-1
Sheffield United	46	11	9	26	44	79	42	0-3	1-2	1-0	0-2	1-2	1-2	0-3	3-1	1-0	1-2	3-1	2-1	2-0	1-3	2-1	0-2	2-0	1-0	1-3	2-2	2-1	0-0		0-4
Scunthorpe United	46	12	6	28	43	87	42	4-1	0-1	1-0	2-4	0-2	1-0	1-4	0-0	1-2	0-3	1-5	0-2	1-1	2-0	2-1	1-0	0-0	2-0	3-0	1-3	0-3	3-3	2-1	

6/08/2010 - 7/05/2011 • ‡ Qualified for the play-offs • Top scorers: **24** - Danny Graham, Watford • **21** - Shane Long, Reading & Grant Holt, Norwich

Play-off semi-finals: Nottingham Forest 0-0 1-3 **Swansea City** • **Reading** 0-0 3-0 Cardiff City

Play-off final: **Swansea City** 4-2 Reading. Wembley, 30-05-2011, Att: 86 581, Ref: Dowd. Scorers - Sinclair 3 [21p 22 80p], Dobbie [40] for Swansea; Allen OG [49], Mills [57] for Reading

ENGLAND 2010–11

COCA-COLA FOOTBALL LEAGUE ONE (3)

Result columns (left to right): Brighton, South'pton, Hudd'field, MK Dons, Peter'boro, B'mouth, Orient, Exeter, Rochdale, Colchester, Brentford, Carlisle, Charlton, Yeovil, Sheff Wed, Hartlepool, Tranmere, Oldham, Notts Co, Walsall, Dagenham, Bristol Rov, Plymouth, Swindon

Team	Pl	W	D	L	F	A	Pts	Results
Brighton & Hove Alb	46	28	11	7	85	40	95	1-2 2-3 3-1 2-0 1-1 5-0 3-0 2-2 2-1 0-4 3-1 1-2 0-2 0-4 1-2 0-2 1-1 0-2 1-4 3-2 2-4 0-2 1
Southampton	46	28	8	10	86	38	92	0-0 4-1 4-1 3-2 2-0 1-1 4-0 0-2 0-0 2-1 0-2 0-3 0-2 0-2 0-2 0-2 0-1 0-0 3-1 4-0 1-0 0-1 4-1
Huddersfield Town ‡	46	25	12	9	77	48	87	2-1 2-0 1-1 4-1 2-2 2-2 0-1 0-0 4-4 2-0 3-1 4-2 1-0 0-1 0-0 0-3 0-1 0-2 1-0 1-3 2-0 0
Peterborough Utd ‡	46	23	10	13	106	75	79	0-3 4-4 4-2 2-1 3-3 2-2 3-0 2-1 1-1 2-1 6-0 1-5 2-2 5-3 4-0 2-1 5-2 3-4 1-5 0-3 0-2 1 5-4
Milton Keynes Dons‡	46	23	8	15	67	60	77	1-0 2-0 1-3 1-0 2-0 2-3 1-0 1-1 1-1 1-3 2-2 0-3 2-1 4-1 2-0 0-0 2-1 1-1 2-0 2-0 1-3 2-1
Bournemouth ‡	46	19	14	13	75	54	71	1-0 1-3 1-1 5-1 3-2 1-3 3-0 1-2 1-2 2-2 0-0 0-1 1-2 3-0 3-3 3-3 0-2 1-3 3-2
Leyton Orient	46	19	13	14	71	62	70	0-0 0-2 1-2 2-1 2-2 2-2 3-0 2-1 4-2 1-0 0-0 1-3 1-5 4-0 1-0 0-3 1-0 2-0 0-0 1-4 1-2 0-3 0
Exeter City	46	20	10	16	66	71	70	1-2 1-2 1-4 2-1 2-1 1-2 0-2 1 1-0 2-2 4-2 3-5 1-1 2-1 1-2 0-3 1-2 1-2 2-1 2-1 1-0 0
Rochdale	46	18	14	14	63	55	68	2-2 2-0 3-0 2-2 1-4 0-0 1-0 1-0 1-2 0-1 2-3 2-0 0-1 2-1 1-1 0-3 2-3 2-3 1-1 1-3 3
Colchester United	46	16	14	16	57	63	62	1-1 0-2 0-3 1-2 0-1 2-1 1-4 2-0 1-2 3-3 0-0 1-2 3-3 0-0 1-2 0-2 0-2 2-2 1-1 1-2 1-0 2-1
Brentford	46	17	10	19	55	62	61	0-1 0-3 0-1 2-1 0-2 1-2 1-1 1-3 1-1 2-1 2-1 1-2 1-2 1-0 2-0 1-3 1-1 1-2 2-1 1-0 2-0 0-1
Carlisle United	46	16	11	19	60	62	59	0-0 3-2 2-2 0-1 4-1 1-0 0-1 2-2 1-4 1-2 0 3-4 0-2 0-1 1-0 2-0 2-2 2-1 0-1 3-0 2-4 0-1 1-0 0
Charlton Athletic	46	15	14	17	62	66	59	0-4 1-1 0-1 3-2 1-0 3-1 1-1 3-3 1-1 0-0 1-1 3 3-2 1-0 0-1 1-1 1-0 0-1 2-2 1-1 2-0 1-2 1-2 0-2 4
Yeovil Town	46	16	11	19	56	66	59	0-1 1-1 1-1 0-2 1-0 2-2 2-1 1-3 0-1 4-2 2-0 1-0 0-1 0-2 3-1 1-1 2-1 1-1 1-3 0-1 1-0 3-3
Sheffield Wed'day	46	16	10	20	67	67	58	1-0 0-1 0-2 1-4 2-2 1-1 1-0 1-2 2-0 2-1 1-3 0-1 2-2 2 2-0 4-0 0-0 1-3 0-2 0-6 2-2 4-3 1
Hartlepool	46	15	12	19	47	65	57	3-1 0-0 0-1 2-0 0-1 2-2 0-1 2-3 0-2 1-0 3-0 0-0 4-2 1-3 1-0 5 1-1 4-2 1-2 1-0 1-2 2-2 0-2
Tranmere Rovers	46	15	11	20	53	60	56	1-1 2-0 0-2 1-0 4-2 0-3 1-2 4-0 1-1 2-4 0-1 1-1 0-3 0-0 1 2-0 1-3 3-2 0-0 1-1 0-0 2
Oldham Athletic	46	13	17	16	53	62	56	0-1 0-6 1-0 0-5 1-2 2-1 1-3 3-1 2-0 0-2 1-0 0-0 2-3 4-0 0-0 3-0 1-1 1-1 1-4 2-2 0
Notts County	46	14	8	24	46	60	50	1-1 1-3 0-3 0-1 2-0 0-2 3-2 0-2 1-2 2-0 1-0 1-1 0-4 0-0 2-3 0-0 1-0 2 1-1 1-0 0-1 2-0 1-0
Walsall	46	12	12	22	56	75	48	1-3 1-0 2-4 1-3 1-2 0-2 1-0 2-2 0-1 0-0 1-3 2-2 1-2 0-0 1-1 5-2 1-4 1-1 0-3 1-0 6-1 2-1 1-2
Dagenham & Red.	46	12	11	23	52	70	47	0-1 1-3 1-1 0-2 0-1 1-2 2-0 1-1 0-1 4-1 3-0 1-2 1-1 1-1 1-2 2-0 1-3 1-1 0-2 0-1 3-1 0-2 1-2
Bristol Rovers	46	11	12	23	48	82	45	2-4 0-4 0-1 2-1 2-1 0-0 3-0 2-2 1-0 1-0 0-1 1-2 2-1 1-0 0-0 1-1 2-1 2-0 2-2 2-3 3-1
Plymouth Argyle §10	46	15	7	24	51	74	42	0-2 1-3 2-1 0-3 1-0 1-2 1-4 2-0 0-1 2-1 1-2 1-2 2-0 0-3 2-0 1-1 3-0 2-1 1-2 0-2 1-3 1 1-0
Swindon Town	46	9	14	23	50	72	41	1-2 1-0 1-0 1-0 1-1 2-2 0-0 1-1 0-1 1-0 0-2 1-1 0-0 2-1 2-0 0-1 1-2 1-2 1-2 3

7/08/2010 • 7/05/2011 • ‡ Qualified for the play-offs • § = points deducted • Top scorer: **26** - Craig Mackail-Smith SCO, Peterborough
Play-off semi-finals: Milton Keynes Dons 3-2 0-2 **Peterborough Utd** • Bournemouth 1-1 3-3 2-4p **Huddersfield Town**
Final: **Peterborough** 3-0 Huddersfield Town. Old Trafford, 29-05-2011, Att: 48 410, Ref: Tanner. Scorers - Rowe [78], Mackail-Smith [80], McCann [85]

ENGLAND 2010–11

COCA-COLA FOOTBALL LEAGUE TWO (4)

Result columns (left to right): Chesterfield, Bury, Wycombe, Shrewsbury, Accrington, Stevenage, Torquay, Gillingham, Rotherham, Crewe Alex, Port Vale, Oxford Utd, Southend, Aldershot, Macc'field, Northants, Cheltenham, Bradford C, Burton Alb, Morecambe, Hereford, Barnet, Lincoln, Stockport

Team	Pl	W	D	L	F	A	Pts	Results
Chesterfield	46	24	14	8	85	51	86	2-3 4-1 4-3 5-2 1-0 1-3 1-5 0-5 5-2 0-1 2-1 2-2 2-1 2-1 2-1 0-2 4 0-2 1 2-0 2 4-0 2-1 4-1
Bury	46	23	12	11	82	50	81	1-1 1-3 1-0 3-0 0-1 2-5 4-1 1-3 0-1 0-1 1-2 2-1 1-2 3-0 1-1 0-1 0-1 1-2 0-1 0-0 1
Wycombe Wanderers	46	22	14	10	69	50	80	1-2 1-0 2-2 1-2 0-1 1-3 1-0 1-0 2-0 1-1 0-0 3-2 1-2 2-2 2-2 1-1 0-4 1-2 0-2 1-4 2-2 2-0
Shrewsbury Town ‡	46	22	13	11	72	49	79	0-0 0-3 1-1 0-0 1-0 1-1 0-0 0-1 2-3 0-1 1-1 1-4 1-3 1-1 1-3 1-3 0-1 3-4 0-2 1-2 0-2 0
Accrington Stanley ‡	46	18	19	9	73	55	73	2-2 1-0 1-1 1-3 1-0 1-0 7-4 2-3 3-2 0-0 3-0 1-0 0-3 0-1 2-3 4-2 3-0 1-1 4-0 3-1 3-0 3-0
Stevenage ‡	46	18	15	13	62	45	69	0-0 3-3 0-2 1-1 2-2 0-0 2-2 3-0 1-1 0-0 1-0 0-0 1-2 2-2 2-0 1-4 0-2 1-2 1-2 0-0 1-4 2-2 1-3 1
Torquay United ‡ §1	46	17	18	11	74	53	68	0-0 3-4 0-0 5-0 0-0 2-0 1-1 1-1 2-1 0-0 3-4 1-0 1-1 3-3 0-2 1-2 0-1 0-3 1-1 3-1 2-0 2-0
Gillingham	46	17	17	12	67	57	68	0-2 1-1 0-2 2-0 3-1 1-0 1-1 3-1 1-3 3-0 0-0 0-0 2-1 2-4 1-0 1-1 2-0 1-0 1-0 0-2 4-0 1-2 1
Rotherham United	46	17	15	14	75	60	66	1-0 0-0 3-4 1-3 2-0 1-1 3-1 0-1 3-1 5-0 2-1 1-2 1-1 2-1 2-6 4-0 0-3 3-0 1-0 0-0 0-2 1-4 0
Crewe Alexandra	46	18	11	17	87	65	65	2-0 3-0 3-0 1-2 0-0 0-1 3-3 1-3 1-0 2-1 1-1 0-3 1-1 2-0 8-1 2-1 4-1 1-2 1-0 1-7 0-1 1-2 0
Port Vale	46	17	14	15	54	49	65	1-1 0-0 2-1 1-0 2-0 1-3 1-2 0-0 1-0 2-1 1-2 1-1 0-2 1-1 1-0 1-2 1-2 1-7 2-1 1-0 0-2 1-1 2
Oxford United	46	17	12	17	58	60	63	0-0 1-2 2-2 3-1 0-0 1-2 0-2 0-1 2-1 2-1 2-1 0-2 0-1 2-1 3-1 1-1 2-1 3-0 4-0 0-1 2-1 0-1
Southend United	46	16	13	17	62	56	61	2-3 1-1 3-2 0-2 1-1 1-0 2-1 2-2 0-0 2-1 3-2 1 0-0 4-1 1-1 1-2 4-0 1-1 2-3 4-0 2-1 1-0 1
Aldershot Town	46	14	19	13	54	54	61	0-2 1-3 0-0 3-0 1-1 1-1 1-0 1-2 2-3 2-1 2-1 0 0-0 1-1 0-2 1-0 1-2 2-1 1-3 1-0 2-0 2-1 0
Macclesfield Town	46	14	13	19	59	73	55	1-1 2-4 0-1 0-1 2-0 4-3 2-4 0-2 1-0 0-0 3-3 2-0 0-0 2-0 0-0 2-1 2-0 1-2 1-0 1-1 1-1 1-0 2
Northampton Town	46	11	19	16	63	71	52	1-2 2-4 1-2 3-0 0-2 0-2 2-2 1-2 6-2 0-0 2-1 2-1 1-0 1 1-2 0 2-3 3 3-4 0-0 2-1 2
Cheltenham Town	46	13	13	20	56	77	52	0-3 0-2 1-2 0-1 1-2 1-0 2-2 1-2 1-1 3-2 0-0 1-0 2-1 2-0 1-1 0 4-0 2-1 1-1 0-3 1-1 2-2 1
Bradford City	46	15	7	24	43	68	52	0-1 1-0 1-0 1-2 1-1 1-0 0-3 0-1 2-1 1-5 0-2 5-0 0-0 2-2 1-0 1-1 1-3 1 1-1 0-1 1-0 1 3-2 3
Burton Albion	46	12	15	19	56	70	51	1-0 1-3 1-2 0-0 0-1 1-0 2-3 1-3 1-2 4-1 1-0 0-0 0-3 1-1 2-3 2-1 1-2 0-3 0 3-2 3-0 1-4-3 1-2 1
Morecambe	46	13	12	21	54	73	51	1-1 4-0 3-1 0-1 2-0 0-2 1-1 1-0 0-0 3-2 1-1 1-1 2-1 2-1 1-0 1-2 1-2 2-1 2-5 0
Hereford United §3	46	12	17	17	50	66	50	3-0 0-3 0-0 2-1 1-4 2-2 0-0 0-1 1-0 1-0 1-0 2-1 3-2 2-2 2-1 1-1 1-1 1-0 0-2 1 1-2 0 1-3 0
Barnet	46	12	12	22	58	77	48	2-2 1-1 0-1 1-1 2-0 0-3 0-3 1-2 1-4 2-1 1-0 2-2 0-2 1-2 1-0 4-1 3-1 0-2 0-0 1-2 2-0 4-2 1 3
Lincoln City	46	13	8	25	45	81	47	0-2 0-5 1-2 1-5 0-0 1-0 2-0 4-0 6-1 1-1 0-3 1-2 1-0 3-2 1-0 2-0 2-2 1-0 3-1 1-1 1-0 0-0 2 0-3 0-0
Stockport County	46	9	13	24	48	96	40	1-1 2-1 0-0 4-2 2-2 2-1 1-1 5-3 3-3 3-0 5-2 1-2 1-2 2-1 4-2 2-1 1-1 1-0 0-0 0-5 2-1 3-4

7/08/2010 - 7/05/2011 • ‡ Qualified for the play-offs • § = points deducted • Top scorer: **26** - Clayton Donaldson, Crewe Alexandra
Play-off semi-finals: **Stevenage** 2-0 1-0 Accrington Stanley • **Torquay Utd** 2-0 0-0 Shrewsbury Town
Play-off final: **Stevenage** 1-0 Torquay Utd. Old Trafford, 28-05-2011, Att: 11 484, Ref: Deadman. Scorer - Mousinho [41]

ENGLAND 2010-11

FOOTBALL CONFERENCE BLUE SQUARE PREMIER (5)

Team	Pl	W	D	L	F	A	Pts
Crawley Town	46	31	12	3	93	30	**105**
AFC Wimbledon ‡	46	27	9	10	83	47	**90**
Luton Town ‡	46	23	15	8	85	37	**84**
Wrexham ‡	46	22	15	9	66	49	**81**
Fleetwood Town ‡	46	22	12	12	68	42	**78**
Kidderminster H §5	46	20	17	9	74	60	**72**
Darlington	46	18	17	11	61	42	**71**
York City	46	19	14	13	55	50	**71**
Newport County	46	18	15	13	78	60	**69**
Bath City	46	16	15	15	64	68	**63**
Grimsby Town	46	15	17	14	72	62	**62**
Mansfield Town	46	17	10	19	73	75	**61**
Kettering Town	46	15	13	18	64	75	**58**
Rushden & D §5	46	16	14	16	65	62	**57**
Gateshead	46	14	15	17	65	68	**57**
Hayes & Yeading	46	15	6	25	57	81	**51**
Cambridge United	46	11	17	18	53	61	**50**
Barrow	46	12	14	20	52	67	**50**
Tamworth	46	12	13	21	62	83	**49**
Forest Green	46	10	16	20	53	72	**46**
Southport	46	11	13	22	56	77	**46**
Altrincham	46	11	11	24	47	87	**44**
Eastbourne Boro	46	10	9	27	62	104	**39**
Histon §5	46	8	9	29	41	90	**28**

Results grid (opponents in order: Crawley T, Wimbledon, Luton T, Wrexham, Fleetwood T, Kidminster, Darlington, York C, Newport Co, Bath C, Grimsby T, Mansfield T, Kettering T, Rushden, Gateshead, Hayes & Y, Cambridge, Barrow, Tamworth, Forest Green, Southport, Altrincham, Eastbourne, Histon):

- Crawley Town: 3-1 1-1 3-2 1-2 1-0 1-0 1-0 1-2 3-2 1-0 2-0 2-1 4-0 2-1 5-2 3-0 3-2 3-1 1-0 7-0 3-1 5-0
- AFC Wimbledon: 2-1 · 0-0 1-1 0-1 2-0 2-1 2-2 4-0 2-1 2-1 3-2 1-0 1-0 3-1 3-0 2-0 3-0 1-1 5-0 4-1 3-0 2-0
- Luton Town: 1-2 3-0 · 1-1 1-4 1-4 0-5 0-1 3-1 1-1 0-2 0-2 2-3 0-2 2-1 2-0 0-0 2-0 6-1 6-0 2-1 3-0 5-1
- Wrexham: 0-0 1-2 1-0 · 0-0 2-2 1-1 1-1 0-2 0-2 0-1 1-2 0-1 1-2 7-0 2-1 0-1 1-4 2-2 1-2 1-2 1-2 1-4-0
- Fleetwood Town: 1-2 1-0 3-1 0-1 · 1-1 0-2 1-1 2-1 3-0 3-0 4-1 1-0 0-1 2-2 1-0 2-2 0-2 1-2 0-2 0-3 1-0 1-1-1
- Kidderminster H: 0-0 2-0 3-3 1-0 2-1 · 1-2 0-0 2-3 1-0 3-2 1-3 4-1 1-0 2-1 3-1 0-2 0-2 2-1 0-3 4-2 1-2 1-2-2
- Darlington: 1-1 0-0 2-2 0-1 4-0 1-0 · 1-1 2-0 2-1 0-2 2-0 2-0 0-1 1-1 0-3 1-0 3-1 1-1 0-3 0-1 6-1 3-1
- York City: 1-1 4-1 1-0 1-1 1-0 1-2 0-0 · 2-1 1-1 0-2 1-0 1-2 0-2 1-2 0-0 0-1 2-2 1-2 0-3 0-1 0-1-0
- Newport County: 0-1 3-3 1-1 1-1 3-3 0-2 1-4 0-1 · 1-2 2-1 1-0 1-2 1-3 2-1 2-1 1-5 0-1 5-1 3-1 2-0 2-1 3-3 2-2
- Bath City: 0-2 2-0 0-0 2-1 1-0 2-0 2-2 2-2 2-0 · 2-1 2-0 1-1 2-1 1-0 0-1 5-1 4-1 0-1 2-0 4-2 1-2 2-1 1-2-1
- Grimsby Town: 0-0 2-1 2-0 2-1 1-2 3-3 0-1 0-0 2-0 2-2 · 7-2 2-1 1-1 2-2 1-2 1-1 1-1 2-1 1-1 1-0 1-1 2-2-1
- Mansfield Town: 1-4 2-5 0-0 2-3 2-5 1-2 1-1 5-0 3-2 0-0 2-1 · 1-1 2-1 3-2 3-1 0-1 0-1 0-1 3-1 3-2 2-0 1-4 0-1-0
- Kettering Town: 0-0 1-2 1-3 1-2 1-1 1-0 0-0 1-1 2-0 2-1 1-2 0-2 · 0-1 1-4 2-1 2-2 1-1 0-1 2-1 3-1 3-3 3-3 0-4-3
- Rushden & D: 0-1 1-0 0-1 2-2 1-1 2-1 2-1 2-1 0-4 0-1 5-1 4-1 1-0 · 1-2 0-2 1-1 2-2 2-2 1-2 2-2 2-2 0-2-0
- Gateshead: 0-0 0-2 1-0 0-1 0-2 2-2 2-0 3-1 7-1 1-0 0-1 0-0 2-2 · 1-0 2-3 3-0 3-1 1-1 1-0 2-0 3-0 2-0
- Hayes & Yeading: 0-3 0-0 1-0 3-1 2-0 4-3 2-1 2-1 2-2 1-0 3-4 0-3 2-3 3-3-1 · 2-0 2-0 2-1 3-4 1-0 0-1 2-1 1-2
- Cambridge United: 2-2 1-2 0-0 1-3 0-1 1-2 0-1 1-0 1-1 2-1 1-1 1-5 3-0 0-0 2-5 0-1 0 · 3-1 3-3 1-1 0-0 4-0 2-0 0-0
- Barrow: 1-1 2-0 0-1 0-1 0-2 2-1 1-0 2-1 0-1 0-1 2-2 2-5 0-2 0-1 3-2 0-1 2-3 · 2-0 2-3 0-1 1-1 4-0 1-1
- Tamworth: 0-3 2-5 3-1 1-1 0-2 2-2 1-1 1-3 3-2 2-2 2-1 0-2 3-1 1-1 2-1 1-2 1-2 3-1 · 2-1 0-1 1-0 4-2 0-1
- Forest Green: 0-3 0-0 0-1 3-0 1-1 1-1 2-1 0-0 0-0 3-3 2-1 0-2 2-2 1-1 0-1 1-2 3-4 0 · 0-0 1-0 3-4 0-1
- Southport: 0-4 0-1 2-1 0-1 1-0 2-4 1-0 2-2 1-2 3-2 2-1 2-1 2-2 5-1 0-0 1-0 1-2 4-2 1-4-0 · 1-0 1-3 3-1
- Altrincham: 0-1 0-2 0-1 0-0 1-0 1-2 2-2 0-0 1-3 0-3 2-2 0-4 3-2 2-0 4-3 2-2 2-1 1-4 2-2 2-0 2-0 0-2 1-1 · 3-4 0-3
- Eastbourne Boro: 1-2 2-3 2-4 4-3 0-6 1-1 1-2 1-0 0-2 0-2 3-1 3-1 3-0 2-0 3-5 0-0 2-0 2-1 4-0 0-4 1-5-0 · 2-2
- Histon: 0-2 0-4 0-4 1-1 1-0 0-1 0-1 1-2 0-0 1-2 1-6 2-3 0-3 0-2 1-3 0-1 0-2 3-1 1-1 2-0 3-2 1-3 0-1-1 ·

14/08/2010 - 30/04/2011 • ‡ = points deducted for the play-offs • § = points deducted • Rushden & Diamonds relegated at the end of the season
Top scorer: 37 - Matt Tubbs, Crawley Town • 25 - Alan Connell, Grimsby Town • 23 - Danny Kedwell, AFC Wimbledon
Play-off semi-finals: Fleetwood Town 0-2 1-6 **AFC Wimbledon** • Wrexham 0-3 1-2 **Luton Town**
Play-off final: **AFC Wimbledon** 0-0 4-3p Luton Town. Eastlands, Manchester, 21-05-2011, Att: 18 195, Ref: Adcock

---

ENGLAND 2010-11 FOOTBALL CONFERENCE BLUE SQUARE NORTH (6)

Team	Pl	W	D	L	F	A	Pts
Alfreton Town	40	29	5	6	97	33	**92**
AFC Telford United ‡	40	23	13	4	71	29	**82**
Boston United ‡	40	23	10	7	72	33	**79**
Eastwood Town	40	22	7	11	82	50	**73**
Guiseley ‡	40	20	13	7	56	41	**73**
Nuneaton Town ‡	40	21	9	10	66	44	**72**
Solihull Moors	40	18	10	12	66	49	**64**
Droylsden	40	17	9	14	69	67	**60**
Blyth Spartans	40	16	10	14	61	54	**58**
Stalybridge Celtic	40	16	9	15	64	55	**57**
Workington	40	16	6	18	52	60	**54**
Harrogate Town	40	13	11	16	53	66	**50**
Corby Town	40	13	10	17	58	80	**49**
Gloucester City	40	14	5	21	49	63	**47**
Hinckley United	40	13	7	20	76	76	**46**
Worcester City	40	12	10	18	49	55	**46**
Vauxhall Motors	40	12	9	19	52	71	**45**
Gainsborough Tr'ty	40	12	5	23	50	74	**41**
Hyde	40	10	6	24	44	73	**36**
Stafford Rangers	40	8	8	24	39	78	**32**
Redditch United §5	40	2	8	30	30	105	**9**
Ilkeston Town				Expelled after 7 games			

14/08/2010 - 30/04/2011 • ‡ Qualified for the play-offs
§ = points deducted
Play-off semis: Nuneaton Town 1-1 1-2 **AFC Telford Utd** • Guiseley 1-0 2-3 Boston United
Play-off final: **AFC Telford United** 3-2 Guiseley

ENGLAND 2010-11 FOOTBALL CONFERENCE BLUE SQUARE SOUTH (6)

Team	Pl	W	D	L	F	A	Pts
Braintree Town	42	27	8	7	78	33	**89**
Farnborough ‡	42	25	7	10	83	47	**82**
Ebbsfleet United ‡	42	22	12	8	75	51	**78**
Chelmsford City ‡	42	23	8	11	82	50	**77**
Woking ‡	42	22	10	10	63	42	**76**
Welling United §5	42	24	8	10	81	47	**75**
Dover Athletic	42	22	8	12	80	51	**74**
Eastleigh	42	22	6	14	74	53	**72**
Havant & Wat'ville	42	16	10	16	56	51	**58**
Dartford	42	15	12	15	60	59	**57**
Bromley	42	15	12	15	49	61	**57**
Weston-Super-Mare	42	15	8	19	56	67	**53**
Basingstoke Town	42	13	10	19	50	63	**49**
Boreham Wood	42	12	11	19	56	67	**47**
Staines Town	42	11	14	17	48	63	**47**
Bishops Stortford	42	13	6	23	48	79	**45**
Dorchester Town	42	10	14	18	49	59	**44**
Hampton & Rich'd	42	9	15	18	43	61	**42**
Maidenhead United	42	10	10	22	43	70	**40**
Thurrock	42	8	13	21	50	77	**37**
Lewes	42	9	9	24	34	70	**36**
St Albans City §10	42	7	13	22	39	75	**24**

14/08/2010 - 30/04/2011 • ‡ Qualified for the play-offs
§ = points deducted
Play-off semis: Chelmsford City 1-4 1-2 **Ebbsfleet United** • Woking 0-1 1-1 **Farnborough**
Play-off final: Farnborough 2-4 **Ebbsfleet United**

ENGLAND 2010–11 ISTHMIAN LEAGUE RYMAN PREMIER (7)

	Pl	W	D	L	F	A	Pts
Sutton United	42	26	9	7	76	33	**87**
Tonbridge Angels‡	42	22	10	10	71	45	**76**
Bury Town ‡	42	22	10	10	67	49	**76**
Lowestoft Town ‡	42	20	15	7	68	30	**75**
Harrow Borough ‡	42	22	7	13	77	51	**73**
Canvey Island	42	21	10	11	69	51	**73**
Kingstonian	42	21	9	12	66	50	**72**
Concord Rangers	42	21	8	13	72	55	**71**
Cray Wanderers	42	20	9	13	72	46	**69**
AFC Hornchurch	42	19	12	11	60	46	**69**
Billericay Town	42	20	9	13	61	81	**69**
Wealdstone	42	16	10	16	58	54	**58**
Carshalton Ath	42	14	10	18	49	57	**52**
Tooting &Mitcham	42	13	10	19	63	85	**49**
Hendon	42	12	10	20	61	81	**46**
Margate	42	11	12	19	52	64	**45**
Horsham	42	11	11	20	43	77	**44**
Hastings United	42	9	11	22	50	65	**38**
Aveley	42	10	8	24	35	62	**38**
Maidstone United	42	9	10	23	43	75	**37**
Croydon Ath	42	10	4	28	44	95	**31**
Folkestone Inv	42	5	12	25	34	68	**27**

21/08/2010 - 7/05/2011 • ‡ Play-offs
Play-off semis: **Tonbridge** 3-2 Harrow
Bury 1-2 **Lowestoft**
Play-off final: **Tonbridge** 4-3 Lowestoft

ENGLAND 2010–11 SOUTHERN LEAGUE ZAMARETTO PREMIER (7)

	Pl	W	D	L	F	A	Pts
Truro City	40	27	6	7	91	35	**87**
Hednesford T ‡	40	26	5	9	82	38	**83**
Salisbury City ‡	40	23	10	7	82	45	**79**
Cambridge City ‡	40	24	7	9	74	40	**79**
Leamington ‡	40	24	6	10	68	39	**78**
Chesham Utd	40	20	11	9	64	35	**71**
Chippenham Town	40	18	14	8	54	41	**68**
Stourbridge	40	18	8	14	72	61	**62**
Brackley Town	40	16	10	14	67	47	**58**
Swindon S'marine	40	17	7	16	56	58	**58**
Bashley	40	14	10	16	55	63	**52**
Evesham Utd	40	14	9	17	54	49	**51**
Cirencester Town	40	13	8	19	59	67	**47**
Oxford City	40	11	12	17	48	54	**45**
Hemel Hempstead	40	13	6	21	50	59	**45**
Banbury Utd	40	11	8	21	44	67	**40**
Bedford Town	40	10	7	23	41	76	**37**
Weymouth	40	12	8	20	55	85	**34**
Didcott Town	40	7	11	22	39	69	**32**
Tiverton Town	40	7	8	25	33	77	**29**
Halesowen Town	40	5	9	26	24	107	**24**
Windsor & Eton				Expelled in Feb 2011			

14/08/2009 - 3/05/2011 • ‡ Play-offs
Play-off semis: **Hednesford** 3-1 Leamington
Salisbury 1-0 Cambridge City
Play-off final: **Salisbury** 2-2 3-2p Hednesford

ENGLAND 2010–11 NORTHERN LEAGUE EVO-STIK PREMIER (7)

	Pl	W	D	L	F	A	Pts
Halifax Town	42	30	8	4	108	36	**98**
Colwyn Bay ‡	42	24	7	11	67	56	**79**
Bradford Park Av‡	42	23	8	11	84	55	**77**
FC Utd M'chester‡	42	24	4	14	76	53	**76**
North Ferriby Utd‡	42	22	7	13	78	51	**73**
Buxton	42	20	10	12	71	52	**70**
Kendal Town	42	21	5	16	80	77	**68**
Marine	42	20	7	15	74	64	**67**
Worksop Town	42	21	6	15	72	54	**66**
Chasetown	42	20	6	16	76	59	**66**
Matlock Town	42	20	6	16	74	59	**66**
Northwich Victoria	42	18	9	15	66	55	**63**
Stocksbridge PS	42	17	6	19	75	75	**57**
Ashton United	42	16	5	21	57	62	**53**
Mickleover Sports	42	15	7	20	70	76	**52**
Whitby Town	42	14	9	19	58	77	**51**
Nantwich Town	42	13	7	22	68	90	**46**
Frickley Athletic	42	11	11	20	43	68	**44**
Burscough	42	12	7	23	56	73	**43**
Hucknall Town	42	11	10	21	57	80	**43**
Ossett Town	42	9	5	28	45	103	**32**
Retford United	42	5	2	35	31	111	**17**

21/08/2010 - 3/05/2011 • ‡ Play-offs
Play-off semis: **Colwyn Bay** 2-0 North Ferriby
Bradford PA 0-2 **FC United**
Play-off final: **Colwyn Bay** 1-0 FC United

MEDALS TABLE

		Overall			League			Cup			LC			Europe			
		G	S	B	G	S	B	G	S	B	G	S	B	G	S	B	City/Town
1	Liverpool	40	24	24	18	12	7	7	6	9	**7**	3	3	8	3	5	Liverpool
2	Manchester United	38	27	28	19	14	6	11	7	9	4	4	4	4	2	9	Manchester
3	Arsenal	27	24	24	13	8	7	10	7	9	2	5	7	2	4	1	London
4	Aston Villa	20	16	17	7	10	2	7	3	10	5	3	5	1			Birmingham
5	Tottenham Hotspur	17	9	27	2	4	9	8	1	9	4	3	6	3	1	3	London
6	Chelsea	16	11	25	4	4	5	6	4	9	4	2	4	2	1	7	London
7	Everton	15	17	20	9	7	7	5	8	11		2	2	1			Liverpool
8	Newcastle United	11	10	8	4	2	4	6	7	3		1		1	1		Newcastle
9	Manchester City	10	8	10	2	3	4	5	4	2	2	1	3	1		1	Manchester
10	Blackburn Rovers	10	3	18	3	1	3	6	2	10	1		5				Blackburn
11	Wolverhampton Wanderers	9	10	14	3	5	6	4	4	6	2		1		1	1	Wolverhampton
12	Nottingham Forest	9	5	14	1	2	4	2	1	9	4	2		2		1	Nottingham
13	Sunderland	8	8	18	6	5	8	2	2	8		1	2				Sunderland
14	Sheffield Wednesday	8	5	19	4	1	7	3	3	10	1	1	2				Sheffield
15	Leeds United	7	12	13	3	5	2	1	3	4	1	1	3	2	3	4	Leeds
16	West Bromwich Albion	7	9	12	1	2	1	5	6	10	1	2	1				West Bromwich
17	Sheffield United	5	4	8	1	2		4	2	7			1				Sheffield
18	The Wanderers	5						5									London
19	Preston North End	4	11	5	2	6	2	2	5	3							Preston
20	Huddersfield Town	4	7	6	3	3	3	1	4	2			1				Huddersfield
21	Bolton Wanderers	4	5	12		3	4	3	1	7	1	1	1				Bolton
22	West Ham United	4	5	10		1		3	2	2		2	6	1	1	1	London
23	Portsmouth	4	3	3	2		1	2	3	2							Portsmouth
24	Leicester City	3	7	5		1	1		4	4	3	2					Leicester
25	Derby County	3	6	16	2	3	4	1	3	9			2		1		Derby
26	Burnley	3	4	14	2	2	5	1	2	5			4				Burnley
27	Ipswich Town	3	2	9	1	2	3	1		2			4	1			Ipswich
28	Birmingham City	2	5	10				2	7		2	1	2		2	1	Birmingham
29	Old Etonians	2	4					2	4								Eton

FA CUP (SPONSORED BY E.ON) 2010–11

Third Round

Manchester City	2	4
Leicester City *	2	2
Sunderland *	1	
Notts County	2	
Blackburn Rovers *	1	
Queens Park Rangers	0	
Sheffield United *	1	
Aston Villa	3	
Everton	5	
Scunthorpe United *	1	
Ipswich Town	0	
Chelsea *	7	
Stevenage *	3	
Newcastle United	1	
West Bromwich Albion	0	
Reading *	1	
Arsenal *	1	3
Leeds United	1	1
Dover Athletic	0	
Huddersfield Town *	2	
Swansea City *	4	
Colchester United	0	
Norwich City *	0	
Leyton Orient	1	
Crawley Town *	2	
Derby County	1	
Carlisle United	0	
Torquay United *	1	
Southampton *	2	
Blackpool	0	
Liverpool	0	
Manchester United *	1	
Bolton Wanderers *	2	
York City	0	
Hull City *	2	
Wigan Athletic	3	
Tottenham Hotspur *	3	
Charlton Athletic	0	
Peterborough United	2	
Fulham *	6	
Sheffield Wednesday	3	
Bristol City *	0	
Wycombe Wanderers *	0	
Hereford United	1	
Coventry City *	2	
Crystal Palace	1	
Millwall *	1	
Birmingham City	4	
West Ham United *	2	
Barnsley	0	
Preston North End *	1	
Nottingham Forest	2	
Burton Albion *	2	
Middlesbrough	1	
Port Vale	2	
Burnley *	4	
Brighton & Hove Albion *	3	
Portsmouth	1	
Hartlepool United	1	
Watford *	4	
Wolverhampton Wanderers	2	5
Doncaster Rovers *	2	0
Cardiff City	1	0
Stoke City *	1	2

Fourth Round

Manchester City	1	5
Notts County *	1	0
Blackburn Rovers	1	
Aston Villa *	3	
Everton *	1 1	4p
Chelsea	1 1	3p
Stevenage *	1	
Reading	2	
Arsenal *	2	
Huddersfield Town	1	
Swansea City *	1	
Leyton Orient	2	
Crawley Town	1	
Torquay United *	0	
Southampton *	1	
Manchester United	2	
Bolton Wanderers *	0	1
Wigan Athletic	0	0
Tottenham Hotspur	0	
Fulham *	4	
Sheffield Wednesday *	4	
Hereford United	1	
Coventry City	2	
Birmingham City *	3	
West Ham United *	3	
Nottingham Forest	2	
Burton Albion	1	
Burnley *	3	
Brighton & Hove Albion	1	
Watford *	0	
Wolverhampton Wanderers *	0	
Stoke City	1	

Fifth Round

Manchester City *	3
Aston Villa	0
Everton *	0
Reading	1
Arsenal	1 5
Leyton Orient *	1 0
Crawley Town	0
Manchester United *	1
Bolton Wanderers	1
Fulham *	0
Sheffield Wednesday	0
Birmingham City *	3
West Ham United *	5
Burnley	1
Brighton & Hove Albion	0
Stoke City *	3

* Home team

FA CUP (SPONSORED BY E.ON) 2010–11

Quarter–finals　　　　　　　**Semi–finals**　　　　　　　Final

Manchester City *	1
Reading	0

Manchester City	1
Manchester United	0

Arsenal	0
Manchester United *	2

Manchester City	1
Stoke City ‡	0

Bolton Wanderers	3
Birmingham City *	2

Bolton Wanderers	0
Stoke City	5

FA CUP FINAL 2011

Wembley Stadium, London, 14-05-2011, 15:00, Att: 88 643, Ref: Martin Atkinson

Manchester City	1	Yaya Toure [71]
Stoke City	0	

West Ham United	1
Stoke City *	2

Man City - Joe Hart - Micah Richards, Vincent Kompany, Joleon Lescott, Aleksandar Kolarov - Nigel de Jong, Gareth Barry (Adam Johnson 73) - David Silva (Patrick Vieira 90), Yaya Toure, Mario Balotelli - Carlos Tevez (c) (Pablo Zabaletta 88). Tr: Roberto Mancini
Stoke - Thomas Sorensen - Andy Wilkinson●, Ryan Shawcross (c), Robert Huth●, Marc Wilson - Jermaine Pennant, Glenn Whelan (Danny Pugh 85), Rory Delap (John Carew 81), Matthew Etherington (Dean Whitehead 62) - Jonathan Walters, Kenwyne Jones. Tr: Tony Pulis

‡ Qualified for the UEFA Europa League
Semi-finals played at Wembley Stadium, London

CARLING LEAGUE CUP 2010-11

Second Round

Birmingham City *	3
Rochdale	2
Blackpool	3
Milton Keynes Dons *	4
Everton *	5
Huddersfield Town	1
Hull City	1
Brentford *	2
Burnley	3
Morecambe *	1
Southampton *	0
Bolton Wanderers	1
Blackburn Rovers *	3
Norwich City	1
Aston Villa	Bye
Manchester United	Bye
Sheffield Wednesday	2
Scunthorpe United *	4
Notts County	2
Watford *	1
Southend United	1
Wolverhampton Wanderers *	2
Stoke City *	2
Shrewsbury Town	1
Port Vale	0
Fulham *	6
Sunderland *	2
Colchester United	0
Oxford United	0
West Ham United *	1
Ipswich Town	1
Crewe Alexandra *	0
Middlesbrough	1
Millwall *	2
Liverpool	Bye
Reading *	2 2p
Northampton Town	2 4p
Leicester City	2
Leeds United *	1
Crystal Palace	1 3p
Portsmouth *	1 4p
Manchester City	Bye
Leyton Orient *	0
West Bromwich Albion	2
Wigan Athletic	3
Hartlepool United *	0
Bradford City *	1
Preston North End	2
Peterborough United *	2
Cardiff City	1
Tranmere Rovers *	1
Swansea City	3
Newcastle United	3
Accrington Stanley *	2
Chelsea	Bye
Tottenham Hotspur	Bye
Arsenal	Bye

Third Round

Birmingham City *	3
Milton Keynes Dons	1
Everton	1 3p
Brentford *	1 4p
Burnley *	1
Bolton Wanderers	0
Blackburn Rovers	1
Aston Villa *	3
Manchester United	5
Scunthorpe United *	2
Notts County	2
Wolverhampton Wanderers *	4
Stoke City *	2
Fulham	0
Sunderland *	1
West Ham United	2
Ipswich Town	2
Millwall *	1
Liverpool *	1 2p
Northampton Town	1 4p
Leicester City	2
Portsmouth *	1
Manchester City	1
West Bromwich Albion *	2
Wigan Athletic *	2
Preston North End	1
Peterborough United *	1
Swansea City	3
Newcastle United	4
Chelsea *	3
Tottenham Hotspur *	1
Arsenal	4

Fourth Round

Birmingham City *	1 4p
Brentford	1 3p
Burnley	1
Aston Villa *	2
Manchester United *	3
Wolverhampton Wanderers	2
Stoke City	1
West Ham United *	3
Ipswich Town *	3
Northampton Town	1
Leicester City *	1
West Bromwich Albion	4
Wigan Athletic *	2
Swansea City	0
Newcastle United *	0
Arsenal	4

* Home team/Home team in the first leg

CARLING LEAGUE CUP 2010-11

Quarter-finals   **Semi-finals**   **Final**

Birmingham City *	2
Aston Villa	1

Birmingham City	1	3
West Ham United *	2	1

Manchester United	0
West Ham United *	4

Birmingham City ‡		2
Arsenal		1

Ipswich Town *	1
West Bromwich Albion	0

Ipswich Town *	1	0
Arsenal	0	3

CARLING LEAGUE CUP FINAL 2011
Wembley Stadium, London, 27-02-2011, 16:00, Att: 88 851, Referee: Mike Dean

Birmingham City	2 Zigic 28, Martins 89
Arsenal	1

Wigan Athletic	0
Arsenal *	2

Birmingham City - Ben Foster - Stephen Carr, Roger Johnson, Martin Jiranek, Liam Ridgewell - Sebastian Larsson●, Barry Ferguson●, Keith Fahey (Obafemi Martins 83) - Criag Gardner (Jean Beausejour 50), Lee Bowyer - Nikola Zigic (Cameron Jerome● 92+). Tr: Alex McLeish
Arsenal - Wojciech Szczesny - Bacary Sagna, Johan Djourou, Laurent Koscielny●, Gael Clichy● - Alexandre Song, Jack Wilshere - Tomas Rosicky, Samir Nasri, Andrei Arshavin (Marouane Chamakh 77) - Robin van Persie (c) (Nicklas Bendtner 69). Tr: Arsene Wenger

‡ Qualified for the UEFA Europa League

JOHNSTONE'S PAINT FOOTBALL LEAGUE TROPHY 2010-11

Second Round		Third Round		Quarter-finals (regional semi-finals)		Semi-finals (regional finals)		Final	
Carlisle United *	2 4p	Carlisle United *	3	Carlisle United *	3	Carlisle United *	4 0	Carlisle United	1
Port Vale	2 3p	Crewe Alexandra	1	Sheffield Wednesday	1	Huddersfield Town	0 3	Brentford	0
Macclesfield Town *	2								
Crewe Alexandra	4								
Hartlepool United *	1	Hartlepool United	1						
Bradford City	0	Sheffield Wednesday *	4						
Chesterfield	2 7p								
Sheffield Wednesday *	2 8p								
Tranmere Rovers *	0 4p	Tranmere Rovers	1	Tranmere Rovers *	0				
Stockport County	0 3p	Bury *	0	Huddersfield Town	2				
Shrewsbury Town	0 5p								
Bury *	0 6p								
Rotherham United	1	Rotherham United *	2						
Burton Albion *	2	Huddersfield Town	5						
Peterborough United	2								
Huddersfield Town *	3								
Exeter City	3	Exeter City	2	Exeter City	2 5p	Exeter City	1 1		
Hereford United *	0	Plymouth Argyle *	1	Bristol Rovers *	2 4p	Brentford *	1 2		
Cheltenham Town *	0								
Plymouth Argyle	2								
Wycombe Wanderers	2	Wycombe Wanderers	3						
Colchester United *	0	Bristol Rovers	6						
Aldershot Town	0								
Bristol Rovers *	1								
Charlton Athletic	2	Charlton Athletic	1	Charlton Athletic	0 1p				
Milton Keynes Dons *	1	Southend United *	0	Brentford *	0 3p				
Barnet *	1								
Southend United	3								
Swindon Town *	2	Swindon Town *	1 2p						
Torquay United	0	Brentford	1 4p						
Leyton Orient *	0 4p								
Brentford	0 5p								

* Home team/home team in the first leg

TROPHY FINAL

Wembley Stadium, London
3-04-2011, 13:30
Att: 40 476, Ref: Salisbury
Scorer - Peter Murphy 12
Carlisle - Moore - Woodman (O'Connor 88), Osborne, Neilson, Legge● - Saunders, Weston (Grabban 78), Diagouraga●●◆87, Reed● (Bean 46) - Alexander, Schlupp. Tr: Forster
Brentford - Collin - Simek, Murphy, Robson● - Michali(● - Thirwell (c), Taiwo (Loy 88), Marshall (Noble 23), Berrett - Zoko (Madden 67), Curran. Tr: Abbott

CLUB BY CLUB GUIDE TO THE 2010-11 SEASON IN ENGLAND

ARSENAL 2010–11

Mth	Date	Opponent	Res	Score	Comp	Scorers	Att
Aug	15	Liverpool	D	1-1	PL	OG 90	44 722
Aug	21	Blackpool	W	6-0	PL	Walcott 3 12 39 58, Arshavin 32p, Diaby 49, Chamakh 83	60 032
Aug	28	Blackburn	W	2-1	PL	Walcott 20, Arshavin 51	25 059
Sep	11	Bolton	W	4-1	PL	Koscielny 24, Chamakh 58, Song 78, Vela 83	59 876
Sep	15	Braga	W	6-0	CLgH	Fabregas 2 9p 53, Arshavin 30, Chamakh 34, Vela 2 69 84	59 333
Sep	18	Sunderland	D	1-1	PL	Fabregas 13	38 950
Sep	21	Tottenham	W	4-1	LCr3	Lansbury 15, Nasri 2 92p 96p, Arshavin 105	35 883
Sep	25	West Brom	L	2-3	PL	Nasri 2 75 90	60 025
Sep	28	Partizan	W	3-1	CLgH	Arshavin 15, Chamakh 71, Squillaci 82	29 348
Oct	3	Chelsea	L	0-2	PL		41 828
Oct	16	B'ham City	W	2-1	PL	Nasri 41p, Chamakh 47	60 070
Oct	19	Shakhtar	W	5-1	CLgH	Song 19, Nasri 42, Fabregas 60p, Wilshere 66, Chamakh 69	60 016
Oct	24	Man City	W	3-0	PL	Nasri 20, Song 66, Bendtner 88	47 393
Oct	27	Newcastle	W	4-0	LCr4	OG 45, Walcott 2 53 88, Bendtner 83	33 157
Oct	30	West Ham	W	1-0	PL	Song 88	60 086
Nov	3	Shakhtar	L	1-2	CLgH	Walcott 10	51 153
Nov	7	Newcastle	L	0-1	PL		60 059
Nov	10	Wolves	W	2-0	PL	Chamakh 2 1 90	27 329
Nov	14	Everton	W	2-1	PL	Sagna 36, Fabregas 48	36 279
Nov	20	Tottenham	L	2-3	PL	Nasri 9, Chamakh 27	60 102
Nov	23	Braga	L	0-2	CLgH		14 809
Nov	27	Aston Villa	W	4-2	PL	Arshavin 39, Nasri 45, Chamakh 56, Wilshere 90	38 544
Nov	30	Wigan	W	2-0	LCqf	OG 41, Bendtner 65	59 525
Dec	4	Fulham	W	2-1	PL	Nasri 2 14 76	60 049
Dec	8	Partizan	W	3-1	CLgH	V. Persie 30p, Walcott 73, Nasri 77	58 845
Dec	13	Man Utd	L	0-1	PL		75 227
Dec	27	Chelsea	W	3-1	PL	Song 44, Fabregas 51, Walcott 53	60 112
Dec	29	Wigan	D	2-2	PL	Arshavin 39, Bendtner 44	17 014
Jan	1	B'ham City	W	3-0	PL	V. Persie 13, Nasri 58, OG 66	24 341
Jan	5	Man City	D	0-0	PL		60 085
Jan	12	Leeds Utd	D	1-1	FAr3	Fabregas 90p	59 520
Jan	12	Ipswich	L	0-1	LCsf		29 146
Jan	15	West Ham	W	3-0	PL	V. Persie 2 13 77p, Walcott 41	32 682
Jan	19	Leeds Utd	W	3-1	FAr3	Nasri 5, Sagna 35, V. Persie 76	38 232
Jan	22	Wigan	W	3-0	PL	V. Persie 3 22 58 86	59 552
Jan	25	Ipswich	W	3-0	LCsf	Bendtner 61, Koscielny 64, Fabregas 77	59 387
Jan	30	Hudd'field	W	2-1	FAr4	OG 20, Fabregas 86p	59 375
Feb	1	Everton	W	2-1	PL	Arshavin 70, Koscielny 75	60 014
Feb	5	Newcastle	D	4-4	PL	Walcott 1, Djourou 3, V. Persie 2 10 26	51 561
Feb	12	Wolves	W	2-0	PL	V. Persie 2 16 56	60 050
Feb	16	Barcelona	W	2-1	CLr2	V. Persie 78, Arshavin 83	59 927
Feb	20	Orient	D	1-1	FAr5	Rosicky 53	9 136
Feb	23	Stoke	W	1-0	PL	Squillaci 8	60 041
Feb	27	B'ham City	L	1-2	LCf	V. Persie 39	88 851
Mar	2	Orient	W	5-0	FAr5	Chamakh 7, Bendtner 3 29 43 62p, Clichy 75	59 361
Mar	5	Sunderland	D	0-0	PL		60 081
Mar	8	Barcelona	L	1-3	CLr2	OG 53	95 486
Mar	12	Man Utd	L	0-2	FAqf		74 693
Mar	19	West Brom	D	2-2	PL	Arshavin 70, V. Persie 77	25 729
Apr	2	Blackburn	D	0-0	PL		60 087
Apr	10	Blackpool	W	3-1	PL	Diaby 18, Eboue 51, V. Persie 90	16 030
Apr	17	Liverpool	D	1-1	PL	V. Persie 90	60 029
Apr	20	Tottenham	D	3-3	PL	Walcott 4, Nasri 12, V. Persie 40	36 138
Apr	24	Bolton	L	1 2	PL	V. Persie 48	26 881
May	1	Man Utd	W	1-0	PL	Ramsey 56	60 107
May	8	Stoke	L	1-3	PL	V. Persie 81	27 478
May	15	Aston Villa	L	1-2	PL	V. Persie 90	60 023
May	22	Fulham	D	2-2	PL	V. Persie 29, Walcott 89	25 674

4th Att: 1 140 480 • Av: 60 025 (+0.16%) • The Emirates 60 361 (99%)

See Page 268 for the Arsenal league appearances and goalscorers

ASTON VILLA 2010–11

Mth	Date	Opponent	Res	Score	Comp	Scorers	Att
Aug	14	West Ham	W	3-0	PL	Downing 15, Petrov 40, Milner 66	36 604
Aug	19	Rapid	D	1-1	ELpo	Bannan 12	16 891
Aug	22	Newcastle	L	0-6	PL		43 546
Sep	26	Rapid	L	2-3	ELpo	Agbonlahor 22, Heskey 77	29 980
Sep	29	Everton	W	1-0	PL	Young.L 9	34 725
Sep	13	Stoke	L	1-2	PL	Downing 35	25 899
Sep	18	Bolton	D	1-1	PL	Young.A 13	34 655
Sep	22	Blackburn	W	3-1	LCr3	Heskey 59, Young.A 2 75 77	18 753
Sep	26	Wolves	W	2-1	PL	Downing 25, Heskey 88	27 511
Sep	2	Tottenham	L	1-2	PL	Albrighton 16	35 871
Oct	16	Chelsea	D	0-0	PL		40 122
Oct	23	Sunderland	L	0-1	PL		41 506
Oct	27	Burnley	W	2-1	LCr4	Heskey 86, Downing 96	34 618
Oct	31	B'ham City	D	0-0	PL		40 688
Nov	6	Fulham	D	1-1	PL	Albrighton 42	23 654
Nov	10	Blackpool	W	3-2	PL	Downing 28, Delfouneso 58, Collins 87	34 330
Nov	13	Man Utd	D	2-2	PL	Young.A 72p, Albrighton 76	40 073
Nov	21	Blackburn	L	0-2	PL		21 848
Nov	27	Arsenal	L	2-4	PL	Clark 2 52 71	38 544
Dec	1	B'ham City	L	1-2	LCqf	Agbonlahor 30	27 679
Dec	6	Liverpool	L	0-3	PL		39 079
Dec	11	West Brom	W	2-1	PL	Downing 26, Heskey 80	37 015
Dec	26	Tottenham	L	1-2	PL	Albrighton 82	39 411
Dec	28	Man City	L	0-4	PL		46 716
Dec	2	Chelsea	D	3-3	PL	Young.A 41p, Heskey 47, Clark 90	41 222
Dec	5	Sunderland	L	0-1	PL		32 627
Jan	8	Sheff Utd	W	3-1	FAr3	Walker 9, Albrighton 33, Petrov 90	16 888
Jan	16	B'ham City	D	1-1	PL	Collins 73	22 287
Jan	22	Man City	W	1-0	PL	Bent 18	37 315
Jan	25	Wigan	W	2-1	PL	Agbonlahor 50, Young.A 61p	16 442
Jan	29	Blackburn	D	3-1	FAr4	Clark 11, Pires 35, Delfouneso 42	26 067
Feb	1	Man Utd	L	1-3	PL	Bent 59	75 256
Feb	5	Fulham	D	2-2	PL	OG 13, Walker 72	35 899
Feb	12	Blackpool	D	1-1	PL	Agbonlahor 10	16 000
Feb	26	Blackburn	W	4-1	PL	Young.A 2 49p 82, OG 62, Downing 64	34 309
Mar	2	Man City	L	0-3	FAr5		25 570
Mar	5	Bolton	L	2-3	PL	Bent 15, Albrighton 64	22 533
Mar	19	Wolves	W	1-0	PL		38 965
Mar	2	Everton	D	2-2	PL	Bent 2 47 68	37 619
Mar	10	Newcastle	W	1-0	PL	Collins 24	37 090
Apr	16	West Ham	W	2-1	PL	Bent 37, Agbonlahor 90	34 672
Apr	23	Stoke	D	1-1	PL	Bent 43	35 235
Apr	30	West Brom	L	1-2	PL	OG 4	25 889
May	7	Wigan	D	1-1	PL	Young.A 17	36 293
May	15	Arsenal	W	2-1	PL	Bent 2 11 15	60 023
May	22	Liverpool	W	1-0	PL	Downing 33	42 785

9th Att: 706 685 • Av: 37 193 (-3.58%) • Villa Park 42 582 (87%)

VILLA LEAGUE APPEARANCES/GOALS 2010-11

Goalkeepers Brad Friedel USA 38

Defenders Nathan Baker 4/0 • Habib Beye SEN 2+1/0 • Ciaran Clark IRL 16+3/3 • James Collins WAL 31+1/3 • Carlos Cuellar ESP 10+2/0 • Richard Dunne IRL 32/0 • Eric Lichaj USA 3+2/0 • Kyle Walker 15/1 • Stephen Warnock 19/0 • Luke Young 23/1

Midfield Marc Albrighton 20+9/5 • Barry Bannan SCO 7+5/0 • Michael Bradley USA 0+3/0 • Fabian Delph 4+3/0 • Stewart Downing 38/7 • Chris Herd AUS 1+5/0 • Jonathan Hogg 5/0 • Stephen Ireland IRL 6+4/0 • Daniel Johnson • Jean Makoun CMR 7/0 • James Milner 1/1 • Stilian Petrov BUL 23+4/1 • Robert Pires FRA 2+7/0 • Nigel Reo-Coker 24+6/0 • Moustapha Salifou TOG • Steven Sidwell 1+3/0 • Ashley Young 34/7

Forwards Gabriel Agbonlahor 17+9/3 • Darren Bent 16/9 • John Carew NOR 6+4/0 • Nathan Delfouneso 2+9/1 • Emile Heskey 11+8/3 • Andreas Weimann AUT 0+1/0

Coach Kevin MacDonald • Gerard Houllier FRA (8/09/10)

KEY

CS = Community Shield • PL = FA Premier League (Barclays Premier League) • FA = FA Cup • LC = Carling League Cup • CL = UEFA Champions League • EL = Europa League
See page 13 for further explanations

BIRMINGHAM CITY 2010–11

Aug	14 Sunderland	D	2-2	PL	Dann [77], Ridgewell [88]	38 390
	21 Blackburn	W	2-1	PL	Gardner 2 [57 71]	**21 394**
	26 Rochdale	W	3-2	LCr2	McFadden [28p], Murphy [48], Derbyshire [53]	6 431
Sep	29 Bolton	D	2-2	PL	Johnson [4], Gardner [51]	18 139
	12 Liverpool	D	0-0	PL		27 333
	18 West Brom	L	1-3	PL	Jerome [15]	23 062
	21 MK Dons	W	3-1	LCr3	Hleb [24], Zigic [26], Gardner [28]	9 450
	25 Wigan	D	0-0	PL		22 186
Oct	2 Everton	L	0-2	PL		23 138
	16 Arsenal	L	1-2	PL	Zigic [33]	60 070
	23 Blackpool	W	2-0	PL	Ridgewell [37], Zigic [57]	26 850
	26 Brentford	D	1-1	LCr4	Phillips [90]. W 4-3p	15 166
	31 Aston Villa	D	0-0	PL		40 688
Nov	6 West Ham	D	2-2	PL	Jerome [64], Ridgewell [73]	26 474
	9 Stoke	L	2-3	PL	Fahey [74], Jerome [76]	26 381
	13 Man City	D	0-0	PL		44 321
	20 Chelsea	W	1-0	PL	Bowyer [17]	24 357
Dec	27 Fulham	D	1-1	PL	Larsson [20]	24 391
	1 Aston Villa	W	2-1	LCqf	Larsson [12p], Zigic [84]	27 679
	4 Tottenham	D	1-1	PL	Gardner [81]	25 770
	12 Wolves	L	0-1	PL		25 150
	28 Man Utd	L	0-1	PL		28 242
	1 Arsenal	L	0-3	PL		24 341
Jan	4 Blackpool	W	2-1	PL	Hleb [24], Dann [89]	14 550
	8 Millwall	W	4-1	FAr3	Derbyshire 2 [17 45], Murphy [27], Jerome [72]	9 841
	11 West Ham	L	1-2	LCsf	Ridgewell [56]	34 754
	16 Aston Villa	D	1-1	PL	Johnson [49]	22 287
	22 Man Utd	L	0-5	PL		75 326
	26 West Ham	W	3-1	LCsf	Bowyer [59], Johnson [79], Gardner [94]	27 519
Feb	29 Coventry	W	3-2	FAr4	Bentley [35], Parnaby [67], Phillips [73]	16 669
	2 Man City	D	2-2	PL	Zigic [24], Gardner [77p]	24 379
	6 West Ham	W	1-0	PL	Zigic [65]	32 927
	12 Stoke	W	1-0	PL	Zigic [90]	33 660
	15 Newcastle	L	0-2	PL		**28 270**
	19 Sheff Wed	W	3-0	FAr5	Beausejour [6], Martins [18], Murphy [53]	14 607
Mar	27 Arsenal	W	2-1	LCf	Zigic [28], Martins [89]	88 851
	5 West Brom	L	1-3	PL	Beausejour [48]	27 013
	9 Everton	D	1-1	PL	Beausejour [17]	33 974
	12 Bolton	L	2-3	FAqf	Jerome [38], Phillips [80]	23 699
	19 Wigan	L	1-2	PL	Ridgewell [6]	16 421
Apr	2 Bolton	W	2-1	PL	Phillips [4], Gardner [59]	26 142
	9 Blackburn	D	1-1	PL	Bowyer [32]	28 426
	16 Sunderland	W	2-0	PL	Larsson [41], Gardner [66]	28 108
	20 Chelsea	L	1-3	PL	Larsson [77p]	40 848
	23 Liverpool	L	0-5	PL		44 734
May	1 Wolves	D	1-1	PL	Larsson [27]	26 072
	7 Newcastle	L	1-2	PL	Bowyer [45]	47 409
	15 Fulham	L	0-2	PL		27 759
	22 Tottenham	L	1-2	PL	Gardner [79]	36 119

18th   Att: 483 775 • Av: 25 461 (+0.85%) • St Andrew's 30 079 (84%)

BLACKBURN ROVERS 2010–11

Aug	14 Everton	W	1-0	PL	Kalinic [15]	25 869
	21 B'ham City	L	1-2	PL	N'Zonzi [54]	21 394
	24 Norwich	W	3-1	LCr2	Mame Diouf 3 [29 80 84]	9 235
	28 Arsenal	L	1-2	PL	Mame Diouf [27]	25 059
Sep	11 Man City	D	1-1	PL	Kalinic [25]	44 246
	18 Fulham	D	1-1	PL	Samba [30]	23 759
	22 Aston Villa	L	1-3	LCr3	Givet [34]	18 753
	25 Blackpool	W	2-1	PL	OG [20], Emerton [90]	15 901
Oct	2 Stoke	L	0-1	PL		25 515
	18 Sunderland	D	0-0	PL		21 894
	24 Liverpool	L	1-2	PL	OG [51]	43 328
	30 Chelsea	L	1-2	PL	Benjani [22]	25 836
Nov	6 Wigan	W	2-1	PL	Pedersen [58], Roberts [68]	24 413
	10 Newcastle	W	2-1	PL	Pedersen [3], Roberts [82]	41 053
	13 Tottenham	L	2-4	PL	Nelsen [80], Givet [90]	35 700
	21 Aston Villa	W	2-0	PL	Pedersen 2 [45 65]	**21 848**
	27 Man Utd	L	1-7	PL	Samba [84]	74 850
Dec	4 Wolves	W	3-0	PL	Dunn [28], Emerton [43], Nelsen [55]	22 314
	12 Bolton	L	1-2	PL	Mame Diouf [87]	24 471
	18 West Ham	D	1-1	PL	Nelsen [51]	21 934
	26 Stoke	L	0-2	PL		24 440
	28 West Brom	W	3-1	PL	Kalinic 2 [2 54], Mame Diouf [62]	24 440
Jan	1 Sunderland	L	0-3	PL		36 242
	5 Liverpool	W	3-1	PL	Olsson [32], Benjani 2 [38 57]	24 522
	8 QPR	W	1-0	FAr3	Hoilett [77]	10 284
	15 Chelsea	L	0-2	PL		40 846
	23 West Brom	W	2-0	PL	OG [41], Hoilett [47]	24 057
	29 Aston Villa	L	1-3	FAr4	Kalinic [18]	26 067
Feb	2 Tottenham	L	0-1	PL		23 253
	5 Wigan	L	3-4	PL	Roberts [23], Samba [58], Dunn [81p]	18 567
	12 Newcastle	D	0-0	PL		26 781
	26 Aston Villa	L	1-4	PL	Kalinic [80]	34 309
Mar	5 Fulham	L	2-3	PL	Hanley [45], Hoilett [65]	25 687
	19 Blackpool	D	2-2	PL	Samba [49], Hoilett [90]	27 209
	2 Arsenal	D	0-0	PL		60 087
Apr	9 B'ham City	D	1-1	PL	Hoilett [45]	28 426
	16 Everton	L	0-2	PL		33 857
	25 Man City	L	0-1	PL		23 529
May	30 Bolton	W	1-0	PL	Olsson [20]	28 985
	7 West Ham	D	1-1	PL	Roberts [13]	33 789
	14 Man Utd	D	1-1	PL	Emerton [20]	**29 867**
	22 Wolves	W	3-2	PL	Roberts [23], Emerton [38], Hoilett [45]	29 009

15th   Att: 474 995 • Av: 24 999 (-1.69%) • Ewood Park 31 154 (80%)

BLACKBURN LEAGUE APPEARANCES/GOALS 2010-11
Goalkeepers Mark Bunn 2+1 • Paul Robinson 36
Defenders Pascal Chimbonda FRA 3+3/0 • Gael Givet FRA 29/1 • Grant
Hanley SCO 5+2/1 • Phil Jones 24+2/0 • Michel Salgado ESP 36/0 •
Ryan Nelsen NZL 28/3 • Martin Olsson SWE 25+4/2 •
Christopher Samba CGO 33/4
Midfield Keith Andrews IRL 2+3/0 • David Dunn 17+10/2 •
Brett Emerton AUS 24+6/4 • Herold Goulon FRA 1+3/0 • Vince Grella
AUS 4+1/0 • David Hoilett CAN 17+7/5 • Jermaine Jones USA 15/0 •
Amine Koumba ALG 0+1/0 • Jason Lowe 0+1/0 • Josh Morris 0+4/0 •
Steven N'Zonzi FRA 13+8/1 • Morten Pedersen NOR 27+8/4
Forwards El Hadji Diouf SEN 18+2/0 • Mame Diouf SEN 17+9/3 •
Nikola Kalinic CRO 15+3/5 • Benjani Mwaruwari ZIM 6+12/3 •
Jason Roberts GRN 13+12/5 • Ruben Rochina ESP 1+3/0 •
Roque Santa Cruz PAR 7+2/0
Coach Sam Allardyce • Steve Kean SCO (22/12/10)

BIRMINGHAM LEAGUE APPEARANCES/GOALS 2010-11
Goalkeepers Colin Doyle IRL 0+1 • Ben Foster 38
Defenders Stephen Carr IRL 38/0 • Scott Dann 20/2 • Curtis
Davies 2+4/0 • Martin Jiranek CZE 10/0 • Roger Johnson 38/2 • David
Murphy 3+7/0 • Stuart Parnaby 5/0 • Liam Ridgewell 36/4
Midfield Jean Beausejour CHI 9+8/2 • David Bentley 9+4/0 • Lee
Bowyer 24+5/4 • Keith Fahey IRL 19+5/1 • Barry Ferguson SCO 35/0 •
Craig Gardner 25+4/8 • Aliaksandr Hleb BLR 13+6/1 • Sebastian
Larsson SWE 31+4/4 • Jordan Mutch 3/0
Forwards Matt Derbyshire 4+9/0 • Cameron Jerome 30+4/3 • Obafemi
Martins NGA 3+1/0 • James McFadden SCO 3+1/0 • Garry O'Connor
SCO 2+1/0 • Kevin Phillips 5+9/1 • Nikola Zigic SRB 13+12/5
Coach Alex McLeish SCO

ARSENAL LEAGUE APPEARANCES/GOALS 2010-11
Goalkeepers Manuel Almunia ESP 8 • Lukasz Fabianski POL 14 •
Jens Lehmann GER 1 • Wojciech Szczesny POL 15
Defenders Gael Clichy FRA 33/0 • Johan Djourou SUI 20+2/1 •
Emmanuel Eboue CIV 8+5/1 • Kieran Gibbs 4+3/0 •
Laurent Koscielny FRA 30/2 • Bakari Sagna FRA 33/1 • Sebastien
Squillaci FRA 20+2/1 • Thomas Vermaelen BEL 5/0
Midfield Denilson BRA 6+10/0 • Abou Diaby FRA 13+3/2 • Jay
Emmanuel-Thomas 0+1/0 • Cesc Fabregas ESP 22+3/3 • Samir Nasri
FRA 28+2/10 • Aaron Ramsey WAL 5+2/1 • Tomas Rosicky CZE 8+13/0
• Alexandre Song CMR 30+1/4 • Jack Wilshere 31+4/1
Forwards Andrey Arshavin RUS 25+12/6 • Nicklas
Bendtner DEN 3+14/2 • Marouane Chamakh MAR 18+11/7 • Robin van
Persie NED 19+6/18 • Carlos Vela MEX 0+4/1 • Theo Walcott 19+9/9
Coach Arsene Wenger FRA

BLACKPOOL 2010–11

	Date	Opponent		Score	Comp	Scorers	Att
Aug	14	Wigan	W	4-0	PL	T-Fletcher 16, Harewood 2 37 42, Baptiste 76	16 152
	21	Arsenal	L	0-6	PL		60 032
	24	MK Dons	L	3-4	LCr2	Ormerod 55, Sylvestre 58, Adam 82p	7 458
	28	Fulham	D	2-2	PL	OG 71, Varney 76	15 529
Sep	11	Newcastle	W	2-0	PL	Adam 44p, Campbell 90	49 597
	19	Chelsea	L	0-4	PL		41 761
	25	Blackburn	L	1-2	PL	Phillips 85	15 901
Oct	3	Liverpool	W	2-1	PL	Adam 29p, Varney 45	43 156
	17	Man City	L	2-3	PL	Harewood 78, T-Fletcher 90	16 116
	23	B'ham City	L	0-2	PL		26 850
Nov	1	West Brom	W	2-1	PL	Adam 12p, Varney 63	15 210
	6	Everton	D	2-2	PL	Eardley 10, Vaughan 48	16 094
	10	Aston Villa	L	2-3	PL	Harewood 45, Campbell 85	34 330
	13	West Ham	D	0-0	PL		31 194
	20	Wolves	W	2-1	PL	Varney 3, Harewood 44	15 922
Dec	2	Bolton	D	2-2	PL	Evatt 28, Varney 58	25 851
	11	Stoke	W	1-0	PL	Campbell 48	26 879
	28	Sunderland	W	2-0	PL	Campbell 2 50 90	42 892
Jan	1	Man City	L	0-1	PL		47 296
	4	B'ham City	L	1-2	PL	Campbell 68	14 550
	8	South'ton	L	0-2	FAr3		21 464
	12	Liverpool	W	2-1	PL	T-Fletcher 12, Campbell 69	16 089
	15	West Brom	L	2-3	PL	Vaughan 11, T-Fletcher 80	25 316
	22	Sunderland	L	1-2	PL	Adam 86p	16 037
	25	Man Utd	L	2-3	PL	Cathcart 15, Campbell 44	15 574
Feb	2	West Ham	L	1-3	PL	Adam 42	15 095
	5	Everton	L	3-5	PL	Baptiste 37, Puncheon 62, Adam 64	38 202
	12	Aston Villa	D	1-1	PL	Grandin 14	16 000
	22	Tottenham	W	3-1	PL	Adam 18p, Campbell 44, Ormerod 80	16 069
	26	Wolves	L	0-4	PL		29 086
Mar	7	Chelsea	L	1-3	PL	Puncheon 86	15 584
	19	Blackburn	D	2-2	PL	Adam 2 25p 29	27 209
	3	Fulham	L	0-3	PL		25 692
Apr	10	Arsenal	L	1-3	PL	T-Fletcher 52	16 030
	16	Wigan	L	1-3	PL	Campbell 83	16 030
	23	Newcastle	D	1-1	PL	Campbell 32	16 003
	30	Stoke	D	0-0	PL		16 003
	7	Tottenham	D	1-1	PL	Adam 76p	35 585
May	14	Bolton	W	4-3	PL	Campbell 2 9 45, Puncheon 19, Adam 63	15 979
	22	Man Utd	L	2-4	PL	Adam 40, T-Fletcher 57	75 400

19th Att: 299 815 • Av: 15 779 (+83.24%) • Bloomfield Road 16 220 (97%)

BOLTON WANDERERS 2010–11

	Date	Opponent		Score	Comp	Scorers	Att
Aug	14	Fulham	D	0-0	PL		20 352
	21	West Ham	W	3-1	PL	OG 48, Elmander 2 68 84	32 533
	24	South'ton	W	1-0	LCr2	Klasnic 31	10 251
	29	B'ham City	D	2-2	PL	Davies.K 71p, Blake 81	18 139
Sep	11	Arsenal	L	1-4	PL	Elmander 44	59 876
	18	Aston Villa	D	1-1	PL	Davies.K 35	34 655
	21	Burnley	L	0-1	LCr3		17 602
	26	Man Utd	D	2-2	PL	Knight 6, Petrov 67	23 926
Oct	2	West Brom	D	1-1	PL	Elmander 64	22 846
	16	Stoke	W	2-1	PL	Lee 21, Klasnic 90	22 975
	23	Wigan	D	1-1	PL	Elmander 66	17 100
	31	Liverpool	L	0-1	PL		25 171
Nov	6	Tottenham	W	4-2	PL	Davies.K 2 31 76p, Steinsson 57, Petrov 90	20 255
	10	Everton	D	1-1	PL	Klasnic 79	31 808
	13	Wolves	W	3-2	PL	OG 2, Elmander 62, Holden 67	27 508
	20	Newcastle	W	5-1	PL	Davies.K 2 18p 90p, Lee 38, Elmander 2 50 71	22 203
	27	Blackpool	D	2-2	PL	Petrov 76, Davies.M 89	25 851
Dec	4	Man City	L	0-1	PL		46 860
	12	Blackburn	W	2-1	PL	Muamba 65, Holden 88	24 471
	18	Sunderland	L	0-1	PL		35 101
	26	West Brom	W	2-0	PL	Taylor 40, Elmander 86	23 413
	29	Chelsea	L	0-1	PL		40 982
	1	Liverpool	L	1-2	PL	Davies 43	35 400
	5	Wigan	D	1-1	PL	Moreno 54	18 852
	8	York	W	2-0	FAr3	Davies.K 83, Elmander 89	13 120
Jan	15	Stoke	L	0-2	PL		26 809
	24	Chelsea	L	0-4	PL		22 837
	29	Wigan	D	0-0	FAr4		14 950
	2	Wolves	W	1-0	PL	Sturridge 90	18 944
	5	Tottenham	L	1-2	PL	Sturridge 55	36 197
Feb	13	Everton	W	2-0	PL	Cahill 10, Sturridge 67	22 986
	16	Wigan	W	1-0	FAr4	Klasnic 66	7 515
	20	Fulham	W	1-0	FAr5	Klasnic 19	19 571
	26	Newcastle	D	1-1	PL	Sturridge 38	48 062
Mar	5	Aston Villa	W	3-2	PL	Cahill 2 45 75, Klasnic 86	22 533
	12	B'ham City	W	3-2	FAqf	Elmander 21, Davies.K 66p, Lee 90	23 699
	19	Man Utd	L	0-1	PL		75 486
	2	B'ham City	L	1-2	PL	Elmander 71	26 142
	9	West Ham	W	3-0	PL	Sturridge 2 14 50, Lee 20	25 857
	17	Stoke	L	0-5	FAsf		75 064
Apr	24	Arsenal	W	2-1	PL	Sturridge 38, Cohen 90	26 881
	27	Fulham	L	0-3	PL		23 222
	30	Blackburn	L	0-1	PL		28 985
	7	Sunderland	L	1-2	PL	Klasnic 87	22 597
May	14	Blackpool	L	3-4	PL	Davies.K 6, Taylor 24, Sturridge 53	15 979
	22	Man City	L	0-2	PL		26 285

8th Att: 434 528 • Av: 22 869 (+4.52%) • Reebok Stadium 28 101 (81%)

BLACKPOOL LEAGUE APPEARANCES/GOALS 2010-11

Goalkeepers Matt Gilks SCO 18 • Mark Halstead 0+1 • Richard Kingson GHA 19+1 • Paul Rachubka 1+1
Defenders Alex Baptiste 19+2/2 • Chris Basham 1+1/0 • Craig Cathcart NIR 28+2/1 • Stephen Crainey SCO 31/0 • Neil Eardley WAL 30+1/1 • Rob Edwards 1+1/0 • Ian Evatt 36+2/1 • Dekil Keinan ISR 3+3/0
Midfield Charlie Adam SCO 34+1/12 • David Carney AUS 5+6/0 • Ishmel Demontagnac 0+1/0 • Jason Euell JAM 1+2/0 • Matt Phillips 6+21/1 • Jason Puncheon 6+5/3 • Andy Reid IRL 2+3/0 • Keith Southern 11+10/0 • Ludovic Sylvestre FRA 6+2/0 • Gary Taylor-Fletcher 29+2/6 • David Vaughan WAL 35/2
Forwards James Beattie 5+4/0 • Dudley Junior Campbell 30+1/13 • Elliot Grandin FRA 21+2/1 • Marlon Harewood 7+9/5 • Sergey Kornilenko BLR 3+3/0 • Brett Ormerod 6+13/1 • Luke Varney 24+6/5
Coach Ian Holloway

BOLTON LEAGUE APPEARANCES/GOALS 2010-11

Goalkeepers Adam Bogdan HUN 3+1 • Jussi Jaaskelainen FIN 35
Defenders Gary Cahill 36/3 • Mark Connolly IRL • Zat Knight 34/1 • Marcos Alonso ESP 4/0 • Andy O'Brien IRL 1+1/0 • Sam Ricketts WAL 14+3/0 • Paul Robinson 35/0 • Gretar Steinsson ISL 23/1 • David Wheater 5+2/0
Midfield Tamir Cohen ISR 3+5/1 • Mark Davies 9+15/1 • Sean Davis 1/0 • Ricardo Gardner JAM 3+2/0 • Stuart Holden USA 26/2 • Lee Chung Yong KOR 25+6/3 • Fabrice Muamba 32+4/1 • Martin Petrov BUL 18+10/3 • Matthew Taylor 22+14/2
Forwards Robert Blake 0+8/1 • Kevin Davies 37/8 • Johan Elmander SWE 37/10 • Ivan Klasnic CRO 0+22/4 • Rodrigo Moreno ESP 4+13/1 • Daniel Sturridge 11+1/8
Coach Owen Coyle IRL

CHELSEA 2010–11

	Date	Opponent	Res	Comp	Scorers	Att
Aug	8	Man Utd	L 1-3	CS	Kalou 82	84 623
	14	West Brom	W 6-0	PL	Malouda 2 6 90, Drogba 3 45 55 68, Lampard 63	41 589
	21	Wigan	W 6-0	PL	Malouda 34, Anelka 2 48 52, Kalou 2 78 90, Benayoun 94+	14 476
	28	Stoke	W 2-0	PL	Malouda 32, Drogba 77p	40 931
Sep	11	West Ham	W 3-1	PL	Essien 2 2 83, Kalou 17	33 014
	15	Zilina	W 4-1	CLgF	Essien 13, Anelka 2 24 28, Sturridge 48	10 829
	19	Blackpool	W 4-0	PL	Kalou 1, Malouda 2 12 41, Drogba 30	41 761
	22	Newcastle	L 3-4	LCr3	Van Aanholt 6, Anelka 2 70 86p	41 511
	25	Man City	L 0-1	PL		47 203
	28	Marseille	W 2-0	CLgF	Terry 7, Anelka 28p	40 675
Oct	3	Arsenal	W 2-0	PL	Drogba 40, Alex 85	41 828
	16	Aston Villa	D 0-0	PL		40 122
	19	Sp. Moskva	W 2-0	CLgF	Zhirkov 24, Anelka 43	70 012
	23	Wolves	W 2-0	PL	Malouda 23, Kalou 81	41 752
	30	Blackburn	W 2-1	PL	Anelka 39, Ivanovic 84	25 836
Nov	3	Sp. Moskva	W 4-1	CLgF	Anelka 49, Drogba 62p, Ivanovic 2 66 92+	40 477
	7	Liverpool	L 0-2	PL		44 238
	10	Fulham	W 1-0	PL	Essien 30	41 593
	14	Sunderland	L 0-3	PL		41 072
	20	B'ham City	L 0-1	PL		24 357
	23	Zilina	W 2-1	CLgF	Sturridge 51, Malouda 86	40 266
	28	Newcastle	D 1-1	PL	Kalou 45	46 469
Dec	4	Everton	D 1-1	PL	Drogba 42p	41 642
	8	Marseille	L 0-1	CLgF		50 604
	12	Tottenham	D 1-1	PL	Drogba 70	35 787
	27	Arsenal	L 1-3	PL	Ivanovic 57	60 112
	29	Bolton	W 1-0	PL	Malouda 60	40 982
Jan	2	Aston Villa	D 3-3	PL	Lampard 23p, Drogba 84, Terry 89	41 222
	5	Wolves	L 0-1	PL		26 432
	9	Ipswich	W 7-0	FAr3	Kalou 33, Sturridge 2 33 52, OG 41, Anelka 49, Lampard 2 78 79	41 654
	15	Blackburn	W 2-0	PL	Ivanovic 57, Anelka 76	40 846
	24	Bolton	W 4-0	PL	Drogba 11, Malouda 41, Anelka 56, Ramires 74	22 837
	29	Everton	D 1-1	FAr4	Kalou 75	28 376
Feb	1	Sunderland	W 4-2	PL	Lampard 15p, Kalou 23, Terry 60, Anelka 90	37 855
	6	Liverpool	L 0-1	PL		**41 829**
	14	Fulham	D 0-0	PL		25 685
	19	Everton	D 1-1	FAr4	Lampard 104, L 3-4p	41 113
	22	København	W 2-0	CLr2	Anelka 2 17 54	36 713
Mar	1	Man Utd	W 2-1	PL	Luiz 54, Lampard 79p	41 825
	7	Blackpool	W 3-1	PL	Terry 20, Lampard 2 63p 66	15 584
	16	København	D 0-0	CLr2		36 454
	20	Man City	W 2-0	PL	Luiz 78, Ramires 90	41 741
	2	Stoke	D 1-1	PL	Drogba 33	27 508
	6	Man Utd	L 0-1	CLqf		37 915
	9	Wigan	W 1-0	PL	Malouda 66	**40 734**
Apr	12	Man Utd	L 1-2	CLqf	Drogba 77	74 672
	16	West Brom	W 3-1	PL	Drogba 22, Kalou 26, Lampard 45	25 163
	20	B'ham City	W 3-1	PL	Malouda 2 3 62, Kalou 26	40 848
	23	West Ham	W 3-0	PL	Lampard 44, Torres 84, Malouda 90	41 656
	30	Tottenham	W 2-1	PL	Lampard 45, Kalou 89	41 681
May	8	Man Utd	L 1-2	PL	Lampard 69	75 445
	15	Newcastle	D 2-2	PL	Ivanovic 2, Alex 83	41 739
	22	Everton	L 0-1	PL		38 712

2nd Att: 787 271 • Av: 41 435 (+0.03%) • Stamford Bridge 42 449 (97%)

EVERTON 2010–11

	Date	Opponent	Res	Comp	Scorers	Att
Aug	14	Blackburn	L 0-1	PL		25 869
	21	Wolves	D 1-1	PL	Cahill 43	37 767
	25	Hudd'field	W 5-1	LCr2	Fellaini 8, Rodwell 16, Beckford 50p, Saha 77, Osman 85	28 901
	29	Aston Villa	L 0-1	PL		34 725
Sep	11	Man Utd	D 3-3	PL	Pienaar 39, Cahill 90, Arteta 90	36 556
	18	Newcastle	L 0-1	PL		38 019
	21	Brentford	D 1-1	LCr3	Coleman 6, L 3-4p	8 960
	25	Fulham	D 0-0	PL		25 598
Oct	2	B'ham City	W 2-0	PL	OG 54, Cahill 90	23 138
	17	Liverpool	W 2-0	PL	Cahill 34, Arteta 50	**39 673**
	23	Tottenham	D 1-1	PL	Baines 17	35 967
	30	Stoke	W 1-0	PL	Yakubu 67	35 513
Nov	6	Blackpool	D 2-2	PL	Cahill 13, Coleman 50	16 094
	10	Bolton	D 1-1	PL	Beckford 90	**31 808**
	14	Arsenal	L 1-2	PL	Cahill 89	36 279
	22	Sunderland	D 2-2	PL	Cahill 5, Arteta 83	37 331
	27	West Brom	L 1-4	PL	Cahill 42	35 237
Dec	4	Chelsea	D 1-1	PL	Beckford 86	41 642
	11	Wigan	D 0-0	PL		32 853
	20	Man City	W 2-1	PL	Coleman 4, Baines 19	45 028
	28	West Ham	D 1-1	PL	Coleman 42	33 422
Jan	1	Stoke	L 0-2	PL		27 418
	5	Tottenham	W 2-1	PL	Saha 3, Coleman 76	34 124
	8	Sc'thorpe	W 5-1	FAr3	Saha 4, Beckford 33, Coleman 58, Fellaini 73, Baines 83	7 028
	16	Liverpool	D 2-2	PL	Distin 46, Beckford 52	44 795
	22	West Ham	D 2-2	PL	Bilyaletdinov 77, Fellaini 90	34 179
	29	Chelsea	D 1-1	FAr4	Saha 62	28 376
Feb	1	Arsenal	L 1-2	PL	Saha 24	60 014
	8	Blackpool	W 5-3	PL	Saha 4 20 47 76 84, Beckford 79	38 202
	13	Bolton	L 0-2	PL		22 986
	19	Chelsea	D 1-1	FAr4	Baines 119, W 4-3p	41 113
	26	Sunderland	W 2-0	PL	Beckford 2 8 39	37 776
Mar	1	Reading	L 0-1	FAr5		29 976
	5	Newcastle	W 2-1	PL	Osman 31, Jagielka 36	50 128
	9	B'ham City	D 1-1	PL	Heitinga 35	33 974
	19	Fulham	W 2-1	PL	Coleman 36, Saha 49	33 239
Apr	2	Aston Villa	D 2-2	PL	Osman 28, Baines 83p	37 619
	9	Wolves	W 3-0	PL	Beckford 21, Neville 39, Bilyaletdinov 45	28 352
	16	Blackburn	W 2-0	PL	Osman 54, Baines 75p	35 857
	23	Man Utd	L 0-1	PL		75 300
	30	Wigan	D 1-1	PL	Baines 78p	17 051
May	7	Man City	W 2-1	PL	Distin 66, Osman 72	37 351
	14	West Brom	L 0-1	PL		25 838
	22	Chelsea	W 1-0	PL	Beckford 75	38 712

7th Att: 684 738 • Av: 36 038 (-1.87%) • Goodison Park 40 157 (89%)

CHELSEA LEAGUE APPEARANCES/GOALS 2010-11
Goalkeepers Petr Cech CZE 38
Defenders Alex BRA 12+3/2 • Ryan Bertrand 0+1/0 • Jose Bosingwa POR 13+7/0 • Jeffrey Bruma NED 1+1/0• Ashley Cole 38/0 • David Luiz BRA 11+1/2 • Paulo Ferreira POR 12+9/0 • Branislav Ivanovic SRB 32+2/4 • John Terry 33/3
Midfield Yossi Benayoun ISR 1+6/1 • Michael Essien GHA 32+1/3 • Frank Lampard 23+1/10 • Florent Malouda FRA 33+5/13 Joshua McEachran 1+8/0 • John Mikel NGA 28/0 • Ramires BRA 22+7/2 • Yuriy Zhirkov RUS 6+6/0
Forwards Nicolas Anelka FRA 27+5/6 • Didier Drogba CIV 30+6/12 Salomon Kalou CIV 16+15/10 • Gael Kakuta FRA 1+4/0 • Daniel Sturridge 0+13/0 • Fernando Torres ESP 8+6/1
Coach Carlo Ancelotti ITA

EVERTON LEAGUE APPEARANCES/GOALS 2010-11
Goalkeepers Tim Howard USA 38
Defenders Leighton Baines 38/5 • Seamus Coleman IRL 25+9/5 Sylvain Distin FRA 38/2 • Johnny Heitinga NED 23+4/1 • Tony Hibbert 17+3/0 • Phil Jagielka 31+2/1 • Phil Neville 31/1
Midfield Mikel Arteta ESP 29/3 • Diniyar Bilyaletdinov RUS 10+16/2 Tim Cahill AUS 22+5/8 • Marouane Fellaini BEL 19+1/1 • Adam Forshaw 0+1/0 • Leon Osman 20+6/4 • Steven Pienaar RSA 18/1 Jack Rodwell 14+10/0
Forwards Victor Anichebe NGA 8+8/0 • Yakubu Ayegbeni NGA 7+7/1 Jose Baxter 0+1/0 • Jermaine Beckford 14+18/8 • Magaye Gueye FRA 2+3/0 • Louis Saha 14+8/7 • James Vaughan 0+1/0 Apostolos Vellios GRE 0+3/0
Coach David Moyes SCO

FULHAM 2010–11

	14 Bolton	D	0-0	PL		20 352
Aug	22 Man Utd	D	2-2	PL	Davies 57, Hangeland 90	25 643
Aug	25 Port Vale	W	6-0	LCr2	Gera 2 10 45, Dembele 26, Zamora 2 36 66, Dempsey 70	9 031
	28 Blackpool	D	2-2	PL	Zamora 35, Etuhu 87	15 529
Sep	11 Wolves	W	2-1	PL	Dembele 2 48 90	25 280
	18 Blackburn	D	1-1	PL	Dempsey 56	23 759
	21 Stoke	L	0-2	LCr3		12 778
	25 Everton	D	0-0	PL		25 598
	2 West Ham	D	1-1	PL	Dempsey 33	34 589
Oct	16 Tottenham	L	1-2	PL	Kamara 30	25 615
	23 West Brom	L	1-2	PL	OG 9	25 625
	30 Wigan	W	2-0	PL	Dempsey 2 30 44	25 448
	6 Aston Villa	D	1-1	PL	Hangeland 90	23 654
	10 Chelsea	L	0-1	PL		41 593
Nov	13 Newcastle	D	0-0	PL		44 686
	21 Man City	L	1-4	PL	Gera 69	25 694
	27 B'ham City	D	1-1	PL	Dempsey 53	24 391
	4 Arsenal	L	1-2	PL	Kamara 30	60 049
Dec	11 Sunderland	D	0-0	PL		24 462
	26 West Ham	L	1-3	PL	Hughes 11	25 332
	28 Stoke	W	2-0	PL	Baird 2 4 11	26 954
	1 Tottenham	L	0-1	PL		35 603
	4 West Brom	W	3-0	PL	Davies 45, Dempsey 56, Hangeland 65	23 654
Jan	8 Peter'boro	W	6-2	FAr3	Kamara 3 32 59 76, Etuhu 45, Gera 66, Greening 89	15 936
	15 Wigan	D	1-1	PL	Johnson 86	18 820
	22 Stoke	W	2-0	PL	Dempsey 2 33 56p	23 766
	26 Liverpool	L	0-1	PL		40 466
	30 Tottenham	W	4-0	FAr4	Murphy 2 11p 14p, Hangeland 23, Dembele 45	21 829
	2 Newcastle	W	1-0	PL	Duff 67	25 620
	5 Aston Villa	D	2-2	PL	Johnson 52, Dempsey 78	35 899
Feb	14 Chelsea	D	0-0	PL		25 685
	20 Bolton	L	0-1	FAr5		19 571
	27 Man City	D	1-1	PL	Duff 48	43 077
Mar	5 Blackburn	W	3-2	PL	Duff 2 37 59, Zamora 89p	25 687
	19 Everton	L	1-2	PL	Dempsey 62	33 239
	3 Blackpool	W	3-0	PL	Zamora 2 23 28, Etuhu 73	25 692
	9 Man Utd	L	0-2	PL		75 339
Apr	23 Wolves	D	1-1	PL	Johnson 80	28 825
	27 Bolton	W	3-0	PL	Dempsey 2 15 48, Hangeland 65	23 222
	30 Sunderland	W	3-0	PL	Kakuta 33, Davies 2 61 72	39 576
	9 Liverpool	L	2-5	PL	Dembele 57, Sidwell 86	25 693
May	15 B'ham City	W	2-0	PL	Hangeland 2 5 49	27 759
	22 Arsenal	D	2-2	PL	Sidwell 26, Zamora 56	25 674

8th Att: 475 810 • Av: 25 042 (+4.74%) • Craven Cottage 25 700 (97%)

LIVERPOOL 2010–11

Jy	29 Rabotnicki	W	2-0	ELp3	N'Gog 2 17 58	18 000
	5 Rabotnicki	W	2-0	ELp3	N'Gog 22, Gerrard 40p	31 202
	15 Arsenal	D	1-1	PL	N'Gog 46	44 722
	19 Trabzonspor	W	1-0	ELpo	Babel 45	40 941
Aug	23 Man City	L	0-3	PL		47 087
	26 Trabzonspor	W	2-1	ELpo	OG 83, Kuyt 88	18 630
	29 West Brom	W	1-0	PL	Torres 66	41 194
	12 B'ham City	D	0-0	PL		27 333
	16 Steaua	W	4-1	ELgK	Cole 1, N'Gog 2 55p 90, Lucas 81	25 665
Sep	19 Man Utd	L	2-3	PL	Gerrard 2 64p 70	75 213
	22 Northants	D	2-2	LCr3	Jovanovic 9, N'Gog 116, L 2-4p	22 577
	25 Sunderland	D	2-2	PL	Kuyt 5, Gerrard 64	43 626
	30 Utrecht	D	0-0	ELgK		23 662
	3 Blackpool	L	1-2	PL	Kyrgiakos 53	43 156
	17 Everton	L	0-2	PL		39 673
Oct	21 Napoli	D	0-0	ELgK		52 910
	24 Blackburn	W	2-1	PL	Kyrgiakos 48, Torres 53	43 328
	31 Bolton	W	1-0	PL	Rodriguez 87	25 171
	4 Napoli	W	3-1	ELgK	Gerrard 3 76 88p 89	33 892
	7 Chelsea	W	2-0	PL	Torres 2 11 44	44 238
Nov	10 Wigan	D	1-1	PL	Torres 7	16 754
	13 Stoke	L	0-2	PL		27 286
	20 West Ham	W	3-0	PL	Johnson 17, Kuyt 27p, Rodriguez 38	43 024
	28 Tottenham	L	1-2	PL	Skrtel 42	35 962
	2 Steaua	D	1-1	ELgK	Jovanovic 19	13 639
	6 Aston Villa	W	3-0	PL	N'Gog 14, Babel 16, Rodriguez 56	39 079
Dec	11 Newcastle	L	1-3	PL	Kuyt 50	50 137
	15 Utrecht	D	0-0	ELgK		37 878
	29 Wolves	L	0-1	PL		41 614
	1 Bolton	W	2-1	PL	Torres 49, Cole 90	35 400
	5 Blackburn	L	1-3	PL	Gerrard 81	24 522
	9 Man Utd	L	0-1	FAr3		74 727
Jan	2 Blackpool	L	1-2	PL	Torres 3	16 089
	16 Everton	D	2-2	PL	Meireles 29, Kuyt 68p	44 795
	22 Wolves	W	3-0	PL	Torres 2 37 90, Meireles 50	41 614
	26 Fulham	W	1-0	PL	OG 52	40 466
	2 Stoke	W	2-0	PL	Meireles 47, Suarez 79	40 254
	6 Chelsea	W	1-0	PL	Meireles 69	41 829
Feb	12 Wigan	D	1-1	PL	Meireles 24	44 609
	17 Sp Praha	D	0-0	ELr2		17 569
	24 Sp Praha	W	1-0	ELr2	Kuyt 86	42 929
	27 West Ham	L	1-3	PL	Johnson 84	34 941
	6 Man Utd	W	3-1	PL	Kuyt 3 34 39 65	44 753
	10 Braga	L	0-1	ELr3		12 991
Mar	18 Braga	D	0-0	ELr3		37 494
	20 Sunderland	W	2-0	PL	Kuyt 34p, Suarez 77	47 207
	2 West Brom	L	1-2	PL	Skrtel 50	26 196
	11 Man City	W	3-0	PL	Carroll 2 13 35, Kuyt 34	44 776
Apr	17 Arsenal	D	1-1	PL	Kuyt 90	60 029
	23 B'ham City	W	5-0	PL	Rodriguez 3 7 66 73, Kuyt 24, Cole 86	44 734
	1 Newcastle	W	3-0	PL	Rodriguez 10, Kuyt 59p, Suarez 65	44 923
May	9 Fulham	W	5-2	PL	Rodriguez 3 17 70, Kuyt 16, Suarez 75	25 693
	15 Tottenham	L	0-2	PL		44 893
	22 Aston Villa	L	0-1	PL		42 785

6th Att: 813 584 • Av: 42 820 (-0.10%) • Anfield 45 276 (94%)

FULHAM LEAGUE APPEARANCES/GOALS 2010-11
Goalkeepers Mark Schwarzer AUS 31 • David Stockdale 7
Defenders Chris Baird NIR 25+4/2 • Matthew Briggs 3/0 • Rafik Halliche ALG 0+1/0 • Brede Hangeland NOR 37/6 • Aaron Hughes NIR 38/1 • Stephen Kelly IRL 8+2/0 • Paul Konchesky 1/0 • John Paintsil GHA 15+1/0 • Carlos Salcido MEX 22+1/0 • Philippe Senderos SUI 3/0
Midfield Simon Davies WAL 25+5/4 • Clint Dempsey USA 35+2/12 • Kagisho Dikgacoi RSA 0+1/0 • Damien Duff IRL 22+2/4 • Dickson Etuhu NGA 23+5/2 • Jonathan Greening 6+4/0 • Danny Murphy 37/0 • Bjorn Helge Riise NOR 0+3/0 • Steven Sidwell 10+2/2
Forwards Moussa Dembele BEL 22+2/3 • Zoltan Gera HUN 10+17/1 Eidur Gudjohnsen ISL 4+6/0 • Andy Johnson 15+12/3 • Eddie Johnson USA 1+10/0 • Gael Kakuta FRA 2+5/1 • Diomansy Kamara SEN 7+3/2 Bobby Zamora 9+5/5
Coach Mark Hughes WAL

LIVERPOOL LEAGUE APPEARANCES/GOALS 2010-11
Goalkeepers Pepe Reina ESP 38
Defenders Daniel Agger DEN 12+4/0 • Jamie Carragher 28/0 • Fabio Aurelio BRA 7+7/0 • John Flanagan 7/0 • Glen Johnson 28/2 • Martin Kelly 10+1/0 • Paul Konchesky 15/0 • Sotirios Kyrgiakos GRE 10+6/2 Jack Robinson 1+1/0 • Martin Skrtel SVK 38/2 • Danny Wilson SCO 1+1/0
Midfield Joe Cole 9+11/2 • Steven Gerrard 20+1/4 • Lucas Leiva BRA 32+1/0 • Javier Mascherano ARG 1/0 • Christian Poulsen DEN 9+3/0 • Raul Meireles POR 32+1/5 • Maxi Rodriguez ARG 24+4/10 • Jonjo Shelvey 0+15/0 • Jay Spearing 10+1/0
Forwards Ryan Babel NED 1+8/1 • Andy Carroll 5+2/2 • Dani Pacheco ESP 0+1/0 • Nathan Eccleston 0+1/0 • Milan Jovanovic SRB 5+5/0 • Dirk Kuyt NED 32+1/13 • David N'Gog FRA 9+16/2 Luis Suarez URU 12+1/4 • Fernando Torres ESP 22+1/9
Coach Roy Hodgson • Kenny Dalglish SCO (8/01/11)

MANCHESTER CITY 2010–11

Mo	Date	Opponent	R	Score	Comp	Scorers	Att
Aug	14	Tottenham	D	0-0	PL		35 928
	19	Timisoara	W	1-0	ELpo	Balotelli 72	24 695
	23	Liverpool	W	3-0	PL	Barry 13, Tevez 2 52 68	47 087
	26	Timisoara	W	2-0	ELpo	Wright-Phillips 43, Boyata 59	23 542
	29	Sunderland	L	0-1	PL		38 610
Sep	11	Blackburn	D	1-1	PL	Vieira 56	44 246
	16	RB Salzburg	W	2-0	ELgA	Silva 8, Jo 63	25 150
	19	Wigan	W	2-0	PL	Tevez 43, Toure.Y 70	15 525
	22	West Brom	L	1-2	LCr3	Jo 19	10 418
	25	Chelsea	W	1-0	PL	Tevez 59	47 203
	30	Juventus	D	1-1	ELgA	Johnson 37	35 212
Oct	3	Newcastle	W	2-1	PL	Tevez 18p, Johnson 75	46 067
	17	Blackpool	W	3-2	PL	Tevez 2 67 79, Silva 89	16 116
	21	Lech Poznan	W	3-1	ELgA	Adebayor 3 13 25 73	33 388
	24	Arsenal	L	0-3	PL		**47 393**
	30	Wolves	L	1-2	PL	Adebayor 23p	25 971
Nov	4	Lech Poznan	L	1-3	ELgA	Adebayor 51	42 590
	7	West Brom	W	2-0	PL	Balotelli 2 20 27	23 013
	10	Man Utd	D	0-0	PL		47 210
	13	B'ham City	D	0-0	PL		44 321
	21	Fulham	W	4-1	PL	Tevez 2 6 56, Zabaleta 32, Toure.Y 34	25 694
	27	Stoke	D	1-1	PL	Richards 81	27 405
Dec	1	RB Salzburg	W	3-0	ELgA	Balotelli 2 18 65, Johnson 78	37 552
	4	Bolton	W	1-0	PL	Tevez 4	46 860
	11	West Ham	W	3-1	PL	Toure.Y 30, OG 73, Johnson 81	32 813
	16	Juventus	D	1-1	ELgA	Jo 77	6 992
	20	Everton	L	1-2	PL	OG 72	45 028
	26	Newcastle	W	3-1	PL	Barry 2, Tevez 2 5 81	51 635
	28	Aston Villa	W	4-0	PL	Balotelli 3 8p 27 55p, Lescott 13	46 716
Jan	1	Blackpool	W	1-0	PL	Johnson 34	47 296
	5	Arsenal	D	0-0	PL		60 085
	9	Leicester	D	2-2	FAr3	Milner 22, Tevez 44	31 200
	15	Wolves	W	4-3	PL	Toure.K 40, Tevez 2 49 66, Toure.Y 49	46 672
	18	Leicester	W	4-2	FAr3	Tevez 15, Vieira 37, Johnson 38, Kolarov 90	27 755
	22	Aston Villa	L	0-1	PL		37 315
	30	Notts Co	D	1-1	FAr4	Dzeko 80	16 587
Feb	2	B'ham City	D	2-2	PL	Tevez 4, Kolarov 41	24 379
	5	West Brom	W	3-0	PL	Tevez 3 17p 22 39p	46 846
	12	Man Utd	L	1-2	PL	Silva 65	75 322
	15	Aris	D	0-0	ELr2		18 812
	20	Notts Co	W	5-0	FAr4	Vieira 2 37 58, Tevez 84, Dzeko 89, Richards 90	27 276
	24	Aris	W	3-0	ELr2	Dzeko 2 7 12, Toure.Y 75	36 748
	27	Fulham	D	1-1	PL	Balotelli 26	**43 077**
Mar	2	Aston Villa	W	3-0	FAr5	Tevez.Y 5, Balotelli 25, Silva 70	25 570
	5	Wigan	W	1-0	PL	Silva 38	44 864
	10	Dy. Kyiv	L	0-2	ELr3		16 315
	13	Reading	W	1-0	FAqf	Richards 74	41 150
	17	Dy. Kyiv	W	1-0	ELr3	Kolarov 39	27 816
	20	Chelsea	L	0-2	PL		41 741
Apr	3	Sunderland	W	5-0	PL	Johnson 9, Tevez 15p, Silva 63, Vieira 67, Toure.Y 73	44 197
	11	Liverpool	L	0-3	PL		44 776
	16	Man Utd	W	1-0	FAsf	Toure.Y 52	86 549
	25	Blackburn	W	1-0	PL	Dzeko 75	23 529
May	1	West Ham	W	2-1	PL	De Jong 11, Zabaleta 14	44 511
	7	Everton	L	1-2	PL	Toure.Y 29	37 351
	10	Tottenham	W	1-0	PL	OG 30	47 029
	14	Stoke	W	1-0	FAf	Toure.Y 73	88 643
	17	Stoke	W	3-0	PL	Tevez 2 14 65, Lescott 53	45 103
	22	Bolton	W	2-0	PL	Lescott 43, Dzeko 62	26 285

3rd   Att: 872 195 • Av: 45 880 (+0.81%) • Etihad Stadium 47 726 (96%)

MANCHESTER UNITED 2010–11

Mo	Date	Opponent	R	Score	Comp	Scorers	Att
Aug	8	Chelsea	W	3-1	CS	Valencia 41, Hernandez 76, Berbatov 90	84 623
	16	Newcastle	W	3-0	PL	Berbatov 33, Fletcher 42, Giggs 85	75 221
	22	Fulham	D	2-2	PL	Scholes 11, OG 84	25 643
	28	West Ham	W	3-0	PL	Rooney 33p, Nani 50, Berbatov 69	75 061
Sep	11	Everton	D	3-3	PL	Fletcher 44, Vidic 48, Berbatov 65	36 556
	14	Rangers	D	0-0	CLgC		74 408
	19	Liverpool	W	3-2	PL	Berbatov 3 42 59 84	75 213
	22	Scunthorpe	W	5-2	LCr3	Gibson 23, Smalling 36, Owen 2 49 71, Park 54	9 077
	26	Bolton	D	2-2	PL	Nani 23, Owen 74	23 926
	29	Valencia	W	1-0	CLgC	Hernandez 85	34 946
Oct	2	Sunderland	D	0-0	PL		41 709
	16	West Brom	D	2-2	PL	Hernandez 5, Nani 25	75 272
	20	Bursapor	W	1-0	CLgC	Nani 7	72 610
	2	Stoke	W	2-1	PL	Hernandez 2 27 86	27 372
	26	Wolves	W	3-2	LCr4	Bebe 56, Park 70, Hernandez 90	46 083
	30	Tottenham	W	2-0	PL	Vidic 31, Nani 84	75 223
Nov	2	Bursapor	W	3-0	CLgC	Fletcher 48, Obertan 73, Bebe 77	19 050
	6	Wolves	W	2-1	PL	Park 2 45 90	75 285
	10	Man City	D	0-0	PL		47 210
	13	Aston Villa	D	2-2	PL	Macheda 81, Vidic 85	40 073
	20	Wigan	W	2-0	PL	Evra 45, Hernandez 76	74 181
	24	Rangers	W	1-0	CLgC	Rooney 87p	49 764
	27	Blackburn	W	7-1	PL	Berbatov 5 2 26 47 62 70, Park 23,	74 850
Dec	7	Valencia	D	1-1	CLgC	Anderson 62	74 513
	13	Arsenal	W	1-0	PL	Park 41	75 227
	26	Sunderland	W	2-0	PL	Berbatov 2 5 57	75 269
	28	B'ham City	D	1-1	PL	Berbatov 58	28 242
Jan	1	West Brom	W	2-1	PL	Rooney 3, Hernandez 75	25 499
	4	Stoke	W	2-1	PL	Hernandez 27, Nani 62	**73 401**
	9	Liverpool	W	1-0	FAr3	Giggs 2p	74 727
	16	Tottenham	D	0-0	PL		35 828
	22	B'ham City	W	5-0	PL	Berbatov 3 2 31 53, Giggs 45, Nani 76	75 326
	25	Blackpool	W	3-2	PL	Berbatov 2 72 88, Hernandez 74	15 574
	29	South'ton	W	2-1	FAr4	Owen 65, Hernandez 75	28 792
Feb	1	Aston Villa	W	3-1	PL	Rooney 2 1 45, Vidic 64	75 256
	5	Wolves	L	1-2	PL	Nani 3	28 811
	12	Man City	W	2-1	PL	Nani 41, Rooney 78	75 322
	19	Crawley	W	1-0	FAr5	Brown 28	74 778
	1	Marseille	D	0-0	CLr2		57 957
	26	Wigan	W	4-0	PL	Hernandez 2 17 74, Rooney 84,	18 140
Mar	1	Chelsea	L	1-2	PL	Rooney 30 Fabio 87	41 825
	6	Liverpool	L	1-3	PL	Hernandez 90	44 753
	12	Arsenal	W	2-0	FAqf	Fabio 28, Rooney 49	74 693
	15	Marseille	W	2-1	CLr2	Hernandez 2 5 75	73 996
	19	Bolton	W	1-0	PL	Berbatov 88	**75 486**
Apr	2	West Ham	W	4-2	PL	Rooney 3 65 73 79p, Hernandez 84	34 546
	6	Chelsea	W	2-1	CLqf	Rooney 24	37 915
	9	Fulham	W	2-0	PL	Berbatov 12, Valencia 32	75 339
	12	Chelsea	W	2-1	CLqf	Hernandez 43, Park 77	74 672
	16	Man City	L	0-1	FAsf		86 549
	19	Newcastle	D	0-0	PL		49 025
	27	Schalke	W	2-0	CLsf	Giggs 67, Rooney 69	54 142
May	1	Arsenal	L	0-1	PL		60 107
	4	Schalke	W	4-1	CLsf	Valencia 25, Gibson 31, Anderson 2 72 76	74 687
	8	Chelsea	W	2-1	PL	Hernandez 1, Vidic 69	75 445
	14	Blackburn	D	1-1	PL	Rooney 73p	29 867
	22	Blackpool	W	4-2	PL	Park 21, Anderson 62, OG 74, Owen 81	75 400
	28	Barcelona	L	1-3	CLf	Rooney 87	87 695

1st   Att: 1 427 077 • Av: 75 109 (+0.33%) • Old Trafford 75 769 (99%)

MAN CITY LEAGUE APPEARANCES/GOALS 2010-11

Goalkeepers Joe Hart 38
Defenders Jerome Boateng GER 14+2/0 • Dedryk Boyata BEL 5+2/0 • Wayne Bridge 1+2/0 • Aleksandar Kolarov SRB 20+4/1 • Vincent Kompany BEL 37/0 • Joleon Lescott 20+2/3 • Ryan McGivern NIR 0+1/0 • Micah Richards 16+2/1 • Kolo Toure CIV 21+1/1 • Reece Wabara 0+1/0
Midfield Gareth Barry 31+2/2 • David Silva ESP 30+5/4 • Nigel de Jong NED 30+2/1 • Adam Johnson 13+16/4 • James Milner 21+5/2 • Abdul Razak CIV 0+1/0 • Yaya Toure CIV 35/6 • Patrick Vieira FRA 4+11/2 • Shaun Wright-Phillips 2+5/0 • Pablo Zabaleta ARG 21+5/2
Forwards Emmanuel Adebayor TOG 2+6/1 • Mario Balotelli ITA 12+5/6 • Edin Dzeko BIH 8+7/2 • Jo BRA 3+9/0 • Roque Santa Cruz PAR 0+1/0 • Carlos Tevez ARG 30+1/21
Coach Roberto Mancini ITA

MAN UTD LEAGUE APPEARANCES/GOALS 2010-11

Goalkeepers Tomasz Kuszczak POL 5 • Edwin van der Sar NED 33
Defenders Wes Brown 4+3/0 • Jonny Evans NIR 11+2/0 • Patrice Evra FRA 34+1/1 • Fabio BRA 5+6/1 • Rio Ferdinand 19/0 • Gary Neville 3/0 • John O'Shea IRL 18+2/0 • Rafael BRA 15+1/0 • Chris Smalling 11+5/0 • Nemanja Vidic SRB 35/5
Midfield Anderson BRA 14+4/1 • Michael Carrick 23+5/0 • Darren Fletcher 22+4/2 • Darron Gibson IRL 6+6/0 • Ryan Giggs WAL 19+6/2 • Owen Hargreaves 0+1/0 • Nani POR 31+2/9 • Park Ji Sung KOR 13+4/5 • Paul Scholes 16+6/1 • Luis Valencia ECU 8+2/1
Forwards Bebe POR 2+4/0 • Dimitar Berbatov BUL 24+8/21 • Javier Hernandez MEX 15+12/13 • Federico Macheda 2+5/1 • Gabriel Obertan FRA 3+4/0 • Michael Owen 1+10/2 • Wayne Rooney 25+3/11
Coach Alex Ferguson SCO

NEWCASTLE UNITED 2010-11

	Date	Opponent		Score	Comp	Scorers	Att
Aug	16	Man Utd	L	0-3	PL		75 221
	22	Aston Villa	W	6-0	PL	Barton 13, Nolan 2 32 87, Carroll 3 33 67 90	43 546
	25	Accrington	W	3-2	LCr2	Taylor 36, Ameobi 51, Lovenkrands 68	4 098
	28	Wolves	D	1-1	PL	Carroll 63	27 745
Sep	11	Blackpool	L	0-2	PL		49 597
	18	Everton	W	1-0	PL	Ben Arfa 45	38 019
	22	Chelsea	W	4-3	LCr3	Ranger 27, Taylor 32, Ameobi 2 49 90	41 511
	26	Stoke	L	1-2	PL	Nolan 43p	41 915
Oct	3	Man City	L	1-2	PL	Gutierrez 24	46 067
	16	Wigan	D	2-2	PL	Ameobi 72, Coloccini 90	44 415
	23	West Ham	W	2-1	PL	Nolan 23, Carroll 69	34 486
	27	Arsenal	L	0-4	LCr4		33 157
	31	Sunderland	W	5-1	PL	Nolan 3 26 34 75, Ameobi 2 45p 70	**51 988**
Nov	7	Arsenal	W	1-0	PL	Carroll 45	60 059
	10	Blackburn	L	1-2	PL	Carroll 47	**41 053**
	13	Fulham	D	0-0	PL		44 686
	20	Bolton	L	1-5	PL	Carroll 52	22 203
	28	Chelsea	D	1-1	PL	Carroll 6	46 469
Dec	5	West Brom	L	1-3	PL	Lovenkrands 90	23 486
	11	Liverpool	W	3-1	PL	Nolan 15, Barton 90, Carroll 90	50 137
	26	Man City	L	1-3	PL	Carroll 72	51 635
	28	Tottenham	L	0-2	PL		35 927
	2	Wigan	W	1-0	PL	Ameobi 18	15 277
Jan	5	West Ham	W	5-0	PL	Best 3 18 39 60, Nolan 45, Lovenkrands 63	42 387
	8	Stevenage	L	1-3	FAr3	Barton 90	6 644
	16	Sunderland	D	1-1	PL	Nolan 52	47 869
	22	Tottenham	D	1-1	PL	Coloccini 59	51 010
	2	Fulham	L	0-1	PL		25 620
Feb	5	Arsenal	D	4-4	PL	Barton 2 68p 83p, Best 75, Tiote 88	51 561
	12	Blackburn	D	0-0	PL		26 781
	15	B'ham City	W	2-0	PL	Lovenkrands 2, Best 50	28 270
	26	Bolton	D	1-1	PL	Nolan 13	48 062
Mar	5	Everton	L	1-2	PL	Best 23	50 128
	19	Stoke	L	0-4	PL		27 505
	2	Wolves	W	4-1	PL	Nolan 22, Ameobi 45, Lovenkrands 50, Gutierrez 90	49 939
Apr	10	Aston Villa	D	1-1	PL		37 090
	19	Man Utd	D	0-0	PL		49 025
	23	Blackpool	D	1-1	PL	Lovenkrands 17	16 003
	1	Liverpool	L	0-3	PL		44 923
May	7	B'ham City	W	2-1	PL	Ameobi 36p, Taylor 43	47 409
	15	Chelsea	D	2-2	PL	Gutierrez 10, Taylor 90	41 739
	22	West Brom	D	3-3	PL	Taylor 16, Lovenkrands 39, OG 47	51 678

12th Att: 906 640 • Av: 47 718 (+9.98%) • St James' Park 52 387 (91%)

STOKE CITY 2010-11

	Date	Opponent		Score	Comp	Scorers	Att
Aug	14	Wolves	L	1-2	PL	Faye 55	27 850
	21	Tottenham	L	1-2	PL	Fuller 25	27 243
	24	Shrewsbury	W	2-1	LCr2	Walters 26, Tuncay 37	11 995
	28	Chelsea	L	0-2	PL		40 931
Sep	13	Aston Villa	W	2-1	PL	Jones 80, Huth 90	25 899
	18	West Ham	D	1-1	PL	Jones 48	27 028
	21	Fulham	W	2-0	LCr3	Higginbotham 23, Jones 79	12 778
	26	Newcastle	W	2-1	PL	Jones 67, OG 85	41 915
Oct	2	Blackburn	W	1-0	PL	Walters 48	25 515
	16	Bolton	L	1-2	PL	Delap 47	22 975
	24	Man Utd	L	1-2	PL	Tuncay 81	27 372
	27	West Ham	L	1-3	LCr4	Jones 6	25 304
	30	Everton	L	0-1	PL		35 513
Nov	6	Sunderland	L	0-2	PL		36 541
	9	B'ham City	W	3-2	PL	Huth 44, Fuller 71, Whitehead 85	26 381
	13	Liverpool	W	2-0	PL	Fuller 56, Jones 90	27 286
	20	West Brom	W	3-0	PL	Etherington 55p, Walters 2 85p 90	24 164
	27	Man City	D	1-1	PL	Etherington 90	27 405
Dec	4	Wigan	D	2-2	PL	Huth 18, Etherington 31	15 100
	11	Blackpool	L	0-1	PL		26 879
	26	Blackburn	W	2-0	PL	Huth 51, Wilson 90	25 440
	28	Fulham	L	0-2	PL		26 954
Jan	1	Everton	W	2-0	PL	Jones 23, OG 69	27 418
	4	Man Utd	L	1-2	PL	Whitehead 50	73 401
	8	Cardiff	D	1-1	FAr3	Tuncay 45	18 629
	15	Bolton	W	2-0	PL	Higginbotham 37, Etherington 63p	26 809
	18	Cardiff	W	2-0	FAr3	Walters 2 91 115	13 671
	22	Fulham	L	0-2	PL		23 766
	30	Wolves	W	1-0	FAr4	Huth 81	11 967
	2	Liverpool	L	0-2	PL		40 254
Feb	5	Sunderland	W	3-2	PL	Carew 32, Huth 2 83 90	26 008
	12	B'ham City	L	0-1	PL		23 660
	19	Brighton	W	3-0	FAr5	Carew 14, Walters 22, Shawcross 43	21 312
	23	Arsenal	L	0-1	PL		60 041
	28	West Brom	D	1-1	PL	Delap 53	**25 019**
Mar	5	West Ham	L	0-3	PL		33 066
	13	West Ham	W	2-1	FAqf	Huth 12, Higginbotham 63	24 550
	19	Newcastle	W	4-0	PL	Walters 29, Pennant 47, Higginbotham 49, Fuller 90	27 505
Apr	2	Chelsea	D	1-1	PL	Walters 8	27 508
	9	Tottenham	L	2-3	PL	Etherington 27, Jones 41	32 702
	17	Bolton	W	5-0	FAsf	Etherington 11, Huth 17, Jones 30, Walters 2 68 81	75 064
	23	Aston Villa	D	1-1	PL	Jones 20	35 235
	26	Wolves	W	3-0	PL	Jones 16, Shawcross 45, Pennant 50	27 030
	30	Blackpool	D	0-0	PL		16 003
May	8	Arsenal	W	3-1	PL	Jones 28, Pennant 40, Walters 82	27 478
	14	Man City	L	0-1	FAf		88 643
	17	Man City	L	0-3	PL		45 103
	22	Wigan	L	0-1	PL		**27 566**

13th Att: 510 303 • Av: 26 858 (-1.12%) • Britannia Stadium 27 740 (97%)

NEWCASTLE LEAGUE APPEARANCES/GOALS 2010-11

Goalkeepers Steve Harper 18 • Tim Krul NED 20+1/0
Defenders Sol Campbell 4+3/0 • Fabricio Coloccini ARG 35/2 • Jose Enrique ESP 36/0 • James Perch 9+3/0 • Danny Simpson 30/0 • Ryan Taylor 3+2/0 • Steven Taylor 12+2/3 • Mike Williamson 28+1/0
Midfield Joey Barton 32/4 • Hatem Ben Arfa FRA 3+1/1 • Shane Ferguson NIR 3+4/0 • Dan Gosling 0+1/0 • Danny Guthrie 11+3/0 • Jonas Gutierrez ARG 34+3/3 • Stephen Ireland IRL 0+2/0 • Kazenga LuaLua COD 0+2/0 • Kevin Nolan 30/12 • Wayne Routledge 10+7/0 • Cheik Tiote CIV 26/1
Forwards Sammy Ameobi 0+1/0 • Shola Ameobi 21+7/6 • Leon Best IRL 9+2/6 • Andy Carroll 18+1/11 • Shefki Kuqi FIN 0+6/0 • Peter Lovenkrands DEN 18+7/6 • Nile Ranger 1+23/0 • Alan Smith 7+4/0 • Xisco ESP 0+2/0
Coach Chris Hughton • Alan Pardew (9/12/10)

STOKE LEAGUE APPEARANCES/GOALS 2010-11

Goalkeepers Asmir Begovic BIH 28 • Thomas Sorensen DEN 10
Defenders Danny Collins WAL 23+2/0 • Danny Higginbotham 9+1/2 • Robert Huth 35/6 GER • Ryan Shawcross 36/1 • Ryan Shotton 0+2/0 • Andrew Wilkinson 21+1/0 • Marc Wilson IRL 21+7/1
Midfield Rory Delap IRL 33+4/2 • Salif Diao SEN 3+5/0 • Matthew Etherington 30+2/5 • Abdoulaye Faye SEN 12+2/1 • Jermaine Pennant 26+3/3 • Danny Pugh 5+5/0 • Michael Tonge 0+2/0 • Glenn Whelan IRL 14+15/0 • Dean Whitehead 31+6/2
Forwards John Carew NOR 7+3/1 • Ricardo Fuller JAM 9+19/4 • Kenwyne Jones TRI 33+1/9 • Eidur Gudjohnsen ISL 0+4/0 • Mamady Sidibe MLI 0+2/0 • Tuncay Sanli TUR 5+9/1 • Jon Walters IRL 27+9/6
Coach Tony Pulis WAL

SUNDERLAND 2010–11

Mon	Day	Opponent	Res	Score	Comp	Scorers	Att
Aug	14	B'ham City	D	2-2	PL	Bent 24p OG 56	38 390
	21	West Brom	L	0-1	PL		23 624
	24	Colchester	W	2-0	LCr2	Bent 2 19 37	13 532
	29	Man City	W	1-0	PL	Bent 90p	38 610
	11	Wigan	D	1-1	PL	Gyan 66	15 844
Sep	18	Arsenal	D	1-1	PL	Bent 90	38 950
	21	West Ham	L	1-2	LCr3	Gyan 41	21 907
	25	Liverpool	D	2-2	PL	Bent 2 25p 48	43 626
	2	Man Utd	D	0-0	PL		41 709
Oct	18	Blackburn	D	0-0	PL		21 894
	23	Aston Villa	W	1-0	PL	OG 25	41 506
	31	Newcastle	L	1-5	PL	Bent 90	51 988
	6	Stoke	W	2-0	PL	Gyan 2 9 87	36 541
	9	Tottenham	D	1-1	PL	Gyan 67	35 843
Nov	14	Chelsea	W	3-0	PL	Onuoha 45, Gyan 52, Welbeck 87	41 072
	22	Everton	D	2-2	PL	Welbeck 2 23 70	37 331
	27	Wolves	L	2-3	PL	Bent 67, Welbeck 77	25 112
	5	West Ham	W	1-0	PL	Henderson 34	36 940
	11	Fulham	D	0-0	PL		24 462
Dec	18	Bolton	W	1-0	PL	Welbeck 32	**35 101**
	26	Man Utd	L	0-2	PL		75 269
	28	Blackpool	L	0-2	PL		42 892
	1	Blackburn	W	3-0	PL	Welbeck 11, Bent 19, Gyan 89	36 242
	5	Aston Villa	W	1-0	PL	Bardsley 80	32 627
Jan	8	Notts Co	L	1-2	FAr3	Bent 81p	17 582
	16	Newcastle	D	1-1	PL	Gyan 90	**47 864**
	22	Blackpool	W	2-1	PL	Richardson 2 15 36	16 037
	1	Chelsea	L	2-4	PL	Bardsley 3, Richardson 27	37 855
Feb	5	Stoke	L	2-3	PL	Richardson 3, Gyan 48	26 008
	12	Tottenham	L	1-2	PL	Gyan 11	40 986
	26	Everton	L	0-2	PL		37 776
Mar	5	Arsenal	D	0-0	PL		60 081
	20	Liverpool	L	0-2	PL		47 207
	3	Man City	L	0-5	PL		44 197
	9	West Brom	L	2-3	PL	OG 10, Bardsley 31	41 586
Apr	16	B'ham City	L	0-2	PL		28 108
	23	Wigan	W	4-2	PL	Gyan 55, Henderson 2 66 77, Sessegnon 73p	39 650
	30	Fulham	L	0-3	PL		39 576
	7	Bolton	W	2-1	PL	Zenden 45, OG 90	22 597
May	14	Wolves	L	1-3	PL	Sessegnon 34	41 273
	22	West Ham	W	3-0	PL	Zenden 17, Sessegnon 51, Riveros 90	32 792

10th   Att: 760 214 • Av: 40 011 (-0.85%) • Stadium of Light 49 000 (81%)

TOTTENHAM HOTSPUR 2010–11

Mon	Day	Opponent	Res	Score	Comp	Scorers	Att
Aug	14	Man City	D	0-0	PL		35 928
	17	Young Boys	L	2-3	CLpo	Bassong 42, Pavlyuchenko 83	30 166
	21	Stoke	W	2-1	PL	Bale 2 19 30	27 243
	25	Young Boys	W	4-0	CLpo	Crouch 3 5 61 78p, Defoe 32	34 709
	28	Wigan	L	0-1	PL		35 101
	11	West Brom	D	1-1	PL	Modric 26	23 642
	14	W Bremen	D	2-2	CLgA	OG 12, Crouch 18	30 344
	18	Wolves	W	3-1	PL	Van der Vaart 77p, Pavlyuchenko 87, Hutton 90	35 940
Sep	21	Arsenal	L	1-4	LCr3	Keane 49	35 883
	25	West Ham	L	0-1	PL		34 190
	29	Twente	W	4-1	CLgA	Van der Vaart 47, Pavlyuchenko 2 50p 64p, Bale 85	32 318
	2	Aston Villa	W	2-1	PL	Van de Vaart 2 45 75	35 871
	16	Fulham	W	2-1	PL	Pavlyuchenko 31, Huddlestone 64	25 615
Oct	20	Inter	L	3-4	CLgA	Bale 3 52 90 91+	49 551
	23	Everton	D	1-1	PL	Van der Vaart 20	35 967
	30	Man Utd	L	0-2	PL		75 223
	2	Inter	W	3-1	CLgA	Van der Vaart 18, Crouch 61, Pavlyuchenko 89	34 103
	6	Bolton	L	2-4	PL	Hutton 79, Pavlyuchenko 87	20 255
	9	Sunderland	D	1-1	PL	Van der Vaart 64	35 843
Nov	13	Blackburn	W	4-2	PL	Bale 2 16 76, Pavlyuchenko 42, Crouch 69	35 700
	20	Arsenal	W	3-2	PL	Bale 50, Van der Vaart 67p, Kaboul 86	60 102
	24	W Bremen	W	3-0	CLgA	Kaboul 6, Modric 45, Crouch 79	33 546
	28	Liverpool	W	2-1	PL	OG 65, Lennon 90	35 962
	4	B'ham City	D	1-1	PL	Bassong 19	25 770
	7	Twente	D	3-3	CLgA	OG 12, Defoe 2 47 59	30 400
Dec	12	Chelsea	D	1-1	PL	Pavlyuchenko 15	35 787
	26	Aston Villa	W	2-1	PL	Van der Vaart 2 23 67	39 411
	28	Newcastle	W	2-0	PL	Lennon 57, Bale 81	35 927
	1	Fulham	W	1-0	PL	Bale 42	35 603
	5	Everton	L	1-2	PL	Van der Vaart 11	34 124
	9	Charlton	W	3-0	FAr3	Townsend 49, Defoe 2 58 60	35 698
Jan	16	Man Utd	D	0-0	PL		35 828
	22	Newcastle	D	1-1	PL	Lennon 90	51 010
	30	Fulham	L	0-4	FAr4		21 829
	2	Blackburn	W	1-0	PL	Crouch 3	23 253
	5	Bolton	W	2-1	PL	Van der Vaart 6p, Kranjcar 90	**36 197**
Feb	12	Sunderland	W	2-1	PL	Dawson 44, Kranjcar 57	40 986
	15	Milan	W	1-0	CLr2	Crouch 80	75 652
	22	Blackpool	L	1-3	PL	Pavlyuchenko 90	16 069
	6	Wolves	D	3-3	PL	Defoe 2 30 35, Pavlyuchenko 48	28 669
Mar	9	Milan	D	0-0	CLr2		34 320
	19	West Ham	D	0-0	PL		36 010
	2	Wigan	D	0-0	PL		18 578
	5	Real Madrid	L	0-4	CLqf		71 657
	9	Stoke	W	3-2	PL	Crouch 2 11 34, Modric 18	**32 702**
Apr	13	Real Madrid	L	0-1	CLqf		34 311
	20	Arsenal	D	3-3	PL	Van der Vaart 2 7 70p, Huddlestone 44	36 138
	23	West Brom	D	2-2	PL	Pavlyuchenko 27, Defoe 67	36 160
	30	Chelsea	L	1-2	PL	Sandro 19	41 681
	7	Blackpool	D	1-1	PL	Defoe 89	35 585
May	10	Man City	L	0-1	PL		47 029
	15	Liverpool	W	2-0	PL	Van der Vaart 9, Modric 56p	44 893
	22	B'ham City	W	2-1	PL	Pavlyuchenko 2 49 90	36 119

5th   Att: 678 368 • Av: 35 703 (-0.25%) • White Hart Lane 36 230 (98%)

SUNDERLAND LEAGUE APPEARANCES/GOALS 2010-11

Goalkeepers Craig Gordon SCO 15 • Simon Mignolet BEL 23
Defenders Marcos Angeleri ARG 0+2/0 • Phil Bardsley SCO 32+2/3 Titus Bramble 22+1/0 • Paulo da Silva Par 1/0 • Ahmed El Mohamadi EGY 26+10/0 • Anton Ferdinand 23+4/0 • Louis Laing 0+1/0 • John Mensah GHA 15+3/0 • Nedum Onuoha 31/1 • Michael Turner 15/0
Midfield Lee Cattermole 22+1/0 • Jack Colback 6+5/0 • Jordan Cook 0+3/0 • Jordan Henderson 37/3 • Steed Malbranque FRA 24+11/0 • David Meyler IRL 4+1/0 • Sulley Ali Muntari GHA 7+2/0 • Andy Reid IRL 0+2/0 • Kieran Richardson 23+3/4 • Cristian Riveros PAR 5+7/1 Stephane Sessegnon BEN 13+1/3 • Boudewijn Zenden NED 10+17/2
Forwards Darren Bent 20/8 • Frazier Campbell 3/0 • Asamoah Gyan GHA 20+1/10 • Craig Lynch 0+2/0 • Ryan Noble 0+3/0 Martyn Waghorn 0+2/0 • Danny Welbeck 21+5/6
Coach Steve Bruce

SPURS LEAGUE APPEARANCES/GOALS 2010-11

Goalkeepers Carlo Cudicini ITA 8 • Heurelho Gomes BRA 30
Defenders Benoit Assou-Ekotto CMR 30/0 • Gareth Bale WAL 29+1/7 Sebastien Bassong CMR 7+5/1 • Vedran Corluka CRO 13+2/0 • Michael Dawson 24/1 • William Gallas FRA 26+1/0 • Alan Hutton SCO 19+2/2 Younes Kaboul FRA 19+2/1 • Ledley King 6/0 • Kyle Walker 0+1/0
Midfield David Bentley 1+1/0 • Tom Huddlestone 13+1/2 • Jermaine Jenas 14+5/0 • Niko Kranjcar CRO 2+11/2 • Aaron Lennon 25+9/3 Luka Modric 32/3 • Wilson Palacios HON 16+5/0 • Steven Pienaar RSA 5+3/0 • Danny Rose 4/0 • Sandro BRA 11+8/1 Rafael van der Vaart NED 28/13
Forwards Peter Crouch 20+14/4 • Jermain Defoe 16+6/4 Giovanni Dos Santos MEX 0+3/0 • Robbie Keane IRL 2+5/0 Roman Pavlyuchenko RUS 18+11/10
Coach Harry Redknapp

WEST BROMWICH ALBION 2010-11

	Date	Opponent		Score	Comp	Scorers	Att
Aug	14	Chelsea	L	0-6	PL		41 589
	21	Sunderland	W	1-0	PL	Odemwingie 81	23 624
	24	Orient	W	2-0	LCr2	Ibanez 29, Wood 90	2 349
	29	Liverpool	L	0-1	PL		41 194
Sep	1	Tottenham	D	1-1	PL	Brunt 40	23 642
	18	B'ham City	W	3-1	PL	OG 51, Odemwingie 59, Olsson 70	23 062
	22	Man City	W	2-1	LCr3	Zuiverloon 55, Cox 57	10 418
	25	Arsenal	W	3-2	PL	Odemwingie 50, Jara 52, Thomas 73	60 025
Oct	2	Bolton	D	1-1	PL	Morrison 78	22 846
	16	Man Utd	D	2-2	PL	OG 50, Tchoyi 55	75 272
	23	Fulham	W	2-1	PL	Mulumbu 17, Fortune 40	25 625
	26	Leicester	W	4-1	LCr4	Cox 2 21 90, Tchoyi 62, Reid 79	16 957
Nov	1	Blackpool	L	1-2	PL	Mulumbu 84	15 210
	7	Man City	L	0-2	PL		23 013
	10	West Ham	D	2-2	PL	Odemwingie 38p, Ibanez 72	33 023
	13	Wigan	L	0-1	PL		16 085
	20	Stoke	L	0-3	PL		24 164
	27	Everton	W	4-1	PL	Scharner 16, Brunt 26, Tchoyi 75, OG 87	35 237
Dec	1	Ipswich	L	0-1	LCqf		11 363
	5	Newcastle	W	3-1	PL	Tchoyi 32, Odemwingie 2 71 89	23 486
	11	Aston Villa	L	1-2	PL	Scharner 90	37 015
	26	Bolton	L	0-2	PL		23 413
	28	Blackburn	L	1-3	PL	Thomas 17	24 440
Jan	1	Man Utd	L	1-2	PL	Morisson 14	25 499
	4	Fulham	L	0-3	PL		23 654
	8	Reading	L	0-1	FAr3		13 005
	15	Blackpool	W	3-2	PL	Odemwingie 2 38 87, Morisson 52	25 316
	23	Blackburn	L	0-2	PL		24 057
Feb	1	Wigan	D	2-2	PL	Odemwingie 5, Fortune 79	25 358
	5	Man City	L	0-3	PL		46 846
	12	West Ham	D	3-3	PL	Dorrans 3, Thomas 8, OG 32	23 916
	20	Wolves	D	1-1	PL	Vela 90	26 170
	28	Stoke	D	1-1	PL	Vela 87	25 019
Mar	5	B'ham City	W	3-1	PL	Mulumbu 47, Morisson 58, Scharner 72	27 013
	19	Arsenal	D	2-2	PL	Reid 3, Odemwingie 58	25 729
	2	Liverpool	W	2-1	PL	Brunt 2 62p 89p	26 196
Apr	9	Sunderland	W	3-2	PL	Odemwingie 29, Mulumbu 54, Scharner 72	41 586
	16	Chelsea	L	1-3	PL	Odemwingie 17	25 163
	23	Tottenham	D	2-2	PL	Odemwingie 5, Cox 81	36 160
	30	Aston Villa	W	2-1	PL	Odemwingie 60, Mulumbu 84	25 889
May	8	Wolves	L	1-3	PL	Odemwingie 55p	28 510
	14	Everton	W	1-0	PL	Mulumbu 10	25 838
	22	Newcastle	D	3-3	PL	Tchoyi 3 62 71 90	51 678

11th Att: 468 976 • Av: 24 682 (+11.19%) • The Hawthorns 26 484 (93%)

WEST HAM UNITED 2010-11

	Date	Opponent		Score	Comp	Scorers	Att
Aug	14	Aston Villa	L	0-3	PL		36 604
	21	Bolton	L	1-3	PL	Noble 79p	32 533
	24	Oxford	W	1-0	LCr2	Parker 90	20 902
	28	Man Utd	L	0-3	PL		75 061
Sep	11	Chelsea	L	1-3	PL	Parker 85	33 014
	18	Stoke	D	1-1	PL	Parker 32	27 028
	21	Sunderland	W	2-1	LCr3	Piquionne 35, Obinna 59	21 907
	25	Tottenham	W	1-0	PL	Piquionne 29	34 190
Oct	2	Fulham	D	1-1	PL	Piquionne 51	34 589
	16	Wolves	D	1-1	PL	Noble 52p	28 582
	23	Newcastle	L	1-2	PL	Cole 12	34 486
	27	Stoke	W	3-1	LCr4	Parker 84, Da Costa 96, Obinna 118	25 304
	30	Arsenal	L	0-1	PL		60 086
Nov	6	B'ham City	D	2-2	PL	Piquionne 48, Behrami 58	26 474
	10	West Brom	D	2-2	PL	Parker 43, Piquionne 50p	33 023
	13	Blackpool	D	0-0	PL		31 194
	20	Liverpool	L	0-3	PL		43 024
	27	Wigan	W	3-1	PL	Behrami 35, Obinna 56, Parker 75	34 178
		Man Utd	W	4-0	LCqf	Spector 2 22 37, Cole 2 55 67	33 551
Dec	5	Sunderland	L	0-1	PL		36 940
	11	Man City	L	1-3	PL	Tomkins 89	32 813
	18	Blackburn	D	1-1	PL	Stanislas 78	21 934
	26	Fulham	W	3-1	PL	Cole 2 37 73, Piquionne 45	25 332
	28	Everton	D	1-1	PL	OG 16	33 422
Jan	1	Wolves	W	2-0	PL	OG 51, Sears 79	33 500
	5	Newcastle	L	0-5	PL		42 387
	8	Barnsley	W	2-0	FAr3	Spector 29, Piquionne 90	32 159
	11	B'ham City	W	2-1	LCsf	Noble 13, Cole 78	34 754
	15	Arsenal	L	0-3	PL		32 682
	22	Everton	D	2-2	PL	Spector 26, Piquionne 85	34 179
	26	B'ham City	L	1-3	LCsf	Cole 32	27 519
	30	Nottm For	W	3-2	FAr4	Obinna 2 3 4 42 52p	29 287
	2	Blackpool	W	3-1	PL	Obinna 2 24 44, Keane 87	15 095
	6	B'ham City	L	0-1	PL		32 927
Feb	12	West Brom	D	3-3	PL	Ba 2 51 83, Cole 58	23 916
	21	Burnley	W	5-1	FAr5	Hitzlsperger 23, Cole 2 48 50, Reid 59, Sears 90	30 000
	27	Liverpool	W	3-1	PL	Parker 22, Ba 45, Cole 90	34 941
Mar	5	Stoke	W	3-0	PL	Ba 21, Da Costa 30, Hitzlsperger 83	33 066
	13	Stoke	L	1-2	FAqf	Piquionne 30	24 550
	19	Tottenham	D	0-0	PL		36 010
Apr	2	Man Utd	L	2-4	PL	Noble 2 11p 24p	34 546
	9	Bolton	L	0-3	PL		25 857
	16	Aston Villa	L	1-2	PL	Keane 2	34 672
	23	Chelsea	L	0-3	PL		41 656
	1	Man City	L	1-2	PL	Ba 33	44 511
May	7	Blackburn	D	1-1	PL	Hitzlsperger 78	33 789
	15	Wigan	L	2-3	PL	Ba 2 12 26	22 043
	22	Sunderland	L	0-3	PL		32 792

20th Att: 636 357 • Av: 33 492 (-0.57%) • Upton Park 35 303 (94%)

WEST BROM LEAGUE APPEARANCES/GOALS 2010-11

Goalkeepers Scott Carson 32 • Boaz Myhill WAL 6
Defenders Marek Cech SVK 14+1/0 • James Hurst 1/0 • Pablo Ibanez ESP 8+2/1 • Gonzalo Jara CHI 24+5/1 • Abdoulaye Meite CIV 10/0 • Jonas Olsson SWE 24/1 • Steven Reid IRL 13+10/1 • Nicky Shorey 25+3/0 • Gabriel Tamas ROU 22+4/0
Midfield Giles Barnes 1+13/0 • Chris Brunt NIR 34/4 • Graham Dorrans SCO 16+5/1 • Ishmael Miller 0+6/0 • James Morrison SCO 26+5/4 • Youssuf Mulumbu COD 34/6 • Paul Scharner AUT 33/4 • Somen Tchoyi CMR 7+16/6 • Jerome Thomas 32+1/3 • George Thorne 0+1/0 • Gianni Zuiverloon NED 1+1/0
Forwards Roman Bednar CZE 1+3/0 • Simon Cox IRL 8+11/1 • Marc-Antoine Fortune FRA 14+11/2 • Peter Odemwingie NGA 29+3/15 • Carlos Vela MEX 3+5/2 • Chris Wood NZL 0+1/0
Coach Roberto Di Matteo ITA • Roy Hodgson (11/02/11)

WEST HAM LEAGUE APPEARANCES/GOALS 2010-11

Goalkeepers Ruud Boffin BEL 1 • Robert Green 37
Defenders Tal Ben Haim ISR 8/0 • Wayne Bridge 15/0 • Manuel Da Costa POR 14+2/1 • Daniel Gabbidon WAL 24+2/0 • Herita Ilunga COD 10+1/0 • Lars Jacobsen DEN 22+2/0 • Radoslav Kovac CZE 7+6/0 • Winston Reid NZL 3+4/0 • Jonathan Spector USA 10+4/1 • Jordan Spence 2/0 • James Tomkins 18+1/1 • Matthew Upson 30/0
Midfield Valon Behrami SUI 6+1/2 • Luis Boa Morte POR 19+3/0 • Jack Collison WAL 2+1/0 • Kieron Dyer 8+3/0 • Julien Faubert FRA 7+2/0 • Thomas Hitzlsperger GER 11/2 • Mark Noble 25+1/4 • Gary O'Neil 7+1/0 • Scott Parker 30+2/5 • Junior Stanislas 4+2/1
Forwards Demba Ba SEN 10+2/7 • Pablo Barrera MEX 6+8/0 • Carlton Cole 21+14/5 • Alessandro Diamanti ITA 0+1/0 • Zavon Hines JAM 4+5/0 • Robbie Keane IRL 5+4/2 • Benny McCarthy RSA 0+6/0 • Frank Nouble 0+2/0 • Victor Obinna NGA 17+8/3 • Frederic Piquionne FRA 26+8/6 • Freddie Sears 9+2/1
Coach Avram Grant ISR

WIGAN ATHLETIC 2010–11

	Date	Opponent	Res	Score	Comp	Scorers	Att
Aug	14	Blackpool	L	0-4	PL		16 152
	21	Chelsea	L	0-6	PL		14 476
	24	Hartlepool	W	3-0	LCr2	OG 3, Gomez 76, Moses 86	3 196
	28	Tottenham	W	1-0	PL	Rodallega 80	35 101
Sep	11	Sunderland	D	1-1	PL	Alcaraz 87	15 844
	19	Man City	L	0-2	PL		15 525
	22	Preston	W	2-1	LCr3	Gomez 87, N'Zogbia 90	6 987
	25	B'ham City	D	0-0	PL		22 186
Oct	2	Wolves	W	2-0	PL	Gomez 65, Rodallega 86	14 042
	16	Newcastle	D	2-2	PL	N'Zogbia 2 22 23	44 415
	23	Bolton	D	1-1	PL	Rodallega 59	17 100
	26	Swansea	W	2-0	LCr4	Boselli 51, Watson 90p	11 705
	30	Fulham	L	0-2	PL		25 448
Nov	6	Blackburn	L	1-2	PL	N'Zogbia 75	24 413
	10	Liverpool	D	1-1	PL	Rodallega 52	16 754
	13	West Brom	W	1-0	PL	Moses 70	16 085
	20	Man Utd	L	0-2	PL		74 181
	27	West Ham	L	1-3	PL	Cleverley 86	34 178
	30	Arsenal	L	0-2	LCqf		59 525
Dec	4	Stoke	D	2-2	PL	OG 29, Cleverley 40	15 100
	11	Everton	D	0-0	PL		32 853
	26	Wolves	W	2-1	PL	Rodallega 9, Cleverley 20	26 901
	29	Arsenal	D	2-2	PL	Watson 18p, OG 81	17 014
	2	Newcastle	L	0-1	PL		15 277
Jan	5	Bolton	D	1-1	PL	Stam 80	18 852
	8	Hull	W	3-2	FAr3	Diame 2 21 77, McManaman 56	10 433
	15	Fulham	D	1-1	PL	Rodallega 57	18 820
	22	Arsenal	L	0-3	PL		59 552
	25	Aston Villa	L	1-2	PL	McCarthy 80	16 442
	29	Bolton	D	0-0	FAr4		14 950
Feb	1	West Brom	D	2-2	PL	N'Zogbia 20, Watson 43	25 358
	5	Blackburn	W	4-3	PL	McCarthy 2 35 56, Rodallega 50, Watson 65p	18 567
	12	Liverpool	D	1-1	PL	Gohouri 65	44 609
	16	Bolton	L	0-1	FAr4		7 515
Mar	26	Man Utd	L	0-4	PL		18 140
	5	Man City	L	0-1	PL		44 864
	19	B'ham City	W	2-1	PL	Cleverley 25, Figueroa 90	16 421
	2	Tottenham	D	0-0	PL		18 578
	9	Chelsea	L	0-1	PL		40 734
Apr	16	Blackpool	W	3-1	PL	Rodallega 3, N'Zogbia 45, OG 66	16 030
	23	Sunderland	L	2-4	PL	Diame 52, Di Santo 90	39 650
	30	Everton	D	1-1	PL	N'Zogbia 21	17 051
May	7	Aston Villa	D	1-1	PL	N'Zogbia 10	36 293
	15	West Ham	W	3-2	PL	N'Zogbia 2 57 90, Sammon 68	22 043
	22	Stoke	W	1-0	PL	Rodallega 78	27 566

16th Att: 319 431 • Av: 16 812 (-6.63%) • DW Stadium 25 138 (66%)

WOLVERHAMPTON WANDERERS 2010–11

	Date	Opponent	Res	Score	Comp	Scorers	Att
Aug	14	Stoke	W	2-1	PL	Jones 37, Fletcher 38	27 850
	21	Everton	D	1-1	PL	Ebanks-Blake 74	37 767
	24	Southend	W	2-1	LCr2	Milijas 27p, Stearman 120	10 284
	28	Newcastle	D	1-1	PL	Ebanks-Blake 43	27 745
Sep	11	Fulham	L	1-2	PL	Van Damme 9	25 280
	18	Tottenham	L	1-3	PL	Fletcher 45	35 940
	21	Notts Co	W	4-2	LCr3	Milijas 83p, Fletcher 92, Doyle 2 105 119	11 516
	26	Aston Villa	L	1-2	PL	Jarvis 62	27 511
Oct	2	Wigan	L	0-2	PL		14 042
	16	West Ham	D	1-1	PL	Jarvis 10	28 582
	23	Chelsea	L	0-2	PL		41 752
	26	Man Utd	L	2-3	LCr4	Elokobi 60, Foley 76	46 083
	30	Man City	W	2-1	PL	Milijas 30, Edwards 57	25 971
Nov	6	Man Utd	L	1-2	PL	Ebanks-Blake 65	75 285
	10	Arsenal	L	0-2	PL		27 329
	13	Bolton	L	2-3	PL	Foley 69, Fletcher 77	27 508
	20	Blackpool	L	1-2	PL	Doyle 87	15 922
	27	Sunderland	W	3-2	PL	Foley 50, Hunt 81, Ebanks-Blake 89	25 112
Dec	4	Blackburn	L	0-3	PL		22 314
	12	B'ham City	W	1-0	PL	Hunt 45	25 150
	26	Wigan	L	1-2	PL	Fletcher 87	26 901
	29	Liverpool	W	1-0	PL	Ward 56	41 614
	1	West Ham	L	0-2	PL		33 500
Jan	5	Chelsea	W	1-0	PL	OG 5	26 432
	8	Doncaster	D	2-2	FAr3	Milijas 38, Hunt 58p	8 616
	15	Man City	L	3-4	PL	Milijas 12, Doyle 68p, Zubar 86	46 672
	18	Doncaster	W	5-0	FAr3	Fletcher 5, Bia 61, Doyle 66, Jarvis 74, Jones 90	10 031
	22	Liverpool	L	0-3	PL		28 869
	30	Stoke	L	0-1	FAr4		11 967
Feb	2	Bolton	L	0-1	PL		18 944
	5	Man Utd	W	2-1	PL	Elokobi 10, Doyle 40	28 811
	12	Arsenal	L	0-2	PL		60 050
	20	West Brom	D	1-1	PL	O'Hara 40	26 170
	26	Blackpool	W	4-0	PL	Jarvis 3, O'Hara 54, Ebanks-Blake 2 79 90	29 086
Mar	6	Tottenham	D	3-3	PL	Doyle 2 20 40p, Fletcher 87	28 669
	19	Aston Villa	W	1-0	PL	Jarvis 38	38 965
	2	Newcastle	L	1-4	PL	Ebanks-Blake 58	49 939
Apr	9	Everton	L	0-3	PL		28 352
	3	Fulham	D	1-1	PL	Fletcher 22	28 825
	26	Stoke	L	0-3	PL		27 030
May	1	B'ham City	D	1-1	PL	Fletcher 7p	26 072
	8	West Brom	W	3-1	PL	Fletcher 2 15 47, Guedioura 28	28 510
	14	Sunderland	W	3-1	PL	Craddock 23, Fletcher 54, Elokobi 78	41 273
	22	Blackburn	L	2-3	PL	O'Hara 73, Hunt 87	29 009

17th Att: 526 222 • Av: 27 695 (-2.36%) • Molineux 29 195 (94%)

WIGAN LEAGUE APPEARANCES/GOALS 2010-11

Goalkeepers Ali Al Habsi OMA 34 • Chris Kirkland 4 • Mike Pollitt 0+1
Defenders Antolin Alcaraz PAR 34/1 • Emmerson Boyce BRB 20+2/0
Gary Caldwell SCO 22/0 • Steven Caldwell SCO 9+2/0 • Maynor
Figueroa HON 32+1/1 • Steve Gohouri CIV 26+1/1 • Piscu ESP 1/0
Ronnie Stam NED 17+8/1
Midfield Tom Cleverley 19+6/4 • Momo Diame SEN 30+6/1 • Jordi
Gomez ESP 9+4/1 • James McArthur SCO 3+15/0 • James
McCarthy IRL 24/3 • Charles N'Zogbia FRA 32+2/9 • Hendry
Thomas HON 22+2/0 • Ben Watson 23+6/3
Forwards Mauro Boselli ARG 5+3/0 • Franco Di Santo ARG 9+16/1
Callum McManaman 0+3/0 • Victor Moses NGA 8+13/1
Hugo Rodallega COL 34+2/9 • Conor Sammon IRL 1+6/1
Coach Roberto Martinez ESP

WOLVES LEAGUE APPEARANCES/GOALS 2010-11

Goalkeepers Marcus Hahnemann USA 14 • Wayne Hennessey WAL 24
Defenders Christophe Berra SCO 31+1/0 • Jody Craddock 14+1/1
George Elokobi CMR 23+4/2 • Kevin Foley IRL 30+3/2
Michael Mancienne 13+3/0 • Steven Mouyokolo FRA 2+2/0
Richard Stearman 27+4/0 • Jelle Van Damme BEL 4+2/1
Stephen Ward IRL 27+7/1
Midfield Dave Edwards WAL 12+3/1 • Adlene Guedioura ALG 4+6/1
Greg Halford 0+2/0 • Adam Hammill 7+3/0 • Karl Henry 28+1/0
Stephen Hunt IRL 14+6/3 • Matthew Jarvis 34+3/4 • David
Jones 11+1/1 • Michael Kightly 1+3/0 • Nenad Milijas SRB 20+3/2
Geoffrey Mujangi Bia BEL 0+1/0 • Jamie O'Hara 13+1/3
Forwards Marcus Bent 0+3/0 • Kevin Doyle IRL 25+1/5
Sylvain Ebanks-Blake 11+19/7 • Steven Fletcher SCO 15+14/10
Andy Keogh IRL 0+1/0 • Sam Vokes WAL 0+2/0
Coach Mick McCarthy IRL

EQG – EQUATORIAL GUINEA

FIFA/COCA-COLA WORLD RANKING

'93	'94	'95	'96	'97	'98	'99	'00	'01	'02	'03	'04	'05	'06	'07	'08	'09	'10	'11	'12
-	-	-	-	-	195	188	187	190	192	160	171	171	109	85	123	135	165	150	

	2011												High	Low	Av
Jan	Feb	Mar	Apr	May	Jun	Jul	Aug	Sep	Oct	Nov	Dec		High	Low	Av
164	165	148	142	142	149	155	154	152	155	151	150		64	195	156

Equatorial Guinea played host to the 2012 CAF Africa Cup of Nations, sharing the duty with neighbours Gabon and like them upsetting the form book by reaching the quarter-finals. It was their maiden performance at the finals and made them the smallest country to compete at the tournament. Despite their lowly status on the FIFA/Coca-Cola World Ranking, Equatorial Guinea rode a tide of fevered emotion to reach the last eight in a satisfying performance that matched the considerable financial commitment to the tournament. The former Spanish colony achieved arguably the biggest upset in Nations Cup finals history when they beat Senegal in their second group game to ensure they advanced to the knockout stage after just two matches. The 2-1 win, achieved with an extraordinary long-range winner from fullback Kily, came against a backdrop of thunderous support in the newly-built stadium in Bata. Just four days earlier the stadium had played host to the opening ceremony of the tournament, followed by another exciting late win for Equatorial Guinea in the opening game against Libya. 'Nzalang Nacional' were eventually eliminated in the quarter-finals by Cote d'Ivoire, but to get that far had been a wonderful and unexpected achievement that brought this oil-rich and historically secretive nation into the limelight.

CAF AFRICA CUP OF NATIONS RECORD
1957-1988 DNE 1990 DNQ 1992-2000 DNE 2002-2010 DNQ **2012** 7 QF (Hosts)

FEDERACION ECUATOGUINEANA DE FUTBOL (FEGUIFUT)

Avenida de Hassan II,
☏ Apartado postal 1017, Malabo
☎ +240 222274048
✆ +240 333096565
✉ fefmanga@yahoo.es
🖥 www.feguifut.net
FA 1960 CON 1986 FIFA 1986
P Bonifacio Manga
GS Candido Nsue

FIFA BIG COUNT 2006

Total players	25 590
% of population	4.74%
Male	25 240
Female	350
Amateurs 18+	1 400
Unregistered	3 300
Professionals	230
Referees	50
Admin & coaches	65
Number of clubs	18
Number of teams	48

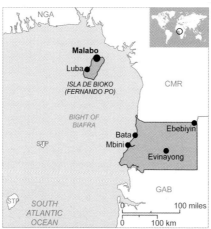

MAJOR CITIES/TOWNS

		Population
1	Bata	219 302
2	Malabo	175 365
3	Ebebiyin	31 827
4	Aconibe	14 182
5	Añisoc	13 657
6	Evinayong	8 924
7	Luba	8 042
8	Mongomo	6 979
9	Mengomeyen	6 700
10	Micomeseng	6 310
11	Niefang	5 495
12	Cogo	5 417
13	Rebola	5 354
14	Nsok	5 335
15	Bidjabidjan	4 837
16	Mbini	4 690
17	Nsork	4 246
18	Ayene	3 922
19	Palea	3 824

REPUBLICA DE GUINEA ECUATORIAL • REPUBLIC OF EQUATORIAL GUINEA

Capital Malabo	Population 633 441 (165)	% in cities 39%
GDP per capita $37 300 (29)	Area km² 28 051 km² (145)	GMT +/- +1
Neighbours (km) Cameroon 189, Gabon 350 • Coast 296		

RECENT INTERNATIONAL MATCHES PLAYED BY EQUATORIAL GUINEA

2006	Opponents		Score	Venue	Comp	Scorers	Att	Referee
3-09	Liberia	W	2-1	Malabo	CNq	Juan Epitie [24], Rodolfo Bodipo [88]		Agbenyega GHA
7-10	Cameroon	L	0-3	Yaounde	CNq			Daami TUN
2007								
5-03	Congo	L	1-2	N'Djamena	CMr1	Desire Pierre [18]		
9-03	Gabon	D	1-1	N'Djamena	CMr1	Ibrahima Toure [44p]		
25-03	Rwanda	W	3-1	Malabo	CNq	Andre Moreira [29], Juvenal Edjogo [75], Juan Epitie [81]		Louzaya CGO
2-06	Rwanda	L	0-2	Kigali	CNq			Auda EGY
17-06	Liberia	D	0-0	Monrovia	CNq			Diouf SEN
9-09	Cameroon	W	1-0	Malabo	CNq	Juvenal Edjogo [39]		Sidibe MLI
21-11	Niger	D	1-1	Malabo	Fr	Rodolfo Bodipo		
2008								
1-06	Sierra Leone	W	2-0	Malabo	WCq	Falcao Carolino [47], Juan Epitie [57]	13 000	Codjia BEN
7-06	South Africa	L	1-4	Atteridgeville	WCq	Juvenal Edjogo [78p]	10 000	Diouf SEN
15-06	Nigeria	L	0-1	Malabo	WCq		15 200	Mendy GAM
21-06	Nigeria	L	0-2	Abuja	WCq		20 000	Ambaya LBY
6-09	Sierra Leone	L	1-2	Freetown	WCq	Rodolfo Bodipo [83p]	22 000	Doue CIV
11-10	South Africa	L	0-1	Malabo	WCq		6 500	Djaoupe TOG
2009								
28-03	Cape Verde Islands	L	0-5	Sal	Fr			
25-04	Mali	L	0-3	Bamoko	Fr			
6-06	Estonia	L	0-3	Tallinn	Fr		2 150	Malzinskas LTU
2010								
11-08	Morocco	L	1-2	Rabat	Fr	Anselmo Eyegue [38]		
12-10	Botswana	L	0-2	Malabo	Fr			
2011								
8-02	Chad	W	2-0	Malabo	Fr	Daniel Ekedo [53p], OG [74]		
29-03	Gambia	W	1-0	Malabo	Fr	Thierry Fidjeu [42]		
3-09	Burkina Faso	L	0-1	Bobo Dioulasso	Fr			
7-09	Central African Rep	W	3-0	Malabo	Fr	Randy [20p], Samuel Itondo 2 [44 83]		
7-10	Gabon	L	0-2	Cannes	Fr			
11-10	Cameroon	D	1-1	Malabo	Fr	Doulla Viera [31]		
11-11	Madagascar	W	2-0	Malabo	WCq	Juvenal [20p], Randy [74p]	10 000	Otogo-Castane GAB
15-11	Madagascar	L	1-2	Antananarivo	WCq	Doulla Viera [24]		
2012								
6-01	South Africa	D	0-0	Bata	Fr			
21-01	Libya	W	1-0	Bata	CNr1	Javier Balboa [87]	35 000	Doue CIV
25-01	Senegal	W	2-1	Bata	CNr1	Randy [61], Kily [93+]	35 000	Abdel Rahman SUD
29-01	Zambia	L	0-1	Malabo	CNr1		44 000	Benouza ALG
4-02	Côte d'Ivoire	L	0-3	Malabo	CNqf		12 500	Maillet SEY

Fr = Friendly match • CN = CAF African Cup of Nations • CM = CEMAC Cup • WC = FIFA World Cup
q = qualifier • r1 = first round group • qf = quarter-final

ERI – ERITREA

FIFA/COCA-COLA WORLD RANKING

'93	'94	'95	'96	'97	'98	'99	'00	'01	'02	'03	'04	'05	'06	'07	'08	'09	'10	'11	'12
-	-	-	-	-	189	169	158	171	157	155	169	169	140	132	162	163	177	190	

						2011								High	Low	Av
Jan	Feb	Mar	Apr	May	Jun	Jul	Aug	Sep	Oct	Nov	Dec			High	Low	Av
178	178	178	181	181	186	188	189	190	190	184	190			121	190	162

Eritrea entered the 2014 FIFA World Cup qualifiers but were eliminated in November 2011 after losing 4-2 on aggregate over two matches to Rwanda. It ended a brief run of international activity which has been sorely lacking for the Red Sea state in recent years. The defection of players seeking political asylum during trips elsewhere on the continent at both national team, youth team and club level, had led to a restriction on entries by Eritrean teams in international competitions. In preparation for the World Cup qualifiers the national team had a friendly match at home to Sudan in August but did not play again before the two-legged qualifying tie against Rwanda. The first leg in Asmara ended in a 1-1 draw but Rwanda assembled a three goal lead in the return match in Kigali four days later before Abraham Tedros got a late consolation goal for Eritrea. The year ended with Eritrea plummeting to their lowest ever place in the FIFA Coca Cola World Rankings, They finished 2011 in 190th place, down from 177 at the end of 2010. No clubs were entered into CAF's annual competitions in 2011 while the national team also did not go to December's East and Central African Senior Challenge Cup tournament in Tanzania and did not enter in the 2013 CAF Africa Cup of Nations preliminaries.

CAF AFRICA CUP OF NATIONS RECORD
1957-1998 DNE **2000-2008** DNQ **2010-2012** DNQ

ERITREAN NATIONAL FOOTBALL FEDERATION (ENFF)

Sematat Avenue 29-31, PO Box 3665, Asmara
☎ +291 1 120335
📠 +291 1 126821
✉ enff@tse.com.er

FA 1996 CON 1998 FIFA 1998
P Tesfaye Gebreyesus Dsue
GS Mekonen Ghidey Tesfaye

FIFA BIG COUNT 2006

Total players	381 218
% of population	7.96%
Male	307 799
Female	73 419
Amateurs 18+	6 524
Youth under 18	21
Unregistered	694
Professionals	0
Referees	239
Admin & coaches	1 314
Number of clubs	24
Number of teams	258

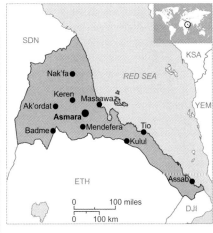

MAJOR CITIES/TOWNS

		Population
1	Asmara	648 530
2	Assab	92 155
3	Keren	74 465
4	Mitsiwa	47 799
5	Addi Ugri	19 096
6	Barentu	17 820
7	Addi K'eyih	15 902
8	Ginda	14 075
9	Edd	13 709
10	Dek'emhare	13 343
11	Ak'ordat	10 784
12	Addi Kwala	8 225
13	Sen'afe	7 311
14	Teseney	4 570

HAGERE ERTRA • STATE OF ERITREA

Capital Asmara	Population 5 647 168 (109)	% in cities 21%
GDP per capita $700 (223)	Area km² 117 600 km² (100)	GMT +/- +3
Neighbours (km) Djibouti 109, Ethiopia 912, Sudan 605 • Coast 2234		

RECENT INTERNATIONAL MATCHES PLAYED BY ERITREA

2005	Opponents	Score		Venue	Comp	Scorers	Att	Referee
28-11	Zanzibar †	L	0-3	Kigali	CCr1			
30-11	Rwanda	L	2-3	Kigali	CCr1	Suleiman Muhamoul 2		
2-12	Burundi	D	0-0	Kigali	CCr1			
4-12	Tanzania	L	0-1	Kigali	CCr1			
2006								
2-09	Kenya	W	2-1	Nairobi	CNq	Origi OG 15, Shimangus Yednekatchew 67		Lwanja MWI
7-10	Swaziland	D	0-0	Asmara	CNq			Gasingwa RWA
2007								
7-01	Yemen	L	1-4	Sana'a	Fr			
25-03	Angola	L	1-6	Luanda	CNq	Misgina Besirat 73		Evehe CMR
21-05	Sudan	W	1-0	Asmara	Fr	Shimangus Yednekatchew 46		
26-05	Sudan	D	1-1	Asmara	Fr			
2-06	Angola	D	1-1	Asmara	CNq	Hamiday Abdelkadir 15		Marange ZIM
16-06	Kenya	W	1-0	Asmara	CNq	Berhane Arega 80		Abdelrahman SUD
9-09	Swaziland	D	0-0	Manzini	CNq			Ssegonga UGA
30-11	Sudan	L	0-1	Omdurman	Fr			
3-12	Sudan	L	0-1	Omdurman	Fr			
9-12	Rwanda	L	1-2	Dar es Salaam	CCr1	Berhane Arega 38		
11-12	Djibouti	W	3-2	Dar es Salaam	CCr1	Berhane Arega 6, Shimangus Yednekatchew 42, Binam Fissehaye 68		
14-12	Uganda	W	3-2	Dar es Salaam	CCr1	Elmon Yeamekibron 2 53 64, Samuel Ghebrehine 82		
17-12	Burundi	L	1-2	Dar es Salaam	CCqf	Berhane Arega 20		
2008								
No international matches played in 2008								
2009								
1-12	Zimbabwe †	D	0-0	Nairobi	CCr1			
3-12	Rwanda	L	1-2	Nairobi	CCr1	Yosief Tzerezghi 83		
5-12	Somalia	W	3-1	Nairobi	CCr1	Isaias Andberhian 25p, Filmon Tseqay 27, OG 60		
8-12	Tanzania	L	0-4	Nairobi	CCqf			
2010								
No international matches played in 2010								
2011								
19-08	Sudan	L	0-3	Asmara	Fr			
11-11	Rwanda	D	1-1	Asmara	WCq	Tesfalem Tekle 35	6 000	Keita MLI
15-11	Rwanda	L	1-3	Kigali	WCq	Abraham Tedros 89	10 000	Bondo BOT

CN = CAF African Cup of Nations • CC = CECAFA Cup • WC = FIFA World Cup • q = qualifier • r1 = first round group • † Not a full international

ESP – SPAIN

FIFA/COCA-COLA WORLD RANKING

'93	'94	'95	'96	'97	'98	'99	'00	'01	'02	'03	'04	'05	'06	'07	'08	'09	'10	'11	'12
5	2	4	8	11	15	4	7	7	3	3	5	5	12	4	1	1	1	1	

	2011												High	Low	Av
Jan	Feb	Mar	Apr	May	Jun	Jul	Aug	Sep	Oct	Nov	Dec			
1	1	1	1	1	1	1	2	1	1	1	1	1	25	5

For the second year running Barcelona and Real Madrid were in a different class to the rest of their opponents in La Liga, finishing over 20 points clear of Valencia in third place. Indeed, it could be claimed that the pair were in a different class to every other team in Europe and that the UEFA Champions League semi-final between the two would have been a more fitting final. In the battle between Pep Guardiola and Jose Mourinho it was the former who came out on top with Barcelona winning both the league and the European Cup. In the league they finished four points clear of Real despite Ronaldo scoring an astonishing 41 goals in just 32 starts for Real who topped the 100 goal mark for the second year running. Barcelona, however, had world footballer of the year Lionel Messi who scored 53 in all competitions, including both in their crucial 2-0 Champions League semi-final victory over Real and then another in the final at Wembley where Barcelona demolished Manchester United to win the title for the third time in six years. Real's consolation was beating Barcelona 1-0 in the Spanish Cup Final although they dropped the trophy from the top of the bus taking them on a celebratory tour of Madrid which then ran over it. Meanwhile, the national team qualified with ease for the Euro 2012 finals although there were unexpected defeats in friendlies.

UEFA EUROPEAN CHAMPIONSHIP RECORD

1960 DNE **1964** 1 Winners (Hosts) 1968 QF 1972 DNQ 1976 QF **1980** 7 r1 **1984** 2 F **1988** 6 r1 1992 DNQ
1996 6 QF **2000** 5 QF **2004** 10 r1 **2008** 1 Winners **2012** Qualified

REAL FEDERACION ESPANOLA DE FUTBOL (RFEF).

Ramon y Cajal
s/n Apartado postale 385, Las Rozas 28230, Madrid
☎ +34 91 4959800
📠 +34 91 4959801
✉ rfef@rfef.es
🖥 www.rfef.es
FA 1913 CON 1954 FIFA 1904
P Angel Maria Villar Llona
GS Jorge Perez

FIFA BIG COUNT 2006

Total players	2 834 190
% of population	7.02%
Male	2 536 103
Female	298 087
Amateurs 18+	136 132
Unregistered	1 915 000
Professionals	1 331
Referees	9 573
Admin & coaches	53 000
Number of clubs	18 092
Number of teams	39 811

MAJOR CITIES/TOWNS

		Population
1	Madrid	3 119 376
2	Barcelona	1 641 281
3	Valencia	890 020
4	Sevilla	706 146
5	Zaragoza	658 434
6	Málaga	570 055
7	Murcia	440 303
8	Palma	384 097
9	Las Palmas	378 356
10	Bilbao	354 726
11	Córdoba	327 809
12	Valladolid	317 149
13	Alacante	305 523
14	Vigo	294 682
15	Gijón	276 280
16	La Coruña	243 838
34	San Sebastian	184 790
124	Irun	62 743
159	Villarreal	45 214

REINO DE ESPANA • KINGDOM OF SPAIN

Capital	Madrid	Population	40 525 002 (32)	% in cities	77%
GDP per capita	$34 600 (36)	Area km²	505 370 km² (51)	GMT + / -	+1
Neighbours (km)	Andorra 63, France 623, Gibraltar 1, Portugal 1214, Morocco 16 • Coast 4964				

RECENT INTERNATIONAL MATCHES PLAYED BY SPAIN

2009	Opponents		Score	Venue	Comp	Scorers	Att	Referee
12-08	Macedonia	W	3-2	Skopje	Fr	Torres [52], Pique [54], Riera [56]	25 000	Vink NEN
5-09	Belgium	W	5-0	La Coruña	WCq	David Silva 2 [41 67], Villa 2 [49 85], Pique [50]	30 441	Layec FRA
9-09	Estonia	W	3-0	Merida	WCq	Fabregas [33], Cazorla [82], Mata [92+]	14 362	Oriekhov UKR
10-10	Armenia	W	2-1	Yerevan	WCq	Fabregas [33], Mata [64]	10 500	Jech CZE
14-10	Bosnia-Herzegovina	W	5-2	Zenica	WCq	Pique [13p], David Silva [14], Negredo 2 [50 55], Mata [81]	13 500	Plautz AUT
14-11	Argentina	W	2-1	Madrid	Fr	Xabi Alonso 2 [16 86p]	54 000	Kelly IRL
18-11	Austria	W	5-1	Vienna	Fr	Fabregas [10], Villa 2 [20 45], Guiza [56], Hernandez [57]	32 000	Meyer GER
2010								
3-03	France	W	2-0	Paris	Fr	Villa [21], Sergio Ramos [45]	79 021	Thomson SCO
29-05	Saudi Arabia	W	3-2	Innsbruck	Fr	Villa [31], Xabi Alonso [59], Llorente [90]	7 200	Einwaller AUT
3-06	Korea Republic	W	1-0	Innsbruck	Fr	Navas [85]	17 400	Schorgenhofer AUT
8-06	Poland	W	6-0	Murcia	Fr	Villa [12], Silva [14], Xabi Alonso [52], Fabregas [58], Torres [76], Pedro [81]	30 000	Koukoulakis GRE
16-06	Switzerland	L	0-1	Durban	WCr1		62 453	Webb ENG
21-06	Honduras	W	2-0	Johannesburg	WCr1	Villa 2 [17 51]	54 386	Nishimura JPN
25-06	Chile	W	2-1	Pretoria	WCr1	Villa [24], Iniesta [37]	41 958	Rodriguez MEX
29-06	Portugal	W	1-0	Cape Town	WCr2	Villa [63]	62 955	Baldassi ARG
3-07	Paraguay	W	1-0	Johannesburg	WCqf	Villa [83]	55 359	Batres GUA
7-07	Germany	W	1-0	Durban	WCsf	Puyol [73]	60 960	Kassai HUN
11-07	Netherlands	W	1-0	Johannesburg	WCf	Iniesta [116]	84 490	Webb ENG
11-08	Mexico	D	1-1	Mexico City	Fr	Silva [90]	105000	Moreno PAN
3-09	Liechtenstein	W	4-0	Vaduz	ECq	Torres 2 [18 54], Villa [26], Silva [62]	6 100	Yoldirim TUR
7-09	Argentina	L	1-4	Buenos Aires	Fr	Llorente [84]	65 600	Ruiz COL
8-10	Lithuania	W	3-1	Salamanca	ECq	Llorente 2 [47 56], Silva [79]	16 800	Rocchi ITA
12-10	Scotland	W	3-2	Glasgow	ECq	Villa [44p], Iniesta [55], Llorente [79]	51 322	Busacca SUI
17-11	Portugal	L	0-4	Lisbon	Fr		38 000	Gautier FRA
2011								
9-02	Colombia	W	1-0	Madrid	Fr	Silva [86]	70 000	Trutz SVK
25-03	Czech Republic	W	2-1	Granada	ECq	Villa 2 [69 72p]	16 301	Kassai HUN
29-03	Lithuania	W	3-1	Kaunas	ECq	Xavi [19], OG [70], Mata [83]	9 180	Duhamel FRA
4-06	USA	W	4-0	Boston	Fr	Cazorla 2 [28 41], Negredo [32], Torres [73]	64 121	Silvera URU
7-06	Venezuela	W	3-0	Puerto La Cruz	Fr	Villa [5], Pedro [20], Xabi Alonso [45]	36 000	Buckley PER
10-08	Italy	L	1-2	Bari	Fr	Xabi Alonso [37p]	50 000	Brych GER
2-09	Chile	W	3-2	St Gall	Fr	Iniesta [55], Fabregas 2 [71 90]	14 605	Laperriere SUI
6-09	Liechtenstein	W	6-0	Logrono	ECq	Negredo 2 [33 37], Xavi [44], Ramos [52], Villa 2 [59 79]	15 660	Lechner AUT
7-10	Czech Republic	W	2-0	Prague	ECq	Mata [7], Xabi Alonso [23]	18 800	Tagliavento ITA
11-10	Scotland	W	3-1	Alicante	ECq	Silva 2 [6 44], Villa [54]	27 559	Johannesson SWE
12-11	England	L	0-1	London	Fr		87 189	De Bleeckere BEL
15-11	Costa Rica	D	2-2	San Jose	Fr	Silva 2 [82 90]	30 000	Navarro CAN

Fr = Friendly match • EC = UEFA EURO 2012 • WC = FIFA World Cup
q = qualifier • r1 = first round group • r2 = second round • qf = quarter-final • sf = semi-final • f = final

SPAIN NATIONAL TEAM HISTORICAL RECORDS

Caps

127 - Iker Casillas 2000- • **126** - Andoni Zubizarreta 1985-98 • **107** - Xavi 2000- • **102** - Raul 1996-2006 • **98** - Carles Puyol 2000- • **92** - Xabi Alonso 2003- • **91** - Fernando Torres 2003- • **89** - Fernando Hierro 1989-2002 • **82** - Sergio Ramos 2005- & David Villa 2005- • **81** - Jose Antonio Camacho 1975-88 • **75** - Rafael Gordillo 1978-88 • **69** - Emilio Butragueno 1984-92 & Carlos Marchena 2002- • **68** - Luis Arconada 1977-85 • **66** - Michel 1985-92 • **63** - Andres Iniesta 2006- • **62** - Luis Enrique 1991-2002; Miguel Angel Nadal 1991-2002 & Cesc Fabregas 2006- • **60** - Victor Munoz 1981-88 & Joan Capdevila 2002-

Goals

51 - David Villa 2005- • **44** - Raul 1996-2006 • **29** - Fernando Hierro 1989-2002 • **27** - Fernando Morientes 1998-2007 & Fernando Torres 2003- • **26** - Emilio Butragueno 1984-92 • **23** - Alfredo di Stefano 1957-61 & Julio Salinas 1986-96 • **21** - Michel 1985-92 • **20** - Telmo Zarra 1945-71 • **17** - Isidro Langara 1932-36 • **16** - Pirri 1966-78 & Luis Regueiro 1927-36 • **15** - Santillana 1975-85

Past Coaches

Francisco Bru 1920 • Julian Ruete 1921-22 • Pedro Parages 1923-24 • Fernando Gutierrez Alzaga 1925 • Ricardo Cabot Montalt 1925 • Ezequiel Montero Roman 1926-27 • Fred Pentland 1929 • Jose Maria Mateos 1929-33 • Amadeo Garcia Salazar 1934-36 • Eduardo Teus Lopez 1941-42 • Jacinto Quincoces 1945 • Paulino Alcantara 1951 • Ricardo Zamora 1952 • Pedro Escartin Moran 1952-61 • Helenio Herrera 1959-62 • Jose Villalonga 1962-66 • Domingo Balmanya 1966-68 • Luis Molowny 1969 • Miguel Munoz 1969 • Ladislao Kubala 1969-80 • Jose Santamaria 1980-82 • Luis Suarez 1988-91 • Vicente Miera 1991-92 • Javier Clemente 1992-98 • Jose Antonio Camacho 1998-2002 • Inaki Saez 2002-04 • Luis Aragones 2004-08 • Vicente del Bosque 2008-

SPAIN 2010–11

LIGA BBVA — PRIMERA DIVISION

	Pl	W	D	L	F	A	Pts
Barcelona †	38	30	6	2	95	21	96
Real Madrid †	38	29	5	4	102	33	92
Valencia †	38	21	8	9	64	44	71
Villarreal †	38	18	8	12	54	44	62
Sevilla ‡	38	17	7	14	62	61	58
Athletic Bilbao ‡	38	18	4	16	59	55	58
Atlético Madrid ‡	38	17	7	14	62	53	58
RCD Espanyol	38	15	4	19	46	55	49
Osasuna	38	13	8	17	45	46	47
Sporting Gijón	38	11	14	13	35	42	47
Málaga	38	13	7	18	54	68	46
Racing Santander	38	12	10	16	41	56	46
Real Zaragoza	38	12	9	17	40	53	45
Levante	38	12	9	17	41	52	45
Real Sociedad	38	14	3	21	49	66	45
Getafe	38	12	8	18	49	60	44
RCD Mallorca	38	12	8	18	41	56	44
Deportivo La Coruña	38	10	13	15	31	47	43
Hércules	38	9	8	21	36	60	35
Almería	38	6	12	20	36	70	30

Results matrix (home team in left column; opponents left→right: Barcelona, Real Madrid, Valencia, Villarreal, Sevilla, Ath. Bilbao, At. Madrid, Espanyol, Osasuna, Sp. Gijón, Málaga, Racing, Zaragoza, Levante, Sociedad, Getafe, Mallorca, Deportivo, Hércules, Almería):

	Bar	RM	Val	Vil	Sev	Bil	AtM	Esp	Osa	SpG	Mál	Rac	Zar	Lev	Soc	Get	Mal	Dep	Hér	Alm
Barcelona		5-0	2-1	3-1	5-0	2-1	3-0	2-0	2-0	1-0	4-1	3-0	1-0	2-1	5-0	2-1	1-1	0-0	0-2	3-1
Real Madrid	1-1		2-0	4-2	1-0	5-1	2-0	3-0	1-0	0-1	7-0	6-1	2-3	2-0	4-1	4-0	1-0	6-1	2-0	8-1
Valencia	0-1	3-6		5-0	0-1	2-1	1-1	2-1	3-3	0-0	4-3	1-0	1-1	0-0	3-0	2-0	1-2	2-0	2-0	2-1
Villarreal	0-1	1-3	1-1		1-0	4-1	2-0	4-0	4-2	1-1	1-1	2-0	1-0	0-1	2-1	2-1	3-1	1-0	1-0	2-0
Sevilla	1-1	2-6	2-0	3-2		4-3	3-1	1-2	1-0	3-0	0-0	1-1	3-1	4-1	3-1	1-3	1-2	0-0	1-0	1-3
Athletic Bilbao	3-1	0-3	1-2	0-1	2-0		1-2	2-1	1-0	3-0	1-1	2-1	2-1	3-2	2-1	3-0	3-0	1-2	3-0	1-0
Atlético Madrid	1-2	1-2	1-2	3-1	2-2	0-2		2-3	3-0	4-0	0-3	0-0	1-0	4-1	3-0	2-0	3-0	2-0	2-1	1-1
RCD Espanyol	1-5	0-1	2-2	0-1	2-3	2-1	2-2		1-0	1-0	1-0	2-4	0-2	4-1	4-1	3-1	1-2	2-0	0-0	0-0
Osasuna	0-3	1-0	1-0	1-0	3-2	1-2	2-3	4-0		1-0	3-0	3-1	0-0	1-1	3-1	0-0	1-1	0-0	3-0	0-0
Sporting Gijón	1-1	0-1	0-2	1-1	2-0	2-2	1-0	1-0	1-0		1-2	2-1	0-0	1-1	1-3	2-0	2-0	2-2	2-0	1-0
Málaga	1-3	1-4	1-3	2-3	1-2	1-1	0-3	2-0	0-1	2-0		4-1	1-2	1-0	1-2	2-2	3-0	0-0	3-1	3-1
Racing Santander	0-3	1-3	1-1	2-2	3-2	1-2	2-1	0-0	4-1	1-1	1-2		2-0	1-1	2-1	0-1	1-0	3-0	1-0	1-0
Real Zaragoza	0-2	1-3	4-0	0-3	1-2	2-1	0-1	1-0	1-3	2-2	3-5	1-1		1-0	2-1	2-1	3-2	1-0	0-1	1-0
Levante	1-1	0-0	0-1	1-2	1-4	1-2	2-0	1-0	2-1	0-0	3-1	3-1	1-2		2-1	2-0	1-1	1-2	2-1	1-0
Real Sociedad	2-1	1-2	1-2	1-0	2-3	2-0	2-4	1-0	1-0	2-1	0-2	1-0	2-1	1-1		1-1	1-0	3-0	1-3	2-0
Getafe	1-3	2-3	2-4	1-0	1-0	2-2	1-1	1-3	2-0	3-0	0-0	1-1	1-4	1-0	4-0		3-0	4-1	3-0	2-0
RCD Mallorca	0-3	0-1	2-0	0-2	2-1	0-3	4-0	1-2	0-0	4-2	0-0	1-1	0-2	1-2	0-2	0-0		0-0	3-0	4-1
Deportivo La Coruña	0-4	0-0	0-2	1-0	3-2	1-0	1-3	0-0	0-1	1-3	0-2	0-0	0-0	1-2	1-2	2-2	1-0		1-0	0-2
Hércules	0-3	1-3	1-2	2-2	0-0	1-4	1-0	0-0	4-0	4-0	4-1	2-3	2-1	3-1	2-1	0-0	2-2	1-0		1-2
Almería	0-8	1-1	0-3	0-0	0-1	1-3	2-2	3-2	3-2	1-1	1-1	1-1	1-0	1-2	2-2	3-3	1-1	1-1	1-1	

28/08/2010 - 21/05/2011 • † Qualified for the UEFA Champions League • ‡ Qualified for the Europa Cup

Top scorers: **40** - Cristiano Ronaldo POR, Real Madrid • **31** - Lionel Messi ARG, Barcelona • **20** - Sergio Aguero ARG, At. Madrid • Alvaro Negredo, Sevilla • **18** - Fernando Llorente, Athletic Bilbao • Giuseppe Rossi ITA, Villarreal • Roberto Soldado, Valencia • David Villa, Barcelona • **15** - Karim Benzema FRA, Real Madrid • **14** - Salomon Rondon VEN, Málaga

SPAIN 2010–11

SEGUNDA DIVISION A (2)

	Pl	W	D	L	F	A	Pts
Real Betis	42	25	8	9	85	44	83
Rayo Vallecano	42	23	10	9	73	48	79
Barcelona B	42	20	11	11	85	62	71
Elche ‡	42	18	15	9	55	42	69
Granada ‡	42	18	14	10	71	47	68
Celta Vigo ‡	42	17	16	9	62	43	67
Real Valladolid ‡	42	19	9	14	65	51	66
Xerez	42	17	9	16	60	64	60
Alcorcón	42	17	7	18	57	52	58
Numancia	42	17	6	19	65	63	57
Girona	42	15	12	15	58	56	57
Recreativo Huelva	42	12	20	10	44	37	56
Cartagena	42	16	8	18	48	63	56
Huesca	42	13	16	13	39	45	55
Las Palmas	42	13	15	14	56	71	54
Córdoba	42	13	13	16	58	63	52
Villarreal B	42	15	6	21	43	63	51
Gimnàstic Tarragona	42	12	13	17	37	45	49
Salamanca	42	13	7	22	46	68	46
Tenerife	42	9	11	22	42	66	38
Ponferradina	42	5	19	18	36	63	34
Albacete	42	7	11	24	35	64	32

Results (vs opponents left→right: Real Betis, Rayo Vallecano, Barcelona B, Elche, Granada, Celta Vigo, Valladolid, Xerez, Alcorcón, Numancia, Girona, Recreativo, Cartagena, Huesca, Las Palmas, Córdoba, Villarreal B, Gimnàstic, Salamanca, Tenerife, Ponferradina, Albacete):

Team	Results →
Real Betis	4-0 2-1 4-4 1-1 2-1 3-1 3-0 4-1 2-1 0-1 5-0 3-1 4-1 3-1 2-1 1-0 1-0 3-1 3-0 2-0
Rayo Vallecano	1-0 2-3 1-2 1-2 1-3 3-0 3-0 1-0 3-2 2-0 0-0 3-1 3-1 4-0 2-0 4-2 3-0 4-2 3-0 1-1 3-3
Barcelona B	0-3 1-2 2-0 4-0 1-1 0-0 2-1 2-0 1-0 1-2 1-1 0-1 2-1 3-0 0-1 3-5 4-1 4-1 4-0 5-1 3-1 1-2 1-...
Elche	0-2 1-2 1-1 0-0 1-3 2-2 4-1 1-0 1-0 0-0 1-0 1-2 3-0 2-2 2-1 0-1 0-3 1-1 0-2 0-1-0
Granada	3-0 1-1 4-1 3-3 1-1 0-1 5-0 3-0 0-2 1-2 1-2 0-5 2-1 1-3 0-6 1-0 1-2 1-2 0-3-0
Celta Vigo	1-1 0-0 1-2 2-2 1-1 1-2 1-1 3-0 4-0 0-4 0-3 3-0 1-2 2-0 3-2 0-3 0-1 0-1 0-1 3-1
Real Valladolid	1-0 2-2 1-2 0-2 3-3 2-1 2-0 4-5 1-0 4-0 0-1 2-0 3-0 5-1 3-1 0-1 0-2 2-2 1-1-1
Xerez	2-3 0-1 1-0 0-1 2-1 4-0 0-0 1-0 3-1 1-1 1-4 1-3 2-1 1-3 3-1 2-2 0-2 0-0 0-4-2
Alcorcón	3-3 2-0 1-3 0-1 2-0 1-0 3-1 3-1 3-1 2-0 0-0 0-1 5-0 2-1 1-2 1-1 4-0 3-2 2-0 2-0
Numancia	1-2 0-3 4-6 2-0 3-2 1-3 3-3 0-2 4-0 1-2 2-0 3-1 4-0 1-0 1-2 1-1 0-3 2-2 1-3 0-0-1
Girona	0-1 1-3 0-2 2-2 2-0 1-1 2-0 4-2 3-1 2-0 0-0 1-1 3-1 1-1 2-1 2-3 2-1 1-1 4-2 3-0 3-0
Recreativo Huelva	1-3 1-1 1-1 0-0 0-0 1-0 1-1 0-1 0-4 3-0 0-1 1-2 1-2 1-0 0-0 2-3 0-1 0-0
Cartagena	2-1 2-4 5-1 0-1 2-1 0-4 1-1 2-1 0-1 0-1 3-0 2-0 5-2 1-2 2-0 2-2 1-0 1-0 1-1 1-1
Huesca	1-1 4-1 1-2 2-0 1-2 1-0 1-3 1-0 0-0 1-1 0-0 0-2 0-3 0-1 1-0 1-0 1-0 0-1 1-1-0
Las Palmas	2-2 1-2 2-1 1-1 2-0 0-3 4-1 0-0 1-1 2-0 1-1 0-1 2-2 3-2 2-1 1-0 1-0 2-1 0-2-1
Córdoba	1-1 2-3 2-0 0-0 0-0 1-0 0-2 2-1 3-3 2-0 2-0 0-0 1-0 2-2 0-3 3-5 1-... 3-5-1
Villarreal B	1-0 1-2 2-3 1-1 2-1 2-2 2-0 1-2 4-1 0-0 1-2 0-2 0-1 0-3 0-3 0-2 0-1 0-2 1-0 1-0
Gimnàstic Tarragona	3-0 1-0 1-1 0-0 3-1 2-1 0-0 2-2 0-1 0-2 0-0 0-2 0-0 0-0 0-1 1-1 2-0 1-0 0-1
Salamanca	0-3 0-1 2-3 5-4 1-2 1-1 0-5 2-3 1-2 2-1 0-0 1-2 0-1 4-2 1-1 0-1 1-2 2-1 1-0
Tenerife	0-3 2-1 1-4 1-0 2-2 0-2 3-2 2-2 1-1 0-1 3-1 3-1 0-1 1-0 1-1 2-0 2-1 1-1 1-1-0
Ponferradina	1-1 0-1 2-0 1-0 0-0 0-1 1-1 2-1 2-0 4-1 1-1 2-0 4-1 0-0 0-2 3-0 1-5 1-3 2-1 2-1
Albacete	2-1 1-1 2-2 0-2 2-1 0-1 1-1 1-1 1-2 1-1 1-2 0-3 1-0 1-1 0-0 2-0 1-0-1

27/08/2010 - 4/06/2011 • ‡ Qualified for the play-offs • Barcelona B ineligible for promotion

Top scorer: **32** - Jonathan Soriano, Barcelona B • **27** - Javi Guerra, Valladolid • **25** - Ruben Castro, Betis • **24** - Alexandre Geijo SUI, Granada
Play-off semi-finals: Celta 1-0 0-1 4-5p **Granada** • Valladolid 1-0 1-3 **Elche** • Play-off final: **Granada** 0-0 1-1 Elche. Granada promoted on away goals. 1st leg. Nuevo Los Carmenes, Granada, 15-06-2011, Att: 16 200, Ref: Zamorano • 2nd leg. Martinez Valero, Elche, 18-06-2011, Att: 36 000, Ref: Torres. Scorers - Xumetra [82] for Elche; Ighalo [28] for Granada

SPAIN 2010–11
SEGUNDA DIVISION B (3)
GROUP 1

	Pl	W	D	L	F	A	Pts
Lugo †	38	22	9	7	64	39	75
Guadalajara ‡	38	21	10	7	62	25	73
Real Madrid Castilla ‡	38	21	8	9	73	38	71
Leganés ‡	38	20	9	9	54	35	69
Universidad LPGC	38	18	8	12	41	43	62
Rayo Vallecano B	38	16	10	12	41	34	58
Getafe B	38	15	9	14	45	45	54
Alcalá	38	13	13	12	38	39	52
Celta B	38	15	7	16	43	52	52
Vecindario	38	13	12	13	37	53	51
Atlético B	38	13	11	14	43	43	50
Montañeros	38	13	10	15	50	53	49
Cacereño	38	11	15	12	34	33	48
Coruxo	38	11	14	13	40	41	47
Badajoz	38	12	11	15	41	44	47
Conquense ‡	38	11	14	13	47	43	47
Deportivo B	38	12	9	17	47	57	45
Pontevedra	38	10	9	19	38	49	39
Extremadura	38	8	8	22	29	50	32
Cerro Reyes	38	5	4	29	20	71	19

28/08/2010 - 15/05/2011 • † Championship playoff
‡ Play-offs • Universidad LPGC relegated

SPAIN 2010–11
SEGUNDA DIVISION B (3)
GROUP 2

	Pl	W	D	L	F	A	Pts
Eibar †	38	21	10	7	58	32	73
Mirandés ‡	38	20	12	6	52	24	72
Deportivo Alavés ‡	38	18	12	8	63	43	66
Real Unión Irún ‡	38	19	8	11	51	35	65
Palencia	38	17	12	9	44	28	63
Logroñés	38	18	9	11	44	32	63
Osasuna B	38	16	10	12	49	39	58
Oviedo	38	15	13	10	45	34	58
Lemona	38	13	14	11	42	38	53
Gimnástica Torrelavega	38	13	13	12	34	41	52
Real Sociedad B	38	12	15	11	34	37	51
Bilbao Athletic	38	9	19	10	29	37	46
Zamora	38	11	10	17	46	56	43
Cultural Leonesa	38	9	16	13	42	48	43
Guijuelo	38	7	18	13	39	44	39
Caudal Deportivo ‡	38	9	11	18	29	38	38
La Muela	38	8	14	16	36	56	38
Peña Sport	38	9	9	20	30	56	36
Sporting de Gijón B	38	7	13	18	26	54	34
Barakaldo	38	4	12	22	27	48	24

28/08/2010 - 15/05/2011 • † Championship playoff
‡ Play-offs

SEGUNDA DIVISION B (3) CHAMPIONSHIP PLAY-OFFS

Semi-finals: **Sabadell** 0-0 1-1 Eibar • **Real Murcia** 2-0 0-1 Lugo
Final: Sabadell 1-0 0-1 8-9p **Real Murcia** • Sabadell and Murcia promoted • Eibar and Lugo join regular play-offs in the second round

SPAIN 2010–11
SEGUNDA DIVISION B (3)
GROUP 3

	Pl	W	D	L	F	A	Pts
Sabadell †	38	19	12	7	42	24	69
Badalona ‡	38	17	14	7	40	26	65
Alcoyano ‡	38	17	12	9	46	32	63
Orihuela ‡	38	17	12	9	41	30	63
Lleida	38	17	9	12	46	30	60
L'Hospitalet	38	16	12	10	58	34	60
Sant Andreu	38	13	16	9	37	29	55
Dénia	38	14	13	11	34	38	55
Alicante	38	12	17	9	40	32	53
Castellón	38	15	8	15	39	42	53
Ontinyent	38	14	9	15	35	32	51
Teruel	38	12	14	12	37	32	50
Atlético Baleares	38	11	16	11	43	38	49
Gandía	38	12	13	13	36	45	49
Sporting Mahonés	38	12	9	17	35	54	45
Benidorm ‡	38	10	12	16	32	45	42
Alzira	38	8	16	14	34	40	40
Atlètica Gramenet	38	10	6	22	37	67	36
Mallorca B	38	7	13	18	36	48	34
Santiboià	38	7	7	24	35	65	28

29/08/2010 - 15/05/2011 • † Championship playoff
‡ Play-offs • Alicante and Castellón relegated

SPAIN 2010–11
SEGUNDA DIVISION B (3)
GROUP 4

	Pl	W	D	L	F	A	Pts
Real Murcia †	38	24	10	4	68	21	82
Sevilla Atlético ‡	38	21	11	6	82	40	74
Melilla ‡	38	21	9	8	53	28	72
Cádiz ‡	38	21	6	11	61	37	69
San Roque	38	18	9	11	42	35	63
Ceuta	38	16	12	10	52	42	60
Roquetas	38	16	11	11	48	36	59
Real Jaén	38	14	14	10	39	29	56
Ecija	38	15	9	14	41	45	54
Lucena	38	14	10	14	42	40	52
Caravaca	38	13	10	15	41	40	49
Puertollano	38	12	12	14	40	50	48
Almería B	38	12	10	16	38	46	46
Polideportivo Ejido	38	11	11	16	41	51	44
Lorca Atlético	38	12	7	19	37	55	43
Real Betis B ‡	38	10	12	16	36	45	42
Alcalá	38	11	7	20	30	52	40
Unión Estepona	38	8	16	14	37	45	40
Yeclano Deportivo	38	5	12	21	28	63	27
Jumilla	38	5	4	29	16	72	19

28/08/2010 - 15/05/2011 • † Championship playoff
‡ Play-offs

SEGUNDA DIVISION B (3) PLAY-OFFS

FIRST ROUND: Melilla 1-1 0-1 **Deportivo Alavés** • Castilla 0-2 2-2 **Alcoyano** • Leganés 2-1 0-1 **Badalona** • Cadiz 2-0 1-4 **Mirandés** • Real Unión Irun 2-1 0-3 **Sevilla Atlético** • Orihuela 0-2 1-1 **Guadalajara** • **SECOND ROUND:** Deportivo Alavés 0-0 1-2 **Lugo** • **Alcoyano** 0-0 1-1 Eibar • **Mirandés** 1-0 0-0 Badalona • **Guadalajara** 4-1 1-3 Sevilla Atlético • **THIRD ROUND:** Alcoyano 1-0 1-0 Lugo • **Guadalajara** 0-1 2-1 Mirandés • Alcoyano & Guadalajara promoted • Relegation play-offs: **Conquense** 2-0 1-2 Caudal • Benidorm 1-1 1-3 **Betis B** • Caudal & Benidorm relegated

MEDALS TABLE

		Overall			League			Cup		Europe			City
		G	S	B	G	S	B	G	S	G	S	B	
1	Real Madrid	60	44	18	31	20	7	18	19	11	5	11	Madrid
2	Barcelona	57	37	22	21	22	12	25	9	11	6	10	Barcelona
3	Athletic Bilbao	31	20	10	8	7	10	23	12		1		Bilbao
4	Atlético Madrid	20	20	19	9	8	12	9	9	2	3	7	Madrid
5	Valencia	17	18	9	6	6	9	7	9	4	3		Valencia
6	Real Zaragoza	8	7	6		1	4	6	5	2	1	2	Zaragoza
7	Sevilla	8	6	4	1	4	4	5	2	2			Sevilla
8	RCD Espanyol	4	7	4			4	4	5		2		Barcelona
9	Real Sociedad	4	7	3	2	3	2	2	4			1	San Sebastián
10	Deportivo La Coruña	3	5	6	1	5	4	2				2	La Coruña
11	Real Betis Balompié	3	2	2	1		2	2	2				Sevilla
12	Real Union Irún	3	1					3	1				Irún
13	RCD Mallorca	1	3	2			2	1	2		1		Palma
14	Arenas Guecho Bilbao	1	3	1			1	1	3				Bilbao
15	Racing Irún	1						1					Irún
16	Sporting Gijón		3	1		1	1		2				Gijón
17	Celta Vigo		3						3				Vigo
18	Las Palmas		2	1		1	1						Las Palmas
19	Español Madrid		2						2				Madrid
	Getafe		2						2				Madrid
	Real Valladolid		2						2				Valladolid
22	Villarreal		1	4		1	1					3	Villarreal
23	Racing Santander		1	1		1	1						Santander
24	Deportivo Alavés		1								1		Vitoria
	Basconia		1						1				Basauri
	Castellon		1						1				Castellon
	Castilla		1						1				Madrid
	Elche		1						1				Elche
	España Barcelona		1						1				Barcelona
	Europa		1						1				Barcelona
	Gimnastica Madrid		1						1				Madrid
	Granada		1						1				Granada
	Osasuna		1						1				Pamplona
	Racing Ferrol		1						1				Ferrol
	Recreativo Huelva		1						1				Huelva
	Sabadell		1						1				Sabadell
	Real Vigo Sporting		1						1				Vigo
38	Real Oviedo			3			3						Oviedo
39	Tenerife			1								1	Tenerife

COPA DEL REY 2010–11

Third Elimination Round

Sant Andreu *	0
Real Murcia	1
Xerez	2
Elche *	1
Huesca	0
Real Valladolid *	1
Universidad LPGC	1
Lucena *	0
Cádiz	0
Polideportivo Ejido *	1
Logroñés	2
Badajoz *	0
Real Unión Irún *	1
Orihuela	0
Córdoba *	2
Rayo Vallecano	1
Real Betis	2 5p
Granada *	2 4p
Ponferradina	1 1p
Alcorcón *	1 3p
Ceuta	2 7p
Melilla *	2 6p

Round of 32

Real Madrid	0	5
Real Murcia *	0	1
Xerez *	2	2
Levante	3	1
RCD Espanyol	2	1
Real Valladolid *	0	1
Universidad LPGC *	0	1
Atlético Madrid	5	1
Villarreal	1	2
Polideportivo Ejido *	1	0
Logroñés *	0	1
Valencia	3	4
Málaga	0	3
Hércules *	0	2
Real Unión Irún *	0	1
Sevilla	4	6
Almería	3	2
Real Sociedad *	2	1
Sporting Gijón	1	2
RCD Mallorca *	3	2
Córdoba *	2	1
Racing Santander	0	3
Osasuna *	1	1
Deportivo La Coruña	1	2
Real Betis *	0	2
Real Zaragoza	1	1
Portugalete *	1	0
Getafe	1	0
Athletic Bilbao	1	2
Alcorcón *	0	0
Ceuta *	0	1
Barcelona	2	5

Round of 16

Real Madrid *	8	0
Levante	0	2
RCD Espanyol	0	1
Atlético Madrid *	1	1
Villarreal	0	4
Valencia *	0	2
Málaga	3	0
Sevilla *	5	3
Almería *	4	4
RCD Mallorca	3	3
Córdoba *	1	1
Deportivo La Coruña	1	3
Real Betis *	1	3
Getafe	2	1
Athletic Bilbao	0	1
Barcelona *	0	1

* Home team/home team in the first leg

COPA DEL REY 2010-11

Quarter–finals   **Semi–finals**   **Final**

Real Madrid *   3   1
Atlético Madrid   1   0

Real Madrid   1   2
Sevilla *   0   0

Villarreal *   3   0
Sevilla   3   3

Real Madrid   1
Barcelona   0

Almería *   1   3
Deportivo La Coruña   0   2

Almería   0   0
Barcelona *   5   3

COPA DEL REY FINAL 2011

Mestalla, Valencia, 20-04-2011, 20:30, Att: 55 000, Ref: Undiano

Real Betis   0   3
Barcelona *   5   1

Real Madrid   1   Cristiano Ronaldo [103]
Barcelona   0

Real - Iker Casillas (c) - Alvaro Arbeloa, Sergio Ramos, Ricardo Carvalho (Ezequiel Garay 120), Marcelo - Pepe• - Xabi Alonso•, Sami Khedira (Esteban Granero 104) - Mesut Ozil (Emmanuel Adebayor• 70), Cristiano Ronaldo, Angel di Maria••♦120. Tr: Jose Mourinho
Barca - Jose Manuel Pinto - Daniel Alves, Javier Mascherano, Gerard Pique, Adriano• - Sergio Busquets (Ibrahim Afellay 108) - Xavi, Andres Iniesta - Pedro•, Lionel Messi•, David Villa (Seydou Keita 106). Tr: Josep Guardiola

CLUB BY CLUB GUIDE TO THE 2010-11 SEASON IN SPAIN

ALMERIA 2010–11

Month	Day	Opponent	Res	Score	Comp	Scorers	Att
Aug	29	Osasuna	D	0-0	PD		14 147
	13	Sociedad	D	2-2	PD	Piatti 20, Ulloa 90	11 000
Sep	18	Espanyol	L	0-1	PD		24 345
	22	Levante	L	0-1	PD		9 900
	26	Deportivo	W	2-0	PD	Uche 2 4 19	14 000
	3	Malaga	D	1-1	PD	Uche 76	11 400
	17	Racing	L	0-1	PD		14 005
Oct	24	Hercules	D	1-1	PD	Ulloa 84	10 167
	28	Sociedad	W	3-2	CRr4	Goitom 66, Ulloa 2 71 88	15 377
	31	At. Madrid	D	1-1	PD	Piatti 45	35 000
	7	Sp. Gijon	D	1-1	PD	Corona 16	9 693
	10	Sociedad	W	2-1	CRr4	Goitom 21, Ulloa 48	
Nov	13	Ath. Bilbao	L	0-1	PD		34 000
	20	Barcelona	L	0-8	PD		13 000
	28	Valencia	L	1-2	PD	Ulloa 90	35 000
	5	Zaragoza	D	1-1	PD	Piatti 78	16 000
Dec	11	Sevilla	W	3-1	PD	Vargas 48, Piatti 2 81 90	35 000
	19	Getafe	L	2-3	PD	Uche 7, Ulloa 24	9 000
	22	Mallorca	W	4-3	CRr5	Ulloa 3 6 28 72, Uche 65	1 500
	3	Villarreal	L	0-2	PD		18 000
	6	Mallorca	W	4-3	CRr5	Piatti 2 1 42, Juanma Ortiz 2 3 34	9 569
	9	Mallorca	L	1-4	PD	Crusat 66	15 800
	13	Deportivo	W	1-0	CRqf	Juanma Ortiz 35	3 447
Jan	16	Real Madrid	D	1-1	PD	Ulloa 60	13 893
	19	Deportivo	W	3-2	CRqf	Corona 19, Crusat 20, Goitom 55p	8 000
	23	Osasuna	W	3-2	PD	Garcia 8, Ulloa 2 11 55	8 000
	26	Barcelona	L	0-5	CRsf		49 875
	29	Sociedad	L	0-2	PD		23 500
	2	Barcelona	L	0-3	CRsf		16 000
Feb	13	Espanyol	W	3-2	PD	Silva 5, Uche 7, Bernardello 18	9 300
	13	Levante	L	0-1	PD		12 000
	20	Deportivo	D	1-1	PD	Piatti 48	12 000
	28	Malaga	L	1-3	PD	Feghouli 8	26 000
	3	Racing	D	1-1	PD	Crusat 64	15 000
Mar	6	Hercules	W	2-1	PD	Feghouli 70, M'Bami 73	18 000
	12	At. Madrid	D	2-2	PD	Crusat 49, Goitom 77	13 228
	20	Sp. Gijon	L	0-1	PD		25 700
	4	Ath. Bilbao	L	1-3	PD	Piatti 6	10 564
Apr	9	Barcelona	L	1-3	PD	Corona 50	80 452
	16	Valencia	L	0-3	PD		10 562
	25	Zaragoza	L	0-1	PD		27 000
	1	Sevilla	L	0-1	PD		8 427
	7	Getafe	L	0-2	PD		17 000
May	11	Villarreal	D	0-0	PD		5 500
	15	Mallorca	W	3-1	PD	Uche 5, Juanma Ortiz 15, Piatti 32	5 000
	21	Real Madrid	L	1-8	PD	Uche 33	50 000

20th Att: 201 634 • Av: 10 612 (-15.5%) • Mediterraneo 22 000 (48%)

ATHLETIC BILBAO 2010–11

Month	Day	Opponent	Res	Score	Comp	Scorers	Att
Aug	28	Hercules	W	1-0	PD	Llorente 46	24 000
	11	At. Madrid	L	1-2	PD	Llorente 88	39 600
Sep	18	Sp. Gijon	D	2-2	PD	Gurpegi 29, Llorente 58	20 000
	21	Mallorca	W	3-0	PD	Lopez 44, San Jose 62p, Perez 90	35 000
	25	Barcelona	L	1-3	PD	Gabilondo 90	34 053
	2	Valencia	L	1-2	PD	Gabilondo 90	45 000
	17	Zaragoza	W	2-1	PD	Iraola 11, Llorente 23	30 000
Oct	24	Sevilla	L	3-4	PD	Llorente 2 73 77, Gabilondo 90	40 000
	28	Alcorcon	W	1-0	CRr4	Gurpegi 55	4 500
	31	Getafe	W	3-0	PD	Iraola 6, San Jose 12p, Gabilondo 83	32 000
	7	Villarreal	L	1-4	PD	Llorente 6	22 000
Nov	10	Alcorcon	W	2-0	CRr4	Gabilondo 26, Orbaiz 90	18 000
	13	Almeria	W	1-0	PD	Llorente 10	34 000
	20	Real Madrid	L	1-5	PD	Llorente 40	79 500
	28	Osasuna	W	1-0	PD	Gurpegi 90	35 000
	5	Sociedad	L	0-2	PD		30 000
Dec	12	Espanyol	W	2-1	PD	Llorente 73, Lopez 78	35 000
	18	Levante	W	2-1	PD	Gabilondo 10, Javi Martinez 73	18 000
	21	Barcelona	D	0-0	CRr5		45 207
	2	Deportivo	L	1-2	PD	Llorente 86	35 000
	5	Barcelona	D	1-1	CRr5	Llorente 85	40 000
	8	Malaga	D	1-1	PD	Javi Martinez 90	20 000
Jan	15	Racing	W	2-1	PD	Javi Martinez 7, Muniain 10	36 000
	24	Hercules	W	3-0	PD	Javi Martinez 5, Llorente 59, Muniain 64	30 000
	30	At. Madrid	W	2-0	PD	Toquero 2 45 64	35 000
	5	Sp. Gijon	W	3-0	PD	Lopez 16p, Toquero 27, Llorente 73	39 000
	14	Mallorca	L	0-1	PD		11 600
	20	Barcelona	L	1-2	PD	Iraola 50p	83 533
	27	Valencia	L	1-2	PD	Llorente 14	35 000
	2	Zaragoza	L	1-2	PD	Llorente 18	17 000
Mar	6	Sevilla	W	2-0	PD	OG 66, Iraola 88p	37 000
	14	Getafe	D	2-2	PD	OG 69, Vera 90	6 000
	20	Villarreal	L	0-1	PD		37 000
	4	Almeria	W	3-1	PD	Muniain 29, Toquero 52, Orbaiz 61	10 564
Apr	9	Real Madrid	L	0-3	PD		38 000
	17	Osasuna	W	2-1	PD	Llorente 69, Muniain 90	18 239
	23	Sociedad	W	2-1	PD	Muniain 18, Toquero 29	38 000
	2	Espanyol	L	1-2	PD	Susaeta 42	23 023
	7	Levante	W	3-2	PD	Toquero 30, Lopez 48p, Llorente 63	40 000
May	10	Deportivo	L	1-2	PD	Toquero 3	34 000
	15	Malaga	D	1-1	PD	Lopez 65p	36 000
	21	Racing	W	2-1	PD	Lopez 19, Llorente 20	22 000

6th Att: 675 653 • Av: 35 560 (-2.7%) • San Mamés 39 750 (89%)

ALMERIA LEAGUE APPEARANCES/GOALS 2010-11

Goalkeepers Diego Alves BRA 33 • Esteban 5
Defenders Santiago Acasiete PER 17+3/0 • Carlos Garcia 33/1
Michael Jakobsen DEN 14+2/0 • Lillo 1+1/0 • Luna 13/0
Michel Macedo BRA 30+1/0 • Hernan Pellerano ARG 7+1/0 • Rigo 1/0
Marcelo Silva URU 21/1
Midfield Hernan Bernardello ARG 33/1 • Corona 21+9/2
Albert Crusat 30+4/3 • Sofiane Feghouli FRA 4+5/2 • Juanito 5+4/0
Juanma Ortiz 24+2/1 • Modeste M'Bami CMR 28+2/1 • Nieto 0+1/0
Jose Ortiz 0+16/0 • Diego Valeri ARG 2+7/0 • Fabian Vargas COL 12+8/1
Forwards Henok Goitom SWE 8+18/1 • Pablo Piatti ARG 34+1/8
Kalu Uche NGA 26+6/7 • Leonardo Ulloa ARG 16+18/7
Coach Juanma Lillo • Jose Luis Oltra (24/11/10) • Roberto Olabe (5/4/11)

KEY

SC = Supercopa • USC = UEFA Super Cup •
PD = Primera Division • CR = Copa del Rey •
CL = UEFA Champions League • EL = Europa
League
See page 13 for further explanations

ATHLETIC LEAGUE APPEARANCES/GOALS 2010-11

Goalkeepers Gorka Iraizoz 37 • Raul Fernandez 1
Defenders Aitor Ocio 3+1/0 • Fernando Amorebieta 16+1/0
Jon Aurtenetxe 9+1/0 • Mikel Balenziaga 1/0 • Borja Ekiza 21/0
Andoni Iraola 37/4 • Koikili 16/0 • Mikel San Jose 30+1/2
Ustaritz 8+2/0 • Xabi Castillo 10+1/0
Midfield David Lopez 17+11/6 • Igor Gabilondo 10+19/5
Carlos Gurpegi 28+3/2 • Igor Martinez 5+3/0 • Ander Iturraspe 5+12/0
Javi Martinez 35/4 • Markel Susaeta 15+13/1
Forwards Oscar de Marcos 3+10/0 • Diaz de Cerio 0+2/0 • Ibai 0+3/0
Fernando Llorente 37+1/18 • Iker Muniain 30+5/5
Gaizka Toquero 26+4/7 • Ion Velez 0+5/0 • Urko Vera 0+5/1
Coach Joaquin Caparros

ATLETICO LEAGUE APPEARANCES/GOALS 2010-11

Goalkeepers David De Gea 38
Defenders Antonio Lopez 15+2/0 • Alvaro Dominguez 17+2/2
Filipe BRA 23+4/1 • Diego Godin URU 25/0 • Luis Perea COL 28/0
Pulido 2/0 • Tomas Ujfalusi CZE 32/0 • Valera 11+4/1
Midfield Elias BRA 10+5/2 • Fran Merida 6+11/0 • Juanfran 5+10/1
Jurado 1/1 • Koke 8+9/2 • Mario Suarez 18+9/2 • Noguera 0+2/0
Paulo Assuncao BRA 17+7/0 • Raul Garcia 18+11/1 • Jose Antonio
Reyes 34/6 • Simao POR 15+1/4 • Tiago POR 28+3/4
Forwards Kun Aguero ARG 31+1/20 • Diego Costa BRA 13+15/6
Diego Forlan URU 23+9/8
Coach Quique Flores

ATLETICO MADRID 2010–11

Aug	27	Inter	W	2-0	USC	Reyes 62, Aguero 82	18 500
	30	Sp. Gijon	W	4-0	PD	Jurado 11, Forlan 2 39 63, Simao 90	50 000
Sep	11	Ath. Bilbao	W	2-1	PD	Forlan 11, Tiago 80	39 600
	16	Aris	L	0-1	ELgB		16 699
	19	Barcelona	L	1-2	PD	Garcia 25	54 851
	22	Valencia	D	1-1	PD	Simao 19	50 000
	26	Zaragoza	W	1-0	PD	Costa 20	35 000
	30	Leverkusen	D	1-1	ELgB	Simao 51p	28 052
Oct	3	Sevilla	L	1-3	PD	Costa 58	40 000
	16	Getafe	W	2-0	PD	Simao 38, Costa 73	54 000
	21	Rosenborg	W	3-0	ELgB	Godin 17, Aguero 66, Costa 78	28 472
	24	Villarreal	L	0-2	PD		21 000
	27	Univ. LPGC	W	5-0	CRr4	Godin 24, Aguero 2 41 53, Costa 48, Merida 84	13 161
	31	Almeria	D	1-1	PD	Aguero 33	35 000
Nov	4	Rosenborg	W	2-1	ELgB	Aguero 3, Tiago 84	14 250
	7	Real Madrid	L	0-2	PD		79 500
	10	Univ. LPGC	D	1-1	CRr4	Merida 75	5 000
	13	Osasuna	W	3-0	PD	Forlan 2 26 70, Aguero 41	43 000
	21	Sociedad	W	4-2	PD	Forlan 71, Aguero 2 79 82, Simao 90p	24 000
	27	Espanyol	L	2-3	PD	Tiago 45, Aguero 66	39 000
Dec	1	Aris	L	2-3	ELgB	Forlan 11, Aguero 16	21 154
	4	Levante	L	0-2	PD		11 804
	11	Deportivo	W	2-0	PD	Aguero 2 8 35	35 000
	16	Leverkusen	D	1-1	ELgB	Merida 72	18 093
	19	Malaga	W	3-0	PD	Tiago 2 22 69, Dominguez 66	20 000
	22	Espanyol	W	1-0	CRr5	Simao 33p	18 000
Jan	3	Racing	D	0-0	PD		35 000
	6	Espanyol	D	1-1	CRr5	Aguero 25	25 212
	10	Hercules	L	1-4	PD	Reyes 89	24 000
	13	Real Madrid	L	1-3	CRqf	Forlan 7	77 000
	17	Mallorca	W	3-0	PD	Valera 12, Forlan 33, Reyes 90	30 000
	20	Real Madrid	L	0-1	CRqf		53 000
	23	Sp. Gijon	L	0-1	PD		22 000
	30	Ath. Bilbao	L	0-2	PD		35 000
Feb	5	Barcelona	L	0-3	PD		84 766
	12	Valencia	L	1-2	PD	Reyes 3	40 000
	19	Zaragoza	W	1-0	PD	Aguero 66	17 000
	26	Sevilla	D	2-2	PD	Koke 47, Reyes 76	48 000
Mar	2	Getafe	D	1-1	PD	Elias 81	10 000
	5	Villarreal	W	3-1	PD	Reyes 5, Aguero 69, Forlan 72	30 000
	12	Almeria	D	2-2	PD	Aguero 2 39 60	13 228
	19	Real Madrid	L	1-2	PD	Aguero 86	53 000
Apr	3	Osasuna	W	3-2	PD	Costa 3 39 61 63	15 686
	10	Sociedad	W	3-0	PD	Filipe 12, Suarez 45, Aguero 78	50 000
	17	Espanyol	D	2-2	PD	Koke 2, Aguero 49	28 110
	24	Levante	W	4-1	PD	Elias 19, Aguero 2 50 70p, OG 84	38 040
	30	Deportivo	W	1-0	PD	Aguero 80	34 000
May	7	Malaga	L	0-3	PD		40 000
	10	Racing	L	1-2	PD	Suarez 11	16 000
	15	Hercules	W	2-1	PD	Dominguez 2, Reyes 71	20 000
	21	Mallorca	W	4-3	PD	Aguero 3 12 59 81, Juanfran 18	23 800

7th Att: 764 891 • Av: 40 257 (-2.1%) • Vicente Calderón 54 851 (73%)

BARCELONA 2010–11

Aug	14	Sevilla	L	1-3	SC	Ibrahimovic 21	38 000
	21	Sevilla	W	4-0	SC	OG 14, Messi 3 25 43 90	67 414
	29	Racing	W	3-0	PD	Messi 3, Iniesta 33, Villa 62	19 095
Sep	11	Hercules	L	0-2	PD		79 363
	14	Panath'kos	W	5-0	CLgD	Messi 2 22 45, Villa 33, Pedro 78, Alves 93+	69 738
	19	At. Madrid	W	2-1	PD	Messi 13, Pique 33	54 851
	22	Sp. Gijon	W	1-0	PD	Villa 49	66 947
	25	Ath. Bilbao	W	3-1	PD	Keita 55, Xavi 74, Busquets 90	34 053
	29	Rubin	D	1-1	CLgD	Villa 60p	23 950
Oct	3	Mallorca	D	1-1	PD	Messi 21	79 085
	16	Valencia	W	2-1	PD	Iniesta 47, Puyol 63	87 995
	20	Kobenhavn	W	2-0	CLgD	Messi 2 19 92+	75 852
	23	Zaragoza	W	2-0	PD	Messi 2 42 66	26 000
	26	Ceuta	W	2-0	CRr4	Maxwell 16, Pedro 25	6 000
	30	Sevilla	W	5-0	PD	Messi 2 4 64, Villa 2 24 90, Alves 24	81 020
Nov	2	Kobenhavn	D	1-1	CLgD	Messi 31	37 049
	7	Getafe	W	3-1	PD	Messi 23, Villa 35, Pedro 64	15 000
	10	Ceuta	W	5-1	CRr4	Nolito 2, Milito 7, Pedro 50, Krkic 63, Messi 68	38 971
	13	Villarreal	W	3-1	PD	Villa 22, Messi 2 58 83	80 766
	20	Almeria	W	8-0	PD	Messi 3 17 37 67, Iniesta 19, OG 27, Pedro 35, Krkic 2 62 73	13 000
	24	Panath'kos	W	3-0	CLgD	Pedro 2 27 69, Messi 62	58 466
	29	Real Madrid	W	5-0	PD	Xavi 10, Pedro 18, Villa 2 55 58, Jeffren 90	98 772
Dec	4	Osasuna	W	3-0	PD	Pedro 26, Messi 2 65 84p	19 602
	7	Rubin	W	2-0	CLgD	Fontas 51, Vazquez 83	50 436
	12	Sociedad	W	5-0	PD	Villa 9, Iniesta 33, Messi 2 47 87, Krkic 90	74 931
	18	Espanyol	W	5-1	PD	Pedro 2 19 60, Xavi 30, Villa 2 76 84	40 010
	21	Ath. Bilbao	D	0-0	CRr5		45 207
Jan	2	Levante	W	2-1	PD	Pedro 2 47 59	71 681
	5	Ath. Bilbao	D	1-1	CRr5	Abidal 75	40 000
	8	Deportivo	W	4-0	PD	Villa 26, Messi 52, Iniesta 80, Pedro 81	32 000
	12	Betis	W	5-0	CRqf	Messi 3 44 62 73, Pedro 76, Keita 83	59 498
	16	Malaga	W	4-1	PD	Iniesta 8, Villa 2 18 74, Pedro 36	71 576
	19	Betis	L	1-3	CRqf	Messi 38	35 000
	22	Racing	W	3-0	PD	Pedro 2, Messi 33p, Iniesta 56	70 072
	26	Almeria	W	5-0	CRsf	Messi 2 16 19, Villa 11, Pedro 31, Keita 88	49 875
	29	Hercules	W	3-0	PD	Pedro 43, Messi 2 87 89	30 000
Feb	2	Almeria	W	3-0	CRsf	Adriano 35, Thiago 56, Afellay 66	16 000
	5	At. Madrid	W	3-0	PD	Messi 3 17 28 79	84 766
	12	Sp. Gijon	D	1-1	PD	Villa 80	28 000
	16	Arsenal	L	1-2	CLr2	Villa 26	59 927
	20	Ath. Bilbao	W	2-1	PD	Villa 4, Messi 78	83 533
	26	Mallorca	W	3-0	PD	Messi 38, Villa 57, Pedro 66	21 227
Mar	2	Valencia	W	1-0	PD	Messi 77	50 800
	5	Zaragoza	W	1-0	PD	Keita 43	78 965
	8	Arsenal	W	3-1	CLr2	Messi 2 45 71p, Xavi 69	95 486
	13	Sevilla	D	1-1	PD	Krkic 30	45 000
	19	Getafe	W	2-1	PD	Alves 17, Krkic 50	81 913
	2	Villarreal	W	1-0	PD	Pique 67	23 000
Apr	6	Shakhtar	W	5-1	CLqf	Iniesta 2, Alves 34, Pique 53, Keita 61, Xavi 86	86 518
	9	Almeria	W	3-1	PD	Messi 2 53p 90, Thiago 64	80 452
	12	Shakhtar	W	1-0	CLqf	Messi 43	51 759
	16	Real Madrid	D	1-1	PD	Messi 53p	79 500
	20	Real Madrid	L	0-1	CRf		55 000
	23	Osasuna	W	2-0	PD	Villa 24, Messi 88	73 285
	27	Real Madrid	W	2-0	CLsf	Messi 2 76 87	71 657
	30	Sociedad	L	1-2	PD	Thiago 29	30 000
May	3	Real Madrid	D	1-1	CLsf	Pedro 54	95 701
	8	Espanyol	W	2-0	PD	Iniesta 29, Pique 48	89 994
	11	Levante	W	1-0	PD	Keita 28	20 000
	15	Deportivo	D	0-0	PD		70 044
	21	Malaga	W	3-1	PD	Krkic 44p, Afellay 76, Bartra 85	28 000
	28	Man Utd	W	3-1	CLf	Pedro 27, Messi 54, Villa 69	87 695

1st Att: 1 505 160 • Av: 79 218 (+1.5%) • Camp Nou 99 354 (79%)

BARCELONA LEAGUE APPEARANCES/GOALS 2010-11

Goalkeepers Pinto 6 • Victor Valdes 32
Defenders Eric Abidal FRA 23+3/0 • Adriano BRA 11 ı 1/0
Andreu Fontas 5+1/0 • Marc Bartra 2/1 • Dani Alves BRA 31+4/2
Martin Montoya 1+1/0 • Maxwell BRA 19+6/0 • Gabriel Milito ARG 8+2/0
Gerard Pique 29+2/3 • Carles Puyol 17/1
Midfield Ibrahim Afellay NED 7+9/1 • Sergio Busquets 25+3/1
Jonathan MEX 1+1/0 • Andres Iniesta 32+2/8
Seydou Keita MLI 15+20/3 • Javier Mascherano ARG 18+9/0
Oriol Romeu 0+1/0 • Sergi Roberto 1/0 • Thiago 6+6/2 • Xavi 29+2/3
Forwards David Villa 32+2/18 • Jeffren 4+4/1 • Bojan Krkic 9+18/6
Lionel Messi ARG 31+2/31 • Nolito 0+2/0 • Pedro 24+9/13
Coach Josep Guardiola

DEPORTIVO LA CORUNA 2010-11

	Date	Opponent	Res	Score	Comp	Scorers	Att
Ag	29	Zaragoza	D	0-0	PD		15 000
	12	Sevilla	D	0-0	PD		35 000
Sep	20	Getafe	D	2-2	PD	Guardado 2 [50p] [57p]	13 000
	23	Villarreal	L	0-1	PD		16 000
	26	Almeria	L	0-2	PD		14 000
	3	Real Madrid	L	1-6	PD	Rodriguez [78]	67 000
	17	Osasuna	D	0-0	PD		12 000
Oct	25	Sociedad	L	0-3	PD		23 040
	28	Osasuna	D	1-1	CRr4	Saul [70]	11 268
	31	Espanyol	W	3-0	PD	Adrian [28], Lopo [76], Colotto [87]	10 000
	7	Levante	W	2-1	PD	Riki [10], Aythami [52]	10 000
	10	Osasuna	W	2-1	CRr4	Riki [53], Nouioui [64]	8 000
Nov	14	Mallorca	D	0-0	PD		15 000
	21	Malaga	W	3-0	PD	Adrian [22p], Colotto [30], Alvarez [83]	10 000
	28	Racing	L	0-1	PD		12 086
	6	Hercules	W	1-0	PD	Nouioui [73]	14 000
Dec	11	At. Madrid	L	0-2	PD		35 000
	18	Sp. Gijon	D	1-1	PD	Aythami [12]	20 000
	21	Córdoba	D	1-1	CRr5	Riki [17p]	5 000
	2	Ath. Bilbao	W	2-1	PD	Adrian 2 [22p] [52]	35 000
	5	Córdoba	W	3-1	CRr5	Adrian 3 [90p] [102] [120p]	5 000
	8	Barcelona	L	0-4	PD		32 000
Jan	13	Almeria	L	0-1	CRqf		3 447
	16	Valencia	L	0-2	PD		40 000
	19	Almeria	L	2-3	CRqf	Alvarez [44p], Adrian [51]	8 000
	23	Zaragoza	L	0-1	PD		22 000
	29	Sevilla	D	3-3	PD	Nouioui 2 [15] [62], Laure [87]	14 000
	5	Getafe	L	1-4	PD	Riki [68p]	10 000
Feb	13	Villarreal	W	1-0	PD	Lopo [60]	14 000
	20	Almeria	D	1-1	PD	Aranzubia [90]	12 000
	26	Real Madrid	D	0-0	PD		34 600
	2	Osasuna	D	0-0	PD		13 437
Mar	7	Sociedad	W	2-1	PD	Riki [41], Adrian [52]	14 000
	13	Espanyol	L	0-2	PD		24 819
	20	Levante	L	0-1	PD		18 000
	3	Mallorca	W	2-1	PD	Xisco [55], Nouioui [67]	22 000
	10	Malaga	D	0-0	PD		27 000
Apr	17	Racing	W	2-0	PD	Nouioui [45], Xisco [49]	31 000
	24	Hercules	L	0-1	PD		20 000
	30	At. Madrid	L	0-1	PD		34 000
	7	Sp. Gijon	D	2-2	PD	Adrian 2 [9] [40]	25 000
May	10	Ath. Bilbao	W	1-0	PD	OG 2 [22] [71]	34 000
	15	Barcelona	D	0-0	PD		70 044
	21	Valencia	L	0-2	PD		34 600

18th   Att: 390 200 • Av: 20 536 (+0.9%) • Riazor 34 600 (59%)

RCD ESPANYOL 2010-11

	Date	Opponent	Res	Score	Comp	Scorers	Att
Ag	29	Getafe	W	3-1	PD	Osvaldo 2 [34] [55], Datolo [90]	23 421
	12	Villarreal	L	0-4	PD		16 000
Sep	20	Almeria	W	1-0	PD	Callejon [48]	24 345
	21	Real Madrid	L	0-3	PD		70 000
	26	Osasuna	W	1-0	PD	Alvaro [25]	26 820
	2	Sociedad	L	0-1	PD		25 000
	17	Mallorca	W	1-0	PD	Luis Garcia [32p]	13 000
Oct	24	Levante	W	2-1	PD	Datolo [13], Callejon [81]	20 000
	27	Valladolid	W	2-0	CRr4	Alvaro 2 [37] [55]	7 900
	31	Deportivo	L	0-3	PD		10 000
	6	Malaga	W	1-0	PD	Marquez 2	22 000
	9	Valladolid	D	1-1	CRr4	Osvaldo [68]	10 120
Nov	14	Racing	D	0-0	PD		13 105
	21	Hercules	W	3-0	PD	Verdu [15], Osvaldo [81p], Luis Garcia [90p]	26 110
	27	At. Madrid	W	3-2	PD	Luis Garcia [22p], Verdu [54], Osvaldo [78]	39 000
	5	Sp. Gijon	W	1-0	PD	Luis Garcia [70]	26 000
Dec	12	Ath. Bilbao	L	1-2	PD	Osvaldo [33]	35 000
	18	Barcelona	L	1-5	PD	Osvaldo [63]	40 010
	22	At. Madrid	L	0-1	CRr5		18 000
	2	Valencia	L	1-2	PD	OG [45]	30 000
	6	At. Madrid	D	1-1	CRr5	Luis Garcia [90]	25 212
Jan	9	Zaragoza	W	4-0	PD	Osvaldo [8], Luis Garcia [30p], Alvaro [34], Sergio Garcia [87]	32 000
	15	Sevilla	W	2-1	PD	Callejon 2 [41] [78]	35 000
	23	Getafe	W	3-1	PD	Luis Garcia [54], Callejon [60], Sergio Garcia [64]	11 000
	30	Villarreal	L	0-1	PD		24 244
	5	Almeria	L	2-3	PD	Verdu [34], Alvaro [49]	9 300
	13	Real Madrid	L	0-1	PD		40 500
Feb	20	Osasuna	L	0-4	PD		18 000
	26	Sociedad	W	4-1	PD	OG [42], Sergio Garcia [54], Callejon [81], Marquez [90]	26 400
	1	Mallorca	L	1-2	PD	Alvaro [19]	20 134
	6	Levante	L	0-1	PD		13 600
Mar	13	Deportivo	W	2-0	PD	Alonso [62], Verdu [81]	24 819
	20	Malaga	L	0-2	PD		27 000
	3	Racing	L	1-2	PD	Osvaldo [37p]	24 427
	10	Hercules	D	0-0	PD		21 000
Apr	17	At. Madrid	D	2-2	PD	Osvaldo 2 [38] [58]	28 110
	24	Sp. Gijon	L	0-1	PD		21 000
	2	Ath. Bilbao	W	2-1	PD	Osvaldo [35], Alonso [76]	23 023
	8	Barcelona	L	0-2	PD		89 994
May	11	Valencia	D	2-2	PD	Osvaldo [19], Galan [76]	28 000
	15	Zaragoza	L	0-1	PD		34 000
	21	Sevilla	L	2-3	PD	Osvaldo [54], Verdu [73]	26 000

8th   Att: 506 403 • Av: 26 652 (-8.7%) • Cornellà-El Prat 40 500 (65%)

DEPORTIVO LEAGUE APPEARANCES/GOALS 2010-11
Goalkeepers Aranzubia 32/1 • Manu 6
Defenders Aythami 17+2/2 • Diego Colotto ARG 36/2
David Rochela 2/0 • Laure 21+1/1 • Lopo 33/2 • Manuel Pablo 30/0
Claudio Morel PAR 14+1/0 • Knut Rindaroy NOR 3+1/0
Diego Seoane 8+3/0 • Ze Castro POR 4+2/0
Midfield Antonio Tomas 20+1/0 • Yves Desmarets FRA 9+3/0 • Andres
Guardado 18+2/2 • Juan Dominguez 9+11/0 • Juan Rodriguez 29+2/1
Juca BRA 1+7/0 • Michel 7+1/0 • Pablo Alvarez 3+14/1
Ruben Perez 31+1/0 • Saul 8+5/0 • Juan Carlos Valeron 9+12/0
Forwards Adrian 31+5/7 • Dioni 1+3/0 • Lassad Nouioui FRA 16+17/5
Riki 8+11/3 • Jose Sand ARG 2+3/0 • Jonathan Urreta URU 5+1/0
Xisco 5+4/2
Coach Miguel Angel Lotina

ESPANYOL LEAGUE APPEARANCES/GOALS 2010-11
Goalkeepers Cristian Alvarez ARG 5 • Carlos Kameni CMR 33
Defenders Victor Alvarez 0+1/0 • Chica 28+1/0 • David Garcia 16+1/0
• Forlin ARG 21/0 • Galan 21+1/1 • Jordi Amat 23+3/0
Raul Rodriguez 8+2/0 • Victor Ruiz 15/0 • Didac Vila 12+1/0
Midfield Baena 13+2/0 • Jesus Datolo ARG 3+11/2
Ivan De la Pena 0+2/0 • Aldo Duscher ARG 14+5/0 • Isaias 0+4/0
Javi Lopez 18+7/0 • David Lopez 0+4/0 • Eric Lopez 0+1/0
Manu 1+6/0 • Javier Marquez 26+3/2 • Verdu 36+1/5
Forwards Ivan Alonso URU 10+10/2 • Alvaro 8+22/4
Jose Callejon 36+1/6 • Coro 0+1/0 • Luis Garcia 36+1/6
Pablo Osvaldo ITA 22+2/13 • Rui Fonte POR 0+11/0
Sergio Garcia 13+8/3 • Thievy FRA 0+2/0
Coach Mauricio Pochettino ARG

GETAFE 2010–11

	Date	Opponent	Res	Score	Comp	Scorers	Att
Aug	19	APOEL	W	1-0	ELpo	Parejo 43	4 235
	26	APOEL	D	1-1	ELpo	Cata Diaz 99	18 643
	29	Espanyol	L	1-3	PD	OG 62	23 421
Sep	12	Levante	W	4-1	PD	Gavilan 2 5 89, Colunga 11, Arizmendi 90	11 000
	16	OB Odense	W	2-1	ELgH	Arizmendi 51, Pedro Rios 81	2 420
	20	Deportivo	D	2-2	PD	OG 33, Arizmendi 69	13 000
	23	Malaga	L	0-2	PD		11 000
	26	Racing	W	1-0	PD	Sanchez 16	13 077
	30	Young Boys	L	0-2	ELgH		12 830
	3	Hercules	W	3-0	PD	Parejo 21, Del Moral 43, Miku 82	11 000
Oct	16	At. Madrid	L	0-2	PD		54 000
	21	Stuttgart	L	0-1	ELgH		17 400
	24	Sp. Gijon	W	3-0	PD	Boateng 9, Colunga 51p, Marcano 60	11 000
	27	Portugalete	D	1-1	CRr4	Sardinero 6	4 000
	31	Ath. Bilbao	L	0-3	PD		32 000
Nov	4	Stuttgart	L	0-3	ELgH		3 459
	7	Barcelona	L	1-3	PD	Del Moral 70p	15 000
	11	Portugalete	D	0-0	CRr4		
	14	Valencia	L	0-2	PD		35 000
	22	Zaragoza	D	1-1	PD	Colunga 49p	10 000
	27	Sevilla	W	3-1	PD	Del Moral 57p, Miku 59, Pedro Rios 77	24 000
Dec	1	OB Odense	D	1-1	ELgH	Pedro Rios 17	5 599
	5	Mallorca	W	3-0	PD	Pedro Rios 2 20 28, Parejo 79	9 000
	11	Villarreal	W	1-0	PD	Albin 89	10 000
	16	Young Boys	W	1-0	ELgH	Sardinero 15	1 631
	19	Almeria	W	3-2	PD	Del Moral 29, Miku 48, Boateng 71	9 000
	22	Betis	W	2-1	CRr5	Miku 27, Pedro Rios 35	20 000
Jan	3	RealMadrid	L	2-3	PD	Parejo 29, Albin 85	11 000
	6	Betis	L	1-3	CRr5	Casquero 90	8 000
	9	Osasuna	D	0-0	PD		17 000
	15	Sociedad	L	0-4	PD		10 000
	23	Espanyol	L	1-3	PD	Miku 13	11 000
	29	Levante	L	0-2	PD		10 500
Feb	5	Deportivo	W	4-1	PD	Colunga 2 19 26, Miku 45, Pedro Rios 57	10 000
	13	Malaga	D	2-2	PD	Miku 8, Colunga 24	25 000
	20	Racing	L	0-1	PD		8 000
	27	Hercules	D	0-0	PD		17 000
Mar	2	At. Madrid	D	1-1	PD	Del Moral 3	10 000
	6	Sp. Gijon	L	0-2	PD		23 000
	14	Ath. Bilbao	D	2-2	PD	Del Moral 2 58 85	6 000
	19	Barcelona	L	1-2	PD	Del Moral 88	81 913
Apr	2	Valencia	L	2-4	PD	Del Moral 13, Sardinero 87	12 000
	11	Zaragoza	L	1-2	PD	Casquero 45	25 000
	16	Sevilla	W	1-0	PD	Miku 76	13 000
	24	Mallorca	L	0-2	PD		14 668
May	1	Villarreal	L	1-2	PD	Pedro Rios 32	16 000
	7	Almeria	W	2-0	PD	Colunga 5, Pedro Rios 53	17 000
	10	RealMadrid	L	0-4	PD		55 000
	15	Osasuna	W	2-0	PD	OG 66, Pedro Rios 90	16 500
	21	Sociedad	D	1-1	PD	Diaz 9	32 000

16th Att: 212 500 • Av: 11 184 (-4.1%) • Coliseum 17 700 (63%)

HERCULES 2010–11

	Date	Opponent	Res	Score	Comp	Scorers	Att
Ag	28	Ath. Bilbao	L	0-1	PD		24 000
Sep	11	Barcelona	W	2-0	PD	Valdez 2 26 59	79 363
	19	Valencia	L	1-2	PD	Trezeguet 42p	28 000
	22	Zaragoza	D	0-0	PD		18 000
	26	Sevilla	W	2-0	PD	Trezeguet 2 21p 38	17 000
Oct	3	Getafe	L	0-3	PD		11 000
	18	Villarreal	D	2-2	PD	Valdez 26, Trezeguet 40	20 000
	24	Almeria	D	1-1	PD	Valdez 38	10 167
	27	Malaga	D	0-0	CRr4		10 000
	30	RealMadrid	L	1-3	PD	Trezeguet 3	28 000
Nov	7	Osasuna	L	0-3	PD		14 130
	11	Malaga	L	2-3	CRr4	Portillo 31, Aguilar 62	
	14	Sociedad	W	2-1	PD	Trezeguet 47, Drenthe 52	18 000
	21	Espanyol	L	0-3	PD		26 110
	28	Levante	W	3-1	PD	Valdez 2 40 67, Trezeguet 62	16 000
Dec	6	Deportivo	L	0-1	PD		14 000
	12	Malaga	W	4-1	PD	Trezeguet 66, Drenthe 69p, Paz 72, Koki 81	17 000
	20	Racing	D	0-0	PD		17 000
	3	Mallorca	L	0-3	PD		9 000
Jan	10	At. Madrid	W	4-1	PD	Tote 11, Valdez 23, Thomert 32, Trezeguet 44	24 000
	15	Sp. Gijon	L	0-2	PD		17 000
	24	Ath. Bilbao	L	0-3	PD		30 000
	29	Barcelona	L	0-3	PD		30 000
Feb	6	Valencia	L	0-2	PD		40 000
	13	Zaragoza	W	2-1	PD	Farinos 80, Trezeguet 89	20 000
	20	Sevilla	L	0-1	PD		38 000
	27	Getafe	D	0-0	PD		17 000
Mar	2	Villarreal	L	0-1	PD		15 000
	6	Almeria	L	1-2	PD	Paz 51	18 000
	12	RealMadrid	L	0-2	PD		71 000
	20	Osasuna	L	0-4	PD		17 000
Apr	3	Sociedad	W	3-1	PD	Portillo 70, Drenthe 2 84 90	24 000
	10	Espanyol	D	0-0	PD		21 000
	17	Levante	L	1-2	PD	Trezeguet 82	14 098
	24	Deportivo	W	1-0	PD	Tiago Gomes 60	20 000
	1	Malaga	L	1-3	PD	Valdez 4	29 000
May	7	Racing	L	2-3	PD	Sendoa 40, Tiago Gomes 43	20 000
	11	Mallorca	D	2-2	PD	Sendoa 2 12 42	10 000
	15	At. Madrid	L	1-2	PD	Trezeguet 67	20 000
	21	Sp. Gijon	D	0-0	PD		18 000

19th Att: 383 000 • Av: 20 157 (+51.2%) • Jose Rico Perez 30 000 (67%)

GETAFE LEAGUE APPEARANCES/GOALS 2010-11

Goalkeepers Jordi Codina 22+1 • Oscar Ustari ARG 16
Defenders Cata Diaz 35/1 • Mane 30+1/0 • Ivan Marcano 26+3/1
Pedro Mario 2/0 • Miguel Torres 37/0 • Rafa Lopez 17+2/0
Midfield Derek Boateng GHA 30+2/2 • Borja 4+9/0
Francisco Casquero 15+12/1 • Jaime Gavilan 15+3/2
Pedro Mosquera 4+10/0 • Daniel Parejo 28+8/3 • Pedro Rios 27+4/7
Pablo Pintos URU 4+2/0 • Victor Sanchez 21+8/1
Forwards Adrian Colunga 22+7/7 • Juan Albin URU 4+14/2
Angel Arizmendi 7+12/2 • Adrian Corpa 0+1/0 • Manu del Moral 28+2/9
Miku VEN 24+7/7 • Adrian Sardinero 4+6/1
Coach Michel

HERCULES LEAGUE APPEARANCES/GOALS 2010-11

Goalkeepers Alba 1+1 • Calatayud 34 • Piet Velthuizen NED 3
Defenders David Cortes 34/0 • Royston Drenthe NED 15+2/4
Juanra 13+1/0 • Paco Pena 28/0 • Noe Pamarot FRA 28+1/0 • Paz 29/2
Corneliu Pulhac ROU 9/0 • Sergio Rodriguez 10+3/0
Mohamed Sarr SEN 2/0
Midfield Abel Aguilar COL 33+1/0 • Farinos 11+1/1
Matias Fritzler ARG 22+4/0 • Kiko 21+13/1 • Rufete 3+11/0
Sendoa 7+16/3 • Tiago Gomes POR 25+3/2
Forwards Cristian 2+17/0 • Luis Carlos 0+1/0
Javier Portillo 11+15/1 • Olivier Thomert FRA 12+6/1 • Tote 15+6/1
David Trezeguet FRA 28+3/12 • Nelson Valdez PAR 22+3/8
Coach Esteban Vigo • Miroslav Dukic SRB (23/03/2011)

LEVANTE 2010–11

	Day	Opponent	Res	Score	Comp	Scorers	Att
Ag	28	Sevilla	L	1-4	PD	Suarez [11p]	10 241
	12	Getafe	L	1-4	PD	Jorda [14]	11 000
Sep	19	Villarreal	L	1-2	PD	Caicedo [90]	11 500
	22	Almeria	W	1-0	PD	Sergio [39]	9 900
	25	Real Madrid	D	0-0	PD		18 326
	3	Osasuna	D	1-1	PD	Sergio [79]	16 000
Oct	17	Sociedad	W	2-1	PD	Del Horno [60], Caicedo [66]	11 200
	24	Espanyol	L	1-2	PD	Stuani [84]	20 000
	27	Xerez	W	3-2	CRr4	Stuani 2 [60 81], Larrea [88]	4 029
	1	Mallorca	L	1-2	PD	Stuani [26]	11 000
	7	Deportivo	L	1-2	PD	Juanlu [73]	10 000
Nov	10	Xerez	L	1-2	CRr4	Caicedo [44]	5 000
	14	Malaga	L	0-1	PD		25 000
	21	Racing	W	3-1	PD	Caicedo 2 [23 26], Stuani [42]	10 421
	28	Hercules	L	1-3	PD	Suarez [41]	16 000
Dec	4	At. Madrid	W	2-0	PD	Nano [3], Caicedo [59]	11 804
	12	Sp. Gijon	D	1-1	PD	Caicedo [71]	18 000
	18	Ath. Bilbao	L	1-2	PD	Caicedo [21]	18 000
	22	Real Madrid	L	0-8	CRr5		60 000
	2	Barcelona	L	1-2	PD	Stuani [80]	71 681
Jan	6	Real Madrid	W	2-0	CRr5	Xisco Munoz [62p], Sergio [86]	12 387
	9	Valencia	L	0-1	PD		19 000
	15	Zaragoza	L	0-1	PD		20 000
	22	Sevilla	L	1-4	PD	Xisco Nadal [58]	35 000
	29	Getafe	W	2-0	PD	Valdo [47], Caicedo [54]	10 500
Feb	5	Villarreal	L	0-2	PD	Valdo [48]	20 000
	13	Almeria	W	1-0	PD	Caicedo [53]	12 000
	19	Real Madrid	L	0-2	PD		65 000
	27	Osasuna	W	2-1	PD	Ballesteros [44], Caicedo [50]	11 747
Mar	2	Sociedad	D	1-1	PD	Del Horno [77]	20 000
	6	Espanyol	W	1-0	PD	Caicedo [27]	13 600
	13	Mallorca	D	1-1	PD	Juanlu [37]	11 722
	20	Deportivo	W	1-0	PD	Suarez [90]	18 000
	3	Malaga	W	3-1	PD	Stuani 2 [6 71], Suarez [9]	11 000
Apr	10	Racing	D	1-1	PD	Jorda [89]	15 000
	17	Hercules	W	2-1	PD	Suarez [5], Juanlu [43]	14 098
	24	At. Madrid	L	1-4	PD	Caicedo [39p]	38 040
	1	Sp. Gijon	D	0-0	PD		16 000
	7	Ath. Bilbao	L	2-3	PD	Stuani [77], Nano [85]	40 000
May	11	Barcelona	D	1-1	PD	Caicedo [41]	20 000
	15	Valencia	D	0-0	PD		45 000
	21	Zaragoza	L	1-2	PD	Stuani [79]	19 102

14th Att: 260 261 • Av: 13 697 (+61.8%) • Ciutat de Valencia 25 534 (53%)

MALAGA 2010–11

	Day	Opponent	Res	Score	Comp	Scorers	Att
Ag	28	Valencia	L	1-3	PD	Fernandez [45]	30 000
	12	Zaragoza	W	5-3	PD	Fernando 2 [2 28], Juanmi 2 [7 29], Owusu-Abeyie [35]	20 000
Sep	19	Sevilla	L	1-2	PD	Rondon [14]	25 000
	23	Getafe	W	2-0	PD	Rondon [54], Apono [61p]	11 000
	27	Villarreal	L	2-3	PD	Eliseu [4], Rondon [30]	25 000
	3	Almeria	D	1-1	PD	Owusu-Abeyie [50]	11 400
Oct	16	Real Madrid	L	1-4	PD	Stadsgaard [55]	30 000
	24	Osasuna	L	0-3	PD		14 000
	27	Hercules	D	0-0	CRr4		10 000
	31	Sociedad	L	1-2	PD	Juanmi [77]	18 000
	6	Espanyol	L	0-1	PD		22 040
Nov	11	Hercules	W	3-2	CRr4	Eliseu [11], Edinho [16], Fernandez [90]	
	14	Levante	W	1-0	PD	Eliseu [64]	25 000
	21	Deportivo	L	0-3	PD		10 000
	28	Mallorca	L	0-2	PD		12 254
Dec	5	Racing	W	4-1	PD	Eliseu [28], Recio [43], Rondon 2 [52 55]	22 500
	12	Hercules	L	1-4	PD	Fernandez [12]	17 000
	19	At. Madrid	L	0-3	PD		20 000
	22	Sevilla	L	3-5	CRr5	Rondon 2 [19 26], Owusu-Abeyie [41]	18 000
	2	Sp. Gijon	W	2-1	PD	Weligton [45], Apono [59p]	18 000
	5	Sevilla	L	0-3	CRr5		12 000
Jan	8	Ath. Bilbao	D	1-1	PD	Demichelis [81]	20 000
	16	Barcelona	L	1-4	PD	Duda [68]	71 576
	22	Valencia	L	3-4	PD	Rondon 2 [10 35], Baptista [79]	35 000
	29	Zaragoza	L	1-2	PD	Duda [16]	25 000
	6	Sevilla	D	0-0	PD		36 000
Feb	13	Getafe	D	2-2	PD	Baptista [80p], Rondon [90]	25 000
	20	Villarreal	D	1-1	PD	Fernandez [82]	20 000
	28	Almeria	W	3-1	PD	Maresca [52], Rondon [78], Juanmi [90]	26 000
	3	Real Madrid	L	0-7	PD		56 000
Mar	6	Osasuna	L	0-1	PD		24 000
	13	Sociedad	W	2-0	PD	Duda [25], Rondon [58]	24 000
	20	Espanyol	W	2-0	PD	Rondon 2 [8 26]	27 000
	3	Levante	L	1-3	PD	Fernandez [61]	11 000
Apr	10	Deportivo	D	0-0	PD		27 000
	16	Mallorca	W	3-0	PD	Fernandez [26], Baptista 2 [40 57]	27 000
	24	Racing	W	2-1	PD	Baptista [32], Fernandez [35]	14 009
	1	Hercules	W	3-1	PD	Baptista 2 [5 76], Rondon [73]	29 000
	7	At. Madrid	W	3-0	PD	Rondon [29], Baptista [35], Maresca [84]	40 000
May	10	Sp. Gijon	W	2-0	PD	Baptista [10], Eliseu [68]	30 000
	15	Ath. Bilbao	D	1-1	PD	Recio [42]	36 000
	21	Barcelona	L	1-3	PD	Fernandez [31]	28 000

11th Att: 483 500 • Av: 25 447 (+8.5%) • La Rosaleda 28 963 (87%)

LEVANTE LEAGUE APPEARANCES/GOALS 2010-11

Goalkeepers Manolo Reina 18 • Gustavo Munua URU 20
Defenders Sergio Ballesteros 35/1 • Cerra 7+2/0
Asier Del Horno 21+1/2 • Javi Venta 33/0 • Juanfran 22+1/0
Nano 28+4/2 • Miquel Robuste 4+3/0 • Hector Rodas 5/0
Midfield Nacho Gonzalez URU 2+1/0 • Juanlu 28+2/3
Gorka Larrea 2+4/0 • Adrian Lois 0+1/0 • Mono 0+1/0 • Jefferson
Montero ECU 4+7/0 • Miguel Pallardo 21+6/0 • Sergio 9+5/2
Valdo CPV 25+4/2 • Vicente Iborra 14+2/0 • Xavier Torres 34+1/0
Forwards Felipe Caicedo ECU 22+5/13 • Rafa Jorda 7+10/2 • Christian
Stuani URU 11+19/8 • Ruben Suarez 18+9/5 • Wellington
Silva BRA 0+2/0 • Xisco Munoz 16+10/0 • Xisco Nadal 12+13/1
Coach Luis Garcia Plaza

MALAGA LEAGUE APPEARANCES/GOALS 2010-11

Goalkeepers Arnau 7+2 • Asenjo 5 • Wilfredo Caballero ARG 15
Galatto BRA 4 • Ruben 7
Defenders Martin Demichelis ARG 18/1 • Ivan Gonzalez 4+2/0
Helder Rosario POR 3/0 • Jesus Gamez 30/0 • Juanito 5+1/0
Manolo 7+2/0 • Manu 5+2/0 • Patrick Mtiliga DEN 17+2/0
Kris Stadsgaard DEN 23+2/1 • Weligton BRA 31/1
Midfield Apono 26+1/2 • Cala 0+1/0 • Camacho 12+3/0
Duda POR 20/3 • Eliseu POR 34+1/4 • Fernando 12+9/2
Enzo Maresca ITA 9+11/2 • Portillo 7+10/0 • Edu Ramos 1+4/0
Recio 18+5/2 • Sandro Silva BRA 12+12/0
Forwards Nabil Baha MAR 4+1/0 • Edinho POR 1+7/0
Sebastian Fernandez URU 21+9/7 • Juanmi 6+11/4
Julio Baptista BRA 11/9 • Albert Luque 0+3/0
Quincy Owusu-Abeyie GHA 15+10/2 • Jose Rondon VEN 28+2/14
Coach Juan Ramon Lopez Muniz • Jesualdo Ferreira POR (17/06/10) •
Manuel Pellegrini CHI (2/11/10)

RCD MALLORCA 2010–11

Mo	Day	Opponent		Score	Comp	Scorers	Att
Ag	29	Real Madrid	D	0-0	PD		22 867
	12	Sp. Gijon	L	0-2	PD		20 000
Sep	18	Osasuna	W	2-0	PD	Castro 25p, De Guzman 90	12 000
	21	Ath. Bilbao	L	0-3	PD		35 000
	26	Sociedad	W	2-0	PD	Cavenaghi 2 7 62	11 000
Oct	3	Barcelona	D	1-1	PD	N'Sue 43	79 085
	17	Espanyol	L	0-1	PD		13 000
	23	Valencia	W	2-1	PD	Castro 2 7p 29	45 000
	27	Sp. Gijon	W	3-1	CRr4	Cavenaghi 2 12 33, Ruben 90	9 774
	1	Levante	W	2-1	PD	Pereira 64, Webo 84	11 000
	7	Zaragoza	L	2-3	PD	Webo 19, Pereira 61	21 000
Nov	11	Sp. Gijon	D	2-2	CRr4	N'Sue 2 10 15	15 000
	14	Deportivo	D	0-0	PD		15 000
	21	Sevilla	W	2-1	PD	Pereira 36, Webo 90	40 000
	28	Malaga	W	2-0	PD	Webo 50, Castro 55	12 254
	5	Getafe	L	0-3	PD		9 000
Dec	12	Racing	L	0-1	PD		12 350
	18	Villarreal	L	1-3	PD	De Guzman 28	15 000
	22	Almeria	L	3-4	CRr5	De Guzman 22, Victor 44, Webo 88	1 500
	3	Hercules	W	3-0	PD	N'Sue 38, Victor 41, Pereira 51	9 000
	6	Almeria	L	3-4	CRr5	Cavenaghi 2 70 77, Pereira 76	9 569
Jan	9	Almeria	W	4-1	PD	Ramis 12, Victor 37, N'sue 67, Pereira 88	15 800
	17	At. Madrid	L	0-3	PD		30 000
	23	Real Madrid	L	0-1	PD		74 000
	29	Sp. Gijon	L	0-4	PD		11 336
	5	Osasuna	D	1-1	PD	Castro 37	15 403
Feb	14	Ath. Bilbao	W	1-0	PD	Webo 11	11 600
	21	Sociedad	L	0-1	PD		20 000
	26	Barcelona	L	0-3	PD		21 227
	1	Espanyol	W	2-1	PD	Webo 63, N'Sue 83	20 134
Mar	5	Valencia	L	1-2	PD	Ramis 31p	14 000
	13	Levante	D	1-1	PD	Ramis 60	11 722
	19	Zaragoza	W	1-0	PD	De Guzman 67	13 200
	3	Deportivo	L	1-2	PD	Webo 27	22 000
	9	Sevilla	D	2-2	PD	Ienaga 16, De Guzman 43	16 170
Apr	16	Malaga	L	0-3	PD		27 000
	24	Getafe	W	2-0	PD	Nunes 25, Ienaga 67	14 668
	1	Racing	L	0-2	PD		15 185
	8	Villarreal	D	0-0	PD		13 000
May	11	Hercules	D	2-2	PD	Victor 76, Webo 80	10 000
	15	Almeria	L	1-3	PD	Webo 42	5 000
	21	At. Madrid	L	3-4	PD	De Guzman 62p, Webo 2 71 90	23 800

17th Att: 273 272 • Av: 14 382 (+6.9%) • Son Moix 23 142 (62%)

OSASUNA 2010–11

Mo	Day	Opponent		Score	Comp	Scorers	Att
Ag	29	Almeria	D	0-0	PD		14 147
	11	Real Madrid	L	0-1	PD		73 600
	18	Mallorca	L	0-2	PD		12 000
Sep	21	Sociedad	W	3-1	PD	Pandiani 38, Camunas 42, Aranda 75	18 715
	26	Espanyol	L	0-1	PD		26 820
	3	Levante	D	1-1	PD	Pandiani 72	16 000
	17	Deportivo	D	0-0	PD		12 000
Oct	24	Malaga	W	3-0	PD	Nekounam 2p, Shojaei 37, Aranda 56	14 000
	28	Deportivo	D	1-1	CRr4	Juanfran 68	11 268
	31	Racing	L	1-4	PD	Nekounam 58p	13 281
	7	Hercules	W	3-0	PD	Monreal 40, Lolo 56, Vadocz 90	14 130
Nov	10	Deportivo	L	1-2	CRr4	Lekic 62	8 000
	13	At. Madrid	L	0-3	PD		43 000
	21	Sp. Gijon	W	1-0	PD	Shojaei 54	14 570
	28	Ath. Bilbao	L	0-1	PD		35 000
	4	Barcelona	L	0-3	PD		19 602
Dec	13	Valencia	D	3-3	PD	Juanfran 40, Flano 60, Aranda 87	28 000
	19	Zaragoza	D	0-0	PD		15 000
	2	Sevilla	L	0-1	PD		36 500
	9	Getafe	D	0-0	PD		17 000
Jan	15	Villarreal	L	2-4	PD	Vadocz 47, Calleja 71	18 000
	23	Almeria	L	2-3	PD	Aranda 24, Lekic 90	8 000
	30	Real Madrid	W	1-0	PD	Camunas 62	17 131
	5	Mallorca	D	1-1	PD	Flano 8	15 403
	13	Sociedad	L	0-1	PD		28 000
Feb	20	Espanyol	W	4-0	PD	Nekounam 2 14 55p, Lolo 80, Soriano 88	18 000
	27	Levante	L	1-2	PD	Pandiani 41	11 747
	2	Deportivo	W	1-0	PD		13 437
	6	Malaga	W	1-0	PD	Sergio 90	24 000
Mar	13	Racing	W	3-1	PD	Sola 20, Nekounam 24p, Soriano 50	15 854
	20	Hercules	W	4-0	PD	Camunas 10, Nelson 36, Vadocz 61, Sola 66	17 000
	3	At. Madrid	L	2-3	PD	Sola 31, Nekounam 80p	15 686
Apr	10	Sp. Gijon	L	0-1	PD		24 000
	17	Ath. Bilbao	L	1-2	PD	Sola 51	18 239
	23	Barcelona	L	0-2	PD		73 285
	1	Valencia	W	1-0	PD	OG 59	18 575
May	7	Zaragoza	W	3-1	PD	Camunas 62, Sergio 70, Sola 81	34 500
	11	Sevilla	W	3-2	PD	Sola 2 46 87, Lekic 90	19 500
	15	Getafe	L	0-2	PD		16 500
	21	Villarreal	W	1-0	PD	Cejudo 41	19 436

9th Att: 314 425 • Av: 16 548 (-0.3%) • Reyno de Navarra 19 800 (83%)

MALLORCA LEAGUE APPEARANCES/GOALS 2010-11
Goalkeepers Dudu Aouate ISR 35 • German Lux ARG 3+1
Defenders Ayoze 19/0 • Corrales 1+1/0 • Jose Nunes POR 34/1
Kevin 18+1/0 • Pablo Cendros 29+2/0 • Ramis 33/3
Ratinho BRA 7/0 • Ruben 7+5/0
Midfield Chori Castro URU 25+8/5 • Jonathan de Guzman NED 33/5
Akihiro Ienaga JPN 3+11/2 • Joao Victor BRA 21+b/0 • Marti 33+1/0
Marti Crespi 3+2/0 • Mickael Pereira FRA 24+11/5 • Pina 1+8/0
Sergio Tejera 10+6/0
Forwards Fernando Cavenaghi ARG 7+4/2 • Emilio N'Sue 34+4/4
Sergi 1+4/0 • Victor 9+15/3 • Pierre Webo CMR 28+6/11
Coach Gregorio Manzano • Michael Laudrup DEN (2/07/10)

OSASUNA LEAGUE APPEARANCES/GOALS 2010-11
Goalkeepers Ricardo 38
Defenders Damia 22+5/0 • Josetxo 6+3/0 • Lolo 23+4/2
Miguel Flano 28+2/2 • Monreal 31/1 • Nelson BRA 25+4/1
Oier 2+1/0 • Sergio 22/2
Midfield Alvaro Cejudo 13/1 • Xavi Annunziata 0+1/0 • Calleja 4+14/1
Camunas 30+1/4 • Juanfran 18/1 • Javad Nekounam IRN 26/6
Punal 32+1/0 • Ruper 0+4/0 • Masoud Shojaei IRN 14+4/2
Soriano 23+7/2 • Timor 0+1/0 • Krisztian Vadocz 12+19/3
Forwards Aranda 15+5/4 • Coro 4+2/0 • Dejan Lekic SRB 5+22/2
Walter Pandiani URU 13+8/3 • Sola 12+4/7
Coach Jose Antonio Camacho • Jose Luis Mendilibar (14/02/11)

REAL MADRID 2010–11

Mth	Date	Opponent	Res	Score	Comp	Scorers	Att
Ag	29	Mallorca	D	0-0	PD		22 867
	11	Osasuna	W	1-0	PD	Carvalho 48	73 600
	15	Ajax	W	2-0	CLgG	OG 31, Higuain 73	69 639
	18	Sociedad	W	2-1	PD	Di Maria 51, Ronaldo 74	32 000
Sep	21	Espanyol	W	3-0	PD	Ronaldo 29p, Higuain 79, Benzema 88	70 000
	25	Levante	D	0-0	PD		18 326
	28	Auxerre	W	1-0	CLgG	Di Maria 81	19 525
	3	Deportivo	W	6-1	PD	Ronaldo 2 4 89, Ozil 24, Di Maria 34, Higuain 53, OG 60	67 000
	16	Malaga	W	4-1	PD	Higuain 2 30 65, Ronaldo 2 45 50p	30 000
Oct	19	Milan	W	2-0	CLgG	Ronaldo 13, Ozil 14	71 657
	23	Racing	W	6-1	PD	Higuain 10, Ronaldo 4 15 27 47 55p, Ozil 63	80 000
	26	Real Murcia	D	0-0	CRr4		20 674
	30	Hercules	W	3-1	PD	Di Maria 52, Ronaldo 2 82 86	28 000
	3	Milan	D	2-2	CLgG	Higuain 45, Leon 94+	76 357
	7	At. Madrid	W	2-0	PD	Carvalho 13, Ozil 19	79 500
	10	Real Murcia	W	5-1	CRr4	Granero 4, Higuain 45, Ronaldo 75, Benzema 85p, Alonso 89	75 000
Nov	14	Sp. Gijon	W	1-0	PD	Higuain 82	25 500
	20	Ath. Bilbao	W	5-1	PD	Higuain 19, Ronaldo 3 30 62 90p, Ramos 57p	79 500
	23	Ajax	W	4-0	CLgG	Benzema 36, Arbeloa 44, Ronaldo 2 70 81p	48 491
	29	Barcelona	L	0-5	PD		98 772
	4	Valencia	W	2-0	PD	Ronaldo 2 73 87	75 000
	8	Auxerre	W	4-0	CLgG	Benzema 3 12 72 88, Ronaldo 49	54 917
Dec	12	Zaragoza	W	3-1	PD	Ozil 15, Ronaldo 44, Di Maria 47	35 000
	19	Sevilla	W	1-0	PD	Di Maria 77	65 000
	22	Levante	W	8-0	CRr5	Benzema 3 6 32 69, Ozil 10, Ronaldo 3 45 72 74, Leon 89	60 000
	3	Getafe	W	3-2	PD	Ronaldo 2 11p 57, Ozil 19	11 000
	6	Levante	L	0-2	CRr5		12 387
	9	Villarreal	W	4-2	PD	Ronaldo 3 9 45 79, Kaka 82	68 000
	13	At. Madrid	W	3-1	CRqf	Ramos 14, Ronaldo 61, Ozil 90	77 000
Jan	16	Almeria	D	1-1	PD	Granero 77	13 893
	20	At. Madrid	W	1-0	CRqf	Ronaldo 23	53 000
	23	Mallorca	W	1-0	PD	Benzema 61	74 000
	26	Sevilla	W	1-0	CRsf	Benzema 17	40 000
	30	Osasuna	L	0-1	PD		17 131
	2	Sevilla	W	2-0	CRsf	Ozil 82, Adebayor 90	75 000
	6	Sociedad	W	4-1	PD	Kaka 8, Ronaldo 2 21 42, Adebayor 89	74 000
Feb	13	Espanyol	W	1-0	PD	Marcelo 24	40 500
	19	Levante	W	2-0	PD	Benzema 6, Carvalho 41	65 000
	22	Lyon	D	1-1	CLr2	Benzema 65	40 299
	26	Deportivo	D	0-0	PD		34 600
	3	Malaga	W	7-0	PD	Benzema 2 27 62, Di Maria 36, Marcelo 45, Ronaldo 3 51 68p 77	56 000
	6	Racing	W	3-1	PD	Adebayor 24, Benzema 2 27 75	18 444
Mar	12	Hercules	W	2-0	PD	Benzema 2 24 56	71 000
	16	Lyon	W	3-0	CLr2	Marcelo 37, Benzema 66, Di Maria 76	70 034
	19	At. Madrid	W	2-1	PD	Benzema 11, Ozil 33	53 000
	2	Sp. Gijon	L	0-1	PD		77 000
	5	Tottenham	W	4-0	CLqf	Adebayor 2 4 57, Di Maria 72, Ronaldo 87	71 657
	8	Ath. Bilbao	W	3-0	PD	Kaka 2 13p 54p, Ronaldo 70	38 000
	13	Tottenham	W	1-0	CLqf	Ronaldo 50	34 311
Apr	16	Barcelona	D	1-1	PD	Ronaldo 82p	79 500
	20	Barcelona	W	1-0	CRf	Ronaldo 103	55 000
	23	Valencia	W	6-3	PD	Benzema 23, Higuain 3 31 42 53, Kaka 2 39 62	47 500
	27	Barcelona	L	0-2	CLsf		71 657
	30	Zaragoza	L	2-3	PD	Ramos 62, Benzema 85	67 000
	3	Barcelona	D	1-1	CLsf	Marcelo 64	95 701
	7	Sevilla	W	6-2	PD	Ramos 21, Ronaldo 4 31 65 70 75, Kaka 42	36 000
May	10	Getafe	W	4-0	PD	Ronaldo 3 24 58 90p, Benzema 77	55 000
	15	Villarreal	W	3-1	PD	Marcelo 17, Ronaldo 2 22 90	22 000
	21	Almeria	W	8-1	PD	Ronaldo 2 4 77, Adebayor 3 31 52 73, Benzema 2 48 63, Joselu 87	50 000

2nd — Att: 1 326 100 • Av: 69 794 (-6.7%) • Bernabéu 80 354 (86%)

REAL SOCIEDAD 2010–11

Mth	Date	Opponent	Res	Score	Comp	Scorers	Att
Ag	29	Villarreal	W	1-0	PD	Prieto 57	25 000
	13	Almeria	D	2-2	PD	Tamudo 8, Sutil 33	11 000
Sep	18	RealMadrid	L	1-2	PD	Tamudo 62	32 000
	21	Osasuna	L	1-3	PD	Tamudo 16	18 715
	26	Mallorca	L	0-2	PD		11 000
	2	Espanyol	W	1-0	PD	OG 85	25 000
Oct	17	Levante	L	1-2	PD	Sarpong 78	11 200
	25	Deportivo	W	3-0	PD	Llorente 17, Griezmann 70, Agirretxe 86	23 040
	28	Almeria	L	2-3	CRr4	Sarpong 7, Elustondo 31	15 377
	31	Malaga	W	2-1	PD	Griezmann 43, Llorente 55	18 000
	6	Racing	W	1-0	PD	Llorente 7	24 665
	10	Almeria	L	1-2	CRr4	Agirretxe 51	
Nov	14	Hercules	L	1-2	PD	Griezmann 16	18 000
	21	At. Madrid	L	2-4	PD	Llorente 12, Rivas 86	24 000
	28	Sp. Gijon	W	3-1	PD	Prieto 11, Zurutuza 45, Aranburu 45	19 000
	5	Ath. Bilbao	W	2-0	PD	Prieto 26p, OG 49	30 000
Dec	12	Barcelona	L	0-5	PD		74 931
	18	Valencia	L	1-2	PD	Prieto 23p	22 000
	3	Zaragoza	L	1-2	PD	Prieto 33	20 000
	8	Sevilla	L	2-3	PD	Rivas 23, Llorente 44	17 000
Jan	15	Getafe	W	4-0	PD	Prieto 10p, Griezmann 33, Aranburu 2 88 90	10 000
	23	Villarreal	L	1-2	PD	Aranburu 30	15 000
	29	Almeria	W	2-0	PD	Agirretxe 45, Tamudo 78	23 500
	6	RealMadrid	L	1-4	PD	OG 72	74 000
Feb	13	Osasuna	L	1-0	PD	Tamudo 74	28 000
	20	Mallorca	L	1-0	PD	Tamudo 56	20 000
	26	Espanyol	L	1-4	PD	Estrada 43	26 400
	2	Levante	D	1-1	PD	Zurutuza 53	20 000
Mar	7	Deportivo	L	1-2	PD	Agirretxe 65	14 000
	13	Malaga	L	0-2	PD		24 000
	20	Racing	L	1-2	PD	Griezmann 72	16 681
	3	Hercules	L	1-3	PD	Ifran 90	24 000
	10	At. Madrid	L	0-3	PD		50 000
Apr	17	Sp. Gijon	W	2-1	PD	Griezmann 2 32 79	26 000
	23	Ath. Bilbao	L	1-2	PD	OG 31	38 000
	30	Barcelona	W	2-1	PD	Ifran 70, Prieto 82p	30 000
	7	Valencia	L	0-3	PD		30 000
May	11	Zaragoza	W	2-1	PD	Tamudo 24, Aranburu 88	26 000
	15	Sevilla	L	1-3	PD	Agirretxe 73	40 000
	21	Getafe	D	1-1	PD	Sutil 65	32 000

15th — Att: 476 205 • Av: 25 063 (+26.6%) • Anoeta 32 076 (78%)

SOCIEDAD LEAGUE APPEARANCES/GOALS 2010-11
Goalkeepers Claudio Bravo CHI 38
Defenders Ansotegi 32/1 • Carlos Martinez 25/0
Alberto de la Bella 28+2/0 • Vadim Demidov NOR 12+1/0
Labaka 9+5/0 • Mikel Gonzalez 30+2/0
Midfield Aranburu 27+5/5 • Dani Estrada 18+1/1 • Elustondo 13+5/0
Asier Illarramendi 2+1/0 • Markel Bergara 9+10/0 • Xabi Prieto 36+1/7
Rivas 31+1/2 • Jeffrey Sarpong NED 1+15/1 • Sutil 4+13/2
Zurutuza 30+6/2
Forwards Agirretxe 1+10/3 • Antoine Griezmann FRA 34+3/7 • Diego
Ifran URU 3+7/2 • Llorente 15+3/5 • Tamudo 20+11/7 • Viguera 0+5/0
Coach Martin Lasarte

REAL LEAGUE APPEARANCES/GOALS 2010-11
Goalkeepers Adan 2+1 • Iker Casillas 35 • Jerzy Dudek POL 1
Jesus 0+1 • Mejias 0+1
Defenders Alvaro Arbeloa 20+6/0 • Ezequiel Garay ARG 4+1/0
Marcelo BRA 31+1/3 • Nacho 2/0 • Pepe POR 25+1/0 • Raul
Albiol 13+7/0 • Ricardo Carvalho POR 31+2/3 • Sergio Ramos 30+1/3
Midfield Alex 0+1/0 • Canales 3+7/0 • Angel Di Maria ARG 29+6/6
Lassana Diarra FRA 19+7/0 • Mahamadou Diarra MLI 0+3/0 • Fernando
Gago ARG 1+3/0 • Esteban Granero 8+11/1 • Juan Carlos 0+1/0
Kaka BRA 11+3/7 • Sami Khedira GER 20+5/0 • Mesut Ozil GER 30+6/6
Pedro Leon 0+6/0 • Xabi Alonso 29+5/0
Forwards Emmanuel Adebayor TOG 6+8/5
Karim Benzema FRA 20+13/15 • Cristiano Ronaldo POR 32+2/41
Gonzalo Higuain ARG 16+1/10 • Joselu 0+1/1 • Morata 0+1/0
Coach Manuel Pellegrini • Jose Mourinho POR (28/05/10)

RACING SANTANDER 2010–11

Month	Date	Opponent	Res	Score	Comp	Scorers	Att
Aug	29	Barcelona	L	0-3	PD		19 095
	11	Valencia	L	0-1	PD		45 000
Sep	19	Zaragoza	W	2-0	PD	Henrique 76, Nahuelpan 90	13 475
	23	Sevilla	D	1-1	PD	Pinillos 54	30 000
	26	Getafe	L	0-1	PD		13 077
	3	Villarreal	L	0-2	PD		19 000
	17	Almeria	W	1-0	PD	Munitis 33	14 005
Oct	23	Real Madrid	L	1-6	PD	Diop 73	80 000
	27	Córdoba	L	0-2	CRr4		5 000
	31	Osasuna	W	4-1	PD	Bakircioglu 28, Rosenberg 2 35 62, Torrejon 85	13 281
	6	Sociedad	L	0-1	PD		24 665
Nov	9	Córdoba	W	3-1	CRr4	Bolado 25, Bakircioglu 72, Bedia 102	6 293
	14	Espanyol	D	0-0	PD		13 105
	21	Levante	L	1-3	PD	Lacen 88	10 421
	28	Deportivo	W	1-0	PD	Rosenberg 61	12 086
Dec	5	Malaga	L	1-4	PD	Rosenberg 45	22 500
	12	Mallorca	W	1-0	PD	Serrano 90	12 350
	20	Hercules	D	0-0	PD		17 000
	3	At. Madrid	D	0-0	PD		35 000
Jan	9	Sp. Gijon	D	1-1	PD	OG 30	19 000
	15	Ath. Bilbao	L	1-2	PD	Bolado 74	36 000
	22	Barcelona	L	0-3	PD		70 072
	31	Valencia	D	1-1	PD	Nahuelpan 33	16 308
	5	Zaragoza	L	0-1	PD	Christian 14	22 000
Feb	12	Sevilla	W	3-2	PD	Christian 12, OG 19, Arana 90	14 054
	20	Getafe	W	1-0	PD	Pinillos 88p	8 000
	27	Villarreal	D	2-2	PD	Nahuelpan 3, Dos Santos 68	16 385
	3	Almeria	D	1-1	PD	Colsa 37	15 000
Mar	6	Real Madrid	L	1-3	PD	Bakircioglu 70	18 444
	13	Osasuna	L	1-3	PD	Rosenberg 57	15 854
	20	Sociedad	W	2-1	PD	Bakircioglu 43, Dos Santos 77	16 681
	3	Espanyol	W	2-1	PD	Colsa 50, Dos Santos 75	24 427
Apr	10	Levante	D	1-1	PD	OG 32	15 000
	17	Deportivo	L	0-2	PD		31 000
	24	Malaga	L	1-2	PD	Rosenberg 73	14 009
	1	Mallorca	W	2-0	PD	Rosenberg 13, Bakircioglu 43	15 185
	7	Hercules	W	3-2	PD	Dos Santos 2 14 41, Henrique 45	20 000
May	10	At. Madrid	W	2-1	PD	Bakircioglu 38, Rosenberg 48	16 000
	15	Sp. Gijon	L	1-2	PD	Fernandez 32	26 000
	21	Ath. Bilbao	L	1-2	PD	Bakircioglu 87	22 000

12th | Att: 298 190 • Av: 15 694 (-4.1%) • El Sardinero 22 271 (70%)

RACING LEAGUE APPEARANCES/GOALS 2010-11

Goalkeepers Mario Fernandez 1+3/1 • Tono 37
Defenders Christian 13+2/2 • Cisma 27+5/0 • Alvaro Gonzalez 3+1/0 • Henrique BRA 35/2 • Osmar Barba 2+2/0 • Pinillos 19+1/2 • Waldo Ponce CHI 22/0 • Torrejon 36/1
Midfield Edu Bedia 0+6/0 • Adrian Gonzalez 16+6/0 • Arana 5+9/1 • Colsa 30+1/2 • Papakouli Diop SEN 13+6/1 • Francis 20+4/0 • Julian Luque 1+6/0 • Medhi Lacen ALG 24+9/1 • Oscar Serrano 0+4/1 • Ramon Arcas 1/0 • Tato 1+1/0 • Alexandros Tziolis GRE 8+2/0
Forwards Kennedy Bakircioglu SWE 30+2/6 • Ivan Bolado 7+12/1 • Giovani Dos Santos MEX 9+7/5 • Munitis 33+3/1 • Ariel Nahuelpan ARG 15+15/3 • Markus Rosenberg SWE 29+4/8 • Mohammed Tchite BEL 1/0
Coach Miguel Angel Portugal • Marcelino (9/02/11)

SEVILLA 2010–11

Month	Date	Opponent	Res	Score	Comp	Scorers	Att
Aug	14	Barcelona	W	3-1	SC	Luis Fabiano 62, Kanoute 2 73 83	38 000
	18	Braga	L	0-1	CLpo		16 646
	21	Barcelona	L	0-4	SC		67 414
	24	Braga	L	3-4	CLpo	Luis Fabiano 60, Navas 84, Kanoute 91+	31 350
	28	Levante	W	4-1	PD	Konko 2 12 62, Negredo 28p, Renato 88	10 241
Sep	12	Deportivo	D	0-0	PD		35 000
	16	PSG	L	0-1	ELgl		24 960
	19	Malaga	W	2-1	PD	Alfaro 20, Caceres 45	25 000
	23	Racing	D	1-1	PD	Negredo 13p	30 000
	26	Hercules	L	0-2	PD		17 000
	30	Dortmund	W	1-0	ELgl	Cigarini 45	49 100
	3	At. Madrid	W	3-1	PD	Negredo 29, Perotti 35, Kanoute 35	40 000
	17	Sp. Gijon	L	0-2	PD		20 000
	21	KarpatyLviv	W	1-0	ELgl	Kanoute 34	27 925
Oct	24	Ath. Bilbao	W	4-3	PD	Luis Fabiano 2 35 62, Kanoute 2 45p 80p	40 000
	27	Real Unión	W	4-0	CRr4	Negredo 2 45 68, Alfaro 89, Jose Carlos 90	4 500
	30	Barcelona	L	0-5	PD		81 020
Nov	4	KarpatyLviv	W	4-0	ELgl	Alfaro 2 9 42, Cigarini 31, Negredo 51	21 394
	8	Valencia	W	2-0	PD	Negredo 54, Alfaro 77	30 000
	10	Real Unión	W	6-1	CRr4	Alfaro 15, Rodri 27, Bernardo 41, Cigarini 60, J. Carlos 73, Acosta 88	10 000
	14	Zaragoza	W	2-1	PD	Luis Fabiano 29, Negredo 90	28 000
	21	Mallorca	L	1-2	PD	Luis Fabiano 88	40 000
	27	Getafe	L	1-3	PD	Kanoute 30	24 000
	2	PSG	L	2-4	ELgl	Kanoute 2 32 36	18 783
	5	Villarreal	L	0-1	PD		20 000
Dec	11	Almeria	L	1-3	PD	Kanoute 83	35 000
	15	Dortmund	D	2-2	ELgl	Romaric 31, Kanoute 34	27 062
	19	Real Madrid	L	0-1	PD		65 000
	22	Malaga	W	5-3	CRr5	Alfaro 11, Negredo 32, Romaric 2 66 80, Capel 82	18 000
	2	Osasuna	W	1-0	PD	Kanoute 36	36 500
	5	Malaga	W	3-0	CRr5	Romaric 51, Perotti 65, Luis Fabiano 90	12 000
Jan	8	Sociedad	W	3-2	PD	Kanoute 2 25 65, Luis Fabiano 63	17 000
	12	Villarreal	D	3-3	CRqf	Negredo 2 39 60, Alexis 88	18 000
	15	Espanyol	L	1-2	PD	Negredo 90	35 000
	18	Villarreal	W	3-0	CRqf	Renato 7, Kanoute 47, Alexis 50	29 000
	22	Levante	W	4-1	PD	Luis Fabiano 3 28 43p 68, Escude 39	35 000
	26	Real Madrid	L	0-1	CRsf		40 000
	29	Deportivo	D	3-3	PD	Negredo 2 63 79, Escude 74	14 000
	2	Real Madrid	L	0-2	CRsf		75 000
Feb	6	Malaga	D	0-0	PD		36 000
	12	Racing	L	2-3	PD	Fazio 40, Luis Fabiano 83p	14 054
	1	Porto	L	1-2	ELr2	Kanoute 65	21 555
	20	Hercules	W	1-0	PD	Rakitic 21	38 000
	23	Porto	W	1-0	ELr2	Luis Fabiano 71	35 609
	26	At. Madrid	D	2-2	PD	Negredo 41, Rakitic 66	48 000
Mar	1	Sp. Gijon	W	3-0	PD	Luis Fabiano 28p, Perotti 35, Negredo 65	25 000
	6	Ath. Bilbao	L	0-2	PD		37 000
	13	Barcelona	D	1-1	PD	Navas 45	45 000
	20	Valencia	W	1-0	PD	Rakitic 70	40 000
	3	Zaragoza	W	3-1	PD	Perotti 43, Kanoute 56p, Negredo 90p	30 000
Apr	9	Mallorca	D	2-2	PD	Negredo 31p, Rakitic 68	16 170
	16	Getafe	L	0-1	PD		35 000
	24	Villarreal	W	3-2	PD	Rakitic 9, Negredo 14, Romaric 62	35 000
	1	Almeria	W	1-0	PD	Renato 58	8 427
	7	Real Madrid	L	2-6	PD	Negredo 2 61 84	36 000
May	11	Osasuna	L	2-3	PD	Negredo 2 26 28	19 500
	15	Sociedad	W	3-1	PD	Kanoute 2 54 60, Negredo 86	40 000
	21	Espanyol	W	3-2	PD	Negredo 2 62, Kanoute 45	26 000

5th | Att: 665 500 • Av: 35 026 (-10.0%) • Sánchez Pizjuán 45 500 (76%)

SEVILLA LEAGUE APPEARANCES/GOALS 2010-11

Goalkeepers Javi Varas 19+2 • Andres Palop 19
Defenders Alexis 21/0 • Bernardo COL 1/0 • Martin Caceres URU 24+1/1 • Mouhamadou Dabo FRA 21+3/0 • Ivica Dragutinovic SRB 0+2/0 • Julien Escude FRA 27+1/2 • Federico Fazio ARG 17+2/1 • Antonin Luna 2/0 • Fernando Navarro 30/0 • Sergio Sanchez 6+1/0
Midfield Lautaro Acosta ARG 2+8/0 • Alejandro Alfaro 8+12/2 • Diego Capel 17+10/0 • Jose Carlos 2+4/0 • Luca Cigarini ITA 5+1/0 • Tiberio Guarente ITA 3+4/0 • Abdoulay Konko FRA 4+2/0 • Jesus Navas 15/1 • Gary Medel CHI 15/0 • Diego Perotti ARG 27+4/3 • Ivan Rakitic CRO 13/5 • Renato BRA 12+12/2 • Romaric CIV 19+7/1 • Didier Zokora CIV 17+6/0
Forwards Alvaro Negredo 29+9/20 • Frederic Kanoute MLI 19+9/12 • Arouna Kone CIV 0+1/0 • Luis Alberto 1+1/0 • Luis Fabiano BRA 16+5/10 • Rodri 2+3/0
Coach Antonio Alvarez • Gregorio Manzano (26/09/10)

SPORTING GIJON 2010–11

Mo	Date	Opponent	Res	Score	Comp	Scorers	Att
Ag	30	At. Madrid	L	0-4	PD		50 000
	12	Mallorca	W	2-0	PD	Botia 47, Diego Castro 86p	20 000
Sep	18	Ath. Bilbao	D	2-2	PD	De las Cuevas 13, Sangoy 23	20 000
	22	Barcelona	L	0-1	PD		66 947
	25	Valencia	L	0-2	PD		17 000
	2	Zaragoza	D	2-2	PD	OG 33, Diego Castro 49p	14 000
	17	Sevilla	W	2-0	PD	Sangoy 6, Diego Castro 51	20 000
Oct	24	Getafe	L	0-3	PD		11 000
	27	Mallorca	L	1-3	CRr4	Barral 60	9 774
	31	Villarreal	D	1-1	PD	Diego Castro 69p	20 000
	7	Almeria	D	1-1	PD	Novo 73	9 693
	11	Mallorca	D	2-2	CRr4	Bilic 25, Muniz 63	15 000
Nov	14	Real Madrid	L	0-1	PD		25 500
	21	Osasuna	L	0-1	PD		14 570
	28	Sociedad	L	1-3	PD	Arnolin 3	19 000
	5	Espanyol	L	0-1	PD		26 000
Dec	12	Levante	D	1-1	PD	Eguren 79	18 000
	18	Deportivo	D	1-1	PD	Diego Castro 89	20 000
	2	Malaga	L	1-2	PD	Diego Castro 42p	18 000
	9	Racing	D	1-1	PD	Diego Castro 90	19 000
Jan	15	Hercules	W	2-0	PD	Barral 1, Cases 31	17 000
	23	At. Madrid	W	1-0	PD	Barral 51	22 000
	29	Mallorca	W	4-0	PD	Andre Castro 2 3 66, OG 60, Novo 87	11 336
	5	Ath. Bilbao	L	0-3	PD		39 000
Feb	12	Barcelona	D	1-1	PD	Barral 16	28 000
	19	Valencia	D	0-0	PD		40 000
	26	Zaragoza	D	0-0	PD		23 500
	1	Sevilla	L	0-3	PD		25 000
Mar	6	Getafe	W	2-0	PD	De las Cuevas 32, Andre Castro 41	23 000
	13	Villarreal	D	1-1	PD	Andre Castro 90p	20 000
	20	Almeria	W	1-0	PD	De las Cuevas 13	25 700
	2	Real Madrid	W	1-0	PD	De las Cuevas 79	77 000
Apr	10	Osasuna	W	1-0	PD	Barral 66	24 000
	17	Sociedad	L	1-2	PD	De las Cuevas 69	26 000
	24	Espanyol	W	1-0	PD	Novo 71	21 000
	1	Levante	D	0-0	PD		16 000
	7	Deportivo	D	2-2	PD	Ayoze 35p, Barral 90p	25 000
May	10	Malaga	L	0-2	PD		30 000
	15	Racing	W	2-1	PD	De las Cuevas 44, Novo 52	26 000
	21	Hercules	D	0-0	PD		18 000

10th Att: 412 700 • Av: 21 721 (+1.2%) • El Molinón 29 800 (72%)

VALENCIA 2010–11

Mo	Date	Opponent	Res	Score	Comp	Scorers	Att
Ag	28	Malaga	W	3-1	PD	Aduriz 10, Joaquin 2 70 74	30 000
	11	Racing	W	1-0	PD	Maduro 45	45 000
Sep	14	Bursaspor	W	4-0	CLgC	Tino Costa 16, Aduriz 41, Hernandez 68, Soldado 76	25 000
	19	Hercules	W	2-1	PD	Mata 2, Hernandez 23	28 000
	22	At. Madrid	D	1-1	PD	Aduriz 83	50 000
	25	Sp. Gijon	W	2-0	PD	Topal 7, Soldado 10	17 000
	29	Man Utd	L	0-1	CLgC		34 946
	2	Ath. Bilbao	W	2-1	PD	Aduriz 11, Vicente 90	45 000
	16	Barcelona	L	1-2	PD	Hernandez 38	87 995
Oct	20	Rangers	D	1-1	CLgC	Edu 46	45 153
	23	Mallorca	L	1-2	PD	Soldado 36p	45 000
	27	Logroñés	W	3-0	CRr4	Aduriz 2 55 60, Vicente 79	8 000
	30	Zaragoza	D	1-1	PD	OG 43	38 000
	2	Rangers	W	3-0	CLgC	Soldado 2 33 71, Tino Costa 90	26 821
	8	Sevilla	L	0-2	PD		30 000
	11	Logroñés	W	4-1	CRr4	Isco 2 24 43, Vicente 34, Feghouli 86	5 000
Nov	14	Getafe	W	2-0	PD	Tino Costa 8, Navarro 63	35 000
	20	Villarreal	D	1-1	PD	Aduriz 20	23 000
	24	Bursaspor	W	6-1	CLgC	Mata 17p, Soldado 2 21 55, Aduriz 30, Joaquin 37, Dominguez 78	31 225
	28	Almeria	W	2-1	PD	Soldado 2 26 63	35 000
	4	Real Madrid	L	0-2	PD		75 000
	8	Man Utd	D	1-1	CLgC	Hernandez 32	74 513
Dec	13	Osasuna	D	3-3	PD	Soldado 24, Stankevicius 32, Aduriz 42	28 000
	18	Sociedad	W	2-1	PD	Tino Costa 45, Aduriz 90	22 000
	21	Villarreal	D	0-0	CRr5		20 000
	2	Espanyol	W	2-1	PD	Aduriz 29, Mata 90	30 000
	6	Villarreal	L	2-4	CRr5	Banega 5, Soldado 23	20 000
	9	Levante	W	1-0	PD	Mata 83	19 000
Jan	16	Deportivo	W	2-0	PD	Mathieu 78, Hernandez 90	40 000
	22	Malaga	W	4-3	PD	Mata 17p, Soldado 53, Banega 67, Aduriz 90	35 000
	31	Racing	D	1-1	PD	Tino Costa 78	16 308
	6	Hercules	W	2-0	PD	Aduriz 43, Tino Costa 53	40 000
Feb	12	At. Madrid	W	2-1	PD	Joaquin 2 41 86	40 000
	15	Schalke	D	1-1	CLr2	Soldado 17	42 703
	19	Sp. Gijon	D	0-0	PD		40 000
	27	Ath. Bilbao	W	2-1	PD	Mata 71, Jonas 81	35 000
	2	Barcelona	L	0-1	PD		50 800
Mar	5	Mallorca	W	2-1	PD	Hernandez 2 33 56	14 000
	9	Schalke	L	1-3	CLr2	Ricardo Costa 17	53 517
	12	Zaragoza	L	0-4	PD		30 000
	20	Sevilla	L	0-1	PD		40 000
	2	Getafe	W	4-2	PD	Soldado 4 46 64 66 77	12 000
Apr	10	Villarreal	W	5-0	PD	Soldado 2 14 75, Mata 2 56 73, Banega 62	45 000
	16	Almeria	W	3-0	PD	Soldado 51, Stankevicius 67, Alba 81	10 562
	23	Real Madrid	L	3-6	PD	Soldado 60, Jonas 80, Alba 85	47 500
	1	Osasuna	L	0-1	PD		18 575
	7	Sociedad	W	3-0	PD	Soldado 2 17 37, Jonas 25	30 000
May	11	Espanyol	D	2-2	PD	Soldado 9, Mata 25	28 000
	15	Levante	D	0-0	PD		45 000
	21	Deportivo	W	2-0	PD	Aduriz 4, Soldado 90	34 600

3rd Att: 764 300 • Av: 40 226 (-2.1%) • Mestalla 55 000 (73%)

SPORTING LEAGUE APPEARANCES/GOALS 2010-11
Goalkeepers Ivan Cuellar 13 • Juan Pablo 24+1 • Raul 1
Defenders Gregory Arnolin FRA 23/1 • Alberto Botia 27+1/1
Canella 15+2/0 • Guiller 0+1/0 • Javi Poves 0+1/0 • Jorge 2+3/0
Jose Angel 22+3/0 • Sastre 7+1/0
Midfield Sergio Alvarez 3+4/0 • Ayoze 6+7/1 • Carmelo 9+9/0
Andre Castro POR 11+5/4 • Miguel De las Cuevas 30+7/6
Diego Castro 26+2/7 • Sebastian Eguren URU 28+3/1
Ivan Hernandez 24+1/0 • Lora 35+1/0 • Marcos Landeira 0+2/0
Sergio Matabuena 3+1/0 • Nacho Cases 16+1/1
Cristian Portilla 0+1/0 • Rivera 31/0
Forwards Mate Bilic CRO 3+15/0 • David Barral 24+10/5
Juan Muniz 0+1/0 • Luis Moran 6+9/0 • Nacho Novo 15+15/4
Gaston Sangoy ARG 14+5/2
Coach Manolo Preciado

VALENCIA LEAGUE APPEARANCES/GOALS 2010-11
Goalkeepers Cesar Sanchez 15+1 • Guaita 19+2 • Moya 4
Defenders Bruno 17+2/0 • David Navarro 16+1/1
Angel Dealbert 10+4/0 • Jordi Alba 14+13/2
Hedwiges Maduro NED 17+1/1 • Jeremy Mathieu FRA 27+2/1
Luis Miguel POR 20+4/0 • Ricardo Costa POR 29/0
Marius Stankevicius LTU 19+2/2
Midfield David Albelda 12+4/0 • Ever Banega ARG 19+9/2
Tino Costa ARG 17+7/4 • Sofiane Feghouli 0+3/0 • Manuel
Fernandes POR 5+2/0 • Isco 0+4/0 • Joaquin 24+5/4 • Pablo
Hernandez 20+7/5 • Mehmet Topal TUR 21+2/1 • Vicente 5+9/1
Forwards Artiz Aduriz 20+9/10 • Alejandro Dominguez ARG 3+6/0
Jonas BRA 8+5/3 • Juan Manuel Mata 31+2/8
Roberto Soldado 26+8/18
Coach Unai Emery

VILLARREAL 2010–11

	Date	Opponent		Score	Comp	Scorers	Att
Aug	19	Mogilev	W	5-0	ELpo	Marchena 10, Cazorla 17, Borja 35, Cani 44, Nilmar 74	7 913
	26	Mogilev	W	2-1	ELpo	Nilmar 45, Ruben 90	6 542
	29	Sociedad	L	0-1	PD		25 000
Sep	12	Espanyol	W	4-0	PD	Rossi 2 23 55p, Borja 31, Nilmar 77	16 000
	16	D Zagreb	L	0-2	ELgD		17 021
	19	Levante	W	2-1	PD	Nilmar 2 16 42	11 500
	23	Deportivo	W	1-0	PD	Nilmar 34	16 000
	27	Malaga	W	3-2	PD	Cazorla 2 20 33, Rossi 24	25 000
	30	ClubBrugge	W	2-1	ELgD	Rossi 41, Rodriguez 56	14 900
Oct	3	Racing	W	2-0	PD	Nilmar 9, Rossi 14	19 000
	18	Hercules	D	2-2	PD	Capdevilla 29, Borja 63	20 000
	21	PAOK	W	1-0	ELgD	Ruben 38	14 760
	24	At. Madrid	W	2-0	PD	Cani 9, Rossi 52	21 000
	27	Ejido	D	1-1	CRr4	Altidore 44	3 500
	31	Sp. Gijon	D	1-1	PD	Rossi 90p	20 000
	4	PAOK	L	0-1	ELgD		22 779
Nov	7	Ath. Bilbao	W	4-1	PD	Nilmar 39, Cazorla 45, Rossi 84, Montero 90	22 000
	10	Ejido	W	2-0	CRr4	Montero 17, Altidore 90	9 000
	13	Barcelona	L	1-3	PD	Nilmar 26	80 766
	20	Valencia	D	1-1	PD	Rossi 73	23 000
	27	Zaragoza	W	3-0	PD	Senna 9, Cazorla 18, Nilmar 65	15 000
	2	D Zagreb	W	3-0	ELgD	Rossi 2 25p 80, Ruben 62	11 911
	5	Sevilla	W	1-0	PD	Nilmar 30	20 000
Dec	11	Getafe	L	0-1	PD		10 000
	15	ClubBrugge	W	2-1	ELgD	Rossi 2 30 34p	16 265
	18	Mallorca	W	3-1	PD	Cazorla 11, Rossi 35p, Nilmar 51	15 000
	21	Valencia	D	0-0	CRr5		20 000
	3	Almeria	W	2-0	PD	Catala 22, Borja 58	18 000
	6	Valencia	W	4-2	CRr5	Cazorla 47, Rossi 2 49p 90, Ruben 63	20 000
	9	RealMadrid	L	2-4	PD	Cani 7, Ruben 18	68 000
	12	Sevilla	D	3-3	CRqf	Cani 24, Rossi 29, Ruben 55	18 000
Jan	15	Osasuna	W	4-2	PD	Ruben 22, Cani 50, Capdevilla 65, Rodriguez 84	18 000
	18	Sevilla	L	0-3	CRqf		29 000
	23	Sociedad	W	2-1	PD	Rossi 2 41 47	15 000
	30	Espanyol	W	1-0	PD	Rossi 44	24 244
	5	Levante	L	0-1	PD		20 000
	13	Deportivo	L	0-1	PD		14 000
Feb	17	Napoli	D	0-0	ELr2		47 529
	20	Malaga	D	1-1	PD	Ruben 36	20 000
	24	Napoli	W	2-1	ELr2	Nilmar 42, Rossi 45	21 061
	27	Racing	D	2-2	PD	Ruben 66, Nilmar 90	16 385
	2	Hercules	W	1-0	PD	Rossi 22	15 000
	5	At. Madrid	L	1-3	PD	Rossi 34	30 000
Mar	10	Leverkusen	W	3-2	ELr3	Rossi 42, Nilmar 2 70 94+	20 126
	13	Sp. Gijon	D	1-1	PD	Rossi 29	20 000
	17	Leverkusen	W	2-1	ELr3	Cazorla 33, Rossi 61	19 779
	20	Ath. Bilbao	W	1-0	PD	Ruben 58	37 000
	2	Barcelona	L	0-1	PD		23 000
	7	Twente	W	5-1	ELqf	Marchena 23, Borja 43, Nilmar 2 45 81, Rossi 55	19 094
Apr	10	Valencia	L	0-5	PD		45 000
	14	Twente	W	3-1	ELqf	Rossi 60p, Ruben 84p, Cani 90	23 500
	18	Zaragoza	W	1-0	PD	Rossi 71p	16 000
	24	Sevilla	L	2-3	PD	Marchena 57, Rossi 73	35 000
	28	Porto	L	1-5	ELsf	Cani 45	44 719
	1	Getafe	W	2-1	PD	Cani 61, Rossi 74	16 000
	5	Porto	W	3-2	ELsf	Cani 17, Capdevilla 75, Rossi 80p	18 523
May	8	Mallorca	D	0-0	PD		13 000
	11	Almeria	D	0-0	PD		5 500
	15	RealMadrid	L	1-3	PD	Cani 51	22 000
	21	Osasuna	L	0-1	PD		19 436

4th | Att: 355 000 • Av: 18 684 (+6.3%) • El Madrigal 25 000 (74%)

REAL ZARAGOZA 2010–11

	Date	Opponent		Score	Comp	Scorers	Att
Aug	29	Deportivo	D	0-0	PD		15 000
	12	Malaga	L	3-5	PD	Edmilson 41, Perez 68, Herrera 82	20 000
Sep	19	Racing	L	0-2	PD		13 475
	22	Hercules	D	0-0	PD		18 000
	26	At. Madrid	L	0-1	PD		35 000
	2	Sp. Gijon	D	2-2	PD	S-Pongolle 2 56 61	14 000
	17	Ath. Bilbao	L	1-2	PD	Braulio 90	30 000
Oct	23	Barcelona	L	0-2	PD		30 000
	27	Real Betis	W	1-0	CRr4	Gabi 61p	15 000
	30	Valencia	D	1-1	PD	Lanzaro 3	38 000
	7	Mallorca	W	3-2	PD	Lafita 57, Bertolo 84, Gabi 90p	21 000
	10	Real Betis	L	1-2	CRr4	Jarosik 15	11 000
Nov	14	Sevilla	L	1-2	PD	Bertolo 53	28 000
	22	Getafe	D	1-1	PD	Bertolo 34	10 000
	27	Villarreal	L	0-3	PD		15 000
	5	Almeria	D	1-1	PD	Gabi 67p	16 000
Dec	12	RealMadrid	L	1-3	PD	Gabi 54p	35 000
	19	Osasuna	D	0-0	PD		15 000
	3	Sociedad	W	2-1	PD	S-Pongolle 10, Braulio 90	20 000
	9	Espanyol	L	0-4	PD		32 000
Jan	15	Levante	W	1-0	PD	Gabi 45	20 000
	23	Deportivo	W	1-0	PD	Boutahar 38	22 000
	29	Malaga	W	2-1	PD	Bertolo 40, S-Pongolle 87	25 000
	5	Racing	D	1-1	PD	Boutahar 40	22 000
Feb	13	Hercules	L	1-2	PD	Braulio 4	20 000
	19	At. Madrid	L	0-1	PD		17 000
	25	Sp. Gijon	D	0-0	PD		23 500
	2	Ath. Bilbao	W	2-1	PD	Jarosik 49, Uche 56	17 000
	5	Barcelona	L	0-1	PD		78 965
Mar	12	Valencia	W	4-0	PD	Jarosik 5, Herrera 40, Gabi 2 65p 75p	30 000
	19	Mallorca	L	0-1	PD		13 200
	3	Sevilla	L	1-3	PD	Jarosik 47	30 000
	11	Getafe	W	2-1	PD	Ponzio 14, Bertolo 35	25 000
Apr	18	Villarreal	L	0-1	PD		16 000
	25	Almeria	W	1-0	PD	OG 70	27 000
	30	RealMadrid	W	3-2	PD	Lafita 2 41 77, Gabi 55p	67 000
	8	Osasuna	L	1-3	PD	Lafita 15	34 500
May	11	Sociedad	L	1-2	PD	Gabi 54	26 000
	15	Espanyol	W	1-0	PD	Ponzio 54	34 000
	21	Levante	W	1-0	PD	Gabi 2 38 73	19 102

13th | Att: 445 500 • Av: 23 447 (-5.4%) • La Romareda 34 596 (67%)

ZARAGOZA LEAGUE APPEARANCES/GOALS 2010-11
Goalkeepers Leo Franco ARG 21+2 • Toni Doblas 17+1
Defenders Matteo Contini ITA 24/0 • Paulo da Silva PAR 10+3/0
Carlos Diogo URU 33/0 • Edmilson BRA 8+4/1
Maurizio Lanzaro ITA 17/1 • Ivan Obradovic SRB 19+1/0
Paredes 16+3/0 • Adam Pinter HUN 4+5/0
Midfield Ander Herrera 30+3/2 • Nicolas Bertolo ARG 25+11/5
Said Boutahar MAR 12+9/2 • Gabi 36/10 • Jiri Jarosik CZE 36/3
Jorge Lopez 12+15/0 • Lafita 22+8/4 • Guirane N'Daw SEN 3+6/0
Leonardo Ponzio ARG 30+2/2
Forwards Braulio 12+15/3 • Kevin 2+1/0 • Marco Perez COL 3+13/1
Florent Sinama-Pongolle FRA 15+9/4 • Ikechukwu Uche NGA 11+3/1
Coach Jose Aurelio Gay • Javier Aguirre MEX (17/11/10)

VILLARREAL LEAGUE APPEARANCES/GOALS 2010-11
Goalkeepers Diego Lopez 38
Defenders Angel 18/0 • Joan Capdevila 31+1/2 • Carlos Tomas 1/0
Catala 9+6/1 • Cicinho BRA 0+6/0 • Gonzalo Rodriguez ARG 20+3/1
Joan Uriol 1+5/0 • Kiko 2+2/0 • Carlos Marchena 27+1/1
Mario 20+1/0 • Mateo Musacchio ARG 27+4/0 • Mario Perez 0+1/0
Midfield Borja Valero 34+1/3 • Bruno Soriano 36+1/0 • Cani 25+9/5
Santi Cazorla 34+3/5 • Cristobal 1+1/0 • Javier Matilla 3+8/0 • Marcos
Gullon 1/0 • Marcos Senna 15+5/1 • Jefferson Montero ECU 0+9/1
Nacho Insa 0+1/0 • Mubarak Wakaso GHA 1+10/0
Forwards Jozy Altidore USA 0+3/0 • Nicki Bille Nielsen DEN 0+1/0
Marco Ruben ARG 12+18/5 • Nilmar BRA 27+4/11
Giuseppe Rossi ITA 35+1/18
Coach Juan Carlos Garrido

EST – ESTONIA

FIFA/COCA-COLA WORLD RANKING

'93	'94	'95	'96	'97	'98	'99	'00	'01	'02	'03	'04	'05	'06	'07	'08	'09	'10	'11	'12
109	119	129	102	100	90	70	67	83	60	68	81	76	106	124	119	102	82	57	

	2011															
	Jan	Feb	Mar	Apr	May	Jun	Jul	Aug	Sep	Oct	Nov	Dec		High	Low	Av
	86	87	82	74	75	79	79	86	58	59	58	57		57	137	93

For so long regarded as the weakest national team of the trio of ex-Soviet Baltic states, Estonia are beginning to make their presence felt and that was particularly true in the qualifiers for Euro 2012 where they made it to the play-offs, having finished second behind Italy in what was a tough group. Consistency remains a problem - as illustrated by the run of five consecutive defeats in the middle of 2011 - but the team pulled out the stops when it mattered to squeeze past Serbia and Slovenia after winning their final three qualifiers. That meant a play-off against the Republic of Ireland where once again Estonia were let down by their home form - a 4-0 defeat at the hands of the Irish in the first leg in Tallinn rendering the second game almost meaningless. Estonia's record cap winner may have missed out on the current success of the side, but Martin Reim continued to make waves in club football with Flora Tallinn. Having coached them to the league title in 2010, Reim then led them to the double in 2011. The season was notable for the 46 goals scored by Aleksanders Cekulajevs in 35 matches for Trans Narva as well as the failure of Levadia Tallinn to make the top three for the first time since being formed in 1999. Also, spare a thought for Ajax Lasnamae who were just eight goals shy of conceding 200 in the season.

UEFA EUROPEAN CHAMPIONSHIP RECORD

1960-1992 DNE (Played as part of the Soviet Union) 1996-2012 DNQ

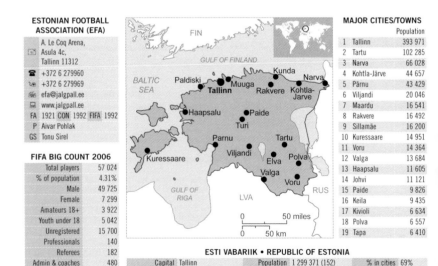

ESTONIAN FOOTBALL ASSOCIATION (EFA)

A. Le Coq Arena,
Asula 4c,
Tallinn 11312
☎ +372 6 279960
📠 +372 6 279969
✉ efa@jalgpall.ee
🖥 www.jalgpall.ee
FA 1921 CON 1992 FIFA 1992
P Aivar Pohlak
GS Tonu Sirel

FIFA BIG COUNT 2006

Total players	57 024
% of population	4.31%
Male	49 725
Female	7 299
Amateurs 18+	3 922
Youth under 18	5 042
Unregistered	15 700
Professionals	140
Referees	182
Admin & coaches	480
Number of clubs	138
Number of teams	671

MAJOR CITIES/TOWNS

		Population
1	Tallinn	393 971
2	Tartu	102 285
3	Narva	66 028
4	Kohtla-Järve	44 657
5	Pärnu	43 429
6	Viljandi	20 046
7	Maardu	16 541
8	Rakvere	16 492
9	Sillamäe	16 200
10	Kuressaare	14 951
11	Voru	14 364
12	Valga	13 684
13	Haapsalu	11 605
14	Johvi	11 121
15	Paide	9 826
16	Keila	9 435
17	Kivioli	6 634
18	Polva	6 557
19	Tapa	6 410

ESTI VABARIIK • REPUBLIC OF ESTONIA

Capital	Tallinn	Population	1 299 371 (152)	% in cities	69%
GDP per capita	$21 400 (57)	Area km²	45 228 km² (132)	GMT +/-	+2
Neighbours (km)	Latvia 343, Russia 290 • Coast 3794				

RECENT INTERNATIONAL MATCHES PLAYED BY ESTONIA

2009	Opponents	Score		Venue	Comp	Scorers	Att	Referee
11-02	Kazakhstan	L	0-2	Antalya	Fr		200	Gocek TUR
28-03	Armenia	D	2-2	Yerevan	WCq	Vassiljev 38, Zenjov 67	3 000	Wilmes LUX
1-04	Armenia	W	1-0	Tallinn	WCq	Puri 83	5 200	Zimmermann SUI
29-05	Wales	L	0-1	Llanelli	Fr		4 071	Thorisson ISL
6-06	Equatorial Guinea	W	3-0	Tallinn	Fr	Vikmae 8, Voskoboinikov 35, Zenjov 90	2 150	Malzinskas LTU
10-06	Portugal	D	0-0	Tallinn	Fr		6 350	Svendsen DEN
12-08	Brazil	L	0-1	Tallinn	Fr		8 550	Ingvarsson SWE
5-09	Turkey	L	2-4	Kayseri	WCq	Voskoboinikov 7, Vassiljev 52	28 569	Skjerven NOR
9-09	Spain	L	0-3	Merida	WCq		14 362	Oriekhov UKR
10-10	Bosnia-Herzegovina	L	0-2	Tallinn	WCq		6 450	Rizzoli ITA
14-10	Belgium	W	2-0	Tallinn	WCq	Piiroja 30, Vassiljev 67	4 680	Vollquartz DEN
14-11	Albania	D	0-0	Tallinn	Fr		2 110	Kancleris LTU
30-12	Angola	W	1-0	Vila Real	Fr	Saag 78	200	Almeida POR
2010								
3-03	Georgia	L	1-2	Tbilisi	Fr	Purje 83	40 000	Banari MDA
21-05	Finland	W	2-0	Tallinn	Fr	Oper 5, Post 55	5 650	Vad HUN
26-05	Croatia	D	0-0	Tallinn	Fr		3 000	Svendsen DEN
19-06	Latvia	D	0-0	Kaunas	BC		300	Mazeika LTU
20-06	Lithuania	L	0-2	Kaunas	BC		600	Sipailo LVA
11-08	Faroe Islands	W	2-1	Tallinn	ECq	Saag 91+, Piiroja 93+	5 470	Vucemilovic CRO
3-09	Italy	L	1-2	Tallinn	ECq	Zenjov 31	8 600	Velasco ESP
7-09	Uzbekistan	D	3-3	Tallinn	Fr	Purje 25, Vassiljev 2 62 71p	2 055	Jones WAL
8-10	Serbia	W	3-1	Belgrade	ECq	Kink 63, Vassiljev 73, OG 91+	12 000	Layushkin RUS
12-10	Slovenia	L	0-1	Tallinn	ECq		5 722	Skjerven NOR
17-11	Liechtenstein	D	1-1	Tallinn	Fr	Vassiljev 57p	1 909	Gvardis RUS
18-12	China PR	L	0-3	Zhuhai	Fr		8 500	Ko Hyung Jin KOR
22-12	Qatar	L	0-2	Doha	Fr			
2011								
25-03	Uruguay	W	2-0	Tallinn	Fr	Vassiljev 61, Zahovaiko 65	6 817	Munukka FIN
29-03	Serbia	D	1-1	Tallinn	ECq	Vassiljev 84	5 185	Nijhuis NED
3-06	Italy	L	0-3	Modena	ECq		19 434	Tudor ROU
7-06	Faroe Islands	L	0-2	Toftir	ECq		1 715	Munukka FIN
19-06	Chile	L	0-4	Santiago	Fr		20 000	Vasquez URU
23-06	Uruguay	L	0-3	Rivera	Fr		25 000	Laverni ARG
10-08	Turkey	L	0-3	Istanbul	Fr		20 000	Probert ENG
2-09	Slovenia	W	2-1	Ljubljana	ECq	Vassiljev 29p, Purje 81	15 480	Studer SUI
6-09	Northern Ireland	W	4-1	Tallinn	ECq	Vunk 28, Kink 32, Zenjov 60, Saag 93+	8 660	Stalhammar SWE
7-10	Northern Ireland	W	2-1	Belfast	ECq	Vassiljev 2 77p 84	12 604	Grafe GER
11-10	Ukraine	L	0-2	Tallinn	Fr		4 501	Malek POL
11-11	Republic of Ireland	L	0-4	Tallinn	ECpo		10 500	Kassai HUN
15-11	Republic of Ireland	D	1-1	Dublin	ECpo	Vassiljev 57	51 151	Kuipers NED

Fr = Friendly match • EC = UEFA EURO 2012 • BC = Baltic Cup • WC = FIFA World Cup • q = qualifier

ESTONIA NATIONAL TEAM HISTORICAL RECORDS

Caps
157 - Martin Reim 1992-2007 • 143 - Marko Kristal 1992-2005 • 120 - Mart Poom 1992-2009 • 118 - Andres Oper 1995- • 114 - Kristen Viikmae 1997- • 103 - Indrek Zelinski 1994-2010 • 99 - Raio Piiroja 1998- • 94 - Sergei Terehhov 1997-2007 • 86 - Marek Lemsalu 1992-2007 • 83 - Andrei Stepanov 1999- • 80 - Urmas Kirs 1991-2000 • 74 - Enar Jaager 2002- & Joel Lindpere 1999-

Goals
36 - Andres Oper 1995- • 27 - Indrek Zelinski 1994-2010 • 21 - Eduard Ellman-Eelma 1921-35 • 18 - Richard Kuremaa 1933-40 • 17 - Arnold Pihlak 1920-31 • 15 - Kristen Viikmae 1997- • 14 - Georg Siimenson 1932-39 & Martin Reim 1992-2007

Past Coaches
Ferenc Konya HUN 1924 • Ferenc Nagy HUN 1925 • Antal Mally HUN 1927 • Fritz Kerr AUT 1930 • Albert Vollrat 1932 • Bernhard Rein 1934 • Antal Mally HUN 1935 • Bernhard Rein 1936-38 • Elmar Saar 1939-40 • Uno Piir 1992-93 • Roman Ubakivi 1994-95 • Aavo Sarap 1995 • Teitur Thordarson ISL 1996-99 • Tarmo Ruutli 1999-2000 • Arno Pijpers NED 2000-04 • Jelle Goes NED 2004-07 • Viggo Jensen DEN 2007 • Tarmo Ruutli 2008-

ESTONIA 2011

MEISTRILIIGA

	Pl	W	D	L	F	A	Pts	Flora	Nomme Kalju	Trans Narva	Levadia	Sillamäe	Paide LM	Tammeka	Viljandi	Kuressaare	Ajax
Flora Tallinn †	36	26	8	2	100	24	86	—	3-3 1-0	3-0 1-1	0-1 3-0	2-2 4-0	2-1 2-1	1-0 3-2	0-0 4-0	3-0 2-1	6-0 13-1
Nomme Kalju ‡	36	24	7	5	82	23	79	0-1 3-0	—	1-1 1-0	1-1 1-1	1-2 3-0	0-0 1-2	4-0 3-1	3-0 2-1	1-1 3-0	4-0 3-0
Trans Narva ‡	36	22	7	7	107	29	73	0-2 1-1	1-3 3-2	—	1-1 0-2	1-0 2-3	3-0 3-0	4-1 4-0	5-0 5-0	4-0 4-0	7-0 14-0
Levadia Tallinn	36	21	10	5	76	25	73	1-1 1-1	1-3 0-1	2-1 1-1	—	4-1 3-2	0-1 0-0	2-3 0-2	2-1 2-0	2-1 4-0	3-0 6-0
Sillamäe Kalev	36	17	3	16	77	59	54	0-1 0-6	1-1 0-3	0-3 2-5	1-2 0-2	—	2-0 4-0	2-3 5-1	2-0 5-0	1-1 3-0	7-0 7-0
Paide Linnameeskond	36	13	6	17	40	51	45	1-2 1-4	0-3 0-5	0-1 0-1	0-0 0-3	1-0 0-0	—	2-2 2-1	2-1 2-0	4-1 1-0	0-4 2-2
Tammeka Tartu	36	11	6	19	57	75	39	0-0 1-4	2-3 0-1	1-1 1-4	0-5 0-4	1-4 2-0	2-2 1-2	—	1-1 1-3	2-1 1-0	5-0 9-0
Tulevik Viljandi	36	8	6	22	37	69	30	0-2 2-4	0-3 0-3	0-0 1-3	0-1 0-0	2-3 3-2	1-0 1-1	1-2 0-3	—	2-0 0-2	3-1 8-0
FC Kuressaare	36	7	5	24	28	68	26	0-1 0-3	0-1 0-2	0-2 0-2	1-5 0-0	0-1 1-2	1-0 2-1	4-1 0-2	0-2 3-0	—	1-1 0-0
Ajax Lasnamäe	36	0	4	32	11	192	4	0-3 0-11	0-3 0-7	0-7 0-12	1-4 0-7	1-5 0-7	1-2 0-6	0-3 0-3	0-0 0-4	2-2 3-5	—

5/03/2011 - 5/11/2011 • † Qualified for the UEFA Champions League • ‡ Qualified for the Europa Cup
Relegation play-off: Infonet 0-1 1-4 Kuressaare • Top scorers: 46 - Aleksandrs Cekulajevs LVA, Trans • 22 - Tarmo Neemelo, Kalju & Albert Prosa, Tammeka • 21 - Henri Anier, Flora • 20 - Vitali Leitan, Levadia • 17 - Maksim Gruznov, Trans • 16 - Juri Jevdokimov, Kalju & Kristen Vikmae, Kalju

ESTONIA 2011 ESILIIGA (2)

	Pl	W	D	L	F	A	Pts
Tallinna Kalev	36	21	10	5	102	39	73
Tallinna Infonet	36	19	11	6	101	47	68
Tamme Auto Kivioli	36	21	4	11	73	61	67
Levadia Tallinn-2	36	16	12	8	67	43	60
Flora Tallinn-2	36	17	7	12	70	51	58
FC Puuma	36	15	9	12	81	72	54
Lootus Kohtla-Järve	36	9	11	16	59	75	38
Vaprus Pärnu	36	8	11	17	55	63	35
TJK Legion	36	7	6	23	44	104	27
Warrior Valga	36	3	7	26	34	131	16

6/03/2011 - 6/11/2011
Relegation play-off: Tammeka Tartu-2 1-0 0-1 5-4p Pärnu
Second teams of the major clubs ineligible for promotion

MEDALS TABLE

		Overall			League			Cup	
		G	S	B	G	S	B	G	S
1	Flora Tallinn	14	10	3	9	6	3	5	4
2	Levadia Tallinn	13	4	2	7	3	2	6	1
3	TVMK Tallinn	3	5	5	1	3	5	2	2
4	Lantana Tallinn	3	4	5	2	1	5	1	3
5	Norma Tallinn	3	2		2	1		1	1
6	Tallinna Sadam	2	2	1		2	1	2	
7	Trans Narva	1	4	5		1	5	1	3
8	Levadia II Tallinn	1						1	
9	Tulevik Viljandi			3			1		2
10	EP Jõhvi			2			1		1
	Nomme Kalju			2			1		1
12	Tammeka Tartu			1					1
	Kalev Sillamäe			1			1		

EESTI KARIKAS 2010–11

Round of 16

Flora Tallinn *	1
Lootus Kohtla-Järve	0
Sillamäe Kalev-2	0
Raasiku Joker *	3
Tartu HaServ *	1
Ganvix Türi	0
Nomme United	1
Ajax Lasnamäe *	4
Sillamäe Kalev *	12
Tamme Auto Kivioli	1
Kohtla-Järve Alko	0
Hiiumaa Emmaste *	4
Tallinna Kalev *	2
Tammeka Tartu-2	1
Tammeka Tartu *	0
Trans Narva	1

Quarter-finals

Flora Tallinn *	w-o
Raasiku Joker	
Tartu HaServ *	0
Ajax Lasnamäe	4
Sillamäe Kalev	1
Hiiumaa Emmaste *	0
Tallinna Kalev	0
Trans Narva *	1

Semi-finals

Flora Tallinn *	6
Ajax Lasnamäe	0
Sillamäe Kalev *	1 16p
Trans Narva	1 17p

Final

Flora Tallinn	2
Trans Narva	0

CUP FINAL

A. Le Coq Arena, Tallinn
10-05-2011
Scorers - Markus Jurgenson 48, Alo Dupikov 78 for Flora

* Home team • ‡ Qualified for the Europa Cup

ETH – ETHIOPIA

FIFA/COCA-COLA WORLD RANKING

'93	'94	'95	'96	'97	'98	'99	'00	'01	'02	'03	'04	'05	'06	'07	'08	'09	'10	'11	'12
96	115	105	108	126	145	142	133	155	138	130	151	112	92	105	103	122	124	135	

2011												High	Low	Av
Jan	Feb	Mar	Apr	May	Jun	Jul	Aug	Sep	Oct	Nov	Dec	High	Low	Av
124	123	124	127	128	136	139	140	133	135	137	135	86	155	122

Ethiopia made it through the preliminary round of qualifying in Africa for the 2014 FIFA World Cup in Brazil after overcoming neighbours Somalia 5-0 on aggregate. It was a much needed boost for the game in the country after a run of disappointing results. The Ethiopians finished third in their 2012 CAF Africa Cup of Nations qualifying group behind Guinea and Nigeria after two wins over Madagascar and an encouraging draw at home with Nigeria saw them amass seven points. The 'Walyas' went through three coaches in the year, starting with Iffy Onoura who left after the 4-0 defeat to Nigeria in March. He was followed in the hot seat by Tom Saintfiet but the Belgian quit at the end of the Nations Cup qualifiers after just five matches. His replacement Sewnet Bishaw returned to the helm for the World Cup matches against Somalia as well as for the East and Central African Senior Challenge Cup in Tanzania. The tournament proved to be a big disappointment after draws with Sudan and Malawi and a defeat to Kenya saw the team go out after the first round. A poor start to the Premier League campaign cost defending champions Saint George dear - despite conceding just one goal in their final 18 matches. The title went instead to Ethiopian Coffee - or Bunna in Amharic - although Saint George did beat Muger Cement 3-1 in the Cup Final.

CAF AFRICA CUP OF NATIONS RECORD
1957 2 **1959** 3 **1962** 1 Winners (Hosts) **1963** 3 **1965** 6 r1 **1968** 4 SF (Hosts) **1970** 8 r1
1972-1974 DNQ **1976** 5 r1 (Hosts) **1978-1980** DNQ **1982** 8 r1 **1984** DNQ **1986** DNE **1988** Withdrew **1990** DNQ
1992 Withdrew **1994-1998** DNQ **2000** Withdrew **2002-2008** DNQ **2010** Disqualified **2012** DNQ

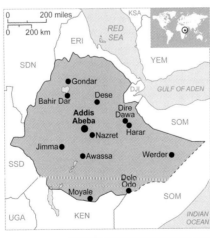

ETHIOPIAN FOOTBALL FEDERATION (EFF)

Addis Abeba Stadium,
PO Box 1080,
Addis Abeba
☎ +251 11 5156205
📠 +251 11 5515899
📧 effl@ethionet.et
🖥 www.ethiopianfootball.org
FA 1943 CON 1957 FIFA 1953
P Sahilu Gebremariam
GS Ashenafi Ejigu

FIFA BIG COUNT 2006

Total players	3 474 245
% of population	4.65%
Male	3 309 020
Female	165 225
Amateurs 18+	21 225
Youth under 18	35 000
Unregistered	520 000
Professionals	20
Referees	10 100
Admin & coaches	300 500
Number of clubs	1 000
Number of teams	3 000

MAJOR CITIES/TOWNS

		Population
1	Addis Abeba	3 230 771
2	Dire Dawa	317 010
3	Nazret	262 462
4	Gondar	223 080
5	Dese	193 705
6	Mek'ele	193 567
7	Bahir Dar	191 804
8	Jimma	182 422
9	Debre Zeyit	150 454
10	Awassa	144 029
11	Harar	137 123
12	Jijiga	112 002
13	Shashemenne	106 938
14	Debre Mark'os	97 983
15	Assela	97 048
16	Nek'emte	97 005
17	Arba Minch	83 299
18	Kembolcha	79 002
19	Gode	77 792

FEDERAL DEMOCRATIC REPUBLIC OF ETHIOPIA

Capital	Addis Abeba	Population	85 237 338 (14)	% in cities	17%
GDP per capita	$900 (214)	Area km²	1 104 300 km² (27)	GMT +/-	+3
Neighbours (km)	Djibouti 349, Eritrea 912, Kenya 861, Somalia 1600, Sudan 1606				

RECENT INTERNATIONAL MATCHES PLAYED BY ETHIOPIA

2010	Opponents		Score	Venue	Comp	Scorers	Att	Referee
5-09	Guinea	L	1-4	Addis Abeba	CNq	Umed Ukuri [29]		Mnkantjo ZIM
10-10	Madagascar	W	1-0	Antananarivo	CNq	Fikru Teferra [56]		Ngosi MWI
29-11	Uganda	L	1-2	Dar es Salaam	CCr1	Shemeles Bekele [24]		
2-12	Kenya	W	2-1	Dar es Salaam	CCr1	Shemeles Bekele 2 [25 44]		
4-12	Malawi	D	1-1	Dar es Salaam	CCr1	Umed Ukuri [70]		
7-12	Zambia	W	2-1	Dar es Salaam	CCqf	OG [17], Umed Ukuri [70]		
12-12	Uganda	L	3-4	Dar es Salaam	CC3p	Umed Ukuri 2 [2 33], Tesfaye Alebachew [67]		
2011								
27-03	Nigeria	L	0-4	Abuja	CNq			Jedidi TUN
28-05	Sudan	L	1-2	Addis Abeba	Fr	Chala Diriba		
5-06	Nigeria	D	2-2	Addis Abeba	CNq	Salhadin Said 2 [45 50]		
4-09	Guinea	L	0-1	Conakry	CNq			
4-10	Malawi	D	0-0	Addis Abeba	Fr			
8-10	Madagascar	W	4-2	Addis Abeba	CNq	Umed Ukuri [31], Aden Girma [56], Fikru Teferra [59], Shemeles Bekele [73]		
12-11	Somalia	D	0-0	Djibouti	WCq		3 000	Hassan Ourouke DJI
16-11	Somalia	W	5-0	Addis Abeba	WCq	Omod Okwury [5], Shemeles Bekele 2 [62 65], Getaneh Kebede 2 [87 92+]	22 000	Kordi TUN
28-11	Sudan	D	1-1	Dar es Salaam	CCr1	Getaneh Kebede [34]		
30-11	Kenya	L	0-2	Dar es Salaam	CCr1			
2-12	Malawi	D	1-1	Dar es Salaam	CCr1	Aden Girma [16p]		

Fr = Friendly match • CN = CAF African Cup of Nations • CC = CECAFA Cup • WC = FIFA World Cup • q = qualifier • † Not an official International

ETHIOPIA 2010–11

PREMIER LEAGUE

	Pl	W	D	L	F	A	Pts	Eth. Coffee	Saint George	Dedebit	SidamaCoffee	Defence	Awassa City	Adama City	Harar Beer	Muger Cem't	EEPCO	CBE	Dire Dawa C	Trans Ethiopia	Sebeta City	Nyala	Fincha Sugar
Ethiopian Coffee †	30	17	10	3	52	28	61		0-0	2-1	1-2	1-0	2-0	5-2	1-0	2-0	3-1	1-0	3-0	1-1	2-1	1-2	3-1
Saint George ‡	30	17	9	4	44	16	60	2-2		1-0	0-0	1-1	2-2	3-0	2-1	1-0	0-0	2-0	0-2	5-0	1-1	1-2	3-0
Dedebit	30	18	4	8	62	29	58	1-2	3-1		0-0	5-2	4-2	7-1	2-0	2-0	3-0	1-0	2-0	5-3	3-2	2-0	4-0
Sidama Coffee	30	13	14	3	32	16	53	1-1	0-0	1-0		0-1	1-1	0-0	1-1	1-0	0-0	0-0	3-2	3-0	1-0	2-0	2-0
Defence Mekelakeya	30	15	8	7	51	37	53	3-5	0-2	2-1	1-0		1-1	1-1	1-1	3-0	1-4	1-0	1-0	1-0	0-0	4-1	8-1
Awassa City	30	10	11	9	39	36	41	3-1	0-1	0-2	1-1	2-1		1-0	1-1	2-2	1-1	2-0	3-0	1-0	0-1	1-0	1-1
Adama City	30	10	9	11	30	39	39	1-2	2-1	1-0	0-2	1-1	2-0		0-0	1-1	1-0	0-1	1-1	2-0	2-1	2-3	3-1
Muger Cement	30	10	7	13	24	30	37	1-3	0-0	0-1	0-1	0-0	2-1	0-0	1-0		1-0	1-0	2-0	1-0	1-0	0-1	2-0
Harar Beer	30	7	15	8	27	26	36	0-0	0-1	2-1	1-1	2-1	0-0	1-1		1-0	1-0	0-0	2-0	3-1	2-2	1-1	2-2
EEPCO Mebrat Hail	30	9	9	12	35	35	36	0-2	0-1	2-3	1-1	1-1	2-1	0-2	1-0	2-2		2-0	5-1	1-0	2-2	2-1	3-0
Banks	30	9	9	12	33	39	36	1-1	0-4	2-2	1-2	2-4	1-1	3-1	1-1	3-2	3-2		0-1	1-1	1-0	1-0	1-0
Dire Dawa City	30	10	6	14	25	41	36	1-1	0-2	2-1	0-2	0-1	1-0	2-0	1-0	1-0	1-1	0-1		1-1	1-0	2-1	2-0
Trans Ethiopia	30	9	8	13	29	40	35	1-1	0-1	0-2	1-0	1-2	3-3	0-2	0-0	2-1	1-0	1-1	3-0		1-1	2-0	1-0
Sebeta City	30	9	7	14	30	37	34	1-1	0-2	0-3	1-2	2-3	1-4	0-1	2-0	1-1	1-0	2-1	2-0	0-1		1-0	1-0
Lideta Nyala	30	5	7	18	29	55	22	1-2	0-3	0-0	1-1	2-5	1-2	2-0	0-3	1-2	1-1	2-6	2-2	2-3	1-3		0-0
Finchaa Sugar	30	0	11	19	14	52	11	0-0	0-1	1-1	1-1	0-1	1-2	0-0	1-1	0-1	0-1	2-2	1-1	0-1	0-1	2-2	

24/10/2010 - 27/06/2011 • † Qualified for the CAF Champions League • ‡ Qualified for the CAF Confederations Cup

MENGISTU WORKU ETHIOPIA CUP 2011

Quarter-finals		Semi-finals		Final	
Saint George	1				
Adama City	0	Saint George	0 6p		
Defence Mekelakeya	1	Harar Beer	0 5p		
Harar Beer	2			Saint George	3
EEPCO Mebrat Hail	p			Muger Cement	1
Ethiopian Coffee	p	EEPCO Mebrat Hail	1	Addis Abeba, 5-11-2011	
Sidama Coffee	0	Muger Cement	2	Scorers - Shimelis Bekele 2 [36 66], Sula Matouvu [74] for St George; Kibrete Ayele [44] for Muger	
Muger Cement	1				

FIJ – FIJI

FIFA/COCA-COLA WORLD RANKING

'93	'94	'95	'96	'97	'98	'99	'00	'01	'02	'03	'04	'05	'06	'07	'08	'09	'10	'11	'12
107	120	139	157	146	124	135	141	123	140	149	135	135	150	131	106	132	152	161	

2011													High	Low	Av
Jan	Feb	Mar	Apr	May	Jun	Jul	Aug	Sep	Oct	Nov	Dec		High	Low	Av
151	151	152	156	155	156	156	141	147	149	158	161		94	170	135

Despite the 2011 season being well underway, the fate of the 2010 league title was still being hotly disputed midway through the year. Although Ba had won the title a point ahead of rivals Lautoka, the latter were declared champions in March 2011 after they were awarded a win against Rewa - having originally drawn the match 1-1 - after Rewa had fielded an ineligible player. Those two extra points were enough for Lautoka to leapfrog Ba. Ba then launched their own appeal, which proved successful, and so in July they were awarded the title again. Ba left no room for doubt in the 2011 campaign, although it did take a spectacular collapse by Labasa in the final month of the season to ensure a record 17th league success. The two met in the penultimate game of the campaign with Ba's 5-0 win proving the decisive moment of the season. The football tournament of the 2011 Pacific Games in Noumea, New Caledonia was the focus for the Fiji national team during the year but they missed out on reaching the final for only the third time since the mid-1970s. They looked to have achieved their target when they took the lead in the semi-final tie against the Solomon Islands with just 20 minutes to go but they couldn't hold on and were knocked out by a Henry Fa'arodo penalty in extra-time.

FIFA WORLD CUP RECORD
1930-1978 DNE 1982 DNQ 1986 DNE 1990-2010 DNQ

FIJI FOOTBALL
ASSOCIATION (FFA)

Taramati Street,
Vatuwaqa,
PO Box 2514, Suva
☎ +679 3300453
📠 +679 3304642
✉ bobkumar@fijifootball.com.fj
🖥 www.fijifootball.com
FA 1938 CON 1966 FIFA 1963
P Rajesh Patel
GS Mohamed Sheik Ibrahim

FIFA BIG COUNT 2006

Total players	49 688
% of population	5.48%
Male	46 338
Female	3 350
Amateurs 18+	11 188
Youth under 18	17 300
Unregistered	8 200
Professionals	0
Referees	117
Admin & coaches	2 929
Number of clubs	400
Number of teams	2 000

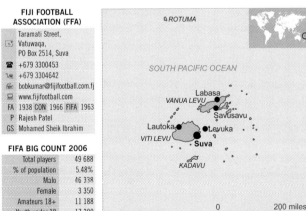

MAJOR CITIES/TOWNS

		Population
1	Nasinu	88 013
2	Suva	85 919
3	Lautoka	54 356
4	Nausori	52 451
5	Nadi	45 519
6	Labasa	28 083
7	Lami	20 461
8	Ba	16 040
9	Sigatoka	9 826
10	Savusavu	7 446
11	Vatukoula	5 616
12	Navua	5 151
13	Rakiraki	5 078
14	Levuka	4 394
15	Tavua	2 457
16	Deuba	1 881
17	Pacific Harbour	1 874
18	Seaqaqa	888
19	Navouvalu	557

MATANITU KO VITI • REPUBLIC OF THE FIJI ISLANDS

Capital	Suva	Population	944 720 (157)	% in cities	52%
GDP per capita	$3 800 (159)	Area km²	18 274 km² (156)	GMT +/-	+12
Neighbours (km)	Coast 1129		

RECENT INTERNATIONAL MATCHES PLAYED BY FIJI

2009	Opponents	Score	Venue	Comp	Scorers	Att	Referee
No international matches played in 2009							
2010							
No international matches played in 2010							
2011							
13-07	Vanuatu	W 2-0	Labasa	Fr	Bolaitoga 13, Naqeleca 90		
15-07	Vanuatu	L 1-2	Lautoka	Fr	Avinesh 46		
17-08	Samoa	W 3-0	Navua	Fr	Krishna 29, Kainihewe 33, Dau 88		
18-08	Samoa	W 5-1	Suva	Fr	Krishna 3 2 38 51, Tiwa 2 61 73		
27-08	Tahiti	W 3-0	Boulari	PGr1	Waqa 28, OG 44, Rokotakala 86		Kerr NZL
30-08	Kiribati †	W 9-0	Boulari	PGr1	Krishna 3 17p 56 86, Suwamy 47, Avinesh 52, Dunadamu 2 63 72, OG 91+, Manuca 92+		Ambassa NCL
3-09	Cook Islands	W 4-1	Boulari	PGr1	Krishna 24, Kainihewe 35, Dunadamu 57p, Suwamy 69		Ambassa NCL
5-09	Papua New Guinea	W 2-0	Boulari	PGr1	Suwamy 37, Kainihewe 45		Billon NCL
7-09	Solomon Islands	L 1-2	Lifou	PGsf	Dunadamu 69		Jacques TAH
9-09	Tahiti	L 1-2	Boulari	PG3p	Avinesh 58		Billon NCL

OC = Oceania Nations Cup • SP = South Pacific Games • WC = FIFA World Cup
q = qualifier • r1 = first round group • sf = semi-final • f = final • † Not a full international

FIJI 2011

NEW WORLD NATIONAL FOOTBALL LEAGUE

	Pl	W	D	L	F	A	Pts	Ba	Labasa	Lautoka	Navua	Rewa	Suva	Savusavu	Nadi	Tavua	Nadroga	U-20/U-23
Ba †	20	16	1	3	58	10	**49**		5-0	3-1	1-1	3-0	3-1	4-0	3-2	2-0	6-0	5-0
Labasa	20	13	3	4	32	18	**42**	2-1		2-1	2-0	1-1	1-0	0-1	1-1	0-6	4-0	2-1
Lautoka	20	13	1	6	47	24	**40**	1-0	0-3		1-3	5-1	8-1	4-1	1-1	4-0	1-0	2-1
Navua	20	11	5	4	30	15	**38**	0-1	0-0	0-1		0-0	4-0	0-0	4-0	1-0	3-2	3-1
Rewa	20	8	6	6	25	27	**30**	0-2	0-5	2-0	1-1		0-3	1-0	1-1	0-0	1-1	6-0
Suva	20	9	1	10	23	27	**28**	0-1	0-1	3-1	0-2	0-1		1-1	4-0	**2-0**	0-1	2-1
Savusavu	20	7	3	10	15	25	**24**	1-0	0-1	0-1	0-1	0-3	0-1		1-0	1-0	1-0	1-3
Nadi	20	6	5	9	18	31	**23**	0-5	0-3	0-1	1-2	0-1	1-0	2-0		1-0	4-2	2-1
Tavua	20	5	2	13	25	31	**17**	0-5	0-1	1-3	1-0	4-1	1-2	2-3	1-1		1-0	7-0
Nadroga	20	3	3	14	15	47	**12**	1-5	0-3	2-6	0-1	1-3	0-2	1-1	0-0	2-1		0-3
Fiji U-20/23	20	4	0	16	18	51	**12**	0-3	1-0	0-5	3-4	0-2	0-1	0-3	0-1	2-0	1-2	

12/02/2011 - 27/11/2011 • † Qualified for the O-League • Match in bold awarded

BATTLE OF THE GIANTS 2011

Semi-finals

Rewa	1
Navua	0

Labasa	0
Suva	2

Finals

Rewa	0 4p
Suva	0 3p

Ratu Cakobau Park, Nausori, 15-08-2011

FA CUP TOURNAMENT 2011

Semi-finals

Rewa	1
Nadi	0

Latoka	0
Labasa	1

Finals

Rewa	1
Labasa	0

Churchill Park, Lautoka
13-06-2011
Scorer - James Naka 50

INTERDISTRICT CHAMPIONSHIP

Semi-finals

Labasa	1
Lautoka	0

Suva	0
Ba	1

Finals

Labasa	1
Ba	0

TFL National Stadium, Suva
16-10-2011
Scorer - Maciu Dunadamu 50

MEDALS TABLE

		Overall		Lg	ID		BoG		FACT	OFC
		G	S	G	G	S	G	B		
1	Ba	61	23	17	22	16	14	6	8	1
2	Lautoka	22	17	3	16	9	1	5	2 3	
3	Nadi	20	22	8	6	15	5	4	1 2	1
4	Suva	17	21	2	11	15	3	4	1 2	
5	Rewa	15	11		9	7	5	3	1 1	
6	Nadroga	11	5	3	3	3	3		2 2	
7	Labassa	9	15	2	3	3	1	5	3 7	
8	Navua	5	3		1		1	2	3 1	
9	Tavua	2	3		1			2	1 1	
10	Nasinu	1	6		1	3		2	1	
11	Taileva		1			1				
12	Rakiraki		1			1				

FIN – FINLAND

FIFA/COCA-COLA WORLD RANKING

'93	'94	'95	'96	'97	'98	'99	'00	'01	'02	'03	'04	'05	'06	'07	'08	'09	'10	'11	'12
45	38	44	79	60	55	56	59	46	43	40	43	46	52	36	55	55	83	86	

	Jan	Feb	Mar	Apr	May	Jun	Jul	Aug	Sep	Oct	Nov	Dec		High	Low	Av
2011	80	78	78	81	81	76	75	79	72	78	88	86		33	88	52

HJK Helsinki dominated club football in 2011, winning a spectacular league and cup double. Their third consecutive league title came thanks to a record number of points, games won and goals scored while the veteran Jari Litmanen scored a vital extra-time goal in their victory over KuPS in the Cup Final. Off the field financial troubles and a major match fixing investigation had a major impact on the season with two clubs - AC Oulu and Tampere United - thrown out of the top division. Tampere's involvement with a Singaporean company saw the Finnish FA take away their license completely and having lost in the final of the pre-season League Cup to Honka, their season came to an end with little sign that they would play again. Finland seems to have been a magnet for match fixing in recent years with many of the trails leading back to Singapore according to FIFA's head of Security Chris Eaton. Wilson Raj Perumal, a Singaporean match-fixer was convicted along with seven Zambians and two Georgian players from RoPS Rovaniemi. A disappointing qualifying campaign for Euro 2012 saw four different coaches at the helm but Mixu Paatelainen faces a difficult job as he prepares the team for perhaps the most difficult World Cup qualifying group anywhere in the world in which Finland were paired with France and Spain.

UEFA EUROPEAN CHAMPIONSHIP RECORD
1960-1964 DNE 1968-2012 DNQ

**SUOMEN PALLOLIITTO
(SPL/FBF)**

Urheilukatu 5,
PO Box 191,
Helsinki 00251
☎ +358 9 742151
📠 +358 9 4543352
📧 anne.toivomaki@palloliitto.fi
🖥 www.palloliitto.fi
FA 1907 CON 1954 FIFA 1908
P Sauli Niinisto
GS Kimmo Lipponen

FIFA BIG COUNT 2006

Total players	362 469
% of population	6.93%
Male	304 398
Female	58 251
Amateurs 18+	26 555
Youth under 18	101 334
Unregistered	120 000
Professionals	360
Referees	2 655
Admin & coaches	14 300
Number of clubs	990
Number of teams	4 258

MAJOR CITIES/TOWNS

		Population
1	Helsinki	571 838
2	Espoo	241 741
3	Tampere	210 450
4	Vantaa	194 638
5	Turku	176 346
6	Oulu	132 629
7	Lahti	99 477
8	Kuopio	91 431
9	Jyväskylä	85 362
10	Pori	76 274
11	Lappeenranta	59 213
12	Rovaniemi	58 624
13	Vaasa	58 388
14	Joensuu	57 682
15	Kotka	54 159
16	Hämeenlinna	49 055
17	Mikkeli	48 894
18	Porvoo	48 255
51	Valkeakoski	20 366

SUOMEN TASAVALTA • REPUBLIC OF FINLAND

Capital	Helsinki	Population	5 250 275 (113)	% in cities	63%
GDP per capita	$37 000 (31)	Area km²	338 145 km² (64)	GMT +/-	+2
Neighbours (km)	Norway 727, Sweden 614, Russia 1313 • Coast 1250				

RECENT INTERNATIONAL MATCHES PLAYED BY FINLAND

2008	Opponents	Score	Venue	Comp	Scorers	Att	Referee
6-02	Greece	L 1-2	Nicosia	Fr	Litmanen [66]	500	Kailis CYP
26-03	Bulgaria	L 1-2	Sofia	Fr	Litmanen [22p]	2 500	Tudor ROU
29-05	Turkey	L 0-2	Duisburg	Fr		15 036	Kinhofer GER
2-06	Belarus	D 1-1	Helsinki	Fr	Kallio [90]	6 474	Skomina SVN
20-08	Israel	W 2-0	Tampere	Fr	Johansson 2 [43 88]	4 929	
10-09	Germany	D 3-3	Helsinki	WCq	Johansson [33], Vayrynen [43], Sjolund [53]	37 150	Kassai HUN
11-10	Azerbaijan	W 1-0	Helsinki	WCq	Forssell [61p]	22 124	Collum SCO
15-10	Russia	L 0-3	Moscow	WCq		28 000	Vassaras GRE
19-11	Switzerland	L 0-1	St Gall	Fr		11 500	Kulbakov RUS
2009							
4-02	Japan	L 1-5	Tokyo	Fr	Porokara [50]	34 532	Huang Junjie CHN
11-02	Portugal	L 0-1	Faro-Loule	Fr		19 834	Bertolini SUI
28-03	Wales	W 2-0	Cardiff	WCq	Johansson [43], Kuqi [91+]	22 604	Iturralde ESP
1-04	Norway	L 2-3	Oslo	Fr	Johansson [39], Alexei Eremenko [91+]	16 239	Styles ENG
6-06	Liechtenstein	W 2-1	Helsinki	WCq	Forssell [33], Johansson [71]	20 319	Kovarik CZE
10-06	Russia	L 0-3	Helsinki	WCq		37 028	Plautz AUT
12-08	Sweden	L 0-1	Stockholm	Fr		15 212	Fautrel FRA
5-09	Azerbaijan	W 2-1	Lenkoran	WCq	Tihinen [74], Johansson [85]	12 000	Trifonos CYP
9-09	Liechtenstein	D 1-1	Vaduz	WCq	Litmanen [74p]	3 132	Panic BIH
10-10	Wales	W 2-1	Helsinki	WCq	Porokara [5], Moisander [77]	14 000	Mazic SRB
14-10	Germany	D 1-1	Hamburg	WCq	Johansson [11]	51 500	Atkinson ENG
2010							
18-01	Korea Republic	L 0-2	Malaga	Fr		270	Fernandez ESP
3-03	Malta	W 2-1	Ta'qali	Fr	Roman Eremenko [66p], Vayrynen [69]	800	Bergonzi ITA
21-05	Estonia	L 0-2	Tallinn	Fr		5 650	Vad HUN
29-05	Poland	D 0-0	Kielce	Fr		14 200	Avram ROU
11-08	Belgium	W 1-0	Turku	Fr	Porokara [13]	7 451	Hamer LUX
3-09	Moldova	L 0-2	Chisinau	ECq		10 300	Malek POL
7-09	Netherlands	L 1-2	Rotterdam	ECq	Forssell [18]	25 000	Nikolaev POL
12-10	Hungary	L 1-2	Helsinki	ECq	Forssell [86]	18 532	Kelly IRL
17-11	San Marino	W 8-0	Helsinki	ECq	Vayrynen [39], Hamalainen 2 [49 67], Forssell 3 [51 59 78], Litmanen [71p], Porokara [73]	8 192	Matejek POL
2011							
9-02	Belgium	D 1-1	Ghent	Fr	Porokara [90]	12 000	Zimmermann SUI
29-03	Portugal	L 0-2	Aveiro	Fr		13 737	Studer SUI
3-06	San Marino	W 1-0	Serravalle	ECq	Forssell [41]	1 218	Sipailo LVA
7-06	Sweden	L 0-5	Stockholm	ECq		32 128	Gautier FRA
10-08	Latvia	W 2-0	Riga	Fr	Hamalainen [58], Furuholm [88]	5 314	Bezborodov RUS
2-09	Moldova	W 4-1	Helsinki	ECq	Hamalainen 2 [11 43], Forssell [52p], OG [70]	9 056	Kakos GRE
6-09	Netherlands	L 0-2	Helsinki	ECq		21 580	Grafe GER
7-10	Sweden	L 1-2	Helsinki	ECq	Toivio [73]	23 257	Clattenburg ENG
11-10	Hungary	D 0-0	Budapest	ECq		25 169	Undiano ESP
15-11	Denmark	L 1-2	Esbjerg	Fr	Alexei Eremenko [18]	14 132	Jakobsson ISL

Fr = Friendly match • EC = UEFA EURO 2012 • WC = FIFA World Cup • q = qualifier

FINLAND NATIONAL TEAM HISTORICAL RECORDS

Caps
137 - Jari Litmanen 1989-2010 • **105** - Jonatan Johansson 1996-2010 & Sami Hyypia 1992-2010 • **100** - Ari Hjelm 1983-96 • **98** - Joonas Kolkka 1994- • **81** - Mikael Forssell 1999- • **83** - Erkka Petaja 1983-94 • **76** - Arto Tolsa 1964-81 & Hannu Tihinen 1997-2009 • **75** - Toni Kuivasto 1997- • **71** - Mika Nurmela 1992-2007 • **70** - Mika-Matti Paatelainen 1986-2000

Goals
32 - Jari Litmanen 1989-2010 • **26** - Mikael Forssell 1999- • **22** - Jonatan Johansson 1996-2010 • **20** - Ari Hjelm 1983-96 • **18** - Mika-Matti Paatelainen 1986-2000 • **17** - Verner Eklof 1919-27 • **16** - Aulis Koponen 1924-35 & Gunnar Astrom 1923-37 • **14** - Alexei Eremenko 2003- • **13** - William Kanerva 1922-38; Jorma Vaihela 1947-54 & Kai Pahlman 1954-68 • **12** - Kalevi Lehtovirta 1947-59

Past Coaches
Jarl Ohman 1922 • Ferdinand Fabra GER 1936-1937 • Gabor Obitz HUN 1939 • Axel Martensson SWE 1945 • Niilo Tammisalo 1946 • Aatos Lehtonen 1947-1955 • Kurt Weinreich GER 1955-1958 • Aatos Lehtonen 1959-1961 • Olavi Laaksonen 1962-1974 • Martti Kosma 1975 • Aulis Rytkonen 1975-1978 • Esko Malm 1979-1981 • Martti Kuusela 1982-1987 • Jukka Vakkila 1988-1992 • Tommy Lindholm 1993-1994 • Jukka Ikalainen 1994-1996 • Richard Moller Nielsen DEN 1996-1999 • Antti Muurinen 2000-2005 • Jyrki Heliskoski 2005 • Roy Hodgson ENG 2006-2007 • Stuart Baxter SCO 2008-10 • Olli Huttunen 2010-11 • Markku Kanerva 2011 • Mika-Matti Paatelainen 2011

FINLAND 2011

VEIKKAUSLIIGA (1)

	Pl	W	D	L	F	A	Pts	HJK	Inter	JJK	Honka	TPS	KuPS	IFK	MyPa-47	VPS	Haka	Jaro	RoPS
HJK Helsinki †	33	26	3	4	86	23	81		1-0 4-2	6-2 0-0	2-1	6-0	4-1 1-0	1-0	4-1	3-0 2-0	5-2	1-0 6-0	5-1 5-0
Inter Turku ‡	33	16	9	8	70	44	57	1-1		2-0 2-1	4-0 2-2	0-0	4-4	2-0 2-0	1-1 5-2	3-1	6-1 1-1	2-0	3-0 6-2
JJK Jyväskylä ‡	33	14	12	7	60	48	54	0-2	1-0		2-2	1-1	2-0 1-2	2-1 2-0	1-0 4-0	2-0 1-2	4-2 2-1	3-3	3-0
Honka Espoo	33	13	14	6	57	40	53	0-2 1-1	2-3	0-0 2-2		1-2 1-1	3-1	2-0	1-1 2-0	1-1	1-1	4-1 1-1	1-0 5-2
TPS Turku	33	13	11	9	48	44	50	2-0 2-1	2-1 1-1	2-3 2-2	2-4		5-0	2-0	2-1 1-1	1-1	2-0 1-2	1-3 2-1	2-1
KuPS Kuopio ‡	33	10	10	13	44	55	40	2-4	0-1 2-1	4-4	0-2 1-4	1-1 2-0		2-1 2-1	2-0 2-0	2-1 4-2	1-2	1-1	1-0
IFK Mariehamn	33	10	8	15	39	47	38	2-0 0-2	1-0	2-2	1-0 1-1	0-1 0-3	2-2		1-1	0-1	2-1	3-1 5-2	3-3 5-2
MyPa-47 Anjalankoski	33	11	5	17	39	52	38	0-2 0-1	2-3	2-1	0-1	0-0	1-0	0-2 0-1		1-0 2-3	3-0 2-0	2-1	0-4 2-0
VPS Vaasa	33	8	13	12	32	44	37	0-2	3-3 0-0	1-1	1-1 0-1	2-1 3-2	1-1	1-0 1-1	1-2		1-1 1-2	0-0	2-1
Haka Valkeakoski	33	10	7	16	36	60	37	0-5 1-3	2-0	0-2 1-2	2-2	0-4	1-0 2-1	0-2 1-1	2-1	1-2 4-0		3-1	2-0 0-1
Jaro Pietarsaari	33	7	10	16	49	64	31	1-0	1-3 3-2	1-1 2-3	2-2	1-1	1-1 1-1	4-0	1-5 2-4	2-0 0-1	1-2 1-1		8-2
RoPS Rovaniemi	33	5	8	20	39	78	23	1-4	3-4	1-2 3-3	1-2	1-1 3-1	0-0 1-1	1-1	2-1	1-1 0-0	1-2	1-0 0-2	

2/05/2011 - 29/10/2011 • † Qualified for the UEFA Champions League • ‡ Qualified for the Europa League
Top scorers: **22** - Timo Furuholm, Inter • **16** - Akseli Pelvas, HJK; Tamas Gruborovics HUN, JJK & Mika Ojala Inter • **15** - Henri Lehtonen, Inter; Berat Sadik, HJK & Demba Savage GAM, Honka • **14** - Babatunde Wusu NGA, JJK

LEAGUE CUP 2011

Quarter-finals		Semi-finals		Final	
Honka Espoo *	2				
Jaro Pietarsaari	0	Honka Espoo *	2		
Inter Turku	1 5p	JJK Jyväskylä	1		
JJK Jyväskylä *	1 6p			Honka Espoo	3
HJK Helsinki *	4			Tampere Utd	0
KuPS Kuopio	3	HJK Helsinki	0 0p	Espoo, 23-04-2011	
TPS Turku	0	Tampere Utd *	0 3p	Scorers - Nicholas Otaru [20],	
Tampere Utd *	1	* Home team		Demba Savage 2 [67 76]	

MEDALS TABLE

		Overall			League			Cup		LC
		G	S	B	G	S	B	G	S	
1	HJK Helsinki	39	20	11	**24**	13	11	11	5	**4** 2
2	Haka	22	10	10	9	7	10	**12**	3	1
3	TPS Turku	11	18	9	8	12	9	3	5	1
4	Reipas Lahti	10	9	3	3	6	3	7	3	
5	HPS Helsinki	10	7	2	9	6	2	1	1	
6	Tampere Utd	9	5	3	5	1	3	3	3	1 1
7	KuPS Kuopio	8	10	1	5	9	1	2	1	1
	FC Lahti	8	10	1	5	4	1	2	4	1 2
9	HIFK Helsinki	7	8	4	7	7	4		1	
10	KTP Kotka	6	4	2	2		2	4	3	1
11	VPS Vaasa	4	7	1	2	5	1		1	2 1
12	MyPa-47	4	5	3	1	5	3	3		
13	Abo IFK Turku	4	5	1	3	5	1	1		
14	Kronshagen IF	4	2	3	4	1	3		1	
15	IFK Vaasa	3	2	2	3	2	2			
16	Alliansi Vantaa	3	2		1			1	1	2
	Inter Turku	3	2		1	1		1	1	1 1
18	Honka Espoo	2	5			2			3	2
19	MP Mikkeli	2	3			3		2		

FINLAND 2011

YKKONEN (2)

	Pl	W	D	L	F	A	Pts	Lahti	OPS	AC Oulu	PK-35	Viikingit	KooTeePee	Hämeenlinna	JIPPO	HIFK	PS Kemi	PoPa	KPV	FC Espoo
FC Lahti	24	16	4	4	50	18	52		1-2	1-2	1-1	2-1	2-0	4-0	2-1	1-0	3-1	4-0	1-0	3-0
OPS-jp Oulu	24	15	4	5	46	26	49	1-1		0-1	1-2	1-1	1-2	0-0	1-0	3-0	2-1	7-0	2-0	3-1
AC Oulu	24	14	6	4	51	22	48	2-0	6-2		1-2	2-1	3-1	0-0	1-1	1-1	3-0	4-0	0-1	7-0
PK-35 Vantaa	24	13	5	6	38	19	44	1-1	1-3	0-2		0-0	1-0	2-1	1-0	3-2	5-0	3-0	5-0	1-0
Viikingit Helsinki	24	13	4	7	50	28	43	1-0	4-3	5-2	U-U		1-0	0-2	2-1	4-0	2-0	3-1	8-1	1-1
KooTeePee Kotka	24	13	2	9	37	26	41	2-3	1-2	2-0	0-0	1-2		2-3	1-0	3-1	3-0	3-0	2-1	
FC Hämeenlinna	24	9	6	9	30	34	33	1-3	0-2	0-4	0-2	1-0	0-1		1-1	0-0	1-0	1-3	5-2	2-3
JIPPO Joensuu	24	6	12	6	24	20	30	0-0	0-0	1-1	1-0	2-1	1-0	2-2		0-0	2-0	1-2	1-1	3-0
HIFK Helsinki	24	8	5	11	26	30	29	0-2	1-2	1-3	1-0	3-2	0-2	0-1	1-1		0-1	3-1	4-0	3-0
PS Kemi	24	5	4	15	25	43	19	1-2	0-1	2-2	3-0	1-3	1-3	1-3	2-2	0-1		0-0	4-0	2-0
PoPa Pori	24	6	1	17	23	58	19	1-4	0-2	0-2	0-3	1-5	1-2	2-3	0-2	1-2	4-2		2-0	1-0
KPV Kokkola	24	4	4	16	19	58	16	0-2	2-3	1-1	0-4	0-1	2-4	0-3	0-0	1-1	0-1	1-0		4-1
FC Espoo	24	3	5	16	19	56	14	0-7	1-2	0-1	2-1	3-2	1-1	0-0	1-1	0-2	1-1	1-3	2-3	

28/04/2011 - 22/10/2011

SUOMEN CUP 2011

Sixth Round

Team	Score
HJK Helsinki	Bye
KooTeePee Kotka	0
SJK Seinajoki *	3
Jaro Pietarsaari	4
ViPa*	1
AC Oulu	0
MyPa-47 Anjalankoski *	2
JJK Jyväskylä	Bye
FC Hämeenlinna	0
PK-35 Vantaa *	2
TPS Turku *	2 5p
VPS Vaasa	2 4p
FC Espoo	1
FC Lahti *	2
IFK Mariehamn	8
LPS Laajasalo*	0
Honka Espoo	Bye
Tampere United	Bye
JBK Pietarsaari	0 2p
JIPPO Joensuu *	0 4p
Haka Valkeakoski	0 4p
Inter Turku*	0 2p
MaPS	1
GBK Kokkola *	3
IF Gnistan *	3
Sudet Kouvola	0
EIF Ekenäs*	0
KuPS Kuopio	2

Round of 16

Team	Score
HJK Helsinki	4
SJK Seinajoki*	0
Jaro Pietarsaari	1
MyPa-47 Anjalankoski *	3
JJK Jyväskylä	8
PK-35 Vantaa*	0
TPS Turku*	0
FC Lahti *	2
IFK Mariehamn *	1
Honka Espoo	0
Tampere United	1
JIPPO Joensuu *	2
Haka Valkeakoski	2
GBK Kokkola*	0
IF Gnistan*	2
KuPS Kuopio	6

Quarter-finals

Team	Score
HJK Helsinki	2
MyPa-47 Anjalankoski*	1
JJK Jyväskylä	3
FC Lahti *	4
IFK Mariehamn *	4
JIPPO Joensuu	0
Haka Valkeakoski*	0
KuPS Kuopio	2

Semi-finals

Team	Score
HJK Helsinki *	3
FC Lahti	0
IFK Mariehamn*	0
KuPS Kuopio	3

Final

Team	Score
HJK Helsinki	2
KuPS Kuopio ‡	1

CUP FINAL

Sonera (Töölö), Helsinki
24-09-2011; Att: 5125; Ref: Jouni Hyytia
Scorers - Jari Litmanen 108, Alexander Ring 116 for HJK; Markus Joenmaki 119 for KuPS
HJK - Ville Wallen - Tuomas Kansikas•, Mathias Lindstrom, Mikko Sumusalo - Rami Hakanpaa, Joel Perovuo, Erfani Zeneli (Aki Riihilahti• 97), Sebastian Sorsa (Cheyne Fowler 112), Alexander Ring - Berat Sadik, Akseli Pelvas (Jari Litmanen 80). Tr: Antti Muurinen
KuPS - Mikko Vilmunen - Pyry Karkkainen•, Alain Bono, Joni Nissinen (Atte Hoivala 4), Markus Joenmaki - Juho Nykanen (Olajide Williams 111), Tero Taipale, Patrice Ollo - Miikka Ilo, Ilja Venalainen (Fikru-Teferra Lemessa 61), Dickson Nwakaeme•. Tr: Esa Pekonen

League Cup semi-finalists given a bye to the round of 16 • * Home team in the first leg • ‡ Qualified for the Europa League

FRA – FRANCE

FIFA/COCA-COLA WORLD RANKING

'93	'94	'95	'96	'97	'98	'99	'00	'01	'02	'03	'04	'05	'06	'07	'08	'09	'10	'11	'12
15	19	8	3	6	2	3	2	1	2	2	2	5	4	7	11	7	18	15	

					2011									
	Jan	Feb	Mar	Apr	May	Jun	Jul	Aug	Sep	Oct	Nov	Dec	High	Low	Av
	18	19	18	19	19	15	16	15	12	15	15	15	1	27	7

2011 was dominated by the purchase of Paris Saint-Germain by Qatar Sports Investments in what many see as a game changer for French football. Of the so-called 'Big Five' leagues of western Europe, the French have always lagged behind the Spanish, Italians, English and Germans. Many of the top French professionals play abroad and success in European competition has been limited. The 1998 World Cup triumph changed the somewhat negative attitude of the French public towards football - especially in Paris - and PSG intend to build on that to make the club capable of challenging for honours, not only in France but in Europe too. Former Milan and Inter coach Leonardo was installed as general manager and a number of high profile signings followed, including coach Carlo Ancellotti at the end of the year. All this rather overshadowed the wonderful achievement of Lille in not only winning their first championship for 57 years but also completing the double by winning the French cup for the first time in 56 years. The French national team qualified for the finals of Euro 2012 as coach Laurent Blanc brought some sense of stability to a team still reeling from the aftermath of their 2010 World Cup debacle. They were chased hard by Bosnia-Herzegovina, but a 1-1 draw between the two in the final game saw France through.

UEFA EUROPEAN CHAMPIONSHIP RECORD

1960 4 SF **1964** QF **1968** QF **1972-1980** DNQ **1984** 1 Winners (Hosts) **1988** DNQ
1992 6 r1 **1996** 4 SF **2000** 1 Winners **2004** 6 QF **2008** 15 r1 **2012** Qualified

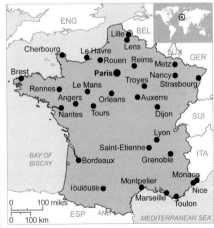

FEDERATION FRANÇAISE DE FOOTBALL (FFF)

87, Boulevard de Grenelle, Paris 75738

☎ +33 1 44317300
📠 +33 1 44317373
✉ webmaster@fff.fr
🖥 fff.fr

FA 1919 CON 1954 FIFA 1904
P Noel Le Graet
GS Alain Christnacht

FIFA BIG COUNT 2006

Total players	4 190 040
% of population	6.88%
Male	3 851 161
Female	338 879
Amateurs 18+	753 244
Youth under 18	1 034 046
Unregistered	1 233 100
Professionals	1 825
Referees	27 782
Admin & coaches	257 941
Number of clubs	18 823
Number of teams	111 760

MAJOR CITIES/TOWNS

		Population
1	Paris	2 183 500
2	Marseille	782 687
3	Lyon	485 872
4	Toulouse	453 217
5	Nice	332 817
6	Nantes	280 989
7	Strasbourg	279 152
8	Montpellier	257 712
9	Lille	254 149
10	Bordeaux	239 768
11	Rennes	210 404
12	Reims	203 950
13	Le Havre	181 051
14	Angers	179 574
15	Saint-Etienne	171 257
16	Toulon	169 176
17	Grenoble	160 226
167	Auxerre	42 389
188	Lens	39 493

REPUBLIQUE FRANCAISE • FRENCH REPUBLIC

Capital	Paris	Population	64 057 792 (21)	% in cities	77%
GDP per capita	$33 300 (39)	Area km²	551 500 km² (42)	GMT +/-	+1
Neighbours (km)	Andorra 56, Belgium 620, Germany 451, Italy 488, Luxembourg 73, Monaco 4, Spain 623, Switzerland 573 • Coast 4668				

RECENT INTERNATIONAL MATCHES PLAYED BY FRANCE

2009	Opponents	Score		Venue	Comp	Scorers	Att	Referee
11-02	Argentina	L	0-2	Marseilles	Fr		60 000	Eriksson SWE
28-03	Lithuania	W	1-0	Kaunas	WCq	Ribery [67]	8 700	Braamhaar NED
1-04	Lithuania	W	1-0	Paris	WCq	Ribery [75]	79 543	Webb ENG
2-06	Nigeria	L	0-1	St-Etienne	Fr		25 000	Bennett ENG
5-06	Turkey	W	1-0	Lyon	Fr	Benzema [39p]	32 000	Grafe GER
12-08	Faroe Islands	W	1-0	Tórshavn	WCq	Gignac [41]	2 974	Koukoulakis GRE
5-09	Romania	D	1-1	Paris	WCq	Henry [48]	78 209	Bebek CRO
9-09	Serbia	D	1-1	Belgrade	WCq	Henry [36]	49 256	Rosetti ITA
10-10	Faroe Islands	W	5-0	Guingamp	WCq	Gignac 2 [34 39], Gallas [53], Anelka [85], Benzema [87]	16 755	Malek POL
14-10	Austria	W	3-1	Paris	WCq	Benzema [18], Henry [26p], Gignac [66]	78 099	Proenca POR
14-11	Republic of Ireland	W	1-0	Dublin	WCq	Anelka [72]	74 103	Brych GER
18-11	Republic of Ireland	D	1-1	Paris	WCq	Gallas [103]	79 145	Hansson SWE
2010								
3-03	Spain	L	0-2	Paris	Fr		79 021	Thomson SCO
26-05	Costa Rica	W	2-1	Lens	Fr	OG [22], Valbuena [83]	40 000	Bezborodov RUS
30-05	Tunisia	D	1-1	Rades/Tunis	Fr	Gallas [62]	55 000	El Raay LBY
4-06	China PR	L	0-1	Saint-Pierre	Fr		10 043	Proenca POR
11-06	Uruguay	D	0-0	Cape Town	WCr1		64 100	Nishimura JPN
17-06	Mexico	L	0-2	Polokwane	WCr1		35 370	Al Ghamdi KSA
22-06	South Africa	L	1-2	Bloemfontein	WCr1	Malouda [70]	39 415	Ruiz COL
11-08	Norway	L	1-2	Oslo	Fr	Ben Arfa [48]	15 165	Velasco ESP
3-09	Belarus	L	0-1	Paris	ECq		76 395	Collum SCO
7-09	Bosnia-Herzegovina	W	2-0	Sarajevo	ECq	Benzema [72], Malouda [78]	28 000	Brych GER
9-10	Romania	W	2-0	Paris	ECq	Remy [83], Gourcuff [93+]	79 299	Proenca POR
12-10	Luxembourg	W	2-0	Metz	ECq	Benzema [22], Gourcuff [76]	24 710	Jug SVN
17-11	England	W	2-1	London	Fr	Benzema [16], Valbuena [55]	85 495	Larsen DEN
2011								
9-02	Brazil	W	1-0	Paris	Fr	Benzema [55]	79 712	Stark GER
25-03	Luxembourg	W	2-0	Luxembourg	ECq	Mexes [28], Gourcouf [72]	8 400	Hagen NOR
29-03	Croatia	D	0-0	Paris	Fr		60 000	Kelly IRL
3-06	Belarus	D	1-1	Minsk	ECq	Malouda [22]	26 500	Fernandez ESP
6-06	Ukraine	W	4-1	Donetsk	Fr	Gameiro [58], Martin 2 [87 90], Kaboul [89]	11 200	Clattenburg ENG
9-06	Poland	W	1-0	Warsaw	Fr	OG [12]	32 000	Kuipers NED
10-08	Chile	D	1-1	Montpellier	Fr	Remy [20]	30 000	Atwell ENG
2-09	Albania	W	2-1	Tirana	ECq	Benzema [11], M'Vila [18]	15 600	Nikolaev RUS
6-09	Romania	D	0-0	Bucharest	ECq		49 137	Webb ENG
7-10	Albania	W	3-0	Paris	ECq	Malouda [11], Remy [38], Reveillere [67]	65 239	Koukoulakis GRE
11-10	Bosnia-Herzegovina	D	1-1	Paris	ECq	Nasri [78p]	78 467	Thomson SCO
11-11	USA	W	1-0	Paris	Fr	Remy [72]	70 018	Koukoulakis GRE
15-11	Belgium	D	0-0	Paris	Fr		52 825	Muniz ESP

Fr = Friendly match • EC = UEFA EURO 2008/2012 • WC = FIFA World Cup
q = qualifier • r1 = first round group • r2 = second round • qf = quarter-final • sf = semi-final • f = final

FRANCE NATIONAL TEAM HISTORICAL RECORDS

Caps — 142 - Lilian Thuram 1994-2008 • 123 - Thierry Henry 1997- • 116 - Marcel Desailly 1993-2004 • 108 - Zinedine Zidane 1994-2006 • 107 - Patrick Vieira 1997-2009 • 103 - Didier Deschamps 1989-2000 • 97 - Laurent Blanc 1989-2000 & Bixente Lizarazu 1992-2004 • 92 - Sylvain Wiltord 1999-2006 • 87 - Fabien Barthez 1994-2006 • 84 - William Gallas 2002- • 82 - Manuel Amoros 1982-92 & Youri Djorkaeff 1993-2002 • 79 - Robert Pires 1996-2004 • 76 - Maxime Bossis 1976-86 • 73 - Florent Malouda 2004- • 72 - Michel Platini 1976-87

Goals — 51 - Thierry Henry 1997- • 41 - Michel Platini 1976-87 • 34 - David Trezeguet 1998-2008 • 31 - Zinedine Zidane 1994-2006 • 30 - Just Fontaine 1953-60 & Jean-Pierre Papin 1986-95 • 28 - Youri Djorkaeff 1993-2002 • 26 - Sylvain Wiltord 1999-2006 • 22 - Jean Vincent 1953-61 • 21 - Jean Nicolas 1933-38 • 20 - Paul Nicolas 1920-31 & Eric Cantona 1987-95 • 19 - Jean Baratte 1944-52 • 18 - Roger Piantoni 1952-61 & Raymond Kopa 1952-62 • 16 - Larent Blanc 1989-2000 • 15 - Eugene Maes 1911-13 & Herve Revelli 1973-77

Past Coaches — Gaston Barreau 1919-45 • Gabriel Hanot 1945-49 • Paul Baron & Pierre Pibarot 1949-53 • Pierre Pibarot 1953-54 • Jules Bigot & Albert Batteux 1954-56 • Albert Batteux 1956-60 • Albert Batteux & Henri Guerin 1960-64 • Henri Guerin 1964-1966 • Jose Arribas ESP & Jean Snella 1966 • Just Fontaine 1967 • Louis Dugauguez 1967-1968 • Georges Boulogne 1969-1973 • Stefan Kovacs 1973-1975 • Michel Hidalgo 1976-1984 • Henri Michel 1984-1988 • Michel Platini 1988-1992 • Gerard Houllier 1992-1993 • Aime Jacquet 1994-1998 • Roger Lemerre 1998-2002 • Jacques Santini 2002-2004 • Raymond Domenech 2004-2010 • Laurent Blanc 2010-

FRANCE 2010–11

LIGUE 1 ORANGE

Team	Pl	W	D	L	F	A	Pts
Lille OSC †	38	21	13	4	68	36	76
Olympique Marseille †	38	18	14	6	62	39	68
Olympique Lyonnais †	38	17	13	8	61	40	64
Paris Saint-Germain ‡	38	15	15	8	56	41	60
Sochaux-Montbéliard ‡	38	17	7	14	60	43	58
Stade Rennais ‡	38	15	11	12	38	35	56
Girondins Bordeaux	38	12	15	11	42	41	51
Toulouse FC	38	14	8	16	37	35	50
AJ Auxerre	38	10	19	9	45	41	49
AS Saint-Etienne	38	12	13	13	46	47	49
FC Lorient	38	12	13	13	46	48	49
Valenciennes FC	38	10	18	10	45	41	48
AS Nancy-Lorraine	38	13	9	16	43	48	48
Montpellier-Hérault	38	12	11	15	32	43	47
SM Caen	38	11	13	14	46	51	46
Stade Brestois	38	11	13	14	36	43	46
OGC Nice	38	11	13	14	33	48	46
AS Monaco	38	9	17	12	36	40	44
Racing Club Lens	38	7	14	17	35	58	35
AC Arlés-Avignon	38	3	11	24	21	70	20

7/08/2010 - 29/05/2011 • † Qualified for the UEFA Champions League • ‡ Qualified for the Europa League

Top scorers: **25** - Moussa Sow SEN, Lille • **22** - Kevin Gameiro, Lorient • **17** - Gregory Pujol, Valenciennes; Youssef El Arabi MAR, Caen & Lisandro Lopez ARG, Lyon • **16** - Loic Remy, Marseille • **15** - Gervinho CIV, Lille; Ideye Brown NGA, Sochaux & Modibo Maiga MLI, Sochaux • **14** - Nene BRA, PSG • **13** - Dimitri Payet, St-Etienne • **12** - Park Chu Young KOR, Monaco • **11** - Andre Ayew GHA, Marseille

FRANCE 2010–11

LIGUE 2 ORANGE

Team	Pl	W	D	L	F	A	Pts
Evian-Thonon Gaillard	38	18	13	7	63	41	67
AC Ajaccio	38	17	13	8	45	37	64
Dijon FCO	38	17	11	10	55	40	62
Le Mans FC	38	17	11	10	48	37	62
CS Sedan Ardennes	38	15	14	9	57	37	59
Angers SCO	38	14	15	9	41	32	57
Clermont Foot	38	12	16	10	51	49	52
US Boulogne CO	38	13	13	12	35	41	52
Le Havre AC	38	12	13	13	43	38	49
Stade de Reims	38	12	13	13	53	51	49
FC Istres	38	12	13	13	45	47	49
Tours FC	38	13	10	15	52	59	49
FC Nantes	38	11	14	13	38	40	47
LB Châteauroux	38	12	11	15	41	47	47
Stade Lavallois	38	11	14	13	36	43	47
ES Troyes AC	38	13	7	18	35	45	46
FC Metz	38	10	15	13	43	40	45
Vannes Olympique	38	12	8	18	39	61	44
Nîmes Olympique	38	9	10	19	35	46	37
Grenoble Foot 38	38	7	12	19	36	60	33

6/08/2010 - 27/05/2011 • Top scorers: **23** - Sebastian Ribas URU, Dijon • **21** - Thorstein Helstad NOR, Le Mans • **20** - Sloan Privat, Clermont

FRANCE 2010-11

NATIONAL (3)

	Pl	W	D	L	F	A	Pts	Bastia	Amiens	Guingamp	Strasbourg	Cannes	Fréjus	Beauvais	Rouen	Orléans	Créteil	Luzenac	Paris	Niort	Pacy	Colmar	Gap	Bayonne	Rodez	Plabennec	Alfortville	Gueugnon
SC Bastia	40	27	10	3	81	24	**91**		1-0	2-0	1-0	0-0	1-0	5-1	0-0	0-2	2-1	1-0	3-0	2-1	0-0	3-0	5-0	4-2	0-0	6-1	1-1	3-0
Amiens SFC	40	24	12	4	58	27	**84**	1-0		2-1	1-1	2-0	1-0	2-0	2-1	0-0	2-1	1-1	2-0	2-1	2-0	1-0	1-0	1-1	5-1	1-0	3-1	3-2
En Avant Guingamp	40	23	11	6	87	36	**80**	2-5	1-2		0-0	4-0	3-1	3-0	1-0	4-1	5-1	4-1	2-0	2-0	2-1	2-0	5-0	2-2	3-1	3-1	6-3	5-0
RC Strasbourg	40	20	17	3	56	27	**77**	1-1	1-1	2-1		3-3	3-0	1-0	1-1	2-0	1-1	1-0	0-0	0-0	1-0	2-0	2-1	2-0	2-1	0-0	4-0	2-1
AS Cannes	40	18	14	8	51	35	**68**	2-1	1-1	0-0	1-0		1-1	0-0	3-2	4-2	1-0	2-0	0-0	1-0	0-0	2-1	0-1	3-0	2-0	1-0	3-0	2-1
Fréjus Saint-Raphaël	40	19	10	11	56	41	**67**	1-1	0-1	1-1	1-2	0-0		1-0	1-0	1-1	3-0	1-0	3-1	1-0	1-0	1-1	2-1	3-0	2-1	2-0	2-1	**3-0**
AS Beauvais Oise	40	15	16	9	53	48	**61**	1-4	0-0	2-2	2-1	2-1	1-1		1-1	1-2	0-0	0-0	3-2	4-2	3-2	0-0	1-1	3-0	3-2	0-0	2-2	3-1
FC Rouen	40	15	14	11	54	44	**59**	0-1	2-0	0-2	1-2	2-0	1-1	1-1		0-1	3-0	0-0	1-1	1-0	3-2	2-1	2-0	3-1	1-1	2-0	2-1	1-0
US Orléans	40	13	14	13	43	40	**53**	0-2	0-0	1-1	1-1	1-1	3-0	2-3	2-2		0-0	1-0	1-1	1-1	2-0	2-0	4-0	0-1	0-1	2-1	0-1	1-0
US Créteil-Lusitanos	40	13	12	15	41	48	**51**	1-2	1-3	1-2	0-0	2-2	0-1	0-1	0-0	0-1		3-0	0-0	4-2	1-0	0-2	1-1	1-0	3-1	0-0	3-2	2-0
US Luzenac	40	12	13	15	39	44	**49**	1-5	1-1	1-1	1-1	1-0	0-1	1-1	2-2	4-2	0-0		2-1	0-0	0-0	0-1	3-0	1-1	2-0	2-0	4-0	2-0
Paris FC	40	11	16	13	45	46	**49**	1-2	1-0	1-1	2-2	1-1	1-1	2-2	2-0	1-3	2-2	1-0		1-0	2-0	0-1	1-0	0-2	3-1	1-1	5-1	**3-0**
Chamois Niortais FC	40	13	10	17	46	46	**49**	2-0	2-2	1-0	0-2	0-2	0-3	1-2	2-1	0-0	3-1	2-3	0-0		0-2	1-1	2-0	4-0	3-2	2-0	2-0	3-0
Pacy Vallée-d'Eure §2	40	13	8	19	41	47	**45**	1-2	2-1	0-1	0-0	1-0	2-3	0-2	2-4	0-0	2-3	0-0	2-0	1-0		2-1	2-1	2-1	0-1	1-1	1-0	3-4
SR Colmar	40	11	11	18	34	48	**44**	0-0	0-0	0-3	1-2	0-3	3-2	1-2	0-0	1-0	1-2	3-1	0-2	0-3	1-2		4-2	0-1	1-0	0-0	0-0	0-0
Gap FC	40	11	10	19	44	62	**43**	0-2	0-1	0-0	1-1	2-3	2-2	2-1	1-3	2-1	1-2	2-0	0-1	1-1	1-0	2-2		4-0	4-0	3-1	1-1	1-0
Aviron Bayonnais	40	11	10	19	36	58	**43**	1-2	0-2	0-0	1-2	2-0	2-1	0-1	3-3	2-1	0-1	0-1	0-0	2-1	0-1	1-1	3-0		3-1	1-0	0-4	0-0
Rodez Aveyron	40	11	7	22	41	63	**40**	0-0	0-2	0-2	0-3	0-2	3-2	2-1	4-2	1-0	0-1	2-0	2-2	1-1	1-0	0-1	1-2	0-0		1-1	4-0	0-2
Stade Plabennecois	40	9	12	19	33	52	**39**	0-3	0-0	1-1	0-2	0-0	1-3	0-0	0-1	1-1	1-0	2-0	2-1	1-2	1-3	2-1	1-1	2-0	3-1		1-2	**3-0**
Alfortville	40	6	10	24	36	79	**28**	0-4	2-4	0-6	1-3	0-0	1-2	0-0	1-2	0-2	1-1	1-2	2-1	0-1	1-1	0-1	0-0	1-1	0-2	0-2		**3-0**
FC Gueugnon	40	3	7	30	21	81	**16**	1-4	1-2	1-2	1-1	2-4	2-1	**0-3**	0-0	0-1	0-1	0-2	1-1	0-0	**0-3**	**0-3**	**0-3**	0-2	0-0	0-3	0-2	

6/08/2010 - 27/05/2011 • § = points deducted • Gueugnon folded after 32 matches. Their matches in bold were awarded

Top scorers: **21** - Thibault Giresse, Guingamp • **20** - David Suarez, Bastia • **16** - Jan Koller CZE, Cannes

MEDALS TABLE

		Overall			League			Cup		LC		Europe		
		G	S	B	G	S	B	G	S	G	S	G	S	B
1	Olympique Marseille	22	21	7	9	10	5	**10**	8	2		1	3	2
2	AS Saint-Etienne	16	7	3	**10**	3	2	6	3				1	1
3	Paris Saint-Germain	14	12	6	2	6	3	8	4	**3**	1	1	1	3
4	AS Monaco	13	12	14	7	5	10	5	4	1	1		2	4
5	Girondins Bordeaux	12	19	6	6	9	4	3	6	**3**	3		1	2
6	Olympique Lyonnais	12	8	8	7	3	6	4	3	1	2			2
7	FC Nantes Atlantique	11	13	4	8	7	2	3	5		1			2
8	Lille OSC	10	11	3	4	7	3	6	4					
9	Stade de Reims	8	6	4	6	3	4	2	1				2	
10	OGC Nice	7	5		4	3		3	1		1			
11	Racing Club Paris	6	4	5	1	2	5	5	2					
12	Racing Club Strasbourg	6	4	3	1	1	3	3	3	2				
13	FC Sochaux-Montbéliard	5	7	5	2	3	4	2	3	1	1			1
14	AJ Auxerre	5	1	6	1		5	4	1					1
15	Red Star 93 Paris	5	1					5	1					
16	FC Sète	4	4	1	2		1	2	4					
17	FC Metz	3	3	1		1	1	2	1	1	1			
18	Racing Club Lens	2	8	3	1	4	2		3	1	1			1
19	CS Sedan Ardennes	2	3	2			2	2	3					
20	Stade Rennais	2	3					2	3					
21	CO Roubaix-Tourcoing	2	2	1	1		1	1	2					
22	CAS Généraux	2						2						
	AS Nancy-Lorraine	2						1		1				
24	SC Bastia	1	4	1			1	1	2		1		1	
25	Montpellier HSC	1	2	1			1	1	1		1			
26	Toulouse FC	1	1	2		1	2	1						
	Le Havre AC	1	1	1			1	1	1					
28	AS Cannes	1	1			1		1						
	En Avant Guingamp	1	1					1	1					
	FC Lorient	1	1					1			1			
	Cercle Athlétique Paris	1	1					1	1					
	SO Montpellier	1	1					1	1					

COUPE DE LA LIGUE 2010-11

Third Round		Fourth Round		Quarter-finals		Semi-finals		Final	
Olympique Marseille	3ye	Olympique Marseille	1						
Stade Rennais	1	En Avant Guingamp *	0						
En Avant Guingamp	3			Olympique Marseille *	2				
FC Lorient	1	FC Lorient	1 3p	AS Monaco	1				
Stade Brestois	0	AS Monaco *	1 5p						
Racing Club Lens	0					Olympique Marseille	2		
AS Monaco	1					AJ Auxerre *	0		
AS Saint-Etienne	2	AS Saint-Etienne *	1						
OGC Nice	0	Girondins Bordeaux	0	AS Saint-Etienne	0				
AS Nancy-Lorraine	1			AJ Auxerre *	2				
Girondins Bordeaux	2								
SC Bastia	2	SC Bastia	0					Olympique Marseille	1
Sochaux-Montbéliard	0	AJ Auxerre *	4					Montpellier-Hérault	0
AJ Auxerre	3ye								
Paris Saint-Germain	3ye	Paris Saint-Germain	2						
		Olympique Lyonnais *	1						
Olympique Lyonnais	3ye			Paris Saint-Germain	3				
US Boulogne CO	2	US Boulogne CO	0	Valenciennes FC *	1				
Toulouse FC	1	Valenciennes FC *	4						
Nîmes Olympique	1 4p					Paris Saint-Germain	0		
Valenciennes FC	1 5p					Montpellier-Hérault *	1		
Lille OSC	3ye	Lille OSC *	4						
		SM Caen	1	Lille OSC	1				
AC Arlés-Avignon	0			Montpellier-Hérault *	2				
SM Caen	1								
AJ Ajaccio	3	AJ Ajaccio	0						
Le Havre AC	0	Montpellier-Hérault *	2						
Montpellier-Hérault	3ye								

* Home team • Ligue 1 clubs enter in the third round

COUPE DE LA LIGUE FINAL
Stade de France, Paris
23-04-2011, 20.45, Att. 78 511, Ref. Gautier
Scorer – Taiwo 80

OM – Steve Mandanda (c) - Rod Fanni,
Souleymane Diawara, Gabriel Heinze, Taye
Taiwo - Stephane Mbia (Charles Kabore● 7) -
Benoit Cheyrou, Lucho Gonzalez (Fabrice
Abriel 85) - Mathieu Valbuena (Jordan
Ayew 90), André-Pierre Gignac, Andre Ayew.
Tr: Didier Deschamps
Montpellier - Laurent Pionnier - Garry Bocaly●,
Mapou Yanga-M'Biwa, Benjamin Stambouli,
Cyril Jeunechamp - Younes Belhanda, Joris
Marveaux (Banjali-Fode Koita 89), Romain
Pitau (c) (Hasan Kabze 73), Jamel Saihi -
Olivier Giroud, Souleymane Camara (Geoffrey
Dernis 83). Tr: Rene Girard

COUPE DE FRANCE 2010–11

Round of 64

Team	Score
Lille OSC	3
US Forbach *	1
AJ Auxerre	1
ES Wasquehal *	2
US Raon-l'Étape *	4
SA Sézanne	0
UA Cognac	1
FC Nantes *	3
FC Metz	3
ES Troyes AC *	2
AC Arlés-Avignon *	1 2p
CS Sedan Ardennes	1 4p
Vendée Fontenay	3
US Avranches *	1
Vannes Olympique	1
FC Lorient *	4
Stade de Reims *	1
Montpellier-Hérault	0
AS Saint-Étienne *	0
Clermont Foot	2
Vaulx-en-Velin *	1 5p
Jura Sud	1 4p
AS Cannes	0
Stade Rennais *	7
JA Drancy	0 7p
US Montagnarde *	0 6p
Amiens SC	2 4p
US Boulogne CO *	2 5p
Olympique Lyonnais	1
SM Caen *	0
US Créteil-Lusitanos *	1 5p
OGC Nice	1 6p
Angers SCO *	2
Valenciennes FC	1
FC Rouen	1
Girondins Bordeaux *	3
Evian-Thonon Gaillard *	3
Olympique Marseille	1
AS Poissy *	1
RC Strasbourg	2
Sochaux-Montbéliard	1
Jarville JF *	0
Toulouse FC *	1
Paris FC	2
Stade Brestois	1
Issy-les-Moulineaux *	0
AS Monaco	1 2p
SO Chambéry *	1 3p
Le Mans FC	3
US Chauvigny *	1
Le Poire-sur-Vie	0
AS Cherbourg *	1
Nîmes Olympique *	3
Fréjus Saint-Raphaël	2
Aurillac FCA *	2 3p
AS Nancy-Lorraine	2 4p
FC Martigues *	2
Cheminots Paray	1
Trelissac FC *	0
US Quevilly	1
SU Agen *	2
Poitiers FC	0
Racing Club Lens	1
Paris Saint-Germain *	5

Round of 32

Team	Score
Lille OSC	1
ES Wasquehal *	0
US Raon-l'Étape	1
FC Nantes *	2
FC Metz	1
CS Sedan Ardennes *	0
Vendée Fontenay *	0
FC Lorient	1
Stade de Reims	3
Clermont Foot *	1
Vaulx-en-Velin * ‡‡	0
Stade Rennais	2
JA Drancy	1
US Boulogne CO *	0
Olympique Lyonnais	0
OGC Nice *	1
Angers SCO *	1
Girondins Bordeaux	0
Evian-Thonon Gaillard	0
RC Strasbourg *	1
Sochaux-Montbéliard *	2
Paris FC	1
Stade Brestois	1 3p
SO Chambéry *	1 4p
Le Mans FC	1
AS Cherbourg *	0
Nîmes Olympique *	1
AS Nancy-Lorraine	2
FC Martigues	1 5p
US Quevilly *	1 3p
SU Agen *	2
Paris Saint-Germain	3

Round of 16

Team	Score
Lille OSC *	1 3p
FC Nantes	1 2p
FC Metz	0
FC Lorient *	3
Stade de Reims	4
Stade Rennais *	3
JA Drancy * ††	0
OGC Nice	1
Angers SCO *	2
RC Strasbourg	0
Sochaux-Montbéliard	1
SO Chambéry *	2
Le Mans FC	2
AS Nancy-Lorraine *	1
FC Martigues *	1
Paris Saint-Germain	4

* Home team • ‡ Played at Stade Lille-Metropioe • ‡‡ Played at the Stade de Balmont, Lyon

COUPE DE FRANCE 2010–11

Quarter-finals   Semi-finals   Final

| Lille OSC * | 0 5p |
| FC Lorient | 0 3p |

| Lille OSC | 2 |
| OGC Nice * | 0 |

| Stade de Reims * | 2 |
| **OGC Nice** | 3 |

| Lille OSC | 1 |
| Paris Saint-Germain ‡ | 0 |

| **Angers SCO** | 3 |
| SO Chambéry * † | 0 |

| Angers SCO * | 1 |
| **Paris Saint-Germain** | 3 |

COUPE DE FRANCE FINAL 2011

Stade de France, Paris, 14-05-2011, 20:45, 79 000, Clement Turpin

| Lille OSC | 1 | Obraniak [89] |
| **Paris Saint-Germain** * | 2 |

Paris St-Germain   0

LOSC - Mickael Landreau - Mathieu Debuchy, Adil Rami, Aurelien Chedjou, Franck Beria - Rio Mavuba (c) - Idrissa Gana Gueye (Tulio de Melo 63), Yohan Cabaye - Gervinho, Moussa Sow (Ludovic Obraniak 79), Eden Hazard (Stephane Dumont 89). Tr: Rudi Garcia

| Le Mans FC | 0 |
| **Paris Saint-Germain** * | 2 |

PSG - Gregory Coupet - Ceara, Zoumana Camara, Mamadou Sakho, Siaka Tiene● - Clement Chantome, Claude Makelele (c) (Jeremy Clement 48) - Mathieu Bodmer (Mevlut Erdinc 69) - Ludovic Giuly (Adama Toure 90), Guillaume Hoarau, Nene●. Tr: Antoine Kombouaré

† Played in Grenoble • †† Played in Seine-Saint-Denis
‡ Qualified for the Europa League

CLUB BY CLUB GUIDE TO THE 2010-11 SEASON IN FRANCE

ARLES-AVIGNON 2010–11

Mon	Date	Opponent	Res	Score	Comp	Scorers	Att
Aug	7	Sochaux	L	1-2	L1	Dja Djedje [11]	10 381
	14	Lens	L	0-1	L1		10 881
	21	Toulouse	L	1-2	L1	Dja Djedje [64]	16 233
	28	Rennes	L	0-1	L1		9 364
Sep	11	PSG	L	0-4	L1		19 025
	18	Marseille	L	0-3	L1		**15 003**
	22	Caen	L	0-1	LCr3		4 357
	25	Montpellier	L	1-3	L1	Kermorgant [61]	13 748
Oct	2	Auxerre	L	0-4	L1		12 459
	16	Brest	D	0-0	L1		12 406
	24	Lyon	D	1-1	L1	Dja Djedje [36]	11 547
	30	Lorient	L	0-2	L1		15 758
Nov	6	Caen	W	3-2	L1	Germany [24], Diawara 2 [33 76p]	7 430
	13	Monaco	D	0-0	L1		5 161
	21	Bordeaux	L	2-4	L1	Meriem [22], Bouazza [89]	9 285
	27	Val'ciennes	L	0-3	L1		9 829
Dec	4	Nancy	D	1-1	L1	Dja Djedje [8]	**7 295**
	11	Lille	L	0-1	L1		7 955
	18	St-Etienne	L	0-2	L1		21 883
	22	Nice	D	0-0	L1		9 085
Jan	8	Sedan	D	1-1	CFr9	Kermorgant [94]. L 2-4p	2 093
	15	Rennes	L	0-4	L1		19 857
	29	PSG	L	1-2	L1	Ndiaye [57]	8 576
Feb	5	Marseille	L	0-1	L1		47 737
	12	Montpellier	D	0-0	L1		8 489
	19	Auxerre	D	1-1	L1	Ndiaye [65]	10 316
	26	Brest	D	1-1	L1	Ghilas [37]	7 410
Mar	6	Lyon	L	0-5	L1		36 786
	12	Lorient	D	3-3	L1	Meriem [6], Kermorgant [64], Cabella [80]	7 397
	20	Caen	L	0-2	L1		14 715
Apr	2	Monaco	L	0-2	L1		9 203
	9	Bordeaux	D	0-0	L1		24 250
	17	Val'ciennes	L	0-1	L1		7 652
	24	Nancy	D	0-0	L1		18 873
	30	Lille	L	0-5	L1		16 937
May	7	St-Etienne	L	0-1	L1		10 471
	11	Nice	L	2-3	L1	Cabella [39], Diawara [93+]	7 526
	15	Toulouse	W	1-0	L1	Ghilas [20]	7 568
	21	Lens	W	1-0	L1	Kermorgant [44]	28 705
	29	Sochaux	L	1-3	L1	Cabella [28]	7 880

20th Att: 174 950 • Av: 9 207 (+124.8%) • Parc des Sports 17 518 (52%)

ARLES LEAGUE APPEARANCES/GOALS 2010-11
Goalkeepers Cyrille Merville 19 • Vincent Plante 17+1
Naby Yattara GUI 2
Defenders Loic Abenzoar 10+2/0 • Bobo Balde GUI 13/0
Amin El Erbate MAR 8/0 • Jean-Alain Fanchone 16+5/0 • Fabien
Laurenti 26/0 • Gregory Lorenzi 12/0 • Alvaro Mejia ESP 12/0
Deme N'Diaye SEN 25+8/2 • Francisco Pavon ESP 26/0
Bakary Soro CIV 24+4/0
Midfield Jamel Ait Ben Idir 21+4/0 • Rachid Aliaoui 0+1/0
Thomas Ayasse 19+4/0 • Angelos Basinas GRE 3+1/0 • Hameur
Bouazza 3+6/1 • Remy Cabella 5+12/3 • Emmanuel Correze 4+4/0
Gael Germany MTQ 16+3/1 • Kamel Ghilas ALG 11+8/2 • Clement
Martinez 0+1/0 • Camel Meriem 31+1/2 • Sebastien Piocelle 15+4/0
Romain Rocchi 13+4/0
Forwards Angelos Charisteas 3+3/0 • Kaba Diawara GUI 10+10/3
Franck Dja Djedje CIV 30+4/4 • Anthony Guise 0+1/0
Jonathan BRA 0+3/0 • Yann Kermorgant 20+6/3 • Chafik Najih 1+1/0
Benjamin Psaume 3+11/0
Coach Michel Estevan • Jean-Louis Saez (16/09/10) • Faruk
Hadzibegic BIH (2/10/10)

KEY
SC = Trophée des Champions (played in Tunis) •
L1 = Ligue 1 • CF = Coupe de France •
LC = Coupe de la Ligue • CL = UEFA Champions
League • EL = Europa League
See page 13 for further explanations

AUXERRE 2010–11

Mon	Date	Opponent	Res	Score	Comp	Scorers	Att
Aug	7	Lorient	D	2-2	L1	Pedretti [20], Le Tallec [58]	8 958
	14	Brest	D	1-1	L1	Pedretti [83]	12 209
	17	Zenit	L	0-1	CLpo		21 405
	21	Val'ciennes	D	1-1	L1	Jelen [69]	8 020
	25	Zenit	W	2-0	CLpo	Hengbart [9], Jelen [53]	15 277
	29	Monaco	L	0-2	L1		6 677
Sep	11	Caen	D	1-1	L1	Pedretti [19]	8 956
	15	Milan	L	0-2	CLgG		69 317
	19	Lille	L	0-1	L1		14 827
	25	Nancy	D	2-2	L1	Oliech 2 [1 11]	**7 664**
	28	Real Madrid	L	0-1	CLgG		19 525
Oct	2	Arlés	W	4-0	L1	Traore [18], Pedretti [44], Contout [58], Birsa [82]	12 459
	16	Bordeaux	L	0-1	L1		10 270
	19	Ajax	L	1-2	CLgG	Birsa [56]	51 383
	24	PSG	W	3-2	L1	Mignot [4], Contout [11], Quercia [24]	27 523
	27	Bastia	W	4-0	LCr4	Quercia [8], Sammaritano 2 [24 78], Hengbart [68]	7 557
	30	Nice	W	2-0	L1	Birsa [43], Pedretti [78]	9 286
Nov	3	Ajax	W	2-1	CLgG	Sammartiano [9], Langil [84]	9 089
	9	St-Etienne	W	2-0	LCqf	Pedretti [16p], Dudka [48p]	7 906
	14	Rennes	W	2-1	L1	Birsa [67], Quercia [86]	9 089
	20	St-Etienne	D	1-1	L1	Mignot [28]	21 830
	23	Milan	L	0-2	CLgG		19 244
	28	Toulouse	L	1-2	L1	Traore [56]	10 326
Dec	4	Lens	D	1-1	L1	Mignot [87]	27 147
	8	Real Madrid	L	0-4	CLgG		54 917
	11	Marseille	D	1-1	L1	Birsa [40p]	16 104
	18	Montpellier	D	1-1	L1	Traore [76]	14 842
	22	Lyon	D	1-1	L1	Quercia [46]	38 838
Jan	8	Wasquehal	L	1-2	CFr9	Coulibaly [12]	3 093
	15	Monaco	D	1-1	L1	Quercia [26]	9 319
	19	Marseille	L	0-2	LCsf		17 025
	29	Caen	L	0-2	L1		13 224
Feb	6	Lille	D	1-1	L1	Dudka [86]	10 965
	12	Nancy	L	1-3	L1	Jelen [55]	14 102
	19	Arlés	D	1-1	L1	Jelen [84]	10 316
	26	Bordeaux	L	0-3	L1		23 105
Mar	5	PSG	W	1-0	L1	Chafni [86]	12 045
	12	Nice	L	0-1	L1		7 582
	19	Sochaux	W	2-0	L1	Jelen 2 [18 64]	16 213
Apr	2	Rennes	D	0-0	L1		27 743
	9	St-Etienne	D	2-2	L1	Oliech [42], Dudka [80p]	**17 298**
	16	Toulouse	W	1-0	L1	Dudka [92+]	33 853
	24	Lens	D	1-1	L1	Boly [6]	12 980
May	1	Marseille	D	1-1	L1	Jung [77]	53 578
	7	Montpellier	W	1-0	L1	Contout [79]	13 004
	11	Lyon	W	4-0	L1	Oliech [20], Traore 2 [45 50], Hengbart [79]	12 007
	15	Val'ciennes	D	1-1	L1	Jung [87]	12 079
	21	Brest	L	0-1	L1		11 922
	29	Lorient	W	2-1	L1	OG [25], Birsa [49]	15 750

9th Att: 214 742 • Av: 11 302 (-8.4%) • L'Abbé-Deschamps 21 379 (52%)

AUXERRE LEAGUE APPEARANCES/GOALS 2010-11
Goalkeepers Olivier Sorin 38
Defenders Jeremy Berthod 11+6/0 • Willy Boly 8/1 • Adama
Coulibaly MLI 38/0 • Stephane Grichting SUI 24+1/0 • Cedric
Hengbart 27+1/1 • Onanga Itoua 2/0 • Jean-Pascal Mignot 16+1/3
Amadou Sidibe MLI 9+1/0
Midfield Valter Birsa SVN 27+6/5 • Kamel Chafni MAR 16+6/1
Dariusz Dudka POL 29/3 • Steeven Langil 3+7/0 • Delvin
Ndinga CGO 25+1/0 • Benoit Pedretti 20/5 • Frederic
Sammaritano 10+17/1 • Prince Segbefia TOG 3+1/0
Alain Traore BFA 18+2/5
Forwards Maxime Bourgeois 0+3/0 • Roy Contout 25+4/3 • Ireneusz
Jelen POL 18+3/5 • Jung Jo Guk KOR 1+14/2 • Anthony Le Tallec 8+14/1
Dennis Oliech KEN 28+5/4 • Julien Quercia 14+5/4
Coach Jean Fernandez

GIRONDINS BORDEAUX 2010–11

Mon	Date	Opponent	Res	Score	Comp	Scorers	Att
Aug	8	Montpellier	L	0-1	L1		21 810
	15	Toulouse	L	1-2	L1	Plasil 48	31 614
	22	PSG	W	2-1	L1	Diarra 67, Cianni 94+	30 073
	29	Marseille	D	1-1	L1	Modeste 88	**32 805**
Sep	12	Nice	L	1-2	L1	Modeste 96+p	10 309
	19	Lyon	W	2-0	L1	Diarra 60, Jussie 92+	29 890
	22	Nancy	W	2-1	LCr3	Bellion 11, Modeste 70	14 605
	25	Caen	D	0-0	L1		19 467
Oct	2	Lorient	W	1-0	L1	Ciani 26	23 944
	16	Auxerre	W	1-0	L1	Modeste 19	10 270
	23	Brest	L	0-2	L1		24 960
	26	St-Etienne	L	0-1	LCr4		24 841
Nov	2	Monaco	D	2-2	L1	OG 10, Jussie 74	5 023
	6	Val'ciennes	D	1-1	L1	Maazou 86	21 679
	13	Nancy	W	2-1	L1	Sane.L 22, Wendel 88	22 640
	21	Arlés	W	4-2	L1	Modeste 3 35p 59 88, Gouffran 39	9 285
	27	Lille	D	1-1	L1	OG 51	26 066
Dec	5	St-Etienne	D	2-2	L1	Ben Khalfallah 30, Fernando 89	19 008
	12	Rennes	D	0-0	L1		**19 991**
	19	Sochaux	D	1-1	L1	Jussie 28	12 030
	22	Lens	D	2-2	L1	Diarra 67, Gouffran 92+	24 014
	8	Rouen	W	3-1	CFr9	Modeste 30, Diabate 2 50 81	8 797
Jan	16	Marseille	L	1-2	L1	Modeste 74p	48 147
	22	Angers	L	0-1	CF10		16 021
	30	Nice	W	2-0	L1	Sane.L 38, Modeste 57	20 251
Feb	6	Lyon	D	0-0	L1		35 909
	6	Caen	L	1-2	L1	Modeste 49	21 857
	19	Lorient	L	1-5	L1	Fernando 40	15 513
	26	Auxerre	W	3-0	L1	Diarra 13, Modeste 53p, Plasil 79	23 105
Mar	8	Brest	W	3-1	L1	Wendel 49, Plasil 67, Diabate 92+	14 034
	13	Monaco	L	0-1	L1		26 811
	19	Val'ciennes	D	2-2	L1	Jussie 81, Ciani 84	11 072
	2	Nancy	D	0-0	L1		19 022
	9	Arlés	D	0-0	L1		24 250
Apr	16	Lille	D	1-1	L1	Sow 58	17 073
	24	St-Etienne	W	2-0	L1	Plasil 15, Diabate 89	29 657
	30	Rennes	D	0-0	L1		22 010
May	7	Sochaux	L	0-4	L1		24 143
	11	Lens	L	0-1	L1		28 209
	18	PSG	W	2-0	L1	Diabate 6p	25 648
	21	Toulouse	L	0-2	L1		18 429
	29	Montpellier	W	2-0	L1	Diabate 15, Wendel 37	21 045

7th Att: 474 370 • Av: 24 967 (-14.7%) • Chaban-Delmas 34 694 (71%)

STADE BRESTOIS 2010–11

Mon	Date	Opponent	Res	Score	Comp	Scorers	Att
Aug	7	Toulouse	L	0-2	L1		14 653
	14	Auxerre	D	1-1	L1	Roux 26	12 209
	21	Lyon	L	0-1	L1		32 720
	28	Caen	W	2-0	L1	Roux 75, Licka 78p	15 490
Sep	12	Lorient	D	0-0	L1		14 480
	18	Nancy	W	2-0	L1	Micola 70, Toure 93+	14 159
	21	Lorient	L	0-1	LCr3		11 309
	26	Val'ciennes	W	1-0	L1	Roux 77	11 520
	2	Monaco	W	1-0	L1	Grougi 71	5 431
Oct	16	Arlés	D	0-0	L1		12 406
	23	Bordeaux	W	2-0	L1	Poyet 6, Lesoimer 80	24 960
	30	St-Etienne	W	2-0	L1	Licka 77, Poyet 84	15 047
Nov	7	Lille	L	1-3	L1	Poyet 62	16 225
	13	Sochaux	D	1-1	L1	Roux 38	12 960
	20	Rennes	L	1-2	L1	Grougi 92+p	28 879
	30	Lens	W	4-1	L1	Poyet 11, Baysse 19, Grougi 2 65 80	13 761
Dec	5	PSG	L	1-3	L1	Roux 54	28 058
	11	Montpellier	D	0-0	L1		11 933
	18	Nice	D	1-1	L1	Martial 14	9 248
	22	Marseille	D	0-0	L1		15 154
	9	Issy	W	1-0	CFr9	Martial 99	3 000
Jan	15	Caen	L	1-3	L1	Grougi 45p	11 971
	22	Chambéry	D	1-1	CF10	Grougi 107, L 3-4p	3 500
	29	Lorient	L	0-2	L1		15 469
	30	Nancy	W	2-1	L1	Ayite 44, Grougi 88	12 280
Feb	6	Val'ciennes	L	0-3	L1		10 682
	19	Monaco	W	2-0	L1	Ayite 2 14 89	13 271
	26	Arlés	D	1-1	L1	Toure 49	7 410
Mar	6	Bordeaux	L	1-3	L1	Ferradj 87	14 034
	12	St-Etienne	L	0-2	L1		20 706
	19	Lille	L	1-2	L1	Lesoimier 18	13 354
	2	Sochaux	L	1-2	L1	Grougi 62p	10 982
	9	Rennes	W	2-0	L1	Roux 29, Grougi 55	15 127
Apr	16	Lens	D	1-1	L1	Ayite 60	30 713
	24	PSG	D	2-2	L1	Toure 37, Grougi 45	14 550
	1	Montpellier	D	0-0	L1		13 837
	7	Nice	D	0-0	L1		14 336
	11	Marseille	L	0-3	L1		46 313
May	16	Lyon	D	1-1	L1	Licka 76	14 527
	21	Auxerre	W	1-0	L1	Toure 63	11 922
	29	Toulouse	L	0-2	L1		14 515

16th Att: 257 435 • Av: 13 549 (+75.9%) • Francis-Le Bié 15 097 (89%)

BORDEAUX LEAGUE APPEARANCES/GOALS 2010-11

Goalkeepers Cedric Carrasso 34+1 • Kevin Olimpa 2 • Ulrich Rame 3+1
Defenders Matthieu Chalme 19+2/0 • Michael Ciani 27+2/3
Henrique BRA 0+2/0 • Florian Marange 11+1/0 • Marc Planus 9+2/0
Ludovic Sane 34/2 • Salif Sane 3/0 • Vujadin Savic SRB 7/1
Benoit Tremoulinas 30+1/0
Midfield Floyd Ayite • Fahid Ben Khalfallah TUN 26+6/1 • Evan
Chevalier 0+1/0 • Alou Diarra 31/4 • Pierre Ducasse 4+6/0 • Remy
Elissalde 0+1/0 • Fernando BRA 34+1/2 • Yoann Gourcuff 2+1/0
Jaroslav Plasil CZE 37/4 • Wendel BRA 26+5/3
Forwards Andre BRA 1+7/0 • David Bellion 0+2/0 • Fernando
Cavenaghi ARG 2/0 • Cheick Diabate MLI 7+9/4 • Yoan
Gouffran 15+7/2 • Jussie BRA 21+10/4 • Moussa Maazou NIG 5+10/1
Anthony Modeste 27+10/10 • Henri Saivet 1+5/0
Coach Laurent Blanc • Jean Tigana (25/05/10) • Eric Bedouet (7/05/11)

BREST LEAGUE APPEARANCES/GOALS 2010-11

Goalkeepers Steeve Elana 38
Defenders Moise Apanga GAB 28+2/0 • Paul Baysse 29+2/1
Ousmane Coulibaly 5+2/0 • Omar Daf SEN 28/0 • Filippos
Darlas GRE 2/0 • Ahmed Kantari MAR 32/0 • Gregory Lorenzi 0+2/0
Johan Martial 7/1 • Theophile N'Iame CMR 0+2/0
Midfield Yoann Bigne 4+5/0 • Anthony Bova 0+2/0 • Oscar
Ewolo CGO 32+3/0 • Brahim Ferradj 21+5/1 • Bruno Grougi 25+8/9
Benoit Lesoimier 28+5/2 • Mario Licka CZE 27+8/3 • Granddi
Ngoyi 17+8/0 • Richard Soumah 8+5/0 • Fodie Traore 1+3/0
Forwards Jonathan Ayite TOG 9+5/4 • Tomas Micola CZE 10+7/1
Romain Poyet 24+8/4 • Nolan Roux 26+2/6 • Larsen Toure GUI 17+5/4
Coach Alex Dupont

SM CAEN 2010–11

Month	Date	Opponent	Res	Score	Comp	Scorers	Att
Aug	7	Marseille	W	2-1	L1	Seube 52, El Arabi 86	55 790
Aug	15	Lyon	W	3-2	L1	El Arabi 2, Yatabare 16, N'Diaye 77	19 937
Aug	22	Montpellier	D	0-0	L1		16 738
Aug	28	Brest	L	0-2	L1		15 490
Sep	11	Auxerre	D	1-1	L1	El Arabi 92+	8 956
Sep	18	Lorient	W	1-0	L1	El Arabi 41	15 522
Sep	22	Arlés	W	1-0	LCr3	Traore 76	4 357
Sep	25	Bordeaux	D	0-0	L1		19 467
Oct	2	Val'ciennes	L	1-2	L1	El Arabi 71	10 469
Oct	16	Monaco	D	0-0	L1		16 285
Oct	23	St-Etienne	D	1-1	L1	El Arabi 38	31 715
Oct	27	Lille	L	1-4	LCr4	Yatabare 13	9 685
Oct	30	Nancy	L	2-3	L1	El Arabi 13, Traore 54	14 016
Nov	6	Arlés	L	2-3	L1	El Arabi 10, Traore 66	7 430
Nov	13	Lille	L	2-5	L1	El Arabi 40, Traore 88	14 997
Nov	20	PSG	L	1-2	L1	El Arabi 85	26 190
Nov	28	Sochaux	L	0-3	L1		13 420
Dec	4	Toulouse	L	0-1	L1		30 275
Dec	11	Nice	D	0-0	L1		**12 350**
Dec	22	Rennes	W	1-0	L1	Hamouma 9	14 500
Jan	8	Lyon	L	0-1	CFr9		10 227
Jan	15	Brest	W	3-1	L1	Nivet 11, El Arabi 81p, Hamouma 87	11 971
Jan	22	Lens	L	0-2	L1		33 564
Jan	29	Auxerre	W	2-0	L1	Nivet 59, Traore 86	13 224
Feb	5	Lorient	L	0-2	L1		13 438
Feb	12	Bordeaux	W	2-1	L1	Traore 10, Hamouma 90	21 857
Feb	19	Val'ciennes	D	2-2	L1	Nivet 47, Yatabare 65	13 648
Feb	26	Monaco	D	2-2	L1	El Arabi 67, Mollo 71	5 142
Mar	5	St-Etienne	W	1-0	L1	El Arabi 92+	17 763
Mar	12	Nancy	L	0-2	L1		16 282
Mar	20	Arlés	W	2-0	L1	Mollo 79, El Arabi 85	14 715
Apr	2	Lille	L	1-3	L1	El Arabi 85	16 898
Apr	9	PSG	L	1-2	L1	Hamouma 94+	18 981
Apr	16	Sochaux	L	2-3	L1	El Arabi 9, Hamouma 89	11 338
Apr	24	Toulouse	D	1-1	L1	Hamouma 29	15 563
May	1	Nice	W	4-0	L1	Hamouma 2 34 89, Mollo 45, El Arabi 91+	7 895
May	7	Lens	D	1-1	L1	Niang 2	20 294
May	11	Rennes	D	1-1	L1	Niang 54	20 044
May	15	Montpellier	W	2-0	L1	Hamouma 27, Traore 69	15 737
May	21	Lyon	D	0-0	L1		37 026
May	29	Marseille	D	2-2	L1	Mollo 7, Niang 45	**20 540**

15th Att: 304 365 • Av: 16 019 (+21.3%) • Michel d'Ornano 22 864 (70%)

RACING CLUB LENS 2010–11

Month	Date	Opponent	Res	Score	Comp	Scorers	Att
Aug	7	Nancy	L	1-2	L1	Maoulida 72	31 392
Aug	14	Arlés	W	1-0	L1	Pollet 69	10 881
Aug	21	Monaco	D	2-2	L1	OG 73, Roudet 83	32 905
Aug	28	St-Etienne	L	1-3	L1	Jemaa 93+	27 520
Sep	11	Lille	L	1-4	L1	Boukari 61	36 811
Sep	18	Val'ciennes	D	1-1	L1	Boukari 90	13 669
Sep	22	Monaco	L	0-1	LCr3		4 661
Sep	26	PSG	L	0-2	L1		28 676
Oct	2	Sochaux	L	0-3	L1		11 115
Oct	17	Rennes	D	0-0	L1		30 224
Oct	23	Nice	W	1-0	L1	Jemaa 91+	29 436
Oct	30	Toulouse	D	1-1	L1	Yahia 28	16 453
Nov	7	Montpellier	W	2-0	L1	Hermach 4, Akale 41	30 502
Nov	13	Marseille	D	1-1	L1	Eduardo 58	50 073
Nov	21	Lyon	L	1-3	L1	Akale 24	32 518
Nov	30	Brest	L	1-4	L1	Eduardo 44	13 761
Dec	4	Auxerre	D	1-1	L1	Yahia 30	**27 147**
Dec	11	Lorient	L	0-3	L1		15 347
Dec	22	Bordeaux	D	2-2	L1	Eduardo 15, Boukari 45	24 014
Jan	8	PSG	L	1-5	CFr9	Eduardo 82p	10 000
Jan	15	St-Etienne	W	2-1	L1	Roudet 82p, OG 83	32 260
Jan	22	Caen	W	2-0	L1	Hermach 20, Maoulida 55	33 564
Jan	29	Lille	L	0-1	L1		17 451
Feb	5	Val'ciennes	D	1-1	L1	Jemaa 37	32 290
Feb	12	PSG	D	0-0	L1		32 919
Feb	19	Sochaux	L	2-3	L1	Jemaa 36, Yahia 59	30 338
Feb	26	Rennes	L	0-2	L1		22 745
Mar	5	Nice	D	0-0	L1		8 235
Mar	12	Toulouse	L	0-1	L1		29 483
Mar	19	Montpellier	W	4-1	L1	Akale 19, OG 30, Roudet 33, Jemaa 62	14 579
Apr	3	Marseille	L	0-1	L1		**40 859**
Apr	10	Lyon	L	0-3	L1		34 429
Apr	16	Brest	D	1-1	L1	Hermach 20	30 713
Apr	24	Auxerre	D	1-1	L1	Roudet 49	12 980
Apr	30	Lorient	L	2-3	L1	Demont 34, Eduardo 36	31 554
May	7	Caen	D	1-1	L1	Varane 37	20 294
May	11	Bordeaux	W	1-0	L1	Hermach 86	28 209
May	15	Monaco	L	1-0	L1	Moukandjo 14	6 444
May	21	Arlés	L	0-1	L1		28 705
May	29	Nancy	L	0-4	L1		19 026

19th Att: 597 586 • Av: 31 452 (-8.1%) • Felix-Bollaert 41 233 (76%)

CAEN LEAGUE APPEARANCES/GOALS 2010-11

Goalkeepers Thomas Bosmel 3 • Alexis Thebaux 35
Defenders Pablo Barzola ARG 11+1/0 • Thomas Heurtaux 29+2/0 Romain Inez 18+2/0 • Branko Lazarevic SRB 4+1/0 • Nicolas Seube 29/1 • Jeremy Sorbon 24+1/0 • Gregory Tafforeau 16/0
Midfield Anthony Deroin 0+4/0 • Romain Hamouma 31+1/9 • Gregory Leca 24+2/0 • Damien Marcq 22+6/0 • Yohan Mollo 27+8/4 • Thibault Moulin 4+13/0 • Ismaila N'Diaye 5+6/1 • Benjamin Nivet 24+7/3 Gregory Proment 6+1/0 • Alexandre Raineau 21+2/0 Rajiv van la Parra NED 1+5/0 • Sambou Yatabare MLI 18+7/2
Forwards Youssef El Arabi MAR 36+2/17 • Benjamin Morel 2+6/0 M'Baye Niang 4+3/3 • Kandia Traore CIV 24+14/6
Coach Franck Dumas

LENS LEAGUE APPEARANCES/GOALS 2010-11

Goalkeepers Hamdi Kasraoui TUN 6+1 • Vedran Runje CRO 32
Defenders Serge Aurier 24+3/0 • Henri Bedimo CMR 31+4/0 Zakarya Bergdich 2/0 • Eric Chelle SEN 15+1/0 • Franck Queudrue 8+1/0 • Marco Ramos POR 2+1/0 • Romain Satre 1/0 Darnel Situ 0+1/0 • Alassane Toure 10+2/0 • Raphael Varane 22+1/2 Alaeddine Yahia TUN 32+2/3
Midfield Kanga Akale CIV 21+9/3 • Abdoulrazak Boukari 14+4/3 Alexandre Coeff 0+1/0 • Yohan Demont 30+3/1 Adil Hermach MAR 30+1/4 • Steven Joseph-Monrose 2+8/0 Sidi Keita MLI 6+1/0 • Geoffrey Kondogbia 1+2/0 Nenad Kovacevic SRB 13+3/0 • Sebastien Roudet 29+3/4 Gregory Sertic 11+12/0 • Samba Sow MLI 7+3/0
Forwards Eduardo BRA 24+8/4 • Issam Jemaa TUN 20+6/5 Toifilou Maoulida 20+12/2 • Kevin Monnet-Paquet 3/0 Abdelhakim Omrani 0+2/0 • David Pollet BEL 2+14/1
Coach Jean-Guy Wallemme • Ladislau Boloni ROU (2/01/11)

LILLE OSC 2010–11

Mon	Date	Opponent	Res	Score	Comp	Scorers	Att
Aug	7	Rennes	D	1-1	L1	Sow 62	21 442
	15	PSG	D	0-0	L1		15 790
	19	Vaslui	D	0-0	ELpo		3 821
	22	Sochaux	D	0-0	L1		11 436
	26	Vaslui	W	2-0	ELpo	Cabaye 70p, Chedjou 81	16 876
	29	Nice	D	1-1	L1	Hazard 67p	16 659
Sep	11	Lens	W	4-1	L1	Gervinho 2 23 87, Frau 2 79 81	36 811
	16	Sporting	L	1-2	ELgC	Frau 57	14 457
	19	Auxerre	W	1-0	L1	Sow 90	14 827
	26	Toulouse	D	1-1	L1	Gervinho 27	15 101
	30	Gent	D	1-1	ELgC	Frau 20	8 755
Oct	3	Montpellier	W	3-1	L1	Sow 2 19 32, Gervinho 80	15 195
	17	Lyon	L	1-3	L1	Sow 52	34 976
	21	Levski	W	1-0	ELgC	Chedjou 50	14 646
	24	Marseille	L	1-3	L1	Cabaye 26	17 305
	27	Caen	W	4-1	LCr4	Cabaye 2 7 44p, Gervinho 53, Hazard 74	9 685
Nov	30	Val'ciennes	L	1-1	L1	OG 86	12 391
	4	Levski	D	2-2	ELgC	Tulio 35, OG 88	17 440
	7	Brest	W	3-1	L1	Sow 41, Gervinho 51, Hazard 75	16 225
	10	Montpellier	L	1-2	LCqf	Hazard 68	5764
	13	Caen	W	5-2	L1	Sow 3 25 34 45, Gervinho 91+, Beria 93+	14 997
	21	Monaco	W	2-1	L1	Frau 39, Obraniak 78	16 454
	27	Bordeaux	D	1-1	L1	Sow 35	26 066
Dec	1	Sporting	L	0-1	ELgC		16 569
	5	Lorient	W	6-3	L1	Sow 3 11 49 82, OG 18, Gervinho 58, Frau 88	14 239
	11	Arlés	W	1-0	L1	Tulio 93+	7 955
	16	Gent	W	3-0	ELgC	Obraniak 30, Frau 56, Sow 89	15 285
	22	St-Etienne	D	1-1	L1	Sow 72	16 783
Jan	8	Forbach	W	3-1	CFr9	Hazard 31, Chedjou 48, Gervinho 74	6 000
	15	Nice	W	2-0	L1	Gervinho 44, Sow 50	6 975
	19	Nancy	W	3-0	L1	Gervinho 2 47 61, Hazard 49	16 145
	23	Wasquehal	W	1-0	CF10	Tulio 40	15 778
	29	Lens	W	1-0	L1	Tulio 68	**17 451**
	2	Nantes	D	1-1	CF11	Hazard 43, W 3-2p	9 302
Feb	6	Auxerre	D	1-1	L1	Sow 9	10 965
	13	Toulouse	W	2-0	L1	Gervinho 38, Tulio 95+	15 941
	17	PSV	D	2-2	ELr2	Gueye 6, Tulio 31	16 951
	20	Montpellier	L	0-1	L1		16 934
	24	PSV	L	1-3	ELr2	Frau 23	28 500
	27	Lyon	D	1-1	L1	Sow 8	17 166
Mar	2	Lorient	D	0-0	CFqf	W 5-3p	13 705
	6	Marseille	W	2-1	L1	Hazard 10, Frau 91+	52 960
	13	Val'ciennes	W	2-1	L1	Sow 39, Hazard 92+	17 083
	19	Brest	W	2-1	L1	Gervinho 39, Sow 53	13 354
	2	Caen	W	3-1	L1	Chedjou 30, Hazard 61, Sow 73	16 898
	2	Monaco	L	0-1	L1		7 986
Apr	16	Bordeaux	D	1-1	L1	Sow 58	17 073
	19	Nice	W	2-0	CFsf	Hazard 44, Gervinho 46	17 135
	24	Lorient	D	1-1	L1	Debuchy 42	16 335
	30	Arlés	W	5-0	L1	Gervinho 2 6 45, Debuchy 49p, Cabaye 84, Rozehnal 89	16 937
May	7	Nancy	W	1-0	L1	Hazard 45	18 037
	10	St-Etienne	W	2-1	L1	Tulio 15, Mavuba 67	22 176
	14	PSG	W	1-0	CFf	Obraniak 89	79 000
	18	Sochaux	W	1-0	L1	Gervinho 53	16 813
	21	PSG	D	2-2	L1	Obraniak 5, Sow 59	40 404
	29	Rennes	W	3-2	L1	Sow 3 36p 61 76	17 111

1st Att: 312 095 • Av: 16 426 (+9.9%) • Métropole 17 963 (91%)

LORIENT 2010–11

Mon	Date	Opponent	Res	Score	Comp	Scorers	Att
Aug	7	Auxerre	D	2-2	L1	Diarra 7, Robert 68	8 958
	14	Nice	L	1-2	L1	Jouffre 11	15 201
	21	Marseille	L	0-2	L1		53 389
	28	Lyon	W	2-0	L1	Gameiro 8p, Kitambala 66	14 814
Sep	12	Brest	D	0-0	L1		14 480
	18	Caen	L	0-1	L1		15 522
	21	Brest	W	1-0	LCr3	Kitambala 45	11 309
	25	Monaco	W	2-1	L1	Gameiro 5, Kitambala 89	16 018
	2	Bordeaux	L	0-1	L1		23 944
Oct	17	Val'ciennes	W	2-1	L1	Gameiro 13p, Diarra 25	**14 541**
	23	Nancy	L	0-1	L1		14 614
	26	Monaco	D	1-1	LCr4	Diarra 118, L 3-5p	4 889
	30	Arlés	W	2-0	L1	Gameiro 55, Kitambala 77	15 758
Nov	6	St-Etienne	W	2-1	L1	Gameiro 2 22 82	27 861
	20	Sochaux	L	0-2	L1		9 266
	27	Rennes	W	2-0	L1	Romao 61, Morel 86	15 369
	5	Lille	L	3-6	L1	Gameiro 2 7 45, Kitambala 57	14 239
Dec	11	Lens	W	3-0	L1	Amalfitano 49, Kitambala 56, Mvuemba 74	15 347
	18	Toulouse	L	0-3	L1		26 027
	21	Montpellier	D	0-0	L1		16 126
Jan	8	Vannes	W	4-1	CFr9	Fanchone 37, Kitambala 58, Diarra 90, Romao 91+	12 065
	15	Lyon	L	0-3	L1		32 722
	22	Fontenay	W	1-0	CF10	Autret 107	5 550
	29	Brest	W	2-0	L1	Gameiro 2 62 70	15 469
	1	Metz	W	3-0	CF11	Gameiro 2 52 91+, Diarra 83	9 000
Feb	5	Caen	W	2-0	L1	Amalfitano 21, Gameiro 86	13 438
	12	Monaco	L	1-3	L1	Gameiro 22	4 921
	19	Bordeaux	W	5-1	L1	Amalfitano 14, Gameiro 3 35 38 88, Mvuemba 62p	15 513
	26	Val'ciennes	D	0-0	L1		10 350
Mar	2	Lille	D	0-0	CFqf	L 3-5p	13 160
	5	Nancy	D	0-0	L1		16 063
	12	Arlés	D	3-3	L1	Amalfitano 19, Diarra 45, Gameiro 53	7 397
	19	St-Etienne	D	0-0	L1		16 045
Apr	2	PSG	D	0-0	L1		27 226
	9	Sochaux	D	1-1	L1	Morel 35	15 104
	16	Rennes	W	2-1	L1	Gameiro 51, Coquelin 62	28 261
	24	Lille	D	1-1	L1	Gameiro 69	16 335
	30	Lens	W	3-2	L1	Gameiro 2 20 83, Amalfitano 92+p	31 554
May	7	Toulouse	D	0-0	L1		15 705
	11	Montpellier	L	1-3	L1	Ecuele 22	13 945
	15	Marseille	D	2-2	L1	Kone 47, Gameiro 80	**16 956**
	21	Nice	L	0-2	L1		10 366
	29	Auxerre	L	1-2	L1	Gameiro 20	15 750

11th Att: 297 058 • Av: 15 635 (+28%) • Stade du Moustoir 18 110 (86%)

LILLE LEAGUE APPEARANCES/GOALS 2010-11
Goalkeepers Mickael Landreau 38
Defenders Franck Beria 25+2/1 • Aurelien Chedjou CMR 31+3/1
Mathieu Debuchy 35/2 • Emerson BRA 17+3/0 • Adil Rami 36/0
David Rozehnal CZE 10+3/1 • Pape Souare SEN 1+1/0
Jerry Vandam 1+1/0
Midfield Florent Balmont 26+1/0 • Yohan Cabaye 36/2 • Stephane
Dumont 1+11/0 • Idrissa Gueye SEN 2+9/0 • Rio Mavuba 38/1
Ludovic Obraniak POL 5+21/2
Forwards Pierre-Alain Frau 10+19/5 • Gervinho CIV 33+2/15 • Eden
Hazard BEL 35+3/7 • Emil Lyng DEN 0+1/0 • Moussa Sow SEN 33+3/25
Tulio de Melo 5+22/4 • Omar Wade SEN 0+3/0
Coach Rudi Garcia

LORIENT LEAGUE APPEARANCES/GOALS 2010-11
Goalkeepers Fabien Audard 29 • Lionel Cappone 9+2 • Benjamin
Lecomte 0+2
Defenders Maxime Baca 27+2/0 • Gregory Bourillon 32+1/0
Bruno Ecuele GAB 31/1 • Lamine Kone 6+2/1 • Arnaud Lo Lan 10+6/0
Jeremy Morel 28+1/2 • Franco Sosa ARG 11+2/0
Midfield Morgan Amalfitano 38/5 • Mathias Autret 0+7/0
Francis Coquelin 13+11/1 • Sigamary Diarra MLI 28+6/3
Cheick Doukoure 1+5/0 • Yann Jouffre 5+8/1
Olivier Monterrubio 0+1/0 • Remi Mulumba 0+1/0
Arnold Mvuemba 33+1/2 • Alaixys Romao TOG 33/1
Forwards Sebastian Dubarbier ARG 1+5/0 • James Fanchone 2+9/0
Kevin Gameiro 36/22 • Lynel Kitambala 24+3/6 • Kevin
Monnet-Paquet 22+9/0 • Fabien Robert 0+4/1 • Gilles Sunu 0+9/0
Coach Christian Gourcuff

OLYMPIQUE LYONNAIS 2010–11

	7	Monaco	D	0-0	L1		35 275
Aug	15	Caen	L	2-3	L1	Gomis 2 6 23	19 937
	21	Brest	W	1-0	L1	Makoun 19	32 720
	28	Lorient	L	0-2	L1		14 814
Sep	11	Val'ciennes	D	1-1	L1	Pied 26	35 925
	14	Schalke	W	1-0	CLgG	Bastos 21	35 552
	19	Bordeaux	L	0-2	L1		29 890
	25	St-Etienne	L	0-1	L1		39 408
	29	Hapoel TA	W	3-1	CLgG	Bastos 2 7p 36, Pjanic 94+	12 226
Oct	2	Nancy	W	3-2	L1	Lopez 37, Briand 2 55 75	17 252
	17	Lille	W	3-1	L1	Lopez 2 3 56p, Gourcuff 41	34 976
	20	Benfica	W	2-0	CLgG	Briand 21, Lisandro 51	36 816
	24	Arlés	D	1-1	L1	Briand 47	11 547
	27	PSG	L	1-2	LCr4	Briand 38	26 587
	30	Sochaux	W	2-1	L1	Bastos 31, Lacazette 69	33 992
Nov	2	Benfica	D	3-4	CLgG	Gourcuff 74, Gomis 85, Lovren 95+	37 394
	6	Rennes	D	1-1	L1	Bastos 54	28 357
	14	Nice	W	1-0	L1	Pied 30	32 672
	21	Lens	W	3-1	L1	Gomis 2 64 73, Lopez 89	32 518
	24	Schalke	L	0-3	CLgG		51 132
	28	PSG	D	2-2	L1	Cissokho 54, Gomis 87	34 965
Dec	4	Montpellier	W	2-1	L1	Lopez 2 5 94+	18 990
	7	Hapoel TA	D	2-2	CLgG	Lisandro 62, Lacazette 88	32 245
	12	Toulouse	W	2-0	L1	Lopez 5, Gomis 35	32 547
	19	Marseille	D	1-1	L1	Lopez 35	54 290
	22	Auxerre	D	1-1	L1	OG 45	38 838
Jan	8	Caen	W	1-0	CFr9	Diakhate 74	10 227
	15	Lorient	W	3-0	L1	Gomis 2 41 58, Kallstrom 54	32 722
	23	Nice	L	0-1	CF10		5 606
	29	Val'ciennes	L	1-2	L1	Bastos 70	11 065
Feb	6	Bordeaux	D	0-0	L1		35 909
	12	St-Etienne	W	4-1	L1	Gomis 28, OG 40, Bastos 69, Briand 91+	34 686
	18	Nancy	W	4-0	L1	Gourcuff 37, Pied 76, Pjanic 86, Briand 89	**31 957**
	22	Real Madrid	D	1-1	CLr2	Gomis 83	40 299
	27	Lille	D	1-1	L1	Kallstrom 26	17 166
Mar	6	Arlés	W	5-0	L1	Lopez 3 14 51 55, Pjanic 18, Bastos 93+	36 786
	12	Sochaux	W	2-0	L1	Lopez 22, Pjanic 64	17 879
	16	Real Madrid	L	0-3	CLr2		70 034
	19	Rennes	D	1-1	L1	Gomis 36	35 504
Apr	3	Nice	D	2-2	L1	Kallstrom 22, Lopez 45	8 856
	10	Lens	W	3-0	L1	OG 55, Briand 61, Lopez 91+	34 429
	17	PSG	L	0-1	L1		40 133
	27	Montpellier	W	3-2	L1	Ederson 23, Lopez 55, Gourcuff 90	34 849
May	1	Toulouse	L	0-2	L1		20 785
	8	Marseille	W	3-2	L1	Lopez 25p, Delgado 69, Cris 84	**39 548**
	11	Auxerre	L	0-4	L1		12 007
	16	Brest	D	1-1	L1	Licka 76	14 527
	21	Caen	D	0-0	L1		37 026
	29	Monaco	W	2-0	L1	Diakhate 67, Lopez 82	11 140

3rd Att: 670 048 • Av: 35 266 (-1.5%) • Stade de Gerland 41 044 (85%)

OLYMPIQUE MARSEILLE 2010–11

Jy	28	PSG	D	0-0	SC	W 5-4p	57 000
	7	Caen	L	1-2	L1	Samassa 77	**55 790**
Aug	14	Val'ciennes	L	2-3	L1	Taiwo 82p, Ayew.A 85	15 637
	21	Lorient	W	2-0	L1	Heinze 6, Taiwo 71	53 389
	29	Bordeaux	D	1-1	L1	Lucho 12	32 805
	12	Monaco	D	2-2	L1	Valbuena 42, OG 80	49 384
	15	Sp Moskva	L	0-1	CLgG		45 729
Sep	18	Arlés	W	3-0	L1	Cheyrou 32, Ayew.A 2 37 54	15 003
	25	Sochaux	W	2-1	L1	Taiwo 19, Lucho 61	49 895
	28	Chelsea	L	0-2	CLgG		40 675
	2	St-Etienne	D	1-1	L1	Gignac 27	35 003
Oct	16	Nancy	W	1-0	L1	Remy 27	48 306
	19	Zilina	W	1-0	CLgG	Diawara 48	49 250
	24	Lille	W	3-1	L1	Remy 2 53 80, Lucho 71	17 305
	27	Guingamp	W	1-0	LCr4	Ayew.A 42	17 037
	3	Zilina	W	7-0	CLgG	Gignac 3 12 21 54, Heinze 24, Remy 36, Lucho 2 52 63	9 664
	7	PSG	L	1-2	L1	Lucho 30	40 234
Nov	10	Monaco	W	2-1	LCqf	Ayew.A 42, Azpilicueta 60	17 765
	13	Lens	D	1-1	L1	Mbia 6	50 073
	20	Toulouse	W	1-0	L1	Ayew.A 88	30 258
	23	Sp Moskva	W	3-0	CLgG	Valbuena 18, Remy 54, Brandao 68	43 217
	27	Montpellier	W	4-0	L1	Lucho 20, Cheyrou 28, Valbuena 65, Remy 92+	51 137
Dec	1	Rennes	D	0-0	L1		50 057
	5	Nice	L	0-1	L1		12 415
	8	Chelsea	W	1-0	CLgG	Brandao 81	50 604
	11	Auxerre	D	1-1	L1	Remy 8	16 104
	19	Lyon	D	1-1	L1	Valbuena 51	54 290
	22	Brest	D	0-0	L1		15 154
	9	Evian TG	L	1-3	CFr9	OG 58	12 246
Jan	16	Bordeaux	W	2-1	L1	Gignac 23, Brandao 45	48 147
	19	Auxerre	W	2-0	LCsf	Brandao 45, Gignac 68	17 025
	30	Monaco	D	0-0	L1		10 991
	5	Arlés	W	1-0	L1	Gignac 55	47 737
	5	Sochaux	W	2-1	L1	Gignac 2 45 70	19 905
Feb	19	St-Etienne	W	2-1	L1	Lucho 69, Remy 79	53 494
	23	Man Utd	D	0-0	CLr2		57 957
	27	Nancy	W	2-1	L1	Ayew.A 2 45 87	20 019
	6	Lille	L	1-2	L1	Remy 60	52 960
	11	Rennes	W	2-0	L1	Remy 3, Lucho 80	29 002
Mar	15	Man Utd	L	1-2	CLr2	OG 82	73 996
	20	PSG	W	2-1	L1	Heinze 16, Ayew.A 35	52 792
	3	Lens	W	1-0	L1	Cheyrou 68	40 859
	10	Toulouse	D	2-2	L1	Remy 30, Gignac 84	50 698
Apr	17	Montpellier	W	2-1	L1	Gignac 69, Taiwo 82p	25 119
	23	Montpellier	W	1-0	LCf	Taiwo 80	78 511
	27	Nice	W	4-2	L1	Ayew.A 3 30 60 90, Ayew.J 78	49 574
	1	Auxerre	D	1-1	L1	Valbuena 56	53 578
	8	Lyon	L	2-3	L1	Lucho 70, Remy 78	39 548
May	11	Brest	W	3-0	L1	Remy 12, Ayew.J 59, Heinze 81	**46 313**
	15	Lorient	D	2-2	L1	Remy 14, Gignac 88	16 956
	21	Val'ciennes	D	2-2	L1	Ayew.A 34, Remy 37	52 923
	29	Caen	D	2-2	L1	Remy 2 68 88	20 540

2nd Att: 970 537 • Av: 51 081 (+2.0%) • Vélodrome 60 013 (85%)

LYON LEAGUE APPEARANCES/GOALS 2010-11
Goalkeepers Hugo Lloris 37 • Remy Vercoutre 1
Defenders Aly Cissokho 30/1 • Cris BRA 19+1/1
Pape Diakhate SEN 23+1/1 • Lamine Gassama SEN 3+1/0
Thimothee Kolodziejczak 7+1/0 • Dejan Lovren CRO 26+2/0
Anthony Reveillere 35/0
Midfield Cesar Delgado ARG 9+10/1 • Ederson BRA 5+3/2 • Maxime
Gonalons 15+8/0 • Yoann Gourcuff 20+4/3 • Clement Grenier 2+5/0
Kim Kallstrom SWE 29+4/3 • Jean Makoun CMR 11+2/1
Michel Bastos BRA 22+6/5 • Jeremy Pied 7+17/3 • Miralem
Pjanic BIH 16+14/3 • Enzo Reale 1/0 • Jeremy Toulalan 27+1/0
Forwards Jimmy Briand 22+11/6 • Bafetimbi Gomis 28+7/10
Alexandre Lacazette 0+8/1 • Lisandro Lopez ARG 24+3/17
Harry Novillo 1/0
Coach Claude Puel

MARSEILLE LEAGUE APPEARANCES/GOALS 2010-11
Goalkeepers Steve Mandanda 38
Defenders Azpilicueta ESP 12+3/0 • Souleymane Diawara SEN 27/0
Rod Fanni 19/0 • Gabriel Heinze ARG 31/3 • Hilton BRA 6+2/0
Taye Taiwo NGA 29+1/4
Midfield Fabrice Abriel 4+18/0 • Hatem Ben Arfa 0+1/0 • Benoit
Cheyrou 27+7/3 • Edouard Cisse 21+2/0 • Lucho Gonzalez ARG 33+3/8
Charles Kabore BFA 22+12/0 • Stephane Mbia CMR 24+2/1
Leyti N'Diaye SEN 3+1/0 • Matthieu Valbuena 26+6/4
Forwards Andre Ayew GHA 32+6/11 • Jordan Ayew GHA 5+17/2
Brandao BRA 13+6/1 • Andre-Pierre Gignac 20+10/8 • Guy
Gnabouyou 0+1/0 • Mamadou Niang SEN 2/0 • Loic Remy 24+7/15
Coach Didier Deschamps

MONACO 2010–11

Mth	Date	Opponent	Res	Score	Comp	Scorers	Att
Aug	7	Lyon	D	0-0	L1		35 275
	17	Montpellier	D	0-0	L1		8 917
	21	Lens	D	2-2	L1	Niculae 19, Aubameyang 70	32 905
	29	Auxerre	W	2-0	L1	Niculae 52, Aubameyang 59	6 677
Sep	12	Marseille	D	2-2	L1	Niculae 15, Park 79	49 384
	18	Toulouse	D	0-0	L1		6 070
	22	Lens	W	1-0	LCr3	Niculae 83p	4 661
	25	Lorient	L	1-2	L1	Mbokani 26	16 018
Oct	2	Brest	L	0-1	L1		5 431
	16	Caen	D	0-0	L1		16 285
	23	Val'ciennes	L	0-2	L1		5 121
	26	Lorient	D	1-1	LCr4	Hansson 99. W 5-3p	4 889
Nov	2	Bordeaux	D	2-2	L1	Park 49, Coutadeur 65	5 023
	7	Nancy	W	4-0	L1	Malonga 2 55 62, Park 2 81 87	14 745
	10	Marseille	L	1-2	LCqf	Coutadeur 22p	17 765
	13	Arlés	D	0-0	L1		5 161
	21	Lille	L	1-2	L1	Adriano 57	16 454
	27	Nice	D	1-1	L1	Park 76	9 134
Dec	4	Rennes	L	0-1	L1		20 829
	12	St-Etienne	L	0-2	L1		6 694
	18	PSG	D	2-2	L1	Puygrenier 32, Niculae 88	32 842
	22	Sochaux	W	2-1	L1	Malonga 8, Park 93+	4 984
Jan	8	Chambéry	D	1-1	CFr9	Malonga 19. L 2-3p	3 500
	15	Auxerre	D	1-1	L1	Adriano 71	9 319
	30	Marseille	D	0-0	L1		10 991
Feb	6	Toulouse	L	0-2	L1		24 662
	12	Lorient	W	3-1	L1	Lolo 3, Mangani 56, Park 94+	4 921
	19	Brest	L	0-2	L1		13 271
	26	Caen	D	2-2	L1	Park 2 35p 62	5 142
Mar	5	Val'ciennes	D	0-0	L1		11 859
	13	Bordeaux	W	1-0	L1	Adriano 22	26 811
	20	Nancy	L	0-1	L1		5 446
		Arlés	W	2-0	L1	Moukandjo 29, Park 66	9 203
Apr	9	Lille	W	1-0	L1	Park 12	7 986
	16	Nice	L	2-3	L1	Gosso 28, Park 75	8 988
	24	Rennes	W	1-0	L1	Welcome 72	6 569
	1	St-Etienne	D	1-1	L1	Welcome 30	23 656
	7	PSG	D	1-1	L1	Adriano 24	9 338
May	11	Sochaux	L	0-3	L1		14 524
	15	Lens	L	0-2	L1	Moukandjo 14	6 444
	21	Montpellier	W	1-0	L1	Moukandjo 56	17 998
	29	Lyon	L	0-2	L1		11 140

18th Att: 131 189 • Av: 6 905 (-12.6%) • Stade Louis II 18 521 (37%)

MONTPELLIER 2010–11

Mth	Date	Opponent	Res	Score	Comp	Scorers	Att
Jy	29	Györi ETO	W	1-0	ELpo	Giroud 32	7 000
Aug	5	Györi ETO	L	0-1	ELpo	L 3-4p	9 928
	8	Bordeaux	W	1-0	L1	Bocaly 47	21 810
	17	Monaco	D	0-0	L1		8 917
	22	Caen	D	0-0	L1		16 738
	28	Val'ciennes	W	1-0	L1	Giroud 29	11 122
Sep	11	Nancy	L	1-2	L1	Estrada 49	14 427
	18	St-Etienne	L	0-3	L1		30 406
	25	Arlés	W	3-1	L1	Giroud 2 42 48, Camara 82	13 748
Oct	3	Lille	L	1-3	L1	Giroud 23p	15 195
	16	Sochaux	W	2-0	L1	Yanga-Mbiwa 30, Belhanda 44	13 967
	23	Rennes	W	1-0	L1	Marveaux 43	22 688
	26	Ajaccio	W	2-0	LCr4	Kabze 32, Koita 89	6 616
	31	PSG	D	1-1	L1	Estrada 42	19 967
Nov	7	Lens	L	0-2	L1		30 502
	10	Lille	W	2-1	LCqf	Kabze 2 28 52	5 764
	13	Toulouse	W	1-0	L1	Giroud 20	15 175
	20	Nice	W	1-0	L1	Giroud 83	6 826
	27	Marseille	L	0-4	L1		51 137
Dec	4	Lyon	L	1-2	L1	Spahic 80	18 990
	11	Brest	D	0-0	L1		11 933
	18	Auxerre	D	1-1	L1	Belhanda 58	14 842
	21	Lorient	D	0-0	L1		16 126
	8	St. de Reims	L	0-1	CFr9		5 018
Jan	15	Val'ciennes	W	2-1	L1	Giroud 80, El Kaoutari 81	13 560
	18	PSG	W	1-0	LCsf	Giroud 117	17 641
	30	Nancy	W	2-1	L1	Camara 8, Bocaly 59	13 536
	5	St-Etienne	L	1-2	L1	Martin 86	18 035
Feb	12	Arlés	D	0-0	L1		8 489
	20	Lille	W	1-0	L1	Belhanda 84	16 934
	26	Sochaux	D	0-0	L1		12 085
	5	Rennes	L	0-1	L1		15 165
Mar	13	PSG	D	2-2	L1	Giroud 2 47 59	23 605
	19	Lens	L	1-4	L1	Bocaly 57	14 579
	2	Toulouse	W	1-0	L1	Camara 75	12 123
	10	Nice	D	1-1	L1	Dernis 42	14 245
Apr	17	Marseille	L	1-2	L1	Giroud 64	25 119
	23	Marseille	L	0-1	LCf		78 511
	27	Lyon	L	2-3	L1	Giroud 30, Camara 84	34 849
	1	Brest	D	0-0	L1		13 877
	7	Auxerre	L	0-1	L1		13 004
May	11	Lorient	W	3-1	L1	Giroud 26, Estrada 52, Saihi 64	13 945
	15	Caen	L	0-2	L1		15 737
	21	Monaco	L	0-1	L1		17 998
	29	Bordeaux	L	0-2	L1		21 045

14th Att: 313 081 • Av: 16 478 (-8.4%) • Stade de la Mosson 32 950 (50%)

MONACO LEAGUE APPEARANCES/GOALS 2010-11
Goalkeepers Sebastien Chabbert 4+2 • Stephane Ruffier 34
Defenders Adriano BRA 32/4 • Laurent Bonnart 24+1/0
Petter Hansson SWE 28+2/0 • Layvin Kurzawa 5/0 • Igor Lolo CIV 9+9/1
Thomas Mangani 20+4/1 • Cedric Mongongu COD 14+5/0
Vincent Muratori 14+3/0 • Nicolas N'Koulou CMR 26+4/0
Sebastien Puygrenier 28+3/1 • Djimi Traore MLI 5+2/0
Midfield Alejandro Alonso ARG 3+1/0 • Frederic Bulot GAB 3+5/0
Mathieu Coutadeur 11+7/1 • Mahamadou Diarra MLI 9/0
Pascal Feindouno GUI 2+3/0 • Jean-Jacques Gosso CIV 10+4/1
Lukman Haruna NGA 12+5/0 • Gregory Lacombe 4+4/0
Cris Malonga 9+7/1 • Nampalys Mendy 13+1/0
Forwards Pierre Aubameyang GAB 17+2/2 • Serge Gakpe TOG 2+8/0
Valere Germain 6+2/0 • Moussa Maazou NIG 0+1/0
Kevin Malcuit 0+1/0 • Dieumerci Mbokani COD 9+1/1
Benjamin Moukandjo CMR 13+3/3 • Daniel Niculae ROU 13+4/4
Park Chu Young KOR 32+1/12 • Yannick Sagbo CIV 0+1/0
Georgie Welcome HON 5+8/2
Coach Guy Lacombe • Laurent Banide (10/01/11)

MONTPELLIER LEAGUE APPEARANCES/GOALS 2010-11
Goalkeepers Geoffrey Jourdren 37 • Laurent Pionnier 1
Defenders Garry Bocaly 27+2/3 • Xavier Collin 2+1/0 • Nenad
Dzodic SRB 3/0 • Abdelhamid El Kaoutari MAR 18+7/1 • Cyril
Jeunechamp 31/0 • Emir Spahic BIH 23/1 • Benjamin
Stambouli 14+12/0 • Mapou Yanga-Mbiwa CTA 36/1
Midfield Younes Belhanda MAR 28+8/3 • Geoffrey Dernis 14+11/1
Marco Estrada CHI 26+4/3 • Gregory Lacombe 0+3/0
Jonas Martin 0+5/0 • Joris Marveaux 30+5/1 • Romain Pitau 27+3/0
Jamel Saihi TUN 5+9/1
Forwards Karim Ait Fana 9+10/0 • Romain Armand 0+1/0
Souleymane Camara SEN 28+8/4 • Olivier Giroud 33+4/12 • Hasan
Kabze TUR 16+6/0 • Bengali-Fode Koita 1+4/0 • John Utaka NGA 9+2/0
Coach Rene Girard

NANCY 2010–11

	7	Lens	W	2-1	L1	Feret [27], Berenguer [83]	31 392
	14	Rennes	L	0-3	L1		14 512
Aug	21	Nice	D	1-1	L1	Alo'o Efoulou [85]	7 711
	28	Toulouse	L	0-2	L1		14 335
	11	Montpellier	W	2-1	L1	Bakar [5], Traore [34]	14 427
	18	Brest	L	0-2	L1		14 159
Sep	22	Bordeaux	L	1-2	LCr3	Diakite [61]	14 605
	25	Auxerre	D	2-2	L1	Cuvillier [17], Vahirua [36]	7 664
	2	Lyon	L	2-3	L1	Andre Luiz [57], Feret [70]	17 252
	16	Marseille	L	0-1	L1		48 306
Oct	23	Lorient	W	1-0	L1	Feret [8]	14 614
	30	Caen	W	3-2	L1	Hadji [36p], OG [39], Traore [69]	14 016
	7	Monaco	L	0-4	L1		14 745
Nov	13	Bordeaux	L	0-2	L1	Alo'o Efoulou [83]	22 640
	20	Val'ciennes	W	2-0	L1	Andre Luiz [29], Vahirua [74]	14 083
	27	St-Etienne	D	1-1	L1	Vahirua [68]	14 381
	4	Arlés	D	1-1	L1	Hadji [26]	7 295
Dec	11	Sochaux	W	1-0	L1	Andre Luiz [74]	**13 401**
	22	PSG	W	2-0	L1	Hadji 2 [66 83]	17 845
	9	Aurillac	D	2-2	CFr9	Feret [20], Andre Luiz [42], W 4-3p	4 800
	15	Toulouse	L	0-1	L1		12 107
Jan	19	Lille	L	0-3	L1		16 145
	22	Nimes	W	2-1	CFl0	Feret 2 [68 108]	6 743
	30	Montpellier	L	1-2	L1	Hadji [2]	13 536
	2	Le Mans	L	1-2	CFl1	Diakite [32]	5 023
	5	Brest	L	1-2	L1	OG [74]	12 280
Feb	12	Auxerre	W	3-1	L1	Feret [9], Cuvillier [15], Hadji [47]	14 102
	18	Lyon	L	0-4	L1		31 957
	27	Marseille	L	1-2	L1	Feret [34]	**20 019**
	5	Lorient	D	0-0	L1		16 063
Mar	12	Caen	W	2-0	L1	N'Guemo [38], Traore [85]	16 282
	20	Monaco	W	1-0	L1	Andre Luiz [19]	5 446
	2	Bordeaux	D	0-0	L1		19 022
	9	Val'ciennes	D	1-1	L1	Vahirua [92+]	10 607
Apr	16	St-Etienne	L	1-2	L1	Andre Luiz [40]	24 274
	24	Arlés	D	0-0	L1		18 873
	30	Sochaux	L	0-1	L1		14 082
	7	Lille	L	0-1	L1		18 037
	10	PSG	D	2-2	L1	N'Guemo [21p], Hadji [68]	27 675
May	15	Nice	W	3-0	L1	Hadji [34], Berenguer [76], Traore [86]	19 401
	21	Rennes	W	2-0	L1	Traore [16], Feret [92+]	24 250
	29	Lens	W	4-0	L1	Berenguer 2 [29 49], OG [45], Vahirua [92+]	19 026

13th Att: 307 625 • Av: 16 191 (-0.8%) • Marcel Picot 20 087 (80%)

OGC NICE 2010–11

	7	Val'ciennes	D	0-0	L1		7 833
	14	Lorient	W	2-1	L1	Gace [12], Remy [70]	15 201
Aug	21	Nancy	D	1-1	L1	Fae [27]	7 711
	29	Lille	D	1-1	L1	Fae [34p]	16 659
	12	Bordeaux	W	2-1	L1	Mouloungui [35], Bamogo [94+]	10 309
	18	Sochaux	L	0-4	L1		9 744
Sep	22	St-Etienne	L	0-2	LCr3		13 468
	25	Rennes	L	1-2	L1	Ljuboja [26]	7 577
	3	PSG	D	0-0	L1		22 595
	17	St-Etienne	W	2-1	L1	Mounier [47], Ben Saada [67]	9 306
Oct	23	Lens	L	0-1	L1		29 436
	30	Auxerre	L	0-2	L1		9 286
	7	Toulouse	W	2-0	L1	Ljuboja [17], Ben Saada [92+]	7 636
Nov	14	Lyon	L	0-1	L1		32 672
	20	Montpellier	L	0-1	L1		6 826
	27	Monaco	D	1-1	L1	Mouloungui [85]	9 134
	5	Marseille	W	1-0	L1	Fae [92+]	**12 415**
Dec	11	Caen	D	0-0	L1		12 350
	18	Brest	D	1-1	L1	Ljuboja [7]	9 248
	22	Arlés	D	0-0	L1		9 085
	6	Créteil	D	1-1	CFr9	Mouloungui [18], W 7-6p	2 500
Jan	15	Lille	L	0-2	L1		6 975
	23	Lyon	W	1-0	CFl0	Clerc [98]	5 606
	30	Bordeaux	L	0-2	L1		20 251
	2	Drancy	W	1-0	CFl1	Mounier [42]	6 000
	5	Sochaux	W	1-0	L1	Pejcinovic [29]	**6 699**
Feb	13	Rennes	L	0-2	L1		18 387
	20	PSG	L	0-3	L1		8 655
	26	St-Etienne	W	2-0	L1	Coulibaly [55], Mounier [85]	19 793
	1	St. de Reims	W	3-2	CFqf	Ljuboja [31], Mouloungui 2 [48 114]	19 763
	5	Lens	D	0-0	L1		8 235
Mar	12	Auxerre	W	1-0	L1	Mouloungui [62]	7 582
	19	Toulouse	D	1-1	L1	OG [93+]	12 356
	3	Lyon	D	2-2	L1	Mouloungui [91+], Civelli [93+]	8 856
	10	Montpellier	D	1-1	L1	OG [73]	14 245
Apr	16	Monaco	W	3-2	L1	Mounier [21], Civelli [46], Mouloungui [59]	8 988
	19	Lille	L	0-2	CFsf		17 135
	27	Marseille	L	2-4	L1	Traore [42], Civelli [93+]	49 574
	1	Caen	L	0-4	L1		7 895
	7	Brest	D	0-0	L1		14 336
	11	Arlés	W	3-2	L1	Ljuboja 2 [31 76], Clerc [55]	7 526
May	15	Nancy	L	0-3	L1		19 401
	21	Lorient	W	2-0	L1	Mouloungui 2 [1 16]	10 366
	29	Val'ciennes	L	1-2	L1	Mouloungui [87]	15 193

17th Att: 160 638 • Av: 8 455 (-2.9%) • Stade du Ray 18 696 (45%)

NANCY LEAGUE APPEARANCES/GOALS 2010-11

Goalkeepers Gennaro Bracigliano 7 • Damien Gregorini 31
Defenders Andre Luiz BRA 34/5 • Michael Chretien MAR 26/0 • Reynald Lemaitre 23+2/0 • Jordan Loties 24+1/0 • Joel Sami 20+3/0
Midfield Pascal Berenguer 15+3/4 • Jonathan Brison 28+6/0 • Aatif Chahechouhe 1+4/0 • Alexandre Cuvillier 17+8/2 • Samba Diakite 16+7/0 • Julien Feret 36/6 • Benjamin Gavanon 16+7/0 • Massadio Haidara 7+3/0 • Ziri Hammar 0+1/0 • Chris Malonga CGO 0+2/0 • Alfred N'Diaye 10+4/0 • Landry N'Guemo CMR 30+3/2 • Fouad Rachid 0+2/0 • Bakaye Traore MLI 19+10/5
Forwards Paul Alo'o Efoulou MLI 3+5/2 • Djamel Bakar 10+10/1 • Youssouf Hadji MAR 25+1/8 • Benjamin Jeannot 5+4/0 • Marama Vahirua 15+10/5
Coach Pablo Correa URU

NICE LEAGUE APPEARANCES/GOALS 2010-11

Goalkeepers Lionel Letizi 3+1 • David Ospina COL 35
Defenders Alain Cantareil 1+3/0 • Renato Civelli ARG 31/3 • Francois Clerc 29/1 • Drissa Diakite MLI 24+5/0 • Ismael Gace 12+6/1 • Larrys Mabiala COD 6+3/0 • Kevin Malaga 0+1/0 • Gregory Paisley 8/0 • Nemanja Pejcinovic SRB 32/1/1
Midfield Chaouki Ben Saada TUN 15+12/2 • Kafoumba Coulibaly CIV 33+1/1 • Didier Digard 21+3/0 • Émerse Fae CIV 23+1/3 • David Hellebuyck 4+5/0 • Cyril Hennion 0+1/0 • Anthony Mounier 33+1/3 • Lloyd Pallun 3+3/0 • Julien Sable 29+3/0 • Abdou Traore MLI 14+9/1
Forwards Adeilson BRA 0+1/0 • Mamadou Bagayoko MLI 1+4/0 • Stephane Bahoken 0+1/0 • Habib Bamogo BFA 2+9/1 • David Bellion 9+1/0 • Esmael Goncalves 0+1/0 • Danijel Ljuboja SRB 22+8/5 • Eric Mouloungui GAB 26+8/8 • Mickael Pote BEN 0+8/0 • Abeiku Quansah GHA 0+5/0 • Loic Remy 2/1
Coach Eric Roy

PARIS SAINT-GERMAIN 2010-11

Date	Opponent	Res	Score	Comp	Scorers	Att
Jul 28	Marseille	D	0-0	SC	L 4-5p	57 000
Aug 7	St-Etienne	W	3-1	L1	Erdinc [5], OG [42], Nene [83]	22 689
Aug 15	Lille	D	0-0	L1		15 790
Aug 19	Maccabi TA	W	2-0	ELpo	Luyindula [3], Hoarau [60]	10 322
Aug 22	Bordeaux	L	1-2	L1	Hoarau [76]	30 073
Aug 26	Maccabi TA	L	3-4	ELpo	Hoarau [40p], Giuly [64], Nene [90p]	8 674
Aug 29	Sochaux	L	1-3	L1	Hoarau [50]	12 222
Sep 11	Arlés	W	4-0	L1	Hoarau [18], Sakho [29], Nene 2 [49] [56]	19 025
Sep 16	Sevilla	W	1-0	ELgJ	Nene [76]	24 960
Sep 19	Rennes	D	0-0	L1		28 606
Sep 26	Lens	W	2-0	L1	OG [49], Nene [93+]	28 676
Sep 30	Karpaty	W	2-0	ELgJ	Jallet [4], Nene [20]	11 295
Oct 3	Nice	D	0-0	L1		22 595
Oct 16	Toulouse	W	2-0	L1	Sakho [11], Erdinc [56]	20 437
Oct 21	B Dortmund	D	1-1	ELgJ	Chamtome [87]	50 200
Oct 24	Auxerre	L	2-3	L1	Nene 2 [1] [68p]	27 523
Oct 27	Lyon	W	2-1	LCr4	Bodmer [86], Giuly [101]	26 587
Oct 31	Montpellier	D	1-1	L1	Giuly [37]	19 967
Nov 4	B Dortmund	D	0-0	ELgJ		26 204
Nov 7	Marseille	W	2-1	L1	Erdinc [9], Hoarau [19]	40 234
Nov 10	Val'ciennes	W	3-1	LCqf	Camara [9], Jallet [27], Luyindula [51]	7 395
Nov 14	Lorient	D	1-1	L1	Nene [90]	15 422
Nov 20	Caen	W	2-1	L1	Hoarau [40], Erdinc [50]	26 190
Nov 28	Lyon	D	2-2	L1	Cissokho [54], Gomis [87]	34 965
Dec 2	Sevilla	W	4-2	ELgJ	Bodmer [17], Hoarau 2 [20] [47], Nene [45]	18 783
Dec 5	Brest	W	3-1	L1	Nene [5], Bodmer [59], Giuly [77]	28 058
Dec 11	Val'ciennes	W	2-1	L1	Nene 2 [47] [84]	11 136
Dec 15	Karpaty	D	1-1	ELgJ	Luyindula [39]	14 230
Dec 18	Monaco	D	2-2	L1	Nene 2 [40] [52]	32 842
Dec 22	Nancy	L	0-2	L1		17 845
Jan 8	Lens	W	5-1	CFr9	Camara [20], Nene [50], Hoarau 2 [53p] [62], Luyindula [75]	10 000
Jan 15	Sochaux	W	2-1	L1	Sakho [16], Giuly [23]	28 201
Jan 18	Montpellier	L	0-1	LCsf		17 641
Jan 23	Agen	W	3-2	CF10	Bodmer [13], Luyindula [47], Hoarau [50]	11 000
Jan 29	Arlés	W	2-1	L1	Erdinc 2 [17] [49]	8 576
Feb 2	Martigues	W	4-1	CF11	Hoarau 3 [15] [79] [91+], Luyindula [64]	7 500
Feb 5	Rennes	L	0-1	L1		26 001
Feb 12	Lens	D	0-0	L1		32 919
Feb 17	BATE	D	2-2	ELr2	Erdinc [30], Luyindula [89]	6 000
Feb 20	Nice	W	3-0	L1	Giuly [24], Hoarau [44], Armand [74]	8 655
Feb 24	BATE	D	0-0	ELr2		17 717
Feb 27	Toulouse	W	2-1	L1	Armand [28], OG [38]	29 860
Mar 2	Le Mans	W	2-0	CFqf	Bahebeck [108], Kebano [117]	12 760
Mar 5	Auxerre	L	0-1	L1		12 045
Mar 10	Benfica	L	1-2	ELr3	Luyindula [14]	33 928
Mar 13	Montpellier	D	2-2	L1	Hoarau [11], OG [13]	23 605
Mar 17	Benfica	D	1-1	ELr3	Bodmer [35]	40 193
Mar 20	Marseille	L	1-2	L1	Chantome [27]	52 792
Apr 2	Lorient	D	0-0	L1		27 226
Apr 9	Caen	W	2-1	L1	Jallet [13], Chantome [69]	18 981
Apr 17	Lyon	W	1-0	L1	Camara [76]	40 133
Apr 20	Angers	W	3-1	CFsf	Bodmer [22], Nene [50], Hoarau [62]	17 000
Apr 24	Brest	D	2-2	L1	Bodmer [20], OG [87]	14 550
Apr 30	Val'ciennes	W	3-1	L1	Nene [10], Bodmer [22], Sakho [88]	29 158
May 7	Monaco	D	1-1	L1	Erdinc [51]	9 338
May 10	Nancy	D	2-2	L1	Erdinc [4], Camara [45]	27 675
May 14	Lille	L	0-1	CFf		79 000
May 18	Bordeaux	L	0-1	L1		25 648
May 21	Lille	D	2-2	L1	Hoarau [45], Bodmer [73]	40 404
May 29	St-Etienne	D	1-1	L1	Bodmer [91+p]	25 874

4th Att: 557 016 • Av: 29 317 (-11.9%) • Parc des Princes 47 428 (61%)

STADE RENNAIS 2010-11

Date	Opponent	Res	Score	Comp	Scorers	Att
Aug 7	Lille	D	1-1	L1	Bangoura [25]	21 442
Aug 14	Nancy	W	3-0	L1	Montano [50], Brahimi [58], Bangoura [87]	14 512
Aug 21	St-Etienne	D	0-0	L1		24 731
Aug 28	Arlés	W	1-0	L1	Montano [28]	9 364
Sep 11	Sochaux	W	2-1	L1	T-Catherine [5], Mangane [93+]	17 504
Sep 19	PSG	D	0-0	L1		28 606
Sep 22	Guingamp	L	1-3	LCr3	Kembo-Ekoko [4]	7 828
Sep 25	Nice	W	2-1	L1	Dalmat [7], Montano [77]	7 577
Oct 3	Toulouse	W	3-1	L1	Danze [45], Mangane [77], Marveaux [81p]	21 711
Oct 17	Lens	D	0-0	L1		30 224
Oct 23	Montpellier	L	0-1	L1		22 688
Nov 6	Lyon	D	1-1	L1	Kembo-Ekoko [5]	28 357
Nov 14	Auxerre	L	1-2	L1	Kembo-Ekoko [70]	9 089
Nov 20	Brest	W	2-1	L1	Kembo-Ekoko [39], Leroy [82]	28 879
Nov 27	Lorient	L	0-2	L1		15 369
Dec 1	Marseille	D	0-0	L1		50 057
Dec 4	Monaco	W	1-0	L1	Montano [64p]	20 829
Dec 12	Bordeaux	D	0-0	L1		19 991
Dec 18	Val'ciennes	W	1-0	L1	Kana-Biyik [93+]	20 112
Dec 22	Caen	L	0-1	L1		14 500
Jan 9	Cannes	W	7-0	CFr9	Tettey 2 [15] [64], Montano 2 [20] [24], M'Vila [30], Camara [69], Brahimi [77]	6 331
Jan 15	Arlés	W	4-0	L1	Tettey [23], Brahimi 2 [37] [56], M'Vila [91+p]	19 857
Jan 23	Vaulx	W	2-0	CF10	Tettey [49], Brahimi [73]	4 000
Jan 29	Sochaux	L	1-5	L1	Boukari [54]	11 833
Feb 1	St.de Reims	L	3-4	CF11	Boukari [37], Leroy 2 [71] [78]	7 399
Feb 5	PSG	W	1-0	L1	Brahimi [19]	26 001
Feb 13	Nice	W	2-0	L1	Montano [52], Boukari [58p]	18 387
Feb 20	Toulouse	W	2-1	L1	M'Vila [45], Montano [88p]	21 379
Feb 26	Lens	W	2-0	L1	Boukari [14], Montano [70]	22 745
Mar 5	Montpellier	W	1-0	L1	Boukari [27]	15 165
Mar 11	Marseille	L	0-2	L1		29 002
Mar 19	Lyon	D	1-1	L1	Gomis [36]	35 504
Apr 2	Auxerre	D	0-0	L1		27 743
Apr 9	Brest	L	0-2	L1		15 127
Apr 16	Lorient	L	1-2	L1	Dalmat [23]	28 261
Apr 24	Monaco	L	0-1	L1		6 569
Apr 30	Bordeaux	D	0-0	L1		22 010
May 8	Val'ciennes	L	0-2	L1		11 429
May 11	Caen	D	1-1	L1	Mangane [44]	20 044
May 15	St-Etienne	W	2-1	L1	Montano [11], Leroy [44]	22 580
May 21	Nancy	L	0-2	L1		24 250
May 29	Lille	L	2-3	L1	OG [26], Montano [82]	17 111

6th Att: 444 553 • Av: 23 398 (+3.2%) • Route de Lorient 31 127 (75%)

PSG LEAGUE APPEARANCES/GOALS 2010-11
Goalkeepers Gregory Coupet 15 • Apoula Edel ARM 23+1
Defenders Sylvain Armand 31+2/2 • Zoumana Camara 14+3/2
Ceara BRA 14+6/0 • Christophe Jallet 35/1 • Tripy Makonda 1+3/0
Mamadou Sakho 35/4 • Siaka Tiene CIV 27+2/0 • Sammy Traore MLI 0+2/0
Midfield Mathieu Bodmer 21+7/5 • Clement Chantome 26/2
Jeremy Clement 8+16/0 • Loic Landre 0+1/0 • Claude Makelele 33/0
Nene BRA 35/14
Forwards Jean-Christophe Bahebeck 1+9/0 • Mevlut Erdinc TUR 29+5/8
Ludovic Giuly 30+5/4 • Guillaume Hoarau 31+2/9 • Neeskens
Kebano 1+2/0 • Mateja Kezman SRB 0+1/0 • Peguy Luyindula 4+19/0
Jean-Eudes Maurice 0+10/0 • Stephane Sessegnon BEN 4+10/0
Coach Antoine Kombouare

RENNES LEAGUE APPEARANCES/GOALS 2010-11
Goalkeepers Johann Carrasso 1 • Nicolas Douchez 37
Defenders John Boye GHA 8+2/0 • Rod Fanni 11/0 • Jean-Armel Kana-Biyik 27+1/1 • Kader Mangane SEN 29/3 • Samuel Souprayen 14+2/0
Kevin Theophile-Catherine 25+1/2
Midfield Abdoulrazak Boukari TOG 18/4 • Yacine Brahimi 14+8/4
Stephane Dalmat 30+3/2 • Romain Danze 38/1 • Tongo
Doumbia 9+10/0 • Yassine Jebbour 3+3/0 • Fabien Lemoine 7+11/0
Jerome Leroy 22+12/2 • Yann M'Vila 37/2 • Georges Mandjeck CMR 7+15/0
Sylvain Marveaux 9+1/1 • Alexander Tettey NOR 15+2/1
Forwards Ismael Bangoura GUI 1+3/2 • Abdoul Camara 5+19/0
Asamoah Gyan GHA 2+1/0 • Franck Julienne 0+1/0 • Jires Kembo-Ekoko COD 16+7/3 • Victor Montano COL 31+1/9 • John Verhoek 2+5/0
Coach Frederic Antonetti

SAINT-ETIENNE 2010–11

	Date	Opponent	Res	Score	Comp	Scorers	Att
Aug	7	PSG	L	1-3	L1	Payet 39	22 689
	14	Sochaux	W	3-2	L1	OG 6, Perrin 2 57 64	24 053
	21	Rennes	D	0-0	L1		24 731
	28	Lens	W	3-1	L1	Payet 3 5 79 85	27 520
Sep	11	Toulouse	W	1-0	L1	Batlles 34	19 336
	18	Montpellier	W	3-0	L1	Payet 2 21 66, Riviere 32	30 406
	22	Nice	W	2-0	LCr3	Landrin 14, Bergessio 39	13 468
	25	Lyon	W	1-0	L1	Payet 75	39 408
Oct	2	Marseille	D	1-1	L1	Batlles 59	**35 003**
	17	Nice	L	1-2	L1	Payet 11p	9 306
	23	Caen	D	1-1	L1	Riviere 82	31 715
	26	Bordeaux	W	1-0	LCr4	N'Daw 11	24 841
	30	Brest	L	0-2	L1		15 047
Nov	6	Lorient	L	1-2	L1	Sako 56	27 861
	9	Auxerre	L	0-2	LCqf		7 906
	20	Auxerre	D	1-1	L1	Perrin 54	21 830
	27	Nancy	D	1-1	L1	Perrin 52	14 381
Dec	1	Val'ciennes	D	1-1	L1	Riviere 15	10 940
	5	Bordeaux	D	2-2	L1	Ebondo 67, Bocanegra 69	**19 008**
	12	Monaco	W	2-0	L1	Batlles 20, Sako 78	6 694
	18	Arlés	W	2-0	L1	Batlles 51, Riviere 52	21 883
	22	Lille	D	1-1	L1	Sako 75p	16 783
Jan	8	Clermont	L	0-2	CFr9		12 260
	15	Lens	L	1-2	L1	OG 78	32 260
	29	Toulouse	W	2-1	L1	Sako 2 18 32	19 102
Feb	5	Montpellier	W	2-1	L1	Riviere 2 12 36	18 035
	12	Lyon	L	1-4	L1	Bocanegra 13	34 686
	19	Marseille	L	1-2	L1	Landrin 94+	53 494
	26	Nice	L	0-2	L1		19 793
Mar	5	Caen	L	0-1	L1		17 763
	12	Brest	W	2-0	L1	Sako 34p, Payet 88	20 706
	19	Lorient	D	0-0	L1		16 045
Apr	3	Val'ciennes	D	1-1	L1	Payet 58	24 702
	9	Auxerre	D	2-2	L1	Riviere 27, Aubameyang 70	17 298
	16	Nancy	W	2-1	L1	Payet 2 57 65	24 274
	24	Bordeaux	L	0-2	L1		29 657
May	1	Monaco	D	1-1	L1	Payet 11	23 656
	7	Arlés	W	1-0	L1	Alonso 33p	10 471
	10	Lille	L	1-2	L1	Riviere 5	22 176
	15	Rennes	L	1-2	L1	Sako 28	22 580
	21	Sochaux	L	1-2	L1	Aubameyang 9	19 930
	29	PSG	D	1-1	L1	Guilavogui 70	25 874

10th Att: 476 828 • Av: 25 096 (-4.7%) • Geoffroy-Guichard 35 616 (70%)

SOCHAUX 2010–11

	Date	Opponent	Res	Score	Comp	Scorers	Att
Aug	7	Arlés	W	2-1	L1	Butin 17, Faty 54	10 381
	14	St-Etienne	L	2-3	L1	Boudebouz 66, Martin 67	24 053
	22	Lille	D	0-0	L1		11 436
	29	PSG	W	3-1	L1	Maiga 14, Ideye 20, Perquis 45	12 222
Sep	11	Rennes	L	1-2	L1	Perquis 37	17 504
	18	Nice	W	4-0	L1	Ideye 45, Boudebouz 66, Martin 78, Maiga 89	9 744
	22	Bastia	L	0-2	LCr3		5 750
	25	Marseille	L	1-2	L1	Maurice-Belay 76	49 895
Oct	2	Lens	W	3-0	L1	Maiga 13, Ideye 45, Perquis 73	11 115
	16	Montpellier	L	0-2	L1		13 967
	23	Toulouse	L	1-3	L1	Tulasne 91+	11 198
	30	Lyon	L	1-2	L1	Ideye 66	33 992
Nov	6	Auxerre	D	1-1	L1	Maiga 82	11 020
	13	Brest	D	1-1	L1	Ideye 22	12 960
	20	Lorient	W	2-0	L1	Maiga 44, Ideye 59	9 266
	28	Caen	W	3-0	L1	Perquis 41, Ideye 50, Maurice-Belay 63	13 420
Dec	4	Val'ciennes	W	2-1	L1	Carlao 15, Maiga 55	**9 188**
	11	Nancy	L	0-1	L1		13 401
	19	Bordeaux	D	1-1	L1	Ideye 35	12 030
	22	Monaco	L	1-2	L1	OG 47	4 984
Jan	8	Jarville	W	1-0	CFr9	Ideye 82	10 573
	25	PSG	L	1-2	L1	Maiga 14	28 201
	21	Paris FC	W	2-1	CF10	Maiga 36, Martin 49	3 975
	29	Rennes	W	5-1	L1	Maiga 2 19 85, Martin 43, Ideye 52, Boudebouz 73p	11 833
Feb	2	Chambéry	L	1-2	CF11	Ideye 20	3 500
	5	Nice	L	0-1	L1		6 699
	12	Marseille	L	1-2	L1	Ideye 44	19 905
	19	Lens	W	3-2	L1	Maurice-Belay 6, Maiga 30, Boudebouz 67	30 338
	26	Montpellier	D	0-0	L1		12 085
Mar	5	Toulouse	W	1-0	L1	Maiga 64	14 126
	12	Lyon	L	0-2	L1		17 879
	19	Auxerre	L	0-2	L1		16 213
Apr	2	Brest	W	2-1	L1	Boudebouz 7p, Ideye 91+	10 982
	9	Lorient	D	1-1	L1	Drame 25	15 104
	16	Caen	W	3-2	L1	Drame 13, Maiga 2 81 86	11 338
	24	Val'ciennes	D	1-1	L1	OG 12	12 229
	30	Nancy	W	1-0	L1	Butin 11	14 082
May	7	Bordeaux	W	4-0	L1	Ideye 2 9 30, Perquis 11, Boudebouz 22	24 143
	11	Monaco	W	3-0	L1	Sauget 22, Maiga 24, Boudebouz 84	14 524
	18	Lille	L	0-1	L1		16 813
	21	St-Etienne	W	2-1	L1	Ideye 2 4 72	**19 930**
	29	Arlés	W	3-1	L1	Boudebouz 17p, Nogueira 50, Maiga 83	7 880

5th Att: 240 158 • Av: 12 640 (-5.1%) • Auguste Bonal 20 005 (63%)

ST-ETIENNE LEAGUE APPEARANCES/GOALS 2010-11

Goalkeepers Jeremy Janot 36 • Jessy Moulin 2+1
Defenders Yoann Andreu 0+1/0 • Mustapha Bayal SEN 19/0 • Johan Benalouane 0+1/0 • Carlos Bocanegra USA 34/2 • Albin Ebondo 29+1/1 • Faouzi Ghoulam 10+2/0 • Sylvain Marchal 19/0 • Sylvain Monsoreau 30+1/0 • Loris Nery 10+4/0
Midfield Alejandro Alonso ARG 11+3/1 • Laurent Batlles 22+10/4 • Josua Guilavogui 17+5/1 • Christophe Landrin 11+14/1 • Blaise Matuidi 34/0 • Guirane N'Daw SEN 2+3/0 • Dimitri Payet 28+5/13 • Loic Perrin 27/4 • Bakary Sako 32+6/7
Forwards Pierre Aubameyang GAB 8+6/2 • Gonzalo Bergessio ARG 5+11/0 • Yoric Ravet 0+2/0 • Emmanuel Riviere 31+4/8 • Idriss Saadi 0+9/0 • Boubacar Sanogo CIV 1+12/0
Coach Christophe Galtier

SOCHAUX LEAGUE APPEARANCES/GOALS 2010-11

Goalkeepers Pierrick Cros 13 • Matthieu Dreyer 10+1 • Teddy Richert 15
Defenders Jeremie Brechet 20/0 • Boukary Drame SEN 23+3/2 • Jacques Faty SEN 23+1/1 • Maxime Josse 6+5/0 • Yassin Mikari TUN 5+1/0 • Damien Perquis POL 35/5 • Mathicu Peybernes 4+3/0 • David Sauget 38/1
Midfield Kevin Anin 23+1/0 • Ryad Boudebouz ALG 37+1/8 • Carlao BRA 19+5/1 • Marvin Martin 37/3 • Vincent Nogueira 4+19/1 • Loic Poujol 1+6/0 • Rafael Dias POR 0+3/0 • Geoffrey Tulasne 1+1/1
Forwards Cedric Bakambu 0+9/0 • Ideye Brown NGA 33+2/15 • Edouard Butin 5+13/2 • Modibo Maiga MLI 35+1/15 • Nicolas Maurice-Belay 31+6/3 • Vaclav Sverkos CZE 0+4/0
Coach Francis Gillot

TOULOUSE 2010–11

	Date	Opponent	Res	Score	Comp	Scorers	Att
Aug	7	Brest	W	2-0	L1	Braaten 35, Machado 85p	14 653
	15	Bordeaux	W	2-1	L1	Braaten 45, Didot 83	31 614
	21	Arlés	W	2-1	L1	Braaten 36, Didot 62	16 233
	28	Nancy	W	2-0	L1	Capoue 69, Tabanou 93+	14 335
Sep	11	St-Etienne	L	0-1	L1		19 336
	18	Monaco	D	0-0	L1		6 070
	22	Boulogne	L	1-2	LCr3	Sissoko 77	3 931
	26	Lille	D	1-1	L1	Devaux 75	15 101
Oct	3	Rennes	L	1-3	L1	Sissoko 88	21 711
	16	PSG	L	0-2	L1		20 437
	23	Sochaux	W	3-1	L1	Congre 2 73 89, Cetto 80	11 198
	30	Lens	D	1-1	L1	Machado 6p	16 453
Nov	7	Nice	L	0-2	L1		7 636
	13	Montpellier	L	0-1	L1		15 175
	20	Marseille	L	0-1	L1		30 258
	28	Auxerre	W	2-1	L1	Braaten 8, Santander 35	10 326
Dec	4	Caen	W	1-0	L1	Santander 65	30 275
	12	Lyon	L	0-2	L1		32 547
	18	Lorient	W	3-0	L1	Machado 2 15 60, Santander 67	26 027
	22	Val'ciennes	L	1-2	L1	Sissoko 35	9 852
Jan	7	Paris FC	L	1-2	CFr9	Mansare 65	6 384
	15	Nancy	W	1-0	L1	Tabanou 28	12 107
	29	St-Etienne	L	1-2	L1	Tabanou 51	19 102
Feb	6	Monaco	W	2-0	L1	Sissoko 2 48 76	24 662
	13	Lille	L	0-2	L1		15 941
	20	Rennes	L	1-2	L1	OG 61	21 379
	27	PSG	L	1-2	L1	Tabanou 62	29 860
Mar	5	Sochaux	L	0-1	L1		14 126
	12	Lens	W	1-0	L1	Santander 75	29 483
	19	Nice	D	1-1	L1	Santander 27	12 356
	2	Montpellier	L	0-1	L1		12 123
Apr	10	Marseille	D	2-2	L1	Braaten 45, Cetto 61	50 698
	16	Auxerre	L	0-1	L1		33 853
	24	Caen	D	1-1	L1	Sissoko 39p	15 563
	1	Lyon	W	2-0	L1	Cetto 29, OG 68	20 785
	7	Lorient	D	0-0	L1		15 705
	11	Val'ciennes	D	0-0	L1		17 475
May	15	Arlés	L	0-1	L1		7 568
	21	Bordeaux	W	2-0	L1	Cetto 27, Capoue 55	18 429
	29	Brest	W	2-0	L1	Pentecote 2 3 63	14 515

8th Att: 376 068 • Av: 19 793 (+3.2%) • Municipal 35 575 (55%)

VALENCIENNES 2010–11

	Date	Opponent	Res	Score	Comp	Scorers	Att
Aug	7	Nice	D	0-0	L1		7 833
	14	Marseille	W	3-2	L1	Danic 48, Pujol 2 53 62	15 637
	21	Auxerre	D	1-1	L1	Danic 66	8 020
	28	Montpellier	L	0-1	L1		11 122
Sep	11	Lyon	D	1-1	L1	Bong 69	35 925
	18	Lens	D	1-1	L1	Samassa 55	13 669
	21	Nîmes	D	1-1	LCr3	Cohade 95+, W 5-4p	5 062
	26	Brest	L	0-1	L1		11 520
Oct	2	Caen	W	2-1	L1	Pujol 24, Samassa 29	10 469
	17	Lorient	L	1-2	L1	Danic 4	14 541
	23	Monaco	W	2-0	L1	Pujol 2 32 52	5 121
	26	Boulogne	W	4-0	LCr4	Aboubakar 3 11 65 84, Bong 37	7 378
	31	Lille	L	1-2	L1	Pujol 88	12 391
Nov	6	Bordeaux	D	1-1	L1	Ducourtioux 18	21 679
	10	PSG	L	1-3	LCqf	Dossevi 3	7 395
	20	Nancy	L	0-2	L1		14 083
	27	Arlés	W	3-0	L1	Pujol 20, Sanchez Moreno 78, Danic 82	9 829
Dec	1	St-Etienne	D	1-1	L1	Danic 76	10 940
	4	Sochaux	L	1-2	L1	Sanchez Moreno 65	9 188
	11	PSG	L	1-2	L1	Aboubakar 82	11 136
	18	Rennes	L	0-1	L1		20 112
	22	Toulouse	W	2-1	L1	Angoua 44, Danic 45	9 852
	8	Angers	L	1-2	CFr9	OG 58	5 261
Jan	15	Montpellier	L	1-2	L1	Dossevi 49	13 560
	29	Lyon	W	2-1	L1	Bisevac 51, Pujol 58	11 065
	5	Lens	D	1-1	L1	Dossevi 39	32 290
Feb	13	Brest	W	3-0	L1	Ducourtioux 14, Bisevac 22, Pujol 69	10 682
	19	Caen	D	2-2	L1	Pujol 80, Langil 88	13 648
	26	Lorient	D	0-0	L1		10 350
	5	Monaco	D	0-0	L1		11 859
Mar	13	Lille	L	1-2	L1	Pujol 59	17 083
	19	Bordeaux	D	2-2	L1	Danic 2 36 59	11 072
	3	St-Etienne	D	1-1	L1	Pujol 49	24 702
	9	Nancy	D	1-1	L1	Pujol 43	10 607
Apr	17	Arlés	W	1-0	L1	Pujol 68	7 652
	24	Sochaux	D	1-1	L1	Kadir 10	12 229
	30	PSG	L	1-3	L1	Pujol 14	29 158
	8	Rennes	W	2-0	L1	Kadir 18, Danic 53	11 429
	11	Toulouse	D	0-0	L1		17 475
May	15	Auxerre	D	1-1	L1	Kadir 80	12 079
	21	Marseille	D	2-2	L1	Kadir 33, Gomis 66	52 923
	29	Nice	L	2-1	L1	Pujol 2 48 69	15 193

12th Att: 221 610 • Av: 11 664 (-3.8%) • Stade Nungesser 16 547 (70%)

Valenciennes moved to their new Stade du Hainaut (25 172) in July 2011

TOULOUSE LEAGUE APPEARANCES/GOALS 2010-11
Goalkeepers Ali Ahamada 8+1 • Mathieu Valverde 29 • Marc Vidal 1+1
Defenders Mauro Cetto ARG 25/4 • Daniel Congre 37/2 • Mohamed Fofana MLI 21/0 • Adrian Gunino URU 29/0 • Cheikh M'Bengue 25/0 • Dany Nounkeu CMR 0+1/0
Midfield Wissam Ben Yedder 0+4/0 • Daniel Braaten NOR 21+11/5 • Etienne Capoue 37/2 • Antoine Devaux 23+5/1 • Etienne Didot 36/2 • Fode Mansare MLI 6+19/0 • Paulo Machado POR 29+4/4 • Adrien Regattin 0+3/0 • Pantxi Sirieix 1+11/0 • Moussa Sissoko 32+4/5 • Franck Tabanou 32+2/4
Forwards Andre-Pierre Gignac 1/0 • Soren Larsen DEN 0+2/0 • Xavier Pentecote 2+4/2 • Federico Santander PAR 18+5/5 • Ahmed Soukouna 1+1/0 • Yannis Tafer 4+12/0
Coach Alain Casanova

VALENCIENNES LEAGUE APPEARANCES/GOALS 2010-11
Goalkeepers Nicolas Penneteau 38
Defenders Brou Angoua CIV 30+1/1 • Bodo Balde GUI 12+3/0 • Milan Bisevac SRB 32/2 • Gaetan Bong CMR 22/1 • David Ducourtioux 33+4/2 • Rudy Mater 26+3/0 • Nicolas Pallois 4+7/0 • Rafael Schmitz BRA 3+2/0
Midfield Fahid Ben Khalfallah TUN 2+1/0 • Lilian Bochet 0+1/0 • Renaud Cohade 27+4/0 • Gael Danic 31+5/9 • Mathieu Dossevi 17+7/2 • Remi Gomis 26+3/1 • Foued Kadir ALG 11+1/4 • Steeven Langil 0+7/1 • Guillaume Loriot 3+1/0 • Nicolas Mirin 6+4/0 • Nam Tae Hee KOR 11+7/0 • Jose Saez 11+8/0 • Carlos Sanchez COL 27+1/2
Forwards Vincent Aboubakar CMR 4+13/1 • Kama Massampu 0+2/0 • Gregory Pujol 33/17 • Mamadou Samassa 9+9/2
Coach Philippe Montanier

FRO – FAROE ISLANDS

FIFA/COCA-COLA WORLD RANKING

'93	'94	'95	'96	'97	'98	'99	'00	'01	'02	'03	'04	'05	'06	'07	'08	'09	'10	'11	'12
115	133	120	135	117	125	112	117	117	114	126	131	132	181	194	184	117	136	116	

						2011									
Jan	Feb	Mar	Apr	May	Jun	Jul	Aug	Sep	Oct	Nov	Dec		High	Low	Av
134	135	135	136	136	114	112	111	126	122	116	116		94	198	133

There was a sense of disappointment in Faroese football when national team coach Brian Kerr decided not to renew his contract at the end of the Euro 2012 qualifying campaign with the Irishman deciding to return home after two and a half years in the job. He had helped the team achieve a couple of notable results and although they finished bottom of their Euro 2012 qualifying group, the 2-1 win over Estonia was their first in the competition for 16 years. It also made up for the earlier loss against the Estonians who had scored two injury-time goals to deny the Faroes a win. His replacement Lars Olsen comes with a good pedigree - the former Brøndby, Randers and OB Odense coach was captain of the victorious Danish team that won the European Championship in 1992. In club football there was a sense of deja-vu, especially as far as EB/Streymur were concerned. In the league they finished runners-up yet again - the fifth time in six seasons - and won the cup again - for the fourth time in five seasons. They beat IF Fuglafjordur 3-0 in the Cup Final with goals from Arnbjorn Hansen and Daniel Udson but they were beaten to the championship by B'36 Tórshavn who won their first title for six years on the 75th anniversary of the club. Defending campions HB Tórshavn had a poor season and only just avoided relegation.

UEFA EUROPEAN CHAMPIONSHIP RECORD
1960-1988 DNE 1992-2012 DNQ

THE FAROE ISLANDS'
FOOTBALL ASSOCIATION
(FSF)

 Gundadalur, PO Box 3028, Tórshavn 110

☎ +298 351979
📠 +298 319079
📧 fsf@football.fo
🖥 www.football.fo
FA 1979 CON 1988 FIFA 1988
P Christian Andreasen
GS Niklas A Lidarenda

FIFA BIG COUNT 2006

Total players	8 094
% of population	17.13%
Male	6 290
Female	1 804
Amateurs 18+	1 654
Youth under 18	4 040
Unregistered	2 000
Professionals	0
Referees	60
Admin & coaches	990
Number of clubs	23
Number of teams	303

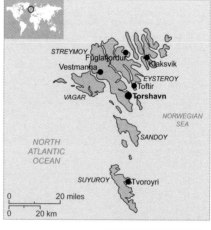

MAJOR CITIES/TOWNS
Population

1	Tórshavn	12 194
2	Klaksvík	4 628
3	Hoyvík	3 200
4	Argir	1 891
5	Fuglafjørður	1 580
6	Vágur	1 406
7	Vestmanna	1 238
8	Tvøroyri	1 213
9	Miðvágur	1 030
10	Sørvágur	988
11	Leirvík	885
12	Saltangará	882
13	Sandavágur	838
14	Strendur	834
15	Kollafjørður	829
16	Toftir	788
17	Skáli	711
18	Hvalba	663
19	Eiði	648

FOROYAR • FAROE ISLANDS

Capital Tórshavn	Population 48 856 (208)	% in cities 41%
GDP per capita $31 000 (43)	Area km² 1 393 km² (182)	GMT +/- 0
Neighbours (km) Coast 1117		

RECENT INTERNATIONAL MATCHES PLAYED BY THE FAROE ISLANDS

2006	Opponents	Score		Venue	Comp	Scorers	Att	Referee
14-05	Poland	L	0-4	Wronki	Fr		4 000	Prus USA
16-08	Georgia	L	0-6	Toftir	ECq		2 114	Ross NIR
2-09	Scotland	L	0-6	Glasgow	ECq		50 059	Egorov RUS
7-10	Lithuania	L	0-1	Tórshavn	ECq		1 982	Buttimer IRL
11-10	France	L	0-5	Sochaux	ECq		19 314	Corpodean ROU
2007								
24-03	Ukraine	L	0-2	Toftir	ECq		717	Skomina SVN
28-03	Georgia	L	1-3	Tbilisi	ECq	Rógvi Jacobsen [57]	12 000	Saliy KAZ
2-06	Italy	L	1-2	Tórshavn	ECq	Rógvi Jacobsen [77]	5 800	Malek POL
6-06	Scotland	L	0-2	Toftir	ECq		4 100	Kasnaferis GRE
12-09	Lithuania	L	1-2	Kaunas	ECq	Rógvi Jacobsen [93+]	5 500	Georgiev BUL
13-10	France	L	0-6	Tórshavn	ECq		1 980	Rossi SMR
17-10	Ukraine	L	0-5	Kyiv	ECq		5 000	Jakov ISR
21-11	Italy	L	1-3	Modena	ECq	Rógvi Jacobsen [83]	16 142	Meyer GER
2008								
16-03	Iceland	L	0-3	Kopavogur	Fr		400	Skjerven NOR
4-06	Estonia	L	3-4	Tallinn	Fr	Holst 2 [63 66], Olsen [70]	2 300	Stalhammar SWE
20-08	Portugal	L	0-5	Aveiro	Fr		22 000	Shandor UKR
6-09	Serbia	L	0-2	Belgrade	WCq		9 615	Nikolaev RUS
10-09	Romania	L	0-1	Tórshavn	WCq		805	Strahonja CRO
11-10	Austria	D	1-1	Tórshavn	WCq	Lokin [47]	1 890	Ceferin SVN
15-10	Lithuania	L	0-1	Kaunas	WCq		5 000	Kapitanis CYP
2009								
22-03	Iceland	W	2-1	Kopavogur	Fr	Benjaminsen [22], Antonuisson OG [42]	553	Riley ENG
10-06	Serbia	L	0-2	Tórshavn	WCq		2 896	Levi ISR
12-08	France	L	0-1	Tórshavn	WCq		2 974	Koukoulakis GRE
5-09	Austria	L	1-3	Graz	WCq	Andreas Olsen [82]	12 300	Borg MLT
9-09	Lithuania	W	2-1	Toftir	WCq	Suni Olsen [13], Arnbiorn Hansen [34]	1 942	Vad HUN
10-10	France	L	0-5	Guingamp	WCq		16 755	Malek POL
14-10	Romania	L	1-3	Piatra-Neamt	WCq	Bo [83]	13 000	Gvardis RUS
2010								
21-03	Iceland	L	0-2	Kopavogur	Fr		312	Larsen DEN
4-06	Luxembourg	D	0-0	Hesperange	Fr		713	Bertolini SUI
11-08	Estonia	L	1-2	Tallinn	ECq	Edmundsson [26]	5 470	Vucemilovic CRO
3-09	Serbia	L	0-3	Tórshavn	ECq		1 847	Toussaint LUX
7-09	Italy	L	0-5	Florence	ECq		19 266	Kulbakov BLR
8-10	Slovenia	L	1-5	Ljubljana	ECq	Mouritsen [93+]	15 750	Todorov BUL
12-10	Northern Ireland	D	1-1	Toftir	ECq	Holst [60]	1 921	Zimmermann SUI
16-11	Scotland	L	0-3	Aberdeen	Fr		10 873	Van Boekel NED
2011								
3-06	Slovenia	L	0-2	Toftir	ECq		974	Drachta AUT
7-06	Estonia	W	2-0	Toftir	ECq	Benjaminsen [43p], Hansen.A [47]	1 715	Munukka FIN
10-08	Northern Ireland	L	0-4	Belfast	ECq		13 183	Aleckovic BIH
2-09	Italy	L	0-1	Tórshavn	ECq		5 654	Bognar HUN
6-09	Serbia	L	1-3	Belgrade	ECq	Benjaminsen [37]	7 500	Amirkhanyan ARM

Fr = Friendly match • EC = UEFA EURO 2008/2012 • WC = FIFA World Cup • q = qualifier

FAROE ISLANDS NATIONAL TEAM HISTORICAL RECORDS

Caps
83 - Oli Johannesen 1992-2007 • 71 - Jakup Mikkelsen 1995- • 68 - Frodi Benjaminsen 1999- • 65 - Jens Martin Knudsen 1988-2006 • 62 - Julian Johnsson 1995-2006 & Jakup a Borg 1998- • 57 - John Petersen 1995-2004 • 54 - Allan Morkore 1990-2001 • 52 - Rogvi Jacobsen 1999- • 51 - Ossur Hansen 1992-2002

Goals
10 - Rogvi Jacobsen 1999- • 9 - Todi Jonsson 1991-2005 • 8 - John Petersen 1995-2004 & Uni Arge 1992-2002 • 5 - Frodi Benjaminsen 1999- • 4 - Julian Johnsson 1995-2006, Suni Olsen 2001- & Jan Allan Muller 1988-98

Past Coaches
Pall Gudlaugsson ISL 1988-93 • Johan Melle Nielsen & Jogvan Nordbud 1993 • Allan Simonsen DEN 1994-2001 • Henrik Larsen DEN 2002-05 • Jogvan Martin Olsen 2006-08 • Hedin Askham 2009 • Brian Kerr 2009-11 • Lars Olsen DEN 2011-

FAROE ISLANDS 2011

VODAFONEDEILDIN

	Pl	W	D	L	F	A	Pts	B'36	EB	Víkingur	NSI	KI	B'68	IF	HB	07	B'71
B'36 Tórshavn †	27	21	4	2	63	28	67		1-0 1-2	2-0	4-3	4-1	1-0	1-1 3-0	4-1 3-2	1-0	4-1 2-1
EB/Streymur Eidi ‡	27	19	3	5	66	32	60	2-1		2-1 3-3	2-2 5-1	2-0 3-0	3-2	1-0 1-0	3-1	1-0 2-1	5-1 1-0
Víkingur Gøtu/Leirvík ‡	27	18	5	4	61	31	59	1-1 0-2	2-1		3-2 1-2	2-1	2-1 4-1	1-0 4-0	3-1	1-1 5-1	3-2
NSI Runavík ‡	27	11	8	8	58	47	41	2-3 1-2	2-2	0-1		3-3	1-0 2-1	1-1 1-2	2-1 2-1	9-0 1-0	1-1
KI Klaksvík	27	10	4	13	48	50	34	0-2 0-3	1-3	0-1 1-4	1-2 5-1		3-1 5-3	2-0	2-2	1-2	1-2
B'68 Toftir	27	9	5	13	44	44	32	2-2 2-3	1-0 3-2	1-2	1-1	3-0		3-4 0-1	0-0 1-0	1-1	3-1
IF Fuglafjørdur	27	8	4	15	36	44	28	1-1	0-4 0-2	1-2	1-1	0-1 0-1	3-1		3-0 7-1	1-2 1-2	1-2 3-2
HB Tórshavn	27	7	5	15	46	56	26	1-3	3-2 3-4	1-2 2-2	0-0	1-4 1-3	3-3	3-1		5-0	2-0 5-0
07 Vestur	27	6	6	15	30	65	24	0-3 2-3	1-7	1-1	4-6	3-3 2-2	0-1 0-1	1-0	1-0		2-1 2-2
B'71 Sandur	27	3	2	22	25	80	11	2-3	1-2	0-3 1-4	1-6 1-3	0-6 0-1	0-5 0-3	1-4	0-2	2-0	

9/04/2011 - 12/10/2011 • † Qualified for the UEFA Champions League • ‡ Qualified for the Europa League
Top scorers: 21 - Finnur Justinussen, Víkingur • 18 - Klæmint Olsen, NSI • 17 - Lukasz Cieslewicz POL, B'36

FAROE ISLANDS 2011
1. DEILD (2)

	Pl	W	D	L	F	A	Pts
FC Sudoroy	27	22	4	1	88	23	70
TB Tvøroyri	27	19	4	4	81	26	61
AB Argir	27	19	4	4	80	25	61
Skála	27	12	4	11	54	43	40
NSI Runavík 2	27	12	2	13	61	68	38
HB Tórshavn 2	27	10	3	14	43	56	33
Víkingur Gøtu/Leirvík 2	27	9	4	14	48	58	31
EB/Streymur Eidi 2	27	10	1	16	44	73	31
FC Hoyvík	27	8	2	17	40	66	26
07 Vestur 2	27	0	0	27	16	117	0

9/04/2011 - 22/10/2011

MEDALS TABLE

		Overall			League			Cup	
		G	S	B	G	S	B	G	S
1	HB Tórshavn	47	25	4	21	14	4	26	11
2	KI Klaksvík	22	10	8	17	2	8	5	8
3	B'36 Tórshavn	14	14	6	9	4	6	5	10
4	TB Tvøroyri	12	10		7	5		5	5
5	GI Gøtu	12	6	4	6	3	4	6	3
6	EB/Streymur	5	6		1	5		4	1
7	NSI Runavík	3	5	1	1	1	1	2	4
8	B'68 Toftir	3	2	6	3	1	6		1
9	FC Sudoroy (ex VB)	2	3	2	1		2	1	3
10	B'71 Sandur	2	2	1	1		1	1	2
11	IF Fuglafjørdur	1	6		1				6
12	SI Sørvagur	1			1				
13	Víkingur Gøtu/Leirvík	1		2				2	1
14	Skála		1	1		1	1		
	LIF Leirvik		1						1
16	Royn Valba	1							1
	MB Midvágur			1			1		

FFA CUP 2011

Round of 16		Quarter–finals		Semi–finals		Final	
EB/Streymur Eidi	2						
B'36 Tórshavn *	0	**EB/Streymur Eidi**	3				
B'71 Sandur	0	NSI Runavík *	0				
NSI Runavík *	2			**EB/Streymur Eidi**	0 3		
Víkingur Gøtu/Leirvík	2			B'68 Toftir *	0 2		
HB Tórshavn *	0	Víkingur Gøtu/Leirvík *	2 2p				
FC Hoyvík	0	**B'68 Toftir**	2 4p				
B'68 Toftir *	5					**EB/Streymur Eidi ‡**	3
07 Vestur *	3					IF Fuglafjørdur	0
FC Sudoroy	0	**07 Vestur** *	1				
Undrid FF *	0	KI Klaksvík	0				
KI Klaksvík	2			07 Vestur	0 2		
AB Argir *	1			**IF Fuglafjørdur** *	1 1		
TB Tvøroyri	0	AB Argir	1				
Skála	0	**IF Fuglafjørdur** *	7	‡ Qualified for the Europa League			
IF Fuglafjørdur *	6			* Home team/Home team in the first leg			

CUP FINAL

Vid Djupumyrar, Klaksvik
5-08-2011, Att: 2278, Ref: Muller
Scorers - Arnbjorn Hansen 2 [10] [90],
Daniel Udsen [55p] for EB

First round: **Skála** 7-2 Royn Hvalba • **TB Tvøroyri** 2-0 FF Giza • **Undrid FF** 6-0 MB Midvágur

GAB – GABON

FIFA/COCA-COLA WORLD RANKING

'93	'94	'95	'96	'97	'98	'99	'00	'01	'02	'03	'04	'05	'06	'07	'08	'09	'10	'11	'12
60	64	67	46	63	82	74	89	102	121	111	109	104	95	104	62	48	39	77	

2011												High	Low	Av
Jan	Feb	Mar	Apr	May	Jun	Jul	Aug	Sep	Oct	Nov	Dec			
40	61	60	59	59	60	60	67	67	68	77	77	30	125	81

Gabon were successful co-hosts of the 2012 CAF Africa Cup of Nations, putting on an excellent tournament and playing some exciting football. But there was no fairytale ending for the home side as they lost on post-match penalties in the quarter-finals, giving away a lead with just minutes left in their match against Mali. It put a dampener on the final week of the tournament as the support for the Gabonese side had transformed the usually timid Libreville into a city of fevered expectation. Gabon surprised everyone by winning all three games in a tough first round group containing Morocco, Tunisia and outsiders Niger. The goals of Pierre-Emerick Aubameyang proved the catalyst for Gabon's success so it was ironic that it was his miss that saw them lose the penalty shootout against Mali. The hope is that the hosting of the Nations Cup, and the lavish spending by the oil-rich state on the footballing infrastructure will lead to a lasting legacy for the game in a country that has often been luke-warm in its attitude towards football. Gabon's under-23's certainly got into the spirit of the occasion when they won the African Championship in Morocco at the end of 2011. The Gabonese were rank outsiders but beat the hosts 2-1 in the final after coming back from a goal down to score through Landry Obiang and Allen Nono.

CAF AFRICA CUP OF NATIONS RECORD

1957-1970 DNE 1972 DNQ 1974-1976 DNE 1978 DNQ 1980-1982 DNE 1984-1992 DNQ **1994** 12 r1 **1996** 7 QF
1998 DNQ **2000** 15 r1 **2002-2008** DNQ **2010** 10 r1 **2012** 5 QF (Co-hosts)

FEDERATION GABONAISE DE FOOTBALL (FGF)

Boite postale 181, Libreville

☎ +241 704985
📠 +241 704992
✉ fegafoot@hotmail.fr
🖥 www.les-pantheres.com
FA 1962 CON 1967 FIFA 1963
P Placide Engandzas
GS Barthelemy Moussadji

FIFA BIG COUNT 2006

Total players	69 800
% of population	4.90%
Male	69 800
Female	0
Amateurs 18+	5 500
Youth under 18	2 800
Unregistered	5 500
Professionals	0
Referees	100
Admin & coaches	900
Number of clubs	60
Number of teams	220

MAJOR CITIES/TOWNS

		Population
1	Libreville	732 885
2	Port-Gentil	138 378
3	Masuku	54 466
4	Oyem	39 132
5	Moanda	38 220
6	Mouila	28 483
7	Lambaréné	26 257
8	Tchibanga	24 547
9	Koulamoutou	20 563
10	Makokou	17 203
11	Bitam	13 053
12	Tsogni	12 621
13	Gamba	12 585
14	Mounana	11 130
15	Ntoum	10 862
16	Nkan	10 808
17	Lastoursville	10 572
18	Okandja	9 070
19	Ndendé	7 860

REPUBLIQUE GABONAISE • GABONESE REPUBLIC

Capital	Libreville	Population	1 514 993 (151)	% in cities	85%
GDP per capita	$14 200 (81)	Area km²	267 667 km² (76)	GMT +/-	+1
Neighbours (km)	Cameroon 298, 1903, Equatorial Guinea 350 • Coast 885				

RECENT INTERNATIONAL MATCHES PLAYED BY GABON

2007	Opponents	Score		Venue	Comp	Scorers	Att	Referee
7-03	Congo	D	2-2	N'Djamena	CMr1	Ambourouet [62], Akiremy [89]		
9-03	Equatorial Guinea	D	1-1	N'Djamena	CMr1	Akiremy [15]		
11-03	Chad	W	2-1	N'Djamena	CMsf	Akiremy 2 [44 56]		
16-03	Congo	L	0-1	N'Djamena	CMf			
17-06	Madagascar	W	2-0	Antananarivo	CNq	Akiremy [20], Meye [89]		
21-08	Benin	D	2-2	Paris	Fr	Nzigou [4], Mouloungui [42p]		
8-09	Côte d'Ivoire	D	0-0	Libreville	CNq			Damon RSA
2008								
25-03	Congo DR	D	0-0	Aubervilliers	Fr			
7-06	Libya	L	0-1	Tripoli	WCq		30 000	Chaibou NIG
14-06	Ghana	W	2-0	Libreville	WCq	Meye [45], Stephane Nguema [59]	13 000	Benouza ALG
22-06	Ghana	L	0-2	Accra	WCq		29 040	Damon RSA
28-06	Lesotho	W	2-0	Libreville	WCq	Fabrice Do Marcolino 2 [45 63]	15 000	Mendy GAM
19-08	Mali	W	1-0	Mantes-La-Ville	Fr	Meye [30]		
7-09	Lesotho	W	3-0	Bloemfontein	WCq	Ecuele [56], Meye [72], Mbanangoye [94+]	1 500	Abd El Fatah EGY
11-10	Libya	W	1-0	Libreville	WCq	Mbanangoye [82]	26 000	Bennett RSA
18-11	Guinea	D	3-3	Compiegne	Fr	Stephane Nguema 2 [13 55], Mouloungui [30]		
2009								
28-03	Morocco	W	2-1	Casablanca	WCq	Pierre Aubameyang [34], Meye [45]	38 000	Diatta SEN
6-06	Togo	W	3-0	Libreville	WCq	Ecuele [11], Meye [67], Brou [81]	20 000	Lwanja MWI
11-08	Benin	D	1-1	Dieppe	Fr	Pierre Aubameyang [1]		
5-09	Cameroon	L	0-2	Libreville	WCq		10 000	Ndinya KEN
9-09	Cameroon	L	1-2	Yaoundé	WCq	Cousin [90]	38 000	Bennaceur TUN
10-10	Morocco	W	3-1	Libreville	WCq	Erbate OG [43], Moulougui [65], Cousin [70]	14 000	Doue CIV
14-11	Togo	L	0-1	Lomé	WCq		10 000	Seechurn MRI
2010								
6-01	Mozambique	W	2-0	Bloemfontein	Fr	Fanuel Massingue [5], Cousin [76]		
13-01	Cameroon	W	1-0	Lubango	CNr1	Cousin [17]	15 000	Bennett RSA
17-01	Tunisia	D	0-0	Lubango	CNr1		16 000	Codjia BEN
21-01	Zambia	L	1-2	Benguela	CNr1	Fabrice Do Marcolino [83]	5 000	Benouza ALG
19-05	Togo	W	3-0	Ajaccio	Fr	Pierre Aubameyang [16], OG [27], Do Marcolino [80]		
11-08	Algeria	W	2-1	Algiers	Fr	Cousin [35], Pierre Aubameyang [55]		Rouaissi MAR
6-09	Burkina Faso	D	1-1	Cannes	Fr	Roger Issakounia [52]		
8-10	Oman	L	0-1	Muscat	Fr			
12-10	Saudi Arabia	L	0-1	Istanbul	Fr			
17-11	Senegal	L	1-2	Saint-Gratien	Fr	Pierre Aubameyang [29]		
2011								
9-02	Congo DR	W	2-0	Mantes la Ville	Fr	Stephane N'Guema [24], Daniel Cousin [53p]		
7-06	Gambia	L	0-1	Moanda	Fr			
10-08	Guinea	D	1-1	St Leu La Foret	Fr	Bruno Mbanangoye [41]		
6-09	Niger	W	1-0	Nice	Fr	Bruno Ecuele [44]		
7-10	Equatorial Guinea	W	2-0	Cannes	Fr	Roguy Meye [43], Levy Clement Madinda [59]		
10-11	Brazil	L	0-2	Libreville	Fr			Hlungwani RSA
15-11	Ghana	L	1-2	St Leu La Foret	Fr	Eric Mouloungui [44]		
2012								
9-01	Burkina Faso	D	0-0	Bitam	Fr			
16-01	Sudan	D	0-0	Franceville	Fr			
23-01	Niger	W	2-0	Libreville	CNr1	Pierre Aubameyang [31], Stephane N'Guema [42]	38 000	Maillet SEY
27-01	Morocco	W	3-2	Libreville	CNr1	Pierre Aubameyang [76], Daniel Cousin [79], Bruno Mbanangoye [96+]	35 000	Gassama GAM
31-01	Tunisia	W	1-0	Franceville	CNr1	Pierre Aubameyang [61]	22 000	Doue CIV
5-02	Mali	D	1-1	Libreville	CNqf	Eric Mouloungui [54], L 4-5p	30 000	Haimoudi ALG

Fr = Friendly match • CN = CAF African Cup of Nations • CM = CEMAC Cup • WC = FIFA World Cup
q = qualifier • r1 = first round group • sf = semi-final • 3p = third place play-off • f = final

GABON 2010-11

CHAMPIONNAT NATIONAL DE D1 (LINAF)

	Pl	W	D	L	F	A	Pts	Missile	Mangasport	Pélican	Mounana	Sogéa	USB	CMS	Mbilanzambi	Stade Mandji	Sapins	FC 105	USO	RSC	Estuaire
Missile FC Libreville	26						**53**		0-0	2-1	3-2	0-1			1-2	5-1	3-1	3-1	7-0	2-2	
Mangasport Moanda	26						**48**			0-2	2-3	**0-0**		1-0	0-0	2-1	4-1	1-0	1-1	**0-0**	2-0
AS Pélican	26						**40**	0-0	3-2					0-2		2-1	3-1	0-0	2-1	0-0	2-0
CF Mounana	26						**38**	0-1	1-1	2-1			2-1	0-1		3-1	3-0		2-3	0-0	**0-0**
Sogéa FC	26						**36**		1-1	0-3	1-2			1-0	1-1	1-0	0-0	2-0		1-1	0-2
US Bitam	26						**36**	2-1	1-1	1-1	2-2	3-0		2-1	2-0	2-1	2-0	1-1	2-1		2-0
Cercle Mbéri Sportif	26						**35**	1-5		0-0			0-0	1-2	3-0		0-0	1-0	4-0	1-3	4-0
US Mbilanzambi	26						**30**	1-1	1-2		3-2	2-3		0-0		0-2		0-1	3-1	2-0	2-1
AS Stade Mandji	26						**27**	1-3	1-2	1-1	1-3			0-0	2-1			0-0	2-1		0-2
Sapins FC	26						**26**			1-3	0-4	0-0		1-0		4-3				1-1	
FC 105 Libreville	26						**24**	0-1			0-0		0-2		0-0	1-0	2-3	0-0		2-1	0-1	
US Oyem	26						**22**	1-1			2-2	0-0	0-4	**0-0**	2-3			0-0		1-1	2-1
RSC	26						**22**	0-2	1-2	0-2	1-1	0-4		1-2		1-3			1-0		
En Avant Estuaire	26						**17**			0-2	2-2	0-1	0-2	1-0	3-2	1-2				3-0	

27/11/2010 - 3/08/2011 • † Qualified for the CAF Champions League • ‡ Qualified for the CAF Confederation Cup • Championship suspended

MEDALS TABLE

		Overall			Lge	Cup	Africa			City
		G	S	B	G	G	G	S	B	
1	FC 105	14			9	5				Libreville
2	Mangasport	12			6	6				Moanda
3	US Mbilanzambi (USM)	9			5	4				Libreville
4	AS Sogara	6	1		5	1	1			Port-Gentil
5	Mbilinga	6		1	1	5			1	Port-Gentil
6	US Bitam	5			2	3				Bitam
7	En Avant Estuaire (ex Téléstar)	3				3				Libreville
	Stade Mandji	3			1	2				Port-Gentil
	Vautour Mangoungou	3			2	1				Libreville
10	Aigle Royale	2			2					Libreville
	Olympique Sportif	2			2					Libreville
	Petrosport	2			1	1				Port-Gentil
13	Anges ABC	1			1					Libreville
	Jeunesse AC (JAC)	1			1					Libreville
	AS Police	1			1					Libreville
	AS Solidarité	1			1					Libreville
	Zalang COC	1			1					Libreville
	AO Evizo	1					1			Lambaréné
	Missile FC	1			1					Libreville

COUPE DU GABON INTERCLUBS 2011

Round of 16		Quarter-finals		Semi-finals		Final	
Mangasport Moanda	2						
En Avant Estuaire	1	**Mangasport Moanda**	4				
TS Bourgeons	1	CF Mounana	0				
CF Mounana	2			**Mangasport Moanda**	2		
RSC Libreville	1			Missile FC Libreville	0		
Ibinga FC	0	RSC Libreville	2				
FC Sapin	1	**Missile FC Libreville**	4				
Missile FC Libreville	7					**Mangasport Moanda** ‡	1
US Oyem	3					AS Pélican	0
Rails FC	0	**US Oyem**	1				
Ecole	0	Cercle Mbéri Sportif	0			CUP FINAL	
Cercle Mbéri Sportif	6						
Renaissance d'Oyem	1 4p			US Oyem	0 2p	Stade Monédang de Sibang,	
FC 105 Libreville	1 1p	Renaissance d'Oyem	0	**AS Pélican**	0 4p	Libreville, 7-08-2011	
US Mounana	4p	**AS Pélican**	3			Scorer - Castel Kawadi	
AS Pélican	5p			‡ Qualified for the CAF Confederation Cup			

GAM – GAMBIA

FIFA/COCA-COLA WORLD RANKING

'93	'94	'95	'96	'97	'98	'99	'00	'01	'02	'03	'04	'05	'06	'07	'08	'09	'10	'11	'12
125	117	112	128	132	135	151	155	148	143	138	154	164	134	117	88	116	100	116	

						2011									
Jan	Feb	Mar	Apr	May	Jun	Jul	Aug	Sep	Oct	Nov	Dec	**High**	**Low**	**Av**
106	108	107	103	103	105	102	107	125	111	118	116	**65**	**166**	**129**

Gambia ended their relationship with Belgian coach Paul Put after failing in their ambition of reaching a first-ever CAF Africa Cup of Nations finals. They finished behind Burkina Faso in their qualifying group after a 3-1 win over Namibia had seen them get off to a perfect start. That, however, was their only win of the campaign. Gambia played five friendlies in 2011 with a 3-0 home win over the Democratic Republic of Congo the highlight of the year, but they remained firmly outside of the top 100 in the FIFA/Coca-Cola World Ranking. 2010 club champions Ports Authority competed in the CAF Champions League but neighbours Diaraf Dakar dispatched them in the first round, 3-1 on aggregate. The 2011 league season saw Ports Authority relinquish their league crown to Brikama United, who had only been promoted to the first division two seasons previously. Brikama, who played their home matches on an artificial pitch, were the first club from outside of the capital Banjul to take the championship since its inception in 1969. It was not a season that the majority of fans will care to remember though. Of the 132 games played, 79 featured one goal or less with over a quarter of the matches finishing 0-0. None of the teams could manage more than a goal-a-game on average. GAMTEL beat Ports Authority 2-0 in the Cup Final.

CAF AFRICA CUP OF NATIONS RECORD

1957-1974 DNE   1976 DNQ   1978 DNE   1980-1988 DNQ   1990 DNE   1992 DNQ   1994 DNE   1996 Withdrew   1998-2000 DNE   2002-2012 DNQ

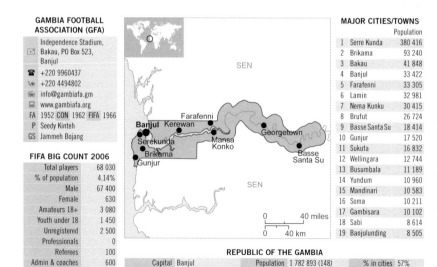

GAMBIA FOOTBALL ASSOCIATION (GFA)

Independence Stadium, Bakau, PO Box 523, Banjul

☎ +220 9960437
📠 +220 4494802
📧 info@gambiafa.gm
🖥 www.gambiafa.org

FA 1952 CON 1962 FIFA 1966
P Seedy Kinteh
GS Jammeh Bojang

FIFA BIG COUNT 2006

Total players	68 030
% of population	4.14%
Male	67 400
Female	630
Amateurs 18+	3 080
Youth under 18	1 450
Unregistered	2 500
Professionals	0
Referees	100
Admin & coaches	600
Number of clubs	50
Number of teams	200

MAJOR CITIES/TOWNS

		Population
1	Serre Kunda	380 416
2	Brikama	93 240
3	Bakau	41 848
4	Banjul	33 422
5	Farafenni	33 305
6	Lamin	32 981
7	Nema Kunku	30 415
8	Brufut	26 724
9	Basse Santa Su	18 414
10	Gunjur	17 520
11	Sukuta	16 832
12	Wellingara	12 744
13	Busumbala	11 189
14	Yundum	10 960
15	Mandinari	10 583
16	Soma	10 211
17	Gambisara	10 102
18	Sabi	8 614
19	Banjulunding	8 505

REPUBLIC OF THE GAMBIA

Capital Banjul	Population 1 782 893 (148)	% in cities 57%
GDP per capita $1300 (202)	Area km² 11 295 km² (166)	GMT +/- 0
Neighbours (km) Senegal 740 • Coast 80		

RECENT INTERNATIONAL MATCHES PLAYED BY GAMBIA

2008	Opponents	Score	Venue	Comp	Scorers	Att	Referee
1-06	Liberia	D 1-1	Monrovia	WCq	Mustapha Jarjue [17]	35 000	Keita GUI
8-06	Senegal	D 0-0	Banjul	WCq		24 500	Ncobo RSA
14-06	Algeria	W 1-0	Banjul	WCq	Mustapha Jarjue [19p]	18 000	Coulibaly MLI
20-06	Algeria	L 0-1	Blida	WCq		25 000	Ndume GAB
6-09	Liberia	W 3-0	Banjul	WCq	Njogu Demba 2 [10 76], Ousman Jallow [26]	10 000	Ambaya LBY
11-10	Senegal	D 1-1	Dakar	WCq	Aziz Corr Nyang [85]	50 000	Bennaceur TUN
2009							
No international matches played in 2009							
2010							
3-01	Angola	D 1-1	Vila Real	Fr	Ebrima Sawaneh [4]		
9-01	Tunisia	W 2-1	Rades/Tunis	Fr	Cherno Samba [57], Sainey Nyassi [85]		
30-05	Mexico	L 1-5	Bayreuth	Fr	Ebrima Sohna [65]		
4-09	Namibia	W 3-1	Banjul	CNq	Sainey Nyassi [10], Momoudou Ceesay [12], Ousman Jallow [34]		Ragab Omar LBY
9-10	Burkina Faso	L 1-3	Ouagadougou	CNq	Momoudou Ceesay [75]		Osman EGY
2011							
9-02	Guinea-Bissau	L 1-3	Lisbon	Fr	Momoudou Ceesay [27]		
29-03	Equatorial Guinea	L 0-1	Malabo	Fr			
7-06	Gabon	W 1-0	Moanda	Fr	Njogu Demba-Nyren [77p]		
24-07	Liberia	L 2-3	Monrovia	Fr	Foday Trawally 2		
10-08	Congo DR	W 3-0	Bakau	Fr	Tijan Jaiteh [19], Demba Savage [24], Momoudou Ceesay [12]		
3-09	Namibia	L 0-1	Windhoek	CNq			
8-10	Burkina Faso	D 1-1	Bakau	CNq	Mamadou Danso [59]		

Fr = Friendly match • CN = CAF African Cup of Nations • WC = FIFA World Cup • q = qualifier

GFA CUP 2011

Quarter-finals		Semi-finals		Final	
GAMTEL	6				
Watermann	0	GAMTEL	1 1		
Wallidan	0	Real Banjul	1 0		
Real Banjul	2			GAMTEL	2
Armed Forces				Ports Authority	0
		Armed Forces	0		
Young Africans	0	Ports Authority	1		
Ports Authority	3				

Cup Final: Serrekunda East Mini-Stadium, 1-10-2011
Scorers - Matarr Nyan [33], Asaan Ceesay [81]

MEDALS TABLE

		Overall	Lge	Cup	City
		G	G	G	
1	Wallidan	37	15	22	Banjul
2	Real Banjul	11	8	3	Banjul
3	Ports Authority	7	6	1	Banjul
4	White Phantoms	6		6	
5	Hawks	5	2	3	Banjul
6	Augustians	4	2	2	Banjul
	GAMTEL	4		4	Banjul
	Starlight	4	2	2	Banjul
9	Armed Forces	2	2		Banjul
	Arrance	2		2	
11	Brikama United	1	1		Brikama

GAMBIA 2011

GFA LEAGUE FIRST DIVISION

	Pl	W	D	L	F	A	Pts	Brikama Utd	Real Banjul	Ports	GAMTEL	Armed Forces	Wallidan	Y'ng Africans	Bakau Utd	Samger	Steve Biko	Interior	Africell
Brikama United	22	12	7	3	22	12	43		1-0	2-1	1-0	2-1	0-0	1-0	0-0	2-1	0-0	1-0	3-0
Real Banjul	22	10	10	2	17	7	40	2-1		1-0	0-0	1-0	0-0	1-1	2-0	1-1	0-0	2-0	0-1
Ports Authority	22	9	8	5	19	13	35	0-0	1-1		1-0	2-1	1-0	0-1	2-0	0-0	1-1	2-1	1-0
GAMTEL	22	8	9	5	22	16	33	2-0	0-0	2-3		0-0	1-0	0-0	1-0	4-1	0-0	0-1	1-0
Armed Forces	22	7	10	5	17	12	31	0-0	0-0	0-0	3-1		1-0	0-0	2-0	2-0	0-0	1-1	2-1
Wallidan	22	6	8	8	9	15	26	1-1	0-0	1-0	0-3	1-0		0-0	0-1	0-1	1-1	1-0	2-1
Young Africans	22	4	12	6	10	11	24	0-1	0-1	0-0	3-1	0-1	0-0		0-0	0-0	0-0	0-0	1-2
Bakau United	22	5	9	8	15	19	24	0-1	0-1	0-0	1-1	1-1	0-1	1-1		1-0	1-0	1-1	1-1
Samger	22	5	8	9	12	19	23	0-1	1-1	2-1	1-2	0-0	1-1	2-1	0-0		0-0	0-0	0-0
Steve Biko	22	3	13	6	11	14	22	0-0	0-1	0-2	1-1	0-1	2-0	0-1	3-1	0-2		1-1	0-0
Interior	22	3	12	7	13	18	21	3-2	0-0	0-1	0-0	1-1	2-0	0-0	0-2	0-1	1-1		2-1
Africell	22	4	6	12	14	25	18	1-2	1-2	0-0	1-2	1-0	0-0	0-1	1-4	2-0	0-1	0-0	

6/03/2011 - 31/07/2011 • † Qualified for the CAF Champions League

GEO – GEORGIA

FIFA/COCA-COLA WORLD RANKING

'93	'94	'95	'96	'97	'98	'99	'00	'01	'02	'03	'04	'05	'06	'07	'08	'09	'10	'11	'12
-	92	79	95	69	52	66	66	58	90	93	104	104	94	77	108	124	73	73	

2011												High	Low	Av
Jan	Feb	Mar	Apr	May	Jun	Jul	Aug	Sep	Oct	Nov	Dec			
72	71	72	56	57	56	57	63	64	67	74	73	42	156	85

There were first time winners of both the league and the cup in 2011 with Zestafoni claiming the league title thanks to a 20-match unbeaten run from early November which only came to an end after they had secured the title. Zestafoni's challenge had not been that surprising with their star striker Nikoloz Gelashvili topping the scoring charts for the second time in three seasons, but FC Gagra's Cup Final win over Torpedo Kutaisi was entirely unexpected. Not only did they become the first team from outside of the top flight to win a trophy but they also beat four of the top six finishers in the top division to do it. It took an own goal in extra-time from Torpedo Kutaisi's Sevasti Todua to win the trophy and it turned out to be a double celebration as Gagra were also promoted back to the Umaglesi Liga. The national team had a disappointing end to their Euro 2012 qualifying campaign when after having remained unbeaten in their first five games they then proceeded to lose four of the final five. That left the team just one place off the bottom of a group that coach Temuri Ketsbaia would have had high hopes of securing a play-off spot in. Georgia's 2014 FIFA World Cup qualifying group offers little prospect of doing that after the draw paired them with two of the past four World Cup winners in France and Spain.

UEFA EUROPEAN CHAMPIONSHIP RECORD
1960-1992 DNE (played as part of the Soviet Union) **1996-2012** DNQ

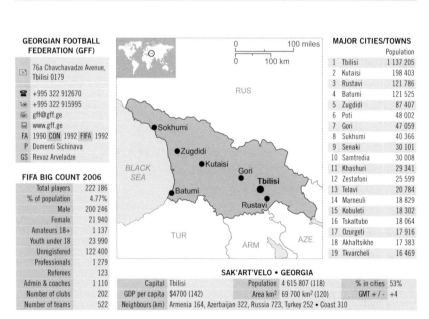

GEORGIAN FOOTBALL FEDERATION (GFF)

	76a Chavchavadze Avenue, Tbilisi 0179
☎	+995 322 912670
📠	+995 322 915995
✉	gff@gff.ge
🖳	www.gff.ge
FA	1990 CON 1992 FIFA 1992
P	Domenti Sichinava
GS	Revaz Arveladze

FIFA BIG COUNT 2006

Total players	222 186
% of population	4.77%
Male	200 246
Female	21 940
Amateurs 18+	1 137
Youth under 18	23 990
Unregistered	122 400
Professionals	1 279
Referees	123
Admin & coaches	1 110
Number of clubs	202
Number of teams	522

MAJOR CITIES/TOWNS

		Population
1	Tbilisi	1 137 205
2	Kutaisi	198 403
3	Rustavi	121 786
4	Batumi	121 525
5	Zugdidi	87 407
6	Poti	48 002
7	Gori	47 059
8	Sukhumi	40 366
9	Senaki	30 101
10	Samtredia	30 008
11	Khashuri	29 341
12	Zestafoni	25 599
13	Telavi	20 784
14	Marneuli	18 829
15	Kobuleti	18 302
16	Tskaltubo	18 064
17	Ozurgeti	17 916
18	Akhaltsikhe	17 383
19	Tkvarcheli	16 469

SAK'ART'VELO • GEORGIA

Capital	Tbilisi	Population	4 615 807 (118)	% in cities	53%
GDP per capita	$4700 (142)	Area km²	69 700 km² (120)	GMT +/-	+4
Neighbours (km)	Armenia 164, Azerbaijan 322, Russia 723, Turkey 252 • Coast 310				

RECENT INTERNATIONAL MATCHES PLAYED BY GEORGIA

2008	Opponents	Score	Venue	Comp	Scorers	Att	Referee
6-02	Latvia	L 1-3	Tbilisi	Fr	Kaladze [46]	6 000	Shmolik BKR
26-03	Northern Ireland	L 1-4	Belfast	Fr	Healy OG [55]	15 000	Wilmes LUX
27-05	Estonia	D 1-1	Tallinn	Fr	Kenia [82]	2 500	Vejlgaard DEN
31-05	Portugal	L 0-2	Viseu	Fr		8 500	Meir ISR
20-08	Wales	W 2-1	Swansea	Fr	Kenia [67], Gotsiridze [90]	6 435	Jug SVN
6-09	Republic of Ireland	L 1-2	Mainz	WCq	Kenia [92+]	4 500	Szabo HUN
10-09	Italy	L 0-2	Udine	WCq		27 164	Einwaller AUT
11-10	Cyprus	D 1-1	Tbilisi	WCq	Kobiashvili [73]	40 000	Matejek CZE
15-10	Bulgaria	D 0-0	Tbilisi	WCq		32 250	Kuipers NED
19-11	Romania	L 1-2	Bucharest	Fr	Martsvaladze [11]	2 000	Vassaras GRE
2009							
11-02	Republic of Ireland	L 1-2	Dublin	WCq	Iashvili [1]	45 000	Hyytia FIN
28-03	Cyprus	L 1-2	Larnaca	WCq	Kobiashvili [71p]	1 500	Fautrel FRA
1-04	Montenegro	D 0-0	Tbilisi	WCq		16 000	Malcolm NIR
6-06	Moldova	L 1-2	Tbilisi	Fr	Khizanishvili [85]	8 000	Salyi KAZ
10-06	Albania	D 1-1	Tirana	Fr	Dvalishvili [2]	2 000	Stavrev MKD
12-08	Malta	L 0-2	Ta'Qali	Fr			Kailis CYP
5-09	Italy	L 0-2	Tbilisi	WCq		32 000	Borski POL
9-09	Iceland	L 1-3	Reykjavik	Fr	Dvalishvili [33]	4 726	Trefoloni ITA
10-10	Montenegro	L 1-2	Podgorica	WCq	Dvalishvili [45]	5 420	Dereli TUR
14-10	Bulgaria	L 2-6	Sofia	WCq	Dvalishvili [34], Kobiashvili [51p]	700	Jakobsson ISL
2010							
3-03	Estonia	W 2-1	Tbilisi	Fr	Kobiashvili [45p], Siradze [90]	40 000	Banari MDA
25-05	Cameroon	D 0-0	Linz	Fr		3 500	Brugger AUT
11-08	Moldova	D 0-0	Chisinau	Fr		3 000	Shvetsov UKR
3-09	Greece	D 1-1	Piraeus	ECq	Iashvili [3]	14 794	Clos ESP
7-09	Israel	D 0-0	Tbilisi	ECq		45 000	Kever SUI
8-10	Malta	W 1-0	Tbilisi	ECq	Siradze [91+]	38 000	Black NIR
12-10	Latvia	D 1-1	Riga	ECq	Siradze [74]	4 330	Neves POR
17-11	Slovenia	W 2-1	Koper	Fr	Guruli [67], Ananidze [68]	4 000	Whitby WAL
2011							
9-02	Armenia	W 2-1	Limassol	Fr	Iashvili [22], Siradze [34]		Giannis CYP
26-03	Croatia	W 1-0	Tbilisi	ECq	Kobiashvili [90]	55 000	Tagliavento ITA
29-03	Israel	L 0-1	Tel Aviv	ECq		13 716	Fautrel FRA
3-06	Croatia	L 1-2	Split	ECq	Kankava [17]	28 000	Johannesson SWE
10-08	Poland	L 0-1	Lubin	Fr		12 310	Shandor UKR
2-09	Latvia	L 0-1	Tbilisi	ECq		15 422	Trattou CYP
6-09	Malta	D 1-1	Ta'Qali	ECq	Kankava [15]	5 000	Van Boekel NED
11-10	Greece	L 1-2	Tbilisi	ECq	Targamadze [19]	7 824	Orsato ITA
11-11	Moldova	W 2-0	Tbilisi	Fr	Kobakhidze [36], Ananidze [39p]		Aliyev AZE

Fr = Friendly match • EC = UEFA EURO 2012 • WC = FIFA World Cup • q = qualifier

GEORGIA NATIONAL TEAM HISTORICAL RECORDS

Caps

100 - Levan Kobiashvili 1996- • **83** - Kakha Kaladze 1996- • **79** - Zurab Khizanishvili 1999- • **69** - Giorgi Nemsadze 1992-2004 • **67** - Aleksander Iashvili 1996- • **62** - Gocha Jamarauli 1994-2004 • **60** - Shota Arveladze 1992-2007 • **59** - Levan Tskitishvili 1995-2009 • **55** - Giorgi Demetradze 1996-2007 • **54** - Giorgi Kinkladze 1992-2005 • **52** - Temuri Ketsbaia 1994-2003

Goals

26 - Shota Arveladze 1992-2007 • **17** - Temuri Ketsbaia 1994-2003 • **15** - Aleksander Iashvili 1996- • **12** - Giorgi Demetradze 1996-2007 & Levan Kobiashvili 1996- • **9** - Mikheil Kavelashvili 1994-2002 • **8** - Giorgi Kinkladze 1992-2005 & David Siradze 2004-

Past Coaches

Giga Norakidze 1992 • Aleksandr Chivadze 1993-96 • Vladimir Gutsaev 1996 • David Kipiani 1997 • Vladimir Gutsaev 1998-99 • Johan Boskamp 1999 • David Kipiani & Revaz Dzodzuashvili 2000-01 • Aleksandr Chivadze 2001-03 • Ivo Susak 2003 • Merab Jordania 2003 • Gocha Tqhebuchava 2004 • Alain Giresse 2004-05 • Gayoz Darsadze 2005 • Klaus Toppmoller 2006-08 • Hector Cuper 2008-09 • Temuri Ketsbaia 2010-

GEORGIA 2010–11

UMAGLESI LIGA

	Pl	W	D	L	F	A	Pts	Zestafoni	Dinamo	Olimpi	Torpedo	WIT Georgia	Baia	Kolkheti	Sioni	Spartaki	Samtredia
FC Zestafoni	36	24	6	6	72	19	78		0-1 1-0	1-0 2-0	2-1 1-0	3-0 4-0	6-1 3-0	2-0 0-0	4-0 0-0	4-0 2-0	7-0 4-1
Dinamo Tbilisi	36	21	9	6	55	22	72	2-1 0-0		1-1 2-0	1-0 1-2	2-0 1-1	0-0 2-1	5-0 4-2	2-1 0-1	0-1 1-3	2-7-1
Olimpi Rustavi	36	20	6	10	52	31	66	1-0 1-2	1-0 1-0		0-0 1-1	2-1 2-1	2-0 2-0	2-0 0-1	3-1 2-1	2-0 1-0	3-0 4-0
Torpedo Kutaisi	36	14	13	9	31	22	55	1-0 0-0	1-1 0-0	1-1 2-1		0-1 0-0	1-0 2-0	0-0 1-0	0-0 2-0	1-0 1-0	0-0 2-1
WIT Georgia Tbilisi	36	14	6	16	35	41	48	0-2 1-1	0-1 0-2	0-4 0-1	1-0 2-1		2-1 1-1	5-1 0-1	1-0 3-0	0-1 1-1	4-2 2-0
Baia Zugdidi	36	13	5	18	36	51	44	2-1 1-3	0-0 1-2	0-1 3-1	1-0 1-0	1-0 1-0		2-1 1-0	2-2 1-0	1-1 2-0	3-1 4-1
Kolkheti Poti	36	10	10	16	25	47	40	0-2 1-4	1-3 0-2	5-1 0-0	0-1 1-1	2-0 0-2	1-0 2-1		0-0 1-0	1-0 0-0	1-0 2-1
Sioni Bolnisi	36	10	9	17	27	45	39	1-3 1-0	1-0 0-2	2-1 1-0	0-0 1-4	0-0 1-2	1-3 1-0	0-0 2-0		2-0 1-1	1-0 5-0
Spartaki Tskhinvali	36	7	11	18	32	42	32	1-1 1-2	0-0 1-3	2-3 0-2	1-2 2-2	1-2 0-1	2-0 3-0	4-0 0-0	3-0 3-0		2-2 1-0
FC Samtredia	36	6	7	23	27	72	25	1-3 0-1	1-0 1-2	1-1 0-4	1-0 0-1	1-0 0-1	3-1 3-0	1-1 0-0	0-1 1-1	1-0 0-0	

14/08/2010 - 22/05/2011 • † Qualified for the UEFA Champions League • ‡ Qualified for the Europa League
Relegation play-offs: Chikhura Sachkhere 1-2 **Spartaki Tskhinvali** • **Dila Gori** 2-0 Samtredia
Top scorers: **18** - Nikoloz Gelashvili, Zestafoni • **16** - Irakli Modebadze, Olimpi • **13** - Giorgi Megreladze, Baia/Torpedo & Rati Tsinamdzgvrishvili, Zestafoni • **12** - Jaba Dvali, Zestafoni • **8** - Levan Khmaladze, Dinamo & Aleksandre Koshkadze, Dinamo

GEORGIA 2010–11 PIRVELI LIGA (2)

	Pl	W	D	L	F	A	Pts
FC Gagra	32	23	6	3	73	19	75
Merani Martvili	32	22	7	3	60	15	73
Dila Gori	32	20	9	3	58	21	69
Chikhura Sachkhere	32	20	6	6	58	25	66
Dinamo Batumi	32	18	9	5	66	18	63
Guria Lanchkhuti	32	14	14	4	50	59	46
Kolkheti Khobi	32	12	10	10	30	34	46
Imereti Khoni	32	11	4	17	36	43	37
Meshakhte Tqibuli	32	10	5	17	32	48	35
Norchi Dinamo Tbilisi	32	10	5	17	39	58	35
Chkherimela Kharagauli	32	7	14	11	35	45	35
Adeli Batumi	32	10	2	20	38	54	32
Mertskhali Ozurgeti	32	8	8	16	41	68	32
Samgurali Tskhaltubo	32	8	6	18	38	64	30
Skuri Tsalenjikha	32	8	5	19	28	52	29
FC Chiatura	32	8	5	19	28	69	29
Lokomotivi Tbilisi	32	7	7	18	30	48	28

28/08/2010 - 23/05/2011

MEDALS TABLE

		Overall			League			Cup		Europe		
		G	S	B	G	S	B	G	S	G	S	B
1	Dinamo Tbilisi	22	6	5	13	4	5	9	2			
2	Torpedo Kutaisi	5	7	2	3	3	2	2	4			
3	Lokomotivi Tbilisi	3	3	1		2	1	3	1			
	WIT Georgia Tbilisi	3	3	1	2	3	1	1				
5	FC Zestafoni	2	3	2	1			2		1	3	
6	Olimpi Rustavi	2	1	3	2			3		1		
7	Ameri Tbilisi	2	1	1				1		2	1	
8	Dinamo Batumi	1	5	1				1	1	1	4	
9	Sioni Bolnisi	1	2		1	1				1		
	Guria Lanchkhuti	1	2					2		1		
11	FC Gagra	1								1		
12	Tskhumi Sukhumi		3					1			2	
13	Kolkheti-1913 Poti		2	3				2	3			
14	Gorda Rustavi		1	2						2		1
15	Margveti Zestafoni		1			1						
	Samgurali		1							1		
	FC Samtredia		1			1						
	Shevardeni 1906		1					1				
19	Alazani Gurdzhaani			1				1				

GEORGIAN CLUBS IN THE SOVIET UNION

		G	S	B	G	S	B	G	S	G	S	B
6	Dinamo Tbilisi	4	11	13	2	5	13	2	6	1		1

SAKARTVELOS TASI 2010–11

Round of 16		Quarter-finals		Semi-finals		Final	
FC Gagra *	1						
Kolkheti Poti	0	**FC Gagra** *	1 2 4p				
Chikhura Sachkhere *	0	Dinamo Tbilisi	2 1 2p				
Dinamo Tbilisi	4			**FC Gagra** *	3 4		
Spartaki Tskhinvali *	1			WIT Georgia Tbilisi	0 2		
FC Samtredia	0	Spartaki Tskhinvali	1 0				
Skuri Tsalenjikha *	1	**WIT Georgia Tbilisi** *	2 1				
WIT Georgia Tbilisi	2					**FC Gagra**	1
FC Zestafoni	2					Torpedo Kutaisi	0
Dinamo Batumi *	1	**FC Zestafoni** *	3 0				
Lokomotivi Tbilisi *	0	Metalurgi Rustavi	0 0				
Metalurgi Rustavi	2			FC Zestafoni	0 0		
Sioni Bolnisi	0 4p			**Torpedo Kutaisi** *	1 0		
Merani Martvili *	0 2p	Sioni Bolnisi *	0 0				
Baia Zugdidi	0	**Torpedo Kutaisi**	1 0				
Torpedo Kutaisi *	1						

CUP FINAL
Boris Paichadze, Tbilisi, 26-05-2011, Att: 15 000, Ref: Kvaratskhelia
Scorer - Sevasti Todua OG [115]

* Home team in the first leg • ‡ Qualified for the Europa League

GER – GERMANY

FIFA/COCA-COLA WORLD RANKING

'93	'94	'95	'96	'97	'98	'99	'00	'01	'02	'03	'04	'05	'06	'07	'08	'09	'10	'11	'12
1	5	2	2	2	3	5	11	12	4	12	19	16	6	5	2	6	3	3	

2011												High	Low	Av
Jan	Feb	Mar	Apr	May	Jun	Jul	Aug	Sep	Oct	Nov	Dec			
3	3	3	4	3	3	3	3	3	3	3	3	1	22	6

After a Euro 2012 qualifying campaign that saw the national team win all 10 group matches, the Germans look to have built a team capable of winning honours at both continental and world level. It was a stunning achievement for coach Joachim Low, one of just three coaches still in his job from a previous finals in the competition. Germany have never gone more than three European Championships without winning it but with their last success in England in 1996 the pressure is on to maintain that record. 2011 saw Germany host the FIFA Women's World Cup but despite huge and enthusiastic crowds, the German women's team failed to live up to expectations and were knocked out in the quarter-finals by eventual winners Japan. In club football Borussia Dortmund surprised everyone by becoming the youngest winners of the Bundesliga. Jurgen Klopp's youthful side claimed the first title for the club in nine years, denying second place Bayer Leverkusen that elusive first title. It proved to be a good year for the Ruhr with Dortmund's neighbours Schalke winning the DFB Cup. In the final they thrashed second division MSV Duisburg 5-0 in the Olympiastadion and further made up for a wretched season in the league by reaching the semi-finals of the UEFA Champions League, where they lost 6-1 on aggregate to Manchester United.

UEFA EUROPEAN CHAMPIONSHIP RECORD

1960-1964 DNE **1968** DNQ **1972** 1 Winners **1976** 2 F **1980** 1 Winners **1984** 5 r1 **1988** 3 SF (Hosts)
1992 2 F **1996** 1 Winners **2000** 14 r1 **2004** 12 r1 **2008** 2 F **2012** Qualified

DEUTSCHER FUSSBALL-BUND (DFB)

Otto-Fleck-Schneise 6,
Postfach 71 02 65,
Frankfurt 60528
☎ +49 69 67880
📠 +49 69 6788266
✉ info@dfb.de
🖥 www.dfb.de
FA 1900 CON 1954 FIFA 1904
P Wolfgang Niersbach
GS Helmut Sandrock

FIFA BIG COUNT 2006

Total players	16 308 946
% of population	19.79%
Male	14 438 313
Female	1 870 633
Amateurs 18+	4 221 170
Youth under 18	2 081 912
Unregistered	10 000 000
Professionals	864
Referees	81 372
Admin & coaches	77 800
Number of clubs	25 922
Number of teams	170 480

MAJOR CITIES/TOWNS

		Population
1	Berlin	3 418 983
2	Hamburg	1 773 537
3	Munich/München	1 360 717
4	Cologne/Köln	1 001 499
5	Frankfurt	653 746
6	Stuttgart	596 337
7	Dortmund	586 344
8	Düsseldorf	582 784
9	Essen	578 549
10	Bremen	549 597
11	Dresden	523 592
12	Hanover	517 553
13	Leipzig	513 810
14	Nuremberg	503 786
15	Duisburg	494 215
26	Gelsenkirchen	262 063
27	Mönch'gladbach	257 896
62	Wolfsburg	121 088
83	Kaiserslautern	97 168

BUNDESREPUBLIK DEUTSCHLAND • FEDERAL REPUBLIC OF GERMANY

Capital	Berlin	Population	82 329 758 (16)	% in cities	74%
GDP per capita	$35 500 (33)	Area km²	357 022 km² (62)	GMT +/-	+1
Neighbours (km)	Austria 784, Belgium 167, Czech Republic 646, Denmark 68, France 451, Luxembourg 138, Netherlands 577, Poland 456, Switzerland 334 • Coast 2389				

RECENT INTERNATIONAL MATCHES PLAYED BY GERMANY

2009 Opponents	Score		Venue	Comp	Scorers	Att	Referee
11-02 Norway	L	0-1	Düsseldorf	Fr		42 000	Messner AUT
28-03 Liechtenstein	W	4-0	Leipzig	WCq	Ballack [4], Jansen [8], Schweinsteiger [47], Podolski [50]	43 368	Ishchenko UKR
1-04 Wales	W	2-0	Cardiff	WCq	Ballack [11], Williams OG [48]	26 064	Hauge NOR
29-05 China PR	D	1-1	Shanghai	Fr	Podolski [8]	25 000	Lee KOR
2-06 UAE	W	7-2	Dubai	Fr	Westermann [29], Gomez 4 [35 45 47 90], Trochowski [39], Juma OG [52]	7 000	Darwish JOR
12-08 Azerbaijan	W	2-0	Baku	WCq	Schweinsteiger [12], Klose [54]	22 500	Kelly IRL
5-09 South Africa	W	2-0	Leverkusen	Fr	Gomez [35], Ozil [77]	29 569	Circhetta SUI
9-09 Azerbaijan	W	4-0	Hanover	WCq	Ballack [14p], Klose 2 [55 65], Podolski [71]	35 369	Kakos GRE
10-10 Russia	W	1-0	Moscow	WCq	Klose [35]	72 100	Busacca SUI
14-10 Finland	D	1-1	Hamburg	WCq	Podolski [90]	51 500	Atkinson ENG
18-11 Côte d'Ivoire	D	2-2	Gelsenkirchen	Fr	Podolski 2 [11p 90]	33 015	Kuipers NED
2010							
3-03 Argentina	L	0-1	Munich	Fr		65 152	Atkinson ENG
13-05 Malta	W	3-0	Aachen	Fr	Cacau 2 [16 58], OG [61]	27 000	Hamer LUX
29-05 Hungary	W	3-0	Budapest	Fr	Podolski [5p], Gomez [69], Cacau [73]	14 000	Larsen DEN
3-06 Bosnia-Herzegovina	W	3-1	Frankfurt	Fr	Lahm [50], Schweinsteiger 2 [73p 77p]	48 000	Rizzoli ITA
13-06 Australia	W	4-0	Durban	WCr1	Podolski [8], Klose [26], Muller [68], Cacau [70]	62 660	Rodriguez EX
18-06 Serbia	L	0-1	Port Elizabeth	WCr1		38 294	Undiano ESP
23-06 Ghana	W	1-0	Johannesburg	WCr1	Ozil [60]	83 391	Simon BRA
27-06 England	W	4-1	Bloemfontein	WCr2	Klose [20], Podolski [32], Muller 2 [67 70]	40 510	Larrionda URU
3-07 Argentina	W	4-0	Cape Town	WCqf	Muller [3], Klose 2 [68 89], Friedrich [74]	64 100	Irmatov UZB
7-07 Spain	L	0-1	Durban	WCsf		60 960	Kassai HUN
10-07 Uruguay	W	3-2	Port Elizabeth	WC3p	Muller [19], Jansen [56], Khedira [82]	36 254	Archundia MEX
11-08 Denmark	D	2-2	Copenhagen	Fr	Gomez [19], Helmes [73]	19 071	Kelly IRL
3-09 Belgium	W	1-0	Brussels	ECq	Klose [51]	41 126	Hauge NOR
7-09 Azerbaijan	W	6-1	Cologne	ECq	Westermann [28], Podolski [44], Klose 2 [45 92+], OG [53], Badstuber [86]	43 751	Strombergsson SWE
8-10 Turkey	W	3-0	Berlin	ECq	Klose 2 [42 87], Ozil [79]	74 244	Webb ENG
12-10 Kazakhstan	W	3-0	Astana	ECq	Klose [48], Gomez [76], Podolski [85]	18 000	Tudor ROU
17-11 Sweden	D	0-0	Gothenburg	Fr		21 959	Velasco ESP
2011							
9-02 Italy	D	1-1	Dortmund	Fr	Klose [16]	60 196	Braamhaar NED
26-03 Kazakhstan	W	4-0	Kaiserslautern	ECq	Klose 2 [3 88], Muller.T 2 [25 43]	47 849	Stavrev MKD
29-03 Australia	L	1-2	Monchengladbach	Fr	Gomez [26]	30 152	Lannoy FRA
29-05 Uruguay	W	2-1	Sinsheim	Fr	Gomez 2 [20], Schurrle [35]	25 655	Benquerenca POR
3-06 Austria	W	2-1	Vienna	ECq	Gomez 2 [44 90]	47 500	Busacca SUI
7-06 Azerbaijan	W	3-1	Baku	ECq	Ozil [29], Gomez [40], Schurrle [93+]	30 000	Koukoulakis GRE
10-08 Brazil	W	3-2	Stuttgart	Fr	Schweinster [61p], Gotze [67], Schurrle [80]	54 767	Kassai HUN
2-09 Austria	W	6-2	Gelsenkirchen	ECq	Klose [8], Ozil 2 [23 47], Podolski [28], Schurrle [83], Gotze [88]	53 313	Tagliavento ITA
6-09 Poland	D	2-2	Gdansk	Fr	Kroos [68p], Cacau [96+]	38 000	Orsato ITA
7-10 Turkey	W	3-1	Istanbul	ECq	Gomez [35], Muller.T [66], Schweinsteiger [86p]	49 532	Atkinson ENG
11-10 Belgium	W	3-1	Dusseldorf	ECq	Ozil [30], Schurrle [33], Gomez [48]	48 483	Moen NOR
11-11 Ukraine	D	3-3	Kyiv	Fr	Kroos [38], Rolfes [65], Muller.T [77]	69 720	Velasco ESP
15-11 Netherlands	W	3-0	Hamburg	Fr	Muller.T [15], Klose [26], Ozil [66]	51 500	Cakir TUR

Fr = Friendly match • EC = UEFA EURO 2012 • WC = FIFA World Cup • q = qualifier • r1 = first round group • r2 = second round etc

GERMANY NATIONAL TEAM HISTORICAL RECORDS

Caps
150 - Lothar Matthaus 1980-2000 • **113** - Miroslav Klose 2001- • **108** - Jurgen Klinsmann 1987-98 • **105** - Jurgen Kohler 1986-98 • **103** - Franz Beckenbauer 1965-77 • **101** - Thomas Haßler 1988-2000 • **98** - Michael Ballack 1999- • **96** - Berti Vogts 1967-78 • **95** - Sepp Maier 1966-79; Karl-Heinz Rummenigge 1976-86 & Lukas Podolski 2004- • **90** - Rudi Voller 1982-94 & Bastian Schweinsteiger 2004-

Goals
68 - Gerd Muller 1966-74 • **63** - Miroslav Klose 2001- • **47** - Jurgen Klinsmann 1987-98 & Rudi Voller 1982-94 • **45** - Karl-Heinz Rummenigge 1976-86 • **43** - Uwe Seeler 1954-70 & Lukas Podolski 2004- • **42** - Michael Ballack 1999- • **37** - Oliver Bierhoff 1996-2002 • **33** - Fritz Walter 1940-58 • **32** - Klaus Fischer 1977-82 • **30** - Ernst Lehner 1933-42 • **29** - Andreas Moller 1988-99 • **27** - Edmund Conen 1934-42 • **24** - Richard Hofmann 1927-33 • **23** - Lothar Matthaus 1980-2000 & Bastian Schweinsteiger 2004-

Past Coaches
Committee 1908-28 • Otto Nerz 1928-36 • Sepp Herberger 1936-64 • Helmut Schon 1964-78 • Jupp Derwall 1978-84 • Franz Beckenbauer 1984-90 • Berti Vogts 1990-98 • Erich Ribbeck 1998-2000 • Rudi Voller 2000-04 • Jurgen Klinsmann 2004-06 • Joachim Low 2006-

GERMANY 2010-11

1. BUNDESLIGA

	Pl	W	D	L	F	A	Pts	Bor. Dortmund	Leverkusen	Bayern München	Hannover 96	1.FSV Mainz	1.FC Nürnberg	Kaiserslautern	Hamburger SV	SC Freiburg	1.FC Köln	TSG Hoffenheim	VfB Stuttgart	Werder Bremen	Schalke 04	VfL Wolfsburg	Gladbach	Eint. Frankfurt	FC St Pauli
Borussia Dortmund †	34	23	6	5	67	22	75		0-2	2-0	4-1	1-1	2-0	5-0	2-0	3-0	1-0	1-1	1-1	2-0	0-0	2-0	4-1	3-1	2-0
Bayer Leverkusen †	34	20	8	6	64	44	68	1-3		1-1	2-0	0-1	0-0	3-1	1-1	2-2	3-2	2-1	4-2	2-2	2-0	3-0	3-6	2-1	2-1
Bayern München †	34	19	8	7	81	40	65	1-3	5-1		3-0	1-2	3-0	5-1	6-0	4-2	0-0	4-0	2-1	0-0	4-1	2-1	1-0	4-1	3-0
Hannover 96 ‡	34	19	3	12	49	45	60	0-4	2-2	3-1		2-0	3-1	3-0	3-2	3-0	2-1	2-0	2-1	4-1	0-1	1-0	0-1	2-1	0-1
1.FSV Mainz ‡	34	18	4	12	52	39	58	0-2	0-1	1-3	0-1		3-0	2-1	0-1	1-1	2-0	4-2	2-0	1-1	0-1	1-0	1-0	3-0	2-1
1.FC Nürnberg	34	13	8	13	47	45	47	0-2	1-0	1-1	3-1	0-0		1-3	2-0	1-2	3-1	1-2	2-1	1-3	2-1	2-1	0-1	3-0	5-0
1.FC Kaiserslautern	34	13	7	14	48	51	46	1-1	0-1	2-0	0-1	0-1	0-2		1-1	2-1	1-1	2-2	3-3	3-2	5-0	0-0	3-0	0-3	2-0
Hamburger SV	34	12	9	13	46	52	45	1-1	2-4	0-0	0-0	2-4	1-1	2-1		0-2	6-2	2-1	4-2	4-0	2-1	1-3	1-1	1-0	0-1
SC Freiburg	34	13	5	16	41	50	44	1-2	0-1	1-2	1-3	0-1	1-1	0-1	1-0		3-2	3-2	2-1	1-3	1-2	2-1	3-0	0-1	1-3
1.FC Köln	34	13	5	16	47	62	44	1-2	2-0	3-2	4-0	4-2	1-0	1-3	3-2	1-0		1-1	1-3	3-0	2-1	1-0	0-4	1-0	1-0
TSG Hoffenheim	34	11	10	13	50	50	43	1-0	2-2	1-2	4-0	1-2	1-1	3-2	0-0	0-1	1-1		1-2	4-1	2-0	1-3	3-2	1-0	2-2
VfB Stuttgart	34	12	6	16	60	59	42	1-3	1-4	3-5	2-1	1-0	1-4	2-4	3-0	0-1	0-1	1-1		6-0	1-0	1-1	7-0	1-2	2-0
Werder Bremen	34	10	11	13	47	61	41	2-0	2-2	1-3	1-1	0-2	2-3	3-2	2-1	4-2	2-1	1-1	2-1		1-1	0-1	1-0	0-3	0-3
Schalke 04 ‡	34	11	7	16	38	44	40	1-3	0-1	2-0	1-2	1-3	1-1	0-1	0-1	1-0	3-0	0-1	2-2	4-0		0-1	1-0	2-2	2-1
VfL Wolfsburg	34	9	11	14	43	48	38	0-3	2-3	1-1	2-0	3-4	1-2	1-2	0-1	2-1	4-1	2-2	2-0	0-0	2-2		2-1	1-1	2-2
B. Mönchengladbach ‡‡	34	10	6	18	48	65	36	1-0	1-3	3-3	1-2	2-3	1-1	0-1	2-0	2-0	5-1	2-0	2-3	1-4	2-1	1-1		0-4	1-2
Eintracht Frankfurt	34	9	7	18	31	49	34	1-0	0-3	1-0	0-3	2-1	2-0	0-0	1-3	0-1	0-2	0-4	0-2	1-1	0-0	0-3	0-1		2-1
FC St Pauli	34	8	5	21	35	68	29	1-3	0-1	1-8	0-1	2-4	3-2	1-0	1-1	2-2	3-0	0-1	1-2	1-3	0-2	1-1	3-1	1-3	

20/08/2010 - 14/05/2011 • † Qualified for the UEFA Champions League • ‡ Qualified for the Europa League
‡‡ Relegation play-off: **Borussia Mönchengladbach** 1-0 1-1 VfL Bochum
Top scorers: **28** - Mario Gomez, Bayern • **22** - Papiss Cisse SEN, Freiburg • **17** - Milivoje Novakovic SVN, Köln • **16** - Lucas Barrios PAR, Dortmund; Theofanis Gekas GRE, Frankfurt & Srdan Lakic CRO, Kaiserslautern • **15** - Andre Schurrle, Mainz • **14** - Didier Koman Ya CIV, Hannover • **13** - Lukas Podolski, Köln & Raul ESP, Schalke • **12** - Thomas Muller, Bayern & Arjen Robben NED, Bayern • **11** - Mladen Petric CRO, Hamburg

GERMANY 2010-11

2. BUNDESLIGA (2)

	Pl	W	D	L	F	A	Pts	Hertha BSC	FC Augsburg	VfL Bochum	Greuther Fürth	Erzgebirge Aue	Energie Cottbus	For. Düsseldorf	MSV Duisburg	1860 München	All. Aachen	Union Berlin	SC Paderborn	FSV Frankfurt	FC Ingolstadt	Karlsruher SC	VfL Osnabrück	RW Oberhausen	Arm. Bielefeld
Hertha BSC Berlin	34	23	5	6	69	28	74		2-1	0-2	2-0	2-0	2-2	4-2	0-2	1-2	0-0	1-2	2-0	3-1	3-1	4-0	4-0	3-2	3-1
FC Augsburg	34	19	8	7	58	27	65	1-1		0-1	0-0	0-2	2-0	1-0	2-0	1-2	1-2	1-1	1-0	2-1	2-0	3-1	2-2	2-0	3-0
VfL Bochum †	34	20	5	9	49	35	65	0-2	0-2		0-2	2-0	1-0	2-0	3-1	3-2	1-1	3-0	3-0	1-0	1-4	1-1	2-1	2-1	3-1
SpVgg Greuther Fürth	34	17	10	7	47	27	61	0-2	1-1	1-1		1-2	3-1	1-1	2-1	1-0	1-1	1-0	2-0	1-0	0-4	3-0	0-0	1-0
Erzgebirge Aue	34	16	8	10	40	37	56	0-2	3-2	1-0	0-0		1-2	1-0	1-0	1-0	3-1	1-3	1-0	1-1	3-1	1-0	2-1	3-0
Energie Cottbus	34	16	7	11	65	52	55	0-1	1-1	2-1	1-1	6-0		2-0	3-1	0-0	3-3	0-0	3-1	1-2	5-5	2-0	3-1	2-0
Fortuna Düsseldorf	34	16	5	13	49	39	53	1-2	1-0	0-1	1-0	3-0	3-1		1-0	1-2	3-0	6-0	3-1	1-2	5-5	2-0	3-0	2-0
MSV Duisburg	34	15	7	12	53	38	52	0-1	0-0	0-2	3-1	2-2	1-0		2-1	3-2	0-1	1-3	4-1	3-0	4-1	3-0	4-1	0-1	3-0
TSV 1860 München §2	34	14	10	10	50	36	50	1-0	0-2	1-3	3-0	0-0	4-0	1-1	1-1		2-1	1-0	0-1	3-3	1-1	5-1	3-1	1-1	1-0
Alemannia Aachen	34	13	9	12	58	60	48	0-5	1-3	1-3	2-2	1-5	2-3	0-0	2-2	2-1		2-2	2-0	2-1	4-2	2-1	4-0	1-1
1.FC Union Berlin	34	11	9	14	39	45	42	1-1	0-0	0-1	1-1	4-2	1-0	2-0	0-0	1-2	1-2		0-2	2-0	1-1	3-3	2-1	2-2
SC Paderborn 07	34	10	9	15	32	47	39	1-0	1-1	0-0	0-4	0-1	0-5	3-0	0-0	3-2	1-3	2-0		2-2	1-1	3-0	1-0	0-0	3-1
FSV Frankfurt	34	11	5	18	41	54	38	1-1	0-1	0-1	0-0	0-2	3-2	1-0	4-0	2-1	1-3	2-1	1-0		1-7	1-7	4-0	2-1
FC Ingolstadt 04	34	9	10	15	40	46	37	1-1	1-4	3-0	0-0	1-2	3-0	1-1	2-1	1-0	1-2	0-1	1-0	1-2		1-1	0-1	1-2	1-0
Karlsruher SC	34	8	9	17	46	72	33	2-6	0-1	0-2	1-1	1-1	1-0	2-2	3-1	2-4	3-0	3-2	2-1	0-2	1-4		2-2	4-0	1-0
VfL Osnabrück ‡	34	8	7	19	40	62	31	2-0	0-2	1-3	0-2	3-2	2-0	2-3	1-3	0-1	1-3	4-1	2-1	1-1	2-1	1-0		3-1	0-0
Rot-Weiß Oberhausen	34	7	7	20	30	65	28	1-3	0-3	3-1	1-4	1-2	0-4	1-2	0-0	0-0	1-3	0-2	2-0	1-0	1-1	2-1	1-0		3-0
Arminia Bielefeld §3	34	4	8	22	28	65	017	1-3	0-2	2-2	1-4	0-1	1-2	0-2	1-3	0-3	1-3	1-1	1-1	1-1	1-0	2-1	2-1	3-3	

20/08/2010 - 15/05/2011 • § = Points deducted
† Promotion play-off (see Bundesliga) • ‡ Relegation play-off: **Dynamo Dresden** 1-1 3-1 Vfl Osnabrück
Top scorers: **25** - Nils Petersen, Cottbus • **20** - Benjamin Auer, Aachen • **16** - Benjamin Lauth, 1860 München

GERMANY 2010–11

3. BUNDESLIGA (3)

Column key: BS = Braunschweig, HR = Hansa Rostock, DD = Dyn. Dresden, WW = SV Wehen, RWE = Rot-Weiß Erfurt, SAA = Saarbrücken, OFF = Offenbach, REG = Regensburg, HDH = Heidenheim, VfB2 = VfB Stuttgart-2, KOB = TuS Koblenz, SAN = SV Sandhausen, BAB = SV Babelsberg, UNT = Unterhaching, CZJ = Carl Zeiss Jena, AAL = VfR Aalen, BUR = W. Burghausen, BR2 = W. Bremen-2, BM2 = B. München-2, AHL = Rot-Weiss Ahlen

Team	Pl	W	D	L	F	A	Pts	BS	HR	DD	WW	RWE	SAA	OFF	REG	HDH	VfB2	KOB	SAN	BAB	UNT	CZJ	AAL	BUR	BR2	BM2	AHL
Eint. Braunschweig	38	26	7	5	81	22	85	–	2-1	2-1	1-2	4-0	1-0	2-1	2-0	4-0	2-1	4-1	2-0	1-1	3-0	6-0	2-0	3-0	1-2	2-0	2-0
Hansa Rostock	38	24	6	8	70	36	78	2-1	–	1-0	3-1	3-0	2-1	0-0	5-0	2-1	0-1	2-0	0-1	3-0	7-2	2-1	3-0	1-1	2-0	0-2	2-0
1.FC Dynamo Dresden	38	19	8	11	55	37	65	1-1	2-2	–	3-0	1-3	3-0	2-0	1-1	0-0	1-1	1-0	3-1	0-1	4-0	2-0	1-0	2-0	1-1	3-1	3-0
SV Wehen Wiesbabden	38	18	10	10	55	39	64	0-2	1-2	2-2	–	0-1	2-1	1-2	2-0	5-2	2-1	1-0	2-0	0-3	0-2	1-1	3-3	0-1	1-1	3-0	0-0
Rot-Weiß Erfurt	38	18	7	13	63	45	61	3-1	0-1	3-0	0-0	–	1-2	3-1	0-1	0-1	2-3	0-2	1-4	2-4	2-0	2-1	1-0	1-1	2-1	2-0	4-0
1.FC Saarbrücken	38	17	8	13	61	51	59	0-3	3-0	3-2	0-0	1-3	–	2-0	0-0	3-4	1-0	0-0	3-1	3-1	2-3	1-3	3-2	2-1	1-0	4-1	0-0
Offenbacher Kickers	38	16	9	13	52	45	57	2-2	3-2	2-3	0-0	2-1	2-0	–	2-1	1-0	2-2	0-0	1-2	2-1	1-0	0-2	2-0	2-0	3-1	4-1	1-2
SSV Jahn Regensburg	38	13	13	12	35	41	52	0-3	2-2	0-1	0-0	0-0	2-2	0-2	–	2-1	1-2	0-2	0-0	1-3	0-0	0-1	1-2	0-2	0-0	1-2	
1.FC Heidenheim	38	14	9	15	59	58	51	1-4	1-2	3-0	0-2	1-1	2-0	1-0	1-0	–	0-3	1-1	1-1	5-1	2-0	0-0	4-1	3-1	3-1	3-0	
VfB Stuttgart-2	38	12	15	11	48	48	51	0-0	3-0	1-0	3-3	3-1	2-2	0-2	1-2	2-1	–	1-2	0-1	1-1	1-1	3-2	1-1	1-0	3-2	0-0	5-1
TuS Koblenz	38	13	10	15	38	46	49	0-2	0-2	0-1	3-2	1-1	1-2	0-1	0-2	4-0	2-0	–	3-0	1-0	1-1	1-0	1-0	0-4	0-0	1-3	0-0
SV Sandhausen	38	11	13	14	43	46	46	0-2	1-2	4-1	0-0	3-2	3-1	0-2	2-2	1-2	0-1	0-0	–	0-0	0-0	2-1	3-1	5-1	1-0	5-0	
SV Babelsberg 03	38	12	10	16	39	47	46	0-3	0-2	1-1	0-0	1-1	0-2	2-0	0-1	4-3	3-0	0-1	0-0	–	0-4	4-1	3-1	0-2	2-0	1-0	0-0
SpVgg Unterhaching	38	11	12	15	39	55	45	0-1	3-0	0-1	3-1	0-2	1-1	0-0	1-1	0-1	1-1	1-1	1-0		–	1-1	2-0	2-0	2-0	0-4	0-0
Carl Zeiss Jena	38	11	11	16	43	62	44	2-2	1-3	1-0	1-0	1-3	0-7	1-0	1-2	2-1	1-1	2-2	3-0	0-0	1-2	–	0-0	1-0	1-1	1-1	3-3
VfR Aalen	38	9	14	15	40	52	41	0-0	1-1	1-0	1-2	0-4	1-1	1-1	2-3	2-1	1-1	1-2	0-0	3-0	0-0	1-1	–	1-0	1-1	2-2	3-0
Wacker Burghausen	38	9	10	19	46	66	37	0-0	0-1	4-0	2-1	1-1	0-3	4-4	3-0	0-1	2-2	3-4	3-1	1-4	1-2	1-2	3-2	–			
Werder Bremen-2	38	8	12	18	33	56	36	0-5	0-2	0-3	1-4	1-2	2-0	0-0	0-1	0-1	1-1	0-2	1-1	1-0	3-0	0-1	1-1	1-1	–	2-0	3-1
Bayern München-2	38	7	9	22	30	54	30	1-0	0-0	1-2	0-1	1-0	0-0	1-0	0-2	2-3	1-1	1-0	1-2	1-0	1-2	0-1	1-1	0-1		–	2-3
Rot-Weiss Ahlen §3	38	11	9	18	45	69	39	0-3	0-2	0-1	4-1	4-3	0-2	3-3	2-0	3-1	2-0	2-3	1-1	0-2	1-1	3-0	4-2	0-1	1-1	2-0	–

23/07/2010 - 14/05/2011 • § = points deducted • TuS Koblenz relegated along with Ahlen who were demoted to last place
Top scorers: **19** - Dominick Kumbela COD, Braunschweig & Patrick Meyer, Heidenheim • **17** - Alexander Esswein, Dresden & Matthew Taylor USA, Ahlen

GERMANY 2010–11

REGIONALLIGA NORD (4)

Column key: CHE = Chemnitzer FC, WOB = VfL Wolfsburg-2, LUB = VfB Lübeck, RBL = RB Leipzig, HAL = Hallescher FC, KIE = Holstein Kiel, HBE = Hertha BSC-2, HSV = Hamburger SV-2, H96 = Hannover 96-2, COT = En. Cottbus-2, ZFC = ZFC Meuselwitz, MAG = 1.FC Magdeburg, WIL = Wilhelmshaven, PLA = VFC Plauen, HAV = TSV Havelse, BS2 = Braunschweig-2, OBE = FC Oberneuland, TÜR = Türkiyemspor

Team	Pl	W	D	L	F	A	Pts	CHE	WOB	LUB	RBL	HAL	KIE	HBE	HSV	H96	COT	ZFC	MAG	WIL	PLA	HAV	BS2	OBE	TÜR
Chemnitzer FC	34	25	7	2	82	23	82	–	1-1	6-0	1-0	0-0	0-2	3-1	6-0	2-2	4-2	1-0	3-0	1-0	2-1	5-0	1-0	3-1	4-0
VfL Wolfsburg-2	34	23	6	5	59	28	75	0-4	–	3-1	1-0	2-2	1-1	2-0	2-1	1-0	3-1	3-0	0-0	2-1	3-1	2-1	1-0	2-1	1-0
VfB Lübeck	34	21	6	7	58	36	69	0-0	3-1	–	0-0	3-2	2-0	1-1	3-0	2-0	2-3	2-0	0-2	1-2	2-1	1-0	1-0	3-2	5-0
RB Leipzig	34	18	10	6	57	29	64	1-1	0-1	2-1	–	2-0	1-5	2-0	3-0	1-1	3-2	3-0	2-1	3-2	1-0	2-0	4-0	3-0	1-1
Hallescher FC	34	16	10	8	51	34	58	0-1	0-2	2-2	0-0	–	0-3	1-1	0-2	1-0	1-0	3-1	0-2	1-1	3-1	1-3	1-1	3-1	4-0
KSV Holstein Kiel	34	15	10	9	65	36	55	0-2	1-1	2-2	1-2	1-1	–	5-0	0-0	3-1	0-1	1-0	0-1	3-2	1-3	6-1	5-0	1-1	8-0
Hertha BSC Berlin-2	34	15	7	12	47	49	52	2-0	0-2	1-2	1-1	2-2	2-2	–	0-1	1-3	2-2	0-0	3-1	1-1	3-2	3-0	4-2	1-0	
Hamburger SV-2	34	14	7	13	57	49	49	3-4	0-1	1-1	0-1	1-2	1-3	4-4	–	3-2	2-2	2-0	1-1	4-0	1-2	2-0	2-1	4-0	
Hannover 96-2	34	13	7	14	56	47	46	1-2	1-0	0-1	0-3	1-2	1-0	2-2		–	0-2	1-1	0-3	9-2	3-2	3-1	0-0	1-0	4-1
Energie Cottbus-2	34	13	6	15	49	51	45	0-1	0-5	1-3	3-1	0-3	0-1	3-0	1-1	1-0	–	0-1	2-0	3-0	2-0	1-2	2-0	6-1	1-0
ZFC Meuselwitz	34	12	6	16	41	53	42	0-4	2-1	1-3	3-3	0-1	2-1	0-1	1-2	2-1	2-0	–	1-1	3-1	3-1	2-2	2-0	1-3	4-0
1.FC Magdeburg	34	11	8	15	37	46	41	1-6	1-2	0-2	2-1	1-3	2-0	1-1	2-0	1-0	0-2	2-0	–	1-1	0-2	1-2	3-2	1-0	1-1
SV Wilhelmshaven	34	11	8	15	48	61	41	1-5	1-0	0-2	1-1	0-1	0-0	3-1	3-1	1-0	3-1	1-0	3-1	–	2-0	6-1	1-2	1-5	2-2
VFC Plauen	34	11	6	17	43	48	39	1-1	1-2	0-1	0-2	1-2	2-0	3-1	1-2	2-3	0-0	0-1	3-1	2-0	–	1-1	3-1	3-1	3-0
TSV Havelse	34	10	5	19	45	67	35	0-2	1-1	1-2	0-0	0-3	0-1	0-1	1-0	0-2	3-0	3-1	3-3	1-4	1-0	–	1-0	6-2	4-0
Eint. Braunschweig-2	34	7	8	19	31	54	29	2-2	0-1	0-1	0-0	1-1	2-5	3-0	0-5	1-1	3-3	1-2	1-0	0-0	0-1	2-0	–	4-0	4-1
FC Oberneuland	34	8	4	22	46	77	28	1-2	0-5	2-0	0-4	2-0	2-3	0-2	0-2	0-4	2-2	4-1	0-0	1-2	2-2	2-1	0-2	–	6-0
Türkiyemspor §3	34	0	5	29	12	96	2	0-2	2-4	0-3	0-3	0-4	0-0	0-2	0-3	0-5	1-2	0-1	0-1	0-2	1-1	1-4	0-0	1-2	–

6/08/2010 - 28/05/2011 • § = points deducted
Top scorers: **25** - Benjamin Forster, Chemnitzer • **18** - Marc Heider, Kiel • **16** - Daniel Frahn, RB Leipzig & Bastian Henning, Lübeck

GERMANY 2010–11

REGIONALLIGA WEST (4)

Team	Pl	W	D	L	F	A	Pts	Pr'ßen Münster	Eintracht Trier	Lotte	Kaiserslautern-2	Gladbach-2	Dortmund-2	Köln-2	Wuppertaler	Verl	Wiedenbrück	Schalke-2	Elversberg	Mainz-2	Bochum-2	Leverkusen-2	Düsseldorf-2	Homburg	Bielefeld-2
Preußen Münster	34	22	6	6	56	24	72		3-1	2-1	2-1	3-0	0-2	3-0	2-2	0-1	3-0	3-0	1-0	2-1	2-2	2-0	0-1	3-0	2-0
Eintracht Trier	34	18	8	8	58	34	62	1-1		1-1	0-1	1-2	2-0	2-2	2-4	1-0	2-0	1-0	2-0	2-2	0-0	3-1	3-0	3-1	2-0
Sportfreunde Lotte	34	17	11	6	43	29	62	1-0	2-0		1-1	0-0	1-3	3-1	2-0	0-0	1-0	1-0	2-2	0-0	3-0	1-0	2-1	2-0	0-2
1.FC Kaiserslautern-2	34	16	11	7	53	36	59	3-0	0-2	0-1		0-0	2-1	3-1	4-1	1-1	1-1	2-1	1-1	0-1	4-1	5-1	0-4	1-1	2-1
B. Mönchengladbach-2	34	16	11	7	53	41	59	1-0	0-4	5-2	1-1		2-1	3-1	0-2	3-2	2-2	0-1	1-0	1-1	3-0	0-0	1-1	1-1	1-0
Borussia Dortmund-2	34	15	7	12	56	47	52	1-1	0-2	1-1	0-2	1-0		0-0	2-1	0-1	2-3	2-0	1-3	3-2	2-1	4-3	2-0	1-1	1-1
1.FC Köln-2	34	13	12	9	61	43	51	0-3	2-2	0-1	2-2	1-1	3-1		1-1	3-0	2-0	1-1	7-0	1-0	3-0	1-0	2-1	2-3	5-2
Wuppertaler SV	34	14	8	12	52	59	50	1-1	1-3	1-0	0-1	1-1	3-1	3-2		1-0	2-0	2-4	1-3	2-0	1-0	3-4	2-2	1-0	1-1
SC Verl	34	12	12	10	40	34	48	1-2	1-1	0-0	1-3	1-2	2-0	2-2	4-1		3-0	4-1	1-0	0-2	2-3	3-2	2-0	0-0	0-0
SC Wiedenbrück	34	13	7	14	50	55	46	0-2	2-0	1-1	3-1	1-3	1-3	2-5	2-3	0-0		1-0	2-2	2-2	5-3	1-3	5-1	2-0	2-1
FC Schalke 04-2	34	12	8	14	34	45	44	1-1	2-2	0-1	1-0	1-0	1-5	1-0	3-0	3-1	0-1		0-0	0-2	2-1	1-1	0-0	1-0	1-1
SV Elversberg	34	10	13	11	39	44	43	0-2	2-0	1-1	1-1	1-4	1-1	1-3	2-2	1-2	2-3	0-0		1-2	3-0	1-0	2-1	1-0	0-0
1.FSV Mainz 05-2	34	11	8	15	48	51	41	1-2	0-2	3-1	0-0	2-1	1-2	1-1	1-2	0-0	0-3	3-0	1-1		0-3	3-0	1-5	1-3	3-0
VfL Bochum-2	34	8	10	16	49	64	34	1-2	0-3	1-1	2-3	4-4	2-1	0-0	2-2	1-1	2-2	2-3	0-2	4-2		4-0	2-3	0-0	1-4
Bayer Leverkusen-2	34	9	6	19	43	58	33	0-2	0-1	1-2	0-1	1-2	1-3	0-0	2-0	1-3	1-0	4-1	1-1	3-1	0-0		2-1	1-1	6-2
Fortuna Düsseldorf-2	34	8	7	19	41	55	31	0-1	3-1	1-2	1-1	2-4	2-2	0-3	4-0	0-1	0-1	1-0	1-1	2-5	0-2	2-1		0-0	0-1
FC 08 Homburg	34	7	9	18	29	49	30	0-2	0-3	1-2	2-3	0-1	0-2	0-0	2-3	0-0	2-0	1-2	0-2	2-0	0-2	1-3	2-1		2-1
Arminia Bielefeld-2	34	5	6	23	30	67	21	0-1	1-3	0-3	0-2	2-3	1-5	1-4	1-2	0-0	0-2	1-2	0-1	0-4	1-3	2-0	1-0	2-3	

6/08/2010 - 28/05/2011

Top scorers: **18** - Robert Mainka, Wiedenbrück • **15** - Alban Meha ALB, Trier & Andrew Wooten USA, Kaiserslautern

GERMANY 2010–11

REGIONALLIGA SUD (4)

Team	Pl	W	D	L	F	A	Pts	Darmstadt	Kickers	Hessen Kassel	Greuther Fürth-2	Hoffenheim-2	Eint.Frankfurt-2	Freiburg-2	TSV München-2	Pfullendorf	Karlsruher-2	Nürnberg-2	Worms	Memmingen	Sonnenhof	FSV Frankfurt-2	Wiesbaden-2	Ulm	Weiden
SV Darmstadt 98	30	18	8	4	50	26	62		1-1	3-2	3-1	2-0	2-1	2-5	1-1	0-2	1-0	1-1	1-0	4-0	1-0	2-0	4-1	3-0	
Stuttgarter Kickers	30	17	7	6	54	28	58	1-0		2-4	0-1	1-0	2-1	2-1	1-3	2-0	2-2	1-2	1-1	2-0	2-1	7-2	3-0	2-2	
KSV Hessen Kassel	30	16	6	8	59	37	54	1-0	0-0		0-1	3-4	3-2	3-1	4-2	2-0	3-2	0-0	3-0	3-0	3-0	1-0	6-0	4-0	2-1
SpVgg Greuther Fürth-2	30	14	6	10	51	42	48	1-1	0-2	1-1		1-1	1-3	2-4	5-1	1-2	2-2	6-1	1-1	0-2	3-0	2-1	2-3	3-1	6-0
TSG Hoffenheim-2	30	13	7	10	60	40	46	1-1	1-1	3-0	2-3		1-2	1-1	2-0	1-2	1-5	1-0	2-6	0-0	1-4	0-5	5-1		
Eintracht Frankfurt-2	30	14	4	12	56	48	46	2-3	0-4	2-0	1-2	1-1		3-1	4-0	4-2	1-1	1-4	4-3	0-2	5-0	1-0	1-2	0-2	1-0
SC Freiburg-2	30	12	7	11	65	54	43	1-2	1-0	1-1	4-1	3-3	0-3		5-3	5-1	2-1	3-3	1-2	2-0	0-2	1-4	1-3	3-2	3-0
TSV 1860 München-2	30	11	8	11	39	54	41	0-3	1-5	2-0	1-0	0-1	1-0	0-3		1-1	1-0	5-2	4-2	1-1	0-1	1-1	3-1	3-1	
SC Pfullendorf	30	12	4	14	40	43	40	0-0	0-0	2-1	0-0	3-1	1-3	0-1	1-2		1-3	0-2	0-1	2-0	2-0	3-0	5-1	2-1	
Karlsruher SC-2	30	10	9	11	42	37	39	1-3	0-1	0-0	2-4	1-0	4-0	1-1	0-0	1-2		1-1	1-0	0-1	1-1	1-0	2-2	2-1	
1.FC Nürnberg 2	30	10	7	13	43	46	37	0-1	1-2	1-2	4-4	1-2	2-3	3-0	0-1	1-0	1-2		1-0	1-1	2-1	2-3	2-0	4-0	
VfR Wormatia Worms	30	10	6	14	40	45	36	1-2	3-0	2-0	1-1	1-5	1-2	0-5	6-0	2-1	1-2	0-1		0-0	1-1	1-1	2-0	1-0	4-1
FC Memmingen	30	9	9	12	33	50	36	1-1	1-1	4-2	2-1	0-3	1-3	1-0	3-3	4-1	2-2	2-1	0-3		0-1	1-0	2-0	1-1	0-2
Sonnenhof Großaspach	30	8	9	13	29	44	33	1-1	0-3	1-1	0-1	1-1	2-2	3-3	0-1	1-4	3-1	0-2	1-2	0-0		1-1	1-1	1-1	
FSV Frankfurt-2	30	6	8	16	31	52	26	0-1	0-2	1-4	0-1	1-3	1-1	2-2	0-0	3-1	1-4	2-0	2-0	4-1	0-2		0-0	1-3	2-2
SV Wehen Wiesbaden-2	30	5	5	20	25	71	20	0-3	1-3	0-3	0-2	2-5	1-0	2-7	1-1	0-1	1-0	1-1	1-2	2-2	1-3	2-0		4-1	
SSV Ulm 1846	0	0	0	0	0	0	0	3-0	2-1	3-2	3-2	0-4	3-5	1-3	2-1	1-1	1-4	0-0	2-1	0-0	0-1	0-1	4-2		
SpVgg Weiden	0	0	0	0	0	0	0	1-1	0-1		0-0			0-2	2-4		1-1		0-1			2-0	2-1		

4/08/2010 - 28/05/2011 • Weiden withdrew in December 2010. Ulm withdrew at the end of the season

Top scorers: **19** - Kai Herdling, Hoffenheim • **18** - Simon Brandstetter, Freiburg • **17** - Christian Bickel, Freiburg

GERMANY 2010-11   OBERLIGA (5)

BAYERN	Pl	Pts
FC Ismaning	34	66
FC Ingolstadt 04-2	34	63
TSV 1860 Rosenheim	34	53
TSV Buchbach	34	53
Würzburger FV	34	52
SV Seligenporten	34	52
SpVgg Unterhaching-2	34	51
Eintracht Bamberg	34	51
1.FC Schweinfurt 05	34	50
TSV Großbardorf	34	45
FSV Erlangen-Bruck	34	45
TSV 1896 Rain am Lech	34	44
TSV Aindling	34	43
SV Heimstetten	34	43
SpVgg Bayern Hof	34	41
SpVgg Bayreuth	34	41
SV Schalding-Heining	34	32
Freier TuS Regensburg	34	23

BREMEN	Pl	Pts
Werder Bremen 3	30	75
Bremer SV	30	69
SG Aumund-Vegesack	30	67
FC Bremerhaven	30	62
Blumenthaler SV	30	53
1.FC Burg	30	45
FC Bremerhaven	30	43
Brinkumer SV	30	40
TuS Schwachhausen	30	33
Habenhauser FV	30	32
TSV Wulsdorf	30	30
VfL Bremen	30	30
FC Oberneuland-2	30	28
Türkspor Bremen	30	25
TSV Melchiorshausen	30	21
SC Weyhe	30	16

NRW	Pl	Pts
Rot-Weiss Essen	32	71
TSV Germania Windeck	32	66
Fortuna Köln	32	61
Almemannia Aachen 2	32	52
Schwarz-Weiß Essen	32	51
SSVg. Velbert	32	49
Sportfreunde Siegen	32	48
MSV Duisburg 2	32	44
VfB Speldorf	32	42
SV Schermbeck	32	42
VfB Homberg	32	38
SV Bergisch Gladbach	32	37
Westfalia Herne	32	36
FC Wegberg-Beeck	32	36
VfB Hüls	32	36
Westfalia Rhynern	32	31
SpVgg Erkenschwick	32	17
1. FC Kleve	32	0

HESSEN	Pl	Pts
Bayern Alzenau	34	66
SC Waldgirmes	34	58
KSV Baunatal	34	58
1.FC Eschborn	34	57
Kickers Offenbach-2	34	54
OSC Vellmar	34	53
Viktoria Urberach	34	53
Eintracht Stadtallendorf	34	53
FSV Fernwald	34	50
Eintracht Wetzlar	34	47
Rot-Wieß Darmstadt	34	45
1.FC 04 Darmstadt	34	45
SV Buchonia Flieden	34	45
Rot-Weiss Frankfurt	34	42
RSV Würges	34	42
Hünfelder SV	34	32
1.FC Schwalmstadt	34	31
VfB Marburg	34	21

HAMBURG	Pl	Pts
FC St Pauli-2	34	83
TSV Buchholz	34	68
Curslack-Neuengamme	34	62
SC Condor Hamburg	34	57
FC Altona 93	34	54
Eintracht Norderstedt	34	52
ASV Bergedorf 85	34	52
Meiendorfer SV	34	51
Victoria Hamburg	34	50
Germania Schnelsen	34	45
SV Rugenbergen	34	45
Niendorfer TSV	34	40
Oststeinbeker SV	34	39
Uhlenhorster Paloma	34	32
HSV Barmbek-Uhlenhorst	34	32
Wedeler TSV	34	32
Concordia Hamburg	34	31
Bramfelder SV	34	24

NORDOST - NORD	Pl	Pts
Torgelower SV Greif	30	69
Hansa Rostock-2	30	69
Berlin Ankaraspor Kulübü	30	66
TSG Neustrelitz	30	58
1.FC Union Berlin-2	30	51
FSV Optik Rathenow	30	46
BFC Dynamo	30	45
Brandenburger SC Süd	30	41
FC Anker Wismar	30	39
Malchower SV	30	37
SV Germania	30	34
Lichterfelder FC Berlin	30	30
SV Altlüdersdorf	30	28
Tennis Borussia Berlin	30	22
Reinickendorfer Füchse	30	21
Ludwigsfelder FC	30	20

NORDOST - SUD	Pl	Pts
VfB Germania Halberstadt	30	72
VfB Auerbach	30	57
FSV Budissa Bautzen	30	52
Rot-Weiß Erfurt-2	30	48
SG Dynamo Dresden-2	30	41
FSV 63 Luckenwalde	30	41
FC Erzgebirge Aue-2	30	41
1. FC Lokomotive Leipzig	30	39
FSV Zwickau	30	37
FC Sachsen Leipzig	30	36
Chemnitzer FC-2	30	34
FSV Wacker 03 Gotha	30	34
FC Carl Zeiss Jena-2	30	33
VfL Halle 1896	30	33
SC Borea Dresden	30	32
1.FC Magdeburg-2	30	26

NIEDERSACHSEN	Pl	Pts
SV Meppen	38	81
BV Cloppenburg	38	77
VfL Osnabrück-2	38	72
Kickers Emden	38	71
VfV Hildesheim	38	67
VfB Oldenburg	38	65
Goslarer SC 08	38	62
Schwarz-Weiß Rehden	38	62
Eintracht Nordhorn	38	56
SC Langenhagen	38	55
Osterholz-Scharmbeck	38	53
TSV Ottersberg	38	51
Hansa Lüneburg	38	49
TuS Heeslingen	38	47
Arminia Hannover	38	45
Eintracht Northeim	38	38
SV Drochtersten/Assel	38	36
Ramlingen/Ehlershausen	38	33
Teutonia Uelzen	38	24
TuS Güldenstern Stade	38	13

SC'WIG-HOLSTEIN	Pl	Pts
VfR Neumünster	34	82
SV Eichede	34	67
FC Sylt	34	63
VfB Lübeck-2	34	59
NTSV Strand 08	34	56
ETSV Weiche Flensburg	34	53
Holstein Kiel 2	34	53
TSV Kropp	34	51
SV Henstedt-Ulzburg	34	48
Flensburg 08	34	47
Heikendorfer SV	34	47
FT Eider Büdelsdorf	34	42
SV Todesfelde	34	40
Heider SV	34	39
PSV Union Neumünster	34	34
TSV Bordesholm	34	27
Eckernförder SV	34	21
Schleswig 06	34	21

B-WURTTEMBERG	Pl	Pts
SV Waldhof Mannheim	36	83
FC Nöttingen	36	78
FC 08 Villingen	36	65
SpVgg Neckarelz	36	58
1. FC Normannia Gmünd	36	55
Stuttgarter Kickers-2	36	54
FV Illertissen	36	52
FC Astoria Walldorf	36	51
VfL Kirchheim unter Teck	36	50
TSG Balingen	36	50
Kehler FV	36	46
FSV Hollenbach	36	45
Bahlinger SC	36	45
SSV Reutlingen	36	45
SGV Freiberg	36	44
TSG Weinheim	36	38
VfB Neckarrems	36	35
ASV Durlach	36	24
SV Linx	36	18

SUDWEST	Pl	Pts
SC Idar-Oberstein	36	67
FK Pirmasens	36	63
SG 06 Betzdorf	36	60
SC Hauenstein	36	58
SVN 1929 Zweibrücken	36	55
SF Köllerbach	36	55
Borussia Neunkirchen	36	54
TuS Mechtersheim	36	53
SV Elversberg-2	36	50
Eintracht Trier-2	36	47
SpVgg Wirges	36	47
Alemannia Waldalgesheim	36	46
SV Roßbach	36	46
1.FC Saarbrücken-2	36	45
SV Gonsheim	36	45
Rot-Weiß Hasborn	36	44
SG Bad Breisig	36	37
SV Auersmacher	36	36
Sportfreunde Eisbachtal	36	33

MEDALS TABLE

		Overall			League			Cup		Europe			
		G	**S**	**B**	**G**	**S**	**B**	**G**	**S**	**G**	**S**	**B**	**City**
1	Bayern München	43	14	16	22	8	5	15	2	6	4	11	Munich
2	Schalke 04	13	16	5	7	9	2	5	7	1		3	Gelsenkirchen
3	1.FC Nürnberg	13	5	1	9	3		4	2			1	Nuremburg
4	Hamburger SV	11	15	6	6	8	2	3	4	2	3	4	Hamburg
5	Werder Bremen	11	12	8	4	7	5	6	4	1	1	3	Bremen
6	Borussia Dortmund	11	8	8	7	4	5	2	2	2	2	3	Dortmund
7	B. Mönchengladbach	10	7	8	5	2	5	3	2	2	3	3	Mönchengladbach
8	VfB Stuttgart	8	8	6	5	4	4	3	2		2	2	Stuttgart
9	1.FC Köln	7	15	9	3	8	2	4	6		1	7	Cologne
10	1.FC Kaiserslautern	6	9	4	4	4	2	2	5			2	Kaiserslautern
11	Eintracht Frankfurt	6	4	7	1	1	5	4	2	1	1	2	Frankfurt
12	Lokomotive Leipzig (VfB)	4	2		3	2		1					Leipzig
13	Dresdner SC	4	1		2	1		2					Dresden
14	Fortuna Düsseldorf	3	7	2	1	1	2	2	5		1		Düsseldorf
15	Karlsruher SC	3	3	1	1	1		2	2			1	Karlsruhe
16	TSV München 1860	3	3		1	2		2			1		Munich
17	SpVgg Fürth	3	1		3	1							Fürth
18	Hannover 96	3			2			1					Hanover
19	Bayer 04 Leverkusen	2	8	4		5	3	1	2	1	1	1	Leverkusen
20	Hertha BSC Berlin	2	7	5	2	5	4		2			1	Berlin
21	Viktoria 89 Berlin	2	2		2	2							Berlin
22	Rot-Weiss Essen	2	1		1			1	1				Essen
23	SK Rapid Wien	2			1			1					Vienna - AUT
24	Holstein Kiel	1	2		1	2							Kiel
	Karlsruher FV	1	2		1	2							Karlsruhe
	Kickers Offenbach	1	2			2		1					Offenbach
27	Blau-Weiß Berlin	1	1		1	1							Berlin
	First Vienna	1	1			1		1					Vienna - AUT
	VfL Wolfsburg	1	1		1							1	Wolfsburg
30	KFC Uerdingen 05	1		2			1	1				1	Krefeld
31	Eint. Braunschweig	1		1	1	1							Braunschweig
32	Freiburger FC	1			1								Freiburg
	Schwarz-Weiss Essen	1						1					Essen
	VfR Mannheim	1			1								Mannheim
35	MSV Duisburg		6	1		2			4			1	Duisburg
36	TSV Alemania Aachen		4			1			3				Aachen
37	1.FC Saarbrücken		2			2							Saarbrücken
	FSV Frankfurt		2			1			1				Frankfurt
	Stuttgarter Kickers		2			1			1				Stuttgart
	VfL Bochum		2						2				Bochum
	1.FC Union Berlin		2			1			1				Berlin
42	Admira Wien		1			1							Vienna - AUT
	Borussia Neunkirchen		1						1				Neunkirchen
	DFC Prag		1			1							Prague - CZE
	Energie Cottbus		1						1				Cottbus
	Fortuna Köln		1						1				Cologne
	Hertha BSC Berlin am		1						1				Berlin
	1.FC Phorzheim		1			1							Pforzheim
	LSV Groß Hamburg		1			1							Hamburg
	Preußen Münster		1			1							Münster
	Waldhof Mannheim		1						1				Mannheim
52	SC Freiburg			1			1						Freiburg

Leading East German Clubs (1948-91)

		Overall			League			Cup		Europe			
		G	**S**	**B**	**G**	**S**	**B**	**G**	**S**	**G**	**S**	**B**	**City**
1	Dynamo Dresden	15	12	8	8	8	6	7	4			1	Dresden
2	Dynamo Berlin	13	10	4	10	4	3	3	6			1	Berlin
3	1.FC Magdeburg	11	2	6	3	2	6	7		1			Magdeburg
4	Viktoria 91 Frankfurt	8	7	1	6	4	1	2	3				Frankfurt/Oder
5	Carl Zeiss Jena	7	13	6	3	9	5	4	3		1	1	Jena
6	Sachsenring Zwickau	5	1	4	2		3	3	1			1	Zwickau
7	Lokomotive Leipzig	4	8	9		3	8	4	4		1	1	Leipzig

DFB POKAL 2010-11

First Round		Second Round		Third Round	
Schalke 04	2				
VfR Aalen *	1	Schalke 04	1		
SC Paderborn 07	0	FSV Frankfurt *	0		
FSV Frankfurt *	2			Schalke 04	1
SpVgg Greuther Fürth	2			FC Augsburg *	0
Eintracht Braunschweig *	1	SpVgg Greuther Fürth *	2		
SV Sandhausen *	4 1p	FC Augsburg	4		
FC Augsburg	4 3p				
Offenbacher Kickers *	3				
VfL Bochum	0	Offenbacher Kickers *	0 4p		
Wacker Burghausen *	0	Borussia Dortmund	0 2p		
Borussia Dortmund	3			Offenbacher Kickers *	0
SV Elversberg *	0 5p			1.FC Nürnberg	2
Hannover 96	0 4p	SV Elversberg *	0		
Eintracht Trier *	0	1.FC Nürnberg	3		
1.FC Nürnberg	2				
Alemannia Aachen	2				
Schwarz-Weiß Essen *	1	Alemannia Aachen *	2		
Berlin Ankaraspor Kulübü *	1	1.FSV Mainz	1		
1.FSV Mainz	2			Alemannia Aachen *	1 5p
Hamburger SV	5			Eintracht Frankfurt	1 3p
Torgelower SC Greif *	1	Hamburger SV	2		
SV Wilhelmshaven *	0	Eintracht Frankfurt *	5		
Eintracht Frankfurt	4				
VfB Stuttgart	2				
SV Babelsberg 03 *	1	VfB Stuttgart	3		
FC St Pauli	0	Chemnitzer FC *	1		
Chemnitzer FC *	1			VfB Stuttgart *	3
Werder Bremen	4			Bayern München	6
Rot-Weiss Ahlen *	0	Werder Bremen	1		
Germania Windeck *	0	Bayern München *	2		
Bayern München	4				
Energie Cottbus	2				
TuS Heeslingen *	1	Energie Cottbus *	2		
FC Oberneuland *	0	SC Freiburg	1		
SC Freiburg	1			Energie Cottbus	3
SC Victoria Hamburg *	1			VfL Wolfsburg *	1
Rot-Weiß Oberhausen	0	SC Victoria Hamburg *	1		
Preußen Münster *	1	VfL Wolfsburg	3		
VfL Wolfsburg	2				
Borussia Mönchengladbach	3				
Erzgebirge Aue *	1	Borussia Mönchengladbach *	1 5p		
FK Pirmasens *	1	Bayer Leverkusen	1 4p		
Bayer Leverkusen	11			Borussia Mönchengladbach	0
FC Ingolstadt 04 *	2			TSG Hoffenheim *	2
Karlsruher SC	0	FC Ingolstadt 04	0		
Hansa Rostock *	0	TSG Hoffenheim *	1		
TSG Hoffenheim	4				
1.FC Kaiserslautern	3				
VfL Osnabrück *	2	1.FC Kaiserslautern *	3		
SSV Jahn Regensburg *	1 5p	Arminia Bielefeld	0		
Arminia Bielefeld	1 6p			1.FC Kaiserslautern	4
Hertha BSC Berlin	2			TuS Koblenz *	1
SC Pfullendorf *	0	Hertha BSC Berlin	1		
Fortuna Düsseldorf	0	TuS Koblenz *	2		
TuS Koblenz *	1				
1.FC Köln	2				
ZFC Meuselwitz *	0	1.FC Köln *	3		
SC Verl *	1	TSV 1860 München	0		
TSV 1860 München	2			1.FC Köln *	1
Hallescher FC *	1			MSV Duisburg	2
1.FC Union Berlin	0	Hallescher FC *	0		
VfB Lübeck *	0	MSV Duisburg	3		
MSV Duisburg	2				

DFB POKAL 2010–11

| Quarter–finals | Semi–finals | Final |

Schalke 04 * 3
1.FC Nürnberg 2

Schalke 04 1
Bayern München * 0

Alemannia Aachen * 0
Bayern München 4

Schalke 04 ‡ 5
MSV Duisburg 0

Energie Cottbus * 1
TSG Hoffenheim 0

Energie Cottbus 1
MSV Duisburg * 2

1.FC Kaiserslautern 0
MSV Duisburg * 2

DFB POKAL FINAL 2011
Olympiastadion, Berlin, 21-05-2011, 20:00, Att: 75708, Wolfgang Stark

Schalke 04 5 Draxler [18], Howedes [42], Huntelaar 2 [22][70],
MSV Duisburg 0 Jurado [55]

Schalke - Manuel Neuer (c) - Benedikt Howedes, Kyriakos Papadopoulos, Christoph Metzelder, Hans Sarpei (Sergio Escudero 43) - Peer Kluge (Atsuto Uchida 81), Jose Manuel Jurado - Jefferson Farfan, Julian Draxler (Joel Matip 72) - Raul, Klaas-Jan Huntelaar. Tr: Ralf Rangnick
Duisburg - David Yelldell - Benjamin Kern (Maurice Exslager 77), Daniel Reiche (Filip Trojan 60), Branimir Bajic, Olivier Veigneau - Goran Sukalo - Sefa Yılmaz, Ivica Banovic, Ivica Grlic (c), Olcay Sahan - Manuel Schaffler. Tr: Milan Sasic

* Home team • ‡ Qualified for the UEFA Europa League

CLUB BY CLUB GUIDE TO THE 2010-11 SEASON IN GERMANY

BAYER LEVERKUSEN 2010–11

	Date	Opponent	Res	Score	Comp	Scorers	Att
	14	Pirmasens	W	11-1	DPr1	Kießling 2 36 60, Helmes 3 46 58 65, Renato 63, Sam 2 67 88, Derdiyok 2 84 90, Vidal 86p	8 254
Aug	19	Tavriya	W	3-0	ELpo	Kadlec 2 1 83, Ballack 90p	13 000
	22	B Dortmund	W	3-1	BL	Barnetta 19, Renato 22	73 300
	26	Tavriya	W	3-1	ELpo	Vidal 51p, OG 74, Castro 90	10 700
	29	Gladbach	L	3-6	BL	Derdiyok 24, Vidal 58p, Kießling 70	30 210
Sep	11	Hannover	D	2-2	BL	Derdiyok 62, Helmes 90	40 852
	16	Rosenborg	W	4-0	ELgB	Helmes 3 4 58 61, Reinartz 38	13 065
	19	Nürnberg	D	0-0	BL		23 963
	22	E Frankfurt	W	2-1	BL	Bender 9, Vidal 91+p	24 404
	25	Stuttgart	W	4-1	BL	Hyypia 19, Vidal 21, Balitsch 69, Sam 88	38 300
	30	At. Madrid	D	1-1	ELgB	Derdiyok 39	28 052
Oct	3	W Bremen	D	2-2	BL	Helmes 16, Derdiyok 78	30 210
	16	Wolfsburg	W	3-2	BL	Rolfes 2 72 82, Vidal 75p	30 000
	21	Aris	D	0-0	ELgB		16 372
	24	Mainz	L	0-1	BL		30 210
	27	Gladbach	D	1-1	DPr2	Derdiyok 107, W 5-4p	34 570
	30	Schalke	W	1-0	BL	Sam 65	61 673
Nov	4	Aris	W	1-0	ELgB	Vidal 90	18 265
	7	Kaiser'tern	W	3-1	BL	Sam 2 38 84, Helmes 68	29 794
	13	St Pauli	W	1-0	BL	Renato 81	24 387
	20	Bayern M	D	1-1	BL	Vidal 45p	30 210
	27	Hoffenheim	D	2-2	BL	Sam 8, Vidal 10p	29 250
	1	Rosenborg	W	1-0	ELgB	Sam 35	11 096
Dec	5	Köln	W	3-2	BL	Helmes 21, Barnetta 55, Reinartz 61	30 210
	11	Hamburg	W	4-2	BL	Sam 30, Vidal 61, Renato 2 66 78	51 225
	16	At. Madrid	D	1-1	ELgB	Helmes 69	18 093
	19	Freiburg	D	2-2	BL	Vidal 16p, Helmes 75	22 421
Jan	14	B Dortmund	L	1-3	BL	Kießling 80	30 210
	23	Gladbach	W	3-1	BL	Kadlec 37, Castro 2 45 73	36 696
	28	Hannover	W	2-0	BL	Vidal 21, Rolfes 42	28 013
Feb	5	Nürnberg	L	0-1	BL		34 113
	12	E Frankfurt	W	3-0	BL	Rolfes 8, Renato 32, Balitsch 84	42 600
	17	Metalist	W	4-0	ELr2	Derdiyok 23, Castro 72, Sam 2 90 92+	35 150
	20	Stuttgart	W	4-2	BL	Kießling 2 6 90, Castro 41, Reinartz 81	28 851
	24	Metalist	W	2-0	ELr2	Rolfes 47, Ballack 70	16 212
	27	W Bremen	D	2-2	BL	Derdiyok 42, Rolfes 67	37 500
Mar	5	Wolfsburg	W	3-0	BL	Bender 21, Renato 29, Kießling 45	28 115
	10	Villarreal	L	2-3	ELr3	Kadlec 33, Castro 72	20 126
	13	Mainz	W	1-0	BL	Renato 82	20 300
	17	Villarreal	L	1-2	ELr3	Derdiyok 82	19 779
	20	Schalke	W	2-0	BL	Derdiyok 19, OG 28	30 210
Apr	2	Kaiser'tern	W	1-0	BL	Sam 70	46 050
	10	St Pauli	W	2-1	BL	Kießling 66, Bender 77	30 210
	17	Bayern M	L	1-5	BL	Derdiyok 62	69 000
	23	Hoffenheim	W	2-1	BL	Kadlec 40, Vidal 51	29 313
	30	Köln	L	0-2	BL		50 000
May	7	Hamburg	D	1-1	BL	Kießling 54	30 210
	14	Freiburg	W	1-0	BL	Balitsch 45	24 000

2nd Att: 486 764 • Av: 28 633 (-2.3%) • BayArena 30 210 (94%)

BAYERN MUNCHEN 2010–11

	Date	Opponent	Res	Score	Comp	Scorers	Att
	7	Schalke	W	2-0	SC	Muller 75, Klose 81	30 662
Aug	16	G Windeck	W	4-0	DPr1	Klose 44, Ribery 45, Kroos 84, Gomez 85	41 100
	20	Wolfsburg	W	2-1	BL	Muller 9, Schweinsteiger 91+	69 000
	27	Kaiser'tern	L	0-2	BL		49 780
	11	W Bremen	D	0-0	BL		69 000
Sep	15	Roma	W	2-0	CLgE	Muller 79, Klose 83	66 000
	18	Köln	D	0-0	BL		69 000
	21	Hoffenheim	W	2-1	BL	Muller 62, Van Buyten 91+	30 150
	25	Mainz	L	1-2	BL	OG 45	69 000
	28	Basel	W	2-1	CLgE	Schweinsteiger 2 56p 89	37 500
Oct	3	B Dortmund	L	0-2	BL		80 720
	16	Hannover	W	3-0	BL	Gomez 3 21 77 90	69 000
	19	Cluj	W	3-2	CLgE	OG 2 32 37, Gomez 77	64 000
	22	Hamburg	D	0-0	BL		57 000
	26	W Bremen	W	2-1	DPr2	Schweinsteiger 2 27 74	64 000
	29	Freiburg	W	4-2	BL	Demichelis 39, Gomez 61, Tymoshchuk 72, Kroos 80	69 000
Nov	3	Cluj	W	4-0	CLgE	Gomez 3 12 24 71, Muller 90	14 097
	6	Gladbach	D	3-3	BL	Gomez 2, Schweinsteiger 40, Lahm 84	54 057
	14	Nürnberg	W	3-0	BL	Gomez 2 10 75, Lahm 57p	69 000
	20	Leverkusen	D	1-1	BL	Gomez 34	30 210
	23	Roma	L	2-3	CLgE	Gomez 2 33 39	42 789
	27	E Frankfurt	W	4-1	BL	Tymoshchuk 2 29 88, Muller 59, Gomez 61	69 000
Dec	4	Schalke	L	0-2	BL		61 673
	8	Basel	W	3-0	CLgE	Ribery 2 35 50, Tymoshchuk 37	64 000
	11	St Pauli	W	3-0	BL	Altintop 16, Lahm 71p, Ribery 79	69 000
	19	Stuttgart	W	5-3	BL	Gomez 3 31 52 54, Muller 36, Ribery 43	40 500
Jan	22	Stuttgart	W	6-3	DPr3	Ottl 6, Gomez 8, Klose 2 52 86, Muller 81, Ribery 90	40 500
	15	Wolfsburg	D	1-1	BL	Muller 7	30 000
	22	Kaiser'tern	W	5-1	BL	Robben 45, Gomez 3 46 80 85, Muller 91+	69 000
	29	W Bremen	W	3-1	BL	Robben 64, OG 75, Klose 86	40 500
Feb	26	Aachen	W	4-0	DPqf	Gomez 26, Muller 2 75 80, Robben 88	32 190
	5	Köln	L	2-3	BL	Gomez 22, Altintop 43	50 000
	12	Hoffenheim	W	4-0	BL	Gomez 2, Muller 15, Robben 2 63 81	69 000
	19	Mainz	W	3-1	BL	Schweinsteiger 9, Muller 50, Gomez 77	20 300
	23	Inter	W	1-0	CLr2	Gomez 90	75 925
	26	B Dortmund	L	1-3	BL	Gustavo 15	69 000
Mar	2	Schalke	L	0-1	DPsf		69 000
	5	Hannover	L	1-3	BL	Robben 55	49 000
	12	Hamburg	W	6-0	BL	Robben 3 40 47 55, Ribery 64, Muller 79, OG 85	69 000
	15	Inter	L	2-3	CLr2	Gomez 21, Muller 31	66 000
	19	Freiburg	W	2-1	BL	Gomez 9, Ribery 88	24 000
	2	Gladbach	W	1-0	BL	Robben 77	69 000
Apr	9	Nürnberg	D	1-1	BL	Muller 4	48 548
	17	Leverkusen	W	5-1	BL	OG 7, Gomez 3 28 44 45, Ribery 75	69 000
	23	E Frankfurt	D	1-1	BL	Gomez 88p	51 500
	30	Schalke	W	4-1	BL	Robben 6, Muller 2 13 84, Gomez 19	69 000
May	7	St Pauli	W	8-1	BL	Gomez 3 10 52 86, Van Buyten 32, Robben 2 54 84, Ribery 2 74 88	24 487
	14	Stuttgart	W	2-1	BL	Gomez 36, Schweinsteiger 70	69 000

3rd Att: 1 173 000 • Av: 69 000 (0%) • Allianz Arena 69 000 (100%)

LEVERKUSEN LEAGUE APPEARANCES/GOALS 2010-11

Goalkeepers Rene Adler 32 • Fabian Giefer 2
Defenders Gonzalo Castro 19+4/3 • Manuel Friedrich 17+2/0
Sami Hyypia FIN 20+1/1 • Michal Kadlec CZE 30+2/2
Daniel Schwaab 28+2/0 • Domagoj Vida CRO 0+1/0
Midfield Hanno Balitsch 9+15/3 • Michael Ballack 13+4/0 • Tranquillo
Barnetta SUI 19+5/2 • Lars Bender 10+17/3 • Stefan Reinartz 29+2/2
Renato Augusto BRA 26+1/7 • Simon Rolfes 21+7/5
Sidney Sam 26+4/7 • Arturo Vidal CHI 31+2/10
Forwards Eren Derdiyok SUI 18+14/6 • Patrick Helmes 8+3/5
Nicolai Jørgensen DEN 1+8/0 • Stefan Kießling 15+7/7
Coach Jupp Heynckes

BAYERN LEAGUE APPEARANCES/GOALS 2010-11

Goalkeepers Hans Jorg Butt 22+1 • Thomas Kraft 12
Defenders Holger Badstuber 21+2/0 • Edson Braafheid NED 2+1/0
Breno BRA 7+6/0 • Diego Contento 12+2/0 • Martin Demichelis
ARG 3+3/1 • Philipp Lahm 34/3 • Daniel Van Buyten BEL 18+3/2
Midfield David Alaba AUT 0+2/0 • Hamit Altintop TUR 8+6/2
Toni Kroos 19+8/1 • Luiz Gustavo BRA 13+1/1 • Andreas Ottl 9+6/0
Danijel Pranjic CRO 22+6/0 • Franck Ribery FRA 22+3/7
Bastian Schweinsteiger 31+1/4 • Anatoliy Tymoshchuk UKR 23+3/3
Mark van Bommel NED 12+1/0
Forwards Mario Gomez 27+5/28 • Miroslav Klose 9+11/1 • Thomas
Muller 32+2/12 • Ivica Olic CRO 3+3/0 • Arjen Robben NED 13+1/12
Coach Louis van Gaal NED

BORUSSIA DORTMUND 2010-11

	Day	Opponent		Score	Comp	Scorers	Att
Aug	14	Burghausen	W	3-0	DPr1	Barrios 4, Subotic 13, Großkrey	
	19	Karabakh	W	4-0	ELpo	Kagawa 2 [13 40], Barrios 2 [20 29]	47 800
	22	Leverkusen	L	0-2	BL		73 300
	26	Karabakh	W	1-0	ELpo	Barrios 90	15 000
	29	Stuttgart	W	3-1	BL	OG 5, Barrios 26, Gotze 37	40 500
Sep	11	Wolfsburg	W	2-0	BL	Sahin 50, Kagawa 67	73 600
	16	Karpaty	W	4-3	ELpo	Sahin 12p, Gotze 2 [27 90], Barrios 87	28 045
	19	Schalke	W	3-1	BL	Kagawa 2 [20 58], Lewandowski 86	60 069
	22	Kaiser'tern	W	5-0	BL	Barrios 2 [31 87], Großkreutz 38, Hummels 65, Lewandowski 75	70 100
	25	St Pauli	W	3-1	BL	Großkreutz 2 [17 60], Kagawa 50	24 082
	30	Sevilla	L	0-1	ELgJ		49 100
Oct	3	Bayern M	W	2-0	BL	Barrios 51, Sahin 60	80 720
	15	Köln	W	2-1	BL	Blaszczykowski 20, Sanhin 91+	50 000
	21	PSG	D	1-1	ELgJ	Sahin 50p	50 200
	24	Hoffenheim	D	1-1	BL	Da Silva 90	80 720
	27	K.Offenbach	D	0-0	DPr2	L 2-4p	25 000
	31	Mainz	W	2-0	BL	Gotze 26, Barrios 67	20 300
Nov	4	PSG	D	0-0	ELgJ		26 204
	7	Hannover	W	4-0	BL	Kagawa 11, Barrios 72, Lewandowski 80, Blaszczykowski 91+	49 000
	12	Hamburg	W	2-0	BL	Kagawa 49, Barrios 70	80 720
	20	Freiburg	W	2-1	BL	Lewandowski 75, OG 78	24 000
	27	Gladbach	W	4-1	BL	Subotic 45, Kagawa 52, Großkreutz 76, Barrios 88	79 200
Dec	2	Kapaty	W	3-0	ELgJ	Kagawa 5, Hummels 49, Lewandowski 89	40 100
	5	Nürnberg	W	2-0	BL	Hummels 23, Lewandowski 88	48 548
	11	W Bremen	W	2-0	BL	Sahin 9, Kagawa 70	80 720
	15	Sevilla	D	2-2	ELgJ	Kagawa 4, Subotic 49	27 062
	18	E Frankfurt	L	0-1	BL		51 500
Jan	14	Leverkusen	W	3-1	BL	Großkreutz 2 [49 53], Gotze 55	30 210
	22	Stuttgart	D	1-1	BL	Gotze 43	80 720
	29	Wolfsburg	W	3-0	BL	Barrios 2, Sahin 40, Hummels 70	30 000
Feb	4	Schalke	D	0-0	BL		80 720
	12	Kaiser'tern	D	1-1	BL	Bender 82	49 780
	19	St Pauli	W	2-0	BL	Barrios 39, OG 49	80 720
	26	Bayern M	W	3-1	BL	Barrios 9, Sahin 18, Hummels 60	69 000
	4	Köln	W	1-0	BL	Lewandowski 44	80 720
Mar	12	Hoffenheim	L	0-1	BL		30 150
	19	Mainz	D	1-1	BL	Hummels 8	80 720
	2	Hannover	W	4-1	BL	Gotze 59, Barrios 2 [64 73], Großkreutz 83	80 720
	9	Hamburg	D	1-1	BL	Blaszczykowski 92+	57 000
Apr	17	Freiburg	W	1-0	BL	Gotze 23, Lewandowski 43, Großkreutz 83	80 720
	23	Gladbach	L	0-1	BL		54 057
	30	Nürnberg	W	2-0	BL	Barrios 32, Lewandowski 43	80 720
May	7	W Bremen	L	0-2	BL		40 600
	14	E Frankfurt	W	3-1	BL	Barrios 2 [68 90], OG 72	80 720

1st Att: 1 345 560 • Av: 79 151 (+2.4%) • Westfalenstadion 80 720 (98%)

BORUSSIA MONCHENGLADBACH 2010-11

	Day	Opponent		Score	Comp	Scorers	Att
Aug	14	Aue	W	3-1	DPr1	Bradley 38, Idrissou 64, Reus 87	12 652
	21	Nürnberg	D	1-1	BL	Idrissou 31	42 202
	29	Leverkusen	W	6-3	BL	Herrmann 2 [20 44], Brouwers 40, Arango 56, Idrissou 60, Reus 69	30 210
Sep	11	E Frankfurt	L	0-4	BL		45 315
	18	Stuttgart	L	0-7	BL		39 500
	22	St Pauli	L	1-2	BL	Arango 25	41 080
	25	Schalke	D	2-2	BL	Daems 15, Bradley 43	61 673
	2	Wolfsburg	D	1-1	BL	Marx 65	40 423
	17	Hoffenheim	L	2-3	BL	Bobadilla 12, Idrissou 91+	30 150
Oct	23	W Bremen	L	1-4	BL	OG 67	53 511
	27	Leverkusen	D	1-1	DPr2	Idrissou 109, W 5-4p	34 570
		Kaiser'tern	L	0-3	BL		49 167
	6	Bayern M	D	3-3	BL	Herrmann 5, Reus 56, Camargo 61	54 057
Nov	13	Köln	W	4-0	BL	Bobadilla 2 [51 90], Bradley 70, Camargo 82	50 000
	20	Mainz	L	2-3	BL	Reus 2 [53 69]	45 472
	3	B Dortmund	L	1-4	BL	Reus 33	79 200
	4	Hannover	L	1-2	BL	Bradley 17	37 195
Dec	12	Freiburg	L	0-3	BL		22 700
	17	Hamburg	L	1-2	BL	Camargo 48	42 253
	21	Hoffenheim	L	0-2	DPr3		23 500
	15	Nürnberg	W	1-0	BL	Neustadter 8	37 464
Jan	23	Leverkusen	L	1-3	BL	Stranzl 65	36 696
	30	E Frankfurt	W	1-0	BL	Camargo 85	43 700
	5	Stuttgart	L	2-3	BL	Dante 29, Camargo 32	39 132
Feb	12	St Pauli	L	1-3	BL	Camargo 8	24 487
	20	Schalke	W	2-1	BL	Reus 12, Idrissou 23	51 592
	25	Wolfsburg	L	1-2	BL	Daems 74p	28 763
	5	Hoffenheim	W	2-0	BL	Daems 64p, Camargo 70	35 350
Mar	12	W Bremen	D	1-1	BL	Dante 92+	40 500
	18	Kaiser'tern	L	0-1	BL		47 696
	2	Bayern M	L	0-1	BL		69 000
	10	Köln	W	5-1	BL	Arango 29, Reus 2 [34 39], Daems 65p, Nordtveit 67	53 104
Apr	15	Mainz	L	0-1	BL		20 300
	23	B Dortmund	W	1-0	BL	Idrissou 36	54 057
	30	Hannover	W	1-0	BL	Reus 76	48 800
	7	Freiburg	W	2-0	BL	Hanke 80, Reus 82	49 072
May	14	Hamburg	D	1-1	BL	Arango 41	57 000
	19	Bochum	W	1-0	BLpo	Camargo 93+	54 057
	22	Bochum	D	1-1	BLpo	Reus 72	28 650

16th Att: 768 207 • Av: 45 189 (-2.7%) • Borussia-Park 54 057 (83%)

KEY
BL = Bundesliga • DP = DFB Pokal
(German Cup) • CL = UEFA Champions
League • EL = Europa League
See page 13 for further explanations

DORTMUND LEAGUE APPEARANCES/GOALS 2010-11
Goalkeepers Mitchell Langerak AUS 1 • Roman Weidenfeller 33
Defenders Dede BRA 0+4/0 • Felipe Santana BRA 5+8/0
Mats Hummels 32/5 • Patrick Owomoyela 5+1/0
Lukász Piszczek POL 29+4/0 • Marcel Schmelzer 34/0
Neven Subotic SRB 31/1
Midfield Sven Bender 29+2/1 • Jakub Blaszczykowski POL 15+14/3
Antonio da Silva BRA 5+17/1 • Markus Feulner 0+6/0
Mario Gotze 29+4/6 • Kevin Großkreutz 32+2/8
Shinji Kagawa JPN 17+1/8 • Sebastian Kehl 3+3/0
Nuri Sahin TUR 30/6
Forwards Lucas Barrios PAR 29+3/16
Robert Lewandowski POL 15+18/8 • Dimitar Rengelov BUL 0+1/0
Marco Stiepermann 0+4/0 • Mohamed Zidan EGY 0+8/0
Coach Jurgen Klopp

GLADBACH LEAGUE APPEARANCES/GOALS 2010-11
Goalkeepers Logan Bailly BEL 15 • Christofer Heimeroth 13
Marc-Andre ter Stegen 6
Defenders Bamba Anderson BRA 11+2/0 • Roel Brouwers NED 10+5/1
Jan-Ingwer Callsen Brooker 3 1 1/0 • Filip Daems BEL 34/4
Dante BRA 17+1/2 • Tobias Levels 22/0 • Sebastian Schachten 7+6/0
Martin Stranzl AUT 17/1 • Jens Wissing 2+1/0
Midfield Juan Arango VEN 24+1/4 • Michael Bradley USA 17+2/3
Michael Fink 4+2/0 • Patrick Herrmann 15+9/3 • Tony Jantschke 10+1/0
Thorben Marx 19+8/1 • Marcel Meeuwis NED 0+2/0
Neustadter 20+4/1 • Havard Nordtveit NOR 15+1/1 • Marco Reus 32/10
Forwards Raul Bobadilla ARG 8+6/3 • Igor de Camargo BEL 14+5/7
Mike Hanke 10+4/1 • Mohamadou Idrissou CMR 26+7/5
Elias Kachunga 0+2/0 • Karim Matmour ALG 3+15/0
Coach Michael Frontzeck • Lucien Favre SUI

EINTRACHT FRANKFURT 2010–11

Month	Day	Opponent		Result	Comp	Scorers	Att
Aug	13	Wil'shaven	W	4-0	DPr1	Amanatidis 21, Tzavellas 38, Ochs 59, Altintop 89	6 485
	21	Hannover	L	1-2	BL	Kohler 27	37 212
	28	Hamburg	L	1-3	BL	Ochs 37	51 500
Sep	11	Gladbach	W	4-0	BL	Kohler 24, Gekas 2 36 64, Ochs 50	45 315
	17	Freiburg	L	0-1	BL		40 600
	22	Leverkusen	L	1-2	BL	Gekas 18	24 404
	25	Nürnberg	W	2-0	BL	Gekas 17, Chris 88	43 100
Oct	3	Stuttgart	W	2-1	BL	Gekas 18, Chris 69	40 200
	17	Kaiser'tern	W	3-0	BL	Gekas 2 45 67, Meier 83	49 780
	23	Schalke	D	0-0	BL		51 500
	27	Hamburg	W	5-2	DPr2	Caio 13, Gekas 2 21 45, OG 65, Altintop 87p	39 400
Nov	30	St Pauli	W	3-1	BL	Gekas 2 42p 70, Caio 90	24 330
	6	Wolfsburg	W	3-1	BL	Gekas 2 26 55p, Schwegler 38	43 800
	13	W Bremen	D	0-0	BL		35 300
	20	Hoffenheim	L	0-4	BL		44 300
	27	Bayern M	L	1-4	BL	Gekas 33	69 000
Dec	4	Mainz	W	2-1	BL	Russ 35, Gekas 84p	51 500
	11	Köln	L	0-1	BL		45 000
	18	B Dortmund	W	1-0	BL	Gekas 87	51 500
Jan	22	Aachen	D	1-1	DPr3	Fenin 99. L 3-5p	32 160
	16	Hannover	L	0-3	BL		39 300
	21	Hamburg	L	0-1	BL		50 239
	30	Gladbach	L	0-1	BL		43 700
Feb	6	Freiburg	D	0-0	BL		21 900
	12	Leverkusen	L	0-3	BL		42 600
	18	Nürnberg	L	0-3	BL		40 853
	27	Stuttgart	L	0-2	BL		47 400
Mar	5	Kaiser'tern	D	0-0	BL		49 400
	12	Schalke	L	1-2	BL	Tzavellas 70	61 673
	19	St Pauli	W	2-1	BL	Gekas 2 34p 77	50 500
Apr	3	Wolfsburg	D	1-1	BL	Meier 59	29 125
	8	W Bremen	D	1-1	BL	Fenin 83	51 500
	16	Hoffenheim	L	0-1	BL		30 150
	23	Bayern M	D	1-1	BL	Rode 53	51 500
	30	Mainz	L	0-3	BL		20 300
May	7	Köln	L	0-2	BL		51 500
	14	B Dortmund	L	1-3	BL	Rode 46	80 720

17th Att: 805 200 • Av: 47 365 (+0.4%) • Waldstadion 51 500 (92%)

SC FREIBURG 2010–11

Month	Day	Opponent		Result	Comp	Scorers	Att
Aug	14	Obern'land	W	1-0	DPr1	Cisse 13	2 306
	21	St Pauli	L	1-3	BL	Cisse 78	24 000
	28	Nürnberg	W	2-1	BL	Cisse 2 41p 53	36 780
Sep	11	Stuttgart	W	2-1	BL	Cisse 58, Schuster 72	23 000
	17	E Frankfurt	W	1-0	BL	Rosenthal 89	40 600
	22	Schalke	L	1-2	BL	Cisse 69	24 500
	26	Wolfsburg	L	1-2	BL	Cisse 36	26 204
Oct	2	Köln	W	3-2	BL	Rosenthal 2 4 11, Cisse 70	22 100
	16	W Bremen	L	1-2	BL	Schuster 62	34 500
	23	Kaiser'tern	W	2-1	BL	Cisse 35	24 500
	26	E Cottbus	L	1-2	DPr2	Cisse 66	8 050
	29	Bayern M	L	2-4	BL	Reisinger 64, OG 87	69 000
Nov	6	Mainz	W	1-0	BL	Cisse 64p	22 400
	14	Hoffenheim	W	1-0	BL	Cisse 91+	30 150
	20	B Dortmund	L	1-2	BL	OG 27	24 000
	27	Hannover	L	0-3	BL		34 108
Dec	4	Hamburg	W	1-0	BL	Cisse 3	24 000
	12	Gladbach	W	3-0	BL	Cisse 2 19 59, Barth 41	22 700
	19	Leverkusen	D	2-2	BL	Rosenthal 24, Reisinger 65	22 421
Jan	15	St Pauli	D	2-2	BL	Cisse 2 61 75	24 051
	22	Nürnberg	D	1-1	BL	Flum 32	20 000
	30	Stuttgart	W	1-0	BL	Flum 24	38 600
Feb	6	E Frankfurt	D	0-0	BL		21 900
	12	Schalke	L	0-1	BL		60 439
	19	Wolfsburg	W	2-1	BL	Reisinger 43, Cisse 69	19 200
	26	Köln	L	0-1	BL		45 500
Mar	6	W Bremen	L	1-3	BL	Cisse 49p	24 000
	12	Kaiser'tern	L	1-2	BL	OG 21	41 015
	19	Bayern M	L	1-2	BL	Cisse 17	24 000
	2	Mainz	D	1-1	BL	Cisse 1	20 000
Apr	9	Hoffenheim	W	3-2	BL	Schuster 23, Cisse 60p, Butscher 78	24 000
	17	B Dortmund	L	0-3	BL		80 720
	21	Hannover	L	1-3	BL	Rosenthal 79	24 000
	30	Hamburg	W	2-0	BL	Cisse 2 16 88	52 985
May	7	Gladbach	L	0-2	BL		49 072
	14	Leverkusen	L	0-1	BL		24 000

9th Att: 392 300 • Av: 23 076 (+0.7%) • Dreisamstadion 24 493 (94%)

EINTRACHT LEAGUE APPEARANCES/GOALS 2010-11
Goalkeepers Ralf Fahrmann 14+1 • Oka Nikolov MKD 20
Defenders Chris BRA 5+2/2 • Julian Dudda 1/0 • Maik Franz 23/0 Sebastian Jung 33/0 • Kevin Kraus 1/0 • Patrick Ochs 29/2 • Nikola Petlovic SRB 1/0 • Marco Russ 31/1 • Giorgios Tzavellas GRE 25/1 Aleksandar Vasoski MKD 6+5/0
Midfield Caio BRA 12+15/1 • Ricardo Clark USA 8+3/0 • Sonny Kittel 2+6/0 • Benjamin Kohler 28+2/2 • Umit Korkmaz AUT 0+2/0 Alexander Meier 20+4/2 • Sebastian Rode 11/2 Pirmin Schwegler SUI 32/1 • Marcel Steinhofer 0+4/0 Marcel Titsch-Rivero 0+1/0
Forwards Halil Altintop TUR 26+8/0 • Ioannis Amanatidis GRE 6+13/0 Martin Fenin CZE 6+18/1 • Theofanis Gekas GRE 31+3/16 Marcel Heller 3+7/0
Coach Michael Skibbe • Christoph Daum

FREIBURG LEAGUE APPEARANCES/GOALS 2010-11
Goalkeepers Oliver Baumann 30 • Simon Pouplin FRA 4
Defenders Oliver Barth 28+1/1 • Felix Bastians 29/0 • Heiko Butscher 22+3/1 • Pavel Krmas CZE 5+1/0 • Mensur Mujdza BIH 32/0 Daniel Sereinig SUI 0+2/0 • Omer Toprak TUR 18+6/0 Daniel Williams USA 1+6/0
Midfield Yacine Abdessadki MAR 20+1/0 • Ivica Banovic CRO 1+1/0 Daniel Caligiuri 11+12/0 • Johannes Flum 10+2/2 • Cedric Makiadi COD 34/0 • Maximilian Nicu ROU 17+6/0 • Zvonko Pamic CRO 0+2/0 • Anton Putsila BLR 21+4/0 • Jan Rosenthal 19+3/5 Jonathan Schmid FRA 0+1/0 • Julian Schuster 26/3
Forwards Squipon Bektasi ALB 0+1/0 • Papiss Cisse SEN 32/22 Jonathan Jager FRA 4+8/0 • Erik Jendrisek SVK 5+3/0 Stefan Reisinger 3+19/4 • Kisho Yano 2+13/0
Coach Robin Dutt

HAMBURGER SV 2010–11

Aug	15	Torgel. Greif	W	5-1	DPr1	Van Nistelrooy 3 34 65 67, Guerrero 53, Jarolim 81	8 000
	21	Schalke	W	2-1	BL	Van Nistelrooy 2 46 83	57 000
	28	E Frankfurt	W	3-1	BL	Mathijsen 61, Van Nistelrooy 81, Guerrero 89	51 500
Sep	11	Nürnberg	D	1-1	BL	Mathijsen 61	54 099
	19	St Pauli	D	1-1	BL	Petric 88	24 360
	22	Wolfsburg	L	1-3	BL	Choupo-Moting 27	50 231
	25	W Bremen	L	2-3	BL	Van Nistelrooy 59, Pitroipa 63	36 300
	2	Kaiser'tern	W	2-1	BL	Kacar 45, Choupo-Moting 84	57 000
Oct	16	Mainz	W	1-0	BL	Guerrero 89	20 300
	22	Bayern M	D	0-0	BL		57 000
	27	E Frankfurt	L	2-5	DPr2	Petric 2 23 66	39 400
	30	Köln	L	1-3	BL	Petric 15, Son 24	50 000
Nov	6	Hoffenheim	W	2-1	BL	Westermann 45, Petric 83	54 162
	12	B Dortmund	L	0-2	BL		80 720
	20	Hannover	L	2-3	BL	Son 2 40 54	49 000
	27	Stuttgart	W	4-2	BL	Trochowski 3, Pitroipa 29, Petric 36, Van Nistelrooy 60	53 055
Dec	4	Freiburg	L	0-1	BL		24 000
	11	Leverkusen	L	2-4	BL	OG 49, Elia 79	51 225
	17	Gladbach	W	2-1	BL	Elia 46, Trochowski 72	42 253
	15	Schalke	W	1-0	BL	Van Nistelrooy 53	61 673
Jan	1	E Frankfurt	W	1-0	BL	Petric 65	50 239
	29	Nürnberg	L	0-2	BL		36 202
	12	Wolfsburg	W	1-0	BL	Petric 33p	30 000
Feb	16	St Pauli	L	0-1	BL		57 000
	19	W Bremen	W	4-0	BL	Petric 42, Guerrero 2 64 79, Ben-Hatira 87	54 121
	26	Kaiser'tern	D	1-1	BL	Jansen 54	45 682
Mar	6	Mainz	L	2-4	BL	Jansen 17, Petric 59	49 462
	12	Bayern M	L	0-6	BL		69 000
	19	Köln	W	6-2	BL	Petric 3 11 38 43, Ben Hatira 31, Kacar 51, Ze Roberto 57p	57 000
Apr	2	Hoffenheim	D	0-0	BL		30 150
	9	B Dortmund	D	1-1	BL	Van Nistelrooy 39p	57 000
	16	Hannover	D	0-0	BL		57 000
	23	Stuttgart	L	0-3	BL		39 000
May	30	Freiburg	L	0-2	BL		52 985
	7	Leverkusen	D	1-1	BL	Westermann 2	30 210
	14	Gladbach	D	1-1	BL	Ben-Hatira 71	57 000

8th | Att: 925 579 • Av: 54 446 (-1.5%) • Volksparkstadion 57 000 (95%)

HANNOVER 96 2010–11

Aug	14	Elversberg	D	0-0	DPr1	L 4-5p	2 700
	21	E Frankfurt	W	2-1	BL	Rausch 21, Ya Konan 75	37 212
	28	Schalke	W	2-1	BL	Rausch 31, Abdellaoue 49	61 226
Sep	11	Leverkusen	D	2-2	BL	Ya Konan 20, Abdellaoue 50	40 852
	18	Wolfsburg	L	0-2	BL		30 000
	21	W Bremen	W	4-1	BL	OG 11, Ya Konan 53, Schulz 79, Abdellaoue 92+	43 127
	26	Kaiser'tern	W	1-0	BL	Abdellaoue 33	40 115
Oct	1	St Pauli	L	0-1	BL		49 000
	16	Bayern M	L	0-3	BL		69 000
	23	Köln	W	2-1	BL	Ya Konan 2 4 15	44 214
	31	Hoffenheim	L	0-4	BL		28 450
Nov	7	B Dortmund	L	0-4	BL		49 000
	13	Mainz	W	1-0	BL	Pinto 44	20 000
	20	Hamburg	W	3-2	BL	Stindl 31, Schulz 58, Hanke 91+	49 000
	27	Freiburg	W	3-0	BL	Schlaudraff 15, Ya Konan 73, Hanke 89	34 108
Dec	4	Gladbach	W	2-1	BL	Hanke 73, Ya Konan 75	37 195
	10	Stuttgart	W	2-1	BL	Ya Konan 2 35 76	36 207
	18	Nürnberg	L	1-3	BL	Pinto 75p	33 111
Jan	16	E Frankfurt	W	3-0	BL	Abdellaoue 15, Schulz 21, Ya Konan 89	39 300
	22	Schalke	L	0-1	BL		49 000
	28	Leverkusen	L	0-2	BL		28 013
Feb	5	Wolfsburg	W	1-0	BL	Pinto 5	37 213
	13	W Bremen	D	1-1	BL	Ya Konan 26	39 500
	19	Kaiser'tern	W	3-0	BL	Schlaudraff 2 17 57	35 412
	26	St Pauli	W	1-0	BL	Schulz 89	24 487
Mar	5	Bayern M	W	3-1	BL	Abdellaoue 16, Rausch 51, Pinto 62	49 000
	11	Köln	L	0-4	BL		46 500
	19	Hoffenheim	W	2-1	BL	Ya Konan 38, Abdellaoue 53	47 200
Apr	2	B Dortmund	L	1-4	BL	Abdellaoue 56	80 720
	9	Mainz	W	2-0	BL	Ya Konan 45p, Pinto 59	48 000
	16	Hamburg	D	0-0	BL		57 000
	21	Freiburg	W	3-1	BL	Abdellaoue 24, Schlaudraff 31, Rausch 58	24 000
	30	Gladbach	L	0-1	BL		48 800
May	7	Stuttgart	L	1-2	BL	Stindl 66	39 000
	14	Nürnberg	W	3-1	BL	Haggui 30, Rausch 61, Ya Konan 78p	49 000

4th | Att: 746 345 • Av: 43 903 (+14.7%) • Niedersachsen 49 000 (89%)

TSG HOFFENHEIM 2010–11

Month	Date	Opponent		Score	Comp	Scorers	Att
Aug	14	H Rostock	W	4-0	DPr1	Ba 14, Ibisevic 2 18 32, Mlapa 28	12 600
	21	W Bremen	W	4-1	BL	Ba 20, Mlapa 37, Ibisevic 40, Salihovic 43	30 150
	28	St Pauli	W	1-0	BL	Vorsah 87	23 794
Sep	10	Schalke	W	2-0	BL	Vorsah 37, Salihovic 93+	30 150
	18	Kaiser'tern	D	2-2	BL	Luiz Gustavo 39, Sigurdsson 77	44 453
	21	Bayern M	L	1-2	BL	Ibisevic 1	30 150
	24	Köln	D	1-1	BL	Ba 54	45 000
Oct	2	Mainz	L	2-4	BL	Ba 41, Sigurdsson 64	20 300
	17	Gladbach	W	3-2	BL	Ba 46, OG 67, Salihovic 82p	30 150
	24	B Dortmund	D	1-1	BL	Ba 9	80 720
	27	Ingolstadt	W	1-0	DPr2	Ba 63	10 500
	31	Hannover	W	4-0	BL	Sigurdsson 2 45 48p, Ba 51, Mlapa 71	28 450
Nov	6	Hamburg	L	1-2	BL	Salihovic 6p	54 162
	14	Freiburg	L	0-1	BL		30 150
	20	E Frankfurt	W	4-0	BL	Vukcevic 31, Ibisevic 2 69 71, Mplapa 90	44 300
	27	Leverkusen	D	2-2	BL	Ibisevic 38, Sigurdsson 94+p	29 250
Dec	4	Stuttgart	D	1-1	BL	Salihovic 11	36 800
	11	Nürnberg	D	1-1	BL	Compper 55	30 150
	18	Wolfsburg	D	2-2	BL	Luiz Gustavo 34, Sigurdsson 40	24 512
	21	Gladbach	W	2-0	DPr3	Sigurdsson 35, Ba 63	23 500
Jan	15	W Bremen	L	1-2	BL	Vukcevic 87	37 274
	23	St Pauli	D	2-2	BL	Compper 29, Alaba 90	29 300
	29	Schalke	W	1-0	BL	Vorsah 4	60 569
	26	E Cottbus	L	0-1	DPqf		15 220
Feb	5	Kaiser'tern	W	3-2	BL	Sigurdsson 27, Rudy 39, Ibisevic 61	30 150
	12	Bayern M	L	0-4	BL		69 000
	19	Köln	D	1-1	BL	OG 48	30 000
	26	Mainz	L	1-2	BL	Alaba 83	29 000
Mar	5	Gladbach	L	0-2	BL		35 350
	12	B Dortmund	W	1-0	BL	Ibisevic 63	30 150
	19	Hannover	L	0-2	BL		47 200
	2	Hamburg	D	0-0	BL		30 150
Apr	9	Freiburg	L	2-3	BL	Ibisevic 34p, Babel 42	24 000
	16	E Frankfurt	W	1-0	BL	Firmino 77	30 150
	23	Leverkusen	L	1-2	BL	Sigurdsson 28	29 313
	30	Stuttgart	L	1-2	BL	Mlapa 14	30 150
May	7	Nürnberg	W	2-1	BL	Firmino 40, Sigurdsson 86	48 548
	14	Wolfsburg	L	1-3	BL	Firmino 49	30 150

11th Att: 507 800 • Av: 29 871 (+0.6%) • Rhein-Neckar-Arena 30 150 (99%)

1.FC KAISERSLAUTERN 2010–11

Month	Date	Opponent		Score	Comp	Scorers	Att
Aug	13	Osnabrück	W	3-2	DPr1	Lakic 90, Hoffer 2 106 111	15 500
	21	Köln	W	3-1	BL	Lakic 2 70 84, Ilicevic 88	49 200
	27	Bayern M	W	2-0	BL	Ilicevic 36, Lakic 37	49 780
Sep	12	Mainz	L	1-2	BL	Lakic 20	20 300
	18	Hoffenheim	D	2-2	BL	Hoffer 2 46 75	44 453
	22	B Dortmund	L	0-5	BL		70 100
	26	Hannover	L	0-1	BL		40 115
	2	Hamburg	L	1-2	BL	Lakic 3	57 000
Oct	17	E Frankfurt	L	0-3	BL		49 780
	23	Freiburg	L	1-2	BL	Moravek 8	24 500
	26	Bielefeld	W	3-0	DPr2	Lakic 3 11 42 48	17 159
	30	Gladbach	W	3-0	BL	Tiffert 71, Nemec 83, Lakic 88	49 167
Nov	7	Leverkusen	L	1-3	BL	Dick 15	29 794
	13	Stuttgart	D	3-3	BL	Micanski 58, Ilicevic 76, Abel 78	46 904
	20	Nürnberg	W	3-1	BL	Rivic 4, Ilicevic 12, Lakic 33	40 711
	27	Schalke	W	5-0	BL	Lakic 2 8 56, Amedick 39, Ilicevic 76p, Moravek 88	49 474
Dec	3	St Pauli	L	0-1	BL		24 337
	11	Wolfsburg	D	0-0	BL		38 181
	18	W Bremen	W	2-1	BL	Lakic 2 1 52	35 135
	16	Köln	D	1-1	BL	Moravek 51	42 295
	19	Koblenz	W	4-1	DPr3	Lakic 3 54 59 65, Nemec 64	15 000
	22	Bayern M	L	1-5	BL	Moravek 62	69 000
	26	MSV D'burg	L	0-2	DPqf		22 917
Jan	29	Mainz	L	0-1	BL		46 649
	5	Hoffenheim	L	2-3	BL	Hoffer 57, Rodnei 59	30 150
Feb	12	B Dortmund	D	1-1	BL	Moravek 90	49 780
	19	Hannover	L	0-3	BL		35 412
	26	Hamburg	D	1-1	BL	Jansen 54	45 682
Mar	5	E Frankfurt	D	0-0	BL		49 400
	12	Freiburg	W	2-1	BL	Nemec 34, Hoffer 92+	41 015
	18	Gladbach	W	1-0	BL	OG 61	47 696
	2	Leverkusen	L	0-1	BL		46 050
Apr	9	Stuttgart	W	4-2	BL	Lakic 2 17 79, Hoffer 68, Rivic 86	39 000
	16	Nürnberg	L	0-2	BL		49 780
	23	Schalke	W	1-0	BL	Lakic 42	61 673
	29	St Pauli	W	2-0	BL	Tiffert 29, Abel 68	49 780
May	7	Wolfsburg	W	2-1	BL	Lakic 25, Amedick 44	30 000
	14	W Bremen	W	3-2	BL	Nemec 7, Rodnei 9, Lakic 30	49 780

7th Att: 788 665 • Av: 46 392 (+31.1%) • Fritz-Walter 49 780 (93%)

HOFFENHEIN LEAGUE APPEARANCES/GOALS 2010-11
Goalkeepers Daniel Haas 9 • Tom Starke 25
Defenders Andreas Beck 33/0 • Edson Braafheid NED 9+1/0 • Marvin Compper 32/2 • Christian Eichner 2+2/0 • Manuel Gulde 0+1/0 • Andreas Ibertsberger AUT 18+2/0 • Matthias Jaissle 4+5/0 • Josip Simunic CRO 7+3/0 • Jannik Vestergaard DEN 0+1/0 • Isaac Vorsah GHA 29+1/3
Midfield David Alaba AUT 17/2 • Dominik Kaiser 0+1/0 • Luiz Gustavo BRA 17/2 • Roberto Firmino BRA 5+6/3 • Sebastian Rudy 29+3/1 • Sejad Salihovic BIH 24+2/5 • Gylfi Sigurdsson ISL 10+19/9 • Tobias Weis 13+4/0
Forwards Demba Ba SEN 15+2/6 • Ryan Babel NED 15/1 • Vedad Ibisevic BIH 25+6/8 • Peniel Mlapa 18+12/4 • Chinedu Obasi NGA 2+3/0 • Prince Tagoe GHA 0+6/0 • Denis Thomalla 0+4/0
Coach Ralf Rangnick • Marco Pezzaiuoli

KAISERSLAUTERN LEAGUE APPEARANCES/GOALS 2010-11
Goalkeepers Tobias Sippel 25 • Kevin Trapp 9
Defenders Mathias Abel 19/2 • Martin Amedick 23+3/2 • Alexander Bugera 11+1/0 • Florian Dick 27/1 • Leon Jessen DEN 23+4/0 • Thanos Petsos GRE 16+4/0 • Rodnei BRA 26/2
Midfield Jiri Bilek CZE 14+1/0 • Pierre De Wit 7+6/0 • Danny Fuchs 0+1/0 • Ivo Ilicevic CRO 19+2/5 • Oliver Kirch 23+6/0 • Jan Moravek CZE 23+6/5 • Stiven Rivic CRO 7+5/2 • Bastian Schulz 1+2/0 • Christian Tiffert 33/2 • Clemens Walch AUT 5+7/0
Forwards Chadli Amri ALG 1+5/0 • Adam Hlousek CZE 12+1/1 • Erwin Hoffer AUT 11+13/5 • Srdan Lakic CRO 30+1/16 • Ilian Micanski BUL 2+8/1 • Adam Nemec SVK 7+17/3
Coach Marco Kurz

1.FC KOLN 2010-11

Mon	Day	Opponent		Score	Comp	Scorers	Att
Aug	15	Meuselwitz	W	2-0	DPr1	Yalcin 6, Novakovic 45	9 018
	21	Kaiser'tern	L	1-3	BL	Novakovic 8	49 200
	28	W Bremen	L	2-4	BL	Podolski 37, McKenna 93+	35 500
Sep	12	St Pauli	W	1-0	BL	Yalcin 17	50 000
	18	Bayern M	D	0-0	BL		69 000
	21	Mainz	L	0-2	BL		20 300
	24	Hoffenheim	D	1-1	BL	Podolski 17	45 000
Oct	2	Freiburg	L	2-3	BL	Mohamad 22, Matuszczyk 50	22 100
	15	B Dortmund	L	1-2	BL	Podolski 82	50 000
	23	Hannover	L	1-2	BL	Lanig 85	44 214
	26	TSV M'chen	W	3-0	DPr2	Lanig 58, Novakovic 79, Podolski 83	24 500
	30	Hamburg	W	3-2	BL	Novakovic 3 11 29 84	50 000
Nov	6	Nürnberg	L	1-3	BL	Geromel 16	41 789
	13	Gladbach	L	0-4	BL		50 000
	21	Stuttgart	W	1-0	BL	Podolski 82p	39 500
	28	Wolfsburg	D	1-1	BL	Novakovic 51	43 000
Dec	5	Leverkusen	L	2-3	BL	Geromel 27, Lanig 65	30 210
	11	E Frankfurt	W	1-0	BL	Clemens 56	45 000
	18	Schalke	L	0-3	BL		61 673
Jan	22	MSV D'burg	L	1-2	DPr3	Terodde 84	44 500
	16	Kaiser'tern	D	1-1	BL	Podolski 29	42 295
	22	W Bremen	W	3-0	BL	Podolski 2 7 84, Matuszczyk 33	45 100
	29	St Pauli	L	0-3	BL		24 355
Feb	5	Bayern M	W	3-2	BL	Clemens 55, Novakovic 2 62 73	50 000
	13	Mainz	W	4-2	BL	Podolski 2 3 55, Novakovic 2 43 60	44 000
	19	Hoffenheim	D	1-1	BL	Mohamed 69	30 000
	26	Freiburg	W	1-0	BL	Podolski 89	45 500
Mar	4	B Dortmund	L	0-1	BL		80 720
	11	Hannover	W	4-0	BL	Petit 36, Podolski 60, Novakovic 2 79 89	46 500
	19	Hamburg	L	2-6	BL	Jajalo 50, Podolski 62	57 000
Apr	3	Nürnberg	W	1-0	BL	Novakovic 92+	49 000
	10	Gladbach	L	1-5	BL	Novakovic 50	53 104
	16	Stuttgart	L	1-3	BL	Novakovic 68	50 000
	24	Wolfsburg	L	1-4	BL	Freis 40	30 000
	30	Leverkusen	W	2-0	BL	Novakovic 2 67 82	50 000
May	7	E Frankfurt	W	2-0	BL	Chihi 24, Podolski 93+p	51 500
	14	Schalke	W	2-1	BL	Novakovic 25, Jajalo 60	50 000

10th Att: 812 300 • Av: 47 782 (-0.6%) • RheinEnergie 50 000 (95%)

1.FSV MAINZ 2010-11

Mon	Day	Opponent		Score	Comp	Scorers	Att
Aug	15	Ankaraspor	W	2-1	DPr1	Holtby 2 38 70	1 120
	22	Stuttgart	W	2-0	BL	Allagui 26, Rasmussen 47	20 300
	28	Wolfsburg	W	4-3	BL	Rasmussen 39, Soto 48, Schurrle 58, Szalai 85	26 116
Sep	12	Kaiser'tern	W	2-1	BL	Bungert 71, Schurrle 74	20 300
	18	W Bremen	W	2-0	BL	Risse 53, Schurrle 61	34 023
	21	Köln	W	2-0	BL	Holtby 2 72 91+	20 300
	25	Bayern M	W	2-1	BL	Allagui 15, Szalai 77	69 000
Oct	2	Hoffenheim	W	4-2	BL	Allagui 2, Szalai 47, OG 59, Schurrle 74p	20 300
	16	Hamburg	L	0-1	BL		20 300
	24	Leverkusen	W	1-0	BL	Ivanschitz 70	30 210
	27	Aachen	L	1-2	DPr2	Szalai 68	25 657
	31	B Dortmund	L	0-2	BL		20 300
Nov	6	Freiburg	L	0-1	BL		22 400
	13	Hannover	L	0-1	BL		20 000
	20	Gladbach	W	3-2	BL	Schurrle 64, Allagui 2 76 88	45 472
	26	Nürnberg	W	3-0	BL	Schurrle 27, Noveski 54, Allagui 86	20 300
Dec	4	E Frankfurt	L	1-2	BL	Schurrle 42p	51 500
	12	Schalke	L	0-1	BL		20 300
	18	St Pauli	W	4-2	BL	Schurrle 2 11 28, Szalai 41, Caligiuri 83	24 235
Jan	15	Stuttgart	L	0-1	BL		33 500
	22	Wolfsburg	L	0-1	BL		18 900
	29	Kaiser'tern	W	1-0	BL	Holtby 23	46 649
	5	W Bremen	D	1-1	BL	Schurrle 19	20 300
Feb	13	Köln	L	2-4	BL	Allagui 31, Sliskovic 89	44 000
	13	Bayern M	L	1-3	BL	Allagui 84	69 000
	26	Hoffenheim	W	2-1	BL	Ivanschitz 23, Soto 86	29 000
Mar	6	Hamburg	W	4-2	BL	Schurrle 2 56 82, OG 61, Heller 88	49 462
	13	Leverkusen	L	0-1	BL		20 300
	19	B Dortmund	D	1-1	BL	Sliskovic 89	80 720
Apr	2	Freiburg	D	1-1	BL	Allagui 74	20 000
	9	Hannover	L	0-2	BL		48 000
	15	Gladbach	W	1-0	BL	Schurrle 87	20 300
	24	Nürnberg	D	0-0	BL		48 548
	30	E Frankfurt	W	3-0	BL	Ivanschitz 26, Soto 2 38 44	20 300
May	7	Schalke	W	3-1	BL	Schurrle 52, Holtby 82, Noveski 85	60 309
	14	St Pauli	W	2-1	BL	Schurrle 58p, Allagui 82	20 300

5th Att: 343 100 • Av: 20 182 (+0.4%) • am Bruchweg 24 493 (82%)

KOLN LEAGUE APPEARANCES/GOALS 2010-11
Goalkeepers Faryd Mondragon COL 12 • Michael Rensing 17
Miro Varvodic CRO 5/0
Defenders Andrezinho BRA 6+2/0 • Miso Brecko SVN 28+1/0
Christian Eichner 17/0 • Geromel BRA 27/2 • Tomoaki Makino JPN 1+4/0
Kevin McKenna CAN 2+5/1 • Youssef Mohamad LIB 28/2
Stephan Salger 5/0 • Christopher Schorch 1+3/0
Midfield Adil Chihi MAR 4+7/1 • Christian Clemens 22+5/2 • Fabrice
Ehret FRA 16+5/0 • Mato Jajalo CRO 24+6/2 • Martin Lanig 24+4/2
Adam Matuszczyk POL 16+8/2 • Slawomir Peszko POL 11/0
Petit POR 23+1/1 • Kevin Pezzoni 15+5/0 • Wilfried Sanou BFA 0+3/0
Reinhold Yabo 1+3/0 • Taner Yalcin 5+11/1
Forwards Sebastian Freis 8+5/1 • Alexandru Ionita ROU 0+8/0
Milivoje Novakovic SVN 24+4/17 • Lukas Podolski 32/13
Simon Terodde 0+5/0 • Jose Vunguidica ANG 0+1/0
Coach Zvonimir Soldo CRO • Volker Finke

MAINZ LEAGUE APPEARANCES/GOALS 2010-11
Goalkeepers Heinz Muller 10 • Martin Pieckenhagen 0+1
Christian Wetklo 24
Defenders Niko Bungert 26+2/1 • Malik Fathi 17+2/0 • Christian
Fuchs AUT 30+1/0 • Eugen Gopko 0+1/0 • Jan Kirchhoff 8+2/0 • Zsolt
Low HUN • Nikolce Noveski MKD 32/2 • Bo Svensson DEN 19/0
Radoslav Zabavnik SVK 10+2/0
Midfield Marco Caligiuri 17+5/1 • Florian Heller 7+12/1 • Lewis
Holtby 23+7/4 • Andreas Ivanschitz AUT 13+7/3 • Jared Jeffrey USA
Miroslav Karhan SVK 9+4/0 • Eugen Polanski POL 25+3/0 • Marcel
Risse 12+13/1 • Jan Simak CZE 0+1/0 • Elkin Soto COL 21+5/4
Forwards Sami Allagui TUN 18+10/10 • Haruna Babangida NGA 1/0
Morten Rasmussen DEN 3+2/2 • Andre Schurrle 26+7/15
Petar Sliskovic CRO 1+8/2 • Adam Szalai HUN 14+6/4
Coach Thomas Tuchel

1.FC NURNBERG 2010–11

	Date	Opponent	Result	Comp	Scorers	Att
Aug	15	E Trier	W 2-0	DPr1	Bunjaku 15, Ekici 89	5 200
	21	Gladbach	D 1-1	BL	Hegeler 15	42 202
	28	Freiburg	L 1-2	BL	Schieber 14	36 780
Sep	11	Hamburg	D 1-1	BL	Pinola 82p	54 099
	19	Leverkusen	D 0-0	BL		23 963
	22	Stuttgart	W 2-1	BL	Schieber 3, Pinola 91+	36 790
	25	E Frankfurt	L 0-2	BL		43 100
Oct	2	Schalke	W 2-1	BL	Frantz 62, Wolf 84	48 548
	16	St Pauli	L 2-3	BL	Ekici 48, Wolf 62	24 343
	23	Wolfsburg	W 2-1	BL	Gundogan 11, Frantz 63	40 127
	27	Elversberg	W 3-0	DPr2	Schieber 43, Pinola 50p, Simons 74	3 600
	30	W Bremen	W 3-2	BL	Gundogan 2 45 73, Ekici 47	35 500
Nov	6	Köln	W 3-1	BL	Hegeler 11, Gundogan 43, Schieber 90	41 789
	14	Bayern M	L 0-3	BL		69 000
	20	Kaiser'tern	L 1-3	BL	Mak 67	40 711
	26	Mainz	L 0-3	BL		20 300
Dec	5	B Dortmund	L 0-2	BL		48 548
	11	Hoffenheim	D 1-1	BL	Eigler 87	30 150
	18	Hannover	W 3-1	BL	OG 28, Wolf 31, Schieber 82	33 111
	19	Offenbach	W 2-0	DPr3	Simons 2 20 66	24 000
	15	Gladbach	L 0-1	BL		37 464
Jan	22	Freiburg	D 1-1	BL	Schieber 56	20 000
	25	Schalke	L 2-3	DPqf	Schieber 2 4 32	49 191
	29	Hamburg	W 2-0	BL	Simons 59p, Cohen 70	36 202
	5	Leverkusen	W 1-0	BL	Eigler 59	34 113
Feb	12	Stuttgart	W 4-1	BL	Simons 11, Schieber 28, Chandler 51, Ekici 63	38 000
	18	E Frankfurt	W 3-0	BL	Schieber 67, Mak 87, Cohen 90	40 853
	26	Schalke	L 1-2	BL	Hegeler 37	61 431
Mar	5	St Pauli	W 5-0	BL	Wollscheid 3, Eigler 4 14 17 86 88	45 109
	12	Wolfsburg	W 2-1	BL	Wollscheid 45, Nilsson 92+	27 316
	19	W Bremen	L 1-3	BL	Gundogan 30	48 548
Apr	3	Köln	L 0-1	BL		49 000
	9	Bayern M	L 1-2	BL	Eigler 60	48 548
	16	Kaiser'tern	W 2-0	BL	Eigler 34, Mak 92+	49 780
	24	Mainz	D 0-0	BL		48 548
	30	B Dortmund	L 0-2	BL		80 720
May	7	Hoffenheim	L 1-2	BL	Wollscheid 16	48 548
	14	Hannover	L 1-3	BL	Weißmeier 25	49 000

6th   Att: 714 337 • Av: 42 020 (-0.8%) • Frankenstadion 48 548 (86%)

FC SANKT PAULI 2010–11

	Date	Opponent	Result	Comp	Scorers	Att
Aug	14	Chemnitzer	L 0-1	DPr1		10 431
	21	Freiburg	W 3-1	BL	Boll 83, Sukuta-Pasu 89, Bartels 91+	24 000
Sep	28	Hoffenheim	L 0-1	BL		23 794
	12	Köln	L 0-1	BL		50 000
	19	Hamburg	D 1-1	BL	Boll 77	24 360
	22	Gladbach	W 2-1	BL	Asamoah 66, Bruns 71p	41 080
	25	B Dortmund	L 1-3	BL	Hennings 25	24 082
Oct	1	Hannover	W 1-0	BL	Ebbers 6	49 000
	16	Nürnberg	W 3-2	BL	Asamoah 45, Ebbers 59, Bruns 82	24 343
	24	Stuttgart	L 0-2	BL		40 000
	30	E Frankfurt	L 1-3	BL	Zambrano 5	24 330
Nov	5	Schalke	L 0-3	BL		61 673
	13	Leverkusen	L 0-1	BL		24 387
	21	Wolfsburg	D 1-1	BL	Thorant 28	24 150
	28	W Bremen	L 0-3	BL		36 400
Dec	3	Kaiser'tern	W 1-0	BL	OG 48	24 337
	11	Bayern M	L 0-3	BL		69 000
	18	Mainz	L 2-4	BL	Lehmann 2 33p 63	24 235
	15	Freiburg	D 2-2	BL	Ebbers 13, Asamoah 68	24 051
Jan	23	Hoffenheim	D 2-2	BL	Kruse 51, Asamoah 82	29 300
	29	Köln	W 3-0	BL	Takyi 2 30 36, Bruns 76p	24 355
	12	Gladbach	W 3-1	BL	Kruse 37, Asamoah 52, Lehmann 57	24 487
Feb	16	Hamburg	W 1-0	BL	Asamoah 59	57 000
	19	B Dortmund	L 0-2	BL		80 720
	26	Hannover	L 0-1	BL		24 487
	5	Nürnberg	L 0-5	BL		45 109
Mar	13	Stuttgart	L 1-2	BL	Boll 18	24 487
	19	E Frankfurt	L 1-2	BL	Takyi 42	50 500
	1	Schalke	L 0-2	BL		24 487
Apr	10	Leverkusen	L 1-2	BL	Takyi 58	30 210
	16	Wolfsburg	D 2-2	BL	Naki 60, Lehmann 77	30 000
	23	W Bremen	L 1-3	BL	Bartels 90	24 487
	29	Kaiser'tern	L 0-2	BL		49 780
May	7	Bayern M	L 1-8	BL	Egger 78	24 487
	14	Mainz	L 1-2	BL	Lehmann 42	20 300

18th   Att: 413 336 • Av: 24 314 (+16.5%) • Millerntor 24 487 (99%)

NURNBERG LEAGUE APPEARANCES/GOALS 2010-11

Goalkeepers Raphael Schafer 34 • Alexander Stephan 0+1
Defenders Pascal Bieler 3+1/0 • Timothy Chandler USA 11+3/1
Dominic Maroh 6+2/0 • Per Nilsson SWE 14+5/1 • Javier
Pinola ARG 27+1/2 • Marvin Plattenhardt 4+5/0 • Andreas Wolf 30/3
Philipp Wollscheid 18+1/3
Midfield Almog Cohen ISR 19+6/2 • Mehmet Ekici TUR 29+3/3 • Mike
Frantz 10+4/2 • Ilkay Gundogan 21+4/5 • Jens Hegeler 29+5/3 • Juri
Judt 24/0 • Markus Mendler 1+5/0 • Marek Mintal SVK 0+17/0 • Timmy
Simons BEL 34/0 • Dario Vidosic AUS 1+4/0 • Julian Wießmeier 1/1
Forwards Nassim Ben Khalifa SUI 0+1/0 • Isaac Boakye GHA 0+2/0
Albert Bunjaku SUI 3/0 • Christian Eigler 21+11/8 • Robert
Mak SVK 6+16/3 • Rubin Okotie AUT 0+4/0 • Julian Schieber 28+1/7
Coach Dieter Hecking

ST PAULI LEAGUE APPEARANCES/GOALS 2010-11

Goalkeepers Mathias Hain 3+1 • Thomas Kessler 26
Benedikt Pliquett 5
Defenders Davidson Drobo-Ampem GHA 0+1/0 • Marcel Eger 4+3/1
Ralph Gunesch 20/0 • Jan-Philipp Kalla 4+1/0
Florian Lechner 9+1/0 • Fabio Morena 7/0 • Bastian Oczipka 20/0
Carsten Rothenbach 13/0 • Markus Thorandt 29/1 • Moritz Volz 8+1/0
Carlos Zambrano CAN 19+1/1
Midfield Fabian Boll 28/3 • Florian Bruns 11+19/3 • Dennis
Daube 7+6/0 • Petar Filipovic 0+1/0 • Max Kruse 27+6/2 • Matthias
Lehmann 33/5 • Timo Schultz 0+4/0 • Charles Takyi 19+5/4
Forwards Gerald Asamoah 21+6/6 • Fin Bartels 23+8/2 • Marius
Ebbers 21+10/3 • Rouwen Hennings 10+6/1 • Deniz Naki 6+14/1
Richard Sukuta-Pasu 1+8/1
Coach Holger Stanislawski

FC SCHALKE 04 2010–11

Mth	Day	Opponent	Res	Score	Comp	Scorers	Att
	7	Bayern M	L	0-2	SC		30 662
Aug	16	Aalen	W	2-1	DPr1	Farfan 2 [43 46]	13 452
	21	Hamburg	L	1-2	BL	Farfan [80]	57 000
	28	Hannover	L	1-2	BL	Jones [82]	61 226
	10	Hoffenheim	L	0-2	BL		30 150
	14	Lyon	L	0-1	CLgB		35 552
Sep	19	B Dortmund	L	1-3	BL	Huntelaar [89]	60 069
	22	Freiburg	W	2-1	BL	Rakitic [9], Huntelaar [87]	24 500
	25	Gladbach	D	2-2	BL	Huntelaar [52], Raul [87]	61 673
	29	Benfica	W	2-0	CLgB	Farfan [73], Huntelaar [85]	50 436
	2	Nürnberg	L	1-2	BL	Huntelaar [74]	48 458
	16	Stuttgart	D	2-2	BL	Edu [29], Huntelaar [80p]	61 673
Oct	20	Hapoel TA	W	3-1	CLgB	Raul 2 [3 58], Jurado [68]	50 900
	23	E Frankfurt	D	0-0	BL		51 500
	26	FSV Fr'kfurt	W	1-0	DPr2	Jurado [12]	10 826
	30	Leverkusen	L	0-1	BL		61 673
	2	Hapoel TA	D	0-0	CLgB		13 094
	5	St Pauli	W	3-0	BL	Raul 2 [14 81], Huntelaar [53]	61 673
Nov	13	Wolfsburg	D	2-2	BL	Edu [39], Huntelaar [75]	30 000
	20	W Bremen	W	4-0	BL	Metzelder [22], Raul 3 [45 56 71]	61 673
	24	Lyon	W	3-0	CLgB	Farfan [13], Huntelaar 2 [20 89]	51 132
	27	Kaiser'tern	L	0-5	BL		49 474
Dec	4	Bayern M	W	2-0	BL	Jurado [58], Howedes [67]	61 673
	7	Benfica	W	2-1	CLgB	Jurado [19], Howedes [81]	23 348
	12	Mainz	W	1-0	BL	Farfan [30]	20 300
	18	Köln	W	3-0	BL	Raul 3 [30 50 87]	61 673
	21	Augsburg	W	1-0	DPr3	Farfan [84]	30 660
Jan	15	Hamburg	L	0-1	BL		61 673
	22	Hannover	W	1-0	BL	Raul [33]	49 000
	29	Hoffenheim	L	0-1	BL		60 569
	25	Nürnberg	W	3-2	DPqf	Gavranovic [14], Rakitic [58], Drexler [119]	49 191
Feb	4	B Dortmund	D	0-0	BL		80 720
	12	Freiburg	L	0-1	BL	Farfan [49]	60 439
	15	Valencia	D	1-1	CLr2	Raul [64]	42 703
	20	Gladbach	L	1-2	BL	Kluge [2]	51 592
	26	Nürnberg	D	1-1	BL	Raul [52]	61 431
	2	Bayern M	W	1-0	DPsf	Raul [15]	69 000
	5	Stuttgart	L	0-1	BL		39 000
Mar	9	Valencia	W	3-1	CLr2	Farfan 2 [40 94+], Gavranovic [52]	53 517
	12	E Frankfurt	W	2-1	BL	Jurado [45p], Charisteas [84]	61 673
	20	Leverkusen	L	0-2	BL		30 210
	1	St Pauli	W	2-0	BL		24 487
	5	Inter	W	5-2	CLqf	Matip [17], Edu 2 [40 75], Raul [53], OG [57]	72 770
Apr	9	Wolfsburg	W	1-0	BL	Jurado [76]	61 673
	13	Inter	W	2-1	CLqf	Raul [45], Howedes [81]	54 142
	16	W Bremen	D	1-1	BL	Edu [63]	40 500
	23	Kaiser'tern	L	0-1	BL		61 673
	26	Man Utd	L	0-2	CLsf		54 142
	30	Bayern M	L	1-4	BL	OG [8]	69 000
	4	Man Utd	L	1-4	CLsf	Jurado [35]	74 687
May	7	Mainz	L	1-3	BL	Huntelaar [47]	60 309
	14	Köln	L	1-2	BL	Raul [87]	50 000
	21	MSV D'burg	W	5-0	DPf	Draxler [18], Huntelaar 2 [22 70], Howedes [42], Jurado [55]	75 708

14th — Att: 1 042 446 • Av: 61 320 (0%) • Veltins-Arena 61 673 (99%)

VFB STUTTGART 2010–11

Mth	Day	Opponent	Res	Score	Comp	Scorers	Att
	29	Molde	W	3-2	ELp3	Rudy [27], Kuzmanovic [74], Harnik [82]	3 270
	5	Molde	D	2-2	ELp3	Pogrebnyak [54], Gebhart [90]	11 500
	14	Babelsberg	W	2-1	DPr1	Cacau 2 [21 25]	5 805
Aug	19	Slovan	W	1-0	ELpo	Harnik [88]	8 120
	22	Mainz	L	0-2	BL		20 300
	26	Slovan	D	2-2	ELpo	Gebhart [56], Gentner [65]	14 000
	29	B Dortmund	L	1-3	BL	Cacau [69]	40 500
	11	Freiburg	L	1-2	BL	Pogrebnyak [27]	23 000
	16	Young Boys	W	3-0	ELgH	Cacau [23p], Gentner [59], Tasci [90]	13 800
Sep	18	Gladbach	W	7-0	BL	Pogrebnyak 3 [2 55 60], Niedermeier [21], Kuzmanovic [64], Delpierre [73], Marica [80]	39 500
	22	Nürnberg	L	1-2	BL	Cacau [85]	36 790
	25	Leverkusen	L	1-4	BL	Kuzmanovic [52]	38 300
	30	Odense	W	2-1	ELgH	Kuzmanovic [71], Harnik [86]	8 854
	3	E Frankfurt	L	1-2	BL	Pogrebnyak [85]	40 200
Oct	16	Schalke	D	2-2	BL	Gebhart [15], Harnik [74]	61 673
	21	Getafe	W	1-0	ELgH	Marica [5]	17 400
	24	St Pauli	W	2-0	BL	Niedermeier [19], Kuzmanovic [79]	40 000
	27	Chemnitzer	W	3-1	DPr2	Harnik 3 [79 106 118]	17 145
	30	Wolfsburg	L	0-2	BL		29 043
	4	Getafe	W	3-0	ELgH	Marica [26], Gebhart [64], Harnik [76]	3 459
Nov	7	W Bremen	W	6-0	BL	Marica [10], Cacau 2 [31 45], Gentner [68], Niedermeier [73], Boka [86]	39 500
	13	Kaiser'tern	D	3-3	BL	Boka [19], Cacau [32], Gentner [50p]	46 904
	21	Köln	L	0-1	BL		39 500
	27	Hamburg	L	2-4	BL	Marica [9], Gentner [46]	53 055
	1	Young Boys	L	2-4	ELgH	Pogrebnyak [48], Schipplock [68]	18 627
	4	Hoffenheim	D	1-1	BL	Harnik [34]	36 800
	10	Hannover	L	1-2	BL	Niedermeier [74]	36 207
Dec	16	Odense	W	5-1	ELgH	Gebhart [20], OG [48], Gentner [65], Pogrebnyak [70], Marica [90]	14 000
	19	Bayern M	L	3-5	BL	Harnik 2 [50 64], Gentner [71]	40 500
	22	Bayern M	L	3-6	DPr3	Pogrebnyak 2 [32 45], Delpierre [77]	40 500
	15	Mainz	L	0-1	BL	Harnik [79]	33 500
Jan	22	B Dortmund	D	1-1	BL	Pogrebnyak [84]	80 720
	30	Freiburg	L	0-1	BL		38 600
	5	Gladbach	W	3-2	BL	Pogrebnyak [51], Harnik [56], Gebhart [87p]	39 132
Feb	12	Nürnberg	L	1-4	BL	Funk [45]	38 000
	17	Benfica	L	1-2	ELr2	Harnik [21]	44 852
	20	Leverkusen	L	2-4	BL	Harnik [16], Kuzmanovic [52]	28 851
	24	Benfica	L	0-2	ELr2		25 800
	27	E Frankfurt	W	2-0	BL	Harnik [64], Hajnal [68]	47 400
	5	Schalke	W	1-0	BL	Kuzmanovic [15p]	39 000
Mar	13	St Pauli	W	2-1	BL	Kuzmanovic [23], Schipplock [87]	24 487
	20	Wolfsburg	D	1-1	BL	Niedermeier [90]	38 500
	2	W Bremen	D	1-1	BL	Hajnal [13]	40 500
	9	Kaiser'tern	L	2-4	BL	Kuzmanovic [26p], Pogrebnyak [39]	39 000
Apr	16	Köln	W	3-1	BL	Trasch [51], Harnik [53], Kuzmanovic [63p]	50 000
	23	Hamburg	W	3-0	BL	Cacau 2 [6 88], Gentner [78]	39 000
	30	Hoffenheim	W	2-1	BL	Cacau [63], Kuzmanovic [68p]	30 150
	7	Hannover	W	2-1	BL	Hajnal [58], Okazaki [61]	39 000
May	14	Bayern M	L	1-2	BL	Okazaki [24]	69 000

12th — Att: 659 400 • Av: 38 788 (-5.6%) • Mercedes-Benz 60 441 (64%)

SCHALKE LEAGUE APPEARANCES/GOALS 2010-11

Goalkeepers Manuel Neuer 34

Defenders Avelar BRA 2+1/0 • Sergio Escudero ESP 5+1/0 • Benedikt Howedes 30/1 • Joel Matip CMR 14+12/0 • Christoph Metzelder 32/1 • Christian Pander 1+3/0 • Kyriakos Papadopoulos GRE 10+8/0 • Nicolas Plestan FRA 3/0 • Hans Sarpei GHA 6+3/0 • Atsuto Uchida JPN 24+2/0

Midfield Anthony Annan GHA 8+1/0 • Alexander Baumjohann 3+6/0 Ciprian Deac ROU 2/0 • Julian Draxler 3+12/1 • Hao Junmin CHN 2+4/0 Jermaine Jones USA 10/1 • Jurado ESP 21+7/3 • Ali Karimi IRN 0+1/0 Peer Kluge 18+4/1 • Christoph Moritz 8+4/0 • Vasilis Pliatsikas GRE 1/0 Ivan Ratic CRO 14+2/1 • Lukas Schmitz 21+2/0

Forwards Angelos Charisteas GRE 1+3/1 • Edu BRA 15+13/3 Jefferson Farfan PER 26+2/3 • Mario Gavranovic SUI 4+4/0 • Klaas-Jan Huntelaar NED 22+2/8 • Erik Jendrisek SVK 0+3/0 • Raul ESP 34/13

Coach Felix Magath • Ralf Rangnick

STUTTGART LEAGUE APPEARANCES/GOALS 2010-11

Goalkeepers Sven Ulreich 34

Defenders Ermin Bicakcic 1/0 • Arthur Boka CIV 18+5/2 Khalid Boularouz NED 13+3/0 • Stefano Celozzi 6+1/0 • Philipp Degen SUI 4+1/0 • Matthieu Delpierre FRA 15+3/1 • Cristian Molinaro ITA 24+3/0 • Georg Niedermeier 25+4/5 • Serdar Tasci 26/0

Midfield Mamadou Bah GUI 2/0 • Mauro Camoranesi ITA 3+4/0 Daniel Didavi 4+4/0 • Elson BRA 2+1/0 • Patrick Funk 7+2/1 Timo Gebhart 15+10/2 • Christian Gentner 23+8/5 • Tamas Hajnal HUN 11+1/3 • Zdravko Kuzmanovic SRB 27+5/9 Christian Trasch 34/1

Forwards Johan Audel FRA 0+3/0 • Cacau 24+3/8 • Martin Harnik AUT 17+15/9 • Ciprian Marica ROU 8+5/3 • Shinji Okazaki JPN 12/2 Pavel Pogrebnyak RUS 18+8/8 • Sven Schipplock 1+11/1

Coach Christian Gross SUI • Bruno Labbadia

WERDER BREMEN 2010–11

Mon	Date	Opponent	Res	Score	Comp	Scorers	Att
Aug	14	RW Ahlen	W	4-0	DPr1	Pizarro[28], Almeida[63], Borowski[68], Marin[82]	9 120
	18	Sampdoria	W	3-1	CLpo	Fritz[51], Frings[67p], Pizarro[69]	25 276
	21	Hoffenheim	L	1-4	BL	Frings[3p]	
	24	Sampdoria	L	2-3	CLpo	Rosenberg[93+], Pizarro[100]	25 574
	28	Köln	W	4-2	BL	Frings[33p], Arnautovic 2[36][91], Almeida[74]	35 500
Sep	11	Bayern M	D	0-0	BL		69 000
	14	Tottenham	D	2-2	CLgA	Almeida[43], Marin[47]	30 344
	18	Mainz	L	0-2	BL		34 023
	21	Hannover	L	1-4	BL	Frings[36p]	43 127
	25	Hamburg	W	3-2	BL	OG[25], Almeida 2[28][85]	36 300
	29	Inter	L	0-4	CLgA		48 126
Oct	3	Leverkusen	D	2-2	BL	Almeida[53], Marin[62]	30 210
	16	Freiburg	W	2-1	BL	Hunt[33], Almeida[73]	34 500
	20	Twente	D	1-1	CLgA	Arnautovic[80]	23 248
	23	Gladbach	W	4-1	BL	Marin[5], Wesley[12], Hunt[51], Pizarro[75]	53 511
	26	Bayern M	L	1-2	DPr2	Pizarro[2]	64 000
	30	Nürnberg	L	2-3	BL	Almeida[5], Pizarro[92+]	35 500
Nov	2	Twente	L	0-2	CLgA		30 200
	7	Stuttgart	L	0-6	BL		39 500
	13	E Frankfurt	D	0-0	BL		35 300
	20	Schalke	L	0-4	BL		61 673
	24	Tottenham	L	0-3	CLgA		33 546
	28	St Pauli	W	3-0	BL	Almeida 3[1][20][64]	36 400
Dec	4	Wolfsburg	D	0-0	BL		30 000
	7	Inter	W	3-0	CLgA	Prodl[39], Arnautovic[49], Pizarro[88]	30 400
	11	B Dortmund	L	0-2	BL		80 720
	18	Kaiser'tern	L	1-2	BL	Hunt[34p]	35 135
Jan	15	Hoffenheim	W	2-1	BL	Pizarro[36], Frings[92+]	37 274
	22	Köln	L	0-3	BL		45 100
	29	Bayern M	L	1-3	BL	Mertesacker[46]	40 500
Feb	5	Mainz	D	1-1	BL	Pizarro[92+]	20 300
	13	Hannover	D	1-1	BL	Mertesacker[50]	39 500
	19	Hamburg	L	0-4	BL		54 121
	27	Leverkusen	D	2-2	BL	OG[82], Prodl[91+]	37 500
Mar	6	Freiburg	W	3-1	BL	Wagner[12], Pizarro[76], Marin[93+]	24 000
	12	Gladbach	D	1-1	BL	Wagner[39]	40 500
	19	Nürnberg	W	3-1	BL	Wagner 2[27p][89p], Pizarro[50]	48 548
Apr	2	Stuttgart	D	1-1	BL	Frings[34]	40 500
	8	E Frankfurt	D	1-1	BL	OG[58]	51 500
	16	Schalke	D	1-1	BL	Wagner[59]	40 500
	23	St Pauli	W	3-0	BL	OG[51], Pizarro 2[73][75]	24 487
	29	Wolfsburg	L	0-1	BL		40 000
May	7	B Dortmund	W	2-0	BL	Silvestre[5], Pizarro[63]	40 600
	14	Kaiser'tern	L	2-3	BL	Frings[43], Arnautovic[55]	49 780

13th Att: 639 532 • Av: 37 620 (+4.4%) • Weserstadion 42 100 (89%)

VFL WOLFSBURG 2010–11

Mon	Date	Opponent	Res	Score	Comp	Scorers	Att
Aug	15	Pr Münster	W	2-1	DPr1	Cicero[80], Grafite[88]	15 050
	20	Bayern M	L	1-2	BL	Dzeko[55]	69 000
	28	Mainz	L	3-4	BL	Dzeko 2[23][27], Diego[30]	26 116
Sep	11	B Dortmund	L	0-2	BL		73 600
	18	Hannover	W	2-0	BL	Diego[55], Dzeko[67]	30 000
	22	Hamburg	W	3-1	BL	Dzeko[15], Grafite 2[71][78]	50 231
	26	Freiburg	W	2-1	BL	Grafite 2[25][64]	26 204
Oct	2	Gladbach	D	1-1	BL	Kahlenberg[27]	40 423
	16	Leverkusen	L	2-3	BL	Diego[9], Grafite[68]	30 000
	23	Nürnberg	L	1-2	BL	Grafite[29]	40 127
	26	V Hamburg	W	3-1	DPr2	Pekarik[17], Josue[52], Schafer[55]	8 370
	30	Stuttgart	W	2-0	BL	Dzeko 2[6][76]	29 043
Nov	6	E Frankfurt	L	1-3	BL	Dejagah[66]	43 800
	13	Schalke	D	2-2	BL	Grafite[11], Dzeko[33]	30 000
	21	St Pauli	L	1-3	BL	Dzeko[54]	24 150
	28	Köln	D	1-1	BL	Cicero[81]	43 000
Dec	4	W Bremen	D	0-0	BL		30 000
	11	Kaiser'tern	D	0-0	BL		38 181
	18	Hoffenheim	D	2-2	BL	Diego[75], Dzeko[90]	24 512
	22	Cottbus	L	1-3	DPr3	Dzeko[56]	10 801
Jan	15	Bayern M	D	1-1	BL	Riether[86]	30 000
	22	Mainz	W	1-0	BL	Kjær[82]	18 900
	29	B Dortmund	L	0-3	BL		30 000
Feb	5	Hannover	L	0-1	BL		37 213
	12	Hamburg	L	0-1	BL		30 000
	19	Freiburg	L	1-2	BL	Helmes[28]	19 200
	25	Gladbach	W	2-1	BL	Diego 2[37][45]	28 763
Mar	5	Leverkusen	L	0-3	BL		28 115
	12	Nürnberg	L	1-2	BL	Mandzukic[22]	27 316
	20	Stuttgart	D	1-1	BL	Grafite[39]	38 500
Apr	3	E Frankfurt	D	1-1	BL	Mandzukic[85]	29 125
	9	Schalke	L	0-1	BL		61 673
	16	St Pauli	D	2-2	BL	Mandzukic[39], Polak[88]	30 000
	24	Köln	W	4-1	BL	Mandzukic 2[14][39], Dejagah 2[58][88]	30 000
	29	W Bremen	W	1-0	BL	Riether[22]	40 000
May	7	Kaiser'tern	L	1-2	BL	Mandzukic[6]	30 000
	14	Hoffenheim	W	3-1	BL	Mandzukic 2[60][73], Grafite[78]	30 150

15th Att: 491 079 • Av: 28 887 (-1.2%) • Volkswagen Arena 30 000 (96%)

WERDER LEAGUE APPEARANCES/GOALS 2010-11

Goalkeepers Sebastian Mielitz 5+1 • Tim Wiese 29

Defenders Leon Balogun 0+3/0 • Sebastian Boenisch POL 1/0 • Clemens Fritz 23+5/0 • Per Mertesacker 30/2 • Petri Pasanen FIN 23+1/0 • Sebastian Prodl AUT 25/1 • Dominik Schmidt 7+5/0 • Mikael Silvestre FRA 26/1

Midfield Philipp Bargfrede 23+5/0 • Tim Borowski 10+2/0 • Torsten Frings 32/6 • Aaron Hunt 21+8/3 • Said Husejinovic BIH 0+4/0 • Daniel Jensen DEN 3+8/0 • Felix Kroos 3+2/0 • Marko Marin 28+6/3 • Predrag Stevanovic SRB 1+2/0 • Florian Trinks 4+4/0 • Wesley BRA 18+2/1

Forwards Marko Arnautovic AUT 15+10/3 • Denni Avdic SWE 2+5/0 • Onur Ayik 0+1/0 • Hugo Almeida POR 7+6/9 • Claudio Pizarro PER 20+2/9 • Lennart Thy 0+2/0 • Sandro Wagner 12+11/5

Coach Thomas Schaaf

WOLFSBURG LEAGUE APPEARANCES/GOALS 2010-11

Goalkeepers Diego Benaglio SUI 28 • Marwin Hitz SUI 5+1 • Andre Lenz 1

Defenders Andrea Barzagli ITA 17/0 • Arne Friedrich 15/0 • Fabian Johnson USA 1+5/0 • Sergej Karimow KAZ • Simon Kjær DEN 32/1 • Alexander Madlung 4+16/0 • Peter Pekarik SVK 19+4/0

Midfield Cicero BRA 14+7/1 • Tolga Cigerci 5+1/0 • Diego BRA 30/6 • Makoto Hasebe JPN 19+4/0 • Josue BRA 26/0 • Thomas Kahlenberg DEN 8+6/1 • Koo Ja Cheol KOR 1+9/0 • Zvjezdan Misimovic BIH 0+1/0 • Jan Polak CZE 9+3/1 • Sascha Riether 28/2 • Karim Ziani ALG 4+1/0

Forwards Ashkan Dejagah 10+13/3 • Edin Dzeko BIH 17/10 • Grafite BRA 22+6/9 • Patrick Helmes 5+3/1 • Mario Mandzukic CRO 15+9/8 • Dieumerci Mbokani COD 2+5/0 • Tuncay Sanli TUR 3+1/0

Coach Lorenz-Gunther Kostner • Felix Magath

GHA – GHANA

FIFA/COCA-COLA WORLD RANKING

'93	'94	'95	'96	'97	'98	'99	'00	'01	'02	'03	'04	'05	'06	'07	'08	'09	'10	'11	'12
37	26	29	25	57	48	48	57	59	61	78	77	50	28	43	25	34	16	29	

2011														
	Jan	Feb	Mar	Apr	May	Jun	Jul	Aug	Sep	Oct	Nov	Dec	High	Low	Av
	16	15	16	15	15	33	36	36	37	33	29	29	14	89	43

Ghana's long quest for a fifth Africa Cup of Nations title has now passed the 30-year mark after their heavily fancied side missed out on success at the 2012 finals in Equatorial Guinea and Gabon. A star-studded Ghana squad, despite the absence of Michael Essien and Kevin-Prince Boateng, looked physically strong and imposing as they marched to the semi-finals but were then upset 1-0 by Zambia. A squandered penalty by Asamoah Gyan early in the game in Bata brought back memories of his miss at the 2010 FIFA World Cup finals which cost the Black Stars a semi-final place. Ghana's loss in the third place playoff against Mali put further pressure on coach Goran Stevanovic just one year after he took over the job. At club level, Berekum Chelsea won a first-ever league title, running away with the race almost from the start of the season and finishing 10 points ahead of runners-up AshantiGold. Formed in 2000 and named after the English club, the team returned home to Berekum in 2010 from nearby Bechem and the move paid dividends with the unexpected championship triumph. There were also surprise winners in the Ghana FA Cup when second division FC Nania, owned by former African Footballer of the Year Abedi Pele, beat Asante Kotoko 1-0 in the final with an extra time goal from substitute Evans Omani.

CAF AFRICA CUP OF NATIONS RECORD

1957-1959 DNE **1962** DNQ **1963** 1 Winners (hosts) **1965** 1 Winners **1968** 2 F **1970** 2 F **1972-1976** DNQ
1978 1 Winners (hosts) **1980** 5 r1 **1982** 1 Winners **1984** 6 r1 **1986-1990** DNQ **1992** 2 F **1994** 5 QF **1996** 4 SF **1998** 11 r1
2000 8 QF (hosts) **2002** 7 QF **2004** DNQ **2006** 10 r1 **2008** 3 SF (hosts) **2010** 2 F **2012** 4 SF

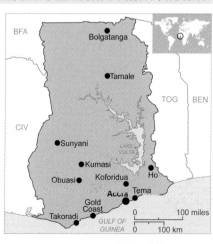

GHANA FOOTBALL ASSOCIATION (GFA)

General Secretariat,
South East Ridge,
PO Box AN 19338, Accra
☎ +233 302660380
📠 +233 302668590
📧 info@ghanafa.org
🖥 www.ghanafa.org
FA 1957 CON 1958 FIFA 1958
P Kwesi Nyantakyi
GS Emmanuel Gyimah

FIFA BIG COUNT 2006

Total players	987 500
% of population	4.42%
Male	987 600
Female	0
Amateurs 18+	16 500
Youth under 18	11 000
Unregistered	110 000
Professionals	0
Referees	800
Admin & coaches	4 400
Number of clubs	280
Number of teams	1 650

MAJOR CITIES/TOWNS

		Population
1	Accra	2 365 018
2	Kumasi	1 852 449
3	Tamale	447 349
4	Takoradi	308 266
5	Ashiaman	271 850
6	Tema	175 717
7	Cape Coast	175 710
8	Teshie	175 237
9	Sekondi	171 032
10	Obuasi	166 950
11	Madina	133 015
12	Koforidua	109 489
13	Wa	93 394
14	Techiman	87 407
15	Nungua	85 764
16	Tema New Town	84 470
17	Sunyani	81 716
18	Ho	81 532
19	Dome	71 757

REPUBLIC OF GHANA

Capital	Accra	Population	23 832 495 (47)	% in cities	50%
GDP per capita	$1500 (198)	Area km²	238 533 km² (81)	GMT +/-	0
Neighbours (km)	Burkina Faso 549, Cote d'Ivoire 668, Togo 877 • Coast 539				

RECENT INTERNATIONAL MATCHES PLAYED BY GHANA

2010	Opponents	Score		Venue	Comp	Scorers	Att	Referee
5-01	Malawi	D	0-0	Manzini	Fr		2 000	Fakudze SWZ
15-01	Côte d'Ivoire	L	1-3	Cabinda	CNr1	Asamoah Gyan 93+	23 000	Damon RSA
19-01	Burkina Faso	W	1-0	Luanda	CNr1	Andre Ayew 30	8 000	Maillet SEY
24-01	Angola	W	1-0	Luanda	CNqf	Asamoah Gyan 15	50 000	Benouza ALG
28-01	Nigeria	W	1-0	Luanda	CNsf	Asamoah Gyan 21	7 500	Bennett RSA
31-01	Egypt	L	0-1	Luanda	CNf		50 000	Coulibaly MLI
3-03	Bosnia-Herzegovina	L	1-2	Sarajevo	Fr	Sulley Muntari 22	10 000	Batinic CRO
1-06	Netherlands	L	1-4	Rotterdam	Fr	Asamoah Gyan 78	45 000	Moen NOR
5-06	Latvia	W	1-0	Milton Keynes	Fr	Quincy Owusu-Abeyie 88	8 108	Clattenburg ENG
13-06	Serbia	W	1-0	Pretoria	WCr1	Asamoah Gyan 85p	38 833	Baldassi ARG
19-06	Australia	D	1-1	Rustenburg	WCr1	Asamoah Gyan 25p	34 812	Rosetti ITA
23-06	Germany	L	0-1	Johannesburg	WCr1		83 391	Simon BRA
26-06	USA	W	2-1	Rustenburg	WCr2	Kevin Prince Boateng 5, Asamoah Gyan 93	34 976	Kassai HUN
2-07	Uruguay	D	1-1	Johannesburg	WCqf	Sulley Muntari 45	84 017	Benquerenca POR
11-08	South Africa	L	0-1	Johannesburg	Fr		45 000	
5-09	Swaziland	W	3-0	Lobamba	CNq	Andre Ayew 13, Prince Tagoe 69, Hans Sarpei 80		Seechurn MRI
10-10	Sudan	D	0-0	Kumasi	CNq		39 000	Damon RSA
17-11	Saudi Arabia	D	0-0	Dubai	Fr			
2011								
8-02	Togo	W	4-1	Antwerp	Fr	Dominic Adiyah 10, Jonathan Mensah 60, OG 69, Samuel Inkoom 83		
27-03	Congo	W	3-0	Brazzaville	CNq	Prince Tagoe 24, Dominic Adiyiah 44, Sulley Muntari 82		Bennett RSA
29-03	England	D	1-1	London	Fr	Asamoah Gyan 90	80 102	Cakir TUR
3-06	Congo	W	3-1	Kumasi	CNq	Isaac Vorsah 62, Prince Tagoe 66, Emmanuel Agyemang-Badu 78		
7-06	Korea Republic	L	1-2	Jeonju	Fr	Asamoah Gyan 63	41 271	Irmatov UZB
2-09	Swaziland	W	2-0	Accra	CNq	Asamoah Gyan 8, Emmanuel Agyemang-Badu 78		
5-09	Brazil	L	0-1	London	Fr		25 700	Dean ENG
8-10	Sudan	W	2-0	Khartoum	CNq	Asamoah Gyan 11, John Mensah 20		
11-10	Nigeria	D	0-0	Watford	Fr		5 000	Clattenburg ENG
15-11	Gabon	W	2-1	St Leu La Foret	Fr	Emmanuel Agyemang-Badu 15, Derek Asamoah 90		
2012								
24-01	Botswana	W	1-0	Franceville	CNr1	John Mensah 25	5 000	Diatta SEN
28-01	Mali	W	2-0	Franceville	CNr1	Asamoah Gyan 64, Andre Ayew 71	7 000	Haimoudi ALG
1-02	Guinea	D	1-1	Franceville	CNr1	Emmanuel Agyemang-Badu 27	5 500	Bennett RSA
5-02	Tunisia	W	2-1	Franceville	CNqf	John Mensah 9, Andre Ayew 100	8 000	Alioum CMR
8-02	Zambia	L	0-1	Bata	CNsf		12 000	Benouza ALG
11-02	Mali	L	0-2	Malabo	CN3p		15 000	Grisha EGY

Fr = Friendly match • CN = CAF African Cup of Nations • WC = FIFA World Cup
q = qualifier • r1 = first round group • r2 = second round •qf = quarter-final • sf = semi-final • 3p = third place play-off

GHANA NATIONAL TEAM HISTORICAL RECORDS

Caps	**90** -Richard Kingson 1996-
Goals	**33** - Abedi Pele 1982-98
Past Coaches	George Ainsley ENG 1958-59 • Andreas Sjoberg SWE 1959-62 • Jozsef Ember HUN 1963 • Charles Gyamfi 1963-65 • Carlos Alberto Pereira BRA 1967 • Karl-Heinz Marotzke GER 1968-70 • Nicolae Dumitru ROU 1974-74 • Karl Weigang GER 1974-75 • Sampaio BRA 1977-78 • Fred Osam-Duodu 1978-81 • Charles Gyamfi 1982-83 • Emmanuel Afranie 1984 • Herbert Addo 1984 • Rudi Gutendorf GER 1986-87 • Fred Osam-Duodu 1988-89 • Burkhard Ziese GER 1990-92 • Otto Pfister GER 1992-93 • Fred Osam-Duodu 1993 • Jorgen Larsen DEN 1993-94 • Edward Aggrey-Fynn 1994 • Petre Gavrilla ROU 1995 • Ismael Kurtz BRA 1996 • Sam Arday 1996-97 • Rinus Israel NED 1997-98 • Giuseppe Dossena ITA 1999-2000 • Fred Osam-Duodu 2000 • Cecil Jones 2001 • Fred Osam-Duodu 2001-02 • Milan Zivadinovic SRB 2002 • Emmanuel Afranie 2002, Burkhard Ziese GER 2003 • Ralf Zumdick GER 2003 • Mariano Barreto 2004 • Sam Arday 2004 • Ratomir Dujkovic SRB 2004-06 • Claude Le Roy FRA 2006-08 • Sellas Tetteh 2008 • Milovan Rajevac SRB 2008-10 • Kwasi Appiah 2010 • Goran Stevanovic SRB 2011-

GHANA 2010-11

GLO PREMIER LEAGUE

	Pl	W	D	L	F	A	Pts	Chelsea	AshantiGold	Asante Kotoko	Medeama	Aduana Stars	Liberty Pros	Hearts of Oak	New Edubiase	Heart of Lions	Arsenal	Ebusua Dwarfs	All Stars	Mighty Jets	King Faisal	RTU	BA Stars
Berekum Chelsea †	30	18	3	9	33	26	57		0-0	1-0	1-0	1-0	2-0	1-0	3-0	0-0	2-0	1-0	2-1	2-1	1-0	1-0	2-0
AshantiGold	30	13	8	9	24	14	47	3-0		0-1	0-0	1-0	2-0	1-0	2-0	1-1	1-0	0-0	3-0	1-1	2-0	1-0	
Asante Kotoko	30	13	7	10	36	27	46	2-3	0-0		0-1	3-0	2-3	0-1	1-2	0-0	2-1	1-0	2-1	1-0	2-1	2-1	3-1
Medeama	30	12	10	8	35	31	46	0-1	1-1	0-1		1-1	2-1	1-0	3-1	1-1	2-1	0-0	2-2	2-1	2-1	2-1	3-1
Aduana Stars	30	12	9	9	20	18	45	1-0	1-0	2-0	1-0		0-0	0-0	1-2	1-0	2-1	1-1	1-0	1-0	2-0	1-0	1-0
Liberty Professionals	30	12	7	11	31	29	43	0-1	2-0	0-4	0-1	0-0		1-2	2-1	2-1	1-1	2-2	3-1	0-1	0-1	2-0	4-0
Hearts of Oak	30	13	4	13	26	22	43	1-1	1-0	0-2	2-3	1-0	0-1		0-1	0-1	1-0	3-0	2-1	1-0	0-1	3-0	
New Edubiase United	30	11	10	9	33	32	43	2-0	1-0	1-1	4-2	0-0	0-0	0-2		2-1	3-1	0-0	0-0	0-0	2-2	1-0	4-1
Heart of Lions	30	10	11	9	22	21	41	2-0	0-1	2-2	0-0	2-0	1-0	1-1	0-0		2-0	1-0	0-0	0-0	1-0	1-0	1-2
Berekum Arsenal	30	11	8	11	30	34	41	4-3	1-0	0-0	2-0	1-1	0-1	0-1	3-1	0-0		1-0	1-0	2-1	0-0	1-0	1-1
Ebusua Dwarfs	30	11	8	11	30	24	41	3-1	2-1	1-0	1-2	1-0	1-1	0-0	1-1	1-2	5-0		1-0	1-0	3-0	3-0	1-0
Wa All Stars	30	10	9	11	29	29	39	2-0	1-0	0-2	1-1	1-0	2-0	1-0	2-0	1-2	2-2	0-0		2-0	1-0	1-1	3-1
Mighty Jets	30	11	4	15	24	30	37	0-1	0-1	2-0	2-1	1-0	1-2	1-0	2-1	0-0	2-1	1-0	1-1		0-1	1-0	2-1
King Faisal Babes	30	10	6	14	26	32	36	1-0	0-0	3-2	2-2	0-1	0-1	1-2	3-0	1-0	1-0	1-2	1-3	2-1		0-0	1-0
Real Tamale United	30	9	6	15	24	26	33	1-2	0-1	0-0	1-0	1-1	0-0	2-1	0-0	3-0	0-1	4-0	2-0	1-0	2-1		3-0
Brong Ahafo Stars §3	30	7	4	19	16	44	22	2-0	1-0	0-0	0-0	0-0	0-2	0-1	0-3	1-0	0-2	1-0	1-0	1-0	1-2	0-1	1-0

5/09/2010 - 5/06/2011 • † Qualified for the CAF Champions League • § = points deducted

MEDALS TABLE

		Overall			League			Cup			Africa			City
		G	S	B	G	S	B	G	S	B	G	S	B	
1	Asante Kotoko	31	24	7	21	14	4	8	3		2	7	3	Kumasi
2	Hearts of Oak	30	17	8	19	11	6	9	4		2	2	2	Accra
3	Great Olympics	5	4	6	2	3	5	3	1			1		Accra
4	Real Republicans	5		1	1			4			1			Accra
5	Ashanti Gold	4	7	3	3	5	3	1	1			1		Obuasi
6	Cornerstones	2	6			4		2	2					Kumasi
7	Eleven Wise	2	5	3	1	3	3	1	2					Sekondi
8	Sekondi Hasaacas	2	4	2	1	3	1	1	1			1		Sekondi
9	Cape Coast Dwarfs	2	3	5	1	1	5	1	2					Cape Coast
10	Okwahu United	1	3	2		1	2	1	2					Nkawkaw
11	Ghapoha Tema	1	1					1	1					Tema
12	Aduana Stars	1			1									Dormaa Ahenkro
	Berekum Chelsea	1			1									Berekum
	Nania	1						1						Accra
	Voradep Ho	1						1						Ho
16	Real Tamale United		5	3		2	3		3					Tamale

MTN GHANA FA CUP 2011

First round		Quarter-finals		Semi-finals		Final	
Nania	2						
Unity FC	0	**Nania**	1				
Berekum Arsenal	0	D'International	0				
D'International	1			**Nania**	2 5p		
Bolga All Stars	1 5p			Berekum Chelsea	2 3p		
Stark FC	1 4p	Bolga All Stars	0				
Eleven Wise	0	**Berekum Chelsea**	1				
Berekum Chelsea	2					**Nania** ‡	1
Wa All Stars	0 5p					Asante Kotoko	0
Universal Stars	0 4p	**Wa All Stars**	3				
Sporting Mirren	0	Medeama	1			**CUP FINAL**	
Medeama	1			Wa All Stars	0 4p		
Heart of Lions	1 4p			**Asante Kotoko**	0 5p	Accra Sports Stadium, Accra	
New Edubiase United	1 3p	Heart of Lions	1			24-07-2011	
Aduana Stars	2 10p	**Asante Kotoko**	3			Scorer - Evans Omani [107]	
Asante Kotoko	2 11p			‡ Qualified for the CAF Confederation Cup			

GNB – GUINEA-BISSAU

FIFA/COCA-COLA WORLD RANKING

'93	'94	'95	'96	'97	'98	'99	'00	'01	'02	'03	'04	'05	'06	'07	'08	'09	'10	'11	'12
131	122	118	133	148	165	173	177	174	183	186	190	186	191	171	186	194	147	163	

2011												High	Low	Av
Jan	Feb	Mar	Apr	May	Jun	Jul	Aug	Sep	Oct	Nov	Dec			
147	146	136	136	136	145	151	150	163	167	160	163	115	195	166

After a shock win over Kenya at the start of the 2012 CAF Africa Cup of Nations qualifiers, Guinea-Bissau continued to gain experience and build up their competitiveness but they were unable to conjure up any more wins in their group. That surprise win in September 2010 was followed by five straight defeats at the hands of Angola, Uganda and by the Kenyans in the return match in Nairobi. The former Portuguese colony had traditionally been an infrequent participant in continental competition, hamstrung by a lack of financial resources, but there is now funding for a team who are getting better with each match. For the first time since 1993, Guinea-Bissau took part in a friendly match when they played two games in Lisbon - including a 3-1 win over Gambia in February that saw Cicero score a first-ever hat trick for the country. Coach Norton de Matos has made good use of a large group of players who play their club football in Portugal but the year ended in disappointment with defeat by just a single goal on aggregate to Togo in a preliminary round tie in the 2014 FIFA World Cup qualifiers. The first leg in Bissau was a 1-1 draw and the return in Togo a narrow 0-1 loss. Atletico Bissora won the league while cup honours went to Desportivo Mansaba who beat Binar 3-1 in the final thanks to a hat trick by Lentine.

CAF AFRICA CUP OF NATIONS RECORD

1957-1992 DNE **1994** DNQ **1996** Withdrew **1998-2004** DNE **2006** DNQ **2008** DNE **2010-2012** DNQ

FEDERAÇAO DE FUTEBOL DA GUINE-BISSAU (FFGB)

	Alto Bandim (Nova Sede),
✉	Case Postale 375, Bissau 1035
☎	+245 3201918
📠	+245 3206915
@	ffgb_bissau@hotmail.com
💻	
FA	1974 CON 1986 FIFA 1986
P	Jose Lobato
GS	Simao Da Rocha

FIFA BIG COUNT 2006

Total players	71 900
% of population	4.99%
Male	71 900
Female	0
Amateurs 18+	1 100
Youth under 18	1 200
Unregistered	7 500
Professionals	0
Referees	100
Admin & coaches	300
Number of clubs	40
Number of teams	110

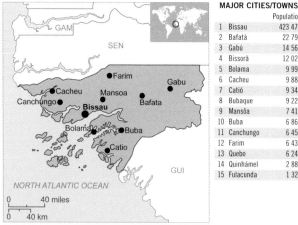

MAJOR CITIES/TOWNS

		Population
1	Bissau	423 478
2	Bafatá	22 791
3	Gabú	14 561
4	Bissorã	12 027
5	Bolama	9 998
6	Cacheu	9 882
7	Catió	9 342
8	Bubaque	9 229
9	Mansôa	7 414
10	Buba	6 867
11	Canchungo	6 456
12	Farim	6 439
13	Quebo	6 243
14	Quinhámel	2 885
15	Fulacunda	1 321

REPUBLICA DA GUINE-BISSAU • REPUBLIC OF GUINEA-BISSAU

Capital	Bissau	Population	1 533 964 (150)	% in cities	30%
GDP per capita	$600 (224)	Area km²	36 125 km² (137)	GMT +/-	0
Neighbours (km)	Guinea 386, Senegal 338 • Coast 350				

RECENT INTERNATIONAL MATCHES PLAYED BY GUINEA-BISSAU

2002	Opponents	Score		Venue	Comp	Scorers	Att	Referee
No international matches played after June 2002								
2003								
10-10	Mali	L	1-2	Bissau	WCq	Dionisio Fernandes [50]	22 000	Sowe GAM
14-11	Mali	L	0-2	Bamako	WCq		13 251	Seydou MTN
2004								
No International matches played in 2004								
2005								
18-11	Guinea	D	2-2	Conakry	ACr1	Manuel Fernandes 2 [35p 49]		
20-11	Sierra Leone	D	1-1	Conakry	ACr1	Agostino Soares [62]		
25-11	Senegal †	D	1-1	Conakry	ACsf			
27-11	Mali †	L	0-1	Conakry	AC3p			
2006								
No international matches played in 2006								
2007								
17-10	Sierra Leone	L	0-1	Freetown	WCq		25 000	Mana NGA
17-11	Sierra Leone	D	0-0	Bissau	WCq		12 000	Lamptey GHA
2-12	Sierra Leone	W	2-0	Bissau	ACr1	Emiliano [8], Suleimane [49]		
7-12	Cape Verde	D	1-1	Bissau	ACsf	Adilson [7]. L 2-3p		
2008								
No international matches played in 2008								
2009								
No international matches played in 2009								
2010								
4-09	Kenya	W	1-0	Bissau	CNq	Dionisio [76]		Bennaceur TUN
9-10	Angola	L	0-1	Luanda	CNq			Coulibaly MLI
16-11	Cape Verde Islands	L	1-2	Lisbon	Fr	Cicero [27]		
2011								
9-02	Gambia	W	3-1	Lisbon	Fr	Cicero 3 [78 90 94+]		
26-03	Uganda	L	0-1	Bissau	CNq			
4-06	Uganda	L	0-2	Kampala	CNq			
3-09	Kenya	L	1-2	Nairobi	CNq	Ailton [81]		
8-10	Angola	L	0-2	Bissau	CNq			
11-11	Togo	D	1-1	Bissau	WCq	Basile de Carvalho [38]	3 000	Diedhiou SEN
15-11	Togo	L	0-1	Lome	WCq		25 000	Mohamadou CMR

AC = Amilcar Cabral Cup • CN = CAF African Cup of Nations • WC = FIFA World Cup
q = qualifier • r1 = first round group • sf = semi-final • 3p = third place play-off • † Not a full international

GUINEA-BISSAU 2011
I DIVISAO

	Pl	W	D	L	F	A	Pts
Atlético Bissorã	16						32
Os Balantas Mansôa	16						31
SB Benfica	16						27
FC Cuntum	16						27
Sporting Bafatá	16						22
Sporting CB	16						21
Sport Portos	16						20
Mavegro FC	16						20
Binar FC	10						6
FC Canchungo				Disqualified			

/01/2011 - 4/06/2011

TACA DA GUINE-BISSAU FINAL
Estadio Lino Correia, Bissau, 11-06-2011
Desportivo Mansabá   3-1   Binar FC
Scorers - Lentine 3 [11 34 54] for Desportivo; Wie [22] for Binar

GRE – GREECE

FIFA/COCA-COLA WORLD RANKING

'93	'94	'95	'96	'97	'98	'99	'00	'01	'02	'03	'04	'05	'06	'07	'08	'09	'10	'11	'12
34	28	34	35	42	53	34	42	57	48	30	18	16	16	11	20	13	11	14	

						2011									
Jan	Feb	Mar	Apr	May	Jun	Jul	Aug	Sep	Oct	Nov	Dec		High	Low	Av
11	10	10	12	12	12	13	14	11	8	14	14		8	66	28

Replacing Otto Rehagell as the Greek national team coach was never going to be an easy job for Portugal's Fernando Santos but against a backdrop of a political crisis and austerity measures that were having a profound effect on Greek society, he got off to the best possible start by remaining unbeaten for his first 17 matches in charge and taking Greece to the finals of the 2012 European Championship. The Greeks won a potentially tricky group two points ahead of Croatia, whom they beat 2-0 in a crucial qualifier in Piraeus towards the end of the campaign. Greece rose to a record high of eight in the FIFA/Coca-Cola World Ranking although a defeat to Romania in front of just 800 fans in Austria at the end of the year saw them slip back out of the top ten. It was the first defeat suffered by Greece since the World Cup in South Africa and the first defeat under Santos. The Greek Super League saw familiar champions as Olympiacos won their 13th title in 15 seasons but there was a first trophy in nine years for AEK, the forgotten member of the 'big three' clubs from Athens. Theirs has been a turbulent recent history off the field with financial troubles and the failure to replace their Nea Filadelfeia stadium, which was demolished in 2003, but the cup triumph ended the longest barren spell for the club for over half a century.

UEFA EUROPEAN CHAMPIONSHIP RECORD

1960 r1 1964 DNE 1968-1976 DNQ **1980** 8 r1 1984-2000 DNQ **2004** 1 Winners **2008** 16 r1 **2012** Qualified

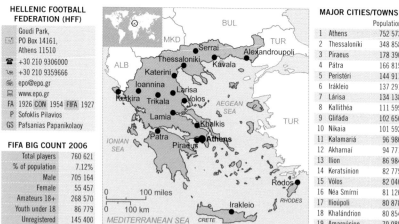

HELLENIC FOOTBALL FEDERATION (HFF)

Goudi Park,
PO Box 14161,
Athens 11510
☎ +30 210 9306000
📠 +30 210 9359666
✉ epo@epo.gr
🖥 www.epo.gr
FA 1926 CON 1954 FIFA 1927
P Sofoklis Pilavios
GS Pafsanias Papanikolaoy

FIFA BIG COUNT 2006

Total players	760 621
% of population	7.12%
Male	705 164
Female	55 457
Amateurs 18+	268 570
Youth under 18	86 779
Unregistered	145 400
Professionals	1 818
Referees	3 230
Admin & coaches	10 100
Number of clubs	5 571
Number of teams	5 899

MAJOR CITIES/TOWNS

		Population
1	Athens	752 573
2	Thessaloníki	348 858
3	Piraeus	178 390
4	Pátra	166 815
5	Peristéri	144 911
6	Irákleio	137 291
7	Lárisa	134 138
8	Kallithéa	111 595
9	Glifáda	102 656
10	Nikaia	101 592
11	Kalamariá	96 986
12	Akharnaí	94 771
13	Ilion	86 984
14	Keratsínion	82 775
15	Vólos	82 046
16	Néa Smírni	81 126
17	Ilioúpoli	80 878
18	Khalándrion	80 854
19	Amaroúsion	79 088

ELLINIKI DHIMOKRATIA • HELLENIC REPUBLIC

Capital Athens	Population 10 737 428 (74)	% in cities 61%
GDP per capita $32 100 (40)	Area km² 131 957 km² (96)	GMT +/- +2
Neighbours (km) Albania 282, Bulgaria 494, Turkey 206, Macedonia FYR 246 • Coast 13 676		

RECENT INTERNATIONAL MATCHES PLAYED BY GREECE

2009	Opponents	Score		Venue	Comp	Scorers	Att	Referee
11-02	Denmark	D	1-1	Piraeus	Fr	Gekas [62]		Undiano ESP
28-03	Israel	D	1-1	Ramat Gan	WCq	Gekas [41]	38 000	Rosetti ITA
1-04	Israel	W	2-1	Irákleio	WCq	Salpingidis [32], Samaras [66p]	22 794	Benquerença POR
12-08	Poland	L	0-2	Bydgoszcz	Fr		19 000	Sagara JPN
5-09	Switzerland	L	0-2	Basel	WCq		38 500	De Bleeckere BEL
9-09	Moldova	D	1-1	Chisinau	WCq	Gekas [33]	9 870	Stalhammar SWE
10-10	Latvia	W	5-2	Athens	WCq	Gekas 4 [4 47p 57 91+], Samaras [73]	18 981	Ovrebo NOR
14-10	Luxembourg	W	2-1	Athens	WCq	Torosidis [30], Gekas [33]	13 932	Ceferin SVN
14-11	Ukraine	D	0-0	Athens	WCpo		39 045	Duhamel FRA
18-11	Ukraine	W	1-0	Donetsk	WCpo	Salpingidis [31]	31 643	Benquerença POR
2010								
3-03	Senegal	L	0-2	Volos	Fr		10 000	Skomina SVN
25-05	Korea DPR	D	2-2	Altach	Fr	Katsouranis [2], Charisteas [48]	3 000	Schorgenhofer AUT
2-06	Paraguay	L	0-2	Winterthur	Fr		5 200	Circhetta SUI
12-06	Korea Republic	L	0-2	Port Elizabeth	WCr1		31 513	Hester NZL
17-06	Nigeria	W	2-1	Bloemfontein	WCr1	Salpingidis [44], Torosidis [71]	31 593	Ruiz COL
22-06	Argentina	L	0-2	Polokwane	WCr1		38 891	Irmatov UZB
11-08	Serbia	W	1-0	Belgrade	Fr	Salpingidis [45]	10 000	Teixeira ESP
3-09	Georgia	D	1-1	Piraeus	ECq	Spiropoulos [72]	14 794	Clos ESP
7-09	Croatia	D	0-0	Zagreb	ECq		24 399	Larsen DEN
8-10	Latvia	W	1-0	Piraeus	ECq	Torosidis [58]	13 520	Damato ITA
12-10	Israel	W	2-1	Piraeus	ECq	Salpingidis [22], Karagounis [63p]	16 935	Hansson SWE
17-11	Austria	W	2-1	Vienna	Fr	Samaras [49], Fotakis [81]	16 200	Kever SUI
2011								
9-02	Canada	W	1-0	Larissa	Fr	Fetfatzidis [63]		Moen NOR
26-03	Malta	W	1-0	Ta'Qali	ECq	Torosidis [92+]	10 605	Weiner GER
29-03	Poland	D	0-0	Larissa	Fr		12 000	Atkinson ENG
4-06	Malta	W	3-1	Piaeus	ECq	Fetfatzidis 2 [7 63], Papadopoulos [26]	14 746	Gil POL
7-06	Ecuador	D	1-1	New York	Fr	Tziolis [16]	39 656	Geiger USA
10-08	Bosnia-Herzegovina	D	0-0	Sarajevo	Fr		12 000	Dabanovic MNE
2-09	Israel	W	1-0	Tel Aviv	ECq	Ninis [60]	13 100	Thomson SCO
6-09	Latvia	D	1-1	Riga	ECq	Papadopoulos [84]	5 415	Todorov BUL
7-10	Croatia	W	2-0	Piraeus	ECq	Samaras [71], Gekas [79]	27 200	Webb ENG
11-10	Georgia	W	2-1	Tbilisi	ECq	Fotakis [79], Charisteas [85]	7 824	Orsato ITA
11-11	Russia	D	1-1	Piraeus	Fr	Katsouranis [60]		Chapron FRA
15-11	Romania	L	1-3	Altach	Fr	Karagounis [34]	800	Gangl AUT

Fr = Friendly match • EC = UEFA EURO 2012 • WC = FIFA World Cup • q = qualifier • r1 = First round group

GREECE NATIONAL TEAM HISTORICAL RECORDS

Caps
120 - Theodoros Zagorakis 1994-2007 • **114** - Giorgos Karagounis 1999- • **100** - Angelos Basinas 1999-2009 • **96** - Stratos Apostolakis 1986-98 • **90** - Antonis Nikopolidis 1999-2008 • **88** - Angelos Charisteas 2001- & Kostas Katsouranis 2003- • **78** - Dimitris Saravakos 1982-94 • **77** - Stelios Giannakopoulos 1997-2008 & Tasos Mitropoulos 1978-94 • **76** - Panagiotis Tsalouchidis 1987-95 • **75** - Nikos Anastopoulos 1977-88 • **74** - Nikos Liberopoulos 1996- • **72** - Giourkas Seitaridis 2002-

Goals
29 - Nikos Anastopoulos 1977-88 • **25** - Angelos Charisteas 2001- • **22** - Dimitris Saravakos 1982-94 • **21** - Mimis Papaioannou 1963-78 & Theofanis Gekas 2005- • **18** - Nikos Machlas 1993-2002 • **17** - Demis Nikolaidis 1995-2004 • **16** - Panagiotis Tsalouchidis 1987-95

Past Coaches
Ioannis Kalafatis 1920 • Apostolos Nikolaidis 1929 • Jan Kopsiva CZE 1929-30 • Svejik CZE 1930 • Jan Kopsiva CZE 1930 • Committee 1930-31 • Lefteris Panourglas 1932 • Kostas Negrepontis 1933-34 • Apostolos Nikolaidis 1934-35 • Kostas Konstantaras 1935 • Kischler AUT 1936 • Kostas Konstantaras 1936-37 • Kostas Negrepontis 1938 • Bucket ENG 1938 • Kostas Negrepontis 1948-50 • Antonis Migiakis 1951 • Ioannis Chelmis 1951 • Nikos Katrantzos 1951 • Kostas Negrepontis & Antonis Migiakis 1952 • Antonis Migiakis 1952-53 • Kostas Negrepontis 1953 • Ioannis Chelmis 1954 • Antonis Migiakis 1954-55 • Ioannis Chelmis 1955 • Kostas Andritsos 1956 • Rino Martini ITA 1957-58 • Antonis Migiakis 1958 • Paul Barone FRA 1959-60 • Tryfonas Tzanetis 1960-61 • Antonis Migiakis 1961 • Tryfonas Tzanetis 1962-64 • Lakis Petropoulos & Ioannis Magiras 1964-65 • Panos Markovits 1966-67 • Lakis Petropoulos 1967 • Kostas Karapatis 1968 • Dan Georgiadis 1968-69 • Lakis Petropoulos 1969-71 • Bily Bingham NIR 1971-73 • Alketas Panagoulias 1973-76 • Lakis Petropoulos 1976-77 • Alketas Panagoulias 1977-81 • Christos Archontidis 1982-84 • Miltos Papapostolou 1984-88 • Alekos Sofianidis 1988-89 • Antonis Georgiadis 1989-91 • Stefanos Petritsis 1992 • Antonis Georgiadis 1992 • Alketas Panagoulias 1992-94 • Kostas Polychroniou 1994-98 • Anghel Iordanescu ROU 1998-99 • Vassilis Daniil 1999-2001 • Nikos Christidis 2001 • Otto Rehhagel GER 2001-10 • Fernando Santos POR 2010-

GREECE 2010–11

SUPER LEAGUE

Team	Pl	W	D	L	F	A	Pts	Olympiacos	Panathinaikos	AEK	PAOK	Olymp Volos	Aris	Kavala	Ergotelis	Xánthi	Panionios	Atromitos	Kérkira	Asteras	Larisa	Panserraikos	Iraklis
Olympiacos †	30	24	1	5	65	18	73		2-1	6-0	3-0	3-1	1-0	3-1	3-0	1-0	5-0	2-0	2-1	2-0	3-0	6-0	4-2
Panathinaikos †	30	18	6	6	47	26	60	2-1		3-1	1-0	0-1	1-0	4-2	2-0	1-1	2-1	4-2	1-1	2-1	1-0	1-1	2-0
AEK Athens ‡	30	15	5	10	46	37	50	1-0	1-0		4-0	0-4	1-2	1-0	3-1	1-0	1-1	0-0	1-0	0-0	2-2	4-0	2-0
PAOK Thessaloníki ‡	30	14	6	10	32	29	48	2-1	0-1	2-1		1-1	0-1	0-2	2-0	2-1	3-1	1-0	0-1	2-0	1-0	1-0	3-2
Olympiacos Volou - R ‡	30	12	11	7	40	28	47	0-1	3-2	3-1	0-3		1-1	1-1	0-1	3-0	0-0	1-1	2-0	1-0	1-1	1-1	3-0
Aris Thessaloníki	30	13	6	11	29	29	45	1-2	0-1	0-4	0-0	2-1		1-0	1-0	0-2	0-2	0-1	2-0	2-0	1-0	1-1	3-1
Kavala - R	30	10	10	10	29	27	40	0-1	2-2	2-1	0-1	0-1	0-1		3-1	1-1	2-1	3-0	1-1	1-0	1-0	1-0	0-0
Ergotelis	30	11	6	13	32	38	39	0-2	1-4	2-3	1-2	0-0	0-0	2-1		1-0	2-0	1-0	1-1	3-0	0-1	2-1	2-0
Xánthi	30	9	9	12	29	35	36	0-3	0-2	0-2	1-0	1-0	1-2	1-1	0-1		1-1	2-2	3-0	2-1	1-0	1-1	2-0
Panionios	30	8	11	11	25	35	35	1-1	1-1	1-0	1-0	0-1	1-0	1-1	0-1	0-2		1-0	0-1	0-1	0-0	3-3	0-0
Iraklis Thessaloníki - R	30	7	14	9	22	28	35	2-1	1-3	2-0	0-0	0-0	1-0	0-1	1-1	1-1	1-1	1-0	0-0	0-0	1-0	1-1	
Atromitos	30	7	13	10	30	34	34	3-1	0-1	1-1	2-2	2-2	0-0	0-0	1-1	1-1	1-2		1-1	4-2	0-0	3-0	2-1
Kérkira	30	9	6	15	30	40	33	0-2	0-2	2-1	2-1	1-3	3-4	1-1	1-0	1-1	1-2	0-0		3-1	1-2	1-0	3-0
Asteras Tripolis	30	7	10	13	21	29	31	0-1	0-0	0-3	0-0	2-1	1-2	0-1	3-0	1-2	3-1	0-0	1-1		0-2	1-1	0-2
Larisa	30	5	10	15	29	47	25	0-1	2-0	2-3	1-2	2-2	2-2	0-0	3-3	3-0	0-1	2-1	1-0	1-1		0-2	2-1
Panserraikos	30	6	6	18	22	48	24	0-1	1-0	1-3	1-1	2-2	1-0	0-4	2-1	1-1	1-2	0-1	0-2	0-1	1-0		1-0

27/08/2010 - 17/04/2011 • † Qualified for the UEFA Champions League • ‡ Qualified for the Europa League
Olympiakos Volou and Kavala found guilty of match fixing and relegated. Iraklis found guilty of forgery and relegated
Top scorers: **20** - Djibril Cisse FRA, Panathinaikos • **14** - Kevin Mirallas BEL, Olympiacos • **13** - David Fuster ESP, Olympiacos • **12** - Rafik Djebbour ALG, AEK/Olympiacos • **10** - Benjamin Onwuachi NGA, Kavala

GREECE 2010–11 FOOTBALL LEAGUE (2)

	Pl	W	D	L	F	A	Pts
Panetolikos	34	23	6	5	47	19	75
PAS Giannina	34	22	8	4	55	17	74
OFI Crete †	34	21	6	7	42	20	69
Trikala - R	34	18	6	10	42	23	60
Levadiakos - P †	34	17	9	8	48	33	60
Doxa Dramas - P †	34	16	8	10	51	28	56
Diagoras Rhodos †	34	15	7	12	36	36	52
Panthrakikos	34	13	8	13	36	38	47
Veria	34	12	8	14	37	42	44
Pierikos Katerini	34	11	10	13	39	43	43
Agrotikos Asteras	34	11	7	16	34	41	40
Ethnikos Asteras	34	9	11	14	27	38	38
Illioupoli	34	10	6	18	29	50	36
Thrasivoulos	34	9	9	16	33	36	36
Anagennisi Karditsas	34	9	6	19	20	43	33
Ionikos	34	8	9	17	25	51	33
Ethnikos Piraeus	34	8	8	18	28	48	32
Kallithea	34	3	10	21	27	54	19

12/09/2010 - 15/05/2011 • † Play-offs

CHAMPIONS LEAGUE PLAY-OFFS

	Pl	W	D	L	F	A	Pts	Pan	PAOK	AEK	OV
Panathinaikos §3	6	3	1	2	9	5	13		1-0	1-1	3-0
PAOK Thessaloníki	6	4	0	2	11	8	12	2-1		2-1	5-1
AEK Athens §1	6	2	1	3	6	6	8	0-2	3-0		1-0
Olympiacos Volos	6	2	0	4	5	12	6	2-1	1-2	1-0	

12/05/2011 - 25/05/2011 • § = bonus points • Panathinaikos qualified for the Champions League, PAOK, AEK & Olympiacos Volou for the Europa League

FOOTBALL LEAGUE PROMOTION PLAY-OFFS

	Pl	W	D	L	F	A	Pts	OFI	Lev	DD	DR
OFI Crete §4	6	4	2	0	12	5	18		1-1	3-0	3-0
Levadiakos §2	6	4	1	1	12	2	15	0-1		3-0	4-0
Doxa Dramas §1	6	1	2	3	5	13	6	3-3	0-3		1-1
Diagoras Rhodos	6	0	1	5	2	12	1	1-2	0-1	0-1	

14/07/2011 - 1/08/2011 • § = bonus points • OFI Crete promoted • Levadiakos and Doxa were promoted on October 2011

Trikala, Anagennisi Karditsa, Ionikos and Ethnikos Piraeus found guilty of forgery and relegated. Ilioupoli found guilty of match fixing and relegated.

MEDALS TABLE

		Overall			League			Cup		Europe			City
		G	S	B	G	S	B	G	S	G	S	B	
1	Olympiacos	62	28	10	38	17	10	24	11				Piraeus
2	Panathinaikos	37	31	19	20	20	17	17	10		1	2	Athens
3	AEK	24	26	16	11	19	15	13	7			1	Athens
4	PAOK	6	17	9	2	5	9	4	12				Thessaloníki
5	Aris	4	11	8	3	3	8	1	8				Thessaloníki
6	Larissa	3	3		1	1		2	2				Larissa
7	Panionios	2	6	3				2	3		2	4	Athens
8	Iraklis	1	7	2				3	2		1	4	Thessaloníki
9	OFI Crete	1	2	2				1	2		1	1	Irákleio
10	Ethnikos	1	2					2					Piraeus
11	Kastoria	1						1					Kastoria

KYPELLO ELLADOS 2010-11

Fourth Round		Fifth Round		Quarter-finals		Semi-finals		Final	
AEK Athens	5	**AEK Athens**	4	**AEK Athens**	2 2	**AEK Athens** *	0 1	**AEK Athens** ‡	3
Panthrakikos *	1	Larisa *	0	Panathinaikos *	0 3	PAOK Thessaloniki	0 0	Atromitos	0
Ethnikos Piraeus *	0								
Larisa	1								
Trikala *	1 4p	**Trikala**	2						
Aris Thessaloniki	1 2p	Panathinaikos *	3						
Kozani *	0								
Panathinaikos	5								
Olympiacos	1	**Olympiacos**	1	**Olympiacos** *	1 0				
Ilioupoli *	0	Asteras Tripolis *	0	PAOK Thessaloniki	1 1				
Pierikos Katerini *	1								
Asteras Tripolis	3								
PAS Giannina *	1	**PAS Giannina**	1						
Ergotelis	0	PAOK Thessaloniki *	2						
Eordaikos 2007 *	1								
PAOK Thessaloniki	2								
Olympiacos Volou	1	**Olympiacos Volou** *	2	**Olympiacos Volou**	2 1	**Olympiacos Volou**	1 0		
OFI Crete *	0	Panserraikos	0	Kérkira *	0 2	**Atromitos** *	2 0		
Aetos Skydra *	0								
Panserraikos	2								
Iraklis Thessaloniki	2	**Iraklis Thessaloniki** *	1 0 3p						
Panetolikos *	0	**Kérkira**	1 0 5p						
Veria *	0								
Kérkira	1								
Diagoras Rhodos *	3	**Diagoras Rhodos**	1 1	**Diagoras Rhodos**	0 0				
Panionios	1	Ethnikos Asteras *	1 0	**Atromitos** *	2 1				
Xánthi	0 2p								
Ethnikos Asteras *	0 4p								
Kavala	2	Kavala	0						
Panachaiki 2005 *	0	**Atromitos** *	1						
Anagennisi Giannitsa *	1								
Atromitos	3								

Superleague clubs enter in the fourth round • * Home team/home team in the first leg • ‡ Qualified for the Europa League

CUP FINAL

Olympic, Athens, 30-04-2011, 20:30
Att: 43 000. Ref: Anastasios Kakos
Scorers – Liberopoulos [29], Baha [78], Kafes [85]
AEK - Sebastian Saja - Nikos Georgeas, Nikos Karabelas, Kostas Manolas, Traianos Dellas - Papa Bouba Diop•, Grigoris Makos•, Panagiotis Lagos - Ismael Blanco (Pantelis Kafes• 70), Ignacio Scocco (Nabil Baha 33), Nikos Liberopoulos (c)•. Tr: Manolo Jimenez
Atromitos - Charles Itandje - Vangelis Nastos, Ioannis Skondras•, Marcin Baszczynski, Marcelo Oliveira (Marcelo Sarmiento 83) - Kostas Nebegleras (c)•, Stelios Sfakianakis, Andreas Tatos - Marek Saganowski (Brito 66), Henri Camara (Massamba Sambou 89), Ilias Anastasakos. Tr: Giorgos Donis

GRN – GRENADA

FIFA/COCA-COLA WORLD RANKING

'93	'94	'95	'96	'97	'98	'99	'00	'01	'02	'03	'04	'05	'06	'07	'08	'09	'10	'11	'12
143	142	141	127	111	117	121	143	133	131	154	144	151	163	176	118	138	94	134	

							2011												
Jan	Feb	Mar	Apr	May	Jun	Jul	Aug	Sep	Oct	Nov	Dec		High	Low	Av
94	92	94	99	98	117	120	118	120	116	106	134		88	176	133

Having qualified for two consecutive CONCACAF Gold Cups, Grenada set off on the road to Brazil 2014 hoping to make an impact in the FIFA World Cup qualifiers for the first time. There was to be no repeat of their Gold Cup heroics, however, as they finished bottom of their group some 14 points behind winner Guatemala. Grenada weren't disgraced and there was a morale boosting win over Belize in Belmopan having earlier lost to them at home, but the warning signs had been there during the 2011 Gold Cup which had been staged before the World Cup qualifiers kicked-off. Grenada lost 4-0 to Jamaica in their opening match which was followed by a 7-1 hammering at the hands of Honduras before bowing out with a 4-0 defeat by Guatemala. The step up in class for Mike Adams' side proved to be too much and there can be little doubt that the Caribbean Cup remains the pinnacle of the team's ambitions, especially in emulating their achievement in reaching the final in 2008 and the semi-final in 2010. In club football, the 2011 Premier Division was won by Hard Rock who finished a point ahead of defending champions Paradise. It was the first title won by the club, while the premier cup competition - the Waggy T Super Knock Out - was won by Carib Hurricanes who beat GBSS 7-6 on penalties after a 2-2 draw.

FIFA WORLD CUP RECORD
1930-1978 DNE 1982 DNQ 1986-1994 DNE 1998-2014 DNQ

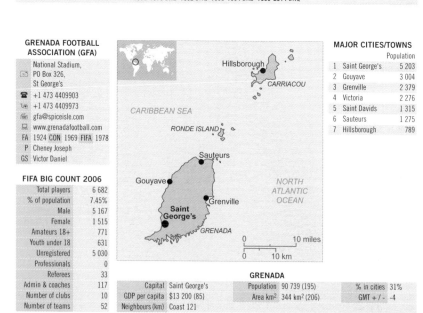

GRENADA FOOTBALL ASSOCIATION (GFA)

National Stadium,
PO Box 326,
St George's

☎ +1 473 4409903
📠 +1 473 4409973
✉ gfa@spiceisle.com
🖥 www.grenadafootball.com
FA 1924 CON 1969 FIFA 1978
P Cheney Joseph
GS Victor Daniel

FIFA BIG COUNT 2006

Total players	6 682
% of population	7.45%
Male	5 167
Female	1 515
Amateurs 18+	771
Youth under 18	631
Unregistered	5 030
Professionals	0
Referees	33
Admin & coaches	117
Number of clubs	10
Number of teams	52

MAJOR CITIES/TOWNS

Population
1	Saint George's	5 203
2	Gouyave	3 004
3	Grenville	2 379
4	Victoria	2 276
5	Saint Davids	1 315
6	Sauteurs	1 275
7	Hillsborough	789

GRENADA

Capital Saint George's	Population 90 739 (195)	% in cities 31%
GDP per capita $13 200 (85)	Area km² 344 km² (206)	GMT + / - -4
Neighbours (km) Coast 121		

RECENT INTERNATIONAL MATCHES PLAYED BY GRENADA

2010	Opponents		Score	Venue	Comp	Scorers	Att	Referee
26-11	Martinique	D	1-1	Fort de France	CCr1	Kithson Bain [29]	5 000	Bogle JAM
28-11	Trinidad and Tobago	W	1-0	Fort de France	CCr1	Kithson Bain [69]	500	Cruz CRC
30-11	Cuba	D	0-0	Fort de France	CCr1		2 000	Bogle JAM
3-12	Jamaica	L	1-2	Fort de France	CCsf	Kithson Bain [13]	4 000	Taylor BRB
5-12	Cuba	L	0-1	Fort de France	CC3p		4 000	Lopez GUA
2011								
27-03	St Kitts and Nevis	D	0-0	Basseterre	Fr		1 000	Matthew SKN
2-04	St Kitts and Nevis	L	0-1	St George's	Fr		3 500	Bedeau GRN
27-05	Antigua and Barbuda	D	2-2	St George's	Fr	Clive Murray 2 [3 47]	3 500	Bedeau GRN
29-05	Panama	L	0-2	Panama City	Fr		5 000	Perea PAN
6-06	Jamaica	L	0-4	Carson/LA	GCr1		21 550	Toledo USA
10-06	Honduras	L	1-7	Miami	GCr1	Clive Murray [19]	18 057	Gantar CAN
13-06	Guatemala	L	0-4	Harrison/NY	GCr1		25 000	Toledo USA
2-09	Belize	L	0-3	St George's	WCq		2 600	Rubalcaba CUB
18-09	St Vincent/Grenadines	L	1-2	Kingstown	WCq	Cassim Langaigne [76]	2 500	Ward CAN
7-10	Belize	W	4-1	Belmopan	WCq	Shane Rennie [37], Marcus Julien [37], Lancaster Joseph [50], Clive Murray [80]	1 200	Jarquin NCA
15-10	St Vincent/Grenadines	D	1-1	St George's	WCq	Clive Murray [92+]	2 000	Willett ATG
11-11	Guatemala	L	0-3	Guatemala City	WCq		24 000	Andino HON
15-11	Guatemala	L	1-4	St George's	WCq	Shane Rennie [37p]	200	Angela ARU

Fr = Friendly match • CC = Digicel Caribbean Cup • WC = FIFA World Cup • q = qualifier • r1 = first round group • sf = semi-final • f = final

GRENADA 2011

PREMIER DIVISION	Pl	W	D	L	F	A	Pts	Hard Rock	Paradise	GBSS	QPR	Eagles	Hurricanes	Chantimelle	Fontenoy	Ball Dogs	South Stars
Hard Rock	18	12	3	3	33	13	39		3-1	0-0	3-1	1-0	2-1	1-0	0-1	3-0	3-0
ASOMS Paradise	18	12	2	4	49	21	38	1-1		0-2	1-1	1-3	1-2	3-0	4-1	3-1	5-1
Grenada Boys SS	18	10	4	4	25	13	34	1-0	1-0		1-0	1-0	0-1	1-2	3-0	1-0	3-0
Queens Park Rangers	18	8	4	6	25	18	28	0-1	1-3	0-0		2-0	2-1	1-2	1-1	1-0	4-0
Eagles Super Strikers	18	8	3	7	34	28	27	2-2	0-2	5-2	2-0		4-1	4-3	1-2	3-0	3-2
Carib Hurricane	18	8	2	8	29	29	26	2-5	1-3	1-3	0-1	1-1		2-0	2-0	6-2	1-3
Chantimelle	18	7	2	9	27	28	23	2-0	1-2	0-3	2-2	0-3	1-2		1-0	2-1	6-0
Fontenoy United	18	6	3	9	21	28	21	0-1	1-2	0-1	0-3	4-1	0-3	1-1		2-0	3-0
Ball Dogs	18	4	2	12	21	33	14	1-4	1-2	1-1	1-2	2-0	0-0	2-1	1-2		5-0
South Stars	18	1	3	14	13	66	6	0-3	0-13	1-1	0-3	2-2	1-2	0-3	3-3	0-3	

4/06/2011 - 30/10/2011

WAGGY T SUPER KNOCK OUT 2011

First round		Quarter–finals		Semi–finals		Final	
Carib Hurricane	1 5p						
Ball Dogs	1 4p	**Carib Hurricane**	2 5p				
St David's United	0	Queens Park Rangers	2 3p				
Queens Park Rangers	7			**Carib Hurricane**	2		
Honved	1 5p			ASOMS Paradise	1		
Maran	1 4p	Honved	1				
Mt Moritz	1	**ASOMS Paradise**	2				
ASOMS Paradise	2					**Carib Hurricane**	2 7p
Hard Rock	1					Grenada Boys SS	2 6p
Red Out	0	**Hard Rock**	4				
Idlers	1 4p	Glovers Spice Boys	0			CUP FINAL	
Glovers Spice Boys	1 5p			Hard Rock	1 3p		
Fontenoy United	1			**Grenada Boys SS**	1 4p	National Stadium	
Grand Mal	1 2p	Fontenoy United	0			3-12-2011	
Sunjets	0	**Grenada Boys SS**	3				
Grenada Boys SS	2						

Third Place: **Paradise** 0-0 7-6p Hard Rock

GUA – GUATEMALA

FIFA/COCA-COLA WORLD RANKING

'93	'94	'95	'96	'97	'98	'99	'00	'01	'02	'03	'04	'05	'06	'07	'08	'09	'10	'11	'12
120	149	145	105	83	73	73	56	67	78	77	71	56	105	106	109	121	118	90	

	2011														
	Jan	Feb	Mar	Apr	May	Jun	Jul	Aug	Sep	Oct	Nov	Dec	High	Low	Av
	117	126	125	125	124	118	116	113	109	99	90	90	50	163	91

Guatemala got their 2014 FIFA World Cup qualifying campaign off to a great start with six wins out of six to qualify for the penultimate round of qualifying in CONCACAF, prompting the belief that the team could potentially break their World Cup duck and qualify for the finals in Brazil. The older stalwarts such as MLS-based captain Carlos Ruiz are being joined by a younger generation of players such as Chicago Fire's Marco Pappa but their experience in both the 2011 Copa Centroamericana and the 2011 CONCACAF Gold Cup show there may still be some ground to make up before they can make a serious challenge. In the Gold Cup Guatemala lost to Jamaica in the group stage and only squeezed through into the quarter-finals as one of the third place teams with the best record. Although they took the lead against Mexico through Ruiz in the quarter-final, Guatemala were knocked out by goals in the second half through De Nigris and Javier Hernandez. At home, the two championship finals played in 2011 were both contested by Comunicaciones and Municipal. Having won the first 6-0 on aggregate, Comunicaciones were looking to complete a hat-trick of championships and to win both titles in the same year for the first time, but they lost 4-0 on aggregate to their great rivals with Municipal crowned for a record 29th time.

FIFA WORLD CUP RECORD
1930-1954 DNE 1958-1962 DNQ 1966 DNE 1970-2010 DNQ

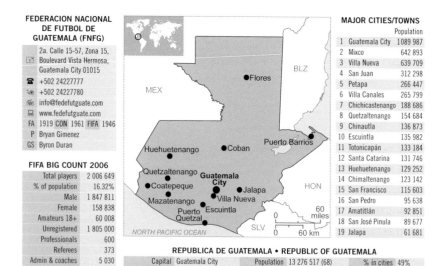

FEDERACION NACIONAL DE FUTBOL DE GUATEMALA (FNFG)

2a. Calle 15-57, Zona 15,
Boulevard Vista Hermosa,
Guatemala City 01015
☎ +502 24227777
📠 +502 24227780
✉ info@fedefutguate.com
🖥 www.fedefutguate.com
FA 1919 CON 1961 FIFA 1946
P Bryan Gimenez
GS Byron Duran

FIFA BIG COUNT 2006

Total players	2 006 649
% of population	16.32%
Male	1 847 811
Female	158 838
Amateurs 18+	60 008
Unregistered	1 805 000
Professionals	600
Referees	373
Admin & coaches	5 030
Number of clubs	138
Number of teams	225

MAJOR CITIES/TOWNS

		Population
1	Guatemala City	1089 987
2	Mixco	642 893
3	Villa Nueva	639 709
4	San Juan	312 298
5	Petapa	266 447
6	Villa Canales	265 799
7	Chichicastenango	188 686
8	Quetzaltenango	154 684
9	Chinautla	136 873
10	Escuintla	135 982
11	Totonicapán	133 184
12	Santa Catarina	131 746
13	Huehuetenango	129 252
14	Chimaltenango	123 142
15	San Francisco	115 603
16	San Pedro	95 638
17	Amatitlán	92 851
18	San José Pinula	89 677
19	Jalapa	61 681

REPUBLICA DE GUATEMALA • REPUBLIC OF GUATEMALA

Capital	Guatemala City	Population	13 276 517 (68)	% in cities 49%
GDP per capita	$5300 (136)	Area km²	108 889 km² (106)	GMT + / - -6
Neighbours (km)	Belize 266, El Salvador 203, Honduras 256, Mexico 962 • Coast 400		

RECENT INTERNATIONAL MATCHES PLAYED BY GUATEMALA

2009	Opponents	Score	Venue	Comp	Scorers	Att	Referee
17-01	Haiti	W 1-0	Fort Pierce	Fr	Villatoro [64]	5 000	Jurisvic USA
25-01	Costa Rica	L 1-3	Tegucigalpa	UCr1	Mynor Lopez [51]	3 000	Rodriguez MEX
27-01	Panama	L 0-1	Tegucigalpa	UCr1		1 000	Aguilar SLV
29-01	Nicaragua	L 0-2	Tegucigalpa	UC5p		150	Moncada HON
11-02	Venezuela	L 1-2	Maturin	Fr	Dwight Pezzarossi [50]	10 000	Perluzzo VEN
28-06	Mexico	D 0-0	San Diego	Fr		27 094	Navarro CAN
30-06	Canada	L 0-3	Oxnard	Fr		200	Singh USA
2010							
3-03	El Salvador	W 2-1	Los Angeles	Fr	Marco Pappa [44], Jonny Brown [83]	10 000	Salazar USA
31-05	South Africa	L 0-5	Polokwane	Fr		38 000	Ibrahim NIG
4-09	Nicaragua	W 5-0	Fort Lauderdale	Fr	Transito Montepeque 2 [30 58], Carlos Figueroa [36], Fredy Thompson [42], Yony Flores [54]	5 000	Vaughn USA
7-09	Japan	L 1-2	Osaka	Fr	Mario Rodriguez [22]	44 541	Archundia MEX
7-09	El Salvador	W 2-0	Washington DC	Fr	Fredy Thompson [45], Transito Montepeque [81]	12 246	Marrufo USA
9-10	Belize	W 4-2	San Jose	Fr	Jonny Brown [20], Mario Castellanos [50], Dwight Pezzarossi [69], Carlos Figueroa [74]	5 500	Bermudez SLV
12-10	Honduras	L 0-2	Los Angeles	Fr		10 000	Hernandez USA
17-11	Guyana	W 3-0	Kennesaw	Fr	Transito Montepeque [23], Guillermo Ramirez 2 [30 64]	4 124	Okulaja USA
2011							
16-01	Costa Rica	L 0-2	Panama City	UCr1		1 500	Moreno PAN
18-01	Honduras	L 1-3	Panama City	UCr1	Guillermo Ramirez [24]	10 000	Aguilar SLV
21-01	Nicaragua	W 2-1	Panama City	UCr1	Carlos Ruiz [45], Manuel Leon [66]	5 000	Garcia MEX
28-03	Bolivia	D 1-1	Mazatenango	Fr	Carlos Ruiz [41]	6 154	Aguilar SLV
1-06	Venezuela	L 0-2	Guatemala City	Fr		13 000	Ruano SLV
6-06	Honduras	D 0-0	Carson/LA	GCr1		21 550	Chacon MEX
10-06	Jamaica	L 0-2	Miami	GCr1		18 057	Quesada CRC
13-06	Grenada	W 4-0	Harrison/NY	GCr1	Jose Del Aguila [16], Marco Pappa [22], Carlos Ruiz [54], Carlos Gallardo [59]	25 000	Toledo USA
18-06	Mexico	L 1-2	East Rutherford/NY	GCqf	Carlos Ruiz [5]	78 807	Campbell JAM
2-09	St Vincent/Grenadines	W 4-0	Guatemala City	WCq	Marco Pappa [15], Yony Flores [31], Mario Rodriguez [53], Freddy Garcia [71]	24 000	Andino HON
6-09	Belize	W 2-1	Belmopan	WCq	Gustavo Cabrera [4], Mynor Lopez [75]	3 027	Mejia SLV
7-10	St Vincent/Grenadines	W 3-0	Kingstown	WCq	Mario Rodriguez 2 [44 58], Dwight Pezzarossi [71]	3 000	Brea CUB
11-10	Belize	W 3-1	Guatemala City	WCq	Carlos Gallardo [8p], Mynor Lopez [65], Carlos Ruiz [78p]	21 107	Penaloza MEX
11-11	Grenada	W 3-0	Guatemala City	WCq	Freddy Garcia 2 [1 31], Angelo Padilla [45]	13 710	Brizan TRI
15-11	Grenada	W 4-1	St George's	WCq	Nicko Williams OG [67], Fredy Thompson [77], Guillermo Ramirez [84], Lyndon Joseph OG [90]	200	Angela ARU

Fr = Friendly match • UC = UNCAF Cup/Copa Centroamericana • GC = CONCACAF Gold Cup • WC = FIFA World Cup
q = qualifier • r1 = first round group • qf = quarter-final • sf = semi-final • 3p = third place play-off • 5p = 5th place play-off

GUATEMALA NATIONAL TEAM HISTORICAL RECORDS

Caps
104 - Guillermo Ramirez 1997- • **101** - Gustavo Cabrera 2001- • **92** - Carlos Ruiz 1998- • **87** - Juan Carlos Plata 1996-2010 • **85** - Fredy Thompson 2001- • **82** -Julio Giron 1992-2006 • **80** - Edgar Estrada 1995-2003 • **77** - Gonzalo Romero 2000- • **71** - Fredy Garcia 2000-08 • **69** - Erick Miranda 1991-2001 • **66** - Juan Manuel Funes 1985-2000 • **62** - Mario Rodriguez 2003- • **60** - Martin Machon 1992-2006

Goals
45 - Carlos Ruiz 1998- • **35** - Juan Carlos Plata 1996- • **23** - Fredy Garcia 1998- • **15** - Juan Manuel Funes 1985-2000

Past Coaches
Jimmy Elliott ENG 1935 • Manuel Felipe Carrera 1946 • Jose Alberto Cevasco ARG 1948 • Enrique Natalio Pascal Palomini ARG 1950 • Juan Aguirre 1953 • Alfredo Cuevas ARG 1955-57 • Jose Alberto Cevasco ARG 1960-61 • Afro Geronazzo ARG 1961 • Cesar Viccino ARG 1965 • Ruben Amorin URU 1967 • Cesar Viccino ARG 1968-69 • Lorenzo Ausina Tur ESP 1969 • Carmelo Faraone ARG 1971 • Afro Geronazzo ARG 1971-72 • Ruben Amorin URU 1972 • Nestor Valdez CHI 1972 • Ruben Amorin URU 1976 • Carlos Cavagnaro ARG 1976 • Carlos Wellman 1976 • Jose Ernesto Romero 1979 • Ruben Amorin URU 1980 • Carlos Cavagnaro ARG 1983 • Dragoslav Sekularac YUG 1984-85 • Julio Cesar Cortes URU 1987 • Jorge Roldan 1988 • Ruben Amorin URU 1989-90 • Haroldo Cordon 1991 • Miguel Angel Brindisi ARG 1992 • Jorge Roldan 1995 • Juan Ramon Veron ARG 1996 • Horacio Cordero ARG 1996 • Miguel Angel Brindisi ARG 1997-98 • Carlos Bilardo & Eduardo Lujan ARG 1998 • Benjamin Monterroso 1999 • Carlos Miloc URU 2000 • Julio Cesar Cortes URU 2000-03 • Victor Manuel Aguado MEX 2003 • Ramon Maradiaga HON 2004-05 • Hernan Dario Gomez COL 2006-08 • Ramon Maradiaga HON 2008 • Benjamin Monterroso 2008-09 • Ever Almeida PAR 2010-

GUATEMALA 2010–11

LIGA NACIONAL TORNEO CLAUSURA

	Pl	W	D	L	F	A	Pts	Municipal	Heredia	Com'ciones	Malacateco	Mictlán	Peñarol	Juventud	Xelajú	Marquense	USAC	Suc'péquez	Xinabajul
Municipal †	22	11	4	7	33	20	37		1-0	1-2	2-2	3-0	1-0	2-1	4-0	3-1	0-1	0-0	4-0
Deportivo Heredia †	22	11	4	7	32	19	37	1-0		2-0	2-0	1-1	3-1	0-0	5-0	2-1	1-1	1-0	2-0
Comunicaciones †	22	11	3	8	39	28	36	0-1	2-4		2-0	1-2	3-0	2-0	2-0	2-4	4-1	2-0	5-1
Malacateco †	22	11	3	8	32	25	36	1-0	2-0	1-3		3-1	4-1	1-0	3-0	2-1	1-0	2-1	3-0
Mictlán †	22	10	5	7	24	23	35	2-1	1-0	1-1	2-1		2-0	1-0	0-0	1-0	0-0	2-1	3-0
Peñarol La Mesilla †	22	10	3	9	35	36	33	2-1	4-1	3-1	2-2	2-0		1-1	1-0	3-1	4-1	2-1	2-0
Juventud Retalteca	22	9	3	10	25	21	30	0-1	1-4	1-2	0-1	2-1	2-1		4-0	3-0	2-0	1-0	3-1
Xelajú	22	8	6	8	25	34	30	3-0	1-0	2-2	1-0	3-0	1-0	0-2		2-2	2-2	3-2	1-1
Deportivo Marquense	22	8	5	9	28	30	29	1-1	0-2	1-1	1-0	0-2	2-3	1-0	2-2		2-0	3-0	1-0
USAC	22	6	8	8	22	23	26	1-1	2-1	0-1	2-0	1-1	5-0	0-2	1-0	0-1		0-0	4-0
Suchitepéquez	22	6	5	11	21	28	23	1-2	0-0	2-1	2-1	2-1	4-3	2-0	0-2	1-1	0-0		2-0
Xinabajul	22	4	5	13	11	40	17	1-4	1-0	1-0	2-2	1-0	0-0	0-0	1-2	0-2	0-0	1-0	

15/01/2011 - 24/04/2011 • † Qualified for the play-offs • Top two receive a bye to the semi-finals
USAC and Xinabajul were relegated with the worst record over the 2010-11 season

CLAUSURA 2010–11 PLAY-OFFS

Semi-finals   **Finals**
Comunicaciones *   2 0
Deportivo Heredia   0 1   **Comunicaciones** * †   3 3
Malacateco *   0 0   Municipal   0 0
Municipal   0 1   (finals 13-05-2011 & 15-05-2011)

Play-offs first round: Peñarol 0-1 0-7 **Comunicaciones**
Mictlán 2-1 0-2 **Malacateco**
† Qualified for the CONCACAF Champions League • * Home team in first leg • Top scorer: **7** - Oscar Isaula, Malacateco

APERTURA 2011–12 PLAY-OFFS

Semi-finals   **Finals**
Municipal *   3 0
Suchitepéquez   1 1   **Municipal** * †   2 2
Xelajú   0 2   Comunicaciones   0 0
Comunicaciones *   3 1   (finals 15-12-2011 & 18-12-2010)

Play-offs first round: Heredia 1-1 0-0 **Comunicaciones**
Municipal 2-0 0-0 Marquense
† Qualified for the CONCACAF Champions League • * Home team in first leg • Top scorers: **10** - Juan Valenzuela, Zacapa & Henry Hernandez COL, Heredia

MEDALS TABLE

		Overall			League			Cup		Cent Am		
		G	S	B	G	S	B	G	S	G	S	B
1	Deportivo Municipal	37	20	7	29	17	6	7	2	1	1	1
2	Comunicaciones	30	22	10	24	21	7	5		1	2	3
3	Aurora	10	9	6	8	8	5	2	1			1
4	Xelajú	6	6	2	5	4	1	1	2			1
5	Deportivo Jalapa	5	1		2			3	1			
6	Suchitepéquez	3	6	2	1	5	1	2	1			1
7	Tip Nac	3	1		3	1						
8	Cobán Imperial	1	6	2	1	3	2			3		
9	Juventud Retalteca	1	3	2		2	2	1	1			
10	IRCA	1		2				2	1			
11	Hospicio	1		1				1	1			
	Amatitlan	1		1				1	1			
13	Deportivo Marquense	3			3							
14	Universidad	1	4		1	4						
15	Antigua	1	1		1	1						

GUATEMALA 2011–12

LIGA NACIONAL TORNEO APERTURA

	Pl	W	D	L	F	A	Pts	Suc'péquez	Xelajú	Marquense	Com'ciones	Heredia	Municipal	Peñarol	Malacateco	Zacapa	Juventud	Mictlán	Petapa
Suchitepéquez †	22	14	1	7	34	21	43		1-0	2-0	1-0	1-0	2-1	1-0	4-1	2-0	2-0	3-0	2-1
Xelajú †	22	11	5	6	30	23	38	1-0		2-2	1-0	1-0	2-1	2-1	3-0	4-1	1-0	2-1	2-1
Deportivo Marquense †	22	9	9	4	31	20	36	1-0	2-2		1-0	3-1	0-3	3-1	1-1	4-0	1-0	4-0	3-0
Comunicaciones †	22	8	11	3	27	20	35	1-0	1-1	0-0		3-1	0-0	2-2	3-1	4-3	1-0	1-1	2-1
Deportivo Heredia †	22	10	5	7	35	30	35	1-0	1-0	3-2	2-2		3-1	2-1	2-0	2-0	1-1	5-1	1-0
Municipal †	22	8	10	4	37	22	34	0-1	1-1	0-0	1-1	3-1		2-0	5-0	2-0	4-2	2-1	3-0
Peñarol La Mesilla	22	8	7	7	36	31	31	6-2	3-1	0-0	0-1	2-0	2-2		3-1	2-1	2-0	2-1	2-1
Malacateco	22	4	10	8	29	42	22	2-2	2-2	2-0	1-1	2-2	3-3	2-2		1-1	3-1	0-0	2-1
Deportivo Zacapa	22	5	6	11	27	43	21	1-4	1-2	2-2	1-1	2-1	2-2	2-0	2-1		2-2	2-1	2-0
Juventud Retalteca	22	4	8	10	24	33	20	1-3	1-0	0-0	1-1	2-3	0-0	1-1	2-1	2-0		4-1	1-1
Mictlán	22	5	5	12	23	39	20	1-0	1-0	0-1	1-2	1-0	0-0	3-3	0-1	2-1	3-1		1-0
Deportivo Petapa	22	3	9	10	24	33	18	2-0	2-0	1-1	0-0	1-1	1-1	1-1	2-2	0-1	2-2	4-3	

10/07/2011 - 27/11/2011 • † Qualified for the play-offs • Top two receive a bye to the semi-finals

GUI – GUINEA

FIFA/COCA-COLA WORLD RANKING

'93	'94	'95	'96	'97	'98	'99	'00	'01	'02	'03	'04	'05	'06	'07	'08	'09	'10	'11	'12
63	66	63	73	65	79	91	80	108	120	101	86	79	23	33	39	73	46	80	

							2011									
	Jan	Feb	Mar	Apr	May	Jun	Jul	Aug	Sep	Oct	Nov	Dec		High	Low	Av
	46	46	45	62	62	66	68	69	76	75	79	80		22	123	72

Guinea showed glimpses of their enormous potential, unveiled a new pacey style to their play and equalled a long-standing record at the 2012 CAF Africa Cup of Nations finals in Gabon and Equatorial Guinea but still did not make it past the first round. 'Syli Nationale' were drawn in a tough group in Franceville, Gabon where they beat Botswana 6-1 to equal the record for the biggest winning margin in the tournament's history. But their opening group game loss to Mali - a match they dominated - cost them a place in the quarter-finals. They had to beat group favourites Ghana in their last game to have any chance to go through to the quarter-finals but ended the match down to 10 men and played out a 1-1 draw. Coach Michel Dussuyer could take much satisfaction from the performance of his young squad who will have high hopes for the FIFA World Cup qualifiers. Guinea had caused a major sensation in the qualifying competition when a goal from Ibrahima Traore deep in stoppage time in Abuja eliminated Nigeria from the finals and Traore is among an exciting group of players that also includes Mamadou Dioulde Bah, Sadio Diallo and Abdoul Razzagui Camara, the former French under-21 international. In club football, Horoya deposed defending champions Fello Star Labe by a single goal to win their first title for a decade.

CAF AFRICA CUP OF NATIONS RECORD

1957-1962 DNE 1963 Disqualified 1965-1968 DNQ 1970 6 r1 1972 DNQ 1974 5 r1 1976 2 r2 1978 DNQ 1980 7 r1 1982-1992 DNQ 1994 11 r1 1996 DNQ 1998 9 r1 2000 DNQ 2002 Disqualified 2004 7 QF 2006 6 QF 2008 8 QF 2010 DNQ 2012 9 r1

FEDERATION GUINEENNE DE FOOTBALL (FGF)

PO Box 3645, Conakry

☎ +224 20 455878
🖷 +224 20 455879
📧 guineefoot59@yahoo.fr
🌐 feguifoot.net
FA 1960 CON 1962 FIFA 1962
P Salifou Camara
GS Ibrahima Barry

FIFA BIG COUNT 2006

Total players	410 100
% of population	4.23%
Male	406 600
Female	3 500
Amateurs 18+	10 100
Youth under 18	8 000
Unregistered	90 000
Professionals	0
Referees	433
Admin & coaches	2 400
Number of clubs	150
Number of teams	700

MAJOR CITIES/TOWNS

		Population
1	Conakry	1 931 184
2	Guékédou	250 288
3	Nzérékoré	237 753
4	Kankan	207 390
5	Kindia	189 907
6	Boké	126 668
7	Kissidougou	125 303
8	Fria	119 722
9	Faranah	93 608
10	Macenta	92 569
11	Kamsar	90 341
12	Coyah	86 352
13	Mamou	78 615
14	Lola	67 815
15	Labé	59 110
16	Kérouane	38 224
17	Yomou	31 787
18	Siguiri	28 150

REPUBLIQUE DE GUINEE • REPUBLIC OF GUINEA

Capital	Conakry	Population	10 057 975 (81)	% in cities	34%
GDP per capita	$1100 (208)	Area km²	245 857 km² (78)	GMT +/-	0
Neighbours (km)	Cote d'Ivoire 610, Guinea-Bissau 386, Liberia 563, Mali 858, Senegal 330, Sierra Leone 652, Coast 320				

RECENT INTERNATIONAL MATCHES PLAYED BY GUINEA

2009	Opponents	Score	Venue	Comp	Scorers	Att	Referee
12-08	Egypt	D 3-3	Cairo	Fr	Souleymane Youla 2 [30] [40], Kaba Diawarra [48]		
5-09	Malawi	L 1-2	Blantyre	WCq	Oumar Kalabane [37]	15 000	Codjia BEN
11-10	Burkina Faso	L 1-2	Accra	WCq	Mamadou Bah [82]	5 000	Ambaya LBY
14-11	Côte d'Ivoire	L 0-3	Abidjan	WCq		28 000	Marange ZIM
2010							
11-08	Mali	W 2-0	Marignane	Fr	Kamil Zayatte [52], Kevin Constant [34]		
5-09	Ethiopia	W 4-1	Addis Abeba	CNq	Ibrahima Yattara [37], Oumar Kalabane [45], Karamoko Cisse [61], Kamil Zayatte [75]		Mnkantjo ZIM
10-10	Nigeria	W 1-0	Conakry	CNq	Kevin Constant [5]		El Ahrach MAR
17-11	Burkina Faso	L 1-2	Mantes-La-Ville	Fr	Karamoko Cisse [10]		
2011							
9-02	Senegal	L 0-3	Dakar	Fr			
27-03	Madagascar	D 1-1	Antananarivo	CNq	Mamadou Bah [80]		Mpanisi ZAM
5-06	Madagascar	W 4-1	Conakry	CNq	Oumar Kalabane [6], Ibrahima Bangoura [17], Abdoulaye Diallo [60], Dianbobo Balde [62]		
10-08	Gabon	D 1-1	St Leu la Foret	Fr	Sadio Diallo [77]		
4-09	Ethiopia	W 1-0	Conakry	CNq	Dianbobo Balde [33]		
6-09	Venezuela	L 1-2	Caracas	Fr	Ibrahima Camara [79p]	14 000	Gambetta PER
8-10	Nigeria	D 2-2	Abuja	CNq	Ibrahima Bangoura [63], Ibrahima Traore [102+]		
11-11	Senegal	L 1-4	Mantes La Ville	Fr	Pascal Feindouno [89p]		
15-11	Burkina Faso	D 1-1	Mantes La Ville	Fr	Ibrahima Conte [90]		
2012							
24-01	Mali	L 0-1	Franceville	CNr1		10 000	Jedidi TUN
28-01	Botswana	W 6-1	Franceville	CNr1	Abdoulaye Diallo 2 [16] [27], Abdoul Camara [41], Ibrahima Traore [45], Mamadou Bah [84], Naby Soumah [86]	4 000	El Ahrach MAR
1-02	Ghana	D 1-1	Franceville	CNr1	Abdoul Camara [45]	5 500	Bennett RSA

Fr = Friendly match • CN = CAF African Cup of Nations • AC = Amilcar Cabral Cup • WC = FIFA World Cup
q = qualifier • r1 = first round group • sf = semi-final • f = final • † = not a full international

GUINEA 2010 CHAMPIONNAT NATIONAL	Pl	W	D	L	F	A	Pts
Fello Star Labé	26	13	7	6	23	10	**46**
Atlético Coléah	26	11	9	6	27	15	**42**
Horoya AC Conakry	26	9	12	5	18	7	**39**
Hafia FC Conakry	26	10	9	7	18	16	**39**
ASFAG	26	11	6	9	18	19	**39**
Baraka Djoma	26	9	11	6	19	17	**38**
Baté Nafadji	26	9	7	10	17	17	**34**
Espoir Labé	26	9	6	11	18	24	**33**
Ashanti GB Siguiri	26	9	6	11	10	18	**33**
Etoile de Guinée	26	8	7	11	19	23	**31**
ASM Sangarédi	26	6	13	7	11	15	**31**
AS Kaloum Star	26	6	10	10	14	17	**28**
CI Kamsar	26	6	9	11	10	22	**27**
Satellite FC	26	5	10	11	18	19	**25**

18/12/2009 - 24/08/2010

GUINEA 2011 CHAMPIONNAT NATIONAL	Pl	W	D	L	F	A	Pts
Horoya AC Conakry †	22	13	5	4	35	17	**44**
Fello Star Labé	22	13	5	4	38	19	**44**
Atlético Coléah	22	11	2	9	25	23	**35**
Baraka Djoma	22	9	7	6	26	25	**34**
Ashanti GB Siguiri	22	8	8	6	18	16	**32**
ASFAG	22	7	9	6	19	17	**30**
Baté Nafadji	22	7	6	9	22	23	**27**
Espoir Labé	22	6	9	7	25	27	**27**
Hafia FC Conakry	22	7	6	9	18	21	**27**
Sankaran	22	5	10	7	16	17	**25**
Etoile de Guinée	22	5	6	11	17	36	**21**
Séquence	22	2	5	15	7	25	**11**

3/02/2011 - 28/08/2011
† Qualified for the CAF Champions League

COUPE NATIONALE 2011

Quarter-finals		Semi-finals		Final	
Séquence	1				
Fello Star Labé	0	**Séquence**	2		
AS Kaloum Star	1 6p	Atlético Coléah	0		
Atlético Coléah	1 7p			**Séquence** ‡	3
Santoba	2			Ashanti GB Siguiri	1
Baté Nafadji	1	Santoba	1 5p	Stade du Septembre 28, Conakry	
Noramba	0 5p	**Ashanti GB Siguiri**	1 6p	2-10-2011. Scorers - Naby Kéita [26],	
Ashanti GB Siguiri	0 6p	‡ Qualified for CAF Confederation Cup		François Tinkiano [34p], Athanas Tinkiano [75]; Malick Youla [82]	

GUM – GUAM

FIFA/COCA-COLA WORLD RANKING

'93	'94	'95	'96	'97	'98	'99	'00	'01	'02	'03	'04	'05	'06	'07	'08	'09	'10	'11	'12
-	-	-	188	191	198	200	200	199	199	200	201	2005	204	198	201	201	184	188	192

	2011												High	Low	Av
	Jan	Feb	Mar	Apr	May	Jun	Jul	Aug	Sep	Oct	Nov	Dec	High	Low	Av
	188	188	188	194	195	195	195	197	186	187	189	192	182	205	197

The Guam national team found itself at the centre of controversy when they entered a team for the 2011 Pacific Games in Noumea. Their presence meant that the tournament could not be used as part of the OFC qualifiers for the 2014 FIFA World Cup in Brazil as Guam are members of the Asian Football Confederation and not the Oceania body. Ironically Guam had decided not to enter the World Cup qualifiers in their own confederation, which given the heavy defeats inflicted by the Solomon Islands and New Caledonia in the Pacific Games may have been a wise decision. There was, however, a victory to celebrate in the tournament - a 2-0 win over American Samoa, and that was followed by a 1-1 draw with Tuvalu as Guam finished fifth out of the six teams in their group. At home, club football was dominated by Cars Plus Football Club who won the curtailed 2011 championship with a 100 per cent record in the 10 games played. They also won a short tournament played in the autumn before the 2011-12 championship kicked off in October, beating Guam Shipyard 4-1 in the final, but they fell just short of a clean sweep of trophies when they narrowly failed to land the 2011 Beck's GFA Cup. In the final they lost 2-1 to Quality Distributors who won the trophy for the third time in the four year history of the tournament.

FIFA WORLD CUP RECORD
1930-1998 DNE 2002 DNQ 2006-2014 DNE

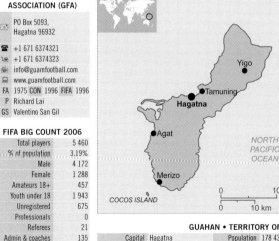

GUAM FOOTBALL ASSOCIATION (GFA)

PO Box 5093,
Hagatna 96932

☎ +1 671 6374321
📠 +1 671 6374323
📧 info@guamfootball.com
🌐 www.guamfootball.com
FA 1975 CON 1996 FIFA 1996
P Richard Lai
GS Valentino San Gil

FIFA BIG COUNT 2006

Total players	5 460
% of population	3.19%
Male	4 172
Female	1 288
Amateurs 18+	457
Youth under 18	1 943
Unregistered	675
Professionals	0
Referees	21
Admin & coaches	135
Number of clubs	13
Number of teams	195

MAJOR CITIES/TOWNS

		Population
1	Tamuning	11 809
2	Yigo	10 533
3	Mangilao	10 071
4	Astumbo	6 536
5	Ordot	4 968
6	Barrigada	4 957
7	Agat	4 780
8	Anderson Air Force Base	4 556
9	Mongmong	4 229
10	Agana Heights	3 953
11	Dededo	3 487
12	Talofofo	3 180
13	Chalan Pago	2 977
14	Morbo Annex	2 344
15	Yona	2 330
16	Apra Harbor	2 265
17	Sinajana	2 123
18	Finegayan Station	1 957

GUAHAN • TERRITORY OF GUAM

Capital	Hagatna	Population 178 430 (187)	% in cities 93%
GDP per capita	$15 000 (74)	Area km² 544 km² (195)	GMT +/- +10
Neighbours (km)	Coast 125		

RECENT INTERNATIONAL MATCHES PLAYED BY GUAM

2007	Opponents		Score	Venue	Comp	Scorers	Att	Referee
17-06	Chinese Taipei	L	0-10	Macau	EACq		10	Wan Daxue CHN
21-06	Hong Kong	L	1-15	Macau	EACq	Mendiola [33]	300	Matsuo JPN
23-06	Mongolia	L	2-5	Macau	EACq	Pangelinan [2], Mendiola [8]	100	Wan Daxue CHN
2008								
2-04	Sri Lanka	L	1-5	Taipei	CCq	Mendiola [62]	300	Kovalenko UZB
4-04	Chinese Taipei	L	1-4	Taipei	CCq	Pangelinan [17]	850	Win Cho MYA
6-04	Pakistan	L	2-9	Taipei	CCq	Pangelinan [74], Iltaf OG [80]	200	Auda Lazim IRQ
2009								
11-03	Mongolia	W	1-0	Manenggon Hills	EACq	Mendiola [9]		Kim Jong Hyeuk KOR
13-03	Northern Marianas †	W	2-1	Manenggon Hills	EACq	Borja [10], Mariano [68]		Cheng Oi Cho HKG
15-03	Macao	D	2-2	Manenggon Hills	EACq	Borja [36], Cunliffe [90]		Kim Jong Hyeuk KOR
23-08	Korea DPR	L	2-9	Kaohsiung	EACq	Borja [1], Cunliffe [20]	2 000	Matsuo JPN
25-08	Chinese Taipei	L	2-4	Kaohsiung	EACq	Borja 2 [5 26]	7 500	Matsuo JPN
27-08	Hong Kong	L	0-12	Kaohsiung	EACq		1 500	Tojo JPN
2010								
No international matches played in 2010								
2011								
27-08	Solomon Islands	L	0-7	Noumea	PGr1			Varman FIJ
30-08	New Caledonia	L	0-9	Noumea	PGr1			Zitouni TAH
1-09	American Samoa	W	2-0	Noumea	PGr1	Napitu [49], Merfalen [70]		George VAN
3-09	Vanuatu	L	1-4	Noumea	PGr1	Cunliffe [14]		Kerr NZL
5-09	Tuvalu †	D	1-1	Noumea	PGr1	Cunliffe [18p]		Zitouni TAH

EAC = East Asian Championship • AC = AFC Asian Cup • CC = AFC Challenge Cup
q = qualifier • r1 = first round group • † Not an official international

GUAM 2010–11

BUDWEISER SOCCER LEAGUE DIVISION ONE	Pl	W	D	L	F	A	Pts	Car Plus	Quality Distributors	Fuji-Ichiban	Guam Shipyard	Strykers	Carpet Masters
Cars Plus	10	10	0	0	55	6	30		1-0	4-1	5-1	9-2	5-1
Quality Distributors	10	6	1	3	40	20	19	0-3		1-1	3-2	4-5	8-0
Fuji-Ichiban Espada	10	6	1	3	36	17	19	1-2	1-2		6-2	6-1	10-1
Guam Shipyard	10	2	1	7	15	38	7	0-8	1-7	1-4		1-1	4-2
Ben Moore Strykers	10	2	1	7	22	45	7	0-9	3-6	1-2	0-2		8-1
Carpet Masters	10	2	0	8	17	59	6	0-9	3-9	2-4	2-1	5-1	

27/02/2011 - 1/05/2011
Top scorers: 15 - Elias Merfalen, Cars Plus • 14 - Scott Spindel, Quality Distributors • 13 - Kyle Burry, Benjamin Moore Strykers

BECK'S GFA CUP 2011

First round		Quarter–finals		Semi–finals		Final	
Quality Distributors	8						
Han Ma Um	0	Quality Distributors	11				
Big Blue 2	2	Strykers	1				
Strykers	3			Quality Distributors	4		
Sinajana Ambassadors	3			MDA Cobras	1		
Fuji-Ichiban Espada	2	Sinajana Ambassadors	3				
Ben Moore Strykers	3	MDA Cobras	7				
MDA Cobras	4					Quality Distributors	2
Guam Shipyard	16					Cars Plus	1
Doosan FC	0	Guam Shipyard	5				
Guahan ICRC	1	Rovers FC	1			CUP FINAL	
Rovers FC	5			Guam Shipyard	4 1p		
Sidekicks	13			Cars Plus	4 3p	GFA Field, Harmon	
Samurai Strykers	1	Sidekicks	0			15-06-2011	
United FC	0	Cars Plus	8			Scorers - Scott Spindel 2 for Quality	
Cars Plus	13					Distributors; OG for Cars Plus	

3rd Place: MDA Cobras beat Guam Shipyard

GUY – GUYANA

FIFA/COCA-COLA WORLD RANKING

'93	'94	'95	'96	'97	'98	'99	'00	'01	'02	'03	'04	'05	'06	'07	'08	'09	'10	'11	'12
136	154	162	153	168	161	171	183	178	169	182	182	167	100	128	131	127	109	91	

						2011								High	Low	Av
Jan	Feb	Mar	Apr	May	Jun	Jul	Aug	Sep	Oct	Nov	Dec			High	Low	Av
111	112	109	110	110	116	114	114	116	97	97	91			86	185	149

The Guyana national team got off to a flying start in the 2014 FIFA World Cup qualifiers, sensationally winning their group ahead of favourites Trinidad and Tobago to qualify for the next round. The Guyanese won four of their first five matches including a shock 2-1 win over Trinidad in Georgetown in the penultimate group game. However, they were then drawn in a difficult group in the next round containing Mexico, Costa Rica and El Salvador. When the Guyana Football Federation introduced the GFF Super League for clubs in 2009, it was hoped that the competition would give a better structure to football in the country which until then had been based around cup competitions and local tournaments, but after two seasons the Super League failed to make an appearance in 2011. Of the major cup tournaments played, the usually pre-eminent Kashif and Shanghai Cup was undermined by a lack of clubs from Georgetown and by the fact that it was won by Trinidad's Caledonia AIA. A tournament largely made up of clubs from the capital - the Banks Beer Knockout Cup - was staged at the same time, with the final also played on New Year's Day. It was won by the 2010 GFF Super League champions Alpha United. In the final they beat the unfortunate Fruta Conquerors - their third defeat in a final over the course of the year.

FIFA WORLD CUP RECORD
1930-1974 DNE 1978-1998 DNQ 2002 DNE 2006-2010 DNQ

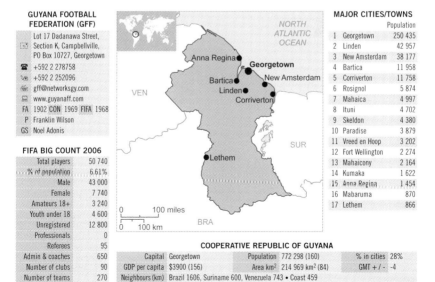

GUYANA FOOTBALL FEDERATION (GFF)

Lot 17 Dadanawa Street, Section K, Campbellville, PO Box 10727, Georgetown

☎ +592 2 278758
📠 +592 2 252096
✉ gff@networksgy.com
🖥 www.guyanaff.com
FA 1902 CON 1969 FIFA 1968
P Franklin Wilson
GS Noel Adonis

FIFA BIG COUNT 2006

Total players	50 740
% of population	6.61%
Male	43 000
Female	7 740
Amateurs 18+	3 240
Youth under 18	4 600
Unregistered	12 800
Professionals	0
Referees	95
Admin & coaches	650
Number of clubs	90
Number of teams	270

MAJOR CITIES/TOWNS

		Population
1	Georgetown	250 435
2	Linden	42 957
3	New Amsterdam	38 177
4	Bartica	11 958
5	Corriverton	11 758
6	Rosignol	5 874
7	Mahaica	4 997
8	Ituni	4 702
9	Skeldon	4 380
10	Paradise	3 879
11	Vreed en Hoop	3 202
12	Fort Wellington	2 274
13	Mahaicony	2 164
14	Kumaka	1 622
15	Anna Regina	1 454
16	Mabaruma	870
17	Lethem	866

COOPERATIVE REPUBLIC OF GUYANA

Capital	Georgetown	Population	772 298 (160)	% in cities	28%
GDP per capita	$3900 (156)	Area km²	214 969 km² (84)	GMT +/-	-4
Neighbours (km)	Brazil 1606, Suriname 600, Venezuela 743 • Coast 459				

RECENT INTERNATIONAL MATCHES PLAYED BY GUYANA

2008	Opponents	Score		Venue	Comp	Scorers	Att	Referee
8-08	Dominica	W	3-0	Georgetown	CCq	Codrington 2 [20 43], Edmonds [36]	3 000	Forde BRB
10-08	Surinam	D	1-1	Georgetown	CCq	Peters [90]	10 000	Forde BRB
3-09	Trinidad and Tobago	L	0-3	Port of Spain	Fr		1 000	Brizan TRI
21-09	Antigua and Barbuda	L	0-3	St John's	Fr		3 500	Willett ATG
5-11	St Kitts and Nevis	D	1-1	Macoya	CCq	Richardson [35]	750	Cambridge VIN
7-11	Antigua and Barbuda	L	1-2	Macoya	CCq	Jerome [45]	500	Minyetty DOM
9-11	Trinidad and Tobago	D	1-1	Macoya	CCq	Richardson [58p]	1 000	Minyetty DOM
2009								
3-06	Antigua and Barbuda	L	1-2	Paramaribo	Fr	Parks [34]	1 700	Wijngaarde SUR
28-10	Surinam	W	1-0	Paramaribo	Fr	Millington [66]	2 000	Jauregui ANT
30-10	Netherlands Antilles	W	1-0	Paramaribo	Fr	Millington [29]	500	Pinas SUR
1-11	French Guiana †	W	1-0	Paramaribo	Fr	Archer [57]	1 000	Wijngaarde SUR
2010								
26-09	Trinidad and Tobago	D	1-1	Providence	Fr	Dwight Peters [43]	9 000	Lancaster GUY
13-10	St Lucia	W	1-0	Paramaribo	CCq	Christopher Bourne [10]	550	Davis TRI
15-10	Netherlands Antilles	W	3-2	Paramaribo	CCq	Dwight Peters [15], Anthony Abrams [45], Walter Moore [58]	750	Matthew SKN
17-10	Suriname	W	2-0	Paramaribo	CCq	Walter Moore [18p], Devon Millington [90]	2 800	Davis TRI
2-11	Haiti	D	0-0	Marabella	CCq		880	Taylor BRB
4-11	Trinidad and Tobago	L	1-2	Port of Spain	CCq	Shawn Beveney [78]	1 100	Legister JAM
6-11	St Vincent/Grenadines	W	2-0	Port of Spain	CCq	Devon Millington [57], Sean Cameron [81]	850	Taylor BRB
17-11	Guatemala	L	0-3	Kennesaw	Fr		4 124	Okulaja USA
27-11	Guadeloupe	D	1-1	Riviere-Pilote	CCr1	Dwain Jacobs [86]	2 500	Davis TRI
29-11	Antigua and Barbuda	L	0-1	Riviere-Pilote	CCr1		3 000	Wijngaarde SUR
1-12	Jamaica	L	0-4	Riviere-Pilote	CCr1		3 000	Cruz CRC
2011								
20-05	Barbados	W	1-0	Linden	Fr	Chris Bourne [86]	300	Lancaster GUY
22-05	Barbados	W	3-2	Georgetown	Fr	Rishawn Sandiford [28], Colin Nelson [61p], Anani Mohamed [69]	2 500	Young GUY
29-05	Barbados	D	1-1	Bridgetown	Fr	OG [76]	2 055	Taylor BRB
24-08	India	W	2-1	Georgetown	Fr	Vurlon Mills [19], Walter Moore [62]	2 500	Lancaster GUY
2-09	Barbados	W	2-0	Georgetown	WCq	Shawn Beveney [26], Charles Pollard [73]	4 500	St Catherine LCA
6-09	Bermuda	W	2-1	Georgetown	WCq	Vurlon Mills 2 [50 60]	3 500	Geiger USA
7-10	Barbados	W	2-0	Bridgetown	WCq	Anthony Abrams [73], Chris Nurse [87]	2 500	Georges HAI
11-10	Bermuda	D	1-1	Prospect	WCq	Ricky Shakes [81]	2 573	Angela ARU
11-11	Trinidad and Tobago	W	2-1	Georgetown	WCq	Ricky Shakes [10], Leon Cort [81]	18 000	Wijngaarde SUR
15-11	Trinidad and Tobago	L	0-2	Port of Spain	WCq		2 000	Mejia SLV

Fr = Friendly match • CC = Digicel Caribbean Cup • WC = FIFA World Cup • q = qualifier • † Not a full international

MAYOR'S CUP 2011

First round		Quarter–finals		Semi–finals		Final	
Camptown	1						
Bakewell Buxton	0	Camptown	1				
Beacon		Western Tigers	0				
Western Tigers				Camptown	2		
Santos				Alpha United	0		
Victoria Kings		Santos					
BV/Triumph United	0	Alpha United					
Alpha United	8					Camptown	2
Pele	5					Fruta Conquerors	0
Seawall	1	Pele					
Den Amstel	2	Riddim Squad				CUP FINAL	
Riddim Squad	3			Pele	1		
Guyana Defence Force	6			Fruta Conquerors	2	21-04-2011	
Monedderlust	0	Guyana Defence Force	1			Scorer - Peter Parks [12], Devon	
New Amsterdam Utd	0	Fruta Conquerors	2			Forde [88] for Camptown	
Fruta Conquerors	1			Third place: Pele 1-0 Alpha United			

BANKS BEER KNOCKOUT CUP 2011–12

First round		Quarter–finals		Semi–finals		Final	
Alpha United	11						
Charlestown United	0	Alpha United	2				
University of Guyana	1	Riddim Squad	0				
Riddim Squad	3			Alpha United	2		
GFC	2			Camptown	0		
Houston Stars	0	GFC	0				
Northern Rangers	0	Camptown	1				
Camptown	2					Alpha United	1
Beacon	5					Fruta Conquerors	0
Flamingo	1	Beacon	6				
Guyana Defence Force		Black Pearl	1			CUP FINAL	
Black Pearl	w-0			Beacon	1		
Santos	4			Fruta Conquerors	2	1-01-2012	
Banks DIH All Stars	2	Santos	1 2p			Scorer - Andrew Murray 80 for Alpha United	
Police	0	Fruta Conquerors	1 4p				
Fruta Conquerors	2			Third place: Beacon 3-0 Camptown			

WESTERN TIGERS SUPER 8 CUP 2011

Quarter-finals		Semi-finals		Final	
Pele	0 p				
Santos	0 p	Pele	5		
GFC	0	Western Tigers	0		
Western Tigers	3			Pele	1
Guyana Defence Force	2 4p			Fruta Conquerors	0
Camptown	2 2p	Guyana Defence Force	2		
Riddim Squad	1	Fruta Conquerors	5	30-01-2011	
Fruta Conquerors	3	3rd Place: GDF 3-0 Western Tigers			

KASHIF & SHANGHAI CUP 2011–12

First round		Quarter–finals		Semi–finals		Final	
Caledonia AIA (TRI)	10						
New Amsterdam Utd	1	Caledonia AIA	3				
Grove Hi-Tec	2	Victoria Kings	1				
Victoria Kings	3			Caledonia AIA	3		
Caribbean Utd (BRB)	2			Milerock	1		
Winners Connection	0	Caribbean Utd	0				
Seawall	0	Milerock	2				
Milerock	2					Caledonia AIA	2
Amelia's Ward	2 4p					Pele	0
Western Tigers	2 3p	Amelia's Ward	3				
BV/Triumph United	0	Buxton Stars	0			CUP FINAL	
Buxton Stars	1			Amelia's Ward	1		
Mill Ballers	1 3p			Pele	3	1-01-2012	
Rosignol United	1 0p	Mill Ballers	1			Scorers - Devon Jorsling 74, Jamaal Gay 83 for Caledonia AIA	
Timehri Panthers	0	Pele	3				
Pele	10			Third place: Milerock 2-0 Amelia's Ward			

Preliminary Round: **Buxton Stars** 2-1 Den Amstel • **Seawall** 2-1 Topp XX • **Grove Hi-Tec** 1-1 5-3p Netrockers • **Mill Ballers** 2-1 Kuru Kuru Warriors

HAI – HAITI

FIFA/COCA-COLA WORLD RANKING

'93	'94	'95	'96	'97	'98	'99	'00	'01	'02	'03	'04	'05	'06	'07	'08	'09	'10	'11	'12
145	132	153	114	125	109	99	84	82	72	96	95	98	102	69	102	90	90	81	

2011												High	Low	Av
Jan	Feb	Mar	Apr	May	Jun	Jul	Aug	Sep	Oct	Nov	Dec	High	Low	Av
90	96	99	98	96	89	117	116	108	107	78	81	66	155	103

Haiti started their qualifying campaign for the 2014 FIFA World Cup in Brazil in blistering style, scoring 17 goals in their opening three games in a group they were favourites to win. In their fourth game, however, against Curacao in Willemstad, they could only draw 2-2 and they proved to be two crucial points lost as they fought Antigua and Barbuda for a place in the next round. With the two meeting each other in the final two matches, Haiti needed to get something out of the first of those games in Antigua but they lost 1-0 in St John's and their quest for a first appearance in the finals since 1974 was over. Given the problems still facing the country in the aftermath of the earthquake in 2010, football has been a healthy diversion for much of the country but this was one good-news story that didn't materialise. It has been remarkable how quickly the clubs have got back into the swing of league competion and over the course of 17 months four league campaigns were organised to make up for lost time. Victory, from the capital Port au Prince, followed up their 2010 Cup triumph by winning the second of the four tournaments but all the others were won by teams from St Marc - Tempete winning two and Baltimore the other. There was no cup played in 2011 but Aigle Noir won a short knockout competition for the top eight teams from the 2010-11 season.

FIFA WORLD CUP RECORD

1930 DNE 1934 DNQ 1938-1950 DNE 1954 DNQ 1958-1966 DNE 1970 DNQ **1974** 15 r1 1978-1986 DNQ 1990 DNE 1994-2014 DNQ

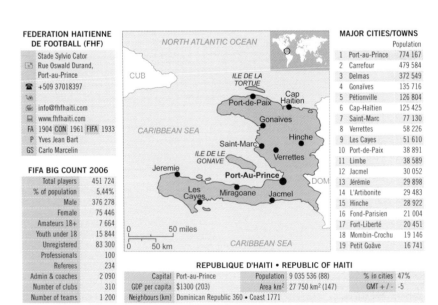

FEDERATION HAITIENNE DE FOOTBALL (FHF)

	Stade Sylvio Cator
	Rue Oswald Durand, Port-au-Prince
☎	+509 37018397
✉	info@fhfhaiti.com
	www.fhfhaiti.com
FA	1904 CON 1961 FIFA 1933
P	Yves Jean Bart
GS	Carlo Marcelin

FIFA BIG COUNT 2006

Total players	451 724
% of population	5.44%
Male	376 278
Female	75 446
Amateurs 18+	7 664
Youth under 18	15 844
Unregistered	83 300
Professionals	100
Referees	234
Admin & coaches	2 090
Number of clubs	310
Number of teams	1 200

NORTH ATLANTIC OCEAN
CUB
ILE DE LA TORTUE
Port-de-Paix   Cap Haïtien
Gonaives
CARIBBEAN SEA
Hinche
Saint-Marc
ILE DE LE GONAVE
Verrettes
Jeremie
Port-Au-Prince
DOM
Les Cayes   Miragoane   Jacmel
0   50 miles
0   50 km
CARIBBEAN SEA

MAJOR CITIES/TOWNS

Population

1	Port-au-Prince	774 167
2	Carrefour	479 584
3	Delmas	372 549
4	Gonaïves	135 716
5	Pétionville	126 804
6	Cap-Haïtien	125 425
7	Saint-Marc	77 130
8	Verrettes	58 226
9	Les Cayes	51 610
10	Port-de-Paix	38 891
11	Limbe	38 589
12	Jacmel	30 052
13	Jérémie	29 898
14	L'Artibonite	29 483
15	Hinche	28 922
16	Fond-Parisien	21 004
17	Fort-Liberté	20 451
18	Mombin-Crochu	19 146
19	Petit Goâve	16 741

REPUBLIQUE D'HAITI • REPUBLIC OF HAITI

Capital	Port-au-Prince	Population	9 035 536 (88)	% in cities	47%
GDP per capita	$1300 (203)	Area km²	27 750 km² (147)	GMT + / -	-5
Neighbours (km)	Dominican Republic 360 • Coast 1771				

RECENT INTERNATIONAL MATCHES PLAYED BY HAITI

2009	Opponents	Score		Venue	Comp	Scorers	Att	Referee
17-01	Guatemala	L	0-1	Fort Pierce	Fr		5 000	Jurisvic USA
11-02	Colombia	L	0-2	Pereira	Fr		20 000	Ruiz COL
31-03	Panama	L	0-4	La Chorrera	Fr		4 500	Amaya PAN
23-05	Jamaica	D	2-2	Fort Lauderdale	Fr	Jean Jerome [39], Leonel Saint-Preux [66]	12 000	Marrufo USA
19-06	Panama	D	1-1	Port-au-Prince	Fr	Philbert Merceus [74]	2 000	Grant HAI
27-06	Syria	L	1-2	Montreal	Fr	Leonel Saint-Preux [29]	4 649	Petrescu CAN
4-07	Honduras	L	0-1	Seattle	GCr1		15 387	Rodriguez MEX
8-07	Grenada	W	2-0	Washington DC	GCr1	Fabrice Noel [13], James Marcelin [79]	26 079	Moreno PAN
11-07	USA	D	2-2	Foxboro	GCr1	Vaniel Sirin [46], Mones Cherry [48]	24 137	Quesada CRC
19-07	Mexico	L	0-4	Dallas	GCqf		85 000	Campbell JAM
2010								
5-05	Argentina	L	0-4	Cutral Co	Fr		16 500	Osses CHI
2-11	Guyana	D	0-0	Marabella	CCq		880	Taylor BRB
4-11	St Vincent/Grenadines	W	3-1	Port of Spain	CCq	Sony Norde [45], Leonel Saint-Preux [62], Ricardo Charles [83]	1 100	Campbell JAM
6-11	Trinidad and Tobago	L	0-4	Port of Spain	CCq		850	Campbell JAM
18-11	Qatar	W	1-0	Doha	Fr	Jean Monuma [53]	5 000	Al Awaji KSA
2011								
9-02	El Salvador	L	0-1	San Salvador	Fr		15 000	Espana GUA
2-09	US Virgin Islands	W	6-0	Port au Prince	WCq	James Marcelin [18], Jean Maurice [27], Pierre Listner [44], Jean Monuma [61], Jean Alexandre 2 [65 78]	12 000	Cruz CRC
6-09	Curacao	W	4-2	Willemstad	WCq	Kevin Lafrance [37], James Marcelin [58], Wilde Guerrier [61], Angelo Zimmerman OG [75]	5 000	Solis CRC
7-10	US Virgin Islands	W	7-0	Frederiksted	WCq	Jean Maurice 3 [5 66 82p], Kim Jaggy [11], Kervens Belfort 2 [57 74p], Reginal Goreux [64]	406	Holder CAY
11-10	Curacao	D	2-2	Port au Prince	WCq	Jean Maurice [25p], Kervens Belfort [60]	7 800	Clarke LCA
11-11	Antigua and Barbuda	L	0-1	St John's	WCq		8 000	Pineda HON
15-11	Antigua and Barbuda	W	2-1	Port au Prince	WCq	Judelin Aveska 60, Kervens Belfort [67]	3 000	Toledo USA

Fr = Friendly match • CC = Digicel Caribbean Cup • GC = CONCACAF Gold Cup • WC = FIFA World Cup
q = qualifier • r1 = first round group stage • sf = semi-final • f = final • † Not a full international

HAITI NATIONAL TEAM HISTORICAL RECORDS

Past Coaches: Ernst Nono Baptiste 1999 • Emmanuel Sanon 1999-2000 • Jorge Castelli ARG 2001-02 • Andres Cruciani ARG 2002-03 • Fernando Clavijo USA 2003-05 • Luis Armelio Garcia CUB 2006-07 • Wagneau Eloi 2008 • Jairo Rios Rendon COL 2009-10 • Edson Tavares BRA 2010-

HAITI 2010–11

CHAMPIONNAT CLOTURE	Pl	W	D	L	F	A	Pts	Victory	America	Carrefour	Baltimore	Saint-Louis	Cavaly	Tempête	Mirebalais	Capoise	Don Bosco	Racing	Violette	Aigle Noir	Eclair	Racing Club	Dynamite
Victory SC †	15	8	3	4	22	13	27		3-1	0-0			1-0				2-2		1-0	1-2	4-0	
America Cayes	15	8	3	4	22	10	27			4-0			0-0		1-0	3-0			3-0			3-0
AS Carrefour	15	6	7	2	17	12	25				1-1	3-1	0-0	2-1	1-1	1-0					1-0	4-0
Baltimore St Marc	15	6	6	3	14	9	24	0-1	0-0			1-0	1-0		0-0		0-0			2-0	3-1	
AS Saint-Louis	15	6	5	4	14	13	23	1-0	2-1							0-0		2-2		0-0	0-0	1-0	3-0
Cavaly Léogâne	15	5	7	3	11	5	22					0-1			0-0	2-0	0-0	2-0				0-0	2-1
Tempête St Marc	15	5	7	3	16	13	22	4-2	2-2		0-0	1-0	1-1		1-0	1-0			1-0				
AS Mirebalais	15	5	6	4	13	11	21	3 0				0-0						1-1	1-1	1-0	1-0	3-1	
AS Capoise	15	5	5	5	13	17	20	0-0			1-0				2-1			2-0	1-1	2-1	1-1		
Don Bosco	15	4	8	3	17	10	20		0-1	1-1		4-0			2-2	3-0	1-2				1-1		
Racing Gônaïves	15	5	5	5	12	15	20	0-1	1-0	0-1	1-1			1-0			0-0			1-1	3-2	1-0
Violette AC	15	5	3	7	17	19	18		0-2	2-2	1-2	1-3	0-2				1-0	2-0		2-0	2-1	
Aigle Noir	15	4	4	7	7	17	16			0-0			0-2	0-0			0-0	0-1	2-1		1-0	1-0	
Eclair Gônaïves	15	4	4	7	12	18	16		0-1	1-0			0-0	2-1			0-2						4-0
Racing Club Haïtien	15	4	3	8	15	19	15	0-3	2-0		2-1			0-0		4-1					1-2		1-0
Dynamite St Marc	15	1	2	12	9	30	5	0-3			1-2			1-1	0-1	1-1	0-1		1-3	4-0			

22//10/2010 - 30/01/2011 • Matches in bold awarded • Don Bosco, Eclair, Violette and Dynamite relegated • † Qualified for the CFU Club Championship

SUPER HUIT 2011

Quarter-finals		Semi-finals		Final	
Aigle Noir	0 9p				
America Cayes	0 9p	**Aigle Noir** ‡	2 5p		
Victory FC	1	AS Capoise	2 5p		
AS Capoise	2			**Aigle Noir**	2
Baltimore St Marc	1			AS Mirebalais	0
AS Carrefour	0	Baltimore St Marc	0 2p	20-02-2011	
Tempête St Marc	0 7p	**AS Mirebalais**	0 4p		
AS Mirebalais	0 8p	‡ Won on lots			

Played between the eight teams with the best overall record from the 2010-11 Ouverture and Cloture
Trophée des Champions: **Tempête St Marc** 2-0 Victory FC (played between the Ouverture and Cloture winners)

HAITI 2011

CHAMPIONNAT OUVERTURE

	Pl	W	D	L	F	A	Pts	Baltimore	Victory	Capoise	America	Aigle Noir	Mirebalais	Saint-Louis	Tempête	Cavaly	Valencia	FICA	Racing	Carrefour	Racing Club	Triomphe
Baltimore St Marc †	14	8	6	0	14	2	30		3-0	0-0				1-0		1-0	2-0	1-0	1-0		0-0	
Victory SC	14	8	3	3	16	6	27	0-2		2-0	3-0	0-1	0-0		3-1							
AS Capoise	14	8	1	5	13	11	25								1-0	0-0	1-0	2-0	1-0	2-0		1-0
America Cayes	14	6	4	4	18	12	22			0-1		3-2	1-0		1-0		5-2				2-0	4-0
Aigle Noir	14	5	4	5	10	11	19	0-0			2-1				0-1		0-0	1-1	1-0			2-0
AS Mirebalais	14	5	3	6	8	10	18	0-0		1-0				1-0	2-1	1-0				2-0	0-0	
AS Saint-Louis	14	5	3	6	9	10	18	0-1		1-0					1-0	0-0					1-0	3-0
Tempête St Marc	14	4	6	4	18	12	18	1-1						3-0		1-1	1-1	3-2	3-0			4-0
Cavaly Léogâne	14	3	8	3	9	7	17					0-0	1-1	0-1	3-1					2-0	0-0	1-0
Valencia Léogâne	14	4	5	5	11	12	17			0-1			0-0	2-0	**3-0**	0-0			1-0	2-0		
FICA	14	4	5	5	10	10	17	1-2			1-0				1-0	1-1	1-1			2-0		1-0
Racing Gônaïves	14	4	5	5	9	18	17			1-0	2-1	1-1	0-0				0-0	0-0			1-0	3-0
AS Carrefour	14	3	6	5	11	10	15			0-0				0-0		0-0			7-0			1-0
Racing Club Haïtien	14	3	4	7	6	12	13		0-1	1-2			1-0	1-0		1-1		0-0	0-0			
Triomphe Liancourt	14	3	1	10	4	23	10	0-1		0-3					1-0	1-0		1-0		1-2	0-2	

1/05/2011 - 12/08/2011 • † Qualified for the CFU Club Championship • Matches in bold awarded • Triomphe and Racing Gônaïves relegated

HAITI 2011

CHAMPIONNAT CLOTURE

	Pl	W	D	L	F	A	Pts	Tempête	Victory	Cavaly	Baltimore	Racing Club	FICA	Valencia	Aigle Noir	Carrefour	Saint-Louis	Capoise	America	Mirebalais	Triomphe	Racing
Tempête St Marc †	14	9	4	1	20	7	31		1-1			2-1					2-0	1-0	1-1	2-0	2-1	
Victory SC	14	6	6	2	15	6	24						1-1	1-1	1-0		2-1	2-0			3-0	3-0
Cavaly Léogâne	14	6	4	4	9	9	22	0-1	0-0		1-0		1-0	1-0				1-0	0-0			
St Marc	14	6	4	4	12	9	22	0-1	0-0							1-0	1-0			1-1	2-0	
Racing Club Haïtien	14	5	6	3	20	13	21			1-1	3-2					2-2	3-0	1-1			2-0	5-1
FICA	14	5	5	4	10	6	20	1-1						0-1	1-0	1-0		0-0				2-0
Valencia Léogâne	14	5	5	4	11	6	20	1-0							1-0	0-0	0-1				3-0	3-0
Aigle Noir	14	6	2	6	7	9	20	0-4	1-0	0-1			2-0			0-0			0-0	1-0		
AS Carrefour	14	4	5	5	12	13	17					2-1			0-3		1-2	1-0	2-0		0-0	3-0
AS Saint-Louis	14	5	2	7	8	13	17						1-2		0-0	0-0		1-0		1-0	2-0	1-0
AS Capoise	14	3	8	3	8	6	17				0-0		0-0		0-1		0-1		1-0	2-0		2-0
America Cayes	14	4	4	6	16	11	16	1-0			0-1	0-1	0-0			0-0	2-1					10-1
AS Mirebalais	14	3	6	5	8	9	15			0-1	0-0		0-0		1-0	1-1		1-0			3-0	
Triomphe Liancourt	14	2	4	8	7	22	14	0-0		1-0							0-1	2-2	2-1			1-0
Racing Gônaïves	14	1	3	10	8	32	6	1-2	4-1	1-1							0-1	0-0		0-0		

11/09/2011 - 11/12/2011 • † Qualified for the CFU Club Championship

HKG – HONG KONG

FIFA/COCA-COLA WORLD RANKING

'93	'94	'95	'96	'97	'98	'99	'00	'01	'02	'03	'04	'05	'06	'07	'08	'09	'10	'11	'12
112	98	111	124	129	136	122	123	137	150	142	133	117	117	125	151	143	146	169	

2011												High	Low	Av
Jan	Feb	Mar	Apr	May	Jun	Jul	Aug	Sep	Oct	Nov	Dec			
146	143	140	147	146	145	154	154	156	156	168	169	90	169	129

A government-supported overhaul of football in the former British colony saw the Hong Kong Football Association appoint a new chief executive, a new head coach and make moves to implement sweeping changes at all levels of the game. Former Melbourne Victory coach Ernie Merrick was placed at the helm of the national side at the start of 2012 while Gordon McKie, previously the head of the Scottish Rugby Football Union, was placed in charge of the day-to-day running of the administrative and commercial side of the game. Among the tasks for Merrick was a need to improve the territory's youth development structure and the flow of young players into a team that has slipped further down the FIFA/Coca-Cola World Ranking. Hong Kong struggled in 2011 at international level, losing convincingly to Saudi Arabia in the second phase of qualifying for the FIFA World Cup finals in Brazil. In club football, Hong Kong's most successful side South China were close to completing a clean sweep of all four trophies on offer during the season. They won both the FA Cup and the League Cup but lost in the final of the Senior Shield on penalties to Citizen and finished second to Kitchee in an incredibly tight race for the league championship. It was Kitchee's fourth title overall and their first since 1964.

FIFA WORLD CUP RECORD
1930-1970 DNE 1974-2014 DNQ

THE HONG KONG FOOTBALL ASSOCIATION LTD (HKFA)

55 Fat Kwong Street, Homantin, Kowloon
☎ +852 27129122
📠 +852 27604303
✉ hkfa@hkfa.com
🌐 www.hkfa.com
FA 1914 CON 1954 FIFA 1954
P Timothy Tsun Ting Fok
GS Vincent Yuen

FIFA BIG COUNT 2006

Total players	149 956
% of population	2.16%
Male	139 960
Female	9 996
Amateurs 18+	2 203
Youth under 18	1 762
Unregistered	50 780
Professionals	211
Referees	149
Admin & coaches	910
Number of clubs	82
Number of teams	582

MAJOR CITIES/TOWNS

		Population
1	Sha Tin, NT	628 000
2	Eastern, HKI	616 000
3	Kwun Tong, Kw	562 000
4	Tuen Mun, NT	488 000
5	Kwai Tsing, NT	477 000
6	Yuen Long, NT	449 000
7	Wong Tai Sin, Kw	444 000
8	Kowloon City	381 000
9	Sham Shui Po, Kw	353 000
10	Sai Kung, NT	327 000
11	Tai Po, NT	310 000
12	North, NT	298 000
13	Southern, HKI	290 000
14	Yau Tsim Mong, Kw	282 000
15	Tsuen Wan, NT	275 000
16	Central & Western	261 000

Kw = Kowloon
NT = New Territories
HKI = Hong Kong Island

XIANGGANG TEBIE XINGZHENGQU •HONG KONG SPECIAL ADMINISTRATIVE REGION

Capital Victoria	Population 7 055 071 (100)	% in cities 100%
GDP per capita $43 800 (15)	Area km² 1 104 km² (183)	GMT +/- +8
Neighbours (km) China 30 • Coast 733		

RECENT INTERNATIONAL MATCHES PLAYED BY HONG KONG

2009	Opponents	Score	Venue	Comp	Scorers	Att	Referee
21-01	Bahrain	L 1-3	Hong Kong	ACq	Cheng Siu Wai 90	6 013	Vo Minh Tri VIE
28-01	Yemen	L 0-1	Sana'a	ACq		10 000	Al Hilali OMA
23-08	Chinese Taipei	W 4-0	Kaohsiung	EAq	Lee Wai Lim 38, Chan Wai Ho 45, Chan Siu Ki 60, Ambassa Guy 63	12 000	Tojo JPN
25-08	Korea DPR	D 0-0	Kaohsiung	EAq		100	Kim Jong Hyeok KOR
27-08	Guam	W 12-0	Kaohsiung	EAq	Man Pei Tak 5, Wong Chin Hung 15, Chan Siu Ki 4 18 35 75 77, Chao Pengfei 3 37 71 92+, Leung Chun Pong 41, Poon Yiu Cheuk 89, Chan Wai Ho 90	1 500	Tojo JPN
8-10	Japan	L 0-6	Shizuoka	ACq		16 028	Torky IRN
18-11	Japan	L 0-4	Hong Kong	ACq		13 254	Green AUS
2010							
6-01	Bahrain	L 0-4	Manama	ACq		1 550	Balideh QAT
7-02	Korea Republic	L 0-5	Tokyo	EAC		2 728	Sato JPN
11-02	Japan	L 0-3	Tokyo	EAC		16 368	Zhao Liang CHN
14-02	China PR	L 0-2	Tokyo	EAC		16 439	Kim Jong Hyeok KOR
3-03	Yemen	D 0-0	Hong Kong	ACq		1 212	Minh Tri Vo VIE
4-10	India	W 1-0	Pune	Fr	Li Haiqiang 76	8 000	Patwal IND
9-10	Philippines	W 4-2	Kaohsiung	Fr	Chan Man Fai 5, Xu Deshuai 31, Lo Kwan Yee 84, Ju Yingzhi 91+	650	Kao Jung Fang TPE
10-10	Macau	W 4-0	Kaohsiung	Fr	Tam Lok Hin 38, Xu Deshuai 52, Lam Hok Hei 2 72 74	1 200	Yu Ming Hsun TPE
12-10	Chinese Taipei	D 1-1	Kaohsiung	Fr	Lo Kwan Yee 75p	3 000	Kao Tsai Hu TPE
17-11	Paraguay	L 0-7	Hong Kong	Fr		6 250	Mohd Salleh MAS
2011							
9-02	Malaysia	L 0-2	Kuala Lumpur	Fr			
3-06	Malaysia	D 1-1	Hong Kong	Fr	Chan Siu Ki 59	586	
23-07	Saudi Arabia	L 0-3	Dammam	WCq		20 354	Tseytlin UZB
28-07	Saudi Arabia	L 0-5	Hong Kong	WCq		1 402	Minh Tri Vo VIE
30-09	Philippines	D 3-3	Kaohsiung	Fr	Lee Wai Lim 2, Cheng Lai Hin 22, Au Yeung Yiu Chung 86		
2-10	Macau	W 5-1	Kaohsiung	Fr	Sham Kwok Keung 2 19 75, Chan Siu Ki 43, Wong Chin Hung 2 50 81		
4-10	Chinese Taipei	W 6-0	Kaohsiung	Fr	Chan Siu Ki 15, Kwok Kin Pong 25, Chan Wai Ho 40, Lee Hong Lim 2 42 68, Lo Kwan Yee 76		

Fr = Friendly match • EAC = East Asian Championship • AC = AFC Asian Cup • WC = FIFA World Cup • q = qualifier

HONG KONG NATIONAL TEAM HISTORICAL RECORDS

Past Coaches

Tom Sneddon ENG 1954-56 • Lai Shiu Wing 1958-67 • Chu Wing Keung 1967 • Tang Sum 1968 • Lau Tim 1968 • Hui King Shing 1969-70 • Chan Fai Hung 1970-72 • Ho Ying Fun 1973-75 • Franz van Balkom NED 1976-77 • Chan Yong Chong MAS 1978-79 • Peter McParland ENG 1980 • George Knobel NED 1980 • Lo Tak Kuen 1981 • Kwok Ka Ming 1982-90 • Wong Man Wai 1992 • Chan Hung Ping 1993 • Khoo Luan Khen MAS 1994-95 • Tsang Wai Chung 1996 • Kwok Ka Ming 1997 • Sebastian Araujo BRA 1998 • Chan Hung Ping 1999-2000 • Arie van der Zouwen NED 2000-01 • Casemiro Mior BRA 2002 • Lai Sun Cheung 2003-07 • Lee Kin Wo 2007 • Dejan Antonic SRB & Goran Paulic CRO 2008-09 • Kim Pan Gon KOR 2009 • Liu Chun Fai 2010 • Tsang Wai Chung 2010-11 • Liu Chun Fai 2011-12 • Ernie Merrick SCO 2012-

LEAGUE CUP 2010-11

Quarter-finals		Semi-finals		Final	
South China	4				
Tuen Mun	1	**South China**	4		
Tai Chung	1	Kitchee	2		
Kitchee	4			**South China**	2
Hong Kong FC	2			TSW Pegasus	1
Wofoo Tai Po	1	Hong Kong FC	1		
Rangers	2	**TSW Pegasus**	2		
TSW Pegasus	3			Yuen Long, 27-03-2011	
				Scorers -	

1st round: Citizen 0-1 **Fourway Rangers** • **South China** 2-1 Sun Hei SC

HONG KONG 2010–11

COOLPOINT VENTILATION FIRST DIVISION

	Pl	W	D	L	F	A	Pts	Kitchee	South China	TSW Pegasus	Sun Hei	Tai Po	Citizen	Fourway Rangers	Tuen Mun	Tai Chung	HKFC
Kitchee †	18	14	2	2	52	16	**44**		2-0	1-4	3-1	2-1	3-1	2-1	3-0	7-0	6-0
South China	18	14	1	3	41	19	**43**	3-4		2-1	2-1	0-1	2-0	2-1	0-0	4-0	2-1
TSW Pegasus	18	10	1	7	40	28	**31**	0-0	2-3		0-4	0-1	1-0	2-3	2-1	2-1	5-1
Sun Hei	18	8	3	7	36	32	**27**	0-4	1-3	4-3		1-0	4-5	0-0	2-1	3-0	3-1
Tai Po	18	8	3	7	37	21	**27**	0-3	1-2	4-3	0-0		2-3	2-2	7-1	3-1	1-1
Citizen	18	7	5	6	29	31	**26**	1-1	1-2	0-4	2-2	1-0		1-1	0-0	3-1	4-1
Fourway Rangers	18	7	4	7	41	36	**25**	0-2	1-3	1-2	5-2	0-5	5-2		3-1	5-4	7-1
Tuen Mun	18	5	3	10	16	30	**18**	1-2	0-1	0-2	3-1	1-2	1-1	1-0		1-0	1-0
Tai Chung	18	3	2	13	19	49	**11**	1-0	1-6	0-1	0-4	1-0	0-1	2-2	1-3		4-2
Hong Kong FC	18	1	2	15	20	69	**5**	2-7	1-4	2-6	0-3	0-6	1-3	2-4	2-1	2-2	

4/09/2010 - 23/05/2011 • † Qualified for the AFC Cup
Top scorers: 12 - Jordi Tarres ESP, Kitchee & Makhosonke Bhengu RSA, Fourway Rangers • 11 - Itaparica BRA, Pegasus

HONG KONG 2010–11 SECOND DIVISION

	Pl	W	D	L	F	A	Pts
Sham Shui Po	22	16	4	2	57	15	52
Pontic	22	17	1	4	80	27	52
Double Flower	22	13	4	5	46	29	43
Shatin	22	13	3	6	40	29	42
Happy Valley	22	11	2	9	38	35	35
Southern District	22	9	6	7	37	33	33
Biu Chun	22	9	4	9	37	38	31
Wing Yee	22	8	3	11	38	50	27
Kwai Tsing	22	5	3	14	26	50	18
Yuen Long	22	5	3	14	26	41	18
Fukien	22	5	2	15	21	56	17
Lucky Mile	22	3	1	18	21	64	10

12/09/2010 - 17/04/2011

SENIOR SHIELD 2010–11

Quarter–finals		Semi–finals		Final	
Citizen	5				
SunHei	0	**Citizen**	2		
Kitchee	1 10p	Rangers	0		
Rangers	1 11p			**Citizen**	3 4p
Wofoo Tai Po	1			South China	3 2p
TSW Pehasus	0	Wofoo Tai Po	0	Hong Kong Stadium
Tai Chung	0	**South China**	3	16-01-2011, 4694
South China	4			Scorers - Festus 44, Sham

Kwok Keung 55, Tam Lok Hin for Citizen; Li Haiqiang 13, Joel 23, Giovane 36 for South China

1st round: Hong Kong FC 0-1 **Wofoo Tai Po** • Citizen 1-0 Tuen Mun

FA CUP 2010–11

Quarter–finals		Semi–finals		Final	
South China	3				
Citizen	1	**South China**	3		
Rangers	2	Sun Hei	1		
Sun Hei	3			**South China**	2
TSW Pegasus	7			Wofoo Tai Po	1
Tai Chung	1	TSW Pegasus	2	Hong Kong Stadium
Tuen Mun	0	**Wofoo Tai Po**	4	29-05-2011, 3829
Wofoo Tai Po	4			Scorers - Chan Wai Ho 12,

Mateja Kezman 103 for South China; Ye Jia 40 for Wofoo Tai Po

1st round: Hong Kong FC 0-2 **Sun Hei** • Kitchee 1-1 4-5p **Tuen Mun** • † Qualified for the AFC Cup

MEDALS TABLE

		Overall		Lge		FAC		Shield		VC		LC		Asia	
		G	S	G	B	G	B	G	B	G	B	G	B	G	S
1	South China	73	39	31	16	10	4	21	11	8	7	3			1
2	Seiko	29	8	9	3	6	1	8	2	8	2				
3	Eastern	16	9	4	2	3	1	7	2	2	4				
4	Happy Valley	15	38	6	16	2	5	5	9	1	3	1	5		
5	Kitchee	12	13	4	6		1	5	5			2	1		
6	Sun Hei	11	8	3	2	3	1	1	4			4	1		
7	Rangers	9	8	1		2	3	4	2	2	2		1		
	Sing Tao	9	8	1	4		1	6	2	2	1				
9	Double Flower	6	11	2	2	3	2		4	1	3				
10	Bulova	5	4		2	2	1	1	1	2	1				

HON – HONDURAS

FIFA/COCA-COLA WORLD RANKING

'93	'94	'95	'96	'97	'98	'99	'00	'01	'02	'03	'04	'05	'06	'07	'08	'09	'10	'11	'12
40	53	49	45	73	91	69	46	27	40	49	59	41	56	53	40	37	59	53	

2011												High	Low	Av
Jan	Feb	Mar	Apr	May	Jun	Jul	Aug	Sep	Oct	Nov	Dec			
56	39	38	43	43	44	51	50	53	57	54	53	20	95	51

On the face of it 2011 was a good year for the Honduran national team. They won the Copa Centroamericana in February and then reached the semi-finals of the CONCACAF Gold Cup in June, but overall the results during the year were not hugely impressive. After the Copa Centroamericana success, coach Juan Castillo ended his short spell in charge and was replaced by the Colombian Luis Fernando Suarez, who had led Ecuador to the 2006 World Cup finals. In the Gold Cup, despite reaching the semi-finals, Honduras won just one match - a 7-1 thrashing of Grenada - but that was followed by a 1-0 defeat at the hands of Jamaica. A penalty shoot-out victory over rivals Costa Rica saw them qualify for the semi-finals for the third time in four tournaments but they were then beaten 2-0 by Mexico. One of the emerging stars of the team, Jerry Bengtson, had an outstanding domestic season with his club Motagua, who were winners of the first championship played during the year. His two goals in the second leg of the final away to Olimpia, secured the club's first title since 2006 and only their second over the past decade. In the second half of the year it was back to business as usual for Olimpia, the most successful team in the country, as they beat Real España in the final to win their 24th championship.

CONCACAF GOLD CUP RECORD

1991 F r/u **1993** r1 **1996** r1 **1998** r1 **2000** QF **2002** DNQ **2003** r1 **2005** SF **2007** QF **2009** SF **2011** SF

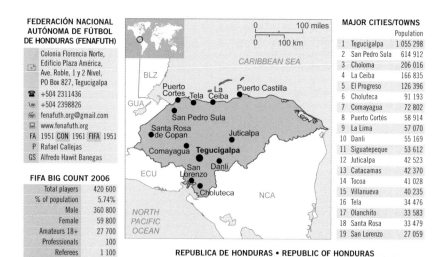

FEDERACIÓN NACIONAL AUTÓNOMA DE FÚTBOL DE HONDURAS (FENAFUTH)

Colonia Florencia Norte, Edificio Plaza América, Ave. Roble, 1 y 2 Nivel, PO Box 827, Tegucigalpa

☎ +504 2311436
📠 +504 2398826
✉ fenafuth.org@gmail.com
🖥 www.fenafuth.org
FA 1951 CON 1961 FIFA 1951
P Rafael Callejas
GS Alfredo Hawit Banegas

FIFA BIG COUNT 2006

Total players	420 600
% of population	5.74%
Male	360 800
Female	59 800
Amateurs 18+	27 700
Professionals	100
Referees	1 100
Admin & coaches	5 700
Number of clubs	220
Number of teams	1 100

MAJOR CITIES/TOWNS

		Population
1	Tegucigalpa	1 055 298
2	San Pedro Sula	614 912
3	Choloma	206 016
4	La Ceiba	166 835
5	El Progreso	126 396
6	Choluteca	91 193
7	Comayagua	72 802
8	Puerto Cortés	58 914
9	La Lima	57 070
10	Danli	55 169
11	Siguatepeque	53 612
12	Juticalpa	42 523
13	Catacamas	42 370
14	Tocoa	41 028
15	Villanueva	40 235
16	Tela	34 476
17	Olanchito	33 583
18	Santa Rosa	33 479
19	San Lorenzo	27 059

REPUBLICA DE HONDURAS • REPUBLIC OF HONDURAS

Capital Tegucigalpa	Population 7 792 854 (93)	% in cities 48%
GDP per capita $4400 (152)	Area km² 112 090 km² (102)	GMT + / - -6
Neighbours (km) Guatemala 256, El Salvador 342, Nicaragua 922 • Coast 820		

RECENT INTERNATIONAL MATCHES PLAYED BY HONDURAS

2010	Opponents	Score		Venue	Comp	Scorers	Att	Referee
23-01	USA	W	3-1	Carson	Fr	Carlos Pavon [19p], Jerry Palacios [37], Roger Espinoza [53]	18 626	Archundia MEX
3-03	Turkey	L	0-2	Istanbul	Fr		22 000	Olsiak SVK
21-04	Venezuela	L	0-1	San Pedro Sula	Fr		40 000	Moreno PAN
27-05	Belarus	D	2-2	Villach	Fr	Julio De Leon [25], George Welcome [71]	400	Eisner AUT
2-06	Azerbaijan	D	0-0	Zell Am See	Fr		1 000	Drachta AUT
5-06	Romania	L	0-3	St Velt an der Glan	Fr		1 500	Grobelnik AUT
16-06	Chile	L	0-1	Nelspruit	WCr1		32 664	Maillet SEY
21-06	Spain	L	0-2	Johannesburg	WCr1		54 386	Nishimura JPN
25-06	Switzerland	D	0-0	Bloemfontein	WCr1		28 042	Baldassi ARG
4-09	El Salvador	D	2-2	Los Angeles	Fr	Oscar Garcia [58], Roger Rojas [86]. W 4-3p	15 000	Stoica USA
7-09	Canada	L	1-2	Montreal	Fr	Erick Norales [34]	7 525	Geiger USA
9-10	New Zealand	D	1-1	Auckland	Fr	Walter Martinez [64]	18 153	O'Leary NZL
12-10	Guatemala	W	2-0	Los Angeles	Fr	Roger Rojas [21], George Welcome [80]	10 000	Hernandez USA
17-11	Panama	L	0-2	Panama City	Fr		3 646	Cruz CRC
18-12	Panama	W	2-1	San Pedro Sula	Fr	Johny Leveron 2 [7 44]	3 000	Rodas GUA
2011								
14-01	Costa Rica	D	1-1	Panama City	UCr1	Ramon Nunez [90]	6 000	Garcia MEX
18-01	Guatemala	W	3-1	Panama City	UCr1	Ramon Nunez [13], Jorge Claros 2 [42 88]	10 000	Aguilar SLV
21-01	El Salvador	W	2-0	Panama City	UCsf	Johnny Leveron [78], Marvin Chavez [90]	5 000	Quesada CRC
23-01	Costa Rica	W	2-1	Panama City	UCf	Walter Martinez [8], Emil Martinez [52]	2 000	Lopez GUA
9-02	Ecuador	D	1-1	La Ceiba	Fr	Carlo Costly [8]. L 4-5p	15 100	Lopez GUA
25-03	Korea Republic	L	0-4	Seoul	Fr		31 224	Sato JPN
29-03	China PR	L	0-3	Wuhan	Fr		10 000	Iemoto JPN
29-05	El Salvador	D	2-2	Houston	Fr	Carlo Costly [44], Jerry Bengtson [49p]	25 380	Villareal USA
6-06	Guatemala	D	0-0	Carson/LA	GCr1		21 550	Chacon MEX
10-06	Grenada	W	7-1	Miami	GCr1	Jerry Bengtson 2 [26 37], Carlo Costly 3 [28 67 71], Walter Martinez [88], Alfredo Mejia [93+]	18 057	Gantar CAN
13-06	Jamaica	L	0-1	Harrison/NY	GCr1		25 000	Aguilar SLV
18-06	Costa Rica	D	1-1	East Rutherford/NY	GCqf	Jerry Bengtson [49]. W 4-2p	78 807	Moreno PAN
22-06	Mexico	L	0-2	Houston	GCsf		70 627	Lopez GUA
10-08	Venezuela	W	2-0	Fort Lauderdale	Fr	Carlo Costly 2 [57 68]	20 000	Vaughn USA
3-09	Colombia	L	0-2	East Rutherford/NY	Fr		15 000	Gonzalez USA
6-09	Paraguay	L	0-3	San Pedro Sula	Fr		20 000	Aguilar SLV
8-10	USA	L	0-1	Miami	Fr		21 170	Campbell JAM
11-10	Jamaica	W	2-1	La Ceiba	Fr	Jerry Bengtson [1], Mario Martinez [54]	18 000	Moreno PAN
14-11	Serbia	W	2-0	San Pedro Sula	Fr	Jerry Bengtson 2 [4 29]	20 000	Rodas GUA

Fr = Friendly match • UC = UNCAF Cup/Copa Centroamericana • GC = CONCACAF Gold Cup • WC = FIFA World Cup
q = qualifier • r1 = first round group • qf = quarter-final • 5p = fifth place play-off • sf = semi-final • f = final

HONDURAS NATIONAL TEAM HISTORICAL RECORDS

Caps
137 - Amado Guevara 1994-• **101** - Carlos Pavon 1993-• **98** - Noel Valladares 2000-• **88** - Milton Nunez 1994-2008 • **85** - Danilo Turcios 1999-& Ivan Guerrero 1999-• **84** - Maynor Figueroa 2003-• **83** - Julio Cesar de Leon 1999-• **76** - Wilson Palacios 2003-• **71** - Samuel Caballero 1998-2008

Goals
58 - Carlos Pavon 1993-2010 • **35** - Wilmer Velasquez 1996-2007 • **34** - Milton Nunez 1994-2008 • **29** - Amado Guevara 1994-2010 • **28** - Nicolas Suazo 1991-98 • **20** - Carlo Costly 2007-• **18** - Saul Martinez 2001-08 • **17** - Eduardo Bennett 1991-2000 • **16** - David Suazo 1999-• **15** - Julio Cesar de Leon 1999-• **13** - Jairo Martinez 1998-

Past Coaches
Flavio Ortega 1991-92 • Estanislao Malinowski URU 1993-94 • Carlos Carranza 1995-96 • Miguel Company PER 1997-98 • Ramon Maradiaga 1999-02 • Bora Milutinovic SRB 2003-04 • Jose de la Paz Herrera 2005 • Flavio Ortega 2006 • Reinaldo Rueda COL 2006-10 • Juan de Dios Castillo MEX 2010-11 • Luis Fernando Suarez COL 2011-

HONDURAS 2010–11

TORNEO CLAUSURA

	Pl	W	D	L	F	A	Pts	Olimpia	Motagua	Vida	Marathón	España	Necaxa	Hispano	Savio	Platense	Victoria
Olimpia †	18	9	6	3	24	11	33		1-1	2-1	1-1	1-0	2-0	6-0	2-1	1-0	3-1
Motagua †	18	8	7	3	25	17	31	2-1		2-0	1-0	2-3	1-1	0-0	4-1	1-1	0-2
Vida †	18	7	5	6	23	18	26	0-0	0-0		2-1	0-1	3-1	1-1	5-3	4-1	2-1
Marathón †	18	7	4	7	21	17	25	0-1	0-1	2-1		2-0	2-2	2-1	1-0	0-1	3-0
Real España	18	6	7	5	25	25	25	0-0	2-1	0-1	2-2		2-2	1-1	1-1	2-1	2-3
Necaxa	18	5	9	4	25	24	24	1-0	0-1	0-0	1-0	2-1		2-2	4-0	1-0	2-2
Hispano	18	5	9	4	16	18	24	1-0	0-0	0-0	0-0	2-3	2-0		2-0	1-0	2-1
Deportivo Savio	18	5	5	8	25	36	20	0-0	3-3	1-0	2-1	3-3	2-2	1-0		4-2	2-1
Platense	18	4	5	9	21	29	17	1-1	1-3	2-1	1-2	0-1	1-1	1-1	2-0		2-2
Victoria	18	3	5	10	25	35	14	1-2	1-2	0-2	0-2	1-1	3-3	0-0	3-1	3-4	

16/01/2011 - 15/05/2011 • † Qualified for the play-offs
Play-off final details: 1st leg. Tiburcio Andino, Tegucigalpa, 8-05-2011, Att: 12 462, Ref: Raul Castro. Scorers - Amado Guevara ^{42}, Jerry Bengtson ^{68} for Motagua; Douglas Caetano ^{10}, Ramiro Bruschi ^{74} for Olimpia • 2nd leg. Tiburcio Andino, Tegucigalpa, 15-05-2011, Att: 23 326. Ref: Hector Rodriguez. Scorers - Jerry Bengtson 2 $^{16\ 93+}$, Guevara 46 for Motagua; Fabio de Souza ^{29} for Olimpia
Top scorers (including play-offs): 15 - Jerry Bengtson, Motagua • 12 - Ney Costa BRA, Savio • 9 - Elmer Zelaya, Victoria
Hispano relegated with the worst aggregate record for the 2010-11 season • Olimpia qualified for the CONCACAF Champions League

CLAUSURA 2010–11 PLAY-OFFS

Semi-finals			Finals			
Motagua ‡	0	3				
Vida *	1	2	**Motagua * †**	2	3	
Marathón *	1	0	Olimpia	2	1	
Olimpia ‡	0	1				

† Qualified for the CONCACAF Champions League • * Home team in first leg • ‡ Qualified on season record • **Motagua** are Clausura champions

MEDALS TABLE

		Overall			Lge		Cent Am			City
		G	S	B	G	B	G	S	B	
1	Olimpia	26	20	1	24	17	2	2	1	Tegucigalpa
2	Motagua	12	9		12	9				Tegucigalpa
3	Real España	10	11	1	10	11			1	San Pedro Sula
4	Marathón	8	12	1	8	11			1	San Pedro Sula
5	Platense	2	3		2	3				Puerto Cortés
	Vida	2	3		2	3				La Ceiba
7	Victoria	1	1		1	1				La Ceiba
8	UNAH			3		2	1			Choluteca
9	At. Morazán	1			1					
	Petrotela	1			1					

APERTURA 2011–12 PLAY-OFFS

Semi-finals			Finals			
Olimpia *	1	0				
Marathón	0	0	**Olimpia * †**	1	2	
Vida *	0	1	Real España	0	0	
Real España	1	4				

Play-offs first round: Necaxa 1-1 0-1 **Olimpia** • Savio 2-1 1-2 **Vida**
† Qualified for the CONCACAF Champions League • * Home team in first leg • **Olimpia** are Apertura champions

HONDURAS 2011–12

TORNEO APERTURA

	Pl	W	D	L	F	A	Pts	España	Marathón	Olimpia	Vida	Savio	Necaxa	Motagua	Platense	Victoria	Choloma
Real España †	18	9	7	2	25	13	34		1-1	2-0	1-0	2-2	2-2	0-1	1-0	0-0	2-0
Marathón †	18	9	4	5	32	19	31	2-0		0-2	1-2	5-0	3-0	2-1	1-0	3-2	1-1
Olimpia †	18	7	5	6	16	11	26	0-1	1-0		4-1	1-1	0-1	1-1	1-0	1-2	2-0
Vida †	18	7	5	6	19	21	26	1-1	1-2	0-0		2-0	1-0	2-0	3-1	1-0	2-2
Deportivo Savio †	18	6	6	6	22	25	24	1-1	1-1	0-0	2-0		1-2	0-3	2-0	2-0	3-1
Necaxa †	18	6	5	7	16	20	23	1-3	1-0	0-0	0-1	1-2		1-0	1-1	1-0	0-0
Motagua	18	6	4	8	20	19	22	0-2	1-4	0-1	3-0	2-1	1-1		3-0	3-0	0-0
Platense	18	6	3	9	14	23	21	0-0	0-3	1-0	2-0	1-0	3-2	1-0		2-1	1-1
Victoria	18	5	4	9	21	25	19	1-2	2-2	0-2	1-1	1-2	2-1	2-1	2-0		4-0
Atlético Choloma	18	3	9	6	18	27	18	1-4	3-1	1-0	1-1	2-2	0-1	1-1	3-1	1-1	

7/08/2011 - 17/12/2011 • † Qualified for the play-offs (top two qualify for the semi-finals)
Play-off final details: 1st leg. Tiburcio Andino, Tegucigalpa, 11-12-2011, Att: 23 807, Ref: Geovanny Mendoza. Scorer - Carlos Mejia ^{84} for Olimpia • 2nd leg. Francisco Morazon, San Pedro Sula, 17-12-2011, Att: 18 000, Ref: Hector Rodriguez. Scorer - Carlos Mejia 2 $^{82\ 84}$ for Olimpia
Top scorers (including play-offs): 15 - Claudio Cardozo URU, Marathón • 9 - Jerry Bengtson, Motagua • 7 - Charles Cordoba COL, Vida

HUN – HUNGARY

FIFA/COCA-COLA WORLD RANKING

'93	'94	'95	'96	'97	'98	'99	'00	'01	'02	'03	'04	'05	'06	'07	'08	'09	'10	'11	'12
50	61	62	75	77	46	45	47	66	56	72	64	74	62	50	47	54	42	37	

						2011									High	Low	Av
	Jan	Feb	Mar	Apr	May	Jun	Jul	Aug	Sep	Oct	Nov	Dec			High	Low	Av
	41	37	36	52	52	45	47	45	27	36	37	37			27	87	57

There were first-time winners in both the league and the cup in 2011 as defending champions and cup winners Debrecen failed to win a trophy for the first season since 2004. The league title went to Videoton. They were coached by the veteran Gyorgy Mezey who had led Hungary to the 1986 World Cup in Mexico - their last appearance at a major tournament. The club had been rescued by businessman Istvan Garancsi in 2007, a year after winning the cup as Fehérvár, and reverted to the name under which they had reached the 1985 UEFA Cup final. They almost pulled off the double but lost an entertaining Cup Final to Kecskeméti for whom Central African Republic striker Foxi scored a hat-trick. Before the final Videoton had informed Mezey that they would not be extending his contract, a fact that no doubt helped undermine their quest for the double. It was yet another bad year for Budapest, most notably the relegation of MTK - the second most successful club in Hungarian football - and clubs from the capital have now won just three trophies in the past seven seasons. The national team impressed over the course of 2011, winning seven of their 11 games but once again they failed to win the games that really mattered, their two defeats at the hands of the Netherlands meaning that they finished third in their UEFA Euro 2011 qualifying group.

UEFA EUROPEAN CHAMPIONSHIP RECORD
1960 r1 **1964** 3 SF **1968** QF **1972** 4 SF **1976-2012** DNQ

HUNGARIAN FOOTBALL FEDERATION (MLSZ)

Kanai ut. 314/24,
Budapest 1112

☎ +36 1 5779500
✆ +36 1 5779503
✉ mlsz@mlsz.hu
🖥 www.mlsz.hu
FA 1901 CON 1954 FIFA 1906
P Sandor Csanyi
GS Marton Vagi

FIFA BIG COUNT 2006

Total players	527 326
% of population	5.28%
Male	477 368
Female	49 958
Amateurs 18+	61 208
Youth under 18	63 744
Unregistered	203 100
Professionals	468
Referees	3 615
Admin & coaches	7 150
Number of clubs	2 748
Number of teams	4 631

MAJOR CITIES/TOWNS

		Population
1	Budapest	1 656 358
2	Debrecen	205 042
3	Miskolc	174 574
4	Szeged	161 725
5	Pécs	155 402
6	Györ	130 391
7	Nyíregyháza	115 113
8	Kecskemét	105 498
9	Székesfehérvár	104 486
10	Szombathely	79 976
11	Szolnok	74 604
12	Tatabánya	71 840
13	Kaposvár	66 332
14	Békéscsaba	64 372
15	Érd	63 547
16	Zalaegerszeg	60 622
17	Veszprém	60 225
18	Sopron	56 219
19	Eger	56 036

MAGYAR KOZTARSASAG • REPUBLIC OF HUNGARY

Capital	Budapest	Population	9 905 596 (82)	% in cities 68%
GDP per capita	$19 800 (63)	Area km²	93 028 km² (109)	GMT + / - +1
Neighbours (km)	Austria 366, Croatia 329, Romania 443, Serbia 166, Slovakia 676, Slovenia 102, Ukraine 103		

RECENT INTERNATIONAL MATCHES PLAYED BY HUNGARY

2009	Opponents	Score		Venue	Comp	Scorers	Att	Referee
11-02	Israel	L	0-1	Tel Aviv	Fr		9 500	Borski POL
28-03	Albania	W	1-0	Tirana	WCq	Torghelle [38]	12 000	Kuipers NED
1-04	Malta	W	3-0	Budapest	WCq	Hajnal [7], Gera [81], Juhasz [93+]	34 400	Sukhina RUS
12-08	Romania	L	0-1	Budapest	Fr		9 000	Vnuk SVK
5-09	Sweden	L	1-2	Budapest	WCq	Huszti [79p]	40 169	Rizzoli ITA
9-09	Portugal	L	0-1	Budapest	WCq		42 000	Lannoy FRA
10-10	Portugal	L	0-3	Lisbon	WCq		50 115	Hamer LUX
14-10	Denmark	W	1-0	Copenhagen	WCq	Buzsaky [35]	36 956	Meyer GER
14-11	Belgium	L	0-3	Ghent	Fr		8 000	Piccirillo FRA
2010								
3-03	Russia	D	1-1	Gyor	Fr	Vanczak [39]	10 000	Vucemilovic CRO
29-05	Germany	L	0-3	Budapest	Fr		14 000	Larsen DEN
5-06	Netherlands	L	1-6	Amsterdam	Fr	Dzsudzsak [6]	45 000	Meyer GER
11-08	England	L	1-2	London	Fr	OG [62]	72 024	Lannoy FRA
3-09	Sweden	L	0-2	Stockholm	ECq		32 304	Atkinson ENG
7-09	Moldova	W	2-1	Budapest	ECq	Rudolf [50], Koman [66]	9 209	Kovarik CZE
8-10	San Marino	W	8-0	Budapest	ECq	Rudolf 2 [11 25], Szalai 3 [18 27 48], Koman [60], Dzsudzsak [89], Gera [93+p]	10 596	Kaasik EST
12-10	Finland	W	2-1	Helsinki	ECq	Szalai [50], Dzsudzsak [94+]	18 532	Kelly IRL
17-11	Lithuania	W	2-0	Szekesfehervar	Fr	Priskin [61], Dzsudzsak [80]	4 500	Nijhuis NED
2011								
9-02	Azerbaijan	W	2-0	Dubai	Fr	Rudolf [37], Hajnal [81]	500	Al Zarooni UAE
25-03	Netherlands	L	0-4	Budapest	ECq		25 311	Velasco ESP
29-03	Netherlands	L	3-5	Amsterdam	ECq		51 700	Moen NOR
3-06	Luxembourg	W	1-0	Luxembourg	Fr	Szabics [53]	1 213	Arnason ISL
7-06	San Marino	W	3-0	Serravalle	ECq		1 915	Radovanovic MNE
10-08	Iceland	W	4-0	Budapest	Fr	Koman [32], Rudolf [45], Dzsudzsak [59], Elek [88]	12 000	Stark GER
2-09	Sweden	W	2-1	Budapest	ECq		23 500	Skomina SVN
6-09	Moldova	W	2-0	Chisinau	ECq		10 500	Bebek CRO
11-10	Finland	D	0-0	Budapest	ECq		25 169	Undiano ESP
11-11	Liechtenstein	W	5-0	Budapest	Fr	Priskin 2 [10 20], Dzsudzsak [76], Koman [79], Feczesin [89]	23 000	Balaj ROU
15-11	Poland	L	1-2	Poznan	Fr	Priskin [78]	7 500	Kaasik EST

Fr = Friendly match • EC = UEFA EURO 2012 • WC = FIFA World Cup • q = qualifier

HUNGARY NATIONAL TEAM HISTORICAL RECORDS

Caps

101 - Jozsek Bozsik 1947-62 • **92** - Laszlo Fazekas 1968-83 • **86** - Gyula Grosics 1947-62 • **85** - Ferenc Puskas 1945-56 & Gabor Kiraly 1998- • **82** - Imre Garaba 1980-91 • **81** - Sandor Matrai 1956-67 • **77** - Ferenc Sipos 1957-66 • **76** - Ferenc Bene 1962-79 & Mate Fenyvesi 1954-66 • **75** - Florian Albert 1959-74 & Karoly Sandor 1949-64 • **73** - Zoltan Gera 2002- • **72** - Lajos Tichy 1955-64 • **70** - Jozsef Kiprich 1984-95 & Tibor Nyilasi 1975-85 • **69** - Nandor Hidegkuti 1945-58 • **68** - Imre Schlosser 1906-27 & Sandor Kocsis 1948-56

Goals

84 - Ferenc Puskas 1945-56 • **75** - Sandor Kocsis 1948-56 • **59** - Imre Schlosser 1906-27 • **51** - Lajos Tichy 1955-64 • **42** - Gyorgy Sarosi 1931-43 • **39** - Nandor Hidegkuti 1945-58 • **36** - Ferenc Bene 1962-79 • **32** - Gyula Zsengeller 1935-47 & Tibor Nyilasi 1975-85 • **31** - Florian Albert 1959-74 • **29** - Ferenc Deak 1946-49 • **28** - Jozsef Kiprich 1984-95 • **27** - Karoly Sandor 1949-64 • **26** - Jozsef Takacs 1923-33 • **25** - Geza Toldi 1929-40 • **24** - Istvan Avar 1929-35 & Laszlo Fazekas 1968-83 • **21** - Mihaly Pataki 1912-20 & Zoltan Gera 2002-

Past Coaches

Ferenc Gillemot 1902-04 • Ferenc Stobbe 1904-06 • Alfred Hajos 1906 • Ferenc Stobbe 1907-08 • Frigyes Minder 1908-11 • Ede Herczog 1911-14 • Frigyes Minder 1914-17 • Akos Fehery 1918-19 • Frigyes Minder 1919 • Jozsef Harsady 1920 • Lajos Tibor 1920 • Gyula Kiss 1921-24 • Odon Holits 1924 • Lajos Mariassy 1924-26 • Gyula Kiss 1926-28 • Janos Foldessy 1928-29 • Mihaly Pataki 1930 • Frigyes Minder 1930 • Lajos Mariassy 1930-32 • Odon Nadas 1932-34 • Karoly Dietz 1934-39 • Denes Ginzery 1939-41 • Jozsef Fabian 1941 • Denes Ginzery 1941 • Jozsef Fabian 1942 • Kalman Vaghy 1942-43 • Tibor Gallowich 1945-48 • Gusztav Sebes 1949-56 • Marton Bukovi, Lajos Baroti & Karoly Lakat 1956-57 • Karoly Sos 1957 • Lajos Baroti 1957-66 • Rudolf Illovszky 1966-67 • Karoly Sos 1968-69 • Jozsef Hoffer 1970-71 • Rudolf Illovszky 1971-74 • Jozsef Bozsik 1974 • Ede Moor 1974-75 • Janos Szocs 1975 • Lajos Baroti 1975-78 • Ferenc Kovacs 1978-79 • Karoly Lakat 1979-80 • Kalman Meszoly 1980-83 • Gyorgy Mezey 1983-86 • Imre Komora 1986 • Jozsef Verebes 1987 • Jozsef Garami 1987 • Laszlo Balint 1988 • Gyorgy Mezey 1988 • Bertalan Bicskei 1989 • Kalman Meszoly 1990-91 • Robert Glazer 1991 • Imre Jenei ROU 1992-93 • Ferenc Puskas 1993 • Jozsef Verebes 1993-94 • Kalman Meszoly 1994-95 • Janos Csank 1996-97 • Bertalan Bicskei 1998-01 • Imre Gellei 2001-03 • Lothar Matthaus GER 2004-05 • Peter Bozsik 2006 • Peter Varhidi 2006-08 • Erwin Koeman NED 2008-2010 • Sandor Egervari 2010-

HUNGARY 2010-11

SOPRONI LIGA NB I

	Pl	W	D	L	F	A	Pts	Videoton	Paks	Ferencváros	ZTE	Debrecen	Ujpest	Kaposvár	Haladás	Győr	Honvéd	Vasas	Kecskemét	Pápa	Siófok	MTK	Szolnok
Videoton †	30	18	7	5	59	29	61		2-1	1-1	3-0	2-1	1-0	3-1	3-1	2-1	0-2	3-0	2-2	4-0	2-0	2-1	3-1
Paksi SE ‡	30	17	5	8	54	37	56	1-0		3-2	2-2	2-2	2-1	2-3	2-1	2-1	0-1	3-0	2-0	4-0	0-0	1-1	3-1
Ferencvárosi TC ‡	30	15	5	10	50	43	50	0-5	2-1		4-4	1-1	1-0	1-0	2-1	3-0	1-3	0-1	2-1	3-0	1-2	3-0	1-0
Zalaegerszegi TE	30	14	6	10	51	47	48	1-2	1-0	2-1		1-1	2-1	3-5	1-1	1-1	2-1	2-1	2-1	3-1	2-1	1-0	2-1
Debreceni VSC	30	12	10	8	53	43	46	3-1	2-1	2-1	2-1		1-1	3-1	1-2	1-1	2-2	3-1	6-2	2-0	2-3	3-1	4-0
Ujpesti FC	30	13	6	11	50	38	45	1-0	2-3	6-0	4-2	2-2		3-2	3-1	0-0	3-1	2-2	2-1	2-1	1-1	2-1	1-0
Kaposvári Rákóczi	30	13	4	13	41	42	43	1-4	1-2	2-1	2-1	0-0	0-1		1-0	3-0	0-0	0-1	2-1	3-2	3-0	2-1	0-1
Szombathelyi Haladás	30	11	8	11	42	36	41	2-0	1-2	1-1	0-0	3-0	0-2	2-0		3-3	1-1	3-0	1-0	1-0	4-0	2-0	3-1
Győri ETO	30	10	11	9	40	35	41	1-1	1-1	1-0	0-1	3-0	2-1	2-0	2-2		3-0	0-1	2-1	0-1	1-0	1-1	4-2
Budapest Honvéd	30	11	7	12	36	39	40	2-2	1-0	0-1	1-0	1-0	1-4	1-0	3-1	1-1		0-0	1-2	2-4	0-1	1-2	0-0
Vasas SC	30	11	7	12	34	46	40	0-0	2-3	1-3	2-0	1-5	1-0	1-3	2-1	2-1	3-2		1-1	1-1	3-0	1-1	3-0
Kecskeméti TE ‡	30	11	3	16	51	56	36	2-4	0-1	1-2	1-0	3-0	4-3	4-1	1-0	3-3	2-1	3-1		0-1	2-3	3-0	4-2
Lombard Pápa TFC	30	10	5	15	39	52	35	1-2	1-2	0-5	4-3	1-1	3-1	1-1	5-1	2-1	0-1	2-1	4-1		0-1	0-2	0-0
Bodajk FC Siófok	30	8	10	12	29	41	34	1-1	1-3	1-1	0-4	4-1	1-1	0-0	0-0	0-1	1-3	0-0	1-2	0-1		0-0	1-1
MTK Hungária	30	8	6	16	35	49	30	0-3	3-4	1-3	3-4	0-0	1-0	0-2	0-3	0-0	3-1	4-0	4-2	2-1	1-2		1-0
Szolnoki MAV	30	5	6	19	26	56	21	1-1	3-1	2-3	1-3	1-2	1-0	1-2	0-0	0-3	0-2	0-1	2-1	2-2	0-4	2-1	

30/07/2010 - 22/05/2011 • † Qualified for the UEFA Champions League • ‡ Qualified for the UEFA Cup
Top scorers: 24 - Andre Alves BRA, Videoton • 15 - Andre Schembri MLT, Ferencvaros & Daniel Bode, Paks • 14 - Adamo Coulibaly FRA, Debrecen • 13 - Lorant Olah, Kaposvar & Attila Tokoli, Kecskemet • 12 - Patrik Tischler, MTK

HUNGARY 2010-11 — NB II NYUGATI (WEST)

	Pl	W	D	L	F	A	Pts
Pécsi MFC	30	21	3	6	55	17	66
Gyirmót SE	30	19	6	5	62	29	63
Videoton-Puskas Akad.	30	18	4	8	58	32	58
Bajai LSE	30	17	3	10	51	38	54
BKV Előre	30	13	9	8	38	37	48
FC Ajka	30	13	7	10	47	35	46
FC Tatabánya	30	13	7	10	47	39	46
Kozármisleny SE	30	13	6	11	41	37	45
Győri ETO II	30	13	3	14	42	47	42
Szigetszentmiklosi TK	30	12	6	12	45	40	42
Budaörsi SC	30	11	8	11	42	41	41
Ferencvárosi TC II	30	10	4	16	36	35	34
Barcsi FC	30	9	6	15	35	61	33
Veszprém FC	30	10	0	20	33	54	30
Honvéd II	30	4	6	20	24	57	18
Kaposvölgye VSC	30	4	2	25	21	78	14

14/08/2010 - 11/06/2011

HUNGARY 2010-11 — NB II KELETI (EAST)

	Pl	W	D	L	F	A	Pts
Diósgyőri VTK	30	22	2	6	66	23	68
Mezokövesdi SE	30	19	5	6	48	20	62
Nyíregyháza Spartacus	30	18	6	6	66	23	60
Dunakanyar-Vac FC	30	18	6	6	47	27	60
MTK-Hungária II	30	16	7	7	48	34	55
Békéscsabai Elore FC	30	11	10	9	45	40	43
Vecsési FC	30	10	8	12	36	37	38
Debreceni VSC II	30	10	7	13	37	45	37
Ujpesti FC II	30	9	8	13	43	58	35
Rákospalotai EAC	30	9	6	15	30	38	33
Kazincbarcika SC	30	8	8	14	37	60	31
Ceglédi VSE	30	8	6	16	46	61	30
Makói FC	30	8	6	16	30	54	30
Hajdúböszörményi TE	30	7	9	14	29	42	30
Oroszházai FC	30	7	9	14	32	52	30
Bocsi KSC	30	5	7	18	27	53	22

14/08/2010 - 11/06/2011

MEDALS TABLE

		Overall			League			Cup		Europe			City
		G	S	B	G	S	B	G	S	G	S	B	
1	Ferencvárosi TC	49	45	23	28	34	21	20	9	1	2	2	Budapest
2	MTK Hungária FC	35	23	16	23	20	15	12	2	1		1	Budapest
3	Ujpest FC	28	28	20	20	21	18	8	6	1		2	Budapest
4	Budapest-Honvéd FC	20	22	5	13	12	5	7	10				Budapest
5	Vasas SC	10	5	14	6	2	13	4	3			1	Budapest
6	Debreceni VSC	9	3	3	5	1	3	4	2				Debrecen
7	Győri ETO FC	7	5	6	3	2	5	4	3			1	Győr
8	Csepel SC	4		2	4		2						Budapest
9	Videoton FC Fehérvár	2	6	3	1	2	3	1	3		1		Székesfehérvár
10	Diósgyőri VTK	2	3	1			1	2	3				Miskolc
11	Budapest TC	2	2	3	2	1	3	1					Budapest
12	Dunakanyar-Vac FC	1	5		1	2				3			Vác
13	Pécsi MFC	1	3	1		1	1	1	2				Pécs
14	Zalaegerszeg TE	1	1	1	1			1					Zalaegerszeg

MAGYAR KUPA 2010-11

Fourth Round		Round of 16			Quarter-finals			Semi-finals			Final	
Kecskeméti TE	3	Kecskeméti TE	3	3	Kecskeméti TE *	5	1	Kecskeméti TE *	5	0	Kecskeméti TE ‡	3
Tiszakanyár SE *	0	Debreceni VSC *	0	1	Bodajk FC Siófok	1	1	Zalaegerszegi TE	1	0	Videoton	2
Nagyecsed RSE *	1 7p											
Debreceni VSC	1 8p											
Ferencvárosi TC	5	Ferencvárosi TC	1	2								
Rákospalotai EAC *	0	Bodajk FC Siófok *	3	1								
BKV Előre *	1											
Bodajk FC Siófok	2											
MTK Hungária	5	MTK Hungária *	0	1	MTK Hungária *	0	1					
Cegládi VSE *	0	Győri ETO	0	1	Zalaegerszegi TE	0	2					
Barcsi FC *	0											
Győri ETO	7											
Vasas SC	3	Vasas SC *	0	0								
Tisza Volán *	1	Zalaegerszegi TE	6	3								
Honvéd II *	1											
Zalaegerszegi TE	2											
Kaposvári Rákóczi	2	Kaposvári Rákóczi *	1	1	Kaposvári Rákóczi	3	2	Kaposvári Rákóczi *	0	0		
Dunaharaszti MTK *	1	Paksi SE	0	0	Ujpesti FC *	2	2	Videoton	1	4		
Pécsi MFC *	1											
Paksi SE	0											
Lombard Pápa TFC	1 3p	Lombard Pápa TFC *	1	1								
Gyirmót SE *	1 2p	Ujpesti FC	3	3								
Bocsi KSC *	1											
Ujpesti FC	5											
Budapest Honvéd	3	Budapest Honvéd	3	7	Budapest Honvéd *	1	0					
Putnok Varosi *	1	Egri FC *	0	0	Videoton	1	4					
Tiszabecs LC *	1											
Egri FC	3											
Szombathelyi Haladás	5	Szombathelyi Haladás	0	1								
Lipot SK *	2	Videoton *	3	3								
Bajai LSE *	2											
Videoton	4											

CUP FINAL

Puskas Ferenc, Budapest
17-05-2011. Att: 5000. Ref: Zoltan Ivanyi
Scorers - Foxi Kethevoama 3 [2 14 80] for
Kecskemet; OG [48], Nikolic [82] for Videoton
Kecskemet - Ladislav Rybansky - Bela Balogh,
SSinisa Radanovic, David Mohl, Attila Gyagya,
Gabor Bori, Codiong Ebala, Foxi Kethevoama
(Vladan Savic 93+), Vladan Cukic (Lajos
Bertus 91+), Francis Litsingi•, Attila Tokoli•
(Sindou Dosso 87). Tr: Tomislav Sivic
Videoton - Zsolt Sebok - Tamas Vasko, Pal
Lazar, Zoltan Liptak, Gyorgy Sandor, Balazs
Farkas (Denes Szakaly 60), Attila Polonkai•
(Dusan Vasiljevic 46), Akos Elek, Andras
Gosztonyi (Laszlo Lencse 70), Andre Alves,
Nemanja Nikolic. Tr: Gyorgy Mezey

* Home team in the first leg • ‡ Qualified for the Europa League

IDN – INDONESIA

FIFA/COCA-COLA WORLD RANKING

'93	'94	'95	'96	'97	'98	'99	'00	'01	'02	'03	'04	'05	'06	'07	'08	'09	'10	'11	'12
106	134	130	119	91	87	90	97	87	110	91	91	109	153	133	139	120	127	142	

						2011								
Jan	Feb	Mar	Apr	May	Jun	Jul	Aug	Sep	Oct	Nov	Dec	**High**	**Low**	**Av**
125	129	128	130	130	132	137	131	139	140	144	142	**76**	**153**	**113**

The death of two fans in a crush at the final of the 2011 South East Asian Games between Indonesia and Malaysia in Jakarta brought to a tragic end a year in which the game in Indonesia was be beset by all manner of problems. A threat by FIFA to ban the football federation from all competitions was dropped when a new president and executive were elected mid-way through the year, but problems still remained. A breakaway league - the Liga Primer Indonesia - that had been formed prior to the resolution of the crisis was designated as the country's national championship by the new administration. However, the Indonesia Super League, which had previously been used to determine the champions, continued to operate and under a ruling passed by the Court of Arbitration for Sport in Lausanne, the 2011 champions Persipura Jayapura were admitted into the qualifying rounds of the 2012 AFC Champions League. The political fall-out surrounding the regime change at the PSSI also engulfed the national team, with Austrian coach Alfred Riedl replaced by Dutchman Wim Rijsbergen, who took over for the country's unsuccessful qualifying campaign for the 2014 FIFA World Cup. Rijsbergen was then appointed technical director at the start of 2012 and replaced as coach by Aji Santoso.

FIFA WORLD CUP RECORD
1930-1934 DNE **1938** 15 r1 1950-1954 DNE 1958 DNQ 1962-1970 DNE 1974-2014 DNQ

FOOTBALL ASSOCIATION OF INDONESIA (PSSI)

Gelora Bung Karno,
Pintu X-XI, Senayan,
PO Box 2305, Jakarta 10023
☎ +62 21 5704762
📠 +62 21 5734386
✉ pssi@pssi-football.com
🖥 www.pssi-football.com
FA 1930 CON 1954 FIFA 1952
P Djohar Arifin Husin
GS Tri Goestoro

FIFA BIG COUNT 2006

Total players	7 094 260
% of population	2.89%
Male	7 094 260
Female	0
Amateurs 18+	2 560
Youth under 18	62 600
Unregistered	6 982 300
Professionals	800
Referees	669
Admin & coaches	400
Number of clubs	73
Number of teams	73

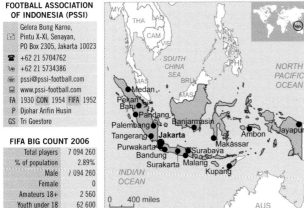

MAJOR CITIES/TOWNS

		Population
1	Jakarta	8 579 263
2	Surabaya	2 336 843
3	Medan	1 772 833
4	Bekasi	1 724 003
5	Bandung	1 601 767
6	Tangerang	1 495 586
7	Depok	1 442 313
8	Makasar	1 440 539
9	Semarang	1 283 279
10	Palembang	1 271 855
11	Padang	960 184
12	BandarLampung	916 561
13	Bogor	834 098
14	Pekan Baru	763 275
15	Malang	755 371
16	Yogyakarta	703 753
17	Banjarmasin	606 831
18	Surakarta	563 208
19	Manado	508 585

REPUBLIK INDONESIA • REPUBLIC OF INDONESIA

Capital Jakarta	Population 240 271 522 (4)	% in cities 52%
GDP per capita $3900 (155)	Area km² 1 904 569 km² (16)	GMT +/- +7
Neighbours (km) Timor-Leste 228, Malaysia 1782, Papua New Guinea 820 • Coast 54716		

RECENT INTERNATIONAL MATCHES PLAYED BY INDONESIA

2008 Opponents	Score	Venue	Comp	Scorers	Att	Referee
5-12 Myanmar	W 3-0	Jakarta	AFFr1	Budi Sunarsono [24], Firman Utina [28], Bambang Pamungkas [64]	40 000	Ramachandran MAS
7-12 Cambodia	W 4-0	Jakarta	AFFr1	Budi Sunarsono 3 [15 54 70], Bambang Pamungkas [76]	30 000	Nafeez MAS
9-12 Singapore	L 0-2	Jakarta	AFFr1		50 000	Ramachandran MAS
16-12 Thailand	L 0-1	Jakarta	AFFsf		70 000	Vo Minh Tri VIE
20-12 Thailand	L 1-2	Bangkok	AFFsf	OG [9]	40 000	Hadimin BRU
2009						
19-01 Oman	D 0-0	Muscat	ACq		13 000	Shamsuzzaman BAN
28-01 Australia	D 0-0	Jakarta	ACq		50 000	Abdul Bashir SIN
4-11 Singapore	L 1-3	Singapore	Fr	Eka Ramdani [12]		
14-11 Kuwait	L 1-2	Kuwait City	ACq	Bambang Pamungkas [33]	16 000	Kovalenko UZB
18-11 Kuwait	D 1-1	Jakarta	ACq	Budi Sunarsono [45]	36 000	Tojo JPN
2010						
6-01 Oman	L 1-2	Jakarta	ACq	Boaz Salossa [45]	45 000	Mohd Salleh MAS
3-03 Australia	L 0-1	Brisbane	ACq		20 422	Ogiya JPN
8-10 Uruguay	L 1-7	Jakarta	Fr	Boaz Salossa [18]	25 000	Daud SIN
12-10 Maldives	W 3-0	Bandung	Fr	Oktavianus Maniani [30], Yongki Aribowo [74], Tony Sucipto [90]	13 000	Palaniyandi SIN
21-11 Timor-Leste	W 6-0	Palembang	Fr	Muhammad Ridwan [12], Oktavianus Maniani [26], Cristian Gonzales 2 [37 46], Bambang Pamungkas [70], Yongki Aribowo [83]		
24-11 Chinese Taipei	W 2-0	Palembang	Fr	Cristian Gonzales [10], Firman Utina [18p]		Singh SIN
1-12 Malaysia	W 5-1	Jakarta	AFFr1	OG [22], Cristian Gonzales [33], Muhammad Ridwan [52], Arif Suyono [76], Irfan Bachdim [94+]	62 000	Vo Min Tri VIE
4-12 Laos	W 6-0	Jakarta	AFFr1	Firman Utina 2 [26p 51], Muhammad Ridwan [33], Irfan Bachdim [63], Arif Suyono [77], Oktavianus Maniani [82]	70 000	Daud SIN
7-12 Thailand	W 2-1	Jakarta	AFFr1	Bambang Pamungkas 2 [82 91+]	65 000	Sato JPN
16-12 Philippines	W 1-0	Jakarta	AFFsf	Cristian Gonzales [32]	70 000	Moradi IRN
19-12 Philippines	W 1-0	Jakarta	AFFsf	Cristian Gonzales [43]	88 000	Ebrahim BHR
26-12 Malaysia	L 0-3	Kuala Lumpur	AFFf		70 000	Toma JPN
29-12 Malaysia	W 2-1	Jakarta	AFFf	Mohammad Nasuha [72], Muhammad Ridwan [88]	88 000	Green AUS
2011						
23-07 Turkmenistan	D 1-1	Ashgabat	WCq	Muhammad Ilham [30]	7 500	Torky IRN
28-07 Turkmenistan	W 4-3	Jakarta	WCq	Cristian Gonzales 2 [9 19], Mohammad Nasuha [43], Muhammad Ridwan [76]	88 000	Williams AUS
22-08 Palestine	W 4-1	Surakarta	Fr	Hariono [65], Cristian Gonzales [70], Bambang Pamungkas 2 [77 85]	25 000	
27-08 Jordan	L 0-1	Amman	Fr			
2-09 Iran	L 0-3	Tehran	WCq		75 800	Toma JPN
6-09 Bahrain	L 0-2	Jakarta	WCq		85 000	Lee Min Hu KOR
7-10 Saudi Arabia	D 0-0	Kuala Lumpur	Fr		150	
11-10 Qatar	L 2-3	Jakarta	WCq	Cristian Gonzales 2 [27 35]	28 000	Bashir SIN
11-11 Qatar	L 0-4	Doha	WCq		6 500	Basma SYR
15-11 Iran	L 1-4	Jakarta	WCq	Bambang Pamungkas [44]	6 000	Tan Hai CHN

Fr = Friendly match • AFF = ASEAN Football Federation Championship • AC = AFC Asian Cup • WC = FIFA World Cup
q = qualifier • r1 = first round group • sf = semi-final • f = final

INDONESIA NATIONAL TEAM HISTORICAL RECORDS

Caps
83 - Bambang Pamungkas 1999-

Goals
37 - Bambang Pamungkas 1999- • 31 - Kurniawan Dwi Yulianto 1995-2005 • 16 - Budi Sudarsono 2001- & Rochy Putiray 1991-2004

Past Coaches
Johannes van Mastenbroek NED 1938 • Choo Seng Quee SIN 1951-53 • Antun Pogacnik YUG 1954-64 • EA Mangindaan 1966-70 • Endang Witarsa 1970 • Djamiaat Dalhar 1971-72 • Suwardi Arland 1972-74 • Aang Witarsa 1974-75 • Wiel Coerver NED 1975-76 • Suwardi Arland 1976-78 • Frans Van Balkom NED 1978-79 • Marek Janota 1979-80 • Bernd Fischer GER 1980-81 • Harry Tjong 1981-82 • Sinyo Aliandoe 1982-83 • M. Basri, Iswadi Idris and Abdul Kadir 1983-84 • Bertje Matulapelwa 1985-87 • Anatoli Polosin URS 1987-91 • Ivan Toplak YUG 1991-93 • Romano Matte ITA 1993-95 • Danurwindo 1995-96 • Henk Wullems NED 1996-97 • Rusdy Bahalwan 1998 • Bernard Schumm 1999 • Nandar Iskandar 1999-00 • Benny Dollo 2000-01 • Ivan Kolev BUL 2002-04 • Peter Withe ENG 2004-07 • Ivan Kolev BUL 2007 • Benny Dollo 2008-10 • Alfred Riedl AUT 2010-11 • Wim Rijsbergen NED 2011-12 • Aji Santoso 2012-

INDONESIA 2010–11

DJARUM INDONESIA SUPER LEAGUE (ISL)

	Pl	W	D	L	F	A	Pts	Persipura	Arema	Persija	Semen	Sriwijaya	Persisam	Persib	Persiwa	Persela	Persiba	PSPS	Pelita Jaya	Deltas	Persijap	Bontang
Persipura Jayapura †	28	17	9	2	63	23	60		6-1	2-1	1-1	3-2	2-0	5-1	1-1	3-0	3-1	4-1	2-1	2-0	1-0	8-1
Arema Indonesia ‡	28	15	7	6	52	25	52	1-0		2-1	3-1	1-1	2-0	2-0	4-0	1-0	3-0	4-2	1-0	3-0	2-0	8-0
Persija Jakarta	28	15	7	6	52	28	52	1-1	2-1		1-1	0-0	7-2	3-0	0-0	2-0	5-1	3-0	1-0	2-0	3-0	4-1
Semen Padang	28	12	12	4	41	27	48	1-1	2-0	1-0		2-1	3-1	1-1	3-0	1-0	2-1	1-0	4-0	3-0		2-2
Sriwijaya Palembang	28	13	7	8	43	32	46	0-0	1-1	3-3	5-0		3-1	4-1	2-1	0-0	2-1	2-1	2-1	1-0	2-0	4-1
Persisam Putra	28	13	3	12	39	45	42	1-2	2-1	1-0	1-1	4-1		1-0	5-2	4-1	4-1	2-0	1-0	1-0	1-1	1-2
Persib Bandung	28	11	6	11	44	43	39	2-2	1-1	2-3	1-1	1-0	4-1		5-2	2-1	5-1	0-1	1-0	4-0	4-1	3-0
Persiwa Wamena	28	10	8	10	43	50	38	1-1	1-0	2-0	0-0	2-0	1-1	3-0		0-0	3-1	2-0	3-3	2-0	3-1	4-2
Persela Lamongan	28	10	7	11	30	31	37	0-1	0-0	0-0	1-0	1-0	4-1	1-1	5-1		1-0	3-0	1-1	1-0	1-0	4-1
Persiba Balikpapan	28	9	7	12	41	44	34	1-0	0-0	0-1	1-1	0-1	2-0	2-0	4-0	4-0		3-2	3-1	4-0	0-0	1-1
PSPS Pekanbaru §3	28	10	3	15	38	47	30	1-2	1-1	2-2	2-1	0-1	0-1	1-0	0-3	2-1	2-2		1-0	1-0	5-0	6-2
Pelita Jaya Karawang	28	8	5	15	31	36	29	0-5	1-0	0-1	2-2	1-0	0-1	1-2	4-0	2-2	1-1	2-3		3-0	2-0	1-0
Delta Putra Sidoarjo	28	9	2	17	34	52	29	1-1	1-1	1-2	0-3	3-1	4-0	4-1	2-1	2-0	4-3	0-2			5-3	3-2
Persijap Jepara	28	7	7	14	28	50	28	1-3	2-3	4-1	1-1	1-1	1-0	1-1	3-2	0-2	1-1	1-0	1-0	2-1		2-1
Bontang	28	3	6	19	33	79	15	1-1	0-5	1-3	1-1	2-3	0-1	0-1	3-3	2-0	3-5	0-1	1-2	2-1	1-1	

26/09/2009 - 19/06/2011 • † Qualified for the AFC Champions League • ‡ Qualified for the AFC Cup • § = points deducted
Relegation play-off: Bontang 2-3 **Persidafon**
Top scorers: **22** - Boaz Solossa, Persipura • **16** - Francisco Barreto PAR, Persiba & Edward Wilson Junior LBR, Semen • **15** - Kenji Adachihara JPN, Bontang • **13** - Marcio Souza BRA, Deltras; Greg Nwokolo NGA, Persija; Boakay Eddie Foday LBR, Persiwa & Julio Lopez CHI, Persisam • **12** - Dzumafo Herman Epandi CMR, PSPS & Bambang Pamungkas, Persija • **11** - Cristiano Lopes BRA, Deltras & Budi Sudarsono, Sriwijaya • **10** - Keith Gumbs SKN, Sriwijaya & Ferdinand Sinaga, Persiwa • **9** - Cristian Gonzales, Persib

INDONESIA 2011

LIGA PRIMER INDONESIA

	Pl	W	D	L	F	A	Pts	Persebaya	Persema	PSM	Jakarta FC	Medan	Batavia	Bali	Persibo	Semarang	Minangkabau	Atjeh	Bintang	Bogor	Solo	Bandung	Mataram	Manado	Tangerang	Cendrawasih
Persebaya 1927	18	12	4	2	42	13	40		4-0	3-2				4-0		4-1	2-0						2-1	3-1		0-0
Persema Malang	18	12	4	2	35	17	40			2-1	2-1	1-1	1-0	1-1	2-0	1-1		4-1					5-2	2-1		
PSM Makassar	18	10	4	4	36	18	34	4-0				1-4	2-1			2-0	2-0	3-0	4-1				1-1	0-0		5-1
Jakarta FC 1928	18	9	5	4	33	20	32	0-1								2-1	0-1		3-1		3-0		3-1	3-0		2-2
Medan Chiefs	18	9	5	4	26	20	32	0-0						2-2	0-2			2-0	2-1				3-0	2-0		
Batavia Union	18	8	7	3	32	23	31	0-0			1-1	1-1				2-0	2-1	1-2	3-2				4-1	3-2		
Bali Devata	18	8	5	5	22	17	29	2-1		2-3	1-1		0-1			1-1	2-0		1-0					1-0	2-2	3-1
Persibo Bojonegoro	18	8	5	5	25	22	29					5-1	0-2	1-1		3-1	0-0		2-1			2-1	2-1	2-0		
Semarang United	18	9	1	8	18	21	28	0-1				0-1	2-1	1-0			2-1			3-2			0-0	1-0		1-0
Minangkabau FC	18	8	5	5	21	20	27	0-5			1-0	2-2		1-1		1-0			1-0					4-1	3-1	3-1
Atjeh United	18	8	2	8	23	24	26	1-0				0-1			1-1	2-0				1-0			2-0	2-1		4-1
Bintang Medan	18	6	4	8	29	30	22	1-1				0-1	1-2	2-2		1-0		1-0			2-1			3-0	3-1	
Bogor Raya FC	18	6	3	9	22	24	21			1-2	2-0	2-4		2-0	1-1	2-1	0-0				0-4		5-0	3-0		
Solo FC	18	4	4	10	19	29	16			0-2	1-5	1-4	0-1		0-3			1-0		3-1			7-3			0-0
Bandung FC	18	4	4	10	22	33	16			0-1	1-1		1-1		0-1	0-1	3-1	1-0		2-2			5-3			1-2
Real Mataram	18	4	4	10	27	41	16	2-6				1-1			3-2	0-1		1-2		3-1		1-1			2-2	2-1
Manado United	18	3	6	9	19	36	15	0-0				1-2		2-1	0-2			2-2		1-0		1-1				3-0
Tangerang Wolves	18	2	5	11	19	36	11	0-4				0-2	2-3	3-3			2-4		1-1		0-0		1-1	2-0		
Cendrawasih Papua	18	1	4	13	18	44	7	1-5				0-0		1-2	1-2				3-2	1-2			1-2	2-4		

8/01/2011 - 20/11/2011
Top scorers: **13** - Juan Manuel Cortes ARG, Batavia; Fernando Soler ARG, Real Mataram & Laakkad Abdelhadi MAR, Medan Chiefs

INDONESIA 2010–11
DIVISIE UTAMA (2) GROUP 1

	Pl	W	D	L	F	A	Pts
Persiraja Banda Aceh ‡	24	15	3	6	43	25	48
PSAP Sigli ‡	24	14	5	5	53	20	47
PSMS Medan ‡	24	14	3	7	36	25	45
Persita Tangerang	24	12	7	5	42	18	43
Persipasi Bekasi	24	13	4	7	38	21	43
Persih Tembilahan	24	13	3	8	31	32	42
Persitara Jakarta	24	9	6	9	29	34	33
Persikabo Bogor	24	8	6	10	34	34	30
PSLS Lhokseumawe	24	7	8	9	24	24	29
Bengkulu City	24	7	6	11	20	35	27
Pro Duta	24	5	8	11	26	32	23
PSSB Bireuen	24	4	6	14	19	35	18
Persires Rengat	24	1	3	20	12	72	6

19/11/2010 - 30/04/2011 • ‡ Qualified for the play-offs

INDONESIA 2010–11
DIVISIE UTAMA (2) GROUP 2

	Pl	W	D	L	F	A	Pts
Mitra Kukar ‡	24	15	2	7	38	20	47
Persiram Raja Ampat ‡	24	11	9	4	26	20	42
Gresik United ‡	24	12	4	8	27	16	40
Perseman Manokwari	24	12	3	9	22	15	39
PSIM Yogyakarta	24	12	3	9	26	22	39
Persik Kediri	24	11	3	10	25	21	36
Persikab Kabupaten	24	10	5	9	33	30	35
PSIS Semarang	24	10	5	9	22	22	35
PSCS Cilacap	24	9	5	10	25	26	32
Persemalra	24	10	1	13	32	30	31
PPSM Sakti Magelang	24	9	3	12	18	26	30
Persikota Tangerang	24	6	8	10	18	24	26
Persis Solo	24	1	5	18	8	48	0

19/11/2010 - 30/04/2011 • ‡ Qualified for the play-offs

INDONESIA 2010–11
DIVISIE UTAMA (2) GROUP 3

	Pl	W	D	L	F	A	Pts
Persifadon Dafonsoro ‡	24	15	3	6	51	17	48
Persiba Bantul ‡	24	13	5	6	52	20	44
PSBI Blitar	24	12	3	9	29	24	39
Persigo Gorontalo	24	11	3	10	30	30	36
Barito Putra	24	11	2	11	30	23	35
Persiku Kudus	24	11	1	12	30	36	34
Persekam Metro	24	11	1	12	28	37	34
Perseru Serui	24	9	4	11	30	31	31
Persipro Probolinggo	24	9	4	11	23	35	31
PSS Sleman	24	9	4	11	22	40	31
Persebaya Surabaya	24	11	0	13	32	40	30
PSIR Rembang	24	9	3	12	23	35	30
Mojokerto Putra	24	6	5	13	22	34	23

19/11/2010 - 30/04/2011 • ‡ Qualified for the play-offs

MEDALS TABLE

		Overall		Lge		Cup		
		G	S	G	S	G	S	City
1	Persija	11	6	11	5		1	Jakarta
2	Persis	8	1	8	1			Solo
3	Persebaya	7	11	7	11			Surabaya
4	Tiga Berlian	7	1	4	1	3		Palembang
5	Persib	6	8	6	8			Bandung
	PSM	6	8	6	8			Makassar
7	PSMS	6	7	6	7			Medan
8	Persipura	4	5	4	2		3	Jayapura
9	Arema	4	3	2	1	2	2	Malang
10	Sriwijaya	4		1		3		Palembang
11	Pelita Jaya	3	5	3	2		3	Karawang
12	Mitra Kukar	3	2	3	1		1	Tenggarong
13	Arseto	2	1	1	1	1		Solo
	PSIS	2	1	2	1			Semarang
15	Persik	2		2				Kediri
16	PSIM	1	5	1	5			Yogyakarta
17	Petrokimia	1	1	1	1			Gresik
	Bandung Raya	1	1	1	1			Bandung
	Gelora Dewata	1	1		1		1	Denpasar
20	Persiraja	1		1				Banda Aceh
	Warna Agung	1		1				Jakarta
	Semen Padang	1				1		Indarung
	Makassar Utama	1					1	Makassar

DIVISIE UTAMA (2) PLAY-OFFS (DELAPAN BESAR)

First round

Group A

	Pl	W	D	L	F	A	Pts	PBA	GU	PRA
Persifadon Dafonsoro	3	2	1	0	7	4	7	1-1	3-2	3-1
Persiraja Banda Aceh	3	1	1	1	3	4	4		2-1	0-2
Gresik United	3	1	0	2	6	7	3			3-2
Persiram Raja Ampat	3	1	0	2	5	6	3			

Group B

	Pl	W	D	L	F	A	Pts	PB	PSAP	PSMS
Mitra Kukar	3	2	1	0	4	1	7	0-0	1-0	3-1
Persiba Bantul	3	0	3	0	3	3	3		0-0	3-3
PSAP Sigli	3	0	2	1	1	2	2			1-1
PSMS Medan	3	0	2	1	5	7	2			

12/05/2011 - 25/05/2011 • Persiba, Persiraja and Mitra promoted to ISL. Persifadon entered play-off (see ISL)

Semi-finals

Persiba Bantul
Persifadon Dafonsoro

Mitra Kukar
Persiraja Banda Aceh

Final

Persiba Bantul	1
Persiraja Banda Aceh	0

3rd place play-off

Mitra Kukar	2
Persifadon Dafonsoro	1

IND – INDIA

'93	'94	'95	'96	'97	'98	'99	'00	'01	'02	'03	'04	'05	'06	'07	'08	'09	'10	'11	'12
100	109	121	120	112	110	106	122	121	127	127	132	127	157	143	143	134	142	162	

	2011												High	Low	Av
	Jan	Feb	Mar	Apr	May	Jun	Jul	Aug	Sep	Oct	Nov	Dec			
	144	145	145	145	144	147	153	158	163	160	162	162	94	165	128

Indian football generated significant column inches in the world's press in early 2012 with the announcement of a league featuring global stars and an auction styled on cricket's Indian Premier League. World Cup winner Fabian Cannavaro and former Liverpool star Robbie Fowler were amongst those due to feature in Premier League Soccer, which was to be played in the football hotbed of West Bengal. However, opposition from the All India Football Federation and a lack of top grade facilities were believed to be behind the postponement of the league, the latter highlighting issues that had been raised by former national team coach Bob Houghton. The Englishman was hounded out of his position at the helm of the national side following their appearance at the AFC Asian Cup finals in Qatar at the start of 2011 and he was replaced, first by Armando Colaco and then by Savio Medeira. Under Medeira, India once again won the South Asian Football Federation Championship, handing surprise package Afghanistan a 4-0 defeat in the 2011 final in New Delhi to claim the crown for a record sixth time. In club football, Salgoacar were the team of the season, winning both the I-League and the Federation Cup ahead of East Bengal. The third major tournament of the year, the Durand Cup was won by Salgoacar's Goan rivals Churchill Brothers.

FIFA WORLD CUP RECORD
1930-1982 DNE 1986 DNQ 1990 DNE 1994-2014 DNQ

ALL INDIA FOOTBALL FEDERATION (AIFF)

Football House, Sector 19,
Phase 1 Dwarka,
New Delhi 110075
☎ +91 11 28041430
🖷 +91 11 28041434
✉ aiff@the-aiff.com
🖥 www.the-aiff.com
FA 1937 CON 1954 FIFA 1948
P Praful Patel
GS Kushal Das

FIFA BIG COUNT 2006

Total players	20 587 900
% of population	1.88%
Male	19 020 900
Female	1 567 000
Amateurs 18+	71 000
Youth under 18	313 500
Unregistered	2 212 000
Professionals	400
Referees	17 640
Admin & coaches	21 000
Number of clubs	6 500
Number of teams	12 000

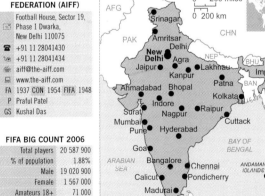

MAJOR CITIES/TOWNS

		Population
1	Mumbai/Bombay	13 922 125
2	Delhi/Dilli	12 259 230
3	Bangalore	5 310 318
4	Calcutta/Kolkata	5 080 519
5	Madras/Chennai	4 590 267
6	Hyderabad	4 025 335
7	Ahmadabad	3 913 793
8	Pune	3 337 481
9	Surat	3 233 988
10	Kanpur	3 144 267
11	Jaipur	3 102 808
12	Lakhnau	2 685 528
13	Nagpur	2 403 239
14	Patna	1 814 012
15	Indore	1 811 513
16	Bhopal	1 752 244
17	Thana	1 739 697
18	Ludhiana	1 701 212
19	Agra	1 638 209

BHARATIYA GANARAJYA • REPUBLIC OF INDIA

Capital	New Delhi	Population	1 166 079 217 (2)	% in cities	29%
GDP per capita	$2900 (167)	Area km²	3 287 263 km² (7)	GMT +/-	+5.5
Neighbours (km)	Bangladesh 4053, Bhutan 605, China 3380, Myanmar 1463, Nepal 1690, Pakistan 2912 • Coast 7000				

RECENT INTERNATIONAL MATCHES PLAYED BY INDIA

2008 Opponents	Score	Venue	Comp	Scorers	Att	Referee
30-07 Afghanistan	W 1-0	Hyderabad	CCr1	Lawrence [92+]	300	Iemoto JPN
1-08 Tajikistan	D 1-1	Hyderabad	CCr1	Tuchiev OG [61]	350	Shamsuzzaman BAN
3-08 Turkmenistan	W 2-1	Hyderabad	CCr1	Bhutia 2 [54 80]	1 000	Jasim UAE
7-08 Myanmar	W 1-0	Hyderabad	CCsf	Chetri [82]	1 500	Shamsuzzaman BAN
13-08 Tajikistan	W 4-1	Delhi	CCf	Chetri 3 [9 23 75], Bhutia [18]	10 000	Kovalenko UZB
2009						
14-01 Hong Kong	L 1-2	Hong Kong	Fr	Bhutia [80]	1 200	
19-08 Lebanon	L 0-1	New Delhi	Fr			Hannan BAN
23-08 Kyrgyzstan	W 2-1	New Delhi	Fr	Bhutia [43], Chetri [58p]		
26-08 Sri Lanka	W 3-1	New Delhi	Fr	Bhutia [25], Gouramangi Singh [69], Dias [85]		Adil MDV
29-08 Syria	L 0-1	New Delhi	Fr			Adil MDV
31-08 Syria	D 1-1	New Delhi	Fr	Renedy Singh [114]. W 5-4p	20 000	Adil MDV
2010						
4-09 Thailand	L 0-1	Bangkok	Fr			
8-09 Thailand	L 1-2	New Delhi	Fr	Pradeep [60]		
15-09 Namibia	W 2-0	New Delhi	Fr	Wadoo [28], Pereira [54]		Patwal IND
4-10 Hong Kong	L 0-1	Pune	Fr		8 000	Patwal IND
8-10 Vietnam	W 3-1	Pune	Fr	Chetri 3 [25 49 72]		Dinesh IND
13-10 Yemen	L 3-6	Pune	Fr	Pereira [21], Yadav [49], Surkurmar Singh 92+		Patwal IND
11-11 Iraq	L 0-2	Sharjah	Fr			
14-11 Kuwait	L 1-9	Abu Dhabi	Fr	Rafi [69]		
18-11 UAE	L 0-5	Dubai	Fr			
2011						
10-01 Australia	L 0-4	Doha	ACr1		11 749	Badwawi UAE
14-01 Bahrain	L 2-5	Doha	ACr1	Gouramangi Singh [9], Chetri [52]	11 032	Mohd Salleh MAS
18-01 Korea Republic	L 1-4	Doha	ACr1	Chetri [12p]	11 366	Al Ghamdi KSA
21-03 Chinese Taipei	W 3-0	Petaling Jaya	CCq	Jeje Lalpekhlua [32], Sunil Chetri [76], Jewel Shaikh [88]	50	Abdul Wahab MAS
23-03 Pakistan	W 3-1	Petaling Jaya	CCq	Jeje Lalpekhlua 2 [67 94+], Steven Dias [90]	100	Alrshaidat JOR
25-03 Turkmenistan	D 1-1	Petaling Jaya	CCq	Jeje Lalpekhlua [60]	200	Abdul Wahab MAS
10-07 Maldives	D 1-1	Male	Fr	Sunil Chetri [18]		
23-07 UAE	L 0-3	Al Ain	WCq		3 179	Al Dosari QAT
28-07 UAE	D 2-2	New Delhi	WCq	Jeje Lalpekhlua [74], Gouramangi Moirangthem 92+	13 000	Bashir SIN
21-08 Trinidad & Tobago	L 0-3	Port of Spain	Fr		6 600	Campbell JAM
24-08 Guyana	L 1-2	Georgetown	Fr	Steven Dias [36]	2 500	Lancaster GUY
13-11 Malaysia	D 1-1	Guwahati	Fr	Syed Nabi [88]	20 000	
16-11 Malaysia	W 3-2	Calcutta	Fr	Sunil Chetri 2 [39 53], Jeje Lalpekhlua [47]	2 500	.
29-11 Zambia	L 0-5	Margao	Fr			
3-12 Afghanistan	D 1-1	New Delhi	SAFr1	Sunil Chetri [10]		
5-12 Bhutan	W 5-0	New Delhi	SAFr1	Syed Nabi [29], Clifford Miranda 2 [44 58], Sunil Chetri 2 [69 84]		
7-12 Sri Lanka	W 3-0	New Delhi	SAFr1	Jeje Lalpekhlua [50], Sunil Chetri [70], OG [93+]		
9-12 Maldives	W 3-1	New Delhi	SAFsf	Syed Nabi [24], Sunil Chetri 2 [70p 91+]		
11-12 Afghanistan	W 4-0	New Delhi	SAFf	Sunil Chetri [71p], Clifford Miranda [79], Jeje Lalpekhlua [80], Sushil Singh [95+]		

Fr = Friendly match • SAF = South Asian Football Federation Cup • CC - AFC Confederation Cup • AC = AFC Asian Cup • WC = FIFA World Cup
q = qualifier • r1 = first round group • qf = quarter-final • sf = semi-final • f = final

INDIA NATIONAL TEAM HISTORICAL RECORDS

Caps
110 - Shabbir Ali 1974-84 • **107** - Bhaichung Bhutia 1995- • **84** - PK Banerjee 1952-67 • **82** - Mahesh Gawli 1997-2011

Goals
65 - PK Banerjee 1952-67 • **43** - Bhaichung Bhutia 1995- • **40** - IM Vijayan 1989-2004 • **35** - Shabbir Ali 1974-84 • **35** - Sunil Chetri 2005-

Past Coaches
Syed Abdul Rahim 1950-62 • Harry Wright ENG 1963-64 • Pradip Kumar Banerjee 1981-82 • Bob Bootland ENG 1983 • Milovan Ciric YUG 1984 • Barry Ford AUS 1984 • Pradip Kumar Banerjee 1985 • Syed Nayeemuddin 1986 • Amal Dutta 1987 • Jozsef Gelei HUN 1990-91 • Syed Nayeemuddin 1992 • Jiri Pesek CZE 1993-94 • Rustam Akramov UZB 1995-96 • Syed Nayeemuddin 1997-98 • Sukhvinder Singh 1999-02 • Stephen Constantine ENG 2002-05 • Syed Nayeemuddin 2005-06 • Bob Houghton ENG 2006-11 • Armando Colaco 2011 • Savio Medeira 2011-

INDIA 2010–11

ONGC I-LEAGUE	Pl	W	D	L	F	A	Pts	Salgoacar	East Bengal	Dempo	Churchill Bros	Pune	Mohun Bagan	Mumbai	Chirag Utd	Indian Arrows	Viva Kerala	Air India	HAL	JCT Mills	ONGC
Salgoacar †	26	18	2	6	58	27	56		3-2	1-3	4-3	0-1	1-3	2-3	4-3	5-0	4-0	0-1	3-0	2-0	5-0
East Bengal †	26	15	6	5	44	21	51	1-0		3-2	2-2	1-0	2-1	1-2	2-1	4-0	3-0	6-1	1-0	3-0	1-0
Dempo Sports Club	26	15	5	6	63	33	50	1-3	0-1		2-0	2-1	4-1	1-0	1-1	5-2	3-3	14-0	2-4	2-0	2-0
Churchill Brothers	26	14	8	4	57	31	50	1-2	2-1	1-1		2-3	2-0	3-1	2-1	6-0	1-1	2-0	3-0	3-1	3-3
Pune	26	9	9	8	32	27	36	0-1	2-1	3-2	0-1		1-1	1-1	1-1	3-0	4-4	2-1	0-1	4-0	1-0
Mohun Bagan	26	8	10	8	34	32	34	2-2	1-1	2-2	0-0	0-0		2-0	0-1	2-0	2-1	2-0	1-2	2-0	1-2
Mumbai FC	26	9	7	10	24	28	34	0-1	1-1	0-1	1-5	2-0	0-0		0-0	1-2	2-0	2-1	1-0	1-1	1-0
Chirag United	26	5	14	7	31	36	29	1-4	0-0	2-4	3-5	1-0	1-1	0-1		2-1	1-1	0-0	1-0	0-0	4-2
Indian Arrows	26	7	8	11	31	49	29	1-3	1-1	1-1	1-2	0-0	5-4	1-1	0-0		0-1	2-1	2-1	0-0	1-1
Viva Kerala	26	6	9	11	30	36	27	0-3	0-1	0-2	0-1	1-1	2-0	1-0	1-1	0-1		7-1	1-1	4-1	0-0
Air India	26	5	9	12	25	57	24	1-1	0-3	4-0	2-2	0-0	1-1	0-1	1-1	2-5	1-1		1-1	1-0	0-0
HAL Bangalore	26	6	6	14	18	40	24	0-1	1-1	0-3	0-3	1-2	1-1	1-0	1-1	0-4	0-1	1-3		0-0	1-0
JCT Mills	26	6	6	14	17	35	24	0-2	0-1	1-2	1-1	2-1	0-1	1-0	2-2	2-0	1-0	2-0	0-1		1-0
ONGC Mumbai	26	5	9	12	25	40	24	0-1	1-0	0-1	1-1	1-1	1-3	2-2	2-2	1-1	1-0	1-2	4-0	2-1	

3/12/2010 - 1/06/2011 • † Qualified for the AFC Cup

Top scorer: **30** - Ranty Martins NGA, Dempo • **23** - Odafe Onyeka NGA, Churchill • **18** - Ryuji Sueoka JPN, Salgoacar • **17** - Beto BRA, Dempo & Tolgay Ozbey AUS, East Bengal • **15** - Yusif Yakubu GHA, Salgoacar • **13** - Jeje Lalpekhlua, Indian Arrows • **12** - Kayne Vincent NZL, Churchill

INDIA 2010–11
NATIONAL LEAGUE 2ND DIVISION

	Pl	W	D	L	F	A	Pts
Shillong Lajong	7	5	1	1	12	6	16
Sporting Clube Goa	7	4	2	1	10	6	14
Vasco Sports Club	7	4	1	2	13	8	13
Ar-Hima FC	7	3	2	2	11	8	11
United Sikkim	7	2	4	1	9	9	10
Royal Wahingdoh	7	1	2	4	12	13	5
Mohammedan Sporting	7	1	1	5	4	9	4
Southern Samity	7	1	1	5	4	16	4

24/04/2011 - 13/05/2011

33RD FEDERATION CUP 2011

First round group stage

Group A (Pune)	Pl	W	D	L	F	A	Pts	RW	CB	MB
Shillong Lajong	3	2	0	1	5	4	6	1-0	1-3	3-1
Royal Wahingdoh	3	2	0	1	4	3	6		2-1	2-1
Churchill Brothers	3	1	1	1	4	3	4			2-2
Mohun Bagan	3	0	1	2	2	5	1			

Group B (Pune)	Pl	W	D	L	F	A	Pts	IA	Mu	HAL
Salgoacar	3	2	1	0	7	0	7	3-0	0-0	4-0
Indian Arrows	3	2	0	1	3	4	6		2-1	1-0
Mumbai FC	3	1	1	1	3	3	4			2-1
HAL Bangalore	3	0	0	3	1	7	0			

Group C (Kolkata)	Pl	W	D	L	F	A	Pts	De	Pu	MS
East Bengal	3	2	1	0	4	2	7	1-0	2-1	1-1
Dempo Sports Club	3	1	0	2	4	4	3		1-2	3-1
Pune	3	1	1	1	3	3	4			0-0
Mohammedan Sporting	3	0	2	1	2	4	2			

Group D (Kolkata)	Pl	W	D	L	F	A	Pts	SCG	AI	CU
Prayag United	3	2	1	0	3	1		2-1	0-0	1-0
Sporting Clube Goa	3	2	0	1	4	3			2-1	1-0
Air India	3	1	1	1	4	4				3-2
Chirag United	3	0	0	3	2	5				

Semi–finals

Salgoacar	1
Shillong Lajong	0

Prayag United	1
East Bengal	2

† Qualified for the AFC Cup
Semi–finals played in Kolkata
17/09/2011 - 29/09/2011

Final

Salgoacar	3
East Bengal †	1

CUP FINAL

Salt Lake Stadium, Kolkata
29-09-2011, 18:00
Att: 85 000, Ref: Kumar
Scorers - Chidi Edeh [5], Francis Fernandes [17], Ryuji Sueoka [67] for Salgoacar; Alan Gow [26] for East Bengal

124TH DURAND CUP 2011

First round group stage

Group A	Pl	W	D	L	F	A	Pts	Sa	BSF
Prayag United	2	2	0	0	4	0	**6**	2-0	2-0
Salgoacar	2	1	0	1	1	2	**3**		1-0
BSF	2	0	0	2	0	3	**0**		

Group B	Pl	W	D	L	F	A	Pts	US	IAF
Shillong Lajong	2	2	0	0	5	2	**6**	3-1	2-1
United Sikkim	2	1	0	1	4	3	**3**		3-0
Indian Air Force	2	0	0	2	1	5	**0**		

Group C	Pl	W	D	L	F	A	Pts	AI	ONG
Pune	2	1	1	0	3	2	**4**	2-1	1-1
Air India	2	1	0	1	4	2	**3**		3-0
ONGC	2	0	1	1	1	4	**1**		

Group D	Pl	W	D	L	F	A	Pts	MS	AR
Churchill Brothers	2	2	0	0	7	0	**6**	2-0	5-0
Mohammedan Sporting	2	1	0	1	1	2	**3**		1-0
Army Red	2	0	0	2	0	6	**0**		

Semi–finals

Churchill Brothers	4
Shillong Lajong	1

Pune	0
Prayag United	2

Played in New Delhi
4/10/2011 - 15/10/2011

Final

Churchill Brothers	0 5p
Prayag United	0 4p

CUP FINAL

Ambedkar, New Delhi
15-10-2011

MEDALS TABLE

		Overall			League			FC		D Cup	St		Asia			City	DOF
		G	S	B	G	S	B	G	S	G	S		G	S	B		
1	Mohun Bagan	32	27	2	3	2	1	13	5	16	20	26			1	Kolkata	1889
2	East Bengal FC	25	22	2	3	4	2	7	8	15	10	31				Kolkata	1920
3	JCT Mills	8	8	1	1	1	1	2		5	7	9				Phagwara	1971
4	Salgoacar SC	8	4	2	2	1	2	4	3	2		18				Vasco, Goa	
5	Border Security Force	8	3					1	1	7	2	3				Jalandhar	1962
6	Mahindra United	6	6	2	1		2	2	3	3	3	12				Mumbai	1955
7	Dempo Sports Club	6	4	1	4	1	1	1	3	1		10				Panjim, Goa	1968
8	Churchill Brothers SC	3	7	2	1	5	2			2	2	6				Salcete, Goa	1988
9	Mohammedan Sporting	3	6					2	3	1	3	11				Kolkata	1892
10	Kerala Police	2						2				5				Thiruv'puram	
11	Indian Telephone Ind.	1						1				18				Bangalore	
	Chirag United	1								1						Kolkata	1927
13	Sporting Clube de Goa		4	1		1	1	2		1		1				Goa	1999
14	Mafatlal Hills		2					2									
15	Prayag United		1							1						Kerala	1983
	Tata Football Academy		1							1						Jamshedpur	1983
	Shillong Lajong		1					1								Shillong	1951
18	Vasco Sports Club			2			2					6				Vasco, Goa	2007
19	Pune FC			1			1									Balewadi	1952

FC = Federation Cup • D Cup = Durand Cup • St = State championship (not included in overall total)

IRL – REPUBLIC OF IRELAND

FIFA/COCA-COLA WORLD RANKING

'93	'94	'95	'96	'97	'98	'99	'00	'01	'02	'03	'04	'05	'06	'07	'08	'09	'10	'11	'12
10	9	28	36	47	56	35	31	17	14	14	12	24	49	35	38	35	36	22	

						2011									
Jan	Feb	Mar	Apr	May	Jun	Jul	Aug	Sep	Oct	Nov	Dec		High	Low	Av
35	35	34	34	34	31	33	31	29	25	21	22		6	57	28

The Republic of Ireland qualified for the finals of the European Championship for only the second time in their history, Giovanni Trapattoni inspiring the team to a play-off victory over Estonia and a place in the finals in Poland and the Ukraine. Once again the goals of Robbie Keane proved vital and in the 2-0 victory over Macedonia in June 2011 he became the first player from the British Isles to score 50 goals in an international career. The draw for the finals landed the Irish in the most difficult group, alongside Trapattoni's compatriots Italy, Croatia and world champions Spain. They will hope to rekindle the fighting spirit of the Jack Charlton era and banish the memories of the internal disputes which tarnished the 2002 FIFA World Cup campaign - their last appearance at the finals of a major tournament. In club football, Shamrock Rovers successfully defended their league title while Sligo Rovers did the same in the FAI Cup, where once again goalkeeper Ciaran Kelly was the hero for Sligo. In the 2010 final he had saved four penalties in the shoot-out. Against Shelbourne in the 2011 final, he was brought on just before the end and saved two of the three Shelbourne penalties. Derry City celebrated their return to the top flight by winning the League Cup - their tenth triumph since first winning the trophy 21 years previously.

UEFA EUROPEAN CHAMPIONSHIP RECORD
1960 pr 1964 QF 1968-1984 DNQ **1988** 5 r1 1992-2008 DNQ **2012** Qualified

THE FOOTBALL ASSOCIATION OF IRELAND (FAI)

National Sports Campus, Abbotstown, Dublin 15
☎ +353 1 8999500
🖷 +353 1 8999501
✉ info@fai.ie
🌐 www.fai.ie
FA 1921 CON 1954 FIFA 1923
P Paddy McCaul
GS John Delaney

FIFA BIG COUNT 2006

Total players	421 644
% of population	10.38%
Male	390 444
Female	31 200
Amateurs 18+	77 870
Youth under 18	174 498
Unregistered	98 800
Professionals	476
Referees	1 020
Admin & coaches	6 310
Number of clubs	5 629
Number of teams	15 025

MAJOR CITIES/TOWNS

		Population
1	Dublin	1 064 376
2	Cork	193 328
-	Londonderry	83 652
3	Galway	76 433
4	Waterford	49 094
5	Swords	38 711
6	Limerick	38 439
7	Dundalk	35 867
8	Bray	32 436
9	Drogheda	32 221
10	Navan	29 437
11	Ennis	26 205
12	Kilkenny	23 369
13	Tralee	22 945
14	Naas	21 418
15	Newbridge	20 614
16	Mullingar	20 202
17	Carlow	19 999
18	Sligo	18 926

EIRE • IRELAND

Capital Dublin	Population 4 203 200 (125)	% in cities 61%
GDP per capita $45 500 (11)	Area km² 70 273 km² (119)	GMT +/- 0
Neighbours (km) United Kingdom (Northern Ireland) 360 • Coast 1448		

RECENT INTERNATIONAL MATCHES PLAYED BY THE REPUBLIC OF IRELAND

2008	Opponents		Score	Venue	Comp	Scorers	Att	Referee
20-08	Norway	D	1-1	Oslo	Fr	Keane [44]	16 037	Whitby WAL
6-09	Georgia	W	2-1	Mainz	WCq	Doyle [13], Whelan [70]	4 500	Szabo HUN
10-09	Montenegro	D	0-0	Podgorica	WCq		12 000	Kaldma EST
15-10	Cyprus	W	1-0	Dublin	WCq	Keane [5]	55 833	Tudor ROU
19-11	Poland	L	2-3	Dublin	Fr	Hunt [88p], Andrews [91+]	50 566	Jakobsson ISL
2009								
11-02	Georgia	W	2-1	Dublin	WCq	Keane 2 [73p 78]	45 000	Hyytia FIN
28-03	Bulgaria	D	1-1	Dublin	WCq	Dunne [1]	60 002	Bebek CRO
1-04	Italy	D	1-1	Bari	WCq	Keane [88]	48 000	Stark GER
29-05	Nigeria	D	1-1	London	Fr	Keane [38]	11 263	Collum SCO
6-06	Bulgaria	D	1-1	Sofia	WCq	Dunne [24]	38 000	Larsen DEN
12-08	Australia	L	0-3	Limerick	Fr		19 000	Burrull ESP
5-09	Cyprus	W	2-1	Nicosia	WCq	Doyle [5], Keane [83]	5 191	Einwaller AUT
8-09	South Africa	W	1-0	Limerick	Fr	Lawrence [37]	11 300	Thomson SCO
10-10	Italy	D	2-2	Dublin	WCq	Whelan [8], St Ledger [87]	70 640	Hauge NOR
14-10	Montenegro	D	0-0	Dublin	WCq		50 212	Hrinak SVK
14-11	France	L	0-1	Dublin	WCpo		74 103	Brych GER
18-11	France	D	1-1	Paris	WCpo	Keane [33]	79 145	Hansson SWE
2010								
2-03	Brazil	L	0-2	London	Fr		40 082	Dean ENG
25-05	Paraguay	W	2-1	Dublin	Fr	Doyle [7], Lawrence [39]	16 722	Laperriere SUI
28-05	Algeria	W	3-0	Dublin	Fr	Green [31], Keane 2 [51 86]	16 888	Braamhaar NED
11-08	Argentina	L	0-1	Dublin	Fr		45 200	Rasmussen DEN
3-09	Armenia	W	1-0	Yerevan	ECq	Fahey [76]	8 600	Szabo HUN
7-09	Andorra	W	3-1	Dublin	ECq	Kilbane [15], Doyle [41], Keane [54]	40 283	Trattou CYP
8-10	Russia	L	2-3	Dublin	ECq	Keane [72p], Long [78]	50 411	Blom NED
12-10	Slovakia	D	1-1	Zilina	ECq	St Ledger [16]	10 892	Undiano ESP
17-11	Norway	L	1-2	Dublin	Fr	Long [5p]	25 000	Jakobsson ISL
2011								
8-02	Wales	W	3-0	Dublin	Fr	Gibson [60], Duff [66], Fahey [82]	19 783	Courtney NIR
26-03	Macedonia FYR	W	2-1	Dublin	ECq	McGeady [2], Keane [21]	33 200	Vad HUN
29-03	Uruguay	L	2-3	Dublin	Fr	Long [15], Fahey [48p]	20 200	Ennjimi FRA
24-05	Northern Ireland	W	5-0	Dublin	Fr	Ward [24], Keane 2 [37 54p], OG [45], Cox [80]	12 083	Thomson SCO
29-05	Scotland	W	1-0	Dublin	Fr	Keane [23]	17 694	Whitby WAL
4-06	Macedonia FYR	W	2-0	Skopje	ECq	Keane 2 [8 37]	29 500	Meyer GER
7-06	Italy	W	2-0	Liege	Fr	Andrews [36], Cox [90]	21 516	Gumienny BEL
10-08	Croatia	D	0-0	Dublin	Fr		20 179	Hagen NOR
2-09	Slovakia	D	0-0	Dublin	ECq		35 480	Proenca POR
6-09	Russia	D	0-0	Moscow	ECq		49 515	Brych GER
7-10	Andorra	W	2-0	Andorra La Vella	ECq	Doyle [8], McGeady [20]	860	Kovarik CZE
11-10	Armenia	W	2-1	Dublin	ECq	OG [43], Dunne [59]	45 200	Iturralde ESP
11-11	Estonia	W	4-0	Tallinn	ECpo	Andrews [13], Walters [67], Keane 2 [71 88p]	10 500	Kassai HUN
15-11	Estonia	D	1-1	Dublin	ECpo	Ward [32]	51 151	Kuipers NED

Fr = Friendly match • EC = UEFA EURO 2012 • WC = FIFA World Cup • q = qualifier • po = play-off

REPUBLIC OF IRELAND NATIONAL TEAM HISTORICAL RECORDS

Caps

120 - Shay Given 1996- • **114** - Robbie Keane 1998- • **110** - Kevin Kilbane 1997- • **102** - Steve Staunton 1988-2002 • **94** - Damien Duff 1998- • **91** - Niall Quinn 1986-2002 • **88** - Tony Cascarino 1986-2000 • **83** - Paul McGrath 1985-97 • **80** - Pat Bonner 1981-96 • **74** - John O'Shea 2001- • **73** - Ray Houghton 1986-98 • **72** - Kenny Cunningham 1996-2005 & Liam Brady 1975-90 • **71** - Kevin Moran 1980-94, Frank Stapleton 1977-90 & Richard Dunne 2000- • **70** - Andy Townsend 1989-97 • **69** - John Aldridge 1986-97

Goals

53 - Robbie Keane 1998- • **21** - Niall Quinn 1986-2002 • **20** - Frank Stapleton 1977-90 • **19** - Don Givens 1969-82; Tony Cascarino 1986-2000 & John Aldridge 1986-97 • **14** - Noel Cantwell 1954-67 • **13** - Jimmy Dunne 1930-39 & Gerry Daly 1973-87

Past Coaches

Doug Livingstone SCO 1951-53 • Alex Stevenson 1953-55 • Johnny Carey 1955-67 • Noel Cantwell 1967 • Charlie Hurley 1967-69 • Mick Meagan 1969-71 • Liam Tuohy 1971-73 • Sean Thomas 1973 • Johnny Giles 1973-80 • Alan Kelly Snr 1980 • Eoin Hand 1980-85 • Jack Charlton ENG 1986-95 • Mick McCarthy 1996-2002 • Don Givens 2002 • Brian Kerr 2003-05 • Steve Staunton 2006-07 • Don Givens 2007-08 • Giovanni Trapattoni ITA 2008-

REPUBLIC OF IRELAND 2011

EIRCOM LEAGUE OF IRELAND PREMIER DIVISION

	Pl	W	D	L	F	A	Pts	Shamrock R	Sligo Rovers	Derry City	St Pat's	Bohemians	Bray Wand	Dundalk	UCD	Drogheda Utd	Galway Utd
Shamrock Rovers †	36	23	8	5	69	24	77		1-0	1-2	1-1	1-0	2-0	1-0	1-0	1-1	0-1 5-2	3-1 2-2	3-1 6-0	3-0 4-0	4-0 4-0
Sligo Rovers ‡	36	22	7	7	73	19	73	0-1 2-0		3-0 1-1	2-0 0-0	1-2 1-2	3-1 3-0	1-0 5-0	4-0 4-2	2-0 2-0	3-0 7-1
Derry City ‡	36	18	14	4	63	23	68	0-0 1-0	0-1 0-0		1-1 2-0	3-0 0-0	1-1 1-1	2-0 0-0	7-0 2-1	2-0 2-2	6-0 4-0
St Patrick's Athletic ‡	36	17	12	7	62	35	63	0-0 1-1	2-1 1-0	1-1 1-1		0-0 1-1	2-3 1-0	3-2 2-2	1-1 2-2	3-0 4-0	5-2 6-1
Bohemians	36	17	9	10	39	27	60	1-1 0-1	0-0 0-3	0-2 0-1	0-1 0-0		1-1 2-1	0-1 3-1	1-0 2-0	1-0 2-0	0-1 2-0
Bray Wanderers	36	15	6	15	53	50	51	1-0 1-2	0-0 0-3	1-2 1-2	0-1 0-3	1-3 1-2		1-5 1-0	2-1 4-0	2-1 1-2	2-0 4-0
Dundalk	36	11	11	14	50	53	44	1-1 1-2	1-1 1-1	1-0 0-2	1-2 0-2	0-0 1-3	0-0 2-2		3-1 2-0	1-2 1-0	3-2 6-1
University College	36	10	4	22	42	80	34	1-6 1-2	2-1 0-1	0-2 2-2	1-3 2-1	0-2 2-0	0-1 1-2	0-2 3-0		2-1 5-4	3-0 2-1
Drogheda United	36	7	4	25	32	77	25	0-4 0-1	0-3 0-3	2-2 0-3	1-4 4-3	0-1 0-2	0-1 1-4	1-2 2-2	0-1 3-1		1-1 1-0
Galway United	36	1	3	32	20	115	6	0-1 2-3	0-1 0-8	1-4 0-3	0-3 0-2	0-2 0-3	0-3 0-6	0-3 2-2	0-0 3-4	1-2 1-2	

4/03/2011 - 28/10/2011 • † Qualified for the UEFA Champions League • ‡ Qualified for the Europa League
Relegation play-off: Monaghan United 2-0 3-1 Galway United
Top scorers: 22 - Eamon Zayed LBY, Derry • 20 - Eoin Doyle, Sligo • 15 - Danny North ENG, St Pat's & Gary Twigg SCO, Shamrock • 13 - Mark Quigley, Dundalk • 12 - Matthew Blinkhorn ENG, Sligo • 11 - Chris Fagan, Bohemians • 10 - Karl Sheppard, Shamrock

REPUBLIC OF IRELAND 2011
FIRST DIVISION (2)

	Pl	W	D	L	F	A	Pts
Cork City	30	20	9	1	73	26	69
Shelbourne	30	22	2	6	62	24	68
Monaghan United	30	21	4	5	60	27	67
Limerick	30	20	6	4	49	22	66
Waterford United	30	13	3	14	37	31	42
Longford Town	30	12	4	14	38	41	40
Mervue United	30	10	4	16	37	45	34
Athlone Town	30	9	5	16	25	53	32
Finn Harps	30	8	4	18	29	45	28
Wexford Youths	30	4	2	24	29	69	14
Salthill Devon	30	2	5	23	18	74	11

4/03/2011 - 29/10/2011

MEDALS TABLE

		Overall			League			Cup		LC	
		G	S	B	G	S	B	G	B	G	B
1	Shamrock Rovers	42	28	12	17	14	12	24	9	1	5
2	Shelbourne	21	25	11	13	11	11	7	11	1	3
3	Bohemian FC	21	24	14	11	14	14	7	7	3	3
4	Dundalk	21	19	6	9	10	6	8	5	4	4
5	Derry City	16	10	3	2	4	3	4	4	10	2
6	Cork Athletic	12	8	2	7	2	2	5	6		
7	St. Patrick's Athletic	11	13	2	7	4	2	2	7	2	2
8	Waterford United	10	12	8	6	4	8	2	7	2	1
9	Drumcondra	10	9	4	5	5	4	5	4		
10	Sligo Rovers	8	12	6	2	3	6	4	6	2	3
11	Cork City	7	10	5	2	5	5	2	3	3	2
12	Limerick	7	6	3	2	2	3	2	3	3	1
13	Athlone Town	6	3	3	2	1	3	1		3	2
14	St. James' Gate	4	3		2	1		2	2		
15	Drogheda United	3	3	4	1	1	4	1	2	1	
16	Cork Hibernians	3	3	3	1	1	3	2	2		
17	Galway United	3	3	1		1	1	1	1	2	1
18	Longford Town	3	3					2	2	1	1

LEAGUE OF IRELAND CUP 2011

Round of 16		Quarter–finals		Semi–finals		Final	
Derry City *	2						
Mervue United	1	Derry City	3				
Drogheda United *	2	University College *	0				
University College	3			Derry City *	3 5p		
Shelbourne *	4			Sligo Rovers	3 3p		
Bohemians	2	Shelbourne *	1				
Cockhill Celtic *	0	Sligo Rovers	2				
Sligo Rovers	4					Derry City	1
Limerick *	1					Cork City	0
Waterford United	0	Limerick *	5				
Dundalk	1	Monaghan United	0				
Monaghan United *	2			Limerick	1		
St Patrick's Athletic *	1 3p			Cork City *	3		
Shamrock Rovers	1 1p	St Patrick's Athletic	1				
Wexford Youths *	0	Cork City *	2				
Cork City	1						

CUP FINAL
Turner's Cross, Cork
24-09-2011, Ref: Tuite
Scorer - Eamon Zayed 67p for Derry City

* Home team

FA OF IRELAND CUP 2011

Third Round

Team	Score
Sligo Rovers *	3
Pike Rovers	2
Everton AFC	1
Monaghan United *	4
University College	2
Cherry Orchard *	1
Athlone Town	0
Shamrock Rovers *	4
Dundalk *	4
Galway United	1
Mervue United	0
Drogheda United *	4
Longford Town *	0 1
Finn Harps	0 0
Douglas Hall	0
Bohemians *	3
St Patrick's Athletic	3
Crumlin United *	0
New Ross Celtic	0
Waterford United *	3
Wexford Youths *	4
Derry City	1
Midleton *	0
Cork City	2
Limerick	4
Sacred Heart *	2
Youghal United *	1
Bray Wanderers	3
Sheriff YC	2
Salthill Devon *	1
Greystones *	1
Shelbourne	3

Round of 16

Team	Score
Sligo Rovers *	0 4
Monaghan United	0 0
University College	2 0
Shamrock Rovers *	2 6
Dundalk	1 2
Drogheda United *	1 1
Longford Town *	1
Bohemians	3
St Patrick's Athletic	3
Waterford United *	0
Wexford Youths *	0
Cork City	1
Limerick	4
Bray Wanderers *	0
Sheriff YC * ‡‡	0
Shelbourne	3

Quarter-finals

Team	Score
Sligo Rovers *	1
Shamrock Rovers	0
Dundalk *	0 0
Bohemians	0 1
St Patrick's Athletic	1
Cork City *	0
Limerick	3
Shelbourne *	4

Semi-finals

Team	Score
Sligo Rovers	1
Bohemians *	0
St Patrick's Athletic	1 1
Shelbourne *	1 3

Final

Team	Score
Sligo Rovers ‡	1 4p
Shelbourne	1 1p

PENALTIES

Sligo	Shel	
Doyle		✓
	Bermingham	✓
Ryan		✓
	Dawson	✗
Keane		✓
	James	✗
Cretaro		✓

CUP FINAL

Aviva Stadium, Dublin, 6-11-2011, 15:30
Att: 21 662. Ref: Richie Winter
Scorers - Iarflaith Davoren [48] for Sligo; Philly Hughes [30] for Shelbourne
Sligo - Brendan Clarke (Ciaran Kelly 120) - Alan Keane, Gavin Peers•, Jason McGuinness, Iarflaith Davoren - John Dillon (Matthew Blinkhorn 60), Danny Ventre, Richie Ryan (c), Aaron Greene• - John Russell (Raffaele Cretaro 78) - Eoin Doyle. Tr: Paul Cook
Shelbourne - Dean Delaney - Ian Ryan, Andrew Boyle, Stephen Paisley•, Sean Byrne - Brendan McGill (Karl Bermingham 120), John Sullivan (Conan Byrne, 59), Kevin Dawson•, Barry Clancy••◆36 - David Cassidy (Colm James 117) - Philip Hughes•. Tr: Alan Mathews

‡‡ Sherriff won the match 3-2 but were disqualified. Shelbourne were awarded the tie 3-0 • = Home team • ‡ Qualified for the Europa League

IRN – IRAN

FIFA/COCA-COLA WORLD RANKING

'93	'94	'95	'96	'97	'98	'99	'00	'01	'02	'03	'04	'05	'06	'07	'08	'09	'10	'11	'12
59	75	108	83	46	27	49	37	29	33	28	20	19	38	41	43	64	66	45	

2011													High	Low	Av
Jan	Feb	Mar	Apr	May	Jun	Jul	Aug	Sep	Oct	Nov	Dec		High	Low	Av
65	44	43	46	47	50	54	53	50	42	45	45		15	122	47

The departure of Afshin Ghotbi in the aftermath of Iran's elimination at the AFC Asian Cup finals in Qatar in early 2011 was followed by the coup of capturing the services of former Real Madrid coach Carlos Queiroz. The Portuguese made an immediate impact, building on the work of Ghotbi by steering Iran into the final phase of Asia's qualifying tournament for the 2014 FIFA World Cup in Brazil with an unbeaten record in a group that also featured Qatar, Bahrain and Indonesia. Of the 15 matches played in 2011, the quarter-final defeat in the Asian Cup at the hands of Korea proved to be the only loss of the year. In club football, Sepahan claimed the Iran Pro League title in what turned out to be a three-way battle for the crown with neighbours Zob Ahan and Tehran giants Esteghlal. Persepolis finished fourth but they won the cup after beating Malavan 4-3 on aggregate in the final. Once again the AFC Champions League proved to be a disappointment as Iranian clubs continue to search for a first title in the competition since the creation of the format in 2002. Both Zob Ahan and Sepahan progressed to the knockout phase but neither made it beyond the quarter-finals and you have to go back to 1993 and the title won by Pas to find the last time an Iranian team were crowned champions of Asia.

FIFA WORLD CUP RECORD

1930-1970 DNE   1974 DNQ   **1978** 14 r1   1982-1986 DNE   1990-1994 DNQ   **1998** 20 r1   2002 DNQ   **2006** 26 r1   2010 DNQ

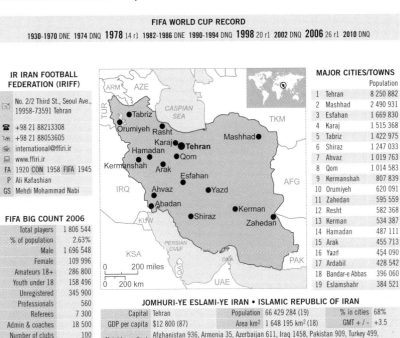

IR IRAN FOOTBALL FEDERATION (IRIFF)

No. 2/2 Third St., Seoul Ave., 19958-73591 Tehran

☎ +98 21 88213308
📠 +98 21 88053605
📧 international@ffiri.ir
🖥 www.ffiri.ir
FA 1920 CON 1958 FIFA 1945
P Ali Kafashian
GS Mehdi Mohammad Nabi

FIFA BIG COUNT 2006

Total players	1 806 544
% of population	2.63%
Male	1 696 548
Female	109 996
Amateurs 18+	286 800
Youth under 18	158 496
Unregistered	345 900
Professionals	560
Referees	7 300
Admin & coaches	18 500
Number of clubs	100
Number of teams	270

MAJOR CITIES/TOWNS

		Population
1	Tehran	8 250 882
2	Mashhad	2 490 931
3	Esfahan	1 669 830
4	Karaj	1 515 368
5	Tabriz	1 422 975
6	Shiraz	1 247 033
7	Ahvaz	1 019 763
8	Qom	1 014 583
9	Kermanshah	807 839
10	Orumiyeh	620 091
11	Zahedan	595 559
12	Resht	582 368
13	Kerman	534 387
14	Hamadan	487 111
15	Arak	455 713
16	Yazd	454 090
17	Ardabil	428 542
18	Bandar-e Abbas	396 060
19	Eslamshahr	384 521

JOMHURI-YE ESLAMI-YE IRAN • ISLAMIC REPUBLIC OF IRAN

Capital	Tehran	Population	66 429 284 (19)	% in cities	68%
GDP per capita	$12 800 (87)	Area km²	1 648 195 km² (18)	GMT +/-	+3.5
Neighbours (km)	Afghanistan 936, Armenia 35, Azerbaijan 611, Iraq 1458, Pakistan 909, Turkey 499, Turkmenistan 992 • Coast 2440				

RECENT INTERNATIONAL MATCHES PLAYED BY IRAN

2009	Opponents		Score	Venue	Comp	Scorers	Att	Referee
12-08	Bosnia-Herzegovina	W	3-2	Sarajevo	Fr	Shojaei [79], Borhani [86], Teymourian [90]		
31-08	Bahrain	L	2-4	Manama	Fr	Zandi 2 [37 83p]		
5-09	Uzbekistan	D	0-0	Tashkent	Fr		9 500	Irmatov UZB
10-11	Iceland	W	1-0	Tehran	Fr	Ansarifard [54]		Waleed QAT
14-11	Jordan	W	1-0	Tehran	ACq	Nekounam [72]	15 000	Nishimura JPN
18-11	Macedonia FYR	D	1-1	Tehran	Fr	Teymourian [36]	3 000	Moradi IRN
22-11	Jordan	L	0-1	Amman	ACq		11 000	Al Badwawi UAE
2010								
2-01	Korea DPR	W	1-0	Doha	Fr	Madanchi [43]	1 000	Maillet SEY
6-01	Singapore	W	3-1	Singapore	ACq	Aghili [11p], Madanchi [12], Rezaei [62]	7 356	Sun Baojie CHN
3-03	Thailand	W	1-0	Tehran	ACq	Nekounam [90]	17 000	Balideh QAT
11-08	Armenia	W	3-1	Yerevan	Fr	Aghily 2 [68 90p], Nosrati [71]	3 000	Kvartskhelia GEO
3-09	China PR	W	2-0	Zhengzhou	Fr	Teymourian [38], Gholami [63]	20 000	Kim Jong Hyeok KOR
7-09	Korea Republic	W	1-0	Seoul	Fr	Shojaei [35]	38 642	Mohd Salleh MAS
24-09	Bahrain	W	3-0	Amman	WAr1	Aghili 2 [36 38], Oladi [47]	5 000	Al Ghafari JOR
28-09	Oman	D	2-2	Amman	WAr1	Meydavoudi [15], Teymourian [52]	2 000	Ko Hyung Jin KOR
1-10	Iraq	W	2-1	Amman	WAsf	Hosseini [57], Gholami [82]	10 000	Matsuo JPN
3-10	Kuwait	L	1-2	Amman	WAf	Meydavoudi [95+]	4 000	Al Ghafari JOR
7-10	Brazil	L	0-3	Abu Dhabi	Fr		15 000	Al Marzouqi UAE
28-12	Qatar	D	0-0	Doha	Fr		2 000	Szabo HUN
2011								
2-01	Angola	W	1-0	Al Rayyan	Fr	Nekounam [90]	BCD	
11-01	Iraq	W	2-1	Al Rayyan	ACr1	Rezaei [42], Mobali [84]	10 478	Irmatov UZB
15-01	Korea DPR	W	1-0	Doha	ACr1	Ansarifard [63]	6 488	Shukralla BHR
19-01	UAE	W	3-0	Doha	ACr1	Afshin [67], Nori [83], OG [93+]	5 012	Kim Dong Jin KOR
22-01	Korea Republic	L	0-1	Doha	ACqf		7 111	Irmatov UZB
9-02	Russia	W	1-0	Abu Dhabi	Fr	Khalatbari [90]	5 000	Albadwawi UAE
17-07	Madagascar	W	1-0	Tehran	Fr	Hosseini [18]	10 000	Mombini IRN
23-07	Maldives	W	4-0	Tehran	WCq	Ansari 2 [4 62], Karimi [67], Daghighi [86]	20 195	Mahapab THA
28-07	Maldives	W	1-0	Male	WCq	Khalatbari [45]	9 000	Kim Sang Woo KOR
2-09	Indonesia	W	3-0	Tehran	WCq	Nekounam 2 [53 74], Timotian [87]	75 800	Toma JPN
6-09	Qatar	D	1-1	Doha	WCq	Aghili [46]	8 125	Choi Myung Yong KOR
5-10	Palestine	W	7-0	Tehran	Fr	Ghazi [45], Ansarifard [49], Nekounam [55], Montazeri [59], Nouri [70], Kazemian 2 [58 90]	5 000	Mozaffari IRN
11-10	Bahrain	W	6-0	Tehran	WCq	Hosseini [31], Jabari [34], Aghili [42], Timotian [61], Ansari [75], Rezaei [83]	82 000	Green AUS
11-11	Bahrain	D	1-1	Manama	WCq	Jabari [92+]	18 000	Bashir SIN
15-11	Indonesia	W	4-1	Jakarta	WCq	Midavoodi [7], Jabari [21], Rezaei [25], Nekounam [73]	6 000	Tan Hai

Fr = Friendly match • WA = West Asian Federation Championship • AC = AFC Asian Cup • WC = FIFA World Cup • q = qualifier

IRAN NATIONAL TEAM HISTORICAL RECORDS

Caps
149 - Ali Daei 1993-2006 • 124 - Javad Nekounam 2000- • 118 - Ali Karimi 1998- • 111 - Mehdi Mahdavikia 1996-2009 • 89 - Hossein Kaebi 2002- • 87 - Karim Bagheri 1993-2010 • 82 - Hamid Reza Estili 1990-2000 • 80 - Javad Zarincheh 1987-2000 & Mohammad Nosrati 2002- • 79 - Ahmad Reza Abedzadeh 1987-98

Goals
109 - Ali Daei 1993-2006 • 50 - Karim Bagheri 1993-2010 • 37 - Ali Karimi 1998- • 30 - Javad Nekounam 2000- • 19 - Gholam Hossein Mazloomi 1969-77 & Farshad Pious 1984-1994 • 18 - Ali Ashgar Modir Roosta 1990-98 • 15 - Vahid Hashemian 1998-2009

Past Coaches
Hossein Sadaghiani 1950 • Mostafa Salimi 1951-52 • Edmund Masayufskei AUT 1956-57 • Hossein Sadaghiani 1958 • Ferenc Meszaros HUN 1959 • Hossein Fekri 1962-66 • Gyorgy Szucs HUN 1966 • Hossein Fekri 1967 • Mahmoud Bayati 1968 • Zdravko Rajkov YUG 1969 • Mahmoud Bayati 1970 • Igor Netto URS 1970 • Parviz Dehdari 1971 • Mohammad Ranjbar 1972 • Mahmoud Bayati 1973 • Danny McLennan SCO 1974 • Frank O'Farrell IRL 1974-75 • Heshmat Mohajerani 1976-78 • Hassan Habibi 1982 • Naser Ebrahimi 1982 • Jalal Cheraghpour 1982 • Ahmad Tousi 1983-84 • Mahmoud Yavari 1984 • Nasser Ebrahimi 1984-85 • Parviz Dehdari 1986-89 • Reza Vatankhah 1989 • Mehdi Monajati 1989 • Ali Parvin 1989-93 • Hassan Habibi 1994-95 • Stanko Poklepovic CRO 1994 • Mayeli Kohan 1996-97 • Valdeir Viera BRA 1997 • Tomislav Ivic CRO 1998 • Jalal Talebi 1998 • Mansour Pourheidari 1998-2000 • Jalal Talebi 2000 • Ademar Braga 2000-01 • Miroslav Blazevic CRO 2001 • Branko Ivankovic CRO 2002 • Homayoun Shahrokhi 2003 • Branko Ivankovic CRO 2003-6 • Amir Ghalenoei 2006-07 • Parviz Mazloomi 2007 • Mansour Ebrahimzadeh 2008 • Ali Daei 2008-09 • Erich Rutemoller GER 2009 • Mayeli Kohan 2009 • Gholam Peyrovani 2009 • Afshin Ghotbi 2009-11 • Carlos Queiroz POR 2011-

IRAN 2010–11 — IRAN PRO LEAGUE

	Pl	W	D	L	F	A	Pts	Sepahan	Esteghlal T	Zob Ahan	Persopolis	Teraktor-Sazi	Foolad	Sanat-Mes	Mes	Malavan	Sanat-Naft	Saba	Saipa	Shahrdari	Naft Tehran	Rah Ahan	Hamedan	Paykan	Steel Azin
Sepahan †	34	18	12	4	56	29	**66**		1-1	2-0	0-0	1-0	3-2	1-1	0-0	2-0	0-0	4-1	1-0	2-0	1-0	2-2	2-1	3-2	5-0
Esteghlal Tehran †	34	18	11	5	55	34	**65**	4-3		1-2	1-0	1-2	1-2	0-0	2-0	6-2	2-0	3-2	0-0	3-1	2-1	1-0	3-2	3-0	2-2
Zob Ahan †	34	18	9	7	49	31	**63**	1-0	1-1		0-3	0-0	1-1	2-0	3-0	6-0	2-1	0-2	2-1	2-0	2-1	0-0	1-0	2-1	2-0
Persepolis †	34	17	7	10	50	36	**58**	1-4	0-1	2-0		1-0	3-1	0-0	2-3	2-0	1-4	2-1	0-0	3-1	2-1	0-0	1-1	5-1	2-1
Teraktor-Sazi Tabriz	34	15	12	7	42	29	**57**	1-3	1-1	1-2	1-0		1-1	1-0	2-0	3-1	1-2	2-2	1-0	3-1	1-2	3-1	0-1	2-1	3-0
Foolad Ahvaz	34	14	12	8	58	36	**54**	1-1	4-1	2-2	1-1	1-1		1-0	1-0	4-1	0-0	2-1	4-0	2-1	1-0	0-0	5-2	6-0	0-1
Mes Kerman	34	13	13	8	41	30	**52**	3-2	1-1	1-2	1-0	1-1	1-0		1-0	2-0	2-1	1-0	5-2	0-0	3-0	2-0	0-0	1-1	1-0
Malavan	34	13	9	12	33	32	**48**	0-0	0-1	1-0	2-1	2-0	1-0	2-1		2-1	2-0	2-3	0-0	1-1	3-2	1-0	3-0	2-0	0-1
Sanat-Naft Abadan	34	13	3	18	36	54	**42**	0-1	2-0	2-1	0-1	1-3	2-2	1-0	2-1		3-1	1-0	1-1	1-0	1-0	0-1	2-0	2-1	2-0
Saba Qom	34	9	14	11	39	40	**41**	1-1	1-1	1-2	2-1	0-0	1-1	1-1	1-0	0-0		1-1	4-4	2-2	0-1	5-2	1-1	2-1	1-0
Saipa	34	8	13	13	42	47	**37**	2-1	0-0	0-2	0-1	1-1	5-5	2-4	1-1	1-0	1-0		0-1	0-0	2-1	0-1	2-1	1-1	2-2
Shahrdari Tabriz	34	8	13	13	45	53	**37**	1-2	2-3	1-1	1-1	1-1	0-2	2-1	2-1	3-2	0-1	2-2		1-0	2-2	1-0	2-2	2-4	3-0
Naft Tehran	34	7	15	12	38	44	**36**	0-0	0-0	1-2	1-5	1-1	0-3	1-1	0-0	5-1	0-0	0-0	3-1		2-2	1-0	4-1	4-1	2-2
Shahin Bushehr	34	8	11	15	31	37	**35**	0-0	0-0	1-1	1-2	0-0	2-0	1-1	0-1	1-2	0-0	1-1	0-1	0-1		2-0	0-1	2-1	1-1
Rah Ahan	34	8	11	15	29	39	**35**	1-1	0-1	2-2	2-3	0-1	1-0	2-2	2-0	0-2	0-2	0-0	0-0	0-1	1-0	1-1		2-1	0-3	0-0
Hamedan-Paas	34	8	11	15	30	48	**35**	0-1	0-2	2-1	1-2	0-0	0-0	1-0	1-1	1-0	1-0	2-2	1-1	1-1	1-2	1-0		1-0	1-1
Paykan Tehran	34	9	6	19	38	60	**33**	2-4	1-3	0-0	3-0	1-2	0-2	1-2	1-1	1-0	3-2	1-0	1-0	1-3	0-1	1-0	3-1		3-1
Steel Azin Tehran	34	6	10	18	30	63	**28**	1-2	1-3	0-2	0-2	0-1	2-1	1-1	0-0	2-1	3-1	1-5	1-6	1-1	0-2	2-2	3-0	0-0	

26/07/2010 - 20/05/2011 • † Qualified for the AFC Champions League

Top scorers: **24** - Reza Norouzi, Foolad • **22** - Edinho BRA, Mes Kerman • **19** - Karim Ansarifard, Saipa • **18** - Ibrahima Toure SEN, Sepahan • **14** - Saeed Daghighi, Shahrdari; Mehrdad Oladi, Malavan & Arash Borhani, Esteghlal • **13** - Rouhollah Arab, Sanat Naft & Seyed Hosseini, Zob Ahan

IRAN 2010–11 — AZADEGAN LEAGUE GROUP A (2)

	Pl	W	D	L	F	A	Pts
Damash Gilan	26	13	9	4	39	24	**48**
Moghavemat Sepasi †	26	12	5	9	24	18	**41**
Shahrdari Yasuj	26	11	6	9	28	26	**39**
Naft Masjed Soleyman	26	8	11	7	33	32	**35**
Shahrdari Bandar Abbas	26	9	8	9	26	26	**35**
Etka Tehran	26	9	7	10	30	28	**34**
Gol Gohar Sirjan	26	8	10	8	29	27	**34**
Tarbyat Badani Yazd	26	6	15	5	24	22	**33**
Mes Rafsanjan	26	8	8	10	20	25	**32**
Hamyari Arak	26	8	8	10	20	28	**32**
Sanati Kaveh	26	7	10	9	27	32	**31**
Machine Sazi	26	7	10	9	30	36	**31**
Payam Mashhad	26	9	5	12	30	30	**29**
Foolad Natanz	26	6	10	10	30	36	**28**

22/09/2010 - 10/05/2011 • † Qualified for the play-off

Promotion play-off:
Moghavemat Sepasi 2-0 4-0 Aluminium Hormozgan

IRAN 2010–11 — AZADEGAN LEAGUE GROUP B (2)

	Pl	W	D	L	F	A	Pts
Mes Sarcheshme	26	14	6	6	34	14	**48**
Alumin'm Hormozgan†	26	13	9	4	29	19	**48**
Gostaresh Foolad	26	14	6	6	28	22	**48**
Nassaji Mazandaran	26	11	9	6	34	17	**42**
AbooMoslem	26	11	9	6	28	20	**42**
Shirin-Faraz	26	8	11	7	17	19	**35**
Sanat Sari	26	8	11	7	18	24	**35**
IranJavan	26	8	9	9	29	26	**33**
Bargh Shiraz	26	7	11	8	24	25	**32**
Payam Shiraz	26	5	12	9	20	22	**27**
Foolad Yadz	26	7	6	13	23	38	**27**
Damash Tehran	26	6	7	13	22	29	**25**
Esteghlal Ahvaz	26	6	6	14	20	33	**24**
Sepidrood Rasht	26	4	8	14	21	39	**20**

22/09/2010 - 10/05/2011 • † Qualified for the play-off

MEDALS TABLE

		Overall			League			Cup			Asia			City
		G	S	B	G	S	B	G	S	G	S	B	
1	Persepolis	15	9	7	**9**	7	4	**5**	1	1	1	3	Tehran
2	Esteghlal	14	13	7	7	8	4	**5**	3	2	2	3	Tehran
3	Pas	6	5	2	5	5	2	1				Tehran
4	Sepahan	6	2	2	3	1	2	3		1		Esfahan
5	Saipa	4		2	3		2	1				Karaj
6	Malavan	3	4	2			2	3	4			Bandar Anzali
7	Zob Ahan	2	5	2		3	2	2	1	1		Esfahan
8	Bahman	1	4			2		1	2			Karaj
9	Moghavemat Sepasi	1	2	1			1	1	2			Shiraz
10	Saba Battery	1	1	1			1	1	1			Qom
11	Bargh	1	1					1	1			Shiraz
12	Foolad	1		2	1		2					Ahvaz
13	Shahin	1						1				Ahvaz

JAAM HAZFI 2010–11

Second Stage - First Round

Team	Score
Persepolis *	5
Naft Mahmoudabad	1
Saipa	1
Damash Gilan *	3
Rah Ahan *	w-o
Sanat-Naft Abadan	
Machine Sazi *	1
Sepahan	3
Steel Azin Tehran	3
Omran Kish *	2
Mes Kerman *	0
Naft Masjed Soleyman	1
Shahrdari Bandar Abbas *	2
Saba Qom	1
Sepidrood Rasht	1
Foolad Ahvaz *	2
Esteghlal Tehran	4
Hamedan-Paas *	1
Payam Mashhad	
Shahin Bushehr *	w-o
Sanati Kaveh	0 4p
Paykan Tehran *	0 2p
Zob Ahan *	0
Shahrdari Yasuj	1
Teraktor-Sazi Tabriz *	w-o
Moghavemat Sepasi	
Behineh Rahbar Abadeh	0
Shahrdari Tabriz *	6
Foolad Natanz *	3
Naft Tehran	2
IranJavan *	2
Malavan	3

Round of 16

Team	Score
Persepolis	2
Damash Gilan *	1
Rah Ahan	0
Sepahan *	4
Steel Azin Tehran *	2
Naft Masjed Soleyman	1
Shahrdari Bandar Abbas	
Foolad Ahvaz *	w-o
Esteghlal Tehran *	1
Shahin Bushehr	0
Sanati Kaveh	0
Shahrdari Yasuj *	1
Teraktor-Sazi Tabriz *	5
Shahrdari Tabriz *	2
Foolad Natanz	0
Malavan *	3

Quarter-finals

Team	Score
Persepolis *	0 4p
Sepahan	0 2p
Steel Azin Tehran *	0
Foolad Ahvaz	2
Esteghlal Tehran *	2
Shahrdari Yasuj	0
Teraktor-Sazi Tabriz *	0 4p
Malavan	0 5p

Semi-finals

Team	Score
Persepolis	1
Foolad Ahvaz *	0
Esteghlal Tehran	1
Malavan *	2

Final

Persepolis †	4	0
Malavan	2	1

CUP FINAL 1ST LEG

Azadi, Tehran, 7-06-2011, 19:45
Att: 82 300, Ref: Faghani. Scorers -
Noormohammadi 47, Norouzi 63, Nouri 2 71 86p for
Persepolis; Rostami 34, Nozhati 69 for Malavan
Persepolis - Alireza Haghighi - Saman
Aghazamani (Alireza Mohammad● 71), Mojtaba
Shiri, Alireza Noormohammadi, Ebrahim
Shakouri● - Maziar Zare - Hamidreza Aliasgari,
Hossein Badamaki (Shpejtim Arifi 87),
Mohammad Nouri - Hadi Norouz● - Vahid
Hashemian● (c) (Amir Hossein Feshangchi 64).
Tr: Ali Daei
Malavan - Ali Hasani Sefat - Alen Basic●, Saeed
Salarzadeh, Ali Reza Ramezani, Abolhassan
Jafari◆37, Mohammad Rostami●●◆88, Pejman
Nouri (c), Mohsen Mosalman●, Mehdi
Daghagheleh (Babak Pourgholami 44),
Mohammed Nozhati●, Mehrdad Oladi
(Mohammad Heidari 78). Tr: Farhad Pourgholami

CUP FINAL 2ND LEG

Takhti, Bandar Anzali, 10-06-2011, 17:00
Att: 20 000, Ref: Mombini
Scorer - Oladi 19 for Malavan
Malavan - Ali Hasani Sefat - Hadi Tamini●,
Babak Pourgholami●, Saeed Salarzadeh,
Mohammad Hamrang● (Aziz Maeboudi 78),
Pejman Nouri (c), Mohsen Mosalman, Mehdi
Daghagheleh, Ali Reza Ramezani, Mohammad
Heidari, Mehrdad Oladi. Tr: Farhad Pourgholami
Persepolis - Alireza Haghighi● - Saman
Aghazamani, Mojtaba Shiri (Sepehr Heidari 13),
Alireza Noormohammadi, Ebrahim Shakouri
(Saeid Hallafi 83) - Maziar Zare - Hamidreza
Aliasgari, Mohammad Nouri, Hossein
Badamaki● - Vahid Hashemian● (c), Shpejtim
Arifi (Amir Hossein Feshangchi 53). Tr: Ali Daei

Esteghlal Tehran	1
Malavan *	2

Preliminary Round: ● = Home team · † Qualified for the AFC Champions League

IRQ – IRAQ

FIFA/COCA-COLA WORLD RANKING

'93	'94	'95	'96	'97	'98	'99	'00	'01	'02	'03	'04	'05	'06	'07	'08	'09	'10	'11	'12
65	88	110	98	68	94	78	79	72	53	43	44	54	83	68	72	88	101	78	

					2011									
	Jan	Feb	Mar	Apr	May	Jun	Jul	Aug	Sep	Oct	Nov	Dec	High	Low	Av
	98	88	88	89	89	95	108	109	107	91	81	78	39	139	78

The arrival of the Brazilian Zico as coach at the end of August 2011 galvanised an Iraq national team that has struggled in recent years to live up to its Asian Cup winning exploits of 2007. Still leaning heavily on the talents of Younus Mahmood and Nashat Akram, the Iraqis have set their sights on a place at the 2014 FIFA World Cup in Brazil for what would be only their second appearance in the finals. Wolfgang Sidka did not have his contract renewed at the end of his one-year tenure, during which the German had steered the team to the quarter-finals of the AFC Asian Cup in Qatar and past Yemen in a preliminary round of World Cup qualifying. Zico's appointment coincided with a strong run of form for the Iraqis, with the team comfortably securing a place in the final group stage of qualifying for Brazil. Iraqi club football saw a major reorganisation for the 2011-12 championship with the creation of a single top division of 20 teams. Earlier in the year Al Zawra'a had beaten Arbil on penalties in the play-off between the winners of the northern and southern groups to win the national title. Iraqi clubs featured in the AFC Cup for the first time in 2011, having failed to meet the criteria to play in the AFC Champions League. Arbil reached the last four of the tournament where they lost 5-3 on aggregate to Al Kuwait.

FIFA WORLD CUP RECORD
1930-1970 DNE **1974** DNQ **1978** DNE **1982** DNQ **1986** 23 r1 **1990-2010** DNQ

IRAQI FOOTBALL ASSOCIATION (IFA)

Al Shaab Stadium,
PO Box 484,
Baghdad
☎ +964 740 0601245
info@ifa.iq
www.ifa.iq
FA 1948 CON 1971 FIFA 1950
P Najeh Al Obaidi
GS Ahmed Ali Tariq

FIFA BIG COUNT 2006

Total players	540 000
% of population	2.02%
Male	500 100
Female	39 900
Amateurs 18+	6 600
Youth under 18	7 900
Unregistered	100 000
Professionals	0
Referees	600
Admin & coaches	2 300
Number of clubs	110
Number of teams	170

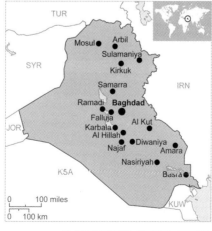

MAJOR CITIES/TOWNS

		Population
1	Baghdad	5 337 684
2	Mosul	2 803 999
3	Basra	1 871 994
4	Arbil	1 190 251
5	Kirkuk	850 787
6	Najaf	828 207
7	Sulamaniya	759 508
8	Al Hillah	528 008
9	Karbala	509 819
10	Amara	465 707
11	Diwaniya	455 473
12	Qubba	421 730
13	Falluja	309 868
14	Ramadi	290 535
15	Al Kut	289 084
16	Nasiriyah	257 091
17	Dahuk	241 033
18	Zakhu	186 129
19	Tall Afar	168 228

AL JUMHURIYAH AL IRAQIYAH • REPUBLIC OF IRAQ

Capital Baghdad	Population 28 945 657 (40)	% in cities 67%
GDP per capita $3200 (162)	Area km² 438 317 km² (58)	GMT +/- +3
Neighbours (km) Iran 1458, Jordan 181, Kuwait 240, Saudi Arabia 814, Syria 605, Turkey 352 • Coast 58		

RECENT INTERNATIONAL MATCHES PLAYED BY IRAQ

2010	Opponents	Score	Venue	Comp	Scorers	Att	Referee
16-09	Jordan	L 1-4	Amman	Fr	Nashat Akram [59]		
21-09	Oman	W 3-2	Amman	Fr	Samal Saeed [56], Nashat Akram [68], Ahmad Manajid [19]		
25-09	Yemen	W 2-1	Amman	WAr1	Samal Saeed [49], Hawar Mohammed [72]	3 000	
29-09	Palestine	W 3-0	Amman	WAr1	Mustafa Karim 2 [15 76], Nashat Akram [86p]	4 000	
1-10	Iran	L 1-2	Amman	WAsf	Mustafa Karim [71]		
12-10	Qatar	W 2-1	Doha	Fr	Emad Mohammed 2 [11 57]		
11-11	India	W 2-0	Sharjah	Fr	Mustafa Karim [17p], Mahdi Karim [66]		
17-11	Kuwait	D 1-1	Abu Dhabi	Fr	Younis Mahmoud [45]		
23-11	UAE	D 0-0	Aden	GCr1			Al Qahtani KSA
26-11	Bahrain	W 3-2	Aden	GCr1	Alaa Abdul-Zahra 2 [23 57], Hawar Mohammed [90p]		Allabany YEM
29-11	Oman	D 0-0	Abyan	GCr1			Younis EGY
2-12	Kuwait	D 2-2	Aden	GCsf	Hawar Mohammed [6], Alaa Abdul Zahra [14]. L 4-5p		Shaaban EGY
18-12	Syria	L 0-1	Sulaymaniyah	Fr			
22-12	Syria	W 1-0	Damascus	Fr	Salam Shakir [88]		
28-12	Saudi Arabia	W 1-0	Dammam	Fr	Younis Mahmoud [24]		
2011							
2-01	China PR	L 2-3	Doha	Fr	Younis Mahmoud 2 [44 50]		
11-01	Iran	L 1-2	Al Rayyan	ACr1	Younis Mahmoud [13]	10 478	Irmatov UZB
15-01	UAE	W 1-0	Al Rayyan	ACr1	Walid Abbas OG [93+]	7 233	Nishimura JPN
19-01	Korea DPR	W 1-0	Al Rayyan	ACr1	Karrar Jassim [22]	4 111	Mohd Salleh MAS
22-01	Australia	L 0-1	Doha	ACqf		7 889	Abdou QAT
26-03	Korea DPR	W 2-0	Sharjah	Fr	Alaa Abdul Zahra 2 [53 71]		
29-03	Kuwait	L 0-1	Sharjah	Fr			
29-06	Syria	L 1-2	Arbil	Fr	Alaa Abdul Zahra [80]		
13-07	Kuwait	L 0-2	Amman	Fr			
16-07	Jordan	D 1-1	Amman	Fr	Mustafa Karim [15]. L 4-5p		
23-07	Yemen	W 2-0	Arbil	WCq	Hawar Mohammed [10], Alaa Abdul Zahra [64]	20 000	Kovalenko UZB
28-07	Yemen	D 0-0	Al Ain	WCq		1 500	Basma SYR
19-08	Qatar	W 1-0	Doha	Fr	Salam Shakir [35]		
2-09	Jordan	L 0-2	Arbil	WCq		24 000	Shukralla BHR
6-09	Singapore	W 2-0	Singapore	WCq	Alaa Abdul Zahra [50], Younis Mahmoud [86]	5 505	Tojo JPN
11-10	China PR	W 1-0	Shenzhen	WCq	Younis Mahmoud [45]	25 021	Mozaffari IRN
11-11	China PR	W 1-0	Doha	WCq	Younis Mahmoud [92+]	5 000	Green AUS
15-11	Jordan	W 3-1	Amman	WCq	Nashat Akram 2 [55 81], Qusai Munir [65]	13 000	Albadwawi UAE
13-12	Bahrain	L 0-3	Doha	PGr1			Abdurahaman SUD
16-12	Qatar	D 0-0	Doha	PGr1			Haimoudi ALG

Fr = Friendly • WA = West Asian Federation Championship • AC = AFC Asian Cup • GC = Gulf Cup • PG = Pan Arab Games • WC = FIFA World Cup
q = qualifier • r1 = first round group • qf = quarter-final • sf = semi-final • f = final

IRAQ NATIONAL TEAM HISTORICAL RECORDS

Past Coaches

Dhia Habib 1951 • Ismail Mohammed 1957 • Shawqi Aboud 1959 • Hadi Abbas 1959 • Shawqi Aboud 1963-64 • Adil Basher 1964 • Shawqi Aboud 1965 • Adil Basher 1966 • Jalil Shihab 1967 • Abdelilah Mohammed Hassan 1968 • Adil Basher 1968 • Ljubomir Kokeza YUG 1969 • Yuri Illichev URS 1969-71 • Adil Basher 1971-72 • Abdelilah Mohammed Hassan 1972 • Gyula Teleki HUN 1973 • Thamir Muhsin 1973 • Wathiq Naji 1974 • Jalil Shihab 1974 • Thamir Muhsin 1974 • Wathiq Naji 1975 • Danny McLennan SCO 1975-76 • Lenko Grcic YUG 1976-78 • Jamal Salih 1978 • Emmanuel Baba 1978-80 • Wathiq Naji 1980 • Anwar Jassam 1980 • Vojo Gardasevic YUG 1981 • Douglas Aziz 1981 • Emmanuel Baba 1981-84 • Anwar Jassam1985 • Akram Ahmad Salman 1985 • Wathiq Naji 1985 • Jorge Vieira BRA 1985 • Edu BRA 1986 • Ze Mario BRA 1986 • Evaristo de Macedo BRA - 1986 • Akram Ahmad Salman 1986 • Emmanuel Baba 1987-88 • Jamal Salih 1988 • Emmanuel Baba1988-89 • Anwar Jassam1989-90 • Yuri Morozov URS 1990 • Adnan Dirjal 1992-93 • Emmanuel Baba 1993 • Anwar Jassam 1995-96 • Emmanuel Baba 1996 • Yahya Alwan 1996-97 • Ayoub Odisho 1997 • Emmanuel Baba 1997 • Akram Ahmad Salman 1998 • Najih Humoud 1999 • Adnan Hamad 2000 • Milan Zivadinovic SRB 2000-01 • Adnan Hamad 2001 • Rudolf Belin CRO 2001 • Adnan Hamad 2002 • Bernd Stange GER 2002-04 • Adnan Hamad 2004 • Akram Ahmad Salman 2005-07 • Jorvan Vieira BRA 2007 • Egil Olsen NOR 2007-08 • Adnan Hamad 2008 • Jorvan Vieira BRA 2008-09 • Radhi Shenaishil 2009 • Bora Milutinovic SRB 2009 • Nadhim Shaker 2009-10 • Wolfgang Sidka GER 2010-11 • Zico BRA 2011-

IRAQ 2010–11

PREMIER LEAGUE GROUP A (NORTH)

	Pl	W	D	L	F	A	Pts	Arbil	Al Sina'a	Zakho	Kahrabaa	Karkh	Duhok	Al Naft	Al Shurta	Mosul	Ramadi	Peshmerga	Diyala	Samara'a	Al Jaish
Arbil † ‡	26	17	5	4	54	21	56		3-1	2-1	1-0	3-1	2-1	3-0	2-0	4-0	2-1	1-1	4-0	2-0	5-0
Al Sina'a	26	16	7	3	31	17	55	2-1		1-0	1-0	3-1	3-2	0-0	0-0	2-1	1-0	2-1	1-0	3-1	1-0
Zakho	26	16	5	5	38	21	53	2-0	2-1		1-0	2-0	2-1	2-1	1-1	1-1	2-0	2-1	3-1	1-0	1-0
Kahrabaa	26	12	7	7	32	22	43	2-2	1-1	1-2		1-1	0-2	0-0	0-2	2-1	2-1	4-1	2-0	3-2	1-0
Karkh	26	10	11	5	35	27	41	1-1	1-1	4-2	2-2		4-0	1-1	0-0	0-0	1-0	2-2	3-1	3-0	1-0
Duhok	26	12	4	10	36	28	40	1-0	0-1	1-1	0-1	2-1		1-2	1-0	2-1	4-0	3-2	3-0	2-0	1-1
Al Naft Baghdad	26	10	9	7	25	23	39	0-2	0-0	1-0	0-1	0-0	3-0		2-0	1-1	2-1	2-1	1-1	1-2	1-0
Al Shurta	26	8	11	7	28	23	35	3-1	1-1	0-0	0-3	0-0	1-0	2-0		1-2	4-0	2-0	1-1	3-1	2-1
Mosul	26	8	11	7	29	29	35	2-2	0-1	2-2	1-0	1-2	1-2	1-1	0-0		1-1	1-0	1-1	3-1	1-0
Ramadi	26	7	7	12	28	40	28	2-5	1-0	1-0	0-0	1-2	0-0	3-2	2-1	1-3		1-0	1-1	1-1	5-1
Peshmerga	26	5	7	14	19	31	22	0-1	0-1	0-3	0-0	1-1	1-0	0-1	2-1	0-0	1-0		1-0	0-0	3-0
Diyala	26	3	10	13	15	33	19	0-0	0-0	0-1	0-1	0-1	0-0	0-1	1-1	0-0	1-2	1-0		1-0	2-1
Samara'a	26	4	6	16	24	44	18	0-2	1-2	1-2	0-2	3-1	1-2	1-1	0-0	2-3	2-2	2-1	2-1		1-1
Al Jaish	26	1	6	19	12	47	9	0-3	0-1	0-2	1-3	0-1	0-5	0-1	2-2	0-1	1-1	0-0	2-2	1-0	

PREMIER LEAGUE GROUP A (SOUTH)

	Pl	W	D	L	F	A	Pts	Al Zawra'a	Al Quwa Al Jawiya	Baghdad FC	Al Mina'a	Karbala	Al Najaf	Masafi	Al Talaba	Nafit Janob	Nafit Maysan	Diwaniya	Al Nasiriya	Hassanin	Hindiya
Al Zawra'a † ‡	26	19	5	2	45	15	62		1-0	0-0	2-1	1-0	1-0	3-0	2-0	4-2	0-0	5-0	3-0	2-1	2-1
Al Quwa Al Jawiya	26	19	3	4	47	13	60	2-0		0-0	2-1	2-0	2-0	3-0	2-1	2-0	1-0	3-0	2-1	1-0	4-0
Baghdad FC	26	13	8	5	32	17	47	0-1	0-2		1-1	1-1	2-1	0-0	0-0	2-1	2-1	2-0	3-0	2-0	1-0
Al Mina'a	26	12	9	5	33	21	45	3-1	2-1	0-0		0-1	0-0	2-0	2-0	0-0	1-1	3-1	1-0	2-0	1-0
Karbala	26	13	6	7	23	17	45	1-2	1-0	1-3	0-0		1-0	1-0	1-0	3-1	0-0	0-2	2-0	1-0	0-0
Al Najaf	26	11	9	6	34	20	42	1-1	0-0	1-2	1-0	2-0		1-0	4-1	1-1	2-1	4-1	3-1	2-0	5-1
Masafi Baghdad	26	12	5	9	22	28	41	0-2	1-5	1-0	1-2	0-0	2-2		1-0	0-0	1-0	1-0	1-0	1-0	2-1
Al Talaba	26	9	11	6	33	25	38	0-0	0-0	1-0	4-2	2-2	0-0	1-1		1-1	2-2	1-1	1-0	6-0	3-0
Nafit Al Janob	26	9	10	7	28	24	37	1-2	1-0	2-1	0-0	0-1	0-0	0-1	3-3		3-1	3-0	0-0	0-0	1-0
Nafit Maysan	26	6	7	13	20	29	25	1-1	1-2	0-1	1-3	1-0	1-0	0-1	0-2	0-2		1-0	**3-0**	0-1	2-1
Diwaniya	26	5	6	15	25	45	21	1-2	1-3	2-4	2-2	0-1	1-1	1-2	0-1	1-1	1-0		3-0	3-2	1-0
Al Nasiriya	26	3	5	18	13	38	14	0-1	0-2	0-2	1-1	0-1	0-0	0-2	0-0	0-1	2-2	3-1		2-0	2-0
Hassanin	26	3	4	19	7	39	13	0-2	0-2	0-2	0-1	0-2	1-2	1-2	0-1	1-0	0-0	0-0	1-0		0-0
Hindiya	26	2	4	20	16	47	10	0-4	2-4	1-1	1-2	0-2	0-1	0-1	1-2	0-1	0-1	0-1	2-2	2-1	3-1

26/11/2010 - 9/08/2011 • † Qualified for the championship play-off • ‡ Qualified for the AFC Cup • Match in bold awarded

Top scorers: **17** - Louay Salah, Arbil • **13** - Amjad Radhi, Al Quwa • **12** - Mahdi Karim, Arbil; Hammadi Ahmed, Al Quwa & Husam Ibrahim, Al Mina'a

CHAMPIONSHIP FINAL 2011

Al Shaab, Baghdad, 15-08-2011

Al Zawra'a　0-0 5-4p　Arbil

3rd Place: Al Sina'a 1-0 Al Quwa Al Jawiya

MEDALS TABLE

		Overall			League			Cup		Asia			City
		G	S	B	G	S	B	G	S	G	S	B	
1	Al Zawra'a	26	8	2	12	6	2	14	1		1		Baghdad
2	Al Quwa Al Jawia	11	12	9	6	9	9	5	3				Baghdad
3	Al Talaba	7	14	5	5	7	5	2	6		1		Baghdad
4	Al Karkh	5	3	1	3	2	1	2			1		Daghdad
5	Al Jaish	3	6		1	2		2	4				Baghdad
6	Arbil FC	3	1	2	3	1	1					1	Arbil
7	Al Shurta	2	9	8	2	3	8		5		1		Baghdad
8	Al Mina'a	1	1	1	1	1	1						Basra
9	Al Sina'a		1	3			3				1		Baghdad
10	Duhok	1		1	1		1						Duhok
11	Salah al Deen	1			1								Tikrit
12	Al Najaf		3	2		3	2						Najaf
13	Al Shabab		3	1			1		3				Baghdad

ISL – ICELAND

FIFA/COCA-COLA WORLD RANKING

'93	'94	'95	'96	'97	'98	'99	'00	'01	'02	'03	'04	'05	'06	'07	'08	'09	'10	'11	'12
47	39	50	60	72	64	43	50	52	58	58	93	94	93	90	83	92	112	104	

						2011									
Jan	Feb	Mar	Apr	May	Jun	Jul	Aug	Sep	Oct	Nov	Dec		High	Low	Av
113	114	115	116	116	122	121	124	106	108	104	104		37	124	72

KR Reykjavík have had to take a back seat in recent recent years but 2011 saw them re-kindle some of the fighting spirit that has made them the most successful club in the country. With just one trophy in the previous seven seasons, KR stormed to a league and cup double under their new coach Runar Kristinsson. He played for the club for ten years before moving abroad but remarkably for Iceland's record cap winner, this was Kristinsson's first title with the club. KR lost just once all season and won the cup by beating Thór 2-0 in the final although their opponents did hit the bar five times during the match. At national team level, the qualifiers for Euro 2012 were not a great success with Iceland finishing a long way off the leading trio of Denmark, Portugal and Norway and only just above Cyprus at the bottom. A 1-0 win over the Cypriots in the penultimate game ensured that they avoided the wooden spoon and there are promising signs with the appointment of the veteran Swede Lars Lagerback as coach and the emergence of a talented generation of youth players who made it through to the finals of the the U-21 championship in Denmark. To qualify for the finals they had beaten Germany 4-1 in their group and once there beat hosts Denmark 3-1, just missing out on the semi-finals on goal difference.

UEFA EUROPEAN CHAMPIONSHIP RECORD
1960 DNE 1964 r1 1968-1972 DNE 1976-2012 DNQ

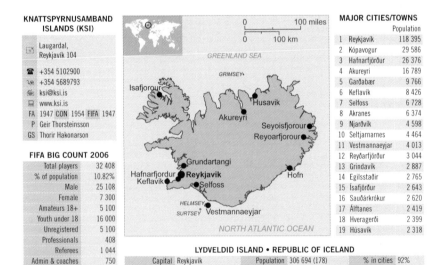

KNATTSPYRNUSAMBAND ISLANDS (KSI)

Laugardal, Reykjavík 104

☎ +354 5102900
📠 +354 5689793
📧 ksi@ksi.is
🖥 www.ksi.is
FA 1947 CON 1954 FIFA 1947
P Geir Thorsteinsson
GS Thorir Hakonarson

FIFA BIG COUNT 2006

Total players	32 408
% of population	10.82%
Male	25 108
Female	7 300
Amateurs 18+	5 100
Youth under 18	16 000
Unregistered	5 100
Professionals	408
Referees	1 044
Admin & coaches	750
Number of clubs	97
Number of teams	870

MAJOR CITIES/TOWNS
Population

1	Reykjavík	118 395
2	Kópavogur	29 586
3	Hafnarfjörður	26 376
4	Akureyri	16 789
5	Garðabær	9 766
6	Keflavík	8 426
7	Selfoss	6 728
8	Akranes	6 374
9	Njarðvík	4 598
10	Seltjarnarnes	4 464
11	Vestmannaeyjar	4 013
12	Reyðarfjörður	3 044
13	Grindavík	2 887
14	Egilsstaðir	2 765
15	Ísafjörður	2 643
16	Sauðárkrókur	2 620
17	Álftanes	2 419
18	Hveragerði	2 399
19	Húsavík	2 318

LYDVELDID ISLAND • REPUBLIC OF ICELAND

Capital	Reykjavik	Population	306 694 (178)	% in cities	92%
GDP per capita	$42 300 (17)	Area km²	103 000 km² (107)	GMT +/-	0
Neighbours (km)	Coast 4970				

RECENT INTERNATIONAL MATCHES PLAYED BY ICELAND

2008	Opponents	Score		Venue	Comp	Scorers	Att	Referee
2-02	Belarus	L	0-2	Ta'Qali	Fr			
4-02	Malta	L	0-1	Ta'Qali	Fr			
6-02	Armenia	W	2-0	Ta'Qali	Fr	Gudmundsson 45, Thorvaldsson 72		Attard MLT
16-03	Faroe Islands	W	3-0	Kopavogur	Fr	Saevarsson.J 45, OG 72, Gudmundsson 80	400	Skjerven NOR
26-03	Slovakia	W	2-1	Zilina	Fr	Thorvaldsson 71, Gudjohnsen 82	4 120	Lehner AUT
28-05	Wales	L	0-1	Reykjavik	Fr		5 322	McCourt NIR
20-08	Azerbaijan	D	1-1	Reykjavik	Fr	Steinsson 58	5 133	Evans WAL
6-09	Norway	D	2-2	Oslo	WCq	Helguson 39, Gudjohnsen 69	17 254	Yefet ISR
10-09	Scotland	L	1-2	Reykjavik	WCq	Gudjohnsen 77p	9 767	Gumieny BEL
11-10	Netherlands	L	0-2	Rotterdam	WCq		37 500	Trefoloni ITA
15-10	Macedonia FYR	W	1-0	Reykjavik	WCq	Veigar Gunnarsson 15	5 527	Dereli TUR
19-11	Malta	W	1-0	Corradino	Fr	Helgusson 66		
2009								
11-02	Liechtenstein	W	2-0	La Manga	Fr	Smarason 28, Gudjohnsen 47	150	Reinert FRO
22-03	Faroe Islands	L	1-2	Kopavogur	Fr	Saevarsson 91+	553	Riley ENG
1-04	Scotland	L	1-2	Glasgow	WCq	Indridi Sigurdsson 54	42 259	Einwaller AUT
6-06	Netherlands	L	1-2	Reykjavik	WCq	Kristian Sigurdsson 88	9 635	Dean ENG
10-06	Macedonia FYR	L	0-2	Skopje	WCq		7 000	Ennjimmi FRA
12-08	Slovakia	D	1-1	Reykjavik	Fr	Kristian Sigurdsson 60	5 099	Christoffersen DEN
5-09	Norway	D	1-1	Reykjavik	WCq	Gudjohnsen 29	7 321	Tudor ROU
9-09	Georgia	W	3-1	Reykjavik	WCq	Johannsson 14, Skulason 18, Veigar Gunnarsson 55p	4 726	Trefoloni ITA
13-10	South Africa	W	1-0	Reykjavik	Fr	Veigar Gunnarsson 50	3 253	Moen NOR
10-11	Iran	L	0-1	Tehran	Fr			Waleed QAT
14-11	Luxembourg	D	1-1	Luxembourg	Fr	Johannsson 63	913	Van Boekel NED
2010								
3-03	Cyprus	D	0-0	Larnaca	Fr			Yordanov.N BUL
21-03	Faroe Islands	W	2-0	Kopavogur	Fr	Vilhjalmsson 10, Sigthorsson 37	312	Larsen DEN
24-03	Mexico	D	0-0	Charlotte	Fr		63 227	Geiger USA
29-05	Andorra	W	4-0	Reykjavik	Fr	Helguson 2 32p 51, Veigar Gunnarsson 87p, Sigthorsson 88	2 567	Reinert FRO
11-08	Liechtenstein	D	1-1	Reykjavik	Fr	Gislason 20	3 000	Buttimer IRL
3-09	Norway	L	1-2	Reykjavik	ECq	Helguson 38	6 137	Banti ITA
7-09	Denmark	L	0-1	Copenhagen	ECq		18 908	McDonald SCO
12-10	Portugal	L	1-3	Reykjavik	ECq	Helguson 17	9 767	Einwaller AUT
17-11	Israel	L	2-3	Tel Aviv	Fr	Finnbogason 79, Sigthorsson 85	4 500	Spathas GRE
2011								
26-03	Cyprus	D	0-0	Nicosia	ECq		2 088	Ceferin SVN
4-06	Denmark	L	0-2	Reykjavik	ECq		7 629	Aydinus TUR
10-08	Hungary	L	0-4	Budapest	Fr		12 000	Stark GER
2-09	Norway	L	0-1	Oslo	ECq		22 381	Hategan ROU
6-09	Cyprus	W	1-0	Reykjavik	ECq	Sigthorsson 5	5 267	Jovanetic SRB
7-10	Portugal	L	3-5	Porto	ECq	Jonasson 2 48 68, Gylfi Sigurdsson 94+p	35 715	Nijhuis NED

Fr = Friendly match • EC = UEFA EURO 2012 • WC = FIFA World Cup • q = qualifier

ICELAND NATIONAL TEAM HISTORICAL RECORDS

Caps
104 - Runar Kristinsson 1987-2004 • **86** - Hermann Hreidarsson 1996- • **80** - Gudni Bergsson 1984-2003 • **74** - Brynjar Bjorn Gunnarsson 1997-2009 & Birkir Kristinsson 1988-2004 • **73** - Arnor Gudjohnsen 1979-97 • **72** - Olafur Thordarson 1984-96 • **71** - Arnar Gretarsson 1991-2004 & Arni Gautur Arason 1998- • **70** - Atli Edvaldsson 1976-91 • **69** - Saevar Jonsson 1980-92 • **67** - Marteinn Geirsson 1971-82

Goals
24 - Eidur Gudjohnsen 1996- • **17** - Rikhardur Jonsson 1947-65 • **14** - Rikhardur Dadason 1991-2004 & Arnor Gudjohnsen 1979-97 • **13** - Thordur Gudjonsson 1993-2004 • **12** - Tryggvi Gudmundsson 1997-2008 • **11** - Petur Petursson 1978-90 & Matthias Hallgrimsson 1968-77

Past Coaches
Frederick Steele & Murdo McDougall 1946 • Roland Bergstrom SWE 1947 • Fritz Buchloh GER 1949 • Oli B. Jonsson 1951 • Franz Kohler 1953 • Karl Gudmundsson 1954-56 • Alexander Wier 1957 • Oli B. Jonsson 1958 • Karl Gudmundsson 1959 • Oli B. Jonsson 1960 • Karl Gudmundsson 1961 • Rikhardur Jonsson 1962 • Karl Gudmundsson 1963-66 • Reynir Karlsson 1967 • Walter Pfeiffer 1968 • Rikhardur Jonsson 1969-71 • Duncan McDowell 1972 • Eggert Johannesson 1972 • Henning Enoksen DEN 1973 • Tony Knapp ENG 1974-77 • Juri Ilitchev URS 1978-79 • Gudni Kjartansson 1980-81 • Johannes Atlason 1982-83 • Tony Knapp ENG 1984-85 • Siegfried Held GER 1986-89 • Gudni Kjartansson 1989 • Bo Johansson SWE 1990-91 • Asgeir Eliasson 1991-95 • Logi Olafsson 1996-97 • Gudjon Thordarson 1997-99 • Atli Edvaldsson 2000-03 • Asgeir Sigurvinsson & Logi Olafsson 2003-05 • Eyjolfur Sverrisson 2006-07 • Olafur Johannesson 2007-11 • Lars Lagerback 2011-

ICELAND 2011

URVALSDEILD (1)

	Pl	W	D	L	F	A	Pts	KR	FH	IBV	Stjarnan	Valur	Breidablik	Fylkir	Keflavík	Fram	Grindavík	Thór	Vikingur
KR Reykjavík †	22	13	8	1	44	22	47		2-0	2-2	1-1	1-1	4-0	3-2	1-1	2-1	1-1	3-1	3-2
FH Hafnarfjördur ‡	22	13	5	4	48	31	44	2-1		4-2	3-0	3-2	4-1	2-2	1-0	1-1	7-2	2-0	1-1
IBV Vestmannæyjar ‡	22	12	4	6	37	27	40	1-1	3-1		2-1	1-1	1-1	1-2	2-1	1-0	0-2	3-1	2-0
Stjarnan Gardabær	22	10	7	5	51	35	37	1-1	4-0	3-2		5-0	3-2	4-1	2-3	2-2	2-1	5-1	0-0
Valur Reykjavík	22	10	6	6	28	23	36	0-0	1-0	0-1	1-1		2-0	3-1	0-1	1-0	1-1	2-1	2-1
Breidablik	22	7	6	9	34	42	27	2-3	0-1	1-2	4-3	1-1		3-1	2-1	1-1	2-1	4-1	2-6
Fylkir Reykjavík	22	7	4	11	34	44	25	0-3	3-5	1-3	2-3	2-1	1-2		2-1	0-0	2-3	1-1	2-1
Keflavík	22	7	3	12	27	32	24	2-3	1-1	0-2	4-2	0-2	1-1	1-2		1-0	1-2	2-1	2-1
Fram Reykjavík	22	6	6	10	20	28	24	1-2	1-2	0-2	2-5	3-1	1-0	0-0	1-0		1-1	0-1	2-1
Grindavík	22	5	8	9	26	37	23	0-3	1-3	2-0	2-2	0-2	1-1	1-4	0-2	1-2		4-1	0-0
Thór Akureyri ‡	22	6	3	13	28	41	21	1-2	2-2	2-1	0-1	0-3	1-2	2-0	2-1	3-0	0-0		6-1
Vikingur Reykjavík	22	3	6	13	24	39	15	0-2	1-3	1-3	1-1	0-1	2-2	1-3	2-1	0-1	0-0	2-0	

2/05/2011 - 1/10/2011 • † Qualified for the UEFA Champions League • ‡ Qualified for the Europa League
Top scorers: **15** - Gardar Johannsson, Stjarnan • **13** - Atli Bjornsson, FH • **12** - Halldor Bjornsson, Stjarnan & Kjartan Finnbogason, KR

ICELAND 2011 — 1.DEILD (2)

	Pl	W	D	L	F	A	Pts
IA Akranes	22	16	3	3	53	17	51
Selfoss	22	15	2	5	44	22	47
Haukar Hafnarfjördur	22	10	6	6	33	23	36
Vikingur Olafsvík	22	10	4	8	35	26	34
Fjölnir Reykjavík	22	8	8	6	34	38	32
Bl/Bolungarvík	22	9	4	9	27	37	31
Thróttur Reykjavík	22	9	3	10	34	45	30
KA Akureyri	22	9	2	11	32	40	29
IR Reykjavík	22	6	4	12	27	42	22
Leiknir Reykjavík	22	5	5	12	31	32	20
Grótta Seltjarnarnes	22	4	8	10	16	29	20
HK Kópavogur	22	3	7	12	23	38	16

13/05/2011 - 17/09/2011

MEDALS TABLE

		Overall			League			Cup		City
		G	S	B	G	S	B	G	S	
1	KR Reykjavik	37	32	12	25	27	12	12	5	Reykjavik
2	Valur	29	20	18	20	17	18	9	3	Reykjavik
3	IA Akranes	27	21	13	18	12	13	9	9	Akranes
4	Fram	25	27	16	18	17	16	7	10	Reykjavik
5	Keflavik IF	8	8	7	4	3	7	4	5	Keflavik
6	IBV Vestmannæyjar	7	12	9	3	6	9	4	6	Vestmannæyjar
7	FH Hafnarfjördur	7	10	1	5	7	1	2	3	Hafnarfjördur
8	Vikingur	6	8	8	5	7	8	1	1	Reykjavik
9	Fylkir	2	2	1		2	1	2		Reykjavik
10	Breidablik UBK	2	1	1	1		1	1	1	Kópavogur
11	KA Akureyri	1	3		1				3	Akureyri
12	IBA Akureyri	1	4			4		1		Akureyri
13	Fjölnir		2						2	Reykjavik
14	Leiftur	1	3			3		1		Olafsfjördur
15	Grindavik	1	2						1	Grindavik
	Thór Akureyri	1	2						1	Akureyri
17	Vidir Gardur	1							1	Gardi

BIKARKEPPNI 2011

Round of 16

KR Reykjavík *	2
FH Hafnarfjördur	0
Haukar Hafnarfjördur *	1
Keflavík	3
Thróttur Reykjavík *	3
Fram Reykjavík	1
Breidablik	1
BÍ/Bolungarvík *	4
IBV Vestmannæyjar	3
Valur Reykjavík *	2
Hamar Hveragerdi	2
Fjölnir Reykjavík *	3
Grindavík *	2
HK Kópavogur	1
Vikingur Reykjavík	1
Thór Akureyri *	3

Quarter–finals

KR Reykjavík *	3
Keflavík	2
Thróttur Reykjavík	2
BÍ/Bolungarvík *	3
IBV Vestmannæyjar	2
Fjölnir Reykjavík *	1
Grindavík	1
Thór Akureyri *	2

Semi–finals

KR Reykjavík	4
BÍ/Bolungarvík *	1
IBV Vestmannæyjar	0
Thór Akureyri *	2

Final

KR Reykjavík	2
Thór Akureyri ‡	0

CUP FINAL
Laugardalsvøllur, Reykjavik
13-08-2011, 5327, Valgeirsson
Scorers - Gunnar Gudmundsson OG [45], Baldur Sigurdsson [82] for KR

* Home team • ‡ Qualified for the Europa League

ISR – ISRAEL

FIFA/COCA-COLA WORLD RANKING

'93	'94	'95	'96	'97	'98	'99	'00	'01	'02	'03	'04	'05	'06	'07	'08	'09	'10	'11	'12
57	42	42	52	61	43	26	41	49	46	51	48	44	44	26	18	26	50	37	

						2011									
Jan	Feb	Mar	Apr	May	Jun	Jul	Aug	Sep	Oct	Nov	Dec	**High**	**Low**	**Av**
50	52	58	33	33	30	32	32	38	38	37	37	**15**	**71**	**41**

For the second year running Maccabi Haifa and Hapoel Tel Aviv were a cut above the other teams in the Israeli Premier League but having won the double in 2010, Hapoel had to be content with just the cup in 2011 as Maccabi reclaimed the league crown they had last won in 2006. Maccabi had ended the regular season five points ahead of Hapoel, but with the points totals being cut and rounded up that was down to just two as the five extra matches kicked-off. After the first match Hapoel found themselves at the top of the table but Maccabi won the match between the two in the next game and held on to secure their 12th title. The two clubs also met in the Cup Final where an early goal by Salim Tuama won the cup for Hapoel and denied Maccabi what would have been their first cup win since 1998 and their first double for 20 years. It was a fitting farewell for Hapoel coach Eli Guttman who stood down at the end of the season having missed several months of the season after suffering a heart attack. Before they year was out, however, he was back in the game, this time as national team coach after the contract of Luis Fernandes wasn't renewed following an unsuccessful Euro 2012 qualifying campaign in which the Israelis had never managed to keep pace with either Greece or Croatia in their group.

UEFA EUROPEAN CHAMPIONSHIP RECORD
1960-1992 DNE (not a member of UEFA) **1996-2012** DNQ

THE ISRAEL FOOTBALL ASSOCIATION (IFA)

- Ramat-Gan Stadium, 299 Aba Hilell Street, Ramat Gan 52134
- ☎ +972 3 6171500
- 📠 +972 3 5702044
- ✉ karens@football.org.il
- 🖥 www.football.org.il
- FA 1928 CON 1992 FIFA 1929
- P Avi Luzon
- GS Ori Shilo

FIFA BIG COUNT 2006

Total players	283 866
% of population	4.47%
Male	251 516
Female	32 350
Amateurs 18+	8 423
Youth under 18	33 883
Unregistered	77 000
Professionals	1 360
Referees	1 350
Admin & coaches	10 800
Number of clubs	280
Number of teams	1 400

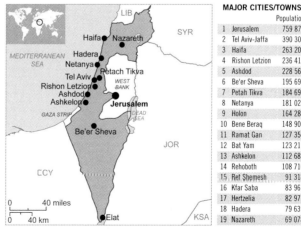

MAJOR CITIES/TOWNS
Population

1	Jerusalem	759 873
2	Tel Aviv-Jaffa	390 300
3	Haifa	263 208
4	Rishon Letzion	236 411
5	Ashdod	228 564
6	Be'er Sheva	195 695
7	Petah Tikva	184 695
8	Netanya	181 028
9	Holon	164 285
10	Bene Beraq	148 908
11	Ramat Gan	127 354
12	Bat Yam	123 211
13	Ashkelon	112 682
14	Rehoboth	108 710
15	Bet Shemesh	91 318
16	Kfar Saba	83 967
17	Hertzelia	82 971
18	Hadera	79 639
19	Nazareth	69 078

MEDINAT YISRA'EL • STATE OF ISRAEL

Capital Jerusalem	Population 7 233 701 (97)	% in cities 92%
GDP per capita $28 600 (48)	Area km² 22 072 km² (152)	GMT + / - +2
Neighbours (km) Egypt 266, Gaza Strip 51, Jordan 238, Lebanon 79, Syria 76, West Bank 307 • Coast 273		

RECENT INTERNATIONAL MATCHES PLAYED BY ISRAEL

2008 Opponents	Score		Venue	Comp	Scorers	Att	Referee
6-02 Romania	W	1-0	Tel Aviv	Fr	Golan 25	8 000	Duarte Gomez POR
26-03 Chile	W	1-0	Tel Aviv	Fr	Benayoun 30	24 463	Velasco ESP
20-08 Finland	L	0-2	Tampere	Fr		4 929	
6-09 Switzerland	D	2-2	Ramat Gan	WCq	Benayoun 73, Sahar 92+	29 600	Hansson SWE
10-09 Moldova	W	2-1	Chisinau	WCq	Golan 39, Saban 45	10 500	Muniz ESP
11-10 Luxembourg	W	3-1	Luxembourg	WCq	Benayoun 2p, Golan 54, Toama 81	3 562	Egorov RUS
15-10 Latvia	D	1-1	Riga	WCq	Benayoun 50	7 100	Hrinak SVK
19-11 Côte d'Ivoire	D	2-2	Tel Aviv	Fr	Barda 18, Golan 24	27 167	
2009							
11-02 Hungary	W	1-0	Tel Aviv	Fr	Benayoun 77	9 500	Borski POL
28-03 Greece	D	1-1	Ramat Gan	WCq	Golan 55	38 000	Rosetti ITA
1-04 Greece	L	1-2	Iraklio	WCq	Barda 58	22 794	Benquerença POR
12-08 Northern Ireland	D	1-1	Belfast	Fr	Barda 27	10 250	Valgeirsson ISL
5-09 Latvia	L	0-1	Ramat Gan	WCq		20 000	Kircher GER
9-09 Luxembourg	W	7-0	Ramat Gan	WCq	Barda 3 9 21 43, Baruchyan 15, Golan 58, Sahar 2 62 84	7 038	Svendsen DEN
10-10 Moldova	W	3-1	Ramat Gan	WCq	Barda 2 22 70, Ben Dayan 65	8 700	Blom NED
14-10 Switzerland	D	0-0	Basel	WCq		38 500	Tudor ROU
2010							
26-05 Uruguay	L	1-4	Montevideo	Fr	Rafaelov 30	60 000	Osses CHI
30-05 Chile	L	0-3	Concepcion	Fr		25 000	Arias PAR
2-09 Malta	W	3-1	Tel Aviv	ECq	Benayoun 3 7 64p 75	17 365	Ennjimi FRA
7-09 Georgia	D	0-0	Tbilisi	ECq		45 000	Kever SUI
9-10 Croatia	L	1-2	Tel Aviv	ECq	Shechter 81	33 421	Stark Ger
12-10 Greece	L	1-2	Piraeus	ECq	OG 59	16 935	Hansson SWE
17-11 Iceland	W	3-2	Tel Aviv	Fr	Damari 2 5 14, Rafaelov 27	4 500	Spathas GRE
2011							
9-02 Serbia	L	0-2	Tel Aviv	Fr		8 000	Nikolaev RUS
26-03 Latvia	W	2-1	Tel Aviv	ECq	Barda 16, Kayal 81	10 801	Mazic SRB
29-03 Georgia	W	1-0	Tel Aviv	ECq	Ben Haim II 59	13 716	Fautrel FRA
4-06 Latvia	W	2-1	Riga	ECq	Benayoun 19, Ben Haim I 43p	6 147	Kelly IRL
10-08 Côte d'Ivoire	L	3-4	Geneva	Fr	Shechter 76, Melikson 2 79 87p	2 000	
2-09 Greece	L	0-1	Tel Aviv	ECq		13 100	Thomson SCO
6-09 Croatia	L	1-3	Zagreb	ECq	Hemed 44	13 688	Velasco ESP
11-10 Malta	W	2-0	Ta'Qali	ECq	Refaelov 11, Gershon 93+	2 164	Duarte POR

Fr = Friendly match • EC = UEFA EURO 2012 • WC = FIFA World Cup • q = qualifier

ISRAEL NATIONAL TEAM HISTORICAL RECORDS

Caps
94 - Arik Benado 1995-2007 • **88** - Alon Harazi 1992-2006 • **85** - Yossi Benayoun 1998- & Amir Schelach 1992-2001 • **84** - Mordechai Spiegler **(57)** 1963-77 • **83** - Nir Klinger **(76)** 1987-97 • **80** - Avi Nimni 1992-2006 • **78** - Tal Banin 1990-2002; Itzhak Shum **(53)** 1969-81 & Eyal Berkovic 1992-2004 • **74** - Walid Badir 1997-2007 • **72** - Alon Hazan 1990-2000 • **70** - Itzik Visoker **(43)** 1963-76

Goals
33 - Mordechai Spiegler 1963-77 • **24** - Yehoshua Feigenbaum 1966-77 & Yossi Benayoun 1998- • **23** - Ronen Harazi 1992-99 • **22** - Nahum Stelmach 1956-68 • **21** - Gidi Damti 1971-81 • **18** - Giora Spiegel 1965-80 & Yehoshua Glazer 1949-61

Past Coaches
Egon Pollack AUT 1948 • Lajos Hess 1949 • Vladislav Scali HUN 1950 • Jerry Beit haLevi 1953-54 • Jack Gibbons ENG 1956 • Jerry Beit haLevi 1957 • Moshe Varon 1958 • Gyula Mandi HUN 1959-63 • George Ainsley ENG 1963-64 • Yosef Mirmovich YUG 1964 • Gyula Mandi HUN 1964 • Yosef Mirmovich 1964-65 • Milovan Ciric 1965-68 • Emmanuel Scheffer 1968-70 • Edmond Schmilovich 1970-73 • David Schweitzer 1973-77 • Emmanuel Scheffer 1978-79 • Jack Mansell ENG 1980-81 • Yosef Mirmovich 1983-86 • Miljenko Mihic YUG 1986-88 • Itzhak Schneor & Ya'akov Grundman 1988-92 • Shlomo Scharf 1992-2000 • Richard Moller Nielsen DEN 2000-02 • Avram Grant 2002-06 • Dror Kashtan 2006-10 • Eli Ohana 2010 • Luis Fernandez FRA 2010-11 • Eli Guttman 2011-

Appearances and goals in brackets are totals in games recognised as full internationals by FIFA

ISRAEL 2010-11

LIGAT HA'AL

	Pl	W	D	L	F	A	Pts	Maccabi H	Hapoel TA	Maccabi TA	Bnei Yehuda	Ironi	Maccabi N	Maccabi PT	Hapoel Acre	Hapoel BS	Hapoel Haifa	Beitar	Ashdod	Bnei Sakhnin	Hapoel PT	Hapoel Ashk	Hapoel RG
Maccabi Haifa †	35	24	8	3	63	28	**45**		0-2	3-0	1-0	3-2	3-0	1-0	3-1	2-2	0-0	3-3	1-1	1-0	2-0	3-0	3-2
Hapoel Tel Aviv ‡	35	21	7	7	72	36	**38**	4-1		1-0	0-1	2-4	2-1	2-0	4-1	3-2	5-0	0-0	0-2	1-0	2-0	5-1	4-0
Maccabi Tel Aviv ‡	35	18	6	11	53	40	**35**	0-1	1-1		2-0	0-1	0-3	1-1	2-2	0-2	0-1	1-0	4-1	4-0	2-1	2-0	2-0
Bnei Yehuda Tel Aviv ‡	35	15	10	10	42	34	**31**	2-3	0-1	2-0		3-1	1-1	2-0	1-0	0-0	3-2	2-1	0-0	2-0	2-0	2-0	0-0
Ironi Kiriat Shmona	35	14	10	11	57	45	**28**	0-1	1-1	4-0	2-2		3-0	2-2	2-2	1-0	1-3	0-1	3-0	2-0	3-1	2-2	1-0
Maccabi Netanya	35	12	13	10	47	47	**27**	1-1	1-3	0-2	0-0	1-1		2-2	1-3	1-0	1-1	4-1	2-0	1-0	3-3	3-0	2-0
Maccabi Petah Tikva	33	13	10	10	57	41	**28**	1-3	1-2	2-2	3-0	0-0	2-0		1-1	0-1	2-3	2-1	2-2	1-2	2-3	4-0	4-1
Hapoel Acre	33	12	11	10	49	45	**27**	0-2	2-2	3-1	3-1	3-0	0-0	1-1		2-3	2-1	3-0	1-2	0-0	3-0	1-0	0-0
Hapoel Be'er Sheva	33	11	9	13	41	43	**23**	1-1	0-3	0-1	0-1	1-1	1-2	2-1	0-2		0-2	1-2	5-0	1-0	0-0	1-0	2-0
Hapoel Haifa	33	12	8	13	40	43	**22**	0-2	1-0	0-0	2-0	1-4	1-2	1-1	1-1	1-1		0-2	2-0	4-1	3-2	1-2	2-0
Beitar Jerusalem	35	12	9	14	38	35	**26**	0-0	1-0	0-1	1-1	1-0	0-0	0-2	2-0	5-1	1-0		0-0	0-0	0-2	4-0	3-2
FC Ashdod	35	10	11	14	42	55	**25**	1-2	3-3	1-2	1-2	2-2	1-0	1-3	3-1	0-3	0-0	3-0		0-0	1-2	3-2	2-2
Bnei Sakhnin	35	9	8	18	25	44	**23**	1-2	1-3	1-3	0-1	1-0	1-1	2-3	0-1	1-1	1-3	1-0	0-2		1-1	2-0	0-0
Hapoel Petah Tikva	35	10	8	17	42	58	**22**	0-1	1-5	0-1	2-1	1-3	1-1	1-4	2-2	3-1	2-0	1-0	3-1	0-1		0-2	2-0
Hapoel Ashkelon	35	9	5	21	33	66	**19**	0-3	0-2	2-4	0-0	0-1	0-4	0-1	0-0	3-4	0-0	2-1	4-1	1-0	3-1		1-1
Hapoel Ramat Gan	35	3	9	23	24	65	**10**	3-1	0-1	0-3	1-1	0-3	0-1	0-2	3-2	0-0	1-2	0-0	1-2	1-2	1-1	0-4	

21/08/2010 - 21/05/2011 • † Qualified for the UEFA Champions League • ‡ Qualified for the Europa League • Points halved after 30 matches
Relegation play-off: **Hapoel Petah Tikva** 4-1 1-0 Hapoel Kfar Saba
Top scorers: **21** - Toto Tamuz, Hapoel Tel Aviv • **18** - Eden Ben Basat, Hapoel Haifa & Eliran Atar, Maccabi Tel Aviv • **17** - Moshe Ohayon, Ashdod •
16 - Pedro Galvan ARG, Bnei Yehuda & Ben Sahar, Hapoel Tel Aviv • **15** - Omer Damari, Maccabi Petah Tikva

ISRAEL 2010-11
LIGA LEUMIT (2)

	Pl	W	D	L	F	A	Pts
Ironi Ramat Hasharon	35	19	11	5	55	28	**38**
Ironi Rishon Letzion	35	18	8	9	57	31	**36**
Hapoel Kfar Saba	35	20	9	6	54	36	**36**
Maccabi Hertzelia	35	17	10	8	41	21	**35**
Hapoel Ranana	35	14	11	10	43	27	**30**
Sektzia Nes Tziona	35	13	11	11	31	29	**27**
Hapoel Herzelia	33	15	8	10	46	37	**30**
Hapoel Bnei Lod	33	11	13	9	36	31	**24**
Hapoel Upper Nazareth	33	12	11	10	46	41	**22**
Beitar/Shimshon TA	33	9	9	15	44	47	**19**
Hapoel Nazareth Illit	35	12	7	16	43	46	**23**
Maccabi Be'er Sheva	35	8	14	13	33	42	**22**
Ironi Bat Yam	35	7	15	13	29	54	**22**
Hakoah Ramat Gan	35	7	12	16	32	50	**21**
Maccabi Ironi Jatt	35	4	11	20	27	66	**14**
Ahva Arraba	35	6	8	21	21	62	**10**

20/08/2010 - 20/05/2011 • Relegation play-off:
Maccabi Kabilio Jaffa 1-2 1-1 **Hakoah Ramat Gan**

Top group play-offs: Maccabi TA 3-1 Ironi KS • Maccabi Haifa 1-2 Maccabi
Netanya • Hapoel TA 2-1 Bnei Yehuda • Maccabi Netanya 3-3 Ironi KS • Bnei
Yehuda 1-3 Maccabi TA • Maccabi Haifa 2-0 Hapoel TA • Hapoel TA 2-2 Maccabi
Netanya • Ironi KS 1-2 Bnei Yehuda • Maccabi TA 0-2 Maccabi Haifa • Hapoel TA
2-2 Maccabi TA • Maccabi Netanya 0-4 Bnei Yehuda • Maccabi Haifa 2-0 Ironi KS
• Maccabi TA 4-1 Maccabi Netanya • Beni Yehuda 1-1 Maccabi Haifa • Ironi KS
2-1 Hapoel TA
Middle group play-offs: Hapoel Haifa 1-2 Hapoel BS • Maccabi PT 4-1 Hapoel
Acre • Hapoel Haifa 0-2 Maccabi PT • Hapoel BS 2-3 Hapoel Acre • Maccabi PT
1-1 Hapoel BS • Hapoel Acre 2-1 Hapoel Haifa
Relegation group play-offs: Ashdod 4-1 Hapoel Ashkelon • Beitar Jerusalem 5-1
Hapoel RG • Hapoel PT 1-1 Bnei Sakhnin • Beitar Jerusalem 3-0 Hapoel PT •
Hapoel RG 2-0 Hapoel Ashkelon • Bnei Sakhnin 1-0 Ashdod • Ashdod 0-0 Beitar
Jerusalem • Hapoel PT 1-2 Hapoel RG • Hapoel Ashkelon 2-1 Bnei Sakhnin •
Hapoel PT 1-1 Ashdod • Beitar Jerusalem 0-1 Hapoel Ashkelon • Hapoel RG 1-2
Bnei Sakhnin • Bnei Sakhnin 1-0 Beitar Jerusalem • Hapoel Ashkelon 0-3 Hapoel PT
• Ashdod 1-0 Hapoel RG

MEDALS TABLE

		Overall			League			Cup		Asia/Eur			City
		G	S	B	G	S	B	G	S	G	S	B	
1	Maccabi Tel Aviv	42	20	9	18	9	9	22	11	2			Tel Aviv
2	Hapoel Tel Aviv	27	21	6	12	12	6	14	8	1	1		Tel Aviv
3	Maccabi Haifa	17	15	5	12	6	5	5	9				Haifa
4	Beitar Jerusalem	13	9	5	6	6	5	7	3				Jerusalem
5	Hapoel Petach Tikva	8	15	4	6	9	4	2	6				Petach Tikva
6	Maccabi Netanya	6	6	4	5	4	4	1	2				Netanya
7	Hapoel Haifa	4	7	8	1	2	8	3	5				Haifa
8	Hakoah Ramat Gan	4	1	1	2		1	2	1				Ramat Gan
9	Hapoel Kfar Saba	4			1			3					Kfar Saba
10	Bnei Yehuda Tel Aviv	3	7	2	1	3	2	2	4				Tel Aviv
11	Hapoel Beer Sheva	3	2	5	2		5	1	2				Beer Sheva
12	Maccabi Petach Tikva	2	5	1		3	1	2	2				Petach Tikva

G'VIAA H'AMEDINA (STATE CUP) 2010-11

Eighth Round

Team	Score
Hapoel Tel Aviv	7
Maccabi Ironi Kiryat Ata*	0
Ironi Bat Yam	0
Hapoel Ashkelon*	1
Hapoel Rishon Letzion*	3
Bnei Sakhnin	1
Hapoel Ramat Gan*	0
Beitar Jerusalem	1
Hapoel Ranana	2
Hakoah Ramat Gan*	0
Hapoel Acre*	0
Maccabi Ironi Jatt	2
Hapoel Be'er Sheva	4
Hapoel Afula*	1
Maccabi Akhi Nazareth	0
Ironi Kiriat Shmona*	1
Maccabi Netanya*	4
Bnei Yehuda Tel Aviv	1
Hapoel Petah Tikva*	3
Maccabi Hertzelia*	2
Maccabi Tamra	0
Maccabi Petah Tikva*	0
FC Ashdod	1
Mac'bi Daliyat Al Karmel	0
Hapoel Haifa*	2
Maccabi Ironi Netivot	0
Sektzia Nes Tziona*	1
Hapoel Jerusalem*	2
Maccabi Be'er Sheva	0
Hapoel Kfar Saba*	0
Maccabi Haifa	3

Round of 16

Team	Score
Hapoel Tel Aviv*	2
Hapoel Ashkelon	1
Hapoel Rishon Letzion	0
Beitar Jerusalem*	2
Hapoel Ranana*	3
Maccabi Ironi Jatt	0
Hapoel Be'er Sheva	0
Ironi Kiriat Shmona*	4
Maccabi Netanya*	1
Hapoel Petah Tikva	0
Maccabi Hertzelia*	0
FC Ashdod	2
Hapoel Haifa	3
Sektzia Nes Tziona*	1
Hapoel Jerusalem	1
Maccabi Haifa*	2

Quarter-finals

Team	Score
Hapoel Tel Aviv*	1
Beitar Jerusalem	0
Hapoel Ranana*	0
Ironi Kiriat Shmona	1
Maccabi Netanya*	1 4p
FC Ashdod	1 1p
Hapoel Haifa*	1
Maccabi Haifa	3

Semi-finals

Team	Score
Hapoel Tel Aviv*	2
Ironi Kiriat Shmona	0
Maccabi Netanya*	2
Maccabi Haifa	3

Final

Team	Score
Hapoel Tel Aviv ‡	1
Maccabi Haifa	0

CUP FINAL

National Stadium, Ramat Gan
25-05-2011, Att: 40 000. Ref: Meir Levi
Scorer - Salim Tuama [2] for Hapoel

Hapoel - Vincent Enyeama - Omri Kenda, Walid Badir, Bevan Fransman, Dedi Ben Dayan, Avihai Yadin, Shay Abutbol, Eran Zahavi, Salim Tuama (Victor Maree 79), Toto Tamuz (Elroi Cohen 77), Ben Sahar (Ma'aran Al Lala 90). Tr: Eli Gutman

Maccabi - Nir Davidovich - Eyal Meshumar, Arik Benado, Andriy Pylyavskiy, Tsepo Masilela, Gustavo Boccoli (Muhammad Ghdir 72), Seydou Yahaya, Yaniv Katan, Lior Refaelov (Shlomi Azulay 79), Tomer Hemed, Vladimer Dvalishvili (Idan Vered 52). Tr: Elisha Levi

Premier League clubs enter in the eighth round • * Home team • ‡ Qualified for the UEFA Europa League

ITA – ITALY

FIFA/COCA-COLA WORLD RANKING

'93	'94	'95	'96	'97	'98	'99	'00	'01	'02	'03	'04	'05	'06	'07	'08	'09	'10	'11	'12
2	4	3	10	9	7	14	4	6	13	10	10	12	2	3	4	4	14	9	

2011															
Jan	Feb	Mar	Apr	May	Jun	Jul	Aug	Sep	Oct	Nov	Dec		High	Low	Av
14	13	11	9	9	6	8	7	6	6	9	9		1	16	7

By winning the 2011 title Milan ended a six-season barren spell on the domestic front and although they have gone longer without winning the Scudetto - they won just one between 1969 and 1987 - the latest was probably the hardest to bear given that city rivals Inter collected five championships and three Coppa Italia's in those six seasons. Under coach Massimiliano Allegri, Milan put an end to that nightmare run thanks to two vital wins over second-place Inter, the second coming at the beginning of April when Inter's surge in form had reduced Milan's lead to just two points. After having played Roma in five of the previous six Coppa Italia finals, Inter beat Palermo 3-1 in the 2011 final, their victory ensuring they maintained their record of having won a trophy in each of the past six seasons. They didn't, however, retain their UEFA Champions League crown in what was an awful season for Italian clubs in Europe and from the 2012-13 season the Italians have lost their fourth Champions League spot to Germany. Corruption in Italian football once more reared its ugly head when Operation Last Bet - Calcio scommesse - revealed large-scale match fixing in Serie B and Lega Pro Prima Divisione games. A number of well-known figures, including former Lazio striker Giuseppe Signori, were implicated with Signori receiving a five-year ban.

UEFA EUROPEAN CHAMPIONSHIP RECORD
1960 DNE **1964** r2 **1968** 1 Winners **1972** QF **1976** DNQ **1980** 4 3p/o **1984** DNQ **1988** 4 SF **1992** DNQ
1996 10 r1 **2000** 2 F **2004** 9 r1 **2008** 8 QF **2012** Qualified

FEDERAZIONE ITALIANA GIUOCO CALCIO (FIGC)

Via Gregorio Allegri 14, Roma 00198

☎ +39 06 84912542
📠 +39 06 84912526
✉ international@figc.it
🖥 www.figc.it
FA 1898 CON 1954 FIFA 1905
P Giancarlo Abete
GS Antonio Di Sebastiano

FIFA BIG COUNT 2006

Total players	4 980 296
% of population	8.57%
Male	4 688 929
Female	291 367
Amateurs 18+	877 602
Youth under 18	557 453
Unregistered	3 207 700
Professionals	3 541
Referees	24 981
Admin & coaches	53 500
Number of clubs	16 128
Number of teams	80 864

MAJOR CITIES/TOWNS

		Population
1	Rome	2 491 807
2	Milan	1 324 927
3	Naples	959 303
4	Turin	862 469
5	Palermo	647 870
6	Genoa	585 060
7	Florence	378 158
8	Bologna	371 940
9	Bari	304 594
10	Catania	289 838
11	Venice	265 493
12	Verona	263 899
13	Messina	236 530
14	Padova	215 258
15	Trieste	198 389
16	Brescia	195 448
17	Taranto	190 548
18	Parma	186 566
49	Udine	97 669

REPUBBLICA ITALIANA • ITALIAN REPUBLIC

Capital	Rome	Population	58 126 212 (23)	% in cities	68%
GDP per capita	$31 400 (41)	Area km²	301 340 km² (71)	GMT +/-	+1
Neighbours (km)	Austria 430, France 488, San Marino 39, Slovenia 199, Switzerland 740 • Coast 7600				

RECENT INTERNATIONAL MATCHES PLAYED BY ITALY

2009	Opponents	Score		Venue	Comp	Scorers	Att	Referee
15-06	USA	W	3-1	Pretoria	CCr1	Rossi 2 58 94+, De Rossi 72	34 341	Pozo CHI
18-06	Egypt	L	0-1	Johannesburg	CCr1		52 150	Hansson SWE
21-06	Brazil	L	0-3	Pretoria	CCr1		41 195	Archundia MEX
12-08	Switzerland	D	0-0	Basel	Fr		31 500	Kircher GER
5-09	Georgia	W	2-0	Tbilisi	WCq	Kaladze OG 2 56 66	32 000	Borski POL
9-09	Bulgaria	W	2-0	Turin	WCq	Grosso 11, Iaquinta 40	26 122	Meyer GER
10-10	Republic of Ireland	D	2-2	Dublin	WCq	Camoranesi 26, Gilardino 90	70 640	Hauge NOR
14-10	Cyprus	W	3-2	Parma	WCq	Gilardino 3 78 81 92+	15 009	Yefet ISR
14-11	Netherlands	D	0-0	Pescara	Fr		17 134	Circhetta SUI
18-11	Sweden	W	1-0	Cesena	Fr	Chiellini 29	18 260	Skomina SVN
2010								
3-03	Cameroon	D	0-0	Monte Carlo	Fr		10 752	Ennjimi FRA
3-06	Mexico	L	1-2	Brussels	Fr	Bonucci 89	30 000	Verbist BEL
5-06	Switzerland	D	1-1	Geneva	Fr	Quagliarella 14	30 000	Piccirillo FRA
14-06	Paraguay	D	1-1	Cape Town	WCr1	De Rossi 63	62 869	Archundia MEX
20-06	New Zealand	D	1-1	Nelspruit	WCr1	Iaquinta 29p	38 229	Batres GUA
24-06	Slovakia	L	2-3	Johannesburg	WCr1	Di Natale 81, Quagliarella 92+	53 412	Webb ENG
10-08	Cote d'Ivoire	L	0-1	London	Fr		11 176	Atkinson ENG
3-09	Estonia	W	2-1	Tallinn	ECq	Cassano 60, Bonucci 63	8 600	Velasco ESP
7-09	Faroe Islands	W	5-0	Florence	ECq	Gilardino 11, De Rossi 22, Cassano 27, Quagliarella 81, Pirlo 90	19 266	Kulbakov BLR
8-10	Northern Ireland	D	0-0	Belfast	ECq		15 200	Chapron FRA
12-10	Serbia	W	3-0	Genoa	ECq	Match abanadoned after six minutes at 0-0	28 000	Thomson SCO
17-11	Romania	D	1-1	Klagenfurt	Fr	OG 82	14 000	Einwaller AUT
2011								
9-02	Germany	D	1-1	Dortmund	Fr	Rossi 81	60 196	Braamhaar NED
25-03	Slovenia	W	1-0	Ljubljana	ECq	Thiago Motta 73	15 790	Brych GER
29-03	Ukraine	W	2-0	Kyiv	Fr	Rossi 27, Matri 81	18 000	Nikolaev RUS
3-06	Estonia	W	3-0	Modena	ECq	Rossi 21, Cassano 39, Pazzini 68	19 434	Tudor ROU
7-06	Republic of Ireland	L	0-2	Liege	Fr		21 516	Gumienny BEL
10-08	Spain	W	2-1	Bari	Fr	Montolivo 11, Aquilani 84	50 000	Brych GER
2-09	Faroe Islands	W	1-0	Torshavn	ECq	Cassano 11	5 654	Bognar HUN
6-09	Slovenia	W	1-0	Florence	ECq	Pazzini 85	18 000	Moen NOR
7-10	Serbia	D	1-1	Belgrade	ECq	Marchisio 2	35 000	Proenca POR
11-10	Northern Ireland	W	3-0	Pescara	ECq	Cassano 2 21 53, OG 74	19 480	Mateu ESP
11-11	Poland	W	2-0	Wroclaw	Fr	Balotelli 30, Pazzini 60	42 771	Duhamel FRA
15-11	Uruguay	L	0-1	Rome	Fr		42 000	Duarte POR

Fr = Friendly match • EC = UEFA EURO 2012 • WC = FIFA World Cup • q = qualifier • r1 = first round group • qf = quarter-finals

ITALY NATIONAL TEAM HISTORICAL RECORDS

Caps
136 - Fabio Cannavaro 1997- • 126 - Paolo Maldini 1988-2002 • 112 - Dino Zoff 1968-83 & Gianluigi Buffon 1997- • 98 - Gianluca Zambrotta 1999- • 94 - Giacinto Facchetti 1963-77 • 91 - Alessandro Del Piero 1995-2008 • 81 - Franco Baresi 1982-94, Giuseppe Bergomi 1982-98; Marco Tardelli 1976-85 & Andrea Pirlo 2002- • 79 - Demetrio Albertini 1991-2002 • 78 - Alessandro Nesta 1996-2006 & Gaetano Scirea 1975-86 • 73 - Giancarlo Antognoni 1974-83; Antonio Cabrini 1978-87 & Gennaro Gattuso 2000-

Goals
35 - Luigi Riva 1965-74 • 33 - Giuseppe Meazza 1930-39 • 30 - Silvio Piola 1935-52 • 27 - Roberto Baggio 1988-2004 & Alessandro Del Piero 1995-2008 • 25 - Adolfo Baloncieri 1920-30, Filippo Inzaghi 1997-2007 & Alessandro Altobelli • 23 - Christian Vieri 1997-2005 & Francesco Graziani 1975-83 • 22 - Alessandro Mazzola 1963-74 • 20 - Paolo Rossi 1977-86 • 19 - Roberto Bettega 1975-83

Past Coaches
Committee 1910-12 • Vittorio Pozzo 1912 • Committee 1912-24 • Vittorio Pozzo 1924 • Committee 1924-25 • Augusto Rangone 1925-28 • Carlo Carcano 1928-29 • Vittorio Pozzo 1929-48 • Committe - Novo, Bardelli, Copernico & Biancone 1949-59 • Committee - Beretta, Busini & Combi 1951 • Committee - Beretta & G. Meazza 1952-53 • Committee - Czeizler, Schiavio & Piola 1953-54 • Committee - Marmo, Pasquale, Tentorio, Schiavio & Foni 1954-56 • Committee - Foni, Pasquale, Schiavio, Tentorio, Marmo, Biancone 1957-58 • Committee - Ferrari, Mocchetti & Biancone 1958-59 • Giuseppe Viani 1960 • Giovanni Ferrari 1960-61 • Giovanni Ferrari & Paolo Mazza 1962 • Edmondo Fabbri 1962-66 • Helenio Herrera & Ferruccio Valcareggi 1966-67 • Ferruccio Valcareggi 1967-74 • Fulvio Bernardini 1974-75 • Fulvio Bernardini & Enzo Bearzot 1975-77 • Enzo Bearzot 1977-86 • Azeglio Vicini 1986-91 • Arrigo Sacchi 1991-96 • Cesare Maldini 1997-98 • Dino Zoff 1998-2000 • Giovanni Trapattoni 2000-04 • Marcello Lippi 2004-06 • Roberto Donadoni 2006-08 • Marcello Lippi 2008-10 • Cesare Prandelli 2010-

ITALY 2010-11

SERIE A

	Pl	W	D	L	F	A	Pts	Milan	Inter	Napoli	Udinese	Lazio	Roma	Juventus	Palermo	Fiorentina	Genoa	Chievo	Parma	Catania	Cagliari	Cesena	Bologna	Lecce	Sampdoria	Brescia	Bari
Milan †	38	24	10	4	65	24	82		3-0	3-0	4-4	0-0	0-1	1-2	3-1	1-0	1-0	3-1	4-0	1-1	4-1	2-0	1-0	4-0	3-0	3-0	1-1
Internazionale †	38	23	7	8	69	42	76	0-1		3-1	2-1	2-1	5-3	0-0	3-2	3-1	5-2	2-0	5-2	3-1	1-0	3-2	4-1	1-0	1-1	1-1	4-0
Napoli †	38	21	7	10	59	39	70	1-2	1-1		1-2	4-3	2-0	3-0	1-0	0-0	1-0	1-3	2-0	1-0	2-1	2-0	4-1	1-0	4-0	0-0	2-2
Udinese †	38	20	6	12	65	43	66	0-0	3-1	3-1		2-1	1-1	2-0	4-2	1-2	1-0	1-2	0-0	2-0	1-1	1-0	1-1	4-0	2-0	0-0	1-0
Lazio ‡	38	20	6	12	55	39	66	1-1	3-1	2-0	3-2		0-2	0-1	2-0	2-0	4-2	1-2	1-0	1-1	2-1	1-0	3-1	1-2	1-0	1-0	1-0
Roma ‡	38	18	9	11	59	52	63	0-0	1-0	0-2	2-0	2-0		0-2	2-3	3-2	2-1	1-0	2-2	4-2	3-0	0-0	2-2	0-3	1-1	1-1	1-0
Juventus	38	15	13	10	57	47	58	0-1	1-0	0-2	2-1	2-1	1-1		1-3	1-1	3-2	2-1	4-2	2-4	2-3	3-1	0-2	4-0	3-3	2-1	2-1
Palermo ‡	38	15	5	16	58	63	56	1-0	1-2	2-1	0-7	0-1	3-1	2-1		2-4	1-0	1-3	3-1	3-1	0-0	2-2	4-1	2-2	3-0	1-0	2-1
Fiorentina	38	12	15	11	49	44	51	1-2	1-2	1-1	5-2	1-2	2-2	0-0	1-2		1-0	1-0	2-0	3-0	1-0	1-0	1-1	1-1	1-0	0-0	3-2	2-1
Genoa	38	14	9	15	45	47	51	1-1	0-1	0-1	2-4	0-0	4-3	0-2	1-0	1-1		1-3	3-1	1-0	0-1	3-2	1-0	4-2	2-1	3-0	2-1
Chievo Verona	38	11	13	14	38	40	46	1-2	2-1	2-0	0-2	0-1	2-2	1-1	0-0	0-1	0-0		2-1	0-2	0-1	2-0	1-0	0-0	0-1	0-0	
Parma	38	11	13	14	39	47	46	0-1	2-0	1-3	2-1	1-1	0-0	1-0	3-1	1-1	1-1	0-0		2-0	1-2	2-2	0-0	1-1	0-2	1-0	2-1
Catania	38	12	10	16	40	52	46	0-2	1-2	1-1	1-0	1-4	2-1	1-3	4-0	0-0	2-1	1-1	2-1		2-0	2-0	1-1	3-2	1-0	1-0	1-0
Cagliari	38	12	9	17	44	51	45	0-1	0-1	0-1	0-4	1-0	5-1	1-3	3-1	1-2	0-1	4-1	1-1	3-0		0-2	2-0	3-2	0-0	1-1	2-1
Cesena	38	11	10	17	38	50	43	2-0	1-2	1-4	0-3	1-0	0-1	2-2	1-2	2-2	0-0	1-1	1-1	1-0		0-2	1-0	0-1	1-0	1-1	1-0
Bologna §3	38	11	12	15	35	52	42	0-3	0-0	0-2	2-1	3-1	0-1	0-0	1-0	1-1	1-2	1-0	0-1	0-2	2-0	2-2		2-0	1-1	1-0	0-4
Lecce	38	11	8	19	46	66	41	1-1	1-1	2-1	2-0	2-4	1-2	2-0	2-4	1-0	1-3	3-2	1-1	1-0	3-3	1-1	0-1		2-3	2-1	0-1
Sampdoria	38	8	12	18	33	49	36	1-1	0-2	1-2	0-0	2-0	2-1	0-0	1-2	2-1	0-0	0-1	0-0	0-1	2-3	3-1	1-2		3-3	3-0	
Brescia	38	7	11	20	34	52	32	0-1	1-1	0-1	1-0	2-2	1-1	1-3	2-2	0-0	0-3	0-1	2-1	2-1	2-3	1-2	2-1	0-0		2-0	
Bari	38	5	9	24	27	56	24	2-3	0-3	0-2	0-2	0-2	3-1	0-1	1-1	0-0	1-2	0-1	1-1	0-0	1-1	0-2	1-1	2-1	2-1		

28/08/2010 - 22/05/2011 • † Qualified for the UEFA Champions League • ‡ Qualified for the UEFA Europa League • § Points deducted
Top scorers: **28** - Antonio Di Natale, Udinese • **26** - Edson Cavani URU, Napoli • **21** - Samuel Eto'o CMR, Inter • **20** - Alessandro Matri, Cagliari/Juventus • **19** - Marco Di Vaio, Bologna • **17** - Giampaolo Pazzini, Inter/Sampdoria • **15** - Francesco Totti, Roma • **14** - Zlatan Ibrahimovic SWE, Milan; Pato BRA, Milan & Robinho BRA, Milan • **13** - Antonio Floro Flores, Genoa/Udinese

ITALY 2010-11

SERIE B (2)

	Pl	W	D	L	F	A	Pts	Atalanta	Siena	Novara	Varese	Padova	Reggina	Livorno	Torino	Empoli	Modena	Crotone	Vicenza	Pescara	Cittadella	Grosseto	Sassuolo	Ascoli	Albinoleffe	Piacenza	Triestina	Portosummaga	Frosinone
Atalanta	42	22	13	7	61	35	79		0-0	1-1	0-0	4-1	1-1	0-2	2-1	1-2	1-0	2-0	2-0	1-0	2-2	0-1	0-2	1-3	1-3	0-4	0-4	1-0	0
Siena	42	21	14	7	67	35	77	1-0		1-1	5-0	2-1	4-0	2-2	0-0	0-2	0-2	2-0	2-1	3-1	3-1	4-0	3-0	2-1	2-1	3-0	1-2	3-0	
Novara ‡	42	18	16	8	63	38	70	2-0	2-2		1-1	1-1	3-1	4-1	1-0	1-2	3-3	0-3	0-1	2-2	1-0	0-1	0-3	0-2	2-2	0-0	0-2	1	
Varese ‡	42	16	20	6	51	34	68	0-0	1-0	3-1		0-0	1-0	3-0	0-3	0-1	1-1	0-1	1-0	3-2	1-1	1-3	0-1	0-4	0-1	0-3	3		
Padova ‡	42	15	17	10	63	48	62	1-1	0-0	1-2	3		4-0	3-2	1-1	2-2	1-1	0-4	1-3	1-2	1-3	0-1	0-3	1-2	0-0	0-0	1-3	1-3	1
Reggina ‡	42	15	16	11	46	40	61	1-1	1-1	0-0	4-0	0-3		1-1	1-1	0-0	4-0	0-3	2-1	0-0	1-1	0-0	2-1	0-0	1-1	0-2	1-1	0-2	1
Livorno	42	15	14	13	49	46	59	2-1	1-1	1-0	0-0	3-3	0		2-1	2-1	0-1	1-2	0-1	1-3	0-1	0-4	1-1	1-2	1-0	1-3	0-0	2-1	
Torino	42	15	13	14	49	48	58	1-2	1-1	1-0	1-0	2-0	2-1	1-0		2-1	3-2	1-2	1-3	1-1	1-1	0-1	2-2	1-1	1-0	1-2	0-2	1-1	2
Empoli	42	13	18	11	46	39	57	3-0	3-0	0-0	1-1	2-2	1-0	0-0	1-1		0-1	0-0	0-1	0-0	2-0	1-0	0-1	1-0	3-1	1-1	1-1	2-3	2-1
Modena	42	12	19	11	46	51	55	1-2	0-1	2-0	1-0	1-2	1-1	1-1	0-0	1-1		2-1	1-0	1-1	1-1	1-1	0-2	1-0	2-2	3-2	2-3	1-2	1
Crotone	42	13	15	14	45	50	54	2-2	1-2	0-3	1-0	1-0	0-0	1-1	1-3	2-3	1		2-0	1-1	1-0	0-2	0-1	0-0	1-0	1-2	1-2	0-4	1
Vicenza	42	15	9	18	44	54	54	1-1	2-1	0-0	1-2	1-0	1-0	0-1	0-1	1-1	1-1	1-2		2-2	1-0	0-1	1-1	1-0	1-0	3-1	2-0	4-1	1-0
Pescara	42	14	11	17	44	48	53	0-2	1-1	2-1	0-0	2-0	0-0	2-1	0-1	0-0	2-1	0-1	0		1-0	4-2	1-0	1-2	2-0	2-2	0-0	4-2	1-1
Cittadella	42	12	15	15	50	54	51	0-1	0-0	0-2	2-3	1-1	2-2	0-2	1-2	3-1	1-1	1-0	0-1	3-2		1-1	1-1	0-0	1-0	4-3	0-4	1-1	1-1
Grosseto	42	12	15	15	43	50	51	1-1	0-1	0-0	3-1	0-1	0-0	0-0	0-2	1-3	1-2	1-2	3-1	1		1-0	0-0	3-0	1-3	0-2	0-3	1-2	0
Sassuolo	42	13	12	17	42	46	51	0-2	4-3	0-1	1-0	3-2	1-0	1-2	1-0	1-1	0-2	2-1	2-0	1-1	1-1		0-1	1-0	1-1	0-0	0-1	5-3	
Ascoli §6	42	14	14	14	41	48	50	1-1	3-?	1-1	0-0	1-0	2-1	1-5	0-4	0-0	1-1	2-2	2-1	1-1	0-0	1-1	2-0	0		2-0	3-1	3-0	1-0	3-1
Albinoleffe ‡	42	13	10	19	55	66	49	2-3	1-0	3-1	3-1	2-1	1-1	3-0	3-1	2-2	0-0	0-1	1-2	2-1	2-1	3-1	1-3	1-1		3-3	1-1	1-0	2-1
Piacenza ‡	42	11	13	18	50	63	46	3-2	0-1	1-2	2-1	2-2	3-2	0-1	1-1	2-1	0-2	2-4	0-1	0-2	4-0	1-0	2-4	3-3		2-2	1-2	1-1	
Triestina	42	8	11	23	34	57	40	0-1	0-1	1-1	1-0	0-0	4-0	0-0	1-1	2-2	3-0	0-1	1-0	3-2	0-1	2-1	0-1	1-0	1		0-0	2-2	
Portosummaga	42	10	10	22	39	63	40	1-2	1-4	1-5	1-1	1-1	1-1	2-0	0-1	0-1	1-1	2-3	1-0	1-2	2-0	1-1	1-0	2-1	1-0	2-1	0-1	2	0-1
Frosinone	42	8	14	20	46	64	38	0-1	0-1	1-1	1-0	1-1	1-1	2-0	2-1	0-2	3-1	1-2	3-4	0-1	1-1	1-0	0-1	2-1	1-2	1-1	1-1	0-1	

20/08/2010 - 29/05/2011 • ‡ = promotion/relegation play-off • Top scorer: **23** - Federico Piovaccari, Cittadella
Play-off semis: Reggina 0-0 2-2 **Novara** (Novara qualified on higher league position) • **Padova** 1-0 3-3 Varese
Play-off final: Padova 0-0 0-2 **Novara** • Novara promoted
Relegation play-off: Piacenza 0-0 2-2 Albinoleffe (Albinoleffe won on higher league position) • Piacenza relegated

ITALY 2010–11

LEGA PRO PRIMA DIVISIONE GROUP A (3)

	Pl	W	D	L	F	A	Pts	Gubbio	Sorrento	Salernitana	Verona	Spezia	Lumezzane	Reggiana	Como	SPAL	Cremonese	Bassano Virtus	Pavia	Ravenna	Pergocrema	Monza	Südtirol	Paganese	Alessandria
Gubbio §1	34	20	6	8	48	31	65		1-0	3-1	2-1	2-1	0-1	2-1	1-1	1-1	1-0	1-1	1-0	0-0	0-2	4-0	4-0	3-1	1-0
Sorrento ‡	34	16	10	8	61	43	58	2-1		2-2	1-0	2-0	2-0	4-3	3-0	2-1	2-3	0-1	0-0	3-2	4-0	1-0	3-2	1-0	4-3
Salernitana ‡ §5 R¹	34	17	8	9	49	39	54	2-1	1-4		2-1	1-0	0-1	1-1	2-0	3-0	2-1	2-0	3-1	1-1	1-0	2-0	2-1	2-0	1-1
Verona ‡	34	12	14	8	42	30	50	1-2	1-1	2-1		1-0	1-0	0-0	2-3	1-1	1-1	0-0	4-2	0-0	2-1	1-1	4-0	2-0
Spezia §1	34	12	12	10	38	33	47	2-0	2-1	2-1	1-0		0-0	2-0	1-1	0-0	1-2	1-0	2-2	4-1	1-1	3-0	1-0	1-0	1-1
Lumezzane §1	34	12	11	11	34	34	46	0-2	1-2	1-3	1-1	1-2		2-2	2-2	1-0	2-2	3-1	1-1	0-0	1-1	1-0	1-0	2-0	0-3
Reggiana	34	12	9	13	36	37	45	0-1	3-1	0-1	0-0	1-1	0-2		1-1	0-2	3-0	0-1	2-1	3-0	1-0	3-2	2-2	2-1	1-0
Como §1	34	10	15	9	41	40	44	0-1	3-2	2-1	1-1	2-1	3-0	0-2		2-3	1-0	0-1	4-2	1-2	1-1	2-4	0-0	0-0	0-0
SPAL §1	34	11	11	12	39	37	43	1-0	0-0	1-2	1-1	1-2	0-2	2-0	1-2		1-1	1-0	1-0	3-0	0-1	0-0	2-2	3-1	1-1
Cremonese	34	9	15	10	37	38	42	5-1	0-0	1-1	1-2	2-2	1-0	0-1	2-2	1-4		0-0	2-1	1-0	0-0	2-0	0-0	2-0	1-1
Bassano Virtus	34	10	12	12	26	29	42	0-1	2-1	0-1	1-0	0-0	0-1	0-0	2-2	2-3	0-0		0-0	2-0	1-0	2-1	0-0	1-0	0-1
Pavia	34	9	12	13	34	45	39	1-1	5-4	1-2	1-1	2-1	1-4	2-0	1-1	1-0	0-1	1-1		1-1	1-0	1-0	2-1	1-0	1-1
Ravenna ‡ §7 R¹	34	10	12	12	33	40	35	2-1	2-2	1-1	0-1	0-1	2-1	0-0	1-1	1-1	0-0	1-1	2-0		3-1	1-0	0-1	1-0	0-1
Pergocrema ‡ §1	34	7	15	12	30	35	35	1-1	0-0	2-0	0-0	2-2	0-0	0-1	1-0	1-1	2-1	1-2	1-2	1-2		1-1	3-0	0-0	1-1
Monza ‡	34	7	11	16	34	49	32	2-3	1-1	3-3	1-5	0-0	0-1	0-0	0-1	2-1	2-2	2-0	2-0	1-1	2-2		3-4	0-0	0-2
Südtirol ‡	34	7	11	16	28	43	32	0-2	0-2	0-1	0-0	0-0	1-1	1-3	0-2	1-1	1-0	0-2	1-1	2-2	0-0	1-1		2-1	1-2
Paganese	34	8	8	18	17	36	32	0-2	0-0	0-1	2-1	0-1	1-0	0-0	1-0	1-0	2-1	1-1	0-0	0-2	1-2	1-0			1-0
Alessandria ‡ §2 R¹	34	15	12	7	40	28	55	2-0	3-3	3-1	2-1	3-1	1-1	0-1	0-0	1-0	1-0	1-0	1-0	2-1	2-1	0-0	0-0	1-0	

22/08/2010 - 15/05/2011 • ‡ Entered play-offs • § Points deducted • R¹ Relegated due to bankruptcy, financial or match fixing issues
Promotion play-off semi-finals: **Verona** 2-0 1-0 Sorrento • **Salernitana** 1-1 3-1 Alessandria • Final: **Verona** 2-0 0-1 Salernitana • Verona promoted
Relegation play-offs: Südtirol 1-0 1-2 **Ravenna** • Monza 1-0 0-1 **Pergocrema** • Südtirol and Monza relegated due to worse season records but both spared after Salernitana and Ravenna were later relegated. Alessandria were demoted to last place for match fixing

LEGA PRO CHAMPIONSHIP

Gubbio   1-1 0-1   **Nocerina**

Nocerina are Lega Pro Prima Divisione Champions

ITALY 2010–11

LEGA PRO PRIMA DIVISIONE GROUP A (3)

	Pl	W	D	L	F	A	Pts	Nocerina	Benevento	At. Roma	Taranto	Juve Stabia	Foggia	Lucchese	V. Lanciano	Siracusa	Pisa	Barletta	Gela	Andria BAT	Cosenza	Ternana	Foligno	Viareggio	Cavese
Nocerina	34	21	9	4	52	30	72		3-3	2-1	1-0	1-2	3-1	2-1	1-1	0-0	3-2	2-1	1-0	1-0	2-1	1-0	3-1	3-1	0-0
Benevento ‡	34	17	10	7	53	40	61	1-1		2-0	0-0	1-1	4-3	2-1	3-5	1-0	1-0	1-2	2-1	2-0	3-1	1-0	2-0	2-2	1-0
Atletico Roma ‡ R¹	34	17	6	11	52	33	57	2-3	3-0		1-0	1-0	3-3	1-2	0-0	2-1	3-1	3-0	1-2	0-1	4-1	0-0	1-2	2-1	6-0
Taranto ‡	34	14	13	7	36	28	55	2-1	3-1	0-1		1-0	2-1	1-1	2-2	2-1	2-2	2-1	3-2	1-0	1-0	1-3	1-0	1-0
Juve Stabia ‡	34	16	7	11	43	35	55	2-2	2-1	3-2	0-3		0-2	4-1	1-0	5-0	1-0	1-0	0-1	3-1	2-1	2-0	0-2	1-0	2-1
Foggia §2	34	14	5	15	67	58	45	0-1	2-1	3-1	0-0	4-1		2-3	5-2	0-2	3-1	0-2	2-1	1-2	4-0	4-4	2-2	2-1
Lucchese R¹	34	12	8	14	42	38	44	0-0	1-2	0-2	0-1	0-0	4-2		2-0	4-2	1-1	2-0	3-0	1-1	0-1	4-0	3-0	0-0	1-0
Virtus Lanciano	34	9	17	8	28	31	44	1-2	1-0	1-0	0-0	1-0	5-3	0-0		1-0	1-1	1-1	1-0	1-0	0-2	0-0	1-2	1-2	0-2
Siracusa	34	12	8	14	32	38	44	2-0	1-0	0-1	1-0	1-1	1-0	1-0	0-0		2-2	1-0	2-0	0-1	1-1	2-2	2-1	2-1	1-0
Pisa	34	10	13	11	39	40	43	1-1	1-0	0-2	2-1	1-1	1-2	2-0	1-1	2-0		2-2	4-0	2-1	2-0	2-3	0-0	1-0	1-0	1-0
Barletta	34	9	13	12	32	38	40	1-2	1-1	0-0	0-0	0-2	1-2	1-0	0-1	1-1		0-0	3-2	2-0	1-2	0-0	0-0	3-3
Gela R¹	34	10	10	14	31	42	40	2-1	0-1	1-2	0-0	0-0	2-1	3-0	1-1	1-0	2-1	0-1		2-1	1-3	0-0	0-0	0-0	2-1
Andria BAT	34	10	9	15	31	37	39	0-1	1-1	1-1	0-0	0-1	0-1	1-1	0-0	1-0	3-0	0-0	4-1		1-1	0-1	2-1	0-0	1-0
Cosenza ‡ §6 R¹	34	10	14	10	36	38	38	1-1	1-2	1-0	0-0	2-1	1-0	2-4	1-1	1-2	0-0	1-1	2-0	0-1		1-1	1-0	2-1	0-0
Ternana ‡ §2	34	9	11	14	30	45	36	0-3	1-3	1-2	3-3	2-1	3-2	0-1	0-0	2-1	1-0	2-0	2-0	2-3	0-0		0-2	3-2	1-1
Foligno ‡ §4	34	8	11	15	36	45	31	0-1	2-2	0-1	0-0	1-1	2-1	1-0	1-1	1-1	1-1	0-2	1-4	0-1	0-0	0-0		2-0	0-1
Viareggio ‡	34	6	13	15	30	44	31	0-1	1-2	1-1	2-0	0-2	0-4	1-1	3-1	1-0	1-1	1-1	1-1	0-2	1-1	1-0	1-3		1-1
Cavese §6 R¹	34	8	11	15	31	41	29	0-2	2-3	0-2	1-1	2-0	0-3	1-0	0-3	3-1	0-1	1-0	1-1	3-0	2-2	0-0	2-2	2-0	

22/08/2010 - 15/05/2011 • ‡ Entered play-offs • § Points deducted • R¹ Relegated due to bankruptcy, financial or match fixing issues
Promotion play-off semi-finals: **Juve Stabia** 1-0 1-1 Benevento • Taranto 0-1 3-2 **At. Roma** • Final: **Juve Stabia** 0-0 2-0 At. Roma • Juve promoted
Relegation play-offs: **Viareggio** 3-1 1-0 Cosenza • **Foligno** 1-0 1-1 Ternana • Cosenza and Ternana relegated. Ternana later spared due to various forced relegations including that of Cosenza

		Overall			League			Cup		Europe			City
		G	S	B	G	S	B	G	S	G	S	B	
1	Juventus	42	32	19	27	20	13	9	4	6	8	6	Turin
2	Milan	32	24	22	18	13	18	5	6	9	5	4	Milan
3	Internazionale	31	23	22	18	14	14	7	6	6	3	8	Milan
4	Torino	13	17	7	8	9	6	5	7		1	1	Turin
5	Roma	13	20	7	3	11	5	9	7	1	2	2	Rome
6	Genoa 1893	10	5	2	9	4	1	1	1			1	Genoa
7	Fiorentina	9	11	7	2	5	5	6	3	1	3	2	Florence
8	Bologna	9	4	5	7	4	3	2				2	Bologna
9	Lazio	8	8	5	2	6	4	5	1	1	1	1	Rome
10	Pro Vercelli	7	1		7	1							Vercelli
11	Napoli	6	8	8	2	4	7	3	4	1		1	Naples
12	Sampdoria	6	6	4	1	1	3	4	3	1	2	1	Genoa
13	Parma	6	4	3		1	2	3	2	3	1	1	Parma
14	Hellas-Verona	1	3		1				3				Verona
15	Atalanta	1	2	1				1	2			1	Bergamo
	Venezia	1	2	1		1	1	1	1				Venice
	Vicenza	1	2	1		2		1				1	Vicenza
18	Cagliari	1	1	1	1	1						1	Cagliari
19	Casale	1			1								Casale Monferrato
	Novese	1			1								Novi Ligure
	Vado	1						1					Vado Ligure
22	Palermo		3						3				Palermo
23	US Milanese		2	1		2	1						Milan
	Udinese		2	1		1	1		1				Udine
25	Alba		2			2							Rome
	Livorno		2			2							Livorno
27	Alessandria		1	1			1		1				Alessandria
	Padova		1	1			1		1				Padua
29	Ancona		1						1				Ancona
	Catanzaro		1						1				Catanzaro
	Fortitudo		1			1							Rome
	Novara		1						1				Novarra
	Perugia		1			1							Perugia
	Pisa		1			1							Pisa
	Savoia		1			1							Torre Annunziata
	SPAL Ferrara		1						1				Ferrara
37	Modena			1			1						Modena

MEDALS TABLE

COPPA ITALIA 2010-11

Third Round		Fourth Round		Round of 16	
				Internazionale *	3
Vicenza *	1			Genoa	2
Ascoli	0	Vicenza	1		
Grosseto	1	Genoa *	3		
Genoa *	2				
Bologna *	3				
Modena	2	Bologna	3		
Piacenza	0	Cagliari *	0		
Cagliari *	3			Bologna	1
				Napoli *	2
				Juventus *	2
Brescia *	1			Catania	0
Cittadella	0	Brescia	1		
Varese	3	Catania *	5		
Catania *	4				
Lazio *	3				
Portosummaga	0	Lazio *	3		
Crotone *	0	AlbinoLeffe	0		
AlbinoLeffe	1			Lazio	1
				Roma *	2
				Milan *	3
Livorno	1			Bari	0
Atalanta *	0	Livorno	1		
Torino	1	Bari *	4		
Bari *	3				
Udinese *	4				
Padova	0	Udinese *	2		
Siena	2	Lecce	1		
Lecce *	3			Udinese	2 4p
				Sampdoria *	2 5p
				Parma *	2
Reggina	4			Fiorentina	1
Frosinone *	2	Reggina	0		
Empoli	0	Fiorentina *	3		
Fiorentina *	1				
Chievo Verona *	2				
Sassuolo	0	Chievo Verona *	3		
Cesena *	1	Novara	0		
Novara	3			Chievo Verona	0
				Palermo *	1

Clubs playing in Europe enter in the round of 16

COPPA ITALIA 2010-11

Quarter–finals   **Semi–finals**   **Final**

Internazionale	0 5p
Napoli *	0 4p

Internazionale	1 1
Roma *	0 1

Juventus *	0
Roma	2

Internazionale	3
Palermo ‡	1

Milan	2
Sampdoria *	1

Milan *	2 1
Palermo	2 2

Parma	0 4p
Palermo *	0 5p

COPPA ITALIA FINAL 2011

Stadio Olimpico, Rome, 29-05-2011, 21:00, Att: 70 000, Ref: Emidio Morganti

Internazionale	3	Eto'o 2 [26 76], Milito [92+]
Palermo	1	Munoz [88]

Inter - Julio Cesar - Yuto Nagamoto, Lucio, Andrea Ranocchia, Cristian Chivu - Dejan Stankovic - Javier Zanetti (c), Wesley Sneijder (Diego Milito 87), Thiago Motta (McDonald Mariga 83) - Giampaolo Pazzini (Goran Pandev 61), Samuel Eto'o. Tr: Leonardo

Palermo - Salvatore Sirigu - Mattia Cassani (c), Ezequiel Munoz●●◆57, Dorin Goian (Moris Carrozzieri● 24), Federico Balzaretti - Giulio Migliaccio, Afriyie Acquah● (Fabrizio Miccoli 55), Antonio Nocerino - Josip Ilicic, Abel Hernandez (Mauricio Pinilla 79), Javier Pastore. Tr: Delio Rossi

‡ Qualified for the UEFA Europa League
* Home team/Home team in the first leg

CLUB BY CLUB GUIDE TO THE 2010-11 SEASON IN ITALY

BARI 2010–11

Month	No	Opponent	Res	Score	Comp	Scorers	Att
Sep	29	Juventus	W	1-0	SA	Donati [43]	**45 162**
	12	Napoli	D	2-2	SA	Barreto [12], Castillo [88]	27 214
	19	Cagliari	D	0-0	SA		17 945
	22	Inter	L	0-4	SA		61 093
	26	Brescia	W	2-1	SA	Rivas [16], Barreto [55p]	16 833
Oct	3	Genoa	L	1-2	SA	Barreto [52p]	22 358
	17	Lazio	L	0-2	SA		22 779
	23	Fiorentina	L	1-2	SA	Parisi [90]	23 874
	28	Torino	W	3-1	ICr3	Caputo [4], Parisi [64], Pulzetti [70]	6 076
	31	Udinese	L	0-2	SA		15 701
Nov	7	Milan	L	2-3	SA	Kutuzov [65], Barreto [90]	35 780
	10	Chievo	D	0-0	SA		8 822
	14	Parma	L	0-1	SA		15 500
	21	Catania	L	0-1	SA		11 573
	28	Cesena	D	1-1	SA	Caputo [64]	15 182
Dec	1	Livorno	W	4-1	ICr4	Rana [25], Masiello [51], Rivas [55], D'Alessandro [73]	1 601
	5	Sampdoria	L	0-3	SA		20 877
	12	Roma	L	0-1	SA		28 187
	19	Palermo	D	1-1	SA	Masiello [54p]	17 000
	6	Lecce	W	1-0	SA	Okaka [78]	BCD
Jan	9	Bologna	L	0-2	SA		17 000
	16	Juventus	L	1-2	SA	Rudolf [57]	18 882
	20	Milan	L	0-3	ICr5		9 391
	30	Napoli	L	0-2	SA		17 879
Feb	1	Cagliari	L	1-2	SA	Okaka [14]	14 000
	3	Inter	L	0-3	SA		36 121
	6	Brescia	L	0-2	SA		3 000
	13	Genoa	D	0-0	SA		14 812
	20	Lazio	L	0-1	SA		32 492
	27	Fiorentina	D	1-1	SA	Ghezzal [86]	14 739
Mar	6	Udinese	L	0-1	SA		15 904
	13	Milan	D	1-1	SA	Rudolf [39]	61 363
	20	Chievo	L	1-2	SA	Ghezzal [41p]	8 822
	3	Parma	W	2-1	SA	Parisi [64], Alvarez [90]	18 195
Apr	10	Catania	D	1-1	SA	Gazzi [33]	14 638
	17	Cesena	L	0-1	SA		15 699
	23	Sampdoria	L	0-1	SA		14 881
May	1	Roma	L	2-3	SA	Bentivoglio [25p], Huseklepp [42]	**1 592**
	7	Palermo	L	1-2	SA	Bentivoglio [7]	19 808
	15	Lecce	L	0-2	SA		16 329
	22	Bologna	W	4-0	SA	Grandolfo 3 [28 47 54], Huseklepp [78]	18 658

20th Att: 358 695 • Av: 18 878 (-26.2%) • San Nicola 58 270 (32%)

BOLOGNA 2010–11

Month	No	Opponent	Res	Score	Comp	Scorers	Att
Sep	30	Inter	D	0-0	SA		28 439
	12	Lazio	L	1-3	SA	Mudingayi [78]	22 462
	19	Roma	D	2-2	SA	Di Vaio 2 [77 90]	29 599
	22	Udinese	W	2-1	SA	Gimenez [16], Di Vaio [90]	14 220
	26	Catania	D	1-1	SA	Di Vaio [40]	10 913
Oct	3	Sampdoria	D	1-1	SA	Britos [65]	15 431
	17	Palermo	L	1-4	SA	Di Vaio [66]	23 587
	24	Juventus	D	0-0	SA		28 785
	27	Modena	W	3-2	ICr3	Ramirez 2 [60 89], Radovanovic [84]	4 960
	31	Cagliari	L	0-2	SA		10 000
Nov	6	Lecce	W	2-0	SA	Di Vaio [84], Gimenez [85]	13 954
	10	Genoa	L	0-1	SA		21 913
	14	Brescia	W	1-0	SA	Di Vaio [58]	**13 304**
	21	Napoli	L	1-4	SA	Meggiorini [68]	39 626
	25	Cagliari	W	3-0	ICr4	Meggiorini [32], Ramirez [84], Gimenez [90]	3 950
Dec	5	Cesena	W	2-0	SA	Di Vaio [31], Britos [87]	15 680
	8	Chievo	W	2-1	SA	Britos [39], Di Vaio [93+]	13 764
	12	Milan	L	0-3	SA		24 915
	19	Parma	D	0-0	SA		13 265
	6	Fiorentina	D	1-1	SA	Di Vaio [5]	15 000
Jan	9	Bari	W	2-0	SA	Ekdal [38], Di Vaio [69]	17 000
	15	Inter	L	1-4	SA	Gimenez [76]	52 724
	18	Napoli	L	1-2	ICr5	Meggiorini [56p]	33 806
	23	Lazio	W	3-1	SA	Ramirez [36], Di Vaio 2 [39 90]	14 295
	2	Udinese	D	1-1	SA	Di Vaio [63]	14 000
Feb	6	Catania	W	1-0	SA	Portanova [41]	15 000
	13	Sampdoria	L	1-3	SA	Paponi [64]	20 924
	19	Palermo	W	1-0	SA	Paponi [90]	21 219
	23	Roma	L	0-1	SA		19 663
	26	Juventus	W	2-0	SA	Di Vaio 2 [48 66]	20 843
Mar	6	Cagliari	D	2-2	SA	Di Vaio [29p], Ramirez [93+]	25 134
	13	Lecce	W	1-0	SA	Ramirez [33]	6 958
	20	Genoa	D	1-1	SA	Di Vaio [28]	19 149
	2	Brescia	L	1-3	SA	Di Vaio [30]	10 000
Apr	10	Napoli	L	0-2	SA		**34 092**
	17	Chievo	L	0-2	SA		10 846
	23	Cesena	L	0-2	SA		21 458
May	1	Milan	L	0-1	SA		74 121
	8	Parma	D	0-0	SA		19 879
	15	Fiorentina	D	1-1	SA	Ramirez [50]	21 026
	22	Bari	L	0-4	SA		18 658

16th Att: 377 359 • Av: 19 861 (-1.4%) • Renato Dall'Ara 39 444 (50%)

KEY

SC = Supercoppa (played in Beijing) • SA = Serie A • IC = Coppa Italia • CL = UEFA Champions League • EL = Europa League

See page 13 for further explanations

BARI LEAGUE APPEARANCES/GOALS 2010-11

Goalkeepers Jean-Francois Gillet BEL 36 • Daniele Padelli 2
Defenders Nicola Belmonte 25+1/0 • Kamil Glik POL 15+1/0 Andrea Masiello 36/1 • Alessandro Parisi 27/2 • Andrea Raggi 14+2/0 Michele Rinaldi 2+4/0 • Marco Rossi 27+3/0
Midfield Sergio Almiron ARG 21+4/0 • Edgar Alvarez HON 18+11/1 Simone Bentivoglio 16/2 • Paul Codrea ROU 4+2/0 Marco Crimi 1+2/0 • Massimo Donati 23+8/1 Gianluca Galasso 3+1/0 • Alessandro Gazzi 29+2/1 Erik Huseklepp NOR 12+2/2 • Jaime ESP 5+5/0 • Kamil Kopunek SVK 4+1/0 • Salvatore Masiello 6/0 • Nico Pulzetti 11+4/0 Emanuel Rivas ARG 9+13/1 • Nicola Strambelli 1+2/0
Forwards Barreto BRA 13/4 • Francesco Caputo 5+7/1 • Jose Castillo ARG 4+10/1 • Marco D'Alessandro 1+10/0 • Abdelkader Ghezzal ALG 15+5/2 • Francesco Grandolfo 1+2/3 • Vitaliy Kutuzov BLR 13+1/1 • Stefano Okaka 6+4/2 • Luigi Rana 2+1/0 Gergely Rudolf HUN 11+2/2
Coach Giampiero Ventura • Bortolo Mutti (10/02/11)

BOLOGNA LEAGUE APPEARANCES/GOALS 2010-11

Goalkeepers Cristiano Lupatelli 0+1 • Emiliano Viviano 38
Defenders Miguel Britos URU 33/3 • Nicolo Cherubin 9+3/0 Andrea Esposito 8+3/0 • Gyorgy Garics 15/0 • Vangelis Moras GRE 17+2/0 • Archimede Morleo 7+2/0 Daniele Portanova 33/1 • Matteo Rubin 28+1/0
Midfield Antonio Busce 10+6/0 • Federico Casarini 18+14/0 Francesco Della Rocca 23+4/0 • Albin Ekdal SWE 19+3/1 • Rene Krhin SVN 2+2/0 • Gaby Mudingayi BEL 32/1 • Massimo Mutarelli 7+8/0 • Diego Perez URU 27/0 • Ivan Radovanovic SRB 6+4/0 Gaston Ramirez URU 16+9/4 • Luca Siligardi 4+8/0
Forwards Marco Di Vaio 38/19 • Henry Gimenez URU 8+18/3 Riccardo Meggiorini 14+15/1 • Daniele Paponi 6+8/2
Coach Alberto Malesani (1/09/10)

BRESCIA 2010–11

	Date	Opponent	Res	Score	Comp	Scorers	Att
Sep	29	Parma	L	0-2	SA		12 630
	12	Palermo	W	3-2	SA	Dallamano 4, Eder 28, Caracciolo 44p	8 100
	19	Chievo	W	1-0	SA	Diamanti 30	9 370
	22	Roma	W	2-1	SA	Hetemaj 13, Caracciolo 65p	12 000
	26	Bari	L	1-2	SA	Kone 30	16 833
	3	Lazio	L	0-1	SA		29 555
	17	Udinese	L	0-1	SA		5 397
Oct	24	Lecce	L	1-2	SA	Caracciolo 19	6 837
	27	Cittadella	W	1-0	ICr3	Diamanti 30	688
	31	Napoli	L	0-1	SA		6 008
	6	Inter	D	1-1	SA	Caracciolo 14	58 183
	10	Juventus	D	1-1	SA	Diamanti 73	20 000
Nov	14	Bologna	L	0-1	SA		13 304
	21	Cagliari	L	1-2	SA	Caracciolo 20p	3 893
	25	Catania	L	1-5	ICr4	Feczesin 18	3 500
	28	Genoa	D	0-0	SA		3 532
	4	Milan	L	0-3	SA		41 418
Dec	12	Sampdoria	W	1-0	SA	Cordova 13	11 043
	19	Catania	L	0-1	SA		9 283
	6	Cesena	L	1-2	SA	Eder 50	5 000
	9	Fiorentina	L	2-3	SA	Diamanti 30, Cordova 45	20 664
Jan	16	Parma	W	2-0	SA	Bega 45, Diamanti 88	9 980
	22	Palermo	L	0-1	SA		21 152
	30	Chievo	L	0-3	SA		8 500
	2	Roma	D	1-1	SA	Eder 69	26 590
	6	Bari	W	2-0	SA	Diamanti 17p, Caracciolo 90	3 000
Feb	13	Lazio	L	0-2	SA		6 269
	20	Udinese	D	0-0	SA		14 000
	27	Lecce	D	2-2	SA	Caracciolo 16, Zoboli 18	4 677
	6	Napoli	D	0-0	SA		29 146
Mar	11	Inter	D	1-1	SA	Caracciolo 85	**27 000**
	20	Juventus	L	1-2	SA	Eder 42	19 162
	2	Bologna	W	3-1	SA	Hetemaj 4, Zoboli 8, Caracciolo 66p	10 000
Apr	10	Cagliari	D	1-1	SA	Caracciolo 61	10 000
	17	Genoa	L	0-3	SA		21 540
	23	Milan	L	0-1	SA		22 123
	1	Sampdoria	D	3-3	SA	Eder 50, Caracciolo 2 58 84	6 512
May	8	Catania	L	1-2	SA	Diamanti 90	8 000
	15	Cesena	L	0-1	SA		18 626
	22	Fiorentina	D	2-2	SA	Eder 19, Accardi 88	3 000

19th Att: 177 522 • Av: 9 343 (+118.3%) • Mario Rigamonti 27 547 (33%)

CAGLIARI 2010–11

	Date	Opponent	Res	Score	Comp	Scorers	Att
Sep	29	Palermo	D	0-0	SA		28 612
	11	Roma	W	5-1	SA	Conti 8, Matri 2 23p 47, Acquafresca 38, Lazzari 88	18 000
	19	Bari	D	0-0	SA		17 945
	22	Sampdoria	D	0-0	SA		10 000
	26	Juventus	L	2-4	SA	Matri 2 20 81	19 394
	3	Chievo	D	0-0	SA		7 800
	17	Inter	L	0-1	SA		20 000
Oct	24	Lazio	L	1-2	SA	Matri 59	32 417
	27	Piacenza	W	3-0	ICr3	Nene 2 38 45, Acquafresca 60	3 000
	31	Bologna	W	2-0	SA	Nene 51, Nainggolan 79	10 000
	7	Udinese	D	1-1	SA	Conti 12	14 056
	10	Napoli	L	0-1	SA		15 000
Nov	14	Genoa	L	0-1	SA		10 000
	21	Brescia	W	2-1	SA	Matri 63, Conti 66	3 893
	25	Bologna	L	0-3	ICr4		3 950
	28	Lecce	W	3-2	SA	Matri 2 6 15, Canini 28	8 000
	5	Fiorentina	L	0-1	SA		21 644
Dec	12	Catania	W	3-0	SA	Nene 3 11 27 71	15 000
	18	Cesena	L	0-1	SA		12 851
	6	Milan	L	0-1	SA		**23 000**
	9	Parma	W	2-1	SA	Acquafresca 2 22 32	12 185
Jan	16	Palermo	W	3-1	SA	Matri 23, OG 47, Biondini 54	8 000
	22	Roma	L	0-3	SA		28 249
	30	Bari	W	2-1	SA	Matri 2 8 12	14 000
	2	Sampdoria	W	1-0	SA	Nainggolan 37	21 000
	5	Juventus	L	1-3	SA	Acquafresca 51	20 000
Feb	13	Chievo	W	4-1	SA	Conti 18, Canini 29, Nene 2 43 71	15 000
	19	Inter	L	0-1	SA		47 672
	27	Lazio	W	1-0	SA	OG 40	8 000
	6	Bologna	D	2-2	SA	Cossu 59, Ragatzu 83	25 134
Mar	13	Udinese	L	0-4	SA		10 000
	20	Napoli	L	1-2	SA	Acquafresca 56	44 497
	3	Genoa	W	1-0	SA	Acquafresca 16	22 141
Apr	10	Brescia	D	1-1	SA	Cossu 22	10 000
	17	Lecce	D	3-3	SA	Acquafresca 2 20 72, Conti 67	12 672
	23	Fiorentina	L	1-2	SA	Cossu 46	10 000
	1	Catania	L	0-2	SA		4 599
May	8	Cesena	L	0-2	SA		6 000
	14	Milan	L	1-4	SA	Cossu 38	80 018
	22	Parma	D	1-1	SA	OG 55	**5 000**

14th Att: 235 000 • Av: 12 368 (-9.1%) • Sant'Elia 23 486 (52%)

BRESCIA LEAGUE APPEARANCES/GOALS 2010-11
Goalkeepers Michele Arcari 22 • Nicola Leali 1 • Matteo Sereni 15
Defenders Pietro Accardi 6+2/1 • Francesco Bega 25+2/1
Gaetano Berardi SUI 24+3/0 • Simone Dallamano 12+2/1
Fabio Daprela SUI 6+4/0 • Sebastian de Maio FRA 0+2/0 • Victor
Mareco PAR 6+2/0 • Gilberto Martinez CRC 19/0 • Marco
Zambelli 25+3/0 • Jonathan Zebina FRA 26+2/0 • Davide Zoboli 18/2
Midfield Davide Baiocco 13+8/0 • Alessandro Budel 4+0/0
Nicolas Cordova CHI 17+4/2 • Antonio Filippini 11+4/0 • Perparim
Hetemaj FIN 28+2/2 • Panagiotis Kone GRE 23+8/1 • Lorenzo
Tassi 0+1/0 • Adam Vass HUN 15+5/0 • Nana Welbeck GHA 0+1/0
Cristiano Zanetti 8/0
Forwards Andrea Caracciolo 30+3/12 • Alessandro Diamanti 29+3/6
Eder BRA 27+8/6 • Robert Feczesin HUN 0+2/0
Jonathas BRA 2+4/0 • Davide Lanzafame 1+12/0
Davide Possanzini 5+12/0 • Riccardo Taddei 0+4/0
Coach Giuseppe Iachini • Mario Beretta (6/12/10) • Giuseppe
Iachini (30/01/11)

CAGLIARI LEAGUE APPEARANCES/GOALS 2010-11
Goalkeepers Michael Agazzi 38 • Ivan Pelizzoli 0+1
Defenders Alessandro Agostini 34/0 • Lorenzo Ariaudo
Davide Astori 36/0 • Michele Canini 36/2 • Gabriele Perico 21+6/0
Francesco Pisano 15+3/0
Midfield Davide Biondini 35+2/1 • Pablo Ceppelini URU 0+3/0
Daniele Conti 27+2/5 • Andrea Cossu 35/4 • Simon Laner 3+15/0
Andrea Lazzari 20+10/1 • Radja Nainggolan BEL 33+3/2
Alex Pinardi 3+4/0 • Mikhail Sivakov BLR 0+2/0
Forwards Robert Acquafresca 27+10/8 • Alessandro Matri 19+3/11
Simone Missiroli 5+11/0 • Nene BRA 18+9/6
Daniele Ragatzu 4+14/1
Coach Pierpaolo Bisoli (23/06/10) • Roberto Donadoni (16/11/10)

CATANIA 2010–11

	Date	Opponent	Res	Score	Comp	Scorers	Att
Sep	29	Chievo	L	1-2	SA	Ricchiuti 22	7 329
	12	Parma	W	2-1	SA	Mascara 12p, Antenucci 82p	11 208
	18	Milan	D	1-1	SA	Capuano 27	42 637
	22	Cesena	W	2-0	SA	Silvestre 23, Lopez 59	11 418
	26	Bologna	D	1-1	SA	OG 66	10 913
Oct	3	Lecce	L	0-1	SA		7 270
	17	Napoli	D	1-1	SA	Gomez 69	13 136
	24	Genoa	L	0-1	SA		21 858
	27	Varese	W	4-3	ICr3	Pesce 12, Antenucci 26, Morimoto 56, Spolli 116	2 372
	31	Fiorentina	D	0-0	SA		13 990
Nov	7	Sampdoria	D	0-0	SA		20 778
	10	Udinese	W	1-0	SA	Lopez 60	12 418
	14	Palermo	L	1-3	SA	Terlizzi 46	25 532
	21	Bari	W	1-0	SA	Terlizzi 83	11 573
	25	Brescia	W	5-1	ICr4	Martinho 12, Lopez 2 54 87, Pesce 58, Antenucci 83	3 500
	28	Lazio	D	1-1	SA	Silvestre 44	22 451
Dec	5	Juventus	L	1-3	SA	Morimoto 36	16 556
	12	Cagliari	L	0-3	SA		15 000
	19	Brescia	W	1-0	SA	Lopez 33	9 283
	6	Roma	L	2-4	SA	Silvestre 29, Lopez 37	32 148
	9	Inter	L	1-2	SA	Gomez 71	15 089
Jan	13	Juventus	L	0-2	ICr5		5 441
	16	Chievo	D	1-1	SA	Lopez 29p	12 788
	22	Parma	L	0-2	SA		12 316
	29	Milan	L	0-2	SA		16 613
Feb	2	Cesena	D	1-1	SA	Lopez 9	13 522
	6	Bologna	L	0-1	SA		15 000
	13	Lecce	W	3-2	SA	Silvestre 45, Lodi 2 80 85	13 810
	20	Napoli	L	0-1	SA		47 422
	27	Genoa	W	2-1	SA	Lopez 51, Bergessio 56	12 538
Mar	6	Fiorentina	L	0-3	SA		20 813
	13	Sampdoria	W	1-0	SA	Llama 75	9 283
	20	Udinese	L	0-2	SA		16 000
	3	Palermo	W	4-0	SA	OG 48, Bergessio 61, Ledesma 67, Pesce 77	19 136
Apr	10	Bari	D	1-1	SA	Lopez 44	14 638
	17	Lazio	L	1-4	SA	Schelotto 46	14 014
	23	Juventus	D	2-2	SA	Gomez 81, Lodi 90	23 461
	1	Cagliari	W	2-0	SA	Silvestre 78, Bergessio 82	4 599
May	8	Brescia	W	2-1	SA	Silvestre 27, Bergessio 75	8 000
	15	Roma	W	2-1	SA	Bergessio 78, Gomez 90	19 083
	22	Inter	L	1-3	SA	Ledesma 66	56 072

13th Att: 247 448 • Av: 13 023 (-16.9%) • Angelo Massimino 23 420 (55%)

CESENA 2010–11

	Date	Opponent	Res	Score	Comp	Scorers	Att
Sep	28	Roma	D	0-0	SA		33 000
	11	Milan	W	2-0	SA	Bogdani 31, Giaccherini 44	21 058
	19	Lecce	W	1-0	SA	Bogdani 55	14 277
	22	Catania	L	0-2	SA		11 418
	26	Napoli	L	1-4	SA	Parolo 48	16 250
Oct	2	Udinese	L	0-1	SA		13 968
	17	Parma	D	1-1	SA	Bogdani 17	14 292
	24	Chievo	L	1-2	SA	OG 44	9 800
	27	Novara	L	1-3	ICr3	Schelotto 45	2 194
	31	Sampdoria	L	0-1	SA		14 884
Nov	7	Juventus	L	1-3	SA	Jimenez 11	35 290
	10	Lazio	W	1-0	SA	Parolo 84	15 279
	13	Fiorentina	L	0-1	SA		20 340
	21	Palermo	L	1-2	SA	Bogdani 24	14 068
	28	Bari	D	1-1	SA	Colucci 62p	15 182
Dec	5	Bologna	L	0-2	SA		15 680
	18	Cagliari	W	1-0	SA	Jimenez 17	**12 851**
	6	Brescia	W	2-1	SA	Jimenez 33, Ceccarelli 41	5 000
	9	Genoa	D	0-0	SA		13 857
	16	Roma	L	0-1	SA		19 834
Jan	19	Inter	L	2-3	SA	Bogdani 23, Giaccherini 29	52 507
	23	Milan	L	0-2	SA		37 952
	30	Lecce	D	1-1	SA	Bogdani 92+	6 643
	2	Catania	D	1-1	SA	Jimenez 31	13 522
	6	Napoli	L	0-2	SA		34 565
Feb	13	Udinese	L	0-3	SA		16 704
	20	Parma	D	2-2	SA	Rosina 31, Sammarco 79	14 095
	27	Chievo	W	1-0	SA	Jimenez 90p	14 084
	6	Sampdoria	W	3-2	SA	Parolo 43, Giaccherini 2 46 48	21 215
Mar	12	Juventus	D	2-2	SA	Jimenez 41p, Parolo 80	21 932
	19	Lazio	L	0-1	SA		20 409
	3	Fiorentina	D	2-2	SA	Jimenez 18, Caserta 86	17 876
	10	Palermo	D	2-2	SA	Parolo 91+, Giaccherini 95+	22 375
Apr	17	Bari	W	1-0	SA	Bogdani 48	15 699
	23	Bologna	W	2-0	SA	Giaccherini 48, Malonga 84	21 458
	30	Inter	L	1-2	SA	Budan 56	**22 158**
	8	Cagliari	W	2-0	SA	Jimenez 54, Malonga 84	6 000
May	15	Brescia	W	1-0	SA	Giaccherini 60	18 626
	22	Genoa	L	2-3	SA	Bogdani 49p, Jimenez 86	26 655

15th Att: 312 912 • Av: 16 469 (+32.1%) • Dino Manuzzi 23 860 (69%)

CATANIA LEAGUE APPEARANCES/GOALS 2010-11

Goalkeepers Mariano Andujar ARG 37 • Andrea Campagnolo 1
Defenders Pablo Alvarez ARG 20+3/0 • Blazej Augustyn POL 5+1/0
Giuseppe Bellusci 6+3/0 • Ciro Capuano 22+1/1
Giovanni Marchese 11+1/0 • Alessandro Potenza 19+1/0
Matias Silvestre ARG 36/6 • Nicolas Spolli ARG 23+2/0
Christian Terlizzi 9+3/2
Midfield Marco Biagianti 15/0 • Ezequiel Carboni ARG 24+4/0
Gennaro Delvecchio 2+5/0 • Alejandro Gomez ARG 30+6/4
Mariano Izco ARG 11+7/0 • Pablo Ledesma ARG 25+7/2 • Cristian
Llama ARG 5+10/1 • Francesco Lodi 10+6/3 • Simone Pesce 5+3/1
Rafael Martinho BRA 5+6/0 • Adrian Ricchiuti ARG 19+12/1 • Ezequiel
Schelotto ARG 9+5/1 • Fabio Sciacca 3+1/0
Forwards Mirco Antenucci 2+12/1 • Gonzalo Bergessio ARG 12+1/5
Maxi Lopez ARG 32+3/8 • Giuseppe Mascara 16+2/1
Takayuki Morimoto JPN 4+8/1
Coach Marco Giampaolo (30/05/10) • Diego Simeone ARG (19/01/11)

CESENA LEAGUE APPEARANCES/GOALS 2010-11

Goalkeepers Francesco Antonioli 37 • Alex Calderoni 1
Defenders Yohan Benalouane FRA 10+5/0 • Hernan
Dellafiore ARG 4+3/0 • Ivan Fatic MNE 0+2/0 • Felipe BRA 7/0
Maurizio Lauro 23+7/0 • Yuto Nagamoto JPN 16/0
Maximiliano Pellegrino ARG 24+6/0 • Davide Santon 9+2/0
Steve von Bergen SUI 34/0
Midfield Stephen Appiah GHA 13+1/0 • Fabio Caserta 19+6/1
Luca Ceccarelli 25+7/1 • Giuseppe Colucci 32+1/1 • Nicolas
Gorobsov ARG 1/0 • Luis Jimenez CHI 30+1/9 • Marco Parolo 37/5
Luigi Piangerelli 0+5/0 • Alessandro Rosina 4+6/1 • Paolo
Sammarco 7+8/1 • Ezequiel Schelotto ARG 11+6/0
Forwards Erjon Bogdani ALB 29+6/8 • Igor Budan CRO 6+11/1
Emanuele Giaccherini 34+2/7 • Odion Ighalo NGA 0+3/0
Dominique Malonga FRA 5+17/2 • Roope Riski FIN 0+1/0
Alejandro Rodriguez 0+1/0
Coach Massimo Ficcadenti

CHIEVO VERONA 2010–11

	Date	Opp	Res	Score	Comp	Scorers	Att
Sep	29	Catania	W	2-1	SA	Moscardelli 15, Pellissier 84p	7 329
	12	Genoa	W	3-1	SA	Moscardelli 45, Marcolini 56, Pellissier 73	23 258
	19	Brescia	L	0-1	SA		9 370
	22	Napoli	W	3-1	SA	Pellissier 2 22 75, Fernandes 58	46 037
	26	Lazio	L	0-1	SA		8 500
	3	Cagliari	D	0-0	SA		7 800
	16	Milan	L	1-3	SA	OG 70	49 170
Oct	24	Cesena	W	2-1	SA	Cesar 31, Thereau 91+	9 800
	28	Sassuolo	W	2-0	ICr3	Mandelli 44, Moscardelli 80	1 611
	31	Parma	D	0-0	SA		13 562
	7	Fiorentina	L	0-1	SA		21 236
	10	Bari	D	0-0	SA		8 822
Nov	14	Sampdoria	D	0-0	SA		20 526
	21	Inter	W	2-1	SA	Pellissier 29, Moscardelli 82	19 268
	30	Novara	W	3-0	ICr4	Granoche 2 23 35, De Paula 83	1 251
	4	Roma	D	2-2	SA	Moscardelli 61, Granoche 83	11 447
Dec	8	Bologna	L	1-2	SA	Cesar 49	13 764
	12	Lecce	L	2-3	SA	Bogliacino 55, Mandelli 94+	5 824
	19	Juventus	D	1-1	SA	Pellissier 92+	22 819
	6	Udinese	L	0-2	SA		14 000
	9	Palermo	D	0-0	SA		12 000
Jan	12	Parma	L	0-1	ICr5		6 602
	16	Catania	D	1-1	SA	Pellissier 65	12 788
	23	Genoa	D	0-0	SA		17 284
	30	Brescia	W	3-0	SA	Pellissier 2 45 93+, Mandelli 46	8 500
	2	Napoli	W	2-0	SA	Moscardelli 20, Sardo 50	11 000
	6	Lazio	D	1-1	SA	Cesar 64	21 700
Feb	13	Cagliari	L	1-4	SA	Thereau 84	15 000
	20	Milan	L	1-2	SA	Fernandes 61	29 404
	27	Cesena	L	0-1	SA		14 084
	6	Parma	D	0-0	SA		10 536
Mar	13	Fiorentina	L	0-1	SA		10 489
	20	Bari	W	2-1	SA	Pellissier 38, Moscardelli 49	8 822
	3	Sampdoria	D	0-0	SA		14 456
	9	Inter	L	0-2	SA		61 456
Apr	17	Bologna	W	2-0	SA	Constant 15, Marcolini 83	10 846
	23	Roma	L	0-1	SA		27 319
	1	Lecce	W	1-0	SA	Rigoni 58	10 825
	9	Juventus	D	2-2	SA	Uribe 68, Sardo 69	23 740
May	15	Udinese	L	0-2	SA		19 031
	22	Palermo	W	3-1	SA	Pellissier 40, Constant 67, Pulzetti 80	20 888

11th Att: 251 026 • Av: 13 211 (+10.6%) • Bentegodi 39 211 (33%)

FIORENTINA 2010–11

	Date	Opp	Res	Score	Comp	Scorers	Att
Sep	29	Napoli	D	1-1	SA	D'Agostino 50	25 025
	12	Lecce	L	0-1	SA		8 979
	18	Lazio	L	1-2	SA	Ljajic 19p	20 868
	22	Genoa	D	1-1	SA	Gilardino 11	23 101
	26	Parma	W	2-0	SA	Ljajic 61p, De Silvestri 76	21 126
	3	Palermo	L	1-2	SA	Gilardino 58	22 795
	17	Sampdoria	L	1-2	SA	Marchionni 6	22 738
Oct	23	Bari	W	2-1	SA	Donadel 34, Gilardino 82	23 874
	26	Empoli	W	1-0	ICr3	Babacar 119	7 734
	31	Catania	D	0-0	SA		13 990
	7	Chievo	W	1-0	SA	Cerci 81	21 236
	10	Roma	L	2-3	SA	Gilardino 69, D'Agostino 90	28 532
	13	Cesena	W	1-0	SA	Gilardino 59	20 340
Nov	20	Milan	L	0-1	SA		47 549
	27	Juventus	D	1-1	SA	OG 4	21 740
	30	Reggina	W	3-0	ICr4	Babacar 29, Marchionni 44, Cerci 47	4 904
	5	Cagliari	W	1-0	SA	Mutu 52	21 644
Dec	11	Udinese	L	1-2	SA	Santana 31	14 107
	14	Parma	L	1-2	ICr5	Santana 114	3 517
	6	Bologna	D	1-1	SA	Santana 67	16 000
	9	Brescia	W	3-2	SA	Gilardino 72, Santana 86, Ljajic 86	20 664
Jan	15	Napoli	D	0-0	SA		49 443
	23	Lecce	D	1-1	SA	Gilardino 56	20 292
	29	Lazio	L	0-2	SA		20 655
	2	Genoa	W	1-0	SA	Santana 40	20 129
	6	Parma	D	1-1	SA	D'Agostino 49p	13 588
Feb	13	Palermo	W	4-2	SA	Gilardino 36, Camporese 70, OG 78, Montolivo 88	24 571
	16	Inter	L	1-2	SA	Pasqual 33	31 595
	20	Sampdoria	D	0-0	SA		21 723
	27	Bari	D	1-1	SA	Gilardino 21	14 739
	6	Catania	W	3-0	SA	Mutu 2 21 24, Gilardino 61	20 813
Mar	13	Chievo	W	1-0	SA	Vargas 48	10 489
	20	Roma	D	2-2	SA	Mutu 21, Gamberini 34	23 634
	3	Cesena	D	2-2	SA	Gilardino 35, Montolivo 69	17 876
Apr	10	Milan	L	1-2	SA	Vargas 79	32 677
	17	Juventus	D	0-0	SA		34 483
	23	Cagliari	W	2-1	SA	Cerci 2 45 50	10 000
	1	Udinese	W	5-2	SA	Vargas 9, D'Agostino 2 21 51, Cerci 2 71 86	8 527
May	8	Inter	L	1-3	SA	Gilardino 74	55 879
	15	Bologna	D	1-1	SA	Cerci 20	21 026
	22	Brescia	D	2-2	SA	Vargas 2, Cerci 75	3 000

9th Att: 432 471 • Av: 22 761 (-17.1%) • Artemio Franchi 35 575 (63%)

CHIEVO LEAGUE APPEARANCES/GOALS 2010-11

Goalkeepers Stefano Sorrentino 37 • Lorenzo Squizzi 1+1
Defenders Marco Andreolli 27+1/0 • Bostjan Cesar SVN 29+3/3
Nicholas Frey FRA 19+2/0 • Bojan Jokic SVN 13+2/0 • Davide
Mandelli 16+4/2 • Andrea Mantovani 31/0 • Santiago
Morero ARG 3+2/0 • Gennaro Sardo 20+7/2
Midfield Simone Dentivoglio 0+4/0 • Mariano Bogliacino URU 23+11/1
Kevin Constant GUI 27+5/2 • Milos Dimitrijevic SRB 2/0 • Gelson
Fernandes SUI 24+5/2 • Roberto Guana 15+4/0 • Luciano BRA 3+1/0
Michele Marcolini 14+12/2 • Nico Pulzetti 3+4/1 • Luca Rigoni 27+2/1
Fernando Uribe COL 0+6/1
Forwards Marcos De Paula BRA 0+3/0 • Diego Farias BRA 0+1/0
Pablo Granoche URU 5+13/1 • Davide Moscardelli BEL 21+13/6
Sergio Pellissier 35/11 • Cyril Thereau FRA 15+8/2
Coach Stefano Pioli (10/06/10)

FIORENTINA LEAGUE APPEARANCES/GOALS 2010-11

Goalkeepers Vlada Avramov SRB 1 • Artur Boruc POL 26
Sebastien Frey FRA 11
Defenders Michele Camporese 7+2/1 • Gianluca Comotto 16+4/0
Lorenzo De Silvestri 23+3/1 • Felipe BRA 2+3/0 • Alessandro
Gamberini 35/1 • Per Kroldrup DEN 17+2/0 • Cesare Natali 16+4/0
Manuel Pasqual 33+1/1
Midfield Valon Behrami SUI 15+2/0 • Mario Bolatti ARG 1+9/0
Gaetano D'Agostino 12+8/5 • Marco Donadel 26+3/1 • Nikola
Gulan SRB 3+3/0 • Adem Ljajic SRB 14+12/3 • Marco
Marchionni 13+11/1 • Riccardo Montolivo 29/2 • Cristiano
Piccini 0+1/0 • Amidu Salifu GHA 0+1/0 • Mario Santana ARG 22+6/4
Juan Vargas PER 19+5/4 • Cristiano Zanetti 4+2/0
Forwards Khouma Babacar SEN 3+15/0 • Alessio Cerci 17+7/7
Alberto Gilardino 35/12 • Adrian Mutu ROU 18+2/4 • Haris
Seferovic SUI 0+1/0 • Papa Waigo SEN 0+1/0
Coach Sinisa Mihajlovic SRB (3/06/10)

GENOA 2010–11

	Date	Opponent		Score	Comp	Scorers	Att
Sep	28	Udinese	W	1-0	SA	Mesto 80	14 500
	12	Chievo	L	1-3	SA	Destro 6	23 258
	19	Parma	D	1-1	SA	Toni 28p	13 619
	22	Fiorentina	D	1-1	SA	Mesto 17	23 101
	25	Milan	L	0-1	SA		41 909
Oct	3	Bari	W	2-1	SA	Palacio 36, Toni 95+	22 358
	16	Roma	L	1-2	SA	Rudolf 78	30 958
	24	Catania	W	1-0	SA	Rossi 68	21 858
	20	Grosseto	W	2-1	ICr3	Toni 2 83p 119	3 000
	29	Inter	L	0-1	SA		27 566
Nov	7	Palermo	L	0-1	SA		24 368
	10	Bologna	W	1-0	SA	Milanetto 81	21 913
	14	Cagliari	W	1-0	SA	Ranocchia 83	10 000
	21	Juventus	L	0-2	SA		27 474
	24	Vicenza	W	3-1	ICr4	Toni 2 86p 92, Destro 97	5 000
	28	Brescia	D	0-0	SA		3 532
Dec	5	Lecce	W	3-1	SA	Toni 55, Ranocchia 76, Rossi 94+	6 197
	11	Napoli	L	0-1	SA		24 288
	6	Lazio	D	0-0	SA		22 090
Jan	9	Cesena	D	0-0	SA		13 867
	12	Inter	L	2-3	ICr5	Kharja 54p, Sculli 90	15 254
	16	Udinese	L	2-4	SA	Milanetto 45, Destro 58	21 448
	23	Chievo	D	0-0	SA		17 284
	30	Parma	W	3-1	SA	Palacio 16p, OG 43, Kaladze 45	24 000
Feb	2	Fiorentina	L	0-1	SA		20 129
	6	Milan	D	1-1	SA	Flores 45	26 000
	13	Bari	D	0-0	SA		14 812
	16	Sampdoria	W	1-0	SA	Rafinha 55	25 001
	20	Roma	W	4-3	SA	Palacio 2 52 74, Paloschi 2 68 86	22 180
	27	Catania	L	1-2	SA	Flores 19	12 538
Mar	6	Inter	L	2-5	SA	Palacio 40, Boselli 91+	56 322
	13	Palermo	W	1-0	SA	Flores 77	21 657
	20	Bologna	D	1-1	SA	Dainelli 43	19 149
	3	Cagliari	L	0-1	SA		22 141
Apr	10	Juventus	L	2-3	SA	OG 7, Flores 57	23 018
	17	Brescia	W	3-0	SA	Rafinha 59, OG 70, Antonelli 93+	21 540
	23	Lecce	W	4-2	SA	Flores 2 10 62, Palacio 2 43 54	**21 369**
	30	Napoli	L	0-1	SA		52 495
May	8	Sampdoria	W	2-1	SA	Flores 45, Boselli 96+	**29 465**
	14	Lazio	L	2-4	SA	Palacio 12, Flores 89	27 178
	22	Cesena	W	3-2	SA	Palacio 2 6 17, Palacio 45	26 655

10th Att: 450 361 • Av: 23 703 (-6.5%) • Luigi Ferraris 36 685 (64%)

GENOA LEAGUE APPEARANCES/GOALS 2010-11

Goalkeepers Eduardo POR 37 • Mattia Perin 1
Defenders Luca Antonelli 5+5/1 • Chico ESP 7+8/0 • Domenico Criscito 36/0 • Dario Dainelli 33+1/1 • Kakha Kaladze GEO 23+3/1 • Francesco Modesto 0+1/0 • Emiliano Moretti 9+9/0 • Diego Polenta URU 0+1/0 • Rafinha BRA 28+6/2 • Andrea Ranocchia 16/2
Midfield Bosko Jankovic SRB 3+3/0 • Houssine Kharja MAR 8+5/0 • Abdoulay Konko MAR 11+2/0 • Juraj Kucka SVK 15+2/0 • Giandomenico Mesto 32+4/2 • Miguel Veloso POR 15+5/0 • Omar Milanetto POR 28+3/2 • Marco Rossi 32/2 • Franco Zuculini ARG 1+3/0
Forwards Yiadom Boakye GHA 0+4/0 • Mauro Boselli ARG 1+6/2 • Mattia Destro 5+11/2 • Antonio Floro Flores 18/10 • Enej Jelenic SVN 0+2/0 • Rodrigo Palacio ARG 24+3/9 • Raffaele Palladino 3+2/0 • Alberto Paloschi 3+9/2 • Gergely Rudolf HUN 4+8/1 • Giuseppe Sculli 4+4/0 • Luca Toni 16/3
Coach Gian Piero Gasperini • Davide Ballardini (8/11/10)

INTER LEAGUE APPEARANCES/GOALS 2010-11
Cont'd

Forwards Denis Alibec ROU 0+2/0 • Jonathan Biabiany FRA 9+5/0 • Samuel Eto'o CMR 35/21 • Diego Milito ARG 16+7/5 • Goran Pandev MKD 17+10/2 • Giampaolo Pazzini 14+3/11
Coach Rafa Benitez ESP (10/06/10) • Leonardo BRA (24/12/10)

INTERNAZIONALE 2010–11

	Date	Opponent		Score	Comp	Scorers	Att
Aug	21	Roma	W	3-1	SC	Pandev 41, Eto'o 2 70 81	65 860
	27	At. Madrid	L	0-2	USC		18 500
	30	Bologna	D	0-0	SA		28 439
Sep	11	Udinese	W	2-1	SA	Lucio 7, Eto'o 67	62 014
	14	Twente	D	2-2	CLgA	Sneijder 13, Eto'o 41	23 800
	19	Palermo	W	2-1	SA	Eto'o 2 62 70	27 291
	22	Bari	W	4-0	SA	Milito 2 27 86, Eto'o 2 50p 63p	61 093
	25	Roma	L	0-1	SA		45 109
	29	W Bremen	W	4-0	CLgA	Eto'o 3 21 27 81, Sneijder 34	48 126
	3	Juventus	D	0-0	SA		78 883
Oct	17	Cagliari	W	1-0	SA	Eto'o 39	20 000
	20	Tottenham	W	4-3	CLgA	Zanetti 2, Eto'o 2 11p 35, Stankovic 14	49 551
	24	Sampdoria	D	1-1	SA	Eto'o 80	56 415
	29	Genoa	W	1-0	SA	Muntari 45	27 566
Nov	2	Tottenham	L	1-3	CLgA	Eto'o 80	34 103
	6	Brescia	D	1-1	SA	Eto'o 73p	58 183
	10	Lecce	D	1-1	SA	Milito 76	14 583
	14	Milan	L	0-1	SA		**80 018**
	21	Chievo	L	1-2	SA	Eto'o 92+	19 268
	24	Twente	W	1-0	CLgA	Cambiasso 55	29 466
	28	Parma	W	5-2	SA	Stankovic 3 18 19 75, Cambiasso 23, Motta 72	49 787
Dec	3	Lazio	L	1-3	SA	Pandev 74	39 710
	7	W Bremen	L	0-3	CLgA		30 400
	15	Seongnam	W	3-0	CWsf	Stankovic 3, Zanetti 32, Milito 73	35 995
	18	TP Mazembe	W	3-0	CWf	Pandev 13, Eto'o 17, Biabiany 85	42 174
	6	Napoli	W	3-1	SA	Motta 2 3 55, Cambiasso 37	60 515
	9	Catania	W	2-1	SA	Cambiasso 2 74 79	15 089
	12	Genoa	W	3-2	ICr5	Eto'o 2 15 43, Mariga 59	15 254
Jan	15	Bologna	W	4-1	SA	Stankovic 20, Milito 30, Eto'o 2 63 72	52 724
	19	Cesena	W	3-2	SA	Eto'o 14, Milito 15, Chivu 45	52 507
	23	Udinese	L	1-3	SA	Stankovic 16	26 036
	26	Napoli	D	0-0	ICqf	W 5-4p	40 580
	30	Palermo	W	3-2	SA	Pazzini 2 57 73, Eto'o 76p	58 000
	3	Bari	W	3-0	SA	Kharja 70, Pazzini 94+, Sneijder 96+	36 121
	6	Roma	W	5-3	SA	Sneijder 3, Eto'o 2 35 63p, Motta 71, Cambiasso 90	62 344
Feb	13	Juventus	L	0-1	SA		24 485
	16	Fiorentina	W	2-1	SA	OG 6, Pazzini 62	31 595
	19	Cagliari	W	1-0	SA	Kharja 8	**47 672**
	23	Bayern M	L	0-1	CLr2		75 925
	27	Sampdoria	W	2-0	SA	Sneijder 73, Eto'o 94+	24 417
	6	Genoa	W	5-2	SA	Pazzini 50, Eto'o 2 51 57, Pandev 71, Nagatomo 84	56 322
Mar	11	Brescia	D	1-1	SA	Eto'o 18	27 000
	15	Bayern M	W	3-2	CLr2	Eto'o 4, Sneijder 63, Pandev 88	66 000
	20	Lecce	W	1-0	SA	Pazzini 52	62 477
	2	Milan	L	0-3	SA		80 018
	5	Schalke	L	2-5	CLqf	Stankovic 1, Milito 34	72 770
	9	Chievo	W	2-0	SA	Cambiasso 66, Maicon 84	61 456
Apr	13	Schalke	L	1-2	CLqf	Motta 49	54 142
	16	Parma	L	0-2	SA		17 504
	19	Roma	W	1-0	ICsf	Stankovic 45	23 979
	23	Lazio	W	2-1	SA	Sneijder 40, Eto'o 53	57 830
	30	Cesena	W	2-1	SA	Pazzini 2 92+ 95+	22 139
May	8	Fiorentina	W	3-1	SA	Pazzini 25, Cambiasso 28, Coutinho 77	55 879
	11	Roma	D	1-1	ICsf	Eto'o 58	33 094
	15	Napoli	D	1-1	SA	Eto'o 15	57 400
	22	Catania	W	3-1	SA	Pazzini 2 15 48, Nagatomo 63	56 072
	29	Palermo	W	1-0	ICf	Eto'o 2 26 76, Milito 92+	70 000

2nd Att: 1 130 191 • Av: 59 484 (+5.8%) • San Siro 80 074 (74%)

INTER LEAGUE APPEARANCES/GOALS 2010-11

Goalkeepers Luca Castellazzi 13+2 • Julio Cesar BRA 25
Defenders Cristian Chivu ROU 24/1 • Ivan Cordoba COL 15+7/0 • Lucio BRA 30+1/1 • Maicon BRA 28/1 • Marco Materazzi 6+2/0 • Yuto Nagatomo JPN 10+3/2 • Felice Natalino 1+1/0 • Obiora Nwankwo NGA 0+2/0 • Andrea Ranocchia 17+1/0 • Walter Samuel ARG 8+2/0 • Davide Santon 5+7/0 • Javier Zanetti ARG 35/0
Midfield Esteban Cambiasso ARG 28+2/7 • Coutinho BRA 8+5/1 • Houssine Kharja MAR 10+5/2 • Mancini BRA 0+2/0 • MacDonald Mariga KEN 2+10/0 • Motta 15+4/4 • Sulley Ali Muntari GHA 1+7/1 • Joel Obi NGA 2+8/0 • Wesley Sneijder NED 22+3/4 • Dejan Stankovic SRB 22+4/5

JUVENTUS 2010–11

	Date	Opponent	Res	Score	Comp	Scorers	Att
Jy	29	Shamrock	W	2-0	ELp3	Amauri 2 3 75	6 000
	5	Shamrock	W	1-0	ELp3	Del Piero 74	17 579
Aug	19	Sturm Graz	W	2-1	ELpo	Bonucci 15, Amauri 91+	15 322
	26	Sturm Graz	W	1-0	ELpo	Del Piero 53	15 585
	29	Bari	L	0-1	SA		45 162
	12	Sampdoria	D	3-3	SA	Marchisio 43, Pepe 50, Quagliarella 67	23 949
	16	Lech	D	3-3	ELgA	Chiellini 2 45 50, Del Piero 68	10 837
Sep	19	Udinese	W	4-0	SA	OG 18, Quagliarella 24, Marchisio 43, Iaquinta 77	20 757
	23	Palermo	L	1-3	SA	Iaquinta 87	20 607
	26	Cagliari	W	4-2	SA	Krasic 3 13 34 70, Bonucci 57	19 394
	30	Man City	D	1-1	ELgA	Iaquinta 11	35 212
	3	Inter	D	0-0	SA		78 883
Oct	17	Lecce	W	4-0	SA	Aquilani 13, Melo 34p, Quagliarella 44, Del Piero 82	23 373
	21	Salzburg	D	1-1	ELgA	Krasic 47	19 200
	24	Bologna	D	0-0	SA		28 785
	30	Milan	W	2-1	SA	Quagliarella 24, Del Piero 65	76 768
	4	Salzburg	D	0-0	ELgA		12 162
	7	Cesena	W	3-1	SA	Del Piero 31p, Quagliarella 43, Iaquinta 87	20 534
Nov	10	Brescia	D	1-1	SA	Quagliarella 71	20 000
	13	Roma	D	1-1	SA	Iaquinta 35	23 869
	21	Genoa	W	2-0	SA	OG 18, Krasic 23	27 474
	27	Fiorentina	D	1-1	SA	Pepe 82	21 740
	1	Lech	D	1-1	ELgA	Iaquinta 84	42 590
	5	Catania	W	3-1	SA	Pepe 34, Quagliarella 2 44 57	16 556
Dec	12	Lazio	W	2-1	SA	Chiellini 2, Krasic 90	20 098
	16	Man City	D	1-1	ELgA	Giannetti 43	6 992
	19	Chievo	D	1-1	SA	Quagliarella 31	22 819
	6	Parma	L	1-4	SA	Legrottaglie 59	23 873
	9	Napoli	L	0-3	SA		58 666
	13	Catania	W	2-0	ICr5	Krasic 34, Pepe 54	5 441
Jan	16	Bari	W	2-1	SA	Del Piero 43, Aquilani 79	**18 882**
	23	Sampdoria	D	0-0	SA		25 933
	27	Roma	L	0-2	ICqf		18 300
	30	Udinese	L	1-2	SA	Marchisio 60	22 000
	2	Palermo	L	1-2	SA	Marchisio 36	25 000
	5	Cagliari	W	3-1	SA	Matri 2 21 75, Toni 84	20 000
Feb	13	Inter	W	1-0	SA	Matri 30	24 485
	20	Lecce	L	0-2	SA		9 000
	26	Bologna	L	0-2	SA		20 843
	5	Milan	L	0-1	SA		**24 908**
Mar	12	Cesena	D	2-2	SA	Matri 2 19 35	21 932
	20	Brescia	W	2-1	SA	Krasnic 23, Del Piero 68	19 162
	3	Roma	W	2-0	SA	Matri 74	50 952
Apr	10	Genoa	W	3-2	SA	OG 49, Matri 63, Toni 83	23 137
	17	Fiorentina	D	0-0	SA		34 483
	23	Catania	D	2-2	SA	Del Piero 2 19p 38	23 461
	2	Lazio	W	1-0	SA	Pepe 87	42 070
May	9	Chievo	D	2-2	SA	Del Piero 13p, Matri 55	23 740
	15	Parma	L	0-1	SA		17 259
	22	Napoli	D	2-2	SA	Chiellini 47, Matri 84	23 389

7th Att: 421 444 • Av: 22 181 (-4.4%) • Olimpico 27 994 (79%)

LAZIO 2010–11

	Date	Opponent	Res	Score	Comp	Scorers	Att
	29	Sampdoria	L	0-2	SA		21 504
	12	Bologna	W	3-1	SA	Mauri 68, Rocchi 75, Hernanes 90p	22 462
	18	Fiorentina	W	2-1	SA	Ledesma 31, Kozak 67	20 868
Sep	22	Milan	D	1-1	SA	Floccari 81	41 246
	26	Chievo	W	1-0	SA	Zarate 69	8 500
	3	Brescia	W	1-0	SA	Mauri 45	29 555
	17	Bari	W	2-0	SA	Hernanes 52, Floccari 61	22 779
Oct	24	Cagliari	W	2-1	SA	Floccari 22, Mauri 53	32 417
	27	P'Summaga	W	3-0	ICr3	Gonzalez 8, Kozak 36, Bresciano 54	4 529
	31	Palermo	W	1-0	SA	Andre Dias 27	29 539
	7	Roma	L	0-2	SA		**52 121**
	11	Cesena	L	0-1	SA		15 279
	14	Napoli	W	2-0	SA	Zarate 15, Floccari 61	24 487
Nov	21	Parma	D	1-1	SA	Floccari 45	13 986
	25	AlbinoLeffe	W	3-0	ICr4	Garrido 14, Stenardo 44, Del Nero 86	4 000
	28	Catania	D	1-1	SA	Hernanes 45	22 451
	3	Inter	W	3-1	SA	Biava 26, Zarate 53, Hernanes 89	39 710
Dec	12	Juventus	L	1-2	SA	Zarate 14	20 098
	19	Udinese	W	3-2	SA	Hernanes 2, Biava 52, OG 89	20 644
	6	Genoa	D	0-0	SA		22 090
	9	Lecce	L	1-2	SA	Mauri 47	25 621
Jan	16	Sampdoria	W	1-0	SA	Kozak 84	21 833
	19	Roma	L	1-2	ICr5	Hernanes 57p	40 637
	23	Bologna	L	1-3	SA	Floccari 5	14 295
	29	Fiorentina	W	2-0	SA	Kozak 2 69p 73	20 655
	1	Milan	D	0-0	SA		38 809
	6	Chievo	D	1-1	SA	Hernanes 45	21 700
Feb	13	Brescia	W	2-0	SA	Gonzalez 7, Kozak 58	6 269
	20	Bari	W	1-0	SA	Hernanes 6	32 492
	27	Cagliari	L	0-1	SA		8 000
	6	Palermo	W	2-0	SA	Sculli 2 7 18	24 251
Mar	13	Roma	L	0-2	SA		48 955
	19	Cesena	W	2-0	SA	Zarate 1	**20 409**
	3	Napoli	L	3-4	SA	Mauri 29, Andre Dias 57, OG 68	57 155
	10	Parma	W	2-0	SA	Hernanes 23, Floccari 77	31 208
Apr	17	Catania	W	4-1	SA	Hernanes 40, Mauri 56, Floccari 78, Zarate 90	14 014
	23	Inter	L	1-2	SA	Zarate 24p	57 830
	2	Juventus	L	0-1	SA		42 070
	8	Udinese	L	1-2	SA	Kozak 76	22 044
May	14	Genoa	W	4-2	SA	Biava 7, Rocchi 52, Hernanes 2 56 66	27 178
	22	Lecce	W	4-2	SA	Rocchi 7, Zarate 2 35 54p, OG 63	18 218

5th Att: 552 510 • Av: 29 079 (-20.4%) • Olimpico 72 698 (40%)

JUVENTUS LEAGUE APPEARANCES/GOALS 2010-11
Goalkeepers Gianluigi Buffon 16 • Marco Storari 22+1
Defenders Andrea Barzagli 14+1/0 • Leonardo Bonucci 32+2/1
Giorgio Chiellini 32/2 • Fabio Grosso 17+2/0 • Zdenek
Grygera CZE 9+4/0 • Nicola Legrottaglie 2+3/1 • Marco Motta 19+3/0
Leandro Rinaudo 1/0 • Frederik Sorensen DEN 12+5/0
Armand Traore SEN 7+3/0
Midfield Alberto Aquilani 31+2/2 • Paolo De Ceglie 6+1/0 • Albin
Ekdal SWE 0+1/0 • Felipe Melo BRA 28+1/1 • Manuel Giandonato 2/0 • Milos
Krasic SRB 33/7 • Claudio Marchisio 32/4 • Simone Pepe 22+8/4
Hasan Salihamidzic BIH 1+9/0 • Mohamed Sissoko MLI 4+14/0
Forwards Amauri 5+4/0 • Filippo Boniperti 0+1/0 • Alessandro
Del Piero 19+14/8 • Niccolo Giannetti 1/0 • Vincenzo Iaquinta 8+11/4
Davide Lanzafame 0+3/0 • Alberto Libertazzi 0+1/0
Jorge Martinez URU 6+8/0 • Alessandro Matri 15+1/9
Fabio Quagliarella 17/9 • Luca Toni 5+9/2
Coach Luigi Delneri (19/05/10)

LAZIO LEAGUE APPEARANCES/GOALS 2010-11
Goalkeepers Tommaso Berni 2 • Fernando Muslera URU 36
Defenders Andre Dias BRA 33/2 • Giuseppe Biava 35/3 • Luis
Cavanda ANG 2+1/0 • Mobido Diakite FRA 4+4/0 • Garrido ESP 8+2/0
Stephan Lichtsteiner SUI 33+1/0 • Stefan Radu ROU 26/0
Guglielmo Stendardo 6+8/0
Midfield Mark Bresciano AUS 7+13/0 • Cristian Brocchi 25+6/0
Pasquale Foggia 2+7/0 • Alvaro Gonzalez URU 8+11/1
Hernanes BRA 35+1/11 • Cristian Ledesma 30+4/1
Matuzalem BRA 18+4/0 • Stefano Mauri 26+3/6
Lionel Scaloni ARG 5+7/0
Forwards Simone Del Nero 1+1/0 • Sergio Floccari 25+5/8
Libor Kozak CZE 6+13/6 • Tommaso Rocchi 6+11/3
Giuseppe Sculli 11+2/2 • Mauro Zarate ARG 28+7/9
Coach Edoardo Reja

LECCE 2010–11

	No	Opponent	Res	Score	Comp	Scorers	Att
Sep	9	Milan	L	0-4	SA		37 177
	12	Fiorentina	W	1-0	SA	Di Michele [9]	8 979
	19	Cesena	L	0-1	SA		14 277
	22	Parma	D	1-1	SA	Jeda [31p]	7 957
	26	Palermo	D	2-2	SA	Giacomazzi [8], Corvia [46]	22 378
Oct	3	Catania	W	1-0	SA	Corvia [36]	7 270
	17	Juventus	L	0-4	SA		23 373
	24	Brescia	W	2-1	SA	Ofere [54], Di Michele [61]	6 837
	27	Siena	W	3-2	ICr3	Bertolacci [43], Corvia [51], Chevanton [61]	1 832
	30	Roma	L	0-2	SA		36 692
Nov	6	Bologna	L	0-2	SA		13 954
	10	Inter	D	1-1	SA	Olivera [79]	14 583
	14	Udinese	L	0-4	SA		2 817
	21	Sampdoria	L	2-3	SA	Di Michele [72], Diamoutene [83]	6 609
	24	Udinese	L	1-2	ICr4	Chevanton [17]	2 733
	28	Cagliari	L	2-3	SA	Olivera [54], Di Michele [81]	8 000
Dec	5	Genoa	L	1-3	SA	Ofere [45]	6 197
	12	Chievo	W	3-2	SA	Ofere [16], Piatti 2 [45 69]	5 824
	19	Napoli	L	0-1	SA		44 113
Jan	6	Bari	L	0-1	SA		BCD
	9	Lazio	W	2-1	SA	OG [39], Grossmuller [73]	25 621
	16	Milan	L	0-1	SA	Olivera [82]	15 926
	23	Fiorentina	D	1-1	SA	Di Michele [29]	20 292
	30	Cesena	D	1-1	SA	Corvia [11]	6 643
Feb	2	Parma	W	1-0	SA	Chevanton [91+]	11 975
	6	Palermo	L	2-4	SA	Giacomazzi [17], Jeda [50]	9 176
	13	Catania	L	2-3	SA	Jeda [56], Munari [61]	13 810
	20	Juventus	W	2-0	SA	Mesbah [32], Bertolacci [48]	9 000
	27	Brescia	D	2-2	SA	Corvia [30], Munari [70]	4 677
Mar	4	Roma	L	1-2	SA	Giacomazzi [75]	10 488
	13	Bologna	D	0-1	SA		6 958
	20	Inter	L	0-2	SA		62 477
Apr	3	Udinese	W	2-0	SA	Bertolacci 2 [48 65]	10 196
	10	Sampdoria	W	2-1	SA	Di Michele [39], Olivera [66]	26 531
	17	Cagliari	D	3-3	SA	Mesbah [49], Fabiano [88], Corvia [93+]	12 672
	23	Genoa	L	2-4	SA	Di Michele 2 [3 30]	21 369
	1	Chievo	L	0-1	SA		10 825
May	8	Napoli	W	2-1	SA	Corvia [49p], Chevanton [89]	14 406
	15	Bari	W	2-0	SA	Jeda 2 [52 80]	16 329
	22	Lazio	L	2-4	SA	Coppola [33], Piatti [41]	18 218

17th   Att: 177 938 • Av: 9 365 (+9.7%) • Via del Mare 33 876 (27%)

MILAN 2010–11

	No	Opponent	Res	Score	Comp	Scorers	Att
Sep	29	Lecce	W	4-0	SA	Pato 2 [16 28], Thiago [23], Inzaghi [90]	37 177
	11	Cesena	L	0-2	SA		21 058
	15	Auxerre	W	2-0	CLgG	Ibrahimovic 2 [66 69]	69 317
	18	Catania	D	1-1	SA	Inzaghi [45]	42 637
	22	Lazio	D	1-1	SA	Ibrahimovic [66]	41 246
	25	Genoa	W	1-0	SA	Ibrahimovic [49]	41 909
	28	Ajax	D	1-1	CLgG	Ibrahimovic [37]	51 276
Oct	2	Parma	W	1-0	SA	Pirlo [26]	19 615
	16	Chievo	W	3-1	SA	Pato 2 [17 30], Robinho [93+]	49 170
	19	Real Madrid	L	0-2	CLgG		71 657
	25	Napoli	W	2-1	SA	Robinho [22], Ibrahimovic [72]	53 901
	30	Juventus	L	1-2	SA	Ibrahimovic [82]	76 768
Nov	3	Real Madrid	D	2-2	CLgG	Ibrahimovic 2 [68 78]	76 357
	7	Bari	W	3-2	SA	Ambrosini [4], Flamini [31], Pato [72]	35 780
	10	Palermo	W	3-1	SA	Pato [19], Ibrahimovic [77p], Robinho [82]	38 903
	14	Inter	W	1-0	SA	Ibrahimovic [5p]	80 018
	20	Fiorentina	W	1-0	SA	Ibrahimovic [5]	47 549
	23	Auxerre	W	2-0	CLgG	Ibrahimovic [64], Ronaldinho [91+]	19 244
	27	Sampdoria	D	1-1	SA	Robinho [43]	26 820
Dec	4	Brescia	W	3-0	SA	Boateng [4], Robinho [28], Ibrahimovic [31]	41 418
	8	Ajax	L	0-2	CLgG		72 960
	12	Bologna	W	3-0	SA	Boateng [9], Robinho [35], Ibrahimovic [60]	24 915
	18	Roma	L	0-1	SA		53 769
Jan	6	Cagliari	W	1-0	SA	Strasser [85]	23 000
	9	Udinese	D	4-4	SA	Pato 2 [45 82], OG [78], Ibrahimovic [93+]	39 405
	16	Lecce	D	1-1	SA	Ibrahimovic [49]	15 926
	20	Bari	W	3-0	ICr5	Ibrahimovic [19], Merkel [45], Robinho [66]	9 391
	23	Cesena	W	2-0	SA	OG [45], Ibrahimovic [92+]	37 952
	26	Sampdoria	W	2-1	ICqf	Pato 2 [17 21]	11 458
	29	Catania	W	2-0	SA	Robinho [58], Ibrahimovic [85]	16 613
Feb	1	Lazio	D	0-0	SA		38 809
	6	Genoa	D	1-1	SA	Pato [29]	26 000
	12	Parma	W	4-0	SA	Seedorf [8], Cassano [17], Robinho 2 [62 65]	46 119
	15	Tottenham	L	0-1	CLr2		75 652
	20	Chievo	W	2-1	SA	Robinho [25], Pato [82]	29 404
	28	Napoli	W	3-0	SA	Ibrahimovic [50p], Boateng [77], Pato [79]	77 276
Mar	5	Juventus	W	1-0	SA	Gattuso [68]	24 908
	9	Tottenham	D	0-0	CLr2		34 320
	13	Bari	D	1-1	SA	Cassano [82]	61 363
	19	Palermo	L	0-1	SA		25 116
Apr	2	Inter	W	3-0	SA	Pato 2 [1 62], Cassano [90p]	80 018
	10	Fiorentina	W	2-1	SA	Seedorf [8], Pato [41]	32 677
	16	Sampdoria	W	3-0	SA	Seedorf [20], Cassano [54p], Robinho [62]	60 028
	20	Palermo	D	2-2	ICsf	Ibrahimovic [4], Emanuelson [76]	20 022
	23	Brescia	W	1-0	SA	Robinho [82]	22 123
May	1	Bologna	W	1-0	SA	Flamini [7]	74 121
	7	Roma	D	0-0	SA		58 083
	10	Palermo	L	1-2	ICsf	Ibrahimovic [94+]	33 414
	14	Cagliari	W	4-1	SA	Robinho 2 [22 35], Gattuso [24], Seedorf [77]	80 018
	22	Udinese	D	0-0	SA		29 644

1st   Att: 1 024 409 • Av: 53 916 (+25.5%) • San Siro 80 074 (67%)

LECCE LEAGUE APPEARANCES/GOALS 2010-11
Goalkeepers Massimiliano Benassi 1 • Antonio Rosati 37+1
Defenders Davide Brivio 17+5/0 • Souleymane Diamoutene MLI 1+1/1
Giulio Donati 10+4/0 • Fabiano BRA 27+1/1 • Stefano Ferrario 18+2/0
Alberto Giuliatto 9+3/0 • Gustavo BRA 19+5/0 • Andrea Rispoli 9+4/0
Simone Sini 1+1/0 • Nenad Tomovic SRB 16/0
Midfield Andrea Bertolacci 10/3 • Manuel Coppola 1+13/1
Guillermo Giacomazzi URU 30+2/3 • Carlos Grossmuller URU 18+5/1
Djamel Mesbah ALG 29+5/2 • Gianni Munari 27+7/2
Ignacio Piatti ARG 14+11/3 • Giuseppe Vives 29+4/0
Forwards Ernesto Chevanton URU 3+11/2 • Daniele Corvia 12+18/6
David Di Michele 22+1/8 • Jeda BRA 22+3/5 • Edward Ofere NGA 6+5/3
Ruben Olivera URU 30+1/4
Coach Luigi De Canio

MILAN LEAGUE APPEARANCES/GOALS 2010-11
Goalkeepers Christian Abbiati 35 • Marco Amelia 3+1
Flavio Roma 0+1
Defenders Luca Antonini 18+4/0 • Daniele Bonera 15+1/0 • Didac
Vila ESP 1/0 • Marek Jankulovski CZE 3+2/0 • Nicola Legrottaglie 0+1/0
Alessandro Nesta 26/0 • Massimo Oddo 3+4/0 • Sokratis
Papastathopoulos GRE 3+2/0 • Thiago Silva 33/1
Mario Yepes COL 11+2/0 • Gianluca Zambrotta 15/0
Midfield Ignazio Abate 26+3/0 • Massimo Ambrosini 16+2/1 • Kevin
Prince Boateng GHA 18+8/3 • Urby Emanuelson NED 2+7/0
Mathieu Flamini FRA 14+8/2 • Gennaro Gattuso 28+3/2 • Alexander
Merkel GER 6/0 • Andrea Pirlo 12+5/1 • RonaldInho BRA 7+4/0
Clarence Seedorf NED 23+7/4 • Rodney Strasser SLE 1+2/1
Mark van Bommel NED 14/0

MILAN LEAGUE APPEARANCES/GOALS 2010-11
Cont'd
Forwards Giacomo Beretta 0+1/0 • Marco Borriello 1/0 • Antonio
Cassano 9+8/4 • Zlatan Ibrahimovic SWE 29/14 • Filippo Inzaghi 1+5/2
Nnamdi Oduamadi NGA 0+1/0 • Pato BRA 19+6/14
Robinho BRA 26+8/14
Coach Massimiliano Allegri (25/06/10)

NAPOLI 2010-11

	Day	Opponent	Res	Score	Comp	Scorers	Att
Aug	19	Elfsborg	W	1-0	ELpo	Lavezzi 45	33 534
Aug	26	Elfsborg	W	2-0	ELpo	Cavani 2 29 38	10 621
Aug	29	Fiorentina	D	1-1	SA	Cavani 7	25 025
Sep	12	Bari	D	2-2	SA	Cavani 30, Cannavaro 87	27 214
Sep	16	Utrecht	D	0-0	ELgK		25 897
Sep	19	Sampdoria	W	2-1	SA	Hamsik 84, Cavani 86	23 566
Sep	22	Chievo	L	1-3	SA	Cannavaro 9	46 037
Sep	26	Cesena	W	4-1	SA	Lavezzi 72, Hamsik 81p, Cavani 2 88 90	16 250
Sep	30	Steaua	D	3-3	ELgK	Vitale 44, Hamsik 73, Cavani 90	10 203
Oct	3	Roma	W	2-0	SA	Hamsik 72, OG 83	44 782
Oct	17	Catania	D	1-1	SA	Cavani 39	13 136
Oct	21	Liverpool	D	0-0	ELgK		52 910
Oct	25	Milan	L	1-2	SA	Lavezzi 78	53 901
Oct	31	Brescia	W	1-0	SA	Lavezzi 77	6 008
Nov	4	Liverpool	L	1-3	ELgK	Lavezzi 28	33 892
Nov	7	Parma	W	2-0	SA	Cavani 2 19 86	**26 931**
Nov	10	Cagliari	W	1-0	SA	Lavezzi 94+	15 000
Nov	14	Lazio	L	0-2	SA		24 487
Nov	21	Bologna	W	4-1	SA	Maggio 2, Hamsik 2 37 48, Cavani 74	39 626
Nov	28	Udinese	L	1-3	SA	Hamsik 58	15 087
Dec	2	Utrecht	D	3-3	ELgK	Cavani 3 5 42 70p	22 500
Dec	6	Palermo	W	1-0	SA	Maggio 95+	48 307
Dec	11	Genoa	W	1-0	SA	Hamsik 25	24 288
Dec	15	Steaua	W	1-0	ELgK	Cavani 90	40 631
Dec	19	Lecce	W	1-0	SA	Cavani 93+	44 113
Dec	6	Inter	L	1-3	SA	Pazienza 25	60 515
Jan	9	Juventus	W	3-0	SA	Cavani 3 20 26 53	**58 666**
Jan	15	Fiorentina	D	0-0	SA		49 443
Jan	18	Bologna	W	2-1	ICr5	Yebda 9, Lavezzi 23	33 806
Jan	23	Bari	W	2-0	SA	Lavezzi 38, Cavani 87	17 879
Jan	26	Inter	D	0-0	ICqf	L 4-5p	40 580
Jan	30	Sampdoria	W	4-0	SA	Cavani 3 17 45p 57, Hamsik 48	48 084
Feb	2	Chievo	L	0-2	SA		11 000
Feb	6	Cesena	W	2-0	SA	Cavani 13, Sosa 91+	34 565
Feb	12	Roma	W	2-0	SA	Cavani 2 49p 83	32 354
Feb	17	Villarreal	D	0-0	ELr2		47 529
Feb	20	Catania	W	1-0	SA	Zuniga 25	47 422
Feb	24	Villarreal	L	1-2	ELr2	Hamsik 18	21 061
Feb	28	Milan	L	0-3	SA		77 276
Mar	6	Brescia	D	0-0	SA		29 146
Mar	13	Parma	W	3-1	SA	Hamsik 52, Lavezzi 56, Maggio 87	16 273
Mar	20	Cagliari	W	2-1	SA	Cavani 2 49p 61	44 497
Apr	3	Lazio	W	4-3	SA	Dossena 60, Cavani 3 62 81p 88	57 155
Apr	10	Bologna	W	2-0	SA	Mascara 30, Hamsik 45p	34 092
Apr	17	Udinese	L	1-2	SA	Mascara 94+	56 757
Apr	21	Palermo	L	1-2	SA	Cavani 2p	26 778
Apr	30	Genoa	W	1-0	SA	Hamsik 83	52 495
May	8	Lecce	L	1-2	SA	Mascara 67	14 406
May	15	Inter	D	1-1	SA	Zuniga 45	57 400
May	22	Juventus	D	2-2	SA	Maggio 22, Lucarelli 71	23 389

3rd | Att: 866 561 • Av: 45 608 (-0.1%) • San Paolo 60 240 (75%)

PALERMO 2010-11

	Day	Opponent	Res	Score	Comp	Scorers	Att
Aug	19	Maribor	W	3-0	ELpo	Maccarone 37p, Hernandez 39, Pastore 77	28 416
Aug	26	Maribor	L	2-3	ELpo	Hernandez 2 62 68	12 200
Aug	29	Cagliari	D	0-0	SA		28 612
Sep	12	Brescia	L	2-3	SA	Pastore 23, Balzaretti 83	8 100
Sep	16	Sparta	L	2-3	ELgF	Maccarone 38, Hernandez 83	13 766
Sep	19	Inter	L	1-2	SA	Ilicic 28	27 291
Sep	23	Juventus	W	3-1	SA	Pastore 2, Ilicic 62, Bovo 85	20 607
Sep	26	Lecce	D	2-2	SA	Pinilla 53, Maccarone 90	22 378
Sep	30	Lausanne	W	1-0	ELgF	Migliaccio 79	9 772
Oct	3	Fiorentina	W	2-1	SA	Ilicic 20, Pastore 37	22 795
Oct	17	Bologna	W	4-1	SA	Pastore 17, Ilicic 24, Pinilla 47, Bacinovic 83	23 587
Oct	21	CSKA M'kva	L	0-3	ELgF		17 548
Oct	24	Udinese	L	1-2	SA	Pinilla 83	14 714
Oct	31	Lazio	L	0-1	SA		29 539
Nov	4	CSKA M'kva	L	1-3	ELgF	Maccarone 10	11 980
Nov	7	Genoa	W	1-0	SA	Pinilla 42	24 368
Nov	10	Milan	L	1-3	SA	Bacinovic 63	38 903
Nov	14	Catania	W	3-1	SA	Pastore 3 34 47 85	25 532
Nov	21	Cesena	W	2-1	SA	Ilicic 11, Miccoli 51	14 068
Nov	28	Roma	W	3-1	SA	Miccoli 20, Ilicic 61, Nocerino 65	**29 597**
Dec	2	Sparta	D	2-2	ELgF	Rigoni 23, Pinilla 60p	8 623
Dec	6	Napoli	L	0-1	SA		48 307
Dec	11	Parma	W	3-1	SA	Pinilla 51, Miccoli 61, OG 88	25 817
Dec	15	Lausanne	W	1-0	ELgF	Munoz 84	7 150
Dec	19	Bari	D	1-1	SA	Ilicic 45	17 000
Jan	6	Sampdoria	W	3-0	SA	Miccoli 37, Migliaccio 50, Maccarone 79	26 020
Jan	9	Chievo	D	0-0	SA		12 000
Jan	12	Chievo	W	1-0	ICr5	Miccoli 80p	6 602
Jan	16	Cagliari	L	1-3	SA	Pastore 50	8 000
Jan	22	Brescia	W	1-0	SA	Bovo 87	21 152
Jan	25	Parma	D	0-0	ICqf	W 5-4p	15 335
Jan	30	Inter	L	2-3	SA	Miccoli 5, Nocerino 36	58 000
Feb	2	Juventus	W	2-1	SA	Miccoli 7, Migliaccio 20	25 000
Feb	6	Lecce	W	4-2	SA	Miccoli 45, Pastore 57, Hernandez 60, Ilicic 62	9 176
Feb	13	Fiorentina	L	2-4	SA	Pastore 7, Nocerino 48	24 571
Feb	19	Bologna	L	0-1	SA		21 219
Feb	27	Udinese	L	0-7	SA		22 831
Mar	6	Lazio	L	0-2	SA		24 251
Mar	13	Genoa	L	0-1	SA		21 657
Mar	19	Milan	W	1-0	SA	Goian 10	25 116
Apr	3	Catania	L	0-4	SA		19 136
Apr	10	Cesena	D	2-2	SA	Kurtic 5, Pinilla 36	22 375
Apr	20	Roma	W	3-2	SA	Pinilla 43p, Hernandez 2 84 90	33 851
Apr	25	Milan	D	2-2	ICsf	Pastore 14, Hernandez 53	20 022
Apr	23	Napoli	W	2-1	SA	Balzaretti 37, Bovo 45p	26 778
May	1	Parma	L	1-3	SA	Pastore 56	14 315
May	7	Bari	W	2-1	SA	Miccoli 39, Bovo 53	**19 808**
May	10	Milan	W	2-1	ICsf	Migliaccio 57, Bovo 73p	33 414
May	15	Sampdoria	W	2-1	SA	Miccoli 45, Pinilla 86	24 221
May	22	Chievo	L	1-3	SA	Nocerino 15	20 888
May	29	Inter	L	1-3	ICf	Munoz 88	70 000

8th | Att: 471 260 • Av: 24 803 (-0.9%) • Renzo Barbera 37 242 (66%)

NAPOLI LEAGUE APPEARANCES/GOALS 2010-11

Goalkeepers Morgan De Sanctis 38

Defenders Salvatore Aronica 19+7/0 • Hugo Campagnaro ARG 30+1/0 • Paolo Cannavaro 31+1/2 • Cribari BRA 6+3/0 • Andrea Dossena 31+2/1 • Gianluca Grava 12+1/0 • Christian Maggio 33/4 • Fabiano Santacroce 10+1/0 • Victor Ruiz ESP 6/0 • Juan Zuniga COL 15+12/2

Midfield Manuele Blasi 1+1/0 • Walter Gargano URU 29+7/0 • Marek Hamsik SVK 36+1/11 • Raffaele Maiello 1+2/0 • Michele Pazienza 30+1/1 • Jose Sosa ARG 7+17/1 • Luigi Vitale 2+4/0 • Hassan Yebda ALG 15+14/0

Forwards Edinson Cavani URU 32+3/26 • Nicolao Dumitru 0+9/0 • Ezequiel Lavezzi ARG 29+2/6 • Cristiano Lucarelli 1+8/1 • Giuseppe Mascara 4+10/3

Coach Walter Mazzarri

PALERMO LEAGUE APPEARANCES/GOALS 2010-11

Goalkeepers Francesco Benussi 1 • Salvatore Sirigu 37

Defenders Sinisa Andelkovic SVN 7/0 • Federico Balzaretti 33/2 • Cesare Bovo 31+1/4 • Morris Carrozzieri 0+1/0 • Mattia Cassani 32/0 • Matteo Darmian 0+5/0 • Santiago Coroia ARG 2+1/0 • Dorin Goian ROU 12+4/1 • Ezequiel Munoz ARG 32+2/0

Midfield Afriyie Acquah GHA 3+8/0 • Armin Bacinovic SVN 29+4/2 • Josip Ilicic SVN 30+4/8 • Joao Pedro BRA 0+1/0 • Pajtim Kasami SUI 4+10/0 • Jasmin Kurtic 2+2/1 • Fabio Liverani 4+8/0 • Giulio Migliaccio 35/2 • Antonio Nocerino 38/8 • Javier Pastore ARG 34+1/11 • Nicola Rigoni 1+3/0

Forwards Abel Hernandez URU 12+10/3 • Massimo Maccarone 3+15/2 • Fabrizio Miccoli 17+4/9 • Michele Paolucci 0+2/0 • Mauricio Pinilla CHI 13+9/8

Coach Delio Rossi • Serse Cosmi (28/02/11) • Delio Rossi (3/04/11)

PARMA 2010–11

	Opp		Res	Comp	Scorers	Att
Sep	29 Brescia	W	2-0	SA	Bojinov [11], Morrone [45]	12 630
	12 Catania	L	1-2	SA	Giovinco [91+]	11 208
	19 Genoa	D	1-1	SA	Zaccardo [72]	13 619
	22 Lecce	D	1-1	SA	Crespo [69]	7 957
	26 Fiorentina	L	0-2	SA		21 126
Oct	2 Milan	L	0-1	SA		**19 615**
	17 Cesena	D	1-1	SA	Zaccardo [28]	14 292
	24 Roma	D	0-0	SA		13 937
	31 Chievo	D	0-0	SA		13 562
Nov	7 Napoli	L	0-2	SA		26 931
	11 Sampdoria	W	1-0	SA	Bojinov [84]	16 009
	14 Bari	W	1-0	SA	Candreva [33]	15 500
	21 Lazio	D	1-1	SA	Crespo [23]	13 986
	28 Inter	L	2-5	SA	Crespo 2 [4 36]	49 787
Dec	5 Udinese	W	2-1	SA	Crespo 2 [24p 55]	12 223
	11 Palermo	L	1-3	SA	Lucarelli [7]	25 817
	14 Fiorentina	W	2-1	ICr4	Crespo 2 [115 117]	3 517
	19 Bologna	D	0-0	SA		13 265
	6 Juventus	W	4-1	SA	Giovinco 2 [41 47], Crespo [62], Palladino [92+]	23 873
Jan	9 Cagliari	L	1-2	SA	Giovinco [54]	12 185
	16 Brescia	L	0-2	SA		9 980
	22 Catania	W	2-0	SA	Candreva [57], Giovinco [62]	12 316
	25 Genoa	L	1-3	SA	Crespo [33]	24 000
	30 Palermo	D	0-0	ICqf	L 4-5p	15 335
Feb	2 Lecce	L	0-1	SA		**11 975**
	6 Fiorentina	D	1-1	SA	Amauri [15]	13 588
	12 Milan	L	0-4	SA		46 119
	20 Cesena	D	2-2	SA	Crespo [64p], Palladino [89]	14 095
	27 Roma	D	2-2	SA	Amauri 2 [74 79]	28 499
Mar	6 Chievo	D	0-0	SA		10 536
	13 Napoli	L	1-3	SA	Palladino [29]	16 273
	20 Sampdoria	W	1-0	SA	Zaccardo [65]	21 895
	3 Bari	L	1-2	SA	Amauri [80]	18 195
Apr	10 Lazio	L	0-2	SA		31 208
	16 Inter	W	2-0	SA	Giovinco [35], Amauri [86]	17 504
	23 Udinese	W	2-0	SA	Amauri 2 [13 91+]	19 518
	1 Palermo	W	3-1	SA	Dzemaili 2, Modesto [18], Candreva [89]	14 315
May	8 Bologna	D	0-0	SA		19 879
	15 Juventus	W	1-0	SA	Giovinco [64]	17 259
	22 Cagliari	D	1-1	SA	Bojinov [34]	5 000

12th Att: 276 551 • Av: 14 555 (-18.2%) • Ennio Tardini 27 906 (52%)

ROMA 2010–11

	Opp		Res	Comp	Scorers	Att
Aug	21 Inter	L	1-3	SC	Riise [21]	65 860
	28 Cesena	D	0-0	SA		33 000
	11 Cagliari	L	1-5	SA	De Rossi [18]	18 000
	15 Bayern M	L	0-2	CLgE		66 000
Sep	19 Bologna	D	2-2	SA	Borriello [8], OG [59]	29 599
	22 Brescia	L	1-2	SA	Borriello [84]	12 000
	25 Inter	W	1-0	SA	Vucinic [92+]	45 109
	28 Cluj	W	2-1	CLgE	Mexes [69], Borriello [71]	30 252
	3 Napoli	L	0-2	SA		44 782
Oct	6 Genoa	W	2-1	SA	Borriello [34], Brighi [53]	30 958
	19 Basel	L	1-3	CLgE	Borriello [21]	22 365
	24 Parma	D	0-0	SA		13 937
	30 Lecce	W	2-0	SA	Burdisso.N [62], Vucinic [76]	36 692
	3 Basel	W	3-2	CLgE	Menez [16], Totti [26p], Greco [76]	36 375
Nov	7 Lazio	W	2-0	SA	Borriello [52p], Vucinic [87p]	52 121
	10 Fiorentina	W	3-2	SA	Fabio [45], Borriello [51], Perrotta [77]	28 532
	23 Juventus	D	1-1	SA	Totti [45p]	23 869
	20 Udinese	W	2-0	SA	Menez [24], Borriello [56]	28 391
	23 Bayern M	W	3-2	CLgE	Borriello [49], De Rossi [81], Totti [84p]	42 789
	28 Palermo	L	1-3	SA	Totti [92+]	29 597
Dec	4 Chievo	D	2-2	SA	Fabio 2 [26 44]	11 447
	8 Cluj	D	1-1	CLgE	Borriello [21]	12 800
	12 Bari	W	1-0	SA	Juan [30]	28 187
	18 Milan	W	1-0	SA	Borriello [69]	53 769
	6 Catania	W	4-2	SA	Borriello 2 [5 47], Vucinic 2 [86 93+]	32 148
Jan	9 Sampdoria	L	1-2	SA	Vucinic [18]	22 802
	16 Cesena	W	1-0	SA	OG [88]	19 834
	19 Lazio	W	2-1	ICr5	Boriello [53p], Fabio [77]	40 637
	22 Cagliari	W	3-0	SA	Totti [21p], Perrotta [70], Menez [92+]	28 249
	27 Juventus	W	2-0	ICqf	Vucinic [65], Taddei [90]	18 300
Feb	2 Brescia	D	1-1	SA	Borriello [58]	**26 590**
	6 Inter	L	3-5	SA	Fabio [13], Vucinic [75], Loria [81]	62 344
	12 Napoli	L	0-2	SA		32 354
	16 Shakhtar	L	2-3	CLr2	OG [26], Menez [61]	35 873
	20 Genoa	L	3-4	SA	Mexes [6], Burdisso [16], Totti [51]	22 180
	23 Bologna	W	1-0	SA	De Rossi [45]	19 663
	27 Parma	D	2-2	SA	Totti [19p], Juan [36]	28 499
Mar	4 Lecce	W	2-1	SA	Vucinic [32], Pizarro [90p]	10 488
	8 Shakhtar	L	0-3	CLr2		46 543
	13 Lazio	W	2-0	SA	Totti 2 [70 92+p]	48 955
	20 Fiorentina	D	2-2	SA	Totti 2 [27p 52]	23 634
	3 Juventus	L	0-2	SA		50 952
Apr	9 Udinese	W	2-1	SA	Totti 2 [57p 94+]	24 981
	16 Palermo	L	2-3	SA	Totti [20p], Vucinic [92+]	33 851
	19 Inter	L	0-1	ICsf		23 979
	23 Chievo	W	1-0	SA	Perrotta [4]	27 319
	1 Bari	W	3-2	SA	Totti 2 [30 57p], Rosi [94+]	1 592
	7 Milan	D	0-0	SA		**58 083**
May	11 Inter	D	1-1	ICsf	Borriello [85]	33 094
	15 Catania	L	1-2	SA	Loria [14]	19 083
	22 Sampdoria	W	3-1	SA	Totti [30], Vucinic [70], Borriello [86]	28 944

6th Att: 656 412 • Av: 34 548 (-12.3%) • Olimpico 72 698 (47%)

PARMA LEAGUE APPEARANCES/GOALS 2010-11
Goalkeepers Antonio Mirante 36 • Nicola Pavarini 2+1
Defenders Angelo BRA 10+11/0 • Luca Antonelli 12/0 • Hernan Dellafiore ARG 0+1/0 • Rolf Feltscher VEN 2+1/0 • Alessandro Lucarelli 32/1 • Francesco Modesto 13+2/1 • Obiora Nwankwo NGA 0+1/0 • Massimo Paci 18+1/0 • Gabriel Paletta ARG 26+1/0 • Marco Pisano 2+3/0 • Cristian Zaccardo 34/3
Midfield Antonio Candreva 23+8/3 • Manuel Coppola 0+1/0 • Blerim Dzemaili SUI 26+4/1 • Filipe Oliveira POR 0+1/0 • Daniele Galloppa 5+6/0 • Massimo Gobbi 30+4/0 • Fernando Marques ESP 12+1/0 • Stefano Morrone 30+4/1 • Toni Calvo ESP 0+3/0 • Francesco Valiani 31+4/0 • Ze Eduardo BRA 0+2/0
Forwards Amauri 11/7 • Valeri Bojinov BUL 13+18/3 • Hernan Crespo ARG 16+13/9 • Gregoire Defrel FRA 0+1/0 • Sebastian Giovinco 28+2/7 • Raffaele Palladino 6+5/3 • Alberto Paloschi 0+1/0
Coach Pasquale Marino (2/06/10) • Franco Colomba (5/04/11)

ROMA LEAGUE APPEARANCES/GOALS 2010-11
Goalkeepers Doni BRA 14+2 • Julio Sergio BRA 18 • Bogdan Lobont ROU 6
Defenders Guillermo Burdisso ARG 0+2/0 • Nicolas Burdisso ARG 28/2 • Marco Cassetti 31+1/0 • Paolo Castellini 4+2/0 • Cicinho BRA 3+3/0 • Juan BRA 29+2/2 • Simone Loria 2+4/2 • Philippe Mexes FRA 21+1/1 • John Arne Riise NOR 32/0
Midfield Matteo Brighi 13+12/1 • Daniele De Rossi 28/2 • Fabio Simplicio BRA 18+6/4 • Alessandro Florenzi 0+1/0 • Leandro Greco 8+5/0 • Simone Perrotta 22+3/3 • David Pizarro CHI • Aleandro Rosi 7+9/1 • Taddei BRA 12+11/0
Forwards Adriano BRA 2+3/0 • Marco Borriello 25+9/11 • Gianluca Caprari 0+2/0 • Julio Baptista BRA 0+7/0 • Jeremy Menez FRA 23+9/2 • Stefano Okaka 0+4/0 • Francesco Totti 29+3/15 • Mirko Vucinic MNE 22+6/10
Coach Claudio Raneiri • Vincenzo Montella (21/02/11)

SAMPDORIA 2010–11

	Date	Opponent	Res	Score	Comp	Scorers	Att
Aug	18	W Bremen	L	1-3	CLpo	Pazzini 90	25 276
	24	W Bremen	W	3-2	CLpo	Pazzini 2 8 13, Cassano 85	25 574
	29	Lazio	W	2-0	SA	Cassano 59p, Guberti 71	21 504
Sep	12	Juventus	D	3-3	SA	Pozzi 2 36 73, Cassano 64	23 949
	16	PSV	D	1-1	ELgl	Cacciatore 25	17 500
	19	Napoli	L	1-2	SA	Cassano 78p	23 566
	22	Cagliari	D	0-0	SA		10 000
	26	Udinese	D	0-0	SA		21 478
	30	Debreceni	W	1-0	ELgl	Pazzini 18p	12 159
Oct	3	Bologna	D	1-1	SA	OG 45	15 431
	17	Fiorentina	W	2-1	SA	Ziegler 81, Cassano 81	22 738
	21	M Kharkov	L	1-2	ELgl	Koman 32	34 580
	24	Inter	D	1-1	SA	Guberti 62	56 415
	31	Cesena	W	1-0	SA	Pazzini 92+	14 884
Nov	4	M Kharkov	D	0-0	ELgl		13 259
	7	Catania	D	0-0	SA		20 778
	11	Parma	L	0-1	SA		16 009
	14	Chievo	D	0-0	SA		20 526
	21	Lecce	W	3-2	SA	Pazzini 3 8 40p 88	6 609
	27	Milan	D	1-1	SA	Pazzini 60	26 820
Dec	1	PSV	L	1-2	ELgl	Pazzini 45	12 131
	5	Bari	W	3-0	SA	Pazzini 17p, Guberti 2 56 61	20 877
	12	Brescia	L	0-1	SA		11 043
	16	Debreceni	L	0-2	ELgl		5 500
	6	Palermo	L	0-3	SA		26 020
	9	Roma	W	2-1	SA	Pozzi 57, Guberti 84	22 802
Jan	6	Lazio	L	0-1	SA		21 833
	19	Udinese	D	2-2	ICr5	Macheda 32, Pazzini 109p, W 5-4p	5 082
	23	Juventus	L	0-3	SA		25 933
	26	Milan	L	1-2	ICqf	Guberti 51	11 458
	30	Napoli	L	0-4	SA		48 084
Feb	2	Cagliari	L	0-1	SA		21 000
	2	Udinese	L	0-2	SA		14 383
	13	Bologna	W	3-1	SA	Palombo 8, Gastaldello 11, Maccarone 15	20 924
	16	Genoa	L	0-1	SA		25 001
	20	Fiorentina	D	0-0	SA		21 723
	27	Inter	L	0-2	SA		24 417
Mar	6	Cesena	L	2-3	SA	Vota 83, Maccarone 90p	21 215
	13	Catania	L	0-1	SA		9 283
	20	Parma	L	0-1	SA		21 895
	3	Chievo	D	0-0	SA		14 456
Apr	10	Lecce	L	1-2	SA	Maccarone 69	26 531
	16	Milan	L	0-3	SA		60 028
	23	Bari	W	1-0	SA	Pozzi 59p	14 881
May	1	Brescia	D	3-3	SA	Pozzi 55, Tissone 63, Mannini 91+	25 555
	8	Genoa	L	1-2	SA	Pozzi 66	29 465
	15	Palermo	L	1-2	SA	Biabiany 50	24 221
	22	Roma	L	1-3	SA	Mannini 26	28 944

18th Att: 437 781 • Av: 23 041 (-8.2%) • Luigi Ferraris 36 685 (62%)

UDINESE 2010–11

	Date	Opponent	Res	Score	Comp	Scorers	Att
Aug	28	Genoa	L	0-1	SA		14 500
	11	Inter	L	1-2	SA	Flores 31	62 014
Sep	19	Juventus	L	0-4	SA		20 757
	22	Bologna	L	1-2	SA	Di Natale 9	14 220
	26	Sampdoria	D	0-0	SA		21 478
	2	Cesena	W	1-0	SA	Benatia 93+	13 968
	17	Brescia	W	1-0	SA	Corradi 80	5 397
Oct	24	Palermo	W	2-1	SA	Benatia 9, Di Natale 54p	14 714
	27	Padova	W	4-0	ICr3	Flores 21, Corradi 2 26 57, Angella 43	3 000
	31	Bari	W	2-0	SA	Sanchez 16, Isla 60	15 701
	7	Cagliari	D	1-1	SA	Flores 44	14 056
	10	Catania	L	0-1	SA		12 418
Nov	14	Lecce	W	4-0	SA	Di Natale 3 11 24 40, Flores 56	2 817
	20	Roma	L	0-2	SA		28 391
	24	Lecce	W	2-1	ICr4	Corradi 78p, Flores 119	2 733
	28	Napoli	W	3-1	SA	Di Natale 3 16p 45 57	15 087
Dec	5	Parma	L	1-2	SA	Di Natale 35	12 223
	11	Fiorentina	W	2-1	SA	Armero 63, Di Natale 80	14 107
	19	Lazio	L	2-3	SA	Sanchez 50, Denis 61	20 644
	6	Chievo	W	2-0	SA	Sanchez 14, Di Natale 25	14 000
	9	Milan	D	4-4	SA	Di Natale 2 35 66, Sanchez 53, Denis 89	39 405
Jan	16	Genoa	W	4-2	SA	Armero 27, Di Natale 56, Denis 70, Denis 90	21 448
	19	Sampdoria	D	2-2	ICr5	Isla 90, Denis 91. L 4-5p	5 082
	23	Inter	W	3-1	SA	Zapata 21, Di Natale 25, Domizzi 09	26 036
	30	Juventus	W	2-1	SA	Zapata 67, Sanchez 85	22 000
Feb	2	Bologna	D	1-1	SA	Domizzi 76	14 000
	5	Sampdoria	W	2-0	SA	Sanchez 18, Di Natale 39	14 383
	13	Cesena	W	3-0	SA	Di Natale 2 41 75, Gokhan 69	16 704
	20	Brescia	D	0-0	SA		14 000
	27	Palermo	W	7-0	SA	Di Natale 3 10 41 60p, Sanchez 4 19 28 42 48	22 831
Mar	6	Bari	W	1-0	SA	Di Natale 76p	15 904
	13	Cagliari	W	4-0	SA	Benatia 43, Sanchez 44, Di Natale 2 48 54	10 000
	20	Catania	W	2-0	SA	Gokhan 22, Di Natale 74p	16 000
	3	Lecce	L	0-2	SA		10 196
Apr	9	Roma	L	1-2	SA	Di Natale 88	24 981
	17	Napoli	W	2-1	SA	Gokhan 55, Denis 61	56 757
	20	Parma	L	0-2	SA		19 518
	1	Fiorentina	L	2-5	SA		24 604
May	8	Lazio	W	2-1	SA	Di Natale 2 35 42	22 044
	15	Chievo	W	2-0	SA	Isla 28, Asamoah 75	19 031
	22	Milan	D	0-0	SA		29 644

4th Att: 320 516 • Av: 16 869 (-0.9%) • Friuli 41 652 (40%)

SAMPDORIA LEAGUE APPEARANCES/GOALS 2010-11
Goalkeepers Gianluca Curci 35 • Angelo da Costa BRA 3+1
Defenders Pietro Accardi 4+5/0 • Fabrizio Cacciatore 5/0 • Daniele Gastaldello 28+1/1 • Stefano Lucchini 26/0 • Gilberto Martinez CRC 8+1/0 • Massimo Volta 20+5/1 • Luciano Zauri 26+1/0
Midfield Doniolo Doccena 17+5/0 • Stefano Guberti 29+7/5 • Vladimir Koman 14+12/0 • Zsolt Laczko HUN 7+2/0 • Daniele Mannini 18+12/2 • Pedro Obiang ESP 0+4/0 • Marco Padalino SUI 0+1/0 • Angelo Palombo 34/1 • Andrea Poli 13+8/0 • Fernando Tissone ARG 20+2/1 • Reto Ziegler SUI 32+2/1
Forwards Jonathan Biabiany FRA 8+8/1 • Antonio Cassano 7/4 Bruno Fornaroli URU 0+1/0 • Massimo Maccarone 15+2/3 • Federico Macheda 3+11/0 • Guido Marilungo 8+2/0 • Giampaolo Pazzini 18+1/6 Nicola Pozzi 14+8/6 • Simone Zaza 0+2/0
Coach Domenico Di Carlo (26/05/10) • Alberto Cavasin (7/03/11)

UDINESE LEAGUE APPEARANCES/GOALS 2010-11
Goalkeepers Emanuele Belardi 3 • Samir Handanovic SVN 35
Defenders Gabrielle Angella 1+7/0 • Mehdi Benatia FRA 34/3 • Andrea Coda 16+6/0 • Juan Cuadrado COL 3+6/0 • Maurizio Domizzi 28+2/2 • Mauricio Isla CHI 34/2 • Giovanni Pasquale 10+7/0 • Cristian Zapata COL 35/2
Midfield Almen Abdi SUI 6+13/0 • Emmanuel Agyemang GHA 2+6/0 • Pablo Armero COL 29+2/2 • Kwadwo Asamoah GHA 37+1/2 • Cristian Battocchio 0+1/0 • Joel Ekstrand SWE 0+1/0 • Gokhan Inler SUI 35/3 • Giampiero Pinzi 30+4/1
Forwards Bernardo Corradi 0+18/1 • German Denis ARG 8+17/4 Antonio Di Natale 35+4/28 • Antonio Floro Flores 10+2/3 Alexis Sanchez CHI 27+14/12 • Matej Vydra CZE 0+2/0
Coach Francesco Guidolin (24/05/10)

JAM – JAMAICA

FIFA/COCA-COLA WORLD RANKING

'93	'94	'95	'96	'97	'98	'99	'00	'01	'02	'03	'04	'05	'06	'07	'08	'09	'10	'11	'12
80	96	56	32	39	33	41	48	53	51	46	49	42	57	97	65	81	58	54	

						2011							High	Low	Av
Jan	Feb	Mar	Apr	May	Jun	Jul	Aug	Sep	Oct	Nov	Dec			High	Low	Av
59	59	48	64	55	38	44	43	45	50	47	54			27	116	58

In May 2010 the area of Tivoli Gardens in the Jamaican capital of Kingston came to world attention when 70 people were killed as security forces sought to capture drug-lord Christopher Coke. A year later former prime minister Edward Seaga, the president of local football team Tivoli Gardens FC, dedicated his team's league and cup double to the dead and injured. Coached by Glendon 'Admiral' Bailey, Tivoli beat St George's 3-0 in the Cup Final a week after having beaten Boys' Town 1-0 in a winner-takes-all final match of the season. That secured a record-equalling fifth league title for Tivoli Gardens but there remains a reluctance for the top Jamaican clubs to test themselves against the elite of the Caribbean with 2010 champions Harbour View declining to take part in the 2011 CFU Club Championship. There was no such reluctance on the part of the national team. Having been crowned Caribbean champions in December 2010 they represented the region with some style at the 2011 CONCACAF Gold Cup in the USA. They won all three of their first round games against Grenada, Guatemala and Honduras, without conceding a goal to qualify for a quarter-final against the hosts. Unfortunately for Jamaica, the USA played their best game of the tournament to win 2-0 and but for keeper Donovan Rickets it may have been more.

FIFA WORLD CUP RECORD

1930-1962 DNE 1966-1970 DNQ 1974 DNE 1978 DNQ 1982 DNE 1986-1994 DNQ **1998** 22 r1 2002-2010 DNQ

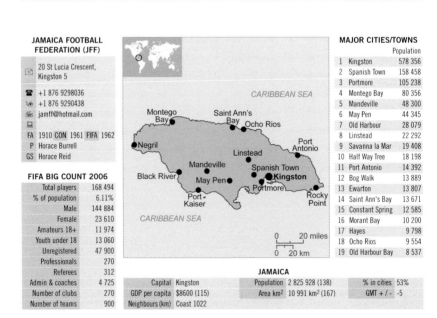

JAMAICA FOOTBALL FEDERATION (JFF)

20 St Lucia Crescent, Kingston 5

☎ +1 876 9298036
📠 +1 876 9290438
✉ jamff@hotmail.com

FA 1910 CON 1961 FIFA 1962
P Horace Burrell
GS Horace Reid

FIFA BIG COUNT 2006

Total players	168 494
% of population	6.11%
Male	144 884
Female	23 610
Amateurs 18+	11 974
Youth under 18	13 060
Unregistered	47 900
Professionals	270
Referees	312
Admin & coaches	4 725
Number of clubs	270
Number of teams	900

MAJOR CITIES/TOWNS

		Population
1	Kingston	578 356
2	Spanish Town	158 458
3	Portmore	105 238
4	Montego Bay	80 356
5	Mandeville	48 300
6	May Pen	44 345
7	Old Harbour	28 079
8	Linstead	22 292
9	Savanna la Mar	19 408
10	Half Way Tree	18 198
11	Port Antonio	14 392
12	Bog Walk	13 889
13	Ewarton	13 807
14	Saint Ann's Bay	13 671
15	Constant Spring	12 585
16	Morant Bay	10 200
17	Hayes	9 798
18	Ocho Rios	9 554
19	Old Harbour Bay	8 537

JAMAICA

Capital Kingston	Population 2 825 928 (138)	% in cities 53%
GDP per capita $8600 (115)	Area km² 10 991 km² (167)	GMT + / - -5
Neighbours (km) Coast 1022		

RECENT INTERNATIONAL MATCHES PLAYED BY JAMAICA

2008	Opponents	Score		Venue	Comp	Scorers	Att	Referee
3-12	Barbados	W	2-1	Kingston	CCr1	Austin [76], Shelton [82]	20 000	Aguilar SLV
5-12	Grenada	W	4-0	Montego Bay	CCr1	Vernan [6], Shelton [18], Williams [53], Phillips [78]	4 000	Moreno PAN
7-12	Trinidad and Tobago	D	1-1	Treawny	CCr1	Vernan [46]	20 000	Moreno PAN
11-12	Guadeloupe †	W	2-0	Kingston	CCsf	Thompson [11], Shelton [57]	23 000	Aguilar SLV
14-12	Grenada	W	2-0	Kingston	CCf	Shelton 2 [16p 70p]	22 000	Brizan TRI
2009								
11-02	Nigeria	D	0-0	London	Fr		8 000	Dean ENG
23-05	Haiti	D	2-2	Fort Lauderdale	Fr	Addlery [29], Stewart [88]	12 000	Marrufo USA
30-05	El Salvador	D	0-0	Washington DC	Fr		30 313	Prus USA
7-06	Panama	W	3-2	Kingston	Fr	Johnson [44], Hodges [50], Daley [90]	12 000	Whittaker CAY
28-06	Cayman Islands	W	4-1	Grand Cayman	Fr	Bayliss [22], Wolfe [43], Daley [68], Morrison [82]	900	Holder CAY
3-07	Canada	L	0-1	Carson	GCr1		27 000	Vaughn USA
7-07	Costa Rica	L	0-1	Columbus	GCr1		7 059	Marrufo USA
10-07	El Salvador	W	1-0	Miami	GCr1	Cummings [69]	17 269	Hospedales TRI
12-08	Ecuador	D	0-0	New Jersey	Fr		21 360	Prus USA
16-08	St Kitts and Nevis	W	1-0	Basseterre	Fr	Hodges [55]	5 000	Willett SKN
17-11	South Africa	D	0-0	Bloemfontein	Fr		15 000	Andria'harisoa MAD
2010								
31-01	Canada	W	1-0	Kingston	Fr	Shelton [67]	18 000	Hospedales TRI
10-02	Argentina	L	1-2	Mar Del Plata	Fr	Johnson [46]	20 000	Rivera PER
28-04	South Africa	L	0-2	Offenbach	Fr		562	Sippel GER
11-08	Trinidad and Tobago	W	3-1	Macoya	Fr	Richards [7], Austin [30p], Bryan [52]	4 500	Taylor BRB
5-09	Costa Rica	W	1-0	Kingston	Fr	Johnson [66]	15 000	Brizan TRI
7-09	Peru	L	1-2	Fort Lauderdale	Fr	Cummings [18]	5 217	Vaughn USA
10-10	Trinidad and Tobago	W	1-0	Kingston	Fr	Richards [19p]	7 000	Archundia MEX
17-11	Costa Rica	D	0-0	Fort Lauderdale	Fr		4 000	Renso USA
27-11	Antigua and Barbuda	W	3-1	Riviere-Pilote	CCr1	Shelton 2 [14 37], Richards [40]	3 000	Wijngaarde SUR
29-11	Guadeloupe †	W	2-0	Riviere-Pilote	CCr1	Francis [53], Johnson [93+]	3 000	Lopez GUA
1-12	Guyana	W	4-0	Riviere-Pilote	CCr1	Richards [42], Morgan 2 [49 75], Vernan [90]	3 000	Cruc CRC
3-12	Grenada	W	2-1	Fort de France	CCsf	Richards [7], Smith [96]	4 000	Taylor BRB
5-12	Guadeloupe †	D	1-1	Riviere-Pilote	CCf	Cummings [32]. W 5-4p	4 000	Wijngaarde SUR
2011								
25-03	Venezuela	L	0-2	Montego Bay	Fr		6 000	Wijngaarde SUR
29-03	El Salvador	W	3-2	San Salvador	Fr	Dane Richards 2 [24 26], Omar Cummings [53]	15 000	Rodas GUA
6-06	Grenada	W	4-0	Carson	GCr1	Luton Shelton [21], Ryan Johnson [39], Demar Phillips [79], Omar Daley [84]	21 550	Toledo USA
10-06	Guatemala	W	2-0	Miami	GCr1	Demar Phillips 2 [65 77]	18 057	Quesada CRC
13-06	Honduras	W	1-0	Harrison	GCr1	Ryan Johnson [35]	25 000	Aguilar SLV
19-06	USA	L	0-2	Washington DC	GCqf		45 424	Rodriguez.M MEX
10-08	China PR	L	0-1	Hefei	Fr		60 000	Lee Min Hu KOR
2-09	Ecuador	L	2-5	Quito	Fr	Omar Cummings [55], Demar Phillips [66]	6 000	Buitriago COL
6-09	Colombia	L	0-2	Fort Lauderdale	Fr		8 000	Dellavie USA
11-10	Honduras	L	1-2	La Ceiba	Fr	Demar Phillips [45]	18 000	Moreno PAN

Fr = Friendly match • CC = Digicel Caribbean Cup • GC = CONCACAF Gold Cup • WC = FIFA World Cup
q = qualifier • r1 = first round group • qf = quarter-final • † Not a full international

JAMAICA NATIONAL TEAM HISTORICAL RECORDS

Caps	**120** - Ian Goodison 1996- • **109** - Ricardo Gardner 1997-2009 • **107** - Durrant Brown 1984-1998 • **105** - Theodore Whitmore 1993-2005
Goals	**31** - Luton Shelton 2004- • **28** - Paul Young 1993-98 • **27** - Onandi Lowe 1994-2004 • **24** - Theodore Whitmore 1993-2005 • **19** - Walter Boyd 1991-2001
Past Coaches	Geoffrey Maxwell 1989-90 • Carl Brown 1990-94 • Rene Simoes BRA 1994-2000 • Sebastiao Lazaroni BRA 2000 • Clovis De Oliveira BRA 2000-01 • Carl Brown 2001-04 • Sebastian Lazaroni BRA 2004 • Wendell Downswell 2004-06 • Carl Brown 2006 • Bora Milutinovic 2006-07 • Theodore Whitmore 2007-08 • Rene Simoes BRA 2008 • Theodore Whitmore 2008 • John Barnes ENG 2008-09 • Theodore Whitmore 2009-

JAMAICA 2010–11

DIGICEL PREMIER LEAGUE

	Pl	W	D	L	F	A	Pts	Tivoli G'ns	Boys' Town	Harbour V	Waterhouse	Portmore U	Village Utd	Reno	Sporting	Arnett G'ns	Humble L	St George's	Benfica
Tivoli Gardens	38	20	12	6	52	27	**72**		0-2 1-0	1-0 0-0	1-1 1-0	1-1 1-1	4-0 0-0	2-1 1-1	0-1 1-0	1-1	1-0	3-0 2-1	5-0
Boys' Town	38	19	11	8	39	28	**68**	1-0 0-1		2-1 1-2	1-1 0-2	1-1 1-1	0-0 1-2	1-0 0-0	0-1 0-0	0-2	2-1	4-2 2-0	1-1
Harbour View	38	17	10	11	43	28	**61**	3-2 0-0	5-1 0-0		1-1 1-0	1-0 1-0	0-1 4-0	1-0	0-0	0-1 1-0	1-0 2-0	2-0	0-1 3-1
Waterhouse	38	14	9	15	38	35	**51**	1-0 1-2	0-1 0-2	1-0 0-1		1-1 1-0	2-2 0-0	1-0 2-1	0-1	2-0 1-1	1-0	3-1 0-1	4-1 4-0
Portmore United	38	12	12	14	31	34	**48**	2-0 0-0	0-1 2-0	0-0 0-0	1-0 1-0		3-0 0-2	2-1	1-0	0-0 0-1	2-1 0-3	1-0	3-0
Village United	38	12	11	15	43	49	**47**	1-1 1-3	1-2 0-1	2-0 3-0	2-0 3-2	1-1 5-1		0-1	0-3 1-1	2-2 0-0	0-1 2-1	0-1	1-2
Reno	38	13	11	14	39	37	**50**	1-0	0-0	1-2 2-1	1-1	0-1 1-2	1-1 0-3		1-1	0-0	2-0 2-0	2-1 1-2	4-1
Sporting Central Acad.	38	11	14	13	39	36	**47**	1-2	1-1	0-1 2-2	0-2 0-0	0-1 1-1	4-3	0-1 1-1		3-0 4-0	1-1 2-4	1-1 1-1	0-0 0-3
Arnett Gardens	38	11	14	13	38	36	**47**	0-1 2-2	1-0 1-1	0-0	3-1	2-1	1-0	0-3 1-1	0-2 2-0		1-1 0-0	0-0 0-1	1-0 1-2 0
Humble Lions	38	12	10	16	35	32	**46**	1-1 0-3	0-1 0-1	1-1	1-2 2-0	0-1	3-0	1-1 0-1	1-0 0-1	0-0 1		2-0 3-1	1-0 0-2
St George's	38	13	7	18	29	41	**46**	0-1	1-0	1-2 0-0	1-0	1-1 1-0	0-1 0-1	2-2 0-0	1-0 0-1	0-2 0-1 0-0	0		0-1 1-1
Benfica	38	10	7	21	34	77	**37**	1-3 2-3	2-1 1-1	0-4	0-0	2-1 0-1	2-2 0-0	3-2 0-1	1-2 0-1	1-2 1-0	1-0 7-2	1-1 2	

29/08/2010 – 1/05/2011 • Top scorer: **17** – Kirk Ramsey, Arnett Gardens

JFF FLOW CHAMPIONS CUP 2010–11

Round of 16		Quarter–finals		Semi–finals		Final	
Tivoli Gardens	2 3p						
Harbour View	2 1p	**Tivoli Gardens** *	1				
Monymusk	0	Fraziers Whip	0				
Fraziers Whip				**Tivoli Gardens** *	1		
Arnett Gardens	1			Boys' Town	0		
Downs	0	Arnett Gardens	0				
Humble Lions		**Boys' Town** *	1				
Boys' Town						**Tivoli Gardens**	3
Sandals Whitehouse	2					St George's	0
Montpelier	0	**Sandals Whitehouse** *	1 4p				
Benfica	1 1p	Santos	1 1p			**CUP FINAL**	
Santos	1 4p			Sandals Whitehouse	0		
Portmore United	4			**St George's** *	3	Tony Spaulding Sports Complex	
Sporting Central Acad.	2	Portmore United	0			8-05-2011	
Waterhouse	2 1p	**St George's** *	1			Scorers - Keammar Daley [43], Jameel	
St George's	2 4p				* Home team	Thompson [89], Navion Boyd [90]	

MEDALS TABLE

		Overall			League		Cup		City/Town
		G	S	B	G	S	G	S	
1	Portmore United (ex Hazard Utd)	8	6		4	3	4	3	Portmore
	Tivoli Gardens	8	6		5	4	3	2	Kingston
3	Harbour View	7	7		3	5	4	2	Kingston
4	Boys' Town	5	5		3	4	2	1	Kingston
5	Reno	5	3		3	3	2		Savannah del Mar
6	Santos	5	1		5	1			Kingston
7	Waterhouse	4	3		2	2	2	1	Kingston
8	Arnett Gardens	3	5		3	4		1	Kingston
9	Seba United	3	4		2	4	1		Montego Bay
10	Wadadah	2	2		2			2	Montego Bay
11	Violet Kickers	2	1		2			1	Montego Bay
12	Olympic Gardens	2					2		Kingston
13	Cavalier	1	3		1	3			Kingston
14	Jamaica Defence Force	1			1				Kingston
	Naggo's Head	1			1		2		Portmore
16	Black Lions		1		1				
	Constant Spring		1		1				Constant Spring
	Humble Lions		1				1		Clarendon
	Rivoli United		1				1		Spanish Town
	St George's		1		1				
	Thunderbolts		1		1				
	Village United		1				1		Falmouth

JOR – JORDAN

FIFA/COCA-COLA WORLD RANKING

'93	'94	'95	'96	'97	'98	'99	'00	'01	'02	'03	'04	'05	'06	'07	'08	'09	'10	'11	'12
87	113	143	146	124	126	115	105	99	77	47	40	86	95	120	124	111	104	82	

						2011									
Jan	Feb	Mar	Apr	May	Jun	Jul	Aug	Sep	Oct	Nov	Dec		High	Low	Av
107	84	80	92	93	83	91	92	85	81	82	82		37	152	100

Jordan's national team continued to establish itself in the upper echelons of Asian football during the course of 2011, following up their appearance at the finals of the AFC Asian Cup finals in Qatar by reaching the final phase of qualifying for the 2014 FIFA World Cup. Under Iraqi coach Adnan Hamed, who has overseen the development of the team since 2009, the Jordanians secured a place amongst the final 10 teams in Asia fighting for a place in Brazil. They were drawn alongside Australia, Iraq, Japan and Oman in a five-team group which sees the top two qualify automatically for the finals. The realistic hope, perhaps, would be a third-place finish and the chance to meet the winners of the Oceania qualifiers for a place in Brazil. In club football, Al Wihdat underlined their current dominance at home by winning the championship for the fifth time in the past seven years. They relegated the usually powerful Al Faysali to a distant second place in the league and then won the JFA Cup by beating Mansheyat Bani Hasan 3-1 in the final. The Amman-based club also reached the semi-finals of the AFC Cup, a competition that Jordanian clubs won three times in the first four editions. Wihdat missed out on adding their name to the list of winners after they were eliminated 2-1 on aggregate by Nasaf of Uzbekistan, who went on to win the competition.

FIFA WORLD CUP RECORD
1930-1982 DNE 1986-2010 DNQ

JORDAN FOOTBALL ASSOCIATIOM (JFA)

Al-Hussein Youth City,
PO Box 962024,
Amman 11196
☎ +962 6 5657662
🖷 +962 6 5657660
✉ info@jfa.com.jo
🖳 www.jfa.com.jo
FA 1949 CON 1970 FIFA 1958
P HRH Prince Ali Al Hussein
GS Khalil Al Salem

FIFA BIG COUNT 2006

Total players	121 191
% of population	2,05%
Male	112 856
Female	8 335
Amateurs 18+	3 637
Youth under 18	1 163
Unregistered	40 250
Professionals	21
Referees	161
Admin & coaches	6 070
Number of clubs	93
Number of teams	146

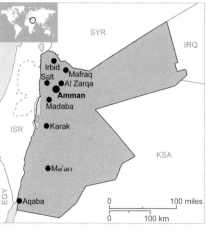

MAJOR CITIES/TOWNS

		Population
1	Amman	1 155 710
2	Al Zarqa	460 007
3	Russeifa	309 152
4	Irbit	302 061
5	Quaismeh	198 777
6	Khelda	179 928
7	Wadi Essier	159 554
8	Khraibet Essooq	133 849
9	Aqaba	99 265
10	Ramtha	92 461
11	Salt	91 385
12	Madaba	86 372
13	Jbaiha	85 732
14	Swaileh	72 705
15	Al Muqabalayn	70 421
16	Mshairfet Ras	60 013
17	Mafraq	58 447
18	Sahab	55 562
19	Um Qsair	54 341

AL MAMLAKAH AL URDUNIYAH AL HASHIMIYA • HASHEMITE KINGDOM OF JORDAN

Capital Amman	Population 6 342 948 (104)	% in cities 78%
GDP per capita $5200 (139)	Area km² 89 342 km² (111)	GMT +/- +2
Neighbours (km) Iraq 181, Israel 238, Saudi Arabia 744, Syria 375, West Bank 97		

RECENT INTERNATIONAL MATCHES PLAYED BY JORDAN

2009	Opponents		Score	Venue	Comp	Scorers	Att	Referee
5-09	Malaysia	D	0-0	Amman	Fr			
9-09	New Zealand	L	1-3	Amman	Fr	Hatem Aqel [2]		
10-10	Kuwait	L	1-2	Cairo	Fr	Amer Deeb [64]		
14-10	UAE	L	1-3	Dubai	Fr	Abdullah Deeb [60p]		
14-11	Iran	L	0-1	Tehran	ACq		15 000	Nishimura JPN
22-11	Iran	W	1-0	Amman	ACq	Amer Deeb [78]	11 000	Albadwawi USA
30-12	China PR	D	2-2	Jinan	Fr	Mahmoud Shelbaieh 2 [71 78]		
2010								
6-01	Thailand	D	0-0	Bangkok	ACq		15 000	Williams AUS
25-02	Azerbaijan	L	0-2	Amman	Fr			Shaaban EGY
3-03	Singapore	W	2-1	Amman	ACq	Odai Alsaify [9], Bashar Yaseen [60]	17 000	Abdou QAT
16-09	Iraq	W	4-1	Amman	Fr	Ahmad Al Zugheir [6], Abdullah Deeb [19], Hassouneh Qasem [69], Amer Deeb [73]		
19-09	Bahrain	W	2-0	Zarqa	Fr	Moayad Abukeshek [22], Abdullah Deeb [52]		
24-09	Syria	D	1-1	Amman	WArl	Amer Deeb [13]	18 000	
28-09	Kuwait	D	2-2	Amman	WArl	Hasan Abdel Fattah 2 [38 51]	18 000	
16-11	Cyprus	D	0-0	Amman	Fr		3 500	Ebrahim BHR
28-12	Bahrain	L	1-2	Dubai	Fr	Baha Suleiman [60]		
2011								
2-01	Uzbekistan	D	2-2	Sharjah	Fr	Amer Deeb [33], Odai Al Saify [75]		Hashmi UAE
9-01	Japan	D	1-1	Doha	ACr1	Hasan Abdel Fattah [45]	6 255	Abdul Bashir SIN
13-01	Saudi Arabia	W	1-0	Al Rayyan	ACr1	Baha Suleiman [42]	17 349	Albadwawi UAE
17-01	Syria	W	2-1	Doha	ACr1	Ali Dyab OG [30], Odai Alsaify [59]	9 849	Abdou QAT
21-01	Uzbekistan	L	1-2	Doha	ACqf	Bashar Yaseen [58]	16 073	Abdul Bashir SIN
26-03	Kuwait	D	1-1	Sharjah	Fr	Hasan Abdel Fattah [23p]		
29-03	Korea DPR	D	1-1	Sharjah	Fr	Hasan Abdel Fattah [29]		
5-07	Syria	L	1-3	Istanbul	Fr	Amer Deeb [10]		
8-07	Yemen	W	4-0	Istanbul	Fr	Ahmad Ibrahim [62], Hasan Abdel Fattah [65], Shadi Abu Hashhash [90], Abdullah Deeb [92+]		
13-07	Saudi Arabia	D	1-1	Amman	Fr	Hasan Abdel Fattah [9]. L 3-4p		
16-07	Iraq	D	1-1	Amman	Fr	Mohammad Al Dumeiri [5]. W 5-4p		
23-07	Nepal	W	9-0	Amman	WCq	Hasan Mahmoud 4 [7 72 83 90], Amer Khalil 2 [20 57], Ahmad Ibrahim 2 [20 62], Abdallah Salim [24]	17 000	Jahanbazi IRN
28-07	Nepal	D	1-1	Kathmandu	WCq	Saeed Almurjan [53]	20 000	Fan Qi CHN
22-08	Tunisia	D	3-3	Amman	Fr	Abdullah Deeb 2 [20 52], Ahmad Hayel [47]		
27-08	Indonesia	W	1-0	Amman	Fr	Abdullah Deeb [55]		
2-09	Iraq	W	2-0	Arbil	WCq	Hasan Mahmoud [43], Abdallah Salim [47]	24 000	Shukralla BHR
6-09	China PR	W	2-1	Amman	WCq	Baha Suleiman [49], Amer Khalil [56]	19 000	Irmatov UZB
6-10	Thailand	D	0-0	Bangkok	Fr			
11-10	Singapore	W	3-0	Singapore	WCq	Abdallah Salim [11], Anas Bani Yaseen [54], Ahmad Ibrahim [64]	3 799	Choi Myung Yong KOR
11-11	Singapore	W	2-0	Amman	WCq	Ahmad Ibrahim [15], Amer Khalil [65]	19 000	Williams AUS
15-11	Iraq	L	1-3	Amman	WCq	Hasan Mahmoud [17]	13 000	Albadwawi UAE

Fr = Friendly match • WA = West Asian Federation Championship • AC = AFC Asian Cup • WC = FIFA World Cup
q = qualifier • r1 = first round group

JORDAN NATIONAL TEAM HISTORICAL RECORDS

Caps
91 - Faisal Ibrahim 2000- • **84** - Bashar Bani Yaseen 1999- • **83** - Hatem Aqel 2000- • **76** - Amer Deeb 2002 • **74** - Amer Shafia 2002- • **72** - Mahmoud Shelbaieh 2002- • **70** - Hassouneh Al Sheikh 1997-2010

Goals
32 - Mahmoud Shelbaieh 2002- • **20** - Abdullah Deeb 2007- & Hassan Abdel Fattah 2004- • **16** - Rafat Ali 1996-2008 • **14** - Odai Al Saify 2007- & Amer Deeb 2002-

Past Coaches
Branko Smiljanic SRB 2000-02 • Mahmoud El Gohary EGY 2002-07 • Nelo Vingada POR 2007-09 • Adnan Hamad 2009-

JORDAN 2010–11

PROFESSIONAL LEAGUE

	Pl	W	D	L	F	A	Pts	Al Wihdat	Al Faysali	Shabab	Al Buq'aa	Mansheyat	Al Yarmouk	Al Ramtha	Al Jazeera	Al Arabi	Al Hussein	Kfarsoum	Al Ahli
Al Wihdat ‡	20	16	3	1	42	16	51		1-0	3-1	2-0	**0-3**	2-1	2-0	5-1	3-1	5-2	1-0	
Al Faysali ‡	20	9	7	4	26	19	34	0-3		2-1	2-0	0-1	1-1	0-0	0-0	3-2	1-1	2-0	*2-1*
Shabab Al Ordon	20	9	6	5	38	26	33	0-0	1-3		4-3	5-0	0-3	3-1	1-0	1-0	1-1	8-1	
Al Buq'aa	20	8	7	5	34	28	31	2-3	2-1	1-1		2-1	3-0	3-0	3-2	1-1	3-1	1-0	*3-0*
Mansheyat B. Hasan	20	7	6	7	25	26	27	0-1	1-2	2-2	0-0		2-1	2-2	2-1	0-0	1-0	0-0	*0-0*
Al Yarmouk	20	7	5	8	32	31	26	0-1	1-1	1-2	2-2	2-4		3-1	1-3	3-1	2-1	1-2	
Al Ramtha	20	6	5	9	16	24	23	0-3	0-1	1-1	0-1	1-0	1-3		3-0	1-0	1-1	1-0	*2-1*
Al Jazeera	20	6	4	10	26	33	22	2-2	1-2	0-3	3-3	2-1	0-1	1-0		0-1	3-3	2-0	*3-1*
Al Arabi	20	4	7	9	23	29	19	2-3	1-3	4-1	1-1	0-2	2-2	0-0	2-1		1-1	0-0	*1-1*
Al Hussein	20	2	9	9	20	32	15	1-2	0-0	0-2	0-0	2-0	2-4	0-1	0-2	3-2		0-0	*0-0*
Kfarsoum	20	2	9	9	13	31	15	0-0	2-2	0-0	4-3	3-3	0-0	0-2	0-2	0-2	1-1		
Al Ahli			Excluded after 15 rounds					*0-1*	*1-4*	*0-3*			*2-3*	*1-1*	*2-2*	*1-2*		*2-5*	

20/08/2010 - 22/04/2011 • ‡ Qualified for the AFC Cup • Relegation play-off: Al Hussein 1-3 **Kfarsoum** • Matches in italics void

JORDAN 2010–11
FIRST DIVISION (2)

Group A	Pl	W	D	L	F	A	Pts
Shabab Al Hussein †	12	7	4	1	29	10	25
That Ras †	12	7	2	3	25	10	23
Al Ittihad Al Ramtha	12	5	1	6	28	23	16
Shehan	12	4	3	5	21	23	15
Al Badiah Al Wosta	12	3	4	5	14	22	13
Al Qouqazy	12	3	4	5	10	22	13
Shabab Al Muhatah	12	4	0	8	18	35	12

Group B	Pl	W	D	L	F	A	Pts
Ain Karem †	12	8	2	2	22	9	26
Al Jaleel †	12	7	3	2	24	13	24
Al Sareeh	12	5	4	3	17	13	19
Al Salt	12	4	3	5	18	19	15
Al Tora	12	4	1	7	17	23	13
Al Sheikh Hussein	12	3	2	7	13	20	11
Al Karmel	12	3	1	8	14	28	10

Final Round	Pl	W	D	L	F	A	Pts
Al Jaleel	3	2	0	1	5	3	6
That Ras	3	1	2	0	3	2	5
Shabab Al Hussein	3	1	1	1	2	3	4
Ain Karem	3	0	1	2	3	5	1

† Qualified for final round

MEDALS TABLE

		Overall			Lge		Cup		FAS		Asia			City
		G	S	B	G	S	G	S	G	S	G	S	B	
1	Al Faysali	55	11		31		16	5	6	5	2	1		Amman
2	Al Wihdat	28	10	3	12		9	4	7	6			3	Amman
3	Al Ramtha	9	10	1	2		2	9	5	1			1	Irbid
4	Al Ahli	8	1		8		1							Amman
5	Al Jazeera	6	2		3		1	1	2	1				Amman
6	Shabab Al Ordon	5	2		1		2	2	1				1	Zarqa
7	Al Hussein	3	12					5	3	7				Irbid
8	Amman	3	1		1				2	1				Amman
9	Al Arabi	1	2				1	1	1					Irbid
10	Jordan	1			1									Amman
	Kfarsoum	1							1					
	Al Yarmouk	1							1					Irbid
13	Al Buq'aa			3				1		2				Amman
	Shabab Al Hussein			3				1		2				Amman
15	Al Jalil			1		1								
	Al Qadisiya			1				1						
	Mansheyat			1						1				B.Hasan

JFA CUP 2010–11

First Round

		Quarter-finals			Semi-finals			Final	
Al Wihdat *	4								
Ain Karem	0	**Al Wihdat** *	2	1					
Al Ahli	0	Al Yarmouk	0	1					
Al Yarmouk *	1				**Al Wihdat** *	3	1		
Al Jazeera *	4				Kfarsoum	0	0		
Al Jaleel	1	Al Jazeera	0	0					
Al Buq'aa *	0 4p	**Kfarsoum** *	0	1					
Kfarsoum	0 5p							**Al Wihdat**	3
Al Arabi *	3							Mansheyat B. Hasan	1
That Ras	0	**Al Arabi**	3	0					
Al Hussein *	0	Al Faysali *	2	1	Al Arabi	0	2		
Al Faysali	1				**Mansheyat B. Hasan** *	1	1		
Al Ramtha	3								
Shabab Al Hussein *	0	Al Ramtha *	0 0 2p						
Shabab Al Ordon *	2 3p	**Mansheyat B. Hasan**	0 0 4p						
Mansheyat B. Hasan	2 4p								

* Home team in the first leg

CUP FINAL
International, Amman
20-05-2011
Scorers - Rafat Ali 2 [4p] [20], Ahmad KashKash [88] for Wihdat; Nabel Abu Ali 40p for Mansheyat. Rafat Ali (AW) & Malik Rashed (MBH) Sent off [90]

JPN – JAPAN

FIFA/COCA-COLA WORLD RANKING

'93	'94	'95	'96	'97	'98	'99	'00	'01	'02	'03	'04	'05	'06	'07	'08	'09	'10	'11	'12
43	36	31	21	14	20	57	38	34	22	29	17	15	47	34	35	43	29	19	

2011												High	Low	Av
Jan	Feb	Mar	Apr	May	Jun	Jul	Aug	Sep	Oct	Nov	Dec			
29	17	15	13	14	13	14	15	15	17	19	19	9	62	31

The 2011 Japanese football season was played against the background of the catastrophic March 11 earthquake and tsunami, which happened after just one round of matches had been played. The J.League's schedule was heavily disrupted in the aftermath and the subsequent rescheduling of games led to the national team withdrawing from a planned appearance at the Copa America. Clubs along Japan's east coast, including top flight sides Kashima Antlers and Vegalta Sendai, were most adversely affected by the disaster, with former champions Kashima struggling throughout 2011. Kashiwa Reysol, from a working class suburb on the edge of Tokyo, became the first club in J.League history to win the J.League title just 12 months after successfully claiming the second division crown as they held off a late surge by defending champions Nagoya Grampus. History was also made in the Emperor's Cup which saw two second division sides contest the final for the first time with FC Tokyo beating Kyoto Sanga 4-2 on New Year's Day. While the men's national team celebrated victory in the AFC Asian Cup in Qatar in January, the women's team - the Nadeshiko - underlined Japan's continuing development in all aspects of the game by winning the FIFA Women's World Cup in Germany, defeating the USA in the final amid emotional scenes.

FIFA WORLD CUP RECORD

1930-1950 DNE 1954 DNQ 1958 DNE 1962 DNQ 1966 DNE 1970-1994 DNQ **1998** 31 r1 **2002** 9 r2 (hosts) **2006** 28 r1 **2010** 9 r2

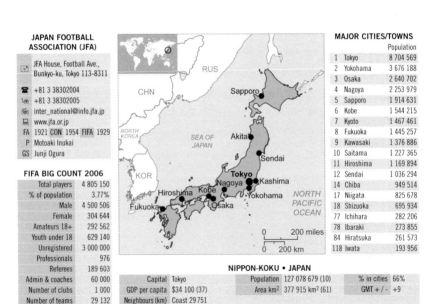

JAPAN FOOTBALL ASSOCIATION (JFA)

JFA House, Football Ave.,
Bunkyo-ku, Tokyo 113-8311

☎ +81 3 38302004
📠 +81 3 38302005
📧 inter_national@info.jfa.jp
🖥 www.jfa.or.jp
FA 1921 CON 1954 FIFA 1929
P Motoaki Inukai
GS Junji Ogura

FIFA BIG COUNT 2006

Total players	4 805 150
% of population	3.77%
Male	4 500 506
Female	304 644
Amateurs 18+	292 562
Youth under 18	629 140
Unregistered	3 000 000
Professionals	976
Referees	189 603
Admin & coaches	60 000
Number of clubs	1 000
Number of teams	29 132

MAJOR CITIES/TOWNS

		Population
1	Tokyo	8 704 569
2	Yokohama	3 676 188
3	Osaka	2 640 702
4	Nagoya	2 253 979
5	Sapporo	1 914 631
6	Kobe	1 544 215
7	Kyoto	1 467 461
8	Fukuoka	1 445 257
9	Kawasaki	1 376 886
10	Saitama	1 227 365
11	Hiroshima	1 169 894
12	Sendai	1 036 294
14	Chiba	949 514
17	Niigata	825 678
18	Shizuoka	695 934
77	Ichihara	282 206
78	Ibaraki	273 855
84	Hiratsuka	261 573
118	Iwata	193 956

NIPPON-KOKU • JAPAN

Capital Tokyo	Population 127 078 679 (10)	% in cities 66%
GDP per capita $34 100 (37)	Area km² 377 915 km² (61)	GMT +/- +9
Neighbours (km) Coast 29 751		

RECENT INTERNATIONAL MATCHES PLAYED BY JAPAN

2009	Opponents	Score	Venue	Comp	Scorers	Att	Referee
5-09	Netherlands	L 0-3	Enschede	Fr		23 750	Skomina SVN
9-09	Ghana	W 4-3	Utrecht	Fr	Nakamura.K [53], Tamada [78], Okazaki [79], Inamoto [83]	2 506	Blom NED
8-10	Hong Kong	W 6-0	Shizuoka	ACq	Okazaki 3 [18 75 78], Nagamoto [29], Nakazawa [51], Tanaka.MT [67]	16 028	Torky IRN
10-10	Scotland	W 2-0	Yokohama	Fr	Berra OG [83], Honda [90]	61 285	Kim KOR
14-10	Togo	W 5-0	Miyagi	Fr	Okazaki 3 [5 8 65], Morimoto [11], Honda [85]	32 852	Mikulski POL
14-11	South Africa	D 0-0	Port Elizabeth	Fr			Baltazar ANG
18-11	Hong Kong	W 4-0	Hong Kong	ACq	Hasebe [33], Sato [75], Nakamura.S [84], Okazaki [91+]	13 254	Green AUS
2010							
6-01	Yemen	W 3-2	Sana'a	ACq	Hirayama 3 [42 55 79]	10 000	Albadwawi UAE
2-02	Venezuela	D 0-0	Oita	Fr		27 009	Fan Qi CHN
6-02	China PR	D 0-0	Tokyo	EAF		25 964	Delovski AUS
11-02	Hong Kong	W 3-0	Tokyo	EAF	Tamada 2 [41 82], Tanaka.MT [65]	16 368	Zhao Liang CHN
14-02	Korea Republic	L 1-3	Tokyo	EAF	Endo [23p]	42 951	Delovski AUS
3-03	Bahrain	W 2-0	Toyota	ACq	Okazaki [36], Honda [92+]	38 042	Abdul Bashir SIN
7-04	Serbia	L 0-3	Osaka	Fr		46 270	Choi Myung Yong KOR
24-05	Korea Republic	L 0-2	Saitama	Fr		57 873	Attwell ENG
30-05	England	L 1-2	Graz	Fr	Tanaka.MT [7]	15 326	Eisner AUT
4-06	Côte d'Ivoire	L 0-2	Sion	Fr		4 919	Studer SUI
14-06	Cameroon	W 1-0	Bloemfontein	WCr1	Honda [39]	30 620	Benquerenca POR
19-06	Netherlands	L 0-1	Durban	WCr1		62 010	Baldassi ARG
24-06	Denmark	W 3-1	Rustenburg	WCr1	Honda [17], Endo [30], Okazaki [87]	27 967	Damon RSA
29-06	Paraguay	D 0-0	Pretoria	WCr2	L 3-5p	36 742	De Bleeckere BEL
4-09	Paraguay	W 1-0	Yokohama	Fr	Kagawa [70]	65 157	Rodriguez.M MEX
7-09	Guatemala	W 2-1	Osaka	Fr	Morimoto 2 [12 20]	44 541	Archundia MEX
8-10	Argentina	W 1-0	Saitama	Fr	Okazaki [19]	57 735	Gil POL
12-10	Korea Republic	D 0-0	Seoul	Fr		62 503	Irmatov UZB
2011							
9-01	Jordan	D 1-1	Doha	ACr1	Yoshida [92+]	6 255	Abdul Bashir SIN
13-01	Syria	W 2-1	Doha	ACr1	Hasebe [35], Honda [82p]	10 453	Torky IRN
17-01	Saudi Arabia	W 5-0	Al Rayyan	ACr1	Okazaki 3 [8 13 80], Maeda 2 [19 51]	2 022	Irmatov UZB
21-01	Qatar	W 3-2	Doha	ACqf	Kagawa 2 [29 71], Inoha [90]	19 479	Mohd Salleh MAS
25-01	Korea Republic	D 2-2	Doha	ACsf	Maeda [36], Hosogai [97]. W 3-0p	16 171	Al Ghamdi KSA
29-01	Australia	W 1-0	Doha	ACf	Lee [109]	37 174	Irmatov UZB
1-06	Peru	D 0-0	Niigata	Fr		39 048	Webb ENG
7-06	Czech Republic	D 0-0	Yokohama	Fr		65 856	Atkinson ENG
10-08	Korea Republic	W 3-0	Sapporo	Fr	Kagawa 2 [34 54], Honda [52]	38 263	Irmatov UZB
2-09	Korea DPR	W 1-0	Saitama	WCq	Yoshida [94+]	62 000	Albadwawi UAE
6-09	Uzbekistan	D 1-1	Tashkent	WCq	Okazaki [65]	32 000	Al Ghamdi KSA
7-10	Vietnam	W 1-0	Kobe	Fr	Lee [24]	27 522	Mahapab THA
11-10	Tajikistan	W 8-0	Osaka	WCq	Havenaar 2 [11 47], Okazaki 2 [19 74], Komano [35], Kagawa 2 [41 68], Nakamura.K [56]	44 688	Williams AUS
11-11	Tajikistan	W 4-0	Dushanbe	WCq	Konno [36], Okazaki 2 [61 92+], Maeda [82]	18 000	Kim Dong Jin KOR
15-11	Korea DPR	L 0-1	Pyongyang	WCq		50 000	Shukralla BHR

Fr = Friendly match • EAF - East Asian Federation Cup • AC = AFC Asian Cup • WC = FIFA World Cup • q = qualifier

JAPAN NATIONAL TEAM HISTORICAL RECORDS

Caps 122 - Masami Ihara 1988-99 • 117 - Yoshikatsu Kawaguchi 1997- • 113 - Yasuhito Endo 2002- • 112 - Yuji Nakazawa 1999- • 98 - Shunsuke Nakamura 2000-10 • 89 - Kazuyoshi Miura 1990-2000 • 83 - Junichi Inamoto 2000- • 82 - Alessandro dos Santos 2002-06 • 70 - Satoshi Tsunami 1980-95 • 77 - Seigo Narazaki 1998-2010 • 72 - Keiji Tamada 2004-

Goals 55 - Kunishige Kamamoto 1964-77 & Kazuyoshi Miura 1990-2000 • 28 - Takuya Takagi 1992-97 • 26 - Shiji Okazaki 2008- • 24 - Shunsuke Nakamura 2000-10 & Hirome Hara 1978-88 • 23 - Naohiro Takahara 2000-08 • 21 - Masashi Nakayama 1990-2003

Past Coaches Hirokazu Ninomiya 1951 • Shigemaru Takenokoshi 1951-56 • Hidetoki Takahashi 1957 • Taizo Kawamoto 1958 • Shigemaru Takenokoshi 1958-59 • Dettmar Cramer (Technical Director) 1960-64 • Hidetoki Takahashi 1960-62 • Ken Naganuma 1962-70 • Shunichiro Okano 1970-72 • Ken Naganuma 1972-76 • Hiroshi Ninomiya 1976-78 • Yukio Shimomura 1979-80 • Masashi Watanabe 1980 • Saburo Kawabuchi 1980-1981 • Takaji Mori 1981-1986 • Yoshinobu Ishii 1986-1987 • Kenzo Yokoyama 1988-1992 • Hans Ooft 1992-1993 • Falcão 1993-94 • Shu Kamo 1995-1997 • Takeshi Okada 1997-1998 • Philippe Troussier 1998-2002 • Zico 2002-2006 • Ivica Osim 2006-2007 • Takeshi Okada 2007-2010 • Alberto Zaccheroni 2010-

JAPAN 2011

J.LEAGUE DIVISION 1

	Pl	W	D	L	F	A	Pts	Kashiwa	Nagoya	Gamba	Vegalta	Yokohama	Kashima	Sanfrecce	Jubilo	Vissel	Shimizu	Kawasaki	Cerezo	Omiya	Albirex	Urawa	Ventforet	Avispa	Montedio
Kashiwa Reysol †	34	23	3	8	65	42	72		2-1	2-4	1-0	2-0	2-1	3-1	0-3	3-0	3-0	3-2	1-1	1-3	4-0	3-1	2-1	3-2	1-0
Nagoya Grampus †	34	21	8	5	67	36	71	0-0		4-1	0-1	1-1	2-1	3-2	2-1	3-1	1-1	2-0	3-1	2-2	4-0	1-1	4-1	5-2	3-0
Gamba Osaka †	34	21	7	6	78	51	70	2-0	2-2		1-0	2-1	1-0	5-3	2-2	3-2	2-2	6-3	2-1	2-0	2-1	1-0	0-2	2-0	3-2
Vegalta Sendai	34	14	14	6	39	25	56	0-0	1-1	2-1		1-1	0-1	0-0	3-3	2-0	0-0	0-0	2-1	0-1	2-0	1-0	4-0	1-0	2-1
Yokohama F-Marinos	34	16	8	10	46	40	56	0-2	1-1	1-1	1-3		1-1	1-1	1-0	1-0	1-1	2-1	2-1	1-0	1-0	1-0	1-2	4-0	2-1
Kashima Antlers	34	13	11	10	53	40	50	0-1	1-1	1-4	3-0	0-3		2-0	2-0	1-1	2-2	2-1	3-3	1-2	0-0	0-1	6-0	3-1	3-0
Sanfrecce Hiroshima	34	14	8	12	52	49	50	1-3	0-3	4-1	0-0	3-2	2-1		3-1	1-0	4-0	2-3	1-3	4-2	1-0	0-0	1-1	0-0	3-2
Jubilo Iwata	34	13	8	13	53	45	47	6-1	0-1	1-2	1-1	1-2	1-2	1-1		3-0	2-1	2-1	0-4	1-2	1-0	1-1	2-1	4-1	4-0
Vissel Kobe	34	13	7	14	44	45	46	0-4	0-1	0-4	1-1	2-0	0-1	1-0	3-1		1-1	1-0	4-1	0-1	2-1	1-0	4-2	0-0	2-0
Shimizu S-Pulse	34	11	12	11	42	51	45	1-2	2-0	1-3	1-0	0-0	0-0	0-1	0-0	1-5		2-3	3-3	3-0	2-1	1-0	3-0	1-0	2-1
Kawasaki Frontale	34	13	5	16	52	53	44	3-2	1-2	2-1	1-2	3-0	3-2	2-0	1-0	0-3	1-1		1-2	0-1	1-2	0-1	2-2	3-2	2-0
Cerezo Osaka	34	11	10	13	67	53	43	5-0	2-3	1-1	1-1	0-1	1-3	5-4	2-3	0-3	4-0	3-3		0-1	1-1	3-1	0-4	7-1	6-0
Omiya Ardija	34	10	12	12	38	48	42	0-1	2-3	2-2	2-1	1-1	0-1	2-0	1-1	1-4	0-5	0-0	1-1		2-3	1-2	3-1	2-0	0-1
Albirex Niigata	34	10	9	15	38	46	39	0-3	0-1	2-2	1-1	4-2	2-2	0-1	1-1	1-0	4-0	1-1	1-0	3-2		2-3	1-2	3-1	2-0
Urawa Reds	34	8	12	14	36	43	36	1-3	3-0	1-1	0-0	0-2	2-2	1-1	0-3	2-3	1-3	2-0	1-1	0-1	1-1		2-0	3-0	0-1
Ventforet Kofu	34	9	6	19	42	63	33	1-4	3-1	4-3	1-2	1-2	1-1	0-2	0-1	1-1	1-2	0-1	0-2	1-1	3-0	3-2		2-1	1-1
Avispa Fukuoka	34	6	4	24	34	75	22	0-2	0-3	2-3	0-3	0-1	1-2	2-1	1-2	2-2	2-2	2-1	0-3	1-0	0-3	1-2	1-0		0-2
Montedio Yamagata	34	5	6	23	24	64	21	2-1	0-2	0-5	0-1	0-2	0-2	1-3	1-1	2-0	1-1	0-1	0-0	0-1	0-1	0-0	3-1	0-5	

5/03/2011 - 3/12/2011 • † Qualified for the AFC Champions League
Top scorers: **20** - Joshua Kennedy AUS, Nagoya • **17** - Mike Havenaar, Ventforet • **15** - Leandro Domingues BRA, Kashiwa; Lee Keun Ho KOR, Gamba & Tadanari Lee, Sanfrecce • **14** - Shingo Akamine, Vegalta; Ryoichi Maeda, Jubilo & Keiji Tamada, Nagoya • **13** - Bruno Lopes BRA, Albirex & Junya Tanaka, Kashiwa • **12** - Hidetaka Kanazono, Jubilo; Yu Kobayashi, Kawasaki & Yuzo Tashiro, Kashima

JAPAN 2011

J.LEAGUE DIVISION 2

	Pl	W	D	L	F	A	Pts	FC Tokyo	Sagan	Consadole	Tokushima	Verdy	JEF United	Kyoto	Giravanz	Thespa	Tochigi	Kumamoto	Oita	Fagiano	Shonan	Ehime	Kataller	Mito	Yokohama	Gainare	Gifu
FC Tokyo	38	23	8	7	67	22	77		1-0	0-0	1-0	1-1	1-0	6-1	2-0	1-0	0-0	5-0	1-2	3-0	1-1	1-1	1-1	1-0	2-0	3-0	4-0
Sagan Tosu	38	19	12	7	68	34	69	0-0		1-0	1-1	3-1	1-0	2-1	2-3	1-2	1-2	2-2	1-6	0-2	0-1	2-0	1-2	1-2	1-2	1-0	1-0
Consadole Sapporo	38	21	5	12	49	32	68	2-1	0-1		0-0	4-2	4-0	2-1	0-0	1-0	0-3	0-2	0-2	0-1	3-1	3-1	0-4	1-0	1-2	4-1	0-0
Tokushima Vortis	38	19	8	11	51	38	65	0-2	0-3	0-2		2-2	1-0	2-1	0-3	0-0	4-1	0-1	2-2	4-0	2-2	3-1	1-1	4-1	1-0	4-1	2-0
Tokyo Verdy	38	16	11	11	69	45	59	1-0	1-3	2-4	2-1		0-1	1-0	0-1	3-0	0-5	2-4	2-2	4-0	2-3	3-1	1-1	4-1	3-7	2-0	3-0
JEF United Chiba	38	16	10	12	46	39	58	3-0	3-3	2-0	0-1	1-1		0-1	1-0	2-3	2-2	1-3	2-2	1-2	0-2	1-0	0-0	2-2	1-0	1-1	0-3
Kyoto Sanga	38	17	7	14	50	45	58	1-4	0-0	4-0	1-2	1-0	2-1		1-0	3-1	1-1	0-2	0-2	3-1	1-0	0-0	0-0	2-1	1-1	1-0	3-1
Giravanz Kitakyushu	38	16	10	12	45	46	58	1-0	0-0	0-3	1-1	1-0	2-1	0-1		1-0	1-0	2-1	3-1	1-0	2-2	2-1	1-0	2-2	0-2	2-2	1-0
Thespa Kusatsu	38	16	9	13	51	51	57	2-1	0-0	2-1	2-0	0-0	3-1	2-4	2-2		4-0	1-1	1-2	1-0	0-0	2-2	1-1	0-5	4-2	2-0	2-1
Tochigi SC	38	15	11	12	44	39	56	2-1	0-0	1-0	1-2	4-0	1-0	2-1	2-1	1-1		0-1	2-1	0-0	0-3	1-2	1-2	0-0	2-1	1-0	0-1
Rosso Kumamoto	38	13	12	13	33	44	51	0-1	0-0	1-0	0-1	1-1	0-1	1-1	2-0	0-1	0-0		0-1	2-1	1-0	1-2	1-1	1-1	2-1	0-1	2-0
Oita Trinita	38	12	14	12	42	45	50	1-2	2-1	2-0	1-2	2-2	4-0	0-0	0-0	2-2	2-3	2-1		1-0	3-1	2-1	2-0	1-0	2-1	0-2	1-2
Fagiano Okayama	38	13	9	16	43	58	48	0-2	4-1	0-1	0-0	4-0	1-2	1-3	0-1	2-2	4-0	0-0	1-1		1-1	1-1	1-0	1-1	0-2	1-1	1-2
Shonan Bellmare	38	12	10	16	46	48	46	1-2	1-0	0-2	1-2	1-3	2-0	0-1	1-1	2-0	0-1	0-2	2-5	1-1		1-1	2-0	3-2	0-1	0-1	7-1
Ehime FC	38	10	14	14	44	54	44	0-5	2-2	2-0	0-1	2-1	0-2	0-3	1-2	2-2	1-1	1-1	2-3	0-0	1-1		1-0	0-1	0-0	3-2	2-0
Kataller Toyama	38	11	10	17	36	53	43	1-0	0-3	1-2	0-2	1-5	1-2	1-1	1-2	2-3	1-3	1-1	1-0	0-2	2-3	2-1		2-0	0-2	4-2	1-0
Mito Hollyhock	38	11	9	18	40	49	42	1-0	0-2	1-2	2-1	1-1	1-0	2-2	0-3	1-0	2-2	0-0	0-1	1-1	0-0	3-1	3-0		0-1	3-1	1-2
Yokohama FC	38	11	8	19	40	54	41	0-1	1-2	1-2	0-1	2-1	1-1	1-1	1-2	2-2	2-0	0-1	2-2	0-1	3-2	0-1	1-2	1-0		0-1	1-1
Gainare Tottori	38	8	7	23	36	60	31	1-5	3-6	1-0	0-2	0-1	0-1	2-1	0-1	1-1	0-5	0-1	0-0	1-4	0-2	4-0	0-1	0-1	0-1		1-1
FC Gifu	38	6	6	26	39	83	24	0-2	4-4	1-3	0-2	1-3	0-3	2-3	1-3	0-1	0-1	1-1	0-1	1-3	0-1	1-1	1-2	1-4	3-2	2-3	

5/03/2011 - 3/12/2011
Top scorers: **24** - Yohei Toyoda, Sagan • **16** - Takuma Abe, Verdy • **14** - Masaki Fukai, JEF United & Manabu Saito, Ehime • **12** - Ricardo Lobo BRA, Tochigi & Yoshihiro Uchimura, Consadole • **11** - Yasuhito Morishima, Oita

JAPAN 2011

9TH JAPAN FOOTBALL LEAGUE (JFL) (3)

Team	Pl	W	D	L	F	A	Pts	Sagawa S	Nagano	Machida	Matsumoto	V-Varen	Honda	Zweigen	Honda Lock	FC Ryukyu	Tochigi	Sanuki	Sagawa P	MIO	Blaublitz	Yokogawa	Arte	JEF United	Sony
Sagawa Shiga	33	23	1	9	60	34	70		2-1	3-3	2-1	0-1	3-2	0-1	1-2	2-1	2-1	2-0	1-2	1-0	2-1	1-0	2-1	4-0	2-0
Nagano Parceiro	33	19	6	8	51	27	63	0-1		1-0	1-1	0-0	0-0	0-3	1-1	3-1	2-1	2-1	0-0	4-1	4-1	0-2	1-0	4-0	
Machida Zelvia -P	33	18	7	8	61	28	61	2-1	2-2		3-1	3-0	1-0	2-0	4-0	5-1	0-0	2-0	2-0	6-0	1-1	1-2	1-3	1-0	*0-0*
Matsumoto Yamaga -P	33	17	8	8	60	38	59	1-2	2-1	2-0		1-1	1-1	2-0	2-0	1-0	3-1	2-2	6-0	3-2	1-2	2-2	1-2	1-1	*0-3*
V-Varen Nagasaki	33	15	11	7	61	44	56	2-1	0-2	5-1	1-1		1-1	0-2	1-1	1-3	2-2	0-1	6-0	2-1	2-2	1-0	1-2	3-3	*0-1*
Honda FC	33	15	7	11	40	36	52	0-1	0-3	0-4	3-0	0-2		2-1	3-3	2-1	2-0	1-1	2-1	2-0	1-1	2-0	2-1	1-1	*0-0*
Zweigen Kanazawa	33	13	8	12	49	40	47	0-2	1-2	1-1	1-2	3-3	1-0		2-3	0-3	1-1	1-2	4-1	1-1	1-2	0-1	1-0	4-0	
Honda Lock	33	12	11	10	47	45	47	0-3	1-2	0-1	0-2	1-3	3-2	1-1		0-4	2-2	1-0	6-1	2-1	1-1	0-1	1-2	2-0	
FC Ryukyu	33	14	4	15	47	51	46	2-1	0-4	0-0	0-1	1-3	1-0	1-1	0-2		4-0	2-0	0-4	1-4	0-1	1-1	3-2	0-2	*4-0*
Tochigi Uva	33	12	9	12	40	43	45	1-3	0-2	1-0	1-2	4-0	1-3	0-1	1-0	2-2		1-0	1-0	3-2	1-1	1-0	0-0	3-0	*3-2*
Kamatamare Sanuki	33	11	7	15	39	49	40	1-2	1-0	0-3	4-2	1-1	0-1	1-2	1-1	2-1	1-1		3-2	1-2	2-1	1-0	3-1	1-1	
Sagawa Printing	33	11	5	17	43	61	38	0-2	2-0	0-2	1-1	2-3	0-1	0-0	1-2	4-1	1-2	2-1		2-1	2-0	2-1	2-2	0-1	*1-2*
MIO Biwako Kusatsu	33	11	5	17	43	65	38	1-4	3-1	1-6	0-2	0-6	1-0	2-0	0-2	1-2	1-1	1-1	2-2		1-2	4-1	3-1	1-0	
Blaublitz Akita	33	10	7	16	38	52	37	1-2	0-2	2-1	3-2	0-2	0-2	1-3	0-3	0-1	2-1	2-0	2-3	1-2		0-1	0-1	2-1	*1-0*
Yokogawa Musashino	33	9	9	15	33	37	36	0-1	0-2	0-0	0-2	3-4	0-1	3-3	0-0	1-2	0-1	2-0	0-0	3-3			0-1	4-0	*1-1*
Arte Takasaki	33	9	7	17	39	55	34	4-3	0-1	0-1	1-0	1-5	0-1	1-3	0-3	2-2	1-2	1-1	2-3	0-1	0-1	2-2		*2-1*	*1-1*
JEF United Club	33	4	7	22	27	63	19	3-1	0-1	0-2	0-2	1-2	1-2	0-2	0-3	0-2	0-1	3-3	2-3	3-1	1-1	0-1	2-3		
Sony Sendai	17	3	7	7	14	24	16	*0-0*	*0-2*	*1-0*	*0-2*	*1-1*	*1-1*	*1-1*	*1-4*	*1-1*				*3-0*	*1-1*	*1-1*		*0-0*	

23/04/2011 - 11/12/2011 • Matches in italics for Sony Sendai are not included in the final standings

Top scorers: **20** - Masatoshi Matsuda, Blaublitz • **19** - Ryota Arimitsu, V-Varen & Tetsuya Kijima, Matsumoto • **16** - Yoshinori Katsumata, Machida

MEDALS TABLE

	Team	Overall G	S	B	J.League G	S	B	JSL G	S	B	EC G	S	JLC G	S	B	Asia G	S	B	City	Former name	Formed
1	Tokyo Verdy	16	8	1	2	1		5	3		5	3	3	1		1		1	Tokyo	Yomiuri	1969
2	Kashima Antlers	15	7	3	7	2	2				4	2	4	3				1	Ibaraki	Sumitomo	1947
3	Yokohama F.Marinos	14	8	2	3	2	1	2	4		6	1				2	1	1	Yokohama	Nissan	1972
4	Urawa Reds	13	15	6	1	3		4	6	5	6	3	1	3		1		1	Saitama	Mitsubishi	1950
5	Jubilo Iwata	9	10	3	3	3			1		3		2	2		2	3	1	Iwata	Yamaha	1970
6	JEF United	9	4	6				2	1		4		4	2		2	1	1	Ichihara	Furukawa	1946
7	Sanfrecce Hiroshima	8	13	2		1		5	1	1	3	10		1				1	Hiroshima	Toyo Kogyo/Mazda	1938
8	Cerezo Osaka	7	12	2		1		4	4	1	3	8							Osaka	Yanmar	1957
9	Shonan Bellmare	7	5	3				3	1	3	3	4		1					Hiratsuka	Fujita	1968
10	Gamba Osaka	6	3	6	1	1	6				3	1	1	1		1			Osaka	Matsushita	1980
11	Kashiwa Reysol	5	4	7	1			2			1	1	5	2	3	1			Kashiwa	Hitachi	1940
12	Shimizu S-Pulse	3	8	3	1	2					1	4	1	3		1		1	Shimizu		1991
13	Nagoya Grampus	3	4	3	1	2	2				2	1				1	1		Nagoya	Toyota	1939
14	Yokohama Flugels	3	2	3				1			1	1	2	1		1		1	Yokohama	All Nippon	
15	FC Tokyo	3									1		2						Tokyo	Tokyo Gas	1935
	Yawata/Nippon Steel	1	5	2				2	2		1	3							Kitakyushu		1950
17	Nippon Kokan	1	4					3			1	1							Kawasaki		1912
18	Kyoto Sanga	1	1								1	1							Kyoto	Kyoto Shiko	1922
19	Oita Trinita	1											1						Oita		1994
20	Kawasaki Frontale		6			3									3				Kawasaki	Fujitsu	1955
21	Honda		2						2										Hamamatsu		1971

The creation of the J.League saw all of the company teams change their names as listed above • In 1998 Yokohama Marinos merged with Yokohama Flugels (previously All Nippon Airways) to form Yokohama F.Marinos. Disgruntled Flugel's fans then formed Yokohama FC in protest

JSL = Japan Soccer League (1965-92) • EC = Emperor's Cup • JLC = J.League Cup • Keio University are the Emperor's Cup record holders with 9

EMPEROR'S CUP 2011

Second Round		Third Round		Fourth Round	
FC Tokyo *	4				
FC Kagoshima	0	FC Tokyo *	2		
Sanyo Electric Sumoto	0	Vissel Kobe	1		
Vissel Kobe *	8			FC Tokyo	1
Gamba Osaka *	2			Mito Hollyhock *	0
Sagawa Shiga	0	Gamba Osaka *	2		
Consadole Sapporo *	2	Mito Hollyhock	3		
Mito Hollyhock	3				
Ehime FC *	2				
FC Ryukyu	0	Ehime FC	1		
Zweigen Kanazawa	2	Sanfrecce Hiroshima *	0		
Sanfrecce Hiroshima *	4			Ehime FC *	1
Tokyo Verdy *	7			Urawa Reds	3
V-Varen Nagasaki	1	Tokyo Verdy	1		
Miyazaki Sangyo-keiei Univ'ty	1	Urawa Reds *	2		
Urawa Reds *	4				
Shimizu S-Pulse *	2				
FC Gifu Second	0	Shimizu S-Pulse *	5		
Rosso Kumamoto	0	Gainare Tottori	0		
Gainare Tottori *	3			Shimizu S-Pulse *	2
Jubilo Iwata *	1			JEF United Chiba	0
Dezzola Shimane	0	Jubilo Iwata *	0		
Fukushima United	0	JEF United Chiba	1		
JEF United Chiba *	3				
Vegalta Sendai *	2				
Sony Sendai	1	Vegalta Sendai *	3		
Kochi University	0	Avispa Fukuoka	1		
Avispa Fukuoka *	3			Vegalta Sendai	1 2p
Fagiano Okayama	1			Cerezo Osaka *	1 4p
Thespa Kusatsu *	0	Fagiano Okayama	0		
Hokkaido University	0	Cerezo Osaka *	3		
Cerezo Osaka *	6				
Yokohama F-Marinos *	3				
Kamatamare Sanuki	1	Yokohama F-Marinos *	3		
Honda Lock	1	Tochigi SC	0		
Tochigi SC *	2			Yokohama F-Marinos *	4
Albirex Niigata *	5			Matsumoto Yamaga	0
Toyama Shinjo Club	0	Albirex Niigata *	0		
Yokohama FC	0	Matsumoto Yamaga	1		
Matsumoto Yamaga *	2				
Kashiwa Reysol *	2				
Tochigi Uva	0	Kashiwa Reysol *	6		
Machida Zelvia	1	Ventforet Kofu	1		
Ventforet Kofu *	2			Kashiwa Reysol	3 8p
Giravanz Kitakyushu	1			Nagoya Grampus *	3 9p
FC Gifu *	0	Giravanz Kitakyushu	0		
Suzuka Rampole	0	Nagoya Grampus *	1		
Nagoya Grampus *	6				
Shonan Bellmare *	2				
Fagiano Okayama Next	1	Shonan Bellmare	3		
Omiya Ardija *	1 3p	Fukuoka University *	0		
Fukuoka University	1 5p			Shonan Bellmare	1
Oita Trinita *	1			Kawasaki Frontale *	0
Tokushima Vortis	0	Oita Trinita	0		
Arte Takasaki	1	Kawasaki Frontale *	4		
Kawasaki Frontale *	2				
Kashima Antlers *	2				
University of Tsukuba	0	Kashima Antlers *	2		
Sagan Tosu	3 2p	Kataller Toyama	1		
Kataller Toyama *	3 4p			Kashima Antlers *	0
Montedio Yamagata *	2			Kyoto Sanga	1
Blaublitz Akita	0	Montedio Yamagata *	2		
Sagawa Printing	0	Kyoto Sanga	3		
Kyoto Sanga *	3				

J.League clubs join in the second round • * Home team

EMPEROR'S CUP 2011

Quarter–finals   Semi–finals   Final

| FC Tokyo * | 1 |
| Urawa Reds | 0 |

| FC Tokyo †† | 1 |
| Cerezo Osaka | 0 |

| Shimizu S-Pulse | 2 5p |
| Cerezo Osaka * | 2 6p |

| FC Tokyo † | 4 |
| Kyoto Sanga | 2 |

| Yokohama F-Marinos | 0 4p |
| Nagoya Grampus * | 0 3p |

| Yokohama F-Marinos | 2 |
| Kyoto Sanga ‡ | 4 |

91ST EMPEROR'S CUP FINAL 2011
National Stadium, Tokyo, 1-01-2012, 14:00, Att: 41 974, Ref: Yuichi Nishimura

| Shonan Bellmare | 0 |
| Kyoto Sanga * | 1 |

| FC Tokyo | 4 | Yasuyuki Konno 15, Masato Morishige 36, Lucas 2 42 66 |
| Kyoto Sanga | 2 | Hiroki Nakayama 13, Yuya Kubo 71 |

FC Tokyo - Shuichi Gonda - Yuhei Tokunaga - Masato Morishige, Yasuyuki Konno (c), Kenta Mukuhara - Hideto Takahashi, Yohei Kajiyama, Naohiro Ishikawa (Hokuto Nakamura 88), Tatsuya Yazawa (Roberto Cesar 75) - Naotake Hanyu (Tatsuya Suzuki 71), Lucas. Tr: Kiyoshi Okuma
Kyoto - Yuichi Mizutani - Koken Kato (Shogo Shimohata 76), Jun Ando, Shun Morishita, Takayuki Fukumura - Jung Woo Young, Atsutaka Nakamura (Taisuke Nakamura 58), Kohei Kudo, Hiroki Nakayama (c) - Takumi Miyayoshi, Dutra (Yuya Kubo 54). Tr: Takeshi Oki

‡ Played at National Stadium, Tokyo
†† Played at Nagai Stadium, Osaka
† Qualified for the AFC Champions League

J.LEAGUE YAMAZAKI NABISCO CUP 2011

First Round

- Kashima Antlers — Bye
- Kawasaki Frontale — 2 3
- Sanfrecce Hiroshima * — 2 1
- Vissel Kobe — 1 1
- Yokohama F-Marinos * — 1 2
- Albirex Niigata — Bye
- Ventforet Kofu * — 1 0
- Shimizu S-Pulse — 0 2
- Nagoya Grampus — Bye
- Gamba Osaka — Bye
- Vegalta Sendai — 1 2
- Kashiwa Reysol * — 0 1
- Avispa Fukuoka — 0 0
- Jubilo Iwata * — 2 3
- Cerezo Osaka — Bye
- Omiya Ardija — Bye
- Montedio Yamagata — 0 1
- Urawa Reds * — 2 2

Second Round

- Kashima Antlers — Bye
- Kawasaki Frontale — 0 3
- Yokohama F-Marinos * — 4 2
- Albirex Niigata — 1 3
- Shimizu S-Pulse * — 2 1
- Nagoya Grampus — Bye
- Gamba Osaka — Bye
- Vegalta Sendai * — 0 0
- Jubilo Iwata — 0 3
- Cerezo Osaka — Bye
- Omiya Ardija — 0 1
- Urawa Reds * — 2 2

Quarter-finals

- Kashima Antlers * — 3
- Yokohama F-Marinos — 2
- Albirex Niigata — 3
- Nagoya Grampus * — 5
- Gamba Osaka * — 3
- Jubilo Iwata — 1
- Cerezo Osaka * — 1
- Urawa Reds — 2

Semi-finals

- Kashima Antlers — 2
- Nagoya Grampus * — 1
- Gamba Osaka — 1
- Urawa Reds * — 2

Final

- Kashima Antlers — 1
- Urawa Reds — 0

CUP FINAL

National Stadium, Tokyo
1-01-2012, 13:10, Att: 46 599, Ref: Minoru Tojo
Scorer - Yuya Osako 105 for Kashima
Kashima - Hitoshi Sogahata● - Toru Araiba, Alex Santos● (Fellype Gabriel 76), Koji Nakata, Mitsuo Ogasawara (Chikashi Masuda 91), Takuya Nozawa, Takesji Aoki●●80, Yasushi Endo (Yuzo Tashiro 63), Gaku Shibasaki, Yuya Osako, Shinzo Koroki. Tr: Oswaldo de Oliveira
Urawa - Nobuhiro Kato - Nobuhisa Yamada (Keisuke Tsuboi 107), Tsadaki Hirakawa, Mitsuru Nagata, Mizuki Hamada, Keita Suzuki (Shuto Kojima 91), Yosuke Kashiwagi, Tsukasa Umesaki● (Shunki Takahashi● 76), Naoki Yamada●●80, Sergio Escudero, Genki Haraguchi. Tr: Takafumi Hori

* Home team/home team in the 1st leg

CLUB BY CLUB GUIDE TO THE 2011 SEASON IN JAPAN

ALBIREX NIIGATA 2011

Mon	Date	Opponent	Res	Comp	Scorers	Att
Mar	5	Avispa	W 3-0	JL	Michael 52, Bruno Lopes 69, Fujita 75	10 254
Apr	24	Jubilo	D 1-1	JL	Cho 6p	33 662
	29	Cerezo	D 1-1	JL	Bruno Lopes 3	9 014
	3	Vissel	W 1-0	JL	Bruno Lopes 74	30 610
	7	Omiya	D 0-0	JL		9 094
May	14	Kashiwa	L 0-3	JL		25 312
	21	Gamba	L 1-2	JL	Michael 77	15 978
	28	Urawa	D 1-1	JL	Suzuki 70	25 272
	11	Sanfrecce	L 0-1	JL		22 196
	15	Nagoya	L 0-4	JL		6 793
Jun	18	Vegalta	D 1-1	JL	Mikado 72	23 602
	22	Yokohama	L 0-1	JL		8 109
	25	Cerezo	D 1-1	JL	Bruno Lopes 76	24 947
	2	Montedio	W 2-0	JL	Tanaka 2 13 49	23 408
	6	Ventforet	L 1-2	JL	Bruno Lopes 52	13 644
Jul	10	Kashima	W 2-1	JL	Bruno Lopes 59p, Cho 88	10 602
	16	Shimizu	L 1-2	JL	Ishikawa 5	13 599
	23	Kawasaki	W 1-0	JL	Bruno Lopes 53	25 420
	30	Montedio	W 1-0	JL	Tanaka 62	10 461
	6	Shimizu	W 4-0	JL	Michael 2 40 77, Cho 67, Chiba 94+	37 830
Aug	14	Urawa	L 2-3	JL	Michael 54p, Bruno Lopes 94p	37 375
	20	Vissel	L 1-2	JL	Gonzaga 4	11 340
	24	Omiya	D 0-0	JL		18 175
	27	Sanfrecce	L 0-1	JL		14 852
	10	Kashima	D 2-2	JL	Homma 44, Bruno Lopes 67	25 819
	14	Shimizu	L 1-2	LCr2	Homma 6	6 939
Sep	17	Vegalta	L 0-2	JL		16 046
	24	Jubilo	L 0-1	JL		9 251
	28	Shimizu	W 3-1	LCr2	Bruno Lopes 36, Tanaka 55, Michael 58	10 024
	1	Yokohama	W 4-2	JL	Cho 20, Sakai 59, Michael 60, Bruno Lopes 72	24 439
	5	Nagoya	L 3-5	LCqf	Bruno Lopes 63, Kawamata 93+, Kikuchi 98	4 108
Oct	12	Toyama	W 5-0	ECr2	Bruno Lopes 17, Kawamata 2 21 76, Kogure 23, Uchida 94+	3 597
	16	Kawasaki	W 2-1	JL	Bruno Lopes 2 59 70	16 903
	23	Avispa	W 3-1	JL	Homma 2, Cho 2 64 82	27 107
	29	Kashiwa	L 0-4	JL		10 623
Nov	16	Matsumoto	L 0-1	ECr3		4 842
	19	Gamba	D 2-2	JL	Mikado 45, Bruno Lopes 70	22 990
	27	Ventforet	L 0-3	JL		13 361
Dec	3	Nagoya	L 0-1	JL		26 300

14th Att: 442 836 • Av: 26 049 (-14.7%) • Big Swan 42 300

AVISPA FUKUOKA 2011

Mon	Date	Opponent	Res	Comp	Scorers	Att
Mar	5	Albirex	L 0-3	JL		10 254
	23	Shimizu	L 0-1	JL		11 025
Apr	29	Kashima	L 1-2	JL	Nakamachi 40	12 147
	3	Vegalta	L 0-1	JL		15 859
	7	Yokohama	L 2-3	JL	Jogo 2 31 42	13 520
May	15	Gamba	L 2-3	JL	Sueyoshi 18, Okamoto 62	18 403
	21	Jubilo	L 1-4	JL	Okamoto 86	12 372
	29	Nagoya	L 2-5	JL	Okamoto 26p, Shigematsu 66	11 132
	5	Jubilo	L 0-2	LCr1		9 440
	11	Cerezo	L 0-3	JL		6 020
Jun	15	Vissel	D 0-0	JL		6 151
	18	Kashiwa	L 0-2	JL		6 087
	22	Urawa	L 0-3	JL		20 240
	25	Jubilo	L 1-2	JL	Naruoka 78	5 865
	2	Ventforet	W 1-0	JL	Tanaka 17	6 585
Jul	9	Kawasaki	L 2-3	JL	Okamoto 2 71 77	16 686
	13	Omiya	W 1-0	JL	Naruoka 42	4 028
	18	Sanfrecce	D 0-0	JL		9 864
	24	Montedio	L 0-2	JL		7 004
	27	Jubilo	L 0-3	LCr1		4 411
Aug	31	Nagoya	L 0-3	JL		19 421
	7	Gamba	L 0-2	JL		13 389
	14	Kawasaki	W 2-1	JL	Jogo 2 69 85	9 581
	20	Kashiwa	L 2-3	JL	Okamoto 7, Jogo 73	8 470
	24	Vissel	D 2-2	JL	Matsuura 60, Shigematsu 90	6 119
	28	Kashima	L 0-6	JL		13 434
Sep	10	Yokohama	L 0-1	JL		15 818
	17	Ventforet	L 1-2	JL	Okamoto 47	9 100
	25	Sanfrecce	W 2-1	JL	Sueyoshi 40, Naruoka 75	12 540
	1	Omiya	W 2-0	JL	Matsuura 48, Jogo 69	7 214
Oct	8	Kochi Univ	W 3-0	ECr2	Nakamachi 14, Matsuura 31, Takahashi 64	938
	15	Vegalta	L 0-3	JL		7 191
	23	Albirex	L 1-3	JL	Takahashi 88	27 107
	3	Shimizu	D 2-2	JL	Ramazotti 66, Nakamachi 68	12 632
Nov	16	Vegalta	L 1-3	ECr3	Okamoto 68	4 831
	19	Montedio	W 5-0	JL	Suzuki 2, Matsuura 11, Nakamachi 36, Ushinohama 2 89 90	5 053
	26	Urawa	L 1-2	JL	Okamoto 32	17 117
Dec	3	Cerezo	L 1-7	JL	Jogo 32	11 009

17th Att: 177 054 • Av: 10 415 (+18%) • Level-5 Stadium 22 563

KEY

SC = Fuji Xerox Super Cup • JL = J.League •
LC = J. League Yamazaki Nabisco Cup • EC =
Emperor's Cup • CL = AFC Champions League
See page 13 for further explanations

ALBIREX LEAGUE APPEARANCES/GOALS 2011

Goalkeepers Masaaki Higashiguchi 14 • Hideaki Ozawa 16+1 • Yohei Takeda 4

Defenders Naoki Ishikawa 20+2/1 • Shigeto Masuda 0+2/0 • Kazunari Ōno 4+3/0 • Daisuke Suzuki 20+4/1 • Jun Uchida 4+1/0 • Yusuke Murakami 14+1/0

Midfield Kazuhiko Chiba 27+2/1 • Seiya Fujita 14+4/1 • Ayato Hasebe 0+1/0 • Isao Homma 34/2 • Masaru Kato 0+2/0 • Naoya Kikuchi 21+2/0 • Yoshiyuki Kobayashi 14+10/0 • Fumiya Kogure 6+13/0 • Michael BRA 25+5/6 • Yuta Mikado 26+7/2 • Atomu Tanaka 22+3/3

Forwards Bruno Lopes BRA 33/13 • Cho Young Cheol KOR 21+4/6 • Kengo Kawamata 5+18/0 • Hideo Oshima 2+3/0 • Noriyoshi Sakai 4+2/0 • Anderson Gonzaga BRA 5+6/1

Coach Hisashi Kurosaki

AVISPA LEAGUE APPEARANCES/GOALS 2011

Goalkeepers Ryuichi Kamiyama 17 • Yuji Rokutan 17

Defenders Kim Min Jae KOR 15+3/0 • Shogo Kobara 20/0 • Yosuke Miyaji 1+2/0 • Daiki Niwa 30/0 • Makoto Tanaka 8/0 • Takumi Wada 20+1/0 • Iatsunori Yamagata 30+1/0 • Kazuki Yamaguchi 11+3/0

Midfield Hisashi Jogo 29+2/7 • Takuya Matsuura 31+1/3 • Kosuke Nakamachi 18+6/2 • Sho Naruoka 22+5/3 • Toshiya Sueyoshi 27+2/2 • Jun Suzuki 23+7/1 • Taku Ushinohama 0+4/2

Forwards Hideya Okamoto 19+11/8 • Kentaro Shigematsu 8+17/2 • Norihisa Shimizu 2+3/0 • Yutaka Takahashi 3+18/2 • Yusuke Tanaka 23+8/1 • Masato Yoshihara 0+4/0 • Ramazotti BRA 0+4/1

Coach Yoshiyuki Shinoda

CEREZO OSAKA 2011

	Date	Opponent	Res		Comp	Scorers	Att
Mar	2	Arema	W	2-1	CLgG	Rodrigo Pimpao 2 [14 76]	10 856
	5	Gamba	L	1-2	JL	Kurata [73]	20 055
	16	Shandong	L	0-2	CLgG		20 821
Apr	5	Jeonbuk	W	1-0	CLgG	Inui [53]	11 351
	20	Jeonbuk	L	0-1	CLgG		7 892
	24	Montedio	D	0-0	JL		
	29	Albirex	D	1-1	JL	Inui [41]	9 014
	3	Arema	W	4-0	CLgG	Kiyotake [31], Rodrigo Pimpao [43], Inui 2 [46 61]	4 000
	7	Vegalta	D	1-1	JL	Komatsu [90]	11 576
	10	Shandong	W	4-0	CLgG	Rodrigo Pimpao [39], Kiyotake [47], Inui [73], Kurata [81]	9 035
May	15	Urawa	D	1-1	JL	Kiyotake [35]	31 571
	20	Kawasaki	D	3-3	JL	Kiyotake [52], Rodrigo Pimpao [54], Martinez [81]	7 712
	24	Gamba	W	1-0	CLr2	Takahashi [88]	16 463
	29	Omiya	L	0-1	JL		5 351
	11	Avispa	W	3-0	JL	Rodrigo Pimpao [9], Kurata [44], Kiyotake [75]	6 020
	15	Yokohama	L	0-1	JL		9 098
Jun	18	Ventforet	W	2-0	JL	Komatsu [85], Bando [90]	8 402
	22	Nagoya	L	2-3	JL	Rodrigo Pimpao [43], Inui [90]	7 875
	25	Albirex	D	1-1	JL	Sakemoto [90]	24 947
	2	Kashiwa	W	5-0	JL	Inui [17], Rodrigo Pimpao [23], Martinez [67], Bando [83], Kurata [90]	13 741
	10	Sanfrecce	W	3-1	JL	Kurata [33], Kiyotake [49] Komatsu [51]	11 615
Jul	13	Jubilo	L	2-3	JL	Kim [49], Maruhashi [74]	8 076
	16	Vissel	L	1-4	JL	Kim [67]	14 961
	23	Shimizu	W	4-0	JL	Kim 2 [53 78], Kurata [59p], Inui [90]	11 254
	31	Kashima	L	1-3	JL	Inui [22]	28 039
	6	Kawasaki	W	2-1	JL	Kiyotake [11], Kurata [36]	15 781
	13	Gamba	D	1-1	JL	Kim [76]	37 172
Aug	17	Kashima	L	1-2	JL	Kim [53]	11 251
	20	Shimizu	D	3-3	JL	Bando 3 [76p 77 87]	12 823
	24	Yokohama	L	1-2	JL	Sugimoto [59]	10 480
	28	Urawa	W	3-1	JL	Yamaguchi [48], Ogihara [87], Kurata [90]	26 248
	10	Sanfrecce	W	5-4	JL	Kiyotake [46], Bando 3 [55 57 77], Kim [72]	20 160
	14	Jeonbuk	W	4-3	CLqf	Bando [29], Kiyotake 2 [56 81], Kim [64p]	15 450
Sep	18	Omiya	D	0-0	JL		9 781
	23	Montedio	W	6-0	JL	Bando [24], Fujimoto [28] Sakemoto [46], Ogihara [49], Lopes [85], Otake [87p]	10 609
	27	Jeonbuk	L	1-6	CLqf	Komatsu [71]	16 423
	2	Vegalta	L	1-2	JL	Komatsu [87p]	16 407
	5	Urawa	L	1-2	LCqf	Lopes [73]	6 736
Oct	12	Hokkaido	W	6-0	ECr2	OG [24], Lopes 2 [30 78], Sugimoto [71], Komatsu [81], Otake [86]	2 116
	15	Ventforet	L	0-4	JL		7 501
	23	Jubilo	W	4-0	JL	Ogihara 2 [37 63], Kurata [49], Bando [90]	9 513
	3	Nagoya	L	1-3	JL	Komatsu [36p]	23 677
Nov	16	Fagiano	W	3-0	ECr3	Bando 2 [52 93+], Sugimoto [92+]	3 631
	20	Vissel	L	0-3	JL		16 030
	26	Kashiwa	D	1-1	JL	Uemoto [48]	11 107
	3	Avispa	W	7-1	JL	Fujimoto [10], Kiyotake [35], Kim [40], Kurata 2 [45p 50], Sugimoto [52], Murata [76]	11 009
Dec	17	Vegalta	D	1-1	ECr4	Murata [115], W 4-2p	5 316
	24	Shimizu	D	2-2	ECqf	Kim [11], Kiyotake [93], W 6-5p	8 252
	29	FC Tokyo	L	0-1	ECsf		11 982

12th Att: 240 465 • Av: 14 145 (-5.8%) • Nagai Ball Gall Field 17 518

GAMBA OSAKA 2011

	Date	Opponent	Res		Comp	Scorers	Att
Mar	1	Melbourne	W	5-1	CLgE	Takei [4], Adriano [7p], Lee [10], Futagawa [62], Kim [90]	12 949
	5	Cerezo	W	2-1	JL	Adriano [65], Endo [76]	20 055
	15	Tianjin	L	1-2	CLgE	Lee [30]	26 866
Apr	5	Jeju Utd	L	1-2	CLgE	Nakazawa [23]	2 167
	20	Jeju Utd	W	3-1	CLgE	Adriano 2 [26 48], Takei [88]	11 398
	24	Sanfrecce	L	1-4	JL	Kawanishi [87]	18 788
	29	Montedio	W	3-2	JL	Adriano 2 [22 37], Lee [86]	17 052
	4	Melbourne	D	1-1	CLgE	Nakazawa [43]	7 437
	11	Tianjin	W	2-0	CLgE	Endo [74], Usami [90p]	7 939
May	15	Avispa	W	3-2	JL	Adriano [30p], Usami [53], Futagawa [57]	18 403
	21	Albirex	W	2-1	JL	Adriano 2 [8.88]	15 978
	24	Cerezo	L	0-1	CLr2		16 463
	29	Kawasaki	L	1-2	JL	Adriano [51p]	14 056
	11	Shimizu	D	2-2	JL	Adriano [15], Usami [57]	16 315
	15	Vegalta	L	1-2	JL	Adriano [65]	14 519
	18	Yokohama	W	2-1	JL	Endo [9], Yamaguchi [26]	18 001
Jun	22	Kashiwa	W	4-2	JL	Endo [13], Hirai [51], Lee [62], Shimohira [90]	9 882
	26	Sanfrecce	W	5-3	JL	Nakazawa [3], Endo [34], Hirai [55], Sasaki [78], Takagu [85]	16 845
	2	Uwara	D	1-1	JL	Usami [56]	42 331
	10	Omiya	W	3-2	JL	Lee [5], Nakazawa [75], Kim [77]	11 982
	13	Vissel	W	3-2	JL	Futagawa [45], Usami [63], Lee [79]	15 244
Jul	16	Ventforet	L	3-4	JL	Lee [15], Hirai [19], Nakazawa [66]	14 126
	23	Jubilo	D	2-2	JL	Yamaguchi [7], Lee [55]	11 364
	27	Kashima	W	4-1	JL	Takei [7], Lee 2 [80 88], Rafinha [83]	13 298
	30	Jubilo	W	2-1	JL	Nakazawa [26], Rafinha [72]	13 515
	7	Avispa	W	2-0	JL	Rafinha [25], OG [75]	13 389
	13	Cerezo	D	1-1	JL	Nakazawa [79]	37 172
	17	Nagoya	D	2-2	JL	Rafinha [45], Kim [74]	15 951
Aug	20	Kawasaki	W	6-3	JL	Hirai [17], Kim [28], Rafinha 3 [47p 88 90], Myojin [78]	12 119
	24	Kashiwa	W	2-0	JL	Otsuka [81], Hirai [82]	12 635
	28	Vissel	W	4-0	JL	Takei [28], Kim [55], Lee [70], Futagawa [90]	17 177
	10	Omiya	W	2-0	JL	Lee [43], Rafinha [77]	15 106
Sep	18	Yokohama	D	1-1	JL	Rafinha [58]	37 725
	24	Ventforet	L	0-2	JL		19 882
	2	Urawa	W	1-0	JL	Lee [28]	20 053
	3	Jubilo	W	3-1	LCqf	Sasaki [43], Rafinha [67], OG [76]	4 112
	9	Urawa	L	1-2	LCsf	Otsuka [90+3]	23 879
Oct	12	Sagawa Sh	W	2-0	ECr2	Kawanishi, Kim	2 932
	15	Nagoya	L	1-4	JL	Myojin [26]	17 481
	22	Montedio	W	5-0	JL	Futagawa [30], Lee [35], Fujihara [60], Rafinha [76], Kawanishi [89]	13 573
	3	Kashima	W	1-0	JL	Rafinha [57]	20 991
Nov	16	Mito	L	2-3	ECr3	Kim [40], Sasaki [65]	2 938
	19	Albirex	D	2-2	JL	Kawanishi 2 [77 83]	22 990
	26	Vegalta	W	1-0	JL	Lee [25]	18 001
Dc	3	Shimizu	W	3-1	JL	Lee 2 [32 39], Futagawa [52]	18 670

3rd Att: 278 981 • Av: 16 411 (-1.4%) • Osaka Expo'70 21 000

CEREZO LEAGUE APPEARANCES/GOALS 2011

Goalkeepers Kim Jin Hyeon KOR 34
Defenders Teruyuki Moniwa 33/0 • Takahiro Ogihara 10/4 • Hiroyuki Omata 3+1/0 • Taikai Uemoto 24+1/1
Midfield Masaki Chugo 22+2/0 • Kota Fujimoto 12+7/2 • Takashi Inui 13+1/5 • Kim Bo Kyung KOR 25+2/8 • Hiroshi Kiyotake 23+2/7 • Shu Kurata 30+3/10 • Masato Kurogi 2+3/0 • Martinez BRA 21/2 • Yusuke Maruhashi 30+2/1 • Kazuya Murata 0+6/1 • Noriyuki Sakemoto 17+5/2 Daisuke Takahashi 17/0 • Hotaru Yamaguchi 6+11/1 • Yohei Otake 1+4/1
Forwards Ryuji Bando 7+14/10 • Rui Komatsu 10+13/5 Ryo Nagai 4+6/0 • Rodrigo Pimpao BRA 14/4 • Kenyu Sugimoto 6+9/2 Fabio Lopes BRA 11+3/1
Coach Levir Culpi BRA

GAMBA LEAGUE APPEARANCES/GOALS 2011

Goalkeepers Yosuke Fujigaya 34
Defenders Hiroki Fujihara 10+2/1 • Akira Kaji 28+2/0 • Kim Jon Ya 2+1/0 • Sota Nakazawa 27/5 • Takumi Shimohira 21/1 • Kazumichi Takagi 8+5/1 • Tatsuya Uchida 3+2/0 • Satoshi Yamaguchi 30/2
Midfield Yasuhito Endo 31+2/4 • Takahiro Futagawa 28+4/5 Hideo Hashimoto 1+3/0 • Tomokazu Myojin 25+2/2 • Kotaro Omori 0+1/0 Hayato Sasaki 3+18/1 • Takuya Takei 30+3/2 • Takashi Usami 13+1/4 Shigeru Yokotani 1+10/0
Forwards Shoki Hirai 11+10/5 • Shota Kawanishi 1+7/4 Kim Seung Yong 14+14/4 • Lee Keun Ho 31+1/15 • Shohei Otsuka 0+1/0 Rafinha BRA 15+2/11 • Adriano BRA 8/9 • Afonso BRA 0+5/0
Coach Akira Nishino

JUBILO IWATA 2011

		Opp	Res	Sc	Comp	Scorers	Att
Apr	5	Ventforet	W	1-0	JL	Yamamoto.K 81	10 254
	24	Albirex	D	1-1	JL	Gilsinho 68	33 662
	29	Sanfrecce	D	1-1	JL	Kanazono 73	11 319
	3	Kawasaki	L	0-1	JL		18 449
	7	Montedio	W	4-0	JL	Maeda 2 2 45, Yamazaki 13, Yamada 60	8 960
May	14	Vegalta	D	3-3	JL	Yamada 58, Yamazaki 61, Kanazono 90	11 544
	21	Avispa	W	4-1	JL	Yamazaki 5, Maeda 2 32 49, Yamamoto.K 35	12 372
	28	Shimizu	D	0-0	JL		12 678
	5	Avispa	W	2-0	LCr1	Yamazaki 13, Kobayashi 63	9 440
	11	Nagoya	L	0-1	JL		12 067
Jun	15	Kashiwa	W	3-0	JL	Kanazono 20, Maeda 2 45 59	7 803
	18	Kashima	L	0-2	JL		11 830
	22	Omiya	L	1-2	JL	Maeda 1	6 386
	25	Avispa	W	2-1	JL	Kanazono 17, Yamada 43	5 865
	3	Vissel	W	3-0	JL	Nasu 54, Kanazono 72, OG 73	7 706
	9	Yokohama	L	1-2	JL	Nasu 17	11 226
Jul	13	Cerezo	W	3-2	JL	Kanazono 63, Komano 77, Yamada 80	8 076
	17	Urawa	D	1-1	JL	Maeda 90p	18 623
	23	Gamba	D	2-2	JL	Kanazono 37, Yamada 70	11 364
	27	Avispa	W	3-0	LCr1	Kaga 31, Gilsinho 66, Arata 83	4 411
	30	Gamba	L	1-2	JL	Nasu 49	13 515
Aug	7	Nagoya	L	1-2	JL	Kanazono 19	14 230
	14	Kashiwa	W	6-1	JL	Yamamoto.S 33, Fujita 43, Souto 2 49 57, Kanazono 65, Suganuma 86	12 472
	20	Yokohama	L	0-1	JL		24 518
	24	Vegalta	D	1-1	JL	OG 71	8 693
	27	Omiya	L	0-2	JL		10 013
	10	Shimizu	W	2-1	JL	Komano 45, Maeda 62	30 516
Sep	14	Vegalta	D	0-0	LCr2		7 360
	17	Sanfrecce	L	1-3	JL	Maeda 25	11 894
	24	Albirex	W	1-0	JL	Arata 90	9 251
	28	Vegalta	W	3-0	LCr2	Maeda 7, Yamamoto.S 2 81 86	6 339
	1	Montedio	D	1-1	JL	Maeda 57	7 475
Oct	5	Gamba	L	1-2	LCqf	Nasu 7	4 112
	12	Fukushima	W	3-0	ECr2	Arata 3 33 71 83	2 019
	15	Kashima	L	1-2	JL	Kanazono 68	8 313
	23	Cerezo	L	0-4	JL		9 513
	3	Urawa	W	3-0	JL	Maeda 2 13 67, Yamazaki 54	34 623
Nov	16	JEF United	L	0-1	ECr3		2 548
	19	Ventforet	W	2-1	JL	Kanazono 2 2 10	7 244
	27	Vissel	L	1-3	JL	Maeda 80	17 187
Dec	3	Kawasaki	W	2-1	JL	Gilsinho 2 17 43	12 349

8th Att: 299 525 • Av: 11 796 (-2.8%) • Yamaha Stadium 16 893

KASHIMA ANTLERS 2011

		Opp	Res	Sc	Comp	Scorers	Att
Feb	26	Nagoya	D	1-1	SC	Nozawa 66. L 1-3p	35 963
Mar	2	Shanghai	D	0-0	CLgH		20 036
	6	Omiya	D	3-3	JL	Inoha 47, Iwamasa 58, OG 90	23 262
	6	Suwon	D	1-1	CLgH	Nakata 71	7 689
	13	Sydney	W	3-0	CLgH	Nozawa 41, Gabriel 51, Koroki 90	7 320
Apr	19	Suwon	D	1-1	CLgH	Tashiro 55	4 619
	23	Yokohama	L	0-3	JL		15 688
	29	Avispa	W	2-1	JL	Osako 59, Iwamasa 71	12 147
	3	Shanghai	W	2-0	CLgH	Koroki 2 32 80	11 954
	10	Sydney	W	2-1	CLgH	Osako 64, Nozawa 84	3 164
May	15	Kawasaki	L	2-3	JL	Endo 50, Carlao 90	19 643
	21	Urawa	D	2-2	JL	Nishi 13, Masuda 62	37 521
	25	Seoul	L	0-3	CLr2		12 725
	29	Sanfrecce	L	1-2	JL	Koroki 18	8 049
	11	Montedio	W	2-0	JL	Koroki 35, Iwamasa 40	11 012
	15	Ventofret	L	0-1	JL		7 810
Jun	18	Jubilo	W	2-0	JL	Koroki 6, Tashiro 64	11 830
	22	Vissel	W	1-0	JL	Tashiro 37	9 705
	25	Kawasaki	D	2-2	JL	Tashiro 31, Nakata 45	17 409
	2	Shimizu	D	0-0	JL		15 528
	10	Albirex	L	1-2	JL	Nozawa 56p	10 602
Jul	13	Nagoya	L	1-2	JL	Osako 2	12 845
	17	Vegalta	W	3-0	JL	Masuda 13, Nozawa 18, Tashiro 69	11 364
	23	Kashiwa	L	1-2	JL	Tashiro 57	30 807
	27	Gamba	L	1-4	JL	Masuda 19	13 298
	31	Cerezo	W	3-1	JL	Tashiro 2 38 45, Ogasawara 90	28 039
Aug	6	Montedio	W	3-1	JL	Nozawa 16, Osako 24, Araiba 58	13 139
	13	Vegalta	W	1-0	JL	Gabriel 29p	19 224
	17	Cerezo	W	2-1	JL	Osako 56, Masuda 74	11 251
	20	Sanfrecce	W	2-0	JL	Iwamasa 65, Nozawa 87	16 237
	24	Ventforet	D	1-1	JL	Tashiro 61	11 340
	28	Avispa	W	6-0	JL	Tashiro 2 19 88, Endo 2 45 80, Iwamasa 48, Nakata 57	13 434
Sep	10	Albirex	D	2-2	JL	Iwamasa 74, Tashiro 79	25 819
	18	Nagoya	D	1-1	JL	Masuda 77	22 258
	24	Urawa	D	0-0	JL		25 106
	2	Kashiwa	L	0-1	JL		21 466
	5	Yokohama	W	3-2	LCqf	Koroki 49, Osako 73, Tashiro 111	4 804
Oct	9	Nagoya	W	2-1	LCsf	Osako 50, Shibasaki 107	8 562
	12	Un Tsukuba	W	2-0	ECr2	Tashiro 33	3 468
	15	Jubilo	W	2-1	JL	Tashiro 54, OG 70	8 313
	22	Vissel	D	1-1	JL	Nozawa 63p	13 248
	29	Urawa	W	1-0	LCf	Osako 70	46 599
Nov	3	Gamba	L	0-1	JL		20 991
	16	Kataller	W	2-1	ECr3	Koroki 28, Nozawa 101	3 465
	19	Omiya	D	1-1	JL	Koroki 90	9 537
	26	Shimizu	W	3-0	JL	Gabriel 50, Nozawa 69, Alex 73	21 524
Dec	3	Yokohama	W	1-0	JL	Osako 32	26 973
	17	Kyoto	L	0-1	ECr4		5 671

6th Att: 274 655 • Av: 16 156 (-22.9%) • Kashima Stadium 40 728

JUBILO LEAGUE APPEARANCES/GOALS 2011

Goalkeepers Yoshikatsu Kawaguchi 34
Defenders Yoshiaki Fujita 31/1 • Kenichi Kaga 29/0 • Jo Kanazawa 0+8/0 • Masahiro Koga 6+2/0 • Yuichi Komano 34/2 • Lee Gang Jin KOR 2+2/0 Daisuke Nasu 33/3 • Ryu Okada 0+4/0 • Park Joo Ho KOR 11/0
Midfield Keisuke Funatani 3+3/0 • Yuki Kobayashi 33/0 • Norihiro Nishi 9+1/0 • Hiroki Yamada 28+1/5 • Kosuke Yamamoto 18+5/2 Shuto Yamamoto 15+13/1 • Rodrigo Souto BRA 12/2
Forwards Tomoyuki Arata 0+13/1 • Gilsinho BRA 14+15/3 • Hidetaka Kanazono 17+11/12 • Ryoichi Maeda 28/14 • Minoru Suganuma 0+11/1 Ryohei Yamazaki 17+2/4
Coach Masaaki Yanagishita

KASHIMA LEAGUE APPEARANCES/GOALS 2011

Goalkeepers Hitoshi Sogahata 34
Defenders Toru Araiba 19+4/1 • Masahiko Inoha 7+3/1 • Daiki Iwamasa 28/6 • Koji Nakata 25+1/2 • Takefumi Toma 1+1/0
Midfield Takeshi Aoki 16+7/0 • Shoma Doi 0+2/0 • Yasushi Endo 24+6/3 Fellype Gabriel BRA 14+2/2 • Takuya Honda 0+3/0 • Kenji Koyano 0+3/0 Chikashi Masuda 27+5/5 • Masashi Motoyama 2+11/0 Daigo Nishi 24/2 • Takuya Nozawa 34/6 • Mitsuo Ogasawara 23+8/1 Gaku Shibasaki 6+7/0 • Tarta BRA 0+7/0
Forwards Alex BRA 26+4/1 • Carlao BRA 1+4/1 • Shinzo Koroki 25+11/4 Yuya Osako 20+5/5 • Igor Sartori BRA 0+2/0 • Yuzo Tashiro 16+6/12
Coach Oswaldo de Oliveira BRA

KASHIWA REYSOL 2011

	Date	Opponent	Res	Score	Comp	Scorers	Att
Mar	5	Shimizu	W	3-0	JL	Wagner 21, Park 65, Domingues 68	10 390
	23	Omiya	W	1-0	JL	Domingues 55	8 441
Apr	29	Ventofert	W	2-1	JL	Tanaka 59, Kitajima 64	10 319
	3	Montedio	L	1-2	JL	Kitajima 70	10 414
	7	Urawa	W	3-1	JL	Kitajima 2 I 83, Wagner 21	24 222
May	15	Albirex	W	3-0	JL	Wagner 23, Kondo 61, Kudo 81	25 312
	21	Nagoya	D	0-0	JL		21 506
	28	Vissel	W	3-0	JL	Tanaka 2 21 24, Domingues 73	6 855
	5	Vegalta	L	0-1	LCr1		8 769
	11	Yokohama	W	2-0	JL	Tanaka 26, Kitajima 37	17 597
Jun	15	Jubilo	L	0-3	JL		7 803
	18	Avispa	W	2-0	JL	Tanaka 39, Hyodo 90	6 087
	22	Gamba	L	2-4	JL	Tanaka 10, Domingues 67	9 882
	25	Ventforet	W	4-1	JL	Tanaka 2 28 34, Wagner 2 61 82	10 450
	2	Cerezo	L	0-5	JL		13 741
	9	Vegalta	W	1-0	JL	Sawa 90	10 324
	13	Sanfrecce	W	3-1	JL	Domingues 10, Kitajima 55, Kudo 90	7 887
Jul	16	Kawasaki	L	2-3	JL	OG 53, Domingues 70	19 619
	23	Kashima	W	2-1	JL	Kitajima 33, Domingues 79	30 807
	27	Vegalta	L	1-2	LCr1	Kitajima 16	10 439
	31	Vegalta	D	0-0	JL		15 315
	6	Yokohama	W	2-0	JL	Domingues 8, Wagner 66	11 051
	14	Jubilo	L	1-6	JL	Domingues 38	12 472
Aug	20	Avispa	W	3-2	JL	Domingues 19, Kudo 42, Hayashi 67	8 470
	24	Gamba	L	0-2	JL		12 635
	28	Kawasaki	W	3-2	JL	Kudo 61, Tanaka 2 73 78	10 703
	10	Nagoya	W	2-1	JL	Tanaka 65, Sawa 70	10 914
Sep	17	Vissel	W	4-0	JL	Kudo 4, Wagner 57, Tanaka 72, Park 77	4 253
	25	Omiya	L	1-3	JL	Domingues 63	10 875
	2	Kashima	W	1-0	JL	Kudo 31	21 466
Oct	8	Tochigi	W	2-0	ECr2	Masushima 4, Domingues 59	3 110
	16	Montedio	W	1-0	JL	Wagner 33	10 361
	22	Sanfrecce	W	3-1	JL	Wagner 68, Kitajima 2 82 87	14 450
	3	Albirex	W	4-0	JL	Domingues 2 7p 34, Wagner 55, Tanaka 90	10 623
Nov	16	Ventforet	W	6-1	ECr3	Wagner 10, Kudo 26, Kitajima 29, Hashimoto 37, Tanaka 2 67 80	3 950
	20	Shimizu	W	2-1	JL	Kudo 62, Domingues 84	19 584
	26	Cerezo	D	1-1	JL	Domingues 65	11 107
Dec	3	Urawa	W	3-1	JL	Wagner 29, Hashimoto 38, Barada 76	54 441
	8	Auckland	W	2-0	CWr1	Tanaka 37, Kudo 40	18 754
	11	Monterrey	D	1-1	CWqf	Domingues 53. W.4-3p	27 525
	14	Santos	L	1-3	CWsf	Sakai 54	29 173
	18	Al Sadd	D	0-0	CW3p	L 3-5p	60 527
	21	Nagoya	D	3-3	ECr4	Domingues 2 41 115, Kudo 66. L 8-9p	5 618

1st   Att: 202 593 • Av: 11 917 (+47.1%) • Hitachi Stadium 15 900

KAWASAKI FRONTALE 2011

	Date	Opponent	Res	Score	Comp	Scorers	Att
Mar	5	Montedio	W	2-0	JL	Yajima 34, Noborizato 38	18 673
	23	Vegalta	L	1-2	JL	Tanaka 37	15 030
Apr	29	Nagoya	L	0-2	JL		4 556
	3	Jubilo	W	1-0	JL	Kobayashi 90	18 449
	7	Vissel	L	0-1	JL		10 364
	15	Kashima	W	3-2	JL	Juninho 10, Yamase 31, Kobayashi 78	19 643
May	20	Cerezo	D	3-3	JL	Yamase 17, Yajima 29, Kobayashi 72	7 712
	29	Gamba	W	2-1	JL	Nakamura 61 90	14 056
	5	Sanfrecce	D	2-2	LCr1	Yamase 2, Komiyama 88	12 498
	11	Ventforet	D	2-2	JL	Kobayashi 34, Yamase 49	13 111
	15	Omiya	W	5-0	JL	Tasaka 41, Igawa 44, Kobayashi 64, Yajima 71, Yamase 78	7 003
Jun	18	Sanfrecce	W	2-0	JL	Yajima 35, Kikuchi 58	13 605
	22	Shimizu	W	3-2	JL	Inamoto 4, Yamase 13, Kobayashi 81	12 217
	25	Kashima	D	2-2	JL	Tashiro 31, Nakata 45	17 409
	3	Yokohama	L	1-2	JL	OG 22	29 980
	9	Avispa	W	3-2	JL	Inamoto 38, Nakamura 45, Juninho 66	16 686
	13	Urawa	L	0-2	JL		24 293
Jul	16	Kashima	W	3-2	JL	Yajima 4, Kobayashi 30, Juninho 61p	19 619
	23	Albirex	L	0-1	JL		25 420
	27	Sanfrecce	W	3-1	LCr1	Kobayashi 2 10 62, Noborizato 54	11 067
	30	Urawa	L	0-1	JL		20 047
	6	Cerezo	L	1-2	JL	Noborizato 64	15 781
	14	Avispa	L	1-2	JL	Kobayashi 25	9 581
Aug	20	Gamba	L	3-6	JL	Yajima 30, Nakamura 40, Yamase 45	12 119
	24	Nagoya	L	1-2	JL	Kusukami 66	19 754
	28	Kashima	L	2-3	JL	Tasaka 50, Juninho 54	10 703
	11	Vissel	L	0-3	JL		14 918
	14	Yokohama	L	0-4	LCr2		9 859
	17	Montedio	W	1-0	JL	Kobayashi 53	10 333
Sep	24	Shimizu	D	1-1	JL	Juninho 65	20 973
	28	Yokohama	W	3-2	LCr2	Tasaka 40, Juninho 86, Yamase 95+	10 528
	1	Ventforet	W	1-0	JL	Kobayashi 25	11 377
	8	Arte	W	2-1	ECr2	Kobayashi 61, Tasaka 105	3 308
Oct	16	Albirex	L	1-2	JL	Juninho 89	16 903
	22	Vegalta	D	0-0	JL		15 224
	3	Omiya	L	0-1	JL		17 556
	16	Oita	W	4-0	ECr3	Kobayashi 25, Tasaka 55, Kusukami 77, Yajima 84	4 747
Nov	19	Sanfrecce	W	3-2	JL	Kobayashi 45, Yokoyama 84, Yajima 90	12 041
	26	Yokohama	W	3-0	JL	OG 49, Juninho 2 77 84	19 972
Dec	3	Jubilo	L	1-2	JL	Juninho 52	12 349
	17	Shonan	L	0-1	ECr4		8 291

11th   Att: 294 776 • Av: 17 340 (-6.5%) • Todoroki 25 000

KASHIWA LEAGUE APPEARANCES/GOALS 2011
Goalkeepers Kazushige Kirihata 8 • Takanori Sugeno 26
Defenders Wataru Hashimoto 21+4/1 • Naoya Kondo 31+1/1 • Yohei Kurakawa 0+1/0 • Tatsuya Masushima 23+2/0 • Yusuke Murakami 5/0 • Takanori Nakajima 1+2/0 • Park Dong Hyuk KOR 16+1/2 Hiroki Sakai 26+1/0
Midfield An Young Hak PRK 1+1/0 • Akimi Barada 16+11/1 • Akihiro Hyodo 6+10/1 • Jorge Wagner BRA 29+2/11 • Ryoichi Kurisawa 31/0 Leandro Domingues BRA 30/15 • Koki Mizuno 0+10/0 Hidekazu Otani 24+3/0 • Yuki Otsu 9+1/0
Forwards Ryohei Hayashi 1+9/1 • Hideaki Kitajima 18+5/9 • Masato Kudo 16+8/7 • Roger Barada 0+2/0 • Masakatsu Sawa 11+12/2 • Junya Tanaka 25+5/13
Coach Nelsinho Baptista BRA

KAWASAKI LEAGUE APPEARANCES/GOALS 2011
Goalkeepers Takashi Aizawa 17 • Shunsuke Ando 4 • Rikihiro Sugiyama 13
Defenders Akito Fukumori 0+2/0 • Yusuke Igawa 2+1/1 • Hiroki Ito 7+3/0 • Takanobu Komiyama 24+1/0 • Yuki Saneto 8+4/0 • Jun Sonoda 0+2/0 • Yudai Tanaka 6/0 • Yusuke Tanaka 30/2 • Tomonobu Yokoyama 3+7/1
Midfield Junichi Inamoto 12/2 • Kosuke Kikuchi 30+1/1 • Jumpei Kusukami 7+12/1 • Kengo Nakamura 26+4/4 • Ryota Oshima 4+5/0 • Kosei Shibasaki 31/0 • Yusuke Tasaka 18+7/2 • Koji Yamase 30+4/6
Forwards Juninho BRA 27+5/9 • Yu Kobayashi 14+18/12 • Satoshi Kukino 0+6/0 • Masaru Kurotsu 0+1/0 • Yuki Natsume 0+3/0 • Kyohei Noborizato 12+7/2 • Takuro Yajima 24+6/7
Coach Naoki Soma

MONTEDIO YAMAGATA 2011

Month	Date	Opponent	Res	Score	Comp	Scorers	Att
Mar	5	Kawasaki	L	0-2	JL		18 673
	24	Cerezo	D	0-0	JL		8 551
	29	Gamba	L	2-3	JL	Sato 69, Miyamoto 79	17 052
Apr	3	Kashiwa	W	2-1	JL	Ishii 61, Hasegawa 83	10 414
	7	Jubilo	L	0-4	JL		8 960
	14	Omiya	L	0-1	JL		7 435
	22	Vegalta	L	0-1	JL		18 008
	28	Ventforet	D	1-1	JL	Ito 26	7 582
May	5	Urawa	L	0-2	LCr1		23 275
	11	Kashima	L	0-2	JL		11 012
	15	Shimizu	L	1-2	JL	Okubo 88p	10 745
	18	Vissel	W	2-0	JL	Okubo 53, Ito 83	6 587
	22	Sanfrecce	L	2-3	JL	Okubo 33p, Ota 72	7 593
	25	Yokohama	L	0-2	JL		7 667
Jun	2	Albirex	L	0-2	JL		23 408
	6	Urawa	D	0-0	JL		8 303
	13	Yokohama	L	1-2	JL	Miyazaki 57	7 104
	17	Nagoya	L	0-2	JL		11 757
	24	Avispa	W	2-0	JL	Akiba 30, Hasegawa 72	7 004
	27	Urawa	L	1-2	LCr1	Kawashima 25	5 012
	30	Albirex	L	0-1	JL		10 461
Jul	6	Kashima	L	1-3	JL	Ota 49	13 139
	13	Ventforet	W	3-1	JL	Maeda 37, Yamazaki 2 55 87	7 940
	20	Omiya	D	1-1	JL	Ota 77	7 730
	24	Shimizu	D	1-1	JL	Yamazaki 80	6 942
	27	Vegalta	L	1-2	JL	Okubo 30	19 087
Aug	11	Urawa	W	1-0	JL	Yamazaki 2	27 709
	17	Kawasaki	L	0-1	JL		10 333
	23	Cerezo	L	0-6	JL		10 609
Sep	1	Jubilo	D	1-1	JL	Ito 3	7 475
	8	Blaublitz	W	2-0	ECr2	Shimomura 23, Hasegawa 38	2 425
	16	Kashiwa	L	0-1	JL		10 361
	22	Gamba	L	0-5	JL		13 573
Oct	3	Vissel	L	0-2	JL		11 420
Nov	16	Kyoto	L	2-3	ECr3	Hasegawa 7, Miyazaki 9	1 849
	19	Avispa	L	0-5	JL		5 053
	26	Nagoya	L	0-3	JL		26 481
Dec	3	Sanfrecce	L	1-3	JL		7 016

18th Att: 158 527 • Av: 9 325 (-20.3%) • ND Soft Stadium 20 315

NAGOYA GRAMPUS 2011

Month	Date	Opponent	Res	Score	Comp	Scorers	Att
Feb	26	Kashima	D	1-1	SC	Masukawa 54 3-1p	35 963
Mar	1	Hangzhou	L	0-2	CLgF		28 674
	5	Yokohama	D	1-1	JL	Kennedy 90p	27 153
	6	FC Seoul	L	1-1	CLgF	Nagai 14	7 348
Apr	12	Al Ain	W	4-0	CLgF	Kanazaki 2 27 45, OG 61, Fujimoto 77	5 914
	19	FC Seoul	W	2-0	CLgF	Kanazai 26, Nagai 81	10 927
	24	Urawa	L	0-3	JL		42 767
	29	Kawasaki	W	2-0	JL	Tamada 2 34 82	4 556
May	4	Hangzhou	W	1-0	CLgF	Fujimoto 77p	13 767
	7	Shimizu	D	1-1	JL	Tamada 8	11 559
	11	Al Ain	L	1-3	CLgF	Fujimoto 49	892
	15	Ventforet	L	1-3	JL	Fujimoto 39	14 075
	21	Kashiwa	D	0-0	JL		21 506
	25	Suwon	L	0-2	CLr2		11 036
	29	Avispa	W	5-2	JL	Kennedy 23, Tamada 2 51 90, Fujimoto 81, Burzanovic 87	11 132
Jun	11	Jubilo	W	1-0	JL	Tamada 89	12 067
	15	Albirex	W	4-0	JL	Tamada 28, Kennedy 2 37 83, Tanaka 90	6 793
	18	Omiya	D	2-2	JL	Isomura 45, Kennedy 52p	8 345
	22	Cerezo	W	3-2	JL	Isomura 14, Tamada 44, Kennedy 73	7 875
	25	Urawa	D	1-1	JL	Isomura 45	28 515
Jul	2	Vegalta	D	1-1	JL	OG 65	18 533
	9	Vissel	W	1-0	JL	Nakamura 84	17 568
	13	Kashima	W	2-1	JL	Kennedy 35, Burzanovic 79	12 845
	17	Montedio	W	2-0	JL	Tamada 43, Kennedy 57	11 757
	23	Sanfrecce	W	3-2	JL	Tulio Tanaka 15, Kennedy 67, Masukawa 80	11 904
	31	Avispa	W	3-0	JL	Tamada 51, Fujimoto 73, Kennedy 53p	19 421
Aug	7	Jubilo	W	2-1	JL	Ogawa 28, Nagai 73	14 230
	13	Sanfrecce	W	3-0	JL	Ogawa 23, Kennedy 39, Nagai 90	7 099
	17	Gamba	D	2-2	JL	Burzanovic 56, Kennedy 85	15 951
	20	Vegalta	L	0-1	JL		13 365
	24	Kawasaki	W	2-1	JL	Kennedy 2 75 78	19 754
	28	Ventforet	W	4-1	JL	Tamada 32, Kennedy 34, Fujimoto 2 45 69	19 061
Sep	10	Kashiwa	L	1-2	JL	Tamada 17	10 914
	18	Shimizu	D	1-1	JL	Tulio Tanaka 82	22 258
	23	Vissel	W	3-1	JL	Tulio Tanaka 10, Fujimoto 61, Kennedy 86	15 987
Oct	2	Shimizu	L	0-2	JL		20 181
	5	Albirex	W	5-3	LCqf	Kanazaki 15, Nagai 2 91+ 105, Hashimoto 114, Tulio Tanka 121	4 108
	9	Kashima	L	1-2	LCsf	Tulio Tanaka 80	8 562
	12	Suzuka	W	6-0	ECr2	Burzanovic 2 14 35, Hashimoto 19, Arai 42, Tanaka 78, Taguchi 88	2 280
	15	Gamba	W	4-1	JL	Nakamura 2 11 68, Fujimoto 2 49 84	17 481
	22	Omiya	W	3-2	JL	Tulio Tanaka 3, Tamada 77, Kennedy 84p	9 200
Nov	3	Cerezo	W	3-1	JL	Fujimoto 24, Kennedy 42, Nagai 76	23 677
	16	Giravanz	W	1-0	ECr3	Ogawa 57	2 840
	19	Yokohama	W	2-1	JL	Ogawa 13, Kennedy 83	23 023
	26	Montedio	W	3-0	JL	Kennedy 7, Tulio Tanaka 2 39 45	26 481
Dec	3	Albirex	W	1-0	JL	Tamada 54	26 300
	21	Kashiwa	D	3-3	ECr4	Nagai 2 77 96, Masukawa 88, W 9-8p	5 618
	24	Yokohama	D	0-0	ECqf	L 3-4p	8 728

2nd Att: 284 590 • Av: 16 741 (-16.2%) • Mizuho 27 000

MONTEDIO LEAGUE APPEARANCES/GOALS 2011
Goalkeepers Kenta Shimizu 18 • Yuki Uekusa 16
Defenders Hidenori Ishii 30/1 • Tatsuya Ishikawa 16+2/0 • Ryo Kobayashi 18+0/0 • Kazuya Maeda 20+1/1 • Takuya Miyamoto 26+2/1 • Kei Nakano 0+1/0 • Shogo Nishikawa 10+1/0 • Takuya Sonoda 12+4/0
Midfield Masaru Akiba 25+6/1 • Yuji Funayama 15+4/0 • Tatsuya Furuhashi 4+8/0 • Tomoyasu Hirose 10+9/0 • Shun Ito 11+10/3 • Daichi Kawashima 2+11/0 • Kohei Miyazaki 6+7/2 • Katsuyuki Miyazawa 22+3/0 • Tetsuro Ota 21+5/3 • Kentaro Sato 24+3/1 • Tomi Shimomura 11+9/0 • Takumi Yamada 5/0
Forwards Yu Hasegawa 16+6/2 • Tomotaka Kitamura 5/0 • Tetsuya Okubo 17+3/4 • Masato Yamazaki 14/4
Coach Shinji Kobayashi

NAGOYA LEAGUE APPEARANCES/GOALS 2011
Goalkeepers Seigo Narazaki 24 • Yoshihari Takagi 10+1
Defenders Shohei Abe 30+2/0 • Alex 4+7/0 • Mitsuru Chiyotanda 5+12/0 • Takahiro Masukawa 33/1 • Marcus Tulio Tanaka 31/6
Midfield Igor Burzanovic MNE 8+14/3 • Danilson Cordoba COL 21+2/0 • Jungo Fujimoto 32+1/9 • Sho Hanai 0+1/0 • Koji Hashimoto 0+3/0 • Ryota Isomura 6+14/3 • Mu Kanazaki 3+9/0 • Naoshi Nakamura 23+4/3 • Yoshizumi Ogawa 34/3 • Taishi Taguchi 0+3/0 • Hayuma Tanaka 34/1 • Teruki Tanaka 0+1/0 • Makito Yoshida 1+4/0 • Keiji Yoshimura 3+3/0
Forwards Joshua Kennedy AUS 31/20 • Hikaru Kuba 1+1/0 • Kensuke Nagai 8+19/3 • Keiji Tamada 32/14
Coach Dragan Stojkovic SRB

OMIYA ARDIJA 2011

	Day	Opp	Res	Score	Comp	Scorers	Att
M	6	Kashima	D	3-3	JL	Lee 2 [11 64], Ueda [49]	23 262
Apr	23	Kashwia	L	0-1	JL		8 441
	29	Vissel	W	1-0	JL	Lee [35]	10 502
	3	Ventforet	D	1-1	JL	Higashi [15]	12 056
	7	Albirex	D	0-0	JL		9 094
May	14	Montedio	W	1-0	JL	Higashi [28]	7 435
	22	Shimizu	L	1-4	JL	Rafael [90]	6 668
	29	Cerezo	W	1-0	JL	Rafael [14]	5 351
	11	Urawa	D	2-2	JL	Rafael [37], Fukaya [53]	12 221
	15	Kawasaki	L	0-5	JL		7 003
Jun	18	Nagoya	D	2-2	JL	Aoki 2 [67 90]	8 345
	22	Jubilo	W	2-1	JL	Murakami [15], Kanakubo [90]	6 386
	26	Vissel	D	1-1	JL	Higashi [83]	5 627
	3	Sanfrecce	L	0-1	JL		8 526
	10	Gamba	L	2-3	JL	Ishihara 2 [45 59]	11 982
Jul	13	Avispa	L	0-1	JL		4 028
	17	Yokohama	D	1-1	JL	Rafael [74]	11 037
	23	Veglta	W	1-0	JL	Lee [52]	12 018
	30	Yokohama	L	1-2	JL	Rafael [36]	21 214
	7	Vegalta	D	2-2	JL	Rafael [14], Pimpao [40]	9 979
	13	Shimizu	L	0-3	JL		16 768
Aug	20	Montedio	D	1-1	JL	Ishihara [73]	7 730
	24	Albirex	D	0-0	JL		18 175
	27	Jubilo	W	2-0	JL	Higashi [72], Watanabe [76]	10 013
	10	Gamba	L	0-2	JL		15 106
	14	Urawa	L	0-2	LCr2		3 036
Sep	18	Cerezo	D	0-0	JL		9 781
	25	Kashiwa	W	3-1	JL	Rafael 2 [5 56], Aoki [77]	10 875
	28	Urawa	L	1-2	LCr2	Kanazawa [73]	8 982
	1	Avispa	L	0-2	JL		7 214
Oct	10	Fukuoka Un	D	1-1	ECr2	Ueda [70], L 3-5p	1 500
	15	Urawa	W	1-0	JL	Rafael [84]	34 654
	22	Nagoya	L	2-3	JL	Higashi [54], Rafael [66]	9 200
	3	Kawasaki	W	1-0	JL	Higashi [2]	17 556
Nov	19	Kashima	L	1-1	JL	Lee [67]	9 537
	26	Sanfrecce	L	2-4	JL	Kanazawa [53], Lee [88]	16 779
Dc	3	Ventforet	W	3-1	JL	Ishihara [13], Higashi 2 [29 47]	10 628

13th Att: 154 681 • Av: 9 099 (-17.7%) • NACK5 Stadium 15 500

SANFRECCE HIROSHIMA 2011

	Day	Opp	Res	Score	Comp	Scorers	Att
M	5	Vegalta	D	0-0	JL		18 709
Apr	24	Gamba	W	4-1	JL	Lee [1], Morisaki [11], Mikic [36], Sato [76]	18 788
	29	Jubilo	D	1-1	JL	Lee [68p]	11 319
	3	Shimizu	W	1-0	JL	Mujiri [70]	18 847
	7	Ventforet	D	1-1	JL	Sato [73p]	12 481
May	14	Yokohama	W	3-2	JL	Lee 2 [17 33], Mujiri [67]	17 004
	21	Vissel	L	0-1	JL		15 520
	29	Kashima	W	2-1	JL	Morisaki 2 [9 90]	8 049
	5	Kawasaki	D	2-2	LCr1	Hattori [41], Mujiri [61]	12 498
	11	Albirex	W	1-0	JL	Sato [89]	22 196
	15	Urawa	D	0-0	JL		13 707
Jun	18	Kawasaki	L	0-2	JL		13 605
	22	Montedio	W	3-2	JL	Sato [27], Lee [43], Morisaki [80p]	7 593
	26	Gamba	L	3-5	JL	Morisaki [45], Nakajima [74], Mujiri [90]	16 845
	3	Omiya	W	1-0	JL	Morita [50]	8 526
	10	Cerezo	L	1-3	JL	Lee [2]	11 615
	13	Kashiwa	L	1-3	JL	Sato [7]	7 887
Jul	18	Avispa	D	0-0	JL		9 864
	23	Nagoya	L	2-3	JL	Lee [7], Aoyama [85]	11 904
	27	Kawasaki	L	1-3	LCr1	Sato [39]	11 067
	30	Shimizu	W	4-0	JL	Lee [4], OG [40], Mujiri [83], Lee [89]	16 816
	6	Ventforet	W	2-0	JL	Lee [19], Sato [74]	11 193
	13	Nagoya	L	0-3	JL		7 099
Aug	20	Kashima	L	0-2	JL		16 237
	24	Urawa	D	1-1	JL	Lee [58]	27 947
	27	Albirex	W	1-0	JL	Mujiri [82]	14 852
	10	Cerezo	L	4-5	JL	Mikic [22], Takahagi [33], Sato 2 [44 90]	20 160
Sep	17	Jubilo	W	3-1	JL	Lee 2 [3 57], Sato [20p]	11 894
	25	Avispa	L	1-2	JL	Mizumoto [90]	12 540
	1	Vissel	W	1-0	JL	Nakajima [90]	12 706
Oct	8	Zweigen	W	4-2	ECr2	Sato 2 [2 86], Yokotake [30], Mizumoto [45]	3 858
	15	Yokohama	D	1-1	JL	Mujiri [87]	20 174
	22	Kashiwa	L	1-3	JL	Lee [57]	14 450
	3	Vegalta	D	0-0	JL		17 215
	16	Ehime	L	0-1	ECr3		3 171
Nov	19	Kawasaki	L	2-3	JL	Takahagi [10], Moriwaki [67], Aoyama [71]	12 041
	26	Omiya	W	4-2	JL	Tomic [41], Sato [45p], Lee [64], Aoyama [71]	16 779
Dc	3	Montedio	W	3-1	JL	Moriwaki [54], Sato [76], Yamagishi [88]	7 016

7th Att: 224 447 • Av: 13 203 (-9.3%) • Big Arch 50 000

OMIYA LEAGUE APPEARANCES/GOALS 2011
Goalkeepers Takashi Kitano 34
Defenders Yuki Fukaya 25+2/1 • Kim Young Kwon KOR 26+1/0 • Kazuhiro Murakami 26+3/1 • Arata Sugiyama 15+4/0 • Shusuke Tsubouchi 12+7/0
Midfield Takuya Aoki 34/3 • Chikara Fujimoto 20+6/0 • Hayato Hashimoto 6+3/0 • Keigo Higashi 23+4/8 • Jun Kanakubo 3+7/1 • Yosuke Kataoka 14+1/0 • Norio Suzuki 1/0 • Kota Ueda 31/1 • Daigo Watanabe 13+10/1
Forwards Naoki Ishihara 5+20/4 • Lee Chun Soo KOR 24+3/6 • Rafael BRA 31/10 • Shintaro Shimizu 0+4/0 • Daisuke Watabe 19+4/0 • Rodrigo Pimpao BRA 6+3/1
Coach Jun Suzuki

SANFRECCE LEAGUE APPEARANCES/GOALS 2011
Goalkeepers Shusaku Nishikawa 34
Defenders Hiroki Mizumoto 18/1 • Kohei Morita 12+3/1 • Ryota Moriwaki 27/2
Midfield Toshihiro Aoyama 19+8/2 • Kota Hattori 9+8/0 • Hironori Ishikawa 1+10/0 • Takuya Marutani 1+5/0 • Mihael Mikic CRO 29+2/2 • Kazuyuki Morisaki 32/0 • Koji Morisaki 28+2/5 • David Mujiri GEO 11+23/6 • Koji Nakajima 31+2/2 • Yojiro Takahagi 23+8/2 • Ante Tomic CRO 4+5/1 • Satoru Yamagishi 23+7/1 • Tsubasa Yokotake 7+5/0
Forwards Tadanari Lee 31+1/15 • Hisato Sato 33/11 • Masato Yamazaki 0+8/0
Coach Mihailo Petrovic AUS

SHIMIZU S-PULSE 2011

Month	Date	Opponent	Res	Score	Comp	Scorers	Att
M	5	Kashiwa	L	0-3	JL		10 390
Apr	23	Avispa	W	1-0	JL	Omae 80	11 025
	29	Yokohama	D	1-1	JL	Omae 80p	33 436
	3	Sanfrecce	L	0-1	JL		18 847
	7	Nagoya	D	1-1	JL	Brosque 18	11 559
May	14	Vissel	L	1-5	JL	Takahara 77	14 350
	22	Omiya	W	4-1	JL	Brosque 39, Takahara 2 50 59, Tsujio 69	6 668
	28	Jubilo	D	0-0	JL		12 678
	5	Ventforet	L	0-1	LCr1		10 466
	11	Gamba	D	2-2	JL	Ota 47, Omae 50	16 315
Jun	15	Montedio	W	2-1	JL	Takahara 68, Brosque 90p	10 745
	18	Urawa	W	3-1	JL	Bosnar 2 25 86, Takahara 64	31 921
	22	Kawasaki	L	2-3	JL	Brosque 20, Ono 44p	12 217
	26	Vegalta	W	1-0	JL	Brosque 81	13 081
	2	Kashima	D	0-0	JL		15 528
	9	Ventforet	W	2-1	JL	Ono 29, Omae 45	12 114
	13	Vegalta	D	0-0	JL		11 585
Jul	16	Albirex	W	2-1	JL	Ono 57, Takahara 90	13 599
	23	Cerezo	L	0-4	JL		11 254
	27	Ventforet	W	2-0	LCr1	Ono 48, Takagi 65	11 641
	30	Sanfrecce	L	0-4	JL		16 816
	6	Albirex	L	0-4	JL		37 830
	13	Omiya	W	3-0	JL	Edamura 48, Ono 54, Takahara 78	16 768
Aug	20	Cerezo	D	3-3	JL	Ono 8, Takagi 80, Takahara 89	12 823
	24	Montedio	D	1-1	JL	Iwashita 55	6 942
	27	Yokohama	D	0-0	JL		17 162
	10	Jubilo	L	1-2	JL	Omae 63	30 516
	14	Albirex	W	2-1	LCr2	Omae 16, Alex 74	6 939
Sep	17	Urawa	W	1-0	JL	Omae 63	21 524
	24	Kawasaki	D	1-1	JL	Brosque 56	20 973
	28	Albirex	L	1-3	LCr2	Omae 25	10 024
	2	Nagoya	W	2-0	JL	Omae 73, Brosque 84	20 181
	8	Gifu	W	2-0	ECr2	Takeuchi 44, Omae 45	3 648
Oct	15	Vissel	D	1-1	JL	Bosnar 55	12 706
	23	Ventforet	W	3-0	JL	Takagi 36, Ono 45, Omae 66	19 832
	3	Avispa	D	2-2	JL	Iwashita 61p, Bosnar 64	12 632
Nov	16	Gainare	W	5-0	ECr3	Iwashita 27, Takahara 45, Sugiyama 70, Nagai 79, Yamamoto 81	3 618
	20	Kashiwa	L	1-2	JL	Bosnar 43	19 584
	26	Kashima	L	0-3	JL		21 542
	3	Gamba	L	1-3	JL	Ito 9	18 670
Dec	17	JEF United	W	2-0	ECr4	Brosque 49, Ito 62	6 855
	24	Cerezo	D	2-2	ECqf	Ono 23, Takagi 103. L 5-6p	8 252

10th Att: 268 614 • Av: 15 801 (-12.2%) • The Outsourcing Stadium 17 518

URAWA REDS 2011

Month	Date	Opponent	Res	Score	Comp	Scorers	Att
M	6	Vissel	L	0-1	JL		19 913
Apr	24	Nagoya	W	3-0	JL	Richardez 31, Tanaka 31, Haraguchi 78	42 767
	29	Vegalta	L	0-1	JL		18 456
	3	Yokohama	L	0-2	JL		47 056
	7	Kashiwa	L	1-3	JL	Haraguchi 90	24 222
May	15	Cerezo	D	1-1	JL	Haraguchi 8	31 571
	21	Kashima	D	2-2	JL	Takasaki 67, Mazola 69	37 521
	28	Albirex	D	1-1	JL	Edmilson 22	25 272
	5	Montedio	W	2-0	LCr1	Edmilson 45, Haraguchi 89	23 275
	11	Omiya	D	2-2	JL	Edmilson 56p, Haraguchi 78	12 221
Jun	15	Sanfrecce	D	0-0	JL		13 707
	18	Shimizu	L	1-3	JL	Umesaki 80	31 921
	22	Avispa	W	3-0	JL	Suzuki 53, Richardez 73, Edmilson 90	20 240
	25	Nagoya	D	1-1	JL	Mazola 90p	28 515
	2	Gamba	D	1-1	JL	Haraguchi 77	42 331
	6	Montedio	D	0-0	JL		8 303
	13	Kawasaki	W	2-0	JL	Haraguchi 57, Nagata 79	24 293
Jul	17	Jubilo	D	1-1	JL	Kashiwagi 29	18 623
	23	Ventforet	W	2-0	JL	Hirakawa 53, Kashigawa 73	31 369
	27	Montedio	W	2-1	LCr1	Kashiwagi 48, Despotovic 74	5 012
	30	Kawasaki	W	1-0	JL	OG 10	20 047
	6	Vissel	L	2-3	JL	Tanaka 47, Mazola 77	32 231
Aug	14	Albirex	W	3-2	JL	Haraguchi 9, Nagata 38, Yamada 61	37 375
	20	Ventforet	L	2-3	JL	Kashiwagi 23, Escudero 83	21 589
	24	Sanfrecce	D	1-1	JL	Haraguchi 54	27 947
	28	Cerezo	L	1-3	JL	Takasaki 78	26 248
	1	Montedio	L	0-1	JL		27 709
	14	Omiya	W	2-0	LCr2	Richardez 52, Haraguchi 65	3 036
Sep	17	Shimizu	L	0-1	JL		21 524
	24	Kashima	D	0-0	JL		25 106
	28	Omiya	W	2-1	LCr2	Despotovic 2 6 23	8 982
	2	Gamba	L	0-1	JL		20 053
	5	Cerezo	W	2-1	LCqf	OG 9, Despotovic 83,	6 736
	9	Gamba	W	2-1	LCsf	Umesaki 21, Escudero 38	23 879
Oct	12	Miyazaki Un	W	4-1	ECr2	OG 14, Mazola 18, Hara 55, Takasaki 76	4 849
	15	Omiya	L	0-1	JL		34 654
	22	Yokohama	W	2-1	JL	Haraguchi 50, Umesaki 61	27 527
	29	Kashima	L	0-1	LCf		46 599
	3	Jubilo	L	0-3	JL		34 263
Nov	16	Tokyo Verdy	W	2-1	ECr3	Hara 2 56 86	7 427
	19	Vegalta	D	0-0	JL		30 891
	26	Avispa	W	2-1	JL	Kashiwagi 45, Richardez 63p	17 177
	3	Kashiwa	L	1-3	JL	Kashiwagi 53	54 441
Dec	17	Ehime	W	3-1	ECr4	Richardez 9, Hara 38, Kashiwagi 77	9 234
	24	FC Tokyo	L	0-1	ECqf		11 612

15th Att: 576 477 • Av: 33 910 (-15%) • Saitama 2002 Stadium 63 700

SHIMIZU LEAGUE APPEARANCES/GOALS 2011
Goalkeepers Kempei Usui 14 • Kaito Yamamoto 20
Defenders Eddy Bosnar AUS 32/5 • Yasuhiro Hiraoka 20+4/0 • Koicuko Iwashita 27+2/2 • Arata Kodama 0+2/0 • Taisuke Muramatsu 16+3/0 • Naoya Okane 1/0 • Kosuke Ota 33+1/1 • Shinji Tsujio 27/1
Midfield Takuma Edamura 16+11/6 • Calvin Jong-a-Pin NED 11/0 • Daigo Kobayashi 3+9/0 • Freddie Ljungberg SWE 5+3/0 • Shinji Ono 24+2/6 • Kota Sugiyama 2+8/0 • Ryo Takeuchi 1/0 • Masaki Yamamoto 9+5/0
Forwards Alex Brosque AUS 28+5/7 • Sho Ito 8+3/1 • Atomu Nabeta 2+5/0 • Yuichiro Nagai 2+15/0 • Genki Omae 31+3/8 • Toshiyuki Takagi 19+10/2 • Naohiro Takahara 23+5/8
Coach Afshin Ghotbi IRN

URAWA LEAGUE APPEARANCES/GOALS 2011
Goalkeepers Nobuhiro Kato 26 • Norihiro Yamagishi 8+1
Defenders Jun Anyama 0+1/0 • Mizuki Hamada USA 3+1/0 • Mitsuru Nagata 34/2 • Koji Noda 5+5/0 • Takuya Okamoto 0+1/0 • Matthew Spiranovic AUS 23+2/0 • Keisuke Tsuboi 4+1/0 • Tomoya Ugajin 13+1/0 • Nobuhisa Yamada 16+8/0
Midfield Tadaaki Hirakawa 24/1 • Yosuke Kashiwagi 29+2/5 • Shuto Kojima 5+1/0 • Marcio Richardez BRA 28+2/3 • Keita Suzuki 26/1 • Shunki Takahashi 26+1/0 • Tsukasa Umesaki 6+7/2 • Naoki Yamada 12+6/1
Forwards Edmilson BRA 11+1/3 • Sergio Escudero ESP 11+9/1 • Kazuki Hara 4+6/0 • Genki Haraguchi 28+2/9 • Mazola BRA 2+19/3 • Hiroyuki Takasaki 5+10/2 • Tatsuya Tanaka 16+6/2 • Ranko Despotovic SRB 9+5/0
Coach Zeljko Petrovic MNE

VEGALTA SENDAI 2011

Mon	Date	Opponent	Res	Score	Comp	Scorers	Att
M	5	Sanfrecce	D	0-0	JL		18 709
Apr	23	Kawasaki	W	2-1	JL	Ota 73, Kamata 87	15 030
	29	Urawa	W	1-0	JL	Ota 40	18 456
	3	Avispa	W	1-0	JL	Akamine 78	15 859
	7	Cerezo	D	1-1	JL	Ota 30	11 576
May	14	Jubilo	D	3-3	JL	Sugai 5, Akamine 10, Kakuda 87	11 544
	22	Montedio	W	1-0	JL	Sugai 53	18 008
	28	Yokohama	D	1-1	JL	Akamine 20	15 181
	5	Kashiwa	W	1-0	LCr1	Nakashima 90+3	8 769
	11	Vissel	D	1-1	JL	Akamine 21	13 034
	15	Gamba	W	2-1	JL	Sugai 53, Akamine 86	14 519
Jun	18	Albirex	D	1-1	JL	Sugai 90	23 602
	22	Ventforet	W	4-0	JL	Ryang 19, Watanabe 36, Akamine 69, Nakashima 75	11 356
	26	Shimizu	L	0-1	JL		13 081
	2	Nagoya	D	1-1	JL	Ryang 44	18 533
	9	Kashiwa	L	0-1	JL		10 324
	13	Shimizu	D	0-0	JL		11 585
Jul	17	Kashima	L	0-3	JL		17 120
	23	Omiya	L	0-1	JL		12 018
	27	Kashiwa	W	2-1	LCr1	Kakuda 47, Tomita 90+3	10 439
	31	Kashiwa	D	0-0	JL		15 315
	7	Omiya	D	2-2	JL	Akamine 55, Sugai 77	9 979
Aug	13	Kashima	L	0-1	JL		19 224
	20	Nagoya	W	1-0	JL	Sugai 17	13 365
	24	Jubilo	L	0-1	JL	Akamine 48	8 693
	27	Montedio	W	2-1	JL	Akamine 3, Ryang 12	19 087
	11	Ventforet	W	2-1	JL	Ota 55, Akamine 79	11 176
	14	Jubilo	D	0-0	LCr2		7 360
Sep	17	Albirex	W	2-0	JL	Akamine 58, Ryang 75p	16 046
	24	Yokohama	W	3-1	JL	Kakuda 10, Yanagisawa 12, Akamine 55	23 204
	28	Jubilo	L	0-3	LCr2		6 339
Oct	2	Cerezo	W	2-1	JL	Watanabe 21, Sugai 40	16 407
	8	SonySendai	W	2-1	ECr2	Ota 74, Muto 114	5 714
	15	Avispa	W	3-0	JL	Matsushita 2 21 68, Muto 82	7 191
	22	Kawasaki	D	0-0	JL		15 224
	3	Sanfrecce	D	0-0	JL		17 215
Nov	16	Avispa	W	3-1	ECr3	Tamura 2 18 22, Nakashima 82	4 831
	19	Urawa	D	0-0	JL		30 891
	26	Gamba	L	0-1	JL		18 001
Dec	3	Vissel	W	2-0	JL	Akamine 2 19 80	18 575
	17	Cerezo	D	1-1	ECr4	Muto 98. L 2-4p	5 316

4th Att: 266 144 • Av: 15 656 (-9.6%) • Yurtec Stadium 20 000

VENTFORET KOFU 2011

Mon	Date	Opponent	Res	Score	Comp	Scorers	Att
M	5	Jubilo	L	0-1	JL		10 254
Apr	23	Vissel	D	1-1	JL	Daniel 65	6 893
	29	Kashiwa	L	1-2	JL	Havenaar 42p	10 319
	3	Omiya	D	1-1	JL	Abe 53	12 056
	7	Sanfrecce	D	1-1	JL	Havenaar 10	12 481
May	15	Nagoya	W	3-1	JL	Abe 28, Havenaar 71, Matsuhashi 77	14 075
	21	Yokohama	L	0-4	JL		17 751
	28	Montedio	D	1-1	JL	Havenaar 21	7 582
	5	Shimizu	W	1-0	LCr1	Havenaar 66	10 466
	11	Kawasaki	D	2-2	JL	Abe 40, Havenaar 54	13 111
Jun	15	Kashima	W	1-0	JL	Havenaar 90	7 810
	18	Cerezo	L	0-2	JL		8 402
	22	Vegalta	L	0-4	JL		11 356
	25	Kashima	L	1-4	JL	Havenaar 58	10 450
	2	Avispa	L	0-1	JL		6 585
	6	Albirex	W	2-1	JL	Paulinho 41, Ishihara 71	13 644
	9	Shimizu	L	1-2	JL	Paulinho 42	12 114
Jul	16	Gamba	W	4-3	JL	Havenaar 2 20 70, Uchiyama 31, Paulinho 68	14 126
	23	Urawa	L	0-2	JL		31 369
	27	Shimizu	L	0-2	LCr1		11 641
	30	Vissel	L	2-4	JL	Paulinho 52, Kim 58	9 231
Aug	6	Sanfrecce	L	0-2	JL		11 193
	13	Montedio	L	1-3	JL	Paulinho 32	7 940
	20	Urawa	W	3-2	JL	Paulinho 2 13 43, Havenaar 19	21 589
	24	Kashima	D	1-1	JL	Abe 74	11 959
	28	Nagoya	L	1-4	JL	Havenaar 9	19 061
Sep	11	Vegalta	L	1-2	JL	Havenaar 83	11 176
	17	Avispa	W	2-1	JL	Havenaar 4, Paulinho 28p	9 100
	24	Gamba	W	2-0	JL	Paulinho 62, Havenaar 90	19 882
	1	Kawasaki	L	0-1	JL		11 377
	8	Machida	W	2-1	ECr2	Uchiyama 6, Paulinho 36	3 421
Oct	15	Cerezo	W	4-0	JL	Paulinho 2, Havenaar 2 28 63, Inzuka 90	7 501
	23	Shimizu	L	0-3	JL		19 832
	3	Yokohama	L	1-2	JL	Havenaar 67	15 315
Nov	16	Kashima	L	1-6	ECr3	Yabu 13	3 950
	19	Jubilo	L	1-2	JL	Izawa 16	7 244
	27	Albirex	W	3-0	JL	Katagiri 37, Yabu 66, Kashiwa 82	13 361
Dec	3	Omiya	L	1-3	JL	Izawa 25	10 628

16th Att: 205 808 • Av: 12 106 (-2.4%) • Yamanashi 17 000

VEGALTA LEAGUE APPEARANCES/GOALS 2011
Goalkeepers Takuto Hayashi 34
Defenders Cho Byong Kuk KOR 28/0 • Junya Hosokawa 0+3/0 Makoto Kakuda 29/2 • Jiro Kamata 33/1 • Park Joo Sung KOR 27/0 Naoki Sugai 30/7 • Kodai Watanabe 7+3/2
Midfield Toshihiro Matsushita 15+11/2 • Max BRA 0+2/0 Yoshiaki Ota 21+9/4 • Ryang Yong Gi PRK 31+3/4 • Daisuke Saito 0+3/0 Kunimitsu Sekiguchi 27+3/0 • Yoshiki Takahashi 10+9/0 Naoya Tamura 12+7/0 • Shingo Tomita 26+5/0 • Diego BRA 0+5/0
Forwards Shingo Akamine 31/14 • Yuki Muto 0+5/1 • Takayuki Nakahara 0+9/0 • Yuki Nakashima 2+18/1 • Atsushi Yanagisawa 10+7/1 Marquinhos BRA 1/0
Coach Makoto Teguramori

VENTFORET LEAGUE APPEARANCES/GOALS 2011
Goalkeepers Hikori Aratani 13/0 • Kota Ogi 21+2
Defenders Daniel BRA 28/1 • Daisuke Ichikawa 19+3/0 Teruaki Kobayashi 7+4/0 • Daisuke Tomita 17+1/0 • Takuma Tsuda 4+2/0 Toshihiko Uchiyama 19+1/1 • Yutaka Yoshida 23/0
Midfield Yuki Horigome 0+3/0 • Kazunari Hosaka 4+4/0 • Yusuke Inuzuka 3+2/1 • Katsuya Ishihara 14+2/1 • Teruyoshi Ito 23+5/0 • Atsushi Izawa 13+1/2 • Yoshifumi Kashiwa 16+13/1 • Genki Nagasato 13+1/0 Tomoya Uchida 7+2/0 • Yuji Yabu 4+8/1 • Hideomi Yamamoto 30/0 Rudnei BRA 0+2/0
Forwards Yoshiro Abe 14+10/4 • Davi BRA 3+7/0 • Mike Havenaar 32/17 Atsushi Katagiri 15+14/1 • Kim Sin Young KOR 3+3/1 Masaru Matsuhashi 8+4/1 • Paulinho BRA 21+7/10
Coach Toshiya Miura • Satoru Sakuma

VISSEL KOBE 2011

Mth	Date	Opponent	Res	Score	Comp	Scorers	Att
Apr	6	Urawa	W	1-0	JL	Popo 74	19 913
	23	Ventforet	D	1-1	JL	Okubo 41	6 893
	29	Omiya	L	0-1	JL		10 502
May	3	Albirex	L	0-1	JL		30 610
	7	Kawasaki	W	1-0	JL	Park 68	10 364
	14	Shimizu	W	5-1	JL	Okubo 2 18 57, Tokura 2 34 75, Botti 90	14 350
	21	Sanfrecce	W	1-0	JL	Tanaka 36	15 520
	28	Kashiwa	L	0-3	JL		6 855
Jun	5	Yokohama	D	1-1	LCr1	Rogerinho 90+3	8 101
	11	Vegalta	D	1-1	JL	Mogi 89	13 034
	15	Avispa	D	0-0	JL		6 151
	18	Montedio	L	0-2	JL		6 587
	22	Kashima	L	0-1	JL		9 705
	26	Omiya	D	1-1	JL	Okubo 53	5 627
	3	Jubilo	L	0-3	JL		7 706
	9	Nagoya	L	0-1	JL		17 568
	3	Gamba	L	2-3	JL	Popo 68, Park 80	15 244
Jul	16	Cerezo	W	4-1	JL	Matsuoka 2, Popo 54, Park 57, Okubo 89	14 961
	23	Yokohama	L	0-1	JL		15 402
	27	Yokohama	L	1-2	LCr1	Yoshida	5 204
	30	Ventforet	W	4-2	JL	Ishibitsu 11, Yoshida 2 24 49, Tanaka 82	9 231
Aug	6	Urawa	W	3-2	JL	Yoshida 2 14 19, Okubo 90	32 231
	13	Yokohama	W	2-0	JL	Okubo 34, Popo 88	13 930
	20	Albirex	W	2-1	JL	Yoshida 30, Matsuoka 60	11 340
	24	Avispa	D	2-2	JL	Popo 6, Yoshida 24	6 119
	28	Gamba	L	0-4	JL		17 177
Sep	11	Kawasaki	W	3-0	JL	Yoshida 39, Park 51, Okubo 88	14 918
	17	Kashiwa	L	0-4	JL		4 253
	23	Nagoya	L	1-3	JL	Park 4	15 987
	1	Sanfrecce	L	0-1	JL		12 706
Oct	10	Sanyo	W	8-0	ECr2	Morioka 3 22 32 46, Matsuoka 26, Popo 2 31 55, Park 58, Botti 68	2 471
	15	Shimizu	D	1-1	JL	Morioka 85	12 706
	22	Kashima	D	1-1	JL	Popo 54	13 248
	3	Montedio	W	2-0	JL	Yoshida 30, Popo 44	11 420
Nov	16	FC Tokyo	L	1-2	ECr3	Komoto 37	5 937
	20	Cerezo	W	3-0	JL	Yoshida 11, Kitamoto 53, Okubo 90	16 030
	27	Jubilo	W	3-1	JL	Kitamoto 19, Soma 25, Morioka 87	17 187
Dc	3	Vegalta	L	0-2	JL		18 575

9th Att: 224 962 • Av: 13 233 (+3.1%) • Home's Stadium 30 132

YOKOHAMA F-MARINOS 2011

Mth	Date	Opponent	Res	Score	Comp	Scorers	Att
Apr	5	Nagoya	D	1-1	JL	Hyodo 63	27 153
	23	Kashima	W	3-0	JL	Ogura 3, Kurihara 2 76 90	15 688
	29	Shimizu	D	1-1	JL	Hyodo 85	33 436
May	3	Urawa	W	2-0	JL	Watanabe 70, Oguro 90	47 056
	7	Avispa	W	3-2	JL	Watanabe 46, Ono 2 77 81	13 520
	14	Sanfrecce	L	2-3	JL	Nakazawa 43, Nakamura 69	17 004
	21	Ventforet	W	4-0	JL	Taniguchi 11, Watanabe 17, Oguro 2 25 40	17 751
	28	Vegalta	D	1-1	JL	Taniguchi 68	15 181
	5	Vissel	D	1-1	LCr1	Aoyama 74	8 101
Jun	11	Kashima	L	0-2	JL		17 597
	15	Cerezo	W	1-0	JL	Kim 81	9 098
	18	Gamba	L	1-2	JL	Kim 87	18 001
	22	Albirex	W	1-0	JL	Hyodo 31p	8 019
	26	Montedio	W	2-0	JL	Kurihara 44, Watanabe 90	7 667
	3	Kawasaki	W	2-1	JL	Oguro 37, Watanabe 70	29 980
	9	Jubilo	W	2-1	JL	Watanabe 35, Nakamura 51p	11 226
	13	Montedio	W	2-1	JL	Watanabe 1, Kim 90	7 104
Jul	17	Omiya	D	1-1	JL	Ono 37	11 037
	23	Vissel	W	1-0	JL	Hyodo 63	15 402
	27	Vissel	W	2-1	LCr1	Kurihara 44, Taniguchi 78	5 204
	30	Omiya	W	2-1	JL	Oguro 2 53 65	21 214
Aug	6	Kashiwa	L	0-2	JL		11 051
	13	Vissel	L	0-2	JL		13 930
	20	Jubilo	W	1-0	JL	Ono 84	24 518
	24	Cerezo	W	2-1	JL	Hyodo 15, Nakamura 44	10 480
	27	Shimizu	D	0-0	JL		17 162
	10	Avispa	W	1-0	JL	Hasegawa 11	15 818
Sep	14	Kawasaki	W	4-0	LCr2	Hyodo 6, Watanabe 24, Oguro 2 69 91+	9 859
	18	Gamba	D	1-1	JL	Hyodo 20	37 725
	24	Vegalta	L	1-3	JL	Kobayashi 3	23 204
	28	Kawasaki	L	2-3	LCr2	Taniguchi 25, Oguro 64	10 528
	1	Albirex	L	2-4	JL	Kurihara 71, Amano 90	24 439
Oct	5	Kashima	L	2-3	LCqf	OG 1, Watanabe 11	4 804
	12	Sanuki	W	3-1	ECr2	Hyodo 86, Taniguchi 88, Oguro 93+	2 905
	15	Sanfrecce	D	1-1	JL	Oguro 75	20 174
	22	Urawa	L	1-2	JL	Oguro 4	27 527
Nov	3	Ventforet	W	2-1	JL	Oguro 86, Moriya 89	15 315
	16	Tochigi	W	3-0	ECr3	Oguro 2 33 80, Nakamura 94+	3 951
	19	Nagoya	L	1-2	JL	Nakamura 71	23 023
	26	Kawasaki	L	0-3	JL		19 972
Dec	3	Kashima	D	1-1	JL	Oguro 32	26 973
	17	Matsumoto	W	4-0	ECr4	Ono 3 28 73 75, Nakamura 87	10 120
	24	Nagoya	D	0-0	ECqf	W 4-3p	8 728
	29	Kyoto	L	2-4	ECsf	Watanabe 42, Nakazawa 95+	14 467

5th Att: 357 647 • Av: 21 038 (-18%) • Nissan Stadium 72 327

VISSEL LEAGUE APPEARANCES/GOALS 2011
Goalkeepers Kenta Tokushige 34
Defenders Kenji Haneda 2+4/0 • Keisuke Hayashi 2/0
Yosuke Ishibitsu 15+1/1 • Kunie Kitamoto 34/2 • Hiroyuki Komoto 32/0
Gakuto Kondo 19/0 • Tsuneyasu Miyamoto 2+2/0 • Tsubasa Oya 2/0
Takahito Soma 6+2/1
Midfield Kenji Baba 0+1/0 • Botti BRA 21+5/1 • Ryosuke
Matsuoka 21+1/2 • Masatoshi Mihara 15+3/0 • Ryota Morioka 4+17/2
Kang Jo Park 23+4/5 • Popo BRA 21+11/7 • Rogerinho BRA 7+4/0
Hideo Tanaka 23+3/2
Forwards Koki Arita 0+10/0 • Lee Jae Min KOR 1+2/0
Kohei Mishima 0+4/0 • Hiroto Mogi 25+2/1 • Keijiro Ogawa 7+5/0
Yoshito Okubo 26+4/9 • Ken Tokura 6+8/2 • Takayuki Yoshida 26+3/9
Bae Chun Suk KOR 0+3/0
Coach Masahiro Wada

YOKOHAMA LEAGUE APPEARANCES/GOALS 2011
Goalkeepers Yota Akimoto 1 • Hiroki Iikura 33
Defenders Takashi Amano 2+11/1 • Naoaki Aoyama 7+3/0
Yasuhiro Hato 14+2/0 • Takashi Kanai 21/0 • Kun-Hoan Kim KOR 0+30/3
Yuzo Kobayashi 32/1 • Yuzo Kurihara 29+1/4 • Yuji Nakazawa 33/1
Eijiro Takeda 0+1/0
Midfield Aria Jasuru Hasegawa 12+11/1 • Shingo Hyodo 34/6
Kenta Kano 2+8/0 • Rei Matsumoto 0+1/0 • Kentaro Moriya 2+2/1
Shunsuke Nakamura 23+1/4 • Shohei Ogura 33/1 • Hiroyuki Taniguchi 33/2
Forwards Masashi Oguro 24+4/10 • Yuji Ono 20+8/4
Kazuma Watanabe 19+11/7
Coach Kazushi Kimura

KAZ – KAZAKHSTAN

FIFA/COCA-COLA WORLD RANKING

'93	'94	'95	'96	'97	'98	'99	'00	'01	'02	'03	'04	'05	'06	'07	'08	'09	'10	'11	'12
-	153	163	156	107	102	123	120	98	117	136	147	137	135	112	137	125	138	138	

					2011									
Jan	Feb	Mar	Apr	May	Jun	Jul	Aug	Sep	Oct	Nov	Dec	High	Low	Av
137	137	132	140	139	126	126	126	132	129	138	138	98	166	129

Since independence from the Soviet Union in 1991 the cities of Shymkent and Karagandy have lived in the shadows of both Almaty and Astana as far as football is concerned. In 2011, however, that changed as Shakhter Karagandy won their first silverware by winning the Kazakh championship and Ordabasy Shymkent broke their duck by beating the outgoing champions Tobol 1-0 in the Cup Final. It has been a tough job for the clubs in the country to create a stable framework in order to meet the UEFA licensing criteria and this has had the effect of levelling the playing field. Remarkably, in the 20 Cup Finals played since independence there have been 14 different winners whilst the league has been won by eight different clubs. Shakhter were trailing surprise package Zhetysu by two points with two games to go when the teams met in Taldykorgan, but a 2-0 victory saw them take the lead and then clinch the title on the last day of the season with a 2-0 win at home to Astana. In the qualifiers for Euro 2012, Kazakhstan finished with the wooden spoon in their admittedly difficult group. After four straight defeats in their opening matches coach Bernd Storck was eventually replaced by Miroslav Beranek who managed a win over Azerbaijan and a draw with Austria in their remaining two home matches.

UEFA EUROPEAN CHAMPIONSHIP RECORD
1960-1992 DNE (Played as part of the Soviet Union) **1996-2004** DNE (as a member of the AFC) **2008-2012** DNQ

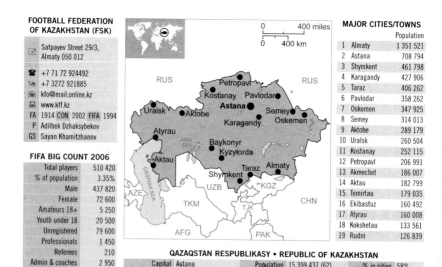

FOOTBALL FEDERATION OF KAZAKHSTAN (FSK)

Satpayev Street 29/3, Almaty 050 012

☎ +7 71 72 924492
🖷 +7 3272 921885
✉ kfo@mail.online.kz
🖥 www.kff.kz
FA 1914 CON 2002 FIFA 1994
P Adilbek Dzhaksybekov
GS Sayan Khamitzhanov

FIFA BIG COUNT 2006

Total players	510 420
% of population	3.35%
Male	437 820
Female	72 600
Amateurs 18+	5 250
Youth under 18	20 500
Unregistered	79 600
Professionals	1 450
Referees	210
Admin & coaches	2 950
Number of clubs	43
Number of teams	300

MAJOR CITIES/TOWNS

		Population
1	Almaty	1 351 521
2	Astana	708 794
3	Shymkent	461 798
4	Karagandy	427 906
5	Taraz	406 262
6	Pavlodar	358 262
7	Oskemen	347 925
8	Semey	314 013
9	Aktobe	289 179
10	Uralsk	260 504
11	Kostanay	252 115
12	Petropavl	206 991
13	Akmechet	186 007
14	Aktau	182 799
15	Temirtau	179 035
16	Ekibastuz	160 492
17	Atyrau	160 008
18	Kokshetau	133 561
19	Rudni	126 839

QAZAQSTAN RESPUBLIKASY • REPUBLIC OF KAZAKHSTAN

Capital Astana	Population 15 399 437 (62)	% in cities 58%
GDP per capita $11 500 (96)	Area km² 2 724 900 km² (9)	GMT +/- +4 +5

Neighbours (km) China 1533, Kyrgyzstan 1224, Russia 6846, Turkmenistan 379, Uzbekistan 2203

RECENT INTERNATIONAL MATCHES PLAYED BY KAZAKHSTAN

2007	Opponents		Score	Venue	Comp	Scorers	Att	Referee
22-08	Finland	L	1-2	Tampere	ECq	Byakov [23]	13 047	Kassai HUN
8-09	Tajikistan	D	1-1	Almaty	Fr	Nurdauletov [54]		
12-09	Belgium	D	2-2	Almaty	ECq	Byakov [39], Smakov [77p]	18 100	Tudor ROU
13-10	Poland	L	1-3	Warsaw	ECq	Byakov [20]	11 040	Berntsen NOR
17-10	Portugal	L	1-2	Almaty	ECq	Byakov [93+]	25 057	Wegeref NED
21-11	Armenia	W	1-0	Yerevan	ECq	Ostapenko [64]	3 100	Fautrel FRA
24-11	Serbia	L	0-1	Belgrade	ECq		500	Vasaras GRE
2008								
3-02	Azerbaijan	D	0-0	Antalya	Fr			Kamil TUR
6-02	Moldova	L	0-1	Antalya	Fr		300	Lehner AUT
26-03	Armenia	L	0-1	Pernis	Fr			Vink NED
23-05	Russia	L	0-6	Moscow	Fr		10 000	
27-05	Montenegro	L	0-3	Podgorica	Fr		9 000	Tusin LUX
20-08	Andorra	W	3-0	Almaty	WCq	Ostapenko 2 [14 30], Uzdenov [44]	7 700	Banari MDA
6-09	Croatia	L	0-3	Zagreb	WCq		17 424	Johannesson SWE
10-09	Ukraine	L	1-3	Almaty	WCq	Ostapenko [68]	17 000	Brych GER
11-10	England	L	1-5	London	WCq	Kukeyev [68]		
2009								
11-02	Estonia	W	2-0	Antalya	Fr	Baltiyev 2 [33 82]	200	Gocek TUR
1-04	Belarus	L	1-5	Almaty	WCq	Abdulin [10]	19 000	Jech CZE
6-06	England	L	0-4	Almaty	WCq		24 000	Jakobsson ISL
10-06	Ukraine	L	1-2	Kyiv	WCq	Nusserbayev [18]	11 500	Paixao POR
9-09	Andorra	W	3-1	Andorra La Vella	WCq	Khizhnichenko 2 [14 35], Baltiyev [29]	510	Toussaint LUX
10-10	Belarus	L	0-4	Brest	WCq		9 530	Ennjimmi FRA
14-10	Croatia	L	1-2	Astana	WCq	Khizhnichenko [26]	10 250	Circhetta SUI
2010								
3-03	Moldova	L	0-1	Antalya	Fr		500	Bezborodov RUS
11-08	Oman	W	3-1	Astana	Fr	Karpovich [20], Zhumaskaliev [43], OG [62]		Irmatov UZB
3-09	Turkey	L	0-3	Astana	ECq		15 800	Vad HUN
7-09	Austria	L	0-2	Salzburg	ECq		22 500	Strahonja CRO
8-10	Belgium	L	0-2	Astana	ECq		8 500	Borski POL
12-10	Germany	L	0-3	Astana	ECq		18 000	Tudor ROU
2011								
9-02	Belarus	D	1-1	Antalya	Fr	Ostapenko [88]	1 500	Banari MDA
26-03	Germany	L	0-4	Kaiserslautern	ECq		47 849	Stavrev MKD
3-06	Azerbaijan	W	2-1	Astana	ECq	Gridin 2 [57 68]	10 000	Norris SCO
10-08	Syria	D	1-1	Astana	Fr	Kukeev [70]	13 500	Egorov RUS
2-09	Turkey	L	1-2	Istanbul	ECq	Konysbayev [55]	47 756	Turpin FRA
6-09	Azerbaijan	L	2-3	Baku	ECq	Ostapenko [20], Yevstigneyev.V [77]	9 112	Hermansen DEN
7-10	Belgium	L	1-4	Brussels	ECq	Nurdauletov [86p]	29 758	Mazic SRB
11-10	Austria	D	0-0	Astana	ECq		11 000	Kaasik EST

Fr = Friendly match • EC = UEFA EURO 2008/2012 • WC = FIFA World Cup • q = qualifier • BCD = behind closed doors

KAZAKHSTAN NATIONAL TEAM HISTORICAL RECORDS

Caps
73 - Ruslan Baltiyev 1997-2009 • **59** - Samat Smakov 2000-11 • **54** - Nurbol Zhumaskaliyev 2001- • **51** - Andrey Karpovich 2000- •
38 - David Loriya 2000-11 • **35** - Alexandr Kuchma 2000- & Farkhadbek Irismetov 2004- • **34** - Alexandr Familtsev 1997-2006 •
32 - Dmitry Byakov 2000-08 • **30** - Sergei Ostapenko 2007- • **29** - Maxim Zhalmagambetov 2004-08

Goals
13 - Ruslan Baltiyev 1997-2009 • **12** - Viktor Zubarev 1997-2002 • **8** - Dmitry Byakov 2000-08 • **6** - Igor Avdeyev 1996-2005; Oleg
Litvinenko 1997-2006; Nurbol Zhumaskaliyev 2001- & Sergei Ostapenko 2007-

Past Coaches
Bakhtiar Baiseitov 1992 • Baurzhan Baimukhammedov 1994 • Serik Berdalin 1995-97 • Sergei Gorokhovadatskiy 1998 • Voit Talgaev 2000
• Vladimir Fomichev 2000 • Vakhid Masudov 2001-02 • Leonid Pakhomov RUS 2003-04 • Sergey Timofeev 2004-05 • Arno Pijpers NED
2006-08 • Bernd Storck GER 2008-10 • Miroslav Beranek CZE 2011-

KAZAKHSTAN 2011

SUPERLIGA ALMA TV

	Pl	W	D	L	F	A	Pts	Shakhter	Zhetysu	FK Aktobe	Astana	Irtysh	Ordabasy	Tobol	Kaisar	FK Taraz	FK Atyrau	Kairat	Vostock
Shakhter Karagandy †	32	19	6	7	52	29	42		3-3	2-1	1-0	2-1	0-0	2-0	2-0	3-0	0-2	4-2	2-0
Zhetysu Taldykorgan ‡	32	19	5	8	51	27	38	1-0		3-2	2-0	1-0	1-0	4-1	3-0	3-2	2-0	0-1	3-0
FK Aktobe ‡	32	15	9	8	53	31	34	0-1	1-1		1-1	7-2	2-0	2-1	6-1	0-0	2-0	3-0	3-0
Lokomotiv Astana	32	16	7	9	50	37	33	2-0	1-2	0-2		1-0	1-3	3-1	5-1	1-0	3-2	6-1	2-0
Irtysh Pavlodar	32	15	5	12	50	50	32	2-1	2-1	2-3	2-1		3-0	5-0	3-1	2-0	3-0	1-1	3-1
Ordabasy Shymkent ‡	32	11	10	11	41	36	28	1-0	0-0	0-1	1-2	0-1		1-0	1-1	0-1	1-1	2-0	0-0
Tobol Kostanay	32	14	3	15	48	44	32	1-2	1-0	1-2	0-1	4-1	1-3		3-0	2-1	3-0	2-1	0-0
Kaisar Kyzylorda	32	10	5	17	29	53	27	0-1	0-4	0-2	2-4	1-0	1-2	0-3		4-1	1-0	2-0	1-1
FK Taraz	32	10	5	17	30	39	25	0-1	0-1	0-2	1-2	0-1	1-1	1-0	1-3		1-0	2-1	3-1
FK Atyrau	32	8	10	14	28	43	24	1-4	1-0	1-1	0-0	1-0	1-1	0-2	2-1	0-0		0-1	2-1
Kairat Almaty	32	8	8	16	30	49	22	2-1	0-1	3-0	2-3	1-3	0-3	0-0	3-0	0-0	2-0		1-1
Vostock Oskemen	32	5	11	16	23	47	17	1-2	0-0	0-0	0-0	1-2	0-4	2-2	1-3	2-0	0-0	1-1	

6/03/2011 – 29/10/2011 • † Qualified for the UEFA Champions League • ‡ Qualified for the Europa League
Top scorers: 16 - Ulugbek Bakaev UZB, Zhetysu • 15 - Sergei Khizhnichenko, Shakhter • 12 - Malick Mane SEN, Aktobe; Dragan Bogavac, Astana & Sergey Gridin, Tobol • 11 - Daurenbek Tazhimbetov, Ordabasy

KAZAKHSTAN 2011 PERVAIA (2)

	Pl	W	D	L	F	A	Pts
Sunkar Kaskelen	32	24	5	3	62	19	77
Okzhetpes Kokshetau	32	21	6	5	59	25	69
Ilie-Saulet	32	18	5	9	42	23	59
Akzhayuk Uralsk	32	16	8	8	54	30	53
Ekibastuzetc	32	15	7	10	47	34	52
Bulak Talgar	32	15	5	12	39	32	50
FK Astana 64	32	14	8	10	48	38	50
Ak Bulak Talgar	32	12	11	9	38	31	47
Aktobe-Zhas	32	13	7	12	56	53	46
Tarlan Shymkent	32	11	10	11	38	34	43
Cesna Almaty	32	13	4	15	47	50	43
Kaspiy Aktau	32	10	7	15	33	42	37
Lashin Taraz	32	8	10	14	31	39	34
Kyzylzhar Pet'pavlovsk	32	8	10	14	38	54	31
Spartak Semey	32	7	8	17	33	56	29
Gefest Karagandy	32	7	3	22	24	61	24
CSKA Almaty	32	2	2	28	17	85	8

24/04/2011 - 23/10/2011

MEDALS TABLE

		Overall			League			Cup		City
		G	S	B	G	S	B	G	S	
1	Kairat Almaty	7	2	3	2		3	5	2	Almaty
2	Irtysh Pavlodar	6	5	5	5	3	5	1	2	Pavlodar
3	FK Astana	6	2	1	3		1	3	2	Astana
4	FK Aktobe	5	3	1	4	2	1	1	1	Aktobe
5	FK Semey	4		1	3		1			Semey
6	Tobol Kostanay	2	6	3	1	4	3	1	2	Kostanay
7	FK Taraz	2	4		1	2		1	2	Taraz
8	Ordabasy Shymkent	1	3	1		1	1	1	2	Oskemen
9	Shakhter Karagandy	1	2	3		1	3		2	Atyrau
10	Vostock Oskemen	1	2					1	2	Kyzylorda
	FK Atyrau	1	2			2				Almaty
12	Kaisar Kyzylorda	1	1					1	1	Astana
	FK Almaty	1	1					1	1	Almaty
	Lokomotiv Astana	1	1			1		1		Petropavl
15	Dostyk Almaty	1								Shymkent
16	Yesil-Bogatyr Petropavl	3	1		2	1			1	Karagandy
17	Ekibastuzetc	2						2		Ekibastuz
18	Zhetysu Taldykorgan	1						1		Taldykorgan
19	Gornyak Khromtau		1					1		Khromtau

KUBOK KAZAKHSTANA 2011

First round		Quarter-finals		Semi-finals		Final	
Ordabasy Shymkent *	2						
Kaisar Kyzylorda	1	Ordabasy Shymkent	3				
Tarlan Shymkent *	0	Sunkar Kaskelen *	1				
Sunkar Kaskelen	1			Ordabasy Shymkent	1 3		
Shakhter Karagandy	3			FK Taraz *	3 0		
Kazakhmys Satpayev *	0	Shakhter Karagandy *	2				
Akzhayuk Uralsk	1	FK Taraz	4				
FK Taraz *	4					Ordabasy Shymkent ‡	1
Irtysh Pavlodar	5					Tobol Kostanay	0
Kyzylzhar P'pavlovsk *	2	Irtysh Pavlodar *	1				
Gefest Karagandy *	0	Okzhetpes Kokshetau	0				
Okzhetpes Kokshetau	1			Irtysh Pavlodar *	1 2		
Kairat Almaty	1 4p			Tobol Kostanay	1 3		
Lokomotiv Astana *	1 2p	Kairat Almaty	0				
FK Atyrau	2	Tobol Kostanay *	1				
Tobol Kostanay *	3						

CUP FINAL
Astana Arena, Astana
13-11-2011, 8500, Duzmambetov
Scorer - Mukhtar Mukhtarov [40] for Ordabasy

* Home team/Home team in first leg • ‡ Qualified for the Europa League

KEN – KENYA

FIFA/COCA-COLA WORLD RANKING

'93	'94	'95	'96	'97	'98	'99	'00	'01	'02	'03	'04	'05	'06	'07	'08	'09	'10	'11	'12
74	83	107	112	89	93	103	108	104	81	72	74	89	127	110	68	98	120	120	

	2011												High	Low	Av
	Jan	Feb	Mar	Apr	May	Jun	Jul	Aug	Sep	Oct	Nov	Dec	High	Low	Av
	126	127	129	124	123	130	130	133	131	136	133	120	68	137	99

After a miserable start to their CAF Africa Cup of Nations qualifying campaign, the Harambee Stars rallied in 2011 with two wins, an away draw and a narrow loss in Angola but they were always off the pace in their bid to reach the finals and finished third in the group. A routine FIFA World Cup qualifier against the Seychelles in November saw Kenya win 7-0 on aggregate - including three goals in two games for captain Denis Oliech. But they ended the year in disappointing fashion at the annual CECAFA Cup in Tanzania in December, losing to Sudan and Malawi in the group stage and embarrassingly failing to make the quarter-finals. Zedekiah Otieno started the year in charge but lasted 10 months to be replaced by Francis Kimanzi, who returned to the job in November. In club football, a tightly contested Premier League was only decided right at the end of the season with Tusker edging defending champions Ulinzi Stars by a single point. Ugly scenes marred the FKL Cup semi-final between arch-rivals Gor Mahia and AFC Leopards - less than a year after seven fans died in a stampede at a match between the two. Gor Mahia won 1-0 to qualify for the final where they then beat Sofapaka. It was a record eighth cup triumph for the club in the various guises in which cup football has been played since the first tournament in 1964.

CAF AFRICA CUP OF NATIONS RECORD

1957-1959 DNE 1962-1970 DNQ **1972** 6 r1 1974-1982 DNQ 1984 DNE 1986 DNQ
1988 8 r1 **1990** 7 r1 **1992** 12 r1 1994 DNQ 1996 DNE 1998-2002 DNQ **2004** 13 r1 2006-2012 DNQ

FOOTBALL KENYA LTD

FKF Complex Centre, Moi
Sports Complex, Kasarani
PO Box 12705-00400 NRB
Nairobi 00400
☎ +254 20 2644630
📠 +254 20 2644632
📧 info@fk.co.ke
🖥 www.fkf.co.ke
FA 1960 CON 1968 FIFA 1960
P Sam Nyamweya
GS Omondi Aduda

FIFA BIG COUNT 2006

Total players	2 041 102
% of population	5.88%
Male	1 952 326
Female	88 776
Amateurs 18+	25 906
Youth under 18	49 141
Unregistered	1 003 000
Professionals	55
Referees	3 700
Admin & coaches	48 310
Number of clubs	690
Number of teams	3 450

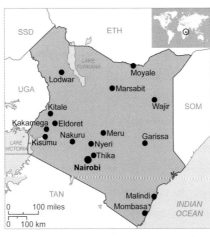

MAJOR CITIES/TOWNS

		Population
1	Nairobi	3 141 065
2	Mombasa	888 454
3	Nakuru	275 723
4	Eldoret	248 042
5	Kisumu	228 032
6	Ruiru	130 016
7	Thika	102 847
8	Kitale	79 984
9	Malindi	78 731
10	Kakamega	71 140
11	Bungoma	69 658
12	Kilifi	59 976
13	Garissa	56 533
14	Mumias	55 737
15	Busia	51 204
16	Meru	50 921
17	Nyeri	49 442
18	Homa Bay	45 139
19	Narok	45 078

JAMHURI YA KENYA • REPUBLIC OF KENYA

Capital	Nairobi	Population	39 002 772 (33)	% in cities	22%
GDP per capita	$1600 (193)	Area km²	580 367 km² (48)	GMT +/-	+3
Neighbours (km)	Ethiopia 861, Somalia 682, Sudan 232, Tanzania 769, Uganda 933 • Coast 536		

RECENT INTERNATIONAL MATCHES PLAYED BY KENYA

2010	Opponents	Score		Venue	Comp	Scorers	Att	Referee
29-11	Malawi	L	2-3	Dar es Salaam	CCr1	John Baraza [34], Fred Ajwang [45]		
2-12	Ethiopia	L	1-2	Dar es Salaam	CCr1	Fred Ajwang [85]		
5-12	Uganda	L	0-2	Dar es Salaam	CCr1			
2011								
5-01	Sudan	W	1-0	Cairo	Fr	Collins Okoth [17p]		
8-01	Congo DR	L	0-1	Cairo	Fr			
14-01	Egypt	L	1-5	Cairo	Fr	Kevin Opondo [67]		
17-01	Congo DR	L	0-1	Ismailia	Fr			
9-02	South Africa	L	0-2	Rustenburg	Fr			
26-03	Angola	W	2-1	Nairobi	CNq	Jamal Mohammed [53], McDonald Mariga [87]		
29-03	Nigeria	L	0-3	Abuja	Fr			
5-06	Angola	L	0-1	Luanda	CNq			Maillet SEY
25-06	Sudan	L	1-2	Nairobi	Fr	Dennis Oliech [10]		
10-08	Botswana	L	0-1	Gaborone	Fr			
3-09	Guinea-Bissau	W	2-1	Nairobi	CNq	Mike Baraza [58], Dennis Oliech [93+]		
8-10	Uganda	D	0-0	Kampala	CNq			
11-11	Seychelles	W	3-0	Roche Caiman	WCq	Pascal Ochieng [41], Dennis Oliech 2 [75] [81]	2 000	Batte UGA
15-11	Seychelles	W	4-0	Nairobi	WCq	Brian Mandela [19], Dennis Oliech [36], Titus Mulama [45], Victor Wanyama [74]	5 000	Gomes RSA
28-11	Malawi	L	0-2	Dar es Salaam	CCr1			
30-11	Ethiopia	W	2-0	Dar es Salaam	CCr1	Bob Mugalia [13], Victor Ochieng [44]		
3-12	Sudan	L	0-1	Dar es Salaam	CCr1			

Fr = Friendly match • CN = CAF African Cup of Nations • CC = CECAFA Cup • WC = FIFA World Cup • q = qualifier • r1 = first round group

KENYA 2011

PREMIER LEAGUE

	Pl	W	D	L	F	A	Pts	Tusker	Ulinzi Stars	Sofapaka	Gor Mahia	Leopards	SonySugar	Posta	Chemelil	KCB	Thika Utd	West'n Stima	Mathare Utd	Karuturi	Nairobi City	Bandari	Congo Utd
Tusker †	30	17	7	6	34	17	58		1-2	0-1	0-0	2-0	1-0	1-2	2-1	0-0	0-1	1-0	2-1	0-0	2-1	1-0	1-0
Ulinzi Stars	30	16	9	5	38	20	57	1-0		2-1	0-0	0-1	1-0	3-0	4-1	1-1	1-1	2-1	2-0	0-0	1-2	3-1	2-0
Sofapaka	30	15	7	8	42	23	52	1-0	2-0		0-0	3-1	1-2	0-2	3-2	0-0	4-1	5-0	2-1	0-0	0-0	2-0	5-0
Gor Mahia	30	12	12	6	27	22	48	0-0	1-0	0-0		3-1	2-1	3-1	0-0	2-2	1-0	1-0	1-1	1-1	0-1	1-0	1-2
AFC Leopards	30	13	7	10	36	27	46	1-2	1-0	3-1	3-0		1-2	3-1	1-1	0-1	0-2	1-0	2-2	1-0	2-1	2-1	2-0
SonySugar	30	13	5	12	33	33	44	0-2	0-0	0-1	1-0	0-3		2-0	2-1	1-0	1-0	3-1	3-2	0-0	3-2	1-1	
Posta Rangers	30	11	10	9	33	31	43	1-1	1-1	1-3	3-0	0-0	3-0		2-0	1-3	1-0	0-0	0-0	1-0	2-1	1-0	0-0
Chemelil Sugar	30	10	11	9	30	27	41	0-3	0-0	0-0	0-1	1-1	2-0	3-0		3-2	4-1	0-0	1-1	2-0	0-0	0-0	1-0
Kenya Com'cial Bank	30	11	7	12	38	32	40	1-2	0-1	0-1	1-0	0-0	0-0	2-2	1-2		3-2	0-1	3-2	0-1	2-0	4-1	4-0
Thika United	30	11	6	13	36	39	39	0-2	1-1	2-1	1-3	1-2	1-1	1-1	1-0	1-2		1-1	4-1	3-1	2-1	3-0	2-0
Western Stima	30	9	10	11	21	28	37	0-2	1-2	0-0	0-1	1-0	2-2	2-1	0-0	1-0	2-1		1-0	0-1	1-1	2-1	1-0
Mathare United	30	7	13	10	32	35	34	1-1	0-1	3-1	0-0	1-0	1-0	0-0	0-0	2-3	1-1	3-3		3-0	0-0	3-0	1-0
Karuturi Sports	30	8	10	12	19	28	34	1-1	1-1	1-0	1-1	0-0	1-0	0-0	0-1	1-0	0-1	0-0	1-1		1-0	0-1	2-0
Nairobi City Stars	30	8	7	15	28	34	31	0-1	1-2	1-0	0-1	1-2	0-3	1-1	0-2	3-1	0-1	0-0	2-0	4-1		2-2	4-0
Bandari Mombasa	30	9	4	17	22	39	31	0-1	0-2	1-3	1-0	0-0	1-0	1-0	1-2	0-0	1-0	1-0	0-1	1-0	4-1		3-2
Congo United	30	5	5	20	18	52	20	1-2	1-2	0-1	2-2	1-0	1-4	0-4	1-0	0-1	3-0	0-1	1-1	1-2	1-0	0-0	

26/02/2011 - 26/11/2011 • † Qualified for the CAF Champions League

FKL CUP 2011

Quarter-finals		Semi-finals		Final	
Gor Mahia	1				
Finlays	0	**Gor Mahia**	1		
Congo United	0	AFC Leopards	0		
AFC Leopards	1			**Gor Mahia**	1
Thika United	5			Sofapaka	0
Kaya Zosi	0	Thika United	1	Nairobi City Stadium	
KRA	1	**Sofapaka**	2	26-10-2011	
Sofapaka	2			Scorer - Edwin Lavatsa [31] for Gor Mahia	

MEDALS TABLE

		Overall	Lge	Cup
		G	G	G
1	Gor Mahia	21	12	8
2	Leopards	19	12	7
3	Tusker (ex Breweries)	12	9	3
4	Luo Union	5	2	3
5	Ulinzi Stars	4	4	
6	Mathare United	3	1	2
7	Sofapaka	2	1	1

Gor Mahia have also won the African Cup Winners Cup

KGZ – KYRGYZSTAN

FIFA/COCA-COLA WORLD RANKING

'93	'94	'95	'96	'97	'98	'99	'00	'01	'02	'03	'04	'05	'06	'07	'08	'09	'10	'11	'12
-	166	172	168	140	151	159	174	164	171	157	150	157	139	139	158	159	174	191	

	2011														
	Jan	Feb	Mar	Apr	May	Jun	Jul	Aug	Sep	Oct	Nov	Dec	High	Low	Av
	175	175	174	160	170	169	180	177	178	186	188	191	119	191	158

The 2010 Krygyz league winners Neftchi Kochkorta progressed to the finals of the AFC President's Cup but failed in their bid to add to the two titles won by compatriots Dordoi-Dynamo in the competition in 2006 and 2007. Neftchi earned their place in the six-team final tournament by seeing off the challenge of Bangladesh's Abahani Limited and Don Bosco from Sri Lanka, but once there they finished second behind Cambodia's Phnom Penh Crown in their group to miss out on a place in the final against hosts Taipower. Neftchi's season was a tale of what might have been as they relinquished their domestic crown to Dordoi Dynamo, while Abdish-Ata Kant beat them 1-0 in the final of the Kyrgyzstan Cup. A victory for the national team over Cambodia in the qualifiers for the 2012 AFC Challenge Cup was the country's only success on the international stage during 2011 but defeats in the other two group matches ensured Kyrgyzstan did not qualify for the finals in Nepal. In the qualifiers for the 2014 FIFA World Cup in Brazil, Kyrgyzstan were drawn against fellow Central Asian nation Uzbekistan in a preliminary round tie. A 4-0 defeat in Tashkent was followed by a 3-0 loss in the return in Bishkek in what was the team's first match in the Kyrgyz capital for over three years - and only their 10th overall in 19 years of international football.

FIFA WORLD CUP RECORD
1930-1994 DNE **1998-2014** DNQ

FOOTBALL FEDERATION OF KYRGYZ REPUBLIC (FFKR)

 Kurenkeeva Street 195, PO Box 1484, Bishkek 720 040,
☎ +996 312 374911
📠 +996 312 374911
📧 media@ffkr.kg
🌐 www.ffkr.kg
FA 1992 CON 1994 FIFA 1994
P Aibek Alybaev
GS Nurtazin Djetybaev

FIFA BIG COUNT 2006

Total players	124 477
% of population	2.39%
Male	116 605
Female	7 872
Amateurs 18+	7 985
Youth under 18	460
Unregistered	50 500
Professionals	0
Referees	69
Admin & coaches	1 425
Number of clubs	100
Number of teams	500

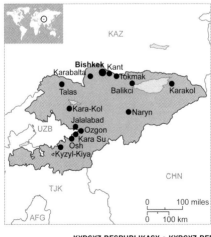

MAJOR CITIES/TOWNS

		Population
1	Bishkek	930 377
2	Osh	235 861
3	Jalalabad	78 739
4	Karakol	68 589
5	Tokmak	60 371
6	Karabalta	55 215
7	Balikci	44 084
8	Ozgön	39 667
9	Naryn	39 409
10	Talas	34 404
11	Kizil-Kiya	28 061
12	Bazarkurgon	27 991
13	Tashkömür	22 310
14	Gulcha	22 034
15	Colponata	19 884
16	Karakol	19 008
17	Toktogul	18 918
18	Kant	18 290
19	Kara-Su	16 727

KYRGYZ RESPUBLIKASY • KYRGYZ REPUBLIC

Capital Bishkek	Population 5 431 747 (112)	% in cities 36%
GDP per capita $2200 (184)	Area km² 199 951 km² (86)	GMT +/- +6
Neighbours (km) China 858, Kazakhstan 1224, Tajikistan 870, Uzbekistan 1099		

RECENT INTERNATIONAL MATCHES PLAYED BY KYRGYZSTAN

2009 Opponents	Score	Venue	Comp	Scorers	Att	Referee
28-03 Nepal	D 1-1	Kathmandu	CCq	Mirlan Murzaev [86p]	15 000	Jahanbazi IRN
30-03 Palestine	D 1-1	Kathmandu	CCq	Mirlan Murzaev [20p]	2 000	Yu Ming Hsun
25-07 China PR	L 0-3	Tianjin	Fr			
20-08 Syria	L 0-2	New Dehli	Fr			Singh IND
23-08 India	L 1-2	New Dehli	Fr	Mirlan Murzaev [90]		
25-08 Lebanon	D 1-1	New Dehli	Fr	Anton Zemlianuhin [48]		Hannan BAN
28-08 Sri Lanka	W 4-1	New Dehli	Fr	Anton Zemlianuhin [34], Ildar Amirov [45], Mirlan Murzaev [65], Rustem Usanov [70]		Singh IND
2010						
17-02 India †	W 2-1	Colombo	CCr1	Ildar Amirov [15], Anton Zemlianuhin [32]	800	Shukralla BHR
19-02 Korea DPR	L 0-4	Colombo	CCr1		300	El Haddad LIB
21-02 Turkmenistan	L 0-1	Colombo	CCr1		100	El Haddad LIB
2011						
21-03 Tajikistan	L 0-1	Male	CCq		4 000	Mohamed UAE
23-03 Maldives	L 1-2	Male	CCq	OG [87]	9 000	Al Awaji KSA
25-03 Cambodia	W 4-3	Male	CCq	Aziz Sydykov [5], Rustem Usanov [45], Cholponbek Esenkul uulu 2 [80 85]	1 000	Zhao Liang CHN
23-07 Uzbekistan	L 0-4	Tashkent	WCq		20 257	Balideh QAT
28-07 Uzbekistan	L 0-3	Bishkek	WCq		14 700	Abdulnabi BHR

Fr = Friendly match • CC = AFC Challenge Cup • WC = FIFA World Cup • † Not a full international
q = qualifier • r1 = first round group • qf = quarter-final • sf = semi-final

KYRGYZSTAN NATIONAL TEAM HISTORICAL RECORDS

Caps
38 - Vyacheslav Amin 2000-09 & Ruslan Sydykov 1997-2009 • **37** - Vadim Kharchenko 2003- • **30** - Vladimir Salo 1994-2004 • **29** - Zakir Djalilov • **27** - Valeriy Berezovskii & Ruslan Djamshidov 1999- • **26** - Igor Kudrenko 2001-08 • **25** - Marat Djumakeev 1992-2001

Goals
4 - Mirlan Murzaev 2009- • **3** - Sergey Chikishev 2003-04; Sergey Kutsov 1996-2001; Farhad Khaytbaev 1994-2000; Zamirbek Zhumagulov 1992-2003; Ruslan Djamshidov 1999- ; Cholponbek Esenkul uulu 2007- ; Anton Zemlianuhin 2007-

Coaches
Meklis Koshaliyev 1992-96 • Evgeniy Novikov 1997-2001 • Nematzhan Zakirov 2003-05 • Boris Podkorytov 2006 • Nematzhan Zakirov 2007-08 • Anarbek Ormombekov 2009-11 • Marat Djumakeev 2011-

KYRGYZSTAN 2011

PREMIER LEAGUE

	Pl	W	D	L	F	A	Pts	Dordoi	Neftchi	Abdish-Ata	Alga	Alay	Ysyk-Kol
Dordoi-Dynamo †	20	15	3	2	54	12	48		0-0 2-0	4-0 3-0	5-2 4-1	0-0 2-0	2-1 3-0
Neftchi Kochkorata	20	12	5	3	32	14	41	0-0 0-4		2-0 2-1	1-1 1-0	2-2 2-1	4-0 3-0
Abdish-Ata Kant	20	10	4	6	37	24	34	3-0 3-2	0-0 1-0		0-0 2-0	2-1 2-3	2-0 3-0
Alga Bishkek	20	7	5	8	29	36	26	2-4 1-1	0-3 1-2	3-2 2-2		2-1 2-1	3-2 3-0
Alay Osh	20	5	3	12	25	36	18	0-4 1-4	1-2 0-2	0-1 1-1	3-1 1-1		3-1 3-0
Ysyk-Kol Karakol	20	1	0	19	8	63	3	0-4 0-3	0-1 0-3	1-9 0-3	1-3 0-3	2-0 0-3	

17/04/2011 - 16/10/2011 • † Qualified for the AFC President's Cup • Yssk-Kol withdrew after 10 games. Their remaining matches were awarded 3-0
Top scorers: **12** - Vladimir Verevkin, Alga • **10** - Kayumzhan Sharipov, Dordoi • **9** - David Tetteh GHA, Dordoi

KYRGYZSTAN CUP 2011

Semi-finals		Finals	
Abdish-Ata Kant	7		
Alay Osh	4		
		Abdish-Ata Kant	1
		Neftchi Kochkorata	0
Dordoi-Dynamo	1		
Neftchi Kochkorata	2		

MEDALS TABLE

		Overall			League			Cup		Asia		
		G	S	B	G	S	B	G	S	G	S	B
1	Alga Bishkek	14	7		5	6		9	1			
2	Dordoi-Dynamo	14	5	3	7	1	3	5		2	4	
3	Abdish-Ata Kant	3	4	2		4	2	3				
4	Dinamo Bishkek	3	2		3	1			1			
5	Kant-Oil	2			2							
6	Zhashtyk Kara-Su	1	9	5	1	2	5		7			
7	Neftchi Kochkorata	1	3		1	1			2			
8	AiK Bishkek	1	2	2		2	2	1				
9	Semetey Kyzyl-Kiya	1	2	1		1	1	1	1			
10	Metallurg Kadamjay	1	1		1				1			
11	Ak-Maral Tokmak	1		1				1	1			
12	Alay Osh		6	5		5			6			

KOR – KOREA REPUBLIC

FIFA/COCA-COLA WORLD RANKING

'93	'94	'95	'96	'97	'98	'99	'00	'01	'02	'03	'04	'05	'06	'07	'08	'09	'10	'11	'12
41	35	46	44	27	17	51	40	42	20	22	22	29	51	42	42	52	40	32	

2011														
Jan	Feb	Mar	Apr	May	Jun	Jul	Aug	Sep	Oct	Nov	Dec	High	Low	Av
38	32	29	31	31	26	28	33	29	29	32	32	17	62	36

South Korean football faced its most challenging year ever after a number of match-fixing stories emerged during 2011 with the scandal tragically leading to the suicides of two players and a coach. Chung Jung Kwan, a former midfielder for Jeonbuk, took his life and left a note speaking of his shame, while Lee Soo Chul, the coach of Sanju Sangmu Phoenix, was sacked in July for his involvement and then took his life in October. In all nearly 50 players were arrested as the authorities sought to clean up the image of the game. Many of the matches being investigated were in the K-League Cup which was identified as an easy target for the fixers as the least important of the competitions played. As a result the tournament was discarded for the 2012 season. On the field the 2011 K-League title was won by Jeonbuk who beat Ulsan - winners of the tarnished K-League Cup - 4-2 on aggregate in the final. Jeonbuk almost pulled off a K-League and AFC Champions League double but lost to Qatar's Al Sadd in the final of the Champions League in Jeonju on post-match penalties after a 2-2 draw. Jeonbuk's Choi Kang Hee was appointed national team coach at the end of the year although he is officially only on-loan to the national association until the end of the 2014 FIFA World Cup qualifiers in which finish in mid-2013.

FIFA WORLD CUP RECORD

1930-1950 DNE **1954** 15 r1 **1958** DNE **1962** DNQ **1966** DNE **1970-1982** DNQ
1986 20 r1 **1990** 22 r1 **1994** 20 r1 **1998** 30 r1 **2002** 4 SF (co-hosts) **2006** 17 r1 **2010** 15 r2

KOREA FOOTBALL ASSOCIATION (KFA)

1-131 Sinmunno, 2-ga, Jongno-Gu, Seoul 110-062

☎ +82 2 7377538
📠 +82 2 7352755
📧 kfainfo@kfa.or.kr
🖥 www.kfa.or.kr
FA 1928 CON 1954 FIFA 1948
P Cho Chung Yun
GS Kim Joo Sung

FIFA BIG COUNT 2006

Total players	1 094 227
% of population	2.24%
Male	1 021 677
Female	72 550
Amateurs 18+	12 372
Youth under 18	18 205
Unregistered	423 100
Professionals	550
Referees	948
Admin & coaches	3 700
Number of clubs	96
Number of teams	864

MAJOR CITIES/TOWNS

		Population
1	Seoul	9 660 532
2	Busan	3 351 991
3	Incheon	2 533 513
4	Daegu	2 413 599
5	Goyang	1 518 319
6	Daejeon	1 437 093
7	Suwon	1 374 548
8	Gwangju	1 360 225
9	Seongnam	1 023 219
10	Ulsan	957 963
12	Bucheon	810 980
13	Jeonju	720 987
15	Anyang	623 289
16	Jeongju	619 781
10	Changwon	618 370
19	Kimhae	417 161
35	Gimpo	220 543
48	Gwangyang	138 012
63	Seogwipo	92 056

TAEHAN-MIN'GUK • REPUBLIC OF KOREA

Capital Seoul	Population 48 508 972 (25)	% in cities 81%
GDP per capita $27 700 (50)	Area km² 99 720 km² (108)	GMT + / - +9
Neighbours (km) Korea DPR 238 • Coast 2413		

RECENT INTERNATIONAL MATCHES PLAYED BY KOREA REPUBLIC

2010	Opponents	Score	Venue	Comp	Scorers	Att	Referee
9-01	Zambia	L 2-4	Johannesburg	Fr	Kim Jung Woo [35], Koo Ja Cheol [83]	2 000	Gornes RSA
18-01	Finland	W 2-0	Malaga	Fr	Oh Beom Seok [39], Lee Jung Soo [61]	270	Fernandez ESP
22-01	Latvia	W 1-0	Malaga	Fr	Kim Jae Sung [55]	150	Velasco ESP
7-02	Hong Kong	W 5-0	Tokyo	EAC	Kim Jung Woo [10], Koo Ja Cheol [24], Lee Dong Gook [32], Lee Seung Yeoul [37], No Byung Jun [93+]	2 728	Sato JPN
10-02	China PR	L 0-3	Tokyo	EAC		3 629	Ng Kai Lam HKG
14-02	Japan	W 3-1	Tokyo	EAC	Lee Dong Gook [33p], Lee Seung Yeoul [39], Kim Jae Sung [70]	42 951	Delovski AUS
3-03	Côte d'Ivoire	W 2-0	London	Fr	Lee Dong Gook [4], Kwak Tae Hwi [90]	6 000	Mariner ENG
16-05	Ecuador	W 2-0	Seoul	Fr	Lee Seung Ryul [71], Lee Chung Yong [83]	62 209	Wongkamdee THA
24-05	Japan	W 2-0	Saitama	Fr	Park Ji Sung [6], Park Chu Young [90]	57 873	Attwell ENG
30-05	Belarus	L 0-1	Kufstein	Fr		1 000	Brugger AUT
3-06	Spain	L 0-1	Innsbruck	Fr		17 400	Schorgenhofer AUT
12-06	Greece	W 2-0	Port Elizabeth	WCr1	Lee Jung Soo [7], Park Ji Sung [52]	31 513	Hester NZL
17-06	Argentina	L 1-4	Johannesburg	WCr1	Lee Chung Yong [45]	82 174	De Bleeckere BEL
22-06	Nigeria	D 2-2	Durban	WCr1	Lee Jung Soo [38], Park Chu Young [49]	61 874	Benquerenca POR
26-06	Uruguay	L 1-2	Port Elizabeth	WCr2	Lee Chung Yong [68]	30 597	Stark GER
11-08	Nigeria	W 2-1	Suwon	Fr	Yoon Bit Garam [17], Choi Hyo Jin [44]	40 331	Nishimura JPN
7-09	Iran	L 0-1	Seoul	Fr		38 642	Mohd Salleh MAS
12-10	Japan	D 0-0	Seoul	Fr		62 503	Irmatov UZB
30-12	Syria	W 1-0	Abu Dhabi	Fr	Ji Dong Won [83]	500	Al Marzouqi UAE
2011							
10-01	Bahrain	W 2-1	Doha	ACr1	Koo Ja Cheol 2 [40 52]	6 669	Al Hilali OMA
14-01	Australia	D 1-1	Doha	ACr1	Koo Ja Cheol [24]	15 526	Abdou QAT
18-01	India	W 4-1	Doha	ACr1	Ji Dong Won 2 [6 23], Koo Ja Cheol [9], Son Heung Min [81]	11 366	Al Ghamdi KSA
22-01	Iran	W 1-0	Doha	ACqf	Yoon Bit Garam [105]	7 111	Irmatov UZB
25-01	Japan	D 2-2	Doha	ACsf	Li Sung Yueng [23p], Hwang Jae Won [120]. L 0-3p	16 171	Al Ghamdi
28-01	Uzbekistan	W 3-2	Doha	AC3p	Koo Ja Cheol [18], Ji Dong Won 2 [28 39]	8 199	Abdul Bashir SIN
9-02	Turkey	D 0-0	Trabzon	Fr		20 000	Boyko UKR
25-03	Honduras	W 4-0	Seoul	Fr	Lee Jung Soo [28], Kim Jung Woo [44], Park Chu Young [83], Lee Keun Ho [90]	31 224	Sato JPN
3-06	Serbia	W 2-1	Seoul	Fr	Park Chu Young [10], Kim Young Kwon [54]	40 000	Albadwawi UAE
7-06	Ghana	W 2-1	Jeonju	Fr	Ji Dong Won [10], Koo Ja Cheol [90]	41 271	Irmatov UZB
10-08	Japan	L 0-3	Sapporo	Fr		38 263	Irmatov UZB
2-09	Lebanon	W 6-0	Goyang	WCq	Park Chu Young 3 [8 45 67], Ji Dong Woon 2 [66 85], Kim Jung Woo [82]	37 655	Abdul Bashir SIN
6-09	Kuwait	D 1-1	Kuwait City	WCq	Park Chu Young [9]	20 000	Torky IRN
7-10	Poland	D 2-2	Seoul	Fr	Park Chu Young 2 [66 76]	40 000	Shukralla BHR
11-10	UAE	W 2-1	Suwon	WCq	Park Chu Young [55], OG [64]	28 689	Tan Hai CHN
11-11	UAE	W 2-0	Dubai	WCq	Lee Keun Ho [88], Park Chu Young [93+]	8 272	Irmatov UZB
15-11	Lebanon	L 1-2	Beirut	WCq	Koo Ja Cheol [20]	35 000	Al Ghamdi KSA

Fr = Friendly match • AC = AFC Asian Cup • EAC = East Asian Championship • WC = FIFA World Cup
q = qualifier • r1 = first round group • qf = quarter-final • sf = semi-final • 3p = third place play-off

KOREA REPUBLIC NATIONAL TEAM HISTORICAL RECORDS

Caps 136 - Hong Myung Bo 1990-2002 • 133 - Lee Woon Jae 1994- • 123 - Yoo Sang Chul 1994-2005 • 121 - Cha Bum Kun 1972-86 • 120 - Lee Young Pyo 1999- • 104 - Kim Tae Young 1992-2004 • 103 - Hwang Seon Hong 1993-2002 • 97 - Kim Nam Il 1998- • 96 - Park Ji Sung 2000- • 95 - Choi Soon Hoo 1980-91 & Ha Seok Joo 1991-2001 • 92 - Cho Young Jeung 1975-86 & Park Sung Hwa 1974-84 • 89 - Choi Jong Duk 1975-86 & Seo Jung Won 1990-2001 • 88 - Park Kyung Hoon 1981-90 • 84 - Huh Jung Moo 1974-86 • 83 - Seol Ki Hyeon 2000-09 • 81 - Lee Dong Gook 1998- • 80 - Cho Gwang Rae 1975-86 • 79 - Lee Chun Soo 2000- • 77 - Kim Joo Sung 1985-96 • 76 - Ko Jung Woon 1989-95

Goals 55 - Cha Bum Kun 1972-86 • 50 - Hwang Seon Hong 1993-2002 • 30 - Choi Soon Hoo 1980-91 • 29 - Huh Jung Moo 1974-86 & Kim Do Hoon 1994-2003 • 27 - Choi Yong Soo 1995-2003 & Lee Tae Hoo 1980-91 • 25 - Lee Dong Gook 1998- • 24 - Lee Young Moo 1974-82 & Park Sung Hwa 1974-84 • 23 - Ha Seok Joo 1991-2001 • 22 - Chung Hae Won 1980-90

Past Coaches For coaches prior to 1984 see Oliver's Almanack of World Football 2011 • Mun Jeong-Sik 1984-85 • Kim Jung-Nam 1985-86 • Park Jong-Hwan 1986-88 • Kim Jung-Nam 1988 • Lee Hoi-Taek 1988-90 • Lee Cha-Man 1990 • Park Jong-Hwan 1990-91 • Ko Jae-Wook 1991 • Kim Ho 1992-94 • Anatoliy Byshovets RUS 1994-95 • Park Jong-Hwan 1995 • Huh Jung-Moo 1995 • Jeong Byeong-Tak 1995 • Ko Jae-Wook 1995 • Park Jong-Hwan 1996-97 • Cha Bum-Kun 1997-98 • Kim Pyung-Seok 1998 • Huh Jung-Moo 1998-2000 • Guus Hiddink NED 2001-02 • Kim Ho-Gon 2002 • Humberto Coelho POR 2003-04 • Park Seong-Hwa 2004 • Jo Bonfrere NED 2004-05 • Dick Advocaat NED 2005-06 • Pim Verbeek NED 2006-07 • Huh Jung-Moo 2007-10 • Cho Kwang-Rae 2010-

KOREA REPUBLIC 2011

K-LEAGUE OVERALL

	Pl	W	D	L	F	A	Pts	Jeonbuk	Pohang	Seoul	Suwon	Busan	Ulsan	Chunnam	Gyeongnam	Jeju	Seongnam	Gwangju	Daegu	Incheon	Sangju	Daejeon	Gangwon
Jeonbuk Hyundai Motors †	30	18	9	3	67	32	63		3-1	2-2	0-0	5-2	1-0	0-1	2-0	3-2	2-0	6-1	2-2	4-2	5-1	0-0	1-0
Pohang Steelers ‡	30	17	8	5	59	33	59	3-2		1-2	2-0	3-2	2-0	1-1	1-0	2-1	1-1	5-1	2-2	2-2	4-3	7-0	0-0
FC Seoul ‡‡	30	16	7	7	56	38	55	3-1	1-1		0-2	2-1	1-1	1-0	3-1	2-1	3-1	4-1	0-2	1-1	3-2	4-1	6-3
Suwon Samsung Bluewings ‡‡	30	17	4	9	51	33	55	2-2	2-1	1-0		1-2	2-1	1-2	1-2	2-0	3-2	2-1	4-1	1-0	3-0	4-0	2-0
Busan I'Park ‡‡	30	13	7	10	49	43	46	2-3	2-1	1-1	4-3		2-0	3-0	0-1	3-1	1-0	1-1	2-2	1-0	3-3	1-0	2-0
Ulsan Hyundai Horang-i ‡‡	30	13	7	10	33	29	46	0-0	2-1	1-2	1-1	1-0		2-0	0-0	0-1	3-2	2-1	2-1	1-1	3-1	1-2	1-0
Chunnam Dragons	30	11	10	9	33	29	43	1-1	0-1	3-0	3-1	1-1	0-1		2-0	1-1	0-0	0-2	3-1	0-0	0-1	2-0	1-0
Gyeongnam FC	30	12	6	12	41	40	42	1-3	2-3	0-3	0-2	3-2	1-0	1-2		1-1	2-2	1-0	3-0	2-1	0-1	7-1	0-0
Jeju United	30	10	10	10	44	45	40	0-0	1-3	0-3	3-2	2-1	1-2	0-1	2-3		2-1	2-1	3-0	2-1	3-3	3-3	1-0
Seongnam Ilhwa Chunma	30	9	8	13	43	47	35	1-0	1-3	2-0	1-1	2-0	3-2	3-2	1-1	2-2		1-3	1-0	2-2	2-3	2-1	3-1
Gwangju Sangmu Phoenix	30	9	8	13	32	43	35	1-1	0-1	1-0	0-1	2-2	0-0	0-0	0-2	2-2	2-0		3-2	0-1	0-0	2-1	2-0
Daegu FC	30	8	9	13	35	46	33	1-2	1-1	2-1	1-2	2-3	0-0	1-0	2-1	0-2	2-1	1-2		2-0	0-0	1-1	1-0
Incheon United	30	6	14	10	31	40	32	2-6	0-1	1-1	2-1	0-0	0-2	1-1	2-2	0-0	2-1	2-2	1-1		0-0	2-0	0-0
Sangju Sangmu	30	7	8	15	36	53	29	0-3	1-3	3-4	1-0	1-2	1-2	0-1	1-3	1-1	1-3	0-0	2-0	2-0		0-0	0-0
Daejeon Citizen	30	6	9	15	31	59	27	2-3	0-0	1-1	1-3	1-3	1-0	4-4	2-0	0-0	0-2	1-0	2-2	1-2	1-3		1-0
Gangwon FC	30	3	6	21	14	45	15	0-3	0-2	0-2	0-1	1-0	1-2	1-1	0-1	2-4	1-1	0-1	1-0	1-3	2-0	0-3	

5/03/2011 - 30/10/2011 • † Qualified for the play-off final • ‡ Qualified for the play-off semi-final • ‡‡ Qualified for the play-off first round
Top scorers: **22** - Dejan Damjanovic MNE, Seoul • **16** - Lee Dong Gook, Jeonbuk • **15** - Kim Jung Woo, Sangju/Seongnam • **14** - Santos BRA, Jeju • **13** - Mota BRA, Pohang • **10** - Kim Dong Chan, Jeonbuk & Mauricio Molina COL, Seoul
First round: FC Seoul 1-3 **Ulsan**; **Suwon** 1-0 Busan I'Park • Second round: Suwon 1-1 1-3p **Ulsan** • Semi-final: Pohang 0-1 **Ulsan**

K-LEAGUE FINAL 2011 1ST LEG

Ulsan Munsu, Ulsan, 30-11-2011, Att: 25 375, Ref: Lee Sam Ho

Ulsan	1	Kwak Tae Hwi 63
Jeonbuk	2	Eninho 2 52p 79

Ulsan - Kim Young Kwang - Kwak Tae Hwi, Lee Jae Sung•, Lee Yong, Lee Ho, Juan Velez, Choi Jae Soo, Seul-Ki Go• (Park Seung Il 82), Seol Ki Hyeon, Kim Shin Woo, Lucio. Tr: Kim Ho Gon
Jeonbuk - Kim Min Sik - Kim Sang Sik, Cho Sung Hwan•, Sim Woo Yeon, Choi Chul Soon, Park Won Jae, Lee Seung Hyun (Krunoslav Lovrek 70), Eninho, Jung Hoon (Son Seung Joon 90), Lee Dong Gook, Luiz Henrique (Jeong Seong Hoon 70). Tr: Choi Kang Hee

K-LEAGUE FINAL 2011 2ND LEG

World Cup Stadium, Jeonju, 4-12-2011, Att: 33 554, Ref: Choi Kwang Bo

Jeonbuk	2	Eninho 59p, Luiz 68
Ulsan	1	Seol Ki Hyeon 56

Jeonbuk - Kim Min Sik - Kim Sang Sik, Cho Sung Hwan, Sim Woo Yeon, Choi Chul Soon, Park Won Jae, Eninho•, Jung Hoon• (Jeong Seong Hoon 54), Lee Dong Gook (Lee Seung Hyun 84), Seo Jung Jin (Son Seung Joon 65), Luiz Henrique•. Tr: Choi Kang Hee
Ulsan - Kim Young Kwang - Kang Min Soo, Kwak Tae Hwi, Lee Yong, Lee Ho, Juan Velez• (Kim Dong Suk 73), Choi Jae Soo•, Seol Ki Hyeon, Kim Shin Wook (Lee Jin Ho 89), Lucio, Seung Il Park (Ko Chang Hyeon 83). Tr: Kim Ho Gon

Jeonbuk Hyundai Motors win the 2011 K–League and qualify for the AFC Champions League along with Pohang Steelers, Ulsan Hyundai and KFA Cup winners Seongnam Ilhwa Chunma

KOREA REPUBLIC 2011 KOREA NATIONAL LEAGUE (2) OVERALL STANDINGS

	Pl	W	D	L	F	A	Pts
Ulsan Mipo Dolphins	26	17	2	7	53	34	53
Goyang Kookmin Bank	26	13	8	5	37	25	47
Gangneung City	26	12	10	4	40	25	46
Busan Kyotong	26	11	8	7	29	27	41
Changwon City	26	11	7	8	37	36	40
Incheon Korail	26	11	6	9	29	23	39
Suwon City	26	8	11	7	28	23	35
Daejeon HNP	26	9	8	9	40	38	35
Cheonan City	26	9	8	9	31	31	35
Gimhae City	26	10	3	13	39	44	33
Yongin City	26	5	11	10	22	32	26
Ansan Hallelujah	26	5	8	13	25	42	23
Mokpo City	26	5	6	15	25	36	21
Chungju Hummel	26	5	6	15	25	44	21

12/03/2011 - 29/10/2011 • ‡ Qualified for play-offs
Play-offs first round: **Gangneung City** 3-2 Incheon Korail; Busan Kyotong 0-1 **Changwon City**
Play-off second round: Gangneung City 1-3 **Changwon City**
Play-off semi-finals: **Koyang KB** 2-1 Changwon City
Play-off final: Goyang KB 1-1 0-1 **Ulsan Dolphins**

MEDALS TABLE

	Overall			League			Cup			LC			Asia		
	G	S	B	G	S	B	G	S	B	G	S	B	G	S	B
1 Suwon S. Bluewings	15	6	4	4	2	3	3	3		6			2	1	1
2 Seongnam I. Chunma	14	11	1	7	3		2	3		3	3		2	2	1
3 Pohang Steelers	11	9	4	4	4	3	2	3		2	2	1	3		
4 Busan I'Park	9	9	7	4	3	2	1	1		3	5	4	1		1
5 FC Seoul	7	10	1	4	5					2	4	1	1		
6 Ulsan Hyundai	7	10	7	2	6	4		1		5	3	1			2
7 Jeonbuk Hyundai	6	4	2	2			3	1		1	1		1	2	1
8 Jeju United	4	7	4	1	4	4		1		3	2				
9 Chunnam Dragons	3	6	1		1	1	3	1		3			1		
10 Daejeon Citizen	1	1					1			1					
11 Gimpo Halleluyah	1			1											
12 Gyeongnam FC	1	1					1			1					
13 Incheon United	1									1					
Ulsan Mipo Dolphins	1						1								

HANA BANK KOREAN FA CUP 2011

First Round

Seongnam Ilhwa Chunma *	3
Mokpo City	0
Yeonsei University	1
Incheon United *	2
Jeonbuk Hyundai Motors *	2
Kyung Hee University	1
Cheonan City *	1
Busan I'Park	2
FC Seoul *	4
Yongin City	0
Gyeongnam FC	1
Busan Kyotong *	0
Ulsan Mipo Dolphins	3
Daegu FC *	2
Daejeon HNP	0
Pohang Steelers *	2
Ulsan Hyundai Horang-i *	1
Ansan Hallelujah	0
Gangneung City *	1
Sangju Sangmu Phoenix	2
Daejeon Citizen	3
Gimhae City *	0
Chungju Hummel *	0 3p
Gangwon FC	0 4p
Chunnam Dragons *	1
Konkuk University	0
Goyang Kookmin Bank	2
Jeju United *	4
Suwon City	2
Gwangju FC *	1
Pocheon	1
Suwon Samsung B'wings *	3

Second Round

Seongnam Ilhwa Chunma	2
Incheon United *	0
Jeonbuk Hyundai Motors *	1
Busan I'Park	2
FC Seoul	1
Busan Kyotong *	0
Ulsan Mipo Dolphins	0
Pohang Steelers *	2
Ulsan Hyundai Horang-i *	2
Sangju Sangmu Phoenix	1
Daejeon Citizen	1 3p
Gangwon FC *	1 4p
Chunnam Dragons *	1
Jeju United	0
Suwon City *	0
Suwon Samsung Bluewings	1

Quarter-finals

Seongnam Ilhwa Chunma *	2
Busan I'Park	1
FC Seoul	2
Pohang Steelers *	4
Ulsan Hyundai Horang-i *	3
Gangwon FC	0
Chunnam Dragons	0
Suwon Samsung B'wings *	1

Semi-finals

Seongnam Ilhwa Chunma *	3
Pohang Steelers	0
Ulsan Hyundai Horang-i	2
Suwon Samsung B'wings *	3

Final

Seongnam Ilhwa Chunma *†	1
Suwon Samsung Bluewings	0

CUP FINAL

Seongnam Tancheon, Seongnam
15-10-2011, Att: 14,756, Ref:
Scorer: Cho Dong Geon 77 for Seongnam
Seongnam - Ha Kang Jin - Sasa Ognenovski, Kim Tae Yoon, Hing Chul, Park Jin Po - Heverton, Kim Sung Hwan, Jo Jae Cheol, Jeon Sung Chan - Everton, Dzenan Radoncic. Tr: Shin Tae Yong
Suwon - Jung Sung Ryong - Oh Beom Seok, Mato Neretljak, Yang Sang Min, Kwak Hee Ju - Park Hyun Beom, Lee Sang Ho, Oh Jang Eun, Lee Yong Rae - Yeom Ki Hun, Stevica Ristic. Tr: Yoon Seong Hyo

* Home team • † Qualified for the AFC Champions League

POSCO K-LEAGUE CUP 2011

First Round Groups

Group A

	Pl	W	D	L	F	A	Pts	PS	Gy	SIC	IU	Da	DC
Pohang Steelers	5	4	0	1	11	3	12			2-0	4-1		0-1
Gyeongnam FC	5	3	1	1	7	2	10	1-2			1-0		3-0
Seongnam Ilhwa Chunma	5	2	2	1	4	3	8		0-0		1-1	1-0	3-0
Incheon United	5	1	2	2	6	5	5			0-0		0-0	
Daegu FC	5	1	2	2	5	5	5	0-2	0-2		0-2		
Daejeon Citizen	5	0	1	4	1	11	1	0-3				1-1	

Group B

	Pl	W	D	L	F	A	Pts	BIP	UHH	CD	Ga	SSP	Gw
Busan I'Park	5	4	0	1	7	3	12		2-1		1-0	2-1	1-0
Ulsan Hyundai Horang-i	5	4	0	1	8	1	12	2-1		1-0			1-0
Chunnam Dragons	5	3	1	1	7	6	10		1-0				
Gangwon FC	5	1	1	3	6	9	4	0-2		0-0		5-0	2-3
Sangju Sangmu Phoenix	5	1	0	4	9	12	3	1-0			0-0		2-1
Gwangju FC	5	1	0	4	4	12	3	1-2		0-2			

Quarter-finals

Ulsan Hyundai Horang-i *	4
Jeonbuk Hyundai Motors	1

FC Seoul	0
Gyeongnam FC *	1

Suwon Samsung Bluewings	0 4p
Jeju United *	0 2p

Pohang Steelers *	1
Busan I'Park	2

Semi-finals

Ulsan Hyundai Horang-i *	4
Gyeongnam FC	2

Suwon Samsung Bluewings	1
Busan I'Park *	2

Final

Ulsan Hyundai Horang-i *	3
Busan I'Park	2

CUP FINAL

Munsu, Ulsan, 13-07-2011,
Att: 21 853, Ref: Lee Min Hu
Scorers - Ko Chang Hyeon 38, Seol Ki Hyeon 45, Kang Jin Ouk 58 for Ulsan;
Yang Dong Hyun 2 71 77 for Busan

Ulsan - Kim Young Kwang • Kang Min Soo •, Kang Jin Ouk, Kwak Tae Hwi, Lee Yong (Lee Jae Sung 72) - Lee Ho, Juan Velez, Choi Jae Soo, Ko Chang Hyeon • (Kim Shin Wook 57), Go Seul Ki • - Seol Ki Hyeon (Park Seung Il 83). Tr: Kim Ho Gon
Busan - Jeon Sang Wook - Iain Fyfe •, Kim Chang Soo, Choo Sung Ho •, Park Hee Do (Yang Dong Hyun 45), Kim Han Yoon (Han Ji Ho 22) (Yoon Dong Min 57), Park Tae Min, Yu Ho Jun, Lim Sang Hyub, Park Jong Woo, Han Sang Woon •. Tr: Ahn Ik Soo

Top scorer: **11** - Kim Shin Wook, Ulsan • FC Seoul, Jeonbuk, Suwon & Jeju received byes to the quarter-finals due to AFC Champions League committments • * Home team

BUSAN I'PARK 2011

	Date	Opponent		Score	Comp	Scorers	Att
Mar	6	Jeju	L	1-2	KL	Park Hee Do 12	4 172
	13	Sangju	D	3-3	KL	Han Sang Woon 5, Fyfe 84, Lee Won Gyu 94+	29 267
	16	Ulsan	L	1-2	LCgB	OG 58	4 856
	20	Jeonbuk	L	2-5	KL	Yang Dong Hyun 18, Lim Sang Hyub 30	9 747
Apr	3	Seongnam	L	0-2	KL		6 438
	6	Gwangju	W	1-0	LCgB	Han Ji Ho 83	1 502
	10	Seoul	D	1-1	KL	Yang Dong Hyun 73	5 208
	16	Daegu	D	2-2	KL	Han Sang Woon 25, Yang Dong Hyun 80p	3 111
	20	Sangju	W	2-1	LCgB	Han Ji Ho 30, Kim Han Yoon 54	1 038
	24	Daejeon	W	3-1	KL	Kim Eung Jin 16, Kim Han Yoon 53, Han Sang Woon 70	14 895
	30	Chunnam	W	3-0	KL	Lim Sang Hyub 33, Lee Jung Ho 31, Han Sang Woon 79	2 515
May	5	Gangwon	W	2-0	LCgB	Choo Sung Hi 30, Choi Jin Ho 66	13 724
	8	Pohang	W	2-1	KL	Kim Chang Soo 30, Han Sang Woon 43	10 272
	11	Chunnam	W	1-0	LCgB	Lee Jong Won 32	602
	15	Incheon	D	0-0	KL		6 208
	18	Cheonan	W	2-1	FAr1	OG 36, Yoon Dong Min 66	1 550
	21	Suwon	W	2-1	KL	Lee Jung Ho 12, Yang Dong Hyun 88p	18 714
	28	Gwangju	D	1-1	KL	Lim Sang Hyub 65	6 564
Jun	11	Gangwon	L	0-1	KL		5 373
	15	Jeonbuk	W	2-1	FAr2	Han Sang Woon 2 55 64	4 328
	18	Gyeongnam	L	2-3	KL	Yang Dong Hyun 63, Han Sang Woon 75	8 137
	25	Ulsan	W	2-0	KL	Lim Sang Hyub 53, Yang Dong Hyun 61	2 336
	29	Pohang	W	2-1	LCqf	Yoon Dong Min 10, Park Hee Do 20	6 288
	2	Seongnam	W	1-0	KL	Han Sang Woon 18	6 019
	6	Suwon	W	2-1	LCsf	Lim Sang Hyub 43, Kim Han Yoon 91+	1 878
Jul	9	Daegu	W	3-2	KL	OG 61, Lim Sang Hyub 86, Han Sang Woon 91+	1 027
	13	Ulsan	L	2-3	LCf	Yang Dong Hyun 2 71 77	21 853
	16	Sangju	W	2-1	KL	Han Ji Ho 38, Park Tae Min 74	8 352
	23	Suwon	W	4-3	KL	Lim Sang Hyub 45, Yang Dong Hyun 70, Fagner 2 77 86	8 143
	27	Seongnam	L	1-2	FAqf	Han Sang Woon 13p	928
Aug	6	Pohang	L	2-3	KL	Lim Sang Hyub 39, Fagner 89p	16 355
	13	Incheon	W	1-0	KL	Fagner 25p	5 613
	21	Chunnam	D	1-1	KL	Park Jong Woo 21	7 651
	27	Jeonbuk	L	2-3	KL	Han Sang Woon 9, Fagner 47	6 695
Sep	11	Daejeon	W	1-0	KL	Fagner 30	3 124
	18	Seoul	L	1-2	KL	Eder Baiano 42	33 663
	25	Gwangju	D	2-2	KL	Yoon Dong Min 76, Yang Dong Hyun 81	3 156
Oct	2	Gyeongnam	L	0-1	KL		8 691
	16	Jeju	W	3-1	KL	Park Jong Woo 34, Lim Sang Hyub 2 42 60	4 835
	22	Ulsan	L	0-1	KL		11 257
	30	Gangwon	W	2-0	KL	Han Ji Ho 35, Yang Dong Hyun 90p	6 237
Nv	20	Suwon	L	0-1	KLpo		23 903

5th Att: 108 630 • Av: 7 242 • Busan Asiad 53 864

CHUNNAM DRAGONS 2011

	Date	Opponent		Score	Comp	Scorers	Att
Mar	6	Jeonbuk	W	1-0	KL	Gong Young Sun 22	17 932
	13	Pohang	L	0-1	KL		19 247
	16	Sangju	W	1-0	LCgB	Lee Hyun Seung 21	1 143
	20	Seoul	W	3-0	KL	Reina 36, Lee Jong Ho 76, Kim Young Wook 90	3 622
Apr	2	Daegu	L	0-1	KL		4 892
	6	Gangwon	D	0-0	LCgB		5 150
	10	Seongnam	D	0-0	KL		8 099
	17	Gyeongnam	W	2-1	KL	Indio 2 73p 90	7 319
	20	Gwangju	W	2-0	LCgB	Cornthwaite 35, Nam Jun Jae 90	847
	23	Sangju	L	0-1	KL		7 809
	30	Busan	L	0-3	KL		2 515
May	4	Ulsan	W	1-0	LCgB	Cornthwaite 51	4 243
	7	Suwon	W	2-1	KL	Ji Dong Won 48, Lee Hyun Seung 57	38 068
	11	Busan	L	0-1	LCgB		602
	14	Daejeon	W	2-0	KL	Shin Young Jun 68, Reina 89	4 149
	18	Konkuk Un	W	1-0	FAr1	Indio 62	1 104
	21	Jeju	W	1-0	KL	Ji Dong Won 63	3 260
	28	Ulsan	L	0-1	KL		7 828
Jun	11	Incheon	D	1-1	KL	Ji Dong Won 29	7 498
	15	Jeju	W	1-0	FAr2	Weslley 117	2 297
	18	Gwangju	D	0-0	KL		4 086
	26	Gangwon	W	1-0	KL	Kim Myung Jung 25	2 924
	2	Daejeon	D	4-4	KL	Weslley 2 45 52, Wan Lee 54, Lee Byung Yoon 90	6 761
Jul	10	Suwon	W	3-1	KL	Shin Young Jun 62, Yoon Suk Young 75, Weslley 84	5 080
	17	Daegu	W	3-1	KL	Kim Myung Jung 2, Shin Young Jun 55, Reina 99+p	6 955
	23	Ulsan	L	0-2	KL		32 157
	27	Suwon	L	0-1	FAqf		5 867
Aug	7	Incheon	D	0-0	KL		1 368
	13	Seoul	L	0-1	KL		19 566
	21	Busan	D	1-1	KL	Kim Myung Jung 36	7 651
	27	Sangju	W	1-0	KL	Lee Hyun Seung 62	9 135
Sep	11	Gyeongnam	W	2-0	KL	Cornthwaite 60, Lee Hyun Seung 71	3 479
	18	Jeju	D	1-1	KL	Kim Myung Jung 46	8 249
	25	Seongnam	L	2-3	KL	Ahn Jae Joon 45, Hwang Do Yeon 77	4 225
	2	Gangwon	D	1-1	KL	Wessley 43	3 543
Oct	16	Gwangju	L	0-2	KL		6 235
	22	Pohang	D	1-1	KL	Lee Jong Ho 54	10 362
	30	Jeonbuk	D	1-1	KL	Kim Myung Jung 17	10 115

7th Att: 102 810 • Av: 6 854 • Gwangyang Stadium 14 284

BUSAN LEAGUE APPEARANCES/GOALS 2011
Goalkeepers Lee Beom Young 14 • Jeon Sang Wook 17
Defenders Hong Seong Yo 1+3/0 • Iain Fyfe AUS 8/1
Lee Jung Ho 11+1/2 • Lee Yo Han 12+3/0 • Bas van den Brink NED 0+2/0 • Choo Sung Hi 5+1/0 • Lee Won Gyu 3/1 • Kim Chang Soo 29/1
Kim Eung Jin 12/1 • Yoo Ji Hun 5/0 • Eder Baiano BRA 12/1
Hwang Jae Hun 11/0 • Lee Dong Won 5+1/0 • Lee Sang Hong 9/0
Midfield Kim Keun Chul 3/0 • Lee Gil Hoon 1/0 • Lim Sang Hyub 27+1/9
Yu Ho Jun 8+5/0 • Kim Ik Hyun 0+3/0 • Park Jong Woo 25/2
Lee Jong Won 0+1/0 • Park Hee Do 9+1/1 • Park Tae Min 17+1/1
Lee Sung Woon 4+2/0 • Yoon Dong Min 1+12/1
Jeong Min Hyeong 1+4/0 • Kim Han Yoon 22/1 • Choi Kwang Hee 5+5/0
Forwards Felipe Azevedo BRA 5/0 • Yang Dong Hyun 6+19/9
Han Sang Woon 23+5/9 • Han Ji Ho 19+8/2 • Choi Jin Ho 1+7/0
Fagner BRA 10+1/6
Coach Ahn Ik Soo

CHUNNAM LEAGUE APPEARANCES/GOALS 2011
Goalkeepers Lee Woon Jae 30
Defenders Lee Sang Ho 8/0 • Yoon Suk Young 18+1/1
Ahn Jae Joon 26+1/1 • Robert Cornthwaite AUS 17/1
Bang Dae Jong 6+4/0 • Lee Jun Ki 2+2/0 • Lee Wan 16/1
Hwang Do Yeon 6+2/1 • Jeong Jun Yeon 12+2/0
Midfield Kim Hyung Ho 8/0 • Kim Young Wook 4+17/1
Lee Hyun Seung 21+3/3 • Song Jung Hyun 7+2/0 • Lee Seung Hee 26/0
Baek Seung Min 0+1/0 • Javier Reina COL 20+1/3 • Yoo Ji No 15+1/0
Jung Keun Hee 1/0 • Shin Young Jun 10+9/3 • Park Young Joon 0+2/0
Lee Byung Yoon 0+5/1
Forwards Kim Myung Jung 22+2/5 • Ji Dong Won 10+1/3
Indio BRA 5+10/2 • Jung Yoon Sung 4+1/0 • Weslley BRA 22+2/4
Nam Jun Jae 4+1/0 • Gong Young Sun 7/1 • Kim Hyung Pil 0+2/0
Lee Jong Ho 3+15/2
Coach Jung Hae Seong

DAEGU FC 2011

Mon	Day	Opponent	Res	Score	Comp	Scorers	Att
Mar	5	Gwangju	L	2-3	KL	Hwang Il Soo 54, Cho Hyung Ik 64	36 241
	13	Gangwon	W	1-0	KL	Song Je Heon 20	13 427
	16	Gyeongnam	L	0-2	LCgA		952
	20	Incheon	D	1-1	KL	Lee Ji Nam 31	5 326
Apr	2	Chunnam	W	1-0	KL	Lee Ji Nam 90	4 892
	6	Incheon	D	0-0	LCgA		2 351
	9	Gyeongnam	W	2-1	KL	Kim Hyun Sung 30, Song Chang Ho 90	6 537
	16	Busan	D	2-2	KL	Song Je Heon 22, Song Chang Ho 77	3 111
	20	Pohang	W	1-0	LCgA	Hwang Il Soo 11	7 817
	24	Jeonbuk	L	1-2	KL	Thiago 67	6 348
	30	Ulsan	L	1-2	KL	Juninho 18	5 609
May	5	Seongnam	L	0-2	LCgA		9 744
	8	Jeju	L	0-3	KL		3 547
	11	Daejeon	D	1-1	LCgA	Hwang Il Soo 29	1 775
	18	Dolphins	L	2-3	FAr1	Cho Hyung Ik 53, Kim Hyun Sung 53	812
	21	Seoul	W	2-0	KL	Lee Sang Deok 44, Ahn Seong Min 67	14 817
	28	Pohang	D	2-2	KL	Ahn Seong Min 39, Thiago 45	14 469
Jun	5	Sangju	D	0-0	KL		3 053
	11	Daejeon	D	1-1	KL	Ahn Seong Min 56	2 037
	18	Suwon	L	1-4	KL	Kim Hyun Sung 12	17 145
	25	Seongnam	W	2-1	KL	Juninho 22p, Thiago 92+	1 127
Jul	2	Sangju	L	2-1	KL	Kim Min Goo 29, Kim Hyun Sung 29	11 635
	9	Busan	L	2-3	KL	Yoo Kyoung Youl 35, Hwang Il Soo 69	1 027
	17	Chunnam	L	1-3	KL	Song Je Heon 37	6 955
	23	Pohang	D	1-1	KL	Kim Hyun Sung 92+	5 427
Aug	6	Jeju	L	0-2	KL		4 128
	13	Jeonbuk	D	2-2	KL	Kim Hyun Sung 58, Matheus 87	14 914
	27	Seongnam	L	0-1	KL		3 899
Sep	9	Seoul	W	2-1	KL	Kim Hyun Sung 2 31 34	5 612
	17	Daejeon	D	2-2	KL	Song Je Heon 2 2p 25	12 952
	24	Suwon	L	1-2	KL	Song Je Heon 90	14 326
	2	Incheon	W	2-0	KL	Song Je Heon 2 47 61	3 215
	9	Gwangju	L	1-2	KL	Yoo Kyoung Youl 63	20 187
Oct	16	Gyeongnam	L	0-3	KL		5 138
	23	Gangwon	L	0-1	KL		8 826
	30	Ulsan	D	0-0	KL		5 814

12th Att: 97 157 • Av: 6 477 • Daegu Stadium 66 422 & Civic 19 467

DAEJEON CITIZEN 2011

Mon	Day	Opponent	Res	Score	Comp	Scorers	Att
Mar	6	Ulsan	W	2-1	KL	Wagner 2 19 52	34 758
	12	Seoul	D	1-1	KL	Wagner 14	32 340
	16	Incheon	L	0-3	LCgA		4 256
	20	Gyeongnam	W	2-0	KL	Wagner 49, Hwang Jae Jun 75	8 209
Apr	3	Gangwon	W	3-0	KL	Kim Seong Jun 78, Park Seong Ho 2 86 90	12 317
	6	Pohang	L	0-3	LCgA		4 785
	10	Jeju	D	0-0	KL		16 788
	16	Sangju	D	0-0	KL		7 624
	20	Seongnam	L	0-1	LCgA		1 534
	24	Busan	L	1-3	KL	Han Jae Woong 26	14 895
	1	Gwangju	L	1-2	KL	Kim Chang Hoon 44	2 351
May	5	Gyeongnam	L	0-3	LCgA		11 826
	8	Incheon	L	1-2	KL	Wagner 65	13 178
	11	Daegu	D	1-1	LCgA	Hwang Il Soo 29	1 775
	14	Chunnam	L	0-2	KL		4 149
	18	Gimhae	W	3-0	FAr1	Park Sung Ho 13, Han Jae Woong 59, Kim Ba Woo 87	600
	22	Pohang	D	0-0	KL		31 423
	29	Jeonbuk	L	2-3	KL	Hwang Jin San 19, Park Seong Ho 37p	12 241
Jun	11	Daegu	D	1-1	KL	OG 61	2 037
	15	Gangwon	D	1-1	FAr2	Chang Seong Ho 77. L 3-4p	3 212
	18	Seongnam	L	1-2	KL	Hwang Jin San 65	8 712
	25	Suwon	L	1-3	KL	Park Seong Ho 64	4 771
Jul	2	Chunnam	D	4-4	KL	Weslley 2 45 52, Wan Lee 54, Lee Byung Yoon 90	6 761
	9	Pohang	L	0-7	KL		5 473
	16	Gyeongnam	L	1-7	KL	Lee Wong Hee 78	11 256
	23	Gangwon	W	1-0	KL	Cho Hong Kyu 54	14 382
Aug	6	Suwon	L	0-4	KL		24 451
	13	Jeju	D	3-3	KL	Park Seong Ho 2 26 45, Lee Ho 83	10 597
	20	Ulsan	W	1-0	KL	Wagner 15	9 230
	27	Incheon	L	0-2	KL		4 619
	11	Busan	L	0-1	KL		3124
Sep	17	Daegu	D	2-2	KL	Kim Seong Jun 33, Park Seong Ho 86	12 952
	24	Seoul	L	1-4	KL	Lee Sang Hyup 70	30 286
	1	Seongnam	L	0-2	KL		10 351
Oct	16	Sangju	L	1-3	KL	Park Seong Ho 7	8 591
	22	Jeonbuk	D	0-0	KL		13 721
	30	Gwangju	W	1-0	KL	Baba 62	17 441

15th Att: 213 553 • Av: 14 236 • Daejeon World Cup Stadium 40 535

KEY

KL = K-League • FA = Korean FA Cup • LC =
K-League Cup • CL = AFC Champions League
See page 13 for further explanations

DAEGU LEAGUE APPEARANCES/GOALS 2011

Goalkeepers Baek Min Cheol 10 • Lee Yang Jong 1 • Park Jun Hyuk 19
Defenders Kang Yong 8+1/0 • Yoo Kyoung Youl 16+1/2
Son Han Bok 23/0 • Lee Ji Nam 20+6/2 • Yoon Si Ho 19+1/0
Park Jong Jin 17/0 • Lee Sang Dok 13/1 • Ahn Jae Hoon 17+1/0
Midfield Oh Joo Hyun 1/0 • Kim Ki Hee 11+1/0
Uhn Byung Hoon 5+3/0 • Ahn Seong Min 8/3 • Juninho BRA 15/2
Hwang Il Soo 16+11/2 • Choi Ho Jung 2+4/0 • Song Chang Ho 17+7/2
Kim Dae Yeol 7/0 • Lee Hyung Sang 0+4/0 • Kim Yoo Sung 3+3/0
Ahn Sang Hyun 7+6/0
Forwards Matheus BRA 2+7/1 • Cho Hyung Ik 13/1
Han Dong Won 3+9/0 • Kim Hyun Sung 23+3/7
Thiago Quirino BRA 7+5/3 • Kim Min Goo 8+10/1
Song Je Heon 19+4/8
Coach Lee Young Jin

DAEJEON LEAGUE APPEARANCES/GOALS 2011

Goalkeepers Choi Eun Seong 28 • Shin Jun Bae 0+1 • Choi Hyun 2
Defenders Park Jung Hye 10/0 • Kim Han Sup 18/0
Park Gun Young 5+2/0 • Kim Young Bin 8+1/0 • Cho Hong Kyu 5+2/1
Lee Ho 24+1/1 • Yang Jung Min 1+2/0 • Lee Woong Hee 6+7/1
Lee Sang Hee 3/0 • Hwang Jae Hun 14/1
Midfield Kim Seong Jun 29/2 • Lee Hyun Woong 6/0
Kang Gu Nam 0+3/0 • Kim Chang Hoon 28/1 • Yuta Baba JPN 3+3/1
Kim Ba Woo 3+3/0 • Kang In Jun 0+1/0 • Park Min Geun 9+6/0
Jeon Bo Hun 1+4/0 • Kim Tae Yeon 10+1/0 • Lee Joong Won 0+4/0
Kim Joo Hyung 0+1/0 • Kim Do Yeon 1+6/0 • Noh Yong Hoon 10/0
Ko Dae Woo 0+4/0 • Han Deok Hee 11+3/1 • Zijian Bai CHN 0+9/0
Hwang Jin San 18+10/2
Forwards Wagner BRA 25+2/7 • Wesley BRA 0+1/0
Park Seong Ho 28/8 • Kim Jin Sol 0+2/0 • Hwang Hun Hee 0+1/0
Han Jae Woong 23/3 • Lee Sang Hyup 1+6/1 • Kwak Chang He 1/0
Coach Yoo Sang Chul

GANGWON FC 2011

Mar	5	Gyeongnam	L	0-1	KL	15 497
	13	Daegu	L	0-1	KL	13 427
	16	Gwangju	W	5-0	LCgB	Seo Dong Hyeon 50, Kwon Soon Hyung 66, Kim Young Hoo 2 86 93+, Lee Chang Hoon 90 — 2 320
	20	Jeju	L	0-1	KL	3152
Apr	3	Daejeon	L	0-3	KL	12 317
	6	Chunnam	D	0-0	LCgB	5 150
	10	Ulsan	L	0-1	KL	7 349
	15	Suwon	L	0-2	KL	19 121
	20	Ulsan	L	1-2	LCgB	Seo Dong Hyeon 84 — 983
	23	Incheon	L	1-3	KL	Kim Young Hoo 44 — 3 511
	30	Pohang	D	0-0	KL	10 466
May	5	Busan	L	0-2	LCgB	13 724
	8	Seongnam	D	1-1	KL	Kim Young Hoo 20 — 3 177
	11	Sangju	L	1-2	LCgB	Ha Jung Hun 6 — 5 445
	14	Gwangju	L	0-1	KL	5 733
	18	Chungju	D	0-0	FAr1	W 4-3p — 2 212
	21	Jeonbuk	L	0-1	KL	8 720
	28	Sangju	D	0-0	KL	11 324
Jun	11	Busan	W	1-0	KL	OG 42 — 5 373
	15	Daejeon	D	1-1	FAr2	Dzakmic 40. W 4-3p — 3 212
	18	Seoul	L	0-2	KL	11 347
	26	Chunnam	L	0-1	KL	2 924
Jul	2	Jeju	L	2-4	KL	Lee Eul Young 38, Kim Young Ho 42 — 3 207
	9	Gwangju	L	0-2	KL	9 876
	16	Ulsan	L	1-2	KL	Lee Jung Woon 38 — 4 020
	23	Daejeon	L	0-1	KL	14 382
	27	Ulsan	L	0-3	FAqf	1 327
Aug	6	Jeonbuk	L	0-3	KL	2 017
	13	Pohang	L	0-2	KL	2 240
	20	Incheon	D	0-0	KL	5 786
	27	Seoul	L	3-6	KL	Yoon Jun Ha 74, Seo Dong Hyeon 85p, Kim Jin Ryong 90 — 23 921
Sep	10	Sangju	W	2-0	KL	Seo Dong Hyeon 2, Jung Sung Min 82 — 3 360
	18	Suwon	L	0-1	KL	3 508
	24	Gyeongnam	D	0-0	KL	9 036
Oct	1	Chunnam	D	1-1	KL	Oh Jae Seok 90 — 3 543
	8	Seongnam	L	1-3	KL	Kim Young Hoo 53 — 3 010
	23	Daegu	W	1-0	KL	Kim Jin Ryong 54 — 8 826
	30	Busan	L	0-1	KL	6 237

16th — Att: 87 676 • Av: 5 845 • Wonju Stadium 20 000

GWANGJU FC 2011

Mar	5	Daegu	W	3-2	KL	Park Gi Dong 2 52 84, Kim Dong Sub 81p — 36 241
	12	Suwon	L	1-2	KL	Kim Dong Sub 3 — 31 506
	16	Gangwon	L	0-5	LCgB	2 320
	20	Ulsan	L	1-2	KL	Kim Dong Sub 37 — 5 175
Apr	2	Pohang	L	0-1	KL	15 627
	6	Busan	L	0-1	LCgB	1 502
	9	Sangju	D	0-0	KL	7 253
	16	Jeonbuk	L	1-6	KL	Joao Paulo 85 — 8 455
	20	Chunnam	L	0-2	LCgB	847
	24	Seoul	W	1-0	KL	Joao Paulo 36 — 4 127
May	1	Daejeon	W	2-1	KL	Lee Seung Ki 8, Joao Paulo 36 — 2 351
	5	Sangju	W	3-2	LCgB	Kim Seong-Min 2 13 90, Yoo Dong Min 60 — 8 972
	8	Gyeongnam	L	0-1	KL	8 625
	11	Ulsan	L	1-2	LCgB	Yoo Jong Hyun 14 — 568
	14	Gangwon	W	1-0	KL	Kim Dong Sub 23 — 5 733
	18	Suwon City	L	1-2	FAr1	Yoo Jong Hyun 58 — 457
	22	Incheon	L	0-1	KL	7 210
	28	Busan	D	1-1	KL	Joao Paulo 90 — 6 564
Jun	11	Seongnam	W	2-0	KL	Lee Seung Ki 72, Joao Paulo 80 — 4 132
	18	Chunnam	D	0-0	KL	4 086
	25	Jeju	L	1-2	KL	Yoo Dong Min 90 — 1 191
Jul	2	Incheon	D	2-2	KL	Kim Dong Sub 42, Joao Paulo 84 — 6 387
	9	Gangwon	W	2-0	KL	Lee Seung Ki 2 29 60 — 9 876
	16	Jeonbuk	D	1-1	KL	Lee Seung Ki 57 — 3 248
	23	Seoul	L	1-4	KL	Kim Dong Sub 71 — 21 124
Aug	6	Gyeongnam	L	0-2	KL	2 874
	13	Sangju	L	0-2	KL	6 735
	27	Jeju	D	2-2	KL	Lee Seng ki 11, Heo Jae Won 40 — 3 285
Sep	10	Pohang	L	1-5	KL	Park Gi Dong 39 — 10 165
	17	Seongnam	W	3-1	KL	Lee Seung Ki 3p, Kim Dong Sub 44, Joao Paulo 90 — 5 589
	25	Busan	D	2-2	KL	Lee Seung Ki 60, Yoo Jong Hyun 90 — 3 156
Oct	2	Ulsan	D	0-0	KL	3 426
	9	Daegu	W	2-1	KL	Jung Woo In 11, Ahn Sung Nam 36 — 20 187
	16	Chunnam	W	2-0	KL	Joao Paulo 74, Ahn Sung Nam 90 — 6 235
	23	Suwon	L	0-1	KL	24 778
	30	Daejeon	L	0-1	KL	17 441

11th — Att: 131 670 • Av: 8 778 • Gwangju World Cup Stadium 44 118

GANGWON LEAGUE APPEARANCES/GOALS 2011
Goalkeepers Kim Keun Bae 8 • Yoo Hyun 22
Defenders Park Sang Jin 18+3/0 • Kwak Kwang Seon 24/0
Park Woo Hyun 5+1/0 • Park Ji Yong 10/0 • Oh Jae Seok 21+1/1
Kim Oh Kyu 1/0 • Lee Jung Woon 11/0 • Stipe Lapic CRO 1/0
Lee Min Kyu 10+2/0 • Kim Jin Hwan 14+1/0 • Lee Jun Hyung 0+2/0
Midfield Lee Sang Don 21/0 • Muhamed Dzakmic BIH 14/0
Lee Eul Yong 17+2/1 • Baek Jong Hwan 12+5/0
Mateas Delic CRO 3+7/0 • Kwon Soon Hyung 18+4/0
Jang Hyuk Jin 1+4/0 • Lee Chang Hoon 10+2/0 • Ha Jung Hun 0+4/0
Park Tae Woong 10+2/0 • Kim Jung Joo 2+2/0 • Lee Woo Hyuk 1+6/0
Kim Eun Hu 1+2/0
Forwards Kim Young Hoo 21+7/4 • Yoon Jun Ha 14+12/1
Chung Kyung Ho 8+2/0 • Kim Jin Ryong 7+5/2
Jung Sung Min 4+6/1 • Seo Dong Hyeon 20+5/2
Coach Kim Sang Ho

GWANGJU LEAGUE APPEARANCES/GOALS 2011
Goalkeepers Park Ho Jin 30
Defenders Jung Woo In 20+2/1 • Park Byung Joo 20+1/0
Lee Yong 27/0 • Kim Su Beom 16+4/0 • Lim Ha Ram 7+4/0
Heo Jae Won 26+1/1
Midfield Lim Sun Young 10+5/0 • Kim Eun Seon 24/0
Lee Seung Ki 25/8 • Ahn Dong Hyuk 6+14/0 • Cho Woo Jin 0+8/0
Park Hyun 1/0 • Kim Hong Il 0+1/0 • Park Hee Sung 19+4/0
Ahn Sung Nam 19+2/2
Forwards Kim Dong Sub 23/7 • Park Gi Dong 27/3
Yoo Dong Min 1+15/1 • Yoo Jong Hyun 20+3/1 • Kim Sung Min 0+3/0
Alessandro Celin BRA 1/0 • Joao Paulo BRA 7+20/8 • Vinicius 1+1/0
Coach Choi Man Hee

GYEONGNAM FC 2011

Mar	5	Gangwon	W	1-0	KL	Yoon Bit Garam [45]	15 497
	13	Ulsan	W	1-0	KL	Lucio [55]	16 749
	16	Daegu	W	2-0	LCgA	Kim Young Woo [32], Lucio [70]	952
	20	Daejeon	L	0-2	KL		8 209
Apr	3	Incheon	W	2-1	KL	Yun Il Lok [3], Lucio [63]	8 672
	6	Seongnam	D	0-0	LCgA		1 411
	9	Daegu	L	1-2	KL	Yoon Bit Garam [85p]	6 537
	17	Chunnam	L	1-2	KL	Kim In Han [31]	7 319
	20	Incheon	W	1-0	LCgA	Kim In Han [83]	1 321
	24	Suwon	W	2-1	KL	Han Kyung In [50], Kim In Han [54]	20 315
	30	Seongnam	D	2-2	KL	Lucio [41], Kim Young Woo [82]	2 317
May	5	Daejeon	W	3-0	LCgA	Han Kyung In [31], Yoon Bit Garam [57], Lucio [90]	11 826
	8	Gwangju	W	1-0	KL	Kim Young Woo [75]	8 625
	11	Pohang	L	1-2	LCgA	Ahn Hyun Sik [68]	961
	15	Seoul	L	1-3	KL	Kim In Han [44]	26 008
	18	Busan Kyo.	L	1-2	FAr1	Han Kyung In [67]	459
	21	Sangju	L	0-1	KL		8 247
	29	Jeju	D	1-1	KL	DeVere [59]	8 498
Jun	11	Jeonbuk	L	0-2	KL		14 115
	18	Busan	W	3-2	KL	Lee Kyung Ryul [70], Lee Hun [85], Kim Tae Wook [89]	8 137
	25	Pohang	L	2-3	KL	Le Hun [29p], Yun Il Lok [64]	1 214
	29	Seoul	W	1-0	LCqf	Yoon Bit Garam [26]	2 469
Jul	3	Ulsan	D	0-0	KL		3 376
	6	Ulsan	L	2-4	LCsf	Lee Hyo Gyun [16], Lee Dong Geun [80]	2 589
	9	Jeju	W	3-2	KL	Yun Il Lok [78], Yoon Bit Garam [81], Kim In Han [92+]	6 326
	16	Daejeon	W	7-1	KL	Yoon Bit Garam [11p], Lee Hyo Gyun [15], Lee Hun [18], Park Min [42], DeVere [57], Gil [86], Lucio [90]	11 256
	23	Incheon	D	2-2	KL	Lee Hyo Gyun [53], Jung Dae Sun [57]	6 768
Aug	6	Gwangju	W	2-0	KL	Seo Sang Min [7], Yoon Bit Garam [69]	2 874
	13	Suwon	L	0-2	KL		7 809
	20	Seongnam	D	1-1	KL	Lee Kyung Ryul [17]	5 195
	27	Pohang	L	0-1	KL		15 359
Sep	11	Chunnam	L	0-2	KL		3 479
	18	Jeonbuk	L	1-3	KL	Kang Seung Jo [42]	10 536
	24	Gangwon	D	0-0	KL		9 036
Oct	2	Busan	W	1-0	KL	Roni [17]	8 691
	16	Daegu	W	3-0	KL	Gil 2 [43 80], Yun Il Lok [72]	5 138
	22	Sangju	W	3-1	KL	Yoon Bit Garam [31], Seo Sang Min [48], Kim Joo Young [69]	3 245
	30	Seoul	L	0-3	KL		9 068

8th Att: 136 021 • Av: 9 207 • Changwon Football Center 15 500

INCHEON UNITED 2011

Mar	5	Sangju	L	0-2	KL		15 042
	12	Jeju	D	0-0	KL		27 831
	16	Daejeon	W	3-0	LCgA	Kim Myung Woon [39], Yoo Byung Soo [49], Kapadze [74]	4 256
	20	Daegu	D	1-1	KL	Giaretta [45]	5 326
Apr	3	Gyeongnam	L	1-2	KL	Yoo Byung Soo [23]	8 672
	6	Daegu	D	0-0	LCgA		2 351
	9	Pohang	D	2-2	KL	Kapadze [35], Yoo Byung Soo [84]	16 762
	17	Seongnam	W	2-1	KL	Kim Jae Woong [1], Park Joon Tae [90]	8 278
	20	Gyeongnam	L	0-1	LCgA		1 321
	23	Gangwon	W	3-1	KL	Kim Jae Woong [63], Yoo Byung Soo [65], Park Joon Tae [78]	3 511
	30	Jeonbuk	L	2-6	KL	Han Gyo Won [2], Bae Hyo Sung [83]	1 127
May	5	Pohang	L	1-4	LCgA	Luizinho [88p]	16 671
	8	Daejeon	W	2-1	KL	Park Joon Tae [75], Kim Jae Woong [75]	13 178
	11	Seongnam	D	1-1	LCgA	Kim Jae Woong [17]	1 024
	15	Busan	D	0-0	KL		6 208
	18	Yeonei Un.	W	2-1	FAr1	Yoo Joon Soo [5], Lee Yun Pyo [64]	428
	22	Gwangju	W	1-0	KL	Han Gyo Won [73]	7 210
	29	Suwon	W	2-1	KL	Jang Won Seok [3], Kapadze [33p]	10 582
Jun	11	Chunnam	D	1-1	KL	Jang Won Seok [9]	7 498
	15	Seongnam	L	0-2	FAr2		1 027
	18	Ulsan	D	1-1	KL	Luizinho [33]	23 897
	25	Seoul	D	1-1	KL	Han Gyo Won [39]	15 315
Jul	2	Gwangju	D	2-2	KL	Park Joon Tae [48], Chun Jae Ho [72]	6 452
	10	Seongnam	D	2-2	KL	OG [46], Kapadze [83]	3 147
	16	Suwon	L	0-1	KL		17 088
	23	Gyeongnam	D	2-2	KL	Fabio Bahia [73], Park Joon Tae [78]	6 768
Aug	7	Chunnam	D	0-0	KL		1 368
	13	Busan	L	0-1	KL		5 613
	20	Gangwon	D	0-0	KL		5 786
	27	Daejeon	W	2-0	KL	Jung Hyuk [7], Fabio Bahia [83]	4 619
Sep	9	Jeonbuk	L	2-4	KL	Jung In Hwan [9], Elionar [51]	8 334
	17	Pohang	L	0-1	KL		6 728
	24	Ulsan	L	0-2	KL		5 141
Oct	2	Daegu	L	0-2	KL		3 215
	16	Seoul	D	1-1	KL	Jung In Hwan [62]	6 822
	22	Jeju	L	1-2	KL	Kapadze [34]	4 879
	30	Sangju	D	0-0	KL		4 331

13th Att: 113 432 • Av: 7 562 • Incheon Munhak 49 084

GYEONGNAM LEAGUE APPEARANCES/GOALS 2011
Goalkeepers Kim Byung Ji **30**
Defenders Ahn Hyun Sik **10/0** • Park Jae Hong **19+3/0**
Kim Joo Young **4/1** • Luke DeVere AUS **30/2** • Lee Hye Gang **4+2/0**
Lee Kyung Ryul **14+6/2** • Park Min **5+3/1** • Lee Jae Myung **12+1/0**
Loo Yong Ki **21+1/0** • Koh Rao So 0 **i1/0** • Kim Jong Soo **1/0**
Midfield Kim Tae Wook **13+1/1** • Kang Seung Jo **9/1**
Kim Young Woo **12+1/2** • Yoon Bit Garam **23+2/6** • Kim In Han **18+5/4**
Seo Sang Min **13+6/2** • Lee Dong Geun **0+2/0** • Yun Il Lok **13+8/4**
Choi Young Jun **9+4/0** • Kim Jin Hyun **3+2/0** • Park Chang Heon **3/0**
Forwards Wilmar Gil COL **7+3/3** • Roni BRA **7+3/1** • Lucio BRA **4+3/4**
Ahn Seong Bin **0+2/0** • Lee Hun **13+1/3** • Jeong Da Hooeon **28/0**
Lee Hyo Gyun **9+3/2** • Kang Chul Min **0+1/0** • Han Kyung In **10+8/1**
Jung Seung Yong **1+2/0** • Jung Dae Sun **2+9/1** • Feitosa BRA **2+4/0**
Coach Choi Jin Han

INCHEON LEAGUE APPEARANCES/GOALS 2011
Goalkeepers Song Yoo Geol **11** • Yoon Ki Won **5** • Kwon Jung Hyuk **14**
Defenders Kim Young Bin **0+1/0** • Kim Han Sup **8/0**
Jang Won Seok **21+1/2** • Diego Giaretta **5+1/1** • Bae Hyo Sung **28+1/1**
Lee Yun Pyo **21+1/0** • Jung In Hwan **22/2** • Jeon Jun Hyung **6+2/0**
Jang Kyung Jin **9+3/0** • Park Tae Su **0+1/0** • Ahn Tae Eun **5+2/0**
Lim Joong Yong **0+1/0**
Midfield Fabio Bahia BRA **25+4/2** • Lee Jae Kwon **24+3/0**
Jung Hyuk **11+4/1** • Almir BRA **3+2/0** • Lee Jong Hyun **0+2/0**
Ahn Jae Gon **3+2/0** • Kim Jae Woong **10+5/3** • Chun Jae Ho **19+1/1**
Timur Kapadze UZB **25+3/4** • Shin Dong Hyuk **0+1/0**
Cho Beom Seok **2+1/0** • Kyung Deuk Ji **1+1/0**
Forwards Kim Myung Woon **6+3/0** • Yoo Byung Soo **9+3/3**
Luizinho BRA **6+1/1** • Elionar Bombinha BRA **6/1** • Yoo Jun Su **7+7/0**
Kwon Hyuk Jin **0+1/0** • Han Gyo Won **17+10/3** • Park Joon Tae **1+22/5**
Coach Huh Jung Moo

JEJU UNITED 2011

		Opponent		Score	Comp	Scorers	Att
Mar	1	Tianjin	L	0-1	CLgE		5 245
	6	Busan	W	2-1	KL	Santos 27, Bae Ki Jong 62	4 172
	12	Incheon	D	0-0	KL		27 831
	15	Melbourne V	W	2-1	CLgE	Park Hyun Beom 41, Lee Hyun Ho 84	4 825
	20	Gangwon	W	1-0	KL	OG 68	3 152
Apr	2	Sangju	D	3-3	KL	Kim In Ho 24, Junior 32, Kang Soo Il 90	2 054
	5	Gamba	W	2-1	CLgE	Shin Young Rok 55, Bae Ki Jong 65	2 167
	10	Daejeon	D	0-0	KL		16 788
	16	Pohang	L	1-3	KL	Kim In Ho 47	2 078
	20	Gamba	L	1-3	CLgE	Shin Young Rok 68	11 398
	24	Seongnam	W	2-1	KL	Park Hyun Beom 10, OG 74	2 813
	30	Seoul	L	1-2	KL	Park Hyun Beom 37	9 797
May	4	Tianjin	L	0-3	CLgE		26 683
	8	Daegu	W	3-0	KL	Santos 27, Kim Eung Jung 77, Bae Ki Jong 89	3 547
	11	Melbourne V	D	1-1	CLgE	Kim Eung Jung 25	1 519
	15	Ulsan	W	1-0	KL	Park Hyun Beom 59	21 755
	18	Goyang KB	W	4-2	FArl	Santos 54, Park Hyun Beom 62, Kim Eung Jung 66, Kang Su Il 86	800
	21	Chunnam	L	0-1	KL		3 260
	29	Gyeongnam	D	1-1	KL	Jair 30	8 498
Jun	11	Suwon	W	3-2	KL	Jair 45, Santos 63, Kwon Yong Nam 90	2 712
	15	Chunnam	L	0-1	FAr2		2 297
	18	Jeonbuk	L	2-3	KL	Santos 2 11 66	15 939
	25	Gwangju	W	2-1	KL	Santos 54, Bae Ki Jong 92+	1 191
	29	Suwon	D	0-0	LCqf	L 2-4p	2 822
Jul	2	Gangwon	W	2-1	KL	Kim Eun Jung 2 5 81, Lee Hyun Ho 28, Santos 85	3 207
	9	Gyeongnam	L	2-3	KL	Park Hyun Beom 42p, Santos 58	6 326
	16	Seongnam	D	2-2	KL	Park Hyun Beom 2 76p 83	3 591
	23	Sangju	D	1-1	KL	Kim Eun Jung 89	8 451
	6	Daegu	W	2-0	KL	Kim Young Sin 30, Lee Hyun Ho 63	4 128
Aug	13	Daejeon	D	3-3	KL	Santos 2 31 59, Kang Soo Il 47	10 597
	20	Seoul	L	0-3	KL		12 775
	27	Gwangju	D	2-2	KL	Kwon Yong Nam 70, Kim Eun Jung 78	3 285
Sep	10	Ulsan	L	1-2	KL	Santos 45	2 523
	18	Chunnam	D	1-1	KL	Kim Eun Jung 66	8 249
	24	Jeonbuk	D	0-0	KL		7 059
Oct	2	Pohang	L	1-2	KL	Santos 66	12 139
	16	Busan	L	1-3	KL	Yang Juna 85	4 835
	22	Incheon	W	2-1	KL	Kang Soo Il 38, Santos 68p	4 879
	30	Suwon	L	0-2	KL		20 197

9th • Att: 69 138 • Av: 4 609 • Jeju World Cup Stadium 35 657

JEJU LEAGUE APPEARANCES/GOALS 2011
Goalkeepers Kim Ho Jun 24 • Jeon Tae Hyun 6
Defenders Kang Min Hyuk 18+2/0 • Kim In Ho 10+1/2 • Ma Chul Jun 10+5/0 • Hong Jeong Ho 16/0 • Kang Junu 19+4/0 • Yoon Won Il 1+4/0
Midfield Park Jin Ok 19+2/0 • Park Hyun Beom 18/6 • Yang Juna 6/1
Choi Won Kwon 14+1/0 • Kim Young Sin 15+8/1 • Oh Seung Beom 29/0
Kim Tae Min 1+2/0 • Kim Jun Yub 2/0 • Lee Hyun Ho 19+8/2
Moon Min Kwi 1/0
Forwards Kang Soo Il 5+19/3 • Shin Young Rok 3+5/0
Jair BRA 9+2/2 • Bae Ki Jong 23+3/3 • Kim Eun Jung 27+3/6
Nam Jun Jae 1+2/0 • Felipinho BRA 1/0 • Lee Sang Hyup 2+1/0
Bae Il Hwan 0+1/0 • Ahn Jong Hoon 0+1/0 • Kwon Yong Nam 3+7/2
Shim Young Sung 0+6/0 • Santos Junior BRA 28+1/14
Coach Park Kyung Hoon

JEONBUK HYUNDAI MOTORS 2011

		Opponent		Score	Comp	Scorers	Att
Mar	2	Shandong	W	1-0	CLgG	Park Won Jae 59	3 826
	6	Chunnam	L	0-1	KL		17 932
	12	Seongnam	W	1-0	KL	Sim Woo Yeon 36	9 571
	16	Arema	W	4-0	CLgG	Kim Jee Wong 26, Huang Bowen 78, Luiz Henrique 2 81 88	30 000
	20	Busan	W	5-2	KL	Lee Dong Gook 2 32 64, Kim Jee Woong 41, Lee Seung Hyun 73, Jeong Seong Hoon 79	9 747
Apr	2	Seoul	L	1-3	KL	Lee Dong Gook 81	27 406
	5	Cerezo	L	0-1	CLgG		11 351
	10	Suwon	D	0-0	KL		26 597
	16	Gwangju	W	6-1	KL	Kim Jee Wong 17, Kim Dong Chan 27, Lee Seung Hyun 30, Lee Dong Gook 38, Huang Bowen 42, Lovrek 79	8 455
	20	Cerezo	W	1-0	CLgG	Lee Dong Gook 77	7 892
	24	Daegu	W	2-1	KL	Kim Dong Chan 23, Kim Jee Woong 38	6 348
	30	Incheon	W	6-2	KL	Lim You Hwan 13, Lee Dong Gook 2 14 70, Eninho 58, Jeong Song Hoon 79, Kim Dong Chan 90	1 127
May	3	Shandong	W	2-1	CLgG	Lee Dong Gook 2 31 52	17 343
	7	Ulsan	W	1-0	KL	Kim Dong Chan 51	22 723
	10	Arema	W	6-0	CLgG	Lovrek 3 1 45 60, Kim Dong Chan 9, Jeong Seong Hoon 28, Kang Seung Jo 77	6 439
	15	Pohang	L	2-3	KL	Lee Dong Gook 39, Park Won Jae 44	16 732
	18	Kyung He	W	2-1	FAr1	Eninho 47, Luiz Henrique 59	1 273
	21	Gangwon	W	1-0	KL	Lovrek 24	8 720
	24	Tianjin	W	3-0	CLr2	Eninho 2 33 84, Lee Seung Hyun 44	5 254
	29	Daejeon	W	3-2	KL	Lee Dong Gook 2 28 83, Lee Seung Hyun 90	12 241
Jun	11	Gyeongnam	W	2-0	KL	Eninho 29, Lee Dong Gook 76	14 115
	15	Busan	L	1-2	FAr2	Cho Sung Hwan 3	4 328
	18	Jeju	W	3-2	KL	Eninho 65, OG 82, Luiz Henrique 89	15 939
	25	Sangju	W	3-0	KL	Cho Sung Hwan 18, Luiz Henrique 32, Lee Seung Hyun 90	4 765
	29	Ulsan	L	1-4	LCqf	Park Jung Hoon 19	2 153
Jul	3	Seoul	D	2-2	KL	Eninho 30p, Lee Seung Hyun 45	15 879
	10	Ulsan	D	0-0	KL		10 572
	16	Gwangju	D	1-1	KL	OG 63	3 248
	24	Seongnam	W	2-0	KL	OG 16, Kim Dong Chan 64	16 298
	6	Gangwon	W	3-0	KL	Kim Dong Chan 3 1 8 19	2 017
Aug	13	Daegu	D	2-2	KL	Eninho 38, Sim Woo Yeon 71	14 914
	21	Pohang	W	3-1	KL	Lee Dong Gook 3 64p 79 91+	21 253
	27	Busan	W	3-2	KL	Huang Bowen 39, Lim You Hwan 57, Jeong Seong Hoon 57	6 695
Sep	9	Incheon	W	4-2	KL	Eninho 25, Kim Dong Chan 56, Jeong Seong Hoon 2 78 89	8 334
	14	Cerezo	L	3-4	CLqf	Lee Dong Gook 2 6 45, Cho Sung Hwan 58	15 450
	18	Gyeongnam	W	3-1	KL	Luiz Henrique 2 21 37, Lee Dong Gook 34p	10 536
	24	Jeju	D	0-0	KL		7 059
	27	Cerezo	W	6-1	CLqf	Eninho 31, Kim Dong Chan 77, Lee Dong Gook 4 49 56 65 91+	16 423
Oct	3	Sangju	W	5-1	KL	Lee Dong Gook 2 28 88, Lee Seung Hyun 2 45 60, Eninho 67	11 609
	8	Suwon	D	2-2	KL	Choi Chul Soon 16, Eninho 84	13 004
	19	Al Ittihad	W	3-2	CLsf	Eninho 2, Son Seung Joon 57, Cho Sung Hwan 77	16 942
	22	Daejeon	D	0-0	KL		13 721
	26	Al Ittihad	W	2-1	CLsf	Eninho 2 22 36	17 069
	30	Chunnam	D	1-1	KL	Kim Dong Chan 66	10 115
Nov	5	Al Sadd	D	2-2	CLf	Eninho 17, Lee Seung Hyun 92+. L 2-4p	41 805
	30	Ulsan	W	2-1	KLf	Eninho 2 52p 79	25 375
Dc	4	Ulsan	W	2-1	KLf	Eninho 60p, Luiz Henrique 69	33 554

1st • Att: 259 790 • Av: 16 236 • Jeonju World Cup Stadium 43 348

JEONBUK LEAGUE APPEARANCES/GOALS 2011
Goalkeepers Kim Min Sik 17 • Yeom Dong Gyun 14 • Lee Bum Soo 1
Defenders Sim Woo Yeon 21/2 • Kim Sang Sik 21+1/0
Son Seung Joon 4+4/0 • Cho Sung Hwan 27/1 • Lim You Hwan 11/2
Choi Chul Soon 23/1 • Lee Kwang Hyun 1+2/0 • Kim Jae Hwan 2/0
Midfield Jin Kyung Sun 5+2/0 • Kim Young Woo 7/0
Eninho BRA 21+5/11 • Lee Seung Hyun 17+12/7 • Jung Hoon 22/0
Kang Seung Jo 0+4/0 • Huang Bowen CHN 18+2/2
Kim Jee Woong 12/3 • Jeon Kwang Hwan 6/0 • Park Won Jae 27/0
Forwards Jeong Seong Hoon 7+19/5 • Luiz Henrique BRA 17+7/5
Kim Dong Chan 11+11/10 • Krunoslav Lovrek CRO 9+16/2
Lee Dong Gook 26+3/16 • Kim Hyung Bum 1+2/0 • Seo Jung Jin 4+5/0
Coach Choi Kang Hee

POHANG STEELERS 2011

Mon	Date	Opponent	Res	Score	Comp	Scorers	Att
Mar	5	Seongnam	D	1-1	KL	Mota 3	17 353
	13	Chunnam	W	1-0	KL	Adriano 78	19 247
	16	Seongnam	W	2-0	LCgA	Jung Seok Min 58, Kim Tae Su 69	7 211
	20	Suwon	W	2-0	KL	Kim Jae Sung 21, Shin Hyung Min 89	14 812
Apr	2	Gwangju	W	1-0	KL	Shin Hyung Min 54	15 627
	6	Daejeon	W	3-0	LCgA	Adriano 2 17 23, No Byung Jun 87	4 785
	9	Incheon	D	2-2	KL	Hwang Jin Sung 2 5 49	16 762
	16	Jeju	W	3-1	KL	Hwang Jin Sung 2 12 73, No Byung Jun 30	2 078
	20	Daegu	L	0-1	LCgA		7 817
	23	Ulsan	W	2-0	KL	Cho Chan Ho 80, Adriano 87	14 394
	30	Gangwon	D	0-0	KL		10 466
May	5	Incheon	W	4-1	LCgA	Ko Mu Yeol 9, Cho Chan Ho 2 11 28, Kim Gi Dong 35	16 671
	8	Busan	L	1-2	KL	Mota 45	10 272
	11	Gyeongnam	W	2-1	LCgA	Kim Gi Dong 27p, Mota 80	961
	15	Jeonbuk	W	3-2	KL	Shin Hyung Min 56, Adriano 2 73 80p	16 732
	18	Daejeon HNP	W	2-0	FAr1	Ko Mu Yeol 26, Cho Chan Ho 82	2 596
	22	Daejeon	D	0-0	KL		31 423
	28	Daegu	D	2-2	KL	Kim Jae Sung 7, Kim Gi Dong 19p	14 469
	1	Seoul	D	1-1	KL	Hwang Jin Sung 47	44 358
	15	Dolphins	W	1-0	FAr2	Mota 25	1 820
Jun	18	Sangju	W	4-3	KL	Ko Mu Yeol 49, Kim Tae Su 73, Mota 80, Asamoah 88	12 254
	25	Gyeongnam	W	3-2	KL	Asamoah 25, Mota 2 57 71	1 214
	29	Busan	L	1-2	LCqf	Jung Seok Min 69	6 288
	2	Suwon	L	1-2	KL	Kim Jae Sung 45	27 152
Jul	9	Daejeon	W	7-0	KL	Kim Jae Sung 6, Hwang Jin Sung 31, Mota 2 32 39, Shin Kwang Hoon 57, Ko Mu Yeol 70, Kim Gi Dong 88p	5 473
	17	Seoul	L	1-2	KL	Ko Mu Yeol 34	18 115
	23	Daegu	D	1-1	KL	Kim Jae Sung 44	5 427
	27	Seoul	W	4-2	FAqf	Asamoah 31, Mota 64, No Byung Jun 2 99 108	10 419
Aug	6	Busan	W	3-2	KL	OG 15, Ko Mu Yeol 20, Asamoah 83	16 355
	13	Gangwon	W	2-0	KL	Ko Mu Yeol 50, Asamoah 59	2 240
	21	Jeonbuk	L	1-3	KL	No Byung Jun 68	21 253
	24	Seongnam	L	0-3	FAsf		5 752
	27	Gyeongnam	W	1-0	KL	No Byung Jun 76	15 359
Sep	10	Gwangju	W	5-1	KL	Mota 2 37p 52, Ko Mu Yeol 2 56 69, No Byung Jun 84	10 165
	17	Incheon	W	1-0	KL	Mota 6p	6 728
	25	Sangju	W	3-1	KL	Adriano 21, Mota 45, Shin Hyung Min 90	4 352
Oct	2	Jeju	W	2-1	KL	Mota 4, Asamoah 24	12 139
	16	Ulsan	L	1-2	KL	Asamoah 83	23 875
	22	Chunnam	D	1-1	KL	Mota 89	10 362
	30	Seongnam	W	3-1	KL	Ko Mu Yeol 2 56 74p, Cho Chan Ho 74	3 211
Nv	26	Ulsan	L	0-1	KLsf		21 317

2nd   Att: 226 527 • Av: 14 157 • Pohang Steel Yard 25 000

SANGJU SANGMU PHOENIX DRAGONS 2011

Mon	Date	Opponent	Res	Score	Comp	Scorers	Att
Mar	5	Incheon	W	2-0	KL	Kim Jung Woo 2 5 53	15 042
	13	Busan	D	3-3	KL	Cho Young Tae 29, Choi Hyo Jin 38, Kim Jung Woo 86	29 267
	16	Chunnam	L	0-1	LCgB		1 143
	20	Seongnam	W	3-2	KL	Jang Nam Seok 2 65 66, Kim Jung Woo 68	2 893
Apr	2	Jeju	D	3-3	KL	Kim Jung Woo 2 2 39, Ko Cha Won 85	2 054
	6	Ulsan	L	1-2	LCgB	Kim Jung Woo 82	3 323
	9	Gwangju	D	0-0	KL		7 253
	16	Daejeon	D	0-0	KL		7 624
	20	Busan	L	1-2	LCgB	Kim Chi Woo 92+	1 038
	23	Chunnam	W	1-0	KL	Kim Jung Woo 3	7 809
	30	Suwon	W	1-0	KL	Ko Cha Won 71	5 948
May	5	Gwangju	L	2-3	LCgB	Kim Dong Hyun 24, Kim Jung Woo 61	8 972
	8	Seoul	L	3-4	KL	OG 21, Choi Hyo Jin 46, Kim Jung Woo 74	9 170
	11	Gangwon	W	2-1	LCgB	Kim Dong Hyun 52, Kim Jung Woo 93+	5 445
	18	Gangneung	W	2-1	FAr1	Kim Cheol Ho 2 66 117	2 000
	21	Gyeongnam	W	1-0	KL	OG 81	8 247
	28	Gangwon	D	0-0	KL		11 324
Jun	5	Daegu	D	0-0	KL		3 053
	11	Ulsan	L	1-2	KL	Kim Jung Woo 15	10 573
	15	Ulsan	L	1-2	FAr2	Kim Jung Woo 23	1 385
	18	Pohang	L	3-4	KL	Kim Jung Woo 13p, Jang Nam Seok 38, Ko Cha Won 90	12 254
	25	Jeonbuk	L	0-3	KL		4 765
	2	Daegu	L	1-2	KL	Kim Jung Woo 9	11 635
Jul	9	Seoul	L	2-3	KL	Kim Jung Woo 34p, Kim Min Soo 85	28 034
	16	Busan	L	1-2	KL	Kim Cheol Ho 34	8 352
	23	Jeju	D	1-1	KL	Kim Jung Woo 60	8 451
	6	Seongnam	L	1-2	KL	Kim Jung Woo 74	8 867
Aug	13	Gwangju	W	2-0	KL	Ryu Chang Hyun 14, Kim Jung Woo 90	6 735
	20	Suwon	L	0-3	KL		26 989
	27	Chunnam	L	0-1	KL		9 153
Sep	10	Gangwon	L	0-2	KL		3 360
	17	Ulsan	L	1-3	KL	Lee Sung Jae 57	6 573
	25	Pohang	L	1-3	KL	Kim Yong Tae 73	4 352
	3	Jeonbuk	L	1-5	KL	Lee Sung Jae 55	11 609
Oct	16	Daejeon	W	3-1	KL	Ko Cha Won 28, Kim Chi Woo 33, Kim Min Soo 36	8 591
	22	Gyeongnam	L	1-3	KL	Ryu Chang Hyun 85	3 245
	30	Incheon	D	0-0	KL		4 331

14th   Att: 125 236 • Av: 8 349 • Sangju Civic Stadium 20 000

POHANG LEAGUE APPEARANCES/GOALS 2011

Goalkeepers Shin Hwa Yong 24 • Hwang Gyo Chung 0+1 • Kim Da Sol 7
Defenders Kim Gwang Seok 31/0 • Lee Won Jae 0+2/0
Kim Won Il 14+4/0 • Jung Hong Yeon 1+3/0 • Shin Kwang Hoon 25/1
Kim Hyung Il 17+2/0 • Yoon Won Il 1/0 • Kim Dae Ho 11+1/0
Midfield Park Hee Chul 13+1/0 • Kim GI Dong 2+12/2
Kim Jae Sung 28+1/5 • Hwang Jin Sung 24+3/6 • Kim Tae Su 16+6/1
Kim Jung Kyum 8/0 • Shin Hyung Min 28/4 • Jang Hyun Kyu 1+1/0
Cho Chan Ho 6+13/2 • Shin Jin Ho 1+1/0 • Lee Seul Ki 0+1/0
Jung Seok Min 0+2/0
Forwards Derek Asamoah GHA 24+3/7 • Mota BRA 26+2/13 • Ko Mu Yeol 17+7/9 • Kim Sun Woo 0+1/0 • No Byung Jun 9+20/4 • Adriano Chuva BRA 7+5/4
Coach Hwang Sun Hong

SANGJU LEAGUE APPEARANCES/GOALS 2011

Goalkeepers Kwon Soon Tae 15 • Kim Jee Hyuk 11 • Lee Sang Gi 3+1
Defenders Choi Hyo Jin 25/0 • Oh Chang Sik 1/0 • Yoon Yeo San 11/0
Kim Seon Woo 5+2/0 • Hwang Ji Yoon 0+1/0 • Kim Chi Gon 18/0
Kim Joo Hwan 7/0 • Yoon Shin Young 7+6/0 • Lee Jong Chan 5/0
Kang Min Woo 0+3/0 • Lcc Yoon Ui 1/0
Midfield Kim Young Sam 13/0 • Kim Min Oh 9/0 • Kim Chi Woo 26/1
Lee Jong Min 15+6/0 • Kim Jung Woo 20+1/15 • Jung Kyung Ho 9/0
Kim Cheol Ho 27/1 • Byung Woong 1+4/0 • Ko Cha Won 18+10/4
Kim Ji Min 4+2/0 • Oh Won Jong 0+3/0 • Kim Yong Tae 15+2/1
Oh Bong Jin 0+2/0 • Kim Bum Joon 4+6/0 • Hwang Byung In 4/0
Forwards Jang Nam Seok 15/3 • Cho Yong Tae 7+1/1
Ryu Chang Hyun 12+6/2 • Ju Kwang Youn 2+1/0
Kim Dong Hyun 1+5/0 • Kim Min Soo 7+8/2 • Lee Je Kyu 4+4/0
Kwak Chul Ho 2+5/0 • Lee Sung Jae 6+4/2
Coach Lee Soo Chul • Kim Tae Wan (12/07/11)

SEONGNAM ILHWA CHUNMA 2011

Mon	Date	Opponent		Score	Comp	Scorers	Att
Mar	5	Pohang	D	1-1	KL	Kim Jin Ryong 62	17 353
	12	Jeonbuk	L	0-1	KL		9 571
	16	Pohang	L	0-2	LCgA		7 211
	20	Sangju	L	2-3	KL	Song Ho Young 4, Ognenovski 90p	2 893
Apr	3	Busan	W	2-0	KL	Cho Dong Geon 54, Hong Chul 56	6 438
	6	Gyeongnam	D	0-0	LCgA		1 411
	10	Chunnam	D	0-0	KL		8 099
	17	Incheon	L	1-2	KL	Hong Jin Sub 79	8 278
	20	Daejeon	W	1-0	LCgA	Cho Dong Geon 85	1 534
	24	Jeju	L	1-2	KL	Namkung Do 90p	2 813
	30	Gyeongnam	D	2-2	KL	OG 13, Cho Dong Geon 35p	2 317
May	5	Daegu	W	2-0	LCgA	Hong Chul 80, Kim Deok Il 85	9 744
	8	Gangwon	D	1-1	KL	Hong Chul 22	3 177
	11	Incheon	D	1-1	LCgA	Hong Jin Sub 24	1 024
	15	Suwon	D	1-1	KL	Ognenovski 58	12 131
	18	Mokpo	W	3-0	FAr1	Ognenovski 42, Namkung Do 51, Jo Jae Cheol 78	518
	22	Ulsan	L	2-3	KL	Cho Dong Geon 2 26 45	8 576
	29	Seoul	W	2-0	KL	Cho Dong Geon 77, Kim Jin Ryong 90	10 314
Jun	11	Gwangju	L	0-2	KL		4 132
	15	Incheon	W	2-0	FAr2	Cho Dong Geon 47, Everton 66	1 027
	18	Daejeon	W	2-1	KL	Jeon Sung Chan 27, Cho Dong Geon 73	8 712
	25	Daegu	L	1-2	KL	Namkung Do 76	1 127
Jul	2	Busan	L	0-6	KL		6 019
	10	Incheon	D	2-2	KL	OG 57, Song Ho Young 87	3 147
	16	Jeju	D	2-2	KL	Heverton 19, Everton 22	3 591
	24	Jeonbuk	L	0-2	KL		16 298
	27	Busan	W	2-1	FAqf	Heverton 5, Radoncic 90	928
Aug	6	Sangju	W	3-1	KL	Namkung Do 28, Radoncic 63, Everton 86	8 867
	14	Ulsan	W	3-2	KL	Jeon Sung Chan 17, Everton 21, Heverton 79	5 026
	20	Gyeongnam	D	1-1	KL	Everton 20	5 195
	24	Pohang	W	3-0	FAsf	Ognenovski 39, Cho Dong Keon 45, Radoncic 65	5 752
	27	Daegu	W	1-0	KL	Cho Dong Geon 19p	3 899
Sep	10	Suwon	L	2-3	KL	Ognenovski 2 49 90	15 787
	17	Gwangju	L	1-3	KL	Radoncic 70	5 589
	25	Chunnam	W	3-2	KL	Heverton 2 21p 89, Everton 44	4 225
Oct	1	Daejeon	W	2-0	KL	Hong Chul 11, Heverton 14	10 351
	8	Gangwon	W	3-1	KL	Radoncic 1, Kim Sung Hwan 9	3 010
	15	Suwon	W	1-0	FAf	Cho Dong Keon 76	14 756
	23	Seoul	L	1-3	KL	Jeon Sung Chan 64	42 909
	30	Pohang	L	1-3	KL	Ognenovski 58p	3 211

10th   Att: 86 952 • Av: 5 796 • Tancheon Sports Complex 19 000

FC SEOUL 2011

Mon	Date	Opponent		Score	Comp	Scorers	Att
Mar	2	Al Ain	W	1-0	CLgF	Damjanovic 25	5 128
	6	Suwon	L	0-2	KL		51 606
	12	Daejeon	D	1-1	KL	OG 37	32 340
	15	Hangzhou	W	3-0	CLgF	Damjanovic 17, Ou Kyoung Jun 71, Molina 80	6 103
	20	Chunnam	L	0-3	KL		3 622
Apr	2	Jeonbuk	W	3-1	KL	Damjanovic 2 21 85, Molina 23	27 406
	6	Nagoya	D	1-1	CLgF	Choi Hyun Tae 63	7 348
	10	Busan	D	1-1	KL	Ko Yo Han 37	5 208
	16	Ulsan	L	1-1	KL	Ha Dae Sung 83	28 418
	19	Nagoya	L	0-2	CLgF		10 927
	24	Gwangju	L	0-1	KL		4 127
	30	Jeju	W	2-1	KL	Park Yong Ho 58, Ko Myong Jin 82	9 797
May	4	Al Ain	W	3-0	CLgF	Ko Yo Han 17, Damjanovic 2 40 73	23 623
	8	Sangju	W	4-3	KL	Damjanovic 3 8 35 73, Hyun Young Min 88	9 170
	11	Hangzhou	D	1-1	CLgF	Bang Seung Hwan 67	12 178
	15	Gyeongnam	W	3-1	KL	Damjanovic 11, Ko Yo Han 2 71 90	26 008
	18	Yongin City	W	4-0	FAr1	Choi Jong Han 57, Damjanovic 2 64 83, Adi 71	3 733
	21	Daegu	L	0-2	KL		14 817
	25	Kashima	W	3-0	CLr2	Bang Seung Hwan 38, Damjanovic 55, Ko Myong Jin 92+	12 725
	29	Seongnam	L	0-2	KL		10 314
Jun	11	Pohang	D	1-1	KL	Damjanovic 9	44 358
	15	Busan Kyo.	W	1-0	FAr2	Djeparov 45	1 014
	18	Gangwon	W	2-0	KL	Ha Dae Sung 24, Molina 45	11 347
	25	Incheon	D	1-1	KL	Damjanovic 40	15 315
	29	Gyeongnam	L	0-1	LCqf		2 469
Jul	3	Jeonbuk	D	2-2	KL	Kang Joon Hoon 82, Damjanovic 82	15 879
	9	Sangju	W	3-2	KL	Damjanovic 2 55 66, Bang Seung Hwan 94+	28 034
	17	Pohang	W	2-1	KL	Damjanovic 2 8 24	18 115
	23	Gwangju	W	4-1	KL	Damjanovic 2 6 22, Choi Jong Hwan 33, Molina 43	21 124
	27	Pohang	L	2-4	FAqf	Damjanovic 51, Molina 73	10 419
Aug	6	Ulsan	W	2-1	KL	Choi Hyun Tae 8, Ko Myong Jin 75	12 107
	13	Chunnam	W	1-0	KL	Molina 94+	19 566
	20	Jeju	W	3-0	KL	Damjanovic 2 42 88, Ha Dae Sun 75	12 775
	27	Gangwon	W	6-3	KL	Molina 3 9 60 83, Damjanovic 2 18 48, Lee Seung Ryul 71	23 921
Sep	9	Daegu	L	1-2	KL	Bang Seung Hwan 53	5 612
	14	Al Ittihad	L	1-3	CLqf	Choi Tae Uk 82	16 790
	18	Busan	W	2-1	KL	Kim Dong Jin 64, Kang Jung Hoon 90	33 663
	24	Daejeon	W	4-1	KL	Damjanovic 3 3 17 71, Molina 84	30 286
	27	Al Ittihad	W	1-0	CLqf	Molina 85	15 000
Oct	3	Suwon	L	0-1	KL		44 537
	16	Incheon	D	1-1	KL	Molina 75	6 822
	23	Seongnam	W	3-1	KL	Kim Tae Hwan 37, Damjanovic 77, Molina 90	42 909
	30	Gyeongnam	W	3-0	KL	Ha Dae Sung 3 60 78 86	22 468
Nv	19	Ulsan	L	1-3	KLpo	Damjanovic 59	30 799

3rd   Att: 448 027 • Av: 28 001 • Seoul World Cup Stadium 66 806

SEONGNAM LEAGUE APPEARANCES/GOALS 2011

Goalkeepers Ha Kang Jin 27 • Jung San 1 • Kang Sung Kwan 2
Defenders Yun Young Sun 14+2/0 • Sasa Ognenovski AUS 23+1/5
Park Jin Po 28/0 • Jeong Ho Jeong 7/0 • Kim Tae Youn 25/0
Yong Hyun Jin 9+3/0 • Hong Chul 19+1/3
Midfield Jo Jae Cheol 26+2/0 • Jean BRA 3/0 • Lee Chang Hoon 4+4/0
Kim Sung Hwan 29/1 • Namkung Woong 2+3/0 • Heverton BRA 12/6
Jeon Sung Chan 21+1/3 • Park Sang Hee 6+2/0 • Lim Se Hyun 3+1/0
Kim Tae Wang 0+1/0 • Hong Jin Sub 7+7/1
Forwards Cho Dong Geon 24+3/7 • Dzenan Radoncic MNE 4+6/3 • Sim
Jae Myung 2+3/0 • Song Ho Young 5+10/2 • Namkung Do 6+12/3 •
Kim Deok Il 1+2/0 • Kim Jin Ryong 7+4/2 • Han Geu Ru 1+3/0 •
Everton Santos BRA 18+7/5 • Kim Jung Woo 0+2/0
Coach Shin Tae Young

SEOUL LEAGUE APPEARANCES/GOALS 2011

Goalkeepers Kim Yong Dae 29 • Han Il Goo 2 • Yoo Sang Hoon 0+1
Defenders Kim Dong Woo 14+1/0 • Kim Dong Jin 6+3/1
Adilson BRA 30/0 • Hyun Young Min 25+1/1 • Park Yong Ho 15+3/1
Lee Jung Youl 0+2/0 • Kim Tae Hwan 9+7/1
Midfield Mauricio Molina COL 28+1/10 • Moon Ki Han 6+6/0
Ha Dae Sung 16+2/6 • Yeo Hyo Jin 7+2/0 • Han Tae You 3/0
Ko Yo Han 19/3 • Ko Myong Jin 23+1/2 • Choi Jong Hwan 6+1/1
Lee Gyu Ro 12+2/0 • Kang Jung Hoon 0+8/2 • Choi Hyun Tae 23+4/1
Server Djeparov UZB 15/0
Forwards Ou Kyoung Jun 2+6/0 • Dejan Damjanovic MNE 29+1/24
Bang Seung Hwan 7+9/2 • Bae Hae Min 0+3/0
Lee Seung Ryul 6+12/1 • Choi Tae Uk 4+9/0
Ko Kwang Min 3+3/0 • Lee Jae An 2+5/0
Coach Hwangbo Kwan • Choi Yong Soo (26/04/11)

SUWON SAMSUNG BLUEWINGS 2011

Mon	Date	Opponent	Res	Score	Comp	Scorers	Att
Mar	2	Sydney	D	0-0	CLgF		7 095
	6	Seoul	W	2-0	KL	Geynrikh 42, Oh Jang Eun 60	51 606
	12	Gwangju	W	2-1	KL	Neretljak 2 78 83p	31 506
	16	Shanghai	W	4-0	CLgF	Ha Tae Goon 3 6 62 77, Oh Jang Eun 45	5 393
	20	Pohang	L	0-2	KL		14 812
Apr	2	Ulsan	W	2-1	KL	Oh Jang Eun 54, Neretljak 90p	26 234
	6	Kashima	D	1-1	CLgF	Yeom Ki Hun 67	7 689
	10	Jeonbuk	D	0-0	KL		26 597
	15	Gangwon	W	2-0	KL	Neretljak 44, Choi Sung Kuk 56	19 121
	19	Kashima	D	1-1	CLgF	Yeom Ki Hun 47	4 619
	24	Gyeongnam	L	1-2	KL	OG 65	20 315
	30	Sangju	L	0-1	KL		5 948
May	3	Sydney	W	3-1	CLgF	Ha Tae Goon 34, Neretljak 50, Yeom Ki Hun 80	9 495
	7	Chunnam	L	1-2	KL	Kwak Hee Ju 24	38 068
	10	Shanghai	W	3-0	CLgF	Ha Tae Goon 2 13 56, Shin Se Gye 90	6 730
	15	Seongnam	D	1-1	KL	Geynrikh 90	12 131
	18	Pocheon	W	3-1	FAr1	Bergson 61, Park Jong Jin 69, Choi Sung Kuk 78	2 832
	21	Busan	L	1-2	KL	OG 66	18 714
	25	Nagoya	W	2-0	CLr2	Yeom Ki Hun 24, Lee Sang Ho 58	11 036
	29	Incheon	L	1-2	KL	Yeom Ki Hun 17	10 582
Jun	11	Jeju	L	2-3	KL	Geynrikh 7, Park Jong Jin 66	2 712
	15	Suwon City	W	1-0	FAr2	Oh Jang Eun 27	2 642
	18	Daegu	W	4-1	KL	Yeom Ki Hun 3 15 63p 66, Marcel 27	17 145
	25	Daejeon	W	3-1	KL	Yang Juna 11, Lee Sang Ho 40, Ha Tae Goon 90	4 771
	29	Jeju	D	0-0	LCqf	W 4-2p	2 822
Jul	2	Pohang	W	2-1	KL	Marcel 2 4 68	27 152
	6	Busan	L	1-2	LCsf	Yang Juna 8	1 878
	10	Chunnam	L	1-3	KL	Ristic 45	5 080
	16	Incheon	W	1-0	KL	Ristic 35	17 088
	23	Busan	L	3-4	KL	Ristic 23p, Lee Sang Ho 80, Ha Tae Goon 84	8 143
	27	Chunnam	W	1-0	FAqf	Lee Yong Rae 25	5 867
Aug	6	Daejeon	W	4-0	KL	Kwak He Ju 9, Yeom Ki Hun 57, Lee Sang Ho 2 70 93+	24 451
	13	Gyeongnam	W	2-0	KL	Ristic 20, Kwak Hee Ju 71	7 809
	20	Sangju	W	3-0	KL	Yeom Ki Hun 19p, Ristic 31, Lee Sang Ho 90p	26 989
	24	Ulsan	W	3-2	FAsf	Ristic 75, Neretljak 82, Park Hyun Beom 111	14 698
	27	Ulsan	D	1-1	KL	Oh Jang Eun 72	21 753
Sep	10	Seongnam	W	3-2	KL	Ristic 15, Yeom Ki Hun 25, Oh Jang Eun 86	15 787
	14	Zob Ahan	D	1-1	CLqf	Park Hyun Beom 68	7 659
	18	Gangwon	W	1-0	KL	Neretljak 8	3 508
	24	Daegu	W	1-0	KL	Yeom Ki Hun 23, Lee Sang Ho 75	14 326
	28	Zob Ahan	W	2-1	CLqf	Yang Sang Min 77, Neretljak 99p	7 250
	3	Seoul	W	1-0	KL	Ristic 78	44 537
	8	Jeonbuk	D	2-2	KL	Yeom Ki Hun 20, Neretljak 34p	13 004
Oct	15	Seongnam	L	0-1	FAf		14 756
	19	Al Sadd	L	0-2	CLsf		9 864
	23	Gwangju	W	1-0	KL	Ristic 10	24 778
	26	Al Sadd	W	1-0	CLsf	Oh Jang Eun 7	10 800
	30	Jeju	W	2-0	KL	Neretljak 31, Ristic 90	20 197
Nov	20	Busan	W	1-0	KLpo	Ha Tae Goon 45	23 903
	23	Ulsan	D	1-1	KLpo	Neretljak 84p	15 862

4th Att: 400 073 • Av: 23 533 • Suwon World Cup Stadium 44 959

ULSAN HYUNDAI 2011

Mon	Date	Opponent	Res	Score	Comp	Scorers	Att
Mar	6	Daejeon	L	1-2	KL	Kim Shin Wook 80	34 758
	13	Gyeongnam	L	0-1	KL		16 749
	16	Busan	W	2-1	LCgB	Kim Shin Wook 2 20 46	4 856
	20	Gwangju	W	2-1	KL	Kwak Tae Hwi 2 67 86	5 175
	2	Suwon	L	1-2	KL	Kim Shin Wook 67	26 234
Apr	6	Sangju	W	2-1	LCgB	Lee Jin Ho 2 12 52	3 323
	10	Gangwon	W	1-0	KL	Lee Jae Sung 90	7 349
	16	Seoul	D	1-1	KL	Kwak Tae Hwi 64	28 418
	20	Gangwon	W	2-1	LCgB	Kim Shin Wook 25, Seol Ki Hyon 34p	983
	23	Pohang	L	0-2	KL		14 394
	30	Daegu	W	2-1	KL	Go Seul Ki 45, Kim Shin Wook 52	5 609
May	4	Chunnam	L	0-1	LCgB		4 243
	7	Jeonbuk	L	0-1	KL		22 723
	11	Gwangju	W	2-1	LCgB	Kim Shin Wook 2 9 39	568
	15	Jeju	L	0-1	KL		21 755
	18	Ansan	W	1-0	FAr1	OG 65	350
	22	Seongnam	W	3-2	KL	Kim Shin Wook 13, Seol Ki Hyeon 32p, Kwak Tae Hwi	8 576
	28	Chunnam	W	1-0	KL	Kang Min Soo 14	7 828
	11	Sangju	W	2-1	KL	Go Seul Ki 14, Kwak Tae Hwi 88	10 573
Jun	15	Sangju	W	2-1	FAr2	Lee Ho 30, Go Seul Ki 113	1 385
	18	Incheon	D	1-1	KL	Ko Chang Hyeon 45	23 897
	25	Busan	L	0-2	KL		2 336
	29	Jeonbuk	W	4-1	LCqf	Kim Shin Wook 2 26 30, Choi Jae Soo 41, Jung Dae Sun 53	2 153
Jul	3	Gyeongnam	D	0-0	KL		3 376
	6	Gyeongnam	W	4-2	LCsf	Kim Shin Wook 4 47 66 78 88	2 589
	10	Jeonbuk	D	0-0	KL		10 572
	13	Busan	W	3-2	LCf	Ko Chang Hyeon 38, Seol Ki Hyeon 45, Kang Jin Ouk 58	21 853
	16	Gangwon	W	2-1	KL	Kim Shin Wook 54, Lee Jin Ho 78	4 020
	23	Chunnam	W	2-0	KL	Kim Shin Wook 39, Seol Ki Hyeon 58p	32 157
	27	Gangwon	W	3-0	FAqf	Go Seul Ki 3 7 30 50	1 327
Aug	6	Seoul	L	1-2	KL	Kang Min Soo 77	12 107
	14	Seongnam	L	2-3	KL	Go Seul Ki 2 60 82	5 026
	20	Daejeon	L	0-1	KL		9 230
	24	Suwon	L	2-3	FAsf	Seol Ki Hyeon 2 58 74	14 698
	27	Suwon	D	1-1	KL	Lee Jin Ho 34	21 753
	10	Jeju	W	2-1	KL	Kwak Tae Hwi 2 31 72	2 523
Sep	17	Sangju	W	3-1	KL	Lee Jin Ho 30, Kwak Tae Hwi 71, Park Seung Il 79	6 573
	24	Incheon	W	2-0	KL	Seol Ki Hyeon 69, Park Seung Il 81	5 141
	2	Gwangju	D	0-0	KL		3 436
Oct	16	Pohang	W	2-1	KL	Go Seul Ki 21, Ko Chang Hyeon 90	23 875
	22	Busan	W	1-0	KL	Go Seul Ki 71	11 257
	30	Daegu	D	0-0	KL		5 814
	19	Seoul	W	3-1	KLpo	Kwak Tae Hwi 18, Kim Shin Wook 35, Go Seul Ki 60	30 799
Nov	23	Suwon	D	1-1	KLpo	Kim Shin Wook 23	15 862
	26	Pohang	W	1-0	KLsf	Seol Ki Hyeon 72	21 317
Dc	30	Jeonbuk	L	1-2	KLf	Kwak Tae Hwi 63	25 375
	4	Jeonbuk	W	1-0	KLf	Seol Ki Hyeon 54	33 554

6th Att: 254 164 • Av: 15 885 • Ulsan Munsu 44 102

SUWON LEAGUE APPEARANCES/GOALS 2011
Goalkeepers Jung Sung Ryong 30 • Yang Dong Won 2
Defenders Mato Neretljak CRO 25/8 • Yang Sang Min 17+6/0
Oh Beom Seok 28/0 • Woo Seung Je 5+8/0 • Hwang Jae Won 9/0
Choi Sung Hwan 8+10/0 • Kwak Hee Ju 19/3 • Min Sang Ki 0+1/0
Midfield Park Hyun Beom 22+1/0 • Lee Yong Rae 28/0
Lee Sang Ho 27+1/6 • Oh Jang Eun 29+1/4 • Lee Kyung Hwan 0+1/0
Hong Soon Hak 12/0 • Cho Ji Hoon 1/0 • Park Jong Jin 14+6/1
Yang Juna 4+2/1 • Im Kyung Hyun 2+1/0 • Shin Se Gye 8+2/0
Forwards Marcel 10+1/3 • Diego BRA 1+3/0 • Choi Sung Kuk 7+5/1
Stevica Ristic MKD 13/9 • Bergson BRA 1+6/0 • Lee Hyun Jin 0+6/0
Aleksandar Geynrikh UZB 6+13/3 • Cho Yong Tae 0+2/0
Yeom Ki Hun 21+9/9 • Ha Tae Goon 5+12/3
Coach Yoon Seong Hyo

ULSAN LEAGUE APPEARANCES/GOALS 2011
Goalkeepers Kim Young Kwang 28 • Kim Seung Gyu 1+1
Choi Moo Rim 1 • Chung Yoo Suk 5
Defenders Lee Yong 16+6/0 • Park Byung Gyu 3+3/0
Kang Min Soo 18+7/2 • Kwak Tae Hwi 34/10 • Lee Jae Sung 22+1/1
Kang Jin Ouk 11+3/0 • Vinicius BRA 0+1/0
Midfield Choi Jae Soo 31+3/0 • Ko Chang Hyeon 20+6/2
Magnum BRA 4/0 • Song Chong Gug 13/0 • Kim Young Sam 3/0
Go Seul Ki 28+1/7 • Juan Estiven Velez COL 27+3/0
Kim Jong Kuk 0+2/0 • Kim Dong Suk 3+5/0
Forwards Kim Shin Wook 25+10/8 • Seol Ki Hyeon 34/5
Naji Majrashi KSA 0+7/0 • Lucio BRA 10+5/0 • Moon Dae Seong 1+1/0
Lee Jin Ho 6+14/3 • Jung Dae Sun 1+6/7 • Park Seung Il 11+8/2
Coach Kim Ho Gon

KSA – SAUDI ARABIA

FIFA/COCA-COLA WORLD RANKING

'93	'94	'95	'96	'97	'98	'99	'00	'01	'02	'03	'04	'05	'06	'07	'08	'09	'10	'11	'12
38	27	54	37	33	30	39	36	31	38	26	28	33	64	61	48	63	81	96	

					2011										
Jan	Feb	Mar	Apr	May	Jun	Jul	Aug	Sep	Oct	Nov	Dec		High	Low	Av
78	81	79	88	88	92	92	87	97	98	98	96		21	98	45

Saudi Arabia's dramatic slide from the pinnacle of Asian football continued as the Frank Rijkaard-coached national team was knocked out of the qualifying tournament for the 2014 FIFA World Cup finals in Brazil. The Saudis, already reeling from a dismal performance at the AFC Asian Cup finals in Qatar in early 2011, suffered further ignominy when they finished third in their qualifying group behind Australia and Oman. For a country that had appeared in four World Cups between 1994 and 2006, the failure to qualify for a second successive finals was regarded as a disaster. The fact that they didn't even make it to the final round of qualifying in Asia was seen as a national humiliation. Saudi clubs also seem to be losing ground in the AFC Champions League. Al Ittihad in 2006 were the last team to be crowned Asian champions and in the 2011 tournament they almost made it back to the final but were knocked out by Korea's Jeonbuk after losing both legs in the semi-final by the odd goal. At home Al Hilal won a league and cup double for the third time in four years and they did it without losing a game. Their 5-0 victory over Al Wahda in the final of the Crown Prince Cup was a record score for the final. Hilal did lose one match during the season - a semi-final defeat in the increasingly prestigious Champions Cup, a tournament won by Al Ahli.

FIFA WORLD CUP RECORD
1930-1974 DNE 1978-1990 DNQ **1994** 12 r2 **1998** 28 r1 **2002** 32 r1 **2006** 28 r1 2010-2014 DNQ

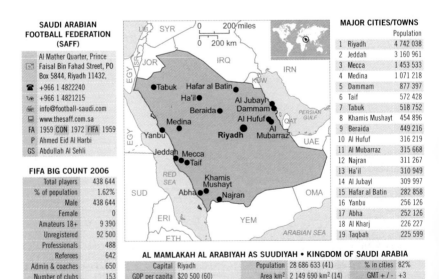

SAUDI ARABIAN FOOTBALL FEDERATION (SAFF)

Al Mather Quarter, Prince
Faisal Bin Fahad Street, PO
Box 5844, Riyadh 11432,

☎ +966 1 4822240
📠 +966 1 4821215
✉ info@football-saudi.com
🖥 www.thesaff.com.sa
FA 1959 CON 1972 FIFA 1959
P Ahmed Eid Al Harbi
GS Abdullah Al Sehli

FIFA BIG COUNT 2006

Total players	438 644
% of population	1.62%
Male	438 644
Female	0
Amateurs 18+	9 390
Unregistered	92 500
Professionals	488
Referees	642
Admin & coaches	650
Number of clubs	153
Number of teams	780

MAJOR CITIES/TOWNS

		Population
1	Riyadh	4 742 038
2	Jeddah	3 160 961
3	Mecca	1 453 533
4	Medina	1 071 218
5	Dammam	877 397
6	Taif	572 428
7	Tabuk	518 752
8	Khamis Mushayt	454 896
9	Beraida	449 216
10	Al Hufuf	316 219
11	Al Mubarraz	315 668
12	Najran	311 267
13	Ha'il	310 949
14	Al Jubayl	309 997
15	Hafar al Batin	282 858
16	Yanbu	256 126
17	Abha	252 126
18	Al Kharj	226 227
19	Taqbah	225 599

AL MAMLAKAH AL ARABIYAH AS SUUDIYAH • KINGDOM OF SAUDI ARABIA

Capital Riyadh		Population 28 686 633 (41)	% in cities 82%
GDP per capita $20 500 (60)		Area km² 2 149 690 km² (14)	GMT +/- +3
Neighbours (km) Iraq 814, Jordan 744, Kuwait 222, Oman 676, Qatar 60, UAE 457, Yemen 1458 • Coast 2640			

RECENT INTERNATIONAL MATCHES PLAYED BY SAUDI ARABIA

2010	Opponents		Score	Venue	Comp	Scorers	Att	Referee
21-05	Congo DR	W	2-0	Schwaz	Fr	Ahmed Al Fraidi 33, Sultan Al Numari 74		
25-05	Nigeria	D	0-0	Wattens	Fr		1 000	Einwaller AUT
29-05	Spain	L	2-3	Innsbruck	Fr	Osama Hawsawi 17, Mohammad Al Sahlawi 74	7 200	Einwaller AUT
11-08	Togo	W	1-0	Riyadh	Fr	Saud Kariri 43		
9-10	Uzbekistan	W	4-0	Jeddah	Fr	Mohannad Aseri 2 30p 45, Taisser Al Jassam 57, Saleh Bashir 86		
12-10	Bulgaria	L	0-2	Istanbul	Fr		100	
12-10	Gabon	W	1-0	Istanbul	Fr	Alaa Al Rishani 4		
16-11	Uganda	D	0-0	Dubai	Fr			
17-11	Ghana	D	0-0	Dubai	Fr			
22-11	Yemen	W	4-0	Aden	GCr1	Osama Al Harbi 4, Mohammad Al Shalhoub 58, Mohanad Aseri 71p, Mishal Al Saeed 90		Al Marzouqi UAE
25-11	Kuwait	D	0-0	Abyan	GCr1			Ogiya JPN
28-11	Qatar	D	1-1	Aden	GCr1	OG 89		Al Marzouqi UAE
2-12	UAE	W	1-0	Aden	GCsf	Ahmad Abbas 55		Ogiya JPN
5-12	Kuwait	L	0-1	Aden	GCf			Al Harrasi OMA
28-12	Iraq	L	0-1	Dammam	Fr			
31-12	Bahrain	W	1-0	Manama	Fr	Osama Hawsawi 66		
2011								
4-01	Angola	D	0-0	Dammam	Fr			
9-01	Syria	L	1-2	Al Rayyan	ACr1	Taisser Al Jassam 60	15 768	Kim Dong Jin KOR
13-01	Jordan	L	0-1	Al Rayyan	ACr1		17 349	Albadwawi UAE
17-01	Japan	L	0-5	Al Rayyan	ACr1		2 022	Irmatov UZB
13-07	Jordan	D	1-1	Amman	Fr	Nassir Al Shamrani 94+ . W 4-3p		
16-07	Kuwait	L	0-1	Amman	Fr			
23-07	Hong Kong	W	3-0	Dammam	WCq	Nassir Al Shamrani 2 45 47, Osama Al Harbi 45	20 354	Tseytlin UZB
28-07	Hong Kong	W	5-0	Hong Kong	WCq	Hassan Fallatah 34, Mohammed Noor 71p, Nassir Al Shamrani 73, Mohammed Al Sahlawi 79, Osama Hawsawi 93+	1 402	Minh Tri Vo VIE
2-09	Oman	D	0-0	Seeb	WCq		14 000	Abdou QAT
6-09	Australia	L	1-3	Dammam	WCq	Nassir Al Shamrani 66	15 000	Nishimura JPN
7-10	Indonesia	D	0-0	Kuala Lumpur	Fr			
11-10	Thailand	D	0-0	Bangkok	WCq		42 000	Irmatov UZB
11-11	Thailand	W	3-0	Riyadh	WCq	Naif Hazazi 59, Ahmed Al Fraidi 80, Mohammed Noor 89p	32 500	Liu Kwok Man HKG
15-11	Oman	D	0-0	Riyadh	WCq		62 740	Torky IRN

Fr = Friendly match • AC = AFC Asian Cup • GC = Gulf Cup • WC = FIFA World Cup • q = qualifier • r1 = first round group • sf = semi-final • f = final

SAUDI ARABIA NATIONAL TEAM HISTORICAL RECORDS

Caps
177 -Mohammed Al Deayea 1990-2006 • **161** - Sami Al Jaber 1992-2006 • **139** - Majed Abdullah 1978-94 • **138** - Mohammed Al Khilaiwi 1990-2001 • **122** - Abdullah Zubromawi 1993-2002 • **106** - Hussein Sulimani 1996-2009

Goals
118 - Majed Abdullah 1978-94

Past Coaches
Abdul Rahman Fawzi EGY 1957-62 • Ali Chaouach TUN 1962-70 • George Seknas ENG 1970-72 • Taha Ismail EGY 1972-74 • Abdo Saleh Washash EGY 1974 • Ferenc Puskas HUN 1975 • Bill McGarry ENG 1976-77 • Danny Allison ENG 1978 • David Wallit ENG 1979 • Rubens Minelli BRA 1980 • Mario Zagallo BRA 1981-84 • Khalil Ibrahim Al Zayani 1984-86 • Kosia Tastilo URU 1986 • Osvaldo BRA 1987 • Carlos Galletti BRA 1988 • Omar Borras URU 1988 • Carlos Alberto Parreira BRA 1988-90 • Metin Turel TUR 1990 • Caldinho Garcia BRA 1992 • Veloso BRA 1992 • Candinho BRA 1993 • Leo Beenhakker NED 1993-94 • Mohammed Al Kharashy 1994 • Ivo Wortmann BRA 1994 • Jorge Solari ARG 1994 • Mohammed Al Kharashy 1995 • Ze Mario BRA 1995-96 • Nelo Vingada POR 1996-97 • Otto Pfister GER 1998 • Carlos Alberto Parreira BRA 1998 • Mohammed Al Kharashy 1998 • Otto Pfister GER 1999 • Milan Macala CZE 1999-2000 • Nasser Al Johar 2000 • Slobodan Santrac SRB 2001 • Nasser Al Johar 2001-02 • Gerard van der Lem NED 2002-04 • Nasser Al Johar 2004 • Gabriel Calderon ARG 2004-05 • Marcos Paqueta BRA 2006-07 • Helio dos Anjos BRA 2007-08 • Nasser Al Johar 2008-09 • Jose Peseiro POR 2009-11 • Nasser Al Johar 2011

SAUDI ARABIA 2010–11

ZAIN SAUDI PREMIER LEAGUE

Team	Pl	W	D	L	F	A	Pts	Hilal	Ittihad	Ittifaq	Shabab	Nasr	Ahli	Taawun	Faysali	Fat'h	Ra'ed	Najran	Wahda	Qadisiya	Hazm
Al Hilal †	26	19	7	0	52	18	64		0-0	1-0	2-1	1-1	3-3	1-0	5-1	2-0	2-1	2-1	2-1	0-0	3-0
Al Ittihad †	26	13	12	1	49	23	51	0-0		2-1	2-2	5-2	2-0	0-1	3-3	2-0	3-0	2-0	1-1	2-2	4-0
Al Ittifaq †	26	15	3	8	45	30	48	2-3	2-1		1-0	3-0	4-3	1-0	1-0	2-2	2-2	1-0	3-0	1-0	2-1
Al Shabab	26	13	7	6	42	30	46	0-2	1-1	2-1		2-0	2-1	4-1	4-1	0-0	0-2	0-1	4-3	3-1	1-0
Al Nasr	26	11	10	5	44	34	43	0-1	2-2	2-1	0-0		2-1	2-2	3-2	4-2	1-0	6-1	0-1	0-0	2-1
Al Ahli †	26	11	4	11	48	41	37	1-1	3-1	5-1	1-2	0-0		1-1	3-0	1-2	1-2	2-1	3-2	2-1	1-0
Al Taawun	26	9	8	9	37	31	35	2-2	0-1	0-1	4-1	2-2	2-1		4-1	0-0	1-0	2-3	1-2	1-1	2-0
Al Faysali	26	10	5	11	39	47	35	2-3	0-2	1-0	0-1	1-1	3-2	2-1		1-2	1-3	4-2	1-0	2-1	3-1
Al Fat'h	26	8	7	11	27	35	31	1-2	0-0	1-0	1-1	1-1	0-2	1-3	0-1		1-1	2-0	2-1	1-3	3-0
Al Ra'ed	26	7	9	10	31	40	30	0-4	1-2	0-3	2-2	1-1	2-3	0-0	0-0	1-2		3-2	3-2	1-4	2-0
Najran	26	8	2	16	33	52	26	0-3	2-2	2-4	1-2	0-1	2-1	0-3	0-1	2-1	0-0		1-5	2-1	4-0
Al Wahda	26	6	6	14	43	44	24	1-3	1-2	0-1	1-2	1-3	1-3	0-0	3-3	3-0	2-3	2-0		0-0	8-1
Al Qadisiya	26	4	11	11	31	39	23	0-2	1-1	0-3	1-1	1-3	1-3	4-1	2-2	0-1	1-1	2-3	1-1		1-0
Al Hazm	26	1	3	22	13	70	6	0-2	0-3	1-4	0-4	2-5	1-3	0-3	0-3	2-1	0-0	0-3	1-1	2-2	

14/08/2010 – 15/05/2011 • † Qualified for the AFC Champions League

Top scorers: 17 - Nasser Al Shamrani, Shabab • 16 - Victor Simoes BRA, Ahli • 14 - Yousef Al Salem, Ittifaq & Mohanad Aseri, Wahda

SAUDI ARABIA 2010–11 FIRST DIVISION (2)

Team	Pl	W	D	L	F	A	Pts
Hajr	30	19	6	5	51	32	63
Al Ansar	30	15	10	5	40	24	55
Al Riyadh	30	16	4	10	38	29	52
Abha	30	13	12	5	59	43	51
Al Khaleej	30	14	7	9	44	36	49
Al Watani	30	11	13	6	44	34	46
Al Ta'ee	30	11	10	9	33	33	43
Dhemk	30	10	9	11	51	47	39
Ohod	30	12	3	15	40	46	39
Hitteen	30	9	10	11	48	39	37
Al Urooba	30	10	7	13	44	55	37
Al Jeel	30	9	8	13	36	45	35
Al Sho'ala	30	9	7	14	36	46	34
Al Adala	30	7	11	12	33	41	32
Al Rabi'a	30	5	7	18	37	60	22
Al Najma	30	4	8	18	32	56	20

23/09/2010 – 11/05/2011

CHAMPIONS CUP 2011

First round

Al Ahli	3	0
Al Shabab	0	1
Al Ittifaq	1	4
Al Wahda *	2	3
Al Hilal *	2	3
Al Faysali	1	0
Al Nasr *	3	1
Al Ittihad	3	1

Semi-finals

Al Ahli	2	4
Al Wahda *	2	1
Al Hilal *	0	1
Al Ittihad	3	1

Final

Al Ahli †	0 4p
Al Ittihad	0 2p

Final – Jeddah
24-06-2011

† Qualified for the AFC Champions League

* Home team in 1st leg • 3rd Place: Hilal 6-3 Wahda

MEDALS TABLE

	Team	Overall			Lge		Cup		CC	Asia			City
		G	S	B	G	S	G	S		G	S	B	
1	Al Hilal	32	20	3	13	10	15	7	1	4	2	3	Riyadh
2	Al Ittihad	22	19	3	8	7	10	8	1	3	1	3	Jeddah
3	Al Ahli	16	13		2	5	13	7	1			1	Jeddah
4	Al Nasr	14	13		6	5	7	6			1	2	Riyadh
5	Al Shabab	11	12	1	5	5	3	6	2	1	1	1	Riyadh
6	Al Ittifaq	4	8		2	2	2	6					Dammam

CROWN PRINCE CUP 2010–11

First Round

Al Hilal *	4	
Najran	0	
Hajr *	1 2p	
Al Ahli	1 4p	
Al Riyadh *	4	
Al Hazm	0	
Al Qadisiya	1	
Al Nasr	5	
Al Ittifaq	2	
Al Fat'h *	1	
Al Taawun	0	
Al Ittihad *	3	
Al Ra'ed	3	
Al Shabab *	2	
Al Faysali	1 2p	
Al Wahda *	1 4p	

Quarter-finals

Al Hilal *	2 4p
Al Ahli	2 3p
Al Riyadh *	1
Al Nasr	2
Al Ittifaq *	3
Al Ittihad	1
Al Ra'ed *	1 2p
Al Wahda	1 4p

Semi-finals

Al Hilal *	2
Al Nasr	0
Al Ittifaq	2 2p
Al Wahda *	2 3p

Final

Al Hilal	5
Al Wahda	0

CUP FINAL

King Abdul Aziz, Mecca
15-04-2011
Scorers – Ahmad Ali [24], Abdullah Al Zori [60], Mohammed Al Shalhoub [69], Christian Wilhelmsson [71], Nawaf Al Aabed [80]

* Home team

KUW – KUWAIT

FIFA/COCA-COLA WORLD RANKING

'93	'94	'95	'96	'97	'98	'99	'00	'01	'02	'03	'04	'05	'06	'07	'08	'09	'10	'11	'12
64	54	84	62	44	24	82	74	74	83	48	54	72	78	119	127	104	102	99	

						2011										
	Jan	Feb	Mar	Apr	May	Jun	Jul	Aug	Sep	Oct	Nov	Dec		High	Low	Av
	99	101	103	100	100	100	95	95	99	96	100	99		24	128	77

Kuwait were one of the highest profile national teams to crash out in the early stages of qualifying for the 2014 FIFA World Cup in Brazil. The team struggled to build on the promise shown in capturing the West Asian Football Federation Championship title in Jordan in 2010 and finishing third in their group behind Korea Republic and Lebanon. Kuwait did claim the bronze medal at the Pan Arab Games at the end of the year, but that will have been scant consolation for football fans in the country. In club football, Kuwait's demotion from the AFC Champions League to the AFC Cup has certainly increased the competitiveness of the Kuwaiti sides and in the 2011 AFC Cup Al Kuwait narrowly missed out on winning back the title they won in 2009. They made it through to a second final in three years but lost 2-1 to Uzbekistan's Nasaf Karshi in a match played in their opponents home stadium. Earlier in the year Al Kuwait had won the Crown Prince Cup by defeating Kitan in the final but it was Al Qadisiya who dominated the season at home. They started the year by winning the Federation Cup and then finished four points ahead of Al Kuwait in the Premier League to complete a hat-trick of titles. Qadisiya were knocked out in the semi-finals of the end of season Emir Cup, however, by Kazma who then went on to beat Al Kuwait 1-0 in the final.

FIFA WORLD CUP RECORD
1930-1970 DNE 1974-1978 DNQ **1982** 21 r1 1986-2014 DNQ

KUWAIT FOOTBALL ASSOCIATION (KFA)

Block 5, Street 101, Building 141 A Jabriya, PO Box Hawalli 4020, Kuwait 32071

☎ +965 22 549770
📠 +965 22 549955
📧 info@kfa.org.kw
🖥 www.kfa.org.kw
FA 1952 CON 1962 FIFA 1962
P Shk. Talal Fahad Al Sabah
GS Saho Al Shammari

FIFA BIG COUNT 2006

Total players	45 800
% of population	1.89%
Male	45 800
Female	0
Youth under 18	1 100
Unregistered	6 600
Professionals	0
Referees	100
Admin & coaches	300
Number of clubs	40
Number of teams	110

MAJOR CITIES/TOWNS

		Population
1	Jaleeb al Shuyukh	187 884
2	Subbah al Salem	152 780
3	Al Qurayn	141 372
4	Salmiya	138 158
5	Farwaniya	97 640
6	Sulaibiah	88 766
7	Hawalli	87 254
8	Fahaheel	79 779
9	Tayma	76 251
10	Al Fardaws	74 205
11	Al Kuwayt	74 180
12	Al Qasr	64 724
13	Ardiya	62 148
14	Reqa	60 827
15	Abrak Khitan	53 698
16	Zahar	48 364
17	Doha	46 697
18	Mangaf	45 590
19	Al Ahmadi	44 696

DAWLAT AL KUWAYT • STATE OF KUWAIT

Capital	Kuwait City	Population	2 691 158 (139)	% in cities	98%
GDP per capita	$57 500 (6)	Area km²	17 818 km² (157)	GMT + / -	+3
Neighbours (km)	Iraq 240, Saudi Arabia 222 • Coast 499				

RECENT INTERNATIONAL MATCHES PLAYED BY KUWAIT

2010	Opponents	Score		Venue	Comp	Scorers	Att	Referee
2-12	Iraq	D	2-2	Aden	GCsf	Bader Al Mutwa [1], Fahad Al Enezi [58]. W 5-4p		Shaaban EGY
5-12	Saudi Arabia	W	1-0	Aden	GCf	Waleed Ali Jumah [94]		Al Harrasi OMA
24-12	Korea DPR	W	2-1	6th October City	Fr	Ahmed Al Rashidi [29], Musaed Neda [90]		
27-12	Korea DPR	D	2-2	6th October City	Fr	Ahmad Ajab Al Azemi [23], Talal Al Amer [57]		
31-12	Zambia	W	4-0	Suez	Fr	Yousef Nasser [19], Fahad Al Enezi 2 [21 33], Bader Al Mutwa [25]		
2011								
8-01	China PR	L	0-2	Doha	ACr1		7 423	Williams AUS
12-01	Uzbekistan	L	1-2	Doha	ACr1	Bader Al Mutwa [50p]	3 481	Shukralla BHR
16-01	Qatar	L	0-3	Doha	ACr1		28 339	Abdul Bashir SIN
14-02	Bahrain	D	0-0	Manama	Fr			
26-03	Jordan	D	1-1	Sharjah	Fr	Hamad Al Enezi [38p]		
29-03	Iraq	W	1-0	Sharjah	Fr	Hussain Al Moussawi [2]		
2-07	Lebanon	W	6-0	Beirut	Fr	Musaed Neda 2 [23 33], Yousef Al Sulaiman 2 [54 68], Waleed Jumah 2 [62 78]		
6-07	Oman	D	1-1	Beirut	Fr	Yousef Al Sulaiman [45]		
13-07	Iraq	W	2-0	Amman	Fr	Fahad Awadh [66], Hussain Fadel [84]		
16-07	Saudi Arabia	W	1-0	Amman	Fr	Bader Al Mutwa [70]		
23-07	Philippines	W	3-0	Kuwait City	WCq	Yousef Naser [17], Mesaed Al Enezi [68], Fahad Al Ebrahim [85]	20 000	Abu Loum JOR
28-07	Philippines	W	2-1	Manila	WCq	Yousef Naser [63], Waleed Jumah [85]	13 000	Liu Kwok Man HKG
10-08	Korea DPR	D	0-0	Kuwait City	Fr			
27-08	Oman	L	0-1	Muscat	Fr			
2-09	UAE	W	3-2	Al Ain	WCq	Yousef Naser 2 [7 65], Bader Al Mutwa [51]	8 715	Basma SYR
6-09	Korea Republic	D	1-1	Kuwait City	WCq	Hussain Ali [54]	20 000	Torky IRN
11-10	Lebanon	D	2-2	Beirut	WCq	Mesaed Al Enezi [51], OG [89]	32 000	Toma JPN
4-11	Bahrain	L	0-1	Kuwait City	Fr			
11-11	Lebanon	L	0-1	Kuwait City	WCq		17 500	Kovalenko UZB
15-11	UAE	W	2-1	Kuwait City	WCq	Fahad Al Enezi [50], OG [68]	10 000	Al Hilali OMA
22-12	Palestine	W	3-0	Doha	PG3p	Hussain Al Moussawi [92], Fahad Al Rashidi [94], Bader Al Mutwa [119]		

Fr = Friendly match • AC = AFC Asian Cup • GC = Gulf Cup • PG = Pan Arab Games • WC = FIFA World Cup • q = qualifier

KUWAIT NATIONAL TEAM HISTORICAL RECORDS

Caps — **134** - Bashar Abdullah 1996-2008 • **109** - Wael Sulaiman Al Habashi 1986-96 & Nohair Al Shammari • **108** - Jamal Mubarak 1994-2004

Goals — **75** - Bashar Abdullah 1996-2008

Coaches — Milan Macala CZE 1996-99 • Dusan Uhrin CZE 1999-2001 • Berti Vogts GER 2001-02 • Radojko Avramovic SRB 2002-03 • Paulo Cesar Carpegiani BRA 2003-04 • Mohammed Ibrahem 2004 • Slobodan Pavkovic SRB 2005 • Mohammed Ibrahem 2005 • Mihai Stoichita ROU 2005-06 • Saleh Zakaria 2006-07 • Rodion Gacanin CRO 2007-08 • Mohammed Ibrahim 2008-09 • Goran Tufegdzic SRB 2009-

FEDERATION CUP 2010-11

Group 1	Pl	W	D	L	F	A	Pts	Qa	Na	Ka	Ar	Sa	Kh	Ya
Al Qadisiya	12	8	3	1	32	17	27		1-4	1-1	2-2	2-1	4-1	9-2
Al Nasr	12	8	2	2	26	11	26	1-3		0-3	4-0	2-0	4-0	2-0
Kazma	12	6	3	3	30	10	21	1-2	1-2		0-0	7-1	1-1	5-0
Al Arabi	12	5	4	3	21	17	19	0-1	1-1	1-4		2-1	0-0	4-0
Salmiya	12	4	2	6	17	22	14	0-2	1-1	2-1	2-3		2-1	1-1
Khitan	12	1	2	9	9	31	5	2-3	1-2	0-5	0-5	0-3		0-1
Al Yarmouk	12	1	2	9	9	36	5	2-2	0-3	0-1	2-3	0-3	1-3	

Group 2	Pl	W	D	L	F	A	Pts	Ku	Ta	Sa	Fe	Ja	So	Sh
Al Kuwait	12	7	3	2	23	11	24		3-1	5-1	3-0	1-1	3-0	2-0
Al Tadamon	12	6	2	4	21	20	20	2-1		1-1	1-3	2-0	1-0	4-1
Al Sahel	12	5	3	4	23	24	18	1-1	5-2		4-1	2-2	2-0	2-1
Fehayheel	12	4	4	4	18	20	16	1-2	2-0	1-1		1-2	2-2	2-2
Jahra	12	3	5	4	15	16	14	0-1	1-1	0-3	2-0		4-0	1-1
Solaybeekhat	12	4	2	6	20	23	14	4-1	2-0	5-1	1-3	2-3		2-1
Al Shabab	12	2	3	7	19	25	9	1-2	2-4	4-1	2-3	2-0	2-2	

Semi-finals		Final	
Al Qadisiya	4		
Al Tadamon	0		
		Al Qadisiya	2
		Al Nasr	0
Al Kuwait	0 2p	**CUP FINAL**	
Al Nasr	0 4p	Al Kuwait Sports Club, Kuwait City 13-01-2011	

6/09/2010 - 13-01-2011

KUWAIT 2010-11

PREMIER LEAGUE

	Pl	W	D	L	F	A	Pts	Qadisiya	Al Kuwait	Arabi	Kazma	Jahra	Nasr	Salmiya	Sahel
Al Qadisiya †	21	16	3	2	47	10	51		2-2 2-0	2-0	1-0 0-0	1-1	2-1 2-0	4-0 1-0	5-0
Al Kuwait	21	14	5	2	46	17	47	3-0		0-2 1-0	3-1 1-0	4-1	4-0 1-0	1-1	6-1
Al Arabi	21	12	3	6	28	19	39	0-2 0-3	1-5		0-1	2-0 1-0	3-0 0-0	4-0	4-2
Kazma	21	11	5	5	28	14	38	1-0	1-1	0-0 1-0		4-0 1-0	1-3 1-0	1-1	2-0 2-1
Jahra	21	5	4	12	14	31	19	0-4 0-1	0-1 1-3	1-1	1-2		1-1 2-1	0-0	1-0 2-1
Al Nasr	21	4	4	13	18	34	16	1-3	0-4	1-2	0-0	1-0		1-2 2-3	0-1 4-1
Salmiya	21	3	5	13	17	36	14	1-2	1-2 2-2	0-1 1-2	0-2 0-2	2-1 0-1	0-1 0-1		1-1 0-2
Al Sahel	21	3	3	15	16	53	12	0-2 0-8	1-1 0-1	0-1 0-3	1-6	0-1	1-1	3-2	

20/08/2010 - 8/04/2011 • ‡ Qualified for the AFC Cup • Relegation play-off: **Salmiya 2-1 Khitan** • Top scorer: **15** - Firas Al Khatib SYR, Qadisiya

KUWAIT 2010-11 FIRST DIVISION (2)

	Pl	W	D	L	F	A	Pts
Al Shabab	20	10	6	4	36	21	36
Khitan	20	9	5	6	28	25	32
Al Tadamon	20	8	7	5	35	26	31
Solaybeekhat	20	7	2	11	33	42	23
Fehayheel	20	3	11	6	31	40	20
Al Yarmouk	20	5	5	10	26	35	20

22/08/2010 - 2/04/2011

MEDALS TABLE

	Overall			League			EC		CPC		FC	Asia		
	G	S	B	G	S	B	G	S	G	S		G	S	B
1 Al Arabi	36	17	4	**16**	3	4	**15**	11	5	2	1			
2 Al Qadisiya	36	16	5	14	7	4	13	7	**6**	1	**3**		1	1
3 Al Kuwait	26	20	3	10	5	3	9	9	5	4	1 1	1	1	
4 Kazma	12	14	5	4	4	5	7	8	1	1	1			
5 Salmiya	7	11	5	4	5	5	2	6	1					

CROWN PRINCE CUP 2010-11

First Round		Quarter-finals		Semi-finals		Final	
Al Kuwait	Bye						
		Al Kuwait	3				
Al Tadamon	0	Fehayheel	1				
Fehayheel	1			**Al Kuwait**	2		
Jahra	1			Al Arabi	1		
Kazma	0	Jahra	2				
Al Yarmouk	0	**Al Arabi**	3				
Al Arabi	7					**Al Kuwait**	2
Al Shabab	3					Khitan	1
Salmiya	1	**Al Shabab**	2				
		Al Qadisiya	1			**CUP FINAL**	
Al Qadisiya	Bye			Al Shabab	0		
Solaybeekhat	4			**Khitan**	1	Al Kuwait Sports Club, Kuwait City	
Al Sahel	1	Solaybeekhat	1			15-05-2011	
Al Nasr	1	**Khitan**	2				
Khitan	3						

EMIR CUP 2010-11

First Round		Quarter-finals		Semi-finals		Final	
Kazma	1						
Al Tadamon	0	**Kazma**	3				
Salmiya	1	Khitan	2				
Khitan	3			**Kazma**	1		
Al Shabab	1			Al Qadisiya	0		
Al Arabi	0	Al Shabab	2				
		Al Qadisiya	5				
Al Qadisiya	Bye					**Kazma**	1
Al Nasr	3					Al Kuwait	0
Al Yarmouk	0	**Al Nasr**	2				
Solaybeekhat	0	Jahra	0			**CUP FINAL**	
Jahra	3			Al Nasr	1		
Fehayheel	1			**Al Kuwait**	3	Al Kuwait Sports Club, Kuwait City	
Al Sahel	0	Fehayheel	0	3rd place:		7-06-2011	
		Al Kuwait	4				
Al Kuwait	Bye						

LAO – LAOS

FIFA/COCA-COLA WORLD RANKING

'93	'94	'95	'96	'97	'98	'99	'00	'01	'02	'03	'04	'05	'06	'07	'08	'09	'10	'11	'12
146	160	152	147	143	144	156	165	162	170	167	162	170	151	176	169	178	169	174	

	2011												High	Low	Av
Jan	Feb	Mar	Apr	May	Jun	Jul	Aug	Sep	Oct	Nov	Dec			
168	169	169	175	174	174	177	180	182	181	175	174	134	190	163

Laos's positive showing in recent years - reaching the semi-finals of the South East Asian Games in 2009 on home soil and an encouraging performance at the AFF Suzuki Cup a year later - was matched in 2011 when they gained a notable scalp in the 2014 FIFA World Cup qualifiers. Laos were drawn against neighbours Cambodia in the first round of Asian qualifying, but after a 4-2 defeat in the first leg in Phnom Penh the team rallied brilliantly in the return in Vientiane to pull the tie back to 6-6 on aggregate. That meant extra-time during which Laos scored twice more to win the game 6-2, their record victory in an international, to take them through to the next round and a tie against China. Laos looked like springing one of the biggest upsets of the year when they took a 2-0 lead inside the first 31 minutes of the first leg in Kunming, but they quickly ran out of steam and were brushed aside by the Chinese 7-2 on the day and 13-3 on aggregate. The country's under-23 team competed at the 2011 edition of the South East Asian Games in Jakarta but missed out on a place in the knockout phase of the competition after winning just once - against Timor-Leste - and finishing fourth in their six-team group at the multi-sport event. The Ministry of Public Works and Transport were the Laos league champions in 2011 while Banks won the cup.

FIFA WORLD CUP RECORD
1930-1998 DNE 2002-2006 DNQ 2010 DNE

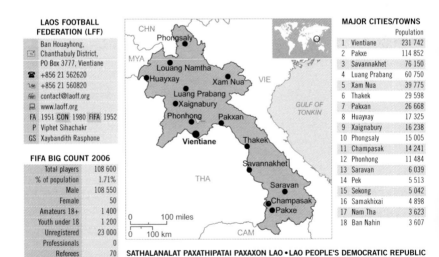

LAOS FOOTBALL FEDERATION (LFF)
Ban Houayhong,
Chanthabuly District,
PO Box 3777, Vientiane
☎ +856 21 562620
📠 +856 21 560820
📧 contact@laoff.org
🖥 www.laoff.org
FA 1951 CON 1980 FIFA 1952
P Viphet Sihachakr
GS Xaybandith Rasphone

FIFA BIG COUNT 2006

Total players	108 600
% of population	1.71%
Male	108 550
Female	50
Amateurs 18+	1 400
Youth under 18	1 200
Unregistered	23 000
Professionals	0
Referees	70
Admin & coaches	350
Number of clubs	50
Number of teams	150

MAJOR CITIES/TOWNS

		Population
1	Vientiane	231 742
2	Pakxe	114 852
3	Savannakhet	76 150
4	Luang Prabang	60 750
5	Xam Nua	39 775
6	Thakek	29 598
7	Pakxan	26 668
8	Huayxay	17 325
9	Xaignabury	16 238
10	Phongsaly	15 005
11	Champasak	14 241
12	Phonhong	11 484
13	Saravan	6 039
14	Pek	5 513
15	Sekong	5 042
16	Samakhixai	4 898
17	Nam Tha	3 623
18	Ban Nahin	3 607

SATHALANALAT PAXATHIPATAI PAXAXON LAO • LAO PEOPLE'S DEMOCRATIC REPUBLIC

Capital Vientiane	Population 6 834 942 (102)	% in cities 31%
GDP per capita $2100 (186)	Area km² 236 800 km² (83)	GMT + / - +7
Neighbours (km) Cambodia 541, China 423, Myanmar 235, Thailand 1754, Vietnam 2130		

RECENT INTERNATIONAL MATCHES PLAYED BY LAOS

2006	Opponents	Score		Venue	Comp	Scorers	Att	Referee
12-11	Philippines	W	2-1	Bacolod	AFFq	Sisomephone [47], Phaphouvanin [49]		
14-11	Cambodia	D	2-2	Bacolod	AFFq	Soukhavong [30], Sisomephone [35]		
16-11	Timor Leste	W	3-2	Bacolod	AFFq	Saysongkham [34], Phothilath [61], Saynakhonevieng [91+]		
18-11	Brunei Darussalam	W	4-1	Bacolod	AFFq	Saysongkham [6], Phaphouvanin [17], Leupvisay [43], Phothilath [55]		
2007								
13-01	Indonesia	L	1-3	Singapore	AFFr1	Xaysongkham [13]		
15-01	Singapore	L	0-11	Singapore	AFFr1		5 224	U Hla Tint MYA
17-01	Vietnam	L	0-9	Singapore	AFFr1		1 005	
22-08	Lesotho	L	1-3	Petaling Jaya	Fr	Visay Phaphouvanin		
25-08	Myanmar	L	0-1	Kuala Lumpur	Fr			
2008								
17-10	Cambodia	L	2-3	Phnom Penh	AFFq	Luanglath [30], Leupvisay [30]		
21-10	Philippines	W	2-1	Phnom Penh	AFFq	Luanglath [56], Phaphouvanin [59]		
23-10	Brunei Darussalam	W	3-2	Phnom Penh	AFFq	Phaphouvanin [8], Singto [89], Saynakhonevieng [93+]		
25-10	Timor-Leste	W	2-1	Phnom Penh	AFFq	Singto [7], Phaphouvanin [50]		
6-12	Malaysia	L	0-3	Phuket	AFFr1		5 000	Nitrorejo IDN
8-12	Thailand	L	0-6	Phuket	AFFr1		10 000	Hadimin BRU
10-12	Vietnam	L	0-4	Phuket	AFFr1			Cho Win MYA
2009								
No international matches played in 2009								
2010								
22-10	Cambodia	D	0-0	Vientiane	AFFq			Abdul Wahab MAS
24-10	Philippines	D	2-2	Vientiane	AFFq	Soukaphone [29], Kanyala [41]		Pechsri THA
26-10	Timor-Leste	W	6-1	Vientiane	AFFq	Kovanh [11], Soukaphone [17], Lamnao [47p], Konekham [59], Kanyala [61], Ketsada [78]		Phung Dinh Dung VIE
1-12	Thailand	D	2-2	Jakarta	AFFr1	Inthammavong [54], Sysomvang [82]		Sato JPN
4-12	Indonesia	L	0-6	Jakarta	AFFr1		70 000	Daud SIN
7-12	Malaysia	L	1-5	Palembang	AFFr1	Lamnao [8]		Vo Minh Tri VIE
2011								
10-02	Chinese Taipei	L	2-5	Kaohsiung	CCq	Ketsada [65], Phattana [73]	1 000	Ng Chiu Kok HKG
16-02	Chinese Taipei	D	1-1	Vientiane	CCq	Vongchiengkham [82]	15 300	Abdul Wahab MAS
29-06	Cambodia	L	2-4	Phnom Penh	WCq	Phomsouvanh 2 [10 61]	25 000	Jahanbazi IRN
3-07	Cambodia	W	6-2	Vientiane	WCq	Singto 2 [19 55], Sayavutthi [34], Syphasay [46], Phaphouvanin [94], Sysomvang [112]	9 000	Sato JPN
23-07	China PR	L	2-7	Kunming	WCq	Vongchiengkham [5], Phaphouvanin [31]	13 500	Delovski AUS
28-07	China PR	L	1-6	Vientiane	WCq	Phaphouvanin [47]	13 000	Shamsuzzaman BAN

AFF = ASEAN Football Federation Championship • AC = AFC Asian Cup 2004 • WC = FIFA World Cup • q = qualifier • r1 = first round group

LBR – LIBERIA

FIFA/COCA-COLA WORLD RANKING

'93	'94	'95	'96	'97	'98	'99	'00	'01	'02	'03	'04	'05	'06	'07	'08	'09	'10	'11	'12
123	127	87	94	94	108	105	95	73	88	110	123	135	115	145	139	161	160	123	

						2011									
Jan	Feb	Mar	Apr	May	Jun	Jul	Aug	Sep	Oct	Nov	Dec	High	Low	Av
159	158	160	159	157	125	125	123	128	121	123	123	66	164	114

Liberia were due to kick-off their 2014 FIFA World Cup qualifying campaign with a preliminary tie over two legs against Mauritius but the Lone Star advanced to the group stage without kicking a ball after their opponents withdrew. It was a financial windfall too with considerable savings on the costs it would have taken to play a tie on the other side of the continent. It was one of the few highlights of 2011 for Liberia, who had finished last in their qualifying group for the 2012 CAF Africa Cup of Nations. A 1-0 win over the Cape Verde Islands in Monrovia in June was the only success for the national team in the qualifiers. Italian Robert Landi took over as national team coach from former Hungarian international Bertalan Bicskei who took sick leave early in the year and then passed away in July. The death of the coach followed that of 20-year-old Patrick Doeplah, whose body was found at a house in Monrovia the day after he had returned to the country to participate in a training camp with the under-23 side ahead of the 2012 Olympic Games qualifiers. Doeplah, who had been playing club football in Israel, suffered a presumed heart attack. In Club football, LISCR FC, or Liberia Ship Corporate Registry Football Club, won a first-ever Premier League title while Invincible Eleven beat holders Barrack Young Controllers 1-0 in the Cup Final.

CAF AFRICA CUP OF NATIONS RECORD

1957-1965 DNE **1968** DNQ **1970-1974** DNE **1976** DNQ **1978-1980** DNE **1982** DNQ **1984** DNE **1986-1990** DNQ
1992 DNE **1994** DNQ **1996** 9 r1 **1998-2000** DNQ **2002** 10 r1 **2004-2012** DNQ

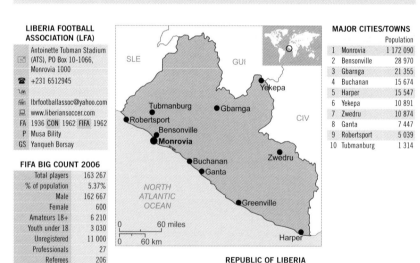

LIBERIA FOOTBALL ASSOCIATION (LFA)

Antoinette Tubman Stadium
(ATS), PO Box 10-1066,
Monrovia 1000
☎ +231 6512945
📠
📧 lbrfootballassoc@yahoo.com
💻 www.liberiansoccer.com
FA 1936 CON 1962 FIFA 1962
P Musa Bility
GS Yanqueh Borsay

FIFA BIG COUNT 2006

Total players	163 267
% of population	5.37%
Male	162 667
Female	600
Amateurs 18+	6 210
Youth under 18	3 030
Unregistered	11 000
Professionals	27
Referees	206
Admin & coaches	450
Number of clubs	45
Number of teams	125

MAJOR CITIES/TOWNS

		Population
1	Monrovia	1 172 090
2	Bensonville	28 970
3	Gbarnga	21 355
4	Buchanan	15 674
5	Harper	15 547
6	Yekepa	10 891
7	Zwedru	10 874
8	Ganta	7 447
9	Robertsport	5 039
10	Tubmanburg	1 314

REPUBLIC OF LIBERIA

Capital Monrovia	Population 3 441 790 (132)	% in cities 60%
GDP per capita $500 (226)	Area km² 111,369 km² (103)	GMT +/- 0
Neighbours (km) Guinea 563, Cote d'Ivoire 716, Sierra Leone 306 • Coast 579		

RECENT INTERNATIONAL MATCHES PLAYED BY LIBERIA

2006	Opponents		Score	Venue		Comp	Scorers	Att	Referee
3-09	Equatorial Guinea	L	1-2	Malabo		CNq	Krangar [35]		Agbenyega GHA
8-10	Rwanda	W	3-2	Monrovia		CNq	Doe [27], Makor [68], Williams [76]		Olatunde NGA
2007									
24-03	Cameroon	L	1-3	Yaoundé		CNq	Doe [39]		Djaoupe TOG
3-06	Cameroon	L	1-2	Monrovia		CNq	Mennoh [65]		Coulibaly MLI
17-06	Equatorial Guinea	D	0-0	Monrovia		CNq			Diouf SEN
8-09	Rwanda	L	0-4	Kigali		CNq			Mwanza ZAM
2008									
26-03	Sudan	W	2-0	Omdurman		Fr	Lomell [46], Mennoh [57]		
24-04	Oman	L	0-1	Muscat		Fr			
30-04	Sierra Leone	W	3-1	Paynesville		Fr	Krangar [21], Laffor [58], Zortiah [86]		
27-05	Libya	L	2-4	Tripoli		Fr	Lomell [56], Zortiah [88]		
1-06	Gambia	D	1-1	Monrovia		WCq	Makor [82]	35 000	Keita GUI
6-06	Algeria	L	0-3	Blida		WCq		40 000	Lemghambodj MTN
15-06	Senegal	D	2-2	Monrovia		WCq	Williams [74], Makor [85]	18 000	Djaoupe TOG
21-06	Senegal	L	1-3	Dakar		WCq	Williams [89]	40 000	Chaibou NIG
6-09	Gambia	L	0-3	Banjul		WCq		10 000	Ambaya LBY
11-10	Algeria	D	0-0	Monrovia		WCq		2 000	Ahmed Auda EGY
2009									
No international matches played in 2009									
2010									
5-09	Zimbabwe	D	1-1	Paynesville		CNq	Sekou Oliseh [68]		Codjia BEN
9-10	Mali	L	1-2	Bamako		CNq	Theo Weeks [42]		Djaoupe TOG
2011									
26-03	Cape Verde Islands	L	2-4	Praia		CNq	Patrick Wleh [38], Alseny Keita [85]		Lemghaifry MTN
5-06	Cape Verde Islands	W	1-0	Paynesville		CNq	Francis Doe [31]		
24-07	Gambia	W	3-2	Monrovia		Fr	James Roberts [3], Vatalis Sieh [58], Marcus Marcauley		
10-08	Angola	D	0-0	Monrovia		Fr			
14-08	Niger	D	0-0	Monrovia		Fr			
4-09	Zimbabwe	L	0-3	Harare		CNq			
8-10	Mali	D	2-2	Paynesville		CNq	Dioh Williams [2], Patrick Wleh [90]		

CN = CAF African Cup of Nations • WC = FIFA World Cup • q = qualifier

LIBERIA NATIONAL TEAM HISTORICAL RECORDS

Coach

George Weah & Dominic Vava 2000-02 • Kadalah Kromah 2002-04 • Joseph Sayon 2004-06 • Shawky El Din 2006 • Joe Nagbe 2006-08 • Antoine Hey 2008-09 • Bertalan Bicskei 2010-11 • Roberto Landi 2011-12 • Thomas Kojo 2012-

LBY – LIBYA

FIFA/COCA-COLA WORLD RANKING

'93	'94	'95	'96	'97	'98	'99	'00	'01	'02	'03	'04	'05	'06	'07	'08	'09	'10	'11	'12
152	167	175	184	147	147	131	116	116	104	83	61	80	99	95	82	115	72	63	

2011															
	Jan	Feb	Mar	Apr	May	Jun	Jul	Aug	Sep	Oct	Nov	Dec	High	Low	Av
	71	70	71	58	58	63	63	64	62	65	63	63	58	187	113

2011 saw the dramatic fall of Muammar Gaddafi's long standing regime in Libya, the outbreak of a civil war and the suspension of all football in the country. But against this backdrop the Libyan national team wrote one of the most unlikely success stories in the history of the game by qualifying for the 2012 CAF Africa Cup of Nations finals in Gabon and Equatorial Guinea. Coached by the pragmatic Brazilian Marcos Paqueta, Libya did not lose a single game despite playing at home just once. The uprising led to the suspension of league activity while Paqueta and his Brazilian support staff fled Tripoli and lost all contact with the federation after the headquarters were hit during NATO bombings of the capital. Yet the persistent coach made his own way to Cairo for a crucial 1-0 win over Mozambique in September where a scratch team made up mostly of players from liberated areas in and around Benghazi kept the dream alive. A draw in Zambia in their last game confirmed Libya's extraordinary qualification for the finals. Once at the finals the Libyans were desperately unlucky not to progress from the group stage. After losing the opening match of the tournament to hosts Equatorial Guinea, they held eventual winners Zambia to a 2-2 draw and then beat pre-tournament favourites Senegal 2-1, Ihaab Boussefi scoring a late winner for Libya.

CAF AFRICA CUP OF NATIONS RECORD

1957-1965 DNE **1968** DNQ **1970** DNE **1972** DNQ **1974-1980** DNE **1982** 2 F (hosts)
1984-1986 DNQ **1988-1998** DNE **2000-2004** DNQ **2006** 14 r1 **2008-2010** DNQ **2012** 10 r1

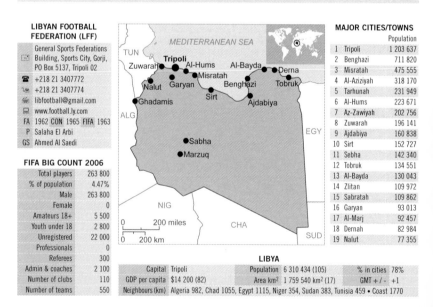

LIBYAN FOOTBALL FEDERATION (LFF)

General Sports Federations Building, Sports City, Gorji, PO Box 5137, Tripoli 02
☎ +218 21 3407772
📠 +218 21 3407774
✉ libfootball@gmail.com
🖥 www.football.ly.com
FA 1962 CON 1965 FIFA 1963
P Salaha El Arbi
GS Ahmed Al Saedi

FIFA BIG COUNT 2006

Total players	263 800
% of population	4.47%
Male	263 800
Female	0
Amateurs 18+	5 500
Youth under 18	2 800
Unregistered	22 000
Professionals	0
Referees	300
Admin & coaches	2 100
Number of clubs	110
Number of teams	550

MAJOR CITIES/TOWNS

		Population
1	Tripoli	1 203 637
2	Benghazi	711 820
3	Misratah	475 555
4	Al-Aziziyah	318 170
5	Tarhunah	231 949
6	Al-Hums	223 671
7	Az-Zawiyah	202 756
8	Zuwarah	196 141
9	Ajdabiya	160 838
10	Sirt	152 727
11	Sebha	142 340
12	Tobruk	134 551
13	Al-Bayda	130 043
14	Zlitan	109 972
15	Sabratah	109 862
16	Garyan	93 013
17	Al-Marj	92 457
18	Dernah	82 984
19	Nalut	77 355

LIBYA

Capital	Tripoli	Population	6 310 434 (105)	% in cities	78%
GDP per capita	$14 200 (82)	Area km²	1 759 540 km² (17)	GMT +/-	+1
Neighbours (km)	Algeria 982, Chad 1055, Egypt 1115, Niger 354, Sudan 383, Tunisia 459 • Coast 1770				

RECENT INTERNATIONAL MATCHES PLAYED BY LIBYA

2007	Opponents	Score		Venue	Comp	Scorers	Att	Referee
7-02	Algeria	L	1-2	Algiers	Fr	Younus Al Shibani [48]		
20-03	Mauritania	D	0-0	Tripoli	Fr			
25-03	Namibia	W	2-1	Tripoli	CNq	Salem Rewani [12], Tarek Tayeb [66]		Abdelrahman SUD
27-05	Botswana	D	0-0	Gaborone	Fr			
2-06	Namibia	L	0-1	Windhoek	CNq			Ncobo RSA
17-06	Ethiopia	W	3-1	Tripoli	CNq	Ahmed Zuwai 2 [10 47], Salem Rewani [22]		Saadallah TUN
22-08	Sudan	L	0-1	Khartoum	Fr			
8-09	Congo DR	D	1-1	Kinshasa	CNq	Khaled Hussein [51]		Djaoupe TOG
16-10	Bahrain	L	0-2	Al Muharraq	Fr			
18-11	Saudi Arabia	W	2-1	Ismailia	Fr	Osama Al Fazzani [24], Omar Dawood [94+]		
21-11	Egypt	D	0-0	Port Said	Fr			
2008								
26-03	Uganda	D	1-1	Kampala	Fr	Younus Al Shibani [89]		
22-05	Zambia	D	2-2	Tripoli	Fr	Osama Salah 2 [13 61]		
27-05	Liberia	W	4-1	Tripoli	Fr	Ali Rahuma [4], Omar Dawood [11], Mohamed El Mughrby [77], Ali Rahuma [82]		
1-06	Ghana	L	0-3	Kumasi	WCq		27 908	Maillet SEY
7-06	Gabon	W	1-0	Tripoli	WCq	Brou OG [5]	30 000	Chaibou NIG
15-06	Lesotho	W	1-0	Bloemfontein	WCq	Ahmed Saad Osman [85]	3 500	Marange ZIM
20-06	Lesotho	W	4-0	Tripoli	WCq	Osama Salah [3], Omar Dawood [50], Younus Al Shibani [68], Hesham Shaban [80]	30 000	Trabelsi TUN
20-08	Senegal	D	0-0	Tripoli	Fr			
24-08	Chad	W	3-0	Tripoli	Fr	Omar Dawood [19], Mohamed Esnani [77], Nader Kara [80]		
28-08	Niger	W	6-2	Tripoli	Fr	Mohamed El Mughrby 2 [34 76], Ahmed Masli [44], Mohamed Zubya [87]		
5-09	Ghana	W	1-0	Tripoli	WCq	Ahmed Saad Osman [86]	45 000	Coulibaly MLI
11-10	Gabon	L	0-1	Libreville	WCq		26 000	Bennett RSA
2009								
11-02	Uruguay	L	2-3	Tripoli	Fr	Mohamed Esnani [31], Osama Salah [57]		
5-10	Kuwait	D	1-1	Cairo	Fr	Ahmed Kerwaa [88]		
2010								
6-01	Benin	L	0-1	Cotonou	Fr			
3-03	Mali	W	2-1	Tripoli	Fr	Mohamed El Mughrby [35p], Khalid Al Deelawi [81]		
5-09	Mozambique	D	0-0	Maputo	CNq			Bangoura GUI
10-10	Zambia	W	1-0	Tripoli	CNq	Ahmed Saad Osman [36]		Gassama GAM
17-11	Niger	D	1-1	Tripoli	Fr	Mohamed Al-Ghandour [69]. W 4-1p		
2011								
9-02	Benin	W	3-2	Tripoli	Fr	Ahmed Zuway [4], Abdullah Al Sharif [16], Ahmed Saad Osman [35]		
28-03	Comoros	W	3-0	Bamako	CNq	Walid Mhadeb [20], Ahmed Wafa [70], Djamal Mahamat [82]		Diatta SEN
5-06	Comoros	D	1-1	Mitsamiouli	CNq	Ihaab Boussefi [43]		
3-09	Mozambique	W	1-0	Cairo	CNq	Djamal Mahamat [28]		
8-10	Zambia	D	0-0	Chingola	CNq			
15-11	Belarus	D	1-1	Dubai	Fr	Ahmed Saad Osman [32]	250	Mohamed UAE
2012								
16-01	Côte d'Ivoire	L	0-1	Abu Dhabi	Fr			
21-01	Equatorial Guinea	L	0-1	Bata	CNr1		35 000	Doue CIV
25-01	Zambia	D	2-2	Bata	CNr1	Ahmed Saad Osman 2 [4 47]	1 500	Coulibaly MLI
29-01	Senegal	W	2-1	Bata	CNr1	Ihaab Boussefi 2 [6 84]	10 000	Seechurn MRI

Fr = Friendly match • CN = CAF African Cup of Nations • WC = FIFA World Cup • q = qualifier • r1 = first round

LIBYA 2010–11

FIRST DIVISION

	Pl	W	D	L	F	A	Pts	Ittihad	Ahly T	Ahly B	Akhdar	Tirsana	Medina	Darnes	Khaleej Sirt	Nasr	Hilal	Olympique	Wahda	Tahaddi	Shat	Najma	Swihli
Al Ittihad	15	12	3	0	32	7	39		1-0		2-0	1-1		3-0		2-1	1-0					3-0	
Al Ahly Tripoli	15	10	3	2	24	11	33			1-0	1-0	2-0	0-0		3-1		1-1	3-3				2-0	
Al Ahly Benghazi	15	9	4	2	19	9	31	1-1				2-1	2-1	2-0	1-0	0-0	1-1			2-1			
Al Akhdar	15	7	3	5	27	18	24		2-0				2-0	2-3		4-1	2-1	1-1				4-0	4-1
Al Tirsana	15	6	5	4	16	11	23							0-0		2-0	1-1	2-1	0-0	4-0	2-0		2-1
Al Medina	15	6	4	5	21	14	22	0-1							2-1	1-1		4-0	4-0	2-1	0-1		
Darnes	15	5	6	4	15	16	21		2-4			2-1	0-0			2-0	1-0		1-1			2-1	
Khaleej Sirt	15	6	2	7	24	31	20									1-3	4-1	1-1	2-2	1-0	3-1	2-1	1-0
Al Nasr	14	5	2	7	16	17	17	2-1							1-2		1-1	2-2	2-0		1-0	2-0	
Al Hilal Benghazi	15	3	7	5	9	17	16		1-1		1-1	1-0			2-4	0-3		0-0			1-0		1-1
Olympique	15	2	9	4	16	19	15	0-1			0-0	3-1					1-1		1-1		0-0	2-0	2-2
Al Wahda	15	3	6	6	16	21	15	2-3	1-2	0-1	2-2				4-3		0-0				0-2		2-2
Al Tahaddi	15	3	5	7	11	20	14	2-2	0-2			0-0		0-0		1-0	1-1				1-2	1-1	1-1
Al Shat	15	3	3	9	12	27	12	0-4	0-1	0-4	1-0	0-0		0-1		2-3						1-1	
Al Najma	15	2	4	9	10	24	10			0-1			1-1	2-1				0-0	1-0	0-1	1-3		1-1
Al Swihli	14	0	8	6	10	16	8	0-1	0-1	1-2	1-2		1-1	0-0			1-1	0-0					

9/08/2010 - 4/02/2011

MEDALS TABLE

		Overall			Lge	Cup		Africa			City
		G	S	B	G	G	S	G	S	B	
1	Al Ittihad	23	4	3	17	6	4			3	Tripoli
2	Al Ahly	15		1	10	5				1	Tripoli
3	Al Ahly	6			4	2					Benghazi
4	Al Medina	4	3		3	1	3				Tripoli
5	Al Nasr	4		1	1	3				1	Benghazi
6	Al Tahaddi	3	1		3		1				Benghazi
7	Al Mahalah	2			2						Tripoli
	Al Shat	2			1	1					Tripoli
9	Al Hilal	1	3			1	3				Benghazi
10	Olympique	1	1		1		1				Az-Zawiyah
11	Al Dahra	1			1						Tripoli
	Khaleej Sirt	1				1					Sirt
13	Al Akhdar		3				3				Al Bayda
14	Al Swihli		1				1				Misurata
	Ittihad Al Asskari		1				1				
	Al Jamarek		1				1				Tripoli
	Al Tirsana		1				1				Tripoli
	Al Yarmouk		1				1				

LCA – ST LUCIA

FIFA/COCA-COLA WORLD RANKING

'93	'94	'95	'96	'97	'98	'99	'00	'01	'02	'03	'04	'05	'06	'07	'08	'09	'10	'11	'12
139	157	114	134	142	139	152	135	130	112	130	114	128	160	180	176	186	181	185	

	2011												High	Low	Av
Jan	Feb	Mar	Apr	May	Jun	Jul	Aug	Sep	Oct	Nov	Dec		108	192	144
181	181	182	185	185	185	183	184	185	179	184	185				

2011 proved to be another difficult year for the St Lucia national team although their 2014 FIFA World Cup qualifying campaign got off to a great start. In a preliminary round tie against Aruba they staged a stirring comback which saw them qualify for the group stage. St Lucia travelled to Oranjestad in the first leg and just after half-time found themselves 2-1 up. The game then ran away from them and Alain Providence's team were left with a 4-2 defeat to overturn in the return at home. A hat-trick from Jamil Joseph helped to do just that but their 4-2 win - only their second victory since 2004 - meant a penalty shoot-out against the Arubans which they won 5-4. The first group stage was a different story altogether for the St Lucians. They did manage to pick up one point, against St Kitts, but there were heavy defeats against Puerto Rico and especially Canada, whose 7-0 victory in Gros Islet equalled their best-ever win set previously in 1904. In club football the Gold Division of the National League was played to a league format without the play-offs at the end and it was won by Vempers Sports Athletic Dramatic Club - VSADC for short. They finished ahead of defending champions Northern United who took part in the 2011 CFU Club Championship, losing to Walking Boyz Co in the first round.

FIFA WORLD CUP RECORD
1930-1990 DNE 1994-2014 DNQ

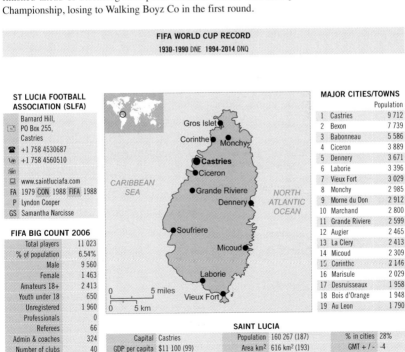

ST LUCIA FOOTBALL ASSOCIATION (SLFA)

Barnard Hill,
PO Box 255,
Castries
☎ +1 758 4530687
📠 +1 758 4560510
✉
🖥 www.saintluciafa.com
FA 1979 CON 1988 FIFA 1988
P Lyndon Cooper
GS Samantha Narcisse

FIFA BIG COUNT 2006

Total players	11 023
% of population	6.54%
Male	9 560
Female	1 463
Amateurs 18+	2 413
Youth under 18	650
Unregistered	1 960
Professionals	0
Referees	66
Admin & coaches	324
Number of clubs	40
Number of teams	125

MAJOR CITIES/TOWNS

		Population
1	Castries	9 712
2	Bexon	7 739
3	Babonneau	5 586
4	Ciceron	3 889
5	Dennery	3 671
6	Laborie	3 396
7	Vieux Fort	3 029
8	Monchy	2 985
9	Morne du Don	2 912
10	Marchand	2 800
11	Grande Riviere	2 599
12	Augier	2 465
13	La Clery	2 413
14	Micoud	2 309
15	Corinthe	2 146
16	Marisule	2 029
17	Desruisseaux	1 958
18	Bois d'Orange	1 948
19	Au Leon	1 790

SAINT LUCIA

Capital	Castries	Population	160 267 (187)	% in cities 28%
GDP per capita	$11 100 (99)	Area km²	616 km² (193)	GMT + / - -4
Neighbours (km)	Coast 158		

RECENT INTERNATIONAL MATCHES PLAYED BY ST LUCIA

2006	Opponents		Score	Venue	Comp	Scorers	Att	Referee
28-07	Guyana	L	2-3	Linden	Fr	Titus Elva [62], Levi Gilbert [70]	1 800	Lancaster GUY
30-07	Guyana	L	0-2	Georgetown	Fr		3 500	James GUY
27-09	Jamaica	L	0-4	Kingston	CCq		4 000	Tamayo CUB
29-09	Haiti	L	1-7	Kingston	CCq	Germal Valcin [90p]	3 000	Callendar BRB
1-10	St Vincent/Grenadines	L	0-8	Kingston	CCq		3 000	Tamayo CUB

2007

No international matches played in 2007

2008

6-02	Turks and Caicos Isl	L	1-2	Providenciales	WCq	Nyhime Gilbert [92+]	2 200	Whittaker CAY
26-03	Turks and Caicos Isl	W	2-0	Vieux Fort	WCq	Kenwin McPhee [28], Titus Elva [85]	1 200	Forde BRB
18-05	Antigua and Barbuda	L	1-6	St John's	Fr	Barnet Bledman [91+]	4 000	Willett ATG
14-06	Guatemala	L	0-6	Guatemala City	WCq		24 600	Archundia MEX
21-06	Guatemala	L	1-3	Los Angeles	WCq	Kenwin McPhee [45]	12 000	Wijngaarde SUR

2009

No international matches played in 2009

2010

10-09	St Vincent/Grenadines	L	1-5	Vieux Fort	Fr	Jamil Joseph [10]	400	St Catherine LCA
21-09	Trinidad and Tobago	L	0-3	St John's	Fr		205	St Catherine LCA
23-09	Antigua and Barbuda	L	0-5	St John's	Fr		500	Willett ATG
13-10	Guyana	L	0-1	Paramaribo	CCq		550	Davis TRI
15-10	Suriname	L	1-2	Paramaribo	CCq	Zacchaeus Polius [77]	750	Baptiste DMA
17-10	Netherlands Antilles	D	2-2	Paramaribo	CCq	Zacchaeus Polius 2 [7 35]	2 800	Willet ATG

2011

8-07	Aruba	L	2-4	Oranjestad	WCq	Kevin Edward [20], Cliff Magnam Valcin [46]	300	Foster CAY
12-07	Aruba	W	4-2	Castries	WCq	Jamil Joseph 3 [14 29 74], Kurt Frederick [74]. W 5-4p	500	Lancaster GUY
21-08	Barbados	L	0-4	Bridgetown	Fr		3 500	Skeete BRB
2-09	Canada	L	1-4	Toronto	WCq	Tremain Paul [7]	11 500	Marrufo USA
6-09	St Kitts and Nevis	L	2-4	Gros Islet	WCq	Zaine Pierre [65], Cliff Magnam Valcin [84]	2 005	Thomas JAM
7-10	Canada	L	0-7	Gros Islet	WCq	Match awarded to Canada	1 005	Vidal PAN
11-10	St Kitts and Nevis	D	1-1	Basseterre	WCq	Cliff Magnam Valcin [74]	1 000	Skeete BRB
11-11	Puerto Rico	L	0-4	Bayamon	WCq	Match awarded to Puerto Rico	350	Holder BRB
14-11	Puerto Rico	L	0-3	Mayaguez	WCq		1 050	Willett ATG

Fr = Friendly match • CC = Digicel Caribbean Cup • WC = FIFA World Cup • q = qualifier

BLACKHEART/KASHIF & SHANGHAI FOOTBALL TOURNAMENT 2011

First Round		Quarter-finals		Semi-finals		Final	
Anse La Raye	3						
Babonneauu	0	Anse La Raye	1				
Micoud	2 4p	Desruisseaux	0				
Desruisseaux	2 2p			Anse La Raye	4		
Vieux Fort North	1			Mon Repos	1		
Mabouya Valley	0	Vieux Fort North	0				
Gros Ilet	1	Mon Repos	1				
Mon Repos	2					Anse La Raye	1
Dennery	4					Canaries	0
Laborie	0	Dennery	2				
South Castries	1	Soufrière	1				
Soufrière	2			Dennery	2 1p		
Marchland	2			Canaries	2 4p		
Central Castries	1	Marchland	1				
Vieux Fort South	1	Canaries	4	3rd place: Dennery 4-3 Mon Repos			
Canaries	2						

CUP FINAL

12-06-2011

LES – LESOTHO

FIFA/COCA-COLA WORLD RANKING

'93	'94	'95	'96	'97	'98	'99	'00	'01	'02	'03	'04	'05	'06	'07	'08	'09	'10	'11	'12
138	135	149	162	149	140	154	136	126	132	120	144	145	160	154	161	150	170	147	

						2011									
Jan	Feb	Mar	Apr	May	Jun	Jul	Aug	Sep	Oct	Nov	Dec		High	Low	Av
170	171	168	177	176	178	184	185	160	162	148	147		120	185	145

Lesotho returned to international action in 2011 after a hiatus of some 20 months having made a decision to divert the money usually used to support the national team into developing a promising generation of players at under-20 level. Lesotho had surprisingly qualified for the African U-20 Championship and had high hopes of qualification for the FIFA U-20 World Cup in Colombia. At the finals in South Africa, however, Lesotho failed to win a game. The wisdom of the experiment came under further question when the under-20 coach Leslie Notsi moved up to the national side but instead of taking the bulk of his players with him to form a new-look team, he picked just a handful of the youngsters. His decision looked justified when Lesotho successfully progressed through the first phase of Africa's qualifiers for the 2014 FIFA World Cup, beating Burundi 3-2 on aggregate in November. In club football, Lesotho Correctional Services finally lived up to their billing as the country's most exciting side by taking the Premier League on goal difference from Lesotho Defence Force. The two sides played each other in final fixture of the campaign with a 1-1 draw being enough to ensure the title for the prison guards. Their coach Mafa Ramakau, a former national team mentor, has now won nine championships with different clubs in his long career.

CAF AFRICA CUP OF NATIONS RECORD

1957-1972 DNQ 1974 DNQ 1976-1978 DNE 1980-1982 DNQ 1984-1992 DNE 1994 DNQ 1996 Withdrew 1998 DNE 2000-2010 DNQ 2012 DNE

LESOTHO FOOTBALL ASSOCIATION (FAL)

Old Polo Ground,
PO Box 1879,
Maseru-100
☎ +266 22311879
✆ +266 22310586
✉ fal@leo.co.ls
🖳 www.lesothofootball.com
FA 1932 CON 1964 FIFA 1964
P Salemane Phafane
GS Mofihli Makoele

FIFA BIG COUNT 2006

Total players	110 000
% of population	5.44%
Male	109 900
Female	100
Amateurs 18+	27 200
Youth under 18	2 300
Unregistered	5 500
Professionals	0
Referees	100
Admin & coaches	2 200
Number of clubs	110
Number of teams	1 000

MAJOR CITIES/TOWNS

		Population
1	Maseru	247 237
2	Hlotse	44 148
3	Mafeteng	39 876
4	Teyateyaneng	26 554
5	Maputsoa	23 037
6	Mohale's Hoek	21 869
7	Qacha's Nek	16 606
8	Quthing	6 453
9	Mokhotlong	5 980
10	Butha Buthe	5 868
11	Thaba-Tseka	4 767

KINGDOM OF LESOTHO

Capital	Maseru	Population	2 130 819 (142)	% in cities	25%
GDP per capita	$1600 (194)	Area km²	30 355 km² (141)	GMT +/-	+2
Neighbours (km)	South Africa 909				

RECENT INTERNATIONAL MATCHES PLAYED BY LESOTHO

2008	Opponents		Score	Venue	Comp	Scorers	Att	Referee
8-06	Ghana	L	2-3	Bloemfontein	WCq	Sello Musa [89], Lehlohonolo Seema [90]	8 000	Gasingwa RWA
15-06	Libya	L	0-1	Bloemfontein	WCq		3 500	Marange ZIM
20-06	Libya	L	0-4	Tripoli	WCq		30 000	Trabelsi TUN
28-06	Gabon	L	0-2	Libreville	WCq		15 000	Mendy GAM
20-07	Malawi	L	0-1	Secunda	CCr1			Seechurn MRI
22-07	Namibia	D	1-1	Secunda	CCr1	Thabane Rankara [80]		Seechurn MRI
24-07	Comoros	W	1-0	Secunda	CCr1	Moli Lesesa [50]		Labrosse SEY
30-08	Botswana	L	0-1	Gaborone	Fr			
7-09	Gabon	L	0-3	Bloemfontein	WCq		1 500	Abd El Fatah
11-10	Ghana	L	0-3	Sekondi	WCq		20 000	Rahman SUD
2009								
1-04	Botswana	D	0-0	Maseru	Fr			
19-06	Swaziland	D	1-1	Manzini	Fr	Thapelo Tale [72]		
21-06	Swaziland	D	1-1	Lobamba	Fr	Thapelo Mokhele [41]		
12-08	Zimbabwe	D	1-1	Bulawayo	Fr	Thabo Motsweli [31p]		
11-09	Malaysia	L	0-5	Kuala Lumpur	Fr			
19-10	Zimbabwe	D	2-2	Harare	CCr1	Thabiso Maile 2 [50p 90p]		Ramocha BOT
21-10	Mauritius	W	1-0	Harare	CCr1	Mophane Boakang [88]		Ngosi MWI
2010								
No international matches played in 2010								
2011								
20-08	Swaziland	D	0-0	Maseru	Fr			
22-08	Swaziland	L	0-1	Maseru	Fr			
30-08	Botswana	W	2-1	Gaborone	Fr			
31-10	Namibia	D	0-0	Windhoek	Fr			
6-11	Congo DR	L	0-3	Pretoria	Fr			
11-11	Burundi	W	1-0	Maseru	WCq	Lehlomela Ramabele [82]	5 000	Shikongo NAM
15-11	Burundi	D	2-2	Bujumbura	WCq	Thapelo Tale [16], Bokang Mothoana [22]	7 200	Raphael MWI
21-12	Botswana	L	0-3	Rustenburg	Fr			

Fr = Friendly match • CN = CAF African Cup of Nations • CC = COSAFA Castle Cup • WC = FIFA World Cup • q = qualifier • r1 = first round group

LESOTHO 2010-11

BUDDIE PREMIER LEAGUE

	Pl	W	D	L	F	A	Pts	LCS Maseru	LDF Maseru	Bantu United	Linare	Matlama	LMPS Maseru	Likhopo	Lioli	Maduma	Joy	Mphatlalatsane	Lerotholi	Swallows	Mabeoana
LCS Maseru †	26	15	10	1	43	17	55		1-2	2-2	2-0	0-0	2-0	4-2	1-1	5-1	3-2	1-0	2-1	2-0	1-0
LDF Maseru	26	16	7	3	39	19	55	1-1		2-1	2-2	3-2	3-2	1-0	2-1	3-1	0-1	2-2	2-0	1-0	1-0
Bantu United	26	14	6	6	36	23	48	1-1	0-0		1-0	1-2	1-1	1-2	1-0	2-0	2-0	3-1	1-0	3-0	1-0
Linare	26	12	8	6	37	24	44	0-0	0-1	1-2		1-0	1-1	2-2	1-1	0-1	0-0	3-1	3-1	2-1	6-2
Matlama	26	10	10	6	27	18	40	0-1	0-0	1-0	2-1		1-1	0-1	0-0	0-0	1-1	1-1	1-0	4-1	2-1
LMPS Maseru	26	10	8	8	34	28	38	0-1	0-0	3-0	0-2	0-2		0-0	1-1	2-1	2-2	3-2	2-0	1-2	3-1
Likhopo	26	10	7	9	27	27	37	0-0	1-0	0-2	1-3	1-1	0-1		0-0	0-2	2-1	2-1	1-2	2-0	3-0
Lioli	26	9	9	8	25	22	36	0-0	0-1	2-1	0-1	0-0	1-0	1-2		4-2	1-0	3-1	1-0	1-0	2-0
Maduma	26	9	9	8	31	33	36	2-3	1-0	1-2	1-1	1-0	2-2	1-2	0-0		3-1	3-3	3-1	2-1	1-0
Joy	26	8	9	9	24	24	33	0-1	1-1	0-1	0-1	0-0	1-0	2-1	3-1	0-0		1-0	0-0	1-0	1-0
Mphatlalatsane	26	4	11	11	29	37	23	1-1	1-2	1-1	0-1	2-3	1-3	1-0	3-1	0-0	0-0		2-0	2-0	0-0
Lerotholi Polytechnic	26	6	5	15	17	34	23	0-3	0-2	1-2	1-1	1-0	0-2	0-1	0-0	0-0	2-1	2-2		2-1	0-1
Mazenod Swallows	26	2	7	17	15	42	13	0-0	0-3	1-3	1-2	0-1	1-3	0-0	1-0	0-0	2-2	1-1	0-2		1-1
Mabeoana	26	1	6	19	13	49	9	1-5	1-4	1-1	0-2	0-3	0-1	1-1	1-3	1-2	0-3	0-0	0-1	1-1	

11/09/2010 - 29/05/2011 • † Qualified for the CAF Champions League • Match in bold awarded

LIB – LEBANON

FIFA/COCA-COLA WORLD RANKING

'93	'94	'95	'96	'97	'98	'99	'00	'01	'02	'03	'04	'05	'06	'07	'08	'09	'10	'11	'12
108	129	134	97	90	85	111	110	93	119	115	105	125	126	134	150	148	154	111	

						2011									
Jan	Feb	Mar	Apr	May	Jun	Jul	Aug	Sep	Oct	Nov	Dec		High	Low	Av
169	172	169	178	178	177	159	160	146	146	111	111		85	178	120

Lebanon's progress to the final phase of qualifying for the 2014 FIFA World Cup finals was one of the biggest stories in Asian football throughout 2011 and early 2012. Their place amongst the final 10 teams in Asia fighting for a place in the finals in Brazil was unlikely in itself but it also came against the backdrop of a run of poor results which had seen the team lose six out of the first seven games played during the year. However, the return of German coach Theo Bucker transformed the fortunes of the team, despite a heavy 6-0 loss against Korea Republic in the first match of their qualifying group. The UAE were convincingly beaten 3-1 at home in the next match but it was the away win over Kuwait and the extraordinary 2-1 victory over the Koreans in Beirut which really grabbed the headlines and saw them through to the final round. There they face Korea again along with Iran, Uzbekistan and Qatar in the knowledge that a place in the top two would take the team to the finals in Brazil. In club football, Al Ahed continued their recent rise in fortunes when they won the Premier League for the third time in four seasons. Ahed also broke new ground when they beat Safa 3-0 in the FA Cup Final. It was their fourth cup triumph in eight seasons but it won them the double for the first time in the club's history.

FIFA WORLD CUP RECORD
1930-1990 DNE 1994-2010 DNQ

LEBANESE FOOTBALL ASSOCIATION (FLFA)

	Verdun Street -
	Bristol Radwan Center, PO Box 4732, Beirut
☎	+961 1 745745
📠	+961 1 349529
✉	libanfa@cyberia.net.lb
💻	
FA	1933 CON 1964 FIFA 1935
P	Hachem Haydar
GS	Jehad Shahaf

FIFA BIG COUNT 2006

Total players	318 485
% of population	8.22%
Male	318 385
Female	100
Amateurs 18+	12 240
Youth under 18	6 130
Unregistered	300 000
Professionals	50
Referees	184
Admin & coaches	3 311
Number of clubs	178
Number of teams	877

MAJOR CITIES/TOWNS

		Population
1	Beirut	2 006 452
2	Tripoli	190 793
3	Juniyah	99 581
4	Baalbek	81 842
5	Sidon (Saida)	58 364
6	Zahlah	53 627
7	Kafr Ass	50 478
8	Alayh	45 074
9	Jubayl	44 807
10	Sur (Tyre)	41 824
11	Nabatiyat	35 333
12	Riyak	29 648
13	Talabaya	28 046
14	Ad Damur	27 216
15	Al Hirmil	23 834
16	Ber Al Yaas	23 338
17	Arsal	17 081
18	Bint Jubayl	16 686
19	Amzit	15 629

AL JUMHURIYAH AL LUBNANIYAH • LEBANESE REPUBLIC

Capital	Beirut	Population 4 017 095 (126)	% in cities 87%
GDP per capita	$11 100 (98)	Area km² 10 400 km² (169)	GMT + / - +2
Neighbours (km) Israel 79, Syria 375 • Coast 225			

RECENT INTERNATIONAL MATCHES PLAYED BY LEBANON

2007 Opponents	Score		Venue	Comp	Scorers	Att	Referee
16-06 Syria	L	0-1	Amman	WAr1			
20-06 Jordan	L	0-3	Amman	WAr1			
23-09 UAE	D	1-1	Dubai	Fr	Mahmoud El Ali [17]		
8-10 India	W	4-1	Sidon	WCq	Roda Antar [33], Mohammad Ghaddar 2 [62 76], Mahmoud El Ali [63]	500	Al Fadhli KUW
30-10 India	D	2-2	Goa	WCq	Mohammad Ghaddar 2 [76p 88]	10 000	Mujghef JOR
2008							
2-01 Kuwait	L	2-3	Kuwait City	Fr	Mohammad Ghaddar [14p], Mahmoud El Ali [41]		
20-01 China PR	D	0-0	Zhongshan	Fr			
28-01 Jordan	L	1-4	Amman	Fr	Tarek El Ali [77]		
6-02 Uzbekistan	L	0-1	Beirut	WCq		800	Al Hilali OMA
26-03 Singapore	L	0-2	Singapore	WCq		10 118	Takayama JPN
9-04 Maldives	W	4-0	Beirut	ACq	Mahmoud El Ali [5], Ali Yaacoub [11], Abbas Ali Atwi [13p], Mohammad Ghaddar [40]		
23-04 Maldives	W	2-1	Male	ACq	Mohamed Korhani [9], Nasrat Al Jamal [74]		
27-05 Qatar	L	1-2	Doha	Fr	Mohammad Ghaddar [20]		
2-06 Saudi Arabia	L	1-4	Riyadh	WCq	Mahmoud El Ali [42]	8 000	Al Fadhli KUW
7-06 Saudi Arabia	L	1-2	Riyadh	WCq	Mohammad Ghaddar [93+]	2 000	Tongkhan THA
14-06 Uzbekistan	L	0-3	Tashkent	WCq		7 000	Breeze AUS
22-06 Singapore	L	1-2	Beirut	WCq	Khaizan OG [62]	500	Moradi IRN
2009							
14-01 Vietnam	L	1-3	Hanoi	ACq	Akram Moghrabi [73]	13 000	Toma JPN
21-01 Thailand	L	1-2	Phuket	Fr	Mahmoud El Ali [50]	15 000	Veerapool THA
23-01 Korea DPR	W	1-0	Phuket	Fr	Abbas Atwi [2p]		
28-01 Syria	L	0-2	Saida	ACq		300	Balideh QAT
1-04 Namibia	D	1-1	Saida	Fr	Zakaria Shararah [72]		
19-08 India	W	1-0	New Dehli	Fr	Ali Al Saadi [4]		Abdul Hannan BAN
22-08 Sri Lanka	L	3-4	New Dehli	Fr	Akram Moghrabi 9, Ali Al Saadi 45, Korhani [97+p]		Rowan IND
25-08 Kyrgyzstan	D	1-1	New Dehli	Fr	Abbas Atwi [56]		Abdul Hannan BAN
27-08 Syria	L	0-1	New Dehli	Fr			Rowan IND
14-11 China PR	L	0-2	Beirut	ACq		2 000	Albadwawi UAE
22-11 China PR	L	0-1	Zheijang	ACq		21 520	Breeze AUS
2010							
6-01 Vietnam	D	1-1	Saida	ACq	Mahmoud El Ali [19]	50	Kovalenko UZB
3-03 Syria	L	0-4	Damascus	ACq		16 000	Kim Dong Jin KOR
2011							
2-07 Kuwait	L	0-6	Beirut	Fr			
9-07 Oman	L	0-1	Beirut	Fr			
17-07 UAE	L	2-6	Al Ain	Fr	Mahmoud El Ali 2 [29 67]		
23-07 Bangladesh	W	4-0	Beirut	WCq	Hassan Maatouk [16], Mahmoud El Ali [27], Ali Al Saadi [55], Tarek El Ali [64]	2 000	Auda IRQ
28-07 Bangladesh	L	0-2	Dhaka	WCq		11 000	Aonrak THA
17-08 Syria	L	2-3	Saida	Fr	Hassan Maatouk [18], Mohammad Ghaddar [71]		
2-09 Korea Republic	L	0-6	Goyang	WCq		37 655	Abdul Bashir SIN
6-09 UAE	W	3-1	Beirut	WCq	Mohammad Ghaddar [37p], Akram Moghrabi [52], Roda Antar [83]	4 000	Faghani IRN
11-10 Kuwait	D	2-2	Beirut	WCq	Hassan Maatouk 2 [15 86p]	32 000	Toma JPN
11-11 Kuwait	W	1-0	Kuwait City	WCq	Mahmoud El Ali [57]	17 500	Kovalenko UZB
15-11 Korea Republic	W	2-1	Beirut	WCq	Ali Al Saadi [4], Abbas Ali Atwi [32]	35 000	Al Ghamdi KSA

Fr = Friendly match • WA = West Asian Cup • AR = Arab Cup • AC = AFC Asian Cup • WC = FIFA World Cup • q = qualifier
r1 = first round group

LEBANON NATIONAL TEAM HISTORICAL RECORDS

Past Coaches

Joseph Nalbandian 1958-69 • Joseph Abou Murad 1971-73 • Adnan Meckdache 1974-76 • Joseph Abou Murad 1976-78 • Adnan Meckdache 1987-92 • Adnan Al Shargi 1993 • Terry Yorath WAL 1995-97 • Dietmar Werner GER 1998 • Mahmoud Saad EGY 1998-2000 • Josip Skoblar CRO 2000 • Theo Bucker GER 2000-01 • Richard Tardi 2002 • Mohammad Qwid SYR 2004-05 • Adnan Al Shargi 2005 • Emile Rustom 2005-06 • Adnan Meckdache 2006-08 • Emile Rustom 2009-11 • Theo Bucker 2011-

LEBANON 2010-11

PREMIER LEAGUE

	Pl	W	D	L	F	A	Pts	Ahed	Safa	Nijmeh	Ansar	Mabarra	Racing	Akhaa	Salam Sour	Shabab S	Tadamon	Shabab G	Islah
Al Ahed ‡	22	17	4	1	51	18	55		1-0	5-0	2-2	2-1	0-1	1-0	2-0	3-1	2-0	2-0	3-0
Safa ‡	22	14	3	5	38	21	45	2-3		1-3	1-0	3-1	0-0	3-1	3-1	1-0	3-0	3-0	1-0
Al Nijmeh	22	13	5	4	34	19	44	0-2	2-1		0-1	1-1	1-0	2-1	2-0	2-1	1-0	5-0	3-2
Al Ansar	22	12	7	3	40	15	43	0-0	2-1	1-1		3-2	0-0	3-0	6-0	3-0	1-0	1-2	2-1
Al Mabarra	22	10	6	6	34	26	36	2-2	2-2	1-0	1-1		2-1	0-0	3-0	3-2	2-0	1-3	2-0
Racing Club Beirut	22	7	8	7	26	20	29	3-4	0-1	0-0	2-0	2-1		2-2	2-0	0-0	0-0	1-1	4-0
Al Akhaa Al Ahli Aley	22	6	6	10	17	25	24	0-1	1-1	0-1	0-1	1-1	2-1		1-0	2-1	1-0	1-1	1-0
Salam Sur (Tyre)	22	7	2	13	19	45	23	1-5	1-3	0-3	0-5	1-0	1-0	2-1		2-1	3-2	3-0	2-0
Shabab Al Sahel	22	6	4	12	21	33	22	1-2	1-2	0-0	0-5	1-3	2-1	1-0	1-1		0-1	2-0	3-2
Al Tadamon Sur (Tyre)	22	4	8	10	15	23	20	2-2	1-2	1-1	0-0	1-0	1-2	0-1	1-1	3-0		0-0	1-1
Shabab Al Ghazieh	22	5	5	12	17	37	20	2-3	0-2	1-4	0-0	0-2	1-3	2-0	1-0	0-1	0-1		1-1
Al Islah	22	0	4	18	14	44	4	0-4	1-2	0-2	2-3	0-1	2-2	0-1	1-1	0-2	0-1	1-2	

9/10/2010 - 24/04/2011 • ‡ Qualified for AFC Cup
Top scorers: **15** - Hassan Maatouk, Al Ahed • **13** - Tarek El Ali, Mabarra • **11** - Mahmoud El Ali, Al Ahed • **10** - Akram Moghrabi, Nijmeh

ELITE CUP 2011

Semi-finals

Al Ahed	4
Al Mabarra	1
Racing Club Beirut	0
Safa	4

Finals

Al Ahed	4
Safa	2

Sports City, Beirut
24-09-2011

MEDALS TABLE

		Overall			Lge	Cup		Asia			City
		G	S	B	G	G	S	G	S	B	
1	Al Ansar	25	3		13	12	3				Beirut
2	Al Nijmeh	12	6	2	7	5	5	1	2		Beirut
3	Homenetmen	10	3		7	3	3				Beirut
4	Al Nahda	9	1		5	4	1				
5	Al Ahed	7	2		3	4	2				Beirut
6	Homenmen	4	4		4	4					Beirut
7	Racing Club	3	2		3	2					Beirut
8	Shabiba Al Mazra	3	1		1	2	1				Beirut
	Sika	3	1		3	1					Beirut
10	American University	3			3						Beirut
11	Safa SC	2	8			2	7			1	Beirut
12	Tripoli SC	2	1		1	1	1				Tripoli
	Helmi Sport	2	1			2	1				
14	Shabab Al Sahel	1	2			1	2				Beirut
15	Al Tadamon Sur	1	1			1	1				Tyre
	Al Mabarra	1	1			1	1				
17	Al Bourj	1				1					

FA CUP 2010-11

Round of 16

Al Ahed *	2
Shabab Al Ghazieh	1
Al Tadamon Sur *	0
Al Akhaa Al Ahli	1
Salam Zgharta	2
Al Tadamon Beirut *	0
Salam Sur *	0
Shabab Al Sahel	4
Al Ansar	4
Al Mahabba Trables *	0
Racing Club Beirut *	1
Al Mabarra	2
Al Nijmeh *	3
Al Shabab Trables	0
Al Islah	0 2p
Safa *	0 3p

Quarter-finals

Al Ahed	5
Al Akhaa Al Ahli *	1
Salam Zgharta	0
Shabab Al Sahel *	2
Al Ansar *	w/o
Al Mabarra	
Al Nijmeh *	0
Safa	1

Semi-finals

Al Ahed *	2
Shabab Al Sahel	1
Al Ansar	1
Safa *	2

Final

Al Ahed	3
Safa ‡	0

CUP FINAL

18-05-2011
Scorers - Mahmoud El Ali 2 [30] [72], Ali Bazzi [90]

* Home team • ‡ Qualified for AFC Cup

LIE – LIECHTENSTEIN

FIFA/COCA-COLA WORLD RANKING

'93	'94	'95	'96	'97	'98	'99	'00	'01	'02	'03	'04	'05	'06	'07	'08	'09	'10	'11	'12
160	156	157	154	158	159	125	147	150	147	148	142	122	158	122	149	154	148	132	

	2011													High	Low	Av
	Jan	Feb	Mar	Apr	May	Jun	Jul	Aug	Sep	Oct	Nov	Dec		High	Low	Av
	148	147	143	153	153	120	118	119	118	126	130	132		118	165	145

Only twice before - in 1981 and 2007 - has the national team of Liechtenstein won two games during the course of a year but they equalled that in 2011 with a 1-0 victory over San Marino in a friendly and with an impressive 2-0 win over Lithuania in the qualifiers for Euro 2012, a result that took Liechtenstein to a record high of 118 in the FIFA/Coca-Cola World Ranking. A decade previously the match against San Marino would have been a real battle of the minnows but Liechtenstein have moved on since then, making the most of the resources available to them. Wins may be a rarity but as they showed in the return match against Lithuania they are perfectly capable of resolute defending for a draw which is what they achieved in Kaunas. The other highlight of the season came in a friendly against Switzerland in Vaduz in which Mario Frick became the first player from Liechtenstein to reach 100 caps for his country. In club football, FC Vaduz romped home to a 13th consecutive cup triumph scoring 21 goals in their three matches and they continued to impress in the Swiss Challenge League, just missing out on promotion to the Super League. Eric Orie's team finished only two points behind Servette in the play-off spot as they fought to regain their place in the top flight of Swiss football.

UEFA EUROPEAN CHAMPIONSHIP RECORD
1960-1992 DNE   1996-2012 DNQ

LIECHTENSTEINER FUSSBALLVERBAND (LFV)

Landstrasse 149,
Postfach 165,
Vaduz 9490
☎ +423 2374747
📠 +423 2374748
📧 info@lfv.li
🖥 www.lfv.li
FA 1934 CON 1992 FIFA 1976
P Reinhard Walser
GS Roland Ospelt

FIFA BIG COUNT 2006

Total players	3 315
% of population	9.75%
Male	2 990
Female	325
Amateurs 18+	795
Youth under 18	1 400
Unregistered	310
Professionals	10
Referees	34
Admin & coaches	240
Number of clubs	7
Number of teams	95

MAJOR CITIES/TOWNS

		Population
1	Schaan	5 747
2	Vaduz	5 070
3	Triesen	4 674
4	Balzers	4 450
5	Eschen	4 141
6	Mauren	3 718
7	Triesenberg	2 566
8	Ruggell	1 920
9	Gamprin	1 463
10	Schellenberg	1 032
11	Planken	387

FUERSTENTUM LIECHTENSTEIN • PRINCIPALITY OF LIECHTENSTEIN

Capital	Vaduz	Population	34 761 (210)	% in cities	14%
GDP per capita	$118 000 (1)	Area km²	160 km² (218)	GMT + / -	+1
Neighbours (km)	Austria 34, Switzerland 41				

RECENT INTERNATIONAL MATCHES PLAYED BY LIECHTENSTEIN

2009	Opponents	Score		Venue	Comp	Scorers	Att	Referee
11-02	Iceland	L	0-2	La Manga	Fr		150	Reinert FRO
28-03	Germany	L	0-4	Leipzig	WCq		43 368	Ishchenko UKR
1-04	Russia	L	0-1	Vaduz	WCq		5 679	McKeon IRL
6-06	Finland	L	1-2	Helsinki	WCq	Mario Frick 13	20 319	Kovarik CZE
12-08	Portugal	L	0-3	Vaduz	Fr		5 525	Bertolini SUI
5-09	Russia	L	0-3	St Petersburg	WCq		21 000	Constantin ROU
9-09	Finland	D	1-1	Vaduz	WCq	Michele Polverino 75	3 132	Panic BIH
10-10	Azerbaijan	L	0-2	Vaduz	WCq		1 635	Radovanovic NME
14-10	Wales	L	0-2	Vaduz	WCq		1 858	Kaldma EST
14-11	Croatia	L	0-5	Vinkovci	Fr		10 000	Fabian HUN
2010								
11-08	Iceland	D	1-1	Reykjavik	Fr	Michael Stocklasa 70	3 000	Buttimer IRL
3-09	Spain	L	0-4	Vaduz	ECq		6 100	Yildirim TUR
7-09	Scotland	L	1-2	Glasgow	ECq	Mario Frick 47	37 050	Shvestov UKR
12-10	Czech Republic	L	0-2	Vaduz	ECq		2 555	Sukhina RUS
17-11	Estonia	D	1-1	Tallinn	Fr	Mario Frick 35	1 909	Gvardis RUS
2011								
9-02	San Marino	W	1-0	Serravalle	Fr	Michele Polverino 57		Banti ITA
29-03	Czech Republic	L	0-2	Ceske Budejovice	ECq		6 600	Hategan ROU
3-06	Lithuania	W	2-0	Vaduz	ECq	Philippe Erne 7, Michele Polverino 36	1 886	Kuchin KAZ
10-08	Switzerland	L	1-2	Vaduz	Fr	Marco Ritzberger 51	5 444	Eisner AUT
2-09	Lithuania	D	0-0	Kaunas	ECq		3 500	Johnsen NOR
6-09	Spain	L	0-6	Logrono	ECq		15 660	Lechner AUT
8-10	Scotland	L	0-1	Vaduz	ECq		5 636	Hagen NOR
11-11	Hungary	L	0-5	Budapest	Fr		23 000	Balaj ROU

Fr = Friendly match • EC = UEFA EURO 2012 • WC = FIFA World Cup • q = qualifier

LIECHTENSTEINER NATIONAL TEAM HISTORICAL RECORDS

Caps	**104** - Mario Frick 1993- • **97** - Martin Stocklasa 1996- • **90** - Peter Jehle 1998- • **81** - Thomas Beck 1998- • **78** - Daniel Hasler 1993-2007 • **73** - Martin Telser 1996-2007 • **72** - Ronny Buchel 1998-2010 • **70** - Michael Stocklasa 1998- • **68** - Franz Burgmeier 2001-
Goals	**16** - Mario Frick 1993- • **7** - Franz Burgmeier 2001- • **5** - Martin Stocklasa 1996- & Thomas Beck 1998- • **2** - Michele Polverino 2007- • **2** - Michael Stocklasa 1998- ; Fabio D'Elia 2001- & Benjamin Fischer 2005-
Past Coaches	Dietrich Weise GER 1994-96 • Alfred Riedl AUT 1997-98 • Ralf Loose GER 1998-2003 • Walter Hormann AUT 2003-04 • Martin Andermatt SUI 2004-06 • Hans-Peter Zaug SUI 2006-

LIECHTENSTEINER CUP 2010–11

Second Preliminary round		Quarter-finals		Semi-finals		Final
FC Vaduz	Bye					
		FC Vaduz	8			
FC Schaan	1	FC Ruggell	1			
FC Ruggell	2					
				FC Vaduz	8	
USV Eschen/Mauren-2	Bye			FC Triesenberg	0	
		USV Eschen/Mauren-2	1			
FC Schaan	0	**FC Triesenberg**	2			
FC Triesenberg	1					**FC Vaduz ‡**	5
FC Balzers	Bye					USV Eschen/Mauren	0
		FC Balzers	13			
USV Eschen/Mauren-3	1	FC Triesen	1			**CUP FINAL**
FC Triesen	4			FC Balzers	1	Rheinparkstadion, Vaduz
FC Balzers-3	4			**USV Eschen/Mauren**	2	25-04-2011, Att: 2155, Ref: Hanni
FC Triesen-2	1	FC Balzers-3	0			Scorers - David Harrer 38, Mario
		USV Eschen/Mauren	6			Sara 52, Roland Schwegler 64,
USV Eschen/Mauren	Bye			‡ Qualified for the Europa League		Arlan 73, Diego Ciccone 92+

LTU – LITHUANIA

FIFA/COCA-COLA WORLD RANKING

'93	'94	'95	'96	'97	'98	'99	'00	'01	'02	'03	'04	'05	'06	'07	'08	'09	'10	'11	'12
85	59	43	48	45	54	50	85	97	100	101	100	100	69	59	51	62	55	92	

	2011														
	Jan	Feb	Mar	Apr	May	Jun	Jul	Aug	Sep	Oct	Nov	Dec	High	Low	Av
	55	55	54	47	48	58	58	56	75	85	94	92	37	118	72

After a promising start to their Euro 2012 qualifying group, Lithuania saw their campaign fall to pieces after having put themselves in contention for a play-off spot in a group that was always going to be won by Spain. A defeat at the hands of Liechtenstein in Vaduz was followed by a draw against the same opponents at home in Kaunas, and in the end Lithuania stood just a point ahead of Liechtenstein in the final standings. That spelt the end for coach Raimondas Zutautas and he was replaced at the start of 2012 by the Romanian-born Hungarian Csaba Laszlo. In club football, newly promoted FBK Kaunas were expected to follow up their sensational season in 2010 and challenge the dominance of Ekranas Panevezys. Between them the two clubs have won every championship since 1999 but FBK failed to deliver and were relegated after being denied a licence for the 2012 season. Instead, Ekranas won a fourth consecutive championship with all of them coming under coach Valdas Urbonas. It was their sixth overall and thanks to their 4-2 win over Banga in the Cup Final, they now stand just two trophies shy of FBK's record haul of 12 in the league and cup. In the Cup Final against Banga, Ekranas were 2-0 down before staging a great comeback to win 4-2 after extra-time.

UEFA EUROPEAN CHAMPIONSHIP RECORD
1960-1992 DNE (Played as part of the Soviet Union) **1996-2012** DNQ

LITHUANIAN FOOTBALL FEDERATION (LFF)

📮 Seimyniskiu 15, Vilnius 09312

☎ +370 52638741
📠 +370 52638740
📧 info@lff.lt
🖥 www.lff.lt
FA 1922 CON 1992 FIFA 1992
P Liutauras Varanavicius
GS Julius Kvedaras

FIFA BIG COUNT 2006

Total players	135 874
% of population	3.79%
Male	119 020
Female	16 854
Amateurs 18+	3 510
Youth under 18	9 764
Unregistered	38 100
Professionals	340
Referees	195
Admin & coaches	1 370
Number of clubs	64
Number of teams	367

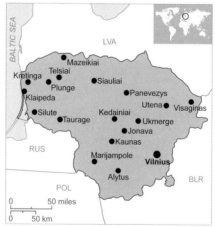

MAJOR CITIES/TOWNS

		Population
1	Vilnius	543 859
2	Kaunas	352 440
3	Klaipeda	183 436
4	Siauliai	127 105
5	Panevėzys	113 230
6	Alytus	68 263
7	Marijampolé	46 998
8	Mazeikiai	40 525
9	Jonava	34 203
10	Utena	32 592
11	Kédainiai	31 000
12	Telsiai	29 868
13	Visaginas	28 061
14	Tauragé	27 754
15	Ukmerge	27 426
16	Plungé	23 145
17	Kretinga	21 548
18	Siluté	20 903
19	Radviliskis	19 454

LIETUVOS RESPUBLIKA • REPUBLIC OF LITHUANIA

Capital	Vilnius	Population 3 555 179 (130)	% in cities 67%
GDP per capita	$17 800 (69)	Area km² 65 300 km² (122)	GMT +/- +2
Neighbours (km)	Belarus 680, Latvia 576, Poland 91, Russia 227 • Coast 90		

RECENT INTERNATIONAL MATCHES PLAYED BY LITHUANIA

2008	Opponents	Score		Venue	Comp	Scorers	Att	Referee
26-03	Azerbaijan	W	1-0	Vilnius	Fr	Klimavicius [38]	1 500	Satchi MDA
27-05	Czech Republic	L	0-2	Prague	Fr		14 220	Hrinak SVK
31-05	Estonia	W	1-0	Jurmala	BC	Mizigurskis [89]	1 300	Lajuks LVA
1-06	Latvia	L	1-2	Riga	BC	Beniusis [81]	3 300	Kaldma EST
4-06	Russia	L	1-4	Burghausen	Fr	Savenas [24]	2 850	Sippel GER
20-08	Moldova	W	3-0	Vilnius	Fr	Poskus 2 [23 54], Danilevicius [61]	2 000	Kaasik EST
6-09	Romania	W	3-0	Cluj	WCq	Stankevicius [31], Mikoliunas [69], Kalonas [86]	14 000	Kelly IRL
10-09	Austria	W	2-0	Marijampole	WCq	Danilevicius 2 [52 58]	4 500	Tagliavento ITA
11-10	Serbia	L	0-3	Belgrade	WCq		22 000	Mejuto ESP
15-10	Faroe Islands	W	1-0	Kaunas	WCq	Danilevicius [20]	5 000	Kapitanis CYP
19-11	Moldova	D	1-1	Tallinn	Fr	Savenas [72p]	100	Tohver EST
22-11	Estonia	D	1-1	Kuressaare	Fr	Kavaliauskas [35]	1 000	Nieminen FIN
2009								
7-02	Poland	D	1-1	Faro-Loule	Fr	Klimavicius [26]	150	Gomes POR
11-02	Andorra	W	3-1	Albufeira	Fr	Velicka [44], Boar [53], Kavaliauskas [83]		Xistra POR
28-03	France	L	0-1	Kaunas	WCq		8 700	Braamhaar NED
1-04	France	L	0-1	Paris	WCq		79 543	Webb ENG
6-06	Romania	L	0-1	Marijampole	WCq		5 850	Eriksson SWE
12-08	Luxembourg	W	1-0	Luxembourg	Fr	Danilevicius [40]	1 000	Black NIR
9-09	Faroe Islands	L	1-2	Toftir	WCq	Danilevicius [22p]	1 942	Vad HUN
10-10	Austria	L	1-2	Innsbruck	WCq	Stankevicius [66]	14 200	Gumienny BEL
14-10	Serbia	W	2-1	Marijampole	WCq	Kalonas [20p], Stankevicius [68p]	2 000	Guenov BUL
2010								
25-05	Ukraine	L	0-4	Kharkov	Fr		42 000	Sukhina RUS
18-06	Latvia	D	0-0	Kaunas	BC		1 000	Kaasik EST
20-06	Estonia	W	2-0	Kaunas	BC	Savenas [31p], Rimkevicius [90]	600	Sipailo LVA
11-08	Belarus	L	0-2	Kaunas	Fr		3 500	Satchi MDA
3-09	Scotland	D	0-0	Kaunas	ECq		5 248	Cakir TUR
7-09	Czech Republic	W	1-0	Olomouc	ECq	Sernas [27]	12 038	Yefet ISR
8-10	Spain	L	1-3	Salamanca	ECq	Sernas [54]	16 800	Rocchi ITA
17-11	Hungary	L	0-2	Szekesfehervar	Fr		4 500	Nijhuis NED
2011								
25-03	Poland	W	2-0	Kaunas	Fr	Mikoliunas [18], Cesnauskis [29]	5 000	Treimanis LVA
29-03	Spain	L	1-3	Kaunas	ECq	Stankevicius [57]	9 180	Duhamel FRA
3-06	Liechtenstein	L	0-2	Vaduz	ECq		1 886	Kuchin KAZ
7-06	Norway	L	0-1	Oslo	Fr		12 945	Attwell ENG
10-08	Armenia	W	3-0	Kaunas	Fr	Klimavicius [8], Cesnauskis [75], Beniusis [78]		Sipailo LVA
2-09	Liechtenstein	D	0-0	Kaunas	ECq		3 500	Johnsen NOR
6-09	Scotland	L	0-1	Glasgow	ECq		34 071	Jakobsson ISL
11-10	Czech Republic	L	1-4	Kaunas	ECq	Sernas [68p]	4 000	Fernandez ESP

Fr = Friendly match • EC = UEFA EURO 2012 • BC = Baltic Cup • WC = FIFA World Cup • q = qualifier

LITHUANIA NATIONAL TEAM HISTORICAL RECORDS

Caps	84 - Andrius Skerla 1996- • 76 - Deividas Semberas 1996- • 69 - Tomas Danilevicius 1998- • 65 - Aurelijus Skarbalius 1991-2005 • 61 - Gintaras Stauce 1992-2004 • 59 - Marius Stankevicius 2001- • 58 - Zydrunas Karcemarskas 2002- • 56 - Edgaras Jankauskas 1995-2008; Andrius Tereskinas 1991-2000 & Tomas Zvirgzdauskas 1998-2008 • 51 - Igoris Morinas 1997-2007
Goals	19 - Tomas Danilevicius 1998- • 12 - Antanas Lingis 1928-38 • 10 - Edgaras Jankauskas 1995-2008 • 9 - Virginijus Baltusnikas 1990-98 • 8 - Jaroslavas Citavicius 1926-33; Valdas Ivanauskas 1992-2000; Darius Maciulevicius 1991-2005 & Robertas Poskus 1999-
Past Coaches	Benjaminas Zelkevicius 1990-91 • Algimantas Liubinskas 1992-94 • Benjaminas Zelkevicius 1995-97 • Kestutis Latoza 1998-99 • Robertas Tautkus 1999 • Stasys Stankus 1999-2000 • Julius Kvedaras 2000 • Benjaminas Zelkevicius 2000-03 • Algimantas Liubinskas 2003-08 • Jose Couceiro POR 2008-09 • Raimondas Zutautas 2010-11 • Csaba Laszlo 2012-

LITHUANIA 2011

A LYGA

	Pl	W	D	L	F	A	Pts	Ekranas	Zalgiris	Suduva	Siauliai	Kruoja	Banga	Tauras	Dainava	Mazeikiai	FBK	Atlantas	Klaipeda
Ekranas Panevezys †	33	24	8	1	68	14	80		1-2	1-0 2-2	1-0	0-0	1-1 1-0	1-0	1-0	5-0	3-0 3-1	7-0 2-1	2-2 5-0
Zalgiris Vilnius ‡	33	22	6	5	56	17	72	0-1 1-2		3-1	0-0	1-0 2-0	3-1 0-0	1-0 1-0	2-1	1-1	3-0 2-0	8-1 3-0	5-0 3-0
Suduva Marijampole ‡	33	19	8	6	70	19	65	0-0	1-1 2-0		0-0 0-0	0-1 2-0	1-0	3-0	6-1 1-1	3-0 4-0	3-0	5-2 13-0	2-1
KFK Siauliai	33	16	11	6	45	30	59	0-0 0-0	0-0	1-0		1-0	0-4	1-3 2-0	1-0 1-3	1-0	2-1 2-2	3-1 3-1	4-0 5-0
Kruoja Pakruojis	33	13	10	10	43	34	49	0-4	0-2	0-1 0-1	1-2 1-1		0-0	1-1	0-1	2-1 2-0	0-4	0-0 2-0	6-0
Banga Gargzdai	33	13	7	13	51	37	46	1-4	0-1	0-1 0-2	3-1	1-2 1-2		1-1	1-2 3-1	0-1 2-0	1-1	3-0 5-0	3-1
Tauras Taurage	33	11	12	10	50	38	45	0-0 0-1	1-1 1-2	0-2 1-1	6-2 0-0	2-2 0-2	3-1 0-0		2-1 2-2	1-1	3-1 1-1	4-2 6-0	6-1 2-1
Dainava Alytus	33	13	6	14	53	54	45	0-3	1-5	0-2	1-3	0-6 1-1	0-1 0-0	2-2 2-4		1-2	2-0 3-0	1-0 7-0	5-1
FK Mazeikiai	33	9	9	15	36	54	36	1-2 1-2	2-0	0-1	0-0	0-0	1-5 0-2	1-4 2-2	0-0 2-2		1-1	3-2 2-0	1-0
FBK Kaunas §6	33	8	8	17	41	53	26	0-1	0-1	0-3	2-1	0-1	3-1 1-1	2-0 1-1	0-1 0-2	0-0		4-0	2-2 5-1
Atlantas Klaipeda	33	3	2	28	28	121	11	0-4	0-3	0-2 0-2	1-2	0-3	1-2 2-4	1-0	2-5 0-5	2-3	2-0 3-4		1-3 2-2
FC Klaipeda	33	2	3	28	19	89	9	0-1	0-1	0-2 0-1	0-1	1-2	0-3 0-5	1-0 0-2	0-1 0-3	2-4	0-2 1-2	0-4	

12/03/2011 - 6/11/2011 • † Qualified for the UEFA Champions League • ‡ Qualified for the Europa League • § = points deducted
Top scorers: 19 - Deivydas Matulevicius, Zalgiris • 17 - Arsenij Buinickij, Dainava & Goran Jerkovic CRO, Tauras • 13 - Tadas Eliosius, Suduva

LITHUANIA 2010
LFF 1 LYGA (2)

	Pl	W	D	L	F	A	Pts
FK Vilnius	24	17	3	4	56	13	54
Nevezis Kedainiai	24	16	1	7	64	21	49
Atletas Kaunas	24	12	6	6	57	38	42
FK Trakai	24	12	6	6	48	33	42
Lietava Jonava	24	7	8	9	40	29	29
Lifosa Kedainiai	24	7	7	10	46	73	28
Venta Kursenai	24	7	4	13	43	59	25
FK Silute	24	6	4	14	22	50	22
Minija Kretinga	24	3	3	18	17	77	12

9/04/2011 - 22/10/2011

MEDALS TABLE

		Overall			League			Cup	
		G	S	B	G	S	B	G	S
1	FBK Kaunas	12	4	1	8	2	1	4	2
2	Ekranas Panevezys	10	6	4	6	3	4	4	3
3	Zalgiris Vilnius	8	14	3	3	9	3	5	5
4	Kareda Siauliai	4	2		2	2		2	
5	Inkaras Kaunas	3	2	1	2		1	1	2
6	Atlantas Klaipeda	2	3	3		2	3	2	1
7	Suduva Marijampole	2	3	3		2	3	2	1
8	Sirijus Klaipeda	2	1	1	1		1	1	1
9	Neris Vilnius	1	1			1		1	
10	ROMAR Mazeikiai	1		1	1		1		
11	Vetra Vilnius		5	3		1	3		4
12	Panerys Vilnius		1	1		1	1		
13	Banga Gargzdai		1						
	Tauras Siauliai		1						1
	Tauras Taurage		1						1

LFF TAURE 2010–11

Round of 16		Quarter–finals		Semi–finals		Final	
Ekranas Panevezys	Bye						
		Ekranas Panevezys	1				
Kruoja Pakruojis	2	Vidzgiris Alytus *	0				
Vidzgiris Alytus *	4			Ekranas Panevezys	2 2		
Suduva Marijampole	Bye			KFK Siauliai *	0 2		
		Suduva Marijampole	0				
		KFK Siauliai *	1				
KFK Siauliai	Bye					Ekranas Panevezys	4
FBK Kaunas *	3					Banga Gargzdai ‡	2
Atletas Kaunas	0	FBK Kaunas	3				
		Tauras Taurage *	2				
Tauras Taurage	Bye			FBK Kaunas *	0 1		
FC Klaipeda	2			Banga Gargzdai	5 1		
Granitas Vilnius *	1	FC Klaipeda	0				
Nevezis Kedainiai	3	Banga Gargzdai *	2				
Banga Gargzdai *	4						

* Home team in the first leg
‡ Qualified for the Europa League

CUP FINAL
Alytus Stadium, Alytus
14-05-2011, Att: 1800,
Ref: Atmanavicius
Scorers - Radavicius 30, Varnas 55,
Matovic 107, Velicka 115 for Ekranas;
Zelmikas 11, Urbaitis 13 for Banga

LUX – LUXEMBOURG

FIFA/COCA-COLA WORLD RANKING

'93	'94	'95	'96	'97	'98	'99	'00	'01	'02	'03	'04	'05	'06	'07	'08	'09	'10	'11	'12
111	128	100	123	138	143	124	139	142	148	153	155	150	186	149	121	128	134	128	

	2011														
	Jan	Feb	Mar	Apr	May	Jun	Jul	Aug	Sep	Oct	Nov	Dec	High	Low	Av
	132	131	117	126	125	128	128	128	114	118	127	128	93	195	137

The recent improvement in the results of the Luxembourg national team have been helped to a large degree by the infusion of players who have taken up citizenship in the Duchy, players like the Portuguese Daniel da Mota and the Congolese Joel Kitenge. Da Mota who has played his club football in Luxembourg since 2001 got the year off to a cracking start when he scored twice in a 2-1 victory over Slovakia in February. Unfortunately that was just a friendly but Luxembourg did manage to win a game in their Euro 2012 qualifying group with a 2-1 victory at home to Albania thanks to goals from Aurelien Joachim and Gilles Bettmer - both of whom were born and bred in the country. An earlier draw at home to Belarus meant they finished with four points although they still ended bottom of their group. In club football, Da Motta had a fantastic season with F'91 Dudelange who reclaimed their league crown from Jeunesse. Along with Frenchman Tomasz Gruszczynski, the pair formed a lethal strike duo as Dudelange finished 12 points ahead of their closest rivals Fola Esch. It was the club's tenth title since first winning the championship in 2000. They almost claimed a fourth double but lost 1-0 in the Cup Final to the holders FC Differdange 03, the goal coming from Portuguese midfielder Pedro Ribeiro.

UEFA EUROPEAN CHAMPIONSHIP RECORD
1960 DNE 1964 QF 1968-2012 DNQ

FEDERATION LUXEMBOURGEOISE DE FOOTBALL (FLF)

PO Box 5,
Monderange 3901
☎ +352 4886651
📠 +352 48866582
✉ flf@football.lu
🖥 www.football.lu
FA 1908 CON 1954 FIFA 1910
P Paul Philipp
GS Joel Wolff

FIFA BIG COUNT 2006

Total players	47 580
% of population	10.03%
Male	44 626
Female	2 954
Amateurs 18+	15 806
Youth under 18	11 874
Unregistered	4 100
Professionals	300
Referees	264
Admin & coaches	1 050
Number of clubs	111
Number of teams	746

MAJOR CITIES/TOWNS

		Population
1	Luxemburg	75 375
2	Esch-sur-Alzette	28 950
3	Dudelange	18 473
4	Schifflange	8 364
5	Bettembourg	7 627
6	Pétange	7 371
7	Ettelbruck	6 466
8	Diekirch	6 343
9	Strassen	6 026
10	Bertrange	5 634
11	Fousbann	5 509
12	Belvaux	5 449
13	Differdange	5 431
14	Soleuvre	5 116
15	Mamer	5 066
16	Wiltz	5 021
17	Echternach	4 901
18	Rodange	4 803
19	Obercorn	4 786

GRAND DUCHE DE LUXEMBOURG

Capital	Luxembourg	Population	491 775 (169)	% in cities	82%
GDP per capita	$81 200 (3)	Area km²	2 586 km² (178)	GMT +/-	+1
Neighbours (km)	Belgium 148, France 73, Germany 138				

RECENT INTERNATIONAL MATCHES PLAYED BY LUXEMBOURG

2007	Opponents		Score	Venue	Comp	Scorers	Att	Referee
22-08	Georgia	D	0-0	Luxembourg	Fr		1 123	Weatherall NIR
8-09	Slovenia	L	0-3	Luxembourg	ECq		2 012	Berezka UKR
12-09	Bulgaria	L	0-3	Sofia	ECq		4 674	Demirlek TUR
13-10	Belarus	W	1-0	Gomel	ECq	Fons Leweck [95+]	14 000	Svendsen DEN
17-10	Romania	L	0-2	Luxembourg	ECq		3 584	Brych GER
17-11	Netherlands	L	0-1	Rotterdam	ECq		45 000	Hansson SWE
2008								
30-01	Saudi Arabia	L	1-2	Riyadh	Fr	Rene Peters [87p]	2 000	
26-03	Wales	L	0-2	Luxembourg	Fr		1 879	Kuipers NED
27-05	Cape Verde Islands	D	1-1	Luxembourg	Fr	Fons Leweck [77]	2 051	Radovanovic MNE
20-08	Macedonia FYR	L	1-4	Luxembourg	Fr	Joel Kitenge [73]	885	Brugger AUT
6-09	Greece	L	0-3	Luxembourg	WCq		4 596	Hermansen DEN
10-09	Switzerland	W	2-1	Zurich	WCq	Jeff Strasser [27], Fons Leweck [87]	20 500	Filipovic SRB
11-10	Israel	L	1-3	Luxembourg	WCq	Rene Peters [14]	3 562	Egorov RUS
15-10	Moldova	D	0-0	Luxembourg	WCq		2 157	Borski POL
19-11	Belgium	D	1-1	Luxembourg	Fr	Mario Mutsch [47]		Riley ENG
2009								
28-03	Latvia	L	0-4	Luxembourg	WCq		2 516	Whitby WAL
1-04	Latvia	L	0-2	Riga	WCq		6 700	Aydinus TUR
12-08	Lithuania	L	0-1	Luxembourg	Fr		1 000	Black NIR
5-09	Moldova	D	0-0	Chisinau	WCq		7 820	Mazeika LTU
9-09	Israel	L	0-7	Ramat Gan	WCq		7 038	Svendsen DEN
10-10	Switzerland	L	0-3	Luxembourg	WCq		8 031	Iturralde ESP
14-10	Greece	L	1-2	Athens	WCq	Papadopoulos OG [90]	13 932	Ceferin SVN
14-11	Iceland	D	1-1	Luxembourg	Fr	Kim Kintziger [75]	913	Van Boekel NED
2010								
3-03	Azerbaijan	L	1-2	Luxembourg	Fr	Jeff Strasser [33]	874	Kari FIN
4-06	Faroe Islands	D	0-0	Hesperange	Fr		713	Bertolini SUI
11-08	Wales	L	1-5	Llanelli	Fr	Joel Kitenge [44]	4 904	Gestranius FIN
3-09	Bosnia-Herzegovina	L	0-3	Luxembourg	ECq		7 327	Banari MDA
7-09	Albania	L	0-1	Tirana	ECq		10 000	Trutz SVK
8-10	Belarus	D	0-0	Luxembourg	ECq		1 857	Stavrev MKD
12-10	France	L	0-2	Metz	ECq		24 710	Jug SVN
17-11	Algeria	D	0-0	Luxembourg	Fr		7 033	Sippel GER
2011								
9-02	Slovakia	W	2-1	Luxembourg	Fr	Daniel Da Mota 2 [60 81]		Thual FRA
25-03	France	L	0-2	Luxembourg	ECq		8 400	Hagen NOR
29-03	Romania	L	1-3	Piatra-Neamt	ECq	Lars Gerson [22]	13 500	Gocek TUR
3-06	Hungary	L	0-1	Luxembourg	Fr		1 213	Arnason ISL
7-06	Belarus	L	0-2	Minsk	ECq		9 500	Salmanov AZE
10-08	Portugal	L	0-5	Faro	Fr			Mateu ESP
2-09	Romania	L	0-2	Luxembourg	ECq		2 812	Karasev RUS
6-09	Albania	W	2-1	Luxembourg	ECq	Gilles Bettmer [27], Aurelien Joachim [78]	2 132	Kari FIN
7-10	Bosnia-Herzegovina	L	0-5	Zenica	ECq		12 000	Evans WAL
15-11	Switzerland	L	0-1	Luxembourg	Fr		852	Delferiere BEL

Fr = Friendly match • EC = UEFA EURO 2008/2012 • WC = FIFA World Cup • q = qualifier

LUXEMBOURG NATIONAL TEAM HISTORICAL RECORDS

Caps	**98** - Jeff Strasser 1993- • **88** - Carlo Weis 1978-98 • **82** - Rene Peters 2000- • **77** - Francois Konter 1955-69 • **73** - Roby Langers 1980-98 & Eric Hoffmann 2002-10 • **69** - Manuel Cardoni 1993-2004 • **67** - Ernest Brenner 1955-65 • **64** - Marcel Bossi 1980-93 & Jeff Saibene 1986-2001 • **63** - Gilbert Dresch 1975-87 • **58** - Jean-Paul Girres 1980-92 • **57** - Fernand Brosius 1956-66 • **56** - Nicolas Kettel 1946-59
Goals	**16** - Leon Mart 1936-45 • **15** - Gustave Kemp 1937-45 • **14** - Camille Libar 1938-47 • **13** - Nicolas Kettel 1946-59 • **12** - Francois Muller 1949-54 • **11** - Leon Letsch 1947-62 • (Totals include all matches and not just full internationals)
Past Coaches	Ernst Melchior 1969-72 • Louis Pilot 1978-84 • Paul Philipp 1985-2001 • Allan Simonsen 2001-04 • Guy Hellers 2004-10 • Luc Holz 2010-

LUXEMBOURG 2010-11

BGL LIGUE DIVISION NATIONALE

	Pl	W	D	L	F	A	Pts	Dudelange	Fola Esch	Käerjeng	Differdange	Progrès	Grevenmacher	Pétange	Jeunesse	RM Hamm	Swift	Racing Union	Wiltz	Etzella	Canach
F91 Dudelange †	26	19	2	5	76	23	59		3-0	1-2	3-4	5-1	0-3	3-0	2-0	4-2	2-0	3-2	15-0	4-1	2-0
Fola Esch ‡	26	14	5	7	48	28	47	0-3		2-0	1-2	1-1	1-1	1-1	3-2	1-1	4-2	3-0	4-0	5-0	1-2
UN Käerjeng 97 ‡	26	13	5	8	53	35	44	1-3	1-2		2-2	3-4	5-1	0-0	1-1	1-0	4-1	1-1	5-1	6-1	5-0
FC Differdange 03 ‡	26	12	7	7	51	37	43	0-1	0-3	2-1		1-2	2-2	1-1	3-0	3-1	3-0	0-2	4-4	1-2	4-0
Progrès Niedercorn	26	12	5	9	43	43	41	1-5	2-1	2-1	2-4		1-3	1-2	1-3	5-2	2-0	1-0	0-1	3-2	2-0
CS Grevenmacher	26	11	6	9	43	39	39	0-3	1-2	0-0	0-2	1-2		1-0	2-2	1-2	1-3	1-0	4-1	1-2	1-1
CS Pétange	26	10	8	8	37	36	38	1-0	1-0	1-0	1-4	1-0	2-2		1-1	2-5	1-3	2-2	5-1	2-1	2-3
Jeunesse d'Esch	26	10	7	9	40	37	37	1-0	1-1	4-0	1-2	2-2	1-3	2-1		2-1	4-1	0-1	0-2	0-1	2-0
RM Hamm Benfica	26	11	3	12	47	46	36	0-1	1-2	1-2	2-0	0-1	3-2	2-2	1-3		2-0	0-4	4-0	1-0	4-1
Swift Hesperange	26	9	4	13	38	49	31	0-3	0-2	2-3	0-0	2-2	2-3	0-0	1-2	4-2		2-1	2-1	4-2	2-0
Racing Union	26	8	5	13	38	38	29	0-2	0-2	1-3	1-1	0-0	0-2	4-1	0-1	0-0			1-3	5-1	4-2
FC Wiltz 71	26	8	2	16	38	78	26	1-5	2-1	0-1	2-1	0-3	2-3	2-1	2-4	1-3	1-3	1-4		1-2	1-1
Etzella Ettelbruck	26	5	6	15	31	60	21	1-1	1-2	0-1	2-2	2-2	0-4	0-2	0-0	2-2	2-3	2-3	1-3		1-1
Jeunesse Canach	26	5	5	16	28	62	20	2-2	0-3	2-4	1-3	1-0	0-1	1-3	1-1	2-4	2-1	3-2	1-5	1-2	

8/08/2010 - 21/05/2011 • † Qualified for the UEFA Champions League • ‡ Qualified for the Europa League
Relegation play-off: **US Hostert** 1-1 6-4p FC Wiltz 71 • Top scorer: **18** - Sanel Ibrahimovic BIH, Wiltz

LUXEMBOURG 2010-11 EHRENPROMOTION (2)

	Pl	W	D	L	F	A	Pts
Union Kayl Tetange	26	20	2	4	59	31	62
US Rumelange	26	20	2	4	47	22	62
US Hostert	26	16	4	6	50	32	52
Victoria Rosport	26	15	4	7	61	39	49
CS Obercorn	26	14	5	7	50	30	47
Young Boys Diekirch	26	12	4	10	42	39	40
FC 72 Erpeldange	26	11	4	11	57	46	37
FC Mondercange	26	10	4	12	40	34	34
US Mondorf-les-Bains	26	6	7	13	34	46	25
Koeppchen W'dange	26	6	7	13	32	46	25
Sporting Steinfort	26	6	5	15	24	45	23
Green Boys	26	4	9	13	31	67	21
Avenir Beggen	26	5	4	17	30	54	19
Minerva Lintgen	26	3	7	16	25	51	16

22/08/2010 - 21/05/2011
Relegation play-offs: Steinfort 0-1 **Muhlenbach Lusitanos**
Green Boys 0-1 **Mamer**

MEDALS TABLE

		Overall			League			Cup		
		G	S	B	G	S	B	G	S	B
1	Jeunesse Esch/Alzette	40	23	15	28	12	15	12	11	
2	Red Boys Differdange	21	19	14	6	10	14	15	9	
3	AC Spora Luxembourg	19	18	10	11	10	10	8	8	
4	Union Luxembourg	16	18	12	6	8	12	10	10	
5	Stade Dudelange	14	13	6	10	6	6	4	7	
6	Avenir Beggen	13	9	3	6	5	3	7	4	
7	F'91 Dudelange	13	8		9	4		4	4	
8	Fola Esch	8	9	4	5	8	4	3	1	
9	Progres Niedercorn	7	8	8	3	5	8	4	3	
10	CS Grevenmacher	5	12	4	1	7	4	4	5	
11	US Hollerich	5	3	2	5	3	2			
12	Aris Bonnevoie	4	6	2	3	1	2	1	5	
13	US Rumelange	2	5	1		3	1	2	2	
14	Sporting Club Luxembourg	2	3	2	2	3	2			
15	The National Schifflange	2	3		1	2		1	1	
16	Alliance Dudelange	2	2			1		2	1	
17	FC Differdange 03	2	1	1		1	1		2	
18	Racing Club Luxembourg	2	3			1		3	1	

COUPE DE LUXEMBOURG 2010-11

Round of 16

FC Differdange 03 *	3
RM Hamm Benfica	1
US Rumelange *	0
Jeunesse Canach	2
CS Grevenmacher	2
UN Käerjeng 97 *	0
Progrès Niedercorn *	2
Racing Union	3
Jeunesse d'Esch	4
Sporting Steinfort *	1
Flaxweiler/Beyren	1
Union Kayl Tetange	2
Fola Esch	2
Etzella Ettelbruck *	1
Swift Hesperange	1
F91 Dudelange *	2

Quarter-finals

FC Differdange 03 *	5
Jeunesse Canach	0
CS Grevenmacher	1
Racing Union *	4
Jeunesse d'Esch	4
Union Kayl Tetange *	1
Fola Esch *	1
F91 Dudelange	2

Semi-finals

FC Differdange 03	2
Racing Union *	0
Jeunesse d'Esch *	0
F91 Dudelange	2

Final

FC Differdange 03 ‡	1
F91 Dudelange	0

CUP FINAL

Josy Barthel, Luxembourg
29-05-2011, Ref: Bourgnon

Scorer - Pedro Ribeiro 24

* Home team • ‡ Qualified for the Europa League

LVA – LATVIA

FIFA/COCA-COLA WORLD RANKING

'93	'94	'95	'96	'97	'98	'99	'00	'01	'02	'03	'04	'05	'06	'07	'08	'09	'10	'11	'12
86	69	60	82	75	77	62	92	106	79	51	65	69	90	86	67	45	78	68	

	2011														
	Jan	Feb	Mar	Apr	May	Jun	Jul	Aug	Sep	Oct	Nov	Dec	High	Low	Av
	76	76	75	76	78	82	84	84	74	75	68	68	45	111	74

Aleksandrs Starkovs' return to Skonto Riga in 2010 had an immediate impact with the club winning their first title for six years, but his departure at the end of the year to coach FK Baku in Azerbaijan had an equally dramatic effect as Skonto could only finish in fourth place in the 2011 championship. Instead it was Ventspils who took the honours in both league and cup. They, along with west coast neighbours Liepajas Metalurgs, have benefitted most from the decline of Skonto in recent years and the two met in the Cup Final with Ventspils winning 3-1 in Riga in May. Ventspils had appointed Russian coach Sergei Podpaly at the start of the season and he added the league title at the end of the year with Metalurgs once again consigned to the runners-up spot. There was some comfort for Skonto when they beat Ventspils in the final of the Baltic Cup as Latvian clubs once again dominated the competition. The match finished 1-1 with Skonto winning the penalty shoot-out 5-4. Although Starkovs had left to coach in Azerbaijan, he did retain his role as national team coach, but the Latvians had a miserable time in their Euro 2012 qualifying group as they finished well off the pace. Wins over Georgia and Malta did little to lift the spirits with just a single point won against the top three of Greece, Croatia and Israel.

UEFA EUROPEAN CHAMPIONSHIP RECORD
1960-1992 DNE (Played as part of the Soviet Union) **1996-2000** DNQ **2004** 14 r1 **2008-2012** DNQ

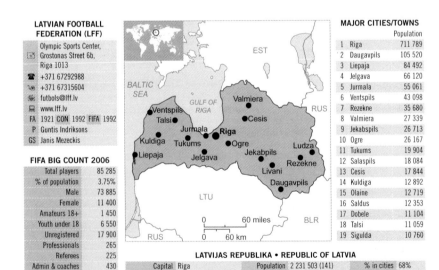

LATVIAN FOOTBALL FEDERATION (LFF)

Olympic Sports Center,
Grostonas Street 6b,
Riga 1013

☎ +371 67292988
📠 +371 67315604
✉ futbols@lff.lv
🖥 www.lff.lv
FA 1921 CON 1992 FIFA 1992
P Guntis Indriksons
GS Janis Mezeckis

FIFA BIG COUNT 2006

Total players	85 285
% of population	3.75%
Male	73 885
Female	11 400
Amateurs 18+	1 450
Youth under 18	6 550
Unregistered	17 900
Professionals	265
Referees	225
Admin & coaches	430
Number of clubs	68
Number of teams	420

MAJOR CITIES/TOWNS

		Population
1	Riga	711 789
2	Daugavpils	105 520
3	Liepaja	84 492
4	Jelgava	66 120
5	Jurmala	55 061
6	Ventspils	43 098
7	Rezekne	35 680
8	Valmiera	27 339
9	Jekabspils	26 713
10	Ogre	26 167
11	Tukums	19 904
12	Salaspils	18 084
13	Cesis	17 844
14	Kuldiga	12 892
15	Olaine	12 719
16	Saldus	12 353
17	Dobele	11 104
18	Talsi	11 059
19	Sigulda	10 760

LATVIJAS REPUBLIKA • REPUBLIC OF LATVIA

Capital	Riga	Population	2 231 503 (141)	% in cities	68%
GDP per capita	$17 300 (72)	Area km²	64 589 km² (123)	GMT +/-	+2
Neighbours (km)	Belarus 171, Estonia 343, Lithuania 576, Russia 292 • Coast 498				

RECENT INTERNATIONAL MATCHES PLAYED BY LATVIA

2008	Opponents		Score	Venue	Comp	Scorers	Att	Referee
6-02	Georgia	W	3-1	Tbilisi	Fr	Karlsons [7], Stepanovs [16], Astafjevs [34]		Shmolik BLR
26-03	Andorra	W	3-0	Andorra la Vella	Fr	Ivanovs [10], Pereplotkins [24], Rimkus [41]		Rubinos Perez ESP
30-05	Estonia	W	1-0	Riga	BC	Laizans [48p]	4 500	Zuta LTU
1-06	Lithuania	W	2-1	Riga	BC	Pereplotkins [57], Alunderis OG [77]	3 300	Kaldma EST
20-08	Romania	L	0-1	Urziceni	Fr		10 000	Ovrebo NOR
6-09	Moldova	W	2-1	Tiraspol	WCq	Karlsons.G [8], Astafjevs [22]	4 300	Courtney NIR
10-09	Greece	L	0-2	Riga	WCq		8 600	Chapron FRA
11-10	Switzerland	L	1-2	St Gall	WCq	Ivanovs [71]	18 026	Batista POR
15-10	Israel	D	1-1	Riga	WCq	Kolesnicenko [89]	7 100	Hrinak SVK
12-11	Estonia	D	1-1	Tallinn	Fr	Grebis [75]	2 000	Sandmoen NOR
2009								
11-02	Armenia	D	0-0	Limassol	Fr		150	
28-03	Luxembourg	W	4-0	Luxembourg	WCq	Karlsons [24], Cauna [48], Visnakovs [72], Pereplotkins [86]	2 516	Whitby WAL
1-04	Luxembourg	W	2-0	Riga	WCq	Zigajevs [43], Verpakovskis [75]	6 700	Aydinus TUR
12-08	Bulgaria	L	0-1	Sofia	Fr		2 000	Pamporidis GRE
5-09	Israel	W	1-0	Ramat Gan	WCq	Gorkss [59]	20 000	Kircher GER
9-09	Switzerland	D	2-2	Riga	WCq	Cauna [62], Astafjevs [75]	8 600	Kralovec CZE
10-10	Greece	L	2-5	Athens	WCq	Verpakovskis 2 [12 40]	18 981	Ovrebo NOR
14-10	Moldova	W	3-2	Riga	WCq	Rubins 2 [32 44], Grebis [76]	3 800	Hyytia FIN
14-11	Honduras	L	1-2	Tegucigalpa	Fr	Kolesnicenko [45p]		Quesada CRC
2010								
22-01	Korea Republic	L	0-1	Malaga	Fr		150	Velasco ESP
5-06	Ghana	L	0-1	Milton Keynes	Fr		8 108	Clattenburg ENG
18-06	Lithuania	D	0-0	Kaunas	BC		1 000	Kaasik EST
19-06	Estonia	D	0-0	Kaunas	BC		300	Mazeika LTU
11-08	Czech Republic	L	1-4	Liberec	Fr	Cauna [90]	7 456	Dankovsky UKR
3-09	Croatia	L	0-3	Riga	ECq		7 600	Kuipers NED
7-09	Malta	W	2-0	Ta'Qali	ECq	Gorkss [43], Verpakovskis [85]	6 255	Asumaa FIN
8-10	Greece	L	0-1	Piraeus	ECq		13 520	Damato ITA
12-10	Georgia	D	1-1	Riga	ECq	Cauna [91+]	4 330	Neves POR
17-11	China PR	L	0-1	Kunming	Fr		7 500	Ko Hyung Jin KOR
2011								
26-03	Israel	L	1-2	Tel Aviv	ECq	Gorkss [62]	10 801	Mazic SRB
4-06	Israel	L	1-2	Riga	ECq	Cauna [62p]	6 147	Kelly IRL
7-06	Austria	L	1-3	Graz	Fr	Mihadjuks [49]	8 500	Evans WAL
10-08	Finland	L	0-2	Riga	Fr		5 314	Bezborodov RUS
2-09	Georgia	W	1-0	Tbilisi	ECq	Cauna [64]	15 422	Trattou CYP
6-09	Greece	D	1-1	Riga	ECq	Cauna [19]	5 415	Todorov BUL
7-10	Malta	W	2-0	Riga	ECq	Visnakovs.A [33], Rudnevs [83]	4 315	Trutz SVK
11-10	Croatia	L	0-2	Rijeka	ECq		8 370	Gautier FRA

Fr = Friendly match • EC = UEFA EURO 2012 • BC = Baltic Cup • WC = FIFA World Cup
q = qualifier • po = play-off • r1 = first round group

LATVIA NATIONAL TEAM HISTORICAL RECORDS

Caps	**167** - Vitalijs Astafjevs 1992-2010 • **117** - Andrejs Rubins 1998- • **108** - Juris Laizans 1998- • **106** - Imants Bleidelis 1995-07 • **105** - Mihails Zemlinskis 1992-2005 • **100** - Igors Stepanovs 1995- • **90** - Maris Verpakovskis 1999- • **86** - Aleksandrs Kolinko 1997- • **81** - Andrejs Stolcers 1994-2005 • **75** - Marian Pahars 1996-2007 • **73** - Vitas Rimkus 1995-2008 • **70** - Oleg Blagonadezdins 1992-2004
Goals	**28** - Maris Verpakovskis 1999- • **24** - Eriks Petersons 1929-39 • **16** - Vitalijs Astafjevs 1992-2010 • **15** - Marian Pahars 1996-2007 & Juris Laizans 1998- • **14** - Alberts Seibelis 1925-39 • **13** - Ilja Vestermans 1935-38 • **12** - Mihails Zemlinskis 1992-2005
Past Coaches	Janis Gilis 1992-97 • Revaz Dzodzuashvili GEO 1998-99 • Gary Johnson ENG 1999-2001 • Aleksandrs Starkovs 2001-04 • Jurijs Andrejevs 2004-07 • Aleksandrs Starkovs 2007-

LATVIA 2011

VIRSLIGA

	Pl	W	D	L	F	A	Pts	Ventspils	Metalurgs	Daugava	Skonto	FC Jurmala	Jelgava	Gulbene	FK Jurmala	Olimps/RFS
FK Ventspils †	32	22	5	5	75	19	71		0-1 1-2	2-1 2-1	0-1 0-0	4-0 2-0	4-0 0-0	4-0 1-1	4-0 4-1	4-0 4-0
Liepajas Metalurgs ‡	32	22	4	6	74	26	70	0-0 2-1		2-0 1-3	0-1 0-0	1-0 1-1	0-1 2-0	1-2 6-2	4-1 6-1	4-1 7-1
Daugava Daugavpils ‡	32	19	6	7	58	30	63	0-3 1-1	2-1 0-1		1-1 0-0	1-1 3-0	1-1 2-1	3-1 2-1	1-0 2-1	2-0 2-0
Skonto Riga	32	17	9	6	62	21	60	1-3 0-1	0-2 0-1	1-1 1-0		0-1 1-1	4-0 2-1	2-1 5-0	2-0 3-0	4-0 6-0
FC Jurmala	32	12	8	12	45	42	44	0-1 2-3	1-3 1-4	0-2 2-1	1-2 1-1		1-1 2-0	4-1 2-0	0-2 2-0	4-0 6-1
FK Jelgava	32	13	4	15	47	54	43	2-0 1-2	1-3 3-2	1-3 1-2	1-2 1-4	0-2 0-2		3-1 3-0	1-0 4-1	5-1 2-1
FB Gulbene	32	7	7	18	39	67	28	0-2 0-3	0-0 0-1	0-2 2-4	1-0 1-1	1-1 0-2	3-0 2-3		1-1 4-1	2-1 3-0
FK Jurmala	32	5	6	21	34	75	21	0-3 1-2	0-5 1-2	1-3 0-3	0-4 2-2	3-1 0-0	2-3 1-1	5-3 2-2		2-1 4-0
Olimps/RFS Riga	32	1	3	28	19	117	6	0-8 1-6	1-4 0-3	0-6 1-3	0-4 0-7	2-2 1-2	1-3 1-3	1-3 1-1	0-0 2-1	

2/04/2011 - 5/11/2011 • † Qualified for the UEFA Champions League • ‡ Qualified for the Europa League
Relegation play-off: Olimps/RFS 1-2 0-2 Spartaks
Top scorer: **22** - Nathan Junior BRA, Skonto • **21** - Mamuka Ghonghadze GEO, Daugava • **16** - Jurgis Kalns Metalurgs & Vladislavs Kozlovs, Jelgava

LATVIA 2011
PIRMALIGA (2)

	Pl	W	D	L	F	A	Pts
FC Metta	24	17	5	2	61	14	56
Liepajas Metalurgs-2	24	17	2	5	87	30	53
FK Spartaks	24	16	4	4	74	20	52
Rigas Futbola Skola	24	16	3	5	68	25	51
SFK Varaviksne	24	12	3	9	56	39	39
FK Ventspils-2	24	9	7	8	45	32	34
FK Rezekne/BJSS	24	9	3	12	41	51	30
Daugava Daugavpils-2	24	8	5	11	37	47	29
FK Auda	24	8	4	12	35	48	28
FK Valmiera	24	9	1	14	33	49	28
FK Tukums	24	5	7	12	35	54	22
FK Jelgava-2	24	5	5	14	30	61	20
Ogres/FK33	24	0	1	23	19	151	1

29/04/2011 - 6/11/2011

MEDALS TABLE

		Overall			League			Cup		
		G	S	B	G	S	B	G	S	City
1	Skonto Riga	22	7	3	15	1	3	7	6	Riga
2	FK Ventspils	9	6	5	4	5	5	5	1	Ventspils
3	Liepajas Metalurgs	8	13	4	2	8	4	1	5	Liepaja
4	FK Jelgava	3	2	2		2	2	3		Jelgava
5	Dinaburg Daugavpils	1	3	2		1	2	1	2	Daugavpils
6	Olimpija Riga	1	1			1		1		Riga
7	FK Riga	1		1			1	1		Riga
	Daugava Daugavpils	1		1			1	1		Daugavpils
9	Daugava Riga		5			3			2	Riga

LATVIJAS KAUSS 2010–11

Round of 16		Quarter-finals		Semi-finals		Final	
FK Ventspils	2						
FK Spartaks	1	**FK Ventspils**	2				
Tranzits Ventspils	1	Daugava Riga	1				
Daugava Riga	3			**FK Ventspils**	2		
Skonto Riga	3			Daugava Daugavpils	0		
FB Gulbene	2	Skonto Riga	0 0p				
FK Salaspils	0	**Daugava Daugavpils**	0 3p				
Daugava Daugavpils	10					**FK Ventspils**	3
FK Jurmala	0 7p					Liepajas Metalurgs	1
Olimps/RFS Riga	0 6p	**FK Jurmala**	3				
Jauniba Riga	0 6p	FK Valmiera	1				
FK Valmiera	0 7p			FK Jurmala	1		
FK Jelgava	1			**Liepajas Metalurgs**	2		
FC Metta	2	FK Jelgava	0				
Blazma Rezekne	0	**Liepajas Metalurgs**	1	‡ Qualified for the Europa League			
Liepajas Metalurgs	1						

CUP FINAL

Skonto, Riga, 15-05-2011,
Att: 1112, Ref: Treimanis
Scorers - Olegs Laizans [35], Ahmed
Abdultaofik 2 [44] [71] for Ventspils;
Antons Jemelins [78p] for Metalurgs

MAC – MACAU

FIFA/COCA-COLA WORLD RANKING

'93	'94	'95	'96	'97	'98	'99	'00	'01	'02	'03	'04	'05	'06	'07	'08	'09	'10	'11	'12
166	175	180	172	157	174	176	180	180	188	184	188	192	185	190	196	187	193	197	

2011												High	Low	Av
Jan	Feb	Mar	Apr	May	Jun	Jul	Aug	Sep	Oct	Nov	Dec			
193	193	181	184	184	183	190	192	191	191	193	197	156	197	181

The Macau national team took part in three tournaments during the course of 2011 but in the seven matches played six ended in defeat. Victory over Cambodia in the second leg of the qualifying round for the 2012 AFC Challenge Cup was the only success Macau's international footballers managed to achieve in yet another disappointing year for the former Portuguese colony. However, that 3-2 win counted for little as it was not enough to overturn a 3-1 deficit from the opening match in Phnom Penh with the Cambodians qualifying for the next round instead. A heavy defeat at the hands of Vietnam over two legs also accounted for Macau in the first round of qualifying for the 2014 FIFA World Cup. Against clearly stronger opponents they crashed out 13-1 on aggregate as their search for a first World Cup win since 1997 continues. Windsor Arch Ka I continued their domination of club football by retaining the league title, although they were pushed to the final day of the season by Monte Carlo. Monte Carlo's challenge was fuelled by the goals of Brazilian striker Kamilo Oliveira da Silva, who finished the season as top scorer before moving to join Hong Kong league side Sham Shui Po. The Macau U-23 side, who have been fielding a team in the league since 2005, took third place well adrift of the leading duo.

FIFA WORLD CUP RECORD
1930-1978 DNE 1982-1986 DNQ 1990 DNE 1994-2014 DNQ

MACAU FOOTBALL ASSOCIATION (AFM)

Avenida Wai Leong Taipa, University of Science and Technology, Football Field, Block I, Taipa, Macau

☎ +853 28830287
📠 +853 28830409
📧 macaufa@macau.ctm.net
🖥 www.macaufa.com
FA 1939 CON 1976 FIFA 1976
P Vitor Lup Kwan Cheung
GS Kam Vai Choi

FIFA BIG COUNT 2006

Total players	14 123
% of population	3.12%
Male	13 423
Female	700
Amateurs 18+	4 130
Unregistered	1 750
Professionals	1
Referees	51
Admin & coaches	703
Number of clubs	96
Number of teams	120

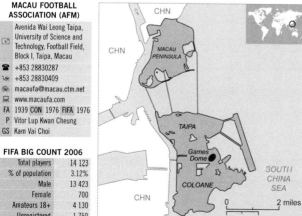

MAJOR CITIES/TOWNS

		Population
1	Macau	559 846

AOMEN TEBIE XINGZHENGQU • MACAU SPECIAL ADMINISTRATIVE REGION

Capital	Macau	Population	559 846 (167)	% in cities	100%
GDP per capita	$30 000 (45)	Area km²	28 km² (235)	GMT +/-	+8
Neighbours (km)	China 0.3 • Coast 41				

RECENT INTERNATIONAL MATCHES PLAYED BY MACAU

2007 Opponents	Score	Venue	Comp	Scorers	Att	Referee
10-06 Hong Kong	L 1-2	Hong Kong	Fr	Chan Kin Seng 29		
17-06 Mongolia	D 0-0	Macau	EAq		300	Matsuo JPN
21-06 Korea DPR	L 1-7	Macau	EAq	Chan Kin Seng 46	300	Wan Daxue CHN
24-06 Chinese Taipei	L 2-7	Macau	EAq	De Sousa 48, Leong Chong In 78	200	Kim Eui Soo KOR
8-10 Thailand	L 1-6	Bangkok	WCq	Chan Kin Seng 23	11 254	Chynybekov KGZ
15-10 Thailand	L 1-7	Macau	WCq	Chan Kin Seng 92+	500	Recho SYR
2008						
25-05 Nepal	L 2-3	Phnom Penh	CCq	Che Chi Man 29p, Chan Kin Seng 59	2 000	Vo Minh Tri VIE
28-05 Cambodia	L 1-3	Phnom Penh	CCq	Che Chi Man 65	3 000	Kurbanov TKM
19-11 Hong Kong	L 1-9	Macau	Fr			
2009						
11-03 Nth Mariana Islands	W 6-1	Manenggon Hills	EAq	Chan Kin Seng 2 13 24, Ho Man Hou 2 33 90, Leong Chong In 40, Loi Wai Hong 62		Sato JPN
13-03 Mongolia	L 1-2	Manenggon Hills	EAq	Ho Man Hou 79		Fan Qi CHN
15-03 Guam	D 2-2	Manenggon Hills	EAq	Chan Kin Seng 2 10 51	1 400	Kim Jong Hyeuk KOR
7-04 Mongolia	W 2-0	Macau	CCpr	Chan Kin Seng 22, Leong Chong In 24	500	Perera SRI
14-04 Mongolia	L 1-3	Ulaan-Baatar	CCpr	Chan Kin Seng 39	3 000	Yu Ming Hsun TPE
16-04 Myanmar	L 0-4	Dhaka	CCq		3 600	Mashentsev KGZ
28-04 Cambodia	L 1-2	Dhaka	CCq	Che Chi Man 75	6 000	Saleem MDV
30-04 Bangladesh	L 0-3	Dhaka	CCq		8 700	Mashentsev KGZ
2010						
9-10 Chinese Taipei	L 1-7	Kaohsiung	Fr	Leong Ka Hang 82	1 000	
10-10 Hong Kong	L 0-4	Kaohsiung	Fr		1 200	Yu Ming Hsun TPE
12-10 Philippines	L 0-5	Kaohsiung	Fr		700	Yu Ming Hsun TPE
2011						
9-02 Cambodia	L 1-3	Phnom Penh	CCq	Leong Ka Hang 80	2 000	Win Cho MYA
16-02 Cambodia	W 3-2	Macau	CCq	Vernon Wong 62, Leong Ka Hang 73, Alves Vinicio 75	100	Perea SRI
29-06 Vietnam	L 0-6	Ho Chi Minh City	WCq		20 000	Mashentsev KGZ
3-07 Vietnam	L 1-7	Macau	WCq	Leong Ka Hang 59	500	Auda IRQ
30-09 Chinese Taipei	L 0-3	Kaohsiung	Fr			
2-10 Hong Kong	L 1-5	Kaohsiung	Fr	Leong Ka Hang 82		
4-10 Philippines	L 0-2	Kaohsiung	Fr			

Fr = Friendly match • EA = East Asian Championship • AC = AFC Asian Cup • CC = AFC Challenge Cup • WC = FIFA World Cup
q = qualifier • r1 = first round group

MACAU 2011

CAMPEONATO 1° DIVISAO LIGA DE ELITE	Pl	W	D	L	F	A	Pts	Ka I	Monte Carlo	Macau U-23	Porto	Lam Pak	Policia	Hong Ngai	Lam Ieng	Hoi Fan	Artilheiros
Windsor Arch Ka I	18	15	0	3	88	24	45		4-2	0-3	5-2	4-2	2-1	7-1	5-1	7-0	12-0
Monte Carlo	18	14	2	2	80	16	44	3-2		1-2	3-1	5-1	5-1	7-0	3-0	5-1	5-0
Macau U-23	18	10	6	2	34	16	36	0-2	0-2		0-0	1-1	0-0	2-0	1-0	2-1	4-0
FC Porto	18	9	5	4	45	30	32	5-2	1-1	2-2		1-0	2-3	3-0	0-1	3-0	3-3
Lam Pak	18	9	2	7	46	30	29	1-2	0-2	0-1	1-3		3-1	2-1	5-2	2-2	6-1
Policía	18	7	3	8	21	33	24	0-3	0-0	1-5	0-3	1-2		2-1	1-0	1-0	2-1
Hong Ngai	18	6	1	11	41	57	19	2-6	0-8	2-2	1-3	1-6	1-2		3-0	2-1	6-1
Lam Ieng	18	4	2	12	29	55	14	0-4	2-10	0-2	3-4	1-4	1-1	1-4		5-1	5-2
Hoi Fan	18	2	4	12	28	69	9	1-8	1-6	3-3	3-3	1-4	3-2	2-7	2-4		3-3
Artilheiros Pau Peng	18	0	3	15	22	104	3	0-13	0-12	1-4	2-6	0-6	1-2	2-9	3-3	2-3	

14/01/2011 - 26/06/2011 • Top scorer: **38** - Kamilo Oliveira da Silva, Monte Carlo

MAD – MADAGASCAR

FIFA/COCA-COLA WORLD RANKING

'93	'94	'95	'96	'97	'98	'99	'00	'01	'02	'03	'04	'05	'06	'07	'08	'09	'10	'11	'12
89	111	132	140	163	150	134	114	122	101	118	147	149	184	149	135	158	155	160	

	2011												High	Low	Av
Jan	Feb	Mar	Apr	May	Jun	Jul	Aug	Sep	Oct	Nov	Dec			
154	155	156	138	138	138	150	152	158	165	157	160	81	188	136

Madagascar were eliminated early in the 2014 FIFA World Cup qualifiers, losing 2-3 on aggregate to Equatorial Guinea at the first stage of qualifying for the finals in Brazil. After a run of eight losses and two draws over 15 months, a narrow 2-1 win in the second leg for 'Barea' was welcome but it was not enough to overturn the 2-0 defeat in the first leg in Malabo. Frenchman Jean Paul Rabier had been fired in February after losing the opening two matches in the 2012 CAF African Cup of Nations qualifiers, and was replaced as coach by Maurice Mosa, whose third spell in charge lasted just seven months. He departed after the disappointing results at the Indian Ocean Island Games in the Seychelles where Madagascar failed to beat non-FIFA members Mayotte and Reunion. Franck Rajaonarisamba took over for the last two games of the Nations Cup preliminaries but lost his job after the World Cup setback. Japan Actuel's FC won the national Champions League in emphatic style, winning all three games at the end of the season play-offs featuring the provincial champions from Madagascar's regional leagues. The team from Manjakaray were coached by Abdou Bin Amidou to a first-ever title and a place in the 2012 CAF Champions League. Just weeks earlier CNaPS Sport had won the Malagasy Cup after a post-match penalty shoot out victory over Tana FC.

CAF AFRICA CUP OF NATIONS RECORD

1957-1970 DNE 1972-1974 DNQ 1976-1978 DNE 1980-1988 DNQ 1990 DNE 1992 DNQ 1994 DNE 1996 Withdrew 1998 DNE 2000-2012 DNQ

FEDERATION MALAGASY DE FOOTBALL (FMF)

26 rue de Russie, Isoraka,
PO Box 4409,
Antananarivo 101
☎ +261 20 2268374
🖷 +261 20 2268373
✉ fmf@blueline.mg

FA 1961 CON 1963 FIFA 1964
P Ahmad
GS Stanislas Rakotomalala

FIFA BIG COUNT 2006

Total players	826 420
% of population	4.44%
Male	787 470
Female	38 950
Amateurs 18+	16 650
Youth under 18	13 700
Unregistered	27 000
Professionals	0
Referees	680
Admin & coaches	4 108
Number of clubs	220
Number of teams	880

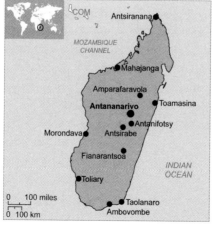

MAJOR CITIES/TOWNS

		Population
1	Antananarivo	1 612 632
2	Toamasina	219 669
3	Antsirabé	192 499
4	Fianarantsoa	179 302
5	Mahajanga	162 807
6	Toliary	120 790
7	Antsiranana	86 421
8	Antanifotsy	75 485
9	Ambovombe	70 740
10	Amparafaravola	55 578
11	Taolanaro	47 791
12	Ambatondrazaka	46 532
13	Mananara	44 455
14	Soavinandriana	43 237
15	Mahanoro	43 021
16	Soanierana Ivongo	42 364
17	Faratsiho	40 148
18	Vavatenina	39 824
19	Morondava	38 963

REPUBLIQUE DE MADAGASCAR • REPUBLIC OF MADAGASCAR

Capital	Antananarivo	Population	20 653 556 (55)	% in cities	29%
GDP per capita	$1000 (212)	Area km²	587 041 km² (46)	GMT +/-	+3
Neighbours (km)	Coast 4828				

RECENT INTERNATIONAL MATCHES PLAYED BY MADAGASCAR

2006 Opponents	Score	Venue	Comp	Scorers	Att	Referee
2-09 Gabon	L 0-4	Libreville	CNq			Diatta SEN
2007						
25-03 Côte d'Ivoire	L 0-3	Antananarivo	CNq			Maillet SEY
28-04 Zimbabwe	L 0-1	Maputo	CCr1			Faduco MOZ
29-04 Seychelles	W 5-0	Maputo	CCr1	Voavy 3 [11 14 69], Ramiadamanana [62], Andriatsima [84]		Mpopo LES
3-06 Côte d'Ivoire	L 0-5	Bouaké	CNq			Louzaya CGO
17-06 Gabon	L 0-2	Antananarivo	CNq			Mlangeni SWZ
29-07 Congo DR	D 0-0	Antananarivo	Fr			
14-08 Comoros	W 3-0	Antananarivo	Fr	Voavy 2 [70 89], Ramiadamanana [90]		
14-10 Comoros	W 6-2	Antananarivo	WCq	Andriatsima 4 [30 40 49p 57], Rakotomandimby [65], Tsaralaza [79]	7 754	Kaoma ZAM
17-11 Comoros	W 4-0	Moroni	WCq	Nomenjanahary 2 [37 51], Rakotomandimby [61], Robson [73]	1 610	Damon RSA
2008						
9-03 Mauritius	W 2-1	Curepipe	Fr	Rabemananjara 2 [77 81]		
31-05 Botswana	D 0-0	Gaborone	WCq		11 087	Kaoma ZAM
8-06 Côte d'Ivoire	D 0-0	Antananarivo	WCq			Labrosse SEY
15-06 Mozambique	D 1-1	Antananarivo	WCq	Mamihasindrahona [91p]	15 501	Ebrahim RSA
22-06 Mozambique	L 0-3	Maputo	WCq		20 000	Maillet SEY
19-07 Swaziland	D 1-1	Witbank	CCr1	Robson [65]		Nhlapo RSA
21-07 Seychelles	D 1-1	Witbank	CCr1	Rabenandrasana [23]		Kaoma ZAM
23-07 Mauritius	W 2-1	Witbank	CCr1	Rabenandrasana [52], Rabemananjara [63]		Marange ZIM
30-07 Mozambique	L 1-2	Thulamahashe	CCsf	Rabemananjara		Marange ZIM
3-08 Zambia	L 0-2	Thulamahashe	CC3p			
7-09 Botswana	W 1-0	Antananarivo	WCq	Rabemananjara [24]	20 000	Seechurn MRI
11-10 Côte d'Ivoire	L 0-3	Abidjan	WCq		24 000	Benouza ALG
2009						
19-09 South Africa	L 0-1	Kimberley	Fr			
2010						
29-08 Comoros	W 1-0	Mahajanga	Fr			
5-09 Nigeria	L 0-2	Calabar	CNq			Jedidi TUN
10-10 Ethiopia	L 0-1	Antananarivo	CNq			Ngosi MWI
2011						
27-03 Guinea	D 1-1	Antananarivo	CNq	Rajoarimanana [17]		
5-06 Guinea	L 1-4	Conakry	CNq	Arsene [24]		
17-07 Iran	L 0-1	Tehran	Fr			
4-08 Mayotte †	D 1-1	Praslin	IOGr1	Rajoarimanana [36]	1 800	Camille SEY
6-08 Reunion †	L 1-2	Mahe	IOGr1	Rajoarimanana [22]	1 000	Seechurn MRI
4-09 Nigeria	L 0-2	Antananarivo	CNq			
8-10 Ethiopia	L 2-4	Addis Abeba	CNq	Razafimandimby [3], Nomenjanahary [57]		
11-11 Equatorial Guinea	L 0-2	Malabo	WCq		10 000	Otogo-Castane GAB
15-11 Equatorial Guinea	W 2-1	Antananarivo	WCq	Rajoarimanana [54], Ramanamahefa [90]	5 000	Nunkoo MRI

Fr = Friendly match • CN = CAF African Cup of Nations • CC = COSAFA Cup • WC = FIFA World Cup • † Not a full international
q = qualifier • r1 = first round group • sf = semi-final • 3p = third place play-off

MADAGASCAR 2011
THB CHAMPIONS LEAGUE
FIRST STAGE

Group A - Toliara	Pl	W	D	L	F	A	Pts
Capricorne ‡	5	5	0	0	9	3	15
Ihosy ‡	5	4	0	1	10	7	12
FC2A Amboasary	5	2	0	3	1	1	6
Vohipeno	5	2	0	3	5	7	6
Fomelo	5	2	0	3	3	6	6
Rohondroho	5	0	0	5	4	8	0

Group B - Antsirabe	Pl	W	D	L	F	A	Pts
Académie Ny Antsika ‡	5	5	0	0	16	0	15
Japan Actuel's ‡	5	4	0	1	12	4	12
AS Port	5	2	0	3	3	6	6
RDN Arivonimamo	5	2	0	3	2	10	6
Briamdat	5	1	0	4	4	6	3
FCCM Vangaindrano	5	1	0	4	4	15	3

Group C - Toamasina	Pl	W	D	L	F	A	Pts
CNaPS Sport Itasy ‡	5	5	0	0	20	3	15
FCE Atsinanana ‡	5	4	0	1	13	4	12
HZAM Amparafaravola	5	3	0	2	7	7	9
Tsiroanomamandidy	5	2	0	3	3	8	6
AJS Sainte Marie	5	1	0	4	3	12	3
ACFM Fandriana	5	0	0	5	5	17	0

Group D - Antsiranana	Pl	W	D	L	F	A	Pts
Ajesaia Antananarivo ‡	5	3	0	2	7	4	9
ASCUM Boeny ‡	5	3	0	2	3	2	9
Racing Nosy Be	5	3	0	2	6	5	9
Fitamy Mampikony	5	3	0	2	7	7	9
Maeva	5	2	0	3	2	4	9
Joël Sava	5	1	0	4	2	5	9

18/09/2011 - 25/09/2011 • ‡ Qualified for the second stage

MADAGASCAR 2011
THB CHAMPIONS LEAGUE
SECOND STAGE

Group A - Toamasina	Pl	W	D	L	F	A	Pts
Académie Ny Antsika ‡	3	3	0	0	5	1	9
Capricorne ‡	3	2	0	1	3	3	6
ASCUM Boeny	3	1	0	2	2	3	3
FCE Atsinanana	3	0	0	3	2	5	0

Group B -	Pl	W	D	L	F	A	Pts
CNaPS Sport Itasy ‡	3	3	0	0	11	1	9
Japan Actuel's ‡	3	2	0	1	14	5	6
Ajesaia Antananarivo	3	1	0	2	5	2	3
Ihosy	3	0	0	3	2	24	0

19/10/2011 - 23/10/2011 • ‡ Qualified for the final stage

MADAGASCAR 2011
THB CHAMPIONS LEAGUE
FINAL STAGE (POULE DES AS)

Final Stage -	Pl	W	D	L	F	A	Pts	CSI	ANA	Cap
Japan Actuel's †	3	3	0	0	7	2	9	2-1	3-1	2-0
CNaPS Sport Itasy	3	2	0	1	5	2	6		1-0	3-0
Académie Ny Antsika	3	0	1	2	2	5	1			1-1
Capricorne	3	0	1	2	1	6	1			

23/11/2011 - 27/11/2011 • † Qualified for the CAF Champions League

TELMA COUPE DE MADAGASCAR 2011

Round of 16		Quarter-finals		Semi-finals		Final	
CNaPS Sport Itasy	5						
FC GRE Antalaha	1	CNaPS Sport Itasy	9				
Ajesaia Antananarivo	1	Antafana Toamasina	0				
Antafana Toamasina	2			CNaPS Sport Itasy	1 4p		
FC Toamasina	2			Adema Antananarivo	1 3p		
ASCUM Mahajanga	1	FC Toamasina	0				
FCM Ilakaka	0	Adema Antananarivo	2				
Adema Antananarivo	4					CNaPS Sport Itasy	1 5p
Académie Ny Antsika	2					Tana FC ‡	1 4p
FC Lazio	1	Académie Ny Antsika	1				
St Michel	3	Terrible Côte Ouest	0				
Terrible Côte Ouest	0			Académie Ny Antsika	1 2p		
3FB Toliara	2			Tana FC	1 4p		
AS Comato	1	3FB Toliara	0				
FC Prescoi United	1	Tana FC	2				
Tana FC	3			‡ Qualified for the CAF Confederation Cup			

CUP FINAL

Stade Mahamasina,
20-11-2011, 7000
Scorers - Damien [60] for CNaPS,
Lanto [39] for Tana

MAR – MOROCCO

FIFA/COCA-COLA WORLD RANKING

'93	'94	'95	'96	'97	'98	'99	'00	'01	'02	'03	'04	'05	'06	'07	'08	'09	'10	'11	'12
30	33	38	27	15	13	24	28	36	35	38	33	36	39	39	41	67	79	61	

2011												High	Low	Av
Jan	Feb	Mar	Apr	May	Jun	Jul	Aug	Sep	Oct	Nov	Dec	High	Low	Av
77	74	66	72	73	63	63	61	59	56	60	61	10	95	37

Morocco qualified top of their group for the 2012 Africa Cup of Nations qualifiers and went to the finals in Equatorial Guinea and Gabon as one of the hot favourites, only to crash out after their first two matches. It was a performance that left the team shell-shocked and came as a hammer blow to the reputation of their Belgian coach Eric Gerets, who had taken much of the credit for a perceived overhaul and revival in the form of the side. Exciting young players like Younes Belhanda, Oussama Assaidi and Adel Taarabt reflect a wealth of talent at Gerets' disposal but for all the flair and flamboyance they got caught out in the cauldron of competition. There was much better news at club level where Moroccan teams continued their push for trophies in continental competition. Maghreb Fes became the third Moroccan side to win the CAF Confederation Cup in the eight year history of the competition after beating Tunisia's Club Africain on penalties in the 2011 final. In the CAF Champions League Wydad Casablanca made it through to the final - the first Moroccan side to do so since neighbours Raja in 2002 - but they lost to Esperance of Tunisia 1-0 on aggregate. It was a double-winning season for Maghreb Fes after they won the Coupe du Trone at the end of the year while league honours went to Raja for the second time in three seasons.

CAF AFRICA CUP OF NATIONS RECORD

1957-1962 DNQ 1963 DNQ 1965-1968 DNE 1970 DNQ 1972 5 r1 1974 DNE 1976 1 Winners 1978 6 r1 1980 SF 3 (hosts) 1982-1984 DNQ 1986 4 SF 1988 4 SF 1990 DNQ 1992 9 r1 1994-1996 DNQ 1998 7 QF 2000 9 r1 2002 9 r1 2004 2 F 2006 13 r1 2008 11 r1 2010 DNQ 2012 12 r1

FEDERATION ROYALE MAROCAINE DE FOOTBALL (FRMF)

51 Bis Avenue Ibn Sina, Agdal, Case Postale 51, Rabat 10 000

☎ +212 37 672706
🖷 +212 37 671070
✉ contact@frmf.ma
🖥 www.frmf.ma

FA 1955 CON 1966 FIFA 1960
P Ali Fassi Fihri
GS Tarik Najem

FIFA BIG COUNT 2006

Total players	1 628 016
% of population	4.90%
Male	1 553748
Female	74 268
Amateurs 18+	40 010
Unregistered	165 000
Professionals	601
Referees	2 007
Admin & coaches	6 644
Number of clubs	563
Number of teams	2 815

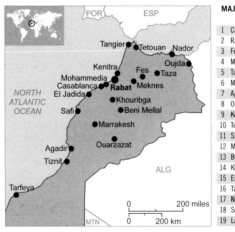

MAJOR CITIES/TOWNS

		Population
1	Casablanca	3 269 962
2	Rabat	1 787 307
3	Fes	1 024 587
4	Marrakesh	903 589
5	Tangier	746 516
6	Meknes	586 197
7	Agadir	556 324
8	Oujda	423 444
9	Kenitra	395 808
10	Tetouan	347 052
11	Safi	301 693
12	Mohammedia	201 880
13	Beni Mellal	179 565
14	Khouribga	172 775
15	El Jadida	160 791
16	Taza	150 761
17	Nador	142 349
18	Settat	129 747
19	Larache	116 051

AL MAMLAKAH AL MAGHRIBIYAH • KINGDOM OF MOROCCO

Capital	Rabat	Population	34 859 364 (35)	% in cities	56%
GDP per capita	$4500 (148)	Area km²	446 550 km² (57)	GMT +/-	0
Neighbours (km)	Algeria 1559, Western Sahara 443, Spain 16 • Coast 1835				

RECENT INTERNATIONAL MATCHES PLAYED BY MOROCCO

2008	Opponents	Score	Venue	Comp	Scorers	Att	Referee
21-01	Namibia	W 5-1	Accra	CNr1	Alloudi 3 [2 5 28], Sektioui [39p], Zerka [74]		Evehe CMR
24-01	Guinea	L 2-3	Accra	CNr1	Aboucherouane [60], Ouaddou [89]		Damon RSA
28-01	Ghana	L 0-2	Accra	CNr1			Sowe GAM
26-03	Belgium	W 4-1	Brussels	Fr	Alloudi [14], Sektoui [34], El Zhar [85], Benjelloun [89]	24 000	Nijhuis NED
31-05	Ethiopia	W 3-0	Casablanca	WCq	Benjelloun [4], Aboucherouane [13], Kharja [85]	5 000	Diatta SEN
7-06	Mauritania	W 4-1	Nouackhott	WCq	Sektioui [9], Benjelloun [37], Safri [58], Kharja [79]	9 500	Lamptey GHA
14-06	Rwanda	L 1-3	Kigali	WCq	Safri [78]	12 000	Evehe CMR
21-06	Rwanda	W 2-0	Casablanca	WCq	Safri [12p], El Zhar [49]	2 500	Benouza ALG
20-08	Benin	W 3-1	Rabat	Fr	Kharja [21], Safri [57], Zerka [78]		
6-09	Oman	D 0-0	Muscat	Fr			
11-10	Mauritania	W 4-1	Rabat	WCq	Safri [35], Youssef Hadji 2 [55 60], Zemmama [65]	1 472	Aboubacar CIV
19-11	Zambia	W 3-0	Rabat	Fr	Kharja [3], Sektioui [24], Baha [62]		
2009							
11-02	Czech Republic	D 0-0	Casablanca	Fr		38 000	Alakim TUN
28-03	Gabon	L 1-2	Casablanca	WCq	El Hamdaoui [83]	38 000	Diatta SEN
31-03	Angola	W 2-0	Lisbon	Fr	Taarabt [9], Chamakh [51]		
7-06	Cameroon	D 0-0	Yaounde	WCq		35 000	Seechurn MRI
20-06	Togo	D 0-0	Rabat	WCq		22 000	Kaoma ZAM
12-08	Congo	D 1-1	Rabat	Fr	El Ahmadi [44]		
6-09	Togo	D 1-1	Lome	WCq	Taarabt [92+]	24 651	Ssegonga UGA
10-10	Gabon	L 1-3	Libreville	WCq	Taarabt [88]	14 000	Doue CIV
14-11	Cameroon	L 0-2	Fes	WCq		17 000	Bennett RSA
2010							
11-08	Equatorial Guinea	W 2-1	Rabat	Fr	Youssef Hadji 2 [65 79]		
4-09	Central African Rep	D 0-0	Rabat	CNq			Coulibaly MLI
9-10	Tanzania	W 1-0	Dar es Salaam	CNq	El Hamdaoui [42]		Seechurn MRI
17-11	Northern Ireland	D 1-1	Belfast	Fr	Chamakh [55]	15 000	Hagen NOR
2011							
9-02	Niger	W 3-0	Marrakech	Fr	Boussoufa 2 [16 82p], El Bakkali [91+]		
27-03	Algeria	L 0-1	Annaba	CNq			Seechurn MRI
4-06	Algeria	W 4-0	Marrakech	CNq	Benatia [27], Chamakh [39], Youssef Hadji [60], Assaidi [69]		Doue CIV
10-08	Senegal	W 2-0	Dakar	Fr	Kharja [10], El Arabi [25]		
4-09	Central African Rep	D 0-0	Bangui	CNq			
9-10	Tanzania	W 3-1	Marrakech	CNq	Chamakh [20], Taarabt [69], Boussoufa [89]		
11-11	Uganda	L 0-1	Marrakech	Fr			
13-11	Cameroon	D 1-1	Marrakech	Fr	Amrabat [90]. L 2-4p		
2012							
23-01	Tunisia	L 1-2	Libreville	CNr1	Kharja [86]	18 000	Bennett RSA
27-01	Gabon	L 2-3	Libreville	CNr1	Kharja 2 [24 90p]	22 000	Doue CIV
31-01	Niger	W 1-0	Libreville	CNr1	Belhanda [78]	4 000	Nampiandraza MAD

Fr = Friendly match • CN = CAF African Cup of Nations • WC = FIFA World Cup
q = qualifier • r1 = first round group • qf = quarter-final • sf = semi-final • f = final

MOROCCO NATIONAL TEAM HISTORICAL RECORDS

Caps · **115** - Noureddine Naybet 1990-2006

Goals · **42** - Ahmed Faras 1965-79

Past Coaches · Larbi Ben Barek, Abdelkader Lohkmiri & Mohamed Kadmiri 1957-61) • Mohamed Massoun & Kader Firoud 1961-64 • Mohamed Massoun & Abderrahmane Belmahjoub 1964-67 • Cluzeau FRA & Abdellah Settati 1968-70 • Blagoja Vidinic YUG 1970-71 • Abderrahmane Belmahjoub 1971 • Jose Barinaga ESP 1972 • Abdallah El Emmani 1972-76 • Gheorghe Mardarescu ROU 1976-77 • Abdallah Ben Barek 1977 • Cluzeau FRA 1979 • Just Fontaine FRA 1979-81 • Yabram Hamidouch 1981 • Jose Faria BRA 1983-88 • Jaime Valente BRA 1988-89 • Antonio Angelillo ARG 1989-90 • Werner Olk GER 1990-92 • Abdelkhalek Louzani 1992 • Abdellah Ajri Blinda 1993-94 • Mohammed Lamari 1994 • Gilson Nunez BRA 1995 • Henri Michel FRA 1995-2000 • Henryk Kasperczak POL 2000 • Mustapha Madih 2001 • Humberto Coelho POR 2002 • Badou Zaki 2002-05 • Philippe Troussier FRA 2005 • Mohamed Fakhir 2005-07 • Henri Michel FRA 2007-08 • Roger Lemerre FRA 2008-09 • Hassan Moumen 2009-10 • Eric Gerets BEL 2010-

MOROCCO 2010–11

CHAMPIONNAT DU GNF1

	Pl	W	D	L	F	A	Pts	RCA	MAS	WAC	OCK	OCS	FAR	FUS	MAT	HUS	DHJ	JSM	CRH	KAC	WAF	KACM	CKT
Raja Casablanca †	30	18	6	6	45	23	60		2-1	1-2	2-1	4-1	2-1	0-0	2-1	2-0	1-1	2-0	2-0	1-0	3-0	2-0	2-1
Maghreb Fès †	30	14	11	5	34	23	53	2-1		2-1	0-0	2-2	1-2	2-1	0-0	0-0	3-1	1-0	0-0	1-1	3-0	1-1	1-0
Wydad Casablanca ‡	30	13	12	5	31	18	51	1-1	3-1		1-2	1-0	1-1	0-2	1-2	1-1	1-1	0-2	2-2	0-0	2-0	0-0	0-0
Olympique Khouribga	30	14	8	8	31	20	50	1-2	2-1	1-0		2-0	1-0	1-0	2-0	0-0	2-1	1-0	0-0	1-0	1-0	2-0	0-0
Olympique Safi	30	12	13	5	31	25	49	1-0	2-1	0-1	1-1		1-0	1-0	1-1	1-0	2-2	1-1	1-0	2-0	1-1	1-1	1-0
FAR Rabat	30	10	10	10	28	27	40	1-1	1-1	1-1	0-2	1-2		0-2	1-1	2-3	0-0	4-2	1-0	0-1	1-1	0-0	1-0
FUS Rabat	30	8	14	8	22	21	38	1-1	0-0	0-1	2-1	0-0	0-1		1-1	1-1	2-0	2-1	1-1	0-1	1-1	1-1	0-0
MA Tétouan	30	8	12	10	26	28	36	1-2	1-1	0-1	2-1	0-1	2-1	1-0		1-0	0-0	0-0	0-2	0-0	1-0	0-1	1-1
HUS Agadir	30	8	12	10	22	24	36	1-1	0-1	0-0	1-0	1-2	0-1	0-1	1-1		0-1	1-0	1-1	1-1	1-0	0-0	1-0
Difaa El Jadida	30	7	14	9	25	25	35	1-0	0-0	0-1	0-0	0-0	0-1	0-0	1-1	0-1		2-0	0-1	2-0	2-2	1-1	3-2
JS Massira	30	8	10	12	24	35	34	1-0	1-2	0-1	1-1	3-3	1-1	0-0	2-1	1-3	1-0		0-0	2-1	2-2	0-2	0-0
Chabab Rif Hoceima	30	6	15	9	21	24	33	1-2	0-1	0-0	1-0	0-2	0-0	2-2	3-2	0-0	1-0	0-1		0-0	1-1	1-1	1-1
Kénitra AC	30	6	14	10	16	24	32	1-2	0-0	0-0	3-2	1-0	1-0	0-0	0-0	2-1	1-2	0-1	0-2		0-0	0-0	1-1
Wydad Fès	30	6	13	11	21	30	31	0-3	0-1	0-1	1-0	0-0	0-1	1-1	1-0	0-0	1-1	1-2	1-1	0-0		0-0	3-1
Kawkab Marrakech	30	4	16	10	19	25	28	1-0	0-1	0-0	1-1	1-1	0-1	3-0	2-2	1-2	0-0	0-1	0-2	0-0	0-1		2-1
Chabab Kasba Tadla	30	4	8	18	17	41	20	0-1	1-2	0-3	0-2	0-0	0-3	0-1	1-0	2-1	1-3	1-1	1-0	0-1	0-3	2-1	

20/08/2010 - 28/05/2011 • † Qualified for the CAF Champions League • ‡ Qualified for the CAF Confederation Cup

MOROCCO 2010–11
CHAMPIONNAT DU GNF2

	Pl	W	D	L	F	A	Pts
COD Meknès	34	16	16	2	35	10	64
IZ Khemisset	34	17	10	7	43	29	61
Union Aït Melloul	34	16	13	5	42	24	61
CAY Berrechid	34	15	14	5	33	20	59
TAS Casablanca	34	13	11	10	26	25	50
Mouloudia Oujda	34	12	11	11	29	29	47
US Mohammedia	34	12	10	12	28	28	46
Chabab Houara	34	11	13	10	28	29	46
Rachad Bernoussi	34	10	13	11	27	29	43
Racing Casablanca	34	10	12	12	38	36	42
IR Tanger	34	9	13	12	28	33	40
AS Salé	34	10	9	15	38	39	39
TUS Temara	34	7	18	9	25	26	39
Stade Marocain	34	8	15	11	18	24	39
Raja Al Hoceima	34	8	11	15	18	29	35
IR Fkih Ben Salah	34	9	8	17	27	39	35
Chabab Mohammedia	34	6	15	13	25	33	33
Hilal Nador	34	3	16	15	18	44	25

21/08/2010 - 22/05/2011

MEDALS TABLE

			Overall			League			Cup		Africa		
			G	S	B	G	S	B	G	S	G	S	B
1	FAR Rabat	FAR	25	11	7	12	5	5	11	4	2	2	2
2	Wydad Casablanca	WAC	23	15	10	12	7	8	9	6	2	2	2
3	Raja Casablanca	RCA	20	12	10	10	7	9	6	4	4	1	1
4	Kawkab Marrakech	KACM	9	8	3	2	6	3	6	2	1		
5	Maghreb Fès	MAS	8	11	2	4	3	2	3	8	1		
6	FUS Rabat	FUS	6	4	1	2	1		5	2	1		
7	KAC Kénitra	KAC	5	5	1	4	2	1	1	3			
8	Mouloudia Oujda	MCO	5	2	3	1	1	3	4	1			
9	Olympic Casablanca	OC	3	1		1	1		2				
10	Olympique Khouribga	OCK	2	6	3	1	2	3	1	4			
11	Rennaisance Settat	RSS	2	5	3	1	2	3	1	3			
12	Chabab Mohammedia	SCCM	2	2	1	1			1	1	2		
	COD Meknès	CODM	2	2	1	1			1	1	2		
14	Hassania Agadir	HUSA	2	2		2					2		
15	Racing Casablanca	RAC	1	2					2		1		

COUPE DU TRONE 2011

Round of 16

Round of 16		Quarter–finals		Semi–finals		Final	
Maghreb Fès	1						
Kawkab Marrakech *	0	Maghreb Fès	1				
Chabab Kasba Tadla	0	HUS Agadir *	0				
HUS Agadir *	1			Maghreb Fès *	1 3p		
FUS Rabat	2			Wydad Casablanca	1 2p		
Kénitra AC *	0	FUS Rabat *	1 4p				
JSM Laâyoune *	1	Wydad Casablanca	1 5p				
Wydad Casablanca	4					Maghreb Fès	1
Difaa El Jadida *	2					COD Meknès ‡	0
CS Toulal	0	Difaa El Jadida *	2				
Chabab Mohammedia*	0	Chabab Rif Hoceima	1				
Chabab Rif Hoceima	1			Difaa El Jadida	0		
US Mohammedia	2			COD Meknès *	1		
AS Salé *	1	US Mohammedia	1				
Olympique Safi	0 3p	COD Meknès *	2				
COD Meknès *	0 4p						

* Home team • ‡ Qualified for the CAF Confederation Cup

CUP FINAL

Moulay Abdallah, Rabat
17-12-2011
Scorer - Jefferson 75 for MAS Fès

MAS – MALAYSIA

FIFA/COCA-COLA WORLD RANKING

'93	'94	'95	'96	'97	'98	'99	'00	'01	'02	'03	'04	'05	'06	'07	'08	'09	'10	'11	'12
79	89	106	96	87	113	117	107	111	128	116	120	123	152	159	156	160	144	148	

						2011							High	Low	Av
Jan	Feb	Mar	Apr	May	Jun	Jul	Aug	Sep	Oct	Nov	Dec		**High**	**Low**	**Av**
142	140	138	144	143	144	145	146	147	151	155	148		**75**	**170**	**121**

Malaysia continued to assert their newly-found dominance at regional level as the country's under-23 team retained the gold medal at the football tournament in the biennial multi-sport South East Asian Games in Jakarta in late 2011. A penalty shoot-out win over bitter rivals Indonesia in the final saw the Malaysians win their third regional trophy in as many years as they seek to match Thailand as the top nation in south east Asia. The SEA Games gold came a year after the full national side won the AFF Suzuki Cup but there was a major setback when neighbours Singapore knocked them out of the 2014 FIFA World Cup qualifiers. The Malaysians had only just squeezed past a weak Chinese Taipei team on away goals in the first round of qualifying but in the second round they then lost 5-3 in the first leg in Singapore and could only draw the return in Kuala Lumpur to tumble out of the tournament. In club football, Kelantan won the Malaysian Super League for the first time but were denied a league and cup double when a Jamaluddin own goal in extra-time handed Terengganu the Malaysian FA Cup before a huge crowd just shy of 90,000 in the national stadium in Kuala Lumpur. The ever-popular Malaysia Cup was won in 2011 by Negeri Sembilan who denied Terengganu a cup double after beating them 2-1 in the final.

FIFA WORLD CUP RECORD
1930-1970 DNE 1974-2014 DNQ

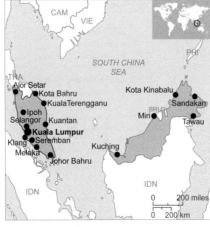

FOOTBALL ASSOCIATION OF MALAYSIA (FAM)

3rd Floor Wisma FAM, Jalan SS5A/9, Kelana Jaya, Petaling Jaya 47301

☎ +60 3 78733100
📠 +60 3 78757984
📧 gensecfam@gmail.com
🖥 www.fam.org.my
FA 1933 CON 1954 FIFA 1956
P HRH Sultan Ahmad Shah
GS Azzuddin Bin Ahmad

FIFA BIG COUNT 2006

Total players	585 730
% of population	2.40%
Male	549 300
Female	36 430
Amateurs 18+	1 430
Youth under 18	7 300
Unregistered	259 800
Professionals	600
Referees	1 810
Admin & coaches	10 000
Number of clubs	11-
Number of teams	550

MAJOR CITIES/TOWNS

		Population
1	Kuala Lumpur	1 468 984
2	Subang Jaya	1 321 672
3	Klang	1 055 207
4	Johor Bahru	895 509
5	Ampang Jaya	756 309
6	Ipoh	702 464
7	Kuching	658 562
8	Shah Alam	617 149
9	Kota Kinabalu	579 304
10	Petaling Jaya	543 415
11	Batu Sembilan	515 961
12	Sandakan	479 121
13	Kajang-Sungai	428 131
14	Seremban	419 536
15	Kuantan	407 778
17	Kuala Terengganu	286 433
18	Kota Bahru	277 301
20	Selangor	265 297
25	Alor Setar	213 624

MALAYSIA

Capital	Kuala Lumpur	Population	25 715 819 (46)	% in cities	70%
GDP per capita	$15 200 (75)	Area km²	329 847 km² (66)	GMT +/-	+8
Neighbours (km)	Brunei 381, Indonesia 1782, Thailand 506 • Coast 4675				

RECENT INTERNATIONAL MATCHES PLAYED BY MALAYSIA

2008 Opponents	Score	Venue	Comp	Scorers	Att	Referee
6-06 Indonesia	D 1-1	Surabaya	Fr	Adan [34]		
22-07 India	D 1-1	Hyderabad	Fr	Indra Putra [75]		
10-10 Pakistan	W 4-1	Kuala Lumpur	Fr	Safee Sali [42], Zaquan Abd Radzak [60], Hairuddin Omar [70], Muhymeen [81]		
15-10 Nepal	W 4-0	Petaling Jaya	Fr	Indra Putra [20], Safee Sali 2 [25 48], Muhymeen [52]	1 000	Junji Huang CHN
20-10 Afghanistan	W 6-0	Petaling Jaya	Fr	Ashaari Shamsuddin 2 [21 64], Nizaruddin Yusof [41], Zaquan Abd Radzak [44], Safee Sali [85], Hairuddin [87]	3 000	
23-10 Myanmar	W 4-0	Kuala Lumpur	Fr	Indra Putra 2 [26 76p], Safee Sali [61], Amirul Hadi [83]	20 000	Mahapab THA
18-11 Myanmar	L 1-4	Yangon	Fr	Amirul Hadi [75]	30 000	
29-11 Singapore	D 2-2	Petaling Jaya	Fr	Amirul Hadi [22], Hardi Jaafar [74]		
6-12 Laos	W 3-0	Phuket	AFFr1	Safee Sali 2 [68 87], Indra Putra [73]	5 000	Nitrorejo IDN
8-12 Vietnam	L 2-3	Phuket	AFFr1	Indra Putra 2 [20 85]		Palaniyandi SIN
10-12 Thailand	L 0-3	Phuket	AFFr1		15 000	Abdul Bashir SIN
2009						
21-01 UAE	L 0-5	Kuala Lumpur	ACq		10 000	Williams AUS
12-08 Kenya	D 0-0	Kuala Lumpur	Fr			
15-08 China PR	D 0-0	Kuala Lumpur	Fr			
30-08 Saudi Arabia	L 1-2	Riyadh	Fr	Shakir [85]		
5-09 Jordan	D 0-0	Amman	Fr			
11-09 Lesotho	W 5-0	Kuala Lumpur	Fr	Zaquan Abd Razak [41], Norshahrul Talaha [44], Manaf 2 [78 90], Amirul Hadi [88]		
14-11 Uzbekistan	L 1-3	Tashkent	ACq	Zaquan Abd Razak [68]	5 000	Moradi IRN
18-11 Uzbekistan	L 1-3	Kuala Lumpur	ACq	Baddrol Bin Bakhtiar [70]	2 000	Tan Hai CHN
2010						
6-01 UAE	L 0-1	Dubai	ACq		3 500	Basma SYR
27-02 Yemen	W 1-0	Kuala Lumpur	Fr	Baddrol Bin Bakhtiar [55]		
3-09 Oman	L 0-3	Doha	Fr			
1-12 Indonesia	L 1-5	Jakarta	AFFr1	Norshahrul Talaha [18]	62 000	Vo Min Tri VIE
4-12 Thailand	D 0-0	Jakarta	AFFr1			Win Cho MYA
7-12 Laos	W 5-1	Palembang	AFFr1	Amri Yahyah 2 [4 40], Mohd Zainal [73], Norshahrul Talaha [77], Mahalli Jasuli [90]		Vo Min Tri VIE
15-12 Vietnam	W 2-0	Kuala Lumpur	AFFsf	Safee Sali 2 [60 79]	45 000	Sun Baojie CHN
18-12 Vietnam	D 0-0	Hanoi	AFFsf		40 000	Kim Sang Woo KOR
26-12 Indonesia	W 3-0	Kuala Lumpur	AFFf	Safee Sali 2 [61 73], Ashaari Shamsuddin [68]	70 000	Toma JPN
29-12 Indonesia	L 1-2	Jakarta	AFFf		80 000	Green AUS
2011						
9-02 Hong Kong	W 2-0	Kuala Lumpur	Fr	Safiq Bin Rahim [43], Amirul Hadi Zainal [90]		
3-06 Hong Kong	D 1-1	Hong Kong	Fr	Hadi Bin Yahaya [65]		
18-06 Myanmar	W 2-0	Kota Bahru	Fr	Amirul Hadi Zainal [28], Baddrol Bin Bakhtiar [55]		
29-06 Chinese Taipei	W 2-1	Kuala Lumpur	WCq	Safiq Bin Rahim [29], Mohamad Abd Radzak [54]	45 000	Mahapab THA
3-07 Chinese Taipei	L 2-3	Taipei	WCq	Mohamad Abd Radzak [8], Safiq Bin Rahim [40]	16 768	Minh Tri Vo VIE
23-07 Singapore	L 3-5	Singapore	WCq	Safee Sali 2 [17 1], Hadi Bin Yahaya [70]	6 000	Shukralla BHR
28-07 Singapore	D 1-1	Kuala Lumpur	WCq	Safee Sali [57]	90 000	Takayama JPN
7-10 Australia	L 0-5	Canberra	Fr			
13-11 India	D 1-1	Guwahati	Fr	Safiq Bin Rahim [44]		
16-11 India	L 2-3	Calcutta	Fr	Safee Sali 2 [45 60]		

Fr = Friendly match • AFF = ASEAN Football Federation Championship • AC = AFC Asian Cup • WC = FIFA World Cup
q = qualifier • r1 = first round group • sf = semi-final • 3p = third place play-off • † not a full international

MALAYSIA NATIONAL TEAM HISTORICAL RECORDS

Past Coaches — Neoh Boon Hean • Edwin Dutton • Choo Seng Quee SIN • Otto Westphal GER • C. De Silva • Peter Velappan • Abdul Ghani Minhat 1969 • Harold Hassall ENG • Dave McLaren AUS 1970-71 • Jalil Che Din 1972 • M. Kuppan 1973-77 • Jalil Che Din 1974 • Chow Kwai Lam 1978 • Karl-Heinz Weigang GER 1979-82 • M. Chandran 1982-83 • Frank Lord ENG 1983-85 • Mohamad Bakar 1985-86 • Jozef Venglos CZE 1986-87 • Abdul Rahman Ibrahim 1987 • Richard Bate ENG 1988 • M. Chandran 1988 • Trevor Hartley ENG 1989 • Ahmad Shafie 1990 • Rahim Abdullah 1991 • Ken Worden AUS 1992-93 • Claude Le Roy FRA 1994-95 • Hatem Souisi TUN 1995 • Wan Jamak Wan Hassan 1996-97 • Hatem Souisi 1998 • Abdul Rahman Ibrahim 1998-2000 • Allan Harris 2001-04 • K. Rajagopal1 2004 • Bertalan Bicskei HUN 2004-05 • Norizan Bakar 2005-07 • Bhaskaran Sathianathan 2007-09 • Rajagopal Krishnasamy 2009-

MALAYSIA 2011

MALAYSIAN SUPER LEAGUE (MSL)

	Pl	W	D	L	F	A	Pts	Kelantan	Terengganu	Selangor	Kedah	U-23	Perak	Johor FC	Negeri	PBDKT	Sabah	Felda Utd	KLFA	Pahang	Perlis
Kelantan FA ‡	26	17	5	4	52	21	56		1-1	1-0	2-0	2-1	1-0	4-1	3-0	1-2	0-0	6-0	2-0	1-0	4-0
Terengganu FA	26	16	5	5	54	26	53	0-3		1-1	0-1	3-1	3-0	3-0	3-0	3-2	3-0	1-0	4-0	5-0	3-1
Selangor FA	26	16	4	6	42	24	52	0-2	3-2		2-0	1-2	1-0	3-2	2-0	0-2	1-0	2-1	1-1	2-1	7-1
Kedah FA	26	13	6	7	25	20	45	1-1	2-1	0-2		1-2	0-0	1-0	1-1	1-0	0-0	1-0	0-0	1-0	2-0
Harimau Muda A	26	12	7	7	38	28	43	2-2	1-2	1-2	0-1		1-1	2-2	1-1	3-1	2-0	1-1	1-0	3-1	1-1
Perak FA	26	10	10	6	31	24	40	4-0	1-1	0-0	1-3	1-1		1-0	2-0	2-0	1-1	1-0	5-3	0-0	2-1
Johor FC	26	8	10	8	26	28	34	0-1	2-1	0-0	0-1	0-1	1-1		0-0	2-1	3-0	0-0	0-0	2-1	2-1
Negeri Sembilan FA	26	8	8	10	29	32	32	0-0	1-1	1-2	0-2	1-0	3-1	2-1		4-0	1-0	0-1	0-1	3-1	2-0
PBDKT T-Team FC	26	9	4	13	35	40	31	4-3	0-1	2-1	3-1	1-3	0-0	1-1	1-3		3-0	2-0	2-3	0-0	3-0
Sabah FA	26	7	7	12	24	32	28	1-2	1-2	1-2	1-0	0-2	2-1	0-1	2-0	1-3		2-1	3-0	2-0	2-2
Felda United FC	26	7	7	12	22	34	28	1-3	2-6	0-1	1-2	2-0	0-1	0-0	2-2	2-0	1-1		2-1	2-1	2-0
Kuala Lumpur FA	26	6	8	12	23	34	26	0-2	1-2	1-3	0-1	0-1	1-1	1-2	1-1	3-1	1-0	0-0		0-0	3-0
Pahang FA	26	5	7	14	19	36	22	2-0	1-2	2-1	0-1	0-2	0-2	0-0	1-1	1-0	2-2	0-0	0-2		3-1
Perlis FA	26	2	4	20	20	61	10	1-5	1-3	0-2	0-1	1-3	1-2	2-2	3-2	2-1	0-1	0-1	0-0	1-2	

29/01/2011 - 6/07/2011 • ‡ Qualified for the AFC Cup • Harimau Muda A is the Malaysia U-21 team
Top scorers: 20 - Abdul Hadi Yahya, Terengganu • 19 - Norshahrul Idlan Talaha, Kelantan • 13 - Abdul Manaf Mamat, Terengganu

MALAYSIA 2011 PREMIER LEAGUE (2)

	Pl	W	D	L	F	A	Pts
PKNS FC	22	18	3	1	51	7	57
Sarawak FA	22	15	3	4	51	16	48
PDRM FA	22	12	3	7	36	28	39
Johor FA	22	11	3	8	37	25	36
Sime Darby FC	22	10	5	7	22	12	35
USM FC	22	11	2	9	32	30	35
ATM FA	22	9	7	6	26	22	34
Muar Mun'pal Council	22	8	4	10	29	42	28
Pos Malaysia FC	22	7	6	9	26	36	27
Harimau Muda B	22	5	5	12	24	28	20
Sinar Dimaja MS FC	22	3	2	17	22	63	11
Penang FA	22	1	1	20	14	61	4

31/01/2011 - 1/07/2011 • Harimau Muda B is the national U-20 development team and is ineligible for promotion

MEDALS TABLE

		Overall			League			MCup		FAC		Asia		
		G	S	B	G	S	B	G	S	G	S	G	S	B
1	Selangor FA	43	20	1	6	2	1	32	15	5	2	1		
2	FA of Singapore	26	19		2			24	19					
3	Perak FA	11	15	3	2	1	3	7	11	2	3			
4	Kedah FA	10	10	1	3	3	1	4	6	3	1			
5	Penang FA	8	13		3	2		4	9	1	2			
6	Pahang FA	8	7		5	2		2	4	1	1			
7	Kuala Lumpur FA	8	2		2			3	1	3	1			
8	Negeri Sembilan FA	6	4	3	1	1	3	3	3	2				
9	Johor FA	4	1					2	1	1				
10	Terengganu FA	3	9	1		3	1	1	4	2	2			
11	Perlis FA	3	5	2	1	1	2	2	1		3			
12	Sabah FA	2	6	2	1		2		3	1	3			
13	Kelantan FA	2	6	1	1	1	1	1	3		2			
14	Sarawak FA	2	3	1	1		1	1	2					
15	Brunei D'salam	1	1					1	1					

MALAYSIA CUP 2011

First Round Groups

Group A	Pl	W	D	L	F	A	Pts	Pe	Sa	Ke	Jo
Perak	6	4	2	0	9	5	14		2-1	2-1	2-1
Sabah	6	3	1	2	10	6	10	0-0		0-1	3-1
Kedah	6	2	6	2	9	8	8	1-1	1-2		3-3
Johor FA	6	0	1	5	7	16	1	1-2	1-4	0-2	

Group B	Pl	W	D	L	F	A	Pts	NS	Te	PK	SD
Negeri Sem'lan	6	4	1	1	10	4	13		1-0	0-2	5-0
Terengganu	6	4	1	1	8	3	13	0-0		3-2	1-0
PKNS	6	3	0	3	7	6	9	1-2	0-1		1-0
Sime Darby	6	0	0	6	1	13	0	1-2	0-3	0-1	

Group C	Pl	W	D	L	F	A	Pts	Ke	FU	Jo	Sa
Kelantan	6	4	1	1	11	4	13		2-0	2-1	4-0
Felda United	6	3	1	2	6	4	10	2-0		1-1	1-0
Johor FC	6	2	2	2	7	8	8	1-1	0-2		3-1
Sarawak	6	1	0	5	2	11	3	0-2	1-0	0-1	

Group D	Pl	W	D	L	F	A	Pts	PT	Se	KL	PD
PBDKT T-Team	6	4	1	1	15	4	13		1-0	1-1	4-0
Selangor	6	3	1	2	9	5	10	1-2		2-1	2-0
Kuala Lumpur	6	2	3	1	7	4	9	2-1	0-0		0-0
PDRM	6	0	1	5	1	19	1	0-6	1-4	0-3	

Quarter-finals

Negeri Sem'lan	0	3
Felda United *	1	0
Sabah *	1	1
PBDKT T-Team	2	2
Selangor *	3	1
Perak	1	0
Kelantan FA	1	2
Terengganu *	3	2

Semi-finals

Negeri Sem'lan	4	2
PBDKT T-Team*	2	1
Selangor FA *	0	1
Terengganu	2	2

Final

Negeri Sem'lan	2
Terengganu	1

CUP FINAL
Shah Alam, Selangor, 29-10-2011, Att: 60 000, Ref: Mohd Shokri Nor Scorers - Subramaniam Kunanlan 81, Hairuddin Omar 86 for Negeri; Mohd Ashaari Shamsuddin 59 for Terengganu

* Home team in the 1st leg

MALAYSIA FA CUP 2011

First Round		Round of 16		Quarter-finals			Semi-finals			Final	
Terengganu FA	2	Terengganu FA	3	Terengganu FA	3	1	Terengganu FA	3	2	Terengganu FA ‡	2
USM FC*	1	ATM FA*	2	Perak FA*	2	3	Pahang FA*	2	0	Kelantan FA	1
Sarawak FA	0										
ATM FA*	2	Sime Darby FC	0								
Sime Darby FC	5	Perak FA*	3								
Malacca FA*	0										
PDRM FA*	1	Kuala Lumpur FA	0 4p	Kuala Lumpur FA*	1	0					
Perak FA	4	Negeri Sembilan FA*	0 2p	Pahang FA	2	0					
Kuala Lumpur FA*	3										
Pos Malaysia FC	0	PKNS FC*	1								
Negeri Sembilan FA	Bye	Pahang FA	3								
PKNS FC*	5										
Muar Mun'pal Council	0	Selangor FA*	2	Selangor FA*	3	2	Selangor FA*	1	1		
Sabah FA	1	Harimau Muda B	1	Johor FA	1	1	Kelantan FA	5	1		
Pahang FA*	2										
Selangor FA	Bye	Harimau Muda A*	1								
Melodi Jaya SC*	0	Johor FA	2								
Harimau Muda B	4										
Harimau Muda A*	4	Felda United FC*	1	Felda United FC	2	0					
SDMS Kepala Batas FC	0	Kedah FA	0	Kelantan FA*	2	3					
Penang FA*	1										
Johor FA	5	Johor FC*	0								
Felda United FC	2	Kelantan FA	1								
Perlis FA*	0										
Kedah FA	Bye										
Johor FC*	5										
KL Spa FC	0										
PBDKT T-Team FC*	1 5p										
Kelantan FA	1 6p										

* Home team/home team in the first leg • ‡ Qualified for the AFC Cup

CUP FINAL

National Stadium, Bukit Jalil, Kuala Lumpur 11-06-2011. Att: 87 500. Ref: Mohd Salleh Scorers - Jamaluddin OG 98+, Nordin Alias 110 for Terengganu; Azwan Roya 79 for Kelantan

Terengganu - Mohd Sharbinee - Hariri Mohd Safii, Mohd Zubir Azmi, Marzuki Yusof (c), Mazlizam Mohamad - Joseph Kalang Tie, Ismail Faruqi (Nordin Alias 80), Reeshafiq Alwi, Mohd Ashaari - Abdul Manaf Mamat, Abdul Hadi Yahya. Tr: Irfan Bakti

Kelantan - Khairul Fahmi - Mohd Daudsu Jamaluddin, Mohd Farisham Ismail, Subraminiam, Zairul Fitree Ishak - Khairul Izuan Rosli (Ramzul Zahini), Suppiah Chanturu, Shakir Shaari, Azwan Roya - Badrul Radzi, Norshahrul Idlan Talaha. Tr: M Karathu

MDA – MOLDOVA

'93	'94	'95	'96	'97	'98	'99	'00	'01	'02	'03	'04	'05	'06	'07	'08	'09	'10	'11	'12
-	118	109	117	131	116	93	94	103	111	106	114	107	86	52	97	94	84	136	

						2011									
Jan	Feb	Mar	Apr	May	Jun	Jul	Aug	Sep	Oct	Nov	Dec		High	Low	Av
84	81	87	86	86	85	85	88	122	123	135	136		37	149	102

Sheriff Tiraspol's spectacular 10-year reign as Moldovan champions came to a surprising end in 2011when they were finally deposed by Dacia, a club from the capital Chisinau. Dacia almost certainly benefitted from Sheriff's preoccupation with a Europa League campaign which saw them qualify for the group stage for the second year running, but Dacia did have an incredible season. They lost just once in the 39-game campaign, finishing nine points ahead of Sheriff to claim their first-ever trophy. There were also first-time winners of the cup with Iskra-Stal from the town of Rîbnita beating Olimpia Balti 2-1 in the final after having knocked out of Sheriff in the semi-finals. For Sheriff - double winners for the three previous seasons - it was a hugely disappointing year as they finished bottom of their 2010-11 Europa League group and they failed to get past the qualifying rounds in the 2011-12 tournament. In the qualifiers for Euro 2012 the national team could only finish above minnows San Marino in what was one of the tougher groups. Their Romanian coach Gavril Balint was replaced after the campaign by Ion Caras who returned for his third spell in charge, having coached the newly independent nation from 1991 until 1997. Drawn in a difficult 2014 FIFA World Cup qualifying group containing England, he set a target of fourth place.

UEFA EUROPEAN CHAMPIONSHIP RECORD
1960-1992 DNE (Played as part of the Soviet Union) **1996-2012** DNQ

FOOTBALL ASSOCIATION OF MOLDOVA (FMF)

Federatia Moldoveneasca de Fotbal, Str. Tricolorului nr. 39, Chisinau MD-2012
☎ +373 22 210413
📠 +373 22 210432
✉ fmf@fmf.md
🖥 www.fmf.md
FA 1990 CON 1992 FIFA 1994
P Pavel Cebanu
GS Nicolai Cebotari

FIFA BIG COUNT 2006

Total players	168 570
% of population	3.77%
Male	147 430
Female	21 140
Amateurs 18+	6 629
Youth under 18	2 603
Unregistered	66 150
Professionals	543
Referees	151
Admin & coaches	560
Number of clubs	86
Number of teams	2 036

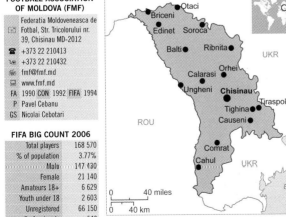

MAJOR CITIES/TOWNS

		Population
1	Chisinau	586 151
2	Tiraspol	143 977
3	Balti	100 176
4	Tighina	98 001
5	Ribnita	50 345
6	Ungheni	31 344
7	Cahul	30 487
8	Soroca	23 484
9	Edinet	21 944
10	Orhei	21 878
11	Comrat	20 750
12	Causeni	20 433
13	Dubasari	20 199
14	Ocnita	18 556
15	Ciadir Lunga	17 523
16	Straseni	17 459
17	Floresti	15 324
18	Ialoveni	14 311
36	Otaci	8 400

REPUBLICA MOLDOVA • REPUBLIC OF MOLDOVA

Capital Chisinau	Population 4 320 748 (122)	% in cities 42%
GDP per capita $2500 (172)	Area km² 33 851 km² (139)	GMT +/- +2
Neighbours (km) Romania 450, Ukraine 940		

RECENT INTERNATIONAL MATCHES PLAYED BY MOLDOVA

2008 Opponents	Score	Venue	Comp	Scorers	Att	Referee
6-02 Kazakhstan	W 1-0	Antalya	Fr	Bugaev 13	300	Lehner AUT
24-05 Croatia	L 0-1	Rijeka	Fr		7 000	Ceferin SVN
28-05 Armenia	D 2-2	Tiraspol	Fr	Arakelyan OG 42, Alexeev 74	3 653	Ischenko UKR
20-08 Lithuania	L 0-3	Vilnius	Fr		2 000	Kaasik EST
6-09 Latvia	L 1-2	Tiraspol	WCq	Alexeev 76	4 300	Courtney NIR
10-09 Israel	L 1-2	Chisinau	WCq	Picusciac 1	10 500	Muniz ESP
11-10 Greece	L 0-3	Piraeus	WCq		13 684	Berntsen NOR
15-10 Luxembourg	D 0-0	Luxembourg	WCq		2 157	Borski POL
18-11 Estonia	L 0-1	Tallinn	Fr		1 500	Larsen DEN
19-11 Lithuania	D 1-1	Tallinn	Fr	Bugalov 65	100	Tohver EST
2009						
11-02 Macedonia FYR	D 1-1	Antalya	Fr	Andronic 60	600	Salyi KAZ
28-03 Switzerland	L 0-2	Chisinau	WCq		10 500	McDonald SCO
1-04 Switzerland	L 0-2	Geneva	WCq		20 100	Rocchi ITA
6-06 Georgia	W 2-0	Tbilisi	Fr	Sofroni 7, Golovatenco 57	8 000	Salyi KAZ
10-06 Belarus	D 2-2	Borisov	Fr	Calincov 77, Andronic 82	2 000	Mazeika LTU
12-08 Armenia	W 4-1	Yerevan	Fr	Golovatenco 2 34 64, Andronic 82, Epureanu 90p	1 000	Silagava GEO
5-09 Luxembourg	D 0-0	Chisinau	WCq		7 820	Mazeika LTU
9-09 Greece	D 1-1	Chisinau	WCq	Andronic 90	9 870	Stalhammar SWE
10-10 Israel	L 1-3	Ramat Gan	WCq	Calincov 92+	8 700	Blom NED
14-10 Latvia	L 2-3	Riga	WCq	Ovseannicov 25, Sofroni 90	3 800	Hyytia FIN
2010						
3-03 Kazakhstan	W 1-0	Antalya	Fr	Epureanu 65	500	Bezborodov RUS
26-05 Azerbaijan	D 1-1	Seekirchen	Fr	Cojocari 81	200	Lechner AUT
29-05 UAE	L 2-3	Anif	Fr	Tigirlas 14, Bulgaru 80	200	Schorgenhofer AUT
11-08 Georgia	D 0-0	Chisinau	Fr		3 000	Shvestov UKR
3-09 Finland	W 2-0	Chisinau	ECq	Suvorov 69, Doros 74	10 300	Malek POL
7-09 Hungary	L 1-2	Budapest	ECq	Suvorov 79	9 209	Kovarik CZE
8-10 Netherlands	L 0-1	Chisinau	ECq		10 500	Meyer GER
12-10 San Marino	W 2-0	Serravalle	ECq	Josan 20, Doros 86p	714	Courtney NIR
2011						
6-02 Poland	L 0-1	Vila Real	Fr		250	Dos Anjos POR
9-02 Andorra	W 2-1	Lagos	Fr	Picusceac 66, Bugaev 90		Lopes POR
29-03 Sweden	L 1-2	Stockholm	ECq	Suvorov 92+	25 544	Kircher GER
3-06 Sweden	L 1-4	Chisinau	ECq	Bugaev 61	10 500	Marriner ENG
10-08 Cyprus	L 2-3	Nicosia	Fr	Armas 23, Ovsyannikov 45	2 000	Mazic SRB
2-09 Finland	L 1-4	Helsinki	ECq	Alexeev 85	9 056	Kakos GRE
6-09 Hungary	L 0-2	Chisinau	ECq		10 500	Bebek CRO
7-10 Netherlands	L 0-1	Rotterdam	ECq		47 226	Jug SV
11-10 San Marino	W 4-0	Chisinau	ECq	Zmeu 30, OG 62, Suvorov 66, Andronic.G 87	6 534	Reinert FRO
11-11 Georgia	L 0-2	Tbilisi	Fr			Aliyev AZE

Fr = Friendly match • EC = UEFA EURO 2012 • WC = FIFA World Cup • q = qualifier

MOLDOVA NATIONAL TEAM HISTORICAL RECORDS

Caps: 74 - Radu Rebeja 1991-2008 • **69** - Serghei Clescenco 1991-2006 • **55** - Valeriu Catinsus 1999-2009 • **53** - Ion Testemitanu 1991-2007 • 52 - Serghei Rogaciov 1996-2007 • **46** - Serghei Epureanu 1996-2006 & Serghei Stroenco 1992-2007

Goals: 11 - Serghei Clescenco 1991-2006 • **9** - Serghei Rogaciov 1996-2007 • **8** - Iurie Miterev 1992-2006 • **7** - Serghei Dadu 2002- • **6** - Viorel Frunza 2002-08 • **5** - Igor Bugaiov 2007- & Ion Testemitanu 1991-2007

Past Coaches: Ion Caras 1991-92 • Eugen Piunovschi 1992 • Ion Caras 1992-97 • Ivan Daniliant 1998-99 • Alexandru Matiura 1999-2001, Alexandru Spiridon 2001 • Viktor Pasulko UKR 2002-06 • Anatol Teslev 2006-07 • Igor Dobrovolski RUS 2007-09 • Gavril Balint Rou 2010-11 • Ion Caras 2012-

MOLDOVA 2010-11

PREMIER LEAGUE

Team	Pl	W	D	L	F	A	Pts	Dacia	Sheriff	Milsami	Zimbru	Iskra-Stali	Olimpia	Tiraspol	CSCA Rapid	Academia	Costuleni	Nistru	Sfintul	Gagauziya	Dinamo
Dacia Chisinau †	39	27	11	1	66	16	92		0-0 1-1	0-0	1-1 1-0	0-0	3-1 2-0	2-0	1-0	3-1 2-0	3-1	1-1 2-0	7-0 3-0	1-0	5-0 3-1
Sheriff Tiraspol ‡	39	24	11	4	81	16	83	3-0		2-0 2-1	1-0	1-0 2-1	1-1	3-0 0-0	4-0 2-1	1-1	1-1 4-0	1-0	4-0 6-0	3-0 5-1	2-0
Milsami Orhei ‡	39	23	9	7	71	23	78	1-2 0-0	0-1		1-0 1-2	0-0	0-0 2-1	5-1	3-0	1-1 1-0	2-0	5-0 1-2	2-1 4-0	2-1	1-1 7-2
Zimbru Chisinau	39	22	10	7	56	20	76	0-1	1-1 1-0	0-0		0-1	0-0 0-0	1-0 0-1	0-0 1-0	1-0	2-1	2-0	2-1 3-0	1-0 3-1	6-1
Iskra-Stal Rîbnita ‡	39	21	11	7	62	26	74	0-0	0-1	2-2 2-1	0-0		0-0 4-2	1-0	0-0 3-2	5-0	1-1 2-1	4-0	3-1	1-0 4-0	6-1
Olimpia Balti	39	21	11	7	59	31	74	1-2	0-0 1-0	0-0	1-1	0-1 2-1		0-4	0-3 3-0	2-1 3-2	4-1	0-0 1-0	4-1	1-1 1-0	4-2 1-0
FC Tiraspol	39	17	6	16	57	45	57	0-0 0-1	0-3	1-2	0-1	0-2	0-0 1-2		1-3	1-0 0-0	2-1	3-0 4-0	1-0	1-0 5-0	4-1 7-0
CSCA Rapid Ghidighici	39	15	10	14	39	37	55	0-2 0-0	1-1	0-1	0-1 0-0	0-0 1-2	1-1	2-0		2-0 4-2	1-0	1-0 3-2	2-0 1-3	2-1	2-0 2-0
Academia Chisinau	39	14	10	15	44	37	52	0-0	1-1	0-1	0-1	0-0	0-1	0-0 1-2	1-1		2-0	0-1 1-0	2-0	0-3	2-1 0-0
FC Costuleni	39	7	6	26	23	68	27	1-2	0-1	0-0	0-7 0-3	0-2 1-3	0-1	0-1 1-2	0-0 1-2	0-0		1-5	2-1 2-0	0-3	2-1 0-0
Nistru Otaci	39	7	4	28	33	75	25	1-1	0-3 1-3	0-1	1-5 2-4	0-1	0-2 0-3	4-2	0-4	0-1 1-0	1-0		3-0	1-0	2-0 4-0
Sfintul G. Suruceni	39	6	7	26	30	83	25	0-2	1-1	0-4	0-3	2-2	0-2	0-2 0-1	0-0 1-1	0-2 1-2	2-2 0-2	1-1 1-1		2-2 1-3	1-2 2-0
Gagauziya Comrat	39	7	2	30	38	89	23	1-4	0-2	0-4	0-2	0-3	0-4 0-3	1-2	1-3 1-2	1-2	1-3	0-3 0-3	2-1 5-1		5-4
Dinamo Bender	39	6	4	29	25	118	22	0-2	0-7 0-7	0-3 1-0	1-6	0-1	0-8 0-2	0-3 0-1	1-5	1-1 0-0	1-0	3-2 0-2	0-4	1-0	

24/07/2010 - 22/05/2011 • † Qualified for the UEFA Champions League • ‡ Qualified for the Europa League
Top scorers: **26** - Gheorghe Boghiu, Milsami • **21** - Ghenadie Orbu, Dacia • **19** - Mahai Cojusea, Gagauziya • **16** - Alexandru Popovici, Iskra-Stal

MOLDOVA 2010-11 DIVIZIA A (2)

	Pl	W	D	L	F	A	Pts
Lokomotiva Balti	28	17	8	3	59	23	59
Ursidos Chisinau	28	16	10	2	63	17	58
Dinamo Auto Tiraspol	28	17	6	5	52	26	57
Intersport-Aroma	28	15	9	4	53	20	54
Sheriff-2 Tiraspol	28	15	5	8	64	26	50
Lilcora Chisinau	28	14	6	8	55	38	48
FC Cahul 2005	28	13	5	10	35	40	44
CSCA Buiucani	28	12	6	10	56	45	42
Zimbru-2 Chisinau	28	9	7	12	38	33	34
Speranta C. Veche	28	9	7	12	32	45	34
MIPAN-Voran Chisinau	28	9	2	17	45	72	29
Sfintul-2	28	7	4	17	28	48	25
Dinamo-2 Bender	28	5	6	17	27	60	21
Olimp Ungheni	28	4	7	17	31	75	19
Olimpia-2 Tiligul	28	4	0	24	16	86	12

8/08/2010 - 4/06/2011 • No Promotion

MEDALS TABLE

		Overall			League			Cup		City
		G	S	B	G	S	B	G	S	
1	Sheriff Tiraspol	17	3		10	2		7	1	Tiraspol
2	Zimbru Chisinau	13	7	2	8	5	2	5	2	Chisinau
3	Tiligul-Tiras	3	8	3		6	3	3	2	Tiraspol
4	FC Tiraspol	3	3	4	1	1	4	2	2	Tiraspol
5	Nistru Otaci	1	11	3		3	3	1	8	Otaci
6	Dacia Chisnau	1	5	1	1	2	1		3	Chisinau
7	Iskra-Stal Ribnita	1	1	1	1	1		1		Ribnita
8	Bugeac Comrat	1	1					1	1	Comrat
9	Olimpia Balti	1	2			2			1	Balti
10	Dinamo Chisinau	1							1	Chisinau
11	Codru Calarasi	1				1			1	Calarasi
	Moldova Boroseni	1				1			1	Boroseni
	Milsami Orhei	1				1			1	Orhei

CUPA MOLDOVEI 2010-11

Round of 16

Iskra-Stal Rîbnita	1
Ursidos Chisinau *	0
Lilcora Chisinau *	0
CSCA Rapid Ghidighici	3
FC Tiraspol *	1 5p
Milsami Orhei	1 4p
FC Costuleni	0
Sheriff Tiraspol *	3
Dacia Chisinau	4
Nistru Otaci *	1
Zimbru Chisinau	1 8p
FC Cahul 2005 *	1 9p
Academia Chisinau	4
Izvoras 67 *	0
Sfintul G. Suruceni	0
Olimpia Balti *	1

Quarter-finals

Iskra-Stal Rîbnita	1 2
CSCA Rapid G'ghici *	1 0
FC Tiraspol *	2 0
Sheriff Tiraspol	3 2
Dacia Chisinau	0 7
FC Cahul 2005 *	0 0
Academia Chisinau	0 0
Olimpia Balti *	2 1

Semi-finals

Iskra-Stal Rîbnita	0 3
Sheriff Tiraspol *	1 0
Dacia Chisinau *	0 1
Olimpia Balti	1 2

Final

Iskra-Stal Rîbnita ‡	2
Olimpia Balti	1

* Home team/home team in the first leg • ‡ Qualified for the Europa League

CUP FINAL
Zimbru, Chisinau
26-05-2011, Ref: Gheciu
Scorers - Olexandr Suchu [11], Evgheny Gorodetchi [25] for Iskra-Stal; Gheorghii Ovseannicov [22] for Olimpia

MDV – MALDIVES

FIFA/COCA-COLA WORLD RANKING

'93	'94	'95	'96	'97	'98	'99	'00	'01	'02	'03	'04	'05	'06	'07	'08	'09	'10	'11	'12
148	162	169	176	160	166	143	154	147	152	141	139	133	158	151	154	137	162	173	

	2011														
	Jan	Feb	Mar	Apr	May	Jun	Jul	Aug	Sep	Oct	Nov	Dec	High	Low	Av
	161	160	161	143	148	151	160	162	166	162	166	173	126	183	154

The Maldives long ago shrugged off the embarrassment associated with their record 17-0 defeat at the hands of Iran in qualifying for the 1998 FIFA World Cup finals, so when the two nations were paired again in the second round of qualifying for Brazil 2014, the Indian Ocean islanders had the opportunity to prove just how far they had progressed in the intervening years. A 5-0 aggregate defeat over two legs underlined that the Maldives are no longer the whipping boys they once were in Asian football. At the end of 2011 the team once again showed its strength at a regional level with their run to the semi-finals of the South Asian Football Federation Championship. Draws against Nepal and Pakistan were followed by a 3-1 win over Bangladesh which saw them qualify from the group stage. Their progress to the final, however, was halted by tournament hosts and defending champions India. In club football, VB Sports won the Dhivehi League and then ended the season by claiming the FA Cup after a classic final against Maziya which finished 6-4 - Ali Ashfaq scoring four of the goals. Just prior to that, however, they had been knocked out of the President's Cup, thus failing to make a clean sweep of the three trophies during the season. Instead it was Victory who claimed the President's Cup - for the 21st time in the club's history.

FIFA WORLD CUP RECORD
1930-1994 DNE 1998-2014 DNQ

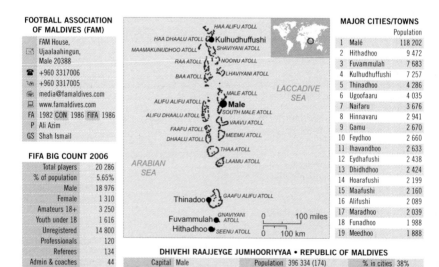

FOOTBALL ASSOCIATION OF MALDIVES (FAM)

	FAM House, Ujaalaahingun, Male 20388
☎	+960 3317006
📠	+960 3317005
✉	media@famaldives.com
🖥	www.famaldives.com
FA	1982 CON 1986 FIFA 1986
P	Ali Azim
GS	Shah Ismail

FIFA BIG COUNT 2006

Total players	20 286
% of population	5.65%
Male	18 976
Female	1 310
Amateurs 18+	3 250
Youth under 18	1 616
Unregistered	14 800
Professionals	120
Referees	134
Admin & coaches	44
Number of clubs	60
Number of teams	367

MAJOR CITIES/TOWNS

		Population
1	Malé	118 202
2	Hithadhoo	9 472
3	Fuvammulah	7 683
4	Kulhudhuffushi	7 257
5	Thinadhoo	4 286
6	Ugoofaaru	4 035
7	Naifaru	3 676
8	Hinnavaru	2 941
9	Gamu	2 670
10	Feydhoo	2 660
11	Ihavandhoo	2 633
12	Eydhafushi	2 438
13	Dhidhdhoo	2 424
14	Hoarafushi	2 199
15	Maafushi	2 160
16	Alifushi	2 089
17	Maradhoo	2 039
18	Funadhoo	1 988
19	Meedhoo	1 888

DHIVEHI RAAJJEYGE JUMHOORIYYAA • REPUBLIC OF MALDIVES

Capital Male	Population 396 334 (174)	% in cities 38%
GDP per capita $4500 (149)	Area km² 298 km² (209)	GMT + / - +5
Neighbours (km) Coast 644		

RECENT INTERNATIONAL MATCHES PLAYED BY THE MALDIVES

2006	Opponents	Score		Venue	Comp	Scorers	Att	Referee
No international matches played in 2006								
2007								
2-10	Oman	L	0-1	Muscat	Fr			
8-10	Yemen	L	0-3	Sana'a	WCq		3 000	Mansour LIB
28-10	Yemen	L	0-2	Male	WCq		8 900	Sarkar IND
2008								
9-04	Lebanon	L	0-4	Beirut	ACq			
23-04	Lebanon	L	1-2	Male	ACq	Shamveel Qasim [22]		
3-06	Pakistan	W	3-0	Male	SAFr1	Mohamed Shifan [45], Ahmed Thariq [48], Akram OG [90]		
5-06	Nepal	W	4-1	Male	SAFr1	Ismail Mohamed 2 [10 47], Ibrahim Fazeel 2 [51 62]		
7-06	India	L	0-1	Male	SAFr1			
11-06	Sri Lanka	W	1-0	Colombo	SAFsf	Ibrahim Fazeel [70]		
14-06	India	W	1-0	Colombo	SAFf	Mukhtar Naseer [87]		
2009								
28-03	Sri Lanka	D	1-1	Colombo	Fr	Ibrahim Fazeel [19]		
14-04	Turkmenistan	L	1-3	Male	CCq	Ibrahim Fazeel [61p]	9 000	Al Ghafary JOR
16-04	Philippines	W	3-2	Male	CCq	Ibrahim Fazeel [26p], Ali Ashfaq [45], Mukhthar Naseer [82]	9 000	Faghani IRN
18-04	Bhutan	W	5-0	Male	CCq	Ali Ashfaq 2 [4 36], Ibrahim Fazeel [45p 47], Mohamed Umair [80]	9 000	Lazeem IRQ
5-12	Nepal	D	1-1	Dhaka	SAFr1	Ahmed Thariq [61]		
7-12	Afghanistan	W	3-1	Dhaka	SAFr1	Ahmed Thariq [52], Ali Ashfaq 2 [69 89]		
9-12	India †	W	2-0	Dhaka	SAFr1	Ahmed Thariq [15], Ibrahim Fazeel [82]		
11-12	Sri Lanka	W	5-1	Dhaka	SAFsf	Ahmed Thariq [21], Ibrahim Fazeel 2 [63 85p], Ali Ashfaq [76], Ali Ashad [87]		
13-12	India †	D	0-0	Dhaka	SAFf	L 1-3p		
2010								
12-10	Indonesia	L	0-3	Bandung	Fr			
2011								
21-03	Cambodia	W	4-0	Male	CCq	Mukhthar Naseer [2], Ali Ashfaq 3 [41 84 88]	8 000	Zhao Liang CHN
23-03	Kyrgyzstan	W	2-1	Male	CCq	Ali Ashadh [5], Shamveel Qasim [22]	9 000	Al Awaji KSA
25-03	Tajikistan	D	0-0	Male	CCq		9 000	Mohamed UAE
7-06	Singapore	L	0-4	Singapore	Fr			
10-07	India	D	1-1	Male	Fr	Mukhtaar Naseer		
23-07	Iran	L	0-4	Tehran	WCq		20 195	Mahapab THA
28-07	Iran	L	0-1	Male	WCq		9 000	Kim Sang Woo KOR
4-08	Mauritius	D	1-1	Praslin	IOGr1	Mohamed Arif [32]	1 800	Rakotonjanahary MAD
6-08	Comoros	D	2-2	Roche Caiman	IOGr1	Ahmed Thariq [4], Ibrahim Fazeel [45p]	1 000	Dubec REU
9-08	Seychelles	L	1-5	Roche Caiman	IOGr1	Shamveel Qasim [26]	5 500	Rakotonjanahary MAD
22-11	Seychelles	W	3-0	Male	Fr	Ahmed Thariq 2 [13 45], Ali Ashfaq [78]		
24-11	Seychelles	W	2-1	Male	Fr	Ibrahim Fazeel 2 [85 92+p]		
2-12	Nepal	D	1-1	New Delhi	SAFr1	Ali Ashfaq [45]		Singh SIN
4-12	Pakistan	D	0-0	New Delhi	SAFr1			Robesh SRI
6-12	Bangladesh	W	3-1	New Delhi	SAFr1	Ahmed Thariq 2 [6 17], Ali Ashfaq [70]		Tufaylieh SYR
9-12	India	L	1-3	New Delhi	SAFsf	Shamveel Qasim [60]		Faizullin KGZ

Fr = Friendly match • SAF = South Asian Football Federation Cup • CC = AFC Challenge Cup • AC = AFC Asian Cup • WC = FIFA World Cup
q = qualifier • r1 = first round group • sf = semi-final • f = final • † Not a full international

MALDIVES NATIONAL TEAM HISTORICAL RECORDS

Coach | Yordan Stoikov BUL 1999 • Victor Stanculescu ROU 1999-2000 • Jozef Jankech SVK 2001-03 • Manuel Gomes POR 2004 • Yordan Stoikov BUL 2005-06 • Jozef Jankech SVK 2007-08 • Teoman Yamanlar TUR 2008-09 • Istvan Urbanyi HUN 2009-10 • Andres Cruciani ARG 2010-11 • Istvan Urbanyi HUN 2011-

MALDIVES 2011

DHIRAAGU DHIVEHI LEAGUE

	Pl	W	D	L	F	A	Pts	VB Sports	Victory	Maziya	New Radiant	Eagles	Valencia	AYL	Vyansa
VB Sports ‡	19	15	2	2	61	12	47		4-0 1-0	4-1 0-2	3-2 1-0	9-0 8-1	2-0 3-0	6-1	4-0
Victory ‡	19	10	5	4	43	28	35	2-2		2-1 2-2	3-2 1-6	2-0 2-2	2-0 2-0	0-0	7-1
Maziya	19	10	5	4	31	21	35	1-2	3-1		1-0 3-0	2-0 3-0	0-4 1-1	1-1	2-0
New Radiant	19	9	4	6	41	24	31	2-1	1-1	1-1		0-2 2-1	4-2 2-2	3-1	1-0
Eagles	19	5	3	11	16	49	18	0-0	1-5	0-2	0-7		1-1 3-2	1-2	0-1
Valencia	19	4	5	10	25	37	17	0-4	1-2	1-1	0-0	1-2		4-2	3-2
All Youth Linkage	14	3	2	9	13	36	11	0-6	1-5	1-2	0-5	0-1	1-2		2-0
Vyansa	14	2	0	12	9	32	6	0-1	0-4	1-2	1-3	0-1	3-1	0-1	

30/03/2011 - 24/09/2011 • Top four qualify for the President's Cup • ‡ Qualified for the AFC Cup

PRESIDENT'S CUP 2011

Preliminary round	Semi–final	Final
	Victory 2	
	VB Sports 1	
		Victory 2
		New Radiant 1
	VB Sports 2	
Maziya 1	**New Radiant** 3	
New Radiant 2		

Final: Galolhu, Malé, 23-10-2011. Scorers - Ibrahim Fazeel [74], Fauzan Habeeb [108] for Victory;
Ahmed Thariq [44] for New Radiant

FA CUP 2011

Quarter–finals	Semi–finals	Final
VB Sports w/o		
Vyansa	**VB Sports** 2	
Eagles 1	New Radiant 1	
New Radiant 2		**VB Sports** 6
Victory 7		Maziya 4
Riverside 1	Victory 1	
Valencia 1	**Maziya** 2	
Maziya 2	Third place: Victory 3-1 New Radiant	

Final: Galolhu, Malé, 31-10-2011, Ref: Al Hoish (KSA). Scorers - Ali Ashfaq 4 [50p 64 71 94],
Ali Ashad [57], Qasim Shamweel [108] for VB; Rasheed [11], Mohamed Umair 3 [30 80p 82] for Maziya

MEDALS TABLE

		Overall			Lge	PC	FAC		CW	Asia			Town
		G	S	B	G	G	G	S	G	G	S	B	
1	Victory SC	30	3		2	21	4	3	3				Malé
2	New Radiant SC	22	7	1	1	7	10	7	4			1	Malé
3	Club Valencia	20	8		5	5	4	8	6				Malé
4	VB Sports	12	3		3	3	6	3					Malé
5	Hurriyya	1	2		1		2						Malé
6	Maziya		1				1						

VB Sports previosly known as Club Lagoons and Island FC • LGE = Dhivehi League • PC = President's Cup
(also known historically as the National Championship) • FAC = FAC Cup • CW = Cup Winners Cup

MEX – MEXICO

FIFA/COCA-COLA WORLD RANKING

'93	'94	'95	'96	'97	'98	'99	'00	'01	'02	'03	'04	'05	'06	'07	'08	'09	'10	'11	'12
16	15	12	11	5	10	10	12	9	8	7	7	5	20	15	26	17	27	21	

						2011									
Jan	Feb	Mar	Apr	May	Jun	Jul	Aug	Sep	Oct	Nov	Dec		High	Low	Av
27	27	27	26	28	9	20	20	20	22	20	21		4	33	13

Mexico won just about everything on offer within the CONCACAF region in 2011 as well as the FIFA U-17 World Cup which the country staged during June and July. It was the second time that the Mexicans had won the U-17 world title, following on from their 2005 triumph in Peru. The week before the finals kicked-off, the senior national team beat neighbours USA to retain the CONCACAF Gold Cup, winning all six matches on the way to the title. In the final Mexico found themselves two goals down before staging a valiant comeback to win the match 4-2. There was also a CONCACAF U-20 title to celebrate with the one dampener coming in the Copa America in Argentina in which an experimental team finished bottom of the rankings. At club level there was continued domination of the CONCACAF Champions League by Mexican clubs with Monterrey beating Real Salt Lake in the final in what was the sixth straight success for Mexico. At home there was a long-overdue title for Monterrey's cross-town rivals Tigres UANL who won the championship for only the third time in their history by beating Santos 4-1 on aggregate in the final at the end of the year. Another university-based club, Pumas UNAM, had won the championship played in the first half of the year. In the final they overcame Morelia 3-2 over the two legs.

CONCACAF GOLD CUP RECORD
1991 SF **1993** Winners **1996** Winners **1998** Winners **2000** QF **2002** QF **2003** Winners **2005** QF **2007** F **2009** Winners **2011** Winners

FEDERACION MEXICANA DE FUTBOL ASOCIACION, A.C. (FMF)

Colima No. 373, Colonia Roma, Mexico D.F. 06700
☎ +52 55 52410166
📠 +52 55 52410191
✉ ddemaria@femexfut.org.mx
🖥 www.femexfut.org.mx
FA 1927 CON 1961 FIFA 1929
P Justino Compean
GS Decio De Maria

FIFA BIG COUNT 2006

Total players	8 479 595
% of population	7.89%
Male	7 151 688
Female	1 327 907
Amateurs 18+	186 954
Youth under 18	129 006
Unregistered	7 000 000
Professionals	4 593
Referees	522
Admin & coaches	32 600
Number of clubs	302
Number of teams	16 957

MAJOR CITIES/TOWNS

		Population
1	Mexico City	8 587 132
2	Ecatepec	1 956 531
3	Guadalajara	1 605 520
4	Tijuana	1 595 681
5	Juárez	1 585 034
6	Puebla	1 483 341
7	Nezahualcóyotl	1 216 077
8	León	1 197 771
9	Monterrey	1 113 114
10	Zapopan	1 060 417
11	Naucalpan	846 554
12	Guadalupe	767 167
13	Mérida	760 249
14	Chihuahua	750 039
16	San Luis Potosí	718 137
17	Aguascalientes	712 682
19	Cancún	700 394
30	Toluca	571 143
33	Torreon	540 078

ESTADOS UNIDOS MEXICANOS • UNITED MEXICAN STATES

Capital	Mexico City	Population	111 211 789 (11)	% in cities 77%
GDP per capita	$14 300 (79)	Area km²	1 964 375 km² (15)	GMT +/- -6
Neighbours (km)	Belize 250, Guatemala 962, US 3141 • Coast 9330		

RECENT INTERNATIONAL MATCHES PLAYED BY MEXICO

2010	Opponents	Score		Venue	Comp	Scorers	Att	Referee
24-02	Bolivia	W	5-0	San Francisco	Fr	Barrera [3], Hernandez 2 [13 20], Luna [18], Aguilar [51]	20 000	Vaughn USA
3-03	New Zealand	W	2-0	Pasadena	Fr	Hernandez [54], Vela [57]	90 526	Marrufo USA
17-03	Korea DPR	W	2-1	Torreon	Fr	Blanco [51], Hernandez [69]	30 000	Moreno PAN
24-03	Iceland	D	0-0	Charlotte	Fr		70 000	Geiger USA
7-05	Ecuador	D	0-0	New Jersey	Fr		77 507	Depiero CAN
10-05	Senegal	W	1-0	Chicago	Fr	Medina [60]	60 610	Salazar USA
13-05	Angola	W	1-0	Houston	Fr	Guardado [52]	70 099	Toledo USA
16-05	Chile	W	1-0	Mexico City	Fr	Medina [13]	100 000	Geiger USA
24-05	England	L	1-3	London	Fr	Franco [45]	88 638	Toma JPN
26-05	Netherlands	L	1-2	Freiburg	Fr	Hernandez [73]	22 000	Graefe GER
30-05	Gambia	W	5-1	Bayreuth	Fr	Hernandez 2 [18 50], Bautista 2 [59 74], Medina [80]	15 000	Brych GER
3-06	Italy	W	2-1	Brussels	Fr	Vela [17], Medina [84]	30 000	Verbist BEL
11-06	South Africa	D	1-1	Johannesburg	WCr1	Rafael Marquez [79]	84 490	Irmatov UZB
17-06	France	W	2-0	Polokwane	WCr1	Hernandez [64], Blanco [79p]	35 370	Al Ghamdi KSA
22-06	Uruguay	L	0-1	Rustenburg	WCr1		33 425	Kassai HUN
27-06	Argentina	L	1-3	Johannesburg	WCr2	Hernandez [71]	84 377	Rosetti ITA
11-08	Spain	D	1-1	Mexico City	Fr	Hernandez [10]	100 000	Moreno PAN
4-09	Ecuador	L	1-2	Guadalajara	Fr	OG [40]	43 800	Quesada CRC
7-09	Colombia	W	1-0	Monterrey	Fr	Hernandez [89]	43 000	Pineda HON
12-10	Venezuela	D	2-2	Juarez	Fr	Hernandez [33], Dos Santos [60]	20 000	Aguilar SLV
2011								
9-02	Bosnia-Herzegovina	W	2-0	Atlanta	Fr	OG [48], Pacheco [54]	45 000	Marrufo USA
26-03	Paraguay	W	3-1	Oakland	Fr	Hernandez.J 2 [6 34], Guardado [28]		Ward CAN
29-03	Venezuela	D	1-1	San Diego	Fr	De Nigris [62]		Salazar USA
28-05	Ecuador	D	1-1	Seattle	Fr	Torres [7]	50 305	Jurisevic USA
1-06	New Zealand	W	3-0	Denver	Fr	Dos Santos 2 [22 30], De Nigris [43]	45 401	Vaughn USA
5-06	El Salvador	W	5-0	Arlington	GCr1	Juarez [55], De Nigris [58], Hernandez.J 3 [60 67 95+p]	80 108	Wijngaarde SUR
9-06	Cuba	W	5-0	Charlotte	GCr1	Hernandez.J 2 [36 76], Dos Santos 2 [63 68], De Nigris [65]	46 012	Campbell JAM
12-06	Costa Rica	W	4-1	Chicago	GCr1	Marquez [16], Guardado 2 [19 25], Barrera [38]	62 000	Moreno PAN
18-06	Guatemala	W	2-1	New York	GCqf	De Nigris [48], Hernandez.J [66]	78 807	Campbell JAM
22-06	Honduras	W	2-0	Houston	GCsf	De Nigris [92], Hernandez.J [99]	70 627	Lopez GUA
25-06	USA	W	4-2	Pasadena	GCf	Barrera 2 [29 50], Guardado [36], Dos Santos [76]	93 420	Aguilar SLV
4-07	Chile	L	1-2	Mendoza	CAr1	Araujo [40]	25 000	Soto VEN
8-07	Peru	L	0-1	Mindoza	CAr1		10 000	Pezzotta ARG
12-07	Uruguay	L	0-1	La Plata	CAr1		36 000	Orozco BOL
10-08	USA	D	1-1	Philadelphia	Fr	Peralta [17]	30 132	Bogle JAM
2-09	Poland	D	1-1	Warsaw	Fr	Hernandez.J [35]	18 000	Deaconu ROU
4-09	Chile	W	1-0	Barcelona	Fr	Guardado [79]	7 210	Muniz ESP
11-10	Brazil	L	1-2	Torreon	Fr	OG [10]	30 000	Mejia SLV
11-11	Serbia	W	2-0	Queretaro	Fr	Salcido [3], Hernandez.J [89p]	34 000	Lopez GUA

Fr = Friendly match • GC = CONCACAF Gold Cup • CA = Copa America • CC = FIFA Confederations Cup • WC = FIFA World Cup
q = qualifier • r1 = first round group • r2 = second round • qf = quarter-final • sf = semi-final • f = final

MEXICO NATIONAL TEAM HISTORICAL RECORDS

Caps
177 - Claudio Suarez 1992-2006 • **145** - Pavel Pardo 1996-2009 • **129** - Jorge Campos 1991-2003 • **121** - Ramon Ramirez 1991-2000 & Gerardo Torrado 1999- • **119** - Cuauhtemoc Blanco 1995- • **108** - Alberto Garcia-Aspe 1988-2002 • **98** - Oswaldo Sanchez 1996- & Rafael Marquez 1997- • **90** - Carlos Hermosillo 1984-97 • **89** - Jared Borgetti 1997-2008 • **85** - Luis Hernandez 1995-2002 • **84** - Zague 1988-2002; Salvador Carmona 1996-2005 & Duilio Davino 1996-2006 • **82** - Gustavo Pena 1961-74 • **81** - Miguel Espana 1984-94 & Carlos Salcido • **80** - Ricardo Osorio 2003- • **79** - Juan Palencia 1996-2009 • **78** - Luis Garcia 1991-99 • **70** - Jesus Arellano 1996-2006

Goals
46 - Jared Borgetti 1997-2008 • **39** - Cuauhtemoc Blanco 1995- • **35** - Carlos Hermosillo 1984-97 & Luis Hernandez 1995-2002 • **31** - Enrique Borja 1966-75 • **30** - Zague 1988-2001 • **29** - Luis Flores 1983-93; Luis Garcia 1991-98 & Hugo Sanchez 1977-98 • **28** - Benjamin Galindo 1983-97 • **21** - Francisco Fonseca 2004-08 & Alberto Garcia-Aspe 1988-2002 • **19** - Javier Fragoso 1965-70 • **16** - Isidoro Diaz 1960-70 & Ricardo Pelaez 1989-99 • **15** - Horacio Casarin 1937-56; Ramon Ramirez 1991-2000 & Omar Bravo 2003-

Past Coaches
For coaches prior to 1983 see Oliver's Almanack of World Fooyball 2011 • Bora Milutinovic YUG 1983-86 • Mario Velarde 1987-89 • Alberto Guerra 1989 • Manuel Lapuente 1990-91 • Cesar Luis Menotti ARG 1991-92 • Miguel Mejia Baron 1993-95 • Bora Milutinovic YUG 1995-97 • Manuel Lapuente 1997-2000 • Mario Carrillo 1999 • Gustavo Vargas 1999 • Enrique Meza 2000-01 • Javier Aguirre 2001-02 • Ricardo La Volpe ARG 2002-06 • Hugo Sanchez 2006-08 • Jesus Ramirez 2008 • Sven-Goran Eriksson SWE 2008-09 • Javier Aguirre 2009-10 • Enrique Meza 2010 • Efrain Flores 2010 • Jose Manuel de la Torre 2010-

MEXICO 2010-11 PRIMERA DIVISION NACIONAL (CLAUSURA)

Grupo 1

	Pl	W	D	L	F	A	Pts
Tigres UANL †	17	10	5	2	26	9	35
Monterrey †	17	7	5	5	23	20	26
Guadalajara †	17	6	7	4	23	15	25
Santos Laguna	17	7	2	8	23	23	23
Estudiantes Tecos	17	4	5	8	21	34	17
Necaxa	17	3	6	8	10	15	15

Grupo 2

	Pl	W	D	L	F	A	Pts
Atlante †	17	8	3	6	28	17	27
América †	17	8	2	7	31	28	26
Atlas	17	6	5	6	19	19	23
San Luis	17	4	9	4	20	18	21
Toluca	17	5	6	6	28	27	21
Pachuca	17	4	6	7	16	25	18

Grupo 3

	Pl	W	D	L	F	A	Pts
Pumas UNAM †	17	10	5	2	27	13	35
Morelia †	17	9	4	4	31	24	31
Cruz Azul †	17	7	5	5	25	20	26
Puebla	17	5	3	9	16	26	18
Querétaro	17	4	4	9	16	35	16
Jaguares	17	4	2	11	15	30	14

8/01/2011 - 1/05/2011 • † Qualified for the play-offs
Top scorers (inc play-offs): **13** - Angel Reyna, América & Rafael Marquez Lugo, Morelia • **10** - Wilmer Aguirre PER, San Luis; Hector Mancilla CHI, UANL & Emanuel Villa ARG, Cruz Azul

MEXICO 2011-12 PRIMERA DIVISION NACIONAL (APERTURA)

	Pl	W	D	L	F	A	Pts
Guadalajara †	17	8	6	3	24	18	30
Cruz Azul	17	8	5	4	21	14	29
Tigres UANL	17	7	7	3	22	13	28
Santos Laguna	17	8	3	6	29	25	27
Jaguares	17	7	5	5	28	23	26
Pachuca	17	7	5	5	28	25	26
Morelia	17	7	5	5	25	22	26
Querétaro	17	8	2	7	23	21	26
Pumas UNAM	17	7	4	6	19	25	25
San Luis	17	6	6	5	23	20	24
Monterrey	17	7	3	7	27	26	24
Puebla	17	6	4	7	26	29	22
Toluca	17	4	8	5	19	27	20
Atlante	17	5	4	8	24	28	19
Tijuana	17	3	9	5	21	23	18
Estudiantes Tecos	17	6	0	11	24	30	18
América	17	3	6	8	26	31	15
Atlas	17	2	6	9	20	30	12

22/07/2011 - 6/11/2011 • † Qualified for the play-offs
Top scorers (inc play-offs): **11** - Ivan Alonso URU, Toluca • **10** - Carlos Bueno URU, Querétaro & Oribe Peralta, Santos • **8** - Christian Benitez ECU, América; Enrique Esqueda, Pachuca; Marco Fabian, Guadalajara & Jackson Martinez COL, Jaguares

CLAUSURA 2010-11 PLAY-OFFS

Quarter–finals			Semi–finals			Final		
UNAM †	1	2						
Monterrey *	3	0	UNAM	1	2			
Tigres UNAL	1	1	Guadalajara *	1	0			
Guadalajara *	3	1				UNAM	1	2
Cruz Azul *	2	0				Morelia	1	1
Atlante	1	0	Cruz Azul *	2	0			
América *	1	2	Morelia	0	3			
Morelia	2	3						

* Home team in 1st leg • † Qualified on overall record

CLAUSURA 2010-11 FINAL

Estadio Morelos, Morelia, 19-05-2011, 20:30, Att: 40 000, Ref: Roberto Garcia
Morelia   1   Rojas [72]
Pumas UNAM   1   Palencia [68]

Morelia - Federico Vilar (c) - Enrique Perez, Adrian Aldrete, Joel Huiqui - Jorge Gastelum, Joao Rojas, Jaime Lozano - Elias Hernandez, Aldo Leao - Rafael Marquez Lugo, Luis Gabriel Rey (Manuel Perez 86). Tr: Tomas Boy
UNAM - Alejandro Palacios - Efrain Velarde●, Marco Antonio Palacios, Dario Veron (c), Luis Fernando Fuentes - Israel Castro, David Cabrera● (Leandro Augusto 59) - Dante Lopez, Martin Bravo (Juan Carlos Cacho 59) - Javier Cortes, Francisco Palencia (Jehu Chiapas 71). Tr: Guillermo Vazquez

Olimpico, Mexico City, 22-05-2011, 12:00, Att: 63 000, Ref: Marco Rodriguez
Pumas UNAM   2   Palencia [14p], Cortes [77]
Morelia   1   Lozano [25p]

UNAM - Alejandro Palacios● - Efrain Velarde●, Luis Fernando Fuentes (Leandro Augusto 54), Dario Veron●, Marco Antonio Palacios - Javier Cortes, David Cabrera - Israel Castro (c), Juan Francisco Palencia (Juan Carlos Cacho 71) - Martin Bravo (Carlos Emilio Orrantia 46), Dante Lopez. Tr: Guillermo Vazquez
Morelia - Federico Vilar● (c) - Enrique Perez, Adrian Aldrete, Joel Huiqui - Jorge Gastelum (Luis Miguel Noriega● 56), Joao Rojas● (Manuel Perez 90), Jaime Lozano - Elias Hernandez (Luis Gabriel Rey 79), Aldo Leao - Rafael Marquez Lugo, Miguel Sabah●. Tr: Tomas Boy

APERTURA 2011-12 PLAY-OFFS

Quarter–finals			Semi–finals			Final		
Tigres UANL	1	3						
Pachuca *	0	0	Tigres UANL	0	1			
Guadalajara	1	0	Querétaro *	0	0			
Querétaro *	2	0				Tigres UANL	1	3
Morelia *	2	2				Santos *	0	1
Cruz Azul	1	1	Morelia *	2	2			
Jaguares *	2	1	Santos †	1	3			
Santos	2	2						

* Home team in 1st leg • † Qualified on overall record

APERTURA 2011-12 FINAL

1st leg. Nueva Corona, Torreón, 8-12-2011, Att: 30 000, Ref: Paul Delgadillo
Santos Laguna   0
Tigres UANL   1   Alvarez [8]

Santos - Oswaldo Sanchez● - Jorge Estrada● (Carlos Morales● 45), Cesar Ibanez, Santiago Hoyos, Felipe Baloy●, Juan Rodriguez◆(Christian Suárez (Jaime Toledo 61), Carlos Quintero (Osmar Mares 45), Jose Cardenas, Rodolfo Salinas, Oribe Peralta. Tr: Benjamin Galindo
UANL - Enrique Palos - Israel Jimenez, Juninho, Hugo Ayala, Jorge Torres, Carlos Salcido, Danilinho, Damian Alvarez, Manuel Viniegra (Jesus Duenas 88), Lucas Lobos, Hector Mancilla (Alan Pulido 72). Tr: Ricardo Ferretti

2nd leg. Universitario, Monterrey, 11-12-2011, Att: 43 000, Ref: Marco Rodriguez
Tigres UANL   3   Mancilla [52], Danilinho [63], Pulido [87]
Santos Laguna   1   Peralta [30]

UANL - Enrique Palos - Israel Jimenez◆68, Juninho, Hugo Ayala, Jorge Torres●, Carlos Salcido, Danilinho● (Jose Rivas 89), Damian Alvarez, Manuel Viniegra (David Toledo 87), Lucas Lobos●, Hector Mancilla● (Alan Pulido 79). Tr: Ricardo Ferretti
Santos - Oswaldo Sanchez◆12 - Cesar Ibanez, Santiago Hoyos, Osmar Mares, Felipe Baloy◆68, Christian Suarez, Carlos Morales● (Daniel Luduena 66), Carlos Quintero● (Miguel Becerra 15), Jose Cardenas (Candido Ramirez 66), Rodolfo Salinas●, Oribe Peralta. Tr: Benjamin Galindo

MEXICO 2010-11

PRIMERA DIVISION NACIONAL RESULTS AND RELEGATION TABLE

Team	Pl	Pts	Av	Toluca	Monterrey	Cruz Azul	Pumas UNAM	Morelia	América	Santos Laguna	Pachuca	Guadalajara	Tigres UANL	San Luis	Atlante	Puebla	Atlas	Estudiantes	Jaguares	Querétaro	Necaxa
Toluca	102	171	1.6765		1-1	0-0	1-1	1-6	2-1	3-1	1-1	1-2	1-1	1-2	1-1	2-1	0-0	4-4	2-0	2-0	2-3
Monterrey	102	169	1.6569	2-0		2-4	5-2	1-1	2-1	1-1	2-0	2-3	0-0	0-2	1-0	1-1	2-0	3-2	1-1	2-0	2-1
Cruz Azul	102	162	1.5882	1-0	3-0		3-3	2-3	1-0	3-0	4-1	1-1	3-2	1-0	2-0	1-0	2-1	4-1	2-0	3-0	0-0
Pumas UNAM	102	159	1.5588	2-1	3-2	2-0		1-0	0-2	2-0	0-0	1-1	2-0	0-1	2-2	4-1	1-1	5-1	1-0	3-0	2-0
Morelia	102	156	1.5294	1-2	0-2	1-1	0-1		0-2	0-0	1-3	1-1	0-3	3-3	2-1	3-3	1-0	4-1	2-1	6-0	1-0
América	102	152	1.4902	4-3	0-0	0-2	0-1	1-2		3-2	0-2	0-0	1-2	3-0	1-1	5-4	1-1	4-1	3-0	3-1	1-1
Santos Laguna	102	152	1.4902	2-0	1-2	3-0	4-0	0-1	2-3		1-1	1-1	0-2	1-3	2-1	4-0	3-1	1-0	1-0	0-2	2-1
Pachuca	102	149	1.4608	0-0	2-2	0-4	3-2	1-1	3-0	0-3		1-1	2-3	0-0	0-4	1-0	1-2	3-1	3-0	2-1	1-1
Guadalajara	102	144	1.4118	0-0	2-3	0-0	0-0	0-1	3-0	0-1	4-1		0-0	1-1	2-0	0-0	2-2	3-0	0-3	2-0	1-0
Tigres UANL	102	140	1.3725	0-1	0-1	2-0	2-0	0-1	1-1	1-0	4-2	1-1		1-1	2-0	3-0	3-0	5-0	0-0	0-1	1-0
San Luis	102	128	1.2549	1-2	1-1	0-0	0-1	1-0	1-2	1-1	1-0	0-1	1-0		2-1	3-0	1-1	3-2	0-0	3-2	1-0
Atlante	102	126	1.2353	2-1	1-2	3-0	0-2	2-0	0-1	1-4	1-3	2-1	1-1	0-0		2-0	3-1	0-1	5-1	1-0	1-1
Puebla	102	123	1.2059	1-1	1-2	2-0	2-0	0-1	0-2	2-2	0-1	3-1	1-1	3-2	1-1		2-0	2-0	1-0	2-0	1-0
Atlas	102	121	1.1863	0-1	1-0	1-3	0-0	5-0	0-2	1-2	1-2	1-1	2-2	2-1	3-1	1-0		1-1	2-0	2-1	0-1
Estudiantes Tecos	102	121	1.1863	4-2	3-2	0-3	2-2	1-1	1-3	1-3	1-0	1-0	0-0	3-2	0-1	1-3	2-1		0-0	0-0	0-2
Jaguares	102	116	1.1373	1-1	1-4	2-3	3-1	0-0	2-2	1-2	2-0	1-0	0-1	2-1	2-0	4-0	2-1	0-2		4-1	1-1
Querétaro	68	74	1.0882	0-5	0-0	1-1	2-1	0-3	0-1	5-2	1-1	2-2	2-2	3-2	1-4	2-1	2-1	1-0	1-1		1-0
Necaxa	34	31	0.9118	1-1	0-1	2-1	0-1	0-0	1-0	1-0	1-2	1-2	0-2	0-2	1-2	1-0	0-1	2-2	0-1	2-2	

The relegation averages are worked out over three years. This table lists the results of the 2010-11 season - the Apertura played in the second half of 2010 and the Clausura in the first half of 2011. For details of the Apertura see Oliver's Almanack of World Football 2011. The Apertura results are in the shaded boxes

MEDALS TABLE

#	Team	Overall G	S	B	League G	S	B	Cup G	S	B	CON'CAF G	S	B	Sth Am	City
1	América	25	14	9	14	10	5	6	3		5		1	1 3	Mexico City
2	Real Club España	20	5	4	15	5	4	5							
3	Necaxa	16	8	9	7	7	7	7			2	1	1	1	Aguascalientes
4	Cruz Azul	15	14	1	8	9		2	2		5	2	1	1	Mexico City
5	Guadalajara	14	17	9	11	9	4	2	5		1	2	1	1 4	Guadalajara
6	Toluca	14	8	5	10	5	2	2	1		2	2	2	1	Toluca
7	Pachuca	14	7	6	7	7	5	2			4		1	1	Pachuca
8	UNAM Pumas	11	8	1	7	6		1			3	1	1	1	Mexico City
9	Asturias	11	4	3	3	4	3	8							
10	Atlante	10	13	3	5	8	3	3	4		2	1			Mexico City
11	León	10	10	6	5	5	4	5	4			1	2		León
12	Reforma	8	3	2	6	3	2	2							
13	Puebla	7	4	3	2	2	3	4	2		1				Puebla
14	Monterrey	6	5	5	4	3	2	1	2		1			3	Monterrey
15	Atlas	5	4	4	1	3	4	4	1						Guadalajara
16	Tigres UANL	5	4	1	3	3		2	1				1		Monterrey
17	Santos Laguna	4	5	2	4	5							1	1	Torreón
18	Zacatepec	4	3	1	2	1	1	2	2						Zacatepec
19	UAG Tecos	3	6		1	4		1	2		1				Zapopan
20	Veracruz	3	3	3	2		3	1	3						Veracruz
21	Club Mexico	3	1	1	1	1	1	2							
22	Marte	3		1	3		1								Xochitepec
23	Tampico Madero	2	4		1	2		1	2						Tampico Madero
24	British Club	2	3	5	1	3	5	1							
25	Moctezuma	2	3			3		2							
26	Oro Jalisco	1	6		1	5			1						
	Monarcas Morelia	1	6		1	3			1			2			Morelia
28	Rovers	1	1	1	1	1	1								
29	Mexico Cricket Club	1			1										
	Orizaba	1			1										

MKD – FYR MACEDONIA

FIFA/COCA-COLA WORLD RANKING

'93	'94	'95	'96	'97	'98	'99	'00	'01	'02	'03	'04	'05	'06	'07	'08	'09	'10	'11	'12
-	90	94	86	92	59	68	76	89	85	92	92	87	54	58	56	65	76	103	

	2011														
	Jan	Feb	Mar	Apr	May	Jun	Jul	Aug	Sep	Oct	Nov	Dec	High	Low	Av
	81	79	83	85	85	98	96	90	94	93	103	103	46	147	79

For the third year running there were first-time champions in the Macedonian league with Shkendija claiming the title in their first season after being promoted to the top flight. That was remarkable in itself but politically it was an explosive development in Macedonian football as the club provides a focus for Albanian nationalism within the country. Based in Tetovo close to the Albanian border, the club was formed in 1979 as a focal point for the large Albanian community in Yugoslavia but was soon banned after stirring nationalist unrest. Re-instated in the Macedonian league, the club has worked its way up the ladder and their fans have become the most notorious in the league. There are few visiting fans to the Gradski Stadium in Tetovo where incidents such as the burning of Macedonian flags are common and hard to control. League runners-up Metalurg Skopje also won their first trophy when they claimed the Cup after a 2-0 win over Shkendija's bitter cross-town rivals Teteks. In the qualifiers for Euro 2012, the national team had a change of coach halfway through what was a disappointing campaign when John Toshack replaced Mirsad Jonuz in the summer. The Macedonians won just twice - as expected in the two games against Andorra - finishing well behind the other four teams in the group.

UEFA EUROPEAN CHAMPIONSHIP RECORD

1960-1992 DNE (Played as part of Yugoslavia) **1996-2012** DNQ

FOOTBALL FEDERATION OF MACEDONIA (FFM)

8-ma Udarna brigada 31-a,
PO Box 84,
Skopje 1000
☎ +389 23 129291
📠 +389 23 165448
📧 ffm@ffm.com.mk
🖥 www.ffm.com.mk
FA 1908 CON 1994 FIFA 1994
P Haralampie Hadji-Risteski
GS Igor Klimper

FIFA BIG COUNT 2006

Total players	93 896
% of population	4.58%
Male	82 546
Female	11 350
Amateurs 18+	14 530
Youth under 18	7 760
Unregistered	19 000
Professionals	356
Referees	740
Admin & coaches	1 125
Number of clubs	456
Number of teams	615

MAJOR CITIES/TOWNS

		Population
1	Skopje	480 678
2	Kumanovo	114 283
3	Bitola	85 622
4	Tetovo	75 045
5	Prilep	73 648
6	Veles	57 623
7	Ohrid	55 021
8	Gostivar	52 406
9	Stip	48 425
10	Strumica	45 591
11	Kavadarci	38 944
12	Struga	37 656
13	Kocani	34 668
14	Kicevo	32 161
15	Lipkovo	29 259
16	Saraj	26 726
17	Zelino	26 586
18	Radovis	25 387
47	Kratavo	9 906

REPUBLIKA MAKEDONIJA • REPUBLIC OF MACEDONIA

Capital Skopje	Population 2 066 718 (144)	% in cities 67%
GDP per capita $9100 (111)	Area km² 25 713 km² (149)	GMT +/- +1
Neighbours (km) Albania 151, Bulgaria 148, Greece 246, Kosovo 159, Serbia 62		

RECENT INTERNATIONAL MATCHES PLAYED BY FYR MACEDONIA

2008	Opponents	Score		Venue	Comp	Scorers	Att	Referee
6-02	Serbia	D	1-1	Skopje	Fr	Novevski [58]	12 000	
26-03	Bosnia-Herzegovina	D	2-2	Zenica	Fr	Maznov 2 [40 45]		Svilokos CRO
26-05	Poland	D	1-1	Reutlingen	Fr	Maznov [45]	2 200	Brych GER
20-08	Luxembourg	W	4-1	Luxembourg	Fr	Pandev 2 [6 45], Grozdanoski [33], Naumoski [49]	885	Brugger AUT
6-09	Scotland	W	1-0	Skopje	WCq	Naumoski [5]	9 000	Kralovec CZE
10-09	Netherlands	L	1-2	Skopje	WCq	Pandev [77]	11 000	Gilewski POL
15-10	Iceland	L	0-1	Reykjavík	WCq		5 527	Dereli TUR
19-11	Montenegro	L	1-2	Podgorica	Fr	Popov [85]		Panic BIH
2009								
11-02	Moldova	D	1-1	Antalya	Fr	Pandev [54]	600	Saliy KAZ
1-04	Netherlands	L	0-4	Amsterdam	WCq		47 750	Rasmussen DEN
6-06	Norway	D	0-0	Skopje	WCq		7 000	Tagliavento ITA
10-06	Iceland	W	2-0	Skopje	WCq	Stojkov [9], Ivanovski [85]	7 000	Ennjimmi FRA
12-08	Spain	L	2-3	Skopje	Fr	Pandev 2 [8 33]	25 000	Vink NED
5-09	Scotland	L	0-2	Glasgow	WCq		50 214	Stark GER
9-09	Norway	L	1-2	Oslo	WCq	Grncarov [79]	14 766	Paixao POR
11-10	Qatar	W	2-1	Skopje	Fr	Pandev 2 [25 40]	5 000	Georgiev BUL
14-11	Canada	W	3-0	Strumica	Fr	Sedloski [48], Pandev 2 [61p 90p]	6 000	Genov BUL
18-11	Iran	D	1-1	Tehran	Fr	Pandev [49]	3 000	Moradi IRN
2010								
3-03	Montenegro	W	2-1	Skopje	Fr	Naumoski [27], Pandev [31]	7 000	Janku ALB
29-05	Azerbaijan	W	3-1	Villach	Fr	Trickovski [8], Despotovski [66], Djurovski [88]	100	Drabek AUT
2-06	Romania	W	1-0	Bischofshofen	Fr	Sikov [28]	1 000	Krassnitzer AUT
11-08	Malta	D	1-1	Ta'Qali	Fr	Trickovski [36]		Rossi SMR
3-09	Slovakia	L	0-1	Bratislava	ECq		5 980	Circhetta SUI
7-09	Armenia	D	2-2	Skopje	ECq	Gjurovski [42], Naumoski [96+p]	9 000	Berntsen NOR
8-10	Andorra	W	2-0	Andorra La Vella	ECq	Naumoski [42], Sikov [60]	550	Mazeika LTU
12-10	Russia	L	0-1	Skopje	ECq		10 500	Johannesson SWE
17-11	Albania	D	0-0	Korce	Fr		12 000	Gocek TUR
22-12	China PR	L	0-1	Guangzhou	Fr		8 000	
2011								
9-02	Cameroon	L	0-1	Skopje	Fr		3 000	Kalugjerovic MNE
26-03	Republic of Ireland	L	1-2	Dublin	ECq	Trickovski [45]	33 200	Vad HUN
4-06	Republic of Ireland	L	0-2	Skopje	ECq		29 500	Meyer GER
10-08	Azerbaijan	W	1-0	Baku	Fr	Pandev [57]		Kulbakov BLR
2-09	Russia	L	0-1	Moscow	ECq		31 028	Yildirim TUR
6-09	Andorra	W	1-0	Skopje	ECq	Ivanovski [59]	5 000	Whitby WAL
7-10	Armenia	L	1-4	Yerevan	ECq	Sikov [86]	14 403	Schorgenhofer AUT
11-10	Slovakia	D	1-1	Skopje	ECq	Noveski [79]	4 100	Chapron FRA
15-11	Albania	D	0-0	Prilep	Fr		4 500	Vincic SVN

Fr = Friendly match • EC = UEFA EURO 2012 • WC = FIFA World Cup • q = qualifier

FYR MACEDONIA NATIONAL TEAM HISTORICAL RECORDS

Caps
100 - Goce Sedloski 1996-2010 • 78 - Velice Sumulikoski 2002- • 73 - Artim Sakiri 1996-2006 • 70 - Igor Mitreski 2001- • 61 - Goran Pandev 2001- • 59 - Petar Milosevski 1998-2009 • 50 - Vlatko Grozdanoski 2001- • 48 - Georgi Hristov 1995-2003 & Nikolce Noveski 2004- • 44 - Ilco Naumoski 2003- & Toni Micevski 1993-2002 • 43 - Goran Maznov 2001- & Vlade Lazarevski

Goals
24 - Goran Pandev 2001- • 16 - Georgi Hristov 1995-2003 • 15 - Artim Sakiri 1996-2009 • 10 - Goran Maznov 2001- • 9 - Ilco Naumoski 2003- • 8 - Goce Sedloski 1996- & Sasa Ciric 1996-2002 • 5 - Aco Stojkov 2002- ; Mitko Stojkovski 1994-2002 & Zoran Boskovski 1993-98

Past Coaches
Andon Doncevski 1993-95 • Gjoko Hadzievski 1996-99 • Dragan Kanatlarovski 1999-2001 • Gjore Jovanovski 2001-02 • Nikola Ilievski 2002-03 • Dragan Kanatlarovski 2003-05 • Slobodan Santrac SRB 2005 • Boban Babunski 2005-06 • Srecko Katanec SVN 2006-09 • Mirsad Jonuz 2009-11 • John Toshack 2011-

FYR MACEDONIA 2010-11

PRVATA FUDBALSKA LIGA

Team	Pl	W	D	L	F	A	Pts	Results (vs Shk, Met, Ren, Rab, Sil, Tur, Tet, Bre, Sko, Nap, Var, Pel)
Shkendija Tetovo †	33	21	9	3	65	23	72	3-0 2-2 4-1 3-0 2-1 3-0 1-0 3-0 0-0 3-1 2-0 1-0 3-0 4-1 3-1 2-0 4-1
Metalurg Skopje ‡	33	17	10	6	48	24	61	1-1 2-0 0-0 0-1 1-2 3-0 1-1 0-1 1-1 0-3 0-3 0-2-1 1-2 1-0 4-0 5-0
Renova Cepciste ‡	33	17	9	7	54	31	60	1-0 1-1 1-0 1-1 2-2 3-1 2-1 0-0 2-1 4-2 2-0 1-1 5-0 4-1 4-0 1-0 2-0
Rabotnicki Skopje ‡	33	15	10	8	53	31	55	1-1 2-2 1-1 1-1 0-0 2-1 3-1 1-2 2-1 3-1 7-0 1-1 1-1 0-0 2-0 3-0 1-2
Sileks Kratovo	33	13	8	12	39	38	47	1-1 0-1 2-1 2-0 2-0 2-0 0-2 0-0 3-1 3-0 0-0 1-1 2-1 1-0 0-1 2-1
Turnovo	33	13	6	14	35	35	45	0-1 0-2 1-3 2-0 1-1 0-2 4-0 2-0 1-0 0-2 2-0 1-0 1-0 0-0 3-0 1-1 3-0
Teteks	33	12	8	13	38	36	44	1-0 0-0 1-1 0-1 1-1 0-2 1-0 2-0 0-2 2-1 2-1 2-1 3-2 2-1 3-0 6-1
Bregalnica Stip	33	12	5	16	33	49	41	2-1 0-2 1-2 3-1 1-4 0-2 2-2 1-0 1-0 1-0 0-0 4-2 0-0 2-0 4-0
Skopje	33	9	10	14	36	39	37	3-3 2-2 0-0 0-1 2-0 0-1 2-1 1-1 3-0 1-2 1-0 0-3 1-0 1-0 2-0 4-1
Napredok Kicevo	33	10	7	16	30	48	37	1-1 0-1 1-2 1-0 2-0 0-5 1-0 0-1 1-0 1-1 1-0 0-0 2-0 1-3 2-1 3-1 2-0
Vardar Skopje	33	9	5	19	24	44	29	0-2 1-2 0-1 0-2 1-0 1-3 2-1 1-1 2-0 1-2 1-1 1-0 0-0 2-1 1-0 1-0
Pelister Bitola	33	5	3	25	25	83	18	0-1 1-3 0-0 0-1 0-5 0-3 1-3 2-3 2-0 1-4 1-1 2-0 5-4 1-1 1-2 1-0

31/07/2010 - 28/05/2011 • † Qualified for the UEFA Champions League • ‡ Qualified for the Europa League

Relegation play-off: **Napredok Kicevo** 2-0 Tikves • Skopje 1-4 **Miravci**. Miravci declined promotion saving Vardar from relegation

Top scorers: **20** - Hristijan Kirovski, Skopje • **19** - Borce Manevski, Rabotnicki • **13** - Ferhan Hasani, Skendija • **12** - Ersen Sali, Skendija & Aleksandar Temelkov • **11** - Boban Jancevski, Renova & Izair Emini, Skendija

FYR MACEDONIA 2010-11 — VTORA LIGA (2)

Team	Pl	W	D	L	F	A	Pts
11 Oktomvri Prilep	26	16	6	4	50	19	54
Ohrid 2004	26	16	5	5	51	21	53
Tikves Kavadarci	26	13	9	4	45	27	48
Miravci	26	14	4	8	43	22	46
Belasica Strumica	26	13	4	9	39	26	43
Rinija	26	10	9	7	25	19	39
Drita Bogovinje	26	9	8	9	37	29	35
Gorno Lisice	26	11	2	13	41	49	35
Lokomotiva Skopje	26	9	4	13	27	46	31
Ohrid Lote	26	9	2	15	40	49	29
Vlazrimi Kicevo §1	26	8	4	14	28	56	27
Novaci	26	5	7	14	22	37	22
Cementarnica	26	4	10	12	20	41	22
Vlaznimi TL Struga	26	6	4	16	24	51	22

8/08/2010 - 29/05/2011 • § = points deducted

MEDALS TABLE

		Overall			League			Cup		City
		G	S	B	G	S	B	G	S	
1	Vardar Skopje	10	3	3	5	2	3	5	1	Skopje
2	Sloga Jugomagnat	6	7	2	3	2	2	3	5	Skopje
3	Sileks Kratovo	5	6		3	5		2	1	Kratovo
4	Rabotnicki Skopje	5	3	1	3	2	1	2	1	Skopje
5	Pobeda Prilep	3	4	4	2	2	4	1	2	Prilep
6	Makedonija Skopje	2	2	2	1	1	2	1	1	Skopje
7	Pelister Bitola	1	2	1			1	1	2	Bitola
8	Cementarnica Skopje	1	1	1			1	1	1	Skopje
9	Metalurg Skopje	1	1	1	1	1	1			Skopje
10	Shkendija Tetovo	1	1		1				1	Tetovo
	Teteks	1	1					1	1	Tetovo
12	Renova Cepciste	1	2	1	1	2	1			Tetovo
13	Baskimi Kumanovo	1						1		Kumanovo
14	Milano Kumanovo		3			2			1	Kumanovo
15	Belasica Strumica		2			2				Strumica
16	Madzari Skopje	1						1		Skopje
	Napredok Kicevo	1						1		Kicevo
18	Balkan Skopje		1						1	Skopje
	Balkan Stokokomerc		1						1	Skopje

MAKEDONSKI CUP 2010-11

Round of 16

Metalurg Skopje	0 1 7p
11 Oktomvri Prilep *	1 0 6p
Miravci	0 0 3p
Lokomotiva Skopje *	0 0 4p
Bregalnica Stip *	0 2
Pelister Bitola	0 0
Vlaznimi TL Struga	0 2
Napredok Kicevo *	4 0
Tikves Kavadarci	3 0
Osogovo Kocani *	0 1
Renova Cepciste	0 0
Vardar Skopje *	1 1
Horizont Turnovo	3 1
Rinija *	0 0
Sileks Kratovo *	0 0
Teteks	1 2

Quarter-finals

Metalurg Skopje	3 1
Lokomotiva Skopje *	0 1
Bregalnica Stip *	0 0
Napredok Kicevo	1 1
Tikves Kavadarci	1 4
Vardar Skopje *	4 0
Horizont Turnovo *	1 0
Teteks	2 1

Semi-finals

Metalurg Skopje *	0 2
Napredok Kicevo	0 0
Tikves Kavadarci *	0 0
Teteks	0 6

Final

Metalurg Skopje ‡	2
Teteks	0

CUP FINAL
Goce Delcev, Prilep
24-05-2011, Att: 3000, Ref: Boshkov
Scorers - Marko Kostencovski [14], Aleksandar Tenekedziev [65] for Metalrg

* Home team in the first leg • ‡ Qualified for the Europa League

MLI – MALI

FIFA/COCA-COLA WORLD RANKING

'93	'94	'95	'96	'97	'98	'99	'00	'01	'02	'03	'04	'05	'06	'07	'08	'09	'10	'11	'12
70	52	52	67	80	70	72	98	112	73	54	51	63	36	46	45	47	67	67	

	2011												High	Low	Av
	Jan	Feb	Mar	Apr	May	Jun	Jul	Aug	Sep	Oct	Nov	Dec			
	68	85	85	70	70	78	77	81	62	68	67	67	35	117	64

Mali finished top of their qualifying group for the 2012 CAF Africa Cup of Nations and went on to an unexpected third place at the finals in Equatorial Guinea and Gabon. This was despite new coach Alain Giresse having to overhaul the team during the qualifiers and then play the finals with a weakened squad beset with injury problems. Giresse promoted a number of younger players to the side which meant that established players such as captain Mahamadou Diarra, Frederic Kanoute and midfield hard man Momo Sissoko didn't feature in his plans. The coach did, however, persuade Barcelona's Seydou Keita to return to the national team following his one-man protest over money and match arrangements during the preceding 18 months. Keita's first game back was the vital 3-0 qualifying win over the Cape Verde Islands in Bamako and with the emergence at the 2012 tournament of a promising new generation led by the likes of Abdou Traore, Cheikh Tidiane Diabate, Samba Diakite and Samba Sow, will give Mali confidence for their 2014 FIFA World Cup qualifying campaign. At home, Stade Malien continued to dominate the league when they won the title for the ninth time in 12 years but they missed out on the double when Club Olympique Bamako beat them 2-1 after extra-time in the Cup Final.

CAF AFRICA CUP OF NATIONS RECORD

1957-1963 DNE 1965-1970 DNQ **1972** 2 F 1974-1976 DNQ **1978** Disqualified 1980 DNE 1982-1986 DNQ 1988 DNE 1990-1992 DNQ **1994** 4 SF 1996-2000 DNQ **2002** 4 SF **2004** 4 SF 2006 DNQ **2008** 10 r1 **2010** 9 r1 **2012** 3 SF

FEDERATION MALIENNE DE FOOTBALL (FMF)

Avenue du Mali, Hamdallaye
ACI 2000, PO Box 1020,
Bamako 12582

☎ +223 2238844
📠 +223 2224254
📧 malifoot@afribone.net.ml

FA 1960 CON 1963 FIFA 1962
P Hammadoun Kola Cisse
GS Boubacar Thiam

FIFA BIG COUNT 2006

Total players	1 391 625
% of population	11.88%
Male	1 363 775
Female	27 850
Amateurs 18+	5 100
Youth under 18	9 075
Unregistered	1 352 450
Professionals	0
Referees	575
Admin & coaches	5 503
Number of clubs	140
Number of teams	700

MAJOR CITIES/TOWNS

		Population
1	Bamako	1 728 444
2	Sikasso	192 400
3	Kayes	133 101
4	Ségou	104 987
5	Mopti	103 428
6	Nioro	92 387
7	Koutiala	79 502
8	Markala	76 914
9	Kati	51 105
10	Kolokani	48 679
11	Gao	46 608
12	Bougouni	36 527
13	Timbuktu	35 638
14	Banamba	31 817
15	Niono	30 838
16	San	30 028
17	Nara	28 822
18	Koulikoro	28 222

REPUBLIQUE DE MALI • REPUBLIC OF MALI

Capital	Bamako	Population	12 666 987 (70)	% in cities 32%
GDP per capita	$1100 (209)	Area km²	1 240 192 km² (24)	GMT + / - 0
Neighbours (km)	Algeria 1376, Burkina Faso 1000, Guinea 858, Cote d'Ivoire 532, Mauritania 2237, Niger 821, Senegal 419			

RECENT INTERNATIONAL MATCHES PLAYED BY MALI

2008	Opponents	Score		Venue	Comp	Scorers	Att	Referee
10-01	Egypt	L	0-1	Abu Dhabi	Fr			
21-01	Benin	W	1-0	Sekondi	CNr1	Kanoute [49p]		Damon RSA
25-01	Nigeria	D	0-0	Sekondi	CNr1			El Arjoun MAR
29-01	Côte d'Ivoire	L	0-3	Accra	CNr1			Maillet SEY
1-06	Congo	W	4-2	Bamoko	WCq	Seydou Keita 2 [1 61], Adama Coulibaly [32], Soumaila Coulibaly [42]	40 000	Bennaceur TUN
7-06	Chad	W	2-1	N'Djamena	WCq	Kanoute 2 [4 22]	15 000	Aguidissou BEN
14-06	Sudan	L	2-3	Khartoum	WCq	Kanoute 2 [63 94+]	15 000	Abdelfattah EGY
22-06	Sudan	W	3-0	Bamoko	WCq	Kanoute [23], Seydou Keita 2 [58 66]	25 000	Doue CIV
19-08	Gabon	L	0-1	Mantes-La-Ville	Fr			
7-09	Congo	L	0-1	Brazzaville	WCq		16 000	Haimoudi ALG
11-10	Chad	W	2-1	Bamako	WCq	Sidi Yaya Keita 2 [44 82]	40 000	Keita GUI
18-11	Algeria	D	1-1	Rouen	Fr	Cheick Diabate [13]		
2009								
11-02	Angola	W	4-0	Bois-Guillaume	Fr	Ismail Coulibaly [14], Yatabare [18], Kanoute [35], Seydou Keita [66]		
28-03	Sudan	D	1-1	Omdurman	WCq	Kanoute [19]	35 000	Maillet SEY
25-04	Equatorial Guinea	W	3-0	Bamako	Fr	Sekou Camara [18], Idrissa Traore [38], Diamoutene [86]		
7-06	Ghana	L	0-2	Bamako	WCq		40 000	Evehe CMR
21-06	Benin	W	3-1	Bamako	WCq	Maiga [29], Mamadou Diallo [76], Kanoute [84]	40 000	Abd El Fatah EGY
12-08	Burkina Faso	W	3-0	Le Petit Quevilly	Fr	Mamadou Diallo 2 [20 35], Maiga [25]		
6-09	Benin	D	1-1	Cotonou	WCq	Samassa [72]	33 000	Damon RSA
11-10	Sudan	W	1-0	Bamako	WCq	Kanoute [89]	15 000	Benouza ALG
15-11	Ghana	D	2-2	Kumasi	WCq	Fane [23], Ndiaye [68]	39 000	Diatta SEN
27-12	Korea DPR	L	0-1	Doha	Fr			
30-12	Iran	W	2-1	Doha	Fr	Ndiaye [29], Bakaye Traore [30]		
2010								
2-01	Qatar	D	0-0	Doha	Fr			
4-01	Egypt	L	0-1	Dubai	Fr			
10-01	Angola	D	4-4	Luanda	CNr1	Seydou Keita 2 [79 93+], Kanoute [88], Yattabare [94+]	45 000	Abd El Fatah EGY
14-01	Algeria	L	0-1	Luanda	CNr1		4 000	Ssegonga UGA
18-01	Malawi	W	3-1	Cabinda	CNr1	Kanoute [1], Seydou Keita [3], Bagayoko [85]	21 000	Seechurn MRI
3-03	Libya	L	1-2	Tripoli	Fr	Bakary Coulibaly [15]		
11-08	Guinea	L	0-2	Marignane	Fr			
4-09	Cape Verde Islands	L	0-1	Praia	CNq			Benouza ALG
9-10	Liberia	W	2-1	Bamako	CNq	Abdou Traore [2], OG [51]		Djaoupe TOG
17-11	Congo DR	W	3-1	Evreux	Fr	Maiga [48], Abdou Traore [54], Ndiaye [75p]		
2011								
8-02	Côte d'Ivoire	L	0-1	Valence	Fr			
26-03	Zimbabwe	W	1-0	Bamako	CNq	Cheick Diabate [24]		Gassama GAM
5-06	Zimbabwe	L	1-2	Harare	CNq	Mahamane Traore [49]		
10-08	Tunisia	L	2-4	Monastir	Fr	Modibo Maiga [45], Cheick Diabate [56]		Keita GUI
3-09	Cape Verde Islands	W	3-0	Bamako	CNq	Cheick Diabate 2 [27 30], Mahamane Traore [50]		Diatta SEN
8-10	Liberia	D	2-2	Paynesville	CNq	Cheick Diabate [16], Cedric Kante [87]		
11-11	Burkina Faso	D	1-1	St Leu La Foret	Fr	Seydou Keita [47]		
2012								
24-01	Guinea	W	1-0	Franceville	CNr1	Bakaye Traore [30]	10 000	Jedidi TUN
28-01	Ghana	L	0-2	Franceville	CNr1		7 000	Haimoudi ALG
1-02	Botswana	W	2-1	Libreville	CNr1	Garra Dembele [56], Seydou Keita [74]	20 000	Abdul Rahman SUD
5-02	Gabon	D	1-1	Libreville	CNqf	Cheick Diabate [85], W 5-4p	30 000	Haimoudi ALG
8-02	Côte d'Ivoire	L	0-1	Libreville	CNsf		32 000	Bennett RSA
11-02	Ghana	W	2-0	Malabo	CN3p	Cheick Diabate 2 [23 80]	15 000	Grisha EGY

Fr = Friendly match • CN = CAF African Cup of Nations • WC = FIFA World Cup • q = qualifier

MALI 2011

PREMIERE DIVISION

	Pl	W	D	L	F	A	Pts	Stade Malien	Djoliba	Réal	ASKO	COB	Jeanne d'Arc	Duguwolofila	O. Créateurs	Bakaridjan	CSK	ASB	Police	USFAS	CASS
Stade Malien †	26	18	5	3	46	12	59		1-0	1-1	2-0	0-0	5-0	0-0	1-0	4-1	4-0	3-0	2-1	1-0	5-1
Djoliba †	26	14	7	5	37	19	49	1-0		2-1	0-0	0-0	1-1	3-2	0-1	3-0	3-2	2-1	0-2	4-1	2-0
Réal Bamako ‡	26	12	9	5	35	20	45	1-0	1-0		3-0	2-0	0-0	1-1	3-1	0-0	1-0	1-1	1-1	1-1	4-0
AS Korofina Bamako	26	11	8	7	24	21	41	0-2	1-1	1-1		1-0	2-0	0-0	2-1	3-0	1-2	0-0	1-0	1-0	1-1
Club Olympique ‡	26	9	11	6	29	23	38	0-2	0-0	1-1	1-0		0-1	0-0	2-2	1-2	2-0	2-0	0-0	2-2	1-0
Jeanne d'Arc	26	10	6	10	32	32	36	1-2	0-2	1-2	0-0	2-0		3-2	1-1	2-1	0-2	0-1	2-3	2-0	1-0
Duguwolofila Koulikoro	26	8	12	6	31	31	36	0-0	0-0	1-0	2-1	2-3	2-2		2-1	2-2	3-1	2-0	0-4	0-0	2-1
Onze Créateurs	26	9	5	12	40	39	32	1-0	1-4	4-1	2-0	1-2	0-2	4-1		1-4	3-0	4-0	3-2	2-3	0-1
Bakaridjan Ségou	26	8	7	11	28	35	31	0-2	3-2	1-0	1-2	1-1	1-1	0-0	0-1		0-2	1-0	3-1	0-1	2-0
Centre Salif Keita	26	9	4	13	29	40	31	1-2	0-3	0-1	1-2	1-1	0-3	1-1	1-1	1-1		1-2	1-0	2-1	1-0
AS Bamako	26	8	7	11	27	38	31	0-0	0-1	1-0	0-0	0-1	1-5	1-1	3-2	0-0	3-1		3-0	2-2	5-2
AS Police Bamako	26	8	6	12	34	35	30	0-2	1-2	1-2	1-2	0-3	2-0	1-0	1-1	2-1	0-2	6-1		1-1	0-0
USFAS Bamako	26	6	8	12	34	44	26	3-4	0-0	1-2	0-2	1-4	1-0	2-3	2-2	3-2	1-3	1-0	1-3		1-1
CAS Sévaré	26	2	5	19	13	50	11	0-1	0-1	0-4	0-1	2-2	1-2	0-2	1-0	0-1	1-3	0-2	1-1	0-5	

22/11/2010 - 17/07/2011 • † Qualified for the CAF Champions League • ‡ Qualified for the CAF Confederation Cup • Match in bold awarded

MEDALS TABLE

		Overall			Lge	Cup		Africa			
		G	S	B	G	G	S	G	S	B	City
1	Djoliba AC	40	10	3	21	19	10			3	Bamako
2	Stade Malien	35	10		17	17	9	1	1		Bamako
3	Real Bamako	15	8		5	10	7		1		Bamako
4	Club Olympique	3	2			3	2				Bamako
5	AS Bamako	1	1			1	1				Bamako
6	AS Sigui Kayes	1				1					Kayes
7	Avenir Ségou		4				4				Ségou
8	AS Nianan Koulikoro		3				3				Koulikoro
9	Kayésienne		2				2				Kayes
	USFAS Bamako		2				2				Bamako

COUPE DU MALI 2011

Round of 16		Quarter-finals		Semi-finals		Final	
Club Olympique	2						
Centre Salif Keita	1	Club Olympique	0 3p				
Réal Bamako	2	Bakaridjan Ségou	0 2p				
Bakaridjan Ségou	0			Club Olympique	0 3p		
Onze Créateurs	4			Djoliba	0 1p		
CAS Sévaré	0	Onze Créateurs	0				
USFAS Bamako	0	Djoliba	2				
Djoliba	1					Club Olympique ‡	2
AS Korofina Bamako	9					Stade Malien	1
Attar Kidal	1	AS Korofina Bamako	2				
AS Bamako	1	Mamahira	1				
Mamahira	2			AS Korofina Bamako	1 4p		
Reveil Club	1			Stade Malien	1 5p		
Sigui Kayes	0	Reveil Club	0				
Duguwolofila	1	Stade Malien	8				
Stade Malien	6						

CUP FINAL

Modibo Keita, Bamako, 23-07-2011,
Att: 5000, Ref: Teixeira (ESP)
Scorers - Bassoma Sangare [7], Melvin
Kicmett [115] for COB; Souleymane
Dembele [82] for Stade

‡ Qualified for the CAF Confederation Cup

MLT – MALTA

'93	'94	'95	'96	'97	'98	'99	'00	'01	'02	'03	'04	'05	'06	'07	'08	'09	'10	'11	'12
83	78	90	122	133	130	116	119	131	122	129	134	118	119	136	147	146	164	156	

						2011							High	Low	Av
Jan	Feb	Mar	Apr	May	Jun	Jul	Aug	Sep	Oct	Nov	Dec				
163	163	156	163	161	161	173	167	154	158	155	156		66	173	124

For a club that was once the most successful in the country, Floriana's Cup Final triumph was a welcome return to winning ways. It was their first trophy since 1994 and it was won thanks to a last-gasp Ivan Wood's goal against Valletta in the final. Remarkably, that was the only game Valletta lost all season - in the league, the cup and in Europe. Coached by Jesmond Zerafa, Valletta were simply unbeatable right up until the last minute of the last game they played during the season. They were knocked out of Europe by Poland's Ruch Chorzow but only on away goals after two draws, and they won 18 of their 28 league matches to finish comfortably above Floriana in second place. It was a fitting end to the career of Valletta's long-serving captain Gilbert Agius who since first appearing for the club in 1990 has won seven winners medals in both the league and the cup. One area in which some of the Valletta players were less than invincible, however, was for the Malta national team which once again had a poor qualifying campaign, this time in the qualifiers for Euro 2012. They managed to pick up just one point in their 10 games - a 1-1 draw at home to Georgia - a record that saw saw coach John Buttigieg and his assistant Carmen Busuttil removed from their posts.

UEFA EUROPEAN CHAMPIONSHIP RECORD
1960 DNE 1964 r1 1968 DNE 1972-2012 DNQ

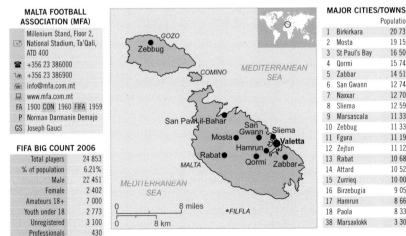

MALTA FOOTBALL ASSOCIATION (MFA)

	Millenium Stand, Floor 2,
⌂	National Stadium, Ta'Qali, ATD 400
☎	+356 23 386000
📠	+356 23 386900
✉	info@mfa.com.mt
🖥	www.mfa.com.mt
FA	1900 CON 1960 FIFA 1959
P	Norman Darmanin Demajo
GS	Joseph Gauci

FIFA BIG COUNT 2006

Total players	24 853
% of population	6.21%
Male	22 451
Female	2 402
Amateurs 18+	7 000
Youth under 18	2 773
Unregistered	3 100
Professionals	430
Referees	99
Admin & coaches	2 105
Number of clubs	51
Number of teams	325

MAJOR CITIES/TOWNS

		Population
1	Birkirkara	20 737
2	Mosta	19 152
3	St Paul's Bay	16 507
4	Qormi	15 743
5	Zabbar	14 519
6	San Gwann	12 741
7	Naxxar	12 704
8	Sliema	12 595
9	Marsascala	11 335
10	Zebbug	11 335
11	Fgura	11 196
12	Zejtun	11 129
13	Rabat	10 684
14	Attard	10 523
15	Zurrieq	10 002
16	Birzebugia	9 057
17	Hamrun	8 665
18	Paola	8 330
38	Marsaxlokk	3 302

REPUBBLIKA TA' MALTA • REPUBLIC OF MALTA

Capital	Valletta	Population	405 165 (173)	% in cities 94%
GDP per capita	$24 600 (52)	Area km²	316 km² (207)	GMT +/- +1
Neighbours (km)	Coast 196		

RECENT INTERNATIONAL MATCHES PLAYED BY MALTA

2008 Opponents	Score	Venue	Comp	Scorers	Att	Referee
2-02 Armenia	L 0-1	Ta'Qali	Fr			
4-02 Iceland	W 1-0	Ta'Qali	Fr	Frendo [18]		
6-02 Belarus	L 0-1	Ta'Qali	Fr			Tshagharyan ARM
26-03 Liechtenstein	W 7-1	Ta'Qali	Fr	Mifsud 5 [2p 17 21p 59 69], Pace [35], Said [86]		Collum SCO
30-05 Austria	L 1-5	Graz	Fr	Mifsud [41]	14 200	Krajnc SVN
20-08 Estonia	L 1-2	Tallinn	Fr	Azzopardi [9]	2 700	Gilewski POL
6-09 Portugal	L 0-4	Ta'Qali	WCq		11 000	Blom NED
10-09 Albania	L 0-3	Tirana	WCq		7 400	Schoergenhofer AUT
11-10 Denmark	L 0-3	Copenhagen	WCq		33 124	Paniashvili GEO
15-10 Hungary	L 0-1	Ta'Qali	WCq		4 797	Valgeirsson ISL
19-11 Iceland	L 0-1	Corradino	Fr			Demarco ITA
2009						
11-02 Albania	D 0-0	Ta'Qali	WCq		2 041	Deaconu ROU
28-03 Denmark	L 0-3	Ta'Qali	WCq		6 235	Mikulski POL
1-04 Hungary	L 0-3	Budapest	WCq		34 400	Sukhina RUS
5-06 Czech Republic	L 0-1	Jablonec	Fr		6 019	Fautrel FRA
10-06 Sweden	L 0-4	Gothenburg	WCq		25 271	Murray SCO
12-08 Georgia	W 2-0	Ta'Qali	Fr	Mifsud 2 [64 73]		Kailis CYP
4-09 Cape Verde Islands	L 0-2	Ta'Qali	Fr			Banti ITA
9-09 Sweden	L 0-1	Ta'Qali	WCq		4 705	McCourt NIR
10-10 Angola	L 1-2	Vila Real	Fr	Cohen [13]		Almeida POR
14-10 Portugal	L 0-4	Guimaraes	WCq		29 350	Kelly IRL
18-11 Bulgaria	L 1-4	Paola	Fr	Mifsud [46]		Nijhuis NED
2010						
3-03 Finland	L 1-2	Ta'Qali	Fr	Mifsud [17]		Bergonzi ITA
13-05 Germany	L 0-3	Aachen	Fr		27 000	Hamer LUX
11-08 FYR Macedonia	D 1-1	Ta'Qali	Fr	Mifsud [47]		Rossi ITA
2-09 Israel	L 1-3	Tel Aviv	ECq	Pace [38]	17 365	Ennjimi FRA
7-09 Latvia	L 0-2	Ta'Qali	ECq		6 255	Asumaa FIN
8-10 Georgia	L 0-1	Tbilisi	ECq		38 000	Black NIR
17-11 Croatia	L 0-3	Zagreb	ECq		9 000	Gomes POR
2011						
9-02 Switzerland	D 0-0	Ta'Qali	Fr		3 000	Stamatis CYP
26-03 Greece	L 0-1	Ta'Qali	ECq		10 605	Weiner GER
4-06 Greece	L 1-3	Piraeus	ECq	Mifsud [54]	14 746	Gil POL
10-08 Central African Rep	W 2-1	Ta'Qali	Fr	Mifsud 2 [2p 44]		Ozkalfa TUR
2-09 Croatia	L 1-3	Ta'Qali	ECq	Mifsud [38]	6 150	Chapron FRA
6-09 Georgia	D 1-1	Ta'Qali	ECq	Mifsud [25]	5 000	Van Boekel NED
7-10 Latvia	L 0-2	Riga	ECq		4 315	Trutz SVK
11-10 Israel	L 0-2	Ta'Qali	ECq		2 164	Paixao POR

Fr = Friendly match • EC = UEFA EURO 2012 • WC = FIFA World Cup • q = qualifier

MALTA NATIONAL TEAM HISTORICAL RECORDS

Caps

121 - David Carabott 1987-2005 • 120 - Gilbert Agius 1993- • 111 - Carmel Busuttil 1982-2001 • 103 - Joe Brincat 1988-2004 • 95 - John Buttigieg 1984-2000 • 91 - Brian Said 1996- • 90 - Silvio Vella 1988-2000 • 87 - Michael Mifsud 2000- • 74 - Michael Degiorgio 1981-92 • 70 - Hubert Suda 1988-2003 • 69 - Jeffrey Chetcuti 1994-2005

Goals

30 - Michael Mifsud 2000- • 23 - Carmel Busuttil 1982-2001 • 12 - David Carabott 1987-2005 • 8 - Gilbert Agius 1993- & Hubert Suda 1988-2003 • 6 - Kristian Laferla 1986-98; Raymond Xuereb 1971-85 & Joe Brincat 1988-2004 • 5 - George Mallia 1999- & Brian Said 1996-

Past Coaches

Joe A. Griffiths 1957-61 • Carm Borg 1961-64 • Janos Bedl HUN 1966 • Tony Formosa 1966 • Joseph Attard 1969 • Saviour Cuschieri 1970 • Victor Scerri 1973 • Terrenzio Polverini ITA 1974-76 • John Calleja 1976-78 • Victor Scerri 1978-83 • Guentcho Dobrev BUL 1984-87 • Horst Heese GER 1988-91 • Pippo Psaila 1991-93 • Pietro Ghedin ITA 1993-95 • Robert Gatt 1996 • Milorad Kosanovic YUG 1996-97 • Josif Ilic YUG 1997-2001 • Sigfried Held GER 2001-03 • Horst Heese GER 2003-06 • Dusan Fitzel CZE 2006-09 • John Buttigieg 2009-11

MALTA 2010–11

PREMIER LEAGUE

	Pl	W	D	L	F	A	Pts	Valletta	Floriana	Birkirkara	Marsaxlokk	Tarxien	Hamrun Sp	Sliema W	Qormi	Hibernians	Vittoriosa
Valletta (22) †	28	18	10	0	59	17	42		0-0 3-0	3-1 1-1	0-0 1-1	5-2 2-2	1-1 5-0	4-0	1-0	2-0	3-0
Floriana (15) ‡	28	14	5	9	46	32	34	0-2 1-1		0-1 3-0	0-1 1-1	0-2 5-1	3-1 2-0	0-1	4-3	1-3	0-0
Birkirkara (14) ‡	28	11	9	8	42	40	29	2-2 0-1	0-2 1-5		2-5 2-0	0-0 3-0	2-0 2-2	2-2	1-4	3-1	1-1
Marsaxlokk (14)	28	9	11	8	45	43	26	0-2 0-1	0-3 4-0	2-0 1-4		2-4 2-4	2-1 6-3	0-0	0-1	2-2	2-2
Tarxien Rainbows (12)	28	10	7	11	41	45	23	0-2 0-1	3-1 1-2	0-0 1-3	0-0 0-1		3-1 3-3	2-1	1-1	2-0	1-0
Hamrun Spartans (12)	28	7	6	15	44	66	16	0-2 1-1	1-2 0-2	1-1 1-1	2-3 2-4	3-1 1-4		3-2	2-1	2-4	2-0
Sliema Wanderers (11)	24	10	7	7	37	31	26	1-4	0-1	1-4	1-1	1-1	3-1		0-0 4-1	4-0 0-1	4-3 2-0
Qormi (11)	24	7	7	10	37	43	18	0-4	0-1	0-2	2-2	2-1	1-3	0-0 0-4		1-0 5-2	2-2 2-2
Hibernians (8)	24	6	6	12	34	46	17	2-2	1-1	1-2	2-2	3-1	3-4	0-0 2-3	0-0 4-3		1-2 2-1
Vittoriosa Stars (6)	24	3	6	15	26	48	10	2-3	1-6	0-1	1-1	0-1	2-3	0-1 1-2	2-4 1-4	2-0 1-0	

11/09/2010 - 7/05/2011 • † Qualified for the UEFA Champions League • ‡ Qualified for the Europa League • Points taken forward for the final round in brackets • Top scorers: 17 - Alfred Effiong NGA, Marsaxlokk • 16 - Terrence Scerri, Valletta • 14 - Gaetan Spiteri, Hamrun Spartans

MALTA 2010–11 FIRST DIVISION (2)

	Pl	W	D	L	F	A	Pts
Balzan Youth	18	15	2	1	42	16	47
Mqabba	18	10	5	3	38	16	35
Mosta	18	9	5	4	42	22	32
Melita	18	9	5	4	31	21	32
Lija Athletic	18	7	3	8	24	25	24
St George's	18	6	6	6	25	28	24
St Andrews	18	5	5	8	20	28	20
Dingli Swallows	18	5	3	10	20	36	18
Pietà Hotspurs	18	4	4	10	34	37	16
Msida St Joseph §4	18	0	2	16	5	52	-2

23/10/2010 - 1/05/2011 • § = points deducted

MEDALS TABLE

	Overall			League			Cup		City
	G	S	B	G	S	B	G	S	
1 Sliema Wanderers	46	50	19	26	31	19	20	19	Sliema
2 Floriana	44	24	13	25	12	13	19	12	Floriana
3 Valletta	32	29	20	20	16	20	12	13	Valletta
4 Hibernians	18	19	9	10	9	9	8	10	Paola
5 Hamrun Spartans	13	13	13	7	10	13	6	3	Hamrun
6 Birkirkara	7	9	6	3	6	6	4	3	Birkirkara
7 Rabat Ajax	3	2	1	2	1	1	1	1	Rabat
8 St. Georges	1	6	5	1	4	5		2	Cospicua
9 Zurrieq	1	2	2			2	1	2	Zurrieq
10 Marsaxlokk	1	2	1	1	1	1		1	Marsaxlokk
Melita St. Julians	1	2	1		1	1		1	Melita
12 Gzira United	1		1		1		1		Gzira
13 KOMR Militia	1			1					

FA TROPHY 2010–11

Round of 16		Quarter-finals		Semi-finals		Final	
Floriana	1						
Mosta	0	Floriana	1 5p				
		Qormi	1 3p	Floriana	2		
Qormi	Bye			Birkirkara	1		
Sliema Wanderers	Bye						
		Sliema Wanderers	3 1p				
		Birkirkara	3 3p			Floriana ‡	1
Rirkirkara	Bye					Valletta	0
Tarxien Rainbows	3						
Hamrun Spartans	2	Tarxien Rainbows	4				
Marsaxlokk	0	Vittoriosa Stars	2				
Vittoriosa Stars	3			Tarxien Rainbows	0		
Hibernians	3			Valletta	1		
St Andrews	2	Hibernians	0				
		Valletta	1				
Valletta	Bye			‡ Qualified for the Europa League			

CUP FINAL

National, Ta'Qali
22-05-2011

Scorer - Ivan Woods 89 for Floriana

MNE – MONTENEGRO

FIFA/COCA-COLA WORLD RANKING

'93	'94	'95	'96	'97	'98	'99	'00	'01	'02	'03	'04	'05	'06	'07	'08	'09	'10	'11	'12
-	-	-	-	-	-	-	-	-	-	-	-	-	-	172	112	74	25	51	

						2011									
Jan	Feb	Mar	Apr	May	Jun	Jul	Aug	Sep	Oct	Nov	Dec		High	Low	Av
25	25	25	24	24	16	17	19	26	39	51	51		16	199	93

For a team that has been playing its football as an independent nation for just five years, Montenegro's achievement in reaching the play-offs for Euro 2012 was extraordinary. It was achieved on the back of an excellent start to the campaign at the end of 2010, because of the eight matches played in 2011 Montenegro's only victory came in a friendly against Uzbekistan. However, they did play a great game against England at the end of the campaign - a 2-2 draw ensuring their qualification for a play-off against the Czech Republic. A place in the finals at their first attempt proved to be a step too far with the Czechs winning both legs and the Montenegrins will go into their 2014 FIFA World Cup qualifying group with Serbia's Branko Brnovic in charge after Zlatko Kranjcar was replaced following the defeat to Wales in September. At home, Mogren Budva became the first team to win a second league title as Buducnost finished as runners-up for the fourth time in the five years that the championship has been staged. The two finished tied on 73 points but with two wins in the three games played between each other, Mogren won on the better head-to-head record. They were denied the double after losing to Rudar on penalties in the Cup Final. For Rudar it was a third Cup Final victory and a record fourth trophy overall.

UEFA EUROPEAN CHAMPIONSHIP RECORD

1960-2004 DNE (Played as Yugoslavia) 2008 DNE 2012 DNQ

FOOTBALL ASSOCIATION OF MONTENEGRO (FAM)

Fudbalski savez Crne Gore,
Ulica 19. Decembar 13,
PO Box 275,
Podgorica 81000
☎ +382 20 445600
📠 +382 20 445660
✉ info@fscg.me
🖳 www.fscg.me
FA 1931 CON 2007 FIFA 2007
P Dejan Savicevic
GS Momir Djurdjevac

FIFA BIG COUNT 2006

Total players	N/A
% of population	N/A
Male	N/A
Female	N/A
Youth under 18	N/A
Unregistered	N/A
Professionals	N/A
Referees	N/A
Admin & coaches	N/A
Number of clubs	N/A
Number of teams	N/A

MAJOR CITIES/TOWNS

		Population
1	Podgorica	145 192
2	Niksic	58 712
3	Pljevlja	21 354
4	Bijelo Polje	15 357
5	Bar	15 112
6	Cetinje	14 569
7	Herceg Novi	13 361
8	Budva	13 093
9	Berane	11 498
10	Ulcinj	11 056
11	Tivat	10 056
12	Rozaje	9 130
13	Dobrota	8 533
14	Danilovgrad	5 574
15	Tuzi	4 564
16	Bijela	4 102
17	Mojkovac	3 938
18	Skaljari	3 874
19	Igalo	3 785

CRNA GORA • MONTENEGRO

Capital Podgorica	Population 672 180 (164)	% in cities 60%
GDP per capita $10 100 (104)	Area km² 13 812 km² (161)	GMT +/- +1
Neighbours (km) Albania 172, Bosnia-Herzegovina 225, Croatia 25, Kosovo 79, Serbia 124 • Coast 293		

INTERNATIONAL MATCHES PLAYED BY MONTENEGRO

2007	Opponents	Score		Venue	Comp	Scorers	Att	Referee
24-03	Hungary	W	2-1	Podgorica	Fr	Vucinic 64p, Burzanovic 82p	11 000	Kranjc SVN
1-06	Japan	L	0-2	Shizuoka	Fr		28 635	Svendsen DEN
3-06	Colombia	L	0-1	Matsumoto	Fr		10 070	Ogiya JPN
22-08	Slovenia	D	1-1	Podgorica	Fr	Vucinic 28p		
12-09	Sweden	L	1-2	Podgorica	Fr	Vucinic 15	9 000	Brugger AUT
17-10	Estonia	W	1-0	Tallinn	Fr	Vucinic 41	2 000	Fröjdfeldt SWE
2008								
26-03	Norway	W	3-1	Podgorica	Fr	Burzanovic 7, Boskovic 37, Dalovic 59	9 000	Stavrev MKD
27-05	Kazakhstan	W	3-0	Podgorica	Fr	Dalovic 2 15 45, Drincic 21	9 000	Tusin LUX
31-05	Romania	L	0-4	Bucharest	Fr		8 000	Tudor ROU
20-08	Hungary	D	3-3	Budapest	Fr	Jovetic 2 45p 68, Vukevic 51	4 913	Havrilla SVK
6-09	Bulgaria	D	2-2	Podgorica	WCq	Vucinic 61, Jovetic 82p	9 000	Oriekhov UKR
10-09	Republic of Ireland	D	0-0	Podgorica	WCq		12 000	Kaldma EST
15-10	Italy	L	1-2	Lecce	WCq	Vucinic 19	20 162	Proenca POR
19-11	Macedonia FYR	W	2-1	Podgorica	Fr	Dzudovic 24, Jovetic 33p		Panic BIH
2009								
28-03	Italy	L	0-2	Podgorica	WCq		10 500	Atkinson ENG
1-04	Georgia	D	0-0	Tbilisi	WCq		16 000	Malcolm NIR
6-06	Cyprus	D	2-2	Larnaca	WCq	Damjanovic 2 65 77	3 000	Velasco ESP
12-08	Wales	W	2-1	Podgorica	Fr	Jovetic 31p, Dalovic 45	5 000	Mazic SRB
5-09	Bulgaria	L	1-4	Sofia	WCq	Jovetic 9	7 543	Asumaa FIN
9-09	Cyprus	D	1-1	Podgorica	WCq	Vucinic 56p	4 000	Zimmermann SUI
10-10	Georgia	W	2-1	Podgorica	WCq	Batak 14, Delibasic 78	5 420	Dereli TUR
14-11	Republic of Ireland	D	0-0	Dublin	WCq		50 212	Hrinal SVK
18-11	Belarus	W	1-0	Podgorica	Fr	Vucinic 80	5 000	Stavrev MKD
2010								
3-03	FYR Macedonia	L	1-2	Skopje	Fr	Basa 62	7 000	Janku ALB
25-05	Albania	L	0-1	Podgorica	Fr		7 000	Strahonja CRO
29-05	Norway	L	1-2	Oslo	Fr	Vucinic 82	13 132	Eriksson SWE
11-08	Northern Ireland	W	2-0	Podgorica	Fr	Dalovic 2 43 59	5 000	Jovanetic SRB
3-09	Wales	W	1-0	Podgorica	ECq	Vucinic 30	7 442	Kakos GRE
7-09	Bulgaria	W	1-0	Sofia	ECq	Zverotic 36	9 470	Bezborodov RUS
8-10	Switzerland	W	1-0	Podgorica	ECq	Vucinic 68	10 750	Iturralde ESP
12-10	England	D	0-0	London	ECq		73 451	Grafe GER
17-11	Azerbaijan	W	2-0	Podgorica	Fr	Pejovic 62, Beciraj 74	3 000	Stavrev MKD
2011								
25-03	Uzbekistan	W	1-0	Podgorica	Fr	Vukevic 90	6 000	Glodovic SRB
4-06	Bulgaria	D	1-1	Podgorica	ECq	Djalovic 53	11 500	Yefet ISR
10-08	Albania	L	2-3	Tirana	Fr	Savic 2 40 49	5 500	Genov BUL
2-09	Wales	L	1-2	Cardiff	ECq	Jovetic 71	8 194	Banti ITA
7-10	England	D	2-2	Podgorica	ECq	Zverotic 45, Delibasic 91+	11 340	Stark GER
11-10	Switzerland	L	0-2	Basel	ECq		19 997	Benquerenca POR
11-11	Czech Republic	L	0-2	Prague	ECpo		14 560	Atkinson ENG
15-11	Czech Republic	L	0-1	Podgorica	ECpo		11 000	Rizzoli ITA

Fr = Friendly match • EC = UEFA EURO 2012 • WC = FIFA World Cup • q = qualifier

MONTENEGRO NATIONAL TEAM HISTORICAL RECORDS

Caps
30 - Simon Vukcevic 2007- • **28** - Elsad Zverotic 2008- • **27** - Savo Pavicevic 2007- ; Milan Jovanovic 2007- & Vladimir Bozovic 2007- • **26** - Milorad Petkovic 2007- • **25** - Mirko Vucinic 2007- ; Radomir Salovic 2007 - & Radoslav Batak 2007-

Goals
11 - Mirko Vucinic 2007- • **7** - Radomir Dalovic 2007- & Stevan Jovetic 2007-

Past Coaches
Zoran Filipovic 2007-10 • Zlatko Kranjcar 2010-11 • Branko Brnovic 2011-

MONTENEGRO 2010–11

PRVA CRNOGORSKA LIGA

	Pl	W	D	L	F	A	Pts	Mogren	Buducnost	Rudar	Zeta	Mladost	Decic	Grbalj	Lovcen	Petrovac	Mornar	Sutjeska	Bar
Mogren Budva †	33	22	7	4	60	24	73	—	2-0 1-2	1-0	0-0 2-0	1-0	5-0 4-1	0-0 2-0	0-0	3-1	2-0 2-0	4-1	3-1 1-2
Buducnost Podgorica ‡	33	22	7	4	58	29	73	1-2	—	0-1 2-1	0-0	3-3 2-0	2-2	2-1	2-0 1-0	4-3 1-3	1-3 3-2	2-1 3-0	1-0
Rudar Pljevlja ‡	33	16	7	10	44	29	55	4-0 0-1	0-2	—	2-1 2-2	2-1	1-0 2-0	0-1 4-3	1-1	3-0	2-1 1-1	3-0	0-0 2-2
Zeta Golubovci ‡	33	12	13	8	36	29	49	1-2	0-2 2-2	1-0	—	2-1 1-0	0-0	1-0	2-0 2-1	1-0 0-1	4-0 3-0	3-1	0-0 2-0
Mladost Podgorica	33	10	11	12	36	35	41	2-2 1-1	0-2	2-0 1-3	2-0	—	0-0	1-0	1-2 3-1	1-1	1-1 1-0	0-1 5-1	1-0 3-1
Decic Tuzi	33	10	9	14	24	33	39	0-1	0-2 0-0	1-0	0-0 3-0	1-0 2-0	—	1-0	2-0 2-0	0-2	2-0 0-1	1-0	1-1 1-1
Grbalj Radanovici	33	10	8	15	30	35	38	0-1	1-3 1-0	0-1	1-1 1-1	0-1 2-2	0-2 0-0	—	1-0	1-2	1-0	0-0	5-0 3-0
Lovcen Cetinje	33	9	10	14	29	36	37	0-1 0-1	1-3	1-0 2-2	0-2	0-0	2-2	1-0 1-0	—	0-0	3-2 2-2	1-1	0-1 1-0
OFK Petrovac	33	8	11	14	26	38	35	0-0 1-1	0-2	0-1	2-0	0-0	0-0	0-1 1-2	1-0	—	1-1	1-1	0-3 0-0
Mornar Bar	33	9	7	17	25	45	34	0-5	1-2	0-1	0-0	0-0	1-0	0-0 2-1	0-1 2-1	1-0	—	2-1 3-1	1-0 1-1
Sutjeska Niksic	33	9	7	17	32	54	34	1-4 3-1	1-2	0-0 2-1	1-1	2-1 2-0	2-1	1-2	1-2 0-2	1-1	2-0	—	2-0 3-1
OFK Bar	33	7	11	15	30	43	32	2-4	0-0 1-2	0-2	0-0 3-3	1-2	0-0 3-0	1-0 0-0	2-5	1-1	1-0	2-0 0-1	—

14/08/2010 - 28/05/2011 • † Qualified for the UEFA Champions League • ‡ Qualified for the Europa League
Relegation play-offs: Jedinstvo 0-0 0-1 Sutjeska • Mornar 1-1 0-0 Berane
Top scorers: 20 - Ivan Vukovic, Buducnost • 19 - Zarko Korac, Zeta • 16 - Bozo Markovic, Sutjeska • 13 - Ivica Jovanovic SRB, Rudar

MONTENEGRO 2010–11
II LIGA (2)

	Pl	W	D	L	F	A	Pts
Bokelj Kotor	33	24	5	4	61	22	77
Jedinstvo Bijelo Polje ‡	33	14	11	8	33	28	53
FK Berane ‡	33	15	6	12	46	32	51
Bratstvo Cijevna	33	14	6	13	46	34	48
Iskra Bugojno	33	12	11	10	39	40	47
Kom Podgorica	33	12	9	12	37	31	45
Ibar Rozaje	33	10	14	9	33	33	44
Celik Niksic	33	11	9	13	37	34	42
Jezero Plav	33	10	10	13	38	57	39
Zabjelo Podgorica	33	7	13	13	34	48	34
Otrant Ulcinj	33	6	12	15	36	56	30
Pljevlja 1997	33	5	10	18	25	50	25

15/08/2010 - 28/05/2011 • ‡ Promotion play-off

MEDALS TABLE

	Overall G	S	B	League G	S	B	Cup G	S	City
1 Rudar Pljevlja	4	1		1	1		3		Pljevlja
2 Mogren Budva	3	1	2	2	2		1	1	Budva
3 Buducnost Podgorica	1	6		1	4			2	Podgorica
4 Zeta Golubovci	1	1		1	1				Golubovci
5 OFK Petrovac	1						1		Petrovac
6 Sutjeska Niksic	1	1		1			1		Niksic
7 Lovcen Cetinje	1						1		Cetinje
8 Grbalj Radanovici					1				Radanovici

KUPA CRNE GORE 2010–11

Round of 16

Rudar Pljevlja *	2 2
Crvena stijena	0 1
Iskra Bugojno	1 0
Sutjeska Niksic *	2 2
Decic Tuzi	0 2
Mladost Podgorica	0 1
Pljevlja 1997	0 0
Zeta Golubovci *	1 3
OFK Petrovac *	3 2
Jezero Plav	0 0
Gornja Zeta	0 0
Buducnost Podgorica	4 6
OFK Bar *	1 1
Mornar Bar	0 1
Bokelj Kotor	0 0
Mogren Budva	3 1

Quarter-finals

Rudar Pljevlja *	0 2
Sutjeska Niksic	0 1
Decic Tuzi *	0 0
Zeta Golubovci	0 2
OFK Petrovac	0 2
Buducnost Podgorica *	0 0
OFK Bar *	1 1
Mogren Budva	1 2

Semi-finals

Rudar Pljevlja *	1 2
Zeta Golubovci	0 2
OFK Petrovac	0 0
Mogren Budva *	2 2

Final

Rudar Pljevlja	2 5p
Mogren Budva	2 4p

CUP FINAL
Pod Goricom, Podgorica, 25-05-2011, Att: 4000, Ref: Spasojevic
Scorers - Nedjelko Vlahovic [53], Veselin Bojic [97p] for Rudar; Ardijan Dokaj [15p], Marko Cetkovic [112] for Mogren

* Home team in the first leg • ‡ Qualified for the Europa League

MGL – MONGOLIA

FIFA/COCA-COLA WORLD RANKING

'93	'94	'95	'96	'97	'98	'99	'00	'01	'02	'03	'04	'05	'06	'07	'08	'09	'10	'11	'12
-	-	-	-	-	196	198	196	187	193	179	185	179	181	178	192	171	182	168	

2011													High	Low	Av
Jan	Feb	Mar	Apr	May	Jun	Jul	Aug	Sep	Oct	Nov	Dec		High	Low	Av
182	182	183	179	179	179	163	160	163	167	166	168		160	200	184

The fixture list for the Mongolian national team is largely confined to the qualifying tournaments of just three competitions - the FIFA World Cup, the AFC Challenge Cup and the East Asian Championship. That meant that after a dark year in 2010 with no matches played, 2011 saw a return to international action with the Mongolians drawn against Myanmar in the 2014 FIFA World Cup qualifiers and against the Philippines in the 2012 AFC Challenge Cup. In a sign of the growing technical level of the game in the country, both home legs were won although a combined crowd of just 6,000 for the two matches shows the progress still to be made in winning over the public to football. Despite the wins, Mongolia didn't make it through to the next round of either competition after losing both ties on aggregate by the odd goal. FC Ulaanbaatar, meanwhile, claimed the Niislel Lig title despite only finishing in third place in the standings at the end of the regular season. Three points separated the top five teams, with Ulaanbaatar DS topping the table ahead of Khasiin Khulguud, FC Ulaanbaatar and Khoromkhon, with Erchim missing out on a place in the play-offs by virtue of goal difference. FC Ulaanbaatar then saw off Khasiin Khulguud over two legs in the semi-finals before defeating Ulaanbaatar DS 1-0 in the final to win the title for the first time.

FIFA WORLD CUP RECORD
1930-1998 DNE 2002-2014 DNQ

MONGOLIA FOOTBALL FEDERATION (MFF)

PO Box 259,
Ulaan-Baatar 210646

☎ +976 11 345968
🖷 +976 11 345966
✉ mongolianff@the-mff.mn
🖳 the-mff.mn
FA 1959 CON 1998 FIFA 1998
P Ganbold Buyannemekh
GS Terbaatar Dambiijav

FIFA BIG COUNT 2006

Total players	51 200
% of population	1.81%
Male	51 200
Female	0
Amateurs 18+	800
Youth under 18	3 020
Unregistered	11 000
Professionals	200
Referees	30
Admin & coaches	73
Number of clubs	10
Number of teams	70

MAJOR CITIES/TOWNS

		Population
1	Ulaan Baatar	922 127
2	Erdenet	90 353
3	Darchan	78 254
4	Choybalsan	46 525
5	Saynshand	31 784
6	Olgiy	31 747
7	Moron	29 536
8	Ulaan Gom	29 529
9	Hovd	29 486
10	Uliastay	27 657
11	Suche Baatar	25 906
12	Bayanhongor	24 148
13	Arvaiheer	21 929
14	Dzuunharaa	19 949
15	Tsetserleg	19 875
16	Altay	19 344
17	Dzuunmod	19 024
18	Bulgan	18 239
19	Nalajh	17 311

MOGOL ULS • MONGOLIA

Capital	Ulaan-Baatar	Population	3 041 142 (136)	% in cities	57%
GDP per capita	$3200 (163)	Area km²	1 564 116 km² (19)	GMT +/-	+8
Neighbours (km)	China 4677, Russia 3543				

RECENT INTERNATIONAL MATCHES PLAYED BY MONGOLIA

2005 Opponents	Score	Venue	Comp	Scorers	Att	Referee
5-03 Hong Kong	L 0-6	Taipei	EAq			
7-03 Korea DPR	L 0-6	Taipei	EAq			
9-03 Guam	W 4-1	Taipei	EAq	Tugsbayer 2 [31] [34], Bayarzorig [46], Buman-Uchral [81]		
13-03 Chinese Taipei	D 0-0	Taipei	EAq			
2006						
No international matches played in 2006						
2007						
17-06 Macau	D 0-0	Macau	EAq		300	Matsuo JPN
19-06 Korea DPR	L 0-7	Macau	EAq		300	Ogiya JPN
23-06 Guam	W 5-2	Macau	EAq	OG [24], Davaa 2 [37] [42], Bayasgalan [46], Batchuluun [75]	100	Wan Daxue CHN
21-10 Korea DPR	L 1-4	Ulaan-Baatar	WCq	Selenge [93+]	4 870	Takayama JPN
28-10 Korea DPR	L 1-5	Pyongyang	WCq	Lumbengarav Donorov [41]	5 000	Gosh BAN
2008						
No international matches played in 2008						
2009						
11-03 Guam	L 0-1	Manenggon Hills	EAq			Kim Jong Hyeuk KOR
13-03 Macau	W 2-1	Manenggon Hills	EAq	Norjmoo Tsedenbal [67], Lumbengarav Donorov [69]		Fan Qi CHN
15-03 Northern Marianas†	W 4-1	Manenggon Hills	EAq	Lumbengarav Donorov [16], Badrakhzaya Sukhbaatar [42], Norjmoo Tsedenbal [71], Ariunbold Batsaikhan [90]	700	Sato JPN
7-04 Macau	L 0-2	Macau	CCq		500	Perera SRI
14-04 Macau	W 3-1	Ulaan-Baatar	CCq	Munkhbaatar Altankhuu [55], OG [77], Lumbengarav Donorov [89]	3 000	Yu Ming Hsun TPE
2010						
No international matches played in 2010						
2011						
9-02 Philippines	L 0-2	Bacolod	CCq		20 000	Yu Ming Hsun TPE
15-03 Philippines	W 2-1	Ulaan-Baatar	CCq	Lumbengarav Donorov [22], Garidmagnai Bayasgalan [35]	3 000	Ko Hyung Jin KOR
29-06 Myanmar	W 1-0	Ulaan-Baatar	WCq	Tsend-Ayush Khurelbaatar [48]	3 500	Kim Jong Hyeok KOR
3-07 Myanmar	L 0-2	Yangon	WCq		18 000	Liu Kwok Man HKG

EA = EAFF East Asian Championship • AC = AFC Asian Cup • CC = AFC Challenge Cup • WC = FIFA World Cup • q = qualifier

MONGOLIA 2011

NIISLEL LIG FIRST STAGE

	Pl	W	D	L	F	A	Pts	Ulaanbaatar DS	Khulguud	FC Ulaanbaatar	Khoromkhon	Erchim	Selenge Press	Khangarid	Mazaalai
Ulaanbaatar DS †	14	7	3	4	23	15	24		4-3	1-0	1-0	1-2	3-1	2-2	0-0
Khasiin Khulguud †	14	7	1	6	27	24	22	1-0		2-3	1-2	1-0	1-4	3-1	3-0
FC Ulaanbaatar †	14	6	3	5	35	24	21	0-0	1-3		3-4	3-0	7-2	4-1	2-0
Khoromkhon †	14	5	6	3	20	22	21	1-0	1-1	3-3		0-0	2-4	1-0	3-2
Erchim	14	6	3	5	23	20	21	2-0	3-1	3-6	1-1		2-3	1-2	3-0
Selenge Press	14	5	3	6	30	33	18	2-4	3-1	3-2	1-1	2-3		2-2	1-2
Khangarid	14	3	5	6	20	26	14	1-3	2-3	2-1	4-0	0-3	1-1		1-1
Mazaalai	14	2	6	6	9	23	12	0-4	0-3	0-0	1-1	0-0	2-1	1-1	

1/05/2011 - 1/09/2011 • † Qualified for the play-offs

FINAL STAGE PLAY-OFFS

Semi-finals			Finals	
FC Ulaanbaatar	1	1		
Khasiin Khulguud	0	2		
			FC Ulaanbaatar	1
			Ulaanbaatar DS	0
Khoromkhon	3	0		
Ulaanbaatar DS	2	2	18-09-2011	

MOZ – MOZAMBIQUE

FIFA/COCA-COLA WORLD RANKING

'93	'94	'95	'96	'97	'98	'99	'00	'01	'02	'03	'04	'05	'06	'07	'08	'09	'10	'11	'12
104	94	76	85	67	80	101	112	128	125	127	126	130	128	75	95	72	96	105	

						2011									
	Jan	Feb	Mar	Apr	May	Jun	Jul	Aug	Sep	Oct	Nov	Dec	High	Low	Av
	92	94	93	96	94	106	103	99	115	110	105	105	66	134	103

Mozambique had a major sporting year with their hosting of the All-Africa Games in Maputo in August although any hopes of a footballing gold medal disappeared quickly. Both the men's and women's team lost all of their group games and were eliminated at the first hurdle. After qualifying for the 2010 CAF Africa Cup of Nations, the Mambas had high hopes of making it to the 2012 finals in Equatorial Guinea and Gabon but finished a disappointing third in their group behind Zambia and Libya. Defeat at home to Zambia in March effectively ended their chances with any outside hopes laid to rest on an emotional evening in Cairo in September against a Libyan team celebrating the liberation of their country. Defeat led to the departure of Dutch coach Mart Nooij. He was replaced by the German Gert Engels who steered Mozambique through a 2014 FIFA World Cup qualifier against the Comoros Islands. The 5-1 aggregate success saw Mozambique through to the group stage of qualifying in Africa. Liga Muculmana retained their league crown with a runaway eight point lead over second placed Maxaquene while relegation for army club Matchedje ended a run in the top flight stretching back to the first national league in 1978. Ferroviario Maputo won the cup with an easy three goal victory in the final against Chingale from Tete Province.

CAF AFRICA CUP OF NATIONS RECORD

1957-1980 DNE 1982-1984 DNQ **1986** 8 r1 1988-1994 DNQ **1996** 14 r1 **1998** 16 r1 2000-2008 DNQ **2010** 15 r1 2012 DNQ

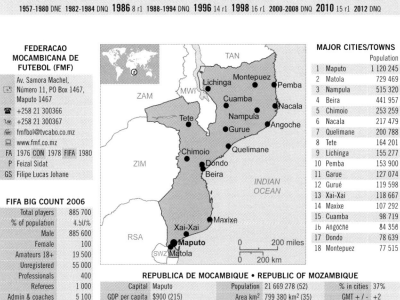

FEDERACAO MOCAMBICANA DE FUTEBOL (FMF)

Av. Samora Machel,
Número 11, PO Box 1467,
Maputo 1467
☎ +258 21 300366
📠 +258 21 300367
✉ fmfbol@tvcabo.co.mz
🌐 www.fmf.co.mz
FA 1976 CON 1978 FIFA 1980
P Feizal Sidat
GS Filipe Lucas Johane

FIFA BIG COUNT 2006

Total players	885 700
% of population	4.50%
Male	885 600
Female	100
Amateurs 18+	19 500
Unregistered	55 000
Professionals	400
Referees	1 000
Admin & coaches	5 100
Number of clubs	170
Number of teams	850

MAJOR CITIES/TOWNS

		Population
1	Maputo	1 120 245
2	Matola	729 469
3	Nampula	515 320
4	Beira	441 957
5	Chimoio	253 259
6	Nacala	217 479
7	Quelimane	200 788
8	Tete	164 201
9	Lichinga	155 277
10	Pemba	153 900
11	Garue	127 074
12	Gurué	119 598
13	Xai-Xai	118 667
14	Maxixe	107 292
15	Cuamba	98 719
16	Angòche	84 358
17	Dondo	78 639
18	Montepuez	77 515

REPUBLICA DE MOCAMBIQUE • REPUBLIC OF MOZAMBIQUE

Capital	Maputo	Population 21 669 278 (52)	% in cities 37%
GDP per capita	$900 (215)	Area km² 799 380 km² (35)	GMT +/- +2
Neighbours (km)	Malawi 1569, South Africa 491, Swaziland 105, Tanzania 756, Zambia 419, Zimbabwe 1231 • Coast 2470		

RECENT INTERNATIONAL MATCHES PLAYED BY MOZAMBIQUE

2007 Opponents	Score		Venue	Comp	Scorers	Att	Referee
20-08 Zimbabwe	D	0-0	Beira	Fr	W 3-1p		
8-09 Tanzania	W	1-0	Dar es Salaam	CNq	Tico-Tico [2]		Guezzaz MAR
29-09 Zambia	L	0-3	Atteridgeville	CCsf			Bennett RSA
2008							
13-01 South Africa	L	0-2	Durban	Fr			
21-05 Lesotho	L	2-3	Maputo	Fr	Fanuel [9], Tico-Tico [43]		
1-06 Côte d'Ivoire	L	0-1	Abidjan	WCq		20 000	Auda EGY
8-06 Botswana	L	1-2	Maputo	WCq	Miro [60]	30 000	Faudze SWZ
15-06 Madagascar	D	1-1	Antananarivo	WCq	Dario [33]	15 501	Ebrahim RSA
22-06 Madagascar	W	3-0	Maputo	WCq	Tico-Tico [23], Carlitos [52], Domingues [64]	20 000	Maillett SEY
27-07 Botswana	W	2-0	Secunda	CCqf	Momed Hagi [18], Txuma [89]		Katjimune NAM
30-07 Madagascar	W	2-1	Thulamahashe	CCsf	Tico-Tico [19], Momed Hagi [66]		Marange ZIM
20-08 Swaziland	W	3-0	Maputo	Fr	Dario 2 [4 12], Domingues [35]		
7-09 Côte d'Ivoire	D	1-1	Maputo	WCq	Miro [56]	35 000	El Achiri MAR
11-10 Botswana	W	1-0	Gaborone	WCq	Genito [6]	2 000	Seck SEN
19-11 Tanzania	L	0-1	Dar es Salaam	Fr			
2009							
11-02 Malawi	W	2-0	Maputo	Fr	Dario [31], Domingues [90]		
29-03 Nigeria	D	0-0	Maputo	WCq		35 000	Eyob ERI
6-06 Tunisia	L	0-2	Rades/Tunis	WCq		30 000	Djaoupe TOG
20-06 Kenya	L	1-2	Nairobi	WCq	Domingues [49]	15 000	Keita GUI
12-08 Swaziland	W	1-0	Maputo	Fr	Miro [39]		
6-09 Kenya	W	1-0	Maputo	WCq	Tico-Tico [66]	35 000	Coulibaly MLI
11-10 Nigeria	L	0-1	Abuja	WCq		13 000	Abdel Rahman SUD
25-10 Malawi	W	1-0	Harare	CCqf	Josemar [35]		Ramocha BOT
29-10 Zambia	L	0-2	Bulawayo	CCsf			Ramocha BOT
14-11 Tunisia	W	1-0	Maputo	WCq	Dario [83]	30 000	Doue CIV
19-12 Malawi	L	0-1	Tete	Fr			
28-12 Zambia	L	0-1	Johannesburg	Fr			
2010							
6-01 Gabon	L	0-2	Bloemfontein	Fr			
12-01 Benin	D	2-2	Benguela	CNr1	Miro [29], Fumo [54]	15 000	Abdel Rahman SUD
16-01 Egypt	L	0-2	Benguela	CNr1		16 000	Djaoupe TOG
20-01 Nigeria	L	0-3	Lubango	CNr1		10 000	Coulibaly MLI
3-03 Botswana	L	0-1	Maputo	Fr			
8-06 Portugal	L	0-3	Johannesburg	Fr		34 000	Dyer RSA
11-08 Swaziland	W	2-1	Maputo	Fr	Domingues [9p], Miro [51]		
5-09 Libya	D	0-0	Maputo	CNq			Bangoura GUI
9-10 Comoros	W	1-0	Moroni	CNq	Josemar [90]		Ibada TAN
2011							
9-02 Botswana	D	1-1	Maputo	Fr	Miro [58]		
27-03 Zambia	L	0-2	Maputo	CNq			
23-04 Tanzania	W	2-0	Maputo	Fr	Jerry Sitoe 2 [17 48]		
4-06 Zambia	L	0-3	Chingola	CNq			
3-09 Libya	L	0-1	Cairo	CNq			Omar EGY
8-10 Comoros	W	3-0	Maputo	CNq	Maninho [6], Dario [18p], Domingues [40]		
11-11 Comoros	W	1-0	Mitsamiouli	WCq	Miro [54p]	3 000	Jane LES
15-11 Comoros	W	4-1	Maputo	WCq	Domingues [26], Jerry Sitoe [45], Whiskey [59], Clesio Bauque [84]	10 000	Ruzive ZIM

Fr = Friendly match • CN = CAF African Cup of Nations • CC = COSAFA Cup • WC = FIFA World Cup • q = qualifier

MOZAMBIQUE 2011

CAMPEONATO NACIONAL DA 1ª DIVISAO

	Pl	W	D	L	F	A	Pts	L Muçulmana	Maxaquene	Songo	Costa do Sol	Ferroviário M	Ferroviário N	Chingale	Vilankulo	Desportivo	Ferroviário B	Incomáti	Matchedje	A Muçulmano	Sporting
Liga Muçulmana †	26	19	4	3	48	18	61		1-1	0-0	0-1	2-1	2-0	1-0	2-1	1-0	4-1	2-0	4-1	1-0	8-2
Maxaquene	26	15	8	3	45	14	53	1-2		2-1	0-0	1-1	3-0	5-0	1-0	4-0	2-1	2-0	0-0	0-0	5-1
HCB Songo	26	10	11	5	28	13	41	2-0	1-1		2-0	1-1	3-0	1-1	1-0	0-1	3-0	0-0	0-0	0-0	5-1
Costa do Sol	26	11	6	9	31	25	39	0-1	0-3	0-1		2-2	2-1	1-0	0-1	2-1	2-0	2-0	2-1	2-1	6-3
Ferroviário Maputo ‡	26	10	7	9	36	32	37	1-1	1-1	1-0	2-1		1-2	2-1	0-1	1-2	3-3	2-0	3-2	3-1	1-0
Ferroviário Nampula	26	10	6	10	28	26	36	0-2	0-0	1-0	0-0	2-0		1-2	1-1	0-0	1-2	1-0	2-0	2-1	5-2
Chingale Tete	26	9	9	8	19	23	36	1-0	2-0	1-0	1-0	2-1	0-0		3-3	0-2	1-0	1-0	0-1	0-0	0-0
Vilankulo	26	10	5	11	26	25	35	1-2	0-2	1-1	2-1	0-1	0-2	0-1		2-3	2-0	1-0	4-1	0-0	2-0
Desportivo Maputo	26	10	5	11	23	25	35	1-3	0-1	0-2	0-1	1-1	1-0	1-0	0-1		0-0	0-1	3-0	2-1	0-0
Ferroviário Beira	26	6	13	7	21	25	31	0-0	3-2	1-1	0-0	2-0	0-0	1-1	0-0	0-0		0-0	0-0	3-1	0-1
Incomáti Xinavane	26	8	5	13	11	25	29	0-1	0-1	0-1	0-4	1-0	1-1	2-0	0-0	0-2	1-1		0-1	0-0	0-0
Matchedje Maputo	26	7	6	13	21	36	27	0-1	0-4	0-1	1-1	1-3	2-0	0-0	2-1	1-0	0-0	1-2		1-2	1-2
Atlético Muçulmano	26	5	6	15	20	37	21	2-5	0-2	0-0	1-0	1-4	2-5	0-0	1-0	1-4	0-1	0-1	1-2		3-0
Sporting Beira	26	4	5	17	20	53	17	1-3	0-1	1-1	1-1	1-0	0-1	1-1	1-2	1-0	1-3	0-1	0-1	1-0	

5/03/2011 - 20/11/2011 • † Qualified for the CAF Champions League • ‡ Qualified for the CAF Confederation Cup

MEDALS TABLE

		Overall G	Lge G	Cup G	Cup S	City/Town
1	Costa do Sol	20	9	11	3	Maputo
2	Ferroviário Maputo	14	9	5	4	Maputo
3	Maxaquene	13	4	9	3	Maputo
4	Desportivo Maputo	8	6	2	1	Maputo
5	Matchedje	3	2	1	1	Maputo
6	Ferroviário Nampula	2	1	1	1	Nampula
7	Liga Muçulmana	2	2			Maputo
8	Têxtil Púnguè	1	1		3	Beira
	Textáfrica Chimoio	1	1		3	Chimoio
10	Palmeiras Beira	1		1	3	Beira
11	Ferroviário Beira	1		1	2	Beira
12	Clube de Gaza	1		1		Xai-Xai
13	Atlético Muçulmano	1		1		Matola
14	Chingale Tete				2	Tete

TACA NACIONAL 2011

Round of 16

Ferroviário Maputo	1
Desportivo Maputo	0
Djuba	0
Vilankulo	4
Ferroviário Nampula	2
Sporting Nampula	0
1° de Maio	0
Maxaquene	4
Palmeiras Quelimane	3
Leões de Vumba	0
Matchedje Beira	0
Ferroviário Beira	6
Costa do Sol	2
Clube de Gaza	1
HCB Songo	1
Chingale Tete	2

Quarter-finals

Ferroviário Maputo	0 5p
Vilankulo	0 4p
Ferroviário Nampula	0
Maxaquene	1
Palmeiras Quelimane	2
Ferroviário Beira	1
Costa do Sol	1 4p
Chingale Tete	1 5p

Semi-finals

Ferroviário Maputo	3
Maxaquene	1
Palmeiras Quelimane	0
Chingale Tete	2

Final

Ferroviário Maputo ‡	3
Chingale Tete	0

CUP FINAL

Estadio Nacional de Zimpeto, Maputo,
26-11-2011, Ref: Joao Armando
Scorers - Luis 3, Rachid 81, Clesio 86

‡ Qualified for the CAF Confederation Cup

Cup Final line-ups: **Ferro** - Pinto - Chico, Zabula, Butana, Fredy, Whisky, Rachid, Tchitcho, Imo, Luis (Clesio), Sonito. Tr: Nacir Armando
Chingale Tete - Joaquim - Elisio, Fred, Louis, Tony, Ze, Ernesto (Mauro), Hilario, Hagi (Mauricio), Alone (Magaba), Paulo. Tr: Sergio Faife

MRI – MAURITIUS

FIFA/COCA-COLA WORLD RANKING

'93	'94	'95	'96	'97	'98	'99	'00	'01	'02	'03	'04	'05	'06	'07	'08	'09	'10	'11	'12
133	146	154	150	151	148	118	118	124	126	123	140	143	138	158	170	181	191	194	

	2011												High	Low	Av
Jan	Feb	Mar	Apr	May	Jun	Jul	Aug	Sep	Oct	Nov	Dec		High	Low	Av
191	191	191	189	189	189	195	188	188	189	191	194		116	195	146

Mauritius slumped to an all-time low in 2011 in the FIFA/Coca-Cola World Ranking after another miserable year for the national team. They finished without a point from their 2012 CAF Africa Cup of Nations qualifying campaign and although 'Club M' had a tough group, paired with the might of Cameroon, the Democratic Republic of Congo and Senegal, they conceded 22 goals in six matches and they looked far from competitive. The Indian Ocean Island Games in the Seychelles in August offered some respite from a four-year and 20-match winless streak but they only won against the Comoros Islands in their group, before beating non-FIFA members Mayotte on post-match penalties in the semi-final. In the gold medal game, Mauritius and hosts Seychelles played out a 1-1 draw before the home team won on penalties. The team was pulled out of the 2014 FIFA World Cup qualifiers and the 2013 CAF Africa Cup of Nations preliminary campaign in order to reflect on a future strategy for the game. For the second year running Mauritius also declined to enter any clubs in African competition for 2012 while at home AS Port Louis 2000 won a shortened league campaign in 2011 that was a prelude to the launch of a new 10-team professional league which kicked-off at the end of January 2012.

CAF AFRICA CUP OF NATIONS RECORD
1957-1965 DNE 1968-1972 DNQ **1974** 8 r1 1976-1986 DNQ 1988 DNE 1990-2012 DNQ

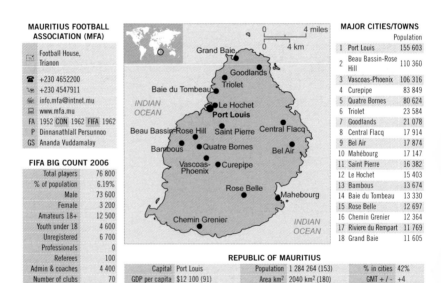

MAURITIUS FOOTBALL ASSOCIATION (MFA)

Football House, Trianon

☎ +230 4652200
📠 +230 4547911
✉ info.mfa@intnet.mu
🖥 www.mfa.mu
FA 1952 CON 1962 FIFA 1962
P Dinnanathlall Persunnoo
GS Ananda Vuddamalay

FIFA BIG COUNT 2006

Total players	76 800
% of population	6.19%
Male	73 600
Female	3 200
Amateurs 18+	12 500
Youth under 18	4 600
Unregistered	6 700
Professionals	0
Referees	100
Admin & coaches	4 400
Number of clubs	70
Number of teams	700

MAJOR CITIES/TOWNS
Population

1	Port Louis	155 603
2	Beau Bassin-Rose Hill	110 360
3	Vascoas-Phoenix	106 316
4	Curepipe	83 849
5	Quatre Bornes	80 624
6	Triolet	23 584
7	Goodlands	21 078
8	Central Flacq	17 914
9	Bel Air	17 874
10	Mahébourg	17 147
11	Saint Pierre	16 382
12	Le Hochet	15 403
13	Bambous	13 674
14	Baie du Tombeau	13 330
15	Rose Belle	12 697
16	Chemin Grenier	12 364
17	Riviere du Rempart	11 769
18	Grand Baie	11 605

REPUBLIC OF MAURITIUS

Capital	Port Louis	Population	1 284 264 (153)	% in cities	42%
GDP per capita	$12 100 (91)	Area km²	2040 km² (180)	GMT +/-	+4
Neighbours (km)	Coast 177				

RECENT INTERNATIONAL MATCHES PLAYED BY MAURITIUS

2006 Opponents	Score		Venue	Comp	Scorers	Att	Referee
3-09 Tunisia	D	0-0	Curepipe	CNq			Ncobo RSA
7-10 Seychelles	L	1-2	Roche Caiman	CNq	Kervin Godon [53]		Raolimanana MAD
2007							
21-03 Côte d'Ivoire	L	0-3	Bellevue	Fr			
25-03 Sudan	L	1-2	Curepipe	CNq	Ricardo Naboth [61]		Mwanza ZAM
26-05 Swaziland	D	0-0	Mbabane	CCr1	W 6-5p		Labrosse SEY
27-05 South Africa	L	0-2	Mbabane	CCr1			Mufeti NAM
2-06 Sudan	L	0-3	Omdurman	CNq			Lwanja MWI
16-06 Tunisia	L	0-2	Rades/Tunis	CNq			Benouza ALG
14-08 Seychelles	W	3-0	Antananarivo	Fr	Giovanni Jeannot 2 [24 64], Kersley Appou [40]		
9-09 Seychelles	D	1-1	Curepipe	CNq	Christopher Perle [62]		Mwandike TAN
2008							
9-03 Madagascar	L	1-2	Curepipe	Fr	Wesley Marquette [68]		
31-05 Tanzania	D	1-1	Dar es Salaam	WCq	Wesley Marquette [39]	35 000	Marange ZIM
8-06 Cameroon	L	0-3	Curepipe	WCq		2 400	Martins ANG
15-06 Cape Verde Islands	L	0-1	Curepipe	WCq		1 400	Kaoma ZAM
22-06 Cape Verde Islands	L	1-3	Praia	WCq	Andy Sophie [67]	2 850	Coulibaly MLI
19-07 Seychelles	L	0-7	Witbank	CCr1			Kaoma ZAM
21-07 Swaziland	D	1-1	Witbank	CCr1	Johan Marmitte [35]		Nhlapo RSA
23-07 Madagascar	L	1-2	Witbank	CCr1	Wesley Marquette [34]		Marange ZIM
6-09 Tanzania	L	1-4	Curepipe	WCq	Wesley Marquette [13]	103	Ndinya KEN
11-10 Cameroon	L	0-5	Yaounde	WCq		12 000	Lemghambodj MTN
2009							
2-10 Egypt	L	0-4	Cairo	Fr			
17-10 Zimbabwe	L	0-3	Harare	CCr1			Ebrahim RSA
21-10 Lesotho	L	0-1	Harare	CCr1			Ngosi MWI
2010							
4-09 Cameroon	L	1-3	Bellevue	CNq	Jonathan Bru [45p]		Damon RSA
9-10 Senegal	L	0-7	Dakar	CNq			Bennett RSA
2011							
27-03 Congo DR	L	0-3	Kinshasa	CNq			Solomon NGA
5-06 Congo DR	L	1-2	Bellevue	CNq	Jonathan Bru [11p]		Kalyoto MWI
4-08 Maldives	D	1-1	Praslin	IOGr1	Fabrice Pithia [9]	1 800	Rakotonjanahary MAD
6-08 Seychelles	L	1-2	Roche Caiman	IOGr1	Fabrice Pithia [77]	6 500	Rassuhi MAY
9-08 Comoros	W	2-0	Praslin	IOGr1	Fabrice Pithia [35], Gurty Calambe [87]	300	Rassuhi MAY
11-08 Mayotte †	D	0-0	Roche Caiman	IOGsf	W 5-4p	2 500	Adelaid COM
13-08 Seychelles	D	1-1	Roche Caiman	IOGf	Jerry Louis [62], L 3-4p	10 000	Dubec REU
3-09 Cameroon	L	0-5	Yaounde	CNq			Bangoura GUI
9-10 Senegal	L	0-2	Bellevue	CNq			

Fr = Friendly match • CN = CAF African Cup of Nations • CC = COSAFA Cup • IOG = Indian Ocean Games • WC = FIFA World Cup
q = qualifier • r1 = first round group • † Not an official international

MAURITIUS 2011

BARCLAYS PREMIER LEAGUE

	Pl	W	D	L	F	A	Pts	ASPL 2000	ASVP	Savanne	Pamplemousses	PAS Mates	Cercle	Rivière Rempart	Petite Rivière	CSSC	Entente	CTNFB	Highlands	Faucon Flacq
AS Port-Louis 2000	12	10	0	2	29	8	**30**					2-1	2-1				3-0		3-0	5-0
AS Vacoas-Phoenix	12	9	2	1	29	5	**29**	1-0				4-2	0-1	2-0				6-0	3-0	2-0
Savanne SC	12	7	1	4	23	17	**22**	2-4	0-0			0-2					3-2		1-0	3-1
Pamplemousses SC	12	6	3	3	22	15	**21**	2-1	1-1	1-5		4-0			0-1	2-1	1-1	1-1	4-0	2-0
Pointe-aux-Sables	12	6	1	5	23	20	**19**													
Cercle de Joachim	12	5	3	4	13	15	**18**			2-1	1-2	1-2			0-4	1-1	1-0			
AS Rivière Rempart	12	5	1	6	11	11	**16**	0-1		0-2		3-2	0-1		1-2	0-1			3-0	
Petite Rivière Noire	12	4	3	5	16	16	**15**	**0-3**	0-1	2-0		0-2				1-0	1-1		1-1	1-1
Curepipe Starlight	12	3	4	5	11	15	**13**	0-2	0-3	2-3		2-1					0-0		1-2	
Entente Boulet Rouge	12	2	4	6	12	23	**10**		1-6			3-2		1-2	1-1	0-2			1-2	
CTNFB	12	1	6	5	14	27	**9**	1-3		1-3		1-4		0-0	4-3	1-1	1-1		2-2	2-2
US Highlands	12	2	3	7	8	22	**9**					0-0	0-1							
Faucon Flacq SC	12	1	3	8	10	27	**6**					2-5	2-2	0-1		0-2	0-1		2-1	

26/02/2011 - 26/06/2011 • Match in bold awarded • Top ten qualify for the new professional league to start in 2012

REPUBLIC CUP 2011

Quarter–finals		Semi–finals		Final	
Pamplemousses SC	4				
Faucon Flacq SC	2	**Pamplemousses SC**	4		
		PAS Mates	3		
PAS Mates				**Pamplemousses SC**	3
Entente Boulet Rouge				Petite Rivière Noire	1
		Entente Boulet Rouge	0		
US Highlands	1	**Petite Rivière Noire**	2		
Petite Rivière Noire	5				

CUP FINAL

Stade Anjalay, Belle Vue
13-03-2011, Att: 1000
Scorers - OG [24], Ratovonirina 2 [30] [39] for PSS; Calambe [13] for PRN

MSR – MONTSERRAT

FIFA/COCA-COLA WORLD RANKING

'93	'94	'95	'96	'97	'98	'99	'00	'01	'02	'03	'04	'05	'06	'07	'08	'09	'10	'11	'12
-	-	-	-	-	-	201	202	203	203	204	202	202	198	201	201	203	203	206	

					2011									
Jan	Feb	Mar	Apr	May	Jun	Jul	Aug	Sep	Oct	Nov	Dec	**High**	**Low**	**Av**
203	203	202	202	202	203	203	203	203	203	204	206	**196**	**206**	**202**

Montserrat national team coach Kenny Dyer once again rallied his troops, bringing together a disparate group of footballers from all four corners of the globe to take part in a preliminary round qualifier for the 2014 FIFA World Cup in Brazil. Three of the players were based in Montserrat with others coming from the USA, Australia and the UK. Port Vale's Anthony Griffith was the player with the highest profile to make the trip to Trinidad for the first leg of the tie against Belize, a match that had to be played away from Montserrat as the changing rooms at Sturge Park were still not finished. That was a disappointment for the MFA who rated the pitch at the new facility as one of the best in the region. Dyer, who works as a coach in a soccer academy in the USA, had less than a week to prepare the team and they lost 5-2 with both goals coming from Jay Lee Hodgson, a player based with Shepshed Dynamo in the Northern Premier League in England. Montserrat's opponents Belize were in the midst of a bitter dispute between their football federation and the government which saw the second leg delayed and moved to Honduras where, despite a 3-1 defeat, Hodgson scored another goal to make him the top scorer in the history of the Monserrat national team with three goals.

FIFA WORLD CUP RECORD
1930-1998 DNE   2002-2010 DNQ

MONTSERRAT FOOTBALL ASSOCIATION INC. (MFA)

PO Box 505, Blakes

☎ +1 664 4951043

✉ mfainc@candw.ms

FA 1994 CON 1996 FIFA 1996
P Vincent Cassell
GS TBD

FIFA BIG COUNT 2006

Total players	700
% of population	7.42%
Male	600
Female	100
Amateurs 18+	100
Youth under 18	100
Unregistered	100
Professionals	0
Referees	6
Admin & coaches	0
Number of clubs	0
Number of teams	10

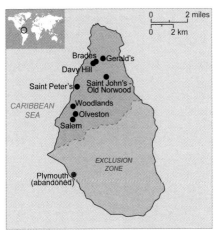

MAJOR CITIES/TOWNS

		Population
1	Brades	1 305
2	Saint Peter's	794
3	Saint John's-Old Norwood	728
4	Salem	552
5	Blakes Estate	492
6	Davy Hill	427
7	Olveston	381
8	Happy Hill	359
9	Woodlands	315
10	Gerald's	269
11	Plymouth	0

MONTSERRAT

Capital Plymouth	Population 5 097 (228)	% in cities 14%
GDP per capita $3400 (160)	Area km² 102 km² (225)	GMT +/- -4
Neighbours (km) Coast 40		

INTERNATIONAL MATCHES PLAYED BY MONTSERRAT

1991	Opponents		Score	Venue	Comp	Scorers	Att	Referee
10-05	St Lucia	L	0-3	Vieux Fort	CCq			
14-05	Anguilla	D	1-1	Vieux Fort	CCq			
1992								
15-04	Antigua and Barbuda	L	0-5	Basseterre	CCq			
17-04	St Kitts and Nevis	L	0-10	Basseterre	CCq			
1993								
No international matches played in 1993								
1994								
23-02	St Kitts and Nevis	L	1-9	Basseterre	CCq			
25-02	Antigua and Barbuda	L	0-8	Basseterre	CCq			
1995								
26-03	Anguilla	W	3-2	Plymouth	CCq	Ian Edwards, Julian Wade, Everton Morris		
2-04	Anguilla	W	1-0	The Valley	CCq	Curt Webb		
1-05	St Vincent/Grenadines	L	0-9	Kingstown	CCq			
7-05	St Vincent/Grenadines	L	0-11	Plymouth	CCq			
1996-1998								
No international matches played in 1996, 1997 & 1998								
1999								
5-02	British Virgin Islands	L	1-3	Road Town	CCq	Curt Webb		
7-02	British Virgin Islands	L	0-3	Road Town	CCq			
2000								
15-03	Dominican Republic	L	0-3	San Cristobal	WCq		2 000	
19-03	Dominican Republic	L	1-3	Port of Spain	WCq	Wayne Dyer [88]	50	
2001								
6-02	Saint-Martin †	L	1-3	Marigot	CCq			
8-02	Anguilla	L	1-4	Marigot	CCq	Joseph Morris [53]		
2002								
30-06	Bhutan	L	0-4	Thimphu	Fr		25 000	
2003								
No international matches played in 2003								
2004								
29-02	Bermuda	L	0-13	Hamilton	WCq		3 000	Kennedy USA
21-03	Bermuda	L	0-7	Plymouth	WCq		250	Charles DMA
31-10	St Kitts and Nevis	L	1-6	Basseterre	CCq	Curt Adams [81]		Bedeau GRN
2-11	Antigua and Barbuda	L	4-5	Basseterre	CCq	Tesfaye Bramble [36], Ruel Fox [41], Junior Mendes [50], Vladimir Farrell [61]		Phillip GRN
4-11	St Lucia	L	0-3	Basseterre	CCq	Not played. St Lucia awarded the match 3-0		
2005								
No international matches played in 2005								
2006								
No international matches played in 2006								
2007								
No international matches played in 2007								
2008								
26-03	Surinam	L	1-7	Macoya	WCq	Vladimir Farrell [48]	100	Aguilar SLV
2009								
No international matches played in 2009								
2010								
6-10	St Vincent/Grenadines	L	0-7	Kingstown	CCq		5 000	Pinas PUR
8-10	Barbados	L	0-5	Kingstown	CCq		350	Pinas PUR
10-10	St Kitts And Nevis	L	0-4	Kingstown	CCq		1 100	Elskamp SUR
2011								
15-06	Belize	L	2-5	Couva	WCq	Jay Lee Hodgson 2 [44 86]	100	Willett ATG
17-07	Belize	L	1-3	San Pedro Sula	WCq	Jay Lee Hodgson [58]	150	Reyna GUA

Fr = Friendly match • CC = Digicel Caribbean Cup • WC = FIFA World Cup • q = qualifier • † Not an official international. All matches played before Montserrat joined FIFA in 1996 are not considered as full internationals by FIFA

MTN – MAURITANIA

FIFA/COCA-COLA WORLD RANKING

'93	'94	'95	'96	'97	'98	'99	'00	'01	'02	'03	'04	'05	'06	'07	'08	'09	'10	'11	'12
144	137	85	113	135	142	160	161	177	180	165	175	178	133	130	158	169	180	204	

	2011												High	Low	Av
Jan	Feb	Mar	Apr	May	Jun	Jul	Aug	Sep	Oct	Nov	Dec			
176	176	174	180	180	183	187	190	193	200	201	204	85	204	152

Mauritania were the only African country who failed to enter the 2014 FIFA World Cup qualifiers and have now played just a single game over a three year period since 2008. They had also withdrawn from the 2012 CAF Africa Cup of Nations qualifiers after losing six successive games in 2008. The hiatus from international competition did not extend to club level, however, with CF Cansado being hammered in the first round of the 2011 CAF Champions League. They lost 7-0 away in the first leg to former winners ASEC Abidjan of Cote d'Ivoire and conceded two more in the return leg at home in Nouakchott. But there was a major morale boosting triumph in the CAF Confederation Cup where Tevragh Zeina eliminated AS Real Bamako of Mali in the first round in a shock upset. The 1-0 aggregate triumph was followed by a solid showing against former African champions JS Kabylie in the next round although the Mauritanian team lost 3-1 on aggregate. At home, Cansado failed to hold onto their league title, finishing 10 points behind winners FC Nouadhibou and runners-up Tevragh Zeina. Both teams finished on 38 points and scored 25 goals each but Nouadhibou took the title after conceding only six to Tevragh Zeina's seven. Consolation for Tevragh Zeina was cup success, beating ACS Ksar 2-0 in July's final in the capital.

CAF AFRICA CUP OF NATIONS RECORD
1957-1978 DNE 1980-1982 DNQ 1984 DNE 1986 DNQ 1988-1990 DNE 1992 DNQ
1994 DNE 1996-1998 DNQ 2000 DNE 2002-2010 DNQ 2012 DNQ

FEDERATION DE FOOT-BALL DE LA REPUBLIQUE ISLAMIQUE DE MAURITANIE (FFM)

- ✉ BP 566, Nouakchott
- ☎ +222 35 241860
- 📠 +222 35 241861
- @ dmassa59@yahoo.fr
- 🖥 www.ffrim.com
- FA 1961 CON 1968 FIFA 1964
- P Ahmed Ould Abderrahmane
- GS Massa Diarra

FIFA BIG COUNT 2006

Total players	137 920
% of population	4.34%
Male	137 920
Female	0
Amateurs 18+	3 520
Youth under 18	1 600
Unregistered	14 300
Professionals	0
Referees	177
Admin & coaches	700
Number of clubs	68
Number of teams	250

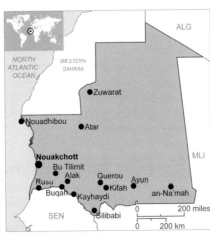

MAJOR CITIES/TOWNS

		Population
1	Nouakchott	798 725
2	Nouadhibou	83 277
3	Kifah	80 612
4	Rusu	72 400
5	Kayhaydi	54 593
6	Zuwarat	50 949
7	an-Na'mah	41 583
8	Bu Tilimit	37 812
9	Silibabi	33 084
10	Atar	31 958
11	Buqah	27 859
12	Tinbadgah	27 562
13	Guérou	27 031
14	Magta' Lahjar	26 026
15	Alak	25 140
16	Ayun	24 991
17	Tintane	19 118
18	Tijiqjah	18 375
19	Adel Bagrou	16 004

AL JUMHURIYAH AL ISLAMIYAH AL MURITANIYAH • ISLAMIC REPUBLIC OF MAURITANIA

Capital	Nouakchott	Population	3 129 486 (135)	% in cities	41%
GDP per capita	$2100 (187)	Area km²	1 030 700 km² (29)	GMT +/-	0
Neighbours (km)	Algeria 463, Mali 2237, Senegal 813, Western Sahara 1561 • Coast 754				

RECENT INTERNATIONAL MATCHES PLAYED BY MAURITANIA

2006 Opponents	Score	Venue	Comp	Scorers	Att	Referee
3-09 Botswana	W 4-0	Nouakchott	CNq	Seydou Mbodji [3], Moussa Karamoko 2 [8 23], Yohan Langlet [83]		Djaoupe TOG
8-10 Burundi	L 1-3	Bujumbura	CNq	Mohamed Benyachou [51]		Abdelrahman SUD
21-12 Lebanon	D 0-0	Beirut	ARr1			Al Jannaz BHR
24-12 Sudan	L 0-2	Beirut	ARr1			Ebel KUW
27-12 Somalia	W 8-2	Beirut	ARr1			
2007						
20-03 Libya	D 0-0	Tripoli	Fr			
25-03 Egypt	L 0-3	Cairo	CNq			Benouza ALG
3-06 Egypt	D 1-1	Nouakchott	CNq	Yohan Langlet [70]		Sowe GAM
16-06 Botswana	L 1-2	Gaborone	CNq	Yohan Langlet [74]		Gasingwa RWA
13-10 Burundi	W 2-1	Nouakchott	CNq	Dominique Da Silva [32], Ahmed Teguedi [47]		Aboubacar CIV
2008						
31-05 Rwanda	L 0-3	Kigali	WCq		12 000	Doue CIV
7-06 Morocco	L 1-4	Nouakchott	WCq	Ahmed Teguedi [82p]	9 500	Lamptey GHA
13-06 Ethiopia	L 0-1	Nouakchott	WCq		5 000	Ambaya EGY
22-06 Ethiopia	L 1-6	Addis Abeba	WCq	Voulani Ely [44]	13 000	Lwanja MWI
6-09 Rwanda	L 0-1	Nouackchott	WCq		1 000	Bennaceur TUN
11-10 Morocco	L 1-4	Rabat	WCq	Ahmed Teguedi [67]	1 472	Aboubacar CIV
2009						
No international matches played in 2009						
2010						
11-08 Palestine	D 0-0	Nouakchott	Fr			
2011						
No international matches played in 2011						

Fr = Friendly match • CN = CAF African Cup of Nations • AR = Arab Cup • WC = FIFA World Cup • q = qualifier • r1 = first round group

MAURITANIA 2011

CHAMPIONNAT NATIONAL

	Pl	W	D	L	F	A	Pts	Nouadhibou	Tevragh Zeina	Concorde	Cansado	Ksar	Kédia	Imraguens	Tidjikja	Police
FC Nouadhibou	16	12	2	2	25	6	38		2-1	4-0	1-0	0-1	1-0	3-0	2-2	1-0
Tevragh Zeina	16	12	2	2	25	7	38	1-0		1-0	2-1	1-0	1-0	1-2	1-0	3-1
ASAC Concorde	16	9	1	6	26	16	28	0-0	0-3		2-4	2-0	4-0	1-0	0-2	3-0
CF Cansado	16	8	4	4	22	16	28	0-1	0-0	2-1		1-1	1-0	1-1	2-2	2-0
ACS Ksar	16	7	2	7	20	23	23	0-2	1-3	0-4	3-2		0-1	2-1	2-0	4-1
Kédia Zouératt	16	6	1	9	10	17	19	0-3	0-1	0-1	1-2	2-1		2-1	1-0	2-0
Imraguens	16	4	2	10	13	27	14	1-2	0-5	0-4	1-2	1-2	1-0		2-0	1-2
Tidjikja	16	2	6	8	11	19	12	0-2	0-1	0-2	0-1	2-2	0-0	0-0		1-1
ASC Police	16	1	2	13	5	26	5	0-1	0-0	0-2	0-1	0-1	0-1	0-1	0-2	

23/10/2010 - 18/06/2011 • No relegation. League expanded to 14 teams for 2012

COUPE DU PRESIDENT DE LA REPUBLIQUE 2011

Quarter–finals		Semi–finals		Final	
Tevragh Zeina	1 9p				
ASAC Concorde	1 8p	**Tevragh Zeina**	6		
FC Sahel	1 3p	Talhaya Rosso	1		
Talhaya Rosso	1 4p			**Tevragh Zeina**	2
FC Nouadhibou	1 5p			ACS Ksar	0
Kédia Zouératt	1 4p	FC Nouadhibou	0		
ACS Kiffa	2	**ACS Ksar**	1		
ACS Ksar	3				

Olympique, Nouakchott, 9-07-2011
Scorers - Cheikh Biyaye [1], Ely
Cheikh Ould Voulany [22]

MWI – MALAWI

FIFA/COCA-COLA WORLD RANKING

'93	'94	'95	'96	'97	'98	'99	'00	'01	'02	'03	'04	'05	'06	'07	'08	'09	'10	'11	'12
67	82	89	88	97	89	114	113	120	95	105	109	106	104	138	104	99	86	94	

	2011												High	Low	Av
	Jan	Feb	Mar	Apr	May	Jun	Jul	Aug	Sep	Oct	Nov	Dec	High	Low	Av
	91	89	89	78	72	71	72	73	78	87	87	94	67	138	99

Conceding a goal in the last minute of their final qualifier in the 2012 CAF Africa Cup of Nations preliminaries cost Malawi a place at a second successive tournament. They gave up a goal to Karl Max Barthelemy in the 94th minute of their match against bottom-placed Chad in N'Djamena and as a result Tunisia grabbed top spot and qualification right at the death. Malawi had needed to win the game and were 2-1 ahead right into the final exchanges of the game. Having played at the 2010 finals in Angola, Malawi looked to have benefitted tremendously from the experience as they put together a competent qualifying campaign for the 2012 finals with consistent team selection under coach Kinnah Phiri, among the longest serving on the continent. The Flames held Togo and Tunisia to away draws, beat the Togolese at home but then could only draw against Tunisia at home in their penultimate qualifier. Had they won Malawi would have ensured their trip to the tournament in Equatorial Guinea and Gabon. There was a guest participation at the end-of-year East and Central African Senior Challenge Cup in Dar-es-Salaam where Malawi got as far as the quarter-finals, before losing 1-0 to hosts Tanzania. At home there were trophies in 2011 for Escom United in the Super League, Moyale Barracks in the Standard Bank Cup and Wanderers in the Presidential Cup.

CAF AFRICA CUP OF NATIONS RECORD
1957-1974 DNE **1976-1982** DNQ **1984** 7 r1 **1986-2008** DNQ **2010** 12 r1 **2012** DNQ

FOOTBALL ASSOCIATION OF MALAWI (FAM)

	Cimwembe Technical Centre,
✉	Off Cimwembe Road
	PO Box 51657, Limbe
☎	+265 1 987201
📠	+265 1 875109
@	generalsecretary@fam.mw
🖥	www.fam.mw
FA	1966 CON 1968 FIFA 1967
P	Walter Nyamilandu Manda
GS	Suzgo Nyirenda

FIFA BIG COUNT 2006

Total players	515 800
% of population	3.96%
Male	515 600
Female	200
Amateurs 18+	11 400
Youth under 18	8 700
Unregistered	29 700
Professionals	0
Referees	600
Admin & coaches	1 800
Number of clubs	70
Number of teams	120

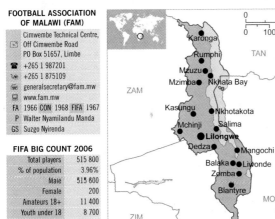

MAJOR CITIES/TOWNS

		Population
1	Lilongwe	922 894
2	Blantyre	760 064
3	Mzuzu	187 151
4	Zomba	105 264
5	Kasungu	64 433
6	Mangochi	54 509
7	Karonga	44 112
8	Salima	42 651
9	Nkhotakota	34 741
10	Liwonde	31 218
11	Rumphi	29 803
12	Nsanje	28 246
13	Mzimba	27 778
14	Mchinji	27 135
15	Balaka	25 169
16	Mulanje	21 890
17	Luchenza	16 350
18	Dedza	15 681
19	Nkhata Bay	15 294

DZIKO LA MALAWI • REPUBLIC OF MALAWI

Capital	Lilongwe	Population	14 268 711 (66)	% in cities	19%
GDP per capita	$800 (220)	Area km²	118 484 km² (99)	GMT +/-	+2
Neighbours (km)	Mozambique 1569, Tanzania 475, Zambia 837		

RECENT INTERNATIONAL MATCHES PLAYED BY MALAWI

2008	Opponents	Score		Venue	Comp	Scorers	Att	Referee
20-07	Lesotho	W	1-0	Secunda	CCr1	Msowoya [75]		Rajindraparsad MRI
22-07	Comoros	W	1-0	Secunda	CCr1	Kondowe [62]		Marange ZIM
24-07	Namibia	L	0-1	Secunda	CCr1			Marange ZIM
5-09	Djibouti	W	3-0	Djibouti	WCq	Msowoya [30], Chavula [63], Nyondo [67]	700	Carvalho ANG
30-09	South Africa	L	0-3	Johannesburg	Fr			
11-10	Congo DR	W	2-1	Blantyre	WCq	Ngambi [56], Msowoya [83]	50 000	Codjia BEN
2009								
11-02	Mozambique	L	0-2	Maputo	Fr			
21-03	Uganda	L	1-2	Kampala	Fr	Nyondo [37]		
29-03	Côte d'Ivoire	L	0-5	Abidjan	WCq		34 000	Haimoudi ALG
30-05	Rwanda	W	2-0	Blantyre	Fr	Msowoya 2 [63 82]		
6-06	Burkina Faso	L	0-1	Blantyre	WCq		25 000	Bennaceur TUN
21-06	Guinea	L	1-2	Conakry	WCq	Msowoya [88]	14 000	Abdul Rahman SUD
6-07	Swaziland	W	3-1	Blantyre	Fr	Maziya OG [19], Wadabwa 2 [43 86]		
5-09	Guinea	W	2-1	Blantyre	WCq	Msowoya 2 [46 59]	15 000	Codjia BEN
10-10	Côte d'Ivoire	D	1-1	Blantyre	WCq	Ngwira [64]	25 000	El Achiri MAR
25-10	Mozambique	L	0-1	Harare	CCqf			Ramocha BOT
14-11	Burkina Faso	L	0-1	Ouagadougou	WCq		20 000	Abd El Fatah EGY
19-12	Mozambique	W	1-0	Tete	Fr	Nyirenda [88]		
29-12	Egypt	D	1-1	Cairo	Fr	Msowoya [87]		
2010								
5-01	Ghana	D	0-0	Manzini	Fr			
11-01	Algeria	W	3-0	Luanda	CNr1	Mwafulirwa [17], Kafoteka [35], Banda [48]	1 000	Diatta SEN
14-01	Angola	L	0-2	Luanda	CNr1		48 500	Doue CIV
18-01	Mali	L	1-3	Luanda	CNr1	Mwafulirwa [58]	21 000	Seechurn MRI
3-03	Zimbabwe	L	1-2	Harare	Fr	Makandawire [13]		
12-05	Yemen	L	0-1	Sana'a	Fr			
9-07	Togo	D	1-1	Lome	CNq	Mwakasungula [18]		Bennett RSA
11-08	Botswana	D	1-1	Blantyre	CNq	Banda [75]		Carvalho ANG
4-09	Tunisia	D	2-2	Rades/Tunis	CNq	Msowoya [45], Kanyenda [82p]		Lamptey GHA
9-10	Chad	W	6-2	Blantyre	CNq	Zakazaka [13], Kanyenda 2 [21 52], Msowoya 2 [68 79], Ngambi [85]		Kirwa KEN
17-11	Rwanda	W	2-1	Blantyre	Fr	Banda [56], Nyirenda [76]		
29-11	Kenya	W	3-2	Dar es Salaam	CFr1	Nyirenda [1], Banda 2 [26 81]		
2-12	Uganda	D	1-1	Dar es Salaam	CFr1	Nyirenda [2]		
4-12	Ethiopia	D	1-1	Dar es Salaam	CFr1	Kabichi [27]		
2011								
9-02	Namibia	W	2-1	Windhoek	Fr	Wadabwa [41], Harawa [82]		
26-03	Togo	W	1-0	Blantyre	CNq	Chavula [18]		
29-05	Swaziland	D	1-1	Manzini	Fr	Nyondo [56]		
5-06	Botswana	D	0-0	Lobatse	CNq			
6-07	Namibia	L	0-1	Mzuzu	Fr			
3-09	Tunisia	D	0-0	Blantyre	CNq			
4-10	Ethiopia	D	0-0	Addis Abeba	Fr			
8-10	Chad	D	2-2	N'Djamena	CNq	Ngambi [35], Nyirenda [81]		
28-11	Kenya	W	2-0	Dar es Salaam	CFr1	Banda [23], Kamwendo [66p]		
30-11	Sudan	D	0-0	Dar es Salaam	CFr1			
2-12	Ethiopia	D	1-1	Dar es Salaam	CFr1	Kabichi [27]		
6-12	Tanzania	L	0-1	Dar es Salaam	CFqf			

Fr = Friendly match • CN = CAF African Cup of Nations • CC = COSAFA Cup • CF = CECAFA Cup • WC = FIFA World Cup
q = qualifier • r1 = first round group • qf = quarter-final • sf = semi-final • f = final

MALAWI 2010–11

SUPER LEAGUE

	Pl	W	D	L	F	A	Pts	Escom United	Silver Strikers	Moyale Barracks	CIVO United	MTL Wanderers	Blue Eagles	Bullets	Tigers FC	Zomba United	Red Lions	Blantyre United	MAFCO	Juke Box	Blackpool	Eagle Strikers
Escom United	28	17	7	4	58	21	58		1-1	1-2	1-1	1-1	4-0	0-0	3-0	4-1	1-0	2-1	4-0	3-1	1-1	6-0
Silver Strikers	28	15	9	4	45	23	54	2-2		1-2	1-0	1-2	1-1	0-1	1-1	2-0	3-0	1-1	2-0	1-0	1-0	5-0
Moyale Barracks	28	15	6	7	47	31	51	1-2	1-1		2-0	2-2	1-0	0-0	0-0	3-2	0-0	3-1	2-1	4-2	3-3	1-0
CIVO United	28	14	8	6	34	19	50	3-0	2-0	1-0		1-0	1-0	1-0	1-1	1-0	1-0	1-0	5-0	3-0	0-0	2-1
MTL Wanderers	28	13	7	8	43	32	46	0-1	1-1	5-0	1-1		2-0	3-0	1-2	0-3	2-3	0-2	1-2	2-1	1-0	1-1
Blue Eagles	28	13	7	8	34	30	46	1-0	2-2	2-0	2-0	0-1		2-1	1-1	0-2	1-1	1-2	2-1	2-0	2-1	3-1
Bullets	28	11	8	9	29	26	41	0-2	1-2	2-1	1-0	3-1	0-0		2-0	1-2	0-0	2-0	4-3	1-0	3-1	2-2
Tigers FC	28	10	7	11	36	36	37	0-4	2-3	0-2	1-2	0-2	0-1	1-0		6-1	2-0	0-1	3-2	1-1	2-0	2-1
Zomba United	28	9	8	11	36	42	35	1-5	1-2	1-3	1-1	1-2	0-0	2-2	3-1		0-0	1-0	1-2	3-0	0-0	3-1
Red Lions	28	8	10	10	28	31	34	0-2	1-3	2-1	0-0	2-2	2-3	0-0	0-1	1-1		2-1	2-0	3-1	0-1	1-3
Blantyre United	28	9	6	13	31	41	33	1-2	0-1	2-1	2-2	1-1	1-1	2-1	1-6	2-3	0-0		1-3	2-1	2-0	1-2
MAFCO	28	7	7	14	31	45	28	2-1	0-1	0-2	2-2	0-1	1-2	0-1	2-2	1-1	1-1	0-0		2-1	0-1	4-1
Juke Box	28	7	4	17	23	43	25	1-3	0-0	0-4	1-0	1-2	0-1	0-0	0-1	1-0	0-1	3-1	0-0		2-0	1-0
Blackpool §1	28	6	6	16	22	39	23	0-0	1-5	0-2	2-1	1-2	1-0	0-1	0-0	0-1	0-4	1-2	1-2	1-2		4-0
Eagle Strikers	28	4	4	20	23	61	16	0-2	0-1	0-4	0-1	1-4	3-4	1-0	1-0	1-1	1-2	0-1	0-0	2-3	0-2	

11/06/2010 - 27/02/2011 • § = points deducted

STANDARD BANK CUP 2010–11

Quarter-finals
Moyale Barracks
Escom United
CHANCO
CIVO United

Semi-finals
Moyale Barracks 0 2
ESCOM United 0 2

CHANCO 0
CIVO United 6

Final
Moyale Barracks 0 5p
CIVO United 0 3p

Mzuzu Stadium
30-01-2011, Att: 20 000

MEDALS TABLE

		Overall	Lge	Cup	City/Town
		G	G	G	
1	Bullets	45	11	34	Blantyre
2	Wanderers	24	4	20	Blantyre
3	Silver Strikers	16	3	13	Lilongwe
4	MDC United	9	1	8	Blantyre
5	Tigers	7	1	6	Blantyre
6	CIVO United	5	1	4	Lilongwe
7	Moyale Barracks	3		3	Mzuzu
	Red Lions	3		3	Zomba
	Sucoma	3		3	Chikwawa
	MITCO	3		3	Lilongwe
	Michuru Castles	3		3	Blantyre
	Escom United	3	2	1	Blantyre

PRESIDENTIAL CUP 2011

First Round
MTL Wanderers
Escom United
Hard Hammers
Blue Eagles
Moyale Barracks 1
Cobbe Barracks 2
Red Lions
Tigers 2
Silver Strikers 3
CIVO United 1
Ntaja Medicals 0
Amazon 1
MAFCO 3

Quarter-finals
MTL Wanderers 2
Hard Hammers 0

Blue Eagles 0 2p
Cobbe Barracks 0 3p

Red Lions 2 4p
Silver Strikers 2 1p

CIVO United 2 4p
MAFCO 2 5p

Semi-finals
MTL Wanderers 3
Cobbe Barracks 1

Red Lions 0 2p
MAFCO 0 4p

Final
MTL Wanderers 1
MAFCO 0

CUP FINAL
Kamuzo, Blantyre
25-06-2011, Att: 50 000
Scorer - Anthony Banda 93+ for Wanderers

MYA – MYANMAR

'93	'94	'95	'96	'97	'98	'99	'00	'01	'02	'03	'04	'05	'06	'07	'08	'09	'10	'11	'12
110	124	115	104	114	115	126	124	151	162	140	144	147	154	157	156	140	149	172	

						2011									
	Jan	Feb	Mar	Apr	May	Jun	Jul	Aug	Sep	Oct	Nov	Dec	High	Low	Av
	149	149	161	162	166	167	165	168	168	170	169	172	97	172	137

Myanmar's 2014 FIFA World Cup qualifying campaign was marked by huge controversy when the second leg of their tie against Oman was abandoned just before half-time after supporters in the Thuwunna Youth Training Centre stadium in Rangoon repeatedly hurled objects on to the field. The trouble came after the award of a penalty in the 39th minute which had seen the Omanis go 2-0 ahead on the day and 4-0 on aggregate. Oman were awarded the tie and Myanmar were then banned from entering the 2018 FIFA World Cup qualifiers, although that was later overturned on appeal. There was disappointment for club side Yadanarbon who had sensationally won the AFC President's Cup in 2010. They made it to the finals of the 2011 tournament in Chinese Taipei but then failed to progress beyond the group stage. There was, however, a very exciting climax to the 2011 National League season in Myanmar. Yangon United and Ayeyawady United met on the final day but despite preserving their unbeaten record for the season, a 2-2 draw was not enough for Ayeyawady to win the championship which went instead to their opponents from the capital. A Charles Obi goal six minutes from time secured the draw for Yangon, who then went on to complete the league and cup double by beating Nay Pyi Taw 5-0 in the MFF Cup Final.

FIFA WORLD CUP RECORD
1930-2006 DNE 2010 DNQ

MYANMAR FOOTBALL FEDERATION (MFF)

National Football Training Centre, Thuwunna Thingankyun, Township, PO Box 11070, Yangon

☎ +951 500123
📠 +951 527797
✉ adm_mff@mff-ma.com
🖥 www.myanmarfootball.org
FA 1947 CON 1954 FIFA 1957
P Zaw Zaw
GS Aung Tin

FIFA BIG COUNT 2006

Total players	1 122 039
% of population	2.37%
Male	1 043 159
Female	78 880
Amateurs 18+	104 405
Unregistered	214 380
Professionals	0
Referees	830
Admin & coaches	2 920
Number of clubs	598
Number of teams	4 200

MAJOR CITIES/TOWNS

		Population
1	Yangon	4 994 082
2	Mandalay	1 363 655
3	Mawlamyine	502 459
4	Bago	270 214
5	Pathein	262 786
6	Monywa	202 983
7	Meiktila	200 584
8	Mergui	197 856
9	Sittwe	197 125
10	Taunggyi	174 154
11	Myingyan	160 203
12	Dawei	156 227
13	Pyay	149 625
14	Henzada	149 583
15	Lashio	142 496
16	Pakokku	142 478
17	Thaton	141 948
18	Maymyo	132 612
19	Thayetmyo	128 124

PYIDAUNGZU MYANMA NAINGNGANDAW • UNION OF MYANMAR

Capital	Yangon	Population	48 137 741 (26)	% in cities	33%
GDP per capita	$1200 (206)	Area km²	676 578 km² (40)	GMT +/-	+6.5

Neighbours (km) Bangladesh 193, China 2185, India 1463, Laos 235, Thailand 1800 • Coast 1930

RECENT INTERNATIONAL MATCHES PLAYED BY MYANMAR

2008	Opponents	Score		Venue	Comp	Scorers	Att	Referee
5-12	Indonesia	L	0-3	Jakarta	AFFr1		40 000	Ramachandran MAS
7-12	Singapore	L	1-3	Jakarta	AFFr1	Min Tun Myo [28]	21 000	Phung VIE
9-12	Cambodia	W	3-2	Bandung	AFFr1	Mo Win [29], Win Thein Yaza [35], Min Tun Myo [85]		Martinez PHI
2009								
26-04	Macau	W	4-0	Dhaka	CCq	Khin Maung Lwin [3], Win Thein Yaza [15], Phyo Oo Pyaye [48], Min Tun Myo [59]	3 600	Mashentsev KGZ
28-04	Bangladesh	W	2-1	Dhaka	CCq	Pai Soe 2 [68] [77]	14 000	Matsuo JPN
30-04	Cambodia	W	1-0	Dhaka	CCq	Win Thein Yaza [94+]	2 500	Mozaffari IRN
2010								
16-02	Sri Lanka	W	4-0	Colombo	CCr1	Thi Ha Kyaw [39], Paing Yan [71], Pai Soe [81], Min Tun Myo [87]	3 000	Faghani IRN
18-02	Bangladesh	W	2-1	Colombo	CCr1	Tun Win Tun [16], Pai Soe [32]	500	Al Yarimi YEM
20-02	Tajikistan	L	0-3	Colombo	CCr1		100	Shukralla BHR
24-02	Korea DPR	L	0-5	Colombo	CCsf		400	Al Yarimi YEM
27-02	Tajikistan	L	0-1	Colombo	CC3p		300	El Haddad LIB
2-12	Vietnam	L	1-7	Hanoi	AFFr1	Kyaw Moe Aung [16]	40 000	Patwal IND
5-12	Singapore	L	1-2	Hanoi	AFFr1	Khin Maung Lwin [13]		Tao Ranchang CHN
8-12	Philippines	D	0-0	Nam Dinh	AFFr1			Patwal IND
2011								
21-03	Philippines	D	1-1	Yangon	CCq	Khin Maung Lwin [93+]	5 000	
23-03	Bangladesh	L	0-2	Yangon	CCq		3 000	
25-03	Palestine	L	1-3	Yangon	CCq	Zaw Htat Aung [25p]	1 500	Abdulhusin BHR
18-06	Malaysia	L	0-2	Kota Bahru	Fr			
29-06	Mongolia	L	0-1	Ulaan-Baatar	WCq		3 500	Kim Jong Hyeok KOR
3-07	Mongolia	W	2-0	Yangon	WCq	Paing Soe [62], Mai Aih Naing [88]	18 000	Liu Kwok Man HKG
14-07	Thailand	L	0-1	Buriram	Fr			
15-07	Thailand	D	1-1	Buriram	Fr	Paing Soe [63]		
23-07	Oman	L	0-2	Seeb	WCq	Awarded 3-0 to Oman	6 300	Sabbagh LIB
28-07	Oman	L	0-2	Yangon	WCq	Abandoned 45 mins. Awarded 3-0 to Oman	30 000	Sato JPN

Fr = Friendly match • AFF = AFF Championship • CC = AFC Challenge Cup • q = qualifier • r1 = 1st round group • † Not a full international

MYANMAR 2011

MYANMAR NATIONAL LEAGUE

	Pl	W	D	L	F	A	Pts	Yangon Utd	Ayeyawady Utd	Zeyar Shwe	Kanbawza	Okktha Utd	Nay Pyi Taw	Magway	S. Myanmar Utd	Yadanarbon	Manaw Myay	Rakhapura Utd	Zwekapin Utd
Yangon United †	22	17	3	2	50	15	**54**		0-0	3-2	3-0	4-0	1-0	4-1	1-1	2-1	1-0	4-0	3-0
Ayeyawady United	22	15	7	0	41	11	**52**	2-2		3-0	1-0	1-1	0-0	0-0	1-0	1-1	2-1	3-0	2-0
Zeyar Shwe Myay	22	14	3	5	46	25	**45**	3-1	1-1		4-1	2-1	2-0	4-2	3-0	3-1	1-2	3-2	1-0
Kanbawza	22	9	6	7	27	21	33	3-0	0-1	0-0		1-0	1-0	1-1	1-1	1-0	1-0	3-1	4-1
Okktha United	22	9	6	7	27	26	33	1-2	1-3	1-2	1-1		1-0	1-2	1-0	1-1	0-0	1-1	3-1
Nay Pyi Taw	22	8	6	8	33	28	30	0-2	1-2	2-1	1-1	2-3		0-2	1-1	2-0	7-2	1-1	3-1
Magway	22	8	6	8	32	32	30	0-3	0-1	0-1	2-1	0-2	0-0		1-1	3-2	4-2	0-1	1-0
Southern Myanmar Utd	22	5	10	7	23	25	25	0-2	0-1	1-1	1-0	1-2	2-2	2-2		1-0	0-0	1-2	2-0
Yadanarbon	22	6	5	11	28	31	23	0-3	0-2	1-2	2-1	2-3	0-1	2-2	1-1		1-0	1-0	6-0
Manaw Myay	22	4	6	12	18	33	18	1-3	1-3	2-1	1-1	0-2	1-3	0-1	1-1	0-1		0-0	2-0
Rakhapura United	22	4	6	12	24	42	18	0-2	2-5	1-3	0-1	0-0	2-4	3-2	1-4	1-1	0-0		2-3
Zwekapin United	22	1	0	21	11	71	3	0-4	0-6	0-6	0-4	0-1	2-3	1-6	1-2	1-4	0-2	0-4	

15/01/2011 - 5/10/2011 • † Qualified for the AFC President's Cup • Top scorer: Lappe Lappe, Okkthar United

NAM – NAMIBIA

FIFA/COCA-COLA WORLD RANKING

'93	'94	'95	'96	'97	'98	'99	'00	'01	'02	'03	'04	'05	'06	'07	'08	'09	'10	'11	'12
156	123	116	103	86	69	80	87	101	123	144	158	161	116	114	115	113	138	121	

					2011								High	Low	Av
	Jan	Feb	Mar	Apr	May	Jun	Jul	Aug	Sep	Oct	Nov	Dec			
	138	138	140	141	140	153	140	143	119	127	121	121	68	167	118

Namibia's efforts to get a ticket to the 2012 CAF Africa Cup of Nations finals through the back door failed just weeks before the kick-off of the tournament in Equatorial Guinea and Gabon. Namibia had protested six months earlier that opponents Burkina Faso has used an ineligible player in their qualifying match in Windhoek but after two appeals and a ruling from the Court for Arbitration in Sport in Switzerland, they were unsuccessful. They strongly believed in the legitimacy of their case with regard to the Cameroon-born defender Herve Zengue who had been given a Burkina Faso passport, and they spent considerable resources in their cause. Namibia had ended their three-team qualifying group in last place after losing three of their four games. That saw a change of coach with Brian Isaacs replaced by Bernard Kaanjuka, who immediately instigated an overhaul of the 'Brave Warriors' squad. He replaced many of the foreign-based players, putting his faith in a younger crop of emerging talent and it paid off at the end of the year when Namibia beat Djibouti both home and away in a one-sided 8-0 aggregate triumph in their 2014 FIFA World Cup qualifier. Windhoek club Black Africa won the Premier League for their first championship since 1999 but kept up their record as the side with most post-independence titles.

CAF AFRICA CUP OF NATIONS RECORD
1957-1994 DNE **1996** DNQ **1998** 14 r1 **2000-2006** DNQ **2008** 14 r1 **2010-2012** DNQ

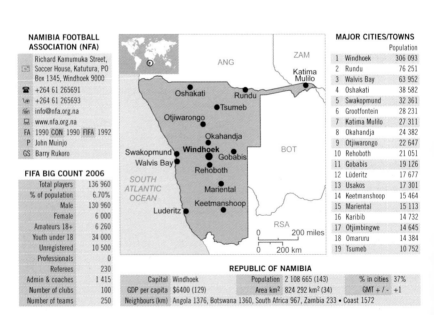

NAMIBIA FOOTBALL ASSOCIATION (NFA)

Richard Kamumuka Street, Soccer House, Katutura, PO Box 1345, Windhoek 9000
☎ +264 61 265691
📠 +264 61 265693
📧 info@nfa.org.na
🖥 www.nfa.org.na
FA 1990 CON 1990 FIFA 1992
P John Muinjo
GS Barry Rukoro

FIFA BIG COUNT 2006

Total players	136 960
% of population	6.70%
Male	130 960
Female	6 000
Amateurs 18+	6 260
Youth under 18	34 000
Unregistered	10 500
Professionals	0
Referees	230
Admin & coaches	1 415
Number of clubs	100
Number of teams	250

MAJOR CITIES/TOWNS

		Population
1	Windhoek	306 093
2	Rundu	76 251
3	Walvis Bay	63 952
4	Oshakati	38 582
5	Swakopmund	32 361
6	Grootfontein	28 231
7	Katima Mulilo	27 311
8	Okahandja	24 382
9	Otjiwarongo	22 647
10	Rehoboth	21 051
11	Gobabis	19 126
12	Lüderitz	17 677
13	Usakos	17 301
14	Keetmanshoop	15 464
15	Mariental	15 113
16	Karibib	14 732
17	Otjimbingwe	14 645
18	Omaruru	14 384
19	Tsumeb	10 752

REPUBLIC OF NAMIBIA

Capital	Windhoek	Population	2 108 665 (143)	% in cities	37%
GDP per capita	$6400 (129)	Area km²	824 292 km² (34)	GMT +/-	+1
Neighbours (km)	Angola 1376, Botswana 1360, South Africa 967, Zambia 233 • Coast 1572		

RECENT INTERNATIONAL MATCHES PLAYED BY NAMIBIA

2007	Opponents	Score		Venue	Comp	Scorers	Att	Referee
6-02	Botswana	L	0-1	Gaborone	Fr			
25-03	Libya	L	1-2	Tripoli	CNq	Colin Benjamin [85]		
26-05	Zambia	L	1-2	Windhoek	Fr	Letu Shatimuene [89]		
2-06	Libya	W	1-0	Windhoek	CNq	Colin Benjamin [4]		Ncobo RSA
16-06	Congo DR	D	1-1	Windhoek	CNq	Michael Pienaar [38]		Mwanza ZAM
6-07	Malawi	W	2-1	Blantyre	Fr	Gerson Katjatenja [23], Rudolph Bester [65]		
28-07	Botswana	L	0-1	Gaborone	CCr1			Lwanja MWI
29-07	Lesotho	W	3-2	Gaborone	CCr1	Tara Katupose [53], Brian Brendell 2 [67 77]		Disang BOT
8-09	Ethiopia	W	3-2	Addis Abeba	CNq	Rudolph Bester 2 [64 81], Tara Katupose [89]		Auda EGY
17-10	Morocco	L	0-2	Tanger	Fr			
2-11	Saudi Arabia	L	0-1	Riyadh	Fr			
17-11	Tunisia	L	0-2	Rades	Fr			
2008								
5-01	Egypt	L	0-3	Aswan	Fr			
12-01	Senegal	L	1-3	Dakar	Fr	Brian Brendell [62]		
21-01	Morocco	L	1-5	Accra	CNr1	Brian Brendell [23]		Evehe CMR
24-01	Ghana	L	0-1	Accra	CNr1			Bennaceur TUN
28-01	Guinea	D	1-1	Sekondi	CNr1	Brian Brendell [80]		Ssegonga UGA
26-03	Malawi	L	1-3	Windhoek	Fr	Tulongeni Tuyeni [53]		
31-05	Kenya	W	2-1	Windhoek	WCq	Wilko Risser [14], Costa Khaiseb [89]	6 000	Ssegonga UGA
8-06	Zimbabwe	L	0-2	Harare	WCq		27 979	Lwanja MWI
14-06	Guinea	L	1-2	Windhoek	WCq	Rudolph Bester [42]	5 000	Imiere NGA
22-06	Guinea	L	0-4	Conakry	WCq		15 000	Monteiro Lopes CPV
20-07	Comoros	W	3-0	Secunda	CCr1	Lazarus Kaimbi [25], Quinton Jacobs 2 [43 74]		Labrosse SEY
22-07	Lesotho	D	1-1	Secunda	CCr1	Jamu Ngatjizeko [23]		Seechurn MRI
24-07	Malawi	W	1-0	Secunda	CCr1	Lazarus Kaimbi [50]		Marange ZIM
6-09	Kenya	L	0-1	Nairobi	WCq		40 000	Hicuburundi BDI
11-10	Zimbabwe	W	4-2	Windhoek	WCq	Wilko Risser 2 [18 53], Rudolph Bester [30], Paulus Shipanga [43]	4 000	Coulibaly MLI
2009								
21-03	Botswana	D	0-0	Keetmanshoop	Fr			
1-04	Lebanon	D	1-1	Saida	Fr	Rudolph Bester [70]		
4-04	Angola	D	0-0	Dundo	Fr			
6-06	Congo DR	W	4-0	Windhoek	Fr	Quinton Jacobs [34], Rudolph Bester [49], Heinrich Isaacks 2 [73 84]		
5-09	Swaziland	D	1-1	Windhoek	Fr	Rudolph Bester [28]		
25-10	Zambia	L	0-1	Harare	CCqf			Ebrahim RSA
2010								
3-03	South Africa	D	1-1	Durban	Fr	Rudolph Bester [42]	35 000	Nguluwe MWI
21-03	Botswana	D	0-0	Windhoek	Fr			
4-09	Gambia	L	1-3	Banjul	CNq	Wilko Risser [90]		Ragab LBY
15-09	India	L	0-2	New Delhi	Fr			
2011								
9-02	Malawi	L	1-2	Windhoek	Fr	Wilko Risser [35]		
16-03	Botswana	D	1-1	Maun	Fr	Eslin Kamuhanga [33]		
26-03	Burkina Faso	L	0-4	Ouagadougou	CNq			Cordier CHA
4-06	Burkina Faso	L	1-4	Windhoek	CNq	Tangeni Shipahu [83]		
6-07	Malawi	W	1-0	Mzuzu	Fr	Sydney Urikhob [85]		
3-09	Gambia	W	1-0	Windhoek	CNq	Tangeni Shipahu [83]		
31-10	Lesotho	D	0-0	Windhoek	Fr			
11-11	Djibouti	W	4-0	Djibouti	WCq	Rudolph Bester 2 [13 52], Lazarus Kaimbi [50], Sadney Urikhob [88]	3 000	Bamlak ETH
15-11	Djibouti	W	4-0	Windhoek	WCq	Heinrich Isaacks [17], Lazarus Kaimbi 2 [34 58], Sadney Urikhob [88]	2 145	Chirinda MOZ
22-12	Angola	D	0-0	Lubango	Fr			

Fr = Friendly match • CN = CAF African Cup of Nations • CC = COSAFA Cup • WC = FIFA World Cup • q = qualifier • r1 = first round group

NAMIBIA 2010–11

MTC PREMIER LEAGUE

	Pl	W	D	L	F	A	Pts	Black Africa	Ramblers	Pirates	African Stars	Tigers	Arrows	SK Windhoek	Civics	Blue Waters	Gunners	Blue Boys	Oshakati City
Black Africa	22	15	2	5	41	19	47		1-0	2-1	0-0	1-0	1-0	2-0	3-0	2-1	6-1	4-2	5-2
Ramblers	22	10	5	7	22	15	35	0-2		2-3	1-0	0-1	1-0	0-0	1-1	0-1	2-1	3-0	3-0
Orlando Pirates	22	10	5	7	30	24	35	1-0	1-0		0-0	2-1	1-2	1-2	2-1	1-2	3-1	3-0	2-1
African Stars	22	8	9	5	23	16	33	1-1	0-1	2-1		0-2	1-0	0-0	1-2	2-2	1-1	2-0	2-0
United Africa Tigers	22	9	4	9	27	20	31	1-0	0-1	0-1	0-0		1-1	2-0	3-0	3-3	0-1	1-2	5-1
Eleven Arrows	22	9	4	9	28	22	31	1-3	1-1	2-1	0-0	2-1		2-1	3-0	1-0	1-1	2-3	5-1
SK Windhoek	22	9	4	9	23	26	31	1-2	0-1	2-0	1-1	2-1	0-2		0-0	2-1	1-0	0-2	4-2
Civics	22	8	5	9	18	27	29	0-1	0-0	0-2	0-4	1-0	2-1	0-2		0-0	1-0	5-2	1-1
Blue Waters	22	8	4	10	27	30	28	3-2	0-1	0-0	0-1	0-1	2-1	3-1	1-0		2-3	2-1	2-0
Mighty Gunners	22	7	5	10	25	33	26	2-1	0-2	1-1	0-1	1-1	1-0	4-2	0-1	3-0		1-1	3-1
Blue Boys	22	7	3	12	28	39	24	1-2	2-1	2-2	2-4	0-1	0-1	0-2	0-1	2-1	3-0		3-1
Oshakati City	22	5	4	13	22	43	19	1-0	1-1	1-1	2-0	1-2	1-0	0-1	0-2	3-1	2-0	0-0	

24/09/2009 - 21/05/2011

MEDALS TABLE

	Club	Overall G	S	B	Lge G	S	Cup G	S	City/Town
1	Black Africa	8	2		5		3	2	Winhoek
2	Chief Santos	6			2		4		Tsumeb
3	Civics	5	2		3		2	2	Windhoek
4	African Stars	4	2		2		2	2	Windhoek
	Orlando Pirates	4	2		1		3	2	Windhoek
6	Blue Waters	4	1		3		1	1	Walvis Bay
7	United Africa Tigers	2	5				2	5	Windhoek
8	Eleven Arrows	2	1		1		1	1	Windhoek
9	Ramblers	2			1		1		Okahandja
	Liverpool	2			1		1		Walvis Bay
11	Life Fighters		2					2	Otjiwarongo
	Young Ones		2					2	Windhoek
13	SK Windhoek		1					1	Windhoek

LEO NFA CUP 2011

Round of 16		Quarter–finals		Semi–finals		Final	
Eleven Arrows	9						
Pescanova	1	Eleven Arrows	0 4p				
Young Eleven	0	Rundu Chiefs	0 2p				
Rundu Chiefs	2			Eleven Arrows	1		
African Stars	2			Orlando Pirates	0		
Hotspurs	0	African Stars	0				
Oshakati City	1	Orlando Pirates	1				
Orlando Pirates	2					Eleven Arrows ‡	2
Black Africa	3					Civics	0
Ramblers	0	Black Africa	3				
Young Rangers	2 1p	Golden Bees	0				
Golden Bees	2 3p			Black Africa	1		
Blue Boys	1			Civics	2		
Bingo	0	Blue Boys	0				
Blue Waters	1 6p	Civics	1	Semi-finals played in Windhoek			
Civics	1 7p			‡ Qualified for the CAF Confederation Cup			

CUP FINAL

Khuisebmund, Walvis Bay
28-05-2011
Scorers - Dumisa Jantze 4, Freedom Puriza 70 for Arrows

NCA – NICARAGUA

FIFA/COCA-COLA WORLD RANKING

'93	'94	'95	'96	'97	'98	'99	'00	'01	'02	'03	'04	'05	'06	'07	'08	'09	'10	'11	'12
155	168	174	179	182	188	193	191	188	186	173	158	152	168	161	181	133	158	154	

2011												High	Low
Jan	Feb	Mar	Apr	May	Jun	Jul	Aug	Sep	Oct	Nov	Dec	High	Low
157	161	164	166	166	161	178	179	156	160	153	154	132	193

Nicaragua's FIFA World Cup qualifying campaigns rarely last more than a couple of games but the road to Brazil did set a new landmark for the game in the country - a first-ever victory in a qualifying match. In their group they beat Dominica twice and, but for the withdrawl of the Bahamas, that number could have been even greater. The group was won by Panama, however, and with just the leaders progressing to the next round, Nicaragua's adventure came to an end after just four games. That historic first victory against Dominica came away in Roseau with Raul Leguias and Felix Rodriguez scoring the goals in a 2-0 win. With an expanded national stadium in Managua owned by the federation and a new technical centre in Diriamba, it is hoped that football can start to match baseball in popularity. In club football, Real Esteli won the 2011 championship after a marathon four-game encounter with Deportivo Ferretti. Ferretti had won the apertura at the end of 2010 and they qualified for the final of the clausura where they met Esteli. Had Ferretti won they would have automatically been crowned champions as winners of both stages, but they lost 3-2 on aggregate which saw Esteli take the clausura. That meant the two met again in the championship final which finished 2-2 on aggregate, with Esteli taking the title on penalties.

FIFA WORLD CUP RECORD
1930-1990 DNE 1994-2014 DNQ

FEDERACION NICARAGUENSE DE FUTBOL (FENIFUT)

Porton Principal del Hospital Bautista 1 c. abajo, 1 c. al sur y 1/2 c. abajo Apartado Postal 976 Managua
☎ +505 22227035
📠 +505 22227885
📧 fenifut@yahoo.com
🖥 www.fenifut.org.ni
FA 1931 CON 1968 FIFA 1950
P Julio Rocha Lopez
GS Florencio Leiva

FIFA BIG COUNT 2006

Total players	467 031
% of population	8.38%
Male	408 081
Female	58 950
Unregistered	190 354
Professionals	0
Referees	1 372
Admin & coaches	4 398
Number of clubs	1 270
Number of teams	4 221

MAJOR CITIES/TOWNS

		Population
1	Managua	925 313
2	León	144 179
3	Esteli	97 488
4	Chinandega	93 996
5	Tipitapa	93 080
6	Masaya	93 053
7	Matagalpa	89 132
8	Granada	81 674
9	Ciudad Sandino	75 610
10	Puerto Cabezas	48 491
11	Jinotega	45 580
12	Juigalpa	44 686
13	El Viejo	41 110
14	Bluefields	40 297
15	Ocotal	38 148
16	Diriamba	36 827
17	Chichigalpa	36 186
18	Jinotepe	33 604
19	Mateare	32 114

REPUBLICA DE NICARAGUA • REPUBLIC OF NICARAGUA

Capital Managua	Population 5 891 199 (108)	% in cities 57%
GDP per capita $2900 (165)	Area km² 130 370 km² (97)	GMT +/- -6
Neighbours (km) Costa Rica 309, Honduras 922 • Coast 910			

RECENT INTERNATIONAL MATCHES PLAYED BY NICARAGUA

2006	Opponents	Score		Venue	Comp	Scorers	Att	Referee
	No international matches played in 2006							
2007								
8-02	Guatemala	L	0-1	San Salvador	UCr1		10 000	Pineda HON
10-02	El Salvador	L	1-2	San Salvador	UCr1	Samuel Wilson [53]	20 000	Arredondo MEX
12-02	Belize	W	4-2	San Salvador	UCr1	Emilio Palacios 3 [12 20 68], Milton Bustos [28]	5 000	Quesada CRC
15-02	Honduras	L	1-9	San Salvador	UC5p	Samuel Wilson [31]	3 000	Aguilar SLV
2008								
6-02	Netherlands Antilles	L	0-1	Diriamba	WCq		7 000	Lopez GUA
26-03	Netherlands Antilles	L	0-2	Willemstad	WCq		9 000	Wijngaarde SUR
2009								
22-01	El Salvador	D	1-1	Tegucigalpa	UCr1	Marlon Medina [85]	20 000	Batres GUA
24-01	Honduras	L	1-4	Tegucigalpa	UCr1	Armando Reyes [30]	20 000	Batres GUA
26-01	Belize	D	1-1	Tegucigalpa	UCr1	Juan Barrera [66]	8 000	Moncada HON
29-01	Guatemala	W	2-0	Tegucigalpa	UC5p	Samuel Wilson 2 [39 85]	150	Moncada HON
5-07	Mexico	L	0-2	Oakland	GCr1		32 700	Ward CAN
9-07	Guadeloupe	L	0-2	Houston	GCr1		47 713	Moncada HON
12-07	Panama	L	0-4	Phoenix	GCr1		23 876	Pineda HON
2010								
4-09	Guatemala	L	0-5	Fort Lauderdale	Fr		5 000	Vaughn USA
2011								
14-01	El Salvador	L	0-2	Panama City	UCr1		2 000	Quesada CRC
16-01	Panama	L	0-2	Panama City	UCr1		7 747	Lopez GUA
18-01	Belize	D	1-1	Panama City	UCr1	Denis Espinoza [10p]	10 000	Brea CUB
21-01	Guatemala	L	1-2	Panama City	UC5p	Felix Rodriguez [24]	5 000	Garcia MEX
26-05	Cuba	D	1-1	Havana	Fr	Raul Leguias [44p]	3 500	Brea CUB
28-05	Cuba	L	1-2	Havana	Fr	OG [89]	2 950	Rubalcaba CUB
2-09	Dominica	W	2-0	Roseau	WCq	Raul Leguias [1], Felix Rodriguez [36]	3 000	Legister JAM
6-09	Panama	L	1-2	Managua	WCq	OG [18]	10 521	Reyna GUA
11-10	Panama	L	1-5	Panama City	WCq	Daniel Reyes [88]	10 846	Ventura SLV
11-11	Dominica	W	1-0	Managua	WCq	Raul Leguias [57]	2 100	Cruz CRC

Fr = Friendly match • UC = UNCAF Cup/Copa Centroamericana • GC = CONCACAF Gold Cup • WC = FIFA World Cup • q = qualifier
r1 = first round group • 5p = fifth place play-off

NICARAGUA 2010-11

XXVII CAMPEONATO NACIONAL PRIMERA DIVISION TORNEO CLAUSURA

	Pl	W	D	L	F	A	Pts	Real Estelí	Diriangén	Walter Ferreti	Ocotal	Managua	América	Xilotepelt	Real Madriz
Real Estelí †	14	8	4	2	22	11	28		1-0	1-0	2-1	3-0	2-1	2-2	3-0
Diriangén †	14	7	3	4	24	17	24	1-0		2-0	2-3	0-3	0-1	4-1	1-1
Dep. Walter Ferreti †	14	7	1	6	18	14	22	2-1	0-1		0-1	3-2	0-1	3-1	2-0
Deportivo Ocotal †	14	6	3	5	24	26	21	1-1	4-5	0-1		2-1	4-3	3-3	2-1
Managua FC	14	5	2	7	19	20	17	0-0	0-1	1-3	4-1		2-1	2-2	1-0
América	14	5	2	7	17	23	17	0-1	1-5	1-1	2-0	1-0		3-1	**0-3**
Xilotepelt	14	3	5	6	21	29	14	1-3	1-1	1-3	1-2	1-0	3-1		1-1
Real Madriz	14	2	6	6	12	17	12	2-2	0-0	1-0	0-0	2-3	1-1	1-2	

29/01/2011 - 3/04/2011 • † Qualified for the Clausura play-offs • Match in bold awarded • Xilotepelt and América relegated
See Oliver's Almanack 2011 for Apertura details

CLAUSURA SEMI-FINALS

	Pl	W	D	L	F	A	Pts	RE	WF	Di	DO
Real Estelí †	6	5	0	1	13	2	15		2-0	2-0	5-0
Dep. Walter Ferreti †	6	2	2	2	5	7	8	2-1		3-1	0-0
Diriangén	6	1	2	3	4	8	5	0-2	0-0		3-1
Deportivo Ocotal	6	1	2	3	4	9	5	0-1	3-0	0-0	

10/04/2011 - 8/05/2011 • † Qualified for the Clausura final

CLAUSURA FINAL

Olímpico del IND, Managua, 15-05-2011
Walter Ferreti 1-0 Real Esteli
Scorer - Salvador Garcia OG 51 for Walter Ferreti

Independencia, Esteli, 21-05-2011
Real Esteli 3-1 Walter Ferreti
Scorers - Manuel Rosas 10, Jose Antonio Flores 20, Samuel Wilson 88 for Esteli; Marlon Mancias 68 for Walter Ferreti. Esteli qualified to meet Apertura winners Walter Ferreti (see Oliver's Almanack 2011) in the 2010-11 Grand Final

2010-11 GRAND FINAL

Independencia, Esteli, 4-06-2011
Real Esteli 1-0 Walter Ferreti
Scorer - Samuel Wilson 3 for Esteli

Olimpico del IND, Managua, 12-05-2011
Walter Ferreti 2-1 2-4p **Real Esteli**
Scorers - Marlon Mancia 5, Ismael Reyes 112 for Walter Ferreti; Rudel Calero 96 for Esteli. Real Esteli are champions for the 2010-11 season

MEDALS TABLE

		Overall	Lge	City/Town
		G	G	
1	Diriangén	25	25	Diriamba
2	Real Estelí	10	10	Estelí
3	Santa Cecilia	5	5	Diriamba
4	UCA Managua	4	4	Managua
5	Aduana	3	3	Managua
6	América	3	3	Managua

NICARAGUA 2011-12

XXVIII CAMPEONATO NACIONAL PRIMERA DIVISION TORNEO APERTURA

	Pl	W	D	L	F	A	Pts	Real Estelí	Managua	Walter Ferreti	Chinandega	Diriangén	Juventus	Real Madriz	Ocotal
Real Estelí †	14	10	3	1	21	8	33		0-1	2-1	1-0	1-1	2-1	3-0	1-0
Managua FC †	14	8	1	5	22	15	25	1-2		2-1	0-3	1-3	0-0	3-2	6-0
Dep. Walter Ferreti †	14	7	2	5	28	18	23	0-0	0-1		6-1	1-0	1-2	3-2	4-1
Chinandega FC †	14	7	2	5	16	15	23	0-1	1-0	0-0		0-2	3-0	1-0	2-1
Diriangén	14	6	4	4	19	16	22	0-0	0-3	2-1	0-1		3-3	1-3	0-0
Juventus	14	3	4	7	22	29	13	1-2	0-1	2-5	3-2	1-2		1-2	3-1
Real Madriz	14	3	1	10	20	33	10	1-4	3-1	2-3	0-1	1-2	2-2		1-4
Deportivo Ocotal	14	2	3	9	17	31	9	1-2	1-2	1-2	1-1	0-2	3-3	3-2	

7/08/2011 - 3/11/2011 • † Qualified for the Apertura play-offs

APERTURA SEMI-FINALS

	Pl	W	D	L	F	A	Pts	RE	WF	Ma	Ch
Real Estelí †	6	4	1	1	8	3	13		2-1	0-0	3-0
Dep. Walter Ferreti †	6	2	2	2	12	10	8	1-2		1-1	3-2
Managua FC	6	2	2	2	5	7	8	1-0	1-4		1-0
Chinandega FC	6	1	1	4	6	11	4	0-1	2-2	2-1	

16/11/2011 - 5/12/2011 • † Qualified for the Apertura final

APERTURA FINAL

Olímpico del IND, Managua, 12-12-2011
Walter Ferretti 1-1 Real Esteli
Scorers - Kesler Rizo 70 for Walter Ferretti, Elmer Mejia 3 for Real Esteli

Independencia, Esteli, 17-12-2011
Real Esteli 3-2 Walter Ferreti
Scorers - OG 59, Elmer Mejia 67, Luis Gonzalez 94+ for Real Esteli; Kesler Rizo 40, Darwin Ramirez 70 for Walter Ferretti. Walter Ferretti win the Apertura and qualify for the 2011-12 Grand Final (see Olivers Almanack 2013)

NCL – NEW CALEDONIA

FIFA/COCA-COLA WORLD RANKING

'93	'94	'95	'96	'97	'98	'99	'00	'01	'02	'03	'04	'05	'06	'07	'08	'09	'10	'11	'12
-	-	-	-	-	-	-	-	-	-	-	186	187	176	118	130	147	156	166	

					2011								High	Low
Jan	Feb	Mar	Apr	May	Jun	Jul	Aug	Sep	Oct	Nov	Dec		High	Low
155	153	153	151	151	158	164	165	155	156	163	166		95	188

Since joining FIFA in 2004, New Caledonia has established itself as one of the top footballing nations in the Pacific region and the national team cemented its reputation by once again winning the football tournament of the Pacific Games. New Caledonia's capital Noumea hosted the multi-sport event in August and September 2011 and the gold medal won in football was just one of 120 won by the host country - double that of nearest rival Tahiti. In the final New Caledonia beat the Solomon Islands 2-0 with two early goals from Georges Gope-Fenepej and Marius Bako to retain their title and establish a new record of six golds in the 48-year history of the tournament. In club football, defending champions Magenta had a poor year both at home and in the 2010-11 OFC Champions League. Instead it was Mont-Dore who won both League tournaments played during the course of the year - the championship for the main island of Grand Terre and the smaller national championship. Gaïtcha won the Coupe de Caledonie for the first time in their history when they beat Magenta 2-0 in a rematch of the 2010 final. They were inspired by new signing Pierre Wajoka who opened the scoring in the first minute against his old club and he then set up Yoran Hmuzo for the second. It meant a ninth winners medal for New Caledonia's most celebrated player.

FIFA WORLD CUP RECORD
1930-2002 DNE   2006-2010 DNQ

FEDERATION CALEDONIENNE DE FOOTBALL (FCF)

✉ 7 bis, rue Suffren Quartien Latin, BP 560, Nouméa 99845
☎ +687 272383
📠 +687 263249
✉ fedcalfoot@canl.nc
🖥 www.fedcalfoot.com
FA 1928 CON   FIFA 2004
P   Edmond Bowen
GS Olivier Dokunengo

FIFA BIG COUNT 2006

Total players	9 800
% of population	4.47%
Male	9 150
Female	650
Amateurs 18+	2 500
Youth under 18	2 400
Unregistered	500
Professionals	0
Referees	100
Admin & coaches	200
Number of clubs	100
Number of teams	250

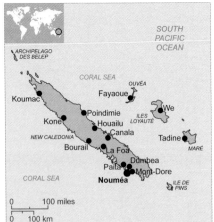

MAJOR CITIES/TOWNS

		Population
1	Nouméa	100 479
2	Mont-Doré	26 549
3	Dumbéa	22 400
4	Païta	15 206
5	Wé	10 549
6	Tadine	7 807
7	Poindimié	5 131
8	Bourail	5 003
9	Koné	4 845
10	Houaïlu	4 664
11	Fayaoué	4 612
12	Canala	3 633
13	Koumac	3 278
14	La Foa	3 141
15	Hienghène	2 862
16	Thio	2 783
17	Ponerihouen	2 778
18	Poya	2 697
19	Voh	2 419

NOUVELLE-CALEDONIE • NEW CALEDONIA

Capital Noumea	Population 227 436 (181)	% in cities 65%
GDP per capita $15 000 (76)	Area km² 18 575 km² (155)	GMT + / - +11
Neighbours (km) Coast 2254		

RECENT INTERNATIONAL MATCHES PLAYED BY NEW CALEDONIA

2006	Opponents	Score		Venue	Comp	Scorers	Att	Referee
No international matches played in 2006								

2007								
17-07	Vanuatu	W	5-3	Noumea	Fr	Mapou 40, Toto 2 47 62, Hmae.J 56, Wajoka 69p		
19-07	Vanuatu	L	0-2	Noumea	Fr			
25-08	Tahiti	W	1-0	Apia	WCq	Wajoka 9p	400	Hester NZL
27-08	Tuvalu †	W	1-0	Apia	WCq	Kabeu 52	250	Sogo SOL
29-08	Cook Islands	W	3-0	Apia	WCq	Kabeu 3 35 51 85	200	Fox NZL
3-09	Fiji	D	1-1	Apia	WCq	Wajoka 44	1 000	Fred VAN
5-09	Solomon Islands	W	3-2	Apia	WCq	Kabeu 37, Toto 54, Mercier 94+	600	Minan PNG
7-09	Fiji	W	1-0	Apia	WCq	Hmae.J 61	400	Hester NZL
17-11	Fiji	D	3-3	Ba	WCq	Djamali 67, Kaudre 83, Hmae.M 88	1 500	O'Leary NZL
21-11	Fiji	W	4-0	Noumea	WCq	Wajoka 28p, Hmae.M 2 30 55, Mapou 59		Breeze AUS

2008								
14-06	Vanuatu	D	1-1	Port Vila	WCq	Djamali 73	4 000	Varman FIJ
21-06	Vanuatu	W	3-0	Noumea	WCq	Wajoka 36, Hmae.M 60, Diaike 87	2 700	Hester NZL
6-09	New Zealand	L	1-3	Noumea	WCq	Hmae.M 55	2 589	Varman FIJ
10-09	New Zealand	L	0-3	Auckland	WCq		8 000	Hauata TAH
24-09	Tahiti	W	1-0	Paris	Fr	Hmae.M 91+		
27-09	Guadeloupe †	L	0-4	Paris	Fr			Alain GYF
30-09	Martinique †	D	1-1	Paris	Fr	Lolohea		Alain GYF
3-10	Mayotte	W	3-2	Paris	Fr	Wajoka 2 53 87p, Kai 58		Touraine GLP

2009								
No international matches played in 2009								

2010								
23-09	Guadeloupe †	D	1-1	Paris	Fr	Hmae.M		Prevot FRA
26-09	Martinique †	L	0-4	Paris	Fr			Tetauira FRA
29-09	Tahiti	D	1-1	Paris	Fr	Watrone 6. L 3-5p		Fouquet FRA

2011								
24-01	Vanuatu	D	0-0	Port Vila	Fr			
3-04	Tahiti	W	3-1	Papeete	Fr	Kabeu 3 29 81 86		
7-04	Tahiti	L	0-1	Papeete	Fr			
27-08	Vanuatu	W	5-0	Noumea	PGr1	Gope-Fenepej 3 5 31 63, Bako 43, Lolohea 51		Achari FIJ
30-08	Guam	W	9-0	Noumea	PGr1	Kai 5 12 26 40 47 91+, Boawe 70, Kaneu 73, Wakanumune 83, Hmae.M 85		Zitouni TAH
1-09	Tuvalu †	W	8-0	Noumea	PGr1	Gorendiawe 15, Kabeu 2 26 35, Gope Fenepej 38, Haeko 50, Lolohea 61, Hmae.M 2 67 85		Kerr NZL
3-09	American Samoa	W	8-0	Noumea	PGr1	Kai 4 10 38 44 66, Haeko 50, Qaeze 55, Vendegou 72, Hmae.M 89		Varman FIJ
5-09	Solomon Islands	L	1-2	Noumea	PGr1	Kai 74		Kerr NZL
7-09	Tahiti	W	3-1	Kone	PGsf	Gope-Fenepej 2 89 108, Hmae 115		Varman FIJ
9-09	Solomon Islands	W	2-0	Noumea	PGf	Gope-Fenepej 9, Bako 11		Kerr NZL

Fr = Friendly match • OC = OFC Oceania Nations Cup • PG = Pacific Games • WC = FIFA World Cup
q = qualifier • r1 = first round group • sf = semi-final • f = final • † Not a full international

NEW CALEDONIA 2011

GRAND TERRE SUPER LIGUE COCA-COLA

	Pl	W	D	L	F	A	Pts	Mont-Dore	Hienghène	Thio Sports	Gaïtcha	Magenta	Lössi	Mouli	Kunié
AS Mont-Dore	14	10	1	3	36	17	45		5-0	4-1	0-1	**2-0**	2-1	3-0	4-3
Hienghène Sports	14	7	3	4	27	26	38	1-2		5-2	1-1	**2-0**	2-1	3-2	2-1
AS Thio Sports	14	7	2	5	26	26	37	0-1	1-1		2-0	2-3	2-1	2-1	2-1
Gaïtcha FCN	13	6	5	2	22	17	36	3-1	2-2	2-4		3-3	2-1	3-1	1-0
AS Magenta	13	6	2	5	24	20	31	2-0	3-0	2-3	n/p		0-0	0-1	2-1
AS Lössi	13	4	3	6	22	22	28	1-1	4-1	3-2	1-1	3-1		4-2	2-3
Mouli Sport	14	3	1	10	20	29	24	1-2	0-1	1-2	1-3	0-2	3-0		1-1
AS Kunié	13	1	3	9	19	39	19	2-7	2-6	1-1	0-0	1-5	n/p	3-6	

12/02/2011 - 24/09/2011 • Top four qualify for the Championnat des Iles • Matches in bold awarded

NEW CALEDONIA 2011

CHAMPIONNAT DES ILES

	Pl	W	D	L	F	A	Pts	Mont-Dore	Thio Sports	Hienghène	Gaïtcha	Qanono
AS Mont-Dore †	8	6	2	0	23	8	28		1-1	3-2	7-1	3-1
AS Thio Sports	8	4	2	2	15	12	22	1-3		2-3	4-1	3-2
Hienghène Sports	8	4	1	3	18	18	21	2-3	1-1		1-5	3-1
Gaïtcha FCN	8	1	2	5	17	25	13	0-0	1-2	3-4		3-3
AS Qanono	8	1	1	6	11	21	12	0-3	0-1	0-2	4-3	

23/10/2011 - 17/12/2011 • † Qualified for the O-League

COUPE DE CALEDONIE 2011

Round of 16		Quarter–finals		Semi–finals		Final	
Gaïtcha FCN	5						
AS Ponoz	0	**Gaïtcha FCN**	2				
USC	4	Tiga Sport	1				
Tiga Sport	7			**Gaïtcha FCN**	2		
AS Qanono	3			AS Thio	0		
CA St Louis	0	AS Qanono	2 1p				
Mouli Sport	1	**AS Thio**	2 3p				
AS Thio	2					**Gaïtcha FCN**	2
AS Lössi	5					AS Magenta	0
AS Goa	2	**AS Lössi**	2				
ASC Boulouparis	0	Hienghène Sport	1			CUP FINAL	
Hienghène Sport	9			AS Lössi	0		
AS Monte Dore	5			**AS Magenta**	1	Stade Numa-Daly, Nouméa	
RC Poindimié	0	AS Mont Dore	1			30-07-2011, Att: 4000	
AS Kunie	1	**AS Magenta**	7			Scorers - Pierre Wajoka [1], Yoran	
AS Magenta	3					Hmuzo [36] for Gaïtcha	

Cup Final line-ups: **Gaïtcha** - Nyikeine - Lolohea (Ausu 79), Bearune.E, Ouka, Bearune.G, Hmuzo, Wajoka (c), Dusy, Bako.M, Bako.Y (Toto 76), Wangane (Siapo 84). Tr: Adrien Ausu • **AS Magenta** - Iona - Ixoee, Forest, Sinedo, Kakou, Gope-Fenepej, Kaudre (c), Read (Henesewene 88), Wea, Gorendiawe (Makalu 55), Jewin (Waheo 88). Tr: Alain Moizan

NED – NETHERLANDS

FIFA/COCA-COLA WORLD RANKING

'93	'94	'95	'96	'97	'98	'99	'00	'01	'02	'03	'04	'05	'06	'07	'08	'09	'10	'11	'12
7	6	6	9	22	11	19	8	8	6	4	6	3	7	9	3	3	2	2	

	2011												
	Jan	Feb	Mar	Apr	May	Jun	Jul	Aug	Sep	Oct	Nov	Dec	High	Low
	2	2	2	2	2	2	2	1	2	2	2	2	1	25

The Dutch national team hit the top of the FIFA/Coca-Cola World Ranking in August 2011 after an incredible run of results which had seen the team win 31 of 40 matches played between September 2008 and October 2011. Of those 40 games just one was lost - the World Cup Final. The Netherlands booked their place in the Euro 2012 finals with ease, winning their first nine games and scoring 37 in the process. At home there was a return to the established order when Ajax won the Eredivisie for the first time since 2004, beating FC Twente in a top-of-the-table title decider on the final day of the season, but there can be little doubt that the club scene has changed for good with Ajax, PSV and Feyenoord no longer in a league of their own. Indeed, Feyenoord have now won the title just three times since the mid-1970s and in October 2010 lost 10-0 against PSV. Much of the levelling of standards has been a result of the astute program of stadium building over the past decade by a number of the smaller clubs who now regularly play to full houses. Twente Enschede embody the new mood in Dutch football and although they may have just missed out on retaining their league title, they did beat Ajax in the Cup Final. Having trailed 2-0, Twente fought back to win 3-2, their winner coming from Marko Janko deep into extra-time.

UEFA EUROPEAN CHAMPIONSHIP RECORD

1960 DNE 1964 r2 1968-1972 DNQ 1976 3 SF 1980 5 r1 1984 DNQ 1988 1 Winners 1992 3 SF 1996 8 QF 2000 3 SF (co-hosts) 2004 4 SF 2008 6 QF 2012 Qualified

KONINKLIJKE NEDERLANDSE VOETBALBOND (KNVB)

Woudenbergseweg 56-58, PO Box 515, Am Zeist 3700
☎ +31 343 499201
📠 +31 343 499189
📧 concern@knvb.nl
🖥 www.knvb.nl
FA 1889 CON 1954 FIFA 1904
P Michael Van Praag
GS Harry Bean

FIFA BIG COUNT 2006

Total players	1 745 860
% of population	10.59%
Male	1 505 604
Female	160 256
Amateurs 18+	562 260
Youth under 18	510 091
Unregistered	250 000
Professionals	1 000
Referees	6 830
Admin & coaches	4 408
Number of clubs	3 656
Number of teams	55 060

MAJOR CITIES/TOWNS

		Population
1	Amsterdam	755 207
2	Rotterdam	590 113
3	s-Gravenhage	489 410
4	Utrecht	296 046
5	Eindhoven	217 469
6	Tilburg	203 927
7	Almere	199 542
8	Groningen	185 514
9	Breda	174 899
10	Nijmegen	161 502
11	Enschede	157 312
12	Apeldoorn	155 307
13	Haarlemmermeer	154 177
14	Haarlem	149 660
17	Arnhem	140 223
18	s-Hertogenbosch	139 133
19	Maastricht	123 550
28	Alkmaar	99 599
70	Kerkrade	48 974

KONINKRIJK DER NEDERLANDEN • KINGDOM OF THE NETHERLANDS

Capital	The Hague	Population	16 715 999 (59)	% in cities	82%
GDP per capita	$40 500 (20)	Area km²	41 543 km² (134)	GMT +/-	+1
Neighbours (km)	Belgium 450, Germany 577 • Coast 451				

RECENT INTERNATIONAL MATCHES PLAYED BY THE NETHERLANDS

2009	Opponents	Score	Venue	Comp	Scorers	Att	Referee
12-08	England	D 2-2	Amsterdam	Fr	Kuyt 10, Van der Vaart 37	48 000	Rizzoli ITA
5-09	Japan	W 3-0	Enschede	Fr	Van Persie 69, Sneijder 73, Huntelaar 87	23 750	Skomina SVN
9-09	Scotland	W 1-0	Glasgow	WCq	Elia 82	51 230	Larsen DEN
10-10	Australia	D 0-0	Sydney	Fr		40 537	Minoru JPN
14-11	Italy	D 0-0	Pescara	Fr		17 134	Chirchetta ITA
18-11	Paraguay	D 0-0	Heerenveen	Fr		25 000	Hrinak SVK
2010							
3-03	USA	W 2-1	Amsterdam	Fr	Kuyt 40p, Huntelaar 73	46 630	Cakir TUR
26-05	Mexico	W 2-1	Freiburg	Fr	Van Persie 2 17 41	22 000	Grafe GER
1-06	Ghana	W 4-1	Rotterdam	Fr	Kuyt 30, Van der Vaart 72, Sneijder 81, Van Persie 87p	45 000	Moen NOR
5-06	Hungary	W 6-1	Amsterdam	Fr	Van Persie 21, Sneijder 55, Robben 2 64 78, Van Bommel 71, Elia 74	45 000	Meyer GER
14-06	Denmark	W 2-0	Johannesburg	WCr1	Agger OG 46, Kuyt 85	83 465	Lannoy FRA
19-06	Japan	W 1-0	Durban	WCr1	Sneijder 53	62 010	Baldassi ARG
24-06	Cameroon	W 2-1	Cape Town	WCr1	Van Persie 36, Huntelaar 83	63 093	Pozo CHI
28-06	Slovakia	W 2-1	Durban	WCr2	Robben 18, Sneijder 84	61 962	Undiano ESP
2-07	Brazil	W 2-1	Port Elizabeth	WCqf	Sneijder 2 53 68	40 186	Nishimura JPN
6-07	Uruguay	W 3-2	Cape Town	WCsf	Van Bronckhorst 18, Sneijder 70, Robben 73	62 479	Irmatov UZB
11-07	Spain	L 0-1	Johannesburg	WCf		84 490	Webb ENG
11-08	Ukraine	D 1-1	Donetsk	Fr	Lens 73	18 051	Skomina SVN
3-09	San Marino	W 5-0	Serravalle	ECq	Kuyt 16p, Huntelaar 3 38 48 66, Van Nistelrooy 90	4 127	Evans WAL
7-09	Finland	W 2-1	Rotterdam	ECq	Huntelaar 2 7 16p	25 000	Nikolaev RUS
8-10	Moldova	W 1-0	Chisinau	ECq	Huntelaar 37	10 500	Meyer GER
12-10	Sweden	W 4-1	Amsterdam	ECq	Huntelaar 2 4 55, Afellay 2 37 59	46 000	Lannoy FRA
17-11	Turkey	W 1-0	Amsterdam	Fr	Huntelaar 52	35 500	Kassai HUN
2011							
9-02	Austria	W 3-1	Eindhoven	Fr	Sneijder 28, Huntellar 48, Kuyt 70p	33 000	Brych GER
25-03	Hungary	W 4-0	Budapest	ECq	Van der Vaart 8, Afellay 45, Kuyt 54, Van Persie 62	25 311	Velasco ESP
29-03	Hungary	W 5-3	Amsterdam	ECq	Van Persie 13, Sneijder 61, Van Nistelrooy 73, Kuyt 2 78 81	51 700	Moen NOR
4-06	Brazil	D 0-0	Goiania	Fr		36 449	Amarilla PAR
8-06	Uruguay	D 1-1	Montevideo	Fr	Kuyt 90. L 3-4p	55 000	Pitana ARG
2-09	San Marino	W 11-0	Eindhoven	ECq	Van Persie 4 7 65 67 79, Sneijder 2 12 87, Heitinga 17, Kuyt 49, Huntelaar 2 56 77, Wijnaldum 90	35 000	Liany ISR
6-09	Finland	W 2-0	Helsinki	ECq	Strootman 29, De Jong 93+	21 580	Grafe GER
7-10	Moldova	W 1-0	Rotterdam	ECq	Huntelaar 40	47 226	Jug SVN
11-10	Sweden	L 2-3	Stockholm	ECq	Huntelaar 23, Kuyt 50	33 066	Cakir TUR
11-11	Switzerland	D 0-0	Amsterdam	Fr		50 000	Eriksson SWE
15-11	Germany	L 0-3	Hamburg	Fr		51 500	Cakir TUR

Fr = Friendly match • EC = UEFA EURO 2012 • WC = FIFA World Cup • q = qualifier • r1 = first round group • qf = quarter-final

NETHERLANDS NATIONAL TEAM HISTORICAL RECORDS

Caps
130 - Edwin van der Sar 1995-2008 • 112 - Frank de Boer 1990-2004 • 106 - Giovanni van Bronckhorst 1996-2010 • 101 - Phillip Cocu 1996-2006 • 93 - Rafael van der Vaart 2001- • 87 - Clarence Seedorf 1994-2008 • 86 - Marc Overmars 1993-2004 • 84 - Aron Winter 1987-2000 & Dirk Kuyt 2004- • 83 - Ruud Krol 1969-83 • 80 - Wesley Sneijder 2003- • 79 - Patrick Kluivert 1994-2004 & Dennis Bergkamp • 78 - Ronald Koeman 1983-94 & Joris Mathijsen 2004- • 74 - Edgar Davids 1994-2005 & John Heitinga 2004- • 73 - Hans van Breukelen 1980-92; Frank Rijkaard 1981-94 & Mark van Bommel 2000- • 72 - Michael Reiziger 1994-2004

Goals
40 - Patrick Kluivert 1994-2004 • 37 - Dennis Bergkamp 1990-2000 • 35 - Faas Wilkes 1946-61 & Ruud van Nistelrooy 1998- • 33 - Abe Lenstra 1940-59 & Johan Cruijff 1966-77 • 30 - Klaas-Jan Huntelaar 2006- • 28 - Beb Bakhuys 1928-37 • 26 - Kick Smit 1935-46 • 25 - Robin van Persie 2005- • 24 - Marco van Basten 1983-92 & Dirk Kuyt 2004- • 23 - Wesley Sneijder 2003- • 19 - Leen Vente 1933-40

Past Coaches
For coaches prior to 1966 see Oliver's Almanack of World Football 2011 • Georg Kessler GER 1966-70 • Frantisek Fadrhonc CZE 1970-74 • Rinus Michels 1974 • George Knobel 1974-76 • Jan Zwartkruis 1976-77 • Ernst Happel AUT 1977-78 • Jan Zwartkruis 1978-81 • Kees Rijvers 1981-84 • Rinus Michels 1984-85 • Leo Beenhakker 1985-86 • Rinus Michels 1986-88 • Thijs Libregts 1988-90 • Leo Beenhakker 1990 • Rinus Michels 1990-92 • Dick Advocaat 1992-95 • Guus Hiddink 1995-98 • Frank Rijkaard 1998-2000 • Louis van Gaal 2000-02 • Dick Advocaat 2002-04 • Marco van Basten 2004-08 • Bert van Marwijk 2008-

NETHERLANDS 2010-11

EREDIVISIE

	Pl	W	D	L	F	A	Pts	Ajax	Twente	PSV	AZ	Groningen	Roda JC	ADO	Heracles	Utrecht	Feyenoord	NEC	Heerenveen	NAC	Graafschap	Vitesse	Excelsior	VVV	Willem II
Ajax †	34	22	7	5	72	30	73		3-1	0-0	4-0	2-0	3-0	0-1	3-0	1-2	2-0	1-1	3-1	3-0	2-0	4-2	4-1	1-0	2-0
FC Twente Enschede †	34	21	8	5	65	34	71	2-2		2-0	1-2	4-2	1-1	3-2	5-0	4-0	2-1	1-1	0-0	2-0	2-0	1-0	2-1	2-1	4-0
PSV Eindhoven ‡	34	20	9	5	79	34	69	0-0	0-1		3-1	1-1	3-1	0-1	5-2	1-0	10-0	3-1	2-2	4-1	6-0	2-1	4-2	3-0	2-1
AZ Alkmaar ‡	34	17	8	9	55	44	59	2-0	2-1	0-4		1-1	1-2	3-1	2-1	1-0	2-1	2-2	2-2	1-1	5-1	3-1	1-1	6-1	3-0
FC Groningen ‡	34	17	6	11	65	52	57	2-2	1-2	0-0	2-0		1-4	3-1	1-4	1-0	2-0	3-1	1-0	2-1	2-1	4-1	2-0	3-2	7-1
Roda JC Kerkrade	34	14	13	7	65	50	55	2-2	0-0	0-0	1-2	1-0		1-1	4-2	1-1	3-0	1-1	0-0	5-1	1-1	4-1	3-0	5-2	2-2
ADO Den Haag ‡	34	16	6	12	63	55	54	3-2	1-2	2-2	0-2	2-4	1-3		3-2	1-0	2-2	5-1	3-1	3-0	2-2	1-0	2-1	3-0	2-1
Heracles Almelo	34	14	7	13	65	56	49	1-4	0-0	0-2	0-0	3-0	1-0	3-0		2-1	1-1	3-2	4-2	4-1	2-0	6-1	4-1	2-2	3-0
FC Utrecht	34	13	8	13	55	51	47	3-0	1-1	1-2	5-1	1-0	1-1	2-3	1-1		0-4	4-0	2-1	3-1	2-2	4-2	2-0	3-2	3-0
Feyenoord	34	12	8	14	53	54	44	1-2	0-1	3-1	0-1	5-1	1-1	2-1	2-1	3-1		1-1	2-2	2-1	0-1	4-0	1-0	3-0	6-1
NEC Nijmegen	34	10	13	11	57	56	43	1-2	2-4	2-2	0-1	3-2	5-0	1-1	1-1	1-1	3-0		2-2	2-2	1-0	0-0	2-0	1-0	3-1
SC Heerenveen	34	10	11	13	60	54	41	1-2	6-2	1-3	0-2	1-4	2-2	0-0	3-2	3-0	0-1	0-0		3-1	4-0	2-1	2-3	2-0	5-0
NAC Breda §1	34	12	5	17	44	60	40	0-3	2-1	4-2	1-1	0-1	1-2	3-2	1-2	3-1	2-0	0-2	0-0		2-0	1-1	1-2	2-0	2-1
De Graafschap	34	9	11	14	31	56	38	0-5	1-1	0-0	2-1	1-1	1-1	3-1	1-0	1-1	0-0	1-1	1-4	3-2		1-3	1-1	3-0	1-0
Vitesse Arnhem	34	9	8	17	42	61	35	0-1	0-3	0-2	1-1	2-1	5-2	3-1	2-0	1-4	1-1	2-1	1-1	0-0	2-0		1-4	2-0	0-0
Excelsior Rotterdam ‡‡	34	10	5	19	45	66	35	2-2	0-2	2-3	2-1	2-2	1-2	1-5	2-1	3-1	3-2	4-2	0-2	1-3	0-0	0-2		1-0	4-0
VVV Venlo ‡‡	34	6	3	25	34	76	21	0-1	1-2	0-3	0-1	3-5	0-4	2-3	1-0	1-2	3-2	1-4	2-2	3-0	1-0	1-5	1-0		0-0
Willem II Tilburg	34	3	6	25	37	98	15	1-3	1-3	2-4	2-1	0-3	4-5	2-4	2-6	3-3	1-1	3-5	4-3	0-1	0-1	1-0	1-1	1-4	

6/08/2010 - 15/05/2011 • † Qualified for the UEFA Champions League • ‡ Qualified for the Europa League • ‡‡ Relegation play-off
Top scorers: 23 - Bjorn Vleminckx BEL, NEC • 21 - Dmitri Bulykin RUS, ADO • 20 - Mads Junker DEN, Roda • 16 - Tim Matavz SVN, Groningen & Balazs Dzsudzsak HUN, PSV • 15 - Kolbeinn Sigthorsson ISL, AZ; Luc Castaignos, Feyenoord; Everton BRA, Heracles; Ola Toivonen SWE, PSV & Ricky van Wolfswinkel, Utrecht • 14 - Marc Janko AUT, Twente; Willy Overtoom, Heracles & Georginio Wijnaldum, PSV
Europa League play-off semi-finals: Heracles 3-2 1-2 Groningen; ADO Den Haag 4-2 2-1 Roda JC • Final: ADO Den Haag 5-1 1-5 4-3p Groningen

NACOMPETITIE

			VVV Venlo	2	2			
MVV Maastricht	2	0	FC Volendam *	1	0	**VVV Venlo**	2	2
FC Volendam *	3	2	Cambuur-Leeuwarden *	2 1 6P		FC Zwolle *	1	2
			FC Zwolle	1 2 7P				
			Helmond Sport	3	1			
FC Den Bosch	1	2	BV Veendam *	3	0	Helmond Sport *	1	2
Go Ahead Eagles *	0	1	FC Den Bosch *	3	1	**Excelsior Rotterdam**	5	4
			Excelsior Rotterdam	3	3	* Home team in 1st leg		

NETHERLANDS 2010-11 — EERSTE DIVISIE

	Pl	W	D	L	F	A	Pts
RKC Waalwijk	34	22	7	5	85	40	73
FC Zwolle † §1	34	20	10	4	69	27	69
Helmond Sport †	34	17	8	9	61	43	59
BV Veendam † §4	34	15	12	7	54	44	53
Cambuur-L'warden † §3	34	15	9	10	64	52	51
FC Volendam †	34	14	9	11	56	50	51
Go Ahead Eagles †	34	13	11	10	58	43	50
FC Den Bosch †	34	11	14	9	56	47	47
Sparta Rotterdam	34	12	7	15	71	65	43
MVV Maastricht † §8	34	14	8	12	44	50	42
FC Dordrecht §4	34	12	9	13	52	56	41
FC Eindhoven	34	10	10	14	41	49	40
FC Emmen	34	8	11	15	48	64	35
Telstar	34	8	10	16	43	54	34
AGOVV Apeldoorn §9	34	11	7	16	54	77	31
Fortuna Sittard §2	34	7	7	20	42	70	26
RBC Roosendaal §3	34	7	8	19	38	66	26
Almere City §6	34	8	7	19	45	84	25

13/08/2010 - 6/05/2011 • † Qualified for Nacompetitie as stage winners • § = points deducted

MEDALS TABLE

		Overall			League			Cup			Europe		
		G	S	B	G	S	B	G	S	B	G	S	B
1	Ajax	54	30	14	30	21	11	18	5		6	3	3
2	PSV Eindhoven	31	20	18	21	13	14	8	7		2		4
3	Feyenoord	28	23	16	14	19	12	11	4		3		4
4	HVV Den Haag	9	3		8			1	3				
5	Sparta Rotterdam	9	2	5	6		5	3	2				
6	HBS Den Haag	5	5		3			2	5				
7	AZ Alkmaar	5	4	6	2	2	5	3	1			1	1
8	Willem II Tilburg	5	2	5	3	1	5	2	1				
9	Quick Den Haag	5			1			4					
10	Twente Enschede	4	8	9	1	3	7	3	4			1	2
11	ADO Den Haag	4	6	4	2		4	2	6				
	Go Ahead Eagles	4	6	4	4	5	4		1				
13	RCH Heemstede	4			2			2					
14	Roda JC Kerkrade	3	6		1	2		2	4				
15	Haarlem	3	3	1	1					1	2	3	
16	FC Utrecht	3	2	1			1	3	2				
17	RAP Amsterdam	3	1		2			1	1				
18	HFC Haarlem	3			3								
19	NAC Breda	2	7	3	1	4	3	1	3				
20	Fortuna Sittard	2	3	1	1	1		2	2				

KNVB BEKER 2010-11

Third Round

Team	Score
FC Twente Enschede	4
VV Capelle	1
Willem II Tilburg	2 4p
FC Zwolle *	2 5p
Rijnsburgse Boys *	4
SV Deurne	2
Flevo Boys *	0
Vitesse Arnhem	6
Roda JC Kerkrade	1 4p
Feyenoord *	1 3p
HSC '21 *	0
Go Ahead Eagles	2
SV Spakenburg *	0 5p
RBC Roosendaal	0 3p
Sparta Rotterdam	0
PSV Eindhoven *	3
FC Groningen	4
VV Haaglandia *	1
Excelsior '31 *	0
ADO Den Haag	2
Dijkse Boys	2 4p
RKSV Groene Ster *	2 1p
ACV	0
SC Genemuiden *	2
FC Volendam	2
HVV Hollandia *	1
NEC Nijmegen	3
FC Dordrecht *	4
AGOVV Apeldoorn	4
VV Gemert *	0
De Graafschap *	1 3p
FC Utrecht	1 4p
RKC Waalwijk *	4
Almere City	1
VVSB *	0
Cambuur-Leeuwarden	2
Heracles Almelo	3
ARC *	0
FC Oss	0
Achilles '29 *	2
Sparta Nijkerk *	2
Kozakken Boys	1
WKE *	0
Excelsior Rotterdam	3
De Treffers *	5
VV Katwijk	1
Voorschoten '97	1
VV Noordwijk *	3
NAC Breda *	3
VVV Venlo	1
FC Emmen *	1
SC Heerenveen	3
SDC Putten *	1 4p
DOVO	1 3p
Fortuna Sittard	1
Telstar *	3
AZ Alkmaar	3
FC Den Bosch *	2
EVV *	3
FC Eindhoven	5
BV Veendam *	2
Helmond Sport	1
MVV Maastricht	0
Ajax *	5

Fourth Round

Team	Score
FC Twente Enschede	1 5p
FC Zwolle *	1 3p
Rijnsburgse Boys	0
Vitesse Arnhem *	3
Roda JC Kerkrade	2
Go Ahead Eagles *	0
SV Spakenburg	0
PSV Eindhoven *	3
FC Groningen *	1 5p
ADO Den Haag	1 4p
Dijkse Boys *	1
SC Genemuiden	9
FC Volendam	2
FC Dordrecht *	1
AGOVV Apeldoorn *	0
FC Utrecht	2
RKC Waalwijk	4
Cambuur-Leeuwarden *	1
Heracles Almelo	3
Achilles '29 *	5
Sparta Nijkerk *	2
Excelsior Rotterdam	1
De Treffers *	0
VV Noordwijk	1
NAC Breda	2
SC Heerenveen *	0
SDC Putten *	0
Telstar	2
AZ Alkmaar *	3
FC Eindhoven	0
BV Veendam	0
Ajax *	3

Fifth Round

Team	Score
FC Twente Enschede *	5
Vitesse Arnhem	0
Roda JC Kerkrade *	1
PSV Eindhoven	3
FC Groningen	3
SC Genemuiden *	2
FC Volendam	0
FC Utrecht *	1
RKC Waalwijk	2 3p
Achilles '29 *	1 1p
Sparta Nijkerk *	3 3p
VV Noordwijk	3 4p
NAC Breda	1
Telstar *	0
AZ Alkmaar	0
Ajax *	1

* Home team • Professional clubs join in the third round

KNVB BEKER 2010-11

Quarter-finals	Semi-finals	Final

FC Twente Enschede *   1 7p
PSV Eindhoven   1 6p

  FC Twente Enschede *   1
  FC Utrecht   0

FC Groningen   2
FC Utrecht *   3

    FC Twente Enschede   3
    Ajax   2

RKC Waalwijk *   6
VV Noordwijk   0

  RKC Waalwijk   1
  Ajax *   5

KNVB BEKER FINAL 2011

Feijenoord Stadion, Rotterdam, 8-05-2011, 18:00, Att: 45 000, Ref: Blom

NAC Breda   1
Ajax *   4

FC Twente	3	Brama [45], Janssen [56], Janko [118]
Ajax	2	De Zeeuw [20], Ebecilio [40]

Twente - Sander Boschker - Peter Wisgerhof (Rasmus Bengtsson 100), Dwight Tiendalli, Bart Buysse, Douglas• - Denny Landzaat, Theo Janssen•, Wout Brama•, Nacer Chadli (Emir Bajrami 92) - Bryan Ruiz, Luuk de Jong• (Marc Janko 106). Tr: Michel Preud'homme
Ajax - Kenneth Vermeer - Jan Vertonghen, Gregory van der Wiel (Dario Cvitanich• 90), Vurnon Anita, Toby Alderweireld - Nicolai Boilesen (Daley Blind• 72), Demy de Zeeuw• (Eyong Enoh• 67), Siem de Jong, Christian Eriksen - Miralem Sulejmani, Lorenzo Ebecilio. Tr: Frank de Boer

CLUB BY CLUB GUIDE TO THE 2010-11 SEASON IN THE NETHERLANDS

ADO DEN HAAG 2010-11

Mon	Date	Opponent	Res	Score	Comp	Scorers	Att
Aug	8	Vitesse	L	1-3	ED	Immers 15	13 400
	15	Roda	L	1-3	ED	Kubik 4	9 859
	22	VVV	W	3-2	ED	Bulykin 2 2 61, Verhoek 88	7 000
	29	PSV	D	2-2	ED	Derijck 56, Kubik 80	11 334
Sep	12	Graafschap	D	2-2	ED	Bulykin 11, Visser 70	11 860
	18	Willem II	W	4-2	ED	Radosavljevic 37, Kubik 2 49 80, Bulykin 90	10 300
	21	Excelsior'31	W	2-0	KBr3	Immers 25, Bulykin 80	1 700
	25	Heracles	W	3-2	ED	Immers 29, Bulykin 2 44 70	14 120
Oct	3	Heerenveen	D	0-0	ED		25 400
	16	Excelsior	W	2-1	ED	Kubik 65, Bulykin 90	14 993
	24	Twente	L	2-3	ED	Bulykin 44, Kubik 54	23 800
	27	Groningen	L	1-3	ED	Immers 12	21 851
	31	Utrecht	W	1-0	ED	Immers 45	10 788
Nov	7	Ajax	W	1-0	ED	Verhoek 44	43 914
	11	Groningen	D	1-1	KBr4	Immers 63, L 4-5p	16 161
	14	NEC	D	1-1	ED	OG 39	12 400
	21	NAC	W	3-0	ED	Bulykin 5, Verhoek 49, Radosavljevic 65	14 500
	28	Feyenoord	L	1-2	ED	Bulykin 45	39 000
Dec	5	AZ	L	0-2	ED		12 000
	11	Roda	D	1-1	ED	Bulykin 13	12 900
	18	Willem II	W	2-1	ED	OG 2 10 52	8 931
Jan	21	Heerenveen	W	3-1	ED	Buijs 12, Vicento 53, Immers 78	11 000
	30	Excelsior	W	5-1	ED	Bulykin 2 20 41, Toornstra 52, Verhoek 65	2 480
Feb	5	PSV	W	1-0	ED	Verhoek 90	35 000
	12	VVV	W	3-0	ED	Toornstra 53, Bulykin 2 63p 83	15 000
	20	Feyenoord	D	2-2	ED	Vicento 81, Bulykin 85	15 000
	26	NAC	L	2-3	ED	Verhoek 25, OG 34	18 700
Mar	5	NEC	W	5-1	ED	Immers 16, Bulykin 28p, Verhoek 49, Toornstra 52, Brouwer 90	14 200
	13	Graafschap	L	0-1	ED		12 300
	20	Ajax	W	3-2	ED	Kubik 31, Immers 76, Derijck 87	15 000
Apr	3	Utrecht	W	3-2	ED	Vicento 39, Radosavljevic 63, Bulykin 66p	19 000
	9	Vitesse	W	1-0	ED	Buijs 28	14 700
	16	AZ	L	1-3	ED	Derijck 67	16 811
	22	Twente	L	1-2	ED	Bulykin 70	12 000
May	1	Groningen	L	2-4	ED	Bulykin 2 25 42p	14 800
	15	Heracles	L	0-3	ED		8 481
	19	Roda	W	4-2	ELpo	Immers 3, Kubik 14, Bulykin 23, Vicento 41	10 960
	22	Roda	W	2-1	ELpo	Pique 31, Verhoek 79	13 900
	26	Groningen	W	5-1	ELpo	Toornstra 3 20 52 71, Immers 66, Leeuwin 83	12 564
	29	Groningen	L	1-5	ELpo	Immers 37. L 3-4p	19 526

7th Att: 220 085 • Av: 12 946 (+10.3%) • Kyocera 15 000 (86%)

ADO LEAGUE APPEARANCES/GOALS 2010-11

Goalkeepers Gino Coutinho 33 • Robert Zwinkels 1
Defenders Ahmed Ammi MAR 18+2/0 • Pascal Bosschaart 18+3/0
Timothy Derijck BEL 33/3 • Christian Kum 27+2/0
Chiro N'Toko BEL 1+3/0 • Mitchell Pique 15+2/0 • Aleksandar
Rankovic SRB 0+3/0 • Christian Supusepa 1+2/0 • Kai van Hese 0+2/0
Midfield Danny Buijs 6+10/2 • Roderick Gielisse 0+4/0
Lex Immers 30/7 • Serhat Koksal TUR 0+1/0 • Ramon Leeuwin 27+3/0
Aleksander Radosavljevic SVN 28+2/3 • Jens Toornstra 34/3
Ricky van den Burgh 6+4/0 • Kevin Visser 3+15/1
Forwards Giorgio Achterberg 0+2/0 • Jarchinio Antonia 0+3/0 • Jordy
Brouwer 0+3/1 • Dmitriy Bulykin RUS 28+2/21 • Santy Hulst 0+1/0
Raily Ignacio 0+1/0 • Frantisek Kubik SVK 26+1/8
Wesley Verhoek 32/7 • Charlton Vicento 7+13/3
Coach John van den Brom

AJAX 2010-11

Mon	Date	Opponent	Res	Score	Comp	Scorers	Att
Jul	28	PAOK	D	1-1	CLp3	Suarez 13	24 151
	31	Twente	L	0-1	SC		25 000
Aug	4	PAOK	D	3-3	CLp3	Suarez 48, De Jong 50, Lindgren 55	24 109
	8	Groningen	D	2-2	ED	El Hamdaoui 2 52 61	22 050
	14	Vitesse	W	4-2	ED	Vertonghen 37, Van der Wiel 40, De jong 46, Anita 57	47 831
	17	Dy. Kyiv	D	1-1	CLpo	Vertonghen 57	16 500
	21	Roda	W	3-0	ED	El Hamdaoui 2 34 72	47 159
	25	Dy. Kyiv	W	2-1	CLpo	Suarez 43, El Hamdaoui 75	50 249
Sep	29	Graafschap	W	5-0	ED	Suarez 3 14 41 85, Emanuelson 69, Eriksen 89	12 550
	11	Willem II	W	2-0	ED	Suarez 2 33p 54p	47 702
	15	Real Madrid	L	0-2	CLgG		69 639
	19	Feyenoord	W	2-1	ED	De Jong 40, El Hamdaoui 57	40 000
	22	MVV	W	5-0	KBr3	El Hamdaoui 2 13 47, Jozefzoon 23, Vertonghen 44, Emanuelson 90	17 363
	25	Twente	D	2-2	ED	El Hamdaoui 15, Enoh 68	24 000
	28	Milan	D	1-1	CLgG	El Hamdaoui 23	51 276
	3	Utrecht	L	1-2	ED	De Jong 90	45 167
Oct	16	NAC	W	3-0	ED	Vertonghen 15, El Hamdaoui 30, Suarez 79	48 370
	19	Auxerre	W	2-1	CLgG	De Zeeuw 7, Suarez 41	51 383
	24	Excelsior	D	2-2	ED	El Hamdaoui 46, Vertonghen 89	3 540
	27	Heerenveen	W	3-1	ED	El Hamdaoui 2 11 47, Anita 84	47 612
	30	Heracles	W	4-1	ED	El Hamdaoui 16, Lindgren 55, Ooijer 78, Sulejmani 81	8 500
Nov	3	Auxerre	L	1-2	CLgG	Alderweireld 79	18 727
	7	ADO	L	0-1	ED		43 914
	11	Veendam	W	3-0	KBr4	Mido 60, Suarez 75, Eriksen 87	22 559
	14	AZ	L	0-2	ED		16 779
	20	PSV	W	0-0	ED		50 082
	23	Real Madrid	L	0-4	CLgG		48 491
	28	VVV	W	2-0	ED	Mido 62, Sulejmani 69	8 000
Dec	4	NEC	D	1-1	ED	Mido 75	22 000
	8	Milan	W	2-0	CLgG	De Zeeuw 57, Alderweireld 66	72 960
	12	Vitesse	W	1-0	ED	Eriksen 11	20 860
	23	AZ	W	1-0	KBr5	Sulejmani 43	29 539
	19	Feyenoord	W	2-0	ED	Alderweireld 31, Sulejmani 77p	51 322
	23	Utrecht	L	0-3	ED		21 000
Jan	27	NAC	W	4-1	KBqf	De Jong 17, Sulejmani 2 34p 83, Anita 82	22 536
	30	NAC	W	3-0	ED	De Jong 13, OG 67, Sulejmani 90	19 000
	4	Graafschap	W	2-0	ED	El Hamdaoui 43	49 137
Feb	13	Roda	D	2-2	ED	Sulejmani 13, De Jong 34	18 936
	17	Anderlecht	W	2-0	ELr2	Alderweireld 32, Eriksen 59, El Hamdaoui 11	21 195
	20	VVV	W	1-0	ED	El Hamdaoui 11	51 078
	24	Anderlecht	W	2-0	ELr2	Sulejmani 2 11 17	42 591
	27	PSV	D	0-0	ED		34 400
Mar	3	Waalwijk	W	5-1	KBsf	Ebecilio 13, El Handaoui 33, De Jong 2 55 85, De Zeeuw 58	28 156
	6	AZ	W	4-0	ED	De Zeeuw 5, De Jong 56, Ebecilio 72, Anita 89	48 328
	10	Sp. Moskva	L	0-1	ELr3		32 841
	13	Willem II	W	2-0	ED	De Jong 47, Vertonghen 80, Eriksen 88	13 500
	17	Sp. Moskva	L	0-3	ELr3		33 631
	20	ADO	L	2-3	ED	Vertonghen 70, Eriksen 85	15 000
Apr	3	Heracles	W	3-0	ED	Oleguer 59, De Jong 65, Ozbiliz 81	50 705
	10	Groningen	W	2-0	ED	Sulejmani 69, Vertonghen 72	51 050
	17	NEC	W	2-1	ED	Sulejmani 45, Alderweireld 66	12 500
	24	Excelsior	W	4-1	ED	Ebecilio 2 13 78, Eriksen 71, De Jong 90	51 185
May	1	Heerenveen	W	2-1	ED	Sulejmani 20, Eriksen 46	26 100
	8	Twente	L	2-3	KBf	De Jong 20, Ebecilio 40	45 000
	15	Twente	W	3-1	ED	De Jong 2 23 78, OG 46	51 738

1st Att: 804 380 • Av: 47 316 (-2.9%) • Amsterdam ArenA 52 960 (89%)

KEY

SC = Super Cup (played in Amsterdam ArenA)
ED = Eredivisie • KB = KNVB Beker
NC = Nacompetitie (relegation play-offs)
CL = UEFA Champions League • EL = Europa
League • See page 13 for further explanations

AZ ALKMAAR 2010–11

Mo	Date	Opponent		Score	Comp	Scorers	Att
Jy	29	IFK Gö'borg	W	2-0	ELp3	Klavan 52, Gudmundsson 56	11 563
	5	IFK Gö'borg	L	0-1	ELp3		10 115
	8	NAC	D	1-1	ED	Falkenburg 57	18 000
Aug	14	Groningen	D	1-1	ED	Martens 87	16 004
	19	Aktobe	W	2-0	ELpo	Holman 20, Wernbloom 27	10 385
	22	PSV	L	1-3	ED	Falkenburg 50	33 200
	26	Aktobe	L	1-2	ELpo	Wernbloom 10	12 600
	29	Excelsior	W	2-1	ED	Sigthorsson 76	15 949
	11	Roda	L	1-2	ED	Elm 27	15 652
	16	Sheriff	W	2-1	ELgE	Gudmundsson 14, Jaliens 82	10 624
Sep	19	NEC	W	1-0	ED	Jonathas 38	12 150
	22	Den Bosch	W	3-2	KBr3	Jonathas 2 32 50, Gudmundsson 34	4 656
	25	Utrecht	W	1-0	ED	Elm 42	16 090
	30	BATE	L	1-4	ELgE	Sigthorsson 89	12 153
	3	Heracles	W	2-1	ED	Sigthorsson 43, Jonathas 88	15 869
	16	VVV	W	1-0	ED	Pelle 90	7 500
	21	Dy. Kyiv	L	1-2	ELgE	Falkenburg 35	12 338
Oct	24	Willem II	W	3-0	ED	Jonathas 11p, Martens 35, Holman 55	16 248
	27	Graafschap	L	1-2	ED	Pelle 49	11 127
	31	Feyenoord	W	2-1	ED	Holman 45, Pelle 60	16 576
	4	Dy. Kyiv	L	0-2	ELgE		15 900
	7	Vitesse	D	1-1	ED	Pelle 47	16 000
Nov	10	Eindhoven	W	3-0	KBr4	Elm 11, Wernbloom 49, Klavan 90	6 523
	14	Ajax	W	2-0	ED	Wernbloom 73, Sigthorsson 77	16 779
	20	Twente	W	2-1	ED	Elm 32, Ortiz 63	23 800
	27	Heerenveen	D	2-2	ED	Wernbloom 7, Sigthorsson 90	16 523
	2	Sheriff	D	1-1	ELgE	Holman 17	3 500
	5	ADO	W	2-0	ED	Elm 39p, Martens 51	12 000
Dec	12	Groningen	L	0-2	ED		22 292
	15	BATE	W	3-0	ELgE	Sigthorsson 2 7 84, Maher 86	13 852
	23	Ajax	L	0-1	KBr5		29 539
	19	NEC	D	2-2	ED	Schaars 30, Falkenburg 35	16 019
Jan	22	Heracles	D	0-0	ED		8 456
	29	VVV	W	6-1	ED	Sigthorsson 5 5 13 26 47 69, Gudmundsson 50	16 128
	5	Excelsior	L	1-2	ED	Sigthorsson 12	3 540
Feb	12	PSV	L	0-4	ED		16 851
	19	Heerenveen	W	2-0	ED	Wernbloom 30, Moreno 68	25 500
	27	Twente	W	2-1	ED	OG 26, Falkenburg 90	16 782
	6	Ajax	L	0-4	ED		48 328
Mar	12	Roda	W	2-1	ED	Sigthorsson 52, Martens 74	14 290
	18	Vitesse	W	3-1	ED	Wernbloom 63, Poulsen 80, Martens 84	16 492
	2	Feyenoord	W	1-0	ED	Benschop 44	47 500
Apr	8	NAC	D	1-1	ED	Elm 32p	16 513
	16	ADO	W	3-1	ED	Sigthorsson 44, Holman 60, Van der Velden 86	16 811
	23	Willem II	L	1-2	ED	Sigthorsson 30	11 700
May	1	Graafschap	W	5-1	ED	Sigthorsson 2 17 52, Holman 45, Pelle 2 66 72	16 585
	15	Utrecht	L	1-5	ED	Martens 65	22 500

4th Att: 277 871 • Av: 16 345 (-0.9%) • AZ Stadion 17 150 (95%)

DE GRAAFSCHAP 2010–11

Mo	Date	Opponent		Score	Comp	Scorers	Att
	7	Excelsior	W	3-0	ED	Poepon 9, Nalbantoglu 60, De Ridder 84	10 995
Aug	14	PSV	L	0-6	ED		33 600
	21	Groningen	L	1-2	ED	Poepon 68	21 552
	29	Ajax	L	0-5	ED		12 550
	12	ADO	D	2-2	ED	Bargas 2 72 87	11 860
Sep	17	Heerenveen	W	3-2	ED	Nalbantoglu 32, Poepon 2 48 84	11 059
	22	Utrecht	D	1-1	KBr3	Overgoor 87, L 3-4p	4 120
	26	VVV	L	0-1	ED		8 000
	3	Feyenoord	D	1-1	ED	Bargas 20	12 550
	16	Utrecht	D	2-2	ED	Bargas 59, De Ridder 89	18 900
Oct	23	Heracles	D	1-1	ED	Hersi 15	11 379
	27	AZ	W	2-1	ED	Poepon 53, Bargas 87	11 127
	30	NAC	L	0-2	ED		18 250
	6	NEC	L	1-4	ED	Nalbantoglu 51	11 749
Nov	20	Roda	W	3-1	ED	Poepon 3 23 25 76	11 004
	24	Willem II	W	1-0	ED	Overgoor 81	8 000
	28	Vitesse	D	1-1	ED	Hersi 23	12 350
	4	Twente	L	0-2	ED		23 500
Dec	11	PSV	D	0-0	ED		12 550
	18	Heerenveen	L	0-4	ED		26 000
	22	Feyenoord	W	1-0	ED	Broekhof 88	41 000
Jan	1	Utrecht	D	0-0	ED		11 890
	4	Ajax	L	0-2	ED		49 137
Feb	13	Groningen	D	1-1	ED	Poepon 51	12 198
	20	Vitesse	L	0-2	ED		16 534
	26	Roda	D	1-1	ED	De Ridder 46	13 100
	4	Willem II	W	2-1	ED	Poepon 80, Bargas 87	12 250
Mar	13	ADO	W	1-0	ED	Poepon 10	12 300
	19	NEC	L	0-1	ED		12 300
	2	NAC	L	1-3	ED	Rose 74	12 250
Apr	9	Excelsior	D	0-0	ED		3 546
	17	Twente	D	1-1	ED	Meijer 89	12 580
	23	Heracles	L	0-2	ED		8 500
May	1	AZ	L	1-5	ED	Jungschlager 84	16 585
	15	VVV	W	1-0	ED	Poepon 6	12 030

14th Att: 202 811 • Av: 11 930 • De Vijverberg 12 600 (95%)

GRAAFSCHAP LEAGUE APPEARANCES/GOALS 2010-11
Goalkeepers Joost Terol 1 • Boy Waterman 33
Defenders Leon Broekhof 16+2/1 • Jordy Buijs 29/0 • Ties Evers 3+7/0
Purrel Frankel 29/0 • Jochem Jansen 1+1/0 • Tyrone Loran ANT 7/0
Muslu Nalbantoglu 15/3 • Jan-Paul Saeijs 10+4/0
Ted van der Pavert 0+2/0 • Vito Wormgoor 24+2/0
Midfield Gregor Breinburg 5+1/0 • Geoffrey Hairemans BEL 2+3/0
Youssouf Hersi 20+2/2 • Peter Jungschlager 30+1/1 • Lion Kaak 0+2/0
Jussi Kujala FIN 10+7/0 • Rogier Meijer 30/1 • Sjoerd Overgoor 4+14/1
Rik Sebens 1+9/0
Forwards Hugo Bargas ARG 16+14/6 • Kaye Coppoolse 1/0 • Steve De
Ridder BEL 23+8/3 • Soufian El Hassnaoui 0+4/0 • Rydell Poepon 32/12
Yuris Rose 32/1
Coach Darije Kalezic BIH

AJAX LEAGUE APPEARANCES/GOALS 2010-11
Goalkeepers Maarten Stekelenburg 26 • Jeroen Verhoeven 2+1 •
Kenneth Vermeer 6
Defenders Toby Alderweireld BEL 26/2 • Vurnon Anita 27+4/3 • Daley
Blind 8+2/0 • Nicolai Boilesen 5+1/0 • Oleguer ESP 2+1/1 • Andre
Ooijer 8+5/1 • Gregory van der Wiel 32/1 • Jan Vertonghen BEL 32/6
Midfield Ismail Aissati MAR 1+1/0 • Roly Bonevacia 1/0 • Siem
de Jong 31+1/12 • Demy de Zeeuw 19+8/1 • Urby Emanuelson 17+1/1
Eyong Enoh CMR 23+4/1 • Christian Eriksen DEN 21+7/6 • Rasmus
Lindgren SWE 7+8/1 • Jody Lukoki COD 0+2/0 • Teemu Tainio 1+1/0
Forwards Geoffrey Castillion 0+1/0 • Dario Cvitanich ARG 1+5/0
Lorenzo Ebecilio 14+2/3 • Mounir El Hamdaoui MAR 25+1/13 • Florian
Jozefzoon 0+4/0 • Mido EGY 1+4/2 • Aras Ozbiliz 3+11/1 • Luis Suarez
URU 13/7 • Miralem Sulejmani SRB 22+10/8 • Marvin Zeegelaar 0+2/0
Coach Martin Jol • Frank de Boer (6/12/10)

AZ LEAGUE APPEARANCES/GOALS 2010-11
Goalkeepers Esteban Alvarado CRC 6 • Joey Didulica CRO 5
Sergio Romero ARG 23
Defenders Kew Jaliens 4+4/0 • Ragnar Klavan EST 27+1/0
Dirk Marcellis 32/0 • Niklas Moisander FIN 29/0 • Hector
Moreno MEX 27/1 • Simon Poulsen DEN 8+6/1 • Gill Swerts BEL 0+1/0
Nick Viergever 11+5/0 • Giliano Wijnaldum 0+1/0
Midfield Rasmus Elm SWE 26+2/5 • Erik Falkenburg 13+6/4 • Brett
Holman AUS 25+1/4 • Adam Maher MAR 0+1/0 • Maarten
Martens BEL 19+5/6 • Celso Ortiz PAR 3+10/1 • Stijn Schaars 29/1
Nick van der Velden 0+10/1 • Pontus Wernbloom SWE 29/4
Forwards Charlison Benschop 7+9/1 • Johann Gudmundsson ISL
19+3/1 • Jonathas BRA 8+3/3 • Graziano Pelle ITA 5+13/6
Kolbeinn Sigthorsson ISL 19+13/15
Coach Gertjan Verbeek

EXCELSIOR ROTTERDAM 2010–11

	Date	Opponent	Res	Score	Comp	Scorers	Att
Aug	7	Graafschap	L	0-3	ED		10 995
	15	Feyenoord	W	3-2	ED	Fernandez 2 29 90, Bovenberg 77	3 600
	20	NEC	W	4-2	ED	Clasie 53, Bovenberg 56, Bergkamp 78, Fernandez 90	3 158
	29	AZ	D	1-1	ED	Fernandez 35	15 949
Sep	11	Heracles	W	2-1	ED	Bergkamp 60, Van Steensel 76	3 000
	18	Groningen	L	0-2	ED		21 300
	22	WKE	W	3-0	KBr3	Fernandez 2 3 11, Nieveld 55	1 500
	26	Vitesse	L	0-2	ED		3 156
Oct	2	Roda	L	1-2	ED	Gudde 38	3 214
	16	ADO	L	1-2	ED	Vincken 45p	14 993
	24	Ajax	D	2-2	ED	Bovenberg 37, Wattamaleo 42	3 540
	27	Utrecht	L	0-2	ED		16 000
	30	Heerenveen	L	0-2	ED		3 514
Nov	6	Twente	L	1-2	ED	Van Steensel 2	23 700
	9	Nijkerk	L	1-2	KBr4	Bovenberg 41	1 900
	13	PSV	L	2-4	ED	Bovenberg 6, Fernandez 70	33 400
	20	VVV	W	1-0	ED	Bergkamp 75	3 000
	27	Willem II	D	1-1	ED	Ramsteijn 51	10 500
Dec	12	Feyenoord	L	0-1	ED		37 500
	15	NAC	L	1-3	ED	Vincken 84	3 188
	18	Groningen	D	2-2	ED	Koolwijk 49p Bovenberg 89	3 045
Jan	23	Roda	L	0-3	ED		12 500
	30	ADO	L	1-5	ED	Vincken 13	2 480
Feb	5	AZ	W	2-1	ED	Vincken 65p, Clasie 79	3 540
	13	NEC	L	0-2	ED		12 000
	19	Willem II	W	4-0	ED	Roorda 2 18 50p, Lagouireh 83, Fernandez 85	3 000
	25	VVV	L	0-1	ED		7 500
Mar	5	PSV	L	2-3	ED	Fernandez 22, De Graaf 90p	3 624
	12	Heracles	L	1-4	ED	Fernandez 75	8 472
	20	Twente	L	0-2	ED		3 540
Apr	2	Heerenveen	W	3-2	ED	Roorda 2 76 81, Lagouireh 90	25 800
	9	Graafschap	D	0-0	ED		3 546
	16	NAC	W	2-1	ED	Bergkamp 20, Fernandez 47	19 000
	24	Ajax	L	1-4	ED	Bovenberg 54	51 185
	1	Utrecht	W	3-1	ED	Roorda 2 25 65, Bergkamp 31	3 546
	15	Vitesse	W	4-1	ED	Fernandez 33, Roorda 2 78p 85, Vincken 90	15 855
	19	Den Bosch	D	3-3	NCsf	Bergkamp 41, Vincken 2 83 84	5 033
May	22	Den Bosch	W	3-1	NCsf	Roorda 19, Koolwijk 85p, Bovenberg 88	3 186
	26	Helmond	W	5-1	NCf	Bergkamp 4, Koolwijk 53p, Fernandez 66, Wattamaleo 71, De Graaf 83	4 200
	29	Helmond	W	4-2	NCf	Bovenberg 2 45 60, Fernandez 2 57 70	3 361

16th Att: 55 691 • Av: 3 276 • Woudestein 3 531 (92%)

FEYENOORD 2010–11

	Date	Opponent	Res	Score	Comp	Scorers	Att
Aug	8	Utrecht	W	3-1	ED	OG 52, Bruins 64, Fer 75	38 000
	15	Excelsior	L	2-3	ED	Vlaar 41, OG 74	3 600
	19	Gent	W	1-0	ELpo	Fer 78	22 500
	22	Heracles	D	1-1	ED	Wijnaldum 71	8 500
	26	Gent	L	0-2	ELpo		8 787
Sep	29	Vitesse	W	4-0	ED	Leerdam 20, Fer 30, Castaignos 75, Wijnaldum 83p	43 000
	12	NAC	L	0-2	ED		17 850
	19	Ajax	L	1-2	ED	Andre Bahia 80	40 000
	22	Roda	D	1-1	KBr3	Cisse 83	24 000
	26	NEC	L	0-3	ED		12 400
Oct	3	Graafschap	D	1-1	ED	Bruins 31p	12 550
	16	Twente	L	0-1	ED		43 000
	24	PSV	L	0-10	ED		33 900
	27	VVV	W	3-0	ED	Wijnaldum 2 65 90, Andre Bahia 83	41 600
	31	AZ	L	1-2	ED	Castaignos 69	16 576
Nov	7	Roda	D	1-1	ED	Castaignos 87	38 000
	14	Heerenveen	D	2-2	ED	Castaignos 11, Cabral 81	39 000
	21	Groningen	L	0-2	ED		21 905
	28	ADO	W	2-1	ED	OG 47, Castaignos 59	39 000
Dec	5	Willem II	D	1-1	ED	Leerdam 36	12 000
	12	Excelsior	W	1-0	ED	Castaignos 21	37 500
	19	Ajax	L	0-2	ED		51 322
Jan	22	Graafschap	L	0-1	ED		41 000
	30	Twente	L	1-2	ED	Swerts 51	23 800
Feb	6	Vitesse	D	1-1	ED	Castaignos 56	15 441
	12	Heracles	W	2-1	ED	Miyaichi 18, Biseswar 33	47 000
	20	ADO	D	2-2	ED	Castaignos 2 30 38	15 000
	27	Groningen	W	5-1	ED	Wijnaldum 4 23 31 48p 83p, Vlaar 87	43 000
Mar	6	Heerenveen	W	1-0	ED	Castaignos 78	26 000
	13	NAC	W	2-1	ED	Castaignos 29, De Vrij 89	46 000
	20	Roda	L	0-3	ED		17 155
	2	AZ	L	0-1	ED		47 500
Apr	10	Utrecht	W	4-0	ED	Fer 8, Leerdam 32, Biseswar 58, Wijnaldum 65	19 000
	17	Willem II	W	6-1	ED	Wijnaldum 2 27 74, Miyaichi 2 29 81, Martins 55, Castaignos 57p	47 000
	24	PSV	W	3-1	ED	Wijnaldum 2 27 83, Castaignos 79	46 000
May	1	VVV	L	2-3	ED	Wijnaldum 68, Castaignos 75	7 500
	15	NEC	D	1-1	ED	Castaignos 43	39 000

10th Att: 716 100 • Av: 42 124 (-4.1%) • Stadion Feijenoord 51 577 (81%)

EXCELSIOR LEAGUE APPEARANCES/GOALS 2010-11
Goalkeepers Cees Paauwe 24 • Nico Pellatz GER 9 • Lex van Haeften 1
Defenders Daan Bovenberg 31/6 • Tim Eekman 3+2/0 • Wouter Gudde 5+12/1 • Miquel Nelom 32/0 • Norichio Nieveld 33/0 • Kaj Ramsteijn 22+3/1 • Leen van Steensel 16+8/2 • Tobias Waisapij 2+3/0
Midfield Adnan Alisic 4+6/0 • Benjamin Baltes GER 5+5/0 • Jordy Clasie 30+2/2 • Edwin de Graaf 4+1/1 • Shabir Isoufi 0+4/0 • Ryan Koolwijk 33/1 • Jerson Ribeiro 0+4/0 • Geert Roorda 11+2/8 Kevin Wattamaleo 19+8/1
Forwards Roland Bergkamp 21+7/5 • Guyon Fernandez 30+1/10 Andrea Fileccia BEL 2+4/0 • Nayib Lagouireh BEL 4+26/2 • Andras Simon HUN 0+1/0 • Tim Vincken 22+2/5 • Marvin Zeegelaar 11+1/0
Coach Alex Pastoor

FEYENOORD LEAGUE APPEARANCES/GOALS 2010-11
Goalkeepers Erwin Mulder 17 • Rob van Dijk 17+1
Defenders Andre Bahia BRA 19+1/2 • Tim de Cler 27+2/0 • Stefan de Vrij 29+1/1 • Kelvin Leerdam 20+2/3 • Michael Lumb DEN 0+2/0 • Bruno Martins 12+3/1 • Gill Swerts BEL 10/1 • Ron Vlaar 26/2
Midfield Adil Auassar 0+3/0 • Luigi Bruins 18+2/2 • Karim El Ahmadi 13+2/0 • Leroy Fer 16+7/3 • Marcel Meeuwis 13/0 • Kamohelo Mokotjo RSA 13+1/0 • Ricky van Haaren 4+8/0 Georginio Wijnaldum 34/14
Forwards Diego Biseswar 21+2/2 • Jerson Cabral 6+17/1 • Luc Castaignos 29+5/15 • Sekou Cisse CIV 0+1/0 • Soren Larsen DEN 0+6/0 Ryo Miyaichi JPN 12/3 • Ruben Schaken 8+3/0 • Krisztian Simon HUN 4+4/0 • Fedor Smolov RUS 5+6/0 • Jhon van Beukering 1+2/0
Coach Mario Been

FC GRONINGEN 2010–11

Mon	Date	Opponent	Res	Score	Comp	Scorers	Att
Aug	8	Ajax	D	2-2	ED	Matavz 72, Pedersen 86	22 050
	14	AZ	D	1-1	ED	Sparv 76	16 004
	21	Graafschap	W	2-1	ED	Granqvist 17p, Enevoldsen 32	21 552
	27	Willem II	W	3-0	ED	Hiariej 37, Enevoldsen 65, Pedersen 67	12 000
Sep	12	Utrecht	W	1-0	ED	Granqvist 85p	21 353
	18	Excelsior	W	2-0	ED	Pedersen 51, Matavz 73	21 300
	22	Haaglandia	W	4-1	KBr3	Ivens 70, Garcia 95, Van de Laak 110, Matavz 113	1 750
	25	PSV	D	1-1	ED	Garcia-Garcia 88	33 200
Oct	3	Twente	L	2-4	ED	Granqvist 28p, Matavz 75	23 800
	17	Heerenveen	W	1-0	ED	Granqvist 46	22 435
	23	NEC	L	2-3	ED	Enevoldsen 70, Andersson 90	12 250
	27	ADO	W	3-1	ED	Ivens 48, Granqvist 58, Van de Lak 89	21 851
Nov	30	VVV	W	5-3	ED	Matavz 2 8 66, Garcia-Garcia 26, OG 59, Van de Lak 75	7 500
	6	NAC	W	2-1	ED	Granqvist 2 17p 44p	21 856
	11	ADO	D	1-1	KBr4	Ivens 83. W 5-4p	16 161
	14	Heracles	L	0-3	ED		8 500
	21	Feyenoord	W	2-0	ED	Matavz 2 13 84	21 905
	27	Roda	L	0-1	ED		13 850
Dec	3	Vitesse	W	4-1	ED	Granqvist 53p, Matavz 63, Andersson 66, Sparv 80	22 099
	12	AZ	W	2-0	ED	Matavz 2 11 90	22 292
	18	Excelsior	D	2-2	ED	Tadic 7, OG 29	3 045
	18	Genemuiden	W	3-2	KBr5	Hiariej 36, Enevoldsen 2 45 62	3 500
Jan	23	Twente	L	1-2	ED	Matavz 33	22 466
	26	Utrecht	L	2-3	KBqf	Matavz 18, Granqvist 49p	10 400
	30	Heerenveen	W	4-1	ED	Ivens 13, Matavz 25, Tadic 2 56 90	26 100
Feb	6	Willem II	W	7-1	ED	Granqvist 26, Stenman 33, Matavz 3 44 55p 71, Enevoldsen 73, Tadic 84	22 091
	13	Graafschap	D	1-1	ED	Holla 32	12 198
	19	Roda	L	1-4	ED	Pedersen 88	22 013
	27	Feyenoord	L	1-5	ED	Pedersen 41	43 000
Mar	6	Heracles	L	1-4	ED	Tadic 12	22 069
	11	Utrecht	L	0-1	ED		19 000
	19	NAC	W	1-0	ED	Granqvist 72	19 000
	3	VVV	W	3-2	ED	Tadic 16, Granqvist 22, Pedersen 45	22 078
Apr	10	Ajax	L	0-2	ED		51 050
	16	Vitesse	L	1-2	ED	Holla 65	17 128
	24	NEC	W	3-1	ED	Enevoldsen 20, Tadic 83, Matavz 89	22 073
	1	ADO	W	4-2	ED	Andersson 2 13 52, Stenman 29, Hiariej 86	14 800
May	15	PSV	D	0-0	ED		22 152
	19	Heracles	L	2-3	ELpo	Ivens 17, Bacuna 57	8 113
	22	Heracles	W	2-1	ELpo	Andersson 29, Ajilore 47	16 059
	26	ADO	L	1-5	ELpo	Ivens 63	12 564
	29	ADO	W	5-1	ELpo	Matavz 2 24 89p, Van Dijk 2 49 59, Bacuna 57, L 3-4p	19 526

5th — Att: 373 635 • Av: 21 979 (+0.4%) • Euroborg 22 579 (97%)

SC HEERENVEEN 2010–11

Mon	Date	Opponent	Res	Score	Comp	Scorers	Att
Aug	7	PSV	L	1-3	ED	Kopic 63	26 100
	14	Twente	D	0-0	ED		23 800
	21	NAC	W	3-1	ED	Dost 2 26 77, OG 59	26 000
	28	NEC	D	2-2	ED	Grindheim 51, Beerens 87	12 150
	11	Vitesse	W	2-1	ED	Beerens 88p, Assaidi 90	26 000
Sep	17	Graafschap	L	2-3	ED	Grindheim 23, Assaidi 54	11 059
	21	Emmen	W	3-1	KBr3	Elm 69, Dost 82, Vayrynen 86	3 127
	25	Roda	D	2-2	ED	Dost 2 15 35	25 800
	3	ADO	D	0-0	ED		25 400
Oct	17	Groningen	L	0-1	ED		22 435
	23	VVV	W	2-0	ED	Dost 50, Vayrynen 53	25 700
	27	Ajax	L	1-3	ED	Dost 25	47 612
	30	Excelsior	W	2-0	ED	Dost 75, Assaidi 88	3 514
Nov	6	Heracles	W	3-2	ED	Breuer 25, Beerens 40p, OG 90	25 500
	9	NAC	L	0-2	KBr4		19 600
	14	Feyenoord	D	2-2	ED	Vayrynen 53	39 000
	21	Willem II	W	5-0	ED	Vayrynen 18, Breuer 2 40 81, Beerens 2 57 61p	25 500
	27	AZ	D	2-2	ED	Vayrynen 53, Janmaat 81	16 523
Dec	5	Utrecht	L	1-2	ED	Beerens 24p	18 211
	12	Twente	W	6-2	ED	Assaidi 3 20 38 86, Elm 63, Narsingh 74, Vayrynen 89p	26 000
	18	Graafschap	W	4-0	ED	Elm 11, Djuricic 34, Narsingh 2 44 66	26 000
Jan	21	ADO	L	1-3	ED	Dost 76	11 000
	30	Groningen	L	1-4	ED	Djuricic 68	26 100
Feb	5	NEC	D	0-0	ED		26 000
	13	NAC	W	2-0	ED	Narsingh 60, Assaidi 82	18 200
	19	AZ	L	0-2	ED		25 500
	26	Willem II	L	3-4	ED	Janmaat 6, Dost 25, Vayrynen 73	11 500
	6	Feyenoord	L	0-1	ED		26 000
Mar	12	Vitesse	D	1-1	ED	Janmaat 87	15 577
	19	Heracles	L	2-4	ED	Vayrynen 35, Haglund 67	8 487
	2	Excelsior	L	2-3	ED	Breuer 2, Dost 31	25 800
Apr	10	PSV	D	2-2	ED	Assaidi 70, Dost 73	33 700
	15	Utrecht	W	3-0	ED	Assaidi 3 18, Narsingh 29, Dost 77	25 000
	23	VVV	D	2-2	ED	Vayrynen 45, Dost 90	7 500
May	1	Ajax	L	1-2	ED	Vayrynen 19	26 100
	15	Roda	D	0-0	ED		15 470

12th — Att: 438 500 • Av: 25 794 (+0.4%) • Abe Lenstra 26 800 (96%)

GRONINGEN LEAGUE APPEARANCES/GOALS 2010-11
Goalkeepers Luciano BRA 30 • Brian Van Loo 4
Defenders Andreas Granqvist SWE 32/11 • Tom Hiariej 21+6/2 • Jonas Ivens BEL 33/2 • Darryl Lachman 2+4/0 • Fredrik Stenman SWE 34/2 • Virgil van Dijk 0+2/0 • Jeroen Voldmato 3 1+3/0
Midfield Oluwafemi Ajilore NGA 4+14/0 • Petter Andersson SWE 6+11/4 Leandro Bacuna 11+13/0 • Thomas Enevoldsen DEN 26+6/5 • Danny Holla 16+4/2 • Maikel Kieftenbeld 29+2/0 • Shkodran Metaj 0+4/0 Tim Sparv FIN 31/2 • Dusan Tadic SRB 34/7
Forwards Gonzalo Garcia-Garcia ESP 8+7/2 • Norair Mamedov 0+5/0 Tim Matavz SVN 24+5/16 • Nicklas Pedersen DEN 21+1/6 Danny Post 0+1/0 • Koen van de Laak 5+11/2
Coach Pieter Huistra

HEERENVEEN LEAGUE APPEARANCES/GOALS 2010-11
Goalkeepers Kenny Steppe BEL 5 • Kevin Stuhr-Ellegaard DEN 28 Brian Vandenbussche BEL 1
Defenders Michel Breuer 31+1/4 • Igor Djuric SRB 4+2/0 • Youssef Fl Akchanui 5+1/0 • Jeffrey Gouweleeuw 6/0 • Daryl Janmaat 20+4/3 Gerry Koning 14+1/0 • Milan Kopic CZE 6+1/1 • Arnold Kruiswijk 21/0
Midfield Filip Djuricic SRB 12+11/2 • Viktor Elm SWE 23+6/3 Christian Grindheim NOR 30/2 • Philip Haglund SWE 5+9/1 • Calvin Jong-a-Pin 28+1/0 • Tobias Kainz AUT 0+1/0 • Quentenm Martinus 0+1/0 • Gert Roorda 0+4/0 • Michal Svec CZE 12+8/0 Mika Vayrynen FIN 30/9
Forwards Ousama Assaidi MAR 30+1/9 • Roy Beerens 23+5/6 • Bas Dost 22+10/13 • Tarik Elyounoussi MAR 1+1/0 • Samir Fazli MKD 0+9/0 Luciano Narsingh 16+8/5 • Michal Papadopulos CZE 1+3/0
Coach Ron Jans

HERACLES ALMELO 2010-11

Aug	7	Willem II	W	3-0	ED	Vejinovic 3, Plet 2 86 90	8 465
	14	VVV	L	0-1	ED		7 200
	22	Feyenoord	D	1-1	ED	Looms 15	8 500
	28	Roda	L	2-4	ED	Vejinovic 64, Overtoom 74	12 240
Sep	11	Excelsior	L	1-2	ED	Fledderus 36	3 000
	19	Twente	D	0-0	ED		8 500
	22	ARC	W	3-0	KBr3	Plet 29, Overtoom 2 34 45	2 500
	25	ADO	L	2-3	ED	Plet 17, Everton 66	14 120
	3	AZ	L	1-2	ED	Overtoom 41	15 869
Oct	17	NEC	W	3-2	ED	Overtoom 45p, Everton 69, Armenteros 88	8 500
	23	Graafschap	D	1-1	ED	Plet 53	11 379
	26	NAC	W	4-1	ED	Armenteros 2, Fledderus 8, Overtoom 28p, Plet 80	8 425
	30	Ajax	L	1-4	ED	Overtoom 38	8 500
Nov	6	Heerenveen	L	2-3	ED	Overtoom 70p, Everton 76	25 500
	11	Achilles	L	3-5	KBr4	Douglas 2 2 51, Everton 30	1 000
	14	Groningen	W	3-0	ED	Armenteros 41, Everton 73, Looms 84	8 500
	20	Vitesse	L	0-2	ED		16 000
	28	Utrecht	W	2-1	ED	OG 55, Overtoom 84p	8 346
Dec	4	PSV	L	2-5	ED	Everton 2 27 62	32 900
	10	VVV	D	2-2	ED	Everton 37, Armenteros 42	8 406
	19	Twente	L	0-5	ED		23 800
Jan	22	AZ	D	0-0	ED		8 456
	28	NEC	D	1-1	ED	Fledderus 63	12 250
	6	Roda	W	1-0	ED	Overtoom 52	8 420
	12	Feyenoord	L	1-2	ED	Fledderus 45	47 000
Feb	18	Utrecht	D	1-1	ED	Cairo 89	19 000
	26	Vitesse	W	6-1	ED	Looms 39, Everton 49, Fledderus 59, Overtoom 2 69p 75p, OG 83	8 475
Mar	6	Groningen	W	4-1	ED	Everton 2 42 65, Armenteros 2 44 89	22 069
	12	Excelsior	W	4-1	ED	Fledderus 32, Quansah 50, Looms 62, Plet 90	8 472
	19	Heerenveen	W	4-2	ED	Everton 20, Armenteros 44, Van der Linden 57, Douglas 59	8 487
Apr	3	Ajax	L	0-3	ED		50 705
	9	Willem II	W	6-2	ED	Everton 3 6 40 58, Overtoom 2 45p 88, Quansah 90	11 700
	17	PSV	L	0-2	ED		8 416
	23	Graafschap	W	2-0	ED	Everton 41, Overtoom 90	8 500
May	1	NAC	W	2-1	ED	Fledderus 70, Plet 74	18 800
	15	ADO	W	3-0	ED	Overtoom 2 72p 85, Armentoros 88	8 481
	19	Groningen	W	3-2	ELpo	Armenteros 2 5 56, Douglas 16	8 113
	22	Groningen	L	1-2	ELpo	Plet 87	16 059

8th Att: 143 849 • Av: 8 462 (+0.05%) • Polman 8 500 (99%)

NAC BREDA 2010-11

Aug	8	AZ	D	1-1	ED	Amoah 79	18 000
	15	Utrecht	L	1-3	ED	Amoah 25	18 000
	21	Heerenveen	L	1-3	ED	Amoah 1	26 000
	28	VVV	W	2-0	ED	Amoah 11, Gorter 26	17 250
	12	Feyenoord	W	2-0	ED	Schilder 2 84 90	17 850
	18	Vitesse	D	0-0	ED		13 450
Sep	23	VVV	W	3-1	KBr3	Leonardo 11, Amoah 67, Boussaboun 82	8 700
	26	Willem II	W	2-1	ED	Luijckx 65, Kolkka 80	18 350
	2	NEC	W	2-0	ED	Amoah 30, Idabdelhay 88	18 059
	16	Ajax	L	0-3	ED		48 370
Oct	22	Roda	L	1-2	ED	Kolkka 36	18 100
	26	Heracles	L	1-4	ED	Luijckx 85	8 425
	30	Graafschap	W	2-0	ED	Penders 58, Gorter 90p	18 250
	6	Groningen	L	1-2	ED	OG 2	21 856
Nov	9	Heerenveen	W	2-0	KBr4	Amoah 48, Schilder 54	19 600
	13	Twente	W	2-1	ED	Boussaboun 81, Amoah 90	18 450
	21	ADO	L	0-3	ED		14 500
	26	PSV	W	4-2	ED	Leonardo 30, Amoah 2 41 79, Boussaboun 50	19 000
Dec	11	Utrecht	W	3-1	ED	Feher 12, OG 56, Luijckx 67	18 400
	15	Excelsior	W	3-1	ED	Amoah 38, Schilder 75, Boussaboun 90	3 188
	18	Vitesse	D	1-1	ED	Gudelj 58	18 000
Jan	18	Telstar	W	1-0	KBr5	Luijckx 27	2 563
	22	NEC	D	2-2	ED	Gudelj 77, Van der Pluijm 90	12 150
	27	Ajax	L	1-4	KBqf	Idabdelhay 8	22 536
	30	Ajax	L	0-3	ED		19 000
Feb	5	VVV	L	0-3	ED		8 000
	13	Heerenveen	L	0-2	ED		18 200
	20	PSV	L	1-4	ED	Lurling 64	33 000
	26	ADO	W	3-2	ED	Schilder 2 4 47, Feher 61	18 700
Mar	5	Twente	L	0-2	ED		23 800
	13	Feyenoord	L	1-2	ED	Jenner 59	46 000
	19	Groningen	L	0-1	ED		19 000
	2	Graafschap	W	3-1	ED	Leonardo 29, Lurling 79, Gorter 85p	12 250
Apr	8	AZ	D	1-1	ED	Gorter 58p	16 513
	16	Excelsior	L	1-2	ED	Boussaboun 26	19 000
	23	Roda	L	1-5	ED	Kolkka 43	14 836
May	1	Heracles	L	1-2	ED	Amoah 18	18 800
	15	Willem II	W	1-0	ED	Jenner 89	11 250

13th Att: 312 409 • Av: 18 377 (+8.6%) • Rat Verlegh 19 000 (96%)

HERACLES LEAGUE APPEARANCES/GOALS 2010-11
Goalkeepers Remko Pasveer 34
Defenders Gaby Jallo SYR 0+1/0 • Mark Looms 31/4 • Birger Maertens BEL 32/0 • Peter Reekers 2+3/0 • Mike te Wierik 2+2/0 • Olivier ter Horst 1+3/0 • Antoine van der Linden 34/1
Midfield Alexander Bannink 0+4/0 • Tim Breukers 32/0 • Thomas Bruns 0+1/0 • Mark Jan Fledderus 27+4/7 • Xander Houtkoop 1+5/0 • Willy Overtoom 35/15 • Kwame Quansah GHA 32/2 • Andrej Rendla SVK 3+7/0 • Ben Rienstra 2+10/0 • Marko Vejinovic 15+12/2
Forwards Anmar Almubaraki IRQ 0+3/0 • Samuel Armenteros SWE 27+5/8 • Ellery Cairo 0+6/1 • Darl Douglas 28+3/1 • Everton BRA 30+3/15 • Glynor Plet 7+15/7
Coach Peter Bosz

NAC BREDA LEAGUE APPEARANCES/GOALS 2010-11
Goalkeepers Jelle ten Rouwelaar 34
Defenders Nemanja Gudelj SRB 19+9/2 • Gabor Horvath HUN 19/0 • Jens Janse 13+4/0 • Milano Koenders 17+7/0 • Tyrone Loran ANT 7+3/0 • Rob Penders 29/1 • Ferne Snoyl 1/0
Midfield Pim Bouwman 0+1/0 • Csaba Feher HUN 22+3/2 • Tim Gilissen 13+5/0 • Donny Gorter 26+5/4 • Kees Kwakman 4/0 • Kees Luijckx 29/3 • Robbert Schilder 32/5 • Marvin van der Pluijm 0+1/0
Forwards Matthew Amoah GHA 27+1/10 • Omer Bayram 1+5/0 • Ali Boussaboun MAR 16+7/4 • Fouad Idabdelhay 5+12/1 • Julian Jenner 3+8/2 • Joonas Kolkka FIN 16+4/3 • Leonardo BRA 23+2/2 • Anthony Lurling 18+4/2 • Alex Schalk 0+1/0
Coach Robert Maaskant • Gert Aandewiel (21/08/10)

NEC NIJMEGAN 2010–11

	Date	Opponent	Res	Comp	Scorers	Att
Aug	7	VVV	W 1-0	ED	Zomer 50	12 250
	15	Willem II	W 5-3	ED	Schone 17, Sibum 67, Vleminckx 3 55p 62 90	11 300
	20	Excelsior	L 2-4	ED	Vleminckx 32, Sibum 73	3 158
	28	Heerenveen	D 2-2	ED	George 48, Schone 50	12 150
Sep	11	PSV	L 1-3	ED	Goossens 39	33 000
	19	AZ	L 0-1	ED		12 150
	23	Dordrecht	L 3-4	KBr3	Chatelle 6, Vleminckx 55, Schone 90	2 200
	26	Feyenoord	W 3-0	ED	Schone 19, Ten Voorde 83, Nuytinck 90	12 400
Oct	2	NAC	L 0-2	ED		18 059
	17	Heracles	L 2-3	ED	Davids 74, Schone 79p	8 500
	23	Groningen	W 3-2	ED	Vleminckx 3 4 11 77	12 250
	26	Roda	D 1-1	ED	Vleminckx 73	12 775
	31	Vitesse	D 0-0	ED		12 500
Nov	6	Graafschap	W 4-1	ED	Will 21, Vleminckx 3 48 61 84	11 749
	14	ADO	D 1-1	ED	Zomer 90	12 400
	21	Utrecht	L 0-4	ED		19 000
	27	Twente	L 2-4	ED	Sibum 9, Vleminckx 74	12 500
Dec	4	Ajax	L 1-1	ED	Nuytinck 78	22 000
	11	Willem II	W 3-1	ED	Vleminckx 11, Schone 55, Goossens 66	12 200
Jan	19	AZ	D 2-2	ED	Vleminckx 2 22 77	16 019
	22	NAC	D 2-2	ED	Vleminckx 39, Goossens 79	12 150
	28	Heracles	D 1-1	ED	Vleminckx 52	12 250
Feb	5	Heerenveen	D 0-0	ED		26 000
	13	Excelsior	W 2-0	ED	Zimling 2 66 80	12 000
	20	Twente	D 1-1	ED	Zimling 7	23 800
	27	Utrecht	D 1-1	ED	Goossens 8	12 150
Mar	5	ADO	L 1-5	ED	Vleminckx 18	14 200
	13	PSV	D 2-2	ED	George 40, Zomer 90	12 300
	19	Graafschap	W 1-0	ED	George 2	12 300
Apr	3	Vitesse	L 1-2	ED	Goossens 66	16 377
	9	VVV	W 4-1	ED	Davids 22, Goossens 2 58 81, Vleminckx 61	7 500
	17	Ajax	L 1-2	ED	Schone 4	12 500
	24	Groningen	L 1-3	ED	Zimling 25	22 073
May	1	Roda	W 5-0	ED	Vleminckx 4 19 55 70 90, Amieux 29	12 500
	15	Feyenoord	D 1-1	ED	Schone 12	39 500

11th Att: 208 950 • Av: 12 291 (-0.8%) • De Goffert 12 470 (98%)

NEC LEAGUE APPEARANCES/GOALS 2010-11
Goalkeepers Gabor Babos HUN 3 • Jasper Cillessen 31
Defenders Remy Amieux FRA 18+2/1 • Bram Nuytinck 31+2/2 • Rens van Eijden 10+4/0 • Mark Otten 12+9/0 • Niels Wellenberg 1+4/0 Nathaniel Will 28/1 • Ramon Zomer 34/3
Midfield Thomas Chatelle BEL 13+14/0 • Lorenzo Davids 26+3/2 John Goossens 28+3/7 • Youri Loen 0+1/0 • Lasse Schone DEN 34/7 Bas Sibum 29+1/3 • Niki Zimling DEN 26/4
Forwards Erton Fejzullahu SWE 1+7/0 • Leroy George 15+7/3 Cayfano Latupeirissa 1+9/0 • Rick ten Voorde 1+15/1 Bjorn Vleminckx BEL 32/23
Coach Wiljan Vloet

PSV EINDHOVEN 2010–11

	Date	Opponent	Res	Comp	Scorers	Att
Aug	7	Heerenveen	W 3-1	ED	Toivonen 2 52 82, Engelaar 90	26 100
	14	Graafschap	W 6-0	ED	Dzsudzsak 4p, Toivonen 3 26 46 55, Amrabat 79, Afellay 84	33 600
	19	Sibir	L 0-1	ELpo		11 500
	22	AZ	W 3-1	ED	Berg 2 43 52, Afellay 90	33 220
	26	Sibir	W 5-0	ELpo	Berg 38, Engelaar 58, Toivonen 63, Dzsudzsak 2 74 90p	20 900
	29	ADO	D 2-2	ED	Derijck 56, Kubik 80	11 334
Sep	11	NEC	W 3-1	ED	Koevermans 46, Afellay 63, Toivonen 69	33 000
	16	Sampdoria	D 1-1	ELgl	Dzsudzsak 90	17 500
	19	Roda	D 0-0	ED		15 690
	22	Sparta	W 3-0	KBr3	Koevermans 2 13 90, Nijland 89	11 000
	25	Groningen	D 1-1	ED	Toivonen 63	33 200
	30	Metalist	W 2-0	ELgl	Dzsudzsak 27p, Berg 30	38 100
Oct	3	VVV	W 3-0	ED	Jonathan 2 55 77, Bouma 62	33 700
	17	Willem II	W 4-2	ED	Dzsudzsak 3, Lens 16, Afellay 44, Jonathan 52	12 500
	21	Debreceni	W 2-1	ELgl	Engelaar 40, Jonathan 66	18 000
	24	Feyenoord	W 10-0	ED	Jonathan 3 24 47 59, Afellay 39, Toivonen 49, Lens 2 55 87, Dzsudzsak 2 62 77p, Engelaar 69	33 900
	27	Vitesse	W 2-0	ED	Jonathan 32, Dzsudzsak 60p	14 148
	30	Twente	L 0-1	ED		34 300
Nov	4	Debreceni	W 3-0	ELgl	Afellay 2, Jonathan 44, Wuytens 88	15 000
	7	Utrecht	W 2-1	ED	Dzsudzsak 2 25 75p	20 461
	10	Spakenburg	W 3-0	KBr4	Koevermans 45, Engelaar 52, Amrabat 65	28 900
	13	Excelsior	W 4-2	ED	Lens 19, Bouma 34, Toivonen 50, Marcelo 78	33 400
	20	Ajax	D 0-0	ED		50 082
	26	NAC	L 2-4	ED	Jonathan 15, Dzsudzsak 33	19 000
Dec	1	Sampdoria	W 2-1	ELgl	Toivonen 2 51 90	12 131
	4	Heracles	W 5-2	ED	Dzsudzsak 36, Toivonen 2 40 74, Afellay 87, Berg 90	32 900
	11	Graafschap	D 0-0	ED		12 550
	16	Metalist	D 0-0	ELgl		15 300
Jan	19	Roda	W 3-1	ED	Lens 5, Berg 53, Dzsudzsak 68	34 000
	22	Roda	W 3-1	KBr5	Toivonen 27, Berg 55, Dzsudzsak 72	6 200
	23	VVV	W 3-0	ED	Bouma 14, Lens 45, Hutchinson 46	8 000
	26	Twente	D 1-1	KBqf	Koevermans 90, L 6-7p	21 000
	29	Willem II	W 2-1	ED	Toivonen 48, Zeefuik 90	32 500
	5	ADO	L 0-1	ED		35 000
Feb	12	AZ	W 4-0	ED	Berg 2 9 77, Dzsudzsak 2 31 66	16 851
	17	Lille	D 2-2	ELr2	Bouma 83, Toivonen 84	16 951
	20	NAC	W 4-1	ED	Dzsudzsak 25, Lens 66, Toivonen 73, Maza 82	33 000
	24	Lille	W 3-1	ELr2	Dzsudzsak 55, Lens 67	28 000
	27	Ajax	D 0-0	ED		34 400
Mar	5	Excelsior	W 3-2	ED	Lens 50, Hutchinson 52, Dzsudzsak 90p	3 624
	10	Rangers	D 0-0	ELr3		26 000
	13	NEC	D 2-2	ED	Dzsudzsak 44, Lens 64	12 300
	17	Rangers	W 1-0	ELr3	Lens 14	35 373
	20	Utrecht	W 1-0	ED	Bakkal 54	33 600
Apr	2	Twente	L 0-2	ED		24 200
	7	Benfica	L 1-4	ELqf	Labyad 80	60 026
	10	Heerenveen	D 2-2	ED	Lens 58, Toivonen 90	33 700
	14	Benfica	D 2-2	ELqf	Dzsudzsak 17, Lens 25	29 500
	17	Heracles	W 2-0	ED	Dzsudzsak 25, Berg 90	8 416
	24	Feyenoord	L 1-3	ED	Toivonen 60	46 000
May	1	Vitesse	W 2-1	ED	Berg 37, Marcelo 63	34 000
	15	Groningen	D 0-0	ED		22 152

3rd Att: 571 400 • Av: 33 612 (+0.5%) • Philips Stadion 35 119 (95%)

PSV LEAGUE APPEARANCES/GOALS 2010-11
Goalkeepers Cassio BRA 0+2 • Andreas Isaksson SWE 34
Defenders Wilfred Bouma 25+1/3 • Stanislav Manolev BUL 20+1/0 Morpolo BRA 26+2/2 • Maza MEX 14+8/2 • Frik Pieters 31/0 Abel Tamata 3/0 • Jagos Vukovic SRB 3+1/0
Midfield Ibrahim Afellay 16+3/7 • Otman Bakkal 12+13/1 Balazs Dzsudzsak HUN 33/16 • Orlando Engelaar 29+1/2 • Atiba Hutchinson CAN 33/2 • Zakaria Labyad 5+2/0 • Funso Ojo BEL 0+2/0 Stijn Wuytens BEL 2+6/0
Forwards Nordin Amrabat 0+6/1 • Marcus Berg SWE 17+8/8 Jonathan BRA 10+1/8 • Danny Koevermans 3+11/1 • Jeremain Lens 31+2/10 • Stefan Nijland 0+4/0 • Ola Toivonen SWE 26+2/15 Genero Zeefuik 1+6/1
Coach Fred Rutten

RODA JC KERKRADE 2010–11

Mon	Day	Opponent	Res	Score	Comp	Scorers	Att
Aug	6	Twente	D	0-0	ED		13 180
	15	ADO	W	3-1	ED	Junker 9p, Delorge 12, Hempte 70	9 859
	21	Ajax	L	0-3	ED		47 159
	28	Heracles	W	4-2	ED	Skoubo 2 6 7, Delorge 19, Junker 80	12 240
Sep	11	AZ	W	2-1	ED	Delorge 6, Janssen 52	15 652
	19	PSV	D	0-0	ED		15 690
	22	Feyenoord	D	1-1	KBr3	Delorge 63. W 4-3p	24 000
	25	Heerenveen	D	2-2	ED	Djoum 69, Junker 75	25 800
Oct	2	Excelsior	W	2-1	ED	Kah 69, Hadouir 88	3 214
	17	Vitesse	W	4-1	ED	Djoum 31, Junker 2 32 36, Janssen 50	13 958
	22	NAC	W	2-1	ED	Djoum 59, Hempte 78	18 100
	26	NEC	D	1-1	ED	Djoum 50	12 775
	31	Willem II	D	2-2	ED	Janssen 2 9 68	13 063
Nov	7	Feyenoord	D	1-1	ED	Junker 24	38 000
	10	GA Eagles	W	2-0	KBr4	Huysegems 72, Meulens 74	3 738
	20	Graafschap	L	1-3	ED	Huysegems 45	11 004
	24	Utrecht	D	1-1	ED	Vormer 25	13 280
	27	Groningen	W	1-0	ED	Djoum 40	13 850
Dec	11	ADO	D	1-1	ED	Janssen 9	12 900
	14	VVV	W	4-0	ED	Janssen 3, Delorge 22, Junker 2 29 80	8 000
	19	PSV	L	1-3	ED	Hadouir 24	34 000
	22	PSV	L	1-3	KBr5	Vormer 42	6 200
Jan	23	Excelsior	W	3-0	ED	Hempte 14, Kah 28, Skoubo 84	12 500
	29	Vitesse	L	2-5	ED	Junker 69	13 277
Feb	6	Heracles	L	0-1	ED		8 420
	13	Ajax	D	2-2	ED	Junker 40, Hadouir 82	18 936
	9	Groningen	W	4-1	ED	Junker 3 15 61 71, Bodor 90	22 013
	26	Graafschap	D	1-1	ED	Skoubo 25	13 100
Mar	1	Utrecht	D	1-1	ED	Junker 32p	19 000
	6	AZ	L	1-2	ED	Junker 72	14 290
	20	Feyenoord	W	3-0	ED	Hadouir 7, Junker 43, OG 90	17 155
	2	Willem II	W	5-4	ED	Kah 49, Skoubo 62, Vormer 2 64 83, De Fauw 75	12 000
Apr	10	Twente	D	1-1	ED	Bodor 76	23 800
	16	VVV	W	5-2	ED	Wielaert 5, Junker 3 15 30 56, Kah 60	16 300
	23	NAC	W	5-1	ED	Hempte 14, Skoubo 17, Junker 2 27 54p, Hadouir 65	14 836
May	1	NEC	L	0-5	ED		12 500
	15	Heerenveen	D	0-0	ED		15 470
	19	ADO	L	2-4	EDpo	Skoubo 27, Meulens 78	10 960
	22	ADO	L	1-2	EDpo	Skoubo 15	13 900

6th Att: 243 523 • Av: 14 325 (-2.9%) • Parkstad Limburg 19 979 (71%)

FC TWENTE 2010–11

Mon	Day	Opponent	Res	Score	Comp	Scorers	Att
Jul	31	Ajax	W	1-0	SC	De Jong 8	25 000
Aug	6	Roda	D	0-0	ED		13 180
	14	Heerenveen	D	0-0	ED		23 800
	21	Vitesse	W	3-0	ED	Janko 58, De Jong 2 66 90	12 422
	29	Utrecht	W	4-0	ED	Janko 2 64 72, De Jong 2 78 84	23 500
Sep	11	VVV	W	2-1	ED	Ruiz 29, Rosales 70	7 000
	14	Inter	D	2-2	CLgG	Janssen 20, OG 30	23 800
	19	Heracles	D	0-0	ED		8 500
	22	Capelle	W	4-1	KBr3	Parker 40, Ruiz 54p, Chadli 58, De Jong 80	2 800
	25	Ajax	D	2-2	ED	Jansen 2 11 62	24 000
	29	Tottenham	L	1-4	CLgG	Chadli 56	32 318
Oct	3	Groningen	W	4-2	ED	Ruiz 2 30 49p, Janko 72, Janssen 88	23 800
	16	Feyenoord	W	1-0	ED	Landzaat 78	43 000
	20	W Bremen	D	1-1	CLgG	Janssen 75	23 248
	24	ADO	W	3-2	ED	Janssen 27, Ruiz 57p, Janko 69	23 800
	27	Willem II	W	3-1	ED	De Jong 2 28 64, Douglas 37	10 400
	30	PSV	W	1-0	ED	Chadli 60	34 300
Nov	2	W Bremen	W	2-0	CLgG	Chadli 81, De Jong 84	30 200
	6	Excelsior	W	2-1	ED	Chadli 26, Janko 75	23 700
	9	Zwolle	D	1-1	KBr4	Chadli 81. W 5-3p	10 500
	13	NAC	L	1-2	ED	Ruiz 21	18 450
	20	AZ	L	1-2	ED	De Jong 17	23 800
	24	Inter	L	0-1	CLgG		29 466
	27	NEC	W	4-2	ED	Ruiz 2 18 44p, Janko 2 40 79	12 500
Dec	4	Graafschap	W	2-0	ED	Janssen 2 7 69	23 500
	7	Tottenham	D	3-3	CLgG	Landzaat 22p, Rosales 56, Chadli 64	24 000
	12	Heerenveen	L	2-6	ED	Chadli 2 32 51	26 000
	21	Vitesse	W	5-0	KBr5	Janssen 2 29 37, De Jong 2 32p 60, Chadli 44	23 000
Jan	19	Heracles	W	5-0	ED	Janko 4 4 45 60 70, De Jong 39	23 800
	23	Groningen	W	2-1	ED	Janko 2 40 81	22 466
	26	PSV	D	1-1	KBqf	Janssen 70p. W 7-6p	21 000
	30	Feyenoord	W	2-1	ED	Brama 76, Ruiz 90	23 800
Feb	6	Utrecht	D	1-1	ED	Chadli 50	21 767
	12	Vitesse	W	1-0	ED	Chadli 39	23 750
	17	Rubin	W	2-0	ELr2	De Jong 77, Wisgerhof 88	657
	20	NEC	D	1-1	ED	Bajrami 27	23 800
	24	Rubin	D	2-2	ELr2	Janssen 45, Douglas 47	23 000
	27	AZ	L	1-2	ED	De Jong 88	16 782
Mar	2	Utrecht	W	1-0	KBsf	Janko 77	21 800
	5	NAC	W	2-0	ED	De Jong 61, Chadli 90	23 800
	10	Zenit	W	3-0	ELr3	De Jong 2 25 90, Landzaat 56	20 750
	13	VVV	W	2-1	ED	Brama 30, John 83	23 800
	17	Zenit	L	0-2	ELr3		18 000
	20	Excelsior	W	2-0	ED	Janssen 2 37 68p	3 540
	2	PSV	W	2-0	ED	Janssen 2 64p 82	24 200
Apr	7	Villarreal	L	1-5	ELqf	Janko 90	19 094
	10	Roda	D	1-1	ED	Janssen 85p	23 800
	14	Villarreal	L	1-3	ELqf	Bajrami 32	23 500
	17	Graafschap	D	1-1	ED	Landzaat 72	12 580
	22	ADO	W	2-1	ED	Ruiz 61, De Jong 85	12 000
May	1	Willem II	W	4-0	ED	De Jong 39, Douglas 50, OG 63, Janssen 77p	24 000
	8	Ajax	W	3-2	KBf	Brama 45, Janssen 56, Janko 118	45 000
	15	Ajax	L	1-3	ED	Janssen 47	51 738

2nd Att: 404 650 • Av: 23 803 (+0.6%) • De Grolsch Veste 24 244 (98%)

RODA JC LEAGUE APPEARANCES/GOALS 2010-11

Goalkeepers Mateusz Prus POL 6 • Przemyslaw Tyton POL 27 Collin van Eijk 1+1
Defenders Davy de Fauw BEL 31/1 • Jimmy Hempte BEL 30/5 • Eelco Horsten 0+4/0 • Pa-Modou Kah NOR 32/4 • Vincent Lachambre BEL 3/0 Ruud Vormer 33/3 • Rob Wielaert 30/1
Midfield Eric Addo GHA 9+4/0 • Boldiszar Bodor HUN 11+15/2 Laurent Delorge BEL 24+1/4 • Arnaud Djoum BEL 19+9/5 • Anouar Hadouir 29/5 • Guus Hupperts 0+2/0 • Willem Janssen 34/6 Sebastian Svard DEN 4+2/0
Forwards Stijn Huysegems BEL 2+11/1 • Mads Junker DEN 32+1/21 Rihairo Meulens 3+15/0 • Wiljan Pluim 0+12/0 • Morten Skoubo DEN 14+6/6 • Aleksandar Stankov MKD 0+1/0 Jeanvion Yulu-Matondo BEL 0+1/0
Coach Harm van Veldhoven BEL

FC TWENTE LEAGUE APPEARANCES/GOALS 2010-11

Goalkeepers Sander Boschker 3+1 • Nikolai Mihailov BUL 31
Defenders Rasmus Bengtsson SWE 8+2/0 • Bart Buysse BEL 10+4/0 Douglas BRA 28/2 • Nicky Kuiper 3+1/0 • Thilo Leugers GER 7+1/0 Oguchi Onyewu USA 7+1/0 • Roberto Rosales VEN 27+2/1 Dwight Tiendalli 13+5/0 • Peter Wisgerhof 31+1/0
Midfield Emir Bajrami SWE 11+1/2 • Alexander Bannink 0+2/0 Steven Berghuis 0+1/0 • Wout Brama 30+1/2 • Arnold Bruggink 0+6/0 David Carney AUS 2+1/0 • Nacer Chadli BEL 30+3/7 Anouar Diba 0+1/0 • Theo Janssen 29+1/13 • Denny Landzaat 19+8/2 Michael Schimpelsberger AUT 3+1/0 • Cheik Tiote CIV 2/0 Dario Vujicevic GER 2+4/0
Forwards Luuk de Jong 31+1/12 • Marc Janko AUT 22+7/14 • Ola John 3+10/1 • Bernard Parker RSA 1+2/0 • Bryan Ruiz CRC 24+3/9
Coach Michel Preud'homme BEL

FC UTRECHT 2010–11

	Date	Opponent	Res	Score	Comp	Scorers	Att
Jul	15	Tiranë	W	4-0	ELp2	Van Wolfswinkel 2 8 27, Asare 30, Mertens 75	9 900
	22	Tiranë	D	1-1	ELp2	Van Wolfswinkel 3	3 000
	29	Luzern	W	1-0	ELp3	Mertens 35	12 100
Aug	5	Luzern	W	3-1	ELp3	Asare 12, Van Wolfswinkel 22, Silberbauer 28	7 125
	8	Feyenoord	L	1-3	ED	Van Wolfswinkel 12	38 000
	15	NAC	W	3-1	ED	Van Wolfswinkel 2 13 81p, Mertens 46	18 000
	19	Celtic	L	0-2	ELpo		35 755
	22	Willem II	W	3-0	ED	Van Wolfswinkel 2 22p 27, Mertens 27	20 000
	26	Celtic	W	4-0	ELpo	Van Wolfswinkel 3 12p 19p 46, Maguire 62	18 240
	29	Twente	L	0-4	ED		23 500
Sep	12	Groningen	L	0-1	ED		21 353
	16	Napoli	D	0-0	ELgK		25 897
	19	VVV	W	3-2	ED	Van Wolfswinkel 2 27p 78, Asare 84	18 100
	22	Graafschap	D	1-1	KBr3	Mulenga 69	4 120
	25	AZ	L	0-1	ED		16 090
	30	Liverpool	D	0-0	ELgK		23 662
Oct	3	Ajax	W	2-1	ED	Van Wolfswinkel 2 6p 14p	45 167
	16	Graafschap	D	2-2	ED	Wuytens 3, Mulenga 13	18 900
	21	Steaua	D	1-1	ELgK	Duplan 60	23 300
	24	Vitesse	W	4-1	ED	OG 3, Mertens 45, Cornelisse 51, Mulenga 56	13 684
	27	Excelsior	W	2-0	ED	Mulenga 6, Van Wolfswinkel 90	16 000
	31	ADO	L	0-1	ED		10 788
Nov	4	Steaua	L	1-3	ELgK	Mertens 33	16 210
	7	PSV	L	1-2	ED	Demouge 81	20 461
	20	AGOVV	W	2-0	KBr4	Duplan 62, Demouge 76	2 880
	21	NEC	W	4-0	ED	Van Wolfswinkel 21p, Duplan 84, Nesu 85, Demouge 90	19 000
	24	Roda	D	1-1	ED	Duplan 61	13 280
	28	Heracles	L	1-2	ED	Cornelisse 73	8 346
Dec	2	Napoli	D	3-3	ELgK	Van Wolfswinkel 2 6 28p, Demouge 35	24 117
	5	Heerenveen	W	2-1	ED	Mertens 34, Wuytens 90	18 211
	11	NAC	L	1-3	ED	Silberbauer 9	18 400
	15	Liverpool	D	0-0	ELgK		37 878
	22	Volendam	W	1-0	KBr5	Maguire 88	10 000
Jan	19	VVV	W	2-1	ED	Demouge 37, Yildirim 90	7 500
	23	Ajax	W	3-0	ED	Duplan 2 22 24, Vorstermans 82	21 000
	26	Groningen	W	3-2	KBqf	Wuytens 12, Mertens 32p, Asare 53	10 400
Feb	1	Graafschap	D	0-0	ED		11 890
	6	Twente	D	1-1	ED	De Kogel 37	21 767
	12	Willem II	D	3-3	ED	Mertens 2 23 55, Vorstermans 90	11 300
	18	Heracles	D	1-1	ED	Van Wolfswinkel 3	19 000
	27	NEC	D	1-1	ED	Van Wolfswinkel 74	12 150
Mar	2	Twente	L	0-1	KBsf		21 800
	6	Roda	D	1-1	ED	De Kogel 82	19 000
	11	Groningen	W	1-0	ED	Demouge 60	19 000
	20	PSV	L	0-1	ED		33 600
Apr	3	ADO	L	2-3	ED	Duplan 34, Strootman 77	19 000
	10	Feyenoord	L	0-4	ED		19 000
	15	Heerenveen	L	0-3	ED		25 000
	24	Vitesse	W	4-2	ED	OG 51, Mertens 52, Strootman 60, Demouge 73	20 500
May	1	Excelsior	L	1-3	ED	Demouge 87	3 546
	15	AZ	W	5-1	ED	Mertens 3 10 12 85, Van Wolfswinkel 2 83 87	22 500

9th | Att: 329 439 • Av: 19 379 (-8.3%) • Galgenwaard 24 426 (79%)

VITESSE ARNHEM 2010–11

	Date	Opponent	Res	Score	Comp	Scorers	Att
Aug	8	ADO	W	3-1	ED	Pluim 45, Nilsson 2 57p 71p	13 400
	14	Ajax	L	2-4	ED	Propper 26, Van Ginkel 43	47 831
	21	Twente	L	0-3	ED		12 422
	29	Feyenoord	L	0-4	ED		43 000
Sep	11	Heerenveen	L	1-2	ED	Propper 76	26 000
	18	NAC	D	0-0	ED		13 450
	21	Flevo Boys	W	6-0	KBr3	Aissati 2 7 16, Barazite 2 49 85, Nilsson 63, Stevanovic 80	3 250
	26	Excelsior	W	2-0	ED	Stevanovic 50, Aissati 62	3 156
Oct	1	Willem II	D	0-0	ED		13 150
	17	Roda	L	1-4	ED	Jenner 58	13 958
	24	Utrecht	L	1-4	ED	Pedersen 61	13 684
	27	PSV	L	0-2	ED		14 148
	31	NEC	D	0-0	ED		12 500
Nov	7	AZ	D	1-1	ED	Aissati 90	16 000
	10	Rijnsburgse	W	3-0	KBr4	Barazite 25, Jenner 45, Propper 78	7 211
	14	VVV	W	5-1	ED	Pluim 11, Jenner 31, Pedersen 2 85 86, Aissati 89	8 000
	20	Heracles	W	2-0	ED	Propper 5, Stevanovic 86	16 000
	28	Graafschap	D	1-1	ED	Pluim 27	12 350
Dec	3	Groningen	L	1-4	ED	Pedersen 79	22 099
	12	Ajax	L	0-1	ED		20 860
	18	NAC	D	1-1	ED	Jenner 30	18 000
	21	Twente	L	0-5	KBr5		23 000
	22	Willem II	L	0-1	ED		11 600
Jan	29	Roda	W	5-2	ED	Matic 16, Van Ginkel 2 23 58, Lopez 45p, Babangida 55	13 277
Feb	6	Feyenoord	D	1-1	ED	Aissati 63p	15 441
	12	Twente	L	0-1	ED		23 750
	20	Graafschap	W	2-0	ED	Bony 72, Matic 84	16 534
	26	Heracles	L	1-6	ED	Kashia 90	8 475
Mar	5	VVV	W	2-0	ED	Van Ginkel 48, OG 90	13 574
	12	Heerenveen	D	1-1	ED	Riverola 43	15 577
	18	AZ	L	1-3	ED	Van Ginkel 44	16 492
	3	NEC	W	2-1	ED	Bony 12, Pedersen 80	16 377
Apr	9	ADO	L	0-1	ED		14 700
	16	Groningen	W	2-1	ED	Bony 71, Kashia 82	17 128
	24	Utrecht	L	2-4	ED	Kashia 54, Tighadouini 86	20 500
	1	PSV	L	1-2	ED	Lopez 79	34 000
May	15	Excelsior	L	1-4	ED	Riverola 62	15 855

15th | Att: 256 877 • Av: 15 110 (-10.9%) • GelreDome 25 000 (60%)

VITESSE LEAGUE APPEARANCES/GOALS 2010-11

Goalkeepers Eloy Room 33 • Piet Velthuizen 1
Defenders Luca Caldirola ITA 8+3/0 • Jeroen Drost 6+1/0 • Guram Kashia GEO 28/3 • Slobodan Rajkovic SRB 24/0 • Civard Sprockel 10/0 • Frank van der Struijk 24+1/0 • Michihiro Yasuda JPN 15/0
Midfield Ismail Aissati MAR 28+1/4 • Alexander Buttner 22+2/0 • Gino Felixdaal 3+4/0 • Ted Heijckman 0+2/0 • Laryea Kingston GHA 1+2/0 • Jordi Lopez ESP 15/2 • Marti Riverola ESP 15/2 • Nemanja Matic SRB 26+1/2 • Rogier Molhoek 0+1/0 • Hayri Pinarci 0+2/0 • Davy Propper 23+6/3 • Dalibor Stevanovic SVN 17+6/2 • Marco van Ginkel 16+10/5
Forwards Haruna Babangida NGA 5+4/0 • Nacer Barazite 5+4/0 • Wilfried Bony CIV 6+1/3 • Roy de Ruiter 0+1/0 • Julian Jenner 10+4/3 • Lasse Nilsson SWE 11+2/2 • Marcus Pedersen NOR 5+11/5 • Wiljan Pluim 10+6/3 • Genaro Snijders 7+8/0 • Adnane Tighadouini 0+2/0
Coach Theo Boss • Albert Ferrer ESP (27/10/10)

UTRECHT LEAGUE APPEARANCES/GOALS 2010-11

Goalkeepers Khali Sinouh MAR 1 • Michel Vorm 33
Defenders Davy Bulthuis 1/0 • Tim Cornelisse 32/2 • Sander Keller 1+2/0 • Gevero Markiet 0+1/0 • Mihai Nesu ROU 26+2/1 • Alje Schut 25+2/0 • Mark van de Maarel 3+2/0 • Mike van der Hoorn 0+1/0 • Ismo Vorstermans 9+1/2 • Jan Wuytens BEL 32/2
Midfield Zakaria Amrani 0+1/0 • Nana Asare GHA 17+1/1 • Jacob Lensky CAN 25+2/0 • Barry Maguire 7+9/0 • Gianluca Nijholt 5+12/0 • Adam Sarota AUS 2+4/0 • Michael Silberbauer DEN 27/1 • Kevin Strootman 14/2 • Michael Zullo AUS 4+2/0
Forwards Evert Brouwers 0+3/0 • Erixon Danso 1+3/0 • Leon de Kogel 2+10/2 • Frank Demouge 12+8/6 • Edouard Duplan FRA 29+1/5 • Anouar Kali 0+2/0 • Loic Loval-Landre FRA 0+1/0 • Dries Mertens BEL 30+1/10 • Jacob Mulenga ZAM 7+2/3 • Tommy Oar AUS 3+4/0 • Ricky van Wolfswinkel 26+3/15 • Attila Yildirim 0+2/1
Coach Ton du Chatinier

VVV VENLO 2010–11

	Opponent	Res		Scorers	Att
Aug	7 NEC	L	0-1	ED	12 250
Aug	14 Heracles	W	1-0	ED	Boymans [11]	7 200
Aug	22 ADO	L	2-3	ED	Ahahaoui [23], Boymans [90]	7 000
Aug	28 NAC	L	0-2	ED		17 250
Sep	11 Twente	L	1-2	ED	Paauwe [42p]	7 000
Sep	19 Utrecht	L	2-3	ED	Boymans 2 [16 72]	18 100
Sep	21 NAC	L	1-3	KBr3	Toth [34]	8 700
Sep	26 Graafschap	W	1-0	ED	Boymans [42]	8 000
Oct	3 PSV	L	0-3	ED		33 700
Oct	16 AZ	L	0-1	ED		7 500
Oct	23 Heerenveen	L	0-2	ED		25 700
Oct	27 Feyenoord	L	0-3	ED		41 600
Oct	30 Groningen	L	3-5	ED	Toth [12], Ahahaoui [50p], Uchebo [86]	7 500
Nov	5 Willem II	W	4-1	ED	Boymans 2 [24p 50], Toth [53], Viana [75]	11 000
Nov	14 Vitesse	L	1-5	ED	Boymans [77p]	8 000
Nov	20 Excelsior	L	0-1	ED		3 000
Nov	28 Ajax	L	0-2	ED		8 000
Dec	10 Heracles	D	2-2	ED	Boymans [62], Uchebo [90]	8 406
Dec	14 Roda	L	0-4	ED		8 000
Dec	19 Utrecht	L	1-2	ED	Leemans [38]	7 500
Jan	23 PSV	L	0-3	ED		8 000
Jan	29 AZ	L	1-6	ED	Musa [37]	16 128
Feb	5 NAC	W	3-0	ED	Musa [2], Chula [58], Ahahaoui [88]	8 000
Feb	12 ADO	L	0-3	ED		15 000
Feb	20 Ajax	L	0-1	ED		51 078
Mar	25 Excelsior	W	1-0	ED	Cullen [1]	7 500
Mar	5 Vitesse	L	0-2	ED		13 574
Mar	13 Twente	L	1-2	ED	De Regt [3]	23 800
Mar	19 Willem II	D	0-0	ED		7 500
Apr	3 Groningen	L	2-3	ED	Vujicevic [41], Cullen [59]	22 078
Apr	9 NEC	L	1-4	ED	Musa [90p]	7 500
Apr	16 Roda	L	2-5	ED	Timisela [84], Uchebo [86]	16 300
Apr	23 Heerenveen	D	2-2	ED	Boymans 2 [86 88]	7 500
Apr	1 Feyenoord	W	3-2	ED	Musa 2 [34 71], Uchebo [80]	7 500
May	15 Graafschap	L	0-1	ED		12 030
May	19 Volendam	W	2-1	NCsf	Cullen [42], Musa [89]	3 122
May	22 Volendam	W	2-0	NCsf	Cullen [6], Boymans [64]	5 500
May	26 Zwolle	W	2-1	NCf	Uchebo 2 [70 79]	8 305
May	29 Zwolle	D	2-2	NCf	Toth [45p], Musa [87]	7 800

17th   Att: 129 200 • Av: 7 600 (+1.8%) • De Koel 8 000 (95%)

WILLEM II TILBURG 2010–11

	Opponent	Res		Scorers	Att
Aug	7 Heracles	L	0-3	ED		8 465
Aug	15 NEC	L	3-5	ED	Hakola [6], Demouge [29], Lasnik [69p]	11 300
Aug	22 Utrecht	L	0-3	ED		20 000
Sep	27 Groningen	L	0-3	ED		12 000
Sep	11 Ajax	L	0-2	ED		47 702
Sep	18 ADO	L	2-4	ED	Rigters [5], Levchenko [52]	10 300
Sep	21 Zwolle	D	2-2	KBr3	Rigters [61], V.d Heijden [83], L 4-5p	6 250
Sep	26 NAC	L	1-2	ED	Landgren [7]	18 350
Oct	1 Vitesse	D	0-0	ED		13 150
Oct	17 PSV	L	2-4	ED	Landgren [10], OG [32]	12 500
Oct	24 AZ	L	0-3	ED		16 248
Oct	27 Twente	L	1-3	ED	Van Zaanen [15]	10 400
Oct	31 Roda	D	2-2	ED	Lasnik [21], Sheotahul [90]	13 063
Nov	5 VVV	L	1-4	ED	Rigters [86]	11 000
Nov	21 Heerenveen	L	0-5	ED		25 500
Nov	24 Graafschap	L	0-1	ED		8 000
Nov	27 Excelsior	D	1-1	ED	Levchenko [89]	10 500
Dec	5 Feyenoord	D	1-1	ED	OG [84]	12 000
Dec	11 NEC	L	1-3	ED	Lasnik [38p]	12 200
Dec	18 ADO	L	1-2	ED	Biemans [51]	8 931
Jan	22 Vitesse	W	1-0	ED	Janga [26]	11 600
Jan	29 PSV	L	1-2	ED	Biemans [17]	32 500
Feb	6 Groningen	L	1-7	ED	Lasnik [51p]	22 091
Feb	12 Utrecht	D	3-3	ED	Van der Heijden [24], Hakola [31], Rigters [89]	11 300
Feb	19 Excelsior	L	0-4	ED		3 000
Feb	26 Heerenveen	W	4-3	ED	Biemans [66], Swinkels [70], Van der Heijden [84], Rigters [89]	11 500
Mar	4 Graafschap	L	1-2	ED	Hakola [78]	12 250
Mar	13 Ajax	L	1-3	ED	Janga [19]	13 500
Mar	19 VVV	D	0-0	ED		7 500
Apr	2 Roda	L	4-5	ED	Lasnik 2 [30p 80], Biemans [57], Rigters [90]	12 000
Apr	9 Heracles	L	2-6	ED	Lasnik [4p], Halilovic [82]	11 700
Apr	17 Feyenoord	L	1-6	ED	Lasnik [20]	47 000
Apr	23 AZ	W	2-1	ED	Lasnik [5], Levchenko [63]	11 700
May	1 Twente	L	0-4	ED		24 000
May	15 NAC	L	0-1	ED		11 250

18th   Att: 192 550 • Av: 11 326 (-11.7%) • Konig Willem II 14 637 (77%)

VENLO LEAGUE APPEARANCES/GOALS 2010-11
Goalkeepers Kevin Begois BEL **15** • Dennis Gentenaar **19**
Defenders Ferry de Regt **26+7/1** • Youssef El Akchaoui MAR **14/0** • Niels
Fleuren **20/0** • Emenike Nkume NGA **8+6/0** • Michael Timisela **29+1/1**
Frank van Kouwen **8+2/0** • Maya Yoshida JPN **18+2/0**
Midfield Josue POR **11+2/0** • Ken Leemans BEL **25+4/1**
Brian Linssen **3+7/0** • Funso Ojo BEL **2+6/0** • Patrick Paauwe **19/1**
Balazs Toth HUN **28+1/2** • Dario Vujicevic GER **15/1**
Forwards Achmed Ahahaoui **22+4/3** • Ruud Boymans **28+2/11**
Robert Cullen JPN **12+3/2** • Jorge Chula POR **11+13/1** • Quins
Kruijsen **4+3/0** • Ahmad Musa NGA **21+2/5** • Rachid Ofrany **0+1/0**
Michael Uchebo NGA **9+14/4** • Diogo Viana POR **6+4/1**
Rick Verbeek **1+7/0**
Coach Jan van Dijk • Willy Boessen (12/01/11)

WILLEM II LEAGUE APPEARANCES/GOALS 2010-11
Goalkeepers Vladan Kujovic SRB **8** • Niki Maenpaa FIN **12**
Davino Verhulst BEL **14**
Defenders Bart Biemans BEL **26+1/4** • Giovanni Gravenbeek **15+3/0**
Denis Halilovic SVN **15+1/1** • Veli Lampi FIN **27+1/0** • Josimar
Lima CPV **0+2/0** • Junior Livramento **1+5/0** • Marlon Pereira **34/0**
Gerrit Pressel GER **4+2/0** • Arjan Swinkels **29/1**
Midfield Ricardo Ippel **12+3/0** • Andreas Landgren SWE **12+1/2**
Andreas Lasnik AUT **32+1/9** • Evgeniy Levchenko UKR **14+5/3**
Jan-Arie van der Heijden **32/2** • Niek Vossebelt **8+10/0**
Jasper Waalkens **0+2/0**
Forwards Frank Demouge **3/1** • Juha Hakola FIN **16+1/3**
Lars Hutten **3+16/0** • Rangelo Janga **9+9/2** • Dragan Jelic SVN **3+2/0**
Maceo Rigters **22+5/5** • Gerson Sheotahul **6+8/1**
David Strihavka CZE **5+6/0** • Rowin van Zaanen **12+7/1**
Coach Gert Heerkes • John Feskens (15/04/11)

NEP – NEPAL

FIFA/COCA-COLA WORLD RANKING

'93	'94	'95	'96	'97	'98	'99	'00	'01	'02	'03	'04	'05	'06	'07	'08	'09	'10	'11	'12
124	138	147	151	155	176	157	166	156	165	165	177	175	170	186	174	152	172	153	

	2011														
	Jan	Feb	Mar	Apr	May	Jun	Jul	Aug	Sep	Oct	Nov	Dec	**High**	**Low**	**Av**
	173	174	172	148	147	147	136	136	135	144	143	153	**124**	**188**	**161**

A run to the semi-finals of the South Asian Football Federation Championship and qualifying for the finals of the AFC Challenge Cup ensured that 2011 would be remembered as one of the better years for the Nepalese national team. Nepal started the year by hosting a qualifying group for the 2012 AFC Challenge Cup and the team made the most of home advantage to finish in second place behind Korea DPR. That saw them through to the finals which the Asian Football Confederation then decided that Nepal should host - the first time the Himalayan kingdom had served as a venue for one of the continent's higher profile events. In mid-year the Nepalese then reached the second round of qualifying for the 2014 FIFA World Cup finals in Brazil, defeating Timor-Leste in the opening round before suffering a bruising 9-0 loss against Jordan in Amman in the next round. It was the one black mark during the year although they did salvage some pride by holding the Jordanians to a 1-1 draw in Kathmandu in the return. At the SAFF Championship in India at the end of the year, Nepal finished second in their group after drawing with Pakistan and the Maldives and beating Bangladesh. In the semi-final, however, they came up against a determined Afghanistan team who beat them 1-0 to deprive the Nepalese a place in the final for the first time.

FIFA WORLD CUP RECORD
1930-1982 DNE 1986-1990 DNQ 1994 DNE 1998-2002 DNQ 2006 DNE 2010-2014 DNQ

ALL-NEPAL FOOTBALL ASSOCIATION (ANFA)

ANFA House, Satobato,
Lalitpur-17, PO Box 12582,
Kathmandu
☎ +977 1 5201060
📠 +977 1 4424314
✉ anfanepal@gmail.com

FA 1951 CON 1971 FIFA 1970
P Ganesh Thapa
GS Dhirendra Kumar Pradhan

FIFA BIG COUNT 2006

Total players	477 800
% of population	1.69%
Male	477 800
Female	0
Amateurs 18+	6 300
Youth under 18	7 200
Unregistered	110 000
Professionals	0
Referees	200
Admin & coaches	2 100
Number of clubs	110
Number of teams	440

MAJOR CITIES/TOWNS

		Population
1	Kathmandu	949 486
2	Pokhara	225 369
3	Lalitpur	210 317
4	Biratnagar	203 018
5	Birganj	161 059
6	Bharatpur	130 696
7	Dhangadhi	129 387
8	Dharan	125 969
9	Janakpur	122 427
10	Butwal	113 658
11	Hetauda	107 859
12	Mahendranagar	98 233
13	Bhaktapur	82 896
14	Siddharthanagar	77 978
15	Triyuga	73 977
16	Nepalganj	66 648
17	Madhyapur Thimi	64 350
18	Gulariya	62 489
19	Mechinagar	60 736

FEDERAL DEMOCRATIC REPUBLIC OF NEPAL

Capital Kathmandu	Population 28 563 377 (42)	% in cities 17%
GDP per capita $1100 (210)	Area km² 147 181 km² (93)	GMT + / - +5.75
Neighbours (km) China 1236, India 1690		

RECENT INTERNATIONAL MATCHES PLAYED BY NEPAL

2008	Opponents	Score	Venue	Comp	Scorers	Att	Referee
31-07	Myanmar	L 0-3	Hyderabad	CCr1		150	Jassim UAE
2-08	Korea DPR	L 0-1	Hyderabad	CCr1		100	Iemoto JPN
4-08	Sri Lanka	W 3-0	Hyderabad	CCr1	Santosh Shahukhala 14, Ju Manu Rai 55, Anjan 68	200	Saleem MDV
15-10	Malaysia	L 0-4	Petaling Jaya	Fr			
17-10	Afghanistan	D 2-2	Petaling Jaya	Fr	Anil Gurung 63, Bijay Gurung 78		
2009							
26-03	Palestine	D 0-0	Kathmandu	CCq		12 000	El Haddad LIB
28-03	Kyrgyzstam	D 1-1	Kathmandu	CCq	Biraj Maharjan 2	15 000	Jahanbazi IRN
29-11	Bhutan	W 2-1	Calcutta	Fr	Anil Gurung 70, Bijay Gurung 80		
5-12	Maldives	D 1-1	Dhaka	SAFr1	Ju Manu Rai 68		
7-12	India †	L 0-1	Dhaka	SAFr1			
9-12	Afghanistan	W 3-0	Dhaka	SAFr1	Anil Gurung 2 55 73, Bijay Gurung 56		
2010							
No international matches played in 2010							
2011							
17-03	Bhutan	W 1-0	Pokhara	Fr	Santosh Shahukhala 29		
19-03	Bhutan	W 2-1	Pokhara	Fr	Bikash Chhetri 24, Bharat Khawas 75		
7-04	Afghanistan	W 1-0	Kathmandu	CCq	Bharat Khawas 27	9 100	Abdul Baki OMA
9-04	Korea DPR	L 0-1	Kathmandu	CCq		22 000	Alabbasi BHR
11-04	Sri Lanka	D 0-0	Kathmandu	CCq		13 500	Adday IRQ
29-06	Timor-Leste	W 2-1	Kathmandu	WCq	Anil Gurung 15p, Jumanu Rai 70	9 000	Sabbagh LIB
2-07	Timor-Leste	W 5-0	Kathmandu	WCq	Anil Gurung 4p, Bhola Silwal 56, Jumanu Rai 59, Jagajeet Shrestha 89, Sujal Shrestha 90	15 000	Lee Min Hu KOR
23-07	Jordan	L 0-9	Amman	WCq		17 000	Jahanbazi IRN
28-07	Jordan	D 1-1	Kathmandu	WCq	Bharat Khawas 80	20 000	Fan Qi CHN
11-10	Philippines	L 0-4	Manila	Fr			
2-12	Maldives	D 1-1	New Delhi	SAFr1	Sandip Rai 51		Singh SIN
4-12	Bangladesh	W 1-0	New Delhi	SAFr1	Sagar Thapa 95+		Kumar IND
6-12	Pakistan	D 1-1	New Delhi	SAFr1	Bharat Khawas 37		Noor Mohamed MAS
9-12	Afghanistan	L 0-1	New Delhi	SAFsf			Tufaylieh SYR

Fr = Friendly match • SAF = South Asian Football Federation Cup • CC = AFC Challenge Cup • AC = AFC Asian Cup
q = qualifier • r1 = first round group • qf = quarter-final • sf = semi-final

NEPAL 2011

MARTYR'S MEMORIAL RED BULL ANFA A DIVISION

	Pl	W	D	L	F	A	Pts	Police	Manang	Jawalakhel	Three Star	Sherpa	Ranipokhari	New Road	Army	Friends	Mahindra	Boudha	Armed Police	Saraswoti	Machhindra	Swoyambhu	Brigade Boys	United Youth	Koilapani
Nepal Police Club †	17	14	2	1	54	7	44		0-1	3-1	1-0	0-0	1-0	3-1	4-1	3-0	4-1	6-0	0-0	5-2	4-0	5-0	5-0	6-0	4-0
Manang Marsyangdi	17	14	2	1	42	7	44			1-0	0-1	2-1	4-0	1-1	1-0	3-1	1-0	2-0	3-0	0-0	3-0	1-0	7-0	5-0	7-3
Jawalakhel Youth Club	17	11	3	3	35	15	36				0-1	1-1	3-2	2-2	1-0	2-1	3-0	3-1	3-0	4-0	1-0	2-0	2-0	3-1	4-1
Three Star Club	17	11	1	5	31	12	34					1-1	0-1	1-0	1-2	2-1	0-1	1-0	0-4	3-1	7-0	2-0	2-0	4-0	4-0
Yeti Himalayan Sherpa	17	9	6	2	45	16	33						1-1	0-2	2-1	1-1	2-0	2-2	4-2	4-0	3-1	1-0	5-0	7-1	9-2
Ranipokhari Corner	17	10	3	4	40	23	33							2-2	4-3	2-0	0-2	5-4	1-0	5-1	1-1	1-0	3-1	5-0	7-0
New Road Team	17	9	5	3	27	15	32								1-4	1-0	2-1	2-0	3-0	2-1	0-0	0-0	1-0	4-0	3-0
Nepal Army Club	17	8	5	4	35	17	29									3-1	4-0	0-0	1-1	5-1	0-0	0-0	2-0	2-0	6-0
Friends Club	17	7	3	7	27	22	24										2-1	0-0	3-2	1-1	2-1	3-0	2-0	4-0	5-0
Mahindra Bansbari	17	6	3	8	20	28	21											3-1	2-1	3-3	0-3	1-0	1-1	0-0	4-1
Boudha FC	17	5	5	7	18	27	20												1-0	2-1	2-0	0-0	0-0	3-0	2-1
Armed Police Force	17	5	3	9	30	26	18													1-0	1-1	0-2	7-0	7-1	4-1
Saraswoti Club	17	4	3	10	26	40	15														1-0	4-1	0-2	3-1	7-1
Machhindra FC	17	3	5	9	20	28	14															1-1	0-2	4-0	7-0
Swoyambhu Club	17	2	5	10	9	27	11																2-1	2-4	1-1
Brigade Boys Club	17	2	4	11	9	41	10																	1-1	1-1
United Youth Club	17	1	3	13	10	61	6																		1-1
Koilapani Polestar	17	0	3	14	12	78	3																		

28/04/2011 - 16/07/2011 • † Qualified for the AFC President's Cup

NGA – NIGERIA

FIFA/COCA-COLA WORLD RANKING

'93	'94	'95	'96	'97	'98	'99	'00	'01	'02	'03	'04	'05	'06	'07	'08	'09	'10	'11	'12
18	12	27	63	71	65	76	52	40	29	35	21	24	9	20	19	22	32	43	

	2011											High	Low	Av
Jan	Feb	Mar	Apr	May	Jun	Jul	Aug	Sep	Oct	Nov	Dec			
32	40	39	38	39	41	43	38	43	44	43	43	5	82	35

Nigeria's Super Eagles have been a regular feature at the CAF Africa Cup of Nations finals since the mid-1970s. Just once since then had they failed to get through the qualifying tournament - in 1986 when they were knocked out by Zambia - until the 2012 tournament that is. Going into their final qualifier, at home to Guinea in Abuja, Nigeria needed to win to make it to the finals in Equatorial Guinea and Gabon. Deep into injury-time they were doing just that until Ibrahima Toure scored an equaliser for Guinea. The 2-2 draw meant Nigeria finished three points behind them in the group and brought a swift close to the tenure of Samson Siasia as coach, replaced by his former FIFA World Cup teammate Stephen Keshi. In club football, Dolphins won the Nigerian Premier League in a close race for the title with Sunshine Stars. Formed in 1988 as Eagle Cement, the Port Harcourt club has quickly established itself as one of the most consistant powers in the country. The title was their third and they have also won the cup four times in a decade that they have dominated along with neighbours Enyimba from the city of Aba just to the north. Enyimba almost made it to a third CAF Champions League final in 2011 but lost in the semi-finals to Morocco's Wydad while Heartland were the Nigerian Federation Cup winners - their first trophy for 18 years.

CAF AFRICA CUP OF NATIONS RECORD
1957-1962 DNE 1963 6 r1 1965 DNE 1968 DNQ 1970 DNE 1972-1974 DNQ 1976 3 r2 1978 3 SF 1980 1 Winners (hosts) 1982 6 r1 1984 2 F 1986 DNQ 1988 2 F 1990 2 F 1992 3 SF 1994 1 Winners 1996 withdrew 1998 DNE 2000 2 F (co-hosts) 2002 3 SF 2004 3 SF 2006 3 SF 2008 7 QF 2010 3 SF 2012 DNQ

NIGERIA FOOTBALL FEDERATION (NFF)
Plot 2033, Olusegun Obasanjo Way, Zone 7, Wuse Abuja, PO Box 5101 Garki, Abuja
☎ +234 9 5237326
nigeria_fa@yahoo.com
www.nigeriaff.com
FA 1945 CON 1959 FIFA 1959
P Aminu Maigari
GS Musa Adamu

FIFA BIG COUNT 2006
Total players	6 653 710
% of population	5.05%
Male	6 344 600
Female	309 110
Amateurs 18+	26 170
Unregistered	565 000
Professionals	2 440
Referees	522
Admin & coaches	32 600
Number of clubs	522
Number of teams	522

MAJOR CITIES/TOWNS
		Population
1	Lagos	9 733 876
2	Ibadan	5 003 747
3	Kano	2 359 248
4	Benin	2 324 188
5	Port Harcourt	1 999 375
6	Kaduna	1 994 242
7	Aba	1 529 729
8	Abuja	1 243 152
9	Maiduguri	1 096 414
10	Ilorin	1 050 031
11	Warri	893 929
12	Onitsha	871 554
13	Akure	804 104
14	Abeokuta	771 585
15	Enugu	698 136
16	Zaria	667 446
17	Oshogbo	647 652
18	Jos	619 122
19	Ife	599 924

FEDERAL REPUBLIC OF NIGERIA
Capital Abuja	Population 149 229 090 (8)	% in cities 48%
GDP per capita $2300 (182)	Area km² 923 768 km² (32)	GMT +/- +1
Neighbours (km) Benin 773, Cameroon 1690, Chad 87, Niger 1497 • Coast 853		

RECENT INTERNATIONAL MATCHES PLAYED BY NIGERIA

2009	Opponents	Score		Venue	Comp	Scorers	Att	Referee
11-02	Jamaica	D	0-0	London	Fr			Dean ENG
29-03	Mozambique	D	0-0	Maputo	WCq		35 000	Eyob ERI
29-05	Republic of Ireland	D	1-1	London	Fr	Eneramo [30]	11 263	Collum SCO
2-06	France	W	1-0	St Etienne	Fr	Akpala [32]	25 000	Bennett ENG
7-06	Kenya	W	3-0	Abuja	WCq	Ike Uche [2], Obinna 2 [72p 77]	60 000	El Achiri MAR
20-06	Tunisia	D	0-0	Rades/Tunis	WCq		45 000	Coulibaly MLI
6-09	Tunisia	D	2-2	Abuja	WCq	Odemwingie [23], Eneramo [80]	52 000	Bennett RSA
11-10	Mozambique	W	1-0	Abuja	WCq	Obinna [93+]	13 000	Abdel Rahman SUD
14-11	Kenya	W	3-2	Nairobi	WCq	Martins 2 [60 81], Yakubu [64]	20 000	Maillet SEY
2010								
12-01	Egypt	L	1-3	Benguela	CNr1	Obassi [12]	18 000	Seechurn MRI
16-01	Benin	W	1-0	Benguela	CNr1	Yakubu [42p]	8 000	Carvalho ANG
20-01	Mozambique	W	3-0	Lubango	CNr1	Odemwingie 2 [45 47], Martins [86]	10 000	Coulibaly MLI
25-01	Zambia	D	0-0	Lubango	CNqf	W 5-4p	10 000	Abd El Fatah EGY
28-01	Ghana	L	0-1	Luanda	CNsf		7 500	Bennett RSA
30-01	Algeria	W	1-0	Benguela	CN3p	Obinna [56]	12 000	Diatta SEN
3-03	Congo DR	W	5-2	Abuja	Fr	Utaka [11], Idehen 2 [28 65], Ezimorah [31], Obinna [52]	5 000	
25-05	Saudi Arabia	D	0-0	Wattens	Fr		1 000	Einwaller AUT
30-05	Colombia	D	1-1	Milton Keynes	Fr	Haruna [70]	BCD	Atkinson ENG
6-06	Korea DPR	W	3-1	Johannesburg	Fr	Yakubu [15], Obinna [62p], Martins [88]	20 000	
12-06	Argentina	L	0-1	Johannesburg	WCr1		55 686	Stark GER
17-06	Greece	L	1-2	Bloemfontein	WCr1	Kalu Uche [16]	31 593	Ruiz COL
22-06	Korea Republic	D	2-2	Durban	WCr1	Kalu Uche [12], Yakubu [69p]	61 874	Benquerenca POR
11-08	Korea Republic	L	1-2	Suwon	Fr	Odemwingie [26]	40 331	Nishimura JPN
5-09	Madagascar	W	2-0	Calabar	CNq	Martins [19], Eneramo [45]		Jedidi TUN
10-10	Guinea	L	0-1	Conakry	CNq			El Ahrach MAR
2011								
9-02	Sierra Leone	W	2-1	Lagos	Fr	Taye Taiwo [15p], Ekigho Ehiosun [45]		
27-03	Ethiopia	W	4-0	Abuja	CNq	Peter Utaka 2 [2 53], Ikechukwu Uche 2 [77 90]		Jedidi TUN
29-03	Kenya	W	3-0	Abuja	Fr	Ikechukwu Uche [2], Victor Obinna 2 [73p 76]		
1-06	Argentina	W	4-1	Abuja	Fr	Ikechukwu Uche 2 [14 40], Victor Obinna [25p], Emmanuel Emenike [52]	30 000	Chaibou NIG
5-06	Ethiopia	D	2-2	Addis Abeba	CNq	Ikechukwu Uche [27], Joseph Yobo [86]		
4-09	Madagascar	W	2-0	Antananarivo	CNq	Joseph Yobo [68], Victor Obinna [72]		Kirwa KEN
6-09	Argentina	L	1-3	Dhaka	Fr	Chidu Obasi [47]	36 000	Shamsuzzaman BAN
8-10	Guinea	D	2-2	Abuja	CNq	Obinna [63], Ikechukwu Uche [77]		
11-10	Ghana	D	0-0	Watford	Fr			
12-11	Botswana	D	0-0	Benin City	Fr			
15-11	Zambia	W	2-0	Kaduna	Fr	Kalu Uche [9], Ikechukwu Uche [90]		

Fr = Friendly match • CN = CAF African Cup of Nations • WC = FIFA World Cup • q = qualifier • r1 = first round group

NIGERIA NATIONAL TEAM HISTORICAL RECORDS

Caps

86 - Nwankwo Kanu 1995-2010 • **80** - Muda Lawal 1976-84 • **63** - • **61** - • **56** - • **54** - • **53** - • **51** - • **49** -

Goals

37 - Rashidi Yekini 1986-98 • **23** - Segun Odegbami 1976-89 • **21** - Yakubu Aiyegbeni 2000- • **18** - Obafemi Martins 2004- • **17** - Sunday Oyarekhua 1971-75 • **14** - Daniel Amokachi 1990-99; Jay-Jay Okocha 1993-2006 & Julius Agahowa 1999- • **13** - Nwankwo Kanu 1995-2010; Samson Siasia 1989-98; Thompson Usiyen 1976-78 & Ikechukwu Uche 2007- • **12** - Asuquo Ekpe 1960-65 & Muda Lawal 1976-84

Past Coaches

John Finch ENG 1949 • Daniel Anyiam 1954-56 • Les Courtier ENG 1956-60 • Moshe Beth-Halevi ISR 1960-61 • George Vardar HUN 1961-63 • George Penna BRA 1963-64 • Daniel Anyiam 1964-65 • Joseph Ember HUN 1965-68 • Peter 'Eto' Amaechina 1969-70 • Heinz Marotze GER 1970-71 • George Penna BRA 1972-73 • Heinz Marotze GER 1974 • Jelisavcic 'Tiki' Tihomir YUG 1974-78 • Otto Gloria BRA 1979-82 • Gottlieb Goller GER 1981 • Adegboyega Onigbinde 1983-84 • Chris Udemezue 1984-86 • Patrick Ekeji 1985 • Paul Hamilton 1987-89 • Manfred Hoener GER 1988-89 • Clemens Westerhof NED 1989-94 • Shaibu Amodu 1994-95 • Jo Bonfere NED 1995-96 • Shaibu Amodu 1996-97 • Philippe Troussier FRA 1997-98 • Monday Sinclair 1997-98 • Bora Milutinovic SRB 1998 • Thijs Libregts NED 1999 • Jo Bonfrere NED 1999-2001 • Shaibu Amodu 2001-02 • Adegboyega Onigbinde 2002 • Christian Chukwu 2002-05 • Augustine Eguavoen 2005-07 • Berti Vogts GER 2007-08 • James Peters 2008 • Shaibu Amodu 2008-10 • Lars Lagerback SWE 2010 • Augustine Eguavoen 2010 • Samson Siasia 2010-11 • Stephen Keshi 2011-

NIGERIA 2010-11

NIGERIAN PREMIER LEAGUE

Team	Pl	W	D	L	F	A	Pts	Dolphin	Sunshine Stars	Warri Wolves	Kano Pillars	Sharks	Enugu Rangers	Enyimba	Kaduna United	Kwara United	Lobi Stars	Heartland	ABS	Gombe United	Niger Tornadoes	Shooting Stars	Ocean Boys	Plateau United	Zamfara United	Crown	JUTH
Dolphin †	38	23	4	11	49	30	73	—	1-0	1-0	1-0	1-0	2-1	1-0	1-0	1-0	1-0	2-0	3-0	3-0	1-0	0-0	3-0	4-0	2-0	2-0	
Sunshine Stars †	38	22	5	11	55	35	71	3-2	—	3-1	3-0	2-0	2-0	2-1	4-1	1-0	2-0	2-1	1-0	3-1	2-0	1-0	2-0	4-0	3-1	2-1	2-0
Warri Wolves ‡	38	19	9	10	44	29	66	4-1	2-0	—	2-1	3-0	1-0	2-0	1-0	1-0	2-1	2-2	1-0	2-1	1-0	1-0	1-0	1-0	3-1	3-0	2-1
Kano Pillars	38	20	5	13	46	31	65	3-2	1-0	1-0	—	1-1	1-0	3-0	2-0	2-1	2-0	3-0	1-0	2-1	0-0	1-0	2-0	5-1	3-0	1-0	1-0
Sharks	38	17	12	9	43	37	63	1-0	2-1	2-0	1-0	—	1-1	2-1	2-1	1-0	1-0	1-0	1-0	1-0	3-1	1-0	1-1	0-2	2-2	4-3	1-1
Enugu Rangers	38	19	5	14	47	30	62	2-2	1-0	0-0	0-1	2-1	—	1-0	3-0	1-0	3-2	1-0	2-0	1-0	4-0	2-0	5-2	1-0	5-1	2-1	4-0
Enyimba	38	19	4	15	44	28	61	3-0	4-0	0-0	1-0	1-0	1-0	—	4-1	3-0	4-0	1-0	1-0	2-0	1-0	1-0	1-0	3-0	1-0	2-1	2-0
Kaduna United	38	16	8	14	42	40	56	2-1	1-0	1-0	1-1	1-1	1-0	1-0	—	3-0	4-2	1-0	1-0	3-0	3-1	2-0	2-0	1-1	2-0	2-1	1-1
Kwara United	38	16	5	17	40	45	53	1-1	3-2	2-0	1-0	3-0	3-2	2-1	1-1	—	1-0	1-0	0-3	1-1	2-0	1-0	2-0	1-1	3-0	2-0	1-0
Lobi Stars	38	15	8	15	34	40	53	2-1	1-1	1-0	1-0	1-1	1-0	1-1	1-2	1-2	—	3-0	0-1	0-0	2-1	1-0	1-0	1-0	1-0	1-0	2-1
Heartland ‡	38	16	4	18	39	35	52	2-0	2-0	0-0	2-0	0-0	3-1	2-0	2-1	2-1	0-0	—	2-0	1-0	2-1	1-0	4-0	2-1	3-0	1-0	4-2
Bukola Babes ABS	38	15	6	17	35	37	51	0-1	0-1	1-0	0-1	1-1	1-0	1-0	2-1	3-0	3-1	1-0	—	3-2	0-1	4-1	2-1	2-2	0-0	1-0	1-0
Gombe United	38	14	8	16	34	37	50	1-0	3-0	1-1	2-1	0-0	0-0	0-2	0-2	1-0	2-0	3-0		—	1-0	1-0	1-0	1-0	2-0	3-1	1-0
Niger Tornadoes	38	13	11	14	35	43	50	1-0	0-0	1-1	1-0	3-2	0-0	1-0	0-0	2-1	1-1	3-1	0-0	1-0	—	2-0	3-0	1-1	1-0	1-0	0-0
Shooting Stars	38	13	8	17	34	39	47	1-1	2-1	1-1	2-1	2-0	0-1	1-0	1-1	1-0	1-0	2-0	1-1	2-1	2-1	—	2-1	1-0	1-3	1-0	
Ocean Boys	38	13	8	17	37	44	47	2-0	2-2	1-1	1-0	1-1	1-0	0-0	2-0	1-1	1-1	1-0	3-0	2-0	2-0	1-0	—	1-1	3-1	2-0	4-1
Plateau United	38	12	8	18	42	49	44	0-1	0-1	2-0	2-2	0-1	0-1	1-0	0-0	7-0	2-0	1-0	1-0	2-1	2-2	1-0	3-1	—	2-0	1-2	1-0
Zamfara United	38	11	6	21	26	58	39	0-1	0-1	1-0	1-1	2-1	1-0	1-0	0-0	1-1	0-2	1-1	1-0	1-0	2-2	2-2	0-1	3-2	—	1-0	1-0
Crown	38	11	4	23	34	48	37	0-1	1-1	1-1	2-0	1-3	0-1	1-2	1-0	1-0	0-1	1-0	0-2	2-0	2-3	2-2	1-0	1-0	3-0	—	1-0
JUTH	38	8	8	22	26	51	32	1-3	0-0	0-1	1-2	0-0	2-0	2-1	1-0	0-2	0-0	1-0	2-2	1-1	2-1	2-1	2-0	0-1	2-0	0-1	—

6/11/2010 - 13/11/2011 • † Qualified for the CAF Champions League • ‡ Qualified for the CAF Confederation Cup

---

FEDERATION CUP 2011

Quarter-finals		Semi-finals		Final	
Heartland	1				
Dolphin	0	**Heartland**	2		
Enugu Rangers	0	Bayelsa United	1		
Bayelsa United	1			**Heartland** ‡	1
Ocean Boys	1			Enyimba	0
Sharks	0	Ocean Boys	1 3p	Teslim Balogun, Lagos	
Kwara United	0	**Enyimba**	1 4p	25-09-2011	
Enyimba	2			Scorer - Chinedu Efugh 40	

Round of 16 played in four groups of four

3rd Place: **Ocean Boys** 2-2 5-4p Bayelsa United

‡ Qualified for the CAF Confederation Cup

MEDALS TABLE

#	Team	Overall			Lge	Cup		Africa			City
		G	S	B	G	G	S	G	S	B	
1	Shooting Stars	15	4	1	5	8	2	2	2	1	Ibadan
2	Enugu Rangers	11	8	4	5	5	7	1	1	4	Enugu
3	Enyimba	10	2	2	6	2	2	2		2	Aba
4	Heartland	7	4	3	5	2	2		2	3	Owerri
5	Dolphin	7	1		3	4			1		Port Harcourt
	Lagos Railways	7	1			7	1				Lagos
7	Bendel Insurance	6	3	2	2	3	2	1	1	2	Benin City
8	BCC Lions	6	2		1	4	1	1	1		Gboko
9	Stationery Stores	5	3	1	1	4	2	1		1	Lagos
10	Julius Berger	4	3		2	2	1	2			Lagos
11	Port Harcourt FC	3	3			3	3				Port Harcourt
12	Leventis United	3	1		1	2		1			Ibadan
13	Lagos ECN	3				3					Lagos
14	Abiola Babes	2	2	1		2	2			1	Mashood
	Kano Pillars	2	2	1	1	1	2			1	Kano

NIG – NIGER

FIFA/COCA-COLA WORLD RANKING

'93	'94	'95	'96	'97	'98	'99	'00	'01	'02	'03	'04	'05	'06	'07	'08	'09	'10	'11	'12
81	70	93	129	150	154	164	182	191	184	164	173	177	147	155	143	163	94	97	

	2011											High	Low	Av
Jan	Feb	Mar	Apr	May	Jun	Jul	Aug	Sep	Oct	Nov	Dec			
94	96	104	97	99	100	98	104	93	95	98	97	68	196	145

Niger benefitted from a large dose of good fortune to qualify for their first-ever CAF Africa Cup of Nations finals, but they looked out of their depth at the 2012 tournament in Gabon where they lost all three of their group games. Niger topped their qualifying group because of a better head to head record against Sierra Leone and South Africa, all of whom finished level on points. South Africa were in prime position to qualify but erroneously believed they would have gone through on goal difference and so contrived to draw their last game with Sierra Leone which saw Niger qualified for the finals instead. Niger's qualification was thanks to their fine form at home where they won all three of their qualifiers, turning their ground in Niamey into something of a fortress. In the finals Frenchman Rolland Courbis had been brought in to advise Harouna Doulla but he took over after Niger lost their opening game to co-hosts Gabon. They were more competitive in the subsequent games against Tunisia and Morocco but again ended up on the losing side. The points gained in the FIFA/Coca Cola World Ranking also meant the Mena Stars went straight into the group phase of Africa's qualifiers for the 2014 FIFA World Cup. At home, Ligue 1 was won by military club AS Garde Nationale who finished nine points clear at the top of the standings.

CAF AFRICA CUP OF NATIONS RECORD
1957-1968 DNE **1970-1972** DNQ **1974** DNE **1976** DNQ **1978-1982** DNE **1984** DNQ **1986-1990** DNE **1992-1994** DNQ
1996 Withdrew **1998** DNE **2000-2010** DNQ **2012** 15 r1

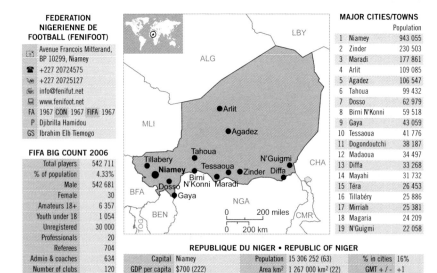

FEDERATION NIGERIENNE DE FOOTBALL (FENIFOOT)

Avenue Francois Mitterand, BP 10299, Niamey
☎ +227 20724575
📠 +227 20725127
✉ info@fenifut.net
🖥 www.fenifoot.net
FA 1967 CON 1967 FIFA 1967
P Djibrilla Hamidou
GS Ibrahim Elh Tiemogo

FIFA BIG COUNT 2006

Total players	542 711
% of population	4.33%
Male	542 681
Female	30
Amateurs 18+	6 357
Youth under 18	1 054
Unregistered	30 000
Professionals	20
Referees	704
Admin & coaches	634
Number of clubs	120
Number of teams	1 010

MAJOR CITIES/TOWNS

		Population
1	Niamey	943 055
2	Zinder	230 503
3	Maradi	177 861
4	Arlit	109 085
5	Agadez	106 547
6	Tahoua	99 432
7	Dosso	62 979
8	Birni N'Konni	59 518
9	Gaya	43 059
10	Tessaoua	41 776
11	Dogondoutchi	38 187
12	Madaoua	34 497
13	Diffa	33 268
14	Mayahi	31 732
15	Téra	26 453
16	Tillabéry	25 886
17	Mirriah	25 381
18	Magaria	24 209
19	N'Guigmi	22 058

REPUBLIQUE DU NIGER • REPUBLIC OF NIGER

Capital	Niamey	Population	15 306 252 (63)	% in cities 16%
GDP per capita	$700 (222)	Area km²	1 267 000 km² (22)	GMT + / - +1
Neighbours (km)	Algeria 956, Benin 266, Burkina Faso 628, Chad 1175, Libya 354, Mali 821, Nigeria 1497			

RECENT INTERNATIONAL MATCHES PLAYED BY NIGER

2008	Opponents	Score		Venue	Comp	Scorers	Att	Referee
31-05	Uganda	L	0-1	Kampala	WCq		25 000	Evehe CMR
8-06	Angola	L	1-2	Niamey	WCq	Ismael Alassane [3]	23 000	Jedidi TUN
14-06	Benin	L	0-2	Niamey	WCq		5 000	Haimoudi ALG
22-06	Benin	L	0-2	Cotonou	WCq		25 000	Niyongabo BDI
28-08	Libya	L	2-6	Tripoli	Fr			
7-09	Uganda	W	3-1	Niamey	WCq	Ilssoufou Alhassane 2 [68 86], Daouda Kamilou [88]	5 000	Lamptey GHA
12-10	Angola	L	1-3	Luanda	WCq	Mallam [19]	3 200	Gasingwa RWA
2009								
No international matches played in 2009								
2010								
19-06	Chad	D	1-1	Niamey	Fr	Koffi Dan Kowa [90]		
11-08	Benin	D	0-0	Porto Novo	Fr			
4-09	South Africa	L	0-2	Nelspruit	CNq			Abdul Rahman SUD
10-10	Egypt	W	1-0	Niamey	CNq	Moussa Maazou [34]		Doue CIV
17-11	Libya	D	1-1	Tripoli	Fr	Moussa Maazou [77]. L 1-4p		
2011								
9-02	Morocco	L	0-3	Marrakech	Fr			
27-03	Sierra Leone	W	3-1	Niamey	CNq	Ilssoufou Alhassane [64], Issa Sidibe [79], Daouda Kamilou [89]		
4-06	Sierra Leone	L	0-1	Freetown	CNq			
10-08	Togo	D	3-3	Niamey	Fr	Moussa Maazou 2 [45 70], Daouda Kamilou [80]		
14-08	Liberia	D	0-0	Monrovia	Fr			
4-09	South Africa	W	2-1	Niamey	CNq	Koffi Kowa [10], Moussa Maazou [47]		
6-09	Gabon	L	0-1	Nice	Fr			
8-10	Egypt	L	0-3	Cairo	CNq			
15-11	Botswana	D	1-1	Niamey	Fr	William N'Gounou [37]		
2012								
23-01	Gabon	L	0-2	Libreville	CNr1		38 000	Maillet SEY
27-01	Tunisia	L	1-2	Libreville	CNr1	William N'Gounou [9]	20 000	Sikazwe ZAM
31-01	Morocco	L	0-1	Libreville	CNr1		4 000	Nampiandraza MAD

Fr = Friendly match • CN = CAF African Cup of Nations • WC = FIFA World Cup • q = qualifier

NIGER 2010-11 LIGUE 1 ORANGE

	Pl	W	D	L	F	A	Pts
AS Garde Nationale	30	18	8	4	52	17	62
Dan Kassawa Maradi	30	15	8	7	36	22	53
AS-FAN Niamey	30	14	6	10	46	24	48
Sahel SC Niamey	30	13	9	8	32	18	48
ASN NIGELEC	30	13	9	8	39	26	48
Akokana Arlit	30	13	9	8	34	22	48
AS Police	30	12	11	7	36	28	47
Olympic FC	30	11	13	6	31	24	46
Jangorzo Maradi	30	11	12	7	32	26	45
Urana	30	11	10	9	31	31	43
AS Douane	30	11	8	11	42	30	41
Alkali Nassara Zinder	30	9	11	10	24	27	38
Racing Boukoki	30	8	10	12	30	38	34
Gendarmerie Nationale	30	6	8	16	25	40	26
Ader Tahoua	30	4	8	20	25	66	10
Malbaza FC	30	0	3	27	8	82	3

7/12/2010 - 23/07/2011

COUPE NATIONALE 2011 FINAL
Stade Seyni Kountche, Niamey, 3-08-2011
Sahel SC Noamey 1-0 Jangorzo Maradi
Scorer - Olache Wassiou [41]

MEDALS TABLE

		Overall	Lge	Cup		City
		G	G	G	S	
1	Sahel SC	22	13	9	2	Niamey
2	Olympic FC	16	11	5	5	Niamey
3	AS-FAN	6	3	3	1	Niamey
	AS Niamey	6	3	3	1	Niamey
	JS Ténéré	6	2	4	1	Niamey
6	Libertie FC	4		4	4	Niamey
7	AS Garde Nationale	4	3	1	2	Niamey
8	Zumunta AC	4	3	1		Niamey
9	Espoir	3	1	2	5	Zinder
10	Jangorzo FC	2	1	1	3	Maradi
11	AS Police	2	1	1		Niamey
12	Akokana FC	1		1	2	Arlit
13	Zindourma	1		1		Zinder
14	Ader FC			3		Niamey
15	Alkali Nassara			1		Zinder
	Magaria			1		Zinder
	AS Maradi			1		Maradi

NIR – NORTHERN IRELAND

FIFA/COCA-COLA WORLD RANKING

'93	'94	'95	'96	'97	'98	'99	'00	'01	'02	'03	'04	'05	'06	'07	'08	'09	'10	'11	'12
39	45	45	64	93	86	84	93	88	103	122	107	103	48	32	52	40	43	88	

	2011												High	Low	Av
	Jan	Feb	Mar	Apr	May	Jun	Jul	Aug	Sep	Oct	Nov	Dec			
	43	38	40	65	65	62	62	59	70	84	89	88	27	124	71

In May 2011 Linfield became only the second club anywhere in the world to reach the 50 league titles mark, joining Glasgow Rangers as members of this very exclusive set. The parallels between the two clubs are striking - supporters of both have long been identified with the unionist communities in their country and until 1949 both had great rivals called Celtic. That was the year that shaped the future of football in Northern Ireland with Belfast Celtic deciding it was unsafe to continue playing following violence at the Boxing Day match between the two. Until then Linfield had won 18 titles to Celtic's 14, but since, winning trophies has been that much easier and for the fifth time in six years Linfield secured the League and Cup double. In the Cup Final they beat Crusaders 2-1 to hold on to their world record for cup wins, although that title is under threat from Liechtenstein's FC Vaduz who are just one behind Linfield's total of 41. Lisburn Distillery were the season's other winners, beating Portadown 2-1 in the League Cup Final to claim the prize for the first time. In the qualifiers for Euro 2012, Northern Ireland had a poor campaign with just two victories to show for their efforts - over Slovenia and the Faroes. Coach Nigel Worthington stepped down afterwards and was replaced by Shamrock Rovers coach Michael O'Neill.

UEFA EUROPEAN CHAMPIONSHIP RECORD
1960 DNE 1964 r2 1968-2012 DNQ

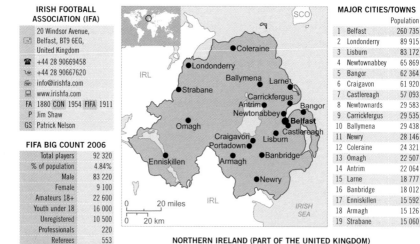

IRISH FOOTBALL ASSOCIATION (IFA)

20 Windsor Avenue,
Belfast, BT9 6EG,
United Kingdom
☎ +44 28 90669458
+44 28 90667620
info@irishfa.com
www.irishfa.com
FA 1880 CON 1954 FIFA 1911
P Jim Shaw
GS Patrick Nelson

FIFA BIG COUNT 2006

Total players	92 320
% of population	4.84%
Male	83 220
Female	9 100
Amateurs 18+	22 600
Youth under 18	16 000
Unregistered	10 500
Professionals	220
Referees	553
Admin & coaches	11 557
Number of clubs	820
Number of teams	1 570

MAJOR CITIES/TOWNS

		Population
1	Belfast	260 735
2	Londonderry	89 915
3	Lisburn	83 172
4	Newtownabbey	65 869
5	Bangor	62 364
6	Craigavon	61 920
7	Castlereagh	57 093
8	Newtownards	29 583
9	Carrickfergus	29 535
10	Ballymena	29 438
11	Newry	28 146
12	Coleraine	24 321
13	Omagh	22 507
14	Antrim	22 064
15	Larne	18 777
16	Banbridge	18 012
17	Enniskillen	15 592
18	Armagh	15 126
19	Strabane	15 060

NORTHERN IRELAND (PART OF THE UNITED KINGDOM)

Capital	Belfast	Population	1 716 942 (149)	% in cities	90%
GDP per capita	$36 700 (32)	Area km²	14 120 km² (160)	GMT +/-	0
Neighbours (km)	Republic of Ireland 360 • Coast 539				

RECENT INTERNATIONAL MATCHES PLAYED BY NORTHERN IRELAND

2008 Opponents	Score	Venue	Comp	Scorers	Att	Referee
6-02 Bulgaria	L 0-1	Belfast	Fr		11 000	McDonald SCO
26-03 Georgia	W 4-1	Belfast	Fr	Lafferty 2 [25] [36], Healy [33], Thompson [87]	15 000	Wilmes LUX
20-08 Scotland	D 0-0	Glasgow	Fr		28 072	Vollquartz DEN
6-09 Slovakia	L 1-2	Bratislava	WCq	Durica OG [81]	5 445	Ivanov.N RUS
10-09 Czech Republic	D 0-0	Belfast	WCq		12 882	Bebek CRO
11-10 Slovenia	L 0-2	Maribor	WCq		12 385	Iturralde ESP
15-10 San Marino	W 4-0	Belfast	WCq	Healy [31], McCann [43], Lafferty [56], Davis [75]	12 957	Kari FIN
19-11 Hungary	L 0-2	Belfast	Fr		6 251	Schoergenhofer AUT
2009						
11-02 San Marino	W 3-0	Serravalle	WCq	McAuley [7], McCann [33], Brunt [63]	1 942	Stankovic SRB
28-03 Poland	W 3-2	Belfast	WCq	Feeney [10], Evans [47], Zewlakow.M OG [62]	13 357	Hansson SWE
1-04 Slovenia	W 1-0	Belfast	WCq	Feeney [73]	13 243	Yefet ISR
6-06 Italy	L 0-3	Pisa	Fr		16 583	Blom NED
12-08 Israel	D 1-1	Belfast	Fr	McCann [19]	10 250	Valgeirsson ISL
5-09 Poland	D 1-1	Chorzow	WCq	Lafferty [38]	38 914	Mejuto ESP
9-09 Slovakia	L 0-2	Belfast	WCq		13 019	Kuipers NED
14-10 Czech Republic	D 0-0	Prague	WCq		8 002	Duhamel FRA
14-11 Serbia	L 0-1	Belfast	Fr		13 500	Toussaint LUX
2010						
3-03 Albania	L 0-1	Tirana	Fr		7 500	Pilav BIH
26-05 Turkey	L 0-2	New Britain	Fr		4 000	Vaughn USA
30-05 Chile	L 0-1	Chillan	Fr		12 000	Prudente URU
11-08 Montenegro	L 0-2	Podgorica	Fr		5 000	Jovanetic SRB
3-09 Slovenia	W 1-0	Maribor	ECq	Evans [70]	12 000	Balaj ROU
8-10 Italy	D 0-0	Belfast	ECq		15 200	Chapron FRA
12-10 Faroe Islands	D 1-1	Toftir	ECq	Lafferty [76]	1 921	Zimmermann SUI
17-11 Morocco	D 1-1	Belfast	Fr	Patterson [86p]	15 000	Hagen NOR
2011						
9-02 Scotland	L 0-3	Dublin	NC		18 742	Connolly IRL
25-03 Serbia	L 1-2	Belgrade	ECq	McAuley [40]	BCD	Gumienny BEL
29-03 Slovenia	D 0-0	Belfast	ECq		14 200	Kuipers NED
24-05 Republic of Ireland	L 0-5	Dublin	NC		15 083	Thomson SCO
27-05 Wales	L 0-2	Dublin	NC		529	Kelly IRL
10-08 Faroe Islands	W 4-0	Belfast	ECq	Hughes [5], Davis [66], McCourt 2 [71] [88]	13 183	AleckovicBIH
2-09 Serbia	L 0-1	Belfast	ECq		15 148	Einwaller AUT
6-09 Estonia	L 1-4	Tallinn	ECq	OG [40]	8 660	Stalhammar SWE
7-10 Estonia	L 1-2	Belfast	ECq	Davis [22]	12 604	Grafe GER
11-10 Italy	L 0-3	Pescara	ECq		19 480	Mateu ESP

Fr = Friendly match • EC = UEFA EURO 2012 • WC = FIFA World Cup • NC = Nations Cup • q = qualifier

NORTHERN IRELAND NATIONAL TEAM HISTORICAL RECORDS

Caps
119 - Pat Jennings 1964-86 • **91** - Mal Donaghy 1980-94 • **89** - David Healy 2000- • **88** - Sammy McIlroy 1972-87 • **87** - Maik Taylor 1999- • **86** - Keith Gillespie 1996-2008 • **79** - Aaron Hughes 1998- • **73** - Jimmy Nicholl 1976-86 • **71** - Michael Hughes 1992-2004 • **67** - David McCreery 1976-90 • **66** - Nigel Worthington • **64** - Martin O'Neill 1972-85 • **63** - Gerry Armstrong 1977-86

Goals
35 - David Healy 2000- • **13** - Billy Gillespie 1913-32 & Colin Clarke 1986-93 • **12** - Joe Bambrick 1928-40; Gerry Armstrong 1977-86; Jimmy Quinn 1985-96 & Iain Dowie 1990-2000 • **11** - Olphie Stanfield 1887-97 • **10** - Billy Bingham 1951-64; Jimmy McIlroy 1952-66; Peter McParland 1954-62 & Johnny Crossan 1960-68

Past Coaches
Peter Doherty 1951-62 • Bertie Peacock 1962-67 • Billy Bingham 1967-71 • Terry Neill 1971-75 • Dave Clements 1975-76 • Danny Blanchflower 1976-79 • Billy Bingham 1980-94 • Bryan Hamilton 1994-98 • Lawrie McMenemy ENG 1998-99 • Sammy McIlroy 2000-03 • Lawrie Sanchez 2004-07 • Nigel Worthington 2007-11 • Michael O'Neill 2012-

NORTHERN IRELAND 2010-11

IFA JJB SPORTS PREMIERSHIP

	Pl	W	D	L	F	A	Pts	Linfield	Crusaders	Glentoran	Cliftonville	Portadown	Distillery	Coleraine	Swifts	Ballymena	Glenavon	Donegal	Newry City
Linfield †	38	26	7	5	80	29	85		8-1 3-1	2-1 3-2	0-0 1-0	4-0 1-0	1-0 2-0	1-0 0-1	1-0	0-0 0-0	1-0	6-2	4-0 1-1
Crusaders ‡	38	23	5	10	78	59	74	2-1 0-1		1-0 2-1	1-3 5-0	3-1 3-1	1-2 4-1	2-0	1-1 2-2	2-1	5-4 1-0	4-5 2-1	2-1
Glentoran ‡	38	20	6	12	63	41	66	0-0 1-2	3-1 2-2		2-0 0-0	1-0 0-1	1-3 2-1	2-0	0-2 0-0	1-2	4-1 2-2	1-0 4-0	2-0
Cliftonville ‡	38	17	7	14	60	56	58	3-1 2-4	2-1 3-0	2-1 1-2		0-1 1-3	1-3 3-2	0-2	2-0 3-2	5-0 2-2	0-2	4-2 2-2	2-1
Portadown	38	15	5	18	49	58	50	1-2 0-4	0-2 0-1	0-1 2-0	2-1 1-0		1-0 1-0	2-0	2-2 2-1	1-3	2-2 1-1	3-0	4-2 2-1
Lisburn Distillery	38	14	6	18	50	66	48	0-4 0-4	2-4 0-1	1-6 0-2	1-1 4-3	2-0 2-1		0-3	4-1	1-1 0-1	2-2	1-3 3-1	2-1
Coleraine	38	17	5	16	51	50	56	0-2	0-3 1-3	1-2 3-1	3-1 3-2	1-3 1-1	0-1 1-2		0-3 2-1	1-0 1-1	0-2 2-1	4-0 3-1	2-0 3-1
Dungannon Swifts	38	14	9	15	50	53	51	2-1 0-4	2-3	1-3	0-1	0-1	2-2 1-2	3-0 1-0		1-2 1-0	2-1 2-2	0-0 3-1	0-0 1-0
Ballymena United	38	12	13	13	48	56	49	3-3	1-1 0-3	0-2 2-3	1-1	3-1 3-1	0-1	0-1 1-1	1-1 0-2		3-3 1-0	0-4 0-3	1-0 1-0
Glenavon	38	12	9	17	60	59	45	0-1 2-2	2-1	0-1	1-2 0-2	1-0	1-1 0-1	1-2 1-2	2-1 1-2	0-2 3-1		3-1 3-0	2-1 2-1
Donegal Celtic	38	8	8	22	55	89	32	1-3 2-0	1-3	0-3	1-1	4-4 0-2	2-1	2-1 1-1	3-4 1-2	2-3 3-3	1-4 3-3		0-3 0-0
Newry City	38	6	8	24	37	65	26	1-2	1-1 2-3	0-0 3-4	0-1 0-2	4-2	1-1 2-1	2-2 0-2	3-0 0-1	0-4 1-1	2-1 0-4	2-1 0-1	

7/08/2010 - 30/04/2011 • † Qualified for the UEFA Champions League • ‡ Qualified for the Europa League

Top scorers: **23** - Peter Thompson, Linfield • **20** - Jordan Owens, Crusaders • **19** - Paul McVeigh, Donegal Celtic • **17** - Daryl Fordyce, Glentoran • **15** - Stuart Dallas, Crusaders & Matty Burrows, Glentoran • **14** - Leon Knight ENG, Coleraine & Gary McCutcheon SCO, Ballymena United

NORTHERN IRELAND 2010-11 IFA CHAMPIONSHIP (2)

	Pl	W	D	L	F	A	Pts
Carrick Rangers	26	18	4	4	57	27	58
Limavady United	26	15	6	5	53	27	51
Dergview	26	15	3	8	51	32	48
Bangor	26	11	8	7	45	38	41
Ballinamallard United	26	11	6	9	45	38	39
HW Welders	26	11	6	9	45	38	39
Ards	26	9	7	10	37	42	34
Institute	26	10	4	12	28	43	34
Larne	26	8	6	12	38	41	30
Loughgall	26	8	6	12	37	48	30
Banbridge Town	26	7	7	12	31	39	28
Glebe Rangers	26	7	7	12	36	46	28
Ballymoney United	26	5	8	13	31	48	23
Ballyclare Comrades	26	5	6	15	28	55	21

7/08/2010 - 10/05/2011

MEDALS TABLE

		Overall			League			Cup		LC	
		G	S	B	G	S	B	G	B	G	B
1	Linfield	100	43	14	50	20	14	41	20	9	3
2	Glentoran	50	48	25	23	24	25	20	19	7	5
3	Belfast Celtic	22	8	8	14	4	8	8	4		
4	Lisburn Distillery	19	15	9	6	8	9	12	7		
5	Cliftonville	12	18	6	3	6	6	8	10	1	2
6	Glenavon	9	21	6	3	10	6	5	10	1	1
7	Portadown	9	18	7	4	9	7	3	7	2	2
8	Crusaders	8	8	4	4	3	4	3	2	1	3
9	Coleraine	7	19	9	1	9	9	5	6	1	4
10	Ballymena United	6	10	5			2	5	6	8	
11	Ards	6	4	8	1	1	8	4	2	1	1
12	Derry City	4	10	3	1	7	3	3	3		
13	Shelbourne Dublin	3	4	1		1	1	3	3		
14	Queen's Island	3	3		1	3		2			
15	Bangor	2	3	2		1	2	1	2	1	
16	Bohemians Dublin	1	5					1	5		
17	Ulster FC	1	3			1		1			
18	Carrick Rangers	1	2					1	2		

CIS INSURANCE LEAGUE CUP 2010-11

Round of 16		Quarter–finals		Semi–finals		Final	
Lisburn Distillery	3						
Institute *	0	**Lisburn Distillery** *	3				
Linfield	1 3p	Newry City	1				
Newry City *	1 4p2			**Lisburn Distillery** *	2 4p		
Ballymena United *	2			Crusaders	2 2p		
Ards	1	Ballymena United *	0				
Loughgall	1	**Crusaders**	2				
Crusaders *	2					**Lisburn Distillery**	2
Glentoran *	5					Portadown	1
Dungannon Swifts	1	**Glentoran**	2				
Glenavon *	1	Cliftonville *	0				
Cliftonville	2			Glentoran *	1		
Coleraine *	3			**Portadown**	2		
Donegal Celtic	2	Coleraine	0				
Carrick Rangers	1	**Portadown** *	2				
Portadown *	2					* Home team	

CUP FINAL

Mourneview Park, Lurgan
2-04-2011, Courtney
Scorers: Scott Davidson [51], David Cushley [88] for Distillery; Matthew Tipton [42] for Portadown

JJB SPORTS IRISH CUP 2010-11

Fifth Round

Team	Score
Linfield *	5
Institute	1
Kilmore Recreation	2 0
Dunmurry Recreation *	2 5
Warrenpoint Town *	1 0 3p
Cliftonville	1 0 1p
Ballymoney United	1
Dungannon Swifts *	5
Coleraine	2
Limavady United *	1
Shankill United	3 1
Carrick Rangers *	3 6
Loughgall *	3
Sport & Leisure Swifts	1
Ballymena United	1 2
Glentoran	1 3
Portadown *	4
Donegal Celtic	3
Ards *	2 0
Harland & Wolff Welders *	2 1
Queen's University *	1
Crumlin United	0
Annagh United *	2
Glenavon	6
Ballinamallard United *	3
Larne	1
Dundela *	1
Lisburn Distillery	4
Nortel	2
Albert Foundry *	0
Newry City	2
Crusaders *	3

Round of 16

Team	Score
Linfield	1 3
Dunmurry Recreation *	1 0
Warrenpoint Town	2
Dungannon Swifts *	4
Coleraine	3
Carrick Rangers *	1
Loughgall	1
Glentoran *	3
Portadown	1 1
Harland & Wolff Welders *	1 0
Queen's University	0
Glenavon *	2
Ballinamallard United	2 4
Lisburn Distillery *	2 2
Nortel	1
Crusaders *	2

Quarter-finals

Team	Score
Linfield	2
Dungannon Swifts *	0
Coleraine	1 3 2p
Glentoran *	1 3 3p
Portadown *	3 3
Glenavon	3 0
Ballinamallard United *	0
Crusaders	5

Semi-finals

Team	Score
Linfield ††	2
Glentoran	0
Portadown *	1
Crusaders †	3

Final

Team	Score
Linfield	2
Crusaders ‡	1

* Home team in the first leg • † Played at Mourneview Park, Lurgan • †† Played at Windsor Park • ‡ Qualified for the Europa League

CUP FINAL

Windsor Park, Belfast

7-05-2011, 15:00. Att: 9000. Ref: Courtney

Scorers - Thompson [78], McAllister [87] for Linfield; Caddell [54] for Crusaders

Linfield - Alan Blayney - Jim Ervin (Jamie Tomelty 75), Stephen Douglas, Chris Casement, Damien Curran, Philip Lowry (Jamie Mulgrew 63), Michael Gault, Robert Garrett, Michael Carvill, Mark McAllister, Peter Thompson. Tr: David Jeffrey

Crusaders - Chris Keenan - Gareth McKeown, Stephen McBride, David Magowan, Colin Coates, Stuart Dallas, Aidan Watson, Chris Morrow (David McMaster 86), Declan Caddell, Jordan Owens, Michael Halliday (David Rainey 79). Tr: Stephen Baxter

NOR – NORWAY

FIFA/COCA-COLA WORLD RANKING

'93	'94	'95	'96	'97	'98	'99	'00	'01	'02	'03	'04	'05	'06	'07	'08	'09	'10	'11	'12
4	8	10	14	13	14	7	14	26	26	42	35	38	50	29	59	32	12	25	

	2011												High	Low	Av
	Jan	Feb	Mar	Apr	May	Jun	Jul	Aug	Sep	Oct	Nov	Dec			
	12	11	11	11	11	11	12	12	23	24	25	25	2	59	23

When Ole Gunnar Solskjær took over as coach of Molde at the start of their centenary year in 2011 few could have predicted the extraordinary impact he would have on the club. Winners of the Norwegian cup in 1994 and 2005, Molde had never won the championship but by the end of the year Solskjær had inspired the team to a first-ever title. After a slow start to the campaign Molde took the lead at the end of June and it was a position they didn't relinquish. It was a great year for the northernmost part of Western Norway and in particular the county of Møre og Romsdal of which Molde is the capital. The largest city in the county is the port of Aalesund and for the second time in three years its people were celebrating their team winning the Norwegian Cup. Coach Kjetil Rekdal has transformed the fortunes of Aalesunds SK and in the 2011 final they beat Brann 2-1 in Oslo with their Costa Rican striker Michael Barrantes responsible for both of the goals. It was not such a happy end to the year for the national team with Egil Olsen's team missing out on the Euro 2012 play-offs on goal difference. The crucial game in their qualifying group proved to be against Denmark in Oslo in March where the Norwegians dropped two crucial points, points that would have taken them above Portugal in second place in the final standings.

UEFA EUROPEAN CHAMPIONSHIP RECORD
1960 r1 1964 r1 1968-1996 DNQ **2000** r1 2004-2012 DNQ

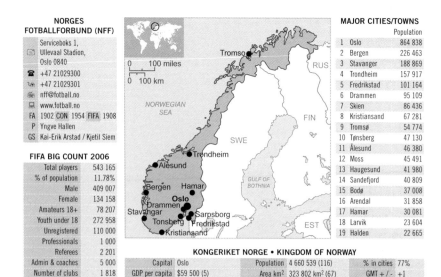

NORGES
FOTBALLFORBUND (NFF)

	Serviceboks 1, Ullevaal Stadion, Oslo 0840
☎	+47 21029300
🖷	+47 21029301
✉	nff@fotball.no
🖥	www.fotball.no
FA	1902 CON 1954 FIFA 1908
P	Yngve Hallen
GS	Kai-Erik Arstad / Kjetil Siem

FIFA BIG COUNT 2006

Total players	543 165
% of population	11.78%
Male	409 007
Female	134 158
Amateurs 18+	78 207
Youth under 18	272 958
Unregistered	110 000
Professionals	1 000
Referees	2 201
Admin & coaches	5 000
Number of clubs	1 818
Number of teams	19 841

MAJOR CITIES/TOWNS
Population

1	Oslo	864 838
2	Bergen	226 463
3	Stavanger	188 869
4	Trondheim	157 917
5	Fredrikstad	101 164
6	Drammen	95 109
7	Skien	86 436
8	Kristiansand	67 281
9	Tromsø	54 774
10	Tønsberg	47 130
11	Ålesund	46 380
12	Moss	45 491
13	Haugesund	41 980
14	Sandefjord	40 809
15	Bodø	37 008
16	Arendal	31 858
17	Hamar	30 081
18	Larvik	23 604
19	Halden	22 665

KONGERIKET NORGE • KINGDOM OF NORWAY

Capital	Oslo	
GDP per capita	$59 500 (5)	
Population	4 660 539 (116)	% in cities 77%
Area km²	323 802 km² (67)	GMT +/- +1
Neighbours (km)	Finland 727, Sweden 1619, Russia 196 • Coast 25 148	

RECENT INTERNATIONAL MATCHES PLAYED BY NORWAY

2008	Opponents	Score		Venue	Comp	Scorers	Att	Referee
6-02	Wales	L	0-3	Wrexham	Fr		7 553	McKeon IRL
26-03	Montenegro	L	1-3	Podgorica	Fr	Carew 72	9 000	Stavrev MKD
28-05	Uruguay	D	2-2	Oslo	Fr	Elyounoussi 55, Riise 84	12 246	Buttimer IRL
20-08	Republic of Ireland	D	1-1	Oslo	Fr	Reginiussen 61	16 037	Whitby WAL
6-09	Iceland	D	2-2	Oslo	WCq	Iversen 2 36p 50	17 254	Yefet ISR
11-10	Scotland	D	0-0	Glasgow	WCq		50 205	Busacca SUI
15-10	Netherlands	L	0-1	Oslo	WCq		23 840	Plautz AUT
19-11	Ukraine	L	0-1	Dnepropetrovsk	Fr		10 000	Lajuks LVA
2009								
11-02	Germany	W	1-0	Dusseldorf	Fr	Grindheim 63	42 000	Messner AUT
28-03	South Africa	L	1-2	Rustenburg	Fr	Pedersen 27	30 000	Fleischer GHA
1-04	Finland	W	3-2	Oslo	Fr	Riise.JA 56, Hoiland 90, Pedersen 92+	16 239	Styles ENG
6-06	Macedonia FYR	D	0-0	Skopje	WCq		7 000	Tagliavento ITA
10-06	Netherlands	L	0-2	Rotterdam	WCq		45 600	Baskakov RUS
12-08	Scotland	W	4-0	Oslo	WCq	Riise.JA 35, Pedersen 2 45 90, Huseklepp 60	24 493	Hamer LUX
5-09	Iceland	D	1-1	Reykjavik	WCq	Riise.JA 11	7 321	Tudor ROU
9-09	Macedonia FYR	W	2-1	Oslo	WCq	Helstad 2, Riise.JA 25	14 766	Paixao POR
10-10	South Africa	W	1-0	Oslo	Fr	Waehler 48	13 504	Collum SCO
14-11	Switzerland	W	1-0	Geneva	Fr	Carew 48p	16 000	Whitby WAL
2010								
3-03	Slovakia	W	1-0	Zilina	Fr	Moldskred 67	9 756	Nijhuis NED
29-05	Montenegro	W	2-1	Oslo	Fr	Grindheim 44, Pedersen 89	13 132	Eriksson SWE
2-06	Ukraine	L	0-1	Oslo	Fr		10 178	Blom NED
11-08	France	W	2-1	Oslo	Fr	Huseklepp 2 51 71	15 165	Velasco ESP
3-09	Iceland	W	2-1	Reykjavik	ECq	Hangeland 58, Abdellaoue 75	6 137	Banti ITA
7-09	Portugal	W	1-0	Oslo	ECq	Huseklepp 21	24 535	Duhamel FRA
8-10	Cyprus	W	2-1	Larnaca	ECq	Riise.JA 2, Carew 42	7 648	Gumienny BEL
12-10	Croatia	L	1-2	Zagreb	Fr	Abdellaoue 21	3 000	Skomina SVN
17-11	Republic of Ireland	W	2-1	Dublin	Fr	Pedersen 34, Huseklepp 86	25 000	Jakobsson ISL
2011								
9-02	Poland	L	0-1	Faro	Fr		500	Dos Anjos POR
26-03	Denmark	D	1-1	Oslo	ECq	Huseklepp 81	24 828	Rocchi ITA
4-06	Portugal	L	0-1	Lisbon	ECq		47 829	Cakir TUR
7-06	Lithuania	W	1-0	Oslo	Fr	Pedersen 84	12 945	Attwell ENG
10-08	Czech Republic	W	3-0	Oslo	Fr	Abdellaoue 2 23 89p, Riise.JA 72	12 734	Black NIR
2-09	Iceland	W	1-0	Oslo	ECq	Abdellaoue 88p	22 381	Hategin ROU
6-09	Denmark	L	0-2	Copenhagen	ECq		37 167	Lannoy FRA
11-10	Cyprus	W	3-1	Oslo	ECq	Pedersen 25, Carew 34, Hogli 65	13 490	Collum SCO
12-11	Wales	L	1-4	Cardiff	Fr	Huseklepp 61	12 600	Grubelnik AUT

Fr = Friendly match • EC = UEFA EURO 2012 • WC = FIFA World Cup • q = qualifier

NORWAY NATIONAL TEAM HISTORICAL RECORDS

Caps	104 - Thorbjorn Svenssen 1947 62 • **100** - Henning Berg 1992-2004 & John Arne Riise 2000- • 97 - Erik Thorstvedt 1982-96 • 91 - John Carew 1998- • 86 - Oyvind Leonhardsen 1990-2003 • 83 - Kjetil Rekdal 1987-2000 • 79 - Steffen Iversen 1998- • 78 - Erik Mykland 1990-2000 • 77 - Svein Grondalen 1973-84 • 76 - Tore Andre Flo 1995-2004 • 75 - Stig Inge Bjornebye 1989-2000 • 75 - Brede Hangeland 2002-
Goals	33 - Jorgen Juve 1928-37 • 26 - Einar Gundersen 1917-28 • 25 - Harald Hennum 1949-60 • 24 - John Carew 1998- • 23 - Ole Gunnar Solskjær 1995-2007 & Tore Andre Flo 1995-2004 • 22 - Gunnar Thoresen 1946-59 • 21 - Steffen Iversen 1998- • 20 - Jan Age Fjortoft 1986-96 • 19 - Odd Iversen 1967-79; Olav Nilsen 1962-71 & Oyvind Leonhardsen 1990-2003
Past Coaches	Willibald Hahn AUT 1953-55 • Ron Lewin ENG 1956-57 • Edmund Majowsky 1958 • Ragnar Larsen 1958 • Kristian Henriksen 1959 • Wilhelm Kment AUT 1960-62 • Ragnar Larsen 1962-66 • Wilhelm Kment AUT 1967-69 • Oivind Johannessen 1970-71 • George Curtis ENG 1972-74 • Kjell Schou-Andreassen & Nils Arne Eggen 1975-77 • Tor Roste Fossen 1978-87 • Tord Grip SWE 1987-88 • Ingvar Stadheim 1988-90 • Egil Olsen 1990-98 • Nils Johan Semb 1998-2003 • Age Hareide 2003-08 • Egil Olsen 2009-

NORWAY 2011

TIPPELIGAEN

	Pl	W	D	L	F	A	Pts	Molde	Tromsø	Rosenborg	Brann	Odd	Haugesund	Vålerenga	Strømgodset	Aalesund	Stabæk	Viking	Fredrikstad	Lillestrøm	Sogndal	Start	Sarpsborg
Molde FK †	30	17	7	6	55	38	58		2-2	0-2	2-2	0-0	3-1	2-1	2-2	5-2	3-2	0-0	2-1	1-0	2-0	5-1	3-1
Tromsø IL ‡	30	15	8	7	56	34	53	0-2		3-1	4-0	2-1	2-0	4-1	2-0	1-0	3-3	3-1	3-1	1-0	0-0	2-0	2-2
Rosenborg BK ‡	30	14	7	9	69	44	49	3-1	3-1		3-6	7-0	0-1	2-0	2-0	2-2	1-2	3-2	2-0	4-4	2-1	4-1	4-0
SK Brann	30	14	6	10	51	49	48	1-3	1-1	2-1		2-0	1-0	1-4	0-0	1-1	2-1	3-2	0-1	2-0	2-0	2-1	1-0
Odd Grenland	30	14	6	10	44	44	48	1-0	3-1	3-3	2-3		1-0	1-1	1-0	2-2	2-3	4-2	2-1	1-3	1-0	0-2	1-0
SK Haugesund	30	14	5	11	55	43	47	5-0	1-1	2-2	3-3	2-1		1-1	5-1	1-0	3-4	2-0	3-2	2-0	4-0	1-0	4-2
Vålerenga IF	30	14	5	11	42	33	47	1-2	2-0	1-0	0-2	0-1	3-2		2-2	2-0	2-0	3-0	1-2	1-1	1-1	2-1	2-0
IF Strømgodset	30	12	9	9	44	43	45	0-1	1-1	3-1	1-0	2-0	3-1	2-1		2-2	1-0	2-2	1-0	3-1	2-1	3-0	5-2
Aalesunds SK ‡	30	12	7	11	36	38	43	1-3	1-0	1-3	3-1	0-1	1-0	2-1	2-1		2-0	2-0	1-2	1-0	1-0	0-0	2-0
Stabæk Fotball	30	11	6	13	44	50	39	1-1	2-4	2-1	1-1	1-3	1-2	1-0	2-0	1-2		0-1	3-1	0-7	0-1	4-1	2-0
Viking FK	30	9	10	11	33	40	37	2-2	2-1	0-0	3-0	1-1	1-1	0-2	0-1	1-0	1-0		2-0	2-0	2-0	1-1	2-2
Fredrikstad FK	30	10	6	14	38	41	36	0-1	0-2	2-0	4-2	0-1	1-0	3-1	1-1	3-1	1-2	0-1		1-1	2-2	1-1	1-1
Lillestrøm SK	30	9	7	14	46	52	34	0-3	3-2	2-5	1-4	1-1	5-0	0-1	4-2	1-1	1-1	2-1	0-0		0-3	2-1	3-1
Sogndal IL	30	8	10	12	24	31	34	2-1	0-0	1-1	1-0	1-4	3-1	0-1	1-1	0-0	0-0	0-0	0-1	2-0		2-0	1-0
IK Start	30	7	5	18	39	61	26	1-2	1-6	1-1	3-1	1-3	1-4	0-2	5-1	2-3	2-4	4-0	3-2	3-0	1-1		1-0
Sarpsborg 08	30	5	6	19	31	65	21	3-0	0-2	0-6	3-5	3-2	0-2	1-1	2-0	1-1	1-1	1-4	2-4	1-0	2-0		

18/03/2011 - 27/11/2011 • † Qualified for the UEFA Champions League • ‡ Qualified for the Europa League
Top scorers: 17 - Mostafa Abdellaoue, Tromsø • 16 - Rade Prica SWE, Rosenborg & Ole Martin Årst, Start • 15 - Kim Ojo NGA, Brann

MEDALS TABLE

		Overall			League			Cup		City
		G	S	B	G	S	B	G	S	
1	Rosenborg BK	31	10	2	22	5	2	9	5	Trondheim
2	Fredrikstad FK	20	16	1	9	9	1	11	7	Fredrikstad
3	Viking SK	13	7	8	8	2	8	5	5	Stavanger
4	Odd Grenland	12	10			2		12	8	Skien
5	Lillestrøm SK	10	16	3	5	8	3	5	8	Lillestrøm
6	SFK Lyn	10	10	4	2	4	4	8	6	Oslo
7	SK Brann	9	13	3	3	5	3	6	8	Bergen
8	FK Skeid Oslo	9	8	1	1	5	1	8	3	Oslo
9	Vålerenga IF	9	5	3	5	3	3	4	2	Oslo
10	FK Sarpsborg	6	6	2			2	6	6	Sarpsborg
11	IF Stromsgodset	6	2	3	1		3	5	2	Drammen
12	Orn FK	4	4					4	4	Horten
13	Molde FK	3	9	3	1	6	3	2	3	Molde

NORWAY 2011

ADECCOLIGAEN (2)

	Pl	W	D	L	F	A	Pts	Hønefoss	Sandnes	Sandefjord	Ranheim	Bodø-Glimt	Hamar'tene	Kongsvinger	Hødd	Bryne	Mjøndalen	Alta	Strømmen	Asker	Nybergsund	Randaberg	Løv-Ham
Hønefoss BK	30	16	9	5	61	28	57		1-0	2-3	2-1	3-2	1-1	2-1	1-1	1-1	3-0	2-0	1-2	0-1	5-3	6-0	2-0
Sandnes Ulf	30	18	2	10	58	32	56	1-0		1-0	2-0	3-0	0-2	3-1	3-0	0-1	4-1	1-2	2-0	4-1	1-0	4-2	6-0
Sandefjord Fotball	30	16	5	9	61	38	53	0-0	1-1		1-1	1-2	1-2	1-2	1-0	1-1	6-0	3-1	2-1	5-1	2-0	4-0	2-1
Ranheim Fotball	30	15	7	8	61	39	52	2-2	0-1	2-1		3-2	1-2	4-0	2-5	2-2	3-0	1-0	4-1	4-0	4-1	3-0	1-0
FK Bodø-Glimt	30	15	7	8	52	38	52	0-0	3-1	1-1	1-1		1-1	4-2	3-1	3-0	1-0	0-0	3-1	3-0	3-0	4-1	0-2
Hamarkameratene	30	14	9	7	52	40	51	1-0	2-2	1-4	0-1	2-2		0-2	2-1	1-2	0-0	2-0	4-2	2-1	1-0	3-0	2-2
Kongsvinger IL	30	14	7	9	50	36	49	2-2	1-0	3-0	3-3	2-0	3-3		1-1	0-2	2-0	1-1	1-1	1-0	1-0	4-1	4-0
IL Hødd	30	13	7	10	54	42	46	0-4	2-1	1-2	0-0	3-0	3-1	0-2		0-1	2-2	3-0	4-0	3-0	3-0	2-1	3-4
Bryne FK	30	11	11	8	47	36	44	0-1	3-5	2-1	3-1	1-2	0-3	0-2	0-1		0-0	2-2	5-0	2-2	2-2	7-0	0-0
Mjøndalen IF	30	10	10	10	42	51	40	2-2	2-1	4-2	1-2	2-4	1-3	2-2	3-0	0-1		3-0	2-1	4-3	5-2	3-1	0-0
Alta IF	30	10	9	11	45	51	39	1-4	0-2	1-2	1-0	3-3	1-5	2-1	2-2	0-0	4-1		1-1	3-4	2-0	4-1	2-0
Strømmen IF	30	9	7	14	43	58	34	0-0	4-2	0-3	2-2	1-2	1-0	1-0	1-1	2-4	0-1	1-2		2-1	2-2	2-1	6-2
Asker Fotball	30	9	7	14	38	56	34	1-2	0-1	2-2	1-1	0-1	1-0	1-1	2-1	0-3	1-1	1-1	1-4		2-0	0-0	3-0
Nybergsund IL-Trysil	30	6	5	19	42	72	23	0-5	2-1	4-2	1-3	0-2	4-0	1-0	3-5	1-2	0-1	2-2	2-6	1-1		3-3	3-1
Randaberg IL	30	4	5	21	37	87	17	0-2	1-2	1-5	1-4	2-0	1-3	0-4	2-2	2-1	1-1	2-2	1-2	2-4	3-2		4-0
Løv-Ham Bergen §1	30	4	5	21	32	71	16	2-5	0-3	1-2	2-5	0-1	2-2	0-1	0-1	0-2	0-0	1-2	3-0	0-1	2-3	4-3	

3/04/2011 - 30/11/2011 • § = points deducted • Top scorer: 18 - Vegard Braaten, Ranheim

NM SAS BRAATHENS CUPEN 2011

Third Round

Team	Score
Aalesunds SK	2
IL Hødd *	1
Kjelsås Fotball *	1
Sarpsborg 08	2
Lillestrøm SK *	0 5p
Sandefjord Fotball	0 4p
Byåsen IL *	3
Rosenborg BK	6
Alta IF	0 5p
Ranheim Fotball *	0 4p
FK Bodø-Glimt	0
Tromsø IL *	3
IF Strømsgodset	2
Mjøndalen IF *	1
Notodden FK *	1
IK Start	2
Fredrikstad FK	4
Lørenskog IF *	0
Kongsvinger IL *	1
Odd Grenland	2
Hønefoss BK *	3
Stabæk Fotball	1
Tiller IL *	1
Molde FK	7
Viking FK *	2
Sandnes Ulf	0
Randaberg IL *	3
SK Haugesund	5
Sogndal IL *	2
Asker Fotball *	0
Åsane Fotball *	0
SK Brann	1

Round of 16

Team	Score
Aalesunds SK *	3
Sarpsborg 08	0
Lillestrøm SK *	2 1p
Rosenborg BK *	2 4p
Alta IF *	1
Tromsø IL	0
IF Strømsgodset	0
IK Start *	1
Fredrikstad FK	2
Odd Grenland *	1
Hønefoss BK	1
Molde FK *	3
Viking FK	3
SK Haugesund *	2
Sogndal IL	2 2p
SK Brann *	2 3p

Quarter-finals

Team	Score
Aalesunds SK *	3
Rosenborg BK	1
Alta IF	0
IK Start *	1
Fredrikstad FK *	3
Molde FK	2
Viking FK *	1 1p
SK Brann	1 3p

Semi-finals

Team	Score
Aalesunds SK *	1
IK Start	0
Fredrikstad FK *	0
SK Brann	2

Final

Team	Score
Aalesunds SK ‡	2
SK Brann	1

CUP FINAL

Ullevaal, Oslo

6-11-2011, Att: 25 032, Ref: Edvartsen

Scorers – Grorud OG 19, Barrantes 38 for Aalesund; Korcsmar 21 for Brann

Aalesund – Sten Grytebust – Einar Jaager, Jonatan Tollas, Daniel Arnefjord (c), Jo Matland – Fredrik Ulvestad, Jason Morrison•, Magnus Olsen (Sander Post 90), Michael Barrantes (Ville Jalasto 87) – Demar Phillips, Edvard Skagestad (Peter Larsen 74). Tr: Kjetil Rekdal

Brann – Piotr Leciejewski – Birkir Sævarsson•, Lars Grorud, Zsolt Korcsmar, Hassan El Fakiri – Rudolph Austin, Maximiliano Bajter• (Tadas Labukas 86), Diego Guastavino – Erik Mjelde (c), Kim Ojo, Bjørnar Holmvik• (Fredrik Haugen• 70). Tr: Rune Skarsfjord

* Home team • ‡ Qualified for the Europa League

NZL – NEW ZEALAND

FIFA/COCA-COLA WORLD RANKING

'93	'94	'95	'96	'97	'98	'99	'00	'01	'02	'03	'04	'05	'06	'07	'08	'09	'10	'11	'12
77	99	102	132	120	103	100	91	84	49	88	95	120	131	95	86	82	63	119	

						2011							High	Low	Av
Jan	Feb	Mar	Apr	May	Jun	Jul	Aug	Sep	Oct	Nov	Dec		High	Low	Av
63	64	56	61	61	97	94	94	89	105	119	119		47	156	96

New Zealand played just three matches in 2011 as Ricki Herbert started preparations for the qualifying tournament for the 2014 FIFA World Cup in Brazil, but victories against teams other than the Pacific island nations remain hard to come by. A solitary win against Serbia in the run-up to the finals in South Africa is all that the All-Whites have achieved since the start of 2010 and in 2011 there were 3-0 defeats at the hands of both Mexico and neighbours Australia. Even within Oceania New Zealand can expect stiffer competition from the likes of New Caledonia, the Solomon Islands and Vanuatu as they search for a place in the finals in Brazil. At home the championship was once again a two-horse race between Auckland City and Waitakere United with Neil Emblen's Waitakere retaining the title for the first time in their history. In the final between the two, a James Pritchard own goal on the stroke of full-time saw Waitakere win 3-2. A week later, however, it was Auckland celebrating after they beat Amicale in the final of the OFC Champions League - a 4-0 victory in the second leg saw them win the trophy for a record third time. There were first-time winners in the annual Chatham Cup - New Zealand's longest-running tournament - with Wairarapa United beating the more experienced Napier City Rovers 1-0 in the final.

FIFA WORLD CUP RECORD

1930-1966 DNE   1970-1978 DNQ   **1982** 23 r1   1986-2006 DNQ   **2010** 22 r1

NEW ZEALAND FOOTBALL (NZF)

North Harbour Stadium,
✉ Stadium Drive, PO Box 301,
043 Albany, Auckland

☎ +64 9 4140175
📠 +64 9 4140176
📧 tracy.brady@nzfootball.co.nz
🖥 www.nzfootball.co.nz
FA 1891 CON 1966 FIFA 1948
P Frank Van Hattum
GS Grant Mckavanagh

FIFA BIG COUNT 2006

Total players	198 757
% of population	4.88%
Male	164 667
Female	34 090
Amateurs 18+	12 067
Youth under 18	79 565
Unregistered	49 500
Professionals	25
Referees	800
Admin & coaches	19 000
Number of clubs	325
Number of teams	7 524

MAJOR CITIES/TOWNS

		Population
1	Auckland	415 400
2	Manukau	400 208
3	Christchurch	373 178
4	North Shore	295 695
5	Waitakere	202 786
6	Wellington	186 122
7	Hamilton	163 757
8	Tauranga	117 085
9	Dunedin	111 855
10	Lower Hutt	97 568
11	Palmerston North	77 177
12	Hastings	63 259
13	Napier	56 891
14	Rotorua	54 070
15	Whangarei	50 272
16	New Plymouth	49 619
17	Porirua	48 761
18	Invercargill	46 320
19	Nelson	43 571

NEW ZEALAND

Capital	Wellington	Population	4 213 418 (124)	% in cities	87%
GDP per capita	$27 900 (49)	Area km²	267 710 km² (75)	GMT +/-	+12
Neighbours (km)	Coast 15 134				

RECENT INTERNATIONAL MATCHES PLAYED BY NEW ZEALAND

2006	Opponents	Score	Venue	Comp	Scorers	Att	Referee
19-02	Malaysia	W 1-0	Christchurch	Fr	Old [87]	10 100	O'Leary NZL
23-02	Malaysia	W 2-1	Albany	Fr	Banks [18], Barron [88]	8 702	Fox NZL
25-04	Chile	L 1-4	Rancagua	Fr	Smeltz [14]	8 000	Osorio CHI
27-04	Chile	L 0-1	La Calera	Fr			Acosta CHI
24-05	Hungary	L 0-2	Budapest	Fr		5 000	Hrinak SVK
27-05	Georgia	W 3-1	Altenkirchen	Fr	Coveny 2 [35 53], Killen [37]	1 000	
31-05	Estonia	D 1-1	Tallinn	Fr	Hay [27]	3 000	Rasmussen DEN
4-06	Brazil	L 0-4	Geneva	Fr		32 000	Laperriere SUI
2007							
7-02	Tahiti	D 0-0	Auckland	Fr			Hester NZL
24-03	Costa Rica	L 0-4	San Jose	Fr		15 000	Rodriguez CRC
28-03	Venezuela	L 0-5	Maracaibo	Fr		12 000	
26-05	Wales	D 2-2	Wrexham	Fr	Smeltz 2 [2 24]	7 819	Skjerven DEN
17-10	Fiji	W 2-0	Lautoka	WCq	Vicelich [37], Smeltz [86]	6 000	Marrufo USA
17-11	Vanuatu	W 2-1	Port Vila	WCq	Smeltz [52], Mulligan [93+]	8 000	Minan PNG
21-11	Vanuatu	W 4-1	Wellington	WCq	Mulligan 2 [14 81], Smeltz 2 [29p 34]	2 500	Jacques TAH
2008							
6-09	New Caledonia	W 3-1	Noumea	WCq	Sigmund [16], Smeltz 2 [66 76]	2 589	Varman FIJ
10-09	New Caledonia	W 3-0	Auckland	WCq	Smeltz 2 [49 76], Christie [69]	8 000	Hauata TAH
19-11	Fiji	L 0-2	Lautoka	WCq		4 500	Fred VAN
2009							
28-03	Thailand	L 1-3	Bangkok	Fr	Elliott [14]		
3-06	Tanzania	L 1-2	Dar es Salaam	Fr	Smeltz [10p]		
6-06	Botswana	D 0-0	Gaborone	Fr			
10-06	Italy	L 3-4	Atteridgeville	Fr	Smeltz [13], Killen 2 [42 57p]	2 000	Bennett RSA
14-06	Spain	L 0-5	Rustenburg	CCr1		21 649	Codjia BEN
17-06	South Africa	L 0-2	Rustenburg	CCr1		36 598	Archundia MEX
20-06	Iraq	D 0-0	Johannesburg	CCr1		23 295	Webb ENG
9-09	Jordan	W 3-1	Amman	Fr	Smeltz 2 [17p 65], Fallon [45]		
10-10	Bahrain	D 0-0	Manama	WCq		37 000	Kassai HUN
14-11	Bahrain	W 1-0	Wellington	WCq	Fallon [45]	36 500	Larrionda URU
2010							
3-03	Mexico	L 0-2	Pasadena	Fr		90 526	Marrufo USA
24-05	Australia	L 1-2	Melbourne	Fr	Killen [16]	55 659	Salazar USA
29-05	Serbia	W 1-0	Klagenfurt	Fr	Smeltz [22]	14 000	Drachta AUT
4-06	Slovenia	L 1-3	Maribor	Fr	Fallon [20]	10 965	Kakkos GRE
15-06	Slovakia	D 1-1	Rustenburg	WCr1	Reid [93+]	23 871	Damon RSA
20-06	Italy	D 1-1	Nelspruit	WCr1	Smeltz [7]	38 229	Batres GUA
24-06	Paraguay	D 0-0	Polokwane	WCr1		34 850	Nishimura JPN
9-10	Honduras	D 1-1	Auckland	Fr	Wood [45]	18 153	O'Leary NZL
12-10	Paraguay	L 0-2	Wellington	Fr		16 477	Cross NZL
2011							
25-03	China PR	D 1-1	Wuhan	Fr	McGlinchey [53]		Toma JPN
1-06	Mexico	L 0-3	Denver	Fr		45 401	Vaughn USA
5-06	Australia	L 0-3	Adelaide	Fr		21 281	Tojo JPN

Fr = Friendly match • OC = OFC Oceania Nations Cup • CC = FIFA Confederations Cup • WC = FIFA World Cup

NEW ZEALAND NATIONAL TEAM HISTORICAL RECORDS

Caps

73 - Ivan Vicelich 1995- • **69** - Simon Elliott 1995- • **64** - Vaughn Coveny 1992-2007 • **61** - Ricki Herbert 1980-89 • **60** - Chris Jackson 1995-2003 • **59** - Brian Turner 1967-82

Goals

28 - Vaughn Coveny 1992-2007 • **22** - Steve Sumner 1976-88 • **21** - Brian Turner 1967-82 • **17** - Shane Smeltz 2003- • **16** - Jock Newall 1951-52 & Keith Nelson 1977-83

Past Coaches

Matthew Robinson AUS 1947-56 • Ken Armstrong ENG 1957-64 • Lou Brocic YUG 1965-66 • Juan Schwanner CHI 1967-68 • Lou Brocic YUG 1969 • Barrie Truman 1970-76 • Wally Hughes 1977-78 • John Adshead ENG 1979-82 • Allan Jones 1983-84 • Kevin Fallon 1985-88 • John Adshead ENG 1989 • Ian Marshall SCO 1990-93 • Bobby Clark SCO 1994-95 • Keith Pritchett SCO 1996-97 • Joe McGrath IRL 1997-98 • Ken Dugdale 1998-2002 • Mick Waitt ENG 2002-04 • Ricki Herbert 2005-

NEW ZEALAND 2010–11

NEW ZEALAND FOOTBALL CHAMPIONSHIP (NZFC)

	Pl	W	D	L	F	A	Pts	Waitakere	Auckland	Wellington	Canterbury	Hawkes Bay	Waikato	Otago Utd	YoungHeart
Waitakere United †	14	12	0	2	39	12	36		0-1	2-0	2-1	1-2	6-1	3-1	6-1
Auckland City †	14	9	3	2	29	12	30	1-3		2-0	0-1	5-0	5-1	0-0	3-1
Team Wellington	14	7	2	5	28	23	23	1-2	0-0		2-4	1-3	3-1	5-0	2-2
Canterbury United	14	6	2	6	20	19	20	0-2	1-2	1-2		0-0	2-2	3-1	1-0
Hawkes Bay United	14	5	4	5	18	22	19	1-3	2-2	2-3	1-2		1-1	3-2	2-1
Waikato	14	4	3	7	21	33	15	1-3	2-3	2-3	1-0	1-0		2-2	3-0
Otago United	14	3	3	8	15	30	12	1-2	0-3	0-3	2-1	0-0	0-1		4-3
YoungHeart Manawatu	14	1	1	12	19	38	4	0-4	1-2	2-3	2-3	0-1	5-2	1-2	

16/10/2010 - 10/04/2011 • Top four qualified for the play-offs • † Qualified for OFC Champions League
Top scorers: **12** - Allan Pearce, Waitakere • **9** - Andy Bevin, Hawkes Bay & Milos Nikolic, Waikato • **8** - Russel Kamo, Canterbury
Play-off Semi-finals: **Waitakere United** 6-2 0-1 Canterbury United; Team Wellington 0-2 1-5 **Auckland City**
Grand Final: **Waitakere United** 3-2 Auckland City. **Waitakere United** are the 2011 NZFC champions
Final details: Douglas Field, Auckland, 10-04-2011, 14:00, Att: 3500, Ref: Peter O'Leary. Scorers - Dakota Lucas 2 [10 37], James Pritchett OG [90] for Waitakere; Aaron Scott OG [26], Manel Exposito [49] for Auckland • **Waitakere** - Jason Rowley, Jason Rowley, Aaron Scott - Martin Bullock, Jake Butler, Ryan De Vries (Michael Gwyther 80), Neil Emblen - Dakota Lucas, Tim Payne (Zane Sole 92+), Allan Pearce. Tr: Neil Emblen • **Auckland** - Jacob Spoonley - Angel Berlanga, Ian Hogg•, James Pritchett, Ivan Vicelich - Alex Feneridis, Stuart Kelly (Luis Corrales 60), Albert Riera (Adam Thomas 80) - Adam Dickinson, Manel Exposito•, Daniel Koprivcic. Tr: Aaron McFarland

MEDALS TABLE (NZFC CLUBS)

	Overall		Lge		OFC		City/Town
	G	S	G	S	G	S	
1 Auckland City	7	1	4	1	3		Auckland
2 Waitakere United	5	4	3	3	2	1	Waitakere
3 Canterbury United		2		2			Christchurch
4 Team Wellington		1		1			Wellington
5 Hawke's Bay United							Napier
Otago United							Dunedin
Waikato FC							Hamilton
YoungHeart Manawatu							Palmerston North

MEDALS TABLE OVERALL (1923-)

		Ov'rall		Lge		Cup		OFC	
		G	S	G	S	G	S	G	S
1	Uni - Mt Wellington	13	13	6	7	7	5		1
2	Christchurch United	12	5	6	2	6	3		
3	Napier City Rovers	8	5	4	3	4	2		
4	Waitakere City	8	3	5	1	3	2		
5	North Shore United	7	9	2	3	5	6		
6	Auckland City	7	1	4	1			3	1
7	Miramar Rangers	6	5	2	4	4	1		
8	Eastern Suburbs	6	4	1	1	5	3		
9	Central United	6	3	2	1	4	2		
10	Waitakere United	5	4	3	3				2
11	Waterside	4	1			4	1		
12	Western	3	5			3	5		
13	Western Suburbs	3	2			3	2		
14	Manurewa	3		1		2			
	Petone	3				3			
	Wellington United	3		3					

CHATHAM CUP 2011

Round of sixteen		Quarter-finals		Semi-finals		Final	
Wairarapa United	1						
Wellington United *	0	**Wairarapa United** *	4				
Central United	0	Waitakere City	1				
Waitakere City *	1			**Wairarapa United**	1		
Dunedin Technical	2			Bay Olympic *	0		
Roslyn-Wakari *	1	Dunedin Technical *	3 3p				
Waitemata	0	**Bay Olympic**	3 5p				
Bay Olympic *	5					**Wairarapa United**	2
Caversham *	6					Napier City Rovers	1
Coastal Spirit	4	**Caversham**	4				
Three Kings United	1	Onehunga Sports *	0			CUP FINAL	
Onehunga Sports *	4			Caversham	1	Memorial Park, Palmerston North	
Manurewa *	1			**Napier City Rovers** *	2	28-08-2011, Ref: Peter O'Leary	
Birkenhead United	0	Manurewa	2			Scorers - Seule Soromon [24], Pita	
Palmerston N'th Marist	0	**Napier City Rovers** *	3			Rabo [86] for Wairarapa; Fergus Neil [67]	
Napier City Rovers *	3					for Napier	

* Home team

OMA – OMAN

FIFA/COCA-COLA WORLD RANKING

'93	'94	'95	'96	'97	'98	'99	'00	'01	'02	'03	'04	'05	'06	'07	'08	'09	'10	'11	'12
97	71	98	91	81	58	92	106	91	96	62	56	91	72	84	96	79	99	85	

2011													High	Low	Av
Jan	Feb	Mar	Apr	May	Jun	Jul	Aug	Sep	Oct	Nov	Dec		High	Low	Av
104	110	110	106	106	107	106	103	105	103	93	85		50	117	86

Oman were one of the success stories in the early stages of qualifying in Asia for the 2014 FIFA World Cup as Paul Le Guen's side overcame both Saudi Arabia and Thailand to find themselves amongst the final 10 nations fighting for a place in Brazil. Oman's form at home in Muscat sealed their place in the final phase of qualifying notably their surprise 1-0 win over Australia and they have been grouped with the Australians again in the final round along with Japan, Iraq and Jordan with the top two guaranteed a place in the finals. The success of the national team was in stark contrast to that of Omani clubs in the second-tier AFC Cup. Al Suwaiq finished bottom of their group while Al Urooba also missed out on a place in the knockout phase of the competition after finishing third in their group behind Lebanon's Al Ahed on goal difference. Creating a stronger and more professional league is at the centre of the development plans of the Omani football association but there is still someway to go before Omani clubs are in a position to make their presence felt in the AFC Cup, let alone the AFC Champions League which is the ultimate objective. Al Suwaiq were back in the 2012 AFC Cup after retaining their league title, finishing three points ahead of Al Urooba while Dhofar won the Sultan Qaboos Cup with a 1-0 victory over Al Ittihad in the final.

FIFA WORLD CUP RECORD
1930-1986 DNE 1990-2010 DNQ

OMAN FOOTBALL ASSOCIATION (OFA)

Seeb Sports Complex,
PO Box 3462,
Ruwi 112
☎ +968 24 533004
📠 +968 24 543023
✉ omanfa@omantel.net.om
🖥 omanfa.com
FA 1978 CON 1979 FIFA 1980
P Khalid Hamad Al Busaidi
GS Hazza Al Saadi

FIFA BIG COUNT 2006

Total players	57 610
% of population	1.86%
Male	57 610
Female	0
Amateurs 18+	3 010
Youth under 18	5 600
Unregistered	11 000
Professionals	0
Referees	105
Admin & coaches	500
Number of clubs	43
Number of teams	129

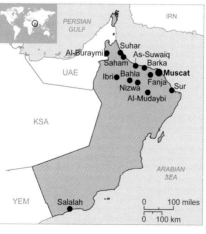

MAJOR CITIES/TOWNS

		Population
1	Muscat	1 152 254
2	Salalah	197 169
3	As-Suwaiq	133 894
4	Suhar	129 737
5	Ibri	122 960
6	Saham	109 763
7	Barka	106 378
8	Ar-Rustaq	101 132
9	Al-Buraymi	96 920
10	Sur	89 863
11	Nizwa	88 021

The Muscat metroplolitan area consists of:

Seeb	299 416
Matrah	229 266
Bawshar	199 505
Qurayyat	54 219
Al Amarat	47 411
Muscat	25 690

SALTANAT UMAN • SULTANATE OF OMAN

Capital	Muscat	Population 3 418 085 (133)	% in cities 72%
GDP per capita	$20 200 (61)	Area km² 309 500 km² (70)	GMT +/- +4
Neighbours (km)	Saudi Arabia 676, UAE 410, Yemen 288 • Coast 2092		

RECENT INTERNATIONAL MATCHES PLAYED BY OMAN

2009	Opponents	Score		Venue	Comp	Scorers	Att	Referee
17-01	Saudi Arabia	D	0-0	Muscat	GCf	W 6-5p		
19-01	Indonesia	D	0-0	Muscat	ACq		13 000	Shamsuzzaman BAN
28-01	Kuwait	W	1-0	Kuwait City	ACq	Hassan Rabia 63	22 000	Al Saeedi UAE
28-03	Senegal	W	2-0	Muscat	Fr	Mohammed Sheiba 10, Saad Obaid 88		
30-05	Egypt	L	0-1	Muscat	Fr			
9-06	Bosnia-Herzegovina	L	1-2	Cannes	Fr	Ahmed Hadid 31		
12-08	Saudi Arabia	W	2-1	Salalah	Fr	Hassan Rabia 2 47 63		
9-09	Qatar	D	1-1	Doha	Fr	Hassan Rabia 63		
14-10	Australia	L	0-1	Melbourne	ACq		20 595	Toma JPN
14-11	Australia	L	1-2	Muscat	ACq	Khalifa Ayil 16	12 000	Sun Baojie CHN
17-11	Brazil	L	0-2	Muscat	Fr			
31-12	Singapore	W	4-1	Singapore	Fr	Fouzi Bashir 15, Yacoob Abdul Karim 20, Hussein Al Hadhri 34, Osama Hadid 69		
2010								
6-01	Indonesia	W	2-1	Jakarta	ACq	Fouzi Bashir 32, Ismail Sulaiman 52	45 000	Mohd Salleh MAS
20-01	Sweden	L	0-1	Muscat	Fr		1 000	Shukralla BHR
3-03	Kuwait	D	0-0	Muscat	ACq		27 000	Moradi IRN
18-05	Yemen	W	1-0	Sana'a	Fr	Ahmed Manaa 24		
11-08	Kazakhstan	L	1-3	Astana	Fr	Hussein Ali 64		Irmatov UZB
3-09	Malaysia	W	3-0	Doha	Fr	Hassan Rabia 3, Amad Ali 2 38 44		
7-09	Qatar	D	1-1	Doha	Fr	Amad Ali 56		
21-09	Iraq	L	2-3	Amman	Fr	Hassan Rabia 42, Osama Hadid 88		
26-09	Bahrain	L	0-2	Amman	WAr1		500	
28-09	Iran	D	2-2	Amman	WAr1	Osma Hadid 40, Yacoob Abdul Karim 45	3 000	
8-10	Gabon	W	1-0	Muscat	Fr	Hassan Rabia 9		
12-10	Chile	L	0-1	Muscat	Fr		9 000	Blooshi KUW
17-11	Belarus	L	0-4	Muscat	Fr		1 000	Al Amri KSA
23-11	Bahrain	D	1-1	Aden	GCr1	Amad Ali 37		Al Enezi KUW
26-11	UAE	D	0-0	Aden	GCr1			Shaaban EGY
29-11	Iraq	D	0-0	Abyan	GCr1			Younis EGY
2011								
29-03	Tunisia	W	2-1	Seeb	Fr	Ahmed Mubarak 2 10p 85p		
6-07	Kuwait	D	1-1	Beirut	Fr	Hassan Rabia 30		
9-07	Lebanon	W	1-0	Beirut	Fr	Hamood Al Sadi 86		
15-07	Syria	D	1-1	Seeb	Fr	Qasim Said 61		
23-07	Myanmar	W	2-0	Seeb	WCq	Amad Ali 22, Ismail Al Ajmi 79. Match awarded 3-0 to Oman	6 300	Sabbagh LIB
28-07	Myanmar	W	2-0	Yangon	WCq	Amad Ali 22, Ahmed Mubarak 39p. Match abandoned and awarded to Oman	30 000	Sato JPN
10-08	Bahrain	D	1-1	Dubai	Fr	Ahmed Hadid 25. Abandoned 65'. Result stood		
27-08	Kuwait	W	1-0	Muscat	Fr	Hussain Al Hadhri 64		
2-09	Saudi Arabia	D	0-0	Seeb	WCq		14 000	Abdou QAT
6-09	Thailand	L	0-3	Bangkok	WCq		19 000	Kim Dong Jin KOR
11-10	Australia	L	0-3	Sydney	WCq		24 732	Kovalenko UZB
4-11	Qatar	D	0-0	Doha	Fr			
11-11	Australia	W	1-0	Muscat	WCq	Amad Ali 18	4 500	Abdulnabi BHR
15-11	Saudi Arabia	D	0-0	Riyadh	WCq		62 740	Torky IRN

Fr = Friendly match • GC = Gulf Cup • WA = West Asian Championship • AC = AFC Asian Cup • WC = FIFA World Cup
q = qualifier • r1 = first round group • sf = semi-final • f = final

OMAN NATIONAL TEAM HISTORICAL RECORDS

Past Coaches — Mamadoh Al Khafaji EGY 1974-76 • George Smith ENG 1979 • Hamed El Dhiab TUN 1980-82 • Mansaf El Meliti TUN 1982 • Paulo Heiki BRA 1984 • Antonio Clemente BRA 1986 • Jorge Vitorio BRA 1986-88 • Karl-Heinz Heddergott GER 1988-89 • Bernd Patzke GER 1990-92 • Heshmat Mohajerani IRN 1992-94 • Rashid Jaber Al Yafi'i 1995-96 • Mahmoud El Gohary EGY 1996 • Jozef Venglos SVK 1996-97 • Ian Porterfield SCO 1997 • Valdeir Vieira BRA 1998-99 • Carlos Alberto Torres BRA 2000-01 • Milan Macala CZE 2001 • Bernd Stange GER 2001 • Rashid Jaber Al Yafi'i 2002 • Milan Macala CZE 2003-05 • Srecko Juricic CRO 2005-06 • Hamad Al Azani 2006 • Milan Macala CZE 2006-07 • Gabriel Calderon ARG 2007-08 • Julio Cesar Ribas URU 2008 • Hamad Al Azani 2008 • Claude Le Roy FRA 2008-11 • Paul Le Guen FRA 2011-

OMAN 2010–11

OFA OMAN MOBILE LEAGUE

	Pl	W	D	L	F	A	Pts	Suwaiq	Urooba	Nahda	Dhofar	Oman Club	Shabab	Salalah	Ahli Sidab	Tali'aa	Muscat	Saham	Nasr
Al Suwaiq ‡	22	12	7	3	31	15	43		2-2	1-1	0-1	1-1	1-0	2-0	1-0	1-0	5-1	2-1	2-1
Al Urooba ‡	22	12	4	6	31	14	40	1-0		1-0	2-0	2-0	3-1	4-1	0-1	0-1	3-0	4-1	5-1
Al Nahda	22	10	8	4	30	18	38	0-1	0-0		1-1	2-1	2-1	2-1	4-0	0-0	3-0	2-3	1-0
Dhofar	22	8	6	8	24	22	30	4-0	0-1	0-2		1-1	2-0	0-0	3-1	3-1	1-1	1-0	0-0
Oman Club	22	7	8	7	24	22	29	1-1	1-2	0-1	1-1		1-2	2-1	1-1	2-0	0-0	1-0	0-0
Al Shabab	22	8	4	10	25	29	28	0-0	1-0	1-1	2-0	1-2		3-1	1-0	4-2	1-3	0-1	3-1
Al Hilal Salalah	22	7	6	9	25	29	27	0-1	2-0	1-1	2-1	0-1	2-1		1-0	3-1	0-3	1-0	3-0
Al Ahli Sidab	22	7	5	10	14	23	26	0-3	0-1	1-2	1-0	1-0	0-1	0-0		0-0	0-0	1-0	1-1
Al Tali'aa	22	6	8	8	27	27	26	0-0	1-0	1-2	4-2	0-0	4-0	3-3	1-2		2-1	3-0	1-1
Muscat	22	6	8	8	23	30	26	0-3	0-0	1-1	2-1	1-3	1-1	1-1	1-2	1-1		3-0	1-0
Saham	22	7	5	10	18	27	26	1-1	0-0	0-0	0-1	3-2	2-1	1-0	2-1	0-0	0-2		2-0
Al Nasr Salalah	22	5	7	10	19	31	22	0-3	1-0	3-2	0-1	1-3	0-0	2-2	0-1	2-1	2-0	1-1	

1/11/2010 - 30/04/2011 • ‡ Qualified for the AFC Cup • Relegation play-off: **Fanja** 0-1 2-1 Muscat

OMAN 2010–11
FIRST DIVISION (2)

Group A

	Pl	W	D	L	F	A	Pts
Fanja	14	7	6	1	21	4	27
Majees	14	8	1	5	22	19	25
Al Salam	14	7	4	3	16	12	25
Al Mudhaibi	14	4	7	3	20	17	19
Khaboora	14	5	4	5	16	16	19
Mirbat	14	5	4	5	14	14	19
Bahla	14	3	2	9	15	25	11
Samail	14	1	4	9	8	25	7

Group B

	Pl	W	D	L	F	A	Pts
Sur	14	8	5	1	21	10	29
Al Masnaah	14	7	7	0	24	9	28
Seeb	14	8	2	4	22	17	26
Sohar	14	7	4	3	23	14	25
Al Ittihad	14	2	6	6	15	19	12
Bashayer	14	3	2	9	11	19	11
Al Wahda	14	2	4	8	11	22	10
Jalan	14	2	4	8	10	27	10

3/11/2010 - 21/04/2011
Play-off semis: Majees 0-2 1-1 **Sur** • **Masnaah** 1-0 4-0 Fanja
3rd Place: Majees 1-2 **Fanja** • Final: **Sur** 0-0 5-3p Masnaah

MEDALS TABLE

		Overall			Lge	Cup	Asia			City
		G	S	B	G	G	G	S	B	
1	Dhofar	17			9	8				Salalah
2	Fanja	15			7	8				Fanja
3	Al Nasr	9			5	4				Salalah
4	Al Ahli	6			1	5				Sidab
	Al Urooba	6				3	3			Sur
6	Sur	5			2	3				Sur
7	Muscat	4			3	1				Muscat
8	Oman Club	3	1		1	2	1			Muscat
9	Seeb	3				3				Seeb
	Al Suwaiq	3			2	1				Al Suwaiq
11	Al Nahda	2	1		2		1			Al Buraimi
12	Al Tali'aa	1				1				Sur
	Saham	1				1				Saham

SULTAN QABOOS CUP 2011

Round of 16		Quarter-finals		Semi-finals		Final	
Dhofar	1						
Al Nahda *	0	**Dhofar**	3 0				
Al Mudhaibi	1 5p	Al Ahli Sidab *	1 0				
Al Ahli Sidab *	1 6p			**Dhofar** *	1 2		
Al Tali'aa	3			Al Hilal Salalah	1 0		
Yankel *	0	Al Tali'aa *	0 1 4p				
Seeb	0 2p	**Al Hilal Salalah**	1 0 5p				
Al Hilal Salalah *	0 4p					**Dhofar**	1
Sur *	2					Al Ittihad	0
Fanja	1	**Sur** *	0 2				
Mirbat	0	Al Urooba	0 1				
Al Urooba *	3			**Sur** *	3 0		
Sohar	1			**Al Ittihad**	3 0		
Oman Club *	0	Sohar *	0 0				
Saham *	1	**Al Ittihad**	0 1				
Al Ittihad	2						

CUP FINAL

Al Saada Stadium, Salalah
26-12-2011
Scorer - Ali Salim 66 for Dhofar

* Home team/Home team in the first leg

PAK – PAKISTAN

FIFA/COCA-COLA WORLD RANKING

'93	'94	'95	'96	'97	'98	'99	'00	'01	'02	'03	'04	'05	'06	'07	'08	'09	'10	'11	'12
142	158	160	173	153	168	179	190	181	178	168	177	158	164	163	165	156	171	179	

						2011							High	Low	Av
Jan	Feb	Mar	Apr	May	Jun	Jul	Aug	Sep	Oct	Nov	Dec		High	Low	Av
171	173	171	168	168	169	171	170	170	173	174	179		141	192	168

Victory over Chinese Taipei in the qualifying rounds for the 2012 AFC Challenge Cup was one of the few bright spots in a disappointing year for Pakistani football as the national team flopped in all three competitions entered in 2011. Despite beating the Taiwanese in their AFC Challenge Cup group held in Malaysia, Pakistan had already lost to both Turkmenistan and India which rendered the victory irrelevant. There was further embarrassment with a 3-0 aggregate defeat at the hands of Bangladesh in the first round of qualifying for the 2014 FIFA World Cup as Pakistan's poor record in the competition continued. Since first taking part in the World Cup qualifiers in 1989 the national team has played 28 times and they have yet to win a game. Of those games 25 have been lost with just 10 goals scored and 113 conceded. The year ended with a trio of draws at the South Asian Football Federation Championship but that wasn't enough to get Zavisa Milosavljevic's team a place in the knockout phase of the regional competition. In club football, Khan Research Labs claimed the league title with ease at the end of the year having earlier beaten KESC 1-0 in the final of the 2011 Pakistan National Football Challenge Cup. It was a fifth trophy in just three seasons for the nuclear scientists who are the best funded and organised club in the country.

FIFA WORLD CUP RECORD
1930-1986 DNE 1990-2014 DNQ

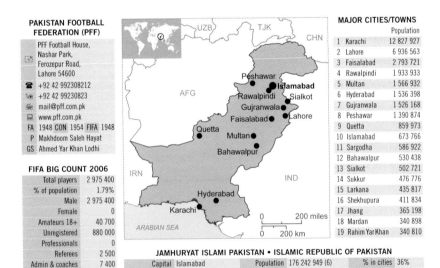

PAKISTAN FOOTBALL FEDERATION (PFF)

PFF Football House,
Nashar Park,
Ferozepur Road,
Lahore 54600

☎ +92 42 992308212
📠 +92 42 99230823
📧 mail@pff.com.pk
🖥 www.pff.com.pk
FA 1948 CON 1954 FIFA 1948
P Makhdoom Saleh Hayat
GS Ahmed Yar Khan Lodhi

FIFA BIG COUNT 2006

Total players	2 975 400
% of population	1.79%
Male	2 975 400
Female	0
Amateurs 18+	40 700
Unregistered	880 000
Professionals	0
Referees	2 500
Admin & coaches	7 400
Number of clubs	720
Number of teams	2 830

MAJOR CITIES/TOWNS

		Population
1	Karachi	12 827 927
2	Lahore	6 936 563
3	Faisalabad	2 793 721
4	Rawalpindi	1 933 933
5	Multan	1 566 932
6	Hyderabad	1 536 398
7	Gujranwala	1 526 168
8	Peshawar	1 390 874
9	Quetta	859 973
10	Islamabad	673 766
11	Sargodha	586 922
12	Bahawalpur	530 438
13	Sialkot	502 721
14	Sukkur	476 776
15	Larkana	435 817
16	Shekhupura	411 834
17	Jhang	365 198
18	Mardan	340 898
19	Rahim Yar Khan	340 810

JAMHURYAT ISLAMI PAKISTAN • ISLAMIC REPUBLIC OF PAKISTAN

Capital	Islamabad	Population	176 242 949 (6)	% in cities	36%
GDP per capita	$2500 (173)	Area km²	796 095 km² (36)	GMT + / -	+5
Neighbours (km)	Afghanistan 2430, China 523, India 2912, Iran 909 • Coast 1046				

RECENT INTERNATIONAL MATCHES PLAYED BY PAKISTAN

2006	Opponents	Score		Venue	Comp	Scorers	Att	Referee
18-02	Palestine	L	0-3	Manama	Fr			
22-02	Jordan	L	0-3	Amman	ACq			Basma SYR
1-03	United Arab Emirates	L	1-4	Karachi	ACq	Muhammad Essa [60]	10 000	Tongkhan THA
2-04	Kyrgyzstan	W	1-0	Dhaka	CCr1	Muhammad Essa [59]	2 500	Shamsuzzaman BAN
4-04	Tajikistan	L	0-2	Dhaka	CCr1		5 000	Tan Hai CHN
6-04	Macau	D	2-2	Dhaka	CCr1	Adeel [12], Muhammad Essa [43]	1 000	Shamsuzzaman BAN
16-08	Oman	L	1-4	Quetta	ACq	Muhammad Essa [79p]	4 000	Torky IRN
6-09	Oman	L	0-5	Muscat	ACq		10 000	Nema IRQ
11-10	Jordan	L	0-3	Lahore	ACq		4 000	Orzuev TJK
15-11	UAE	L	2-3	Abu Dhabi	ACq	Naveed Akram [22], Tanveer Ahmed [67]	6 000	Sarkar IND
2007								
22-10	Iraq	L	0-7	Lahore	WCq		2 500	Chynybekov KGZ
28-10	Iraq	D	0-0	Damascus	WCq		8 000	Al Fadhli KUW
2008								
25-03	Nepal	L	1-2	Pokhara	Fr	Muhammad Essa [21]		
27-03	Nepal	W	2-0	Pokhara	Fr	Muhammad Qasim [46], Muhammad Rasool [90]		
2-04	Chinese Taipei	W	2-1	Taipei	CCq	Muhammad Essa [13], Michael Masih [34]	800	Iemoto JPN
4-04	Sri Lanka	L	1-7	Taipei	CCq	Adnan Farooq Ahmed [17]	300	Kovalenko UZB
6-04	Guam	W	9-2	Taipei	CCq	Jamshed Anwar 2 [9 18], Farooq Shah [28], Muhammad Qasim 3 [44 72 82], Ahmed Tanveer [62], Zahid Hameed [65p], Abdul Rehman [85]	200	Auda Lazim IRQ
3-06	Maldives	L	0-3	Male	SAFr1			
5-06	India	L	1-2	Male	SAFr1	Adnan Farooq Ahmed [88]		
7-06	Nepal	L	1-4	Male	SAFr1	Samar Ishaq [54]		
10-10	Malaysia	L	1-4	Kuala Lumpur	Fr	Arif Mehmood [86]		
2009								
4-04	Chinese Taipei	D	1-1	Colombo	CCq	Adnan Ahmed [53]	400	Tseytlin UZB
6-04	Brunei Darussalam	W	6-0	Colombo	CCq	Safiullah Khan 4 [19 61 68 78], Pathan Khan [31], Adnan Ahmed [84]	200	Orzuev TJK
8-04	Sri Lanka	D	2-2	Colombo	CCq	Safiullah Khan [82], Atif Bashir [84]	3 000	Tseytlin UZB
4-12	Sri Lanka	L	0-1	Dhaka	SAFr1			
6-12	Bangladesh	D	0-0	Dhaka	SAFr1			
8-12	Bhutan	W	7-0	Dhaka	SAFr1	Muhammad Essa 2 [21 54], Reis Ashraf [23], Arif Mehmood 3 [28 35 66], Shabir Khan [45]		
2010								
No international matches played in 2010								
2011								
21-03	Turkmenistan	L	0-3	Petaling Jaya	CCq		150	Bakhshizadeh IRN
23-03	India	L	1-3	Petaling Jaya	CCq	Arif Mehmood [32]	100	Alrshaidat JOR
25-03	Chinese Taipei	W	2-0	Petaling Jaya	CCq	Arif Mehmood [26], Atif Bashir [67]	50	Alrshaidat JOR
29-06	Bangladesh	L	0-3	Dhaka	WCq		5 326	Abu Loum JOR
3-07	Bangladesh	D	0-0	Lahore	WCq		3 500	Abdulnabi BHR
2-12	Bangladesh	D	0-0	New Delhi	SAFr1			Faizullin KGZ
4-12	Maldives	D	0-0	New Delhi	SAFr1			Robesh SRI
6-12	Nepal	D	1-1	New Delhi	SAFr1	Samar Ishaq [49p]		Noor Mohamed MAS

Fr = Friendly match • SAF = South Asian Federation Cup • AC = AFC Asian Cup • CC = AFC Challenge Cup • WC = FIFA World Cup
q = qualifier • r1 = first round group • sf = semi-final • 3p = third place play-off

PAKISTAN 2011

NATIONAL FOOTBALL LEAGUE PREMIER LEAGUE

	Pl	W	D	L	F	A	Pts	KLR	Afghan FC	Army	WAPDA	KESC	Muslim SC	PIA	NBP	HBL	Navy	PAF	KPT	Boloch	PMC Club	Police	PEL
Khan Research Labs †	30	24	5	1	56	10	77		1-2	2-0	0-0	1-0	0-0	1-0	3-1	2-0	0-0	1-1	3-0	3-1	2-0	2-0	3-0
Afghan FC	30	16	9	5	52	24	57	0-0		2-1	1-0	3-2	0-1	1-1	1-0	1-0	2-1	1-1	3-1	4-1	3-0	6-0	3-0
Pakistan Army	30	17	6	7	35	22	57	1-2	2-1		0-0	1-0	1-0	1-0	1-0	0-0	0-0	1-1	2-0	3-1	2-0	0-0	3-0
WAPDA	30	15	7	8	41	25	52	0-1	2-1	0-1		1-1	4-1	3-1	1-0	2-1	3-1	0-1	1-1	2-0	0-2	3-1	3-0
Karachi Electric SC	30	15	6	9	41	30	51	0-1	3-2	2-0	2-1		2-0	2-4	1-0	0-1	1-1	1-1	3-2	1-0	1-1	4-1	1-0
Muslim SC	30	15	6	9	40	33	51	0-4	0-0	1-0	0-0	0-2		1-0	1-0	2-1	1-2	3-0	3-1	2-0	1-0	3-1	3-0
Pakistan Int. Airlines	30	14	7	9	50	33	49	0-4	0-0	3-1	4-1	0-2	1-1		0-2	3-2	2-1	2-0	2-2	2-0	6-2	1-3	3-0
Nat. Bank of Pakistan	30	14	3	13	41	26	45	1-2	1-2	3-0	0-1	3-2	0-2	0-1		1-1	4-1	3-0	0-2	1-0	2-0	6-1	4-1
Habib Bank Ltd	30	10	10	10	34	29	40	0-2	0-0	1-1	0-2	2-1	4-3	0-2	1-0		2-2	0-0	1-0	0-0	1-0	1-0	9-1
Pakistan Navy	30	8	11	11	34	34	35	0-1	1-1	0-2	0-2	1-1	2-0	0-0	0-2	3-0		1-1	6-3	3-1	0-0	2-0	3-0
Pakistan Air Force	30	7	12	11	23	29	33	1-2	0-0	0-1	0-0	0-1	1-2	2-1	0-0	1-0	0-0		4-2	1-0	0-1	3-0	4-1
Karachi Port Trust	30	9	5	16	38	58	32	0-4	0-3	1-2	2-3	1-1	2-2	0-4	0-2	2-3	2-1	1-0		1-1	2-0	3-1	4-1
Boloch Nushki	30	7	7	16	26	40	28	1-2	1-3	0-1	0-0	0-1	3-1	0-4	0-0	0-0	0-0	3-0	1-0		0-0	3-0	3-0
PMC Club Faisalabad	30	7	6	17	17	36	27	0-1	1-0	0-2	0-3	2-1	0-1	0-1	0-2	0-0	1-0	0-0	0-1	1-2		2-0	3-0
Pakistan Police	30	7	3	20	28	63	24	0-1	3-6	2-3	1-0	0-1	1-1	0-0	1-2	0-3	1-2	1-0	1-2	3-1	1-0		1-0
Pak Electron Limited	30	1	5	24	10	74	8	0-3	0-6	0-2	0-2	0-1	1-4	1-1	0-1	0-0	1-0	1-1	0-2	1-3	1-1	1-4	

5/07/2011 - 29/12/2011 • † Qualified for the AFC Presidents Cup
Top scorer: **22** - Jadeed Khan Pathan, Afghan FC

MEDALS TABLE

			All		Lge		Cup	
			G	S	G	S	G	S
1	Pakistan Int. Airlines	PIA	10	6	9	5	1	1
2	WAPDA		8	8	8	5		3
3	Punjab		8	1	8	1		
4	Allied Bank Limited	ABL	7	3	3	2	4	1
5	Pakistan Army		6	8	4	7	2	1
6	Karachi		6	5	6	5		
7	Khan Research Labs	KRL	5	5	2	2	3	3
8	Crescent Textile Mills		4		2		2	
9	Balochistan		3	1	3	1		
10	Pakistan Railways		2	9	2	9		
11	Habib Bank Limited	HBL	2	3	1	3	1	
12	Sindh		2	2	2	2		

PAKISTAN NATIONAL FOOTBALL CHALLENGE CUP 2011

First Round Groups

Group A	Pl	W	D	L	F	A	Pts	WA	Na	NB
ASM FC	3	2	0	1	3	1	6	1-0	0-1	2-0
WAPDA	3	1	1	1	3	3	4		1-1	2-1
Navy	3	1	1	1	3	3	4			1-2
NBP	3	1	0	2	3	5	3			

Group B	Pl	W	D	L	F	A	Pts	AF	ZT	HB
KRL	3	3	0	0	9	0	9	3-0	4-0	2-0
Air Force	3	2	0	1	5	3	6		2-0	3-0
ZTBL	3	1	0	2	1	6	3			1-0
HBL	3	0	0	3	0	6	0			

Group C	Pl	W	D	L	F	A	Pts	KP	Po	PT
PIA	3	3	0	0	5	1	9	2-0	2-1	1-0
KPT	3	2	0	1	2	2	6		1-0	1-0
Police	3	0	1	2	4	6	1			3-3
PTV	3	0	1	2	3	5	1			

Group D	Pl	W	D	L	F	A	Pts	Ar	Ra	PM
KESC	3	2	1	0	7	4	7	0-0	4-3	3-1
Army	3	2	1	0	2	0	7		1-0	1-0
Railway	3	1	0	2	5	6	3			2-1
PMC Club	3	0	0	3	2	6	0			

Quarter-finals

KRL	6
KPT	0

ASM FC	0
Army	2

PIA	3
Air Force	0

WAPDA	0
KESC	2

Semi-finals

KRL	1 4p
Army	1 2p

PIA	1 2p
KESC	1 4p

3rd place: PIA 0-3 **Army**

Final

KRL	1
KESC	0

CUP FINAL

Bohranwali Ground, Faisalabad
27-04-2011
Scorer - Hussnain Abbas [74] for Khan Research Labs

PAN – PANAMA

FIFA/COCA-COLA WORLD RANKING

'93	'94	'95	'96	'97	'98	'99	'00	'01	'02	'03	'04	'05	'06	'07	'08	'09	'10	'11	'12
132	140	126	101	119	131	138	121	109	129	125	100	78	81	67	88	70	64	49	

	2011												High	Low	Av
	Jan	Feb	Mar	Apr	May	Jun	Jul	Aug	Sep	Oct	Nov	Dec			
	67	60	68	68	67	52	65	62	53	53	51	49	49	150	102

For the fourth CONCACAF Gold Cup in succession the USA ended Panama's hopes of a first continental crown, but what made their semi-final exit harder to take was the fact they had beaten the Americans in the first-round group stage. However, qualification for the semi-finals still represented their second best-performance in the tournament and the Panamanians will push the regional superpowers hard in the race to qualify for the 2014 FIFA World Cup in Brazil. They got their campaign of to a perfect start after the Gold Cup when they won all four matches in the first group stage with home and away victories over Nicaragua and Dominica. Coach Julio Dely Valdes saw his side lose just three matches out of the 21 played during the course of 2011 and by the end of the year Panama had risen to a record high of 49 in the FIFA/Coca-Cola World Ranking. At club level, San Francisco won the first of the two championships played during the course of 2011 after beating Chorillo 3-2 in the final in Panama City. It was the second time Chorillo had lost to San Francisco in the final but at the end of the year they were celebrating a first-ever championship, gaining revenge over San Francisco in the play-off semi-finals and then beating Plaza Amador with a comprehensive 4-1 victory in the final.

CONCACAF GOLD CUP RECORD

1991 DNQ **1993** r1 1996 DNQ 1998 DNQ 2000 DNE 2002 DNQ 2003 DNQ **2005** F r/u **2007** QF **2009** QF **2011** SF

FEDERACION PANAMENA DE FUTBOL (FEPAFUT)

Urbanizacion Chanis Calle 153, Edif. Christine PB, Apartado postal 0827-00391 Zona 8, Panama

☎ +507 2333896
✆ +507 2330582
✉ info@fepafut.com
🖳 www.fepafut.com
FA 1937 CON 1961 FIFA 1938
P Pedro Chaluja
GS Jorge Aued

FIFA BIG COUNT 2006

Total players	203 400
% of population	6.37%
Male	176 000
Female	27 400
Amateurs 18+	28 800
Unregistered	30 800
Professionals	300
Referees	300
Admin & coaches	1 700
Number of clubs	570
Number of teams	950

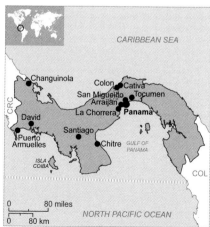

MAJOR CITIES/TOWNS

		Population
1	Panama	425 557
2	San Miguelito	366 201
3	Arraiján	102 355
4	Tocumen	100 800
5	Las Cumbres	93 590
6	David	93 351
7	Colón	87 838
8	La Chorrera	70 297
9	Pacora	63 218
10	Santiago	52 432
11	Chitré	50 122
12	Vista Alegre	47 570
13	Chilibre	38 179
14	Cativá	35 471
15	Nuevo Arraiján	26 861
16	Changuinola	25 496
17	Alcalde Díaz	22 390
18	La Cabima	22 081
19	Puerto Armuelles	20 648

REPUBLICA DE PANAMA • REPUBLIC OF PANAMA

Capital	Panama City	Population	3 360 474 (134)	% in cities	73%
GDP per capita	$11 800 (94)	Area km²	75 420 km² (117)	GMT +/-	-5
Neighbours (km)	Colombia 225, Costa Rica 330 • Coast 2490				

RECENT INTERNATIONAL MATCHES PLAYED BY PANAMA

2009 Opponents	Score	Venue	Comp	Scorers	Att	Referee
23-01 Costa Rica	L 0-3	Tegucigalpa	UCr1		2 000	Campbell JAM
27-01 Guatemala	W 1-0	Tegucigalpa	UCr1	Zapata [31]	1 000	Aguilar SLV
30-01 Honduras	W 1-0	Tegucigalpa	UCsf	Phillips [40]	20 000	Batres GUA
1-02 Costa Rica	D 0-0	Tegucigalpa	UCf	W 5-3p	900	Batres GUA
18-03 Trinidad and Tobago	L 0-1	Marabella	Fr		2 000	Jordan TRI
31-03 Haiti	W 4-0	La Chorrera	Fr	Tejada [4], Blas Perez 3 [57 68 81]	4 500	Amaya PAN
20-05 Argentina	L 1-3	Santa Fe	Fr	Barahona [29]	20 000	Antequera BOL
7-06 Jamaica	L 2-3	Kingston	Fr	Blas Perez [12], Tejada [81]	12 000	Whittaker CAY
19-06 Haiti	D 1-1	Port-au-Prince	Fr	Machada [84]	2 000	Grant HAI
28-06 Honduras	L 0-2	Cary	Fr		3 766	Vaughn USA
5-07 Guadeloupe	L 1-2	Oakland	GCr1	Barahona [68]	32 700	Brizan TRI
9-07 Mexico	D 1-1	Houston	GCr1	Blas Perez [29]	47 713	Aguilar SLV
12-07 Nicaragua	W 4-0	Phoenix	GCr1	Blas Perez [35], Gomez [56], Tejada 2 [77 88]	23 876	Pineda HON
18-07 USA	L 1-2	Philadelphia	GCqf	Blas Perez [45]	32 000	Archundia MEX
2010						
20-01 Chile	L 1-2	Coquimbo	Fr	Roberto Brown [87]	15 000	Vasquez URU
3-03 Venezuela	W 2-1	Barquisimeto	Fr	Roman Torres [9], Blas Perez [51]	37 000	Buitrago COL
11-08 Venezuela	W 3-1	Panama City	Fr	Luis Tejada [75], Blas Perez [88], Edwin Aguilar [90]	2 000	Quesada CRC
3-09 Costa Rica	D 2-2	Panama City	Fr	Luis Tejada 2 [27 38]	23 005	Delgadillo MEX
7-09 Trinidad and Tobago	W 3-0	Panama City	Fr	Edwin Aguilar [13], Luis Tejada [75], Gavilan Gomez [87]	6 645	Cruz CRC
8-10 El Salvador	W 1-0	Panama City	Fr	Blas Perez [61]	16 175	Ruiz COL
12-10 Peru	W 1-0	Panama City	Fr	Gabriel Torres [76]	8 528	Cerdas CRC
26-10 Cuba	L 0-3	Panama City	Fr		2 116	Moreno PAN
17-11 Honduras	W 2-0	Panama City	Fr	Luis Tejada [25], Aramis Haywood [52]	3 646	Cruz CRC
18-12 Honduras	L 1-2	San Pedro Sula	Fr	Edwin Aguilar [40]	3 000	Rodas GUA
2011						
14-01 Belize	W 2-0	Panama City	UCr1	Edwin Aguilar [21], Roberto Brown [28]	10 000	Pineda HON
16-01 Nicaragua	W 2-0	Panama City	UCr1	Armando Cooper [16], Luis Renteria [80]	7 747	Lopez GUA
18-01 El Salvador	W 2-0	Panama City	UCr1	Edwin Aguilar [24], Armando Cooper [78]	10 000	Garcia MEX
21-01 Costa Rica	D 1-1	Panama City	UCsf	Blas Perez [76]. L 2-4p	10 000	Aguilar SLV
23-01 El Salvador	D 0-0	Panama City	UC3p	W 5-4p	2 000	Pineda HON
8-02 Peru	L 0-1	Moquegua	Fr		8 000	Ubriaco URU
25-03 Bolivia	W 2-0	Panama City	Fr	Gabriel Gomez [19], Luis Renteria [83]	4 000	Lopez GUA
29-03 Cuba	W 2-0	Havana	Fr	Luis Renteria [37], Alberto Quintero [80]	6 000	Espana GUA
29-05 Grenada	W 2-0	Panama City	Fr	Gabriel Gomez [2], Alberto Quintero [46]	5 000	Perea PAN
7-06 Guadeloupe †	W 3-2	Detroit	GCr1	Blas Perez [29], Luis Tejada [31], Gabriel Gomez [57p]	28 209	Mejia SLV
11-06 USA	W 2-1	Tampa	GCr1	OG [19], Gabriel Gomez [36]	27 731	Rodriguez.M MEX
14-06 Canada	D 1-1	Kansas City	GCr1	Luis Tejada [91+]	20 109	Lopez GUA
19-06 El Salvador	D 1-1	Washington DC	GCqf	Luis Tejada [90]. W 5-3p	45 424	Quesada CRC
22-06 USA	L 0-1	Houston	GCsf		70 627	Wijngaarde SUR
10-08 Bolivia	W 3-1	Santa Cruz	Fr	Luis Tejada 2 [67 76p], Armando Cooper [90]	10 000	Carrillo PER
2-09 Paraguay	L 0-2	Panama City	Fr		11 000	Pineda HON
6-09 Nicaragua	W 2-1	Managua	WCq	Luis Tejada [7], Blas Perez [50]	10 521	Reyna GUA
7-10 Dominica	W 5-0	Roseau	WCq	Amir Waithe 2 [26 89], Luis Tejada [34], Blas Perez [57], Ricardo Buitrago [62]	4 000	Wijngaarde SUR
11-10 Nicaragua	W 5-1	Panama City	WCq	Luis Tejada 2 [27 64], Blas Perez 3 [48 51 87]	10 846	Ventura SLV
11-11 Costa Rica	W 2-0	Panama City	Fr	Gabriel Gomez [26p], Blas Perez [28]	5 000	Garcia MEX
15-11 Dominica	W 3-0	Panama City	WCq	Rolando Blackburn [6], Ricardo Buitrago [20], Blas Perez [84]	8 000	Vaughn USA

Fr = Friendly match • UC = UNCAF Cup/Copa Centroamericana • GC = CONCACAF Gold Cup • WC = FIFA World Cup • † Not a full international
q = qualifier • r1 = first round group • qf = quarter-final • sf = semi-final • 3p = third place play-off • f = final

PANAMA NATIONAL TEAM HISTORICAL RECORDS

Coaches For coaches prior to 2000 se Oliver's Almanack of World Football 2011 • Miguel Mansilla URU 2000 • Leopoldo Lee 2000 • Ezequiel Fernandez 2000 • Mihai Stoichita ROU 2001 • Carlos Alberto Daluz BRA 2002-03 • Jose Eugenio Hernandez COL 2004-05 • Julio Dely Valdes & Jorge Dely Valdes 2006 • Victor Rene Mendieta 2006 • Alexandre Guimaraes CRC 2006-08 • Gary Stempel ENG 2008-09 • Julio Dely Valdes 2010-

PANAMA 2010-11

LIGA PROFESIONAL DE FUTBOL CLAUSURA

	Pl	W	D	L	F	A	Pts	Chorrillo	San Francisco	San Miguelito	Tauro	Plaza Amador	Veragüense	Chiriquí	Chepo	Arabe Unido	Alianza
Municipal Chorrillo †	18	8	7	3	16	9	31		1-2	0-0	2-0	0-0	1-0	1-0	2-0	1-0	0-0
San Francisco †	18	7	8	3	31	21	29	1-1		2-0	2-0	2-2	2-0	1-1	1-0	2-2	3-0
SportingSan Miguelito†	18	7	6	5	19	14	27	1-0	1-1		0-1	0-1	2-1	2-0	2-2	1-0	4-1
Tauro †	18	7	5	6	25	21	26	1-1	3-3	0-1		1-1	2-0	2-1	2-1	1-1	2-0
Plaza Amador	18	6	8	4	18	17	26	2-2	2-1	1-0	2-1		0-2	0-1	0-1	1-1	1-0
Atlético Veragüense	18	7	4	7	17	17	25	0-1	2-1	1-0	2-1	0-0		3-1	0-2	0-0	1-1
Atlético Chiriquí	18	6	6	6	19	20	24	0-0	2-2	0-0	2-1	3-2	1-1		2-1	0-0	2-0
Chepo	18	6	5	7	21	24	23	2-0	2-2	1-1	1-1	1-1	0-2	0-3		2-1	3-2
Arabe Unido	18	3	8	7	14	16	17	0-1	2-0	1-1	0-2	1-1	0-2	2-0	0-1		3-0
Alianza	18	3	3	12	12	33	12	0-2	0-3	1-3	1-4	0-1	2-0	2-0	2-1	0-0	

28/01/2011 - 14/05/2011 • † Qualified for the play-offs
Play-off final details: Rommel Fernández, Panama City, 14-05-2011, Ref: Roberto Moreno. Scorers - Johan De Avila 10, Roberto Brown 2 83p 91 for San Francisco; Alcibiades Rojas 21, Engie Mitre 42 for Chorrillo
Atlético Veragüense relegated

CLAUSURA 2010-11 PLAY-OFFS

Semi-finals   **Finals**

San Francisco	2	2			
Sp. San Miguelito *	1	1	San Francisco †	3	
Tauro *	1	0	Municipal Chorrillo	2	
Municipal Chorrillo	1	4			

† Qualified for the CONCACAF Champions League • * Home team in first leg • San Francisco are the Clausura champions

APERTURA 2011-12 PLAY-OFFS

Semi-finals   **Finals**

Municipal Chorrillo	2	1			
San Francisco *	0	2	Municipal Chorrillo †	4	
Sp. San Miguelito	2	1	Plaza Amador	1	
Plaza Amador *	3	2			

† Qualified for the CONCACAF Champions League • * Home team in first leg • Chorillo are the Apertura champions

MEDALS TABLE

		Overall		Lge		City/Town
		G	S	G	S	
1	Tauro FC	8	8	8	8	Panama City
2	San Francisco FC	7	6	7	6	La Chorrera
3	Deportivo Arabe Unido	6	3	6	3	Colon
4	CD Plaza Amador	5	3	5	3	Panama City
5	Chorrillo FC	1	2	1	2	Panama City
	AFC Euro Kickers	1	2	1	2	Panama City
7	Panama Viejo FC	1		1		Panama City
8	Sporting Colon		1		1	Colon
	Projusa		1		1	

PANAMA 2011-12

LIGA PROFESIONAL DE FUTBOL APERTURA

	Pl	W	D	L	F	A	Pts	San Miguelito	Chorrillo	San Francisco	Plaza Amador	Chepo	Tauro	Arabe Unido	Alianza	Colón C-3	Chiriquí
SportingSan Miguelito†	18	10	4	4	21	14	34		1-2	0-1	4-3	1-0	1-0	1-0	2-0	2-0	0-0
Municipal Chorrillo †	18	9	5	4	26	19	32	0-1		2-2	2-1	0-1	1-0	0-0	2-2	2-0	0-1
San Francisco †	18	9	4	5	23	19	31	2-2	2-2		0-1	1-2	1-0	3-2	1-0	1-3	2-0
Plaza Amador	18	9	4	5	22	21	31	0-0	2-1	2-1		0-3	1-0	0-0	1-3	2-1	1-0
Chepo	18	9	3	6	24	15	30	0-1	0-1	1-1	0-1		3-0	1-0	2-0	0-0	0-0
Tauro	18	9	1	8	23	16	28	1-1	1-2	1-0	1-2	3-0		0-1	2-1	3 2	1 0
Arabe Unido	18	7	4	7	17	17	25	2-1	0-1	1-2	2-1	1-3	0-1		1-0	0-0	3-1
Alianza	18	3	7	8	20	27	16	2-0	2-4	0-1	0-0	5-3	0-3	1-1		0-0	1-1
Colón C-3	18	2	5	11	13	27	11	0-1	1-2	0-1	1-1	0-1	0-4	0-1	2-2		1-4
Atlético Chiriquí	18	2	5	11	12	26	11	0-1	1-1	0-1	2-3	0-4	0-2	1-2	1-1	1-2	

16/07/2011 - 3/12/2011 • † Qualified for the play-offs
Play-off final details: Rommel Fernández, Panama City, 3-12-2011. Scorers - Rolando Blackburn 2 27 63, Alfredo Phillips 77, Renan Addles 90 for Chorrillo; Javier Caicedo 85 for Plaza Amador
Top scorers: 8 - Delano Welch, Chepo & Cesar Medina, Alianza

PAR – PARAGUAY

FIFA/COCA-COLA WORLD RANKING

'93	'94	'95	'96	'97	'98	'99	'00	'01	'02	'03	'04	'05	'06	'07	'08	'09	'10	'11	'12
61	87	64	38	29	25	17	10	13	18	22	30	30	35	21	17	29	24	24	

	2011														
	Jan	Feb	Mar	Apr	May	Jun	Jul	Aug	Sep	Oct	Nov	Dec	High	Low	Av
	24	24	24	23	23	32	26	25	24	28	24	24	8	103	30

The 2011 Copa America in Argentina is a tournament that Paraguay will not forget in a hurry and not just for the fact that they reached the final for the first time since 1979. It was a performance that showed true grit and determination but which at times bordered on the extraordinary and the downright bizarre. Had they won the final against Uruguay on penalties, the Paraguayans would have become the first team to win a major international title without winning a single game. Three draws had seen them sneak into the quarter-finals on goal difference, although twice they were denied victories - against Venezuela and Brazil - by last minute equalisers. The same opponents were then beaten on penalties on route to the final where their luck finally ran out against Uruguay who claimed the trophy with a 3-0 win. At club level, Cerro Porteño reached the 2011 Copa Libertadores semi-finals before losing to eventual winners Santos, whilst at home the resurgence of Nacional continued when they won the opening championship of the year. The major story of the year, however, was the return to winning ways of Olimpia who won the 2011 Clausura. That ended their longest-ever trophyless run which stretched back to 2000.

COPA AMERICA RECORD

1916-1920 DNE 1921 4/4 1922 2/5 1923 3/4 1924 3/4 1925 3/3 1926 4/5 1927 DNE 1929 2/4 1935 DNE 1937 3/6 1939 3/5 1941 DNE 1942 4/7 1945 DNE 1946 3/6 1947 2/8 1949 2/8 **1953** 1/7 Winners 1955 5/6 1956 5/6 1957 DNE 1959 3/7 1959 5/5 1963 2/7 1967 4/6 1975 7/10 r1 **1979** 1/10 Winners 1983 3/10 SF 1987 9/10 r1 1989 4/10 r2 1991 6/10 r1 1993 8/12 QF 1995 6/12 QF 1997 7/12 QF 1999 6/12 QF (Hosts) 2001 10/12 r1 2004 6/12 QF 2007 5/12 QF 2011 2/12 F

ASOCIACION PARAGUAYA DE FUTBOL (APF)

Estadio de los Defensores del Chaco, Calle Mayor Martinez 1393, Asuncion

☎ +595 21 480120
📠 +595 21 480124
✉ seleccion@apf.org.py
🖥 www.apf.org.py
FA 1906 CON 1921 FIFA 1925
P Juan Angel Napout
GS Arturo Filartiga

FIFA BIG COUNT 2006

Total players	1 037 435
% of population	15.94%
Male	886 966
Female	150 469
Amateurs 18+	53 667
Youth under 18	29 984
Unregistered	950 000
Professionals	590
Referees	802
Admin & coaches	3 200
Number of clubs	1 696
Number of teams	3 500

MAJOR CITIES/TOWNS

		Population
1	Asunción	539 795
2	Ciudad del Este	338 885
3	Luque	293 267
4	Capiatá	291 591
5	San Lorenzo	283 280
6	Limpio	150 879
7	Ñemby	146 409
8	Lambaré	143 479
9	Fernando de la Mora	136 121
10	Itauguá	106 406
11	San Antonio	103 593
12	Mariano Roque Alonso	88 618
13	Villa Elisa	88 459
14	Encarnación	87 581
15	Pedro Juan Caballero	76 816
16	Hernandaríaz	73 115
17	Presidente Franco	68 493
18	Caaguazú	65 263
19	Coronel Oviedo	59 757

REPUBLICA DEL PARAGUAY • REPUBLIC OF PARAGUAY

Capital	Asunción	Population	6 995 655 (101)	% in cities	60%
GDP per capita	$4200 (153)	Area km²	406 752 km² (59)	GMT + / -	-4
Neighbours (km)	Argentina 1880, Bolivia 750, Brazil 1365				

RECENT INTERNATIONAL MATCHES PLAYED BY PARAGUAY

2010	Opponents		Score	Venue	Comp	Scorers	Att	Referee
31-03	South Africa	D	1-1	Asuncion	Fr	Estigarribia [38]	7 738	Fagundes BRA
15-05	Korea DPR	W	1-0	Nyon	Fr	Santa Cruz [85p]	1 000	Bertolini SUI
25-05	Republic of Ireland	L	1-2	Dublin	Fr	Barrios [57]	16 722	Laperriere SUI
30-05	Côte d'Ivoire	D	2-2	Thonon-les-Bains	Fr	Barrios [75], Torres [90]	2 000	Bien FRA
2-06	Greece	W	2-0	Winterthur	Fr	Vera [9], Barrios [25]	5 200	Circhetta SUI
14-06	Italy	D	1-1	Cape Town	WCr1	Antolin Alcaraz [39]	62 869	Archundia MEX
20-06	Slovakia	W	2-0	Bloemfontein	WCr1	Enrique Vera [27], Cristian Riveros [86]	26 643	Maillet SEY
24-06	New Zealand	D	0-0	Polokwane	WCr1		34 850	Nishimura JPN
29-06	Japan	D	0-0	Pretoria	WCr2	W 5-3p	36 742	De Bleeckere BEL
3-07	Spain	L	0-1	Johannesburg	WCqf		55 359	Batres GUA
11-08	Costa Rica	W	2-0	Asuncion	Fr	Vera [8], Riveros [73]	22 000	Beligoy ARG
4-09	Japan	L	0-1	Yokohama	Fr		65 157	Rodriguez MEX
7-09	China PR	D	1-1	Nanjing	Fr	Barrios [8]	30 000	Wang Di CHN
9-10	Australia	L	0-1	Sydney	Fr		25 210	Nishimura JPN
12-10	New Zealand	W	2-0	Wellington	Fr	Valdez [22p], Martinez [28]	16 477	Cross NZL
17-11	Hong Kong	W	7-0	Hong Kong	Fr	Roque Santa Cruz 2 [4 32], Edgar Barreto [30], Jose Ortigoza 2 [46 54], Marcos Riveros [75], Cristian Riveros [90]	6 250	Mohd Salleh MAS
2011								
26-03	Mexico	L	1-3	Oakland	Fr	Cristian Riveros [87]	48 110	Ward CAN
29-03	USA	W	1-0	Nashville	Fr	Oscar Cardozo [18]	29 059	Benigno HON
25-05	Argentina	L	2-4	Resistencia	Fr	Pablo Zeballos [14], Elvis Marecos [55]	24 000	Silvera URU
4-06	Bolivia	W	2-0	Santa Cruz	Fr	Lucas Barrios [34], Federico Santander [73]	27 000	Garay PER
7-06	Bolivia	D	0-0	Ciudad del Este	Fr		15 000	Lopes BRA
11-06	Romania	W	2-0	Asuncion	Fr	Nelson Valdez [2], Roque Santa Cruz [29]	8 000	Larrionda URU
23-06	Chile	D	0-0	Asuncion	Fr		12 000	Oliveira BRA
3-07	Ecuador	D	0-0	Santa Fe	CAr1		20 000	Pezzotta ARG
9-07	Brazil	D	2-2	Cordoba	CAr1	Roque Santa Cruz [54], Nelson Valdez [66]	57 000	Roldan COL
13-07	Venezuela	D	3-3	Salta	CAr1	Antolin Alcaraz [32], Lucas Barrios [62], Cristian Riveros [85]	18 000	Osses CHI
17-07	Brazil	D	0-0	La Plata	CAqf	W 2-0p	36 000	Pezzotta ARG
20-07	Venezuela	D	0-0	Mendoza	CAsf	W 5-3p	8 000	Chacon MEX
24-07	Uruguay	L	0-3	Buenos Aires	CAf		57 921	Fagundes BRA
2-09	Panama	W	2-0	Panama City	Fr	Oscar Cardoza [7], Robin Ramirez [10]	11 000	Pineda HON
6-09	Honduras	W	3-0	San Pedro Sula	Fr	Nestor Camacho [30], Oscar Cardozo 2 [86 90]	20 000	Aguilar SLV
7-10	Peru	L	0-2	Lima	WCq		39 600	Pezzotta ARG
11-10	Uruguay	D	1-1	Asuncion	WCq	Richard Ortiz [92+]	12 922	Seneme BRA
11-11	Ecuador	W	2-1	Asuncion	WCq	Cristian Riveros [47], Dario Veron [57]	11 173	Buitrago COL
15-11	Chile	L	0-2	Santiago	WCq		44 726	Lopes BRA
21-12	Chile	L	2-3	La Serena	Fr	Edgar Benitez [51p], Julio Manzur [56]	12 000	Orozco BOL

Fr = Friendly match • CA = Copa America • WC = FIFA World Cup • q = qualifier • r1 = 1st round • qf = quarter-final

PARAGUAY NATIONAL TEAM HISTORICAL RECORDS

Caps
110 - Carlos Gamarra 1993-2006 • **100** - Denis Caniza 1996-; Roberto Acuna 1993-2011 & Paulo Da Silva 2000- • **95** - Justo Villar 1999- • **89** - Roque Santa Cruz 1999- • **85** - Celso Ayala 1993-2003 • **82** - Jose Cardozo 1991-2006 • **78** - Roberto Fernandez 1976-89 • **77** - Juan Torales 1979-89 • **76** - Cristian Riveros 2005- • **75** - Carlos Bonet 2002- • **74** - Jose Luis Chilavert 1989-2003; Carlos Paredes 1998-2008 & Estanislao Struway 1991-2002 • **70** - Julio Cesar Enciso 1995-2004 • **04** - Julio Cesar Caceres 2002

Goals
25 - Jose Cardozo 1991-2006 & Roque Santa Cruz 1999- • **14** - Cristian Riveros 2005- • **13** - Saturnino Arrua 1969-80 & Julio Cesar Romero 1979-86 • **12** - Carlos Gamarra 1993-2006; Gerardo Rivas 1921-26 & Nelson Valdez 2004-

Past Coaches
Jose Laguna ARG 1921-22 • Manuel Fleitas Solich 1922-29 • Jose Laguna ARG 1929-45 • Manuel Fleitas Solich 1945-46 • Aurelio Gonzalez 1946-47 • Manuel Fleitas Solich 1947-51 • Julio Ramirez 1951-55 • Aurelio Gonzalez 1955-59 • Benjamin Laterza 1959-62 • Manuel Fleitas Solich 1962-65 • Aurelio Gonzalez 1965-74 • Benjamin Benitez 1974-76 • Ramon Rodriguez 1976-80 • Carlos Monin 1980-83 • Ranulfo Miranda 1983-85 • Cayetano Re 1986-88 • Eduardo Manera ARG 1988-89 • Ruben Valdez ESP 1990 • Carlos Kiese 1991-92 • Sergio Markarian URU 1992-93 • Alicio Solalinde 1993-94 • Laszlo Kubala ESP 1995 • Paulo Cesar Carpegiani BRA 1996-98 • Ever Almeida 1998-99 • Sergio Markarian URU 1999-2001 • Cesare Maldini ITA 2001-02 • Anibal Ruiz URU 2002-06 • Raul Amarilla 2006-07 • Gerardo Martino ARG 2007-11 • Francisco Arce 2011-

PARAGUAY 2011

DIVISION PROFESIONAL APERTURA

	Pl	W	D	L	F	A	Pts	Nacional	Olimpia	Libertad	Guaraní	Rubio Nu	Tacuary	Cerro Porteño	3 de Febrero	Independiente	Sol	Luqueño	Caballero
Nacional †	22	14	5	3	34	18	47		1-2	1-2	2-1	3-0	1-0	2-0	1-1	1-0	2-0	0-0	3-1
Olimpia	22	12	6	4	44	22	42	1-2		2-2	4-3	1-3	0-0	0-2	3-1	1-1	2-0	5-0	3-1
Libertad	22	11	6	5	28	18	39	0-1	0-0		0-0	4-1	0-0	1-1	3-0	1-0	1-2	2-1	2-0
Guaraní	22	9	7	6	23	19	34	2-2	0-0	1-2		2-1	1-2	1-0	1-0	2-0	2-0	2-0	2-1
Rubio Nu	22	8	7	7	35	34	31	0-0	0-3	0-1	3-0		0-1	2-2	1-0	2-2	1-0	2-1	1-0
Tacuary	22	6	12	4	17	14	30	0-1	0-0	1-0	0-0	1-0		2-0	1-1	1-1	0-1	3-2	1-1
Cerro Porteño	22	5	9	8	23	29	24	1-2	1-2	1-2	0-0	1-1	1-1		1-1	1-1	1-1	1-0	2-2
3 de Febrero	22	5	8	9	23	31	23	0-2	3-2	3-3	1-1	2-2	0-0	1-2		3-2	0-1	1-0	1-0
Independiente	22	4	10	8	26	29	22	5-1	0-3	2-0	0-0	4-4	1-0	0-1	0-1		1-1	1-1	2-2
Sol de América	22	5	6	11	21	33	21	0-0	0-4	0-1	0-1	3-4	0-0	2-3	3-2	1-0		1-1	1-2
Sportivo Luqueño	22	4	8	10	24	36	20	1-3	1-4	1-0	1-0	2-2	2-2	4-1	2-1	1-1	2-2		1-1
General Caballero	22	4	6	12	21	36	18	1-3	1-2	0-1	0-1	1-5	1-1	1-0	0-0	1-2	3-2	1-0	

29/01/2011 - 5/06/2011 • † Qualified for the Copa Libertadores
Top scorers: 13 - Pablo Zeballos, Olimpia • 12 - Robin Ramirez, Rubio Nu • 10 - Cesar Caceres Canete, 3 de Febrero • 9 - Victor Aquino, Nacional & Juan Ferreyra ARG, Olimpia • 8 - Vladimir Marin COL, Olimpia & Lorenzo Melgarejo, Independiente

PARAGUAY 2011 DIVISION INTERMEDIA (2)

	Pl	W	D	L	F	A	Pts
Cerro Porteño PF	26	13	6	7	43	28	45
Deportivo Carapegua	26	13	6	7	41	29	45
Deportivo Capiatá	26	12	8	6	39	26	44
Deportivo Santaní	26	11	11	4	28	22	44
River Plate	26	9	10	7	32	36	37
General Díaz	26	9	9	8	30	28	36
Atlético Colegiales	26	7	12	7	23	28	33
Sportivo San Lorenzo	26	7	11	8	36	37	32
Fernando de la Mora	26	7	10	9	28	29	31
Sportivo Iteño	26	6	11	9	22	24	29
Sportivo Trinidense	26	7	8	11	22	31	29
Sport Colombia	26	6	10	10	21	26	28
Deportivo Caaguazú	26	5	9	12	29	37	24
12 de Octubre	26	3	13	10	24	37	22

19/03/2011 - 24/09/2011
Play-off: Deportivo Carapegua 1-2 0-0 **Cerro Porteño PF**

MEDALS TABLE

		Overall			Lge		Sth Am			City
		G	S	B	G	S	G	S	B	
1	Olimpia	43	24	8	39	20	4	4	8	Asunción
2	Cerro Porteño	28	28	7	28	28			7	Asunción
3	Libertad	15	20	2	15	20			2	Asunción
4	Guaraní	10	12	1	10	12			1	Asunción
5	Nacional	8	9		8	9				Asunción
6	Sol de América	2	12		2	12				Vila Elisa
7	Sportivo Luqueño	2	4		2	4				Luque
8	Presidente Hayes	1			1					Tacumbu
9	Atlántida		3			3				Asunción
	River Plate		3			3				Asunción
11	12 de Octubre	1			1					Itaugua
12	Atlético Colegiales		1					1		Asunción

PARAGUAY 2011

DIVISION PROFESIONAL CLAUSURA

	Pl	W	D	L	F	A	Pts	Olimpia	Cerro Porteño	Libertad	Nacional	Tacuary	Independiente	Sol	Rubio Nu	Guaraní	Caballero	3 de Febrero	Sportivo Luqueño
Olimpia †	22	14	4	4	38	22	46		1-1	0-2	1-0	3-1	2-2	1-0	2-1	2-0	2-1	4-0	2-0
Cerro Porteño ‡	22	12	7	3	41	22	43	0-0		1-1	1-3	2-1	0-1	2-0	1-1	0-1	5-1	3-0	4-2
Libertad †	22	11	7	4	36	19	40	2-1	0-1		1-1	1-1	2-2	0-2	2-1	3-2	1-0	4-1	2-0
Nacional	22	11	3	8	34	27	36	1-0	1-1	2-1		3-4	2-1	0-1	1-2	5-2	3-0	2-0	2-1
Tacuary ‡	22	7	9	6	31	28	30	2-3	1-2	1-1	1-0		1-0	1-1	1-0	1-2	4-0	2-2	0-0
Independiente	22	7	9	6	29	26	30	0-2	1-3	1-1	3-1	1-0		1-1	3-1	1-1	1-1	2-0	0-0
Sol de América	22	7	7	8	27	30	28	1-3	2-2	0-3	0-1	1-1	3-1		0-0	2-1	4-0	1-3	1-1
Rubio Nu	22	7	6	9	25	29	27	1-1	0-2	0-2	2-3	1-2	1-1	2-0		2-2	0-2	2-1	1-0
Guaraní ‡	22	6	6	10	32	37	24	3-4	0-2	0-3	1-2	0-0	2-2	3-1	2-2		1-2	0-0	2-0
General Caballero	22	7	2	13	29	49	23	1-2	2-4	0-3	2-0	1-1	2-1	1-2	0-1	2-0		3-7	2-1
3 de Febrero	22	4	6	12	29	41	18	0-1	1-1	2-1	1-1	2-3	0-1	2-2	1-2	0-2	5-2		1-1
Sportivo Luqueño	22	3	6	13	18	39	15	3-1	2-3	0-0	1-0	2-2	0-3	1-2	0-2	1-5	1-4	1-0	

29/07/2011 - 18/12/2011 • † Qualified for the Copa Libertadores • ‡ Qualified for the Copa Sudamericana
General Caballero & 3 de Febrero relegated on three season average • Top scorers: 13 - Freddy Bareiro, Cerro Porteno • 12 - Pablo Zeballos, Olimpia • 11 - Hugo Santa Cruz, Caballero • 10 - Federico Santander, Guaraní • 9 - Julio Aguilar, Independiente & Arnaldo Castorino, 3 de Febrero

PER – PERU

FIFA/COCA-COLA WORLD RANKING

'93	'94	'95	'96	'97	'98	'99	'00	'01	'02	'03	'04	'05	'06	'07	'08	'09	'10	'11	'12
73	72	69	54	38	72	42	45	43	82	74	66	66	70	63	75	68	68	35	

2011												High	Low	Av
Jan	Feb	Mar	Apr	May	Jun	Jul	Aug	Sep	Oct	Nov	Dec			
66	68	59	54	54	49	25	26	35	32	35	35	25	91	60

Peru ended a sequence of four consecutive quarter-final exits at the Copa America when they went one better at the 2011 tournament in Argentina, beating Venezuela 4-1 in the third place play-off having lost 2-0 to Uruguay in the semi-finals. There may have been some good fortune in their progress, but inspired by Fiorentina-based captain Juan Manuel Vargas the Peruvians put in their best performance for a number of years. A win over Mexico and a draw with Uruguay ensured that they qualified from their group, setting up a meeting with Colombia in the quater-finals which the Peruvians won with two extra-time goals from Carlos Lobaton and Vargas. At home there were surprise first-time champions when Juan Aurich from the northern city of Chiclayo beat Alianza in the championship final. Although played under a much simpler format and with fewer fixtures than in the previous two seasons, the final was retained, although ironically both clubs finished the campaign on the same number of points. Juan Aurich lost the first leg at home but managed to force a play-off by winning the second in Lima. A penalty shoot-out win in the third match saw the 'Northern Cyclone' take the title away from Lima and its environs for only the second time.

COPA AMERICA RECORD

1916-1926 DNE 1927 3/4 (Hosts) 1929 4/4 1935 3/4 (Hosts) 1937 6/6 **1939** 1/5 Winners (Hosts) 1941 4/5 1942 5/7 1945 DNE
1946 DNE 1947 5/8 1949 3/8 1953 5/7 (Hosts) 1955 3/6 1956 6/6 1957 4/7 (Hosts) 1959 5/7 1959 DNE 1963 5/7 1967 DNE
1975 1/10 Winners 1979 4/10 SF 1983 4/10 SF 1987 6/10 r1 1989 8/10 r1 1991 8/10 r1 1993 5/10 QF 1995 10/12 r1
1997 4/12 SF 1999 8/12 QF 2001 8/12 QF 2004 7/12 QF (Hosts) 2007 7/12 QF 2011 3/12 SF

FEDERACION PERUANA DE FUTBOL (FPF)

Av. Aviación 2085,
San Luis,
Lima 30
☎ +51 1 2258236
📠 +51 1 2261510
✉ fepefutbol@fpf.org.pe
🖥 www.fpf.com.pe
FA 1922 CON 1926 FIFA 1926
P   Manuel Burga
GS Javier Quintana

FIFA BIG COUNT 2006

Total players	1 891 790
% of population	6.68%
Male	1 656 556
Female	235 234
Amateurs 18+	70 050
Youth under 18	166 140
Unregistered	835 000
Professionals	799
Referees	2 663
Admin & coaches	1 519
Number of clubs	1 800
Number of teams	3 000

MAJOR CITIES/TOWNS

		Population
1	Lima	7 902 851
2	Arequipa	904 931
3	Trujillo	825 143
4	Chiclayo	524 630
5	Piura	387 948
6	Iquitos	385 986
7	Cusco	353 686
8	Chimbote	326 455
9	Huancayo	324 188
10	Sullana	287 685
11	Pucallpa	276 304
12	Tacna	247 855
13	Ica	238 383
14	Juliaca	234 660
15	Ayacucho	182 291
16	Huánuco	152 865
17	Chincha Alta	151 228
18	Cajamarca	142 210
25	Huaral	85 423

REPUBLICA DEL PERU • REPUBLIC OF PERU

Capital	Lima	Population	29 546 963 (39)	% in cities	71%
GDP per capita	$8500 (116)	Area km²	1 285 216 km² (20)	GMT + / -	-5

Neighbours (km) Bolivia 1075, Brazil 2995, Chile 171, Colombia 1800, Ecuador 1420 • Coast 2414

RECENT INTERNATIONAL MATCHES PLAYED BY PERU

2009	Opponents	Score		Venue	Comp	Scorers	Att	Referee
6-02	El Salvador	L	0-1	Los Angeles	Fr			
11-02	Paraguay	L	0-1	Lima	Fr			Buckley PER
29-03	Chile	L	1-3	Lima	WCq	Fano 34	48 700	Amarilla PAR
1-04	Brazil	L	0-3	Porto Alegre	WCq		55 000	Pezzotta ARG
7-06	Ecuador	L	1-2	Lima	WCq	Vargas 52	17 050	Torres PAR
10-06	Colombia	L	0-1	Medellin	WCq		32 300	Simon BRA
5-09	Uruguay	W	1-0	Lima	WCq	Rengifo 86	15 000	Chandia CHI
9-09	Venezuela	L	1-3	Puerto La Cruz	WCq	Fuenmayor OG 41	31 703	Vera ECU
10-10	Argentina	L	1-2	Buenos Aires	WCq	Rengifo 89	38 019	Ortube BOL
14-10	Bolivia	W	1-0	Lima	WCq	Fano 54	4 373	Soto VEN
18-11	Honduras	W	2-1	Miami Gardens	Fr	Izaguirre OG 40, Rengifo 63		Jurisevic USA
2010								
4-09	Canada	W	2-0	Toronto	Fr	Jose Carlos Fernandez 68, Jean Tragodara 72	10 619	Jurisevic USA
7-09	Jamaica	W	2-1	Fort Lauderdale	Fr	OG 4, Jose Carlos Fernandez 85	5 217	Vaughn USA
8-10	Costa Rica	W	2-0	Lima	Fr	Luis Ramirez 3, Hernan Rengifo 5	15 000	Ponce ECU
12-10	Panama	L	0-1	Panama City	Fr		8 528	Cerdas CRC
17-11	Colombia	D	1-1	Bogota	Fr	Luis Ramirez 32	6 900	Laverni ARG
2011								
8-02	Panama	W	1-0	Moquegua	Fr	Orlando Contreras 40	8 000	Ubriaco URU
29-03	Ecuador	D	0-0	Den Haag	Fr			Braamhaar NED
1-06	Japan	D	0-0	Niigata	Fr		39 048	Webb ENG
4-06	Czech Republic	D	0-0	Matsumoto	Fr		7 592	Sato JPN
4-07	Uruguay	D	1-1	Mendoza	CAr1	Paolo Guerrero 23	25 000	Roldan COL
8-07	Mexico	W	1-0	Mendoza	CAr1	Paolo Guerrero 82	10 000	Pezzotta ARG
12-07	Chile	L	0-1	Mendoza	CAr1		42 000	Fagundes BRA
16-07	Colombia	W	2-0	Cordoba	CAqf	Carlos Lobaton 101, Juan Vargas 111	30 000	Chacon MEX
19-07	Uruguay	L	0-2	La Plata	CAsf		25 000	Orosco BOL
23-07	Venezuela	W	4-1	La Plata	CA3p	William Chiroque 41, Paolo Guerrero 3 63 89 92+	20 000	Roldan COL
2-09	Bolivia	D	2-2	Lima	Fr	Rinaldo Cruzado 36, Claudio Pizarro 81p	35 000	Soto VEN
5-09	Bolivia	D	0-0	La Paz	Fr		16 670	Arias PAR
7-10	Paraguay	W	2-0	Lima	WCq	Paolo Guerrero 2 46 71	39 600	Pezzotta ARG
11-10	Chile	L	2-4	Santiago	WCq	Claudio Pizarro 49, Jefferson Farfan 60	39 000	Orosco BOL
15-11	Ecuador	L	0-2	Quito	WCq		34 481	Larrionda URU

Fr = Friendly match • CA = Copa América • WC = FIFA World Cup • q = qualifier

PERU NATIONAL TEAM HISTORICAL RECORDS

Caps
127 - Roberto Palacios 1992-2009 • 104 - Hector Chumpitaz 1965-81 • 100 - Jorge Soto PER 1992-2005 • 97 - Juan Jose Jayo 1994-2008 • 95 - Nolberto Solano 1994-2009 • 89 - Ruben Diaz 1972-85 • 84 - Juan Reynoso • 83 - Percy Olivares 1987-2001 • 82 - Jose Velasquez 1972-85 • 81 - Teofilo Cubillas 1968-82 • 75 - Jose Soto 1992-2003 • 74 - Jose Del Solar 1986-2001 • 64 - Juan Carlos Oblitas 1973-85

Goals
26 - Teofilo Cubillas 1968-82 • 24 - Teodoro Fernandez 1935-47 • 20 - Nolberto Solano 1994-2009 • 19 - Roberto Palacios 1992-2009 • 18 - Hugo Sotil 1970-79 • 17 - Oswaldo Ramirez 1969-82 & Paolo Guerrero 2004- • 16 - Franco Navarro 1980-89 • 15 - Pedro Leon 1963-73 & Claudio Pizarro 1999-2007 • 14 - Oscar Gomez Sanchez 1953-59 • 13 - Jorge Alcalde 1935-39 & Jefferson Farfan 2003-

Past Coaches
Pedro Olivieri URU 1927 • Julio Borrelli URU 1929 • Francisco Bru ESP 1930-33 • Telmo Carbajo 1934-35 • Alberto Denegri 1936-37 • Jack Greenwell ENG 1938-39 • Domingo Arrillaga ESP 1940-41 • Angel Fernandez ARG 1942-45 • Jose Arana 1946-47 • Arturo Fernandez 1948-50 • Alfonso Huapaya 1951-52 • William Cook ENG 1953 • Angel Fernandez ARG 1953 • Juan Valdivieso 1954-55 • Arturo Fernandez 1956 • Gyorgy Orth HUN 1957-59 • Jorge de Almeyda BRA 1963 • Dan Georgiadis GRE 1964-65 • Marcos Calderon 1965-67 • Didi BRA 1968-70 • Lajos Baroti HUN 1971-72 • Roberto Scarone URU 1972-73 • Marcos Calderon 1975-79 • Jose Chiarella 1979 • Tim BRA 1980-82 • Juan Jose Tan 1983 • Moises Barack 1984-85 • Roberto Challe 1985-87 • Fernando Cuellar 1987 • Marcos Calderon 1987 • Pepe BRA 1988-89 • Miguel Company 1991 • Vladimir Popovic YUG 1992-93 • Miguel Company 1994-95 • Juan Carlos Oblitas 1996-99 • Francisco Maturana COL 1999-2000 • Julio Cesar Uribe 2000-02 • Paulo Autuori BRA 2003-05 • Freddy Ternero 2005-06 • Franco Navarro 2006 • Julio Cesar Uribe 2007 • Jose del Solar 2007-10 • Sergio Markarian URU 2010-

PERU 2011
PRIMERA DIVISION

	Pl	W	D	L	F	A	Pts	Juan Aurich	Alianza Lima	Sp Huancayo	Un San Martin	León	Un Comercio	Inti Gas	Cienciano	Cobresol	Sp Cristal	Sport Boys	FBC Melgar	César Vallejo	Universitario	CNI	Alianza At.
Juan Aurich †	30	15	11	4	46	21	57		2-0	1-0	1-0	2-0	3-2	3-0	5-0	2-1	2-1	2-2	1-1	2-0	1-0	2-2	2-1
Alianza Lima †	30	16	7	7	44	25	57	1-0		0-2	0-0	2-1	4-1	4-2	2-0	0-0	0-0	3-0	2-0	2-1	0-0	1-0	1-0
Sport Huancayo †	30	15	5	10	49	33	50	0-0	0-2		2-0	1-0	3-1	2-2	2-2	1-5	3-0	3-0	4-1	3-0	1-0	3-1	3-0
Univ. San Martin ‡	30	13	8	9	43	24	47	1-1	4-0	2-1		0-0	5-1	5-0	2-0	0-0	1-1	1-0	2-2	2-1	0-0	1-0	4-0
León de Huanuco ‡	30	14	4	12	37	30	46	2-1	2-0	2-1	1-0		1-0	1-2	4-0	0-1	1-1	1-0	1-0	3-1	2-0	1-3	4-0
Unión Comercio ‡	30	13	6	11	48	42	45	1-1	0-0	2-1	2-1	5-1		3-2	3-1	3-0	1-0	0-0	1-2	5-2	3-2	3-0	2-0
Inti Gas Deportes ‡	30	12	8	10	42	41	44	0-0	0-2	1-2	2-0	1-0	1-0		2-2	3-0	2-0	3-1	2-0	3-0	0-0	4-0	1-0
Cienciano	30	12	4	14	42	46	40	2-1	0-1	1-0	3-2	1-0	2-2	2-1		5-0	0-1	3-0	2-3	1-0	3-0	1-2	4-0
Cobresol	30	9	12	9	31	40	39	1-1	0-5	0-0	0-0	1-1	1-0	3-1	0-0		1-1	2-2	2-1	1-2	1-1	3-1	0-1
Sporting Cristal	30	10	8	12	30	34	38	0-2	1-1	3-0	0-4	0-2	2-1	0-0	1-0	1-1		**3-0**	1-2	2-1	**3-0**	1-1	1-0
Sport Boys	30	10	6	14	26	49	36	0-5	0-5	0-3	1-0	1-1	1-3	3-1	2-0	1-0	0-1		2-1	1-1	2-0	1-0	0-0
FBC Melgar	30	9	7	14	37	44	34	1-1	3-2	2-2	0-1	1-0	1-2	2-2	0-4	1-2	2-1	0-1		3-0	0-0	0-0	0-1
Univ. César Vallejo	30	9	7	14	32	42	34	1-0	1-1	2-0	0-3	1-1	3-3	2-0	3-0	1-0	1-2	2-1			0-0	3-0	0-0
Universitario	30	8	10	12	25	35	34	0-0	2-1	2-1	1-0	2-1	3-0	0-0	5-0	0-1	1-2	2-1	**0-3**	2-2		**0-3**	1-0
Colegio Nacional	30	9	6	15	35	44	33	0-1	**3-0**	1-3	3-1	2-3	0-0	0-1	0-2	2-2	2-1	**3-0**	1-3	1-0	1-1		2-0
Alianza Atlético	30	10	3	17	24	41	33	1-1	0-2	0-2	1-2	1-0	1-0	3-0	3-1	1-2	2-1	1-2	2-1	0-1	3-0	**3-0**	

12/02/2011 - 4/12/2011 • Juan Aurich and Alianza qualified for the final • † Qualified for the Copa Libertadores • ‡ Qualified for the Copa Sudamericana • Matches in bold were awarded • Top scorers: 17 - Luis Tejada PAN, Juan Aurich & Roberto Jimenez, Unión Comercio • 15 - Humberto Osorio COL, Inti Gas & Irven Avila, Sport Huancayo • 14 - Roberto Ovelar PAR, Alianza Lima • 11 - Sergio Ibarra ARG, Cienciano

CHAMPIONSHIP FINAL 2011

1st leg. Elias Aguirre, Chiclayo, 8-12-2011, Att: 19 229, Ref: Buckley

Juan Aurich	1	Zuniga 51
Alianza Lima	2	Arroe 20, Bazan 46

Juan Aurich - Diego Penny - Luis Guadalupe, Nelinho Quina•, Edgar Balbuena, Jorge Molina• (Mauricio Montes 83), Roberto Guizasola, William Chiroque, Eduardo Uribe (Ricardo Ciciliano 46), Renzo Sheput (Pedro Ascoy 46), Ysrael Zuniga•, Luis Tejada. Tr: Diego Umana
Alianza - Salomon Libman• - Edgar Villamarin, Leandro Fleitas, Christian Ramos, Juan Jayo, Joazinho Arroe• (Paolo Hurtado 72), Johnnier Montano• (Oscar Vilchez 63), Luis Trujillo, Edgar Gonzalez, Jorge Bazan (Manuel Corrales 74), Roberto Ovelar•. Tr: Miguel Arrue

CHAMPIONSHIP FINAL 2011

2nd leg. Alejandro Villanueva, Lima, 11-12-2011, Att: 29 846, Ref: Carrillo

Alianza Lima	0	
Juan Aurich	1	Zuniga 63

Alianza - Salomon Libman - Edgar Villamarin•, Leandro Fleitas, Christian Ramos, Johnnier Montano••♦56, Juan Jayo•, Luis Trujillo, Edgar Gonzalez (Cesar Viza 70), Paolo Hurtado (Joazinho Arroe 62), Jorge Bazan••♦56, Roberto Ovelar (Jose Fernandez 46). Tr: Miguel Arrue
Juan Aurich - Diego Penny• - Nelinho Quina, Luis Guadalupe, Edgar Balbuena•, Alfredo Rojas••♦82, Jorge Molina• (Ricardo Ciciliano 46), Roberto Merino•, Roberto Guizasola, William Chiroque (Anderson Cueto 28), Luis Tejada•, Pedro Ascoy (Ysrael Zuniga 46••♦72). Tr: Diego Umana

CHAMPIONSHIP FINAL 2011

Play-off. Estadio Nacional, Lima, 14-12-2011, Att: 29 213, Ref: Rivera

Juan Aurich	0	3p
Alianza Lima	0	1p

Juan Aurich - Diego Penny - Nelinho Quina•, Luis Guadalupe, Edgar Balbuena, Eduardo Uribe (Renzo Sheput 118), Roberto Merino, Roberto Guizasola, Anderson Cueto (Reimond Manco 75), Ricardo Ciciliano•, Pedro Ascoy• (Jorge Molina• 35), Luis Tejada•. Tr: Diego Umana
Alianza - Salomon Libman - Edgar Villamarin, Leandro Fleitas, Christian Ramos, Amilton Prado (Manuel Corrales• 69), Cesar Viza•, Henry Quinteros• (Oscar Vilchez 97), Luis Trujillo, Edgar Gonzalez, Paolo Hurtado• (Cristofer Soto• 46). Tr: Miguel Arrue

PERU 2011 — SEGUNDA DIVISION (2)

	Pl	W	D	L	F	A	Pts
José Gálvez	26	21	3	2	61	20	66
Deportivo Coopsol	26	14	5	7	43	27	47
Alianza Unicachi	26	13	3	10	40	32	42
Sport Ancash	26	17	2	7	50	27	37
Atlético Mineiro	26	8	3	15	35	49	27
Atlético Torino	26	9	3	14	19	40	**29**
Hijos de Acosvinchos	26	8	3	15	29	46	**27**
Univ'dad San Marcos	26	7	6	13	39	56	**27**
América Cochahuayco	26	6	6	14	29	36	**24**
Coronel Bolognesi	26	6	6	14	35	54	**24**

7/05/2011 - 11/12/2011
Relegation play-off: América 1-4 Coronel Bolognesi

COPA PERU 2011

Semi-finals			Finals		
Real Garcilaso	2	2			
Alianza Univ *	3	0			

* Home team in 1st leg

Los Caimanes	1	0	Real Garcilaso *	3	0
Pacífico *	1	1	Pacifico	1	1

Real promoted to the Primera Division

MEDALS TABLE

	Overall			League			Sth Am			City
	G	S	B	G	S	B	G	S	B	
1 Universitario	25	14	18	25	13	14		1	4	Lima
2 Alianza Lima	20	19	12	20	19	9			3	Lima
3 Sporting Cristal	15	16	6	15	15	6		1		Lima
4 Sport Boys	6	7	5	6	7	5				Callao
5 Deportivo Municipal	4	7	6	4	7	6				Lima
6 Univ San Martin	3			3						Lima
7 Atlético Chalaco	2	5	4	2	5	4				Callao
8 Mariscal Sucre	2	2	2	2	2	2				Lima
9 Unión Huaral	2	1		2	1					Huaral
10 Cienciano	1		4			4	1			Cusco
11 Juan Aurich	1	1	3	1	1	3				Chiclayo

PHI – PHILIPPINES

FIFA/COCA-COLA WORLD RANKING

'93	'94	'95	'96	'97	'98	'99	'00	'01	'02	'03	'04	'05	'06	'07	'08	'09	'10	'11	'12
163	171	166	166	175	175	181	179	175	181	189	188	191	171	179	160	167	150	159

2011												High	Low	Av
Jan	Feb	Mar	Apr	May	Jun	Jul	Aug	Sep	Oct	Nov	Dec	**High**	**Low**	**Av**
153	152	151	155	156	159	162	162	166	158	159	159	**149**	**195**	**174**

Football's profile in basketball-mad Philippines continues to rise thanks to the exploits of the national team - the Azkals - in the wake of their run to the semi-finals of the AFF Suzuki Cup in late 2010. Led by a growing band of overseas-born players of Philippines extraction, the team secured a spot in the finals of the 2012 AFF Challenge Cup in Nepal. In the qualifiers they beat Mongolia 3-2 on aggregate in a preliminary round and then finished second behind Palestine in a group played in Myanmar to book their place in the finals. Coached by the German Michael Weiss after the departure early in the year of Englishman Simon McMenemy, the team then also made a small bit of history by winning their first-ever FIFA World Cup match when they beat Sri Lanka 4-0 in Manilla. The 2014 FIFA World Cup qualifiers were only the third that the Philippines had ever entered following on from 1998 and 2002 but they were bundled out of the competition in the following round by Kuwait who won both legs of the tie in a 5-1 aggregate victory. Organising a comprehensive club structure in a country of nearly 100 million inhabitants and 7,107 islands is nigh on impossible but tentative steps have been taken with the establishment of the United Football League which was won for the second year running by the team of the Air Force.

FIFA WORLD CUP RECORD
1930-1994 DNE 1998-2002 DNQ 2006-2010 DNE 2014 DNQ

PHILIPPINE FOOTBALL FEDERATION (PFF)

	No 27 Danny Floro, Corner Capt Henry Javiers Sts., Pasig City, Metro Manila 1600
☎	+63 2 5712870
📠	+63 2 5712872
@	philippine_football_federation @gmail.com
🖥	www.the-pff.com
FA	1907 CON 1954 FIFA 1930
P	Mariano Araneta
GS	Roland Tulay

FIFA BIG COUNT 2006

Total players	1 548 746
% of population	1.87%
Male	1 548 746
Female	120 019
Amateurs 18+	20 910
Unregistered	340 090
Professionals	0
Referees	167
Admin & coaches	132
Number of clubs	75
Number of teams	229

SOUTH CHINA SEA

Manila
Dasmarinas
Batangas
Cabanatuan
Antipolo
PHILIPPINE SEA
Iloilo
Bacolod
Cebu
Mandaue
Butuan
SULU SEA
Cagayan
Iligan
Zamboanga
Davao
BRU
MAS

MAJOR CITIES/TOWNS

		Population
1	Manila	11 165 131
2	Davao	1 627 171
3	Cebu	821 499
4	Zamboanga	762 624
5	Dasmariñas	711 476
6	Dadiangas	657 891
7	Antipolo	628 923
8	Calamba	560 456
9	Cagayan	545 873
10	Bacolod	484 099
11	Bacoor	469 925
12	Iloilo	421 924
13	San Jose	397 951
14	Mandaue	394 174
15	Batangas	388 989
16	Cainta	370 873
17	Iligan	367 763
18	Cabanatuan	357 768
19	Butuan	354 151

REPUBLIKA NG PILIPINAS • REPUBLIC OF THE PHILIPPINES

Capital Manila	Population 97 976 603 (12)	% in cities 65%
GDP per capita $3300 (161)	Area km² 300 000 km² (72)	GMT +/- +8
Neighbours (km) Coast 36 289		

RECENT INTERNATIONAL MATCHES PLAYED BY THE PHILIPPINES

2010	Opponents	Score	Venue	Comp	Scorers	Att	Referee
16-01	Chinese Taipei	D 0-0	Kaohsiung	Fr			
9-10	Hong Kong	L 2-4	Kaohsiung	Fr	Phil Younghusband 2 58p 69	650	Kao Jung Fang TPE
10-10	Chinese Taipei	D 1-1	Kaohsiung	Fr	Ian Araneta 93+	890	Kao Tsai Hu TPE
12-10	Macau	W 5-0	Kaohsiung	Fr	Emilio Caligdong 6, Ian Araneta 3 13 54 90, James Younghusband 48	700	Yu Ming Hsun TPE
22-10	Timor-Leste	W 5-0	Vientiane	AFFq	Ian Araneta 3 27 41 57, Phil Younghusband 30p, Anton Del Rosario 32		Leow SIN
24-10	Laos	D 2-2	Vientiane	AFFq	Phil Younghusband 76p, James Younghusband 94+	2 000	Pechsri THA
26-10	Cambodia	D 0-0	Vientiane	AFFq			Abdul Wahab MAS
2-12	Singapore	D 1-1	Hanoi	AFFr1	Chris Greatwich 93+		Mahapab THA
5-12	Vietnam	W 2-0	Hanoi	AFFr1	Chris Greatwich 38, Phil Younghusband 79	40 000	Napitupulu IDN
8-12	Myanmar	D 0-0	Nam Dinh	AFFr1			Patwal IND
16-12	Indonesia	L 0-1	Jakarta	AFFsf		70 000	Moradi IRN
19-12	Indonesia	L 0-1	Jakarta	AFFsf		88 000	Ebrahim BHR
2011							
9-02	Mongolia	W 2-0	Bacolod	CCq	Emilio Caligdong 43, Phil Younghusband 94+	20 000	Yu Ming Hsun TPE
15-03	Mongolia	L 1-2	Ulaan Baatar	CCq	James Younghusband 4	3 000	Ko Hyung Jin KOR
21-03	Myanmar	D 1-1	Yangon	CCq	James Younghusband 76p	5 000	
23-03	Palestine	D 0-0	Yangon	CCq		500	Adday IRQ
25-03	Bangladesh	W 3-0	Yangon	CCq	Ian Araneta 41, Angel Guirado 2 55 80	200	Kim Jong Hyeok KOR
29-06	Sri Lanka	D 1-1	Colombo	WCq	Nathaniel Burkey 50	4 000	Shamsuzzaman BAN
3-07	Sri Lanka	W 4-0	Manila	WCq	Emilio Caligdong 20, Phil Younghusband 2 43 57p, Angel Guirado 50	12 500	Kim Sang Woo KOR
23-07	Kuwait	L 0-3	Kuwait City	WCq		20 000	Abu Loum JOR
28-07	Kuwait	L 1-2	Manilla	WCq	Stephan Schrock 45	13 000	Liu Kwok Man HKG
30-09	Hong Kong	D 3-3	Kaohsiung	Fr	Phil Younghusband 31p, Emilio Caligdong 2 44 61		
2-10	Chinese Taipei	D 0-0	Kaohsiung	Fr			
4-10	Macau	W 2-0	Kaohsiung	Fr	Emilio Caligdong 2 58 87		
7-10	Singapore	L 0-2	Singapore	Fr			
11-10	Nepal	W 4-0	Manila	Fr	Phil Younghusband 2 43 57p, James Younghusband 30, Matt Hartman 88		

Fr = Friendly match • AFF = ASEAN Football Federation Championship • CC = AFC Challenge Cup • q = qualifier • r1 = 1st round

PHILIPPINES 2010 UNITED FOOTBALL LEAGUE 1

	Pl	W	D	L	F	A	Pts
Philippine Air Force	14	10	3	1	42	17	33
Kaya	14	9	1	4	41	13	28
Union FC	14	8	3	3	24	14	27
Loyola	14	7	1	6	16	19	22
Philippine Army	14	6	3	5	23	15	21
Philippine Navy	14	7	0	7	21	24	21
Green Archers	14	3	1	10	20	42	10
Mendiola United	14	0	0	14	0	42	0
24/01/2010 - 16/06/2010							

PHILIPPINES 2010 UNITED FOOTBALL LEAGUE 2

	Pl	W	D	L	F	A	Pts
Global	14	13	1	0	56	6	40
Manila Nomads	14	10	1	3	50	24	31
Mama Africa FC	14	7	5	2	41	18	26
United South	14	5	2	7	25	38	17
Sunken Garden Utd	14	5	2	7	26	42	17
Manila Lions	14	4	1	9	23	30	13
Manila All-Japan	14	2	2	10	23	49	8
Diliman	14	2	2	10	13	50	8
24/01/2010 - 16/06/2010							

PHILIPPINES 2011 UNITED FOOTBALL LEAGUE 1

	Pl	W	D	L	F	A	Pts
Philippine Air Force	12	8	3	1	30	7	27
Global	12	6	6	0	28	6	24
Philippine Army	12	5	5	2	16	17	20
Kaya	12	5	2	5	13	17	17
Loyola	12	4	3	5	16	24	15
Green Archers	12	2	3	7	12	21	9
Philippine Navy	12	0	2	10	8	31	2
22/01/2011 - 10/06/2011							

PHILIPPINES 2011 UNITED FOOTBALL LEAGUE 2

	Pl	W	D	L	F	A	Pts
Manila Nomads	14	12	1	1	61	12	37
Stallions	14	11	0	3	42	11	33
Pasargad	14	10	0	4	45	21	30
Dolphins United	14	6	3	5	23	19	21
Union International	14	6	0	8	18	46	18
Manila Lions	14	3	1	10	12	35	10
Sunken Garden Utd	14	2	2	10	22	56	8
Manila All-Japan	14	2	1	11	19	42	7
22/01/2011 - 10/06/2011							

PLE – PALESTINE

FIFA/COCA-COLA WORLD RANKING

'93	'94	'95	'96	'97	'98	'99	'00	'01	'02	'03	'04	'05	'06	'07	'08	'09	'10	'11	'12
-	-	-	-	-	184	170	171	145	151	139	126	137	128	165	179	173	177	158	

2011													High	Low	Av
Jan	Feb	Mar	Apr	May	Jun	Jul	Aug	Sep	Oct	Nov	Dec		High	Low	Av
178	178	178	170	171	167	166	157	162	164	164	158		115	191	155

Palestinian football continued to go from strength to strength as the efforts to create a more organised structure within the territories started to pay dividends, most notably with qualification for the 2012 AFC Challenge Cup finals in Nepal by the national team and an historic first appearance at the AFC President's Cup by 2010 club champions Jabal Mukabar. Despite going through three coaches during the course of the year, the Palestine cruised into the finals of the AFC Challenge Cup after wins over Bangladesh and Myanmar saw them top their qualifying group. There were also some creditable performances in the qualifiers for the 2014 FIFA World Cup with a 3-1 aggregate victory over Afghanistan before bowing out against Thailand in the next round. In all an unprecedented 14 matches were played during the year with Murad Eleyan scoring seven of the fifteen goals Palestine scored. His club side Hilal Jerusalem missed out on the West Bank Premier League title after they could only beat title rivals Shabab Al Amari by a single goal instead of the four needed to overtake them on goal difference. Jabal Mukabar only ensured their survival against relegation on the penultimate weekend and their poor form saw them knocked out in the group stage of the 2011 AFC President's Cup although just being there was a triumph in itself.

FIFA WORLD CUP RECORD
1930-1998 DNE 2002-2014 DNQ

PALESTINE FOOTBALL ASSOCIATION (PFA)

✉ PO Box 4373,
Ramallah-Al Bireh

☎ +972 2 2959102
📠 +972 2 2959101
📧 info@pfa.ps
🖥 www.pfa.com
FA 1928 CON 1998 FIFA 1998
P Jibril Al Rajoub
GS Abdelmajeed Hijjeh

FIFA BIG COUNT 2006

Total players	92 160
% of population	2.43%
Male	87 060
Female	5 100
Amateurs 18+	5 500
Youth under 18	13 200
Unregistered	22 100
Professionals	0
Referees	301
Admin & coaches	494
Number of clubs	40
Number of teams	66

MAJOR CITIES/TOWNS

		Population
1	Gaza	674 309
2	Jabaliya	251 324
3	Khan Yunis	250 817
4	Hebron	229 258
5	Nablus	182 734
6	Rafah	181 619
7	al-Nusayrat	89 954
8	Dayr al-Balah	86 229
9	Bayt Lahya	85 096
10	Tulkarm	62 006
11	Qalqilya	61 903
12	Yatta	59 240
13	al-Birah	54 954
14	al-Burayj	50 681
15	Jenin	48 813
16	Bayt Hanun	46 028
17	Bani Suhalyah	45 651
18	Bethlehem	41 176
19	Ramallah	35 439

PALESTINE

Capital	Ramallah
GDP per capita	$2900 (164)
Population	3 636 195 (130)
Area km²	6 200 km² (171)
% in cities	72%
GMT +/-	+2

Neighbours (km) For the West Bank and Gaza: Israel 358, Jordan 97, Egypt 11 • Coast 40

RECENT INTERNATIONAL MATCHES PLAYED BY PALESTINE

2008 Opponents		Score	Venue	Comp	Scorers	Att	Referee
7-08 Iran	L	0-3	Tehran	WAr1		5 000	Delo SYR
9-08 Qatar	L	0-1	Tehran	WAr1			
26-10 Jordan	D	1-1	Ram	Fr	Keshkesh [4]		
2009							
26-03 Nepal	D	0-0	Kathmandu	CCq		12 000	El Haddad LIB
30-03 Kyrgyzstan	D	1-1	Kathmandu	CCq	Said Alsbakhi [29]	2 000	Yu Ming Hsun TPE
10-07 Iraq	L	0-3	Arbil	Fr			
13-07 Iraq	L	0-4	Baghdad	Fr			
18-07 China PR	L	1-3	Tianjin	Fr	Keshkesh [88p]		
10-10 UAE	D	1-1	Dubai	Fr	Al Amour [35]		
2010							
4-06 Sudan	D	1-1	Omdurman	Fr	Jamal [45]		
11-08 Mauritania	D	0-0	Nouakchott	Fr			
27-09 Yemen	L	1-3	Amman	WAr1	Obeid [79]	4 500	
29-09 Iraq	L	0-3	Amman	WAr1		4 000	
2011							
9-02 Tanzania	L	0-1	Dar es Salaam	Fr			
21-03 Bangladesh	W	2-0	Yangon	CCq	Murad Eleyan 2 [46 65]	1 000	
23-03 Philippines	D	0-0	Yangon	CCq		500	Adday IRQ
25-03 Mayanmar	W	3-1	Yangon	CCq	Murad Eleyan 2 [39 90], Ahmed Mahajna [71]	1 500	Abdulhusin BHR
29-06 Afghanistan	W	2-0	Tursunzade	WCq	Murad Eleyan [22], Ismail Alamour [88]	5 000	Al Ghafari JOR
3-07 Afghanistan	D	1-1	Al Ram	WCq	Hussam Wadi [12]	9 000	Al Dosari QAT
23-07 Thailand	L	0-1	Buriram	WCq		17 000	Lee Min Hu KOR
28-07 Thailand	D	2-2	Al Ram	WCq	Murad Eleyan 2 [5 90]	11 500	Abbas BHR
22-08 Indonesia	L	1-4	Surakarta	Fr	Sulaiman Obaid [49]		
5-10 Iran	L	0-7	Tehran	Fr			
6-12 Bahrain	W	1-0	Al Muharraq	Fr	Ali Khatib [66]		
17-12 Sudan	W	2-0	Al Rayyan	Fr	Ali Khatib [39], Ismail Alamour [62]		
20-12 Bahrain	L	1-3	Doha	Fr	Ashraf Alfawaghra [40p]		
22-12 Kuwait	L	0-3	Doha	Fr			

Fr = Friendly match • AC = AFC Asian Cup • CC = AFC Challenge Cup • WA = West Asian Championship • WC = FIFA World Cup • q = qualifier

PALESTINE NATIONAL TEAM HISTORICAL RECORDS

Past Coaches
Ricardo Carugati ARG 1998 • Ricardo Carugati ARG & Azmi Nassar 1999 • Azmi Nassar 2000 • Mansour Hamid El Bouri EGY 2000 • Mustafa Abdel Ghali Yacoub EGY 2001 • Andrzej Wisniewski POL 2002 • Nicola Hadwa Shahwan 2002-04 • Alfred Riedl AUT 2004 • Ghassan Balawi 2004 • Tamas Viczko HUN 2004 • Azmi Nassar 2005-07 • Nelson Dekmak 2007 • Naeem Swerky 2008 • Izzat Hamza 2008-09 • Jamal Daraghmeh 2009 • Mousa Bezaz ALG 2009-11 • Abdel-Nasser Barakat 2011 • Jamal Mahmoud 2011-

PALESTINE 2010-11

WEST BANK PREMIER LEAGUE

	Pl	W	D	L	F	A	Pts	Shabab A	Hilal J	Shabab T	Markaz Balata	Taraji	Shabab K	Jabal	Al-Bireh	Thagafi	Markaz Tulkarm	Hilal A	Markaz Askar
Shabab Al-Am'ari †	22	15	6	1	48	18	51		3-2	2-2	4-2	1-0	5-0	1-1	2-0	3-0	2-1	4-1	4-0
Hilal Jerusalem	22	15	6	1	39	14	51	2-1		0-0	2-0	1-0	1-0	2-0	1-0	3-0	1-1	4-1	2-2
Shabab Al-Thahriyeh	22	11	7	4	40	21	40	0-2	1-1		1-1	4-1	3-0	0-0	4-1	1-1	3-2	5-1	2-0
Markaz Balata	22	10	6	6	34	31	36	0-1	2-5	2-0		2-1	2-1	1-5	1-0	1-1	1-1	2-1	0-0
Taraji Wadi Al-Neiss	22	9	5	8	29	23	32	1-1	1-2	2-1	1-1		3-0	1-0	0-1	1-0	2-0	2-3	2-0
Shabab Al Khaleel	22	7	4	11	24	35	25	1-2	0-2	1-1	2-2	0-0		2-1	2-3	0-2	3-0	1-0	2-1
Jabal Mukabar	22	6	6	10	27	32	24	1-1	0-2	0-1	0-4	0-0	3-4		1-2	1-1	0-2	2-1	2-3
Al-Bireh	22	7	3	12	19	33	24	0-2	0-1	0-1	1-1	0-3	1-1	0-2		0-3	2-2	1-0	0-3
Thagafi Tulkarm	22	5	7	10	26	33	22	0-2	1-1	0-3	1-3	2-2	1-3	1-1	1-2		1-1	1-2	0-1
Markaz Tulkarm	22	5	6	11	27	42	21	2-2	0-1	2-1	0-2	2-4	1-0	1-3	1-4	0-2		0-3	1-0
Hilal Areeha	22	5	5	12	23	37	20	1-1	1-1	1-3	0-1	1-0	0-1	2-3	1-0	1-1	2-4		0-0
Markaz Askar	22	4	5	13	18	35	17	1-2	0-2	1-3	0-3	1-2	1-0	0-1	0-1	1-3	3-3	0-0	

26/08/2010 - 7/05/2011 • † Qualified for the AFC President's Cup • Top scorers: **22** - Eyad Abugharqoud, Al Am'ari & Murad Eleyan, Hilal Jerusalem

PNG – PAPUA NEW GUINEA

FIFA/COCA-COLA WORLD RANKING

'93	'94	'95	'96	'97	'98	'99	'00	'01	'02	'03	'04	'05	'06	'07	'08	'09	'10	'11	'12
-	-	-	169	167	172	183	192	196	167	172	161	166	178	183	201	203	203	193	

2011													High	Low	Av
Jan	Feb	Mar	Apr	May	Jun	Jul	Aug	Sep	Oct	Nov	Dec		High	Low	Av
203	203	202	202	202	203	MD	MD	187	188	190	193		160	203	181

In an effort to reach the final for the first time in the 48-year history of the Pacific Games, Australian coach Frank Farina was brought in by the Papua New Guinea football association for the 2011 tournament in Noumea, New Caledonia. However, despite a 17-1 victory over Kiribati, Papua New Guinea fell at the group stage on goal difference after Tahiti registered an identical scoreline over the hapless Kiribatians. In the final round of fixtures, Tahiti scored six goals in the last 10 minutes against Kiribati to overtake Papua New Guinea and qualify for the semi-finals instead. In the women's tournament, Papua New Guinea enhanced their growing reputation when they beat New Caledonia 2-1 in the final, an injury-time penalty from Linah Honeakil winning the gold medal for her team. In club football, Hekari United continued their complete domination of football in the country, remaining undefeated as they won the National Soccer League for the fifth year in a row. In the final they beat Eastern Stars 4-0 but their luck ran out in the OFC Champions league as they sought to defend the title they won in 2010. A 2-1 defeat at home to eventual finalists Amicale in their first match set the tone for their campaign and they finished bottom of their group - albeit with a positive goal difference and just a four point gap between them and Amicale.

FIFA WORLD CUP RECORD
1930-1994 DNE 1998 DNQ 2002 DNE 2006 DNQ 2010 DNE

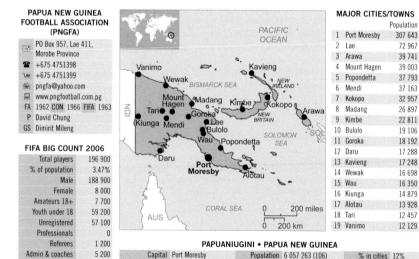

PAPUA NEW GUINEA FOOTBALL ASSOCIATION (PNGFA)

- PO Box 957, Lae 411, Morobe Province
- ☎ +675 4751398
- 📠 +675 4751399
- ✉ pngfa@yahoo.com
- 🖥 www.pngfootball.com.pg
- FA 1962 CON 1966 FIFA 1963
- P   David Chung
- GS Dimirit Mileng

FIFA BIG COUNT 2006

Total players	196 900
% of population	3.47%
Male	188 900
Female	8 000
Amateurs 18+	7 700
Youth under 18	59 200
Unregistered	57 100
Professionals	0
Referees	1 200
Admin & coaches	5 200
Number of clubs	440
Number of teams	1 100

MAJOR CITIES/TOWNS

		Population
1	Port Moresby	307 643
2	Lae	72 967
3	Arawa	39 741
4	Mount Hagen	39 003
5	Popondetta	37 793
6	Mendi	37 163
7	Kokopo	32 957
8	Madang	26 897
9	Kimbe	22 811
10	Bulolo	19 106
11	Goroka	18 192
12	Daru	17 288
13	Kavieng	17 248
14	Wewak	16 698
15	Wau	16 350
16	Kiunga	14 879
17	Alotau	13 928
18	Tari	12 457
19	Vanimo	12 129

PAPUANIUGINI • PAPUA NEW GUINEA

Capital Port Moresby	Population 6 057 263 (106)	% in cities 12%
GDP per capita $2300 (181)	Area km² 462 840 km² (54)	GMT + / - +10
Neighbours (km) Indonesia 820 • Coast 5152		

RECENT INTERNATIONAL MATCHES PLAYED BY PAPUA NEW GUINEA

2007	Opponents	Score	Venue	Comp	Scorers	Att	Referee
13-07	Solomon Islands	L 1-2	Honiara	Fr	Davani		
2008							
No international matches played in 2008							
2009							
No international matches played in 2009							
2010							
No international matches played in 2010							
2011							
27-08	Cook Islands	W 4-0	Boulari	PGr1	Hans 2 [18 50], Muta.D [55], Lepani [85]		Billon NCL
1-09	Tahiti	D 1-1	Boulari	PGr1	Muta.C [15]		Achari FIJ
3-09	Kiribati †	W 17-1	Boulari	PGr1	Kini 3 [13 79 85], Lepani 4 [15 16 54 68], Foster [16], Hans 2 [21 45p], Moka 3 [24 28 41], Yasasa 2 [73 74], Bondaluke [76], Wasi [92+]		Oiaka SOL
5-09	Fiji	L 0-2	Boulari	PGr1			Billon NCL

Fr = Friendly match • PG = Pacific Games • WC = FIFA World Cup • † Not a full international

PAPUA NEW GUINEA 2010–11

NATIONAL SOCCER LEAGUE

	Pl	W	D	L	F	A	Pts	Hekari	Eastern	Tukoko	Besta	Souths	Madang	Gigira
Hekari United †	11	10	1	0	37	10	31		2-1	n/p	4-2	4-1	8-0	6-2
Eastern Stars †	12	8	2	2	34	17	26	1-3		4-0	4-2	2-1	2-0	4-4
Tukoko University †	11	3	5	3	10	13	14	0-1	0-0		0-2	0-0	2-0	1-1
Besta PNG United †	12	3	4	5	26	25	13	1-1	2-3	1-2		2-2	5-2	**3-0**
Petro Souths	12	2	6	4	15	19	12	0-2	0-3	0-0	2-2		2-2	**3-0**
Madang Niupetro Fox	12	2	2	8	16	35	8	2-3	1-5	2-3	2-2	1-3		1-0
Gigira Laitepo Morobe	12	1	4	7	15	34	7	**0-3**	2-5	2-2	3-2	1-1	**0-3**	

30/10/2010 - 1/04/2011 • † Qualified for the play-off semi-finals • Matches in bold awarded

PLAY-OFFS

Semi-finals

Hekari United	5
Besta PNG United	1

Tukoko University	1
Eastern Stars	3

Finals

Hekari United †	4
Eastern Stars	0

† Qualified for OFC Champions League

Final: Lloyd Robson Oval, Port Moresby, 1-04-2011. Scorers - Ian Yanum, Malakai Tiwa 2, Wira Wama for Hekari

MEDALS TABLE

		Overall G S	Lge G S	OFC G S	Town
1	Hekari United	6	5	1	Port Moresby
2	Gelle Hills United	2	2		Port Moresby
3	Rapatona Tigers	1	1		Port Moresby
4	Gigira Rapatona Morobe	1	1		Lae
5	Eastern Stars	1	1		Milne Bay
	Madang Niupetro Fox				Madang
	Tukoko University				Lae

POL – POLAND

FIFA/COCA-COLA WORLD RANKING

'93	'94	'95	'96	'97	'98	'99	'00	'01	'02	'03	'04	'05	'06	'07	'08	'09	'10	'11	'12
28	29	33	53	48	31	32	43	33	34	25	25	22	24	22	34	58	73	66	

2011															
Jan	Feb	Mar	Apr	May	Jun	Jul	Aug	Sep	Oct	Nov	Dec		High	Low	Av
72	71	70	71	71	67	69	65	65	64	66	66		16	73	36

Poland's lowly standing of 66 at the end of 2011 in the FIFA/Coca-Cola World Ranking reflects the national team's lack of competitive action since the end of 2009 rather than any disasterous loss of form in the run up to the finals of Euro 2012. Against the big teams, however, the Poles have struggled and they failed to beat Germany, Italy and France in 2011, all of whom made the journey to Poland during the course of the year to test the water before the finals. Poland will host matches in the impressive redeveloped stadia in Warsaw, Poznan, Wroclaw and Gdansk which along with other stadia that have been redeveloped in recent years, such as Legia's ground in Warsaw and Wisla's ground in Krakow, mean the Ekstraklasa has a fantastic platform from which to develop. The 2011 title went to Wisla Krakow - their third in four years - thanks to a multinational team drawn from 16 nations. They finished ahead of a rejuvinated Slask Wroclaw who were no doubt inspired by the prospect of moving into their new 42,000 capacity Stadion Miejski. Legia Warsaw won the Cup Final on penalties against Lech Poznan and there are signs that Polish clubs could start to make more of an impact in Europe with Lech beating Manchester City in the Europa Cup at their impressive new stadium in Poznan. Exciting times, indeed, for Polish football.

UEFA EUROPEAN CHAMPIONSHIP RECORD

1960 r1   **1964** r1   **1968-2004** DNQ   **2008** 14 r1   **2012** Qualified (as co-hosts)

POLISH FOOTBALL ASSOCIATION (PZPN)

Bitwy Warszawskiej 1920 r.7,
Warsaw 02-366

☎ +48 22 5512253
📠 +48 22 5512240
✉ pzpn@pzpn.pl
🖥 www.pzpn.pl
FA 1919 CON 1954 FIFA 1923
P Grzegorz Lato
GS Zdzislaw Krecina

FIFA BIG COUNT 2006

Total players	2 000 264
% of population	5.19%
Male	1 817 819
Female	182 445
Amateurs 18+	465 854
Youth under 18	185 808
Unregistered	424 300
Professionals	1 202
Referees	11 658
Admin & coaches	60 100
Number of clubs	5 690
Number of teams	13 245

MAJOR CITIES/TOWNS

		Population
1	Warsaw	1 707 566
2	Kraków	755 192
3	Lódz	743 898
4	Wroclaw	631 154
5	Poznan	557 972
6	Gdánsk	453 404
7	Szczecin	405 539
8	Bydgoszcz	357 833
9	Lublin	350 387
10	Katowice	308 170
11	Bialystok	296 227
12	Gdynia	249 946
13	Czestochowa	241 063
14	Radom	223 424
15	Sosnowiec	219 551
16	Torun	204 891
17	Kielce	204 550
18	Zabrze	187 349
36	Chorzow	111 794

RZECZPOSPOLITA POLSKA • REPUBLIC OF POLAND

Capital	Warsaw	Population	38 482 919 (34)	% in cities 61%
GDP per capita	$17 800 (69)	Area km²	312 685 km² (69)	GMT +/- +1
Neighbours (km)	Belarus 605, Czech Republic 615, Germany 456, Lithuania 91, Russia 432, Slovakia 420, Ukraine 428 • Coast 440		

RECENT INTERNATIONAL MATCHES PLAYED BY POLAND

2009	Opponents	Score		Venue	Comp	Scorers	Att	Referee
12-08	Greece	W	2-0	Bydgoszcz	Fr	Obraniak 2 [47 79]	19 000	Sagara JPN
5-09	Northern Ireland	D	1-1	Chorzow	WCq	Lewandowski.M [80]	38 914	Mejuto ESP
9-09	Slovenia	L	0-3	Maribor	WCq		10 226	Collum SCO
10-10	Czech Republic	L	0-2	Prague	WCq		14 010	Larsen DEN
14-10	Slovakia	L	0-1	Chorzow	WCq		5 000	Eriksson SWE
14-11	Romania	L	0-1	Warsaw	Fr		8 000	Mashiah ISR
18-11	Canada	W	1-0	Bydgoszcz	Fr	Rybus [19]	10 400	Christoffersen DEN
2010								
20-01	Thailand	W	3-1	Nak'n Ratchasima	Fr	Glik [43], Malecki [52], Robak [87]	20 000	Mbaga TAN
23-01	Singapore	W	6-1	Nak'n Ratchasima	Fr	Lewandowski.R 2 [26p 37], Iwanski [45p], Brozek.Pi [69], OG [80], Nowak.T [88p]		Amwayi KEN
3-03	Bulgaria	W	2-0	Warsaw	Fr	Blaszczykowski [42], Lewandowski.R [62]	6 800	Kever SUI
29-05	Finland	D	0-0	Kielce	Fr		14 200	Avram ROU
2-06	Serbia	D	0-0	Kufstein	Fr		2 000	Drabek AUT
8-06	Spain	L	0-6	Murcia	Fr		30 000	Koukoulakis GRE
11-08	Cameroon	L	0-3	Szczecin	Fr		17 000	Asumaa FIN
4-09	Ukraine	D	1-1	Lodz	Fr	Jelen [41]	6 500	Irmatov UZB
7-09	Australia	L	1-2	Krakow	Fr	Lewandowski.R [18]	17 000	Bebek CRO
9-10	USA	D	2-2	Chicago	Fr	Matuszczyk [29], Blaszczykowski [72]	31 696	Depiero CAN
12-10	Ecuador	D	2-2	Montreal	Fr	Smolarek [60], Obraniak [70]	1 000	Navarro CAN
17-11	Cote d'Ivoire	W	3-1	Poznan	Fr	Lewandowski.R 2 [19 80], Obraniak [65]	42 000	Toma JPN
10-12	Bosnia-Herzegovina	D	2-2	Antalya	Fr	Pawel Brozek 2 [7 52]	100	Ogretmenoglu TUR
2011								
6-02	Moldova	W	1-0	Vila Real	Fr	Plizga [15]	250	Dos Anjos POR
9-02	Norway	W	1-0	Faro	Fr	Lewandowski.R [18]	500	Dos Anjos POR
25-03	Lithuania	L	0-2	Kaunas	Fr		5 000	Treimanis LVA
29-03	Greece	D	0-0	Larissa	Fr		12 000	Atkinson ENG
5-06	Argentina	W	2-1	Warsaw	Fr	Mierzejewski [26], Pawel Brozek [67]	12 000	Grafe GER
9-06	France	L	0-1	Warsaw	Fr		32 000	Kuipers NED
10-08	Georgia	W	1-0	Lubin	Fr	Blaszczykowski [35]	12 310	Shandor UKR
2-09	Mexico	D	1-1	Warsaw	Fr	Pawel Brozek [27]	18 000	Deaconu ROU
6-09	Germany	D	2-2	Gdansk	Fr	Lewandowski.R [55], Blaszczykowski [90p]	38 000	Orsato ITA
7-10	Korea Republic	D	2-2	Seoul	Fr	Lewandowski.R [29], Blaszczykowski [83]	40 000	Shukralla BHR
11-10	Belarus	W	2-0	Wiesbaden	Fr	Blaszczykowski [31], Lewandowski.R [69]	5 116	Sippel GER
11-11	Italy	L	0-2	Wroclaw	Fr		42 771	Duhamel FRA
15-11	Hungary	W	2-1	Poznan	Fr	Pawel Brozek [37], OG [85]	7 500	Kaasik EST

Fr = Friendly match • EC = UEFA EURO 2008 • WC = FIFA World Cup • q = qualifier • r1 = first round group

POLAND NATIONAL TEAM HISTORICAL RECORDS

Caps
102 - Michal Zewlakow 1998- • 100 - Grzegorz Lato 1971-84 • 97 - Kazimierz Deyna 1968-78 • 96 - Jacek Bak 1993-2008 & Jacek Krzynowek 1999-2009 • 91 - Wladislaw Zmuda 1973-86 • 82 - Antoni Szymanowski 1970-80 • 80 - Zbigniew Boniek 1976-88 • 75 - Wlodzimierz Lubanski 1963-80 • 74 - Tomasz Waldoch 1991-2002 • 72 - Maciej Zurawski 1998-2008 • 70 - Piotr Swierczewski 1992-2003

Goals
48 - Wlodzimierz Lubanski 1963-80 • 45 - Grzegorz Lato 1971-84 • 41 - Kazimierz Deyna 1968-78 • 39 - Ernst Pol 1955-65 • 32 - Andrzej Szarmach 1973-82 • 27 - Gerard Cieslik 1947-58 • 24 - Zbigniew Boniek 1976-88 • 21 - Ernest Willimowski 1934-39 • 20 - Dariusz Dziekanowski 1981-90 & Euzebiusz Smolarek 2002- • 19 - Roman Kosecki 1988-95 • 18 - Lucjan Brychczy 1954-69

Past Coaches
Jozef Szkolnikowski 1921-22 • Jozef Lustgarten 1922 • Kazimierz Glabisz 1923 • Adam Obrubanski 1924 • Tadeusz Kuchar 1925 • Tadeusz Synowiec 1925-27 • Tadeusz Kuchar 1928 • Stefan Loth 1928-31 • Jozef Kaluza 1932-39 • Henryk Reyman 1947 • Andrzej Przeworski 1947 • Zygmunt Alfus 1948 • Andrzej Przeworski 1948 • Mieczyslaw Szymkowiak 1949-50 • Ryszard Koncewicz 1953-56 • Alfred Nowakowski 1956 • Czeslaw Krug 1956 • Henryk Reyman 1957-58 • Czeslaw Krug 1959-62 • Wieslaw Motoczynski 1963-65 • Ryszard Koncewicz 1966 • Antoni Brzezanczyk 1966 • Alfred Nowakowski 1966 • Michal Matyas 1966-67 • Ryszard Koncewicz 1968-70 • Kazimierz Gorski 1971-76 • Jacek Gmoch 1976-78 • Ryszard Kulesza 1978-80 • Antoni Piechniczek 1981-86 • Wojciech Lazarek 1986-89 • Andrzej Strejlau 1989-93 • Leslaw Cmikiewicz 1993 • Henryk Apostel 1994-95 • Wladyslaw Stachurski 1996 • Antoni Piechniczek 1996-97 • Krzysztof Pawlak 1997 • Janusz Wojcik 1997-99 • Jerzy Engel 2000-02 • Zbigniew Boniek 2002 • Pawel Janas 2003-06 • Leo Beenhakker 2006-09 • Stefan Majewski 2009 • Franciszek Smuda 2009-

POLAND 2010–11

LIGA POLSKA ORANGE EKSTRAKLASA

	Pl	W	D	L	F	A	Pts	Wisla	Slask	Legia	Jagiellonia	Lech	Górnik	Polonia	Lechia	Widzew	GKS	Zaglebie	Ruch	Korona	Cracovia	Arka	Polonia
Wisla Krakow †	30	17	5	8	44	29	56		0-0	4-0	2-0	1-0	0-2	0-2	5-2	2-0	3-1	1-0	3-1	2-2	1-0	1-0	2-1
Slask Wroclaw ‡	30	13	10	7	46	34	49	2-0		0-1	0-0	1-2	4-0	2-2	2-1	2-2	4-2	3-1	2-1	0-1	0-0	5-0	0-0
Legia Warszawa ‡	30	15	4	11	45	38	49	2-0	1-2		2-0	2-1	2-1	1-0	0-3	1-0	0-2	2-2	2-3	3-1	2-1	3-0	4-0
Jagiellonia Bialystok ‡	30	14	6	10	38	32	48	2-1	1-1	0-0		2-0	2-0	1-0	1-2	1-3	3-1	2-0	2-1	4-0	4-2	1-0	3-0
Lech Poznan	30	13	6	11	37	23	45	4-1	2-2	1-0	2-0		2-0	2-2	2-0	1-0	0-0	0-1	1-0	4-0	5-0	0-0	1-0
Górnik Zabrze	30	13	6	11	36	40	45	1-0	3-1	1-1	0-1	2-0		0-2	0-0	4-0	1-0	5-1	1-0	2-1	1-0	2-0	1-1
Polonia Warszawa	30	12	8	10	41	26	44	0-1	0-1	3-0	2-0	1-0	0-0		1-2	0-1	0-0	2-1	3-1	1-3	3-0	4-0	2-2
Lechia Gdansk	30	12	7	11	37	36	43	0-3	2-0	2-1	1-2	2-1	5-1	0-0		3-1	0-0	1-2	0-0	0-1	1-0	1-0	2-0
Widzew Lodz	30	11	10	9	41	34	43	0-1	5-2	0-1	4-1	1-1	4-0	0-0	1-0		1-1	2-1	0-0	3-1	2-2	0-0	3-1
GKS Belchatow	30	10	10	10	31	33	40	1-1	0-1	2-0	0-0	1-0	1-1	3-2	1-0	1-0		0-2	3-2	1-0	1-0	1-1	2-0
Zaglebie Lubin	30	10	9	11	31	41	39	0-2	0-1	2-1	0-2	1-0	1-2	1-0	3-1	1-0	1-1		0-0	1-1	0-0	1-0	0-2
Ruch Chorzów	30	10	8	12	29	32	38	2-0	1-2	1-0	0-0	1-0	3-0	0-3	0-0	1-1	2-1	2-2		0-1	1-0	0-0	0-2
Korona Kielce	30	10	7	13	34	49	37	2-2	2-1	1-4	1-1	0-0	1-0	1-3	2-3	1-2	3-1	1-1	0-1		1-0	1-0	3-3
Cracovia	30	8	5	17	37	47	29	0-1	2-3	3-3	3-0	1-0	2-3	3-1	3-0	1-2	3-2	2-2	3-0			2-0	0-1
Arka Gdynia	30	6	10	14	22	43	28	0-1	2-2	2-5	1-0	0-3	2-0	0-0	2-2	1-1	1-0	1-1	0-2	2-1	3-0		2-1
Polonia Bytom	30	6	9	15	29	45	27	2-2	0-0	0-1	3-2	1-2	1-2	0-2	1-1	2-2	1-1	2-0	0-0	1-0	1-1	1-2	

6/08/2010 – 29/05/2011 • † Qualified for the UEFA Champions League • ‡ Qualified for the Europa League
Top scorers: 14 - Tomasz Frankowski, Jagiellonia • 12 - Andrzej Niedzielan, Korana & Abdou Traore, BFA, Lechia • 11 - Artjoms Rudnevs LVA, Lech

MEDALS TABLE

		Overall			League			Cup		Europe		
		G	S	B	G	S	B	G	S	G	S	B
1	Legia Warszawa	22	17	15	8	11	13	14	6			2
2	Górnik Zabrze	20	12	7	14	4	7	6	7	1		
3	Wisla Kraków	18	18	9	14	12	9	4	6			
4	Ruch Chorzów	16	10	8	13	5	8	3	5			
5	Lech Poznan	11	2	4	6		4	5	2			
6	Widzew Lódz	5	7	4	4	7	3	1				1
7	Cracovia	5	2		5	2						
8	Zaglebie Sosnowiec	4	5	2		4	2	4	1			
9	Pogon Lwow	4	3		4	3						
	Polonia Warszawa	4	3		2	3		2				
11	GKS Katowice	3	9	4		4	4	3	5			
12	Slask Wroclaw	3	3	1	1	3	1	2				
13	LKS Lódz	3	2	2	2	1	2	1	1			

POLAND 2010–11

I LIGA POLSKA

	Pl	W	D	L	F	A	Pts	LKS Lodz	Pod'skidzie	Flota	Sandecja	Piast	Pogon	Warta	Leczna	Radzionków	Polkowice	GKS	Kolejarz	Dolcan	Nieciecza	Kluczbork	KSZO	Odra WS	Gorzów
LKS Lodz	34	20	11	3	59	34	71		0-0	1-5	3-1	2-2	2-1	0-0	1-0	4-2	1-0	3-0	2-1	1-0	2-0	2-1	1-0	2-0	2-1
Podbeskidzie	34	20	9	5	53	23	69	1-1		2-1	2-0	0-0	2-1	2-0	3-1	2-1	2-0	2-0	2-0	2-0	0-0	1-0	0-0	1-0	**3-0**
Flota Swinoujscie	34	19	9	6	58	34	66	1-1	1-1		2-1	0-0	1-0	1-0	4-1	4-2	1-1	3-1	0-1	0-1	2-1	2-0	1-0	2-1	**3-0**
Sandecja Nowy Sacz	34	15	11	8	52	34	56	2-2	0-1	2-1		0-0	2-1	3-1	2-0	0-1	3-0	1-1	6-2	2-0	4-0	0-0	3-1	2-1	1-1
Piast Gliwice	34	13	13	8	45	31	52	2-2	2-1	1-2	1-1		0-0	4-0	4-0	0-1	1-0	2-0	3-1	1-1	0-0	2-0	5-0		
Pogon Szczecin	34	14	9	11	55	42	51	1-1	1-3	1-1	1-1	1-1		4-3	3-3	0-0	4-2	3-4	3-0	3-0	1-3	5-1	1-0	3-0	0-0
Warta Poznan	34	14	8	12	42	40	50	4-1	1-1	2-2	2-1	1-0	1-2		1-1	0-2	1-3	2-1	1-3	0-0	1-1	1-2	6-1	1-2	**3-0**
Górnik Leczna	34	14	8	12	44	39	50	1-2	1-0	0-1	1-1	1-1	1-3	0-1		3-0	1-0	1-0	0-0	2-0	1-0	2-0	2-1	2-0	2-1
Ruch Radzionków	34	13	7	14	34	32	46	1-0	3-0	0-1	0-0	3-0	2-0	0-1	3-1		0-1	0-0	2-0	0-1	1-0	1-1	1-0	1-1	0-0
Górnik Polkowice	34	12	6	16	31	39	42	1-1	1-0	1-2	1-1	0-0	0-1	0-0	2-1	1-0		1-1	2-1	1-2	2-1	2-0	1-0	1-2	1-0
GKS Katowice	34	10	11	13	47	57	41	1-3	1-6	5-3	2-3	0-0	1-2	1-1	4-2	1-1	1-0		1-0	1-1	0-0	1-0	2-3	2-0	4-2
Kolejarz Stróze	34	10	8	16	30	43	38	0-1	1-1	1-1	1-2	2-1	0-2	1-0	1-2	0-1	0-0	1-1		1-0	2-0	1-0	1-1	2-0	2-1
Dolcan Zabki	34	10	7	17	33	39	37	0-2	2-0	1-3	1-2	1-2	0-2	1-2	0-1	4-3	2-1	0-1	0-0		5-1	2-0	1-2	1-1	**3-0**
LKS Nieciecza	34	10	7	17	40	53	37	2-3	0-5	2-1	1-0	3-0	1-0	0-1	0-0	1-0	3-0	3-3	3-1	1-0		4-1	3-1	0-1	1-2
MKS Kluczbork	34	8	12	14	36	44	36	1-1	1-2	0-0	0-4	1-2	3-1	4-0	0-0	0-2	3-3	3-1	1-1	1-2	1-1		1-1	0-0	3-2
KSZO Ostrowiec	34	9	9	16	32	43	36	0-2	1-2	0-2	0-0	1-0	0-0	0-1	0-5	2-0	0-2	1-2	3-1	1-0	2-0	2-2		4-0	0-1
Odra Wodzislaw Slaski	34	9	5	20	29	58	32	3-6	1-2	0-1	0-0	0-3	2-0	1-3	2-1	1-2	1-0	1-0	**0-3**	**0-3**	3-2	1-1	3-1		1-3
Gorzów Wielkopolski	34	7	8	19	28	62	29	0-1	1-1	2-4	3-0	**0-3**	**0-3**	0-2	**0-3**	1-0	1-1	3-3	1-0	0-0	0-0	**0-3**	1-2	2-1	

31/07/2010 – 1/06/2011 • Matches in bold awarded • Top scorer: 20 - Charles Nwaogu NGA, Flota

PUCHAR POLSKI 2010-11

Third Round		Fourth Round		Quarter-finals			Semi-finals			Final		
Legia Warszawa	1	Legia Warszawa	2	Legia Warszawa	1	2	Legia Warszawa	1	4	Legia Warszawa ‡	1	5p
Pogon Szczecin *	0	Slask Wroclaw *	1	Ruch Chorzów *	1	0	Lechia Gdansk *	0	0	Lech Poznan	1	4p
MKS Swit *	0											
Slask Wroclaw	0											
OKS 1945 Olsztyn *	2	OKS 1945 Olsztyn *	0 0p									
Odra Wodzislaw Slaski	0	Ruch Chorzów	0 3p									
Ruch Zdzieszowice *	1											
Ruch Chorzów	3											
Jagiellonia Bialystok	1	Jagiellonia Bialystok	1	Jagiellonia Bialystok	0	1						
Flota Swinoujscie *	0	Korona Kielce *	0	Lechia Gdansk *	0	1						
Wigry Suwalki *	0											
Korona Kielce	2											
LKS Lodz *	3	LKS Lodz *	0 1p									
Polonia Bytom	0	Lechia Gdansk	0 3p									
Górnik Zabrze *	0											
Lechia Gdansk	2											
Podbeskidzie *	2	Podbeskidzie *	2	Podbeskidzie	1	2	Podbeskidzie	1	2			
Piast Gliwice	0	GKS Belchatow	0	Wisla Krakow *	0	2	Lech Poznan *	1	3			
Concordia *	0											
GKS Belchatow	1											
Widzew Lodz *	1	Widzew Lodz	0									
Zaglebie Lubin	0	Wisla Krakow *	1									
Dolcan Zabki	0											
Wisla Krakow	1											
Polonia Warszawa	2	Polonia Warszawa	2	Polonia Warszawa	1	1						
Znicz Pruszkow *	0	KSZO Ostrowiec *	0	Lech Poznan *	0	2						
Arka Gdynia	1											
KSZO Ostrowiec *	2											
Cracovia	1	Cracovia *	1									
Gorzów Wielkopolski *	0	Lech Poznan	4									
GKS Tychy *	0											
Lech Poznan	1											

CUP FINAL

Zdzislawa Krzyszkowiaka, Bydgoszcz
3-05-2011. 18:30. Att: 18 200. Ref: Gil
Scorers - Manu 66 for Legia; Injac 29 for Lech
Legia - Wojciech Skaba - Jakub Rzezniczak•,
Jakub Wawrzyniak•, Dickson Choto (Alejandro
Ariel 76), Inaki Astiz (Marcin Komorowski 46) -
Miroslav Radovic, Ivica Vrdoljak•, Maciej Rybus
(Michal Kucharczyk 59), Ariel Borysiuk - Manu,
Michal Hubnik•. Tr: Maciej Skorza
Lech - Krzysztof Kotorowski - Bartosz Bosacki•,
Luis Henriquez, Gregorz Wojtkowiak•, Ivan
Djurdjevic•- Hubert Wolakiewicz, Dmitrije
Injac• (Semir Stilic 69), Jakub Wilk• (Jacek
Kielb 75), Rafal Murawski - Siergiej Kriwiec
(Tomasz Mikolajczak 103), Artoms Rudnevs•.
Tr: Jose Maria Bakero

* Home team/home team in the 1st leg • ‡ Qualified for the Europa League

POR – PORTUGAL

FIFA/COCA-COLA WORLD RANKING

'93	'94	'95	'96	'97	'98	'99	'00	'01	'02	'03	'04	'05	'06	'07	'08	'09	'10	'11	'12
20	20	16	13	30	36	15	6	4	11	17	9	10	8	8	11	5	8	7	

2011													High	Low	Av
Jan	Feb	Mar	Apr	May	Jun	Jul	Aug	Sep	Oct	Nov	Dec				
8	8	9	8	8	7	7	8	5	8	7	7		3	43	13

2011 will forever be associated with FC Porto's heroics both at home and abroad under their astute young coach Andre Villas-Boas or AVB for short. Under his guidance Porto went through the entire 2010-11 league campaign unbeaten - only the third time that has happened in the 73-year history of the league - as well as winning both the cup and the UEFA Europa League. It was a treble to savour for the club as well as for the country as a whole which boasted three of the four semi-finalists in the Europa League and an all-Portuguese final, won by Porto against Braga. Benfica were the other trophy winners of the season - they beat Paços de Ferreira 2-1 in the League Cup Final. The Portuguese national team had an awful start to their Euro 2012 qualifying campaign but Paulo Bento's team made it through to the finals, though once again they needed to beat Bosnia-Herzegovina in a play-off to get there. Portugal failed to win their final game, against Denmark, which would have seen them through automatically but that was a blip in their free-scoring form which saw the team score 21 goals in six games in the second half of the year - six of them coming from Cristiano Ronaldo who will need to repeat his extraordinary club form for his country if Portugal are to make an impact in the finals.

UEFA EUROPEAN CHAMPIONSHIP RECORD

1960 QF 1964 r1 1968-1980 DNQ **1984** SF 1988-1992 DNQ **1996** QF **2000** SF **2004** 2 F (Hosts) **2008** QF **2012** Qualified

FEDERACAO PORTUGUESA DE FUTEBOL (FPF)

Rua Alexandre Herculano, no.58, Apartado 24013, Lisbon 1250-012
☎ +351 21 3252700
🖷 +351 21 3252780
✉ secretario_geral@fpf.pt
🖳 www.fpf.pt
FA 1914 CON 1954 FIFA 1923
P Fernando Gomes Da Silva
GS Angelo Brou

FIFA BIG COUNT 2006

Total players	547 734
% of population	5.16%
Male	488 787
Female	58 947
Amateurs 18+	40 351
Unregistered	210 000
Professionals	1 663
Referees	4 471
Admin & coaches	34 000
Number of clubs	2 284
Number of teams	8 786

MAJOR CITIES/TOWNS

		Population
1	Lisbon	482 678
2	Porto	237 448
3	Amadora	181 377
4	Braga	130 300
5	Setúbal	121 668
6	Queluz	120 811
7	Coimbra	110 764
8	Cacém	109 120
9	Funchal	93 938
10	Mem Martins	89 121
11	Rio de Mouro	65 237
12	Corroios	59 395
13	Aveiro	57 459
14	Odivelas	55 544
15	Amora	55 047
16	Rio Tinto	53 068
17	Leiria	50 087
18	Guimarães	43 062
19	Faro	42 301

REPUBLICA PORTUGUESA • PORTUGUESE REPUBLIC

Capital Lisbon	Population 10 707 924 (75)	% in cities 59%
GDP per capita $22 200 (54)	Area km² 92 090 km² (110)	GMT +/- 0
Neighbours (km) Spain 1214 • Coast 1793		

RECENT INTERNATIONAL MATCHES PLAYED BY PORTUGAL

2009	Opponents	Score	Venue	Comp	Scorers	Att	Referee
11-02	Finland	W 1-0	Faro-Loule	Fr	Cristiano Ronaldo [78p]	19 834	Bertolini SUI
28-03	Sweden	D 0-0	Porto	WCq		40 200	De Bleckere BEL
31-03	South Africa	W 2-0	Lausanne	Fr	Bruno Alves [4], Thwala OG [56]	14 659	Busacca ITA
6-06	Albania	W 2-1	Tirana	WCq	Hugo Almeida [28], Bruno Alves [92+]	13 320	Meyer GER
10-06	Estonia	D 0-0	Tallinn	Fr		6 350	Svendson DEN
12-08	Liechtenstein	W 3-0	Vaduz	Fr		5 525	Bertolini SUI
5-09	Denmark	D 1-1	Copenhagen	WCq	Liedson [86]	37 998	Busacca SUI
9-09	Hungary	W 1-0	Budapest	WCq	Pepe [10]	42 000	Lannoy FRA
10-10	Hungary	W 3-0	Lisbon	WCq	Simao 2 [18 79], Liedson [74]	50 115	Hamer LUX
14-10	Malta	W 4-0	Guimaraes	WCq	Nani [14], Simao [45], Miguel Veloso [52], Edinho [90]	29 350	Kelly IRL
14-11	Bosnia-Herzegovina	W 1-0	Lisbon	WCq	Bruno Alves [31]	60 588	Atkinson ENG
18-11	Bosnia-Herzegovina	W 1-0	Zenica	WCq	Raul Meireles [56]	15 000	Rosetti ITA
2010							
24-05	Cape Verde Islands	D 0-0	Covilha	Fr		6 000	Clos ESP
1-06	Cameroon	W 3-1	Covilha	Fr	Raul Meireles 2 [32 47], Nani [82]	6 125	Weiner GER
8-06	Mozambique	W 3-0	Johannesburg	Fr	Danny [52]	34 000	Dyer RSA
15-06	Côte d'Ivoire	D 0-0	Port Elizabeth	WCr1		37 034	Larrionda URU
21-06	Korea DPR	W 7-0	Cape Town	WCr1	Raul Meireles [29], Simao [53], Hugo Almeida [56], Tiago 2 [60 89], Liedson [81], Cristiano Ronaldo [87]	63 644	Pozo CHI
25-06	Brazil	D 0-0	Durban	WCr1		62 712	Archundia MEX
29-06	Spain	L 0-1	Cape Town	WCr2		62 955	Baldassi ARG
3-09	Cyprus	D 4-4	Guimaraes	ECq	Hugo Almeida [8], Raul Meireles [29], Danny [50], Manuel Fernandes [60]	9 100	Clattenburg ENG
7-09	Norway	L 0-1	Oslo	ECq		24 535	Duhamel FRA
8-10	Denmark	W 3-1	Porto	ECq	Nani 2 [29 30], Cristiano Ronaldo [85]	27 117	Braamhaar NED
12-10	Iceland	W 3-1	Reykjavik	ECq	Cristiano Ronaldo [3], Raul Meireles [27], Postiga [72]	9 767	Einwaller AUT
17-11	Spain	W 4-0	Lisbon	Fr	Carlos Martins [45], Postiga 2 [49 68], Hugo Almeida [90]	38 000	Gautier FRA
2011							
9-02	Argentina	L 1-2	Geneva	Fr	Cristiano Ronaldo [21]	30 000	Busacca SUI
26-03	Chile	D 1-1	Leiria	Fr	Varela [16]	10 694	Blom NED
29-03	Finland	W 2-0	Aveiro	Fr	Ruben Micael 2 [10 71]	13 737	Studer SUI
4-06	Norway	W 1-0	Lisbon	ECq	Helder Postiga [53]	47 829	Cakir TUR
10-08	Luxembourg	W 5-0	Faro	Fr	Helder Postiga [26], Cristiano Ronaldo [44], Fabio Coentrao [47], Hugo Almeida 2 [59 73]		Mateu ESP
2-09	Cyprus	W 4-0	Nicosia	ECq	Cristiano Ronaldo 2 [35p 82], Hugo Almeida [84], Danny [92+]	15 444	Rocchi ITA
7-10	Iceland	W 5-3	Porto	ECq	Nani 2 [13 21], Helder Postiga [44], Joao Moutinho [81], Eliseu [87]	35 715	Nijhuis NED
11-10	Denmark	L 1-2	Copenhagen	ECq	Cristiano Ronaldo [92+]	37 012	Rizzoli ITA
11-11	Bosnia-Herzegovina	D 0-0	Zenica	ECpo		15 292	Webb ENG
15-11	Bosnia-Herzegovina	W 6-2	Lisbon	ECpo	Cristiano Ronaldo 2 [8 53], Nani [24], Helder Postiga 2 [72 82], Miguel Veloso [80]	47 728	Stark GER

Fr = Friendly match • EC = UEFA EURO 2012 • WC = FIFA World Cup • q = qualifier • r1 = first round group • qf = quarter-final

PORTUGAL NATIONAL TEAM HISTORICAL RECORDS

Caps

127 - Luis Figo 1991-2006 • **110** - Fernando Couto 1990-2004 • **94** - Rui Costa 1993-2004 • **88** - Pauleta 1997-2006 • **87** - Cristiano Ronaldo 2003- • **85** - Simao 1998- • **81** - Joao Pinto 1991-2002 • **80** - Vitor Baia 1990-2002 • **79** - Ricardo 2001-08 & Nuno Gomes 1996- • **75** - Ricardo Carvalho 2003- • **73** - Deco 2003- • **70** - Joao Pinto 1983-96 • **66** - Nene 1971-84 • **64** - Eusebio 1961-73 & Humberto 1968-83

Goals

47 - Pauleta 1997-2006 • **41** - Eucobio 1961-73 • **32** - Luis Figo 1991-2006 & Cristiano Ronaldo 2003- • **29** - Nuno Gomes 1996- • **26** - Rui Costa 1993-2004 • **23** - Joao Pinto 1991-2002 • **22** - Nene 1971-84 & Simao 1998- • **19** - Helder Postiga 2003-

Past Coaches

Committee 1921-23 • Ribeiro dos Reis 1925-26 • Candido de Oliveira 1926-29, 1935-45, 1952 • Maia Loureiro 1929 • Laurindo Grijo 1930 • Tavares da Silva 1931, 1945-47, 1951, 1955-57 • Salvador do Carmo 1932-33, 1950, 1953-54 • Virgilio Paula 1947-48 • Armando Sampaio 1949 • Jose Maria Antunes 1957-60, 1962-64 • Armando Ferreira 1961 • Fernando Peyroteo 1961 • Armando Ferreira 1962-64 • Manuel da Luz Afonso 1964-66 • Jose Gomes da Silva 1967 • Jose Maria Antunes 1968-69 • Jose Gomes da Silva 1970-71 • Jose Augusto 1972-73 • Jose Maria Pedroto 1974-76 • Juca 1977-78 • Mario Wilson 1978-80 • Juca 1980-82 • Otto Gloria 1982-83 • Fernando Cabrita 1983-84 • Jose Augusto Torres 1984-86 • Rui Seabra 1986-87 • Juca 1987-89 • Artur Jorge 1990-91 • Carlos Queiroz 1991-93 • Nelo Vingada 1994 • Antonio Oliveira 1994-96 • Artur Jorge 1996-97 • Humberto Coelho 1997-2000 • Antonio Oliveira 2000-02 • Agostinho Oliveira 2002 • Luiz Felipe Scolari 2003-08 • Carlos Queiroz 2008-10 • Paulo Bento 2010-

PORTUGAL 2010–11

LIGA ZON SAGRES

	Pl	W	D	L	F	A	Pts	Porto	Benfica	Sporting	Braga	Vitória SC	Nacional	Paços	Rio Ave	Marítimo	União	Olhanense	Vitória FC	Beira-Mar	Académica	Port'nense	Naval
FC Porto †	30	27	3	0	73	16	**84**		5-0	3-2	3-2	2-0	3-0	3-3	1-0	4-1	5-1	2-0	1-0	3-0	3-1	2-0	3-1
SL Benfica †	30	20	3	7	61	31	**63**	1-2		2-0	1-0	3-0	4-2	2-0	5-2	2-1	3-3	2-0	3-0	2-1	1-2	1-1	4-0
Sporting CP ‡	30	13	9	8	41	31	**48**	1-1	0-2		2-1	2-3	1-1	2-3	1-0	1-0	0-0	0-0	0-1	1-0	2-0	2-1	3-3
Sporting Braga ‡	30	13	7	10	45	33	**46**	0-2	2-1	0-1		3-1	2-0	1-2	1-0	1-0	0-0	3-1	2-2	2-3	5-0	3-1	3-1
Vitória SC Guimarães ‡	30	12	7	11	36	37	**43**	1-1	2-1	1-1	2-1		0-0	1-1	0-0	2-0	1-0	1-0	1-1	1-0	0-2	2-0	1-2
CD Nacional ‡	30	11	9	10	28	31	**42**	0-2	2-1	1-0	1-1	1-3		1-0	1-0	0-0	0-1	0-1	1-0	0-0	1-1	3-1	2-1
Paços de Ferreira	30	10	11	9	35	42	**41**	0-3	1-5	1-0	2-2	2-1	0-1		1-6	1-0	1-1	1-0	2-0	1-1	5-1	2-2	0-0
Rio Ave FC	30	10	8	12	35	33	**38**	0-2	1-2	0-0	2-0	2-3	0-1	3-1		0-0	1-0	0-1	2-0	1-1	2-2	2-0	1-0
CS Marítimo	30	9	8	13	33	32	**35**	0-2	0-1	0-3	1-2	2-0	1-1	1-1	0-1		1-1	4-0	0-1	1-0	1-0	1-1	1-0
União de Leiria	30	9	8	13	25	38	**35**	0-2	0-3	1-2	3-1	1-0	2-1	0-0	1-0	1-3		0-2	1-0	0-3	2-1	0-1	1-0
SC Olhanense	30	7	13	10	24	34	**34**	0-3	1-1	2-2	0-2	0-0	0-0	0-0	2-2	1-1	1-0		3-1	1-1	2-1	2-0	1-3
Vitória FC Setúbal	30	8	10	12	29	42	**34**	0-4	0-2	0-3	0-0	2-1	2-1	1-0	3-3	2-4	4-1	0-0		0-0	0-1	3-1	1-1
SC Beira-Mar	30	7	12	11	32	36	**33**	0-1	1-3	1-1	1-2	3-2	0-2	3-1	1-1	1-1	0-0	1-0	0-0		2-1	0-1	3-1
Académica Coimbra	30	7	9	14	32	48	**30**	0-1	0-1	1-2	0-0	3-1	2-1	0-0	0-1	1-5	0-0	1-1	1-1	3-3		1-0	3-0
Portimonense SC	30	6	7	17	29	49	**25**	2-3	0-1	1-3	0-3	2-1	1-1	0-1	3-1	1-0	1-2	1-1	3-4	1-0	2-2		0-1
Naval 1° de Maio	30	5	8	17	26	51	**23**	0-1	2-1	1-3	0-0	0-3	1-2	1-2	0-1	0-3	0-3	1-1	0-0	2-2	3-1	1-1	

13/08/2010 - 14/05/2011 • † Qualified for the UEFA Champions League • ‡ Qualified for the UEFA Cup
Top scorers: **26** - Hulk BRA, Porto • **16** - Falcao COL, Porto & Joao Tomas, Rio Ave • **12** - Oscar Cardozo PAR, Benfica • **11** - Baba Diawara SEN, Maritimo • **10** - Edgar BRA, Vitória Guimarães & Silvestre Varela POR • **9** - Carlao BRA, Leiria; Claudio Pitbull BRA, Vitória Setúbal; Mario Rondon VEN, Paços; Javier Saviola ARG, Benfica & Leandro Tatu BRA, Beira-Mar

PORTUGAL 2010–11

LIGA DE HONRA (2)

	Pl	W	D	L	F	A	Pts	Gil Vicente	Feirense	Trofense	Oliveirense	Arouca	Leixões	Moreirense	Aves	Santa Clara	Estoril	Freamunde	Penafiel	Belenenses	Sp Covilha	Varzim	Fátima
Gil Vicente FC	30	15	10	5	55	38	**55**		3-2	2-1	0-1	1-1	0-0	2-1	4-2	3-0	2-1	1-1	4-1	1-1	1-1	2-2	3-1
CD Feirense	30	17	4	9	41	31	**55**	0-1		1-0	2-3	2-1	0-0	2-1	0-3	1-0	1-0	0-0	2-1	1-0	2-1	2-1	2-1
CD Trofense	30	15	9	6	41	27	**54**	2-2	0-0		3-2	0-1	0-0	1-0	2-0	3-2	2-1	1-1	1-0	1-2	2-1	2-1	1-1
UD Oliveirense	30	12	9	9	36	35	**45**	2-4	0-1	1-0		2-2	1-0	1-1	1-0	2-0	1-1	1-0	2-0	0-1	1-0	0-1	1-0
FC Arouca	30	11	10	9	47	41	**43**	2-2	2-2	1-3	0-0		1-0	3-0	1-3	1-0	0-0	1-0	6-3	1-1	2-0	3-3	3-0
Leixões SC	30	10	12	8	35	27	**42**	2-0	2-1	1-2	1-1	0-2		0-0	0-0	1-0	1-1	3-1	2-1	1-0	0-1	3-4	3-0
Moreirense FC	30	10	10	10	36	41	**40**	1-1	2-5	2-4	2-0	3-2	0-0		1-0	1-0	1-0	2-1	2-1	2-1	1-1	3-2	2-1
Desportivo Aves	30	10	10	10	35	31	**40**	1-2	0-2	1-1	3-0	3-2	2-2	2-2		2-1	2-1	2-1	0-1	2-0	2-0	1-1	2-0
GD Santa Clara	30	10	8	12	26	29	**38**	3-1	2-1	0-1	1-2	1-1	2-1	1-0	0-0		1-0	1-1	0-3	2-0	3-1	0-0	0-0
GD Estoril-Praia	30	9	11	10	36	31	**38**	1-3	0-1	2-2	2-0	5-2	0-1	2-0	2-0	0-2		1-1	2-0	1-1	3-1	0-0	2-0
SC Freamunde	30	8	13	9	37	39	**37**	0-1	2-1	1-0	0-0	2-2	3-3	1-0	1-0	1-0	2-2		1-4	2-2	5-1	0-0	2-1
SC Penafiel	30	9	9	12	37	44	**36**	2-2	1-0	1-1	3-2	0-1	1-4	1-1	0-0	1-1	0-0	3-2		0-0	1-1	2-2	2-0
Os Belenenses	30	8	11	11	33	36	**35**	2-0	1-2	0-1	3-3	1-0	0-0	1-1	1-1	0-0	0-1	3-0	2-0		1-3	4-2	1-1
Sporting Covilha	30	9	5	16	32	48	**32**	2-1	0-3	0-2	1-3	2-3	2-1	2-1	1-0	0-1	0-1	1-0	0-0	2-0		1-2	3-0
Varzim SC	30	6	13	11	38	48	**31**	1-3	2-0	0-0	1-1	1-0	1-1	1-1	1-1	0-0	2-2	0-2	3-4	1-2	5-2		0-4
CD Fátima	30	5	8	17	29	49	**23**	1-3	1-2	0-2	1-2	1-0	0-2	2-2	0-1	0-0	2-0	2-1	2-2	2-2	1-0	4-2	

28/08/2010 - 29/05/2011 • Top scorers: **15** - Bock, Freamunde • **12** - Henry Antchouet GAB, Moreirense • **11** - Kiko BRA, Arouca; Jeremie N'Jock CMR, Arouca & Miguel Rosa, Belenenses • **10** - Alex Afonso BRA, Estoril; Rafael Lopes, Varzim; Ze Luis CPV, Gil Vicente & Michel BRA, Panafiel

PORTUGAL 2010–11

II DIVISAO CHAMPIONSHIP/PROMOTION PLAY-OFFS (3)

	Pl	W	D	L	F	A	Pts	União	Atlético	Padroense
CF União Madeira	4	2	1	1	5	2	**7**		2-0	2-0
Atlético CP	4	2	0	2	3	6	**6**	1-0		1-0
Padroense FC	4	1	1	2	5	5	**4**	1-1	4-1	

8/05/2011 - 10/06/2011

PORTUGAL 2010-11
II DIVISAO CENTRO (3)

	Pl	W	D	L	F	A	Pts
Padroense FC †	30	16	8	6	44	29	56
Boavista FC	30	16	8	6	46	25	56
CD Tondela	30	16	7	7	46	28	55
Gondomar SC	30	13	11	6	42	26	50
Sertanense FC	30	14	7	9	29	25	49
GD Tourizense	30	13	6	11	48	32	45
Sporting Espinho	30	11	10	9	33	26	43
SC Esmoriz	30	9	11	10	31	38	38
SC Coimbrões	30	11	7	12	38	40	37
Anadia FC	30	10	7	13	32	40	37
Aliados Lordelo	30	9	10	11	28	34	37
Sporting Pombal	30	10	6	14	35	48	36
FC Pampilhosa	30	10	6	14	31	39	36
União da Serra	30	8	10	12	33	36	34
FC Cesarense	30	7	9	14	33	46	30
Eléctrico FC	30	2	7	21	19	56	13

12/09/2010 - 30/04/2011 • † Play-offs

PORTUGAL 2010-11
II DIVISAO NORTE (3)

	Pl	W	D	L	F	A	Pts
CF União Madeira †	30	20	7	3	53	18	67
FC Tirsense	30	15	10	5	40	26	55
GD Chaves	30	13	12	5	34	21	51
AD Fafe	30	13	7	10	40	33	46
AD Lousada	30	13	7	10	46	40	46
CS Marítimo B	30	11	11	8	36	25	44
FC Vizela	30	10	13	7	36	29	43
Macedo de Cavaleiros	30	11	10	9	34	29	43
AD Camacha	30	11	8	11	34	35	41
AD Oliveirense	30	11	8	11	31	37	41
Merelinense FC	30	11	7	12	31	32	40
GD Ribeirão	30	9	12	9	38	29	39
Caniçal	30	9	6	15	32	42	33
CF Andorinha	30	7	7	16	30	55	28
GD Bragança	30	4	6	20	24	53	18
AD Pontassolense	30	2	9	19	20	55	15

12/09/2010 - 30/04/2011 • † Play-offs

PORTUGAL 2010-11
II DIVISAO SUL (3)

	Pl	W	D	L	F	A	Pts
Atlético CP †	30	18	10	2	49	25	64
CD Mafra	30	15	10	5	60	36	55
SCU Torreense	30	16	6	8	36	27	54
CD Pinhalnovense	30	13	11	6	39	29	50
AD Carregado	30	14	5	11	47	40	47
Oriental	30	12	10	8	42	35	46
Louletano DC	30	12	9	9	46	38	45
FC Madalena	30	12	8	10	32	28	44
CD Operário	30	11	9	10	40	40	42
Juventude SC Evora	30	9	12	9	30	34	39
Atlético Reguengos	30	11	5	14	39	47	38
Sporting Farense	30	8	12	10	28	37	36
Casa Pia AC	30	7	7	16	36	49	28
Real SC	30	5	10	15	27	40	25
GD Lagoa	30	5	5	20	19	37	20
SC Praiense	30	3	9	18	26	54	18

12/09/2010 - 30/04/2011 • † Play-offs

MEDALS TABLE

	Overall			League			Cup			Europe		
	G	S	B	G	S	B	G	S	B	G	S	B
1 SL Benfica	61	41	19	32	25	15	27	10		2	6	4
2 FC Porto	49	39	12	25	24	11	20	14		4	1	1
3 Sporting Clube Portugal	38	36	28	18	19	26	19	16		1	1	2
4 OS Belenenses	7	11	14	1	3	14	6	8				
5 Boavista FC	6	4	2	1	3	1	5	1				1
6 Vitória FC Setúbal	3	9	3		1	3	3	8				
7 Académica de Coimbra	1	5			1		1	4				
Sporting Clube Braga	1	5			1		1	3		1		
9 Atlético Clube Portugal	1	3	2			2	1	3				
10 CS Marítimo	1	2					1	2				
11 SC Olhanense	1	1					1	1				
Leixoes SC	1	1					1	1				
SC Beira Mar	1	1					1	1				
14 CF Estrella Amadora	1						1					
15 Vitória SC Guimaraes				5	4			4			5	

TACA DA LIGA BWIN CUP 2010-11

Second Round

Group A	Pl	W	D	L	F	A	Pts	Na	Po	GV	BM
CD Nacional	3	3	0	0	8	3	9		4-1		
FC Porto	3	1	1	1	6	4	4	1-2		3-0	
Gil Vicente FC	3	1	1	1	5	7	4		2-2	2-1	
SC Beira-Mar	3	0	0	3	2	7	0	1-2			

Group B	Pl	W	D	L	F	A	Pts	Be	Ma	DA	Ol
SL Benfica	3	3	0	0	9	2	9		2-0	3-2	
CS Marítimo	3	2	0	1	3	3	6			2-1	
Desportivo Aves	3	1	0	2	4	8	3	0-4			3-2
SC Olhanense	3	0	0	3	4	7	0		0-1		

Group C	Pl	W	D	L	F	A	Pts	PF	SB	VG	Ar
Paços de Ferreira	3	3	0	0	8	5	9		2-1		
Sporting Braga	3	2	0	1	9	4	6	2-3		3-1	
Vitória SC Guimarães	3	1	0	2	3	5	3				1-0
FC Arouca	3	0	0	3	2	8	0	2-3	0-4		

Group D	Pl	W	D	L	F	A	Pts	Sp	Es	Na	Pe
Sporting CP	3	2	0	1	7	2	6		2-0	4-0	
GD Estoril-Praia	3	1	1	1	4	4	4	2-1		0-1	
Naval 1° de Maio	3	1	1	1	3	4	4	2-2			
SC Penafiel	3	1	0	2	1	5	3	0-1			

Semi-finals

SL Benfica	2
Sporting CP	1

CD Nacional	3
Paços de Ferreira	4

Final

SL Benfica	2
Paços de Ferreira	1

LEAGUE CUP FINAL

Estadio Cidade de Coimbra
23-04-2011, 26 222, Proenca

Scorers - Jara [18], Javi Garcia [44] for
Benfica; Luisao OG [52] for Paços

TACA DE PORTUGAL 2010–11

Round of 64

Team	Score
FC Porto *	4
AD Os Limianos	1
CD Operário *	0
Moreirense FC	2
Santa Maria FC *	1
Penalva do Castelo	0
GD Santa Clara	0
Juventude SC Evora *	1
Leixões SC *	3
CD Mafra	2
AD Pontassolense	1
Sporting Espinho *	4
FC Tirsense *	5
UD Sampedrense	1
AD Fafe	0
CD Pinhalnovense *	3
Rio Ave FC *	5
Estrela de Vendas Novas	1
Anadia FC *	1
CD Feirense	2
GD Tourizense *	2
Aliados Lordelo	1
Macedo de Cavaleiros	1
Atlético CP *	3
SC Olhanense	0 4p
Sertanense FC *	0 1p
Padroense FC	1
CD Nacional *	2
Sporting Braga	2
1° de Dezembro *	1
FC Arouca	1
SL Benfica *	5
Académica Coimbra	2
FC Cesarense *	1
SC Mirandela *	1 2p
SC Beira-Mar	1 4p
SCE Bomarralense	†
Louletano DC	†
União de Leiria *	1
União da Madeira	2
Sporting CP	2
GD Estoril-Praia *	1
São João de Ver	1
Paços de Ferreira *	3
CS Marítimo	2
Naval 1° de Maio *	0
Gil Vicente FC *	1 2p
Vitória FC Setúbal	1 4p
Merelinense FC *	2
SC Farense	0
CD Fátima	0 2p
AD Carregado *	0 3p
GD Ribeirão *	2
Os Belenenses	0
Gondomar SC	0 2p
Varzim SC *	0 4p
SCU Torreense	0 5p
GD Lagoa *	0 4p
SC Coimbrões	1
Mondinese FC *	2
Portimonense SC *	2
CD Cinfães	0
Atlético da Malveira	0
Vitória SC Guimarães *	4

Round of 32

Team	Score
FC Porto	1
Moreirense FC *	0
Santa Maria FC	0
Juventude SC Evora *	3
Leixões SC	2
Sporting Espinho *	1
FC Tirsense	0
CD Pinhalnovense *	2
Rio Ave FC *	3
CD Feirense	0
GD Tourizense	2 5p
Atlético CP *	2 6p
SC Olhanense *	1
CD Nacional	0
Sporting Braga	0
SL Benfica *	2
Académica Coimbra	2
SC Beira-Mar *	0
União da Madeira	w-o
Sporting CP *	1
Paços de Ferreira	0
CS Marítimo *	1
Vitória FC Setúbal	2
Merelinense FC *	2
AD Carregado	0
GD Ribeirão	3
Varzim SC *	4
SCU Torreense	2
Mondinese FC *	1
Portimonense SC *	1
Vitória SC Guimarães	2

Round of 16

Team	Score
FC Porto *	4
Juventude SC Evora	0
Leixões SC *	1 4p
CD Pinhalnovense	1 5p
Rio Ave FC *	4
Atlético CP	1
SC Olhanense	0
SL Benfica *	5
Académica Coimbra *	3
União da Madeira	1
Sporting CP	1
Vitória FC Setúbal *	2
Merelinense FC	2
Varzim SC *	1
SCU Torreense	0
Vitória SC Guimarães *	2

† Both teams awarded 3-0 defeats

TAÇA DE PORTUGAL 2010-11

Quarter-finals   **Semi-finals**   Final

FC Porto *	2
CD Pinhalnovense	0

FC Porto *	0	3
SL Benfica	2	1

Rio Ave FC *	0
SL Benfica	2

FC Porto	6
Vitória SC Guimarães ‡	2

Académica Coimbra *	3
Vitória FC Setúbal	2

Académica Coimbra	0	0
Vitória SC Guimarães *	1	0

Merelinense FC *	0
Vitória SC Guimarães	2

TAÇA DE PORTUGAL FINAL 2011

Estadio Nacional, Lisbon, 16-05-2010, 17:00, Att: 25 000, Ref: Pedro Proença

FC Porto	6	Rodriguez 3 [2 45 73], Varela [22], Rolando [35], Hulk [43]
Vitória SC Guimarães	2	Pereira OG [21], Edgar [23]

Porto - Beto - Cristian Sapunaru, Maicon, Rolando, Alvaro Pereira - Fernando● (Freddy Guarin 46) - Fernando Belluschi (Souza 63), Joao Moutinho - James Rodriguez - Silvestre Varela (Mariano Gonzalez 76), Hulk (c)●. Tr: Andre Villas-Boas

Vitoria - Nilson - Leandro Freire, Joao Paulo, Alex (c), Anderson - Renan (Joao Alves 46), Cleber (Jorge Ribeiro 56) - Rui Miguel - Tiago Targino (Marcelo Ioscano 58), Edgar, Faouzi Adbelghni. Tr: Manuel Machado

* Home team/home team in the 1st leg
‡ Qualified for the Europa League

ACADEMICA COIMBRA 2010–11

Aug	15	Benfica	W	2-1	PL	Fidalgo [26], Laionel [90]	48 905
Aug	20	Olhanense	D	1-1	PL	Diogo Gomes [90]	3 009
Aug	29	Beira-Mar	L	1-2	PL	Sougou [60]	3 250
Sep	12	Naval	W	3-0	PL	Sougou [16p], Fidalgo [56], Berger [72]	3 008
Sep	19	Rio Ave	D	2-2	PL	Valente [51], Sougou [62]	1 627
Sep	25	Guimarães	W	3-1	PL	Melo [53], Sougou [80], Laionel [90]	4 506
Oct	1	Leiria	L	1-2	PL	Fidalgo [32]	1 625
Oct	10	Arouca	D	2-2	LCr1	Fidalgo [51], Valente [62]. L 2-4p	407
Oct	17	Cesarense	W	2-1	TPr3	Valente [29], Bischoff [120]	
Oct	23	Nacional	W	2-1	PL	Fidalgo [3], Berger [16]	3 351
Oct	30	Porto	L	0-1	PL		8 103
Nov	6	Portim'ense	D	2-2	PL	Fidalgo [18], Morais [45]	1 094
Nov	10	Arouca	D	1-1	LCr1	Junior Paraiba [18]	554
Nov	13	Sporting	L	1-2	PL	Fidalgo [47]	6 069
Nov	21	Beira-Mar	W	2-0	TPr4	Eder [83], Sougou [88]	1 000
Nov	26	Setúbal	W	1-0	PL	Valente [4]	2 013
Dec	8	Maritimo	L	1-5	PL	Fidalgo [68]	3 349
Dec	17	Braga	L	0-5	PL		7 204
Dec	9	Paços	D	0-0	PL		**2 625**
Jan	12	Un.Madeira	W	3-1	TPr5	Giogo Gomes 2 [42 62], Eder [90]	400
Jan	16	Benfica	L	0-1	PL		**13 264**
Jan	22	Olhanense	L	1-2	PL	Silva [18]	2 116
Jan	28	Setúbal	W	3-2	TPqf	Eder [40], Sougou [44], Bischoff [86p]	3 000
Feb	3	Guimarães	L	0-1	TPsf		10 000
Feb	6	Beira-Mar	D	3-3	PL	Diogo Gomes [6], Sougou [65], Addy [78]	3 286
Feb	13	Naval	L	1-3	PL	Sougou [52p]	988
Feb	20	Rio Ave	L	0-1	PL		2 864
Feb	25	Guimarães	W	2-0	PL	Eder [60], Laionel [90]	11 885
Mar	4	Leiria	D	0-0	PL		3 066
Mar	13	Nacional	D	1-1	PL	Laionel [90]	1 508
Mar	20	Porto	L	1-3	PL	Addy [31]	46 006
Apr	27	Guimarães	D	0-0	TPsf		12 755
Apr	2	Portim'ense	W	1-0	PL	Laionel [59]	3 919
Apr	9	Sporting	L	0-2	PL		24 485
Apr	15	Setúbal	D	1-1	PL	Fidalgo [39]	4 005
May	1	Maritimo	L	0-1	PL		2 150
May	8	Braga	D	0-0	PL		3 951
May	14	Paços	L	1-5	PL	Eder [81]	2 040

14th Att: 68 375 • Av: 4 558 (-11.8%) • Cidade de Coimbra 30 210 (15%)

SC BEIRA-MAR 2010–11

Aug	15	Leiria	D	0-0	PL		2 324
Aug	22	Porto	L	0-3	PL		43 209
Aug	29	Academica	W	2-1	PL	Wilson [45], Djamal [70]	3 250
Sep	13	Setúbal	D	0-0	PL		3 062
Sep	18	Maritimo	D	1-1	PL	Sampaio [50]	2 231
Sep	26	Portim'ense	L	0-1	PL		2 902
Oct	4	Sporting	D	1-1	PL	Renan [38]	13 391
Oct	10	Fátima	D	1-1	LCr1	Tatu [11]	418
Oct	17	Mirandela	D	1-1	TPr3	Ronny [21], W 4-2p	
Oct	23	Paços	D	1-1	PL	Tatu [73]	1 792
Oct	31	Naval	W	3-1	PL	Artur [22p], Tatu [39], Wilson [90]	1 601
Nov	7	Braga	W	3-2	PL	Tatu [24], Ronny 2 [52 68]	10 969
Nov	14	Olhanense	D	1-1	PL	Renan [90]	3 086
Nov	17	Fátima	W	4-1	LCr1	Artur 2 [48 55], Renan [70], Varela [90]	378
Nov	21	Academica	L	0-2	TPr4		1 000
Dec	28	Benfica	L	1-3	PL	Varela [85]	**15 468**
Dec	5	Rio Ave	D	1-1	PL	Tatu [51]	1 413
Dec	18	Guimarães	W	3-2	PL	Tatu [17], Wilson 2 [85 89]	1 755
Dec	2	Gil Vicente	L	1-2	LCr2	Kanu [83]	1 357
Jan	9	Nacional	D	0-0	PL		1 875
Jan	16	Leiria	W	3-0	PL	Ronny [16], Artur [72], Gang Wang [88]	1 037
Jan	9	Porto	L	0-3	LCr2		16 618
Jan	22	Porto	L	0-1	PL		6 956
Feb	29	Nacional	L	1-2	LCr2	Ronny [45]	330
Feb	6	Academica	D	3-3	PL	Djamal [35], Artur [49], Tatu [81]	3 286
Feb	14	Setúbal	D	0-0	PL		**696**
Feb	20	Maritimo	L	0-1	PL		3 212
Feb	27	Portim'ense	L	0-1	PL		2 165
Mar	6	Sporting	L	0-1	PL		16 231
Mar	11	Paços	W	3-1	PL	Tatu [4], Djamal [71], Renan [90]	1 615
Mar	20	Naval	D	2-2	PL	Tatu [23], Artur [45]	1 348
Apr	2	Braga	L	1-2	PL	Tatu [40]	4 021
Apr	10	Olhanense	W	1-0	PL	Wilson [59]	1 032
Apr	17	Benfica	L	1-2	PL	Yartey [90]	25 588
May	1	Rio Ave	D	1-1	PL	Tavares [14]	1 000
May	8	Guimarães	L	0-1	PL		12 533
May	14	Nacional	L	0-2	PL		1 371

13th Att: 60 433 • Av: 4 028 (+104%) • Municipal de Aveiro 30 127 (13%)

ACADEMICA LEAGUE APPEARANCES/GOALS 2011

Goalkeepers Romuald Peiser FRA

Defenders David Addy GHA • Amoreirinha • Markus Berger AUT • Helder Cabral • Luiz Nunes BRA • Orlando • Pedrinho • Pedro Costa • Pape Sow SEN

Midfield Adrien Silva • Amaury Bischoff • Diogo Gomes BRA • Diogo Melo BRA • Diogo Valente • Paulo Grilo • Hugo Morais • Nuno Coelho • Junior Paraiba BRA

Forwards Enrique Carreno ESP • Eder GNB • Laionel BRA • Miguel Fidalgo • Ibrahim Sissoko CIV • Modou Sougou SEN

Coach Jorge Costa (27/12/10) • Ulisses Morais (22/02/11)

BEIRA-MAR LEAGUE APPEARANCES/GOALS 2011

Goalkeepers Rui Rego **30**

Defenders Andre Marques 13+1/0 • Danilo BRA 2/0 • Hugo 26/0 • Kanu BRA 15/0 •Pedro Moreira 28/0 • Ricardo Rocha 1+3/0 • Ruben Lima 1+5/0 • Yohan Tavares FRA 16+5/1 • Luis Tinoco 0+1/0

Midfield Alex Maranhao BRA 0+5/0 • Artur 26/4 • Djamal CHA 27/3 • Jaime 3+2/0 • Joao Luiz BRA 21+3/0 • Renan BRA 28+2/3 • Rui Sampaio 28+2/1 • Sergio Oliveira 1+5/0 • Ishmael Yartey GHA 4+6/1

Forwards Elio 5+4/0 • Leandro Tatu BRA 21+6/9 • Ronny BRA 14+4/3 • Hugo Seixas 1+3/0 • Rui Varela 6+4/1 • Gang Wang CHN 0+14/1 • Wilson 13+14/5

Coach Leonardo Jardim • Rui Bento (1/03/11)

BENFICA LEAGUE APPEARANCES/GOALS 2011

Goalkeepers Julio Cesar BRA **4** • Moreira **2** • Roberto ESP 24+1

Defenders Lionel Carole FRA 6/0 • Fabio Coentrao 23/2 • David Luiz BRA 16/0 • Jardel BRA 5+3/0 • Luis Filipe 3/0 • Luisao BRA 23/1 • Maxi Pereira URU 23+3/0 • Roderick Miranda 4+1/0 • Sidnei BRA 14+2/3

Midfield Pablo Aimar ARG 21+2/5 • Airton BRA 7+8/0 • Carlos Martins 14+11/3 • Cesar Peixoto 9+7/0 • Felipe Menezes BRA 4+3/0 • Jose Fernandez ARG 1+1/0 • Nicolas Gaitan ARG 23+3/7 • Franco Jara ARG 9+17/6 • Javi Garcia ESP 24/2 • Ruben Amorim 6+6/0 • Eduardo Salvio ARG 12+7/4

Forwards Alan Kardec BRA 9+3/3 • Oscar Cardozo PAR 20+2/12 • Nuno Gomes 0+6/4 • Javier Saviola ARG 24/9 • Weldon BRA 0+4/0

Coach Jorge Jesus

SL BENFICA 2010–11

	Date	Opponent	Res	Score	Comp	Scorers	Att
	7	Porto	L	0-2	SC		28 000
Aug	15	Academica	L	1-2	PL	Jara 62	48 905
	21	Nacional	L	1-2	PL	Martins 90	4 568
	28	Setúbal	W	3-0	PL	Cardozo 4, Luisao 44, Aimar 56	36 975
	10	Guimarães	L	1-2	PL	Saviola 32	17 730
	14	Hapoel TA	W	2-0	CLgB	Luisao 21, Cardozo 68	31 512
Sep	19	Sporting	W	2-0	PL	Cardozo 2 13 50	51 899
	25	Maritimo	W	1-0	PL	Coentrao 58	4 200
	29	Schalke	L	0-2	CLgB		50 436
	3	Braga	W	1-0	PL	Martins 73	43 317
	16	Arouca	W	5-1	TPr3	Alan Kardec 2 24 45, Saviola 31, Luisao 66, Gaitan 86	23 449
Oct	20	Lyon	L	0-2	CLgB		36 816
	24	Portim'ense	W	1-0	PL	Javi Garcia 49	12 373
	29	Paços	W	2-0	PL	Aimar 14, Alan Kardec 65p	29 529
	2	Lyon	W	4-3	CLgB	Alan Kardec 20, Coentrao 2 32 67, Javi Garcia 42	37 394
	7	Porto	L	0-5	PL		49 817
Nov	14	Naval	W	4-0	PL	Alan Kardec 10, Gaitan 2 47 62, Nuno Gomes 89	31 143
	24	Hapoel TA	L	0-3	CLgB		11 668
	28	Beira-Mar	W	3-1	PL	Cardozo 2 45p 59, Saviola 65	15 468
	3	Olhanense	W	2-0	PL	Cardozo 42, Saviola 81	25 984
	7	Schalke	L	1-2	CLgB	Luisao 87	23 348
Dec	12	Braga	W	2-0	TPr4	Saviola 38, Aimar 90	26 312
	18	Rio Ave	W	5-2	PL	Aimar 5, Saviola 2 8 52, Salvio 2 62 73	38 456
	2	Maritimo	W	2-0	LCr2	Salvio 25, Saviola 40	20 804
	9	Leiria	W	3-0	PL	Saviola 27, Gaitan 80, Cardozo 90	12 506
	12	Olhanense	W	5-0	TPr5	Saviola 21, Salvio 27, Cardozo 2 39 80, Luisao 80	18 000
Jan	16	Academica	W	1-0	PL	Saviola 18	13 264
	19	Olhanense	W	3-2	LCr2	Javi Garcia 15, Jara 23, Salvio 70	14 897
	22	Nacional	W	4-2	PL	Gaitan 8, Sidnei 20, Cardozo 51, Jara 89	31 255
	26	Rio Ave	W	2-0	TPqf	Cardozo 2 44p 87	10 000
	30	Aves	W	4-0	LCr2	Javi Garcia 36, Jara 70, Nuno Gomes 78, Felipe Menezes 90	4 303
	2	Porto	W	2-0	TPsf	Coentrao 6, Javi Garcia 25	47 512
	6	Setúbal	W	2-0	PL	Gaitan 45, Jara 78	8 605
	13	Guimarães	W	3-0	PL	Sidnei 24, Aimar 49, Martins 90	54 927
Feb	17	Stuttgart	W	2-1	ELr2	Cardozo 70, Jara 81	44 852
	21	Sporting	W	2-0	PL	Salvio 15, Gaitan 63	36 422
	24	Stuttgart	W	2-0	ELr2	Salvio 31, Cardozo 78	25 800
	27	Maritimo	W	2-1	PL	Salvio 81, Coentrao 90	54 991
	2	Sporting	W	2-1	LCsf	Cardozo 34, Javi Garcia 90	49 652
	6	Braga	L	1-2	PL	Saviola 24	18 097
	10	PSG	W	2-1	ELr3	Maxi Pereira 42, Jara 81	33 928
Mar	13	Portim'ense	D	1-1	PL	Nuno Gomes 78	29 711
	17	PSG	D	1-1	ELr3	Gaitan 27	40 193
	21	Paços	W	5-1	PL	Cardozo 5p, Aimar 13, Gaitan 25, Nuno Gomes 2 82 90	3 127
	3	Porto	L	1-2	PL	Saviola 17p	40 433
	7	PSV	W	4-1	ELqf	Aimar 37, Salvio 2 45 52, Saviola 90	60 026
	10	Naval	L	1-2	PL	Alan Kardec 35	4 217
Apr	14	PSV	D	2-2	ELqf	Luisao 45, Cardozo 63p	29 500
	17	Beira-Mar	W	2-1	PL	Sidnei 54, Jara 71	25 588
	20	Porto	L	1-3	TPsf	Cardozo 80p	37 349
	23	Paços	W	2-1	LCf	Jara 18, Javi Garcia 44	26 222
	28	Braga	W	2-1	ELsf	Jardel 50, Cardozo 59	57 778
	1	Olhanense	D	1-1	PL	Jara 4	3 575
May	5	Braga	L	0-1	ELsf		25 384
	8	Rio Ave	W	2-1	PL	Cardozo 2 8 28	2 390
	14	Leiria	D	3-3	PL	Cardozo 41, Javi Garcia 58, Jara 64	29 084

2nd Att: 572 197 • Av: 38 146 (-23.8%) • Estadio da Luz 65 400 (58%)

SPORTING BRAGA 2010–11

	Date	Opponent	Res	Score	Comp	Scorers	Att
Jy	28	Celtic	W	3-0	CLp3	Alan 26p, Echiejile 76, Matheus 88	12 295
	4	Celtic	L	1-2	CLp3	Paulo Cesar 20	53 592
	13	Portim'ense	W	3-1	PL	Matheus 28, Paulo Cesar 45, Leandro Salino 83	13 179
Aug	18	Sevilla	W	1-0	CLpo	Matheus 62	16 646
	21	Setúbal	D	0-0	PL		3 478
	24	Sevilla	W	4-3	CLpo	Matheus 31, Lima 3 58 85 90	31 350
	29	Maritimo	W	1-0	PL	Silvio 45	13 820
	11	Porto	L	2-3	PL	Luis Aguiar 16, Lima 61	47 617
	15	Arsenal	L	0-6	CLgH		59 333
Sep	19	Paços	D	2-2	PL	Moises 11, Luis Aguiar 55	2 725
	24	Naval	W	3-1	PL	Marcio Mossoro 27, OG 50, Paulo Cesar 81	10 276
	28	Shakhtar	L	0-3	CLgH		12 083
	3	Benfica	L	0-1	PL		43 317
	10	1 Dezembro	W	2-1	TPr3		
Oct	19	Partizan	W	2-0	CLgH	Lima 35, Matheus 90	11 454
	23	Olhanense	W	3-1	PL	Marcio Mossoro 49, Lima 2 56 63	11 305
	30	Rio Ave	L	0-2	PL		1 817
	3	Partizan	W	1-0	CLgH	Moises 35	28 295
Nov	7	Beira-Mar	L	2-3	PL	Meyong 76p, Lima 88	10 969
	13	Guimarães	L	1-2	PL	Alan 19	25 651
	23	Arsenal	W	2-0	CLgH	Meyong 2 83 90	14 809
	28	Nacional	W	2-0	PL	Lima 65, Paulo Cesar 90	9 162
	4	Leiria	L	1-3	PL	Matheus 7	1 175
	8	Shakhtar	L	0-2	CLgH		47 627
Dec	12	Benfica	L	0-2	TPr4		26 312
	17	Academica	W	5-0	PL	Paulo Cesar 4, Paulao 25, Keita 35, Meyong 72, Hugo Viana 90	7 204
	3	Guimarães	W	3-1	LCr2	Alan 21p, Lima 42, Meyong 90	8 255
	8	Sporting	L	1-2	PL	Paulo Cesar 17	22 314
	14	Portim'ense	W	3-0	PL	Barbosa 51, Lima 53, Alan 70	1 594
	18	Paços	L	2-3	LCr2	Lima 2 12 80	5 396
	22	Setúbal	D	2-2	PL	Barbosa 55, Guilherme 72	10 439
	30	Arouca	W	4-0	LCr2	Paulao 39, Marcio Mossoro 57, Guilherme 69, Keita 76	865
	5	Maritimo	W	2-1	PL	Barbosa 1, Custodio 65	3 623
	13	Porto	L	0-2	PL		17 478
Feb	17	L. Poznan	L	0-1	ELr2		29 133
	20	Paços	L	1-2	PL	Ukra 34	8 389
	24	L. Poznan	W	2-0	ELr2	Alan 8, Lima 36	10 007
	28	Naval	D	0-0	PL		917
	6	Benfica	W	2-1	PL	Hugo Viana 41, Marcio Mossoro 77	18 097
	10	Liverpool	W	1-0	ELr3	Alan 18p	12 991
Mar	17	Liverpool	D	0-0	ELr3		37 494
	21	Rio Ave	W	1-0	PL	Hugo Viana 73	20 643
	27	Olhanense	W	2-0	PL	Alan 2 13 90p	2 520
		Beira-Mar	W	2-1	PL	OG 68, Meyong 71	4 021
	7	Dy. Kyiv	D	1-1	ELqf	OG 13	16 115
Apr	11	Guimarães	W	3-1	PL	Paulao 62, Ukra 64, Alan 77	25 533
	14	Dy. Kyiv	D	0-0	ELqf		14 839
	18	Nacional	D	1-1	PL	Barbosa 77	1 846
	28	Benfica	L	1-2	ELsf	Vandinho 53	57 778
	1	Leiria	D	0-0	PL		20 332
	5	Benfica	W	1-0	ELsf	Custodio 19	25 384
May	8	Academica	D	0-0	PL		3 951
	14	Sporting	L	0-1	PL		20 804
	18	Porto	L	0-1	ELf		45 391

4th Att: 217 630 • Av: 14 508 (+1.6%) • Municipal 30 152 (13%)

BRAGA LEAGUE APPEARANCES/GOALS 2011

Goalkeepers Artur BRA 18 • Felipe BRA 12
Defenders Anibal Capela 1/0 • Elderson Echiejile NGA 20/0
Kaka BRA 11+1/0 • Leo Fortunato BRA 1+1/0 • Miguel Garcio 16+2/0
Moises BRA 13/1 • Paulao BRA 17+2/2 • Alberto Rodriguez PER 17+1/0
Silvio 20/1
Midfield Luis Aguiar URU 9+3/2 • Custodio 10+3/1
Guilherme BRA 1+4/1 • Helder Barbosa 7+10/4 • Hugo Viana 17+6/3
Leandro Salino BRA 12+7/1 • Andres Madrid ARG 1+4/0 • Marcio
Mossoro BRA 13+8/3 • Vandinho BRA 21+2/0 • Vinicius BRA 1+2/0
Forwards Alan BRA 23+4/5 • Elton BRA 2+4/0 • Ladji Keita SEN 4/1
Lima BRA 25+3/6 • Matheus BRA 9+4/2 • Albert Meyong CMR 2+13/3
Paulo Cesar BRA 15+6/5 • Ukra 12/2
Coach Domingos Paciencia

CS MARITIMO 2010–11

Jul	15	Sp. Fingal	W	3-2	ELp2 Esteves [78], Cherrad [85], Tcho [90] 1 961
Jul	22	Sp. Fingal	W	3-2	ELp2 Alonso [20p], Marquinho [67], Kanu [67] 2 150
Jul	29	Bangor City	W	8-2	ELp3 Tcho 2 [33 79], Danilo Dias 2 [38 75], Diawara 2 [51 77], Kanu [80], Fidelis [90] 2 000
Aug	5	Bangor City	W	2-1	ELp3 Adilson [49], Marquinho [59] 556
Aug	14	Setúbal	L	0-1	PL 4 177
Aug	19	BATE	L	0-3	ELpo 5 230
Aug	22	Sporting	L	0-1	PL 20 828
Aug	26	BATE	L	1-2	ELpo Kanu [90] 2 073
Aug	29	Braga	L	0-1	PL 13 820
Sep	12	Paços	D	1-1	PL Kleber [53] 3 900
Sep	18	Beira-Mar	D	1-1	PL Diawara [37] 2 231
Sep	25	Benfica	L	0-1	PL 4 200
Oct	3	Rio Ave	D	0-0	PL 1 184
Oct	17	Naval	W	2-0	TPr3 Kleber [43], Tcho [78] 150
Oct	24	Naval	W	1-0	PL Roberge [71] 2 820
Oct	31	Olhanense	D	1-1	PL Kleber [5] 2 467
Nov	7	Leiria	D	1-1	PL Kleber [52] 2 907
Nov	12	Nacional	D	0-0	PL 2 856
Nov	21	Setúbal	L	1-2	TPr4 Heldon [82] 1 000
Nov	27	Guimarães	W	2-0	PL Kleber [12p], Diawara [33] 2 920
Dec	8	Academica	W	5-1	PL Tcho [28p], Diawara [49], Marquinho 2 [55 66], Kanu [89] 3 349
Dec	19	Portim'ense	D	1-1	PL Tcho [66p] 3 989
Jan	2	Benfica	L	0-2	LCr2 20 804
Jan	8	Porto	L	1-4	PL Diawara [71] 26 706
Jan	16	Setúbal	W	4-2	PL Sidnei [25], Diawara 2 [55 60], Joao Guilherme [75] 3 466
Jan	19	Aves	W	2-1	LCr2 Luis Olim [3], Tcho [55] 812
Jan	24	Sporting	L	0-3	PL 4 172
Jan	30	Olhanense	W	1-0	LCr2 Danilo Dias [64] 956
Feb	5	Braga	L	1-2	PL Diawara [3] 3 623
Feb	13	Paços	L	0-1	PL 1 017
Feb	20	Beira-Mar	W	1-0	PL Diawara [79] 3 212
Feb	27	Benfica	L	1-2	PL Djalma [75] 54 991
Mar	6	Rio Ave	L	0-1	PL **2 150**
Mar	13	Naval	W	3-0	PL Kleber [23], Djalma [26], Diawara [87] 662
Mar	20	Olhanense	W	4-0	PL Diawara [22], Ben Achour 2 [43 62], Djalma [76] 3 115
Apr	1	Leiria	W	3-1	PL Kleber 2 [38 67], Djalma [59] 709
Apr	8	Nacional	D	1-1	PL Djalma [16] 4 200
Apr	16	Guimarães	L	0-2	PL 8 877
May	1	Academica	W	1-0	PL Diawara [4] **2 150**
May	8	Portim'ense	L	0-1	PL 3 836
May	14	Porto	L	0-2	PL **4 242**

9th Att: 51 586 • Av: 3 439 (-1.5%) • Estadio dos Barreiros 8 922 (38%)

CD NATIONAL 2010–11

Aug	15	Rio Ave	W	1-0	PL Felipe Lopes [68] 1 654
Aug	21	Benfica	W	2-1	PL Luis Alberto [50], Sa [66] **4 568**
Aug	28	Guimarães	L	1-3	PL Bruno Amaro [47] 1 978
Sep	12	Leiria	L	1-2	PL Juninho [55] 868
Sep	20	Porto	L	0-2	PL 3 385
Sep	26	Sporting	D	1-1	PL Danielson [79] 23 372
Oct	3	Portim'ense	W	3-1	PL Claudemir 2 [32 85p], Edgar Costa [32] 1 571
Oct	17	Padroense	W	4-2	TPr3 Mateus [63], Sa 2 [67p 90], Felipe Lopes [88]
Oct	23	Academica	L	1-2	PL Danielson [87] 3 351
Oct	31	Setúbal	W	1-0	PL Sa [24] 1 804
Nov	6	Paços	W	1-0	PL Mateus [89] 989
Nov	12	Maritimo	D	0-0	PL 2 856
Nov	21	Olhanense	L	0-1	TPr4 2 500
Nov	28	Braga	L	0-2	PL 9 162
Dec	7	Naval	W	2-1	PL Claudemir [51p], Nuno Pinto [58] 498
Dec	19	Olhanense	D	0-0	PL 2 045
Dec	2	Porto	W	2-1	LCr2 Anselmo 2 [78 84] 30 018
Jan	9	Beira-Mar	D	0-0	PL 1 875
Jan	16	Rio Ave	W	1-0	PL Diego Barcelos [72] 1 146
Jan	19	Gil Vicente	W	4-1	LCr2 Anselmo 2 [5 85], Luis Alberto [70], Marcio Madeira [79] **417**
Jan	22	Benfica	L	2-4	PL Luis Alberto [76], Mihelic [85] 31 255
Jan	26	Porto	L	0-3	PL 23 212
Jan	29	Beira-Mar	W	2-1	LCr2 Skolnik [18], Luis Alberto [63] 330
Feb	3	Paços	L	3-4	LCsf Diego Barcelos [35], Luis Alberto [44], Thiago Gentil 85p 1 248
Feb	6	Guimarães	D	0-0	PL 12 840
Feb	12	Leiria	L	0-1	PL 1 202
Feb	27	Sporting	W	1-0	PL Mateus [19] 2 640
Mar	7	Portim'ense	D	1-1	PL Skolnik [55] 1 687
Mar	13	Academica	D	1-1	PL Sa [61] 1 508
Mar	20	Setúbal	L	1-2	PL Anselmo [90] 5 272
Apr	4	Paços	W	1-0	PL Edgar Costa [84] 1 147
Apr	8	Maritimo	D	1-1	PL Diego Barcelos [47] 4 200
Apr	18	Braga	D	1-1	PL Luis Alberto [90] 1 846
May	1	Naval	W	2-1	PL Diego Barcelos [24], Claudemir [30p] 723
May	8	Olhanense	L	0-1	PL 3 227
May	14	Beira-Mar	W	2-0	PL Diego Barcelos [3], Edgar Costa [81] 1 371

6th Att: 31 251 • Av: 2 083 (-0.5%) • Estadio da Madeira 5 132 (40%)

MARITIMO LEAGUE APPEARANCES/GOALS 2011

Goalkeepers Marcelo BRA 30

Defenders Alonso BRA 17+5/0 • Briguel 12/0 • Igor Pita 1/0 • Joao Guilherme BRA 10+5/1 • Luciano Amaral BRA 21+1/0 • Valentin Roberge FRA 23+2/1 • Robson BRA 26/0

Midfield Selim Ben Achour TUN 9+2/2 • Dylan Duventru FRA 0+1/0 Heldon CPV 3+12/0 • Luis Olim 0+1/0 • Sergio Marakis RSA 0+1/0 Rafael Miranda BRA 27+2/0 • Ricardo Esteves 17+3/0 • Roberto Sousa BRA 18+3/0 • Tcho BRA 9+9/2

Forwards Adilson BRA 1/0 • Danilo Dias BRA 12+9/0 • Malek Cherrad ALG 1+4/0 • Baba Diawara SEN 29/11 • Djalma 23+4/5 Edinho 2+7/0 • Edivandio CPV 0+2/0 • Fidelis BRA 0+3/0 Kanu BRA 2+5/1 • Kleber BRA 15+3/7 • Evanggelos Mantzios GRE 1/0 Marquinho BRA 9+3/2 • Sidnei CPV 12+3/1

Coach Mitchell van der Gaag NED • Pedro Martins (14/09/10)

NATIONAL LEAGUE APPEARANCES/GOALS 2011

Goalkeepers Rafael Bracalli BRA 30

Defenders Claudemir BRA 20+1/4 • Danielson BRA 30/2 • Felipe Lopes BRA 30/1 • Patacas 10+2/0 • Zarko Tomasevic MNE 4+5/0

Midfield Bruno Amaro 18+7/1 • Joao Aurelio 8+10/0 Juninho BRA 1+3/1 • Luis Alberto BRA 25/3 • Rene Mihelic SVN 9+5/1 Nuno Pinto 15+1/1 • Nejc Pecnik SVN 4+5/0 • Ricardo Fernandes 1/0 Dejan Skolnik SVN 25+1/1 • Danijel Stojanovic CRO 7+1/0 Ivan Todorovic SRB 11+5/0

Forwards Anselmo 5+11/1 • Darko Bodul CRO 1+3/0 • Diego Barcelos BRA 23+1/4 • Edgar Costa 17+8/3 • Marcio Madeira 0+4/0 Mateus ANG 17+6/2 • Orlando Sa 11+5/3 • Pedro Oldoni BRA 1/0 Thiago Gentil BRA 8+2/0

Coach Pedrag Jokanovic SRB • Ivo Vieira (13/03/11)

NAVAL 1° DE MAIO 2010–11

Aug	14	Porto	L	0-1	PL		4 872
	22	Portim'ense	W	1-0	PL	Godemeche [44]	4 707
	30	Sporting	L	1-3	PL	Joao Pedro [75]	**5 201**
Sep	12	Academica	L	0-3	PL		3 008
	19	Setúbal	D	0-0	PL		712
	24	Braga	L	1-3	PL	Fabio Junior [89]	10 276
Oct	3	Paços	L	1-2	PL	Joao Pedro [25]	**384**
	17	Maritimo	L	0-2	TPr3		150
	24	Maritimo	L	0-1	PL		2 820
	31	Beira-Mar	L	1-3	PL	Edvaldo Bolivia [59]	1 601
Nov	7	Olhanense	D	1-1	PL	Edvaldo Bolivia [3]	1 629
	14	Benfica	L	0-4	PL		31 143
	28	Rio Ave	L	0-1	PL		1 204
Dec	7	Nacional	L	1-2	PL	Camora [14]	498
	19	Leiria	L	0-3	PL		579
	3	Sporting	L	0-2	LCr2		11 243
	9	Guimarães	W	2-1	PL	Fabio Junior [71p], Marinho [86]	10 210
Jan	16	Porto	L	1-3	PL	Gomis [88p]	33 109
	19	Estoril	D	2-2	LCr2	Previtali [10], Machado [15]	358
	22	Portim'ense	D	1-1	PL	Previtali [90]	422
	29	Penafiel	W	1-0	LCr2	Joao Pedro [51]	327
	4	Sporting	D	3-3	PL	Fabio Junior [43p], Michel Simplicio [45], Godemeche [67]	20 549
Feb	13	Academica	W	3-1	PL	Gomis [23p], Michel Simplicio [41], Giuliano Amaral [88]	988
	20	Setúbal	D	1-1	PL	Fabio Junior [48]	3 050
	28	Braga	D	0-0	PL		917
Mar	7	Paços	D	0-0	PL		1 480
	13	Maritimo	L	0-3	PL		662
	20	Beira-Mar	D	2-2	PL	Manuel Curto 2 [82p 87p]	1 348
Apr	3	Olhanense	W	3-1	PL	Bruno Moraes 2 [70 73], Edvaldo Bolivia [90]	1 941
	10	Benfica	W	2-1	PL	Bruno Moraes [21], Marinho [82]	4 217
	17	Rio Ave	L	0-1	PL		3 638
May	1	Nacional	L	1-2	PL	Edvaldo Bolivia [41]	723
	8	Leiria	L	0-1	PL		1 436
	14	Guimarães	L	0-3	PL		401

16th   Att: 24 053 • Av: 1 603 (–23.4%) • Municipal 12 630 (12%)

SC OLHANENSE 2010–11

Aug	16	Guimarães	D	0-0	PL		**5 713**
	20	Academica	D	1-1	PL	Yontcha [90p]	3 009
	29	Leiria	W	1-0	PL	Nuno Piloto [20]	2 956
Sep	11	Sporting	D	0-0	PL		25 807
	17	Portim'ense	W	2-0	PL	Paulo Sergio [18], Djalmir [57p]	4 086
	25	Porto	L	0-2	PL		35 430
Oct	2	Setúbal	W	3-1	PL	Mauricio [10], Joao Goncalves [37], Jardel [70]	4 142
	17	Sertanense	D	0-0	TPr3	W 4-1p	1 500
	23	Braga	L	1-3	PL	Mauricio [40]	11 305
	27	Oliveirense	L	0-1	LCr1		525
	31	Maritimo	D	1-1	PL	Yontcha [78]	2 467
Nov	7	Naval	D	1-1	PL	Cadu [51]	1 629
	10	Oliveirense	W	4-1	LCr1	Ismaily [36], Lulinha 2 [44 67], Rui Duarte [65]	2 205
	14	Beira-Mar	D	1-1	PL	Adilson [10]	3 086
	21	Nacional	W	1-0	TPr4	Alexandre [13p]	2 500
Dec	27	Paços	L	0-1	PL		936
	5	Benfica	L	0-2	PL		25 984
	19	Nacional	D	0-0	PL		2 045
	2	Aves	L	2-3	LCr2	Yontcha [46], Toy [86]	498
	9	Rio Ave	W	1-0	PL	Mauricio [22]	1 666
Jan	12	Benfica	L	0-5	TPr5		18 000
	15	Guimarães	L	0-1	PL		10 831
	19	Benfica	L	2-3	LCr2	Djalmir [44], Rui Duarte [56p]	14 897
	22	Academica	W	2-1	PL	Nuno Piloto [22], Rui Duarte [72p]	2 116
	30	Maritimo	L	0-1	LCr2		956
Feb	6	Leiria	W	2-0	PL	Fernandes [19], Paulo Sergio [25]	962
	12	Sporting	D	2-2	PL	Ismaily [64], OG [66]	4 760
	19	Portim'ense	D	1-1	PL	Djalmir [85p]	4 223
Mar	26	Porto	L	0-3	PL		5 296
	6	Setúbal	D	0-0	PL		3 548
	20	Maritimo	L	0-4	PL		3 115
	27	Braga	L	0-2	PL		2 520
Apr	3	Naval	L	1-3	PL	Djalmir [89]	1 941
	10	Beira-Mar	L	0-1	PL		1 032
	16	Paços	D	0-0	PL		**1 851**
May	1	Benfica	D	1-1	PL	Djalmir [90]	3 575
	8	Nacional	W	1-0	PL	Toy [53]	3 227
	14	Rio Ave	D	2-2	PL	Yontcha [57], Dady [80]	1 917

11th   Att: 47 914 • Av: 3 194 (–26.8%) • Jose Arcanjo 10 000 (31%)

NAVAL LEAGUE APPEARANCES/GOALS 2011

Goalkeepers Bruno 1 • Jorge Baptista 2 • Romain Salin FRA 27
Defenders Carlitos 27/0 • Daniel BRA 12/0 • Kevin Gomis FRA 17+4/2
Joao Real 17+2/0 • Jonathas BRA 3/0 • Jose Mario 0+1/0
Illick Lunede GLP 4/0 • Orestes BRA 13+1/0 • Rogerio BRA 16+2/0
Midfield Camora 23+4/1 • Davide 0+1/0 • Giuliano Amaral BRA 4+9/1
Nicolas Godemeche FRA 24/2 • Godinho 2+4/0 • Alexandre
Hauw FRA 10+3/0 • Hugo Machado 10+6/0 • Joao Pedro 11+15/2
Tiago Rosa 2/0
Forwards Bruno Moraes BRA 3+6/3 • Edvaldo Bolivia BOL 27+2/4
Fabio Junior BRA 18+5/4 • Manuel Curto 16+2/2 • Marinho 21+5/2
Michel Simplicio BRA 14+8/2 • Robin Previtali FRA 6+5/1
Coach Victor Zvunka FRA • Rogerio Goncalves (6/10/10)
Carlos Mozer BRA (30/12/10)

OLHANENSE LEAGUE APPEARANCES/GOALS 2011

Goalkeepers Bruno Verissimo 6 • Moretto BRA 13 • Ricardo Batista 11
Defenders Andre Micael 4+1/0 • Anselmo BRA 4+1/1 • Carlos
Fernandes 23/1 • Ismaily BRA 13+4/1 • Jardel BRA 16/1 • Joao
Goncalves 21/1 • Mauricio BRA 26/3 • Mexer MOZ 13+2/0 • Cristian
Suarez CHI 0+1/0
Midfield Esteban Carvajal CHI 0+2/0 • Delson BRA 7+2/0 • Fernando
Alexandre 25/0 • Jorge Goncalves 27+2/0 • Lulinha BRA 2+11/0 • Nuno
Piloto 19/2 • Rui Duarte 14+8/1 • William Tiero GHA 2+2/0 • Pavel
Vieira GNB 0+1/0 • Vinicius BRA 12/0
Forwards Adilson BRA 6+7/1 • Cadu BRA 9+9/1 • Dady CPV 5+2/1 •
Djalmir BRA 9+12/4 • Paulo Sergio 23+1/2 • Toy CPV 5+11/1 • Jean-
Paul Yontcha CMR 9+10/3
Coach Dauto Faquira

PACOS DE FERREIRA 2010–11

	Date	Opponent	Res	Score	Comp	Scorers	Att
Aug	14	Sporting	W	1-0	PL	Rondon 60	**4 845**
	22	Leiria	D	0-0	PL		1 009
	29	Portim'ense	D	2-2	PL	Jorginho 48, Pizzi 75	1 341
Sep	12	Maritimo	D	1-1	PL	Nelson Oliveira 35	3 900
	19	Braga	D	2-2	PL	Baiano 69, Cohene 90	2 725
	27	Setúbal	L	0-1	PL		2 749
Oct	3	Naval	W	2-1	PL	Rondon 46, Nelson Oliveira 50	384
	10	Leixoes	D	1-1	LCr1	Rondon 62	1 382
	17	Sao Joao Ver	W	3-1	TPr3	Pizzi 4, Cohene 2 63 84	
	23	Beira-Mar	D	1-1	PL	Baiano 41	1 792
	29	Benfica	L	0-2	PL		29 529
Nov	6	Nacional	L	0-1	PL		989
	10	Leixoes	W	2-1	LCr1	Amond 8, Nelson Oliveira 62	290
	14	Rio Ave	L	1-3	PL	Rondon 18	1 972
	21	Sporting	L	0-1	TPr4		8 748
	27	Olhanense	W	1-0	PL	Andre Leao 21	**936**
Dec	4	Guimarães	D	1-1	PL	Nelson Oliveira 79	8 551
	19	Porto	L	0-3	PL		3 162
Jan	2	Arouca	W	3-2	LCr2	OG 18, Manuel Jose 55p, Rondon 71	716
	9	Academica	D	0-0	PL		2 625
	15	Sporting	W	3-2	PL	Samuel 28, Manuel Jose 44p, Pizzi 81	17 643
	18	Braga	W	3-2	LCr2	Rondon 29, David Simao 33, Pizzi 61	5 396
	22	Leiria	D	1-1	PL	Pizzi 50	1 254
	30	Guimarães	W	2-1	LCr2	Manuel Jose 41, Cohene 78	1 382
Feb	6	Portim'ense	W	1-0	PL	Nelson Oliveira 87	1 747
	13	Maritimo	W	1-0	PL	Rondon 90	1 017
	20	Braga	W	2-1	PL	Manuel Jose 11p, OG 18	8 389
	26	Setúbal	W	2-0	PL	Rondon 23, Filipe Anunciacao 67	1 610
Mar	3	Nacional	W	4-3	LCsf	Maykon 26, Pizzi 2 42 57, Rondon 51	1 248
	7	Naval	D	0-0	PL		1 480
	11	Beira-Mar	L	1-3	PL	Rondon 61	1 615
	21	Benfica	L	1-5	PL	OG 28	3 127
Apr	4	Nacional	L	0-1	PL		1 147
	10	Rio Ave	L	1-6	PL	Rondon 17	2 000
	16	Olhanense	D	0-0	PL		1 851
	23	Benfica	L	1-2	LCf	OG 52	26 222
	29	Guimarães	W	2-1	PL	Leonel Olimpio 45p, Caetano 85	1 071
	8	Porto	D	3-3	PL	Pizzi 3 47 58 87	48 309
May	14	Academica	W	5-1	PL	Rondon 2 21 33, Ozeia 24, OG 26, Pizzi 43	2 040

7th Att: 28 952 • Av: 1 930 (+16.3%) • Estadio da Mata Real 5 255 (36%)

PACOS LEAGUE APPEARANCES/GOALS 2011
Goalkeepers Antonio Filipe 0+1 • Cassio BRA 29 • Coelho 1
Defenders Baiano BRA 28/2 • Bura 10+3/0 • Javier Cohene PAR 22+1/1 • Jorginho BRA 13/1 • Pedro Queiros 2+2/0 • Samuel BRA 11/1
Midfield Andre Leao 23+2/1 • Bruno BRA 7+3/0 • David Simao 19+6/0 • Filipe Anunciacao 11+4/1 • Leonel Olimpio BRA 28/1 • Manuel Jose 27/2 • Maykon BRA 18+3/0 • Paulo Sousa 1/0
Forwards Alvarinho 0+1/0 • Padraig Amond IRL 0+17/0 • Caetano 7+8/1 • Lucas BRA 0+2/0 • Nelson Oliveira 10+3/4 • Nuno Santos 4+10/0 • Pizzi 22+5/7 • Romeu Torres 0+1/0 • Mario Rondon VEN 24+3/9
Coach Rui Vitoria

PORTO LEAGUE APPEARANCES/GOALS 2011
Goalkeepers Beto 5+1 • Helton BRA 25 • Pawel Kieszek POL 0+1
Defenders Emidio Rafael 5/0 • Jorge Fucile URU 11+5/0 • Maicon BRA 18+3/2 • Nicolas Otamendi ARG 13+2/5 • Rolando 29/0 • Cristian Sapunaru ROU 18+1/0 • Sereno 5+2/0
Midfield Fernando Belluschi ARG 23+3/2 • Andre Castro 0+1/0 • Fernando BRA 18+3/0 • Mariano Gonzalez ARG 1+9/0 • Freddy Guarin COL 12+10/5 • Joao Moutinho 26+1/0 • Alvaro Pereira URU 21/0 • Cristian Rodriguez URU 1+12/1 • Ruben Micael 8+11/0 • Souza BRA 4+8/0
Forwards Radamel Falcao COL 22/16 • Hulk BRA 26/23 • James Rodriguez COL 10+5/2 • Ukra 1+1/0 • Varela 25+1/10 • Walter 3+10/5
Coach Andre Villas-Boas

FC PORTO 2010–11

	Date	Opponent	Res	Score	Comp	Scorers	Att
Aug	7	Benfica	W	2-0	SC	Rolando 3, Falcao 67	28 000
	14	Naval	W	1-0	PL	Hulk 84p	4 872
	19	Genk	W	3-0	ELpo	Falcao 29p, Souza 82, Belluschi 90	13 711
	22	Beira-Mar	W	3-0	PL	Falcao 2 26 81, Belluschi 45	43 209
	26	Genk	W	4-2	CLpo	Hulk 3 36 59p 63, Fernando 53	33 512
	29	Rio Ave	W	2-0	PL	Hulk 2 22 65	5 064
Sep	11	Braga	W	3-2	PL	Varela 2 33 70, Hulk 63	47 617
	16	Rapid	W	3-0	ELgL	Rolando 26, Falcao 65, Micael 77	30 014
	20	Nacional	W	2-0	PL	OG 21, Varela 56	3 385
	25	Olhanense	W	2-0	PL	Otamendi 23, Hulk 45	35 430
	30	CSKA Sofia	W	1-0	ELgL	Falcao 16	17 231
Oct	4	Guimarães	D	1-1	PL	Hulk 37	20 530
	16	Limianos	W	4-1	TPr3	Walter 3 9 60 90, Varela 45	
	21	Besiktas	W	3-1	ELgL	Falcao 26, Hulk 2 59 78	21 722
	25	Leiria	W	5-1	PL	Hulk 2 14 18, Varela 37, Falcao 2 50 75	29 112
Nov	30	Academica	W	1-0	PL	Varela 43	8 103
	4	Besiktas	D	1-1	ELgL	Falcao 36p	34 139
	7	Benfica	W	5-0	PL	Varela 12, Falcao 2 24 28, Hulk 2 80p 90	**49 817**
	14	Portim'ense	W	2-0	PL	Walter 29, Hulk 90p	40 416
	21	Moreirense	W	1-0	TPr4	Falcao 74	5 000
	27	Sporting	D	1-1	PL	Falcao 57	35 063
	2	Rapid	W	3-1	ELgL	Falcao 3 42 85 87	47 600
	6	Setúbal	W	1-0	PL	Hulk 44p	**18 192**
Dec	11	Juventude	W	4-0	TPr5	Falcao 10, Moutinho 39, Pereira 69, Walter 83	26 909
	15	CSKA Sofia	W	3-1	ELgL	Otamendi 22, Micael 54, James Rodriguez 90	22 990
	19	Paços	W	3-0	PL	Otamendi 11, Hulk 90p, Walter 90	3 162
	2	Nacional	L	1-2	LCr2	Hulk 64p	30 018
Jan	8	Maritimo	W	4-1	PL	Guarin 2 37 75, Hulk 60, James Rodriguez 80	26 706
	12	Pinhal'ense	W	2-0	TPqf	Hulk 2 77 90	15 512
	16	Naval	W	3-1	PL	Falcao 44, Hulk 2 45 53	33 109
	19	Beira-Mar	W	3-0	LCr2	Walter 8, Emidio Rafael 18, Fernando 39	16 618
Feb	22	Beira-Mar	W	1-0	PL	Hulk 35p	6 956
	26	Nacional	W	3-0	PL	Hulk 2 4 33, James Rodriguez 45	23 212
	29	Gil Vicente	D	2-2	LCr2	Ruben 45, Emidio Rafael 54	6 547
	2	Benfica	L	0-2	TPsf		47 512
	6	Rio Ave	W	1-0	PL	Varela 6	29 417
	13	Braga	W	2-0	PL	Otamendi 2 45 67	17 478
	17	Sevilla	W	2-1	ELr2	Rolando 58, Guarin 86	21 555
	24	Sevilla	L	0-1	ELr2		35 609
Mar	03	Olhanense	W	3-0	PL	Belluschi 68, Falcao 2 70 90	5 296
	5	Guimarães	W	2-0	PL	Falcao 67, Cristian Rodriguez 90	36 419
	10	CSKA M'kva	W	1-0	ELr3	Guarin 70	19 994
	14	Leiria	W	2-0	PL	Guarin 59, Hulk 90p	3 880
	17	CSKA M'kva	W	2-1	ELr3	Hulk 1, Guarin 24	32 712
	20	Academica	W	3-1	PL	Guarin 54, Maicon 62, Varela 74	46 006
	3	Benfica	W	2-1	PL	Guarin 9, Hulk 26p	40 433
Apr	7	Sp. Moskva	W	5-1	ELqf	Falcao 3 37 84 90, Varela 65, OG 70	38 209
	10	Portim'ense	W	3-2	PL	Hulk 49, Falcao 62, Maicon 85	3 839
	14	Sp. Moskva	W	5-2	ELqf	Hulk 28, Cristian Rodriguez 45, Guarin 47, Falcao 54, Micael 89	17 088
	17	Sporting	W	3-2	PL	Falcao 2 26 50, Walter 87	47 109
	20	Benfica	W	3-1	TPsf	Moutinho 44, Hulk 73, Falcao 75	37 349
	28	Villarreal	W	5-1	ELsf	Falcao 4 49p 67 75 90, Guarin 61	44 719
	1	Setúbal	W	4-0	PL	OG 12, Otamendi 45, Walter 56, Varela 90	4 917
May	5	Villarreal	L	2-3	ELsf	OG 39, Falcao 48	18 523
	8	Paços	D	3-3	PL	Falcao 2 7 53, Hulk 41	48 309
	14	Maritimo	W	2-0	PL	Varela 21, Walter 32	4 242
	18	Braga	W	1-0	ELf	Falcao 44	45 391
	22	Guimarães	W	6-2	TPf	James Rodriguez 3 3 45 74, Varela 22, Rolando 36, Hulk 42	35 000

1st Att: 554 800 • Av: 36 986 (+10.5%) • Estadio do Dragão 65 400 (56%)

PORTIMONENSE SC 2010–11

Aug	13	Braga	L	1-3	PL	Elias 54	13 179
	22	Naval	L	0-1	PL		4 707
	29	Paços	D	2-2	PL	Ivanildo 44, Andre Pinto 55	1 341
Sep	12	Rio Ave	W	3-1	PL	Kadi 32, Pedro Moreira 34, Candeias 65	3 000
	17	Olhanense	L	0-2	PL		4 086
	26	Beira-Mar	W	1-0	PL	Pena 52	2 902
Oct	3	Nacional	L	1-3	PL	Jumisse 31	1 571
	17	Cinfaes	W	2-0	TPr3	Renatinho 28, Dong 84	
	24	Benfica	L	0-1	PL		**12 373**
	28	Aves	L	2-3	LCr1	Renatinho 11, Jumisse 84	256
Nov	1	Guimarães	L	0-2	PL		10 581
	6	Academica	D	2-2	PL	Renatinho 65, Nilson Veiga 66	**1 094**
	10	Aves	D	1-1	LCr1	Renatinho 17	244
	14	Porto	L	0-2	PL		40 416
Dec	21	Guimarães	L	1-2	TPr4	Renatinho 5	694
	29	Leiria	L	1-2	PL	Lito 2	1 177
	5	Sporting	L	1-3	PL	Pires 38	4 585
	19	Maritimo	D	1-1	PL	OG 90	3 989
Jan	7	Setúbal	L	3-4	PL	Lito 28, Pires 32, Ricardo Pessoa 90p	1 224
	14	Braga	L	0-3	PL		1 594
	22	Naval	D	1-1	PL	Ivanildo 4	422
Feb	6	Paços	L	0-1	PL		1 747
	13	Rio Ave	L	0-2	PL		1 339
	19	Olhanense	D	1-1	PL	Lito 31	4 223
	27	Beira-Mar	W	1-0	PL	Ricardo Pessoa 64p	2 165
Mar	7	Nacional	D	1-1	PL	Pedro Moreira 90	1 687
	13	Benfica	D	1-1	PL	Ricardo Pessoa 28p	29 711
	18	Guimarães	W	2-1	PL	Andre Pinto 15, Pires 82	2 961
	2	Academica	L	0-1	PL		3 919
Apr	10	Porto	L	2-3	PL	Ruben 58, Mourad 83	3 839
	17	Leiria	W	1-0	PL	Pedro Silva 63	2 804
	30	Sporting	L	1-2	PL	Pires 68	31 311
May	8	Maritimo	W	1-0	PL	Ivanildo 62	3 836
	14	Setúbal	L	1-3	PL	Pedro Silva 18	5 100

15th Att: 49 607 • Av: 3 307 (+116%) • Municipal 9 544 (34%)

RIO AVE FC 2010–11

Aug	15	Nacional	L	0-1	PL		1 654
	23	Guimarães	D	0-0	PL		9 343
	29	Porto	L	0-2	PL		5 064
Sep	12	Portim'ense	L	1-3	PL	Yazalde 60	3 000
	19	Academica	D	2-2	PL	Joao Tomas 2 28 55	1 627
	26	Leiria	L	0-1	PL		1 474
	3	Maritimo	D	0-0	PL		1 184
Oct	16	Estrela	W	4-1	TPr3	Bruno Gama 45p, Braga 55, Sidnei 79p, Yazalde 88	
	20	Estoril	D	0-0	LCr1		369
	24	Sporting	L	0-1	PL		27 752
	30	Braga	W	2-0	PL	Ze Gomes 72, Joao Tomas 83	1 817
Nov	5	Setúbal	D	3-3	PL	Yazalde 15, Joao Tomas 2 32 90	2 767
	10	Estoril	D	1-1	LCr1	Braga 90, L 3-4p	423
	14	Paços	W	3-1	PL	Joao Tomas 2 24 35, Braga 69	1 972
	21	Feirense	W	3-0	TPr4	Yazalde 31, Braga 59, Tarantini 78	1 000
	28	Naval	W	1-0	PL	Bruno Gama 38	1 204
Dec	5	Beira-Mar	D	1-1	PL	Yazalde 48	1 413
	12	Atlético	W	4-1	TPr5	Yazalde 2 28 36, Bruno Gama 40, Eder 44	1 000
	18	Benfica	L	2-5	PL	Joao Tomas 2 43 71p	38 456
	9	Olhanense	L	0-1	PL		1 666
Jan	22	Nacional	L	0-1	PL		1 146
	16	Guimarães	L	2-3	PL	Joao Tomas 2 49p 76	1 845
	26	Benfica	L	0-2	TPqf		10 000
	6	Porto	L	0-1	PL		29 417
Feb	13	Portim'ense	W	2-0	PL	Joao Tomas 54, Yazalde 60	1 339
	20	Academica	W	1-0	PL	Bruno Gama 90p	2 864
	27	Leiria	W	1-0	PL	Joao Tomas 9	1 683
	6	Maritimo	W	1-0	PL	Braga 78	2 150
Mar	12	Sporting	D	0-0	PL		2 934
	21	Braga	L	0-1	PL		20 643
	3	Setúbal	W	2-0	PL	Yazalde 22, Saulo 90	5 639
Apr	10	Paços	W	6-1	PL	Joao Tomas 2 49 64, Braga 73, Saulo 2 77 80, Tarantini 90	2 000
	17	Naval	W	1-0	PL	Milhazes 13	3 638
	1	Beira-Mar	D	1-1	PL	Tarantini 49	1 000
May	8	Benfica	L	1-2	PL	Braga 89	2 390
	14	Olhanense	D	2-2	PL	Yazalde 9, Joao Tomas 61	1 917

8th Att: 35 865 • Av: 2 391 (-7.9%) • Estadio do Rio Ave 12 815 (18%)

PORTIMONENSE LEAGUE APPEARANCES/GOALS 2011

Goalkeepers Pedro Silva 2 • Ventura 28
Defenders Andre Pinto 26/2 • Joao Di Fabio ITA 14+1/0
Joao Paulo BRA 3/0 • Pedro Alves Silva RRA 21/2 • Ricardo
Nascimento BRA 13/0 • Ricardo Pessoa 29/3 • Ruben 19+1/1
Nilson Veiga CPV 11+1/1
Midfield Andre Vilas Boas 3+1/0 • Elias BRA 21+3/1 • Helder
Castro 6+4/0 • Eduardo Jumisse MOZ 13+1/1 • Pedro Moita 0+1/0
Pedro Moreira 9+12/2 • Angelo Pena VEN 2+3/1 • Soares BRA 15+6/0
Alhassan Wakaso GHA 1+3/0
Forwards Aragoney BRA 1+2/0 • Candeias 27+1/3 • Dong
Fangzhuo CHN 0+3/0 • Helder Pelembe MOZ 3+8/0 • Ivanildo 14+5/3
Calvin Kadi RSA 16+6/1 • Lito CPV 15+7/3 • George Mourad SWE 1+4/1
Patrick BRA 2+6/0 • Pires 11+10/4 • Renatinho 4+1/1
Coach Litos • Carlos Azenha (29/12/10)

RIO AVE LEAGUE APPEARANCES/GOALS 2011

Goalkeepers Mario Felgueiras 7+1 • Paulo Santos 23 • Trigueira 0+1
Defenders Andre Dias 0+1/0 • Eder BRA 8+1/0 • Gaspar 26/0
Jeferson BRA 19/0 • Lionn BRA 7/0 • Milhazes 9+1/1
Tiago Pinto 19+3/0 • Ze Gomes 19+1/1
Midfield Braga 11+10/4 • Bruno China 14/0 • Julio Alves 3+6/0
Mendes 1+8/0 • Ricardo Chaves 13+1/0 • Sidnei BRA 0+9/0
Tarantini 26+2/2 • Vitor Gomes 9+9/0 • Wires BRA 24+1/0
Forwards Bruno Gama 27+2/2 • Cicero 1+12/0 • Fabio Felicio 3+4/0
Joao Tomas 29/16 • Saulo BRA 8+11/3 • Yazalde 24+4/6
Coach Carlos Brito

SPORTING CP 2010–11

	Date	Opponent	Res	Score	Comp	Scorers	Att
Jy	29	Nordsj'lland	W	1-0	ELp3	Vukcevic 24	5 000
	5	Nordsj'lland	W	2-1	ELp3	Postiga 23, Maniche 90	27 152
	14	Paços	L	0-1	PL		4 845
	19	Brøndby	L	0-2	ELpo		20 057
Aug	22	Maritimo	W	1-0	PL	Fernandez 89p	20 828
	26	Brøndby	W	3-0	ELpo	Evaldo 45, Nuno Andre 75, Djalo 90	20 389
	30	Naval	W	3-1	PL	Liedson 41, Fernandez 60p, Djalo 90	5 201
	11	Olhanense	D	0-0	PL		25 807
	16	Lille	W	2-1	ELgC	Vukcevic 11, Postiga 34	14 457
Sep	19	Benfica	L	0-2	PL		51 899
	26	Nacional	D	1-1	PL	Saleiro 65	23 372
	30	Levski	W	5-0	ELgC	Carrico 30, Maniche 43, Salomao 53, Postiga 61, Fernandez 79	15 081
	4	Beira-Mar	D	1-1	PL	Joao Pereira 41	13 391
	16	Estoril	W	2-1	TPr3	Liedson 64, Postiga 79	
Oct	21	Gent	W	5-1	ELgC	Salomao 7, Liedson 2 13 27, Maniche 37, Postiga 60	15 008
	24	Rio Ave	W	1-0	PL	Abel 89	24 775
	31	Leiria	W	2-1	PL	Valdes 2 14 41	4 365
	4	Gent	L	1-3	ELgC	Saleiro 39	8 795
	8	Guimarães	L	2-3	PL	Postiga 17, Vukcevic 30	20 093
Nov	13	Academica	W	2-1	PL	Valdez 9p, Vukcevic 32	6 069
	21	Paços	W	1-0	TPr4	Djalo 45	8 748
	27	Porto	D	1-1	PL	Valdes 38	35 063
	1	Lille	W	1-0	ELgC	Anderson Polga 28	16 569
	5	Portim'ense	W	3-1	PL	Postiga 23, Maniche 42, Andre Santos 45	4 585
Dec	11	Setúbal	L	1-2	TPr5	Liedson 76	6 000
	16	Levski	L	0-1	ELgC		5 226
	20	Setúbal	W	3-0	PL	Djalo 2 20 57, Abel 41	1 849
	3	Naval	W	2-0	LCr2	Vukcevic 69, Liedson 72	11 243
	8	Braga	W	2-1	PL	Salomao 11, Valdes 13	22 314
	15	Paços	L	2-3	PL	Liedson 42, Salomao 62	17 643
Jan	20	Panafiel	W	4-0	LCr2	Joao Pereira 44, Valdes 71p, Zapater 2 83 90	9 489
	24	Maritimo	W	3-0	PL	Zapater 2 44 67, Liedson 76	4 172
	29	Estoril	L	1-2	LCr2	Abel 4	2 420
	4	Naval	D	3-3	PL	Liedson 2 33 90, Postiga 59p	20 549
	12	Olhanense	D	2-2	PL	Postiga 2 27 62	4 760
Feb	17	Rangers	D	1-1	ELr2	Fernandez 89	34 095
	21	Benfica	L	0-2	PL		36 422
	24	Rangers	D	2-2	ELr2	Pedro Mendes 42, Djalo 83	15 375
	27	Nacional	L	0-1	PL		2 640
	2	Benfica	L	1-2	LCsf	Postiga 21	49 652
Mar	6	Beira-Mar	W	1-0	PL	Fernandez 78p	16 231
	12	Rio Ave	D	0-0	PL		2 934
	19	Leiria	D	0-0	PL		15 510
	3	Guimarães	D	1-1	PL	Fernandez 23p	25 531
Apr	9	Academica	W	2-0	PL	Djalo 2 33 35	24 485
	17	Porto	L	2-3	PL	Andre Santos 11, Fernandez 88	47 109
	30	Portim'ense	W	2-1	PL	Postiga 20, Joao Pereira 43	31 311
May	8	Setúbal	L	0-1	PL		35 484
	14	Braga	W	1-0	PL	Djalo 5	20 804

3rd Att: 372 864 • Av: 24 857 (+1.0%) • José Alvalade 50 080 (49%)

UNIAO LEIRIA 2010–11

	Date	Opponent	Res	Score	Comp	Scorers	Att
	15	Beira-Mar	D	0-0	PL		2 324
Aug	22	Paços	D	0-0	PL		1 009
	29	Olhanense	L	0-1	PL		2 956
	12	Nacional	W	2-1	PL	Marcos Paulo 51, N'Gal 57	868
Sep	18	Guimarães	L	0-1	PL		13 551
	26	Rio Ave	W	1-0	PL	Carlao 90p	1 474
	1	Academica	W	2-1	PL	Carlao 79, Zhang 88	1 625
	16	Un.Madeira	L	1-2	TPr3	N'Gal 3	
Oct	20	Gil Vicente	L	2-3	LCr1	Carlao 36, N'Gal 89	1 245
	25	Porto	L	1-5	PL	Carlao 83	29 112
	31	Sporting	L	1-2	PL	Carlao 21	4 365
	7	Maritimo	D	1-1	PL	Carlao 50	2 907
Nov	14	Setúbal	W	1-0	PL	N'Gal 22	905
	20	Gil Vicente	D	1-1	LCr1	Zahovaiko 69	643
	29	Portim'ense	W	2-1	PL	Ze Antonio 56, Carlao 80	1 177
Dec	4	Braga	W	3-1	PL	Carlao 2 20p 27, Silas 88p	1 175
	19	Naval	W	3-0	PL	Carlao 15p, Zhang 64, Amado 90	579
	9	Benfica	L	0-3	PL		12 506
Jan	16	Beira-Mar	L	0-3	PL		1 037
	22	Paços	D	1-1	PL	Vinicius 90	1 254
	6	Olhanense	L	0-2	PL		962
Feb	12	Nacional	W	1-0	PL	Fabricio 43	1 202
	18	Guimarães	L	0-1	PL		848
	27	Rio Ave	L	0-1	PL		1 683
	4	Academica	D	0-0	PL		3 066
Mar	14	Porto	L	0-2	PL		3 880
	19	Sporting	D	0-0	PL		15 510
	1	Maritimo	L	1-3	PL	Joao Silva 64	709
Apr	10	Setúbal	L	1-4	PL	Fabricio 87	6 294
	17	Portim'ense	L	0-1	PL		2 804
	1	Braga	D	0-0	PL		20 332
May	8	Naval	W	1-0	PL	Joao Silva 62	1 436
	14	Benfica	D	3-3	PL	Joao Silva 2 45 89, Leandro Lima 75	29 084

10th Att: 36 108 • Av: 2 407 (-30.9%) • Magalhães Pessoa 30 000 (8%)

SPORTING LEAGUE APPEARANCES/GOALS 2011

Goalkeepers Rui Patricio 30
Defenders Abel 10+2/2 • Anderson Polga BRA 19+1/0
Cedric Soares 2/0 • Daniel Carrico 24/0 • Evaldo BRA 28/0 • Leandro
Grimi ARG 1+1/0 • Joao Pereira 23+1/2 • Nuno Coelho 7+2/0 • Pedro
Silva BRA 1/0 • Marco Torsiglieri ARG 13+3/0
Midfield Andre Santos 26/2 • Cristiano BRA 1+3/0
Matias Fernandez CHI 16+5/5 • Marat Izmailov RUS 2+1/0
Maniche 14+3/1 • Pedro Mendes 6+1/0 • Tales BRA • Jaime
Valdes CHI 17+7/5 • Simon Vukcevic MNE 15+9/2 • William
Carvalho ANG 0+1/0 • Albert Zapater ESP 16+6/2
Forwards Carlos Saleiro 0+27/1 • Diogo Salomao 5+7/2
Helder Postiga 23+2/6 • Liedson 14/5 • Yannick Djalo 17+4/6
Coach Paulo Sergio • Jose Couceiro (26/02/11)

UNIAO LEIRIA LEAGUE APPEARANCES/GOALS 2011

Goalkeepers Andjelko Djuricic SRB 1 • Gottardi BRA 26 • Mika 3
Defenders Bruno Miguel 9+2/0 • Diego Gaucho BRA 6+1/0
Hugo Gomes 15+1/0 • Saidou Panandetiguiri BFA 12+3/0
Patrick Bira 24+1/0 • Mamadou Tall BFA 5+1/0 • Ze Antonio 29/1
Midfield Brigidio 6+19/0 • Bruno Cepeda 0+1/0 • Caca BRA 5+7/0
Diogo Amado 11+4/1 • Manuel Iturra CHI 10+1/0 • Leandro
Lima BRA 13+9/1 • Marco Soares CPV 4+4/0 • Marcos
Paulo BRA 25+1/1 • Paulo Sergio BRA 16+1/0 • Ricardo Pateiro 21+3/0
Silas 12+1/1 • Vinicius BRA 21+2/1
Forwards Carlao BRA 12+1/9 • Carlos Daniel 0+1/0
Fabricio BRA 10+2/2 • Joao Silva 7+5/4 • Serge N'Gal CMR 14+3/2
Rodrigo Silva BRA 3+4/0 • Vjatseslav Zahovaiko EST 2+5/0
Zhang Chengdong CHN 8+6/2
Coach Pedro Caixinha

VITORIA SC GUIMARAES 2010–11

		Opponent	Res	Score	Comp	Scorers	Att
Aug	16	Olhanense	D	0-0	PL		5 713
	23	Rio Ave	D	0-0	PL		9 343
	28	Nacional	W	3-1	PL	Toscano 3 68 87 90	1 978
Sep	10	Benfica	W	2-1	PL	Edgar 17, Rui Miguel 83	17 730
	18	Leiria	W	1-0	PL	Maranhao 72	13 551
	25	Academica	L	1-3	PL	Edgar 55	4 506
Oct	4	Porto	D	1-1	PL	Faouzi 63	20 530
	17	Malveira	W	4-0	TPr3	Toscano 12, Joao Ribeiro 26, Edgar 64, Maranhao 87	
	23	Setúbal	L	1-2	PL	Edgar 73	2 686
Nov	1	Portim'ense	W	2-0	PL	Edgar 40, Maranhao 54	10 581
	8	Sporting	W	3-2	PL	Targino 2 77 79, Bruno Teles 89	20 093
	13	Braga	W	2-1	PL	Maranhao 44, OG 82	25 651
	20	Portim'ense	W	2-1	TPr4	Joao Paulo 50, Edgar 89	694
	27	Maritimo	L	0-2	PL		2 920
Dec	4	Paços	D	1-1	PL	Edgar 36	8 551
	12	Torreense	W	2-0	TPr5	Edgar 16, Toscano 66	3 849
	18	Beira-Mar	L	2-3	PL	Edga 68, Pereirinha 72	1 755
	3	Braga	L	1-3	LCr2	Toscano 4	8 255
	9	Naval	L	1-0	PL	Joao Alves 13	10 210
Jan	15	Olhanense	W	1-0	PL	Joao Ribeiro 50	10 853
	19	Arouca	W	1-0	LCr2	Maranhao 86	6 210
	22	Rio Ave	W	3-2	PL	Edgar 2 9p 89p, Douglas 69	1 845
	27	Merelinense	W	2-0	TPqf	Edgar 30, Cleber Monteiro 45	4 000
	30	Paços	L	1-2	LCr2	Douglas 35	1 382
Feb	3	Academica	W	1-0	TPsf	Faouzi 81	10 000
	6	Nacional	D	0-0	PL		12 840
	13	Benfica	L	0-3	PL		54 927
	18	Leiria	W	1-0	PL	Joao Alves 30	848
	25	Academica	L	0-2	PL		11 885
Mar	5	Porto	L	0-2	PL		36 419
	12	Setúbal	D	1-1	PL	Rui Miguel 27	10 321
	18	Portim'ense	L	1-2	PL	Targino 13	2 961
	27	Academica	D	0-0	TPsf		12 755
Apr	3	Sporting	D	1-1	PL	Joao Paulo 90	25 531
	11	Braga	L	1-3	PL	Edgar 90p	25 533
	16	Maritimo	W	2-0	PL	Rui Miguel 55, Renan 85	8 877
May	2	Paços	L	1-2	PL	Faouzi 18	1 071
	8	Beira-Mar	W	1-0	PL	Toscano 87	12 533
	14	Naval	W	3-0	PL	Jorge Ribeiro 2 33 40, Edgar 77	401
	22	Porto	L	2-6	TPf	OG 21, Edgar 24	35 000

5th Att: 209 235 • Av: 13 949 (-12.2%) • Afonso Henriques 30 165 (46%)

VITORIA FC SETUBAL 2010–11

		Opponent	Res	Score	Comp	Scorers	Att
Aug	14	Maritimo	W	1-0	PL	Jailson 59	4 177
	21	Braga	D	0-0	PL		3 478
	28	Benfica	L	0-3	PL		36 975
Sep	13	Beira-Mar	D	0-0	PL		3 062
	19	Naval	D	0-0	PL		712
	27	Paços	W	1-0	PL	Claudio Pitbull 34	2 749
	2	Olhanense	L	1-3	PL	Silva 57	4 142
	9	Penafiel	L	0-2	LCr1		401
Oct	16	Gil Vicente	D	1-1	TPr3	Zeca 29. W 5-3p	
	23	Guimaraes	W	2-1	PL	Hugo Leal 16, Anderson do O 21	2 686
	31	Nacional	L	0-1	PL		1 804
Nov	5	Rio Ave	D	3-3	PL	Jailson 4, Valdomiro 55, Neca 63	2 767
	10	Penafiel	W	3-1	LCr1	Silva 9, Claudio Pitbull 41, Collin 71. L 1-4p	1 315
	14	Leiria	L	0-1	PL		905
	21	Maritimo	W	2-1	TPr4	Claudio Pitbull 25, Henrique 79	1 000
	26	Academica	L	0-1	PL		2 013
Dec	6	Porto	L	0-1	PL		18 192
	11	Sporting	W	2-1	TPr5	Ney Santos 30, Zeca 34	6 000
	20	Sporting	L	0-3	PL		1 849
Jan	7	Portim'ense	W	4-3	PL	Claudio Pitbull 2 15p 53p, OG 48, Henrique 77	1 224
	16	Maritimo	L	2-4	PL	Claudio Pitbull 2 35 84	3 466
	22	Braga	D	2-2	PL	Djikine 17, Claudio Pitbull 20	10 439
	28	Academica	L	2-3	TPqf	Brasao 17, Collin 88	3 000
Feb	6	Benfica	L	0-2	PL		8 605
	14	Beira-Mar	D	0-0	PL		696
	20	Naval	D	1-1	PL	Neca 26	3 050
	26	Paços	L	0-2	PL		1 610
Mar	6	Olhanense	D	0-0	PL		3 548
	12	Guimarães	D	1-1	PL	William 90	10 321
	20	Nacional	W	2-1	PL	Neca 6, Jailson 79	5 272
	3	Rio Ave	L	0-2	PL		5 639
Apr	10	Leiria	W	4-1	PL	William 27, Neca 46, Claudio Pitbull 75, Jose Pedro 83	6 294
	15	Academica	D	1-1	PL	Claudio Pitbull 81	4 005
	1	Porto	L	0-4	PL		4 917
	8	Sporting	W	1-0	PL	Jailson 55	35 484
May	14	Portim'ense	W	3-1	PL	Neca 31p, Claudio Pitbull 56, Michel 75	5 100

12th Att: 58 813 • Av: 3 920 (-11.1%) • Estadio do Bonfim 25 000 (15%)

GUIMARAES LEAGUE APPEARANCES/GOALS 2011

Goalkeepers Nilson BRA 30
Defenders Anderson Mineiro BRA 4/0 • Bruno Teles BRA 26/1 Edson BRA 13+2/0 • Freire BRA 9+2/0 • Joao Paulo 22/1 • Jorge Ribeiro 11+4/2 • Mahamadou N'Diaye MLI 9/0 • Ricardo CPV 17/0 Tony 1+1/0 • Valdomiro BRA 0+1/0
Midfield Alex 28/0 • Cleber Monteiro BRA 23+1/0 Crivellaro BRA 1+1/0 • Custodio 0+2/0 • Flavio Meireles 3+5/0 Joao Alves 19+3/2 • Joao Pedro BRA 2+4/0 • Joao Ribeiro 21+4/1 Marcelo Toscano BRA 21+4/4 • Bruno Pereirinha 4+6/1 Renan BRA 12/1 • Rui Miguel 8+13/3
Forwards Douglas BRA 4+3/1 • Edgar BRA 23+6/10 • Abdelghani Faouzi MAR 7+9/2 • Maranhao BRA 3+7/3 • Rafael 1+2/0 Targino 7+6/3 • To Mane 0+1/0 • William BRA 0+3/0
Coach Manuel Machado

SETUBAL LEAGUE APPEARANCES/GOALS 2011

Goalkeepers Diego BRA 30 • Matos 0+1
Defenders Anderson do O BRA 18/1 • Aurelien Collin FRA 12+2/0 Michel BRA 6+5/1 • Ney BRA 23/0 • Ricardo Silva 26/0 • Francois Sene SEN 7+4/0 • Tengarrinha 3+4/0 • Valdomiro BRA 19+1/1
Midfield Bruno Gallo BRA 6+3/0 • Mamadou Djikine MLI 2+1/1 • Hugo Leal 23+1/1 • Jose Pedro 10+5/1 • Miguelito 29/0 • Neca 22+3/5 Regula 0+4/0 • Silva BRA 22/1 • Zeca 13+13/0
Forwards Brasao BRA 5+3/0 • Claudio Pitbull BRA 25+1/9 Henrique BRA 9+11/1 • Jailson BRA 8+12/4 • Sassa BRA 7+12/0 William BRA 5+4/2
Coach Manuel Fernandes • Bruno Ribeiro (1/03/11)

PRK – KOREA DPR

FIFA/COCA-COLA WORLD RANKING

'93	'94	'95	'96	'97	'98	'99	'00	'01	'02	'03	'04	'05	'06	'07	'08	'09	'10	'11	'12
62	84	117	144	166	158	172	142	136	124	117	95	82	113	115	113	86	108	110	

	2011											High	Low	Av
Jan	Feb	Mar	Apr	May	Jun	Jul	Aug	Sep	Oct	Nov	Dec			
109	108	113	118	115	119	115	114	121	124	110	110	57	181	120

North Korea's qualification for the 2010 FIFA World Cup finals in South Africa had been a major surprise and they very quickly returned to the margins of the game in Asia after failing to make it through to the final stages of the 2014 qualifiers for Brazil. The tendency to blow hot and cold was illustrated in their World Cup group matches where they managed to beat Japan in Pyongyang but only after having lost there to group winners Uzbekistan. The Koreans finished third, three points behind the Japanese and were knocked out. The World Cup qualifiers came at the end of a year that had started badly with three poor performances at the 2011 AFC Asian Cup in Qatar but there was one bright spot during the year when they made sure of qualifying for the finals of the 2012 AFC Challenge Cup. The Koreans won all three of their qualifying matches in Kathmandu, against hosts Nepal, Afghanistan and Sri Lanka without conceding a goal and they will return to the Nepalese capital in early 2012 to defend the title they won in Sri Lanka in 2010. It could be argued that Korea DPR are caught in no man's land - too good for the weaker nations in the AFC Challenge Cup but not good enough for the top nations in the AFC Asian Cup. It may be a while before they surprise everyone again by qualifying for the World Cup finals but with the Koreans you never can tell.

FIFA WORLD CUP RECORD

1930-1962 DNE   **1966** 8 QF   1970 DNE   1974 DNQ   1978 DNE   1982-1994 DNQ   1998-2002 DNE   2006 DNQ   **2010** 32 r1   2014 DNQ

DPR KOREA FOOTBALL ASSOCIATION (PRK)

Kumsongdong, Kwangbok Street, Mangyongdae Dist., PO Box 56, Pyongyang

☎ +850 2 3814334
📠 +850 2 3814434
📧 chukku-prkfa@hotmail.com
🖥

FA 1945 CON 1974 FIFA 1958
P Ri Jong Mu
GS Kim Jong Man

FIFA BIG COUNT 2006

Total players	502 912
% of population	2.18%
Male	436 956
Female	65 956
Amateurs 18+	7 200
Youth under 18	7 712
Unregistered	170 000
Professionals	0
Referees	360
Admin & coaches	1 498
Number of clubs	170
Number of teams	850

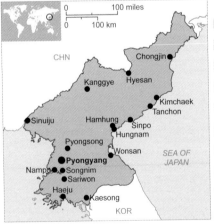

MAJOR CITIES/TOWNS

		Population
1	Pyongyang	3 198 937
2	Hamhung	580 914
3	Nampo	467 044
4	Hungnam	359 613
5	Kaesong	351 503
6	Wonsan	340 174
7	Chongjin	329 382
8	Sinuiju	285 903
9	Haeju	227 231
10	Kanggye	207 807
11	Kimchaek	197 552
12	Sariwon	161 058
13	Songnim	158 441
14	Pyongsong	123 489
15	Hyesan	98 212
16	Sinpo	79 415
17	Hongwon	73 696
18	Chongpyong	72 384
19	Tanchon	71 457

DEMOCRATIC PEOPLE'S REPUBLIC OF KOREA

Capital Pyongyang	Population 22 665 345 (50)	% in cities 63%
GDP per capita $1800 (189)	Area km² 120 538 km² (98)	GMT + / - +9
Neighbours (km) China 1416, Korea Republic 238, Russia 19 • Coast 2495		

RECENT INTERNATIONAL MATCHES PLAYED BY KOREA DPR

2009	Opponents	Score		Venue	Comp	Scorers	Att	Referee
11-02	Saudi Arabia	W	1-0	Pyongyang	WCq	Mun In Guk 29	48 000	Irmatov UZB
28-03	UAE	W	2-0	Pyongyang	WCq	Pak Nam Chol 51, Mun In Guk 93+	50 000	Breeze AUS
1-04	Korea Republic	L	0-1	Seoul	WCq		48 000	Al Hilali OMA
6-06	Iran	D	0-0	Pyongyang	WCq		30 000	Sun Baojie CHN
17-06	Saudi Arabia	D	0-0	Riyadh	WCq		65 000	Basma SYR
23-08	Guam	W	9-2	Kaohsiung	EAq	Kim Yong Jun 8, Pak Nam Chol 12, Mun In Guk 45 An Chol Hyok 4 20 74 78 89, Choe Kum Chol 2 28 41	2 000	Matsuo JPN
25-08	Hong Kong	D	0-0	Kaohsiung	EAq		100	Kim Jong Hyeok KOR
27-08	Chinese Taipei	W	2-1	Kaohsiung	EAq	Jong Tae Se 23p, Ji Yun Nam 61	10 000	Matsuo JPN
13-10	Congo	D	0-0	Le Mans	Fr			
21-11	Zambia	L	1-4	Lusaka	Fr	Mun In Guk 86p	10 129	Mpanisi ZAM
27-12	Mali	W	1-0	Doha	Fr	Hong Yong Jo 55	127	Abdou QAT
30-12	Qatar	W	1-0	Doha	Fr	Choe Chol Man 59	1 223	Shukralla BHR
2010								
2-01	Iran	L	0-1	Doha	Fr		224	Maillet SEY
17-02	Turkmenistan	D	1-1	Colombo	CCr1	Ryang Yong Gi 51	400	Mahapab THA
19-02	Kyrgyzstan	W	4-0	Colombo	CCr1	Pak Song Chol 29, Pak Kwang Ryong 47, Choe Myong Ho 65, Ri Chol Myong 68	300	El Haddad LIB
21-02	India †	W	3-0	Colombo	CCr1	Ryang Yong Gi 2 36 72, Choe Chol Man 57	300	Tan Hai CHN
24-02	Myanmar	W	5-0	Colombo	CCsf	Choe Myong Ho 6, Choe Chol Man 2 12 73, Pak Song Chol 13, Kim Seong Yong 85	400	Al Yarimi YEM
27-02	Turkmenistan	D	1-1	Colombo	CCf	Ryang Yong Gi 75. W 5-4p	3 000	Faghani IRN
6-03	Venezuela	L	1-2	Puerto La Cruz	Fr		10 000	Buitrago COL
17-03	Mexico	L	1-2	Torreon	Fr	Choe Kum Chol 56	30 000	Moreno PAN
22-04	South Africa	D	0-0	Taunusstein-Wehen	Fr		628	Brych GER
15-05	Paraguay	L	0-1	Nyon	Fr		1 000	Bertolini SUI
25-05	Greece	D	2-2	Altach	Fr	Jong Tae Se 2 24 51	3 000	Schorgenhofer AUT
6-06	Nigeria	L	1-3	Johannesburg	Fr	Cha Jong Hyok 64	20 000	
15-06	Brazil	L	1-2	Johannesburg	WCr1	Ji Yun Nam 89	54 331	Kassai HUN
21-06	Portugal	L	0-7	Cape Town	WCr1		63 644	Pozo CHI
25-06	Côte d'Ivoire	L	0-3	Nelspruit	WCr1		34 763	Undiano ESP
24-09	Vietnam	D	0-0	Hanoi	Fr			
2-11	Singapore	W	2-1	Hanoi	Fr	Ri Kwang Chon 80, Hong Yong Jo 90		
6-11	Vietnam	W	2-0	Hanoi	Fr	Myong Cha Hyon 55, Ri Jin Hyok 67		
10-11	Yemen	D	1-1	Aden	Fr	Ri Chol Myong 2		
24-12	Kuwait	L	1-2	6th October City	Fr	Ri Chol Myong 33		
27-12	Kuwait	D	2-2	6th October City	Fr			
31-12	Qatar	W	1-0	Doha	Fr	Ryang Yong Gi 70p		
2011								
4-01	Bahrain	W	1-0	Riffa	Fr	An Chol Hyok 59		
11-01	UAE	D	0-0	Doha	ACr1		3 639	Mohd Salleh MAS
15-01	Iran	L	0-1	Doha	ACr1		6 488	Shukralla BHR
19-01	Iraq	L	0-1	Al Rayyan	ACr1		4 111	Mohd Salleh MAS
26-03	Iraq	L	0-2	Sharjah	Fr			
29-03	Jordan	D	1-1	Sharjah	Fr	Pak Song Chol 32		
7-04	Sri Lanka	W	4-0	Kathmandu	CCq	Choe Kum Chol 2 2 47, Ri Chol Myong 5, Pak Nam Chol 21	2 000	Almarzouq KUW
9-04	Nepal	W	1-0	Kathmandu	CCq	Jong Il Gwan 31	22 000	Alabbasi BHR
11-04	Afghanistan	W	2-0	Kathmandu	CCq	Choe Kum Chol 45, Ri Chol Myong 68	1 000	Abdul Baki OMA
8-06	China PR	L	0-2	Guiyang	Fr		27 000	
10-08	Kuwait	D	0-0	Kuwait City	Fr			
2-09	Japan	L	0-1	Saitama	WCq		62 000	Albadwawi UAE
6-09	Tajikistan	W	1-0	Pyongyang	WCq	Pak Nam Chol 14	28 000	Minh Tri Vo VIE
11-10	Uzbekistan	L	0-1	Pyongyang	WCq		29 000	Faghani IRN
11-11	Uzbekistan	L	0-1	Tashkent	WCq		27 525	El Haddad LIB
15-11	Japan	W	1-0	Pyongyang	WCq	Pak Nam Chol 50	50 000	Shukralla BHR

Fr = Friendly match • CC = AFC Challenge Cup • EA = East Asian Championship • WC = FIFA World Cup • q = qualifier

PUR – PUERTO RICO

FIFA/COCA-COLA WORLD RANKING

'93	'94	'95	'96	'97	'98	'99	'00	'01	'02	'03	'04	'05	'06	'07	'08	'09	'10	'11	'12
105	112	128	149	169	182	186	195	195	198	200	194	195	195	196	142	165	133	108	

2011												High	Low	Av
Jan	Feb	Mar	Apr	May	Jun	Jul	Aug	Sep	Oct	Nov	Dec			
131	130	131	133	132	137	141	144	145	137	106	108	97	202	168

Puerto Rico Islanders once again re-inforced their claim to be the best club side in the Caribbean when they won the CFU Club Championship in May 2011 without having lost a match. It was the second year running that Islanders had remained unbeaten at the tournament following on from their triumph in 2010. At the finals in Georgetown, Guyana, they beat local side Alpha United 3-1 in the semi-final and then Haiti's Tempête by a similar score in the final. Islanders also had another successful season in the USA where they finished second behind Carolina Railhawks in the second tier NASL. That qualified them for the play-offs but they failed to retain the title won in 2010 after losing to Fort Lauderdale in the semi-finals. With so much attention focused on the club, the domestic league struggles for recognition but was won in 2011 by Leones de Ponce who beat regular season champions Sevilla on penalties in the play-off final. The national team also operates to some extent in the shadow of Islanders although its main focus in 2011 was a six-game series in the 2014 FIFA World Cup qualifiers. Grouped with regional giants Canada and minnows St Lucia and St Kitts, Puerto Rico finished in second place as expected behind the Canadians but it wasn't enough to see them through to the next stage.

FIFA WORLD CUP RECORD

1930-1970 DNE 1974 DNQ 1978-1982 DNE 1986-2002 DNQ 2006 DNE 2010-2014 DNQ

FEDERACION PUERTORRIQUENA DE FUTBOL (FPF)

Calle Los Angeles Final
Plaza de Santurce
Apartado postal 367567
San Juan PR 00936

☎ +1 787 7652895
📠 +1 787 7672288
📧 info@fedefutbolpr.com
🖥 www.fedefutbolpr.com
FA 1940 CON 1962 FIFA 1960
P Eric Labrador
GS Frankie Gautier

FIFA BIG COUNT 2006

Total players	222 670
% of population	5.67%
Male	187 470
Female	35 200
Unregistered	43 900
Professionals	45
Referees	601
Admin & coaches	9 016
Number of clubs	75
Number of teams	350

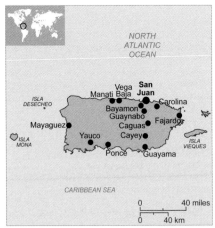

MAJOR CITIES/TOWNS

		Population
1	San Juan	407 386
2	Bayamón	197 009
3	Carolina	167 303
4	Ponce	145 676
5	Caguas	82 148
6	Guaynabo	80 952
7	Mayagüez	72 042
8	Trujillo Alto	54 862
9	Arecibo	47 550
10	Fajardo	33 717
11	Vega Baja	28 930
12	Levittown	28 563
13	Cataño	25 486
14	Guayama	20 749
15	Yauco	20 280
16	Humacao	19 561
17	Candelaria	17 348
18	Cayey	17 263
19	Manatí	15 448

COMMONWEALTH OF PUERTO RICO

Capital	San Juan	Population	3 971 020 (128)	% in cities 98%
GDP per capita	$17 800 (70)	Area km²	13 790 km² (162)	GMT +/- -4
Neighbours (km)	Coast 501			

RECENT INTERNATIONAL MATCHES PLAYED BY PUERTO RICO

2006	Opponents	Score	Venue	Comp	Scorers	Att	Referee
	No international matches played in 2006						
2007							
	No international matches played in 2007						
2008							
16-01	Bermuda	W 2-0	Hamilton	Fr	Taylor Graham [47], Andres Cabrero [67]	500	Mauchette BER
18-01	Bermuda	W 1-0	Hamilton	Fr	Noah Delgado [13]	325	Raynor BER
26-01	Trinidad and Tobago	D 2-2	Bayamon	Fr	Kupono Low [15], Chris Mesaloudis [33]	4 500	Santos PUR
26-03	Dominican Republic	W 1-0	Bayamon	WCq	Petter Villegas [96p]	8 000	Morales MEX
4-06	Honduras	L 0-4	San Pedro Sula	WCq		20 000	Campbell JAM
14-06	Honduras	D 2-2	Bayamon	WCq	Christopher Megaloudis [31], Petter Villegas [41]	5 000	Lopez GUA
2009							
	No international matches played in 2009						
2010							
2-10	Anguilla	W 3-1	Bayamon	CCq	Hansen [28], Megaloudis 2 [32 81]	2 050	Thomas JAM
4-10	Saint Martin †	W 2-0	Bayamon	CCq	Krause [26], Arrieta [80]	1 800	Legister JAM
6-10	Cayman Islands	W 2-0	Bayamon	CCq	Megaloudis [26], Figueroa [89]	3 800	Campbell JAM
22-10	Grenada	L 1-3	St George's	CCq	Nieves [81]	600	Wijngaarde SUR
24-10	Guadeloupe †	L 2-3	St George's	CCq	Megaloudis [65], Villegas [74]	200	Baptiste DMA
26-10	St Kitts and Nevis	L 0-1	St George's	CCq		500	Morrison JAM
2011							
2-09	St Kitts and Nevis	D 0-0	Basseterre	WCq		2 500	Arellano MEX
6-09	Canada	L 0-3	Bayamon	WCq		4 000	Wijngaarde SUR
7-10	St Kitts and Nevis	D 1-1	Bayamon	WCq	Andres Cabrero [37]	2 500	Brizan TRI
11-10	Canada	D 0-0	Toronto	WCq		12 178	Lancaster GUY
11-11	St Lucia	W 4-0	Bayamon	WCq	Cristian Arrieta [4], Hector Ramos 2 [14 46], Andres Carero [54]	350	Holder CAY
15-11	St Lucia	W 3-0	Mayaguez	WCq	Hector Ramos 2 [13 85], Joseph Marrero [87]	1 050	Willet ATG

Fr = Friendly match • CC = Digicel Caribbean Cup • WC = FIFA World Cup • q = qualifier • † Not an official internatiuonal

PUERTO RICO 2011

PUERTO RICO SOCCER LEAGUE	Pl	W	D	L	F	A	Pts	Sevilla	Leones	River Plate	PR Utd	Mayaguez	Huracán
Sevilla †	15	9	4	2	48	17	**31**		2-0	1-0	2-3 3-0	1-3 2-0	10-0 9-0
Leones de Ponce ‡	15	7	5	3	49	22	**26**	4-4 3-3		1-4 2-2	3-1	3-1	5-1 17-0
River Plate Ponce ‡‡	15	7	4	4	62	17	**25**	2-2 1-3	0-1		10-0	2-2	7-0 17-0
Puerto Rico United	15	7	2	6	29	33	**23**	1-1	0-0 0-3	2-1 0-3		6-0 1-3	5-0
Mayaguez ‡‡	15	6	3	6	31	27	**21**	0-2	2-1 2-2	1-3 0-0	0-1		5-0
Caguas Huracán	15	0	0	15	10	113	**0**	0-3	0-4	2-10	1-5 3-4	0-7 3-5	

3/04/2011 - 25/07/2011 • † Qualified for the final • ‡ Qualified for the semi-final • ‡‡ Qualified for the quarter-final (Mayaguez replaced Puerto Rico United who had been suspended)

A-LEAGUE FINALS SERIES

Quarter-final		Semi-final		Grand Final	
River Plate	4				
Mayaguez	1	**Leones de Ponce**	2		
		River Plate	1	**Leones de Ponce**	1 3p
				Sevilla	1 0p

Final series held 27-07-2001 to 31-07-2011

QAT – QATAR

FIFA/COCA-COLA WORLD RANKING

'93	'94	'95	'96	'97	'98	'99	'00	'01	'02	'03	'04	'05	'06	'07	'08	'09	'10	'11	'12
54	60	83	69	70	60	107	102	80	62	65	66	95	58	87	84	86	112	93	

	2011												High	Low	Av
	Jan	Feb	Mar	Apr	May	Jun	Jul	Aug	Sep	Oct	Nov	Dec			
	105	90	90	92	92	93	89	88	100	92	95	93	51	113	78

Al Sadd became the first Qatari club to win the AFC Champions League in its current format although the Doha-based team had been crowned Asian champions back in 1989 under the old system. They defeated former champions Jeonbuk Hyundai Motors in a penalty shootout in the 2011 final in Jeonju. Goalkeeper Mohamed Saqr was the hero for an Al Sadd team that reflected the current landscape in Qatari football, with only one of the starting line-up born in the Gulf state. Qatar's representation in the 2012 edition of the Champions League was increased to four but Al Sadd were not among them after suffering a loss of form in the Qatar Stars League that saw them finish sixth. Lekhwia were surprise first-time winners of the league which was just one of five trophies on offer during the course of the year - all of which were won by different clubs. The Qatar national team saw three different coaches in the wake of Bruno Metsu's exit after the AFC Asian Cup but they still made sure of a place in the final round of qualifying for the 2014 FIFA World Cup in Brazil. Sebastiao Lazaroni steered the team through their first five group matches in the qualifiers but he was replaced by fellow Brazilian Paulo Autuori in early 2012 who sealed a place amongst the final 10 nations seeking a place in Brazil with a draw against Iran.

FIFA WORLD CUP RECORD
1930-1974 DNE 1978-2010 DNQ

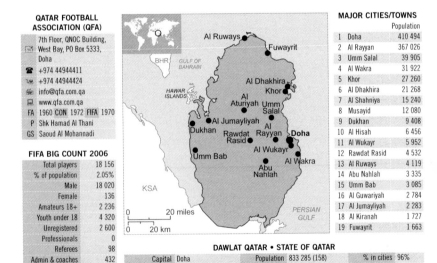

QATAR FOOTBALL ASSOCIATION (QFA)

7th Floor, QNOC Building, West Bay, PO Box 5333, Doha
☎ +974 44944411
📠 +974 44944424
📧 info@qfa.com.qa
🖥 www.qfa.com.qa
FA 1960 CON 1972 FIFA 1970
P Shk Hamad Al Thani
GS Saoud Al Mohannadi

FIFA BIG COUNT 2006

Total players	18 156
% of population	2.05%
Male	18 020
Female	136
Amateurs 18+	2 236
Youth under 18	4 320
Unregistered	2 600
Professionals	0
Referees	98
Admin & coaches	432
Number of clubs	16
Number of teams	160

MAJOR CITIES/TOWNS

		Population
1	Doha	410 494
2	Al Rayyan	367 026
3	Umm Salal	39 905
4	Al Wakra	31 922
5	Khor	27 260
6	Al Dhakhira	21 268
7	Al Shahniya	15 240
8	Musayid	12 080
9	Dukhan	9 408
10	Al Hisah	6 456
11	Al Wukayr	5 952
12	Rawdat Rasid	4 532
13	Al Ruways	4 119
14	Abu Nahlah	3 335
15	Umm Bab	3 085
16	Al Guwariyah	2 784
17	Al Jumayliyah	2 283
18	Al Kiranah	1 727
19	Fuwayrit	1 663

DAWLAT QATAR • STATE OF QATAR

Capital Doha	Population 833 285 (158)	% in cities 96%
GDP per capita $111 000 (2)	Area km² 11 586 km² (165)	GMT + / - +3
Neighbours (km) Saudi Arabia 60 • Coast 563		

RECENT INTERNATIONAL MATCHES PLAYED BY QATAR

2009	Opponents	Score		Venue	Comp	Scorers	Att	Referee
6-06	Australia	D	0-0	Doha	WCq		7 000	Bashir SIN
10-06	Japan	D	1-1	Yokohama	WCq	Ali Yahya 53p	60 256	Mohd Salleh MAS
9-09	Oman	D	1-1	Doha	Fr	Ali Yahya 44		
8-10	Croatia	L	2-3	Rijeka	Fr	Kovac.R OG 43, Soria 69		
11-10	Macedonia FYR	L	1-2	Skopje	Fr	Musa Jama 24		
14-10	Congo DR	D	2-2	Sannois St Gratien	Fr	Ali Yahya 60, Magid Hassan 75		
13-11	Paraguay	W	2-0	Rouen	Fr	Montesin 2 57 81		
17-11	Belgium	L	0-2	Sedan	Fr			
28-12	Iran	W	3-2	Doha	Fr	Ali Yahya 7, Magid Hassan 2 10 94+		
30-12	Korea DPR	L	0-1	Doha	Fr			
2010								
2-01	Mali	D	0-0	Doha	Fr			
3-03	Slovenia	L	1-4	Maribor	Fr	Fabio Cesar 41	4 900	Van Boekel NED
10-08	Bosnia-Herzegovina	D	1-1	Sarajevo	Fr	Wesam Rizik 58p	18 000	Vuckov CRO
3-09	Bahrain	D	1-1	Doha	Fr	Majdi Siddiq 41		
7-09	Oman	D	1-1	Doha	Fr	Fabio Cesar 68		
12-10	Iraq	L	1-2	Doha	Fr	Magid Hassan 33		
18-11	Haiti	L	0-1	Doha	Fr			
22-11	Kuwait	L	0-1	Aden	GCr1			Al Rashid OMA
25-11	Yemen	W	2-1	Abyan	GCr1	Jaralla Al Marri 2 35 55		Abid Iddan IRQ
28-11	Saudi Arabia	D	1-1	Aden	GCr1	Ibrahim Al Ghanim 84		Al Marzouqi UAE
16-12	Egypt	W	2-1	Doha	Fr	Soria 21, OG 43		
22-12	Estonia	W	2-0	Doha	Fr	Soria 2 37 78		
28-12	Iran	D	0-0	Doha	Fr			
31-12	Korea DPR	L	0-1	Doha	Fr			
2011								
7-01	Uzbekistan	L	0-2	Doha	ACr1		37 143	Nishimura JPN
12-01	China PR	W	2-0	Doha	ACr1	Yusef Ahmed 2 27 45	30 778	Kim Dong Jin KOR
16-01	Kuwait	W	3-0	Doha	ACr1	Bilal Mohammed 12, Mohamed El Sayed 16, Fabio Cesar 86	28 339	Abdul Bashir SIN
21-01	Japan	L	2-3	Doha	ACqf	Soria 13, Fabio Cesar 63	19 479	Mohd Salleh MAS
29-03	Russia	D	1-1	Doha	Fr	Kasola Mohammed 4		
23-07	Vietnam	W	3-0	Doha	WCq	Kasola Mohammed 6, Meshal Budawood 51, Yusef Ali 67	6 786	Albadwawi UAE
28-07	Vietnam	L	1-2	Hanoi	WCq	Yusef Ali 17	20 000	Green AUS
19-08	Iraq	L	0-1	Doha	Fr			
25-08	UAE	L	1-3	Al Ain	Fr	Junior Marcone 88		
2-09	Bahrain	D	0-0	Manama	WCq		5 000	Alzarooni UAE
6-09	Iran	D	1-1	Doha	WCq	Mohamed El Sayed 56	8 125	Choi Myung Yong KOR
11-10	Indonesia	W	3-2	Jakarta	WCq	Abdulaziz Al Sulaiti 14, Khalfan Al Khalfan 32, Mohammed Razak 30	28 000	Bashir SIN
4-11	Oman	D	0-0	Doha	Fr			
11-11	Indonesia	W	4-0	Doha	WCq	Mohammed Razak 30, Khalfan Al Khalfan 2 34p 63, Andres Quintana 92+	6 500	Basma SYR
15-11	Bahrain	D	0-0	Doha	WCq		10 509	Nishimura JPN
10-12	Bahrain	D	2-2	Doha	Fr	Jaralla Al Marri 17, Mohammed Razak 34		
16-12	Iraq	D	0-0	Doha	Fr			

Fr = Friendly match • AC = AFC Asian Cup • GC = Gulf Cup • WC = FIFA World Cup

QATAR NATIONAL TEAM HISTORICAL RECORDS

Past Coaches Mohammed Hassan Kheiri 1969-72 • Helmi Hussein Mahmoud 1974 • Frank Wignall ENG 1975-76 • Hassan Othman 1979 • Evaristo de Macedo BRA 1980-86 • Procopio Cardoso BRA 1987-88 • Anatoly Prokopenko URS 1988 • Cabralzinho BRA 1989 • Dino Sani BRA 1989-90 • Evaristo de Macedo BRA 1992 • Ivo Wortmann BRA 1992 • Sebastiao Lapola BRA 1992-93 • Abdul Mallalah 1993 • Dave Mackay SCO 1994-95 • Jorgen Larsen DEN 1995-96 • Jo Bonfrere NED 1996-97 • Dzemal Hadziabdic YUG 1997 • Ze Mario BRA 1998 • Luiz Gonzaga Milioli 1998 • Dzemal Hadziabdic YUG 2000-01 • Paulo Luiz Campos BRA 2001 • Pierre Lechantre FRA 2002-03 • Philippe Troussier FRA 2003-04 • Dzemaludin Musovic BIH 2004-07 • Jorge Fossati URU 2007-08 • Bruno Metsu FRA 2008-11 • Milovan Rajevac SRB 2011 • Sebastiao Lazaroni BRA 2011 • Paulo Autuori

QATAR 2010–11

QATAR STARS LEAGUE

	Pl	W	D	L	F	A	Pts	Lekhwia	Al Gharafa	Al Rayyan	Al Arabi	Qatar SC	Al Sadd	Al Wakra	Al Khritiyat	Umm Salal	Khor	Al Siliya	Al Ahli
Lekhwia	22	15	3	4	40	17	48		0-2	3-1	1-1	1-0	1-2	4-1	0-2	3-0	3-1	4-0	3-0
Al Gharafa	22	14	1	7	51	31	43	0-1		3-3	1-3	0-2	1-0	2-4	5-1	2-0	3-0	3-1	2-0
Al Rayyan	22	12	6	4	39	22	42	2-1	3-2		0-1	1-1	1-1	3-0	2-1	3-0	1-0	4-1	2-0
Al Arabi	22	12	5	5	37	26	41	1-1	1-2	0-4		1-2	2-1	1-3	2-0	2-2	1-1	1-0	4-0
Qatar SC	22	11	7	4	40	26	40	0-1	4-0	2-0	1-1		2-2	1-0	0-0	2-1	3-1	2-2	0-0
Al Sadd	22	11	3	8	32	26	36	0-1	1-3	1-0	0-2	1-3		4-0	3-2	0-1	1-1	3-2	2-0
Al Wakra	22	8	3	11	30	36	27	1-3	0-3	2-2	0-3	0-2	0-1		3-0	2-1	0-0	0-0	2-0
Al Khritiyat	22	7	4	11	27	40	25	1-2	1-4	2-2	1-3	2-3	1-3	1-0		1-0	0-3	1-1	1-1
Umm Salal	22	5	4	13	24	39	19	1-1	2-3	0-2	1-2	4-2	0-3	2-1	2-3		1-1	1-1	1-2
Khor	22	4	7	11	24	33	19	0-2	3-0	0-0	0-1	3-5	3-1	1-2	1-2	1-0		0-0	0-2
Al Siliya	22	3	6	13	25	47	15	0-2	0-3	1-2	5-2	2-2	0-1	2-5	0-2	2-3	3-2		2-1
Al Ahli	22	4	3	15	16	44	15	1-2	1-7	0-1	0-4	3-1	0-1	0-4	0-2	0-1	2-2	3-0	

13/09/2010 - 15/04/2011 • † Qualified for AFC Champions League • Top scorers: 15 - Younis Mahmoud IRQ, Al Gharafa • 14 - Moumouni Dagano BFA, Al Siliya & Bakari Kone CIV, Lekhwia • 12 - Sebastian Soria, Qatar SC • 11 - Yahia Kebe BFA, Al Khritiyat & Mohammed Razak, Lekhwiya • 9 - Jaralla Al Marri, Al Rayyan & Anouar Diba MAR, Al Rayyan • 8 - Juninho BRA, Al Gharafa; Leonardo Pisculichi ARG, Al Arabi & Ali Afif, Al Sadd
Pre-relegation play-off: **Al Ahli** 1-0 Al Siliya. Siliya relegated • Relegation play-off: **Al Ahli** 4-3 Al Shamal

QATAR 2010–11 2ND DIVISION

	Pl	W	D	L	F	A	Pts
Al Jaish	15	13	1	1	48	9	40
Al Shamal	15	9	3	3	27	11	30
Shahaniya	15	6	4	5	17	28	22
Mseimeer	15	5	3	7	25	23	18
Markheya	15	2	5	8	19	35	11
Maitheer	15	1	2	12	6	36	5

26/09/2010 - 10/04/2011

CROWN PRINCE CUP 2011

Semi-finals			Finals	
Al Gharafa	1	5p		
Al Rayyan	1	4p	**Al Gharafa**	2
Lekhwia	0		Al Arabi	0
Al Arabi	1		Qatar SC, 29-04-2011	

Played at the end of the season between the top four teams of the Qatar Stars League

MEDALS TABLE

		Overall			Lge			Cup			CP	SJ	QS	Asia		
		G	S	B	G	S	B	G	S	B				G	S	B
1	Al Sadd	44	6	1	12			12	6		5	12	1	2		1
2	Al Arabi	22	4	1	7			8	3		1	6		1	1	
3	Al Gharafa	20	4		7			6	4		3	3	1			
4	Al Rayyan	17	9	1	7			5	9		3	2				1
5	Qatar SC	13	3		3			3	3		3	4				
6	Al Wakra	7	6		2						6	1	4			
7	Al Oruba	5			5											
8	Al Ahli	4	5					4	5							
9	Umm Salal	3	1	1				1	1			2				1
10	Al Maref	3			3											
11	Khor	2	2								2	1	1			
14	Lekhwia	1			1											

Name changes: Al Gharafa were called Al Ittihad • Kor were previously Al Taawun • Lekhwia were previously Al Shorta • Al Oruba merged with Qatar SC to form Esteqlal but reverted to Qatar SC in 1981 • Cup = Emir Cup • CP = Crown Prince Cup • SJ = Sheikh Jassim Cup • QS = Qatar Stars Cup

EMIR'S CUP 2010–11

Round of 16		Quarter-finals		Semi-finals		Final	
Al Rayyan	Bye						
		Al Rayyan	2				
Al Siliya	0	Qatar SC	1				
Qatar SC	2						
Al Arabi	Bye			**Al Rayyan**	5		
				Al Jaish	0		
		Al Arabi	1				
Al Khritiyat	2	**Al Jaish**	2				
Al Jaish	3						
Lekhwia	Bye					**Al Rayyan** †	2
						Al Gharafa	1
		Lekhwia	4				
Khor	1	Al Wakra	3				
Al Wakra	2						
				Lekhwia	0 4p		
Al Sadd	5			**Al Gharafa**	0 5p		
Umm Salal	2	Al Sadd	1				
		Al Gharafa	3				
Al Gharafa	Bye						

† Qualified for AFC Champions League

CUP FINAL

Khalifa International, Doha
21-05-2011

SHEIKH JASSIM CUP 2011-12

First Round Groups

Group A	Pl	W	D	L	F	A	Pts	Kh	Qa	Ma	Ms
Lekhwiya	4	3	1	0	11	4	10	4-2	0-0	2-0	5-2
Khor	4	2	1	1	9	4	7		0-0	2-0	5-0
Qatar SC	4	0	4	0	2	2	4			1-1	1-1
Markheya	4	1	1	2	3	6	4				2-1
Mseimeer	4	0	1	3	4	13	1				

Group B	Pl	W	D	L	F	A	Pts	Gh	Sa	Si	SH
Al Jaish	4	2	2	0	14	6	8	3-3	3-0	2-2	6-1
Al Gharafa	4	2	1	1	10	4	7		0-1	6-0	1-0
Al Sadd	4	2	0	2	3	7	6			2-1	0-3
Al Siliya	4	1	1	2	5	11	4				2-1
Shahaniya	4	1	0	3	5	9	3				

Group C	Pl	W	D	L	F	A	Pts	Kh	Ra	Sh
Umm Salal	3	2	1	0	7	4	7	3-2	4-2	0-0
Al Khritiyat	3	2	0	1	6	4	6		2-0	2-1
Al Rayyan	3	1	0	2	6	9	3			4-3
Al Shamal	3	0	1	2	4	6	1			

Group D	Pl	W	D	L	F	A	Pts	Wa	Ah	Ma
Al Arabi	3	3	0	0	8	0	9	3-0	2-0	3-0
Al Wakra	3	1	1	1	5	4	4		1-1	4-0
Al Ahli	3	1	1	1	3	4	4			2-1
Maitheer	3	0	0	3	1	9	0			

Semi-finals

Al Arabi	3
Al Jaish	2

Lekhwiya	1
Umm Salal	2

Final

Al Arabi	3
Umm Salal	2

CUP FINAL
Doha Stadium, Doha
24-08-2011

3/08/2011 - 24/08/2011

QATAR STARS CUP 2010-11

First Round Groups

Group A	Pl	W	D	L	F	A	Pts	Sa	Ar	Kh	Wa	Ah
Umm Salal	5	4	0	1	8	2	12	0-2	1-0	2-0	1-0	4-0
Al Sadd	5	3	2	0	13	5	11		2-2	3-1	1-1	5-1
Al Arabi	5	3	1	1	9	3	10			2-0	2-0	3-0
Khor	5	2	0	3	5	9	6				1-0	3-2
Al Wakra	5	1	1	3	5	8	4					4-3
Al Ahli	5	0	0	5	6	20	0					

Group B	Pl	W	D	L	F	A	Pts	Ra	Le	Si	Gh	Kh
Qatar SC	5	3	1	1	12	8	10	0-3	1-1	5-2	4-1	2-1
Al Rayyan	5	3	1	1	9	6	10		1-5	3-0	2-1	0-0
Lekhwiya	5	2	3	0	11	6	9			4-3	1-1	0-0
Al Siliya	5	2	0	3	11	14	6				3-1	3-1
Al Gharafa	5	1	1	3	5	10	4					1-0
Al Khritiyat	5	0	2	3	2	6	2					

Semi-finals

Al Sadd	2	3p
Qatar SC	2	2p

Al Rayyan	0
Umm Salal	1

Final

Al Sadd	1
Umm Salal	0

CUP FINAL
Jassim Bin Hamad, Doha
23-12-2010
Yusef Ahmed 54 for Al Sadd

18/11/2010 - 23/12/2010

ROU – ROMANIA

FIFA/COCA-COLA WORLD RANKING

'93	'94	'95	'96	'97	'98	'99	'00	'01	'02	'03	'04	'05	'06	'07	'08	'09	'10	'11	'12
13	11	11	16	7	12	8	13	15	24	27	29	27	19	13	21	36	56	56	

							2011								
	Jan	Feb	Mar	Apr	May	Jun	Jul	Aug	Sep	Oct	Nov	Dec	High	Low	Av
	56	57	52	41	42	53	53	54	49	55	56	56	3	57	21

Victor Piturca returned in mid-2011 for his third spell in charge of a Romanian national team that has lost its way since qualifying for Euro 2008. Piturca left in 2009 with Romania having failed to qualify for the World Cup in South Africa but his replacement Razvan Lucescu had no better luck in the qualifiers for Euro 2012 and he quit after the tour to South America to return to his job at Rapid. Piturca's task is to take Romania to their first World Cup finals since 1998 although they face a tough group containing Holland and Turkey. At home there were surprise first-time champions in Otelul Galati - the fifth different winners of the league in six seasons and the fourth year in a row that the title has remained outside of Bucharest. Coached by Romania's record cap winner Dorinel Munteanu, Otelul finished four points ahead of FC Timisoara but this was a season beset by financial and licensing problems. Despite finishing second Timisoara were denied a place in the UEFA Champions League and were then relegated after being refused a licence. There was some joy for fans in the capital when Steaua and Dinamo met in the Cup Final for the first time since 1990. Steaua won 2-1 in what was their first trophy for five years and their first Cup Final win since 1999.

UEFA EUROPEAN CHAMPIONSHIP RECORD

1960 QF　1964 r1　1968 DNQ　1972 QF　1976-1980 DNQ　**1984** r1　1988-1992 DNQ　**1996** r1　**2000** QF　2004 DNQ　**2008** r1　2012 DNQ

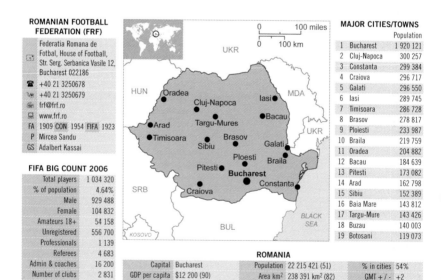

ROMANIAN FOOTBALL FEDERATION (FRF)

Federatia Romana de Fotbal, House of Football, Str. Serg. Serbanica Vasile 12, Bucharest 022186

☎ +40 21 3250678
📠 +40 21 3250679
✉ frf@frf.ro
🖥 www.frf.ro
FA 1909 CON 1954 FIFA 1923
P Mircea Sandu
GS Adalbert Kassai

FIFA BIG COUNT 2006

Total players	1 034 320
% of population	4.64%
Male	929 488
Female	104 832
Amateurs 18+	54 158
Unregistered	556 700
Professionals	1 139
Referees	4 683
Admin & coaches	16 200
Number of clubs	2 831
Number of teams	4 319

MAJOR CITIES/TOWNS

		Population
1	Bucharest	1 920 121
2	Cluj-Napoca	300 257
3	Constanta	299 384
4	Craiova	296 717
5	Galati	296 550
6	Iasi	289 745
7	Timisoara	286 728
8	Brasov	278 817
9	Ploiesti	233 987
10	Braila	219 759
11	Oradea	204 882
12	Bacau	184 639
13	Pitesti	173 082
14	Arad	162 798
15	Sibiu	152 389
16	Baia Mare	143 812
17	Targu-Mure	143 426
18	Buzau	140 003
19	Botosani	119 073

ROMANIA

Capital Bucharest	Population 22 215 421 (51)	% in cities 54%
GDP per capita $12 200 (90)	Area km² 238 391 km² (82)	GMT + / - +2
Neighbours (km) Bulgaria 608, Hungary 443, Moldova 450, Serbia 476, Ukraine 531 • Coast 225		

RECENT INTERNATIONAL MATCHES PLAYED BY ROMANIA

2008	Opponents	Score		Venue	Comp	Scorers	Att	Referee
9-06	France	D	0-0	Zurich	ECr1		30 585	Mejuto Gonzalez ESP
13-06	Italy	D	1-1	Zurich	ECr1	Mutu [55]	30 585	Ovrebø NOR
17-06	Netherlands	L	0-2	Berne	ECr1		30 777	Busacca SUI
20-08	Latvia	W	1-0	Urziceni	Fr	Dica [51]	10 000	Ovrebo NOR
6-09	Lithuania	L	0-3	Cluj	WCq		14 000	Kelly IRL
10-09	Faroe Islands	W	1-0	Tórshavn	WCq	Cocis [59]	805	Strahonja CRO
11-10	France	D	2-2	Constanta	WCq	Petre [5], Goian [16]	12 800	De Bleeckere BEL
19-11	Georgia	W	2-1	Bucharest	Fr	Marica [62], Goian [70]	2 000	Vassaras GRE
2009								
11-02	Croatia	L	1-2	Bucharest	Fr	Marica [22]		Balaj ROU
28-03	Serbia	L	2-3	Constanta	WCq	Marica [50], Stoica [74]	12 000	Trefoloni ITA
1-04	Austria	L	1-2	Klagenfurt	WCq	Tanase [24]	23 000	Thomson SCO
6-06	Lithuania	W	1-0	Marijampole	WCq	Marica [39]	5 850	Eriksson SWE
12-08	Hungary	W	1-0	Budapest	Fr	Ghioane [42]	9 000	Vnuk SVK
5-09	France	D	1-1	Paris	WCq	Escude OG [55]	78 209	Bebek CRO
9-09	Austria	D	1-1	Bucharest	WCq	Bucur [54]	7 505	Atkinson ENG
10-10	Serbia	L	0-5	Belgrade	WCq		39 839	Kapitanis CYP
14-10	Faroe Islands	W	3-1	Piatra-Neamt	WCq	Apostal [16], Bucur [65], Mazilu [87]	13 000	Gvardis RUS
14-11	Poland	W	1-0	Warsaw	Fr	Niculae [59]	8 000	Mashiah ISR
2010								
29-05	Ukraine	L	2-3	Lviv	Fr	Tamas [54], Niculae [63]	22 000	Kralovec CZE
2-06	Macedonia FYR	L	0-1	Bischofshofen	Fr		1 000	Krassnitzer AUT
5-06	Honduras	W	3-0	St Velt An Der Glan	Fr	Niculae [20], Florescu [45], Radoi [76p]	700	Grobelnik AUT
11-08	Turkey	L	0-2	Istanbul	Fr		15 000	Mazic SRB
3-09	Albania	D	1-1	Piatra-Neamt	ECq	Stancu [80]	13 400	Schorgenhofer AUT
7-09	Belarus	D	0-0	Minsk	ECq		26 354	Kralovec CZE
9-10	France	L	0-2	Paris	ECq		79 299	Proenca POR
17-11	Italy	D	1-1	Klagenfurt	Fr	Marica [34]	14 000	Einwaller AUT
2011								
8-02	Ukraine	D	2-2	Paralimni	Fr	Alexa 2 [33 44]. L 2-4p	1 000	Johannesson SWE
9-02	Cyprus	D	1-1	Paralimni	Fr	Torje [56]. W 5-4p	2 500	Shvetov UKR
26-03	Bosnia-Herzegovina	L	1-2	Zenica	ECq	Marica [29]	13 000	Teixeira ESP
29-03	Luxembourg	W	3-1	Piatra-Neamt	ECq	Mutu 2 [24 68], Zicu [78]	13 500	Gocek TUR
3-06	Bosnia-Herzegovina	W	3-0	Bucharest	ECq	Mutu [37], Marica 2 [41 55]	8 200	Eriksson SWE
7-06	Brazil	L	0-1	Sao Paulo	Fr		30 059	Pezzotta ARG
11-06	Paraguay	L	0-2	Asuncion	Fr		8 000	Larrionda URU
10-08	San Marino	W	1-0	Serravalle	Fr	Herea [72]	3 000	Rocchi ITA
2-09	Luxembourg	W	2-0	Luxembourg	ECq	Torje 2 [34 45]	2 812	Karasev RUS
6-09	France	D	0-0	Bucharest	ECq		49 137	Webb ENG
7-10	Belarus	D	2-2	Bucharest	ECq	Mutu 2 [19 51p]	29 486	Kelly IRL
11-10	Albania	D	1-1	Tirana	ECq	Luchin [77]	3 000	Mazeika LTU
11-11	Belgium	L	1-2	Liege	Fr	Niculae [67]	15 000	Ennjimi FRA
15-11	Greece	W	3-1	Altach	Fr	Torje [17], Tanase [61], Chipciu [81]	8 00	Gangl AUT

Fr = Friendly match • EC = UEFA EURO 2008/2012 • WC = FIFA World Cup • q = qualifier • r1 = first round group

ROMANIA NATIONAL TEAM HISTORICAL RECORDS

Caps

134 - Dorinel Munteanu 1991-2007 • **125** - Gheorghe Hagi 1983-2000 • **115** - Gheorghe Popescu 1988-2003 • **108** - Ladislau Boloni 1975-88 • **95** - Dan Petrescu 1989-2000 • **91** - Bogdan Stelea 1988-2005 • **90** - Michael Klein 1981-91 • **84** - Marius Lacatus 1984-98 • **83** - Mircea Rednic 1981-91 • **79** - Razvan Rat 2002- • **78** - Bogdan Lobont 1998- • **77** - Silviu Lung 1979 93

Goals

35 - Gheorghe Hagi 1983-2000 • **34** - Adrian Mutu 2000- • **31** - Iuliu Bodola 1931-39 • **26** - Anghel Iordanescu 1971-81 • **25** - Viorel Moldovan 1993-2005 & Ladislau Boloni 1975-88 • **22** - Rodion Camataru 1978-90 • **21** - Dudu Georgescu 1973-80 & Florin Raducioiu 1988-96 • **20** - Stefan Dobay 1930-39 & Ilie Dumitrescu 1989-98 • **19** - Ioan Ganea 1998-2006

Past Coaches

Valentin Stanescu 1973-75 • Cornel Dragusin 1975 • Stefan Kovacs 1976-79 • Florin Halagian 1979 • Constantin Cernaianu 1979 • Stefan Kovacs 1980 • Valentin Stanescu 1980-1981 • Mircea Lucescu 1981-86 • Emerich Jenei 1986-90 • Gheorghe Constantin 1990 • Mircea Radulescu 1990-92 • Cornel Dinu 1992-93 • Anghel Iordanescu 1993-98 • Victor Piturca 1998-99 • Emerich Jenei 2000 • Ladislau Boloni 2000-01 • Gheorghe Hagi 2001-02 • Anghel Iordanescu 2002-04 • Victor Piturca 2005-09 • Razvan Lucescu 2009-11 • Victor Piturca 2011-

ROMANIA 2010–11
LIGA I BURGER

	Pl	W	D	L	F	A	Pts	Otelul Galati	FC Timisoara	SC Vaslui	Rapid	Steaua	Dinamo	Gaz Metan	Universitatea	Targu Mures	CFR Cluj	Astra Ploesti	FC Brasov	Pandurii	Gloria Bistrita	Universitatea	Victoria	Unirea	Sportul
Otelul Galati †	34	21	7	6	46	25	70		2-1	0-0	1-0	1-0	3-3	2-2	3-0	1-0	1-1	2-1	1-0	2-0	2-1	2-1	1-1	4-1	1-0
FC Timisoara - R	34	17	15	2	63	38	66	2-0		2-1	2-1	0-0	4-1	3-1	2-2	0-0	3-2	2-2	2-0	2-2	2-2	4-0	2-1	3-1	2-1
SC Vaslui †	34	18	11	5	51	28	65	4-0	1-1		1-1	0-3	2-0	3-0	2-0	1-1	5-3	0-0	2-1	3-1	1-0	2-1	1-0	2-0	4-2
Rapid Bucuresti ‡	34	16	11	7	43	22	59	0-0	3-2	2-0		0-0	0-0	2-1	3-0	1-1	2-0	3-0	1-0	1-1	2-0	0-0	7-1	1-0	0-1
Steaua Bucuresti ‡	34	16	9	9	44	27	57	1-0	1-1	1-1	0-1		0-1	0-1	3-0	0-0	2-1	1-0	0-3	2-0	3-1	2-1	2-1	5-0	4-2
Dinamo Bucuresti ‡	34	16	8	10	68	52	56	1-2	0-0	1-2	3-2	2-1		3-2	3-4	4-1	1-2	2-2	2-1	2-2	3-0	2-2	3-1	1-5	5-3
Gaz Metan Medias ‡	34	14	13	7	41	32	55	0-2	2-2	0-0	0-1	0-0	2-1		3-1	0-0	3-2	0-0	0-0	2-0	2-1	1-0	2-2	2-0	3-0
Universitatea Cluj	34	13	8	13	49	56	47	2-1	1-2	1-1	1-2	1-2	2-1	2-2		1-1	1-1	1-0	1-1	1-1	2-1	3-0	2-3	4-2	2-0
Targu Mures	34	12	9	13	34	41	45	1-0	2-3	0-2	1-0	0-1	2-6	1-0	0-2		0-0	1-0	0-1	1-0	2-0	1-4	4-0	1-0	4-1
CFR 1907 Cluj	34	11	12	11	50	45	45	0-1	1-2	1-0	0-1	1-3	1-0	1-1	1-1	1-2		2-2	4-0	2-1	2-2	2-1	2-0	3-0	2-0
Astra Ploesti	34	10	15	9	36	30	45	0-1	1-1	1-1	0-0	1-0	1-2	0-2	1-2	0-0	1-1		3-0	2-0	1-0	2-2	2-0	1-0	2-0
FC Brasov	34	10	13	11	34	40	43	1-0	0-0	1-1	2-0	1-1	2-2	0-0	3-1	1-1	2-2	0-3		3-2	0-1	0-3	1-0	1-1	2-0
Pandurii Targu Jiu	34	9	10	15	36	46	37	0-3	0-1	0-1	0-1	1-1	2-2	0-0	2-0	4-1	2-1	1-0	2-1		0-0	3-1	4-2	0-0	1-0
Gloria Bistrita	34	8	11	15	35	49	35	0-0	3-3	1-1	3-2	1-0	0-2	0-0	2-4	3-1	0-3	1-1	0-0	3-0		1-1	1-0	0-0	1-0
Universitatea Craiova	34	7	9	18	35	48	30	0-1	1-1	0-1	1-1	0-1	0-2	2-1	3-0	2-1	0-0	1-1	1-2	0-2	1-2		1-1	3-0	1-0
Victoria Branesti	34	5	10	19	35	61	25	1-2	0-2	1-3	0-0	0-1	2-4	2-3	0-2	0-0	1-1	1-1	1-1	2-0	2-0	1-0		4-1	1-1
Unirea Urziceni	34	6	7	21	23	63	25	0-3	1-1	2-1	0-0	1-0	0-1	0-1	0-1	1-3	0-3	1-1	1-1	2-1	1-2	2-1			2-1
Sportul Studentesc	34	7	2	25	38	58	23	0-1	2-3	0-1	0-2	1-2	0-1	0-1	2-1	0-2	1-2	3-0	0-1	1-2	2-1	4-2	3-0	2-2	5-1	

23/07/2010 - 21/05/2011 • † Qualified for the UEFA Champions League • ‡ Qualified for the Europa League
Top scorers: 18 - Ianis Zicu, FC Timisoara • 15 - Eric BRA, Medias • 13 - Bogdan Stancu, Steaua; Claudiu Niculescu, Un Cluj & Wesley BRA, Vaslui

ROMANIA 2010–11 LIGA II SERIE 1 (2)

	Pl	W	D	L	F	A	Pts
Ceahlaul Piatra Neamt	30	20	7	3	65	23	67
Concordia Chiajna	30	17	10	3	48	27	61
Sageata Navodari †	30	18	4	8	49	27	58
Delta Tulcea	30	17	4	9	50	37	55
Dunarea Galati	30	13	9	8	44	26	48
CS Otopeni	30	14	4	12	35	38	46
FC Botosani	30	12	6	12	48	46	42
Viitorul Constanta	30	10	11	9	37	37	41
Astra Giurgiu	30	11	8	11	42	44	41
Gloria Buzau	30	9	11	10	33	34	38
FC Snagov	30	11	4	15	36	52	37
Dinamo Bucuresti-2	30	9	7	14	30	44	34
Farul Constanta	30	8	6	16	27	45	30
Steaua Bucuresti-2	30	7	6	17	29	48	27
CF Braila	30	5	6	19	28	47	21
Juventus Bucuresti	30	4	7	19	26	52	19

28/08/2010 - 4/06/2011 • † Play-off

Promotion play-off
Sageata Navodari
0-0 0-2
Vointa Sibiu

ROMANIA 2010–11 LIGA II SERIE 2 (2)

	Pl	W	D	L	F	A	Pts
Petrolul Ploiesti	28	18	5	5	46	22	59
Bihor Oradea	28	17	7	4	43	20	58
CS Mioveni	28	17	6	5	43	19	57
Vointa Sibiu †	28	14	8	6	36	17	50
Alro Slatina	28	14	6	8	46	26	48
CSMS Iasi	28	14	5	9	41	30	47
Ramnicu Valcea	28	11	3	14	35	39	36
UTA Arad	28	13	8	7	48	36	35
Ariesul Turda	28	8	9	11	26	31	33
Gaz Metan Craiova	28	8	7	13	36	39	31
Unirea Alba Iulia	28	8	6	14	22	35	30
Arges Pitesti	28	8	5	15	27	40	29
Muresul Deva	28	7	5	16	31	48	26
ACU Arad	28	6	7	15	18	36	25
Silvania Simleu	28	3	1	24	9	69	10
Minerul Lupeni	0	0	0	0	0	0	0

28/08/2010 - 4/06/2011 • † Play-off

MEDALS TABLE

		Overall			League			Cup		Europe		
		G	S	B	G	S	B	G	S	G	S	B
1	Steaua Bucuresti	46	21	9	23	13	7	22	7	1	1	2
2	Dinamo Bucuresti	31	32	11	19	20	9	12	12			2
3	Rapid Bucuresti	16	19	8	3	14	8	13	5			
4	Universitatea Craiova	10	10	8	4	5	7	6	5			1
5	UT Arad	8	3	1	6	1	1	2	2			
6	Venus Bucuresti	8	1	1	8		1		1			
7	Petrolul Ploiesti	6	4	2	4	3	2	2	1			
	Ripensia Timisoara	6	4	2	4	2	2	2	2			
9	Chinezul Timisoara	6	1		6				1			
10	CFR 1907 Cluj	5		1	2		1	3				
11	Politehnica Timisoara	2	7	5		1	5	2	6			
12	FC Arges Pitesti	2	3	4	2	2	4		1			
13	FC Bihor Oradea	2	3	1	1	2	1	1	1			
14	FCM Resita	2	1		1	1		1				

CUPA ROMANIEI 2010-11

First Round			Second Round			Quarter-finals			Semi-finals			Final	
Steaua Bucuresti	1		Steaua Bucuresti *	1	3p	Steaua Bucuresti	1		Steaua Bucuresti *	0	1	Steaua Bucuresti ‡	2
Gaz Metan Craiova *	0		Sportul Studentesc	1	1p	Rapid Bucuresti *	0		FC Brasov	0	1	Dinamo Bucuresti	1
CS Otopeni	1												
Sportul Studentesc *	3												
Astra Ploesti *	2		Astra Ploesti *	0									
Otelul Galati	1		Rapid Bucuresti	2									
Petrolul Ploiesti	0												
Rapid Bucuresti *	5												
FC Timisoara	3		FC Timisoara *	1	4p	FC Timisoara	0						
Juventus Bucuresti *	1		Vointa Sibiu	1	3p	FC Brasov *	1						
Gaz Metan Medias	1												
Vointa Sibiu *	3												
Universitatea Cluj *	1		Universitatea Cluj	1									
Victoria Branesti	0		FC Brasov *	2									
Chimia Brazi *	0												
FC Brasov	1												
Gloria Bistrita *	3		Gloria Bistrita *	1		Gloria Bistrita	1		Gloria Bistrita *	0	1		
Astra Giurgiu	0		Unirea Urziceni	0		CFR 1907 Cluj *	0		Dinamo Bucuresti	2	5		
Delta Tulcea	0												
Unirea Urziceni *	1												
Targu Mures	1		Targu Mures	0									
Silvania Simleu *	0		CFR 1907 Cluj *	2									
ACU Arad *	0												
CFR 1907 Cluj	1												
Universitatea Craiova *	5		Universitatea Craiova	2		Universitatea Craiova	1	1p					
Minerul Lupeni	0		Pandurii Targu Jiu *	0		Dinamo Bucuresti *	1	3p					
Viitorul Constanta	2												
Pandurii Targu Jiu *	3												
Alro Slatina *	0	4p	Alro Slatina	1									
SC Vaslui	3	3p	Dinamo Bucuresti *	3									
Ceahlaul Piatra Neamt	3												
Dinamo Bucuresti *	2												

CUP FINAL

Siliviu Ploesteanu, Brasov
25-05-2011, 21:15, Att: 7500, Ref: Avram
Scorers - Dica 24, Barboianu OG 51 for Steaua; Torje 22 for Dinamo

Steaua - Ciprian Tatarusanu (c) - Ifeanyi Emeghara, Florin Gardo, George Galamaz, Iasmin Latovlevici - Pablo Brandan - Banel Nicolie, Cristian Tanase• (Valentin Iliev 89), Romeo Surdu - Nicolae Dicu (Eric Bicfalvi 62), Marius Bilasco• (Janos Szekely• 75). Tr: Gabriel Caramarin

Dinamo - Cristian Balgradean - Stefan Barboianu, Dragos Grigore, Cosmin Moti•, Valeriu Bordeanu - Djakaridja Kone (Elis Bakaj• 72) - Gabriel Torje•, Andrei Margaritescu• (George Tucudean 87), Catalin Munteanu, Marius Alexe - Ionel Danciulescu (c) (Liviu Ganea 69). Tr: Ioan Andone

* Home team/home team in the 1st leg • ‡ Qualified for the Europa League

RSA – SOUTH AFRICA

FIFA/COCA-COLA WORLD RANKING

'93	'94	'95	'96	'97	'98	'99	'00	'01	'02	'03	'04	'05	'06	'07	'08	'09	'10	'11	'12
95	56	40	19	31	26	30	20	35	30	36	38	49	67	77	76	85	51	52	

2011													High	Low	Av
Jan	Feb	Mar	Apr	May	Jun	Jul	Aug	Sep	Oct	Nov	Dec			
51	47	46	39	38	47	49	47	51	49	53	52	16	109	47

Just over a year after hosting the FIFA World Cup finals, South Africa suffered the embarrassment of failing to know the rules and sabotaging their own bid to qualify for the 2012 CAF Africa Cup of Nations. The South Africans thought they only needed to draw their last game against Sierra Leone to finish top of their qualifying group on goal difference but the 0-0 draw in Nelspruit saw Niger qualify instead with the better head to head results between the three teams tied at the top. The South African Football Association protested to the Confederation of African Football but then realised they had no grounds for any judicial recourse and hastily withdrew their protest, replacing it with an apology to the country for the blunder. Orlando Pirates won the Premier Soccer League in 2011 although it was a disastrous error by Ajax Cape Town's 41-year-old goalkeeper Hans Vonk that gifted Pirates the title on the last day of the season. Ajax dropped two points against Maritzburg United while Pirates scored a later winner against Golden Arrows to overtake them on goal difference. Pirates actually won every trophy on offer during the course of 2011. A week after having secured the title they beat second division Black Leopards to win the Cup and in the new season won the MTN 8 Cup in September and the League Cup in December.

CAF AFRICA CUP OF NATIONS RECORD

1957-1992 DNE 1994 DNQ **1996** 1 Winners (Hosts) **1998** 2 F **2000** 3 SF **2002** 6 QF
2004 1 r1 **2006** 16 r1 **2008** 13 r1 2010-2012 DNQ

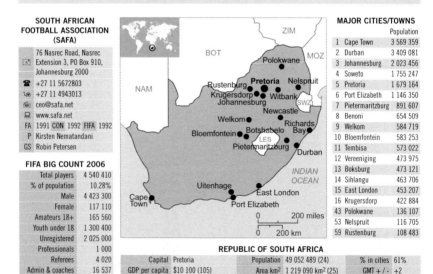

SOUTH AFRICAN FOOTBALL ASSOCIATION (SAFA)

76 Nasrec Road, Nasrec
Extension 3, PO Box 910,
Johannesburg 2000
☎ +27 11 5672803
🖷 +27 11 4943013
✉ ceo@safa.net
🖥 www.safa.net
FA 1991 CON 1992 FIFA 1992
P Kirsten Nematandani
GS Robin Petersen

FIFA BIG COUNT 2006

Total players	4 540 410
% of population	10.28%
Male	4 423 300
Female	117 110
Amateurs 18+	165 560
Youth under 18	1 300 400
Unregistered	2 025 000
Professionals	1 000
Referees	4 020
Admin & coaches	16 537
Number of clubs	450
Number of teams	3 200

MAJOR CITIES/TOWNS

		Population
1	Cape Town	3 569 359
2	Durban	3 409 081
3	Johannesburg	2 023 456
4	Soweto	1 755 247
5	Pretoria	1 679 164
6	Port Elizabeth	1 146 350
7	Pietermaritzburg	891 607
8	Benoni	654 509
9	Welkom	584 719
10	Bloemfontein	583 253
11	Tembisa	573 022
12	Vereeniging	473 975
13	Boksburg	473 121
14	Sihlangu	463 706
15	East London	453 207
16	Krugersdorp	422 884
43	Polokwane	136 107
53	Nelspruit	116 705
59	Rustenburg	108 483

REPUBLIC OF SOUTH AFRICA

Capital	Pretoria	Population	49 052 489 (24)	% in cities 61%
GDP per capita	$10 100 (105)	Area km²	1 219 090 km² (25)	GMT +/- +2
Neighbours (km)	Botswana 1840, Lesotho 909, Mozambique 491, Namibia 967, Swaziland 430, Zimbabwe 225 • Coast 2798		

RECENT INTERNATIONAL MATCHES PLAYED BY SOUTH AFRICA

2009	Opponents		Score	Venue	Comp	Scorers	Att	Referee
14-06	Iraq	D	0-0	Johannesburg	CFr1		48 837	Larrionda URU
17-06	New Zealand	W	2-0	Rustenburg	CFr1	Parker 2 [21] [52]	36 598	Archundia MEX
20-06	Spain	L	0-2	Bloemfontein	CFr1		38 212	Pozo CHI
25-06	Brazil	L	0-1	Johannesburg	CFsf		48 049	Busacca SUI
28-06	Spain	L	2-3	Rustenburg	CF3p	Mphela 2 [73] [93+]	31 788	Breeze AUS
12-08	Serbia	L	1-3	Atteridgeville	Fr	Mphela [90]	10 000	Maullet SEY
5-09	Germany	L	0-2	Leverkusen	Fr		29 569	Circhetta SUI
8-09	Republic of Ireland	L	0-1	Limerick	Fr		11 300	Thomson SCO
19-09	Madagascar	W	1-0	Kimberley	Fr	Mphela [64]		
10-10	Norway	L	0-1	Oslo	Fr		13 504	Collum SCO
13-10	Iceland	L	0-1	Reykjavik	Fr		3 253	Moen NOR
14-11	Japan	D	0-0	Port Elizabeth	Fr		44 000	Baltazar ANG
17-11	Jamaica	D	0-0	Bloemfontein	Fr		15 000	Andriamiharisoa MAD
2010								
27-01	Zimbabwe	W	3-0	Durban	Fr	Tshabalala [49], Mbuyane [76], Thwala [90]	35 000	Nhleko SWZ
3-03	Namibia	D	1-1	Durban	Fr	Mphela [70]	35 000	Nguluwe MWI
31-03	Paraguay	D	1-1	Asuncion	Fr	Tshabalala [71]	7 738	Fagundes BRA
22-04	Korea DPR	D	0-0	Taunusstein-Wehen	Fr		628	Brych GER
28-04	Jamaica	W	2-0	Offenbach/Main	Fr	Moriri [51], Nomvete [85]	562	Sippel GER
16-05	Thailand	W	4-0	Nelspruit	Fr	Tshabalala [22], Mphela 2 [30] [33], Parker [89]	30 000	Kipngetich KEN
24-05	Bulgaria	D	1-1	Johannesburg	Fr	Sangweni [20]	25 000	Kakou RSA
27-05	Colombia	W	2-1	Johannesburg	Fr	Modise [18p], Mphela [58p]	76 000	Kipngetich KEN
31-05	Guatemala	W	5-0	Polokwane	Fr	Mphela 2 [12p] [56p], Letsholonyane [25], Moriri [48], Parker [82]	45 000	Chaibou RSA
5-06	Denmark	W	1-0	Atteridgeville	Fr	Mphela [75]	25 000	Mbata RSA
11-06	Mexico	D	1-1	Johannesburg	WCr1	Tshabalala [55]	84 490	Irmatov UZB
16-06	Uruguay	L	0-3	Pretoria	WCr1		42 658	Busacca SUI
22-06	France	W	2-1	Bloemfontein	WCr1	Khumalo [20], Mphela [37]	39 415	Ruiz COL
11-08	Ghana	W	1-0	Johannesburg	Fr	Mphela [42]	47 000	
4-09	Niger	W	2-0	Nelspruit	CNq	Mphela [12], Parker [45]	40 000	Abdel Rahman SUD
10-10	Sierra Leone	D	0-0	Freetown	CNq		60 000	Lemghaifry MTN
17-11	USA	L	0-1	Cape Town	Fr		52 000	Kirwa KEN
2011								
9-02	Kenya	W	2-0	Rustenburg	Fr	Somma [2], Pienaar [45]	15 000	
26-03	Egypt	W	1-0	Johannesburg	CNq	Mphela [93+]	55 000	Coulibaly MLI
14-05	Tanzania	W	1-0	Dar es Salaam	Fr	Sangweni [44]	5 000	
5-06	Egypt	D	0-0	Cairo	CNq			Jedidi TUN
10-08	Burkina Faso	W	3-0	Johannesburg	Fr	Mphela 2 [14] [51], Tshabalala [19]	10 000	
4-09	Niger	L	1-2	Niamey	CNq	Jali [71]		
8-10	Sierra Leone	D	0-0	Nelspruit	CNq			
12-11	Côte d'Ivoire	D	1-1	Port Elizabeth	Fr	Mphela [53]	28 000	
15-11	Zimbabwe	L	1-2	Harare	Fr	Grobler [28]		

Fr = Friendly match • CN = CAF African Cup of Nations • CC = COSAFA Cup • CF = FIFA Confederations Cup • WC = FIFA World Cup
q = qualifier • r1 = first round group • sf = semi-final • 3p = 3rd place play-off

SOUTH AFRICA NATIONAL TEAM HISTORICAL RECORDS

Caps
105 - Aaron Mokoena 1999- • 79 - Benni McCarthy 1997- & Siyabonga Nomvete 1999- • 74 - Shaun Bartlett 1995-2005 • 73 - John Moshoeu 1992-2004 & Delron Buckley 1999-2008 • 70 - Lucas Radebe 1992-2003 • 67 - Andre Arendse 1995-2004 & Sibusiso Zuma 1998-2008 • 62 - Mark Fish 1993-2004 • 58 - Phil Masinga 1992-2001 & MacBeth Sibaya 2001- • 52 - Neil Tovey 1992-97

Goals
32 - Benni McCarthy 1997- • 29 - Shaun Bartlett 1995-2005 • 22 - Katlego Mphela 2005- • 18 - Phil Masinga 1992-2001 • 16 - Siyabonga Nomvete 1999- • 13 - Sibusiso Zuma 1998-2008 • 10 - Teko Modise 2007- ; Delron Buckley 1999-2008 & Bernard Parker 2007-

Past Coaches
Stanley Tshabalala 1992 • Ephraim Mashaba 1992 • Augusto Palacios PER 1992-94 • Clive Barker 1994-97 • Jomo Sono 1998 • Philippe Troussier FRA 1998 • Trott Moloto 1998-2000 • Carlos Queiroz POR 2000-02 • Jomo Sono 2002 • Ephraim Mashaba 2002-03 • April Phumo 2004 • Stuart Baxter SCO 2004-05 • Ted Dumitru ROU 2005-06 • Pitso Mosimane 2006 • Carlos Alberto Parreira BRA 2007-08 • Joel Santana BRA 2008-09 • Carlos Alberto Parreira BRA 2009-10 • Pitso Mosimane 2010-

SOUTH AFRICA 2010–11

PREMIER SOCCER LEAGUE — THE ABSA PREMIERSHIP

	Pl	W	D	L	F	A	Pts	Pirates	Ajax	Chiefs	Sundowns	Celtic	Wits	SuperSport	Santos	Free State	Platinum S	Arrows	Maritzburg	Swallows	AmaZulu	Vasco	Black Aces
Orlando Pirates †	30	17	9	4	41	23	**60**		3-0	1-3	2-1	2-1	3-2	0-1	0-0	0-0	0-0	2-1	3-1	2-0	1-1	2-0	0-1
Ajax Cape Town	30	18	6	6	50	36	**60**	3-0		1-0	0-1	2-0	3-1	2-1	1-1	1-0	2-0	3-1	2-2	2-0	2-1	1-0	2-1
Kaizer Chiefs	30	17	8	5	45	23	**59**	1-1	4-0		1-0	1-0	1-0	2-0	0-1	1-1	0-0	2-0	3-1	1-0	3-1	2-3	2-0
Mamelodi Sundowns	30	18	4	8	52	28	58	1-2	4-4	2-0		3-1	3-0	2-1	3-1	2-0	1-1	3-2	3-0	2-0	2-3	1-0	3-0
Bloemfontein Celtic	30	14	10	6	37	23	52	1-1	0-0	2-2	1-1		0-0	5-0	1-0	1-0	2-1	1-1	2-0	0-1	3-1	1-1	1-0
Bidvest Wits	30	10	10	10	47	39	40	1-1	2-0	1-1	1-0	1-4		3-0	3-1	2-0	1-1	3-2	1-2	0-1	3-3	6-0	3-0
SuperSport United	30	11	7	12	32	38	40	0-1	1-1	0-2	1-0	2-1	1-2		5-2	0-0	0-2	0-0	1-0	3-0	0-0	3-1	2-1
Santos	30	8	13	9	37	43	37	1-1	3-4	2-2	0-1	0-1	2-1	2-1		3-3	2-2	3-1	1-1	1-1	1-1	1-0	1-0
Free State Stars	30	7	14	9	28	32	35	0-2	2-1	1-0	2-1	0-1	2-2	0-1	0-0		1-1	1-0	4-1	1-3	1-1	1-1	2-1
Platinum Stars	30	6	15	9	34	37	33	1-2	0-3	2-3	0-2	1-1	1-0	0-0	1-1	1-1		0-0	0-0	2-0	2-2	1-1	3-1
Golden Arrows	30	9	6	15	44	49	33	0-2	1-1	1-2	1-3	0-1	1-4	4-2	3-4	2-0	3-3		3-0	2-2	3-2	2-0	3-1
Maritzburg United	30	8	9	13	32	46	33	1-2	3-0	1-1	3-1	0-0	1-1	2-2	1-0	0-2	1-0	0-3		1-0	1-1	2-2	1-0
Moroka Swallows	30	8	8	14	26	40	32	0-2	2-3	0-1	0-2	1-2	1-1	1-1	0-0	1-1	1-0	0-1	1-0		0-4	3-2	3-1
AmaZulu	30	5	15	10	43	45	30	0-0	1-2	1-2	1-1	1-1	1-1	0-1	2-2	0-0	1-0	1-2	3-2	2-2		3-3	4-0
Vasco da Gama	30	7	9	14	35	47	30	1-2	1-2	0-0	0-1	0-1	2-0	0-1	3-0	1-1	3-5	1-0	3-2	0-0	3-1		1-0
Mpuma'ga Black Aces	30	4	3	23	19	53	15	0-1	0-2	0-2	0-2	0-1	1-1	2-1	0-1	1-1	2-3	2-1	1-2	0-2	1-0	2-2	

27/08/2010 – 21/05/2011 • † Qualified for the CAF Champions League

Top scorers: **15** – Knowledge Musona ZIM, Chiefs • **14** – Lehlohonolo Majoro, AmaZulu & Nyasha Mushekwi ZIM, Sundowns • **13** – Katlego Mphela, Sundowns & Bradley Grobler, Platinum Stars • **11** – Diyo Sibisi, Maritzburg; Sibusiso Zuma, Vasco & Collins Mbesuma ZAM, Golden Arrows

SOUTH AFRICA 2010–11 — NATIONAL FIRST DIVISION (2)

Inland	Pl	W	D	L	F	A	Pts
Jomo Cosmos †	21	14	5	2	29	14	47
Black Leopards	21	11	5	5	33	21	38
Pretoria University	21	10	7	4	29	18	37
FC AK	21	7	6	8	27	24	27
Witbank Spurs	21	6	6	9	22	26	24
Dynamos	21	6	3	12	21	37	21
United FC	21	6	5	10	17	24	20
Batau	21	4	3	14	31	45	15

Coastal	Pl	W	D	L	F	A	Pts
Bay United †	21	11	7	3	29	13	40
Thanda Royal Zulu	21	12	3	6	38	27	39
Carara Kicks	21	7	11	3	32	31	32
African Warriors	21	7	9	5	29	25	30
FC Cape Town	21	4	11	6	23	20	23
Blackburn Rovers	21	6	5	10	21	32	23
Nathi Lions	21	3	9	9	27	31	18
Hanover Park	21	4	5	12	23	43	17

10/09/2010 – 8/05/2011 • † Championship play-off

National First Division Championship: Bay United 0-0 0-0 4-5p **Jomo Cosmos**
Jomo Cosmos are First Division champions. Bay United enter the play-offs

Play-off semis: **Bay United** 0-0 4-1 Thanda Royal Zulu
Vasco da Gama 1-1 1-3 **Black Leopards**
Play-off final: Bay United 0-0 0-2 **Black Leopards**
Black Leopards promoted to the Premier Soccer League in place of Vasco

MEDALS TABLE

		Overall			League			Cup		T8		LCup		Africa			City
		G	S	B	G	S	B	G	S	G	S	G	S	G	S	B	
1	Kaizer Chiefs	50	20	5	**10**	6	5	**12**	5	**14**	6	**13**	3				Johannesburg
2	Orlando Pirates	27	22	8	8	5	6	7	7	10	4	1	6	1		2	Johannesburg
3	Mamelodi Sundowns	16	16	3	8	3	3	3	4	3	5	2	3		1		Pretoria
4	Moroka Swallows	7	9	1				1	1	5	1	2	5	2			Johannesburg
5	SuperSport United	6	7	1	3	2	1	2	1	1	2		2				Pretoria
6	Bidvest Wits	6	6	2				2		2	1	2	3	2	2		Johannesburg
7	Jomo Cosmos	5	8	1	1	1		1	4	1	1	2	2	1			Johannesburg
8	Bush Bucks	4	2	1	1	1	1					3	1				Umtata
9	Santos	4	1	1	1	1		2		1							Cape Town
10	Ajax Cape Town	3	8		3			1	1	2		2	2				Cape Town
11	AmaZulu	2	7	2	1	2		6		1	1						Durban
12	Arcadia	2	2	1	1					1	2	1					Pretoria
13	Witbank Aces	2	2					1	1	1	1						Witbank
14	Cape Town Spurs	2	1		1	1		1									Cape Town
15	Bloemfontein Celtic	2		1				1	1	1							Bloemfontein
16	Durban City	2			2												Durban

MTN 8 CUP 2010

First Round		Semi–finals		Final	
Orlando Pirates *	2				
Santos	1	**Orlando Pirates ***	1 1		
Bloemfontein Celtic	0	Kaizer Chiefs	1 0		
Kaizer Chiefs *	1			Orlando Pirates	1 4p
Ajax Cape Town *	1 4p			Moroka Swallows	1 2p
Mamelodi Sundowns	1 3p	Ajax Cape Town *	0 2	Soccer City, Johannesburg	
SuperSport United	2 3p	**Moroka Swallows**	0 3	2-10-2010	
Moroka Swallows *	2 4p	* Home team/home in 1st leg			

TELKOM KNOCK-OUT LEAGUE CUP 2010-11

First Round		Quarter–finals		Semi–finals		Final	
Kaizer Chiefs	2						
AmaZulu *	0	**Kaizer Chiefs ***	2				
Ajax Cape Town *	0	Free State Stars	0	**Kaizer Chiefs ‡**	1		
Free State Stars	1			Santos	0		
Mpuma'ga Black Aces	3						
Moroka Swallows *	1	Mpuma'ga Black Aces	0			**Kaizer Chiefs**	3
Bidvest Wits *	0	**Santos ***	1			Orlando Pirates	0
Santos	1						
Maritzburg United	2					CUP FINAL	
Bloemfontein Celtic *	1	**Maritzburg United ***	2				
Platinum Stars *	0	Mamelodi Sundowns	0	Maritzburg United	0	Soccer City, Johannesburg	
Mamelodi Sundowns	1			**Orlando Pirates ‡‡**	3	3-12-2010	
SuperSport United *	1						
Vasco da Gama	0	SuperSport United *	0				
Golden Arrows *	0	**Orlando Pirates**	3				
Orlando Pirates	1	* Home team • ‡ Played in Polokwane • ‡‡ Played in Durban					

MTN 8 CUP 2011

First Round		Semi–finals		Final	
Orlando Pirates *	1				
Santos	0	**Orlando Pirates ***	3 1		
Bloemfontein Celtic	0	Mamelodi Sundowns	2 1		
Mamelodi Sundowns *	1			**Orlando Pirates**	1
Ajax Cape Town *	5			Kaizer Chiefs	0
SuperSport United	2	Ajax Cape Town	0 1	Soccer City, Johannesburg	
Bidvest Wits	1	**Kaizer Chiefs ***	0 1	10-09-2011	
Kaizer Chiefs *	2	* Home team/home in 1st leg			

TELKOM KNOCK-OUT LEAGUE CUP 2011

First Round		Quarter–finals		Semi–finals		Final	
Orlando Pirates *	2						
Black Leopards	1	**Orlando Pirates**	2				
Mamelodi Sundowns	0	Moroka Swallows *	1				
Moroka Swallows *	3			**Orlando Pirates**	3		
Ajax Cape Town *	1			Golden Arrows *	1		
Free State Stars	0	Ajax Cape Town *	1				
SuperSport United *	0	**Golden Arrows**	2				
Golden Arrows	1					**Orlando Pirates**	3
Santos *	1					Bidvest Wits	1
Maritzburg United	0	**Santos ***	1 4p				
Kaizer Chiefs	1	Platinum Stars	1 3p			CUP FINAL	
Platinum Stars *	2			Santos	0		
Jomo Cosmos *	3			**Bidvest Wits ***	3	Moses Mabhida, Durban	
Bloemfontein Celtic	0	Jomo Cosmos *	0			10-12-2011	
AmaZulu	0	**Bidvest Wits**	1				
Bidvest Wits *	1			* Home team			

NEDBANK FA CUP 2010–11

First Round

Team	Score	
Orlando Pirates *	1	
Mamelodi Sundowns	0	
Future Tigers	0	
United FC *	3	
SuperSport United *	3	
Golden Arrows	1	
Ajax Cape Town	1	
Free State Stars *	2	
AmaZulu *	5	
Real Madrid FC	0	
Cullinan	0	
Carara Kicks *	7	
Witbank Spurs *	3	
Chippa United	2	
Hanover Park	2	
Mpumalanga Black Aces *	4	
Baroka *	2	
Mighty Mega Force	0	
Maritzburg United *	0	
Moroka Swallows	3	
Bidvest Wits *	1	
Santos	0	
Atlie *	2	
Kaizer Chiefs	3	
Vasco da Gama	3	
Amajuba United Killers *	2	
Bloemfontein Celtic *	0	
Platinum Stars	2	
BTX Liverpool *	1	5p
Blackburn Rovers	1	4p
Thanda Royal Zulu	1	
Black Leopards *	2	

Second Round

Team	Score
Orlando Pirates	3
United FC *	1
SuperSport United	0
Free State Stars *	1
AmaZulu *	2
Carara Kicks	0
Witbank Spurs	3
Mpumalanga Black Aces	4
Baroka *	2
Moroka Swallows	1
Bidvest Wits *	0
Kaizer Chiefs	4
Vasco da Gama	2
Platinum Stars *	0
BTX Liverpool *	1
Black Leopards	3

Quarter-finals

Team	Score
Orlando Pirates *	1
Free State Stars	0
AmaZulu *	2
Mpumalanga Black Aces	3
Baroka *	2
Kaizer Chiefs	1
Vasco da Gama	2
Black Leopards *	3

Semi-finals

Team	Score	
Orlando Pirates *		
Mpumalanga Black Aces		
Baroka *	2	1p
Black Leopards	2	3p

Final

Team	Score
Orlando Pirates	3
Black Leopards ‡	1

CUP FINAL

Mombela, Nelspruit
28-05-2011, 15:00, Ref: Harry Lekitlane
Scorers – Chansa [72], Mbuyane 2 [75,89] for Pirates; Mahamutsa OG [54] for Leopards
Pirates - Senzo Meyiwa - Happy Jele, Robyn Johannes, Rooi Mahamutsa, Lucky Lekgwathi (c) - Andile Jali, Oupa Manyisa - Thulasizwe Mbuyane, Isaac Chansa, Tlou Segolela (Clifford Ngobeni 88) - Bongani Ndulula (Mark Mayambela 62). Tr: Ruud Krol
Leopards - Azwindini Maphaha - Moses Kwena ◆87, Simphiwe Vezi, Vincent Mabusela, Edward Ishabalala - Samuel Mabunda (Diala Manaka 79), Raymond Monama (Grant Lungu 88) - Mongezi Bobe (c), Robert Ng'ambi, Khethokwakhe Masiku (Mahlatse Maake 82) - Rodney Ramagalela. Tr: Sunday Chidzambwa

‡ Qualified for the CAF Confederation Cup

* Home team • † played in Olen Park, Potchefstroom • †† played in King's Park, Durban

RUS – RUSSIA

FIFA/COCA-COLA WORLD RANKING

'93	'94	'95	'96	'97	'98	'99	'00	'01	'02	'03	'04	'05	'06	'07	'08	'09	'10	'11	'12
14	13	5	7	12	40	18	21	21	23	24	32	34	22	23	9	12	13	12	

						2011							High	Low	Av
Jan	Feb	Mar	Apr	May	Jun	Jul	Aug	Sep	Oct	Nov	Dec				
13	12	13	18	18	16	17	13	13	13	12	12		3	40	19

Russian football underwent an upheaval in 2011 with a change in the season to run from summer to spring so that clubs could be more competitive in European competition at the start of the year. However, with the long and harsh winters there is little room for manoeuvre in the scheduling as clubs can ill afford to lie idle in the summer months. The decision meant that there was to be a marathon 15-month season running from March 2011 during which three rounds of fixtures would be played with the clubs splitting into championship and relegation groups at the end of 2011. Zenit led the table at the end of the year as their impressive form under coach Luciano Spalletti continued but it was Anzhi Makhachkala who were the subject of headlines around the world. Located on the western shore of the Caspian Sea in the Republic of Dagestan, just to the north of Azerbaijan, Anzhi were bought by Russian billionaire Suleyman Kerimov in January 2011. Flooded with new signings such as Samuel Eto'o, Roberto Carlos and at the start of 2012 with Guus Hiddink as coach, Anzhi just made it into the championship group. In the run up to the 2018 FIFA World Cup Russian club football is likely to change beyond recognition and Kerimov may well be just the first of the oligarchs who decide to spend their money at home rather than abroad.

UEFA EUROPEAN CHAMPIONSHIP RECORD

1960 1 winners **1964** 2 F **1968** 4 SF **1972** 2 F **1976-1984** DNQ **1988** 2 F (as the Soviet Union) **1992** 8 r1 (as the CIS) **1996** 14 r1 **2000** DNQ **2004** 10 r1 **2008** 3 SF **2012** Qualified

FOOTBALL UNION OF RUSSIA (RFU)

House of Football,
Ulitsa Narodnaya 7,
Moscow 115 172
☎ +7 495 9261300
📠 +7 501 9261305
📧 info@rfs.ru
🖥 www.rfs.ru
FA 1912 CON 1992 FIFA 1992
P Sergey Fursenko
GS TBD

FIFA BIG COUNT 2006

Total players	5 802 536
% of population	4.06%
Male	5 105 014
Female	697 522
Amateurs 18+	582 383
Youth under 18	196 170
Unregistered	1 443 800
Professionals	3 724
Referees	36 530
Admin & coaches	223 300
Number of clubs	13 840
Number of teams	55 350

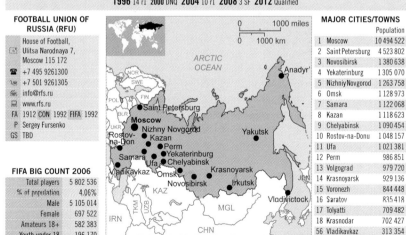

MAJOR CITIES/TOWNS

		Population
1	Moscow	10 494 522
2	Saint Petersburg	4 523 802
3	Novosibirsk	1 380 638
4	Yekaterinburg	1 305 070
5	Nizhniy Novgorod	1 263 758
6	Omsk	1 128 973
7	Samara	1 122 068
8	Kazan	1 118 623
9	Chelyabinsk	1 090 454
10	Rostov-na-Donu	1 048 157
11	Ufa	1 021 381
12	Perm	986 851
13	Volgograd	979 720
14	Krasnoyarsk	929 136
15	Voronezh	844 448
16	Saratov	835 418
17	Tolyatti	709 482
18	Krasnodar	702 427
56	Vladikavkaz	313 354

ROSSIYSKAYA FEDERATSIYA • RUSSIAN FEDERATION

Capital	Moscow	Population	140 041 247 (9)	% in cities	73%
GDP per capita	$16 100 (71)	Area km²	17 098 242 km² (1)	GMT +/-	+2 to +12

Neighbours (km): Azerbaijan 284, Belarus 959, China 3645, Estonia 290, Finland 1313, Georgia 723, Kazakhstan 6846, Korea DPR 17, Latvia 292, Lithuania 227, Mongolia 3441, Norway 196, Poland 432, Ukraine 1576 • Coast 37 653

RECENT INTERNATIONAL MATCHES PLAYED BY RUSSIA

2008	Opponents	Score		Venue	Comp	Scorers	Att	Referee
10-06	Spain	L	1-4	Innsbruck	ECr1	Pavlyuchenko [86]	30 772	Plautz AUT
14-06	Greece	W	1-0	Salzburg	ECr1	Zyryanov [33]	31 063	Rosetti ITA
18-06	Sweden	W	2-0	Innsbruck	ECr1	Pavlyuchenko [24], Arshavin [50]	30 772	De Bleeckere BEL
21-06	Netherlands	W	3-1	Basel	ECqf	Pavlyuchenko [56], Torbinski [112], Arshavin [116]	38 374	Michel SVK
26-06	Spain	L	0-3	Vienna	ECsf		51 428	De Bleeckere BEL
20-08	Netherlands	D	1-1	Moscow	Fr	Zyryanov [78p]	25 000	Frojdfeldt SWE
10-09	Wales	W	2-1	Moscow	WCq	Pavlyuchenko [22p], Pogrebnyak [81]	28 000	Skomina SVN
11-10	Germany	L	1-2	Dortmund	WCq	Arshavin [51]	65 607	Frojdfeldt SWE
15-10	Finland	W	3-0	Moscow	WCq	Pasanen OG [23], Lampi OG [65], Arshavin [88]	28 000	Vassaras GRE
2009								
28-03	Azerbaijan	W	2-0	Moscow	WCq	Pavlyuchenko [32], Zyrianov [71]	62 000	Gumienny BEL
1-04	Liechtenstein	W	1-0	Vaduz	WCq	Zyrianov [38]	5 679	McKeon IRL
10-06	Finland	W	3-0	Helsinki	WCq	Kerzhakov 2 [27 53]	37 028	Plautz AUT
12-08	Argentina	L	2-3	Moscow	Fr	Semshov [17], Pavlyuchenko [78]	28 800	De Bleeckere BEL
5-09	Liechtenstein	W	3-0	St Petersburg	WCq	Berezutsky.V [17], Pavlyuchenko 2 [40p 45p]	21 000	Constantin ROU
9-09	Wales	W	3-1	Cardiff	WCq	Semshov [36], Ignashevich [71], Pavlyuchenko [91+]	14 505	De Sousa POR
10-10	Germany	L	0-1	Moscow	WCq		72 100	Busacca SUI
14-10	Azerbaijan	D	1-1	Baku	WCq	Arshavin [13]	17 000	Webb ENG
14-11	Slovenia	W	2-1	Moscow	WCpo	Bilyaletdinov 2 [40 52]	71 600	Larsen DEN
18-11	Slovenia	L	0-1	Maribor	WCpo		12 510	Hauge NOR
2010								
3-03	Hungary	D	1-1	Gyor	Fr	Bilyaletdinov [59]	10 000	Vucemilovic CRO
11-08	Bulgaria	W	1-0	St Petersburg	Fr	Shirokov [6]	8 200	Rizzoli ITA
3-09	Andorra	W	2-0	Andorra La Vella	ECq	Pogrebnyak 2 [14 64p]	1 100	Borg MLT
7-09	Slovakia	L	0-1	Moscow	ECq		27 052	De Bleeckere BEL
8-10	Republic of Ireland	W	3-2	Dublin	ECq	Kerzakhov [11], Dzagoev [29], Shirokov [50]	50 411	Blom NED
12-10	Macedonia FYR	W	1-0	Skopje	ECq	Kerzhakov [8]	10 500	Johannesson SWE
17-11	Belgium	L	0-2	Voronezh	Fr		31 743	Kaasik EST
2011								
9-02	Iran	L	0-1	Abu Dhabi	Fr		5 000	Albadwawi UAE
26-03	Armenia	D	0-0	Yerevan	ECq		14 800	Thomson SCO
29-03	Qatar	D	1-1	Doha	Fr	Pavlyuchenko [34]	9 000	Al Awaji KSA
4-06	Armenia	W	3-1	St Petersburg	ECq	Pavlyuchenko 3 [26 59 73p]	18 000	Lannoy FRA
7-06	Cameroon	D	0-0	Salzburg	Fr		3 000	Einwaller AUT
10-08	Serbia	W	1-0	Moscow	Fr	Pogrebnyak [53]	27 000	Hategan ROU
2-09	FYR Macedonia	W	1-0	Moscow	ECq	Semshov [41]	31 028	Yildirim TUR
6-09	Republic of Ireland	D	0-0	Moscow	ECq		49 515	Brych GER
7-10	Slovakia	W	1-0	Zilina	ECq	Dzagoev [71]	10 087	Eriksson SWE
11-10	Andorra	W	6-0	Moscow	ECq	Dzagoev 2 [5 44], Ignashevich [26], Pavlyuchenko [30], Glushakov [59], Bilyaletdinov [78]	38 790	Hacmon ISR
11-11	Greece	D	1-1	Piraeus	Fr	Shirokov [2]		Chapron FRA

Fr = Friendly match • EC = UEFA EURO 2008/2012 • WC = FIFA World Cup • q = qualifier
r1 = first round group • qf = quarter-final • sf = semi-final

RUSSIA NATIONAL TEAM HISTORICAL RECORDS

Caps
109 - Viktor Onopko 1992-2004 • **72** - Valeri Karpin 1992-2003 • **71** - Vladimir Beschastnykh 1992-2003 & Sergei Ignashevich 2002- • **67** - Andrei Arshavin 2002- • **65** - Sergei Semak 1997- • **62** - Aleksandr Anyukov 2004- • **60** - Vasili Berezutskiy 2003- • **57** - Aleksandr Kerzhakov 2002- • **56** - Igor Semshov 2002- • **55** - Dmitri Alenichev 1996-2005, Yuri Nikiforov 1993-2002 & Alexey Smertin 1998-2006

Goals
26 - Vladimir Beschastnykh 1992-2003 • **17** - Valeri Karpin 1992-2003 & Aleksandr Kerzhakov 2002- • **16** - Andrei Arshavin 2002- • **15** - Roman Pavlyuchenko 2003- & Dmitri Sychev 2002- • **12** - Igor Kolyvanov 1992-98 • **10** - Sergei Kiryakov 1992-98 & Aleksandr Mostovoi 1992-2004 • **9** - Igor Simutenkov 1994-98 & Dmitriy Bulykin

Past Coaches
Pavel Sadyrin 1992-94 • Oleg Romantsev 1994-96 • Boris Ignatyev 1996-98 • Anatoli Byshovets 1998 • Oleg Romantsev 1999-2002 • Valeri Gazzaev 2002-03 • Georgi Yartsev 2003-05 • Yuri Semin 2005 • Aleksandr Borodyuk 2006 • Guus Hiddink 2006-10 • Dick Advocaat 2010-

RUSSIA 2011–12

PREMIER LEAGUE

	Pl	W	D	L	F	A	Pts	Zenit	CSKA	Dinamo	Spartak M	Lokomotiv	Kuban	Rubin	Anzhi	Krasnodar	Rostov	Terek	Volga	Amkar	Krylya	Spartak N	Tom
Zenit St Petersburg	30	17	10	3	59	25	61		0-3	0-0	3-0	1-1	1-0	2-2	2-0	5-0	4-0	0-0	3-0	1-1	3-0	1-0	4-0
CSKA Moskva	30	16	11	3	58	29	59	0-2		0-4	0-1	3-1	1-1	2-0	3-0	1-1	2-1	2-2	3-1	2-0	2-1	4-0	3-0
Dinamo Moskva	30	16	7	7	51	30	55	1-1	2-2		1-1	4-1	1-0	0-2	2-2	2-1	3-1	6-2	2-0	3-0	1-0	2-0	3-0
Spartak Moskva	30	15	8	7	48	33	53	2-2	2-2	0-2		3-0	1-1	0-0	3-0	4-0	3-2	0-0	1-0	1-2	3-0	1-0	4-0
Lokomotiv Moskva	30	15	8	7	49	30	53	4-2	1-1	3-2	0-2		2-1	1-1	1-2	1-0	1-1	4-0	1-0	4-0	0-0	3-1	3-0
Kuban Krasnodar	30	14	7	9	38	27	49	1-1	0-0	3-1	3-1	0-1		0-2	1-0	0-1	2-0	2-1	5-0	3-2	1-1	1-1	1-3
Rubin Kazan	30	13	10	7	40	27	49	2-3	1-1	3-0	3-0	0-0	0-2		0-3	2-1	1-1	2-0	2-0	1-1	1-0	0-0	4-1
Anzhi Makhachkala	30	13	9	8	38	32	48	0-1	3-5	2-1	2-1	0-1	0-0	1-0		0-0	1-0	2-2	2-1	2-1	3-1	2-0	2-0
FK Krasnodar	30	10	8	12	38	43	38	0-0	1-1	0-1	2-4	1-4	0-2	3-1	2-2		2-0	0-2	4-2	1-0	1-2	2-0	2-2
FK Rostov	30	8	8	14	31	45	32	1-3	1-1	0-2	4-0	0-3	1-2	1-3	1-1	1-3		1-0	1-3	3-0	1-0	0-0	2-1
Terek Groznyi	30	8	7	15	29	45	31	0-1	2-4	0-0	2-4	0-4	1-2	0-1	1-0	2-0	1-1		1-0	1-0	2-0	0-1	2-0
Volga Nizhniy Novgorod	30	8	4	18	24	40	28	0-2	0-2	3-0	0-2	0-0	0-1	1-0	1-2	0-2	0-1	3-1		0-0	2-0	1-0	0-2
Amkar Perm	30	6	9	15	20	39	27	1-3	0-2	0-0	1-0	1-0	3-1	1-1	0-0	0-2	0-1	1-0	1-0		1-1	1-0	1-2
Krylya Sovetov Samara	30	6	9	15	21	43	27	2-5	0-3	1-0	0-1	1-0	1-0	2-2	0-3	0-0	2-2	2-1	0-0	1-1		0-2	2-0
Spartak Nalchik	30	5	9	16	23	40	24	2-2	0-2	2-3	1-1	1-2	0-1	0-1	1-1	2-2	0-1	2-2	1-1	2-1	1-0		1-2
Tom Tomsk	30	4	8	18	19	58	20	2-1	1-1	0-2	1-1	2-2	0-1	0-2	0-0	0-4	1-1	0-1	0-3	0-0	1-1	0-2	

12/03/2011 - 6/11/2011 • Match in bold awarded • The 2011-12 Russian Premier League season is to be played over 18 months in order to realign the Russian season with most of the rest of Europe. After 38 rounds the top eight teams in bold split to play for the championship with the rest playing in a relegation group to be played from 18/11/2011 - 12/05/2012

RUSSIA 2011–12

FIRST DIVISION (2)

	Pl	W	D	L	F	A	Pts	Alania	Mordovia	Shinnik	N Novgorod	SIBIR	Dinamo Bry	Torpedo M	Ural	KamAZ	Yenisey	Khimki	Volgar	SKA-Energiya	Torpedo V	Luch-Energiya	Chernomorets	Baltika	Gazovik	Fakel	Zhemchuzhina
Alania Vladikavkaz	38	21	10	7	50	24	73		4-0	0-1	1-0	1-1	2-1	1-3	1-0	2-0	4-0	1-1	2-0	3-1	1-0	1-0	1-1	2-0	0-0	1-0	3-0
Mordovia Saransk	38	21	10	7	64	44	73	1-2		0-0	3-1	1-0	3-2	2-0	4-2	1-0	2-3	2-1	3-4	2-1	4-0	1-1	2-1	3-1	3-1	3-2	2-1
Shinnik Yaroslavl	38	21	6	11	61	42	69	2-2	0-1		4-1	3-3	5-0	0-4	1-2	3-2	2-0	4-1	3-0	1-2	2-0	0-0	1-0	0-3	2-1	1-0	3-0
FC Nizhniy Novgorod	38	21	5	12	53	40	68	0-3	1-1	3-2		2-1	0-1	1-0	1-5	1-2	0-1	2-0	2-1	2-0	2-0	4-1	1-0	1-0	2-1	3-1	3-0
SIBIR Novosibirsk	38	16	13	9	61	39	61	3-0	2-1	1-0	1-1		4-1	2-0	0-0	1-1	0-1	2-1	5-1	2-2	2-1	2-2	0-0	3-0	1-0	1-2	2-1
Dinamo Bryansk	38	17	9	12	48	40	60	1-0	4-1	0-1	3-2	1-1		0-3	0-0	1-0	2-1	4-2	0-0	2-0	2-1	1-1	0-2	0-1	1-0	1-0	1-0
Torpedo Moskva	38	16	12	10	50	30	60	0-0	1-1	1-0	0-1	1-1	1-0		0-1	2-3	1-0	0-2	2-1	1-1	0-0	2-1	1-1	0-0	4-0	1-1	2-0
Ural Yekaterinburg	38	15	15	8	51	35	60	0-0	0-0	0-2	2-0	3-2	0-0	2-1		2-3	0-0	5-2	0-0	2-0	3-2	1-1	1-0	3-0	1-1	1-1	1-3
KamAZ Chelny	38	17	8	13	48	36	59	2-0	1-2	1-2	0-2	1-1	1-0	3-2	0-1		2-0	1-1	1-0	0-0	3-0	2-0	3-1	0-0	1-3	3-1	1-0
Yenisey Krasnoyarsk	38	14	11	13	45	43	53	0-2	0-0	2-1	2-0	1-1	0-1	1-1	1-1		0-2	0-0	3-0	1-2	0-1	0-0	0-2	1-1	4-2		
FK Khimki	38	13	9	16	47	61	48	0-2	0-6	2-0	1-2	1-3	0-0	2-2	3-1	0-3	1-0		1-1	2-1	3-1	1-0	2-1	1-1	2-1	2-0	3-0
Volgar Astrakhan	38	12	11	15	36	49	47	3-0	0-1	1-1	0-3	1-0	1-5	0-0	0-3	0-2	1-0	1-0		2-0	3-1	0-0	2-2	2-2	1-3	2-0	3-0
SKA Khabarovsk	38	12	11	15	46	57	47	1-1	4-4	0-0	1-1	1-2	0-2	0-1	1-1	1-1	4-3	1-0	1-1		2-0	0-5	1-0	1-1	2-1	1-0	3-1
Torpedo Vladimir	38	12	7	19	45	61	43	0-3	1-2	1-2	1-3	3-2	1-3	3-1	1-0	3-2	0-2	3-3	2-0	3-1		1-1	0-2	1-1	0-0	1-0	3-0
Luch Vladivostock	38	10	12	16	33	40	42	0-1	0-0	2-1	0-0	1-0	0-2	0-2	1-1	0-1	0-0	0-1	2-0	0-1		1-0	0-0	2	1	0	0 0 1
Ch'morets Novorossiysk	38	11	8	19	32	36	41	0-1	0-1	2-3	0-1	1-1	2-1	0-0	1-0	0-1	1-1	1-3	0-2	1-0	0-0	2		1-2	2-0	1-0	0-1
Baltika Kaliningrad	38	9	14	15	31	45	41	0-2	0-0	0-1	0-2	0-1	0-0	0-3	2-2	0-1	2-1	4-1	1-0	0-1	1-3	2-0	1-0		0-0	0-0	0-0
Gazovik Orenburg	38	8	14	16	40	48	38	1-0	1-1	1-2	0-2	2-1	0-0	1-1	0-1	0-0	3-4	1-2	1-3	2-3	1-1	0-0	2-1	1-1		2-1	0-2
Fakel Voronez	38	9	12	20	26	46	39	1-0	0-1	0-0	0-3	0-1	0-0	0-1	0-0	0-0	1-0	1-2	2-1	1-1	3-1	0-2	1-1			3-0	
Zhemchuzhina Sochi	38	8	2	28	22	81	26	0-1	0-3	2-3	1-0	0-3	2-4	0-3	0-3	0-3	1-0	1-0	0-3	2-1	0-3	0-3	0-3	0-3	0-0		

4/04/2011 - 7/11/2011 • The 2011-12 Russian First Division season is to be played over 18 months in order to realign the Russian season with most of the rest of Europe. After 38 rounds the top eight teams in bold split to play for the championship with the rest playing in a relegation group to be played from 11/03/2012 - 26/05/2012

KUBOK ROSSII 2010–11

Fourth Round

Team	Score
CSKA Moskva	Bye
FK Khimki	1 2p
Torpedo Moskva *	1 4p
Krylya Sovetov Samara	Bye
Torpedo Vladimir *	1
Shinnik Yaroslavl	3
Anzhi Makhachkala	Bye
Baltika Kaliningrad	1 2p
Pskov-747 Pskov *	1 4p
Dynamo St Petersburg	0 4p
FC Istra *	0 3p
Zenit St Petersburg	Bye
FK Krasnodar	1
Zhemchuzhina Sochi *	0
Tom Tomsk	Bye
Chernomorets Novorossiysk *	2
Kuban Krasnodar	1
Amkar Perm	Bye
SIBIR Novosibirsk	Bye
Zvezda Ryazan *	0
Avangard Kursk	2
Metallurg Lipetsk *	1
Dinamo Bryansk	0
Spartak Moskva	Bye
FK Rostov	Bye
Rotor Volgograd *	0
Salyut Belgorod	1
Rubin Kazan	Bye
Torpedo Armavir *	0 4p
Volgar Astrakhan	0 5p
Volga Nizhniy Novgorod	1 3p
FC Nizhniy Novgorod *	1 0p
Spartak Nalchik	Bye
Mordovia Saransk	3
Sokol Saratov *	0
Dinamo Moskva	Bye
Saturn Ramenskoe	Bye
SKA Khabarovsk	1 2p
Sakhalin Yuzhno-Sakhalinsk *	1 3p
Terek Groznyi	Bye
Radian-Baikal Irkutsk	0 2p
Luch Vladivostock	0 3p
Gornyal Uchaly *	3
Ural Yekaterinburg	2
Lokomotiv Moskva	Bye
KamAZ Chelny	2
Irtysh Omsk *	0
Alania Vladikavkaz	Bye

Fifth Round

Team	Score
CSKA Moskva	2
Torpedo Moskva *	0
Krylya Sovetov Samara	1
Shinnik Yaroslavl *	2
Anzhi Makhachkala	2
Pskov-747 Pskov *	1
Dynamo St Petersburg *	1
Zenit St Petersburg	3
FK Krasnodar *	2
Tom Tomsk	1
Chernomorets Novorossiysk *	0
Amkar Perm	1
SIBIR Novosibirsk	5
Avangard Kursk *	2
Metallurg Lipetsk *	0
Spartak Moskva	1
FK Rostov	4
Salyut Belgorod *	0
Rubin Kazan	0
Volgar Astrakhan *	1
Volga Nizhniy Novgorod *	5
Spartak Nalchik	0
Mordovia Saransk *	1
Dinamo Moskva	2
Saturn Ramenskoe	1 4p
Sakhalin Yuzhno-Sakhalinsk *	1 3p
Terek Groznyi	0
Luch Vladivostock *	4
Gornyal Uchaly *	1
Lokomotiv Moskva	0
KamAZ Chelny *	0 2p
Alania Vladikavkaz	0 4p

Sixth Round

Team	Score
CSKA Moskva *	1
Shinnik Yaroslavl	0
Anzhi Makhachkala *	2
Zenit St Petersburg	3
FK Krasnodar	1
Amkar Perm *	0
SIBIR Novosibirsk *	0
Spartak Moskva	2
FK Rostov *	2
Volgar Astrakhan	0
Volga Nizhniy Novgorod	1
Dinamo Moskva *	4
Saturn Ramenskoe *	2
Luch Vladivostock	1
Gornyal Uchaly	0 4p
Alania Vladikavkaz *	0 5p

The 16 Premier League teams enter in the fifth round and are drawn away to the 16 qualifiers

KUBOK ROSSII 2010–11

Quarter-finals	Semi-finals	Final

CSKA Moskva 2
Zenit St Petersburg * 0

CSKA Moskva 3 5p
Spartak Moskva * 3 4p

FK Krasnodar 1
Spartak Moskva * 2

CSKA Moskva 2
Alania Vladikavkaz ‡ 1

FK Rostov 2
Dinamo Moskva * 1

FK Rostov * 0 5p
Alania Vladikavkaz 0 6p

Saturn Ramenskoe
Alania Vladikavkaz w-o

KUBOK ROSSI FINAL 2011

Shinnik Stadium, Yaroslavl, 22-05-2011, 19:00, Att: 10 800, Ref: Cladislav Bezborodov

CSKA Moskva 2 Seydou Doumbia 2 [13 69]
Alania Vladikavkaz 1 Neco [23]

CSKA - Igor Akinfeev (c) - Sergei Ignashevich•, Aleksei Berezutski, Kirill Nababkin, Vasili Berezutski - Alan Dzagoev (Keisuke Honda 65), Pavel Mamayev (Tomas Necid 89), Zoran Tosic (Deividas Semberas 83), Evgeni Aldonin•, Seydou Doumbia - Vagner Love. Tr: Leonid Slutsky

Alania - Dmitri Khomich - Ibrahim Gnanou•, Simeon Bulgaru•, Anton Grigoryev•, Dmitri Grachyov• - Roland Gigolayev• (Georgy Gogichayev 71), Jambulad Bazayev• (Atsamaz Burayev 46), Dacosta Goore (Taras Tsarikayev 20), Aslan Dudiyev, Marat Bikmaev - Danilo Neco. Tr: Vladimir Gazzayev

* Home team • ‡ Qualified for the Europa League

RWA – RWANDA

FIFA/COCA-COLA WORLD RANKING

'93	'94	'95	'96	'97	'98	'99	'00	'01	'02	'03	'04	'05	'06	'07	'08	'09	'10	'11	'12
-	-	168	159	172	107	146	128	144	130	109	99	89	121	99	78	102	132	106	

2011												High	Low	Av
Jan	Feb	Mar	Apr	May	Jun	Jul	Aug	Sep	Oct	Nov	Dec			
134	135	133	123	122	134	134	138	143	112	114	106	78	178	127

Rwanda ended 2011 in some style by qualifying for the group stage of the 2014 FIFA World Cup and then reaching the final of the East and Central African Senior Challenge Cup. The double success at the end of the year made up for a disappointing campaign in the 2012 CAF Africa Cup of Nations qualifiers where they finished way behind runaway group winners Cote d'Ivoire. Coach Sellas Tetteh resigned after a 5-0 home defeat to the Ivorians in September and was replaced by the well-travelled Serbian Milutin Sredojevich. On his watch Rwanda beat Eritrea 4-2 on aggregate in November in a preliminary round of World Cup qualifying, and then leading the team to the final of the East and Central African Senior Challenge Cup in Dar es Salaam where they were desperately unlucky not to win the title for the first time since 1999. After a 2-2 draw against Uganda, the Rwandans lost 3-2 on penalties to finish as runners-up for the fourth time in eight years. Rwanda hosted the African U-17 Championships in the capital Kigali and Gisenyi at the start of 2011 and by finishing runners-up to Burkina Faso qualified for the FIFA U-17 World Cup in Mexico in mid-year. Coached by the Frenchman Richard Tardy, Rwanda lost to England and Uruguay but won a consolation point against Canada in their last game at the finals in Mexico.

CAF AFRICA CUP OF NATIONS RECORD

1957-1980 DNE   1982-1984 DNQ   1986-1998 DNE   2000-2002 DNQ   **2004** 9 r1   2006-2012 DNQ

FEDERATION RWANDAISE DE FOOTBALL (FERWAFA)

✉ Boite Postale 2000, Kigali

☎ +250 518525
📠 +250 518523
✉ ferwafa@yahoo.fr
🖥 www.ferwafa.rw
FA 1972 CON 1976 FIFA 1978
P Celestin Ntagungira
GS Michel Gasingwa

FIFA BIG COUNT 2006

Total players	386 400
% of population	4.47%
Male	386 400
Female	0
Amateurs 18+	4 400
Youth under 18	6 500
Unregistered	27 500
Professionals	0
Referees	500
Admin & coaches	1 500
Number of clubs	110
Number of teams	550

MAJOR CITIES/TOWNS

		Population
1	Kigali	965 398
2	Ruhengeri	110 717
3	Gisenyi	106 335
4	Butare	103 312
5	Gitarama	88 031
6	Byumba	74 143
7	Ruhango	70 086
8	Cyangugu	68 031
9	Kabuga	56 973
10	Nyanza	55 806
11	Rwamagana	52 599
12	Kibungo	48 564
13	Kibuye	48 097
14	Gikongoro	34 757
15	Umutara	8 918
16	Nyagatare	3 759

REPUBLIKA Y'U RWANDA • REPUBLIC OF RWANDA

Capital Kigali	Population 10 473 282 (77)	% in cities 18%
GDP per capita $900 (218)	Area km² 26 338 km² (148)	GMT +/- +2
Neighbours (km) Burundi 290, Congo DR 217, Tanzania 217, Uganda 169		

RECENT INTERNATIONAL MATCHES PLAYED BY RWANDA

2008	Opponents	Score		Venue	Comp	Scorers	Att	Referee
6-02	Burundi	D	0-0	Bujumbura	Fr			
31-05	Mauritania	W	3-0	Kigali	WCq	Karekezi [15], Abedi Said [67p], Bokota [72]	12 000	Doue CIV
8-06	Ethiopia	W	2-1	Addis Abeba	WCq	Abedi Said [59], Karekezi [82]	18 000	Ndinya KEN
14-06	Morocco	W	3-1	Kigali	WCq	Abedi Said [15], Bokota [68], Karekezi [93+]	12 000	Evehe CMR
21-06	Morocco	L	0-2	Casablanca	WCq		2 500	Benouza ALG
6-09	Mauritania	W	1-0	Nouakchott	WCq	Bobo [79]	1 000	Bennaceur TUN
19-11	Togo	L	0-1	Lomé	Fr			
2009								
1-01	Uganda	L	0-4	Kampala	CCr1			
5-01	Somalia	W	3-0	Kampala	CCr1	Gasana 2 [20 40], Labama [86]		
7-01	Tanzania	L	0-2	Kampala	CCr1			
9-01	Zanzibar †	W	3-0	Kampala	CCr1	Lomami [12], Mabula [17], Gasana [39]		
28-03	Algeria	D	0-0	Kigali	WCq		22 000	Codjia BEN
30-05	Malawi	L	0-2	Blantyre	Fr			
6-06	Zambia	L	0-1	Chililabombwe	WCq		28 000	Seck SEN
5-07	Egypt	L	0-3	Cairo	WCq		18 000	Imiere NGA
12-08	Tanzania	L	1-2	Kigali	Fr	Mwiseneza [68]		
5-09	Egypt	L	0-1	Kigali	WCq		20 000	Lamptey GHA
11-10	Algeria	L	1-3	Blida	WCq	Mutesa [19]	22 000	Keita GUI
14-11	Zambia	D	0-0	Kigali	WCq		18 000	Ambaya LBY
29-11	Somalia	W	1-0	Nairobi	CCr1	Mwalimu OG [4]		
3-12	Eritrea	W	2-1	Nairobi	CCr1	Ndayishimiye [20], Wolday OG [45]		
5-12	Zimbabwe †	W	1-0	Nairobi	CCr1	Ndayishimiye [20]		
8-12	Zimbabwe †	W	4-1	Nairobi	CCqf	Ndayishimiye [30], Ndamuhanga 2 [67 76], Niyonzima [90]		
10-12	Tanzania	W	2-1	Nairobi	CCsf	Ndayishimiye [68], Mafisango [77]		
13-12	Uganda	L	0-2	Nairobi	CCf			
2010								
7-01	Côte d'Ivoire	L	0-2	Dar es Salaam	Fr			
4-09	Côte d'Ivoire	L	0-3	Abidjan	CNq			Maillet SEY
9-10	Benin	L	0-3	Kigali	CNq			Haimoudi ALG
17-11	Malawi	L	1-2	Blantyre	Fr	Birori [8]		
1-12	Sudan	D	0-0	Dar es Salaam	CCr1			
3-12	Zanzibar	D	0-0	Dar es Salaam	CCr1			
8-12	Tanzania	L	0-1	Dar es Salaam	CCqf			
2011								
26-03	Burundi	W	3-1	Kigali	CNq	Jean-Claude Iranzi [34], Elias Uzamukunda 45p, Eric Gasana [88]		
5-06	Burundi	L	1-3	Bujumbura	CNq	Labama Kamana [48]		
3-09	Côte d'Ivoire	L	0-5	Kigali	CNq			
9-10	Benin	W	1-0	Cotonou	CNq	Medie Kagere [6]		
11-11	Eritrea	D	1-1	Asmara	WCq	Elias Uzamukunda [58]	6 000	Keita MLI
15-11	Eritrea	W	3-1	Kigali	WCq	Olivier Karekezi [4], Jean-Claude Iranzi [70], Labama Kamana [79]	10 000	Bondo BOT
26-11	Tanzania	W	1-0	Dar es Salaam	CCr1	Olivier Karekezi [22]		
29-11	Zimbabwe	W	2-0	Dar es Salaam	CCr1	Medie Kagere 2 [24 82]		
2-12	Djibouti	W	5-2	Dar es Salaam	CCr1	Labama Kamana [3], Jean-Baptiste Mugiraneza [57], Olivier Karekezi 3 [78 80 86]		
5-12	Zanzibar †	W	2-1	Dar es Salaam	CCqf	Jean-Baptiste Mugiraneza [39], Medie Kagere [88]		
8-12	Sudan	W	2-1	Dar es Salaam	CCsf	Jean-Claude Iranzi [6], Olivier Karekezi [78]		
10-12	Uganda	D	2-2	Dar es Salaam	CCf	Medie Kagere 2 [51 79], L 2-3p		

Fr = Friendly match • CN = CAF African Cup of Nations • CC = CECAFA Cup • WC = FIFA World Cup
q = qualifier • r1 = first round group • sf = semi-final • f = final • † Not a full international

RWANDA NATIONAL TEAM HISTORICAL RECORDS

Past Coaches
Rudi Gutendorf GER 1999-2000 • Ratomir Dujkovic SRB 2001-04 • Roger Palmgren SWE 2004-05 • Michael Nees GER 2006-07 • Josip Kuze CRO 2007-08 • Raul Shungu COD 2008 • Branco Tucak CRO 2008-09 • Eric Nhsimiyimana 2009-10 • Sellas Tetteh GHA 2010-11 • Milutin Sredojevic 2011-

RWANDA 2010–11

PRIMUS NATIONAL SOCCER LEAGUE PREMIER DIVISION

	Pl	W	D	L	F	A	Pts	APR	Kiyovu	Police	Etincelles	Jeunesse	Rayon	AS Kigali	Marines	Mukura	Amagaju	Muhanga	Musanze
APR FC †	22	19	2	1	46	9	59		2-1	4-0	3-0	1-1	1-1	0-1	1-0	1-0	3-0	1-0	4-0
Kiyovu Sport ‡	22	12	5	5	32	16	41	1-2		0-2	1-0	1-1	2-0	2-0	4-1	2-0	1-0	2-0	
Police FC Kibungo	22	10	6	6	38	25	36	0-3	0-1		7-1	2-2	1-1	2-2	4-1	1-0	2-0	3-0	5-1
Etincelles Gisenyi	22	8	6	8	26	31	30	0-2	1-1	0-0		2-2	2-0	1-0	3-1	0-1	1-0	1-2	2-0
La Jeunesse	22	6	11	5	22	24	29	0-2	1-1	2-1	0-0		0-0	1-1	1-1	1-0	1-1	1-0	1-3
Rayon Sport	22	7	7	8	25	26	28	2-3	1-2	1-2	3-3	2-1		0-0	3-2	2-1	0-1	1-1	1-0
AS Kigali	22	6	10	6	17	18	28	0-2	1-0	0-0	2-1	0-1	1-0		2-2	3-1	0-1	0-0	0-0
Marines FC Gisenyi	22	6	6	10	28	31	24	2-4	1-1	1-1	2-0	0-2	2-1	0-0		5-0	1-2	2-0	2-0
Mukura Victory	22	7	2	13	18	29	23	0-1	0-2	2-1	0-1	4-1	0-0	1-2	2-1		1-0	1-0	0-1
Amagaju Nyamagabe	22	6	4	12	13	24	22	0-1	2-1	0-1	1-2	0-1	1-2	1-1	0-1	1-0		0-0	1-1
Muhanga Gitarama	22	5	5	12	14	29	20	0-4	0-3	1-2	2-2	1-0	0-1	2-1	2-1	1-1	0-1		1-2
Musanze	22	5	6	11	15	32	18	0-1	1-1	2-1	1-3	1-1	0-3	0-0	0-0	0-2	2-0	0-1	

16/10/2010 - 21/06/2011 • † Qualified for the CAF Champions League • ‡ Qualified for the Confederation Cup

MEDALS TABLE

		Overall G	Lge G	Cup G	City
1	APR FC	22	12	10	Kigali
2	Rayon Sport	15	6	9	Kigali
3	Panthères Noires	9	5	4	Kigali
4	AS Kiyovu Sport	5	3	2	Kigali
5	Mukura Victory	4		4	Butare
6	ATRACO	2	1	1	Kigali
7	Mukungwa	2	2		Ruhengeri
8	Etincelles	1		1	Gisenyi
9	Les Citadins	1		1	Kigali
10	Rwanda FC	1		1	Kigali
		29	33		

COUPE AMAHORO 2011

Round of 16		Quarter-finals		Semi-finals		Final	
APR FC	9						
United Stars	0	**APR FC**	1				
La Jeunesse	0	Kiyovu Sport	0				
Kiyovu Sport	1			**APR FC**	4		
Marines FC Gisenyi	5			AS Kigali	0		
Interforce	1	Marines FC Gisenyi	0 9p				
Etincelles Gisenyi		**AS Kigali**	0 10p				
AS Kigali						**APR FC**	4
Mukura Victory	2					Police FC Kibungo	2
SEC Academy	1	**Mukura Victory**	1 5p				
ASPOR Kigali	1 3p	Muhanga Gitarama	1 4p				
Muhanga Gitarama	1 4p			Mukura Victory	1		
Rayon Sport	9			**Police FC Kibungo**	6		
Pépinière	0	Rayon Sport	2 4p				
Amagaju Nyamagabe	0	**Police FC Kibungo**	2 5p				
Police FC Kibungo	1						

* Home team in the 1st leg • 3rd place: **AS Kigali** 4-3p Mukura Victory

CUP FINAL

Amahoro, Kigali, 19-06-2011

Scorers - Ernest Kwizera 34, Jean-Baptiste Mugiraneza 2 86 95, Victor Nyirenda for APR; Kagere Meddie 16, Ibrahim Ndikumasabo for Police

SAM – SAMOA

FIFA/COCA-COLA WORLD RANKING

'93	'94	'95	'96	'97	'98	'99	'00	'01	'02	'03	'04	'05	'06	'07	'08	'09	'10	'11	'12
-	-	-	177	183	164	180	173	172	163	176	179	182	187	146	176	182	185	149	

2011												High	Low	Av
Jan	Feb	Mar	Apr	May	Jun	Jul	Aug	Sep	Oct	Nov	Dec	**High**	**Low**	**Av**
184	184	185	186	186	187	189	191	203	203	204	149	146	204	175

The decision by FIFA not to sanction the 2011 Pacific Games as the first round of qualifying in Oceania for the 2014 FIFA World Cup in Brazil, saw the Samoa football federation withdraw its teams from the tournament in Noumea, New Caledonia. This was despite the country sending a strong contingent from other sports which brought home 43 gold medals and it left the national team vulnerable when the preliminary round of World Cup qualifying did take place at the end of the year. Samoa hosted the four-team group in Apia but with all three of their opponents having taken part in the Pacific Games the Samoans were under-prepared and it was only thanks to two very late goals in their matches against the Cook Islands and American Samoa that they progressed to the next round. In their opening match against the Cook Islands, Albert Bell scored an injury-time winner and it took an 89th minute winner by Silao Malo against the history-making American Samoans in the final match to make certain of qualifying. In club football, the honours were reversed from the previous year with the 2010 champions Moaulu United winning the 2011 Cup and the 2010 Cup winners Kiwi winning the 2011 championship. The pair dominated the league scoring 163 goals between them and they also met in the Cup Final, which Moaule won 5-2.

FIFA WORLD CUP RECORD
1930-1994 DNE 1998-2010 DNQ

FOOTBALL FEDERATION
SAMOA (FFS)

PO Box 1682,
Apia

☎ +685 29993
✆ +685 27895
✉ tpetana@footballsamoa.ws
🖳 www.footballsamoa.ws
FA 1968 CON 1984 FIFA 1986
P Toetu Petana
GS Sarai Bareman

FIFA BIG COUNT 2006

Total players	5 700
% of population	3.22%
Male	5 400
Female	300
Amateurs 18+	1 100
Youth under 18	1 100
Unregistered	1 100
Professionals	0
Referees	100
Admin & coaches	300
Number of clubs	60
Number of teams	220

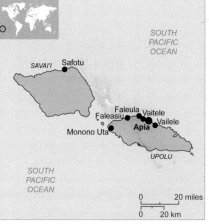

SAVAI'I — Safotu

Faleula — Vaitele
Faleasiu — Vaitele
Monono Uta — Apia

UPOLU

SOUTH PACIFIC OCEAN

0   20 miles
0   20 km

MAJOR CITIES/TOWNS

		Population
1	Apia	36 679
2	Vaitele	7 061
3	Faleasiu	3 780
4	Vailele	3 188
5	Leauvaa	3 145
6	Vaiusu	2 303
7	Faleula	2 197
8	Laulii	2 070
9	Malie	2 004
10	Siusega	1 951
11	Nofoalii	1 823
12	Afega	1 789
13	Fasitoouta	1 765
14	Solosolo	1 686
15	Fagalii	1 650
16	Nuu	1 504
17	Safotu	1 473
18	Manono Uta	1 420
19	Fasito Tai	1 371

MALO SA'OLOTO TUTO'ATASI O SAMOA • INDEPENDENT STATE OF SAMOA

Capital Apia	Population 219 998 (184)	% in cities 23%
GDP per capita $4700 (143)	Area km² 2831 km² (177)	GMT +/- -11
Neighbours (km) Coast 403		

RECENT INTERNATIONAL MATCHES PLAYED BY SAMOA

2004	Opponents	Score	Venue	Comp	Scorers	Att	Referee
5-05	Cook Islands	D 0-0	Auckland	Fr			
10-05	American Samoa	W 4-0	Apia	WCq	Bryce [12], Fasavalu 2 [30] [53], Michael [66]	500	Afu SOL
15-05	Vanuatu	L 0-3	Apia	WCq		650	Breeze AUS
17-05	Fiji	L 0-4	Apia	WCq		450	Diomis AUS
19-05	Papua New Guinea	L 1-4	Apia	WCq	Michael [69]	300	Diomis AUS
2005							
No international matches played in 2005							
2006							
No international matches played in 2006							
2007							
25-08	Vanuatu	L 0-4	Apia	WCq		300	Jacques TAH
27-08	America Samoa	W 7-0	Apia	WCq	Tumua 2 [24] [51], Faaiuaso [29], Cahill 2 [43p] [67], Fonotti [61], Michael [76]	2 800	Minan PNG
29-08	Tonga	W 2-1	Apia	WCq	Faaiuaso [45], Taylor [83]	1 850	Sosongan PNG
3-09	Solomon Islands	L 0-3	Apia	WCq		200	Hester NZL
2008							
No international matches played in 2008							
2009							
No international matches played in 2009							
2010							
No international matches played in 2010							
2011							
17-08	Fiji	L 0-3	Navua	Fr			
18-08	Fiji	L 1-5	Suva	Fr	Albert Bell [53]		
22-11	Cook Islands	W 3-2	Apia	WCq	Luki Gosche 2 [19] [36], Albert Bell [91+]	600	O'Leary NZL
24-11	Tonga	D 1-1	Apia	WCq	Shaun Easthope [43p]	180	Jacques TAH
26-11	American Samoa	W 1-0	Apia	WCq	Silao Malo [89]	800	O'Leary NZL

Fr = Friendly match • WC = FIFA World Cup • q = qualifier

SAMOA 2010–11

SFSF–NC NATIONAL LEAGUE

	Pl	W	D	L	F	A	Pts	Kiwi	Moaula Utd	Adidas	Vaivase-Tai	Central Utd	Moataa	Goldstar	Apia Youth	Lepea	Saints
Kiwi	18	15	3	0	61	13	48		3-1	3-2	1-1	5-1	2-0	3-0	4-2	5-0	5-1
Moaula United	18	14	1	3	102	40	43	0-2		4-7	9-2	3-0	5-3	2-2	5-1	7-4	15-2
Adidas	18	10	3	5	59	40	33	0-5	2-5		2-2	1-4	4-1	6-1	5-2	2-1	3-2
Vaivase-Tai	18	6	6	6	34	37	24	0-0	1-3	1-1		2-3	1-0	1-1	2-1	4-1	2-1
Central United	17	8	0	9	41	58	24	1-7	4-5	0-7	5-1		n/p	0-3	2-5	4-3	**3-0**
Moataa	16	7	1	8	41	40	22	1-4	2-3	1-3	2-0	1-4		3-1	4-2	5-2	n/p
Goldstar Sogi	18	6	4	8	39	38	22	0-2	1-4	1-1	1-0	3-4	1-2		4-0	2-2	7-2
Apia Youth	18	7	1	10	43	55	22	1-5	3-6	3-1	1-6	3-0	2-4	5-2		3-0	3-0
Lepea	18	2	1	15	36	77	7	1-4	0-10	4-7	2-5	7-2	3-9	1-2	1-2		4-1
Togafuafua Saints	17	1	4	12	26	84	7	1-1	1-15	0-5	3-3	2-4	3-3	0-7	4-4	3-0	

17/09/2010 - 4/03/2011 • † Qualified for OFC Champions League • Matches in bold awarded

SAMOA CUP FINAL 2011

Apia, 16-04-2011

Moaula United 5-2 Kiwi

SCO – SCOTLAND

FIFA/COCA-COLA WORLD RANKING

'93	'94	'95	'96	'97	'98	'99	'00	'01	'02	'03	'04	'05	'06	'07	'08	'09	'10	'11	'12
24	32	26	29	37	38	20	25	50	59	54	86	60	25	14	33	46	52	47	

2011													High	Low	Av
Jan	Feb	Mar	Apr	May	Jun	Jul	Aug	Sep	Oct	Nov	Dec				
52	53	50	66	66	61	61	55	52	51	49	47		13	88	39

Rangers completed their first hat-trick of league titles since the late 1990s after edging Celtic in an incredibly tight championship race. They finished just a point ahead of their fierce rivals after a season in which the sectarian tensions between the two clubs often bubbled to the surface - notably with the death threats received by Celtic boss Neil Lennon. Rangers also beat Celtic in the final of the League Cup and the two met in the fifth round of the Scottish Cup, Celtic winning a bad tempered replay in which Lennon and Rangers coach Ally McCoist squared up to each other at the end. Celtic went on the win the final 3-0 against Motherwell to give Lennon his first trophy as Celtic manager but it was a season that the football authorities will want to put behind them quickly. The image of Scottish football also took a massive knock at the start of the 2011-12 season when for the first time in over 50 years interest in European club competition was over before the end of August, although Celtic did receive a reprieve when their Europa League vanquishers were banned. There was worse to come for Rangers whose mountain of debt eventually saw them become one of the highest profile clubs to go into administration. The national team did little to relieve the gloom either, finishing third in their Euro 2012 qualifying group.

UEFA EUROPEAN CHAMPIONSHIP RECORD
1960-1964 DNE **1968-1988** DNQ **1992** r1 **1996** r1 **2000-2012** DNQ

THE SCOTTISH FOOTBALL ASSOCIATION (SFA)

Hampden Park,
Glasgow G42 9AY,
United Kingdom
☎ +44 141 6166000
📠 +44 141 6166001
✉ info@scottishfa.co.uk
🖥 www.scottishfa.co.uk
FA 1873 CON 1954 FIFA 1910
P Campbell Ogilvie
GS Stewart Regan

FIFA BIG COUNT 2006

Total players	420 589
% of population	8.31%
Male	374 075
Female	46 514
Amateurs 18+	39 234
Youth under 18	67 123
Unregistered	302 500
Professionals	4 132
Referees	2 097
Admin & coaches	8 500
Number of clubs	6 600
Number of teams	8 200

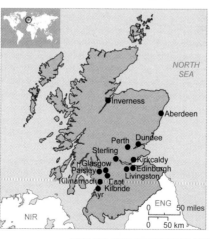

MAJOR CITIES/TOWNS

		Population
1	Glasgow	578 725
2	Edinburgh	449 058
3	Aberdeen	166 927
4	Dundee	141 616
5	East Kilbride	74 604
6	Paisley	71 730
7	Livingston	58 968
8	Cumbernauld	54 003
9	Dunfermline	51 456
10	Hamilton	47 979
11	Kirkcaldy	47 649
12	Ayr	45 899
13	Kilmarnock	45 163
14	Perth	44 201
15	Greenock	42 695
16	Coatbridge	41 454
17	Inverness	41 111
18	Glenrothes	38 862
19	Airdrie	35 309

SCOTLAND (PART OF THE UNITED KINGDOM)

Capital	Edinburgh	Population 5 057 400 (114)	% in cities 89%
GDP per capita	$39 680 (20)	Area km² 77 000 km² (117)	GMT +/- 0
Neighbours (km)	England 164 • Coast 9911		

RECENT INTERNATIONAL MATCHES PLAYED BY SCOTLAND

2007 Opponents	Score	Venue	Comp	Scorers	Att	Referee
8-09 Lithuania	W 3-1	Glasgow	ECq	Boyd [31], McManus [77], McFadden [85]	52 063	Skomina SVN
12-09 France	W 1-0	Paris	ECq	McFadden [64]	43 342	Plautz AUT
13-10 Ukraine	W 3-1	Glasgow	ECq	Miller.K [4], McCulloch [10], McFadden [68]	52 063	Vink NED
17-10 Georgia	L 0-2	Tbilisi	ECq		29 377	Kircher GER
17-11 Italy	L 1-2	Glasgow	ECq	Ferguson [65]	51 301	Mejuto Gonzalez ESP
2008						
26-03 Croatia	D 1-1	Glasgow	Fr	Miller.K [31]	28 821	Hauge NOR
30-05 Czech Republic	L 1-3	Prague	Fr	Clarkson [85]	11 314	Braamhaar NED
20-08 Northern Ireland	D 0-0	Glasgow	Fr		28 072	Vollquartz DEN
6-09 Macedonia FYR	L 0-1	Skopje	WCq		9 000	Kralovec CZE
10-09 Iceland	W 2-1	Reykjavik	WCq	Broadfoot [19], McFadden [59]	9 767	Gumienny BEL
11-10 Norway	D 0-0	Glasgow	WCq		50 205	Busacca SUI
19-11 Argentina	L 0-1	Glasgow	Fr		32 492	Brych GER
2009						
28-03 Netherlands	L 0-3	Amsterdam	WCq		50 000	Duhamel FRA
1-04 Iceland	W 2-1	Glasgow	WCq	McCormack [39], Fletcher.S [65]	42 259	Einwaller AUT
12-08 Norway	L 0-4	Oslo	WCq		24 493	Hamer LUX
5-09 Macedonia FYR	W 2-0	Glasgow	WCq	Brown [56], McFadden [80]	50 214	Stark GER
9-09 Netherlands	L 0-1	Glasgow	WCq		51 230	Larsen DEN
10-10 Japan	L 0-2	Yokohama	Fr		61 285	Kim KOR
14-11 Wales	L 0-3	Cardiff	Fr		13 844	Zimmermann SUI
2010						
3-03 Czech Republic	W 1-0	Glasgow	Fr	Brown [62]	26 530	Fautrel FRA
11-08 Sweden	L 0-3	Stockholm	Fr		25 249	Rocchi ITA
3-09 Lithuania	D 0-0	Kaunas	ECq		5 248	Cakir TUR
7-09 Liechtenstein	W 2-1	Glasgow	ECq	Miller.K [63], McManus [97+]	37 050	Shvetsov UKR
8-10 Czech Republic	L 0-1	Prague	ECq		14 922	Bebek CRO
12-10 Spain	L 2-3	Glasgow	ECq	Naismith.S [58], OG [66]	51 322	Busacca SUI
16-11 Faroe Islands	W 3-0	Aberdeen	Fr	Wilson [24], Commons [31], Mackie [45]	10 873	Van Boekel NED
2011						
9-02 Northern Ireland	W 3-0	Dublin	Fr	Miller [19], McArthur [32], Commons [51]	18 742	Connolly IRL
27-03 Brazil	L 0-2	London	Fr		53 087	Webb ENG
25-05 Wales	W 3-1	Dublin	Fr	Morrison [56], Miller.K [65], Berra [71]	6 036	Crangle NIR
29-05 Republic of Ireland	L 0-1	Dublin	Fr		17 694	Whitby WAL
10-08 Denmark	W 2-1	Glasgow	Fr	OG [22], Snodgrass [44]	17 582	Borg MLT
3-09 Czech Republic	D 2-2	Glasgow	ECq	Miller.K [45], Fletcher.D [82]	51 564	Blom NED
6-09 Lithuania	W 1-0	Glasgow	ECq	Naismith.S [50]	34 071	Jakobsson ISL
8-10 Liechtenstein	W 1-0	Vaduz	ECq	Mackail-Smith [32]	5 636	Hagen NOR
11-10 Spain	L 1-3	Alicante	ECq	Goodwillie [66p]	27 559	Johannesson SWE
11-11 Cyprus	W 2-1	Larnaca	Fr	Miller.K [23], Mackie [57]	2 000	Levi ISR

Fr = Friendly match • EC = UEFA EURO 2008/2012 • WC = FIFA World Cup • q = qualifier

SCOTLAND NATIONAL TEAM HISTORICAL RECORDS

Caps

102 - Kenny Dalglish 1971-86 • **91** - Jim Leighton 1982-98 • **77** - Alex McLeish 1980-93 • **76** - Paul McStay 1983-97 • **72** - Tom Boyd 1990-2001 • **69** - David Weir 1997-2010 • **67** - Christian Dailly 1997-2008 • **65** - Willie Miller 1975-89 • **62** - Danny McGrain 1973-82 • **61** - Richard Gough 1983-93 & Ally McCoist 1985-98 • **58** - John Collins 1988-2000 • **57** - Roy Aitken 1980-92 & Gary McAllister 1990-99 • **55** - Denis Law 1959-74 & Maurice Malpas 1984-93 • **54** - Billy Bremner 1965-76 & Graeme Souness 1976-86

Goals

30 - Kenny Dalglish 1971-86 & Denis Law 1959-74 • **23** - Hughie Gallacher 1924-35 • **22** - Lawrie Reilly 1948-57 • **19** - Ally McCoist 1985-98 • **16** - Kenny Miller 2001- • **15** - Robert Hamilton 1899-1911 & James McFadden 2002- • **14** - Mo Johnston 1984-91

Past Coaches

Committee 1872-54 • Andy Beattie 1954 • Committee 1954-58 • Dawson Walker 1958 • Matt Busby 1958 • Andy Beattie 1959-60 • Ian McColl 1960-65 • Jock Stein 1965-66 • John Prentice 1966 • Malcolm MacDonald 1966-67 • Bobby Brown 1967-71 • Tommy Docherty 1971-72 • Willie Ormond 1973-77 • Ally MacLeod 1977-78 • Jock Stein 1978-85 • Alex Ferguson 1985-86 • Andy Roxburgh 1986-93 • Craig Brown 1993-2002 • Berti Vogts GER 2002-04 • Tommy Burns 2004 • Walter Smith 2004-07 • Alex McLeish 2007 • George Burley 2008-09 • Craig Levein 2009-

SCOTLAND 2010-11

CLYDESDALE BANK PREMIER LEAGUE

	Pl	W	D	L	F	A	Pts	Rangers	Celtic	Hearts	Dundee Utd	Kilmarnock	Motherwell	Inverness CT	St Johnstone	Aberdeen	Hibernian	St Mirren	Hamilton
Rangers †	38	30	3	5	88	29	93		0-2 0-0	1-0 4-0	4-0 2-3	2-1 2-1	4-1 6-0	1-1 1-0	2-1 4-0	2-0	0-3	2-1	4-0
Celtic ‡	38	29	5	4	85	22	92	1-3 3-0		3-0 4-0	1-1 4-1	1-1 2-0	1-0 4-0	2-2	2-0	9-0 1-0	2-1 3-1	4-0 1-0	3-1 2-0
Heart of Midlothian ‡	38	18	9	11	53	45	63	1-2 1-0	2-0 0-3		1-1 2-1	0-3 0-2	0-2 0-0	1-1	1-1 1-0	5-0	1-0	3-0 3-2	2-0
Dundee United ‡	38	17	10	11	55	50	61	0-4 0-2	1-2 1-3	2-0 2-1		1-1 4-2	2-0 4-0	0-0 1-0	3-1 0-3	1-3 1-1	1-0 3-0	1-2	2-1
Kilmarnock	38	13	10	15	53	55	49	2-3 1-5	1-2 0-4	1-2 2-2	1-2 1-1		0-1 3-1	1-2 1-1	1-1	2-0	2-1	2-1 2-0	0-3
Motherwell	38	13	7	18	40	56	46	1-4 0-5	0-1 2-0	1-2 0-1	2-3 3-2	1-2 1-0		1-1	0-0 4-0	1-1 2-1	2-3 2-0	3-1 0-1	1-0
Inverness Caley Thistle	38	14	11	13	51	44	53	1-1	0-1 3-2	1-3 1-1	0-2	1-3	1-2 3-0		1-1 2-0	2-0 0-2	4-2 2-0	1-2 1-0	0-1 1-1
St Johnstone	38	11	11	16	23	43	44	0-2	0-3 0-1	0-2	0-0	0-3 0-0	0-2	1-0 1-0		0-3 0-1	0-0 2-0	1-1 1-2	1-0 0-1
Aberdeen	38	11	5	22	39	59	38	2-3 0-1	0-3	0-1 0-0	0-1	0-1 5-0	1-2	1-2 1-0	0-1 0-2		4-2 0-1	2-0 0-1	4-0 1-0
Hibernian	38	10	7	21	39	61	37	0-3 0-2	0-3	0-2 2-2	2-2	2-1 2-1	2-1	1-1 2-0	0-0 1-2	1-2 1-3		2-0 1-1	1-1 1-2
St Mirren	38	8	9	21	33	57	33	1-3 0-1	0-1	0-2	1-1 1-1	0-2	1-1	1-2 3-3	1-2 0-0	2-1 3-2	1-0 0-1		2-2 3-1
Hamilton Academical	38	5	11	22	24	59	26	1-2 0-1	1-1	0-4 0-2	0-1 1-2	1-1 2-1	0-0 1-3	1-2 0-1	0-1 1-1	1-2 1-0	0-1 0-1	0-1 1-0	

14/08/2010 - 15/05/2011 • † Qualified for the UEFA Champions League • ‡ Qualified for the Europa League • Matches in bold are away matches
Top scorers: 21 - Kenny Miller, Rangers • 20 - Gary Hooper ENG, Celtic • 17 - David Goodwillie, Dundee Utd • 16 - Nikica Jelavic CRO, Rangers • 15 - Adam Rooney, IRL, Inverness; Conor Sammon IRL, Kilmarnock & Anthony Stokes IRL, Hibs (1) Celtic (14) • 14 - Michael Higdon ENG, St Mirren • 13 - Rudolf Skacel CZE, Hearts • 12 - Nick Blackman ENG, Motherwell (10) Aberdeen (2)

SCOTLAND 2010-11

IRN-BRU FIRST DIVISION (2)

	Pl	W	D	L	F	A	Pts	Dunfermline	Raith Rovers	Falkirk	QofS	Partick	Dundee	Morton	Ross County	Cowdenbeath	Stirling Alb
Dunfermline Athletic	36	20	10	6	66	31	70		2-2 2-1	1-3 1-0	6-1 0-0	0-3 1-0	0-2 0-1	3-3 2-1	1-2 1-5	2-0 3-0	4-1
Raith Rovers	36	17	9	10	47	35	60	2-0 2-1		2-1 1-2	0-1 0-1	4-0 0-2	1-2 2-1	1-0 2-1	1-0 1-1	2-1 2-2	0-2 2-1
Falkirk	36	17	7	12	57	41	58	0-1 1-2	0-0 2-1		3-1 0-3	2-0 2-3	3-3 2-2	2-1 1-0	0-1 5-1	2-0 3-0	4-2
Queen of the South	36	14	7	15	54	53	49	2-0 1-3	1-3 0-2	1-5 0-1		2-1 3-3	1-2 3-0	2-0 1-4	3-0 0-1	3-0 2-2	2-2 2-4
Partick Thistle	36	12	11	13	44	39	47	3-1 2-0	0-0 0-3	1-0 1-2	3-1 0-0		1-0 0-0	0-2 0-1	1-1 1-1	0-0 1-1	1-2 6-1
Dundee §25	36	19	12	5	54	34	44	2-2 1-1	0-0 2-0	2-2 0-0	1-0 2-1	3-2		2-1 1-1	3-0 2-2	0-2 2-2	2-4 1
Greenock Morton	36	11	10	15	39	43	43	2-1 0-2	0-1 0-0	0-0 2-2	2-0 0-4	2-0 1-0	0-1 1-3		0-0 2-1	1-2 3-0	0-0 2-0
Ross County	36	9	14	13	30	34	41	0-0 0-1	0-0 0-1	0-1 2-1	1-1 1-1	2-0 2-0	0-0 3-0	1-2 2-2		1-1 3-0	3-1 0-0
Cowdenbeath †	36	9	8	19	41	72	35	0-4 1-2	0-3 0-0	1-2 1-3	2-2 2-1	1-1 2-1	1-3 2-2	0-2 0-2	2-1		5-1 1-0
Stirling Albion	36	4	8	24	32	82	20	3-0 4-1	2-1 1-0	0-4 2-0	4-2 0-3	1-1 0-1	3-2 0-0	0-2 1-3	3-4		

7/08/2010 - 7/05/2011 • † Play-off (see second division) • § = points deducted
Top scorers: 15 - Kris Doolan, Partick & Mark Stewart, Falkirk

SCOTLAND 2010-11

IRN-BRU SECOND DIVISION (3)

	Pl	W	D	L	F	A	Pts	Livingston	Ayr Utd	Forfar Ath	Brechin City	East Fife	Airdrie Utd	Dumbarton	Stenhousemuir	Alloa Ath	Peterhead
Livingston	36	25	7	4	79	33	82		3-2 0-0	2-0 3-0	2-0 0-0	1-1 4-3	2-1 2-0	2-0 1-1	4-1 2-1	3-3 4-0	1-0 5-1
Ayr United †	36	18	5	13	62	55	59	3-1 0-3		0-1 3-1	0-2 2-0	0-4 1-1	1-0 3-1	1-0 2-0	4-3 2-1	1-0 1-2	1-2 2-2
Forfar Athletic †	36	17	8	11	50	48	59	1-0 0-4	4-1 3-2		1-1 2-1	3-2 0-0	1-2 1-2	4-1 2-1	2-0 1-1	1-1 3-1	1-1 2-1
Brechin City †	36	15	12	9	63	45	57	1-3 1-0	0-3 1-0	0-0 0-1		2-3 1-3	3-1 1-2	3-3 6-0	0-3 3-1	1-3 3-2	4-2 3-1
East Fife	36	14	10	12	77	60	52	2-4 1-3	2-3 3-2	1-3 3-0	1-3 0-0		3-3 0-1	6-0 1-3	6-0 1-1	4-1 3-1	2-1 3-1
Airdrie United	36	13	9	14	52	60	48	0-1 2-4	2-2 0-5	2-0 3-1	1-3 0-0	1-3 1-2		1-2 2-1	1-0 2-2	2-0 1-0	2-2 2-3
Dumbarton	36	11	7	18	52	70	40	1-2 0-3	3-2 1-2	1-0 1-3	1-2 4-2	4-2 1-3	1-3 1-1		1-0 0-1	4-1 2-2	3-0 5-2
Stenhousemuir	36	10	8	18	46	59	38	1-2 0-3	3-1 2-1	3-0 0-1	0-0 1-3	1-1 0-2	1-3 1-0	4-0 2-2		0-1 2-3	3-1 4-2
Alloa Athletic †	36	9	9	18	49	71	36	2-2 1-3	4-1 0-1	3-2 0-3	2-2 2-2	3-2 1-3	2-3 1-0	0-2 3-1	0-1 2		2-2 0-0
Peterhead	36	5	11	20	47	76	26	0-0 3-0	2-4 1-2	1-2 1-1	0-5 1-1	2-2 0-2	5-1 2-4	1-0 1-2	2-2 0-3	1-0 4-1	

7/08/2010 - 7/05/2011 • † Play-off • Top scorers: 21 - Mark Roberts, Ayr Utd & Iain Russell, Livingston
Play-off semis: Forfar Athletic 1-4 3-3 Ayr United; Brechin City 2-2 2-0 Cowdenbeath • Final: Ayr United 1-1 2-1 Brechin City

SCOTLAND 2010–11

IRN-BRU THIRD DIVISION (4)

Team	Pl	W	D	L	F	A	Pts	Arbroath	Albion Rov	Queen's Park	Annan Ath	Stranraer	Berwick Rang	Elgin City	Montrose	East Stirling	Clyde
Arbroath	36	20	6	10	80	61	66	—	1-1 3-0	1-0 2-2	0-2 2-1	0-0 2-2	3-2 2-1	2-0 3-5	4-0 4-1	2-0 3-5	3-2 2-0
Albion Rovers †	36	17	10	9	56	40	61	0-2 3-0	—	2-1 1-2	0-0 0-0	1-2 1-0	2-2 0-1	3-1 2-0	3-1 0-2	1-0 2-0	3-1 1-1
Queen's Park †	36	18	5	13	57	43	59	5-2 1-1	0-1 2-1	—	3-0 0-1	1-3 3-3	0-2 1-0	1-1 1-0	1-0 4-1	2-0 2-0	0-1 4-0
Annan Athletic †	36	16	11	9	58	45	59	1-2 3-0	4-1 2-2	2-1 1-2	—	2-2 2-1	1-1 2-3	0-1 2-2	2-2 2-1	3-1 2-1	0-2 1-0
Stranraer	36	15	12	9	72	57	57	4-1 3-4	3-2 1-3	1-0 2-1	2-2 1-1	—	1-1 3-1	2-1 1-1	2-1 2-2	4-1 2-0	3-1 3-0
Berwick Rangers	36	12	13	11	62	56	49	4-1 0-4	1-6 2-2	1-1 3-1	2-2 2-3	2-2 3-3	—	6-2 4-0	1-0 0-1	3-0 1-1	2-1 1-1
Elgin City	36	13	6	17	53	63	45	3-5 3-2	2-2 1-1	4-2 0-1	2-0 2-3	1-2 2-1	1-2 3-2	—	3-2 1-0	0-2 2-0	0-1 0-1
Montrose	36	10	7	19	47	61	37	3-0 0-5	0-2 0-2	1-2 0-2	1-1 0-1	3-3 3-2	1-1 1-1	0-1 1-0	—	0-2 2-0	0-1 0-1
East Stirlingshire	36	10	4	22	33	62	34	1-3 2-5	0-0 1-2	0-1 3-2	1-5 2-0	0-1 0-2	0-0 1-0	0-2 2-1	2-1 1-2	—	0-0 2-0
Clyde	36	8	8	20	37	67	32	1-1 0-3	1-2 0-1	2-3 0-2	0-2 0-2	2-2 4-2	1-4 2-0	1-1 3-3	1-1 2-0	1-2 2-0	—

7/08/2010 - 7/05/2011 • † Play-off • Top scorer: 21 - Gavin Swankie, Arbroath

Play-off semis: Queen's Park 1-1 0-2 **Albion Rovers**; **Annan Athletic** 2-1 0-0 Alloa Athletic • Final: **Albion Rovers** 3-1 1-2 Annan Athletic

MEDALS TABLE

	Team	Overall			League			Cup		LC		Europe			Town/City
		G	S	B	G	S	B	G	S	G	S	G	S	B	
1	Rangers	115	56	19	54	29	17	33	17	27	7	1	3	2	Glasgow
2	Celtic	92	65	21	42	31	17	35	18	14	14	1	2	4	Glasgow
3	Aberdeen	17	28	9	4	13	8	7	8	5	7	1		1	Aberdeen
4	Heart of Midlothian	15	22	17	4	14	17	7	6	4	2				Edinburgh
5	Queen's Park	10	2					10	2						Glasgow
6	Hibernian	9	21	15	4	6	13	2	9	3	6			2	Edinburgh
7	Dundee United	5	12	9	1		8	2	7	2	4	1		1	Dundee
8	Dundee	5	11	3	1	4	1	1	4	3	3			2	Dundee
9	Kilmarnock	4	14	4	1	4	3	3	5		5			1	Kilmarnock
10	Motherwell	4	12	7	1	5	7	2	5	1	2				Motherwell
11	East Fife	4	2	2				1	2	3					Methil
12	St. Mirren	3	5	2				3	3		2			2	Paisley
	Third Lanark	3	5	2	1			2	4		1				Glasgow
14	Dumbarton	3	5		2			1	5						Dumbarton
15	Vale of Leven	3	4					3	4						Alexandria
16	Clyde	3	3	3				3	3						Cumbernauld
17	Dunfermline Athletic	2	6	3				2	2		3			1	Dunfermline
18	Falkirk	2	5	1		2	1	2	2		1				Falkirk
19	Partick Thistle	2	4	3				1	3	1	1				Glasgow
20	Renton	2	3					2	3						Renton
21	Airdrie United	1	7	1		4	1	1	3						Airdrie
22	Morton	1	3	2		1	2	1	1		1				Greenock
23	Raith Rovers	1	2	1			1		1	1	1				Kirkcaldy
24	St. Bernard's	1		1				1	1						Edinburgh
	Livingston	1		1			1			1					Livingston
26	St. Johnstone		2	2							2				Perth
27	Hamilton Academical		2						2						Hamilton
28	Albion Rovers		1						1						Coatbridge
	Ayr United		1								1				Ayr
	Cambuslang		1						1						Cambuslang
	Clydesdale		1						1						Glasgow
	Gretna		1						1						Gretna
	Queen of the South		1						1						Dumfries
	Ross County		1						1						Dingwall
	Thornliebank		1						1						Glasgow

CO-OPERATIVE INSURANCE SCOTTISH LEAGUE CUP 2010-11

Second Round

Rangers	Bye
Clyde	2
Dunfermline Athletic *	3
Hibernian	Bye
Airdrie United	2
Kilmarnock *	6
Dundee United	Bye
St Mirren	3 3p
Ross County *	3 4p
Brechin City *	2 3p
Dundee	2 1p
Motherwell	Bye
Aberdeen	3
Alloa Athletic *	0
Hamilton Academical	0
Raith Rovers *	1
Heart of Midlothian *	4
Elgin City	0
Partick Thistle *	0
Falkirk	1
St Johnstone *	2
Greenock Morton	0
Forfar Athletic	1
Queen of the South *	4
Inverness Caley Thistle *	3
Peterhead	0
Celtic	Bye

Third Round

Rangers *	7
Dunfermline Athletic	2
Hibernian	1
Kilmarnock *	3
Dundee United	2
Ross County *	1
Brechin City *	0
Motherwell	2
Aberdeen *	3
Raith Rovers	2
Heart of Midlothian	3
Falkirk *	4
St Johnstone *	3
Queen of the South	0
Inverness Caley Thistle	0
Celtic *	6

Quarter-finals

Rangers	2
Kilmarnock *	0
Dundee United	0
Motherwell *	1
Aberdeen *	2
Falkirk	1
St Johnstone *	2
Celtic	3

Semi-finals

Rangers	2
Motherwell	1
Aberdeen	1
Celtic	4

Final

Rangers	2
Celtic	1

* Home team ● † Both semi-finals played at Hampden Park, Glasgow

Premier League clubs enter in the second round while those in European competition enter in the third round

LEAGUE CUP FINAL

Hampden Park, Glasgow
20-03-2011, 15:00
Att: 51181, Ref: Craig Thomson
Scorers - Davis 24, Jelavic 98 for Rangers;
Ledley 31 for Celtic

Rangers - Neil Alexander - Steven Whittaker, Madjid Bougherra (Kyle Hutton 82), David Weir (c), Sasa Papac●, Gregg Wylde - Steven Naismith, Steven Davis, Maurice Edu, Kyle Lafferty (Vladimir Weiss 93+) - Nikica Jelavic● (El Haj Diouf● 117). Tr: Walter Smith

Celtic - Fraser Forster - Mark Wilson●, Thomas Rogne (Glenn Loovens 73), Charlie Mulgrew●●, Emilio Izaguirre◆121 - Scott Brown (c) (Ki Sung Yeung 65), Biram Kayal●, Joe Ledley, Kris Commons (Pat McCourt 103) - Gary Hooper, Georgios Samaras. Tr: Neil Lennon

ACTIVE NATION SCOTTISH CUP 2010–11

Third Round

Cove Rangers *	0	
Berwick Rangers	3	
Greenock Morton	2	
Dumbarton *	1	
Beith	2	3
Airdrie United *	2	4
Elgin City *	2	
Livingston	1	
Cowdenbeath	0	
Peterhead *	2	
Sunnybank	0	
Ayr United *	5	
Whitehill Welfare	1	
Montrose *	3	
East Fife *	3	
Forfar Athletic	1	
Stirling Albion *	1	
Partick Thistle	3	
Buckie Thistle	2	
Bo'ness United *	0	
Spartans *	1	
East Stirlingshire	2	
Annan Athletic	2	2
Brechin City *	2	5
Deveronvale	1	
Ross County *	4	
Alloa Athletic *	4	
Raith Rovers	2	
Stranraer *	4	
Girvan	2	
Threave Rovers	2	1
Stenhousemuir *	2	5

Fourth Round

Celtic	2	
Berwick Rangers *	0	
Kilmarnock	0	
Rangers *	3	
Greenock Morton *	2	5
Airdrie United	2	2
Elgin City	0	
Inverness Caley Thistle *	2	
St Mirren *	0	6
Peterhead	0	1
Hibernian *	0	0
Ayr United	0	1
Dunfermline Athletic	2	5
Montrose *	2	3
East Fife	0	
Aberdeen *	6	
St Johnstone	1	
Heart of Midlothian *	0	
Falkirk *	2	0
Partick Thistle	2	1
Buckie Thistle	0	
East Stirlingshire * †	1	
Queen of the South *	1	
Brechin City	2	
Dundee United *	0 0 4p	
Ross County	0 0 3p	
Alloa Athletic	0	
Hamilton Academical *	2	
Stranraer	0	4
Stenhousemuir *	0	3
Dundee *	0	
Motherwell	4	

Fifth Round

Celtic	2	1
Rangers *	2	0
Greenock Morton	1	
Inverness Caley Thistle *	5	
St Mirren	2	
Ayr United *	1	
Dunfermline Athletic	0	
Aberdeen *	1	
St Johnstone *	2	
Partick Thistle	0	
Buckie Thistle *	0	
Brechin City	2	
Dundee United	3	
Hamilton Academical *	1	
Stranraer *	0	
Motherwell	2	

† East Stirlingshire expelled for fielding ineligible player • * Home team

ACTIVE NATION SCOTTISH CUP 2010–11

Quarter–finals	Semi–finals	Final

Celtic 2		
Inverness Caley Thistle * 1		
	Celtic 4	
	Aberdeen 0	
St Mirren * 1 1		
Aberdeen 1 2		
		Celtic ‡ 3
		Motherwell 0
St Johnstone 2 1		
Brechin City * 2 0		
	St Johnstone 0	
	Motherwell 3	
Dundee United * 2 0		
Motherwell 2 3		

Top 16 teams from the previous season enter
in the fourth round. Clubs positioned 17–32
enter in the third round

Both semi-finals played at Hampden Park
‡ Qualified for the Europa League

SCOTTISH FA CUP FINAL 2011

Hampden Park, Glasgow, 21-05-2011, 15:00, Att: 49 618, Ref: Calum Murray

Celtic	3	Ki 32, Craigan OG 76, Mulgrew 88
Motherwell	0	

Celtic - Fraser Forster - Mark Wilson, Glenn Loovens, Daniel Majstorovic●, Emilio
Izaguirre - Scott Brown (c)●, Ki Sung Yeung●, Charlie Mulgrew, Kris Commons
(James Forrest 81) - Gary Hooper (Paddy McCourt 89), Georgios Samaras (Anthony
Stokes 68). Tr: Neil Lennon
Motherwell - Darren Randolph - Tom Hateley, Stephen Craigan●, Shaun
Hutchinson, Steven Hammell (Francis Jeffers 72), Gavin Gunning - Chris Humphrey,
Keith Lasley●, Steve Jennings - Jamie Murphy (Steve Jones 80), John Sutton.
Tr: Stuart McCall

ABERDEEN 2010–11

	Date	Opponent	Res	Comp	Scorers	Att
Aug	14	Hamilton	W 4-0	PL	Hartley 3 19p 40p 65p, Diamond 51	12 005
	21	St Johnstone	W 1-0	PL	Mackie 86	6 523
	24	Alloa Ath	W 3-0	LCr2	Hartley 18p, McArdle 38, Maguire 60	1 649
	28	Kilmarnock	L 0-1	PL		11 287
Sep	11	Dundee Utd	L 1-3	PL	Vernon 26	9 793
	18	Motherwell	D 1-1	PL	Vernon 56	5 251
	22	Raith	W 3-2	LCr3	Hartley 10p, Vernon 2 56 78	5 936
	26	Rangers	L 2-3	PL	Vernon 10, Maguire 30	15 307
	2	Inverness	L 0-2	PL		6 144
	16	Hearts	L 0-1	PL		8 999
Oct	23	Hibernian	W 4-2	PL	Maguire 18, Vernon 2 32 50, Hartley 61p	7 587
	26	Falkirk	W 2-1	LCqf	Hartley 2 64 95+p	6 710
	30	St Mirren	L 1-2	PL	McArdle 57	4 589
	6	Celtic	L 0-9	PL		48 754
Nov	9	Inverness	L 1-2	PL	Velicka 49	5 917
	13	Rangers	L 0-2	PL		44 919
	20	St Johnstone	L 0-1	PL		7 841
	27	Kilmarnock	L 0-2	PL		5 013
	11	Hearts	L 0-5	PL		13 434
Dec	26	Hibernian	W 2-1	PL	Folly 36, Vernon 62	10 115
	29	Hamilton	W 1-0	PL	Vernon 91+	2 968
Jan	1	Dundee Utd	D 1-1	PL	Maguire 35	12 487
	8	East Fife	W 6-0	FAr4	Maguire 3 13 24 42, Vernon 2 30 81, Magennis 90	6 918
	15	St Mirren	W 2-0	PL	Vernon 2 50 67	9 740
	22	Celtic	L 0-1	PL		48 717
	26	Inverness	W 2-0	PL	Jack 44, Blackman 49	4 468
	29	Celtic	L 1-4	LCsf	Vernon 61	38 085
Feb	1	Celtic	L 0-3	PL		12 901
	6	Dunfermline	W 1-0	FAr5	OG 90	5 636
	5	Motherwell	L 1-2	PL	Aluko 3	6 882
	19	Kilmarnock	W 5-0	PL	Vernon 14, Aluko 25, Maguire 59p, McArdle 70, Magennis 82	7 371
	22	Hamilton	W 1-0	PL	Maguire 30p	7 019
	26	Hearts	D 0-0	PL		9 100
Mar	2	St Johnstone	D 0-0	PL		2 909
	7	Dundee Utd	L 1-3	PL	Magennis 51	7 416
	12	St Mirren	D 1-1	FAqf	McArdle 90	4 120
	16	St Mirren	W 2-1	FAqf	Maguire 4, Vernon 46	7 330
	2	Motherwell	L 1-2	PL	Vujadinovic 92+	4 458
	6	St Mirren	L 2-3	PL	OG 47, Milsom 91+	3 489
	9	Hibernian	L 0-1	PL		7 400
Apr	13	Rangers	L 0-1	PL		11 925
	17	Celtic	L 0-4	FAsf		30 381
	25	Hamilton	D 1-0	PL	Blackman 75	2 140
	30	Inverness	W 1-0	PL	Pawlett 75	6 280
May	7	St Mirren	L 0-2	PL		6 361
	10	St Mirren	L 0-2	PL		5 955
	14	Hibernian	W 3-1	PL	Magennis 48, Maguire 2 75 77	11 767

9th   Att: 172 364 • Av: 9 071 (-13.3%) • Pittodrie 21 421 (42%)

ABERDEEN LEAGUE APPEARANCES/GOALS 2011
Goalkeepers Mark Howard ENG 8+1 • Jamie Langfield 30+1
Defenders Myles Anderson ENG 0+1/0 • Andrew Considine 27+1/0
Zander Diamond 32/1 • Jerel Ifil ENG 12+4/0 • Dean Jarvis NIR 0+1/0
Rory McArdle NIR 27+1/2 • David McNamee 9/0
Robert Milsom ENG 17/1 • Clark Robertson 8+6/0
Joe Shaughnessy IRL 1/0 • Steven Smith 15/0 • Stirling Smith 0+1/0
Nikola Vujadinovic MNE 13+5/1
Midfield Nick Blackman ENG 10+5/2 • Yoann Folly FRA 18/1
Ricky Foster 0+1/0 • Ryan Fraser 0+2/0 • Fraser Fyvie 1+4/0
Jack Grimmer 1+1/0 • Hallur Hansson FRO 0+1/0
Paul Hartley 23+1/4 Ryan Jack 26+4/1 • Nicky Low 0+1/0
Peter Pawlett 6+7/1 • Derek Young 20+9/0
Forwards Sone Aluko NGA 27+1/2 • Darren Mackie 7+4/1
Josh Magennis NIR 10+19/3 • Chris Maguire 35/7
Mitchell Megginson 1+5/0 • Michael Paton 4+6/0
Andrius Velicka LTU 1+5/1 • Scott Vernon ENG 29+4/10
Coach Mark McGhee • Craig Brown (10/12/10)

CELTIC 2010–11

	Date	Opponent	Res	Comp	Scorers	Att
Jy	28	Braga	L 0-3	CLp3		12 295
Aug	4	Braga	W 2-1	CLp3	Hooper 52, Juarez 79	53 592
	14	Inverness	W 1-0	PL	McCourt 56	7 547
	19	Utrecht	W 2-0	ELpo	Juarez 19, Samaras 34	35 755
	22	St Mirren	W 4-0	PL	Ledley 5, Maloney 24, Forrest 69, Ki 81	46 812
	26	Utrecht	L 0-4	ELpo		18 240
	29	Motherwell	W 1-0	PL	Murphy 73p	9 207
Sep	11	Hearts	W 3-0	PL	Forrest 28, Maloney 44, McCourt 90	49 023
	19	Kilmarnock	W 2-1	PL	Murphy 41p, Stokes 52	8 645
	22	Inverness	W 6-0	LCr3	Samaras 3 17 37 57, Hooper 21, Stokes 2 74 81	17 429
	25	Hibernian	W 2-1	PL	Brown 5, Loovens 51	48 625
	2	Hamilton	W 3-1	PL	Maloney 2 25 64, Hooper 71	47 446
	17	Dundee Utd	W 2-1	PL	Hooper 2 13 89	11 790
	24	Rangers	L 1-3	PL	Hooper 45	58 874
Oct	27	St Johnstone	W 3-2	LCqf	Stokes 2 8 13, McGinn 12	5 151
	30	St Johnstone	W 2-0	PL	McGinn 2 2 89, Izaguirre 40	6 866
	6	Aberdeen	W 9-0	PL	Stokes 3 26p 45p 74, Hooper 3 28 33 63, OG 61, Ledley 71, McCourt 85p	48 754
Nov	10	Hearts	L 0-2	PL		15 632
	14	St Mirren	W 1-0	PL	Hooper 92+	6 073
	20	Dundee Utd	D 1-1	PL	Hooper 23	47 523
	27	Inverness	D 2-2	PL	Ki 38, McCourt 65	46 096
		Kilmarnock	D 1-1	PL	Rogne 84	44 522
	29	St Johnstone	W 2-0	PL	Cha 91+, Ki 93+	41 522
	29	Motherwell	W 1-0	PL	McCourt 27	40 750
Dec	2	Rangers	W 2-0	PL	Samaras 2 62 70p	50 222
	6	Berwick	W 4-2	FAr4	Majstorovic 17, Brown 82	3 877
	12	Hamilton	D 1-1	PL	Stokes 92+p	5 163
	15	Hibernian	W 3-0	PL	Hooper 44, Stokes 2 50p 65	13 649
Jan	22	Aberdeen	W 1-0	PL		48 717
	26	Hearts	W 4-0	PL	Forrest 7, Stokes 2 53 72, McCourt 85	49 460
	29	Aberdeen	W 4-1	LCsf	Commons 6, Mulgrew 10, Rogne 21, Stokes 34p	38 085
Feb	1	Aberdeen	W 3-0	PL	Hooper 12, Wilson 75, Stokes 78	12 901
	6	Rangers	D 2-2	FAr5	Commons 16, Brown 65	50 230
	13	Dundee Utd	W 3-1	PL	Stokes 16, Wilson 36, Majstorovic 78	11 414
	20	Rangers	W 3-0	PL	Hooper 2 17 27, Commons 70	58 748
	27	Motherwell	L 0-2	PL		9 716
Mar	2	Rangers	W 1-0	FAr5	Wilson 48	57 847
	5	Hamilton	W 2-0	PL	Commons 2 42 52	51 811
	16	Inverness	W 2-1	FAqf	Ledley 2 45 68	6 064
	20	Rangers	L 1-2	LCf	Ledley 31	51 181
	6	Hibernian	W 3-1	PL	Stokes 4, Hooper 2 20p 39	47 809
	9	St Mirren	W 1-0	PL	Commons 78	50 318
	12	St Johnstone	W 1-0	PL	Kayal 45	6 338
Apr	17	Aberdeen	W 4-0	FAsf	Mulgrew 49, Ledley 57, Commons 63p, Maloney 84	30 381
	20	Kilmarnock	W 4-0	PL	Commons 2 4 34, Hooper 31, Stokes 58	9 117
	24	Rangers	D 0-0	PL		50 248
May	1	Dundee Utd	W 4-1	PL	Hooper 23, Kayal 54, Commons 85, Murphy 93+	48 599
	4	Inverness	L 2-3	PL	Commons 2 9 93+p	6 702
	8	Kilmarnock	W 2-0	PL	Brown 45, Commons 68	9 720
	11	Hearts	W 3-0	PL	Hooper 2 12 49, Commons 78	16 681
	15	Motherwell	W 4-0	PL	Hooper 29, Samaras 40, Maloney 52, McCourt 71	57 294
	20	Motherwell	W 3-0	FAf	Ki 32, OG 76, Mulgrew 88	49 618

2nd   Att: 932 703 • Av: 49 089 (+7.6%) • Parkhead 60 355 (81%)

CELTIC LEAGUE APPEARANCES/GOALS 2011
Goalkeepers Fraser Forster ENG 36 • Lukasz Zaluska POL 2
Defenders Cha Du Ri KOR 13+2/1 • Jos Hooiveld NED 4+1/0 • Emilio Izaguirre HON 33/1 • Efrain Juarez MEX 6+7/0 • Glenn Loovens NED 13/1
Daniel Majstorovic SWE 32/1 • Charlie Mulgrew 20+3/0 • Thomas Rogne NOR 14+2/1 • Lewis Toshney 0+1/0 • Mark Wilson 25/2
Midfield Scott Brown 26+2/2 • Marc Crosas ESP 0+1/0 • Oliver Kapo FRA 1+1/0 • Kris Commons 11+3/11 • Gary Hooper ENG 26/20 • Biram Kayal ISR 18+3/2 • Ki Sung Yueng KOR 18+7/3 • Joe Ledley WAL 26+3/2
Freddie Ljungberg SWE 1+6/0 • Shaun Maloney 16+6/5 • Pat McCourt NIR 8+17/7 • Niall McGinn NIR 6+5/2 • Richie Towell IRL 0+1/0
Forwards James Forrest 15+4/3 • Marc-Antoine Fortune FRA 2/0
Daryl Murphy IRL 9+9/3 • Georgios Samaras GRE 16+6/3
Anthony Stokes IRL 22+7/14 • **Coach** Neil Lennon NIR

DUNDEE UNITED 2010–11

Aug	14	St Mirren	D	1-1	PL	Daly [89]	5 618
	19	AEK Athens	L	0-1	ELpo		12 116
	22	Inverness	L	0-4	PL		6 575
	26	AEK Athens	D	1-1	ELpo	Daly [78]	700
	29	Hearts	D	1-1	PL	Gomis [85]	12 898
Sep	11	Aberdeen	W	3-1	PL	Daly [3], OG [7], Goodwillie [9p]	9 793
	18	Rangers	L	0-4	PL		44 786
	22	Ross Cty	W	3-1	LCr3	Goodwillie [61p], OG [101]	2 269
	25	St Johnstone	W	1-0	PL	Goodwillie [61]	7 397
Oct	2	Kilmarnock	W	2-1	PL	Goodwillie [15], Daly [69]	4 633
	17	Celtic	L	1-2	PL	Goodwillie [38]	11 790
	23	Motherwell	L	1-2	PL	Goodwillie [50p]	4 635
	26	Motherwell	L	0-1	LCqf		4 838
	30	Hibernian	W	1-0	PL	Goodwillie [87]	7 377
Nov	6	Hamilton	W	1-0	PL	Goodwillie [76]	2 456
	10	St Mirren	L	1-2	PL	Buaben [86]	5 548
	13	Kilmarnock	D	1-1	PL	Russell [23]	6 597
	20	Celtic	D	1-1	PL	Dillon [94+]	47 523
Dec	29	Hibernian	D	2-2	PL	Goodwillie 2 [2 35]	10 252
	1	Aberdeen	D	1-1	PL	Goodwillie [95+]	12 487
	3	Ross Cty	D	0-0	FAr4		4 041
Jan	12	Motherwell	W	2-0	PL	Russell [53], Goodwillie [90]	4 918
	18	Ross Cty	D	0-0	FAr4	W 4-3p	2 430
	22	Kilmarnock	D	1-1	PL	Kenneth [90]	5 120
	26	St Mirren	D	1-1	PL	Robertson.D [89]	3 095
	30	Hibernian	W	3-0	PL	Daly [13], Conway [48], Russell [80]	6 215
Feb	5	Hamilton	W	3-1	FAr5	Daly [20], Dixon [39], Buaben [59]	2 577
	13	Celtic	L	1-3	PL	Goodwillie [64]	11 414
	19	Hearts	L	1-2	PL	Douglas [6]	15 473
	22	St Johnstone	D	0-0	PL		3 507
	26	Hamilton	D	1-1	PL	Shala [83]	2 011
	1	Inverness	W	2-0	PL	Buaben [75], Robertson.D [90]	3 392
Mar	7	Aberdeen	W	3-1	PL	Douglas [29], Conway [33], Swanson [60]	7 416
	10	Hamilton	W	2-1	PL	Goodwillie [43], Daly [92+]	5 766
	13	Motherwell	D	2-2	FAqf	Goodwillie [40], Daly [73]	7 358
	16	Hearts	W	2-0	PL	Russell 2 [83 93+]	6 718
	19	Inverness	W	1-0	PL	Swanson [43]	6 548
	30	Motherwell	L	0-3	FAqf		8 337
Apr	2	Rangers	W	3-2	PL	Robertson.D [45], Russell [77], Goodwillie [89]	46 697
	6	Motherwell	L	1-2	PL	Russell [79]	3 435
	9	St Johnstone	W	2-0	PL	Russell [45], Robertson.D [85]	6 398
	19	Rangers	L	0-4	PL		11 626
	23	Kilmarnock	W	4-2	PL	Severin [25], Goodwillie 2 [38 47], Conway [49]	5 225
May	1	Celtic	L	1-4	PL	Russell [91+]	48 599
	7	Motherwell	W	4-0	PL	Daly 3 [36 43 49], Watson [88]	5 951
	10	Rangers	L	0-2	PL		49 267
	15	Hearts	W	2-1	PL	Goodwillie [22], Daly [71]	7 119

4th Att: 140 391 • Av: 7 389 (-6.1%) • Tannadice 14 223 (51%)

HAMILTON ACADEMICAL 2010–11

Aug	14	Aberdeen	L	0-4	PL		12 005
	21	Hearts	L	0-4	PL		2 899
	24	Raith	L	0-1	LCr2		1 674
	28	Inverness	W	1-0	PL	Imrie [1]	3 851
	11	Rangers	L	1-2	PL	OG [56]	5 356
Sep	18	Hibernian	D	1-1	PL	Marco Paixao [22]	11 294
	25	Kilmarnock	D	2-2	PL	Marco Paixao [15], Hasselbaink [38]	3 033
	2	Celtic	L	1-3	PL	McLaughlin [3]	47 446
Oct	16	St Mirren	D	2-2	PL	Routledge [39], Imrie [47]	3 577
	23	St Johnstone	L	1-2	PL	Mensing [68p]	2 431
	30	Motherwell	W	1-0	PL	Hasselbaink [15]	4 865
Nov	6	Dundee Utd	L	0-1	PL		2 456
	10	Kilmarnock	L	0-3	PL		4 214
	13	Inverness	L	1-3	PL	Imrie [29]	2 019
	20	Hearts	L	0-2	PL		12 620
	27	St Mirren	D	0-0	PL		2 280
Dec	29	Aberdeen	L	0-1	PL		2 968
	1	Motherwell	D	0-0	PL		3 171
	3	Alloa Ath	W	2-0	FAr4	Hasselbaink [33], Flavio Paixao [90]	1 054
Jan	12	Celtic	D	1-1	PL	Mensing [27]	5 163
	15	Rangers	L	0-4	PL		44 639
	22	Inverness	D	1-1	PL	Sanchez [18]	3 241
	29	Kilmarnock	D	1-1	PL	Antoine-Curier [79]	2 680
	1	St Johnstone	L	0-2	PL		2 631
Feb	5	Dundee Utd	L	1-3	FAr5	Antoine-Curier [46]	2 577
	12	Hearts	L	0-2	PL		2 876
	19	Motherwell	L	0-1	PL		4 407
	22	Aberdeen	L	0-1	PL		7 019
	26	Dundee Utd	D	1-1	PL	Antoine-Curier [33p]	2 011
Mar	1	Hibernian	L	1-2	PL	Flavio Paixao [94+]	2 619
	5	Celtic	L	0-2	PL		51 811
	10	Dundee Utd	L	1-2	PL	Flavio Paixao [26]	5 766
	19	St Johnstone	D	0-0	PL		2 111
	3	St Mirren	L	1-3	PL	Buchanan [43]	4 985
Apr	2	Rangers	L	0-1	PL		4 526
	17	Hibernian	W	2-1	PL	Chambers [9], OG [34]	8 173
	25	Aberdeen	D	1-1	PL	Imrie [64]	2 140
	2	St Mirren	W	1-0	PL	Antoine-Curier [75]	5 037
May	7	Hibernian	W	1-0	PL	Hasselbaink [38]	2 300
	10	St Johnstone	L	0-1	PL		2 253
	14	Inverness	L	1-2	PL	Mensing [50]	2 017

12th Att: 55 056 • Av: 2 897 (-3.6%) • New Douglas Park 6 078 (47%)

DUNDEE UNITED LEAGUE APPEARANCES/GOALS 2011

Goalkeepers Dusan Pernis SVK 38
Defenders Sean Dillon IRL 34/1 • Paul Dixon 28+2/0 • Darren Dods 3/0 Barry Douglas 19+4/2 • Gary Kenneth 26+2/1 • Mihael Kovacevic SUI 2/0 Timothy van der Meulen NED 4+3/0 • Keith Watson 27+2/1
Midfield Stuart Armstrong 2+10/0 • Prince Buaben GHA 29+6/2 • Craig Conway 21+2/3 • Morgaro Gomis FRA 32+2/1 • Jennison Myrie-Williams ENG 0+1/0 • David Robertson 22+8/4 • Scott Robertson 29+5/0 Scott Severin 14+1/1 • Danny Swanson 9+12/2
Forwards Danny Cadamarteri ENG 2+8/0 • Jon Daly IRL 18+11/9 Ryan Dow 0+1/0 • David Goodwillie 37+1/17 • Johnny Russell 21+9/9 Andis Shala GER 1+9/1
Coach Peter Houston

HAMILTON LEAGUE APPEARANCES/GOALS 2011

Goalkeepers Tomas Cerny CZE 37 • Sean Murdoch 1
Defenders Martin Canning 23/0 • Michael Devlin 1/0 David Elebert IRL 17+3/0 • Ziggy Gordon 1/0 • Andy Graham 10+5/0 Brian McQueen 1/0 • Mark McLaughlin 21/1 • Jack Ross 2/0 Jon Routledge ENG 22+2/1
Midfield David Buchanan NIR 27+1/1 • Mark Carrington ENG 6+6/0 James Chambers IRL 6+3/1 • Ali Crawford 9+5/0 Grant Gillespie 8+9/0 • Jim Goodwin IRL 14/0 • David Hopkirk 2+3/0 Jordan Kirkpatrick 2+3/0 • Jim McAlister 15+4/0 Gary McDonald 22+3/0 • Connor Mcglinchey 0+1/0 Simon Mensing GER 30/3 • Alex Neil 8+2/0 • Gavin Skelton ENG 14+2/0 Aaron Wildig ENG 2+1/0 • Kyle Wilkie ENG 3+3/0
Forwards Mickael Antoine-Curier FRA 10+3/4 Damian Casalinuovo ARG 6+13/0 • Tom Elliott ENG 1+6/0 Flavio Paixao POR 26+4/2 • Nigel Hasselbaink NED 21+6/3 Dougie Imrie 35/4 • Lee Kilday 4+1/0 • Derek Lyle 1+3/0 Kieran Millar 0+1/0 • Marco Paixao POR 9+9/2 • Joel Thomas FRA 1+2/0
Coach Billy Reid

HEART OF MIDLOTHIAN 2010–11

	Date	Opponent		Score	Comp	Scorers	Att
Aug	14	St Johnstone	D	1-1	PL	Elliot.C 45	14 562
	21	Hamilton	W	4-0	PL	Elliot.C 2 6 81, Templeton 24, Kyle 76p	2 899
	24	Elgin City	W	4-0	LCr2	Jonsson 11, Kyle 33, Novikovas 59, Robinon 84	4 922
	29	Dundee Utd	D	1-1	PL	Templeton 30	12 898
Sep	11	Celtic	L	0-3	PL		49 023
	18	Inverness	W	3-1	PL	OG 45, Stevenson 55, Elliot.C 69	4 515
	21	Falkirk	L	3-4	LCr3	Kyle 2 67p78, Santana 74	4 216
	25	Motherwell	L	0-2	PL		13 749
Oct	2	Rangers	L	1-2	PL	Skacel 12	15 637
	16	Aberdeen	W	1-0	PL	Kyle 46	8 999
	23	St Mirren	W	3-0	PL	Skacel 3 2 24 92+	12 009
	31	Kilmarnock	L	0-3	PL		13 056
Nov	7	Hibernian	W	2-0	PL	Templeton 19, Elliott.S 67	17 767
	10	Celtic	W	2-0	PL	Black 27, Templeton 58	15 632
	13	St Johnstone	W	2-0	PL	Kyle 64p, Stevenson 94+	4 156
	20	Hamilton	W	2-0	PL	Skacel 32, Templeton 52	12 620
Dec	11	Aberdeen	W	5-0	PL	Templeton 5, Skacel 2 9 58, Elliott.S 51, Novikovas 78	13 434
	14	Motherwell	W	2-1	PL	OG 43, Kyle 60p	3 324
	18	Inverness	D	1-1	PL	Kyle 25p	12 994
	29	St Mirren	W	2-0	PL	Templeton 63, Kyle 82p	4 599
	1	Hibernian	W	1-0	PL	Kyle 86	17 156
Jan	11	St Johnstone	L	0-1	FAr4		6 261
	18	Kilmarnock	W	2-1	PL	Elliott.S 2 73 86	4 996
	22	Rangers	W	1-0	PL	Stevenson 77	16 737
	26	Celtic	L	0-4	PL		49 460
	29	St Johnstone	W	1-0	PL	Skacel 2	13 430
Feb	2	Rangers	L	1-2	PL		44 823
	12	Hamilton	W	2-0	PL	Elliott.S 2 22 47	2 876
	19	Dundee Utd	W	2-0	PL	Skacel 45, Zaliukas 88	15 473
	26	Aberdeen	D	0-0	PL		9 100
Mar	5	Kilmarnock	L	0-2	PL		13 836
	16	Dundee Utd	L	0-2	PL		6 718
	19	St Mirren	W	3-2	PL	Skacel 2 55 93+, Stevenson 82	12 763
	3	Hibernian	D	2-2	PL	Stevenson 24, Elliott.S 83	17 793
Apr	9	Motherwell	D	0-0	PL		13 800
	16	Inverness	D	1-1	PL	Elliott.S 53	4 336
	23	Motherwell	D	3-3	PL	Thomson.C 26p, Skacel 36, Stevenson 52	13 039
	30	Kilmarnock	D	2-2	PL	Skacel 67, OG 76	5 006
May	7	Rangers	L	0-4	PL		46 178
	11	Celtic	L	0-3	PL		16 681
	15	Dundee Utd	L	1-2	PL	Glen 31	7 119

3rd Att: 269 506 • Av: 14 184 (-3.9%) • Tynecastle 17 402 (81%)

HIBERNIAN 2010–11

	Date	Opponent		Score	Comp	Scorers	Att
Jy	29	Maribor	L	0-3	ELp3		9 200
	5	Maribor	L	2-3	ELp3	De Graaf 2 54 89	12 504
Aug	15	Motherwell	W	3-2	PL	Stokes 45, Hanlon 64, Miller 73	5 172
	22	Rangers	L	0-3	PL		17 145
	29	St Mirren	L	0-1	PL		4 480
Sep	11	Inverness	D	1-1	PL	Riordan 8	10 358
	18	Hamilton	D	1-1	PL	Riordan 9	11 294
	22	Kilmarnock	L	1-3	LCr3	Grounds 8	4 074
	25	Celtic	L	1-2	PL	Riordan 54	48 625
Oct	2	St Johnstone	L	0-2	PL		3 819
	16	Kilmarnock	W	2-1	PL	Hogg 2 38 45	11 256
	23	Aberdeen	L	2-4	PL	Nish 63, Bamba 91+	7 587
	30	Dundee Utd	L	0-1	PL		7 377
Nov	7	Hearts	L	0-2	PL		17 767
	10	Rangers	W	3-0	PL	Miller 6, Rankin 19, Dickoh 84	41 514
	13	Motherwell	W	2-1	PL	Riordan 2 14 27	11 178
	20	Inverness	L	2-4	PL	Riordan 66, Miller 78p	4 217
	27	St Johnstone	D	0-0	PL		10 248
Dec	18	Kilmarnock	L	1-2	PL	Riordan 55	4 216
	26	Aberdeen	L	1-2	PL	Riordan 45	10 115
	29	Dundee Utd	D	2-2	PL	Bamba 44, Hanlon 89	10 252
Jan	1	Hearts	L	0-1	PL		17 156
	8	Ayr Utd	D	0-0	FAr4		6 056
	15	Celtic	L	0-3	PL		13 649
	18	Ayr Utd	L	0-1	FAr4		3 826
	22	Motherwell	L	0-2	PL		4 202
	26	Rangers	L	0-2	PL		11 696
	30	Dundee Utd	L	0-3	PL		6 215
Feb	2	St Mirren	W	2-0	PL	Riordan 63, Wotherspoon 93+	9 436
	12	Kilmarnock	W	2-1	PL	Sodje 52, Palsson 70p	11 082
	20	St Mirren	W	1-0	PL	Dickoh 87	3 505
	26	Inverness	W	2-0	PL	Booth 58, Stevenson 89	13 841
Mar	1	Hamilton	W	2-1	PL	Sodje 37, Riordan 75	2 619
	5	St Johnstone	D	1-1	PL	Wotherspoon 80	4 446
	3	Hearts	D	2-2	PL	Miller 35p, Vaz Te 79	17 793
Apr	6	Celtic	L	1-3	PL	Miller 66p	47 809
	9	Aberdeen	W	1-0	PL	Sodje 15	7 400
	17	Hamilton	L	1-2	PL	Sodje 66	8 173
	24	St Mirren	D	1-1	PL	Sodje 26	7 238
	30	St Johnstone	L	1-2	PL	Sodje 23	7 492
May	7	Hamilton	L	0-1	PL		2 300
	11	Inverness	L	0-2	PL		3 344
	14	Aberdeen	L	1-3	PL	Riordan 21	11 767

10th Att: 221 780 • Av: 11 672 (-1.2%) • Easter Road 17 400 (67%)

HEARTS LEAGUE APPEARANCES/GOALS 2011
Goalkeepers Marian Kello SVK 31 • Jamie MacDonald 7
Defenders Darren Barr 11+2/0 • Ismael Bouzid ALG 31+1/0 • Ryan McGowan 3+5/0 • Adrian Mrowiec POL 26+4/0 • Craig Thomson 20+7/1 • Jason Thomson 3+3/0 • Lee Wallace 9/0 • Andy Webster 9/0
Midfield Ian Black 29+3/1 • Andrew Driver 3+10/0 • Jason Holt 0+1/0 • Eggert Jonsson ISL 29/0 • David Obua UGA 7+6/0 • David Palazuelos ESP 31+2/0 • Rudi Skacel CZE 27+2/13 • Ryan Stevenson 18+13/6 • Suso ESP 16+2/0 • Marius Zaliukas LTU 28/1
Forwards Calum Elliot 11+8/4 • Stephen Elliott IRL 21+9/8 • Gary Glen 2+9/1 • Kevin Kyle 16+3/7 • Arvydas Novikovas 1+5/1 • Scott Robinson 1+3/0 • David Smith 0+1/0 • David Templeton 27+6/7
Coach Jim Jefferies

HIBS LEAGUE APPEARANCES/GOALS 2011
Goalkeepers Mark Brown 26 • Jakub Divis CZE 3 • Graeme Smith 3+1 • Graham Stack IRL 6
Defenders Souleymane Bamba FRA 16/2 • Callum Booth 17/1 • Francis Dickoh GHA 27+1/2 • Jonathan Grounds ENG 13/0 • Paul Hanlon 30+3/2 • Michael Hart 16+2/0 • Chris Hogg 6+1/2 • David Stephens WAL 4+4/0 • Scott Taggart 2+1/0 • Steven Thicot FRA 4+3/0
Midfield Edwin de Graaf NED 16+2/0 • Daniel Galbraith 8+14/0 • Lewis Horner ENG 0+1/0 • Kevin McBride 10+1/0 • Liam Miller IRL 30+3/5 • Ian Murray 14+6/0 • Gudlaugur Palsson ISL 15+1/1 • John Rankin 14+3/1 • Martin Scott 8+3/0 • Lewis Stevenson 11+8/1 • Matt Thornhill ENG 5+3/0 • Richie Towell IRL 15+1/0 • David Wotherspoon 26+9/2 • Merouane Zemmama 3+1/0
Forwards Kurtis Byrne IRL 0+3/0 • Darryl Duffy 2+5/0 • Daniel Handling 0+1/0 • Colin Nish 11+9/1 • Derek Riordan 28+5/11 • Akpo Sodje ENG 13+2/6 • Anthony Stokes IRL 3/1 • Valdas Trakys LTU 4+5/0 • Ricardo Vaz Te POR 7+3/1
Coach John Hughes • Colin Calderwood (18/10/10)

INVERNESS CALEDONIAN THISTLE 2010–11

		Opponent		Score	Comp	Scorers	Att
Jy	31	Queen's Pk	W	3-0	LCr1	Cox 22, Odhiambo 55, Tokely 57	1 099
	14	Celtic	L	0-1	PL		**7 547**
Aug	22	Dundee Utd	W	4-0	PL	McCann 34, Rooney 2 51 82p, Duncan 53	6 575
	25	Peterhead	W	3-0	LCr2	Rooney 2 32p 49, Munro 38	1 001
	28	Hamilton	L	0-1	PL		3 851
Sep	11	Hibernian	D	1-1	PL	Rooney 82p	10 358
	18	Hearts	L	1-3	PL	Odhiambo 37	4 515
	22	Celtic	L	0-6	LCr3		17 429
	25	St Mirren	W	2-1	PL	Odhiambo 2 45 50	3 954
Oct	2	Aberdeen	W	2-0	PL	Hayes 19, Rooney 61	6 144
	16	St Johnstone	D	1-1	PL	Hayes 72	4 883
	23	Kilmarnock	W	2-1	PL	Rooney 42p, Hayes 66	4 508
	30	Rangers	D	1-1	PL	Odhiambo 81	43 697
Nov	6	Motherwell	L	1-2	PL	Duff 75	4 054
	9	Aberdeen	W	2-1	PL	Rooney 34p Munro 81	5 917
	13	Hamilton	W	3-1	PL	Rooney 2 49 59, Hayes 52	2 019
	20	Hibernian	W	4-2	PL	Foran 7, Rooney 3 51p 70 80	4 217
	27	Celtic	D	2-2	PL	Foran 70, Munro 83	46 096
Dec	11	Rangers	D	1-1	PL	Hayes 31	6 799
	18	Hearts	D	1-1	PL	Munro 17	12 994
	26	St Mirren	L	1-2	PL	Cox 8	3 819
	29	Kilmarnock	L	1-3	PL	Foran 71	3 735
Jan	2	St Johnstone	L	0-1	PL		3 126
	8	Elgin City	W	2-0	FAr4	Sanchez 89, Rooney 90	2 808
	15	Motherwell	D	0-0	PL		3 728
	18	Rangers	L	0-1	PL		41 623
	22	Hamilton	D	1-1	PL	Sanchez 18	**3 241**
	26	Aberdeen	L	0-2	PL		4 468
Feb	5	Morton	W	5-1	FAr5	Foran 2 19 86, Rooney 2 38 66, Hogg 62	1 893
	12	St Mirren	D	3-3	PL	Rooney 2 6 61, Doran 33	3 203
	19	St Johnstone	W	2-0	PL	Tokely 28, Duncan 62	3 942
	26	Hibernian	L	0-2	PL		13 841
Mar	1	Dundee Utd	L	0-2	PL		3 392
	5	Motherwell	W	3-0	PL	Sutherland 18, Foran 64, MacDonald 72	3 563
	16	Celtic	L	1-2	FAqf	Rooney 44p	6 064
	19	Dundee Utd	L	0-1	PL		6 548
Apr	9	Kilmarnock	D	1-1	PL	Hayes 10	4 518
	16	Hearts	D	1-1	PL	Doran 6	4 336
	25	St Johnstone	W	3-0	PL	Innes 36, Doran 57, Foran 70	2 395
	30	Aberdeen	L	0-1	PL		6 280
May	4	Celtic	W	3-2	PL	OG 7, Munro 53, Sutherland 62	6 702
	7	St Mirren	W	1-0	PL	Rooney 85	3 446
	11	Hibernian	W	2-0	PL	Foran 42, Ross 51	3 344
	14	Hamilton	W	2-1	PL	Foran 44, Rooney 57	2 017

7th Att: 85 998 • Av: 4 526 (+28.9%) • Caledonian 7 780 (58%)

KILMARNOCK 2010–11

		Opponent		Score	Comp	Scorers	Att
	14	Rangers	L	1-2	PL	Hamill 60p	45 739
	22	Motherwell	L	0-1	PL		5 399
Aug	25	Airdrie Utd	W	6-2	LCr2	Sammon 3 4 55 93+, Wright 32, Kelly 64, Sissoko 77	3 066
	28	Aberdeen	W	1-0	PL	Hamill 92+	11 287
	11	St Mirren	W	2-1	PL	Dayton 29, Eremenko 56	6 064
Sep	19	Celtic	L	1-2	PL	Sammon 7	8 645
	22	Hibernian	W	3-1	LCr3	Hamill 2 29 71p, Silva 74	4 074
	25	Hamilton	D	2-2	PL	Hamill 83p, Sammon 89	3 033
	2	Dundee Utd	L	1-2	PL	Sammon 94+	4 633
Oct	16	Hibernian	L	1-2	PL	Silva 2	11 256
	23	Inverness	L	1-2	PL	Miguel 74	4 508
	27	Rangers	L	0-2	LCqf		7 561
	31	Hearts	W	3-0	PL	Wright 45, Sammon 80, Eremenko 82	13 056
Nov	6	St Johnstone	W	3-0	PL	OG 37, Sammon 83, Kelly 94+	3 230
	10	Hamilton	W	3-0	PL	Gordon 34, Sammon 2 46 52	**4 214**
	13	Dundee Utd	D	1-1	PL	Sammon 22	6 597
	20	Rangers	L	2-3	PL	Sammon 2 21 59	10 177
	27	Aberdeen	W	2-0	PL	Sammon 18, Hamill 51p	5 013
Dec	18	Motherwell	W	2-1	PL	Kelly 2 9 43	4 216
	21	Celtic	D	1-1	PL	Sammon 53	44 522
	29	Inverness	W	3-1	PL	Bryson 26, Kelly 68, Hamill 78	3 735
	1	St Mirren	W	2-0	PL	Kelly 64, Bryson 79	6 118
	10	Rangers	L	0-3	FAr4		13 215
Jan	15	St Johnstone	D	1-1	PL	Sammon 60	4 885
	18	Hearts	L	1-2	PL	Miguel 19	4 996
	22	Dundee Utd	D	1-1	PL	Sammon 41	5 120
	29	Hamilton	D	1-1	PL	Sammon 15	2 680
Feb	2	Motherwell	W	1-0	PL	Silva 81	3 640
	12	Hibernian	L	1-2	PL	Hamill 74p	11 082
	19	Aberdeen	L	0-5	PL		7 371
	26	St Mirren	W	2-0	PL	Gros 13, Eremenko 29	5 243
	5	Hearts	W	2-0	PL	Silva 50, Eremenko 56	13 836
Mar	13	Rangers	L	1-2	PL	Hamill 61p	42 417
	19	Motherwell	W	3-1	PL	Pascali 24, Hamill 42p, Kelly 52	4 259
	2	St Johnstone	D	0-0	PL		3 083
	9	Inverness	D	1-1	PL	Kelly 13	4 518
Apr	20	Celtic	L	0-4	PL		9 117
	23	Dundee Utd	L	2-4	PL	Silva 70, Pascali 87	5 225
	30	Hearts	D	2-2	PL	Fowler 55, Agard 86	5 006
	8	Celtic	L	0-2	PL		9 720
May	11	Motherwell	D	1-1	PL	Aubameyang 49	4 101
	15	Rangers	L	1-5	PL	Dayton 65	**16 173**

5th Att: 121 906 • Av: 6 416 (+8.3%) • Rugby Park 18 128 (35%)

INVERNESS LEAGUE APPEARANCES/GOALS 2011
Goalkeepers Ryan Esson 35 • Jonny Tuffey NIR 3
Defenders Kenny Gillet FRA 12+1/0 • Stuart Golabek 1+2/0
Chris Hogg ENG 10/0 • Chris Innes 10+3/1 • Kevin McCann 8/1
Grant Munro 34+1/4 • Graeme Shinnie 19/0 • Ross Tokely 34+1/1
Midfield Gil Blumstein ISR 1+4/0 • Lee Cox ENG 25+2/1
Aaron Doran IRL 11+3/3 • Stuart Duff 33/1 • Russell Duncan 20+4/2
Jonathan Hayes IRL 23+1/6 • Alex MacDonald 2+8/1
Roy McBain 0+2/0 • Gavin Morrison 3+7/0 • Liam Polworth 0+1/0
David Proctor 7+3/0 • Nick Ross 30+4/1
Forwards Richie Foran IRL 30+2/8 • Eric Odhiambo ENG 18+14/4
Adam Rooney IRL 37+1/15 • Dani Sanchez ESP 3+6/1
Shane Sutherland 9+20/2
Coach Terry Butcher ENG

KILMARNOCK LEAGUE APPEARANCES/GOALS 2011
Goalkeepers Cameron Bell 31 • Anssi Jaakkola FIN 7+1/0
Defenders Billy Berntsson SWE 0+4/0 • Tim Clancy IRL 19+2/0
Gary Fisher 0+3/0 • James Fowler 21+5/1 • Ben Gordon 18/1
Garry Hay 17+4/0 • Ryan O'Leary 3/0 • Alex Pursehouse ENG 0+1/0
Mahamadou Sissoko FRA 26+1/0 • Frazer Wright 27/1
Midfield Craig Bryson 33/2 • David Silva POR 17+12/4
James Dayton ENG 7+3/2 • Alexei Eremenko FIN 31/4 • Jamie
Hamill 31+1/8 • Danny Invincibile AUS 3+4/0 • Liam Kelly ENG 30+2/7
Manuel Pascali ITA 34+1/2 • Mehdi Taouil MAR 18+6/0
Forwards Kieran Agard ENG 3+5/1 • Willy Aubameyang FRA 4+2/1
Harry Forrester ENG 3+4/0 • William Gros FRA 8+3/1 • Rory
McKenzie 0+1/0 • Rui Miguel POR 8+13/2 • Connor Sammon 19+4/15
Coach Mixu Paatelainen FIN • Kenny Shiels (25/03/11)

MOTHERWELL 2010–11

Month	Date	Opponent	Res	Score	Comp	Scorers	Att
Jul	15	Breidablik	W	1-0	ELp2	Forbes 63	5 990
Jul	22	Breidablik	W	1-0	ELp2	Murphy 42	1 700
Jul	29	Aalesunds	D	1-1	ELp3	Murphy 46	8 450
Aug	5	Aalesunds	W	3-0	ELp3	Murphy 3, Sutton 13, Page 89	7 721
Aug	15	Hibernian	L	2-3	PL	Sutton 13, Murphy 75p	5 172
Aug	18	OB Odense	L	1-2	ELpo	Hateley 93+	14 911
Aug	22	Kilmarnock	W	1-0	PL	Blackman 37	5 399
Aug	26	OB Odense	L	0-1	ELpo		9 105
Aug	29	Celtic	L	0-1	PL		9 207
Sep	11	St Johnstone	W	2-0	PL	Blackman 3, OG 39	3 254
Sep	18	Aberdeen	D	1-1	PL	Murphy 35	5 251
Sep	21	Brechin	W	2-0	LCr3	Page 2 16 59	903
Sep	25	Hearts	W	3-1	PL	Blackman 58, Sutton 70	13 749
Oct	2	St Mirren	W	3-1	PL	Humphrey 3, Hateley 87p, Murphy 88	4 384
Oct	16	Rangers	L	1-4	PL	Blackman 44	44 609
Oct	23	Dundee Utd	W	2-1	PL	OG 2 1 75	4 635
Oct	26	Dundee Utd	W	1-0	LCqf	Gow 86	4 838
Oct	30	Hamilton	W	1-0	PL		4 865
Nov	6	Inverness	W	2-1	PL	Gow 33, Blackman 43	4 054
Nov	10	St Johnstone	W	4-0	PL	Blackman 3 12 24 45, Sutton 88	3 361
Nov	13	Hibernian	L	1-2	PL	Blackman 10p	11 178
Nov	20	St Mirren	D	1-1	PL	Blackman 74	4 213
Dec	14	Hearts	L	1-2	PL	Lasley 45	**3 324**
Dec	26	Rangers	L	1-4	PL	Sutton 47	9 317
Dec	29	Celtic	L	0-1	PL		40 750
Dec	1	Hamilton	D	0-0	PL		3 171
Jan	9	Dundee	W	4-0	FAr4	Sutton 2 3 47, Jennings 81, Murphy 87	4 285
Jan	12	Dundee Utd	L	0-2	PL		4 918
Jan	15	Inverness	D	0-0	PL		3 728
Jan	22	Hibernian	W	2-0	PL	Murphy 20, Saunders 24	4 202
Jan	26	St Johnstone	L	0-1	PL		2 268
Jan	30	Rangers	L	1-2	LCsf	Lasley 66	23 432
Feb	2	Kilmarnock	L	0-1	PL		3 640
Feb	5	Stranraer	W	2-0	FAr5	Jones 45, Sutton 82	2 042
Feb	12	Rangers	L	0-6	PL		43 789
Feb	15	Aberdeen	W	2-1	PL	Jeffers 14, Murphy 71	6 882
Feb	19	Hamilton	W	1-0	PL	Sutton 36p	4 407
Feb	23	St Mirren	L	0-1	PL		3 613
Feb	27	Celtic	W	2-0	PL	Sutton 2 2 49	**9 716**
Mar	5	Inverness	L	0-3	PL		3 563
Mar	13	Dundee Utd	D	2-2	FAqf	Sutton 2 1 72	7 358
Mar	19	Kilmarnock	L	1-3	PL	Sutton 15	4 259
Mar	30	Dundee Utd	W	3-0	FAqf	Murphy 8, Humphrey 36, Jeffers 63	8 337
Apr	2	Aberdeen	W	2-1	PL	Humphrey 15, Hutchinson 88	4 458
Apr	6	Dundee Utd	W	2-1	PL	Murphy 26, Humphrey 41	3 435
Apr	9	Hearts	D	0-0	PL		13 800
Apr	16	St Johnstone	W	3-0	FAsf	Craigan 5, Murphy 14, Sutton 39	11 920
Apr	23	Hearts	D	3-3	PL	Sutton 2 55 88, Hateley 59	13 039
Apr	30	Rangers	L	0-5	PL		8 968
May	7	Dundee Utd	L	0-4	PL		5 951
May	11	Kilmarnock	D	1-1	PL	Jones 8	4 101
May	15	Celtic	L	0-4	PL		57 294
May	20	Celtic	L	0-3	FAf		49 618

6th • Att: 99 838 • Av: 5 254 (-1.0%) • Fir Park 13 742 (38%)

RANGERS 2010–11

Month	Date	Opponent	Res	Score	Comp	Scorers	Att
Aug	14	Kilmarnock	W	2-1	PL	Miller 16, Naismith 57	45 739
Aug	22	Hibernian	W	3-0	PL	Miller 3 64 69 93+	17 145
Aug	28	St Johnstone	W	2-0	PL	Papac 33, Miller 79	46 109
Aug	11	Hamilton	W	2-1	PL	Jelavic 6, Miller 89	5 356
Aug	14	Man Utd	D	0-0	CLgC		74 408
Sep	18	Dundee Utd	W	4-0	PL	OG 9, Miller 2 68 82, Naismith 77	44 786
Sep	21	Dunfermline	W	7-1	LCr3	Jelavic 2 21 59, Lafferty 3 23 46 71, Bougherra 38, Naismith 77	23 120
Sep	26	Aberdeen	W	3-2	PL	Miller 2 34p 52, Jelavic 67	15 307
Sep	29	Bursaspor	W	1-0	CLgC	Naismith 18	41 905
Sep	2	Hearts	W	2-1	PL	Lafferty 79, Naismith 94+	15 637
Oct	16	Motherwell	W	4-1	PL	Naismith 47, Davis 62, Miller 65, Weiss 67	44 609
Oct	20	Valencia	D	1-1	CLgC	Edu 34	45 153
Oct	24	Celtic	L	1-3	PL	OG 49, Miller 2 55 67	58 874
Oct	27	Kilmarnock	W	2-0	LCqf	Little 25, Naismith 61	7 561
Oct	30	Inverness	D	1-1	PL	Edu 11	43 697
Nov	2	Valencia	L	0-3	CLgC		26 821
Nov	7	St Mirren	W	3-1	PL	OG 48, Naismith 58, Miller 68	5 674
Nov	9	Hibernian	L	0-3	PL		**41 514**
Nov	13	Aberdeen	W	2-0	PL	Miller 21, Weiss 37	44 919
Nov	20	Kilmarnock	W	3-2	PL	Miller 3 42p 55p 63	10 177
Nov	24	Man Utd	L	0-1	CLgC		49 764
Dec	7	Bursaspor	D	1-1	CLgC	Miller 19	9 673
Dec	11	Inverness	D	1-1	PL	Miller 57	6 799
Dec	26	Motherwell	W	4-1	PL	Miller 2 26 61, OG 33, Weiss 51	9 317
Dec	2	Celtic	L	0-2	PL		50 222
Jan	10	Kilmarnock	W	3-0	FAr4	McCulloch 20, Lafferty 37, Whittaker 71p	13 215
Jan	15	Hamilton	W	4-0	PL	Weiss 2 25 46, Whittaker 28p, Edu 82	44 639
Jan	18	Inverness	W	1-0	PL	Davis 45	41 623
Jan	22	Hearts	L	0-1	PL		16 737
Jan	29	Hibernian	W	2-0	PL	Bougherra 26, Jelavic 35	11 696
Jan	30	Motherwell	W	2-1	LCsf	Naismith 75	23 432
Feb	2	Hearts	W	1-0	PL	Lafferty 4	44 823
Feb	6	Celtic	D	2-2	FAr5	Ness 3, Whittaker 41p	50 230
Feb	12	Motherwell	W	6-0	PL	Naismith 5, Jelavic 3 34 37 79, OG 76, Healy 83	43 789
Feb	17	Sporting CP	D	1-1	ELr2	Whittaker 66	34 095
Feb	20	Celtic	L	0-3	PL		58 748
Feb	24	Sporting CP	D	2-2	ELr2	Diouf 20, Edu 90	15 375
Feb	27	St Johnstone	W	4-0	PL	Jelavic 2 5 90, Lafferty 41, Papac 83	43 125
Mar	2	Celtic	L	0-1	FAr5		57 847
Mar	5	St Mirren	W	1-0	PL	Bartley 24	5 405
Mar	8	PSV	D	0-0	ELr3		30 000
Mar	13	Kilmarnock	W	2-1	PL	Diouf 38, OG 87	42 417
Mar	17	PSV	L	0-1	ELr3		35 373
Mar	20	Celtic	W	2-1	LCf	Davis 24, Jelavic 98	51 181
Apr	2	Dundee Utd	L	2-3	PL	Jelavic 18, Naismith 52	46 697
Apr	5	St Johnstone	W	2-0	PL	Lafferty 20, Naismith 83	5 820
Apr	10	Hamilton	W	1-0	PL	Jelavic 44	4 526
Apr	13	Aberdeen	W	1-0	PL	Jelavic 22	11 925
Apr	16	St Mirren	W	2-1	PL	Papac 33, Whittaker 52p	46 392
Apr	19	Dundee Utd	W	4-0	PL	Whittaker 2 23p 60p, Jelavic 72, Lafferty 82	11 626
Apr	24	Celtic	D	0-0	PL		**50 248**
	30	Motherwell	W	5-0	PL	Lafferty 18, Davis 51, Jelavic 65, Naismith 2 76 91+	8 968
My	7	Hearts	W	4-0	PL	Jelavic 23, Lafferty 40, Davis 44, OG 83	46 178
My	10	Dundee Utd	W	2-0	PL	Jelavic 21, Lafferty 25	49 267
My	15	Kilmarnock	W	5-1	PL	Lafferty 3 1 7 53, Naismith 5, Jelavic 49	16 173

1st • Att: 860 793 • Av: 45 304 (-4.3%) • Ibrox 51 082 (88%)

MOTHERWELL LEAGUE APPEARANCES/GOALS 2011

Goalkeepers Lee Hollis 1 • Darren Randolph IRL 37
Defenders Angelis Charalambous CYP 0+1/0
Stephen Craigan NIR 32+3/0 • Gavin Gunning IRL 12+2/0 • Steven Hammell 26+5/0 • Jonathan Page ENG 3+6/0 • Mark Reynolds 19/0
Maurice Ross 5+1/0 • Steven Saunders 22+3/1
Midfield Nick Blackman ENG 15+3/10 • Stuart Carswell 3+1/0
Marc Fitzpatrick 3+2/0 • Ross Forbes 11+12/0 • Alan Gow 9+6/1
Tom Hateley ENG 36+2/2 • Chris Humphrey ENG 33+3/3
Shaun Hutchinson ENG 18+1/1 • Steve Jennings ENG 30/0
Keith Lasley 26/1 • Steven Meechan 0+2/0
Forwards Esteban Casagolda ESP 3+9/0 • Francis Jeffers ENG 8+2/1
Steve Jones NIR 10+2/1 • Robert McHugh 0+1/0
Jamie Murphy 31+4/6 • Jamie Pollock 0+3/0 • Gary Smith 0+1/0
John Sutton ENG 25+10/10
Coach Craig Brown • Stuart McCall (30/12/10)

RANGERS LEAGUE APPEARANCES/GOALS 2011

Goalkeepers Neil Alexander 1 • Allan McGregor 37
Defenders Kyle Bartley ENG 5/1 • Madjid Bougherra ALG 31/1
Kirk Broadfoot 5+3/0 • Ricky Foster 11+4/0 • Kyle Hutton 1+4/0
Sasa Papac BIH 34/3 • Ross Perry • David Weir 37/0 • Andy Webster 1/0
Steven Whittaker 36/4
Midfield Steven Davis NIR 37/4 • Maurice Edu USA 27+6/2
Lee McCulloch 17+4/0 • Steven Naismith 28+3/11 • Jamie Ness 8+3/0
Vladimir Weiss SVK 17+6/5 • Gregg Wylde 9+6/0
Forwards James Beattie ENG 5+2/0 • El-Hadji Diouf SEN 6+9/1 • John Fleck 3+10/0 • David Healy NIR 2+6/1 • Nikica Jelavic CRO 20+3/16
Salim Kerkar FRA 0+1/0 • Kyle Lafferty NIR 23+8/11 • Rory Loy 0+1/0
Kenny Miller 17+1/21 • **Coach** Walter Smith

ST JOHNSTONE 2010–11

	Date	Opponent		Score	Comp	Scorers	Att
Aug	14	Hearts	D	1-1	PL	Parkin [45]	14 562
	21	Aberdeen	L	0-1	PL		6 523
	24	Morton	W	2-0	LCr2	Dobie [22], Davidson [80]	1 530
	28	Rangers	L	1-2	PL	Grainger [25]	46 109
Sep	11	Motherwell	L	0-2	PL		3 254
	18	St Mirren	W	2-1	PL	Jackson [3], Parkin [33]	3 349
	21	Queen OTS	W	3-0	LCr3	Morris [68p], Haber [72], Millar [74]	1 624
	25	Dundee Utd	L	0-1	PL		7 397
Oct	2	Hibernian	W	2-0	PL	Craig [76], Haber [91+]	3 819
	16	Inverness	D	1-1	PL	Samuel [9]	4 883
	23	Hamilton	W	2-1	PL	Parkin [19], Grainger [86]	2 431
	27	Celtic	L	2-3	LCqf	Parkin [31], Davidson [54]	5 151
	30	Celtic	L	0-3	PL		**6 866**
Nov	6	Kilmarnock	L	0-3	PL		3 230
	10	Motherwell	L	0-4	PL		3 361
	13	Hearts	L	0-2	PL		4 156
	20	Aberdeen	W	1-0	PL	OG [82]	7 841
	27	Hibernian	D	0-0	PL		10 248
Dec	11	St Mirren	W	2-1	PL	Parkin [53], Craig [90]	2 701
	26	Celtic	L	0-2	PL		41 522
Jan	2	Inverness	W	1-0	PL	Samuel [85]	3 126
	11	Hearts	W	1-0	FAr4	MacDonald [86]	6 261
	15	Kilmarnock	D	1-1	PL	Taylor [86]	4 885
	22	St Mirren	D	0-0	PL		3 009
	26	Motherwell	W	1-0	PL	Craig [62]	2 268
	29	Hearts	L	0-1	PL		13 430
Feb	1	Hamilton	W	2-0	PL	May 2 [4 46]	2 631
	9	Partick	W	2-0	FAr5	Davidson [42], Craig [57]	2 441
	19	Inverness	L	0-2	PL		3 942
	22	Dundee Utd	D	0-0	PL		3 507
	27	Rangers	L	0-4	PL		43 125
Mar	2	Aberdeen	D	0-0	PL		2 909
	5	Hibernian	D	1-1	PL	OG [46]	4 446
	12	Brechin	D	2-2	FAqf	Millar [48], Invincibile [62]	3 472
	19	Hamilton	D	0-0	PL		2 111
	22	Brechin	W	1-0	FAqf	Samuel [37]	3 891
Apr	2	Kilmarnock	D	0-0	PL		3 083
	5	Rangers	L	0-2	PL		5 820
	9	Dundee Utd	L	0-2	PL		6 398
	12	Celtic	L	0-1	PL		6 338
	16	Motherwell	L	0-3	FAsf		11 920
	25	Inverness	L	0-3	PL		2 395
	30	Hibernian	W	2-1	PL	Craig [74], Moon [92+]	7 492
May	7	Aberdeen	W	2-0	PL	OG [8], Adams [60]	6 361
	10	Hamilton	W	1-0	PL	Craig [29p]	**2 253**
	14	St Mirren	D	0-0	PL		4 230

8th Att: 72 982 • Av: 3 841 (-18.5%) • McDiarmid Park 10 673 (36%)

ST MIRREN 2010–11

	Date	Opponent		Score	Comp	Scorers	Att
Aug	14	Dundee Utd	D	1-1	PL	Lynch [73]	5 618
	22	Celtic	L	0-4	PL		46 812
	25	Ross Co	D	3-3	LCr2	McGregor [44], Higdon [79], McGowan [91+], L 3-4p	1 239
	29	Hibernian	W	1-0	PL	Dargo [58]	4 480
Sep	11	Kilmarnock	L	1-2	PL	Thomson [48]	6 064
	18	St Johnstone	L	1-2	PL	Lynch [37]	3 349
	25	Inverness	L	1-2	PL	McGowan [77]	3 954
Oct	2	Motherwell	L	1-3	PL	Wardlaw [64]	4 384
	16	Hamilton	D	2-2	PL	Higdon 2 [60 73]	3 577
	23	Hearts	L	0-3	PL		12 009
	30	Aberdeen	W	2-1	PL	McAusland [28], Travner [92+]	4 589
	7	Rangers	L	1-3	PL	Higdon [76p]	5 674
	10	Dundee Utd	W	2-1	PL	Higdon 2 [41 65]	5 548
Nov	14	Celtic	L	0-1	PL		6 073
	20	Motherwell	D	1-1	PL	Wardlaw [37]	4 213
	27	Hamilton	D	0-0	PL		2 280
Dec	11	St Johnstone	L	1-2	PL	Higdon [62]	**2 701**
	26	Inverness	W	2-1	PL	Thomson 2 [44 85]	3 819
	29	Hearts	L	0-2	PL		4 599
Jan	3	Kilmarnock	L	0-2	PL		**6 118**
	8	Peterhead	D	0-0	FAr4		2 312
	15	Aberdeen	L	0-2	PL		9 740
	18	Peterhead	W	6-1	FAr4	McGowan 3 [22 33 46], Mooy [31], McQuade 2 [45 56]	1 610
	22	St Johnstone	D	0-0	PL		3 009
	26	Dundee Utd	D	1-1	PL	McGregor [75]	3 095
Feb	2	Hibernian	L	0-2	PL		9 436
	5	Ayr Utd	W	2-1	FAr5	Dargo 2 [7 45]	5 997
	12	Inverness	D	3-3	PL	Higdon [28p], Thomson [29], McGregor [74]	3 203
	20	Hibernian	L	0-1	PL		3 505
	23	Motherwell	W	1-0	PL	Higdon [82]	3 613
	26	Kilmarnock	L	0-2	PL		5 243
Mar	6	Rangers	L	0-1	PL		5 405
	12	Aberdeen	D	1-1	FAqf	McGowan [77]	4 120
	16	Aberdeen	L	1-2	FAqf	OG [87]	7 330
	19	Hearts	L	2-3	PL	Higdon 2 [15 69]	12 763
Apr	2	Hamilton	W	3-1	PL	Higdon 3 [61 64p 71]	4 985
	6	Aberdeen	W	3-2	PL	Higdon [6], Dargo [57], Thomson [68]	3 489
	9	Celtic	L	0-1	PL		50 318
	16	Rangers	L	1-2	PL	McGregor [38]	46 392
	24	Hibernian	D	1-1	PL	Dargo [39p]	7 238
	30	Hamilton	L	0-1	PL		5 037
May	7	Inverness	L	0-1	PL		3 446
	10	Aberdeen	W	1-0	PL	Wardlaw [65]	5 955
	14	St Johnstone	D	0-0	PL		4 230

11th Att: 84 545 • Av: 4 449 (+0.8%) • Greenhill Road 8 023 (55%)

ST JOHNSTONE LEAGUE APPEARANCES/GOALS 2011

Goalkeepers Peter Enckelman FIN 29 • Graeme Smith 9
Defenders Steven Anderson 24+1/0 • Michael Duberry ENG 32+1/0 Graham Gartland IRL 4+3/0 • Danny Grainger ENG 31+2/2 • David MacKay 32/0 • Alan Maybury IRL 23+7/0 • Kevin Rutkiewicz 4+6/0
Midfield Jamie Adams 9+2/1 • Liam Caddis 1+2/0 Liam Craig 29+5/5 • Murray Davidson 33+1/0 Danny Invincibile AUS 8+2/0 • Chris Millar 29+1/0 • Kevin Moon 4+2/1 Jody Morris ENG 23/0 • Cleveland Taylor ENG 11+10/1
Forwards Scott Dobie 1+3/0 • Marcus Haber CAN 5+6/1 • Andy Jackson 10+7/1 • Peter MacDonald 14+10/0 • Stevie May 8+11/2 Steven Milne 1+1/0 • Jennison Myrie-Williams ENG 4+2/0 • Arvydas Novikovas LTU 1+5/0 • Sam Parkin ENG 17+4/4 • Stephen Reynolds 0+5/0 • Jordan Robertson ENG 2+4/0 • Collin Samuel TRI 20+8/2
Coach Derek McInnes

ST MIRREN LEAGUE APPEARANCES/GOALS 2011

Goalkeepers Paul Gallacher 27 • Craig Samson 11
Defenders David Barron 4+5/0 • Ally Love 0+1/0 • Lee Mair 22+2/0 Marc McAusland 24+1/1 • Darren McGregor 36/3 • John Potter 32+2/0 Jure Travner SVN 35+2/1 • David van Zanten IRL 25+3/0
Midfield Garry Brady 3+2/0 • Patrick Cregg IRI 18+4/0 Jim Goodwin IRL 16+1/0 • Nick Hegarty ENG 2+1/0 Michael Higdon ENG 26+2/14 • Mark Lamont 0+1/0 • Sean Lynch 8+6/2 Jamie McCluskey 0+3/0 • Jamie McKernon 0+1/0 Kenny McLean 10+9/0 • Mark McLennan 0+1/0 • Aaron Mooy AUS 7+5/0 Hugh Murray 21+3/0 • Steven Robb 3/0 • Steven Thomson 25+2/5
Forwards Craig Dargo 14+8/3 • Paul McGowan 33/1 Paul McQuade 0+5/0 • Graeme Ramage 0+1/0 • Gareth Wardlaw 16+7/3
Coach Danny Lennon

SDN – SUDAN

FIFA/COCA-COLA WORLD RANKING

'93	'94	'95	'96	'97	'98	'99	'00	'01	'02	'03	'04	'05	'06	'07	'08	'09	'10	'11	'12
119	116	86	74	108	114	132	132	118	106	103	114	92	120	92	93	108	92	113	

2011														
Jan	Feb	Mar	Apr	May	Jun	Jul	Aug	Sep	Oct	Nov	Dec	High	Low	Av
100	106	106	105	106	99	97	98	103	102	112	113	74	137	108

A quarter-final place for Sudan at the 2012 CAF Africa Cup of Nations in Equatorial Guinea and Gabon represented their best performance since winning the tournament in 1970. A 2-1 win over Burkina Faso in Bata was the only game they won but it was their first victory at the finals in 42 years. It also ensured their place in the last eight after edging out Angola on goal difference. The Sudanese then went out in a one-sided quarter-final loss to Zambia but were more than satisfied with their achievement. There were major political changes to the country in 2011 with South Sudan gaining its independence in July. The new country wasted no time in creating a football association and a national team and on July 10, 2011 South Sudan played its first international against Kenyan club side Tusker in the capital Juba. At the CAF Congress in Libreville at the end of the Nations Cup, South Sudan was voted in as the newest member of the organisation. It's open to question, however, if teams from the south will ever be able to match the might of Al Hilal and Al Merreikh, with the former reaching the semi-finals of the 2011 CAF Champions League where they lost to Esperance. It was Al Merreikh, however, who emerged strongest at home by winning the league although they failed to turn up for the Cup Final which was awarded to Hilal.

CAF AFRICA CUP OF NATIONS RECORD

1957 3 1959 2 F 1962 DNQ 1963 2 F 1965-1968 DNQ 1970 1 Winners 1972 7 r1 1974 DNQ 1976 6 r1 1978 DNE 1980 DNQ 1982 DNE 1984 DNQ 1986 DNE 1988-1996 DNQ 1998 Withdrew 2000 DNE 2002-2006 DNQ 2008 16 r1 2010 DNQ 2012 8 QF

SUDAN FOOTBALL ASSOCIATION (SFA)

Baladia Street,
PO Box 437,
Khartoum 11111
☎ +249 183 560088
📠 +249 183 776633
📧 ballafoot@hotmail.com
🖥 www.sudanfootball.com
FA 1936 CON 1957 FIFA 1948
P Mutasim Sirelkhatim
GS Magdi Shams El Din

FIFA BIG COUNT 2006

Total players	1 567 300
% of population	3.80%
Male	1 567 300
Female	0
Amateurs 18+	19 800
Youth under 18	26 500
Unregistered	88 000
Professionals	0
Referees	1 100
Admin & coaches	7 700
Number of clubs	440
Number of teams	2 750

MAJOR CITIES/TOWNS

		Population
1	Omdurman	2 482 917
2	Khartoum	2 316 348
3	Khartoum North	898 224
4	Niyala	531 022
5	Port Sudan	513 792
6	Kassala	474 115
7	Kusti	438 387
8	El Obeid	435 643
9	Wad Madani	368 021
10	Gadaref	366 606
11	El Fasher	286 277
12	Ed De'aein	225 503
13	Rabak	192 136
14	al-Junaynah	186 483

SOUTH SUDAN

1	Juba	231 463
2	Malakal	165 637

UMHURIYAT AS-SUDAN • REPUBLIC OF THE SUDAN

Capital Khartoum	Population 34 206 710 (37)	% in cities 40%
GDP per capita $3000 (170)	Area km² 1 861 484 km² (16)	GMT +/- +3
Neighbours (km)	Central African Republic 175, Chad 1360, Egypt 1273, Eritrea 605, Ethiopia 769, Libya 383, South Sudan 2184, Uganda 435 • Coast 853	

RECENT INTERNATIONAL MATCHES PLAYED BY SUDAN

2008	Opponents	Score		Venue	Comp	Scorers	Att	Referee
20-08	Egypt	W	4-0	Omdurman	Fr	OG 35, Mudathir El Tahir 2 81 90, Ahmed Adil 88		
6-09	Chad	L	1-2	Cairo	WCq	Haytham Kamal 75	4 000	Trabelsi TUN
10-09	Chad	W	3-1	Cairo	WCq	Ahmed Adil 4, Faisal Agab 48p, Saifeldin Ali 76	10 000	Diatta SEN
11-10	Congo	W	2-0	Omdurman	WCq	Mohamed Tahir 30, Faisal Agab 74	27 000	Ambaya LBY
31-12	Kenya	D	0-0	Jinja	CCr1			
2009								
4-01	Djibouti	D	1-1	Jinja	CCr1	El Tayeb El Mahi 16		
6-01	Burundi	L	0-1	Jinja	CCr1			
8-01	Zambia	W	2-0	Kampala	CCr1	Abdelhameed Amarri 33, El Tayeb El Mahi 61		
7-03	Uganda	L	0-2	Khartoum	Fr			
28-03	Mali	D	1-1	Omdurman	WCq	Mudathir El Tahir 23	35 000	Maillet SEY
28-05	Tunisia	L	0-4	Rades/Tunis	Fr			Omar LBY
7-06	Benin	L	0-1	Cotonou	WCq		26 000	Marange ZIM
20-06	Ghana	L	0-2	Omdurman	WCq		30 000	Ambaya LBY
6-09	Ghana	L	0-2	Accra	WCq		38 000	Abd El Fatah EGY
11-10	Mali	L	0-1	Bamako	WCq		15 000	Benouza ALG
14-11	Benin	L	1-2	Omdurman	WCq	Hassan Abakar 45	600	Jedidi TUN
2010								
4-06	Palestine	D	1-1	Omdurman	Fr	Tarek Mukhtar 12		
20-06	Tunisia	L	2-6	Omdurman	Fr	Mudathir El Tahir 59p, Mohannad Tahir 83		
4-09	Congo	W	2-0	Khartoum	CNq	Mudathir El Tahir 2 11 90p		Kaoma ZAM
10-10	Ghana	D	0-0	Kumasi	CNq			Damon RSA
28-11	Zanzibar †	L	0-2	Dar es Salaam	CCr1			
1-12	Rwanda	D	0-0	Dar es Salaam	CCr1			
2011								
5-01	Kenya	L	0-1	Cairo	Fr			
11-01	Congo DR	L	1-2	Cairo	Fr	Mudathir El Tahir 71		
16-01	Tanzania	W	2-0	Cairo	Fr	Hytham Karar 52, Ala'a Eldin Yousif 61		
27-03	Swaziland	W	3-0	Omdurman	CNq	Mohamed Ahmed Bashir 2 2 63, Mudathir El Tahir 71		
28-05	Ethiopia	W	2-1	Addis Abeba	Fr	Bakri Abdel Kader 2		
5-06	Swaziland	W	2-1	Manzini	CNq	Badr Eldin Galag 64, Ala'a Eldin Yousif 88		
25-06	Kenya	W	2-1	Nairobi	Fr	Mohamed Mussa 5, Bakri Abdel Kader 27		
19-08	Eritrea	W	3-0	Asmara	Fr			
26-08	Bahrain	L	0-1	Manama	Fr			
4-09	Congo	W	1-0	Brazzaville	CNq	Bakri Abdel Kader 77		
8-10	Ghana	L	0-2	Khartoum	CNq			
11-11	Cameroon	L	1-3	Marrakech	Fr	Mohamed Tahir 74p		
13-11	Uganda	D	0-0	Marrakech	Fr	L 2-3p		
28-11	Ethiopia	D	1-1	Dar es Salaam	CCr1	Mohamed Tahir 8		
30-11	Malawi	D	0-0	Dar es Salaam	CCr1			
3-12	Kenya	W	1-0	Dar es Salaam	CCr1	Muawia Bashir Koko 25		
5-12	Burundi	W	2-0	Dar es Salaam	CCqf	Amir Rabei Abdelnabi 41, Mohamed Mussa 60		
8-12	Rwanda	L	1-2	Dar es Salaam	CCsf	Ramadan Alagab 68		
10-12	Tanzania	W	1-0	Dar es Salaam	CC3p	Mohamed Sheikh Eldin 84		
17-12	Palestine	L	0-2	Al Rayyan	Fr			
2012								
9-01	Tunisia	L	0-3	Sharjah	Fr			
12-01	Senegal	L	0-1	Dakar	Fr			
16-01	Gabon	D	0-0	Franceville	Fr			
22-01	Côte d'Ivoire	L	0-1	Malabo	CNr1		5 000	Seechurn MRI
26-01	Angola	D	2-2	Malabo	CNr1	Mohamed Ahmed Bashir 2 32 74	2 500	Lemghaifry MTN
30-01	Burkina Faso	W	2-1	Bata	CNr1	Mudathir El Tahir 2 33 79	132	Otogo-Castane GAB
4-02	Zambia	L	0-3	Bata	CNqf		200	Gassama GAM

Fr = Friendly match • CN = CAF African Cup of Nations • CC = CECAFA Cup • WC = FIFA World Cup • † Not a full international
q = qualifier • r1 = first round group • sf = semi-final • f = final

SUDAN 2011

PREMIER LEAGUE

	Pl	W	D	L	F	A	Pts	Merreikh	Hilal O	Amal	Ahly S	Khartoum-3	Hilal K	Ahli K	Nsoor	Mawrada	Nil	Hilal PS	Ittihad	Jazeerat	Hay Al Arab
Al Merreikh †	26	24	1	1	69	10	72		1-0	4-1	3-0	4-0	6-0	1-0	1-0	5-0	2-0	2-0	3-0	4-0	4-0
Al Hilal Omdurman †	26	22	2	2	72	12	68	2-2		1-0	1-0	3-0	6-0	3-2	1-0	2-0	3-0	5-0	2-0	6-0	5-0
Al Amal Atbara ‡	26	12	6	8	28	30	42	2-3	0-4		0-0	2-1	2-1	0-0	2-1	1-0	1-0	2-1	2-0	3-0	2-1
Al Ahly Shendi ‡	26	10	7	9	31	27	37	0-1	1-0	2-0		0-2	0-2	3-2	1-2	2-1	3-2	4-0	3-0	2-2	1-2
Khartoum-3	26	11	4	11	30	34	37	0-1	0-2	0-1	1-1		3-0	3-1	1-0	1-1	2-1	1-1	2-1	1-1	1-0
Al Hilal Kadugli	26	9	6	11	32	44	33	1-2	1-4	2-0	0-1	3-1		2-1	1-2	4-3	0-0	2-0	3-0	1-0	2-2
Al Ahli Khartoum	26	8	7	11	29	33	31	1-0	1-2	3-0	0-3	1-3	1-1		0-1	1-0	1-1	1-2	2-1	2-2	0-0
Al Nsoor	26	8	7	11	16	26	31	1-4	0-5	0-0	1-1	0-1	1-1	0-0		1-0	0-0	0-1	0-1	1-1	1-0
Al Mawrada Omdurman	26	7	7	12	26	35	28	0-3	1-4	3-1	1-1	2-0	0-1	0-0	0-1		1-0	2-0	0-0	0-0	1-1
Al Nil Hasahisa	26	7	7	12	24	33	28	0-2	1-1	1-1	0-0	3-1	4-2	1-2	2-0	1-4		2-1	1-0	0-1	1-0
Al Hilal Port Sudan	26	8	4	14	21	42	28	1-2	0-3	1-1	2-0	2-1	1-1	0-1	0-2	1-2	2-1		1-0	1-1	1-0
Al Ittihad Wad Medani	26	6	8	12	20	31	26	1-2	0-1	1-1	1-1	2-0	1-0	1-3	0-0	2-1	2-0	3-0		1-1	1-1
Jazeerat Al-Feel	26	5	11	10	22	40	26	0-5	0-2	0-1	0-1	1-2	0-0	3-2	2-0	1-1	0-0	3-2	0-0		2-0
Hay Al Arab	26	4	5	17	18	41	20	0-2	2-3	0-2	1-0	0-2	3-1	0-1	0-1	1-2	1-2	0-1	1-1	2-1	

4/03/2011 - 23/11/2011 • † Qualified for the CAF Champions League • ‡ Qualified for the CAF Confederations Cup

MEDALS TABLE

		Overall G	Lge G	Cup G	Africa G	S	B	City
1	Al Merreikh	38	17	20	1	1	2	Omdurman
2	Al Hilal	33	26	7		2	5	Omdurman
3	Al Mawrada	6	1	5			1	Omdurman
4	Burri	1	1					Khartoum
	Al Hilal	1	1					Port Sudan
	Al Ahly	1		1				Wad Medani
	Al Ittihad	1		1				Wad Medani
	Hay Al Arab	1		1				Port Sudan
	Al Nil	1		1				Khartoum

FA CUP 2011

Quarter-finals

Al Hilal Omdurman	3
Al Ittihad Wad Medani	1
Hay Al Arab	1 2p
Al Amal Atbara	1 4p
Al Nsoor	1
Wad Hashem Senar	0
Al Mawrada Omdurman	0
Al Merreikh	4

Semi-finals

Al Hilal Omdurman	2
Al Amal Atbara	1
Al Nsoor	2
Al Merreikh	5

Final

Al Hilal Omdurman	w-o
Al Merreikh	

4/11/2011
Al Hilal awarded the cup after El Merreikh failed to appear for the final

SEN – SENEGAL

FIFA/COCA-COLA WORLD RANKING

'93	'94	'95	'96	'97	'98	'99	'00	'01	'02	'03	'04	'05	'06	'07	'08	'09	'10	'11	'12
56	50	47	58	85	95	79	88	65	27	33	31	30	41	38	50	89	70	44	

						2011								High	Low	Av
	Jan	Feb	Mar	Apr	May	Jun	Jul	Aug	Sep	Oct	Nov	Dec		High	Low	Av
	70	69	69	51	40	43	46	49	42	42	44	44		26	95	56

Senegal were the form team of the 2012 CAF Africa Cup of Nations qualifiers and went into the finals in Equatorial Guinea and Gabon as one of the firm favourites. But the Lions of Teranga had a calamitous campaign, ending without a single point and were the first side to be eliminated. Senegal were two goals down in the first half hour of their opening game against Zambia, eventually losing 2-1 and they then suffered the ignominy of defeat to tiny Equatorial Guinea who were exactly 100 places below them in the FIFA/Coca Cola World Ranking, in what arguably was one of the biggest upsets in Nations Cup history. The final crushing blow was defeat to Libya, ending a disastrous fortnight for the star-studded side. In the qualifiers, Senegal finished top of a group that included two former African champions - Cameroon and the Congo DR. At home there were surprise champions when US Ouakam, a club from the suburbs of Dakar, won a first-ever league title. They were denied the opportunity of winning the double, however, after their cup semi-final against Casa Sport was abandoned due to crowd trouble with the score at 0-0. The match was awarded to Casa who then beat Touré Kounda 1-0 in the final. One of the big stories of the season was the relegation of Jeanne d'Arc, historically one of the most successful teams in the country.

CAF AFRICA CUP OF NATIONS RECORD

1957-1963 DNE **1965** 3 r1 **1968** 5 r1 1970-1978 DNQ 1980 DNE 1982-1984 DNQ **1986** 5 r1 1988 DNQ **1990** 4 SF **1992** 5 QF (Hosts)
1994 8 QF 1996-1998 DNQ **2000** 7 QF **2002** 2 F **2004** 5 QF **2006** 4 SF **2008** 12 r1 2010 DNQ **2012** 13 r1

FEDERATION SENEGALAISE DE FOOTBALL (FSF)

VDN-Ouest-Foire en face du
CICES, Case Postale 13021,
Dakar

☎ +221 33 8692828
📠 +221 33 8200592
📧 fsf@senegalfoot.sn
🖥 www.senegalfoot.sn
FA 1960 CON 1963 FIFA 1962
P Augustin Senghor
GS Victor Cisse

FIFA BIG COUNT 2006

Total players	661 685
% of population	5.52%
Male	661 226
Female	459
Amateurs 18+	15 145
Unregistered	70 000
Professionals	100
Referees	2 960
Admin & coaches	2 064
Number of clubs	191
Number of teams	12 200

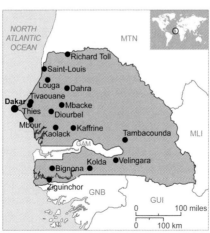

MAJOR CITIES/TOWNS

		Population
1	Dakar	2 535 431
2	Thiès	270 065
3	Mbour	207 286
4	Kaolack	180 409
5	Saint-Louis	175 988
6	Ziguinchor	165 027
7	Diourbel	105 713
8	Louga	85 344
9	Tambacounda	82 412
10	Kolda	65 714
11	Mbacké	57 731
12	Tivaouane	56 345
13	Richard Toll	50 102
14	Joal-Fadiouth	42 024
15	Kaffrine	30 040
16	Dahra	29 590
17	Bignona	26 603
18	Fatick	25 318
19	Vélingara	24 687

REPUBLIQUE DU SENEGAL • REPUBLIC OF SENEGAL

Capital	Dakar	Population	13 711 597 (67)	% in cities	42%
GDP per capita	$1600 (141)	Area km²	196 722 km² (87)	GMT + / -	0
Neighbours (km)	Gambia 740, Guinea 330, Guinea-Bissau 338, Mali 419, Mauritania 813 • Coast 531				

RECENT INTERNATIONAL MATCHES PLAYED BY SENEGAL

2008	Opponents	Score		Venue	Comp	Scorers	Att	Referee
12-01	Namibia	W	3-1	Dakar	Fr	Diomansy Kamara 2 [9 73], Henri Camara [83]		
16-01	Benin	W	2-1	Ouagadougou	Fr	Mendy [13], Gueye [82]		
23-01	Tunisia	D	2-2	Tamale	CNr1	Sall [44], Diomansy Kamara [66]		Nichimura JPN
27-01	Angola	L	1-3	Tamale	CNr1	Abdoulaye Faye [20]		Haimoudi ALG
31-01	South Africa	D	1-1	Kumasi	CNr1	Henri Camara [37]		Kotey GHA
31-05	Algeria	W	1-0	Dakar	WCq	Ibrahima Faye [80]	50 000	Kotey GHA
8-06	Gambia	D	0-0	Banjul	WCq		24 500	Ncobo RSA
15-06	Liberia	D	2-2	Monrovia	WCq	Diouf [47], Gueye [55]	18 000	Djaoupe TOG
21-06	Liberia	W	3-1	Dakar	WCq	Sonko [8], Diouf [32], Henri Camara [63]	40 000	Chaibou NIG
20-08	Libya	D	0-0	Tripoli	Fr			
5-09	Algeria	L	2-3	Blida	WCq	Dia [53], Sougou [91+]	35 000	Maillet SEY
11-10	Gambia	D	1-1	Dakar	WCq	Mangane [65]	50 000	Bennaceur TUN
22-12	Oman	L	0-1	Muscat	Fr			
2009								
28-03	Oman	L	0-2	Muscat	Fr			
1-04	Iran	D	1-1	Tehran	Fr	Papiss Cisse [77]		
12-08	Congo DR	W	2-1	Blois	Fr	Papiss Cisse 2 [66 69]		
5-09	Angola	D	1-1	Portimao	Fr	Mamadou Niang [54]		
14-10	Korea Republic	L	0-2	Seoul	Fr		31 574	Tan Hai CHN
2010								
3-03	Greece	W	2-0	Volos	Fr	Mamadou Niang [71], Guirane N'Daw [80]	10 000	Skomina SVN
10-05	Mexico	L	0-1	Chicago	Fr		60 610	Salazar USA
27-05	Denmark	L	0-2	Aalborg	Fr		14 112	Nijhuis NED
11-08	Cape Verde Islands	W	1-0	Dakar	Fr	Mame Biram Diouf [46]		
5-09	Congo DR	W	4-2	Kinshasa	CNq	Moussa Sow [6], Mamadou Niang 3 [12 22 57p]		Haimoudi ALG
9-10	Mauritius	W	7-0	Dakar	CNq	Papiss Cisse 3 [8 38 76], Mamadou Niang 2 [22 62], Moussa Sow [47], OG [90]		Bennett RSA
17-11	Gabon	W	2-1	Sannois St Gratien	Fr	Papiss Cisse [37], Issiar Dia [57]		
2011								
9-02	Guinea	W	3-0	Dakar	Fr	Papiss Cisse [19], Moussa Sow [60], Dame N'Doye [85]		
26-03	Cameroon	W	1-0	Dakar	CNq	Demba Ba [92+]		
4-06	Cameroon	D	0-0	Yaounde	CNq			
10-08	Morocco	L	0-2	Dakar	Fr			
3-09	Congo DR	W	2-0	Dakar	CNq	Moussa Sow 2 [33 53]		
9-10	Mauritius	W	2-0	Bellevue	CNq	Dame N'Doye [9], Papiss Cisse [26]		
11-11	Guinea	W	4-1	Mantes la Villes	Fr	Guirane N'Daw [12], Souleymane Camara [26], Deme N'Deaye [30p], Mame Biram Diouf [71]		
2012								
12-01	Sudan	W	1-0	Dakar	Fr	Demba Ba [23]		
21-01	Zambia	L	1-2	Bata	CNr1	Dame N'Doye [73]	17 500	Alioum CMR
25-01	Equatorial Guinea	L	1-2	Bata	CNr1	Moussa Sow [89]	35 000	Abdel Rahman SUD
29-01	Libya	L	1-2	Bata	CNr1	Deme N'Diaye [10]	10 000	Seechurn MRI

Fr = Friendly match • CN = CAF African Cup of Nations • WC = FIFA World Cup • q = qualifier • r1 = first round group • qf = quarter-final

SENEGAL NATIONAL TEAM HISTORICAL RECORDS

Past Coaches Peter Schnittger GER 1999-2000 • Bruno Metsu FRA 2000-02 • Guy Stephan FRA 2002-05 • Abdoulaye Sarr 2005-06 • Henryk Kasperczak POL 2006-08 • Lamine N'Diaye 2008 • Amara Traore 2009-12

SENEGAL 2011

CHAMPIONNAT NATIONAL

Team	Pl	W	D	L	F	A	Pts	Ouakem	Diaraf	Casa	La Linguère	Gorée	Niary Tally	Touré Kounda	Douanes	Guédiawaye	DUC	Pikine	Yakaar	Dahra	CSS	Jeanne d'Arc	HLM
US Ouakem †	30	16	7	7	7	14	55		0-2	1-1	0-1	0-1	2-1	2-0	2-0	1-0	0-0	0-1	1-0	1-0	1-0	1-0	1-0
ASC Diaraf	30	11	14	5	31	24	47	0-2		0-0	1-1	2-1	2-2	0-2	1-1	0-0	3-2	0-0	0-0	3-1	1-1	1-0	1-1
Casa Sport ‡	30	12	11	7	33	24	47	0-0	2-4		0-0	1-0	1-0	0-2	5-0	1-1	2-0	0-0	0-1	2-0	3-2	2-1	2-0
ASC La Linguère	30	9	18	3	27	20	45	2-1	1-0	2-2		1-1	2-2	1-1	0-0	0-2	2-0	1-1	1-1	0-0	2-0	2-0	1-0
US Gorée	30	11	10	9	29	22	43	0-2	1-0	0-2	2-0		3-0	2-0	1-0	0-0	1-0	2-0	0-0	1-1	1-0	0-0	0-0
ASC Niary Tally Dakar	30	9	15	6	20	21	42	0-1	0-0	0-0	1-1	2-2		1-0	1-0	1-0	0-1	0-0	1-0	1-0	2-1	0-0	0-0
Touré Kounda Mbour	30	10	10	10	26	23	40	0-0	1-0	2-0	2-2	0-0	0-1		1-0	0-1	0-1	0-0	1-0	0-0	1-0	1-1	2-2
AS Douanes	30	9	12	9	19	22	39	0-1	1-2	1-2	0-0	2-4	1-1	1-0		0-0	0-0	0-0	1-1	0-0	0-0	0-1	1-0
Guédiawaye FC Dakar	30	9	12	9	21	21	39	0-1	0-0	0-0	1-1	1-0	1-1	1-2	0-2		3-1	0-1	1-0	0-3	3-0	0-0	2-0
DUC Dakar	30	10	8	12	27	27	38	0-1	1-2	1-1	0-0	1-3	0-0	0-1	2-0	0-1		1-0	2-0	2-0	0-1	1-1	1-1
AS Pikine	30	7	16	7	21	19	37	0-0	1-1	0-1	0-1	1-1	2-0	2-2	0-1	0-0	0-0		1-1	0-0	3-0	3-2	1-0
ASC Yakaar	30	8	11	11	19	21	35	0-1	1-1	2-2	0-1	1-0	0-1	1-0	0-2	1-0	2-0	2-0		2-0	0-1	0-1	1-0
ASC Dahra	30	7	11	12	17	25	32	1-1	0-0	2-0	0-0	1-0	0-0	0-2	0-1	0-1	1-3	0-2	0-0		0-0	1-0	1-0
CSS Richard Toll	30	6	12	12	15	26	30	1-1	0-1	1-0	1-1	0-0	0-0	0-0	0-1	0-0	0-1	0-0	0-1	2-1		1-1	0-0
Jeanne d'Arc	30	6	11	13	18	30	29	0-2	0-1	1-0	1-0	0-1	2-0	1-3	0-1	0-0	0-3	2-1	1-0	3-2	0-2		0-0
ASC HLM Dakar	30	4	14	12	19	30	26	2-1	1-2	0-1	0-0	2-2	1-1	1-0	0-2	2-2	1-2	1-1	1-1	1-0	0-0	2-1	

18/12/2010 - 14/09/2011 • † Qualified for the CAF Champions League • ‡ Qualified for the CAF Confederation Cup

COUPE NATIONALE 2011

Round of 16

Casa Sport	3
ASC Yakaar	0
ASC HLM Dakar	0
ASEC Ndiambour	2
Renaissance Dakar	1
Laghem	0
Guédiawaye FC Dakar	0 3p
US Ouakem	0 4p
Saint-Louis Foot	1
Etoile Lusitana	0
Cambérène	0
Jeanne d'Arc	1
DUC Dakar	1
Mbaxane	0
ASC Niary Tally Dakar	0
Touré Kounda Mbour	1

Quarter-finals

Casa Sport	1 3p
ASEC Ndiambour	1 2p
Renaissance Dakar	0
US Ouakem	2
Saint-Louis Foot	1
Jeanne d'Arc	0
DUC Dakar	0
Touré Kounda Mbour	1

Semi-finals

Casa Sport †	0
US Ouakem	0
Saint-Louis Foot	0
Touré Kounda Mbour	4

Final

Casa Sport ‡	1
Touré Kounda Mbour	0

CUP FINAL
Demba Diop, Dakar,
24-09-2011, Ref: Seck
Scorer - Aliou Coly 45

† Abandoned 115'. Casa qualified
‡ Qualified for the CAF Confederation Cup

Cup Final line-ups: Casa Sport - Papa Maguette Gningue - Yaya Sonko, Abdoulaye Diallo, Mame Saer Thioune, Mamading Kidiera, Bonaventure Mankabo•, Stephane Badji (c), Aloise Thiaw (Christian Pascal Diatta 80), Emile Paul Tendeng (Siaka Sane 85), Aliou Coly, Assane Drame. Tr: Demba Ramata Ndiaye
Touré Kounda - Ibrahima Diakhate• (c) - Ibou Khole Faye (Aliou Sene 50), Ismaila Diarra Badji•, Abdoulaye Seck, Lamine Fanne, Souleymane Diallo, Abdoulaye Kama, Mame Adama Gueye, Dame Diop•, Thierno Moukhtar Thioune (Madicke Ba 75), Abdoulaye Diakhate (Ibrahima Faye 69). Tr: Lamine Sano

MEDALS TABLE

	Club	Overall G	S	B	Lge G	S	Cup G	S	B	Africa G	S	B	City
1	ASC Diaraf	25	6	1	11		14	6				1	Dakar
2	Jeanne d'Arc	16	5	3	10		6	4			1	3	Dakar
3	AS Douanes	11	2		5		6	2					Dakar
4	US Gorée	7	6	2	3		4	6				2	Gorée, Dakar
5	ASC La Linguère	5	3		1		4	3					Saint-Louis
	SUNEOR	5	3		4		1	3					Diourbel
7	ASF Police	4	3		1		3	3					Dakar
8	ASEC Ndiambour	4	2				3	1				2	Louga
9	Port Autonome	4	1				3	1				1	Dakar
10	US Ouakem	4			1		3						Dakar
11	ASFA Dakar	3	2				3					2	Dakar
12	Olympique Thiès	2	2				2					2	Thiès
13	Casa Sport	2	1				2	1					Ziguinchor
14	Espoir Saint-Louis	2			1		1						Saint-Louis
15	Saltigues	1	1				1	1					Rufisque
	AS Saint-Louisienne	1	1				1	1					Saint-Louis
	Touré Kounda	1	1				1	1					Mbour

SEY – SEYCHELLES

FIFA/COCA-COLA WORLD RANKING

'93	'94	'95	'96	'97	'98	'99	'00	'01	'02	'03	'04	'05	'06	'07	'08	'09	'10	'11	'12
157	175	176	175	181	181	192	188	192	185	163	173	176	130	163	166	178	196	188	

	Jan	Feb	Mar	Apr	May	Jun	Jul	Aug	Sep	Oct	Nov	Dec	High	Low	Av
2011	195	195	195	194	194	190	199	175	177	178	183	188	129	199	175

Seychelles won a first-ever gold at the football tournament of the Indian Ocean Island Games in August, finally achieving a long-held ambition. Under Jean-Louis Ralph the side had trained extensively in South Africa before returning home to provide Africa's smallest nation with a rare success story. Seychelles started slowly with a draw in the opening game against the Comoros Islands but then beat arch-rivals Mauritius and the Maldives to take top place in their group. An extra-time win over Reunion in the semi-finals meant another game against Mauritius in the final. The gold medal match ended 1-1 before the 'Pirates' won the shoot out 4-3 to the delight of the home crowd at Stade Linite in Mahe. Kevin Betsy, the former English Premier League player who had finally agreed to play for Seychelles on the eve of the tournament, scored the opening goal but Mauritius fought back to equalise through Jerry Louis. Goalkeeper Vincent Euphrasie, who had come on for the injured Nelson Sopha, emerged as the hero with two saves in the shoot out. It was back down to earth soon after thanks to a 7-0 aggregate defeat at the hands of Kenya in the 2014 FIFA World Cup qualifiers. There was a clean sweep of trophies for St Michel in club football, winning the President's Cup, Barclays League, Airtel League Cup and Land Marine FA Cup.

CAF AFRICA CUP OF NATIONS RECORD

1957-1988 DNE 1990 DNQ 1992-1996 DNE 1998 DNQ 2000-2002 DNE 2004-2010 DNQ 2012 DNE

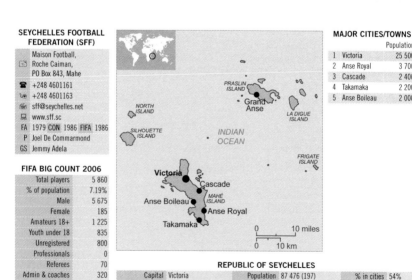

SEYCHELLES FOOTBALL FEDERATION (SFF)

Maison Football,
Roche Caiman,
PO Box 843, Mahe
☎ +248 4601161
📠 +248 4601163
✉ sff@seychelles.net
🖥 www.sff.sc
FA 1979 CON 1986 FIFA 1986
P Joel De Commarmond
GS Jemmy Adela

FIFA BIG COUNT 2006

Total players	5 860
% of population	7.19%
Male	5 675
Female	185
Amateurs 18+	1 225
Youth under 18	835
Unregistered	800
Professionals	0
Referees	70
Admin & coaches	320
Number of clubs	20
Number of teams	60

MAJOR CITIES/TOWNS

		Population
1	Victoria	25 500
2	Anse Royal	3 700
3	Cascade	2 400
4	Takamaka	2 200
5	Anse Boileau	2 000

REPUBLIC OF SEYCHELLES

Capital	Victoria	Population	87 476 (197)	% in cities	54%
GDP per capita	$21 000 (59)	Area km²	455 km² (198)	GMT + / -	+4
Neighbours (km)	Coast 491				

RECENT INTERNATIONAL MATCHES PLAYED BY THE SEYCHELLES

2006	Opponents	Score		Venue	Comp	Scorers	Att	Referee
22-07	Namibia	D	1-1	Katutura	CCr1	Wilnes Brutus [18], W 4-2p		Simisse MRI
23-07	Zambia	L	0-2	Katutura	CCr1			Ngobo RSA
3-09	Sudan	L	0-3	Khartoum	CNq			Kidane ERI
7-10	Mauritius	W	2-1	Roche Caiman	CNq	Wilnes Brutus 2 [23 81]		Raolimanana MAD
2007								
24-03	Tunisia	L	0-3	Victoria	CNq			Ssegonga UGA
28-04	Mozambique	L	0-2	Maputo	CCr1			Mpopo LES
29-04	Madagascar	L	0-5	Maputo	CCr1			Mpopo LES
2-06	Tunisia	L	0-4	Rades/Tunis	CNq			Diatta SEN
16-06	Sudan	L	0-2	Roche Caiman	CNq			Dlamini SWZ
14-08	Mauritius	L	0-3	Antananarivo	Fr			
9-09	Mauritius	D	1-1	Curepipe	CNq	Godfrey Denis [43p]		Mwandike TAN
2008								
1-06	Burundi	L	0-1	Bujumbura	WCq		4 000	Imiere NGA
7-06	Tunisia	L	0-2	Victoria	WCq		2 033	Faduco MOZ
14-06	Burkina Faso	L	2-3	Victoria	WCq	Philip Zialor [47], Don Annacoura [53]	1 000	Seechurn MRI
21-06	Burkina Faso	L	1-4	Ouagadougou	WCq	Bernard St Ange [44]	12 500	Lamptey GHA
19-07	Mauritius	W	7-0	Witbank	CCr1	Colin Laporte [14], Philip Zialor 4 [35 51 59 88], Don Annacoura [66], Trevor Poiret [87]		Kaoma ZAM
21-07	Madagascar	D	1-1	Witbank	CCr1	Godfrey Denis [48]		Kaoma ZAM
23-07	Swaziland	L	0-1	Witbank	CCr1			Katjimune NAM
6-09	Burundi	L	1-2	Victoria	WCq	Philip Zialor [63]	3 000	Djaoupe TOG
11-10	Tunisia	L	0-5	Tunis/Rades	WCq		10 000	Diatta SEN
2009								
18-10	Swaziland	L	1-2	Bulawayo	CCr1	Nelson Laurence [8]		Carvalho ANG
20-10	Comoros	L	1-2	Bulawayo	CCr1	Don Anacoura [54]		Rachide MOZ
22-10	Botswana	L	0-2	Bulawayo	CCr1			Seechurn MRI
2010								
No international matches played in 2010								
2011								
4-08	Comoros	D	0-0	Praslin	IOGr1		1 800	Dubec REU
6-08	Mauritius	W	2-1	Roche Caiman	IOGr1	Nelson Laurence [1], Archille Henriette [28]	6 500	Rassuhi MAY
9-08	Maldives	W	5-1	Roche Caiman	IOGr1	Nelson Laurence [16], Don Anacoura [23], Archille Henriette [62], Alpha Balde 2 [75 80]	5 500	Rakotonjanahary MAD
11-08	Reunion	W	2-1	Roche Caiman	IOGsf	Alex Nibourette [77], Karl Hall [118]	6 500	Ali Saleem MDV
13-08	Mauritius	D	1-1	Roche Caiman	IOGf	W 4-3p. Kevin Betsy [16]	10 000	Dubec REU
11-11	Kenya	L	0-3	Roche Caiman	WCq		2 000	Batte UGA
15-11	Kenya	L	0-4	Nairobi	WCq		5 000	Gomes RSA
22-11	Maldives	L	0-3	Male	Fr			
24-11	Maldives	L	1-2	Male	Fr	Leroy Coralie [49]		

Fr = Friendly match • CN = CAN African Cup of Nations • IOG = Indian Ocean Games • CC = COSAFA Castle Cup • WC = FIFA World Cup
q = qualifier • r1 = first round group

SEYCHELLES 2011

BARCLAYS LEAGUE DIVISION ONE

	Pl	W	D	L	F	A	Pts	St Michel Utd	La Passe	Côte d'Or	Anse Reunion	Light Stars	St Francis	Dynamo	St Louis Suns	St Roch Utd	The Lions
St Michel United	18	13	4	1	42	11	**43**		3-1	1-0	4-2	1-0	2-0	2-0	2-1	6-1	5-1
La Passe	18	12	4	2	44	17	**40**	2-2		2-1	2-0	5-1	2-0	0-0	2-0	**2-0**	5-1
Côte d'Or	18	10	3	5	29	14	**33**	0-1	1-1		0-1	1-0	3-1	1-1	2-1	9-0	2-0
Anse Reunion	18	8	2	8	37	32	**26**	0-2	2-0	1-2		2-1	3-0	4-3	2-2	8-2	1-3
Light Stars	18	6	5	7	36	39	**23**	1-1	2-2	2-2	3-1		2-3	1-0	1-0	2-2	2-3
St Francis	18	6	3	9	27	37	**21**	0-3	0-2	0-1	0-0	5-7		0-2	3-0	4-4	2-1
Northern Dynamo	18	5	4	9	18	30	**19**	0-6	0-4	1-2	2-0	0-2	2-2		0-0	3-2	2-0
St Louis Suns United	18	5	2	11	20	26	**17**	1-0	1-2	0-1	2-1	4-1	1-2	2-0		1-3	3-0
St Roch United	18	4	4	10	34	57	**16**	0-0	3-4	1-0	2-5	5-5	1-3	0-1	2-0		1-2
The Lions	18	5	1	12	23	47	**16**	1-1	0-6	0-1	2-4	2-3	1-2	2-1	2-1	2-5	

24/02/2011 - 8/11/2011 • Match in bold awarded
Relegation play-off: **St Roch United** 2-1 Super Magic Brothers

AIRTEL LEAGUE CUP 2011

Semi-finals

St Michel United	1
St Louis Suns United	0

Light Stars	0
La Passe	4

Final

St Michel United	4
La Passe	2

Stade Linite, Victoria
3-09-2011. Ref: Boniface

Scorers - Jimmy Radafison 2 [26] [34p], Karl Hall 2 [55] [70] for St Michel; Aly [45], Valerie [88]

MEDALS TABLE

		Overall			League			Cup		LC		City
		G	S	B	G	S	B	G	S	G	S	
1	St Michel United	23	6		10	5		8		5	1	Anse aux Pins
2	Red Star	8	6	4	2	2	4	4	3	2	1	Anse aux Pins
3	La Passe	5	7	4	4	3	4		3	1	3	La Passe
4	St Louis Suns Utd †	4	10	4	1	3	4	3	4		3	Victoria
5	Anse Reunion	3	5	3	1	1	3	1	3	1	1	Anse Reunion
6	Seychelles MB	1	1		1			1				Victoria
7	Light Stars		2						1		1	Grand Anse
8	Ascot		1					1				
9	Côte d'Or			1			1					Praslin

LAND MARINE FA CUP 2011

Round of 16

St Michel United	10
Agrics	0

Anse Reunion	
St John Bosco	

Light Stars	4
St Roch United	0

Seychelles MB	0
The Lions	1

Northern Dynamo	5
St Louis Suns United	3

Côte d'Or	1
Beginners	2

Quincy	5
SPDF	3

St Francis	0
La Passe	2

Quarter-finals

St Michel United	7
St John Bosco	1

Light Stars	1
The Lions	2

Northern Dynamo	4
Beginners	1

Quincy	1
La Passe	5

Semi-finals

St Michel United	5
The Lions	2

Northern Dynamo	1
La Passe	2

Final

St Michel United	3
La Passe	1

CUP FINAL

Stade Linite, Victoria
5-11-2011
Scorers - Leeroy Corallie 2 [24] [45], Nelson Laurence [93+] for St Michel; Marcus Labiche [64] for La Passe

All matches played at Stade Linite, Victoria

SIN – SINGAPORE

FIFA/COCA-COLA WORLD RANKING

'93	'94	'95	'96	'97	'98	'99	'00	'01	'02	'03	'04	'05	'06	'07	'08	'09	'10	'11	'12
75	95	104	92	103	81	104	101	115	118	106	112	92	111	126	132	110	140	145	

2011												High	Low	Av
Jan	Feb	Mar	Apr	May	Jun	Jul	Aug	Sep	Oct	Nov	Dec	High	Low	Av
139	142	139	145	144	141	131	129	136	139	152	145	73	152	109

Singapore's football scene received a major boost with news that the island state would from 2012 once again field a team in the Malaysian Cup. The Singaporeans have not played in the tournament since their historic victory in 1994 after which they quit under a cloud during the match fixing scandal that rocked Malaysian football to the core the same year. That led to the creation of the domestic S-League in 1996 but that has struggled to create the same buzz associated with the nation's Malaysia Cup exploits. Reaction to the move was universally positive, with home games sold out as fans both old and young seek to rekindle the atmosphere associated with what are widely seen as the glory days of Singaporean football. Fans were given a foretaste of the return to the Malaysia Cup when Singapore and Malaysia were drawn to face each other in the 2014 FIFA World Cup qualifiers, with Raddy Avramovic's team claiming the spoils in a 6-4 aggregate win over the Malaysians. That earned Singapore a place in the first group stage of qualifying for Brazil, but in a group that also featured Iraq, Jordan and China, the Singaporeans were outgunned and finished with no points from six matches. Tampines Rovers and Home United were the main trophy winners at home, winning the league and cup respectively while Albirex won the League Cup.

FIFA WORLD CUP RECORD
1930-1974 DNE 1978-2014 DNQ

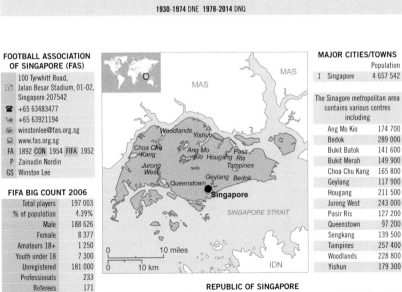

FOOTBALL ASSOCIATION OF SINGAPORE (FAS)

100 Tyrwhitt Road,
Jalan Besar Stadium, 01-02,
Singapore 207542
☎ +65 63483477
📠 +65 63921194
✉ winstonlee@fas.org.sg
🖥 www.fas.org.sg
FA 1892 CON 1954 FIFA 1952
P Zainudin Nordin
GS Winston Lee

FIFA BIG COUNT 2006

Total players	197 003
% of population	4.39%
Male	188 626
Female	8 377
Amateurs 18+	1 250
Youth under 18	7 300
Unregistered	181 000
Professionals	233
Referees	171
Admin & coaches	1 345
Number of clubs	41
Number of teams	104

MAJOR CITIES/TOWNS

	Population
1 Singapore	4 657 542

The Sinagore metropolitan area contains various centres including

Ang Mo Kio	174 700
Bedok	289 000
Bukit Batok	141 600
Bukit Merah	149 900
Choa Chu Kang	165 800
Geylang	117 900
Hougang	211 500
Jurong West	243 000
Pasir Ris	127 200
Queenstown	97 200
Sengkang	139 500
Tampines	257 400
Woodlands	228 800
Yishun	179 300

REPUBLIC OF SINGAPORE

Capital	Singapore	Population	4 657 542 (117)	% in cities	100%
GDP per capita	$51 600 (8)	Area km²	697 km² (192)	GMT + / -	+8
Neighbours (km)	Coast 193				

RECENT INTERNATIONAL MATCHES PLAYED BY SINGAPORE

2008 Opponents	Score		Venue	Comp	Scorers	Att	Referee
14-10 Vietnam	D	0-0	Hanoi	Fr			
29-11 Malaysia	D	2-2	Petaling Jaya	Fr	Aleksandar Duric 2 [10 45]		
5-12 Cambodia	W	5-0	Jakarta	AFFr1	Agu Casmir 2 [44 73], Mustafic Fahrudin [61p], Indra Sahdan Daud [71], Noh Alam Shah [89]	18 000	Mahapab THA
7-12 Myanmar	W	3-1	Jakarta	AFFr1	Noh Alam Shah [1], Agu Casmir 2 [16 74]	21 000	Phung VIE
9-12 Indonesia	W	2-0	Jakarta	AFFr1	Baihakki Khaizan [3], Jiayi Shi [50]	50 000	Ramachandran MAS
17-12 Vietnam	D	0-0	Hanoi	AFFsf		40 000	Ramachandran MAS
21-12 Vietnam	L	0-1	Singapore	AFFsf		55 000	Mohd Salleh MAS
2009							
14-01 Iran	L	0-6	Tehran	ACq		3 000	Mansour LIB
28-01 Jordan	W	2-1	Singapore	ACq	Agu Casmir [21], Noh Alam Shah [63]	6 188	Green AUS
12-08 China PR	D	1-1	Singapore	Fr	Noh Alam Shah [7]. L 3-4p		
22-10 Turkmenistan	W	4-2	Ho Chi Minh City	Fr	Aleksandar Duric 2 [9 38], Masrezwan Masturi [60] Khairul Amri [77]		
24-10 Vietnam	D	2-2	Ho Chi Minh City	Fr	Aleksandar Duric [26], Fazrul Shahul [51]		
4-11 Indonesia	W	3-1	Singapore	Fr	Mustafic Fahrudin [85]		
14-11 Thailand	L	1-3	Singapore	ACq	Mustafic Fahrudin [84p]	22 183	Takayama JPN
18-11 Thailand	W	1-0	Bangkok	ACq	Aleksandar Duric [37]	30 000	Balideh QAT
31-12 Oman	L	1-4	Singapore	Fr	Indra Sahdan Daud [76]		
2010							
6-01 Iran	L	1-3	Singapore	ACq	Noh Alam Shah [31]	7 356	Sun Baojie CHN
17-01 Thailand	L	0-1	Nakhon Ratch'ma	Fr		20 000	Mbaga TAN
20-01 Denmark	L	1-5	Nakhon Ratch'ma	Fr	Fazrul Nawaz [84]		
23-01 Poland	L	1-6	Nakhon Ratch'ma	Fr	Jiayi Shi [39]		Amwayi KEN
3-03 Jordan	L	1-2	Amman	ACq	Noh Alam Shah [48]	17 000	Abdou QAT
11-08 Thailand	L	0-1	Nonthaburi	Fr			Aonrak THA
2-11 Korea DPR	L	1-2	Hanoi	Fr	Aleksandar Duric [41]		
4-11 Vietnam	D	1-1	Hanoi	Fr	Jiayi Shi [24]		
2-12 Philippines	D	1-1	Hanoi	AFFr1	Aleksandar Duric [65]		Mahapab THA
5-12 Myanmar	W	2-1	Hanoi	AFFr1	Aleksandar Duric [62], Casnir [94+]		Tao Ranchang CHN
8-12 Vietnam	L	0-1	Hanoi	AFFr1		40 000	Mahapab THA
2011							
7-06 Maldives	W	4-0	Singapore	Fr	Li Qiu 2 [13p 19], Jiayi Shi [30], Aleksandar Duric [49]		
18-07 Chinese Taipei	W	3-2	Singapore	Fr	Aleksandar Duric 2 [17 54], Fazrul Nawaz [83]		
23-07 Malaysia	W	5-3	Singapore	WCq	Aleksandar Duric 2 [8 81], Li Qiu [22], Mustafic Fahrudin [44], Jiayi Shi [45]	6 000	Shukralla BHR
28-07 Malaysia	D	1-1	Kuala Lumpur	WCq	Jiayi Shi [71]	90 000	Takayama JPN
24-08 Thailand	D	0-0	Bangkok	Fr			
2-09 China PR	L	1-2	Kunming	WCq	Aleksandar Duric [33]	17 000	El Haddad LIB
6-09 Iraq	L	0-2	Singapore	WCq		5 505	Tojo JPN
7-10 Philippines	W	2-0	Singapore	Fr	Shaiful Esah [51], Aleksandar Duric [65]		
11-10 Jordan	L	0-3	Singapore	WCq		3 799	Choi Myung Yong KOR
11-11 Jordan	L	0-2	Amman	WCq		19 000	Williams AUS
15-11 China PR	L	0-4	Singapore	WCq		5 474	Balideh QAT

Fr = Friendly match • AC = AFC Asian Cup • AFF = ASEAN Football Federation Championship • WC = FIFA World Cup
q = qualifier • r1 = first round group • sf = semi-final • f = final

SINGAPORE NATIONAL TEAM HISTORICAL RECORDS

Caps
121 - Aide Iskander 1995-2007 • **115** - Shunmugham Subramani 1996-2007 • **100** - Nasri Nasir 1990-2004

Goals
52 - Fandi Ahmad 1978-97

Past Coaches
Hussein Aljunied 1984-86 • Seak Poh Leong 1986-88 • Jita Singh 1988-89 • Robin Chan 1990-92 • Milous Kvacek CZE 1992 • PN Sivaji 1992-94 • Ken Worden ENG 1994 • Douglas Moore ENG 1994-96 • Barry Whitbread ENG 1996-98 • Vincent Subramaniam 1998-2000 • Jan Poulsen DEN 2000-02 • Radojko Avramovic SRB 2003-

SINGAPORE 2011

S.LEAGUE

	Pl	W	D	L	F	A	Pts	Tampines	Home Utd	SAF	Albirex	Etoile	Gombak	Hougang	Geylang	Lions	Balestier	Tanjong	Woodlands
Tampines Rovers ‡	33	25	3	5	71	25	78		1-1 1-0	1-2		3-1	1-0	1-1	5-2 3-1	0-2	4-1	5-0 5-0	4-1 1-0	5-0
Home United ‡	33	25	2	6	81	29	77	2-0		3-2	2-1 0-4	2-1	3-0 2-1	4-2	2-1 5-0	2-0	5-2	3-1	2-0 2-1
S'pore Armed Forces	33	21	3	9	74	39	66	0-1	2-0 4-0		2-1	1-1 4-1	2-1 1-1-3	0-1	3-1	3-0 3-0	1-0	2-1	7-0
Albirex Niigata	33	20	5	8	80	34	65	0-2 1-3	2-1	6-3 1-0		0-1 1-1 0-0 1-1	5-1	3-1 6-1	4-2	1-0	5-0 1-0	5-0
Etoile FC §5	33	21	4	8	65	36	62	1-2 2-1	2-0	1-0	2-7		2-0	4-2 3-1	3-2	1-2 3-2 0-0 3-0 3-0	6-1	3-0
Gombak United	33	14	6	13	43	41	48	1-1 1-2	1-4	0-1 1-1	1-5	1-0 0-3		0-1 3-1 2-0 2-0	1-2	2-0	3-2	3-0
Hougang United §5	33	15	3	15	55	63	43	2-0	0-5 0-2	1-3	1-1	2-1	3-2		0-2	1-0 1-1 2-2 2-0	4-3	1-0 2-3
Geylang United	33	13	2	18	43	63	41	0-1 0-2	1-3	2-0 3-6	1-0	0-2 2-3	1-0	2-1 1-2		3-3 1-0 0-3 3-2 2-0 2-0	1-0
Young Lions	33	7	6	20	33	54	27	0-1	0-2	0-2	0-5 1-1	1-1	0-2 0-1	2-0	3-2		2-0	0-1	1-2 5-1
Balestier Khalsa	33	7	5	21	28	63	26	0-1	1-1 0-4	0-2 1-3	0-1 1-1-3	0-4	1-2 0-2	2-4	3-1	0-1 1-0		2-0	2-0 2-2
Tanjong Pagar United	33	3	5	25	21	77	14	1-3	0-6 0-3	2-2	1-2	0-2	0-0	0-5 1-3	0-1	0-0 3-1 0-1 1-1-2		0-0 1-1
Woodlands Wellington	33	3	4	26	22	92	13	1-3 0-4	1-5	1-5	0-1 1-5 1-2-0 2-0 1-2-4	1-4	2-2 1-2	0-4	1-0	0-1	

12/02/2011 - 28/11/2011 • ‡ Qualified for the AFC Cup • § = points deducted

Top scorers: **33** - Mislav Karoglan CRO, SAF • **26** - Aleksandar Duric, Tampines • **22** - Shotaro Ihata JPN, Albirex • **21** - Frederic Mendy FRA, Home Utd • **17** - Li Qiu, Home Utd • **15** - Fazrul Nawaz, SAF • **14** - Tatsuro Inui JPN, Albirex & Jordan Webb CAN, Hougang

MEDALS TABLE

		All	Lge	Cup	LC
		G	G	G	G
1	Singapore Armed Forces	19	11	8	
2	Geylang United	18	11	7	
3	Tanjong Pagar United	9	2	7	
	Tampines Rovers	9	6	3	
	Home United	9	3	6	
6	Farrer Park United	4	1	3	
7	Toa Payoh United	2		2	
	Etoile FC	2	1		1
9	Perth Kangaroos	1	1		
	Bangkok Glass	1		1	
	Balestier United	1		1	
	Jurong Town	1		1	
	Woodlands Wellington	1			1
	Gombak United	1			1
	DPMM Brunei	1			1
	Albirex Niigata	1			1

SINGAPORE LEAGUE CUP 2011

Quarter-finals		Semi-finals		Final	
Albirex Niigata	3				
Geylang United	1	**Albirex Niigata**	1 6p		
Gombak United	1	Tampines Rov	1 5p		
Tampines Rov	2			**Albirex Niigata**	0 5p
Home United	1 6p			Hougang Utd	0 4p
Etoile FC	1 5p	Home United	0		
S'pore A. Forces	1	**Hougang Utd**	1	Jalan Basar, 30-07-2011,
Hougang Utd	2			Att: 2259, Ref: Daud

Preliminary round: Hougang Utd 2-0 Woodlands Wellington • Albirex Niigata 3-1 Tanjong Pagar United • Gombak United 2-0 Balestier Khalsa

RHB SINGAPORE CUP 2011

First round		Quarter–finals		Semi–finals		Final	
Home United *	5						
Woodlands Wellington	1	**Home United**	3 0 4p				
Geylang United *	1	Tampines Rovers *	3 0 2p				
Tampines Rovers	2			**Home United** *	1 1		
Gombak United *	2			Etoile FC	1 0		
Balestier Khalsa	1	Gombak United *	0 1				
Tanjong Pagar United	0	**Etoile FC**	1 3				
Etoile FC *	2					**Home United** ‡	1
Hougang United *	1					Albirex Niigata	0
Harimau Muda B	0	**Hougang United** *	3 1				
Pattaya United	1	Okktha United	0 3				
Okktha United ‡‡	2			Hougang United	2 2		
S'pore Armed Forces *	4			**Albirex Niigata** *	2 3		
Phnom Penh Crown	0	S'pore Armed Forces *	0 2 4p	‡‡ Played at Jalan Besar		
South Melbourne	0	**Albirex Niigata**	0 2 5p	3rd place: **Etoile** 3-0 Hougang Utd		
Albirex Niigata ‡	3			* Home Team in the first leg • ‡ Qualified for the AFC Cup		

CUP FINAL

Jalan Besar, Singapore
19-11-2011, Att: 3322, Ref: Hoe
Scorer - Frederic Mendy [118]

SKN – ST KITTS AND NEVIS

FIFA/COCA-COLA WORLD RANKING

'93	'94	'95	'96	'97	'98	'99	'00	'01	'02	'03	'04	'05	'06	'07	'08	'09	'10	'11	'12
166	175	150	121	127	132	137	146	129	109	134	118	129	143	160	152	156	121	116	

	2011												High	Low	Av
Jan	Feb	Mar	Apr	May	Jun	Jul	Aug	Sep	Oct	Nov	Dec				
121	118	119	119	119	121	122	122	123	109	117	116		108	176	136

2011 was a busy year for football in St Kitts and Nevis and it proved to be a relatively successful one too, especially with the spirited performances in the qualifiers for the 2014 FIFA World Cup. The national team had been drawn in a tough group along with Canada, Puerto Rico and St Lucia and with only the top team progressing, making it to the next round would have been a major surprise. It wasn't until the final game, however, against Canada in Toronto, that St Kitts lost. That was their only defeat of the year but of the other five games in the group, four were drawn. A 4-2 win over St Lucia provided a solitary win as the team finished third, a point behind Puerto Rico and seven adrift of the Canadians. In club football, Village Superstars scooped the league and cup double although for much of the season their form had been indifferent. They went into the Final Four play-offs as the team with the worst record but they topped the group and then beat St Paul's 3-0 in the critical third leg of the final. Three weeks earlier they had won a thrilling Cup Final 4-3 against Mantab having already won the newly instituted Easter Cup, played between the four teams with the best record in the second half of the season. Conaree had previously won the first Super Mas Cup played between the four teams with the best record in the first half of the season.

FIFA WORLD CUP RECORD
1930-1994 DNE 1998-2010 DNQ

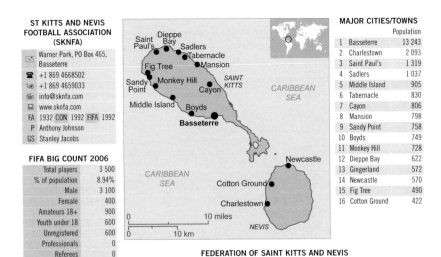

ST KITTS AND NEVIS FOOTBALL ASSOCIATION (SKNFA)

Warner Park, PO Box 465, Basseterre
☎ +1 869 4668502
📠 +1 869 4659033
✉ info@sknfa.com
🖥 www.sknfa.com
FA 1932 CON 1992 FIFA 1992
P Anthony Johnson
GS Stanley Jacobs

FIFA BIG COUNT 2006

Total players	3 500
% of population	8.94%
Male	3 100
Female	400
Amateurs 18+	900
Youth under 18	600
Unregistered	600
Professionals	0
Referees	0
Admin & coaches	100
Number of clubs	30
Number of teams	40

MAJOR CITIES/TOWNS

		Population
1	Basseterre	13 243
2	Charlestown	2 093
3	Saint Paul's	1 319
4	Sadlers	1 037
5	Middle Island	905
6	Tabernacle	830
7	Cayon	806
8	Mansion	798
9	Sandy Point	758
10	Boyds	749
11	Monkey Hill	728
12	Dieppe Bay	622
13	Gingerland	572
14	Newcastle	570
15	Fig Tree	490
16	Cotton Ground	422

FEDERATION OF SAINT KITTS AND NEVIS

Capital	Basseterre	Population	40 131 (209)	% in cities	32%
GDP per capita	$19 100 (65)	Area km²	261 km² (211)	GMT +/-	-4
Neighbours (km)	Coast 135				

RECENT INTERNATIONAL MATCHES PLAYED BY ST KITTS AND NEVIS

2006	Opponents	Score		Venue	Comp	Scorers	Att	Referee
20-09	Barbabdos	D	1-1	St John's	CCq	Atiba Harris [60]	300	Campbell JAM
22-09	Anguilla	W	6-1	St John's	CCq	George Isaac 2 [14 68], Ian Lake 3 [30 46 79], Jevon Francis [81]	500	Phillips GRN
24-09	Antigua and Barbuda	L	0-1	St John's	CCq		2 800	Wijngaarde SUR
2007								
18-11	Antigua and Barbuda	W	3-0	Basseterre	Fr	Jevon Francis [36], Christian OG [43], Aiden Nurse [44]	3 000	Matthew SKN
1-12	Antigua and Barbuda	L	0-2	St John's	Fr		3 800	Willett ATG
14-12	Bermuda	W	2-1	Hamilton	Fr	Jevon Francis [25], Ian Lake [38]	800	Mauchette BER
16-12	Bermuda	L	2-4	Hamilton	Fr	Imran Ponteen [44], Stedro Charles	1 500	Raynor BER
2008								
6-02	Belize	L	1-3	Guatemala City	WCq	Gerard Williams [13]	500	Stennet JAM
26-03	Belize	D	1-1	Basseterre	WCq	Orlando Mitchum [84]	2 000	Brizan TRI
8-06	Antigua and Barbuda	L	0-2	St John's	Fr		4 000	Willett ATG
24-09	British Virgin Islands	W	4-0	Basseterre	CCq	Jevon Francis [15], Zevon Archibald [21], Venton James OG [52], Ian Lake [77]	500	Charles DMA
28-09	Barbados	L	1-3	Basseterre	CCq	George Isaac [13]	500	Charles DMA
5-11	Guyana	D	1-1	Macoya	CCq	Ian Lake [29]	750	Cambridge VIN
7-11	Trinidad and Tobago	L	1-3	Macoya	CCq	Jevon Francis [86]		Wijngaarde SUR
9-11	Antigua and Barbuda	L	3-4	Macoya	CCq	Jevon Francis 3 [57 70 80]	1 000	Wijngaarde SUR
2009								
12-07	Trinidad and Tobago	L	2-3	Basseterre	Fr	Ian Lake [48], Gerard Williams [62]	3 100	Matthew SKN
16-08	Jamaica	L	0-1	Basseterre	Fr		5 000	Willett ATG
5-09	St Vincent/Grenadines	W	3-0	Kingstown	Fr	Stephen Clarke [50], Tishan Hanley [55], Alexis Saddler [81]	3 500	Cambridge VIN
20-09	St Vincent/Grenadines	D	1-1	Basseterre	Fr	Shashi Isaac [10]	1 600	Matthew SKN
2010								
28-08	Antigua and Barbuda	D	1-1	Basseterre	Fr	Ian Lake [30]	500	Matthew SKN
6-10	Barbados	D	1-1	Kingstown	CCq	George Isaac [62]	250	Elskamp SUR
8-10	St Vincent/Grenadines	D	1-1	Kingstown	CCq	Jevon Francis [40]	1 600	Jauregui ANT
10-10	Montserrat	W	4-0	Kingstown	CCq	Alexis Saddler 2 [18 31], Keith Gumbs [21], Ian Lake [90]	1 100	Elskamp SUR
22-10	Guadeloupe	L	1-2	St George's	CCq	Jevon Francis [83p]	300	Taylor BRB
24-10	Grenada	L	0-2	St George's	CCq		500	Morrison JAM
26-10	Puerto Rico	W	1-0	St George's	CCq	Jevon Francis [90]	500	Morrison JAM
2011								
27-03	Grenada	D	0-0	Basseterre	Fr		1 000	Matthew SKN
2-04	Grenada	W	1-0	St George's	Fr	Alexis Saddler [66]	3 500	Bedeau GRN
2-09	Puerto Rico	D	0-0	Basseterre	WCq		2 500	Arellano MEX
6-09	St Lucia	W	4-2	Gros Islet	WCq	Ian Lake [7], Jevon Francis [12], Orlando Mitchum [15], Devaughn Elliott [44]	2 005	Thomas JAM
7-10	Puerto Rico	D	1-1	Bayamon	WCq	Ian Lake [59]	2 500	Brizan TRI
11-10	St Lucia	D	1-1	Basseterre	WCq	Ian Lake [83]	1 000	Skeete BRB
11-11	Canada	D	0-0	Basseterre	WCq		4 000	Bonilla SLV
15-11	Canada	L	0-4	Toronto	WCq		10 235	Cerdas CRC

Fr = Friendly match • CC = Digicel Caribbean Cup • WC = FIFA World Cup • q = qualifier

ST KITTS AND NEVIS NATIONAL TEAM HISTORICAL RECORDS

Past Coaches | Ces Podd 1999-2002 • Elvis Browne 2002-04 • Lenny Lake 2004-07 • Lester Morris 2008-09 • Clinton Percival 2010-

ST KITTS 2010–11

SKNFA DIGICEL SUPER LEAGUE FIRST STAGE

	Pl	W	D	L	F	A	Pts	St Pauls	Newtown	Conaree	Superstars	St Peters	St Thomas	Hotspurs	Mantab	Challengers
St Pauls United †	24	16	4	4	43	20	52		1-0 0-1	2-1 2-1	0-0 2-3	2-0 1-0	2-0 1-2	2-1 2-1	2-0 2-1	2-0 3-0
Newtown United †	24	14	7	3	55	20	49	0-0		1-2 2-2	4-0 1-1	2-2 2-1	4-2 1-0	2-3 3-0	3-0 3-0	5-0 9-0
Conaree United †	24	11	8	5	46	26	41	2-3	0-0		1-1 2-1	3-1 0-1	0-0 1-1	3-1 2-2	0-0 3-1	4-0 2-0
Village Superstars †	24	10	7	7	42	26	37	2-2	0-1	0-1		2-1 2-0	2-0 0-1	2-0 1-1	0-1 4-1	3-3 6-0
St Peters Strikers	24	10	3	11	36	34	33	2-4	0-0	3-2	0-1		0-1 4-1	1-0 3-1	1-0 2-0	1-1 5-0
St Thomas Strikers	24	9	6	9	28	38	33	0-3	1-1	1-5	2-2	5-2		2-1 0-2	0-0 0-0	2-0 2-0
Garden Hotspurs	24	8	6	10	44	35	30	1-1	2-3	0-0	2-1	0-2	4-0		3-1 2-2	1-1 8-0
Mantab United	24	5	4	15	22	46	19	2-1	1-2	2-4	0-3	2-1	2-3	0-3		1-3 3-0
Challengers United	24	1	3	20	16	87	6	0-3	2-5	1-5	0-5	2-3	1-2	1-5	1-2	

29/10/2010 - 21/05/2011 • † Qualified for play-offs

ST KITTS 2010–11

SKNFA DIGICEL SUPER LEAGUE SUPER FOUR PLAY-OFFS

	Pl	W	D	L	F	A	Pts	Superstars	St Pauls	Conaree	Newtown
Village Superstars †	3	2	1	0	6	4	7		3-2		
St Pauls United †	3	2	1	0	3	1	7	1-1			1-0
Conaree United	3	0	1	2	3	5	1		0-1		
Newtown United	3	0	1	2	2	4	1	1-2		1-1	

5/06/2011 - 11/06/2011 • † Qualified for the final

SKNFA DIGICEL SUPER LEAGUE FINAL

Champions	Score	Runners-up
St Pauls United	1-2 2-1 0-3	**Village Superstars**

1st leg. 15-06-2011; 2nd leg. 17-06-2011
Play-off. 21-06-2011. Scorers - Lawrence Ajah Jeffers, Alister Warner, Jevon Francis for Village Superstars

MEDALS TABLE

		Overall G	Lge G	Cup G	Town
1	Newtown United	17	15	2	Basseterre
2	Village Superstars	9	6	3	Basseterre
3	Garden Hotspurs	4	4		Basseterre
4	St Pauls United	2	2		Basseterre
	Cayon Rockets	2	1	1	Cayon

SKNFA CUP 2011

Round of 16

Village Superstars	0 3p
Conaree	0 2p
Molineaux	
Newtown United	
St Peters Strikers	0
St Pauls United	1
Cayon FC	0 3p
Lodge Patriots	0 1p
Basseterre High School	
Mantab United	

Quarter-finals

- **Village Superstars**
- Newtown United
- **St Pauls United**
- **Cayon FC**
- **Mantab United**

Semi-finals

Village Superstars	0 3p
St Pauls United	0 2p
Cayon FC	0
Mantab United	1

Final

Village Superstars	4
Mantab United	3

CUP FINAL

Warner Park, Basseterre, 1-06-2011, Ref: Browne. Scorers - Leroy Clarke [12], Shaquille Pringle [52], Travis Somersall [62], Devaughn Elliott [84] for Superstars; Jermaine Carey 2 [38] [77], Dave Charles [90] for Mantab

SLE – SIERRA LEONE

FIFA/COCA-COLA WORLD RANKING

'93	'94	'95	'96	'97	'98	'99	'00	'01	'02	'03	'04	'05	'06	'07	'08	'09	'10	'11	'12
76	76	58	84	84	111	120	129	138	133	146	160	163	148	156	116	138	125	60	

2011													High	Low	Av
Jan	Feb	Mar	Apr	May	Jun	Jul	Aug	Sep	Oct	Nov	Dec				
123	121	122	121	118	96	93	92	68	63	61	60		51	172	118

Sierra Leone finished joint top of their 2012 CAF Africa Cup of Nations qualifying group but thanks to the head-to-head with South Africa and Niger they missed out on a place in the finals in Equatorial Guinea and Gabon. Sierra Leone lost just once in the group - to Niger - a result that proved vital in the end and there was also a victory over the defending Nations Cup champions Egypt to savour although the Egyptians were already out by then and sent an under-23 side. Coach Lars Olaf Mattsson, imported from Sweden on a part-time basis for national team matches, was not paid for some of his work through the year and in a rare public admission, Sierra Leone's sports ministry apologised and promised to make good the shortfall. Mattsson's appointment had been the subject of a tug of power between government and the football association, who preferred the candidacy of veteran local coach Christian Cole for the job. But as government pay the coach's salary, they got their way. Ports Authority were crowned champions ahead of Kallon FC, the club set up by the former Inter Milan striker Mohamed Kallon. Both clubs lost just once in a season that was shortened to one round of games only. It was Ports seventh title overall, four short of the record held by defending champions East End Lions who finished in fifth place.

CAF AFRICA CUP OF NATIONS RECORD

1957-1972 DNE **1974** DNQ **1976** DNE **1978** DNQ **1980** DNE **1982-1984** DNQ **1986** DNE **1988** DNQ **1990** DNE **1992** DNQ **1994** 10 r1 **1996** 12 r1 **1998** DNE **2000** Disqualified **2002-2012** DNQ

SIERRA LEONE FOOTBALL ASSOCIATION (SLFA)

21 Battery Street, Kingtom, PO Box 672, Freetown

☎ +232 22 240071

✆

📧 starssierra@yahoo.com

🖥 slfa.1hwy.com

FA 1967 CON 1967 FIFA 1967

P Nahim Khadi

GS Abdul Rahman Swaray

FIFA BIG COUNT 2006

Total players	259 630
% of population	4.32%
Male	247 240
Female	12 390
Amateurs 18+	840
Youth under 18	5 640
Unregistered	15 150
Professionals	0
Referees	263
Admin & coaches	2 200
Number of clubs	24
Number of teams	196

GUI

●Kabala

●Kambia
●Rokupr
Port Loko ●Makeni
●Magburaka   Koidu
Lunsar   Koindu
●Freetown   Yengema
●Waterloo   Kailahun●

Segbwema●
Bumpeh● ●Bo
●Kenema
Pondobu●

LBR

NORTH
ATLANTIC
OCEAN

0   50 miles
0   50 km

MAJOR CITIES/TOWNS

		Population
1	Freetown	827 985
2	Bo	206 769
3	Kenema	164 125
4	Makeni	99 549
5	Koidu	91 042
6	Lunsar	23 609
7	Port Loko	22 397
8	Pandebu	19 378
9	Kabala	18 616
10	Waterloo	17 469
11	Kailahun	17 210
12	Magburaka	15 770
13	Segbwema	15 714
14	Koindu	15 659
15	Bumpeh	14 825
16	Yengema	13 225
17	Kambia	12 282
18	Goderich	12 178
19	Rokupr	12 166

REPUBLIC OF SIERRA LEONE

Capital	Freetown	Population	6 440 053 (103)	% in cities	38%
GDP per capita	$900 (217)	Area km²	71 740 km² (118)	GMT +/-	0
Neighbours (km)	Guinea 652, Liberia 306 • Coast 402				

RECENT INTERNATIONAL MATCHES PLAYED BY SIERRA LEONE

2008 Opponents	Score	Venue	Comp	Scorers	Att	Referee
30-04 Liberia	L 1-3	Paynesville	Fr	Kemokai Kallon [65]		
1-06 Equatorial Guinea	L 0-2	Malabo	WCq		13 000	Codjia BEN
7-06 Nigeria	L 0-1	Freetown	WCq		25 000	Korti LBR
14-06 South Africa	W 1-0	Freetown	WCq	Mohammed Kallon [21p]	15 000	Pare BFA
21-06 South Africa	D 0-0	Atteridgeville	WCq		12 000	Evehe CMR
6-09 Equatorial Guinea	W 2-1	Freetown	WCq	Kewullay Conteh [30], Sheriff Suma [73]	22 000	Doue CIV
11-10 Nigeria	L 1-4	Abuja	WCq	Yobo OG [31]	20 000	Kaoma ZAM
2009						
No international matches played in 2009						
2010						
5-09 Egypt	D 1-1	Cairo	CNq	Mustapha Bangura [56]		Diatta SEN
10-10 South Africa	D 0-0	Freetown	CNq			Lemghaifry MTN
2011						
9-02 Nigeria	L 1-2	Lagos	Fr	Mohamed Kabia [89]		
27-03 Niger	L 1-3	Niamey	CNq	Mohamed Bangura [11]		
4-06 Niger	W 1-0	Freetown	CNq	Teteh Bangura [50]		
3-09 Egypt	W 2-1	Freetown	CNq	Sheriff Suma [14], Mohamed Bangura [89p]		
8-10 South Africa	D 0-0	Nelspruit	CNq			

Fr = Friendly match • CN = CAF African Cup of Nations • AC = Amilcar Cabral Cup • WC = FIFA World Cup • q = qualifier

MEDALS TABLE

		Overall G	Lge G	Cup G	City
1	Mighty Blackpool	14	10	4	Freetown
	East End Lions	14	11	3	Freetown
3	Ports Authority	9	7	2	Freetown
4	Kallon FC (inc Fisheries)	5	4	1	Freetown
5	Real Republicans	4	3	1	Freetown
6	Old Edwardians	3	1	2	Freetown
7	Bai Bureh Warriors	2		2	Port Loko
	Kamboi Eagles	2		2	Kenema
9	Freetown United	1	1		Freetown
	Diamond Stars	1		1	Kono
	Wusum Stars	1		1	Bombali
		56	37	19	

SIERRA LEONE 2011

AFRICELL PREMIER LEAGUE

	Pl	W	D	L	F	A	Pts	Ports Authority	Kallon FC	Kamboi Eagles	Wusum Stars	East End Lions	Bo Rangers	Blackpool	Kissy All Stars	Diamond Stars	Freetown City	Edwardians	Central Parade	Nepean Stars	Area Best
Ports Authority †	13	8	4	1	14	6	28				1-0	2-1		2-1	0-0	1-0				
Kallon FC ‡	13	6	6	1	18	7	24	0-0					2-1	0-0	2-2			3-1	2-1		3-0
Kamboi Eagles	13	7	3	3	16	13	24	2-1	0-0				1-1	0-1	1-0	2-0		1-0			3-1
Wusum Stars	13	6	5	2	14	8	23		2-1	2-0		0-2		0-0			2-2	1-1		1-0	2-1
East End Lions	13	6	4	3	16	10	22		0-0	4-1				0-1	3-2			1-1			1-1
Bo Rangers	13	5	6	2	13	5	21	0-0			0-0	2-0		0-0	0-0	0-0		2-0	3-1		
Mighty Blackpool	13	4	7	2	7	3	19								0-0	0-0	0-0		0-0	2-0	
Kissy All Stars	13	3	7	3	10	10	16				0-2							0-0		2-1	
Diamond Stars	13	3	6	4	4	7	15		0-0			0-0	0-1		1-1		0-0	1-0		1-0	
Freetown City	13	3	5	5	10	13	14	0-1	0-2	2-2		0-1	1-0		0-1			2-0	1-1		
Old Edwardians	13	2	6	5	6	11	12	1-1		0-1		0-0		1-0					0-0		2-0
Central Parade	13	2	5	6	7	12	11	0-1			0-2					0-0	0-1			2-0	
Nepean Stars	13	2	1	10	8	21	7	1-3	0-3	1-2		0-2	0-1				3-1	0-0			2-1
Area Best	13	1	1	11	6	23	4	0-1						0-3	0-2	0-2	2-0	0-1		0-1	

26/02/2011 - 10/07/2011 • † Qualified for the CAF Champions League • ‡ Qualified for the CAF Confederation Cup

SLV – EL SALVADOR

FIFA/COCA-COLA WORLD RANKING

'93	'94	'95	'96	'97	'98	'99	'00	'01	'02	'03	'04	'05	'06	'07	'08	'09	'10	'11	'12
66	80	82	65	64	92	96	83	86	94	95	106	124	156	134	111	78	117	69	

	2011													
	Jan	Feb	Mar	Apr	May	Jun	Jul	Aug	Sep	Oct	Nov	Dec	High	Low	Av
	116	98	92	87	87	72	78	75	88	82	69	69	54	169	94

The El Salvador national team showed signs of improvement in 2011 after a number of years in the doldrums. At the CONCACAF Gold Cup they came within a whisker of their best-ever performance and then won all six of their first round group matches in the 2014 FIFA World Cup qualifiers. Under new coach Ruben Israel, El Salvador started the Gold Cup with a heavy 5-0 defeat at the hands of Mexico although a draw with Costa Rica and a 6-1 victory over Cuba saw them through to a quarter-final meeting with Panama. At the RFK Stadium in Washington DC, the Salvadoreans were desperately unlucky not to make it through to the semi-finals for the first time. They had taken a late lead through a Rodolfo Zelaya penalty but then conceded an injury-time equaliser through Luis Tejada before a second penalty shoot-out defeat of the year at the hands of the Panamanians saw them on their way home. At club level there was a welcome return to form for traditional giants Alianza who won the first of the two championships played during the year after beating Deportivo FAS 2-1 in the final. The second went to Isidro-Metapán who since first winning the championship in 2007 have won six titles in just ten campaigns. They beat Once Municipal 1-0 in the final at the Estadio Cuscatlan in San Salvador.

CONCACAF GOLD CUP RECORD

1991 DNQ 1993 DNQ **1996** r1 **1998** r1 2000 DNQ **2002** QF **2003** QF 2005 DNQ **2007** r1 **2009** r1 **2011** QF

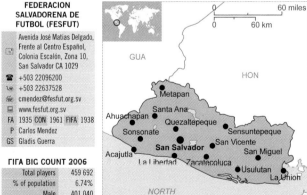

FEDERACION SALVADORENA DE FUTBOL (FESFUT)

Avenida José Matias Delgado, Frente al Centro Español, Colonia Escalón, Zona 10, San Salvador CA 1029
☎ +503 22096200
📠 +503 22637528
✉ cmendez@fesfut.org.sv
🖥 www.fesfut.org.sv
FA 1935 CON 1961 FIFA 1938
P Carlos Mendez
GS Gladis Guerra

FIFA BIG COUNT 2006

Total players	459 692
% of population	6.74%
Male	401 040
Female	58 652
Unregistered	225 900
Professionals	200
Referees	315
Admin & coaches	5 538
Number of clubs	68
Number of teams	2 828

MAJOR CITIES/TOWNS

		Population
1	San Salvador	550 828
2	Soyapango	402 198
3	Santa Ana	189 014
4	San Miguel	174 467
5	Mejicanos	165 652
6	Apopa	136 818
7	N'va San Salvador	131 971
8	Delgado	87 335
9	San Marcos	66 623
10	Sonsonate	63 729
11	Usulután	55 041
12	Cuscatancingo	54 124
13	Cojutepeque	51 348
14	San Martin	48 015
15	Antiguo Cuscatlán	44 829
16	Zacatecoluca	42 234
17	San Vicente	39 742
18	Quezaltepeque	38 348
27	La Libertad	22 890

REPUBLICA DE EL SALVADOR • REPUBLIC OF EL SALVADOR

Capital San Salvador	Population 7 185 218 (99)	% in cities 61%
GDP per capita $6200 (131)	Area km² 21 041 km² (153)	GMT + / - -6
Neighbours (km) Guatemala 203, Honduras 342 • Coast 307		

RECENT INTERNATIONAL MATCHES PLAYED BY EL SALVADOR

2009 Opponents	Score	Venue	Comp	Scorers	Att	Referee
7-08 Colombia	L 1-2	Houston	Fr	Juan Carlos Moscoso [63]	20 418	Marrufo USA
12-08 Trinidad and Tobago	L 0-1	Port of Spain	WCq		16 000	Vaughn USA
5-09 USA	L 1-2	Sandy	WCq	Cristian Castillo [31]	19 066	Pineda HON
9-09 Costa Rica	W 1-0	San Salvador	WCq	Rudis Corrales [91+]	18 000	Archundia MEX
10-10 Mexico	L 1-4	Mexico City	WCq	Julio Martinez [89]	104 000	Batres GUA
14-10 Honduras	L 0-1	San Salvador	WCq		28 000	Salazar USA
2010						
24-02 USA	L 1-2	Tampa	Fr	Rudis Corrales [59]	21 737	Petrescu CAN
3-03 Guatemala	L 1-2	Los Angeles	Fr	Eliseo Quintanilla [89]	10 000	Salazar USA
4-09 Honduras	D 2-2	Los Angeles	Fr	Rodolfo Zelaya 2 [42 90]. L 3-4p	15 000	Stoica USA
8-10 Panama	L 0-1	Panama City	Fr		16 175	Ruiz COL
12-10 Costa Rica	L 1-2	Quesada	Fr	Rafael Burgos [53]	4 000	Rodriguez PAN
2011						
14-01 Nicaragua	W 2-1	Panama City	UCr1	Jaime Alas [71], Rafael Burgos [76]	2 000	Quesada CRC
16-01 Belize	W 5-2	Panama City	UCr1	Osael Romero [15], Rafael Burgos 2 [25 46], Jaime Alas [54], Deris Umanzor [59]	1 500	Cerdas CRC
18-01 Panama	L 0-2	Panama City	UCr1		10 000	Garcia MEX
21-01 Honduras	L 0-2	Panama City	UCsf		5 000	Quesada CRC
23-01 Panama	D 0-0	Panama City	UC3p	L 4-5p	2 000	Pineda HON
9-02 Haiti	W 1-0	San Salvador	Fr	Rafael Burgos [14]	15 000	Espana GUA
24-03 Cuba	W 1-0	Havana	Fr	Denis Alas [74]	3 500	Rodriguez PAN
29-03 Jamaica	L 2-3	San Salvador	Fr	Jaime Alas [41], Mark Blanco [90]	15 000	Rodas GUA
29-05 Honduras	D 2-2	Houston	Fr	Rodolfo Zelaya [73], Rudis Corrales [77]	25 380	Villareal USA
5-06 Mexico	L 0-5	Arlington/Dallas	GCr1		80 108	Wijngaarde SUR
9-06 Costa Rica	D 1-1	Charlotte	GCr1	Rodolfo Zelaya [45]	46 012	Marrufo USA
12-06 Cuba	W 6-1	Chicago	GCr1	Rodolfo Zelaya 2 [13 71], William Romero [29], Lester Blanco [69], Arturo Alvarez [84], Eliseo Quintanilla [94+]	62 000	Brizan TRI
19-06 Panama	D 1-1	Washington DC	GCqf	Rodolfo Zelaya [78p]. L 3-5p	45 424	Quesada CRC
7-08 Venezuela	W 2-1	Washington DC	Fr			
2-09 Dominican Republic	W 3-2	San Salvador	WCq	Rodolfo Zelaya 2 [54 77], Cristian Bautista [63]	25 272	Rodriguez PAN
6-09 Cayman Islands	W 4-1	Georgetown	WCq	Cristian Bautista [49], Luis Anaya 2 [62 80], Moises Garcia [93+]	2 200	Rodas GUA
7-10 Dominican Republic	W 2-1	San Cristobal	WCq	Osael Romero [37p], Mark Blanco [67]	2 323	Cerdas CRC
11-10 Cayman Islands	W 4-0	San Salvador	WCq	Victor Turcios [6], Steve Purdy [13], Jaime Alas [45], Herbert Sosa [88p]	17 570	Cruz CRC
11-11 Suriname	W 3-1	Paramaribo	WCq	Mark Blanco 2 [21 58], Edwin Sanchez [78]	500	Brea CUB
15-11 Suriname	W 4-0	San Salvador	WCq	Osael Romero 2 [33 62], Rafael Burgos 2 [76 83]	9 659	Santos PUR

Fr = Friendly match • UC = UNCAF Cup/Copa Centroamericana • GC = CONCACAF Gold Cup • WC = FIFA World Cup • q = qualifier

EL SALVADOR NATIONAL TEAM HISTORICAL RECORDS

Caps
89 - Luis Guevara Mora 1979-96 • 77 - Marvin Gonzalez 2002- • 74 - Guillermo Rivera 1988-2002 • 72 - Alfredo Pacheco 2002- • 71 - Rudis Corrales 1999- • 68 - Mauricio Cienfuegos 1987-2003 • 66 - Ronald Cerritos 1995-2008 • 65 - Jorge Rodriguez 1994-2005 • 64 - Juan Francisco Barraza 1953-69 • 63 - Ramon Sanchez 2001-

Goals
39 - Raul Diaz Arce 1991-2000 • 22 - Jose Maria Rivas 1979-89 • 21 - Jorge Gonzalez 1976-98 • 17 - Luis Ramirez Zapata 1971-89 • 16 - Norberto Huezo 1973-87; Miguel Cruz 1935-43 & Rudis Corrales 1999- • 14 - Eliseo Quinanilla 2007- • 13 - Juan Francisco Barraza 1953-69 & Ever Hernandez 1976-85 • 12 - Rafael Corado 1943-55 & Gustavo Marroquin 1927-30

Past Coaches
Mark Scott Thompson USA 1930-35 • Pablo Ferre Elias ESP 1935-38 • Maximo Garay ARG 1940-41 • Slade 1941-43 • Amaricano Gonzalez 1943-48 • Rodolfo Orlandini ARG 1949-51 • Marcelo Estrada 1953 • Carbilio Tomasino 1954-59 • Milo Guardado 1959-60 • Conrado Miranda 1961 • Luis Comitante URU 1962-63 • Hernan Vivanco CHI 1965-67 • Rigoberto Guzman 1968 • Gregorio Bundio ARG 1968-70 • Hernan Vivanco CHI 1970 • Conrado Miranda 1971 • Hector D'Angelo ARG 1972 • Jorge Tupinamba BRA 1973 • Pipo Rodriguez 1973-74 • Conrado Miranda 1975 • Marcelo Estrada 1975-76 • Raul Magana 1976 • Aurelio Pinto Beltrao BRA 1976 • Roberto Porta URU 1977 • Julio Contreras Cardona 1977 • Ricardo Tomasino 1978 • Raul Magana 1979 • Pipo Rodriguez 1979-82 • Armando Contreras 1983 • Raul Magana 1984 • Juan Quarterone ARG 1984-85 • Paulo Roberto Cabrera 1986 • Raul Magana 1987 • Milovan Doric YUG 1988 • Miroslav Vukasinovic YUG 1988-89 • Conrado Miranda 1989 • Kiril Dojcinovski YUG 1989 • Oscar Emigdio Benitez 1991 • Jorge Aude URU 1991-92 • Anibal Ruiz URU 1992 • Jorge Vieira BRA 1993-94 • Jose Omar Pastoriza ARG 1995-96 • Armando Contreras 1996-97 • Milovan Doric YUG 1997-98 • Kiril Dojcinovski YUG 1998 • Marinho Peres BRA 1998 • Oscar Emigdio Benitez 1999-2000 • Carlos Recinos 2000-02 • Juan Ramon Paredes 2002-04 • Armando Contreras 2004 • Carlos Cavagnaro ARG 2005 • Miguel Aguilar 2005-06 • Carlos de los Cobos MEX 2006-09 • Jose Luis Rugamas 2010-11 • Ruben Israel URU 2011-

EL SALVADOR 2010-11

PRIMERA DIVISION PROFESIONAL CAMPEONATO CLAUSURA

	Pl	W	D	L	F	A	Pts	Alianza	FAS	I-Metapán	LA Firpo	Aguila	At. Marte	V. Hermosa	UES	Once	At. Balboa
Alianza †	18	8	5	5	32	21	29		4-0	1-4	0-0	4-2	1-0	4-1	5-0	3-0	1-1
Deportivo FAS	18	7	8	3	29	24	29	1-1		1-3	2-0	2-0	2-0	1-1	1-1	2-2	3-0
CD Isidro-Metapán †	18	9	2	7	26	24	29	0-1	2-4		2-1	2-1	2-2	1-0	2-0	2-2	2-1
Luis Angel Firpo †	18	8	4	6	24	15	28	3-0	2-2	2-0		2-1	4-1	1-0	1-1	2-1	4-0
CD Aguila	18	7	6	5	27	21	27	3-2	1-1	2-1	1-0		1-1	1-1	2-0	3-1	2-0
Atlético Marte	18	8	3	7	25	24	27	2-1	1-2	1-2	1-0	3-3		0-1	1-0	5-2	2-0
Vista Hermosa	18	6	8	4	19	15	26	0-0	2-0	3-0	2-0	0-0	0-2		2-2	1-0	0-0
Univ'dad El Salvador	18	3	8	7	14	25	17	1-2	1-2	1-0	0-0	1-0	0-2	2-2		0-0	1-1
Once Municipal	18	2	9	7	17	27	15	1-1	3-3	0-1	1-0	0-0	0-1	1-1	1-1		1-0
Atlético Balboa	18	3	5	10	11	28	14	2-1	0-0	1-0	0-2	0-4	3-0	0-2	1-2	1-1	

22/01/2011 - 21/04/2011 • † Qualified for the play-offs
Top scorers: 17 - Rodolfo Zelaya, Alianza • 12 - Nicolas Munoz, Aguila • 9 - Alcides Bandera URU, Atlético Marte

CLAUSURA PLAY-OFFS

Semi-finals			Finals	
Alianza *	1	1		
Luis Angel Firpo	1	1	Alianza	2
CD Isidro-Metapán *	3	0	Deportivo FAS	1
Deportivo FAS	2	2	* At home in the first leg	

CHAMPIONSHIP FINAL CLAUSURA 2011

Estadio Cuscatlan, San Salvador, 15-05-2011, Att: 23 419, Ref: Marlon Mejia

Alianza	2	Zelaya 2 [41] [74]
Deportivo FAS	1	Velasquez [85]

Alianza - Henry Hernandez - Mauricio Quintanilla, Marcelo Messias•, Edwin Martinez - Cristian Castillo (Jonathan Barrios 91+), Hector Salazar, Roberto Alvarado, Herbert Sosa, Abraham Amaya (Roberto Garcia 69) - Carlos Ayala• (Rafael Burgos 96+), Rodolfo Zelaya◆[87]. Tr: Roberto Gamarra
FAS - Luis Contreras - Victor Velasquez•, Mardoqueo Henriquez (Oscar Ulloa 85), Jose Granadino, Ramon Flores◆[96+] - Roberto Pena, William Maldonado (Marcio Teruel 46), Cristian Alvarez, Juan Moscoso (Carlos Aparicio 72) - Alejandro Bentos•, Williams Reyes. Tr: Agustin Castillo

EL SALVADOR 2011-12

PRIMERA DIVISION PROFESIONAL TORNEO APERTURA

	Pl	W	D	L	F	A	Pts	I-Metapán	FAS	Municipal	Aguila	LA Firpo	Alianza	At. Marte	Juventude	UES	V. Hermosa
CD Isidro-Metapán †	18	11	3	4	32	21	36		0-0	1-1	3-1	4-2	1-0	2-1	0-1	4-2	1-0
Deportivo FAS	18	9	5	4	24	17	32	3-0		2-1	1-3	1-1	2-1	1-0	2-1	1-0	3-1
Once Municipal	18	8	6	4	29	20	30	1-1	1-0		2-0	2-1	1-2	1-1	0-0	0-1	5-0
CD Aguila	18	8	5	5	34	26	29	1-0	1-1	2-2		3-2	1-2	2-0	5-1	3-0	2-2
Luis Angel Firpo	18	8	5	5	30	26	29	1-3	3-1	6-3	2-0		2-2	1-0	2-1	1-1	0-2
Alianza	18	6	6	6	18	17	24	0-1	1-2	0-1	1-1	1-1		0-1	1-0	0-0	2-1
Atlético Marte	18	6	5	7	19	19	23	5-3	0-0	1-1	2-4	0-1	0-2		3-0	2-0	0-0
Juventude Independ'te	18	5	2	11	18	30	17	1-4	1-0	1-2	2-1	2-3	1-2	1-2		3-1	1-1
Univ'dad El Salvador	18	2	8	8	15	29	14	1-3	0-2	1-3	2-2	1-1	1-1	2-2	1-0		0-0
Vista Hermosa	18	1	7	10	11	25	10	0-1	2-2	0-2	1-2	0-1	0-0	0-1	0-1	1-1	

30/07/2011 - 27/11/2011 • † Qualified for the play-offs • 4th place play-off: **LA Firpo** 1-0 Aguia
Top scorers (inc play-offs): 16 - Anel Canales PAN, LA Firpo • 15 - Nicolas Munoz PAN, Aguila & • 14 - Sean Fraser JAM, Once Municipal

APERTURA PLAY-OFFS

Semi-finals			Finals	
Isidro-Metapán	3	3		
LA Firpo *	3	0	Isidro-Metapán	1
Deportivo FAS	0	1	Once Municipal	0
Once Municipal *	1	2	* At home in the first leg	

CHAMPIONSHIP FINAL APERTURA 2011

Estadio Cuscatlan, San Salvador, 18-12-2011, Ref: Elmer Bonilla

Isidro-Metapán	1	Suarez [51]
Once Municipal	0	

I-Metapán - Miguel Montes - Alexander Escobar, Alfredo Pacheco, Milton Molina, Ramon Sanchez•, Jose Alvarado, Paolo Suarez, Hector Mejia, Andres Flores (Edwin Sanchez 94+), Allan Kardeck• (Ernesto Aquino 77), Mark Blanco (Christian Bautista 88). Tr: Edwin Portillo
Municipal - Jasir Deras - Julio Castro, Miguel Solis, Andres Medina, Juan Lazo•, Diego Chavarria, Elder Figueroa••◆[85], Ronald Pimentel, Sean Frazer•, Ricardo Orellana (Pablo Hutt 55), Mario Deras• (Juan Campos 48). Tr: Juan Sarulyte

EL SALVADOR 2010–11
PRIMERA DIVISION
AGGREGATE TABLE

	Pl	W	D	L	F	A	Pts
CD Isidro-Metapán	36	19	6	11	60	51	63
Alianza	36	17	11	8	57	34	62
CD Aguíla	36	16	10	10	48	40	58
Luis Angel Firpo	36	16	11	9	48	32	59
Deportivo FAS	36	11	13	12	48	52	46
Vista Hermosa	36	9	18	9	39	40	45
Atlético Marte	36	12	8	16	47	52	44
Atlético Balboa	36	10	13	13	40	43	43
Univ'dad El Salvador	36	6	15	15	37	52	33
Once Municipal	36	5	14	17	30	52	29

Atlético Balboa relegated due to debts. Once Municipal
remain in the Primera Division

MEDALS TABLE

		Overall			Lge		Cup		Cent Am			
		G	S	B	G	B	G	S	G	S	B	Town/City
1	Deportivo FAS	18	18		17	18			1			Santa Ana
2	CD Aguila	16	10		14	9	1	1	1			San Miguel
3	Alianza FC	10	9	2	9	9			1		2	San Salvador
4	CD Luis Angel Firpo	9	11		9	10	1					Usulután
5	CD Atlético Marte	8	1		8				1			San Salvador
6	AD Isidro Metapán	6	1		6	1						Metapán
7	Once Municipal	3	5		2	5	1					Ahuachapán
8	Hércules	3			3							San Salvador
9	Juventud Olimpica	2	5		2	5						Sonsonate
10	CD Dragon	2	2		2	2						San Miguel
11	CD 33	2			2							San Salvador
	Quequeisque	2			2							La Libertad
13	Chacarita Juniors (Chinameca)	1	1		1	1						San Miguel
	CD Santiagueño	1	1		1	1						Santiago de Maria
	CD Atlético Balboa	1	1			1	1					La Unión
	Libertad FC	1	1		1	1						San Salvador
	San Salvador FC	1	1		1	1						San Salvador
18	CD Platense Municipal	1			1							Zacatecoluca
	CD Vista Hermosa	1			1							Gotera
20	Independiente Nacional		3			2	1					San Vicente
21	Atlante		2			2						
	Excelsior		2			2						Santa Ana
	Municipal Limeño		2			2						Santa Rosa de Lima
	Chalatenango (ex Alacranes)		2			2						Chalatenango
25	Cojutepeque		1			1						Cojutepeque
	El Transito		1			1						La Libertad
	Ferrocarril		1			1						Sonsonate
	Leones		1			1						San Salvador
	Maya		1			1						Quezaltepeque
	Nequepio		1			1						Cuscatlán
	Universidad		1			1						

SMR – SAN MARINO

FIFA/COCA-COLA WORLD RANKING

'93	'94	'95	'96	'97	'98	'99	'00	'01	'02	'03	'04	'05	'06	'07	'08	'09	'10	'11	'12
121	131	951	165	173	179	150	168	158	160	162	164	155	194	197	201	203	203	206	

					2011										
	Jan	Feb	Mar	Apr	May	Jun	Jul	Aug	Sep	Oct	Nov	Dec	**High**	**Low**	**Av**
	203	203	202	202	202	203	203	203	203	203	204	206	**118**	**206**	**170**

If San Marino thought that by organising a friendly against Liechtenstein they could bring an end to their 38-match losing run, they will have been sorely disappointed after losing 1-0 to them in Serravalle. It was San Marino's first friendly match for five years and was played against the last team they beat, but since that victory against Liechtenstein at the end of April 2004, San Marino have played 45 matches and lost every one of them - scoring just five goals and letting in 202. It is a record that has seen them plummet to the absolute bottom of the FIFA/Coca-Cola World Ranking, a position they shared with Montserrat and Andorra in December 2011. A tournament between the three would seem to offer the best opportunity to end a run that increases the world record with every game played and lost. In club football, Tre Fiori won the league for the seventh time after beating Tre Penne in the final for the second year running. Alessandro Giunta scored the only goal of the game for Tre Fiori as they not only won the title for the third year in a row but also became the most successful club side in the history of football in San Marino, overtaking Domagnano's haul of 12 trophies since 1986. In the Coppa Titano, Juvenes/Dogana beat Virtus 4-1 in the final to win the trophy for the second time in three years.

UEFA EUROPEAN CHAMPIONSHIP RECORD
1960-1988 DNE 1992-2012 DNQ

FEDERAZIONE SAMMARINESE GIUOCO CALCIO (FSGC)

Strada di Montecchio 17, San Marino 47890
☎ +378 054 9990515
📠 +378 054 9992348
📧 fsgc@omniway.sm
🖥 www.fsgc.sm
FA 1931 CON 1988 FIFA 1988
P Giorgio Crescentini
GS Luciano Casadei

FIFA BIG COUNT 2006

Total players	2 836
% of population	9.70%
Male	2 421
Female	415
Amateurs 18+	763
Youth under 18	823
Unregistered	650
Professionals	0
Referees	35
Admin & coaches	225
Number of clubs	16
Number of teams	56

MAJOR CITIES/TOWNS

		Population
1	Serravalle	9 894
2	Borgo Maggiore	6 058
3	San Marino	4 433
4	Domagnano	2 872
5	Fiorentino	2 250
6	Acquaviva	1 914
7	Murata	1 580
8	Faetano	1 175
9	Chiesanuova	1 042
10	Montegiardino	837

REPUBBLICA DI SAN MARINO • REPUBLIC OF SAN MARINO

Capital San Marino	Population 30 324 (212)	% in cities 94%
GDP per capita $41 900 (19)	Area km² 61 km² (228)	GMT + / - +1
Neighbours (km) Italy 39		

RECENT INTERNATIONAL MATCHES PLAYED BY SAN MARINO

2004	Opponents		Score	Venue	Comp	Scorers	Att	Referee
28-04	Liechtenstein	W	1-0	Serravalle	Fr	Andy Selva [5]	700	Sammut MLT
4-09	Serbia & Montenegro	L	0-3	Serravalle	WCq		1 137	Kholmatov KAZ
8-09	Lithuania	L	0-4	Kaunas	WCq		4 000	Jareci ALB
13-10	Serbia & Montenegro	L	0-5	Belgrade	WCq		4 000	Isaksen FRO
17-11	Lithuania	L	0-1	Serravalle	WCq		1 457	Nalbandyan ARM
2005								
9-02	Spain	L	0-5	Almeria	WCq		12 580	Clark SCO
30-03	Belgium	L	1-2	Serravalle	WCq	Andy Selva [41]	871	Kasnaferis GRE
4-06	Bosnia-Herzegovina	L	1-3	Serravalle	WCq	Andy Selva [39]	750	Demirlek TUR
7-09	Belgium	L	0-8	Antwerp	WCq		8 207	Stokes IRL
8-10	Bosnia-Herzegovina	L	0-3	Zenica	WCq		8 500	Hamer LUX
12-10	Spain	L	0-6	Serravalle	WCq		3 426	Meyer GER
2006								
16-08	Albania	L	0-3	Serravalle	Fr			
6-09	Germany	L	0-13	Serravalle	ECq		5 090	Dereli TUR
7-10	Czech Republic	L	0-7	Liberec	ECq		9 514	Aliyev AZE
15-11	Republic of Ireland	L	0-5	Dublin	ECq		34 018	Isaksen FRO
2007								
7-02	Republic of Ireland	L	1-2	Serravalle	ECq	Manuel Marani [86]	3 294	Rasmussen DEN
28-03	Wales	L	0-3	Cardiff	ECq		18 752	Tchagharyan ARM
2-06	Germany	L	0-6	Nuremberg	ECq		43 967	Asumaa FIN
22-08	Cyprus	L	0-1	Serravalle	ECq		552	Janku ALB
8-09	Czech Republic	L	0-3	Serravalle	ECq		3 412	Filipovic SRB
12-09	Cyprus	L	0-3	Nicosia	ECq		1 000	Kulbakov BLR
13-10	Slovakia	L	0-7	Dubnica n. Vahom	ECq		2 576	Wilmes LUX
17-10	Wales	L	1-2	Serravalle	ECq	Andy Selva [73]	1 182	Zammit MLT
21-11	Slovakia	L	0-5	Serravalle	ECq		538	Sipailo LVA
2008								
10-09	Poland	L	0-2	Serravalle	WCq		2 374	Zografos GRE
11-10	Slovakia	L	1-3	Serravalle	WCq	Andy Selva [45]	1 037	Kever SUI
15-10	Northern Ireland	L	0-4	Belfast	WCq		12 957	Kari FIN
19-11	Czech Republic	L	0-3	Serravalle	WCq		1 318	Kaasik EST
2009								
11-02	Northern Ireland	L	0-3	Serravalle	WCq		1 942	Stankovic SRB
1-04	Poland	L	0-10	Kielce	WCq		15 200	Kulbakou BLR
6-06	Slovakia	L	0-7	Bratislava	WCq		6 652	Efong Nzolo BEL
12-08	Slovenia	L	0-5	Maribor	WCq		4 400	Meckarovski MKD
9-09	Czech Republic	L	0-7	Uherske Hradiste	WCq		8 121	Amirkhanyan ARM
14-10	Slovenia	L	0-3	Serravalle	WCq		1 745	Szabo HUN
2010								
3-09	Netherlands	L	0-5	Serravalle	ECq		4 127	Evans WAL
7-09	Sweden	L	0-6	Malmo	ECq		21 083	McKeon IRL
8-10	Hungary	L	0-8	Budapest	ECq		10 596	Kaasik EST
12-10	Moldova	L	0-2	Serravalle	ECq		714	Courtney NIR
17-11	Finland	L	0-8	Helsinki	ECq		8 192	Matejek CZE
2011								
9-02	Liechtenstein	L	0-1	Serravalle	Fr			Banti ITA
3-06	Finland	L	0-1	Serravalle	ECq		1 218	Sipailo LVA
7-06	Hungary	L	0-3	Serravalle	ECq		1 915	Radovanovic MNE
10-08	Romania	L	0-1	Serravalle	Fr		3 000	Rocchi ITA
2-09	Netherlands	L	0-11	Eindhoven	ECq		35 000	Liany ISR
6-09	Sweden	L	0-5	Serravalle	ECq		2 946	McLean SCO
11-10	Moldova	L	0-4	Chisinau	ECq		6 534	Reinert FRO

Fr = Friendly match • EC = UEFA EURO 2008/2012 • WC = FIFA World Cup • q = qualifier

SAN MARINO 2010–11

CAMPIONATO SAMMARINESE DI CALCIO

Group A

Team	Pl	W	D	L	F	A	Pts	Pennarossa	La Fiorita	Cosmos	Juvenes/D	Faetano	Fiorentino	Cailungo	Tre Fiori	Libertas	Tre Penne	Murata	Virtus	S. Giovanni	Folgore	Domagnano
Pennarossa †	20	13	3	4	31	15	42		1-2	2-0	0-3	3-2	0-0	1-0	2-1	2-0			5-1		3-0	
La Fiorita †	20	10	6	4	44	28	36	2-1		1-2	0-2	5-1	4-1	0-1	0-0		2-2			6-3		
Cosmos †	20	11	3	6	22	22	36	0-0	0-1		1-0	0-3	2-1	1-0		1-0				2-0	1-2	
Juvenes/Dogana	20	8	5	7	37	31	29	0-1	4-4	0-2		1-3	1-3	4-1	0-1	1-1	3-2		3-1		3-3	
Faetano	20	7	3	10	30	33	24	0-3	1-3	1-3	3-0		0-1	5-0				1-4	0-0	2-4	1-2	
Fiorentino	20	5	4	11	22	37	19	0-1	3-2	1-2	1-2	1-2		1-0					1-3	0-0	0-1	
Cailungo	20	2	4	14	17	40	10	3-0	1-1	1-1	1-3	0-1	2-3					1-3	0-4	0-1	2-2	

Group B

Team	Pl	W	D	L	F	A	Pts	Pennarossa	La Fiorita	Cosmos	Juvenes/D	Faetano	Fiorentino	Cailungo	Tre Fiori	Libertas	Tre Penne	Murata	Virtus	S. Giovanni	Folgore	Domagnano
Tre Fiori †	21	11	6	4	41	26	39			4-1		1-0	4-1	3-3		0-2	1-1	2-3	2-0	1-1	4-0	3-2
Libertas †	21	10	7	4	26	13	37		1-3			0-0	4-1	2-0	0-1		0-0	1-1	1-1	2-0	3-0	1-0
Tre Penne †	21	10	6	5	32	19	36	0-0		0-0		4-0	2-0	0-1	0-1			2-1	3-1	0-1	3-1	2-2
Murata	21	9	8	4	34	19	35	1-1	2-2		0-0				2-1	1-1	0-0		0-1	2-3	1-0	2-0
Virtus	21	8	6	7	32	32	30		0-2		2-2				4-1	0-1	2-3	1-1		0-0	1-0	1-1
San Giovanni	21	9	2	10	29	34	29	0-3		0-2					1-4	0-2	0-1	1-3	4-3		2-0	3-0
Folgore/Falciano	21	3	4	14	21	44	13		0-1	1-3	5-0	1-5	1-3	1-1	3-3	1-1	1-2	0-5	0-1	2-3		2-0
Domagnano	21	0	9	12	17	42	9	1-1	0-1		1-1	2-2				1-3	1-3	0-4	0-2	0-2	1-1	

17/09/2010 - 17/04/2011 • † Qualified for the play-offs • Top scorer (inc play-offs): 13 - Alessandro Giunta, Tre Fiori

PLAY-OFFS WINNERS BRACKET

				FINAL
Tre Fiori	Bye			
		Tre Fiori	2	
		Pennarossa	1	Olimpico, Serravalle
Pennarossa	Bye			26-05-2011
La Fiorita	3		Tre Fiori 2	Scorer - Alessandro Giunta 21
Tre Penne	1	La Fiorita	2	Cosmos 0
Libertas	0	Cosmos	4	
Cosmos	2	Losing teams drop down to the losers bracket		Tre Fiori † 1
				Tre Penne ‡ 0

† Qualified for the UEFA Champions League • ‡ Qualified for the Europa League

PLAY-OFFS LOSERS BRACKET

Teams losing in the losers bracket are eliminated having lost twice overall

				Tre Penne	2
				Cosmos	1
		Tre Penne	3	Tre Penne qualify to meet Tre Fiori in	
		Pennarossa	1	the final • Cosmos qualified for the	
	Tre Penne	2		Europa League	
	La Fiorita	0			
Tre Penne	4				
Libertas	1				

COPPA TITANO 2010–11

Quarter–finals		Semi–finals		Final	
Juvenes/Dogana	3				
Folgore/Falciano	1	Juvenes/Dogana	1		
Tre Fiori	1 3p	Pennarossa	0		
Pennarossa	1 5p			Juvenes/Dogana	4
Murata	5			Virtus	1
Cosmos	0	Murata	0	Olimpico, 30-04-2011	
Domagnano	0	Virtus	2	Scorers - Ceci 17, Santini 30,	
Virtus	1			Hirsch OG 65, Colombini 83	
				for J/D; Hirsch 64 for Virtus	

MEDALS TABLE

		Overall G	Lge G	Cup G
1	Tre Fiori	13	7	6
2	Domagnano	12	4	8
3	Libertas	11	1	10
4	Faetano	6	3	3
	Murata	6	3	3
6	Cosmos	5	1	4
	Juvenes	5		5
	Tre Penne	5		5
9	La Fiorita	3	2	1
	Folgore Falciano	3	3	
	Pennarossa	3	1	2
12	Dogana	2		2
	Juvenes/Dogana	2		2
14	Fiorentino	1	1	

SOL – SOLOMON ISLANDS

FIFA/COCA-COLA WORLD RANKING

'93	'94	'95	'96	'97	'98	'99	'00	'01	'02	'03	'04	'05	'06	'07	'08	'09	'10	'11	'12
149	163	170	171	130	128	144	130	134	142	156	130	140	160	123	163	172	177	180	

2011													High	Low	Av
Jan	Feb	Mar	Apr	May	Jun	Jul	Aug	Sep	Oct	Nov	Dec		High	Low	Av
178	178	178	182	182	180	181	177	178	180	179	180		120	182	149

2011 provided further proof of the progress being made by football in the Solomon Islands with the national team winning the silver medal at the football tournament of the Pacific Games in Noumea, New Caledonia. There was disappointment, however, at missing out on the gold medal - the third time in the past four tournaments that they have lost in the final - and the stark fact remains that the only regional honour won by the team is the 1994 Melanesian Cup. With some of the best known footballers in Pacific Island football such as captain Henry Fa'arodo and striker Benjamin Totori, the Solomons were involved in a tight first round group. They beat hosts New Caledonia but lost to Vanuatu and only progressed at the expense of the latter on goal difference. In the semi-final a Fa'arodo penalty in extra-time saw them through to a final against New Caledonia, but it was the hosts who ran out 2-0 winners. At home, the inaugural S-League was won by Koloale in a tournament played on a traditional league system instead of the usual format of groups followed by knock-out rounds. It proved to be a close race between Koloale and Solomon Warriors but there was consolation for Warriors when they won the S-League cup competition, although they then lost the play-off against Koloale for a place in the OFC Champions League.

FIFA WORLD CUP RECORD
1930-1990 DNE 1994-2010 DNQ

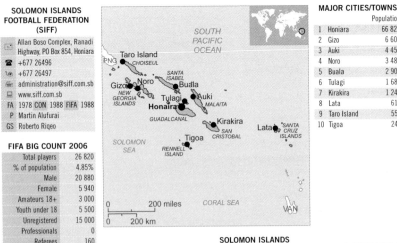

SOLOMON ISLANDS
FOOTBALL FEDERATION
(SIFF)

Allan Boso Complex, Ranadi
Highway, PO Box 854, Honiara
☎ +677 26496
📠 +677 26497
✉ administration@siff.com.sb
🖥 www.siff.com.sb
FA 1978 CON 1988 FIFA 1988
P Martin Alufurai
GS Roberto Riqeo

FIFA BIG COUNT 2006

Total players	26 820
% of population	4.85%
Male	20 880
Female	5 940
Amateurs 18+	3 000
Youth under 18	5 500
Unregistered	15 000
Professionals	0
Referees	160
Admin & coaches	400
Number of clubs	200
Number of teams	500

MAJOR CITIES/TOWNS
Population

1	Honiara	66 824
2	Gizo	6 608
3	Auki	4 455
4	Noro	3 482
5	Buala	2 909
6	Tulagi	1 687
7	Kirakira	1 247
8	Lata	616
9	Taro Island	556
10	Tigoa	243

SOLOMON ISLANDS

Capital Honiara		Population 595 613 (166)		% in cities 18%
GDP per capita $2700 (169)		Area km² 28 896 km² (143)		GMT +/- +11
Neighbours (km) Coast 5313			

RECENT INTERNATIONAL MATCHES PLAYED BY THE SOLOMON ISLANDS

2008	Opponents	Score	Venue	Comp	Scorers	Att	Referee
7-07	Vanuatu	L 1-2	Honiara	Fr			
2009							
No international matches played in 2009							
2010							
No international matches played in 2010							
2011							
7-07	Vanuatu	W 2-1	Honiara	Fr	Lui 61, Totori 64		
9-07	Vanuatu	D 0-0	Honiara	Fr			
27-07	Vanuatu	D 0-0	Port Vila	Fr			
30-07	Vanuatu	L 0-2	Port Vila	Fr			
27-08	Guam	W 7-0	Noumea	PGr1	Fa'arado 2 11 22, Totori 3 24 41p 89, Nawo 72, Paia 86		Varman FIJ
30-08	American Samoa	W 4-0	Noumea	PGr1	Totori 8, Bule 14, Lui 2 28 34		Jacques TAH
1-09	Vanuatu	L 0-1	Noumea	PGr1			Zitouni TAH
3-09	Tuvalu †	W 6-1	Noumea	PGr1	Totori 2 15 41p, Lui 23, Naka 2 37 46, Faisi 91+		Jacques TAH
5-09	New Caledonia	W 2-1	Noumea	PGr1	Nawo 66, Naka 79		Kerr NZL
7-09	Fiji	W 2-1	Lifou	PGsf	Nawo 77, Fa'arodo 93p		Jacques TAH
9-09	New Caledonia	L 0-2	Noumea	PGf			Kerr NZL

Fr = Friendly match • OC = OFC Oceania Nations Cup • SP = South Pacific Games • WC = FIFA World Cup
q = qualifier • r1 = first round group • f = final • † Not a full international

SOLOMON ISLANDS NATIONAL TEAM HISTORICAL RECORDS

Past Coaches Edward Ngara 1995-96 • Wilson Maelaua 1996 • Alexander Napa 1998 • George Cowie SCO 2000-03 • Alan Gillett ENG 2004-05 • Airton Andrioli BRA • Jacob Moli 2010-

SOLOMON ISLANDS 2011

TELEKOM S-LEAGUE

	Pl	W	D	L	F	A	Pts	Koloale	Warriors	Kossa	Western Utd	Malaita Kingz	Hana	Marist Fire	R. Kakamora
Koloale	14	11	2	1	46	12	35		0-3	1-1	3-2	6-0	4-0	6-1	6-0
Solomon Warriors	14	9	4	1	31	13	31	0-1		2-2	2-1	2-2	6-2	1-0	4-1
Kossa	14	6	4	4	24	21	22	2-7	L		2-1	1-0	0-3	3-1	3-0
Western United	14	6	2	6	20	18	20	D	1-1	3-2		2-0	1-3	1-2	1-0
Malaita Kingz	14	4	4	6	10	22	16	1-4	0-2	0-0	0-2		2-1	1-1	2-0
Hana	14	4	3	7	24	24	15	0-1	2-2	1-3	0-1	1-2		2-2	4-0
Marist Fire	14	3	5	6	15	25	14	1-2	0-2	0-3	3-2	0-0	D		2-2
Real Kakamora	14	0	2	12	7	42	2	1-5	1-4	2-2	0-2	L	0-5	0-2	

12/02/2011 - 14/05/2011 • † Qualified for the OFC Champions League play-off • Top scorer: **23** - Benjamin Totori, Koloale

S-LEAGUE CHAMPIONSHIP 2011

Quarter-finals			Semi-finals		Final	
Solomon Warriors	3	3				
Marist Fire	0	0	**Solomon Warriors**	5		
Malaita Kingz	2	0	Western United	1		
Western United	2	0			**Solomon Warriors**	1 4p
Kossa	4	4			Koloale	1 2p
Hana	1	2	Kossa	0	Lawson Tama, Honiara
Real Kakamora	1	1	**Koloale**	2	5-06-2011
Koloale	7	1				

O-LEAGUE PLAY-OFF

Lawson Tama, Honiara, 13-06-2011 & 16-06-2011
Koloale 0-0 3-2 Solomon Warriors
Scorer - Oscar Molina 2

SOM – SOMALIA

FIFA/COCA-COLA WORLD RANKING

'93	'94	'95	'96	'97	'98	'99	'00	'01	'02	'03	'04	'05	'06	'07	'08	'09	'10	'11	'12
-	159	165	178	187	190	197	194	197	190	191	193	184	193	195	200	170	182	189	

	2011												High	Low	Av
	Jan	Feb	Mar	Apr	May	Jun	Jul	Aug	Sep	Oct	Nov	Dec	**High**	**Low**	**Av**
	185	185	186	187	187	188	191	193	193	192	187	189		158	200	186

Somalia's national team spent more than a month in neighbouring Djibouti to prepare for their 2014 FIFA World Cup qualifier and achieved a draw in the first leg of their tie against Ethiopia. Somalia remains a no go for visiting teams and so Djibouti has been the venue for Somali's 'home' matches over the last 18 months. Under coach Alfred Emon the 'Ocean Stars' then travelled to Ethiopia for the return match in Addis Abeba where a 5-0 defeat saw them eliminated from the qualifiers for Brazil. A week later the team was on the road again, this time to the East and Central African Senior Challenge Cup in Tanzania where they lost to Burundi, Uganda and CAF associate members Zanzibar. In the process the Somalis scored only once and conceded 11 goals although they were represented in the final by referee Wiish Hajji Yeberow who took charge of the match between Rwanda and Uganda in Dar-es-Salaam. Despite the continued troubles in the country and the banning of football in some areas controlled by the militant fundamentalist Al Shabab movement, the Somali Football Federation successfully completed an eight-team first division programme, won by Elman. The year ended with a district football tournament in Mogadishu that attracted one of the biggest crowds seen for years at a football match in the capital.

CAF AFRICA CUP OF NATIONS RECORD
1957-1972 DNE **1976** DNQ **1976** DNE **1978** DNQ **1980-1982** DNE **1984-2010** DNQ **2012** DNE

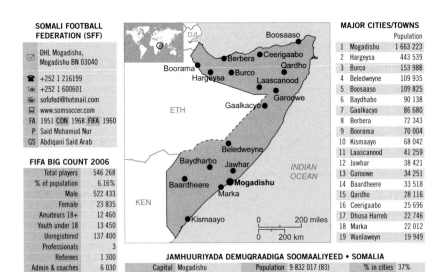

SOMALI FOOTBALL FEDERATION (SFF)

DHL Mogadishu, Mogadishu BN 03040

☎ +252 1 216199
📠 +252 1 600601
📧 sofofed@hotmail.com
🖥 www.somsoccer.com
FA 1951 CON 1968 FIFA 1960
P Said Mohamud Nur
GS Abdiqani Said Arab

FIFA BIG COUNT 2006

Total players	546 268
% of population	6.16%
Male	522 433
Female	23 835
Amateurs 18+	12 460
Youth under 18	13 450
Unregistered	137 400
Professionals	3
Referees	1 300
Admin & coaches	6 030
Number of clubs	48
Number of teams	205

MAJOR CITIES/TOWNS

		Population
1	Mogadishu	1 663 223
2	Hargeysa	443 539
3	Burco	153 988
4	Beledweyne	109 935
5	Boosaaso	109 825
6	Baydhabo	90 138
7	Gaalkacyo	86 680
8	Berbera	72 343
9	Boorama	70 004
10	Kismaayo	68 042
11	Laascaanood	41 259
12	Jawhar	38 421
13	Garoowe	34 251
14	Baardheere	33 518
15	Qardho	28 116
16	Ceerigaabo	25 696
17	Dhusa Harreb	22 746
18	Marka	22 012
19	Wanlaweyn	19 949

JAMHUURIYADA DEMUQRAADIGA SOOMAALIYEED • SOMALIA

Capital Mogadishu	Population 9 832 017 (83)	% in cities 37%
GDP per capita $600 (225)	Area km² 637 657 km² (43)	GMT + / - +3
Neighbours (km) Djibouti 58, Ethiopia 1600, Kenya 682 • Coast 3025		

RECENT INTERNATIONAL MATCHES PLAYED BY SOMALIA

2005	Opponents	Score		Venue	Comp	Scorers	Att	Referee
27-11	Djibouti	W	2-1	Kigali	CCr1	Abdul Hakim [28], Mahmoud Sharki [87]		
29-11	Sudan	L	1-4	Kigali	CCr1	Abdullahi Sheikh Mohamed [37]		
1-12	Uganda	L	0-7	Kigali	CCr1			
5-12	Ethiopia	L	1-4	Kigali	CCr1			
2006								
27-11	Rwanda	L	0-3	Addis Abeba	CCr1			
30-11	Sudan	L	0-3	Addis Abeba	CCr1			
3-12	Uganda	L	0-2	Addis Abeba	CCr1			
21-12	Sudan	L	1-6	Beirut	ARr1	Mohammed Abdulaziz [93+]		
24-12	Lebanon	L	0-4	Beirut	ARr1			
27-12	Mauritania	L	2-8	Beirut	ARr1	Abdulaziz Ali 2 [26 67]		
2007								
16-11	Djibouti	L	0-1	Djibouti	WCq		10 000	Abdul Rahman SUD
10-12	Burundi	L	0-1	Dar es Salaam	CCr1			
12-12	Tanzania	L	0-1	Dar es Salaam	CCr1			
14-12	Kenya	L	0-2	Dar es Salaam	CCr1			
2008								
23-12	Djibouti	W	3-2	Djibouti	Fr	Isse Midnimo, Ali Baashi, Ismail Yusuf		
2009								
1-01	Zanzibar †	L	0-2	Kampala	CCr1			
3-01	Tanzania	W	1-0	Kampala	CCr1	Abshir Cisse [14]		
5-01	Rwanda	L	0-3	Kampala	CCr1			
7-01	Uganda	L	0-4	Kampala	CCr1			
29-11	Rwanda	L	0-1	Nairobi	CCr1			
3-12	Zimbabwe †	L	0-2	Nairobi	CCr1			
5-12	Eritrea	L	1-3	Nairobi	CCr1	Mohamed Hassan [70]		
2010								
28-11	Burundi	L	0-2	Dar es Salaam	CCr1			
30-11	Tanzania	L	0-3	Dar es Salaam	CCr1			
3-12	Zambia	L	0-6	Dar es Salaam	CCr1			
2011								
1-11	Djibouti	L	0-1	Djibouti	Fr			
12-11	Ethiopia	D	0-0	Djibouti	WCq		3 000	Hassan Ourouke DJI
16-11	Ethiopia	L	0-5	Addis Abeba	WCq		22 000	Kordi TUN
25-11	Burundi	L	1-4	Dar es Salaam	CCr1	Khaled Ali [92+]		
28-11	Uganda	L	0-4	Chamazi	CCr1			
1-12	Zanzibar	L	0-3	Dar es Salaam	CCr1			

Fr = Friendly match • CC = CECAFA Cup • AR = Arab Cup • WC = FIFA World Cup
q = qualifier • r1 = first round group • † Not a full international

SOMALIA 2011

SFF FIRST DIVISION

	Pl	W	D	L	F	A	Pts	Elman	SITT	Heegan	Banadir T'com	Horseed	Dekedaha	S/Sheel	Savana
Elman	14	10	1	3	33	10	31		1-0	0-2	1-1	1-2	4-0	4-1	1-0
SITT	14	9	3	2	23	9	30	0-1		1-0	1-1	4-0	3-0	2-0	2-0
Heegan	14	8	2	4	18	13	26	0-4	0-1		1-0	4-3	0-0	2-1	3-0
Banadir Telecom	14	7	4	3	15	8	25	1-0	0-0	0-1		1-2	1-0	2-1	1-0
Horseed	14	5	4	5	20	26	19	0-2	4-4	0-1	0-3		1-1	3-2	0-0
Dekedaha	14	2	4	8	6	22	10	1-5	0-1	0-0	0-1	0-1		0-3	1-1
S/Sheel	14	3	1	10	20	32	10	2-6	2-3	2-1	1-3	2-2	0-1		2-1
Savana	14	1	3	10	7	22	6	0-3	0-1	1-3	0-0	1-2	1-2	2-1	

21/01/2011 - 26/04/2011 • Relegation Play-off: Super Sheel 0-3 Dekedaha

SRB – SERBIA

FIFA/COCA-COLA WORLD RANKING

'93	'94	'95	'96	'97	'98	'99	'00	'01	'02	'03	'04	'05	'06	'07	'08	'09	'10	'11	'12
-	-	-	-	-	-	-	-	-	-	-	-	47	33	27	30	19	23	27	

2011													High	Low	Av
Jan	Feb	Mar	Apr	May	Jun	Jul	Aug	Sep	Oct	Nov	Dec		High	Low	Av
23	23	21	16	16	24	27	29	21	23	27	27		13	47	25

By winning their third double in four years Partizan Belgrade overtook Red Star as the most successful club in Serbia since the break up of Yugoslavia at the start of the 1990s. It was their fourth league title in a row - a first in Serbian football and something that had never happened in Yugoslav times either - but they failed to go through the season unbeaten as they had done in the 2009-10 campaign. The chase for the title proved to be a three-horse race along with Red Star and Vojvodina, and it was Vojvodina who inflicted on Partisan their only two defeats in the league. It wasn't enough to lift them above third place but they did have a chance to win silverware when they met Partizan in the Cup Final. The match, however, was marred by controversy. Vojvodina were upset about decisions going against them, most notably the penalty that put Partizan 2-1 ahead, and in the 81st minute they walked off which meant that the match was awarded 3-0 to Partizan. The national team unsurprisingly failed in its bid to qualify for the European Championship finals for the first time since 2008, unable to reclaim the ground lost in their 3-1 defeat at the hands of Estonia, who made the play-offs instead. Coach Vladimir Petrovic was shown the door at the end of the campaign and replaced by Radovan Curcic.

UEFA EUROPEAN CHAMPIONSHIP RECORD
1960 2 F **1964** r2 **1968** 2 F **1972** QF **1976** 4 SF (Hosts) **1980** DNQ **1984** 8 r1 **1988** DNQ **1992** Qualified but then suspended
1996 DNE **2000** 8 QF (as Yugoslavia) **2004** DNQ (as Serbia and Montenegro) **2008-2012** DNQ (as Serbia)

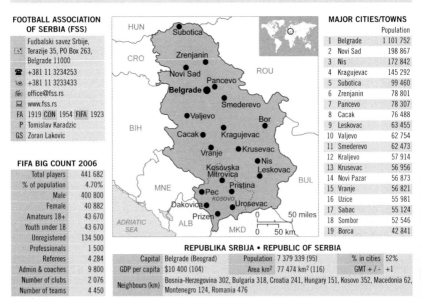

FOOTBALL ASSOCIATION OF SERBIA (FSS)

Fudbalski savez Srbije,
✉ Terazije 35, PO Box 263, Belgrade 11000
☎ +381 11 3234253
📠 +381 11 3233433
📧 office@fss.rs
💻 www.fss.rs
FA 1919 CON 1954 FIFA 1923
P Tomislav Karadzic
GS Zoran Lakovic

FIFA BIG COUNT 2006

Total players	441 682
% of population	4.70%
Male	400 800
Female	40 882
Amateurs 18+	43 670
Youth under 18	43 670
Unregistered	134 500
Professionals	1 500
Referees	4 284
Admin & coaches	9 800
Number of clubs	2 076
Number of teams	4 450

MAJOR CITIES/TOWNS

		Population
1	Belgrade	1 101 752
2	Novi Sad	198 867
3	Nis	172 842
4	Kragujevac	145 292
5	Subotica	99 460
6	Zrenjanin	78 801
7	Pancevo	78 307
8	Cacak	76 488
9	Leskovac	63 455
10	Valjevo	62 754
11	Smederevo	62 473
12	Kraljevo	57 914
13	Krusevac	56 956
14	Novi Pazar	56 873
15	Vranje	56 821
16	Uzice	55 981
17	Sabac	55 124
18	Sombor	52 546
19	Borca	42 841

REPUBLIKA SRBIJA • REPUBLIC OF SERBIA

Capital	Belgrade (Beograd)	Population 7 379 339 (95)	% in cities 52%
GDP per capita	$10 400 (104)	Area km² 77 474 km² (116)	GMT +/- +1
Neighbours (km)	Bosnia-Herzegovina 302, Bulgaria 318, Croatia 241, Hungary 151, Kosovo 352, Macedonia 62, Montenegro 124, Romania 476		

INTERNATIONAL MATCHES PLAYED BY SERBIA

2009	Opponents		Score	Venue	Comp	Scorers	Att	Referee
10-02	Cyprus	W	2-0	Nicosia	Fr	Jovanovic 25, Lazovic 42		Kakkos GRE
11-02	Ukraine	L	0-1	Nicosia	Fr		500	Kakkos GRE
28-03	Romania	W	3-2	Constanta	WCq	Jovanovic 18, Stoica OG 44, Ivanovic 59	12 000	Trefoloni ITA
1-04	Sweden	W	2-0	Belgrade	Fr	Zigic 1, Jankovic 82	17 830	Perez ESP
6-06	Austria	W	1-0	Belgrade	WCq	Milijas 7p	41 000	Vink NED
10-06	Faroe Islands	W	2-0	Tórshavn	WCq	Jovanovic 44, Subotic 69	2 896	Levi ISR
12-08	South Africa	W	3-1	Atteridgeville	Fr	Tosic 2 58 78, Lazovic 69	10 000	Maillet SEY
9-09	France	D	1-1	Belgrade	WCq	Milijas 12p	49 256	Rosetti ITA
10-10	Romania	W	5-0	Belgrade	WCq	Zigic 36, Pantelic 50, Kuzmanovic 77, Jovanovic 2 87 93+	39 839	Kapitanis CYP
14-10	Lithuania	L	1-2	Marijampole	WCq	Tosic 60	2 000	Guenov BUL
14-11	Northern Ireland	W	1-0	Belfast	Fr	Lazovic 57	13 500	Toussaint LUX
18-11	Korea Republic	W	1-0	London	Fr	Zigic 7	5 117	Attwell ENG
2010								
7-04	Japan	W	3-0	Osaka	Fr	Mrda 2 15 23, Tomic 60	46 270	Choi Myung Yong KOR
29-05	New Zealand	L	0-1	Klagenfurt	Fr		14 000	Drachta AUT
2-06	Poland	D	0-0	Kufstein	Fr		2 000	Drabek AUT
5-06	Cameroon	W	4-3	Belgrade	Fr	Krasic 16, Stankovic 25, Milijas 44p, Pantelic 45	30 000	Trattou CYP
13-06	Ghana	L	0-1	Pretoria	WCr1		38 833	Baldassi ARG
18-06	Germany	W	1-0	Port Elizabeth	WCr1	Jovanovic 38	38 294	Undiano ESP
23-06	Australia	L	1-2	Nelspruit	WCr1	Pantelic 84	37 836	Larrionda URU
11-08	Greece	L	0-1	Belgrade	Fr		10 000	Teixeira ESP
3-09	Faroe Islands	W	3-0	Torshavn	ECq	Lazovic 14, Stankovic 18, Zigic 91+	1 847	Toussaint LUX
7-09	Slovenia	D	1-1	Belgrade	ECq	Zigic 86	24 028	Benquerenca POR
8-10	Estonia	L	1-3	Belgrade	ECq	Zigic 60	12 000	Layushkin RUS
12-10	Italy	L	0-3	Genoa	ECq	Match awarded to Italy. Abandoned after 6'	28 000	Thomson SCO
17-11	Bulgaria	W	1-0	Sofia	Fr	Zigic 80	1 500	Avram ROU
2011								
9-02	Israel	W	2-0	Tel Aviv	Fr	Tosic 23, Trivunovic 77	8 000	Nikolaev RUS
25-03	Northern Ireland	W	2-1	Belgrade	ECq	Pantelic 65, Tosic 74	BCD	Gumienny BEL
29-03	Estonia	D	1-1	Tallinn	ECq	Pantelic 38	5 185	Nijhuis NED
3-06	Korea Republic	L	1-2	Seoul	Fr	Petrovic 87	40 000	Albadwawi UAE
7-06	Australia	D	0-0	Melbourne	Fr		28 149	Tojo JPN
10-08	Russia	L	0-1	Moscow	Fr		27 000	Hategan ROU
2-09	Northern Ireland	W	1-0	Belfast	ECq	Pantelic 67	15 148	Einwaller AUT
6-09	Faroe Islands	W	3-1	Belgrade	ECq	Jovanovic 6, Tosic 22, Kuzmanovic 69	7 500	Amirkhanyan ARM
7-10	Italy	D	1-1	Belgrade	ECq	Ivanovic 26	35 000	Proenca POR
11-10	Slovenia	L	0-1	Maribor	ECq		9 848	De Bleeckere BEL
11-11	Mexico	L	0-2	Queretaro	Fr		34 000	Lopez GUA
14-11	Honduras	L	0-2	Honduras	Fr		20 000	Rodas GUA

Fr = Friendly match • EC = UEFA EURO 2012 • WC = FIFA World Cup • q = qualifier

SERBIA NATIONAL TEAM HISTORICAL RECORDS

Caps
102 - Savo Milosevic 1994-2008 & Dejan Stankovic 1998- • **84** - Dragan Stojkovic 1983-2001 • **73** - Predrag Mijatovic 1989-2003 •
64 - Slavisa Jokanovic 1991-2002 • **63** - Sinisa Mihajlovic 1991-2003 • **59** - Mladen Krstajic 1999-2008 & Zoran Mirkovic 1995-2003 •
58 - Darko Kovacevic 1994-2004 • **57** - Nikola Zigic 2004- • **56** - Dejan Savicevic 1986-1999 (internationals played since 1994 only)

Goals
37 - Savo Milosevic 1994-2008 • **28** - Predrag Mijatovic 1989-2003 • **20** - Nikola Zigic 2004- • **19** - Dejan Savicevic 1986-2003 •
17 - Mateja Kezman 2000-2006 • **15** - Dragan Stojkovic 1983-2001 & Dejan Stankovic 1998- • **11** - Danko Lazovic 2002- & Milan Jovanovic
2007- • **10** - Darko Kovacevic 1994-2004 & Marko Pantelic 2003- (internationals played since 1994 only)

Past Coaches
Slobodan Santrac 1994-98 • Milan Zivadinovic 1998-99 • Vujadin Boskov 1999-2000 • Ilija Petkovic 2000-01 • Milovan Doric 2001 •
Vujadin Boskov, Ivan Curkovic & Dejan Savicevic 2001 • Dejan Savicevic 2001-03 • Ilija Petkovic 2003-06 • Javier Clemente ESP 2006-07
• Miroslav Dukic 2007-08 • Radomir Antic 2008-10 • Vladimir Petrovic 2010-11 • Radovan Curcic (caretaker) 2011-

SERBIA 2010–11

JELEN SUPERLIGA

	Pl	W	D	L	F	A	Pts	Partizan	Red Star	Vojvodina	Rad	Spartak	OFK	Sloboda	Javor	Borac	Smederevo	Jagodina	BSK Borca	Hajduk	Metalac	Indjija	Cukaricki
Partizan Beograd †	30	24	4	2	75	21	76		1-0	0-1	3-0	0-0	2-1	5-2	4-1	2-0	5-3	3-0	4-0	2-0	5-0	2-1	4-0
Crvena Zvezda ‡	30	22	4	4	52	18	70	0-1		2-2	2-1	2-2	1-0	5-1	1-0	2-0	1-0	2-1	4-1	3-1	2-0	3-1	4-0
Vojvodina Novi Sad ‡	30	20	7	3	44	14	67	2-0	0-2		2-0	1-0	0-0	3-1	2-0	4-0	4-1	0-0	2-1	2-1	1-1	2-0	3-0
Rad Beograd ‡	30	14	10	6	38	21	52	2-2	0-1	1-0		1-1	2-0	0-0	0-0	3-1	1-0	2-4	5-0	1-0	2-0	2-0	4-0
Spartak Subotica	30	11	10	9	34	27	43	1-2	1-2	0-1	1-2		3-1	2-2	0-0	1-2	2-1	3-2	1-1	1-0	2-0	5-2	2-0
OFK Beograd	30	12	7	11	27	25	43	0-2	0-0	1-0	0-1	2-0		1-0	0-1	2-1	2-2	0-1	1-0	1-0	1-0	2-1	4-0
Sloboda Point Sevojno	30	12	7	11	34	35	43	1-2	0-3	0-0	0-0	0-1	1-0		2-0	0-0	2-1	2-0	2-1	2-2	0-1	1-0	4-0
Javor Ivanjica	30	9	12	9	20	24	39	1-1	0-2	0-1	2-1	0-0	0-0	1-0		1-1	0-0	0-0	0-0	0-0	1-0	2-1	2-0
Borac Cacak	30	9	12	9	22	28	39	0-2	2-0	1-1	0-0	0-0	1-1	1-0	1-1		0-1	1-1	1-0	1-0	1-0	0-0	3-0
FC Smederevo	30	8	11	11	24	31	35	1-4	0-0	0-0	0-0	0-0	1-0	0-0	2-1	0-1		0-0	1-1	1-1	1-0	2-1	2-0
Jagodina	30	8	8	14	26	33	32	0-2	0-2	1-2	1-1	0-1	0-0	0-1	0-1	1-1	1-0		2-0	3-0	0-2	2-0	1-1
BSK Borca	30	7	9	14	20	37	30	0-3	1-3	0-2	0-1	0-0	1-1	0-1	1-0	2-0	0-0	1-0		0-0	1-0	4-0	3-1
Hajduk Kula	30	7	8	15	25	37	29	0-4	2-0	0-1	0-1	1-0	1-2	1-2	2-0	1-1	2-0	1-0	0-1		3-1	1-3	1-1
Metalac G. Milanovic	30	8	5	17	21	38	29	1-1	0-1	0-1	0-0	0-1	2-0	3-2	1-3	0-0	0-3	1-2	2-0	1-1		2-1	1-0
Indjija	30	7	5	18	29	47	26	1-3	0-1	1-2	1-1	2-1	1-2	1-3	1-1	2-0	2-0	2-0	0-0	1-2	1-0		0-0
Cukaricki Stankom	30	0	5	25	10	65	5	2-4	0-1	0-2	0-3	0-2	0-2	1-2	0-1	0-1	0-1	1-3	0-0	1-1	1-2	1-2	

14/08/2010 - 29/05/2011 • † Qualified for the UEFA Champions League • ‡ Qualified for the Europa League
Top scorers: 13 - Andrija Kaluderovic, Red Star & Ivica Iliev, Partizan • 11 - Aboubakar Oumarou CMR, Vojvodina • 9 - Radosav Petrovic, Partizan & Prince Tagoe GHA, Partizan • 8 - Stefan Babovic, Partizan; Cleo BRA, Partizan; Vladimir Jovancic, Rad & Vladimir Torbica, Spartak

SERBIA 2010–11
PRVA LIGA TELEKOM SRBIJA (2)

	Pl	W	D	L	F	A	Pts
BASK Beograd - R	34	24	5	5	54	21	77
Radnicki Kragujevac	34	22	8	4	61	22	74
Novi Pazar	34	21	8	5	66	20	71
Banat Zrenjanin	34	15	11	8	41	31	56
Sindelic Nis	34	15	8	11	41	34	53
Napredak Krusevac	34	13	10	11	35	32	49
Radnicki Sombor	34	13	10	11	30	29	49
Proleter Novi Sad	34	12	9	13	46	40	45
Mladost Lucani	34	11	12	11	29	32	45
Mladi R'nik Pozarevac	34	12	7	15	38	49	43
Novi Sad	34	11	9	14	37	42	42
Bezanija Novi Beograd	34	11	7	16	26	28	40
Teleoptik Zemun	34	9	12	13	35	44	39
Srem Sremska Mitrovica	34	8	12	14	30	43	36
Kolubara Lazarevac §3	34	9	9	16	33	43	33
FK Zemun	34	8	9	17	34	40	33
Radnicki Sid	34	7	5	22	26	50	26
Dinamo Vranje	34	7	5	22	23	65	26

14/08/2010 - 15/06/2011 • § = points deducted
BASK relegated after declining promotion

MEDALS TABLE

	Overall G	S	B	League G	S	B	Cup G	S	City/Town
1 Partizan	19	10	1	12	7	1	7	3	Belgrade
2 Crvena Zvezda	18	15	2	7	11	2	11	4	Belgrade
3 Obilic	1	3	2	1	1	2		2	Belgrade
4 FK Smederevo	1	1	1			1	1	1	Smederevo
5 Zeleznik	1				1		1		Belgrade
6 Vojvodina		5	9		1	9		4	Novi Sad
7 OFK Beograd		1	2			2		1	Belgrade
8 Spartak Subotica		1						1	Subotica
Napredak Krusevac		1						1	Krusevac
Buducnost Dvor		1						1	Banatski Dvor
FK Zemun		1						1	Belgrade
Sevojno		1						1	Sevojno
13 Vozdovac Beograd			1			1			Belgrade
Zeta Golubovci			1			1			Podgorica

From 1992, the season after Croatian clubs left the Yugoslav league

SERBIAN CLUBS IN YUGOSLAVIA UNTIL 1991

	Overall G	S	B	League G	S	B	Cup G	S	Europe G	S	B
1 Crvena Zvedza (Red Star)	31	17	11	18	8	7	12	8	1	1	4
2 Partizan Beograd	16	14	8	11	9	8	5	4		1	
5 OFK Beograd	9	6	5	5	6	4	4				1
8 Vojvodina Novi Sad	2	4	1	2	3	1		1			
10 Yugoslavia Beograd	2	3	3	2	3	3					
17 Nasa Krila Zemun	2						2				
20 FK Radnicki	1	2						2	1		
23 FK Bor	1						1				
Spartak Subotica	1						1				
Trepca Mitrovica	1						1				
29 Radnicki Nis			3			2					1
30 Belgrade Select XI	1								1		
Vozdovac Beograd	1						1				

LAV KUP SRBIJE 2010-11

First Round

Partizan Beograd	6
Mladost Apatin *	0
Napredak Krusevac	0
Proleter Novi Sad *	1
Rad Beograd	2
Donji Srem *	0
Cukaricki Stankom	0
Sindelic Nis *	2
Teleoptik Zemun *	2
OFK Beograd	1
Mokra Gora *	1 8p
FC Smederevo	1 9p
Borac Cacak *	2
Indjija	0
Sloga Kraljevo *	0
Crvena Zvezda	2
Sloboda Point Sevojno	3
Mladi Radnik Pozarevac *	1
Novi Sad	1 3p
Metalac G. Milanovic *	1 5p
Kolubara Lazarevac	0 5p
Hajduk Kula *	0 4p
Novi Pazar	2
Spartak Subotica *	4
Jagodina	2
Bezanija Novi Beograd	0
BSK Borca *	1 3p
Srem Sremska Mitrovica	1 5p
Srem Jakovo *	2 5p
Javor Ivanjica	2 4p
Sloga Petrovac *	0
Vojvodina Novi Sad	2

Round of 16

Partizan Beograd *	3
Proleter Novi Sad	0
Rad Beograd	0 2p
Sindelic Nis *	0 4p
Teleoptik Zemun	0 4p
FC Smederevo *	0 3p
Borac Cacak *	0
Crvena Zvezda *	4
Sloboda Point Sevojno *	2
Metalac G. Milanovic	1
Kolubara Lazarevac	1
Spartak Subotica	2
Jagodina	2
Srem Sremska Mitrovica *	0
Srem Jakovo *	2 6p
Vojvodina Novi Sad	2 7p

Quarter-finals

Partizan Beograd	4
Sindelic Nis *	0
Teleoptik Zemun	1
Crvena Zvezda *	2
Sloboda Point Sevojno *	3
Spartak Subotica	2
Jagodina	0
Vojvodina Novi Sad *	1

Semi-finals

Partizan Beograd *	2	0
Crvena Zvezda	0	1
Sloboda Point Sevojno *	1	0
Vojvodina Novi Sad	2	1

Final

Partizan Beograd	2	(3)
Vojvodina Novi Sad	1	(0)

CUP FINAL

Crvena Zvezda, Belgrade, 11-05-2011
Att: 25 000. Ref: Slobodan Veselinovic
Scorers - Tagoe 17, Vukic 72p for Partizan; Mojsov 63 for Vojvodina
Partizan - Vladimir Stojkovic - Aleksandar Miljkovic, Stefan Savic•, Mladen Krstajic, Marko Jovanovic - Mohamed Kamara - Stefan Babovic, Milan Smiljanic (Radosav Petrovic 82), Nemanja Tomic (Sasa Ilic 73) - Prince Tagoe• Ivica Iliev• (Zvonimir Vukic 62).
Tr: Aleksandar Stanojevic
Vojvodina - Zeljko Brkic - Miroslav Vulicevic, Branislav Trajkovic•, Daniel Mojsov• Vladan Pavlovic - Janko Tumbasevic•, Slobodan Medojevic• - Miroslav Stevanovic (Giorgi Merebashvili 60), Nikola Iazetic• (Aleksandar Katai 74), Brana Ilic• - Aboubakar Oumarou.
Tr: Zoran Milinkovic

Final abandoned after 83' when Vojvodina walked-off with the score at 2-1. Tie awarded 3-0

* Home team/home team in the 1st leg

SRI – SRI LANKA

FIFA/COCA-COLA WORLD RANKING

'93	'94	'95	'96	'97	'98	'99	'00	'01	'02	'03	'04	'05	'06	'07	'08	'09	'10	'11	'12
126	139	135	126	136	134	153	149	143	139	135	140	144	145	167	163	151	163	180	

2011													High	Low	Av
Jan	Feb	Mar	Apr	May	Jun	Jul	Aug	Sep	Oct	Nov	Dec				
162	161	173	173	169	171	176	174	176	177	176	180		122	180	147

2011 proved to be a truly awful year for the Sri Lankan national team which failed to make even a minor impact in the three competitions entered. The team started the year with a poor performance in a 2012 AFC Confederation Cup qualifying group staged in the Nepalese capital Kathmandu. Sri Lanka failed to score in their three matches against the hosts, the defending champions DPR Korea and Afghanistan and finished bottom of the group. There was little joy, either, in the opening round of qualifying for the 2014 FIFA World Cup thanks to a two-legged defeat against the Philippines, including a comprehensive 4-0 loss in the second leg in Manila - the first game ever won in the World Cup by the Filipinos. There was finally a win to celebrate at the end of the year at the South Asian Football Federation Championship in India, but the 3-0 victory over Bhutan was expected and counted for little as both other games in the first group against Afghanistan and India were lost. There was little joy, either for 2010 league champions Don Bosco as the Negombo-based club exited the AFC President's Cup tournament at the earliest point possible, finishing bottom of their four-team group in qualifying. At home, the 2011 championship was won by Ratnam with runners-up Army beating Don Bosco 2-0 to win the Holcim FA Cup.

FIFA WORLD CUP RECORD
1930-1990 DNE 1994-2010 DNQ

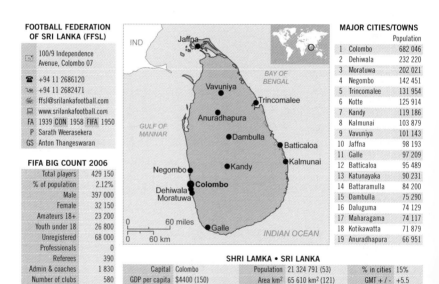

FOOTBALL FEDERATION OF SRI LANKA (FFSL)

100/9 Independence Avenue, Colombo 07

☎ +94 11 2686120
📠 +94 11 2682471
✉ ffsl@srilankafootball.com
🖥 www.srilankafootball.com
FA 1939 CON 1958 FIFA 1950
P Sarath Weerasekera
GS Anton Thangeswaran

FIFA BIG COUNT 2006

Total players	429 150
% of population	2.12%
Male	397 000
Female	32 150
Amateurs 18+	23 200
Youth under 18	26 800
Unregistered	68 000
Professionals	0
Referees	390
Admin & coaches	1 830
Number of clubs	580
Number of teams	1 100

MAJOR CITIES/TOWNS

		Population
1	Colombo	682 046
2	Dehiwala	232 220
3	Moratuwa	202 021
4	Negombo	142 451
5	Trincomalee	131 954
6	Kotte	125 914
7	Kandy	119 186
8	Kalmunai	103 879
9	Vavuniya	101 143
10	Jaffna	98 193
11	Galle	97 209
12	Batticaloa	95 489
13	Katunayaka	90 231
14	Battaramulla	84 200
15	Dambulla	75 290
16	Daluguma	74 129
17	Maharagama	74 117
18	Kotikawatta	71 879
19	Anuradhapura	66 951

SHRI LAMKA • SRI LANKA

Capital	Colombo	Population	21 324 791 (53)	% in cities 15%
GDP per capita	$4400 (150)	Area km²	65 610 km² (121)	GMT + / - +5.5
Neighbours (km)	Coast 1340			

RECENT INTERNATIONAL MATCHES PLAYED BY SRI LANKA

2006	Opponents	Score		Venue	Comp	Scorers	Att	Referee
2-04	Brunei Darusalaam	W	1-0	Chittagong	CCrl	Kasun Weerarathna [74]	2 000	Saidov UZB
4-04	Bhutan	W	1-0	Chittagong	CCrl	Karu [45]		Saidov UZB
6-04	Nepal	D	1-1	Chittagong	CCrl	Izzadeen [19]	2 500	Lee Gi Young KOR
8-04	Chinese Taipei	W	3-0	Chittagong	CCqf	Izzadeen [44], Sanjaya [70], Ratnayaka [90]	2 500	Al Ghatrifi OMA
12-04	Nepal	D	1-1	Chittagong	CCsf	Kasun Weerarathna [65], W 5-3p	2 500	Lee Gi Young KOR
16-04	Tajikistan	L	0-4	Dhaka	CCf		2 000	Moinbini IRN
2007								
21-10	Qatar	L	0-1	Colombo	WCq		6 500	Bashir SIN
28-10	Qatar	L	0-5	Doha	WCq		3 000	Al Ghamdi KSA
2008								
2-04	Guam	W	5-1	Taipei	CCq	Channa Edrib'nage [54], Chathura Weerasinghe 2 [55 64], Safras Mohamed [82], Kasun Weerarathna [91+]	300	Kavalenko UZB
4-04	Pakistan	W	7-1	Taipei	CCq	Chathura Weerasinghe 4 [2 7 9 42], Channa Edribandanage 2 [13p 82], Fernando 2 [72 77]	300	Kavalenko UZB
6-04	Chinese Taipei	D	2-2	Taipei	CCq	Chen Po Liang OG [59], Kasun Weerarathna [86]	900	Iemoto JPN
4-06	Afghanistan	D	2-2	Colombo	SAFrl	Chathura Weerasinghe [8], Channa Edribandanage [80p]		
6-06	Bhutan	W	2-0	Colombo	SAFrl	Chathura Weerasinghe 2 [25 39]		
8-06	Bangladesh	W	1-0	Colombo	SAFrl	Rawme Mohideen [73]		
11-06	Maldives	L	0-1	Colombo	SAFsf			
31-07	Korea DPR	L	0-3	Hyderabad	CCrl		100	Vo Minh Tri VIE
2-08	Myanmar	L	1-3	Hyderabad	CCrl	Kasun Weerarathna [51]	100	Kovalenko UZB
4-08	Nepal	L	0-3	Hyderabad	CCrl		200	Saleem MDV
2009								
28-03	Maldives	D	1-1	Colombo	Fr	Channa Edribandanage [37]		
4-04	Brunei Darussalam	W	5-1	Colombo	CCq	Kasun Weerarathna 4 [4 23 53 67 73], Moh'd Asmeer [32]	700	Zhao Liang CHN
6-04	Chinese Taipei	W	2-1	Colombo	CCq	Kasun Weerarathna [35], Rohana Ruwan Dinesh [39]	1 400	Al Zahrani KSA
8-04	Pakistan	D	2-2	Colombo	CCq	Rohana Ruwan Dinesh [2], Sanjeev Shanmugarajah [88]	3 000	Tseytlin UZB
22-08	Lebanon	W	4-3	New Delhi	Fr	Moh'd Izzadeen 3 [6 80 88], Chathura Weerasinghe [83]		Rowan IND
24-08	Syria	L	0-4	New Delhi	Fr			Singh IND
26-08	India	L	1-3	New Delhi	Fr	Rohana Ruwan Dinesh [62]		Ali Adil MDV
28-08	Kyrgyzstan	L	1-4	New Delhi	Fr	Chathura Weerasinghe [53]		Singh IND
4-12	Pakistan	W	1-0	Dhaka	SAFrl	Chathura Gunarathna [23]		
6-12	Bhutan	W	6-0	Dhaka	SAFrl	Channa Ediri 2 [7 25], Kasun Weerarathna 3 [39 66 78], Chathura Gunarathna [90]		
8-12	Bangladesh	L	1-2	Dhaka	SAFrl	Channa Ediri [42]		
11-12	Maldives	L	1-5	Dhaka	SAFsf	Channa Ediri [62]		
2010								
16-02	Myanmar	L	0-4	Colombo	CCrl		3 000	Faghani IRN
18-02	Tajikistan	L	1-3	Colombo	CCrl	Philip Dalpethado [78]	1 000	Tan Hai CHN
20-02	Bangladesh	W	3-0	Colombo	CCrl	Mohamed Kaiz [7], Chathura Gunarathna [43], Sanjeev Shanmugarajah [79]	600	Mahapab THA
2011								
27-03	Tajikistan	D	2-2	Colombo	Fr	Kaiz Shafraz [12p], Mohamed Zain [80]		
29-03	Tajikistan	L	0-2	Colombo	Fr			
7-04	Korea DPR	L	0-4	Kathmandu	CCq		2 000	Almarzouq KUW
9-04	Afghanistan	L	0-1	Kathmandu	CCq		1 800	Adday IRQ
11-04	Nepal	D	0-0	Kathmandu	CCq		13 500	Adday IRQ
29-06	Philippines	D	1-1	Colombo	WCq	Chathura Wellala [43]	4 000	Shamsuzzaman BAN
3-07	Philippines	L	0-4	Manila	WCq		12 500	Kim Sang Won KOR
3-12	Bhutan	W	3-0	New Delhi	SAFrl	Mohamed Zain [29], Nipuna Bandara 2 [35 65]		Tufaylieh SYR
5-12	Afghanistan	L	1-3	New Delhi	SAFrl	Mohamed Zain [17]		Faizullin KGZ
7-12	India	L	0-3	New Delhi	SAFrl			Faizullin KGZ

Fr = Friendly match • SAF = South Asian Federation Cup • CC = AFC Challenge Cup • WC = FIFA World Cup • q = qualifier

SRI LANKA 2011

DIALOG CHAMPIONS LEAGUE

	Pl	W	D	L	F	A	Pts	Ratnam	Army	Navy	Don Bosco	Renown	Air Force	Police	Blue Star	Saunders	New Youngs	Nandimithra	Java Lane
Ratnam †	22	15	2	5	37	20	47		0-1	0-0	1-1	1-0	3-0	1-0	2-1	0-3	2-1	2-0	2-1
Army	22	11	9	2	31	15	42	0-2		2-1	1-0	0-0	3-1	0-0	3-1	3-1	1-0	6-0	1-0
Navy	22	12	5	5	31	12	41	0-1	0-0		3-0	0-0	2-0	1-0	3-0	**2-0**	0-1	2-1	3-1
Don Bosco	22	10	7	5	27	20	37	4-3	1-1	2-1		2-1	1-1	1-1	1-2	2-0	4-2	0-0	1-0
Renown	22	8	7	7	28	25	31	0-4	2-0	0-0	0-0		0-2	1-2	3-2	2-0	6-0	3-0	1-0
Air Force	22	7	10	5	24	20	31	1-2	1-1	0-1	2-2			1-1	1-0	0-0	1-0	2-0	2-0
Police	22	7	9	6	23	21	30	3-0	0-2	2-1	0-3	1-1	1-1		2-0	1-1	1-1	2-1	3-1
Blue Star	22	7	2	13	23	32	23	0-1	0-1	0-1	1-0	0-2	1-3	1-0		0-0	1-0	7-0	1-1
Saunders	22	4	10	8	18	21	22	1-2	1-1	0-2	1-0	4-0	0-0	0-1	0-1		1-1	0-0	1-1
New Youngs	22	3	8	11	22	42	17	0-3	3-3	1-6	0-1	3-0	4-1	2-2	2-0	1-1		2-2	1-1
Nandimithra	22	3	8	11	19	44	17	1-3	1-1	1-1	0-2	1-3	2-2	1-0	5-2	0-3	0-0		3-2
Java Lane	22	2	9	11	16	27	15	2-1	0-0	0-1	1-2	1-1	1-1	0-0	0-0	1-2	0-0	3-1	

13/08/2011 - 26/02/2012 • † Qualified for the AFC President's Cup • Match in bold awarded

MEDALS TABLE

		Overall G	Lge G	Cup G	Cup S	City
1	Saunders	18	12	6	4	Colombo
2	Ratnam	11	5	6	1	Kotahena
3	Renown	9	4	5	3	Colombo
4	Negombo Youth	3	2	1	2	Negombo
5	Old Bens	2	1	1	2	Colombo
6	Army	2	1	1	1	Colombo
7	Police	1		1	2	Colombo
8	Blue Stars	1	1			Kalutara
	Don Bosco	1	1			Colombo
	Navy	1			1	Colombo
	Pettah United	1	1			Colombo
	York	1			1	Kandy

HOLCIM FA CUP 2011

Round of 16		Quarter-finals		Semi-finals		Final	
Army	3						
Old Bens	1	**Army**	6				
Renown	0 2p	New Young	0				
New Young	0 4p			**Army**	5		
Blue Star	1			Police	0		
Java Lane	0	Blue Star	0				
SLTB	1	**Police**	2				
Police	3					**Army**	2
Nandimithra	2					Don Bosco	0
Matara City	0	**Nandimithra**	1				
Air Force	0	Ratnam	0				
Ratnam	2			Nandimithra	0 2p		
Navy	0 4p			**Don Bosco**	0 3p		
Saunders	0 3p	Navy	0				
Colombo FC	2	**Don Bosco**	2				
Don Bosco	4						

CUP FINAL

9-07-2011
Scorer - Mohamed Izzadeen 2 [38] [46]

STP – SAO TOME E PRINCIPE

FIFA/COCA-COLA WORLD RANKING

'93	'94	'95	'96	'97	'98	'99	'00	'01	'02	'03	'04	'05	'06	'07	'08	'09	'10	'11	'12
-	-	-	-	-	194	187	181	186	191	192	195	197	198	-	-	-	-	196	

2011												High	Low	Av
Jan	Feb	Mar	Apr	May	Jun	Jul	Aug	Sep	Oct	Nov	Dec			
										192	196	179	200	190

Sao Tome e Principe's return to competitive football after an eight year hiatus threatened to be a total disaster after just five minutes of their first match since 2003. The island nation fell two goals behind inside the opening stages of their FIFA World Cup qualifier against Congo at home as their rustiness showed but an overwhelming avalanche of goals did not follow. Sao Tome, who's nickname is 'Seleccao de Falcao e Papagaio', eventually lost 5-0. But within four days they showed a different side as they drew 1-1 away in the second leg in an encouraging reversal of fortune that did not save them from elimination but came as a morale booster. Coach Gustave Clement had lamented a lack of facilities for pre-match preparations but financial restraints have been behind Sao Tome's long-standing isolation from the international game. Sao Tome went into the FIFA World Cup qualifier without any of their contingent of players from Portugal. Instead the majority of players came from Vitoria Riboque, who had won the league title on Sao Tome island just weeks before. Victoria also won the Sao Tome Cup before beating Sundy in the Taca Nacional but they missed out on a clean sweep of all four trophies when Sporting Principe won the Campeonato Nacional played between the champions of Sao Tome and the champions of Principe.

CAF AFRICA CUP OF NATIONS RECORD
1957-1998 DNE **2000-2002** DNQ **2004** DNE **2006** DNQ **2008-2012** DNE

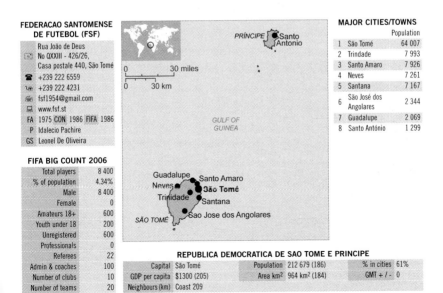

FEDERACAO SANTOMENSE DE FUTEBOL (FSF)

Rua João de Deus
No QXXIII - 426/26,
Casa postale 440, São Tomé
☎ +239 222 6559
📠 +239 222 4231
📧 fsf1954@gmail.com
🖥 www.fsf.st
FA 1975 CON 1986 FIFA 1986
P Idalecio Pachire
GS Leonel De Oliveira

FIFA BIG COUNT 2006

Total players	8 400
% of population	4.34%
Male	8 400
Female	0
Amateurs 18+	600
Youth under 18	200
Unregistered	600
Professionals	0
Referees	22
Admin & coaches	100
Number of clubs	10
Number of teams	20

MAJOR CITIES/TOWNS

		Population
1	São Tomé	64 007
2	Trindade	7 993
3	Santo Amaro	7 926
4	Neves	7 261
5	Santana	7 167
6	São José dos Angolares	2 344
7	Guadalupe	2 069
8	Santo António	1 299

REPUBLICA DEMOCRATICA DE SAO TOME E PRINCIPE

Capital	São Tomé	Population	212 679 (186)	% in cities	61%
GDP per capita	$1300 (205)	Area km²	964 km² (184)	GMT + / -	0
Neighbours (km)	Coast 209				

RECENT INTERNATIONAL MATCHES PLAYED BY SAO TOME E PRINCIPE

2000	Opponents	Score	Venue	Comp	Scorers	Att	Referee
8-04	Sierra Leone	W 2-0	São Tomé	WCq			
22-04	Sierra Leone	L 0-4	Freetown	WCq			
2-07	Gabon	D 1-1	São Tomé	CNq			
15-07	Gabon	L 1-4	Libreville	CNq			
2001							
No international matches played in 2001							
2002							
No international matches played in 2002							
2003							
11-10	Libya	L 0-1	São Tomé	WCq		4 000	Yameogo JPN
12-11	Equatorial Guinea	L 1-3	Malabo	Fr			
16-11	Libya	L 0-8	Benghazi	WCq		20 000	Guirat TUN
2004							
No international matches played in 2004							
2005							
No international matches played in 2005							
2006							
No international matches played in 2006							
2007							
No international matches played in 2007							
2008							
No international matches played in 2008							
2009							
No international matches played in 2009							
2010							
No international matches played in 2010							
2011							
11-11	Congo	L 0-5	São Tomé	WCq		3 000	Ngbokaye CTA
15-11	Congo	D 1-1	Pointe Noire	WCq	Orgando dos Santos [50]	12 000	Mahamat CHA

Fr = Friendly match • CN = CAF African Cup of Nations • WC = FIFA World Cup • q = qualifier

SAO TOME E PRINCIPE 2011

SAO TOME CHAMPIONSHIP

	Pl	W	D	L	F	A	Pts	Vitória	Sporting	Militar	UDRA	UDESCAI	Oque	Barrios Un	Cruz	Guadalupe	Neves	Ribeira	Santana
Vitória FC Riboque	21	15	2	4	35	15	**47**		0-1	0-2	2-1	3-1	1-1	2-1	1-1	2-0	3-2	5-0	3-0
Sporting Club Praia	21	12	4	5	41	23	**40**	0-2		2-1	0-2	2-0	1-2	2-1	1-1	1-1	4-0	7-0	2-1
DM 6 de Setembro	21	11	6	4	39	19	**39**	0-1	2-1		1-1	1-2	1-0	n/p	1-0	4-0	5-0	1-1	4-1
UDRA	21	10	4	7	31	18	**34**	0-1	2-3	0-0		3-0	1-0	1-0	1-2	3-2	0-1	3-0	3-1
UDESCAI Agua Ize	21	9	5	7	16	18	**32**	0-2	2-2	1-0	1-0		0-0	0-1	n/p	1-1	3-1	1-0	0-1
Oque d'El Rei	21	8	6	7	25	16	**30**	2-0	1-2	0-1	n/p	0-1		0-2	5-1	0-0	1-1	0-0	1-0
Barrios Unidos	21	7	8	6	25	22	**29**	2-1	1-1	1-1	1-1	0-1	1-1		1-0	1-1	4-2	1-0	1-1
Cruz Vermelha	21	8	5	8	25	28	**29**	0-1	0-1	0-2	0-0	0-1	3-2	3-2		1-0	1-1	1-1	2-0
Guadalupe	21	6	8	7	20	25	**26**	0-1	2-1	1-1	2-0	0-0	0-2	2-1	1-2		1-0	2-1	1-0
Neves	21	3	8	10	24	37	**17**	n/p	1-2	3-3	0-2	0-0	0-1	1-1	3-0	2-2		0-1	3-0
Ribeira Peixe	21	3	5	13	17	48	**14**	0-1	1-5	2-5	1-2	1-0	0-4	1-1	2-5	n/p	1-1		3-1
Santana	21	2	3	16	15	44	**9**	1-3	n/p	2-3	0-5	0-1	0-2	0-1	1-2	1-1	2-2	2-1	

15/04/2011 - 18/11/2011

CAMPEONATO NACIONAL 2011
Estadio Nacional, São Tomé, 21-12-2011
Sporting Príncipe 2-1 Vitória FC Riboque
Scorer - Artur 2 for Sporting

TACA NACIONAL FINAL 2011
Estadio 13 de Junho, Santo Antonio do Príncipe, 17-12-2011
Vitória FC Riboque 4-1 GD Sundy
Scorers - Vando 2, Maikel, Hitler for Vitória

Sporting Club Príncipe won the Príncipe championship ahead of SO Benfica in second place and GD Sundy in third. GD Sundy won the Príncipe Cup Final 2-1 against SO Benfica. Vitória FC Riboque won the São Tomé Cup Final 2-1 against UDESCAI

SUI – SWITZERLAND

FIFA/COCA-COLA WORLD RANKING

'93	'94	'95	'96	'97	'98	'99	'00	'01	'02	'03	'04	'05	'06	'07	'08	'09	'10	'11	'12
12	7	18	47	62	83	47	58	63	44	44	51	35	17	44	24	18	22	17	

						2011									
Jan	Feb	Mar	Apr	May	Jun	Jul	Aug	Sep	Oct	Nov	Dec		High	Low	Av
22	22	23	25	25	29	30	30	18	18	17	17		3	83	38

There was huge disappointment as the Swiss national team failed to qualify for the finals of Euro 2012, missing out on the tournament for only the second time since 1996. In what was seen as the end to an era, both Alexander Frei, Switzerland's all-time leading scorer, and Hakan Yakin hung up their international boots - Frei after constantly being booed in the home match against Wales. Frei had the satisfaction, however, of leading his club Basel to the league title in yet another photo-finish to the season - a 3-0 win at home to Luzern on the final day securing back-to-back titles. The 2011 Swiss Cup Final threw up a remarkable pairing with FC Sion looking to maintain their perfect record in the final by winning their 12th and Neuchatel looking for their first win in six appearances. Sure enough Sion ran out 2-0 winners, but that marked the start of an ugly episode in Swiss football when Sion were thrown out of the UEFA Europa League after fielding an ineligible player in their match against Celtic - a result of their long-running transfer ban saga following the 2008 signing of Essam El Hadary. More legal cases followed and there were even threats of a Swiss-wide ban by FIFA unless the SFV punished Sion - which they finally did with a 36 point deduction for the 2011-12 league campaign.

UEFA EUROPEAN CHAMPIONSHIP RECORD

1960 DNE 1964 r1 1968-1992 DNQ 1996 r1 2000 DNQ 2004 r1 2008 r1 (co-hosts) 2012 DNQ

SCHWEIZERISCHER FUSSBALL-VERBAND (SFV/ASF)

Worbstrasse 48,
Postfach Bern 3000
☎ +41 31 9508111
✆ +41 31 9508181
✉ sfv.asf@football.ch
🖥 www.football.ch
FA 1895 CON 1954 FIFA 1904
P Peter Gillieron
GS Alex Miescher

FIFA BIG COUNT 2006

Total players	571 700
% of population	7.60%
Male	607 900
Female	63 800
Amateurs 18+	103 700
Youth under 18	127 700
Unregistered	240 000
Professionals	550
Referees	4 783
Admin & coaches	25 300
Number of clubs	1 412
Number of teams	13 005

MAJOR CITIES/TOWNS

		Population
1	Zürich	353 485
2	Geneva	179 019
3	Basel	160 663
4	Berne	121 242
5	Lausanne	118 606
6	Winterthur	96 851
7	Saint Gall	69 713
8	Luzern	57 913
9	Lugano	55 907
10	Biel	49 089
11	Thun	41 754
12	Köniz	37 644
13	La Chaux-de-Fonds	36 853
14	Schaffhausen	33 519
15	Fribourg	33 293
16	Neuchâtel	32 390
17	Chur	32 251
18	Uster	31 296
62	Grenchen	16 060

SCHWEIZ • SUISSE • SVIZZERA • SWITZERLAND

Capital	Bern	Population	7 604 467 (94)	% in cities 73%
GDP per capita	$42 000 (18)	Area km²	41 277 km² (135)	GMT +/- +1
Neighbours (km)	Austria 164, France 573, Italy 740, Liechtenstein 41, Germany 334			

RECENT INTERNATIONAL MATCHES PLAYED BY SWITZERLAND

2008	Opponents	Score		Venue	Comp	Scorers	Att	Referee
7-06	Czech Republic	L	0-1	Basel	ECr1		39 730	Rosetti ITA
11-06	Turkey	L	1-2	Basel	ECr1	Hakan Yakin [32]	39 730	Michel SVK
15-06	Portugal	W	2-0	Basel	ECr1	Hakan Yakin 2 [71 83p]	39 730	Plautz AUT
20-08	Cyprus	W	4-1	Geneva	Fr	Stocker [8], Hakan Yakin [27], Nef [73], Vonlanthen [81]	14 500	Ceferin SVN
6-09	Israel	D	2-2	Ramat Gan	WCq	Hakan Yakin [45], N'Kufo [56]	29 600	Hansson SWE
10-09	Luxembourg	L	1-2	Zurich	WCq	N'Kufo [43]	20 500	Filipovic SRB
11-10	Latvia	W	2-1	St Gall	WCq	Frei [63], N'Kufo [73]	18 026	Batista POR
15-10	Greece	W	2-1	Piraeus	WCq	Frei [41p], N'Kufo [77]	28 810	Medina ESP
19-11	Finland	W	1-0	St Gall	Fr	Ziegler [84]	11 500	Kulbakov RUS
2009								
11-02	Bulgaria	D	1-1	Geneva	Fr	Huggel [45]	9 500	Duarte POR
28-03	Moldova	W	2-0	Chisinau	WCq	Frei [32], Fernandes [92+]	10 500	McDonald SCO
1-04	Moldova	W	2-0	Geneva	WCq	N'Kufo [20], Frei [52]	20 100	Rocchi ITA
12-08	Italy	D	0-0	Basel	Fr		31 500	Kircher GER
5-09	Greece	W	2-0	Basel	WCq	Grichting [84], Padalino [87]	38 500	De Bleeckere BEL
9-09	Latvia	D	2-2	Riga	WCq	Frei [43], Derdiyok [80]	8 600	Kralovec CZE
10-10	Luxembourg	W	3-0	Luxembourg	WCq	Senderos 2 [6 8], Huggel [22]	8 031	Iturralde ESP
14-10	Israel	D	0-0	Basel	WCq		38 500	Tudor ROU
14-11	Norway	L	0-1	Geneva	Fr		16 000	Whitby WAL
2010								
3-03	Uruguay	L	1-3	St Gall	Fr	Gokhan Inler [29p]	12 500	Rizzoli ITA
1-06	Costa Rica	L	0-1	Sion	Fr		11 300	Buttimer IRL
5-06	Italy	D	1-1	Geneva	Fr	Gokhan Inler [10]	30 000	Piccirillo FRA
16-06	Spain	W	1-0	Durban	WCr1	Fernandes [52]	62 453	Webb ENG
21-06	Chile	L	0-1	Port Elizabeth	WCr1		34 872	Al Ghamdi KSA
25-06	Honduras	D	0-0	Bloemfontein	WCr1		28 042	Baldassi ARG
11-08	Austria	W	1-0	Klagenfurt	Fr	Costanzo [73]	18 000	Rubinos ESP
3-09	Australia	D	0-0	St Gall	Fr		14 660	Einwaller AUT
7-09	England	L	1-3	Basel	ECq	Shaqiri [71]	37 500	Rizzoli ITA
8-10	Montenegro	L	0-1	Podgorica	ECq		10 750	Iturralde ESP
12-10	Wales	W	4-1	Basel	ECq	Stocker 2 [8 89], Streller [21], Gokhan Inler [82p]	26 000	Hamer LUX
17-11	Ukraine	D	2-2	Geneva	Fr	Frei 2 [40 62]	11 100	Gumienny BEL
2011								
9-02	Malta	D	0-0	Ta'Qali	Fr		3 000	Stamatis CYP
26-03	Bulgaria	D	0-0	Sofia	ECq		9 600	Collum SCO
4-06	England	D	2-2	London	ECq	Barnetta 2 [32 35]	84 459	Skomina SVN
10-08	Liechtenstein	W	2-1	Vaduz	Fr	Derdiyok [15], OG [34]	5 444	Eisner AUT
6-09	Bulgaria	W	3-1	Basel	ECq	Shaqiri 3 [45 62 90]	16 880	Kralovec CZE
7-10	Wales	L	0-2	Swansea	ECq		12 317	Kuipers NED
11-10	Montenegro	W	2-0	Basel	ECq	Derdiyok [51], Lichtsteiner [65]	19 997	Benquerenca POR
11-11	Netherlands	D	0-0	Amsterdam	Fr		50 000	Eriksson SWE
15-11	Luxembourg	W	1-0	Luxembourg	Fr	Xhaka [9]	852	Delferiere BEL

Fr = Friendly match • EC = UEFA EURO 2008/2012 • WC = FIFA World Cup • q = qualifier • po = play-off

SWITZERLAND NATIONAL TEAM HISTORICAL RECORDS

Caps
117 - Heinz Hermann 1978-91 • **112** - Alain Geiger 1980-96 • **103** - Stephane Chapuisat 1989-2004 • **94** - Johann Vogel 1995-2007 • **87** - Hakan Yakin 2000-11 • **84** - Alexander Frei 2001-11 • **81** - Patrick Muller 1998-2008 • **80** - Severino Minelli 1930-43 • **79** - Andre Egli 1979-94 & Ciriaco Sforza 1991-2001 • **75** - Raphael Wicky 1996-2007 • **72** - Stephane Henchoz 1993-2005 • **71** - Alfred Bickel 1936-54

Goals
42 - Alexander Frei 2001- • **34** - Max Abegglen 1922-37 & Kubilay Turkyilmaz 1988-2001 • **29** - Andre Abegglen 1927-34 & Jacques Fatton 1946-55 • **26** - Adrian Knupp 1989-96 • **23** - Josef Hugi 1951-61 • **22** - Charles Antenen 1948-62 • **21** - Lauro Amado 1935-48 & Stephane Chapuisat 1989-2004 • **20** - Hakan Yakin 2000- • **19** - Robert Ballaman • **15** - Alfred Bickel 1936-54 & Heinz Hermann 1978-91

Past Coaches
Karl Rappan AUT 1960-63 • Alfredo Foni ITA 1964-67 • Erwin Ballabio 1967-69 • Louis Maurer 1970-71 • Rene Hussy 1973-76 • Miroslav Blazevic YUG 1976-77 • Roger Vonlanthen 1977-79 • Leo Walker 1979-80 • Paul Wolfisberg 1981-85 • Daniel Jeandupeux 1986-89 • Uli Stielike GER 1989-91 • Roy Hodgson ENG 1992-95 • Artur Jorge POR 1996 • Rolf Fringer AUT 1996-97 • Gilbert Gress FRA 1998-99 • Enzo Trossero ENG 2000-01 • Jakob Kuhn 2001-08 • Ottmar Hitzfeld GER 2008-

SWITZERLAND 2010–11

AXPO SUPER LEAGUE

	Pl	W	D	L	F	A	Pts	Basel	Zürich	Young Boys	Sion	Thun	Luzern	Grasshopper	Neuchâtel	Bellinzona	St Gallen
FC Basel †	36	21	10	5	76	44	73		3-2 3-1	3-1 2-1	1-1 1-0	1-3 5-1	1-4 3-0	2-2 2-2	4-1 1-0	3-1 2-0	3-0 3-0
FC Zürich †	36	21	9	6	74	44	72	1-4 2-2		2-2 2-1	1-1 2-0	0-1 0-1	0-2 2-2	0-2 0-1	0-3 1-3	0-2 2-5	0-3 1-3
BSC Young Boys ‡	36	15	12	9	65	50	57	2-2 3-3	1-0 4-2		2-1 1-1	2-2 0-1	1-1 3-1	1-0 2-2	0-1 3-2	1-1 4-0	1-1 4-2
FC Sion ‡	36	15	9	12	47	36	54	1-2 3-0	1-1 0-2	2-0 0-2		1-1 1-0	4-1 3-2	2-0 2-0	1-2 0-0	1-1 1-0	0-2 2-0
FC Thun ‡	36	11	16	9	48	43	49	1-1 2-3	1-3 2-3	1-1 1-1	1-0 3-1		1-1 3-3	2-2 0-1	1-2 1-0	0-0 3-1	3-0 0-0
FC Luzern	36	13	9	14	62	57	48	1-1 0-1	1-1 0-5	2-0 1-1	2-3 0-1	1-1 0-1		3-2 1-0	4-2 2-1	6-2 3-2	4-0 1-1
Grasshopper-Club	36	10	11	15	45	54	41	2-1 1-2	1-2 3-1	1-2 3-2	0-4 2-0	0-0 0-0	0-3 2-1		1-1 3-1	2-3 2-2	2-0 1-3
Neuchâtel Xamax	36	8	8	20	44	67	32	1-2 2-2	3-4 1-2	2-4 1-2	0-3 1-0	2-3 1-4	2-1 2-1	1-1 0-0		1-2 1-2	0-1 2-1
AC Bellinzona ††	36	7	11	18	42	75	32	1-0 0-4	1-2 0-1	2-1 1-5	0-2 2-2	2-2 1-1	0-3 2-0	1-1 2-0	3-3 1-1		1-3 1-3
FC St Gallen	36	8	7	21	34	67	31	1-3 0-0	0-3 2-2	1-2 0-2	1-1 0-1	2-1 0-1	1-2 0-4	1-2 1-4	0-2 1-1	3-2 1-0	

17/07/2010 - 25/05/2011 • † Qualified for the UEFA Champions League • ‡ Qualified for the Europa League • †† Relegation play-off
Relegation play-off: Bellinzona 1-0 1-3 Servette
Top scorers: 27 - Alexander Frei, Basel • 16 - Henri Bienvenu CMR, Young Boys • 14 - Mauro Lustrinelli, Bellinzona • 12 - Hakan Yakin Luzern •
10 - Alexandre Alphonse FRA, Zürich; Giovanni Sio CIV, Sion; Admir Mehmedi, Zürich & Marco Streller, Basel

SWITZERLAND 2010–11

CHALLENGE LEAGUE (2)

	Pl	W	D	L	F	A	Pts	Lausanne	Servette	Lugano	Vaduz	Wil	Nyon	Chiasso	Delémont	Biel-Bienne	Wohlen	Aarau	Kriens	Winterthur	Locarno	Schaffh'sen	Yverdon
Lausanne-Sport	30	20	5	5	67	28	65		0-2	3-1	2-0	2-0	1-1	2-1	2-1	3-2	1-2	2-2	4-1	4-0	5-2	4-0	3-0
Servette FC †	30	19	5	6	75	27	62	1-2		0-2	3-1	2-0	3-1	3-0	4-1	2-0	3-0	4-2	6-0	3-3	4-1	6-2	3-1
AC Lugano	30	20	2	8	56	35	62	1-2	0-6		2-1	2-1	1-2	4-1	3-0	2-2	1-1	1-0	2-0	2-3	2-0	2-1	2-1
FC Vaduz	30	19	3	8	59	41	60	1-0	1-4	0-3		3-1	1-5	1-0	6-1	1-1	0-5	2-0	2-1	3-0	2-1	1-0	5-1
FC Wil 1900	30	14	4	12	45	42	46	0-2	0-0	2-1	1-2		2-2	1-2	3-1	3-2	0-3	1-0	2-1	2-1	3-1	2-1	3-1
Stade Nyonnais	30	13	7	10	48	51	46	0-5	0-1	0-1	2-5	0-3		1-0	2-1	1-1	3-2	3-0	2-0	3-3	5-2	1-4	1-0
FC Chiasso	30	12	5	13	34	37	41	1-2	2-1	0-2	0-1	2-1	3-0		1-3	1-2	4-1	1-1	0-0	1-1	1-2	1-0	2-1
SR Delémont	30	12	4	14	47	60	40	1-3	0-3	1-3	1-1	1-0	1-1	3-0		2-1	2-1	3-3	1-1	1-3	1-0	3-2	2-4
FC Biel-Bienne	30	11	6	13	57	57	39	0-4	0-5	2-3	0-4	1-1	5-0	2-1	3-2		0-3	7-1	7-0	3-1	0-2	2-1	3-1
FC Wohlen	30	9	10	11	45	44	37	2-1	0-0	0-3	1-3	2-1	1-2	1-1	3-0	1-1		2-2	1-2	1-1	0-0	5-2	2-1
FC Aarau	30	9	9	12	39	51	36	2-1	0-0	2-0	2-3	1-2	0-4	0-3	5-3	2-0			0-1	1-0	2-0	1-1	2-1
SC Kriens	30	9	6	15	26	50	33	1-3	1-1	0-1	0-1	1-3	1-1	0-2	0-2	3-1	2-0	0-1		2-1	1-1	1-0	1-0
FC Winterthur	30	8	8	14	42	51	32	1-2	3-1	2-1	1-1	3-1	0-0	1-2	1-2	1-0	2-2	1-2	1-3		2-0	0-0	1-2
FC Locarno	30	8	7	15	40	52	31	1-1	3-2	1-2	1-3	1-1	1-0	0-1	3-2	2-2	0-0	1-1	3-0	4-1		3-1	2-3
FC Schaffhausen	30	7	5	18	36	53	26	1-1	1-0	1-2	2-1	1-3	2-3	0-2	1-2	2-2	0-0	2-1	2-1				0-1
Yverdon-Sport	30	6	2	22	27	64	20	0-0	0-2	0-4	0-3	0-2	1-2	0-1	1-4	0-2	2-2	2-0	1-2	0-3	2-1	0-4	

23/07/2010 - 25/05/2011 • † Promotion play-off

MEDALS TABLE

		Overall			League			Cup		Europe			City
		G	S	B	G	S	B	G	S	G	S	B	
1	Grasshopper-Club	45	32	14	27	19	13	18	13			1	Zürich
2	Servette FC	24	28	12	17	16	12	7	12				Geneva
3	FC Basel	24	12	5	14	6	5	10	6				Basel
4	FC Zürich	19	10	9	12	9	7	7	1			2	Zürich
5	BSC Young Boys	17	23	11	11	16	10	6	7			1	Berne
6	Lausanne-Sport	16	16	9	7	8	8	9	8			1	Lausanne
7	FC Sion	14	2	6	2	2	6	12					Sion
8	FC La Chaux-de-Fonds	9	4	7	3	3	7	6	1				La Chaux-de-Fonds
9	AC Lugano	6	9	10	3	5	10	3	4				Lugano
10	FC Aarau	4	3	3	3	1	3	1	2				Aarau
11	Neuchâtel Xamax FC	3	9	9	3	3	9		6				Neuchâtel
12	FC Luzern	3	4	1	1	1	1	2	3				Luzern
13	FC Winterthur	3	4	1	3	2	1		2				Wintherthur
14	FC St Gallen	3	3	3	2		3	1	3				St Gallen

SCHWEIZER CUP / COUPE DE SUISSE 2010-11

Second Round

Team	Score
FC Sion	5
FC Collex-Bossy *	0
Black Stars Basel *	0
AC Lugano	3
FC Wohlen *	5
FC Winterthur	1
FC Gumefens/Sorens *	0
Grasshopper-Club	12
FC Basel	2
Yverdon-Sport *	0
FC Baulmes *	2
Servette FC	5
FC Luzern	2
Stade Nyonnais *	1
ES FC Malley *	0
FC Biel-Bienne	3
FC Zürich	3
FC Locarno *	0
FC Grenchen	0
FC Tuggen *	4
SC Kriens	3
FC Aarau *	2
US Collombey-Muraz *	2
BSC Young Boys	5
FC Thun	3
SC Buochs *	0
FC Schaffhausen *	2
FC St Gallen	6
AC Bellinzona	2
Lausanne-Sport *	0
FC Chiasso	0 3p
Neuchâtel Xamax *	0 4p

Round of 16

Team	Score
FC Sion	3
AC Lugano *	2
FC Wohlen *	1
Grasshopper-Club	2
FC Basel	1 4p
Servette FC *	1 3p
FC Luzern	2 3p
FC Biel-Bienne *	2 5p
FC Zürich	4
FC Tuggen *	0
SC Kriens *	1
BSC Young Boys	2
FC Thun	1
FC St Gallen *	0
AC Bellinzona	0
Neuchâtel Xamax *	1

Quarter-finals

Team	Score
FC Sion	2
Grasshopper-Club *	1
FC Basel	1
FC Biel-Bienne *	3
FC Zürich	4
BSC Young Boys *	3
FC Thun *	1 0p
Neuchâtel Xamax	1 3p

Semi-finals

Team	Score
FC Sion *	2
FC Biel-Bienne	1
FC Zürich *	1 6p
Neuchâtel Xamax	1 7p

Final

Team	Score
FC Sion ‡	2
Neuchâtel Xamax	0

CUP FINAL

St Jakob Park, Basel, 29-05-2011
Att: 37 500. Ref: Jerome Laperriere
Scorers - Sio 2, Vanczak 6 for Sion
Sion - Andris Vanins - Michael Dingsdag, Vilmos Vanczak, Arnaud Buhler (Jonas Elmer 67), Adailton - Fabrizio Zambrella, Didier Crettenand, Goran Obradovic (Rodrigo 87), Serey Die• - Aleksandar Prijovic (Alvaro Dominguez 52), Giovanni Sio•. Tr: Laurent Roussey
Neuchâtel - Jean-Francois Bedenik - Mickael Facchinetti, Stephane Besle, Frederic Page, Gilles Binya - Ibrahima Niasse, Raphael Nuzzolo, Marcos Gelabert (Abdullah Omar 62), Sebastien Wuthrich (Fausto Jorge 46) - Freddy Mveng, Gerard Gohou (Geoffrey Treand 46). Tr: Bernard Challandres

* Home team • ‡ Qualified for the Europa League

SUR – SURINAME

FIFA/COCA-COLA WORLD RANKING

'93	'94	'95	'96	'97	'98	'99	'00	'01	'02	'03	'04	'05	'06	'07	'08	'09	'10	'11	'12
117	104	124	131	145	160	162	164	141	141	158	149	152	122	153	129	144	115	125	

	2011											High	Low	Av
Jan	Feb	Mar	Apr	May	Jun	Jul	Aug	Sep	Oct	Nov	Dec	High	Low	Av
115	117	114	112	112	108	110	110	113	104	122	125	84	168	137

2011 turned out to be a disappointing year for the Suriname national team as they stumbled their way through their 2014 FIFA World Cup qualifying group after having made a promising start. With the experienced Kenneth Jaliens back in the coaching hot seat, the Surinamese looked set for a two-game showdown with El Salvador in the final two group matches but that was before they were surprisingly beaten at home by the Dominican Republic. The defeat rendered the matches against El Salvador almost meaningless and both were lost. In club football it proved to be a memorable year for the town of Moengo with Inter Moengotapoe winning the championship for the fourth time in five seasons and their local rivals Notch FC winning the second division title. But that wasn't the end of the story as far as Notch were concerned as they also won the Cup for the first time in their history. In the final on the artificial pitch at the Franklin Essed Stadion in Paramaribo, they beat league runners-up Walking Boyz Co 4-2 with the prolific Milton Pinas scoring all four goals for Notch. There was less to cheer in the 2011 CFU Club Championship with Inter being knocked-out by Guyana's Milerock whilst Walking Boyz were given a harsh lesson in a 7-0 thrashing by eventual winners Puerto Rico Islanders.

FIFA WORLD CUP RECORD
1930-1958 DNE **1962-1986** DNQ **1990** DNE **1994-2010** DNQ

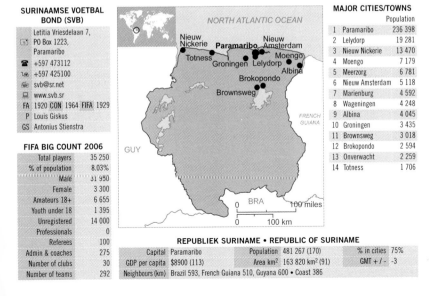

SURINAAMSE VOETBAL BOND (SVB)

Letitia Vriesdelaan 7,
PO Box 1223,
Paramaribo
☎ +597 473112
✆ +597 425100
✉ svb@sr.net
🖥 www.svb.sr
FA 1920 CON 1964 FIFA 1929
P Louis Giskus
GS Antonius Stienstra

FIFA BIG COUNT 2006

Total players	35 250
% of population	8.03%
Male	31 950
Female	3 300
Amateurs 18+	6 655
Youth under 18	1 395
Unregistered	14 000
Professionals	0
Referees	100
Admin & coaches	275
Number of clubs	30
Number of teams	292

NORTH ATLANTIC OCEAN

Nieuw Nickerie · Paramaribo · Nieuw Amsterdam
Totness · Groningen Lelydorp · Moengo
Brokopondo · Albina
Brownsweg

GUY

FRENCH GUIANA

BRA

0   100 miles
0   100 km

MAJOR CITIES/TOWNS

		Population
1	Paramaribo	236 398
2	Lelydorp	19 281
3	Nieuw Nickerie	13 470
4	Moengo	7 179
5	Meerzorg	6 781
6	Nieuw Amsterdam	5 118
7	Marienburg	4 592
8	Wageningen	4 248
9	Albina	4 045
10	Groningen	3 435
11	Brownsweg	3 018
12	Brokopondo	2 594
13	Onverwacht	2 259
14	Totness	1 706

REPUBLIEK SURINAME • REPUBLIC OF SURINAME

Capital	Paramaribo	Population	481 267 (170)	% in cities	75%
GDP per capita	$8900 (113)	Area km²	163 820 km² (91)	GMT +/-	-3
Neighbours (km)	Brazil 593, French Guiana 510, Guyana 600 • Coast 386				

RECENT INTERNATIONAL MATCHES PLAYED BY SURINAME

2011	Opponents	Score		Venue	Comp	Scorers	Att	Referee
2-09	Cayman Islands	W	1-0	Paramaribo	WCq	Friso Mando [11p]	1 000	Skeete BRB
6-09	Dominican Republic	D	1-1	San Cristobal	WCq	Friso Mando [25p]	2 300	Castro HON
23-09	Curacao	W	2-0	Paramaribo	Fr	Stefano Rijssel [25], Milton Pinas [60]	2 000	Botland SUR
25-09	Curacao	D	2-2	Paramaribo	Fr	Evani Esperance [14], Giovanni Drenthe [61]	2 500	Pierau SUR
7-10	Cayman Islands	W	1-0	Georgetown	WCq	Giovanni Drenthe [57]	2 100	Jurisebic USA
11-10	Dominican Republic	L	1-3	Paramaribo	WCq	Naldo Kwasie [81]	1 200	Ward CAN
11-11	El Salvador	L	1-3	Paramaribo	WCq	Evani Esperance [81]	500	Brea CUB
15-11	El Salvador	L	0-4	San Salvador	WCq		9 659	Santos PUR
2-12	Aruba	D	0-0	Paramaribo	Fr		150	Jauregui ANT
4-12	Curacao	W	3-1	Paramaribo	Fr	Stefano Baneti [46], Emilio Limon [76]	50	Angela ARU

Fr = Friendly match • CC = Digicel Caribbean Cup • WC = FIFA World Cup • q = qualifier • † Not a full international

SURINAME 2010–11

HOOFDKLASSE

	Pl	W	D	L	F	A	Pts	WBC	Inter	Transvaal	Leo Victor	Kamal	Excelsior	Robinhood	Boskamp	Voorwarts	Brothers
Walking Boyz Co †	18	14	3	1	47	17	45		2-1	2-1	2-2	2-1	2-0	3-3	3-3	6-1	3-0
Inter Moengotapoe †	18	14	1	3	50	26	43	0-1		2-1	0-0	2-1	3-1	3-1	3-1	5-2	7-1
Transvaal †	18	9	3	6	37	25	30	0-3	0-1		1-4	3-1	4-2	3-1	3-1	3-1	5-0
Leo Victor †	18	7	6	5	34	28	27	0-4	1-3	2-1		0-1	2-2	3-4	3-3	4-0	2-1
Kamal Dewaker †	18	6	5	7	26	27	23	1-2	4-5	1-1	2-3		1-1	1-1	2-1	1-0	2-0
Excelsior †	18	6	5	7	25	27	23	0-3	4-1	0-0	1-0	1-2		5-2	1-0	0-0	3-1
Robinhood	18	5	3	10	32	44	18	2-4	1-2	2-2	2-4	1-2	2-0		2-1	2-3	2-1
Boskamp	18	3	6	9	22	35	15	2-1	1-5	1-4	0-3	1-1	1-1	0-1		3-0	1-1
Voorwarts	18	4	2	12	18	38	14	0-1	2-4	0-1	1-1	2-1	0-2	4-1	1-2		1-0
The Brothers	18	3	4	11	16	40	13	0-3	2-3	1-4	0-0	1-1	3-1	3-2	0-0	1-0	

17/11/2010 - 27/05/2011 • † Top six qualify for the play-off round, the bottom six for the relegation group

SURINAME 2010–11

HOOFDKLASSE CHAMPIONSHIP PLAY-OFFS

	Pl	W	D	L	F	A	Pts	Inter	WBC	Leo Victor	Excelsior	Transvaal	Kamal
Inter Moengotapoe †	10	7	1	2	21	10	22		1-0	2-1	2-1	1-1	3-1
Walking Boyz Co	10	6	0	4	20	14	28	4-3		1-0	3-2	1-2	5-0
Leo Victor	10	5	0	5	22	17	15	0-2	3-2		7-0	3-1	2-1
Excelsior	10	5	0	5	17	27	15	0-4	2-1	6-3		2-1	1-0
Transvaal	10	4	1	5	17	15	13	1-3	1-2	1-0	5-0		1-2
Kamal Dewaker	10	2	0	8	8	22	6	1-0	0-1	1-3	1-3	1-3	

4/06/2011 - 15/09/2011 • † Qualified for the CFU Club Championship

SURINAME 2010–11

HOOFDKLASSE RELEGATION PLAY-OFFS

	Pl	W	D	L	F	A	Pts	Robinhood	Boskamp	Voorwarts	Brothers
Robinhood §3	6	5	0	1	19	6	12		0-2	2-0	4-2
Boskamp	6	3	0	3	10	9	9	1-2		1-2	4-2
Voorwarts †	6	2	1	3	9	15	7	1-5	2-0		3-3
The Brothers	6	1	1	4	12	20	4	0-6	1-2	4-1	

4/06/2011 - 24/07/2011 • § = points deducted • † Relegation play-off
Relegation play-off: Takdier Boys 1-2 1-4 **Voorwarts**

SVB BEKER 2010–11

Final. Franklin Essed Stadion, Paramaribo, 12-06-2011
Notch Moengo 4-2 Walking Boyz Co
Scorer - Milton Pinas 4

SURINAME 2010–11 EERSTE KLASSE

	Pl	W	D	L	F	A	Pts
Notch Moengo	22	17	1	4	52	20	52
Takdier Boys †	22	15	2	5	49	29	47
Boma Star	22	14	3	5	52	30	45
Randjiet Boys	22	14	2	6	61	29	41
SNL	22	12	3	7	54	30	39
FCS Nacional	22	8	4	10	48	53	28
Tammenga	22	9	1	12	45	66	28
Inter Rica	22	7	4	11	40	45	25
De Ster	22	8	1	13	32	50	25
Real Saramacca	22	7	3	12	31	44	24
Jai Hanuman	22	3	5	14	32	47	14
Fortuna 75	22	2	3	17	21	74	9

4/11/2010 - 22/05/2011 • † Play-off

MEDALS TABLE

		Overall	Lge	Cup	CON'CAF		
		G	G	G	G	S	B
1	Robinhood	27	22	5		5	3
2	Transvaal	24	19	3		2	3
3	Voorwarts	6	6				
	Leo Victor	6	5	1			
5	Walking Boyz Co	4	3	1			
	Cicerone	4	4				
7	Inter Moengotapoe	4	4				
8	FCS Nacional	2	1	1			

SVK – SLOVAKIA

FIFA/COCA-COLA WORLD RANKING

'93	'94	'95	'96	'97	'98	'99	'00	'01	'02	'03	'04	'05	'06	'07	'08	'09	'10	'11	'12
150	43	35	30	34	32	21	24	47	55	50	53	45	37	53	44	33	20	40	

2011												High	Low	Av
Jan	Feb	Mar	Apr	May	Jun	Jul	Aug	Sep	Oct	Nov	Dec	High	Low	Av
20	20	22	27	26	28	29	26	39	41	40	40	16	150	40

After the euphoria of their tremendous performance at the 2010 FIFA World Cup finals in South Africa where they beat Italy and reached the knockout phase, Slovakia came down to earth with a bump in the qualifiers for Euro 2012, finishing their group in fourth place behind Russia, the Republic of Ireland and Armenia. Their campaign had started well enough with a victory over Russia and in mid-2011 they were in a position to challenge for a play-off spot but their failure to win any of their final four games - including a 4-0 defeat at home to Armenia - put paid to any lingering hopes. Unlike the the Czech Republic who have qualified for every Euro finals since the two countries split, Slovakia's failure to qualify for Euro 2012 leaves them still waiting for their first appearance. At home, Slovan Bratislava returned to winning ways after a tremendous second half of the season saw them catch and overtake both Senica and defending champions Zilina to claim their sixth league title. Coached by the former Slavia Prague boss Karel Jarolim, Slovan also won the cup after beating Zilina in a thrilling final on penalties. Slovan then made it through to the group stage of the 2011-12 Europa League after knocking out Italian giants Roma in the play-off round under new coach Vladimir Weiss, although they then won just a single point in their group.

UEFA EUROPEAN CHAMPIONSHIP RECORD

1960 3 SF **1964** r1 **1968-1972** DNQ **1976** 1 Winners **1980** 3 **1984-1992** DNQ (as Czechoslovakia) **1996-2012** DNQ

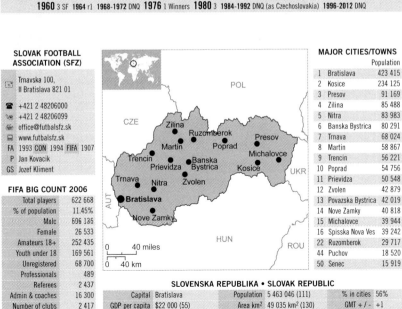

SLOVAK FOOTBALL ASSOCIATION (SFZ)

Trnavska 100,
II Bratislava 821 01

☎ +421 2 48206000
📠 +421 2 48206099
📧 office@futbalsfz.sk
🖥 www.futbalsfz.sk
FA 1993 CON 1994 FIFA 1907
P Jan Kovacik
GS Jozef Kliment

FIFA BIG COUNT 2006

Total players	622 668
% of population	11.45%
Male	596 135
Female	26 533
Amateurs 18+	252 435
Youth under 18	169 561
Unregistered	68 700
Professionals	489
Referees	2 437
Admin & coaches	16 300
Number of clubs	2 417
Number of teams	7 353

MAJOR CITIES/TOWNS

		Population
1	Bratislava	423 415
2	Kosice	234 125
3	Presov	91 169
4	Zilina	85 488
5	Nitra	83 983
6	Banska Bystrica	80 291
7	Trnava	68 024
8	Martin	58 867
9	Trencin	56 221
10	Poprad	54 756
11	Prievidza	50 548
12	Zvolen	42 879
13	Povazska Bystrica	42 019
14	Nove Zamky	40 818
15	Michalovce	39 944
16	Spisska Nova Ves	39 242
22	Ruzomberok	29 717
44	Puchov	18 520
50	Senec	15 919

SLOVENSKA REPUBLIKA • SLOVAK REPUBLIC

Capital	Bratislava	Population	5 463 046 (111)	% in cities	56%
GDP per capita	$22 000 (55)	Area km²	49 035 km² (130)	GMT +/-	+1
Neighbours (km)	Austria 91, Czech Republic 197, Hungary 676, Poland 420, Ukraine 90				

RECENT INTERNATIONAL MATCHES PLAYED BY SLOVAKIA

2008 Opponents	Score	Venue	Comp	Scorers	Att	Referee
20-08 Greece	L 0-2	Bratislava	Fr		4 500	Fabian HUN
6-09 Northern Ireland	W 2-1	Bratislava	WCq	Skrtel [47], Hamsik [70]	5 445	Ivanov.N RUS
10-09 Slovenia	L 1-2	Maribor	WCq	Jakubko [83]	9 900	Moen NOR
11-10 San Marino	W 3-1	Serravalle	WCq	Sestak [33], Kozak [39], Karhan [51]	1 037	Kever SUI
15-10 Poland	W 2-1	Bratislava	WCq	Sestak 2 [84 86]	17 650	Layec FRA
19-11 Liechtenstein	W 4-0	Zilina	Fr	Hamsik 2 [43 72], Vittek [75], Jez [90]	2 010	Oriekhov UKR
2009						
10-02 Ukraine	L 2-3	Limassol	Fr	Vittek 42, Hamsik 69		Kallis CYP
11-02 Cyprus	L 2-3	Nicosia	Fr	Jez [88], Jendrisek [90]	300	
28-03 England	L 0-4	London	Fr		85 512	Hamer LUX
1-04 Czech Republic	W 2-1	Prague	WCq	Sestak [22], Jendrisek [82]	14 956	Undiano ESP
6-06 San Marino	W 7-0	Bratislava	WCq	Cech 2 [3 32], Pekarik [12], Stoch [35], Kozak [42], Jakubko [63], Hanzel [68]	6 652	Efong Nzolo BEL
12-08 Iceland	D 1-1	Reykjavik	Fr	Vittek [35]	5 099	Christoffersen DEN
5-09 Czech Republic	D 2-2	Bratislava	WCq	Sestak [59], Hamsik [73p]	23 800	Ovrebo NOR
9-09 Northern Ireland	W 2-0	Belfast	WCq	Sestak [15], Holosko [67]	13 019	Kuipers NED
10-10 Slovenia	L 0-2	Bratislava	WCq		23 800	Stark GER
14-10 Poland	W 1-0	Chorzow	WCq	Gancarczyk OG [3]	5 000	Eriksson SWE
14-11 USA	W 1-0	Bratislava	Fr	Hamsik [26p]	7 200	Messner AUT
17-11 Chile	L 1-2	Zilina	Fr	Sestak [17]	11 072	Vad HUN
2010						
3-03 Norway	L 0-1	Zilina	Fr		9 756	Nijhuis NED
29-05 Cameroon	D 1-1	Klagenfurt	Fr	Kopunek [6]	10 000	Lechner AUT
5-06 Costa Rica	W 3-0	Bratislava	Fr	OG [16], Vittek [47], Sestak [88p]	12 000	Messner AUT
15-06 New Zealand	D 1-1	Rustenburg	WCr1	Vittek [50]	23 871	Damon RSA
20-06 Paraguay	L 0-2	Bloemfontein	WCr1		26 643	Maillet SEY
24-06 Italy	W 3-2	Johannesburg	WCr1	Vittek 2 [25 73], Kopunek [89]	53 412	Webb ENG
28-06 Netherlands	L 1-2	Durban	WCr2	Vittek [94+]	61 962	Undiano ESP
11-08 Croatia	D 1-1	Bratislava	Fr	Stoch [50]	6 366	Matejek CZE
3-09 FYR Macedonia	W 1-0	Bratislava	ECq	Holosko [91+]	5 980	Circhetta SUI
7-09 Russia	W 1-0	Moscow	ECq	Stoch [27]	27 052	De Bleeckere BEL
8-10 Armenia	L 1-3	Yerevan	ECq	Weiss [37]	8 500	Orsato ITA
12-10 Republic of Ireland	D 1-1	Zilinia	ECq	Durica [36]	10 892	Undiano ESP
17-11 Bosnia-Hercegovina	L 2-3	Bratislava	Fr	Sebo [3], Grajciar [63]	7 822	Mikulski POL
2011						
9-02 Luxembourg	L 1-2	Luxembourg	Fr	Jendrisek [55]	862	Thual FRA
26-03 Andorra	W 1-0	Adorra La Vella	ECq	Sebo [21]	850	Masiah ISR
29-03 Denmark	L 1-2	Trnava	Fr	Holosko [32]	4 927	Fernandez ESP
4-06 Andorra	W 1-0	Bratislava	ECq	Karhan [63]	4 300	Jemini ALB
10-08 Austria	W 2-1	Klagenfurt	Fr	Kucka [21], Jez [30]	13 000	Ceferin SVN
2-09 Republic of Ireland	D 0-0	Dublin	ECq		35 480	Proenca POR
6-09 Armenia	L 0-4	Zilina	ECq		7 238	Borski POL
7-10 Russia	L 0-1	Zilina	ECq		10 087	Eriksson SWE
11-10 FYR Macedonia	D 1-1	Skopje	ECq	Piroska [54]	4 100	Chapron FRA

Fr = Friendly match • EC = UEFA EURO 2012 • WC = FIFA World Cup • q = qualifier • po = play-off

SLOVAKIA NATIONAL TEAM HISTORICAL RECORDS

Caps
107 - Miroslav Karhan 1995- • **79** - Robert Vittek 2001- • **59** - Szilard Nemeth 1996-2006 • **55** - Stanislav Varga 1997-2006 • **53** - Filip Holosko 2005- • **52** - Robert Tomaschek 1994-2001; Radoslav Zabavnik 2003- & Martin Skrtel 2004- • **51** - Jan Durica 2004- & Marek Hamsik 2007- • **48** - Marek Cech 2004- • **45** - Peter Dzurik 1997-2003; Miroslav Konig 1997-2004 & Marek Mintal 2002-09

Goals
23 - Robert Vittek 2001- • **22** - Szilard Nemeth 1996-2006 • **14** - Marek Mintal 2002-09 & Miroslav Karhan 1995- • **12** - Peter Dubovsky 1994-2000 • **11** - Stanislav Sestak 2004- • **9** - Tibor Jancula 1995-2001 & Lubomir Reiter 2001-05 • **8** - Marek Hamsik 2007-

Past Coaches
Jozef Venglos 1993-95 • Jozef Jankech 1995-98 • Dusan Radolsky 1998 • Josef Adamec 1999-2001 • Ladislav Jurkemik 2002-03 • Dusan Galis 2004-06 • Jan Kocian 2006-08 • Vladimir Weiss 2008-

SLOVAKIA 2010-11

SUPER LIGA

	Pl	W	D	L	F	A	Pts	Slovan	Senica	Zilina	Spartak	Dukla	ViOn	Ruzomberok	Nitra	DAC	Kosice	Tatran	Dubnica
Slovan Bratislava †	33	20	8	5	63	22	68		2-2	0-1	1-1 3-0	2-0 3-1	3-0 1-0	3-0 1-0	0-0	1-0 2-0	4-0	4-0	6-1 3-1
FK Senica ‡	33	18	7	8	54	30	61	3-2 1-2		2-1	1-2 4-0	3-0	0-1 2-0	4-0	2-0 3-2	1-1	1-0 1-1	1-1	1-0 0-0
MSK Zilina ‡	33	14	12	7	47	28	54	2-2 0-3	0-0 0-1		1-1	3-3	2-1	1-0	3-1 5-1	2-0 0-0	0-0	2-0 2-1	2-1 0-0
Spartak Trnava ‡	33	13	10	10	40	30	49	1-3	3-0 0-0	1-0 1-1		0-2 0-0	2-0 0-0	4-1	1-1 3-0	0-0	1-0	2-1	4-0
Dukla Banska Bystrica	33	13	9	11	39	32	48	0-0	1-0 3-2	1-2 0-0	1-2 0-0		1-1	1-0 2-0	1-2 2-0	4-1	3-0	3-2	1-0
ViOn Zlaté Moravce	33	12	10	11	35	31	46	1-1	0-0	0-4 2-0	1-0 0-2	3-0 1-2		1-1 3-0	4-1	1-0 1-0	2-3	2-1	2-1
MFK Ruzomberok	33	10	11	12	23	33	41	0-0	1-2	3-2 1-1	0-0 0-0	0-0	1-1 0-0		1-0 2-0	1-0 2-2	1-0	0-1	0-1
FC Nitra	33	11	7	15	30	51	40	1-0 0-1	0-5	0-2 1-0	3-2 0-2	1-1 0-0	1-2	0-2 0-1		1-1	1-0 1-0	3-2	1-1
DAC Dunajská Streda	33	9	9	15	24	39	36	2-1	0-3 2-3	0-3	2-2	1-0 0-0	2-1 3-0	0-1	1-2 1-0		0-0 2-1	2-1	0-0
MFK Kosice	33	8	9	16	28	44	33	2-1	0-4	1-0 0-2	1-3 1-1	2-1	0-1 0-1	0-2 3-0	1-0	4-0		1-0	1-1
Tatran Presov	33	9	6	18	30	49	33	2-1 0-2	0-1 0-1	2-0	0-0 2-1	1-0	1-1	1-2 3-3	1-0	1-1 0-3	1-1		2-1
MFK Dubnica	33	7	10	16	23	47	31	1-1	0-1	2-5 1-0	0-4 1-0	1-0 2-0	0-4 1-0	0-0	1-1	2-1 0-1	0-0	0-1	

17/07/2010 - 25/05/2011 • † Qualified for the UEFA Champions League • ‡ Qualified for the Europa League • Match in bold awarded
Top scorers: **22** - Filip Sebo, Slovan • **18** - Ondrej Smetana CZE, Senica • **10** - Tomas Majtan Zilina; Tomas Oravec, Zilina, Jaroslav Divis, Senica & Koro Kone CIV, Spartak Trnava • **9** - Robert Rak, Nitra • **8** - Marko Milinkovic SRB, Kosice/Slovan & Robert Pich, Dukla/Zilina

SLOVAKIA 2010-11 II LIGA (2)

	Pl	W	D	L	F	A	Pts
AS Trenčín	33	22	6	5	77	30	72
Rimavska Sobota	33	16	6	11	41	35	54
MFK Petrzalka	33	13	12	8	55	36	51
Zemplin Michalovce	33	15	6	12	51	48	51
SFM Senec	33	13	9	11	39	39	48
Tatran Lip'sky Mikulas	33	14	6	13	43	44	48
Bodva Moldava	33	13	8	12	46	40	47
Dolny Kubin	33	13	7	13	45	38	46
LAFC Lucenec	33	11	8	14	41	48	41
MFK Ruzomberok B	33	10	8	15	37	44	38
Slovan Duslo Sala	33	9	6	18	24	44	33
FK Púchov	33	6	4	23	24	77	22

17/07/2010 - 25/05/2011

MEDALS TABLE

		Overall			League			Cup		City
		G	S	B	G	S	B	G	S	
1	Slovan Bratislava	11	3	3	6	2	3	5	1	Bratislava
2	MSK Zilina	5	4	1	5	3	1			Zilina
3	Inter Bratislava	5	2	3	2	2	3	3		Bratislava
4	Artmedia Petrzalka	4	5		2	3		2	2	Bratislava
5	MFK Kosice	3	5	1	2	3	1	1	2	Kosice
6	MFK Ruzomberok	2	1	2	1		2	1	1	Ruzomberok
7	Spartak Trnava	1	6	4		2	4	1	4	Trnava
8	Dukla Banská Bystrica	1	2	2		1	2	1	1	Banská Bystrica
9	Matador Púchov	1	2			1		1	1	Púchov
10	FC Senec	1	1					1	1	Senec
11	1.HFC Humenné	1						1		Humenné
	ViOn Zlaté Moravce	1								Zlaté Moravce
13	Tatran Presov			2					2	Presov
14	DAC Dunajská Streda	1	1			1		1		Dunajská Streda
15	FK Senica	1			1					Senica
	Trans Licartovce	1						1		
17	FC Nitra			1					1	Nitra

MEDALS TABLE FOR SLOVAK CLUBS IN CZECHOSLOVAKIAN FOOTBALL

		Overall			League			Cup		Europe		
		G	S	B	G	S	B	G	S	G	S	B
3	Slovan Bratislava	14	16	3	8	10	3	5	6	1		
5	Spartak Trnava	9	2	2	5	1	1	4	1			1
7	Lokomotíva Kosice	2	1	2				2	1			
8	TJ Internacional	1	6	5	1	3	5		3			
9	1.FC Kosice	1	4	2				1	2	1	3	
14	DAC Dunajská Streda	1	1					1	1			
17	Tatran Presov	4	1					2	1	2		
18	Jednota Trencin	2	1					1	1	1		
20	FC Nitra	1	1					1	1			
22	SK Zilina	1						1				
	Dukla Banská Bystrica	1						1				

SLOVENSKY POHAR 2010-11

Second Round

Team	Score
Slovan Bratislava *	6
FK Púchov	0
Blava Jasl'ske Bohunice *	0
AS Trencín	5
MFK Dubnica	3
SK Kremnicka *	0
FK Senica	
Spartak Myjava *	1
MFK Ruzomberok	0 4p
Zemplin Michalovce *	0 3p
Tatran Presov	1 3p
Odeva Lipany *	1 4p
Spisska Nova Ves *	3
MFK Kosice	0
Slovan Nemsova	0
Spartak Trnava	2
ViOn Zlaté Moravce	5
STK 1914 Samorin *	2
DAC Dunajská Streda	1
MFK Petrzalka *	2
Sport Podbrezova *	2
Dolny Kubin	0
Slovan Duslo Sala *	0
FC Nitra	1
Tatran Lip'sky Mikulas *	2
HFC Humenné *	1
FK Poprad *	0
Dukla Banska Bystrica	1
SFM Senec	3
PSC Pezinok *	0
Vranov nad Toplbu *	0
MSK Zilina	5

Third Round

Team	Score
Slovan Bratislava	1 3p
AS Trencín *	1 2p
MFK Dubnica	0
Spartak Myjava *	1
MFK Ruzomberok	1
Odeva Lipany *	0
Spisska Nova Ves *	0
Spartak Trnava	5
ViOn Zlaté Moravce *	2
MFK Petrzalka	1
Sport Podbrezova *	0
FC Nitra	1
Tatran Lip'sky Mikulas *	0 4p
Dukla Banska Bystrica	0 2p
SFM Senec *	1
MSK Zilina	3

Quarter-finals

Team	Score
Slovan Bratislava	1 2
Spartak Myjava *	0 0
MFK Ruzomberok *	0 0
Spartak Trnava	3 3
ViOn Zlaté Moravce	0 2
FC Nitra *	1 0
Tatran Lip'sky Mikulas *	0 0
MSK Zilina	1 3

Semi-finals

Team	Score
Slovan Bratislava *	2 3
Spartak Trnava	2 2
ViOn Zlaté Moravce	0 1
MSK Zilina *	3 0

Final

Team	Score
Slovan Bratislava	3 5p
MSK Zilina ‡	3 4p

PENALTIES

SB	Zi
✗ Sebo	
	✓ Mraz
✓ Zofcak	
	✓ Guldan
✓ Grendel	
	✓ Pich
✓ Hrdlicka	
	✓ Sourek
✗ Guede	
	✓ Lietava
✗ Dobrotka	
	✗ Ceesay
✓ Dosoudil	
	✗ Gergel

FINAL

Na Stiavnickach, Banská Bystrica
8-05-2011, Att: 2653, Ref: Pavel Kralovec CZE
Scorers - Guldan OG 7, Sebo 2 76 113 for Slovan; Zosak 15, Lietava 40, Mraz 121+ for Zilina
Slovan - Matus Putnocky - Lukas Pauschek, Radek Dosoudil, Martin Dobrotka, Tomas Hrdlicka - Mario Bozic● (Akos Szarka 73) - Marko Milinkovic (Mamadou Bagayoko 60), Karim Guede, Igor Zofcak (c) - Filip Sebo, Kresimir Kordic (Erik Grendel● 46). Tr: Karel Jarolim
Zilina - Martin Dubravka - Ernest Mabouka, Jozef Piacek, Ondrej Sourek, Vladimir Leitner (c) (Robert Pich 107) - Lubomir Guldan - Bello Babatounde, Stefan Zosak (Roman Gergel 84), Tomas Majtan● (Patrik Mraz 63) - Ivan Lietava, Momodou Ceesay●. Tr: Pavel Hapal

* Home team/home team in the 1st leg ‡ Qualified for the Europa League

SVN – SLOVENIA

FIFA/COCA-COLA WORLD RANKING

'93	'94	'95	'96	'97	'98	'99	'00	'01	'02	'03	'04	'05	'06	'07	'08	'09	'10	'11	'12
134	81	71	77	95	88	40	35	25	36	31	42	68	77	83	57	31	17	26	

	2011											High	Low	Av
Jan	Feb	Mar	Apr	May	Jun	Jul	Aug	Sep	Oct	Nov	Dec			
17	16	17	17	17	21	23	23	33	27	26	26	15	134	57

With expectations running high following their appearance at the 2010 FIFA World Cup finals in South Africa, Slovenia had a disappointing qualifying campaign for Euro 2012. They finished fourth in their group, although they were just two points adrift of Estonia in the runners-up spot and but for a calamatous 2-1 defeat at home to the Estonians in the run in, it might have been a very different story. After the qualifiers Matjaz Kek stepped down and was replaced by Slavisa Stojanovic, a coach who had taken NK Domzale to successive titles in 2007 and 2008. His old club won their first trophy since his time in charge when they beat NK Maribor 4-3 in a thrilling 2011 Cup Final - a victory that denied Maribor the double the week after Maribor had emerged victorious in a tight championship race between the two. It was Domzle's first cup triumph but for Maribor the league title was their ninth and they followed it up with an impressive campaign in Europe that saw them qualify for the group stage of the 2011-12 Europa League. They had fallen just short in the 2010-11 campaign after losing to Palermo in the play-offs but made sure with a 3-2 aggregate victory over Scotland's Rangers. Once there, however, they struggled and managed to pick up just a single point in their six group games.

UEFA EUROPEAN CHAMPIONSHIP RECORD
1960-1992 DNE (played as part of Yugoslavia) **1996** DNQ **2000** r1 **2004-2012** DNQ

FOOTBALL ASSOCIATION OF SLOVENIA (NZS)

Nogometna Zveza Slovenije,
Cerinova 4, PO Box 3986,
Ljubljana 1001
☎ +386 1 5300400
✆ +386 1 5300410
✉ fas@nzs.si
🖥 www.nzs.si
FA 1920 CON 1992 FIFA 1992
P Aleksander Ceferin
GS Ales Zavrl

FIFA BIG COUNT 2006

Total players	116 925
% of population	5.82%
Male	107 255
Female	9 670
Amateurs 18+	9 410
Youth under 18	20 831
Unregistered	55 200
Professionals	284
Referees	818
Admin & coaches	5 000
Number of clubs	328
Number of teams	1 060

MAJOR CITIES/TOWNS

		Population
1	Ljubljana	194 727
2	Maribor	88 349
3	Celje	36 723
4	Kranj	34 782
5	Velenje	26 857
6	Koper	24 725
7	Novo mesto	22 941
8	Ptuj	19 014
9	Trbovlje	15 637
10	Kamnik	13 698
11	Jesenice	13 433
12	Domzale	12 465
13	Nova Gorica	12 407
14	Skofja Loka	12 254
15	Murska Sobota	12 135
16	Izola	11 403
17	Kocevje	9 111
18	Postojna	8 867
27	Adajdovscina	6 972

REPUBLIKA SLOVENIJA • REPUBLIC OF SLOVENIA

Capital Ljubljana	Population 2 005 692 (145)	% in cities 48%
GDP per capita $29 600 (47)	Area km² 20 273 km² (154)	GMT + / - +1
Neighbours (km) Austria 330, Croatia 455, Hungary 102, Italy 199 • Coast 46		

RECENT INTERNATIONAL MATCHES PLAYED BY SLOVENIA

2008	Opponents	Score		Venue	Comp	Scorers	Att	Referee
6-02	Denmark	L	1-2	Nova Gorica	Fr	Novakovic [37]	1 700	Kinhofer GER
26-03	Hungary	W	1-0	Zalaegerszeg	Fr	Sisic [59]	7 000	Messner AUT
26-05	Sweden	L	0-1	Gothenburg	Fr		21 118	Collum SCO
20-08	Croatia	L	2-3	Maribor	Fr	Suler [3], Sisic [55p]	11 500	Circhetta SUI
6-09	Poland	D	1-1	Wroclaw	WCq	Dedic [35]	7 300	Jakobsson ISL
10-09	Slovakia	W	2-1	Maribor	WCq	Novakovic 2 [22 81]	9 900	Moen NOR
11-10	Northern Ireland	W	2-0	Maribor	WCq	Novakovic [83], Ljubijankic [84]	12 385	Iturralde ESP
15-10	Czech Republic	L	0-1	Teplice	WCq		15 220	Atkinson ENG
19-11	Bosnia-Herzegovina	L	3-4	Maribor	Fr	Koren [27], Novakovic 2 [64p 75]	10 000	Kari FIN
2009								
11-02	Belgium	L	0-2	Genk	Fr		13 135	Kever SUI
28-03	Czech Republic	D	0-0	Maribor	WCq		12 500	Proenca POR
1-04	Northern Ireland	L	0-1	Belfast	WCq		13 243	Yefet ISR
12-08	San Marino	W	5-0	Maribor	WCq	Koren 2 [19 74], Radosavljevic [39], Kirm [54], Ljubijankic [93+]	4 400	Meckarovski MKD
5-09	England	L	1-2	London	Fr	Ljubijankic [85]	67 232	Eriksson SWE
9-09	Poland	W	3-0	Maribor	WCq	Dedic [13], Novakovic [44], Birsa [62]	10 226	Collum SCO
10-10	Slovakia	W	2-0	Bratislava	WCq	Birsa [56], Pecnik [93+]	23 800	Stark GER
14-10	San Marino	W	3-0	Serravalle	WCq	Novakovic [24], Stevanovic [68], Suler [81]	1 745	Szabo HUN
14-11	Russia	L	1-2	Moscow	WCpo	Pecnik [88]	71 600	Larsen DEN
18-11	Russia	W	1-0	Maribor	WCpo	Dedic [44]	12 510	Hauge NOR
2010								
3-03	Qatar	W	4-1	Maribor	Fr	Novakovic [14], Cesar [30], Kirm [34], Jokic [67]	4 900	Van Boekel NED
4-06	New Zealand	W	3-1	Maribor	Fr	Novakovic 2 [7 30], Kirm [44]	10 965	Kakkos GRE
13-06	Algeria	W	1-0	Polokwane	WCr1	Koren [79]	30 325	Batres GUA
18-06	USA	D	2-2	Johannesburg	WCr1	Birsa [13], Ljubijankic [42]	45 573	Coulibaly MLI
23-06	England	L	0-1	Port Elizabeth	WCr1		36 893	Stark GER
11-08	Australia	W	2-0	Ljubljana	Fr	Dedic [78], Ljubijankic [90]	16 135	Tagliavento ITA
3-09	Northern Ireland	L	0-1	Maribor	ECq		12 000	Balaj ROU
7-09	Serbia	D	1-1	Belgrade	ECq	Novakovic [63]	24 028	Benquerenca POR
8-10	Faeroe Islands	W	5-1	Ljubljana	ECq	Matavz 3 [25 36 65], Novakovic [72p], Dedic [84]	15 750	Todorov BUL
12-10	Estonia	W	1-0	Tallinn	ECq	OG [67]	5 722	Skjerven NOR
17-11	Georgia	L	1-2	Koper	Fr	Cesat [51]	4 000	Whitby WAL
2011								
9-02	Albania	W	2-1	Tirana	Fr	Novakovic [25], Dedic [90p]		Koukoulakis GRE
25-03	Italy	L	0-1	Ljubljana	ECq		15 790	Brych GER
29-03	Northern Ireland	D	0-0	Belfast	ECq		14 200	Kuipers NED
3-06	Faroe Islands	W	2-0	Toftir	ECq	Matavz [29], OG [47]	974	Drachta AUT
10-08	Belgium	D	0-0	Ljubljana	Fr		12 230	Strahonja CRO
2-09	Estonia	L	1-2	Ljubljana	ECq	Matavz [78]	15 480	Studer SUI
6-09	Italy	L	0-1	Florence	ECq		18 000	Moen NOR
11-10	Serbia	W	1-0	Maribor	ECq	Vrsic [45]	9 848	De Bleeckere BEL
15-11	USA	L	2-3	Ljubljana	Fr	Matavz 2 [26 60]	8 140	Schorgenhofer AUT

Fr = Friendly match • EC = UEFA EURO 2012 • WC = FIFA World Cup • q = qualifier • po = play-off

SLOVENIA NATIONAL TEAM HISTORICAL RECORDS

Caps
80 - Zlatko Zahovic 1992-2004 • **74** - Milenko Acimovic 1998-2007 & Ales Ceh 1992-2002 • **71** - Dzoni Novak 1992-2002 • **66** - Marinko Galic 1994-2002 & Aleksander Knavs 1998-2006 • **65** - Mladen Rudonja 1994-2003 • **64** - Amir Karic 1996-2004 • **63** - Miran Pavlin 1994-2004 • **61** - Robert Koren 2003- • **59** - Bostjan Cesar 2003- • **57** - Marko Simeunovic 1992-2004 • **55** - Samir Handanovic 2004-

Goals
35 - Zlatko Zahovic 1992-2004 • **19** - Milvoje Novakovic 2006- • **16** - Saso Udovic 1993-2000 • **14** - Ermin Siljak 1994-2005 • **13** - Milenko Acimovic 1998-2007 • **10** - Primoz Gliha 1993-98 • **8** - Milan Osterc 1997-2002 • **7** - Tim Matavz 2009-

Past Coaches
Bojan Prasnikar 1991-93 • Zdenko Verdenik 1994-97 • Bojan Prasnikar 1998 • Srecko Katanec 1998-2002 • Bojan Prasnikar 2002-04 • Branko Oblak 2004-06 • Matjaz Kek 2007-11 • Slavisa Stojanovic 2011-

SLOVENIA 2010-11

PRVA LIGA

	Pl	W	D	L	F	A	Pts	Maribor	Domzale	Koper	Olimpija	Gorica	Rudar	Triglav	Celje	Nafta	Primorje
NK Maribor †	36	21	12	3	65	25	**75**		1-1 2-0	2-0 1-1	0-0 2-2	3-1 1-2	3-1 2-1	5-0 3-1	2-0 2-0	3-1 0-1	1-1 2-0
Domzale ‡	36	20	7	9	57	35	**67**	0-1 2-2		2-0 1-2	2-1 3-0	1-0 2-0	2-3 2-0	3-0 3-1	1-0 2-0	1-1 3-2	4-1 1-0
FC Koper ‡	36	17	9	10	57	43	**60**	0-1 3-0	2-0 3-1		2-0 2-1	1-0 2-2	2-1 3-3	1-1 0-1	7-3 1-0	0-3 4-1	4-1 2-1
Olimpija Ljubljana ‡	36	15	10	11	59	43	**55**	0-1 0-0	0-1 0-0	1-2 4-0		0-0 1-0	1-3 2-2	1-0 1-3	1-0 3-1	0-1 2-0	3-0 5-0
ND Gorica	36	13	9	14	42	53	**48**	0-2 0-6	0-3 2-1	2-2 0-0	2-2 1-3		1-1 0-0	2-1 1-0	3-3 1-1	1-0 1-0	3-2 4-1
Rudar Velenje	36	12	10	14	55	47	**46**	0-0 2-4	0-1 3-1	2-1 0-1	1-1 1-3	1-2 0-1		5-0 0-0	3-2 1-0	0-0 4-0	3-1 0-1
Triglav 2000 Kranj	36	10	9	17	38	59	**39**	2-2 1-2	1-3 2-4	0-0 0-0	0-5 1-4	2-0 1-0	1-0 1-4		1-1 0-0	2-0 4-0	3-2 2-0
NK Celje	36	9	10	17	41	55	**37**	0-4 0-0	0-1 0-0	2-1 0-3	1-1 1-3	1-0 3-1	5-1 1-0	1-1 2-0		2-4 3-0	3-0 2-3
Nafta Lendava	36	10	7	19	47	67	**37**	0-2 1-1	3-2 2-3	0-2 2-1	2-3 1-2	3-0 1-4	3-3 1-2	2-1 1-1	2-2 0-0		2-1 1-2
Primorje Ajdovscina	36	8	7	21	40	74	**31**	0-0 1-2	0-0 0-0	3-1 1-1	5-1 2-2	0-2 2-3	1-1 0-6	0-3 1-0	2-0 0-1	4-2 1-4	

16/07/2010 - 29/05/2011 • † Qualified for the UEFA Champions League • ‡ Qualified for the Europa League
Play-off: Not played as 2.SNL champions Aluminij declined promotion as did Interblock and Dravinja. Mura were promoted automatically
Top scorers: **16** - Marcos Tavares BRA, Maribor • **13** - Damir Pekic, Domzale & Milan Osterc, Koper • **11** - Joze Benko, Nafta • **10** - Etien Velikonja, Gorica/Maribor; Vito Plut, Maribor/Gorica & Vedran Vinko, Nafta • **9** - Dragan Cadikovski, Celje/Rudar & Dejan Burgar, Triglav

SLOVENIA 2010-11 — 2.SNL (2)

	Pl	W	D	L	F	A	Pts
Aluminij Kidricevo	27	13	9	5	54	22	**48**
Interblock Ljubljana	27	13	8	6	38	25	**47**
Dravinja Kostroj	27	11	10	6	31	23	**43**
Mura Murska Sobota - P	27	12	5	10	42	37	**41**
Drava Ptuj	27	11	6	10	38	41	**39**
Roltek Dob	27	11	5	11	43	44	**38**
Bela Krajina	27	9	10	8	38	39	**37**
Krsko	27	8	7	12	24	35	**31**
Garmin Sencur	27	4	10	13	37	52	**22**
Smartno	27	6	4	17	31	58	**22**

7/08/2010 - 29/05/2011 • Mura promoted after the top three declined promotion on financial grounds

MEDALS TABLE

		Overall			League			Cup		City
		G	**S**	**B**	**G**	**S**	**B**	**G**	**S**	
1	NK Maribor	15	7	3	9	4	3	6	3	Maribor
2	Olimpija Ljubljana	8	6	1	4	3	1	4	3	Ljubljana
3	ND Gorica	6	5	5	4	4	5	2	1	Nova Gorica
4	NK Domzale	3	4		2	3		1	1	Domzale
5	FC Koper	3	2	3	1	1	3	2	1	Koper
6	Interblock Ljubljana	2						2		Ljubljana
7	NK Celje	1	5	1		1	1	1	4	Celje
8	Mura Murska Sobota	1	3	2		2	2	1	1	Murska Sobota
9	Rudar Velenje	1		3			3	1		Velenje
10	Primorje Ajdovscina		5	1		2	1		3	Ajdovscina
11	Korotan Prevalje		1						1	Prevalje
	Aluminij Kidricevo		1						1	Kidricevo
	NK Dravograd		1						1	Dravograd
14	Izola Belvedur			1		1				Izola

POKAL HERVIS 2010–11

First Round

Team	Score
Domzale	4
Malecnik *	1
Krka *	2
Ankaran	5
NK Celje	2
Krsko *	1
Olimpija Ljubljana	Bye
ND Gorica	Bye
Bistrica *	2
Aluminij Kidricevo	0
Primorje Ajdovscina	4
Dogose *	0
Hotiza	0
Interblock Ljubljana	4
FC Koper	Bye
Garmin Sencur	0
Dravinja Kostroj *	1
Rudar Velenje	3
Trnjenik *	1
Postojna *	0
Triglav Gorenjska	3
Nafta Lendava	4
Brda *	2
Mura Murska Sobota	3
Zavrc *	4
Roltek Dob	4
Drava Ptuj *	2
NK Maribor	Bye

Round of 16

Team	Score
Domzale	6
Ankaran *	1
NK Celje	0
Olimpija Ljubljana *	2
ND Gorica	2
Aluminij Kidricevo *	0
Primorje Ajdovscina	2
Interblock Ljubljana *	3
FC Koper	1
Dravinja Kostroj *	0
Rudar Velenje	1
Triglav Gorenjska *	2
Nafta Lendava	3
Zavrc *	0
Roltek Dob *	1 5p
NK Maribor	1 6p

Quarter-finals

Team	Leg 1	Leg 2
Domzale *	0	4
Olimpija Ljubljana	2	0
ND Gorica	2	0
Interblock Ljubljana *	4	0
FC Koper	0	3
Triglav Gorenjska *	1	0
Nafta Lendava *	1	0
NK Maribor	1	4

Semi-finals

Team	Leg 1	Leg 2
Domzale	0	2
Interblock Ljubljana *	0	0
FC Koper *	1	0
NK Maribor	1	1

Final

Team	Score
Domzale ‡	4
NK Maribor	3

FINAL
Stozice, Ljubljana
25-05-2011, Att: 6015, Ref: Damir Skomina
Scorers - Juninho 24, Pekic 2 40 79, Simunovic 52 for Domzale; Filipovic 16, Beric 56, Mezga 63o for Maribor
Domzale - Nejc Vidmar● - Luka Elsner, Darko Zec● (Darko Topic 70), Ivan Knezovic, Tadej Apatic - Dalibor Teinovic●◆76, Marko Drevensek, Juninho, Mato Simunovic - Mitja Zatkovic● (Rok Hanzic 89), Damir Pekic (Jernej Smukavec 78). Tr: Darko Birjukov
Maribor - Matej Radan● - Mitja Resek●, Aleksander Rajcevic●, Jovan Vidovic, Ales Majer (Etien Velikonja 83) - Mitja Viler, Zeljko Filipovic●, Dejan Mezga, Goran Cvijanovic (Matic Crnic 82) - Marcos Tavares●, Robert Beric. Tr: Darko Milanic

* Home team/home team in the 1st leg ● ‡ Qualified for the Europa League

SWE – SWEDEN

FIFA/COCA-COLA WORLD RANKING

'93	'94	'95	'96	'97	'98	'99	'00	'01	'02	'03	'04	'05	'06	'07	'08	'09	'10	'11	'12
9	3	13	17	18	18	16	23	16	25	19	13	14	14	24	32	42	33	18	

					2011								High	Low	Av
Jan	Feb	Mar	Apr	May	Jun	Jul	Aug	Sep	Oct	Nov	Dec		High	Low	Av
33	29	30	29	28	19	19	18	25	14	18	18		2	43	19

After making it to the finals of the European Championship just once in the first 40 years of the competition - as hosts in 1992 - Sweden made sure of their fourth consecutive appearance after qualifying for the finals of Euro 2012 in Poland and the Ukraine. The Swedes were drawn in a tough qualifying group with the Netherlands but although they finished as runners-up they qualified automatically as the second-placed team with the best record after inflicting a rare defeat on the Dutch in the last group match. Qualifying for the finals may have become a Swedish speciality but coach Erik Hamren will need to raise the stakes if the team are to achieve anything once there. In club football, Helsingborg became the eighth different side to win the championship over the past eight seasons. The team from the south-west built on their 2010 cup triumph by not only winning the league but also by retaining the cup after beating Kalmar 3-1 in the final. Coached by the relatively unknown Conny Karlsson they also won the Super Cup at the start of the year to become the first team to win all three trophies in the same year. Once again Swedish clubs made heavy weather of European competition and although Malmo made it to the group stage of the 2011-12 Europa League they picked up just one point in their six games.

UEFA EUROPEAN CHAMPIONSHIP RECORD

1960 DNE **1964** QF **1968-1988** DNQ **1992** 4 SF (Hosts) **1996** DNQ **2000** 14 r1 **2004** 7 QF **2008** 9 r1 **2012** Qualified

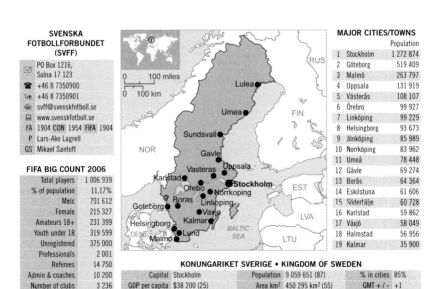

SVENSKA FOTBOLLFORBUNDET (SVFF)

PO Box 1216,
Solna 17 123
☎ +46 8 7350900
📠 +46 8 7350901
✉ svff@svenskfotboll.se
🖥 www.svenskfotboll.se
FA 1904 CON 1954 FIFA 1904
P Lars-Ake Lagrell
GS Mikael Santoft

FIFA BIG COUNT 2006

Total players	1 006 939
% of population	11.17%
Male	701 612
Female	215 327
Amateurs 18+	231 399
Youth under 18	319 599
Unregistered	375 000
Professionals	2 001
Referees	14 750
Admin & coaches	10 200
Number of clubs	3 236
Number of teams	31 000

MAJOR CITIES/TOWNS

		Population
1	Stockholm	1 272 874
2	Göteborg	519 409
3	Malmö	263 797
4	Uppsala	131 919
5	Västerås	108 107
6	Örebro	99 927
7	Linköping	99 229
8	Helsingborg	93 673
9	Jönköping	85 989
10	Norrköping	83 962
11	Umeå	78 448
12	Gävle	69 274
13	Borås	64 364
14	Eskilstuna	61 606
15	Södertälje	60 728
16	Karlstad	59 862
17	Växjö	58 049
18	Halmstad	56 956
19	Kalmar	35 900

KONUNGARIKET SVERIGE • KINGDOM OF SWEDEN

Capital	Stockholm	Population	9 059 651 (87)	% in cities	85%
GDP per capita	$38 200 (25)	Area km²	450 295 km² (55)	GMT +/-	+1
Neighbours (km)	Finland 614, Norway 1619 • Coast 3218				

RECENT INTERNATIONAL MATCHES PLAYED BY SWEDEN

2009	Opponents	Score		Venue	Comp	Scorers	Att	Referee
24-01	USA	L	2-3	Carson	Fr	Nannskog [73], Dahlberg [89]	9 918	Petrescu CAN
28-01	Mexico	W	1-0	Oakland	Fr	Farnerud [52]	46 550	Ward USA
11-02	Austria	W	2-0	Graz	Fr	Elm [58], Kallstrom [63]	11 800	Kassai HUN
28-03	Portugal	D	0-0	Porto	WCq		40 200	De Bleeckere BEL
1-04	Serbia	L	0-2	Belgrade	Fr		17 830	Perez ESP
6-06	Denmark	L	0-1	Stockholm	WCq		33 619	Riley ENG
10-06	Malta	W	4-0	Gothenburg	WCq	Kallstrom [21], Majstorovic [52], Ibrahimovic [56], Berg [58]	25 271	Murray SCO
12-08	Finland	W	1-0	Stockholm	Fr	Elmander [42]	15 212	Fautrel FRA
5-09	Hungary	W	2-1	Budapest	WCq	Mellberg [9], Ibrahimovic [93+]	40 169	Rizzoli ITA
9-09	Malta	W	1-0	Ta'Qali	WCq	Azzopardi OG [82]	4 705	McCourt NIR
10-10	Denmark	L	0-1	Copenhagen	WCq		37 800	Mejuto ESP
14-10	Albania	W	4-1	Stockholm	WCq	Mellberg 2 [6 42], Berg [40], Svensson [86]	25 342	Ivanov.N RUS
18-11	Italy	L	0-1	Cesena	Fr		18 260	Skomina SVN
2010								
20-01	Oman	W	1-0	Muscat	Fr	Svensson [35]	1 000	Shukralla BHR
23-01	Syria	D	1-1	Damascus	Fr	Ranegie [87]	10 000	Najm LIB
3-03	Wales	W	1-0	Swansea	Fr	Elmander [44]	8 258	Black NIR
29-05	Bosnia-Herzegovina	W	4-2	Stockholm	Fr	Toivonen [44], Olsson 2 [68 82], Berg [90]	22 589	Grafe GER
2-06	Belarus	W	1-0	Minsk	Fr	Wilhelmsson [48]	12 000	Nikolaev RUS
11-08	Scotland	W	3-0	Stockholm	Fr	Ibrahimovic [4], Bajrami [39], Toivonen [56]	25 249	Rocchi ITA
3-09	Hungary	W	2-0	Stockholm	ECq	Wernbloom 2 [51 73]	32 304	Atkinson ENG
7-09	San Marino	W	6-0	Malmo	ECq	Ibrahimovic 2 [7 77], OG 2 [11 26], Granqvist [51], Berg [92+]	21 083	McKeon IRL
12-10	Netherlands	L	1-4	Amsterdam	ECq	Granqvist [69]	46 000	Lannoy FRA
17-11	Germany	D	0-0	Gothenburg	Fr		21 959	Velasco ESP
2011								
19-01	Botswana	W	2-1	Cape Town	Fr	Gerndt [30], Svensson [74]	2 000	Hlungwani RSA
22-01	South Africa	D	1-1	Nelspruit	Fr	Hysen [30]		
8-02	Cyprus	W	2-0	Nicosia	Fr	Hysen [26], Berg [45]	2 000	Tudor ROU
9-02	Ukraine	D	1-1	Nicosia	Fr	Elmander [7]. L 4-5p	2 000	Trattou CYP
29-03	Moldova	W	2-1	Stockholm	ECq	Lustig [30], Larsson.S [82]	25 544	Kircher GER
3-06	Moldova	W	4-1	Chisinau	ECq	Toivonen [11], Elmander 2 [30 58], Gerndt [88]	10 500	Marriner ENG
7-06	Finland	W	5-0	Stockholm	ECq	Kallstrom [11], Ibrahimovic 3 [31 35 53], Bajrami [83]	32 128	Gautier FRA
10-08	Ukraine	W	1-0	Kharkov	Fr	Hysen [90]		Tagliavento ITA
2-09	Hungary	L	1-2	Budapest	ECq	Wilhelmsson [60]	23 500	Skomina SVN
6-09	San Marino	W	5-0	Serravalle	ECq	Kallstrom [64], Wilhelmsson 2 [70 93+], Olsson.M [81], Hysen [89]	2 946	McLean SCO
7-10	Finland	W	2-1	Helsinki	ECq	Larsson.S [8], Olsson.M [52]	23 257	Clattenburg ENG
11-10	Netherlands	W	3-2	Stockholm	ECq	Kallstrom [14], Larsson.S [52p], Toivonen [53]	30 066	Cakir TUR
11-11	Denmark	L	0-2	Copenhagen	Fr		18 057	Moen NOR
15-11	England	L	0-1	London	Fr		48 876	Kralovec CZE

Fr = Friendly match • EC = UEFA EURO 2012 • WC = FIFA World Cup • q = qualifier • r1 = first round group • r2 = second round

SWEDEN NATIONAL TEAM HISTORICAL RECORDS

Caps
143 - Thomas Ravelli 1981-97 • 116 - Roland Nilsson 1986-2000 • 115 - Bjorn Nordqvist 1963-78 • 110 - Anders Svensson 1999- • 109 - Niclas Alexandersson 1993-2008 • 106 - Henrik Larsson 1993-2009 • 104 - Olof Mellberg 2000- • 96 - Patrik Andersson 1991-2002 • 94 - Orvar Bergmark 1951-65 • 86 - Teddy Lucic 1995-2006 • 83 - Kennet Andersson 1990-2000 • 80 - Andreas Isaksson 2002- • 78 - Kim Kallstrom 2001- • 77 - Ronnie Hellstrom 1968-80 • 76 - Tobias Linderoth 1999-2008 • 75 - Joachim Bjorklund 1991-2000; Fredrik Ljungberg 1998-2008 & Jonas Thern 1987-97 • 74 - Marcus Allback 1999-2008; Daniel Andersson 1997-2009 & Hakan Mild 1991-2001

Goals
49 - Sven Rydell 1923-32 • 43 - Gunnar Nordahl 1942-48 • 37 - Henrik Larsson 1993-2009 • 32 - Gunnar Gren 1940-58 • 31 - Kennet Andersson 1990-2000 • 29 - Marcus Allback 1999-2008 & Martin Dahlin 1991-2000 • 27 - Agne Simonsson 1957-67 • 26 - Tomas Brolin 1990-95 • 25 - Zlatan Ibrahimovic 2001- • 23 - Per Kaufeldt 1922-29 • 22 - Karl Gustafsson 1908-18 • 21 - Albin Dahl 1920-30 • 20 - Sven Jonasson 1934-40; Erik Persson 1932-39 & Nils-Ake Sandell • 19 - Herbert Karlsson 1919-21 • 18 - Arne Nyberg 1935-46

Past Coaches
Ludvig Kornerup 1908 • Wilhelm Friberg 1909-11 • John Ohlson 1912 • Ruben Gelbord 1912-13 • Hugo Leevin 1914-15 • Frey Svenson 1916 • Anton Johanson 1917-20 • John Pettersson 1921-24 • Jozsef Nagy HUN 1924-27 • John Pettersson 1927-34 • Jozsef Nagy HUN 1934 • John Pettersson 1934-36 • Carl Linde 1937 • Jozsef Nagy HUN 1938 • Gustaf Carlsson 1938-42 • Selection Committee 1942 • Rudolf Kock 1943-46 • George Raynor ENG 1946-54 • Rudolf Kock 1954-56 • George Raynor ENG 1956-58 • Eric Person 1958-61 • George Raynor ENG 1961 • Lennart Nyman 1962-65 • Orvar Bergmark 1966-70 • Georg Ericson 1971-79 • Lars Arnesson 1980-85 • Olle Nordin 1986-90 • Nils Andersson 1990 • Tommy Svensson 1991-97 • Tommy Soderberg 1998-99 • Tommy Soderberg & Lars Lagerback 2000-04 • Lars Lagerback 2004-09 • Erik Hamren 2009-

SWEDEN 2011

ALLSVENSKAN

	Pl	W	D	L	F	A	Pts	Helsingborg	AIK	Elfsborg	Malmö	GAIS	Hacken	IFK Göteborg	Kalmar	Gefle	Mjällby	Djurgården	Orebro	Norrköping	Syrianska	Trelleborg	Halmstad
Helsingborgs IF †	30	18	9	3	55	27	63		1-1	1-0	2-2	1-1	1-1	2-1	1-0	3-0	3-0	3-0	2-0	1-1	1-0	7-3	2-1
AIK Stockholm ‡	30	18	4	8	46	27	58	2-1		0-1	2-0	2-1	2-1	2-0	2-1	0-2	3-0	0-1	1-0	3-0	1-0	3-0	4-0
IF Elfsborg ‡	30	18	3	9	52	32	57	3-2	2-2		3-0	1-3	2-1	3-2	0-0	3-0	4-0	2-1	3-0	2-1	2-1	3-0	3-2
Malmö FF	30	15	9	6	37	30	54	**0-3**	1-1	2-1		2-1	1-0	0-2	2-0	0-0	1-0	1-0	2-1	2-1	1-0	1-1	3-1
GAIS Göteborg	30	16	3	11	47	34	51	1-3	2-0	0-2	2-0		1-0	1-0	1-0	2-3	3-0	2-1	4-1	1-2	1-0	4-0	2-1
BK Hacken Göteborg	30	14	7	9	52	32	49	1-1	3-1	2-0	1-1	2-0		3-1	1-2	0-0	6-0	2-0	1-2	2-2	4-0	1-0	3-1
IFK Göteborg	30	13	6	11	42	34	45	1-2	3-1	1-1	0-0	2-1	2-2		2-0	3-0	0-1	0-4	0-1	1-1	3-0	1-1	3-1
Kalmar FF ‡	30	13	5	12	39	34	44	1-2	1-0	2-1	1-2	2-1	2-0	0-0		0-0	0-3	3-2	4-1	5-0	2-0	3-2	1-0
Gefle IF	30	10	11	9	31	39	41	2-0	0-3	1-0	2-0	1-3	2-2	1-0	1-1		0-0	0-0	0-1	2-0	2-1	1-2	2-1
Mjällby AIF	30	12	4	14	33	39	40	0-1	0-2	2-1	1-1	1-1	1-2	0-2	1-0	5-1		3-0	2-1	0-0	3-0	0-1	2-0
Djurgårdens IF	30	10	6	14	36	40	36	1-1	0-0	0-1	0-1	2-2	1-0	1-2	2-1	1-1	1-0		0-2	1-3	3-0	4-3	2-0
Orebro SK	30	11	3	16	36	46	36	1-1	1-2	0-3	1-2	3-1	4-0	0-2	1-2	2-3	0-2	1-2		2-0	1-0	4-2	1-0
IFK Norrköping	30	9	7	14	32	49	34	0-0	0-1	2-1	0-0	2-0	0-1	2-2	1-2	1-1	0-3	2-1	0-2		2-1	2-1	2-0
Syrianska FC	30	8	4	18	27	44	28	1-2	**3-0**	0-2	0-0	0-2	1-5	1-2	2-1	1-1	3-1	0-0	3-1	3-0		4-1	0-0
Trelleborgs IF	30	7	4	19	39	64	25	1-3	1-2	3-0	2-4	0-1	1-4	2-0	3-2	2-0	1-2	3-2	1-1	1-2	0-1		0-1
Halmstads BK	30	3	5	22	24	58	14	1-2	1-3	1-2	1-5	0-2	0-1	1-2	0-0	2-2	1-0	1-3	0-0	5-4	0-1	1-1	

2/04/2011 - 23/10/2011 • † Qualified for the UEFA Champions League • ‡ Qualified for the Europa League • Matches in bold awarded
Relegation play-off: Angelholm 2-1 1-3 **Syrianska**
Top scorers: **21** - Mathias Ranegie, Häcken/Malmö • **16** - Tobias Hysen, IFK Göteborg • **15** - Teteh Bangura SLE, AIK Stockholm • **14** - Mervan Celik, GAIS Göteborg • **10** - Lasse Nilsson, Elsborg; Wanderson BRA, GAIS Göteborg & Mikael Dahlberg, Gefle

MEDALS TABLE

		Overall			League			Cup			Europe			City
		G	S	B	G	S	B	G	S	B	G	S	B	
1	Malmö FF	30	19	6	16	15	6	14	3			1		Malmö
2	IFK Göteborg	25	16	14	18	10	13	5	6		2	1		Gothenburg
3	AIK Stockholm	19	20	9	11	13	9	8	7					Solna, Stockholm
4	IFK Norrköping	18	14	4	12	10	4	6	4					Norrköping
5	Djurgårdens IF	15	14	8	11	11	8	4	3					Stockholm
6	Örgryte IS Göteborg	15	6	5	14	5	5	1	1					Gothenburg
7	Helsingborgs IF	12	12	8	7	10	8	5	2					Helsingborg
8	IF Elfsborg Borås	7	9	5	5	6	5	2	3					Borås
9	GAIS Göteborg	7	5	3	6	4	3	1	1					Gothenburg
10	Östers IF Växjö	5	7	4	4	3	4	1	4					Växjö

SWEDEN 2011

SUPERETTAN (2)

	Pl	W	D	L	F	A	Pts	Atvidaberg	Sundsvall	Angelholm	Oster	Degerfors	Bro'pojkarna	Falkenbergs	Ljungskile	Assyriska	Landskrona	Hammarby	Jönköping	Värnamo	Brage	Västerås	Qviding
Atvidabergs FF	30	18	3	9	58	31	57		2-0	5-0	0-1	1-2	2-1	4-0	2-2	2-1	1-0	3-1	2-1	5-2	2-0	4-0	4-0
GIF Sundsvall	30	16	7	7	61	29	55	0-1		6-0	2-1	3-0	0-0	4-0	3-0	1-2	2-0	3-3	3-0	2-2	5-0	2-2	4-0
Angelholms FF	30	15	8	7	47	40	53	2-0	1-1		3-0	3-0	3-2	3-2	1-1	2-1	1-2	0-1	2-4	1-1	1-1	3-1	0-0
Osters IF Växjö	30	14	8	8	40	28	50	1-2	0-1	0-2		0-1	2-0	1-0	3-2	4-2	2-3	0-0	2-1	2-0	3-1	0-0	2-1
Degerfors IF	30	14	6	10	53	44	48	1-2	0-2	1-3	3-3		1-0	1-3	2-3	2-3	2-0	3-2	6-1	2-0	5-0	4-1	3-0
IF Brommapojkarna	30	14	5	11	50	38	47	2-2	1-3	0-1	1-0	3-3		2-1	3-1	1-3	1-1	1-0	1-1	1-3	3-0	4-1	4-0
Falkenbergs FF	30	14	3	13	50	43	45	0-2	2-4	1-0	0-4	4-0	1-3		2-0	4-0	5-1	1-1	1-2	4-0	0-2	3-4	3-0
Ljungskile SK	30	12	6	12	48	39	42	1-2	3-1	1-2	0-0	1-3	0-1	1-0		0-0	4-1	2-3	5-1	1-2	5-0	2-1	
Assyriska FF	30	12	5	13	39	41	41	2-0	0-1	2-2	0-0	1-1	0-2	2-1	1-0		1-2	1-0	0-1	3-2	0-2		0-1
Landskrona BoIS	30	11	8	11	36	39	41	3-2	1-2	0-0	1-0	0-0	0-2	0-2	0-0	2-3		3-0	1-0	1-1	1-2	2-1	3-0
Hammarby IF	30	11	7	12	37	40	40	2-0	1-3	0-1	2-1	1-2	1-2	0-0	1-3	0-0	2-1		5-2	1-0	1-0	3-1	2-1
Jönköpings Sodra	30	12	4	14	44	53	40	1-0	2-1	3-0	0-3	0-1	4-2	2-2	2-1	1-1	0-2	0-2		2-3	3-0	5-1	1-0
IFK Värnamo	30	10	9	11	43	51	39	3-3	3-0	1-1	0-1	0-0	2-1	0-2	0-2	3-2	3-1	1-0	2-4		3-1	2-3	0-0
IK Brage	30	7	10	13	30	50	31	1-0	0-0	1-4	0-0	1-1	0-2	2-2	1-1	3-0	0-1	0-0	1-2	2-2		2-0	2-2
Västerås SK	30	7	7	16	39	66	28	0-2	0-0	1-2	1-1	3-5	1-0	1-2	0-1	0-2	3-3	1-2	4-2	2-2	2-1		2-2
Qviding FF	30	1	8	21	17	63	11	1-3	0-2	1-3	0-1	1-0	0-2	0-1	1-4	0-5	1-1	2-2	1-1	0-2	1-2	0-1	

9/04/2011 - 22/10/2011 • Top scorers: **18** - Branimir Hrgota, Jönköpings • **17** - Peter Samuelsson, Degerfors • **15** - Magnus Eriksson, Atvidaberg
Relegation play-offs: IF Sylvia 1-3 2-4 **IK Brage** • Väsby United 0-2 0-1 **IFK Värnamo**

SVENSKA CUPEN 2011

Third Round

Team	Score
Helsingborgs IF	4
Landskrona BoIS*	2
FC Trollhättan*	1
Trelleborgs IF	2
IF Brommapojkarna*	3
Gefle IF	1
IFK Värnamo*	0
IF Elfsborg	1
Atvidabergs FF*	3
AIK Stockholm	0
BK Häcken Göteborg	0 2p
Osters IF Växjö*	0 4p
GAIS Göteborg	3
GIF Sundsvall*	2
Ljungskile SK*	2 2p
Orebro SK	2 4p
IFK Göteborg	6
IF Limhamn/Bunkeflo*	2
IFK Luleå	1 2p
Djurgårdens IF	1 4p
Vasalunds IF*	2
Mjällby AIF	1
Syrianska FC	0 2p
Falkenbergs FF*	0 4p
Malmö FF	4
Jönköpings Södra*	0
Karlstad BK*	1
Halmstads BK	4
IFK Norrköping	3
BKV Norrtälje*	0
IK Sirius*	0
Kalmar FF	1

Fourth Round

Team	Score
Helsingborgs IF*	2
Trelleborgs IF	1
IF Brommapojkarna*	1
IF Elfsborg*	3
Atvidabergs FF*	2
Osters IF Växjö	1
GAIS Göteborg	0
Orebro SK*	1
IFK Göteborg*	3
Djurgårdens IF	0
Vasalunds IF*	0 4p
Falkenbergs FF	0 5p
Malmö FF	3
Halmstads BK*	0
IFK Norrköping*	0
Kalmar FF	2

Quarter-finals

Team	Score
Helsingborgs IF*	2
IF Elfsborg	0
Atvidabergs FF*	0
Orebro SK	3
IFK Göteborg	3
Falkenbergs FF*	2
Malmö FF	1 3p
Kalmar FF*	1 4p

Semi-finals

Team	Score
Helsingborgs IF	3
Orebro SK*	1
IFK Göteborg*	3
Kalmar FF	4

Final

Team	Score
Helsingborgs IF*	3
Kalmar FF ‡	1

FINAL

Olympia, Helsingborg, 5-11-2011
Att: 9513, Ref: Markus Strömbergsson
Scorers - Santos 26, Mahlangu 55, Andersson 80p for Helsingborg; Israelsson 45 for Kalmar
Helsingborg - Pär Hansson (c) - Joseph Baffo (Mattias Lindström 61), Marcus Holgersson, Erlend Hanstveit, Erik Wahlstedt - Christoffer Andersson, Ardian Gashi•, May Mahlangu, Rachid Bouaouzan - Thomas Sorum (Erik Sundin 68), Alvaro Santos (Hannu Patronen 80). Tr: Conny Karlsson
Kalmar - Petter Wasta•- Mattias Johansson, Tobias Carlsson, Markus Thorbjornsson, Stefan Larsson - Tobias Eriksson, Henrik Rydström (c), Erik Israelsson•- Daniel Sobralense••♦86, Ricardo Santos (Mans Söderqvist 81), Daniel Mendes (Abiola Dauda 82). Tr: Nanne Bergstrand

* Home team • ‡ Qualified for the Europe League

SWZ – SWAZILAND

FIFA/COCA-COLA WORLD RANKING

'93	'94	'95	'96	'97	'98	'99	'00	'01	'02	'03	'04	'05	'06	'07	'08	'09	'10	'11	'12
99	125	148	160	165	149	127	137	132	116	114	126	134	148	148	138	135	160	180	

	2011												High	Low	Av
	Jan	Feb	Mar	Apr	May	Jun	Jul	Aug	Sep	Oct	Nov	Dec			
	159	158	159	158	159	157	169	172	169	175	179	180	92	180	137

Swaziland had a disappointing year winning just a solitary international friendly and losing all their competitive matches. That meant that by the end of 2011 the team had slumped to an all-time low of 180 in the FIFA/Coca-Cola World Ranking. They lost in all six group matches in the 2012 CAF Africa Cup of Nations qualifiers and were the eliminated at the first stage of the 2014 FIFA World Cup qualifiers. Swaziland did put up some fight, notably a game performance away against Ghana in Accra where they lost 2-0 in September. But they were beaten at home by Sudan and Congo. In November, they went 3-1 down at home to the Democratic Republic of Congo in the first leg of their FIFA World Cup qualifier and then 5-1 away in the return. The national team, Sihlangu, went through three coaches during the year, starting with Musa Zwane, who was replaced in May by Obed Mlotsa and then in November for the FIFA World Cup qualifiers by Caleb Ngwenya. As a result of the poor performances Swaziland withdrew from the 2013 CAF Africa Cup of Nations qualifiers. Green Mamba won a first-ever league title, but by the narrowest of margins as they edged Manzini Wanderers on the number of goal scored at the end of the season. Royal Leopards won the Cup Final, beating Mhlambanyatsi Rovers 4-3 after extra-time.

CAF AFRICA CUP OF NATIONS RECORD

1957-1984 DNE **1986** DNQ **1988** DNE **1990-1992** DNQ **1994-1998** DNE **2000-2012** DNQ **2013** DNE

NATIONAL FOOTBALL ASSOCIATION OF SWAZILAND (NFAS)

Sigwaca House, Plot 582,
Sheffield Road, PO Box 641,
Mbabane H100

☎ +268 24046852
📠 +268 24046206
✉ info@nfas.org.sz
🖥 www.nfas.org.sz
FA 1968 CON 1976 FIFA 1978
P Adam Mthethwa
GS Frederick Mngomezulu

FIFA BIG COUNT 2006

Total players	54 900
% of population	4.83%
Male	54 900
Female	0
Amateurs 18+	3 300
Unregistered	3 900
Professionals	0
Referees	100
Admin & coaches	800
Number of clubs	60
Number of teams	220

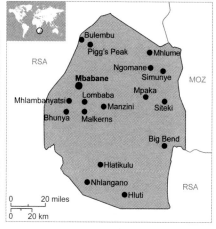

MAJOR CITIES/TOWNS

		Population
1	Manzini	93 374
2	Mbabane	61 391
3	Malkerns	7 902
4	Nhlangano	6 991
5	Mhlume	6 876
6	Big Bend	6 835
7	Siteki	5 910
8	Simunye	5 520
9	Hluti	5 387
10	Pigg's Peak	4 548
11	Ngomane	3 824
12	Lobamba	3 736
13	Mpaka	3 571
14	Vuvulane	3 522
15	Kwalusenl	2 784
16	Bulembu	2 321
17	Hlatikulu	2 271
18	Bhunya	2 187
19	Mhlambanyatsi	2 167

UMBUSO WESWATINI • KINGDOM OF SWAZILAND

Capital	Mbabane	Population	1 123 913 (156)	% in cities 25%
GDP per capita	$4400 (151)	Area km²	17 364 km² (158)	GMT +/- +1
Neighbours (km)	Mozambique 105, South Africa 430		

RECENT INTERNATIONAL MATCHES PLAYED BY SWAZILAND

2006	Opponents	Score		Venue	Comp	Scorers	Att	Referee
26-08	Lesotho	W	3-1	Mbabane	Fr	Mduduzi Mdluli 2 [28] [49], Salebona Jele [64]		
3-09	Angola	L	0-2	Mbabane	CNq			Maillet SEY
7-10	Eritrea	D	0-0	Asmara	CNq			Gasingwa RWA
15-11	Botswana	L	0-1	Gaborone	Fr			
2007								
13-02	Lesotho	W	1-0	Maseru	Fr	Bheki Msimango [5]		
18-03	Lesotho	L	0-1	Lobamba	Fr			
25-03	Kenya	L	0-2	Nairobi	CNq			Seechurn MRI
26-05	Mauritius	D	0-0	Mbabane	CCr1	L 5-6p		Labrosse SEY
27-05	Malawi	W	1-0	Mbabane	CCr1	Mphile Tsabedze [85]		Labrosse SEY
3-06	Kenya	D	0-0	Mbabane	CNq			Katjimune NAM
17-06	Angola	L	0-3	Luanda	CNq			Marange ZIM
9-09	Eritrea	D	0-0	Manzini	CNq			Ssegonga UGA
18-11	Malawi	L	0-3	Manzini	Fr			
2008								
9-02	Botswana	L	1-4	Mbabane	Fr	Tony Tsabedze [77]		
10-02	Lesotho	D	2-2	Mbabane	Fr	Barry Steenkamp [48], Baiano Kunene [58]. L 1-4p		
23-05	Lesotho	D	1-1	Mbabane	Fr	Felix Badenhorst [20]		
8-06	Togo	W	2-1	Mbabane	WCq	Siza Dlamini [55], Collen Salelwako [73]	5 819	Niyongabo BDI
15-06	Zambia	D	0-0	Mbabane	WCq		7 462	Kotey GHA
21-06	Zambia	L	0-1	Chililabombwe	WCq		14 458	Marange ZIM
19-07	Madagascar	D	1-1	Witbank	CCr1	Phinda Dlamini [39]		Nhlapo RSA
21-07	Mauritius	D	1-1	Witbank	CCr1	Gcina Mazibuko [51]		Nhlapo RSA
23-07	Seychelles	W	1-0	Witbank	CCr1	Mfanzile Dlamini [89]		Katjimune NAM
20-08	Mozambique	L	0-3	Maputo	Fr			
11-10	Togo	L	0-6	Accra	WCq		8 000	Evehe CMR
2009								
19-06	Lesotho	D	1-1	Manzini	Fr	Mxolisi Mthethwa [74]		
21-06	Lesotho	D	1-1	Lobamba	Fr	Mfanafuthi Bhembe [83]		
6-07	Malawi	L	1-3	Blantyre	Fr	Thokozani Mkhulisi [77p]		
12-08	Mozambique	L	0-1	Maputo	Fr			
5-09	Namibia	D	1-1	Windhoek	Fr	Mxolisi Mthethwa [38]		
18-10	Seychelles	W	2-1	Bulawayo	CCr1	Mathokoza Twala [72], Mfanzile Dlamini [74]		Carvalho ANG
20-10	Botswana	L	0-1	Bulawayo	CCr1			Seechurn MRI
22-10	Comoros	W	3-0	Bulawayo	CCr1	Mathokoza Twala [37], Mxolisi Mthethwa [46], Mfanzile Dlamini [67]		Carvalho ANG
2010								
11-08	Mozambique	L	1-2	Maputo	Fr	Siza Dlamini [29]		
5-09	Ghana	L	0-3	Lobamba	CNq			Seechurn MRI
10-10	Congo	L	1-3	Brazzaville	CNq	Darren Christie [37]		Ssegonga UGA
27-10	Botswana	L	0-2	Lobatse	Fr			
2011								
9-02	Zambia	L	0-4	Manzini	Fr			
27-03	Sudan	L	0-3	Omdurman	CNq			
25-05	Botswana	D	0-0	Manzini	Fr			
29-05	Malawi	D	1-1	Manzini	Fr	Sidumo Shongwe [69]		
5-06	Sudan	L	1-2	Manzini	CNq	Manqoba Kunene [80]		
31-07	Botswana	L	0-2	Pretoria	Fr			
20-08	Lesotho	D	0-0	Maseru	Fr			
22-08	Lesotho	W	1-0	Maseru	Fr	Mbuso Gina [30]		
2-09	Ghana	L	0-2	Accra	CNq			
8-10	Congo	L	0-1	Lobamba	CNq			
11-11	Congo DR	L	1-3	Lobamba	WCq	Sidumo Shongwe [63]	785	Sikazwe ZAM
15-11	Congo DR	L	1-5	Kinshasa	WCq	Sidumo Shongwe [63]	24 000	Moukoko CGO

Fr = Friendly match • CN = CAF African Cup of Nations • CC = COSAFA Castle Cup • WC = FIFA World Cup • q = qualifier • r1 = first round group

SWAZILAND 2010–11

MTN PREMIER LEAGUE

	Pl	W	D	L	F	A	Pts	Green Mamba	Wanderers	M Sundowns	Highlanders	Swallows	Leopards	Buffaloes	Chiefs	Hellenic	Pirates	Umbelebele	H Sundowns	Rovers	Eleven Men
Green Mamba †	26	15	5	6	52	26	50		1-1	0-0	4-2	1-2	2-0	3-0	1-3	3-0	0-1	2-3	2-1	2-1	2-1
Manzini Wanderers	26	14	8	4	49	23	50	1-0		3-0	1-1	1-2	2-0	2-1	1-2	3-2	3-0	3-1	1-2	2-0	2-1
Manzini Sundowns	26	12	8	6	34	21	44	0-0	1-1		2-2	2-1	1-0	1-0	0-0	2-0	3-0	0-0	0-1	1-1	3-1
Mbabane Highlanders	26	11	8	7	37	31	41	0-0	1-1	1-0		1-3	0-1	1-1	2-2	1-2	1-0	2-1	2-1	1-0	3-1
Mbabane Swallows	26	11	7	8	51	36	40	1-2	1-1	2-1	1-2		1-1	1-1	2-2	5-1	2-1	0-0	0-1	2-0	2-3
Royal Leopards ‡	26	11	6	9	35	26	39	1-2	1-1	2-0	2-0	2-1		0-2	1-2	5-1	0-2	1-2	3-0	2-1	1-0
Young Buffaloes	26	9	9	8	38	28	36	0-4	1-1	0-0	1-2	4-1	0-1		1-1	1-0	1-1	4-0	2-1	1-1	5-0
Malanti Chiefs	26	8	11	7	37	34	35	1-3	0-2	2-4	1-2	2-2	1-1	3-2		2-3	2-2	0-0	0-1	1-1	3-0
Hellenic FC	26	11	2	13	33	44	35	0-1	1-3	2-0	1-0	0-2	1-1	0-4	0-2		4-1	1-0	4-1	2-3	0-2
Moneni Pirates	26	10	4	12	24	32	34	1-0	0-1	0-2	0-3	2-1	0-1	1-0	0-1	0-2		1-0	0-0	2-3	0-0
Umbelebele	26	8	7	11	34	39	31	1-1	2-2	2-5	2-1	2-3	1-0	1-2	1-0	0-1	1-2		6-0	2-2	3-2
Hub Sundowns	26	7	8	11	25	52	29	1-2	0-6	0-3	1-1	2-8	0-5	1-1	0-0	0-0	0-2	1-1		2-1	3-0
Mhlambanyatsi Rovers	26	5	10	11	30	41	25	2-4	2-1	0-1	0-3	1-1	2-2	1-1	0-0	1-2	0-2	2-0	2-2		2-1
Eleven Men in Flight	26	2	3	21	22	68	9	2-10	0-3	0-2	1-2	0-4	1-1	0-2	2-4	1-3	1-3	1-2	0-2	1-1	

22/08/2010 - 22/05/2011 • † Qualified for the CAF Champions League • ‡ Qualified for the CAF Confederation Cup

SWAZILAND 2010–11 NATIONAL FIRST DIVISION (2)

	Pl	W	D	L	F	A	Pts
Tambankulu Callies	20	15	3	2	37	10	48
Masibini Red Lions	20	13	2	5	46	23	41
Manzini Sea Birds	20	11	3	6	36	20	36
Midas City	18	10	4	4	38	11	34
Bush Bucks	19	10	4	5	32	18	34
Illovo FC	20	8	4	8	33	27	28
Motshane FC	19	7	6	6	37	24	27
RSSC United	19	7	6	6	40	28	27
Magwanyane FC	19	5	9	5	15	15	24
Luhleko FC	19	7	3	9	26	29	24
Kontshingila United	19	5	3	11	24	38	18
Manchester United	20	4	4	12	25	40	16
Russian Bombers	20	4	4	12	25	43	16
Mfishane Never Die	20	1	3	16	19	73	6

22/08/2010 - 22/05/2011

MEDALS TABLE

		Overall G	Lge G	Cup G	City/Town
1	Mbabane Highlanders	19	12	7	Mbabane
2	Manzini Wanderers	7	6	1	Manzini
3	Mbabane Swallows	5	3	2	Mbabane
4	Eleven Men in Flight	5	2	3	Siteki
	Manzini Sundowns	5	2	3	Manzini
6	Royal Leopards	5	3	2	Simunye
7	Mhlambanyatsi Rovers	2	1	1	Mhlambanyatsi
	Bulembu Young Aces	2		2	Bulembu
	Moneni Pirates	2		2	Manzini
	Green Mamba	2	1	1	Matsapha
11	Peacemakers	1	1		Mhlume
	Young Buffaloes	1	1		Matsapha
	Hub Sundowns	1		1	
	Malanti Chiefs	1		1	Pigg's Peak
	Mhlume United	1		1	Mhlume

SWAZI BANK CUP 2011

Round of 16		Quarter-finals		Semi-finals		Final	
Royal Leopards	2						
Green Mamba	0	Royal Leopards	2				
Nhlangano Sun	1	Midas Mbabane City	0				
Midas Mbabane City	5			Royal Leopards †	2 0 4p		
Mbabane Swallows	1 5p			Umbelebele	1 0 3p		
Masibini Red Lions	1 3p	Mbabane Swallows	0				
Manzini Wanderers	1	Umbelebele	2				
Umbelebele	7					Royal Leopards ‡	4
Young Buffaloes	2 4p					Mhlambanyatsi Rovers	3
Tambankulu Callies	2 3p	Young Buffaloes	1				
Ludzeludze Killers	0	Moneni Pirates	0				
Moneni Pirates	2			Young Buffaloes	1		
Hub Sundowns	1			Mhlambanyatsi Rovers	2		
Russian Bombers	0	Hub Sundowns	0				
Manzini Sea Birds	1	Mhlambanyatsi Rovers	1				
Mhlambanyatsi Rovers	3						

CUP FINAL

Somhlolo, Mbabane, 3-04-2011
Scorers - Barry Steenkamp 9, Mfanzile Dlamini 48, Mathokoza Thwala 60, Juries Gama 96 for Leopards; Mbuso Gina 2 19 67, Sabelo Sangweni 75 for Rovers

† 1st match abandoned 87' • ‡ Qualified for the CAF Confederation Cup

SYR – SYRIA

FIFA/COCA-COLA WORLD RANKING

'93	'94	'95	'96	'97	'98	'99	'00	'01	'02	'03	'04	'05	'06	'07	'08	'09	'10	'11	'12
82	105	136	115	98	84	109	100	90	91	85	85	98	112	107	105	91	107	114	

	2011													
	Jan	Feb	Mar	Apr	May	Jun	Jul	Aug	Sep	Oct	Nov	Dec	High	Low	Av
	110	104	108	104	104	109	104	97	109	106	115	114	78	145	101

Of all the countries affected by the political change brought about by the Arab Spring, Syria has been perhaps the hardest hit along with Libya. Unsurprisingly, football has had to take a back seat and the league was suspended in March 2011. The national team struggled on briefly but any hopes of building on an encouraging performance at the finals of the AFC Asian Cup in early 2011 were destroyed by an administrative error that saw the national team expelled from the qualifying tournament for the 2014 FIFA World Cup. Punished by FIFA for fielding an ineligible player in their home-and-away win over Tajikistan, the Syrians were not permitted to advance to the third phase of qualifying for Brazil 2014. The incident revolved around striker George Mourad, a Sweden-born player of Syrian decent who had previously represented the land of his birth in a friendly match. On investigation, the Syrian Football Association had not received the required clearance from FIFA to allow Muroud to play and the fixture was awarded to Tajikistan on appeal. The Asian Football Confederation decreed that Syria was unsafe to host games at national or club level, with matches in the final phase of qualifying for the London Olympics and the group stages of the AFC Cup shifted to Amman, the capital of neighbouring Jordan.

FIFA WORLD CUP RECORD
1930-1954 DNE 1958 DNQ 1962-1970 DN E 1974 DNQ 1978 DNE 1982-2010 DNQ

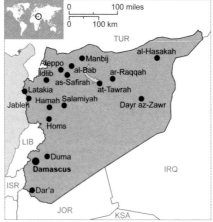

SYRIAN FOOTBALL ASSOCIATION (SFA)

Al Faihaa Sports Complex,
PO Box 421,
Damascus
☎ +963 11 4330451
📠 +963 11 3331511
✉ syrianfa@gmail.com
🖥 www.syrian-soccer.com
FA 1936 CON 1970 FIFA 1937
P Salah Edeen Ramadan
GS Toufik Sarhan

FIFA BIG COUNT 2006

Total players	430 800
% of population	2.28%
Male	430 800
Female	0
Amateurs 18+	4 700
Youth under 18	29 700
Unregistered	214 200
Professionals	0
Referees	700
Admin & coaches	3 600
Number of clubs	170
Number of teams	760

MAJOR CITIES/TOWNS
Population

1	Aleppo	1 693 803
2	Damascus	1 614 297
3	Homs	869 718
4	Hamah	530 994
5	Latakia	366 566
6	Dayr az-Zawr	283 434
7	ar-Raqqah	196 529
8	al-Bab	159 784
9	Idlib	157 427
10	Duma	123 494
11	as-Safirah	117 831
12	Salamiyah	110 042
13	al-Hajar al-Aswad	105 060
14	Tartus	96 401
15	at-Tawrah	95 496
16	al-Qamisl	89 873
17	Ma'arrat-al-Numan	87 742
18	al-Hasakah	82 097
19	Jableh	78 163

AL JUMHURIYAH AL ARABIYAH AS SURIYAH • SYRIAN ARAB REPUBLIC

Capital Damascus	Population 20 178 485 (57)	% in cities 54%
GDP per capita $4600 (146)	Area km² 185 180 km² (88)	GMT + / - +2
Neighbours (km) Iraq 605, Israel 76, Jordan 375, Lebanon 375, Turkey 822 • Coast 193		

RECENT INTERNATIONAL MATCHES PLAYED BY SYRIA

2009	Opponents	Score	Venue	Comp	Scorers	Att	Referee
14-01	China PR	W 3-2	Aleppo	ACq	Maher Al Said 2 8p 24, Firas Al Khatib 39p	7 000	Torky IRN
18-01	Turkmenistan	W 5-1	Kuwait City	Fr	Ali Diab 42, Raja Rafe 53, Tarab Bakri 67, Firas Al Khatib 2 70 83		
23-01	Kuwait	W 3-2	Kuwait City	Fr	Raja Rafe 29p, Feras Ismael 52, Firas Al Khatib 65		
28-01	Lebanon	W 2-0	Saida	ACq	Jehad Alhoussain 37, Firas Al Khatib 77	300	Balideh QAT
1-02	Korea Republic	D 1-1	Dubai	Fr	Yehya Al Rashed 90		Aljunaibi UAE
21-03	Qatar	L 1-2	Aleppo	Fr	Majed Al Haj 79		
27-06	Haiti	W 2-1	Montreal	Fr	Mohamed Al Zeno 8, Firas Al Khatib 26		
20-08	Kyrgyzstan	W 2-0	New Delhi	Fr	Mohamed Al Zeno 9, Abdul Al Agha 72		Patwal IND
24-08	Sri Lanka	W 4-0	New Delhi	Fr	Mohamed Al Zeno 26, Abdulrazak Al Hussein 33, Abdul Al Agha 2 37 55		Patwal IND
27-08	Lebanon	W 1-0	New Delhi	Fr	Mohamed Al Zeno 23		Arumughan IND
29-08	India	W 1-0	New Delhi	Fr	Ali Diab 18		Ali Adil MDV
31-08	India	D 1-1	New Delhi	Fr	Ali Diab 123+ L 4-5p	20 000	Ali Adil MDV
26-10	Kuwait	L 0-1	Al Jahra	Fr			
8-11	Thailand	D 1-1	Bangkok	Fr	Raja Rafe 35p		
14-11	Vietnam	W 1-0	Hanoi	ACq	Raja Rafe 94+	30 000	Williams AUS
18-11	Vietnam	D 0-0	Aleppo	ACq		19 000	Al Hilali OMA
2010							
6-01	China PR	D 0-0	Zheijang	ACq		29 570	Toma JPN
23-01	Sweden	D 1-1	Damascus	Fr	Raja Rafe 5	10 000	Najm LIB
19-02	Kuwait	D 1-1	Al Ain	Fr	Abdelrazaq Al Hussain 81		
3-03	Lebanon	W 4-0	Damascus	ACq	Mohamed Al Zeno 4, Abdul Al Agha 10, Jehad Alhoussain 47, Abdelrazaq Al Hussain 60	16 000	Kim Dong Jin KOR
3-09	Kuwait	L 0-3	Kuwait City	Fr			
7-09	Yemen	L 1-2	Sana'a	Fr	Adib Barakat 29		
24-09	Jordan	D 1-1	Amman	WAr1	Mohamed Al Zeno 82	18 000	
26-09	Kuwait	L 1-2	Amman	WAr1	Ahmad Al Omaier 83	1 500	
8-10	China PR	L 1-2	Kunming	Fr	Adel Abdullah 60		
14-11	Bahrain	W 2-0	Riffa	Fr	Mohamed Al Zeno 48, Oday Jaffal 78		
18-12	Iraq	W 1-0	Sulaymaniyah	Fr	Taha Dyab 86		
22-12	Iraq	L 0-1	Damascus	Fr			
30-12	Korea Republic	L 0-1	Abu Dhabi	Fr		500	Al Marzouqi UAE
2011							
2-01	UAE	L 0-2	Al Ain	Fr		2 400	Abdul BAKI OMA
9-01	Saudi Arabia	W 2-1	Al Rayyan	ACr1	Abdelrazaq Al Hussain 2 38 63	15 768	Kim Dong Jin KOR
13-01	Japan	L 1-2	Doha	ACr1	Firas Al Khatib 76p	10 453	Torky IRN
17-01	Jordan	L 1-2	Doha	ACr1	Mohamed Al Zeno 15	9 849	Abdou QAT
29-06	Iraq	W 2-1	Arbil	Fr	Abdelrazaq Al Hussain 15, Nadim Sabagh 75		
5-07	Jordan	W 3-1	Istanbul	Fr	Feras Ismail 25, Abdelrazaq Al Hussain 40, Maher Al Sayed 88		
15-07	Oman	D 1-1	Seeb	Fr	Feras Ismail 85		
23-07	Tajikistan	L 0-3	Amman	WCq	Orig W 2-1. George Mourad 45, Raja Rafe 77	2 500	Al Ghafari JOR
28-07	Tajikistan	L 0-3	Tursunzade	WCq	Orig W 4-0. Raja Rafe 2 6 35, Nadim Sabagh 53, OG 86		Mashentsev KGZ
10-08	Kazakhstan	D 1-1	Astana	Fr	Nadim Sabagh 63		
17-08	Lebanon	W 3-2	Saida	Fr	Burhan Sahyouni 23, Maher Al Sayed 79, Nadim Sabagh 53		

Fr = Friendly match • WA = West Asian Championship • WG = West Asian Games • AC = AFC Asian Cup • WC = FIFA World Cup
q = qualifier • r1 = first round group • sf = semi-final • 3p = third place play-off • f = final

SYRIA NATIONAL TEAM HISTORICAL RECORDS

Past Coaches: Jalal Talebi IRN 2001-02 • Janusz Wojcik 2003 • Ahmed Rifaat EGY 2003-04 • Miloslav Radenovic SRB 2005-06 • Fajr Ibrahim 2006-08 • Mohamed Qwayed 2008 • Fajr Ibrahim 2008-10 • Ayman Hakeem 2010 • Ratomir Dujkovic SRB 2010 • Tita Valeriu ROU 2010-11 • Claude Le Roy FRA 2011 • Nizar Mahrous 2011

SYRIA 2010-11

PREMIER DIVISION

	Pl	W	D	L	F	A	Pts	Wahda	Karama	Jaish	Ittihad	Shorta	Nwair	Teshrin	Hottin	Wathba	Jazira	Foutoua	Umayya	Taliya	Majd
Al Wahda	15	8	5	2	24	12	29			2-1	1-1		2-0	1-0	4-1	1-1		4-1			1-0
Al Karama	15	8	4	3	24	15	28	2-1			1-0	1-1			3-2	1-1	3-0	1-0	2-1		
Al Jaish	15	8	2	5	17	11	26		1-0			1-0	0-1		1-2	1-0	1-0			1-0	4-0
Al Ittihad	15	7	4	4	21	13	25			2-0			1-1	0-1	2-1	1-0	2-1	2-2	5-0		
Al Shorta	15	7	4	4	20	12	25	0-2		0-0	2-1		3-1		5-0			3-0			2-1
Al Nwair	15	4	8	3	16	15	20	0-1	0-0			1-1			0-0		1-0	2-2	1-1		5-2
Teshrin	15	5	5	5	14	15	20		1-3	0-1		0-0	2-3		0-0	1-1	2-1	2-1			
Hottin	15	6	2	7	22	28	20			3-2	0-2		2-2			2-1	2-1	2-0			2-1
Al Wathba	15	4	6	5	18	20	18				3-2	0-1	3-1					0-0		1-1	2-4
Al Jazira	15	4	5	6	14	15	17	2-2	2-1				0-1	0-0	2-1	0-0			1-0	2-0	
Al Foutoua	15	5	2	8	15	20	17					1-0	0-0	0-1	4-1	1-0				3-0	1-0
Umayya	15	4	4	7	13	21	16	0-0	1-1	0-2					1-0	2-1		2-0			3-1
Al Taliya	15	3	5	7	12	21	14	2-1					0-0	0-1	1-1	1-3	2-1	2-1			
Al Majd	15	2	4	9	17	29	10	1-1		1-3	1-1	3-1				0-1		2-2		0-0	

29/10/2010 - 20/03/2011 • League suspended in March 2011 due to the political situation in Syria. No title was awarded
Top scorers: **10** - Makhete Diop SEN, Karama & Ali Salah Hashim IRQ, Wahda • **9** - Firas Teat, Nwair • **8** - Ahmed Omair, Shorta & Ziad Shaabo, Hottin
AFC Cup play-off: Al Jaish 0-0 0-1 **Al Shorta**

MEDALS TABLE

		Overall G	Lge G	Cup G	Asia G	Asia S	Asia B	City/Town
1	Al Jaish	18	11	6	1			Damascus
2	Al Karama	16	8	8		2		Homs
	Al Ittihad	16	6	9	1			Aleppo
4	Al Foutoua	6	2	4				Dayr az-Zawr
5	Jabala	5	4	1				Jableh
	Al Shorta	5	1	4				Damascus
7	Al Wahda	3	1	2			1	Damascus
	Al Horriya	3	2	1				Aleppo
9	Barada	2	2					Damascus
	Teshrin	2	2					Latakia
	Rmeilan	2		2				
12	Al Ahly	1		1				Cairo
	Hottin	1		1				Latakia
	Al Maghazel	1		1				
	Al Majd	1		1				Damascus
	Al Yarmouk	1		1				Aleppo

FASF CUP 2010-11

Round of 16		Quarter-finals		Semi-finals		Final	
Al Ittihad	6						
Al Shabab	0	**Al Ittihad**	1				
Al Majd	4 3p	Hottin	0				
Hottin	4 4p			**Al Ittihad**	6		
Al Mohafza	3			Al Wahda	1		
Al Karama	2	Al Mohafza	1				
Al Jazira	2	**Al Wahda**	3				
Al Wahda	3					**Al Ittihad** ‡	3
Al Jaish	w-o					Al Wathba	1
Al Taliya		**Al Jaish**	0 3p				
Al Foutoua	0	Al Shorta	0 1p				
Al Shorta	2			Al Jaish	1 3p		
Umayya	w-o			**Al Wathba**	1 4p		
Al Nwair		Umayya	2				
Teshrin	1	**Al Wathba**	4				
Al Wathba	3						

‡ Qualified for the AFC Cup

CUP FINAL
Abbasiyyin, Damascus
3-08-2011
Scorers - Taha Diab, Mohamed Fares, Ahmed Haj Mohamed for Ittihad; Jaja for Wathba

TAH – TAHITI

FIFA/COCA-COLA WORLD RANKING

'93	'94	'95	'96	'97	'98	'99	'00	'01	'02	'03	'04	'05	'06	'07	'08	'09	'10	'11	'12
141	148	156	158	161	123	139	131	127	115	133	124	141	173	162	188	194	184	184	

	2011												High	Low	Av
Jan	Feb	Mar	Apr	May	Jun	Jul	Aug	Sep	Oct	Nov	Dec			High	Low	Av
183	183	184	176	175	176	182	183	184	182	182	184		111	195	151

Tahiti came away with the bronze medal from the football tournament of the 2011 Pacific Games in Noumea, Caledonia, but without ever really impressing during the six matches they played there. The exceptions were the huge 17-1 victory over minnows Kiribati, which ensured qualification for the semi-finals on goal difference at the expense of Papua New Guinea, and in the bronze medal match in which Fiji were beaten 2-1. Not since 1995 have Tahiti - once the powerhouse of football in the Pacific - reached the final and their record of five titles was overtaken by New Caledonia, against whom they lost in the semi-final. Tahiti has always relied on a well-structured club scene to stay at the forefront of football in the region but as more countries set out to improve their leagues, they will no longer have this advantage and in the 2010-11 OFC Champions League Tefana finished bottom of their group. It didn't help that they were grouped with the two clubs from New Zealand - as they have been in three of the past four tournaments - although they did beat the Kiwi champions Waitakere United 3-1 in Faa'a. Tefana ensured that they qualified for the 2011-12 OFC Champions League by retaining their league title, their third in seven years and their fourth overall, finishing comfortably ahead of Dragon in the play-off round.

FIFA WORLD CUP RECORD
1930-1990 DNE 1994-2010 DNQ

FEDERATION TAHITIENNE DE FOOTBALL (FTF)

Rue Coppenrath,
Stade de Fautaua,
BP 50358, Pirae 98716
☎ +689 540954
+689 419629
contact@ftf.pf
www.ftf.pf
FA 1989 CON 1990 FIFA 1990
P Henry Ariiotima
GS Matuanui Ariiotima

FIFA BIG COUNT 2006

Total players	16 396
% of population	6.66%
Male	15 391
Female	1 005
Amateurs 18+	4 429
Youth under 18	5 367
Unregistered	4 500
Professionals	0
Referees	64
Admin & coaches	64
Number of clubs	164
Number of teams	650

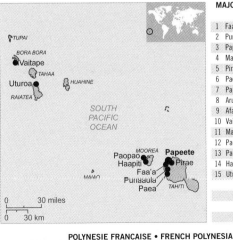

MAJOR CITIES/TOWNS

		Population
1	Faa'a (T)	30 448
2	Punaauia (T)	26 286
3	Papeete (T)	25 980
4	Mahina (T)	14 845
5	Pirae (T)	14 489
6	Paea (T)	12 139
7	Papara (T)	11 121
8	Arue (T)	9 543
9	Afaahiti (T)	5 720
10	Vaitape (BB)	5 182
11	Mataiea (T)	4 580
12	Paopao (M)	4 448
13	Papeari (T)	4 385
14	Haapiti (M)	4 264
15	Uturoa (R)	3 863
	(T) = Tahiti	
	(BB) = Bora Bora	
	(M) = Moorea	
	(R) = Raiatea	

POLYNESIE FRANCAISE • FRENCH POLYNESIA

Capital	Papete	Population	287 032 (179)	% in cities	52%
GDP per capita	$18 000 (68)	Area km²	4167 km² (174)	GMT +/-	-10
Neighbours (km)	Coast 2525				

RECENT INTERNATIONAL MATCHES PLAYED BY TAHITI

2004	Opponents	Score		Venue	Comp	Scorers	Att	Referee
10-05	Cook Islands	W	2-0	Honiara	WCq	Temataua [2], Moretta [80]	12 000	Singh FIJ
12-05	New Caledonia	D	0-0	Honiara	WCq		14 000	Rakaroi FIJ
17-05	Tonga	W	2-0	Honiara	WCq	Wajoka [1], Temataua [78]	400	Sosongan PNG
19-05	Solomon Islands	D	1-1	Honiara	WCq	Simon [30]	18 000	Rakaroi FIJ
29-05	Fiji	D	0-0	Adelaide	WCq		3 000	Farina ITA
31-05	Australia	L	0-9	Adelaide	WCq		1 200	Attison VAN
2-06	Solomon Islands	L	0-4	Adelaide	WCq		50	Rakaroi FIJ
4-06	New Zealand	L	0-10	Adelaide	WCq		200	Shield AUS
6-06	Vanuatu	W	2-1	Adelaide	WCq	Temataua [40], Wajoka [89]	300	Rakaroi FIJ
2005								
No international matches played in 2005								
2006								
No international matches played in 2006								
2007								
25-08	New Caledonia	L	0-1	Apia	WCq		400	Hester NZL
29-08	Tuvalu †	D	1-1	Apia	WCq	Williams [45]	100	Lengeta SOL
1-09	Fiji	L	0-4	Apia	WCq		200	Fox NZL
3-09	Cook Islands	W	1-0	Apia	WCq	Tinorua [64]	100	Aimaasu SAM
2008								
24-09	New Caledonia	L	0-1	Paris	Fr			
27-09	Martinique †	L	0-1	Paris	Fr			
30-09	Guadeloupe †	L	0-1	Paris	Fr			
2009								
No international matches played in 2009								
2010								
23-09	Martinique †	L	1-4	Paris	Fr	Li Fung Kee [27]		Panot FRA
26-09	Guadeloupe †	D	1-1	Paris	Fr	Tehau [57]		Fouquet FRA
29-09	New Caledonia	D	1-1	Paris	Fr	William [30]. W 5-3p		Fouquet FRA
2011								
3-04	New Caledonia	L	1-3	Papeete	Fr	Labayen [61p]		
7-04	New Caledonia	W	1-0	Papeete	Fr	Rochette [72]		
27-08	Fiji	L	0-3	Boulari	PGr1			Kerr NZL
30-08	Cook Islands	W	7-0	Boulari	PGr1	Neuffer [48], Atani [59], OG [69], Chong Hue 2 [73 91+], Poroiae 2 [82p 89]		Oiaka SOL
1-09	Papua New Guinea	D	1-1	Boulari	PGr1	Atani [23]		Achari FIJ
5-09	Kiribati	W	17-1	Boulari	PGr1	Poroiae 2 [16 44p], Chong Hue 4 [19 28 33 46], Araneda [21], Mataitai [53], Ludivion [57], Tehau.T 6 [73 79 85 88 90 91+], Faatiarau [83p], Atani [86]		Oiaka SOL
7-09	New Caledonia	L	1-3	Kone	PGsf	Poroiae [52]		Varman FIJ
9-09	Fiji	W	2-1	Boulari	PG3p	Atani [5], Tehau.L [65]		Billon NCL

Fr = Friendly match • OC = OFC Oceania Cup • SP = South Pacific Games • WC = FIFA World Cup
q = qualifier • r1 = first roundgroup • sf = semi-final • 3p = third place play-off • † Not a full international

TAHITI 2010–11

DIVISION FEDERALE STAGE ONE

	Pl	W	D	L	F	A	Pts	Tefana	Manu Ura	Tamarii Faa'a	Dragon	Vénus	Vaiete	Central	Pirae	Vairao	Excelsior
AS Tefana †	18	15	2	1	52	15	67		1-0	2-1	2-0	4-1	2-2	4-1	1-0	7-0	3-1
AS Manu Ura †	18	14	0	4	41	19	62	2-3		3-1	2-0	2-1	3-0	3-0	5-2	4-1	4-0
AS Tamarii Faa'a †	18	11	3	4	45	29	56	3-3	3-0		3-1	1-2	2-2	3-0	4-2	2-1	4-2
AS Dragon †	18	11	2	5	45	20	55	1-2	3-0	4-1		2-0	5-0	2-1	5-0	1-0	1-1
AS Vénus †	18	7	5	6	23	24	46	1-3	1-2	1-1	3-3		1-0	1-0	0-0	2-0	3-1
AS Vaiete †	18	7	2	9	26	31	43	1-4	1-2	1-2	1-0	2-1		1-2	2-3	4-1	2-1
AS Central Sport	18	7	1	10	29	36	42	1-0	1-2	2-3	3-5	2-2	0-2		4-0	3-1	2-0
AS Pirae	18	4	4	10	28	47	36	0-4	1-3	0-2	0-5	1-1	0-3	3-1		5-3	7-0
AS Vairao	18	2	2	14	22	52	28	0-2	0-2	3-6	0-5	0-1	2-1	2-3	3-3		4-0
AS Excelsior	18	0	3	15	11	49	25	0-5	0-2	0-3	1-2	0-1	0-1	2-3	1-1	1-1	

4/09/2010 - 30/01/2011 • † Qualified for play-offs • Top six split off for a Championship play-off along with the champions of Temanava, while the bottom four join the top four of the second division in a relegation/promotion play-off group • Four points for a win, two points for a draw and one point for a defeat

CHAMPIONSHIP PLAY-OFF

	Pl	W	D	L	F	A	Pts	Tefana	Dragon	Tamarii	Manu Ura	Vaiete	Temanava	Vénus
AS Tefana †	12	9	2	1	26	9	43		3-1	2-4	1-0	2-0	7-0	1-0
AS Dragon	12	6	3	3	20	14	33	0-0		2-0	0-2	3-1	0-0	2-0
AS Tamarii Faa'a	12	6	3	3	29	18	33	1-2	3-4		2-2	4-1	2-0	5-0
AS Manu Ura	12	5	4	3	20	11	31	0-1	2-0	1-1		3-0	2-2	2-0
AS Vaiete	12	2	6	4	21	26	24	1-1	1-1	3-3	3-3		2-2	3-1
AS Temanava	12	1	5	6	10	24	20	0-2	1-3	1-2	1-0	1-1		0-1
AS Vénus	12	1	1	10	9	33	16	2-4	1-4	0-2	0-3	2-5	2-2	

6/02/2011 - 5/06/2011 • † Qualified for the OFC Champions League • Bonus points in brackets

RELEGATION/PROMOTION PLAY-OFF

	Pl	W	D	L	F	A	Pts	Pirae	Central	Roniu	Punaruu	Aorai	Vairao	Olympic	Excelsior
AS Pirae	12	7	2	3	32	20	37		6-4	1-1		4-1	1-3		4-1
AS Central Sport	12	6	1	5	32	24	35	0-2		5-2	0-1	5-2	3-0	2-2	2-0
AS Roniu	12	7	1	4	21	16	34	2-1	3-2		2-1	2-1	2-0	2-1	0-1
AS Punaruu	12	6	3	3	16	16	34	2-1		1-0		1-4	1-0	2-2	0-2
AS Aorai	12	4	0	8	21	30	28	2-3	2-4	0-4	1-2		1-4	2-1	
AS Vairao	12	4	2	6	18	21	27	2-2	2-1		1-2			0-3	1-2
Olympic Mahina	12	3	3	6	18	23	26	2-4	2-4		1-1	0-3	1-3		2-0
AS Excelsior	12	4	2	6	12	20	26	0-3		2-1	2-2	0-2	2-2	0-1	

6/02/2011 - 23/05/2011 • Top four play the 2010-11 season in the Division Federal

MEDALS TABLE

		Overall G	Lge G	Cup G	Town
1	AS Central Sport	38	20	18	Papeete
2	AS Venus	15	9	6	Mahina
3	AS Pirae	15	7	8	Pirae
4	AS Fei Pi	15	7	8	Papeete
5	AS Excelsior	11	7	4	Papeete
6	AS Jeunes Tahitiens	8	3	5	Papeete
7	AS Manu Ura	7	5	2	Papeete
8	AS Tefana	6	3	3	Faa'a
9	AS Dragon	3		3	Papeete
10	AS PTT	3	1	2	Papeete
11	AS Tamarii Punaruu	3	1	2	Papeete
12	AS Arue	2	1	1	Arue
13	CAICT	1		1	
14	Marine	1		1	
15	AS Temanava	1		1	Moorea
16	AS Vaiete	1		1	Papeete

TAN – TANZANIA

FIFA/COCA-COLA WORLD RANKING

'93	'94	'95	'96	'97	'98	'99	'00	'01	'02	'03	'04	'05	'06	'07	'08	'09	'10	'11	'12
98	74	70	89	96	118	128	140	149	153	159	172	165	110	89	99	106	116	137	

						2011									
Jan	Feb	Mar	Apr	May	Jun	Jul	Aug	Sep	Oct	Nov	Dec		High	Low	Av
120	123	121	112	117	127	127	125	127	131	136	137		65	175	122

Tanzania had a very busy year of international action in 2011 but it was only at club level that they achieved any silverware. The Taifa Stars played in four tournaments - the Nile Basin Cup in Egypt, the 2012 CAF Africa Cup of Nations qualifiers, the 2014 FIFA World Cup qualifiers and then finished the year by hosting the East and Central African Senior Challenge Cup. In the FIFA World Cup qualifiers they won 2-1 away in Chad in their first leg of the preliminary round tie but then contrived to lose at home, advancing to the group stage only on the away goals rule. The Tanzanians were hopeful that home advantage would see a repeat success in the East and Central African Senior Challenge Cup but they were beaten 3-1 in the semi-finals by Uganda and then also lost in the third place play-off to Sudan. Dar-es-Salaam also hosted the CECAFA Kagame Inter-Club Cup which saw home rivals Simba and Young Africans reach the final, with Young Africans winning 1-0 to claim the trophy - the first Tanzanian club to do so since Simba in 2002. The two clubs' rivalry continued in the Premier League as well with Young Africans, who are also known as Yanga, pipping Simba to the title on a goal difference of just two. Coached by Sam Timbe, Yanga extended to 22 their record haul of league titles in Tanzania.

CAF AFRICA CUP OF NATIONS RECORD

1957-1965 DNE 1968 Withdrew 1970-1978 DNQ **1980** 8 r1 1982 DNE 1984 DNQ
1986 Withdrew 1988-1992 DNQ 1994 Withdrew 1996-2002 DNQ 2004 Withdrew 2006-2012 DNQ

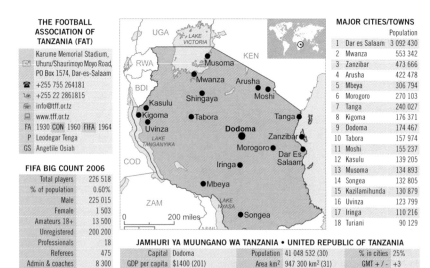

THE FOOTBALL ASSOCIATION OF TANZANIA (FAT)

Karume Memorial Stadium,
Uhuru/Shaurimoyo Moyo Road,
PO Box 1574, Dar-es-Salaam
☎ +255 755 264181
📠 +255 22 2861815
📧 info@tff.or.tz
🖥 www.tff.or.tz
FA 1930 CON 1960 FIFA 1964
P Leodegar Tenga
GS Angetile Osiah

FIFA BIG COUNT 2006

Total players	226 518
% of population	0.60%
Male	225 015
Female	1 503
Amateurs 18+	13 500
Unregistered	200 200
Professionals	18
Referees	475
Admin & coaches	8 300
Number of clubs	200
Number of teams	5 000

MAJOR CITIES/TOWNS

		Population
1	Dar es Salaam	3 092 430
2	Mwanza	553 342
3	Zanzibar	473 666
4	Arusha	422 478
5	Mbeya	306 794
6	Morogoro	270 103
7	Tanga	240 027
8	Kigoma	176 371
9	Dodoma	174 467
10	Tabora	157 974
11	Moshi	155 237
12	Kasulu	139 205
13	Musoma	134 893
14	Songea	132 805
15	Kazilamihunda	130 879
16	Uvinza	123 799
17	Iringa	110 216
18	Turiani	90 129

JAMHURI YA MUUNGANO WA TANZANIA • UNITED REPUBLIC OF TANZANIA

Capital	Dodoma	Population	41 048 532 (30)	% in cities	25%
GDP per capita	$1400 (201)	Area km²	947 300 km² (31)	GMT +/-	+3
Neighbours (km)	Burundi 451, Congo DR 459, Kenya 769, Malawi 475, Mozambique 756, Rwanda 217, Uganda 396, Zambia 338 • Coast 1424				

RECENT INTERNATIONAL MATCHES PLAYED BY TANZANIA

2010	Opponents	Score	Venue	Comp	Scorers	Att	Referee
4-01	Côte d'Ivoire	L 0-1	Dar es Salaam	Fr		60 000	Mbaga TAN
3-03	Uganda	L 2-3	Mwanza	Fr	Nadir Haroub [55], Mrisho Ngasa [58]		
7-06	Brazil	L 1-5	Dar es Salaam	Fr	Jabir Aziz [86]	35 000	Ssegonga UGA
11-08	Kenya	D 1-1	Dar es Salaam	Fr	Mrisho Ngasa [59]		
3-09	Algeria	D 1-1	Blida	CNq	Idrissa Rajab [32]		Djaoupe TOG
9-10	Morocco	L 0-1	Dar es Salaam	CNq			Seechurn MRI
23-11	Kenya	W 1-0	Dar es Salaam	Fr	Gaudence Mwaikimba [1]		
27-11	Zambia	L 0-1	Dar es Salaam	CCr1			Batte UGA
30-11	Somalia	W 3-0	Dar es Salaam	CCr1	Henry Shindika [41p], John Boko [76], Nurdin Bakari [89]		
4-12	Burundi	W 2-0	Dar es Salaam	CCr1	Nurdin Bakari 2 [12 77]		
8-12	Rwanda	W 1-0	Dar es Salaam	CCqf	Shadrack Nsajigwa [62p]		
10-12	Uganda	D 0-0	Dar es Salaam	CCsf	W 5-4p		
12-12	Côte d'Ivoire 'B' †	W 1-0	Dar es Salaam	CCf	Shadrack Nsajigwa [41p]		
2011							
5-01	Egypt	L 1-5	Cairo	Fr	Rashid Gumbo [82]		
8-01	Burundi	D 1-1	Cairo	Fr	Shadrack Nsajigwa [76p]		
11-01	Uganda	D 1-1	Cairo	Fr	Yudah Mugalu [64]		
16-01	Sudan	L 0-2	Cairo	Fr			
9-02	Palestine	W 1-0	Dar es Salaam	Fr	Mrisho Ngassa [63]		
26-03	Central African Rep	W 2-1	Dar es Salaam	CNq	Shaban Nditi [49], Mbwana Samata [91+]		
23-04	Mozambique	L 0-2	Maputo	Fr			
14-05	South Africa	L 0-1	Dar es Salaam	Fr			
5-06	Central African Rep	L 1-2	Bangui	CNq	Shaban Nditi [76]		
3-09	Algeria	D 1-1	Dar es Salaam	CNq	Mbwana Samata [22]		
9-10	Morocco	L 1-3	Marrakech	CNq	Abdi Kassim Sadala [40]		
11-11	Chad	W 2-1	N'Djamena	WCq	Mrisho Ngassa [11], Bakari Hamadi [80]	10 000	Ogunkolade NGA
15-11	Chad	L 0-1	Dar es Salaam	WCq		42 700	Nampiandraza MAD
26-11	Rwanda	L 0-1	Dar es Salaam	CCr1			
29-11	Djibouti	W 3-0	Dar es Salaam	CCr1	Thomas Ulimwengu [2], Mwinyi Kazimoto [37], Rashid Yusuf [85]		
3-12	Zimbabwe	L 1-2	Dar es Salaam	CCr1	Mwinyi Kazimoto [88p]		
6-12	Malawi	W 1-0	Dar es Salaam	CCqf	Nurdin Bakari [37]		
8-12	Uganda	L 1-3	Dar es Salaam	CCsf	Mrisho Ngassa [17]		
10-12	Sudan	L 0-1	Dar es Salaam	CC3p			

Fr = Friendly match • CN = CAF African Cup of Nations • CC = CECAFA Cup • WC = FIFA World Cup
q = qualifier • r1 = first round group • sf = semi-final • f = final • † Not a full international

TANZANIA 2010–11

PREMIER LEAGUE (LIGI KUU TANZANIA BARA)	Pl	W	D	L	F	A	Pts	Yanga	Simba	Azzam	Mtibwa	Kagera	JKT Ruvu	African Lyon	Polisi	Toto Africa	Ruvu SS	Maji Maji	Arusha
Young Africans †	22	14	7	1	32	7	49		1-1	2-1	0-1	2-0	0-0	1-1	2-0	2-0	2-0	1-0	6-1
Simba SC ‡	22	15	4	3	40	17	49	0-1		2-3	4-1	0-0	1-1	2-0	0-1	2-1	2-1	4-1	3-1
Azzam United	22	13	4	5	41	18	43	0-0	1-2		2-2	1-2	0-0	2-1	3-1	3-0	4-1	1-1	5-1
Mtibwa Sugar	22	9	9	4	24	21	36	1-1	0-1	0-4		2-1	0-0	2-0	1-0	1-1	1-1	2-2	3-0
Kagera Sugar	22	9	8	5	22	18	35	0-1	0-2	1-0	1-0		0-1	0-0	1-0	2-2	1-0	0-0	0-0
JKT Ruvu Stars	22	6	10	6	21	21	28	0-0	1-2	0-2	0-0	1-1		1-2	1-1	1-0	1-1	0-1	4-2
African Lyon	22	6	7	9	18	29	25	1-3	0-3	0-3	1-2	2-2	1-2		2-1	1-0	0-0	2-2	1-0
Polisi Dodoma	22	5	6	11	13	22	21	0-1	0-2	0-1	0-0	0-1	0-0	2-0		0-0	1-1	3-2	2-0
Toto Africa	22	5	6	11	19	29	21	0-3	2-2	1-0	1-2	0-2	1-2	1-1	2-0		2-0	0-0	2-1
Ruvu Shooting Stars	22	4	8	10	17	25	20	0-1	0-1	1-2	0-1	2-2	3-2	0-0	2-0	2-1		2-0	0-0
Maji Maji	22	3	7	12	14	26	16	0-0	1-2	0-1	0-1	1-2	0-1	0-1	0-1	2-1	0-0		1-0
Arusha FC	22	3	4	15	13	41	13	0-2	0-2	0-2	1-1	1-3	3-2	0-1	0-0	0-1	1-0	1-0	

21/08/2010 - 10/04/2011 • † Qualified for the CAF Champions League • ‡ Qualified for the CAF Confederation Cup
Top scorer: 18 - Mrisho Ngasa, Azzam

TCA – TURKS AND CAICOS ISLANDS

FIFA/COCA-COLA WORLD RANKING

'93	'94	'95	'96	'97	'98	'99	'00	'01	'02	'03	'04	'05	'06	'07	'08	'09	'10	'11	'12
-	-	-	-	-	-	196	200	200	202	203	203	203	169	181	168	177	187	200	

2011												High	Low	Av
Jan	Feb	Mar	Apr	May	Jun	Jul	Aug	Sep	Oct	Nov	Dec			
186	186	193	193	193	192	193	195	195	194	195	200	158	204	191

The Turks and Caicos Islands national team had seen its FIFA/Coca-Cola World Ranking rise to as high as 158 in February 2008 thanks to a Caribbean Cup win over the Cayman Islands in 2006 and a World Cup qualifying win over St Lucia at the start of 2008. However, with the points gained from those matches assuming less significance and with no further games played, the team found itself hovering near the bottom again as they prepared to take on the Bahamas in a preliminary round of 2014 FIFA World Cup qualifiers. With Star striker and record goalscorer Gavin Glinton making the journey back from his club in Vietnam to play alongside his younger brother Duane - TCI's most capped player - hopes were high of an upset but they were soon dashed in front of a bumper crowd of just over 1000 at the TCIFA's National Academy stadium in Providenciales, Bahamas winning 4-0. There were no goals to celebrate in the return in Nassau either with TCI going down 6-0. With national team games few and far between the league season provides the focus for the game in the country. Run between October and March, it was won for the first time by Provopool who despite not turning up for their fixture against runners-up AFC Academy still finished two points ahead of their rivals. The end of season President's Cup won by AFC National.

FIFA WORLD CUP RECORD
1930-1998 DNE 2002-2010 DNQ

TURKS AND CAICOS ISLANDS FOOTBALL ASSOCIATION (TCIFA)

Tropicana Plaza, Leeward Highway, PO Box 626, Providenciales

☎ +1 649 9415532
🖷 +1 649 9415554
✉ tcifa@tciway.tc
🖳 www.football.tc

FA 1996 CON 1998 FIFA 1998
P Christopher Bryan
GS Sonia Bien-Aime

FIFA BIG COUNT 2006

Total players	2 155
% of population	10.19%
Male	1 540
Female	615
Amateurs 18+	165
Unregistered	1 000
Professionals	0
Referees	12
Admin & coaches	35
Number of clubs	9
Number of teams	9

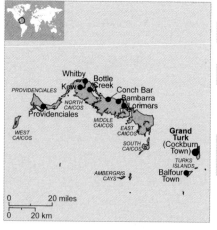

MAJOR TOWNS

Grand Turk
Cockburn Town (3 691)
Salt Cay
Balfour Town
Providenciales
Providenciales
North Caicos
Bottle Creek
Kew
Whitby
Sandy Point
Middle Caicos
Conch Bar
Lorimers
Bambarra
Turks Islands
Balfour Town

TURKS AND CAICOS ISLANDS

Capital	Cockburn Town	Population	22 942 (216)	% in cities	92%
GDP per capita	$11 500 (97)	Area km²	948 km² (185)	GMT +/-	-5
Neighbours (km)	Coast 389				

RECENT INTERNATIONAL MATCHES PLAYED BY TURKS AND CAICOS

2004	Opponents	Score	Venue	Comp	Scorers	Att	Referee
18-02	Haiti	L 0-5	Miami †	WCq		3 000	Stott USA
21-02	Haiti	L 0-2	Hialeah †	WCq		3 000	Valenzuela USA
2005							
No international matches played in 2005							
2006							
2-09	Cuba	L 0-6	Havana	CCq		2 000	Campbell JAM
4-09	Cayman Islands	W 2-0	Havana	CCq	Gavin Glinton 14, Maxime Fleuriot 72	100	Stennett JAM
6-09	Bahamas	L 2-3	Havana	CCq	Gavin Glinton 2 51 72	120	Campbell JAM
2007							
No international matches played in 2007							
2008							
6-02	St Lucia	W 2-1	Providenciales	WCq	David Lowery 31, Gavin Glinton 74	2 200	Whittaker CAY
26-03	St Lucia	L 0-2	Vieux Fort	WCq		1 200	Forde BRB
2009							
No international matches played in 2009							
2010							
No international matches played in 2010							
2011							
2-07	Bahamas	L 0-4	Providenciales	WCq		1 021	Cruz CRC
9-07	Bahamas	L 0-6	Nassau	WCq		1 600	Santos PUR

CC = Digicel Caribbean Cup • WC = FIFA World Cup • q = qualifier • † Both matches played in the USA

TURKS AND CAICOS ISLANDS NATIONAL TEAM HISTORICAL RECORDS

Coach: Luigino Pacetto ITA 1999 • Charlie Cook 2000-03 • Paul Crosbie SCO 2003-04 • Matthew Green ENG 2006-08 • Gary Brough 2011-

TURKS AND CAICOS ISLANDS 2010-11

COXCO MEN'S LEAGUE	Pl	W	D	L	F	A	Pts	Provopool	AFC Academy	AFC National	SWA Sharks
Provopool FC	12	8	0	4	40	29	24		2-0 **0-3**	4-2 4-2	4-0 5-2
AFC Academy	12	7	1	4	35	26	22	1-2 7-5		2-0 2-2	6-1 4-2
AFC National	12	6	1	5	46	34	19	0-6 4-2	1-6 6-2		6-2 7-0
SWA Sharks	12	2	0	10	24	56	6	1-2 7-4	0-1 5-1	2-6 2-10	

23/10/2010 - 8/03/2011 • Match in bold awarded
Top scorers: 20 - Marco Fenelus, AFC National • 15 - Lenford Singh, Provopool • 14 - Bobby Kwatt, AFC Academy

PRESIDENT'S CUP 2011

Group Stage

	Pl	W	D	L	F	A	Pts	Nat	Provo	Acad
SWA Sharks †	3	1	2	0	5	4	5	0-0	1-0	4-4
AFC National †	3	1	1	1	9	4	4		0-4	9-0
Provopool FC	3	1	1	1	6	3	4			2-2
AFC Academy	3	0	2	1	6	15	2			

† Qualified for the final
Played 18/01/2011 - 19/03/2011

Final

AFC National	4
SWA Sharks	2

CUP FINAL
TCIFA National Academy
19-03-2011

TGA – TONGA

FIFA/COCA-COLA WORLD RANKING

'93	'94	'95	'96	'97	'98	'99	'00	'01	'02	'03	'04	'05	'06	'07	'08	'09	'10	'11	'12
-	-	-	164	174	163	178	185	173	175	180	183	185	188	170	188	188	188	176	

2011												High	Low	Av
Jan	Feb	Mar	Apr	May	Jun	Jul	Aug	Sep	Oct	Nov	Dec			
188	188	188	190	190	190	192	194	201	201	202	176	163	202	180

If Tonga's 19-14 victory over France in the 2011 Rugby World Cup in New Zealand in September was the highlight of the year in Tongan sport, the humiliating 2-1 defeat in the 2014 FIFA World Cup qualifiers at the hands of American Samoa ranked at the other end of the spectrum. The Samoans had never won a match and were firmly ensconced at the bottom of the FIFA/Coca-Cola World Ranking and to rub salt into the Tongan wounds, highlights of the match were shown the world over. The result was perhaps a bit harsh on Tonga. They finished in second place in the group after drawing with Samoa and then beating the Cook Islands. Coach Chris Williams had not had the benefit of participation in the football tournament of the 2011 Pacific Games in Noumea, New Caledonia to help his preparations so the haul of four points from the three games represented an achievement and lifted Tonga up to 176 in the rankings. After a year without local football the Major League Premier Division returned and saw SC Lotoha'apai get back to winning ways when they won the title for the first time since 2008. Marist were the team that broke Lotoha'apai's eleven year winning sequence in 2009 but they were beaten 2-1 in the final. They did get some measure of revenge when they beat Lotoha'apai 4-3 in the Cup Final.

FIFA WORLD CUP RECORD
1930-1994 DNE 1998-2010 DNQ

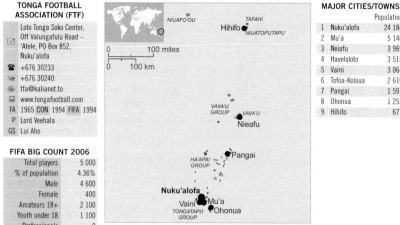

TONGA FOOTBALL ASSOCIATION (FTF)

Loto Tonga Soko Center, Off Valungafulu Road – 'Atele, PO Box 852, Nuku'alofa
☎ +676 30233
📠 +676 30240
✉ tfa@kalianet.to
🖥 www.tongafootball.com
FA 1965 CON 1994 FIFA 1994
P Lord Veehala
GS Lui Aho

FIFA BIG COUNT 2006

Total players	5 000
% of population	4.36%
Male	4 600
Female	400
Amateurs 18+	2 100
Youth under 18	1 100
Professionals	0
Referees	100
Admin & coaches	100
Number of clubs	100
Number of teams	220

MAJOR CITIES/TOWNS

		Population
1	Nuku'alofa	24 184
2	Mu'a	5 140
3	Neiafu	3 969
4	Haveloloto	3 518
5	Vaini	3 064
6	Tofoa-Koloua	2 610
7	Pangai	1 591
8	Ohonua	1 252
9	Hihifo	671

PULE'ANGA TONGA • KINGDOM OF TONGA

Capital	Nuku'alofa	Population	120 898 (188)	% in cities	25%
GDP per capita	$4600 (145)	Area km²	747 km² (189)	GMT +/-	+13
Neighbours (km)	Coast 419				

RECENT INTERNATIONAL MATCHES PLAYED BY TONGA

2002 Opponents	Score	Venue	Comp	Scorers	Att	Referee
No international matches played in 2002 after June						
2003						
1-07 Papua New Guinea	D 2-2	Suva	SPr1	Unaloto-Ki-Atenoa Feao 2 [62] [75]	3 000	Singh FIJ
3-07 New Caledonia	L 0-4	Suva	SPr1		700	Shah FIJ
5-07 Micronesia †	W 7-0	Nausori	SPr1	Ipeni Fonua [5], Maamaloa Tevi [15], Mark Uhatahi 2 [22] [36], Unaloto-Ki-Atenoa Feao 2 [34] [55], Kilifi Uele [72]	1 000	Moli SOL
7-07 Tahiti	L 0-4	Lautoka	SPr1		3 000	Shah FIJ
2004						
10-05 Solomon Islands	L 0-6	Honiara	WCq		12 385	Attison VAN
15-05 Cook Islands	W 2-1	Honiara	WCq	Mark Uhatahi [46], Viliami Vaitaki [61]	15 000	Sosongan PNG
17-05 Tahiti	L 0-2	Honiara	WCq		400	Sosongan PNG
19-05 New Caledonia	L 0-8	Honiara	WCq		14 000	Fred VAN
2005						
No international matches played in 2005						
2006						
No international matches played in 2006						
2007						
27-08 Solomon Islands	L 0-4	Apia	WCq		350	Aimaasu SAM
29-08 Samoa	L 1-2	Apia	WCq	Unaloto-Ki-Atenoa Feao [54]	1 850	Sosongan PNG
1-09 American Samoa	W 4-0	Apia	WCq	Lafaele Moala [38], Pio Palu 2 [56] [63], Kaisani Uhatahi [86]	200	Minan PNG
3-09 Vanuatu	L 1-4	Apia	WCq	Malakai Savieti [50]	50	Minan PNG
2008						
No international matches played in 2008						
2009						
11-06 Cook Islands	D 1-1	Atele	Fr	Mark Uhatahi [35]		
13-06 Cook Islands	L 1-2	Atele	Fr	Mark Uhatahi [48]		
2010						
No international matches played in 2010						
2011						
22-11 American Samoa	L 1-2	Apia	WCq	Unaloto-Ki-Atenoa Feao [88]	150	Achari FIJ
24-11 Samoa	D 1-1	Apia	WCq	Lokoua Taufahema [81]	180	Jacques TAH
26-11 Cook Islands	W 2-1	Apia	WCq	Timote Maamaloa [26], Kinitoni Falatau [90]	200	Ambassa NCL

Fr = Friendly match • SP = South Pacific Games • WC = FIFA World Cup • q = qualifier • r1 = first round group • † Not a full international

TONGA 2010-11 MAJOR LEAGUE PREMIER DIVISION

Semi-finals		Finals	
Lotoha'apai	8		
Longoteme	0		
		Lotoha'apai	2
		Marist	1
Kolofo'ou	0		
Marist	0	3rd place:	
		Kolofo'ou 2-0 Longoteme	

Final: Home of Football, Atele, 9-04-2011. Scorers - Lafaele Moala [28], Kilifi Uele [87] for Lotoha'apai; Kaneti Felela [65p] for Marist

CHALLENGE CUP 2011

Semi-finals		Finals	
Marist	2		
Ngeleia	1		
		Marist	4
		Lotoha'apai	3
Palangi United	2		
Lotoha'apai	5	16-07-2011	

THA – THAILAND

FIFA/COCA-COLA WORLD RANKING

'93	'94	'95	'96	'97	'98	'99	'00	'01	'02	'03	'04	'05	'06	'07	'08	'09	'10	'11	'12
69	85	77	57	54	45	60	61	61	66	60	79	111	137	121	126	105	121	122	

2011												High	Low	Av
Jan	Feb	Mar	Apr	May	Jun	Jul	Aug	Sep	Oct	Nov	Dec			
119	120	117	120	120	123	118	120	117	114	132	122	43	137	83

Buriram PEA swept the board in Thailand as the club backed by influential politician Newin Chidchob claimed all three domestic titles - the Thai Premier League, the Thai FA Cup and the Thai League Cup - to usurp Muangthong United and Chonburi as the new power in the TPL. Under coach Attapol Buspakom, who took BEC Tero Sasana to the final of the 2003 AFC Champions League, Buriram's expensively-assembled squad, playing in a new football-only stadium, was led to glory by young African duo Frank Ohandza and Frank Acheampong. At the start of 2012 the club merged with second division champions Buriram FC, adopting the Buriram United title. The focus of the year for the national team - currently coached by the German Winfried Schaeffer following the departure of Bryan Robson - was the qualifying tournament for the 2014 FIFA World Cup in Brazil. The Thais beat an emerging Palestinian side 3-2 on aggregate in a preliminary round tie but they then struggled in the group stage finishing in last place behind Australia, Oman and Saudi Arabia. After an initial loss to Australia, the Thais showed their usual strength at home to defeat Oman and draw with Saudi Arabia but losses against the Australians, the Saudis and Oman in the second half of the schedule ended any hopes of making progress.

FIFA WORLD CUP RECORD
1930-1970 DNE 1974-2010 DNQ

THE FOOTBALL ASSOCIATION OF THAILAND (FAT)

National Stadium, Gate 3,
Rama 1 Road, Patumwan,
Bangkok 10330

☎ +66 2 2164691
📠 +66 2 2154494
✉ fa_thailand@yahoo.com
🖥 www.fat.org.th
FA 1916 CON 1957 FIFA 1925
P Worawi Makudi
GS Ong-Arj Kosinkar

FIFA BIG COUNT 2006

Total players	1 298 000
% of population	2.01%
Male	1 207 500
Female	90 500
Amateurs 18+	10 700
Unregistered	332 400
Professionals	500
Referees	1 100
Admin & coaches	5 500
Number of clubs	150
Number of teams	1 790

MAJOR CITIES/TOWNS

		Population
1	Bangkok	5 802 832
2	Samut Prakan	446 375
3	Nonthaburi	396 669
4	Udon Thani	228 738
5	Chon Buri	202 292
6	Nakhon Ratchasima	201 685
7	Hat Yai	199 062
8	Phra Pradaeng	196 644
9	Pak Kret	193 071
10	Si Racha	184 893
11	Chiang Mai	184 887
12	Thanyaburi	171 301
13	Khlong Luang	155 444
14	Khon Kaen	140 520
15	Lampang	138 088
16	Nakhon Pathom	128 097
17	Surat Thani	127 309
18	Rayong	126 773
19	Nakhon Si Thammarat	117 441

RATCHA ANACHAK THAI • KINGDOM OF THAILAND

Capital	Bangkok	Population	65 905 410 (20)	% in cities	33%
GDP per capita	$8400 (118)	Area km²	513 120 km² (50)	GMT +/-	+7

Neighbours (km) Myanmar 1800, Cambodia 803, Laos 1754, Malaysia 506 • Coast 3219

RECENT INTERNATIONAL MATCHES PLAYED BY THAILAND

2008 Opponents	Score	Venue	Comp	Scorers	Att	Referee
6-12 Vietnam	W 2-0	Phuket	AFFr1	Sutee Suksomkit [34], Suchao Nutnum [45]	20 000	Abdul Bashir SIN
8-12 Laos	W 6-0	Phuket	AFFr1	Ronnachai Rangsiyo [19], Patiparn Phetphun [30], Arthit Sunthornphit 2 [20 52], Anon Sangsanoi 2 [79 89]	10 000	Hadimin BRU
10-12 Malaysia	W 3-0	Phuket	AFFr1	Sutee Suksomkit [23], Teerasil Dangda 2 [46 76]	15 000	Abdul Bashir SIN
16-12 Indonesia	W 1-0	Jakarta	AFFr1	Teerasil Dangda [6]	70 000	Vo Minh Tri VIE
20-12 Indonesia	W 2-1	Bangkok	AFFsf	Teeratep Winothai [73], Ronnachai Rangsiyo [89]	40 000	Hadimin BRU
24-12 Vietnam	L 1-2	Bangkok	AFFf	Ronnachai Rangsiyo [75]	50 000	Ramachandran MAS
28-12 Vietnam	D 1-1	Hanoi	AFFf	Teerasil Dangda [21]	40 000	Abdul Bashir SIN
2009						
14-01 Jordan	D 0-0	Amman	ACq		5 000	Racho SYR
21-01 Lebanon	W 2-1	Phuket	Fr	Teerasil Dangda [12], Suchao Nutnum [22]		
28-01 Iran	D 0-0	Bangkok	ACq		10 000	Kovalenko UZB
5-02 Saudi Arabia	L 1-2	Sendai	Fr	Teerasil Dangda [89]		
28-03 New Zealand	W 3-1	Bangkok	Fr	Teerasil Dangda 2 [12 74], Tawan Sripan [21]		
8-11 Syria	D 1-1	Bangkok	Fr	Teeratep Winothai [59]		
14-11 Singapore	W 3-1	Singapore	ACq	Sutee Suksomkit 2 [12p 81], Therdsak Chaiman [76]	22 183	Takayama JPN
18-11 Singapore	L 0-1	Bangkok	ACq		30 000	Balideh QAT
29-12 Zimbabwe	W 3-0	Bangkok	Fr	Sutinun Phukhom 2 [27 81], Kirati Keawsombut [84]		
2010						
6-01 Jordan	D 0-0	Bangkok	ACq		15 000	Williams AUS
17-01 Singapore	W 1-0	N'hon Ratchasima	Fr	Sutee Suksomkit [59]		Mbaga TAN
20-01 Poland	L 1-3	N'hon Ratchasima	Fr	Therdsak Chaiman [90p]	20 000	Mbaga TAN
23-01 Denmark	L 0-3	N'hon Ratchasima	Fr			
3-03 Iran	L 0-1	Tehran	ACq		17 000	Balideh QAT
16-05 South Africa	L 0-4	Nelspruit	Fr		30 000	Kipngetich KEN
11-08 Singapore	W 1-0	Nonthaburi	Fr	Sarayoot Chaikamdee [28]		Aonrak THA
4-09 India	W 1-0	Bangkok	Fr	Sarayoot Chaikamdee [72]		Mahapab THA
8-09 India	W 2-1	New Delhi	Fr	Teeratep Winothai [48], Keerati Keawsombut [64]		
1-12 Laos	D 2-2	Jakarta	AFFr1	Sarayoot Chaikamdee 2 [67 91+]		Sato JPN
4-12 Malaysia	D 0-0	Jakarta	AFFr1			Win Cho MYA
7-12 Indonesia	L 1-2	Jakarta	AFFr1	Sukha Suree [68]	65 000	Sato JPN
2011						
14-07 Myanmar	W 1-0	Buriram	Fr	Teerasil Dangda [2]		
15-07 Myanmar	D 1-1	Buriram	Fr	Jakkapan Pornsai [17p]		
23-07 Palestine	W 1-0	Buriram	WCq	Jakkaphan Kaewprom [18]	17 000	Lee Min Hu KOR
28-07 Palestine	D 2-2	Al Ram	WCq	Datsakorn Thonglao 2 [34 93+]	11 500	Abbas BHR
24-08 Singapore	D 0-0	Bangkok	Fr			
2-09 Australia	L 1-2	Brisbane	WCq	Teerasil Dangda [15]	24 540	Balideh QAT
6-09 Oman	W 3-0	Bangkok	WCq	Sompong Soleb [35], Teerasil Dangda [41], OG [91+]	19 000	Kim Dong Jin KOR
6-10 Jordan	D 0-0	Bangkok	Fr			
11-10 Saudi Arabia	D 0-0	Bangkok	WCq		42 000	Irmatov UZB
11-11 Saudi Arabia	L 0-3	Riyadh	WCq		32 500	Liu Kwok Man HKG
15-11 Australia	L 0-1	Bangkok	WCq		19 400	Mozaffari IRN

Fr = Friendly match • AFF = ASEAN Football Federation Championship • AC = AFC Asian Cup • WC = FIFA World Cup • q = qualifier • r1 = 1st round

THAILAND NATIONAL TEAM HISTORICAL RECORDS

Past Coaches: Burkhard Ziese GER 1985-86 • Carlos Roberto de Carvalho BRA 1989-91 • Peter Stubbe GER 1992-94 • Worawit Sumpachanyasathit 1994 • Chatchai Paholpat 1994-95 • Arj-han Srongngamsub 1996 • Thawatchai Sartjakul 1996 • Dettmar Cramer GER 1997 • Withaya Laohakul 1997-98 • Peter Withe ENG 1998-2002 • Carlos Roberto de Carvalho BRA 2003-04 • Chatchai Paholpat 2004-04 • Siegfried Held GER 2004-05 • Charnwit Polcheewin 2005-08 • Peter Reid ENG 2008-09 • Bryan Robson ENG 2009-11 • Winfried Schafer GER 2011-

THAILAND 2011

PROFESSIONAL LEAGUE

	Pl	W	D	L	F	A	Pts	Buriram PEA	Chonburi	Muangthong U	Pattaya Utd	B'kok Glass	Osotspa	Thai Port	BEC Tero	Police Utd	Chiangrai Utd	TTM Phichit	Sisaket	Army Utd	TOT-CAT	Samut	Siam Navy	Sriracha	Khon Kaen
Buriram PEA †	34	26	7	1	64	15	85		3-0	1-0	0-0	2-1	0-0	1-0	1-0	1-1	5-0	6-1	2-1	2-1	1-0	3-0	3-2	1-0	2-0
Chonburi ‡	34	20	9	5	58	29	69	1-1		1-1	2-2	1-0	2-2	0-2	2-0	2-0	0-0	1-0	2-1	5-0	2-1	6-0	2-2	1-0	6-1
Muangthong United	34	17	9	8	54	32	60	0-0	1-2		2-0	6-2	0-0	2-0	1-0	3-1	4-1	3-0	1-0	1-1	2-0	2-0	1-3	1-2	1-0
Pattaya United	34	14	11	9	38	27	53	0-1	1-1	1-0		2-1	0-0	1-1	0-0	0-1	3-0	0-1	1-0	1-0	2-1	3-0	1-2	2-0	3-0
Bangkok Glass	34	15	8	11	55	41	53	0-2	2-0	0-0	0-0		2-0	2-1	2-0	5-3	3-2	4-0	2-0	1-1	1-3	1-2	4-0	3-1	4-0
Osotspa Saraburi	34	12	15	7	47	32	51	0-3	2-2	5-1	2-1	1-0		1-3	1-1	2-0	0-0	3-0	2-1	1-1	4-0	0-0	4-1	1-2	3-0
Thai Port	34	12	9	13	33	38	45	0-1	1-0	0-3	0-2	1-1	0-0		3-2	3-1	1-1	3-1	0-0	0-0	0-1	2-1	3-2	1-3	3-0
BEC Tero Sasana	34	13	6	15	39	35	45	1-2	0-1	2-2	1-0	0-2	1-3	0-0		0-2	3-1	3-0	0-1	1-0	2-3	0-0	2-0	1-0	3-1
Police United	34	11	11	12	36	40	44	2-3	0-0	0-2	0-0	3-1	2-4	0-1	1-0		2-1	1-0	2-2	0-1	1-0	0-1	0-1	3-1	1-2
Chiangrai United	34	11	11	12	47	52	44	2-2	4-3	1-0	3-1	2-2	2-1	1-1	1-3	1-2		2-1	1-0	2-1	2-0	0-0	3-1	1-1	1-1
TTM Phichit	34	12	7	15	38	54	43	0-0	1-0	2-1	1-1	0-1	1-2	2-0	1-2	0-0	3-1		2-2	1-0	0-1	1-2	0-1	2-2	2-1
Sisaket	34	9	12	13	33	39	39	1-0	1-1	1-2	2-0	2-0	2-2	0-1	0-3	1-1	0-0	1-2			2-1	2-0	**2-0**	1-1	2-0
Army United	34	10	9	15	39	40	39	1-3	3-4	3-0	3-3	1-1	1-1	0-1	1-0	0-0	2-1	2-0	1-1		1-0	1-3	2-0	3-1	4-1
TOT-CAT	34	11	4	19	29	55	37	0-4	0-1	1-3	0-2	2-1	0-0	1-0	1-3	1-1	1-1	2-3	0-0	1-0		1-0	2-1	1-0	0-2
Samut Songkhram	34	8	12	14	31	45	36	0-4	0-1	1-3	0-1	1-0	0-0	2-0	1-1	1-1	1-4	2-3	2-1	0-1	3-1		2-0	1-1	1-1
Siam Navy	34	9	6	19	28	51	33	0-1	0-2	0-3	1-2	0-1	0-0	0-1	2-1	1-0	0-1	0-1	1-3	1-1	0-0	1-1		0-1	2-1
Sriracha	34	7	11	16	32	43	32	0-1	1-2	0-0	0-1	2-2	1-1	2-1	0-1	0-1	0-0	1-2	1-1	1-0	0-2	1-1	2-0		4-1
Khon Kaen	34	6	9	19	33	68	27	0-2	0-2	2-2	1-1	0-2	1-1	1-1	0-3	1-2	3-2	2-2	1-1	2-0	4-2	1-2	0-0	2-1	

12/02/2011 - 28/01/2012 • † Qualified for the AFC Champions League • ‡ Qualified for the AFC Cup • Match in bold awarded
Top scorers: 19 - Frank Ohandza CMR, Buriram PEA • 18 - Leandro BRA, Army & Wasan Natasan, Cjiangrai

THAILAND 2011

DIVISION 1 (2)

	Pl	W	D	L	F	A	Pts	Buriram	Chainat	BBCU	PTT Rayong	Songkhla	Bangkok Utd	Saraburi	Raj Pracha	Phuket	Suphanburi	Bangkok FC	Chanthaburi	Rangsit JW	Air Force	Customs	Changmai	RBAC	Thai Honda
Buriram FC	34	25	8	1	84	18	83		5-1	3-0	1-1	0-0	0-0	2-0	7-1	7-0	2-1	2-0	5-1	1-1	6-1	2-1	1-0	3-0	4-2
Chainat	34	21	3	10	68	42	66	2-1		1-2	1-0	2-2	4-2	1-2	4-0	3-0	1-1	1-2	5-0	2-0	7-0	3-0	3-1	1-0	5-1
BBCU	34	18	9	7	39	25	63	0-2	0-1		1-0	0-0	2-1	1-0	2-0	2-1	1-0	2-1	1-0	0-0	3-0	4-2	1-0	0-0	0-0
PTT Rayong	34	17	8	9	54	28	59	0-0	1-1	2-1		5-0	1-2	0-0	1-1	1-0	1-0	1-2	0-1	1-1	2-0	0-2	5-1	2-3	3-0
Songkhla	34	15	11	8	54	39	56	1-1	1-0	1-1	1-1		0-2	2-2	3-0	0-1	1-0	4-0	1-0	2-0	0-2	5-1	2-3	3-0	3-2
Bangkok United	34	15	6	13	54	49	51	0-0	2-1	1-1	3-2	1-2		1-0	1-1	2-1	1-2	1-2	1-2	1-1	0-2	2-3	1-1	1-5	3-1
Saraburi	34	12	14	8	41	31	50	0-0	3-1	0-1	1-1	1-2	1-1		1-1	2-2	1-1	3-0	1-1	1-0	1-0	0-0	1-1	5-2	1-0
Raj Pracha	34	13	7	14	40	54	46	0-2	0-1	2-1	0-3	2-2	2-4	1-0			0-0	2-0	1-2	2-0	1-0	2-1	3-2	1-1	2-1
Phuket	34	11	12	11	45	47	45	0-3	4-1	0-0	3-0	0-0	1-0	0-2	**2-0**		0-1	1-4	0-2	3-1	1-1	1-0	4-0	2-0	6-1
Suphanburi	34	10	14	10	40	37	44	0-2	3-0	0-0	1-2	0-1	1-2	2-0	1-1			2-2	2-1	1-1	0-0	1-0	1-1	1-1	2-1
Bangkok FC	34	13	3	18	56	63	42	1-4	3-1	4-1	1-2	1-2	1-3	0-1	2-4	5-2	1-2		1-2	2-1	3-0	2-3	2-2	1-1	3-1
Chanthaburi	34	11	8	15	39	48	41	0-3	0-1	0-0	2-1	2-2	0-2	2-1	0-2	1-1	2-1	2-1		0-0	1-2	0-1	3-1	6-1	0-2
Rangsit JW	34	10	10	14	31	42	40	1-3	1-2	1-3	0-1	1-0	1-0	1-1	2-1	1-1	1-1	3-2	0-2		1-0	2-1	0-1	0-0	3-2
Air Force United	34	10	10	14	36	53	40	0-1	1-3	0-1	1-1	0-2	2-3	3-3	1-0	1-1	0-0	2-1	3-2	2-2		2-0	3-2	0-1	0-0
Customs United	34	10	6	18	41	55	36	1-3	2-3	1-0	0-1	2-2	1-4	1-1	2-3	2-2	2-2	3-0	1-0	0-1	0-2		2-1	1-0	4-0
Changmai	34	7	9	18	36	55	30	2-1	2-0	1-2	0-1	1-2	2-4	1-1	1-0	0-2	1-1	1-2	1-1	2-0	1-1	1-0		0-1	1-0
RBAC Mittraphap	34	5	10	19	25	61	25	0-2	0-1	0-1	0-5	1-0	2-2	0-2	0-1	0-1	0-4	0-2	1-1	3-2	0-1	1-1	1-2		0-0
Thai Honda	34	6	6	22	33	69	24	0-2	1-2	1-5	0-2	1-3	0-1	0-0	2-1	2-2	0-1	0-1	1-0	0-1	3-1	1-2	3-1	3-3	

12/02/2011 - 26/01/2012 • Matches in bold awarded

THAI FA CUP 2011

Eighth-finals		Quarter-finals		Semi-finals		Final	
Buriram PEA	w-o						
Police United *		**Buriram PEA** *	2				
Sisaket	1	BEC Tero Sasana	0				
BEC Tero Sasana *	2			**Buriram PEA** *	2		
Chainat	0 4p			Army United	0		
Chiangrai United *	0 3p	Chainat	1 4p				
Chonburi	1	**Army United** *	1 5p				
Army United *	2					**Buriram PEA**	1
Songkhla	4					Muangthong United	0
TOT-CAT *	1	**Songkhla**	4				
Samut Songkhram *	0 2p	Loei City *	0			CUP FINAL	
Loei City	0 4p			Songkhla *	2 3p		
Sriracha *	1			**Muangthong United**	2 4p	Suphachalasai, Bangkok	
BBCU	0	Sriracha	0			11-01-2012, Ref: Prapoj Ditsomsri.	
Pattaya United *	0	**Muangthong United** *	4			Scorer - Frank Acheampong 108 for	
Muangthong United	6					Buriram PEA	
					* Home team		

PEA - Sivaruck Tedsungnoen - Apichet Puttan (c), Florent Obama●, Yves Ekwalla Herman●, Theeraton Bunmathan● - Bouba Abbo●, Jakkraphan Kaewprom, Suchao Nuchnum, Rangsan Viwatchaichok● - Frank Acheampong, Frank Ohandza. Tr: Attaphol Buspakom; **Muangthong** - Kawin Thammasatchanan - Ali Diarra, Dagno Siaka●, Nattaporn Phanrit (c)●, Weerawut Kayem● (Anon Sangsanoi 110) - Piyaphon Bantao (Adisak Klinkosoom 95), Naruphol Ar-Romsawa (Jakkraphan Pornsai 58), Pichitphong Choeichiu●, Datsakorn Thonglao● - Teerasil Dangda, Robbie Fowler. Tr: Robbie Fowler

MEDALS TABLE

		All	PL	FAC	Cup	Asia	
		G	G	G	G	G	City
1	Air Force United	16	2	3	11		Rangsit
2	Bangkok Bank	11	1	3	7		Bangkok
3	Thai Port	9		1	8		Bangkok
4	Raj Pracha	9		5	4		Nakhon Pathom
5	Thai Farmers Bank	7		1	4	2	Bangkok
6	Krung Thai Bank	4	2		2		Bangkok
7	Raj Vithi	4			4		Bangkok
8	Buriram PEA	3	2	1			Buriram
9	Vajiravudh College	3			3		Bangkok
10	BEC Tero Sasana	2	2				Bangkok
11	Chonburi	2	1	1			Chonburi
12	Chula United	2	1	1			Bangkok
13	Muangthong Utd	2	2				Nonthaburi

PL = Thai Premier League ● FAC = FA Cup ● Cup = Yai Cup and Khor Royal Cup

THAI LEAGUE CUP 2011

Eighth-finals		Quarter-finals		Semi-finals		Final	
Buriram PEA	0 3						
Changmai *	0 1	**Buriram PEA** *	2 6				
Suphanburi	0 0	BEC Tero Sasana	1 2				
BEC Tero Sasana *	2 0			**Buriram PEA** *	1 2		
Muangthong United *	2 2			Chonburi	0 3		
Kasetsart University	1 2	Muangthong United	2 0				
Sisaket	0 1	**Chonburi** *	3 0				
Chonburi *	1 1					**Buriram PEA**	2
Phattalung *	2 1					Thai Port	0
Trang	1 1	**Phattalung** *	1 3				
Sriracha	1 2	Phuket	0 2			CUP FINAL	
Phuket *	1 3			Phattalung	0 1		
Chiangrai United *	1 1			**Thai Port** *	3 0	Suphachalasai, Bangkok	
Khon Kaen	0 1	Chiangrai United *	1 0			4-02-2012	
Police United *	0 0	**Thai Port**	1 0			Scorer - Rangsan 21, Clarence	
Thai Port	0 2			* Home team in the 1st leg		Bintang 90 for Buriram PEA	

TJK – TAJIKISTAN

FIFA/COCA-COLA WORLD RANKING

'93	'94	'95	'96	'97	'98	'99	'00	'01	'02	'03	'04	'05	'06	'07	'08	'09	'10	'11	'12
-	155	164	163	118	120	119	134	154	168	137	136	141	124	137	146	165	145	139	

2011												High	Low	Av
Jan	Feb	Mar	Apr	May	Jun	Jul	Aug	Sep	Oct	Nov	Dec			
143	141	148	134	134	135	141	153	124	130	139	139	114	180	142

Tajikistan progressed to the group phase of qualifying for the 2014 FIFA World Cup finals in Brazil when preliminary round opponents Syria were thrown out of the competition for fielding an ineligible player. Coach Pulod Kodirov was fired after that loss and was replaced by Alimdzhon Rafikov, who had steered Esteghlal Dushanbe to the finals of the AFC President's Cup earlier in the year. Rafikov's team met Uzbekistan, Japan and DPR Korea and, clearly out of their depth, the Central Asian side predictably finished last in the group without a point to their name. Rafikov, meanwhile, was replaced for the final qualifier by Bosnian coach Kemal Alispahic. Earlier in the year, Tajikistan faced off against teams at their own level as they booked a place in the finals of the 2012 AFC Challenge Cup, the competition contested by the lowest ranked nations within the confederation. The Tajiks won the title in 2006 – the inaugural year of the competition – and have finished in the top three in each of the following two tournaments and they eased through the qualifying rounds in early 2011. Victories over Kyrgyzstan and Cambodia in the Maldives secured them a place in the eight-team finals in Nepal before completing their qualifying campaign with a goalless draw against the group hosts.

FIFA WORLD CUP RECORD
1930-1994 DNE **1998-2010** DNQ

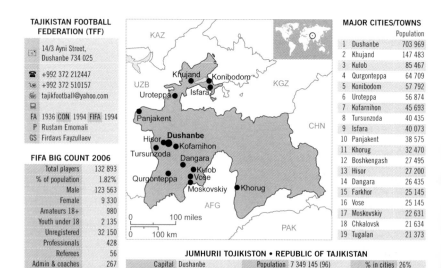

TAJIKISTAN FOOTBALL FEDERATION (TFF)

14/3 Ayni Street, Dushanbe 734 025

☎ +992 372 212447
📠 +992 372 510157
✉ tajikfootball@yahoo.com

FA	1936	CON 1994 FIFA 1994
P	Rustam Emomali	
GS	Firdavs Fayzullaev	

FIFA BIG COUNT 2006

Total players	132 893
% of population	1.82%
Male	123 563
Female	9 330
Amateurs 18+	980
Youth under 18	2 135
Unregistered	32 150
Professionals	428
Referees	56
Admin & coaches	267
Number of clubs	40
Number of teams	260

MAJOR CITIES/TOWNS

		Population
1	Dushanbe	703 969
2	Khujand	147 483
3	Kulob	85 467
4	Qurgonteppa	64 709
5	Konibodom	57 792
6	Uroteppa	56 874
7	Kofarnihon	45 693
8	Tursunzoda	40 435
9	Isfara	40 073
10	Panjakent	38 575
11	Khorug	32 470
12	Boshkengash	27 495
13	Hisor	27 200
14	Dangara	26 435
15	Farkhor	25 145
16	Vose	25 145
17	Moskovskiy	22 631
18	Chkalovsk	21 634
19	Tugalan	21 373

JUMHURII TOJIKISTON • REPUBLIC OF TAJIKISTAN

Capital	Dushanbe	Population	7 349 145 (96)	% in cities 26%
GDP per capita	$1800 (190)	Area km²	143 100 km² (95)	GMT + / - +5
Neighbours (km)	Afghanistan 1206, China 414, Kyrgyzstan 870, Uzbekistan 1161		

RECENT INTERNATIONAL MATCHES PLAYED BY TAJIKISTAN

2010	Opponents	Score	Venue	Comp	Scorers	Att	Referee
2-01	Yemen	W 1-0	Sana'a	Fr	Tukhtasunov [70]		
16-02	Bangladesh	L 0-1	Colombo	CCr1	Rabiev [70]	1 000	Matsuo JPN
18-02	Sri Lanka	W 3-1	Colombo	CCr1	Rabimov [13], Fatkhuloev 2 [32 92+]	1 000	Tan Hai CHN
20-02	Myanmar	W 3-0	Colombo	CCr1	Rabimov [33], Hakimov [52], Rabiev [88]	100	Shukralla BHR
24-02	Turkmenistan	L 0-2	Colombo	CCsf		300	Faghani IRN
27-02	Myanmar	W 1-0	Colombo	CC3p	Hakimov [11]	300	El Haddad LIB
26-06	China PR	L 0-4	Kunming	Fr			
17-11	Afghanistan	W 1-0	Dushanbe	Fr	Choriev [33]		
2011							
21-03	Kyrgyzstan	W 1-0	Male	CCq	OG [88]	4 000	Mohamed UAE
23-03	Cambodia	W 3-0	Male	CCq	Davronov 2, Ergashev [83], Rabimov [89]	550	Patwal IND
25-03	Maldives	D 0-0	Male	CCq		9 000	Mohamed UAE
27-03	Sri Lanka	D 2-2	Colombo	Fr	Rabimov [56], Vasiev [73]		
29-03	Sri Lanka	W 2-0	Colombo	Fr	Ergashev [21], Vasiev [23]		
23-07	Syria	W 3-0	Amman	WCq	Originally L 1-2. Saidov [47]	2 500	Al Ghafari JOR
28-07	Syria	W 3-0	Tursunzade	WCq	Originally L 0-4	9 000	Mashentsev KGZ
2-09	Uzbekistan	L 0-1	Tursunzade	WCq		15 000	Tan Hai CHN
6-09	Korea DPR	L 0-1	Pyongyang	WCq		28 000	Minh Tri Vo VIE
11-10	Japan	L 0-8	Osaka	WCq		44 688	Williams AUS
11-11	Japan	L 0-4	Dushanbe	WCq		18 000	Kim Dong Jin KOR
15-11	Uzbekistan	L 0-3	Tashkent	WCq		5 325	Alzarooni UAE

Fr = Friendly match • AC = AFC Asian Cup • CC = AFC Challenge Cup • WC = FIFA World Cup
q = qualifier • r1 = first round group • qf = quarter-final • sf = semi-final • f = final

TAJIKISTAN NATIONAL TEAM HISTORICAL RECORDS

Past Goals 16 - Yusuf Rabiev 2003- & Numonjon Hakimov 2003- • 10 - Tokhirjon Muminov 1993-2000 • 7 - Djomikhon Mukhidinov 2003- • 6 - Alier Ashurmamadov 1992-2005 & Chukhrat Djabarov 1997-2000

Past Coaches Sharif Nazarov 1992-94 • Vladimir Gulyamkhaydarov 1994-95 • Abdulla Muradov 1996 • Sharif Nazarov 2003 • Zoir Babaev 2004 • Sharif Nazarov 2004-06 • Makhmadjon Khabibulloev 2007 • Pulod Kodirov 2008-11 • Alimzhon Rafikov 2011-12 • Kemal Alispahic BIH 2012-

TAJIKISTAN CUP FINAL 2011
Dushanbe, 26-10-2011
Regar TadAZ 1-0 Esteghlal Dushanbe
Scorer - Jamshed Ismaoilov [64] for Regar

MEDALS TABLE

		Overall			League			Cup		Asia			City
		G	S	B	G	S	B	G	S	G	S	B	
1	Regar TadAZ	15	9	1	7	6		5	3	3		1	Tursunzoda
2	Vakhsh	5	4	5	3	1	4	2	2		1	1	Qurgonteppa
3	Varzob	5	1		3			2	1				Dushanbe
4	Esteghlal	4	1		2			2	1				Dushanbe
5	FK Hujand	3	6	4		3	4	3	3				Khujand
6	SKA Pamir	3	3	1	2	2	1	1	1				Dushanbe
7	Sitora	3	1	1	2	1	1	1					Dushanbe

TAJIKISTAN 2011

PREMIER LEAGUE	Pl	W	D	L	F	A	Pts	Esteghlal	Regar	Ravshan	Energetik	Xayr	SKA Pamir	Hujand	Vakhsh	Parvoz	Shodmon	Guardia
Esteghlal Dushanbe †	40	35	3	2	130	16	108		3-0 3-0	1-0 3-0	3-0 2-1	3-1 3-0	2-0 1-0	2-0 2-2	3-1 4-0	1-0 5-0	6-1 8-0	9-1 10-0
Regar TadAZ	40	30	5	5	108	29	95	1-0 0-0		2-0 2-0	2-0 2-0	1-0 3-0	2-2 1-1	5-0 2-0	4-1 4-2	3-1 3-1	3-1 7-0	4-0 10-1
Ravshan Kulob	40	29	2	9	78	38	89	0-1 0-4	2-0 1-2		2-0 2-1	1-1 2-1	2-1 3-1	2-0 3-0	2-1 3-2	5-0 1-0	4-0 3-0	4-0 3-2
Energetik Dushanbe	40	21	3	16	78	64	66	2-6 0-9	1-4 0-1	0-1 2-3		2-0 2-1	3-2 3-1	0-2 5-1	0-1 2-0	5-1 2-1	3-1 4-2	3-1 5-0
Xayr Vahdat	40	17	3	20	61	59	54	0-1 0-3	0-3 0-3	1-2 0-3	4-2 0-3		3-0 2-1	1-0 3-1	2-1 0-3	3-0 2-1	1-1 8-0	3-0 6-1
SKA Pamir Dushanbe	40	16	4	20	65	69	52	1-3 0-2	0-3 1-4	2-3 0-2	1-3 1-4	0-3 0-1		3-1 5-1	1-1 1-1	3-0 3-0	0-1 1-0	3-2 3-0
FK Hujand	40	15	6	19	56	72	51	0-0 0-3	1-1 1-3	1-1 3-2	1-2 1-3	2-1 3-3	3-4 2-1		3-1 0-0	2-1 1-0	2-1 4-1	3-1 4-0
Vakhsh Qurghonteppa	40	15	5	20	43	51	50	1-0 0-2	0-1 1-0	0-1 0-2	0-1 0-0	0-1 1-0	1-2 2-3	2-0 3-0		1-0 1-0	1-1 3-2	1-0 2-0
Parvoz B'jon Gafurov	40	12	4	24	45	76	40	0-3 0-3	1-1 0-3	3-1 0-0	0-1 0-0	0-3 0-0	2-3 0-2	2-1 3-1	2-1 1-2		0-3 3-1	3-0 5-1
Shodmon Ghissar	40	7	2	31	44	115	23	1-3 1-2	2-4 0-3	0-1 0-1	2-3 1-6	0-2 0-5	0-1 2-3	0-3 1-2	0-3 2-0	1-3 2-3		4-1 4-2
Guardia Dushanbe	40	3	3	34	32	151	12	2-5 0-6	2-1 1-10	0-1 1-6	0-0 1-5	1-5 3-0	0-3 0-5	0-0 2-4	1-0 0-2	2-3 1-1	1-2 2-3	

13/04/2011 - 28/12/2011 • † Qualified for the AFC President's Cup

TKM – TURKMENISTAN

FIFA/COCA-COLA WORLD RANKING

'93	'94	'95	'96	'97	'98	'99	'00	'01	'02	'03	'04	'05	'06	'07	'08	'09	'10	'11	'12
-	108	133	141	134	122	129	125	114	134	99	98	116	155	127	148	141	135	146	

2011												High	Low	Av
Jan	Feb	Mar	Apr	May	Jun	Jul	Aug	Sep	Oct	Nov	Dec			
133	133	154	139	140	143	138	142	141	145	147	146	86	174	130

The schedule of the Turkmenistan national team is largely restricted to matches in the AFC Challenge Cup and the FIFA World Cup and they played in both during the course of 2011. The Turkmens qualified with some comfort for the finals of the 2012 edition of the AFC Challenge Cup as Yazguly Hojageldiyev's side brushed aside Pakistan and Chinese Taipei to join India in the finals in Nepal. The World Cup qualifiers saw them paired in a preliminary round play-off against Indonesia, but despite drawing 1-1 in the first leg at home in Ashgabat, they lost a thrilling game in the return in Jakarta, scoring three late goals in a 4-3 defeat which saw them crash out. In club football, Balkan successfully defended their domestic league crown, finishing two points clear of cup winners HTTU Ashgabat to secure the title for a third time. The Balkanabat-based club also represented Turkmenistan in the 2011 AFC President's Cup and earned a place in the finals of the tournament thanks to victories over WAPDA from Pakistan and Nepal Police Club in a qualifying group. There they came up against hosts Taiwan Power Company who topped the group to make it through to the final. Since the launch of the tournament in 2005 a club from Turkmenistan has yet to make it through to the final of the showpiece event for the smaller nations within the AFC.

FIFA WORLD CUP RECORD
1930-1994 DNE 1998-2010 DNQ

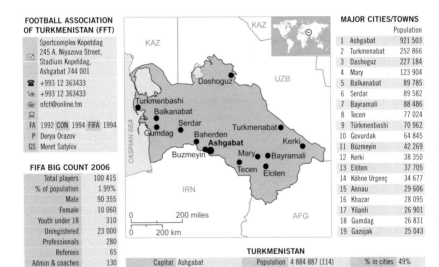

FOOTBALL ASSOCIATION OF TURKMENISTAN (FFT)

Sportcomplex Kopetdag
245 A. Niyazova Street,
Stadium Kopetdag,
Ashgabat 744 001

☎ +993 12 363433
🖷 +993 12 363433
✉ nfct@online.tm

FA	1992	CON	1994	FIFA 1994
P	Derya Orazov		
GS	Meret Satylov		

FIFA BIG COUNT 2006

Total players	100 415
% of population	1.99%
Male	90 355
Female	10 060
Youth under 18	310
Unregistered	23 000
Professionals	280
Referees	65
Admin & coaches	130
Number of clubs	15
Number of teams	98

MAJOR CITIES/TOWNS
Population

1	Ashgabat	921 503
2	Turkmenabat	252 866
3	Dashoguz	227 184
4	Mary	123 904
5	Balkanabat	89 785
6	Serdar	89 582
7	Bayramali	88 486
8	Tecen	77 024
9	Türkmenbashi	70 962
10	Govurdak	64 845
11	Büzmeyin	42 269
12	Kerki	38 350
13	Elöten	37 705
14	Köhne Urgenç	34 677
15	Annau	29 606
16	Khazar	28 095
17	Yilanli	26 901
18	Gumdag	26 831
19	Gazojak	25 043

TURKMENISTAN

Capital	Ashgabat	Population	4 884 887 (114)	% in cities 49%
GDP per capita	$6500 (128)	Area km²	488 100 km² (52)	GMT +/- +5

Neighbours (km) Afghanistan 744, Iran 992, Kazakhstan 379, Uzbekistan 1621 • Caspian Sea 1768

RECENT INTERNATIONAL MATCHES PLAYED BY TURKMENISTAN

2007	Opponents	Score		Venue	Comp	Scorers	Att	Referee
11-10	Cambodia	W	1-0	Phnom Penh	WCq	Karadanov [85]	3 000	Gosh BAN
28-10	Cambodia	W	4-1	Ashgabat	WCq	Nasyrov [41], Gevorkyan 2 [50 66], Karadanov [74]	5 000	Saidov UZB
10-11	Hong Kong	D	0-0	Hong Kong	WCq		2 823	Mujghef JOR
18-11	Hong Kong	W	3-0	Ashgabat	WCq	Nasyrov [42], Bayramov [53], Mirzoev [80]	30 000	Al Hilali OMA
2008								
6-02	Korea Republic	L	0-4	Seoul	WCq		25 738	Najm LIB
26-03	Jordan	L	0-2	Ashgabat	WCq		20 000	Tongkhan THA
18-05	Oman	L	1-2	Nizwa	Fr	Saparov [53]		
2-06	Korea DPR	D	0-0	Ashgabat	WCq		20 000	Al Ghamdi KSA
7-06	Korea DPR	L	0-1	Pyongyang	WCq		25 000	Al Saeedi UAE
14-06	Korea Republic	L	1-3	Ashgabat	WCq	Ovekov [77p]	11 000	Takayama JPN
22-06	Jordan	L	0-2	Amman	WCq		150	Williams AUS
30-07	Tajikistan	D	0-0	Hyderabad	CCr1		150	Kovalenko UZB
1-08	Afghanistan	W	5-0	Hyderabad	CCr1	Ovekov 4 [1 41 77 80], Krendelev [23]	100	Saleem MDV
3-08	India	L	1-2	Hyderabad	CCr1	Orazmamedov [84]	1 000	Jasim UAE
3-10	Mynamar	W	2-1	Ho Chi Minh	Fr			
5-10	Vietnam	W	3-2	Ho Chi Minh	Fr			
2009								
18-01	Syria	L	1-5	Kuwait City	Fr	Bablin [12]		
20-01	Kuwait	L	0-2	Kuwait City	Fr			
14-04	Maldives	W	3-1	Male	CCq	Nasyrov [42], Shamuradov [49], Mirzoyev [68p]	9 000	Al Ghafary JOR
16-04	Bhutan	W	7-0	Male	CCq	Atayev 3 [13 67 79], Chonkayev [16], Urazov [47], Mingazov [62], Mirzoyev [93+]	300	Perera SRI
18-04	Philippines	W	5-0	Male	CCq	OG [26], Shamuradov 2 [54 63], Nasyrov [58], Urazov [65]	400	Al Ghafary JOR
20-10	Vietnam	L	0-1	Ho Chi Minh	Fr			
22-10	Singapore	L	2-4	Ho Chi Minh	Fr	Shamuradov [14p], Ovekov [84]		
2010								
17-02	Korea DPR	D	1-1	Colombo	CCr1	Karadanov [36]	400	Mahapab THA
19-02	India	W	1-0	Colombo	CCr1	Karadanov [24p]	450	Matsuo JPN
21-02	Kyrgyzstan	W	1-0	Colombo	CCr1	Nurmuradov [70]	100	El Haddad LIB
24-02	Tajikistan	W	2-0	Colombo	CCsf	Amanov [33], Urazov [42]	300	Faghani IRN
27-02	Korea DPR	D	1-1	Colombo	CCf	Shamuradov [33]. L 4-5p	3 000	Faghani IRN
2011								
21-03	Pakistan	W	3-0	Petaling Jaya	CCq	Urazov [6], Amanov [46], Karadanov [86]	150	Bakhshizadeh IRN
23-03	Chinese Taipei	W	2-0	Petaling Jaya	CCq	Shamuradov [73], Hangeldiyev [76]	100	Serazitdinov UZB
25-03	India	D	1-1	Petaling Jaya	CCq	Chonkayev [52p]	200	Abdul Wahab MAS
23-07	Indonesia	D	1-1	Ashgabat	WCq	Krendelev [12]	7 500	Torki IRN
28-07	Indonesia	L	3-4	Jakarta	WCq	Amanov [72], Shamuradov [84], Chonkaev [87p]	88 000	Williams AUS

Fr = Friendly match • AC = AFC Asian Cup • CC = AFC Challenge Cup • WC = FIFA World Cup • q = qualifier • r1 = first round group

TURKMENISTAN NATIONAL TEAM HISTORICAL RECORDS

Past Coaches   Bayram Durdiev 1992-96 • Elguja Gugushvili GEO 1996-97 • Tacmirat Agamiradov 1997-98 • Viktor Pozhechevsky UKR 1998-99 • Gurban Berdiev 1999 • Rowsen Muhadov 1999-2000 • Tacmirat Agamiradov 2000-01 • Vladimir Bessonov UKR 2002-03 • Rahim Gurbanmammedov 2003-04 • Boris Grigoryants 2005 • Amangylyc Gocumov 2005-06 • Rahim Gurbanmammedov 2007-09 • Boris Grigoryants 2009-10 • Yazguly Hojageldiyev 2010-

TURKMENISTAN 2011

YOKARY LIGA

Team	Pl	W	D	L	F	A	Pts	Balkan	HTTU	Ashgabat	Merv Mary	Sagadam	Altyn Asyr	Lebap	Ahal	Gara Altyn	Dasoguz
Balkan Balkanabat †	36	26	4	6	78	30	**82**		2-1 2-1	3-0 2-0	1-0 2-1	3-1 2-0	1-0 1-1	3-0 3-2	2-0 5-0	1-0 3-0	8-0 1-1
HTTU Ashgabat	36	25	5	6	85	28	**80**	1-3 1-1		1-0 3-0	2-1 2-0	7-1 3-0	2-1 2-1	4-1 4-1	2-1 7-0	2-0 9-0	4-2 2-1
FK Ashgabat	36	23	4	9	79	41	**72**	4-2 2-1	0-1 1-0		1-0 0-0	5-0 2-2	0-0 1-1	4-1 6-0	2-0 3-2	4-1 5-1	2-0 1-0
Merv Mary	36	20	7	9	63	29	**67**	1-1 2-0	1-0 1-1	0-1 4-0		0-0 2-0	4-1 2-0	0-1 4-2	1-3 0-4	4-0 4-0	4-0 1-1
Sagadam Turkmenbasy	36	17	5	14	43	50	**56**	0-2 1-0	0-2 1-0	0-1 4-2	1-3 3-1		1-0 2-1	1-0 2-0	0-1 2-0	1-0 1-0	2-0 1-0
Altyn Asyr	36	12	9	15	46	42	**44**	0-3 0-1	1-1 0-1	1-2 3-0	1-1 1-2	0-2 2-0		2-2 1-2	1-3 4-0	1-0 5-1	1-0 2-0
Lebap Türkmenabat	36	12	6	18	46	74	**42**	0-3 4-1	0-4 1-1	2-8 1-4	0-1 2-1	0-0 1-1	0-1 2-2		1-0 3-1	2-1 2-1	4-0 1-0
FC Ahal	36	9	4	23	40	82	**31**	3-1 2-4	1-3 0-4	0-2 1-3	1-2 1-3	2-2 1-2	0-0 0-3	2-1 3-2		4-0 2-2	2-1 2-2
Gara Altyn Balkanabat	36	7	3	26	37	83	**24**	1-3 0-2	0-1 1-2	0-1 3-2	0-2 3-3	1-0 3-4	1-1 1-2	4-1 0-2	1-2 4-0		3-0 3-2
FK Dasoguz	36	3	5	28	25	83	**14**	0-4 0-1	1-1 1-3	1-6 0-4	0-1 1-2	2-1 1-4	0-2 1-3	1-1 0-3	0-2 3-0	0-1 3-0	

2/04/2011 - 25/11/2011 • † Qualified for the AFC President's Cup

MEDALS TABLE

	Team	Overall G	Overall S	Overall B	League G	League S	League B	Cup G	Cup S	Asia G	Asia S	Asia B	City
1	Kopetdag Ashgabat	12	6		6	3		6	3				Ashgabat
2	Balkan Balkanabat	6	8	6	3	5	6	3	3				Balkanabat
3	Nisa Ashgabat	5	8	1	4	5	1	1	3				Ashgabat
4	HTTU Ashgabat	5	4	1	3	3		2	1		1		Ashgabat
5	Merv Mary	2	3	3			3	2	3				Mary
6	FK Ashgabat	2	1	4	2		2		1		2		Ashgabat
7	Sagadam Turkmenbasy	2	1	1	1		1	1	1				Turkmenbasy
8	Altyn Asyr	1	2			1		1	1				Asyr
9	FK Dasoguz	1	1					1	1				Dasoguz
10	Garagam Türkmenabad	1		1	1		1						Türkmenabad

TURKMENISTAN CUP 2011

Quarter-finals

HTTU Ashgabat *	2 1	4p
Sagadam Turkmenbasy	1 2	2p
FC Ahal	0	1
Merv Mary *	4	5
Lebap Türkmenabat	1	1
Balkan Balkanabat *	0	1
Altyn Asyr	1	1
FK Ashgabat *	1	2

Semi-finals

HTTU Ashgabat *	0 2
Merv Mary	1 1
Lebap Türkmenabat *	2 0
FK Ashgabat	1 1

* Home team in the first leg

Final

HTTU Ashgabat	0	4p
FK Ashgabat	0	2p

Ahal Stadium, Abadan
30-11-2011, Ref: Saidov

TLS – TIMOR–LESTE

FIFA/COCA-COLA WORLD RANKING

'93	'94	'95	'96	'97	'98	'99	'00	'01	'02	'03	'04	'05	'06	'07	'08	'09	'10	'11	'12
-	-	-	-	-	-	-	-	-	-	-	-	-	198	201	197	200	201	205	

	2011											High	Low	Av
Jan	Feb	Mar	Apr	May	Jun	Jul	Aug	Sep	Oct	Nov	Dec			
201	201	201	200	200	202	202	202	201	201	203	205	197	205	200

Timor-Leste's attempts at raising the profile of football both at home and at a regional level were given a boost at the South East Asian Games in late 2011 by the nation's under-23 team. Making only their second appearance in the competition, Timor-Leste finished third in their five-team group, well adrift of semi-final qualifiers Vietnam and Myanmar, but ahead of Laos - semi-finalists two years previously - Brunei and the Philippines. The full national team, however, remains a work in progress, playing just two competitive fixtures during 2011. Going into their 2014 FIFA World Cup qualifier against Nepal in July, Timor-Leste had only six teams below them in the FIFA/Coca-Cola World Ranking, so it was no surprise when the Nepalese beat them 7-1 on aggregate with both games played in Kathmandu. It was only the second time that Timor-Leste had entered the World Cup and to date all four games have been lost. The East Timorese will, though, be looking forward to the qualifying rounds of the AFF Suzuki Cup, the key regional tournament in South East Asia. The qualifiers kick off in October and the former Portuguese colony will be hoping to progress to the finals for the first time in their history after losing all three of their matches in the preliminary stages of the 2010 competition.

FIFA WORLD CUP RECORD
1930-2006 DNE 2010 DNQ

FEDERACAO FUTEBOL TIMOR-LESTE (FFTL)

	Campo Democracia Ave, Bairo Formosa, PO Box 406, Dili
☎	+670 3310670
📠	+670 3310671
✉	federacao_futebol@yahoo.com
FA	2002 CON 2002 FIFA 2005
P	Francisco Lay
GS	Armandio Sarmento

FIFA BIG COUNT 2006

Total players	15 500
% of population	1.46%
Male	15 500
Female	0
Amateurs 18+	200
Youth under 18	300
Unregistered	0
Professionals	0
Referees	0
Admin & coaches	100
Number of clubs	10
Number of teams	20

MAJOR CITIES/TOWNS

		Population
1	Dili	174 096
2	Dare	20 327
3	Los Palos	17 598
4	Baucau	15 307
5	Ermera	13 768
6	Maliana	12 016
7	Suai	6 729
8	Aubá	6 085
9	Viqueque	5 545
10	Liquiça	4 998
11	Oecussi	4 789
12	Metinaro	4 583
13	Bazartete	3 499
14	Lolotoi	3 440
15	Lautem	3 233
16	Ainaro	3 172
17	Same	2 328
18	Manatuto	1 979
19	Aileu	1 962

REPUBLIKA DEMOKRATIKA TIMOR LOROSA'E • DEMOCRATIC REPUBLIC OF TIMOR-LESTE

Capital Dili	Population 1 131 612 (155)	% in cities 27%
GDP per capita $2300 (180)	Area km² 14 874 km² (159)	GMT +/- +9
Neighbours (km) Indonesia 228 • Coast 706		

RECENT INTERNATIONAL MATCHES PLAYED BY TIMOR–LESTE

2002 Opponents	Score	Venue	Comp	Scorers	Att	Referee
No international matches played before 2003						
2003						
21-03 Sri Lanka	L 2-3	Colombo	ACq			
23-03 Chinese Taipei	L 0-3	Colombo	ACq			
2004						
8-12 Malaysia	L 0-5	Kuala Lumpur	AFFr1			
12-12 Thailand	L 0-8	Kuala Lumpur	AFFr1			
14-12 Philippines	L 1-2	Kuala Lumpur	AFFr1	Anai [14]		
16-12 Myanmar	L 1-3	Kuala Lumpur	AFFr1	Simon Diamantino [15p]		
2005						
No international matches played in 2005						
2006						
12-11 Brunei	L 2-3	Bacolod	AFFq	Adelio Maria Costa [33], Anatacio Belo [77]		
14-11 Philippines	L 0-7	Bacolod	AFFq			
16-11 Laos	L 2-3	Bacolod	AFFq	Antonio Ximenes [82], Adelio Maria Costa [89]		
20-11 Cambodia	L 1-4	Bacolod	AFFq	Adelio Maria Costa [63]		
2007						
21-10 Hong Kong	L 2-3	Gianyar	WCq	Emilio Da Silva 2 [41 69]	1 500	Shaharul MAS
28-10 Hong Kong	L 1-8	Hong Kong	WCq	Emilio Da Silva	1 542	Torky IRN
2008						
17-10 Philippines	L 0-1	Phnom Penh	AFFq		15 000	
19-10 Cambodia	D 2-2	Phnom Penh	AFFq	Anggisu Barbosa [45], Joao Perreira [67p]	12 000	
21-10 Brunei Darussalam	L 1-4	Phnom Penh	AFFq	Rosito Soares [80]		
25-10 Laos	L 1-2	Phnom Penh	AFFq	Alfredo Esteves [44]		
2009						
No international matches played in 2009						
2010						
22-10 Philippines	L 0-5	Vientiane	AFFq			Leow SIN
24-10 Cambodia	L 2-4	Vientiane	AFFq	Chiquito Do Carmo [5], Anggisu Barbosa [85]		Phung Dinh Dung VIE
26-10 Laos	L 1-6	Vientiane	AFFq	Chiquito Do Carmo [9]		
21-11 Indonesia	L 0-6	Palembang	Fr			
2011						
29-06 Nepal	L 1-2	Kathmandu	WCq	Joao Perreira [47]	9 000	Sabbagh LIB
2-07 Nepal	L 0-5	Kathmandu	WCq		15 000	Lee Min Hu KOR

AC = AFC Asian Cup • AFF = ASEAN Football Federation Championship
q = qualifier • r1 = first round group • Matches played before September 2005 are not full internationals

TOG – TOGO

FIFA/COCA-COLA WORLD RANKING

'93	'94	'95	'96	'97	'98	'99	'00	'01	'02	'03	'04	'05	'06	'07	'08	'09	'10	'11	'12
113	86	92	87	78	68	87	81	71	86	94	89	56	60	72	86	71	103	101	

						2011									
Jan	Feb	Mar	Apr	May	Jun	Jul	Aug	Sep	Oct	Nov	Dec	**High**	**Low**	**Av**
101	103	102	109	109	113	123	121	95	94	101	101	**46**	**123**	**82**

Emmanuel Adebayor made a much-anticipated return to the Togo side as they advanced through the preliminary round of Africa's qualifiers for the 2014 FIFA World Cup finals in Brazil. Togo's only genuine world-class star, and a former African Footballer of the Year, had announced his retirement from the international game in the wake of the shooting of the Togo team bus on the eve of the 2010 CAF Africa Cup of Nations. He cited concerns over a lack of security around the team as his reason but was badly shaken by the whole affair. A high-powered delegation of both government and football association officials travelled to London to persuade him back ahead of the two-legged tie against Guinea-Bissau in November. Adebayor missed the first leg away in Bissau, which ended 1-1, but was on hand for the return in Lome, where Serge Gakpe got the only goal of the game for a 2-1 aggregate triumph. For the World Cup qualifiers, Togo sought the services of an expatriate coach, taking former French international Didier Six on a two-match probationary experiment. In the wake of the national team's appearance at the 2006 FIFA World Cup finals, club football has been a major casualty with only two league seasons completed but a new season did kick-off in October 2011 after a gap of over two years.

CAF AFRICA CUP OF NATIONS RECORD

1957-1965 DNQ 1968-1970 DNQ **1972** 7 r1 1974 DNE 1976-1982 DNQ **1984** 8 r1 1986-1988 DNQ 1990 DNE 1992 DNQ 1994 Withdrew
1996 DNQ **1998** 12 r1 **2000** 9 r1 **2002** 12 r1 2004 DNQ **2006** 15 r1 2008 DNQ **2010** Withdrew 2012 DNQ

FEDERATION TOGOLAISE DE FOOTBALL (FTF)

	Route de Kégué, Boite postale 05, Lome
☎	+228 2412535
📠	+228 2258639
✉	ftftogo@gmail.com
💻	
FA 1960	CON 1963	FIFA 1962
P	Gabriel Ameyi
GS	Delali Klussey

FIFA BIG COUNT 2006

Total players	242 400
% of population	4.37%
Male	230 900
Female	11 500
Amateurs 18+	5 200
Youth under 18	4 500
Unregistered	15 600
Professionals	100
Referees	600
Admin & coaches	2 700
Number of clubs	100
Number of teams	620

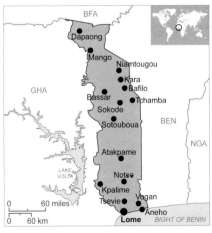

MAJOR CITIES/TOWNS

		Population
1	Lomé	1 565 121
2	Sokodé	112 522
3	Kara	107 889
4	Atakpamé	80 463
5	Kpalimé	77 681
6	Dapaong	54 495
7	Tsévié	50 778
8	Notsé	37 221
9	Aného	27 000
10	Bassar	25 937
11	Mango	25 601
12	Niamtougou	25 599
13	Tchamba	22 485
14	Sotouboua	22 162
15	Vogan	21 523
16	Bafilo	19 851
17	Tabligbo	19 668
18	Badou	13 986
19	Kandé	9 989

REPUBLIQUE TOGOLAISE • TOGOLESE REPUBLIC

Capital Lomé	Population 6 019 877 (107)	% in cities 42%
GDP per capita $900 (216)	Area km² 56 785 km² (125)	GMT +/- 0
Neighbours (km) Benin 644, Burkina Faso 126, Ghana 877 • Coast 56		

RECENT INTERNATIONAL MATCHES PLAYED BY TOGO

2006	Opponents	Score		Venue	Comp	Scorers	Att	Referee
13-06	Korea Republic	L	1-2	Frankfurt	WCr1	Kader Coubadja [31]	48 000	Poll ENG
19-06	Switzerland	L	0-2	Dortmund	WCr1		65 000	Amarilla PAR
23-06	France	L	0-2	Cologne	WCr1		45 000	Larrionda URU
15-08	Ghana	L	0-2	London	Fr			Dean ENG
29-08	Niger	D	1-1	Lomé	Fr	Komlan Amewou [55]		
3-09	Benin	W	2-1	Lomé	CNq	Thomas Dossevi [13], Komlan Amewou [78]		Louzaya CGO
8-10	Mali	L	0-1	Bamako	CNq			Benouza ALG
15-11	Luxembourg	D	0-0	Luxembourg	Fr		1 417	Richards WAL
2007								
7-02	Cameroon	D	2-2	Lomé	Fr	Adekanmi Olufade [25], Emmanuel Adebayor [40]		
25-03	Sierra Leone	W	3-1	Lomé	CNq	Emmanuel Adebayor 2 [38 85], Adekanmi Olufade [62]		Pare BFA
3-06	Sierra Leone	W	1-0	Freetown	CNq	Junior Senaya [48]		Imiere NGA
17-06	Benin	L	1-4	Cotonou	CNq	Adekanmi Olufade [75]		Evehe CMR
22-08	Zambia	W	3-1	Lomé	Fr	Jonathan Ayite 2 [29 41], Adekanmi Olufade [84]		
12-10	Mali	L	0-2	Lomé	CNq			Abdelfattah EGY
18-11	Ghana	L	0-2	Accra	Fr			
21-11	UAE	W	5-0	Accra	Fr	Nouhoun Moutawakilou [19], Sapol Mani [73], OG [77], Thomas Dossevi [83], Emmanuel Adebayor [84]		
2008								
25-03	Guinea	L	0-2	Paris	Fr			
31-05	Zambia	W	1-0	Accra	WCq	Adekanmi Olufade [16]	15 000	Pare BFA
8-06	Swaziland	L	1-2	Mbabane	WCq	Adekanmi Olufade [88]	5 819	Niyongabo BDI
20-08	Congo DR	L	1-2	Dreux	Fr	Emmanuel Adebayor [47p]		
10-09	Zambia	L	0-1	Chililabombwe	WCq		10 500	Damon RSA
11-10	Swaziland	W	6-0	Accra	WCq	Moustapha Salifou [16], Emmanuel Adebayor 4 [29 47 72 85], Adekanmi Olufade [44]	8 000	Evehe CMR
19-11	Rwanda	W	1-0	Lome	Fr	Floyd Ayite [33]		
2009								
11-02	Burkina Faso	D	1-1	Le Petit-Quevilly	Fr	Senah Mangoh [77]		
28-03	Cameroon	W	1-0	Accra	WCq	Emmanuel Adebayor [11]	26 450	Abd El Fatah EGY
6-06	Gabon	L	0-3	Libreville	WCq		20 000	Lwanja MWI
20-06	Morocco	D	0-0	Rabat	WCq		22 000	Kaoma ZAM
12-08	Angola	L	0-2	Lisbon	Fr		7 000	Proenca POR
6-09	Morocco	D	1-1	Lomé	WCq	Moustapha Salifou [3]	24 651	Ssegonga UGA
10-10	Cameroon	L	0-3	Yaoundé	WCq		36 401	Kaoma ZAM
14-10	Japan	L	0-5	Miyagi	Fr		32 852	Mikulski POL
6-11	Bahrain	L	1-5	Manama	Fr	Dove Wome [69]		
14-11	Gabon	W	1-0	Lomé	WCq	Floyd Ayite [71]	10 000	Seechurn MRI
2010								
19-05	Gabon	L	0-3	Ajaccio	Fr			
1-07	Chad	D	2-2	N'Djamena	CNq	Sapol Mani [25], Backer Aloenouvo [68]		Benouza ALG
9-07	Malawi	D	1-1	Lomé	CNq	Backer Aloenouvo [75]		Bennett RSA
11-08	Saudi Arabia	L	0-1	Riyadh	Fr			
4-09	Botswana	L	1-2	Gaborone	CNq	Serge Gakpe [44]		Kagabo RWA
10-10	Tunisia	L	1-2	Lomé	CNq	Sapol Mani [40]		Abdul Rahman SUD
17-11	Chad	D	0-0	Lomé	CNq			Coulibaly MLI
2011								
8-02	Ghana	L	1-4	Antwerp	Fr	Komlan Amewou [50p]		
26-03	Malawi	L	0-1	Blantyre	CNq			
10-08	Niger	D	3-3	Niamey	Fr	Komlan Amewou [2], Kondo Arimiyaou [43], Backer Aloenouvo [60]		
4-09	Botswana	W	1-0	Lome	CNq	Kondo Arimiyaou [23]		
8-10	Tunisia	L	0-2	Rades	CNq			
11-11	Guinea-Bissau	D	1-1	Bissau	WCq	Serge Gakpe [32]	3 000	Diedhiou SEN
15-11	Guinea-Bissau	W	1-0	Lome	WCq	OG [3]	25 000	Mohamadou CMR

Fr = Friendly match • CN = CAF African Cup of Nations • WC = FIFA World Cup • q = qualifier • r1 = first round group

TPE – CHINESE TAIPEI

FIFA/COCA-COLA WORLD RANKING

'93	'94	'95	'96	'97	'98	'99	'00	'01	'02	'03	'04	'05	'06	'07	'08	'09	'10	'11	'12
161	170	178	174	154	169	174	162	170	166	150	155	156	166	169	167	162	153	167	

2011												High	Low	Av
Jan	Feb	Mar	Apr	May	Jun	Jul	Aug	Sep	Oct	Nov	Dec			
152	154	147	160	160	165	166	169	172	166	165	167	144	180	163

Taiwan Power Company converted their long-held domestic dominance into a trophy-winning run in international competition as the Kaohsiung-based club won the 2011 AFC President's Cup. Taipower, as the club is known, defeated Cambodia's Phnom Penh Crown 3-2 in the final at home in Kaohsiung to become the first Taiwanese club to win the competition. They had previously taken part on three occasions but had never progressed beyond the group stage. Taipower also won the Chinese Taipei City A-League, retaining the title they had won the year before for what was their 16th championship in just over 20 years. It was a close-run thing, however, coming on goal difference as both they and Taipei City Tatung went through the season undefeated. The national team had a difficult year in 2011 in both the AFC Challenge Cup and in FIFA World Cup qualifying. They failed to make the finals of the 2012 AFC Challenge Cup in Nepal after losing all three games against India, Turkmenistan and Pakistan, but they could count themselves very unlucky in the World Cup qualifiers for Brazil after being knocked out by a Malaysian team that on paper was much stronger. After losing the first leg 2-1 in Kuala Lumpur, Chinese Taipei won the return 3-2 but went out on away goals.

FIFA WORLD CUP RECORD
1930-1954 DNE 1954 DNQ 1958-1974 DNE 1978-2014 DNQ

CHINESE TAIPEI FOOTBALL ASSOCIATION (CTFA)

Room 210, 2F, 55 Chang Chi Street, Tatung District, Taipei 10363
☎ +886 2 25961185
📠 +886 2 25951594
✉ ctfa7155@ms59.hinet.net
🖥 www.ctfa.com.tw
FA 1924 CON 1954 FIFA 1954
P Lu Kun Shan
GS Chris Wang

FIFA BIG COUNT 2006

Total players	458 460
% of population	1.99%
Male	424 400
Female	34 060
Amateurs 18+	5 960
Unregistered	75 900
Professionals	0
Referees	102
Admin & coaches	374
Number of clubs	60
Number of teams	600

MAJOR CITIES/TOWNS

		Population
1	Taipei	2 655 423
2	Kaohsiung	1 525 999
3	Taizhong	1 078 348
4	Tainan	772 279
5	Banqiao	547 444
6	Zhonghe	414 984
7	Taoyuan	405 289
8	Xinzhu	401 991
9	Xinzhuang	400 647
10	Jilong	389 737
11	Sanchong	380 859
12	Zhongli	367 943
13	Fengshan	343 332
14	Xindian	293 572
15	Jiayi	274 657
16	Zhanghua	239 716
17	Tucheng	237 795
18	Yonghe	236 448
19	Pingdong	217 819

CHINESE TAIPEI

Capital Taipei	Population 22 974 347 (49)	% in cities 69%
GDP per capita $31 100 (42)	Area km² 35 980 km² (138)	GMT +/- +8
Neighbours (km) Coast 1566		

RECENT INTERNATIONAL MATCHES PLAYED BY CHINESE TAIPEI

2008	Opponents	Score		Venue	Comp	Scorers	Att	Referee
2-04	Pakistan	L	1-2	Taipei	CCq	Lo Chi An [5]	800	Iemoto JPN
4-04	Guam	W	4-1	Taipei	CCq	Chang Han [20], Huang Wei Yi [28], Chen Po Liang [33], Chiang Shih Lu [44]	850	Win Cho MYA
6-04	Sri Lanka	D	2-2	Taipei	CCq	Chang Han [28], Tsai Hsien Tang [74]	900	Iemoto JPN
24-05	India	L	0-3	Goa	Fr			
27-05	India	D	2-2	Chennai	Fr	Chen Po Liang [4], Hsieh Meng Hsuan [48]		
2009								
4-04	Pakistan	D	1-1	Colombo	CCq	Chang Han [21]	400	Tseytlin UZB
6-04	Sri Lanka	L	1-2	Colombo	CCq	Huang Wei Yi [80]	1 400	Al Zahrani KSA
8-04	Brunei Darussalam	W	5-0	Colombo	CCq	Chen Po Liang 3 [11 13 58], Huang Wei Yi [30], Kuo Chun Yi [80]	1 000	Al Zahrani KSA
23-08	Hong Kong	L	0-4	Kaohsiung	EAq		12 000	Tojo JPN
25-08	Guam	W	4-2	Kaohsiung	EAq	Chen Po Liang 2 [45 68], Chang Han [61], Lo Chih En [75]	7 500	Matsuo JPN
27-08	Korea DPR	L	1-2	Kaohsiung	EAq	Chang Han [49]	10 000	Matsuo JPN
2010								
16-01	Philippines	D	0-0	Kaohsiung	Fr			
9-10	Macau	W	7-1	Kaohsiung	Fr	Lin Cheng Yi [16], Lo Chih En [43], Lo Chih An [45], Chen Po Hao 2 [46 77], Chang Han [55], Chen Po Liang [67]	1 000	San Hua Nien TPE
10-10	Philippines	D	1-1	Kaohsiung	Fr	Lo Chih An [48]	890	Kao Tsai Hu TPE
12-10	Hong Kong	D	1-1	Kaohsiung	Fr	Lo Chih An [40]	3 000	Kao Tsai Hu TPE
24-11	Indonesia	L	0-2	Palembang	Fr			Singh SIN
2011								
10-02	Laos	W	5-2	Kaohsiung	CCq	Lin Cheng Yi [10], Chang Han 2 [22 56], Chen Po Liang [44], Lo Chih An [49]	1 000	Ng Chiu Kok HKG
16-02	Laos	D	1-1	Vientiane	CCq	Chen Po Liang [65]	15 300	Abdul Wahab MAS
21-03	India	L	0-3	Petaling Jaya	CCq		50	Abdul Wahab MAS
23-03	Turkmenistan	L	0-2	Petaling Jaya	CCq		100	Serazitdinov UZB
25-03	Pakistan	L	0-2	Petaling Jaya	CCq		50	Alrshaidat JOR
29-06	Malaysia	L	1-2	Kuala Lumpur	WCq	Chen Po Liang [76]	45 000	Mahapab THA
3-07	Malaysia	W	3-2	Taipei	WCq	Chang Han [31], Chen Po Liang [44p], Chen Tsan Yuan [75p]	16 768	Minh Tri Vo VIE
18-07	Singapore	L	2-3	Singapore	Fr	Lo Chih An [48], Chiang Shih Lu [62]		
30-09	Macau	W	3-0	Kaohsiung	Fr	Huang Chiu Yi [11], Chen Po Liang [31], Wu Chin Hung [45]		
2-10	Philippines	D	0-0	Kaohsiung	Fr			
4-10	Hong Kong	L	0-6	Kaohsiung	Fr		5 210	

Fr = Friendly match • EA = East Asian Championship • AC = AFC Asian Cup • CC = AFC Challenge Cup • WC = FIFA World Cup • q = qualifier

CHINESE TAIPEI NATIONAL TEAM HISTORICAL RECORDS

Past Coaches
Lee Wai Tong 1954-58 • Law Pak 1977-81 • Chiang Chia 1981-85 • Lo Chih Tsung 1985-88 • Huang Jen Cheng 1988-93 • Chiang Mu Tsai 1994-2000 • Huang Jen Cheng 2000-01 • Lee Po Houng 2001-05 • Dido BRA 2005 • Toshiaki Imai JPN 2005-07 • Chen Sing An 2008-09 • Lo Chih Tsung 2009-

CHINESE TAIPEI 2011

CITY A-LEAGUE

	Pl	W	D	L	F	A	Pts	Taipower	Tatung	NTCPE	Taipei PEC	Ming Chuan	NSTC	Hwa Lian
Taipower ‡	12	9	3	0	47	11	30		1-1	2-0	6-1	5-1	2-1	4-0
Taipei City Tatung	12	9	3	0	39	10	30	2-2		3-1	1-0	2-0	4-1	9-0
NTCPE	12	6	2	4	40	27	20	2-7	2-2		3-2	2-2	5-1	7-0
Taipei PEC	12	5	0	7	22	30	15	2-5	1-5	1-3		3-5	2-0	3-0
Ming Chuan University	12	4	2	6	29	31	14	0-1	2-4	2-5	1-2		3-2	8-1
NSTC	12	3	1	8	28	28	10	1-1	0-2	4-2	1-3	2-3		5-0
Hwa Lian Tsao Tien	12	0	1	11	5	73	1	0-11	0-4	1-8	0-2	2-2	1-10	

13/04/2011 - 1/12/2011 • ‡ Qualified for the AFC President's Cup

TRI – TRINIDAD AND TOBAGO

FIFA/COCA-COLA WORLD RANKING

'93	'94	'95	'96	'97	'98	'99	'00	'01	'02	'03	'04	'05	'06	'07	'08	'09	'10	'11	'12
88	91	57	41	56	51	44	29	32	47	70	63	50	91	81	77	82	89	76	

	2011												High	Low	Av
	Jan	Feb	Mar	Apr	May	Jun	Jul	Aug	Sep	Oct	Nov	Dec			
	87	94	95	94	95	90	88	91	80	79	86	76	25	106	63

Trinidad's Soca Warriors may have had a poor year in 2010 but that was nothing in comparision to the disasterous 2014 FIFA World Cup qualifying campaign they experienced in 2011. With memories of their appearance at the 2006 finals still fresh, Trinidad were expected to be at the very least amongst the final 12 nations in the CONCACAF zone fighting for a place in Brazil but they didn't get past the first group stage - unlike their fellow Caribbean nations Jamaica, Antigua, Cuba and Guyana. Indeed, it was the Guyanese who were responsible for their downfall. Trinidad's campaign started well enough with a win over Bermuda at home and then a victory away to Barbados but they were unexpectedly beaten in their third match, away to Bermuda. It was a defeat that would ultimately cost Otto Pfister's side dear. In the crunch game the Trinidadians travelled to Guyana needing a win but all they could manage was an injury-time consolation goal from Kenwyne Jones in a 2-1 defeat and they were out. Trinidadian clubs also had a lacklustre time in the 2011 CFU Club Championship with Caledonian AIA losing in the quarter-finals to Haiti's Tempête and Defence force losing to the same opponents in the semi-finals. At home there was a realignment of the club calendar with the finish of the 2011 season delayed to May 2012.

FIFA WORLD CUP RECORD
1930-1962 DNE 1966-2002 DNQ **2006** 27 r1 2010 DNQ

TRINIDAD AND TOBAGO FOOTBALL FEDERATION (TTFF)

43 Dundonald Street,
PO Box 400, Port of Spain
☎ +1 868 6237312
📠 +1 868 6238109
📧 richardgroden@aol.com
🖥 www.ttffonline.com
FA 1908 CON 1964 FIFA 1963
P Lennox Watson
GS Richard Groden

FIFA BIG COUNT 2006

Total players	84 600
% of population	7.94%
Male	71 150
Female	13 450
Amateurs 18+	4 250
Youth under 18	11 600
Unregistered	16 000
Professionals	250
Referees	250
Admin & coaches	650
Number of clubs	95
Number of teams	380

MAJOR CITIES/TOWNS

		Population
1	Chaguanas	76 136
2	San Juan	58 815
3	San Fernando	57 032
4	Port of Spain	50 044
5	Arima	37 332
6	Marabella	26 624
7	Tunapuna	18 826
8	Point Fortin	18 748
9	Sangre Grande	17 156
10	Tacarigua	15 973
11	Arouca	12 779
12	Princes Town	10 969
13	Siparia	8 355
14	Couva	5 316
15	Penal	5 058
16	Saint Joseph	4 979
17	Scarborough	4 734
18	Mucurapo	4 542
19	Tabaquite	3 402

REPUBLIC OF TRINIDAD AND TOBAGO

Capital	Port of Spain	Population	1 229 953 (154)	% in cities	13%
GDP per capita	$23 600 (53)	Area km²	5 128 km² (173)	GMT +/-	-4
Neighbours (km)	Coast 362				

RECENT INTERNATIONAL MATCHES PLAYED BY TRINIDAD AND TOBAGO

2009	Opponents	Score		Venue	Comp	Scorers	Att	Referee
11-02	El Salvador	D	2-2	San Salvador	WCq	Carlos Edwards [7], Dwight Yorke [26p]	25 000	Rodriguez MEX
18-03	Panama	W	1-0	Marabella	Fr	Cornell Glen [74p]	2 000	Jordan TRI
28-03	Honduras	D	1-1	Port of Spain	WCq	Khaleem Hyland [88]	23 500	Quesada CRC
1-04	USA	L	0-3	Nashville	WCq		27 958	Moreno PAN
6-06	Costa Rica	L	2-3	Bacolet	WCq	Carlos Edwards [30], Collin Samuel [63]	8 000	Campbell JAM
10-06	Mexico	L	1-2	Mexico City	WCq	Hayden Tinto [45]	92 000	Pineda HON
12-07	St Kitts and Nevis	W	3-2	Basseterre	Fr	Radanfah Abubakr [21], Ataullah Guerra [27], Kerry Baptiste [72]	3 100	Matthew SKN
12-08	El Salvador	W	1-0	Port of Spain	WCq	Cornell Glen [7]	16 000	Vaughn USA
5-09	Honduras	L	1-4	San Pedro Sula	WCq	Kerry Baptiste [86]	38 000	Geiger USA
9-09	USA	L	0-1	Port of Spain	WCq		4 700	Aguilar SLV
10-10	Costa Rica	L	0-4	San Jose	WCq		10 000	Marrufo USA
14-10	Mexico	D	2-2	Port of Spain	WCq	Kerry Baptiste 2 [23p 61]	2 000	Quesada CRC
2010								
5-05	Chile	L	0-2	Iquique	Fr		10 000	Antequera BRA
21-07	Antigua and Barbuda	W	4-1	Macoya	Fr	Kevon Carter 2 [10 30], Kerry Baptiste [18], Devon Jorsling [67]	1 700	Brizan TRI
11-08	Jamaica	L	1-3	Macoya	Fr	Devon Jorsling [28]	4 500	Taylor BRB
7-09	Panama	L	0-3	Panama City	Fr		6 645	Cruz CRC
10-09	Belize	D	0-0	Belmopan	Fr		5 000	Mejia SLV
19-09	Antigua and Barbuda	W	1-0	St John's	Fr	Devon Jorsling [70]	500	Willett ATG
21-09	St Lucia	W	3-0	St John's	Fr	Devon Jorsling [22], Jamal Gay [53], Hughton Hector [86]	205	St Catherine LCA
26-09	Guyana	D	1-1	Providence	Fr	Devon Jorsling [35]	9 000	Lancaster GUY
10-10	Jamaica	L	0-1	Kingston	Fr		7 000	Archundia MEX
2-11	St Vincent/Grenadines	W	6-2	Marabella	CCq	Devon Jorsling 3 [2 35 59], Kerry Baptiste 2 [57 67], Hughton Hector [90]	1 100	Peterkin JAM
4-11	Guyana	W	2-1	Marabella	CCq	Lester Peltier [34], Devorn Jorsling [42]	1 100	Legister JAM
6-11	Haiti	W	4-0	Marabella	CCq	Hughton Hector 2 [4 33], Devon Jorsling [8], Kerry Baptiste [29]	850	Campbell JAM
26-11	Cuba	L	0-2	Fort de France	CCr1		5 000	Lancaster GUY
28-11	Grenada	L	0-1	Fort de France	CCr1		500	Cruz CRC
30-11	Martinique	W	1-0	Fort de France	CCr1	Hughton Hector [47]	2 000	Taylor BRB
2011								
21-08	India	W	3-0	Port of Spain	Fr	Stern John [19p], Darryl Roberts 2 [46 84]	6 600	Campbell JAM
2-09	Bermuda	W	1-0	Port of Spain	WCq	Kenwyne Jones [45]	6 000	Perea PAN
6-09	Barbados	W	2-0	Bridgetown	WCq	Keon Daniel [17], Darryl Roberts [67]	775	Bonilla SLV
7-10	Bermuda	L	1-2	Prospect	WCq	Kevin Molino [82]	2 243	Solis CRC
11-10	Barbados	W	4-0	Port of Spain	WCq	Lester Peltier 3 [6 55 63], Hughtun Hector [90]	3 000	Bogle JAM
11-11	Guyana	L	1-2	Georgetown	WCq	Kenwyne Jones [45 93+]	18 000	Wijngaarde SUR
15-11	Guyana	W	3-0	Port of Spain	WCq	Originally 2-0. Kenwyne Jones [59], Lester Peltier [69]	2 000	Mejia SLV

Fr = Friendly match • CC = Digicel Caribbean Cup • GC = CONCACAF Gold Cup • WC = FIFA World Cup • q = qualifier • r1 = first round group

TRINIDAD AND TOBAGO NATIONAL TEAM HISTORICAL RECORDS

Caps
117 - Angus Eve 1994-2005 • 113 - Stern John 1995-2009 • 101 - Marvin Andrews 1996-2009 • 89 - Dennis Lawrence 2000- • 80 - Carlos Edwards 1999- • 79 - Clayton Ince 1997-2009 • 78 - Russell Latapy 1988-2009 & Densill Theobald • 74 - Arnold Dwarika 1993-2008 • 72 - Dwight Yorke 1989-2009 & Keyeno Thomas 1998-2009 • 70 - Avery John 1996-2009 • 69 - Ansil Elcock 1994-2004 • 67 - Anthony Rougier 1995-2005 • 62 - Cornell Glen 2002- • 61 - Stokely Mason 1996-2004 • 59 - Cyd Gray 2001-08

Goals
70 - Stern John 1995- • 34 - Angus Eve 1994-2005 • 29 - Russell Latapy 1988-2009 • 28 - Arnold Dwarika 1993-2008 • 23 - Cornell Glen 2002- • 22 - Nigel Pierre 1999-2008 • 21 - Leonson Lewis 1988-96 • 19 - Dwight Yorke 1989-2009 • 16 - Steve David 1972-76

Past Coaches
Bertille St. Clair 1997-2000 • Ian Porterfield SCO 2000-01 • Rene Simoes BRA 2001-02 • Hannibal Najjar 2002-03 • Zoran Vranes SRB 2003 • Stuart Charles Fevrier LCA 2003-04 • Bertille St. Clair 2004-05 • Leo Beenhakker NED 2005-06 • Wim Rijsbergen NED 2006-07 • Francisco Maturana COL 2008-09 • Russell Latapy 2009-11 • Otto Pfister GER 2011

FIRST CITIZENS BANK CUP 2010

Quarter–finals		Semi–finals		Final	
Joe Public	2				
North East Stars	0	Joe Public	3		
Caledonia AIA	0	W Connection	1		
W Connection	2			Joe Public	1 3p
Ma Pau	3			Defence Force	1 0p
San Juan Jabloteh	0	Ma Pau	0		
St Ann's Rangers	0 1p	Defence Force	1	23-10-2010	
Defence Force	0 2p				

DIGICEL PRO BOWL 2011

Quarter–finals		Semi–finals		Final	
Joe Public	3				
Police	0	Joe Public	3		
Ma Pau	0	Caledonia AIA	2		
Caledonia AIA	2			Joe Public	1
Defence Force	2			W Connection	0
San Juan Jabloteh	1	Defence Force	0 3p	1-04-2011	
North East Stars	0	W Connection	0 5p	Scorer - Andre Toussaint [11] for	
W Connection	2			Joe Public	

FIRST CITIZENS BANK CUP 2011

First Round Groups   Semi-finals   Semi-finals

Group A	Pl	W	D	L	F	A	Pts	TT	SAR
San Juan Jabloteh †	2	1	1	0	6	5	4	4-4	2-1
T&TEC Sports Club †	2	0	2	0	4	4	2	0-0	
St Ann's Rangers	2	0	1	1	1	2	1		

Semi-finals	
Caledonia AIA	2
San Juan Jabloteh	1

Group B	Pl	W	D	L	F	A	Pts	Cal	NES
W Connection †	2	2	0	0	8	3	6	4-2	4-1
Caledonia AIA †	2	1	0	1	4	4	3	2-0	
North East Stars	2	0	0	2	1	6	0		

† Qualified for the semi-finals

Semi-finals	
W Connection	1 3p
T&TEC Sports Club	1 4p

Semi-finals	
Caledonia AIA	2
T&TEC Sports Club	1

Final. 14-10-2011

TOYOTA CLASSIC 2011

First round		Quarter–finals		Semi–finals		Final	
W Connection	Bye						
		W Connection	1				
Joe Public	1	Angostura Phoenix	0				
Angostura Phoenix	3			W Connection	4		
Caledonia AIA	1			San Juan Jabloteh	2		
Club Sando	0	Caledonia AIA	1				
Real Maracas	0	San Juan Jabloteh	2				
San Juan Jabloteh	5					W Connection	0 5p
St Ann's Rangers	1					T&TEC Sports Club	0 4p
Eagles United	0	St Ann's Rangers	2 3p				
West Side Super Starz	3	North East Stars	2 0p				
North East Stars	4			St Ann's Rangers	1		
Stokely Vale	3			T&TEC Sports Club	2		
WASA	1	Stokely Vale	3				
		T&TEC Sports Club	4				
T&TEC Sports Club	Bye						

CUP FINAL

Manny Ramjohn, Marabella
9-12-2011

TUN – TUNISIA

FIFA/COCA-COLA WORLD RANKING

'93	'94	'95	'96	'97	'98	'99	'00	'01	'02	'03	'04	'05	'06	'07	'08	'09	'10	'11	'12
32	30	22	23	23	21	31	26	28	41	45	35	28	32	47	46	53	45	59	

						2011							High	Low	Av
Jan	Feb	Mar	Apr	May	Jun	Jul	Aug	Sep	Oct	Nov	Dec		High	Low	Av
44	47	44	59	59	57	55	57	61	60	59	59		19	65	35

Tunisia may have lit the spark that set off the fires that fueled the Arab Spring but the country emerged relatively unscathed from the sweeping political changes at home and abroad. The championship was suspended for three months at the start of 2011 but the country ended the year by celebrating two major successes on the football pitch. The African Nations Championship is a national team tournament for home-based players only and Sami Trabelsi's team were winners of the tournament in Sudan in February - Mejdi Traoui, Zouhaier Dhaouadi and Oussama Darragi scoring in a 3-0 win over Angola in the final in Khartoum. They went on to become the nucleus of a new look national side that Trabelsi forged over the year that reached the quarter-finals of the 2012 CAF Africa Cup of Nations. In November leading club side Esperance achieved their long-held ambition of winning the CAF Champions League again, having last won it back in 1994. Losing finalists in 2010, Esperance fought their way back to the 2011 final where they beat Morocco's Wydad Casablanca by the odd goal over the two legs, the Ghanaian Harrison Afful scoring the all-important winner in the second leg in Tunis. It capped a great year for the club which had earlier won both the league and the cup at home.

CAF AFRICA CUP OF NATIONS RECORD

1957-1957 DNE **1962** 3 SF **1963** 5 r1 **1965** 2 F (Hosts) 1968 DNQ 1970-1974 DNE 1976 DNQ **1978** 4 SF 1980 DNE **1982** 7 r1 1984-1992 DNQ **1994** 9 r1 (Hosts) **1996** 2 F **1998** 6 QF **2000** 4 SF **2002** 11 r1 **2004** 1 Winners (Hosts) **2006** 7 QF **2008** 5 QF **2010** 11 r1 **2012** 6 QF

FEDERATION TUNISIENNE DE FOOTBALL (FTF)

Stade annexe d'El Menzah, Cité Olympique, Tunis 1003

☏ +216 71 793760
📠 +216 71 783843
✉ directeur@ftf.org.tn
🖥 www.ftf.org.tn
FA 1956 CON 1960 FIFA 1960
P Mohamed Haddad
GS Ridha Kraiem

FIFA BIG COUNT 2006

Total players	525 264
% of population	5.16%
Male	500 636
Female	24 628
Amateurs 18+	29 404
Youth under 18	20 950
Unregistered	42 435
Professionals	1 075
Referees	998
Admin & coaches	6 626
Number of clubs	250
Number of teams	1 512

MAJOR CITIES/TOWNS

		Population
1	Tunis	741 427
2	Sfax	284 027
3	Ariana	277 114
4	At Tadaman	198 854
5	Sousse	195 100
6	Kairouan	124 505
7	Gabès	123 600
8	Bizerte	118 714
9	El Mourouj	91 693
10	Gafsa	89 492
11	Kasserine	81 443
12	Monastir	80 847
13	Ben Arous	78 601
14	La Marsa	78 585
15	Zarzis	73 142
16	Hammamet	66 065
17	Masakin	65 603
18	Tatouine	65 436
19	Béja	56 517

AL JUMHURIYAH AT TUNISIYAH • TUNISIAN REPUBLIC

Capital Tunis	Population 10 486 339 (76)	% in cities 67%
GDP per capita $7900 (122)	Area km² 163 610 km² (92)	GMT +/- +1
Neighbours (km) Algeria 965, Libya 459 • Coast 1148		

RECENT INTERNATIONAL MATCHES PLAYED BY TUNISIA

2009	Opponents		Score	Venue	Comp	Scorers	Att	Referee
11-02	Netherlands	D	1-1	Radès/Tunis	Fr	Saihi [66]	17 000	Abd El Fatah EGY
28-03	Kenya	W	2-1	Nairobi	WCq	Jemal [6], Jomaa [79]	27 000	Evehe CMR
28-05	Sudan	W	4-0	Radès/Tunis	Fr	Darragi [11], Allagui [17], Jaidi [20], Falhi [55]		Ragab LBY
6-06	Mozambique	W	2-0	Radès/Tunis	WCq	Ben Yahia [21p], Darragi [89]	30 000	Djaoupe TOG
20-06	Nigeria	D	0-0	Radès/Tunis	WCq		45 000	Coulibaly MLI
12-08	Côte d'Ivoire	D	0-0	Sousse	Fr			
6-09	Nigeria	D	2-2	Abuja	WCq	Nabil [24], Darragi [89]	52 000	Bennett RSA
11-10	Kenya	W	1-0	Radès/Tunis	WCq	Jomaa [1]	50 000	Diatta SEN
14-10	Saudi Arabia	L	0-1	Radès/Tunis	Fr			
14-11	Mozambique	L	0-1	Maputo	WCq		30 000	Doue CIV
2010								
9-01	Gambia	L	1-2	Radès/Tunis	Fr	Chermite [94+]		
13-01	Zambia	D	1-1	Lubango	CNr1	Dhaouadi [40]	17 000	Coulibaly MLI
17-01	Gabon	D	0-0	Lubango	CNr1		16 000	Codjia BEN
21-01	Cameroon	D	2-2	Lubango	CNr1	Chermiti [1], Chedjou OG [63]	19 000	Doue CIV
30-05	France	D	1-1	Radès/Tunis	Fr	Jomaa [6]	55 000	El Raay LBY
20-06	Sudan	W	6-2	Omdurman	Fr	Ben Yahia [10], Allagui [37], Haggui [46p], Jomaa 2 [55 57], Akaichi [70]		
1-07	Botswana	L	0-1	Tunis	CNq			Diatta SEN
11-08	Chad	W	3-1	N'Djamena	CNq	Korbi [9], Ben Khalfallah 2 [43 81]		Doue CIV
4-09	Malawi	D	2-2	Rades	CNq	Jomaa 2 [11 26]		Lamptey GHA
10-10	Togo	W	2-1	Lomé	CNq	Jomaa [34], Chermiti [90]		Abdul Rahman SUD
17-11	Botswana	L	0-1	Gaborone	CNq			Kaoma ZAM
2011								
29-03	Oman	L	1-2	Seeb	Fr	Sami Allagui [63]		
29-05	Central African Rep	W	3-0	Sousse	Fr	Oussama Darragi 2 [32p 50], Lamjed Chehoudi [45]		
5-06	Chad	W	5-0	Sousse	CNq	Issam Jemaa 3 [22 44 53], Aymen Abdennour [35], Oussama Darragi [47]		
10-08	Mali	W	4-2	Monastir	Fr	Sami Allagui 2 [19 50], Ammar Jemal [29p], Issam Jemaa [83]		
22-08	Jordan	D	3-3	Amman	Fr	Ammar Jemal 2 [30p 80p], Lamjed Chehoudi [33]		
3-09	Malawi	D	0-0	Blantyre	CNq			
8-10	Togo	W	2-0	Rades	CNq	Walid Hichri [19], Saber Khelifa [79]		
12-11	Algeria	L	0-1	Algiers	Fr			
2012								
9-01	Sudan	W	3-0	Sharjah	Fr	Saber Khelifa [12], Zouheir Dhaouadi [60], Amine Chermiti [83]		
13-01	Côte d'Ivoire	L	0-2	Abu Dhabi	Fr			
23-01	Morocco	W	2-1	Libreville	CNr1	Khaled Korbi [34], Youssef Msakni [76]	18 000	Bennett RSA
27-01	Niger	W	2-1	Libreville	CNr1	Youssef Msakni [4], Issam Jemaa [90]	20 000	Sikazwe ZAM
31-01	Gabon	L	0-1	Franceville	CNr1		22 000	Doue CIV
5-02	Ghana	L	1-2	Franceville	CNqf	Saber Khelifa [41]	8 000	Alioum CMR

Fr = Friendly match • CN = CAF African Cup of Nations • WC = FIFA World Cup • q = qualifier • r1 = first round group • qf = quarter-final

TUNISIA NATIONAL TEAM HISTORICAL RECORDS

Past Coaches Rachid Turki 1956-57 • Hachemi Cherif 1957-60 • Milan Kristic YUG 1960-61 • Frane Matosic YUG 1961-63 • Andre Gerard FRA 1963-65 • Mokhtar Ben Nacef 1965-68 • Rado Radocijic YUG 1968-69 • Beogovic Sereta YUG 1969 • Rado Radocijic YUG 1970 • Hameur Hizem 1970-74 • Andre Nagy HUN 1974-75 • Abdelmajid Chetali 1975-78 • Hameur Hizem 1978-79 • Ahmed Dhib 1979-80 • Hameur Hizem 1980-81 • Ryszard Kulesza POL 1981-83 • Youssef Zouaoui 1984-86 • Jean Vincent FRA 1986-87 • Taoufik Ben Othman 1987-88 • Antoni Piechniczek POL 1988 • Mokhtar Tlili 1988-89 • Antoni Piechniczek POL 1989 • Mrad Moujab 1989-93 • Youssef Zouaoui 1993-94 • Faouzi Benzarti 1994 • Henryk Kasperczak POL 1994-98 • Francesco Scoglio ITA 1998-01 • Eckhard Krautzun GER 2001 • Henri Michel FRA 2001-02 • Ammar Souayah 2002 • Youssef Zouaoui 2002 • Roger Lemerre FRA 2002-08 • Humberto Coelho POR 2008-09 • Faouzi Benzarti 2009-10 • Sami Trabelsi 2010 • Bertrand Marchand FRA 2010 • Faouzi Benzarti 2010-2011 • Ammar Souayah 2011 • Sami Trabelsi 2011-

TUNISIA 2010-11

LIGUE NATIONALE A

	Pl	W	D	L	F	A	Pts	Espérance	Etoile	Sfaxien	Club Africain	Bizertin	Hammam Lif	Stade	Gafsa	Kairouan	Olympique	Marsa	Zarzis	Gabés	H-Sousse
Espérance Tunis †	26	20	4	2	50	18	64		0-0	3-1	2-1	3-0	3-1	5-0	0-0	2-1	1-1	2-1	1-0	2-0	4-0
Etoile du Sahel †	26	19	2	5	49	24	59	5-1		1-0	2-1	3-0	0-1	2-0	1-0	3-2	1-2	3-0	1-0	3-1	2-1
CS Sfaxien ‡	26	12	8	6	32	23	44	0-3	4-1		0-0	1-0	3-1	1-1	1-1	1-1	0-0	1-2	1-1	2-1	2-1
Club Africain ‡	26	8	11	7	35	27	35	2-2	2-0	0-2		2-2	2-0	2-1	1-0	0-0	1-0	0-0	1-2	2-0	2-1
CA Bizertin	26	10	5	11	23	29	35	0-1	0-2	0-3	2-1		0-0	0-0	2-0	2-1	1-0	0-0	1-0	2-0	2-0
CS Hammam Lif	26	9	7	10	23	31	34	0-1	0-2	1-1	0-0	1-0		2-1	3-1	1-4	1-0	3-1	1-0	1-0	1-0
Stade Tunisien	26	8	9	9	26	30	33	0-2	3-1	1-2	1-1	3-0	0-0		1-2	1-1	1-2	2-0	0-0	2-1	0-0
EGS Gafsa	26	8	8	10	28	34	32	0-1	1-1	1-0	4-4	1-0	2-1	1-2		2-0	2-2	0-0	2-1	1-0	3-1
JS Kairouan	26	8	7	11	28	29	31	1-2	1-2	2-1	1-0	1-0	2-2	1-2	2-1		1-1	3-1	2-0	0-0	1-0
Olympique Béjà	26	6	11	9	25	29	29	0-2	2-3	0-1	2-2	3-1	0-0	1-1	2-2	1-0		2-1	0-0	1-3	3-2
AS Marsa	26	7	8	11	26	34	29	1-3	2-4	1-2	1-0	0-0	1-1	0-2	2-0	1-0	0-0		3-1	2-1	2-2
Espérance Zarzis	26	6	9	11	22	24	27	1-2	0-2	0-0	0-0	1-2	4-1	0-0	3-0	1-0	2-0	1-1		3-1	0-1
AS Gabés	26	6	6	14	19	32	24	2-1	0-2	0-1	1-1	1-4	2-0	3-0	2-0	0-0	1-1	1-0	0-0		0-0
ES Hammam-Sousse	26	5	5	16	19	38	20	0-1	0-2	0-1	1-4	1-2	1-0	0-1	1-1	2-0	1-0	0-3	1-1	2-0	

23/07/2010 - 10/07/2011 • † Qualified for the CAF Champions League • ‡ Qualified for the CAF Confederation Cup • § = points deducted
Top scorers: **14** - Ahmed Akaichi, Etoile • **10** - Oussama Darragi, Espérance; Danilo BRA, Etoile & Youssef Msakni, Espérance • **9** - Ayoub Kramti, Gafsa • **7** - Heithem Ben Salem, Bizertin; Michael Eneramo NGA, Espérance & Slema Kazdeoui, Kairouan

TUNISIA 2010-11
LIGUE NATIONAL B (2)

	Pl	W	D	L	F	A	Pts
US Monastir	26	14	9	3	36	20	51
ES Béni Khalled	26	13	7	6	37	29	46
Stade Gabésien	26	11	7	8	35	26	40
LPTA Tozeur	26	12	3	11	31	26	39
AS Djerba	26	9	9	8	30	29	36
EA Mateur	26	9	8	9	20	25	35
CO Transports	26	8	10	8	26	27	34
CS Korba	26	9	7	10	30	32	34
SC Moknine	26	8	7	11	33	35	31
Jendouba Sport	26	7	10	9	26	29	31
AS Kasserine	26	7	10	9	24	28	31
CS Masakin	26	7	9	10	27	31	30
Olympique Kef	26	7	9	10	23	26	30
US Ben Guerdane	26	4	9	13	20	35	21

19/09/2010 - 3/07/2011

MEDALS TABLE

			Overall			League			Cup		Africa			
			G	S	B	G	S	B	G	S	G	S	B	City
1	Espérance Sportive de Tunis	EST	40	20	12	23	10	9	13	6	4	4	3	Tunis
2	Club Africain	CA	22	35	14	10	20	12	11	12	1	3	2	Tunis
3	Etoile Sportive du Sahel	ESS	21	30	15	8	16	15	7	9	6	5		Sousse
4	Club Sportif Sfaxien	CSS	14	8	7	7	1	6	4	5	3	2	1	Sfax
5	Stade Tunisien	ST	10	8	6	4	3	6	6	5				Tunis
6	Avenir Sportif de la Marsa	ASM	5	8	2		1	2	5	7				Marsa, Tunis
7	Club Athlétique Bizertin	CAB	4	3	2	1	2	1	2	1	1		1	Bizerte
8	Club Sportif de Hammam Lif	CSHL	3	1	2	1		1	2	1			1	Hammam Lif
9	Olympique de Béjà	OB	2	2					2	2				Béjà
10	Jeunesse Sportive Kairouan	JSK	1	2		1	1			1				Kairouan
	Sfax Railways Sport	SRS	1	2		1				2				Sfax
12	Club Olympique Transports	COT	1	1	2		1	2	1					Tunis
13	Espérance Sportive de Zarzis	ESZ	1						1					Zarzis
14	Stade Soussien	SS		2			1		1					Sousse
15	EM Mehdia	EMM	1						1					Mehdia
	Union Sportive Monastir	USMo	1						1					Monastir
17	US Tunisien	UST			2			2						Tunis

COUPE DE TUNISIE 2010–11

Round of 32

Team	Score
Espérance Tunis *	1
JS Kairouan	0
CS Masakin *	0
US Ben Guerdane	1
Jendouba Sport *	1
CA Bizertin	0
CS Sfaxien	0
US Monastir *	2
AS Kasserine *	2
Stade Gabésien	0
CS Korba	0
Olympique Béja *	1
Espérance Zarzis *	3
CS Hammam Lif	1
Kalaa Sport	1
Stade Tunisien *	4
EGS Gafsa *	5
Dahmani AC	1
SC Mokine *	2
AS Marsa	2
ES Béni Khalled *	5
Olympique Kef	0
CS Hajeb El Ayoun	0
AS Djerba *	1
AS Gabés *	3
AS Soliman	0
EA Mateur	1
CO Transports *	2
Club Africain	3
AS Ariana *	1
ES Hammam-Sousse	0
Etoile du Sahel *	1

Round of 16

Team	Score
Espérance Tunis *	2
US Ben Guerdane	0
Jendouba Sport *	0 4p
US Monastir	0 5p
AS Kasserine *	1
Olympique Béja	0
Espérance Zarzis	0
Stade Tunisien *	1
EGS Gafsa *	2
AS Marsa	1
ES Béni Khalled *	1
AS Djerba	2
AS Gabés *	3
CO Transports *	1
Club Africain *	1
Etoile du Sahel	2

Quarter-finals

Team	Score
Espérance Tunis	4
US Monastir *	1
AS Kasserine *	0
Stade Tunisien	1
EGS Gafsa	1 4p
AS Djerba *	1 3p
AS Gabés	0
Etoile du Sahel *	1

Semi-finals

Team	Score
Espérance Tunis *	2
Stade Tunisien	0
EGS Gafsa	0
Etoile du Sahel *	2

Final

Team	Score
Espérance Tunis	1
Etoile du Sahel	0

* Home team

CUP FINAL

Stade 7 novembre, Rades
25-07-2011, Ref. Said Kordi
EST - Moez Ben Cherifia - Sameh Derbali, Khalil Chammam●, Walid Hichri●, Mohamed Bachtobji (Ayman Ben Amor 45) - Kkaled Korbi, Mejdi Traou●, Harrison Afful, Youssef Msakni● (Khaled Mouelhi 92+) - Oussama Darragi(c), Wajdi Bouazzi (Khaled Ayari 72). Tr. Nabil Maaloul
ESS - Aymen Mathlouthi● - Hamza Jabnoun, Hatem Bejaoui, Radhouan Felhi, Lamine Diatta - Habib Jacob Meite●, Danillo Bueno●, Lamjed Chehoudi (Lasaad Jaziri 72), Adel Chadly● (Marouane Belghoul 85) - Dos Santos◆16, Ahmed Akaichi. Tr. Monher Kbaier

TUR – TURKEY

FIFA/COCA-COLA WORLD RANKING

'93	'94	'95	'96	'97	'98	'99	'00	'01	'02	'03	'04	'05	'06	'07	'08	'09	'10	'11	'12
52	48	30	31	43	57	29	30	23	9	8	14	11	26	16	10	41	31	28	

	2011												High	Low	Av
	Jan	Feb	Mar	Apr	May	Jun	Jul	Aug	Sep	Oct	Nov	Dec			
	31	31	32	30	30	23	24	24	27	26	28	28	5	67	27

2011 will be a year that Turkish football will be in a hurry to forget with the national team - semi-finalists at Euro 2008 - failing to make the 2012 finals after losing a play-off to Croatia and club football dogged by all manner of corruption and match fixing stories. A number of them concerned 2011 double winners Fenerbahce who were thrown out of the 2011-12 UEFA Champions League as a result. 18 matches played in the Super Lig between February and May 2011 as well as the Turkish Cup Final were initially under investigation but reports suggest the match fixing problem could stretch much further back. It cast a huge shadow over what had been an epic season for Fenerbahce who won 16 of their last 17 games to clinch the title ahead of Trabzonspor on their head-to-head record, coach Aykut Kocaman becoming the first person to win the title with Fenerbahce as both a player and a coach. It was the club's 18th title, moving them one ahead of rivals Galatasaray. A stadium ban at Fenerbahce did, however, produce one of the stories of the year. Instead of playing their league match against Maniaspor in September behind closed doors, the federation came up with the novel idea of just letting in women and children, It turned out to be a spectacular success as 41,000 turned up to cheer the team on to a 1-1 draw.

UEFA EUROPEAN CHAMPIONSHIP RECORD
1960 r1 **1964** r1 **1968-1992** DNQ **1996** r1 **2000** QF **2004** DNQ **2008** SF **2012** DNQ

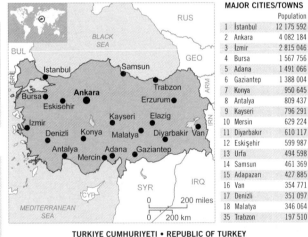

TURKIYE FUTBOL FEDERASYONU (TFF)

Istinye Mah., Darüssafaka
Cad No 45, Kat 2 Sariyer,
Istanbul 34460
☎ +90 212 3622222
📠 +90 212 3234968
✉ intdept@tff.org
🖥 www.tff.org
FA 1923 CON 1962 FIFA 1923
P Yildirim Demiroren
GS Ebru Koksal

FIFA BIG COUNT 2006

Total players	2 748 657
% of population	3.90%
Male	2 402 838
Female	345 819
Amateurs 18+	59 980
Youth under 18	131 916
Unregistered	847 000
Professionals	4 491
Referees	802
Admin & coaches	20 725
Number of clubs	4 298
Number of teams	9 823

MAJOR CITIES/TOWNS

		Population
1	İstanbul	12 175 592
2	Ankara	4 082 184
3	İzmir	2 815 046
4	Bursa	1 567 756
5	Adana	1 491 066
6	Gaziantep	1 388 004
7	Konya	950 645
8	Antalya	809 437
9	Kayseri	796 291
10	Mersin	629 224
11	Diyarbakır	610 117
12	Eskişehir	599 987
13	Urfa	494 598
14	Samsun	461 369
15	Adapazarı	427 885
16	Van	354 771
17	Denizli	351 097
18	Malatya	346 064
35	Trabzon	197 510

TURKIYE CUMHURIYETI • REPUBLIC OF TURKEY

Capital	Ankara	Population	76 805 524 (17)	% in cities 69%
GDP per capita	$11 200 (100)	Area km²	783 562 km² (37)	GMT +/- +2
Neighbours (km)	Armenia 268, Azerbaijan 9, Bulgaria 240, Georgia 252, Greece 206, Iran 499, Iraq 352, Syria 822 • Coast 7200			

RECENT INTERNATIONAL MATCHES PLAYED BY TURKEY

2008	Opponents	Score		Venue	Comp	Scorers	Att	Referee
7-06	Portugal	L	0-2	Geneva	ECr1		29 016	Fandel GER
11-06	Switzerland	W	2-1	Basel	ECr1	Semih Senturk [57], Arda Turan [92+]	39 730	Michel SVK
15-06	Czech Republic	W	3-2	Geneva	ECr1	Arda Turan [75], Nihat Kahveci 2 [87 89]	29 016	Fröjdfeldt SWE
20-06	Croatia	D	1-1	Vienna	ECqf	Semih Senturk [122+]. W 3-1p	51 428	Rosetti ITA
25-06	Germany	L	2-3	Basel	ECsf	Ugur Boral [22], Semih Senturk [86]	39 378	Busacca SUI
20-08	Chile	W	1-0	Izmit	Fr	Halil Altintop [75]		Kakos GRE
6-09	Armenia	W	2-0	Yerevan	WCq	Tuncay Sanli [61], Semih Senturk [77]	30 000	Ovrebo NOR
10-09	Belgium	D	1-1	Istanbul	WCq	Emre Belozoglu [74p]	34 097	Lannoy FRA
11-10	Bosnia-Herzegovina	W	2-1	Istanbul	WCq	Arda Turan [51], Mevlut Erdinc [66]	23 628	Kassai HUN
15-10	Estonia	D	0-0	Tallinn	WCq		6 500	Malek POL
19-11	Austria	W	4-2	Vienna	Fr	Mehmet Aurelio [38], Tuncay Sanli 3 [41 47 62]	23 100	Grafe GER
2009								
11-02	Côte d'Ivoire	D	1-1	Izmir	Fr	Gokhan Unal [11]		Corpodean ROU
28-03	Spain	L	0-1	Madrid	WCq		73 820	Busacca SUI
1-04	Spain	L	1-2	Istanbul	WCq	Semih Senturk [26]	19 617	Riley ENG
2-06	Azerbaijan	W	2-0	Kayseri	Fr	Halil Altintop [70], Ibrahim Uzulmez [75]		Vlk SVK
5-06	France	L	0-1	Lyon	Fr		32 000	Grafe GER
12-08	Ukraine	W	3-0	Kyiv	Fr	Tuncay Sanli [58], Servet Cetin [63], Hamit Altintop [65]		Ceferin SVN
5-09	Estonia	W	4-2	Kayseri	WCq	Tuncay Sanli 2 [27 72], Sercan Yildirim [37], Arda Turan [62]	28 569	Skjerven NOR
9-09	Bosnia-Herzegovina	D	1-1	Zenica	WCq	Emre Belozoglu [4]	14 000	Benquerença POR
10-10	Belgium	L	0-2	Brussels	WCq		30 131	Trefoloni ITA
14-10	Armenia	W	2-0	Bursa	WCq	Halil Altintop [16], Servet Cetin [28]	16 200	Hansson SWE
2010								
3-03	Honduras	W	2-0	Istanbul	Fr	Emre Gungor [41], Hamit Altintop [55]	17 000	Olsiak SVK
22-05	Czech Republic	W	2-1	Harrison	Fr	Arda Turan [31], Nihat Kahveci [48]	16 371	Geiger USA
26-05	Northern Ireland	W	2-0	New Britain	Fr	Sercan Yildirim [48], Semih Senturk [72]	4 000	Vaughn USA
29-05	USA	L	1-2	Philadelphia	Fr	Arda Turan [27]	55 407	Petrescu CAN
11-08	Romania	W	2-0	Istanbul	Fr	Emre Belozoglu [4]	15 000	Mazic SRB
3-09	Kazakhstan	W	3-0	Astana	ECq	Arda Turan [24], Hamit Altintop [26], Nihat Kahveci [76]	15 800	Vad HUN
7-09	Belgium	W	3-2	Istanbul	ECq	Hamit Altintop [48], Semih Senturk [66], Arda Turan [78]	43 538	Skomina SVN
8-10	Germany	L	0-3	Berlin	ECq		74 244	Webb ENG
12-10	Azerbaijan	L	0-1	Baku	ECq		29 500	Deaconu ROU
17-11	Netherlands	L	0-1	Amsterdam	Fr		35 500	Kassai HUN
2011								
9-02	Korea Republic	D	0-0	Trabzon	Fr		20 000	Boyko UKR
29-03	Austria	W	2-0	Istanbul	ECq	Arda Turan [28], Gokhan Gonul [78]	40 420	Kralovec AUT
3-06	Belgium	D	1-1	Brussels	ECq	Burak Yilmaz [22]	44 145	Rizzoli ITA
10-08	Estonia	W	3-0	Istanbul	Fr	Emre Belozoglu [8p], Kazim-Richards 2 [28 35]	20 000	Probert ENG
2-09	Kazakhstan	W	2-1	Istanbul	ECq	Burak Yilmaz [31], Arda Turan [96+]	47 756	Turpin FRA
6-09	Austria	D	0-0	Vienna	ECq		47 500	Undiano ESP
7-10	Germany	L	1-3	Istanbul	ECq	Hakan Balta [79]	49 532	Atkinson ENG
11-10	Azerbaijan	W	1-0	Istanbul	ECq	Burak Yilmaz [60]	32 174	Rasmussen DEN
11-11	Croatia	L	0-3	Istanbul	ECpo		47 000	Brych GER
15-11	Croatia	D	0-0	Zagreb	ECpo		34 000	Proenca POR

Fr = Friendly match • EC = UEFA EURO 2008/2012 • WC = FIFA World Cup • q = qualifier • r1 = first round group

TURKEY NATIONAL TEAM HISTORICAL RECORDS

Caps
119 - Rustu Recber 1994-2009 • **112** - Hakan Sukur 1992-2008 • **102** - Bulent Korkmaz 1990-2005 • **94** - Tugay Kerimoglu 1990-2007 • **90** - Alpay Ozlan 1995-2005 • **80** - Tuncay Sanli 2002- & Emre Belozoglu 2000 • **76** Ogun Tomizkanoglu 1990 2002 • **71** Abdullah Ercan 1992-2003 • **70** - Oguz Cetin 1988-98 • **69** - Nihat Kahveci 2000- • **67** - Hamit Altintop 2004- • **64** - Fatih Akyel 1997-2004 • **60** - Arif Erdem 1994-2003 • **59** - Cetin Servet 2003- • **56** - Recep Cetin 1988-97 & Okan Buruk 1992-2005 • **51** - Fatih Terim 1975-84

Goals
51 - Hakan Sukur 1992-2008 • **22** - Tuncay Sanli 2002- • **21** - Lefter Kucukandonyadis 1948-61 • **19** - Nihat Kahveci 2000- ; Oktay Metin 1956-65 & Turan Cemil 1969-79 • **15** - Zeki-Riza Sporel 1923-32 • **12** - Arda Turan 2006-

Coaches
For coaches prior to 1980 see Oliver's Almanack of World Football 2011 • Ozkan Sumer 1980-81 • Fethi Demircan 1981 • Coskun Ozari 1982-84 • Candan Tarhan 1984 • Yilmaz Gokdel 1984-85 • Kalman Meszoly HUN 1985 • Coskun Ozari 1985-86 • Mustafa Denizli 1987 • Tinaz Tirpan 1988-89 • Fatih Terim 1990 • Sepp Piontek GER 1990-93 • Fatih Terim 1993-96 • Mustafa Denizli 1996-2000 • Senol Gunes 2000-04 • Unal Karaman 2004 • Ersun Yanal 2004-05 • Fatih Terim 2005-09 • Oguz Cetin 2010 • Guus Hiddink NED 2010-11 • Abdullah Avci 2011-

TURKEY 2010-11

TURKCELL SUPER LIG

	Pl	W	D	L	F	A	Pts	Fen	Tra	Bur	Gaz	Bes	Kay	Esk	Gal	Kar	Man	Ant	Ist	Ank	Gen	Siv	Buc	Kon	Kas
Fenerbahçe	34	26	4	4	84	34	82		2-0	0-0	1-0	1-1	2-0	4-2	0-0	2-1	4-2	4-0	2-0	6-0	3-0	1-0	5-2	2-0	2-0
Trabzonspor †	34	25	7	2	69	23	82	3-2		1-0	3-0	1-0	3-3	0-0	2-0	3-0	1-3	0-0	3-1	1-1	3-1	6-1	2-0	1-0	1-0
Bursaspor ‡	34	17	10	7	50	29	61	1-1	0-2		1-4	**0-3**	2-0	2-1	2-0	2-2	2-1	2-3	1-1	0-0	1-0	2-1	1-0	1-0	2-1
Gaziantepspor ‡	34	17	8	9	44	33	59	2-1	1-3	**0-3**		0-0	2-0	2-1	1-0	0-0	1-0	2-1	4-1	3-2	1-1	3-1	2-0	2-2	0-0
Besiktas ‡	34	15	9	10	53	36	54	2-4	1-2	1-0	1-1		4-2	3-1	2-0	1-1	2-3	2-1	0-2	4-0	2-2	2-1	5-1	2-2	1-1
Kayserispor	34	14	9	11	46	44	51	2-0	0-0	1-0	1-2	1-0		2-2	0-0	1-0	1-2	2-2	3-2	1-1	1-1	4-1	2-0	1-3	1-3
Eskisehirspor	34	12	11	11	41	40	47	1-3	0-0	1-1	0-1	2-0	1-2		1-3	1-0	2-1	0-0	1-0	0-0	0-0	2-1	1-0	1-0	4-0
Galatasaray	34	14	4	16	41	46	46	1-2	0-1	0-2	1-0	1-2	1-1	4-2		0-0	0-2	2-1	3-1	2-4	0-2	1-0	1-0	2-0	3-1
Karabükspor	34	12	8	14	46	53	44	0-1	0-4	1-1	3-2	1-4	0-0	1-2	2-1		2-1	2-0	0-2	5-1	3-0	2-1	3-0	2-1	1-3
Manisaspor	34	13	4	17	49	52	43	1-3	1-2	0-2	2-0	0-0	0-2	3-1	2-3	4-2		1-2	1-0	0-3	3-0	4-2	0-1	2-1	
Antalyaspor	34	10	12	12	41	48	42	0-1	0-0	2-2	0-1	0-2	2-1	2-2	3-0	1-2	1-4		1-0	2-2	0-0	1-1	3-3	1-0	3-1
Istanbul BB	34	12	6	16	40	45	42	0-1	1-3	0-0	1-0	2-1	0-0	2-2	3-1	2-1	0-0	1-1		1-4	0-1	1-2	2-1	1-0	3-1
MKE Ankaragücü	34	10	11	13	52	62	41	2-1	0-2	1-5	0-2	1-0	1-1	2-2	3-2	0-0	1-3	2-3	2-2		2-4	1-1	5-3	4-1	3-0
Gençlerbirligi	34	10	10	14	43	51	40	2-4	1-2	1-5	0-0	0-2	4-1	0-1	2-3	2-3	2-0	2-3	2-1	1-0		1-1	1-0	2-1	1-1
Sivasspor	34	8	11	15	43	57	35	3-4	2-3	0-2	1-1	1-0	1-0	1-1	2-1	1-1	5-1	4-2	1-1	0-4	1-1		1-1	1-1	1-1
Bucaspor	34	6	8	20	37	65	26	3-5	1-2	0-2	2-1	0-1	3-3	0-0	0-1	2-1	1-1	1-0	0-2	0-0	3-1	0-4		3-2	4-0
Konyaspor	34	4	12	18	28	49	24	1-4	1-2	0-0	0-2	1-1	0-1	2-1	0-1	2-2	0-0	0-0	0-0	0-2	2-1	1-1	1-1		2-2
Kasimpasa	34	5	8	21	31	71	23	2-6	0-7	0-3	0-1	0-1	1-2	0-2	0-3	1-2	1-4	2-3	2-0	1-3	2-1	1-1	2-0	0-0	

14/08/2010 - 22/05/2011 • † Qualified for the UEFA Champions League • ‡ Qualified for the Europa League • Matches in bold awarded
Top scorers: **28** - Alex BRA, Fenerbahçe • **19** - Burak Yilmaz, Trabzonspor • **15** - Mamadou Niang SEN, Fenerbahçe, Karabükspor • **13** - Necati Ates, Antalyaspor & Umut Bulut, Trabzonspor

PROMOTION PLAY-OFFS

Semi-finals			Final	
Orduspor *	4	3		
Caykur Rizespor	0	3	**Orduspor**	1
Tavsanli Linyitspor *	1	1	Gaziantep BB	0
Gaziantep BB	2	0	* Home team in the 1st leg	

MEDALS TABLE

	Overall			League			Cup		Europe		
	G	S	B	G	S	B	G	S	G	S	B
1 Galatasaray	32	14	17	17	9	16	14	5	1		1
2 Fenerbahçe	22	26	6	18	17	6	4	9			
3 Besiktas	20	20	8	11	14	8	9	6			
4 Trabzonspor	14	13	6	6	8	6	8	5			
5 Altay Izmir	2	5	2				2	5			
6 Gençlerbirligi	2	3	2				2	3			
7 Bursaspor	2	3	1	1			1	3			
MKE Ankaragücü	2	3					2	3			

TURKEY 2010-11

BANK ASYA 1.LIG (2)

	Pl	W	D	L	F	A	Pts	Mersin IY	Samsunspor	Gaziantep BB	Caykur	Orduspor	Tavsanli	Boluspor	Kayseri	Denizlispor	Karsiyaka	Giresunspor	Adanaspor	Kartalspor	Akhisar	Güngörenspor	Altay Izmir	Diyarbakirspor
Mersin Idman Yurdu	32	17	7	8	39	29	58		1-0	1-3	3-0	1-4	1-0	2-0	1-2	2-4	4-0	1-0	0-0	2-1	2-1	1-0	2-3	1-0
Samsunspor	32	16	10	6	45	20	58	1-1		4-0	1-2	1-1	3-0	0-1	0-0	1-1	3-0	1-0	3-1	0-0	0-0	3-0	1-0	3-1
Gaziantep BB †	32	16	9	7	43	26	57	1-0	3-1		3-0	0-0	0-0	2-1	0-0	2-3	1-0	3-0	1-0	0-0	2-0	0-1	3-0	1-0
Caykur Rizespor †	32	15	9	8	36	24	54	3-0	0-1	1-0		3-0	3-1	2-1	2-0	1-0	2-1	1-0	2-1	1-0	0-3	2-2	2-1	1-0
Orduspor †	32	14	12	6	47	29	54	0-1	1-1	2-4	1-1		1-2	0-0	1-0	0-0	1-0	2-1	2-2	0-0	4-0	4-0	1-2	3-1
Tavsanli Linyitspor †	32	13	12	7	32	28	51	0-0	1-1	0-0	2-0	0-0		1-0	1-1	1-0	2-0	1-0	2-1	0-0	3-3	3-1	0-0	4-0
Boluspor	32	14	7	11	46	31	49	2-1	0-1	1-0	0-0	1-2	5-0		0-1	0-2	1-0	3-0	0-1	3-3	3-0	0-1	1-3	1-1
Kayseri Erciyesspor	32	11	15	6	40	29	48	1-1	0-2	2-1	0-0	1-1	2-0	1-1		1-3	1-1	1-1	4-1	2-0	1-0	0-2	1-2	4-0
Denizlispor	32	11	11	10	40	31	44	1-2	0-1	0-1	1-1	0-1	1-0	2-3	1-1		0-0	0-1	1-1	1-1	1-1	2-0	4-1	0-1
Karsiyaka	32	10	11	11	26	34	41	0-0	3-2	1-1	1-0	0-2	1-1	1-1	0-2	2-2		0-1	2-2	1-0	0-0	1-0	0-1	2-0
Giresunspor	32	11	5	16	27	32	38	1-2	0-1	2-0	0-0	0-2	0-1	2-1	1-1	2-0	1-2		2-1	1-0	1-0	3-0	1-0	1-1
Adanaspor	32	8	13	11	41	42	37	0-0	1-1	1-1	2-1	3-1	1-0	1-2	2-2	0-0	0-2	2-2		2-3	2-2	1-0	4-1	2-0
Kartalspor	32	7	13	12	21	29	34	0-1	0-0	2-3	0-1	2-2	1-1	0-3	0-0	2-1	0-2	1-0	0-0		2-0	0-0	0-0	1-0
Akhisar Belediyespor	32	8	9	15	27	39	33	0-1	1-2	1-2	0-2	1-2	0-1	1-0	0-2	1-2	1-2	1-0	1-0	1-0		1-0	1-0	1-1
Güngörenspor	32	7	12	13	19	42	33	0-0	1-0	2-0	0-0	1-1	1-1	1-4	0-2	1-0	0-0	1-0	0-3	2-1	0-0		2-2	1-0
Altay Izmir	32	7	10	15	27	43	31	1-2	0-1	0-0	1-0	0-0	1-2	3-3	2-3	0-2	2-0	0-0	0-0	1-3	0-1	0-0		0-0
Diyarbakirspor	32	1	7	24	10	59	10	0-2	0-5	0-3	0-1	0-3	0-1	0-2	1-1	0-3	0-1	0-2	1-4	2-3	0-2	0-0	0-0	

20/08/2010 - 15/05/2011 • † Qualified for the promotion play-offs

TURKIYE KUPASI 2010-11

Second Round

Gaziantepspor *	4	Türk Telecom	0
Karabükspor	1 4p	**Baypazari Sekerspor***	1 5p
Antalyaspor	2	Orduspor *	1
Eskisehirspor *	1	**Denizlispor**	2
Besiktas *	3	Mersin Idman Yurdu	0
Samsunspor	0	**Gaziantep BB** *	2
Konya Torku	3	Kayseri Erciyesspor *	1
Sivasspor	1	**Manisaspor**	2
Gençlerbirligi *	4	Sebatspor Akçaabat	1
Konyaspor	0	**Bucaspor**	1
MKE Ankaragücü *	3	Tokatspor	1
Hacettepe	0	**Yeni Malatyaspor** *	0
Kasimpasa	4	Menemen	1
Dardanelspor	0	**Istanbul BB** *	1
Karsiyaka *	3	Kayserispor	2
Bandirmaspor	0 3p	**Kitikhanspor**	0 4p

Third round groups

	Pl	W	D	L	F	A	Pts	Gaz	Gal	BS	Ant	Den
Gaziantepspor	4	3	1	0	7	2	10					
Galatasaray	4	2	2	0	7	3	8	3-1			3-1	
Baypazari Sekerspor	4	1	1	2	4	7	4		1-1			2-1
Antalyaspor	4	0	3	1	4	6	3	1-3		0-0		
Denizlispor	4	0	1	3	4	8	1	0-1			2-2	

	Pl	W	D	L	F	A	Pts	Bes	GBB	Tra	KS	Man
Besiktas	4	3	0	1	8	6	9					
Gaziantep BB	4	2	2	0	7	5	8	1-0				2-2
Trabzonspor	4	2	0	2	9	6	7		2-2			3-1
Konya Sekerspor	4	1	1	2	7	9	4	2-3	1-2			1-3
Manisaspor	4	0	0	4	5	10	0	2-3	1-2			

	Pl	W	D	L	F	A	Pts	Gen	Buc	Ank	YM	Fen
Gençlerbirligi	4	2	1	1	6	4	7					4-2
Bucaspor	4	2	1	1	5	4	7	1-2				2-1
MKE Ankaragücü	4	1	3	0	6	4	6	1-2	1-1			
Yeni Malatyaspor	4	1	1	2	3	5	4			0-0		2-1
Fenerbahçe	4	1	0	3	7	10	3	2-1	2-3			

	Pl	W	D	L	F	A	Pts	Kas	IBB	Bur	Kar	Kir
Kasimpasa	4	4	0	0	9	2	12					
Istanbul BB	4	3	0	1	4	3	9	3-1				2-0
Bursaspor	4	1	1	2	4	5	4	1-3				1-0
Karsiyaka	4	1	0	3	5	6	3	0-1				1-1
Kirikhanspor	4	0	1	3	3	9	1	0-2			2-5	

Quarter-finals

Besiktas *	5	3
Gaziantep BB	0	0
Galatasaray	2	0
Gaziantepspor *	3	0
Gençlerbirligi *	2	2
Bucaspor	0	1
Kasimpasa	0	1
Istanbul BB *	0	1

Semi-finals

Besiktas *	3	2
Gaziantepspor	0	2
Gençlerbirligi	1	0
Istanbul BB *	1	3

Final

Besiktas ‡	2	4p
Istanbul BB	2	3p

PENALTIES

IBB		Bes	
✗	Cihan	Almeida	✓
✓	Ekrem	Fernandes	✓
✓	Gokhan Unal	NaAureliosa	✓
✓	Holmen	Hilbert	✗
✗	Metin	Simao	✗

CUP FINAL

Kadir Has, Kayseri
11-05-2011, Att: 28 000, Ref: Yunus Yildirim
Scorers - Quaresma 33, Sivok 78 for Besiktas;
Ibrahim Akin 53p Gokhan Unal 68 for Istanbul
Besiktas - Rustu Recber - Ekrem Dag•, Tomas
Sivok, Mehmet Aurelio, Ismail Koybasi, Manuel
Fernandes, Necip Uysal, Ricardo Quaresma•,
Guti (Roberto Hilbert 106), Simao, Bobo (Hugo
Almeida 56). Tr: Tayfur Havutcu
Istanbul - Kenan Hasagic - Rizvan Sahin, Can
Arat, Metin Depe•, Ekrem Eksioglu, Cihan
Haspolati, Mahmut Tekdemir•, Samuel
Holmen•, Iskender Alin (Tevfik Kose 105), Herve
Tum (Gokhan Unal 56), Ibrahim Akin (Gokhan
Suzen 83). Tr: Abdullah Avci

Galatasaray, Fenerbahçe, Bursaspor and Trabzonspor entered at the group stage • * Home team in the first leg • ‡ Qualified for the Europa League

UAE – UNITED ARAB EMIRATES

FIFA/COCA-COLA WORLD RANKING

'93	'94	'95	'96	'97	'98	'99	'00	'01	'02	'03	'04	'05	'06	'07	'08	'09	'10	'11	'12
51	46	75	60	50	42	54	64	60	89	75	82	85	87	100	110	112	105	130	

	2011												High	Low	Av
	Jan	Feb	Mar	Apr	May	Jun	Jul	Aug	Sep	Oct	Nov	Dec			
	102	111	111	111	111	110	109	108	112	113	120	130	42	130	79

A poor run of form in the second half of 2011 saw the United Arab Emirates crash out of the 2014 FIFA World Cup qualifiers in unexpected fashion as the team lost the first five games in their group. The UAE, who represented Asia at the 1990 finals in Italy, had beaten India 5-2 on aggregate in a preliminary round tie but after a 3-2 defeat at home against Kuwait the team then lost 3-1 in Lebanon, a result that cost coach Srecko Katanec his job. Local coach Abdullah Masfer took over on a caretaker basis, but the team's fortunes did not take a turn for the better, despite avenging the loss against the Lebanese in the final qualifying match in early 2012. The form of the national team belied the improvements being made in Emirati football, with the Olympic team continuing to impress with a squad made up primarily of players that took the silver medal at the Asian Games in Guangzhou in 2010. In club football, Abu Dhabi's Al Jazeera broke their trophy duck in emphatic fashion when they comfortably won the league ahead of Bani-Yas and then beat cross-town rivals Al Wahda 4-0 to win the President's Cup. The form of clubs from the United Arab Emirates in the AFC Champions League continues to be of concern, with all four representatives in the 2011 tournament crashing out in the first round.

FIFA WORLD CUP RECORD
1930-1982 DNE 1986 DNQ **1990** 24 r1 1994-2014 DNQ

UNITED ARAB EMIRATES FOOTBALL ASSOCIATION (UAEFA)

Wadi Al Amrdi Building, 271-574 Near Murshif Park, PO Box 961, Abu Dhabi

☎ +971 2 4445600
📠 +971 2 4448558
✉ info@uaefa.ae
🖥 www.uaefa.ae
FA 1971 CON 1974 FIFA 1972
P Yousuf Al Serkal
GS Yousuf Abdullah

FIFA BIG COUNT 2006

Total players	82 776
% of population	3.18%
Male	82 776
Female	0
Youth under 18	6 689
Unregistered	11 000
Professionals	67
Referees	150
Admin & coaches	836
Number of clubs	31
Number of teams	156

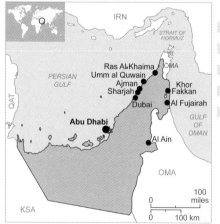

MAJOR CITIES/TOWNS

		Population
1	Dubai	1 770 533
2	Abu Dhabi	896 751
3	Sharjah	845 617
4	Al Ain	651 904
5	Ajman	372 923
6	Ras Al Khaima	171 903
7	Al Fujairah	107 940
8	Umm al Quwain	69 936
9	Khor Fakkan	49 635

AL IMARAT AL ARABIYAH AL MUTTAHIDAH • UNITED ARAB EMIRATES

Capital Abu Dhabi	Population 4 798 491 (115)	% in cities 78%
GDP per capita $44 600 (12)	Area km² 83 600 km² (114)	GMT + / - +4
Neighbours (km) Oman 410, Saudi Arabia 457 • Coast 1318		

RECENT INTERNATIONAL MATCHES PLAYED BY THE UNITED ARAB EMIRATES

2009	Opponents	Score		Venue	Comp	Scorers	Att	Referee
2-06	Germany	L	2-7	Dubai	Fr	Ismael Al Hammadi [53], Nawaf Mubarak [73]	7 000	Darwish JOR
6-06	Korea Republic	L	0-2	Dubai	WCq		4 000	Balideh QAT
10-06	Iran	L	0-1	Tehran	WCq		38 000	Irmatov UZB
10-10	Palestine	D	1-1	Dubai	Fr	Saeed Al Kas [47]		
14-10	Jordan	W	3-1	Dubai	Fr	Mohamed Al Shehhi [35], Ahmad Khamis [56], Mohammed Suroor [80p]		
15-11	Czech Republic	D	0-0	Al Ain	Fr	W 3-2p	5 000	Dalkam JOR
18-11	Iraq	L	0-1	Al Ain	Fr			Osman EGY
16-12	Kuwait	D	0-0	Kuwait City	Fr			
2010								
6-01	Malaysia	W	1-0	Dubai	ACq	Ahmed Khalil [93+]	3 500	Basma SYR
3-03	Uzbekistan	W	1-0	Tashkent	ACq	Sultan Al Menhali [93+]	20 000	Shamsuzzaman BAN
29-05	Moldova	W	3-2	Anif	Fr	Fares Juma [26], Mohamed Al Shehhi [31], Ahmed Khalil [89]	200	Schorgenhofer AUT
5-06	Algeria	L	0-1	Fürth	Fr		12 500	Grafe GER
7-09	Kuwait	W	3-0	Abu Dhabi	Fr	Ahmed Khalil [22], Ismael Matar [42], Saeed Al Kuthairi [91+]		
9-10	Chile	L	0-2	Abu Dhabi	Fr		500	Al Ghamdi KSA
12-10	Angola	L	0-2	Abu Dhabi	Fr			
18-11	India	W	5-0	Dubai	Fr	Saeed Al Kas [15], Amir Mubarak [35], Ali Al Wehaibi 2 [61 73], Ahmed Jumaa [72]		
23-11	Iraq	D	0-0	Aden	GCr1			Al Qatani KSA
26-11	Oman	D	0-0	Aden	GCr1			Shaaban EGY
29-11	Bahrain	W	3-1	Aden	GCr1	Subait Khater [4], Fares Juma [8], Ahmed Juma [64]		Al Marry BHR
2-12	Saudi Arabia	L	0-1	Aden	GCsf			Ogiya JPN
2011								
2-01	Syria	W	2-0	Al Ain	Fr	Saeed Al Kathiri [63], Theyab Awana [89]	2 400	Abdul Baki OMA
5-01	Australia	D	0-0	Al Ain	Fr			Shaban KUW
11-01	Korea DPR	D	0-0	Doha	ACr1		3 639	Mohd Salleh MAS
15-01	Iraq	L	0-1	Al Rayyan	ACr1		7 233	Nishimura JPN
19-01	Iran	L	0-3	Doha	ACr1		5 012	Kim Dong Jin KOR
17-07	Lebanon	W	6-2	Al Ain	Fr	Ahmed Khalil 3 [9 18 54], Mohamed Al Shehhi [22], Hamdan Al Kamali [41], Theyab Awana [79p]		
23-07	India	W	3-0	Al Ain	WCq	Hamdan Al Kamali [21p], Mohamed Al Shehhi [29p], Ismail Al Hammadi [81]	3 179	Al Dosari QAT
28-07	India	D	2-2	New Delhi	WCq	Mohamed Al Shehhi [40], Ali Al Wehaibi [72]	13 000	Bashir SIN
25-08	Qatar	W	3-1	Al Ain	Fr	Hamdan Al Kamali [24p], Ahmed Khalil 2 [50 68]		
2-09	Kuwait	L	2-3	Al Ain	WCq	Ismail Al Hammadi [84], Ahmed Khalil [89]	8 715	Basma SYR
6-09	Lebanon	L	1-3	Beirut	WCq	Mahmoud Al Hammadi [16]	4 000	Faghani IRN
6-10	China PR	L	1-2	Shenzhen	Fr	Eisa Al Marzouqi [86]		
11-10	Korea Republic	L	1-2	Suwon	WCq	Ismael Matar [92+]	28 689	Tan Hai CHN
11-11	Korea Republic	L	0-2	Dubai	WCq		8 272	Irmatov UZB
15-11	Kuwait	L	1-2	Kuwait City	WCq	Ismael Matar [19]	10 000	Al Hilali OMA

Fr = Friendly match • AC = AFC Asian Cup • GC = Gulf Cup • WC = FIFA World Cup • q = qualifier • r1 = first round group • sf = semi-final

UAE NATIONAL TEAM HISTORICAL RECORDS

Caps — **162** - Adnan Al Talyani 1984-97 • **115** - Abdulraheem Jumaa 1998- • **112** - Zuhair Bilal 1988-2002 • **110** - Abdulsalam Jumaa 1997- • **106** - Mushin Faraj 1988-99

Goals — **53** - Adnan Al Talyani 1984-97 • **26** - Ismael Matar 2003-

Past Coaches — Mohammed Sheita EGY 1972-73 • Jumaa Gharib 1973 • Mohammed Sheita EGY 1973-74 • Mimi El Sherbini EGY 1975 • Jumaa Gharib 1975-76 • Dimitri Tadic YUG 1976 • Don Revie ENG 1977-80 • Heshmat Mohajerani IRN 1980-84 • Carlos Alberto Parreira BRA 1984-88 • Mario Zagallo BRA 1988-90 • Bernhard Blaut POL 1990 • Valery Lobanovsky UKR 1990-92 • Antoni Piechniczek POL 1992-95 • Tomislav Ivic CRO 1995-96 • Lori Sandri BRA 1997 • Milan Macala CZE 1997 • Lori Sandri BRA 1998 • Carlos Queiroz POR 1998-99 • Srecko Juricic CRO 1999 • Dr Abdullah Masfar 2000 • Henri Michel FRA 2000-01 • Abdullah Saqr 2001 • Tini Ruijs NED 2001 • Jo Bonfrere NED 2001-02 • Roy Hodgson ENG 2002-04 • Aad De Mos NED 2004-05 • Dick Advocaat NED Aug 2005 • Bruno Metsu FRA 2006-08 • Dominique Bathenay FRA 2008-09 • Srecko Katanec SVN 2009-

UNITED ARAB EMIRATES 2010-11

PRO LEAGUE

	Pl	W	D	L	F	A	Pts	Jazeera	Bani-Yas	Nasr	Shabab	Wahda	Wasl	Sharjah	Ahli	Dubai	Ain	Ittihad	Dhafra
Al Jazeera †	22	16	5	1	64	27	53		4-0	3-0	3-3	0-0	3-1	3-0	5-1	4-2	4-0	5-2	5-3
Bani-Yas †	22	12	5	5	38	24	41	1-1		1-0	2-2	2-1	0-0	1-1	2-1	2-0	3-0	4-2	2-0
Al Nasr †	22	10	5	7	34	30	35	1-2	1-0		3-2	1-3	0-1	1-2	4-0	1-1	0-3	2-0	1-1
Al Shabab †	22	9	7	6	42	32	34	0-2	0-1	2-2		1-1	0-4	1-1	2-2	2-0	3-0	4-1	4-0
Al Wahda	22	8	7	7	44	31	31	2-2	1-3	2-0	5-2		4-0	6-1	1-2	2-2	0-0	3-1	2-4
Al Wasl	22	9	4	9	31	36	31	0-4	2-1	2-3	1-3	2-0		1-2	2-0	1-0	2-2	2-1	2-1
Sharjah	22	8	6	8	30	34	30	1-2	3-5	1-1	0-3	0-0	1-1		2-3	1-0	2-1	3-1	3-0
Al Ahli Dubai	22	7	6	9	30	42	27	2-2	1-0	1-1	1-3	0-2	4-1	2-1		3-1	0-4	2-2	0-0
Dubai	22	8	2	12	33	48	26	1-4	1-4	1-3	0-2	0-5	2-1	1-0	2-1		1-0	3-1	6-4
Al Ain	22	6	7	9	33	35	25	4-1	1-1	1-2	1-1	2-0	0-0	1-1	1-2	4-3		1-4	1-1
Al Ittihad Kalba	22	6	2	14	39	56	20	3-4	2-1	1-2	2-1	5-3	2-3	0-3	2-2	0-1	4-3		1-3
Dhafra	22	3	4	15	27	50	13	0-1	0-2	1-4	0-1	1-1	2-3	0-1	2-0	3-5	0-3	1-2	

26/08/2010 - 5/06/2011 • † Qualified for the AFC Champions League
Top scorers: **18** - Andre Senghor SEN, Bani Yas • **13** - Marcelinho BRA, Sharjah • **12** - Ibrahim Diaky, Jazeera & Bare BRA, Jazeera

UNITED ARAB EMIRATES 2010-11
SECOND DIVISION

GROUP A	Pl	W	D	L	F	A	Pts
Ajman	21	12	4	5	48	29	40
Emirates Club	21	11	4	6	44	31	37
Dibba	21	9	5	7	36	29	32
Al Urooba	21	8	7	6	23	23	31
Al Ahli Fujeira	21	9	4	8	25	31	31
Al Khaleej	21	8	4	9	41	44	28
Al Sha'ab	21	6	7	8	27	33	25
Thaid	21	2	3	16	16	40	9

GROUP B	Pl	W	D	L	F	A	Pts
Al Quwat Al Musalaha	18	13	4	1	52	16	43
Masafi	18	12	3	3	42	16	39
Ras Al Khaima	18	10	5	3	39	17	35
Hatta	18	8	4	6	39	22	28
Al Arabi	18	7	5	6	25	18	26
Dibba Al Hisn	18	8	2	8	32	27	26
Al Jazira Al Hamra	18	6	2	10	22	39	20
Ramms	18	6	2	10	19	46	20
Masfut	18	2	4	12	19	46	10
Al Taawon	18	1	3	14	16	58	6

9/12/2010 - 23/05/2011

MEDALS TABLE

	Overall G	S	B	Lge G	Cup G	Asia G	S	B	City
1 Al Ain	15	1	1	9	5	1	1	1	Al Ain
2 Sharjah	13			5	8				Sharjah
3 Al Ahli	12			5	7				Dubai
4 Al Wasl	9	1		7	2			1	Dubai
5 Al Shabab	7	1		3	4			1	Dubai
6 Al Nasr	6			3	3				Dubai
7 Al Wahda	5	1		4	1			1	Abu Dhabi
8 Al Jazeera	2			1	1				Abu Dhabi
9 Al Sha'ab	1	1			1			1	Sharjah
10 Ajman	1				1				Ajman
Bani Yas	1				1				Abu Dhabi
Emirates Club	1				1				Ras Al Khaima

PRESIDENT'S CUP 2010-11

Round of 16		Quarter-finals		Semi-finals		Final	
Al Jazeera	2						
Al Nasr	1	Al Jazeera	3				
Al Urooba	1	Emirates Club	2				
Emirates Club	4			Al Jazeera	4		
Thaid	2			Al Shabab	1		
Dibba	1	Thaid	0				
Bani-Yas	0	Al Shabab	3				
Al Shabab	2					Al Jazeera	4
Al Wasl	1					Al Wahda	0
Al Quwat Al Musalaha	0	Al Wasl	1				
Dhafra	0	Al Ahli Dubai	0				
Al Ahli Dubai	1			Al Wasl	1		
Masafi	0			Al Wahda	2		
Al Ain ‡	3	Masafi	0				
Ajman	1	Al Wahda	2				
Al Wahda	5						

CUP FINAL
Sheikh Zayed, Abu Dhabi
11-04-2011
Scorers - Bare 2 [12] [80], Oliveira [68], Jumaa [93+] for Jazeera

‡ Al Ain disqualified

UGA – UGANDA

FIFA/COCA-COLA WORLD RANKING

'93	'94	'95	'96	'97	'98	'99	'00	'01	'02	'03	'04	'05	'06	'07	'08	'09	'10	'11	'12
94	93	74	81	109	105	108	103	119	102	103	109	101	103	76	71	75	80	89	

2011												High	Low	Av
Jan	Feb	Mar	Apr	May	Jun	Jul	Aug	Sep	Oct	Nov	Dec			
83	86	86	84	84	77	76	80	82	88	91	89	63	121	96

Uganda came so close to ending their 34-year wait for another appearance at the CAF Africa Cup of Nations finals but failed to win their final match in the 2012 qualifiers and missed out on the finals in Equatorial Guinea and Gabon. The Cranes needed to beat neighbours Kenya in Kampala to finish top of their group but were held to a goalless draw, allowing Angola to leapfrog them into first place. There was a massive burden of expectation on the team but problems on the eve of the game when one of their more experience players, Scottish-based midfielder David Obua, was expelled for not following team orders, also played a role in their failure. Coach Bobby Williamson remained in place despite the setback and took his home-based side to success in the East and Central African Senior Challenge Cup in Tanzania in December. Uganda beat Rwanda 3-2 on post-match penalties after a 2-2 draw in the final of the regional championship. At home, Uganda Revenue Authority won the league at a canter from Kampala City Council but were denied the double when they lost the Cup Final. The team that beat them, Simba, had last won a trophy in 1978 but unlike the national team their 34-year wait came to an end when the beat Uganda Revenue Authority 2-1 in the final in Kampala in June.

CAF AFRICA CUP OF NATIONS RECORD
1957-1959 DNE **1962** 4 SF 1963 DNE 1965 DNQ **1968** 7 r1 1970-1972 DNQ
1974 6 r1 **1976** 8 r1 **1978** 2 F 1980-1982 DNE 1984-1988 DNQ 1990 DNE 1992-2012 DNQ

FEDERATION OF UGANDA FOOTBALL ASSOCIATIONS (FUFA)

FUFA House, Plot No. 879,
Kyadondo Block 8,
Mengo Wakaliga Road,
PO Box 22518, Kampala
☎ +256 41 4272702
📠 +256 41 4272702
✉ fufaf@yahoo.com
🖥 www.fufa.co.ug
FA 1924 CON 1959 FIFA 1959
P Lawrence Mulindwa
GS Edgar Watson Suubi

FIFA BIG COUNT 2006

Total players	1 191 514
% of population	4.23%
Male	1 186 014
Female	5 500
Amateurs 18+	28 000
Professionals	14
Referees	600
Admin & coaches	5 000
Number of clubs	400
Number of teams	2 000

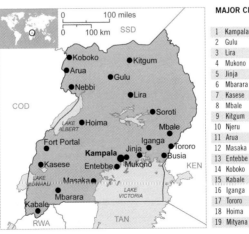

MAJOR CITIES/TOWNS

		Population
1	Kampala	1 560 080
2	Gulu	208 268
3	Lira	174 630
4	Mukono	111 058
5	Jinja	101 604
6	Mbarara	93 969
7	Kasese	91 906
8	Mbale	84 215
9	Kitgum	83 233
10	Njeru	75 380
11	Arua	71 226
12	Masaka	70 273
13	Entebbe	70 052
14	Koboko	59 430
15	Kabale	58 269
16	Iganga	56 074
17	Tororo	55 366
18	Hoima	52 670
19	Mityana	50 612

REPUBLIC OF UGANDA

Capital Kampala	Population 32 369 558 (38)	% in cities 13%
GDP per capita $1300 (204)	Area km² 241 038 km² (80)	GMT +/- +3
Neighbours (km) Congo DR 765, Kenya 933, Rwanda 169, Sudan 435, Tanzania 396		

RECENT INTERNATIONAL MATCHES PLAYED BY UGANDA

2009	Opponents	Score		Venue	Comp	Scorers	Att	Referee
1-01	Rwanda	W	4-0	Kampala	CCr1	Tony Mawejje 59, Simeon Masaba 67p, Brian Omwony 85, Stephen Bengo 87		
3-01	Zanzibar †	D	0-0	Kampala	CCr1			
7-01	Somalia	W	4-0	Kampala	CCr1	Tony Mawejje 2 31 65, Owen Kasule 38, Geofrey Massa 75		
9-01	Tanzania	W	2-1	Kampala	CCr1	Brian Omwony 11, Stephen Bengo 27		
11-01	Burundi	W	5-0	Kampala	CCsf	Brian Omwony 2 30 84, Andrew Mwesigwa 45, Stephen Bengo 46, Geofrey Massa 64		
13-01	Kenya	W	1-0	Kampala	CCf	Brian Omwony 18		
7-03	Sudan	W	2-0	Khartoum	Fr	Brian Omwony 2 9 37		
21-03	Malawi	W	2-1	Kampala	Fr	Brian Omwony 44, Patrick Ochan 57		
31-05	Ghana	L	1-2	Tamale	Fr	Geofrey Serunkuma 88		
29-11	Tanzania	W	2-0	Mumias	CCr1	Owen Kasule 3, Mike Sserumagga 88		
2-12	Burundi	W	2-0	Mumias	CCr1	Geofrey Massa 12, Dan Wagaluka 67		
5-12	Zanzibar †	D	0-0	Nairobi	CCr1			
7-12	Kenya	W	1-0	Nairobi	CCqf	Robert Sentongo 64		
9-12	Zanzibar †	W	2-1	Nairobi	CCsf	Stephen Bengo 2, Hamoud OG 10		
13-12	Rwanda	W	2-0	Nairobi	CCf	Dan Wagaluka 40, Emmanuel Okwi 73		
2010								
3-03	Tanzania	W	3-2	Mwanza	Fr	Sula Matovu 12, Saddam Juma 79, Owen Kasule 84		
11-08	Zambia	D	1-1	Kampala	Fr	Mike Sserumagga 39		
4-09	Angola	W	3-0	Kampala	CNq	David Obua 35, Andrew Mwesigwa 57, Geofrey Serunkuma 88		Osman EGY
9-10	Kenya	D	0-0	Nairobi	CNq			Diatta SEN
7-11	Yemen	D	2-2	Aden	Fr	Mike Sserumagga 32, Patrick Edema 90		
10-11	Bahrain	D	0-0	Riffa	Fr			
16-11	Saudi Arabia	D	0-0	Dubai	Fr			
29-11	Ethiopia	W	2-1	Dar es Salaam	CCr1	Simeon Masaba 35p, Henry Kisseka 46		
2-12	Malawi	D	1-1	Dar es Salaam	CCr1	Okwi Emmanuel 80		
5-12	Kenya	W	2-0	Dar es Salaam	CCr1	Okwi Emmanuel 81, Andrew Mwesigwa 92+p		
8-12	Zanzibar †	D	2-2	Dar es Salaam	CCqf	Mike Sserumaga 13, Okwi Emmanuel 47p. W 5-3p		
10-12	Tanzania	D	0-0	Dar es Salaam	CCsf	L 4-5p		
12-12	Ethiopia	W	4-3	Dar es Salaam	CC3p	Henry Kisseka 5, Okwi Emmanuel 48, Tony Mawejje 53, Sula Matovu 72		
2011								
5-01	Burundi	W	3-1	Cairo	Fr	Manko Kaweesa 33, Noah Ssemakula 55, Owen Kasule 89		
8-01	Egypt	L	0-1	Cairo	Fr			
11-01	Tanzania	D	1-1	Cairo	Fr	Athuman Machupa 24		
14-01	Congo DR	W	1-0	Cairo	Fr	Habib Kavuma 23		
17-01	Egypt	L	1-3	Ismailia	Fr	Ceasar Okhuti 84p		
26-03	Guinea-Bissau	W	1-0	Bissau	CNq	David Obua 22		
4-06	Guinea-Bissau	W	2-0	Kampala	CNq	Godfrey Walusimbi 43, Geofrey Massa 62		
4-09	Angola	L	0-2	Luanda	CNq			
8-10	Kenya	D	0-0	Kampala	CNq			
11-11	Morocco	W	1-0	Marrakech	Fr	Mike Sserumagga 47		
13-11	Sudan	D	0-0	Marrakech	Fr	W 3-2p		
25-11	Zanzibar †	W	2-1	Dar es Salaam	CCr1	Dan Wagaluka 40, Mike Sserumagga 77		
28-11	Somalia	W	4-0	Chamazi	CCr1	Dan Wagaluka 48, Emmanuel Okwi 3 61 76 90		
1-12	Burundi	L	0-1	Dar es Salaam	CCr1			
6-12	Zimbabwe	W	1-0	Dar es Salaam	CCqf	Hamis Kizza 15		
8-12	Tanzania	W	3-1	Dar es Salaam	CCsf	Andrew Mwesigwa 56, Emmanuel Okwi 102, Isaac Isinde 112p		
10-12	Rwanda	D	2-2	Dar es Salaam	CCf	Isaac Isinde 77, Karekezi OG 80. W 3-2p		

Fr = Friendly match • CN = CAF African Cup of Nations • CC = CECAFA Cup • WC = FIFA World Cup
q = qualifier • r1 = first round group • qf = quarter-final • sf = semifinal • 3p = third place play-off • f = final • † Not a full international

UGANDA 2010–11

ECOBANK SUPER LEAGUE

	Pl	W	D	L	F	A	Pts	URA	Kampala CC	Bunamwaya	Simba	Victors	SC Villa	Express	Proline	Police	Masaka	UTODA	Maroons	Fire Masters	Gulu United
URA Kampala †	26	18	5	3	41	15	**59**		1-0	0-0	1-0	2-1	1-0	3-1	2-0	3-0	2-0	3-1	1-0	3-2	3-0
Kampala City Council	26	14	6	6	26	14	**48**	1-2		1-3	1-0	0-0	0-0	2-1	1-0	1-0	2-1	2-0	2-0	0-0	1-0
Bunamwaya Wakiso	26	14	5	7	27	18	**47**	2-1	1-3		0-1	2-0	1-0	2-1	1-1	0-1	1-0	0-1	1-0	0-3	4-0
Simba	26	12	6	8	20	16	**42**	1-2	1-1	1-0		1-1	0-0	1-0	1-1	1-1	1-0	0-1	1-0	1-0	1-0
Victors Jinja	26	10	9	7	33	22	**39**	0-1	0-1	2-1	2-0		1-1	0-1	1-0	2-1	3-1	2-1	0-1	5-2	2-0
SC Villa Kampala	26	9	12	5	22	11	**39**	1-1	0-0	1-1	0-1	0-0		0-0	0-0	1-0	0-1	2-1	2-2	1-0	4-0
Express RE Kampala	26	9	10	7	18	14	**37**	1-1	1-0	0-1	0-1	0-0	0-1		1-1	0-0	1-1	3-0	2-0	1-0	1-0
Proline Buikwe	26	9	9	8	28	24	**36**	0-2	1-2	0-1	1-1	2-1	0-0	0-0		0-2	2-1	2-0	2-0	1-0	2-2
Uganda Police Kampala	26	8	7	11	18	21	**31**	0-1	0-1	0-1	1-0	0-1	1-0	0-0	0-2		1-2	2-1	0-0	0-0	2-0
Masaka Local Council	26	9	4	13	20	27	**31**	1-0	1-0	0-1	0-1	0-0	0-2	0-1	1-0	1-0		1-1	0-1	1-2	1-0
Kampala UTODA	26	7	7	12	19	34	**28**	2-1	1-0	0-0	1-0	1-1	0-3	0-1	0-2	2-1	2-2		0-0	0-0	0-2
Maroons Kampala	26	5	11	10	13	21	**26**	0-0	0-1	1-2	2-1	1-1	0-0	0-0	1-1	0-1	1-0	0-0		1-0	0-0
Fire Masters	26	4	7	15	23	38	**19**	1-4	0-3	0-0	0-1	2-2	0-2	0-1	2-3	2-2	1-2	3-1	1-1		1-2
Gulu United	26	3	4	19	11	44	**13**	0-0	0-1	0-1	0-2	0-5	0-1	0-0	1-4	0-2	1-2	1-2	2-1	0-1	

1709/2010 - 3/06/2011 • † Qualified for the CAF Champions League

MEDALS TABLE

		Overall			Lge	Cup		Africa			City
		G	S	B	G	G	S	G	S	B	
1	SC Villa	24	5		16	8	3	2			Kampala
2	Kampala City Council	16	5	1	8	8	5			1	Kampala
3	Express RE	15	4	1	5	10	4			1	Kampala
4	Uganda Revenue Authority - URA	5	2		4	1	2				Kampala
5	Simba SC	4	4		2	2	3	1			Lugazi
6	Coffee SC	2	2			2	2				
7	Mbale Heroes	2	1			2	1				Mbale
8	Prisons FC	2			2						Kampala
	Victors	2				2					Jinja
10	Nile Breweries	1	4		1		4				Jinja
11	Uganda Commercial Bank	1	3		1		3				Kampala
12	Police FC	1	1		1		1				Jinja
	Uganda Electricity Board - Umeme	1	1			1	1				Jinja
14	Coffee United	1			1						Kakira
	Nsambya	1				1					Kampala
	Bunamwaya	1			1						Wakiso

BELL UGANDA CUP 2011

Round of 16		Quarter–finals		Semi–finals		Final	
Simba	2						
Kampala UTODA	0	**Simba**	2				
Gulu University		Masindi Town Council	1				
Masindi Town Council				**Simba**	1 3p		
Jinja Arsenal				Express RE Kampala	1 2p		
Boroboro Tigers Lira		Jinja Arsenal	0				
Uganda Police	0 2p	**Express RE Kampala**	1				
Express RE Kampala	0 4p					**Simba**	2
Victors Jinja	3					URA Kampala	1
KASE	0	**Victors Jinja**	1				
Baza Holdings		Proline Buikwe	0				
Proline Buikwe				Victors Jinja	0		
Bunamwaya Wakiso	2			**URA Kampala**	1		
Jogoo Young	0	Bunamwaya Wakiso	1 3p				
CRO Mbale		**URA Kampala**	1 4p				
URA Kampala							

CUP FINAL

Nakivubo, Kampala
11-06-2011, Ref: Segonga
Scorers - Robert Omunuk, Richard Lubwama [61] for Simba; Hamis Kiiza for URA

UKR – UKRAINE

FIFA/COCA-COLA WORLD RANKING

'93	'94	'95	'96	'97	'98	'99	'00	'01	'02	'03	'04	'05	'06	'07	'08	'09	'10	'11	'12
90	77	71	59	49	47	27	34	45	45	60	57	40	13	30	15	22	34	55	

	2011														
	Jan	Feb	Mar	Apr	May	Jun	Jul	Aug	Sep	Oct	Nov	Dec	High	Low	Av
	34	34	33	35	35	42	45	48	60	58	55	55	11	132	45

Oleg Blokhin's return as coach in April 2011 gave the flagging Ukraine national team a much needed boost as the country prepared to co-host the Euro 2012 finals. Since being awarded the finals in 2007 there has been continued speculation as to how ready the country would be. With the stadia in Kyiv and Lviv finally finished at the end of 2011, preparations off the pitch looked on course but despite the appointment of Blokhin doubts remained as to how well the team would fare on the pitch. Italy, France, Sweden and the Czech Republic all came to Ukraine to play friendlies and left victorious although there were signs of improvement towards the end of the year, notably the impressive 3-3 draw with Germany and the victory over Austria - games which saw the opening of the stadia in Kyiv and Lviv. Club football in both cities, along with the other Euro 2012 venues in Donetsk and Kharkov, has been left a lasting legacy thanks to the tournament and already Shakhtar Donetsk are reaping the benefits. They retained their league title in 2011 and completed their second double in four years after beating Dynamo Kyiv 2-0 in the Cup Final, leaving the team from the capital without a trophy for the second year running. Shakhter also reached the quarter-finals of the Champions League before losing heavily to eventual winners Barcelona.

UEFA EUROPEAN CHAMPIONSHIP RECORD

1960-1992 DNE (Played as part of the Soviet Union) **1996-2008** DNQ **2012** Qualified (Co-hosts)

FOOTBALL FEDERATION OF UKRAINE (FFU)

Provulok Laboratornyi 7-A,
PO Box 55,
Kyiv 01133

☎ +380 44 5210521
📠 +380 44 5210550
📧 info@ffu.org.ua
🖥 www.ffu.org.ua
FA 1991 CON 1992 FIFA 1992
P Grygoriy Surkis
GS Oleksandr Bandurko

FIFA BIG COUNT 2006

Total players	2 273 017
% of population	4.87%
Male	2 040 756
Female	232 261
Amateurs 18+	25 500
Youth under 18	658 540
Unregistered	314 700
Professionals	2 427
Referees	7 530
Admin & coaches	8 050
Number of clubs	68
Number of teams	6 500

MAJOR CITIES/TOWNS

		Population
1	Kyiv	2 304 511
2	Kharkiv	1 461 234
3	Dnipropetrovsk	1 046 608
4	Odessa	992 669
5	Donetsk	989 569
6	Zaporizhzhya	787 865
7	Lviv	735 417
8	Kryvyi Rih	722 303
9	Mykolayiv	507 710
10	Mariupol	476 263
11	Luhansk	446 411
12	Makiyivka	365 536
13	Vinnytsia	365 227
14	Simferopol	341 281
15	Sevastopol	338 743
16	Kherson	312 536
17	Poltava	305 067
18	Chernihiv	299 989

UKRAYINA • UKRAINE

Capital	Kyiv	Population	45 700 395 (27)	% in cities	68%
GDP per capita	$7400 (124)	Area km²	603 550 km² (45)	GMT + / -	+2
Neighbours (km)	Belarus 891, Hungary 103, Moldova 940, Poland 428, Romania 538, Russia 1576, Slovakia 90 • Coast 2782				

RECENT INTERNATIONAL MATCHES PLAYED BY UKRAINE

2008	Opponents	Score		Venue	Comp	Scorers	Att	Referee
6-02	Cyprus	D	1-1	Nicosia	Fr	Milevskyi [71]	500	Kasnaferis CYP
26-03	Serbia	W	2-0	Odessa	Fr	Shevchenko [54], Nazarenko [57]	8 000	Lajuks LVA
24-05	Netherlands	L	0-3	Rotterdam	Fr		40 000	Circhetta SUI
1-06	Sweden	W	1-0	Stockholm	Fr	Nazarenko [82]	25 203	Einwaller AUT
20-08	Poland	W	1-0	Lviv	Fr	Kravchenko [45]	22 000	Nalbandian ARM
6-09	Belarus	W	1-0	Lviv	WCq	Shevhenko [94+p]	24 000	Rizzoli ITA
10-09	Kazakhstan	W	3-1	Almaty	WCq	Nazarenko 2 [45 80], Shevchenko [54]	17 000	Brych GER
11-10	Croatia	D	0-0	Kharkov	WCq		38 500	Braamhaar NED
19-11	Norway	W	1-0	Dnepropetrovsk	Fr	Seleznov [26p]	10 000	Lajuks LVA
2009								
10-02	Slovakia	W	3-2	Limassol	Fr	Valyayev [10], Seleznov [47], Milevskiy [83p]		Kailis CYP
11-02	Serbia	W	1-0	Nicosia	Fr	Nazarenko [16]	500	Kokas GRE
1-04	England	L	1-2	London	WCq	Shevchenko [74]	87 548	Larsen DEN
6-06	Croatia	D	2-2	Zagreb	WCq	Shevchenko [13], Gay [54]	32 073	Hauge NOR
10-06	Kazakhstan	W	2-1	Kyiv	WCq	Nazarenko 2 [32 47]	11 500	Paixao POR
12-08	Turkey	L	0-3	Kyiv	Fr			Ceferin SVN
5-09	Andorra	W	5-0	Kyiv	WCq	Yarmolenko [18], Milevskiy 2 [45 92+p], Shevchenko [72p], Seleznov [94+p]	14 870	Sipailo LVA
9-09	Belarus	D	0-0	Minsk	WCq		21 727	Kassai HUN
10-10	England	W	1-0	Dnepropetrovsk	WCq	Nazarenko [30]	31 000	Skomina SVN
14-10	Andorra	W	6-0	Andorra La Vella	WCq	Shevchenko [22], Gusev [61], Lima.I OG [69], Rakits Kyy [80], Seleznov [81], Yarmolenko [83]	820	Thomson SCO
14-11	Greece	D	0-0	Athens	WCpo		39 045	Duhamel FRA
18-11	Greece	L	0-1	Donetsk	WCpo		31 643	Benquerença POR
2010								
25-05	Lithuania	W	4-0	Kharkov	Fr	Aliev 2 [10 17], Shevchenko 2 [68p 78]	42 000	Sukhina RUS
29-05	Romania	W	3-2	Lviv	Fr	Aliev [15], Konoplyanka [75], OG [78]	22 000	Kralovec CZE
2-06	Norway	W	1-0	Oslo	Fr	Zozulya [78]	10 178	Blom NED
11-08	Netherlands	D	1-1	Donetsk	Fr	Aliev [75]	18 051	Skomina SVN
4-09	Poland	D	1-1	Lodz	Fr	Seleznev [90]	6 500	Irmatov UZB
7-09	Chile	W	2-1	Kyiv	Fr	Rakitskiy [36], Aliev [52]	10 000	Sevastsyanik BLR
8-10	Canada	D	2-2	Kyiv	Fr	Milevskiy [59], Tymoshchuk [80]	10 000	Mikulski
11-10	Brazil	L	0-2	Derby	Fr		13 088	Atkinson ENG
17-11	Switzerland	D	2-2	Geneva	Fr	Aliev [48], Konoplyanka [75]	11 100	Gumienny BEL
2011								
8-02	Romania	D	2-2	Paralimni	Fr	Rakitskiy [23], Milevskiy [31]. W 4-2p	1 000	Johannesson SWE
9-02	Sweden	D	1-1	Nicosia	Fr	Devic [20p]. 5-4p	2 000	Tudor ROU
29-03	Italy	L	0-2	Kyiv	Fr		18 000	Nikolaev RUS
1-06	Uzbekistan	W	2-0	Kyiv	Fr	Tymoshchuk [54], Voronin [60]		Ozkahya TUR
6-06	France	L	1-4	Donetsk	Fr	Tymoshchuk [53]	11 200	Clattenburg ENG
10-08	Sweden	L	0-1	Kharkov	Fr			Tagliavento ITA
2-09	Uruguay	L	2-3	Kharkov	Fr	Yarmolenko [1], Konoplyanka [44]	30 000	Kuipers NED
6-09	Czech Republic	L	0-4	Prague	Fr		7 322	Trutz SVK
7-10	Bulgaria	W	3-0	Kyiv	Fr	Selin [15], Shevchenko [40], Yarmolenko [82]		Kralovec CZE
11-10	Estonia	W	2-0	Tallinn	Fr	Gusev [45], Aliev [68]	4 501	Malek POL
11-11	Germany	D	3-3	Kyiv	Fr	Yarmolenko [28], Konoplyanka [37], Nazarenko [45]	69 720	Velasco ESP
15-11	Austria	W	2-1	Lviv	Fr	Milevskiy [18], Devic [90]	31 879	Moen NOR

Fr = Friendly match • WC = FIFA World Cup • q = qualifier

UKRAINE NATIONAL TEAM HISTORICAL RECORDS

Caps
101 - Anatoliy Tymoschuk 2000- • **100** - Andriy Shevchenko 1995- • **86** - Olexandr Shovkovskiy 1994-2009 • **75** - Serhiy Rebrov 1992-2006 • **71** - Andriy Gusin 1993-2006 • **68** - Andriy Vorobei 2000-08 • **67** - Andriy Nesmachnyi 2000- • **64** - Andriy Voronin 2002- • **63** - Vladyslav Vashchuk 1996-2007 • **61** - Oleh Gusev 2003- • **58** - Olexandr Holovko 1995-2004 • **54** - Serhiy Popov 1993-2003

Goals
45 - Andriy Shevchenko 1995- • **15** - Serhiy Rebrov 1992-2006 • **11** - Serhiy Nazarenko 2003- • **9** - Andriy Vorobei 2000-08 & Andriy Gusin 1993-2006 • **8** - Tymerlan Guseynov 1993-97 • **7** - Maksym Kalynychenko 2002- & Oleh Gusev 2003-

Past Coaches
Viktor Prokopenko 1992 • Nikolay Pavlov 1992 • Oleh Bazilevich 1993-94 • Nikolay Pavlov 1994 • Jozsef Szabo 1994 • Anatoliy Konkov 1995 • Jozsef Szabo 1996-99 • Valery Lobanovsky 2000-01 • Leonid Buryak 2002-03 • Oleh Blokhin 2003-07 • Olexiy Mykhailychenko 2008-09 • Myron Markevych 2010 • Yuriy Kalitvintsev 2010-

UKRAINE 2010–11

VYSCHA LIHA

	Pl	W	D	L	F	A	Pts	Shakhtar	Dynamo Kyiv	Metalist	Dnipro	Karpaty	Vorskla	Tavriya	Metalurh D	Arsenal	Obolon	Volyn	Zorja	Kryvbas	Illychivets	Sevastopol	Metalurh Z
Shakhtar Donetsk †	30	23	3	4	53	16	72		2-0	2-1	0-0	1-0	1-0	4-1	2-0	4-0	0-1	4-0	1-0	2-0	1-0	5-0	2-1
Dynamo Kyiv †	30	20	5	5	60	24	65	3-0		1-1	0-0	1-0	2-0	2-1	1-0	3-2	0-2	5-1	2-0	3-0	9-0	2-0	2-0
Metalist Kharkiv ‡	30	18	6	6	58	26	60	1-2	1-2		2-2	1-1	2-3	2-3	3-1	2-1	2-1	3-1	3-0	3-4	3-0	4-0	3-0
Dnipro Dnipropetrovsk‡	30	16	9	5	45	19	57	0-1	1-0	0-1		1-0	2-0	2-2	1-2	1-0	3-0	2-0	1-1	1-1	2-0	2-2	3-0
Karpaty Lviv ‡	30	13	9	8	41	34	48	1-0	1-2	0-1	0-0		2-2	1-0	2-1	2-1	3-0	1-0	4-2	2-1	3-1	2-1	1-0
Vorskla Poltava ‡	30	10	9	11	37	32	39	1-1	3-1	0-0	0-2	1-1		0-0	1-1	0-1	0-1	0-1	1-0	3-0	1-3	4-0	2-1
Tavriya Simferopol	30	10	9	11	44	46	39	1-2	1-1	0-1	0-1	3-1	2-2		2-1	0-1	3-1	0-0	0-0	2-1	2-2	2-1	2-0
Metalurh Donetsk	30	11	5	14	36	45	38	0-2	0-2	0-3	3-2	4-1	2-0	2-1		1-5	3-0	0-2	1-1	2-2	0-3	1-0	0-1
Arsenal Kyiv	30	10	7	13	36	38	37	1-3	0-3	0-1	1-2	2-2	0-1	3-1	3-1		1-0	1-1	1-1	1-0	3-1	0-1	1-0
Obolon Kyiv	30	9	7	14	26	38	34	1-0	2-2	0-2	0-1	1-1	0-1	2-1	1-1	1-1		0-1	1-0	1-1	2-0	2-2	1-0
Volyn Lutsk	30	9	7	14	27	49	34	0-1	1-2	1-4	1-1	0-3	0-4	2-2	1-3	0-0	1-0		0-1	0-3	1-1	1-0	1-0
Zorja Luhansk	30	7	9	14	28	40	30	1-3	1-2	0-2	1-1	2-2	1-1	5-3	0-2	0-2	1-0	3-0		1-0	2-2	0-0	0-2
Kryvbas Kryvyi Rih	30	6	11	13	27	45	29	0-2	0-1	0-0	0-3	0-0	1-0	1-4	1-0	1-1	2-2	2-4	0-2		1-0	3-1	0-0
Illychivets Mariupil	30	7	8	15	45	67	29	1-3	3-2	1-4	1-5	2-3	2-6	5-1	1-1	2-2	1-0	2-2	2-2	1-1		4-2	0-0
FC Sevastopol	30	7	6	17	26	48	27	0-1	0-3	0-0	2-1	3-1	0-0	0-1	0-1	0-2	3-1	4-1	0-1	2-2	1-1		1-0
Metalurh Zaporizhya	30	6	6	18	18	40	24	1-1	1-1	0-2	0-3	0-0	2-1	1-2	0-1	1-0	1-0	1-2	0-4	1-0		1-0	

9/07/2010 - 21/05/2011 • † Qualified for the UEFA Champions League • ‡ Qualified for the Europa League
Top scorers: **17** - Yevhen Seleznev, Dnipro • **14** - Marko Devic, Metalist • **13** - Lucky Idahor NGA, Tavriya • **12** - Denys Oliynyk, Metalist

MEDALS TABLE

	Overall			League			Cup		Europe		
	G	S	B	G	S	B	G	S	G	S	B
1 Dynamo Kyiv	22	10	2	13	7		9	3			2
2 Shakhtar Donetsk	14	14		6	10		7	4	1		
3 Chernomorets Odessa	2	2	3		2	3	2				
4 Tavriya Simferopol	2	1		1			1	1			
5 Vorskla Poltava	1						1				
6 Dnipro Dnipropetrovsk	4	4		1	4						3
7 Karpaty Lviv	2	1		1			2				
8 CSCA Kyiv	2						2				
9 Metallist Kharkiv	1	5			5		1				
10 Metalurh Donetsk	1	3			3						

Ukrainian Clubs in the Soviet era

	Overall			League			Cup		Europe		
	G	S	B	G	S	B	G	S	G	S	B
1 Dynamo Kyiv	24	13	5	13	11	3	9	2	2		2
7 Shakhtar	4	6	2		2	2	4	4			
9 Dnipro	3	2	2	2	2	2	1				
13 Zorya	1	2		1				2			
15 Metallist	1	1					1	1			
16 Karpaty	1						1				
21 Chernomorets			1			1					

UKRAINE 2010–11

PERSHA LIHA (2)

	Pl	W	D	L	F	A	Pts	Oleksandrija	Chernomorets	Stal	Krymteplytsja	Lviv	Zakarpattya	Bukovyna	Dynamo-2	Arsenal	Nyva	Tytan	Zirka	Dnister	Naftovyk	Helios	Enerhetyk	Prykarpattija	Feniks
FK Oleksandrija	34	21	6	7	55	25	69		2-1	0-1	1-0	1-0	1-0	1-0	3-0	2-0	2-1	3-0	2-1	2-1	1-1	3-0	2-0	3-0	2-1
Chernomorets Odessa	34	18	11	5	53	26	65	0-2		1-1	4-0	1-1	1-1	3-0	3-1	1-0	0-0	4-0	0-1	1-1	2-1	3-0	4-0	2-1	*
Stal Alchevsk	34	18	8	8	55	31	62	1-0	1-1		1-0	0-0	3-2	4-2	2-2	3-0	1-0	0-0	2-1	1-1	0-1	4-0	3-1	5-0	3-0
Krymteplytsja	34	18	7	9	43	30	61	1-0	1-1	1-2		0-1	0-0	3-1	2-1	4-1	1-1	2-0	3-1	1-1	2-1	1-0	5-1		*
FK Lviv	34	17	8	9	52	28	59	0-3	0-1	0-2	2-1		0-0	2-0	3-0	1-0	4-1	2-0	0-0	1-1	3-0	0-0	2-1	4-2	6-1
Zakarpattya Uzhgorod	34	16	8	10	51	40	56	2-1	0-1	3-2	0-2	2-3		2-2	1-1	2-2	3-0	2-0	0-0	1-0	4-1	2-0	1-1	4-2	3-0
Bukovyna Chernivtsi	34	17	5	12	48	45	56	3-1	3-0	3-1	1-2	0-2	0-0		1-0	2-1	1-0	2-1	1-2	2-2	2-1	0-2	2-1	2-1	*
Dynamo Kyiv-2	34	15	7	12	39	35	52	1-1	2-0	2-1	0-1	1-0	0-1	0-1		0-1	3-1	3-2	0-1	1-0	3-1	1-0	1-1	1-0	1-1
Arsenal Bila Tserkva	34	15	6	13	42	43	51	1-1	2-2	0-0	0-0	1-0	1-3	1-0	0-2		2-1	1-2	2-0	0-0	1-3	2-1	3-2	3-0	*
Nyva Vinnytsia	34	14	8	12	44	42	50	2-2	1-3	2-1	1-0	1-0	2-1	1-1	2-2	3-1		4-0	0-0	3-2	2-2	0-3	2-0	3-0	*
Tytan Armyansk	34	13	5	16	32	42	44	1-0	0-1	2-1	0-0	2-0	0-2	1-0	3-0	2-1	1-2		0-0	0-3	0-1	2-1	0-1	2-0	3-0
Zirka Kirovohrad	34	12	7	15	43	44	43	1-1	0-1	0-1	3-0	3-0	4-0	3-3	1-0	1-0	2-1	1-3		3-1	3-0	1-3	0-0	3-2	0-2
Dnister Ovidiopol	34	10	12	12	39	42	42	1-4	1-2	2-0	0-0	1-3	4-2	2-1	0-1	0-2	1-0	0-0	4-1		1-2	1-0	2-0	2-1	*
Naftovyk-Ukrnafta	34	10	11	13	40	44	41	1-0	0-0	2-0	2-0	0-0	1-1	2-3	2-2	2-3	2-2	4-0	2-0	0-0		1-1	2-3	3-0	1-0
Helios Kharkiv	34	10	10	14	31	44	40	2-2	0-0	0-2	0-0	1-3	1-0	2-1	0-0	0-2	0-0	2-2	2-2	0-0	0-1		0-1	1-0	*
Enerhetyk Burshtyn	34	10	6	18	29	49	36	1-3	1-1	2-0	1-2	0-0	2-1	1-4	2-1	1-0	1-0	0-2	2-0	0-0	1-1	1-1		0-3	1-2
Prykarpattija I-Frank'sk	34	5	1	28	27	82	16	0-3	1-5	0-3	1-2	1-6	1-3	0-1	0-2	1-3	2-2	2-0	2-0	0-2	0-3	*	1-2		
Feniks-Illichovets	34	3	2	29	17	48	8	*	1-3	0-1	2-3	0-3	*	0-1	*	2-4	1-3	*	1-6	1-1	*	1-2	*	*	

17/07/2010 - 11/06/2011 • *Feniks withdrew. Their remaining matches awarded as goalless defeats • Top scorer: **20** - Ruslan Gunchak, Bukovyna

KUBOK UKRAINY 2010-11

First Round		Second Round		Quarter-finals		Semi-finals		Final	
Shakhtar Donetsk *	6								
Kryvbas Kryvyi Rih	0	**Shakhtar Donetsk**	2						
Obolon Kyiv	1	FC Poltava *	0	**Shakhtar Donetsk** *	1				
FC Poltava *	2			Metalurh Zaporizhya	0				
Feniks-Illichovets	1 6p	Feniks-Illichovets *	1			**Shakhtar Donetsk** *	2		
Stal Dniprodxerzhynsk *	1 5p	Metalurh Zaporizhya	2			Dnipro Dnipropetrovsk	1		
Illychivets Mariupil	0								
Metalurh Zaporizhya *	1								
Zorja Luhansk	1	**Zorja Luhansk**	1	Zorja Luhansk *	1 4p				
Prykarpattija I-Frank'sk *	0	Naftovyk-Ukrnafta *	0	**Dnipro Dnipropetrovsk**	1 5p				
Yednist Plysky *	1							**Shakhtar Donetsk**	2
Naftovyk-Ukrnafta	0							Dynamo Kyiv	0
Kremin Kremenchuk *	1	Kremin Kremenchuk *	0						
Shakhtar Sverdlovsk	0	**Dnipro Dnipropetrovsk**	3						
Tavriya Simferopol	1								
Dnipro Dnipropetrovsk *	4								
Arsenal Kyiv	2	**Arsenal Kyiv**	2						
Metalist Kharkiv *	1	FK Oleksandrija *	1	**Arsenal Kyiv**	2				
Metalurh Donetsk	0 3p			Karpaty Lviv *	0				
FK Oleksandrija *	0 5p					Arsenal Kyiv	0		
Vorskla Poltava	2	Vorskla Poltava	0			**Dynamo Kyiv** *	2		
Chernomorets Odessa *	1	**Karpaty Lviv** *	3						
Hirnyk-Sp. Komsomolsk *	0								
Karpaty Lviv	5								
Stal Alchevsk *	3	**Stal Alchevsk** *	1	Stal Alchevsk *	2				
Arsenal Bila Tserkva	1	Volyn Lutsk	0	**Dynamo Kyiv**	3				
Karpaty Yaremche *	4								
Volyn Lutsk	5								
FC Sevastopol	3	FC Sevastopol *	1						
Tytan Armyansk *	1	**Dynamo Kyiv**	2						
Krymteplytsia Molodizhne *	0								
Dynamo Kyiv	1								

CUP FINAL

Yuvileyniy, Sumy
25-05-2011, Att: 27 800, Ref: Victor Shvetsov
Scorers - Eduardo [64], Luiz Adriano [87]
Shakhtar - Andriy Pyatov - Dario Srna(c)•, Tomas Hubschman, Oleksandr Kucher, Yaroslav Rakitskiy - Fernandinho•, Jadson (Henrikh Mkhitaryan 81), Adriano (Douglas Costa 95+), Vyacheslav Shevchuk - Eduardo•◆77, Willian (Alex Teixeira 77). Tr: Mircea Lucescu
Dynamo - Oleksandr Shovkovskiy(c) - Danilo Silva (Betao 58••◆86), Ognjen Vukojevic, Ayila Yussuf•, Goran Popov• - Oleh Husyev, Artem Milevskiy•, Roman Eremenko (Oleksandr Aliyev 70), Yevhen Khacheridi - Andriy Shevchenko, Andriy Yarmolenko. Tr: Yuriy Semin

* Home team • ‡ Qualified for the Europa League

URU – URUGUAY

FIFA/COCA-COLA WORLD RANKING

'93	'94	'95	'96	'97	'98	'99	'00	'01	'02	'03	'04	'05	'06	'07	'08	'09	'10	'11	'12
17	37	32	43	40	76	46	32	22	28	21	16	18	29	28	23	20	7	4	

	2011														
	Jan	Feb	Mar	Apr	May	Jun	Jul	Aug	Sep	Oct	Nov	Dec	High	Low	Av
	7	7	7	7	7	18	5	5	4	4	4	4	4	76	27

2010 had been a fantastic year for Uruguayan football with the national team's epic run to the semi-finals of the World Cup in South Africa, but in many ways 2011 topped even that with their sensational triumph at the 2011 Copa America in Argentina. The 3-0 win over Paraguay in the final in Buenos Aires - thanks to goals from star forwards Luis Suarez and Diego Forlan - meant that Uruguay overtook Argentina as the most successful team in the history of the competition with 15 titles a victory made even sweeter by the fact that they had knocked-out the hosts in the quarter-final. There are also signs that club football is receiving a much-needed boost in the wake of the success of the national team, most notably Peñarol's run to the final of the 2011 Copa Libertadores where they met Santos. The tie was a repeat of the 1962 final and once again Santos ran out winners to deny Peñarol a first continental title since 1987 but it did mark Uruguay's first appearance in the final for 23 years. At home the 2011 title went to Peñarol's great rivals Nacional who beat Defensor 1-0 to clinch the championship - their 43rd overall, just five shy of Peñarol's record haul of 48.

COPA AMERICA RECORD

1916 1/4 Winners **1917** 1/4 Winners 1919 2/4 **1920** 1/4 Winners 1921 3/4 1922 3/5 **1923** 1/4 Winners **1924** 1/4 Winners
1925 DNE **1926** 1/4 Winners 1927 2/4 1929 3/4 **1935** 1/4 Winners 1937 4/6 1939 2/5 1941 2/5 **1942** 1/7 Winners 1945 4/7
1946 4/6 1947 3/8 1949 6/8 1953 3/7 1955 4/6 **1956** 1/6 Winners 1957 3/7 1959 6/7 **1959** 1/5 Winners 1963 DNE **1967** 1/6 Winners
1975 4/10 SF 1979 6/10 r1 **1983** 1/10 Winners **1987** 1/10 Winners 1989 2/10 r2 1991 5/10 r1 1993 7/12 QF **1995** 1/12 Winners
1997 9/12 r1 1999 2/12 F **2001** 4/12 SF **2004** 3/12 SF **2007** 4/12 SF **2011** 1/12 Winners

ASOCIACION URUGUAYA DE FUTBOL (AUF)

Guayabo 1531,
Montevideo 11200

☎ +59 82 4004814
📠 +59 82 4090550
✉ presidencia@auf.org.uy
🖥 www.auf.org.uy
FA 1900 CON 1916 FIFA 1923
P Sebastian Bauza
GS Fernando Caceres

FIFA BIG COUNT 2006

Total players	241 300
% of population	7.03%
Male	214 000
Female	27 300
Amateurs 18+	30 000
Youth under 18	8 000
Unregistered	94 500
Professionals	1 100
Referees	400
Admin & coaches	2 200
Number of clubs	1 210
Number of teams	2 200

MAJOR CITIES/TOWNS

		Population
1	Montevideo	1 328 600
2	Salto	106 286
3	Ciudad de la Costa	101 047
4	Paysandú	77 767
5	Las Piedras	77 484
6	Rivera	69 744
7	Maldonado	63 061
8	Tacuarembó	54 263
9	Melo	53 852
10	Mercedes	44 307
11	Artigas	44 275
12	Minas	39 200
13	San José	39 100
14	Durazno	35 432
15	Florida	33 522
16	San Carlos	28 608
17	Treinta y Tres	27 017
18	Pando	26 869
19	Rocha	26 820

REPUBLICA ORIENTAL DEL URUGUAY • ORIENTAL REPUBLIC OF URUGUAY

Capital	Montevideo	Population	3 494 382 (131)	% in cities	92%
GDP per capita	$12 400 (89)	Area km²	176 215 km² (90)	GMT +/-	-3
Neighbours (km)	Argentina 580, Brazil 1068 • Coast 660				

RECENT INTERNATIONAL MATCHES PLAYED BY URUGUAY

2009	Opponents	Score	Venue	Comp	Scorers	Att	Referee
11-02	Libya	W 3-2	Tripoli	Fr	Eguren [14], Martinez [71], Barragan [75]	50 000	Al Jilali LBY
28-03	Paraguay	W 2-0	Montevideo	WCq	Forlan [28], Lugano [57]	45 000	Simon BRA
1-04	Chile	D 0-0	Santiago	WCq		55 000	Baldassi ARG
6-06	Brazil	L 0-4	Montevideo	WCq		52 000	Laverni ARG
10-06	Venezuela	D 2-2	Puerto Ordaz	WCq	Suarez [60], Forlan [72]	37 000	Fagundes BRA
12-08	Algeria	L 0-1	Algiers	Fr		20 000	Harzi TUN
5-09	Peru	L 0-1	Lima	WCq		15 000	Chandia CHI
9-09	Colombia	W 3-1	Montevideo	WCq	Suarez [7], Scotti [77], Eguren [87]	30 000	Torres PAR
10-10	Ecuador	W 2-1	Quito	WCq	Suarez [69], Forlan [93+p]	42 700	Fagundes BRA
14-10	Argentina	L 0-1	Montevideo	WCq		50 000	Amarilla PAR
14-11	Costa Rica	W 1-0	San Jose	WCpo	Lugano [21]	19 500	Undiano ESP
18-11	Costa Rica	D 1-1	Montevideo	WCpo	Abreu [70]	55 000	Busacca SUI
2010							
3-03	Switzerland	W 3-1	St Gall	Fr	Forlan [35], Suarez [50], Cavani [87]	12 500	Rizzoli ITA
26-05	Israel	W 4-1	Montevideo	Fr	Forlan [15], Pereira [37], Abreu 2 [75 81]	60 000	Osses CHI
11-06	France	D 0-0	Cape Town	WCr1		64 100	Nishimura JPN
16-06	South Africa	W 3-0	Pretoria	WCr1	Forlan 2 [24 80p], Alvaro Pereira [95+]	42 658	Busacca SUI
22-06	Mexico	W 1-0	Rustenburg	WCr1	Suarez [43]	33 425	Kassai HUN
26-06	Korea Republic	W 2-1	Port Elizabeth	WCr2	Suarez 2 [8 80]	30 597	Stark GER
2-07	Ghana	D 1-1	Johannesburg	WCqf	Forlan [55]. W 4-2p	84 017	Benquerenca POR
6-07	Netherlands	L 2-3	Cape Town	WCsf	Forlan [41], Maximiliano Pereira [92+]	62 479	Irmatov UZB
10-07	Germany	L 2-3	Port Elizabeth	WC3p	Cavani [28], Forlan [51]	36 254	Archundia MEX
11-08	Angola	W 2-0	Lisbon	Fr	Cavani [84], Hernandez [90]	1 500	Miguel POR
8-10	Indonesia	W 7-1	Jakarta	Fr	Cavani 3 [35 80 83], Suarez 3 [43 54 69p], Eguren [58]	25 000	Daud SIN
12-10	China PR	W 4-0	Wuhan	Fr	OG [70], Cavani [78], Rodriguez [81], Fernandez [84]	50 000	Lee Dong Jun KOR
17-11	Chile	L 0-2	Santiago	Fr		45 000	Torres PAR
2011							
25-03	Estonia	L 0-2	Tallinn	Fr		6 817	Munukka FIN
29-03	Republic of Ireland	W 3-2	Dublin	Fr	Lugano [12], Cavani [22], Hernandez [40]	20 200	Ennjimi FRA
29-05	Germany	L 1-2	Sinsheim	Fr	Gargano [48]	25 655	Benquerenca POR
8-06	Netherlands	D 1-1	Montevideo	Fr	Suarez [82]. W 4-3p	55 000	Pitana ARG
23-06	Estonia	W 3-0	Rivera	Fr	Caceres [12], OG [55], Lodeiro [72]	25 000	Laverni ARG
4-07	Peru	D 1-1	Mendoza	CAr1	Suarez [45]	25 000	Roldan COL
8-07	Chile	D 1-1	Mendoza	CAr1	Alvaro Pereira [53]	45 000	Amarilla PAR
12-07	Mexico	W 1-0	La Plata	CAr1	Alvaro Pereira [14]	36 000	Orozco BOL
16-07	Argentina	D 1-1	Santa Fe	CAqf	Perez [6]. W 5-4p	47 000	Amarilla PAR
19-07	Peru	W 2-0	La Plata	CAsf	Suarez 2 [52 57]	25 000	Orozco BRA
24-07	Paraguay	W 3-0	Buenos Aires	CAf	Suarez [11], Forlan 2 [41 89]	57 921	Fagundes BRA
2-09	Ukraine	W 3-2	Kharkov	Fr	Gonzalez [43], Lugano [61], Hernandez [87]	30 000	Kuipers NED
7-10	Bolivia	W 4-2	Montevideo	WCq	Suarez [3], Lugano 2 [25 71], Cavani [34]	25 500	Carrillo PER
11-10	Paraguay	D 1-1	Asuncion	WCq	Forlan [68]	12 922	Seneme BRA
11-11	Chile	W 4-0	Montevideo	WCq	Suarez 4 [42 45 67 73]	40 500	Baldassi ARG
15-11	Italy	W 1-0	Rome	Fr	Fernandez [3]	42 000	Duarte POR

Fr = Friendly match • CA = Copa America • WC = FIFA World Cup
q = qualifier • po = play-off • r1 = first round group • qf = quarter-final • sf = semi-final • 3p = third place play-off

URUGUAY NATIONAL TEAM HISTORICAL RECORDS

Caps
84 - Diego Forlan 2002- • **79** - Rodolfo Rodriguez 1976-86 • **74** - Fabian Carini 1999-2009 & Diego Perez 2001- • **72** - Enzo Francescoli 1982-97 • **09** - Alvaro Recoba 1995 2007 • **68** - Angel Romano 1911-27; Pablo Garcia 1997-2008 & Diego Lugano 2003- • **67** - Sebastian Abreu 1996- • **65** - Carlos Aguilera 1982-97 • **61** - Jorge Barrios 1980-92 & Paolo Montero 1991-2005

Goals
32 - Diego Forlan 2002- • **31** - Hector Scarone 1917-30 • **28** - Angel Romano 1911-27 • **27** - Oscar Miguez 1950-58 • **26** - Luis Suarez 2007- & Sebastian Abreu 1996- • **24** - Pedro Petrone 1924-30 • **23** - Carlos Aguilera 1983-97 • **22** - Fernando Morena 1971-83 • **20** - Jose Piendibene 1909-23 • **19** - Severino Varela 1935-42 • **18** - Hector Castro 1926-35 & Carlos Scarone 1909-21

Past Coaches
Coaches prior to 1969 are listed in Oliver's Almanack of World Football 2011 • Juan Hohberg 1969-70 • Hugo Bagnulo 1970-73 • Roberto Porta 1974-74 • Juan Alberto Schiaffino 1974-75 • Jose Maria Rodriguez 1975-77 • Juan Hohberg 1977 • Raul Bentancor 1977-79 • Roque Maspoli 1979-82 • Omar Borras 1982-87 • Roberto Fleitas 1987-88 • Oscar Tabarez 1988-90 • Luis Cubilla 1990-93 • Ildo Maneiro 1993-94 • Hector Nunez 1994-96 • Juan Ahuntchain 1996-97 • Roque Maspoli 1997-98 • Victor Pua 1998-2000 • Daniel Passarella 2000-01 • Victor Pua 2001-03 • Juan Ramon Carrasco 2003-04 • Jorge Fossati 2004-06 • Juan Ferrin 2006 • Oscar Tabarez 2006-

URUGUAY 2010–11

PRIMERA DIVISION PROFESSIONAL TABLA ANUAL

	Pl	W	D	L	F	A	Pts	Rel	Nacional	Defensor	Peñarol	Fénix	Bella Vista	Cerro	Wanderers	Danubio	El Tanque	Central	Liverpool	Racing	River Plate	Rampla Jun	Tacuarembó	Miramar
Nacional † ‡	30	19	6	5	60	31	63	126		3-0	0-0	0-3	1-0	3-0	1-1	2-1	5-2	3-1	0-0	3-0	6-1	0-2	3-0	3-1
Defensor †	30	17	7	6	50	25	58	104	1-2		1-1	5-1	1-2	2-0	1-2	1-1	3-1	1-1	3-0	3-0	4-1	4-1	1-0	2-0
Peñarol †	30	15	7	8	52	37	52	121	0-1	0-1		1-1	2-1	2-1	2-1	1-0	0-0	2-2	1-2	0-1	1-4	1-1	5-0	3-1
Fénix ‡	30	11	12	7	44	35	45	80	2-1	0-1	2-2		2-2	4-0	2-2	1-0	0-1	0-1	0-0	1-1	4-1	3-0	1-1	2-1
Bella Vista ‡	30	12	8	10	40	36	44	88	0-1	1-1	1-2	0-0		0-1	0-1	4-1	1-2	1-1	2-4	1-0	1-0	3-2	3-2	3-2
Cerro	30	10	12	8	34	39	42	82	4-1	2-1	0-2	1-1	2-4		1-1	0-0	2-1	1-5	2-1	1-1	0-0	1-1	2-2	1-1
Wanderers	30	10	11	9	44	33	41	82	1-1	0-1	1-2	2-2	0-2	0-0		1-1	5-1	2-2	1-0	0-1	1-2	2-0	2-0	1-1
Danubio	30	11	8	11	41	40	41	80	0-1	1-1	0-1	1-0	2-0	1-0	0-0		2-0	4-2	3-2	2-0	1-2	3-3	3-1	5-2
El Tanque Sisley	30	12	5	13	40	48	41	82	1-1	0-1	2-4	0-1	0-0	0-2	1-1	3-2		1-0	1-1	1-0	2-1	3-2	0-1	4-1
Central Español	30	10	10	10	47	42	40	74	1-3	2-0	2-3	1-1	0-1	0-0	2-1	1-0	3-5		1-2	1-1	2-0	5-1	0-0	0-1
Liverpool	30	10	10	10	40	39	40	91	0-2	1-2	2-4	2-1	1-1	0-2	0-2	1-1	1-0	2-2		1-0	1-1	3-1	3-0	0-0
Racing CM	30	10	8	12	40	43	38	77	2-2	0-3	2-1	2-4	1-2	1-2	0-2	6-0	2-1	1-1	1-1		2-0	3-2	3-2	1-2
River Plate	30	10	5	15	45	57	35	81	4-2	1-1	2-1	1-2	2-2	3-4	4-2	3-1	1-2	1-3	1-2	1-4		1-2	2-0	2-1
Rampla Juniors	30	7	10	13	38	52	31	77	2-1	1-1	0-1	1-0	1-0	1-4	0-0	4-2	2-2	1-1	1-1	0-0	1-1		1-0	2-0
Tacuarembó	30	7	3	20	27	58	24	58	0-3	1-3	1-5	3-0	1-2	0-1	2-1	0-3	1-2	2-1	3-2	0-2	2-1	1-0		1-1
Miramar Misiones	30	4	8	18	26	53	20	40	2-4	0-1	3-0	0-1	0-0	1-1	0-4	1-2	0-1	0-1	0-4	1-1	1-1	1-2	1-0	

21/08/2010 – 5/06/2011 • † Qualified for the Copa Libertadores • ‡ Qualified for the Copa Sudamericana

Apertura matches are in the shaded boxes • Relegation calculated over two seasons (promoted clubs have season total doubled)

Championship play-offs: Nacional qualified for the final as the overall leading points scorer. The winners of the Apertura (Defensor) and Clausura (Nacional) played off for the right to meet Nacional in the final • Nacional 1-0 Defensor. Nacional won the championship as they had already qualified for the final (details below).

Top scorers: **23** - Santiago Garcia, Nacional • **16** - Cristian Palacios, Peñarol/Central • **12** - Maximiliano Perez ARG, Fénix • **11** - Diego Alonso, Peñarol & Rodrigo Mora, Defensor • **9** - Jean Pierre Barrientos, Racing; Diego Perrone, Danubio; Ignacio Risso, Defensor & Federico Rodriguez, Bella Vista

URUGUAY 2010–11 TORNEO APERTURA

	Pl	W	D	L	F	A	Pts
Defensor †	15	9	3	3	31	13	30
Nacional	15	8	5	2	28	18	29
Bella Vista	15	9	2	4	24	18	29
El Tanque Sisley	15	8	4	3	21	18	28
Danubio	15	7	5	3	24	14	26
Peñarol	15	7	4	4	24	17	25
Wanderers	15	5	6	4	20	16	21
Liverpool	15	5	6	4	18	19	21
Cerro	15	4	7	4	15	17	19
Fénix	15	4	6	5	21	20	18
River Plate	15	5	3	7	16	23	18
Central Español	15	4	5	6	21	25	17
Racing CM	15	3	5	7	14	20	14
Rampla Juniors	15	2	6	7	19	27	12
Miramar Misiones	15	2	5	8	14	23	11
Tacuarembó	15	1	2	12	10	32	5

21/08/2010 – 5/12/2010 • † Qualified for play-off

URUGUAY 2010–11 TORNEO CLAUSURA

	Pl	W	D	L	F	A	Pts
Nacional †	15	11	1	3	32	13	34
Defensor	15	8	4	3	19	12	28
Peñarol	15	8	3	4	28	20	27
Fénix	15	7	6	2	23	15	27
Racing CM	15	7	3	5	26	22	24
Central Español	15	6	5	4	26	17	23
Cerro	15	6	4	5	19	22	22
Wanderers	15	5	5	5	24	17	20
Liverpool	15	5	4	6	22	20	19
Rampla Juniors	15	5	4	6	18	25	19
Tacuarembó	15	6	1	8	17	26	19
River Plate	15	5	2	8	29	34	17
Bella Vista	15	3	6	6	16	18	15
Danubio	15	4	3	8	17	26	15
El Tanque Sisley	15	4	1	10	19	30	13
Miramar Misiones	15	2	3	10	12	30	9

5/02/2011 – 5/06/2011 • † Qualified for play-off

CHAMPIONSHIP FINAL 2011

Centenario, Montevideo,
12-06-2011, 16:00, Att: 50 000, Ref: Dario Ubriaco

Nacional 1 Viudez 19
Defensor 0

Nacional - Rodrigo Munoz - Gabriel Marques•, Alejandro Lembo (c), Sebastian Coates, Alexis Rolin - Facundo Piriz• - Tabare Viudez (Nicolas Vigneri 83), Matias Cabrera, Mauricio Pereyra, Richard Porta (Marcelo Gallardo 66) - Santiago Garcia (Nicolas Lopez 46). Tr: Juan Ramon Carrasco

Defensor - Martin Silva (c) - Damian Suarez, Mario Risso, Nestor Moiraghi•, Adrian Argacha - Eduardo Aranda, Diego Rodriguez•, Sebastian Suarez (Adrian Luna 58◆89), Brahian Aleman (Ignacio Lores 64) - Ignacio Risso (Mauro Vila 69), David Teixeira. Tr: Pablo Repetto

URUGUAY 2010-11 SEGUNDA DIVISION PROFESIONAL (2)

	Pl	W	D	L	F	A	Pts
Rentistas	22	12	6	4	36	18	42
Cerrito	22	11	8	3	39	20	41
Atenas †	22	12	3	7	39	27	39
Boston River †	22	10	7	5	37	25	37
Maldonado †	22	9	10	3	24	17	37
Cerro Largo †	22	8	9	5	30	24	33
Rocha	22	8	6	8	26	32	30
Sud América	22	6	7	9	26	35	25
Huracán	22	5	6	11	25	32	21
Durazno	22	5	5	12	21	47	20
Plaza Colonia	22	6	1	15	28	35	19
Juventud Las Piedras	22	3	6	13	18	37	15

9/10/2010 - 16/04/2011 • † Qualified for play-off

PROMOTION PLAY-OFF

Semi-finals

Cerro Largo	1	1
Atenas	0	0

Maldonado	0	0
Boston River	1	0

Finals

Cerro Largo	2	2	5p
Boston River	2	2	4p

Cerro Largo Promoted

MEDALS TABLE

		Overall			League			Sth Am		
		G	S	B	G	S	B	G	S	B
1	Peñarol	53	47	18	48	40	5	5	7	13
2	Nacional	46	45	22	43	41	12	3	4	10
3	Montevideo Wanderers	4	6	14	4	6	14			
4	Defensor Sporting	4	7	8	4	7	8			
5	River Plate	4	1	1	4	1	1			
6	Danubio	3	4	5	3	4	4			1
7	Rampla Juniors	1	5	14	1	5	14			
8	Bella Vista	1	1	2	1	1	2			
9	Central Español	1		4	1		4			
10	Progreso	1			1					
11	Cerro		1	6		1	6			
12	Universal		1	4		1	4			
13	CA River Plate		1	2		1	2			
14	Albion		1	1		1	1			
15	Rocha		1			1				
16	CA Fénix			3			3			
	Liverpool			3			3			
18	Deutscher			2			2			
	Lito			2			2			
20	Dublin			1			1			
	Huracán			1			1			
	Miramar Misiones			1			1			
	Racing Club de Montevideo			1			1			
	Uruguay Montevideo			1			1			

USA – UNITED STATES OF AMERICA

FIFA/COCA-COLA WORLD RANKING

'93	'94	'95	'96	'97	'98	'99	'00	'01	'02	'03	'04	'05	'06	'07	'08	'09	'10	'11	'12
22	23	19	18	26	23	22	16	24	10	11	11	8	31	19	22	14	18	34	

2011														
Jan	Feb	Mar	Apr	May	Jun	Jul	Aug	Sep	Oct	Nov	Dec	**High**	**Low**	**Av**
18	18	19	22	22	24	30	28	31	34	34	34	4	35	18

Officials at MLS are in no doubt that soccer in America has benefitted hugely from the presence of David Beckham in the past five years, but it has taken him those five years finally to make a significant impact on the pitch after helping LA Galaxy to the 2011 title. With the irrepressible Landon Donovan, Galaxy led the standings at the end of the regular season and then beat New York, Salt Lake and Houston to clinch their first title for six years, Donovan scoring the only goal of the final against Houston. With attendances up yet again there is very real optimism in the game and there was reward for Seattle Sounders - the best supported team in the league - when they completed the first-ever hat-trick of US Open Cup wins, beating Chicago Fire 2-0 in the final. There was disappointment in the CONCACAF Champions League, however, where after becoming the first American club to reach the final for 11 years, Real Salt Lake lost to Monterrey. Having come away from Mexico with a 2-2 draw, they then lost 1-0 in Salt Lake - their first home defeat in 34 matches. The USA national team also lost out to Mexico in the final of the 2011 CONCACAF Gold Cup. It was the third successive tournament that the two had met in the final and before a huge crowd of 93,420 in the Rose Bowl, the USA let slip a 2-0 lead to lose the game 4-2.

CONCACAF GOLD CUP RECORD
1991 Winners **1993** 2 F **1996** 3 SF **1998** 2 F **2000** QF
2002 Winners **2003** 3 SF **2005** Winners **2007** Winners **2009** 2 F **2011** 2 F

US SOCCER FEDERATION (USSF)

US Soccer House,
1801 S. Prairie Avenue,
Chicago IL 60616
☎ +1 312 8081300
📠 +1 312 8081301
✉ communications@ussoccer.org
🖥 www.ussoccer.com
FA 1913 CON 1961 FIFA 1914
P Sunil Gulati
GS Dan Flynn

FIFA BIG COUNT 2006

Total players	24 472 778
% of population	8.20%
Male	17 416 859
Female	7 055 919
Amateurs 18+	260 928
Youth under 18	3 907 065
Unregistered	13 466 000
Professionals	1 513
Referees	140 000
Admin & coaches	656 300
Number of clubs	5 000
Number of teams	400 000

MAJOR CITIES/TOWNS

		Population
1	New York	8 459 053
2	Los Angeles	3 878 732
3	Chicago	2 878 957
4	Houston	2 307 889
5	Phoenix	1 635 801
6	Philadelphia	1 445 991
7	San Antonio	1 402 014
8	San Diego	1 309 752
9	Dallas	1 304 933
10	San Jose	977 894
11	Detroit	901 163
12	Jacksonville	822 422
13	San Francisco	817 244
14	Indianapolis	803 933
15	Austin	792 779
16	Columbus	768 665
17	Fort Worth	751 151
18	Charlotte	723 518
19	Memphis	662 997

UNITED STATES OF AMERICA

Capital Washington DC	Population 307 212 123 (3)	% in cities 82%
GDP per capita $47 500 (10)	Area km² 9 826 675 km² (3)	GMT + / - -5 to -11
Neighbours (km) Canada 8893, Mexico 3141 • Coast 19 924			

RECENT INTERNATIONAL MATCHES PLAYED BY THE USA

2009 Opponents	Score	Venue	Comp	Scorers	Att	Referee
12-08 Mexico	L 1-2	Mexico City	WCq	Davies [9]	104 499	Moreno PAN
5-09 El Salvador	W 2-1	Sandy	WCq	Dempsey [41], Altidore [45]	19 066	Pineda HON
9-09 Trinidad and Tobago	W 1-0	Port of Spain	WCq	Clark [61]	4 700	Aguilar SLV
10-10 Honduras	W 3-2	San Pedro Sula	WCq	Casey 2 [50 66], Donovan [71]	37 000	Moreno PAN
14-10 Costa Rica	D 2-2	Washington DC	WCq	Bradley [71], Bornstein [94+]	26 243	Archundia MEX
14-11 Slovakia	L 0-1	Bratislava	Fr		7 200	Messner AUT
18-11 Denmark	L 1-3	Aarhus	Fr	Cunningham [26]	15 172	Thomson SCO
2010						
23-01 Honduras	L 1-3	Carson	Fr	Goodson [70]	18 626	Archundia MEX
24-02 El Salvador	W 2-1	Tampa	Fr	Ching [75], Kljestan [90]	21 737	Petrescu CAN
3-03 Netherlands	L 1-2	Amsterdam	Fr	Bocanegra [88]	46 630	Cakir TUR
25-05 Czech Republic	L 2-4	East Hartford	Fr	Edu [17], Gomez [66]	36 218	Morales MEX
29-05 Turkey	W 2-1	Philadelphia	Fr	Altidore [58], Dempsey [75]	55 407	Petrescu CAN
5-06 Australia	W 3-1	Roodepoort	Fr	Buddle 2 [4 31], Gomez [90]	6 000	Ebrahim RSA
12-06 England	D 1-1	Rustenburg	WCr1	Dempsey [40]	38 646	Simon BRA
18-06 Slovenia	D 2-2	Johannesburg	WCr1	Donovan [48], Bradley [82]	45 573	Coulibaly MLI
23-06 Algeria	W 1-0	Pretoria	WCr1	Donovan [91+]	35 827	De Bleeckere BEL
26-06 Ghana	L 1-2	Rustenburg	WCr2	Donovan [62p]	34 976	Kassai HUN
10-08 Brazil	L 0-2	New Jersey	Fr		77 223	Brizan TRI
9-10 Poland	D 2-2	Chicago	Fr	Altidore [13], Onyewu [52]	31 696	Depiero CAN
12-10 Colombia	D 0-0	Chester	Fr		8 823	Garcia MEX
17-11 South Africa	W 1-0	Cape Town	Fr	Agudelo [85]	52 000	Kirwa KEN
2011						
22-01 Chile	D 1-1	Carson/LA	Fr	Bunbury [75]	18 580	Chacon MEX
26-03 Argentina	D 1-1	New Jersey	Fr	Agudelo [59]	78 936	Garcia MEX
29-03 Paraguay	L 0-1	Nashville	Fr		29 059	Benigno HON
4-06 Spain	L 0-4	Foxboro/Boston	Fr		64 121	Silvera URU
7-06 Canada	W 2-0	Detroit	GCr1	Altidore [15], Dempsey [62]	28 209	Lopez GUA
11-06 Panama	L 1-2	Tampa	GCr1	Goodson [66]	27 731	Rodriguez.M MEX
14-06 Guadeloupe	W 1-0	Kansas City	GCr1	Altidore [9]	20 109	Solis CRC
19-06 Jamaica	W 2-0	Washington DC	GCqf	Jones [49], Dempsey [79]	45 424	Rodriguez.M MEX
22-06 Panama	W 1-0	Houston	GCsf	Dempsey [77]	70 627	Wijngaarde SUR
25-06 Mexico	L 2-4	Pasadena	GCf	Bradley [8], Donovan [23]	93 420	Aguilar SLV
10-08 Mexico	D 1-1	Philadelphia	Fr	Rogers [73]	30 132	Bogle JAM
2-09 Costa Rica	L 0-1	Carson/LA	Fr		15 798	Molina HON
6-09 Belgium	L 0-1	Brussels	Fr		21 946	Collum SCO
8-10 Honduras	W 1-0	Miami	Fr	Dempsey [36]	21 170	Campbell JAM
11-10 Ecuador	L 0-1	Harrison/NY	Fr		20 707	Aguilar SLV
11-11 France	L 0-1	Paris	Fr		70 018	Koukoulakis GRE
15-11 Slovenia	W 3-2	Ljubljana	Fr	Buddle [9], Dempsey [41], Altidore [43p]	8 140	Schorgenhofer AUT

Fr = Friendly match • GC = CONCACAF Gold Cup • CC = FIFA Confederations Cup • WC = FIFA World Cup
q = qualifier • r1 = first round group • qf = quarter-final • sf = semi-final • f = final

USA NATIONAL TEAM HISTORICAL RECORDS

Caps
164 - Cobi Jones 1992-2004 • **138** - Landon Donovan 2000- • **134** - Jeff Agoos 1988-2003 • **128** - Marcelo Balboa 1988-2000 • **112** - Claudio Reyna 1994-2006 • **110** - Paul Caligiuri 1984-97 • **106** - Eric Wynalda 1990-2000 • **102** - Kasey Keller 1990-2007 • **101** - Earnie Stewart 1990 2004 • **100** - Tony Meola 1988-2006; Joe-Max Moore 1992-2002 & Carlos Bocanegra 2001- • **96** - Alexi Lalas 1990-98 & DaMarcus Beasley 2001- • **95** - Brian McBride 1993-2006 • **90** - John Harkes 1987-2000 • **87** - Frankie Hejduk 1997 2009

Goals
46 - Landon Donovan 2000- • **34** - Eric Wynalda 1990-2000 • **30** - Brian McBride 1993-2006 • **24** - Clint Dempsey 2004-10 & Joe-Max Moore 1992-2002 • **21** - Bruce Murray 1985-93 • **17** - DaMarcus Beasley 2001- & Earnie Stewart 1990-2004 • **15** - Cobi Jones 1992-2004

Past Coaches
Thomas Cahill 1916-24 • George Burford 1924-25 • Nat Agar 1925-26 • George Burford 1928 • Robert Millar 1929-33 • David Gould 1933-34 • Bill Lloyd 1934-37 • Andrew Brown 1947-48 • Walter Giesler 1948-49 • Bill Jeffrey 1949-52 • John Wood 1952-53 • Erno Schwarz 1953-55 • George Meyer 1957 • Jim Reed 1959-61 • John Herberger 1964 • George Meyer 1965 • Phil Woosnam 1968 • Gordon Jago 1969 • Bob Kehoe 1971-72 • Max Wosniak 1973 • Eugene Chyzowych 1973 • Gordon Bradley 1973 • Dettmar Cramer 1974 • Al Miller 1975 • Manny Schellscheidt 1975 • Walter Chyzowych 1976-80 • Bob Gansler 1982 • Alkis Panagoulias 1983-85 • Lothar Osiander 1986-88 • Bob Gansler 1989-91 • John Kowalski 1991 • Bora Milutinovic 1991-95 • Steve Sampson 1995-98 • Bruce Arena 1998-2006 • Bob Bradley 2006-11 • Jurgen Klinsmann 2011-

USA 2011

MAJOR LEAGUE SOCCER REGULAR SEASON

Eastern Conference

	Pl	W	D	L	F	A	Pts	Kansas	Houston	Philadelphia	Columbus	New York	Chicago	DC United	Toronto	NE Revs	LA Galaxy	Seattle	Salt Lake	Dallas	Colorado	Portland	San Jose	Chivas	Vancouver
Sporting Kansas City †	34	13	12	9	50	40	51		3-0	1-1	2-1	2-0	0-0	1-0	4-2	1-1	2-2	1-2	2-0	2-3	1-1	3-1	1-0	1-1	2-1
Houston Dynamo †	34	12	13	9	45	41	49	1-1		0-1	0-2	2-2	1-1	4-1	2-0	1-0	3-1	3-1	3-2	2-2	1-2	2-1	2-1	2-1	3-1
Philadelphia Union †	34	11	15	8	44	36	48	0-0	1-1		1-0	1-0	2-1	3-2	1-1	3-0	1-1	1-1	1-1	2-2	1-2	0-0	1-0	3-2	1-0
Columbus Crew †	34	13	8	13	43	44	47	1-0	2-2	2-1		0-0	0-1	2-1	2-4	3-1	0-1	1-1	2-1	2-0	4-1	1-0	0-0	3-3	2-1
New York Red Bulls †	34	10	16	8	50	44	46	1-0	1-1	1-0	1-1		2-2	0-1	5-0	2-1	2-0	1-0	1-3	2-2	2-2	2-0	3-0	2-3	1-1
Chicago Fire	34	9	16	9	46	45	43	3-2	1-1	1-1	3-2	1-1		1-1	2-0	3-2	1-2	0-0	0-0	1-2	2-0	0-1	2-2	3-2	0-0
DC United	34	9	12	13	49	52	39	0-1	2-2	2-2	3-1	0-4	1-2		3-3	0-1	1-1	2-1	4-1	0-0	1-1	1-1	2-4	2-2	4-0
Toronto FC	34	6	15	13	36	59	33	0-0	2-1	2-6	1-1	1-1	2-2	0-3		2-2	0-0	0-1	1-0	0-1	2-1	2-0	1-1	1-1	1-0
New England Revs	34	5	13	16	38	58	28	3-2	1-1	4-4	0-3	2-2	1-1	2-1	0-0		0-1	1-2	0-2	2-0	0-0	1-1	1-2	2-3	1-0

Western Conference

	Pl	W	D	L	F	A	Pts	Kansas	Houston	Philadelphia	Columbus	New York	Chicago	DC United	Toronto	NE Revs	LA Galaxy	Seattle	Salt Lake	Dallas	Colorado	Portland	San Jose	Chivas	Vancouver
Los Angeles Galaxy †	34	19	10	5	48	28	67	4-1	1-0	1-0	1-0	1-1	2-1	0-0	2-2	1-1		0-0	2-1	3-1	1-0	3-0	2-0	1-0	3-0
Seattle Sounders †	34	18	9	7	56	37	63	1-0	1-1	0-2	6-2	4-2	2-1	3-0	3-0	2-1	0-1		1-2	0-1	4-3	1-1	2-1	0-0	2-2
Real Salt Lake †	34	15	8	11	44	36	53	1-0	0-0	2-1	0-2	3-0	0-3	1-1	3-1	3-3	4-1	1-2		2-0	1-0	1-1	4-0	1-0	2-0
FC Dallas †	34	15	7	12	42	39	52	1-4	0-1	2-0	2-0	0-1	1-1	0-0	1-0	1-0	2-1	0-1	0-0		3-0	4-0	0-2	1-0	2-0
Colorado Rapids †	34	12	13	9	46	42	49	1-1	0-0	1-1	2-0	4-1	1-1	4-1	0-0	2-2	1-3	0-1	0-0	1-0		3-1	1-1	2-2	2-1
Portland Timbers	34	11	9	14	40	48	42	1-2	0-2	1-0	1-0	3-3	4-2	2-3	2-2	3-0	3-0	2-3	1-0	3-2	0-1		1-1	1-0	2-1
San Jose Earthquakes	34	8	14	12	40	45	38	1-1	2-0	0-0	3-0	2-2	2-0	0-2	1-1	2-1	0-0	2-2	0-1	4-2	1-2	1-1		1-2	2-2
Chivas USA	34	8	12	14	41	43	36	2-3	3-0	1-1	0-0	0-0	1-1	0-3	3-0	3-0	0-1	1-2	0-1	1-2	0-1	1-0	2-0		1-1
Vancouver Whitecaps	34	6	10	18	35	55	28	3-3	1-0	1-0	0-1	1-1	4-2	2-1	4-2	1-1	0-4	1-3	3-0	1-2	2-1	1-2	0-1	1-1	

16/03/2011 - 24/10/2011 • † Qualified for the play-offs • Top scorers: **16** - Dwayne De Rosario CAN, DC United & Chris Wondolowski, San Jose • **14** - Thierry Henry FRA, New York • **13** - Andres Mendoza PER, Columbus • **12** - Camilo BRA, Vancouver; Landon Donovan, LA Galaxy; Fredy Montero COL, Seattle & Dominic Oduro GHA, Chicago

MLS PLAY-OFFS 2011

Play-In Round		Conference Semi-finals			Conference Finals		MLS Cup Final	
		Los Angeles Galaxy	1	2				
FC Dallas *	0	New York Red Bulls *	0	1				
New York Red Bulls	2				**Los Angeles Galaxy** *	3		
					Real Salt Lake	1		
		Seattle Sounders	0	2				
		Real Salt Lake *	3	0			**Los Angeles Galaxy** *	1
							Houston Dynamo	0
		Sporting Kansas City	2	2				
Columbus Crew	0	Colorado Rapids *	0	0				
Colorado Rapids *	1				Sporting Kansas City *	0		
					Houston Dynamo	2		
		Philadelphia Union *	1	0				
		Houston Dynamo	2	1				

* Home team/home team in the 1st leg

MLS CUP 2011

Home Depot Center, Carson, Los Angeles
20-11-2011, 18:00, Att: 30 281, Ref: Ricardo Salazar

Los Angeles Galaxy	1	Donovan [72]
Houston Dynamo	0	

LA Galaxy - Josh Saunders - Sean Franklin, Omar Gonzalez, A. J. DeLaGarza, Todd Dunivant - Juninho, David Beckham● - Landon Donovan (c)●, Robbie Keane, Adam Cristman● (Chris Birchall 57), Mike Magee. Tr: Bruce Arena
Houston - Tally Hall - Andre Hainault●, Bobby Boswell●, Geoff Cameron, Jermaine Taylor - Luiz Camargo, Adam Moffat - Danny Cruz (Colin Clark 78), Brian Ching (c), Calen Carr (Carlo Costly 66), Corey Ashe (Je-Vaughn Watson 84). Tr: Dominic Kinnear

USA 2011
NASL (2)

	Pl	W	D	L	F	A	Pts
Carolina RailHawks ‡	28	17	3	8	50	26	54
Puerto Rico Islanders ‡	28	15	7	6	41	32	52
FC Tampa Bay ‡	28	11	8	9	41	36	41
Ft Lauderdale Strikers ‡	28	9	11	8	35	36	38
FC Edmonton ‡	28	10	6	12	35	40	36
NSC Minnesota Stars ‡	28	9	9	10	30	32	36
Montreal Impact	28	9	8	11	35	27	35
Atlanta Silverbacks	28	4	4	20	25	63	16

9/04/2011 - 24/09/2011 • ‡ Qualified for the play-offs
Top scorers: **20** - Etienne Barbara MLT, Carolina • **11** - Pablo Campos BRA, Carolina; Mike Ambersley, Tampa & Jonathan Fana DOM, Puerto Rico

NASL PLAY-OFFS

Quarter-finals	Semi-finals		Final	
Minnesota				
Tampa Bay	**Minnesota**	1 3		
	Carolina	0 4		
			Minnesota	3 1
			Fort Lauderdale	1 0
	Puerto Rico	1 1		
Edmonton	0	**Fort Lauderdale**	3 2	
Fort Lauderdale	5			

Final 1st leg. NSC Stadium, Minnesota, 22-10-2011, Att: 4511. Scorers - Hlavaty [3], Mulholland [53], Rodriguez [72] for Minnesota; Davis OG [53] for Fort Lauderdale
Final 2nd leg. Lockhart Stadium, Fort Lauderdale, 29-10-2011, Att: 2019

USA 2011
USL PRO (3)

American Division	Pl	W	D	L	F	A	Pts
Orlando City ‡	24	15	6	3	36	16	51
Wilmington H'heads ‡	24	14	3	7	42	30	45
Richmond Kickers ‡	24	12	5	7	35	21	41
Charleston Battery ‡	24	10	5	9	24	25	35
Charlotte Eagles	24	9	6	9	32	29	33
Antigua Barracuda	24	9	2	13	32	32	29

National Division	Pl	W	D	L	F	A	Pts
Rochester Rhinos ‡	24	12	4	8	31	23	40
Harrisburg City Isl's ‡	24	10	7	7	37	30	37
Los Angeles Blues ‡	24	8	9	7	34	29	33
Pittsburgh Riverh'ds ‡	24	7	6	11	23	32	27
FC New York	24	6	7	11	27	37	25
Dayton Dutch Lions	24	2	6	16	21	54	12

2/04/2011 - 15/08/2011 • ‡ Qualified for the play-offs
Top scorers: **13** - Jhonny Arteaga COL, New York • **10** - Matthew Delicate ENG, Richmond • **9** - Maxwell Greffin, Orlando; Luke Mulholland ENG, Wilmington & Jose Angulo, Harrisburg

USL PRO PLAY-OFFS

Quarter-finals		Semi-finals		Final	
Orlando *	3				
Charleston	1	**Orlando** *	3		
Wilmington *	0 4p	Richmond	0		
Richmond	0 5p			**Orlando** *	2 3p
Rochester *	4			Harrisburg	2 2p
Pittsburgh	0	Rochester *	1		
Los Angeles	2	**Harrisburg**	2		
Harrisburg *	3	* Home team			

Final: Citrus Bowl, Orlando, 3-09-2011, Att: 11 220, Ref: Bazakos
Scorers - Olum [89], Neal [116p] for Orlando; Noone [95+], Touray [95] for Harrisburg

MEDALS TABLE

		Overall			Lge			Cup			CON'CAF			City
		G	S	B	G	S	G	S	G	S	B			
1	DC United	7	3	6	4	1	2	2	1		6			Washington
2	Los Angeles Galaxy	6	7		3	4	2	2	1	1				Carson/Los Angeles
3	Chicago Fire	5	4	2	1	2	4	2			2			Bridgeview/Chicago
4	Seattle Sounders	3					3							Seattle
5	Columbus Crew	2	2		1		1	2						Columbus
6	Houston Dynamo	2	1	2	2	1					2			Houston
7	Kansas City Wizards	2	1	1	1	1	1				1			Kansas City
8	San Jose Earthquakes	2			2									Santa Clara/San Jose
9	New England Revolution	1	5				4	1	1					Foxboro/Boston
10	FC Dallas	1	3				1	1	2					Frisco/Dallas
11	Colorado Rapids	1	2		1	1			1					Commerce City/Denver
12	Rochester Raging Rhinos	1	1						1	1				Rochester
13	Real Salt Lake	1		1	1						1			Sandy/Salt Lake
14	New York Red Bulls		2				1	1						Harrison/New York
15	Charleston Battery		1					1						Charleston
	Miami Fusion		1											Fort Lauderdale

The record holders for the US Open Cup are Bethlehem Steel and Maccabi Los Angeles with five titles. Along with Chicago Fire, three other clubs have won it four times - Greek American, Philadelphia Ukrainians and Fal Rivver Marksmen. New York Pancyprian-Freedoms have won it three times.

LAMAR HUNT US OPEN CUP 2011

Second Round		Third Round		Quarter-finals		Semi-finals		Final	
Seattle Sounders	Bye	Seattle Sounders *	2	Seattle Sounders *	3	Seattle Sounders *	1	Seattle Sounders *	2
Real Colorado Foxes	1	Kitsap Pumas	1	Los Angeles Galaxy	1	FC Dallas	0	Chicago Fire	0
Kitsap Pumas *	3								
Los Angeles Blues	1	Los Angeles Blues	1						
Ventura County Fusion *	0	Los Angeles Galaxy *	2						
Los Angeles Galaxy	Bye								
Real Salt Lake	Bye	Real Salt Lake *	2	Real Salt Lake	0				
Charlotte Eagles	2	Wilmington Ham'heads	0	FC Dallas *	2				
Wilmington Ham'heads *	3								
Orlando City	1	Orlando City	2						
Charleston Battery *	0	FC Dallas *	3						
FC Dallas	Bye								
Richmond Kickers *	4	Richmond Kickers	2	Richmond Kickers	2	Richmond Kickers	1		
Pittsburgh Riverhounds	1	Columbus Crew *	1	Sporting Kansas City *	0	Chicago Fire *	2		
Columbus Crew	Bye								
Chicago Fire Premier	2	Chicago Fire Premier	0						
Madison 56ers *	0	Sporting Kansas City *	3						
Sporting Kansas City	Bye								
New York Red Bulls	Bye	New York Red Bulls *	2	New York Red Bulls	1				
NY Pancyprian Freedoms	0 5p	FC New York	1	Chicago Fire *	4				
FC New York *	0 6p								
Rochester Rhinos	1	Rochester Rhinos *	0						
Harrisburg City Islanders *	0	Chicago Fire	1						
Chicago Fire	Bye								

* Home team

CUP FINAL

CenturyLink Field, Seattle
4-10-2011, 19:00, Att: 35 615, Ref. Alex Prus
Scorers - Montero 77, Alonso 96+ for Seattle
Seattle - Kasey Keller (c) - James Riley, Jhon Kennedy Hurtado, Jeff Parke, Leonardo Gonzalez - Alvaro Fernandez (Erik Friberg 46), Osvaldo Alonso•, Brad Evans, Lamar Neagle - Fredy Montero, Michael Fucito (Roger Levesque 89). Tr: Sigi Schmid
Chicago - Sean Johnson - Dan Gargan (Sebastian Grazzini 85), Josip Mikulic (Jalil Anibaba• 61), Cory Gibbs, Gonzalo Segares - Logan Pause (c), Pavel Pardo, Daniel Paladini• (Diego Chaves 80), Marco Pappa - Patrick Nyarko•, Dominic Oduro. Tr: Frank Klopas

CLUB BY CLUB GUIDE TO THE 2011 SEASON IN THE USA

CHICAGO FIRE 2011

	Date	Opponent	Res	Score	Comp	Scorers	Att
Mar	19	Dallas	D	1-1	MLS	Chaves 17	20 145
	26	Kansas	W	3-2	MLS	Chaves 34p, Puerari 40, Pappa 59	12 157
	30	Colorado	W	2-1	OCr1	Puerari 45, Anibaba 61	
Apr	9	Seattle	L	1-2	MLS	Chaves 9	36 223
	14	Portland	L	2-4	MLS	OG 66, Pappa 81	18 627
	17	LA Galaxy	L	1-2	MLS	Oduro 89	18 203
	23	Houston	D	1-1	MLS	Chaves 18	12 473
	30	Colorado	D	1-1	MLS	Pappa 42	11 789
	7	Vancouver	D	0-0	MLS		11 680
May	14	Toronto	D	2-2	MLS	Pappa 63, Barouch 75	18 674
	21	Philadelphia	L	1-2	MLS	Oduro 68	18 372
	24	San Jose	D	2-2	OCr2	Barouch 61, Cuesta 76. W 5-4p	4 124
	28	San Jose	D	2-2	MLS	Oduro 56, Gibbs 80	11 926
	4	Seattle	D	0-0	MLS		13 839
	9	Kansas City	D	0-0	MLS		19 925
Jun	12	Columbus	W	1-0	MLS	Nazarit 91+	13 498
	18	NE Revs	D	1-1	MLS	Oduro 31	14 246
	22	Salt Lake	D	0-0	MLS		14 972
	26	New York	D	1-1	MLS	Pappa 57	16 961
	28	Rochester	W	1-0	OCr3	Chaves 37	5 558
	2	Chivas	D	0-0	MLS	Oduro 25	15 152
	9	LA Galaxy	L	1-2	MLS	Nazarit 62	21 762
Jul	12	New York	W	4-0	OCqf	Oduro 7, Cuesta 49, Barouch 2 52 69	4 500
	16	Portland	L	0-1	MLS		16 419
	3	Philadelphia	D	1-1	MLS	Pardo 55	10 557
	7	Vancouver	L	2-4	MLS	Oduro 22, Barouch 81	18 714
	13	New York	D	2-2	MLS	Oduro 16, Grazzini 24	25 177
Aug	18	DC United	D	1-1	MLS	Grazzini 59	15 818
	21	Toronto	W	2-0	MLS	Oduro 18, Gargan 69	12 020
	27	Colorado	W	2-0	MLS	Oduro 18, Gibbs 35	15 211
	30	Richmond	W	2-1	OCsf	Grazzini 32, Oduro 61	8 909
	10	San Jose	L	0-2	MLS		10 525
Sep	17	Chivas	W	3-2	MLS	Gibbs 2, OG 25, Oduro 85	15 246
	25	NE Revs	W	3-2	MLS	Oduro 5p, Oduro 9, Nyarko 30	14 567
	28	Salt Lake	W	3-0	MLS	Pappa 3 9 35 75	20 762
	1	Houston	D	1-1	MLS	Oduro 73	17 544
	4	Seattle	L	0-2	OCf		35 615
Oct	12	Dallas	L	1-2	MLS	Grazzini 85	**10 362**
	15	DC United	W	2-1	MLS	Grazzini 93+, Chaves 95+	16 548
	22	Columbus	W	3-2	MLS	Anibaba 2 11 30, Chaves 81	**20 237**

11th   Att: 242 648 • Av: 14 273 (+2.2%) • Toyota Park 22 000 (64%)

CHIVAS USA 2011

	Date	Opponent	Res	Score	Comp	Scorers	Att
Mar	19	Kansas City	L	2-3	MLS	Conrad 55, Zemanski 84	18 122
	26	Colorado	L	0-1	MLS		13 027
	29	Portland	L	0-2	OCpr		5 061
Apr	2	Toronto	D	1-1	MLS	Moreno 3	18 968
	5	Columbus	D	0-0	MLS		13 385
	16	Vancouver	D	0-0	MLS		20 809
	23	San Jose	W	2-1	MLS	Moreno 45, Trujillo 85	10 525
	30	NE Revs	W	3-0	MLS	LaBrocca 22, Mondaini 45, Moreno 58	14 058
May	7	Salt Lake	L	0-1	MLS		14 365
	15	New York	W	3-2	MLS	Braun 3 5 31 56	16 365
	21	LA Galaxy	L	0-1	MLS		**27 000**
	28	Columbus	D	3-3	MLS	LaBrocca 4, Boyens 37, Flores 57	9 431
	1	Vancouver	D	1-1	MLS	LaBrocca 46	11 753
	4	Portland	W	1-0	MLS	Mondaini 70	14 076
Jun	11	Houston	L	1-2	MLS	Mondaini 7	19 333
	18	Dallas	L	1-2	MLS	Lahoud 71	11 253
	25	Philadelphia	L	2-3	MLS	Umana 28, Braun 77	18 139
	2	Chicago	D	1-1	MLS	LaBrocca 46	15 152
	6	San Jose	W	2-0	MLS	Zemanski 64, LaBrocca 84	**9 425**
	9	Kansas City	D	1-1	MLS	LaBrocca 29	18 467
Jul	16	New York	D	0-0	MLS		14 838
	23	Houston	W	3-0	MLS	Braun 3 32 40 86	11 013
	31	Dallas	L	0-1	MLS		10 023
	6	NE Revs	L	3-2	MLS	Moreno 2 31 80, LaBrocca 58	11 523
	13	Seattle	D	0-0	MLS		36 364
Aug	20	Colorado	D	2-2	MLS	Angel 36, Courtois 86	16 852
	24	Portland	L	0-1	MLS		18 627
	27	Salt Lake	L	0-1	MLS		14 127
	10	DC United	L	0-3	MLS		12 245
Sep	17	Chicago	L	2-3	MLS	Angel 61, LaBrocca 63	15 246
	21	DC United	W	2-0	MLS	Angel 2 57 70	14 849
	24	Toronto	W	3-0	MLS	Angel 2 11 76, Braun 71	14 357
	2	Philadelphia	D	1-1	MLS	Angel 90	16 134
Oct	16	LA Galaxy	L	0-1	MLS		27 000
	22	Seattle	L	1-3	MLS	Estupinan 83	22 137

15th   Att: 252 102 • Av: 14 830 (+15.3%) • Home Depot 27 000 (54%)

KEY TO THE CLUB SECTION

MLS = Major League Soccer • PO = MLS Play-offs • OC = Lamar Hunt US Open Cup • CC = Canadian Championship • CL = CONCACAF Champions League

See Page 13 for further details

CHICAGO MLS APPEARANCES/GOALS 2011

Goalkeepers Jon Conway 6 • Sean Johnson 28
Defenders Jalil Anibaba 27+2/2 • Yamith Cuesta COL 18+2/0 • Cory Gibbs 26/3 • Josip Mikulic CRO 12+2/0 • Dasan Robinson 2+3/0 • Gonzalo Segares CRC 33/0
Midfield Corben Bone 7+3/0 • Dan Gargan 9/1 • Sebastien Grazzini ARG 11/5 • Baggio Husidic BIH 9+9/0 • Marko Maric CRO 0+1/0 • Daniel Paladini 16+7/0 • Marco Pappa GUA 27+2/8 • Pavel Pardo MEX 12+1/1 • Logan Pause 28+1/0 • Bratislav Ristic SRB 5+4/0 • Michael Videira 7+2/0
Forwards Orr Barouch ISR 2+26/2 • Diego Chaves GRE 19+10/6 • Gabe Ferrari 0+3/0 • Cristian Nazarit COL 6+6/2 • Patrick Nyarko GHA 24+6/1 • Dominic Oduro GHA 29+4/12 • Davis Paul 1/0 • Gaston Puerari URU 10+4/1
Coach Carlos De los Cobos MEX • Frank Klopas (30/05/11)

CHIVAS MLS APPEARANCES/GOALS 2011

Goalkeepers Dan Kennedy 32 • Zach Thornton 2
Defenders Andrew Boyens NZL 10+2/1 • Jimmy Conrad 2/1 • David Junior BRA 7+1/0 • Ante Jazic CAN 28/0 • Heath Pearce 29+1/0 • Michael Umana CRC 21+1/1 • Zarek Valentin 24+1/0
Midfield Laurent Courtois FRA 3+8/1 • Simon Elliott NZL 21+3/0 • Jorge Flores 24+1/1 • Blair Gavin 11+7/0 • Nick LaBrocca 34/8 • Michael Lahoud 17+6/1 • Gerson Mayen 1+3/0 • Francisco Mendoza MEX 2+9/0 • Paulo Nagamura BRA 6+5/0 • Mariano Trujillo ARG 1+1/1 • Ben Zemanski 23+5/2
Forwards Juan Pablo Angel COL 9/7 • Tristan Bowen 0+3/0 • Justin Braun 22+7/8 • Chris Cortez 1+8/0 • Victor Estupinan ECU 3+6/1 • Marcos Mondaini ARG 20+4/3 • Alejandro Moreno VEN 22+2/5
Coach Robin Fraser (4/01/11)

COLORADO RAPIDS 2011

	Date	Opponent	Res	Score	Comp	Scorers	Att
Mar	19	Portland	W	3-1	MLS	Larentowicz [8], Cummings [29], Smith [30]	17 139
	26	Chivas	W	1-0	MLS	Amarikwa [32]	13 027
	30	Chicago	L	1-2	OCr1	Akpan [46]	
Apr	3	DC United	W	4-1	MLS	Folan 2 [38] [81], Smith [71], Cummings [92+]	**9 857**
	8	Dallas	L	0-3	MLS		12 261
	13	Salt Lake	L	0-1	MLS		15 513
	22	Seattle	L	0-1	MLS		14 185
	30	Chicago	D	1-1	MLS	Akpan [50]	11 789
May	4	Houston	W	2-1	MLS	Smith [74], Palguta [84]	13 206
	7	NE Revs	D	0-0	MLS		11 755
	14	DC United	D	1-1	MLS	Moor [23]	12 499
	22	Toronto	D	0-0	MLS		13 598
	25	New York	D	2-2	MLS	Larentowicz 2 [26] [31]	18 081
	28	Kansas City	D	1-1	MLS	Casey [13]	16 439
	4	Philadelphia	D	1-1	MLS	Casey [63p]	12 779
Jun	11	Portland	W	1-0	MLS	Moor [92+]	18 627
	18	LA Galaxy	L	1-3	MLS	Casey [64]	**18 277**
	26	Columbus	L	1-4	MLS	Casey [5]	10 771
	3	Houston	D	0-0	MLS		18 203
	6	Kansas City	D	1-1	MLS	Casey [32]	15 209
	9	Vancouver	W	2-1	MLS	Casey [24], Palguta [68]	13 058
Jul	16	Seattle	L	3-4	MLS	Thompson [1], Larentowicz [42], Folan [90]	36 424
	20	New York	W	4-1	MLS	Nyassi 3 [1] [30] [61], Thompson [25]	15 227
	23	NE Revs	D	2-2	MLS	Folan [64p], Kimura [82]	12 273
	29	Philadelphia	W	2-1	MLS	Mastroeni [35], Nyassi [45]	18 770
	5	Columbus	W	2-0	MLS	Mullan [54], Cummings [78]	14 503
	13	San Jose	W	2-1	MLS	Folan [39p], Larentowicz [72]	10 525
Aug	17	I-Metapan	W	3-2	CLgB	Kandji 2 [16] [45], Akpan [50]	4 165
	20	Chivas	D	2-2	MLS	Folan [13], Larentowicz [69]	16 852
	23	RealEspaña	D	1-1	CLgB	Larentowicz [45]	5 841
	27	Chicago	L	0-2	MLS		15 211
	9	LA Galaxy	L	0-1	MLS		20 068
	3	Santos	L	1-4	CLgB	Mullan [77]	9 760
	17	Toronto	L	1-2	MLS	Nyassi [69]	20 318
Sep	21	RealEspaña	L	1-2	CLgB	Akpan [18]	4 512
	24	San Jose	L	1-1	MLS	Moor [71]	17 877
	28	I-Metapan	W	3-1	CLgB	Ababio [31], Amarikwa [49], Cummings [76]	1 920
	1	Dallas	W	1-0	MLS	Moor [26]	13 920
	14	Salt Lake	D	0-0	MLS		16 272
Oct	19	Santos	L	0-2	CLgB		6 000
	22	Vancouver	W	2-1	MLS	Larentowicz [58], Thompson [83]	21 000
	27	Columbus	W	1-0	POr1	Cummings [45]	7 803
	30	Kansas City	L	0-2	POqf		8 601
No	3	Kansas City	L	0-2	POqf		18 565

6th Att: 252 248 • Av: 14 838 (+26.1%) • Dick's Sports Goods 22 385 (66%)

COLUMBUS CREW 2011

	Date	Opponent	Res	Score	Comp	Scorers	Att
Fb	22	Salt Lake	D	0-0	CLqf		4 665
Mar	1	Salt Lake	L	1-4	CLqf	Mendoza [49]	15 405
	19	DC United	L	1-3	MLS	Rogers [79p]	18 132
	26	New York	D	0-0	MLS		10 306
Apr	1	Dallas	W	2-0	MLS	Mendoza [54p], Gaven [90]	14 549
	9	Chivas	D	0-0	MLS		13 385
	16	Kansas City	W	1-0	MLS	Rogers [53]	7 695
	23	Toronto	D	1-1	MLS	Renteria [48]	20 145
	30	Vancouver	W	2-1	MLS	Renteria 2 [51p] [60]	11 298
	7	Seattle	D	1-1	MLS	Renteria [67p]	**7 148**
May	14	San Jose	L	0-3	MLS		9 142
	21	Portland	L	0-1	MLS		18 627
	28	Chivas	D	3-3	MLS	Mendoza 2 [17] [53], Ekpo [64]	9 431
	4	New York	D	1-1	MLS	Balchan [90]	20 393
	8	Salt Lake	W	2-1	MLS	Mendoza [75p], Gardner [81]	9 650
	12	Chicago	L	0-1	MLS		13 498
Jun	18	Houston	W	2-0	MLS	Mendoza [41], Anor [77]	13 039
	26	Colorado	W	4-1	MLS	Gaven [11], Mendoza 2 [17] [47], Heinemann [56]	10 771
	29	Richmond	L	1-2	OCr3	Grossman [35]	1 845
	2	Dallas	L	0-2	MLS		20 704
	6	Vancouver	W	1-0	MLS	Cunningham [90]	19 079
	16	San Jose	D	0-0	MLS		14 109
Jul	20	LA Galaxy	L	0-1	MLS		24 709
	23	Portland	W	1-0	MLS	Gaven [79]	11 246
	30	Salt Lake	W	2-0	MLS	Gaven [5], Heinemann [10]	18 516
	5	Colorado	L	0-2	MLS		14 503
	13	NE Revs	W	3-1	MLS	OG [54], James [75], Renteria [81]	13 041
Aug	20	Philadelphia	W	2-1	MLS	Renteria [37], Mendoza [51p]	13 869
	27	Seattle	L	2-6	MLS	Cunningham [59p], Gardner [73]	36 364
	10	Toronto	L	2-4	MLS	Heinemann [67], Mendoza [87]	13 058
	14	Houston	D	2-2	MLS	Mendoza 2 [64p] [75p]	10 709
Sep	17	Philadelphia	L	0-1	MLS		18 906
	24	LA Galaxy	L	0-1	MLS		**21 203**
	28	Kansas City	L	1-2	MLS	Renteria [34]	17 838
	2	DC United	W	2-1	MLS	OG [47], Gaven [60]	15 566
Oct	15	NE Revs	W	3-0	MLS	Mendoza 2 [30] [62]	16 285
	22	Chicago	L	2-3	MLS	Renteria [73], Duka [80]	20 237
	27	Colorado	L	0-1	POr1		7 803

9th Att: 207 147 • Av: 12 185 (-5.7%) • Crew Stadium 20 455 (59%)

COLORADO MLS APPEARANCES/GOALS 2011

Goalkeepers Matt Pickens 37

Defenders Edward Kwame Adabio 0+1/0 • Miguel Comminges GLP 7/0 • Danny Earls IRL 3+1/0 • Jeff Larentowicz 37/7 • Tyrone Marshall JAM 24+4/0 • Pablo Mastroeni 30/1 • Drew Moor 34/4 • Scott Palguta 6+5/2 • Marvell Wynne 31+1/0

Midfield Kosuke Kimura JPN 36+1 • Ross LaBauex 5+8/0 • Brian Mullan 22+3/1 • Joseph Nane CMR 3+7/0 • Sanna Nyassi GAM 20+9/5 • Jamie Smith SCO 19+2/3 • Wells Thompson 24+9/3 • Anthony Wallace 8+2/0

Forwards Andre Akpan 5+7/1 • Quincy Amarikwa 5+11/1 • Conor Casey 11+3/6 • Omar Cummings JAM 21+8/4 • Caleb Folan ENG 18+10/3 • Macoumba Kandji SEN 1+11/0

Coach Gary Smith

COLUMBUS MLS APPEARANCES/GOALS 2011

Goalkeepers Andy Gruenebaum 2 • Will Hesmer 33

Defenders Rich Balchan 18+1/1 • Shaun Francis JAM 5+1/0 • Andy Iro ENG 2+2/0 • Julius James TRI 32/1 • Chad Marshall 33/0 • Sebastian Miranda CHI 35/0

Midfield Bernardo Anor VEN 6+7/1 • Kevin Burns 15+4/0 • Dilly Duka 17+6/2 • Emmanuel Ekpo NGA 29+3/1 • Josh Gardner 22+1/2 • Eddie Gaven 27/5 • Eric Gehrig 4+4/0 • Leandre Griffit FRA 0+1/0 • Cole Grossman 0+2/0 • Danny O'Rourke 6+1/0 • Robbie Rogers 25+3/2 • Dejan Rusmir SRB 13+5/0 • Tony Tchani CMR 1/0

Forwards Jeff Cunningham 4+17/2 • Tom Heinemann 12+17/3 • Aaron Horton 0+1/0 • Andres Mendoza PER 26+4/13 • Justin Meram 4+12/0 • Emilio Renteria VEN 14+5/8

Coach Robert Warzycha POL

DC UNITED 2011

	Date	Opponent	Res		Comp	Scorers	Att
Mar	19	Columbus	W	3-1	MLS	Wolff 51, Davies 2 63p 77	18 132
	26	NE Revs	L	1-2	MLS	Davies 90p	12 914
Apr	3	Colorado	L	1-4	MLS	Quaranta 70	9 857
	6	Philadelphia	D	2-2	OCpr	Wolff 45, Woolard 111, W 4-2p	2 347
	9	LA Galaxy	D	1-1	MLS	Davies 90p	26 622
	16	Toronto	W	3-0	MLS	Pontius 2 5 73, Davies 11	16 313
	21	New York	L	0-4	MLS		18 052
	26	NE Revs	L	2-3	OCr1	Boskovic 2 73 83	1 843
	29	Houston	L	1-4	MLS	Burch 39	20 577
May	4	Seattle	W	2-1	MLS	Wolff 32, Davies 52	11 254
	7	Dallas	D	0-0	MLS		11 504
	14	Colorado	D	1-1	MLS	Pontius 62p	12 499
	29	Portland	W	3-2	MLS	Kitchen 14, Pontius 75p, Wolff 85	18 627
Jun	3	LA Galaxy	D	0-0	MLS		20 036
	11	San Jose	L	2-4	MLS	Najar 13, Brettschneider 34	14 105
	18	Salt Lake	D	1-1	MLS	Davies 84p	16 841
	25	Houston	D	2-2	MLS	Pontius 31, Davies 73	15 734
Jul	2	Philadelphia	D	2-2	MLS	Wolff 43, Najar 57	13 365
	9	New York	W	1-0	MLS	De Rosario 60	22 200
	16	Dallas	D	0-0	MLS		10 802
	20	NE Revs	L	0-1	MLS		15 597
	30	San Jose	W	2-0	MLS	De Rosario 2 57 67	10 525
Aug	6	Toronto	D	3-3	MLS	De Rosario 3 18 63 88p	11 684
	13	Vancouver	W	4-0	MLS	Pontius 2 45 70, Najar 48, King 81	11 738
	18	Chicago	D	1-1	MLS	Wolff 73	15 818
	21	Kansas City	L	0-1	MLS		15 352
Sep	10	Chivas	W	3-0	MLS	Davies 3 12 15 66	12 245
	17	Seattle	L	0-3	MLS		36 242
	21	Chivas	D	2-2	MLS	De Rosario 39, White 46	14 849
	24	Salt Lake	W	4-1	MLS	Najar 13, De Rosario 3 22 27 31	16 367
	29	Philadelphia	L	2-3	MLS	De Rosario 22, Najar 30	17 963
Oct	2	Columbus	L	1-2	MLS	Woolard 37	15 566
	12	Vancouver	L	1-2	MLS	McDonald 57	17 288
	15	Chicago	L	1-2	MLS	De Rosario 90p	16 548
	19	Portland	D	1-1	MLS	De Rosario 73	14 317
	22	Kansas City	L	0-1	MLS		15 965

13th • Att: 258 332 • Av: 15 196 (+18.5%) • RFK Memorial 45 596 (33%)

FC DALLAS 2011

	Date	Opponent	Res		Comp	Scorers	Att
Mar	19	Chicago	D	1-1	MLS	Rodriguez 18	20 145
	26	San Jose	L	0-2	MLS		11 022
Apr	1	Columbus	L	0-2	MLS		14 549
	8	Colorado	W	3-0	MLS	Ihemelu 26, Ferreira 2 40 46	12 261
	17	Portland	L	2-3	MLS	Ferreira 83, Shea 86	18 627
	23	Vancouver	W	2-1	MLS	John 53, Avila 83	21 000
	1	LA Galaxy	W	2-1	MLS	Castillo 47, Shea 88	21 867
	7	DC United	D	0-0	MLS		11 504
May	11	Toronto	W	1-0	MLS	Hernandez 45p	8 145
	14	Philadelphia	W	2-0	MLS	Shea 29, Castillo 43	12 109
	22	Salt Lake	D	0-0	MLS		10 550
	25	Seattle	W	1-0	MLS	Shea 17	36 026
	28	Houston	D	2-2	MLS	Weaver 43, Clark 88	16 709
Jun	4	NE Revs	W	1-0	MLS	Chavez 68	10 363
	12	Kansas City	L	1-4	MLS	Shea 32	10 450
	18	Chivas	W	2-1	MLS	Shea 23, Jackson 84	11 253
	25	Portland	W	4-0	MLS	Loyd 34, John 39, Shea 58, Luna 87	10 470
	28	Orlando	W	3-2	OCr3	Jackson 38, Villar 50, Rodriguez 95+	1 876
Jul	2	Columbus	W	2-0	MLS	Shea 57, Jackson 76	20 704
	9	Salt Lake	L	0-2	MLS		17 734
	12	Salt Lake	W	2-0	OCqf	Benitez 18, Jackson 54	3 189
	16	DC United	D	0-0	MLS		10 802
	20	Toronto	W	1-0	MLS	Shea 48	21 087
	23	New York	D	2-2	MLS	Chavez 2 51 78	17 276
	28	Alianza	W	1-0	CLpr	Goncalves 70	7 301
	31	Chivas	W	1-0	MLS	Chavez 26	10 023
Aug	3	Alianza	W	1-0	CLpr	Ihemelu 37	3 400
	6	LA Galaxy	L	1-3	MLS	Chavez 8	21 546
	13	Philadelphia	D	2-2	MLS	Maicon 16, Shea 45	18 811
	17	UNAM	W	1-0	CLgC	Chavez 66	4 000
	20	Seattle	L	0-1	MLS		11 635
	24	Toronto	W	1-0	CLgC	Stewart 45	500
	27	Kansas City	W	3-2	MLS	Hernandez 70, Maicon 88, Warshaw 90	20 018
	30	Seattle	L	0-1	OCsf		4 593
Sep	10	NE Revs	L	0-2	MLS		15 498
	14	Tauro	D	1-1	CLgC	Cruz 1	3 001
	17	New York	L	0-1	MLS		17 019
	21	UNAM	L	0-2	CLgC		4 985
	24	Houston	L	0-1	MLS		10 849
	28	Tauro	L	3-5	CLgC	Benitez 22p, Luna 2 84 90p	316
Oct	1	Colorado	L	0-1	MLS		13 920
	12	Chicago	W	2-1	MLS	Jackson 41, Cruz 53	10 362
	15	Vancouver	W	2-0	MLS	Chavez 35, Shea 54	10 222
	18	Toronto	L	0-3	CLgC		2 578
	22	San Jose	L	2-4	MLS	John 45, Luna 90	10 744
	26	New York	L	0-2	POr1		10 017

11th • Att: 218 636 • Av: 12 861 (+34.7%) • Pizza Hut Park 21 193 (60%)

DC UNITED MLS APPEARANCES/GOALS 2011

Goalkeepers Steve Cronin 0+2 • Bill Hamid 28 • Pat Onstad CAN 3 • Joe Willis 3

Defenders Rodrigo Brasesco URU 2+1/0 • Marc Burch 11+0/1 • Chris Korb 12/0 • Ethan White 21+3/1 • Daniel Woolard 26/1 • Jed Zayner 4/0

Midfield Brandon Barklage 0+4/0 • Branko Boskovic MNE 1+3/0 • Austin Da Luz 5+8/0 • Fred BRA 5+12/0 • Dejan Jakovic CAN 15/0 • Stephen King 11+9/1 • Perry Kitchen 30+1/1 • Dax McCarty 11+2/0 • Brandon McDonald 18/1 • Kurt Morsink CRC 2/0 • Andy Najar HON 28+3/5 • Clyde Simms 29/0

Forwards Blake Brettschneider 9+6/1 • Charlie Davies 18+8/11 • Dwayne De Rosario CAN 17+1/13 • Joseph Ngwenya ZIM 7+9/0 • Chris Pontius 25/7 • Santino Quaranta 10+11/1 • Josh Wolff 23+7/5

Coach Ben Olsen

DALLAS MLS APPEARANCES/GOALS 2011

Goalkeepers Kevin Hartman 34 • Chris Seitz 1

Defenders Jair Benitez COL 26+2/0 • Daniel Hernandez 31/2 • Ugo Ihemelu 30+1/2 • Jackson BRA 23+6/3 • George John 32/3 • Zach Loyd 29+2/1 • Jack Stewart 1+1/0 • Bobby Warshaw 4+13/1

Midfield Eric Alexander 16+6/0 • Marvin Chavez HON 31+1/6 • Daniel Cruz COL 6+5/1 • David Ferreira COL 6/3 • Bruno Guarda BRA 5+6/0 • Jeremy Hall 2+2/0 • Andrew Jacobson 23+5/1 • Brek Shea 31+1/11 • Victor Ulloa 1+1/0 • Ricardo Villar BRA 15+6/0

Forwards Fabian Castillo COL 16+6/2 • Maykel Galindo CUB 1+5/0 • Ruben Luna MEX 2+13/2 • Maicon BRA 9+3/2 • Milton Rodriguez COL 5+8/1 • Andrew Wiedeman 0+3/0

Coach Schellas Hyndman

HOUSTON DYNAMO 2011

	Date	Opponent	Res	Score	Comp	Scorers	Att
Mar	19	Philadelphia	L	0-1	MLS		19 385
	25	Seattle	D	1-1	MLS	Cameron [42]	36 204
	3	New York	D	1-1	MLS	Weaver [50]	13 664
	6	Kansas City	L	0-1	OCr1		2 383
Apr	10	Vancouver	W	3-1	MLS	Weaver [37], Boswell [42], Bruin [76]	**12 047**
	17	NE Revs	W	1-0	MLS	Freeman [86]	15 176
	23	Chicago	D	1-1	MLS	Boswell [83]	12 473
	29	DC United	W	4-1	MLS	Bruin 3 [5 41 55], Weaver [60]	20 577
May	4	Colorado	L	1-2	MLS	Clark [71]	13 206
	7	Toronto	L	1-2	MLS	Palmer [87]	20 259
	14	Salt Lake	D	0-0	MLS		16 301
	21	New York	D	2-2	MLS	Davis [12p], Koke [82]	25 314
	25	LA Galaxy	L	0-1	MLS		14 458
	28	Dallas	D	2-2	MLS	Weaver [43], Clark [88]	16 709
	4	San Jose	L	0-2	MLS		9 270
Jun	11	Chivas	W	2-1	MLS	Cameron [28], OG [54]	19 333
	18	Columbus	L	0-2	MLS		13 039
	25	DC United	D	2-2	MLS	Davis [41p], Ching [89]	15 734
	3	Colorado	D	0-0	MLS		18 203
	9	Toronto	W	2-0	MLS	Cruz [51], Cameron [81]	19 085
Jul	16	Kansas City	D	1-1	MLS	Davis [8]	**12 047**
	23	Chivas	L	0-3	MLS		11 013
	30	Seattle	W	3-1	MLS	Clarke [7], Ching 2 [22 70]	18 465
	6	Philadelphia	D	1-1	MLS	Cameron [85]	18 524
Aug	14	Portland	W	2-1	MLS	Moffat [17], Ching [27]	14 475
	17	NE Revs	D	1-1	MLS	Boswell [90]	10 963
	20	Salt Lake	W	3-2	MLS	Ching [47], Boswell [69], Dixon [90]	16 247
	27	Vancouver	L	0-1	MLS		20 226
Sep	10	Kansas City	L	0-3	MLS		14 791
	14	Columbus	D	2-2	MLS	Watson [34], Carr [86]	10 709
	17	San Jose	W	2-1	MLS	Davis [47p], Bruin [80]	18 129
	24	Dallas	W	1-0	MLS	Cameron [87]	10 849
Oct	1	Chicago	D	1-1	MLS	Clarke [33]	17 544
	14	Portland	W	2-0	MLS	Hainault [36], Cruz [59]	20 323
	23	LA Galaxy	W	3-1	MLS	Moffat [28], Boswell [49], Costly [74]	**30 018**
	30	Philadelphia	W	2-1	POqf	Hainault [5], Carr [30]	18 539
Nov	3	Philadelphia	W	1-0	POqf	Ching [45]	24 749
	6	Kansas City	W	2-0	POsf	Hainault [53], Costly [87]	20 839
	20	LA Galaxy	L	0-1	POf		30 281

7th/RU Att: 300 796 • Av: 17 694 (+15.8%) • Robertson 32 000 (55%)

LA GALAXY 2011

	Date	Opponent	Res	Score	Comp	Scorers	Att
Mar	15	Seattle	W	1-0	MLS	Juninho [59]	36 443
	20	NE Revs	D	1-1	MLS	Juninho [39]	27 000
	26	Salt Lake	L	1-4	MLS	Angel [79]	20 507
Apr	2	Philadelphia	W	1-0	MLS	Leonardo [33]	24 998
	9	DC United	D	1-1	MLS	Magee [12]	26 622
	13	Toronto	D	0-0	MLS		22 453
	17	Chicago	W	2-1	MLS	Barrett [42], Gonzalez [72]	18 203
	23	Portland	W	3-0	MLS	Barrett [4], Donovan 2 [8p 67]	23 719
May	1	Dallas	L	1-2	MLS	Donovan [52]	21 867
	7	New York	D	1-1	MLS	Donovan [40]	27 000
	11	Philadelphia	D	1-1	MLS	Donovan [24]	19 178
	14	Kansas City	W	4-1	MLS	Donovan 2 [44 46p], Angel [64], Beckham [87]	19 763
	21	Chivas	W	1-0	MLS	Barrett [26]	27 000
	25	Houston	W	1-0	MLS	Donovan [45p]	**14 458**
	28	NE Revs	W	1-0	MLS	Lopez [69]	21 793
Jun	3	DC United	D	0-0	MLS		20 036
	11	Toronto	D	2-2	MLS	Birchall [3], Angel [91+]	20 675
	18	Colorado	W	3-1	MLS	OG [25], Juninho [42], Barrett [80]	18 277
	25	San Jose	D	0-0	MLS		10 872
	28	LA Blues	W	2-1	OCr3	Gonzalez [75], Magee [81]	3 627
Jul	4	Seattle	D	0-0	MLS		27 000
	9	Chicago	W	2-1	MLS	Donovan [57], Beckham [65]	21 762
	13	Seattle	L	1-3	OCqf	Cristman [37]	4 322
	20	Columbus	W	1-0	MLS	Franklin [70]	24 709
	30	Vancouver	W	4-0	MLS	Donovan 2 [61 74p], Franklin [81], Cristman [89]	27 500
Aug	3	Portland	L	0-3	MLS		18 627
	6	Dallas	W	3-1	MLS	Gonzalez [32], Juninho [62], Magee [81]	21 546
	16	Motagua	W	2-0	CLgA	Cristman [13], Donovan [60]	8 196
	20	San Jose	W	2-0	MLS	Keane [21], Magee [90]	27 000
	25	Alajuelense	W	2-0	CLgA	Gonzalez [37], Barrett [77]	9 855
Sep	5	Kansas City	D	2-2	MLS	Franklin 2 [25 74]	20 512
	9	Colorado	W	1-0	MLS	Donovan [36]	20 068
	13	Morelia	L	1-2	CLgA	Keane [52]	16 000
	17	Vancouver	W	3-0	MLS	Magee 2 [39 75], Keane [64]	22 959
	21	Alajuelense	L	0-1	CLgA		13 377
	24	Columbus	W	1-0	MLS	Barrett [93+]	21 203
	28	Morelia	W	2-1	CLgA	Magee [20], Pereira [90]	7 500
Oct	1	Salt Lake	W	2-1	MLS	Barrett [59], OG [71]	27 000
	4	New York	L	0-2	MLS		25 186
	16	Chivas	W	1-0	MLS	Barrett [53]	27 000
	20	Motagua	W	1-0	CLgA	Pereira [29]	14 000
	23	Houston	L	1-3	MLS	McBean [88]	30 018
	30	New York	W	1-0	POqf	Magee [15]	22 663
Nov	3	New York	W	2-1	POqf	Magee [42], Donovan [74p]	20 000
	6	Salt Lake	W	3-1	POsf	Donovan [23p], Magee [58], Keane [64]	23 437
	20	Houston	W	1-0	POf	Donovan [72]	30 281

1st/W Att: 396 693 • Av: 23 335 (+23.2%) • Home Depot 27 000 (86%)

HOUSTON MLS APPEARANCES/GOALS 2011

Goalkeepers Tally Hall 38

Defenders Bobby Boswell 31+1/5 • Mike Chabala 2+5/0 • Hunter Freeman 22+1/1 • Andrew Hainault CAN 35/3 • Eddie Robinson 2/0 • Kofi Sarkodie 7/0 • Jermaine Taylor JAM 11+4/0

Midfield Corey Ashe 34+2/0 • Geoff Cameron 37/5 • Colin Clark 17+13/4 • Danny Cruz 17+7/2 • Brad Davis 37/4 • Alex Dixon 0+7/1 • Luiz Camargo BRA 10+1/0 • Adam Moffat SCO 16+1/2 • Lovel Palmer JAM 16+3/1 • Je-Vaughn Watson JAM 11+14/1

Forwards Will Bruin 21+7/5 • Calen Carr 8+5/2 • Brian Ching 19+5/6 • Carlos Costly HON 14+7/2 • Jason Garey 2+8/0 • Koke ESP 2+5/1 • Dominic Oduro 0+1/0 • Cameron Weaver 16+11/4

Coach Dominic Kinnear

LA GALAXY MLS APPEARANCES/GOALS 2011

Goalkeepers Brian Perk 1 • Donovan Ricketts JAM 15 • Josh Saunders 22+1

Defenders Gregg Berhalter 8+2/0 • AJ DeLaGarza 34/0 • Todd Dunivant 36/0 • Sean Franklin 29+2/4 • Omar Gonzalez 33/2 • Leonardo BRA 7/1 • Dasan Robinson 1/0 • Ryan Thomas 0+1/0

Midfield David Beckham ENG 29+1/2 • Chris Birchall TRI 18+9/1 • Paolo Cardozo URU 8+10/0 • Landon Donovan 25+2/15 • Frankie Hejduk 6/0 • Hector Jimenez 1+2/0 • Juninho BRA 33/4 • Dan Keat NZL 1+4/0 • Miguel Lopez ARG 14+10/1

Forwards Juan Pablo Angel COL 17+5/3 • Chad Barrett 23+7/7 • Adam Cristman 6+8/1 • Bryan Jordan 5+8/0 • Robbie Keane IRL 7+1/3 • Jovan Kirovski 2+10/0 • Mike Magee 24+6/8 • Jack McBean 1/1

Coach Bruce Arena

NEW ENGLAND REVOLUTION 2011

Mon	Date	Opponent	Res	Score	Comp	Scorers	Att
Mar	20	LA Galaxy	D	1-1	MLS	Joseph [3]	27 000
	26	DC United	W	2-1	MLS	Schilawski [7], Joseph [16p]	12 914
Apr	2	Portland	D	1-1	MLS	McCarthy [22]	7 114
	6	Vancouver	D	1-1	MLS	Stolica [93+]	19 396
	9	Salt Lake	L	0-2	MLS		7 970
	17	Houston	L	0-1	MLS		15 176
	23	Kansas City	W	3-2	MLS	Perovic [12], Joseph [71], Lekic [83]	11 414
	26	DC United	W	3-2	OCr1	Dube 2 [37 47], Koger [67]	
	30	Chivas	L	0-3	MLS		14 058
May	7	Colorado	D	0-0	MLS		11 755
	14	Vancouver	W	1-0	MLS	Joseph [49p]	14 186
	21	San Jose	L	1-2	MLS	Tierney [86]	9 736
	25	Kansas City	L	0-5	OCr2		1 228
	28	LA Galaxy	L	0-1	MLS		**21 793**
Jun	4	Dallas	L	0-1	MLS		10 363
	10	New York	L	1-2	MLS	Boggs [54]	21 201
	15	Toronto	D	0-0	MLS		**6 680**
	18	Chicago	D	1-1	MLS	Lekic [49]	14 246
	26	Seattle	L	1-2	MLS	Nyassi [3]	36 212
Jul	4	Salt Lake	D	3-3	MLS	Lekic [4p], Tierney [16], Joseph [63]	16 139
	17	Philadelphia	L	0-3	MLS		13 414
	20	DC United	W	1-0	MLS	McCarthy [73]	15 597
	23	Colorado	D	2-2	MLS	Feilhaber [25], Joseph [90p]	12 273
	30	Kansas City	D	1-1	MLS	Lekic [38]	17 418
Aug	6	Chivas	L	2-3	MLS	Joseph [69p], Fagundez [86]	11 523
	13	Columbus	L	1-3	MLS	Feilhaber [45]	13 041
	17	Houston	D	1-1	MLS	Cochrane [4]	10 963
	20	New York	D	2-2	MLS	Caraglio 2 [15 37]	18 882
Sep	7	Philadelphia	D	4-4	MLS	Soares [9], Lekic [20p], Zerka [26], Feilhaber [34]	16 148
	10	Dallas	W	2-0	MLS	Joseph [14], Lekic [85]	15 498
	16	Portland	L	0-3	MLS		20 323
	25	Chicago	L	2-3	MLS	Guy 2 [90 92+]	14 567
Oct	1	Seattle	L	1-2	MLS	Fagundez [35]	21 022
	8	San Jose	L	1-2	MLS	Feilhaber [55]	9 111
	15	Columbus	L	0-3	MLS		16 285
	22	Toronto	D	2-2	MLS	Zerka [40], Caraglio [46]	21 600

17th Att: 224 770 • Av: 13 222 (+15.3%) • Gillette Stadium 22 385 (59%)

NEW YORK RED BULL 2011

Mon	Date	Opponent	Res	Score	Comp	Scorers	Att
Mar	19	Seattle	W	1-0	MLS	Agudelo [70]	20 982
	26	Columbus	D	0-0	MLS		10 306
Apr	2	Houston	D	1-1	MLS	Richards [47]	**13 664**
	9	Philadelphia	L	0-1	MLS		19 027
	16	San Jose	W	3-0	MLS	Rodgers 2 [3 14], Henry [87]	14 308
	21	DC United	W	4-0	MLS	Henry 2 [12 38], Lindpere [76], Agudelo [92+]	18 052
	30	Kansas City	W	1-0	MLS	Rodgers [21]	20 636
May	1	LA Galaxy	D	1-1	MLS	Henry [4]	27 000
	15	Chivas	L	2-3	MLS	Henry [20], De Rosario [34p]	16 365
	21	Houston	D	2-2	MLS	Richards [1], Ballouchy [91+]	25 314
	25	Colorado	D	2-2	MLS	Henry [28], Rodgers [33]	18 081
	28	Vancouver	D	1-1	MLS	Rodgers [33]	21 000
Jun	4	Columbus	D	1-1	MLS	Ballouchy [9]	20 393
	10	NE Revs	W	2-1	MLS	OG [37], Henry [50]	21 201
	19	Portland	D	3-3	MLS	Da Luz [5], Henry [73], De Rosario [96+p]	18 627
	23	Seattle	L	2-4	MLS	Richards [30], OG [58]	46 065
	26	Chicago	D	1-1	MLS	Lindpere [40]	16 961
	28	FC New York	W	2-0	OCr3	Hertzog [58], Rooney [65]	2 074
Jul	2	San Jose	D	2-2	MLS	Lindpere 2 [7 85]	41 028
	6	Toronto	W	5-0	MLS	Henry [33], Rodgers [38], Lindpere [52], Agudelo 2 [67 88]	15 269
	9	DC United	L	0-1	MLS		22 200
	12	Chicago	L	0-4	OCqf		4 500
	16	Chivas	D	0-0	MLS		14 838
	20	Colorado	L	1-4	MLS	Henry [67]	15 227
	23	Dallas	D	2-2	MLS	Agudelo [39], Henry [85]	17 276
Aug	6	Salt Lake	L	0-3	MLS		19 081
	13	Chicago	D	2-2	MLS	Henry [9], Lindpere [63]	25 177
	20	NE Revs	D	2-2	MLS	Richards 2 [53 87]	18 882
Sep	10	Vancouver	D	1-1	MLS	Agudelo [68]	19 684
	17	Dallas	W	1-0	MLS	Rodgers [36]	17 019
	21	Salt Lake	L	1-3	MLS	Lindpere [68]	14 266
	24	Portland	W	2-0	MLS	Richards [21], Rodgers [65p]	25 008
Oct	1	Toronto	D	1-1	MLS	Henry [88]	20 132
	4	LA Galaxy	W	2-0	MLS	Rodgers [33], Henry [60]	**25 186**
	15	Kansas City	L	0-2	MLS		19 921
	20	Philadelphia	W	1-0	MLS	OG [8]	25 044
	26	Dallas	W	2-0	POr1	Lindpere [61], Henry [90]	10 016
	30	LA Galaxy	L	0-1	POqf		22 663
Nv	3	LA Galaxy	L	1-2	POqf	Rodgers [4]	20 000

10th Att: 334 740 • Av: 19 691 (+21%) • Red Bull Arena 25 189 (78%)

NEW ENGLAND MLS APPEARANCES/GOALS 2011

Goalkeepers Matt Reis 27 • Bobby Shuttleworth 7

Defenders Kevin Alston 33/0 • Darrius Barnes 22+6/0 • Ryan Cochrane 19+3/1 • Franco Coria ARG 14+4/0 • Didier Domi FRA 8+1/0 • AJ Soares 28/1 • Chris Tierney 25+2/2

Midfield Ousmane Dabo FRA 3/0 • Benny Feilhaber 23/4 • Shalrie Joseph GRN 32/8 • Ryan Kinne 0+1/0 • Stephen McCarthy 18+3/2 • Sainey Nyassi GAM 8+13/1 • Marko Perovic SRB 4/1 • Pat Phelan 15+5/0

Forwards Zak Boggs 16+4/1 • Milton Caraglio ARG 12/3 • Kheli Dube ZIM 0+5/0 • Diego Fagundez URU 3+3/2 • Ryan Guy IRL 6+5/2 • Rajko Lekic DEN 22+1/6 • Kenny Mansally GAM 9+16/0 • Zack Schilawski 13+12/1 • Ilija Stolica SRB 0+2/0 • Moncef Zerka MAR 7/2

Coach Steve Nicol SCO

NEW YORK MLS APPEARANCES/GOALS 2011

Goalkeepers Bouna Coundoul SEN 11+1 • Alex Horwath 1 • Chris Konopka 1 • Frank Rost GER 14 • Greg Sutton CAN 10

Defenders Chris Albright 6+2/0 • Mike Jones 0+1/0 • Stephen Keel 16+3/0 • Rafael Marquez MEX 22/0 • Carlos Mendes 17+3/0 • Roy Miller CRC 33/0 • Tim Ream 31/0

Midfield Stephane Auvray GLP 1+6/0 • Medhi Ballouchy MAR 17+15/2 • Danleigh Borman RSA 1+1/0 • Austin Da Luz 4+3/1 • Matt Kassel 0+2/0 • Joel Lindpere EST 37/8 • Dax McCarty 15+2/0 • Brian Nielsen DEN 0+1/0 • Dane Richards JAM 30/6 • Carl Robinson WAL 0+2/0 • John Rooney ENG 0+5/0 • Jan Gunnar Solli NOR 33/0 • Teemu Tainio FIN 31/0 • Tony Tchani CMR 1+1/0

Forwards Juan Agudelo 12+16/6 • Dwayne De Rosario CAN 12+1/2 • Thierry Henry FRA 29/15 • Corey Hertzog 0+5/0 • Luke Rodgers ENG 22+3/10

Coach Hans Backe SWE

PHILADELPHIA UNION 2011

	Date	Opponent	Res	Score	Comp	Scorers	Att
Mar	19	Houston	W	1-0	MLS	Califf [5]	19 385
	26	Vancouver	W	1-0	MLS	Ruiz [78]	18 591
Apr	2	LA Galaxy	L	0-1	MLS		24 998
	6	DC United	D	2-2	OCpr	Ruiz [18], Carroll [118]	2 347
	9	New York	W	1-0	MLS	Torres [69]	19 027
	16	Seattle	D	1-1	MLS	Ruiz [31]	**15 149**
	30	San Jose	W	1-0	MLS	Le Toux [76]	18 279
May	6	Portland	L	0-1	MLS		18 627
	11	LA Galaxy	D	1-1	MLS	Mwanga [84]	**19 178**
	14	Dallas	L	0-2	MLS		12 109
	21	Chicago	W	2-1	MLS	Farfan.M [64], Ruiz [75]	18 372
	28	Toronto	W	6-2	MLS	Farfan.G [2], Mapp 2 [10 61], Nakazawa [44], Mwanga 2 [71 89]	20 122
Jun	4	Colorado	D	1-1	MLS	Mwanga [66]	12 779
	11	Salt Lake	D	1-1	MLS	Daniel [23]	18 728
	18	Vancouver	L	0-1	MLS		20 168
	22	Kansas City	D	0-0	MLS		9 794
	25	Chivas	W	3-2	MLS	Paunovic [48], Ruiz [69], Mwanga [82]	18 139
Jul	2	DC United	D	2-2	MLS	OG [48], Ruiz [83]	13 365
	9	San Jose	D	0-0	MLS		9 794
	17	NE Revs	W	3-0	MLS	Ruiz [12], Valdes [24], Williams [93+]	13 414
	29	Colorado	L	1-2	MLS	Torres [90]	18 770
Aug	3	Chicago	D	1-1	MLS	Paunovic [34]	10 557
	6	Houston	D	1-1	MLS	McInerney [15]	18 524
	13	Dallas	D	2-2	MLS	Le Toux 2 [34p 85p]	18 811
	20	Columbus	L	1-2	MLS	Paunovic [42]	13 869
	3	Salt Lake	L	1-2	MLS	Le Toux [30]	18 720
	7	NE Revs	D	4-4	MLS	Torres [28], Adu [54], Le Toux 2 [79p 90]	16 148
Sep	10	Portland	D	0-0	MLS		18 504
	17	Columbus	W	1-0	MLS	Le Toux [32]	18 906
	23	Kansas City	D	1-1	MLS	Le Toux [63]	18 778
	29	DC United	W	3-2	MLS	Le Toux 2 [4 15], Farfan.M [57]	17 963
Oct	2	Chivas	D	1-1	MLS	Mapp [59]	16 134
	8	Seattle	W	2-0	MLS	Adu [60], Carroll [70]	36 304
	15	Toronto	D	1-1	MLS	Le Toux [42]	**19 178**
	20	New York	L	0-1	MLS		25 044
	30	Houston	L	1-2	POqf	Le Toux [7]	18 539
Nov	3	Houston	L	0-1	POqf		24 749

8th • Att: 310 394 • Av: 18 258 (+7.4%) • PPL Park 18 500 (98%)

PORTLAND TIMBERS 2011

	Date	Opponent	Res	Score	Comp	Scorers	Att
Mar	19	Colorado	L	1-3	MLS	Cooper [79]	17 139
	26	Toronto	L	0-2	MLS		20 086
	29	Chivas	W	2-0	OCpr	Jewsbury [84], Brunner [86]	5 061
Apr	2	NE Revs	D	1-1	MLS	Jewsbury [39]	7 114
	14	Chicago	W	4-2	MLS	Perlaza 2 [29 48], Wallace [37], OG [84]	18 627
	17	Dallas	W	3-2	MLS	Jewsbury [14], Cooper [35], Wallace [56]	18 627
	23	LA Galaxy	L	0-3	MLS		23 719
	30	Salt Lake	W	1-0	MLS	Cooper [22]	18 627
May	3	San Jose	L	0-1	OCr1		11 412
	6	Philadelphia	W	1-0	MLS	Danso [72]	18 627
	14	Seattle	D	1-1	MLS	Danso [66]	36 593
	21	Columbus	W	1-0	MLS	Brunner [46]	18 627
	29	DC United	L	2-3	MLS	Jewsbury [68p], Perlaza [89]	18 627
Jun	4	Chivas	L	0-1	MLS		14 076
	11	Colorado	L	0-1	MLS		18 627
	19	New York	D	3-3	MLS	Jewsbury [48], Goldthwaite [49], OG [67]	18 627
	25	Dallas	L	0-4	MLS		10 470
Jul	2	Kansas City	L	1-2	MLS	Nagbe [45]	18 627
	10	Seattle	L	2-3	MLS	OG [46], Perlaza [69]	18 627
	16	Chicago	W	1-0	MLS	Jewsbury [24p]	16 419
	23	Columbus	L	0-1	MLS		11 246
	30	Toronto	D	2-2	MLS	Johnson [22], Jewsbury [57p]	18 627
	3	LA Galaxy	W	3-0	MLS	Chabala [27], Perlaza [34], Brunner [68]	18 627
	6	San Jose	D	1-1	MLS	Cooper [23]	10 525
Aug	14	Houston	L	1-2	MLS	Jewsbury [56]	14 475
	17	Kansas City	L	1-3	MLS	Dike [81]	15 271
	20	Vancouver	W	2-1	MLS	Chara [2], Perlaza [31]	18 627
	24	Chivas	W	1-0	MLS	Brunner [44]	18 627
	10	Philadelphia	D	0-0	MLS		18 504
Sep	16	NE Revs	W	3-0	MLS	Chara [10], Cooper [32], Nagbe [66]	20 323
	21	San Jose	D	1-1	MLS	Cooper [9]	18 627
	24	New York	L	0-2	MLS		25 008
	2	Vancouver	W	1-0	MLS	Cooper [25]	21 000
Oct	14	Houston	L	0-2	MLS		20 323
	19	DC United	D	1-1	MLS	Cooper [24]	14 317
	22	Salt Lake	D	1-1	MLS	Danso [91+]	20 378

12th • Att: 320 051 • Av: 18 827 • Jeld-Wen Field 20 323 (92%)

PHILADELPHIA MLS APPEARANCES/GOALS 2011

Goalkeepers Zac MacMath 7+1 • Faryd Mondragon COL 29
Defenders Danny Califf 35/1 • Jordan Harvey 16/0 • Carlos Valdes COL 34/1 • Sheanon Williams 34/1
Midfield Brian Carroll 32/1 • Keon Daniel TRI 9+9/1 • Gabriel Farfan 20+4/1 • Michael Farfan 15+8/2 • Morgan Langley 0+1/0 • Justin Mapp 25+6/3 • Stefani Miglioranzi BRA 12+6/0 • Kyle Nakazawa 14+8/1 • Amobi Okugo 10+5/0 • Zach Pfeffer 2+1/0 • Roger Torres COL 9+18/3
Forwards Freddy Adu 6+7/2 • Sebastien Le Toux FRA 36/12 • Jack McInerney 6+14/1 • Danny Mwanga COD 15+15/5 • Veljko Paunovic SRB 17+1/3 • Carlos Ruiz GUA 13+1/6
Coach Piotr Nowak POL

PORTLAND MLS APPEARANCES/GOALS 2011

Goalkeepers Adin Brown 2 • Jake Gleeson NZL 3+1 • Troy Perkins 29
Defenders Eric Brunner 31+1/3 • Mike Chabala 13+1/1 • Mamadou Danso GAM 23+1/3 • Kerrea Gilbert ENG • Kevin Goldthwaite 3+1/1 • David Horst 11+5/0 • Steve Purdy 8/0
Midfield Eric Alexander 3+3/0 • Kalif Alhassan GHA 27+5/0 • Diego Chara COL 27+1/2 • Jeremy Hall 17/0 • Jack Jewsbury 31/7 • James Marcelin HAI 12+8/0 • Adam Moffat SCO 0+4/0 • Darlington Nagbe 21+7/2 • Lovel Palmer JAM 15/0 • Ryan Pore 2+6/0 • Rodney Wallace CRC 22+3/2 • Sal Zizzo 14+16/0
Forwards Kenny Cooper 29+5/8 • Chinedu Dike 0+11/1 • Eddie Johnson ENG 3+4/1 • Peter Lowry 2+1/0 • Jorge Perlaza COL 26+5/6 • Brian Umony UGA 0+6/0
Coach John Spencer SCO (10/08/10)

REAL SALT LAKE 2011

	Date	Opponent		Score	Comp	Scorers	Att
Fb	22	Columbus	D	0-0	CLqf		4 500
	1	Columbus	W	4-1	CLqf	Saborio 23, Morales 2 36 78, Williams 90	15 405
Mar	15	Saprissa	W	2-0	CLsf	Saborio 9, Espindola 57	16 668
	19	San Jose	W	1-0	MLS	Beckerman 63	10 525
	26	LA Galaxy	W	4-1	MLS	Williams 2, Morales 2 10p 41, Paulo Araujo 68	20 507
	5	Saprissa	L	1-2	CLsf	Olave 60	21 065
	9	NE Revs	W	2-0	MLS	Schuler 27, Paulo Araujo 48	7 970
	13	Colorado	W	1-0	MLS	Espindola 93+	15 513
Apr	20	Monterrey	D	2-2	CLf	Borchers 35, Morales 89	30 247
	27	Monterrey	L	0-1	CLf		20 378
	30	Portland	L	0-1	MLS		18 627
	7	Chivas	W	1-0	MLS	Johnson 87	**14 365**
May	14	Houston	D	0-0	MLS		16 301
	22	Dallas	D	0-0	MLS		10 550
	28	Seattle	L	1-2	MLS	Gonzalez 87	14 674
	4	Vancouver	W	2-0	MLS	Alexandre 32, Espindola 79	15 174
	8	Columbus	L	1-2	MLS	Olave 7	9 650
	11	Philadelphia	D	1-1	MLS	Espindola 52	18 728
Jun	18	DC United	D	1-1	MLS	Espindola 38p	16 841
	22	Chicago	D	0-0	MLS		14 972
	25	Toronto	W	3-1	MLS	Borchers 39, Saborio 2 42 60	15 077
	28	Wilmington	W	2-0	OCr3	Beltran 40, Alexandre 44	7 620
	4	NE Revs	D	3-3	MLS	Johnson 24, Saborio 56p, Espindola 83	16 139
	9	Dallas	W	2-0	MLS	Williams 47, Espindola 94+	17 734
Jul	12	Dallas	L	0-2	OCqf		3 189
	23	San Jose	W	4-0	MLS	Saborio 2 63p 75, Beckerman 78, Olave 83	19 429
	30	Columbus	L	0-2	MLS		18 516
	3	Kansas City	L	0-2	MLS		18 467
	6	New York	W	3-0	MLS	Borchers 14, Gil 44, Saborio 77p	19 081
Aug	13	Toronto	L	0-1	MLS		21 644
	20	Houston	L	2-3	MLS	Espindola 28, Gil 59	16 247
	27	Chivas	W	1-0	MLS	Saborio 11	14 127
	3	Philadelphia	W	2-1	MLS	Beckerman 18, Schuler 26	18 720
	10	Seattle	W	2-0	MLS	OG 13, Saborio 56	35 940
Sep	17	Kansas City	W	1-0	MLS	Borchers 55	19 888
	21	New York	W	3-1	MLS	Saborio 7, Espindola 2 11 21	14 266
	24	DC United	L	1-4	MLS	Saborio 85	16 367
	28	Chicago	L	0-3	MLS		**20 762**
	1	LA Galaxy	L	1-2	MLS	Espindola 45	27 000
	6	Vancouver	L	0-3	MLS		20 113
Oct	14	Colorado	D	0-0	MLS		16 272
	22	Portland	D	1-1	MLS	Saborio 44	20 378
	29	Seattle	W	3-0	POqf	Saborio 2 41 53, Grabavoy 88	17 067
Nov	2	Seattle	L	0-2	POqf		36 021
	6	LA Galaxy	L	1-3	POsf	Saborio 23	23 437

3rd/SF Att: 299 099 • Av: 17 594 (+16.6%) • Rio Tinto 20 008 (87%)

SAN JOSE EARTHQUAKES 2011

	Date	Opponent		Score	Comp	Scorers	Att
Mar	19	Salt Lake	L	0-1	MLS		10 525
	26	Dallas	W	2-0	MLS	Wondolowski 2 6 24	11 022
	2	Seattle	D	2-2	MLS	Dawkins 32, Stephenson 52	10 276
	9	Toronto	D	1-1	MLS	Dawkins 38	8 928
Apr	16	New York	L	0-3	MLS		14 308
	23	Chivas	L	1-2	MLS	Wondolowski 16	10 525
	30	Philadelphia	L	0-1	MLS		18 279
	3	Portland	W	1-0	OCr1	Opara 120	11 412
	11	Vancouver	D	1-1	MLS	Wondolowski 38	15 608
May	12	Columbus	W	3-0	MLS	Wondolowski 50, Lenhart 59, Stephenson 62	9 142
	21	NE Revs	W	2-1	MLS	McLoughlin 71, Convey 83	9 736
	24	Chicago	D	2-2	OCr2	McLoughlin 14, Morrow 43	4 124
	28	Chicago	D	2-2	MLS	Corrales 50, Wondolowski 74	11 926
	4	Houston	W	2-0	MLS	Lenhart 69, Dawkins 71+	9 270
Jun	11	DC United	W	4-2	MLS	Lenhart 3 15 22 59, Dawkins 49	14 105
	17	Kansas City	L	0-1	MLS		18 467
	25	LA Galaxy	D	0-0	MLS		**10 872**
	2	New York	D	2-2	MLS	Stephenson 37, Lenhart 68 †	41 028
	6	Chivas	L	1-2	MLS		9 425
	9	Philadelphia	D	0-0	MLS		9 794
Jul	16	Columbus	D	0-0	MLS		14 109
	20	Vancouver	D	2-2	MLS	Wondolowski 2 3 54	**8 122**
	23	Salt Lake	L	0-4	MLS		19 429
	30	DC United	L	0-2	MLS		10 525
	6	Portland	D	1-1	MLS	Gordon 67	10 525
Aug	13	Colorado	L	1-2	MLS	Gjertsen 22	10 525
	20	LA Galaxy	L	0-2	MLS		27 000
	27	Toronto	D	1-1	MLS	Wondolowski 87	21 117
	10	Chicago	W	2-0	MLS	Wondolowski 10, Corrales 69	10 525
Sep	17	Houston	L	1-2	MLS	Stephenson 40	18 129
	21	Portland	D	1-1	MLS	Stephenson 70	18 627
	24	Colorado	D	1-1	MLS	Wondolowski 18	17 877
	1	Kansas City	D	1-1	MLS	Wondolowski 85	10 525
	8	NE Revs	W	2-1	MLS	Wondolowski 2 8 82	9 111
Oct	15	Seattle	L	1-2	MLS	Wondolowski 25	64 140
	22	Dallas	W	4-2	MLS	Dawkins 2 26 38, Baca 28, Wondolowski 34p	10 744

14th Att: 201 587 • Av: 11 858 (+39.1%) • Buck Shaw 10 525 (92%)

† Played at Stanford Stadium, San Francisco

SALT LAKE MLS APPEARANCES/GOALS 2011
Goalkeepers Kyle Reynish 1 • Nick Rimando 36
Defenders Tony Beltran 20+4/0 • Rauwshan McKenzie 2/0 • Jamison Olave COL 26/2 • Robbie Russell 25+4/0 • Chris Schuler 18+4/2 Dlakc Wagner 1+1/0 • Chris Wingert 25+1/0
Midfield Jean Alexandre HAI 9+10/1 • Yordany Alvarez 4/0 • Kyle Beckerman 30+2/3 • Nat Borchers 31/3 • Luis Gil 14+13/2 • Nelson Gonzalez ARG 2+4/1 • Ned Grabavoy 21+7/1 • Javi Morales ARG 12/2 Paulo Araujo BRA 5+6/2 • Collen Warner 15+8/0 Andy Williams JAM 23+11/2
Forwards Artur Aghasyan ARM 1+3/0 • Chris Agorsor 0+1/0 • Arturo Alvarez SLV 8+8/0 • Cody Arnoux 0+2/0 • Fabian Espindola ARG 28+2/10 Will Johnson CAN 25+3/2 • Alvaro Saborio CRC 25+1/14
Coach Jason Kreis

SAN JOSE MLS APPEARANCES/GOALS 2011
Goalkeepers David Bingham 1 • Jon Busch 33
Defenders Nana Attakora-Gyan CAN 5+1/0 • Bobby Burling 23/0 Ramiro Corrales 29/2 • Victor Cortez • Jason Hernandez 28/0 • Chris Leitch 12+2/0 • Justin Morrow 9/0 • Ike Opara 5+3/0 • Tim Ward 2+1/0
Midfield Anthony Ampaipitakwong 5+7/0 • Rafael Baca 11+4/1 • Steve Beitashour 19/0 • Bobby Convey 19+2/1 • Sam Cronin 22+5/0 • Omar Jasseh GAM 0+1/0 • Brandon McDonald 8+3/0 • Jacob Peterson 5+4/0 Brad Ring 17+4/0 • Khari Stephenson JAM 27+4/5
Forwards Simon Dawkins ENG 19+7/6 • Joey Gjertsen 13+5/1 Alan Gordon 1+1/1 • Maxwell Griffin 0+4/0 • Ryan Johnson JAM 12+2/0 Steven Lenhart 13+1/6 • Matthew Luzunaris 0+6/0 • Ellis McLoughlin 0+10/1 • Scott Sealy TRI 6+5/0 • Chris Wondolowski 30/16 Edmundo Zura ECU 0+1/0
Coach Frank Yallop CAN

SEATTLE SOUNDERS 2011

Mo	#	Opponent	Res	Comp	Scorers	Att
Mar	15	LA Galaxy	L 0-1	MLS		36 443
	19	New York	L 0-1	MLS		20 982
	26	Houston	D 1-1	MLS	Zakuani 80	36 204
Apr	2	San Jose	D 2-2	MLS	Evans 17, White 42	10 276
	9	Chicago	W 2-1	MLS	White 7, Zakuani 24	36 223
	16	Philadelphia	D 1-1	MLS	Fernandez 91+	15 149
	22	Colorado	W 1-0	MLS	Montero 19	14 185
	30	Toronto	W 3-0	MLS	Fernandez 9, Evans 2 52 75p	36 287
May	4	DC United	L 1-2	MLS	Evans 70p	11 254
	7	Columbus	D 1-1	MLS	Montero 7	7 148
	14	Portland	D 1-1	MLS	Fernandez 53	36 593
	21	Kansas City	W 1-0	MLS	Parke 90	36 098
	25	Dallas	L 0-1	MLS		36 026
	28	Salt Lake	W 2-1	MLS	Ianni 71, Neagle 83	14 674
Jun	4	Chicago	D 0-0	MLS		13 839
	11	Vancouver	D 2-2	MLS	Rosales 82, Alonso 84	36 502
	18	Toronto	W 1-0	MLS	Montero 89	21 839
	23	New York	W 4-2	MLS	Friberg 10, Alonso 12, Levesque 2 67 78	46 065
	26	NE Revs	W 2-1	MLS	Wahl 34, Fernandez 40	36 212
	28	Kitsap	W 2-1	OCr3	Fucito 2 39 62	3 811
Jul	4	LA Galaxy	D 0-0	MLS		27 000
	10	Portland	W 3-2	MLS	Montero 2 57 74, Alonso 82p	18 627
	13	LA Galaxy	W 3-1	OCqf	Jaqua 4, Montero 25, Neagle 74	4 322
	16	Colorado	W 4-3	MLS	Fernandez 6, Levesque 47, Montero 82, Rosales 83	36 424
	26	S Francisco	L 0-1	CLpr		700
	30	Houston	L 1-3	MLS	Fernandez 37p	18 465
Aug	3	S Francisco	W 2-0	CLpr	Fernandez 41, Jaqua 98	21 233
	6	Kansas City	W 2-1	MLS	Rosales 90, Neagle 92+	17 493
	13	Chivas	D 0-0	MLS		36 364
	16	Com'ciones	W 4-1	CLgD	Evans 34, Fucito 2 60 66, OG 86	10 017
	20	Dallas	W 1-0	MLS	Rosales 16	11 635
	23	Monterrey	W 1-0	CLgD	Fernandez 38	10 234
	27	Columbus	W 6-2	MLS	Neagle 3 4 21 70, Rosales 16p, Fucito 40, OG 74	36 364
	30	Dallas	W 1-0	OCsf	Montero 40	4 593
Sep	10	Salt Lake	L 1-2	MLS	Montero 45	35 940
	14	Herediano	W 2-1	CLgD	Montero 2 3 54	514
	17	DC United	W 3-0	MLS	Fucito 35, Fernandez 2 45 60	36 242
	20	Herediano	L 0-1	CLgD		10 163
	24	Vancouver	W 3-1	MLS	Evans 33p, Montero 2 63 66	21 000
	27	Com'ciones	D 2-2	CLgD	Alonso 2 44 88	4 500
Oct	1	NE Revs	W 2-1	MLS	Montero 2 36 47	21 022
	4	Chicago	W 2-0	OCf	Montero 77, Alonso 96+	35 615
	8	Philadelphia	L 0-2	MLS		36 364
	15	San Jose	W 2-1	MLS	Ochoa 81, Montero 86	64 140
	18	Monterrey	L 1-2	CLgD	Montero 42	15 866
	22	Chivas	W 3-1	MLS	OG 53, Fernandez 68, Ochoa 73	22 137
	30	Salt Lake	L 0-3	POqf		17 067
No	29	Salt Lake	W 2-0	POqf	Alonso 55, Neagle 61	36 021

2nd   Att: 654 431 • Av: 38 496 (+20.6%) • CenturyLink 36 700 (98%)

SPORTING KANSAS CITY 2011

Mo	#	Opponent	Res	Comp	Scorers	Att
Mar	19	Chivas	W 3-2	MLS	Sassano 2, Bravo 2 45 74	18 122
	26	Chicago	L 2-3	MLS	Besler 51, Bunbury 72	12 157
	2	Vancouver	D 3-3	MLS	Bunbury 2 45 57, Kamara 62	20 518
	6	Houston	W 1-0	OCr1	Sapong 92	2 383
Apr	16	Columbus	L 0-1	MLS		7 695
	23	NE Revs	L 2-3	MLS	Kamara 2 13 69p	11 414
	30	New York	L 0-1	MLS		20 636
	14	LA Galaxy	L 1-4	MLS	OG 39	19 763
	21	Seattle	L 0-1	MLS		36 098
May	25	NE Revs	W 5-0	OCr2	Myers 2 9 19, Sapong 2 24 88, Collin 81	1 228
	28	Colorado	D 1-1	MLS	Smith 75	16 439
	4	Toronto	D 0-0	MLS		19 962
	9	Chicago	D 0-0	MLS		19 925
Jun	12	Dallas	W 4-1	MLS	Zusi 2 27 54, Collin 49, Sassano 77	10 450
	17	San Jose	W 1-0	MLS	Sapong 31	18 467
	22	Philadelphia	D 0-0	MLS		18 127
	25	Vancouver	W 2-1	MLS	Bravo 33p, Julio Cesar 40	18 467
	28	Chicago-2	W 3-0	OCr3	Bunbury 3, Stojcev 58, Kamara 59	4 487
	2	Portland	W 2-1	MLS	Sapong 14, Collin 19	18 627
	6	Colorado	D 1-1	MLS	Zusi 62	15 209
	9	Chivas	D 1-1	MLS	Bravo 93+	18 467
Jul	12	Richmond	L 0-1	OCqf		4 794
	16	Houston	D 1-1	MLS	Collin 90	12 047
	23	Toronto	W 4-2	MLS	Kamara 2 28 33, Bravo 2 37 64	16 382
	30	NE Revs	D 1-1	MLS	Bunbury 89	17 418
	3	Salt Lake	W 2-0	MLS	Espinoza 30, Bunbury 35	18 467
Aug	6	Seattle	L 1-2	MLS	Kamara 20	17 493
	17	Portland	W 3-1	MLS	Zusi 2 25 41, Saad 73	15 271
	21	DC United	W 1-0	MLS	Kamara 20	15 352
	27	Dallas	L 2-3	MLS	Kamara 22, Bravo 67	20 018
	5	LA Galaxy	D 2-2	MLS	Julio Cesar 72, Bravo 92+p	20 512
	10	Houston	W 3-0	MLS	Bunbury 2 9 73, Sapong 79	14 791
Sep	17	Salt Lake	L 0-1	MLS		19 888
	23	Philadelphia	D 1-1	MLS	Bravo 56	18 778
	28	Columbus	W 2-1	MLS	Kamara 14p, OG 74	17 838
	1	San Jose	D 1-1	MLS	Bunbury 86	10 525
Oct	15	New York	W 2-0	MLS	Bunbury 57, Sapong 74	19 921
	22	DC United	W 1-0	MLS	Besler 55	15 965
	30	Colorado	W 2-0	POqf	Bunbury 2 49 59	8 601
Nov	2	Colorado	W 2-0	POqf	Collin 29, Sapong 76	18 565
	6	Houston	L 0-2	POsf		20 839

5th/SF   Att: 302 776 • Av: 17 810 (+96.2%) • Livestrong 18 467 (96%)

SEATTLE MLS APPEARANCES/GOALS 2011

Goalkeepers Kasey Keller 36
Defenders Leonardo Gonzalez CRC 14+2/0 • Jhon Hurtado COL 25/0 • Patrick Ianni 12+4/1 • Jeff Parke 30/1 • James Riley 31/0 • Tyson Wahl 22+1/0
Midfield Osvaldo Alonso CUB 34+1/3 • Servando Carrasco 7+5/0 • Alvaro Fernandez URU 25+6/9 • Erik Friberg SWE 24+4/1 • Michael Fucito 14+7/2 • Lamar Neagle 10+15/6 • Zach Scott 10+3/0 • Amadou Sanyang GAM 0+1/0 • Steve Zakuani COD 6/2
Forwards David Estrada MEX 1+2/0 • Brad Evans 19+3/5 • Nate Jaqua 7+16/0 • Roger Levesque 9+12/3 • Miguel Montano COL 0+2/0 • Fredy Montero COL 29+3/12 • Pat Noonan 2+7/0 • Samuel Ochoa MEX 1+5/2 • Mauro Rosales ARG 22+4/5 • O'Brian White JAM 7/2
Coach Sigi Schmid

KANSAS MLS APPEARANCES/GOALS 2011

Goalkeepers Eric Kronberg 3+1 • Jimmy Nielsen DEN 34
Defenders Olukorede Aiyegbusi ENG 1+2/0 • Matt Besler 35/2 • Aurelien Collin FRA 24+2/4 • Daneil Cyrus TRI 1+1/0 • Michael Harrington 16+6/0 • Julio Cesar BRA 28+2/2 • Scott Lorenz 1/0 • Chance Myers 27+4/0 • Luke Sassano 5+4/2 • Seth Sinovic 23/0 • Shavar Thomas JAM 0+3/0
Midfield Davy Arnaud 16+9/0 • Stephane Auvray FRA 3+3/0 • Birahim Diop SEN 8+11/0 • Roger Espinoza HON 27/1• Jeferson BRA 8+3/0 • Peterson Joseph HAI 0+1/0 • Lawrence Olum 0+1/0 • Craig Rocastle GRN 5+1/0 • Ryan Smith ENG 2+4/1 • Milos Stojcev MNE 11+1/0 • Graham Zusi 28+7/5
Forwards Omar Bravo MEX 26+2/9 • Teal Bunbury 23+9/11 • Kei Kamara SLE 27+6/9 • Soony Saad 0+6/1 • C.J. Sapong 25+12/4
Coach Peter Vermes

TORONTO FC 2011

	Date	Opponent		Score	Comp	Scorers	Att
Mar	19	Vancouver	L	2-4	MLS	De Rosario 20, Maicon 74	22 592
	26	Portland	W	2-0	MLS	Martina 2 14 71	20 086
	2	Chivas	D	1-1	MLS	Gordon 37	18 968
	9	San Jose	D	1-1	MLS	Gordon 27	8 928
	13	LA Galaxy	D	0-0	MLS		22 453
Apr	16	DC United	L	0-3	MLS		16 313
	23	Columbus	D	1-1	MLS	Tchani 41	20 145
	27	Edmonton	W	3-0	CCsf	Santos 2 35 61, Gordon 47	5 781
	30	Seattle	L	0-3	MLS		36 287
	4	Edmonton	W	1-0	CCsf	Gordon 21	17 937
	7	Houston	W	2-1	MLS	Joao Plata 49p, Maicon 81	20 259
	11	Dallas	L	0-1	MLS		8 145
May	14	Chicago	D	2-2	MLS	Joao Plata 9, Maicon 46	18 674
	18	Vancouver	D	1-1	CCf	Santos 73	15 474
	22	Colorado	D	0-0	MLS		13 598
	28	Philadelphia	L	2-6	MLS	Maicon 2 50 59	20 122
	4	Kansas City	D	0-0	MLS		19 962
	11	LA Galaxy	D	2-2	MLS	Gordon 2 68 94+	20 675
	15	NE Revs	D	0-0	MLS		6 680
Jun	18	Seattle	L	0-1	MLS		21 839
	25	Salt Lake	L	1-3	MLS	Maicon 66	15 077
	29	Vancouver	W	1-0	MLS	Soolsma 53p	19 816
	2	Vancouver	W	2-1	CCf	Plata 51p, Yourassowsky 61	18 212
	6	New York	L	0-5	MLS		15 269
	9	Houston	L	0-1	MLS		19 085
Jul	20	Dallas	L	0-1	MLS		21 087
	23	Kansas City	L	2-4	MLS	Koevermans 50, Johnson 72	16 382
	27	Real Esteli	W	2-1	CLpr	Plata 2 56 71	9 241
	30	Portland	D	2-2	MLS	Marosevic 71, Koevermans 81	18 627
	2	Real Esteli	W	2-1	CLpr	Johnson 2 37 47	4 500
	6	DC United	D	3-3	MLS	Marosevic 53, De Guzman 70, Koevermans 85	11 684
Aug	13	Salt Lake	W	1-0	MLS	Joao Plata 77	21 644
	18	Tauro	W	2-1	CLgC	Johnson 22, Deguzman 24	1 905
	21	Chicago	L	0-2	MLS		12 020
	25	Dallas	L	0-1	CLgC		500
	27	San Jose	D	1-1	MLS	Avila 32	21 117
	10	Columbus	W	4-2	MLS	Soolsma 21, Johnson 42, De Guzman 83, Koevermans 90	13 058
Sep	14	UNAM	L	0-4	CLgC		3 382
	17	Colorado	W	2-1	MLS	Koevermans 2 52 60	20 318
	20	Tauro	W	1-0	CLgC	Koevermans 41	10 132
	24	Chivas	L	0-3	MLS		14 357
	27	UNAM	D	1-1	CLgC	Marosevic 35	9 115
	1	New York	D	1-1	MLS	Koevermans 50	20 132
Oct	15	Philadelphia	D	1-1	MLS	Johnson 57	19 178
	18	Dallas	W	3-0	CLgC	Koevermans 28, Plata 2 68 80	2 578
	22	NE Revs	D	2-2	MLS	Soolsma 19, Koevermans 84	21 600

16th Att: 344 535 • Av: 20 267 (+12.3%) • BMO Field 23 000 (88%)

VANCOUVER WHITECAPS 2011

	Date	Opponent		Score	Comp	Scorers	Att
Mar	19	Toronto	W	4-2	MLS	Hassli 2 15 72, Dunfield 26, Harris 63	22 592
	26	Philadelphia	L	0-1	MLS		18 591
Apr	2	Kansas City	D	3-3	MLS	Harris 72, Camilo 2 92+ 93+	20 518
	6	NE Revs	D	1-1	MLS	Hassli 56p	19 396
	10	Houston	L	1-3	MLS	Camilo 38	12 047
	16	Chivas	D	0-0	MLS		20 809
	23	Dallas	L	1-2	MLS	Rochat 25	21 000
	27	Montreal	W	1-0	CCsf	Dunfield 67	8 412
	30	Columbus	L	1-2	MLS	Salgado 69	11 298
	4	Montreal	D	1-1	CCsf	Akloul 113	16 611
May	7	Chicago	D	0-0	MLS		11 680
	11	San Jose	D	1-1	MLS	Chiumiento 91+	15 608
	14	NE Revs	L	0-1	MLS		14 186
	18	Toronto	D	1-1	CCf	Hassli 64	15 474
	28	New York	L	1-1	MLS	Hassli 23p	21 000
	1	Chivas	D	1-1	MLS	Camilo 48	11 753
	4	Salt Lake	L	0-2	MLS		15 174
Jun	11	Seattle	D	2-2	MLS	Hassli 2 29p 86	36 502
	18	Philadelphia	W	1-0	MLS	Rochat 13	20 168
	25	Kansas City	L	1-2	MLS	Camilo 15	18 467
	29	Toronto	L	0-1	MLS		19 816
	2	Toronto	L	1-2	CCf	Camilo 21	18 212
	6	Columbus	D	0-1	MLS		19 079
Jul	9	Colorado	L	1-2	MLS	Camilo 77	13 058
	20	San Jose	D	2-2	MLS	Hassli 2 42 61	8 122
	30	LA Galaxy	L	0-4	MLS		27 500
	7	Chicago	W	4-2	MLS	Hassli 2 1 72, Koffie 23, Camilo 48	18 714
Aug	13	DC United	L	0-4	MLS		11 738
	20	Portland	L	1-2	MLS	Camilo 88	18 627
	27	Houston	W	1-0	MLS	Salinas 86	20 226
	10	New York	D	1-1	MLS	Chiumiento 23	19 684
Sep	17	LA Galaxy	L	0-3	MLS		22 959
	24	Seattle	L	1-3	MLS	Camilo 22	21 000
	2	Portland	L	0-1	MLS		21 000
	6	Salt Lake	W	3-0	MLS	Camilo 2 44p 52p	20 013
Oct	12	DC United	W	2-1	MLS	Camilo 1, Long Tan 46	17 288
	15	Dallas	L	0-2	MLS		10 222
	22	Colorado	L	1-2	MLS	Rochat 49	21 000

18th Att: 347 011 • Av: 20 412 • Empire Field 27 528 (77%)

At the start of October 2011 Vancouver moved to BC Place 22 000

TORONTO MLS APPEARANCES/GOALS 2011

Goalkeepers Stefan Frei SUI 27 • Milos Kocic SRB 7+1
Defenders Nana Attakora-Gyan 4+2/0 • Adrian Cann 12/0 • Kyle Davies USA 0+1/0 • Richard Eckersley ENG 22+1/0 • Ty Harden USA 24+2/0 • Doneil Henry 6+4/0 • Andy Iro ENG 13/0 • Ashtone Morgan 9+5/0 • Dementrius Omphroy USA 0+1/0 • Eddy Viator FRA 2+1/0 • Dicoy Williams JAM 7+1/0 • Mikael Yourassowsky BEL 13+8/0
Midfield Eric Avila USA 8+1/1 • Danleigh Borman RSA 18+4/0 • Oscar Cordon 0+3/0 • Terry Dunfield 2+4/0 • Torsten Frings GER 13/0 • Julian de Guzman 16+3/2 • Dan Gargan USA 12+4/0 • Matt Gold 0+3/0 • Jacob Peterson USA 13/0 • Matthew Stinson 5+8/0 • Nathan Sturgis USA 11+3/0 • Tony Tchani CMR 13/1 • Gianluca Zavarise 4+10/0
Forwards Dwayne De Rosario 2/1 • Alan Gordon USA 8+1/4 • Ryan Johnson JAM 12/3 • Danny Koevermans NED 9+1/8 • Maicon BRA 15+4/6 • Keith Makubuya 0+1/0 • Peri Marosevic USA 4+3/2 • Javier Martina CUW 15+8/2 • Joao Plata ECU 21+5/3 • Nick Soolsma NED 18+5/3
Coach Aron Winter NED (6/01/11)

VANCOUVER MLS APPEARANCES/GOALS 2011

Goalkeepers Joe Cannon USA 20 • Jay Nolly USA 14
Defenders Mouloud Akloul FRA 7+1/0 • Michael Boxall NZL 18+1/0 • Jay DeMerit USA 20+1/0 • Bilal Duckett USA 2+2/0 • Jordan Harvey USA 14+4/0 • Greg Janicki USA 8+1/0 • Jonathan Leathers USA 21+1/0 • Carlyle Mitchell TRI 3/0 • Alexander Morfaw CMR 1+1/0 • Alain Rochat SUI 27+1/3 • Blake Wagner USA 9/0
Midfield Davide Chiumiento SUI 20+6/2 • Terry Dunfield 11+1/1 • Kevin Harmse 1+2/0 • Nizar Khalfan TAN 9+12/1 • Wesley Knight USA 10+2/0 • Gershon Koffie GHA 28+2/1 • Michael Nanchoff USA 1+4/0 • Shea Salinas USA 18+8/1 • Long Tan CHN 4+9/1 • Russell Teibert 5+6/0 • John Thorrington USA 9+2/0 • Peter Vagenas USA 13+3/0
Forwards Jeb Brovsky USA 16+8/0 • Camilo BRA 29+3/12 • Atiba Harris SKN 5/2 • Eric Hassli FRA 21+5/10 • Mustapha Jarju GAM 5+5/0 • Omar Salgado USA 5+9/1
Coach Teitur Thordarson ISL • Tom Soehn (29/05/11)

UZB – UZBEKISTAN

FIFA/COCA-COLA WORLD RANKING

'93	'94	'95	'96	'97	'98	'99	'00	'01	'02	'03	'04	'05	'06	'07	'08	'09	'10	'11	'12
-	78	97	109	79	66	55	71	62	98	81	47	59	45	64	72	76	109	75	

2011															
Jan	Feb	Mar	Apr	May	Jun	Jul	Aug	Sep	Oct	Nov	Dec		High	Low	Av
108	77	76	83	83	85	83	82	79	73	76	75		45	119	76

Since independence in the 1990s Uzbekistan has seen football in the country dominated by three clubs - Neftchi Fergana, Pakhtakor Tashkent and Bunyodkor. It was with some surprise therefore that the first continental title claimed by an Uzbeki club was won by Nasaf from the southern city of Karshi. Before beating Al Kuwait in the 2011 AFC Cup final, Nasaf had never won a trophy at home let alone abroad and were inspired to their triumph by the attacking exploits of the tournament's Most Valuable Player, Arthur Gevorkyan from Turkmenistan, and Ivan Boskovic, the competition's top scorer. Domestic giants Bunyodkor retained their league crown despite lacking the financial might that had previously taken them to the summit of the Uzbek game. Pakhtakor, meanwhile, won the Uzbekistan Cup, defeating Nasaf in the final. Uzbekistan's national team impressed in qualifying for the FIFA World Cup finals as Vadim Abramov's team built on their semi-final run at the AFC Asian Cup in Qatar in 2011. The Uzbeks progressed to the final phase as winners of their group, dropping just two points in a draw in Tashkent against Asian champions Japan. Having been assured of qualification, a ploy by five players to get booked and serve out a suspension in the last match before the next stage backfired when they received increased bans from FIFA.

FIFA WORLD CUP RECORD
1930-1994 DNE 1998-2010 DNQ

UZBEKISTAN FOOTBALL FEDERATION (UFF)

O'zbekiston Futbol Federatsiyasi, Uzbekistanskaya 98/A, Tashkent 100 011

☎ +998 71 2441684
✉ +998 71 2441683
✉ info@the-uff.com
🖥 www.the-uff.com

FA 1946 CON 1994 FIFA 1994
P Mirabror Usmanov
GS Sardor Rakhmatullaev

FIFA BIG COUNT 2006

Total players	730 200
% of population	2.67%
Male	692 500
Female	37 700
Amateurs 18+	4 460
Unregistered	470 300
Professionals	1 580
Referees	350
Admin & coaches	975
Number of clubs	216
Number of teams	24 000

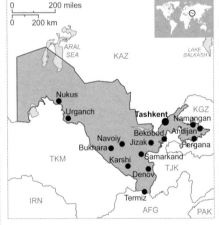

MAJOR CITIES/TOWNS

		Population
1	Tashkent	2 130 904
2	Namangan	434 388
3	Andijan	370 833
4	Samarkand	349 613
5	Nukus	241 652
6	Karshi	232 654
7	Bukhara	232 574
8	Kukon	207 664
9	Fergana	169 403
10	Margilan	166 868
11	Navoiy	160 302
12	Jizak	149 055
13	Termiz	145 070
14	Urganch	142 347
15	Chirchik	127 966
16	Angren	123 190
17	Olmalik	108 887
18	Denov	108 127
19	Khujayli	107 338

OZBEKISTON RESPUBLIKASI • REPUBLIC OF UZBEKISTAN

Capital	Tashkent	Population	27 606 007 (44)	% in cities	%
GDP per capita	$2600 (171)	Area km²	447 400 km² (56)	GMT +/-	+5
Neighbours (km)	Afghanistan 137, Kazakhstan 2203, Kyrgyzstan 1099, Tajikistan 1161, Turkmenistan 1621				

RECENT INTERNATIONAL MATCHES PLAYED BY UZBEKISTAN

2008	Opponents	Score		Venue	Comp	Scorers	Att	Referee
20-08	Oman	L	0-2	Muscat	Fr		1 000	
29-08	Korea DPR	D	0-0	Tashkent	Fr			Saidov UZB
6-09	Qatar	L	0-3	Doha	WCq		8 000	Mohd Salleh MAS
10-09	Australia	L	0-1	Tashkent	WCq		34 000	Al Fadhli KUW
11-10	Korea Republic	L	0-3	Suwon	Fr		21 194	
15-10	Japan	D	1-1	Saitama	WCq	Shatskikh [27]	55 142	Albadwawi UAE
2009								
28-01	UAE	W	1-0	Sharjah	ACq	Farhod Tadjiyev [30]	15 000	Nishimura JPN
1-02	Azerbaijan	D	1-1	Dubai	Fr	Kurbanov [80]		Ali Hamed UAE
11-02	Bahrain	L	0-1	Tashkent	WCq		30 000	Mohd Salleh MAS
28-03	Qatar	W	4-0	Tashkent	WCq	Farhod Tadjiev 3 [34 45 53], Soliev [62]	18 000	Moradi IRN
1-04	Australia	L	0-2	Sydney	WCq		57 292	Albadwawi UAE
1-06	Bosnia-Herzergovina	D	0-0	Tashkent	Fr		15 000	Kovalenko UZB
6-06	Japan	L	0-1	Tashkent	WCq		34 000	Basma SYR
17-06	Bahrain	L	0-1	Manama	WCq		14 100	Moradi IRN
5-09	Iran	D	0-0	Tashkent	Fr		9 500	Irmatov UZB
14-11	Malaysia	W	3-1	Tashkent	ACq	Djeparov [46], Geynrikh 2 [57 65]	5 000	Moradi IRN
18-11	Malaysia	W	3-1	Kuala Lumpur	ACq	Gafurov [32], Nasimov [58], Kapadze [73]	2 000	Tan Hai CHN
2010								
3-03	UAE	L	0-1	Tashkent	ACq		20 000	Shamsuzzaman BAN
25-05	Armenia	L	1-3	Yerevan	Fr	Geynrikh [70]	20 000	Kvaratskhelia GEO
11-08	Albania	L	0-1	Durres	Fr		8 000	Radovanovic MNE
7-09	Estonia	D	3-3	Tallinn	Fr	Shatskikh [40], Geynrikh [55], Salomov [86]	2 055	Jones WAL
9-10	Saudi Arabia	L	0-4	Jeddah	Fr			
12-10	Bahrain	W	4-2	Manama	Fr	Haydarov [5], Navkarov [12], Ahmedov [44], Shatskikh [45]		
25-12	Bahrain	D	1-1	Dubai	Fr	Geynrikh [15]		
2011								
2-01	Jordan	D	2-2	Sharjah	Fr	Hasanov [70], Navkarov [77]		
7-01	Qatar	W	2-0	Doha	ACr1	Ahmedov [59], Djeparov [77]	37 143	Nishimura JPN
12-01	Kuwait	W	2-1	Doha	ACr1	Shatskikh [41], Djeparov [65]	3 481	Shukralla BHR
16-01	China PR	D	2-2	Doha	ACr1	Ahmedov [30], Geynrikh [46]	3 529	Al Hilali OMA
21-01	Jordan	W	2-1	Doha	ACqf	Bakaev 2 [47 49]	16 073	Abdul Bashir SIN
25-01	Australia	L	0-6	Doha	ACsf		24 826	Albadwawi UAE
28-01	Korea Republic	L	2-3	Doha	AC3p	Geynrikh 2 [45p 53]	8 199	Abdul Bashir SIN
25-03	Montenegro	L	0-1	Podgorica	Fr		6 000	Glodovic SRB
1-06	Ukraine	L	0-2	Kyiv	Fr			Ozkahya TUR
5-06	China PR	L	0-1	Kuming	Fr		40 000	Ko Hyung Jin KOR
23-07	Kyrgyzstan	W	4-0	Tashkent	WCq	Geynrikh [28], Bikmaev [48], Djeparov [55], Bakaev [92+]	20 257	Balideh QAT
28-07	Kyrgyzstan	W	3-0	Bishkek	WCq	Karpenko [47], Nasimov 2 [65 90]	14 700	Abdulnabi BHR
2-09	Tajikistan	W	1-0	Tursunzade	WCq	Shatskikh [72]	15 000	Tan Hai CHN
6-09	Japan	D	1-1	Tashkent	WCq	Djeparov [8]	32 000	Al Ghamdi KSA
11-10	Korea DPR	W	1-0	Pyongyang	WCq	Geynrikh [26]	29 000	Faghani IRN
11-11	Korea DPR	W	1-0	Tashkent	WCq	Kapadze [48]	27 525	El Haddad LIB
15-11	Tajikistan	W	3-0	Tashkent	WCq	Tursunov [35], Ahmedov [60], Geynrikh [70]	5 325	Alzarooni UAE

Fr = Friendly match • AC = AFC Asian Cup • WC = FIFA World Cup
q = qualifier • po = play-off • r1 = first round group • qf = quarter-final • po = play-off

UZBEKISTAN NATIONAL TEAM HISTORICAL RECORDS

Caps
89 - Timur Kapadze 2002- • **80** - Server Djeparov 2002- • **68** - Alexander Geynrikh 2002- • **67** - Mirdjalal Kasimov 1992-2005 • **64** - Andrei Fedorov 1994-2006 & Ignaty Nesterov 2002- • **63** - Nikolai Shirshov 1996-2005 & Asror Alikulov 1999-2008 • **59** - Maksim Shatskikh 1999- • **58** - Victor Karpenko 2003- • **54** - Bahtiyor Ashurmatov 1997-2008 • **52** - Fevzi Davletov 1994-2005

Goals
34 - Maksim Shatskikh 1999- • **31** - Mirdjalal Kasimov 1992-2005 • **26** - Alexander Geynrikh 2002- • **20** - Igor Shkvyrin 1992-2000 • **17** - Server Djeparov 2002- • **15** - Jafar Irismetov 1997-2007 • **13** - Nikolai Shirshov 1996-2005

Past Coaches
Makhmud Rahimov 1999-2002 • Viktor Borisov 2000 • Pavel Sadyrin RUS 2000 • Yuri Sarkisyan 2000-04 • Hans-Jurgen Gede GER 2004 • Ravshan Haydarov 2004-05 • Bob Houghton ENG 2005 • Valeri Nepomniachi RUS 2006 • Rauf Inileyev 2007-08 • Mirdjalal Kasimov 2008-10 • Vadim Abramov 2010-

UZBEKISTAN 2011

O'ZBEKISTON CHEMPIONATI OLIY LIGA

	Pl	W	D	L	F	A	Pts	Bunyodkor	Nasaf	Pakhtakor	Neftchi	Mashal	Navbahor	Shurton	Metallurg	Bukhara	Samarkand	Olmalik	Andijan	Kizilgum	Sogdiana
Bunyodkor Tashkent †	26	19	4	3	51	14	61		2-1	2-1	1-0	2-0	1-0	2-0	3-1	3-0	2-0	4-1	3-1	3-1	1-0
Nasaf Karshi †	26	15	8	3	43	15	53	0-0		1-1	3-0	2-0	3-2	5-0	2-0	3-0	0-1	2-1	2-0	2-1	3-1
Pakhtakor Tashkent †	26	15	6	5	33	17	51	0-0	0-0		1-0	1-0	2-1	3-1	0-0	1-0	3-1	1-0	5-1	2-0	1-0
Neftchi Fergana †	26	13	5	8	36	27	44	0-0	1-1	4-1		2-1	1-1	0-0	3-1	2-0	1-0	4-1	3-0	1-0	2-1
Mashal Muborak	26	12	4	10	32	33	40	0-2	1-1	1-0	3-2		2-0	2-1	2-1	2-0	1-0	1-0	4-0	0-0	1-1
Navbahor Namangan	26	9	9	8	26	21	36	1-0	1-1	2-0	0-2	2-0		0-0	1-0	1-0	1-1	0-1	1-1	3-0	2-1
Shurton Guzor	26	9	5	12	29	41	32	1-0	2-1	0-2	4-0	1-4	1-0		2-3	1-1	2-0	2-0	0-0	1-0	3-2
Metallurg Bekobod	26	9	4	13	35	42	31	2-1	0-1	0-1	0-0	3-1	0-0	1-1		3-2	0-1	4-3	4-1	3-1	3-2
FK Bukhara	26	8	7	11	23	38	31	0-4	1-0	0-1	0-0	1-0	2-0	1-1	2-1		2-1	1-0	0-0	2-1	2-1
Samarkand Dinamo	26	8	5	13	23	25	29	0-1	0-1	0-0	2-0	2-0	0-1	3-0	3-1	0-1		0-1	3-1	1-1	2-0
Olmalik FK	26	8	5	13	37	45	29	1-3	0-0	0-1	2-1	2-2	0-3	2-0	4-1	6-1	1-1		2-1	2-1	2-2
FK Andijan	26	7	7	12	29	43	28	1-1	0-4	2-1	2-3	4-0	0-0	3-0	0-1	2-2	2-0	1-0		3-0	2-1
Kizilgum Zarafshon	26	6	6	14	23	40	24	1-3	0-1	0-3	2-1	0-1	0-0	3-2	2-1	0-0	2-1	3-3	2-0		0-0
Sogdiana Jizak	26	4	5	17	32	51	17	1-6	0-2	1-2	0-2	2-3	3-2	2-3	3-1	2-1	0-0	5-2	1-1	0-2	

5/03/2011 – 5/11/2011 • † Qualified for the AFC Champions League
Top scorers: 17 – Milos Trifunovic SRB, Bunyodkor • 16 – Muiddin Mamazulunov TJK, Olmalik • 11 – Lochinbek Soliyev, Andijan & Anvar Berdiyev, Neftchi • 10 – Igor Taran, Shurtan • 9 – Bahodir Pardayev, Sogdiana; Zafar Kholmurodov, Mashal & Shakhboz Erkinov, Shurtan

UZBEKISTAN 2011 BIRINCHI LIGA (2)

	Pl	W	D	L	F	A	Pts
Lokomotiv Tashkent	30	25	4	1	102	11	79
Guliston	30	19	8	3	56	21	65
Yangiyer	30	19	4	7	66	35	61
Erkurgan	30	19	3	8	63	43	60
Horezm Urganch	30	16	8	6	52	26	56
Osiyo Tashkent	30	14	6	10	52	35	48
Mashal Muborak-2	30	13	5	12	42	45	44
Imkon	30	12	4	14	39	50	40
Dinamo Gallakor	30	12	3	15	42	62	39
Jaykhun Nukus	30	11	4	15	35	42	37
Registan	30	10	2	18	40	48	32
Surhon Termiz	30	8	4	18	34	55	28
Bunyodkor Tashkent-2	30	7	6	17	28	46	27
Xiva	30	7	4	19	33	73	25
Kosonsoy Zakovat	30	7	3	20	22	71	24
Oqtepa	30	6	2	22	25	68	20

30/03/2011 – 30/10/2011

MEDALS TABLE

	Overall			League			Cup			Asia		
	G	S	B	G	S	B	G	S	B	G	S	B
1 Pakhtakor Tashkent	19	7	3	8	5	1	11	2				2
2 Neftchi Fergana	7	14	2	5	9	1	2	5				1
3 Bunyodkor Tashkent	6	3	1	4	1		2	2				1
4 Navbahor Namangan	4	1	8	1		8	3	1				
5 Dustlik Tashkent	3			2			1					
6 Nasaf Karshi	1	3	6		1	6		2		1		
7 MHSK Tashkent	1	2	1	1	1	1		1				
8 Mashal Muborak		2	1		1	1		1				
9 Nurafshon Bukhara		1			1							
Samarkand Dinamo		1						1				
Shurton Guzor		1						1				
Temirulchi Kukon		1						1				
13 Traktor Tashkent		1						1				
FK Yangier		1						1				
15 Kizilgum Zarafshon			1			1						
Sogdiana Jizak			1			1						

UZBEKISTAN CUP 2011

Second Round			Quarter–finals			Semi–finals			Final	
Pakhtakor Tashkent *	3	4								
FK Andijan	1	1	**Pakhtakor Tashkent**	1	2					
Kizilgum Zarafshon	0	2	Neftchi Fergana *	0	1					
Neftchi Fergana *	3	2				**Pakhtakor Tashkent**	1	0		
Samarkand Dinamo	0	3				Shurton Guzor *	1	0		
Imkon *	1	1	Samarkand Dinamo	0	3					
Navbahor Namangan *	1	0	**Shurton Guzor ***	4	2				**Pakhtakor Tashkent**	3
Shurton Guzor	2	3							Nasaf Karshi	1
Bunyodkor Tashkent *	5	1								
Erkurgan	0	1	**Bunyodkor Tashkent**	3	2					
Guliston	0	4	Sogdiana Jizak *	1	0					
Sogdiana Jizak *	3	2				Bunyodkor Tashkent *	1 0 3p			
Mashal Muborak *	2	0				**Nasaf Karshi**	0 1 4p			
Lokomotiv Tashkent	1	0	Mashal Muborak *	0	0					
Metallurg Bekobod *	0	0	**Nasaf Karshi**	2	1					
Nasaf Karshi	1	4								

CUP FINAL
Pakhtakor, Tashkent, 13-11-2011
Att: 12 005, Ref: Irmatov
Scorers – Irakli Klimiashvili 2 [5, 82], Aleksandr Kletskov [29] for Pakhtakor; Jahongir Jiamurodov [93+] for Nasaf

* Home team/Home team in the first leg

VAN – VANUATU

FIFA/COCA-COLA WORLD RANKING

'93	'94	'95	'96	'97	'98	'99	'00	'01	'02	'03	'04	'05	'06	'07	'08	'09	'10	'11	'12
164	172	179	180	186	177	184	167	168	156	160	143	146	167	140	141	155	167	174	

						2011									
Jan	Feb	Mar	Apr	May	Jun	Jul	Aug	Sep	Oct	Nov	Dec	High	Low	Av	
166	163	163	165	165	173	169	162	173	174	171	174	131	188	164	

With 12 matches played, 2011 was the busiest year in the history of the Vanuatu national team thanks to an unprecedented number of friendly matches. The tour of the Solomon Islands and then Fiji was to aid preparations for the football tournament of the Pacific Games in Noumea, New Caledonia and the strategy nearly worked. With four of their five group games won, Vanuatu were desperately unlucky not to qualify for the semi-finals, missing out on goal difference after finishing on the same points as both New Caledonia and the Solomon Islands - the failure to wrack up bigger scores against both Guam and Tuvalu costing the side dear. Earlier in the year Vanuatu had backed up its status as one of the major footballing nations in Oceania when club champions Amicale broke new ground by qualifying for the final of the OFC Champions League. After topping a first round group involving the defending champions Hekari United, Amicale faced New Zealand's Auckland City in the final. Despite a goal from the tournament's top goalscorer Fenedy Masauvakalo in the first leg in Port Vila, Amicale went down 2-1 and then lost the tie 6-1 on aggregate. There was more success at home for Amicale after winning the Port Vila League and the smaller National Soccer League, as perennial champions Tafea played second fiddle once again.

FIFA WORLD CUP RECORD
1930-1990 DNE 1994-2010 DNQ

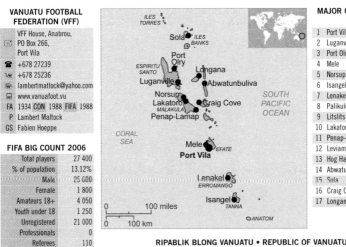

VANUATU FOOTBALL FEDERATION (VFF)

VFF House, Anabrou,
PO Box 266,
Port Vila
☎ +678 27239
📠 +678 25236
✉ lambertmatlock@yahoo.com
🖥 www.vanuafoot.vu
FA 1934 CON 1988 FIFA 1988
P Lambert Maltock
GS Fabien Hoeppe

FIFA BIG COUNT 2006

Total players	27 400
% of population	13.12%
Male	25 600
Female	1 800
Amateurs 18+	4 050
Youth under 18	1 250
Unregistered	21 000
Professionals	0
Referees	110
Admin & coaches	206
Number of clubs	200
Number of teams	400

MAJOR CITIES/TOWNS

		Population
1	Port Vila	47 510
2	Luganville	13 800
3	Port Olry	2 897
4	Mele	2 484
5	Norsup	2 374
6	Isangel	1 695
7	Lenakel	1 473
8	Palikulo	1 450
9	Litslits	1 346
10	Lakatoro	1 247
11	Penap-Lamap	1 236
12	Leviamp	1 180
13	Hog Harbour	1 174
14	Abwatunbuliva	1 071
15	Sola	1 065
16	Craig Cove	1 063
17	Longana	648

RIPABLIK BLONG VANUATU • REPUBLIC OF VANUATU

Capital	Port Vila	Population	218 519 (185)	% in cities	25%
GDP per capita	$4600 (144)	Area km²	12 189 km² (163)	GMT + / -	+11
Neighbours (km)	Coast 2528				

RECENT INTERNATIONAL MATCHES PLAYED BY VANUATU

2007	Opponents		Score	Venue	Comp	Scorers	Att	Referee
17-11	New Zealand	L	1-2	Port Vila	WCq	Naprapol [26]	8 000	Minan PNG
21-11	New Zealand	L	1-4	Wellington	WCq	Sakama [50]	2 500	Jacques TAH
2008								
14-06	New Caledonia	D	1-1	Port Vila	WCq	Mermer [77]	4 000	Varman FIJ
21-06	New Caledonia	L	0-3	Noumea	WCq		2 700	Hester NZL
7-07	Solomon Islands	W	2-1	Honiara	Fr			
6-09	Fiji	L	0-2	Ba	WCq		3 000	Minan PNG
10-09	Fiji	W	2-1	Port Vila	WCq	Sakama [59], Malas [92+]	1 200	O'Leary NZL
2009								
No international matches played in 2009								
2010								
No international matches played in 2010								
2011								
24-01	New Caledonia	D	0-0	Port Vila	Fr			
7-07	Solomon Islands	L	1-2	Honiara	Fr	Michel [89]		
9-07	Solomon Islands	D	0-0	Honiara	Fr			
13-07	Fiji	L	0-2	Labasa	Fr			
15-07	Fiji	W	2-1	Lautoka	Fr	August [7], Tasso [21]		
27-07	Solomon Islands	D	0-0	Port Vila	Fr			
30-07	Solomon Islands	W	2-0	Port Vila	Fr	August [52], Tangis [76]		
27-08	New Caledonia	L	0-5	Noumea	PGr1			Achari FIJ
30-08	Tuvalu †	W	5-1	Noumea	PGr1	Kaltak.J 4 [8 38 45 80], Yelou [49p]		Varman FIJ
1-09	Solomon Islands	W	1-0	Noumea	PGr1	Kaltak.J [92+]		Zitouni TAH
3-09	Guam	W	4-1	Noumea	PGr1	Tangis [50], Tasso [53], Kaltak.J [75], Tari [82]		Kerr NZL
5-09	American Samoa	W	8-0	Noumea	PGr1	Michel 2 [8 22], Garae [43], Kaltak.J 3 [62 70 78], Kaltak.M [64], Aala [73]		Achari FIJ

Fr = Friendly match • WC = FIFA World Cup • PG = Pacific Games • † Not a full international

VANUATU 2010–11

PVFA LIK PREMIA DIVISEN

	Pl	W	D	L	F	A	Pts	Amicale	Tafea	Tupuji	Spirit 08	Shepherds	Teouma	Yatel	Ifira
Amicale	14	12	1	1	41	11	**37**		3-1	3-1	1-0	3-0	4-2	5-2	3-1
Tafea	14	11	1	2	45	13	**34**	1-1		6-2	0-2	6-0	1-0	4-0	8-0
Tupuji Imere	14	8	0	6	29	25	**24**	0-2	1-2		2-1	3-1	3-1	4-1	3-2
Spirit 08	14	7	1	6	21	19	**22**	0-4	0-2	1-2		3-2	1-1	2-1	5-1
Shepherds United	14	6	2	6	18	26	**20**	1-0	2-5	2-1	0-2		2-1	2-0	3-0
Teouma Academy	14	5	3	6	23	21	**18**	1-2	1-3	2-1	2-0	1-1		2-2	2-0
Yatel	14	1	1	12	10	36	**4**	1-5	0-3	**0-3**	0-2	1-2	0-1		2-0
Ifira Black Bird	14	1	1	12	9	45	**4**	0-5	1-3	1-3	1-2	0-0	1-6	1-0	

17/09/2010 - 5/04/2011 • Match in bold awarded

VANUATU 2011

NATIONAL SOCCER LEAGUE

	Pl	W	D	L	F	A	Pts	Amicale	Tafea	Tupuji	Spirit 08	Shepherds	Teouma
Amicale †	6	6	0	0	18	5	**18**		2-1	3-2	n/p	6-1	
Tafea	5	2	1	2	10	6	**7**	1-2		n/p	2-0	5-1	
Tupuji Imere	4	1	1	2	6	7	**4**	0-2	n/p		1-1	n/p	
Spirit 08	5	0	3	2	8	3	**3**	0-3	1-1	n/p		n/p	
Shepherds United	4	0	1	3	4	15	**1**	n/p	n/p	1-3	1-1		
Teouma Academy				Withdrew									

7/04/2011 - 16/06/2011 • † Qualified for the OFC Champions League

VEN – VENEZUELA

FIFA/COCA-COLA WORLD RANKING

'93	'94	'95	'96	'97	'98	'99	'00	'01	'02	'03	'04	'05	'06	'07	'08	'09	'10	'11	'12
93	110	127	111	115	129	110	111	81	69	57	62	67	73	62	65	50	60	39	

	2011												High	Low	Av
	Jan	Feb	Mar	Apr	May	Jun	Jul	Aug	Sep	Oct	Nov	Dec			
	60	63	63	67	68	69	40	44	47	40	39	39	39	129	83

Venezuela were the sensation of the 2011 Copa America in Argentina with the team enjoying its most successful tournament ever. The Vinotinto started their campaign with a draw against Brazil and it was only on goal difference that the Brazilians beat them to top spot in the first round standings after a victory over Ecuador and a thrilling draw with Paraguay in which the Venezuelans scored twice at the very end. An impressive victory over Chile in the quarter-finals was followed by a heart-breaking defeat on penalties in the semi-final against Paraguay. To miss out on a first final in such circumstances was cruel but no longer can Venezuela be regarded as the whipping boys of South American football. With the top players now moving abroad it may be a while before club football matches the exploits of the national team and the 2011 Copa Libertadores was not a good hunting ground with all three Venezuelan representatives failing to reach the knock-out rounds. In the league there was a dramatic last day defeat for the defending champions Caracas at home to Zamora which saw them miss out on the Clausura title which went to Zamora instead. Zamora then took on Apertura winners Deportivo Tachira in the final, which was settled by a single goal in the first leg by Edgar Perez Greco to give Tachira their second title in four years.

COPA AMERICA RECORD

1916-1963 DNE 1967 5/6 1975 10/10 r1 1979 10/10 r1 1983 10/10 r1 1987 10/10 r1 1989 10/10 r1 1991 10/10 r1 1993 11/12 r1
1995 12/12 r1 1997 12/12 r1 1999 12/12 r1 2001 11/12 r1 2004 11/12 r1 2007 6/12 QF (Hosts) 2011 4/12 SF

FEDERACION VENEZOLANA DE FUTBOL (FVF)

Avda. Santos Erminy,
1a Calle las Delicias Torre
Mega II, Sabana Grande,
Caracas 1050
☎ +58 212 7624472
📠 +58 212 7620596
📧 sec_presidencia_fvf@cantv.net
🖥
FA 1926 CON 1965 FIFA 1952
P Rafael Esquivel
GS Serafin Boutureira

FIFA BIG COUNT 2006

Total players	1 490 573
% of population	5.79%
Male	1 270 894
Female	219 679
Amateurs 18+	9 897
Unregistered	516 400
Professionals	546
Referees	832
Admin & coaches	8 300
Number of clubs	717
Number of teams	2 449

MAJOR CITIES/TOWNS

		Population
1	Maracaibo	2 637 443
2	Caracas	1 966 466
3	Valencia	1 855 268
4	Barquisimeto	1 157 843
5	Ciudad Guayana	1 019 336
6	Maracay	628 194
7	Barcelona	621 131
8	Maturín	593 285
9	Petare	568 325
10	Ciudad Bolívar	480 077
11	Turmero	455 679
12	Barinas	428 395
13	Puerto la Cruz	372 800
14	San Cristóbal	364 743
15	Cabimas	351 804
16	Cumaná	333 364
17	Santa Teresa	313 960
18	Mérida	311 314
19	Acarigua	222 321

REPUBLICA BOLIVARIANA DE VENEZUELA • BOLIVARIAN REPUBLIC OF VENEZUELA

Capital	Caracas	Population	26 814 843 (45)	% in cities	93%
GDP per capita	$13 500 (84)	Area km²	912 050 km² (33)	GMT +/-	-4
Neighbours (km)	Brazil 2200, Colombia 2050, Guyana 743 • Coast 2800				

RECENT INTERNATIONAL MATCHES PLAYED BY VENEZUELA

2009	Opponents		Score	Venue	Comp	Scorers	Att	Referee
6-06	Bolivia	W	1-0	La Paz	WCq	Rivero OG [32]	23 427	Vera ECU
10-06	Uruguay	D	2-2	Puerto Ordaz	WCq	Maldonado [9], Rey [74]	37 000	Fagundes BRA
24-06	Mexico	L	0-4	Atlanta	Fr		40 000	Vaughn USA
27-06	Costa Rica	L	0-1	San Jose	Fr		17 000	Zelaya HON
12-08	Colombia	W	2-1	New Jersey	Fr	Rey [34], Vizcarrondo [72]		Prus USA
5-09	Chile	D	2-2	Santiago	WCq	Maldonado [33], Rey [45]	44 000	Ortube BOL
9-09	Peru	W	3-1	Puerto La Cruz	WCq	Fedor 2 [33 52], Vargas [65]	31 703	Vera ECU
10-10	Paraguay	L	1-2	Puerto Ordaz	WCq	Jose Rondon [85]	41 680	Chandia CHI
14-10	Brazil	D	0-0	Campo Grande	WCq		30 000	Carrillo PER
2010								
2-02	Japan	D	0-0	Oita	Fr		27 009	Fan Qi CHN
3-03	Panama	L	1-2	Barquisimeto	Fr	Gonzalez [90p]	37 000	Buitrago COL
6-03	Korea DPR	W	2-1	Puerto La Cruz	Fr	Granados [8], Sanchez [90]	10 000	Buitrago COL
31-03	Chile	D	0-0	Temuco	Fr		20 000	Silvera URU
21-04	Honduras	W	1-0	San Pedro Sula	Fr	Flores [51]	40 000	Moreno PAN
20-05	Aruba	W	3-0	Oranjestad	Fr	Chourio 2 [10 32], Farias [50]	3 500	Jauregui ANT
29-05	Canada	D	1-1	Merida	Fr	Chourio [44]	20 000	Buitrago COL
11-08	Panama	L	1-3	Panama City	Fr	Vizcarrondo [70]	2 000	Quesada CRC
3-09	Colombia	L	0-2	Puerto La Cruz	Fr		30 000	Moreno PAN
7-09	Ecuador	W	1-0	Barquisimeto	Fr	Fedor [86]	37 262	Torres PAN
7-10	Bolivia	W	3-1	Santa Cruz	Fr	Chourio 2 [10 37], Vizcarrondo [28]	35 000	Chaibou NIG
12-10	Mexico	D	2-2	Juarez	Fr	Arango 2 [6 40]	20 000	Aguilar SLV
17-11	Ecuador	L	1-4	Quito	Fr	Maldonado [49p]	9 000	Chaibou NIG
2011								
9-02	Costa Rica	D	2-2	Puerto La Cruz	Fr	Rondon 2 [24 81]	15 000	Gambeta PER
16-03	Argentina	L	1-4	San Juan	Fr	Arismendi [29]	25 000	Puga CHI
25-03	Jamaica	W	2-0	Montego Bay	Fr	Fedor [64], Moreno [67]	6 000	Wijngaarde SUR
29-03	Mexico	D	1-1	San Diego	Fr	Vizcarrondo [73]	60 808	Salazar USA
1-06	Guatemala	W	2-0	Guatemala City	Fr	Fedor [26], Perozo [67]	13 000	Ruano SLV
7-06	Spain	L	0-3	Puerto La Cruz	Fr		36 000	Buckley PER
3-07	Brazil	D	0-0	La Plata	CAr1		35 000	Orozco BOL
9-07	Ecuador	W	1-0	Salta	CAr1	Cesar Gonzalez [62]	12 000	Quesada CRC
13-07	Paraguay	D	3-3	Salta	CAr1	Rondon [5], Fedor [89], Perozo [92+]	18 000	Osses CHI
17-07	Chile	W	2-1	San Juan	CAqf	Vizcarrondo [34], Cuchero [80]	23 000	Vera ECU
20-07	Paraguay	D	0-0	Mendoza	CAsf	L 3-5p	8 000	Chacon MEX
23-07	Peru	L	1-4	La Plata	CA3p	Arango [77]	20 000	Roldan COL
7-08	El Salvador	L	1-2	Washington DC	Fr	Aristeguieta [29]	25 000	Toledo USA
10-08	Honduras	L	0-2	Fort Lauderdale	Fr		20 000	Vaughn USA
2-09	Argentina	L	0-1	Calcutta	Fr		90 000	Rowan IND
6-09	Guinea	W	2-1	Caracas	Fr	Maldonado 2 [25p 39p]	14 000	Gambetta PER
7-10	Ecuador	L	0-2	Quito	WCq		32 278	Osses CHI
11-10	Argentina	W	1-0	Puerto La Cruz	WCq	Amorebieta [62]	35 600	Silvera URU
11-11	Colombia	D	1-1	Barranquilla	WCq	Feltscher [78]	43 953	Ponce ECU
15-11	Bolivia	W	1-0	San Cristobal	WCq	Vizcarrondo [25]	33 351	Buckley PER
22-12	Costa Rica	L	0-2	Barquisimeto	Fr		33 000	Angela USA

Fr = Friendly match • CA = Copa América • WC = FIFA World Cup • q = qualifier

VENEZUELA NATIONAL TEAM HISTORICAL RECORDS

Caps
115 - Jose Manuel Rey 1997- • **103** - Juan Arango 1999- • **91** - Jorge Rojas 1999-2009 • **84** - Miguel Mea Vitali 1999- • **77** - Gabriel Urdaneta 1996-2005 & Luis Vallenilla 1996-2007 • **65** - Ruberth Moran 1996-2007 & Giancarlo Maldonado 2003- • **64** - Leopoldo Jimenez 1999-2005 & Ricardo Paez 2000-07 • **63** - Renny Vega 1999- • **58** - Leonel Vielma 2000-07 • **57** - Rafael Dudamel 1993-2007

Goals
22 - Giancarlo Maldonado 2003- • **19** - Juan Arango 1999- • **14** - Ruberth Moran 1996-2007 • **11** - Jose Manuel Rey 1997- & Daniel Arismendi 2006- • **9** - Gabriel Urdaneta 1996-2005 & Nicolas Fedor 2006-

Past Coaches
Vittorio Godigna ITA 1938 • Alvaro Cartea 1947-48 • Orlando Fantoni BRA 1956 • Rafael Franco ARG 1965-69 • Gregorio Gomez ARG 1969-72 • Walter Roque 1975 • Dan Georgiadis GRE 1975-77 • Jose Hernandez 1979 • Walter Roque 1979-85 • Rafael Santana 1987 • Luis Mendoza 1989 • Carlos Moreno ARG 1989 • Victor Pignanelli 1991 • Ratomir Dujkovic SRB 1992-95 • Lino Alonso 1995 • Rafael Santana 1996 • Eduardo Borrero COL 1997 • Omar Pastoriza ARG 1999-2001 • Richard Paez 2001-07 • Cesar Farias 2007-

VENEZUELA 2010-11 PRIMERA DIVISION TORNEO APERTURA 2010

	Pl	W	D	L	F	A	Pts
Deportivo Táchira †	17	10	6	1	31	11	36
Real Esppor	17	11	3	3	30	11	36
Caracas FC	17	11	2	4	24	15	35
Deportivo Petare	17	9	6	2	25	17	33
Trujillanos FC	17	7	6	4	22	15	27
Aragua FC	17	8	3	6	22	20	27
Deportivo Anzoátegui	17	7	5	5	35	30	26
Yaracuyanos FC	17	6	8	3	20	17	26
Estudiantes Mérida	17	6	4	7	18	22	22
Sport Zulia	17	6	3	8	25	27	21
Mineros de Guayana	17	4	8	5	20	20	20
Monagas SC	17	4	5	8	25	25	17
Zamora FC	17	4	5	8	20	27	17
Atlético Venezuela	17	4	4	9	22	33	16
Deportivo Lara	17	3	7	7	23	28	16
Carabobo FC	17	3	7	7	15	21	16
Atlético El Vigía	17	2	8	7	18	25	14
Caroni	17	2	2	13	7	38	8

8/08/2010-12/12/2010 • † Qualified for the final

VENEZUELA 2010-11 PRIMERA DIVISION TORNEO CLAUSURA 2011

	Pl	W	D	L	F	A	Pts
Zamora FC †	17	13	3	1	37	10	42
Caracas FC	17	12	2	3	32	12	38
Deportivo Anzoátegui	17	8	5	4	27	17	29
Mineros de Guayana	17	9	2	6	27	17	29
Real Esppor	17	8	4	5	16	13	28
Monagas SC	17	7	6	4	22	12	27
Deportivo Petare	17	7	6	4	21	14	27
Trujillanos FC	17	7	4	6	18	16	25
Carabobo FC	17	6	6	5	26	18	24
Aragua FC	17	6	6	5	16	13	24
Yaracuyanos FC	17	6	6	5	18	20	24
Atlético El Vigía	17	7	2	8	35	22	23
Deportivo Lara	17	6	5	6	24	19	23
Deportivo Táchira	17	6	2	9	22	21	20
Sport Zulia	16	5	1	10	14	34	16
Estudiantes Mérida	17	1	5	11	12	32	8
Caroni	16	1	4	11	9	44	7
Atlético Venezuela	17	2	1	14	8	50	7

16/01/2011-15/05/2011 • † Qualified for the final

VENEZUELA 2010-11

AGGREGATE TABLE

	Pl	W	D	L	F	A	Pts	Caracas	Real Esppor	Petare	Táchira	Zamora	Anzoátegui	Trujillanos	Aragua	Yaracuyanos	Mineros	Monagas	Carabobo	Lara	Zulia	El Vigía	Estudiantes	At. Venezuela	Caroni
Caracas FC †	34	23	4	7	56	27	73		3-0	2-2	0-0	0-1	5-1	0-1	1-0	1-2	0-1	1-0	3-0	1-0	5-1	2-1	1-0	4-0	2-2
Real Esppor	34	19	7	8	46	23	64	1-2		0-0	2-2	3-0	3-0	1-1	3-0	2-0	3-2	2-1	1-0	0-0	1-0	2-0	1-0	1-0	3-0
Deportivo Petare	34	16	12	6	46	31	60	2-3	0-0		0-0	0-0	0-0	0-0	1-0	1-1	2-1	2-1	1-1	1-0	1-2	1-0	1-0	5-1	2-1	0-0
Deportivo Táchira †	34	16	8	10	53	32	56	0-1	2-0	1-2		1-2	3-1	1-3	1-0	1-1	1-0	3-1	3-1	4-0	3-1	3-1	4-1	3-0
Zamora FC †	34	16	8	10	53	40	56	0-3	1-0	0-1	1-1		1-1	3-0	1-2	1-0	2-2	2-1	2-2	3-1	5-1	2-1	5-0	1-0
Deportivo Anzoátegui ‡	34	15	10	9	62	47	55	3-0	2-1	2-2	1-0	3-2		3-3	2-4	0-1	1-0	3-1	1-1	2-1	1-0	2-2	2-1	10-0	2-1
Trujillanos FC ‡	34	14	10	10	40	31	52	2-0	0-0	0-1	1-3	2-0	2-0		2-0	1-1	1-1	1-0	1-0	0-0	2-1	3-2	0-1	3-0	2-1
Aragua FC	34	14	10	10	38	33	52	0-1	0-1	2-1	0-1	0-1	0-0	2-1		2-2	1-0	0-0	1-0	2-2	0-1	1-0	3-1	1-2	2-1
Yaracuyanos FC ‡	34	12	14	8	36	38	50	1-0	1-2	1-1	1-0	2-1	1-1	1-1	1-0		2-1	0-0	1-1	1-4	2-0	1-1	1-1	2-0	0-0
Mineros de Guayana	34	13	10	11	47	37	49	0-1	1-3	2-1	1-0	3-1	3-1	3-0	1-1		1-0	1-1	1-1	2-3	1-0	1-1	2-2	2-0
Monagas SC	34	11	11	12	47	37	44	0-1	1-0	2-4	2-0	1-3	1-0	1-2	2-2	4-1	0-0		0-1	1-1	3-2	3-1	6-0	2-2	4-0
Carabobo FC	34	9	13	12	41	39	40	2-2	0-0	0-1	0-2	1-1	1-0	0-0	1-1	1-1	0-2	0-0		2-2	2-3	2-0	3-1	0-2	3-1
Deportivo Lara	34	9	12	13	46	48	39	1-3	1-3	3-0	2-2	2-2	1-1	0-1	1-0	1-3	0-3		0-1	1-1	3-1	0-1	1-1	0-3	1-0
Zulia FC	33	11	4	18	39	62	37	0-1	2-5	1-0	1-0	0-0	1-2	0-0	0-4	2-3	2-1	1-1	1-3	1-0		4-1	1-3	2-1	4-0
Atlético El Vigía	34	9	10	15	41	47	37	1-0	1-0	3-3	0-0	0-3	1-1	0-2	0-0	3-1	1-3	2-1	3-1	1-1	5-1		0-0	4-0	15-0
Estudiantes Mérida	34	7	9	18	28	52	30	1-2	1-0	1-2	2-2	0-4	2-4	1-2	0-0	0-0	0-1	0-0	1-1	1-0	2-1	0-1		4-0	2-1
Atlético Venezuela	34	6	5	23	30	83	23	2-3	0-1	0-2	1-2	1-2	1-4	0-1	1-2	0-3	0-2	1-5	0-4	1-1	1-3	0-3	n/p		1-0
Caroni	33	4	6	23	19	67	18	0-1	0-1	0-3	2-1	4-1	1-7	1-0	0-2	1-0	0-2	0-3	1-3	0-3	n/p	1-0	1-1	0-0	

8/08/2010-15/05/2011 • † Qualified for the Copa Libertadores • ‡ Qualified for the Copa Sudamericana • Apertura matches in shaded boxes
Top scorers: 19 - Daniel Arismendi, Anzoátegui • 17 - Wilmer Jordan Gil COL, Monagas • 13 - Marcelo Refresquini URU, At. Venezuela/Yaracuyanos

CHAMPIONSHIP FINAL 2011

Estadio Agustin Tovar, Barinas
22-05-2011, 18:00, Att: 20 480, Ref: Giovanni Perluzzo

Zamora 0
Deportivo Táchira 1 Perez Greco 40

Zamora - Luis Teran - Nelson Semperena, William Diaz, Moises Galezo (Luilly Garcia 88), Ruben Arocha - Vicente Suanno (c), Jesus Alvarez (Franco Fasciana 71), Jesus Meza (Pedro Ramirez 90), Richard Badillo - Jonathan Copete, Juan Velez. Tr: Jose de Jesus Vera
Táchira - Manuel Sanhouse - Walter Moreno•, Wilker Angel•, Andres Rouga, Layneker Zafra, Jose Yeguez - Pedro Fernandez (c), Diego Guerrero••♦61, Sebastian Hernandez (Mauricio Parra 75) - Edgar Perez Greco (Jorge Casanova• 69), Sergio Herrera (Anderson Arias 86). Tr: Jorge Luis Pinto

CHAMPIONSHIP FINAL 2011

Polideportivo Pueblo Nuevo, San Cristóbal
29-05-2011, 16:30, Att: 37 789, Ref: Jose Luis Hoyo

Deportivo Táchira 0
Zamora U

Táchira - Manuel Sanhouse - Wilker Angel, Walter Moreno, Andres Rouga, Jose Yeguez•, Gerzon Chacon - Pedro Fernandez (c)••♦90, Jorge Casanova, Sebastian Hernandez (John Ospina 80) - Edgar Perez Greco (Julio Gutierrez 73), Sergio Herrera. Tr: Jorge Luis Pinto
Zamora - Roberto Rojas• - Nelson Semperena, William Diaz•, Moises Galezo• - Ruben Arocha• (Franco Fasciana 68), Vicente Suanno (c) (Erlyn Cuica 87), Arles Flores, Richard Badillo, Jesus Meza - Jonathan Copete, Juan Velez. Tr: Jose de Jesus Vera

COPA VENEZUELA 2011

Round of 16		Quarter–finals		Semi–finals		Final	
Mineros de Guayana *	2 2						
Real Esppor	1 3	Mineros de Guayana	1 3				
Deportivo Petare *	1 0	Aragua FC *	0 1				
Aragua FC	1 1			Mineros de Guayana	2 1		
Tucanos de Amazonas *	2 0			Caracas FC *	1 1		
Angostura FC	1 0	Tucanos de Amazonas *	1 0				
Deportivo Anzoátegui *	2 1	Caracas FC	2 1				
Caracas FC	1 3					Mineros de Guayana ‡	2 1
Atlético El Vigía	0 1 3p					Trujillanos FC *	1 0
Deportivo Táchira *	1 0 1p	Atlético El Vigía	0 4				
Loteria del Tachira	0 2	Carabobo FC *	1 0			CUP FINAL	
Carabobo FC *	2 3			Atlético El Vigía	0 0		
Zamora FC	2 2			Trujillanos FC *	1 3		
Deportivo Lara *	3 1	Zamora FC *	1 1			1st leg. 30-11-2011	
Llaneros Guanare *	1 0	Trujillanos FC	3 2			2nd leg. 7-12-2011	
Trujillanos FC	1 1						

* Home team in the 1st leg • ‡ Qualified for the Copa Sudamericana

---

COPA VENEZUELA FINAL 2011

1st leg. Jose Alberto Perez, Valera
30-11-2011, Att: 18 500, Ref: Hector Rojas

Trujillanos 1 Armua 18p
AC Mineros 2 Vallenilla 50, Rojas 52

Trujillanos - Luis Rojas - Ynmer Gonzalez, Victor Valera, Jonathan Espana, Mayker Gonzalez - Hector Alejandro Vasco (Freddy Reyes 85), Arquimedes Figuera, Roberto Armua♦74, Luis Garcia (Ruben Garcia 60), Juan Falcon, Omar Perdomo (Victor Sifontes 70). Tr: Pedro Vera
Mineros - Tito Rojas - Giovanny Romero, Walter Moreno, Jose Manuel Velázquez, Luis Vallenilla - Luis Felipe Chara, Agnel Flores, Alejandro Guerra, Jorge Rojas (Marcos Gutierrez 94+) - Darwin Machis, Julio Gutierrez (Jose Torrealba 80). Tr: Carlos Maldonado

COPA VENEZUELA FINAL 2011

2nd leg. CTE Cachamay, Purto Ordaz
7-12-2011, Att: 41 894, Ref: Maiker Gomez

AC Mineros 1 Guerra 52
Trujillanos 0

Mineros - Tito Rojas - Giovanny Romero, Jose Manuel Velazquez, Walter Moreno, Luis Vallenilla, Luis Felipe Chara, Agnel Flores (Marcos Gutierrez 64), Alejandro Guerra, Jorge Rojas, Julio Gutierrez (Jose Torrealba 85), Darwin Machis. Tr: Carlos Maldonado
Trujillanos - Luis Rojas - Jonnathan Espana♦93+, Victor Valera, Edixon Cuevas• (Ruben Garcia 40), Ynmer Gonzalez, Alejandro Vasco• (Gerardo Mendoza 75), Arquimedes Figuera•, Mayker Gonzalez, Luis Garcia (Julio Ferreira 59), Omar Perdomo, Juan Falcon. Tr: Pedro Vera

---

MEDALS TABLE

		Overall			Lge		Cup		Sth Am			City
		G	S	B	G	B	G	B	G	S	B	
1	Caracas FC	16	4	1	11	2	5	2			1	Caracas
2	Deportivo Galicia	9	6		4	5	5	1				Caracas
3	Deportivo Tachira	8	9		7	8	1	1				San Cristobal
4	Deportivo Petare (ex Italia)	8	8		5	7	3	1				Caracas
5	Portuguesa FC	8	4	1	5	3	3	1			1	Acarigua
6	Unión SC	7	3		7	3						Caracas
7	Dos Caminos SC	6	8		6	7		1				Caracas
8	Deportivo Portugués	6	3		4	2	2	1				Caracas
9	CS Maritimo	6	1		4	1	2					Caracas
10	Estudiantes Merida	5	9		2	7	3	2				Merida
11	Centro Atlético	4	7		4	7						Caracas
12	Loyola SC	4	5		4	5						Caracas
13	Universidad de Los Andes	4	2	1	3	1	1	1			1	Merida
14	Deportivo Venezuela	4			4							Caracas
15	Valencia	3	5		1	2	2	3				Valencia
16	Unión Deportivo Canarias	3	3		1		2	3				Caracas
	Universidad Central	3	3		3	3						Caracas
18	Mineros de Guayana	3	1		1	1	2					Puerto Ordaz
19	Trujillanos	2	5				2	3				Valera
20	La Salle	2	4		2	4						Caracas
	Deportivo Español	2	4		2	3		1				Caracas
22	Zamora FC	2	2			1	2	1				Barinas

VGB – BRITISH VIRGIN ISLANDS

'93	'94	'95	'96	'97	'98	'99	'00	'01	'02	'03	'04	'05	'06	'07	'08	'09	'10	'11	'12
-	-	-	-	180	187	161	172	163	161	175	165	171	190	192	180	191	176	199	

					2011							High	Low	Av
Jan	Feb	Mar	Apr	May	Jun	Jul	Aug	Sep	Oct	Nov	Dec			
177	177	177	183	183	182	186	187	191	192	194	199	160	199	175

The British Virgin Islands were drawn against neighbours the US Virgin Islands in the qualifiers for the 2014 FIFA World Cup in Brazil and with it came the chance for redemption following their Caribbean Cup debacle in October 2010 when they lost 17-0 and 10-0 on successive days against the Dominican Republic and Dominica. It was the fourth time BVI had entered the World Cup and like their neighbours they were yet to win a game so something had to give. Unfortunately for coach Avondale Williams it was his US counterparts who won both games. The first leg in Charlotte Amalie was lost 2-0 and although it looked as if the BVI had secured a draw in the return in Tortola, Reid Klopp scored a goal three minutes into injury time to win the game for the USVI. In the build up to the matches much had been made of the time Andre Villas-Boas had spent as technical director of the BVIFA in 2000-01 - a time when Williams was the main striker for the team - but the fact remains that the BVI will always struggle to make an impact with a population of just over 20,000. At least there is a well-run club scene and all of the players called up for the World Cup qualifiers were based at home. In 2011 the second edition of the national championship was won by Islanders who retained the title won 12 months previously.

FIFA WORLD CUP RECORD
1930-1998 DNE 2002-2014 DNQ

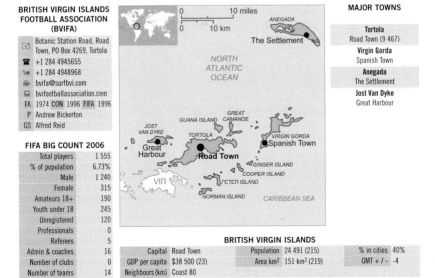

BRITISH VIRGIN ISLANDS FOOTBALL ASSOCIATION (BVIFA)
Botanic Station Road, Road Town, PO Box 4269, Tortola
☎ +1 284 4945655
📠 +1 284 4948968
bvifa@surfbvi.com
bvifootballassociation.com
FA 1974 CON 1996 FIFA 1996
P Andrew Bickerton
GS Alfred Reid

FIFA BIG COUNT 2006

Total players	1 555
% of population	6.73%
Male	1 240
Female	315
Amateurs 18+	190
Youth under 18	245
Unregistered	120
Professionals	0
Referees	5
Admin & coaches	16
Number of clubs	0
Number of teams	14

MAJOR TOWNS
Tortola
Road Town (9 467)
Virgin Gorda
Spanish Town
Anegada
The Settlement
Jost Van Dyke
Great Harbour

BRITISH VIRGIN ISLANDS

Capital Road Town	Population 24 491 (215)	% in cities 40%
GDP per capita $38 500 (23)	Area km² 151 km² (219)	GMT +/- -4
Neighbours (km) Coast 80		

RECENT INTERNATIONAL MATCHES PLAYED BY THE BRITISH VIRGIN ISLANDS

2004	Opponents		Score	Venue	Comp	Scorers	Att	Referee
28-01	Dominica	L	0-1	Tortola	Fr		405	Matthew SKN
30-01	US Virgin Islands	W	5-0	Tortola	Fr	OG [18], Williams [24], Morris 2 [26 56], Ferron [88]	350	Charles DMA
1-02	Dominica	L	1-2	Tortola	Fr	Morris [28]	280	Charles DMA
22-02	St Lucia	L	0-1	Tortola	WCq		800	Stewart JAM
20-03	St Kitts and Nevis	L	0-4	Basseterre	Fr		2 500	Matthew SKN
28-03	St Lucia	L	0-9	Vieux Fort	WCq		665	Corrivault CAN
25-09	US Urgin Islands	W	2-1	Tortola	Fr	Junior Heileger [48], Raul Ettienne [55]	300	Frederick VIR
24-11	St Vincent/Grenadines	D	1-1	Kingstown	CCq	Michael Haynes [53]	300	Prendergast JAM
26-11	Cayman Islands	L	0-1	Kingstown	CCq		1 000	Matthew SKN
28-11	Bermuda	W	2-0	Kingstown	CCq	Venton James 2 [12 24]	400	Matthew SKN
12-12	Trinidad and Tobago	L	0-4	Tortola	CCq		16 000	Arthur LCA
19-12	Tinidad and Tobago	L	0-2	Tunapuna	CCq		2 000	Lancaster GUY
2005								
No international matches played in 2005								
2006								
No international matches played in 2006								
2007								
No international matches played in 2007								
2008								
14-03	US Virgin Islands	D	0-0	Tortola	Fr		300	
15-03	US Virgin Islands	D	1-1	Tortola	Fr		350	
26-03	Bahamas	D	1-1	Nassau	WCq	Rohan Lennon [68]	450	Moreno PAN
30-03	Bahamas	D	2-2	Nassau	WCq	Avondale Williams 2 [72 90p]	940	Suazo DOM
24-09	St Kitts and Nevis	L	0-4	Basseterre	CCq		500	Charles DMA
26-09	Barbados	L	1-2	Basseterre	CCq	Rohan Lennon [23]	150	Baptiste DMA
2009								
5-12	Dominica	L	0-4	Roseau	Fr		600	Baptiste DMA
2010								
25-09	Anguilla	W	2-1	Saint-Martin	Fr	Henroy Mitchell 2 [5 8]	100	
14-10	Dominican Republic	L	0-17	San Cristobal	CCq		200	Lebron PUR
15-10	Dominica	L	0-10	San Cristobal	CCq		200	Santos PUR
2011								
3-07	US Virgin Islands	L	0-2	Charlotte Amalie	WCq		350	Navarro CAN
10-07	US Virgin Islands	L	1-2	Tortola	WCq	Trevor Peters [38]	600	Morrison JAM

Fr = Friendly match • CC = Digicel Caribbean Cup • WC = FIFA World Cup • q = qualifier

BRITISH VIRGIN ISLANDS 2011

BVIFA FOOTBALL LEAGUE

	Pl	W	D	L	F	A	Pts	Islanders	Sugar Boys	Lucian Stars	One Love Utd	Panthers	Wolues	VG United	VG Ballstars	Old Madrid
Islanders	16	13	2	1	66	11	41		4-0	7-0	3-1	3-0	4-1	6-1	2-0	3-0
Sugar Boys	16	9	3	4	44	30	30	3-2		7-4	0-2	3-2	4-3	1-2	1-0	3-0
St Lucian Stars	16	8	3	5	36	42	27	1-9	2-2		3-3	4-3	3-2	**3-0**	2-1	**3-0**
One Love United	16	8	2	6	37	24	26	**0-3**	4-2	0-1		4-2	2-2	4-0	0-1	5-0
HBA Panthers	16	7	4	5	37	30	25	1-1	2-2	2-1	2-0		3-2	5-3	2-2	1-1
Wolues	16	6	3	7	30	32	21	1-1	1-1	3-0	0-4	0-4		2-1	6-1	2-1
Virgin Gorda United	15	4	0	11	17	47	12	0-3	0-7	0-5	**0-3**	1-4	3-0		n/p	**0-3**
Virgin Gorda Ballstars	15	3	2	10	19	34	11	2-4	2-5	1-2	3-0	2-1	0-2	1-3		0-0
Old Madrid	16	2	3	11	14	50	9	0-11	0-3	2-2	2-5	1-3	0-3	0-3	4-3	

26/09/2010 - 5/03/2011 • Matches in bold awarded

VIE – VIETNAM

FIFA/COCA-COLA WORLD RANKING

'93	'94	'95	'96	'97	'98	'99	'00	'01	'02	'03	'04	'05	'06	'07	'08	'09	'10	'11	'12
135	151	122	99	104	98	102	99	105	108	98	103	120	172	142	155	123	137	99	

	2011												High	Low	Av
	Jan	Feb	Mar	Apr	May	Jun	Jul	Aug	Sep	Oct	Nov	Dec			
	136	134	134	135	134	140	143	129	130	134	134	99	84	172	118

Henrique Calisto, the Portuguese coach who steered Vietnam to success at the 2009 AFF Suzuki Cup, stepped down from the helm of the national team in March 2011 to take on the coach's position at Thai Premier League side Muangthong United, ending a fruitful three-year association with the Vietnam Football Federation. In his place, Germany's Falko Goetz was appointed head coach of both the national team and the under-23 side, but the 49-year-old lasted barely six months. Goetz oversaw Vietnam's involvement in qualifying for the 2014 FIFA World Cup finals, which started well with a comprehensive 13-1 aggregate win over Macau. That saw the Vietnamese qualify for a second preliminary round tie, this time against Qatar, but a 3-0 loss in Doha proved costly even though Vietnam won the return in Hanoi 2-1. However, it was the country's performance at the South East Asian Games in Jakarta that brought Goetz's tenure to an end as the Vietnamese were eliminated in the semi-finals by hosts Indonesia. At home, the V-League was won by Song Lam Nghe An, their first title since 2001. SLNA, as they are also known, had won the cup in 2010 but missed out on retaining it - and the double - when they were beaten 3-0 in the 2011 final by Navibank from Saigon, winners of their first-ever trophy.

FIFA WORLD CUP RECORD
1930-1970 DNE **1974** DNQ **1978-1990** DNE **1994-2014** DNQ

VIETNAM FOOTBALL FEDERATION (VFF)

844 National Youth Football Training Centre, Le Quang Dao Str, My Dinh, Tu Liem, Hanoi
☎ +84 43 8452480
📠 +84 43 8233119
📧 thanhhavff@yahoo.com
🌐 www.vff.org.vn
FA 1962 CON 1954 FIFA 1964
P Nguyen Trong Hy
GS Le Bang Ngo

FIFA BIG COUNT 2006

Total players	1 874 350
% of population	2.22%
Male	1 755 000
Female	119 350
Amateurs 18+	20 850
Unregistered	793 200
Professionals	100
Referees	152
Admin & coaches	10 500
Number of clubs	27
Number of teams	10 000

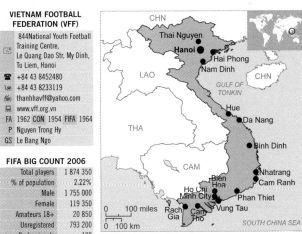

MAJOR CITIES/TOWNS

		Population
1	Ho Chi Minh City	3 873 661
2	Hanoi	1 491 404
3	Hai Phong	635 820
4	Da Nang	490 700
5	Bien Hoa	446 476
6	Hue	305 721
7	Nhatrang	304 167
8	Can Tho	270 754
9	Rach Gia	267 561
10	Vung Tau	235 642
11	Binh Dinh	224 336
12	Nam Dinh	200 516
13	Phan Thiet	169 992
14	Long Xuyen	164 659
15	Buon Ma Thuot	160 360
16	Cam Ranh	155 748
17	Ha Long	155 006
18	Cam Pha	154 894
19	Thai Nguyen	138 555

CONG HOA XA HOI CHU NGHIA VIET NAM • SOCIALIST REPUBLIC OF VIETNAM

Capital Hanoi	Population 86 967 524 (13)	% in cities 28%
GDP per capita $2800 (168)	Area km² 331 210 km² (65)	GMT +/- +7
Neighbours (km) Cambodia 1228, China 1281, Laos 2130 • Coast 3444		

RECENT INTERNATIONAL MATCHES PLAYED BY VIETNAM

2008	Opponents	Score		Venue	Comp	Scorers	Att	Referee
11-06	Indonesia	L	0-1	Surabaya	Fr			
1-10	Mynanmar	L	2-3	Ho Chi Minh City	Fr	Le Cong Vinh 2 [63] [91+]		
5-10	Turkmenistan	L	2-3	Ho Chi Minh City	Fr	Nguyen Minh Phuong [20], Le Cong Vinh [89]		
14-10	Singapore	D	0-0	Hanoi	Fr			
30-10	Korea DPR	D	0-0	Hanoi	Fr			
16-11	Thailand	D	2-2	Hanoi	Fr	Viet Thang [52], Nguyen Minh Phuong [87]		
6-12	Thailand	L	0-2	Phuket	AFFr1		20 000	Abdul Bashir SIN
8-12	Malaysia	W	3-2	Phuket	AFFr1	Pham Thanh Lurong [17], Nguyen Vu Phong 2 [73] [88]		Palaniyandi SIN
10-12	Laos	W	4-0	Phuket	AFFr1	Nguyen Viet Thang [49], Pham Thanh Lurong [63], Huynh Quang Thanh [66], Phan Thanh Binh [81]		Cho Win MYA
17-12	Singapore	D	0-0	Hanoi	AFFsf		40 000	Ramachandran MAS
21-12	Singapore	W	1-0	Singapore	AFFsf	Nguyen Quang Hai [74]	55 000	Mohd Salleh MAS
24-12	Thailand	W	2-1	Bangkok	AFFf	Nguyen Vu Phong [40], Le Cong Vinh [42]	50 000	Ramachandran MAS
28-12	Thailand	D	1-1	Hanoi	AFFf	Le Cong Vinh [93+]	40 000	Abdul Bashir SIN
2009								
14-01	Lebanon	W	3-1	Hanoi	ACq	Nguyen Minh Phuong [11], Le Cong Vinh [30], Nguyen Vu Phong [69]	13 000	Toma JPN
21-01	China PR	L	1-6	Zheijang	ACq		15 300	Kim Dong Jin KOR
31-05	Kuwait	W	1-0	Kuwait City	Fr	Nguyen Trong Hoang [36]		
20-10	Turkmenistan	W	1-0	Ho Chi Minh City	Fr	Nguyen Quang Hai [58]		
24-10	Singapore	D	2-2	Ho Chi Minh City	Fr	Nguyen Quang Hai [18], Vu Nhu Thanh [85p]		
14-11	Syria	L	0-1	Hanoi	ACq		30 000	Williams AUS
18-11	Syria	D	0-0	Aleppo	ACq		19 000	Al Hilali OMA
2010								
6-01	Lebanon	D	1-1	Saida	ACq	Pham Thanh Luong [39]	50	Kovalenko UZB
17-01	China PR	L	1-2	Hanoi	ACq	Le Cong Vinh [76p]	3 000	Abdul Bashir SIN
24-09	Korea DPR	D	0-0	Hanoi	Fr			
8-10	India	L	1-3	Pune	Fr	Vu Nhu Thanh [62]		
12-10	Kuwait	L	1-3	Kuwait City	Fr	Nguyen Minh Phuong [57]		
4-11	Singapore	D	1-1	Hanoi	Fr	Phan Van Tai Em [76]		
6-11	Korea DPR	L	0-2	Hanoi	Fr			
2-12	Myanmar	W	7-1	Hanoi	AFFr1	Nguyen Minh Phuong [30], Nguyen Anh Duc 2 [13] [56], Le Tan Tai [51], Nguyen Trong Hoang 2 [13] [56], Nguyen Vu Phong [94+]	40 000	Patwal IND
5-12	Philippines	L	0-2	Hanoi	AFFr1		40 000	Napitupulu IDN
8-12	Singapore	W	1-0	Hanoi	AFFr1	Nguyen Vu Phong [32]	40 000	Mahaprab THA
15-12	Malaysia	L	0-2	Kuala Lumpur	AFFsf		45 000	Sun Baojie CHN
18-12	Malaysia	D	0-0	Hanoi	AFFsf		40 000	Kim Sang Woo KOR
2011								
29-06	Macau	W	6-0	Ho Chi Minh City	WCq	Le Cong Vinh 3 [20] [36] [42], Phan Thanh Phan [62], Nguyen Ngoc Thanh [67], Nguyen Van Quyet [89]	20 000	Mashentsev KGZ
3-07	Macau	W	7-1	Macau	WCq	Huynh Quang Thanh 2 [2] [86], Nguyen Quang Hai [23], Le Cong Vinh 4 [29] [42] [74] [82]	500	Auda IRQ
23-07	Qatar	L	0-3	Doha	WCq		6 786	Albadwawi UAE
28-07	Qatar	W	2-1	Hanoi	WCq	Nguyen Trong Hoang [60], Nguyen Quang Hai [23]	20 000	Green AUS
7-10	Japan	L	0-1	Kobe	Fr		27 522	Mahapab THA

Fr = Friendly match • AFF = ASEAN Football Federation Championship • AC = AFC Asian Cup • WC = FIFA World Cup
q = qualifier • r1 = first round group • sf = semi-final • 3p = third place play-off

VIETNAM NATIONAL TEAM HISTORICAL RECORDS

Caps
73 - Nguyen Minh Phuong 2002-10

Goals
30 - Le Cong Vinh 2004- & Le Huynh Duc 1995-2004

Past Coaches
Tran Duy Long 1995 • Edson Tavares BRA 1995 • Karl-Heinz Weigang GER 1995-97 • Colin Murphy ENG 1997 • Alfred Riedl AUT 1998-2001 • Henrique Calisto 2002 • Alfred Riedl AUT 2003 • Edson Tavares BRA 2004 • Tran Van Khanh 2004 • Alfred Riedl AUT 2006-07 • Henrique Calisto POR 2008-11 • Mai Duc Chung 2011 • Falko Gotz 2011-

VIETNAM 2011

EXIMBANK V-LEAGUE

	Pl	W	D	L	F	A	Pts	SLNA	T&T Hanoi	Da Nang	Ninh Binh	Dong Thap	Binh Duong	Than Hoa	Navibank	HAGL	Hoa Phat	Khanh Hoa	Hai Phong	Dong Tam	Hanoi ACB
Song Lam Nghe An †	26	15	4	7	48	29	49		1-1	1-0	1-0	6-2	0-1	3-0	3-1	2-2	2-1	4-0	3-1	1-0	2-0
T&T Hanoi	26	13	7	6	51	31	46	0-0		0-2	2-1	7-1	2-2	0-0	4-0	6-2	2-1	1-1	1-0	4-1	3-1
Da Nang	26	12	8	6	49	32	44	3-1	1-3		2-1	2-1	1-1	0-0	2-2	2-1	2-0	1-1	3-1	2-0	3-1
Ninh Binh	26	11	6	9	37	35	39	3-1	1-1	0-4		2-0	2-1	2-2	0-0	3-0	1-1	1-0	2-0	1-2	2-0
Dong Thap	26	10	7	9	38	44	37	3-2	3-1	3-2	2-0		2-0	2-0	0-2	1-1	3-1	2-2	2-0	1-2	3-0
Binh Duong	26	9	9	8	40	42	36	1-4	1-1	1-1	1-1	0-0		4-3	3-1	2-2	2-1	1-3	0-1	2-1	2-0
Than Hoa	26	9	7	10	44	41	34	2-3	1-0	3-3	3-1	3-0	4-1		2-0	2-2	3-1	1-0	1-1	1-2	3-0
Navibank Saigon	26	9	7	10	36	37	34	0-1	2-4	3-3	3-0	0-0	3-2	3-1		2-1	2-0	2-1	2-0	0-1	5-0
Hoang Anh Gia Lai	26	8	8	10	49	46	32	0-1	4-1	1-0	2-3	2-3	1-2	2-2	1-1		1-1	1-0	4-2	3-0	6-1
Hoa Phat Hanoi	26	9	5	12	38	40	32	2-1	2-0	2-4	2-1	1-1	2-1	3-0	2-0	1-2		4-1	1-1	0-1	2-1
Khanh Hoa	26	9	5	12	28	34	32	1-0	1-0	2-1	0-1	4-1	0-2	4-2	1-1	2-1	1-1		0-2	1-0	1-0
Hai Phong	26	7	9	10	28	40	30	1-0	1-3	1-1	2-3	1-1	2-2	2-1	2-0	1-1	2-1	1-0		0-0	2-2
Dong Tam Long An	26	8	6	12	31	44	30	2-2	0-2	0-3	2-2	1-1	1-2	0-3	1-1	4-3	2-3	2-1	1-1		4-1
Hanoi ACB	26	8	2	16	36	58	26	2-3	1-2	2-1	2-3	2-0	3-3	2-1	2-1	1-3	3-2	1-0	5-0	3-1	

22/01/2011 - 21/08/2011 • † Qualified for the AFC Cup

Top scorers: **21** - Gaston Merlo ARG, Da Nang • **19** - Evaldo Goncalves BRA, HAGL • **17** - Samson Kayode NGA, Dong Thap • **16** - Lucas Cantoro ARG, Hanoi ACB • **15** - Pape Omar Faye SEN, Thanh Hoa • **13** - Tomothy Anjembe NGA, Hoa Phat & Gustavo Dourado BRA, Ninh Binh

VIETNAM 2011 SECOND DIVISION

	Pl	W	D	L	F	A	Pts
Saigon FC	26	15	9	2	65	35	54
Kien Giang	26	12	11	3	44	26	47
Binh Dinh	26	13	6	7	31	18	45
Than Quang Ninh	26	11	9	6	45	37	42
An Giang	26	11	4	11	46	46	37
Dong Nai	26	9	9	8	34	35	36
Can Tho	26	11	3	12	33	42	36
T&T Hanoi II	26	8	9	9	38	38	33
Quang Nam	26	7	9	10	30	33	30
Ho Chi Minh City	26	6	10	10	29	36	28
TDC Binh Duong	26	7	7	12	32	43	28
Tay Ninh	26	7	6	13	34	40	27
Nam Dinh	26	5	12	9	29	41	27
Huda Hue	26	4	8	14	31	51	20

20/01/2011 - 20/08/2011

MEDALS TABLE

		Overall			League			Cup		Asia		
		G	S	B	G	S	B	G	S	G	S	B
1	Cang Saigon	6	3	3	4		3	2	3			
2	The Cong Hanoi	5	5	6	5	2	6		3			
3	Song Lam Nghe An	5	4	2	3	3	2	2	1			
4	Cong An Thanh Pho	3	5	2	1	3	2	2	2			
5	Dong Tam Long An	3	4	1	2	3	1	1	1			
6	Binh Duong	3	3	2	2	2	1	1	1			1
	Hai Quan	3	3	2	1	2	2	2	1			
8	Quang Nam Da Nang	2	2	1	1	2						1
9	Hoang Anh Gia Lai	2	1	1	2		1					
	Binh Dinh	2	1	1			1	2	1			
	Da Nang	2	1	1	1	1	1					
12	Hanoi ACB	2	1		1			1	1			
13	Dong Thap	2		1	2		1					
14	Hai Phong	1	4	2		3	2	1	1			
15	Cong An Hanoi	1	3	2	1	1	2		2			
16	Nam Dinh	1	2	1		2	1	1				
17	Hanoi T&T	1	1		1	1						
18	Navibank Saigon	1							1			

VIETNAM CUP 2011

Round of 16

Navibank Saigon	2
T&T Hanoi	0
Binh Dinh	1
Binh Duong	2
Ninh Binh	3
Nam Dinh	1
Da Nang	3 2p
Than Hoa	3 4p
Hoang Anh Gia Lai	0 3p
Hoa Phat Hanoi	0 4p
Than Quang Ninh	1
Khanh Hoa	2
Saigon FC	2
Dong Tam Long An	0
Quang Nam	1
Song Lam Nghe An	2

Quarter-finals

Navibank Saigon	1 10p
Binh Duong	1 9p
Ninh Binh	1 1p
Than Hoa	1 3p
Hoang Anh Gia Lai	3
Khanh Hoa	1
Saigon FC	2
Song Lam Nghe An	4

Semi-finals

Navibank Saigon	2 5p
Than Hoa	2 3p
Hoang Anh Gia Lai	1
Song Lam Nghe An	2

Final

Navibank Saigon †	3
Song Lam Nghe An	0

† Qualified for the AFC Cup

CUP FINAL

Thong Nhat Stadium, Ho Chi Minh
27-08-2011, 15 000, Vo Quang Vinh
Scorers - Nguyen Quang Hai 37, Cao Quang Hurong 2 42 54 for Navibank

VIN – ST VINCENT AND THE GRENADINES

FIFA/COCA-COLA WORLD RANKING

'93	'94	'95	'96	'97	'98	'99	'00	'01	'02	'03	'04	'05	'06	'07	'08	'09	'10	'11	'12
129	144	95	93	122	138	141	127	125	144	169	137	130	85	101	133	152	142	144	

2011												High	Low	Av
Jan	Feb	Mar	Apr	May	Jun	Jul	Aug	Sep	Oct	Nov	Dec			
144	148	148	153	153	154	161	158	158	146	146	144	73	170	131

The St Vincent and Grenadines national team may not have expected to win their 2014 FIFA World Cup qualifying group given that they had been drawn alongside Guatemala, but the aim was to finish above both Grenada and Belize and gain valuable points to move up the FIFA/Coca-Cola World Ranking. Ex-Botswana boss Colwyn Rowe was brought in to see the team through the campaign but after a promising draw in a warm up against Antigua - currently the strongest of the smaller Caribbean islands - the campaign was a disappointment for Vincey Heat. The veteran 36-year old Malaysia-based captain Cornelius Huggins was playing in his fifth tournament but it was youngster Myron Samuel who caught the eye up front playing alongside his namesake and record goalscorer Shandel Samuel. In 2008 Myron had become the youngest player to appear and score for St Vincent, and he opened the scoring in a 2-1 victory over Grenada. He also scored in the return in St George's where Vincey Heat were denied another win by a Grenada equaliser deep into injury-time. A second home defeat - against Belize in the final game - meant St Vincent finished the group in third place. In club football, the NLA Premier League was won for the second year in a row by Avenues United.

FIFA WORLD CUP RECORD
1930-1990 DNE 1994-2010 DNQ

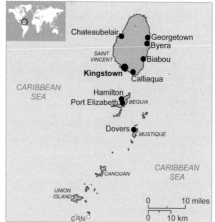

SAINT VINCENT AND THE GRENADINES FOOTBALL FEDERATION (SVGFF)

Nichols Building (2nd Floor), Bentinck Square, Victoria Park, PO Box 1278, Kingstown

☎ +1 784 4561092
🖷 +1 784 4572193
✉ svgfootball@vincysurf.com
🖳 www.svgff.com
FA 1979 CON 1988 FIFA 1988
P Venold Coombs
GS Trevor Huggins

FIFA BIG COUNT 2006

Total players	9 500
% of population	8.06%
Male	8 600
Female	900
Youth under 18	3 300
Professionals	0
Referees	5
Admin & coaches	500
Number of clubs	50
Number of teams	300

MAJOR CITIES/TOWNS

		Population
1	Kingstown	16 532
2	Georgetown	1 443
3	Byera	1 173
4	Biabou	902
5	Port Elizabeth	766
6	Chateaubelair	631
7	Calliaqua	608
8	Hamilton	575
9	Dovers	479

SAINT VINCENT AND THE GRENADINES

Capital	Kingstown	Population	104 574 (192)	% in cities	47%
GDP per capita	$10 200 (103)	Area km²	389 km² (202)	GMT +/-	-4
Neighbours (km)	Coast 84				

RECENT INTERNATIONAL MATCHES PLAYED BY ST VINCENT AND THE GRENADINES

2007	Opponents	Score		Venue	Comp	Scorers	Att	Referee
14-01	Guyana	W	2-0	Marabella	CCr1	Shandel Samuel [4], Sean Glynn [85]	3 000	Angela ARU
16-01	Cuba	L	0-3	Marabella	CCr1		1 700	Angela ARU
18-01	Guadeloupe †	L	0-1	Marabella	CCr1		2 000	Brizan TRI
30-05	Haiti	L	0-3	Port of Spain	Fr		500	Jordan TRI
2008								
13-01	Guyana	L	0-1	Blairmont	Fr		1 300	James GUY
27-01	Guyana	D	2-2	Kingstown	Fr	Randolph Williams [6], George Emerald [80]	2 000	Cambridge VIN
10-02	Grenada	L	1-2	Kingstown	Fr	Alwyn Guy [49]	1 000	Cambridge VIN
13-03	Barbados	L	0-2	Kingstown	Fr		1 050	Cambridge VIN
3-06	Jamaica	L	1-5	Kingston	Fr	Marlon James [56]	20 000	Whittaker CAY
7-06	Cuba	L	0-1	Havana	Fr		400	Duran CUB
15-06	Canada	L	0-3	Kingstown	WCq		5 000	Batres GUA
20-06	Canada	L	1-4	Montreal	WCq	Marlon James [75]	11 500	Aguilar SLV
15-09	Martinique †	L	0-3	Fort de France	CCq		250	George LCA
17-09	Anguilla	W	3-1	Fort de France	CCq	Theon Gordon [35], Darren Hammlet [39], Myron Samuel [80]	100	Fanus LCA
2009								
5-09	St Kitts and Nevis	L	0-3	Kingstown	Fr		3 500	Cambridge VIN
20-09	St Kitts and Nevis	D	1-1	Basseterre	Fr	Wendell Cuffy [47]	1 600	Matthew SKN
2010								
10-09	St Lucia	W	5-1	Vieux Fort	Fr	Norrel George [19], Myron Samuel 2 [21 43], Romano Snagg [57], Wendell Cuffy [72]	400	St Catherine LCA
17-09	Grenada	L	0-1	Kingstown	Fr		350	Gurley VIN
19-09	Grenada	D	0-0	Kingstown	Fr		350	Cambridhe VIN
6-10	Montserrat	W	7-0	Kingstown	CCq	Shandel Samuel 3 [25p 26 66], Damon Francis [56], Cornelius Stewart [63], Chad Balcombe [70], Romano Snagg [89]	5 000	Pinas SUR
8-10	St Kitts and Nevis	D	1-1	Kingstown	CCq	Keith James [73]	1 600	Jauregui ANT
10-10	Barbados	D	0-0	Kingstown	CCq		5 420	Jauregui ANT
2-11	Trinidad and Tobago	L	2-6	Marabella	CCq	Shandel Samuel [28], Cornelius Stewart [45]	1 100	Peterkin JAM
4-11	Haiti	L	1-3	Port of Spain	CCq	Shandel Samuel [64]	1 100	Campbell JAM
6-11	Guyana	L	0-2	Port of Spain	CCq		850	Taylor BRB
2011								
27-05	Barbados	D	0-0	Bridgetown	Fr		3 500	Skeete BRB
26-08	Antigua and Barbuda	L	0-1	St John's	Fr		2 000	Willett ATG
28-08	Antigua and Barbuda	D	2-2	St John's	Fr	Reginald Richardson [21], Shandel Samuel [54p]	2 500	Charles ATG
2-09	Guatemala	L	0-4	Guatemala City	WCq		24 000	Andino HON
11-09	Dominica	W	1-0	Kingstown	Fr	Akeeno Hazelwood [21]	2 500	Cambridge VIN
18-09	Grenada	W	2-1	Kingstown	WCq	Myron Samuel [22], Cornelius Stewart [72]	2 500	Ward CAN
7-10	Guatemala	L	0-3	Kingstown	WCq		3 000	Brea CUB
15-10	Grenada	D	1-1	St George's	WCq	Myron Samuel [22]	2 000	Willett ATG
11-11	Belize	D	1-1	Belmopan	WCq	Cornelius Stewart [11]	300	Skeete BRB
15-11	Belize	L	0-2	Kingstown	WCq		500	Thomas JAM

Fr = Friendly match • CC = Digicel Caribbean Cup • WC = FIFA World Cup • q = qualifier • r1 = first round group • † Not a full international

ST VINCENT AND THE GRENADINES NATIONAL TEAM HISTORICAL RECORDS

Past Coaches: Jorge Ramos BRA 1992 • Lenny Taylor JAM 1995-96 • Bertile St Clair ATG 1996 • Lenny Taylor JAM 2000-01 • Elvis Brown JAM 2002 • Adrian Shaw ENG 2003 • Zoran Vranes SRB 2004-07 • Roger Gurley 2008 • Stewart Hall 2009 • Samuel Carrington 2010 • Colwyn Rowe ENG 2011

VIR – US VIRGIN ISLANDS

FIFA/COCA-COLA WORLD RANKING

'93	'94	'95	'96	'97	'98	'99	'00	'01	'02	'03	'04	'05	'06	'07	'08	'09	'10	'11	'12
-	-	-	-	-	-	194	198	198	197	199	196	196	198	201	195	199	200	178	

2011												High	Low	Av
Jan	Feb	Mar	Apr	May	Jun	Jul	Aug	Sep	Oct	Nov	Dec			
200	200	200	200	200	193	149	149	151	169	177	178	149	202	195

American Samoa may have hogged all the headlines at the end of 2011 after winning their first international match, but the victory by the US Virgin Islands over neighbours British Virgin Islands in July 2011 was no less historic. After joining FIFA in 1998 the USVI had played 24 matches without a win before the two-legged tie against the BVI in the preliminary round of qualifying for the 2014 FIFA World Cup. In front of 350 fans in the Lionel Roberts Stadium in Charlotte Amalie that unwanted record came to an end. The heroes for the USVI in their 2-0 win that day were scorers Alderman Lesmond and Reid Klopp and it was Klopp who a week later secured a dramatic win in the return in Tortola with a goal deep into injury-time. Incredibly, the US Virgin Islands had not only won two games in the space of a week, having won none in the previous 12 years, but they also found themselves with six more games to play. There was little danger, though, of the team adding a third win and sure enough they were on the end of some big defeats against the more powerful teams of Haiti, Antigua and Curacao. However, for Terrence Jones and his team of players drawn from colleges in the USA and from local teams in the USVI, the 2014 World Cup will always be a source of fond memories thanks to their history-making exploits.

FIFA WORLD CUP RECORD
1930-1998 DNE   2002-2010 DNQ

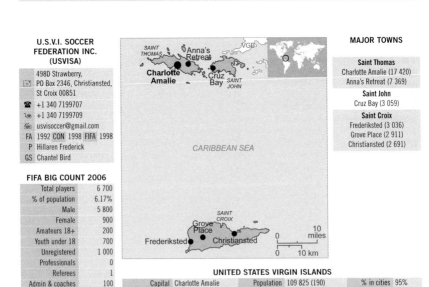

U.S.V.I. SOCCER FEDERATION INC. (USVISA)

498D Strawberry,
PO Box 2346, Christiansted,
St Croix 00851
☎ +1 340 7199707
📠 +1 340 7199709
📧 usvisoccer@gmail.com
FA 1992 CON 1998 FIFA 1998
P Hillaren Frederick
GS Chantel Bird

FIFA BIG COUNT 2006

Total players	6 700
% of population	6.17%
Male	5 800
Female	900
Amateurs 18+	200
Youth under 18	700
Unregistered	1 000
Professionals	0
Referees	1
Admin & coaches	100
Number of clubs	10
Number of teams	20

MAJOR TOWNS

Saint Thomas
Charlotte Amalie (17 420)
Anna's Retreat (7 369)
Saint John
Cruz Bay (3 059)
Saint Croix
Frederiksted (3 036)
Grove Place (2 911)
Christiansted (2 691)

UNITED STATES VIRGIN ISLANDS

Capital	Charlotte Amalie	Population	109 825 (190)	% in cities	95%
GDP per capita	$14 500 (78)	Area km²	1910 km² (181)	GMT +/-	-4
Neighbours (km)	Coast 188				

RECENT INTERNATIONAL MATCHES PLAYED BY THE US VIRGIN ISLANDS

1998	Opponents	Score		Venue	Comp	Scorers	Att	Referee
21-03	British Virgin Isl †	W	1-0	Frederiksted	Fr		300	
1999								
26-02	Turks & Caicos Isl	D	2-2	Frederiksted	CCq	Elvis Stephens [59], Colister Fahie [65]	200	
28-02	Bahamas	D	0-0	Nassau	CCq		200	
2000								
28-01	St Lucia	L	0-9	Frederiksted	Fr		350	
30-01	St Lucia	L	0-2	Frederiksted	Fr		280	
5-03	St Vincent/Grenadines	L	0-9	Kingstown	WCq		4 000	Alexander
19-03	St Vincent/Grenadines	L	1-5	Frederiksted	WCq	Joaquim Santos [72]	425	Forde BRB
2001								
24-03	British Virgin Islands	L	0-2	Tortola	Fr		200	
10-04	Haiti	L	1-12	Port au Prince	CCq	Jonas Verhoff [70]	6 000	Gutierrez
12-04	Guadeloupe †	L	0-11	Port au Prince	CCq		1 500	Grant HAI
14-04	St Lucia	L	1-14	Port au Prince	CCq	Dwight Ferguson [47]	1 000	Charin
2002								
16-08	Dominican Republic	L	1-6	Santo Domingo	CCq	Kevin Sheppard [44]	200	Forde BRB
18-08	Dominican Republic	L	1-5	Santo Domingo	CCq	Kevin Sheppard [69]	200	Laurent
2003								
No international matches played in 2003								
2004								
30-01	British Virgin Islands	L	0-5	Road Town	Fr		350	Charles DMA
31-01	Dominica	L	0-5	Road Town	Fr		550	Matthew SKN
18-02	St Kitts and Nevis	L	0-4	Charlotte Amalie	WCq		225	Brizan TRI
31-03	St Kitts and Nevis	L	0-7	Basseterre	WCq		800	Recinos SLV
25-09	British Virgin Islands	L	1-2	Road Town	Fr	Shane Challenger [65]	300	Frederick VIR
24-11	Haiti	L	0-11	Kingston	CCq		250	Piper TRI
26-11	Jamaica	L	1-11	Kingston	CCq	Victor Lauro [72]	4 200	Piper TRI
28-11	St Martin †	D	0-0	Kingston	CCq		200	Brizan TRI
2005								
No international matches played in 2005								
2006								
27-09	Bermuda	L	0-6	Charlotte Amalie	CCq		150	Small BRB
1-10	Dominican Republic	L	1-6	Charlotte Amalie	CCq	Bryce Pierre [7]	250	Davis TRI
2007								
No international matches played in 2007								
2008								
14-03	British Virgin Islands	D	0-0	Road Town	Fr		300	
15-03	British Virgin Islands	D	1-1	Road Town	Fr		350	
26-03	Grenada	L	0-10	St George's	WCq		3 000	James GUY
2009								
No international matches played in 2009								
2010								
No international matches played in 2010								
2011								
19-06	Anguilla	D	0-0	The Valley	Fr		550	Burton AIA
3-07	British Virgin Islands	W	2-0	Charlotte Amalie	WCq	Alderman Lesmond [7], Reid Klopp [57]	350	Navarro CAN
10-07	British Virgin Islands	W	2-1	Tortola	WCq	Dwayne Thomas [2], Reid Klopp [93+]	600	Morrison JAM
2-09	Haiti	L	0-6	Port au Prince	WCq		12 000	Cruz CRC
6-09	Antigua and Barbuda	L	1-8	Frederiksted	WCq	Jamie Browne [49]	250	Lancaster GUY
7-10	Haiti	L	0-7	Frederiksted	WCq		406	Holder CAY
11-10	Antigua and Barbuda	L	0-10	St John's	WCq		1 500	Matthew SKN
11-11	Curacao	L	0-3	Frederiksted	WCq		210	Navarro CAN
15-11	Curacao	L	1-6	Willemstad	WCq	Keithroy Cornelius [51]	2 000	Legister JAM

Fr = Friendly match • CC = Digicel Caribbean Cup • WC = FIFA World Cup • q = qualifier • † Not a full international

WAL – WALES

FIFA/COCA-COLA WORLD RANKING

'93	'94	'95	'96	'97	'98	'99	'00	'01	'02	'03	'04	'05	'06	'07	'08	'09	'10	'11	'12
29	41	61	80	102	97	98	109	100	52	66	68	71	73	57	60	77	112	48	

2011												High	Low	Av
Jan	Feb	Mar	Apr	May	Jun	Jul	Aug	Sep	Oct	Nov	Dec			
113	116	116	115	114	114	112	117	90	45	50	48	27	117	74

In the last four months of 2011 the Welsh national team began playing to its true potential with players like Tottenham's Gareth Bale, Arsenal's Aaron Ramsey and Liverpool's Craig Bellamy propelling the side over 70 places up the FIFA/Coca-Cola World Ranking with victories over Montenegro, Switzerland, Bulgaria and Norway. Just two weeks after the Norway game, however, the world of football was shocked by the death of the Welsh manager Gary Speed in an apparent suicide. Chris Coleman was given the task of following in his footsteps as the Welsh look to build on the good work Speed did during his brief spell in charge. In club football, Bangor City started the season with a record-breaking 14 successive wins, but looked to have thrown away a first league championship for 16 years after a poor run in March and April left them a point behind The New Saints going into the final match of the season - a crunch title decider between the two. Bangor secured the title with a 1-0 victory, thanks to a second-half Craig Garside goal in what was the final match at their Farrar Road ground. Bangor lost the Cup Final to Llanelli, however, in what was coach Neville Powell's first defeat in the competition since becoming manager in May 2007, ending a 22-match winning streak. For Llanelli it was an historic first triumph in the tournament.

UEFA EUROPEAN CHAMPIONSHIP RECORD

1960 DNE 1964 r1 1968-1972 DNQ 1976 QF 1980-2012 DNQ

THE FOOTBALL ASSOCIATION OF WALES, LTD (FAW)

11/12 Neptune Court,
Vanguard Way, Cardiff,
CF24 5PJ
☎ +44 29 20435830
🖷 +44 29 20496953
✉ info@faw.co.uk
🖵 www.faw.org.uk
FA 1876 CON 1954 FIFA 1910
P Phil Pritchard
GS Jonathan Ford

FIFA BIG COUNT 2006

Total players	173 550
% of population	5.91%
Male	157 550
Female	16 000
Amateurs 18+	35 800
Unregistered	41 000
Professionals	550
Referees	1 120
Admin & coaches	10 200
Number of clubs	1 900
Number of teams	4 500

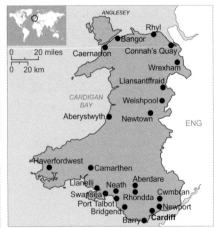

MAJOR CITIES/TOWNS

		Population
1	Cardiff	316 794
2	Swansea	173 870
3	Newport	120 052
4	Rhondda	60 062
5	Barry	53 457
6	Cwmbran	49 608
7	Llanelli	48 890
8	Neath	46 961
9	Wrexham	45 541
10	Bridgend	44 292
11	Pontypool	36 308
12	Port Talbot	34 926
13	Aberdare	34 611
14	Colwyn Bay	31 789
15	Pontypridd	31 614
16	Merthyr Tydfil	29 946
17	Rhyl	26 767
18	Aberystwyth	21 877
188	Llansantffraid	1 889

WALES (PART OF THE UNITED KINGDOM)

Capital	Cardiff	Population	3 004 600 (137)	% in cities	89%
GDP per capita	$30 546 (45)	Area km²	20 779 km² (154)	GMT +/-	0
Neighbours (km)	England 468 • Coast 627				

RECENT INTERNATIONAL MATCHES PLAYED BY WALES

2008	Opponents	Score	Venue	Comp	Scorers	Att	Referee
6-02	Norway	W 3-0	Wrexham	Fr	Fletcher [15], Koumas 2 [62 89]	7 553	McKeon IRE
26-03	Luxembourg	W 2-0	Luxembourg	Fr	Eastwood 2 [37 46]	3 000	Kuipers NED
28-05	Iceland	W 1-0	Reykjavik	Fr	Evans [45]	5 322	McCourt NIR
1-06	Netherlands	L 0-2	Rotterdam	Fr		48 500	Brych GER
20-08	Georgia	L 1-2	Swansea	Fr	Koumas [17]	6 435	Jug SVN
6-09	Azerbaijan	W 1-0	Cardiff	WCq	Vokes [83]	17 106	Stavrev MKD
10-09	Russia	L 1-2	Moscow	WCq	Ledley [67]	28 000	Skomina SVN
11-10	Liechtenstein	W 2-0	Cardiff	WCq	Edwards [42], Frick OG [80]	13 356	Vejlgaard DEN
15-10	Germany	L 0-1	Mönchengladbach	WCq		44 500	Duhamel FRA
19-11	Denmark	W 1-0	Brøndby	Fr	Bellamy [77]	10 271	Weiner GER
2009							
11-02	Poland	L 0-1	Vila Real	Fr		487	Paixao POR
28-03	Finland	L 0-2	Cardiff	WCq		22 604	Iturralde ESP
1-04	Germany	L 0-2	Cardiff	WCq		26 064	Hauge NOR
29-05	Estonia	W 1-0	Llanelli	Fr	Earnshaw [26p]	4 071	Thorisson ISL
6-06	Azerbaijan	W 1-0	Baku	WCq	Edwards [42]	25 000	Strombergsson SWE
12-08	Montenegro	L 1-2	Podgorica	Fr	Vokes [47]	5 000	Mazic SRB
9-09	Russia	L 1-3	Cardiff	WCq	Collins [53]	14 505	De Sousa POR
10-10	Finland	L 1-2	Helsinki	WCq	Bellamy [17]	14 000	Mazic SRB
14-10	Liechtenstein	W 2-0	Vaduz	WCq	Vaughan [16], Ramsey [80]	1 858	Kaldma EST
14-11	Scotland	W 3-0	Cardiff	Fr	Edwards [17], Church [32], Ramsey [35]	13 844	Zimmermann SUI
2010							
3-03	Sweden	L 0-1	Swansea	Fr		8 258	Black NIR
23-05	Croatia	L 0-2	Osijek	Fr		15 000	Vincic SVN
11-08	Luxembourg	W 5-1	Llanelli	Fr	Cotterill [35], Ledley [47p], King [55], Williams [78], Bellamy [82]	4 904	Gestranius FIN
3-09	Montenegro	L 0-1	Podgorica	ECq		7 442	Kakos GRE
8-10	Bulgaria	L 0-1	Cardiff	ECq		14 061	Eriksson SWE
12-10	Switzerland	L 1-4	Basel	ECq	Bale [13]	26 000	Hamer LUX
2011							
8-02	Republic of Ireland	L 0-3	Dublin	Fr		19 783	Courtney NIR
26-03	England	L 0-2	Cardiff	ECq		68 959	Benquerenca POR
25-05	Scotland	L 1-3	Dublin	Fr	Earnshaw [36]	6 036	Thomson SCO
27-05	Northern Ireland	W 2-0	Dublin	Fr	Ramsey [36], Earnshaw [71]	529	Kelly IRL
10-08	Australia	L 1-2	Cardiff	Fr	Blake [83]	6 378	Tohver EST
2-09	Montenegro	W 2-1	Cardiff	ECq	Morison [29], Ramsey [50]	8 194	Banti ITA
6-09	England	L 0-1	London	ECq		77 128	Schorgenhofer AUT
7-10	Switzerland	W 2-0	Swansea	ECq	Ramsey [60p], Bale [71]	12 317	Kuipers NED
11-10	Bulgaria	W 1-0	Sofia	ECq	Bale [45]	11 340	Gil POL
12-11	Norway	W 4-1	Cardiff	Fr	Bale [11], Bellamy [16], Vokes 2 [88 89]	12 600	Grubelnik AUT

Fr = Friendly match • EC = UEFA EURO 2012 • WC = FIFA World Cup • q = qualifier

WALES NATIONAL TEAM HISTORICAL RECORDS

Caps
92 - Neville Southall 1982-98 • **85** - Gary Speed 1990-2004 • **75** - Dean Saunders 1986-2001 • **73** - Peter Nicholas 1979-91 & Ian Rush 1980-96 • **72** - Mark Hughes 1984-99 & Joey Jones 1975-86 • **68** - Ivor Allchurch 1950-66 • **66** - Brian Flynn 1974-84 • **65** - Andy Melville 1989-2004 • **64** - Ryan Giggs 1991-2007 • **62** - David Phillips 1984-98 • **59** - Barry Horne 1988-96, Cliff Jones 1954-70, Kevin Ratcliffe 1981-93 & Terry Yorath 1970-81 • **58** - Craig Bellamy 1998-, Simon Davies 2001- & Leighton Phillips 1971-82

Goals
28 - Ian Rush 1980-96 • 23 - Ivor Allchurch 1950-66 & Trevor Ford 1947-57 • 22 - Dean Saunders 1986-2001 • 17 - Craig Bellamy 1998- • 16 - Mark Hughes 1984-99 & Cliff Jones 1954-70 • 15 - John Charles 1950-65 • 14 - Robert Earnshaw 2002- & John Hartson 1997-2005 • 13 - John Toshack 1969-80 • 12 - Ryan Giggs 1991-2007 & Billy Lewis 1885-1898 • 11 - Billy Meredith 1895-1920

Past Coaches
Committee 1876-1954 • Wally Barnes 1954-55 • Jimmy Murphy 1956-64 • Trevor Morris 1964 • Dave Bowen 1964-74 • Mike Smith ENG 1974-79 • Mike England 1979-87 • David Williams 1988 • Terry Yorath 1988-93 • John Toshack 1994 • Mike Smith ENG 1994-95 • Bobby Gould ENG 1995-99 • Mark Hughes 1999-2004 • John Toshack 2004-10 • Brian Flynn 2010 • Gary Speed 2010-11 • Chris Coleman 2012-

WALES 2010-11

LEAGUE OF WALES

	Pl	W	D	L	F	A	Pts	Bangor City	New Saints	Neath	Llanelli	Prestatyn	Port Talbot	Aberystwyth	Airbus UK	Newtown	Carmarthen	Bala Town	Haverfordwest
Bangor City †	32	22	4	6	80	44	70		4-3	1-0	2-1	1-2	2-0	2-5	2-1	1-2	8-1	2-2	2-1
The New Saints ‡	32	20	8	4	87	34	68	2-2		3-2	3-1	2-3	2-0	3-1	5-2	4-0	6-1	1-1	5-0
Neath Athletic ‡	32	16	10	6	62	41	58	1-2	1-2		1-1	2-2	1-1	0-4	2-1	1-2	1-0	0-1	1-1
Llanelli ‡	32	15	8	9	58	41	53	2-0	2-2	2-1		0-2	1-4	4-0	2-2	3-0	0-3	2-3	2-3
Prestatyn Town	32	10	10	12	44	46	40	4-2	1-2	0-0	0-2		1-1	1-1	1-1	1-2	1-1	2-0	4-0
Port Talbot Town	32	8	12	12	37	48	36	1-2	1-2	0-2	0-0	1-3		1-2	1-0	0-0	3-1	1-1	2-0
Aberystwyth Town	32	11	9	12	42	54	42	1-3	0-1	1-1	0-2	1-0	2-2		1-1	2-2	2-1	2-0	2-2
Airbus UK Broughton	32	11	8	13	53	52	41	1-1	2-2	2-2	1-2	3-4	2-0	3-1		5-3	1-1	0-2	2-4
Newtown	32	8	11	13	40	55	35	0-1	2-2	3-6	0-0	1-0	0-0	0-0	1-0		2-3	1-0	0-1
Carmarthen Town	32	10	5	17	39	64	35	0-1	1-3	0-3	1-3	2-1	1-3	2-3	0-1	1-4		1-2	1-1
Bala Town	32	10	3	19	41	57	33	2-3	3-4	0-2	1-0	2-1	0-0	2-3	2-1	1-2	0-3		4-1
Haverfordwest County	32	5	4	23	30	77	19	1-2	1-4	0-3	0-4	2-3	0-1	0-0	1-3	4-0	0-2	0-1	

13/08/2010 - 30/04/2011 • † Qualified for the UEFA Champions League • ‡ Qualified for the Europa League
Top scorers: **25** - Rhys Griffiths, Llanelli • **19** - Matthew Williams, TNS • **18** - Jamie Reed, Bangor & Lee Trundle ENG, Neath

WALES 2010-11
WELSH LEAGUE DIVISION 1 (2)

	Pl	W	D	L	F	A	Pts
Bryntirion Athletic	30	23	1	6	76	27	70
Afan Lido	30	20	5	5	63	28	65
Cambrian & Clydach V	30	17	6	7	68	37	57
Pontardawe Town	30	15	6	9	54	44	51
Caerau	30	15	4	11	66	52	49
Bridgend Town	30	14	5	11	60	47	47
West End	30	13	6	11	57	47	45
Cardiff Corinthians	30	12	4	14	58	52	40
Taffs Well	30	12	3	15	47	57	39
Aberaman Athletic	30	12	3	15	58	74	39
Goytre United	30	10	8	12	47	53	38
Cwmbran Celtic	30	10	7	13	45	50	37
Barry Town	30	9	8	13	39	55	35
Caldicot Town	30	8	3	19	37	48	27
Garden Village	30	6	7	17	41	75	25
Penrhiwceiber Rangers	30	4	4	22	27	97	16

1/09/2010 - 28/05/2011

WALES 2010-11
CYMRU ALLIANCE (2)

	Pl	W	D	L	F	A	Pts
Connah's Quay	30	23	2	5	89	33	71
Rhyl	30	19	5	6	73	32	62
Cefn Druids	30	18	6	6	60	29	60
Rhos Aelwyd	30	15	6	9	68	64	51
Caersws	30	15	5	10	59	49	50
Llandudno	30	13	10	7	50	35	49
Flint Town United	30	13	7	10	64	55	46
Porthmadog	30	14	4	12	59	54	46
Buckley Town	30	13	6	11	46	48	45
Llangefni Town	30	11	4	15	67	64	37
Penrhyncoch	30	9	10	11	49	56	37
Ruthin Town	30	11	4	15	39	58	37
Guilsfield	30	8	6	16	43	56	30
Rhydymwyn	30	4	6	20	27	82	18
Rhayader Town	30	4	3	23	34	76	15
Welshpool Town §18	30	5	6	19	39	76	3

13/08/2010 - 3/05/2011 • § = points deducted

LOOSEMORES CHALLENGE CUP (LEAGUE CUP) 2010-11

Semi-finals

The New Saints	9	3
Bangor City	0	1
Aberystwyth Town	0	1
Llanelli	1	3

Finals

The New Saints	4
Llanelli	3

Park Hall, Oswestry, 2-05-2011, Att: 310, Ref: Brian James.
Scorers - Aeron Edwards [43], Chris Sharp 2 [75][85], Scott Ruscoe [120] for TNS; Holloway [78], Moses [80], Follows [86] for Llanelli

MEDALS TABLE

		Overall			League			Cup		LC		PC	
		G	S	B	G	S	B	G	S	G	S	G	S
1	Wrexham	28	25					23	22			5	3
2	Cardiff City	23	12	1				22	10			1	2
3	Barry Town	18	3		7	1		6	1	4	1	1	
4	The New Saints	13	7	1	5	5	1	2	2	5			
5	Swansea City	12	10					10	8			2	2
6	Bangor City	11	15	3	3		3	8	9	6			
7	Rhyl	8	11	2	2	2	2	4	4	2	4	1	
8	NEWI Cefn Druids	8	5					8	5				
9	Shrewsbury Town	6	3					6	3				
10	Chirk	5	1					5	1				
11	Chester City	3	10					3	10				
12	Llanelli AFC	3	7	1	1	3	1	1	2	1	1	1	
13	Merthyr Tydfil	3	3					3	3				
14	Oswestry Town	3	1					3	1				
	Caersws	3	1							3	1		
16	Wellington Town	3						3					
17	Newtown	2	6		2			2	4				
18	Newport County	2	4					1	2			1	2
19	Carmarthen Town	2	3	1	1			1	2	1	1		
20	Afan Lido	2	2		1			1	2				
21	Crewe Alexandra	2						2					
22	Cwmbran Town	1	5	2	1	1	2	3		1			
23	UWIC Inter Cardiff	1	4		4			1					
24	Hereford United	1	3					1	3				
25	Connah's Quay	1	2					1	2				
26	Ebbw Vale	1	1	2				2	1			1	
27	Aberystwyth Town	1	1	1	1			1	1				

WELSH CUP 2010–11

Third Round		Fourth Round	Quarter-finals		Semi-finals		Final	
Llanelli *	1	Llanelli	Llanelli *	1	Llanelli †	1	Llanelli ‡	4
Aberystwyth Town	0		Prestatyn Town	0	The New Saints	0	Bangor City	1
Aberaman Athletic *	0	Cefn Druids *						
Cefn Druids	4							
Rhos Aelwyd	2	Rhos Aelwyd *						
Guilsfield *	1							
Cambrian & Clydach V *	2	Prestatyn Town						
Prestatyn Town	3							
Cardiff Grange Harlequins	2	Cardiff Grange Har'quins *	Cardiff Grange Harlequins	0				
Corus Steel *	0		The New Saints *	2				
Newtown *	1	Bridgend Town						
Bridgend Town	2							
Rhyl	1 7p	Rhyl *						
Neath Athletic *	1 6p							
Airbus UK Broughton *	2	The New Saints						
The New Saints	3							
Connah's Quay *	5	Connah's Quay	Connah's Quay *	4	Connah's Quay	0		
Porth	3		UWIC Inter Cardiff	0	Bangor City ††	1		
Goytre United *	2	Carmarthen Town *						
Carmarthen Town	3							
Bala Town	1	Bala Town						
Porthmadog *	0							
Bow Street *	2 5p	UWIC Inter Cardiff *						
UWIC Inter Cardiff	2 6p							
Port Talbot Town	4	Port Talbot Town *	Port Talbot Town *	0				
Gwalchmai *	1		Bangor City	3				
Llanidloes Town	2	Caersws						
Caersws *	4							
Haverfordwest County *	3	Haverfordwest County						
Holyhead Hotspurs	2							
Bryntirion Athletic	1	Bangor City *						
Bangor City *	2							

CUP FINAL

Parc y Scarlets, Llanelli

8-05-2011, 14.30. Att: 1719. Ref: Mark Petch

Scorers - Griffiths 2 [15 60], Moses [20], Venables [64] for Llanelli; Bull [51] for Bangor

Llanelli - Ashley Morris - Kris Thomas, Chris Venables, Stuart Jones, Wyn Thomas - Jason Bowen Jordan Follows 74), Antonio Corbisiero, Rhys Griffiths, Chris Holloway - Craig Moses, Ashley Evans. Tr: Andy Legg

Bangor - Paul Smith - Peter Hoy●, Chris Roberts●, Michael Johnston, Darren Moss - Dave Morley●, Clive Williams (Mark Smyth● 62), Nicky Ward, Chris Jones (Sion Edwards 75) - Les Davies, Alan Bull (Jebb 75). Tr: Neville Powell

* Home team • † Played at Park Hall, Oswestry • †† Played at Belle Vue, Rhyl • ‡ Qualified for the Europa League

YEM – YEMEN

FIFA/COCA-COLA WORLD RANKING

'93	'94	'95	'96	'97	'98	'99	'00	'01	'02	'03	'04	'05	'06	'07	'08	'09	'10	'11	'12
91	103	123	139	128	146	158	160	135	145	132	124	139	141	144	145	130	126	151	

	2011												High	Low	Av
Jan	Feb	Mar	Apr	May	Jun	Jul	Aug	Sep	Oct	Nov	Dec			
127	125	126	127	129	131	135	133	137	149	150	151	90	163	163

The political instability in Yemen throughout 2011 had an impact on football in the country although not as seriously as in some other countries affected by a violent response to the Arab Spring. Only three international matches were played during the year but a full league campaign was completed despite the problems. The league was reduced in size - notably by the withdrawal of 2010 champions Al Saqr - with Urooba cruising to the League title after finishing nine points clear of Al Tilal. It was a first-ever championship for Urooba who are traditionally one of the smaller sides from the capital Sana'a. The major casualty of the political crisis was the President's Cup which was cancelled. That meant that Tilal qualified for the 2012 AFC Cup alongside Urooba, thanks to their league position but both were hamstrung by the AFC's decision that all of their home games in the tournament should be played in neutral venues. That had also been the case for the national team in the 2014 FIFA World Cup qualifiers. Drawn against Iraq in a preliminary round tie, Yemen travelled to Arbil for the first leg which was lost 2-0. Home advantage may well have helped overcome that in the return but before a small crowd in the United Arab Emirates, Yemen could only draw the match 0-0 and their campaign was over for another four years.

FIFA WORLD CUP RECORD

1930-1982 DNE 1986-1990 DNQ (as North Yemen) 1930-1982 DNE 1986-1990 DNQ (as South Yemen) 1994-2010 DNQ

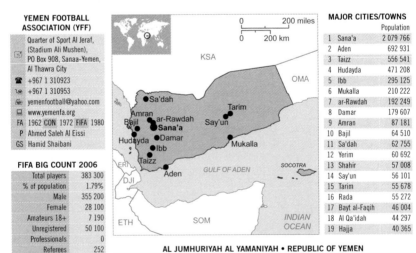

YEMEN FOOTBALL ASSOCIATION (YFF)

Quarter of Sport Al Jeraf, (Stadium Ali Mushen), PO Box 908, Sanaa-Yemen, Al Thawra City
☎ +967 1 310923
📠 +967 1 310953
✉ yemenfootball@yahoo.com
🖳 www.yemenfa.org
FA 1962 CON 1972 FIFA 1980
P Ahmed Saleh Al Eissi
GS Hamid Shaibani

FIFA BIG COUNT 2006

Total players	383 300
% of population	1.79%
Male	355 200
Female	28 100
Amateurs 18+	7 190
Unregistered	50 100
Professionals	0
Referees	252
Admin & coaches	250
Number of clubs	110
Number of teams	220

MAJOR CITIES/TOWNS

		Population
1	Sana'a	2 079 766
2	Aden	692 931
3	Taizz	556 541
4	Hudayda	471 208
5	Ibb	295 125
6	Mukalla	210 222
7	ar-Rawdah	192 249
8	Damar	179 607
9	Amran	87 181
10	Bajil	64 510
11	Sa'dah	62 755
12	Yerim	60 692
13	Shahir	57 008
14	Say'un	56 101
15	Tarim	55 678
16	Rada	55 272
17	Bayt al-Faqih	46 004
18	Al Qa'idah	44 297
19	Hajja	40 365

AL JUMHURIYAH AL YAMANIYAH • REPUBLIC OF YEMEN

Capital	Sana'a	Population	23 822 783 (48)	% in cities	31%
GDP per capita	$2500 (175)	Area km²	527 968 km² (49)	GMT +/-	+3
Neighbours (km)	Oman 288, Saudi Arabia 1458 • Coast 1906				

RECENT INTERNATIONAL MATCHES PLAYED BY YEMEN

2007	Opponents	Score	Venue	Comp	Scorers	Att	Referee
7-01	Eritrea	W 4-1	Sana'a	Fr	Akram Al Worafi [54], Fekri Al Hubaishi [71], Yaser Basuhai [73], Nashwan Al Haggam [79]		
12-01	Bahrain	L 0-4	Dubai	Fr			
17-01	Kuwait	D 1-1	Abu Dhabi	GCr1	Ali Al Omqy [16]		
20-01	UAE	L 1-2	Abu Dhabi	GCr1	Ala Al Sasi [90]		
23-01	Oman	L 1-2	Abu Dhabi	GCr1	Mohammed Salem [9]		
8-10	Maldives	W 3-0	Sana'a	WCq	Mohammed Salem [43], Fekri Al Hubaishi [66], Haitham Thabit [80]	3 000	Mansour LIB
28-10	Maldives	L 0-2	Male	WCq		8 900	Sarkar IND
9-11	Thailand	D 1-1	Sana'a	WCq	Ali Al Nono [43]	12 000	Al Ghamdi KSA
18-11	Thailand	L 0-1	Bangkok	WCq		29 000	Matsumura JPN
2008							
26-01	Bahrain	L 1-2	Manama	Fr	Abdullah Yaslam [67]		
4-04	Tanzania	W 2-1	Sana'a	Fr	Abdullah Yaslam 2 [2 50]		
25-04	Indonesia	L 0-1	Bandung	Fr			
3-05	Oman	D 0-0	Muscat	Fr			
22-05	Sudan	D 1-1	Sana'a	Fr	Muaz Assaj [47]		
2009							
5-01	UAE	L 1-3	Muscat	GCr1	Ali Al Nono [90]		
8-01	Saudi Arabia	L 0-6	Muscat	GCr1			
11-01	Qatar	L 1-2	Muscat	GCr1	Ali Al Nono [30p]		
20-01	Japan	L 1-2	Kumamoto	ACq	Zaher Al Fadhli [47]	32 000	Tan Hai CHN
28-01	Hong Kong	W 1-0	Sana'a	ACq	Akram Al Selwi [51]	10 000	Al Hilali OMA
8-11	Tanzania	D 1-1	Sana'a	Fr	Ali Mubarak [78]		
11-11	Tanzania	W 2-1	Sana'a	Fr	Tamer Hanash [13p], Akram Al Worafi [37]		
18-11	Bahrain	L 0-4	Manama	ACq		1 000	Basma SYR
30-12	Tajikistan	W 2-1	Sana'a	Fr	Khaled Baleid [71], Ali Al Nono [85]		
2010							
2-01	Tajikistan	L 0-1	Sana'a	Fr			
6-01	Japan	L 2-3	Sana'a	ACq	Basem Al Aqel [13], Salem Abbod [39]	10 000	Albadwawi UAE
15-01	Kenya	W 3-1	Sana'a	Fr	Ali Al Nono [45], Ala Al Sasi 2 [48 50]		
20-01	Bahrain	W 3-0	Sana'a	ACq	Ali Al Nono 2 [5 25], Mohammed Al Abidi [86]	7 000	Torky IRN
27-02	Malaysia	L 0-1	Kuala Lumpur	Fr			
3-03	Hong Kong	D 0-0	Hong Kong	ACq		1 212	Minh Tri Vo VIE
12-05	Malawi	W 1-0	Sana'a	Fr			
18-05	Oman	L 0-1	Sana'a	Fr			
7-09	Syria	W 2-1	Sana'a	Fr	Ali Al Nono 2 [18p 55]		
18-09	Zambia	L 0-1	Sana'a	Fr			
25-09	Iraq	L 1-2	Amman	WAr1	Ali Al Nono [10]		
27-09	Palestine	W 3-1	Amman	WAr1	Ali Al Nono 2 [43p 83], Haitham Thabit [63]		
1-10	Kuwait	D 1-1	Amman	WAsf	Ali Al Nono [55], L 3-4p		
13-10	India	W 6-3	Pune	Fr	Haitham Thabit [9], Khaled Baleid [28], Akram Al Worafi [61], Ala Al Sasi 2 [77 88], Yasser Basuhai [93+]		
7-11	Uganda	D 2-2	Sana'a	Fr	Ali Al Nono 2 [9 11]		
10-11	Korea DPR	D 1-1	Sana'a	Fr	Akram Al Worafi [42]		
22-11	Saudi Arabia	L 0-4	Aden	GCr1			Al Marzouqi UAE
25-11	Qatar	L 1-2	Zinjibar	GCr1	Akram Al Worafi [17]		Abid IRQ
28-11	Kuwait	L 0-3	Zinjibar	GCr1			Abbas BHR
2011							
8-07	Jordan	L 0-4	Istanbul	Fr			
23-07	Iraq	L 0-2	Arbil	WCq		20 000	Kovalenko UZB
28-07	Iraq	D 0-0	Al Ain	WCq		1 500	Basma SYR

Fr = Friendly match • GC = Gulf Cup • AC = AFC Asian Cup • WC = FIFA World Cup • q = qualifier • r1 = first round group

YEMEN NATIONAL TEAM HISTORICAL RECORDS

Coach: Milan Zivadinovic SRB 2003-04 • Rabah Saadane ALG 2004-05 • Mohsen Saleh 2007-09 • Hamza Al Jamal 2009 • Sami Hasan Al Nash 2009 • Srecko Jurcic CRO 2009-10 • Amine Al Sunaini 2010-

YEMEN 2011

PREMIER LEAGUE

	Pl	W	D	L	F	A	Pts	Urooba	Tilal	Ahly S	Sha'ab S	Hilal	Sha'ab H	Ittihad	Sha'ab I	Ahly T	Shabab	Wahda
Al Urooba ‡	20	13	5	2	36	18	**44**		2-2	1-1	2-0	1-0	3-0	1-0	2-1	1-0	4-0	2-1
Al Tilal Aden ‡	20	10	5	5	28	19	**35**	1-4		1-0	4-1	0-0	2-1	1-1	3-1	1-0	3-0	2-0
Al Ahly Sana'a	20	9	4	7	26	17	**31**	3-0	2-3		0-1	3-0	0-0	0-1	3-0	1-1	2-1	1-0
Al Sha'ab Sana'a	20	8	5	7	19	23	**29**	0-2	2-1	1-3		2-1	0-1	0-0	2-0	1-1	1-1	3-0
Al Hilal Hudayda	20	7	7	6	18	17	**28**	1-2	0-0	0-0	3-0		1-0	1-0	0-0	0-0	1-0	3-0
Al Sha'ab Hadramaut	20	7	6	7	17	22	**27**	3-3	1-2	1-0	0-1	2-1		1-0	1-0	1-1	0-0	1-0
Al Ittihad Ibb	20	7	5	8	22	22	**26**	1-1	1-0	1-3	3-1	1-3	4-2		0-1	1-0	2-2	0-1
Al Sha'ab Ibb	20	6	6	8	15	22	**24**	2-1	2-0	2-1	0-0	1-1	1-1	0-2		1-0	0-0	0-0
Al Ahly Taizz	20	5	8	7	13	14	**23**	0-1	1-0	1-3	0-1	1-1	0-0	0-0	1-0		1-0	1-1
Al Shabab Al Baydaa	20	5	7	8	21	24	**22**	0-0	0-0	2-0	1-1	4-0	3-2	4-1	0-3			0-2
Al Wahda Sana'a	20	3	2	15	10	27	**11**	2-3	0-2	0-1	0-1	0-1	0-1	1-2	1-2	0-1	1-0	

28/10/2010 - 29/07/2011 • ‡ Qualified for the AFC Cup • 2010 champions Al Saqr withdrew before the season with Al Rasheed and Hassan Abyan
Top scorers: **15** - Tesfaye Tafese ETH, Al Tilal • **9** - Ali Al Nono, Al Ahly Sana'a & Yordanos Abay ETH, Al Saqr

YEMEN 2011
SECOND DIVISION GROUP A (2)

	Pl	W	D	L	F	A	Pts
Al Wahda Aden	18	13	3	2	35	14	**42**
Taliat Taizz	18	12	1	5	30	14	**37**
Shamshan Aden	18	8	5	5	33	18	29
Khanfar	18	7	7	4	26	19	28
Al Ahli Hudayda	18	8	4	6	22	19	28
May 22 Sana'a	17	7	3	7	22	18	24
Salam Al Garfa	16	4	5	7	22	26	17
Doan	17	4	4	9	13	32	16
Rayan Sah	18	3	4	11	17	35	13
Al Jaza'a	16	1	4	11	8	33	7

23/12/2010 - 24/10/2011

YEMEN 2011
SECOND DIVISION GROUP B (2)

	Pl	W	D	L	F	A	Pts
Shula Aden	18	15	0	3	43	7	**45**
Najm Sba	18	12	4	2	30	15	**40**
Al Yarmuk Sana'a	18	10	4	4	34	18	34
Al Tadamun Shabwa	17	7	2	8	21	27	23
Al Nasir Al Dalaa	17	5	7	5	17	14	22
Shabab al Jeel	17	4	9	4	17	16	21
Saioon	17	5	4	8	17	20	19
Al Sharara Lahaj	16	4	4	8	18	29	16
Al Taawun Badan	17	3	4	10	14	32	13
Khusaier Al Mukalla	17	1	2	14	5	38	5

23/12/2010 - 24/10/2011

MEDALS TABLE

		Overall	Lge	Cup		City
		G	G	G	S	
1	Al Ahly	9	6	3		Sana'a
2	Al Hilal	4	2	2	2	Hudayda
	Al Tilal	4	2	2	2	Aden
4	Al Sha'ab	4	2	2	1	Ibb
5	Al Wahda	4	4			Sana'a
6	Al Sha'ab Hadramaut	2		2	3	Mukalla
7	Al Saqr	2	2			Taizz
8	Al Ahli	1		1		Hudayda
	Al Ittihad	1		1		Ibb
	Al Urooba	1	1			Zabid
11	Al Shula			2		Aden
12	Al Rasheed			1		Taizz
	Al Shabab			1		Al Baydaa
	Al Tadamun			1		Shabwa

ZAM – ZAMBIA

FIFA/COCA-COLA WORLD RANKING

'93	'94	'95	'96	'97	'98	'99	'00	'01	'02	'03	'04	'05	'06	'07	'08	'09	'10	'11	'12
27	21	25	20	21	29	36	49	64	67	68	70	58	62	65	72	84	76	79	

	2011														
	Jan	Feb	Mar	Apr	May	Jun	Jul	Aug	Sep	Oct	Nov	Dec	High	Low	Av
	81	102	97	89	90	72	74	76	83	80	79	79	15	102	53

Zambia were crowned African champions after a fairy-tale success story at the 2012 CAF Africa Cup of Nations, overcoming three of the pre-tournament favourites for a deserved triumph. The side, who had fired coach Dario Bonetti just three months before the tournament and re-employed flamboyant Frenchman Herve Renard, beat Senegal to take top place in Group A and then overcame Ghana in the semi-final and Cote d'Ivoire on a penalty shoot-out in the final in Libreville. The success was made poignant by the fact it came just miles from the site of the air crash that wiped out almost their entire team in 1993. Zambia had twice before been Nations Cup runners-up - in 1974 and 1994 - but were not considered one of the fancied sides for 2012. They have, however, been a consistent presence at the Nations Cup having appeared at 11 of the last 12, while eight of their squad had played at the previous four tournaments. The triumph came after the end of a year that at club level had seen Power Dynamos crowned league winners for the first time since 2000. Coached by former international midfielder Beston Chambeshi, Dynamos completed the double in December by beating Konkola Blades in the Cup Final. The hope is that the feel-good factor surrounding the national team triumph will have a knock-on effect at club level.

CAF AFRICA CUP OF NATIONS RECORD

1957-1968 DNE 1970-1972 DNQ **1974** 2 F 1976 DNQ **1978** 5 r1 1980 DNQ **1982** 3 SF 1984 DNQ
1986 7 r1 1988 DNE **1990** 3 SF **1992** 7 QF **1994** 2 F **1996** 3 SF **1998** 10 r1 **2000** 13 r1
2002 14 r1 2004 DNQ **2006** 11 r1 **2008** 9 r1 **2010** 7 QF **2012** 1 Winners

FOOTBALL ASSOCIATION OF ZAMBIA (FAZ)

Football House, Alick Nkhata Road, Long Acres, PO Box 34751, Lusaka

☎ +260 211 250940
📠 +260 211 250946
✉ faz@zamnet.zm
🖥 www.fazfootball.com

FA 1929 CON 1964 FIFA 1964
P Kalusha Bwalya
GS George Kasengele

FIFA BIG COUNT 2006

Total players	1 024 817
% of population	8.91%
Male	992 786
Female	32 031
Amateurs 18+	19 560
Youth under 18	9 050
Unregistered	975 606
Professionals	101
Referees	524
Admin & coaches	11 035
Number of clubs	470
Number of teams	2 350

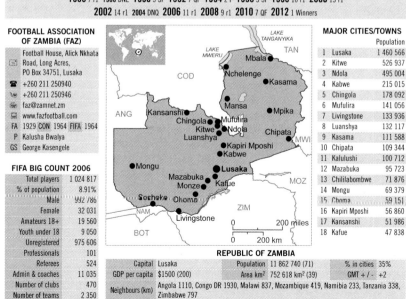

MAJOR CITIES/TOWNS

		Population
1	Lusaka	1 460 566
2	Kitwe	526 937
3	Ndola	495 004
4	Kabwe	215 015
5	Chingola	178 092
6	Mufulira	141 056
7	Livingstone	133 936
8	Luanshya	132 117
9	Kasama	111 588
10	Chipata	109 344
11	Kalulushi	100 712
12	Mazabuka	95 723
13	Chililabombwe	71 876
14	Mongu	69 379
15	Choma	59 151
16	Kapiri Mposhi	56 860
17	Kansanshi	51 986
18	Kafue	47 838

REPUBLIC OF ZAMBIA

Capital	Lusaka	Population	11 862 740 (71)	% in cities 35%
GDP per capita	$1500 (200)	Area km²	752 618 km² (39)	GMT +/- +2
Neighbours (km)	Angola 1110, Congo DR 1930, Malawi 837, Mozambique 419, Namibia 233, Tanzania 338, Zimbabwe 797		

RECENT INTERNATIONAL MATCHES PLAYED BY ZAMBIA

2009 Opponents	Score	Venue	Comp	Scorers	Att	Referee
21-11 Korea DPR	W 4-1	Lusaka	Fr	James Chamanga 3 [10 13 70], Felix Sunzu [90]		
28-11 Kenya	W 2-0	Nairobi	CEr1	James Chamanga [88], Stopila Sunzu [90]		
2-12 Ethiopia	W 1-0	Nairobi	CEr1	James Chamanga [30]		
4-12 Djibouti	W 6-0	Nairobi	CEr1	Kennedy Chola 3 [4 49 89], Felix Sunzu [33], Kebby Hachipaka [65], Charles Siyanga [74]		
7-12 Zanzibar †	D 0-0	Nairobi	CEqf	L 3-4p		
28-12 Mozambique	W 1-0	Johannesburg	Fr	Collins Mbesuma [76]		
2010						
9-01 Korea Republic	W 4-2	Johannesburg	Fr	Felix Katongo [6], Rainford Kalaba [14], James Chamanga [63], Noah Chivuta [72p]	2 000	Gomes RSA
13-01 Tunisia	D 1-1	Lubango	CNr1	Jacob Mulenga [19]	17 000	Coulibaly MLI
17-01 Cameroon	L 2-3	Lubango	CNr1	Jacob Mulenga [8], Chris Katongo [81p]	15 000	Al Ghamdi KSA
21-01 Gabon	W 2-1	Benguela	CNr1	Rainford Kalaba [28], James Chamanga [62]	5 000	Benouza ALG
25-01 Nigeria	D 0-0	Lubango	CNqf	L 4-5p	10 000	Abd El Fatah EGY
26-05 Chile	L 0-3	Calama	Fr		12 000	Favale ARG
11-08 Uganda	D 1-1	Kampala	Fr	OG [22]		
5-09 Comoros	W 4-0	Lusaka	CNq	Rainford Kalaba [5], Fwayo Tembo [21], James Chamanga [30], Emmanuel Mayuka [82]		Eyob ERI
18-09 Yemen	W 1-0	Sana'a	Fr	Rainford Kalaba [15]		
10-10 Libya	L 0-1	Tripoli	CNq			Gassama GAM
27-11 Tanzania	W 1-0	Dar es Salaam	CEr1	Kennedy Mudenda [24]		
30-11 Burundi	D 0-0	Dar es Salaam	CEr1			
3-12 Somalia	W 6-0	Dar es Salaam	CEr1	Felix Sunzu 4 [25 27 43 49p], Alan Mukuka [28], Venecious Mapande [81]		
7-12 Ethiopia	L 1-2	Dar es Salaam	CEqf	Felix Sunuzu [58]		
31-12 Kuwait	L 0-4	Suez	Fr			
2011						
9-02 Swaziland	W 4-0	Manzini	Fr	James Chamanga [15], Collins Mbesuma [47], Isaac Chansa [60], Cifford Mulenga [92+]		
27-03 Mozambique	W 2-0	Maputo	CNq	James Chamanga [15], Emmanuel Mayuka [90]		
4-06 Mozambique	W 3-0	Chingola	CNq	Chris Katongo 2 [47 68], Collins Mbesuma [86]		
10-08 Zimbabwe	L 0-2	Harare	Fr			
4-09 Comoros	W 2-1	Mitsamiouli	CNq	Felix Katongo [23], Emmanuel Mayuka [87]		
8-10 Libya	D 0-0	Chingola	CNq			
15-11 Nigeria	L 0-2	Kaduna	Fr			
29-11 India	W 5-0	Margao	Fr	Jimmy Chisenga [14], Joseph Sitali [56], Bruce Musakanya 3 [69 72 90]		
18-12 Angola	L 0-1	Dundo	Fr			
2012						
14-01 Namibia	D 0-0	Johannesburg	Fr			
21-01 Senegal	W 2-1	Bata	CNr1	Emmanuel Mayuka [12], Rainford Kalaba [20]	17 500	Alioum CMR
25-01 Libya	D 2-2	Bata	CNr1	Emmanuel Mayuka [29], Chris Katongo [54]	1 500	Coulibaly MLI
29-01 Equatorial Guinea	W 1-0	Malabo	CNr1	Chris Katongo [67]	44 000	Benouza ALG
4-02 Sudan	W 3-0	Bata	CNqf	Stopila Sunzu [15], Chris Katongo [66], James Chamanga [86]	200	Gassama GAM
8-02 Ghana	W 1-0	Bata	CNsf	Emmanuel Mayuka [78]	8 000	Alioum CMR
12-02 Côte d'Ivoire	D 0-0	Libreville	CNf	W 8-7p	40 000	Diatta SEN

Fr = Friendly match • CC = COSAFA Cup • CE = CECAFA Cup • CN = CAF African Cup of Nations • WC = FIFA World Cup • BCD = Behind closed doors
q = qualifier • r1 = first round group • qf = quarter-final • sf = semi-final • f = final • † Not an official international

ZAMBIA NATIONAL TEAM HISTORICAL RECORDS

Past Coaches Jochen Figge GER 1992-93 • Godfrey Chitalu 1993 • Ian Porterfield SCO 1993-94 • Roald Poulsen DEN 1994-96 • George Mungwa 1996-97 • Obby Kapita 1997 • Burkhard Ziese GER 1997-98 • Ben Bamfuchile 1998-2001 • Jan Brouwer NED 2001 • Roald Poulsen DEN 2002 • Kalusha Bwalya 2003-06 • Patrick Phiri 2006-08 • Herve Renard FRA 2008-10 • Dario Bonetti ITA 2010-11 • Herve Renard FRA 2011-

ZAMBIA 2011

KONKOLA COPPER MINES PREMIER LEAGUE

	Pl	W	D	L	F	A	Pts	Dynamos	Red Arrows	Konkola	Nchanga	Buffaloes	ZESCO	Nkana	Zanaco	F Rangers	Nakambala	Eagles	Roan	Kabwe	Hotspurs	Nkwazi	Kalewa
Power Dynamos †	30	18	5	7	49	18	59		4-0	2-1	3-0	4-1	0-0	0-1	3-1	0-1	3-0	2-1	1-2	2-0	3-1	5-0	2-0
Red Arrows ‡	30	14	11	5	41	23	53	1-1		1-1	0-0	2-1	0-1	2-1	5-1	1-1	3-0	2-2	1-1	1-0	6-1	3-3	3-0
Konkola Blades	30	13	11	6	28	18	50	1-0	1-0		1-0	0-0	2-0	2-0	0-0	1-1	0-0	0-1	0-0	0-1	0-2	2-1	2-0
Nchanga Rangers	30	14	7	9	23	18	49	0-2	0-0	1-0		0-2	1-0	1-0	2-1	1-2	2-0	1-1	2-0	1-0	1-0	0-0	4-0
Green Buffaloes	30	13	9	8	31	24	48	0-0	0-1	0-1	1-0		1-1	1-0	0-1	1-1	0-1	1-0	3-2	2-1	1-1	1-1	0-0
ZESCO United	30	13	8	9	33	19	47	0-1	0-1	0-1	0-1	1-0		2-1	2-0	0-0	3-0	4-0	0-0	2-0	2-1	0-1	3-0
Nkana	30	13	7	10	35	29	46	0-0	0-2	1-1	0-0	2-0	2-3		0-2	3-0	2-1	0-0	2-1	2-2	1-0	1-1	2-0
Zanaco	30	12	8	10	37	31	44	0-1	0-1	2-3	0-0	1-3	2-1	1-1		2-2	2-0	0-0	2-3	2-0	3-0	5-0	1-0
Forest Rangers	30	10	12	8	30	26	42	0-1	2-0	1-1	2-0	1-2	0-0	1-0	0-1		2-1	0-0	1-2	1-2	0-0	2-1	3-0
Nakambala Leopards	30	12	5	13	24	35	41	2-1	0-1	1-1	1-0	0-1	0-0	1-2	1-2	2-1		1-0	2-0	1-0	1-0	1-0	1-1
Green Eagles	30	9	11	10	21	23	38	2-3	0-0	0-0	0-0	0-1	0-0	2-0	1-2	0-0	0-1		2-0	2-1	1-0	1-0	2-0
Roan United	30	8	10	12	27	35	34	0-3	0-0	1-2	0-1	0-0	1-2	0-1	0-0	3-2	0-1	0-0		1-2	2-1	2-1	3-1
Kabwe Warriors	30	8	6	16	22	28	30	0-1	0-0	1-0	0-1	0-0	1-0	0-1	0-2	0-0	4-0	2-0	1-1		0-0	0-1	3-0
Lime Hotspurs	30	8	6	16	21	34	30	1-1	1-0	1-1	0-1	0-2	0-1	0-2	0-0	1-2	1-0	0-1	0-1	1-0		1-0	1-0
Nkwazi	30	7	7	16	28	53	28	1-0	1-3	0-2	1-0	1-4	2-2	2-4	1-0	0-1	2-2	2-1	1-1	2-1	0-1		1-4
Kalewa	30	4	5	21	17	53	17	1-0	0-1	0-1	1-2	1-2	0-3	1-3	1-1	0-0	1-2	0-1	0-0	1-0	1-0	1-5	3-1	

2/04/2011 - 13/11/2011 • † Qualified for the CAF Champions League • ‡ Qualified for the CAF Confederation Cup

BARCLAYS CUP 2010-11

Quarter-finals

ZESCO United	1
Nakambala Leopards	0
Nkwazi	0
Power Dynamos	1
Lime Hotspurs	0 4p
Nchanga Rangers	0 2p
Green Buffaloes	0
Zanaco	2

Semi-finals

ZESCO United	2
Power Dynamos	0
Lime Hotspurs	0 4p
Zanaco	0 5p

Semis played at A. Davies, Kitwe

Final

ZESCO United	2
Zanaco	0

Nkoloma, Lusaka, 9-04-2011
Scorers - Alfred Luputa [32], Clifford Chipalo [93+] for ZESCO

BARCLAYS CUP 2011

Quarter-finals

Power Dynamos	7
Luena Buffaloes	0
Indeni	0
Red Arrows	2
Nkana	2
Zanaco	0
Nakambala Leopards	0
Konkola Blades	2

Semi-finals

Power Dynamos	2
Red Arrows	0
Nkana	1
Konkola Blades	2

Semis played at Nkoloma, Lusaka

Final

Power Dynamos	2
Konkola Blades	1

Arthur Davies, Kitwe, 4-12-2011
Scorers - Simon Bwalya [20], Mukuka Mulenga [27] for Dynamos; Elson Mkandawire [67] for Konkola

MEDALS TABLE

		Overall			Lg	C	T8	LC	BC	Africa			City
		G	S	B	G	G	G	G	G	G	S	B	
1	Mufulira Wanderers	27		3	9	9	9					3	Mufulira
2	Nkana	24	1	5	11	6	7				1	5	Kitwe
3	Kabwe Warriors	19			5	5	8	1					Kabwe
4	Power Dynamos	18	1		6	6	2	1	2	1		1	Kitwe
5	Green Buffaloes	12			6	1	5						Lusaka
6	Zanaco	11			5	1	3	2					Lusaka
7	Roan United	8			1	4	3						Luanshya
	ZESCO United	8			3	1		1	3				Ndola
9	Nchanga Rangers	6	1		2	1	3					1	Chingola
10	City of Lusaka	5			1	2	2						Lusaka
11	Red Arrows	3			1	1	1						Lusaka
	Konkola Blades	3					3						Chililabombwe

C = Castle/Independence/Mosi Cup • T8 = Top 8 Cup • LC = League Cup (2001-07) • BC = Barclays Cup

ZIM – ZIMBABWE

FIFA/COCA-COLA WORLD RANKING

'93	'94	'95	'96	'97	'98	'99	'00	'01	'02	'03	'04	'05	'06	'07	'08	'09	'10	'11	'12
46	51	59	71	74	74	67	68	68	57	53	60	53	76	87	97	109	119	98	

						2011									
	Jan	Feb	Mar	Apr	May	Jun	Jul	Aug	Sep	Oct	Nov	Dec	High	Low	Av
	117	113	127	129	126	87	86	74	66	74	70	98	40	131	72

On-going revelations of widespread involvement by players and coaches in match fixing when Zimbabwe's national team traveled to Asia for friendly matches during 2011, began to have a serious impact on football in the country. A clean-up campaign instituted by a new regime in charge at the Zimbabwe Football Association has seen some 80 footballers disqualified from playing for the national team and the suspension of coach Norman Mapeza. It was the first step in the investigation and there are expected to be more serious sanctions once it is completed. Mapeza had returned to the coaching role at the start of the year after the abortive attempt to hire Belgian Tom Saintfiet in late 2010. Zimbabwe remained in contention for a Nations Cup berth after a mid-year win at home over Mali but a loss in the Cape Verde Islands in their last game ended their slim hopes. A home-based team were guest competitors at the end of year East and Central African Senior Challenge Cup in Zambia where Zimbabwe lost to eventual winners Uganda in the quarter-finals. A dramatic run in to the Premier League saw Dynamos back at the summit for the first time since 2007. The country's most popular club edged FC Platinum on goal difference on the last day of the campaign and then won the newly created Mbada Diamonds Cup to complete the double.

CAF AFRICA CUP OF NATIONS RECORD

1957-1980 DNE 1982-2002 DNQ **2004** 12 r1 **2006** 12 r1 2008-2012 DNQ

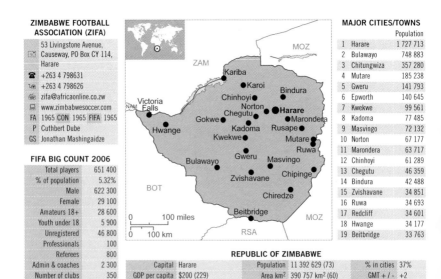

ZIMBABWE FOOTBALL ASSOCIATION (ZIFA)

53 Livingstone Avenue,
Causeway, PO Box CY 114,
Harare
☎ +263 4 798631
📠 +263 4 798626
✉ zifa@africaonline.co.zw
🖥 www.zimbabwesoccer.com
FA 1965 CON 1965 FIFA 1965
P Cuthbert Dube
GS Jonathan Mashingaidze

FIFA BIG COUNT 2006

Total players	651 400
% of population	5.32%
Male	622 300
Female	29 100
Amateurs 18+	28 600
Youth under 18	5 900
Unregistered	46 800
Professionals	100
Referees	800
Admin & coaches	2 300
Number of clubs	350
Number of teams	1 250

MAJOR CITIES/TOWNS

		Population
1	Harare	1 727 713
2	Bulawayo	748 883
3	Chitungwiza	357 280
4	Mutare	185 238
5	Gweru	141 793
6	Epworth	140 645
7	Kwekwe	99 561
8	Kadoma	77 485
9	Masvingo	72 132
10	Norton	67 177
11	Marondera	63 717
12	Chinhoyi	61 289
13	Chegutu	46 359
14	Bindura	42 488
15	Zvishavane	34 851
16	Ruwa	34 693
17	Redcliff	34 601
18	Hwange	34 177
19	Beitbridge	33 763

REPUBLIC OF ZIMBABWE

Capital Harare	Population 11 392 629 (73)	% in cities 37%
GDP per capita $200 (229)	Area km² 390 757 km² (60)	GMT +/- +2
Neighbours (km) Botswana 813, Mozambique 1231, South Africa 225, Zambia 797		

RECENT INTERNATIONAL MATCHES PLAYED BY ZIMBABWE

2008	Opponents		Score	Venue	Comp	Scorers	Att	Referee
11-03	South Africa	L	1-2	Johannesburg	Fr	Gilbert Mushangazhike [12]		
26-03	Botswana	W	1-0	Gaborone	Fr	Cuthbert Malajila [48]		
1-06	Guinea	D	0-0	Conakry	WCq		12 000	Haimoudi ALG
8-06	Namibia	W	2-0	Harare	WCq	Gilbert Mushangazhike 2 [26 85]	27 979	Lwanja MWI
14-06	Kenya	L	0-2	Nairobi	WCq		27 500	Diatta SEN
22-06	Kenya	D	0-0	Harare	WCq		23 000	Kotey GHA
27-07	Zambia	D	0-0	Thulamahashe	CCqf	L 4-5p		Nhlapo RSA
20-08	Botswana	W	1-0	Harare	Fr	Edward Sadomba [30]		
7-09	Guinea	D	0-0	Harare	WCq		23 000	Evehe CMR
10-09	Oman	L	2-3	Muscat	Fr	Pride Tafirenyika [15], Justice Majabvi [67]		
11-10	Namibia	L	2-4	Windhoek	WCq	Esrom Nyandoro [58], Cuthbert Malajila [85]	4 000	Coulibaly MLI
2009								
11-02	Tanzania	D	0-0	Dar es Salaam	Fr			
23-03	Bahrain	L	2-5	Manama	Fr	Ashley Rambanapasi [86p], Tito Marfumo [91+]		
13-05	Jordan	L	0-2	Amman	Fr			
12-08	Lesotho	D	1-1	Bulawayo	Fr	Guthrie Zhokinyu [80]		
17-10	Mauritius	W	3-0	Harare	CCr1	Cuthbert Malajila 2 [48 57], Method Mwanjale [87]		Ebrahim RSA
19-10	Lesotho	D	2-2	Harare	CCr1	Cuthbert Malajila [6], Sello OG [62]		Ramocha BOT
26-10	Botswana	W	1-0	Bulawayo	CCqf	Mthulisi Maphosa [88]		Carvalho ANG
28-10	South Africa †	D	1-1	Harare	CCsf	Phillip Marufu [54]. W 3-2p		Seechurn MRI
1-11	Zambia	W	3-1	Harare	CCf	Nyasha Mushekwi 2 [26 35], Cuthbert Malajila [45]		Carvalho ANG
1-12	Eritrea †	D	0-0	Nairobi	CFr1			
3-12	Somalia †	W	2-0	Nairobi	CFr1	Tapiwa Mangezi [30], Guthrie Zhokinyi [46]		
5-12	Rwanda †	L	0-1	Nairobi	CFr1			
8-12	Rwanda †	L	1-4	Nairobi	CFqf	Lionel Mtizwa [8]		
29-12	Thailand	L	0-3	Bangkok	Fr			
2010								
27-01	South Africa	L	0-3	Durban	Fr		35 000	Nhleko SWZ
3-03	Malawi	W	2-1	Harare	Fr	OG [17], Tafadzwa Rusike [25]		
2-06	Brazil	L	0-3	Harare	Fr		30 000	Martins ANG
4-08	Botswana	L	0-2	Selibe-Phikwe	Fr			
5-09	Liberia	D	1-1	Paynesville	CNq	Knowledge Musona [30]		Codjia BEN
10-10	Cape Verde Islands	D	0-0	Harare	CNq			Ndume GAB
2011								
26-03	Mali	L	0-1	Bamako	CNq			
5-06	Mali	W	2-1	Harare	CNq	Knowledge Musona 2 [45 90p]		
10-08	Zambia	W	2-0	Harare	Fr	Willard Katsande [45], Khama Billiat [47]		
4-09	Liberia	W	3-0	Harare	CNq	Willard Katsande [16], Ovidy Karuru [45], Khama Billiat [85]		
8-10	Cape Verde Islands	L	1-2	Praia	CNq	Knowledge Musona [68]		
15-11	South Africa	W	2-1	Harare	Fr	Knowledge Musona 2 [52 66]		
27-11	Djibouti	W	2-0	Dar es Salaam	CFr1	Donald Ngoma [9], Qadr Amin [73]		
29-11	Rwanda	L	0-2	Dar es Salaam	CFr1			
3-12	Tanzania	W	2-1	Dar es Salaam	CFr1	Donald Ngoma [1], OG [11]		
6-12	Uganda	L	0-1	Dar es Salaam	CFqf			

Fr = Friendly match • CN = CAF African Cup of Nations • CC = COSAFA Cup • CF = CECAFA Cup • WC = FIFA World Cup
q = qualifier • r1 = first round group • qf = quarter-final • sf = semi-final • f = final • † Not a full international

ZIMBABWE 2011

NATIONAL PREMIER SOCCER LEAGUE

	Pl	W	D	L	F	A	Pts	Dynamos	Platinum	Motor Action	Hwange	Gunners	CAPS United	Highlanders	Chicken Inn	Blue Ribbon	Monomatapa	Black Mambas	Shabanie Mine	Masvingo	Saints	Shooting Stars	Kiglon Bird
Dynamos †	30	17	7	6	42	15	58		2-0	2-0	0-0	0-0	2-1	3-1	1-0	1-2	2-0	1-1	2-0	5-1	4-0	1-0	2-0
FC Platinum †	30	17	7	6	44	21	58	0-1		0-0	2-0	0-3	1-1	2-0	1-1	1-0	3-0	3-1	1-0	3-0	1-0	2-0	2-0
Motor Action ‡	30	13	12	5	33	18	51	2-0	2-1		0-0	3-2	2-0	1-0	1-1	0-1	1-0	2-0	3-0	1-1	1-1	0-0	2-0
Hwange ‡	30	14	8	8	31	23	50	0-0	0-1	3-2		0-0	1-0	0-1	2-0	1-0	2-1	1-0	2-1	5-2	1-0	2-0	2-1
Gunners	30	12	8	10	37	30	44	1-3	2-1	0-0	2-1		0-0	1-2	0-1	2-2	1-1	1-0	0-0	1-0	2-1	2-0	0-2
CAPS United	30	12	7	11	44	34	43	0-1	2-2	2-0	0-1	0-3		3-1	1-0	4-1	0-3	1-1	4-0	4-1	5-3	1-0	2-0
Highlanders	30	12	7	11	27	24	43	0-0	1-0	0-2	0-1	2-1	1-0		1-1	1-0	0-0	3-0	0-2	0-0	3-0	1-1	0-0
Chicken Inn	30	10	12	8	32	20	42	0-0	1-1	0-0	2-0	2-0	1-2	1-0		2-2	0-0	1-2	1-0	0-0	1-0	4-1	3-0
Blue Ribbon Stars	30	9	11	10	32	42	38	1-0	0-2	0-1	0-0	1-1	2-0	2-1	1-0		1-1	3-3	1-1	1-0	2-0	1-1	3-0
Monomatapa United	30	7	15	8	27	30	36	0-1	0-2	0-0	0-1	1-5	0-0	1-0	2-1	1-1		3-0	1-1	2-0	2-2	2-2	1-1
Black Mambas	30	10	6	14	34	40	36	1-4	0-3	0-2	1-0	0-1	1-1	1-0	0-1	1-2	0-0		6-0	5-1	3-1	2-1	1-2
Shabanie Mine	30	8	10	12	30	43	34	0-0	1-3	0-0	3-2	1-2	2-0	2-0	0-2	3-3	1-0	1-2		1-0	2-0	1-0	3-1
Masvingo United	30	8	10	12	31	46	34	1-0	1-1	1-3	2-1	3-2	1-0	1-0	0-0	3-0	0-0	1-3	2-2		0-0	2-0	0-3
Zimbabwe Saints	30	5	13	12	23	36	28	1-0	0-0	0-0	1-1	2-1	0-0	0-0	1-0	1-1	1-1	0-0	1-1	0-0		2-2	1-0
Shooting Stars	30	7	6	17	27	45	27	1-4	1-3	1-0	0-1	1-0	2-5	0-1	0-0	2-0	1-2	0-1	1-1	3-0	2-1		3-1
Kiglon Bird	30	5	9	16	22	49	24	1-0	1-2	2-2	0-0	0-1	1-5	0-0	0-5	2-2	0-1	2-0	0-0	0-0	3-2	0-3	

26/03/2011 - 20/11/2011 • † Qualified for the CAF Champions League • ‡ Qualified for the CAF Confederation Cup

BANC ABC SUPER EIGHT 2011

Quarter-finals

Motor Action	2
Monomatapa U	1
Hwange	1
Dynamos	2
Shabanie Mine	1
Gunners	0
CAPS United	0
Highlanders	1

Semi-finals

Motor Action	0 7p
Dynamos	0 6p
Shabanie Mine	0
Highlanders	1

Final

Motor Action	1
Highlanders	0

Barbourfields, Bulawayo
10-09-2011
Scorer - Allan Gahadzikwa [11]
for Motor Action

MEDALS TABLE

		All	Lg	C	IT	LC	S8	
		G	G	G	G	G		City
1	Dynamos	38	19	10	6	2	1	Harare
2	CAPS United	23	4	9	4	5	1	Harare
3	Highlanders	16	7	2	6	1		Bulawayo
4	Zimbabwe Saints	6	2	3	1			Bulawayo
5	Black Rhinos	5	2	1	2			Mutare
	Black Aces	5	2	2		1		Harare
7	Masvingo Utd	4		2	2			Masvingo
8	Hwange	3		3				Hwange
	Arcadia United	3	1	2				Harare
	Bulawayo Rov	3	2	1				Bulawayo
	Motor Action	3	1		1		1	Mutare

Lg = League • C = Castle/Unity/CBZ/Mbada Cup • IT = Independence Trophy/Uhuru Cup • LC = League Cup • S8 = Super Eight

UHURU CUP 2011

Semi-finals

Highlanders	0 4p
Motor Action	0 2p
Gunners	0
Dynamos	2

Finals

Highlanders	0 4p
Dynamos	0 3p

Harare, 18-04-2011

MBADA DIAMONDS CUP 2011

Round of 16

Dynamos	1
CAPS United	0
Hwange	0
Shooting Stars	1
Gunners	2
Masvingo United	0
Black Mambas	0
FC Platinum	1
Zimbabwe Saints	0 6p
Highlanders	0 5p
Chicken Inn	1
Kiglon Bird	3
Blue Ribbon Stars	4
Shabanie Mine	0
Monomatapa United	1
Motor Action	2

Quarter-finals

Dynamos	3
Shooting Stars	0
Gunners	
FC Platinum	
Zimbabwe Saints	9p
Kiglon Bird	8p
Blue Ribbon Stars	0
Motor Action	1

Semi–finals

Dynamos	1
FC Platinum	0
Zimbabwe Saints	0
Motor Action	2

Final

Dynamos	1
Motor Action	0

CUP FINAL

National Stadium, Harare
27-11-2011, Bennett RSA
Scorer - Rodreck Mutuma [79] for Dynamos

## PART THREE

THE CONTINENTAL CONFEDERATIONS

AFC

ASIAN FOOTBALL CONFEDERATION

The most remarkable story of the year in Asian football was without doubt the staggering success of the Japanese women's team, winners of the FIFA Women's World Cup 2011 in Germany. Their penalty shoot-out victory over the USA in the final had added potency coming as it did just a few months after the devastating earthquake and tsunami that struck the country in March. It was the first senior world title for Asian football and came just 10 months after Japan and South Korea had contested the final of the FIFA U-17 Women's World Cup. In the men's game, after the staging of the 2011 AFC Asian Cup in Qatar at the start of the year, the focus turned to qualification for the 2014 FIFA World Cup in Brazil. At the end of the year there were just 13 of the 46 AFC members

THE FIFA BIG COUNT OF 2006 FOR ASIA

	Male	Female		Total
Number of players	80 075 000	5 102 000	Referees and Assistant Referees	263 000
Professionals	11 000		Admin, Coaches, Technical, Medical	410 000
Amateurs 18+	1 531 000		Number of clubs	20 000
Youth under 18	2 322		Number of teams	145 000
Unregistered	81 136 000		Clubs with women's teams	3 000
Total Players	85 849		Players as % of population	2.22%

still in contention for a place in the finals after three rounds of matches had whittled the numbers down. The most notable of the nations to fall early on were China, North Korea and Saudi Arabia and there were some surprise names that made it to the final group stage - notably Lebanon. In club football Al Sadd brought football in Qatar further into the spotlight when they won the 2011 AFC Champions League, beating Jeonbuk Hyundai Motors on penalties in the final. The game was staged in South Korea for the first time since the introduction of the single-match final in 2009 but the home crowd weren't able to celebrate a hat-trick of titles for Korean clubs. Uzbekistan's Nasaf Karshi won the 2011 AFC Cup - the first non-Arab winners in the eight-year history of the tournament - while Taipower from Chinese Taipei were the winners of the 2011 AFC President's Cup.

Asian Football Confederation (AFC)
AFC House, Jalan 1/155B, Bukit Jalil, 57000 Kuala Lumpur, Malaysia
Tel +60 3 89943388   Fax +60 3 89946168
media@the-afc.com   www.the-afc.com
President: Mohamed Bin Hammam QAT   General Secretary: Alex Soosay MAS
AFC Formed: 1954

AFC EXECUTIVE COMMITTEE

President: Mohamed Bin Hammam QAT	Vice-President: Yousuf Al Serkal UAE	Vice-President: Zhang Jilong CHN
Vice-President: Tengku Abdullah Ahmad Shah MAS		Vice-President: Ganesh Thapa NEP
	Hon Treasurer: Farouk Bouzo SYR	
FIFA Vice-President: Prince Ali Bin Al Hussein JOR	FIFA ExCo Member: Worawi Makudi THA	FIFA ExCo Member: Vernon Manilal Fernando SRI

MEMBERS OF THE EXECUTIVE COMMITTEE

Shk. Ali Bin Khalifa Al Khalifa BHR	Hafez I. Al Medlej KSA	Sayyid Khalid Hamed Al Busaidi OMA
Praful Patel IND	Makhdoom Syed Faisal Saleh Hayat PAK	Ali Azim MDV
Lee Boo Aun Winston SIN	Tran Quoc Tuan VIE	Zaw Zaw MYA
Ganbold Buyannemekh MGL	Kohzo Tashima JPN	Richard Lai GUM
	Mahfuza Akhter Kiron BAN	

MAP OF AFC MEMBER NATIONS

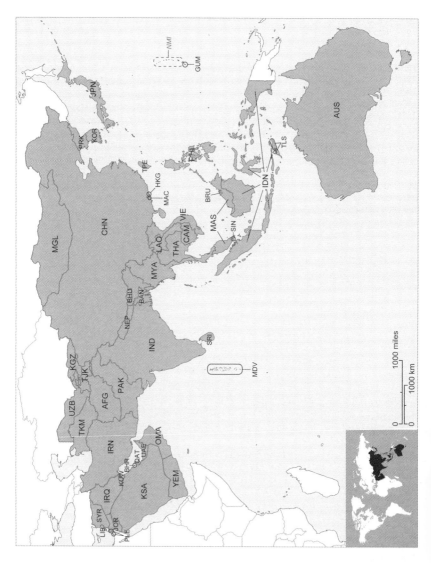

AFC MEMBER ASSOCIATIONS (46)

AFG - **Afghanistan** • AUS - **Australia** • BHR - **Bahrain** • BAN - **Bangladesh** • BHU - **Bhutan** • BRU - **Brunei Darussalam** • CAM - **Cambodia**
CHN - **China PR** • TPE - **Chinese Taipei** • GUM - **Guam** • HKG - **Hong Kong** • IND - **India** • IDN - **Indonesia** • IRN - **Iran** • IRQ - **Iraq**
JPN - **Japan** • JOR - **Jordan** • PRK - **Korea DPR** • KOR - **Korea Republic** • KUW - **Kuwait** • KGZ - **Kyrgyzstan** • LAO - **Laos** • LIB - **Lebanon**
MAC - **Macau** • MAS - **Malaysia** • MDV - **Maldives** • MGL - **Mongolia** • MYA - **Myanmar** • NEP - **Nepal** • OMA - **Oman** • PAK - **Pakistan**
PLE - **Palestine** • PHI - **Philippines** • QAT - **Qatar** • KSA - **Saudi Arabia** • SIN - **Singapore** • SRI - **Sri Lanka** • SYR - **Syria** • TJK - **Tajikistan**
THA - **Thailand** • TLS - **Timor Leste** • TKM - **Turkmenistan** • UAE - **United Arab Emirates** • UZB - **Uzbekistan** • VIE - **Vietnam** • YEM - **Yemen**

AFC PROVISIONAL ASSOCIATE MEMBER ASSOCIATION (1)

MNI - **Northern Mariana Islands** • Not affiliated to FIFA

ASIAN NATIONAL TEAM TOURNAMENTS

AFC ASIAN CUP

Year	Host Country	Winners	Score	Runners-up	Venue
1956	Hong Kong	Korea Republic	2-1	Israel	Government Stadium, Hong Kong
1960	Korea Republic	Korea Republic	3-0	Israel	Hyochang Park, Seoul
1964	Israel	Israel	2-0	India	Bloomfield, Jaffa
1968	Iran	Iran	3-1	Burma	Amjadieh, Tehran
1972	Thailand	Iran	2-1	Korea Republic	Suphachalasai, Bangkok
1976	Iran	Iran	1-0	Kuwait	Azadi, Tehran
1980	Kuwait	Kuwait	3-0	Korea Republic	Kuwait City
1984	Singapore	Saudi Arabia	2-0	China PR	National Stadium, Singapore
1988	Qatar	Saudi Arabia	0-0 4-3p	Korea Republic	Khalifa, Doha
1992	Japan	Japan	1-0	Saudi Arabia	Main Stadium, Hiroshima
1996	UAE	Saudi Arabia	0-0 4-2p	United Arab Emirates	Zayed, Abu Dhabi
2000	Lebanon	Japan	1-0	Saudi Arabia	Camille Chamoun, Beirut
2004	China PR	Japan	3-1	China PR	Workers' Stadium, Beijing
2007	ASEAN co-hosts	Iraq	1-0	Saudi Arabia	Gelora Bung Karno, Jakarta
2011	Qatar	Japan	1-0	Australia	Khalifa International, Doha

From 1956 to 1968 the tournament was played as a league. The result listed is that between the winners and runners-up.

AFC ASIAN CUP MEDALS TABLE

	Country	G	S	B	F	SF
1	Japan	4			4	5
2	Saudi Arabia	3	3		6	6
3	Iran	3		4	2	7
4	Korea Republic	2	3	4	3	6
5	Israel	1	2	1		
6	Kuwait	1	1	1	2	4
7	Iraq	1			1	2
8	China PR		2	2	2	6
9	Utd Arab Emirates		1		1	2
10	Australia		1		1	1
11	India			1		
	Myanmar			1		
13	Thailand			1		1
	Chinese Taipei			1		
	Hong Kong			1		
16	Bahrain					1
	Cambodia					1
	Korea DPR					1
	Uzbekistan					1
		15	15	14	22	44

This table represents the Gold (winners), Silver (runners-up) and Bronze (semi-finalists) placings of countries in the AFC Asian Cup, along with the number of appearances in the final and semi-finals

FOOTBALL TOURNAMENT OF THE ASIAN GAMES

Year	Host Country	Winners	Score	Runners-up	Venue
1951	India	India	1-0	Iran	New Delhi
1954	Philippines	Chinese Taipei	5-2	Korea Republic	Manilla
1958	Japan	Chinese Taipei	3-2	Korea Republic	Tokyo
1962	Indonesia	India	2-1	Korea Republic	Djakarta
1966	Thailand	Burma	1-0	Iran	Bangkok
1970	Thailand	Burma/KoreaRepublic	0-0		Bangkok
1974	Iran	Iran	1-0	Israel	Tehran
1978	Thailand	Korea Rep/Korea DPR	0-0		Bangkok
1982	India	Iraq	1-0	Kuwait	New Dehli
1986	Korea Republic	Korea Republic	2-0	Saudi Arabia	Seoul

FOOTBALL TOURNAMENT OF THE ASIAN GAMES (CONT'D)

Year	Host Country	Winners	Score	Runners-up	Venue
1990	China PR	Iran	0-0 4-1p	Korea DPR	Beijing
1994	Japan	Uzbekistan	4-2	China PR	Hiroshima
1998	Thailand	Iran	2-0	Kuwait	Bangkok
2002	Korea Republic	Iran	2-1	Japan	Busan
2006	Qatar	Qatar	1-0	Iraq	Doha
2010	China PR	Japan	1-0	UAE	Guangzhou

AFC CHALLENGE CUP

Year	Host Country	Winners	Score	Runners-up	Venue
2006	Bangladesh	Tajikistan	4-0	Sri Lanka	Bangabandhu, Dhaka
2008	India	India	4-1	Tajikistan	Ambedkar, Delhi
2010	Sri Lanka	Korea DPR	1-1 5-4p	Turkmenistan	Sugathadasa, Colombo

ASEAN FOOTBALL FEDERATION CHAMPIONSHIP

Year	Host Country	Winners	Score	Runners-up	Venue
1996		Thailand	1-0	Malaysia	
1998	Vietnam	Singapore	1-0	Vietnam	Hanoi Stadium, Hanoi
2000	Thailand	Thailand	4-1	Indonesia	Bangkok
2002	Indonesia/Sin'pore	Thailand	2-2 4-2p	Indonesia	Gelora Senayan, Jakarta
2004	Malaysia/Vietnam	Singapore	3-1 2-1	Indonesia	Jakarta, Singapore
2007	Singapore/Th'land	Singapore	2-1 1-1	Thailand	Singapore, Bangkok
2008	Indonesia/Th'land	Vietnam	2-1 1-1	Thailand	Bangkok, Hanoi
2010	Indonesia/Vietnam	Malaysia	3-0 1-2	Indonesia	Kuala Lumpur, Jakarta

SOUTH ASIAN FOOTBALL FEDERATION CUP

Year	Host Country	Winners	Score	Runners-up	Venue
1993	Pakistan	India	2-0	Sri Lanka	Lahore
1995	Sri Lanka	Sri Lanka	1-0	India	Colombo
1997	Nepal	India	5-1	Maldives	Dasharath Rangashala, Kathmandu
1999	Goa	India	2-0	Bangladesh	Margao
2003	Bangladesh	Bangladesh	1-1 5-3p	Maldives	Bangabandu, Dhaka
2005	Pakistan	India	2-0	Bangladesh	Karachi
2008	Sri Lanka/Maldives	Maldives	1-0	India	Sugathadhasa, Colombo
2009	Bangladesh	India	0-0 3-1p	Maldives	Bangabandu, Dhaka
2011	India	India	4-0	Afghanistan	Jawaharlal Nehru, New Delhi

EAST ASIAN CHAMPIONSHIP

Year	Host Country	Winners	Score	Runners-up	Venue
2003	Japan	Korea Republic	0-0	Japan	International, Yokohama
2005	Korea Republic	China PR	2-2	Japan	World Cup Stadium, Daejeon
2008	China PR	Korea Republic	1-1	Japan	Sports Centre, Chongqing
2010	Japan	China PR	3-0	Korea Republic	Ajinomoto & National, Tokyo

Tournament played as a league. The result listed is that between the winners and runners-up

WEST ASIAN FOOTBALL FEDERATION CHAMPIONSHIP

Year	Host Country	Winners	Score	Runners-up	Venue
2000	Jordan	Iran	1-0	Syria	Malek Abdullah, Amman
2002	Syria	Iraq	3-2	Jordan	Al Abbassiyyine, Damascus
2004	Iran	Iran	4-1	Syria	Tehran
2007	Jordan	Iran	2-1	Iraq	International, Amman
2008	Iran	Iran	2-1	Jordan	Tehran
2010	Jordan	Kuwait	2-1	Iran	King Abdullah, Amman

FOOTBALL TOURNAMENT OF THE SOUTH EAST ASIAN GAMES

Year	Host Country	Winners	Score	Runners-up	Venue
1959	Thailand	Vietnam	3-1	Thailand	Bangkok
1961	Burma	Malaysia	2-0	Burma	Rangoon
1965	Malaysia	Burma	2-2†	Thailand	Kuala Lumpur
1967	Thailand	Burma	2-1	South Vietnam	Bangkok
1969	Burma	Burma	3-0	Thailand	Rangoon
1971	Malaysia	Burma	2-1	Malaysia	Kuala Lumpur
1973	Singapore	Burma	2-1	South Vietnam	Singapore
1975	Thailand	Thailand	2-1	Malaysia	Bangkok
1977	Malaysia	Malaysia	2-0	Thailand	Kuala Lumpur
1979	Indonesia	Malaysia	1-0	Indonesia	Jakarta
1981	Philippines	Thailand	2-1	Malaysia	Manila
1983	Singapore	Thailand	2-1	Singapore	Singapore
1985	Thailand	Thailand	2-0	Singpaore	Bangkok
1987	Indonesia	Indonesia	1-0	Malaysia	Jakarta
1989	Malaysia	Malaysia	3-1	Singapore	Merdeka, Kuala Lumpur
1991	Philippines	Indonesia	0-0 4-3p	Thailand	Manila
1993	Singapore	Thailand	4-3	Myanmar	Singapore
1995	Thailand	Thailand	4-0	Vietnam	Chiang Mai
1997	Indonesia	Thailand	1-1 4-2p	Indonesia	Jakarta
1999	Brunei	Thailand	2-0	Vietnam	Bandar Seri Begawan
2001	Malaysia	Thailand	1-0	Malaysia	Kuala Lumpur
2003	Vietnam	Thailand	2-1	Vietnam	Hanoi
2005	Philippines	Thailand	3-0	Vietnam	Manila
2007	Thailand	Thailand	2-0	Myanmar	Korat
2009	Laos	Malaysia	1-0	Vietnam	Vientiane
2011	Indonesia	Malaysia	1-1 4-3p	Indonesia	Jakarta

† Gold medal shared • Until 2001 the SEA Games featured full national teams but is now a U-23 event

FOOTBALL TOURNAMENT OF THE SOUTH ASIAN GAMES

Year	Host Country	Winners	Score	Runners-up	Venue
1984	Nepal	Nepal	4-2	Bangladesh	Dasharath Rangashala, Kathmandu
1985	Bangladesh	India	1-1 4-1p	Bangladesh	Dhaka
1987	India	India	1-0	Nepal	Salt Lake, Calcutta
1989	Pakistan	Pakistan	1-0	Bangladesh	Islamabad
1991	Sri Lanka	Pakistan	2-0	Maldives	Colombo
1993	Bangladesh	Nepal	2-2 4-3p	India	Dhaka
1995	India	India	1-0	Bangladesh	Madras
1999	Nepal	Bangladesh	1-0	Nepal	Dasharath Rangashala, Kathmandu
2004	Pakistan	Pakistan	1-0	India	Jinnah Stadium, Islamabad
2006	Sri Lanka	Pakistan	1-0	Sri Lanka	Colombo
2010	Bangladesh	Bangladesh	4-0	Afghanistan	Bangabandhu, Dhaka

GULF CUP

Year	Host Country	Winners	Runners-up
1970	Bahrain	Kuwait	Bahrain
1972	Saudi Arabia	Kuwait	Saudi Arabia
1974	Kuwait	Kuwait	Saudi Arabia
1976	Qatar	Kuwait	Iraq
1979	Iraq	Iraq	Kuwait
1982	UAE	Kuwait	Bahrain
1984	Oman	Iraq	Qatar
1986	Bahrain	Kuwait	UAE
1988	Saudi Arabia	Iraq	UAE
1990	Kuwait	Kuwait	Qatar

GULF CUP

Year	Host Country	Winners	Runners-up
1992	Qatar	Qatar	Bahrain
1994	UAE	Saudi Arabia	UAE
1996	Oman	Kuwait	Qatar
1998	Bahrain	Kuwait	Saudi Arabia
2002	Saudi Arabia	Saudi Arabia	Qatar
2004	Kuwait	Saudi Arabia	Bahrain
2005	Qatar	Qatar	Oman
2007	UAE	UAE	Oman
2009	Oman	Oman	Saudi Arabia
2010	Yemen	Kuwait	Saudi Arabia

ASIAN CLUB TOURNAMENTS

AFC CHAMPIONS LEAGUE

Year	Winners	Country	Score	Country	Runners-up
1967	Hapoel Tel Aviv	ISR	2-1	MAS	Selangor
1968	Maccabi Tel Aviv	ISR	1-0	KOR	Yangzee
1970	Taj Club	IRN	2-1	ISR	Hapoel Tel Aviv
1971	Maccabi Tel Aviv	ISR	W-O	IRQ	Police Club
1986	Daewoo Royals	KOR	3-1	KSA	Al Ahly
1987	Furukawa	JPN	4-3	KSA	Al Hilal
1988	Yomiuri	JPN	W-O	KSA	Al Hilal
1989	Al Saad	QAT	2-3 1-0	IRQ	Al Rasheed
1990	Liaoning	CHN	2-1 1-1	JPN	Nissan
1991	Esteghlal SC	IRN	2-1	CHN	Liaoning
1992	Al Hilal	KSA	1-1 4-3p	IRN	Esteghlal SC
1993	Pas	IRN	1-0	KSA	Al Shabab
1994	Thai Farmers Bank	THA	2-1	OMA	Omani Club
1995	Thai Farmers Bank	THA	1-0	QAT	Al Arabi
1996	Ilhwa Chunma	KOR	1-0	KSA	Al Nasr
1997	Pohang Steelers	KOR	2-1	KOR	Ilhwa Chunma
1998	Pohang Steelers	KOR	0-0 6-5p	CHN	Dalian
1999	Jubilo Iwata	JPN	2-1	IRN	Esteghlal SC
2000	Al Hilal	KSA	3-2	JPN	Jubilo Iwata
2001	Suwon Samsung Bluewings	KOR	1-0	JPN	Jubilo Iwata
2002	Suwon Samsung Bluewings	KOR	0-0 4-2p	KOR	Anyang LG Cheetahs
2003	Al Ain	UAE	2-0 0-1	THA	BEC Tero Sasana
2004	Al Ittihad	KSA	1-3 5-0	KOR	Seongnam Ilhwa Chunma
2005	Al Ittihad	KSA	1-1 4-2	UAE	Al Ain
2006	Jeonbuk Hyundai Motors	KOR	2-0 1-2	SYR	Al Karama
2007	Urawa Reds	JPN	1-1 2-0	IRN	Sepahan
2008	Gamba Osaka	JPN	3-0 2-0	AUS	Adelaide United
2009	Pohang Steelers	KOR	2-1	KSA	Al Ittihad
2010	Seongnam Ilhwa Chunma	KOR	3-1	IRN	Zob Ahan
2011	Al Sadd	QAT	2-2 4-2p	KOR	Jeonbuk Hyundai Motors

AFC CHAMPIONS LEAGUE MEDALS TABLE

	Country	G	S	B	F	SF
1	Korea Republic	9	5	6	14	23
2	Japan	5	3	4	8	13
3	Saudi Arabia	4	6	4	10	14
4	Iran	3	4	5	7	14
5	Israel	3	1		4	4
6	Qatar	2	1	2	3	5
7	Thailand	2	1	1	3	4
8	China PR	1	2	3	3	8
9	UAE	1	1	3	2	6
10	Iraq		2		2	4
11	Syria		1	1	1	2
12	Australia		1		1	1
	Malaysia		1		1	1

AFC CHAMPIONS LEAGUE MEDALS TABLE (CONT'D)

	Country	G	S	B	F	SF
	Oman		1		1	1
15	Uzbekistan			4		5
16	Indonesia			1		3
17	Lebanon			1		1
	Korea DPR			1		1
	Kuwait			1		1
20	India					1
	Kazakstan					1
		30	30	37	60	113

This table represents the Gold (winners), Silver (runners-up) and Bronze (semi-finalists) placings of clubs representing the above countries in the AFC Champions League, along with the number of appearances in the final and semi-finals

AFC CHAMPIONS LEAGUE MEDALS TABLE

	Club		G	S	B
1	Pohang Steelers	KOR	3		
2	Esteghlal	IRN	2	2	3
3	Al Hilal	KSA	2	2	2
4	Seongnam Ilhwa Chunma	KOR	2	2	1
5	Al Ittihad	KSA	2	1	1
6	Suwon Samsung Bluewings	KOR	2		1
	Thai Farmers Bank	THA	2		1
8	Maccabi Tel Aviv	ISR	2		
9	Al Saad	QAT	2		
10	Jubilo Iwata	JPN	1	2	
11	Al Ain	UAE	1	1	1
	Liaoning	CHN	1	1	1
	Jeonbuk Hyundai Motors	KOR	1	1	1
14	Hapoel Tel Aviv	ISR	1	1	
15	Busan I'Park	KOR	1		1
	Urawa Reds	JPN	1		1
	Tokyo Verdy	JPN	1		1
18	Gamba Osaka	JPN	1		
	JEF United	JPN	1		
	Pass	IRN	1		
21	Dalian	CHN		1	1
	Al Shabab	KSA		1	1
23	Adelaide United	AUS		1	
	Al Ahli	KSA		1	
	Al Arabi	QAT		1	
	Al Karama	SYR		1	
	Al Nasr	KSA		1	

AFC CHAMPIONS LEAGUE MEDALS TABLE (CONT'D)

	Club		G	S	B
	Al Rasheed	IRQ		1	
	Anyang LG Cheetahs	KOR		1	
	BEC Tero Sasana	THA		1	
	Omani Club	OMA		1	
	Police	IRQ		1	
	Selangor	MAS		1	
	Sepahan	IRN		1	
	Yangzee	KOR		1	
	Yokohama Marinos	JPN		1	
	Zob Ahan	IRN		1	
38	Pirouzi	IRN			3
39	Pakhtakor Tashkent	UZB			2
40	Al Qadisiya	KUW			1
	Al Rayyan	QAT			1
	Al Wasl	UAE			1
	April 25th	PRK			1
	Bunyodkor Tashkent	UZB			1
	Homenetmen	LIB			1
	Nagoya Grampus	JPN			1
	Neftchi Fergana	UZB			1
	Sanfrecce Hiroshima	JPN			1
	Shenzhen	CHN			1
	Tiga Berlian	IDN			1
	Tungsten Mining	KOR			1
	Ulsan Hyundai Horang-i	KOR			1
	Umm Salal	QAT			1
	Al Wahda	UAE			1
			29	29	35

ASIAN CUP WINNERS' CUP

Year	Winners	Country	Score	Country	Runners-up
1991	Pirouzi	IRN	0-0 1-0	BHR	Al Muharraq
1992	Nissan	JPN	1-1 5-0	KSA	Al Nasr
1993	Nissan	JPN	1-1 1-0	IRN	Pirouzi
1994	Al-Qadisiyah	KSA	4-2 2-0	HKG	South China
1995	Yokohama Flugels	JPN	2-1	UAE	Al Shaab
1996	Bellmare Hiratsuka	JPN	2-1	IRQ	Al Talaba
1997	Al Hilal	KSA	3-1	JPN	Nagoya Grampus Eight
1998	Al Nasr	KSA	1-0	KOR	Suwon Samsung Bluewings
1999	Al Ittihad	KSA	3-2	KOR	Chunnam Dragons
2000	Shimizu S-Pulse	JPN	1-0	IRQ	Al Zawra
2001	Al Shabab	KSA	4-2	CHN	Dalian Shide
2002	Al Hilal	KSA	2-1	KOR	Chonbuk Hyundai Motors

CUP WINNERS CUP MEDALS TABLE

	Country	G	S	B	F	SF
1	Saudi Arabia	6	1	3	7	10
2	Japan	5	1	4	6	10
3	Iran	1	1		2	4
4	Korea Republic		3	1	3	4
5	Iraq		2		2	3
6	China PR		1	1	1	3
7	United Arab Emirates		1	1	1	2
8	Bahrain		1		1	1
	Hong Kong		1		1	1
10	Qatar			2		2
11	Thailand			1		2

CUP WINNERS CUP MEDALS TABLE (CONT'D)

	Country	G	S	B	F	SF
12	Indonesia			1		1
	Jordan			1		1
	Vietnam			1		1
15	Uzbekistan					1
	Kuwait					1
	Turkmenistan					1
		12	12	16	24	48

This table represents the Gold (winners), Silver (runners-up) and Bronze (semi-finalists) placings of clubs representing the above countries in the Cup Winners Cup, along with the number of appearances in the final and semi-finals

ASIAN CUP WINNERS CUP MEDALS TABLE

	Club		G	S	B
1	Yokohama Marinos (Nissan)	JPN	2		1
2	Al Hilal	KSA	2		1
3	Pirouzi	IRN	1	1	
	Al Nasr	KSA	1	1	
5	Al Ittihad	KSA	1		2
6	Yokohama Flugels	JPN	1		1
	Shimizu S-Pulse	JPN	1		1
8	Al Qadisiyah	KSA	1		
	Bellmare Hiratsuka	JPN	1		
	Al Shabab	KSA	1		
11	Al Shaab	UAE		1	
	Al Talaba	IRQ		1	
	Al Zawra	IRQ		1	
	Chunnam Dragons	KOR		1	
	Jeonbuk Hyundai Motors	KOR		1	
	Dalian	CHN		1	

ASIAN CUP WINNERS CUP MEDALS TABLE (CONT'D)

	Club		G	S	B
	Muharraq	BHR		1	
	Nagoya Grampus Eight	JPN		1	
	South China	HKG		1	
	Suwon Samsung Bluewings	KOR		1	
21	Al Shabab	UAE			1
	Al Ramtha	JOR			1
	Bangkok Bank	THA			1
	Pupuk Kaltim	IDN			1
	Quang Nam Danang	VIE			1
	Al Arabi	QAT			1
	Al Sadd	QAT			1
	Ulsan Hyundai	KOR			1
	Beijing Guoan	CHN			1
	Kashima Antlers	JPN			1
			12	12	16

AFC CUP

Year	Winners	Country	Score	Country	Runners-up
2004	Al Jaish	SYR	3-2 0-1	SYR	Al Wahda
2005	Al Faysali	JOR	1-0 3-2	LIB	Al Nejmeh
2006	Al Faysali	JOR	3-0 2-4	BHR	Muharraq
2007	Shabab Al Ordun	JOR	1-0 1-1	JOR	Al Faysali
2008	Muharraq	BHR	5-1 5-4	LIB	Safa
2009	Al Kuwait	KUW	2-1	SYR	Al Karama
2010	Al Ittihad Aleppo	SYR	1-1 4-2p	KUW	Al Qadisiya
2011	Nasaf Karshi	UZB	2-1	KUW	Al Kuwait

AFC CUP MEDALS TABLE

	Country	G	S	B	F	SF
1	Jordan	3	1	3	4	7
2	Syria	2	2		4	4
3	Bahrain	1	1	1	2	3
4	Kuwait	1	2		3	3
5	Uzbekistan	1			1	1
6	Lebanon		2	2	2	4
7	Singapore			2		2
	Hong Kong			2		2
9	Maldives			1		1
	India			1		1
	Iraq			1		1
	Oman			1		1
	Thailand			1		1
	Vietnam			1		1
		8	8	16	16	32

This table represents the Gold (winners), Silver (runners-up) and Bronze (semi-finalists) placings of clubs representing the above countries in the AFC Cup, along with the number of appearances in the final and semi-finals

AFC CUP MEDALS TABLE

	Club		G	S	B
1	Al Faysali	JOR	2	1	
2	Al Kuwait	KUW	1	1	
	Muharraq	BHR	1	1	
4	Al Ittihad Aleppo	SYR	1		
	Al Jaish	SYR	1		
	Al Shabab Al Ordun	JOR	1		
	Nasaf Karshi	UZB	1		
8	Al Nijmeh	LIB		1	2
9	Al Karama	SYR		1	
	Al Qadisiya	KUW		1	
	Safa	LIB		1	
	Al Wahda	SYR		1	
13	Al Wihdat	JOR			3
14	Arbil	IRQ			1
	Binh Duong	VIE			1
	Dempo SC	IND			1
	Geylang United	SIN			1
	Home United	SIN			1
	Muangthong United	THA			1
	Al Nahda	OMA			1
	New Radiant	MDV			1
	Riffa	BHR			1
	South China	HGK			1
	Sun Hei	HKG			1
			8	8	16

AFC PRESIDENT'S CUP

Year	Winners	Country	Score	Country	Runners-up
2005	Regar TadAZ	TJK	3-0	KGZ	Dordoi-Dynamo
2006	Dordoi-Dynamo	KGZ	2-1	TJK	Vakhsh Qurgonteppa
2007	Dordoi-Dynamo	KGZ	2-1	NEP	Mahendra Police Club
2008	Regar TadAZ	TJK	1-1 4-3p	KGZ	Dordoi-Dynamo
2009	Regar TadAZ	TJK	2-0	KGZ	Dordoi-Dynamo
2010	Yadanabon	MYA	1-0	KGZ	Dordoi-Dynamo
2011	Kaohsiung Taipower	TPE	3-2	CAM	Phnom Penh Crown

AFC PRESIDENT'S CUP MEDALS TABLE

	Country	G	S	B	F	SF
1	Tajikistan	3	1	2	4	6
2	Kyrgyzstan	2	4		6	6
3	Chinese Taipei	1		1	1	1
4	Myanmar	1			1	1
5	Nepal			1	2	1	3
6	Cambodia			1	1	1	1
7	Turkmenistan			3		3
8	Sri Lanka			2		2
9	Pakistan			1		1
		7	7	12	14	24

This table represents the Gold (winners), Silver (runners-up) and Bronze (semi-finalists) placings of clubs representing the above countries in the AFC President's Cup, along with the number of appearances in the final and semi-finals

AFC PRESIDENT'S CUP MEDALS TABLE

	Club		G	S	B
1	Regar TadAZ	TJK	3		1
2	Dordoi-Dynamo	KGZ	2	4	
3	Kaohsiung Taipower	TPE	1		
	Yadanabon	MYA	1		
5	Nepal Police Club	NEP		1	1
	Vakhsh Qurgonteppa	TJK		1	1
7	Phnom Penh Crown	CAM		1	
	FK Ashgabat	TKM			2
	Blue Star Club	SRI			1
	HTTU Ashgabat	TKM			1
	Khmera	CAM			1
	Ratnam SC	SRI			1
	Tatung	TPE			1
	Three Star Club	NEP			1
	WAPDA	PAK			1
			7	7	12

ASIAN YOUTH TOURNAMENTS

AFC U-19 CHAMPIONSHIP

Year	Host Country	Winners	Score	Runners-up	Venue
1959	Malaysia	Korea Republic	2-1	Malaysia	Kuala Lumpur
1960	Malaysia	Korea Republic	4-0	Malaysia	Kuala Lumpur
1961	Thailand	Burma	0-0†	Indonesia	Bangkok
1962	Thailand	Thailand	2-1	Korea Republic	Bangkok
1963	Malaysia	Burma	2-2†	Korea Republic	Penang
1964	Vietnam	Burma	0-0†	Israel	Saigon
1965	Japan	Israel	5-0	Burma	Tokyo
1966	Philippines	Burma	1-1	Israel	Manila
1967	Thailand	Israel	3-0	Indonesia	Bangkok
1968	Korea Republic	Burma	4-0	Malaysia	Seoul
1969	Thailand	Burma	2-2†	Thailand	Bangkok
1970	Philippines	Burma	3-0	India	Manila
1971	Japan	Israel	1-0	Korea Republic	Tokyo
1972	Thailand	Israel	1-0	Korea Republic	Bangkok
1973	Iran	Iran	2-0	Japan	Tehran
1974	Thailand	Iran	2-2†	India	Bangkok
1975	Kuwait	Iran	0-0†	Iraq	Kuwait City
1976	Thailand	Iran	0-0†	Korea DPR	Bongkok
1977	Iran	Iraq	4-3	Iran	Tehran
1978	Bangladesh	Iraq	1-1†	Korea Republic	Dhaka
1980	Thailand	Korea Republic	4-1‡	Qatar	Bangkok
1982	Thailand	Korea Republic	1-1‡	China PR	Bangkok
1984	UAE	China PR	2-2‡	Saudi Arabia	Abu Dhabi
1986	Saudi Arabia	Saudi Arabia	2-0	Bahrain	Riyadh
1988	Qatar	Iraq	1-1 5-4p	Syria	Doha

AFC U-19 CHAMPIONSHIP (CONT'D)

Year	Host Country	Winners	Score	Runners-up	Venue
1990	Indonesia	Korea Republic	0-0 4-3p	Korea DPR	Jakarta
1992	UAE	Saudi Arabia	2-0	Korea Republic	Dubai
1994	Indonesia	Syria	2-1	Japan	Jakarta
1996	Korea Republic	Korea Republic	3-0	China PR	Suwon
1998	Thailand	Korea Republic	2-1	Japan	Chiang Mai
2000	Iran	Iraq	2-1	Japan	Tehran
2002	Qatar	Korea Republic	1-0	Japan	Doha
2004	Malaysia	Korea Republic	2-0	China PR	Kuala Lumpur
2006	India	Korea DPR	1-1 5-3p	Japan	Kolkata
2008	Saudi Arabia	UAE	2-1	Uzbekistan	Damman
2010	China PR	Korea DPR	3-2	Australia	Zibo

† Title shared between both finalists • ‡ Played on a league system so the match indicated was not a final

AFC U-16 CHAMPIONSHIP

Year	Host Country	Winners	Score	Runners-up	Venue
1984	Qatar	Saudi Arabia	4-3	Qatar	Doha
1986	Qatar	Korea Republic	0-0 5-4p	Qatar	Doha
1988	Thailand	Saudi Arabia	2-0	Bahrain	Bangkok
1990	UAE	Qatar	2-0	UAE	Dubai
1992	Saudi Arabia	China PR	2-2 8-7p	Qatar	Riyadh
1994	Qatar	Japan	1-0	Qatar	Doha
1996	Thailand	Oman	1-0	Thailand	Bangkok
1998	Qatar	Thailand	1-1 3-2p	Qatar	Doha
2000	Vietnam SR	Oman	1-0	Iran	Danang
2002	UAE	Korea Republic	1-1 5-3p	Yemen	Abu Dhabi
2004	Japan	China PR	1-0	Korea DPR	Shizuoka
2006	Singapore	Japan	4-2	Korea DPR	Singapore
2008	Uzbekistan	Iran	2-1	Korea Republic	Tashkent
2010	Uzbekistan	Korea DPR	2-0	Uzbekistan	Tashkent

ASIAN WOMENS TOURNAMENTS

WOMEN'S FOOTBALL TOURNAMENT OF THE ASIAN GAMES

Year	Host Country	Winners	Score	Runners-up	Venue
1990	China PR	China PR	5-0	Japan	Beijing
1994	Japan	China PR	2-0	Japan	Hiroshima
1998	Thailand	China PR	1-0	Korea DPR	Bangkok
2002	Korea Republic	Korea DPR	0-0	China PR	Busan
2006	Qatar	Korea DPR	0-0 4-2p	Japan	Doha
2010	China PR	Australia	1-1 5-4p	Korea DPR	Chengdu

In 1990, 1994 and 2002 the tournament was played as a league. The result listed is that between the winners and runners-up

AFC U-19 WOMEN'S CHAMPIONSHIP

Year	Host Country	Winners	Score	Runners-up	Venue
2002	India	Japan	2-1	Chinese Taipei	
2006	Malaysia	China PR	1-0	Korea DPR	
2007	China PR	Korea DPR	1-0	Japan	Sports Centre, Chongqing
2009	China PR	Japan	2-1	Korea Republic	Hankou Sports Stadium, Wuhan
2011	Vietnam	Japan	2-1	Korea DPR	Thong Nhat, Ho Chi Minh City

AFC U-16 WOMEN'S CHAMPIONSHIP

Year	Host Country	Winners	Score	Runners-up	Venue
2005	Korea Republic	Japan	1-1 3-1p	China PR	Namhae
2007	Malaysia	Korea DPR	3-0	Japan	MPPJ Stadium, Petaling Jaya
2009	Thailand	Korea Republic	4-0	Korea DPR	Supachalasai, Bangkok
2011	China PR	Japan	1-0	Korea DPR	Jiangning Sports Center, Nanjing

In 2011 the U-19 and U-16 tournaments were played as a league. The result listed is that between the winners and runners-up

NATIONAL TEAM TOURNAMENTS IN ASIA 2011

SOUTH ASIAN FOOTBALL FEDERATION CHAMPIONSHIP INDIA 2011

First Round Group Stage

	Pl	W	D	L	F	A	Pts	IND	SRI	BHU
Afghanistan	3	2	1	0	12	3	7	1-1	3-1	8-1
India	3	2	1	0	9	1	7		3-0	5-0
Sri Lanka	3	1	0	2	4	6	3			3-0
Bhutan	3	0	0	3	1	16	0			

	Pl	W	D	L	F	A	Pts	NEP	PAK	BAN
Maldives	3	1	2	0	4	2	5	1-1	0-0	3-1
Nepal	3	1	2	0	3	2	5		1-1	1-0
Pakistan	3	0	3	0	1	1	3			0-0
Bangladesh	3	0	1	2	1	4	1			

Semi-finals

India	3
Maldives	1

Nepal	0
Afghanistan	1

Final

India	4
Afghanistan	0

Held at the Jawaharla Nehru Stadium, New Delhi from 2-12-2011 to 11-12-2011

SOUTH EAST ASIAN GAMES JAKARTA 2011

First Round Group Stage

	Pl	W	D	L	F	A	Pts	IND	SIN	THA	CAM
Malaysia	4	3	1	0	7	2	10	1-0	0-0	2-1	4-1
Indonesia	4	3	0	1	11	2	9		2-0	3-1	6-0
Singapore	4	2	1	1	4	3	7			2-0	2-1
Thailand	4	1	0	3	6	7	3				4-0
Cambodia	4	0	0	4	2	16	0				

	Pl	W	D	L	F	A	Pts	MYA	TLS	LAO	BRU	PHI
Vietnam	5	4	1	0	16	2	13	0-0	2-0	3-1	8-0	3-1
Myanmar	5	4	1	0	13	2	13		1-0	3-2	4-0	5-0
Timor-Leste	5	2	0	3	4	8	6			0-3	2-1	2-1
Laos	5	1	1	3	10	9	4				2-2	2-3
Brunei	5	1	1	3	5	17	4					2-1
Philippines	5	1	0	4	6	14	3					

Semi-finals

Malaysia	1
Myanmar	0

Vietnam	0
Indonesia	2

Final

Malaysia	1	4p
Indonesia	1	3p

3rd Place Play-off

Myanmar	4
Vietnam	1

Held at the Gelora Bung Karno Stadium, Jakarta, Indonesia from 3-11-2011 to 21-11-2011 • U-23 event

WOMEN'S TOURNAMENTS IN ASIA 2011

AFC U-19 WOMEN'S CHAMPIONSHIP VIETNAM 2011

	Pl	W	D	L	F	A	Pts	PRK	CHN	KOR	AUS	VIE
Japan	5	4	1	0	13	3	13	2-1	1-1	3-1	1-0	6-0
Korea DPR	5	4	0	1	13	3	12		4-0	2-1	1-0	5-0
China PR	5	2	2	1	7	8	8			1-1	3-1	2-1
Korea Republic	5	2	1	2	11	9	7				4-2	4-1
Australia	5	1	0	4	7	12	3					4-3
Vietnam	5	0	0	5	5	21	0					

Held in Ho Chi Minh City, Vietnam from 6-10-2011 to 16-10-2011

AFC U-16 WOMEN'S CHAMPIONSHIP CHINA PR 2011

	Pl	W	D	L	F	A	Pts	PRK	CHN	KOR	AUS	THA
Japan	5	5	0	0	18	0	15	1-0	3-0	3-0	1-0	10-0
Korea DPR	5	4	0	1	14	1	12		1-0	4-0	1-0	8-0
China PR	5	2	1	2	11	4	7			0-0	3-0	8-0
Korea Republic	5	2	1	2	7	7	7				4-0	3-0
Australia	5	1	0	4	4	9	3					4-0
Thailand	5	0	0	5	0	33	0					

Held in Nanjing, China PR from 3-11-2011 to 13-11-2011

CLUB TOURNAMENTS IN ASIA 2011

AFC CHAMPIONS LEAGUE 2011

First Round

Round of 16

Group A

Group A		Pl	W	D	L	F	A	Pts	IRN	KSA	QAT	UAE
Sepahan	IRN	6	4	1	1	14	5	**13**		1-1	2-0	5-1
Al Hilal	KSA	6	4	1	1	11	6	**13**	1-2		2-0	3-1
Al Gharafa	QAT	6	2	1	3	6	7	**7**	1-0	0-1		5-2
Al Jazeera	UAE	6	0	1	5	7	20	**1**	1-4	2-3	0-0	

Round of 16: Al Sadd * 1 — Al Shabab 0

Group B

Group B		Pl	W	D	L	F	A	Pts	QAT	KSA	IRN	UZB
Al Sadd	QAT	6	2	4	0	8	6	**10**		1-0	2-2	2-1
Al Nasr	KSA	6	2	2	2	10	7	**8**			2-1	4-1
Esteghlal Tehran	IRN	6	2	2	2	11	10	**8**	1-1	2-1		4-2
Pakhtakor Tashkent	UZB	6	1	2	3	8	14	**5**	1-1	2-2	2-1	

Round of 16: Bunyodkor 1 — Sepahan * 3

Group C

Group C		Pl	W	D	L	F	A	Pts	KSA	UZB	UAE	IRN
Al Ittihad	KSA	6	3	2	1	10	5	**11**		1-1	0-0	3-1
Bunyodkor	UZB	6	2	3	1	8	6	**9**	0-1		3-2	0-0
Al Wahda	UAE	6	1	3	2	6	8	**6**	0-3	1-1		2-0
Persepolis	IRN	6	1	2	3	6	11	**5**	3-2	1-3	1-1	

Round of 16: Zob Ahan * 4 — Al Nasr 1

Group D

Group D		Pl	W	D	L	F	A	Pts	IRN	KSA	UAE	QAT
Zob Ahan	IRN	6	4	1	1	7	3	**13**		0-1	2-1	1-0
Al Shabab	KSA	6	3	2	1	8	4	**11**	0-0		4-1	1-0
Emirates Club	UAE	6	2	0	4	6	10	**6**	0-1	2-1		2-0
Al Rayyan	QAT	6	1	1	4	4	8	**4**	1-3	1-1	2-0	

Round of 16: Nagoya Grampus 0 — Suwon Bluewings * 2

Group E

Group E		Pl	W	D	L	F	A	Pts	JPN	CHN	KOR	AUS
Gamba Osaka	JPN	6	3	1	2	13	7	**10**		2-0	3-1	5-1
Tianjin Teda	CHN	6	3	1	2	8	6	**10**	2-1		3-0	1-1
Jeju United	KOR	6	2	1	3	6	10	**7**	2-1	0-1		1-1
Melbourne Victory	AUS	6	1	3	2	7	11	**6**	1-1	2-1	1-2	

Round of 16: Al Ittihad * 3 — Al Hilal 1

Group F

Group F		Pl	W	D	L	F	A	Pts	KOR	JPN	UAE	CHN
FC Seoul	KOR	6	3	2	1	9	4	**11**		0-2	3-0	3-0
Nagoya Grampus	JPN	6	3	1	2	9	6	**10**	1-1		4-0	1-0
Al Ain	UAE	6	2	1	3	4	9	**7**	0-1	3-1		1-0
Hangzhou Greentown	CHN	6	1	2	3	3	6	**5**	1-1	2-0	0-0	

Round of 16: Kashima Antlers 0 — FC Seoul * 3

Group G

Group G		Pl	W	D	L	F	A	Pts	KOR	JPN	CHN	IDN
Jeonbuk Hy. Motors	KOR	6	5	0	1	14	2	**15**		1-0	1-0	6-0
Cerezo Osaka	JPN	6	4	0	2	11	4	**12**	1-0		4-0	2-1
Shandong Luneng	CHN	6	2	1	3	9	8	**7**	1-2	2-0		5-0
Arema Malang	IDN	6	0	1	5	2	22	**1**	0-4	0-4	1-1	

Round of 16: Cerezo Osaka 1 — Gamba Osaka * 0

Group H

Group H		Pl	W	D	L	F	A	Pts	KOR	JPN	AUS	CHN
Suwon Bluewings	KOR	6	3	3	0	12	3	**12**		1-1	3-1	4-0
Kashima Antlers	JPN	6	3	3	0	9	3	**12**	1-1		2-1	2-0
Sydney FC	AUS	6	1	2	3	6	11	**5**	0-0	0-3		1-1
Shanghai Shenhua	CHN	6	0	2	4	3	13	**2**	0-3	0-0	2-3	

Round of 16: Tianjin Teda 0 — Jeonbuk Hy. Motors * 3

AFC CHAMPIONS LEAGUE 2011

Quarter-finals   **Semi-finals**   **Final**

Al Sadd ‡	3	1
Sepahan *	0	2

Al Sadd	2	0
Suwon Samsung Bluewings *	0	1

Zob Ahan	1	1
Suwon Samsung Bluewings *	1	2

Al Sadd	2	4p
Jeonbuk Hyundai Motors	2	2p

Al Ittihad *	3	0
FC Seoul	1	1

Al Ittihad *	2	1
Jeonbuk Hyundai Motors	3	2

Cerezo Osaka *	4	1
Jeonbuk Hyundai Motors	3	6

* Home team/Home team in the first leg • ‡ First leg awarded 3-0 to Al Sadd after Sepahan fielded an ineligle player. Sepahan had won 1-0

Top scorers: **9** - Lee Dong Gook KOR, Jeonbuk • **7** - Eninho BRA, Jeonbuk • **6** - Ha Tae Gyun KOR, Suwon • **5** - Bader Al Mutwa KUW, Al Nasr; Farhad Majidi IRN, Esteghlal; Dejan Damjanovic MNE, FC Seoul & Ibrahima Toure SEN, Sepahan

AFC CHAMPIONS LEAGUE 2010 QUALIFYING

West Asia Semi-finals

Al Sadd	QAT	5
Al Ittihad	SYR	1

Dempo	IND	Bye

West Asia Final

Al Sadd	2
Dempo	0

East Asia Semi-finals

Al Ain	UAE	Bye

Muangthong United		2 6p
Sriwijaya	IDN	2 7p

East Asia Final

Al Ain	4
Sriwijaya	0

* Home team ● Al Wahda and Singapore Armed Forces qualified for the first round proper

West Asia Qualfying

Semi-Final. Jassim Bin Hamad, Doha
12-02-2011, 17:45, 2000, Faghani IRN

Al Sadd   **5**

Keita 2 [12 30], Leandro 2 [33 67], Siddiq [76]

Saad **Al Sheeb** - Nadir **Belhadj**, Abdulla Koni, Mohammed **Kasola**●, Majdi **Siddiq**, Nasser Nabil **Salem**●, (Talal **Al Bloushi** 63), Wesam **Rizik**, Abdelkarim **Fadlalla**, Yusef **Ali** (Hasan **Al Haidos** 76), **Leandro** (Ali Hasan **Yahya**● 80), Abdulkader **Keita**. Tr: Jorge Fossati

Al Ittihad Aleppo   **1**

Hemidi [82p]

Khaled Haji **Othman** - Ahmad **Kallasi**, Omar **Hemidi**, Abdulkader **Dakka**, Taha **Dyab** (Mohamad **Al Ghabbash** 81), Mohamad **Fares**, Ahmad Haj **Mohamad**, Ayman **Salal**, Jud **Kongnyuy**, Marjan **Jugovic** (Mohamad **Kalaji** 64), Madiou **Konate** (Tamer **Rashed** 81). Tr: Kemal **Alispahic**

Final. Jassim Bin Hamad, Doha
19-02-2011, 17:50, 3841, Kovalenko UZB

Al Sadd   **2**

Keita [33], Leandro [89]

Saad **Al Sheeb** - Mohammed **Kasola**, Lee Jung Soo, Majdi **Siddiq**● (Wesam **Rizik** 61), Talal **Al Bloushi**, Nasser Nabil **Salem**, Abdelkarim **Fadlalla**, Yusef **Ali** (Nadir **Belhadj** 81), Hasan **Al Haidos** (**Leandro** 75), Abdulkader **Keita**, Ali Hasan **Yahya**. Tr: Jorge **Fossati**

Dempo Sports Club   **0**

Subhashish **Chowdhury** - Samir **Naik**, Dominic **Noronha**, Siavash **Samieinia**●, Mahesh **Gawli**, Peter **Carvalho** (Joaquim **Abranches** 77), Climax **Lawrence** (Godwin **Franco** 88), Ogba **Nnanna**, Clifford **Miranda**, Ranty **Soleye**●, **Beto**. Tr: Armando **Colaco**

East Asia Qualfying

Semi-final. Jakabaring, Palembang
12-02-2011, 15:30, 12 000, Bashir SIN

Sriwijaya   **2 7p**

Gumbs [49], Gathuessi [112]

Feri **Rotinsulu** - **Diano**●, Thierry **Gathuessi**●, Achmad **Jufriyanto**, Supardi **Nasir**, Mahyadi **Panggabean**●, **Rendy** (Ardles **Rumbiak**● 82), Mahadirga **Lasut**, Ponaryo **Astaman**, Arif **Suyono** (Budi **Sudarsono**● 75), Rudi **Widodo** (Keith **Gumbs** 36). Tr: Ivan **Kolev**

Muangthong United   **2 6p**

Datsakorn [82], Teerasil [93]

Kawin **Thammasatchanan** - Toni **Kallio**● (Weerawut **Kayem** 56), Panupong **Wongsa**●●♦90, Nattaporn **Phanrit**, Zesh **Rehman** (Naruphol **Ar-Romsawa** 68), Jakkraphan **Pornsai**●, Phichitpong **Choeichiu** (Anon **Sangsanoi** 55), Dagno **Siaka**, Datsakorn **Thonglao**, Teerasil **Dangda**, Christian **Kouakou**. Tr: Rene **Desaeyere**

PENALTIES (SRIWIJAYA WON 7-6)

Gumbs ✓; Datsakorn ✓; Astaman ✓; Jakkraphan ✓; Sudarsono ✓; Anon ✓; Lasut ✓; Naruphol ✓; Diano ✗; Dagno ✗; Gathuessi ✗; Kouakou ✗; Panggabean ✓; Teerasil ✓; Nasir ✓; Nattaporn ✓; Jufriyanto ✓; Weerawut ✗

Final. Jakabaring, Palembang
19-02-2011, 15:30, 12 000, Toma JPN

Sriwijaya   **0**

Feri **Rotinsulu** - Bobby **Satria**●, Thierry **Gathuessi**●, Achmad **Jufriyanto** (Ardiles **Rumbiak** 46), Supardi **Nasir** (Rudi **Widodo** 53) (**Rendy** 76), Mahyadi **Panggabean**, Mahadirga **Lasut**●, Ponaryo **Astaman**, Budi **Sudarsono**, Arif **Suyono**, Keith **Gumbs**. Tr: Ivan **Kolev**

Al Ain   **4**

Haddaf [13], Elias 2 [45p 53], Abdulrahman [50p]

Dawoud **Sulaiman** - Musallem **Fayez**, Fawzi **Fayez**, Fares **Juma**, Ibrahima **Keita**, Ali **Al Wehaibi** (Bandar **Mohamed** 83), Omar **Abdulrahman**● (Mohammed **Abdulrahman** 65), Hazza **Salem**● (Ismaeel **Ahmed** 76), Hamad **Al Marri**, **Elias**●, Haddaf **Abdulla**●. Tr: Alexandre **Gallo**

GROUP A		Pl	W	D	L	F	A	Pts	QAT	IRN	KSA	UAE
Sepahan	IRN	6	4	1	1	14	5	**13**		1-1	2-0	5-1
Al Hilal	KSA	6	4	1	1	11	6	**13**	1-2		2-0	3-1
Al Gharafa	QAT	6	2	1	3	6	7	**7**		1-0	0-1	5-2
Al Jazeera	UAE	6	0	1	5	7	20	**1**	1-4	2-3	0-0	

Mohamed Bin Zayed, Abu Dhabi
1-03-2011, 19:25, 9625, Shukralla BHR

Al Jazeera   0

Ali Khasif - Juma Abdullah•, Saleh Basheer, Abdulla Mousa, Khalid Sebil Lashkari, Yaser Matar, Matias Delgado, Subait Khater, Bare (Khamis Esmaeel 69), Ibrahim Diaky• (Ahmed Jumaa 83), Ricardo Oliveira (Ali Mabkhout 80). Tr: Abel Braga

Al Gharafa   0

Qasem Burhan - Marcone, Hamed Shami (Saud Sabah 80), George Kwesi Semakor, Bilal Mohammed, Ahmed Al Binali, Lawrence Quaye•, Juninho Pernambucano, Younis Mahmoud, Amara Diane (Fahad Al Shammari 78), Mirghani Al Zain• (Othmane El Assas 75) Tr: Bruno Metsu

King Fahd International, Riyadh
1-03-2011, 20:30, 15 000, Irmatov UZB

Al Hilal   1
          Wilhelmsson 93+

Abdullah Alsdairy - Osama Hawsawi, Mirel Radoi, Mohammad Al-Nakhli (Mohammed Al Qarni• 66), Majed Al Marshadi, Shafi Al Dossari (Waleed Al-Gizani 81), Christian Wilhelmsson, Mohammad Al Shalhoub, Ahmed Al Fraidi, Ahmed Ali, Nawaf Al Abed (Essa Al Mehyani 65). Tr: Gabriel Calderon

Sepahan   1
    Toure 51, Januario 60

Mehdi Rahmati - Khosro Heydari (Mehdi Jafarpour 90), Hadi Aghili, Jalal Hosseini, Mohsen Bengar, Omid Ebrahimi, Ahmad Jamshidian•, Ehsan Hajsafi (Hashem Beikzadeh 82), Fabio Januario (Mehdi Karimian 88), Ibrahima Toure, Milorad Janjus. Tr: Amir Ghalenoei

Al Gharafa, Doha
15-03-2011, 18:30, 8310, Kim Dong Jin KOR

Al Gharafa   0

Qasem Burhan - Ibrahim Al Ghanim, Marcone, George Kwesi Semakor, Ahmed Al Binali, Lawrence Quaye, Juninho Pernambucano, Othmane El Assas (Fahad Al Shammari 70), Younis Mahmoud, Amara Diane, Mirghani Al Zain. Tr: Bruno Metsu

Al Hilal   1
          Wilhelmsson 9

Hassan Al Otaibi• - Osama Hawsawi, Abdullah Al Zori•, Mirel Radoi•, Mohammad Al-Nakhli (Salman Al Khaldi 90), Majed Al Marshadi, Khaled Aziz•, Christian Wilhelmsson, Mohammad Al Shalhoub•, Ahmed Al Fraidi (Abdulaziz Al Dosari 60), Ahmed Ali (Yasser Al Khatani• 61). Tr: Gabriel Calderon

Foolad Shahr, Isfahan
15-03-2011, 19:00, 2520, Bashir SIN

Sepahan   5
Jamshidian 2 2 24, Toure 56, Janjus 65, Kazemian 90

Mehdi Rahmati - Khosro Heydari, Hadi Aghili, Jalal Hosseini, Mohsen Bengar, Omid Ebrahimi, Ahmad Jamshidian (Mehdi Karimian 82), Ehsan Hajsafi, Fabio Januario, Ibrahima Toure (Javad Kazemian 86), Milorad Janjus (Reza Enayati 78). Tr: Amir Ghalenoei

Al Jazeera   1
          Bare 54

Ali Khasif - Juma Abdullah, Saleh Basheer, Khalid Sebil Lashkari (Mohammed Marzooq 46), Yaser Matar (Mohamed Al Menhali 80), Saleh Obaid•, Helal Saeed (Khamis Esmaeel 46), Subait Khater, Bare, Ibrahim Diaky, Ricardo Oliveira. Tr: Abel Braga

Foolad Shahr, Isfahan
5-04-2011, 20:00, 5668, Nishimura JPN

Sepahan   2
    Aghili 54p, Jamshidian 66

Mehdi Rahmati - Khosro Heydari (Moharram Navidkia 14), Hadi Aghili, Jalal Hosseini, Mohsen Bengar, Omid Ebrahimi, Ahmad Jamshidian, Ehsan Hajsafi, Fabio Januario (Hossein Papi 90), Ibrahima Toure, Javad Kazemian (Mehdi Jafarpour 84). Tr: Amir Ghalenoei

Al Gharafa   0

Qasem Burhan - Ibrahim Al Ghanim•, Hamed Shami, George Kwesi Semakor, Bilal Mohammed•, Lawrence Quaye, Juninho Pernambucano•, Othmane El Assas, Younis Mahmoud, Amara Diane, Mirghani Al Zain•. Tr: Bruno Metsu

King Fahd International, Riyadh
5-04-2011, 20:45, 13 421, Williams AUS

Al Hilal   3
Kamel 4, Al Khatani 14, Al Shalhoub 94+

Hassan Al Otaibi (Fahad Al Shammari 85) - Osama Hawsawi, Abdullah Al Zori, Mirel Radoi, Lee Young Pyo, Majed Al Marshadi, Christian Wilhelmsson, Mohammad Al Shalhoub, Ahmed Al Fraidi (Abdulaziz Al Dosari 46), Ahmed Ali, Yasser Al Khatani (Nawaf Al Abed 74). Tr: Gabriel Calderon

Al Jazeera   1
          Jumaa 19

Ali Khasif - Saleh Basheer, Mohammed Marzooq, Yaser Matar•, Abdulsalam Jumaa, Sami Rubaiya (Mohamed Al Menhali 46), Saleh Obaid (Mohamed Salem 79), Khamis Esmaeel, Sultan Bargash, Ahmed Jumaa (Ali Mabkhout 68), Abdulla Qasem•. Tr: Abel Braga

Al Gharafa, Doha
20-04-2011, 18:50, 3426, Basma SYR

Al Gharafa   1
          Diane 19

Qasem Burhan - Ibrahim Al Ghanim, Hamed Shami, Bilal Mohammed, Ahmed Al Binali, Lawrence Quaye, Juninho Pernambucano, Othmane El Assas (Muayed Hassan 47), Fahad Al Shammari (Younis Mahmoud 81), Amara Diane, Meshal Abdulla. Tr: Bruno Metsu

Sepahan   0

Mehdi Rahmati - Khosro Heydari, Hadi Aghili (Javad Kazemian 46) (Mehdi Nasiri 89), Jalal Hosseini, Mohsen Bengar••♦57, Moharram Navidkia•, Omid Ebrahimi, Ehsan Hajsafi•, Fabio Januario, Ibrahima Toure, Reza Enayati. Tr: Amir Ghalenoei

Mohamed Bin Zayed, Abu Dhabi
20-04-2011, 19:50, 6154, Toma JPN

Al Jazeera   2
    Mabkhout 44, Qasim 45

Khalid Eisa - Juma Abdullah, Abdulla Mousa•, Khalid Sebil Lashkari, Yaser Matar•, Abdulsalam Jumaa• (Khamis Esmaeel 69), Sami Rubaiya, Helal Saeed (Sultan Bargash• 69), Ahmed Jumaa (Mohamed Al Menhali 74), Abdulla Qasem, Ali Mabkhout. Tr: Abel Braga

Al Hilal   3
Al Khatani 2 56 65, Radoi 77p

Hassan Al Otaibi - Osama Hawsawi, Abdullah Al Zori, Mirel Radoi, Lee Young Pyo, Majed Al Marshadi, Christian Wilhelmsson, Mohammad Al Shalhoub, Ahmed Al Fraidi (Nawaf Al Abed 66), Ahmed Ali (Abdulaziz Al Dosari 80), Yasser Al Khatani (Essa Al Mehyani 90). Tr: Gabriel Calderon

Foolad Shahr, Isfahan
4-05-2011, 20:00, 8833, Tan Hai CHN

Sepahan   1
          Navidkia 55

Mehdi Rahmati - Khosro Heydari, Hadi Aghili, Jalal Hosseini, Moharram Navidkia, Mehdi Karimian (Hossein Papi 62), Omid Ebrahimi, Ehsan Hajsafi, Fabio Januario, Ibrahima Toure, Reza Enayati (Mehdi Jafarpour 71). Tr: Amir Ghalenoei

Al Hilal   1
          Al Zori 46

Hassan Al Otaibi - Osama Hawsawi, Abdullah Al Zori, Mirel Radoi, Lee Young Pyo, Majed Al Marshadi, Salman Al Khaldi, Mohammad Al Shalhoub, Abdulaziz Al Dosari (Sultan Al-Bargan 81), Ahmed Al Fraidi• (Nawaf Al Abed 90), Yasser Al Khatani (Ahmed Ali 73). Tr: Gabriel Calderon

Al Gharafa, Doha
4-05-2011, 19:00, 5786, Kovalenko UZB

Al Gharafa   5
Mahmoud 3 10 62 80, Diane 48, Al Zain 60

Qasem Burhan• - Ibrahim Al Ghanim, Hamed Shami, Bilal Mohammed, Ahmed Al Binali, Juninho Pernambucano• (George Kwesi Semakor 80), Othmane El Assas, Fahad Al Shammari (Lawrence Quaye 64), Younis Mahmoud, Amara Diane, Mirghani Al Zain (Bilal Abdulrahman• 80). Tr: Bruno Metsu

Al Jazeera   2
    Jumaa 31, Ricardo Oliveira 37p

Ali Khasif - Juma Abdullah• (Ali Salem Ahmed Faraj 67), Abdulla Mousa, Khalid Sebil Lashkari•, Abdulsalam Jumaa (Mohammed Marzooq• 69), Sami Rubaiya, Helal Saeed (Sultan Bargash 46), Khamis Esmaeel, Ahmed Jumaa, Ricardo Oliveira, Ali Mabkhout. Tr: Abel Braga

Mohamed Bin Zayed, Abu Dhabi
11-05-2011, 20:00, 2265, Choi Myung Yong KOR

Al Jazeera   1
          Bare 14

Ali Khasif - Abdulla Mousa, Ali Salem Ahmed Faraj, Mohammed Marzooq•, Yaser Matar (Saleh Obaid• 72), Sami Rubaiya (Ali Mabkhout 46), Khamis Esmaeel, Ahmed Jumaa (Matias Delgado 46), Bare•, Ibrahim Diaky, Ahmed Muhad. Tr: Abel Braga

Sepahan   4
Kazemian 32, Toure 2 60 71, Enayati 91+

Mehdi Rahmati - Khosro Heydari• (Mohammad Hassan Rajabzadeh 90), Hadi Aghili, Jalal Hosseini, Mohsen Bengar, Hashem Beikzadeh (Moharram Navidkia 46), Omid Ebrahimi, Ehsan Hajsafi, Fabio Januario, Ibrahima Toure•, Javad Kazemian (Reza Enayati 71). Tr: Amir Ghalenoei

King Fahd International, Riyadh
11-05-2011, 21:05, 19 123, Tojo JPN

Al Hilal   2
    Al Khatani 47, Al Fraidi 82

Hassan Al Otaibi - Osama Hawsawi, Abdullah Al Zori, Mirel Radoi, Lee Young Pyo, Majed Al Marshadi, Mohammad Al Shalhoub (Essa Al Mehyani 80), Abdulaziz Al Dosari (Christian Wilhelmsson 68), Ahmed Al Fraidi, Ahmed Ali (Mohammed Al Qarni 68), Yasser Al Khatani. Tr: Gabriel Calderon

Al Gharafa   0

Qasem Burhan - Ibrahim Al Ghanim, Marcone, Hamed Shami, George Kwesi Semakor (Saad Al Shammari 79), Lawrence Quaye, Bilal Abdulrahman (Amara Diane 62), Othmane El Assas, Fahad Al Shammari, Younis Mahmoud• (Muayed Hassan 77), Mirghani Al Zain. Tr: Bruno Metsu

GROUP B		Pl	W	D	L	F	A	Pts	QAT	KSA	IRN	UZB
Al Sadd	QAT	6	2	4	0	8	6	10		1-0	2-2	2-1
Al Nasr	KSA	6	2	2	2	10	7	8	1-1		2-1	4-0
Esteghlal Tehran	IRN	6	2	2	2	11	10	8	1-1	2-1		4-2
Pakhtakor Tashkent	UZB	6	1	2	3	8	14	5	1-1	2-2	2-1	

Pakhtakor Markaziy, Tashkent
1-03-2011, 17:00, 15 000, Tojo JPN
Pakhtakor Tashkent 2
Karimov [45], Sharofetdinov [61]
Temur Juraev - Bojan Miladinovic, Akbarjon Ismatullaev, Kamoliddin Tadjiev•, Ilhomjon Suyunov•, Kakhi Makharadze, Sherzodbek Karimov, Dilshod Sharofetdinov•, Stanislav Andreev, Sanat Shikhov (Alisher Azizov 75), Dusan Savic (Temurkhuja Abdukholiqov• 79). Tr: Ravshan Haydarov
Al Nasr 2
Al Mutwa [51], OG [88]
Abdullah Al-Anzi - Ahmed Dokhi•, Abdulkarim Al Khaibari, Omar Ibrahim•, Jon McKain•, Ahmed Abbas•, Abdulrahman Al-Qahtani (Saad Al-Harthi 63), Victor Figueroa, Ibrahim Ghaleb, Saud Hamoud Hasan (Mohammad Al-Sahlawi 77), Bader Al Mutwa (Rayan Belal 90). Tr: Dragan Skocic

Azadi, Tehran
1-03-2011, 17:30, 15 000, Kim Dong Jin KOR
Esteghlal Tehran 1
Majidi [27]
Vahid Talebloo - Amir-Hossein Sadeghi, Mehdi Amirabadi•, Hanif Omranzadeh•, Eman Mobali• (Hawar Mulla Mohammed 70), Farzad Ashoubi, Felipe Alves (Esmaeil Sharifat 90), Pejman Montazeri, Farhad Majidi•, Arash Borhani• (Mojtaba Jabbari 81), Mehdi Seyed Salehi. Tr: Parviz Mazloomi
Al Sadd 1
Keita [88]
Saad Al Sheeb - Nadir Belhadj, Abdulla Koni, Mohammed Kasola, Lee Jung Soo, Mesaad Al-Hamad, Talal Al-Bloushi• (Yusef Ali 50), Wesam Rizik•, Abdelkarim Fadlalla (Ali Hasan Yahya 74), Leandro (Majdi Siddiq 90), Abdulkader Keita. Tr: Jorge Fossati

King Fahd International, Riyadh
15-03-2011, 20:30, 12 878, Al Hilali OMA
Al Nasr 2
Sulaimani [60], Al Harthi [81]
Abdullah Al-Anzi - Ahmed Dokhi, Hussein Sulaimani, Omar Ibrahim•, Jon McKain, Ahmed Abbas•, Abdulrahman Al-Qahtani (Mohammad Al-Sahlawi 80), Victor Figueroa• (Khaled Asiri 46), Ibrahim Ghaleb, Saud Hamoud Hasan (Saad Al-Harthi• 54), Bader Al Mutwa. Tr: Dragan Skocic
Esteghlal Tehran 1
Omranzadeh [21]
Vahid Talebloo - Amir-Hossein Sadeghi, Mehdi Amirabadi (Esmaeil Sharifat 67), Hanif Omranzadeh•, Javad Shirzad, Kianoush Rahmati, Felipe Alves (Farzad Ashoubi 61), Hawar Mulla Mohammed, Pejman Montazeri, Farhad Majidi, Mehdi Seyed Salehi (Arash Borhani 84). Tr: Parviz Mazloomi

---

Jassim Bin Hamad, Doha
16-03-2011, 18:05, 3782, Choi Myung Yong KOR
Al Sadd 2
Lee Jung Soo [45], Afif [61]
Mohammed Saqr - Nadir Belhadj, Abdulla Koni, Mohammed Kasola•, Lee Jung Soo, Mesaad Al Hamad, Wesam Rizik, Abdelkarim Fadlalla (Khalfan Ibrahim 59), Leandro (Majdi Siddiq 85), Hasan Al Haidos (Ali Hasan Yahya 59), Abdulkader Keita. Tr: Jorge Fossati
Pakhtakor Tashkent 1
Abdulkholikov [57]
Temur Juraev - Bojan Miladinovic•, Akbarjon Ismatullaev, Kamoliddin Tadjiev♦93+, Ilhomjon Suyunov, Kakhi Makharadze, Sherzodbek Karimov (Sanat Shikhov 88), Dilshod Sharofetdinov, Stanislav Andreev, Vladimir Kozak• (Dusan Savic 62), Temurkhuja Abdukholiqov (Alisher Azizov 87). Tr: Ravshan Haydarov

Jassim Bin Hamad, Doha
5-04-2011, 18:15, 8603, Al Zarooni UAE
Al Sadd 1
Lee Jung Soo [61]
Mohammed Saqr - Nadir Belhadj•♦91+, Abdulla Koni•, Mohammed Kasola, Lee Jung Soo, Nasser Nabil Salem, Wesam Rizik• (Khalfan Ibrahim 59), Abdelkarim Fadlalla, Yusef Ali (Majdi Siddiq 82), Leandro (Hasan Al Haidos 68), Abdulkader Keita•. Tr: Jorge Fossati
Al Nasr 0
Abdullah Al-Anzi - Ahmed Dokhi•, Mohammed Eid♦50, Hussein Sulaimani•, Jon McKain, Victor Figueroa (Abdulaziz Al Azmi 62), Ibrahim Ghaleb•, Mohammad Al-Sahlawi (Ovidiu Petre 53), Saad Al-Harthi (Saud Hamoud Hasan• 77), Bader Al Mutwa, Khaled Asiri•. Tr: Dragan Skocic

Azadi, Tehran
6-04-2011, 17:30, 17 654, Albadwawi UAE
Esteghlal Tehran 4
Hawar [12], Majidi [23], Salehi [57], Borhani [93+]
Mohammad Mohammadi - Amir-Hossein Sadeghi, Hadi Shakourie, Javad Shirzad, Eman Mobali (Mojtaba Jabbari 88), Kianoush Rahmati, Farzad Ashoubi, Hawar Mulla Mohammed (Esmaeil Sharifat 90), Pejman Montazeri, Farhad Majidi (Mehdi Seyed Salehi• 39), Arash Borhani. Tr: Parviz Mazloomi
Pakhtakor Tashkent 0
Temur Juraev• - Igor Krimets, Bojan Miladinovic, Akbarjon Ismatullaev, Ilhomjon Suyunov, Kakhi Makharadze, Dilshod Sharofetdinov (Temurkhuja Abdukholiqov• 61), Stanislav Andreev, Vladimir Kozak, Igor Sergeev (Alisher Azizov 46), Dusan Savic (Sanat Shikhov 81). Tr: Ravshan Haydarov

---

Pakhtakor Markaziy, Tashkent
19-04-2011, 18:00, 7000, Nishimura JPN
Pakhtakor Tashkent 2
Andreev [28], Krimets [88]
Nikita Ribkin - Igor Krimets•, Akbarjon Ismatullaev, Kamoliddin Tadjiev, Ilhomjon Suyunov•, Kakhi Makharadze, Sherzodbek Karimov (Timur Kagirov 90), Stanislav Andreev, Vladimir Kozak, Alisher Azizov (Sanat Shikhov 72), Dusan Savic (Akmal Kholmuradov 90). Tr: Ravshan Haydarov
Esteghlal Tehran 1
Borhani [45]
Mohammad Mohammadi - Amir-Hossein Sadeghi, Hanif Omranzadeh•♦86, Javad Shirzad, Mojtaba Jabbari, Kianoush Rahmati, Farzad Ashoubi, Hawar Mulla Mohammed (Hadi Shakouri 87), Pejman Montazeri, Farhad Majidi (Mehdi Seyed Salehi 80), Arash Borhani• (Esmaeil Sharifat 85). Tr: Parviz Mazloomi

King Fahd International, Riyadh
19-04-2011, 20:40, 18 421, Tan Hai CHN
Al Nasr 1
Sulaimani [75]
Abdullah Al-Anzi - Hussein Sulaimani, Omar Ibrahim, Jon McKain•, Ovidiu Petre, Ahmed Abbas•, Ibrahim Ghaleb, Mohammad Al-Sahlawi, Saad Al-Harthi (Saud Hamoud Hasan 46), Bader Al Mutwa (Victor Figueroa 41), Khaled Asiri (Abdulrahman Al-Qahtani 80). Tr: Dragan Skocic
Al Sadd 1
Siddiq [37]
Mohammed Saqr• - Abdulla Koni, Mohammed Kasola, Lee Jung Soo•, Majdi Siddiq (Dheyab Alinabi 85), Mesaad Al-Hamad, Talal Al-Bloushi•, Abdelkarim Fadlalla•, Yusef Ali (Khalfan Ibrahim 69), Leandro• (Ali Al Mahdi 90), Abdulkader Keita. Tr: Jorge Fossati

Jassim Bin Hamad, Doha
3-05-2011, 18:25, 5060, Williams AUS
Al Sadd 2
Khalfan Ibrahim [54], Leandro [76]
Mohammed Saqr - Nadir Belhadj, Abdulla Koni, Lee Jung Soo•, Majdi Siddiq, Mesaad Al Hamad, Wesam Rizik, Yusef Ali (Hasan Al Haidos 72), Leandro, Abdulkader Keita (Abdelkarim Fadlalla 86), Khalfan Ibrahim (Abdulrab Al Yazidi 90). Tr: Jorge Fossati
Esteghlal Tehran 1
Majidi 2 [6] [37]
Mohammad Mohammadi - Amir-Hossein Sadeghi (Mehdi Amirabadi 90), Hadi Shakouri, Andre Luiz (Mehdi Seyed Salehi 70), Javad Shirzad, Mojtaba Jabbari, Eman Mobali, Kianoush Rahmati•, Hawar Mulla Mohammed• (Farzad Ashoubi 79), Pejman Montazeri, Farhad Majidi. Tr: Parviz Mazloomi

---

King Fahd International, Riyadh
4-05-2011, 20:45, 4034, Green AUS
Al Nasr 4
Hamood [8], Al Mutwa 2 [24] [65], Al Sahlawi [61]
Abdullah Al-Anzi - Ahmed Dokhi, Hussein Sulaimani, Omar Ibrahim, Jon McKain•, Ahmed Abbas (Ovidiu Petre 81), Ibrahim Ghaleb (Saad Al-Harthi 85), Saud Hamoud Hasan (Victor Figueroa 76), Mohammad Al-Sahlawi, Bader Al Mutwa, Khaled Asiri. Tr: Dragan Skocic
Pakhtakor Tashkent 0
Nikita Ribkin - Igor Krimets, Akbarjon Ismatullaev, Timur Kagirov, Akmal Kholmuradov•, Dilshod Sharofetdinov•, Stanislav Andreev, Vladimir Kozak, Sanat Shikhov, Alisher Azizov (Temurkhuja Abdukholiqov 57), Dusan Savic. Tr: Ravshan Haydarov

Pakhtakor Markaziy, Tashkent
11-04-2011, 18:00, 2950, El Haddad LIB
Pakhtakor Tashkent 1
Andreev [60]
Nikita Ribkin (Eldor Tadjibaev 45) - Akbarjon Ismatullaev, Murod Mukhamedov, Akmal Kholmuradov, Ilhomjon Suyunov, Stanislav Andreev, Vladimir Kozak•, Temurkhuja Abdukholiqov, Sanat Shikhov• (Timur Kagirov 78), Alisher Azizov (Bekzod Mirkhaydarov• 82), Dusan Savic. Tr: Ravshan Haydarov
Al Sadd 1
Siddiq [93+]
Saad Al Sheeb - Nadir Belhadj, Abdulla Koni, Taher Zakaria, Majdi Siddiq, Mesaad Al Hamad, Abdulrab Al Yazidi (Khalfan Ibrahim 63), Wesam Rizik, Abdelkarim Fadlalla (Abdulkader Keita 76), Yusef Ali (Leandro 68), Hasan Al Haidos. Tr: Jorge Fossati

Azadi, Tehran
11-04-2011, 18:00, 85 422, Toma JPN
Esteghlal Tehran 2
Majidi [62], Hawar [89]
Mohammad Mohammadi - Amir-Hossein Sadeghi, Mehdi Amirabadi (Hadi Shakouri 77), Javad Shirzad, Mojtaba Jabbari, Eman Mobali (Mehdi Seyed Salehi 55), Kianoush Rahmati, Hawar Mulla Mohammed, Pejman Montazeri, Farhad Majidi, Arash Borhani• (Esmaeil Sharifat 68). Tr: Parviz Mazloomi
Al Nasr 1
Al Mutwa [60]
Abdullah Al-Anzi• - Ahmed Dokhi, Abdou Barnawi•, Mohammed Eid•, Omar Ibrahim, Ahmed Abbas, Ibrahim Ghaleb, Saud Hamoud Hasan (Abdulrahman Al-Qahtani 45) (Victor Figueroa 73), Mohammad Al-Sahlawi (Ovidiu Petre 89), Bader Al Mutwa, Khaled Asiri. Tr: Dragan Skocic

GROUP C		Pl	W	D	L	F	A	Pts	KSA	UZB	UAE	IRN
Al Ittihad	KSA	6	3	2	1	10	5	11		1-1	0-0	3-1
Bunyodkor	UZB	6	2	3	1	8	6	9	0-1		3-2	0-0
Al Wahda	UAE	6	1	3	2	6	8	6	0-3	1-1		2-0
Persepolis	IRN	6	1	2	3	6	11	5	3-2	1-3	1-1	

Al Nahyan, Abu Dhabi
2-03-2011, 20:00, 5622, Williams AUS
Al Wahda 1
Hugo [88]
Mutaz Abdulla - Basheer Saeed•, Haidar Ali (Hugo 64), Mahmoud Khamis, Eisa Ahmed, Hamdan Al Kamali, Magrao, Ismail Matar, Khalid Jalal (Saeed Al Kathiri 87), Mohamed Al Shehhi (Fahed Masoud• 73), Fernando Baiano. Tr: Josef Hickersberger
Bunyodkor 1
Haydarov [85]
Ignatiy Nesterov - Hayrulla Karimov, Slavoljub Dordevic, Sakhob Juraev, Islom Inomov, Azizbek Haydarov•, Shavkat Salomov, Viktor Karpenko (Yannis Mandzukas 76), Asqar Jadigerov, Milos Trifunovic, Anvarjon Solyiev (Kamoliddin Mirzaev 82). Tr: Mirdjalol Kasimov

Prince Abdullah, Jeddah
2-03-2011, 20:35, 10 787, Salleh MAS
Al Ittihad Jeddah 3
Ziaya 2 [13 75], Noor [48p]
Mabrouk Zaid - Redha Tukar, Paulo Jorge, Saleh Al-Saqri, Hamad Al-Montashari, Ahmed Hadid, Saud Khariri, Nuno Assis, Mohammed Noor (Rashid Al-Raheeb 73), Abdelmalek Ziaya (Naif Hazazi 82), Mohammed Ali Al Rashed (Sultan Al-Nemri 67). Tr: Antonio Oliveira
Persepolis 1
Zare [19]
Rahman Ahmadi• - Sepehr Heydari, Ebrahim Shakouri, Alireza Noormohamadi, Maziar Zare•, Hossein Badamaki (Amir Feshangchi 79), Mohammad Nouri, Hamidreza Ali Asgari, Tiago Fraga, Gholamreza Rezaei•, Hadi Norouzi (Vahid Hashemian 57). Tr: Ali Daei

JAR, Tashkent
16-03-2011, 17:00, 6150, Toma JPN
Bunyodkor 0
Ignatiy Nesterov - Akmal Shorakhmedov (Sasa Dordevic• 46), Hayrulla Karimov, Anvar Gafurov, Slavoljub Dordevic, Azizbek Haydarov, Shavkat Salomov (Anvar Rajabov 87), Viktor Karpenko, Asqar Jadigerov•, Milos Trifunovic, Kamoliddin Mirzaev (Anvarjon Solyiev• 56). Tr: Mirdjalol Kasimov
Al Ittihad Jeddah 1
Al Muwallad [34]
Mabrouk Zaid - Redha Tukar, Paulo Jorge, Mishal Al Saeed, Saleh Al-Saqri, Osama Al-Harbi, Manaf Abushgeer, Saud Khariri•, Nuno Assis (Rashid Al-Raheeb 90), Abdelmalek Ziaya (Naif Hazazi 85), Mohammed Ali Al Rashed (Ahmed Hadid 67). Tr: Antonio Oliveira

---

Azadi, Tehran
16-03-2011, 17:30, 15 000, Nishimura JPN
Persepolis 1
Badamaki [66]
Rahman Ahmadi - Sepehr Heydari, Ebrahim Shakouri, Alireza Noormohamadi•, Maziar Zare•, Hossein Badamaki (Amir Feshangchi 65), Mohammad Nouri, Saman Aghazamani, Hamidreza Ali Asgari, Gholamreza Rezaei•, Hadi Norouzi. Tr: Ali Daei
Al Wahda 1
Ameen [54]
Adel Al Hosani - Basheer Saeed, Haidar Ali, Eisa Ahmed, Hamdan Al Kamali•, Magrao, Ismail Matar (Abdulraheem Jumaa 90), Khalid Jalal, Hasan Ameen, Hugo (Saeed Al Kathiri 84), Mohamed Al Shehhi (Yaqoub Al Hosani 89). Tr: Josef Hickersberger

JAR, Tashkent
5-04-2011, 18:00, 7000, Shukralla BHR
Bunyodkor 0
Ignatiy Nesterov - Hayrulla Karimov, Anvar Gafurov (Anvarjon Solyiev 80), Slavoljub Dordevic•, Sakhob Juraev, Azizbek Haydarov, Jovlon Ibrokhimov, Viktor Karpenko, Asqar Jadigerov (Anvar Rajabov 46), Milos Trifunovic, Kamoliddin Mirzaev (Yannis Mandzukas 60). Tr: Mirdjalol Kasimov
Persepolis 0
Alireza Haghighi - Alireza Mohammad•, Sepehr Heydari, Alireza Noormohamadi, Hossein Badamaki, Mohammad Nouri, Saman Aghazamani, Amir Feshangchi (Mojtaba Zarei 73), Hamidreza Ali Asgari•, Vahid Hashemian (Mohammad Mansouri 89), Hadi Norouzi. Tr: Ali Daei

Al Nahyan, Abu Dhabi
5-04-2011, 20:20, 7873, Abdou QAT
Al Wahda 0
Adel Al Hosani - Basheer Saeed•, Haidar Ali (Saeed Al Kathiri 71), Mahmoud Khamis, Eisa Ahmed, Hamdan Al Kamali•, Magrao, Ismail Matar, Khalid Jalal (Fernando Baiano 45), Hugo, Mohamed Al Shehhi (Fahed Masoud 82). Tr: Josef Hickersberger
Al Ittihad Jeddah 3
Ziaya [33], Karimov [71p], Karpenko [95+]
Mabrouk Zaid (Tisir Al-Antaif 88) - Redha Tukar, Paulo Jorge•, Mishal Al Saeed, Saleh Al-Saqri, Osama Al-Harbi, Manaf Abushgeer, Abdelmalek Ziaya• (Ahmed Hadid 66), Mohammed Ali Al Rashed (Naif Hazazi 76). Tr: Antonio Oliveira

---

Azadi, Tehran
20-04-2011, 17:30, 31 765, Balideh QAT
Persepolis 1
Arifi [87]
Alireza Haghighi - Sepehr Heydari, Alireza Noormohamadi, Maziar Zare, Hossein Badamaki (Alireza Mohammad 65◆70), Mohammad Nouri, Saman Aghazamani (Mojtaba Zarei• 74), Amir Feshangchi (Shpejtim Arifi 59), Hamidreza Ali Asgari, Vahid Hashemian, Hadi Norouzi. Tr: Ali Daei
Bunyodkor 3
Rajabov [60], Karimov [71p], Karpenko [95+]
Ignatiy Nesterov - Hayrulla Karimov• (Islom Inomov 87), Anvar Gafurov, Slavoljub Dordevic, Sakhob Juraev• (Sasa Dordevic 77), Azizbek Haydarov, Jovlon Ibrokhimov, Viktor Karpenko, Asqar Jadigerov (Milos Trifunovic• 58), Anvar Rajabov, Kamoliddin Mirzaev. Tr: Mirdjalol Kasimov

Prince Abdullah, Jeddah
20-04-2011, 21:00, 6546, Kim Dong Jin KOR
Al Ittihad Jeddah 0
Mabrouk Zaid - Redha Tukar (Mohammed Ali Al Rashed 88), Paulo Jorge, Mishal Al Saeed, Saleh Al-Saqri (Sultan Al-Nemri 75), Osama Al-Harbi•, Manaf Abushgeer, Ahmed Hadid, Nuno Assis, Mohammed Noor (Naif Hazazi 69), Abdelmalek Ziaya. Tr: Antonio Oliveira
Al Wahda 0
Mutaz Abdulla - Yaqoub Al Hosani (Abdulraheem Jumaa 69), Haidar Ali, Mahmoud Khamis, Magrao•, Ismail Matar, Khalid Jalal, Hasan Ameen, Fahed Masoud (Salem Jasim 76), Hugo, Mohamed Al Shehhi• (Salem Saleh 83). Tr: Josef Hickersberger

Azadi, Tehran
3-05-2011, 17:30, 25 486, Basma SYR
Persepolis 3
Ali Asgari 2 [14 69], Arifi [16]
Alireza Haghighi - Mojtaba Shiri, Sekou Berthe, Alireza Noormohamadi, Maziar Zare•, Hossein Badamaki (Mehdi Shiri 90), Mohammad Nouri, Saman Aghazamani, Hamidreza Ali Asgari, Shpejtim Arifi•, Hadi Norouzi (Amir Feshangchi 87). Tr: Ali Daei
Al Ittihad Jeddah 2
Al Rashid 2 [19 94+]
Mabrouk Zaid - Paulo Jorge, Mishal Al Saeed, Saleh Al-Saqri (Naif Hazazi 71), Hamad Al-Montashari, Osama Al-Harbi•, Manaf Abushgeer (Ahmed Hadid 65), Saud Khariri•, Nuno Assis, Abdelmalek Ziaya (Mohammed Noor 63), Mohammed Ali Al Rashed. Tr: Antonio Oliveira

---

JAR, Tashkent
3-05-2011, 18:00, 7600, Salleh MAS
Bunyodkor 3
Trifunovic 2 [11 35], Soliev [85]
Ignatiy Nesterov - Sasa Dordevic (Islom Inomov 58), Anvar Gafurov, Slavoljub Dordevic, Sakhob Juraev, Azizbek Haydarov, Jovlon Ibrokhimov•, Viktor Karpenko, Anvar Rajabov (Shavkat Salomov 76), Milos Trifunovic, Kamoliddin Mirzaev (Anvarjon Solyiev 70). Tr: Mirdjalol Kasimov
Al Wahda 1
Matar [2], Hugo [54p]
Mutaz Abdulla - Haidar Ali (Eisa Ahmed 79), Mahmoud Khamis, Hamdan Al Kamali, Magrao, Ismail Matar, Khalid Jalal, Hasan Ameen, Fahed Masoud (Salem Saleh 70), Hugo, Mohamed Al Shehhi (Mohamed Al Qahtani 87). Tr: Josef Hickersberger

Al Nahyan, Abu Dhabi
10-05-2011, 20:30, 1900, Al Hilali OMA
Al Wahda 2
Saleh [13], Al Shehhi [70]
Mutaz Abdulla - Yaqoub Al Hosani, Basheer Saeed•, Mahmoud Khamis• (Abdulraheem Jumaa 86), Eisa Ahmed, Hamdan Al Kamali, Hasan Ameen, Fahad Masoud, Hugo, Salem Saleh (Mohamed Al Qahtani 70), Mohamed Al Shehhi (Haidar Ali 75). Tr: Josef Hickersberger
Persepolis 0
Rahman Ahmadi• - Mojtaba Shiri, Sekou Berthe, Alireza Noormohamadi, Hossein Badamaki, Mohammad Nouri, Saman Aghazamani, Hamidreza Ali Asgari•, Tiago Fraga (Mehdi Shiri 46), Shpejtim Arifi (Vahid Hashemian 75), Hadi Norouzi• (Amir Feshangchi 66). Tr: Ali Daei

Prince Abdullah, Jeddah
10-05-2011, 21:10, 7882, Nishimura JPN
Al Ittihad Jeddah 1
Assis [30]
Mabrouk Zaid - Mohammed Salem, Paulo Jorge, Mishal Al Saeed, Hamad Al-Montashari, Ahmed Hadid, Saud Khariri, Nuno Assis, Mohammed Noor (Saleh Al-Saqri 82), Abdelmalek Ziaya (Rashid Al-Raheeb 60), Mohammed Ali Al Rashed (Naif Hazazi 88). Tr: Antonio Oliveira
Bunyodkor 1
Trifunovic [14]
Ignatiy Nesterov - Hayrulla Karimov•, Anvar Gafurov, Slavoljub Dordevic, Sakhob Juraev, Azizbek Haydarov, Jovlon Ibrokhimov (Asqar Jadigerov 56), Viktor Karpenko, Anvar Rajabov (Shavkat Salomov 76), Milos Trifunovic, Kamoliddin Mirzaev (Anvarjon Solyiev 46). Tr: Mirdjalol Kasimov

GROUP D		Pl	W	D	L	F	A	Pts	IRN	KSA	UAE	QAT
Zob Ahan	IRN	6	4	1	1	7	3	13		0-1	2-1	1-0
Al Shabab	KSA	6	3	2	1	8	4	11	0-0		4-1	1-0
Emirates Club	UAE	6	2	0	4	6	10	6	0-1	2-1		2-0
Al Rayyan	QAT	6	1	1	4	4	8	4	1-3	1-1	2-0	

Foolad Shahr, Isfahan
2-03-2011, 18:30, 3480, Kovalenko UZB
Zob Ahan 2
Hosseini [45], Castro [53]
Shahab **Gordan** - Farsheed **Talebi** (Sina Ashori 82), Mohammad Ali **Ahmadi•**, Hossain **Mahini**, Seyed **Hosseini**, Ghasem **Hadadifar•**, Shahin **Kheiri**, Mehdi **Rajabzadeh•**, Mohammad **Khalatbari**, Mohammad **Ghazi•** (Esmail **Farhadi** 65), **Igor** (Jalal **Rafkhaei** 76). Tr: Mansour **Ebrahimsadeh**
Emirates Club 1
Daoudi [39]
Ahmed Ebrahim **Al Zaabi** - Hadef Saif **Al Zaabi**, Mustafa **Saeed**, Ali **Rabeea•** (Faisal **Ali** 70), Mohamed Ali **Al Shehhi**, Amer **Deeb** (Adnan **Hussain** 57), Idris **Faraj•**, Abdulla **Al Balooshi** (Omar **Abdulaziz** 77), Karim **Kerkar**, Nabil **Daoudi**, Hadji **Bougueche**. Tr: Ghazi **Ghrairi**

Ahmed bin Ali, Al Rayyan
2-03-2011, 18:15, 3509, Nishimura JPN
Al Rayyan 1
Itamar [34p]
Saud **Al Hajiri** - Moises, Meshal **Mubarak**, Cho Yong Hyung, Murad **Naji**, Fabio **Cesar**, Rodrigo **Tabata**, Hamid **Ismail•** (Fahad **Khalfan** 74), Daniel **Goma•**, Itamar (Jaralla **Al Marri** 73), Younes **Ali** (Hamad **Al Abedy** 89). Tr: Paulo **Autuori**
Al Shabab 1
Al Shamrani [59]
Waleed **Abdullah** - Abdullah **Al-Astaa**, Marcelo **Tavares**, Hassan **Mouath**, Ziad **Al-Mowalad**, Mesaed **Al Enezi•**, Majed **Al-Marhoum**, Abdulmalek **Al-Khaibri**, Ali **Ataif** (Faisal **bin Sultan** 46), Abdulaziz **bin Saran•** (Omar **Al-Ghamdi** 90), Nasser **Al-Shamrani**. Tr: Enzo **Trossero**

Emirates Club, Ras al Khaimah
16-03-2011, 19:15, 5150, Lee Min Hu KOR
Emirates Club 2
Daoudi [5], Ahmed [24]
Ahmed Ebrahim **Al Zaabi** - Hadef Saif **Al Zaabi•**, Ali **Rabeea**, Mohammed **Ahmed•**, Omar **Abdulaziz•** (Mohamed Ali **Al Shehhi** 68), Amer **Deeb** (Adnan **Hussain•** 84), Idris **Faraj** (Faisal **Ali** 43), Abdulla **Al Balooshi**, Karim **Kerkar**, Nabil **Daoudi**, Hadji **Bougueche**. Tr: Ghazi **Ghrairi**
Al Rayyan 0
Saud **Al Hajiri** - Moises, Meshal **Mubarak**, Cho Yong Hyung, Hamad **Al Abedy** (Abdulla **Afifa** 37), Fabio **Cesar**, Rodrigo **Tabata**, Hamid **Ismail•**, Daniel **Goma•** (Fahad **Khalfan** 82), Itamar•, Jaralla **Al Marri**. Tr: Paulo **Autuori**

Prince Faisal bin Fahd, Riyadh
16-03-2011, 20:00, 3920, Shukralla BHR
Al Shabab 0
Waleed **Abdullah** - Abdullah **Al-Astaa**, Marcelo **Tavares**, Waleed **Jahdali**, Hassan **Mouath**, Abdullah **Al-Shuhail** (Alhassane **Keita** 66), Ziad **Al-Mowalad**, Majed **Al-Marhoum**, Abdulmalek **Al-Khaibri**, Abdulaziz **bin Saran** (Fahad **Hamad** 81), Nasser **Al-Shamrani**. Tr: Enzo **Trossero**
Zob Ahan 0
Shahab **Gordan** - Farsheed **Talebi**, Mohammad Ali **Ahmadi**, Hossain **Mahini**, Seyed **Hosseini•**, Ghasem **Hadadifar**, Shahin **Kheiri**, Mehdi **Rajabzadeh** (Mohammad **Salsali** 90), Mohammad **Khalatbari•**, Mohammad **Ghazi** (Jalal **Rafkhaei** 79), **Igor** (Esmail **Farhadi** 87). Tr: Mansour **Ebrahimsadeh**

Ahmed bin Ali, Al Rayyan
6-04-2011, 18:30, 3009, El Haddad LIB
Al Rayyan 1
Al Marri [13]
Saud **Al Hajiri** - Moises, Meshal **Mubarak**, Cho Yong Hyung, Murad **Naji** (Abdulrahman **Mesbeh** 65), Rami **Fayez** (Mohamed **Saeed** 65), Fabio **Cesar**, Abdulla **Afifa** (Ibrahim **Awal** 87), Rodrigo **Tabata•**, Itamar**•♦60**, Jaralla **Al Marri**. Tr: Paulo **Autuori**
Zob Ahan 3
Khalatbari [11], Castro [24], Hadadifar [71]
Shahab **Gordan•** - Farsheed **Talebi**, Mohammad Ali **Ahmadi**, Hossain **Mahini•**, Seyed **Hosseini**, Ghasem **Hadadifar•**, Shahin **Kheiri** (Majid **Noormohamadi** 87), Mehdi **Rajabzadeh**, Mohammad **Khalatbari**, Esmail **Farhadi** (Mohammad **Ghazi** 89), **Igor** (Mohammad **Salsali** 78). Tr: Mansour **Ebrahimsadeh**

Prince Faisal bin Fahd, Riyadh
6-04-2011, 20:05, 4652, Toma JPN
Al Shabab 4
Keita [2] [45] [50], Muath [74], Shuhail [85]
Waleed **Abdullah** - Marcelo **Tavares•**, Waleed **Jahdali**, Hassan **Mouath**, Ziad **Al-Mowalad** (Abdullah **Al-Shuhail** 76), Mesaed **Al Enezi•**, Ahmed **Otaif**, Abdulmalek **Al-Khaibri**, Ali **Ataif** (Camacho 41), Alhassane **Keita•** (Faisal **bin Sultan** 89), Nasser **Al-Shamrani**. Tr: Enzo **Trossero**
Emirates Club 1
Daoudi [5]
Ahmed Ebrahim **Al Zaabi** - Hadef Saif **Al Zaabi**, Ali **Rabeea** (Khaleel **Abdulla** 84), Faisal **Ali** (Hareb **Al Madhawi** 81), Mohamed Ali **Al Shehhi**, Mubarak **Saeed** (Adnan **Hussain** 59), Amer **Deeb•**, Abdulla **Al Balooshi**, Karim **Kerkar•**, Nabil **Daoudi**, Hadji **Bougueche**. Tr: Ghazi **Ghrairi**

Emirates Club, Ras al Khaimah
19-04-2011, 19:30, 5250, Choi Myung Yong KOR
Emirates Club 2
Bougueche [2] [25] [41]
Ahmed Ebrahim **Al Zaabi•** - Hadef Saif **Al Zaabi•**, Mustafa **Saeed♦57**, Faisal **Ali** (Ali **Rabeea** 62), Mohamed Ali **Al Shehhi**, Hareb **Al Madhawi** (Mohammed **Ahmed** 82), Mubarak **Saeed**, Amer **Deeb** (Nabil **Daoudi** 71), Abdulla **Al Balooshi•**, Karim **Kerkar**, Hadji **Bougueche•**. Tr: Ghazi **Ghrairi**
Al Shabab 1
Bin Saran [45]
Waleed **Abdullah** - Marcelo **Tavares**, Waleed **Jahdali•**, Hassan **Mouath•**, Abdullah **Al-Shuhail**, Ziad **Al-Mowalad•** (Faisal **bin Sultan** 68), Camacho, Ahmed **Otaif•**, Abdulmalek **Al-Khaibri** (Abdullah **Al-Astaa** 78), Alhassane **Keita** (Abdulaziz **bin Saran** 15**••♦76**), Nasser **Al-Shamrani•**. Tr: Enzo **Trossero**

Foolad Shahr, Isfahan
19-04-2011, 20:00, 3351, Tojo JPN
Zob Ahan 1
Farhadi [21]
Shahab **Gordan** - Farsheed **Talebi**, Mohammad Ali **Ahmadi** (Shahin **Kheiri** 90), Mohammad **Salsali•**, Hossain **Mahini**, Seyed **Hosseini**, Mehdi **Rajabzadeh** (Majid **Noormohamadi** 79), Mohammad **Khalatbari**, Esmail **Farhadi**, Jalal **Rafkhaei**, **Igor** (Omid **Abolhassani** 90). Tr: Mansour **Ebrahimsadeh**
Al Rayyan 0
Saud **Al Hajiri** - Moises**••♦92+**, Meshal **Mubarak**, Murad **Naji•** (Abdulrahman **Mesbeh** 71), Fabio **Cesar**, Abdulla **Afifa**, Rodrigo **Tabata•**, Abdul Ghafoor **Murad**, Fahad **Khalfan** (Abdulrahman **Tariq** 84), Mohamed **Salah**, Younes **Ali**. Tr: Paulo **Autuori**

Emirates Club, Ras al Khaimah
3-05-2011, 19:35, 5450, Bashir SIN
Emirates Club 0
Ahmed Ebrahim **Al Zaabi•** - Ali **Rabeea•**, Faisal **Ali**, Mohamed Ali **Al Shehhi**, Hareb **Al Madhawi** (Salem **Mubarak** 82), Mubarak **Saeed** (Khaleel **Abdulla** 88), Adnan **Hussain**, Amer **Deeb**, Abdulla **Al Balooshi•**, Karim **Kerkar**, Hadji **Bougueche•**. Tr: Ghazi **Ghrairi**
Zob Ahan 1
Ghazi [80]
Shahab **Gordan** - Farsheed **Talebi**, Mohammad Ali **Ahmadi•**, Hossain **Mahini**, Seyed **Hosseini**, Ghasem **Hadadifar**, Shahin **Kheiri•**, Mehdi **Rajabzadeh**, Mohammad **Khalatbari•**, Mohammad **Ghazi•** (Jalal **Rafkhaei** 90), **Igor** (Hamid **Shafaat** 90). Tr: Mansour **Ebrahimsadeh**

Prince Faisal bin Fahd, Riyadh
3-05-2011, 20:20, 4000, Al Hilali OMA
Al Shabab 1
Al Shamrani [76]
Waleed **Abdullah** - Marcelo **Tavares**, Naif **Al-Qadi** (Ziad **Al-Mowalad** 39), Hassan **Mouath**, Abdullah **Al-Shuhail** (Abdullah **Al-Astaa** 63), Mesaed **Al Enezi•**, Majed **Al-Marhoum•**, Camacho, Ahmed **Otaif**, Nasser **Al-Shamrani**, Faisal **bin Sultan** (Abdulmalek **Al-Khaibri** 81). Tr: Enzo **Trossero**
Al Rayyan 0
Omar **Bari** - Abdulrahman **Mesbeh**, Meshal **Mubarak**, Cho Yong Hyung, Abdulla **Afifa** (Fahad **Khalfan** 84), Hamid **Ismail**, Daniel **Goma•** (Mohamed **Saeed** 74), Abdul Ghafoor **Murad**, Jaralla **Al Marri** (Abdulrahman **Tariq** 84), Mohamed **Salah**, Younes **Ali•**. Tr: Paulo **Autuori**

Ahmed bin Ali, Al Rayyan
10-05-2011, 18:50, 607, Shukralla BHR
Al Rayyan 2
Ghafoor Murad [74], Alaaeldin [95+]
Omar **Bari•** - Abdulrahman **Mesbeh**, Mohamed **Saeed**, Murad **Naji** (Saleh **Al Zewaidi** 81), Rami **Fayez**, Abdulla **Afifa•**, Abdul Ghafoor **Murad ••♦95+**, Sayaf **Al Korbi** (Hamad **Al Abedy** 77), Fahad **Khalfan** (Ahmed **Alaaeldin** 83), Abdulrahman **Tariq**, Mohamed **Salah**. Tr: Paulo **Autuori**
Emirates Club 1
Mohammed Saeed **Jumaa** - Hadef Saif **Al Zaabi**, Khaleel **Abdulla**, Mohamed Ali **Al Shehhi**, Hareb **Al Madhawi•** (Mohammed **Ahmed** 83), Mubarak **Saeed•**, Amer **Deeb•**, Adel **Al Marzooqi** (Idris **Faraj** 67), Karim **Kerkar**, Nabil **Daoudi**, Salem **Mubarak** (Abdulla **Malalla** 74). Tr: Ghazi **Ghrairi**

Foolad Shahr, Isfahan
10-05-2011, 20:30, 4160, Irmatov UZB
Zob Ahan 0
Mohamad **Bagher** - Farsheed **Talebi**, Mohammad **Salsali**, Hossain **Mahini•**, Seyed Ahmad **Mohammadpour**, Majid **Noormohamadi** (Mehdi **Rajabzadeh** 64), Ghasem **Hadadifar•**, Shahin **Kheiri** (Alireza **Haddadifar** 84), Esmail **Farhadi**, Jalal **Rafkhaei**, **Igor** (Omid **Abolhassani** 71). Tr: Mansour **Ebrahimsadeh**
Al Shabab 1
Bin Sultan [57]
Waleed **Abdullah** - Marcelo **Tavares**, Waleed **Jahdali**, Hassan **Mouath**, Abdullah **Al-Shuhail**, Mesaed **Al Enezi** (Ziad **Al-Mowalad** 86), Majed **Al-Marhoum**, Camacho, Ahmed **Otaif** (Abdulmalek **Al-Khaibri** 90), Nasser **Al-Shamrani**, Faisal **bin Sultan** (Abdullah **Al-Astaa** 77). Tr: Enzo **Trossero**

GROUP E		Pl	W	D	L	F	A	Pts	JPN	CHN	KOR	AUS
Gamba Osaka	JPN	6	3	1	2	13	7	10		2-0	3-1	5-1
Tianjin Teda	CHN	6	3	1	2	8	6	10	2-1		3-0	1-1
Jeju United	KOR	6	2	1	3	6	10	7	2-1	0-1		1-1
Melbourne Victory	AUS	6	1	3	2	7	11	6	1-1	2-1	1-2	

World Cup Stadium, Jeju
1-03-2011, 15:00, 5245, Al Hilali OMA
Jeju United 0
Tianjin Teda 1
Yu Dabao 55

Kim Ho Jun - Kang Min Hyuk, Ma Cheol Jun (Kang Joon Woo 64), Hong Jeong Ho, Park Hyun Beom, Kim Tae Min, Kim Young Shin, Bae Ki Jong (Lee Sang Hyup 68), Kim Eun Jung, Lee Hyun Ho (Shin Young Rok 80), Junior Santos•. Tr: Park Kyung Hoon

Yang Qipeng - Li Weifeng•, Marco Zoric, Bai Yuefeng, Yang Cao, Li Benjian, Wang Xinxin•, Chen Tao (Hu Rentian 88), Obiora Odita (Luciano Olguin 46), Zhang Xiaobin (Kwon Jip 80), Yu Dabao•. Tr: Arie Haan

---

Expo '70, Osaka
1-03-2011, 19:00, 12 949, Albadwawi UAE
Gamba Osaka 5
Takei 4, Adriano 7p, Lee 10, Futagawa 62, Kim Seung Yong 90
Melbourne Victory 1
Muscat 21p

Yosuke Fujigaya - Adriano• (Shigeru Yokotani 81), Kim Jon Ya, Satoshi Yamaguchi (Hiroki Fujiharu 62), Takumi Shimohira•, Akira Kaji, Yasuhito Endo (Kim Seung Yong 71), Takahiro Futagawa, Takashi Usami, Takuya Takei, Lee Keun Ho. Tr: Akira Nishino

Michael Petkovic - Kevin Muscat, Matthew Kemp (Surat Sukha 64), Rodrigo Vargas, Adrian Leijer, Marvin Angulo, Diogo Ferreira (Billy Celeski 15) (Leigh Broxham 76), Tom Pondeljak, Robbie Kruse•. Tr: Ernie Merrick

---

Docklands, Melbourne
15-03-2011, 19:30, 4825, Salleh MAS
Melbourne Victory 1
Allsopp 37
Jeju United 2
Park Hyun Beom 41, Lee Hyun Ho 84

Michael Petkovic - Kevin Muscat, Surat Sukha (Matthew Foschini 66), Matthew Kemp•, Adrian Leijer, Grant Brebner, Marvin Angulo (Carlos Hernandez 58), Tom Pondeljak, Isaka Cernak (Billy Celeski 82), Archie Thompson, Danny Allsopp. Tr: Mehmet Durakovic

Kim Ho Jun - Kang Min Hyuk, Ma Cheol Jun, Hong Jeong Ho, Park Hyun Beom, Kim Tae Min (Kim In Ho 64), Kim Young Shin (Choi Won Kwon 54), Bae Ki Jong (Kang Soo Il 75), Kim Eun Jung, Lee Hyun Ho•, Junior Santos. Tr: Park Kyung Hoon

---

TEDA, Tianjin
15-03-2011, 19:30, 26 866, Balideh QAT
Tianjin Teda 2
Chen Tao 25, Cao Yang 53p
Gamba Osaka 1
Lee Keun Ho 31

Yang Qipeng - Li Weifeng, Marco Zoric•, Bai Yuefeng•, Cao Yang, Li Benjian, Wang Xinxin, Chen Tao (Kwon Jip 90), Zhang Xiaobin• (Wu Weian 86), Yu Dabao (Wu Ze 90), Luciano Olguin. Tr: Arie Haan

Yosuke Fujigaya - Adriano•, Kim Jon Ya, Satoshi Yamaguchi (Kazumichi Takagi 45•), Takumi Shimohira, Akira Kaji, Yasuhito Endo•, Takahiro Futagawa, Takashi Usami (Kim Seung Yong 72), Takuya Takei (Hayato Sasaki 72), Lee Keun Ho. Tr: Akira Nishino

---

World Cup Stadium, Jeju
5-04-2011, 19:30, 2167, Torky IRN
Jeju United 2
Shin Young Rok 53, Bae Ki Jong 64
Gamba Osaka 1
Nakazawa 23

Kim Ho Jun - Kim In Ho, Choi Won Kwon, Ma Cheol Jun, Hong Jeong Ho (Kang Joon Woo 82), Park Hyun Beom, Kim Young Shin (Kang Min Hyuk 86), Shin Young Rok, Bae Ki Jong (Kang Soo Il 77), Lee Hyun Ho, Junior Santos. Tr: Park Kyung Hoon

Yosuke Fujigaya - Adriano, Sota Nakazawa, Kazumichi Takagi (Hayato Sasaki 72), Takumi Shimohira (Shoki Hirai 86), Yasuhito Endo, Takahiro Futagawa (Kim Jon Ya 72), Takashi Usami, Tomokazu Myojin, Kim Seung Yong, Lee Keun Ho. Tr: Akira Nishino

---

TEDA, Tianjin
5-04-2011, 19:30, 25 456, Kovalenko UZB
Tianjin Teda 1
Zoric 19
Melbourne Victory 1
Muscat 52

Yang Qipeng - Li Weifeng, Marco Zoric♦75, Bai Yuefeng, Cao Yang, Li Benjian, Chen Tao (Kwon Jip 56), Wu Weian, Zhang Xiaobin (Liao Bochao 74), Yu Dabao (Obiora Odita 20), Luciano Olguin•. Tr: Arie Haan

Tando Velaphi - Kevin Muscat, Surat Sukha (Diogo Ferreira 72), Matthew Foschini, Adrian Leijer, Leigh Broxham (Billy Celeski 89), Grant Brebner•, Tom Pondeljak (Robbie Kruse 46), Carlos Hernandez, Isaka Cernak, Archie Thompson. Tr: Mehmet Durakovic

---

Docklands, Melbourne
20-04-2011, 19:30, 5693, Faghani IRN
Melbourne Victory 2
Hernandez 44, Muscat 45p
Tianjin Teda 1
Chen Tao 37

Tando Velaphi - Kevin Muscat, Surat Sukha••♦82, Matthew Foschini•, Adrian Leijer, Leigh Broxham, Grant Brebner•, Carlos Hernandez (Diogo Ferreira 90•), Isaka Cernak•, Archie Thompson, Robbie Kruse• (Danny Allsopp 80). Tr: Mehmet Durakovic

Zhao Yanming - Kwon Jip (Wu Weian 20), Li Weifeng (He Yang• 31), Bai Yuefeng, Liao Bochao•, Cao Yang, Li Benjian, Chen Tao, Obiora Odita, Zhang Xiaobin, Yu Dabao• (Luciano Olguin 73). Tr: Arie Haan

---

Expo '70, Osaka
20-04-2011, 19:00, 11 398, Irmatov UZB
Gamba Osaka 3
Adriano 2 26,48, Takei 88
Jeju United 1
Shin Young Rok 67

Yosuke Fujigaya - Adriano, Sota Nakazawa, Satoshi Yamaguchi, Takumi Shimohira (Takuya Takei 73), Yasuhito Endo, Takahiro Futagawa, Takashi Usami (Akira Kaji 73), Tomokazu Myojin, Kim Seung Yong, Lee Keun Ho. Tr: Akira Nishino

Kim Ho Jun - Kim In Ho, Choi Won Kwon, Ma Cheol Jun, Hong Jeong Ho, Park Hyun Beom, Kim Young Shin, Shin Young Rok, Bae Ki Jong (Lee Sang Hyup 78), Lee Hyun Ho (Felipinho 61), Junior Santos (Kim Eun Jung 66). Tr: Park Kyung Hoon

---

Docklands, Melbourne
4-05-2011, 19:30, 7437, Abdou QAT
Melbourne Victory 1
Liejer 12
Gamba Osaka 1
Nakazawa 43

Tando Velaphi - Kevin Muscat•, Rodrigo Vargas, Matthew Foschini, Adrian Leijer, Leigh Broxham, Diogo Ferreira, Carlos Hernandez, Isaka Cernak• (Marvin Angulo 90), Archie Thompson, Danny Allsopp. Tr: Mehmet Durakovic

Yosuke Fujigaya - Adriano (Kazumichi Takagi 66), Sota Nakazawa, Satoshi Yamaguchi, Akira Kaji, Yasuhito Endo, Takahiro Futagawa, Takashi Usami (Takuya Takei 58), Tomokazu Myojin, Kim Seung Yong (Hayato Sasaki 76), Lee Keun Ho. Tr: Akira Nishino

---

TEDA, Tianjin
4-05-2011, 19:30, 26 683, Al Zarooni UAE
Tianjin Teda 3
Olguin 8, Wu Weian 21, Cao Yang 72p
Jeju United 0

Yang Qipeng - Li Weifeng, Bai Yuefeng, Liao Bochao, Cao Yang, Li Benjian, Chen Tao Chen• (Ma Leilei 88 ••♦90), Wu Weian, Obiora Odita• (He Yang 55), Zhang Xiaobin, Luciano Olguin (Mao Biao 86). Tr: Arie Haan

Kim Ho Jun• - Kang Min Hyuk, Kim In Ho•, Hong Jeong Ho, Park Hyun Beom, Kim Tae Min, Kim Young Shin (Jair 78), Shin Young Rok•, Bae Ki Jong, Lee Hyun Ho (Kim Eun Jung 35), Junior Santos (Lee Sang Hyup 83). Tr: Park Kyung Hoon

---

Expo '70, Osaka
11-05-2011, 19:00, 7939, Mozaffarizadeh IRN
Gamba Osaka 2
Endo 74, Usami 94+p
Tianjin Teda 0

Yosuke Fujigaya - Adriano (Shoki Hirai 90), Sota Nakazawa•, Satoshi Yamaguchi, Akira Kaji, Yasuhito Endo, Hayato Sasaki (Takuya Takei 77), Takahiro Futagawa, Tomokazu Myojin, Kim Seung Yong (Takashi Usami 52), Lee Keun Ho. Tr: Akira Nishino

Yang Qipeng♦90 - Li Weifeng, Marco Zoric•, Bai Yuefeng• (Obiora Odita 89), Liao Bochao, Li Benjian•, Chen Tao•, Wu Weian, Zhang Xiaobin (Mao Biao 86), Yu Dabao (Cao Yang 62), Luciano Olguin•. Tr: Arie Haan

---

World Cup Stadium, Jeju
11-05-2011, 19:30, 1519, Kovalenko UZB
Jeju United 1
Kim Eun Jung 25
Melbourne Victory 1
Ferreira 61

Kim Ho Jun - Kim In Ho, Hong Jeong Ho, Kang Joon Woo••♦88, Park Hyun Beom, Kim Young Shin Iair (Kang Soo Il 83), Bae Ki Jong (Felipinho 70), Kim Eun Jung, Lee Hyun Ho (Ma Cheol Jun 57), Junior Santos. Tr: Park Kyung Hoon

Tando Velaphi - Kevin Muscat•, Rodrigo Vargas, Matthew Foschini, Adrian Leijer•, Leigh Broxham, Diogo Ferreira, Carlos Hernandez, Archie Thompson (Billy Celeski 64), Danny Allsopp•, Robbie Kruse (Surat Sukha 88). Tr: Mehmet Durakovic

GROUP F		Pl	W	D	L	F	A	Pts	KOR	JPN	UAE	CHN
FC Seoul	KOR	6	3	2	1	9	4	11		0-2	3-0	3-0
Nagoya Grampus	JPN	6	3	1	2	9	6	10	1-1		4-0	1-0
Al Ain	UAE	6	2	1	3	4	9	7	0-1	3-1		1-0
Hangzhou Greentown	CHN	6	1	2	3	3	6	5	1-1	2-0	0-0	

Zhejiang Yellow Dragon, Hangzhou
1-03-2011, 19:35, 28 674, Abdou QAT

Hangzhou Greentown 2
Ramirez 60, Bali 86

Jiang Bo - Adam **Griffiths** (Wu Wei 42), **Rong** Hao, **Du Wei**, Tang Jiashu•, Matias Masiero• (Fan Xiaodong 70), Sheng Longyuan (Maimaitiyili Bali 60), Sun Ji, Sebastian Vazquez, Wang Song, Luis Ramirez. Tr: Wu Jingui

Nagoya Grampus 0

Seigo Narazaki - Marcus Tulio Tanaka, Takahiro Masukawa, Shohei Abe•, Jungo Fujimoto, Yoshizumi Ogawa (Naoshi Nakamura 65), Keiji Yoshimura, Mu Kanazaki (Kensuke Nagai 65), Hayuma Tanaka, Keiji Tamada (Mitsuru Chiyotanda 81), Joshua Kennedy. Tr: Dragan Stojkovic

---

Tahnoun bin Mohammed, Al Ain
2-03-2011, 19:05, 5128, Faghani IRN

Al Ain 0

Dawoud **Sulaiman** - Musallem **Fayez**, Mohammed **Salem**, Fares Juma, Ibrahima **Keita**, Ali Al Wehaibi (Hamad **Al Marri** 78), Omar **Abdulrahman** (Abdulaziz **Fayez** 46), Rami **Yaslam**, Hazza **Salem** (Bandar **Mohamed** 77), Elias, Haddaf **Abdulla**. Tr: Alexandre Gallo

FC Seoul 1
Damjanovic 25

Kim Yong Dae - **Kim Dong Jin•**, **Adilson**, **Lee Kyu Ro**, Server **Djeparov**, Mauricio **Molina** (Lee Jae An 79), **Ko Yo Han•** (Yeo Hyo Jin 89), **Lee Seung Yeoul** (Kim Hwan 62), **Choi** Hyun Tae, Dejan **Damjanovic**, **Bang Seung Hwan**. Tr: Kwan Hwangbo

---

World Cup Stadium, Seoul
15-03-2011, 20:00, 6103, Irmatov UZB

FC Seoul 3
Damjanovic 16, Ou Kyoung Jun 70, Molina 80

Kim Yong Dae - **Adilson**, **Park Yong Ho**, **Kim Tae Hwan**, **Ou Kyoung Jun** (Moon Ki Han 86), **Hyun Young Min**, **Ko Yo Han**, **Lee Seung Yeoul** (Mauricio Molina 79), **Choi Hyun Tae**, Dejan **Damjanovic**, **Lee Jae An** (Bang Seung Hwan 71). Tr: **Kwan** Hwangbo

Hangzhou Greentown 0

Jiang Bo - Adam **Griffiths**, **Rong** Hao, **Du Wei**, Tang Jiashu (Fan Xiaodong 69), Matias Masiero (Sheng Longyuan 51), Sun Ji, Sebastian Vazquez, Wang Song, Luis Ramirez, Maimaitiyili Bali (Wu Wei 77). Tr: Wu Jingui

---

Mizuho Athletic, Nagoya
6-04-2011, 19:00, 7348, Al Ghamdi KSA

Nagoya Grampus 1
Nagai 14

Seigo Narazaki - Marcus Tulio Tanaka, Takahiro Masukawa, Shohei Abe, Naoshi Nakamura (Alex 79), Jungo Fujimoto (Makito Yoshida 73), Yoshizumi Ogawa, Mu Kanazaki (Mitsuru Chiyotanda 84), Hayuma Tanaka, Joshua Kennedy, Kensuke Nagai. Tr: Dragan Stojkovic

FC Seoul 1
Choi Hyun Tae 61

Kim Yong Dae - **Adilson**, **Yeo Hyo Jin**, **Kim Tae Hwan** (Lee Jae An 63), Server **Djeparov**, Mauricio **Molina** (Kim Dong Jin 85), **Hyun Young Min**, **Moon Ki Han**, **Ko Yo Han** (Kim Tae Hwan 15), **Choi Hyun Tae•**, Dejan **Damjanovic**. Tr: **Hwangbo** Kwan

---

Zhejiang Yellow Dragon, Hangzhou
6-04-2011, 20:00, 26 973, Mozaffarizadeh IRN

Hangzhou Greentown 0

Jiang Bo - Adam **Griffiths**, **Rong** Hao, **Du Wei•**, Tang Jiashu, Matias Masiero (Xie Zhiyu 46), Sheng Longyuan (Fan Xiaodong 89), Sebastian Vazquez, Jiao Zhe, Luis Ramirez, Maimaitiyili Bali (Wang Song 64). Tr: Wu Jingui

Al Ain 0

Ismail **Rabee•**, Musallem **Fayez**, Ismaeel **Ahmed**, Mohammed **Salem**, Fares Juma, Ibrahima **Keita**, Ali Al Wehaibi, Omar **Abdulrahman•**, Rami **Yaslam**, Elias (Haddaf **Abdulla** 89), Valentin **Badea** (Faisal Ali **Hassan** 67). Tr: Alexandre **Gallo**

Mizuho Athletic, Nagoya
12-04-2011, 19:00, 5914, Mohd Salleh MAS

Nagoya Grampus 4
Kanazaki 2 27 45, OG 61, Fujimoto 77

Seigo **Narazaki** - Marcus Tulio Tanaka, Takahiro Masukawa, Shohei Abe, Naoshi Nakamura (Ryota Isomura 83), Jungo Fujimoto, Yoshizumi Ogawa• (Makito Yoshida• 45), Mu Kanazaki• (Keiji Yoshimura 64), Hayuma Tanaka, Joshua Kennedy, Kensuke Nagai. Tr: Dragan Stojkovic

Al Ain 0

Ismail Rabee - Musallem **Fayez**, Ismaeel **Ahmed**, Mohammed Salem, Fares **Juma•**76, Ibrahima **Keita**, Ali Al Wehaibi, Omar **Abdulrahman**, Rami **Yaslam**, Elias (Mohnad Salem 79), Valentin **Badea** (Bandar Mohamed 46). Tr: Alexandre **Gallo**

World Cup Stadium, Seoul
19-04-2011, 20:00, 10 927, Torky IRN

FC Seoul 0

Kim Yong Dae - **Adilson**, **Yeo Hyo Jin**, **Ou Kyoung Jun** (Moon Ki Han 68), Server **Djeparov**, Mauricio **Molina**, **Hyun Young Min**, **Ha Dae Sung** (Lee Jae An 80), **Ko Yo Han** (Kim Tae Hwan 15), **Choi Hyun Tae**, Dejan **Damjanovic•**. Tr: Hwangbo Kwan

Nagoya Grampus 2
Kanazaki 26, Nagai 81

Seigo **Narazaki** - Marcus Tulio Tanaka, Takahiro Masukawa, Shohei Abe, Jungo Fujimoto•, Yoshizumi Ogawa, Keiji Yoshimura, Mu Kanazaki (Mitsuru Chiyotanda 86), Hayuma Tanaka, Makito Yoshida (Ryota Isomura 74), Kensuke Nagai• (Alex 90). Tr: Dragan Stojkovic

---

Tahnoun bin Mohammed, Al Ain
19-04-2011, 19:30, 2324, Kovalenko UZB

Al Ain 1
Abdulrahman 60

Waleed **Salem** - Mohammed **Ayed**, Musallem **Fayez**, Ismaeel **Ahmed**, Mohammed **Salem** (Khaled **Abdulrahman** 83), Ibrahima **Keita**, Ali Al Wehaibi, Omar **Abdulrahman•**, Rami **Yaslam**, Elias (Abdullah **Malalla** 88), Valentin **Badea** (Abdulaziz **Fayez** 74). Tr: Alexandre **Gallo**

Hangzhou Greentown 0

Jiang Bo - Adam **Griffiths**, **Du Wei**, **Li Yan** (Sebastian Vazquez 52•), Matias **Masiero**, **Fan Xiaodong**, **Zheng Kewei** (Tang Jiashu 63), **Jiao Zhe**, **Wang Song**, Luis Ramirez, Zeng Yue (Maimaitiyili Bali 31•). Tr: **Wu** Jingui

---

World Cup Stadium, Seoul
4-05-2011, 20:00, 23 623, Balideh QAT

FC Seoul 3
Ko Yo Han 16, Damjanovic 2 39 72

Han Il Koo - **Adilson**, **Park Yong Ho**, **Lee Kyu Ro•**, Mauricio **Molina**, **Hyun Young Min**, **Ha Dae Sung** (Moon Ki Han 71), **Ko Yo Han** (Lee Jae An 86), **Ko Myong Jin**, **Lee Seung Yeoul** (Server Djeparov 62), Dejan **Damjanovic**. Tr: **Choi** Yong Soo

Al Ain 0

Ismail Rabee - Mohammed **Ayed•**, Khaled **Abdulrahman**, Mohnad **Salem**, Ahmed **Al Shamsi**, Hazza **Salem**, Shehab **Ahmed** (Abdulaziz **Fayez** 50), Hamad **Al Marri•** (Saif **Mohammed** 74), Bandar **Mohamed•**, Mohammed **Abdulrahman•**, Haddaf **Abdulla** (Valentin **Badea** 81). Tr: Alexandre **Gallo**

Zhejiang Yellow Dragon, Hangzhou
11-05-2011, 20:00, 12 178, Faghani IRN

Hangzhou Greentown 1
Zeng Yue 92+

Jiang Bo - Adam **Griffiths**, Tang Jiashu•, **Liu Bin**, Wu Wei (Cao Xuan 56), Xie Zhiyu (Sheng Longyuan 62•), Matias Masiero (Luis Ramirez 71), Fan Xiaodong, Zheng Kewei, Wang Song, Zeng Yue. Tr: **Wu** Jingui

FC Seoul 1
Bang Seung Hwan 66

Han Il Koo - **Adilson**, **Yeo Hyo Jin**, Server **Djeparov**, Mauricio **Molina**, **Hyun Young Min**, **Ha Dae Sung** (Moon Ki Han 86), **Lee Seung Yeoul** (Lee Jae An 59), **Choi Hyun Tae•**, Dejan **Damjanovic**, **Bang Seung Hwan** (Ko Yo Han 90). Tr: **Choi** Yong Soo

---

Tahnoun bin Mohammed, Al Ain
11-05-2011, 19:40, 892, Basma SYR

Al Ain 3
Al Merri 21, Elias 2 39 50p

Dawoud Sulaiman - Musallem **Fayez**, Khaled **Abdulrahman•**, Mohnad Salem, Ibrahima **Keita** (Shehab Ahmed 80), **Al Shamsi**, Hamad **Al Marri**, Elias, Bandar **Mohamed**, Haddaf **Abdulla** (Mohammed Abdulrahman 86), Valentin **Badea** (Hazza **Salem** 74). Tr: Alexandre **Gallo**

Nagoya Grampus 1
Fujimoto 49

Yoshihari **Takagi** - Mitsuru Chiyotanda, Takahiro Masukawa, Shohei Abe, Genta Matsuo•, Jungo Fujimoto, Yoshizumi Ogawa (Teruki Tanaka 84), Koji Hashimoto, Ryota Isomura (Sho Hanai 55), Makito Yoshida (Hikaru Kuba 46), Kensuke Nagai. Tr: Dragan Stojkovic

GROUP G		Pl	W	D	L	F	A	Pts	KOR	JPN	CHN	IDN
Jeonbuk Hy. Motors	KOR	6	5	0	1	14	2	15		1-0	1-0	6-0
Cerezo Osaka	JPN	6	4	0	2	11	4	12	1-0		4-0	2-1
Shandong Luneng	CHN	6	2	1	3	9	8	7	1-2	2-0		5-0
Arema Malang	IDN	6	0	1	5	5	22	1	0-4	0-4	1-1	

World Cup Stadium, Jeonju
2-03-2011, 19:00, 3826, Green AUS

Jeonbuk Hyundai Motors 1
Park Won Jae [59]

Yeom Dong Gyun - Sim Woo Yeon, Kim Sang Sik, Cho Sung Hwan, Choi Chul Soon, Park Won Jae, Eninho, Jung Hun (Krunoslav Lovrek 56), Kim Dong Chan (Jeong Shung Hoon 74), Luis Henrique (Kang Seung Jo 90), Lee Dong Gook. Tr: Choi Kang Hee

Shandong Luneng 0

Yang Cheng - Renato Silva, Zheng Zheng, Ricardo, Zhou Haibin, Cui Peng (Deng Zhuoxiang 85), Wang Yongpo•, Roda Antar, Zhang Chi (Yuan Weiwei• 50), Li Wei• (Han Peng 65), Obina. Tr: Branko Ivankovic

Nagai, Osaka
2-03-2011, 19:00, 10 856, Torky IRN

Cerezo Osaka 2
Rodrigo Pimpao 2 [14 76]

Kim Jin Hyeon - Teruyuki Moniwa, Taikai Uemoto, Masaki Chugo, Takashi Inui (Hiroshi Kiyotake 81), Martinez, Yusuke Maruhashi, Kim Bo Kyung, Daisuke Takahashi, Shu Kurata, Rodrigo Pimpao. Tr: Levir Culpi

Arema Malang 1
Alam Shah [50p]

Achmad Kurniawan - Purwoko Pratono, Zulkifli Syukur, Benny Wahyudi, Waluyo, Muhammad Ridhuan, Esteban Guillen• (Hendra Ridwan 88), Ahmad Bustomi•, Roman Chmelo, Ahmad Amiruddin (Sunarto 84), Noh Alam Shah. Tr: Miroslav Janu

Shandong Stadium, Jinan
16-03-2011, 15:30, 20 821, Al Ghamdi KSA

Shandong Luneng 2
Renato Silva [22], Wang Yongpo [32]

Yang Cheng - Renato Silva, Yuan Weiwei, Zheng Zheng, Ricardo•, Zhou Haibin (Zhang Chi 68), Cui Peng••[83], Wang Yongpo (Wang Tong 90), Roda Antar•, Li Wei (Obina 58), Han Peng. Tr: Branko Ivankovic

Cerezo Osaka 0

Kim Jin Hyeon - Teruyuki Moniwa•, Taikai Uemoto• (Kota Fujimoto 46), Masaki Chugo•, Takashi Inui (Rui Komatsu 46), Martinez, Yusuke Maruhashi, Kim Bo Kyung (Hiroshi Kiyotake 71), Daisuke Takahashi, Shu Kurata, Rodrigo Pimpao. Tr: Levir Culpi

Kanjuruhan, Malang
16-03-2011, 15:30, 30 000, El Haddad LIB

Arema Malang 0

Kurnia Meiga - Purwoko Pratono (Waluyo 81), Zulkifli Syukur, Benny Wahyudi, Leonard Tupamahu, Muhammad Ridhuan, Esteban Guillen, Ahmad Bustomi, Roman Chmelo, Ahmad Amiruddin (Sunarto 64), Yongki Ari Bowo (Wahyu Gunawan•46). Tr: Miroslav Janu

Jeonbuk Hyundai Motors 4
Kim Ji Woong [25], Huang Bowen 2, Luiz Henrique 2 [82 88]

Kim Min Sik - Sim Woo Yeon, Lim You Hwan, Jin Kyung Sun, Lee Seung Hyun, Huang Bowen•, Ha Sung Min (Jeon Kwang Hwan 72), Kim Jee Wong• (Kim Dong Chan 44), Jeong Shung Hoon (Jung Hun• 46), Luis Henrique, Krunoslav Lovrek. Tr: Choi Kang Hee

Kanjuruhan, Malang
5-04-2011, 15:30, 5600, Faghani IRN

Arema Malang 1
Fakhruddin [93+]

Achmad Kurniawan - Juan Revi Auriqto, Purwoko Pratono (Zulkifli Syukur 46), Mochamad Fakhrudin, Benny Wahyudi•, Johan Ahmat Farizi (Waluyo 46), Leonard Tupamahu, Hendra Ridwan• (Muhammad Ridhuan 73), Sunarto, Yongki Ari Bowo, Talaohu. Tr: Miroslav Janu

Shandong Luneng 1
Obina [8]

Yang Cheng - Renato Silva, Yuan Weiwei•, Zheng Zheng, Ricardo•, Zhou Haibin, Cui Peng (Mozhapa Murehemaitijiang• 60), Roda Antar•, Li Wei• (Wang Tong 70), Han Peng, Obina. Tr: Branko Ivankovic

Nagai, Osaka
5-04-2011, 19:00, 11 351, Irmatov UZB

Cerezo Osaka 1
Inui [53]

Kim Jin Hyeon• - Teruyuki Moniwa, Taikai Uemoto, Masaki Chugo, Takashi Inui (Kota Fujimoto 90), Hiroshi Kiyotake (Kazuya Murata 89), Yusuke Maruhashi, Kim Bo Kyung, Daisuke Takahashi, Shu Kurata, Rodrigo Pimpao (Rui Komatsu• 89). Tr: Levir Culpi

Jeonbuk Hyundai Motors 0

Kim Min Sik - Sim Woo Yeon•, Lim You Hwan, Jin Kyung Sun, Lee Seung Hyun (Kim Jee Wong• 73), Kang Seung Jo, Kim Dong Chan•, Ha Sung Min• (Krunoslav Lovrek 57), Park Jung Hoon (Huang Bowen 46), Jeon Kwang Hwan, Jeong Shung Hoon. Tr: Choi Kang Hee

Shandong Stadium, Jinan
20-04-2011, 15:30, 10 059, Albadwawi UAE

Shandong Luneng 5
Deng Zhuoxiang [25], Obina [44], Han Peng [71], Mozhapa [81], Wang Yongpo [92+]

Yang Cheng - Wang Qiang•, Zheng Zheng, Wang Liang•, Ricardo, Zhou Haibin, Cui Peng (Wang Tong 68), Wang Yongpo, Deng Zhuoxiang, Obina (Han Peng 60), Lu Zheng (Mozhapa Murehemaitijiang 75). Tr: Branko Ivankovic

Arema Malang 0

Juan Revi Auriqto - Aji Saka, Purwoko Pratono, Zulkifli Syukur•, Waluyo, Leonard Tupamahu, Muhammad Ridhuan (Sunarto 57), Ahmad Bustomi, Roman Chmelo (Mochamad Fakhrudin 88), Yongki Ari Bowo, Talaohu (Ahmad Amiruddin 46). Tr: Miroslav Janu

World Cup Stadium, Jeonju
20-04-2011, 19:00, 7892, Al Zarooni UAE

Jeonbuk Hyundai Motors 1
Lee Dong Gook [77]

Yeom Dong Gyun - Sim Woo Yeon, Kim Sang Sik•, Cho Sung Hwan•, Park Won Jae, Eninho (Krunoslav Lovrek 60), Lee Seung Hyun, Jung Hun•, Kim Dong Chan (Jeong Shung Hoon 76), Jeon Kwang Hwan (Kang Seung Jo 59), Lee Dong Gook. Tr: Choi Kang Hee

Cerezo Osaka 0

Kim Jin Hyeon - Teruyuki Moniwa, Taikai Uemoto• (Kota Fujimoto 46•), Masaki Chugo, Takashi Inui, Hiroshi Kiyotake, Yusuke Maruhashi, Kim Bo Kyung, Daisuke Takahashi•, Shu Kurata (Martinez• 70), Rodrigo Pimpao (Rui Komatsu 70). Tr: Levir Culpi

Kanjuruhan, Malang
3-05-2011, 15:30, 4000, Al Ghamdi KSA

Arema Malang 0

Kurnia Meiga (Achmad Kurniawan 46), Purwoko Pratono, Zulkifli Syukur, Benny Wahyudi, Waluyo, Muhammad Ridhuan, Esteban Guillen (Juan Revi Auriqto 55), Ahmad Bustomi, Roman Chmelo, Noh Alam Shah, Dendi Santoso (Ahmad Amiruddin 75). Tr: Miroslav Janu

Cerezo Osaka 4
Kiyotake [30], Rodrigo Pimpao [43], Inui 2 [46 60]

Kim Jin Hyeon - Teruyuki Moniwa (Takahiro Ogihara 63), Kota Fujimoto, Masaki Chugo, Takashi Inui, Martinez• (Hotaru Yamaguchi 63), Hiroshi Kiyotake, Yusuke Maruhashi, Daisuke Takahashi (Noriyuki Sakemoto 73), Shu Kurata•, Rodrigo Pimpao. Tr: Levir Culpi

Shandong Stadium, Jinan
3-05-2011, 19:30, 17 343, Mozaffarizadeh IRN

Shandong Luneng 1
Zhou Haibin [40]

Yang Cheng - Wang Qiang•, Yuan Weiwei, Zheng Zheng, Ricardo, Zhou Haibin, Cui Peng, Wang Yongpo (Mozhapa Murehemaitijiang 78), Roda Antar (Wang Tong 60), Deng Zhuoxiang• (Li Wei 71), Obina. Tr: Branko Ivankovic

Jeonbuk Hyundai Motors 2
Lee Dong Gook 2 [31 53]

Yeom Dong Gyun - Sim Woo Yeon, Kim Sang Sik•, Cho Sung Hwan, Choi Chul Soon, Jin Kyung Sun, Eninho• (Krunoslav Lovrek 63), Lee Seung Hyun, Kim Dong Chan (Lim You Hwan 68), Huang Bowen, Lee Dong Gook (Jeong Shung Hoon 80). Tr: Choi Kang Hee

World Cup Stadium, Jeonju
10-05-2011, 15:00, 6439, Abdou QAT

Jeonbuk Hyundai Motors 6
Lovrek 3 [1 45 60], Kim Dong Chan [9], Jeong Seong Hoon [27], Kang Seung Jo [77]

Kim Min Sik• - Lim You Hwan, Lee Kwang Hyeon, Jin Kyung Sun•, Eninho (Kim Hyeung Bum 56), Kang Seung Jo, Kim Dong Chan (Park Jung Hoon 46), Ha Sung Min, Jeong Shung Hoon, Luis Henrique, Krunoslav Lovrek (Kim Jae Hoon 65). Tr: Choi Kang Hee

Arema Malang 0

Achmad Kurniawan - Juan Revi Auriqto•, Zulkifli Syukur (Johan Ahmat Farizi 68), Benny Wahyudi, Waluyo, Leonard Tupamahu•, Muhammad Ridhuan (Sunarto 46), Ahmad Bustomi, Roman Chmelo, Ahmad Amiruddin (Talaohu 46), Noh Alam Shah. Tr: Miroslav Janu

Nagai, Osaka
10-05-2011, 19:00, 9035, Balideh QAT

Cerezo Osaka 4
R'rigo Pimpao [39], Kiyotake [47], Inui [73], Kurata [81]

Kim Jin Hyeon - Teruyuki Moniwa•, Taikai Uemoto, Masaki Chugo (Hotaru Yamaguchi 79), Takashi Inui, Hiroshi Kiyotake, Yusuke Maruhashi, Kim Bo Kyung, Daisuke Takahashi, Rodrigo Pimpao (Shu Kurata 74), Rui Komatsu (Ryo Nagai 74). Tr: Levir Culpi

Shandong Luneng 0

Yang Cheng - Renato Silva•, Zheng Zheng, Ricardo (Obina• 54), Liu Jindong•, Zhou Haibin•, Cui Peng••[75], Wang Yongpo (Li Wei 46), Roda Antar, Deng Zhuoxiang•, Han Peng (Wang Tong 84). Tr: Branko Ivankovic

GROUP H		Pl	W	D	L	F	A	Pts	KOR	JPN	AUS	CHN
Suwon Bluewings	KOR	6	3	3	0	12	3	12		1-1	3-1	4-0
Kashima Antlers	JPN	6	3	3	0	9	3	12	1-1		2-1	2-0
Sydney FC	AUS	6	1	2	3	6	11	5	0-0	0-3		1-1
Shanghai Shenhua	CHN	6	0	2	4	3	13	2	0-3	0-0	2-3	

Sydney Football Stadium, Sydney
2-03-2011, 20:00, 7095, Bashir SIN

Sydney FC 0

Liam **Reddy** - Sebastian **Ryall** (Andrew **Durante** 81), Stephan **Keller**, Matthew **Jurman**•, Scott **Jamieson**, Hirofumi **Moriyasu** (Mark **Bridge** 77), Stuart **Musialik**, Nick **Carle**, Terry **McFlynn**♦33, Bruno **Cazarine**, David **Williams** (Dimitri **Petratos** 70). Tr: Vitezslav **Lavicka**

Suwon Samsung Bluewings 0

Jung Sun Ryong - Mato **Neretljak**•, **Yang** Sang Min, **Oh** Beom Seok, **Hwang** Jae Won, **Lee** Yong Rae, **Oh** Jang Eun, **Park** Jong Jin (**Lee** Hyun Jin 46), **Lee** Sang Ho• (**Woo** Seung Jea 62), **Choi** Sung Kuk (**Kwak** Hee Ju 78), **Yeom** Ki Hun. Tr: **Yoon** Sung Hyo

---

Hongkou, Shanghai
2-03-2011, 20:00, 20 036, Al Ghamdi KSA

Shanghai Shenhua 0

Wang Dalei - **Dai** Lin, **Jiang** Jiajun•, **Wu** Xi, Abdulkader **Dakka**, **Yu** Tao•, **Feng** Renliang, **Jiang** Kun (**Cao** Yunding 75), Facundo Perez **Castro**•, Duvier **Riascos**, Luis **Salmeron** (**Wen** Huyi 77). Tr: **Xi** Zhikang

Kashima Antlers 0

Hitoshi **Sogahata** - Daiki **Iwamasa**, Koji **Nakata**, Toru **Araiba**, Takuya **Nozawa**, **Fellype Gabriel**, Chikashi **Masuda** (Takuya **Honda**•78), Takeshi **Aoki**•, **Alex**, Shinzo **Koroki** (Yuya **Osako** 88), Yuzo **Tashiro** (**Carlao** 80). Tr: Oswaldo **de Oliveira**

World Cup Stadium, Suwon
16-03-2011, 19:30, 5393, Al Zarooni UAE

Suwon Samsung Bluewings 4
Ha Tae Gyun 3 [2 60 76], Oh Jang Eun [42]

Jung Sung Ryong - Mato **Neretljak**, **Yang** Sang Min, **Oh** Beom Seok, **Hwang** Jae Won, **Kwak** Hee Ju, **Lee** Yong Rae (**Lee** Hyun Jin 73), **Oh** Jang Eun (**Lee** Jong Sung 78), **Choi** Sung Kuk (**Woo** Seung Jea 62), **Yeom** Ki Hun, **Ha** Tae Goon. Tr: **Yoon** Sung Hyo

Shanghai Shenhua 0

Wang Dalei - **Dai** Lin• (**Xin** Feng 70), **Jaijun** Jiang•, **Wu** Xi, Abdulkader **Dakka**, **Yu** Tao, **Feng** Renliang (**Cao** Yunding• 46), **Jiang** Kun, Facundo Perez **Castro** (**Wen** Huyi 64), Duvier **Riascos**, Luis **Salmeron**. Tr: **Xi** Zhikang

---

Sydney Football Stadium, Sydney
6-04-2011, 20:00, 7007, Balideh QAT

Sydney FC 1
Carle [12]

Liam **Reddy** - Sebastian **Ryall** (Shannon **Cole** 61), Stephan **Keller**, Matthew **Jurman**, Scott **Jamieson**, Hirofumi **Moriyasu**, Stuart **Musialik**, Nick **Carle**, Bruno **Cazarine** (Dimitri **Petratos**• 74), David **Williams** (Rhyan **Grant** 90), Mark **Bridge**•. Tr: Vitezslav **Lavicka**

Shanghai Shenhua 1
Riascos [6]

Qiu Shenjiong - **Xin** Feng, **Dai** Lin, **Song** Boxuan (**Wen** Huyi• 19), **Wu** Xi•, **Feng** Renliang, **Jiang** Kun (**Zheng** Wei 70), Facundo Perez **Castro**, **Cao** Yunding, Duvier **Riascos**• (Abdulkader **Dakka** 88), Luis **Salmeron**•. Tr: **Xi** Zhikang

---

World Cup Stadium, Suwon
6-04-2011, 19:30, 7689, Al Hilali OMA

Suwon Samsung Bluewings 1
Yeom Ki Hoon [67]

Jung Sung Ryong - Mato **Neretljak** (**Lee** Hyun Jin 79), **Yang** Sang Min•, **Oh** Beom Seok, **Hwang** Jae Won, **Oh** Jang Eun, **Park** Jong Jin• (**Choi** Sung Kuk 58), **Lee** Sang Ho, **Woo** Seung Jea•, **Yeom** Ki Hun, **Ha** Tae Goon. Tr: **Yoon** Sung Hyo

Kashima Antlers 1
Nakata.K [71]

Hitoshi **Sogahata** - Daiki **Iwamasa**, Koji **Nakata**, Toru **Araiba**, Takuya **Nozawa** (Chikashi **Masuda** 88), **Fellype Gabriel** (Yasushi **Endo** 81), Takeshi **Aoki**, Mitsuo **Ogasawara**, **Alex** (Yuzo **Osako** (Masashi **Motoyama** 69), Shinzo **Koroki**. Tr: Oswaldo **de Oliveira**

Sydney Football Stadium, Sydney
13-04-2011, 20:00, 7320, Albadwawi UAE

Sydney FC 0

Liam **Reddy** - Stephan **Keller** (Andrew **Durante** 46), Shannon **Cole**, Matthew **Jurman**, Scott **Jamieson**, Rhyan **Grant**, Hirofumi **Moriyasu** (Joel **Chianese** 80), Stuart **Musialik**, Bruno **Cazarine**, Mark **Bridge**, Dimitri **Petratos** (Kofi **Danning** 56). Tr: Vitezslav **Lavicka**

Kashima Antlers 3
Nozawa [41], Gabriel [51], Koroki [92+]

Hitoshi **Sogahata** - Daiki **Iwamasa**, Koji **Nakata**, Toru **Araiba**, Takuya **Nozawa**, **Fellype Gabriel**, Takeshi **Aoki**, Mitsuo **Ogasawara**, **Alex** (Yuzo **Tashiro** 90), Shinzo **Koroki**, **Carlao** (Masashi **Motoyama**• 70). Tr: Oswaldo **de Oliveira**

Olympic Stadium, Tokyo
19-04-2011, 14:00, 4619, Abdou QAT

Kashima Antlers 1
Tashiro [55]

Hitoshi **Sogahata** - Daiki **Iwamasa**, Koji **Nakata**, Toru **Araiba** (Chikashi **Masuda** 79), Takuya **Nozawa**, **Fellype Gabriel** (Yasushi **Endo** 46), Takeshi **Aoki**, Mitsuo **Ogasawara**, **Alex**, Shinzo **Koroki**•, Yuzo **Tashiro** (Masashi **Motoyama** 59). Tr: Oswaldo **de Oliveira**

Suwon Samsung Bluewings 1
Yeom Ki Hun [48]

Kim Dae Hwan - **Yang** Sang Min, **Oh** Beom Seok, **Hwang** Jae Won•, **Kwak** Hee Ju, **Lee** Yong Rae (**Lee** Hyun Jin 77), **Lee** Sang Ho, **Choi** Sung Kuk (**Park** Jong Jin 29), **Woo** Seung Jea, **Yeom** Ki Hun, **Ha** Tae Goon (**Bergson** 72). Tr: **Yoon** Sung Hyo

---

Hongkou, Shanghai
19-04-2011, 20:00, 10 215, Mohd Salleh MAS

Shanghai Shenhua 2
Jiang Jiajun [8], OG [52]

Qiu Shenjiong - **Xiong** Fei, **Xin** Feng, **Dai** Lin, **Jiang** Jiajun (**Wang** Lin 63), **Wu** Xi (**Cao** Yunding 80), **Jiang** Kun, Facundo Perez **Castro**, Duvier **Riascos**, Luis **Salmeron**• (**Feng** Renliang 80), **Wen** Huyi•. Tr: **Xi** Zhikang

Sydney FC 3
Cazarine 2 [45 59], Bridge [93+]

Liam **Reddy** - Andrew **Durante**•, Shannon **Cole** (Kofi **Danning** 89), Matthew **Jurman**, Scott **Jamieson**•, Hirofumi **Moriyasu** (Rhyan **Grant** 61), Stuart **Musialik**, Nick **Carle**• (Dimitri **Petratos** 75), Terry **McFlynn**•, Bruno **Cazarine**, Mark **Bridge**. Tr: Vitezslav **Lavicka**

Olympic Stadium, Tokyo
3-05-2011, 15:00, 11 954, El Haddad LIB

Kashima Antlers 2
Koroki 2 [32 80]

Hitoshi **Sogahata** - Daiki **Iwamasa**, Koji **Nakata**, Toru **Araiba**, Takuya **Nozawa** (Gaku **Shibasaki** 85), Takeshi **Aoki**, Daigo **Nishi**• (Masahiko **Inoha** 80), Yasushi **Endo**, Mitsuo **Ogasawara**, Yuya **Osako** (**Fellype Gabriel** 67), Shinzo **Koroki**•. Tr: Oswaldo **de Oliveira**

Shanghai Shenhua 0

Wang Dalei• - **Dai** Lin, **Jiang** Jiajun, **Wu** Xi, **Qiu** Tianyi, **Yu** Tao•, **Feng** Renliang (**Zheng** Wei 86), **Kun** Jiang• (**Xiong** Fei 42), Facundo Perez **Castro**, **Cao** Yunding• (**Wang** Guanyi 87), Duvier **Riascos**•. Tr: **Xi** Zhikang

---

World Cup Stadium, Suwon
3-05-2011, 19:30, 9495, Irmatov UZB

Suwon Samsung Bluewings 3
Ha Tae Gyun [34], Neretljak [50], Yeom Ki Hoon [80]

Jung Sung Ryong - Mato **Neretljak**, **Yang** Sang Min, **Oh** Beom Seok, **Hwang** Jae Won, **Kwak** Hee Ju, **Lee** Yong Rae, **Oh** Jang Eun (**Lee** Kyung Hwan 74), **Park** Jong Jin (**Yeom** Ki Hun 60), **Lee** Sang Ho (**Bergson** 84), **Ha** Tae Goon. Tr: **Yoon** Sung Hyo

Sydney FC 1
Cazarine [51]

Liam **Reddy** - Stephan **Keller**•, Andrew **Durante**, Matthew **Jurman**, Scott **Jamieson**•, Hirofumi **Moriyasu** (Rhyan **Grant** 46), Stuart **Musialik** (David **Williams** 62), Nick **Carle**, Terry **McFlynn**, Bruno **Cazarine**, Mark **Bridge** (Kofi **Danning** 79). Tr: Vitezslav **Lavicka**

Olympic Stadium, Tokyo
10-05-2011, 15:00, 3164, Al Ghamdi KSA

Kashima Antlers 2
Osako [64], Nozawa [84]

Hitoshi **Sogahata** - Daiki **Iwamasa**, Koji **Nakata** (Masahiko **Inoha** 29), Toru **Araiba**, Takuya **Nozawa**, Takeshi **Aoki**, Daigo **Nishi**, Yasushi **Endo**, Kenji **Koyano** (**Fellype Gabriel** 60), Mitsuo **Ogasawara**, Yuya **Osako** (**Carlao** 77). Tr: Oswaldo **de Oliveira**

Sydney FC 1
Jurman [26]

Liam **Reddy** - Stephan **Keller**, Andrew **Durante**• (Sebastian **Ryall** 72), Matthew **Jurman**, Scott **Jamieson**•, Rhyan **Grant**, Stuart **Musialik**, Nick **Carle** (Hirofumi **Moriyasu**• 69), Terry **McFlynn** (Kofi **Danning** 87), Bruno **Cazarine**, David **Williams**. Tr: Vitezslav **Lavicka**

Hongkou, Shanghai
10-05-2011, 20:00, 6730, Torky IRN

Shanghai Shenhua 0

Lei Dong - **Xiong** Fei, **Xin** Feng, **Jiang** Jiajun (**Wang** Lin 37), **Wu** Xi (**Feng** Renliang 52), Abdulkader **Dakka**•, **Fan** Lingjiang, **Wang** Guanyi, **Zheng** Wei•, **Wen** Huyi, **Dong** Xuesheng (**Wang** Yun 60). Tr: **Xi** Zhikang

Suwon Samsung Bluewings 3
Ha Tae Gyun 2 [13 55], Shin Se Gye [89]

Jung Sung Ryong - **Choi** Sung Kuk, **Hwang** Jae Won, **Kwak** Hee Ju, **Sin** Se Gye, **Min** Sang Ki, **Lee** Yong Rae, **Hong** Soon Hak, **Cho** Ji Hun (**Lee** Jae Il 76), **Park** Jong Jin• (**Yang** Joon A 74), **Choi** Sung Kuk (**Yeom** Ki Hun 58), **Ha** Tae Goon. Tr: **Yoon** Sung Hyo

ROUND OF SIXTEEN

Jassim Bin Hamad, Doha
25-05-2011, 19:00, 7140, Nishimura JPN

Al Sadd	1
	Koni [12]

Mohammed **Saqr** - Nadir **Belhadj**, Abdulla **Koni**, Lee Jung Soo, Majdi **Siddiq**, Mesaad **Al Hamad•**, Wesam **Rizik•**, Abdelkarim **Fadlalla**, **Leandro•** (Hasan **Al Haidos** 88), Abdulkader **Keita** (Talal **Al Bloushi** 45), Khalfan **Ibrahim** (Yusef **Ali** 61). Tr: Jorge **Fossati**

Al Shabab	0

Waleed **Abdullah** - Marcelo **Tavares**, Waleed **Jahdali**, Hassan **Mouath**, Ziad **Al Mowalad** (Abdullah **Al Shuhail** 76), Majed **Al Marhoum** (Abdullah **Al Astaa** 58), **Camacho**, Ahmed **Otaif**, Abdulmalek **Al Khaibri**, Nasser **Al Shamrani**, Faisal **bin Sultan** (Alhassane **Keita** 57). Tr: Enzo **Trossero**

Foolad Shahr, Isfahan
24-05-2011, 19:30, 6318, Toma JPN

Sepahan	3
	Januario [28], Toure [33], Aghili [69p]

Mehdi **Rahmati** - Khosro **Heydari**, Hadi **Aghili**, Jalal **Hosseini**, Mohsen **Bengar**, Moharram **Navidkia** (Mehdi **Karimian** 90), Omid **Ebrahimi•**, Ehsan **Hajsafi**, Fabio **Januario**, Ibrahima **Toure•**51, Milorad **Janjus** (Reza **Enayati** 90). Tr: Amir **Ghalenoei**

Bunyodkor	1
	Dordevic [57]

Ignatiy **Nesterov** - Hayrulla **Karimov•**, Anvar **Gafurov** (Yannis **Mandzukas** 73), Slavoljub **Dordevic•**, Sakhob **Juraev**, Azizbek **Haydarov•**, Jovlon **Ibrokhimov**, Viktor **Karpenko**, Anvar **Rajabov** (Shavkat **Salomov** 83), Milos **Trifunovic**, Anvarjon **Solyiev•** (Kamoliddin **Mirzaev** 64). Tr: Mirdjalol **Kasimov**

Foolad Shahr, Isfahan
25-05-2011, 19:15, 5711, Choi Myung Yong KOR

Zob Ahan	4
	Ghazi [1], Castro 2 [5 63], Kheiri [74]

Shahab **Gordan** - Farsheed **Talebi**, Mohammad Ali **Ahmadi** (Mohammad **Salsali** 90), Seyed Ahmad **Mohammadpour**, Seyed **Hosseini**, Ghasem **Hadadifar**, Shahin **Kheiri**, Mehdi **Rajabzadeh**, Mohammad **Khalatbari** (Esmail **Farhadi** 80), Mohammad **Ghazi** (Jalal **Rafkhaei** 87), **Igor•**. Tr: Mansour **Ebrahimsadeh**

Al Nasr	1
	Al Mutwa [66]

Abdullah **Al Anzi** (Khalid **Razi** 78) - Ahmed **Dokhi**, Abdou **Barnawi** (Abdulrahman **Al Qahtani** 35), Hussein **Sulaimani•**89, Omar **Ibrahim**, Jon **McKain**, Victor **Figueroa•**, Ibrahim **Ghaleb**, Saud Hamoud **Hasan** (Saad **Al Harthi** 46), Bader **Al Mutwa**, Khaled **Asiri•**. Tr: Dragan **Skocic**

World Cup Stadium, Suwon
25-05-2011, 19:30, 11 036, Abdou QAT

Suwon Samsung Bluewings	2
	Yeom Ki Hun [23], Lee Sang Ho [57]

Jung Sung Ryong - Mato **Neretljak**, Choi Sung Hwan, **Kwak** Hee Ju (**Hwang** Jae Won 64), **Sin** Se Gye, Lee Yong Rae, **Oh** Jang Eun, **Hong** Soon Hak, Lee Sang Ho (**Yang** Joon A 90), **Choi** Sung Kuk (**Woo** Seung Jea 82), **Yeom** Ki Hun. Tr: **Yoon** Sung hyo

Nagoya Grampus	0

Seigo **Narazaki** - Marcus Tulio **Tanaka•**, Shohei **Abe**, Tatsuya **Arai**, Naoshi **Nakamura** (Ryota **Isomura** 76), Jungo **Fujimoto**, Yoshizumi **Ogawa**, Danilson **Cordoba** (Kensuke **Nagai** 43), Hayuma **Tanaka**, Keiji **Tamada** (Teruki **Tanaka** 65), Joshua **Kennedy**. Tr: Dragan **Stojkovic**

Prince Abdullah, Jeddah
24-05-2011, 21:05, 17 150, Kim Dong Jin KOR

Al Ittihad	3
	Nuno Assis 2 [15 59], Ziaya [17]

Mabrouk **Zaid** - Paulo **Jorge**, Mishal **Al Saeed•**, Saleh **Al Saqri**, Hamad **Al Montashari**, Osama **Al Harbi** (Mohammed **Salem** 73), Ahmed **Hadid** (Rashid **Al Raheeb** 85), Saud **Khariri**, Nuno **Assis** (Manaf **Abushgeer** 88), Mohammed **Noor**, Abdelmalek **Ziaya•**. Tr: Antonio **Oliveira**

Al Hilal	1
	Al Dosari [82]

Hassan **Al Otaibi** - Osama **Hawsawi**, Abdullah **Al Zori**, Mirel **Radoi•**, Lee Young Pyo (Nawaf **Al Abed** 66), Majed **Al Marshadi**, Khaled **Aziz** (Ahmed **Ali** 46), Christian **Wilhelmsson**, Mohammad **Al Shalhoub**, Ahmed **Al Fraidi**, Yasser **Al Khahtani** (Abdulaziz **Al Dosari** 66). Tr: Gabriel **Calderon**

World Cup Stadium, Seoul
25-05-2011, 19:30, 12 725, Shukralla BHR

FC Seoul	3
	Bang Seung Hwan [38], Damjanovic [55], Ko Myong Jin [92+]

Kim Yong Dae - **Adilson**, Park Yong Ho, Lee Kyu Ho, Server **Djeparov**, **Hyun** Young Min (**Kim** Dong Jin 90), **Ha** Dae Sung• (**Moon** Ki Han 75), **Ko** Yo Han• (**Kim** Tae Hwan 90), **Ko** Myong Jin, Dejan **Damjanovic**, **Bang** Seung Hwan•. Tr: **Choi** Yong Soo

Kashima Antlers	0

Hitoshi **Sogahata** - Daiki **Iwamasa**, Toru **Araiba**, Masahiko **Inoha**, Takuya **Nozawa**, Chikashi **Masuda** (Yasushi **Endo•** 66), Takeshi **Aoki**, Mitsuo **Ogasawara**, **Alex** (Daigo **Nishi** 79), Shinzo **Koroki**, **Carlao** (Fellype **Gabriel** 46). Tr: Oswaldo **de Oliveira**

Expo '70, Osaka
24-05-2011, 19:00, 16 463, Faghani IRN

Gamba Osaka	0

Yosuke **Fujigaya•** - Sota **Nakazawa**, Akira **Kaji•**, Tatsuya **Uchida**, Yasuhito **Endo**, Takahiro **Futagawa** (Shoki Hirai 90), Takashi **Usami**, Tomokazu **Myojin**, Takuya **Takei**, Lee Keun Ho (Hayato **Sasaki** 67). Tr: Akira **Nishino**

Cerezo Osaka	1
	Takahashi [88]

Kim Jin Hyeon - Taikai **Uemoto**, Kota **Fujimoto**, Takashi **Inui•** (Masaki **Chugo** 46), **Martinez**, Hiroshi **Kiyotake•**, Yusuke **Maruhashi**, Kim Bo Kyung, Daisuke **Takahashi**, Shu **Kurata** (Rui **Komatsu** 46), Rodrigo **Pimpao** (Ryuji **Bando•** 90). Tr: Levir **Culpi**

World Cup Stadium, Jeonju
24-05-2011, 19:00, 5254, Albadwawi UAE

Jeonbuk Hyundai Motors	3
	Eninho 2 [32 84], Lee Seung Hyun [43]

Yeom Dong Gyun - **Sim** Woo Yeon, **Cho** Sung Hwan, **Choi** Chul Soon, **Park** Won Jae, **Eninho**, Lee Seung Hyun (**Kim** Dong Chan 66), **Jung** Hun, **Huang** Bowen, **Luis Henrique** (Krunoslav **Lovrek** 66), **Lee** Dong Gook (**Kim** Hyeung Bum 75). Tr: **Choi** Kang Hee

Tianjin Teda	0

Zhao Yanming - **He** Yang, Li **Weifeng•**, Liao Bochao, Nie Tao (**Zheng** Yi 77), **Cao** Yang, Li **Benjian** (Fan Baiqun 53), Wu Weian, **Ma** Leilei, Zhang Xiaobin (Mao Biao 69), Yu **Dabao•**. Tr: Arie **Haan**

QUARTER-FINALS

Foolad Shahr, Isfahan
14-09-2011, 19:30, 5621, Williams AUS

Sepahan   **1 0**
Ebrahimi [12]. Match awarded to Al Sadd 3-0
Rahman **Ahmadi** - Jalal **Hosseini**, Mohsen **Bengar**,
Hashem **Beikzadeh**, Mehdi **Nasiri•**, Omid **Ebrahimi**,
Ahmad **Jamshidian** (Mehdi **Karimian** 62), Akbar
Imani••♦58, **Fabio Januario** (Moharram **Navidkia** 83),
Emad **Mohammed** (Milorad **Janjus** 70), Mehdi Seyed
Salehi. Tr: Luka **Bonacic**

Al Sadd   **0 3**

Mohammed **Saqr** - Nadir **Belhadj•**, Abdulla **Koni•**, Taher
Zakaria, **Lee** Jung Soo, Mesaad **Al Hamad** (Hasan **Al
Haidos** 66), Talal **Al Bloushi** (Abdulrab **Al Yazidi** 87),
Wesam **Rizik**, Mamadou **Niang**, Abdulkader **Keita**, Khalfan
Ibrahim (Ali Hasan **Yahya** 75). Tr: Jorge **Fossati**

Jassim Bin Hamad, Doha
28-09-2011, 18:20, 6026, Nishimura JPN

Al Sadd   **1**
Niang [86]
Mohammed **Saqr** - Nadir **Belhadj**, Abdulla **Koni•**,
Mohammed **Kasola**, **Lee** Jung Soo, Talal **Al Bloushi**, Nasser
Nabil **Salem**, Wesam **Rizik**, Mamadou **Niang** (Taher
Zakaria 90), Abdulkader **Keita** (Ali Hasan **Yahya** 78),
Khalfan **Ibrahim** (Hasan **Al Haidos** 68). Tr: Jorge **Fossati**

Sepahan   **2**
Emad [7], Ashjari [27]
Reza **Mohammadi** - Hassan **Ashjari•**, Jalal **Hosseini**,
Mohsen **Bengar**, Hashem **Beikzadeh** (Moharram **Navidkia**
76), Abolhassan **Jafari•** (Ahmad **Jamshidian** 46), Mehdi
Karimian (Milorad **Janjus•** 76), Omid **Ebrahimi**, Emad
Mohammed, Farzad **Hatami•**, Mehdi Seyed **Salehi•**.
Tr: Luka **Bonacic**

World Cup Stadium, Suwon
14-09-2011, 19:30, 7659, Toma JPN

Suwon Samsung Bluewings   **1**
Park Hyun Beom [66]
Jung Sung Ryong - Mato **Neretljak**, **Oh** Beom Seok•, **Park**
Hyun Beom, **Lee** Yong Rae, **Oh** Jang Eun, **Hong** Soon Hak,
Diego **Oliveira** (Park Jong Jin•55), **Lee** Sang Ho
(Aleksandr **Geynrikh** 66), Stevica **Ristic•**, **Yeom** Ki Hun.
Tr: **Yoon** Sung hyo

Zob Ahan   **1**
Ghazi [57]
Shahab **Gordan** - Farsheed **Talebi**, Mohammad Ali **Ahmadi**
(Sina **Ashori** 78), Mohammad **Salsali**, Hossain **Mahini**,
Seyed **Hosseini•**, Hawar Mulla **Mohammed**, Hugo
Machado, Esmail **Farhadi** (Felipe **Alves** 90), Mohammad
Ghazi, Igor (Davoud **Haghi** 90). Tr: Mansour
Ebrahimsadeh

Foolad Shahr, Isfahan
28-09-2011, 17:20, 7250, Al Ghamdi KSA

Zob Ahan   **1**
Ghazi [50]
Shahab **Gordan** - Farsheed **Talebi•**, Mohammad Ali
Ahmadi••♦97, Mohammad **Salsali**, Hossain **Mahini**,
Seyed **Hosseini**, Hawar Mulla **Mohammed**, Hugo **Machado**
(Felipe **Alves** 101), Esmail **Farhadi** (Davoud **Haghi** 105),
Mohammad **Ghazi**, Igor (Payam **Sadeghian** 101).
Tr: Mansour **Ebrahimsadeh**

Suwon Samsung Bluewings   **2**
Yang Sang Min [77], Neretljak [99p]
Jung Sung Ryong - Mato **Neretljak**, **Yang** Sang Min, **Oh**
Beom Seok•, **Park** Hyun Beom (**Ha** Tae Goon 120), **Lee**
Yong Rae• (**Choi** Sung Hwan•101), **Oh** Jang Eun, **Hong**
Soon Hak (**Park** Jong Jin 71), **Lee** Sang Ho, Stevica **Ristic**,
Yeom Ki Hun. Tr: **Yoon** Sung Hyo

Prince Abdullah, Jeddah
14-09-2011, 20:35, 16 790, Faghani IRN

Al Ittihad   **3**
Noor [45], Al Muwallad [76], Wendel [92+]
Mabrouk **Zaid** - Rashid **Al Raheeb**, Paulo **Jorge**
(Mohammed **Abusabaan•** 9), Mishal **Al Saeed**, Hamad **Al
Montashari**, Osama **Al Harbi•**, Saud **Khariri•**, Mohammed
Noor, Fahad **Al Enezi** (Saleh **Al Saqri** 80), **Wendel**, Naif
Hazazi•. Tr: Dimitri **Davidovic**

FC Seoul   **1**
Choi Tae Uk [83]
Kim Yong Dae - Kim Dong Woo, **Adilson**, Park Yong Ho•,
Mauricio **Molina**, **Han** Tae You (**Moon** Ki Han 65), **Ko** Myong
Jin, **Choi** Jong Hoan (**Choi** Tae Uk 46), **Choi** Hyun Tae,
Dejan **Damjanovic**, **Bang** Seung Hwan (**Ko** Kwang Min 79).
Tr: **Choi** Yong Soo

World Cup Stadium, Seoul
27-09-2011, 19:30, 15 000, Kovalenko UZB

FC Seoul   **1**
Molina [85]
Kim Yong Dae - Kim Dong Woo, **Kim** Dong Jin, **Adilson•**,
Mauricio **Molina**, **Hyun** Young Min (**Ko** Kwang Min 46), **Ko**
Yo Han, **Ko** Myong Jin, **Choi** Hyun Tae (**Kang** Jung Hun 83),
Dejan **Damjanovic**, **Choi** Tae Uk (**Kim** Tae Hwan 75).
Tr: **Choi** Yong Soo

Al Ittihad   **0**

Mabrouk **Zaid** - Rashid **Al Raheeb**, Mishal **Al Saeed**,
Hamad **Al Montashari•**, Osama **Al Harbi**, Saud **Khariri**,
Mohammed **Noor**, Mohammed **Abusabaan•**, Sultan **Al
Nemri•** (Redha **Tukar** 87), **Wendel**, Naif **Hazazi**
(Abdelmalek **Ziaya** 73). Tr: Dimitri **Davidovic**

Nagai, Osaka
14-09-2011, 19:30, 15 450, Tan Hai CHN

Cerezo Osaka   **4**
Bando [29], Kiyotake 2 [56 81], Kim Bo Kyung [64p]
Kim Jin Hyeon - Takahiro **Ogihara**, Teruyuki **Moniwa**, Taikai
Uemoto, Hiroshi **Kiyotake**, Yusuke **Maruhashi** (Hiroyuki
Omata 74), **Kim** Bo Kyung, Noriyuki **Sakemoto**, Shu
Kurata, Fabio **Lopes** (Kenyu **Sugimoto** 86), Ryuji **Bando**
(Yohei **Otake** 68). Tr: Levir **Culpi**

Jeonbuk Hyundai Motors   **3**
Lee Dong Gook 2 [6 45], Cho Sung Hwan [58]
Kim Min Sik - Kim Sang Sik, **Kim** Young Woo (**Kim** Dong
Chan 76), **Cho** Sung Hwan•, **Lim** You Hwan, **Park** Won
Jae•, **Eninho** (**Choi** Chul Soon 61), Huang **Bowen•**, **Seo**
Jung Jin, Luis **Henrique** (Jeong Shung Hoon 73), **Lee** Dong
Gook. Tr: **Choi** Kang Hee

World Cup Stadium, Jeonju
27-09-2011, 19:00, 16 423, Abdou QAT

Jeonbuk Hyundai Motors   **6**
Eninho [31], Lee Dong Gook 4 [49 55 64 91+],
Kim Dong Chan [76]
Kim Min Sik - **Sim** Woo Yeon•, **Kim** Sang Sik•, **Cho** Sung
Hwan, **Choi** Chul Soon•, **Park** Won Jae, **Eninho•** (**Lee**
Seung Hyun 87), **Jung** Hun, **Seo** Jung Jin (**Kim** Dong
Chan 72), Luis **Henrique** (Krunoslav **Lovrek** 81), **Lee** Dong
Gook. Tr: **Choi** Kang Hee

Cerezo Osaka   **1**
Komatsu [72]
Kim Jin Hyeon - Takahiro **Ogihara**, Teruyuki **Moniwa**,
Hiroyuki **Omata**, Kota **Fujimoto**, Hiroshi **Kiyotake** (Yohei
Otake 67), **Kim** Bo Kyung (Masaki **Chugo** 13) (Rui
Komatsu 57), Noriyuki **Sakemoto**, Shu **Kurata**, Fabio
Lopes, Ryuji **Bando•**. Tr: Levir **Culpi**

SEMI-FINALS

World Cup Stadium, Suwon
19-10-2011, 19:30, 9864, Bashir SIN

Suwon Samsung Bluewings	0

Jung Sung Ryong - Mato Neretljak•, Yang Sang Min•, Choi Sung Hwan, Park Hyun Beom, Lee Yong Rae, Oh Jang Eun (Hong Soon Hak 76), Park Jong Jin (Aleksandr Geynrikh 69), Lee Sang Ho (Ha Tae Goon 73), Stevica Ristic♦89, Yeom Ki Hun. Tr: Yoon Sung Hyo

Al Sadd	2
	Niang 2 70 81

Mohammed Saqr - Nadir Belhadj, Taher Zakaria, Mohammed Kasola•, Lee Jung Soo (Mamadou Niang ••♦90), Talal Al Bloushi, Nasser Nabil Salem (Mesaad Al Hamad 71) (Abdulrab Al Yazidi• 90), Wesam Rizik, Abdulkader Keita♦89, Khalfan Ibrahim. Tr: Jorge Fossati

---

Prince Abdullah, Jeddah
19-10-2011, 20:05, 16 942, Shukralla BHR

Al Ittihad	2
	Hazazi 2 6 18

Mabrouk Zaid - Paulo Jorge, Mishal Al Saeed•, Hamad Al Montashari, Osama Al Harbi•, Saud Khariri, Mohammed Noor (Yahya Hussain Dagriri 83), Sultan Al Nemri (Rashid Al Raheeb 61), Wendel, Naif Hazazi, Abdelmalek Ziaya (Fahad Al Enezi• 35). Tr: Dimitri Davidovic

Jeonbuk Hyundai Motors	3
Eninho 2, Son Seung Joon 57, Cho Sung Hwan 77	

Kim Min Sik - Kim Sang Sik, Son Seung Jun• (Sim Woo Yeon 70), Cho Sung Hwan, Choi Chul Soon, Park Won Jae, Eninho (Lee Seung Hyun 83), Jung Hun, Seo Jung Jin, Luis Henrique, Lee Dong Gook (Kim Dong Chan 34). Tr: Choi Kang Hee

---

Jassim Bin Hamad, Doha
26-10-2011, 18:00, 10 800, Albadwawi UAE

Al Sadd	0

Mohammed Saqr• - Nadir Belhadj (Abdelkarim Fadlalla 87), Abdulla Koni, Taher Zakaria, Ibrahim Majid, Mohammed Kasola, Lee Jung Soo, Talal Al Bloushi, Nasser Nabil Salem (Abdulrab Al Yazidi 71), Hasan Al Haidos (Ali Hasan Yahya 62), Khalfan Ibrahim. Tr: Jorge Fossati

Suwon Samsung Bluewings	1
	Oh Jang Eun 7

Jung Sung Ryong - Mato Neretljak, Yang Sang Min, Oh Beom Seok• (Sin Se Gye• 75), Choi Sung Hwan•, Park Hyun Beom (Park Jong Jin 86), Lee Yong Rae, Oh Jang Eun, Lee Sang Ho (Aleksandr Geynrikh 71), Yeom Ki Hun, Ha Tae Goon•. Tr: Yoon Sung Hyo

---

World Cup Stadium, Jeonju
26-10-2011, 19:00, 17 069, El Haddad LIB

Jeonbuk Hyundai Motors	2
	Eninho 2 22 36

Kim Min Sik - Sim Woo Yeon, Kim Sang Sik, Cho Sung Hwan•, Choi Chul Soon, Park Won Jae, Eninho (Krunoslav Lovrek 62 ••♦88), Jung Hun, Seo Jung Jin (Lee Seung Hyun 80), Jeong Shung Hoon (Kim Dong Chan 64), Luis Henrique•. Tr: Choi Kang Hee

Al Ittihad	1
	Wendel 73

Mabrouk Zaid - Rashid Al Raheeb (Mohammed Ali Al Rashed 88), Paulo Jorge, Mishal Al Saeed, Hamad Al Montashari•, Osama Al Harbi, Saud Khariri•, Mohammed Noor, Mohammed Abusabaan (Fahad Al Enezi 46), Wendel (Saleh Al Saqri 86), Naif Hazazi♦12. Tr: Dimitri Davidovic

AFC Champions League Final	Jeonju World Cup Stadium Jeonju		Saturday 5-11-2011
Kick-off: 19:00	Clear night	17°	Attendance: 41 805

JEONBUK MOTORS   2   2   AL SADD

2 PSO 4

Eninho ¹⁷, Lee Seung Hyun ⁹²⁺   Sim Woo Yeon OG ³⁰, Keita ⁶¹

JEONBUK HYUNDAI MOTORS

Green shirts, Black shorts, Green socks
Tr: Choi Kang Hee

Kim Min Sik

Choi Chul Soon   Sim Woo Yeon   Son Seung Joon   Park Won Jae

Eninho 80   Kim Sang Sik 95+   51 Jung Hoon / Kim Dong Chan   71 Seo Jung Jin / Lee Seung Hyun

71 Luiz Henrique / Lee Dong Gook

Jeong Seong Hoon

95+ Abdul Kader Keita 52 / Ali Afif 100 120 120   Mamadou Niang

74 Khalfan Ibrahim / Hassan Al Haidos 66
Wesam Rizik   Talal Al Bloushi 66

Abdulla Koni

Nadir Belhadj   Lee Jung Soo   53 Mohammed Kasola 21 / Taher Zakaria 80   Ibrahim Majid 73

Mohamed Saqr

Tr: Jorge Fossati URU
White shirts, White shorts, White socks

AL SADD

MATCH OFFICIALS
REFEREE
Ravshan Irmatov UZB
ASSISTANTS
Abdukhamidullo Rasulov UZB
Bahadyr Kochkarov KGZ
4TH OFFICIAL
Tan Hai CHN

(C) Captain † Man of the Match

PENALTIES
Al Sadd	Jeonbuk
✓ Niang	
	Eninho ✓
✓ Al Haidos	
	Kim Dong Chan ✗¹
✗² Lee Jung Soo	
	Park Won Jae ✗¹
✓ Majid	
	Kim Sang Sik ✓
✓ Belhadj	

¹ saved ² hit crossbar

I feel tonight's defeat came from so many chances that we failed to score. I don't feel that my players became complacent after equalising in the last minute. I actually feel that after that goal, our players had much more confidence and maybe could score a goal in extra time to win. I wasn't happy that most people outside of the team made it sound like we were guaranteed to win. I warned my players not to be swayed by outside influence.

Choi Kang Hee

He (Mohamed Saqr) played fantastic today but believe me, it was not the only game that he was fantastic in this competition. Today he had a big game, the Jeonbuk players did not miss the penalties, he saved them. It is different. I really was very worried especially when it went to extra time because, as you can understand, our physical condition to play this game was not the same as normal. When you fly 10 hours two days ago, you need to adapt.

Jorge Fossati

First round groups

Group A (In Phnom Penh CAM)

		Pl	W	D	L	F	A	Pts	CAM	BAN	SRI
Neftchi Kochkorata	KGZ	3	3	0	0	5	0	9	1-0	2-0	2-0
Phnom Penh Crown	CAM	3	2	0	1	4	1	6		1-0	3-0
Abahani Limited	BAN	3	1	0	2	4	4	3			4-1
Don Bosco	SRI	3	0	0	3	1	9	0			

Group B (In Yangon MYA)

		Pl	W	D	L	F	A	Pts	MYA	PLE	BHU
Esteghlal Dushanbe	TJK	3	2	1	0	11	1	7	1-1	2-0	8-0
Yadanarbon	MYA	3	2	1	0	11	4	7		4-3	6-0
Jabal Mukaber	PLE	3	1	0	2	10	6	3			7-0
Yeedzin	BHU	3	0	0	3	0	21	0			

Group C (In Kathmandu NEP)

		Pl	W	D	L	F	A	Pts	TKM	PAK	NEP
Kaohsiung Taipower	TPE	3	2	1	0	5	1	7	1-1	3-0	1-0
Balkan Balkanabat	TKM	3	2	1	0	4	1	7		1-0	2-0
WAPDA	PAK	3	1	0	2	2	4	3			2-0
Nepal Police Club	NEP	3	0	0	3	0	5	0			

Top scorer: **6** - Ho Ming Tsan TPE, Taipower • **5** - Yan Piang MYA, Yadanarbon; Pai Soe MYA, Yadanarbon; Farkhod Tokhirov TJK, Esteghlal; Pavel Pavlov UZB, Neftchi & Kingsley Njoku NGA, PP Crown

Final Tournament groups

	Pl	W	D	L	F	A	Pts	TKM	TJK
Kaohsiung Taipower	2	2	0	0	6	3	6	4-3	2-0
Balkan Balkanabat	2	0	0	1	4	5	1		1-1
Esteghlal Dushanbe	2	0	1	1	1	3	1		

	Pl	W	D	L	F	A	Pts	KGZ	MYA
Phnom Penh Crown	2	2	0	0	6	1	6	2-1	4-0
Neftchi Kochkorata	2	1	0	1	9	4	3		8-2
Yadanarbon	2	0	0	2	2	12	0		

Final

Kaohsiung Taipower	3
Phnom Penh Crown	2

AFC PRESIDENT'S CUP FINAL 2011

National Stadium, Kaohsiung, 25-09-2011, 19:00, 3238, Marai Al Awaji

Kaohsiung Taipower	3	Ho Ming Tsan 2 [2] [47], Chen Po Liang [67]
Phnom Penh Crown	2	Njoku [34], Sovannrithy [82]

Taipower - Pan Wei Chih - Tu Ming Feng, Chen Yu Lin◆94+, Chen Yi Wei (Huang Chiu Ching 87), Liang Chien Wei, Lee Meng Chian - He Ming Chan (Tsai Sheng An 73), Hung Kai Chun, Feng Pao Hsing, Chen Po Liang - Kuo Yin Hung. Tr: Chen Kuei Jen

Crown - Peng Bunchay - Thul Sothearith•, Tieng Tiny• (Sok Sovan 66), Odion Obadin•, Sun Sovanrrithy◆94+ - San Narith◆94+, Sun Sopanha (Hong Ratana 79), Khim Borey (Sok Pheng 69) - Chan Chaya••◆94+, Kouch Sokumpheak, Kingsley Njoku. Tr: David Booth

AFC CUP 2011

First Round

Round of 16

Group A

		Pl	W	D	L	F	A	Pts	UZB	IND	LIB	YEM
Nasaf Karshi	UZB	6	6	0	0	30	4	18		3-0	9-0	7-1
Dempo Sports Club	IND	6	2	1	3	6	19	7	0-4		2-1	2-1
Al Ansar	LIB	6	2	0	4	8	12	6	1-4			2-0	0-2
Al Tilal Aden	YEM	6	1	1	4	9	18	4	2-3	1-4	2-2	

Round of 16: Nasaf Karshi * 2 — Al Faysali 1

Group B

		Pl	W	D	L	F	A	Pts	KUW	UZB	SYR	YEM
Al Qadisiya	KUW	6	4	2	0	15	5	14		4-0	3-2	3-0
Shurton Guzor	UZB	6	2	3	1	10	8	9	1-1		1-1	7-2
Al Ittihad Aleppo	SYR	6	2	2	2	7	7	8	0-2	0-0		2-0
Al Saqr	YEM	6	0	1	5	5	17	1	2-2	0-1	1-2	

Round of 16: Sriwijaya Palembang 0 — Chonburi * 3

Group C

		Pl	W	D	L	F	A	Pts	IRQ	JOR	SYR	KUW
Duhok	IRQ	6	3	2	1	6	3	11		4-2	0-1	1-0
Al Faysali	JOR	6	3	2	1	8	6	11	0-0		2-0	2-1
Al Jaish	SYR	6	3	2	1	8	4	11	0-0	1-1		2-1
Al Nasr	KUW	6	0	0	6	2	11	0	0-1	0-1	0-4	

Round of 16: Duhok * 1 — Dempo Sports Club 0

Group D

		Pl	W	D	L	F	A	Pts	JOR	KUW	IRQ	OMA
Al Wihdat	JOR	6	4	2	0	11	3	14		1-0	0-0	5-1
Al Kuwait	KUW	6	3	1	2	7	6	10	1-3		1-0	0-0
Al Talaba	IRQ	6	1	2	3	4	6	5	0-1	1-2		1-1
Al Suwaiq	OMA	6	0	3	3	5	12	3	1-1	1-3	1-2	

Round of 16: Shurton Guzor 1 — Al Wihdat * 2

Group E

		Pl	W	D	L	F	A	Pts	IRQ	LIB	OMA	SYR
Arbil	IRQ	6	4	2	0	17	4	14		6-2	0-0	1-1
Al Ahed	LIB	6	2	0	4	11	13	6	1-2		2-0	4-1
Al Urooba Sur	OMA	6	1	3	2	4	10	6	0-5	1-0		1-1
Al Karama	SYR	6	1	3	2	8	13	6	0-3	3-2	2-2	

Round of 16: Arbil * 1 — Tampines Rovers 0

Group F

		Pl	W	D	L	F	A	Pts	VIE	IDN	HKG	MDV
Song Lam Nghe An	VIE	6	4	0	2	16	10	12		4-0	1-2	4-2
Sriwijaya Palembang	IDN	6	3	1	2	9	11	10	3-1		3-2	1-1
TSW Pegasus	HKG	6	3	0	3	15	12	9	2-3	1-2		3-0
VB Sports	MDV	6	1	1	4	9	16	4	1-3	2-0	3-5	

Round of 16: Song Lam Nghe An * 1 — Persipura Jayapura 3

Group G

		Pl	W	D	L	F	A	Pts	THA	SIN	VIE	MDV
Muangthong United	THA	6	4	2	0	14	1	14		4-0	4-0	1-0
Tampines Rovers	SIN	6	3	2	1	12	8	11	1-1		3-1	4-0
T & T Hanoi	VIE	6	2	2	2	5	8	8	0-0	1-1		2-0
Victory	MDV	6	0	0	6	1	15	0	0-4	1-3	0-1	

Round of 16: Muangthong United * 4 — Al Ahed 0

Group H

		Pl	W	D	L	F	A	Pts	THA	IDN	HKG	IND
Chonburi	THA	6	4	1	1	18	8	13		4-1	3-0	4-0
Persipura Jayapura	IDN	6	3	2	1	14	9	11	3-0		4-2	4-1
South China	HKG	6	1	2	3	7	14	5	0-3	1-1		1-0
East Bengal	IND	6	0	3	3	9	17	3	4-4	1-1	3-3	

Round of 16: Al Qadisiya * 2 2p — Al Kuwait 2 3p

Top scorers: **10** - Ivan Boskovic MNE, Nasaf • **8** - Firas Al Khatib SYR, Al Qadisiya • **7** - Leandro Carrijo BRA, Pegasus • **6** - Hassan Abdelfattah JOR, Kuwait/Wihdat; Mahmoud Shelbaieh JOR, Wihdat; Aleksandar Duric SIN, Tampines & Pipob On Mo THA, Chonburi

AFC CUP 2011

Quarter-finals	Semi-finals	Final

Nasaf Karshi	1 0 4p	
Chonburi *	0 1 3p	

Nasaf Karshi *	1 1	
Al Wihdat	0 1	

Duhok	1 0	
Al Wihdat *	5 3	

Nasaf Karshi	2	
Al Kuwait	1	

Arbil	2 1	
Persipura Jayapura *	1 0	

Arbil *	0 3	
Al Kuwait	2 3	

AFC CUP FINAL 2011

Markaziy, Karshi, 29-10-2011, 19:00, 15 753, Kim Dong Jin KOR

Nasaf Karshi   2   Shomurodov [62], Pereplotkins [65]

Al Kuwait   1   Kabı [87]

Nasaf - Murod Zukhurov• - Maksud Karimov, Botir Qoraev, Bojan Malisic• - Jahongir Djiyamurodov, Andrejs Pereplotkins, Lutfulla Turaev, Artur Gevorkyan, Erkin Boydullaev - Ilkhom Shomurodov (Fozil Musaev 84), Ivan Boskovic (Artyom Filiposyan 94+). Tr: Anatoliy Demyanenko
Kuwait - Khaled Al Fadhli - Yaqoub Al Taher, Fahad Awadh, Hussain Hakem• (Ali Al Kandari 80), Ahmad Al Subaih• (Abdullah Al Buraiki 61) - Lassana Fane, Rafat Ali, Naser Al Qahtani - Khaled Al Shammari, Rogerio, Boris Kabi•. Tr: Dragan Talajic

Muangthong United	0 0	
Al Kuwait *	1 0	

* Home team/Home team in the first leg

CAF

CONFEDERATION AFRICAINE DE FOOTBALL

The Zambian national team wrote one of the most extraordinary stories in the history of football at the 2012 CAF Africa Cup of Nations in Equatorial Guinea and Gabon. Not only were they surprise winners of the tournament but they won the trophy in Libreville, the scene in 1993 of the plane crash that claimed the lives of a Zambia team that many regard as the best in the history of football in the country. This side will surely rank alongside them now after elevating Zambia to the exclusive list of 14 nations that have won the trophy. They will only be able to enjoy the title of African champions for 12 months, however, as CAF switches the cycle of the biennial tournament by hosting the next finals in South Africa at the start of 2013. Sudan had got 2011 underway by hosting the increasingly popular African Nations Championship, a tournament for national teams

THE FIFA BIG COUNT OF 2006 FOR AFRICA

	Male	Female		Total
Number of players	44 940 000	1 361 000	Referees and Assistant Referees	50 000
Professionals	7 000		Admin, Coaches, Technical, Medical	580 000
Amateurs 18+	926 000		Number of clubs	12 000
Youth under 18	2 156 000		Number of teams	71 000
Unregistered	43 199 000		Clubs with women's teams	1 000
Total Players	46 930 000		Players as % of population	5.16%

made up of home-based players. With one of the strongest leagues on the continent there was little surprise that Tunisia emerged victorious after beating Angola 3-0 in the final in Khartoum. Tunisia's leading club Esperance then claimed the CAF Champions League title in November, with the Ghanaian Harrison Ariful scoring the only goal in the 1-0 aggregate victory over Morocco's Wydad Casablanca. The CAF Confederation Cup also saw a Tunisia - Morocco final with Morocco's Magreb Fes beating Club Africain on post-match penalties after both sides had won their home ties 1-0. In other tournaments, Burkina Faso beat hosts Rwanda in the final of the CAF African U-17 Championship while Nigeria emerged victorious at the CAF African U-20 Championship in South Africa after beating Cameroon 3-2 in the final.

Confédération Africaine de Football (CAF)

PO Box 23, 3 Abdel Khalek Sarwat Street, El Hay El Motamayez, 6th October City, Egypt

Tel +20 2 8371000   Fax +20 2 8370006

info@cafonline.com   www.cafonline.com

President: Issa Hayatou CMR   General Secretary: Hicham El Amrani MAR

CAF Formed: 1957

CAF EXECUTIVE COMMITTEE

President: Issa Hayatou CMR	1st Vice-President: Seyi Memene TOG	2nd Vice-President: Molefi Oliphant RSA

ORDINARY MEMBERS OF THE EXECUTIVE COMMITTEE

Amadou Diakité MLI	Adoum Djibrine CHA	Amos Adamu NGA
Mohamed Raouraoua ALG	Suketu Patel SEY	Hani Abu Rida EGY
Almamy Kabele Camara GUI	Celestin Musabyimana RWA	Thierry Kamach CTA
	Magdi Shams El Din SUD	
Co-opted: Slim Aloulou TUN	FIFA Exco: Jacques Anouma CIV	General Secretary: Hicham El Amrani MAR

MAP OF CAF MEMBER NATIONS

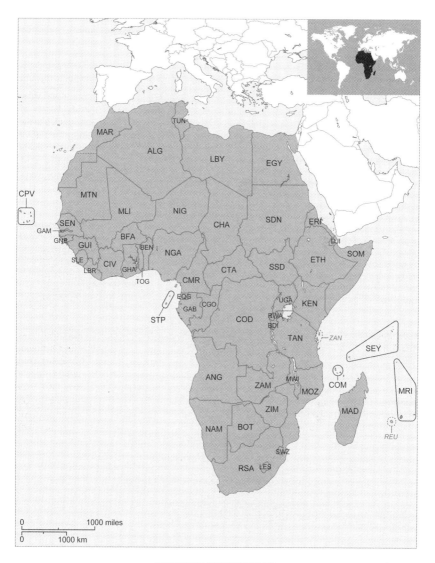

0   1000 miles
0   1000 km

CAF MEMBER ASSOCIATIONS (54)
ALG - **Algeria** • ANG - **Angola** • BEN - **Benin** • BOT - **Botswana** • BFA - **Burkina Faso** • BDI - **Burundi** • CMR - **Cameroon** • CPV - Cape Verde Islands
CTA - **Central African Republic** • CHA - **Chad** • COM - **Comoros** • CGO - **Congo** • COD - **Congo DR** • CIV - **Côte d'Ivoire** • DJI - **Djibouti**
EGY - **Egypt** • EQG - **Equatorial Guinea** • ERI - **Eritrea** • ETH - **Ethiopia** • GAB - **Gabon** • GAM - **Gambia** • GHA - **Ghana** • GUI - **Guinea**
GNB - **Guinea-Bissau** • KEN - **Kenya** • LES - **Lesotho** • LBR - **Liberia** • LBY - **Libya** • MAD - **Madagascar** • MWI - **Malawi** • MLI - **Mali**
MTN - **Mauritania** • MRI - **Mauritius** • MAR - **Morocco** • MOZ - **Mozambique** • NAM - **Namibia** • NIG - **Niger** • NGA - **Nigeria** • RWA - **Rwanda**
STP - **São Tomé e Príncipe** • SEN - **Senegal** • SEY - **Seychelles** • SLE - **Sierra Leone** • SOM - **Somalia** • RSA - **South Africa** • SSD **South Sudan** •
SDN - **Sudan** • SWZ - **Swaziland** • TAN - **Tanzania** • TOG - **Togo** • TUN - **Tunisia** • UGA - **Uganda** • ZAM - **Zambia** • ZIM - **Zimbabwe**

CAF ASSOCIATE MEMBER ASSOCIATIONS (2)
REU - **Reunion** • ZAN - **Zanzibar** • Neither of these two nations is affiliated to FIFA

AFRICAN NATIONAL TEAM TOURNAMENTS

CAF AFRICA CUP OF NATIONS

Year	Host Country	Winners	Score	Runners-up	Venue
1957	Sudan	Egypt	4-0	Ethiopia	Municipal, Khartoum
1959	Egypt	Egypt	2-1	Sudan	Al Ahly Stadium, Cairo
1962	Ethiopia	Ethiopia	2-0	Egypt	Haile Selassie, Addis Abeba
1963	Ghana	Ghana	3-0	Sudan	Accra Stadium, Accra
1965	Tunisia	Ghana	3-2	Tunisia	Zouiten, Tunis
1968	Ethiopia	Congo Kinshasa	1-0	Ghana	Haile Selassie, Addis Abeba
1970	Sudan	Sudan	1-0	Ghana	Municipal, Khartoum
1972	Cameroon	Congo	3-2	Mali	Omnisports, Yaoundé
1974	Egypt	Zaire	2-2 2-0	Zambia	International, Cairo
1976	Ethiopia	Morocco	1-1	Guinea	Addis Abeba Stadium
1978	Ghana	Ghana	2-0	Uganda	Accra Stadium, Accra
1980	Nigeria	Nigeria	3-0	Algeria	Surulere, Lagos
1982	Libya	Ghana	1-1 7-6p	Libya	11th June Stadium, Tripoli
1984	Côte d'Ivoire	Cameroon	3-1	Nigeria	Houphouët Boigny, Abidjan
1986	Egypt	Egypt	0-0 5-4p	Cameroon	International, Cairo
1988	Morocco	Cameroon	1-0	Nigeria	Mohamed V, Casablanca
1990	Algeria	Algeria	1-0	Nigeria	Stade Olympique, Algiers
1992	Senegal	Côte d'Ivoire	0-0 11-10p	Ghana	Stade de l'Amite, Dakar
1994	Tunisia	Nigeria	2-1	Zambia	El Menzah, Tunis
1996	South Africa	South Africa	2-0	Tunisia	Soccer City, Johannesburg
1998	Burkina Faso	Egypt	2-0	South Africa	Stade du 4 Août, Ouagadougou
2000	Ghana/Nigeria	Cameroon	2-2 4-3p	Nigeria	Surulere, Lagos
2002	Mali	Cameroon	0-0 3-2p	Senegal	Stade du 26 Mars, Bamako
2004	Tunisia	Tunisia	2-1	Morocco	Rades, Tunis
2006	Egypt	Egypt	0-0 4-2p	Côte d'Ivoire	International, Cairo
2008	Ghana	Egypt	1-0	Cameroon	Ohene Djan, Accra
2010	Angola	Egypt	1-0	Ghana	Cidade Universitária, Luanda
2012	Eq.Guinea/Gabon	Zambia	0-0 8-7p	Côte d'Ivoire	Stade d'Angondje, Libreville

CAF AFRICA CUP OF NATIONS MEDALS TABLE

	Country	G	S	B	F	SF
1	Egypt	7	1	3	7	11
2	Ghana	4	4	1	8	9
3	Cameroon	4	2	1	6	8
4	Nigeria	2	4	7	6	12
5	Congo DR	2		1	2	4
6	Côte d'Ivoire	1	2	4	3	8
7	Zambia	1	2	3	3	6
8	Tunisia	1	2	1	3	5
9	Sudan	1	2	1	3	2
10	Algeria	1	1	2	2	6
11	South Africa	1	1	1	2	3
12	Morocco	1	1	1	1	4
13	Ethiopia	1	1	1	1	3
14	Congo	1			1	2
15	Mali		1	1	1	5
16	Senegal		1		1	3
17	Uganda		1		1	2
18	Libya		1		1	1
19	Guinea		1			
20	Burkina Faso					1
		28	28	28	52	95

This table represents the Gold (winners), Silver (runners-up) and Bronze (semi-finalists) placings of nations in the Africa Cup of Nations, along with the number of appearances in the final and semi-finals.

FOOTBALL TOURNAMENT OF THE AFRICAN GAMES

Year	Host Country	Winners	Score	Runners-up	Venue
1965	Congo	Congo	0-0 †	Mali	Brazzaville
1973	Nigeria	Nigeria	2-0	Guinea	Lagos
1978	Algeria	Algeria	1-0	Nigeria	Algiers
1987	Kenya	Egypt	1-0	Kenya	Nairobi
1991	Egypt	Cameroon	1-0	Tunisia	Cairo
1995	Zimbabwe	Egypt	3-1	Zimbabwe	Harare
1999	South Africa	Cameroon	0-0 4-3p	Zambia	Johannesburg
2003	Nigeria	Cameroon	2-0	Nigeria	Abuja
2007	Algeria	Cameroon	1-0	Guinea	Algiers
2011	Mozambique	Ghana	1-1 4-2p	South Africa	Maputo

† Decided on number of corner-kicks awarded. Congo won 7-2

CECAFA CUP

Year	Host Country	Winners	Score	Runners-up	Venue
1973	Uganda	Uganda	2-1	Tanzania	
1974	Tanzania	Tanzania	1-1 5-3p	Uganda	
1975	Zambia	Kenya	0-0 5-4p	Malawi	
1976	Zanzibar	Uganda	2-0	Zambia	
1977	Somalia	Uganda	0-0 5-3p	Zambia	
1978	Malawi	Malawi	3-2	Zambia	
1979	Kenya	Malawi	3-2	Kenya	
1980	Sudan	Sudan	1-0	Tanzania	
1981	Tanzania	Kenya	1-0	Tanzania	
1982	Uganda	Kenya	1-1 5-3p	Uganda	
1983	Kenya	Kenya	1-0	Zimbabwe	
1984	Uganda	Zambia	0-0 3-0p	Malawi	Kampala
1985	Zimbabwe	Zimbabwe	2-0	Kenya	Rufaro, Harare
1986	Sudan	Not held			
1987	Ethiopia	Ethiopia	1-1 5-4p	Zimbabwe	
1988	Malawi	Malawi	3-1	Zambia	
1989	Kenya	Uganda	3-3 2-1	Malawi	Nyayo, Nairobi
1990	Zanzibar	Uganda	2-0	Sudan	
1991	Uganda	Zambia	2-0	Kenya	Kampala
1992	Tanzania	Uganda	1-0	Tanzania	Mwanza
1993	Uganda	Not held			
1994	Kenya	Tanzania	2-2 4-3p	Uganda	Nairobi
1995	Uganda	Zanzibar	1-0	Uganda	
1996	Sudan	Uganda	1-0	Sudan	
1997		Not held			
1998	Rwanda	Not held			
1999	Rwanda	Rwanda B	3-1	Kenya	Amahoro, Kigali
2000	Uganda	Uganda	2-0	Uganda B	Nakivubo, Kampala
2001	Rwanda	Ethiopia	2-1	Kenya	Amahoro, Kigali
2002	Tanzania	Kenya	3-2	Tanzania	Memorial, Arusha
2003	Sudan	Uganda	2-0	Rwanda	Khartoum
2004	Ethiopia	Ethiopia	3-0	Burundi	Addis Abeba
2005	Rwanda	Ethiopia	1-0	Rwanda	Amahoro, Kigali
2006	Ethiopia	Zambia	0-0 11-10p	Sudan	Addis Abeba
2007	Tanzania	Sudan	2-2 4-2p	Rwanda	Dar es Salaam
2008	Uganda	Uganda	1-0	Kenya	Kampala
2009	Kenya	Uganda	2-0	Rwanda	Nairobi
2010	Tanzania	Tanzania	1-0	Côte d'Ivoire	Dar es Salaam
2011	Tanzania	Uganda	2-2 3-2p	Rwanda	Dar es Salaam

COSAFA CUP

Year	Host Country	Winners	Score	Runners-up	Venue
1997	Home and away	Zambia	1-1	Namibia	Windhoek
1998	Home and away	Zambia	1-0	Zimbabwe	Harare
1999	Home and away	Angola	1-0 1-1	Namibia	Luanda & Windhoek
2000	Home and away	Zimbabwe	3-0 3-0	Lesotho	Maseru & Bulawayo

COSAFA CUP (CONT'D)

Year	Host Country	Winners	Score	Runners-up	Venue
2001	Home and away	Angola	0-0 1-0	Zimbabwe	Luanda & Harare
2002	Home and away	South Africa	3-1 1-0	Malawi	Blantyre & Durban
2003	Home and away	Zimbabwe	2-1 2-0	Malawi	Blantyre & Harare
2004	Home and away	Angola	0-0 5-4p	Zambia	Lusaka
2005	Home and away	Zimbabwe	1-0	Zambia	Mafikeng
2006	Home and away	Zambia	2-0	Angola	Lusaka
2007	Home and away	South Africa	0-0 4-3p	Zambia	Bloemfontein
2008	South Africa	South Africa	2-1	Mozambique	Thulamahashe
2009	Zimbabwe	Zimbabwe	3-1	Zambia	Harare
2010	Angola	Cancelled			

COUPE CEMAC

Year	Host Country	Winners	Score	Runners-up	Venue
2003	Congo	Cameroon	3-2	Central African Rep.	Brazzaville
2005	Gabon	Cameroon	1-0	Chad	Libreville
2006	Equat. Guinea	Equatorial Guinea	1-1 4-2p	Cameroon	Bata
2007	Chad	Congo	1-0	Gabon	N'Djamena
2008	Cameroon	Cameroon	3-0	Congo	Yaounde
2009	Cent'l African Rep	Central African Rep.	3-0	Equatorial Guinea	Bangui
2010	Congo	Congo	1-1 9-8p	Cameroon	Brazzaville

COPA AMILCAR CABRAL

Year	Host Country	Winners	Score	Runners-up	Venue
1979	Guinea-Bissau	Senegal	1-0	Mali	Bissau
1980	Gambia	Senegal	1-0	Gambia	Banjul
1981	Mali	Guinea	0-0 6-5p	Mali	Bamako
1982	Cape Verde	Guinea	3-0	Senegal	Praia
1983	Mauritania	Senegal	3-0	Guinea-Bissau	Nouakchott
1984	Sierra Leone	Senegal	0-0 5-3p	Sierra Leone	Freetown
1985	Gambia	Senegal	1-0	Gambia	Banjul
1986	Senegal	Senegal	3-1	Sierra Leone	Dakar
1987	Guinea	Guinea	1-0	Mali	Conakry
1988	Guinea-Bissau	Guinea	3-2	Mali	Bissau
1989	Mali	Mali	3-0	Guinea	Bamako
1991	Senegal	Senegal	1-0	Cape Verde Islands	Dakar
1993	Sierra Leone	Sierra Leone	2-0	Senegal	Freetown
1995	Mauritania	Sierra Leone	0-0 4-2p	Mauritania	Nouakchott
1997	Gambia	Mali	1-0	Senegal	Banjul
2000	Cape Verde	Cape Verde Islands	1-0	Senegal	Praia
2001	Mali	Senegal	3-1	Gambia	Bamako
2005	Guinea	Guinea	1-0	Senegal	Conakry
2007	Guinea-Bissau	Mali	2-1	Cape Verde Islands	Bissau

AFRICAN CLUB TOURNAMENTS

CAF CHAMPIONS LEAGUE

Year	Winners	Country	Score	Country	Runners-up
1965	Oryx Douala	CMR	2-1	MLI	Stade Malien
1966	Stade Abidjan	CIV	1-3 4-1	MLI	AS Real Bamako
1967	Tout Puissant Englebert	COD	1-1 2-2	GHA	Asante Kotoko
1968	Tout Puissant Englebert	COD	5-0 1-4	TOG	Etoile Filante
1969	Al Ismaili	EGY	2-2 3-1	COD	Tout Puissant Englebert
1970	Asante Kotoko	GHA	1-1 2-1	COD	Tout Puissant Englebert
1971	Canon Yaoundé	CMR	0-3 2-0 1-0	GHA	Asante Kotoko
1972	Hafia FC Conakry	GUI	4-2 3-2	UGA	Simba FC

CAF CHAMPIONS LEAGUE (CONT'D)

Year	Winners	Country	Score	Country	Runners-up
1973	AS Vita Kinshasa	COD	2-4 3-0	GHA	Asante Kotoko
1974	CARA Brazzaville	CGO	4-2 2-1	EGY	Mehalla Al Kubra
1975	Hafia FC Conakry	GUI	1-0 2-1	NGA	Enugu Rangers
1976	Mouloudia d'Algiers	ALG	3-0 0-3 4-1p	GUI	Hafia FC Conakry
1977	Hafia FC Conakry	GUI	1-0 3-2	GHA	Hearts of Oak
1978	Canon Yaoundé	CMR	0-0 2-0	GUI	Hafia FC Conakry
1979	Union Douala	CMR	0-1 1-0 5-3p	GHA	Hearts of Oak
1980	Canon Yaoundé	CMR	2-2 3-0	COD	AS Bilima
1981	JE Tizi-Ouzou	ALG	4-0 1-0	COD	AS Vita Kinshasa
1982	Al Ahly Cairo	EGY	3-0 1-1	GHA	Asante Kotoko
1983	Asante Kotoko	GHA	0-0 1-0	EGY	Al Ahly Cairo
1984	Zamalek	EGY	2-0 1-0	NGA	Shooting Stars
1985	FAR Rabat	MAR	5-2 1-1	COD	AS Bilima
1986	Zamalek	EGY	2-0 0-2 4-2p	CIV	Africa Sports
1987	Al Ahly Cairo	EGY	0-0 2-0	SUD	Al Hilal
1988	Entente Setif	ALG	0-1 4-0	NGA	Iwuanyanwu Owerri
1989	Raja Casablanca	MAR	1-0 0-1 4-2p	ALG	Mouloudia d'Oran
1990	JS Kabylie	ALG	1-0 0-1 5-3p	ZAM	Nkana Red Devils
1991	Club Africain	TUN	5-1 1-1	UGA	Nakivubo Villa
1992	Wydad Casablanca	MAR	2-0 0-0	SUD	Al Hilal
1993	Zamalek	EGY	0-0 0-0 7-6p	GHA	Asante Kotoko
1994	Espérance Tunis	TUN	0-0 3-1	EGY	Zamalek
1995	Orlando Pirates	RSA	2-2 1-0	CIV	ASEC Mimosas
1996	Zamalek	EGY	1-2 2-1 4-2p	NGA	Shooting Stars
1997	Raja Casablanca	MAR	0-1 1-0 5-4p	GHA	Obuasi Goldfields
1998	ASEC Mimosas	CIV	0-0 4-1	ZIM	Dynamos
1999	Raja Casablanca	MAR	0-0 0-0 4-3p	TUN	Espérance Tunis
2000	Hearts of Oak	GHA	2-1 3-1	TUN	Espérance Tunis
2001	Al Ahly Cairo	EGY	1-1 3-0	RSA	Mamelodi Sundowns
2002	Zamalek	EGY	0-0 1-0	MAR	Raja Casablanca
2003	Enyimba	NGA	2-0 0-1	EGY	Al Ismaili
2004	Enyimba	NGA	1-2 2-1 5-3p	TUN	Etoile du Sahel
2005	Al Ahly Cairo	EGY	0-0 3-0	TUN	Etoile du Sahel
2006	Al Ahly Cairo	EGY	1-1 1-0	TUN	CS Sfaxien
2007	Etoile du Sahel	TUN	0-0 3-1	EGY	Al Ahly Cairo
2008	Al Ahly Cairo	EGY	2-0 2-2	CMR	Cotonsport
2009	TP Mazembe	COD	1-2 1-0	NGA	Heartland
2010	TP Mazembe	COD	5-0 1-1	TUN	Espérance Tunis
2011	Espérance Tunis	TUN	0-0 1-0	MAR	Wydad Casablanca

CAF CHAMPIONS LEAGUE MEDALS TABLE

	Country	G	S	B	F	SF
1	Egypt	12	5	9	17	26
2	Congo DR	5	5	5	10	15
3	Morocco	5	2	3	7	8
4	Cameroon	5	1	6	6	12
5	Tunisia	4	6	4	10	12
6	Algeria	4	1	5	5	10
7	Ghana	3	8	6	11	15
8	Guinea	3	2	3	5	8
9	Nigeria	2	5	10	7	17
10	Côte d'Ivoire	2	2	6	4	9
11	South Africa	1	1	1	2	3
12	Congo	1			1	1
13	Sudan		2	4	2	6
14	Mali		2	1	2	3
	Uganda		2	1	2	3

CAF CHAMPIONS LEAGUE MEDALS TABLE (CONT'D)

	Country	G	S	B	F	SF
16	Zambia		1	6	1	7
17	Togo		1	3	1	4
18	Zimbabwe		1	1	1	1
19	Senegal			5		5
20	Ethiopia			2		2
	Kenya			2		2
22	Angola			1		1
	Libya			1		1
	Tanzania			1		1
		47	47	86	94	172

This table represents the Gold (winners), Silver (runners-up) and Bronze (semi-finalists) placings of clubs representing the above countries in the CAF Champions League, along with the number of appearances in the final and semi-finals

CAF CHAMPIONS LEAGUE MEDALS TABLE

	Club		G	S	B
1	Al Ahly Cairo	EGY	6	2	3
2	Zamalek	EGY	5	1	2
3	TP Mazembe	COD	4	2	2
4	Hafia FC Conakry	GUI	3	2	
5	Raja Casablanca	MAR	3	1	1
6	Canon Yaoundé	CMR	3		2
7	Asante Kotoko	GHA	2	5	3
8	Esperance Tunis	TUN	2	3	3
9	Jeunesse Sportive Kabylie	ALG	2		3
10	Enyimba	NGA	2		2
11	Hearts of Oak	GHA	1	2	1
12	Etoile du Sahel	TUN	1	2	
13	ASEC Mimosas	CIV	1	1	5
14	Ismaily	EGY	1	1	3
15	AS Vita Club Kinshasa	COD	1	1	1
16	Wydad Casablanca	MAR	1	1	
17	FAR Rabat	MAR	1		2
18	Oryx Douala	CMR	1		1
	Union Douala	CMR	1		1
20	CARA Brazzaville	CGO	1		
	Mouloudia Alger	ALG	1		
	Club Africain	TUN	1		
	Entente Setif	ALG	1		
	Orlando Pirates	RSA	1		
	Stade Abidjan	CIV	1		
26	Al Hilal	SUD		2	4
27	Heartland Owerri	NGA		2	2
28	AS Bilima	COD		2	
	Shooting Stars	NGA		2	
30	Nkana Red Devils	ZAM		1	5
31	Enugu Rangers	NGA		1	3
32	Dynamos	ZIM		1	1
	Ghazl Al Mehalla	EGY		1	1
	Mouloudia Oran	ALG		1	1
	CS Sfaxien	TUN		1	1
36	Africa Sports	CIV		1	

CAF CHAMPIONS LEAGUE MEDALS TABLE (CONT'D)

	Club		G	S	B
	Cotonsport	CMR		1	
	Etoile Filante	TOG		1	
	Nakivubo Villa	UGA		1	
	AS Real Bamako	MLI		1	
	Obuasi Goldfields	GHA		1	
	Mamelodi Sundowns	RSA		1	
	Simba FC	UGA		1	
	Stade Malien	MLI		1	
45	US Goree	SEN			2
	AS Kaloum Star	GUI			2
	Lomé I	TOG			2
	Jeanne d'Arc	SEN			2
49	Bendel Insurance	NGA			1
	Kenya Breweries	KEN			1
	Cotton Club	ETH			1
	ASC Diaraf	SEN			1
	Djoliba AC	MLI			1
	Express FC	UGA			1
	Great Olympics	GHA			1
	DC Motema Pembe	COD			1
	Al Ittihad	LBY			1
	Kakimbo FC	GUI			1
	Kano Pillars	NGA			1
	AFC Leopards	KEN			1
	Leopard Douala	CMR			1
	FC Lupopo	COD			1
	Mufulira Wanderers	ZAM			1
	Petro Atlético	ANG			1
	Real Republicans	GHA			1
	St. Georges	ETH			1
	Semassi Sokode	TOG			1
	SC Simba	TAN			1
	Stationery Stores	NGA			1
	Tonnerre Yaoundé	CMR			1
	USM Alger	ALG			1
			46	46	84

CAF CUP WINNERS' CUP

Year	Winners	Country	Score	Country	Runners-up
1975	Tonnerre Yaoundé	CMR	1-0 4-1	CIV	Stella Abidjan
1976	Shooting Stars	NGA	4-1 0-1	CMR	Tonnerre Yaoundé
1977	Enugu Rangers	NGA	4-1 1-1	CMR	Canon Yaoundé
1978	Horoya AC Conakry	GUI	3-1 2-1	ALG	MA Hussein-Dey
1979	Canon Yaoundé	CMR	2-0 6-0	KEN	Gor Mahia
1980	TP Mazembe	COD	3-1 1-0	CIV	Africa Sports
1981	Union Douala	CMR	2-1 0-0	NGA	Stationery Stores
1982	Al Mokaoulum	EGY	2-0 2-0	ZAM	Power Dynamos
1983	Al Mokaoulum	EGY	1-0 0-0	TOG	Agaza Lomé
1984	Al Ahly Cairo	EGY	1-0 0-1 4-2p	CMR	Canon Yaoundé
1985	Al Ahly Cairo	EGY	2-0 0-1	NGA	Leventis United
1986	Al Ahly Cairo	EGY	3-0 0-2	GAB	AS Sogara
1987	Gor Mahia	KEN	2-2 1-1	TUN	Espérance Tunis
1988	CA Bizerte	TUN	0-0 1-0	NGA	Ranchers Bees
1989	Al Merreikh	SUD	1-0 0-0	NGA	Bendel United

CAF CUP WINNERS' CUP

Year	Winners	Country	Score	Country	Runners-up
1990	BCC Lions	NGA	3-0 1-1	TUN	Club Africain
1991	Power Dynamos	ZAM	2-3 3-1	NGA	BCC Lions
1992	Africa Sports	CIV	1-1 4-0	BDI	Vital'O
1993	Al Ahly Cairo	EGY	1-1 1-0	CIV	Africa Sports
1994	DC Motema Pembe	COD	2-2 3-0	KEN	Kenya Breweries
1995	JS Kabylie	ALG	1-1 2-1	NGA	Julius Berger
1996	Al Mokaoulum	EGY	0-0 4-0	COD	Sodigraf
1997	Etoile du Sahel	TUN	2-0 0-1	MAR	FAR Rabat
1998	Espérance Tunis	TUN	3-1 1-1	ANG	Primeiro Agosto
1999	Africa Sports	CIV	1-0 1-1	TUN	Club Africain
2000	Zamalek	EGY	4-1 0-2	CMR	Canon Yaoundé
2001	Kaiser Chiefs	RSA	1-1 1-0	ANG	Inter Luanda
2002	Wydad Casablanca	MAR	1-0 1-2	GHA	Asante Kotoko
2003	Etoile du Sahel	TUN	0-2 3-0	NGA	Julius Berger

Discontinued after the 2003 tournament and replaced by the CAF Confederation Cup

CUP WINNERS CUP MEDALS TABLE

	Country	G	S	B	F	SF
1	Egypt	8		6	8	14
2	Tunisia	4	3	2	7	9
3	Nigeria	3	7	4	10	14
4	Cameroon	3	4	3	7	10
5	Côte d'Ivoire	2	3	2	5	7
6	Congo DR	2	1	2	3	5
7	Kenya	1	2	2	3	5
8	Algeria	1	1	4	2	6
9	Morocco	1	1	2	2	4
10	Zambia	1	1	2	2	4
11	Guinea	1		2	1	3
	Sudan	1		2	1	3
	South Africa	1		2	1	3
14	Angola		2		2	2
15	Ghana		1	2	1	3
16	Burundi		1	1	1	2
	Gabon		1	1	1	2
	Togo		1	1	1	2
19	Libya			3		3
20	Burkina Faso			2		2
	Congo			2		2
	Mali			2		2
	Mozambique			2		2
	Reunion			2		2
25	Benin			1		1
	Madagascar			1		1
	Rwanda			1		1
	Senegal			1		1
	Zimbabwe			1		1
		29	29	58	58	116

This table represents the Gold (winners), Silver (runners-up) and Bronze (semi-finalists) placings of clubs representing the above countries in the Cup Winners Cup, along with the number of appearances in the final and semi-finals

CUP WINNERS CUP MEDALS TABLE

	Club		G	S	B
1	Al Ahly Cairo	EGY	4		
2	Mokawloon	EGY	3		1
3	Africa Sports	CIV	2	2	1
4	Etoile du Sahel	TUN	2		
5	Canon Yaoundé	CMR	1	3	1
6	Gor Mahia	KEN	1	1	1
7	BCC Lions	NGA	1	1	
	Power Dynamos	ZAM	1	1	
	Tonnerre Yaoundé	CMR	1	1	
	Esperance Tunis	TUN	1	1	
11	Horoya AC Conakry	GUI	1		2
	Al Merreikh	SUD	1		2
	Wydad Casablanca	MAR	1		2
14	Daring Club Motema Pembe	COD	1		1
	Shooting Stars	NGA	1		1
	Zamalek	EGY	1		1
17	CA Bizerte	TUN	1		
	Enugu Rangers	NGA	1		
	Jeunesse Sportive Kabylie	ALG	1		
	Kaiser Chiefs	RSA	1		
	TP Mazembe	COD	1		
	Union Douala	CMR	1		
23	Club Africain	TUN		2	1
24	Julius Berger	NGA		2	
25	NA Hussein-Dey	ALG		1	1
	Agaza Lomé	TOG		1	1
	Bendel Insurance	NGA		1	1
28	Asante Kotoko	GHA		1	
	FAR Rabat	MAR		1	
	Inter Clube	ANG		1	
	Kenya Breweries	KEN		1	
	Leventis United	NGA		1	
	Primeiro de Agosto	ANG		1	
	Ranchers Bees	NGA		1	
	Sodigraf	COD		1	
	AS Sogara	GAB		1	
	Stationery Stores	NGA		1	

CUP WINNERS CUP MEDALS TABLE (CONT'D)

Club		G	S	B
Stella Abidjan	CIV		1	
Vital'O	BDI		1	
40 Djoliba AC	MLI			2
Kadiogo	BFA			2
Mufulira Wanderers	ZAM			2
St Louisienne	REU			2
44 Abiola Babes	NGA			1
APR FC	RWA			1
ASEC Mimosas	CIV			1
CR Belouizdad	ALG			1
BFV FC	MAD			1
Blackpool	ZIM			1
Diamant Yaoundé	CMR			1
Dragons de l'Ouème	BEN			1
Al Ahly Tripoli	LBY			1
Al Ittihad	EGY			1
Al Ittihad	LBY			1
Al Nasr	LBY			1
CS Hammam-Lif	TUN			1
Hearts of Oak	GHA			1

CUP WINNERS CUP MEDALS TABLE (CONT'D)

Club		G	S	B
Inter Club	CGO			1
Inter Star	BDI			1
Ismaily	EGY			1
ASC Jeanne d'Arc	SEN			1
Jomos Cosmos	RSA			1
El Kanemi Warriors	NGA			1
Kumbo Strikers	CMR			1
AFC Leopards	KEN			1
Mansoura	EGY			1
Al Masry	EGY			1
Desportivo Maputo	MOZ			1
Maxaquene	MOZ			1
Mbilinga	GAB			1
Orlando Pirates	RSA			1
AS Police	CGO			1
Sekondi Hasaacas	GHA			1
Entente Setif	ALG			1
USM Alger	ALG			1
AS Vita Club Kinshasa	COD			1
		29	29	58

CAF CUP

Year	Winners	Country	Score	Country	Runners-up
1992	Shooting Stars	NGA	0-0 3-0	UGA	Nakivubo Villa
1993	Stella Abidjan	CIV	0-0 2-0	TAN	SC Simba
1994	Bendel Insurance	NGA	0-1 3-0	ANG	Primeiro de Maio
1995	Etoile du Sahel	TUN	0-0 2-0	GUI	Kaloum Star
1996	Kawkab Marrakech	MAR	1-3 2-0	TUN	Etoile du Sahel
1997	Esperance Tunis	TUN	0-1 2-0	ANG	Petro Atlético
1998	CS Sfaxien	TUN	1-0 3-0	SEN	ASC Jeanne d'Arc
1999	Etoile du Sahel	TUN	1-0 1-2	MAR	Wydad Casablanca
2000	JS Kabylie	ALG	1-1 0-0	EGY	Al Ismaili
2001	JS Kabylie	ALG	1-2 1-0	TUN	Etoile du Sahel
2002	JS Kabylie	ALG	4-0 0-1	CMR	Tonnerre Youndé
2003	Raja Casablanca	MAR	2-0 0-0	CMR	Cotonsport Garoua

Discontinued after the 2003 tournament and replaced by the CAF Confederation Cup

CAF CUP MEDALS TABLE

	Country	G	S	B	F	SF
1	Tunisia	4	2	2	6	8
2	Algeria	3			3	3
3	Morocco	2	1		3	3
4	Nigeria	2		3	2	5
5	Côte d'Ivoire	1		3	1	4
6	Cameroon		2	2	2	4
7	Angola		2	1	2	3
8	Egypt		1	2	1	3
9	Tanzania		1	1	1	2
	Uganda		1	1	1	2
11	Guinea		1		1	1
	Senegal		1		1	1
13	Congo DR			2		2

CAF CUP MEDALS TABLE (CONT'D)

	Country	G	S	B	F	SF
14	Congo			1		1
	Ethiopia			1		1
	Kenya			1		1
	Mozambique			1		1
	Reunion			1		1
	Sudan			1		1
	Zambia			1		1
		12	12	24	24	48

This table represents the Gold (winners), Silver (runners-up) and Bronze (semi-finalists) placings of clubs representing the above countries in the CAF Cup, along with the number of appearances in the final and semi-finals

CAF CUP MEDALS TABLE

	Club		G	S	B
1	JS Kabylie	ALG	3		
2	Etoile du Sahel	TUN	2	2	
3	Bendel Insurance	NGA	1		
	Espérance Tunis	TUN	1		
	Kawkab AC Marrakech	MAR	1		
	CS Sfaxien	TUN	1		
	Raja Casablanca	MAR	1		
	Shooting Stars	NGA	1		
	Stella Club Abidjan	CIV	1		
10	Cotonsport	CMR		1	1
11	Ismaily	EGY		1	
	Jeanne d'Arc	SEN		1	
	AS Kaloum	GUI		1	
	Nakivubo Villa	UGA		1	
	Petro Atlétco	ANG		1	
	Primeiro de Maio	ANG		1	
	Simba SC	TAN		1	
	Tonnerre Yaoundé	CMR		1	
	Wydad Casablanca	MAR		1	
20	Africa Sports	CIV			1
	Atletico Sport Aviacao	ANG			1
	CA Bizerte	TUN			1

CAF CUP MEDALS TABLE (CONT'D)

Club		G	S	B
Canon Yaoundé	CMR			1
Club Africain	TUN			1
DC Motema Pembe	COD			1
Enugu Rangers	NGA			1
Ferroviarrio Maputo	MOZ			1
Insurance	ETH			1
Inter Club	CGO			1
Iwuanyanwu Nationale	NGA			1
Jasper United	NGA			1
Kampala CC	UGA			1
Kenya Breweries	KEN			1
Malindi	TAN			1
Al Masry	EGY			1
El Mourada	SUD			1
Nchanga Rangers	ZAM			1
Saint Denis	REU			1
Satelitte	CIV			1
Stade Abidjan	CIV			1
AS Vita Kinshasa	COD			1
Zamalek	EGY			1
		12	12	24

CAF CONFEDERATION CUP

Year	Winners	Country	Score	Country	Runners-up
2004	Hearts of Oak	GHA	1-1 1-1 8-7p	GHA	Asante Kotoko
2005	FAR Rabat	MAR	0-1 3-0	NGA	Dolphin Port Harcourt
2006	Etoile du Sahel	TUN	1-1 0-0	MAR	FAR Rabat
2007	CS Sfaxien	TUN	4-2 1-0	SUD	Al Merreikh
2008	CS Sfaxien	TUN	0-0 2-2	TUN	Etoile du Sahel
2009	Stade Malien	MLI	0-2 2-0 3-2p	ALG	Entente Sétif
2010	FUS Rabat	MAR	0-0 3-2	TUN	CS Sfaxien
2011	Maghreb Fès	MAR	0-1 1-0 6-5p	TUN	Club Africain

CAF CONFEDERATION CUP MEDALS TABLE

	Country	G	S	B	F	SF
1	Tunisia	3	3		6	2
2	Morocco	3	1		4	2
3	Ghana	1	1		2	
4	Mali	1			1	1
5	Nigeria		1	2	1	2
6	Sudan		1	1	1	1
7	Algeria		1		1	1
8	Egypt			1		1
	Libya			1		1
	Angola			1		1
		8	8	6	16	12

This table represents the Gold (winners) and Silver (runners-up) placings of clubs representing the above countries in the CAF Confederation Cup, along with the number of appearances in the final. There were no semi-finals in the Confederation Cup before 2009

CAF CONFEDERATION CUP MEDALS TABLE

	Club		G	S	B
1	CS Sfaxien	TUN	2	1	
2	FAR Rabat	MAR	1	1	
	Etoile du Sahel	TUN	1	1	
4	FUS Rabat	MAR	1		
	Hearts of Oak	GHA	1		
	Stade Malien	MLI	1		
	Maghreb Fès	MAR	1		
8	Entente Sétif	ALG		1	
	Asante Kotoko	GHA		1	
	Dolphin	NGA		1	
	Al Merreikh	SUD		1	
	Club Africain	TUN		1	
13	Bayelsa United	NGA			1
	ENPPI	EGY			1
	Al Hilal	SUD			1
	Al Ittihad	LBY			1
	Sunshire Stars	NGA			1
	InterClube	ANG			1
			8	8	6

CECAFA CLUB CHAMPIONSHIP

Year	Winners	Country	Score	Country	Runners-up
1974	Simba SC	TAN	1-0 †	KEN	Abaluhya FC
1975	Young Africans	TAN	2-0	TAN	Simba SC
1976	Luo Union	KEN	2-1	TAN	Young Africans
1977	Luo Union	KEN	2-1	SOM	Horsed
1978	Kamapala City Council	UGA	0-0 3-2p	TAN	Simba SC
1979	Abaluhya FC	KEN	1-0	UGA	Kampala City Council
1980	Gor Mahia	KEN	3-2	KEN	Abaluhya FC
1981	Gor Mahia	KEN	1-0	TAN	Simba SC
1982	AFC Leopards	KEN	1-0	ZIM	Rio Tinto
1983	AFC Leopards	KEN	2-1	MWI	Admarc Tigers
1984	AFC Leopards	KEN	2-1	KEN	Gor Mahia
1985	Gor Mahia	KEN	2-0	KEN	AFC Leopards
1986	Al Merreikh	SUD	2-2 4-2p	TAN	Young Africans
1987	Nakivubo Villa	UGA	1-0	SUD	Al Merreikh
1988	Kenya Breweries	KEN	2-0	SUD	Al Merreikh
1989	Kenya Breweries	KEN	3-0	TAN	Coastal Union
1990	Not held				
1991	Simba SC	TAN	3-0	UGA	Nikivubo Villa
1992	Simba SC	TAN	1-1 5-4p	TAN	Young Africans
1993	Young Africans	TAN	2-1	UGA	Nakivubo Villa
1994	Al Merreikh	SUD	2-1	UGA	Express FC
1995	Simba SC	TAN	1-1 5-3p	UGA	Express FC
1996	Simba SC	TAN	1-0	RWA	APR FC
1997	AFC Leopards	KEN	1-0	KEN	Kenya Breweries
1998	Rayyon Sport	RWA	2-1	ZAN	Mlandege
1999	Young Africans	TAN	1-1 4-1p	UGA	SC Villa
2000	Tusker FC	KEN	3-1	RWA	APR FC
2001	Tusker FC	KEN	0-0 3-0p	KEN	Oserian
2002	Simba SC	TAN	1-0	BDI	Prince Louis
2003	SC Villa	UGA	1-0	TAN	Simba SC
2004	APR FC	RWA	3-1	KEN	Ulinzi Stars
2005	SC Villa	UGA	3-0	RWA	APR FC
2006	Police FC	UGA	2-1	TAN	Moro United
2007	APR FC	RWA	2-1	UGA	URA Kampala
2008	Tusker	KEN	2-1	UGA	URA Kampala
2009	ATRACO	RWA	1-0	SUD	Al Merreikh
2010	APR FC	RWA	2-0	ETH	Saint George
2011	Young Africans	TAN	1-0	TAN	Simba SC

AFRICAN YOUTH TOURNAMENTS

AFRICAN U–20 CHAMPIONSHIP

Year	Host Country	Winners	Score	Runners-up	Venue
1979		Algeria	2-1 2-3	Guinea	Algiers, Conakry
1981		Egypt	1-1 2-0	Cameroon	Douala, Cairo
1983		Nigeria	2-2 2-1	Côte d'Ivoire	Abidjan, Lagos
1985		Nigeria	1-1 2-1	Tunisia	Tunis, Lagos
1987		Nigeria	2-1 3-0	Togo	Lomé, Lagos
1989		Nigeria	2-1 2-0	Mali	Bamako, Lagos
1991	Egypt	Egypt	2-1	Côte d'Ivoire	Cairo
1993	Mauritius	Ghana	2-0	Cameroon	Bellevue
1995	Nigeria	Cameroon	4-0	Burundi	Lagos
1997	Morocco	Morocco	1-0	South Africa	Meknès
1999	Ghana	Ghana	1-0	Nigeria	Accra

AFRICAN U–20 CHAMPIONSHIP (CONT'D)

Year	Host Country	Winners	Score	Runners-up	Venue
2001	Ethiopia	Angola	2-0	Ghana	Addis Abeba
2003	Burkina Faso	Egypt	4-3	Côte d'Ivoire	Ouagadougou
2005	Benin	Nigeria	2-0	Egypt	Cotonou
2007	Congo	Congo	1-0	Nigeria	Brazzaville
2009	Rwanda	Ghana	2-0	Cameron	Kigali
2011	South Africa	Nigeria	3-2	Cameroon	Johannesburg

AFRICAN U–17 CHAMPIONSHIP

Year	Host Country	Winners	Score	Runners-up	Venue
1995	Mali	Ghana	3-1	Nigeria	Bamako
1997	Botswana	Egypt	1-0	Mali	Gaborone
1999	Guinea	Ghana	3-1	Burkina Faso	Conakry
2001	Seychelles	Nigeria	3-0	Burkina Faso	Victoria
2003	Swaziland	Cameroon	1-0	Sierra Leone	Mbabane
2005	Gambia	Gambia	1-0	Ghana	Bakau
2007	Togo	Nigeria	1-0	Togo	Lome
2009	Algeria	Gambia	3-1	Algeria	Algiers
2011	Rwanda	Burkina Faso	2-1	Rwanda	Kigali

AFRICAN WOMEN'S TOURNAMENTS

CAF AFRICAN WOMEN'S CHAMPIONSHIP

Year	Host Country	Winners	Score	Runners-up	Venue
1991		Nigeria	2-0 4-0	Cameroon	
1995		Nigeria	4-1 7-1	South Africa	
1998	Nigeria	Nigeria	2-0	Ghana	Abeokuta
2000	South Africa	Nigeria	2-0	South Africa	Johannesburg
2002	Nigeria	Nigeria	2-0	Ghana	Lagos
2004	South Africa	Nigeria	5-0	Cameroon	Johannesburg
2006	Nigeria	Nigeria	1-0	Ghana	Warri
2008	Equatorial Guinea	Equatorial Guinea	2-1	South Africa	Malabo
2010	South Africa	Nigeria	4-2	Equatorial Guinea	Daveyton

WOMEN'S FOOTBALL TOURNAMENT OF THE AFRICAN GAMES

Year	Host Country	Winners	Score	Runners-up	Venue
2003	Nigeria	Nigeria	1-0	South Africa	Abuja
2007	Algeria	Nigeria	4-0	South Africa	Algiers
2011	Mozambique	Cameroon	1-0	Ghana	Maputo

AFRICAN WOMEN'S U–20 CHAMPIONSHIP

Year	Host Country	Winners	Score	Runners-up	Venue
2002		Nigeria	6-0 3-2	South Africa	
2004		Nigeria	1-0 0-0	South Africa	

AFRICAN WOMEN'S U–17 CHAMPIONSHIP

Year	Host Country	Winners	Score	Runners-up	Venue
2008	Home & Away	Nigeria	4-2 0-1	Ghana	

NATIONAL TOURNAMENTS IN AFRICA 2011

CAF AFRICAN NATIONS CHAMPIONSHIP SUDAN 2011

First Round Group Stage

Group A	Pl	W	D	L	F	A	Pts	ALG	GAB	UGA
Sudan	3	2	1	0	2	0	**7**	0-0	1-0	1-0
Algeria	3	1	2	0	4	2	**5**		2-2	2-0
Gabon	3	1	1	1	4	4	**4**			2-1
Uganda	3	0	0	3	1	5	**0**			

Group B	Pl	W	D	L	F	A	Pts	NIG	ZIM	GHA
South Africa	3	3	0	0	6	2	**9**	2-0	2-1	2-1
Niger	3	2	0	1	2	2	**6**		1-0	1-0
Zimbabwe	3	1	0	2	2	3	**3**			1-0
Ghana	3	0	0	3	1	4	**0**			

Group C	Pl	W	D	L	F	A	Pts	COD	CIV	MLI
Cameroon	3	3	0	0	5	0	**9**	2-0	2-0	1-0
Congo DR	3	1	1	1	3	4	**4**		2-1	1-1
Côte d'Ivoire	3	1	0	2	2	4	**3**			1-0
Mali	3	0	1	2	1	3	**1**			

Group D	Pl	W	D	L	F	A	Pts	ANG	SEN	RWA
Tunisia	3	2	1	0	6	2	**7**	1-1	2-0	3-1
Angola	3	1	2	0	3	2	**5**		0-0	2-1
Senegal	3	1	1	1	2	2	**4**			2-0
Rwanda	3	0	0	3	2	7	**0**			

Quarter-finals

Tunisia 1
Congo DR 0

South Africa 0
Algeria 2

Sudan 1 4p
Niger 1 3p

Cameroon 0 7p
Angola 0 8p

Semi-finals

Tunisia 1 5p
Algeria 1 3p

Sudan 1 2p
Angola 1 4p

Final

Tunisia 3
Angola 0

3rd Place Play-off

Sudan 1
Algeria 0

Finals played in Khartoum, Omdurman, Port Sudan and Wad Madani, Sudan from 4-02-2011 to 25-02-2011

The CAF African Nations Championship is for national teams comprising African based players only and the matches are not full internationals

REGIONAL TOURNAMENTS IN AFRICA 2011

CECAFA CUP TANZANIA 2011

First round groups

Group A	Pl	W	D	L	F	A	Pts	ZIM	TAN	DJI
Rwanda	3	3	0	0	8	2	**9**	2-0	1-0	5-2
Zimbabwe	3	2	0	1	4	3	**6**		2-1	2-0
Tanzania	3	1	0	2	4	3	**3**			3-0
Djibouti	3	0	0	3	2	10	**0**			

Group B	Pl	W	D	L	F	A	Pts	UGA	ZAN	SOM
Burundi	3	2	1	0	5	1	**7**	1-0	0-0	4-1
Uganda	3	2	0	1	6	2	**6**		2-1	4-0
Zanzibar	3	1	1	1	4	2	**4**			3-0
Somalia	3	0	0	3	1	11	**0**			

Group C	Pl	W	D	L	F	A	Pts	SUD	KEN	ETH
Malawi	3	1	2	0	3	1	**5**	0-0	2-0	1-1
Sudan	3	1	2	0	2	1	**5**		1-0	1-1
Kenya	3	1	0	2	2	3	**3**			2-0
Ethiopia	3	0	2	1	2	4	**2**			

Quarter-finals

Uganda 1
Zimbabwe 0

Malawi 0
Tanzania 1

Sudan 2
Burundi 0

Zanzibar 1
Rwanda 2

Semi-finals

Uganda 3
Tanzania 1

Sudan 1
Rwanda 2

Final

Uganda 2 3p
Rwanda 2 2p

Third place play-off

Sudan 1
Tanzania 0

Top scorers: 5 - Meddie Kagere RWA & Olivier Karekazi RWA

Played in Dar es Salaam, Tanzania from 25-11-2011 to 10-12-2011

CECAFA KAGAME INTER-CLUB CUP TANZANIA 2011

First round groups

Group A

		Pl	W	D	L	F	A	Pts	ERI	BDI	ZAN	RWA
Simba FC	TAN	4	2	2	0	3	0	8	0-0	0-0	1-0	2-0
Red Sea FC	ERI	4	2	1	1	5	3	7	1-0		0-2	4-1
Vital'O	BDI	4	2	1	1	4	2	7		1-0		3-1
Ocean View	ZAN	4	2	0	2	5	4	6				3-2
Etincelles	RWA	4	0	0	4	4	12	0				

Group B

		Pl	W	D	L	F	A	Pts	SUD	UGA	SOM
Yanga	TAN	3	2	1	0	7	4	7	2-2	3-2	2-0
El Merreikh	SUD	3	1	2	0	6	3	5		1-1	3-0
Bunamwaya	UGA	3	1	1	1	7	4	4			4-0
Elman	SOM	3	0	0	3	0	9	0			

Group C

		Pl	W	D	L	F	A	Pts	KEN	RWA	DJI
St George	ETH	3	2	1	0	11	2	7	1-1	3-1	7-0
Ulinzi Stars	KEN	3	1	2	0	10	1	5		0-0	9-0
APR FC	RWA	3	1	1	1	5	3	4			4-0
Ports	DJI	3	0	0	3	0	20	0			

Quarter-finals

Yanga	0	6p
Red Sea FC	0	5p
Vital'O	0	
St George	2	
El Merreikh	1	9p
Ulinzi Stars	1	8p
Bunamwaya	1	
Simba SC	2	

Semi-finals

Yanga	0	5p
St George	0	4p
El Merreikh	1	4p
Simba SC	1	5p

Final

Yanga	1
Simba SC	0

Third place play-off

El Merreikh	2
Saint George	0

Played in Dar es Salaam, Tanzania from 25-06-2011 to 10-07-2011 • Yanga are Young Africans SC

YOUTH TOURNAMENTS IN AFRICA 2011

MEN'S FOOTBALL TOURNAMENT ALL-AFRICA GAMES MOZAMBIQUE 2011

First Round Group Stage

Group A

	Pl	W	D	L	F	A	Pts	GHA	MOZ
South Africa	2	2	0	0	4	1	6	1-0	3-1
Ghana	2	1	0	1	4	4	3		4-3
Mozambique	2	0	0	2	4	7	0		

Group B

	Pl	W	D	L	F	A	Pts	SEN	UGA
Cameroon	2	1	1	0	1	0	4	1-0	0-0
Senegal	2	1	1	0	2	2	3		2-1
Uganda	2	0	1	1	1	2	1		

Semi-finals

Ghana	1	
Cameroon	0	
Senegal	0	5p
South Africa	0	6p

Played as a U-23 tournament

Final

Ghana	1	4p
South Africa	1	2p

Third place play-off

Cameroon	1	5p
Senegal	1	4p

Played at the Estadio Machava, Estadio Maxaquene & Estadio do Zimpeto, Maputo, 4-09-2011 to 17-09-2011

WOMEN'S FOOTBALL TOURNAMENT ALL-AFRICA GAMES MOZAMBIQUE 2011

First Round Group Stage

Group A

	Pl	W	D	L	F	A	Pts	ALG	MOZ
Cameroon	2	2	0	0	4	0	6	3-0	1-0
Algeria	2	1	0	1	7	4	3		7-1
Mozambique	2	0	0	2	1	8	0		
Guinea			Withdrew						

Group B

	Pl	W	D	L	F	A	Pts	RSA	TAN	ZIM
Ghana	3	2	1	0	6	4	7	2-2	2-1	2-1
South Africa	3	1	2	0	8	5	6		2-2	4-1
Tanzania	3	0	2	1	5	6	2			2-2
Zimbabwe	3	0	1	2	4	8	1			

Semi-finals

Cameroon	2
South Africa	0
Algeria	0
Ghana	3

Final

Cameroon	1
Ghana	0

Third place play-off

Algeria	3
South Africa	0

Played at the Estadio Machava, Estadio Maxaquene & Estadio do Zimpeto, Maputo, 4-09-2011 to 17-09-2011

AFRICAN U-20 CHAMPIONSHIP 2011 QUALIFIERS

Preliminary Round			First Round			Second Round		
Mauritius	w-o		Zambia	1	1			
Comoros			**Mauritius**	0	3	Mauritius	0	1
Togo	2	0	**Nigeria**	2	0	Nigeria †	2	2
Guinea	1	1	Guinea	0	1			
Kenya	w-o		Sudan	0	0			
Eritrea			**Kenya**	2	1	Kenya	0	0
Lesotho	6	1	South Africa	0	2	Lesotho †	1	0
Mozambique	1	1	**Lesotho**	2	1			
Senegal	0	1	Morocco	0	0			
Tunisia	0	0	**Senegal**	2	0	Senegal	1	0
Uganda	w-o		**Egypt**	2	0	Egypt †	0	3
Ethiopia			Uganda	0	1			
Chad	5	2	**Mali**	2	2			
Burundi	0	4	Chad	0	0	Mali †	3	0
Equatorial Guinea	0	1	Angola	2	0	Gabon	1	1
Gabon	3	1	**Gabon**	0	3			
			Benin	0	4			
			Burkina Faso	0	2	Benin	0	1
Namibia	w-o		**Ghana**	4	1	Ghana †	2	4
Zimbabwe			Namibia	0	1			
Sierra Leone	2	0	**Gambia**	4	0			
Algeria	0	1	Sierra Leone	1	0	Gambia †	1	1
Malawi	2	1	**Côte d'Ivoire**	1	1	Côte d'Ivoire	0	0
Tanzania	2	3	Tanzania	0	1			
Central African Rep	3	4	**Cameroon**	4	1			
Congo DR	0	1	Central African Rep	0	1	Cameroon †	1	2
			Congo	2	1	Congo	0	0
			Rwanda	0	2			

† Qualified for the finals in Libya/South Africa • Libya qualified as hosts but were replaced by South Africa after the tournament was moved to South Africa • Home teams in the first legs are listed above their opponents • w-o = walk over after opponents withdrew • Matches played between 16-04-2010 and 24-10-2010

CAF AFRICAN U-20 CHAMPIONSHIP SOUTH AFRICA 2011

First Round Group Stage

Group A	Pl	W	D	L	F	A	Pts	EGY	RSA	LES
Mali	3	2	1	0	6	3	7	1-0	4-2	1-1
Egypt	3	2	0	1	3	1	6		1-0	2-0
South Africa	3	1	0	2	4	6	3			2-1
Lesotho	3	0	1	2	2	5	1			

Group B	Pl	W	D	L	F	A	Pts	NGA	GHA	GAM
Cameroon	3	2	1	0	3	1	7	1-0	1-1	1-0
Nigeria	3	2	0	1	4	2	6		2-1	2-0
Ghana	3	0	2	1	3	4	2			1-1
Gambia	3	0	1	2	1	4	1			

Semi-finals

Nigeria	2
Mali	0

Egypt	0 2p
Cameroon	0 4p

Final

Nigeria	3
Cameroon	2

Third place play-off

Egypt	1
Mali	0

Tournament played in Johannesburg, South Africa from 17-04-2011 to 1-05-2011
Nigeria, Cameroon, Egypt and Mali qualified for the FIFA U–20 World Cup in Colombia

AFRICAN U-17 CHAMPIONSHIP 2011 QUALIFIERS

Preliminary Round		First Round		Second Round	
Comoros	1 1	**Reunion**	3 2		
Reunion	3 5	Angola	0 2	Reunion	1 0
Namibia	0 0	South Africa	4 0	**Burkina Faso** †	0 3
South Africa	3 2	**Burkina Faso**	2 2		
Uganda	2 1	Zambia	2 0		
Zambia ‡	0 1	Ghana	1 2	Ghana	2 0 4p
Liberia	1 0	**Senegal**	3 1	**Senegal** †	0 2 5p
Senegal	1 1	Guinea	0 4		
Somalia	3 0	Somalia	0 2		
Kenya	1 0	**Egypt**	3 4	**Egypt** †	w-0
Mauritius	w-0	**Mauritius**	w-0	Mauritius	
Madagascar		Zimbabwe			
		Sierra Leone	w-0		
		Togo		Sierra Leone	2 0
		Benin	1 0	**Côte d'Ivoire** †	2 2
		Côte d'Ivoire	1 0		
Chad	2 0	**Gabon**	2 0		
Gabon	1 1	Algeria	1 0	Gabon	2 0 2p
Congo	1 3	**Congo**	2 1	**Congo** †	0 2 3p
Equatorial Guinea	0 0	Nigeria	0 1		
Sudan	w-0	Sudan	1 2		
Tanzania		**Tunisia**	2 4	Tunisia	3 0
Morocco	w-0	Morocco	1 1	**Gambia** †	1 2
Guinea-Bissau		**Gambia**	0 3		
Lesotho	3 2	Lesotho	0 2		
Mozambique	1 0	**Cameroon**	3 4	Cameroon	0 0
Ethiopia	1 0	Congo DR	1 0	**Mali** †	1 3
Congo DR	1 1	**Mali**	4 2		

† Qualified for the finals in Rwanda • Rwanda qualified as hosts • Home teams in the first legs are listed above their opponents • ‡ Uganda disqualified for using over-aged players • w-o = walk over after opponents withdrew • Matches played between 9-04-2010 and 21-11-2010

CAF AFRICAN U-17 CHAMPIONSHIP RWANDA 2011

First Round Group Stage

Group A	Pl	W	D	L	F	A	Pts	RWA	SEN	EGY
Burkina Faso	3	2	0	1	8	4	**6**	1-2	3-2	4-0
Rwanda	3	2	0	1	3	2	**6**		0-1	1-0
Senegal	3	1	0	2	4	5	**3**			1-2
Egypt	3	1	0	2	2	6	**3**			

Group B	Pl	W	D	L	F	A	Pts	CGO	GAM	MLI
Côte d'Ivoire	3	2	1	0	8	4	**7**	2-2	4-1	2-1
Congo	3	2	1	0	7	3	**7**		3-0	2-1
Gambia	3	1	0	2	2	7	**3**			1-0
Mali	3	0	0	3	2	5	**0**			

Semi-finals

Burkina Faso	1 4p
Congo	1 2p

Côte d'Ivoire	0
Rwanda	1

Final

Burkina Faso	2
Rwanda	1

Third place play-off

Congo	2
Côte d'Ivoire	1

Tournament played in Kigali and Gisenyi, Rwanda from 8-01-2011 to 22-01-2011
Burkina Faso, Rwanda, Congo and Côte d'Ivoire qualified for the FIFA U–17 World Cup in Mexico

CAF AFRICA CUP OF NATIONS EQUATORIAL GUINEA/GABON 2012

Qualifying groups

Group A

	Pl	W	D	L	F	A	Pts	MLI	CPV	ZIM	LBR
Mali	6	3	1	2	9	6	10		3-0	1-0	2-1
Cape Verde Isl	6	3	1	2	7	7	10	1-0		2-1	4-2
Zimbabwe	6	2	2	2	7	5	8	2-1	0-0		3-0
Liberia	6	1	2	3	7	12	5	2-2	1-0	1-1	

Group B

	Pl	W	D	L	F	A	Pts	GUI	NGA	ETH	MAD
Guinea	6	4	2	0	13	5	14		1-0	1-0	4-1
Nigeria	6	3	2	1	12	5	11	2-2		4-0	2-0
Ethiopia	6	2	1	3	8	13	7	1-4	2-2		4-2
Madagascar	6	0	1	5	4	14	1	1-1	0-2	0-1	

Group C

	Pl	W	D	L	F	A	Pts	ZAM	LBY	MOZ	COM
Zambia	6	4	1	1	11	2	13		0-0	3-0	4-0
Libya	6	3	3	0	6	1	12	1-0		1-0	3-0
Mozambique	6	2	1	3	4	6	7	0-2	0-0		3-0
Comoros	6	0	1	5	2	14	1	1-2	1-1	0-1	

Group D

	Pl	W	D	L	F	A	Pts	MAR	CTA	ALG	TAN
Morocco	6	3	2	1	8	2	11		0-0	4-0	3-1
C. African Rep	6	2	2	2	5	5	8	0-0		2-0	2-1
Algeria	6	2	2	2	5	8	8	1-0	2-0		1-1
Tanzania	6	1	2	3	6	9	5	0-1	2-1	1-1	

Group E

	Pl	W	D	L	F	A	Pts	SEN	CMR	COD	MRI
Senegal	6	5	1	0	16	2	16		1-0	2-0	7-0
Cameroon	6	3	2	1	12	5	11	0-0		1-1	5-0
Congo DR	6	2	1	3	10	11	7	2-4	2-3		3-0
Mauritius	6	0	0	6	2	22	0	0-2	1-3	1-2	

Group F

	Pl	W	D	L	F	A	Pts	BFA	GAM	NAM
Burkina Faso	4	3	1	0	12	3	10		3-1	4-0
Gambia	4	1	1	2	5	6	4	1-1		3-1
Namibia	4	1	0	3	3	11	3	1-4	1-0	

Group G

	Pl	W	D	L	F	A	Pts	NIG	RSA	SLE	EGY
Niger	6	3	0	3	6	8	9		2-1	3-1	1-0
South Africa	6	2	3	1	4	2	9	2-0		0-0	1-0
Sierra Leone	6	2	3	1	5	5	9	1-0	0-0		2-1
Egypt	6	1	2	3	5	5	5	3-0	0-0	1-1	

Group H

	Pl	W	D	L	F	A	Pts	CIV	RWA	BDI	BEN
Cote d'Ivoire	6	6	0	0	19	4	18		3-0	2-1	2-1
Rwanda	6	2	0	4	5	15	6	0-5		3-1	0-3
Burundi	6	1	2	3	7	9	5	0-1	3-1		1-1
Benin	6	1	2	3	8	11	5	2-6	0-1	1-1	

Group I

	Pl	W	D	L	F	A	Pts	GHA	SUD	CGO	SWZ
Ghana	6	5	1	0	13	1	16		0-0	3-1	2-0
Sudan	6	4	1	1	8	3	13	0-2		2-0	3-0
Congo	6	2	0	4	5	10	6	0-3	0-1		3-1
Swaziland	6	0	0	6	2	14	0	0-3	1-2	0-1	

Group J

	Pl	W	D	L	F	A	Pts	ANG	UGA	KEN	GNB
Angola	6	4	0	2	7	5	12		2-0	1-0	1-0
Uganda	6	3	2	1	6	2	11	3-0		0-0	2-0
Kenya	6	2	2	2	4	4	8	2-1	0-0		2-1
Guinea-Bissau	6	1	0	5	2	8	3	0-2	0-1	1-0	

Group K

	Pl	W	D	L	F	A	Pts	BOT	TUN	MWI	TOG	CHA
Botswana	8	5	2	1	7	3	17		1-0	0-0	2-1	1-0
Tunisia	8	4	2	2	14	6	14	0-1		2-2	2-0	5-0
Malawi	8	2	6	0	13	8	12	1-1	0-0		1-0	6-2
Togo	8	1	3	4	6	10	6	1-0	1-2	1-1		0-0
Chad	8	0	3	5	7	20	3	0-1	1-3	2-2	2-2	

Final Tournament first Round Group Stage

	Pl	W	D	L	F	A	Pts	EQG	LBY	SEN
Zambia	3	2	1	0	5	3	7	1-0	2-2	2-1
Equat'l Guinea	3	2	0	1	3	2	6		1-0	2-1
Libya	3	1	1	1	4	4	4			2-1
Senegal	3	0	0	3	3	6	0			

	Pl	W	D	L	F	A	Pts	SUD	ANG	BFA
Côte d'Ivoire	3	3	0	0	5	0	9	1-0	2-0	2-0
Sudan	3	1	1	1	4	4	4		2-2	2-1
Angola	3	1	1	1	4	5	4			2-1
Burkina Faso	3	0	0	3	2	6	0			

	Pl	W	D	L	F	A	Pts	TUN	MAR	NIG
Gabon	3	3	0	0	6	2	9	1-0	3-2	2-0
Tunisia	3	2	0	1	4	3	6		2-1	2-1
Morocco	3	1	0	2	4	5	3			1-0
Niger	3	0	0	3	1	5	0			

	Pl	W	D	L	F	A	Pts	MLI	GUI	BOT
Ghana	3	2	1	0	4	1	7	2-0	1-1	1-0
Mali	3	2	0	1	3	3	6		1-0	2-1
Guinea	3	1	1	1	7	3	4			6-1
Botswana	3	0	0	3	2	9	0			

Gabon and Equatorial Guinea qualified automatically as hosts • Togo were initially refused entry but were later re-admitted

CAF AFRICA CUP OF NATIONS EQUATORIAL GUINEA/GABON 2012

Quarter-finals   **Semi-finals**   **Final**

Zambia	3
Sudan	0

Zambia	1
Ghana	0

Tunisia	1
Ghana	2

Zambia	0	8p
Côte d'Ivoire	0	7p

Mali	1	5p
Gabon	1	4p

Mali	0
Côte d'Ivoire	1

Equatorial Guinea	0
Côte d'Ivoire	3

Full match details for the qualifiers and finals
of the 2012 Africa Cup of Nations will appear
in Oliver's Almanack of World Football 2012

Top scorers: **3** - Manucho ANG; Didier Drogba CIV, Pierre-Emerick
Aubameyang GAB; Cheick Diabate MLI; Houssine Kharja MAR;
Christopher Katongo ZAM & Emmanuel Mayuka ZAM

AFRICA CUP OF NATIONS FINAL 2012

Stade d'Angondje, Libreville, 12-02-2011, 20:30, 40 000, Badara Diatta SEN

Zambia   0 8p
Côte d'Ivoire   0 7p

Zambia - Kennedy Mweene - Davies Nkausu, Stophira Sunzu, Hijani Himoonde,
Joseph Musonda (Nyambe Mulenga• 12) (Felix Katongo 74) - Chisamba Lungu,
Isaac Chansa, Nathan Sinkala, Rainford Kalaba - Christopher Katongo (c),
Emmanuel Mayuka. Tr: Herve Renard FRA

Côte d'Ivoire - Boubacar Barry - Jean-Jacques Gosso, Kolo Toure, Sol Bamba•,
Siaka Tiene - Didier Zokora (Didier Ya Konan 75), Yaya Toure (Wilfried Bony 87),
Cheick Tiote• - Gervinho, Salomon Kalou (Max Gradel 63) - Didier Drogba (c).
Tr: Francois Zahoui

Tiote ✓; Chris Katongo ✓; Bony ✓; Mayuka ✓; Bamba ✓; Chansa ✓; Gradel ✓;
Felix Katongo ✓; Drogba ✓; Mweene ✓; Tiene ✓; Sinkala ✓; Ya Konan ✓; Lungu
✓; Kolo Toure ✗¹; Kalaba ✗²; Gervinho ✗²; Sunzu ✓ • ¹ = Saved • ² = Missed

CLUB TOURNAMENTS IN AFRICA IN 2011

ORANGE CAF CHAMPIONS LEAGUE 2011

First Round

Espérance Tunis	TUN	Bye		
Deportivo Mongomo	EQG	0	1	
ASPAC *	BEN	1	1	
Djoliba	MLI	2	2	
East End Lions *	SLE	0	0	
Ports Authority	GAM	1	0	
ASC Diaraf *	SEN	1	2	
ES Sétif	ALG	Bye		
Fello Star Labe *	GUI	1	0	
ASFA/Yennenga	BFA	1	3	
AS Vita Club	COD	1	3	
Zanzibar Ocean View *	ZAN	1	0	
Vital'O *	BDI	2	1	
Cotonsport	CMR	2	1	
Raja Casablanca *	MAR	10		
Tourbillon	CHA	1		
Stade Malien	MLI	Bye		
Motor Action *	ZIM	0 1 4p		
CNaPS Sport Itasy	MAD	1 0 3p		
CF Cansado	MTN	0	0	
ASEC Mimosas *	CIV	7	2	
Club Africain	TUN	2	4	
APR FC *	RWA	2	0	
Ulinzi Stars *	KEN	0	0	
Zamalek	EGY	4	1	
Recreativo Caála *	ANG	2	0	
Saint George	ETH	0	1	
Al Hilal Omdurman	SUD	Bye		
Enyimba	NGA	1	2	
St Michel Ouenzé *	CGO	0	0	
Les Astres Douala	CMR	0 0 3p		
US Bitam *	GAB	0 0 5p		
Jeunesse Abidjan	CIV	0	3	
AS-FAN Niamey *	NIG	0	0	
Al Ittihad Tripoli	LBY	Bye		
ZESCO United *	ZAM	3	1	
Liga Muçulmana	MOZ	0	2	
St Michel United	SEY	0	2	
Young Buffaloes *	SWZ	3	1	
Supersport United *	RSA	2	1	
Matlama	LES	0	2	
Al Ahly Cairo	EGY	Bye		
MC Alger	ALG	1	2	
Olympique Réal *	CTA	1	0	
Dynamos	ZIM	Bye		
El Merreikh	SUD	Bye		
Township Rollers	BOT			
InterClube	ANG	w-o		
TP Mazembe	COD	Bye		
Elan Club *	COM	0	2	
Simba SC	TAN	0	4	
Kano Pillars	NGA	2	1	
Mighty Barrolle *	LBR	1	0	
Aduana Stars	GHA	0	1	
Wydad Casablanca *	MAR	3	0	

Second Round

Espérance Tunis *	5	0
ASPAC	0	2
Djoliba	0	1
ASC Diaraf *	3	1
ES Sétif *	2	4
ASFA/Yennenga	0	3
AS Vita Club *	0	0
Cotonsport	1	2
Raja Casablanca	1	1
Stade Malien *	2	0
Motor Action * ‡‡	0	2p
ASEC Mimosas	0	4p
Club Africain *	4	1
Zamalek	2	2
Recreativo Caála	0	1
Al Hilal Omdurman *	3	1
Enyimba	0	2
US Bitam *	0	1
Jeunesse Abidjan *		
Al Ittihad Tripoli	w-o	
ZESCO United *	5	2
Young Buffaloes	0	0
Supersport United	0	1
Al Ahly Cairo *	2	0
MC Alger	1	3
Dynamos *	4	0
El Merreikh *	2 0 2p	
InterClube	0 2 3p	
TP Mazembe *	3	3
Simba SC	1	2
Kano Pillars	0	0
Wydad Casablanca *	2	0

Third Round

Espérance Tunis *	5	1
ASC Diaraf	0	0
ES Sétif	1	2
Cotonsport *	4	0
Raja Casablanca *	1	5p
ASEC Mimosas ‡‡	1	4p
Club Africain	0	1
Al Hilal Omdurman *	1	1
Enyimba *	1	
Al Ittihad Tripoli ‡‡	0	
ZESCO United *	0	0
Al Ahly Cairo	0	1
MC Alger	1	3
InterClube *	1	2
TP Mazembe ‡	0	2
Wydad Casablanca *	1	0

* Home team in the first leg • Losing teams in the third round enter the Confederation Cup

ORANGE CAF CHAMPIONS LEAGUE 2011

Champions League Stage

Group A	Pl	W	D	L	F	A	Pts	NGA	SUD	CMR	MAR
Enyimba	6	4	2	0	11	5	**14**		2-2	2-0	2-0
Al Hilal	6	2	2	2	6	7	**8**	1-2		2-1	1-0
Cotonsport	6	2	1	3	7	8	**7**	2-3	2-0		2-1
Raja Casablanca	6	0	3	3	1	5	**3**	0-0	0-0	0-0	

Semi-finals

Espérance	1 2
Al Hilal *	0 0

Final

Espérance	0 1
Wydad *	0 0

Enyimba	0 0
Wydad *	1 0

Group B	Pl	W	D	L	F	A	Pts	TUN	MAR	EGY	ALG
Espérance	6	2	4	0	9	4	**10**		0-0	1-0	4-0
Wydad	6	1	4	1	11	9	**7**	2-2		1-1	4-0
Al Ahly	6	1	4	1	7	6	**7**	1-1	3-3		2-0
MC Alger	6	1	2	3	4	12	**5**	1-1	3-1	0-0	

Top scorers: **6** - Edward Sadomba ZIM, Al Hilal • **5** - Youssef Msakni TUN, Espérance & Mouchine Iajour MAR, Wydad

‡ TP Mazembe disqualified for using an ineligible player against Simba SC. Simba played Wydad in a play-off to take Mazembe's place
Wydad Casablanca 3-0 Simba SC. Played at Petro Sport Stadium, Cairo, 28-05-2011. Scorers: Fabrice Ondama [88], Ayoub El Khaliqi [94+], Mouhcine Iajour [96+] for Wydad

‡‡ Played over one leg only due to the political problems in the Côte d'Ivoire and Libya

FIRST ROUND

Rene Pleven d'Akpakpa, Cotonou, 30-01-2011

ASPAC	1	Hyacinthe Sewanou [32]
Dep Mongomo	0	

La Libertad, Bata, 12-02-2011

Dep Mongomo	1	Junior [13], William Dassagate [37]
ASPAC	1	

Brookfields National Stadium, Freetown, 30-01-2011

East End Lions	0	
Djoliba	2	Aliou Bagayoko 2 [66 82]

Hérémakono, Bamoko, 5-03-2011

Djoliba	2	Ousmane Cisse [32], Amadou Karembe [80]
East End Lions	0	

Demba Diop, Dakar, 30-01-2011

ASC Diaraf	1	Ibrahima Ndoye [88]
Ports Authority	1	Hatab Badji [51]

Serrekunda East Mini Stadium, Serrekunda, 12-02-2011

Ports Authority	0	
ASC Diaraf	2	Babacar Ndiour [32], Pape Maka Sarr [82]

Saifoullaye Diallo, Labé, 30-01-2011

Fello Star Labe	1	Diallo Alpha Bacar [60]
ASFA/Yennenga	1	Aly Babo [4]

4 Août, Ouagadougou, 12-02-2011

ASFA/Yennenga	3	Issa Gouo [12], Solomon Asante [41], Abasse
Fello Star Labe	0	Bundu [69]

Amaan, Zanzibar, 30-01-2011

Ocean View	1	OG [88]
AS Vita Club	1	Alfred M'Fongang [76]

Stade des Martyrs, Kinshasa, 27-02-2011

AS Vita Club	3	Yves Mapanda [42], Alfred M'Fongang 2 [70 89]
Ocean View	0	

Prince Louis Rwagasore, Bujumbura, 30-01-2011

Vital'O	2	Tambwe Amissi [20], Sutche Wambo [25]
Cotonsport	2	Jacques Haman [41], Osmaila Baba [73]

Omnisports, Garoua, 6-03-2011

Cotonsport	1	Jacques Haman
Vital'O	1	Ndissaye

Mohamed V, Casablanca, 28-01-2011

Raja Casablanca	10	Abdessamad Ouhakki [10], Hassan Tair 3 [13 28 50], Ismail Belmaalam [19], Bouchaib El Moubarki [25], Mohsine Moutouali [33], Hicham Aboucherouane [63], Lancine Kone [68], Hassan Souari [82]
Tourbillon	1	Habib Mahamat [67]

Rufaro, Harare, 30-01-2011

Motor Action	0	
CNaPS Sport	1	Yvan Rajoarimanana [90]

Mahamasina, Antananarivo, 13-02-2011

CNaPS Sport	0	Motor Action won 4-3p
Motor Action	1	Kudakwashe Musharu [80]

Robert Champroux, Abidjan, 30-01-2011

ASEC Mimosas	7	Robert Sankara [3], Patrick N'Doua [15], Adam Bakayoko 3 [21 28 84], Zahui Okou [77], Jean Imere [87]
CF Cansado	0	

Olympique, Nouakchott, 26-02-2011

CF Cansado	0	
ASEC Mimosas	2	Jean Bougouhi [37], Antoine N'Gossan [87]

Amahoro, Kigali, 29-01-2011

APR FC	2	Alfred Ngabo [43], Eugene Twite [75p]
Club Africain	2	Khaled Melliti [16], Hamza Messaadi [44]

7 Novembre, Rades, 4-03-2011

Club Africain	4	Bilel Ifa [20], Wissem Ben Yahia [49], Ezechiel Ndouassel [73], Youssef Mouihbi [75]
APR FC	0	

Nyayo, Nairobi, 29-01-2011

Ulinzi Stars	0	
Zamalek	4	Mahmoud Fathalla [61p], Hassan Mostafa [69], Mohamed Aoudia [76], Ibrahim Salah [91+]

Military Stadium, Cairo, 27-02-2011

Zamalek	1	Shikabala [58]
Ulinzi Stars	0	

Kuricutelas, Huambo, 30-01-2011

Recreativo Caála	2	Paizinho 2 [28 71]
Saint George	0	

Addis Abeba Stadium, Addis Abeba

Saint George	1	Adane Girma [28]
Recreativo Caála	0	

Alphonse Massemba-Debat, Brazzaville, 30-01-2011

St Michel Ouenzé	0	
Enyimba	1	Nnaemeka Anyanwu [40]

Enyimba International, Aba, 13-02-2011

Enyimba	2	John Lawrence [17], Victor Barnabas [45]
St Michel Ouenzé	0	

Gaston Peyrille, Bitam, 30-01-2011

US Bitam	0	
Les Astres	0	

Réunification, Doula, 5-03-2011

Les Astres	0	US Bitam won 5-3p
US Bitam	0	

General Seyni Kountché, Niamey, 29-01-2011

AS-FAN Niamey	0	
Jeunesse Abidjan	0	

Robert Champroux, Abidjan, 27-02-2011

Jeunesse Abidjan	3	Lacine Traore [36], Djemory Coulibaly [55], Hamadou Diabate [57]
AS-FAN Niamey	0	

Arthur Davies, Kitwe, 29-01-2011

ZESCO United	3	Humphrey Luputa [6], Jackson Mwanza [21], Portipher Zulu [81]
Liga Muçulmana	0	

Liga Muçulmana, Matola, 12-02-2011

Liga Muçulmana	2	Manuel Mablango [25], Dario Monteiro [69]
ZESCO United	1	Portipher Zulu [37]

Mavuso Sports Centre, Manzini, 30-01-2011

Young Buffaloes	3	Vusi Thumbatha [5], Ndoda Mthethwa [59], Sibusiso Dlamini [67]
St Michel United	0	

Linité, Victoria, 13-02-2011

St Michel United	2	
Young Buffaloes	1	Sibusiso Dlamini [67]

Peter Mokaba, Polokwane, 30-01-2011

Supersport Utd	2	Jabulani Maluleke [59], Tebogo Langerman [73]
Matlama	0	

Setsoto, Maseru, 13-02-2011

Matlama	2	Litsepe Marabe [55], Motlalepula Chabeli [59]
Supersport Utd	1	Fikru Lemessa [19]

Barthelemy Boganda, Bangui, 30-01-2011

Olympique Réal	1	Kellebonin [92+]
MC Alger	1	Abdelmalek Mokdad [28]

Stade Rouiba, Rouiba, 11-02-2011

MC Alger	2	Nassim Bouchema [23], Mohamed Derrag [51]
Olympique Réal	0	

Beaumer, Moroni, 29-01-2011

Elan Club	0	
Simba SC	0	

Uhuru, Dar es Salaam, 12-02-2011

Simba SC	4	Mbwana Samata 2 [45 56], Patrick Ochan [47], Amri Kiemba [71]
Elan Club	2	Madaha Mohamed [43], Abdoulkarim Sandjema [63]

Doris Williams, Buchanan, 30-01-2011		
Mighty Barrolle	1	Harris Jimmy [80]
Kano Pillars	2	Morris Chigozie [26], Sheriff Isa [80]

Sani Abacha, Kano, 12-02-2011		
Kano Pillars	1	Gambo Mohammed [29]
Mighty Barrolle	0	

Mohamed V, Casablanca, 30-01-2011		
Wydad	3	Abderahim Benkhajjan [8], Mouhcine Iajour 2 [18 43]
Aduana Stars	0	

Agyeman Badu, Dormaa Ahenkro, 27-02-2011		
Aduana Stars	1	Bernard Dong Bortey [35p]
Wydad	0	

SECOND ROUND

7 Novembre, Rades, 19-03-2011		
Espérance	5	Youssef Msakni 2 [8 15], Dramane Traore [12], OG [25], Oussama Darragi [32]
ASPAC	0	

Rene Pleven d'Akpakpa, Cotonou, 3-04-2011		
ASPAC	2	Adam Wahidi [38], Moukaila Bouraima [76]
Espérance	0	

Demba Diop, Dakar, 20-03-2011		
ASC Diaraf	3	Djibril Sidibe 2 [7 69], Ibrahima N'Doye [42]
Djoliba	0	

Hérémakono, Bamoko, 2-04-2011		
Djoliba	1	Moussa Diallo [58]
ASC Diaraf	1	Moussa N'Diaye [72]

8 Mai 1945, Sétif, 19-03-2011		
ES Sétif	2	Nabil Hemani [8], Lazhar Aissa [47]
ASFA/Yennenga	0	

4 Août, Ouagadougou, 3-04-2011		
ASFA/Yennenga	3	Ali Zoungrana [49], Ocansey Mandela [66p], Mamadou Zongo [80]
ES Sétif	4	Nabil Hemani 2 [26 78], Lazar Aissa [45], Abderahmane Hachoud [95+]

Stade des Martyrs, Kinshasa, 20-03-2011		
AS Vita Club	0	
Cotonsport	1	Hilaire Momi [3]

Omnisports, Garoua, 3-04-2011		
Cotonsport	2	Joel Babanda [35], Hilaire Momi [80]
AS Vita Club	0	

Modibo Keita, Bamako, 19-03-2011		
Stade Malien	2	Mamadou Coulibaly 2 [44 54]
Raja Casablanca	1	Bouchaib El Moubarki [7]

Mohamed V, Casablanca, 28-01-2011		
Raja Casablanca	1	Mamadou Traore [40]
Stade Malien	0	

Rufaro, Harare, 19-03-2011		
Motor Action	0	ASEC won 4-2p
ASEC Mimosas	0	

7 Novembre, Rades, 20-03-2011		
Club Africain	4	Ezechiel Ndouassel [3], Youssef Mouihbi [46], Karim Aouadhi [53], Bilal Ifa [86]
Zamalek	2	Shikabala [30], Ahmed Gaafar [79]

International, Cairo, 2-04-2011		
Zamalek	2	Mahmoud Fathallah [29], Hussein Yasser [45]
Club Africain	1	Wissem Ben Yahia [38], Abandoned 95+ mins

Al Hilal, Omdurman, 20-03-2011		
Al Hilal	3	Osama Ali [22], Mudathir Eltaib 2 [55 80]
Recreativo Caála	0	

Kuricutelas, Huambo, 2-04-2011		
Recreativo Caála	1	Paizinho [28]
Al Hilal	1	Edward Sadomba [68]

Gaston Peyrille, Bitam, 20-03-2011		
US Bitam	0	
Enyimba	0	

Enyimba International, Aba, 13-02-2011		
Enyimba	2	Victor Barnabas, Josiah Maduabuchi [90]
US Bitam	1	

Dag Hammarskjöld, Ndola, 19-03-2011		
ZESCO United	5	Alfred Luputa 3 [5 10 80], Kangwa Chileshe [15], Nicholas Zulu [70]
Young Buffaloes	0	

Mavuso Sports Centre, Manzini, 2-04-2011		
Young Buffaloes	0	
ZESCO United	2	Kangwa Chileshe [47], Luputa Alfred [78]

International, Cairo, 18-03-2011		
Al Ahly Cairo	2	Osama Hosny [3], Dominique Da Silva [84]
Supersport Utd	0	

Peter Mokaba, Polokwane, 2-04-2011		
Supersport Utd	1	Jabulani Maluleke [28]
Al Ahly Cairo	0	

Rufaro, Harare, 20-03-2011		
Dynamos	4	Guthrie Zhokinyi [17], Roderick Mutuma [45], Denver Mukamba [76], Farai Vimisai [83]
MC Alger	1	Reda Babouche [88]

Omar Hammadi, Algiers, 3-04-2011		
MC Alger	3	Brahim Bedbouda 2 [41 90], Abdelmalek Mokdad [76p]
Dynamos	0	

El Merreikh, Omdurman, 19-03-2011		
El Merreikh	2	Mohamed Osman Hanno [16], Faisal Agab [86]
InterClube	0	

Joaquim Dinis, Luanda, 2-04-2011		
InterClube	2	Manucho Barros [15], Pedro Henriques [40p]
El Merreikh	0	InterClube won 3-2p

Stade de la Kenya, Lubumbashi, 20-03-2011		
TP Mazembe	3	Patou Kabangu [11], Narcisse Ekanga [30], Alain Kaluyituka [64]
Simba SC	1	Emmanuel Okwi [75]

National, Dar es Salaam, 3-04-2011		
Simba SC	2	Shija Mkina [59], Mbwana Samata [68]
TP Mazembe	3	Given Singulama [17], Alain Kaluyituka 2 [64 72]

Mohamed V, Casablanca, 20-03-2011		
Wydad	2	Fabrice Ondama 2 [8 84]
Kano Pillars	0	

Sani Abacha, Kano, 3-04-2011		
Kano Pillars	0	
Wydad	0	

THIRD ROUND

El Menzah, Tunis, 23-04-2011

Espérance	5	Dramane Traore [11], Oussama Darragi 2 [14] 32p, Idriss Mhirissi [43], Youssef Msakni [53]
ASC Diaraf	0	

Demba Diop, Dakar, 8-05-2011

ASC Diaraf	0	
Espérance	1	Roger Toindouba [40]

Omnisports, Garoua, 7-05-2011

Cotonsport	4	Ambroise Bitolo [12], Awangue Mbongo [53], Hilaire Momi [70], Lassina Abdou Karim [86]
ES Sétif	1	Lazhar Aissa [34]

8 Mai 1945, Sétif, 13-05-2011

ES Sétif	2	Bouazza Feham [17p], Hocine Metref [58]
Cotonsport	0	

Mohamed V, Casablanca, 7-05-2011

Raja Casablanca	1	Mohsine Moutouali [90]. Raja won 5-4p
ASEC Mimosas	1	Adama Bakayoko [57]

Al Hilal, Omdurman, 24-04-2011

Al Hilal	1	Edward Sadomba [73]
Club Africain	0	

7 Novembre, Rades, 7-05-2011

Club Africain	1	Khaled Melliti [71]. Abandoned 81 mins
Al Hilal	1	Edward Sadomba [18]

Enyimba International, Aba, 8-05-2011

Enyimba	1	Victor Barnabas [66p]
Al Ittihad Tripoli	0	

Dag Hammarskjöld, Ndola, 23-04-2011

ZESCO United	0	
Al Ahly Cairo	0	

International, Cairo, 8-05-2011

Al Ahly Cairo	1	Mohamed Barakat [66]
ZESCO United	0	

Joaquim Dinis, Luanda, 23-04-2011

InterClube	1	Pedro Henriques [9]
MC Alger	1	Zinedine Bensalem [93+]

Omar Hammadi, Algiers, 7-05-2011

MC Alger	3	Youssef Sofiane [5], Abdelmalek Mokdad [45], Brahim Bedbouda [89p]
InterClube	2	Pedro Henriques 2 [43 67]

Mohamed V, Casablanca, 23-04-2011

Wydad	1	Mustapha Allaoui [16]
TP Mazembe	0	

Stade de la Kenya, Lubumbashi, 8-05-2011

TP Mazembe	2	Patou Kabangu [80], Hugues Bedi [93+]
Wydad	0	

GROUP STAGE

GROUP A											
		Pl	W	D	L	F	A	Pts	NGA	SUD	CMR	MAR
Enyimba	NGA	6	4	2	0	11	5	**14**		2-2	2-0	2-0
Al Hilal	SUD	6	2	2	2	6	7	**8**	1-2		2-1	1-0
Cotonsport	CMR	6	2	1	3	7	8	**7**	2-3	2-0		2-1
Raja Casablanca	MAR	6	0	3	3	1	5	**3**	0-0	0-0	0-0	

Stade Mohamed V, Casablanca
16-07-2011, 21:00, Damon RSA

Raja Casablanca	0

Yassine El Had - Zakaria Zerouali•, Mohamed Oulhaj, Rachid Soulaimani•, Ismail Belmaalem - Kouko Guehi, Mamadou Traore, Abdessamad Ouhaki (Abdelhak Talhaoui 76) - Bouchaib El Moubarki, Yassine Salhi (Abdelmoula Berrabah 58), Hassan Souari. Tr: Ilie Balaci

Cotonsport	0

Kassaly Daouda - Amadou Kader, Moussa Souleymanou (Edgard Salli 46), Ambroise Oyongo, Louis Ewonde, Noe Kwin (Baba Ousmaila 18) - Andre Ndame Ndame, Chardin Madila, Michel Balokog - Hilaire Momi, Jacques Haman. Tr: Denis Lavagne

Enyimba International, Aba
17-07-2011, 14:00, Farouk EGY

Enyimba	2
	Valentine Nwabili [49], Uche Kalu [60]

Chijioke Ejiogu - Valentine Nwabili, Nnaemeka Anyanwu, Chidozie Johnson, Samuel Tswanya, Ekene Iwuorie• - Otekpa Eneji•, Josiah Maduabuchi, Uche Kalu, Peter Onoja (Philip Auta 74) - Victor Barnabas (David Tyavkase 68). Tr: Felix Emordi

Al Hilal	2
	Edward Sadomba 2 [23 77]

Goma Genaro Awad - Omar Bakheet, Demba Barry, Abdellatif Saeed - Ala'a Eldin Yousif•, Haitham Mostafa, Mohamed Bashir (Ibrahima Tahir 64), Khalefa Ahmed•, Atir Thomas (Muhannad Tahir 87) - Edward Sadomba, Mudather El Tahir (Bakri Abdi Elkhadir 73). Tr: Milutin Sredojevic

Al Hilal Stadium, Omdurman
29-07-2011, 20:00, Karembe MLI

Al Hilal	1
	Edward Sadomba [65p]

Goma Genaro Awad - Omar Bakheet, Demba Barry, Tag Eldin Ibrahim - Haitham Mostafa, Saif Masawi, Khalefa Ahmed (Ibrahima Toure 84), Atir Thomas, Amir Rabea - Edward Sadomba, Bakri Abdi Elkhadir (Edet Otobong 63). Tr: Milutin Sredojevic

Raja Casablanca	0

Yassine El Had - Zakaria Zerouali, Mohamed Oulhaj•, Ismail Belmaalem, Oumar Diop - Kouko Guehi•, Mamadou Traore, Abdessamad Ouhaki (Yassine Salhi 69), Abdelhak Talhaoui - Hassan Tir, Hassan Souari (Abdelmoula Berrabah 80). Tr: Ilie Balaci

Omnisports, Garoua
30-07-2011, 15:00, Jedidi TUN

Cotonsport 2
Chardin Madila [47], Saidou Idrissa [64]

Kassaly Daouda• - Sebastien Ndzana, Amadou Kader, Louis Ewonde - Abdoul Lancina, Andre Ndame Ndame, Baba Ousmaila, Chardin Madila, Michel Balokog (Idrissa Seidou 63) - Joel Babanda (Moussa Souleymanou 54), Jacques Haman (Noe Kwin 82). Tr: Denis Lavagne

Enyimba 3
Uche Kalu 2 [8 85], Chidozie Johnson [40]

Chijioke Ejiogu - Valentine Nwabili, Chidozie Johnson, Samuel Tswanya, Markson Ojobo• - Otekpa Eneji, Uche Kalu, Rasheed Olabiyi• (David Tyavkase 59), Peter Onoja (Philip Auta 71), Chinedu Udoji - Ifeanyi Ede. Tr: Felix Emordi

---

Enyimba International, Aba
14-08-2011, 14:00, Diatta SEN

Enyimba 2
Uche Kalu [9], Chidozie Johnson [25]

Chijioke Ejiogu - Chidozie Johnson•, Samuel Tswanya, Markson Ojobo, John Agbawu - Otekpa Eneji, Uche Kalu (Musa Mustapha 81), Peter Onoja (Ifeanyi Ede 56), Chinedu Udoji - Junior Osagie (Bernard Okorowanta 56), Philip Auta. Tr: Felix Emordi

Raja Casablanca 0

Yassine El Had - Zakaria Zerouali, Mohamed Oulhaj, Mamadou Traore, Soufiane Talal (Hassan Tir 78), Zakaria Chaabani - Bouchaib El Moubarki, Yassine Salhi• (Abdessamad Ouhaki 66). Tr: Ilie Balaci

---

Al Hilal Stadium, Omdurman
14-08-2011, 22:00, Benouza ALG

Al Hilal 2
Haitham Mustafa [28p], Edet Otobong [82]

El Muez Mahgoub - Omar Bakheet, Demba Barry, Tag Eldin Ibrahim - Ala'a Eldin Yousif (Bakri Abdi Elkhadir• 71), Haitham Mostafa, Saif Masawi, Ibrahima Toure, Khalefa Ahmed - Edward Sadomba, Edet Otobong. Tr: Milutin Sredojevic

Cotonsport 1
Chardin Madila [10]

Kassaly Daouda - Sebastien Ndzana, Louis Ewonde••◆26, Noe Kwin - Abdoul Lancina, Andre Ndame Ndame••◆90, Baba Ousmaila, Chardin Madila, Michel Balokog - Brice Zimbori, Jacques Haman. Tr: Denis Lavagne

---

Stade Mohamed V, Casablanca
26-08-2011, 22:00, Haimoudi ALG

Raja Casablanca 0

Yassine El Had - El Amine Erbate, Zakaria Zerouali, Ismail Belmaalem, Mohamed Chibi - Mamadou Traore (Yassine Salhi 69), Abdelhak Talhaoui, Zakaria Chaabani - Bouchaib El Moubarki (Soufiane Talal 76), Hassan Tir (Abdessamad Ouhaki 80), Hassan Souari. Tr: Ilie Balaci

Enyimba 0

Paul Godwin - Valentine Nwabili, Chidozie Johnson, Samuel Tswanya, Markson Ojobo - Otekpa Eneji, Uche Kalu, Rasheed Olabiyi (Bernard Okorowanta 78), Peter Onoja, Chinedu Udoji - Junior Osagie (Ifeanyi Ede 64). Tr: Felix Emordi

---

Omnisports, Garoua
28-08-2011, 14:00, Kaoma ZAM

Cotonsport 2
Jacques Haman [28], Brice Zimbori [54]

Kassaly Daouda - Sebastien Ndzana, Amadou Kade, Ambroise Oyongo, Noe Kwin - Abdoul Lancina, Baba Ousmaila (Idrissa Seidou 69) (Alexis Yougouda 86), Chardin Madila, Michel Balokog - Brice Zimbori, Jacques Haman (Ewange Mbongo 60). Tr: Denis Lavagne

Al Hilal 0

Goma Genaro Awad - Omar Bakheet (Ala'a Eldin Yousif 61), Demba Barry, Osama Ali (Ibrahima Toure 47), Abdellatif Saeed - Haitham Mostafa, Saif Masawi, Atir Thomas (Mohamed Bashir 67), Khalefa Ahmed - Edward Sadomba, Bakri Abdi Elkhadir. Tr: Milutin Sredojevic

---

Al Hilal Stadium, Omdurman
9-09-2011, 20:30, Bennaceur TUN

Al Hilal 1
Edward Sadomba [5]

El Muez Mahgoub - Omar Bakheet, Demba Barry (Tag Eldin Ibrahim 46) - Ala'a Eldin Yousif (Mudather El Tahir 75), Haitham Mostafa, Saif Masawi, Ibrahima Toure (Muhannad Tahir 79), Atir Thomas, Khalefa Ahmed - Edward Sadomba, Bakri Abdi Elkhadir. Tr: Milutin Sredojevic

Enyimba 2
Valentine Nwabili [68], Samuel Tswanya [92+p]

Paul Godwin - Valentine Nwabili (Samuel Tswanya 83), Emmanuel Anyanwu, Chidozie Johnson, Markson Ojobo - Otekpa Eneji, Josiah Maduabuchi (Henry Uche 56), Uche Kalu, Rasheed Olabiyi, Chinedu Udoji - Ifeanyi Ede. Tr: Felix Emordi

---

Omnisports, Garoua
10-09-2011, 16:00, Mallet SEY

Cotonsport 2
Baba Ousmaila 2 [54 64]

Kassaly Daouda - Sebastien Ndzana, Ambroise Oyongo, Louis Ewonde•, Noe Kwin - Abdoul Lancina, Baba Ousmaila (Ewange Mbongo 75), Chardin Madila, Michel Balokog - Alexis Yougouda, Jacques Haman. Tr: Denis Lavagne

Raja Casablanca 1
Abdessamad Ouhakki [16]

Yassine El Had - El Amine Erbate, Zakaria Zerouali, Ismail Belmaalem•, Mohamed Chibi• - Kouko Guehi, Mamadou Traore, Abdessamad Ouhaki• (Hassan Tir 69), Abdelhak Talhaoui• (Zakaria Chaabani 66) - Bouchaib El Moubarki, Hassan Souari• (Soufiane Talal 59). Tr: Ilie Balaci

---

Stade Mohamed V, Casablanca
18-09-2011, 15:00, Lemghaifry MTN

Raja Casablanca 0

Tarek El Jarmouni - El Amine Erbate, Mohamed Oulhaj, Oumar Diop (Soufiane Talal 61), Mohamed Chibi - Kouko Guehi, Mamadou Traore, Abdelhak Talhaoui (Zakaria Chaabani 66) - Bouchaib El Moubarki (Rachid Soulaimani 82), Yassine Salhi, Hassan Tir. Tr: Ilie Balaci

Al Hilal 0

El Muez Mahgoub - Omar Bakheet, Demba Barry, Osama Ali (Mudather El Tahir 66) - Haitham Mostafa, Saif Masawi, Mohamed Bashir (Muhannad Tahir 57), Atir Thomas, Khalefa Ahmed, Amir Rabea - Edward Sadomba (Bakri Abdi Elkhadir 87). Tr: Milutin Sredojevic

---

Enyimba International, Aba
18-09-2011, 16:00, Maillet SEY

Enyimba 2
Ifeanyi Ede [45p], Valentine Nwabili [86p]

Paul Godwin - Valentine Nwabili, Nnaemeka Anyanwu, Samuel Tswanya - Otekpa Eneji, Uche Kalu, Rasheed Olabiyi, Chinedu Udoji - Ifeanyi Ede, Philip Auta. Tr: Felix Emordi

Cotonsport 0

GROUP B

		Pl	W	D	L	F	A	Pts	TUN	MAR	EGY	ALG
Espérance Tunis	TUN	6	2	4	0	9	4	10		0-0	1-0	4-0
Wydad Casablanca	MAR	6	1	4	1	11	9	7	2-2		1-1	4-0
Al Ahly Cairo	EGY	6	1	4	1	7	6	7	1-1	3-3		2-0
MC Alger	ALG	6	0	2	3	4	12	5	1-1	3-1	0-0	

---

5 Juillet 1962, Algiers
16-07-2011, 18:30, Bennett RSA

MC Alger   **1**
Mohamed Megherbi [17]

Sofiane Azzedine - Abdelkader Besseghir, Hamza Zeddam, Mohamed Megherbi● - Hamza Koudri, Farid Daoud, Billel Attafen, Tayeb Berramla (Sofiane Harkat 85), El Almi Daoudi (Reda Babouche 74) - Herve Oussale●, Zinedine Bensalem. Tr: Abdelhak Meguellati

Espérance Tunis   **1**
Oussama Darragi [7]

Moez Ben Chrifia - Walid Hichri●, Sameh Derbali●, Khalil Chemmam, Banana Yaya - Mejdi Traoui, Wajdi Bouazzi (Harrison Afful 75), Khaled Korbi● - Oussama Darragi, Youssef Msakni●, Yannick N'Djeng (Khaled Ayari 87). Tr: Nabil Maaloul

---

Military Stadium, Cairo
17-07-2011, 21:00, Gassama GAM

Al Ahly Cairo   **3**
Emad Moteab [3], Wael Gomaa [23], Da Silva [75]

Ahmed Abdul Monem - Ahmed Fathi, Wael Gomaa, Sayed Moawad, Sherif Abdul Fadil, Ahmed Al Sayed (Rami Hesham 62) - Hossam Ghaly, Hossam Ashour - Dominique Da Silva (Moataz Eno 79), Emad Moteab, Mohamed Nagi Geddo (Al Sayed Hamdi 71). Tr: Manuel Jose

Wydad Casablanca   **3**
OG [1], Mouhcine Iajour 2 [61 88]

Nadir Lamyaghri - Youssef Rabeh, Mourad Lemsen, Hicham Amrani - Mohamed Berrabah, Ahmed Ajeddou, Said Fettah (Pascal Angan 85), Yassine Lakhal - Fabrice Ondama (Farid Talhaoui 84), Mouhssine Iajour (Adberahim Benkajjane 90), Ayoub El Khaliqi. Tr: Michel Decastel

---

Mohamed V, Casablanca
30-07-2011, 19:00, Abdel Rahman SUD

Wydad Casablanca   **4**
Fabrice Ondama [2], Ahmed Ajeddou [31p], Ayoub El Khaliki [72], Pascal Angan [93+]

Nadir Lamyaghri - Youssef Rabeh, Mourad Lemsen, Hicham Amrani - Mohamed Berrabah●, Ahmed Ajeddou● (Youssef Kaddioui 87), Said Fettah, Yassine Lakhal● (Abdelghani Mouaoui 64), Fabrice Ondama, Mouhssine Iajour (Pascal Angan 81), Ayoub El Khaliqi. Tr: Michel Decastel

MC Alger   **0**

Sofiane Azzedine - Abdelkader Besseghir, Reda Babouche●, Hamza Zeddam, Mohamed Megherbi● - Hamza Koudri, Farid Daoud (Tayeb Berramla 69), Billel Attafen (Seddik Berradja 46), El Almi Daoudi - Herve Oussale●, Zinedine Bensalem. Tr: Abdelhak Meguellati

---

7 Novembre, Rades
30-07-2011, 21:30, Diatta SEN

Espérance Tunis   **1**
Yannick N'Djeng [14]

Moez Ben Chrifia - Harrison Afful, Walid Hichri, Sameh Derbali, Khalil Chemmam - Khaled Mouelhi, Mejdi Traoui●, Wajdi Bouazzi (Bilel Ben Brahim 71) - Oussama Darragi (Oussama Boughanmi 81), Khaled Ayari, Yannick N'Djeng (Mohamed Slema 84). Tr: Nabil Maaloul

Al Ahly Cairo   **0**

Ahmed Abdul Monem - Ahmed Fathi●, Wael Gomaa, Sayed Moawad, Ahmed Al Sayed - Hossam Ghaly●, Mohamed Shawki, Hossam Ashour, Mohamed Aboutrika (Mohamed Fadl 78), Shehab Ahmed (Mohamed Nagi Geddo 44) - Emad Moteab (Al Sayed Hamdi 78). Tr: Manuel Jose

---

International, Cairo
12-08-2011, 22:00, Seechurn MRI

Al Ahly Cairo   **2**
Emad Moteab 2 [9 32]

Ahmed Abdul Monem - Ahmed Fathi●, Wael Gomaa, Sayed Moawad, Sherif Abdul Fadil - Hossam Ghaly●, Mohamed Shawki, Mohamed Aboutrika (Hossam Ashour 71), Rami Hesham - Emad Moteab (Fabio Junior 80), Mohamed Nagi Geddo (Dominique Da Silva 61). Tr: Manuel Jose

MC Alger   **0**

Sofiane Azzedine - Hamza Zeddam, Claude Mobitang, Ahmed Belaid - Seddik Berradja, Hamza Koudri, Farid Daoud (Tayeb Berramla 76), Billel Attafen - Herve Oussale, Mohamed Amroune (El Almi Daoudi 63), Zinedine Bensalem. Tr: Abdelhak Meguellati

---

Mohamed V, Casablanca
14-08-2011, 22:00, Maillet SEY

Wydad Casablanca   **2**
Fabrice Ondama [65], Youssef Kaddioui [78p]

Nadir Lamyaghri - Youssef Rabeh, Mourad Lemsen, Hicham Amrani - Mohamed Berrabah (Pascal Angan 93+), Ahmed Ajeddou (Youssef Kaddioui 65), Said Fettah, Yassine Lakhal● (Abdelghani Mouaaoui 87), Fabrice Ondama, Mouhssine Iajour, Ayoub El Khaliqi. Tr: Michel Decastel

Espérance Tunis   **2**
Wajdi Bouazzi [22], Walid Hicheri [37]

Moez Ben Chrifia - Harrison Afful●, Walid Hichri, Idrissa Coulibaly, Sameh Derbali (Banana Yaya 71), Khalil Chemmam - Khaled Mouelhi, Wajdi Bouazzi (Khaled Ayari 74), Khaled Korbi - Oussama Darragi (Zine Souissi 92+), Yannick N'Djeng●. Tr: Nabil Maaloul

---

El Menzah, Tunis
27-08-2011, Alioum CMR

Espérance Tunis   **0**

Moez Ben Chrifia - Harrison Afful, Walid Hichri, Khalil Chemmam● (Idriss Mhirsi 81), Banana Yaya - Khaled Mouelhi, Wajdi Bouazzi (Sameh Derbali 46), Khaled Korbi - Oussama Darragi (Khaled Ayari 74), Youssef Msakni, Yannick N'Djeng●. Tr: Nabil Maaloul

Wydad Casablanca   **0**

Nadir Lamyaghri - Youssef Rabeh, Adberahim Benkajjane, Mourad Lemsen - Mohamed Berrabah (Pascal Angan 88), Ahmed Ajeddou, Houcine Zidoune● (Younes Mankari● 87), Said Fettah - Fabrice Ondama●, Mouhssine Iajour (Youssef Kaddioui 79), Ayoub El Khaliqi. Tr: Michel Decastel

---

5 Juillet 1962, Algiers
28-08-2011, 22:00, Coulibaly MLI

MC Alger   **0**

Sofiane Azzedine - Abdelkader Besseghir, Reda Babouche, Hamza Zeddam, Claude Mobitang● - Seddik Berradja (Zinedine Bensalem 59), Hamza Koudri, Farid Daoud, Billel Attafen (Mohamed Amroune 89), El Almi Daoudi - Herve Oussale●. Tr: Abdelhak Meguellati

Al Ahly Cairo   **0**

Ahmed Abdul Monem - Wael Gomaa, Sayed Moawad, Sherif Abdul Fadil● (Ahmed Nabil 80), Mohamed Naguib● - Mohamed Shawki, Hossam Ashour, Mohamed Aboutrika (Waleed Soliman 69), Rami Hesham - Emad Moteab (Dominique Da Silva 57), Mohamed Nagi Geddo. Tr: Manuel Jose

---

El Menzah, Tunis
10-09-2011, 19:10, Wokoma NGA

Espérance Tunis   **4**
Mejdi Traoui [8], Yannick N'Djeng 3 [19 43 54]

Moez Ben Chrifia - Harrison Afful●, Walid Hichri (Idrissa Coulibaly 68), Sameh Derbali, Banana Yaya● - Mejdi Traoui, Wajdi Bouazzi, Khaled Korbi - Oussama Darragi (Mohamed Slema 75), Youssef Msakni, Yannick N'Djeng (Khaled Ayari 79). Tr: Nabil Maaloul

MC Alger   **0**

Sofiane Azzedine - Abdelkader Besseghir, Reda Babouche, Hamza Zeddam●, Claude Mobitang, Mohamed Megherbi (Zinedine Bensalem 54) - Hamza Koudri, Farid Daoud●, Billel Attafen (Tayeb Berramla 66), El Almi Daoudi - Mohamed Amroune. Tr: Abdelhak Benchikha

Mohamed V, Casablanca
11-09-2011, 19:30, Doue CIV

Wydad Casablanca   **1**
     Abderahim Benkajjane [47]

Nadir Lamyaghri - Youssef Rabeh, Adberahim Benkajjane•, Mourad Lemsen, Youssef Tourabi (Pascal Angan 88) - Mohamed Berrabah (Ayoub Skouma 46), Said Fettah, Yassine Lakhal - Mouhssine Iajour, Youssef Kaddioui•, Ayoub El Khaliqi•. Tr: Michel Decastel

Al Ahly Cairo   **1**
     Mohamed Nagi Geddo [37]

Ahmed Abdul Monem - Ahmed Fathi, Wael Gomaa, Sayed Moawad, Mohamed Naguib - Mohamed Shawki•, Hossam Ashour, Mohamed Aboutrika (Shehab Ahmed 90), Rami Hesham - Dominique Da Silva (Mohamed Fadl 78), Mohamed Nagi Geddo (Emad Moteab 86). Tr: Manuel Jose

5 Juillet 1962, Algiers
16-09-2011, 19:00, Diatta SEN

MC Alger   **3**
     Reda Babouche 2 [31] [36], Herve Oussale [61]

Sofiane Azzedine - Abdelkader Besseghir, Reda Babouche, Claude Mobitang, Mohamed Megherbi - Hamza Koudri••◆71, Billel Attafen (Ahmed Belaid 85), El Almi Daoudi (Bilal Moumen 81) - Herve Oussale, Mohamed Amroune (Tayeb Berramla 69), Zinedine Bensalem. Tr: Abdelhak Benchikha

Wydad Casablanca   **1**
     Ahmed Ajeddou [79p]

Nadir Lamyaghri - Youssef Rabeh, Mourad Lemsen, Hicham Amrani - Mohamed Berrabah, Ahmed Ajeddou•, Said Fettah◆90, Yassine Lakhal (Youssef Kaddioui 46)- Fabrice Ondama, Mouhssine Iajour, Ayoub El Khaliqi•. Tr: Michel Decastel

International, Cairo
16-09-2011, 20:00, El Raay LBY

Al Ahly Cairo   **1**
     Mohamed Aboutrika [55]

Ahmed Abdul Monem - Ahmed Fathi, Wael Gomaa, Sayed Moawad, Mohamed Naguib (Waleed Soliman 29) - Mohamed Shawki, Hossam Ashour, Mohamed Aboutrika• (Dominique Da Silva 70), Rami Hesham• - Emad Moteab, Mohamed Nagi Geddo (Mohamed Fadl 64). Tr: Manuel Jose

Espérance Tunis   **1**
     Banana Yaya [17]

Moez Ben Chrifia - Walid Hichri, Idrissa Coulibaly•, Khalil Chemmam, Banana Yaya - Mejdi Traoui (Sameh Derbali 54), Wajdi Bouazzi•, Khaled Korbi - Oussama Darragi, Youssef Msakni, Yannick N'Djeng. Tr: Nabil Maaloul

SEMI-FINALS

Al Hilal Stadium, Omdurman
2-10-2011, 20:00, Haimoudi ALG

Al Hilal   **0**

El Muez Mahgoub - Omar Bakheet, Demba Barry, Osama Ali (Mudather El Tahir 29) - Haitham Mostafa (Bakri Abdi Elkhadir 75), Saif Masawi, Khalefa Ahmed, Atir Thomas, Amir Rabea - Edward Sadomba, Muhannad Tahir. Tr: Milutin Sredojevic

Espérance Tunis   **1**
     Youssef Msakni [4]

Moez Ben Chrifia - Harrison Afful, Walid Hichri, Khalil Chemmam, Banana Yaya - Khaled Korbi•, Zine Souissi (Sameh Derbali 66) - Youssef Msakni (Khaled Ayari 86), Yannick N'Djeng (Mohamed Slema 80). Tr: Nabil Maaloul

7 Novembre, Rades
15-10-2011, 19:30, Seechurn MRI

Espérance Tunis   **2**
     Youssef Msakni [52], Wajdi Bouazzi [90]

Moez Ben Chrifia - Harrison Afful (Khaled Korbi 69), Walid Hichri, Sameh Derbali, Khalil Chemmam, Banana Yaya - Khaled Mouelhi, Mejdi Traoui, Wajdi Bouazzi - Youssef Msakni (Safwen Ben Salem 86), Yannick N'Djeng (Mohamed Slema 82). Tr: Nabil Maaloul

Al Hilal   **0**

El Muez Mahgoub - Omar Bakheet, Demba Barry, Abdellatif Saeed - Haitham Mostafa (Mohamed Bashir 71), Saif Masawi, Khalefa Ahmed, Atir Thomas - Edward Sadomba (Ibrahima Toure 65), Muhannad Tahir. Tr: Milutin Sredojevic

Mohamed V, Casablanca
1-10-2011, 19:00, Grisha EGY

Wydad Casablanca   **1**
     Pascal Angan [89]

Nadir Lamyaghri - Youssef Rabeh, Adberahim Benkajjane, Mourad Lemsen• (Pascal Angan 58) - Mohamed Berrabah, Ahmed Ajeddou, Ayoub Skouma (Yassine Lakhal 71), Abderrahmane Mssassi - Fabrice Ondama, Mouhssine Iajour (Youssef Kaddioui 57), Ayoub El Khaliqi. Tr: Michel Decastel

Enyimba   **0**

Paul Godwin• - Valentine Nwabili (Emmanuel Anyanwu 75), Nnaemeka Anyanwu, Chidozie Johnson• (Otekpa Eneji 41), Samuel Tswanya, Markson Ojobo - Uche Kalu, Rasheed Olabiyi•, Peter Onoja (Bernard Okorowanta 94+), Chinedu Udoji• - Ifeanyi Edo. Tr: Felix Emordi

Enyimba International, Aba
16-10-2011, 16:00, Benouza ALG

Enyimba   **0**

Paul Godwin - Valentine Nwabili, Nnaemeka Anyanwu, Chidozie Johnson•, Markson Ojobo - Otekpa Eneji, Josiah Maduabuchi, Uche Kalu•, Peter Onoja (Bernard Okorowanta 56), Chinedu Udoji• - Ifeanyi Ede (Victor Barnabas 74). Tr: Felix Emordi

Wydad Casablanca   **0**

Nadir Lamyaghri - Youssef Rabeh, Mourad Lemsen, Hicham Amrani - Mohamed Berrabah, Ahmed Ajeddou (Yassine Rami 94+), Ayoub Skouma• (Pascal Angan 59), Yassine Lakhal, Abderrahmane Mssassi - Fabrice Ondama (Mouhssine Iajour 80), Ayoub El Khaliqi. Tr: Michel Decastel

CAF Champions League Final 1st Leg	Stade Mohamed V Casablanca	Sunday 6-11-2011
Kick-off: 20:00		Attendance: 50 000

WYDAD 0 0 ESPERANCE

WYDAD CASABLANCA

White shirts with red stripes, White shorts, White socks

Tr: Michel Decastel

Nadir Lamyaghri

Mourad Lemsen   Hicham Amrani **88** Younes Mankari   Youssef Rabeh   Yassine Rami **64** Houcine Zidoune

Said Fettah

Mohamed Berrabah   Yassine Lakhal **70** Youssef Kaddioui   Abderrahmane Mssassi

Fabrice Ondama   Ahmed Ajeddou

Yannick N'Djeng **95+** Mohamed Slema

Youssef Msekni **83** Oussama Darragi

Khaled Korbi   Mejdi Traoui   Khaled Mouelhi   Wajdi Bouazzi **13** **90** Harrison Afful

Khalil Chemmam   Banana Yaya   Walid Hicheri   Idrissa Coulibaly **29**

Moez Ben Cherifa

Tr: Nabil Maaloul

Dark blue shirts, Black shorts, Black socks

ESPERANCE

MATCH OFFICIALS

REFEREE

Neant Alioum CMR

ASSISTANTS

Mekouande Evarist

Yanoussa Moussa

CAF Champions League Final 2nd Leg	Stade 7 Novembre Rades, Tunis	Saturday 12-11-2011
Kick-off: 18:00		Attendance: 50 000

ESPERANCE   1   0   WYDAD

Harrison Afful [21]

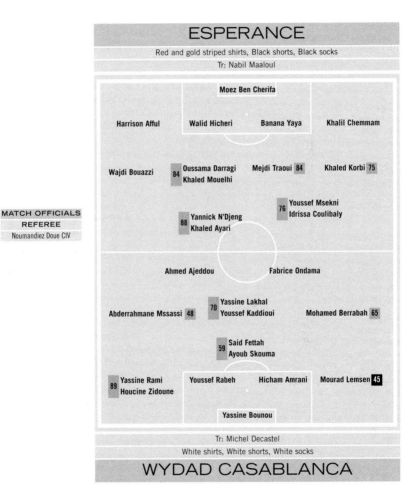

ESPERANCE
Red and gold striped shirts, Black shorts, Black socks
Tr: Nabil Maaloul

Moez Ben Cherifa

Harrison Afful   Walid Hicheri   Banana Yaya   Khalil Chemmam

Wajdi Bouazzi   [84] Oussama Darragi   Mejdi Traoui [84]   Khaled Korbi [75]
                     Khaled Mouelhi

                                          Youssef Msekni
                             [76]   Idrissa Coulibaly
                     [88] Yannick N'Djeng
                         Khaled Ayari

MATCH OFFICIALS
REFEREE
Noumandiez Doue CIV

                Ahmed Ajeddou   Fabrice Ondama

                         Yassine Lakhal
                    [70] Youssef Kaddioui
Abderrahmane Mssassi [48]   Mohamed Berrabah [65]

                         Said Fettah
                    [59] Ayoub Skouma

        [89] Yassine Rami   Youssef Rabeh   Hicham Amrani   Mourad Lemsen [45]
             Houcine Zidoune

                         Yassine Bounou

Tr: Michel Decastel
White shirts, White shorts, White socks

WYDAD CASABLANCA

My number one objective was to win the Champions League. The year before, the team had won the league and then gone on to lose in the final of the Champions League. I told myself that, on behalf of the club, the supporters and the chairman, we had to try to go one better. The Tunisian revolution helped us enormously, because it led to the championship being suspended for two months. That enabled us to remain competitive right up to December.

Nabil Maaloul

We must now turn the page and look to the future. Harrison Afful scored a beautiful goal and we were just unable to equalise. After the sending off of Mourad Lemsen we were at a serious disadvantage. We had to play more defensively with just 10 players but we succeeded in containing Esperance and even had chances to wrap it up. It was a disappointing end to what had been until then a great tournament for Wydad Casablanca.

Michel Decastel

CAF CONFEDERATION CUP 2011

First Round

Team	Country	Score
Maghreb Fès	MAR	1 4
USS Kraké *	BEN	1 1
Dynamic Togolais *	TOG	0 0 2p
Sahel SC Niamey	NIG	0 0 4p
Al Nasr	LBY	2 2 6p
CA Batna *	ALG	2 2 5p
Khartoum-3	SUD	Bye
FUS Rabat	MAR	Bye
Ports Authority	SLE	1 2
Touré Kounda Mbour *	SEN	2 2
AC Léopard Dolisie *	CGO	1 2
Etincelles	RWA	1 0
Primeiro de Agosto	ANG	Bye
Kaduna United	NGA	Bye
CD Ela Nguema	EQG	0 1
Foullah Ediface *	CHA	2 0
AshantiGold	GHA	1 1
Séwé San Pedro *	CIV	0 0
Etoile du Sahel	TUN	Bye
AS Adema *	MAD	0 1
CD Maxaquene	MOZ	0 1
US Sainte-Marienne *	REU	1 0
Bidvest Wits	RSA	0 4
Olympique Béja	TUN	Bye
Centre Salif Keita *	MLI	2 1
Difaa El Jadida	MAR	2 1
Sunshine Stars	NGA	Bye
Diplomate FC8 *	CTA	0 1
Tiko United	CMR	0 3
Africa Sports	CIV	1 1
FC Séquence *	GUI	0 1
Fovu Baham *	CMR	2 1
US Forces Armées	BFA	1 3
Haras Al Hedod	EGY	Bye
Young Africans *	TAN	4 0
Dedebit	ETH	4 2
Victors Jinja	UGA	1 1
Mbabane Highlanders *	SWZ	1 1 1p
KMKM *	ZAN	0 0
DC Motema Pembe	COD	4 2
JS Kabylie	ALG	Bye
Real Bamako	MLI	0 0
Tevragh Zeïna *	MTN	0 1
Al Nil Hasahisa	SUD	Bye
Inter Star	BDI	0 1
Missiles Libreville *	GAB	4 0
St Eloi Lupopo	COD	Bye
Highlanders *	ZIM	1
Nchanga Rangers	ZAM	1
Ismaily	EGY	Bye
Atlético Aviação *	ANG	0 0 4p
Sofapaka	KEN	0 0 5p

Second Round

Team	Score
Maghreb Fès *	0 2
Sahel SC Niamey	0 1
Al Nasr	
Khartoum-3 *	w-o
FUS Rabat *	2 1
Touré Kounda Mbour	0 2
AC Léopard Dolisie	0 1
Primeiro de Agosto *	2 0
Kaduna United *	2 0
Foullah Ediface	0 1
AshantiGold	0 2
Etoile du Sahel *	3 1
AS Adema	1 2
Bidvest Wits *	1 0
Olympique Béja *	2 0
Difaa El Jadida	0 3
Sunshine Stars *	2 1
Tiko United	0 0
Africa Sports *	
US Forces Armées	w-o
Haras Al Hedod *	4 1
Dedebit	0 1
Victors Jinja *	1 0
DC Motema Pembe	1 1
JS Kabylie *	1 2
Tevragh Zeina	0 1
Al Nil Hasahisa *	1 1
Missiles Libreville	1 2
St Eloi Lupopo *	1 2
Nchanga Rangers	0 0
Ismaily *	2 0
Sofapaka	0 4

Third Round

Team	Score
Maghreb Fès *	5 0
Khartoum-3	1 2
FUS Rabat *	1 0
Primeiro de Agosto	1 1
Kaduna United *	w-o
Etoile du Sahel	
AS Adema	0 1
Difaa El Jadida *	3 0
Sunshine Stars *	2 0
US Forces Armées	0 1
Haras Al Hedod *	2 1 3p
DC Motema Pembe	1 2 4p
JS Kabylie	0 3 3p
Missiles Libreville *	3 0 0p
St Eloi Lupopo *	2 0
Sofapaka	1 1

CAF CONFEDERATION CUP 2011

Intermediate Round				Group Stage		Final

FINAL FIRST LEG

Maghreb Fès	MAR	0	2
ZESCO United * †	ZAM	1	0

Stade 7 Novembre, Radès, 19-11-2011, Att: 45 000, Ref: Haimoudi ALG. Scorer - Alexis 7 for Club Africain
Club Africain - Aymen Ben Ayoub - Mohamed Ali Yacoubi, Bilel Ifa, Mehdi Ressaissi, Oussema Hadedi●, Zied Ziadi, Alexis Mendomo, Chaker Regui, Hamza Messadi●, Youssef Mouihbi (Wajdi Mechergui 66), Zouheir Dhaouadi. Tr: Faouzi Benzarti

Primeiro de Agosto	ANG	0	1
ASEC Mimosas * †	CIV	4	1

MAS Fès - Anas Zniti - Mostapha Mrani●, Hamza Hajji, Samir Zekroumi●●♦58, Said Hamouni, Rachid Dehmani, Abdelhadi Halhoul (Brahim Joubari 88), Hamza Bourezzouk, Ali Bamaamer, Youssef El Basri, Chamsseddine Chtaibi (Mohamed Diop 84). Tr: Rachid Taoussi

Kaduna United	NGA	0	3
ES Sétif * †	ALG	1	0

Group A

	Pts	CA	IC	AM	KU
Club Africain	11		2-0	1-0	0-0
InterClube	10	2-1		1-0	4-1
ASEC Mimosas	7	1-1	1-0		2-1
Kaduna Utd	5	0-1	1-1	2-1	

Maghreb Fès	1	1
InterClube *	2	0

Difaa El Jadida	MAR	0	2
InterClube * †	ANG	3	2

Maghreb Fès	0	1	6p
Club Africain	1	0	5p

Sunshine Stars *	NGA	1
Al Ittihad Tripoli * †	LBY	0

Group B

	Pts	MF	SS	MP	JSK
Maghreb Fès	14		1-0	3-0	1-0
Sunshine Stars	11	1-1		2-0	1-0
Motema Pembe	8	1-1	0-0		2-0
JS Kabylie	0	0-1	1-2	0-2	

S'shine Stars*	0	0
Club Africain	1	0

Simba SC * †	TAN	1	0
Motema Pembe	COD	0	2

FINAL SECOND LEG

Complex Sportif, Fès, 4-12-2011, Att: 45 000, Ref: Diatta SEN. Scorer - Tigana 45 for MAS Fès
MAS Fès - Anas Zniti - Rachid Dehmani●, Said Hamouni (Youness El Youssfi 90), Youssef El Basri, Mostapha Mrani, Moussa Tigana, Hamza Hajji, Mohamed Diop, Chamsseddine Chtaibi, Youssef Ayatti (Abdelhadi Halhoul 81), Hamza Bourezzouk. Tr: Rachid Taoussi

JS Kabylie	ALG	0	3
ASC Diaraf * †	SEN	1	0

Club Africain - Aymen Ben Ayoub - Bilel Ifa, Mehdi Meriah (Hamza Agrebi 30), Mehdi Ressaissi●, Mohamed Ali Yacoubi - Alexis Mendomo, Zied Ziadi, Zouheir Dhaouadi, Youssef Mouihbi (Chaker Regui) - Aymen Soltani● (Wajdi Mechergui 62), Ezechiel Ndouassel●♦58. Tr: Faouzi Benzarti

Sofapaka	KEN	0	3
Club Africain * †	TUN	3	1

* Home team in the first leg • † Champions League third round losers that entered at the Intermediate round

FINAL PENALTIES
MAS FÈS WON 6-5

Club Africain	MAS Fès
✗1 Regui	
	Chtaibi ✓
✓ Ifa	
	Hajji ✗2
✓ Yacoubi	
	Youssfi ✓
✓ Agrebi	

(CONTD)

Club Africain	MAS Fès
	Dehmoni ✓
✓ Dhaouadi	
	Bourezzouk ✓
✓ Alexis	
	El Basri ✓
✗1 Ziadi	
	Zniti ✓

✗1 = saved   ✗2 = missed

CONCACAF

CONFEDERATION OF NORTH, CENTRAL AMERICAN AND
CARIBBEAN ASSOCIATION FOOTBALL

Mexico dominated the year in the region, winning all the CONCACAF tournaments that they entered - the Gold Cup, the Champions League and the U-20 championship. The U-17 trophy was the only one that didn't end up in their trophy cabinet but that was because they had already qualified for the FIFA U-17 World Cup as hosts. As if to prove a point the Mexican team went on to claim the world title, beating France and Germany on the way to a 2-0 victory over Uruguay in the final. It was the second time that the Mexicans had won the U-17 world title in six years as football in the country looks to extend its influence beyond the bounds of North and Central America. The region did find itself at the center of controversy off the field during the FIFA presidential election campaign which saw CONCACAF president Jack Warner and general-secretary Chuck Blazer no longer in their positions by the end of the year. Blazer had accused

THE FIFA BIG COUNT OF 2006 FOR NORTH AND CENTRAL AMERICA AND THE CARIBBEAN

	Male	Female		Total
Number of players	33 071 000	10 038 000	Referees and Assistant Referees	172 000
Professionals	9 000		Admin, Coaches, Technical, Medical	961 000
Amateurs 18+	884 000		Number of clubs	17 000
Youth under 18	5 163 000		Number of teams	490 000
Unregistered	36 988 000		Clubs with women's teams	7 000
Total Players	44 242 000		Players as % of population	8.53%

Warner and presidential candidate Mohamed Bin Hamam of offering bribes to Caribbean Football Union officials, a number of whom later received bans of varying lengths. The story somewhat overshadowed the CONCACAF Gold Cup which was held in the aftermath and which produced a repeat final of the previous two tournaments between Mexico and the USA. Before a crowd of 93,420 in Pasadena's Rose Bowl, the Mexicans fell behind to two early American goals but staged a magnificent comeback to win the match 4-2. Earlier in the year it looked as if Mexico's stranglehold on the CONCACAF Champions League might end after Monterrey could only draw the home leg of the final against Real Salt Lake, especially given that Real were unbeaten at home in 34 matches. However, a Humberto Suazo goal on the stroke of half-time denied the Americans and gave Monterrey the title for the first time.

Confederation of North, Central American and Caribbean Association Football (CONCACAF)
725, Fifth Avenue, Trump Tower, 17th Floor, New York, NY 1022, USA
Tel +1 212 3080 044   Fax +1 212 3081 851
mail@concacaf.net   www.concacaf.com
President: Alfredo Hawit Banegas HON   General Secretary: Ted Howard USA
CONCACAF Formed: 1961

CONCACAF EXECUTIVE COMMITTEE
President: Alfredo Hawit Banegas HON
Vice-President: Lisle Austin BRB   Vice-President: Justino Compean MEX
ORDINARY MEMBERS OF THE EXECUTIVE COMMITTEE
Horace Burrell JAM   Ariel Alvarado PAN   Sunil Gulati USA
FIFA Exco: Rafael Salguero GUA   FIFA Exco: Chuck Blazer USA

MAP OF CONCACAF MEMBER NATIONS

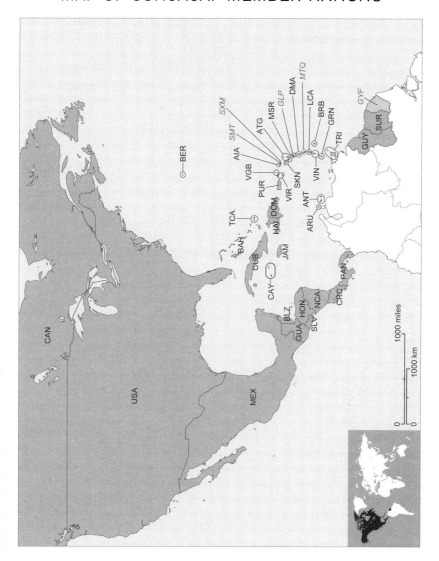

CONCACAF MEMBER ASSOCIATIONS (35)

AIA - Anguilla • ATG - **Antigua and Barbuda** • ARU - **Aruba** • BAH - **Bahamas** • BRB - **Barbados** • BLZ - **Belize** • BER - **Bermuda**
VGB - **British Virgin Islands** • CAN - **Canada** • CAY - **Cayman Islands** • CRC - **Costa Rica** • CUB - **Cuba** • DMA - **Dominica**
DOM - **Dominican Republic** • SLV - **El Salvador** • GRN - **Grenada** • GUA - **Guatemala** • GUY - **Guyana** • HAI - **Haiti** • HON - **Honduras**
JAM - **Jamaica** • MEX - **Mexico** • MSR - **Montserrat** • ANT - **Netherlands Antilles** • NCA - **Nicaragua** • PAN - **Panama** • PUR - **Puerto Rico**
SKN - **St Kitts and Nevis** • LCA - **St Lucia** • VIN - **St Vincent/Grenadines** • SUR - **Suriname** • TRI - **Trinidad and Tobago**
TCA - **Turks and Caicos Islands** • VIR - **US Virgin Islands** • USA - **United States of America**

CONCACAF ASSOCIATE MEMBER ASSOCIATIONS (5)

GYF - **French Guiana** • GLP - **Guadeloupe** • MTQ - **Martinique** • SMT - **Saint Martin** • SMX - **Sint Maarten**
None of these five nations are affiliated to FIFA

CENTRAL AMERICAN, NORTH AMERICAN AND CARIBBEAN NATIONAL TEAM TOURNAMENTS

CONCACAF GOLD CUP

Year	Host Country	Winners	Score	Runners-up	Venue
1991	USA	USA	0-0 4-3p	Honduras	Coliseum, Los Angeles
1993	Mexico/USA	Mexico	4-0	USA	Azteca, Mexico City
1995	USA	Mexico	2-0	Brazil	Coliseum, Los Angeles
1998	USA	Mexico	1-0	USA	Coliseum, Los Angeles
2000	USA	Canada	2-0	Colombia	Coliseum, Los Angeles
2002	USA	USA	2-0	Costa Rica	Rose Bowl, Pasadena
2003	Mexico/USA	Mexico	1-0	Brazil	Azteca, Mexico City
2005	USA	USA	0-0 3-1p	Panama	Giants Stadium, New Jersey
2007	USA	USA	2-1	Mexico	Soldier Field, Chicago
2009	USA	Mexico	5-0	USA	Giants Stadium, New Jersey
2011	USA	Mexico	4-2	USA	Rose Bowl, Pasadena

CONCACAF GOLD CUP MEDALS TABLE

	Country	G	S	B	F	SF
1	Mexico	6	1	1	7	8
2	USA	4	4	2	8	10
3	Canada	1		2	1	3
4	Honduras		1	3	1	4
5	Costa Rica		1	2	1	5
6	Panama		1	1	1	2
7	Jamaica				1	2
8	Guadeloupe			1		1
	Trinidad and Tobago			1		1
10	Guatemala					1
		11	8	12	19	37

This table represents the Gold (winners), Silver (runners-up) and Bronze (semi-finalists) placings in the CONCACAF Gold Cup, along with the number of appearances in the final and semi-finals. It does not include nations from outside of CONCACAF

CCCF CHAMPIONSHIP

Year	Host Country	Winners	Score	Runners-up	Venue
1941	Costa Rica	Costa Rica	3-1	El Salvador	San José
1943	El Salvador	El Salvador	2-1	Guatemala	San Salvador
1946	Costa Rica	Costa Rica	1-4	Guatemala	San José
1948	Guatemala	Costa Rica	2-3	Guatemala	Guatemala City
1951	Panama	Panama	2-0	Costa Rica	Panama City
1953	Costa Rica	Costa Rica	4-1	Honduras	San José
1955	Honduras	Costa Rica	2-1	Netherlands Antilles	Tegucigalpa
1957	Curaçao	Haiti	3-1†	Curaçao	Willemstad
1960	Cuba	Costa Rica	4-1†	Netherlands Antilles	Havana
1961	Costa Rica	Costa Rica	4-0	El Salvador	San José

All tournaments played on a league basis. The result listed is the match played between the top two • † Play-off after both teams finished level

CONCACAF NATIONS CUP

Year	Host Country	Winners	Score	Runners-up	Venue
1963	El Salvador	Costa Rica	4-1	El Salvador	San Salvador
1965	Guatemala	Mexico	2-1	Guatemala	Guatemala City
1967	Honduras	Guatemala	1-0	Mexico	Tegucigalpa
1969	Costa Rica	Costa Rica	1-1	Guatemala	San José
1971	Trinidad & T	Mexico	0-0	Haiti	Port of Spain

All tournaments played on a league basis. The result listed is the match played between the top two

CONCACAF NATIONS CUP/FIFA WORLD CUP QUALIFIERS

Year	Host Country	Winners	Score	Runners-up	Venue
1973	Haiti	Haiti	2-1	Trinidad	Port-au-Prince
1977	Mexico	Mexico	4-1	Haiti	Mexico City
1981	Honduras	Honduras	0-0	El Salvador	Tegucigalpa
1985	Home & Away	Canada	2-1	Honduras	Saint John's
1989	Home & Away	Costa Rica	1-0	USA	San José

All tournaments played on a league basis. The result listed is the match played between the top two

CARIBBEAN CUP

Year	Host Country	Winners	Score	Runners-up	Venue
1989	Barbados	Trinidad & Tobago	2-1	Grenada	Bridgetown
1990	Trinidad	Not completed			
1991	Jamaica	Jamaica	2-0	Trinidad & Tobago	Kingston
1992	Trinidad	Trinidad & Tobago	3-1	Jamaica	Port of Spain
1993	Jamaica	Martinique	0-0 6-5p	Jamaica	Kingston
1994	Trinidad	Trinidad & Tobago	7-2	Martinique	Port of Spain
1995	Cayman/Jamaica	Trinidad & Tobago	5-0	St Vincent/Grenadines	George Town
1996	Trinidad	Trinidad & Tobago	2-0	Cuba	Port of Spain
1997	Antigua/St Kitts	Trinidad & Tobago	4-0	St Kitts and Nevis	St John's
1998	Jamaica/Trinidad	Jamaica	2-1	Trinidad & Tobago	Port of Spain
1999	Trinidad	Trinidad & Tobago	2-1	Cuba	Port of Spain
2001	Trinidad	Trinidad & Tobago	3-0	Haiti	Port of Spain
2005	Barbados	Jamaica	1-0†	Cuba	Waterford
2007	Trinidad	Haiti	2-1	Trinidad & Tobago	Port of Spain
2008	Jamaica	Jamaica	2-0	Grenada	Kingston
2010	Martinique	Jamaica	1-1 5-4p	Guadeloupe	Fort-de-France

† Final tournament played as a league. The match listed is between the top two.

UNCAF CUP/COPA CENTROAMERICANA

Year	Host Country	Winners	Score	Runners-up	Venue
1991	Costa Rica	Costa Rica	2-0†	Honduras	San José
1993	Honduras	Honduras	2-0†	Costa Rica	Tegucigalpa
1995	El Salvador	Honduras	3-0	Guatemala	San Salvador
1997	Guatemala	Costa Rica	1-1†	Guatemala	Mateo Flores, Guatemala City
1999	Costa Rica	Costa Rica	1-0†	Guatemala	San José
2001	Honduras	Guatemala	2-0†	Costa Rica	Tegucigalpa
2003	Panama	Costa Rica	1-1†	Guatemala	Rommel Fernández, Panama City
2005	Guatemala	Costa Rica	1-1 7-6p	Honduras	Mateo Flores, Guatemala City
2007	El Salvador	Costa Rica	1-1 4-1p	Panama	Cuscatlán, San Salvador
2009	Honduras	Panama	0-0 5-3p	Costa Rica	Tiburcio Andino, Tegucigalpa
2011	Panama	Honduras	2-1	Costa Rica	Rommel Fernández, Panama City

† Final tournament played as a league. The match listed is between the top two.

CENTRAL AMERICAN, NORTH AMERICAN AND CARIBBEAN CLUB TOURNAMENTS

CONCACAF CHAMPIONS LEAGUE

Year	Winners	Country	Score	Country	Runners-up
1962	Guadalajara	MEX	1-0 5-0	GUA	Comunicaciones
1963	Racing Club Haïtienne	HAI	W-O	MEX	Guadalajara
1964	Not completed				
1965	Not completed				
1966	Not held				

CONCACAF CHAMPIONS LEAGUE

Year	Winners	Country	Score	Country	Runners-up
1967	Alianza	SLV	1-2 3-0 5-3	ANT	Jong Colombia
1968	Toluca	MEX	W-O †		
1969	Cruz Azul	MEX	0-0 1-0	GUA	Comunicaciones
1970	Cruz Azul	MEX	W-O †		
1971	Cruz Azul	MEX	5-1	CRC	LD Alajuelense
1972	Olimpia	HON	0-0 2-0	SUR	Robinhood
1973	Transvaal	SUR	W-O †		
1974	Municipal	GUA	2-1 2-1	SUR	Transvaal
1975	Atletico Español	MEX	3-0 2-1	SUR	Transvaal
1976	Aguila	SLV	6-1 2-1	SUR	Robinhood
1977	América	MEX	1-0 0-0	SUR	Robinhood
1978	UAG Tecos	MEX	W-O †		
1979	Deportivo FAS	SLV	1-0 8-0	ANT	Jong Colombia
1980	UNAM Pumas	MEX	2-0 ‡	HON	Universidad de Honduras
1981	Transvaal	SUR	1-0 1-1	SLV	Atlético Marte
1982	UNAM Pumas	MEX	2-2 3-0	SUR	Robinhood
1983	Atlante	MEX	1-1 5-0	SUR	Robinhood
1984	Violette	HAI	W-O †		
1985	Defence Force	TRI	2-0 0-1	HON	Olimpia
1986	LD Alajuelense	CRC	4-1 1-1	SUR	Transvaal
1987	América	MEX	2-0 1-1	TRI	Defence Force
1988	Olimpia	HON	2-0 2-0	TRI	Defence Force
1989	UNAM Pumas	MEX	1-1 3-1	CUB	Piñar del Rio
1990	América	MEX	2-2 6-0	CUB	Piñar del Rio
1991	Puebla	MEX	3-1 1-1	TRI	Police FC
1992	América	MEX	1-0	CRC	LD Alajuelense
1993	Deportivo Saprissa	CRC	2-2 ‡	MEX	Leon
1994	Cartagines	CRC	3-2	MEX	Atlante
1995	Deportivo Saprissa	CRC	1-0 ‡	GUA	Municipal
1996	Cruz Azul	MEX	1-1 ‡	MEX	Necaxa
1997	Cruz Azul	MEX	5-3	USA	Los Angeles Galaxy
1998	DC United	USA	1-0	MEX	Toluca
1999	Necaxa	MEX	2-1	CRC	LD Alajuelense
2000	LA Galaxy	USA	3-2	HON	Olimpia
2001	Not completed				
2002	Pachuca	MEX	1-0	MEX	Monarcas Morelia
2003	Toluca	MEX	3-3 2-1	MEX	Monarcas Morelia
2004	LD Alajuelense	CRC	1-1 4-0	CRC	Deportivo Saprissa
2005	Deportivo Saprissa	CRC	2-0 1-2	MEX	UNAM Pumas
2006	América	MEX	0-0 2-1	MEX	Toluca
2007	Pachuca	MEX	2-2 0-0 7-6p	MEX	Guadalajara
2008	Pachuca	MEX	1-1 2-1	CRC	Deportivo Saprissa
2009	Atlante	MEX	2-0 0-0	MEX	Cruz Azul
2010	Pachuca	MEX	1-2 1-0	MEX	Cruz Azul
2011	Monterrey	MEX	2-2 1-0	MEX	Real Salt Lake

† 1968 Toluca were declared champions after Aurora GUA and Transvaal SUR were disqualified • 1970 Cruz Azul were declared champions after Deportivo Saprissa CRC and Transvaal SUR withdrew • 1973 Transvaal were declared champions after LD Alajuelense CRC and Deoprtivo Saprissa CRC withdrew • 1978 UAG Tecos were joint winners with Comunicaciones GUA and Defence Force TRI • 1984 Violette were declared champions after Guadalajara and New York Freedoms were disqualified • ‡ 1980 1993 1995 & 1996 finals played as a league with the match listed between the top two

CONCACAF CHAMPIONS LEAGUE MEDALS TABLE

	Country	G	S	B	F	SF
1	Mexico	27	12	15	39	54
2	Costa Rica	6	5	12	11	23
3	El Salvador	3	1	2	4	6
4	Surinam	2	8	3	10	13
5	Guatemala	2	3	7	5	12
6	Honduras	2	3	3	5	8
7	Trinidad and Tobago	2	3	2	5	7
8	USA	2	2	12	4	16
9	Haiti	2			2	2

CONCACAF CHAMPIONS LEAGUE MEDALS TABLE

	Country	G	S	B	F	SF
10	Netherlands Antilles		2	4	2	6
11	Cuba		2		2	2
12	Martinique			3		3
13	Bermuda			1		1
	Puerto Rico			1		1
		48	41	65	89	154

This table represents the Gold (winners), Silver (runners-up) and Bronze (semi-finalists) placings of clubs representing the above countries in the CONCACAF Champions' Cup, along with the number of appearances in the final and semi-finals.

CONCACAF CHAMPIONS LEAGUE MEDALS TABLE

	Club		G	S	B
1	Cruz Azul	MEX	5	2	1
2	América	MEX	5		1
3	Pachuca	MEX	4		1
4	Deportivo Saprissa	CRC	3	2	7
5	UNAM Pumas	MEX	3	1	1
6	LD Alajuelense	CRC	2	3	4
7	Transvaal	SUR	2	3	
8	Toluca	MEX	2	2	2
9	Olimpia	HON	2	2	1
10	Defence Force	TRI	2	2	
11	Atlante	MEX	2	1	
12	Comunicaciones	GUA	1	2	3
13	Guadalajara	MEX	1	2	1
14	Municipal	GUA	1	1	1
	Necaxa	MEX	1	1	1
16	Los Angeles Galaxy	USA	1	1	
17	DC United	USA	1		6
18	Monterrey	MEX	1		3
19	Alianza	SLV	1		2
20	Aguila	SLV	1		
	Atlético Español	MEX	1		
	CS Cartagines	CRC	1		
	Deportivo FAS	SLV	1		
	Puebla	MEX	1		
	Racing Club Haïtienne	HAI	1		
	UAG Tecos	MEX	1		
	Violette	HAI	1		
28	Robinhood	SUR		5	3

CONCACAF CHAMPIONS LEAGUE MEDALS TABLE

	Club		G	S	B
29	Jong Colombia	ANT		2	1
30	Piñar del Rio	CUB		2	
	Monarcas Morelia	MEX		2	
32	Leon	MEX		1	2
33	Atlético Marte	SLV		1	
	Police FC	TRI		1	
	Real Salt Lake	USA		1	
	Universidad de Honduras	HON		1	
37	Chicago Fire	USA			2
	Houston Dynamo	USA			2
	SUBT	ANT			2
	Trintoc	TRI			2
41	Aurora	GUA			1
	Herediano	CRC			1
	Kansas City Wizards	USA			1
	L'Aiglon	MTQ			1
	Marathon	HON			1
	Pembrooke	BER			1
	Philidelphia Ukrainians	USA			1
	Puerto Rico Islanders	PUR			1
	Real España	HON			1
	Riviere-Pilote	MTQ			1
	US Robert	MTQ			1
	Santos Laguna	MEX			1
	Sithoc	ANT			1
	Suchitepequez	GUA			1
	Tigres UANL	MEX			1
	Xelaju	GUA			1
			48	41	65

TORNEO INTERCLUBES DE UNCAF

Year	Winners	Country	Score	Country	Runners-up
1999	Olimpia	HON	2-0 ‡	CRC	LD Alajuelense
2000	Olimpia	HON	0-0 †	CRC	LD Alajuelense
2001	Municipal	GUA	1-1 †	CRC	Deportivo Saprissa
2002	LD Alajuelense	CRC	4-0 †	PAN	Arabe Unido
2003	Deportivo Saprissa	CRC	3-2	GUA	Comunicaciones
2004	Municipal	GUA	1-0 †	CRC	Deportivo Saprissa
2005	LD Alajuelense	CRC	1-0 0-1 4-2p	HON	Olimpia
2006	Puntarenas FC	CRC	3-2 0-1 3-1p	HON	Olimpia
2007	CD Motagua	HON	1-1 1-0	CRC	Deportivo Saprissa

CFU CLUB CHAMPIONS CUP

Year	Winners	Country	Score	Country	Runners-up
1997	United Petrotin	TRI	2-1	JAM	Seba United
1998	Joe Public	TRI	1-0	TRI	Caledonia AIA
2000	Joe Public	TRI	1-0 †	TRI	W Connection
2003	San Juan Jabloteh	TRI	2-1 1-2 4-2p	TRI	W Connection
2004	Harbour View	JAM	1-1 2-1	JAM	Tivoli Gardens
2005	Portmore United	JAM	1-2 4-0	SUR	Robinhood
2006	W Connection	TRI	1-0	TRI	San Juan Jabloteh
2007	Harbour View	JAM	2-1	TRI	Joe Public
2008	Not held				
2009	W Connection	TRI	2-1	PUR	Puerto Rico Islanders
2010	Puerto Rico Islanders	PUR	1-1 †	TRI	Joe Public
2011	Puerto Rico Islanders	PUR	3-1	HAI	Tempête FC

† Played on a league system. The match listed was between the top two

CENTRAL AMERICAN, NORTH AMERICAN AND CARIBBEAN YOUTH TOURNAMENTS

CONCACAF U-20 TOURNAMENT

Year	Host Country	Winners	Runners-up
1954	Costa Rica	Costa Rica	Panama
1956	El Salvador	El Salvador	Neth. Antilles
1958	Guatemala	Guatemala	Honduras
1960	Honduras	Costa Rica	Honduras
1962	Panama	Mexico	Guatemala
1964	Guatemala	El Salvador	
1970	Cuba	Mexico	Cuba
1973	Mexico	Mexico	Guatemala
1974	Canada	Mexico	Cuba
1976	Puerto Rico	Mexico	Honduras
1978	Honduras	Mexico	Canada

CONCACAF U-20 TOURNAMENT (CONT'D)

Year	Host Country	Winners	Runners-up
1980	USA	Mexico	USA
1982	Guatemala	Honduras	USA
1984	Trinidad	Mexico	Canada
1986	Trinidad	Canada	USA
1988	Guatemala	Costa Rica	Mexico
1990	Guatemala	Mexico	Trinidad
1992	Canada	Mexico	USA
1994	Honduras	Honduras	Costa Rica
1996	Mexico	Canada	Mexico
2009	Trinidad & T	Costa Rica	USA
2011	Guatemala	Mexico	Costa Rica

CONCACAF U-17 TOURNAMENT

Year	Host Country	Winners	Runners-up
1983	Trinidad	USA	Trinidad
1985	Mexico	Mexico	Costa Rica
1987	Honduras	Mexico	USA
1988	Trinidad	Cuba	USA

CONCACAF U-17 TOURNAMENT (CONT'D)

Year	Host Country	Winners	Runners-up
1991	Trinidad	Mexico	USA
1992	Cuba	USA	Mexico
1994	El Salvador	Costa Rica	USA
1996	Trinidad	Mexico	USA
2011	Jamaica	USA	Canada

CENTRAL AMERICAN, NORTH AMERICAN AND CARIBBEAN WOMEN'S TOURNAMENTS

CONCACAF WOMEN'S GOLD CUP

Year	Host Country	Winners	Score	Runners-up	Venue
1991	Haiti	USA	5-0	Canada	Port au Prince
1993	USA	USA	1-0	Canada	Long Island
1994	Canada	USA	6-0	Canada	Montreal
1998	Canada	Canada	1-0	Mexico	Toronto
2000	USA	USA	1-0	Brazil	Foxboro, Boston
2002	USA/Canada	USA	2-1	Canada	Rose Bowl, Pasadena
2006	USA	USA	2-1	Canada	Home Depot Center, Los Angeles
2010	Mexico	Canada	1-0	Mexico	Quintana Roo, Cancun

NATIONAL TEAM TOURNAMENTS 2011

COPA CENTROAMERICANA PANAMA 2011

First Round Group Stage

Group A	Pl	W	D	L	F	A	Pts	SLV	NCA	BLZ
Panama	3	3	0	0	6	0	**9**	2-0	2-0	2-0
El Salvador	3	2	0	1	7	4	**6**		2-0	5-2
Nicaragua	3	0	1	2	1	5	1			1-1
Belize	3	0	1	2	3	8	1			

Group B	Pl	W	D	L	F	A	Pts	CRC	GUA
Honduras	2	1	1	0	4	2	**4**	1-1	3-1
Costa Rica	2	1	1	0	3	1	**4**		2-0
Guatemala	2	0	0	2	1	5	0		

Held in Panama City from 14-01-2011 to 23-01-2011
The top five qualified for the CONCACAF Gold Cup 2011

Semi-finals

Honduras	2
El Salvador	0

Panama	1 2p
Costa Rica	1 4p

Final

Honduras	2
Costa Rica	1

Fifth place play-off

Guatemala	2
Nicaragua	1

Third place play-off

Panama	0 5p
El Salvador	0 4p

Top scorers: **3** - Rafael Burgos SLV & Marco Urena CRC • **2** - Jaime Alas SLV; Armando Cooper PAN; Jorge Claros HON; Ramon Nunez HON & Edwin Aguilar PAN

GROUP A

		Pl	W	D	L	F	A	Pts	SLV	NCA	BLZ
Panama	PAN	3	3	0	0	6	0	**9**	2-0	2-0	2-0
El Salvador	SLV	3	2	0	1	7	4	**6**		2-0	5-2
Nicaragua	NCA	3	0	1	2	1	5	1			1-1
Belize	BLZ	3	0	1	2	3	8	1			

Rommel Fernandez, Panama City
14-01-2011, 17:00, 2000, Quesada CRC
El Salvador 2
Alas.J [71], Burgos [76]
Dagoberto **Portillo** - Xavier **Garcia**•, Marvin **Gonzalez**(c), Victor **Turcios**•, Osael **Romero**, Rafael **Burgos**, Arturo **Alvarez**•, Jaime **Alas** (Dennis **Alas** 76), Reynaldo **Hernandez** (Deris **Umanzor** 41), Andres **Flores** (Edwin **Sanchez**• 58), Luis **Anaya**. Tr: Jose Luis **Rugamas**
Nicaragua 0

Denis **Espinoza**• - Jose **Quijano** (Erick **Tellez** 73), Feliz **Rodriguez**, Norman **Eugarrios**•, Juan **Barrera**, Axel **Villanueva** (Elvis **Figueroa** 46), Milton **Busto**, Samuel **Wilson** (Wilber **Sanchez** 79), Felix **Zeledon**•, Rudel **Calero**, David **Solorzano**(c)•. Tr: Enrique **Llena**

Rommel Fernandez, Panama City
14-01-2011, 21:00, 10 000, Pineda HON
Panama 2
Aguilar [21], Brown [28]
Jaime **Penedo** - Jean Carlos **Cedeno**, Roman **Torres**(c), Gabriel **Gomez** (Amilcar **Henriquez** 62), Edwin **Aguilar** (Marcos **Sanchez** 83), Ricardo **Buitrago**, Roberto **Brown** (Luis **Renteria** 70), Adolfo **Machado**, Eric **Davis**, Armando **Cooper**, Eybir **Bonaga**. Tr: Julio Cesar **Dely Valdes**
Belize 0

Shane **Orio**(c) - Ryan **Simpson** (Ian **Gaynair**• 46), Dalton **Eiley**, Elroy **Kulen**, Elroy **Smith**, Deon **McCaulay**•, Orlando **Jimenez**• (Deris **Benavidez** 72), Evral **Trapp**, Victor **Morales**, Karieem **Haylock** (Luis **Mendez** 86), Daniel **Jimenez**. Tr: Jose **De la Paz**

Rommel Fernandez, Panama City
16-01-2011, 15:00, 1500, Cerdas CRC
Belize 2
Smith [45], Jimenez.O [76]
Shane **Orio**(c) - Ryan **Simpson** (Orlando **Jimenez** 46), Dalton **Eiley**, Elroy **Kulen**, Ian **Gaynair**•, Elroy **Smith**, Deon **McCaulay**, Evral **Trapp** (Deris **Benavidez** 83), Victor **Morales**, Karieem **Haylock** (Luis **Mendez** 59), Daniel **Jimenez**. Tr: Jose **De la Paz**
El Salvador 5
Romero [15], Burgos 2 [25 46], Alas.J [54], Umanzor [59]
Dagoberto **Portillo** - Xavier **Garcia**, Marvin **Gonzalez**(c), Victor **Turcios**, Gilberto **Baires**, Osael **Romero** (Edwin **Sanchez** 71), Rafael **Burgos**, Jose **Alvarez** (Andres **Flores** 57), Deris **Umanzor**, Jaime **Alas** (Herbert **Sosa** 63), Luis **Anaya**. Tr: Jose Luis **Rugamas**

Rommel Fernandez, Panama City
16-01-2011, 19:00, 7747, Lopez GUA
Panama 2
Cooper [16], Renetria [80]
Jaime **Penedo**• - Jean Carlos **Cedeno**, Roman **Torres**(c), Ricardo **Buitrago**, Roberto **Brown** (Marcos **Sanchez** 83), Adolfo **Machado**, Eric **Davis** (Harold **Cummings** 75), Luis **Renteria**, Armando **Cooper**, Amilcar **Henriquez**, Eybir **Bonaga** (Gabriel **Torres** 68). Tr: Julio Cesar **Dely Valdes**
Nicaragua 0

Denis **Espinoza** - Jose **Quijano**, Erick **Tellez**, Feliz **Rodriguez** (Axel **Villanueva** 61), Norman **Eugarrios**, Juan **Barrera**, Samuel **Wilson**• (Mcpherson **Garth** 82), Felix **Zeledon** (Wilber **Sanchez** 74), Rudel **Calero**, Raul **Leguias**, David **Solorzano**(c). Tr: Enrique **Llena**

Rommel Fernandez, Panama City
18-01-2011, 17:00, 10 000, Brea CUB
Nicaragua 1
Espinoza [10p]
Denis **Espinoza** - Jose **Quijano**, Elvis **Figueroa**, Manuel **Gutierrez**• (Felix **Zeledon** 62), Norman **Eugarrios**, Juan Ramon **Barrera** (Wilber **Sanchez** 56), Milton **Busto**, Samuel **Wilson** ♦ 10, Rudel **Caloro**, Raul **Leguias** (Felix **Rodriguez**• 77), David **Solorzano**(c). Tr: Enrique **Llena**
Belize 1
Jimenez.D [81]
Woodrow **West** - Luis **Mendez**, Ryan **Simpson** (Amin **August** 63), Dalton **Eiley**•, Elroy **Kulen**, Elroy **Smith**(c), Deon **McCaulay**, Victor **Morales**, Karieem **Haylock**• (Orlando **Jimenez** 46), Lisbey **Castillo** (Daniel **Jimenez** 46), Deris **Benavidez**. Tr: Jose **De la Paz**

Rommel Fernandez, Panama City
18-01-2011, 21:00, 10 000, Orozco MEX
Panama 2
Aguilar [24], Cooper [78]
Kevin **Melgar** - Harold **Cummings**, Jean Carlos **Cedeno**, Roman **Torres**(c) (Felipe **Baloy** 75), Gabriel **Gomez**, Gabriel **Torres**, Edwin **Aguilar**• (Blas **Perez** 68), Adolfo **Machado** Aramis **Haywood**, Luis **Renteria**, Marcos **Sanchez** (Armando **Cooper** 77). Tr: Julio Cesar **Dely Valdes**
El Salvador 0

Dagoberto **Portillo** - Xavier **Garcia**•, Marvin **Gonzalez**(c), Jose **Henriquez**, Victor **Turcios** (Rafael **Burgos** 75), Osael **Romero** (Gilberto **Baires** 85), Jose **Alvarez** (Andres **Flores** 77), Deris **Umanzor**, Dennis **Alas**, Jaime **Alas**, Mark **Blanco**. Tr: Jose Luis **Rugamas**

GROUP B

		Pl	W	D	L	F	A	Pts		NCA	BLZ
Honduras	HON	2	1	1	0	4	2	4		1-1	3-1
Costa Rica	CRC	2	1	1	0	3	1	4			2-0
Guatemala	GUA	2	0	0	2	1	5	0			

Rommel Fernandez, Panama City
14-01-2011, 19:00, 6000, Orozco MEX

Costa Rica 1
Nunez.V 42

Christian **Gomboa** - Dario **Delgado**, Dave **Myrie**, Celso **Borges**(c), David **Guzman**• (Allen Guevara 46), Randall **Brenes** (Jose Miguel **Cubero** 66), Cesar **Quesada** (Marcos **Urena** 77), Roy **Miller**•, Dennis **Marshall**•, Victor **Nunez**•, Donny **Grant**. Tr: Ricardo **Lavolpe**

Honduras 1
Nunez.R 91+

Noel **Valladares**(c) - Jhony **Palacios**, Johnny **Leveron**, Emil **Martinez**•, Jorge **Claros**, Luis **Ramirez** (Georgie **Welcome** 54), Alfredo **Mejia**, Oscar **Garcia** (Marvin **Chavez** 74), Walter **Martinez** (Ramon **Nunez** 60), Mauricio **Sabillon**, Juan Carlos **Garcia**. Tr: Juan De Dios **Castillo**

Rommel Fernandez, Panama City
16-01-2011, 17:00, 1500, Moreno PAN

Guatemala 0

Luis **Molina** - Cristian **Noriega**•, Yoni **Flores** (Gregory **Ruiz** 57), Carlos **Gallardo**•, Gustavo **Cabrera**, Wilfred **Velazquez**, Guillermo **Ramirez**(c), Fredy **Aguilar** (Transito **Montepeque**• 71), Manuel **Leon** (Carlos **Figueroa** 46), Jaime **Vides**•, Carlos **Ruiz**•. Tr: Ever **Almeida**

Costa Rica 2
Urena 2 48 81

Donny **Grant** - Christian **Gomboa** (Heiner **Mora** 46), Dario **Delgado**, Dave **Myrie**•, Celso **Borges**(c), Marcos **Urena**, Randall **Brenes**, Pedro **Leal** (Jose Miguel **Cubero** 65), Roy **Miller**, Dennis **Marshall**, Victor **Nunez** (Allen Guevara 70). Tr: Ricardo **Lavolpe**

Rommel Fernandez, Panama City
18-01-2011, 19:00, 10 000, Aguilar SLV

Honduras 3
Nunez.R 13, Claros 2 42 88

Noel **Valladares**(c) - Erick **Norales**• (Osman **Chavez** 59), Johnny **Leveron**, Emil **Martinez** (Alexander **Lopez** 82), Jorge **Claros**•, Georgie **Welcome**, Ramon **Nunez**, Alfredo **Mejia**•, Mauricio **Sabillon**, Mario **Martinez** (Marvin **Chavez**• 59), Juan Carlos **Garcia**•. Tr: Juan De Dios **Castillo**

Guatemala 1
Ramirez 24

Luis **Molina** - Cristian **Noriega**, Yoni **Flores**, Carlos **Gallardo**•, Gustavo **Cabrera**•, Wilfred **Velazquez**, Guillermo **Ramirez**(c), Carlos **Figueroa**, Manuel **Leon** (Gregory **Ruiz** 46) (Marco Tulio **Ciani** 70), Jaime **Vides** (Mario **Castellanos** 46), Carlos **Ruiz**. Tr: Ever **Almeida**

5TH PLACE MATCH AND SEMI-FINALS

5/p. Rommel Fernandez, Panama City
21-01-2011, 16:00, 5000, Orozco MEX

Nicaragua 1
Rodriguez 23

Denis **Espinoza** - Jose **Quijano**, Erick **Tellez**, Felix **Zeledon** (Milton **Busto** 75), Norman **Eugarrios**, Juan **Barrera**•, Noriran **Lazo** (Axel **Villanueva** 75), Felix **Rodriguez** (Elvis **Figueroa** 58), Rudel **Calero**, Raul **Leguias**, David **Solorzano**(c). Tr: Enrique **Llena**

Guatemala 2
Ruiz 45, Leon 66

Juan **Paredes** - Cristian **Noriega**, Yoni **Flores**, Gustavo **Cabrera**, Marco Tulio **Ciani** (Gregory **Ruiz** 24) (Edwin **Gonzalez**• 61), Wilfred **Velazquez**, Transito **Montepeque**•, Guillermo **Ramirez**(c) (Riqui **Murga** 61), Carlos **Figueroa**, Manuel **Leon**, Carlos **Ruiz**. Tr: Ever **Almeida**

S/F. Rommel Fernandez, Panama City
21-01-2011, 18:30, 5000, Quesada CRC

Honduras 2
Leveron 78, Chavez 93+

Noel **Valladares**(c) - Osman **Chavez**•, Johnny **Leveron**, Emil **Martinez** (Marvin **Chavez** 62), Jorge **Claros**, Luis **Ramirez**• (Walter **Martinez** 55), Alfredo **Mejia**•, Oscar **Garcia**, Mauricio **Sabillon**, Juan Carlos **Garcia**, Alexander **Lopez** (Mario **Martinez** 72). Tr: Juan De Dios **Castillo**

El Salvador 0

Dagoberto **Portillo** - Marvin **Gonzalez**(c), Victor **Turcios**•, Milton **Molina**, Osael **Romero**, Rafael **Burgos** (Mark **Blanco** 75), Jose **Alvarez** (Andres **Flores** 58), Deris **Umanzor**, Dennis **Alas** (Gilberto **Baires**• 72), Jaime **Alas**, Luis **Anaya**•. Tr: Jose Luis **Rugamas**

S/F. Rommel Fernandez, Panama City
21-01-2011, 21:00, 10 000, Aguilar SLV

Panama 1 2p
Perez 76

Jaime **Penedo** - Jean Carlos **Cedeno**, Roman **Torres**, Gabriel **Gomez**, Blas **Perez**•, Adolfo **Machado**, Eric **Davis** (Gabriel **Torres** 69), Luis **Renteria** (Edwin **Aguilar** 82), Armando **Cooper**, Amilcar **Henriquez**, Felipe **Baloy**(c). Tr: Julio Cesar **Dely Valdes**

Costa Rica 1 4p
Borges 67

Donny **Grant** - Dario **Delgado**, Dave **Myrie**• (Heiner **Mora** 59), Celso **Borges**(c)•, Marcos **Urena**, Randall **Brenes** (Allen **Guevara** 65), Cesar **Quesada**• (Christian **Gomboa** 80), Jose Miguel **Cubero**, Roy **Miller**, Dennis **Marshall**, Victor **Nunez**. Tr: Ricardo **Lavolpe**

PENALTY SHOOT-OUT
PANAMA V COSTA RICA
SEMI-FINAL
COSTA RICA WON 4-2

Perez	✗ ✓	Borges
Torres.G	✓ ✗	Nunez
Gomez	✓ ✓	Urena
Baloy	✗ ✓	Marshall
	✓	Miller

PENALTY SHOOT-OUT
EL SALVADOR V PANAMA
3RD PLACE PLAY-OFF
PANAMA WON 5-4

Alvarez	✗ ✓	Brown
Alas.J	✓ ✓	Torres.G
Blanco	✓ ✓	Davis
Portillo	✓ ✓	Bonaga
Alas.D	✓ ✓	Henriquez

THIRD PLACE MATCH AND FINAL

3/p. Rommel Fernandez, Panama City
23-01-2011, 15:30, 2000, Pineda HON

Panama 0 5p

Jaime **Penedo** - Harold **Cummings**, Roman **Torres**, Gabriel **Gomez** (Eybir **Bonaga** 66), Blas **Perez** (Luis **Renteria**• 83), Gabriel **Torres**, Roberto **Brown**, Adolfo **Machado** (Eric **Davis** 23), Armando **Cooper**, Amilcar **Henriquez**•, Felipe **Baloy**(c). Tr: Julio Cesar **Dely Valdes**

El Salvador 0 4p

Dagoberto **Portillo** - Xavier **Garcia**•, Marvin **Gonzalez**(c)•, Victor **Turcios**, Osael **Romero**• (Gilberto **Baires** 58), Rafael **Burgos** (Mark **Blanco**• 90), Deris **Umanzor**, Dennis **Alas**, Jaime **Alas**, Andres **Flores** (Jose **Alvarez** 71), Luis **Anaya**. Tr: Jose Luis **Rugamas**

Final. R'mel Fernandez, Panama City
23-01-2011, 18:00, 2000, Lopez GUA

Honduras 2
Martinez.W 8, Martinez.E 52

Noel **Valladares**(c) - Osman **Chavez**, Johnny **Leveron**•, Emil **Martinez**• (Marvin **Chavez**), Jorge **Claros**, Ramon **Nunez** (Mariano **Acevedo** 46), Alfredo **Mejia**, Walter **Martinez**, Mauricio **Sabillon**• (Jhony **Palacios**• 78), Juan Carlos **Garcia**, Mario **Martinez**. Tr: Juan De Dios **Castillo**

Costa Rica 1
Urena 73

Donny **Grant** - Dario **Delgado**•◆62, Dave **Myrie**, Celso **Borges**(c), Heiner **Mora**, Marcos **Urena**•, Jose Miguel **Cubero** (Randall **Brenes** 54), Josue **Martinez** (Christian **Gomboa** 66), Roy **Miller**, Dennis **Marshall**, Allen **Guevara** (Cesar **Quesada** 46). Tr: Ricardo **Lavolpe**

CONCACAF GOLD CUP USA 2011

First round groups		Quarter-finals		Semi-finals		Final	
Group A	Pts						
Mexico	9						
Costa Rica	4	**Mexico**	2				
El Salvador	4	Guatemala	1				
Cuba	0			**Mexico**	2		
				Honduras	0		
		Costa Rica	1 2p				
Group B	Pts	**Honduras**	1 4p				
Jamaica	9						
Honduras	4					**Mexico**	4
Guatemala	4					USA	2
Grenada	0						
		Panama	1 3p				
		El Salvador	1 5p				
Group C	Pts			Panama	0		
Panama	7			**USA**	1		
USA	6	Jamaica	0				
Canada	4	**USA**	2				
Guadeloupe	0						

Top scorers: **7** - Javier Hernandez MEX • **4** - Rodolfo Zelaya SLV & Aldo de Nigris MEX • **3** - Marco Urena CRC; Jerry Bengtson HON; Carlo Costly HON; Demar Phillips JAM; Pablo Barrera MEX; Giovani dos Santos MEX; Andres Guardado MEX; Luis Tejada PAN & Clint Dempsey USA

	GROUP A	PL	W	D	L	F	A	PTS	CRC	SLV	CUB
1	Mexico	3	3	0	0	14	1	9	4-1	5-0	5-0
2	Costa Rica	3	1	1	1	7	5	4		1-1	5-0
3	El Salvador	3	1	1	1	7	7	4			6-1
4	Cuba	3	0	0	3	1	16	0			

Cowboys Stadium, Dallas, 5-06-2011, 18:00, 80108, Moreno PAN

Costa Rica   **5**

Urena 2 6 46, Saborio 41, Mora 47, Bolanos 71

Keylor **Navas** - Jose **Salvatierra**, Jhonny **Acosta**, Dennis **Marshall** - Heiner **Mora**, Christian **Bolanos** (Josue **Martinez** 68), Bryan **Oviedo**, Junior **Diaz** - Marco **Urena**• (Joel **Campbell** 56), Celso **Borges**(c), Alvaro **Saborio** (Randall **Brenes** 68). Tr: Ricardo **Lavolpe**

Cuba   **0**

Odelin **Molina** - Alianni **Urgelles**, Reisandry **Fernandez**, Jeniel **Marquez**, Yoel **Colome** - Carlos **Francisco**, Jaime **Colome**(c) - Alberto **Gomez** (Dagoberto **Quesada** 74), Marcel **Hernandez** (Yosniel **Mesa** 78), Alain **Cervantes** - Yaudel **Lahera** (Roberto **Linares** 60). Tr: Raul **Gonzalez**

Cowboys Stadium, Dallas, 5-06-2011, 20:00, 80108, Wijngaarde SUR

Mexico   **5**

Juarez 55, De Nigris 58, Hernandez.J 3 60 67 95+p

Guillermo **Ochoa** - Efrain **Juarez**, Francisco **Rodriguez**•, Hector **Moreno**, Carlos **Salcido** - Pablo **Barrera**, Israel **Castro** (Aldo **De Nigris** 5G), Gerardo **Torrado**(c), Andres **Guardado** (Angel Eduardo **Reyna** 74) - Giovani **Dos Santos** (Rafael **Marquez** 69), Javier **Hernandez**•. Tr: Jose Manuel **De la Torre**

El Salvador   **0**

Miguel **Montes** - Xavier **Garcia**, Luis **Anaya**, Marvin **Gonzalez**(c)♦93+, Reynaldo **Hernandez** - Dennis **Alas**•, Victor **Turcios** (Gilberto **Baires** 60) - Andres **Flores** (Shawn **Martin** 67), Eliseo **Quintanilla**, Jaime **Alas** - Rodolfo **Zelaya** (Rudis **Corrales** 79). Tr: Ruben **Israel**

Bank of America, Charlotte, 9-06-2011, 19:00, 46012, Marrufo USA

Costa Rica   **1**
Brenes [95+]

Keylor **Navas** - Jose **Salvatierra**•, Jhonny **Acosta**•, Dennis **Marshall**, Junior **Diaz** - Heiner **Mora** (Randall **Brenes** 79), Allen **Guevara**, Celso **Borges**(c)•, Christian **Bolanos** (Joel **Campbell** 61) - Marco **Urena** (Bryan **Ruiz** 46), Alvaro **Saborio**. Tr: Ricardo **Lavolpe**

El Salvador   **1**
Zelaya [45]

Miguel **Montes**• - Xavier **Garcia**, Victor **Turcios**•, Luis **Anaya**(c)•, Reynaldo **Hernandez** - Andres **Flores** (Shawn Martin 71), Dennis **Alas**, Jaime **Alas** - Rudis **Corrales** (Eliseo **Quintanilla** 61) - Gilberto **Baires**• (Ramon **Sanchez** 46), Rodolfo **Zelaya**•. Tr: Ruben **Israel**

Bank of America, Charlotte, 9-06-2011, 21:00, 46012, Campbell JAM

Cuba   **0**

Odelin **Molina** - Reisandry **Fernandez**, Hanier **Dranguet**, Jeniel **Marquez**, Yoel **Colome** (Dagoberto **Quesada** 73) - Alberto **Gomez**, Carlos **Francisco**, Jaime **Colome**(c), Alain **Cervantes** (Alianni **Urgelles** 10) - Roberto **Linares** (Yaudel **Lahera** 70), Marcel **Hernandez**. Tr: Raul **Gonzalez**

Mexico   **5**
Hernandez.J 2 [36 76], Dos Santos 2 [63 68], De Nigris [65]

Alfredo **Talavera** - Efrain **Juarez**, Rafael **Marquez**(c) (Jorge **Torres Nilo** 71), Hector **Moreno**, Carlos **Salcido** - Gerardo **Torrado** - Pablo **Barrera** (Aldo **De Nigris** 63), Angel **Reyna**, Andres **Guardado** (Elias **Hernandez** 68) - Giovani **Dos Santos**, Javier **Hernandez**. Tr: Jose Manuel **De la Torre**

Soldier Field, Chicago, 12-06-2011, 18:00, 62000, Brizan TRI

El Salvador   **6**
Zelaya 2 [13 71], Romero [29], Blanco [69], Alvarez [84], Quintanilla [94+]

Miguel **Montes** - Xavier **Garcia**•, Victor **Turcios**, Luis **Anaya**(c), Reynaldo **Hernandez** (Eliseo **Quintanilla** 72) - Andres **Flores** (Arturo **Alvarez** 63), William **Romero**, Dennis **Alas**, Jaime **Alas** - Rudis **Corrales** (Mark **Blanco** 68), Rodolfo **Zelaya**. Tr: Ruben **Israel**

Cuba   **1**
Marquez [83]

Julio **Pichardo** - Alianni **Urgelles**•, Hanier **Dranguet**, Jeniel **Marquez**, Reisandry **Fernandez**• - Carlos **Francisco**, Jaime **Colome**(c) (Francisco **Carrazana** 52) - Alberto **Gomez**, Marcel **Hernandez**, Yoel **Colome** (Dagoberto **Quesada** 75) - Roberto **Linares** (Yaudel **Lahera** 62). Tr: Raul **Gonzalez**

Soldier Field, Chicago, 12-06-2011, 20:00, 62000, Moreno PAN

Mexico   **4**
Marquez [16], Guardado 2 [19 25], Barrera [38]

Alfredo **Talavera** - Efrain **Juarez**•, Rafael **Marquez**(c) (Jorge **Torres Nilo** 70), Hector **Moreno**, Carlos **Salcido** - Pablo **Barrera** (Angel **Reyna** 61), Israel **Castro**, Gerardo **Torrado**, Andres **Guardado**• - Giovani **Dos Santos**, Javier **Hernandez** (Aldo **De Nigris** 84). Tr: Jose Manuel **De la Torre**

Costa Rica   **1**
Urena [69]

Keylor **Navas** - Heiner **Mora** (Oscar **Duarte** 46), Jose **Salvatierra**, Jhonny **Acosta**, Dennis **Marshall**, Junior **Diaz** (Diego **Madrigal** 83) - Allen **Guevara** (Marco **Urena** 46), Celso **Borges**, Christian **Bolanos**• - Bryan **Ruiz**(c), Alvaro **Saborio**. Tr: Ricardo **Lavolpe**

	GROUP B	PL	W	D	L	F	A	PTS		HON	GUA	GRN
1	Jamaica	3	3	0	0	7	0	9		1-0	2-0	4-0
2	Honduras	3	1	1	1	7	2	4			0-0	7-1
3	Guatemala	3	1	1	1	4	2	4				4-0
4	Grenada	3	0	0	3	1	15	0				

Home Depot Center, Carson, 6-06-2011, 21:00, 21550, Toledo USA

Jamaica   **4**
Shelton [21], Johnson [39], Phillips [79], Daley.O [84]

Donovan **Ricketts** - Eric **Vernan**, Dicoy **Williams**•, Shavar **Thomas**(c), Jermaine **Taylor** - Rodolph **Austin** (Keammar **Daley** 69), Jason **Morrison**, Demar **Phillips** - Dane **Richards** (Omar **Daley** 65), Ryan **Johnson**, Luton **Shelton** (Jevaughn **Watson** 79). Tr: Theodore **Whitmore**

Grenada   **0**

Shemel **Louison** - Shane **Rennie** (Bradley **Bubb** 62), Anthony **Modeste**(c), Leon **Johnson**, David **Cyrus**• - Marc **Marshall**, Patrick **Modeste** (Shannon **Phillip** 88) - Ricky **Charles**, Craig **Rocastle** (Lancaster **Joseph** 46), Anthony **Straker** - Delroy **Facey**. Tr: Michael **Adams**

Home Depot Center, Carson, 6-06-2011, 23:00, 21550, Chacon MEX

Honduras   **0**

Noel **Valladares**(c) - Mauricio **Sabillon**, Osman **Chavez** (Johnny **Leveron** 86), Victor **Bernardez**, Brayan **Beckeles** - Oscar **Garcia**, Hendry **Thomas** (Walter **Martinez** 70), Edder **Delgado**, Emil **Martinez** - Jerry **Bengston** (Ramon **Nunez** 70), Carlo **Costly**•. Tr: Luis Fernando **Suarez**

Guatemala   **0**

Ricardo **Jerez** - Carlos **Castrillo** (Henry **Medina** 71••♦79), Cristian **Noriega**, Gustavo **Cabrera**••♦61, Carlos **Gallardo** - Henry David **Lopez** (Jairo **Arreola** 46), Wilfred **Velasquez**, Jose Manuel **Contreras**, Marco **Pappa** (Carlos **Figueroa** 87) - Carlos **Ruiz**(c), Jonathan **Lopez**. Tr: Ever **Almeida**

FIU, Miami, 10-06-2011, 19:00, 18057, Quesada CRC

Jamaica   **2**
Phillips 2 [65 77]

Donovan **Ricketts** - Eric **Vernan**, Dicoy **Williams** (Adrian **Reid** 10), Shavar **Thomas**(c)•, Jermaine **Taylor**• - Rodolph **Austin**• (Damian **Williams** 84), Jason **Morrison**, Demar **Phillips** - Dane **Richards**, Ryan **Johnson** (Keammar **Daley** 63), Luton **Shelton**. Tr: Theodore **Whitmore**

Guatemala   **0**

Ricardo **Jerez** - Elias **Vasquez**, Cristian **Noriega**••♦70, Carlos **Gallardo**, Edwin **Gonzalez** (Marco **Pappa** 46) - Jonathan **Lopez**, Manuel **Leon** (Carlos **Figueroa** 46) (Carlos **Castrillo** 53), Wilfred **Velasquez**, Jose Manuel **Contreras**• - Oscar **Isaula**, Carlos **Ruiz**(c). Tr: Ever **Almeida**

FIU, Miami, 10-06-2011, 21:00, 18057, Gantar CAN

Grenada   **1**
Murray [19]

Shemel **Louison** - Casim **Langaigne**, Shannon **Phillip**, Leon **Johnson**, Anthony **Straker** - Lancaster **Joseph** (Marcus **Julien** 77), Ricky **Charles** (Dwayne **Leo** 46), Anthony **Modeste**(c) (Shane **Rennie** 61), Junior **Williams** - Delroy **Facey**, Clive **Murray**. Tr: Michael **Adams**

Honduras   **7**
Bengtson 2 [26 37], Costly 3 [28 67 71], Martinez.W [88], Mejia [93+]

Noel **Valladares**(c) - Mauricio **Sabillon**, Osman **Chavez**, Victor **Bernardez**, Juan Carlos **Garcia** - Oscar **Garcia**, Hendry **Thomas** (Walter **Martinez** 46), Edder **Delgado**, Emil **Martinez** (Ramon **Nunez** 64) - Jerry **Bengston** (Alfredo **Mejia**• 73), Carlo **Costly**. Tr: Luis Fernando **Suarez**

Red Bull Arena, New York, 13-06-2011, 19:00, 25 000, Toledo USA
Guatemala 4
Del Aguila 16, Pappa 22, Ruiz 54, Gallardo 59

Ricardo **Jerez** - Jonathan **Lopez**, Henry **Medina**, Gustavo **Cabrera**, Carlos **Gallardo** - Wilfred **Velasquez**, Jose Javier **Del Aguila**, Gonzalo **Romero** (Dwight **Pezzarossi** 84), Marco **Pappa** (Manuel **Leon** 88) - Carlos **Ruiz**(c), Henry David **Lopez** (Jairo **Arreola** 46). Tr: Ever **Almeida**

Grenada 0

Shemel **Louison** - Marc **Marshall** (Shannon **Phillip** 65), Anthony **Modeste**(c)•, Leon **Johnson**, Anthony **Straker** - Moron **Phillip**, Ricky **Charles**, Delroy **Facey** (Marcus **Julien** 82), Junior **Williams**• (David **Cyrus** 46) - Clive **Murray**, Bradley **Bubb**. Tr: Michael **Adams**

Red Bull Arena, New York, 13-06-2011, 21:00, 25 000, Aguilar SLV
Honduras 0

Noel **Valladares**(c) - Mauricio **Sabillon**, Osman **Chavez**•, Victor **Bernardez**, Juan Carlos **Garcia** - Oscar **Garcia**, Alfredo **Mejia**•, Edder **Delgado** (Javier **Portillo** 75) - Emil **Martinez** (Walter **Martinez** 46). Jerry **Bengston**, Carlo **Costly** (Ramon **Nunez** 25). Tr: Luis Fernando **Suarez**

Jamaica 1
Johnson 35

Dwayne **Miller** - Omar **Daley** (Eric **Vernan** 84), Adrian **Reid**, Jason **Morrison**, Jermaine **Taylor**(c) - Jevaughn **Watson**• (Navion **Boyd**• 88), Damian **Williams**, Keammar **Daley**•, Demar **Phillips**• - Ryan **Johnson** (Luton **Shelton** 82), Dane **Richards**. Tr: Theodore **Whitmore**

GROUP C	PL	W	D	L	F	A	PTS	USA	CAN	GLP
1 Panama	3	2	1	0	6	4	7	2-1	1-1	3-2
2 USA	3	2	0	1	4	2	6		2-0	1-0
3 Canada	3	1	1	1	2	3	4			1-0
4 Guadeloupe	3	0	0	3	2	5	0			

Ford Field, Detroit, 7-06-2011, 18:00, 28 209, Mejia SLV
Panama 3
Perez 29, Tejada 31, Gomez 57p

Jaime **Penedo** - Adolfo **Machado** (Harold **Cummings** 81), Eduadro Cesar **Dasent**, Felipe **Baloy**(c), Luis **Henriquez** - Armando **Cooper**, Amilcar **Henriquez**, Gabriel **Gomez**, Nelson **Barahona** (Alberto **Quintero** 76) - Blas **Perez**, Luis **Tejada** (Luis **Renteria** 61). Tr: Julio Cesar **Dely Valdes**

Guadeloupe 2
Jovial 2 64 78

Franck **Grandel**• - Michael **Tacalfred**♦37, Eddy **Viator**, Jean-Luc **Lambourde**, Miguel **Comminges** - David **Fleurival**, Stephane **Auvary**(c)• - Loic **Loval**, Gregory **Gendrey** (Brice **Jovial** 46), Cedric **Collet** (Thomas **Gamiette** 57) - Richard **Socrier**•. Tr: Roger **Salnot**

Ford Field, Detroit, 7-06-2011, 20:00, 28 209, Lopez GUA
USA 2
Altidore 15, Dempsey 62

Tim **Howard** - Steve **Cherundolo**, Clarence **Goodson**, Tim **Ream**, Carlos **Bocanegra**(c) - Landon **Donovan**, Michael **Bradley**•, Jermaine **Jones** (Maurice **Edu** 79), Clint **Dempsey** - Juan **Agudelo** (Chris **Wondolowski** 65), Jozy **Altidore** (Sacha **Kljestan** 74). Tr: Bob **Bradley**

Canada 0

Lars **Hirschfeld** - Nikolas **Ledgerwood**, Kevin **McKenna**(c), Andre **Hainault**, Marcel **DeJong** - Terrence **Dunfield** (Jonathan **Beaulieu-Bourgault** 81), Atiba **Hutchinson** - Will **Johnson**• (Ali **Gerba** 65), Dwayne **DeRosario** (Robert **Friend** 81), Joshua **Simpson** - Simeon **Jackson**. Tr: Stephen **Hart**

Raymond James, Tampa, 11-06-2011, 18:00, 27 731, Taylor BRB
Canada 1
De Rosario 50p

Milan **Borjan** - Nikolas **Ledgerwood**, Kevin **McKenna**(c), Andre **Hainault**, Michael **Klukowski** - Terrence **Dunfield**•, Will **Johnson** - Dwayne **DeRosario** (Simeon **Jackson** 63), Julian **DeGuzman** (Pedro **Pacheco** 82), Joshua **Simpson** - Ali **Gerba** (Robert **Friend** 63). Tr: Stephen **Hart**

Guadeloupe 0

Franck **Grandel** - Eddy **Viator**, Stephane **Zubar**•, Jean-Luc **Lambourde**♦4, Miguel **Comminges** - Thomas **Gamiette**, David **Fleurival** (Loic **Loval** 58), Stephane **Auvary**(c), Thery **Racon** (Julien **Ictoi** 65) - Richard **Socrier** (Livio **Nabab**• 73), Brice **Jovial**. Tr: Roger **Salnot**

Raymond James, Tampa, 11-06-2011, 20:00, 27 731, Rodriguez.M MEX
USA 1
Goodson 66

Tim **Howard** - Steve **Cherundolo**, Clarence **Goodson**• (Chris **Wondolowski** 78), Tim **Ream**, Carlos **Bocanegra**(c)• - Landon **Donovan**, Michael **Bradley**, Jermaine **Jones**• (Sacha **Kljestan** 60), Clint **Dempsey** - Juan **Agudelo** (Alejandro **Bedoya**• 61), Jozy **Altidore**•. Tr: Bob **Bradley**

Panama 2
Goodson OG 19, Gomez 36p

Jaime **Penedo**• - Eduadro Cesar **Dasent**, Roman **Torres**, Felipe **Baloy**(c), Luis **Henriquez** - Armando **Cooper** (Alberto **Quintero** 84), Amilcar **Henriquez**, Gabriel **Gomez**, Nelson **Barahona**• (Gabriel **Torres** 70) - Blas **Perez**, Luis **Tejada** (Eybir Olemdo **Bonaga** 81). Tr: Julio Cesar **Dely Valdes**

Livestrong, Kansas City, 14-06-2011, 19:00, 20 109, Lopez GUA
Canada 1
De Rosario 62p

Milan **Borjan** - Nikolas **Ledgerwood**, Kevin **McKenna**(c), Andre **Hainault**, Michael **Klukowski** - Will **Johnson** (Pedro **Pacheco** 84), Terrence **Dunfield** - Dwayne **DeRosario**, Julian **DeGuzman**, Joshua **Simpson**• (Tosaint **Ricketts** 72) - Simeon **Jackson**. Tr: Stephen **Hart**

Panama 1
Tejada 91+

Luis **Mejia** - Adolfo **Machado**, Eduadro Cesar **Dasent**, Felipe **Baloy**(c), Luis **Henriquez** - Alberto **Quintero** (Armando **Cooper** 67), Gabriel **Gomez**, Eybir Olmedo **Bonaga**• (Anibal **Godoy** 78), Eric **Davis** - Blas **Perez**•, Luis **Renteria** (Luis **Tejada** 70). Tr: Julio Cesar **Dely Valdes**

Livestrong, Kansas City, 14-06-2011, 21:00, 20 109, Solis CRC
USA 1
Altidore 9

Tim **Howard** - Steve **Cherundolo**, Clarence **Goodson**, Carlos **Bocanegra**(c), Eric **Lichaj** - Clint **Dempsey**, Michael **Bradley** (Maurice **Edu** 85), Jermaine **Jones**, Landon **Donovan** - Jozy **Altidore** (Sacha **Kljestan** 77), Chris **Wondolowski** (Alejandro **Bedoya** 64). Tr: Bob **Bradley**

Guadeloupe 0

Franck **Grandel** - Michael **Tacalfred**, Stephane **Zubar**•, Eddy **Viator**•, Julien **Ictoi** - Thomas **Gamiette**, Stephane **Auvary**(c)• - Livio **Nabab** (Dimitri **Fautrai** 60), Loic **Loval** (Cedric **Collet** 26), Thery **Racon** (Ludovic **Gotin** 72) - Richard **Socrier**. Tr: Roger **Salnot**

QUARTER-FINALS

Meadowlands, New York, 18-06-2011, 17:00, 78807, Moreno PAN

Costa Rica	1 2p
	Marshall 56

Keylor **Navas** - Jose **Salvatierra●**, Jhonny Acosta, Dennis **Marshall**, Junior **Diaz** (Heiner **Mora** 46) - Celso **Borges**, Bryan **Oviedo**, Christian **Bolanos** (Diego **Madrigal** 69) - Bryan **Ruiz**(c), Alvaro **Saborio**, Marco **Urena** (Joel **Campbell** 108). Tr: Ricardo **Lavolpe**

Honduras	1 4p
	Bengtson 49

Noel **Valladares**(c)● - Mauricio **Sabillon**, Osman Danilo **Chavez**, Victor **Bernardez●**, Juan Carlos **Garcia** - Hendry **Thomas●** (Wilson **Palacios** 94), Roger **Espinoza** (13-Carlo **Costly** 81) - Walter **Martinez** (Ramon **Nunez** 23), Oscar Boniek **Garcia●**, Javier **Portillo●** - Jerry **Bengston**. Tr: Luis Fernando **Suarez**

Meadowlands, New York, 18-06-2011, 20:00, 78807, Campbell JAM

Mexico	2
	De Nigris 48, Hernandez 66

Alfredo **Talavera** - Efrain **Juarez**, Rafael **Marquez**(c)●, Hector **Moreno**, Carlos **Salcido** - Pablo **Barrera** (Jesus Eduardo **Zavala** 82), Israel **Castro** (Aldo **De Nigris** 46), Gerardo **Torrado**, Andres **Guardado** - Giovani **Dos Santos** (Angel Eduardo **Reyna** 77), Javier **Hernandez**. Tr: Jose Manuel **De la Torre**

Guatemala	1
	Ruiz 5

Ricardo **Jerez** - Jonathan **Lopez●**, Cristian Jafeth **Noriega**, Gustavo **Cabrera**, Wilfred Armando **Velasquez●**, Carlos **Gallardo** - Jose Javier **Del Aguila●**, Elias Enco **Vasquez** (Carlos Mauricio **Castrillo** 70), Marco **Pappa** - Carlos **Ruiz**(c), Jairo **Arreola** (Oscar Ovidio **Isaula** 69). Tr: Ever **Almeida**

RFK, Washington, 19-06-2011, 15:00, 45424, Rodriguez.M MEX

USA	2
	Jones 49, Dempsey 79

Tim **Howard** - Steve **Cherundolo**, Clarence **Goodson**, Carlos **Bocanegra**(c), Eric **Lichaj** - Jermaine **Jones●** (Maurice **Edu** 75), Michael **Bradley** - Alejandro **Bedoya** (Landon **Donovan** 65), Sacha **Kljestan**, Clint **Dempsey** - Jozy **Altidore** (Juan **Agudelo** 12). Tr: Bob **Bradley**

Jamaica	0

Donovan **Ricketts** - Adrian **Reid**, Shavar **Thomas**(c), Jermaine **Taylor◆**67 - Eric **Vernan** (Jevaughn **Watson** 63), Rodolph **Austin●**, Jason **Morrison** (Keammar **Daley** 68), Demar **Phillips** - Dane **Richards**, Ryan **Johnson**, Luton **Shelton** (Omar **Daley** 73). Tr: Theodore **Whitmore**

RFK, Washington, 19-06-2011, 18:00, 45424, Quesada CRC

Panama	1 5p
	Tejada 90

Jaime **Penedo** - Adolfo **Machado**, Roman **Torres●**, Felipe **Baloy**(c)●, Luis **Henriquez** (Luis **Renteria●** 85) - Armando **Cooper●** (Alberto **Quintero** 80), Amilcar **Henriquez●**, Gabriel **Gomez** (Anibal **Godoy** 80), Nelson **Barahona** - Luis **Tejada**, Blas **Perez◆**90. Tr: Julio Cesar **Dely Valdes**

El Salvador	1 3p
	Zelaya 78p

Miguel **Montes** - Xavier **Garcia**, Steven **Purdy**, Luis **Anaya**(c)●◆90, Reynaldo **Hernandez●** (Osael **Romero●** 46) - Dennis **Alas**, Victor **Turcios** - Eliseo **Quintanilla** (Arturo **Alvarez** 68), Rudis **Corrales**, Jaime **Alas** (Andres **Flores** 86) - Rodolfo **Zelaya**. Tr: Ruben **Israel**

QUARTER-FINAL PENALTIES CRC V HON

CRC		HON	
✗2	Celso Borges		
		Bryan Ruiz	✓
✗2	Alvaro Saborio		
		Joel Campbell	✗
✓	Carlo Costly		
		Victor Bernardez	✓
✓	Wilson Palacios		
		Jerry Bengston	✓

1 = saved • 2 = missed

QUARTER-FINAL PENALTIES PAN V SLV

PAN		SLV	
✓	Nelson Barahona		
		Luis Renteria	✓
✓	Anibal Godoy		
✓	Amilcar Henriquez		
✓	Luis Tejada		
		Dennis Alas	✗1
✓	William Romero		
		Rodolfo Zelaya	✓
✓	Andres Flores		

SEMI-FINALS

Reliant, Houston, 22-06-2011, 19:00, 70627, Wijngaarde SUR

USA	1
	Dempsey 77

Tim **Howard** - Steve **Cherundolo**, Clarence **Goodson**, Carlos **Bocanegra**(c)●, Eric **Lichaj** - Jermaine **Jones**, Michael **Bradley** - Alejandro **Bedoya**, Sacha **Kljestan** (Landon **Donovan** 46), Clint **Dempsey** - Juan **Agudelo** (Freddy **Adu** 66). Tr: Bob **Bradley**

Panama	0

Jaime **Penedo** - Adolfo **Machado**, Roman **Torres**, Felipe **Baloy**(c), Luis **Henriquez●** - Alberto **Quintero**, Amilcar **Henriquez**, Gabriel **Gomez●** (Anibal **Godoy** 86), Armando **Cooper●** (Luis **Renteria** 71) - Nelson **Barahona** (Gabriel **Torres** 86) - Luis **Tejada**. Tr: Julio Cesar **Dely Valdes**

Reliant, Houston, 22-06-2011, 22:00, 70627, Lopez GUA

Honduras	0

Noel **Valladares**(c) - Mauricio **Sabillon●**, Osman Danilo **Chavez●**, Victor **Bernardez●** (Johnny **Leveron** 46), Juan Carlos **Garcia●** - Hendry **Thomas** - Oscar Boniek **Garcia**, Alfredo **Mejia**, Roger **Espinoza●●◆**114, Javier **Portillo●** (Ramon **Nunez** 60) - Jerry **Bengston** (Carlo **Costly** 70). Tr: Luis Fernando **Suarez**

Mexico	2
	De Nigris 92, Hernandez 99

Alfredo **Talavera** - Efrain **Juarez●**, Rafael **Marquez**(c), Hector **Moreno**, Carlos **Salcido** (Jorge Torres **Nilo** 52) - Pablo **Barrera** (Paul **Aguilar** 102), Israel **Castro**, Gerardo **Torrado●**, Andres **Guardado** (Aldo **De Nigris●** 56) - Giovani **Dos Santos**, Javier **Hernandez**. Tr: Jose Manuel **De la Torre**

CONCACAF Gold Cup Final	Rose Bowl Pasadena	Saturday 25-06-2011
Kick-off: 18:00		Attendance: 93 420

USA   2   4   MEXICO

Michael Bradley [8], Landon Donovan [23]

Pablo Barrera 2 [29] [50], Andres Guardado [36], Giovani Dos Santos [76]

USA

Tr: Bob Bradley

White shirts with blue trimmings, White shorts, White socks

MATCH STATS

USA		MEX
13	Shots	17
4	Shots on goal	8
19	Fouls committed	10
3	Corner kicks	5
0	Caught offside	7
46%	Possession	54%

MATCH OFFICIALS

REFEREE
Joel Aguilar SLV

ASSISTANTS
Hector Vergara CAN
William Torres SLV

4TH OFFICIAL
Walter Lopez GUA

Tim Howard

Steve Cherundolo [11]
Jonathan Bornstein
Clarence Goodson   Carlos Bocanegra(c)   Eric Lichaj

Jermaine Jones [90]   Michael Bradley

Alejandro Bedoya [63]
Juan Agudelo
Freddy Adu [86]
Sacha Kljestan
Clint Dempsey [87]

Landon Donovan [33]

Javier Hernandez   Giovani Dos Santos

Andres Guardado   Gerardo Torrado   Israel Castro   Pablo Barrera [75]
Jesus Zavala

Carlos Salcido [28]
Jorge Torres Nilo [81]
Hector Moreno   Rafael Marquez(c) [43]
Hector Reynoso
Efrain Juarez

Alfredo Talavera

Tr: Jose Manuel De la Torre

Black shirts with red and gold trimmings, Black shorts, Black socks

MEXICO

As a team we made a lot of progress. It was a very good game. It was fast... there was a lot of very good attacking from both sides. I sometimes think a final becomes a real test of both teams going after each other. That was the way we chose to play this game knowing that it would still require good reactions to deal with those situations. Sometimes there are plays where you just have to give credit - Dos Santos' fourth goal was a great piece of skill.

Bob Bradley

I think that if there's something from the team that stood out, it is something that I mentioned in the last press conference - the mentality that the team has to overcome every adversity. I'm going to enjoy the moment, live it, and many more moments will come. In the meantime we just have to enjoy it.

Jose Manuel De la Torre

CLUB TOURNAMENTS 2011

CONCACAF CHAMPIONS LEAGUE 2010–11

Preliminary Round   **Group Phase**

Cruz Azul	MEX	3	6
San Francisco *	PAN	2	0

Group A		Pl	W	D	L	F	A	Pts	USA	MEX	CAN	PAN
Real Salt Lake	USA	6	4	1	1	17	11	**13**		3-1	4-1	2-1
Cruz Azul	MEX	6	3	1	2	15	9	**10**	5-4		0-0	2-0
Toronto FC	CAN	6	2	2	2	5	7	**8**	1-1	2-1		1-0
Arabe Unido	PAN	6	1	0	5	4	14	**3**	2-3	0-6	1-0	

Toronto FC *	CAN	1	2
Motagua	HON	0	2

Santos Laguna	MEX	1	5
SanJuan Jabloteh*	TRI	0	0

Group B		Pl	W	D	L	F	A	Pts	MEX	USA	GUA	TRI
Santos Laguna	MEX	6	4	1	1	19	7	**13**		1-0	6-1	5-1
Columbus Crew	USA	6	4	0	2	10	4	**12**	1-0		1-0	3-0
Municipal	GUA	6	2	2	2	9	13	**8**	2-2	2-1		1-1
Joe Public	TRI	6	0	1	5	7	21	**1**	2-5	1-4	2-3	

Joe Public	TRI	2	4
Brujas Escazú *	CRC	2	2

Marathón	HON	3	1
Tauro *	PAN	0	2

Group C		Pl	W	D	L	F	A	Pts	MEX	CRC	HON	USA
Monterrey	MEX	6	5	1	0	11	4	**16**		1-0	2-0	3-2
Dep. Saprissa	CRC	6	3	1	2	11	7	**10**	2-2		4-1	2-0
Marathón	HON	6	2	0	4	5	11	**6**	0-1	2-1		2-1
Seattle Sounders	USA	6	1	0	5	6	11	**3**	0-2	1-2	2-0	

Seattle Sounders*	USA	1	1
Isidro-Metapán	SLV	0	1

P. Rico Islanders	PUR	4	1
LA Galaxy *	USA	1	2

Group D		Pl	W	D	L	F	A	Pts	HON	MEX	PUR	SLV
Olimpia	HON	6	4	1	1	12	7	**13**		2-1	3-0	2-0
Toluca	MEX	6	3	1	2	15	5	**10**	4-0		3-0	5-0
P. Rico Islanders	PUR	6	2	2	2	8	10	**8**	1-1	3-2		4-1
Deportivo FAS	SLV	6	0	2	4	2	15	**2**	1-4	0-0	0-0	

Deportivo FAS	SLV	1	2
Xelajú	GUA	1	0

Match details for the preliminary round and group phase can be found in *Oliver's Almanack of World Football 2011*

CONCACAF CHAMPIONS LEAGUE 2010-11

Quarter-Finals				Semi-finals			Final		
Monterrey	MEX	1	1						
Toluca	MEX	0	0						
				Monterrey *	2	1			
				Cruz Azul	1	1			
Santos Laguna	MEX	0	1						
Cruz Azul	MEX	2	3						
							Monterrey *	2	1
							Real Salt Lake	2	0
Dep. Saprissa	CRC	1	2						
Olimpia	HON	0	1						
				Dep. Saprissa	0	2			
				Real Salt Lake *	2	1			
Columbus Crew	USA	0	1						
Real Salt Lake	USA	0	4	* Home team in the first leg					

Top scorers: **11** - Javier Orozco MEX, Cruz Azul • **8** - Emanuel Villa ARG, Cruz Azul & Alvaro Saborio CRC, Real Salt Lake • **6** - Hector Mancilla CHI, Toluca • **5** - Jose Maria Cardenas MEX, Santos Laguna; Juan Cuevas ARG, Toluca & Roger Rojas HON, Olimpia • **4** - Christian Gimenez ARG, Cruz Azul; Nicholas Addlery JAM, Puerto Rico Islanders; Claudio Cardoza URU, Marathón; Aldo de Nigris MEX, Monterrey; David Foley ENG, Puerto Rico Islanders; Guillermo Ramirez GUA, Municipal & Humberto Suazo CHI, Monterrey

QUARTER-FINALS

Nemesio Diez, Toluca
23-02-2011, 13 899, Chacon MEX

Toluca 0

Miguel **Centeno** - Francisco **Gamboa**, Diego **Novaretti**, Edgar **Duenas**(c)•, Mario **Mendez** - Carlos **Esquivel**, Antonio **Rios** (Martin **Romagnoli** 53), Carlos **Galeana**, Luis **Arias**♦9 - Raul **Nava** (Nestor **Calderon** 29), Jaimen **Ayovi** (Osvaldo **Gonzalez** 76). Tr: Sergio Lugo **Barron**

Monterrey 1
Martinez [81]

Jonathan **Orozco** - Sergio **Perez**, Hiram **Mier** (Osvaldo **Martinez** 60), Dulio **Davino**, William **Paredes**• - Hector **Morales**, Jesus **Zavala** (Neri **Cardozo** 90), Jose **Arellano**(c)• (Aldo **De Nigris** 45), Luis Ernesto **Perez**, Walter **Ayovi** - Abraham **Carreno**. Tr: Victor Manuel **Vucetich**

Tecnológico, Monterrey
2-03-2011, 17 000, Rodriguez.M MEX

Monterrey 1
Cardozo [87]

Jonathan **Orozco** - Sergio **Perez**, Hiram **Mier**, Jose Maria **Basanta**, William **Paredes** - Hector **Morales**, Jesus **Zavala** (Neri **Cardozo** 78) - Osvaldo **Martinez** (Sergio **Santana** 88), Luis Ernesto **Perez**,Walter **Ayovi** (Jesus Manuel **Corona** 90) - Aldo **De Nigris**. Tr: Victor Manuel **Vucetich**

Toluca 0

Alfredo **Talavera** - Osvaldo **Gonzalez**, Diego **Novaretti**, Edgar **Duenas**(c), Mario **Mendez** - Carlos **Esquivel**, Martin **Romagnoli**, Carlos **Galeana** (Manuel **De La Torre** 19), Nestor **Calderon**• (Isaac **Brizuela** 73) - Emmanuel **Cerda**, Jaimen **Ayovi** (Erbin **Trejo** 76). Tr: Sergio Lugo **Barron**

Estadio Azul, Mexico City
22-02-2011, 14 062, Delgadillo MEX

Cruz Azul 2
Orozco [58], Gimenez [68]

Jose De Jesus **Corona** - Alejandro **Castro**, Horacio **Cervantes**, Nestor **Araujo**, Adrian **Cortes** - Javier **Aquino** (Cesar **Villaluz** 84), Gerardo **Torrado**(c)•, Marcelo Jose **Palau**, Christian **Gimenez** (Isaac **Romo** 80) - Javier **Orozco** (Alam **Bello**• 70), Emmanuel **Villa**•. Tr: Enrique **Meza**

Santos Laguna 0

Oswaldo **Sanchez**(c) - Jorge **Estrada**, Felipe **Baloy**•, Jonathan **Lacerda**, Jose Antonio **Olvera**, Carlos **Morales** - Fernando **Arce**•, Juan Pablo **Rodriguez**, Daniel **Luduena** (Jose **Cardenas** 61) - Carlos Darwin **Quintero** (Oribe **Peralta** 61), Christian **Benitez** (Rodrigo **Ruiz** 83). Tr: Diego **Cocca**

Nuevo Estadio Corona, Torreon
1-03-2011, 25 000, Garcia MEX

Santos Laguna 1
Benitez [71]

Oswaldo **Sanchez**(c) - Jorge **Estrada** (Carlos **Morales** 61), Uriel **Alvarez**, Felipe **Baloy**, Jose Antonio **Olvera** - Fernando **Arce**, Daniel **Luduena** (Rodrigo **Ruiz** 73), Juan Pablo **Rodriguez**, Oribe **Peralta**• (Jose **Cardenas** 53) - Carlos Darwin **Quintero**, Christian **Benitez**•. Tr: Diego **Cocca**

Cruz Azul 3
Villa 2 [36] [52], Gimenez [49]

Jose De Jesus **Corona** - Alejandro **Castro**, Horacio **Cervantes**, Waldo Alonso **Ponce**•, Adrian **Cortes** - Christian **Gimenez**••♦63, Gerardo **Torrado**(c), Marcelo Jose **Palau**•, Javier **Aquino** (Rogelio **Chavez** 77) - Javier **Orozco** (Cesar **Villaluz** 63), Emmanuel **Villa** (Isaac **Romo** 58). Tr: Enrique **Meza**

Ricardo Saprissa, San Jose
24-02-2011, 12 344, Lopez GUA

Deportivo Saprissa 1
Alonso [24]

Victor **Bolivar** - Ricardo **Blanco**, Oscar **Duarte**, Roberto **Wong**, Javier **Loaiza** (Josue **Martinez** 57) - Armando **Alonso**, David **Guzman** (Luis **Cordero** 81), Douglas **Sequeira**• - Walter **Centeno**(c) - Jairo **Arrieta**, Alejandro **Sequeira** (Alonso **Solis** 66). Tr: Juan Manuel **Alvarez**

Olimpia 0

Noel **Valladares**(c)• - Wilfredo **Barahona**, Fabio **De Souza**, Johnny **Palacios**, Juan Carlos **Garcia** - Walter **Castro** (Reynaldo **Tiguath** 90) - Oscar **Garcia**♦10, Miguel Angel **Castillo**•, Bany **Lozano** (Jose Carlos **Dias** 75) - Washington **Bruschi** (Alexander **Lopez** 60), Douglas **Caetano Mattoso**•. Tr: Carlos **Restrepo**

Olimpico, San Pedro Sula
3-03-2011, 20 000, Aguilar SLV

Olimpia 1
Rojas [52]

Noel **Valladares**(c) - Wilfredo **Barahona**, Fabio **De Souza**, Johnny **Palacios**, Juan Carlos **Garcia** - Walter **Castro** (Roger **Rojas** 30) - Alexander **Lopez** (Reynaldo **Tiguath** 46), Miguel Angel **Castillo**, Jose Carlos **Dias**• (Anthony **Lozano** 69) - Washington **Bruschi**, Douglas **Caetano Mattoso**. Tr: Carlos **Restrepo**

Deportivo Saprissa 2
Alonso [25], Cordero [63]

Victor **Bolivar** - Ricardo **Blanco**•, Gabriel **Badilla**, Jose **Mena**•, Roberto **Wong**•, Douglas **Sequeira** - Armando **Alonso**• (Saul **Phillip** 73), Walter **Centeno**(c)•, David **Guzman** (Javier **Loaiza** 85) - Jairo **Arrieta**, Josue **Martinez** (Luis **Cordero** 57). Tr: Juan Manuel **Alvarez**

Crew Stadium, Columbus
22-02-2011, 4500, Marrufo USA

Columbus Crew 0

Raymond **Burse** - Sebastian **Miranda**•, Richard **Balchan**, Andrew **Iro**(c), Joshua **Gardner** (Jeff **Cunningham** 75) - Nicholas **Grossman** - Robbie **Rogers**, Emmanuel **Ekpo**, Eddie **Gaven** (Leandre **Griffit** 63) - Emilio **Renteria**♦73, Andres **Mendoza** (Justin **Meram** 82). Tr: Robert **Warzycha**

Real Salt Lake 0

Nick **Rimando** - Anthony **Beltran**••♦53, Jamison **Olave**, Nathaniel **Borchers**♦73, Christopher **Wingert** - Kyle **Beckerman**(c)• - Ned **Grabavoy** (Andrew **Williams** 82), Javier **Morales**, Will **Johnson** - Alvaro **Saborio**, Edgar **Espindola** (Robert **Russell** 59). Tr: Jason **Kreis**

Rio Tinto, Salt Lake City
1-03-2011, 15 405, Geiger USA

Real Salt Lake 4
Saborio [23], Morales 2 [36] [78], Williams [90]

Nick **Rimando** - Robert **Russell**, Jamison **Olave**, Christopher **Schuler**, Christopher **Wingert** - Kyle **Beckerman**(c) - Andrew **Williams**, Javier **Morales**• (Ned **Grabavoy** 85), Will **Johnson** - Alvaro **Saborio** (Paulo **Araujo** 87), Edgar **Espindola** (Jean **Alexandre** 84). Tr: Jason **Kreis**

Columbus Crew 1
Mendoza [48]

Raymond **Burse** - Sebastian **Miranda**•, Richard **Balchan**, Andrew **Iro**(c), Joshua **Gardner**• (Julius **James** 60) - Nicholas **Grossman** - Robbie **Rogers**, Emmanuel **Ekpo** (Dilaver **Duka** 75), Eddie **Gaven** - Jeff **Cunningham** (Justin **Meram** 63), Andres **Mendoza**•. Tr: Robert **Warzycha**

SEMI-FINALS

Tecnológico, Monterrey
16-03-2011, 22 469, Degadillo MEX

Monterrey **2**

Cardozo [9], Santana [55]

Jonathan **Orozco** - Sergio **Perez**, Hiram **Mier**, Jose Maria **Basanta**•, Ricardo **Osorio** - Jesus **Zavala** - Osvaldo **Martinez** (Humberto **Suazo** 66), Sergio **Santana**• (Abraham **Carreno** 84), Luis Ernesto **Perez**(c)•, Neri **Cardozo** (Walter **Ayovi** 66) - Aldo **De Nigris**•. Tr: Victor Manuel **Vucetich**

Cruz Azul **1**

Cortes [48]

Jose De Jesus **Corona** - Julio **Dominguez** (Marcelo Jose **Palau**• 60), Horacio **Cervantes**•, Waldo Alonso **Ponce**, Adrian **Cortes** - Javier **Aquino**, Cesar **Villaluz**• (Hugo **Droguett**• 46), Gerardo **Torrado**(c), Alejandro **Castro** - Javier **Orozco** (Isaac **Romo** 60) - Emmanuel **Villa**. Tr: Enrique **Meza**

Rio Tinto, Salt Lake City
15-03-2011, 16 668, Wijngaarde SUR

Real Salt Lake **2**

Saborio [9], Espindola [57]

Nick **Rimando** - Robert **Russell**, Jamison **Olave** (Christopher **Schuler** 46), Nathaniel **Borchers**, Anthony **Beltran** - Kyle **Beckerman**(c) - Andrew **Williams** (Ned **Grabavoy** 67), Javier **Morales**, Will **Johnson** - Alvaro **Saborio**, Edgar **Espindola** (Arturo **Alvarez** 87). Tr: Jason **Kreis**

Deportivo Saprissa **0**

Victor **Bolivar** - Ricardo **Blanco**•, Jose **Mena**•, Roberto **Wong**, Gabriel **Badilla**• (Oscar **Duarte** 88) - Armando **Alonso** (Maykol **Ortiz** 77), Douglas **Sequeira**•, David **Guzman** - Walter **Centeno**(c) - Jairo **Arrieta**•, Josue **Martinez** (Luis **Cordero** 71). Tr: Juan Manuel **Alvarez**

Estadio Azul, Mexico City
6-04-2011, 24 574, Chacon MEX

Cruz Azul **1**

Villaluz [23]

Jose De Jesus **Corona** - Julio **Dominguez**, Horacio **Cervantes**, Waldo Alonso **Ponce**••◆77, Fausto **Pinto** (Isaac **Romo** 82) - Christian **Gimenez**, Cesar **Villaluz** (Javier **Aquino** 79), Gerardo **Torrado**(c), Hugo **Droguett** - Javier **Orozco**• (Gonzalo **Pineda** 62) - Emmanuel **Villa**. Tr: Enrique **Meza**

Monterrey **1**

Suazo [80p]

Jonathan **Orozco** - Sergio **Perez**•, Duilio **Davino** (Osvaldo **Martinez** 69), Jose Maria **Basanta**, Ricardo **Osorio** - Sergio **Santana**, Jesus **Zavala**• (Neri **Cardozo** 34), Luis Ernesto **Perez**(c), Walter **Ayovi** - Aldo **De Nigris**, Humberto **Suazo** (Hector **Morales** 82). Tr: Victor Manuel **Vucetich**

Ricardo Saprissa, San Jose
5-04-2011, 21 065, Rodriguez.M MEX

Deportivo Saprissa **2**

Luis Cordero [46], Solis [86p]

Victor **Bolivar** - Oscar **Duarte**, Victor **Cordero**(c), Roberto **Wong** - Armando **Alonso**•, Luis **Cordero**, Saul **Phillip** (Allan **Aleman** 63), David **Guzman** - Walter **Centeno** (Alonso **Solis** 85) - Jairo **Arrieta**, Josue **Martinez** (Alejandro **Sequeira** 69). Tr: Juan Manuel **Alvarez**

Real Salt Lake **1**

Olave [60]

Nick **Rimando** - Robert **Russell**•, Jamison **Olave**•, Nathaniel **Borchers**, Christopher **Wingert** - Kyle **Beckerman**(c) - Andrew **Williams** (Ned **Grabavoy** 57), Javier **Morales**, Will **Johnson** - Alvaro **Saborio**, Edgar **Espindola** (Arturo **Alvarez** 78). Tr: Jason **Kreis**

CONCACAF Champions League Final 1st Leg	Estadio Tecnológico Monterrey	Wednesday 20-04-2011
Kick-off: 22:00		Attendance: 30247

MONTERREY   2 2   REAL SALT LAKE

Aldo de Nigris [18], Humberto Suazo [62p]   Nat Borchers [35], Javier Morales [89]

MONTERREY

Navy blue shirts with white stripes, Navy blue shorts, Navy blue socks

Tr: Victor Manuel Vucetich

Jonathan Orozco

Sergio Perez   Hiram Mier   Jose Maria Basanta   Ricardo Osorio

[69] Sergio Santana / Jesus Arellano   [20] Luis Ernesto Perez (c) / Jesus Zavala [72]   Walter Ayovi   Neri Cardozo

[21] Aldo de Nigris [18] / Osvaldo Martinez   Humberto Suazo

Fabian Espindola   [81] Alvaro Saborio [72] / Arturo Alvarez

Javier Morales

Will Johnson   [60] Ned Grabavoy / Andy Williams [77]

Kyle Beckerman (c) [65]

Chris Wingert   Nat Borchers   Jamison Olave   [81] Robbie Russell / Tony Beltran

Nick Rimando

Tr: Jason Kreis

Gold shirts with claret and blue trimmings, Gold shorts, Claret socks

REAL SALT LAKE

MATCH STATS

Monterrey		Salt Lake
20	Shots	13
8	Shots on goal	6
12	Fouls committed	16
8	Corner kicks	7
4	Caught offside	0
57%	Possession	43%

MATCH OFFICIALS

REFEREE
Joel Aguilar SLV

ASSISTANTS
William Torres SLV
Juan Francisco Zumba SLV

4TH OFFICIAL
Elmer Bonilla SLV

It was a really good game by us, we did enough to win the game. We gave the effort, we made the game. We also made a few errors but nonetheless it makes me feel good to know how Salt Lake plays. They really 'dirtied' up the match. The early substitutions were made because of injuries. No change was made because of tactics.

Victor Manuel Vucetich

We deserved to get a tie here, if not a victory. There's no way we feel like we got lucky coming out of here with a tie. We had two unlucky 'bounces' that they got their goals on - a penalty kick and a missed play but we scored two beautiful goals.

Nick Rimandi

They pinned us back, and pinned us back, and were throwing so many numbers forward. We're not used to seeing that to be honest.

Jason Kreis

CONCACAF Champions League Final 2nd Leg	Rio Tinto Stadium Sandy, Salt Lake City	Wednesday 27-04-2011
Kick-off: 22:00		Attendance: 20 378

REAL SALT LAKE   0   1   MONTERREY

Humberto Suazo [45]

REAL SALT LAKE

Tr: Jason Kreis

Claret shirts with Blue sleeves, Claret shorts, Claret socks

Nick Rimando

Robbie Russell 46 / Tony Beltran   Jamison Olave   Nat Borchers   Chris Wingert

Ned Grabavoy

Andy Williams 64 / Arturo Alvarez   Will Johnson

Javier Morales (c)

Alvaro Saborio   Fabian Espindola 29 / Paulo Araujo 85

Humberto Suazo 90   Sergio Santana 60 / Abraham Carreno

Neri Cardozo 74 / Severo Meza 77   Walter Ayovi   Hector Morales   Osvaldo Martinez 73 / Duilio Davino 73

Ricardo Osorio 74   Jose Maria Basanta (c)   Hiram Mier   Sergio Perez 41

Jonathan Orozco

Tr: Victor Manuel Vucetich

White shirts with blue and black trimmings, White shorts, White socks

MONTERREY

MATCH STATS

Salt Lake		Monterrey
20	Shots	9
4	Shots on goal	1
13	Fouls committed	13
7	Corner kicks	1
2	Caught offside	1
53%	Possession	47%

MATCH OFFICIALS

REFEREE
Roberto Moreno PAN

ASSISTANTS
Daniel Williamson PAN
Jaime Smith PAN

4TH OFFICIAL
Jafeth Perea PAN

The game was lost in minutes 30 to 45. As I told the players last night, when you play a team like Monterrey, if you fall asleep for one play, they punish you. And that one play came right before the halftime. It's a really difficult moment... we haven't lost at home for a long time.

Jason Kreis

I got caught in a one-two for their goal. It just didn't seem to be our night.

Robbie Russell

In the end either team could have won. We were lucky we got the win.

Victor Manuel Vucetich

CFU CLUB CHAMPIONSHIP 2011

Round of 16			Quarter-finals		Semi-finals		Final	
Puerto Rico Islanders	PUR	Bye						
			Puerto Rico Islanders	1 7				
Northern United	LCA	0 1	Walking Boyz Co *	1 0				
Walking Boyz Co	SUR	3 3			Puerto Rico Islanders	3		
River Plate *	PUR	2 0			Alpha United	1		
Bodden Town	CAY	0 1	River Plate	0 2				
Bassa	ATG		Alpha United *	0 3				
Alpha United	GUY	w-o					Puerto Rico Islanders	3
Defence Force	TRI	1 3					Tempête FC	1
Dandy Town Hornets *	BER	1 0	Defence Force	4 3				
Inter Moengotapoe	SUR	1 1	Milerock *	0 0			CUP FINAL	
Milerock *	GUY	0 2			Defence Force	0 2p		
Caledonian AIA	TRI	1 5			Tempête FC	0 4p	National Stadium, Georgetown	
Newtown United *	SKN	0 0	Caledonian AIA *	0 1 2p			27-05-2011	
Centre Bath Estate	DMA		Tempête FC	1 0 3p				
Tempête FC	HAI	w/o	Third place play-off: **Alpha United** 1-1 4-3p Defence Force		* Home team in first leg			

Semi-finals and final played in Providence, Georgetown, Guyana • River Plate played ceded home advantage in both of their ties
Top three qualify for the 2011-12 CONCACAF Champions League

ROUND OF 16

Mindoo Philip Park, Castries
13-03-2011, 16:00, 320, Lancaster GUY

Northern United All Stars	**0**

Randy Poleon - Lennon **Verdant**• (Rico **Daniel** 46), Mogabi **Polius**, Hiram **Hunte**, Troy **Cerry**, Hezron **Justin**, Everton **Lampert**, Francis **Lastic**, Kenwen **McPhee** (Eden **Charles** 17), Troy **Prosper** (Shervon **Jack** 63), Justin **St. Clair**. Tr: F. **McDonald**

Walking Boyz Co	**3**
	Ailton **Paiva** [32], Lupson [45], Felter [49]

Andre **Zebeda** - Franilson **Araujo**, Ferdinard **Jap A Joe**•, Marlon **Felter**, Clifton **Tjin Liep Shie**•, Fabian **Van Dijk**, Ailton **Paiva** (Romario **Sordam** 67), Vano **Sastromedjo**, Sergio **Aroepa**, Rinaldo **Lupson** (Garty **Sordjo** 62), Elias **Afonsoewa** (Clifton **Sandvliet** 82). Tr: Jimmy **Hoepel**

André Kamperveen, Paramaribo
26-03-2011, 20:00, 300, Davis TRI

Walking Boyz Co	**3**
	Aroepa [3], Lupson [40], Afonsoewa [49]

Soeradjkoemar **Somai** - Elias **Afonsoewa**, Iranilson **Araujo**, Sergio **Aroepa**, Marlon **Felter**•, Ferdinard **Jap A Joe**, Rinaldo **Lupson** (Garry **Sordjo** 81), Ailton **Paiva** (Milton **Koenders** 79), Vano **Sastromedjo**•, Clifton **Tjin Liep Shie** (Mitchell **Lynch** 82), Fabian **Van Dijk**. Tr: Andy **Atmodimedjo**

Northern United All Stars	**1**
	St Clair [17]

Randy **Poleon** - Troy **Cerry**, Hiram **Hunte**, Chad **St. Clair** (Troy **Greenidge** 58), Lennon **Verdant** (Rico **Daniel** 71), Francis **Lastic**, Troy **Prosper**, Everton **Lampert**, Victory **Leon**, Mogabi **Polius** (Jonas **Maximus** 46), Dellon **Joseph**. Tr: Marcellus **Lennie**

Mcfield Annex, George Town
18-03-2011, 19:00, 150, Peterkin JAM

Bodden Town	**0**

Levon **Smith**(c) - Craig **Bodden**, Yefrey **Calderon** (Maynor **Rodriguez** 31), Karl **Solomon**, Kareem **James** (Danu **Smith** 70), Charlo **McLean** (Denny **Bailey** 61), Rashad **Rankine**, Naoki **Montoya**, Tevon **Levien**•, Gerome **Graham**, Arvid **Harris**. Tr: Elbert **McLean**

River Plate	**2**
	Megaloudis [2], Francois [63]

Craig Alan **Hill** - Julio Maya **Cruz**, Matia **Maroni**, Nelson **Torres**, Brian **Bayona**, Edwin **Cano**, Juan **Murillo**, Frantz **Francois**, Christopher **Megaloudis**, Petter **Villegas**(c)•, Yessid **Nijim**. Tr: Jorge **Silvetti**

Mcfield Annex, George Town
20-03-2011, 18:00, 275, Peterkin JAM

River Plate	**0**

Craig Alan **Hill** - Julio Maya **Cruz**, Matia **Maroni**, Nelson **Torres**, Brian **Bayona**, Edwin **Cano**•, Juan **Murillo**, Frantz **Francois**, Christopher **Megaloudis**, Petter **Villegas**(c)•, Yessid **Nijim**. Tr: Jorge **Silvetti**

Bodden Town	**1**
	Calderon [75]

Ramon **Sealy** - Craig **Bodden**, Maynor **Rodriguez**, Yefrey **Calderon**(c)•, Karl **Solomon**, Charlo **McLean**• (Anfernee **Wright** 71), Rashad **Rankine** (Kareem **James** 68), Denny **Bailey**•, Tevon **Levien**•, Arvid **Harris**, Jake **Bennett-Rivera** (Gerome **Graham** 53). Tr: Elbert **McLean**

BAA Field, Hamilton
10-03-2011, 20:00, 350, Holder CAY

Dandy Town Hornets	**1**
	Swan [22]

Daniel **Johnson** - George **Dyer**, Fabion **Frankson**•, Keman **Tucker**, Damon **Ming**, Jahmel **Swan**, Jared **Peniston**, Lashun **Dill** (Heys **Wolfe** 81), Seion **Darrell**, Wolde **Maryam-Place** (Shannon **Burchall** 80), Raymond **Beach**(c). Tr: Leroy **Wilson**

Defence Force	**1**
	Narcis [30]

Kevin **Graham** - Rawle **Fletcher**, Michael **Edwards** (Jemel **Sebro** 73), Kerry **Joseph**, Cory **Rivers**(c), Jerwyn **Balthazar** (Balondemu **Julius** 87), Sean **Narcis**• (Kurt **Williams** 80), Dexter **Pacheco**, Rodell **Elcock**, Aklie **Edwards**, Richard **Roy**. Tr: Ross **Russell**

Manny Ramjohn, San Fernando
19-03-2011, 18:00, 500, Thomas JAM

Defence Force	**3**
	Narcis [18], Edwards 2 [73 84]

Kevin **Graham** - Rawle **Fletcher**, Kerry **Joseph** (Jahvon **Neptune** 80), Cory **Rivers**(c), Jerwyn **Balthazar**, Owen **Mathews** (Michael **Edwards** 54), Sean **Narcis**, Dexter **Pacheco** (Anton **Joseph** 65), Rodell **Elcock**, Richard **Roy**, Glynn **Franklin**. Tr: Ross **Russell**

Dandy Town Hornets	**0**

Daniel **Johnson** - George **Dyer**, Jared **Peniston**, Damon **Ming** (Caldre **Burgess** 84), Raymond **Beach**(c), Jahmel **Swan** (Heys **Wolfe** 57), Fabion **Frankson**, Wolde **Maryam-Place** (Shannon **Burchall** 57), Seion **Darrell**•, Keman **Tucker**. Tr: Leroy **Wilson**

MacKenzie Sport Club, Linden
13-03-2011, 19:30, 300, Davis TRI

Milerock	0

Derrick **Carter** - Marlon **Maxius**(c), Devon **Dennis** (Owen **Williams** 90), Clive **Noriega**, Collie **Hercules**, Alester **Johnson**• (Steve **Brewley** 67), Kieron **Cameron**•, Kayode **McKinnon**, Quacy **Johnson**, Keivin **Sullivan**, Oswald **Benjamin** (Ryana **Crandon** 76). Tr: Bryan **Joseph**

Inter Moengotapoe	1
	Brunswijk.J [88]

Rudolf **Daniel** - Morris **Linga**, Patrick **Jimmy**, Fabian **Jeroe**•, Amakitie **Maasie**, Sirano **Amoeferie** (Junglo **Brunswijk** 59), Ives **Vlijter**(c)•, Marlon **Bron** (Jerrel **Adesiba** 73), Ricardo **Misiedjan**, Stefan **Baneti**•, Petrus Eugene **Apanta**•. Tr: Redjo **Sentono**

André Kamperveen, Paramaribo
19-03-2011, 20:00, 1500, Willett ATG

Inter Moengotapoe	1
	Van Dijk [93+]

Rudolf **Daniel** - Morris **Linga**• (Kareem **Kwasie** 83), Patrick **Jimmy**, Fabian **Jeroe**, Amakitie **Maasie**, Gregory **Pokie**, Ives **Vlijter**, Marlon **Bron** (Jerrel **Adesiba** 67), Ronnie **Brunswijk**(c) (Junglo **Brunswijk** 60), Germaine **Van Dijk**•, Petrus Eugene **Apanta**. Tr: Redjo **Sentono**

Milerock	2
	Hercules [5], Jerome [75]

Derrick **Carter**• - Steve **Brewley**•, Marlon **Maxius**(c), Devon **Dennis** (Ryana **Crandon** 67), Clive **Noriega**♦[87], Collie **Hercules**• (Owen **Williams** 90), Kieron **Cameron**, Kayode **McKinnon**, Quacy **Johnson**, Keivin **Sullivan**, Oswald **Benjamin**• (Randy **Jerome** 85). Tr: Bryan **Joseph**

Newtown Stadium, Newtown
10-03-2011, 20:00, 500, Willett ATG

Newtown United	0

Akil **Byron** - Ian **Lake**, Kadeem **Inniss** (Zevon **Archibald** 68), Shashi **Isaac**, Jason **Isaac** (Dylan **Ferdinand** 81), Alexis **Saddler**, Kassal **Greene**, Earl **Jones**, Kareem **Mitchum**, Orlando **Mitchum**, Malivia **Harris**. Tr: Anthony **Isaac**

Caledonian AIA	1
	Rochford [53]

Kevin **Graham** - Nuru Abullah **Muhammad**, Stephen **David**(c), Ryan **Stewart**, Kareem **Joseph**, Jean-Luc **Rochford**, Walter **Moore**, Akim **Armstrong** (Kerry **Daniel** 78), Daneil **Cyrus**, Densill **Theobald**, Keyon **Edwards** (Hayden **Vincent** 89). Tr: Jamaal **Shabazz**

Hasely Crawford, Port of Spain
19-03-2011, 19:30, 1000, Lancaster GUY

Caledonian AIA	5
	Stewart [12], Rochford [43], Joseph [48], Armstrong [54], Woodley [89]

Kevin **Graham** - Nuru Abullah **Muhammad**, Stephen **David**(c), Ryan **Stewart** (Trayon **Bobb** 69), Kareem **Joseph**, Jean-Luc **Rochford** (Kevon **Woodley** 69), Walter **Moore**, Akim **Armstrong**, Daneil **Cyrus**, Densill **Theobald**•, Keyon **Edwards**• (Hayden **Vincent** 79). Tr: Jamaal **Shabazz**

Newtown United	0

Akil **Byron** - Jason **Isaac**•, Kareem **Mitchum**, Orlando **Mitchum**, Alexis **Saddler**, Shashi **Isaac**, Ian **Lake**(c), Malivia **Harris** (Dylan **Ferdinand** 74), Kassal **Greene** (Alston **Francis** 69), Zevon **Archibald** (Kadeem **Inniss** 70), Earl **Jones**•. Tr: Anthony **Isaac**

QUARTER-FINALS

André Kamperveen, Paramaribo
7-05-2011, 20:00, 500, Bogle JAM

Walking Boyz Co	1
	Sandvliet [48]

Soeradjkoemar **Somai** - Iranilson **Araujo**•, Regillo **Kemper**, Marlon **Felter**(c), Ferdinand **Jap A Joe**, Milton **Koenders** (Mitchell **Lynch**• 70), Rinaldo **Lupson**, Ailton **Paiva** (Vano **Sastromedjo** 59), Clifton **Sandvliet** (Elias **Afonsoewa** 59), Clifton **Tjin Liep Shie**, Fabian **Van Dijk**. Tr: Andy **Atmodimedjo**

Puerto Rico Islanders	1
	Cunningham [91+]

Raymond **Burse** - Scott **Jones**, Richard **Martinez**, David **Foley**, Aaron **Pitchkolan**, Jonathan **Fana Frias** (Noah **Delgado** 59), Nicholas **Addlery**(c), Osei **Telesford** (Kevon **Villaroel** 75), Gregory **Richardson** (Joseph **Salem** 37), Jamie **Cunningham**, Jay **Needham**. Tr: Colin **Clarke**

Juan Ramón Loubriel, Bayamón
14-05-2011, 20:00, 500, Morrison JAM

Puerto Rico Islanders	7
	Delgado 2 [5] [8], Pitchkolan [22], Foley [37], Bouraee [44], Fana Frias [56], Salem [88p]

Raymond **Burse** - Richard **Martinez**, Noah **Delgado**(c) (Tyler **Wilson** 69), David **Foley** (Jarad **Van Schaik** 58), Aaron **Pitchkolan**• (Leonardo **Ly** 52), Jonathan **Fana Frias**, Matthew **Bouraee**, Joseph **Salem**, Kevon **Villaroel**, Logan **Emory**, Jay **Needham**. Tr: Colin **Clarke**

Walking Boyz Co	0

Soeradjkoemar **Somai** (Andre **Zebeda** 63) - Ferdinand **Jap A Joe**, Marlon **Felter**(c), Ailton **Paiva**, Vano **Sastromedjo**♦[83], Elias **Afonsoewa** (Gino **Brandon** 69), Garry **Sordjo**, Milton **Koenders**•, Clifton **Tjin Liep Shie** (Mitchell **Lynch** 17), Rinaldo **Lupson**, Sergio **Aroepa**•. Tr: Andy **Atmodimedjo**

Bourda, Georgetown
15-04-2011, 20:00, 500, Brizan TRI

Alpha United	0

Ronson **Williams** - Howard **Lowe**, Melvin **McKenzie**, Dwain **Jacobs**, Issa **McPherson**♦[34], Konata **Mannings**•, Shawn **Bishop** (Shavane **Seaforth**• 61), Travis **Grant**, Dwight **Peters**, Nigel **Codrington** (Anthony **Abrams** 67), Devon **Millington** (Warren **Gilkes** 61). Tr: Wayne **Dover**

River Plate	0

Craig Alan **Hill** - Christopher **Megaloudis**, Frantz **Francois** (Jose **Montoya** 84), Gustavo **Paruolo**, Julio Maya **Cruz**, Martin **Morello**, Matias **Maroni**, Matias **Arce**•, Nelson **Torres**, Petter **Villegas**•, Ruben **Diaz**•. Tr: Jorge **Silvetti**

Bourda, Georgetown
17-04-2011, 15:00, 500, Davis TRI

River Plate	2
	Maroni [78], Diaz [94+]

Craig Alan **Hill** - Christopher **Megaloudis**, Frantz **Francois**, Gustavo **Paruolo**♦[63] (John **Bain** 70), Jose **Montoya**, Martin **Morello**♦[63], Motia **Maroni**•, Matias **Arce**•, Julio Maya **Cruz**, Nelson **Torres** (Edwin **Cano** 74), Ruben **Diaz**. Tr: Jorge **Silvetti**

Alpha United	3
	Peters [55p], Abrams [58], Murray [83]

Ronson **Williams** - Howard **Lowe**, Melvin **McKenzie**•, Dwain **Jacobs**, Konata **Mannings**, Shawn **Bishop** (Warren **Gilkes** 63), Travis **Grant** (Anthony **Abrams** 48), Dwight **Peters**, Nigel **Codrington**, Devon **Millington** (Andrew **Murray**• 71), Shavane **Seaforth**•. Tr: Wayne **Dover**

MacKenzie Sport Club, Linden
10-04-2011, 19:30, 600, Baptiste DMA

Milerock	0

Derrick **Carter** - Marlon **Maxius**(c), Keivin **Sullivan**, Kieron **Cameron**, Devon **Dennis**, Quacy **Johnson**, Steve **Brewley** (Owen **Williams** 65), Oswald **Benjamin** (Randy **Jerome** 73), Kayode **McKinnon**•, Collie **Hercules**, Alester **Johnson** (Ryan **Crandon** 73). Tr: Bryan **Joseph**

Defence Force	4
	Joseph.K [8], Roy [31], Edwards 2 [60] [67]

Kevin **Graham** - Rawle **Fletcher**, Devon **Jordan**•, Kerry **Joseph**, Cory **Rivers**(c), Owen **Mathews** (Michael **Edwards** 51), Sean **Narcis** (Anton **Joseph** 76), Dexter **Pacheco**, Akile **Edwards** (Rodell **Elcock** 20), Richard **Roy**, Akil **Pierre**. Tr: Ross **Russell**

Ato Bolden, Couva
22-04-2011, 18:00, 520, Morrison JAM

Defence Force	3
	Elcock [11], Roy [43] [89]

Kevin **Graham** - Rawle **Fletcher**•, Devin **Jordan**, Kerry **Joseph**, Cory **Rivers**(c), Owen **Mathews** (Ross **Russell** Jr. 65), Sean **Narcis** (Kurt **Williams** 69), Dexter **Pacheco**, Rodell **Elcock**, Richard **Roy**, Akil **Pierre** (Balondemu **Julius** 59). Tr: Ross **Russell**

Milerock	0

Derrick **Carter** - Steve **Brewley** (Germaine **McBean** 67), Marlon **Maxius**(c), Devon **Dennis**, Clive **Nobriga**, Collie **Hercules**, Alester **Johnson** (Owen **Williams** 81), Randy **Jerome**, Ryan **Crandon**• (Jermaine **Granderson** 35), Keivin **Sullivan**, Oswald **Benjamin**. Tr: Bryan **Joseph**

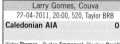

Larry Gomes, Couva
??-04-2011, 20:00, 520, Taylor BRB

Caledonian AIA 0

Victor **Thomas** - Burton **Emmanuel**, Stephen **David**(c), Abdallah **Phillips** (Jean-Luc **Rochford** 71), Kareem **Joseph**, Akim **Armstrong**, Daniel **Cyrus**, Kevon **Woodley** (Hayden **Vincent** 71), Densill **Theobald**, Keyon **Edwards** (Shaquille **Smith** 87), Kemron **Percell**. Tr: Jamaal **Shabazz**

Tempête FC 1
Armstrong OG 5

Guerry **Romondt** - Junior **Etienne•**, Makendy **Duverger** (Ojulesse **Valcourt** 87), Eliphene **Cadet**, Junior **Charles**(c)•, Wisnick **Germinor•**, Chedlin **Francoeur**, Changler **Cadet** (Sony **Abranche** 78), Elie **Paul**, Gregory **Joachim**. Tr: Jean Marie **Dorceus**

Parc Levelt, Saint-Marc
8-05-2011, 16:00, 4552, Angela ARU

Tempête FC 0 3p

Guerry **Romondt** - Makendy **Duverger** (Ojulesse **Valcourt** 120), Shedelin **Francoeur•**, Grand Gregory **Joachin**, Changler **Cadet**, Junior **Etienne**, Vaniel **Sirin** (Junior **Charles** 60), Elie **Paul**, Jackson **Jean**, Ginot **Senat•** (Roobie **Dalusma** 60), Eliphene **Cadet**. Tr: Jean Marie **Dorceus**

Caledonian AIA 1 2p
Armstrong 6

Kevin **Graham** - Daniel **Cyrus•**, Nuru Abdullah **Muhammad•**, Kareem **Joseph**, Sheldon **Emmanuel** (Marcus **Ambrose** 75), Densill **Theobald**, Akim **Armstrong**, Stephen **David**, Abdallah **Phillips**, Keyon **Edwards** (Kevon **Woodley** 89), Cornell **Glenn** (Ryan **Stewart** 62). Tr: Jamaal **Shabazz**

SEMI-FINALS AND THIRD PLACE PLAY-OFF

S/F. National Stadium, Georgetown
25-05-2011, 20:00, 900, Baptiste DMA

Alpha United 1
Jacobs 37

Ronson **Williams** - Adrian **Mitchell•**, Howard **Lowe**(c), Kirk **Duckworth**, Anthony **Bennett**, Dwain **Jacobs**, Dwight **Peters** (Devon **Millington** 60), Issa **McPherson**, Shawn **Bishop** (Travis **Grant** 33), Kelvin **McKenzie**, Nigel **Codrington** (Anthony **Abrams** 62). Tr: Wayne **Dover**

Puerto Rico Islanders 3
Bouraee 23, Fana Frias 108, Foley 116

Raymond **Burse** - Richard **Martinez**, Noah **Delgado**(c) (Jonathan **Fana Frias** 59), David **Foley**, Aaron **Pitchkolan**, Matthew **Bouraee** (Joshua **Hansen** 80), Joseph **Salem**, Osei **Telesford•** (Leonardo **Ly** 105), Kevon **Villaroel**, Logan **Emory**, Jay **Needham**. Tr: Colin **Clarke**

S/F. National Stadium, Georgetown
25-05-2011, 18:00, 900, Willet ATG

Tempête FC 0 4p

Guerry **Romondt** - Makendy **Duverger**, Jackson **Jean** (Junior **Etienne** 83), Eliphene **Cadet** (Valdano **Paul** 68), Junior **Charles**, Sony **Labranche**, Thompson **Amius**(c), Chedlin **Francoeur**, Changler **Cadet**, Elie **Paul**, Grand Gregory **Joachin•**. Tr: Jean Marie **Dorceus**

Defence Force 0 2p

Kevin **Graham** - Rawle **Fletcher**, Devin **Jordan**, Kerry **Joseph**, Cory **Rivers**(c), Owen **Mathews** (Michael **Patrick** 56), Sean **Narcis**, Dexter **Pacheco** (Anton **Joseph•** 58), Rodell **Elcock•**, Richard **Roy**, Akil **Pierre** (Jerwyn **Balthazar** 51). Tr: Ross **Russell**

3/P. National Stadium, Georgetown
27-05-2011, 18:00, 1000, Cambridge VIN

Alpha United 1 4p
Peters 52

Richard **Renolds** - Adrian **Mitchell**, Howard **Lowe**(c), Kris **Camacho**, Kirk **Duckworth**, Dwain **Jacobs**, Dwight **Peters** (Warren **Gilkes** 82), Travis **Grant** (Konta **Manning•** 60), Philbert **Moffatt**, Nigel **Codrington**, Devon **Millington** (Anthony **Abrams** 77). Tr: Wayne **Dover**

Defence Force 1 3p
Roy 58

Kevin **Graham** - Rawle **Fletcher**, Devin **Jordan** (Keston **Williams•** 64), Michael **Edwards** (Balondemu **Julius** 85), Kerry **Joseph**, Cory **Rivers**(c), Anton **Joseph•**, Jerwyn **Balthazar**, Sean **Narcis** (Kurt **Williams** 68••♦90), Rodell **Elcock**, Richard **Roy**. Tr: Ross **Russell**

PENALTY SHOOT-OUT TEMPÊTE V CALEDONIAN QUARTER-FINAL TEMPÊTE WON 3-2		
Charles	✓ ✗	Joseph
Jean	✓ ✓	Stewart
Joachin	✗ ✗	Cyrus
Etienne	✓ ✓	David
	✗	Muhammad

PENALTY SHOOT-OUT TEMPÊTE V DEFENCE SEMI-FINAL TEMPÊTE WON 4-2		
Charles	✓ ✓	Roy
Paul	✓ ✓	Joseph.K
Joachin	✓ ✗	Fletcher
Cadet	✓ ✗	Joseph.A

PENALTY SHOOT-OUT ALPHA UTD V DEFENCE 3RD PLACE PLAY-OFF ALPHA UTD WON 4-3		
Lowe	✗ ✓	Roy
Abrams	✓ ✓	Joseph.K
Manning	✓ ✗	Williams.Ke
Camacho	✓ ✓	Joseph.A
Gilkes	✗ ✗	Rivers
Codrington	✓ ✗	Fletcher

FINAL

National Stadium, Georgetown
27-05:2011, 20:30, 1000, Taylor BRB

Puerto Rico Islanders 3
Needham 24, Fana Frias 2 100 113

Raymond **Burse** - Richard **Martinez**, David **Foley**, Aaron **Pitchkolan•**, Jonathan **Fana Frias**, Matthew **Bouraee** (Scott **Jones** 42), Joseph **Salem** (Jarad **Van Schaik** 71), Osei **Telesford•** (Joshua **Hansen** 90), Kevon **Villaroel♦40**, Logan **Emory**, Jay **Needham**(c). Tr: Colin **Clarke**

Tempête FC 1
Charles 42

Guerry **Romondt♦68** - Makendy **Duverger**, Jackson **Jean** (Ojulesse **Valcourt•** 76), Eliphene **Cadet** (Valdano **Paul** 90), Junior **Charles**, Sony **Labranche**, Thompson **Amius**(c), Chedlin **Francoeur•**, Changler **Cadet** (Tony **Valsaint** 51), Elie **Paul**, Grand Gregory **Joachin**. Tr: Jean Marie **Dorceus**

YOUTH TOURNAMENTS 2011

CONCACAF U-20 CHAMPIONSHIP GUATEMALA 2011 QUALIFYING

Caribbean Groups

Group A	Pl	W	D	L	F	A	Pts	ANT	SKN	VGB
Cuba	3	3	0	0	32	0	**9**	2-0	1-0	29-0
Netherlands Antilles †	3	1	1	1	21	3	**4**		1-1	20-0
St Kitts and Nevis	3	1	1	1	20	2	**4**			19-0
British Virgin Islands	3	0	0	3	0	68	**0**			

Group B	Pl	W	D	L	F	A	Pts	BER	ATG
Guadeloupe	2	1	1	0	5	1	**4**	1-1	4-0
Bermuda †	2	1	1	0	3	1	**4**		2-0
Antigua and Barbuda	2	0	0	2	0	6	**0**		

Group C	Pl	W	D	L	F	A	Pts	GUY	GRN	VIR
Jamaica	3	3	0	0	21	1	**9**	2-0	6-1	13-0
Guyana †	3	2	0	1	8	3	**6**		3-0	5-1
Grenada	3	1	0	2	8	9	**3**			7-0
US Virgin Islands	3	0	0	3	1	25	**0**			

Group D	Pl	W	D	L	F	A	Pts
Trinidad and Tobago	4	4	0	0	16	3	**12**
Suriname †	4	2	0	2	9	6	**6**
Aruba	2	0	0	2	2	7	**0**
St Vincent/Grenadines	2	0	0	2	1	12	**0**

Caribbean Second Round Group

	Pl	W	D	L	F	A	Pts	BER	ANT	GUY
Suriname	3	3	0	0	6	3	**9**	2-1	2-1	2-1
Bermuda	3	1	0	2	5	4	**3**		1-2	3-0
Netherlands Antilles	3	1	0	2	4	5	**3**			1-2
Guyana	3	1	0	2	3	6	**3**			

Central American Groups

	Pl	W	D	L	F	A	Pts	CRC	NCA
Panama	2	2	0	0	2	0	**6**	1-0	1-0
Costa Rica ‡	2	1	0	1	4	1	**3**		4-0
Nicaragua	2	0	0	2	0	5	**0**		

	Pl	W	D	L	F	A	Pts	SLV	BLZ
Honduras	2	2	0	0	7	0	**6**	4-0	3-0
El Salvador ‡	2	1	0	1	6	5	**3**		6-1
Belize	2	0	0	2	1	9	**0**		

‡ Qualified for the Central American Play-off
El Salvador 1-0 1-1 Costa Rica. El Salvador were disqualified for the use of an ineligible player

† Qualified for the Caribbean second round group • As no group host for Caribbean Group D could be determined the group was played in a knockout format over two legs. First round - **Suriname** 3-1 4-2 Aruba; St Vincent/Grenadines 0-8 1-4 **Trinidad & T**. Final - Suriname 1-2 1-2 **Trinidad & T** Cuba Guadeloupe, Jamaica, Trinidad, Suriname, Panama, Honduras and Costa Rica qualified for the finals. Canada, USA and Mexico qualified automatically. Guatemala qualified as hosts

CONCACAF U-20 CHAMPIONSHIP GUATEMALA 2011

Group A	Pts	GUA	JAM
Honduras	**6**	3-1	2-1
Guatemala	3		2-0
Jamaica	0		

Group B	Pts	PAN	SUR
USA	**6**	2-0	4-0
Panama	3		3-0
Suriname	**0**		

Group C	Pts	CAN	GLP
Costa Rica	**6**	3-0	3-0
Canada	3		2-1
Guadeloupe	0		

Group D	Pts	CUB	TRI
Mexico	**6**	3-0	5-0
Cuba	1		0-0
Trinidad & T	1		

Quarter-finals

Mexico	3
Canada	0
Honduras	0
Panama	2
Guatemala	2
USA	1
Cuba	1
Costa Rica	6

Semi-finals

Mexico	4
Panama	1
Guatemala	1
Costa Rica	2

Final

Mexico	3
Costa Rica	1

3rd place play-off: **Guatemala** 0-0 7-6p Panama

FINAL
Mateo Flores, Guatemala City
10-04-2011, 3000, Geiger USA
Scorers - Ulises Davila 2 [18] [52],
Carlos Orrantia [39] for Mexico;
Joseph Mora [17] for Costa Rica

Played in Guatemala City from 28-03-2011 to 10-04-2011 • The four semi-finalists qualify for the 2011 FIFA U-20 World Cup in Colombia

CONCACAF U-17 CHAMPIONSHIP JAMAICA 2011 QUALIFYING

Caribbean Groups

Group A	Pl	W	D	L	F	A	Pts	BER	BAH
Bermuda †	2	1	0	1	5	5	3		5-1
Bahamas	2	1	0	1	2	2	3	1-0	

Group B	Pl	W	D	L	F	A	Pts	ATG	SMT	AIA
St Kitts and Nevis †	3	2	1	0	21	3	7	2-2	7-1	12-0
Antigua and Barbuda	3	2	1	0	17	3	7		5-0	10-1
Saint-Martin	3	1	0	2	5	13	3			4-1
Anguilla	3	0	0	3	2	26	0			

Group C	Pl	W	D	L	F	A	Pts	ANT	ARU	DMA
Guayana †	3	2	1	0	14	2	7	2-2	7-0	5-0
Netherlands Antilles	3	2	1	0	8	3	7		3-0	3-1
Aruba	3	1	0	2	2	11	3			2-1
Dominica	3	0	0	3	2	10	0			

Group D	Pl	W	D	L	F	A	Pts	SUR	GRN	VIN
Barbados †	3	2	1	0	11	2	7	2-2	6-0	3-0
Suriname	3	1	2	0	11	3	5		1-1	8-0
Grenada	3	1	1	1	5	10	4			4-3
St Vincent/Grenadines	3	0	0	3	3	15	0			

Caribbean Second Round Group

Group E	Pl	W	D	L	F	A	Pts	CUB	SKN	BER
Trinidad and Tobago	3	2	1	0	10	1	7	0-0	8-0	2-1
Cuba	3	2	1	0	4	1	7		1-0	3-1
St Kitts and Nevis	3	1	0	2	3	11	3			3-2
Bermuda	3	0	0	3	4	8	0			

Group F	Pl	W	D	L	F	A	Pts	BRB	DOM	GUY
Haiti	3	2	0	1	14	2	6	1-2	6-0	7-0
Barbados	3	2	0	1	8	3	6		0-1	6-1
Dominican Republic	3	2	0	1	2	6	6			1-0
Guyana	3	0	0	3	1	14	0			

Central American Groups

Group A	Pl	W	D	L	F	A	Pts	SLV	NCA
Costa Rica	2	2	0	0	10	1	6	2-1	8-0
El Salvador	2	1	0	1	4	4	3		3-2
Nicaragua	2	0	0	2	2	11	0		

Group B	Pl	W	D	L	F	A	Pts	PAN	GUA
Honduras	2	1	0	1	2	1	3	0-1	2-0
Panama	2	1	0	1	1	1	3		0-1
Guatemala	2	1	0	1	1	2	3		

† Qualified for the Caribbean second round groups • Central American play-off: Nicaragua 0-3 0-1 **Guatemala**
Trinidad, Cuba, Haiti, Barbados, Costa Rica, El Salvador, Honduras, Panama and Guatemala qualified for the finals. Canada and USA qualified automatically. Jamaica qualified as hosts. Mexico did not participate as they had already qualified for the FIFA U-17 World Cup as hosts

CONCACAF U-17 CHAMPIONSHIP JAMAICA 2011

Group A	Pts	SLV	HAI		Quarter-finals		Semi-finals		Final	
Costa Rica	6	3-2	3-1		USA	3				
El Salvador	3		3-0		El Salvador	2				
Haiti	0						USA	2		
							Jamaica	0		
Group B	Pts	PAN	CUB							
USA	6	1-0	3-1		Honduras	1				
Panama	1		0-0		Jamaica	2			USA	3
Cuba	1								Canada	0
Group C	Pts	TRI	GUA							
Jamaica	4	2-2	1-0		Panama	1				
Trinidad & T	4		1-0		Costa Rica	0				
Guatemala	0						Panama	0		
							Canada	1		
Group D	Pts	HON	BRB							
Canada	4	0-0	8-0		Trinidad and Tobago	0				
Honduras	4		2-1		Canada	2				
Barbados	0									

3rd place play-off: **Panama** 1-0 Jamaica

FINAL
Catherine Hall, Montego Bay
27-02-2011, 1130, Wijngaarde SUR
Scorers - Nathan Smith 92, Andrew Oliver 100, Alfred Koroma 120

Played in Montego Bay, Jamaica from 14-02-2011 to 27-02-2011 • The four semi-finalists qualify for the 2011 FIFA U-17 World Cup in Mexico

CONMEBOL

CONFEDERACION SUDAMERICANA DE FUTBOL

95 years after winning the Copa America for the first time, Uruguay added a record 15th title to their name as they proved that their semi-final performance at the 2010 FIFA World Cup in South Africa was no fluke. Throughout much of the past 20 years it looked as if fond memories would be all that football fans in Uruguay had to celebrate - indeed the 2000s were the first decade that the national team or a Uruguayan club had failed to win an international title - but that was more than made up for when 'La Celeste' beat Paraguay 3-0 in the final of the 2011 Copa America in neighbouring Argentina, with strikers Luis Suarez and Diego Forlan once again the toast of Montevideo. Peñarol almost made it an extraordinary double when they reached the final of the Copa Libertadores for the first time in almost a quarter of a century. The final was a rematch of the

THE FIFA BIG COUNT OF 2006 FOR SOUTH AMERICA

	Male	Female		Total
Number of players	24 703	3 074	Referees and Assistant Referees	32 000
Professionals	25 000		Admin, Coaches, Technical, Medical	136 000
Amateurs 18+	980 000		Number of clubs	47 000
Youth under 18	2 346 000		Number of teams	162 000
Unregistered	24 018 000		Clubs with women's teams	1 000
Total involved in football	27 946 000		Players as % of population	7.47%

1962 final against Santos and once again it was the Brazilians who came out on top, Santos winning the trophy for the first time since 1963 when Pele had graced the team. He was in the stands to witness the triumph which came thanks to yet another sparkling performance from star striker Neymar. The fact that a great talent such as Neymar was able to stay in South America and play in the Copa Libertadores is testament to the growing professionalism of club football on the continent. That has been helped by the growing Brazilian economy and the boost that football has received thanks to the 2014 FIFA World Cup being held in Brazil for what will be only the second time that South America will have hosted the tournament since 1962. In the other major competition of the year, the Copa Sudamericana, a sparkling Universidad de Chile side won their first continental title after beating Ecuador's LDU Quito 4-0 on aggregate in the final.

Confederación Sudamericana de Fútbol (CONMEBOL)
Autopista Aeropuerto Internacional y Leonismo Luqueño, Luque, Gran Asuncion, Paraguay
Tel +595 21 645781   Fax +595 21 645791
conmebol@conmebol.com.py   www.conmebol.com
President: Dr Nicolas Leoz PAR   General Secretary: Eduardo Deluca ARG
CONMEBOL formed: 1916

CONMEBOL EXECUTIVE COMMITTEE
President: Dr Nicolas Leoz PAR

Vice-President: Eugenio Figueredo URU	General Secretary: Eduardo Deluca ARG	Treasurer: Romer Osuna BOL

DIRECTORS OF THE EXECUTIVE COMMITTEE

Rafael Esquivel VEN	Nicolas Delfino PER	Oscar Harrison PAR
Nabi Abi Chedid BRA	Luis Chiriboga ECU	Alvaro Fina COL
	Jose Abdalah CHI	

MAP OF CONMEBOL MEMBER NATIONS

CONMEBOL MEMBER ASSOCIATIONS (10)
ARG - **Argentina** • BOL - **Bolivia** • BRA - **Brazil** • CHI - **Chile** • COL - **Colombia**
ECU - **Ecuador** • PAR - **Paraguay** • PER - **Peru** • URU - **Uruguay** • VEN - **Venezuala**

SOUTH AMERICAN
NATIONAL TEAM TOURNAMENTS

COPA AMERICA

Year	Host Country	Winners	Score	Runners-up	Venue
1910	Argentina ††	Argentina	4-1	Uruguay	‡ Racing Club, Buenos Aires
1916	Argentina †	Uruguay	0-0	Argentina	‡ Racing Club, Buenos Aires
1917	Uruguay	Uruguay	1-0	Argentina	‡ Parque Pereira, Montevideo
1919	Brazil	Brazil	1-0	Uruguay	§ Laranjeiras, Rio de Janeiro
1920	Chile	Uruguay	1-1	Argentina	* Sporting Club, Vina del Mar
1921	Argentina	Argentina	1-0	Brazil	* Sportivo Barracas, Buenos Aires
1922	Brazil	Brazil	3-0	Paraguay	§ Laranjeiras, Rio de Janeiro
1923	Uruguay	Uruguay	2-0	Argentina	‡ Parque Central, Montevideo
1924	Uruguay	Uruguay	0-0	Argentina	‡ Parque Central, Montevideo
1925	Argentina	Argentina	2-2	Brazil	‡ Bombonera, Buenos Aires
1926	Chile	Uruguay	2-0	Argentina	* Sport de Nunoa, Santiago
1927	Peru	Argentina	3-2	Uruguay	* Estadio Nacional, Lima
1929	Argentina	Argentina	4-1	Paraguay	* San Lorenzo, Buenos Aires
1935	Peru †	Uruguay	3-0	Argentina	‡ Estadio Nacional, Lima
1937	Argentina	Argentina	2-0	Brazil	‡ San Lorenzo, Buenos Aires
1939	Peru	Peru	2-1	Uruguay	‡ Estadio Nacional, Lima
1941	Chile †	Argentina	1-0	Uruguay	* Estadio Nacional, Santiago
1942	Uruguay	Uruguay	1-0	Argentina	‡ Centenario, Montevideo
1945	Chile †	Argentina	3-1	Brazil	* Estadio Nacional, Santiago
1946	Argentina †	Argentina	2-0	Brazil	‡ Monumental, Buenos Aires
1947	Ecuador	Argentina	6-0	Paraguay	* Estadio Capwell, Guayaquil
1949	Brazil	Brazil	7-0	Paraguay	§ Sao Januario, Rio de Janeiro
1953	Lima	Paraguay	3-2	Brazil	§ Estadio Nacional, Lima
1955	Chile	Argentina	1-0	Chile	‡ Estadio Nacional, Santiago
1956	Uruguay †	Uruguay	1-0	Argentina	‡ Centenario, Montevideo
1957	Peru	Argentina	3-0	Brazil	‡ Estadio Nacional, Lima
1959	Argentina	Argentina	1-1	Brazil	‡ Monumental, Buenos Aires
1959	Ecuador †	Uruguay	5-0	Argentina	* Modelo, Guayaquil
1963	Bolivia	Bolivia	5-4	Brazil	‡ Felix Capriles, Cochabamba
1967	Uruguay	Uruguay	1-0	Argentina	‡ Centenario, Montevideo
1975		Peru	0-1 2-0 1-0	Colombia	Bogota, Lima, Caracas
1979		Paraguay	3-0 0-1 0-0	Chile	Asuncion, Santiago, Buenos Aires
1983		Uruguay	2-0 1-1	Brazil	Montevideo & Salvador
1987	Argentina	Uruguay	1-0	Chile	Monumental, Buenos Aires
1989	Brazil	Brazil	1-0	Uruguay	‡ Maracana, Rio de Janeiro
1991	Chile	Argentina	3-2	Brazil	* Estadio Nacional, Santiago
1993	Ecuador	Argentina	2-1	Mexico	Monumental, Guayaquil
1995	Uruguay	Uruguay	1-1 5-3p	Brazil	Centenario, Montevideo
1997	Bolivia	Brazil	3-1	Bolivia	Hernando Siles, La Paz
1999	Paraguay	Brazil	3-0	Uruguay	Defensores del Chaco, Asuncion
2001	Colombia	Colombia	1-0	Mexico	El Campin, Bogota
2004	Peru	Brazil	2-2 4-2p	Argentina	Estadio Nacional, Lima
2007	Venezuela	Brazil	3-0	Argentina	Pachencho Romero, Maracaibo
2011	Argentina	Uruguay	3-0	Paraguay	Monumental, Buenos Aires

† Extraordinario tournaments are recognised as official tournaments though the teams did not compete for the Copa America • †† Unofficial tournament that is not part of the official records. CONMEBOL refer to it as The South American Championship although it was known at the time as the Copa Centenario • ‡ Tournament played on a league system. The final game was between the top two teams • * Tournament played on a league system. The game listed between the top two teams was not the final match in the tournament • § Tournament played on a league system. The game listed was a play-off after the top two teams finished level on points.

COPA AMERICA MEDALS TABLE

	Country	G	S	B	F	SF
1	Uruguay	15	6	7	5	9
2	Argentina	14	12	4	3	4
3	Brazil	8	11	7	6	8
4	Paraguay	2	6	8	2	3
5	Peru	2		5	1	5
6	Colombia	1	1	3	2	6
7	Bolivia	1	1		1	1
8	Chile		4	5	2	3
9	Mexico		2	3	2	5
10	Honduras			1		1
11	Ecuador					1
	United States					1
	Venezuela					1
		43	43	43	24	46

This table represents the Gold (winners), Silver (runners-up) and
Bronze (semi-finalists) placings of nation in the Copa América,
along with the number of appearances in the final and semi-finals.
It does not include the 1910 tournament and does not distinguish
between official and extraordinario tournaments

SOUTH AMERICAN CLUB TOURNAMENTS

COPA LIBERTADORES DE AMERICA

Year	Winners	Country	Score	Country	Runners-up
1960	Peñarol	URU	1-0 1-1	PAR	Olimpia
1961	Peñarol	URU	1-0 1-1	BRA	Palmeiras
1962	Santos	BRA	2-1 2-3 3-0	URU	Peñarol
1963	Santos	BRA	3-2 2-1	ARG	Boca Juniors
1964	Independiente	ARG	0-0 1-0	URU	Nacional Montevideo
1965	Independiente	ARG	1-0 1-3 4-1	URU	Peñarol
1966	Peñarol	URU	2-0 2-3 4-2	ARG	River Plate
1967	Racing Club	ARG	0-0 0-0 2-1	URU	Nacional Montevideo
1968	Estudiantes LP	ARG	2-1 1-3 2-0	BRA	Palmeiras
1969	Estudiantes LP	ARG	1-0 2-0	URU	Nacional Montevideo
1970	Estudiantes LP	ARG	1-0 0-0	URU	Peñarol
1971	Nacional Montevideo	URU	0-1 1-0 2-0	ARG	Estudiantes LP
1972	Independiente	ARG	0-0 2-1	PER	Universitario
1973	Independiente	ARG	1-1 0-0 2-1	CHI	Colo Colo
1974	Independiente	ARG	1-2 2-0 1-0	BRA	São Paulo FC
1975	Independiente	ARG	0-1 3-1 2-0	CHI	Union Española
1976	Cruzeiro	BRA	4-1 1-2 3-2	ARG	River Plate
1977	Boca Juniors	ARG	1-0 0-1 0-0 5-4p	BRA	Cruzeiro
1978	Boca Juniors	ARG	0-0 4-0	COL	Deportivo Cali
1979	Olimpia	PAR	2-0 0-0	ARG	Boca Juniors
1980	Nacional Montevideo	URU	0-0 1-0	BRA	Internacional
1981	Flamengo	BRA	2-1 0-1 2-0	CHI	Cobreloa
1982	Peñarol	URU	0-0 1-0	CHI	Cobreloa
1983	Grêmio	BRA	1-1 2-1	URU	Peñarol
1984	Independiente	ARG	1-0 0-0	BRA	Grêmio
1985	Argentinos Juniors	ARG	1-0 0-1 1-1 5-4p	COL	América Cali
1986	River Plate	ARG	2-1 1-0	COL	América Cali
1987	Peñarol	URU	0-2 2-1 1-0	COL	América Cali
1988	Nacional Montevideo	URU	0-1 3-0	ARG	Newell's Old Boys
1989	Atlético Nacional Medellín	COL	0-2 2-0 5-4p	PAR	Olimpia
1990	Olimpia	PAR	2-0 1-1	ECU	Barcelona
1991	Colo Colo	CHI	0-0 3-0	PAR	Olimpia

COPA LIBERTADORES DE AMERICA (CONT'D)

Year	Winners	Country	Score	Country	Runners-up
1992	São Paulo FC	BRA	1-0 0-1 3-2p	ARG	Newell's Old Boys
1993	São Paulo FC	BRA	5-1 0-2	CHI	Universidad Catolica
1994	Velez Sarsfield	ARG	1-0 0-1 5-3p	BRA	São Paulo FC
1995	Grêmio	BRA	3-1 1-1	COL	Atlético Nacional Medellin
1996	River Plate	ARG	0-1 2-0	COL	América Cali
1997	Cruzeiro	BRA	0-0 1-0	PER	Sporting Cristal
1998	Vasco da Gama	BRA	2-0 2-1	ECU	Barcelona
1999	Palmeiras	BRA	0-1 2-1 4-3p	COL	Deportivo Cali
2000	Boca Juniors	ARG	2-2 0-0 4-2p	BRA	Palmeiras
2001	Boca Juniors	ARG	1-0 0-1 3-1p	MEX	Cruz Azul
2002	Olimpia	PAR	0-1 2-1 4-2p	BRA	São Caetano
2003	Boca Juniors	ARG	2-0 3-1	BRA	Santos
2004	Once Caldas	COL	0-0 1-1 2-0p	ARG	Boca Juniors
2005	São Paulo FC	BRA	1-1 4-0	BRA	Atlético Paranaense
2006	Internacional	BRA	2-1 2-2	BRA	São Paulo FC
2007	Boca Juniors	ARG	3-0 2-0	BRA	Grêmio
2008	LDU Quito	ECU	4-2 1-3 3-1p	BRA	Fluminense
2009	Estudiantes LP	ARG	0-0 2-1	BRA	Cruzeiro
2010	Internacional	BRA	2-1 3-2	MEX	Guadalajara
2011	Santos	BRA	0-0 2-1	URU	Peñarol

COPA LIBERTADORES MEDALS TABLE

	Country	G	S	B	F	SF
1	Argentina	22	8	32	30	62
2	Brazil	15	15	22	30	52
3	Uruguay	8	8	18	16	34
4	Paraguay	3	3	14	6	20
5	Colombia	2	7	18	9	27
6	Chile	1	5	14	6	20
7	Ecuador	1	2	9	3	12
8	Peru		2	6	2	8
9	Mexico		2	5	2	7
9	Bolivia			3		3
	Venezuela			3		3
		52	52	144	104	248

This table represents the Gold (winners), Silver (runners-up) and
Bronze (semi-finalists) placings of clubs representing the above
countries in the Copa Libertadores, along with the number of
appearances in the final and semi-finals

COPA LIBERTADORES MEDALS TABLE

	Club		G	S	B
1	Independiente	ARG	7		5
2	Boca Juniors	ARG	6	3	4
3	Peñarol	URU	5	5	10
4	Estudiantes La Plata	ARG	4	1	1
5	Nacional Montevideo	URU	3	3	7
6	Olimpia	PAR	3	3	5
7	São Paulo FC	BRA	3	3	3
8	Santos FC	BRA	3	1	3
9	River Plate	ARG	2	2	11
10	Grêmio	BRA	2	2	3
11	Cruzeiro	BRA	2	2	2
12	Internacional	BRA	2	1	2
13	SE Palmeiras	BRA	1	3	2
14	Colo Colo	CHI	1	1	3
15	At. Nacional Medellín	COL	1	1	2

COPA LIBERTADORES MEDALS TABLE (CONT'D)

	Club		G	S	B
16	Flamengo	BRA	1		2
	LDU Quito	ECU	1		2
	Racing Club Avellaneda	ARG	1		2
	Vélez Sarsfield	ARG	1		2
20	Argentinos Juniors	ARG	1		1
21	Once Caldas	COL	1		
	Vasco da Gama	BRA	1		
23	América Cali	COL		4	6
24	Barcelona	ECU		2	5
25	Deportivo Cali	COL		2	2
26	Cobreloa	CHI		2	1
27	Newell's Old Boys	ARG		2	
28	Universidad Catolica	CHI		1	4
29	Universitario	PER		1	3
30	Chivas Guadalajara	MEX		1	2

COPA LIBERTADORES MEDALS TABLE (CONT'D)

	Club		G	S	B
31	Union Española	CHI		1	1
32	Atlético Paranaense	BRA		1	
	Cruz Azul	MEX		1	
	Fluminense	BRA		1	
	São Caetano	BRA		1	
	Sporting Cristal	PER		1	
37	Cerro Porteño	PAR			6
38	CF América	MEX			3
	Millonarios	COL			3
	San Lorenzo de Almagro	ARG			3
	Universidad de Chile	CHI			3
42	Alianza	PER			2
	Botafogo	BRA			2
	Rosario Central	ARG			2
	Libertad	PAR			2
46	Atlético Junior	COL			1
	Atlético Mineiro	BRA			1
	Atlético San Cristobal	VEN			1
	Blooming	BOL			1

COPA LIBERTADORES MEDALS TABLE (CONT'D)

Club		G	S	B
Bolivar	BOL			1
Corinthians	BRA			1
Cúcuta Deportiva	COL			1
Danubio	URU			1
Defensor Lima	PER			1
Deportes Tolima	COL			1
Emelec	ECU			1
Guarani Asuncion	PAR			1
Guarani Campinas	BRA			1
Huracán	ARG			1
Independiente Medellin	COL			1
Independiente Santa Fé	COL			1
Jorge Wilsterman	BOL			1
El Nacional Quito	ECU			1
O'Higgins	CHI			1
Palestino	CHI			1
Portuguesa	VEN			1
ULA Merida	VEN			1
		52	52	144

SUPERCOPA JOAO HAVELANGE

Year	Winners	Country	Score	Country	Runners-up
1988	Racing Club	ARG	2-1 1-1	BRA	Cruzeiro
1989	Boca Juniors	ARG	0-0 0-0 5-3p	ARG	Independiente
1990	Olimpia	PAR	3-0 3-3	URU	Nacional Montevideo
1991	Cruzeiro	BRA	0-2 3-0	ARG	River Plate
1992	Cruzeiro	BRA	4-0 0-1	ARG	Racing Club
1993	São Paulo FC	BRA	2-2 2-2 5-3p	BRA	Flamengo
1994	Independiente	ARG	1-1 1-0	ARG	Boca Juniors
1995	Independiente	ARG	2-0 0-1	BRA	Flamengo
1996	Velez Sarsfield	ARG	1-0 2-0	BRA	Cruzeiro
1997	River Plate	ARG	0-0 2-1	BRA	São Paulo FC

SUPERCOPA MEDALS TABLE

	Country	G	S	B	F	SF
1	Argentina	6	4	4	10	14
2	Brazil	3	5	6	8	14
3	Paraguay	1		2	1	3
4	Uruguay		1	4	1	5
5	Chile			2		2
	Colombia			2		2
		10	10	20	20	40

This table represents the Gold (winners), Silver (runners-up) and Bronze (semi-finalists) placings of clubs representing the above countries in the Supercopa, along with the number of appearances in the final and semi-finals

SUPERCOPA MEDALS TABLE

	Club		G	S	B
1	Cruzeiro	BRA	2	2	2
2	Independiente	ARG	2	1	
3	River Plate	ARG	1	1	2
4	São Paulo FC	BRA	1	1	1
5	Boca Juniors	ARG	1	1	
	Racing Club	ARG	1	1	
7	Olimpia	PAR	1		2
8	Velez Sarsfield	ARG	1		
9	Flamengo	BRA		2	1
10	Nacional Montevideo	URU		1	2
11	Colo Colo	CHI			2
	Peñarol	URU			2
	At. Nacional Medellin	COL			2
14	Argentinos Juniors	ARG			1
	Estudiantes LP	ARG			1
	Santos	BRA			1
	Grêmio	BRA			1
			10	10	20

COPA CONMEBOL

Year	Winners	Country	Score	Country	Runners-up
1992	Atlético Mineiro	BRA	2-0 0-1	PAR	Olimpia
1993	Botafogo	BRA	1-1 2-2 3-1p	URU	Peñarol
1994	São Paulo FC	BRA	6-1 0-3	URU	Peñarol
1995	Rosario Central	ARG	0-4 4-0 4-3p	BRA	Atlético Mineiro
1996	Lanús	ARG	2-0 0-1	COL	Independiente Santa Fé
1997	Atlético Mineiro	BRA	4-1 1-1	ARG	Lanús
1998	Santos	BRA	1-0 0-0	ARG	Rosario Central
1999	Talleres Córdoba	ARG	2-4 3-0	BRA	CSA

COPA CONMEBOL MEDALS TABLE

	Country	G	S	B	F	SF
1	Brazil	5	2	6	7	13
2	Argentina	3	2	4	5	9
3	Uruguay		2		2	2
4	Paraguay		1	1	1	2
	Colombia		1	1	1	2
6	Chile			2		2
7	Ecuador			1		1
	Peru			1		1
		8	8	16	16	32

This table represents the Gold (winners), Silver (runners-up) and Bronze (semi-finalists) placings of clubs representing the above countries in the Copa Conmebol, along with the number of appearances in the final and semi-finals

COPA CONMEBOL MEDALS TABLE

	Club		G	S	B
1	Atlético Mineiro	BRA	2	1	2
2	Lanus	ARG	1	1	
3	Rosario Central	ARG	1	1	1
4	Botafogo	BRA	1		
	Santos	BRA	1		

COPA CONMEBOL MEDALS TABLE (CONT'D)

	Club		G	S	B
	São Paulo FC	BRA	1		
	Talleres Cordoba	ARG	1		
8	Peñarol	URU		2	
9	CSA	BRA		1	
	Independiente Santa Fé	COL		1	
	Olimpia	PAR		1	
12	Corinthians	BRA			1
	Deportes Concepcion	CHI			1
	Gimnasia y Esgrima	ARG			1
	El Nacional Quito	ECU			1
	San Lorenzo	ARG			1
	América Cali	COL			1
	Colón Santa Fé	ARG			1
	Atlético Colegiales	PAR			1
	Sampaio Correa	BRA			1
	São Raimundo	BRA			1
	Vasco da Gama	BRA			1
	Universitario	PER			1
	Universidad de Chile	CHI			1
			8	8	16

COPA MERCOSUR

Year	Winners	Country	Score	Country	Runners-up
1998	Palmeiras	BRA	1-2 3-1 1-0	BRA	Cruzeiro
1999	Flamengo	BRA	4-3	BRA	Palmeiras
2000	Vasco da Gama	BRA	2-0 0-1 4-3	BRA	Palmeiras
2001	San Lorenzo	ARG	0-0 1-1 4-3p	BRA	Flamengo

COPA MERCOSUR MEDALS TABLE

	Country	G	S	B	F	SF
1	Brazil	3	4	3	7	10
2	Argentina	1		3	1	4
3	Paraguay			1		1
	Uruguay			1		1
		4	4	8	8	16

This table represents the Gold (winners), Silver (runners-up) and Bronze (semi-finalists) placings of clubs representing the above countries in the Copa Mercosur, along with the number of appearances in the final and semi-finals

COPA MERCOSUR MEDALS TABLE

	Club		G	S	B
1	Palmeiras	BRA	1	2	
2	Flamengo	BRA	1	1	
3	San Lorenzo	ARG	1		2
4	Vasco da Gama	BRA	1		
5	Cruzeiro	BRA		1	
6	Atlético Mineiro	BRA			1
	Corinthians	BRA			1
	Grêmio	BRA			1
	Olimpia	PAR			1
	Peñarol	URU			1
	River Plate	ARG			1
			4	4	8

COPA MERCONORTE

Year	Winners	Country	Score	Country	Runners-up
1998	Atlético Nacional Medellin	COL	3-1 1-0	COL	Deportivo Cali
1999	América Cali	COL	1-2 1-0	COL	Independiente Santa Fé
2000	Atlético Nacional Medellin	COL	0-0 2-1	COL	Millonarios
2001	Millonários	COL	1-1 1-1 3-1p	ECU	Emelec

COPA MERCONORTE MEDALS TABLE

	Country	G	S	B	F	SF
1	Colombia	4	3	1	7	8
2	Ecuador		1	2	1	3
3	Mexico			3		3
4	Peru			1		1
	Venezuela			1		1
		4	4	8	8	16

This table represents the Gold (winners), Silver (runners-up) and Bronze (semi-finalists) placings of clubs representing the above countries in the Copa Merconorte, along with the number of appearances in the final and semi-finals

COPA MERCONORTE MEDALS TABLE

	Club		G	S	B
1	Atlético Nacional Medellin	COL	2		
2	Millonarios	COL	1	1	1
3	América Cali	COL	1		
4	Emelec	ECU		1	1
5	Deportivo Cali	COL		1	
	Independiente Santa Fé	COL		1	
7	Alianza Lima	PER			1
	Caracas FC	VEN			1
	Chivas Guadalajara	MEX			1
	El Nacional Quito	ECU			1
	Necaxa	MEX			1
	Santos Laguna	MEX			1
			4	4	8

COPA SUDAMERICANA

Year	Winners	Country	Score	Country	Runners-up
2002	San Lorenzo	ARG	4-0 0-0	COL	Atlético Nacional Medellin
2003	Cienciano	PER	3-3 1-0	ARG	River Plate
2004	Boca Juniors	ARG	0-1 2-0	BOL	Bolivar
2005	Boca Juniors	ARG	1-1 1-1 4-3p	MEX	Pumas UNAM
2006	Pachuca	MEX	1-1 2-1	CHI	Colo Colo
2007	Arsenal	ARG	3-2 1-2	MEX	America
2008	Internacional	BRA	1-0 1-1	ARG	Estudiantes LP
2009	LDU Quito	ECU	5-1 0-3	BRA	Fluminense
2010	Independiente	ARG	0-2 3-1 5-3p	BRA	Goiás EC
2011	Universidad de Chile	CHI	1-0 3-0	ECU	LDU Quito

COPA SUDAMERICANA MEDALS TABLE

	Country	G	S	B	F	SF
1	Argentina	5	2	5	7	12
2	Mexico	1	2	2	3	5
3	Brazil	1	2	5	3	8
4	Ecuador	1	1	2	2	4
5	Chile	1	1	1	2	3
6	Peru	1			1	1
7	Colombia		1	2	1	3
8	Bolivia		1	1	1	2
9	Paraguay			1		1
	Uruguay			1		1
		10	10	20	20	40

This table represents the Gold (winners), Silver (runners-up) and Bronze (semi-finalists) placings of countries representing the above countries in the Copa Sudamericana, along with the number of appearances in the final and semi-finals

COPA SUDAMERICANA MEDALS TABLE

	Club		G	S	B
1	Boca Juniors	ARG	2		
2	LDU Quito	ECU	1	1	2
3	Internacional	BRA	1		1
4	Arsenal	ARG	1		
	Cienciano	PER	1		
	Independiente	ARG	1		
	Pachuca	MEX	1		
	San Lorenzo	ARG	1		
	Universidad de Chile	CHI	1		
10	River Plate	ARG		1	2
11	Atlético Nacional Medellin	COL		1	1
	Bolivar	BOL		1	1
13	CF América	MEX		1	
	Colo Colo	CHI		1	
	Estudiantes LP	ARG		1	
	Fluminense	BRA		1	
	Goiás EC	BRA		1	
	Pumas UNAM	MEX		1	
19	Velez Sarsfield	ARG			2

COPA SUDAMERICANA MEDALS TABLE (CONT'D)

	Club		G	S	B
20	Argentinos Juniors	ARG			1
	Atlético Paranaense	BRA			1
	Cerro Porteño	PAR			1
	Guadalajara	MEX			1
	Millonarios	COL			1
	Nacional Montevideo	URU			1

COPA SUDAMERICANA MEDALS TABLE (CONT'D)

Club		G	S	B
Palmeiras	BRA			1
São Paulo FC	BRA			1
Universidad Catolica	CHI			1
Toluca	MEX			1
Vasco da Gama	BRA			1
		10	10	20

SOUTH AMERICAN YOUTH TOURNAMENTS

SUDAMERICANA SUB-20

Year	Host Country	Winners	Runners-up
1954	Venezuela	Uruguay	Brazil
1958	Chile	Uruguay	Argentina
1964	Colombia	Uruguay	Paraguay
1967	Paraguay	Argentina	Paraguay
1971	Paraguay	Paraguay	Uruguay
1974	Chile	Brazil	Uruguay
1975	Peru	Uruguay	Chile
1977	Venezuela	Uruguay	Brazil
1979	Uruguay	Uruguay	Argentina
1981	Ecuador	Uruguay	Brazil
1983	Bolivia	Brazil	Uruguay
1985	Paraguay	Brazil	Paraguay
1987	Colombia	Colombia	Brazil
1988	Argentina	Brazil	Colombia
1991	Venezuela	Brazil	Argentina
1992	Colombia	Brazil	Uruguay
1995	Bolivia	Brazil	Argentina
1997	Chile	Argentina	Brazil
1999	Argentina	Argentina	Uruguay
2001	Ecuador	Brazil	Argentina
2003	Uruguay	Argentina	Brazil
2005	Colombia	Colombia	Brazil
2007	Paraguay	Brazil	Argentina
2009	Venezuela	Brazil	Paraguay
2011	Peru	Brazil	Uruguay

SUDAMERICANA SUB-17

Year	Host Country	Winners	Runners-up
1985	Argentina	Argentina	Brazil
1986	Peru	Bolivia	Brazil
1988	Ecuador	Brazil	Argentina
1991	Paraguay	Brazil	Uruguay
1993	Colombia	Colombia	Chile
1995	Peru	Brazil	Argentina
1997	Paraguay	Brazil	Argentina
1999	Uruguay	Brazil	Paraguay
2002	Peru	Brazil	Argentina
2003	Bolivia	Argentina	Brazil
2005	Venezuela	Brazil	Uruguay
2007	Ecuador	Brazil	Colombia
2009	Brazil	Argentina	Chile
2011	Ecuador	Brazil	Uruguay

From 1985-1988 the championship was a U-16 tournament but
since 1991 it has operated as an U-17 championship

SOUTH AMERICAN WOMEN'S TOURNAMENTS

SOUTH AMERICAN WOMEN'S CHAMPIONSHIP

Year	Host Country	Winners	Runners-up
1991	Brazil	Brazil	Chile
1995	Brazil	Brazil	Argentina
1998	Argentina	Brazil	Argentina
2003	Peru	Brazil	Argentina
2006	Argentina	Argentina	Brazil
2010	Ecuador	Brazil	Colombia

SOUTH AMERICAN WOMEN'S U-20 CHAMPIONSHIP

Year	Host Country	Winners	Runners-up
2004		Brazil	Paraguay
2006	Chile	Brazil	Argentina
2008	Brazil	Brazil	Argentina
2010	Colombia	Brazil	Colombia

SOUTH AMERICAN WOMEN'S U-17 CHAMPIONSHIP

Year	Host Country	Winners	Runners-up
2008	Chile	Colombia	Brazil
2010	Brazil	Brazil	Chile

NATIONAL TEAM TOURNAMENTS
IN SOUTH AMERICA IN 2011

COPA AMERICA ARGENTINA 2011

First round groups		Quarter-finals			Semi-finals			Final	
Group A	Pts								
Colombia	7								
Argentina	5	Uruguay	1	5p					
Costa Rica	3	Argentina	1	4p					
Bolivia	1								
					Uruguay	2			
					Peru	0			
		Colombia	0						
Group B	Pts	**Peru**	2						
Brazil	5								
Venezuela	5					**Uruguay**	3		
Paraguay	3					Paraguay	0		
Ecuador	1								
		Venezuela	2						
		Chile	1						
					Venezuela	0	3p		
Group C	Pts				**Paraguay**	0	5p		
Chile	7								
Uruguay	5	Brazil	0	0p		3rd place play-off			
Peru	4	**Paraguay**	0	2p		**Peru**	4		
Mexico	0					Venezuela	1		

Top scorers: **5** - Paolo Guerrero PER • **4** - Luis Suarez URU • **3** - Sergio Aguero ARG • **2** - Falcao COL & Felipe Caicedo ECU

	GROUP A	PL	W	D	L	F	A	PTS		ARG	CRC	BOL
1	**Colombia**	3	2	1	0	3	0	**7**		0-0	1-0	2-0
2	**Argentina**	3	1	2	0	4	1	**5**			3-0	1-1
3	Costa Rica	3	1	0	2	2	4	**3**				2-0
4	Bolivia	3	0	1	2	1	5	**1**				

Unico, La Plata, 1-07-2011, 21:45, 52 700, Silvera URU

Argentina	1
	Sergio Aguero [76]

Sergio **Romero** - Javier **Zanetti**, Nicolas **Burdisso**, Gabriel **Milito**, Marcos **Rojo** - Ever **Banega**, Javier **Mascherano**(c), Esteban **Cambiasso** (Angel **Di Maria** 46) - Ezequiel **Lavezzi**• (Sergio **Aguero** 71), Lionel **Messi**, Carlos **Tevez**•. Tr: Sergio **Batista**

Bolivia	1
	Edivaldo Rojas [48]

Carlos **Arias** - Ronald **Raldes**(c), Ronald **Rivero**•, Lorgio **Alvarez**, Luis **Gutierrez**• - Jaime **Robles**, Walter **Flores**•, Jhasmani **Campos** (Juan **Arce** 81) - Joselito **Vaca** (Jose **Chavez**• 64) - Edivaldo **Rojas** (Rudy **Cardozo** 90), Marcelo **Moreno Martins**. Tr: Gustavo **Quinteros**

23 de Agosto, Jujuy, 2-07-2011, 15:30, 23 500, Osses CHI

Colombia	1
	Adrian Ramos [44]

Neco **Martinez** - Juan **Zuniga**•, Mario **Yepes**(c), Luis **Perea**, Pablo **Armero** - Gustavo **Bolivar**, Freddy **Guarin**•, Abel **Aguilar** (Hugo **Rodallega** 34) - Dayro **Moreno** (Teofilo **Gutierrez** 70), Radamel **Falcao** (E!kin **Soto** 77), Adrian **Ramos**. Tr: Hernan Dario **Gomez**

Costa Rica	0

Leonel **Moreira** - Jose **Salvatierra**, Johnny **Acosta**, Francisco **Calvo**•, Oscar **Duarte**, Pedro **Leal** - David **Guzman**• (Jose **Cubero** 74), Diego **Madrigal**• (Josue **Martinez** 72) - Randall **Brenes**(c)◆27, Joel **Campbell** (Cesar **Elizondo** 46), Heiner **Mora**. Tr: Ricardo **La Volpe**

Estanislao Lopez, Santa Fe, 6-07-2011, 21:45, 47000, Fagundes BRA
Argentina   0

Sergio **Romero** - Pablo **Zabaleta**, Nicolas **Burdisso**, Gabriel **Milito**, Javier **Zanetti** - Ever **Banega** (Gonzalo **Higuain** 72), Javier **Mascherano**(c), Esteban **Cambiasso** (Fernando **Gago**• 60) - Ezequiel **Lavezzi** (Sergio **Aguero** 61), Lionel **Messi**, Carlos **Tevez**. Tr: Sergio Batista

Colombia   0

Neco **Martinez** - Juan **Zuniga**, Luis **Perea**, Mario **Yepes**(c), Pablo **Armero** - Carlos **Sanchez** - Adrian **Ramos** (Elkin **Soto** 88), Abel **Aguilar**•, Freddy **Guarin**, Dayro **Moreno**• (Aquivaldo **Mosquera** 90) - Radamel **Falcao** (Teofilo **Gutierrez** 87). Tr: Hernan Dario **Gomez**

23 de Agosto, Jujuy, 7-07-2011, 19:15, 23000, Vera ECU
Costa Rica   2
Josue Martinez [59], Joel Campbell [78]

Leonel **Moreira** - Johnny **Acosta**, Oscar **Duarte**•, Francisco **Calvo** - Jose **Salvatierra**•, Pedro **Leal**, David **Guzman**•, Heiner **Mora** (Jose **Cubero** 82), Diego **Madrigal** (Allen **Guevara** 46) - Joel **Campbell**, Josue **Martinez** (Cesar **Elizondo** 80). Tr: Ricardo **La Volpe**

Bolivia   0

Carlos **Arias** - Lorgio **Alvarez**•, Ronald **Raldes**(c), Ronald **Rivero**•♦**69**, Luis **Gutierrez** - Edivaldo **Rojas**, Jaime **Robles** (Jose **Chavez** 66), Walter **Flores**♦**77**, Jhasmani **Campos**• (Nacho **Garcia** 78) - Juan **Arce**, Marcelo **Moreno Martins**•. Tr: Gustavo **Quinteros**

Estanislao Lopez, Santa Fe, 10-07-2011, 16:00, 12000, Chacon MEX
Colombia   2
Radamel Falcao 2 [14 28p]

Luis **Martinez** - Camilo **Zuniga**, Mario **Yepes**(c), Luis **Perea**, Pablo **Armero** - Fredy **Guarin** (Juan **Cuadrado** 50), Carlos **Sanchez**, Abel **Aguilar** - Dayro **Moreno** (Hugo **Rodallega** 46), Radamel **Falcao**, Adrian **Ramos** (Elkin **Soto** 77). Tr: Hernan Dario **Gomez**

Bolivia   0

Carlos **Arias** - Ronald **Raldes**(c), Christian **Vargas**, Santos **Amador**, Lorgio **Alvarez** - Jaime **Robles**, Ronald **Garcia**, Jhasmany **Campos**• - Edivaldo **Rojas** (Joselito **Vaca** 46), Marcelo **Moreno Martins** (Alcides **Pena** 60), Juan Carlos **Arce** (Ricardo **Pedriel** 70). Tr: Gustavo **Quinteros**

Mario Kempes, Cordoba, 11-07-2011, 21:45, 57000, Rivera PER
Argentina   3
Sergio Aguero 2 [45 52], Angel di Maria [63]

Sergio **Romero** - Pablo **Zabaleta**, Nicolas **Burdisso**, Gabriel **Milito**•, Javier **Zanetti**• - Fernando **Gago**, Javier **Mascherano**(c) - Lionel **Messi**, Angel **Di Maria** (Lucas **Biglia**• 79), Sergio **Aguero** (Ezequiel **Lavezzi**• 84) - Gonzalo **Higuain** (Javier **Pastore** 79). Tr: Sergio Batista

Costa Rica   0

Leonel **Moreira** - Oscar **Duarte**•, Jhonny **Acosta**(c), Francisco **Calvo**• (Randall **Brenes** 46) - Jose **Salvatierra**, Pedro **Leal**, Jose **Cubero**, Heiner **Mora**, Cesar **Elizondo** (Luis Miguel **Valle** 56) - Josue **Martinez** (Diego **Madrigal** 46), Joel **Campbell**. Tr: Ricardo **La Volpe**

	GROUP B	PL	W	D	L	F	A	PTS		VEN	PAR	ECU
1	Brazil	3	1	2	0	6	4	5		0-0	2-2	4-2
2	Venezuela	3	1	2	0	4	3	5			3-3	1-0
3	Paraguay	3	0	3	0	5	5	3				0-0
4	Ecuador	3	0	1	2	2	5	1				

Unico, La Plata , 3-07-2011, 16:00, 35000, Orosco BOL
Brazil   0

Julio **Cesar** - Dani **Alves**, **Lucio**(c), Thiago **Silva**•, Andre **Santos** - Lucas **Leiva**, Ramires (Lucas 75) - **Robinho** (Fred 64), Ganso, Neymar - Alexandre **Pato** (Elano 75). Tr: Mano Menezes

Venezuela   0

Renny **Vega** - Roberto **Rosales**, Grenddy **Perozo**, Oswaldo **Vizcarrondo**, Gabriel **Cichero** - Cesar **Gonzalez**• (Giacomo **di Giorgi** 85), Franklin **Lucena**, Tomas **Rincon**, Juan **Arango**(c) - Jose **Rondon**• (Alejandro **Moreno**• 63), Nicolas **Fedor** 'Miku' (Giancarlo **Maldonado** 78). Tr: Cesar **Farias**

Estanislao Lopez, Santa Fe, 3-07-2011, 19:15, 20000, Pezzotta ARG
Paraguay   0

Justo **Villar**(c) - Ivan **Piris**•, Paulo **da Silva**, Dario **Veron**, Aureliano **Torres** - Edgar **Barreto** (Enrique **Vera** 37), Nestor **Ortigoza**, Cristian **Riveros**, Marcelo **Estigarribia** - Roque **Santa Cruz** (Pablo **Zeballos**• 83), Lucas **Barrios** (Nelson **Valdez** 73). Tr: Gerardo **Martino**

Ecuador   0

Marcelo **Elizaga** - Neicer **Reasco**, Norberto **Araujo**, Frickson **Erazo**, Walter **Ayovi**(c) - Antonio **Valencia** (Michael **Arroyo** 46), Edison **Mendez** (David **Quiroz** 81), Segundo **Castillo**, Christian **Noboa** - Christian **Benitez**, Felipe **Caicedo**. Tr: Reinaldo **Rueda**

Mario Kempes, Cordoba, 9-07-2011, 16:00, 57000, Roldan COL
Brazil   2
Jadson [38], Fred [89]

Julio **Cesar** - Dani **Alves**•, **Lucio**(c), Thiago **Silva**, Andre **Santos** - Lucas **Leiva**•, Ramires (Lucas 69) - **Jadson**• (Elano 46), Ganso, Neymar (Fred 81) - Alexandre **Pato**•. Tr: Mano Menezes

Paraguay   2
Roque Santa Cruz [54], Nelson Valdez [66]

Justo **Villar**(c) - Dario **Veron**, Paulo **da Silva**, Antolin **Alcaraz**, Aureliano **Torres** - Nestor **Ortigoza**, Enrique **Vera**, Marcelo **Estigarribia** (Osvaldo **Martinez** 78) - Roque **Santa Cruz**, Lucas **Barrios**• (Nelson **Valdez** 56), Cristian **Riveros** (Victor **Caceres**• 67). Tr: Gerardo **Martino**

Ernesto Martearena, Salta, 9-07-2011, 18:30, 12000, Quesada CRC
Venezuela   1
Cesar Gonzalez [62]

Renny **Vega** - Roberto **Rosales**, Oswaldo **Vizcarrondo**, Grenddy **Perozo**, Gabriel **Cichero** - Cesar **Gonzalez** (Jesus **Meza** 64), Franklin **Lucena**, Tomas **Rincon**, Juan **Arango**(c) - Giancarlo **Maldonado** (Giacomo **di Giorgi** 80), Nicolas **Fedor** 'Miku' (Jose **Rondon** 74). Tr: Cesar **Farias**

Ecuador   0

Marcelo **Elizaga** - Neicer **Reasco**, Norberto **Araujo**, Frickson **Erazo**, Walter **Ayovi**(c) - Segundo **Castillo** (David **Quiroz** 75), Christian **Noboa** - Christian **Benitez**, Edison **Mendez**, Michael **Arroyo** (Edson **Montano** 71) - Felipe **Caicedo**. Tr: Reinaldo **Rueda**

Ernesto Martearena, Salta, 13-07-2011, 19:15, 18 000, Osses CHI

Paraguay 3

Antolin Alcaraz [32], Lucas Barrios [62], Cristian Riveros [85]

Justo Villar(c) - Dario Veron, Antolin Alcaraz, Paulo da Silva, Aureliano Torres - Marcelo Estigarribia (Victor Caceres 84), Cristian Riveros, Nestor Ortigoza, Enrique Vera (Jonathan Santana• 70) - Roque Santa Cruz (Nelson Valdez• 39), Lucas Barrios. Tr: Gerardo Martino

Venezuela 3

Jose Rondon [5], Nicolas Fedor [89], Greddy Perozo [92+]

Renny Vega - Roberto Rosales, Grenddy Perozo•, Oswaldo Vizcarrondo, Gabriel Cichero - Yohandry Orozco (Nicolas Fedor 'Miku' 66), Franklin Luchena, Tomas Rincon(c), Alexander Gonzalez (Giancarlo Maldonado• 75) - Daniel Arismendi (Juan Arango 63), Jose Rondon. Tr: Cesar Farias

---

Mario Kempes, Cordoba, 13-07-2011, 21:45, 39 000, Silvera URU

Brazil 4

Pato 2 [28 61], Neymar 2 [48 71]

Julio Cesar - Maicon, Lucio, Thiago Silva, Andre Santos• - Lucas Leiva, Ramires - Robinho, Ganso (Elias 76), Neymar (Lucas Moura 79) - Alexandre Pato (Fred 84). Tr: Mano Menezes

Ecuador 2

Felipe Caicedo 2 [36 58]

Marcelo Elizaga - Neicer Reasco (Gabriel Achilier 81), Norberto Araujo, Frickson Erazo, Walter Ayovi - Tilson Minda•, Christian Noboa• (Edson Montano 89), Michael Arroyo, Edison Mendez (Narciso Mina 76) - Christian Benitez, Felipe Caicedo. Tr: Reinaldo Rueda

---

	GROUP C	PL	W	D	L	F	A	PTS	URU	PER	MEX
1	Chile	3	2	1	0	4	2	7	1-1	1-0	2-1
2	Uruguay	3	1	2	0	3	2	5		1-1	1-0
3	Peru	3	1	1	1	2	2	4			1-0
4	Mexico	3	0	0	3	1	4	0			

Bicentenario, San Juan, 4-07-2011, 19:15, 25 000, Roldan COL

Uruguay 1

Luis Suarez [45]

Fernando Muslera - Martin Caceres•, Mauricio Victorino, Diego Lugano(c), Maxi Pereira - Nicolas Lodeiro (Cristian Rodriguez 78), Egidio Arevalo Rios, Diego Perez - Edinson Cavani (Abel Hernandez 78), Luis Suarez, Diego Forlan. Tr: Oscar Tabarez

Peru 1

Paolo Guerrero [23]

Raul Fernandez - Renzo Revoredo, Santiago Acasiete•, Alberto Rodriguez, Walter Vilchez(c) - Michael Guevara (Carlos Lobaton 57) - Adan Balbin, Rinaldo Cruzado•, Yoshimar Yotun (Juan Vargas• 59), Luis Advincula (William Chiroque 91+) - Paolo Guerrero•. Tr: Sergio Markarian

---

Bicentenario, San Juan, 4-07-2011, 21:45, 25 000, Soto VEN

Chile 2

Esteban Paredes [66], Arturo Vidal [72]

Claudio Bravo(c)• - Gonzalo Jara, Waldo Ponce, Pablo Contreras - Gary Medel, Arturo Vidal - Mauricio Isla, Matias Fernandez (Carlos Carmona 83), Jean Beausejour (Esteban Paredes 59) - Alexis Sanchez, Humberto Suazo (Marco Estrada 91+). Tr: Claudio Borghi

Mexico 1

Nestor Araujo [40]

Luis Ernesto Michel(c) - Paul Aguilar•, Nestor Araujo, Hector Reynoso, Hiram Mier, Darvin Chavez - Diego Reyes•, Jorge Enriquez, Javier Aquino• (Oribe Peralta 74) - Giovani dos Santos, Rafael Marquez Lugo (Edgar Pacheco• 88). Tr: Luis Tena

---

Malvinas, Mendoza, 8-07-2011, 19:15, 45 000, Amarilla PAR

Uruguay 1

Alvaro Pereira [53]

Fernando Muslera - Maxi Pereira (Sebastian Eguren 85), Diego Lugano(c), Sebastian Coates•, Martin Caceres• - Diego Perez, Egidio Arevalo (Nicolas Lodeiro 79), Alvaro Pereira• - Edinson Cavani (Alvaro Gonzalez• 46), Diego Forlan, Luis Suarez•. Tr: Oscar Tabarez

Chile 1

Alexis Sanchez [64]

Claudio Bravo(c) - Pablo Contreras•, Waldo Ponce, Gonzalo Jara• (Jorge Valdivia 60) - Mauricio Isla, Gary Medel, Arturo Vidal• - Alexis Sanchez•, Luis Jimenez, Jean Beausejour (Carlos Carmona 73) - Humberto Suazo (Esteban Paredes 73). Tr: Claudio Borghi

---

Malvinas, Mendoza, 8-07-2011, 21:45, 10 000, Pezzotta ARG

Peru 1

Paolo Guerrero [82]

Raul Fernandez - Giancarlo Carmona, Santiago Acasiete, Alberto Rodriguez, Walter Vilchez - Adan Balbin, Rinaldo Cruzado (Michael Guevara 76), Carlos Lobaton (Josepmir Ballon 85), Juan Vargas(c) - Paolo Guerrero, Luis Advincula (Yoshimar Yotun 46). Tr: Sergio Markarian

Mexico 0

Luis Ernesto Michel(c) - Paul Aguilar (Edgar Pacheco 46), Nestor Araujo, Hector Reynoso•, Hiram Mier•, Diego Reyes - Darvin Chavez (Miguel Angel Ponce 73), Javier Aquino (Oribe Peralta 85), Jorge Enriquez - Giovani dos Santos, Rafael Marquez Lugo. Tr: Luis Tena

---

Malvinas, Mendoza, 12-07-2011, 19:15, 42 000, Fagundes BRA

Chile 1

Andre Carrillo OG [92+]

Miguel Pinto - Marco Estrada•, Gonzalo Jara, Waldo Ponce - Jean Beausejour♦[61], Francisco Silva (Gary Medel 77), Carlos Carmona, Gonzalo Fierro (Alexis Sanchez 57) - Luis Jimenez - Esteban Paredes (Jorge Valdivia• 57), Humberto Suazo(c). Tr: Claudio Borghi

Peru 0

Salomon Libman• - Renzo Revoredo•, Christian Ramos•, Santiago Acasiete(c) (Walter Vilchez 46), Giancarlo Carmona♦[61], Aldo Corzo• - Josepmir Ballon, Antonio Gonzales (Andre Carrillo 76), Michael Guevara (Carlos Lobaton 69) - William Chiroque, Raul Ruidiaz. Tr: Sergio Markarian

---

Unico, La Plata, 12-07-2011, 21:45, 36 000, Orosco BOL

Uruguay 1

Alvaro Pereira [14]

Fernando Muslera - Maxi Pereira, Diego Lugano(c), Sebastian Coates•, Alvaro Pereira - Alvaro Gonzalez (Nicolas Lodeiro 68), Diego Perez, Egidio Arevalo, Cristian Rodriguez (Sebastian Eguren 83) - Diego Forlan (Sebastian Abreu 89), Luis Suarez. Tr: Oscar Tabarez

Mexico 0

Luis Ernesto Michel(c) - Paul Aguilar• (Oribe Peralta 46), Hiram Mier•, Hector Reynoso, Darvin Chavez - Miguel Ponce (Edgar Pacheco 70), Diego Reyes, Jorge Enriquez, Nestor Araujo - Giovani dos Santos (Javier Aquino 46), Rafael Marquez Lugo•. Tr: Jose Manuel de la Torre

QUARTER-FINALS

Estanislao Lopez, Santa Fe, 16-07-2011, 19:15, 47 000, Amarilla PAR

Argentina   **1 4p**

Gonzalo Higuain [18]

Sergio **Romero** - Pablo **Zabaleta•**, Nicolas **Burdisso•**, Gabriel **Milito•**, Javier **Zanetti** - Fernando **Gago•** (Lucas **Biglia** 97), Javier **Mascherano**(c)**••♦87** - Lionel **Messi**, Angel **Di Maria** (Javier **Pastore** 72), Sergio **Aguero** (Carlos **Tevez•** 84) - Gonzalo **Higuain**. Tr: Sergio **Batista**

Uruguay   **1 5p**

Diego Perez [6]

Fernando **Muslera** - Maxi **Pereira**, Diego **Lugano**(c), Mauricio **Victorino** (Andres **Scotti** 20), Martin **Caceres•** - Alvaro **Gonzalez•**, Diego **Perez••♦38**, Egidio **Arevalo** (Walter **Gargano** 110), Alvaro **Pereira** (Sebastian **Eguren** 110) - Diego **Forlan**, Luis **Suarez**. Tr: Oscar **Tabarez**

Mario Kempes, Cordoba, 16-07-2011, 16:00, 30 000, Chacon MEX

Colombia   **0**

Luis **Martinez** - Camilo **Zuniga**, Mario **Yepes**(c), Luis **Perea**, Pablo **Armero** - Carlos **Sanchez•** (Jackson **Martinez** 111), Fredy **Guarin**, Abel **Aguilar** (Teofilo **Gutierrez** 105) - Dayro **Moreno**, **Falcao**, Adrian **Ramos** (Hugo **Rodallega** 72). Tr: Hernan Dario **Gomez**

Peru   **2**

Carlos Lobaton [101], Juan Vargas [111]

Raul **Fernandez** - Renzo **Revoredo**, Christian **Ramos**, Alberto **Rodriguez•**, Walter **Vilchez**(c) - Adan **Balbin**, Rinaldo **Cruzado** (Josepmir **Ballon** 117), Juan **Vargas** - William **Chiroque** (Yoshimar **Yotun** 95), Paolo **Guerrero**, Luis **Advincula•** (Carlos **Lobaton** 46). Tr: Sergio **Markarian**

Bicentenario, San Juan, 17-07-2011, 19:15, 23 000, Vera ECU

Chile   **1**

Humberto Suazo [69]

Claudio **Bravo**(c) - Gonzalo **Jara** (Esteban **Paredes** 60), Waldo **Ponce**, Pablo **Contreras•** - Gary **Medel•♦82**, Arturo **Vidal•** - Mauricio **Isla•**, Luis **Jimenez** (Carlos **Munoz** 83), Carlos **Carmona** (Jorge **Valdivia** 46) - Alexis **Sanchez**, Humberto **Suazo**. Tr: Claudio **Borghi**

Venezuela   **2**

Oswaldo Vizcarrondo [34], Gabriel Cichero [80]

Renny **Vega** - Roberto **Rosales**, Grenddy **Perozo**, Oswaldo **Vizcarrondo**, Gabriel **Cichero** - Cesar **Gonzalez•** (Alejandro **Moreno** 89), Franklin **Lucena•**, Tomas **Rincon♦93+**, Juan **Arango**(c) - Giancarlo **Maldonado** (Luis **Seijas** 63), Nicolas **Fedor 'Miku'** (Jose **Rondon** 59). Tr: Cesar **Farias**

Unico, La Plata, 17-07-2011, 16:00, 36 000, Pezzotta ARG

Brazil   **0 0p**

Julio **Cesar** - **Maicon•**, **Lucio**(c), Thiago **Silva**, Andre **Santos•** - Lucas **Leiva♦103**, **Ramires** - **Robinho**, **Ganso** (Lucas 100), **Neymar** (Fred 80) - Alexandre **Pato** (Elano 112). Tr: Mano **Menezes**

Paraguay   **0 2p**

Justo **Villar**(c) - Dario **Veron**, Paulo **da Silva**, Antolin **Alcaraz♦103**, Aureliano **Torres** (Elvis **Marecos•** 71) - Victor **Caceres** - Enrique **Vera•** (Edgar **Barreto•** 64), Cristian **Riveros**, Marcelo **Estigarribia•** - Nelson **Valdez**, Lucas **Barrios** (Hernan Perez 83). Tr: Gerardo **Martino**

QUARTER-FINAL PENALTIES ARG v URU

ARG		URU
✓	Messi	
	Forlan	✓
✓	Burdisso	
	Suarez	✓
✗[1]	Tevez	
	Scotti	✓
✓	Pastore	
	Gargano	✓
✓	Higuain	
	Caceres	✓

1 = saved • 2 = missed

QUARTER-FINAL PENALTIES BRA v PAR

BRA		PAR
✗[2]	Elano	
	Barreto	✗[2]
✗[1]	Thiago Silva	
	Estigarribia	✓
✗[2]	Andre Santos	
	Riveros	✓
✗[2]	Fred	

1 = saved • 2 = missed

SEMI-FINALS

Unico, La Plata, 19-07-2011, 21:45, 25 000, Orosco BOL	
Peru	**0**

Raul **Fernandez** - Walter **Vilchez**(c), Santiago **Acasiete**, Alberto **Rodriguez**, Giancarlo **Carmona** - Juan **Vargas♦68**, Rinaldo **Cruzado**, Adan **Balbin●** (Josepmir **Ballon** 90), Yoshimar **Yotun●** (William **Chiroque** 53), Luis **Advincula** (Carlos **Lobaton●** 60) - Paolo **Guerrero**. Tr: Sergio **Markarian**

Uruguay	**2**
	Luis Suarez 2 ⁵² ⁵⁷

Fernando **Muslera** - Maxi **Pereira**, Diego **Lugano**(c)●, Sebastian **Coates**, Martin **Caceres** - Alvaro **Gonzalez**, Walter **Gargano●** (Abel **Hernandez** 70), Egidio **Arevalo**, Alvaro **Pereira** - Diego **Forlan**, Luis **Suarez●** (Sebastian **Eguren** 70). Tr: Oscar **Tabarez**

Malvinas, Mendoza, 20-07-2011, 21:45, 8 000, Chacon MEX	
Paraguay	**0 5p**

Justo **Villar**(c) - Marcos **Caceres**, Paulo **da Silva**, Dario **Veron●**, Ivan **Piris** - Edgar **Barreto** (Marcelo **Estigarribia** 70), Nestor **Ortigoza**, Cristian **Riveros**, Jonathan **Santana●●♦102** - Nelson **Valdez** (Roque **Santa Cruz** 73) (Osvaldo **Martinez** 80), Lucas **Barrios**. Tr: Gerardo **Martino**

Venezuela	**0 3p**

Renny **Vega** - Roberto **Rosales●**, Grenddy **Perozo** (Jose Manuel **Rey** 46), Oswaldo **Vizcarrondo**, Gabriel **Cichero** - Franklin **Lucena**, Cesar **Gonzalez** (Giancarlo **Maldonado** 84), Giacomo **di Georgi**, Juan **Arango**(c) - Alejandro **Moreno** (Nicolas **Fedor 'Miku'** 72), Jose **Rondon**. Tr: Cesar **Farias**

SEMI-FINAL PENALTIES PAR v VEN		
PAR		**VEN**
✓	Ortigoza	
	Maldonado	✓
✓	Barrios	
	Rey	✓
✓	Riveros	
	Lucena	✗¹
✓	Martinez	
	Miku	✓
✓	Veron	

1 = saved • 2 = missed

THIRD PLACE PLAY-OFF

Unico, La Plata, 23-07-2011, 16:00, 20 000, Roldan COL	
Peru	**4**
	William Chiroque ⁴¹, Paolo Guerrero 3 ⁶³ ⁸⁹ ⁹²⁺

Raul **Fernandez** - Christian **Ramos**, Aldo **Corzo**, Alberto **Rodriguez**, Renzo **Revoredo** - Adan **Balbin●**, Yoshimar **Yotun**, Rinaldo **Cruzado●** (Luis **Advincula** 78) - Carlos **Lobaton** (Michael **Guevara** 60), Paolo **Guerrero**(c), William **Chiroque**. Tr: Sergio **Markarian**

Venezuela	**1**
	Juan Arango ⁷⁷

Renny **Vega** - Roberto **Rosales**, Jose Manuel **Rey●**, Oswaldo **Vizcarrondo**, Gabriel **Cichero♦** - Tomas **Rincon**(c)♦58 - Cesar **Gonzalez** (Juan **Arango** 67), Yohandry **Orozco**, Luis Manuel **Seijas** (Franklin **Lucena** 46) - Nicolas **Fedor 'Miku'** (Jose Rondon 61), Giancarlo **Maldonado●**. Tr: Cesar **Farias**

Copa America Final	Estadio Monumental Buenos Aires	Sunday 24-07-2011
Kick-off: 16:00		Attendance: 57 921

URUGUAY 3 0 PARAGUAY

Luis Suarez [11], **Diego Forlan 2** [41] [89]

URUGUAY

Sky blue shirts, Sky blue shorts, Sky blue socks
Tr: Oscar Tabarez

Fernando Muslera

Maximiliano Pereira 29 Diego Lugano (c) Sebastian Coates 85 88 Martin Caceres 17 / Diego Godin

Alvaro Gonzalez 69 Diego Perez 24 / Sebastian Eguren Egidio Arevalo 63 Alvaro Pereira / Edinson Cavani

Diego Forlan Luis Suarez

76 Pablo Zeballos / Lucas Barrios Nelson Valdez

Cristian Riveros 64 Victor Caceres 26 / Marcelo Estigarribia Nestor Ortigoza 64 Enrique Vera 57 / Hernan Perez

Elvis Marecos Dario Veron Paulo da Silva Ivan Piris

Justo Villar (c)

Tr: Gerardo Martino
Red and white striped shirts, Blue shorts, Blue socks

PARAGUAY

MATCH STATS

URU		PAR
11	Shots	4
8	Shots on goal	1
8	Fouls committed	15
11	Corner kicks	4
1	Caught offside	2

MATCH OFFICIALS
REFEREE
Salvio Fagundes BRA
ASSISTANTS
Marcio Eustaquio BRA
Francisco Mondria CHI
4TH OFFICIAL
Enrique Osses CHI

(C) Captain † Man of the Match

This really means so much to me because my grandfather won the Copa America (Juan Carlos Corazo as coach in 1959), my father won it (Pablo Forlan in 1967) and now I have also done it. Three generations of my family have won this trophy.
Diego Forlan

The important thing was that we started the first half well. We scored twice and that was crucial. It was hard for them to make a comeback.
Luis Suarez

In the first-half, Uruguay had more intensity than us. Apart from that, they have two very good strikers who made the difference in the match. The goals scored by Uruguay were really good moves. The movement of the Uruguayan attackers was of an extraordinary quality and that made the difference.
Gerardo Martino

CLUB TOURNAMENTS IN
SOUTH AMERICA IN 2011

COPA SANTANDER LIBERTADORES 2011

Preliminary Round

Grêmio PA	BRA	2	3
Liverpool *	URU	2	1
Union Española	CHI	1	0
Bolívar *	BOL	0	0
Cerro Porteño *	PAR	1	1
Deportivo Petare	VEN	0	1
Jaguares	MEX	2	2
Alianza Lima *	PER	0	0
Deportes Tolima	COL	0	2
Corinthians *	BRA	0	0
Independiente *	ARG	2	0
Deportivo Quito	ECU	0	1

Group Stage

Grupo 1

		Pts	PAR	COL	PER	MEX
Libertad	PAR	14		2-2	5-1	2-0
Once Caldas	COL	7	1-1		0-3	1-1
Universidad San Martín	PER	6	0-1	0-2		2-0
San Luis	MEX	5	1-2	1-1	3-1	

Grupo 2

		Pts	COL	BRA	BOL	PER
Atlético Junior	COL	13		2-1	2-1	1-1
Grêmio PA	BRA	10	2-0		3-0	2-0
Oriente Petrolero	BOL	6	1-2	3-0		2-0
León de Huánuco	PER	5	1-2	1-1	1-0	

Grupo 3

		Pts	MEX	BRA	URU	ARG
CF América	MEX	10		1-0	2-0	2-1
Fluminense	BRA	8	3-2		0-0	2-2
Nacional Montevideo	URU	8	0-0	2-0		0-1
Argentinos Juniors	ARG	7	3-1	2-4	0-1	

Grupo 4

		Pts	CHI	ARG	VEN	CHI
Universidad Católica	CHI	11		0-0	1-3	2-1
Vélez Sarsfield	ARG	10	3-4		3-0	2-1
Caracas	VEN	9	0-2	0-3		2-0
Unión Española	CHI	4	2-2	2-1	1-2	

Grupo 5

		Pts	PAR	BRA	CHI	VEN
Cerro Porteño	PAR	11		1-2	5-2	1-1
Santos	BRA	11	1-1		3-2	3-1
Colo-Colo	CHI	9	2-3	3-2		2-1
Deportivo Táchira	VEN	2	0-2	0-0	2-4	

Grupo 6

		Pts	BRA	MEX	ECU	BOL
Internacional	BRA	13		4-0	2-0	3-0
Jaguares	MEX	9	1-0		2-1	2-0
Emelec	ECU	8	1-1	1-0		1-0
Jorge Wilstermann	BOL	4	1-4	2-1	0-0	

Grupo 7

		Pts	BRA	ARG	COL	PAR
Cruzeiro	BRA	16		5-0	6-1	4-0
Estudiantes LP	ARG	10	0-3		1-0	5-1
Deportes Tolima	COL	8	0-0	1-1		1-0
Guaraní	PAR	0	0-2	1-2	0-2	

Grupo 8

		Pts	ECU	URU	ARG	ARG
LDU Quito	ECU	10		5-0	3-0	2-0
Peñarol	URU	9	1-0		0-1	2-1
Independiente	ARG	8	1-1	3-0		1-3
Godoy Cruz	ARG	7	2-1	1-3	1-1	

* Home team in the first leg

COPA SANTANDER LIBERTADORES 2011

Round of 16			Quarter-finals			Semi-finals			Final		
Santos *	1	0									
CF América	0	0									
			Santos	1	1						
			Once Caldas *	0	1						
Cruzeiro	2	0									
Once Caldas *	1	2									
						Santos *	1	3			
						Cerro Porteño	0	3			
Jaguares *	1	3									
Atlético Junior	1	3									
			Jaguares *	1	0						
			Cerro Porteño	1	1						
Estudiantes LP *	0	0 3p									
Cerro Porteño	0	0 5p									
									Santos	0	2
									Peñarol *	0	1
Vélez Sarsfield *	3	2									
LDU Quito	0	0									
			Vélez Sarsfield *	3	4						
			Libertad	0	2						
Fluminense *	3	0									
Libertad	1	3									
						Vélez Sarsfield	0	2			
						Peñarol *	1	1			
Univ. Católica	2	1									
Grêmio *	1	0									
			Univ. Católica	0	2						
			Peñarol *	2	1						
Internacional	1	1									
Peñarol *	1	2									

* Home team in the first leg

Top scorers: **7** - Roberto Nanni ARG, Cerro Porteño & Wallyson BRA, Cruzeiro • **6** - Neymar BRA, Santos & Lucas Pratto ARG, Univ. Católica • **5** - Maximiliano Moralez ARG, Vélez; Juan Manuel Oliveira URU, Peñarol & Wason Renteria COL, Once Caldas

PRELIMINARY ROUND

Centenario, Montevideo
26-01-2011, 22:00, 13 875, Torres PAR

Liverpool 2

Franco [9], Macchi [25]

Matias Castro - Maximiliano **Montero**, Hugo Souza, Juan **Alvez**, Jhonatan **Souza●** - Maureen **Franco** (Elias **Figueroa** 78), Hernan **Figueredo** (Christian Silvera 88), Mauricio **Felipe**, Carlos **Macchi●** - Nicolas **Guevara** (Johnatan **Blanes●** 46), Emiliano **Alfaro●**. Tr: Eduardo Favaro

Grêmio 2

Andre Lima [6], Douglas [13]

Victor - Gabriel, Paulao●, Rafael Marques●, Gilson● (Diego 81), Lucio - Douglas, Vilson, Fabio Rochemback - Andre Lima● (Lins 87), Junior Vicosa (Vinicius Pacheco 59). Tr: Renato Gaucho

---

Santa Laura, Santiago
3-02-2011, 20:00, 5245, Amarilla PAR

Union Española 0

Rainer Wirth - Rodolfo **Madrid●**, Rafael **Olarra**, Leandro **Delgado**, Luis **Figueroa** - Martin **Liguera**, Braulio **Leal**, Gonzalo **Villagra** - Sebastian **Jaime** (Kevin **Harbottle** 86), Leonardo **Monje**, Fernando **Cordero** (Raul Estevez● 65). Tr: Jose Luis Sierra

Bolívar 0

Marcos **Arguello** - Edemir **Rodriguez**, Pablo **Frontini**, Ronald **Rivero**, Lorgio **Alvarez** - Ronald **Garcia●●♦67**, Walter **Flores●**, Abdon **Reyes** (Diego **Rivero** 27), Rudy **Cardozo** - Jose Marcelo **Gomez** (Juan **Bustillos** 66), Alex **da Rosa●** (Rodrigo **Vargas** 46). Tr: Jorge Habegger

---

Alejandro Villanueva, Lima
26-01-2011, 21:15, 28 285, Pitana ARG

Alianza Lima 0

Salomon **Libman** - Christian **Ramos●**, Edgar **Villamarin**, Leandro **Fleitas●**, Paolo **de la Haza** - Alexander **Sanchez**, Henry **Quinteros** (Cesar **Viza** 46), Edgar **Gonzalez**, Jean **Tragodara** - Roberto **Ovelar** (Cristofer **Soto●** 35), Hernan Gaston **Peirone** (David **Castro** 60). Tr: Gustavo Adolfo **Costas**

Jaguares 2

Pedroza [41], Rodriguez [45p]

Gerardo **Ruiz●** - Miguel Angel **Martinez**, Omar **Flores** - Oscar **Razo●**, Christian **Valdez**, Guillermo **Rojas**, Jorge **Hernandez●**, Ricardo **Esqueda●** (Marvin **Cabrera** 74) - Jorge **Rodriguez** (Alan **Zamora** 79), Damian **Manso** - Jackson **Martinez** (Antonio **Pedroza** 8). Tr: Jose Guadalupe **Cruz**

Manuel Torro, Ibague
2-02-2011, 19:00, 15 014, Silvera URU

Deportes Tolima 2

Santoya [65], Medina [77]

Antony **Silva** - Felix **Noguera**, Yair **Arrechea**, Julian **Hurtado●**, Gerardo **Vallejo** - Rafael **Castillo** (Danny **Santoya** 58), Jhon Fredy **Hurtado**, Gustavo **Bolivar**, Diego **Chara●** - Wilder **Medina** (Luis **Closa** 89), Elkin **Murillo●** (Marlon **Piedrahita** 82). Tr: Hernan **Torres Oliveros**

Corinthians 0

Julio **Cesar** - Alessandro, **Chicao**, Leandro **Castan●**, Fabio **Santos** (Edno 80) - **Jucilei●**, Ralf, **Paulinho** (Luis **Ramirez** 70♦72) - Jorge **Henrique●**, Dentinho (Danilo 69), Ronaldo. Tr: Tite

---

Olimpico, Porto Alegre
2-02-2011, 22:00, 31 426, Pezzotta ARG

Grêmio 3

Andre Lima [37], Vinicius Pacheco 2 [57 73]

Victor - Lucio, Bruno **Collaco**, **Gabriel**, Paulao, Rafael **Marques** - Adilson (Vinicius **Pacheco** 37), Douglas, Fabio Rochemback - Junior **Vicosa●** (Lins 89), Andre Lima (Diego 86). Tr: Renato Gaucho

Liverpool 1

Alfaro [34]

Matias Castro - Jhonatan Souza, Juan Alvez●, Martin Bonjour●, Hugo Souza, Maximiliano Montero (Hernan Figueredo 34) - Carlos Macchi (Renzo Pozzi 75), Mauricio Felipe (Johnatan Blanes 70), David Michel Acosta♦56 - Maureen Franco, Emiliano Alfaro. Tr: Eduardo Favaro

---

General Pablo Rojas, Asuncion
27-01-2011, 20:00, 15 663, Oliveira BRA

Cerro Porteño 1

Nanni [70]

Diego Barreto - Cesar Benitez, Luis Cardozo, Lautaro Formica, Ivan Piris, Mariano Uglessich, Julio dos Santos (Luis Caceres 78), Jorge Nunez (Jonathan Fabbro 63), Javier Villarreal●, Juan Manuel Lucero (Diego Madrigal 69), Roberto Nanni. Tr: Javier Torrente

Deportivo Petare 0

Alan **Liebeskind** - Marcelo Omar **Maidana●**, Andres **Sanchez●**, David **McIntosh●** - Bladimir **Morales●**, Gianfranco **di Julio** (Yohnger **Guerrero** 79), Manuel **Casseres**, Nolberto **Riascos** - Evelio **Hernandez** (Alain **Giroletti** 69), Alex **Sinisterra** (Richard **Blanco** 66), Felix Victor **Guaza**. Tr: Eduardo Sarago

---

Victor Reyna, Tuxtla Gutierrez
1-02-2011, 21:15, 6800, Buitrago COL

Jaguares 2

Pedroza [68], Salazar [74]

Gerardo **Ruiz** - Oscar **Razo**, Miguel Angel **Martinez●**, Ismael **Fuentes**, Marvin **Cabrera** (Christian **Valdez** 51) - Damian **Manso** (Antonio **Salazar** 65), Antonio **Pedroza**, Alan **Zamora** (Ricardo **Esqueda** 57), Jorge **Hernandez●**, Guillermo **Rojas** - Jorge **Rodriguez**. Tr: Jose Guadalupe **Cruz**

Alianza Lima 0

Salomon **Libman●** - Leandro **Fleitas●**, Christian **Ramos●**, Edgar **Villamarin♦29**, Edgar **Gonzalez** - Paolo **de la Haza●**, Luis **Trujillo**, Jean **Tragodara** (David **Castro** 67), Alexander **Sanchez●**, Junior **Viza** (Oscar **Vilchez** 46) - Hernan Gaston **Peirone** (Henry **Quinteros** 84). Tr: Gustavo Adolfo **Costas**

Libertadores de América, Avellaneda
25-01-2011, 21:15, 16 844, Lopes BRA

Independiente 2

Defederico [49], Rodriguez [70]

Hilario **Navarro** - Julian **Velazquez**, Carlos **Matheu**, Eduardo **Tuzzio** - Maximiliano **Velazquez** (Patricio **Rodriguez** 20), Lucas **Mareque**, Roberto **Battion**, Nicolas **Cabrera** - Matias **Defederico** (Cristian **Pellerano** 69) - Andres **Silvera** (Martin **Gomez** 83), Facundo **Parra●**. Tr: Antonio **Mohamed**

Deportivo Quito 0

Marcelo **Elizaga●** - Pedro **Esterilla●** (Michael **Castro** 81), Isaac **Mina**, Luis **Checa●**, Mariano **Mina●** - Juan Carlos **Paredes●**, Segundo **Castillo**, Alex **Bolanos**, Luis **Saritama** - Michael **Quinonez** (Gustavo **Rodas** 66) - Maxi **Bevacqua** (Luis **Perea** 57). Tr: Ruben Dario **Insua**

Hernando Siles, La Paz
27-01-2011, 21:15, 20 433, Rivera PER

Bolívar 0

Marcos **Arguello** - Lorgio **Alvarez**, Ronald **Rivero●**, Pablo **Frontini**, Edemir **Rodriguez** (Ronald **Eguino** 62) - Rudy **Cardozo**, Ronald **Garcia**, Abdon **Reyes** (Marcelo **Gomez** 67), Ze **Carlos●●♦81**, Walter **Flores** (Alex **da Rosa** 55) - William **Ferreira**. Tr: Guillermo Hoyos

Union Española 1

Cordero [17]

Rainer **Wirth●** - Leandro **Delgado**, Rafael **Olarra**, Rodolfo **Madrid●** - Luis **Figueroa**, Braulio **Leal**, Gonzalo **Villagra●**, Martin **Liguera** (Esteban **Gonzalez** 80), Fernando **Cordero** - Sebastian **Jaime** (Diego **Scotti** 72), Leonardo **Monje** (Mario **Aravena** 84). Tr: Jose Luis **Sierra**

Olimpico, Caracas
3-02-2011, 21:00, 2897, Vera ECU

Deportivo Petare 1

Guaza [13]

Alan **Liebeskind** - Marcelo Omar **Maidana●**, Andres **Sanchez**, David **McIntosh** - Bladimir **Morales** (Yohnger **Guerrero** 64), Gianfranco **di Julio**, Rafael **Lobo** (Jhon **Cordoba** 73♦84), Nolberto **Riascos** - Evelio **Hernandez** - Alex **Sinisterra**, Victor **Guaza**. Tr: Eduardo **Sarago**

Cerro Porteño 1

Nanni [34]

Diego **Barreto** - Cesar **Benitez**, Luis **Cardozo**, Mariano **Uglessich**, Ivan **Piris**, Lautaro **Formica●** - Jorge **Nunez**, Javier **Villarreal**, Julio dos Santos (Rodrigo **Burgos** 79) - Juan Manuel **Lucero●** (Jonathan **Fabbro** 66), Roberto **Nanni●** (Freddy **Bareiro** 71). Tr: Javier Torrente

---

Pacaembu, São Paulo
26-01-2011, 22:00, 26 536, Osses CHI

Corinthians 1

Julio **Cesar** - Roberto **Carlos** (Marcelo **Oliveira** 73), Leandro **Castan**, **Chicao**, Alessandro - Jorge **Henrique**, Bruno **Cesar** (Edno 56), **Jucilei●**, Ralf - **Ronaldo**, **Dentinho** (Danilo Fernando 79). Tr: Tite

Deportes Tolima 0

Antony **Silva●** - Gerardo **Vallejo**, Julian **Hurtado**, Felix **Noguera**, Yair **Arrechea●** - Diego **Chara**, Gustavo **Bolivar**, Rafael **Castillo** (Christian **Marrugo** 67), Elkin **Murillo●** (Danny **Santoya** 85) - Wilder **Medina** (Pablo **Gimenez** 77), Jhon Fredy **Hurtado**. Tr: Hernan **Torres Oliveros**

Olimpico Atahualpa, Quito
1-02-2011, 19:45, 12 029, Larrionda URU

Deportivo Quito 1

Quinonez [56]

Marcelo **Elizaga** - Isaac **Mina**, Luis **Checa**, Jairo **Campos** - Juan Carlos **Paredes●** (Michael **Quinonez** 55), Gustavo Ariel **Rodas** (Gonzalo **Rovira** 62), Luis **Saritama**, Segundo **Castillo**, Tilson **Minda●** (Angel **Escobar** 79) - Maxi **Bevacqua**, Luis **Perea**. Tr: Ruben Dario **Insua**

Independiente 0

Hilario **Navarro** - Carlos **Matheu●**, Eduardo **Tuzzio**, Julian **Velazquez** - Nicolas **Cabrera**, Fernando **Godoy** (Cristian **Pellerano** 68), Roberto **Battion**, Lucas **Mareque●** - Matias **Defederico** (Patricio **Rodriguez** 76), Andres **Silvera**, Facundo **Parra** (Maximiliano **Velazquez** 55). Tr: Antonio **Mohamed**

GRUPO 1		PI	W	D	L	F	A	Pts	PAR	COL	PER	MEX
Libertad	PAR	6	4	2	0	13	5	14		2-2	5-1	2-0
Once Caldas	COL	6	1	4	1	7	8	7	1-1		0-3	1-1
Universidad San Martín	PER	6	2	0	4	7	11	6	0-1	0-2		2-0
San Luis	MEX	6	1	2	3	6	9	5	1-2	1-1	3-1	

Alfonso Lastras, San Luis Potosí
15-02-2011, 18:45, 12 198, Buitrago COL

San Luis 1
Cavallo 38

Carlos Trejo• - Sergio Amaury Ponce, Anibal Matellan•, Christian Sanchez, Juan Cuevas, Carlos Hurtado, Noe Maya - Ignacio Torres••♦83 - Wilmer Aguirre, Michael Arroyo, Othoniel Arce (Juan Cavallo• 31). Tr: Ignacio Ambriz

Libertad 0
Pavlovich 18, Aquino 54p

Tobias Vargas - Carlos Bonet, Pedro Portocarrero, Arnaldo Vera, Miguel Samudio• - Jorge Gonzalez• (Rodrigo Rojas• 40), Victor Caceres, Rodolfo Gamarra (Victor Caceres 46), Sergio Aquino - Manuel Maciel (Angel Orue 57), Nicolas Pavlovich. Tr: Javier Luis Torrente

Palogrande, Manizales
16-02-2011, 21:15, 7689, Pezzotta ARG

Once Caldas 0

Luis Martinez - Elkin Calle• (Yedinson Palacios 75), Diego Amaya, Alexis Henriquez•, Luis Nunez (Jhon Pajoy 51) - Carlos Carbonero, Mario Gonzalez, Alexander Mejia, Matias Mirabaje (Carlos Ramirez 46) - Felix Micolta, Dayro Moreno. Tr: Juan Carlos Osorio

Universidad San Martín 3
Arriola 2 37 59, Alemanno 41

Ricardo Farro - Aldo Corzo, Julio Cesar Moreyra, Orlando Contreras, Guillermo Guizasola - Adan Balbin, Carlos Fernandez• (Walter Fretes 88), John Hinostroza, Ronald Quinteros• - German Ariel Alemanno (Gianfranco Labarthe 71), Heber Alberto Arriola•. Tr: Anibal Ruiz

Miguel Grau, Callao
22-02-2011, 19:30, 5000, Seneme BRA

Universidad San Martín 2
Labarthe 84, Marinelli 89

Ricardo Farro - Aldo Corzo, Julio Cesar Moreyra, Orlando Contreras, Guillermo Guizasola - Adan Balbin, Carlos Fernandez (Carlos Marinelli 72), John Hinostroza, Ronald Quinteros - German Ariel Alemanno (Gianfranco Labarthe 72), Heber Alberto Arriola (Christian Cueva 55). Tr: Anibal Ruiz

San Luis 0

Carlos Trejo - Sergio Amaury Ponce, Anibal Matellan, Luis Omar Hernandez, Osmar Mares - Noe Maya•, Jaime Correa, Juan Cuevas (Victor Lojero 76) - Othoniel Arce• (Michael Arroyo 55), Juan Cavallo, Wilmer Aguirre (Juan Medina 66). Tr: Ignacio Ambriz

Palogrande, Manizales
22-02-2011, 21:45, 6226, Laverni ARG

Once Caldas 1
Moreno 28

Luis Martinez - Elkin Calle, Diego Amaya, Alexis Henriquez, Luis Nunez (Diego Arango 78) - Carlos Carbonero•, Carlos Ramirez, Alexander Mejia, Harrison Henao (Jefferson Cuero• 78) - Felix Micolta (Jhon Pajoy 67), Dayro Moreno. Tr: Juan Carlos Osorio

Libertad 1
Ayala 94+

Tobias Vargas - Carlos Bonet, Pedro Portocarrero•, Ignacio Canuto•, Miguel Samudio - Rodrigo Rojas (Victor Ayala• 59), Omar Pouso (Rodolfo Gamarra 59), Victor Caceres, Sergio Aquino - Manuel Maciel (Ariel Nunez 70), Nicolas Pavlovich. Tr: Gregorio Perez

Alfonso Lastras, San Luis Potosí
2-03-2011, 21:15, 6522, Antequera BOL

San Luis 1
Arroyo 17

Cesar Lozano - Sergio Amaury Ponce, Anibal Matellan•, Luis Omar Hernandez, Osmar Mares - Noe Maya, Isai Arredondo (Victor Lojero 72), Juan Cuevas (Carlos Hurtado 81) - Michael Arroyo, Othoniel Arce, Juan Cavallo (Juan Medina 66). Tr: Ignacio Ambriz

Once Caldas 1
Renteria 2

Luis Martinez - Elkin Calle, Diego Amaya•, Alexis Henriquez, Luis Nunez - Harrison Henao• (Mario Gonzalez 71), Carlos Carbonero•, Alexander Mejia, Matias Mirabaje (Felix Micolta 56) - Dayro Moreno, Wason Renteria• (Diego Arango 86). Tr: Juan Carlos Osorio

Dr Nicolás Léoz, Asuncion
8-03-2011, 19:15, 2317, Silvera URU

Libertad 5
Rojas 14, Orue 18, Maciel 28, Ayala 50, Pouso 84

Tobias Vargas - Carlos Bonet (Nelson Romero 88), Pedro Portocarrero, Ignacio Canuto, Miguel Samudio - Victor Ayala, Victor Caceres, Rodrigo Rojas (Omar Pouso 73), Sergio Aquino - Manuel Maciel• (Rodolfo Gamarra 68), Angel Orue. Tr: Gregorio Perez

Universidad San Martín 1
Alemanno 4

Ricardo Farro - Aldo Corzo•, Julio Cesar Moreyra, Orlando Contreras, Guillermo Guizasola - Adan Balbin (Walter Fretes 44), Carlos Fernandez (Carlos Marinelli 46), John Hinostroza, Ronald Quinteros (Christian Cueva 62) - German Ariel Alemanno, Heber Alberto Arriola. Tr: Anibal Ruiz

Miguel Grau, Callao
15-03-2011, 17:15, 1414, Lopes BRA

Universidad San Martín 0

Ricardo Farro - Aldo Corzo, Julio Cesar Moreyra♦24, Orlando Contreras, Guillermo Guizasola - Adan Balbin, Christian Cueva (Diego Nadaya 89), John Hinostroza, Ronald Quinteros (Gianfranco Labarthe 74) - German Ariel Alemanno, Heber Alberto Arriola (Carlos Marinelli 59). Tr: Anibal Ruiz

Libertad 1
Aquino 23p

Tobias Vargas - Carlos Bonet, Pedro Portocarrero, Ignacio Canuto•, Miguel Samudio• - Victor Ayala (Jorge Gonzalez 61), Victor Caceres, Rodrigo Rojas (Omar Pouso 69), Sergio Aquino• - Manuel Maciel, Nicolas Pavlovich (Rodolfo Gamarra 72). Tr: Gregorio Perez

Palogrande, Manizales
15-03-2011, 21:45, 6906, Ponce ECU

Once Caldas 1
Nunez 78

Luis Martinez• - Elkin Calle, Oliver Fula, Alexis Henriquez•88, Luis Nunez• - Carlos Carbonero, Mario Gonzalez (Arnulfo Valentierra• 84), Alexander Mejia• (Harrison Henao 80) - Felix Micolta (Matias Mirabaje 63), Dayro Moreno•, Wason Renteria. Tr: Juan Carlos Osorio

San Luis 1
Medina 93+

Carlos Trejo• - Sergio Amaury Ponce••♦89, Luis Omar Hernandez•, Gabriel de la Vega - Noe Maya, Ignacio Torres, Juan Cavallo (Isai Arredondo 63), Juan Carlos Medina, Juan Cuevas (Juan Isijara 83) - Michael Arroyo•, Victor Lojero. Tr: Ignacio Ambriz

Dr Nicolás Léoz, Asuncion
22-03-2011, 21:15, 1240, Prudente URU

Libertad 2
Pavlovich 2 15 92+

Tobias Vargas - Carlos Bonet, Pedro Portocarrero (Angel Orue 80), Ignacio Canuto•, Miguel Samudio• (Victor Ayala 80) - Victor Caceres, Jorge Gonzalez (Manuel Maciel 62), Rodrigo Rojas, Rodolfo Gamarra, Sergio Aquino - Nicolas Pavlovich. Tr: Gregorio Perez

Once Caldas 2
Renteria 2 11 17

Luis Martinez - Elkin Calle, Diego Amaya, Oliver Fula, Luis Nunez - Carlos Ramirez, Carlos Carbonero• (Felix Micolta 72), Mario Gonzalez• (Harrison Henao 54), Alexander Mejia - Dayro Moreno, Wason Renteria (Matias Mirabaje 81). Tr: Juan Carlos Osorio

Alfonso Lastras, San Luis Potosí
22-03-2011, 20:30, 2750, Abal ARG

San Luis 3
Medina 2, Arroyo 2 13 74

Cesar Lozano - Noe Maya, Anibal Matellan•, Luis Omar Hernandez, Osmar Mares - Ignacio Torres•, Jaime Correa, Juan Carlos Medina (Carlos Hurtado 80), Juan Cuevas (Victor Lojero 70) - Wilmer Aguirre (Juan Cavallo 89), Michael Arroyo•. Tr: Ignacio Ambriz

Universidad San Martín 1
Quinteros 60

Ricardo Farro - Aldo Corzo•, Orlando Contreras, Guillermo Guizasola - Adan Balbin (Christian Cueva 46), Carlos Fernandez, Walter Fretes (Anthony Molina 46), John Hinostroza, Ronald Quinteros♦78 - German Ariel Alemanno, Carlos Ariel Marinelli. Tr: Anibal Ruiz

Dr Nicolás Léoz, Asuncion
19-04-2011, 21:30, 474, Fagundes BRA

Libertad 2
Gonzalez 10, Pavlovich 16

Tobias Vargas - Carlos Bonet, Pedro Portocarrero, Ignacio Canuto, Miguel Samudio - Victor Caceres (Omar Pouso 41), Jorge Gonzalez, Rodrigo Rojas (Rodolfo Gamarra 66), Jose Nunez, Sergio Aquino (Victor Ayala 21) - Nicolas Pavlovich. Tr: Gregorio Perez

San Luis 0

Cesar Lozano - Sergio Amaury Ponce, Anibal Matellan, Christian Sanchez•, Osmar Mares - Isai Arredondo•, Jaime Correa (Daniel Alcantar 55), Juan Medina (Noe Maya 87), Juan Cuevas (Juan Cavallo 82) - Wilmer Aguirre, Michael Arroyo. Tr: Ignacio Ambriz

Miguel Grau, Callao
19-04-2011, 20:30, 1904, Osses CHI

Universidad San Martín 0

Ricardo Farro - Aldo Corzo•, Julio Cesar Moreyra•, Orlando Contreras♦90, Guillermo Guizasola• (Diego Nadaya 77) - Adan Balbin♦81, Cristian Cueva, Carlos Fernandez, John Hinostroza - German Ariel Alemanno• (Benjamin Ubierna 86), Heber Alberto Arriola (Gianfranco Labarthe 46). Tr: Anibal Ruiz

Once Caldas 2
Renteria 16, Mirabaje 76

Luis Martinez - Elkin Calle, Diego Amaya, Alexis Henriquez, Luis Nunez• - Harrison Henao, Alexander Mejia, Carlos Carbonero• (Felix Micolta 85), Matias Mirabaje• (Mario Gonzalez 78) - Dayro Moreno•, Wason Renteria (Oliver Fula 90). Tr: Juan Carlos Osorio

GRUPO 2		Pl	W	D	L	F	A	Pts	COL	BRA	BOL	PER
Atlético Junior	COL	6	4	1	1	9	7	13		2-1	2-1	1-1
Grêmio PA	BRA	6	3	1	2	9	6	10	2-0		3-0	2-0
Oriente Petrolero	BOL	6	2	0	4	7	8	6	1-2	3-0		2-0
León de Huánuco	PER	6	1	2	3	4	8	5	1-2	1-1	1-0	

Heraclio Tapia, Huánuco
17-02-2011, 14:30, 11 115, Oliveira BRA

León de Huánuco 1
Elias 86

Juan Angel Flores - Luis Cardoza•, Jorge Araujo (Jorge Leiva 90), Roller Cambindo - Jair Cespedes, Ever Chavez (Victor Pena 46), Jean Ferrari•, Harrison Otalvaro (Carlos Elias 79), Carlos Zegarra• - Carlos Orejuela, Orlando Rodriguez. Tr: Franco Navarro

Atlético Junior 2
Viafara 23, Bacca 65

Sebastian Viera - Cesar Fawcett•, Anselmo de Almeida, Harold Macias, Sergiu Otalvaro (Juan Valencia• 56) - Jhon Viafara• (Braynner Garcia 61), Jossymar Gomez, Jose Amaya••♦79, Giovanni Hernandez - Carlos Bacca (Julian Barahona• 78), Luis Paez. Tr: Oscar Hector Quintabani

Metropolitano, Barranquilla
24-02-2011, 21:45, 20 348, Rodriguez.M MEX

Atlético Junior 2
Hernandez 28, Viafara 74

Carlos Rodriguez - Cesar Fawcett, Anselmo de Almeida, Harold Macias, Braynner Garcia• - Jossymar Gomez, Jhon Viafara, Giovanni Hernandez - Carlos Bacca, Victor Javier Cortes• (Sherman Cardenas 61) (Julian Barahona 89), Luis Paez (Juan Valencia 80). Tr: Oscar Hector Quintabani

Grêmio 1
Borges 4

Victor - Gabriel, Paulao, Rodolfo, Gilson - Fabio Rochemback, Adilson•, Carlos Alberto• (Bruno Collaco 36), Douglas - Andre Lima• (Junior Vicosa 78). Borges (Vinicius Pacheco 89). Tr: Renato Gaucho

Heraclio Tapia, Huánuco
17-03-2011, 15:00, 9684, Garcia MEX

León de Huánuco 1
Elias 43

Juan Angel Flores - Gianfranco Espinoza, Guillermo Salas, Luis Cardoza•, Roller Cambindo - Jair Cespedes (Victor Pena 67), Jean Ferrari•, Carlos Zegarra - Carlos Orejuela (Orlando Rodriguez 84), Carlos Elias• (Harrison Otalvaro 78), Juan Gonzalez-Vigil. Tr: Franco Navarro

Grêmio 1
Carlos Alberto 54

Victor - Rafael Marques, Gabriel, Lucio, Rodolfo•, Gilson - Fabio Rochemback, Carlos Alberto (Bruno Collaco 72), Douglas - Fernando (Junior Vicosa 35), Borges• (Diego 84). Tr: Renato Gaucho

Olimpico, Porto Alegre
7-04-2011, 19:15, 28 798, Baldassi ARG

Grêmio 2
Lucio 33, Borges 60

Victor - Gabriel, Rafael Marques, Rodolfo•, Bruno Collaco - Fabio Rochemback• (Vinicius Pacheco 69), Adilson•, Lucio (Fernando 82), Douglas, Damian Escudero (Diego 76) - Borges•. Tr: Renato Gaucho

Atlético Junior 0

Sebastian Viera - Cesar Fawcett, Anselmo de Almeida, Harold Macias• (Jose Amaya 45), Sergio Otalvaro• - Jaider Romero••♦67, Juan Valencia, Julian Barahona•, Sherman Cardenas, Giovanni Hernandez (Victor Javier Cortes 80) - Carlos Bacca (Wainer Caneda 87). Tr: Oscar Hector Quintabani

Olimpico, Porto Alegre
17-02-2011, 19:45, 32 791, Prudente URU

Grêmio 3
Douglas 2 43p 70, Gilson 48

Victor - Gabriel, Paulao, Lucio (Maylson 84), Rodolfo, Gilson - Fabio Rochemback, Carlos Alberto• (Adilson 76), Douglas - Andre Lima (Damian Escudero 73), Borges. Tr: Renato Gaucho

Oriente Petrolero 0

Hugo Suarez - Miguel Hoyos, Gustavo Martin Caamano•, Alejandro Schiapparelli (Alejandro Melean 36), Luis Gutierrez - Fernando Saucedo, Jhasmany Campos (Alcides Pena 71), Diego Terrazas (Marcelo Aguirre 57), Joselito Vaca - Mauricio Saucedo•, Juan Carlos Arce. Tr: Gustavo Quinteros

Olimpico, Porto Alegre
3-03-2011, 20:15, 26 455, Osses CHI

Grêmio 3
Andre Lima 41, Borges 54

Victor - Rafael Marques, Gabriel•, Rodolfo (Mario Fernandes 90), Gilson• - Fabio Rochemback•, Adilson, Carlos Alberto (Bruno Collaco 75), Douglas - Andre Lima (Damian Escudero 83), Borges. Tr: Renato Gaucho

León de Huánuco 0

Juan Angel Flores - Gianfranco Espinoza, Jorge Araujo•, Luis Cardoza, Guillermo Salas - Jair Cespedes, Jean Ferrari• (Miguel Cevasco 87), Carlos Zegarra• - Carlos Orejuela, Carlos Elias (Harrison Otalvaro 70), Juan Gonzalez-Vigil (Orlando Rodriguez 65). Tr: Franco Navarro

Metropolitano, Barranquilla
17-03-2011, 21:45, 13 155, Soto VEN

Atlético Junior 2
Bacca 2 64 72p

Carlos Rodriguez - Cesar Fawcett, Anselmo de Almeida•, Harold Macias, Braynner Garcia - Jossymar Gomez (Jaider Romero 46), Sherman Cardenas, Jhon Viafara (Juan Valencia• 83), Luis Paez (Carlos Bacca 46). Tr: Oscar Hector Quintabani

Oriente Petrolero 1
Campos 48

Hugo Suarez (Michael Etulain 84) - Miguel Hoyos, Gustavo Martin Caamano (Alejandro Melean, Luis Gutierrez - Alejandro Schiapparelli•, Marcelo Aguirre••♦57, Jhasmany Campos•, Joselito Vaca - Mauricio Saucedo (Alcides Pena 30), Juan Carlos Arce (Nicolas Fernandez 43). Tr: Gustavo Quinteros

Ramon Tahuichi Aguilera, Santa Cruz
14-04-2011, 21:45, 3360, Ponce ECU

Oriente Petrolero 3
Fernandez 50, Saucedo 75, Arce 79

Michael Etulain - Miguel Hoyos, Gustavo Martin Caamano, Alejandro Schiapparelli, Luis Gutierrez - Marcelo Aguirre, Fernando Saucedo, Diego Terrazas, Walter Veizaga (Jhasmany Campos 65) - Juan Carlos Arce (Alejandro Melean 81), Nicolas Fernandez (Alcides Pena 66). Tr: Gustavo Quinteros

Grêmio 1

Victor - Gabriel, Rafael Marques, Rodolfo♦86, Bruno Collaco (Fernando 32) - Fabio Rochemback•, Adilson (Vinicius Pacheco 57), Lucio, Mario Fernandes (Diego 57), Damian Escudero - Borges. Tr: Renato Gaucho

Heraclio Tapia, Huánuco
23-02-2011, 15:15, 5964, Escalante VEN

León de Huánuco 1
Zegarra 36

Juan Angel Flores - Gianfranco Espinoza, Luis Cardoza, Jair Cespedes•, Roller Cambindo (Jorge Araujo 68) - Jean Ferrari•, Victor Pena, Carlos Zegarra - Carlos Orejuela (Guillermo Salas 87), Carlos Elias (Harrison Otalvaro 61), Juan Gonzalez-Vigil. Tr: Franco Navarro

Oriente Petrolero 0

Hugo Suarez - Miguel Hoyos, Gustavo Martin Caamano (Fernando Saucedo 84), Alejandro Melean, Luis Gutierrez♦90 - Marcelo Aguirre, Jhasmany Campos, Diego Terrazas (Alcides Pena 74), Joselito Vaca• - Mauricio Saucedo, Juan Carlos Arce (Nicolas Fernandez 84). Tr: Gustavo Quinteros

Ramon Tahuichi Aguilera, Santa Cruz
9-03-2011, 18:30, 10 668, Favale ARG

Oriente Petrolero 1
Arce 91+

Hugo Suarez - Miguel Hoyos, Gustavo Martin Caamano•, Alejandro Melean• (Fernando Saucedo 74), Alejandro Schiapparelli - Marcelo Aguirre•, Jhasmany Campos, Diego Terrazas (Alcides Pena 57), Joselito Vaca - Mauricio Saucedo (Nicolas Fernandez 68), Juan Carlos Arce. Tr: Gustavo Quinteros

Atlético Junior 2
Cortes 27, Paez 46

Carlos Rodriguez - Cesar Fawcett, Anselmo de Almeida, Harold Macias•, Braynner Garcia - Jossymar Gomez•, Juan Valencia, Jhon Viafara, Giovanni Hernandez (Sherman Cardenas 85) - Victor Javier Cortes (Vladimir Hernandez 88), Luis Paez (Carlos Bacca 80). Tr: Oscar Hector Quintabani

Ramon Tahuichi Aguilera, Santa Cruz
24-03-2011, 18:30, 2020, Intriago ECU

Oriente Petrolero 2
Pena 16, Campos 77

Michael Etulain - Miguel Hoyos, Gustavo Martin Caamano, Alejandro Melean, Luis Gutierrez - Alejandro Schiapparelli, Jhasmany Campos• (Walter Veizaga 85), Fernando Saucedo (Diego Terrazas 89), Joselito Vaca - Nicolas Fernandez (Juan Carlos Arce• 72), Alcides Pena. Tr: Gustavo Quinteros

León de Huánuco 1

Juan Angel Flores - Gianfranco Espinoza•, Jorge Araujo, Luis Cardoza•, Guillermo Salas - Jair Cespedes (Victor Pena 76), Jean Ferrari•, Harrison Otalvaro, Carlos Zegarra - Juan Gonzalez-Vigil (Jorge Leiva 90), Carlos Orejuela. Tr: Franco Navarro

Metropolitano, Barranquilla
14-04-2011, 20:45, 7626, Vera ECU

Atlético Junior 1
Gomez 75

Sebastian Viera - Anselmo de Almeida, Juan Valencia•, Jhon Valencia, Braynner Garcia - Sergio Otalvaro, Julian Barahona (Cesar Fawcett 46), Sherman Cardenas (Giovanni Hernandez 46), Jossymar Gomez - Victor Javier Cortes (Carlos Bacca 63), Luis Paez. Tr: Oscar Hector Quintabani

León de Huánuco 1
Rodriguez 84

Leonel Cuerdo - Gianfranco Espinoza•, Luis Cardoza• (Ever Chavez 83), Guillermo Salas, Roller Cambindo - Jean Ferrari•, Harrison Otalvaro (Orlando Rodriguez 70), Victor Pena•, Jose Cuero, Carlos Zegarra - Carlos Orejuela (Jair Cespedes 73). Tr: Franco Navarro

GRUPO 3

GRUPO 3		Pl	W	D	L	F	A	Pts	MEX	BRA	URU	ARG
CF América	MEX	6	3	1	2	8	7	10		1-0	2-0	2-1
Fluminense	BRA	6	2	2	2	9	9	8	3-2		0-0	2-2
Nacional Montevideo	URU	6	2	2	2	3	3	8	0-0	2-0		0-1
Argentinos Juniors	ARG	6	2	1	3	9	10	7	3-1	2-4	0-1	

Olímpico, Rio de Janeiro
9-02-2011, 22:00, 15 939, Torres PAR

Fluminense 2
Rafael Moura 2 [57] [73]

Diego - Mariano, Gum, Andre Luis● (Marquinho 73), Carlinhos - Souza (Edwin Valencia 88), Edinho●, Dario Conca, Diguinho, Willians (Rodriguinho 46) - Rafael Moura●. Tr: Muricy Ramalho

Argentinos Juniors 2
Niell 2 [44] [70]

Nicolas Navarro● - Miguel Torren●, Juan Sabia, Santiago Gentiletti● - Gonzalo Prosperi, Juan Mercier, German Basualdo (Mauro Bogado 85), Sergio Escudero (Nicolas Berardo 90) - Gustavo Oberman● (Pablo Hernandez 63), Santiago Salcedo, Franco Niell. Tr: Pedro Troglio

---

Azteca, Mexico City
15-02-2011, 21:00, 18 049, Ruiz COL

CF América 2
Sanchez [3], Vuoso [48]

Guillermo Ochoa - Juan Carlos Valenzuela, Aquivaldo Mosquera●, Oscar Rojas - Daniel Montenegro (Diego Reyes 73), Andres Nicolas Olivera (Angel Reyna 58), Pavel Pardo, Rosinei, Miguel Layun - Vicente Sanchez (Antonio Lopez 71), Vicente Matias Vuoso. Tr: Carlos Reinoso

Nacional Montevideo 0

Leonardo Burian - Gabriel Marques, Alejandro Lembo, Flavio Cordoba, Christian Nunez - Robert Flores●, Facundo Piriz (Maximiliano Calzada 60), Matias Cabrera - Tabare Viudez, Santiago García● (Bruno Fornaroli 63), Richard Porta (Nicolas Vigneri 46). Tr: Juan Ramon Carrasco

---

Olímpico, Rio de Janeiro
23-02-2011, 21:50, 10 017, Amarilla PAR

Fluminense 0

Ricardo Berna - Mariano, Gum, Digao (Araujo 74), Carlinhos - Edwin Valencia (Tarta 61), Leandro Euzebio●, Dario Conca●, Marquinho (Souza 82), Diguinho - Rafael Moura●. Tr: Muricy Ramalho

Nacional Montevideo 0

Leonardo Burian - Gabriel Marques, Alejandro Lembo●, Sebastian Coates, Christian Nunez - Matias Cabrera● (Maximiliano Calzada 57), Facundo Piriz●, Mauricio Pereyra, Nicolas Vigneri - Bruno Fornaroli● (Santiago García● 62), Tabare Viudez (Flavio Cordoba 74). Tr: Juan Ramon Carrasco

---

Diego Maradona, Buenos Aires
24-02-2011, 21:30, 4373, Carrillo PER

Argentinos Juniors 3
Salcedo 2 [45p] [73], Sanchez Prette [93+]

Nicolas Navarro - Miguel Torren (Christian Sanchez Prette 46), Juan Sabia, Santiago Gentiletti - Gonzalo Prosperi, German Basualdo, Pablo Hernandez (Mauro Bogado 46), Sergio Escudero (Nicolas Berardo 82) - Gustavo Oberman●, Santiago Salcedo, Franco Niell. Tr: Pedro Troglio

CF América 1
Montenegro [27]

Guillermo Ochoa - Diego Cervantes●, Juan Carlos Valenzuela, Oscar Rojas● - Daniel Montenegro, Andres Nicolas Olivera (Vicente Sanchez● 69), Pavel Pardo●, Diego Reyes (Daniel Marquez 81), Rosinei (Angel Reyna 76), Miguel Layun - Vicente Matias Vuoso. Tr: Carlos Reinoso

---

Parque Central, Montevideo
2-03-2011, 20:30, 8991, Arias PAR

Nacional Montevideo 0

Leonardo Burian - Gabriel Marques (Richard Porta 84), Alejandro Lembo, Sebastian Coates, Christian Nunez - Matias Cabrera (Tabare Viudez 44), Facundo Piriz, Mauricio Pereyra - Bruno Fornaroli (Jonathan Charquero 70), Santiago García, Horacio Peralta●. Tr: Juan Ramon Carrasco

Argentinos Juniors 1
Niell [21]

Nicolas Navarro - Miguel Torren, Juan Sabia, Santiago Gentiletti - Gonzalo Prosperi, Matias Laba●, Pablo Hernandez (Mauro Bogado 62), Sergio Escudero● - Gustavo Oberman (Christian Sanchez Prette 83), Santiago Salcedo, Franco Niell● (Ciro Ruis● 69). Tr: Pedro Troglio

---

Azteca, Mexico City
2-03-2011, 18:50, 22 099, Roldan COL

CF América 1
Marquez [70]

Guillermo Ochoa - Aquivaldo Mosquera, Juan Carlos Valenzuela, Oscar Rojas - Daniel Montenegro●, Andres Nicolas Olivera (Israel Martinez 70), Pavel Pardo (Angel Reyna 56), Rosinei, Miguel Layun (Daniel Marquez 64) - Vicente Sanchez, Vicente Matias Vuoso. Tr: Carlos Reinoso

Fluminense 0

Ricardo Berna - Mariano, Digao (Souza 82), Gum, Carlinhos - Edwin Valencia (Edinho● 62), Leandro Euzebio, Dario Conca (Araujo 74), Diguinho● - Rafael Moura, Tarta. Tr: Muricy Ramalho

---

Diego Maradona, Buenos Aires
15-03-2011, 21:30, 6834, Osses CHI

Argentinos Juniors 0

Nicolas Navarro - Gonzalo Prosperi, Nicolas Berardo (Pablo Hernandez● 37), Juan Sabia, Santiago Gentiletti - Mauro Bogado (Ciro Ruis 57), Matias Laba, Christian Sanchez Prette (Nicolas Blandi 68), Sergio Escudero● - Santiago Salcedo, Franco Niell. Tr: Pedro Troglio

Nacional Montevideo 1
Garcia [33]

Leonardo Burian - Gonzalo Godoy●, Jadson Viera●, Sebastian Coates, Christian Nunez - Matias Cabrera, Facundo Piriz, Robert Flores (Marcelo Gallardo 57) - Tabare Viudez (Mauricio Pereyra 70), Santiago Garcia, Richard Porta (Maximiliano Calzada 64). Tr: Juan Ramon Carrasco

---

Olímpico, Rio de Janeiro
23-03-2011, 21:50, 13 158, Arias PAR

Fluminense 3
Gum [20], Araujo [79], Deco [86]

Ricardo Berna - Mariano (Deco 52), Digao, Gum●, Julio Cesar (Araujo 74) - Edwin Valencia, Diguinho, Souza - Dario Conca - Fred●, Emerson (Rafael Moura 70). Tr: Enderson Moreira

CF América 2

Armando Navarrete - Diego Cervantes, Juan Carlos Valenzuela, Oscar Rojas● - Daniel Montenegro, Andres Nicolas Olivera● (Pavel Pardo●, Rosinei (Daniel Marquez 89), Miguel Layun - Vicente Sanchez, Vicente Matias Vuoso (Enrique Esqueda 84). Tr: Carlos Reinoso

---

Centenario, Montevideo
6-04-2011, 21:45, 44 952, Ruiz COL

Nacional Montevideo 2
Garcia 2 [50] [66]

Rodrigo Munoz - Gonzalo Godoy●, Jadson Viera, Sebastian Coates, Gabriel Marques - Matias Cabrera (Maximiliano Calzada 71), Facundo Piriz, Mauricio Pereyra (Carlao 54), Tabare Viudez, Santiago García, Jonathan Charquero (Marcelo Gallardo 54●●◆84). Tr: Juan Ramon Carrasco

Fluminense 0

Ricardo Berna - Mariano, Gum, Edinho, Julio Cesar (Araujo 72) - Edwin Valencia, Diguinho (Rafael Moura● 79), Souza (Deco 56) - Dario Conca - Fred, Emerson. Tr: Enderson Moreira

---

Azteca, Mexico City
6-04-2011, 21:50, 19 451, Amarilla PAR

CF América 2
Vuoso [72], Marquez [82]

Guillermo Ochoa● - Diego Cervantes●, Juan Carlos Valenzuela, Aquivaldo Mosquera, Oscar Rojas - Daniel Montenegro, Andres Nicolas Olivera (Angel Reyna● 46), Pavel Pardo (Daniel Marquez● 81), Rosinei, Enrique Esqueda (Vicente Matias Vuoso 46) - Vicente Sanchez. Tr: Carlos Reinoso

Argentinos Juniors 1
Niell [48]

Nicolas Navarro - Miguel Torren●, Juan Sabia, Santiago Gentiletti● - Gonzalo Prosperi, Matias Laba (German Basualdo 77), Juan Mercier, Nicolas Berardo - Ciro Rius (Gustavo Oberman 68), Santiago Salcedo, Franco Niell (Mauro Bogado 74). Tr: Pedro Troglio

---

Centenario, Montevideo
20-04-2011, 21:50, 45 779, Carrillo PER

Nacional Montevideo 0

Rodrigo Munoz - Gonzalo Godoy, Jadson Viera●, Sebastian Coates●, Gabriel Marques● - Mauricio Pereyra (Matias Cabrera 61), Facundo Piriz, Bruno Fornaroli (Carlao 70) - Tabare Viudez, Santiago García, Jonathan Charquero (Anderson 70). Tr: Juan Ramon Carrasco

CF América 0

Guillermo Ochoa - Diego Cervantes, Aquivaldo Mosquera●, Juan Carlos Valenzuela, Diego Reyes, Oscar Rojas● - Daniel Montenegro (Daniel Marquez 82), Andres Nicolas Olivera (Vicente Matias Vuoso 70), Angel Reyna, Rosinei - Vicente Sanchez (Pavel Pardo 82). Tr: Carlos Reinoso

---

Diego Maradona, Buenos Aires
20-04-2011, 21:50, 5706, Roldan COL

Argentinos Juniors 2
Salcedo [25p], Oberman [54]

Nicolas Navarro - Miguel Torren (Gustavo Oberman 46), Juan Sabia, Santiago Gentiletti (Christian Sanchez Prette 77) - Gonzalo Prosperi●, German Basualdo● (Matias Laba 61), Juan Mercier, Sergio Escudero● - Ciro Rius, Santiago Salcedo, Franco Niell. Tr: Pedro Troglio

Fluminense 4
Julio Cesar [17], Fred [40] [88p], Rafael Moura [68]

Ricardo Berna● - Mariano, Gum●, Edinho, Julio Cesar (Tarta 83) - Edwin Valencia, Diguinho● (Araujo 85), Dario Conca, Marquinho - Fred, Rafael Moura (Fernando Bob 90). Tr: Enderson Moreira

GRUPO 4		Pl	W	D	L	F	A	Pts	CHI	ARG	VEN	CHI
Universidad Católica	CHI	6	3	2	1	11	9	11		0-0	1-3	2-1
Vélez Sarsfield	ARG	6	3	1	2	12	7	10	3-4		3-0	2-1
Caracas	VEN	6	3	0	3	7	10	9	0-2	0-3		2-0
Unión Española	CHI	6	1	1	4	7	11	4	2-2	2-1	1-2	

José Amalfitani, Buenos Aires
15-02-2011, 19:30, 7351, Osses CHI

Vélez Sarsfield 3

Moralez [44], Ramirez [59], Martinez [83p]

Marcelo **Barovero** - Fabian **Cubero**•, Omar Fernando **Tobio**, Sebastian **Dominguez**, Emiliano **Papa** - Franco **Razzotti**, Hector **Canteros**, David **Ramirez** (Augusto **Fernandez** 69), Maximiliano **Moralez** (Ivan **Bella** 72) - Juan Manuel **Martinez**, Guillermo **Franco** (Maximiliano **Giusti** 7). Tr: Ricardo **Gareca**

Caracas FC 0

David **Gonzalez** - Giovanny **Romero**, Franklin **Lucena**, Julio **Machado**, Rohel **Briceno** - Juan Francisco **Guerra**, Edgar **Jimenez**• (Luis **Cabezas** 65), Alexander **Gonzalez** (Romulo **Otero**• 85), Nelson **Barahona** (Cesar **Gonzalez** 71), Angelo **Pena**◆12 - Edward **Jimenez**. Tr: Chita **San Vicente**

Santa Laura, Santiago
16-02-2011, 18:45, 10 660, Puga CHI

Unión Española 2

Monje [47], Leal [90p]

Eduardo **Lobos**• - Luis **Figueroa**, Leandro **Delgado**, Rafael **Olarra** (Giovanny **Espinoza** 62), Rodolfo **Madrid** - Braulio **Leal**•, Gonzalo **Villagra**•, Martin **Liguera** (Jose **Perez** 80) - Raul **Estevez** (Kevin **Harbottle** 80), Sebastian **Jaime**, Leonardo **Monje**•. Tr: Jose Luis **Sierra**

Universidad Católica 2

Pratto [66], Meneses [71]

Cristopher **Toselli** - Rodrigo **Valenzuela**•, Alfonso **Parot**, David **Henriquez**• - Juan **Eluchans**, Francisco **Silva**•, Jorge **Ormeno**, Fernando **Meneses**• (Diego **Opazo** 85) - Marcelo **Canete** (Jose **Villanueva**• 59) - Lucas **Pratto** (Tomas **Costa** 75), Roberto **Gutierrez**. Tr: Juan Antonio **Pizzi**

José Amalfitani, Buenos Aires
3-03-2011, 20:15, 8954, Torres PAR

Vélez Sarsfield 3

Ortiz [20], Fernandez [21], Papa [45]

Marcelo **Barovero** - Fabian **Cubero**•, Sebastian **Dominguez**, Fernando **Ortiz**•◆53, Emiliano **Papa** - Franco **Razzotti**, Augusto **Fernandez**, Maximiliano **Moralez** (Fernando **Tobio** 55), Victor **Zapata**• - Juan Manuel **Martinez** (Gaston **Diaz** 79), Maximiliano **Giusti** (Tanque **Silva** 46). Tr: Ricardo **Gareca**

Universidad Católica 4

Pratto 2 [1 87], Costa [73], Pizarro [90]

Cristopher **Toselli** - Hans **Martinez**•, David **Henriquez**, Alfonso **Parot** (Francisco **Pizarro**• 64), Juan **Eluchans** - Fernando **Meneses** (Marcelo **Canete** 79), Jorge **Ormeno**•, Felipe **Gutierrez**, Tomas **Costa** - Lucas **Pratto**, Roberto **Gutierrez** (Pablo **Calandria** 81). Tr: Juan Antonio **Pizzi**

Olímpico, Caracas
3-03-2011, 21:00, 10 120, Vera ECU

Caracas FC 2

Jimenez [39p], Barahona [53]

Renny **Vega** - Giovanny **Romero**, Franklin **Lucena**, Julio **Machado**, Rohel **Briceno**• (Edder **Perez** 80) - Alexander **Gonzalez**, Juan Francisco **Guerra**, Edgar **Jimenez**, Nelson **Barahona**• - Luis **Cabezas** (Daniel **Febles** 86), Josef **Martinez** (Edwards **Jimenez** 76). Tr: Ceferino **Bencomo**

Unión Española 0

Eduardo **Lobos** - Esteban **Gonzalez**, Leandro **Delgado**, Rafael **Olarra** (Giovanny **Espinoza** 57), Fernando **Cordero**• - Braulio **Leal**, Gonzalo **Villagra** (Jose **Perez** 72), Martin **Liguera** - Raul **Estevez**, Sebastian **Jaime** (Kevin **Harbottle** 80), Leonardo **Monje**•. Tr: Jose Luis **Sierra**

San Carlos, Santiago
9-03-2011, 21:45, 13 491, Orozco BOL

Universidad Católica 1

Calandria [53]

Cristopher **Toselli** - Hans **Martinez**••◆70, David **Henriquez**•, Alfonso **Parot** (Marcelo **Canete** 54), Juan **Eluchans**• - Fernando **Meneses**, Jorge **Ormeno**, Felipe **Gutierrez** (Roberto **Gutierrez** 61), Tomas **Costa** - Pablo **Calandria** (Jose **Villanueva** 81), Lucas **Pratto**. Tr: Juan Antonio **Pizzi**

Caracas FC 3

Cabezas 2 [46 49], Barahona [48]

Renny **Vega** - Giovanny **Romero**•, Franklin **Lucena**, Julio **Machado**, Rohel **Briceno** - Alexander **Gonzalez** (Cesar **Gonzalez** 71), Juan Francisco **Guerra**, Edgar **Jimenez**, Nelson **Barahona**, Angelo **Pena** (Josef **Martinez** 80) - Luis **Cabezas** (Daniel **Febles** 88). Tr: Ceferino **Bencomo**

Santa Laura, Santiago
10-03-2011, 19:15, 6209, Seneme BRA

Unión Española 2

Liguera [3], Leal [25]

Eduardo **Lobos** - Leandro **Delgado**, Luis **Figueroa**, Rafael **Olarra**, Fernando **Cordero** - Braulio **Leal**•, Martin **Liguera** (Kevin **Harbottle** 72), Gonzalo **Villagra**• - Raul **Estevez**• (Jose **Perez** 87), Sebastian **Jaime**, Leonardo **Monje** (Diego **Scotti** 70). Tr: Jose Luis **Sierra**

Vélez Sarsfield 1

Ramirez [68]

Marcelo **Barovero** - Fabian **Cubero**•, Omar Fernando **Tobio**, Sebastian **Dominguez**, Emiliano **Papa** - Gaston **Diaz**• (David **Ramirez** 46), Franco **Razzotti** (Hector **Canteros** 84), Maximiliano **Moralez**, Victor **Zapata** (Ricardo **Alvarez**• 64) - Juan Manuel **Martinez**, Tanque **Silva**. Tr: Ricardo **Gareca**

Olímpico, Caracas
22-03-2011, 19:45, 18 232, Delgadillo MEX

Caracas FC 0

Renny **Vega**• - Giovanny **Romero** (Edwards **Jimenez** 70), Franklin **Lucena**, Julio **Machado**, Rohel **Briceno**• Alexander **Gonzalez**, Juan Francisco **Guerra**, Edgar **Jimenez**•, Nelson **Barahona**•◆89, Angelo **Pena** (Cesar **Gonzalez** 77) - Luis **Cabezas** (Josef **Martinez** 66). Tr: Ceferino **Bencomo**

Universidad Católica 2

Villanueva [48], Pratto [84]

Paulo **Garces** - Tomas **Costa**, David **Henriquez**, Alfonso **Parot**, Juan **Eluchans** - Jorge **Ormeno**, Francisco **Silva**, Fernando **Meneses** (Francisco **Pizarro** 68) - Marcelo **Canete**• (Adan **Vergara** 75) - Lucas **Pratto**, Jose **Villanueva**• (Roberto **Gutierrez** 80). Tr: Juan Antonio **Pizzi**

José Amalfitani, Buenos Aires
24-03-2011, 21:45, 5913, Fagundes BRA

Vélez Sarsfield 2

Papa [23], Silva [68]

Marcelo **Barovero** - Fabian **Cubero**• (Gaston **Diaz** 64), Sebastian **Dominguez**, Fernando **Ortiz**•, Emiliano **Papa** - Hector **Canteros**, Maximiliano **Moralez** (Ivan **Bella** 85), David **Ramirez** (Augusto **Fernandez** 46), Victor **Zapata**• - Juan Manuel **Martinez**, Tanque **Silva**. Tr: Ricardo **Gareca**

Unión Española 1

Delgado [33]

Eduardo **Lobos** - Leandro **Delgado**•, Luis **Figueroa**, Rafael **Olarra**, Fernando **Cordero** - Braulio **Leal**, Gonzalo **Villagra**, Martin **Liguera**• (Jose **Perez** 76) - Raul **Estevez**, Sebastian **Jaime**, Leonardo **Monje** (Kevin **Harbottle** 76). Tr: Jose Luis **Sierra**

Santa Laura, Santiago
6-04-2011, 19:30, 5411, Vuaden BRA

Unión Española 1

Jaime [2]

Eduardo **Lobos** - Leandro **Delgado**, Luis **Figueroa** (Esteban **Gonzalez** 72), Rafael **Olarra**, Fernando **Cordero** - Braulio **Leal**, Gonzalo **Villagra**•, Martin **Liguera** - Raul **Estevez**, Sebastian **Jaime**•, Leonardo **Monje** (Kevin **Harbottle** 71). Tr: Jose Luis **Sierra**

Caracas FC 2

Pena [33], Martinez [83]

Renny **Vega** - Giovanny **Romero**, Franklin **Lucena**, Julio **Machado**•, Rohel **Briceno**• - Alexander **Gonzalez**, Juan Francisco **Guerra**•, Edgar **Jimenez**, Angelo **Pena** (Josef **Martinez** 82) - Luis **Cabezas**, Edwards **Jimenez** (Cesar **Gonzalez** 63). Tr: Ceferino **Bencomo**

San Carlos, Santiago
7-04-2011, 21:30, 11 143, Larrionda URU

Universidad Católica 0

Paulo **Garces** - Hans **Martinez**, Adan **Vergara**• (Roberto **Gutierrez** 90), David **Henriquez**, Juan **Eluchans** - Jorge **Ormeno**, Francisco **Silva** (Francisco **Pizarro** 76), Marcelo **Canete**, Fernando **Meneses**, Felipe **Gutierrez** (Jose **Villanueva**• 57) - Lucas **Pratto**. Tr: Juan Antonio **Pizzi**

Vélez Sarsfield 0

Marcelo **Barovero** - Fabian **Cubero**•, Sebastian **Dominguez**, Fernando **Ortiz**, Emiliano **Papa** - Hector **Canteros**•, Augusto **Fernandez**•◆66, Maximiliano **Moralez** (Ivan **Bella** 79), Victor **Zapata** (Maximiliano **Giusti** 86) - Juan Manuel **Martinez** (Ricardo **Alvarez** 69), Tanque **Silva**. Tr: Ricardo **Gareca**

San Carlos, Santiago
14-04-2011, 20:30, 10 118, Osorio CHI

Universidad Católica 2

Calandria [48], Canete [78]

Paulo **Garces** - Rodrigo **Valenzuela**, David **Henriquez**•, Jose **Martinez**, Juan **Eluchans**• - Fernando **Meneses** (Felipe **Gutierrez** 82), Jorge **Ormeno**, Francisco **Silva**• (Tomas **Costa** 68) - Marcelo **Canete** - Pablo **Calandria** (Jose **Villanueva** 71), Lucas **Pratto**. Tr: Juan Antonio **Pizzi**

Unión Española 2

Harbottle [47]

Eduardo **Lobos** - Esteban **Gonzalez**•, Leandro **Delgado** (Francisco **Alarcon** 77), Giovanny **Espinoza**, Rodolfo **Madrid** - Jose **Perez**, Gonzalo **Villagra** (Martin **Liguera** 65), Diego **Scotti**, Kevin **Harbottle** (Nahuel **Donadell** 76) - Fernando **Cordero** - Mario **Aravena**•. Tr: Jose Luis **Sierra**

Olímpico, Caracas
14-04-2011, 19:00, 17 824, Buitrago COL

Caracas FC 0

Renny **Vega** - Giovanny **Romero** (Alexander **Gonzalez** 61), Franklin **Lucena**, Julio **Machado**, Rohel **Briceno** - Nelson **Barahona**•, Juan Francisco **Guerra**, Edwards **Jimenez**, Angelo **Pena**• (Cesar **Gonzalez** 63) - Luis **Cabezas**, Josef **Martinez** (Edgar **Jimenez** 69). Tr: Ceferino **Bencomo**

Vélez Sarsfield 3

Moralez [20], Silva 2 [46 54]

Marcelo **Barovero** - Fabian **Cubero**• (Gaston **Diaz** 58•••85), Sebastian **Dominguez**, Fernando **Ortiz**, Emiliano **Papa** - Ricardo **Alvarez**• (Ivan **Bella** 79), Hector **Canteros**, Maximiliano **Moralez** (Fernando **Tobio** 71), Victor **Zapata** - Juan Manuel **Martinez**, Tanque **Silva**. Tr: Ricardo **Gareca**

GRUPO 5		PI	W	D	L	F	A	Pts	PAR	BRA	CHI	VEN
Cerro Porteño	PAR	6	3	2	1	13	8	11		1-2	5-2	1-1
Santos	BRA	6	3	2	1	11	8	11	1-1		3-2	3-1
Colo-Colo	CHI	6	3	0	3	15	16	9	2-3	3-2		2-1
Deportivo Táchira	VEN	6	0	2	4	5	12	2	0-2	0-0	2-4	

Pueblo Nuevo, San Cristobal
15-02-2011, 20:45, 30 226, Vera ECU

Deportivo Táchira 0

Manuel Sanhouse - Gerson Chacon, Walter Moreno, Andres Rouga, Jose Yeguez - Jorge Casanova (Mauricio Parra 57), Sebastian Hernandez (Yonathan del Valle 77), Diego Guerrero, Pedro Fernandez• - Sergio Herrera, Edgar Perez. Tr: Carlos Maldonado

Santos 0

Rafael - Para (Adriano 74), Edu Dracena, Durval, Leo (Alex Sandro 78), Danilo• - Arouca, Elano, Rodrigo Possebon• - Neymar, Diogo (Ze Eduardo 64). Tr: Adilson Batista

Vila Belmiro, Santos
2-03-2011, 21:50, 6735, Baldassi ARG

Santos 1
Elano 54p

Rafael - Jonathan, Durval, Danilo, Leo•, Edu Dracena - Rodrigo Possebon (Adriano 59), Elano• - Ze Eduardo• (Keirrison 85), Neymar•, Diogo (Alex Sandro 76). Tr: Marcelo Martelotte

Cerro Porteño 1
Nanni 91+p

Diego Barreto• - Ivan Piris, Pedro Benitez•, Luis Cardozo (Freddy Bareiro 82), Cesar Benitez - Jorge Nunez, Rodrigo Burgos•, Luis Caceres (Julio dos Santos 71), Lautaro Formica• - Ivan Torres 55) - Juan Iturbe, Roberto Nanni. Tr: Leonardo Ruben Astrada

Pueblo Nuevo, San Cristobal
6-04-2011, 18:00, 3587, Pezzotta ARG

Deportivo Táchira 0

Manuel Sanhouse - Jose Yeguez•, Andres Rouga•, Walter Moreno, Diego Guerrero (Jorge Casanova 73) - Jose Parra (Sebastian Hernandez 59), Gerson Chacon•, Pedro Fernandez, Julio Gutierrez - Sergio Herrera, Edgar Perez (Yonathan del Valle 68). Tr: Jorge Luis Pinto

Cerro Porteño 2
Nanni 20, Torres 65

Diego Barreto - Ivan Piris, Pedro Benitez, Lautaro Formica• - Luis Cardozo, Javier Villarreal, Rodrigo Burgos• (Mariano Uglessich 83), Ivan Torres (Diego Madrigal 81), Jonathan Fabbro (Julio dos Santos 46), Jorge Luis Rojas - Roberto Nanni. Tr: Leonardo Ruben Astrada

General Pablo Rojas, Asuncion
14-04-2011, 19:30, 12 940, Vazquez URU

Cerro Porteño 1
Benitez 93+

Diego Barreto - Pedro Benitez, Luis Cardozo•, Lautaro Formica (Juan Iturbe 66), Ivan Piris - Ivan Torres (Jorge Nunez 46), Jonathan Fabbro, Jorge Luis Rojas (Juan Manuel Lucero 46), Javier Villarreal, Rodrigo Burgos• - Roberto Nanni. Tr: Leonardo Ruben Astrada

Santos 2
Danilo 11, Maikon Leite 47

Rafael - Jonathan, Edu Dracena•, Durval, Leo - Arouca• (Para 84), Adriano•, Danilo, Ganso - Keirrison (Alex Sandro 76), Diogo (Maikon Leite 31). Tr: Muricy Ramalho

General Pablo Rojas, Asuncion
17-02-2011, 20:00, 14 597, Lopes BRA

Cerro Porteño 5
Nanni 2 1 68p, Dos Santos 6, Iturbe 2 46 85

Diego Barreto - Lautaro Formica, Diego Viera (Cesar Benitez 78), Pedro Benitez, Ivan Piris• - Jonathan Fabbro (Freddy Bareiro• 64), Julio dos Santos (Juan Iturbe 46), Ivan Torres, Rodrigo Burgos, Luis Caceres - Roberto Nanni. Tr: Blas Cristaldo

Colo Colo 2
Jorquera 12, Paredes 73

Juan Castillo• - Andres Scotti•, Alvaro Ormeno, Sebastian Toro• - Paulo Magalhaes, Domingo Salcedo (Mario Salgado 75), Rodrigo Millar, Marco Medel, Cristobal Jorquera, Esteban Paredes - Ezequiel Miralles. Tr: Luis Perez

General Pablo Rojas, Asuncion
10-03-2011, 19:15, 15 499, Ubriaco URU

Cerro Porteño 1
Nanni 27

Diego Barreto - Cesar Benitez, Pedro Benitez, Mariano Uglessich, Ivan Piris - Juan Iturbe (Jonathan Fabbro• 83), Julio dos Santos (Juan Lucero 70), Ivan Torres, Rodrigo Burgos•, Luis Caceres (Jorge Nunez 79) - Roberto Nanni. Tr: Leonardo Ruben Astrada

Deportivo Táchira 1
Herrera 61

Manuel Sanhouse - Gerson Chacon, Walter Moreno•, Andres Rouga•, Jose Yeguez (Julio Gutierrez 66) - Diego Guerrero• (Jorge Casanova 83), Pedro Fernandez•, Sebastian Hernandez - Edgar Perez (Layneker Zafra 66), Wilker Romero•, Sergio Herrera. Tr: Jorge Luis Pinto

Vila Belmiro, Santos
6-04-2011, 21:45, 11 871, Silvera URU

Santos 3
Elano 33, Danilo 35, Neymar 51

Rafael• - Leo•, Durval, Edu Dracena, Para (Bruno Aguiar 84) - Elano• ◆90 (Maikon Leite 78), Danilo - Adriano - Ganso (Alex Sandro 65) - Ze Eduardo◆56, Neymar••◆53. Tr: Marcelo Martelotte

Colo Colo 0

Juan Castillo - Luis Mena (Jose Cabion• 47), Andres Scotti◆56, Nelson Cabrera, Patricio Jerez• - Domingo Salcedo (Daud Gazale 63), Paulo Magalhaes•, Jose Fuenzalida (Diego Rubio 69), Lucas Wilchez - Cristobal Jorquera◆90 - Ezequiel Miralles. Tr: Americo Gallego

Monumental, Santiago
20-04-2011, 19:30, 19 816, Larrionda URU

Colo Colo 2
Jorquera 4, Paredes 20

Francisco Prieto - Lucas Wilchez (Rodrigo Millar 54), Luis Mena• (Jose Fuenzalida 54) (Alvaro Ormeno 64), Andres Scotti, Nelson Cabrera, Paulo Magalhaes• - Jose Cabion, Esteban Paredes, Cristobal Jorquera•, Domingo Salcedo - Ezequiel Miralles•. Tr: Americo Gallego

Cerro Porteño 3
Fabbro 2 42 87, Piris 47

Diego Barreto - Ivan Piris, Pedro Benitez•, Luis Cardozo (Mariano Uglessich 58), Cesar Benitez - Ivan Torres, Javier Villarreal, Jorge Nunez• (Freddy Bareiro 84), Jonathan Fabbro - Roberto Nanni, Juan Manuel Lucero• (Juan Iturbe 74). Tr: Leonardo Ruben Astrada

Pueblo Nuevo, San Cristobal
1-03-2011, 21:00, 15 323, Ponce ECU

Deportivo Táchira 2
Gutierrez 2 86 87

Manuel Sanhouse - Jose Yeguez, Walter Moreno•, Andres Rouga, Gerson Chacon• - Sebastian Hernandez, Pedro Fernandez, Diego Guerrero (Jorge Casanova 79) - Sergio Herrera, Yonathan del Valle (Julio Gutierrez 54), Edgar Perez (Mauricio Parra 46). Tr: Jorge Luis Pinto

Colo Colo 4
Miralles 2 20 45, Paredes 70, Wilchez 82

Juan Castillo - Andres Scotti•, Nelson Cabrera•, Domingo Salcedo• - Jose Cabion• (Paulo Magalhaes 46), Patricio Jerez, Luis Pavez, Rodrigo Millar, Cristobal Jorquera (Lucas Wilchez 70) - Ezequiel Miralles• (Mario Salgado 80), Esteban Paredes. Tr: Americo Gallego

Monumental, Santiago
16-03-2011, 21:50, 26 343, Pezzotta ARG

Colo Colo 3
Paredes 26, Miralles 34, Scotti 42

Juan Castillo - Luis Mena• (Luis Pavez 55), Nelson Cabrera•, Andres Scotti• - Cristobal Jorquera, Jose Fuenzalida, Domingo Salcedo (Lucas Wilchez 66), Patricio Jerez, Jose Cabion• (Alvaro Ormeno 46) - Ezequiel Miralles, Esteban Paredes•. Tr: Americo Gallego

Santos 2
Elano 4, Neymar 48

Rafael - Para•, Edu Dracena, Durval, Leo (Rodrigo Possebon 33), Danilo - Adriano, Elano•, Ganso (Keirrison 44) - Ze Eduardo (Maikon Leite 77), Neymar•. Tr: Marcelo Martelotte

Monumental, Santiago
12-04-2011, 21:30, 17 632, Baldassi ARG

Colo Colo 2
Rubio 2 6 22

Juan Castillo - Patricio Jerez, Nelson Cabrera, Luis Mena, Paulo Magalhaes• - Lucas Wilchez, Jose Fuenzalida, Rodrigo Millar (Alvaro Ormeno 75), Domingo Salcedo• (Jose Cabion 64) - Esteban Paredes•, Diego Rubio (Ezequiel Miralles 61). Tr: Americo Gallego

Deportivo Táchira 1
Perez Greco 4

Manuel Sanhouse - Andres Rouga, Walter Moreno•, Jose Yeguez (Jose Parra 72), Gerson Chacon, Layneker Zafra• - Pedro Fernandez, Diego Guerrero• - Julio Gutierrez (Yonathan del Valle 67), Ebby Perez (Sebastian Hernandez 55), Sergio Herrera. Tr: Jorge Luis Pinto

Pacaembú, São Paulo
20-04-2011, 19:30, 37 701, Pitana ARG

Santos 3
Neymar 4, Jonathan 13, Danilo 72

Rafael - Leo, Durval, Edu Dracena, Jonathan - Elano (Adriano 79), Ganso (Para 84), Danilo, Arouca - Ze Eduardo (Maikon Leite 74), Neymar. Tr: Muricy Ramalho

Deportivo Táchira 1
Chacon 69

Manuel Sanhouse - Gerson Chacon•, Layneker Zafra•, Walter Moreno, Andres Rouga•, Jose Yeguez• - Diego Guerrero (Yonathan del Valle 77), Pedro Fernandez•, Edgar Perez (Mauricio Parra 73), Sebastian Hernandez (Julio Gutierrez 59) - Sergio Herrera. Tr: Jorge Luis Pinto

GRUPO 6		Pl	W	D	L	F	A	Pts	BRA	ARG	COL	PAR
Internacional	BRA	6	4	1	1	14	3	13		4-0	2-0	3-0
Jaguares	MEX	6	3	0	3	6	8	9	1-0		2-1	2-0
Emelec	ECU	6	2	2	2	4	5	8	1-1	1-0		1-0
Jorge Wilstermann	BOL	6	1	1	4	3	11	4	1-4	2-1	0-0	

George Capwell, Guayaquil
16-02-2011, 19:00, 13 589, Pitana ARG

Emelec 1
Gimenez 95+

Javier **Klimowicz** - Oscar **Bagui**, Gabriel **Achilier**, Marcelo **Fleitas•** (Carlos **Quinonez** 77) - Angel **Mena**, Edison **Mendez**, David **Quiroz** (Leandro **Torres** 83), Pedro **Quinonez•** (Polo **Wila** 73), Fernando **Gimenez** - Cristian **Menendez**, Eyal **Strahman**. Tr: Omar **Asad**

Internacional 1
Bolatti 79

Lauro - **Nei**, **Kleber**, **Indio**, Gonzalo **Sorondo** - Mario **Bolatti•** (**Rodrigo** 81), Pablo **Guinazu**, Wilson **Matias**, Andres **D'Alessandro•**, **Ze Roberto•** (Fernando **Cavenaghi** 78) - Leandro **Damiao**. Tr: Celso **Roth**

Beira Rio, Porto Alegre
23-02-2011, 21:50, 26 337, Silvera URU

Internacional 4
Bolatti 2 ¹⁹ ⁴³, Leandro **Damiao** ⁶⁵, Oscar ⁹⁰

Lauro - **Nei**, **Kleber•**, **Indio**, Gonzalo **Sorondo•** - **Ze Roberto•** (**Andrezinho** 85), Pablo **Guinazu**, Mario **Bolatti•**, Wilson **Matias** - Fernando **Cavenaghi** (**Alecsandro** 83), Leandro **Damiao** (Oscar 81). Tr: Celso **Roth**

Jaguares 0

Jorge **Villalpando** - Miguel Angel **Martinez•**, Ismael **Fuentes** (Omar **Flores** 29), Hugo **Sanchez** - Marvin **Cabrera•**, Francisco **Torres** (Antonio **Salazar** 57), Jorge **Hernandez**, Jorge **Rodriguez•••♦**90, Guillermo **Rojas**, Damian **Manso** (Alan **Zamora** 71) - Julio Daniel **Frias**. Tr: Jose Guadalupe **Cruz**

George Capwell, Guayaquil
16-03-2011, 19:50, 11 831, Carrillo PER

Emelec 1
Quiroz 53p

Javier **Klimowicz** - Oscar **Bagui•**, Gabriel **Achilier**, Marcelo **Fleitas•**, Carlos **Quinonez** - Angel **Mena** (Enner **Valencia** 80), Fernando **Gimenez**, David **Quiroz•** (Fernando **Gaibor** 85), Pedro **Quinonez•** - Walter **Iza** (Jose Luis **Quinonez•** 69), Cristian **Menendez•**. Tr: Omar **Asad**

Jaguares 0

Jorge **Villalpando•** - Omar **Flores**, Miguel Angel **Martinez**, Hugo **Sanchez**, Oscar **Razo•**, Christian **Valdez•** - Marvin **Cabrera** (Damian **Manso** 68), Jorge **Hernandez** (Francisco **Torres** 52), Ricardo **Esqueda** (Antonio **Pedroza** 61), Jorge **Rodriguez** - Antonio **Salazar**. Tr: Jose Guadalupe **Cruz**

Félix Capriles, Cochabamba
7-04-2011, 18:15, 1171, Escalante VEN

Jorge Wilstermann 0

Mauro **Machado** - Sergio **Garzon**, Diego **Bengolea** (Juan Carlos **Ojeda** 60), Juan Ignacio **Brown**, **Jusselio** (Marcelo **Carballo** 82) - Christian **Machado**, Ramiro **Rodriguez** **Rendon**, Victor **Melgar** (Ezequiel **Abregu** 55) - Luis Gabriel **Garcia** - Fabio **Lima**, Luis **Toscanini**. Tr: Marcelo **Neveleff**

Emelec 0

Wilmer **Zumba** - Carlos **Quinonez**, Jose Luis **Quinonez**, Gabriel **Achilier•**, Oscar **Bagui** - Angel **Mena** (Enner **Valencia** 61), Pedro **Quinonez**, David **Quiroz**, Fernando **Gimenez** (Armando **Angulo** 75) - Walter **Iza** (Marcos **Caicedo** 69), Cristian **Menendez**. Tr: Omar **Asad**

Victor Reyna, Tuxtla Gutierrez
16-02-2011, 20:15, 6345, Soto VEN

Jaguares 2
Martinez ⁶⁶, Esqueda ⁷⁸

Jorge **Villalpando** - Miguel Angel **Martinez**, Omar **Flores**, Ismael **Fuentes** (Oscar **Razo** 64) - Damian **Manso** (Guillermo **Rojas•** 46), Alan **Zamora** (Edgar **Andrade** 46), Jorge **Hernandez•**, Christian **Valdez•**, Ricardo **Esqueda**, Marvin **Cabrera•** - Antonio **Salazar**. Tr: Jose Guadalupe **Cruz**

Jorge Wilstermann 0

Mauro **Machado** - Lucas **Fernandez•**, Juan Ignacio **Brown**, **Celinho**, Luis **Zapata** (Victor **Melgar** 46) - Ramiro **Rodriguez• Rendon**, Christian **Machado**, Gregorio Ezequiel **Abregu**, Juan Carlos **Ojeda**, Luis Gabriel **Garcia** (Nicolas **Mosquera** 70) - Luis **Toscanini** (**Fabio Lima** 58). Tr: Marcelo **Neveleff**

Victor Reyna, Tuxtla Gutierrez
8-03-2011, 20:45, 5832, Escalante VEN

Jaguares 2
Torres ⁴³ᵖ, Salazar ⁶⁶

Jorge **Villalpando•** - Francisco **Torres** (Edgar **Andrade** 89), Ismael **Fuentes**, Miguel Angel **Martinez** - Oscar **Razo**, Damian **Manso** (Hugo **Sanchez** 83), Christian **Valdez**, Jorge **Hernandez•**, Ricardo **Esqueda**, Guillermo **Rojas** - Julio Daniel **Frias** (Antonio **Salazar** 12). Tr: Jose Guadalupe **Cruz**

Emelec 1
Menendez ⁶⁹

Javier **Klimowicz** - Carlos **Quinonez•**, Gabriel **Achilier**, Jose Luis **Quinonez** (Fernando **Gaibor** 81), Fernando **Gimenez•** - Angel **Mena**, Pedro **Quinonez**, Edison **Mendez**, Leandro **Torres** (Enner **Valencia** 66) - Cristian **Menendez**, Eyal **Strahman** (Armando **Angulo** 71). Tr: Omar **Asad**

Beira-Rio, Porto Alegre
30-03-2011, 21:50, 28 085, Ubriaco URU

Internacional 3
Oscar ¹⁸, D'Alessandro ⁵⁶, Ze Roberto ⁷²

Lauro - **Kleber**, **Indio** (**Rodrigo** 77), **Bolivar**, **Nei** - **Ze Roberto** (Rafael **Sobis** 74), Oscar (**Andrezinho** 82), Pablo **Guinazu**, Wilson **Matias** - Andres **D'Alessandro** - Leandro **Damiao•**. Tr: Celso **Roth**

Jorge Wilstermann 0

Mauro **Machado** - Marcelo **Carballo**, Juan Ignacio **Brown**, **Jusselio** - Lucas **Fernandez••♦**69, Christian **Machado•** (Luis **Toscanini** 60), Ramiro **Rodriguez Rendon**, Luis **Zapata•** - Gregorio Ezequiel **Abregu** (Juan Carlos **Ojeda** 68), Luis Gabriel **Garcia** (Amilcar **Sanchez** 46) - **Fabio Lima**. Tr: Marcelo **Neveleff**

Félix Capriles, Cochabamba
19-04-2011, 19:15, 1510, Quintana PAR

Jorge Wilstermann 2
Fabio Mineiro ⁷⁶, Torres ⁸¹

Mauro **Machado** - Diego **Bengolea** (Ezequiel **Abregu** 60), Juan Ignacio **Brown**, **Jusselio**, Lucas **Fernandez** - Juan Carlos **Ojeda•**, Ramiro **Rodriguez Rendon**, Iani Martin **Veron** (Luis **Toscanini** 60), Nicolas **Torres** - **Fabio Lima•**, Nicolas **Mosquera•** (Luis Gabriel **Garcia** 78). Tr: Marcelo **Neveleff**

Jaguares 1
Torres ⁷

Jorge **Villalpando** - Jaime **Duran** (Diego **Castellanos** 86), Ismael **Fuentes**, Oscar **Razo**, Guillermo **Rojas** (Jesus **Chavez** 82) - Jose Hiber **Ruiz**, Francisco **Torres•**, Ricardo **Esqueda**, Alan **Zamora** - Julio Daniel **Frias♦**51, Antonio **Pedroza**. Tr: Jose Guadalupe **Cruz**

George Capwell, Guayaquil
22-02-2011, 19:30, 11 679, Osorio CHI

Emelec 1
Morante ³³

Javier **Klimowicz** - Oscar **Bagui**, Eduardo **Morante**, Gabriel **Achilier** - Fernando **Gimenez•** (Marcos **Caicedo** 78), Edison **Mendez**, Polo **Wila**, David **Quiroz** (Carlos **Quinonez** 65), Angel **Mena•** - Cristian **Menendez**, Eyal **Strahman** (Leandro **Torres** 72). Tr: Omar **Asad**

Jorge Wilstermann 0

Mauro **Machado** - Lucas **Fernandez•**, Juan Ignacio **Brown**, **Jusselio** - Victor **Melgar**, Gregorio Ezequiel **Abregu**, Iani Martin **Veron** (Oliver **Fernandez•** 46), Christian **Machado**, Juan Carlos **Ojeda**, Luis Gabriel **Garcia** - Luis **Toscanini** (**Fabio Lima•** 72). Tr: Marcelo **Neveleff**

Félix Capriles, Cochabamba
16-03-2011, 18:30, 19 532, Caceres PAR

Jorge Wilstermann 0
Brown ⁸

Mauro **Machado** - Lucas **Fernandez**, Juan Ignacio **Brown**, **Jusselio** - Oliver **Fernandez•** (**Fabio Lima** 56), Luis Gabriel **Garcia**, Victor **Melgar** (Amilcar **Sanchez** 46), Christian **Machado•**, Gregorio Ezequiel **Abregu**, Juan Carlos **Ojeda** (Nicolas **Mosquera** 62) - Luis **Toscanini**. Tr: Marcelo **Neveleff**

Internacional 4
OG ¹⁶, L. **Damiao** ¹⁸, Ze Roberto ²⁴, Kleber ⁸⁰

Lauro - **Kleber**, **Rodrigo**, Gonzalo **Sorondo**, **Nei** - Mario **Bolatti**, Oscar (**Andrezinho** 67), Pablo **Guinazu**, **Tinga** (Wilson **Matias** 46), **Ze Roberto•** - Leandro **Damiao** (Fernando **Cavenaghi** 65). Tr: Celso **Roth**

Victor Reyna, Tuxtla Gutierrez
6-04-2011, 17:30, 7553, Roldan COL

Jaguares 1
Salazar ⁵⁴

Israel **Villasenor•** - Jaime **Duran**, Alan **Zamora** (Damian **Manso** 48), Omar **Flores**, Miguel Angel **Martinez** - Jorge **Hernandez**, Edgar **Andrade**, Jose Hiber **Ruiz** (Christian **Valdez** 66), Francisco **Torres** (Antonio **Salazar** 48), Oscar **Razo**. Tr: Jose Guadalupe **Cruz**

Internacional 0

Lauro - **Kleber**, **Indio**, **Bolivar**, **Nei** - **Ze Roberto** (**Andrezinho** 70), Oscar (Rafael **Sobis** 62), Pablo **Guinazu**, Mario **Bolatti•** (Wilson **Matias** 70) - Andres **D'Alessandro** - Leandro **Damiao•**. Tr: Celso **Roth**

Beira-Rio, Porto Alegre
19-04-2011, 20:15, 36 175, Ruiz COL

Internacional 2
Rafael **Sobis** ⁵¹, Leandro **Damiao** ⁸⁴

Renan - **Kleber•**, **Bolivar**, **Rodrigo**, **Nei** - Andres **D'Alessandro**, **Andrezinho**, Pablo **Guinazu•**, Mario **Bolatti** - Leandro **Damiao•** (**Ze Roberto** 86), Rafael **Sobis** (Fernando **Cavenaghi** 79). Tr: **Falcao**

Emelec 0

Javier **Klimowicz** - Carlos **Quinonez** (Enner **Valencia** 63), Gabriel **Achilier•**, Oscar **Bagui** - Jose Luis **Quinonez**, Fernando **Gaibor** (Eyal **Strahman** 85), Pedro **Quinonez**, Fernando **Gimenez**, David **Quiroz** - Walter **Iza** (Marcos **Caicedo** 73), Cristian **Menendez•**. Tr: Omar **Asad**

GRUPO 7		Pl	W	D	L	F	A	Pts	BRA	ARG	COL	PAR
Cruzeiro	BRA	6	5	1	0	20	1	16		5-0	6-1	4-0
Estudiantes LP	ARG	6	3	1	2	9	11	10	0-3		1-0	5-1
Deportes Tolima	COL	6	2	2	2	5	8	8	0-0	1-1		1-0
Guaraní	PAR	6	0	0	6	2	16	0	0-2	1-2	0-2	

Manuel Toro, Ibagué
15-02-2011, 17:30, 8021, Ponce ECU

Deportes Tolima 1
Santoya 83

Antony Silva - Felix Noguera, Julian Hurtado, Yair Arrechea•, Gerardo Vallejo - Rafael Castillo (Pablo Gimenez 60), Jhon Fredy Hurtado (Danny Santoya 46), Diego Chara, Gustavo Bolivar - Elkin Murillo (Christian Marrugo 77), Wilder Medina. Tr: Hernan Torres Oliveros

Guaraní 0

Pablo Aurrecochea• - Eduardo Javier Filippini, Joel Benitez, Hector Federico Carballo•, Elvis Israel Marecos - Pedro Chavez (Osvaldo Hobecker 57), Angel Ortiz, Miguel Paniagua, Jorge Dario Mendoza - Julian Benitez, Pablo Nicolas Caballero (Fabio Escobar 67). Tr: Felix Dario Leon

---

Unico, La Plata
23-02-2011, 19:30, 29 034, Ubriaco URU

Estudiantes LP 1
Barrientos 44

Agustin Orion• - Facundo Roncaglia, Leandro Desabato, Federico Fernandez, Gabriel Mercado• - Pablo Barrientos• (Leandro Benitez 72), Juan Sebastian Veron, Rodrigo Brana•, Enzo Perez (Maximiliano Nunez• 51) - Gaston Fernandez (Nelson Benitez 84), Leandro Gonzalez. Tr: Alejandro Sabella

Deportes Tolima 0

Antony Silva - Gerardo Vallejo, Yair Arrechea•, Julian Hurtado•, Felix Noguera• - Jhon Fredy Hurtado• (Wilmer Parra 76), Gustavo Bolivar, Diego Chara, Rafael Castillo (Christian Marrugo 46) - Elkin Murillo (Danny Santoya 55), Wilder Medina. Tr: Hernan Torres Oliveros

---

Arena do Jacaré, Sete Lagoas
16-03-2011, 21:50, 8198, Vera ECU

Cruzeiro 6
Montillo 3, Wallyson 31, Roger 2 61 70p, Gilberto 88, Thiago Ribeiro 91+

Fabio - Mauricio Victorino, Gil, Pablo - Walter Montillo (Leandro Guerreiro 80), Roger, Henrique, Marquinhos Parana, Diego Renan (Gilberto 78) - Wellington Paulista• (Thiago Ribeiro 68), Wallyson. Tr: Cuca

Deportes Tolima 0
Marrugo 68

Antony Silva - Felix Noguera• (Hamilton Acuna 74), Julian Hurtado•••87, Wilmer Diaz, Gerardo Vallejo - Rafael Castillo (Danny Santoya 57), Diego Chara, Christian Marrugo•, Gustavo Bolivar• - Elkin Murillo, Wilder Medina (Wilmer Parra 75). Tr: Hernan Torres Oliveros

---

Defensores del Chaco, Asuncion
30-03-2011, 21:50, 119, Osses CHI

Guaraní 0

Joel Silva - Ignacio Ithurralde (Hector Federico Carballo 79), Elvis Israel Marecos, Joel Benitez, Eduardo Javier Filippini - Luis Eladio de la Cruz, Miguel Paniagua, Jorge Dario Mendoza (Fabio Escobar• 69), Christian Sosa - Julian Benitez•, Luis Ovelar (Osvaldo Hobecker 66). Tr: Felix Dario Leon

Cruzeiro 2
Thiago Ribeiro 15, Ortigoza 92+

Fabio - Gilberto, Mauricio Victorino, Gil, Pablo - Roger• (Everton 66), Henrique, Marquinhos Parana - Walter Montillo - Wallyson (Wellington Paulista 65), Thiago Ribeiro (Jose Ortigoza 82). Tr: Cuca

---

Arena do Jacaré, Sete Lagoas
16-02-2011, 22:00, 10 955, Amarilla PAR

Cruzeiro 5
Wallyson 2 1 82, Roger 17, Montillo 2 38 58

Fabio - Mauricio Victorino, Gil•, Pablo - Roger (Dudu 70), Walter Montillo, Henrique•, Marquinhos Parana•, Gilberto (Diego Renan 65) - Wellington Paulista• (Thiago Ribeiro 77), Wallyson. Tr: Cuca

Estudiantes LP 0

Agustin Orion - Federico Fernandez•, Leandro Desabato•, German Re, Gabriel Mercado, Leandro Benitez (Maximiliano Nunez 58) - Rodrigo Brana•, Juan Sebastian Veron, Enzo Perez, Nelson Benitez• - Gaston Fernandez (Rodrigo Lopez 80). Tr: Alejandro Sabella

---

Manuel Toro, Ibagué
2-03-2011, 17:30, 11 233, Larrionda URU

Deportes Tolima 0

Antony Silva - Gerardo Vallejo, Yair Arrechea, Julian Hurtado•, Felix Noguera - Gustavo Bolivar•, Diego Chara, Christian Marrugo - Elkin Murillo (Wilmer Parra 60), Wilder Medina, Danny Santoya. Tr: Hernan Torres Oliveros

Cruzeiro 0

Fabio - Pablo, Gil•, Mauricio Victorino - Walter Montillo, Roger (Dudu 71), Henrique, Marquinhos Parana, Diego Renan (Leandro Guerreiro 79) - Wellington Paulista (Thiago Ribeiro 61), Wallyson. Tr: Cuca

---

Unico, La Plata
17-03-2011, 19:15, 13 318, Vazquez URU

Estudiantes LP 5
Rodrigo Lopez 3 1 18 58, Leandro Gonzalez 2 24 81

Agustin Orion - Facundo Roncaglia♦52, Leandro Desabato•, Federico Fernandez - Raul Iberbia, Juan Sebastian Veron (Matias Sanchez 86), Rodrigo Brana, Gabriel Mercado• - Enzo Perez (Pablo Barrientos 65) - Leandro Gonzalez, Rodrigo Lopez (Maximiliano Nunez 75). Tr: Alejandro Sabella

Guaraní 1
Julian Benitez 79

Pablo Aurrecochea - Ignacio Ithurralde (Joel Benitez 28), Elvis Israel Marecos, Hector Federico Carballo - Tomas Bartomeus (Christian Sosa 69), Miguel Paniagua•, Jorge Dario Mendoza, Eduardo Javier Filippini - Julian Benitez, Osvaldo Hobecker - Luis Ovelar (Fabio Escobar 71). Tr: Felix Dario Leon

---

Defensores del Chaco, Asuncion
13-04-2011, 20:50, 200, Antequera BOL

Guaraní 0

Pablo Aurrecochea - Tomas Bartomeus, Micael Jordane• (Ignacio Ithurralde• 60) Hector Federico Carballo - Miguel Paniagua, Ariel Stark (Julian Benitez• 66), Angel Ortiz, Christian Sosa, Osvaldo Hobecker - Fabio Escobar (Pablo Caballero 61), Luis Ovelar. Tr: Felix Dario Leon

Deportes Tolima 2
Santoya 48, Closa 68

Antony Silva - Marlon Piedrahita, Yair Arrechea, Julian Hurtado, Hamilton Acuna - Luis Closa, Mike Campaz•, Christian Marrugo, Jhon Fredy Hurtado - Roberto Gamarra (Pablo Gimenez 57), Danny Santoya (Wilmer Parra 77). Tr: Hernan Torres Oliveros

---

Arena do Jacaré, Sete Lagoas
22-02-2011, 19:15, 12 067, Orozco BOL

Cruzeiro 4
Wallyson 2 29 63, Farias 85, Thiago Ribeiro 88

Fabio - Gil•, Mauricio Victorino•, Pablo - Walter Montillo•, Roger (Thiago Ribeiro 75), Henrique, Marquinhos Parana, Diego Renan - Wellington Paulista (Ernesto Farias• 62), Wallyson (Dudu 82). Tr: Cuca

Guaraní 0

Pablo Aurrecochea - Eduardo Javier Filippini, Joel Benitez, Hector Federico Carballo, Elvis Israel Marecos, Ignacio Ithurralde (Pedro Chavez 73) (Tomas Bartomeus 80) - Jorge Dario Mendoza (Osvaldo Hobecker 59), Angel Ortiz•, Miguel Paniagua• - Julian Benitez, Fabio Escobar•. Tr: Felix Dario Leon

---

Defensores del Chaco, Asuncion
9-03-2011, 21:45, 1078, Carrillo PER

Guaraní 1
Caballero 43p

Pablo Aurrecochea - Eduardo Javier Filippini, Joel Benitez, Hector Federico Carballo, Elvis Israel Marecos - Jorge Dario Mendoza•, Miguel Paniagua - Juan Aguilar (Christian Sosa 46), Luis Eladio de la Cruz• (Fabio Escobar• 55), Julian Benitez•, Pablo Nicolas Caballero (Luis Ovelar 75). Tr: Felix Dario Leon

Estudiantes LP 2
Barrientos 50, Gonzalez.L 53

Agustin Orion - Federico Fernandez, Leandro Desabato•, Facundo Roncaglia, Gabriel Mercado - Rodrigo Brana, Raul Iberbia, Pablo Barrientos (Nelson Benitez 90), Leandro Benitez, Enzo Perez (Matias Sanchez 74) - Leandro Gonzalez• (Rodrigo Lopez 80). Tr: Alejandro Sabella

---

Manuel Toro, Ibagué
30-03-2011, 17:30, 7797, Rivera PER

Deportes Tolima 1
Noguera 30p

Antony Silva - Felix Noguera (Roberto Gamarra 90), Yair Arrechea, Wilmer Diaz•, Gerardo Vallejo• - Elkin Murillo (Danny Santoya 58), Gustavo Bolivar (Luis Closa 81) - Wilder Medina•, Wilmer Parra. Tr: Hernan Torres Oliveros

Estudiantes LP 1
Federico Fernandez 23

Agustin Orion• - Nelson Benitez•, Leandro Desabato, Federico Fernandez• - Raul Iberbia, Leandro Benitez, Juan Sebastian Veron•, Gabriel Mercado - Enzo Perez - Leandro Gonzalez (Pablo Barrientos 67), Rodrigo Lopez (Dario Stefanatto 90). Tr: Manolo Eduardo Berizzo

---

Unico, La Plata
13-04-2011, 21:50, 14 828, Silvera URU

Estudiantes LP 0

Agustin Orion - Nelson Benitez, German Re, Facundo Roncaglia, Gabriel Mercado (Federico Fernandez 46) - Gabriel Penalba, Dario Stefanatto (Leandro Benitez 77), Maxi Nunez - Pablo Barrientos - Gaston Fernandez (Leandro Gonzalez 63), Juan Pablo Pereyra•. Tr: Alejandro Javier Sabella

Cruzeiro 3
Thiago Ribeiro 10, Wallyson 45, Gilberto 82

Fabio - Gilberto, Mauricio Victorino•, Gil, Pablo• - Roger (Everton 77), Leandro Guerreiro, Henrique, Marquinhos Parana - Wallyson (Jose Ortigoza 87), Thiago Ribeiro (Ernesto Farias 77). Tr: Cuca

GRUPO 8		Pl	W	D	L	F	A	Pts	ECU	URU	ARG	ARG
LDU Quito	ECU	6	3	1	2	12	4	10		5-0	3-0	2-0
Peñarol	URU	6	3	0	3	6	11	9	1-0		0-1	2-1
Independiente	ARG	6	2	2	2	7	8	8	1-1	3-0		1-3
Godoy Cruz	ARG	6	2	1	3	8	10	7	2-1	1-3	1-1	

Malvinas, Mendoza
17-02-2011, 22:15, 19 524, Vazquez URU

Godoy Cruz   **2**
Sanchez.C [16], Sanchez.N [59]

Sebastian Torrico - Zelmar Garcia, Nicolas Sanchez, Leonardo Sigali•, Roberto Russo (Emir Faccioli• 46) - Diego Villar, Ariel Rojas, Nicolas Olmedo•, Carlos Sanchez - Pablo Miranda (Alvaro Navarro 60), Ruben Ramirez (Mariano Donda 90). Tr: Jorge da Silva

LDU Quito   **1**
Reasco [53]

Alexander Dominguez - Jose Valencia (Paul Ambrosi 38), Diego Calderon•, Ulises de la Cruz•, Jorge Guagua - William Araujo• (Miler Bolanos 68), Enrique Vera•, Neicer Reasco• - Patricio Urrutia (Fernando Hidalgo 46♦90) - Luis Bolanos, Carlos Luna. Tr: Edgardo Bauza

---

Libertadores, Avellaneda
24-02-2011, 19:15, 21 354, Fagundes BRA

Independiente   **3**
Parra [46], Pellerano [70], Silvera [85]

Hilario Navarro - Maximiliano Velazquez, Leonel Galeano•, Eduardo Tuzzio, Julian Velazquez - Patricio Rodriguez, Leandro Gracian (Roberto Battion 64), Cristian Pellerano, Nicolas Cabrera - Matias Defederico (Leonel Nunez 73), Facundo Parra (Andres Silvera 66). Tr: Antonio Mohamed

Peñarol   **0**

Fabian Carini - Matias Corujo, Carlos Valdez• (Alejandro Gonzalez 46), Guillermo Rodriguez, Dario Rodriguez - Nicolas Freitas, Luis Aguiar•, Nicolas Domingo, Jonathan Urreta (Fabian Estoyanoff 82) - Juan Olivera (Alejandro Martinuccio 67), Antonio Pacheco. Tr: Diego Aguirre

---

Malvinas, Mendoza
1-03-2011, 20:15, 12 946, Oliveira BRA

Godoy Cruz   **1**
Ramirez [30]

Sebastian Torrico - Zelmar Garcia (Alvaro Navarro 46), Nicolas Sanchez, Leonardo Sigali, Roberto Russo - Diego Villar, Ariel Rojas (Mariano Donda 71), Nicolas Olmedo•, Carlos Sanchez - Fabricio Nunez (Gabriel Oscar Moyano 71), Ruben Ramirez•. Tr: Jorge da Silva

Peñarol   **3**
Olivera 2 [1 41], Aguiar [67]

Sebastian Sosa - Alejandro Gonzalez, Carlos Valdez• (Edison Torres 82), Guillermo Rodriguez, Dario Rodriguez - Matias Corujo, Nicolas Freitas, Luis Aguiar•, Matias Mier (Emiliano Albin• 70) - Alejandro Martinuccio, Juan Olivera (Mauro Guevgeozian 88). Tr: Diego Aguirre

---

Casa Blanca, Quito
3-03-2011, 20:30, 13 768, Ruiz COL

LDU Quito   **3**
Ambrosi [10], Bolanos.M [52], Urrutia [78]

Alexander Dominguez - Paul Ambrossi, Ulises de la Cruz, Neicer Reasco, Banner Caicedo - Ezequiel Gonzalez (Patricio Urrutia 63), Enrique Vera• (William Araujo 73), Diego Calderon - Miller Bolanos, Hernan Barcos (Carlos Luna 81). Tr: Edgardo Bauza

Independiente   **0**

Adrian Gabbarini• - Lucas Mareque, Ivan Velez, Maximiliano Velazquez, Carlos Matheu•, Leonel Galeano• - Leandro Gracian (Patricio Rodriguez 62), Hernan Fredes (Cristian Pellerano 72), Fernando Godoy• - Leonel Nunez, Facundo Parra (Andres Silvera 62). Tr: Antonio Mohamed

---

Centenario, Montevideo
9-03-2011, 20:30, 42 455, Rivera PER

Peñarol   **1**
Aguiar [57]

Sebastian Sosa - Alejandro Gonzalez, Carlos Valdez, Dario Rodriguez - Matias Corujo, Nicolas Freitas•, Luis Aguiar, Jonathan Urreta (Fabian Estoyanoff 59) - Juan Olivera, Matias Mier (Fabian Estoyanoff 59) - Juan Olivera, Antonio Pacheco (Alejandro Martinuccio 77). Tr: Diego Aguirre

LDU Quito   **0**

Alexander Dominguez• - Paul Ambrossi (Jose Valencia 70), Neicer Reasco•, Diego Calderon, Banner Caicedo, Jorge Guagua• - Ezequiel Gonzalez (Patricio Urrutia 87), Fernando Hidalgo (Carlos Luna• 65), Enrique Vera, Ulises de la Cruz - Hernan Barcos•. Tr: Edgardo Bauza

---

Libertadores, Avellaneda
10-03-2011, 21:45, 10 625, Loustau ARG

Independiente   **1**
Parra [15]

Hilario Navarro - Lucas Mareque, Leonel Galeano, Eduardo Tuzzio, Ivan Velez - Patricio Rodriguez, Fernando Godoy, Hernan Fredes (Matias Defederico 59) - Leandro Gracian• - Javir Castillo (Leonel Nunez 59), Facundo Parra. Tr: Antonio Mohamed

Godoy Cruz   **3**
OG [28], Rojas [32], Ramirez [56]

Sebastian Torrico - Zelmar Garcia•, Nicolas Sanchez, Leonardo Sigali, Roberto Russo• - Ariel Rojas (Pablo Miranda 90), Diego Villar, Israel Damonte, Nicolas Olmedo, Carlos Sanchez - Ruben Ramirez (Alvaro Navarro 80). Tr: Jorge da Silva

---

Casa Blanca, Quito
17-03-2011, 19:30, 15 329, Roldan COL

LDU Quito   **5**
Luna [22], Calderon.W 2 [45 78], OG [58], Barcos [63]

Alexander Dominguez - Diego Calderon, Banner Caicedo, Jorge Guagua - Paul Ambrossi, Ulises de la Cruz, Enrique Vera• (Fernando Hidalgo 67♦68), Neicer Reasco - Ezequiel Gonzalez (William Araujo 70) - Hernan Barcos, Carlos Luna (Walter Calderon 25). Tr: Edgardo Bauza

Peñarol   **1**

Sebastian Sosa - Alejandro Gonzalez, Carlos Valdez•, Emiliano Albin, Dario Rodriguez• - Matias Corujo, Nicolas Freitas (Nicolas Domingo 69), Luis Aguiar, Matias Mier (Fabian Estoyanoff 61) - Alejandro Martinuccio, Mauro Guevgeozian (Juan Olivera 61). Tr: Diego Aguirre

---

Malvinas, Mendoza
23-03-2011, 19:30, 11 819, Baldassi ARG

Godoy Cruz   **1**
Ramirez [33]

Sebastian Torrico - Zelmar Garcia, Nicolas Sanchez, Leonardo Sigali•, Roberto Russo - Carlos Sanchez, Nicolas Olmedo•, Israel Damonte•, Diego Villar - Fabricio Nunez (Mariano Donda 74), Ruben Ramirez. Tr: Jorge da Silva

Independiente   **1**
Defederico [1]

Hilario Navarro - Maximiliano Velazquez, Leonel Galeano, Carlos Matheu, Eduardo Tuzzio - Leandro Gracian (Hernan Fredes 55), Federico Mancuello• (Patricio Rodriguez 76), Fernando Godoy•, Nicolas Cabrera - Matias Defederico (Facundo Parra 50), Andres Silvera•. Tr: Antonio Mohamed

---

Centenario, Montevideo
31-03-2011, 21:15, 43 179, Lopes BRA

Peñarol   **2**
Olivera [42], Freitas [70]

Sebastian Sosa - Alejandro Gonzalez•, Carlos Valdez, Dario Rodriguez• - Matias Corujo, Nicolas Freitas, Nicolas Domingo•, Jonathan Urreta, Matias Mier (Fabian Estoyanoff 67) - Juan Olivera (Diego Alonso 90), Antonio Pacheco (Emiliano Albin 74). Tr: Diego Aguirre

Godoy Cruz   **1**
OG [57]

Sebastian Torrico - Zelmar Garcia, Nicolas Sanchez, Leonardo Sigali•, Roberto Russo• - Carlos Sanchez• (Ariel Rojas 60), Nicolas Olmedo, Israel Damonte (Alvaro Navarro 72), Diego Villar• (Fabricio Nunez 79) - Mariano Donda - Ruben Ramirez•. Tr: Jorge da Silva

---

Libertadores, Avellaneda
5-04-2011, 21:15, 13 270, Torres PAR

Independiente   **1**
Nunez [23p]

Fabian Assmann - Lucas Mareque•, Julian Velazquez, Leonel Galeano, Eduardo Tuzzio (Hernan Fredes 79) - Jorge Ivan Perez, Roberto Battion, Fernando Godoy (Leandro Gracian 71) - Patricio Rodriguez (Facundo Parra 70) - Leonel Nunez, Andres Silvera•. Tr: Antonio Mohamed

LDU Quito   **1**
OG [57]

Alexander Dominguez• - Diego Calderon, Banner Caicedo, Jorge Guagua• - Paul Ambrossi, Ulises de la Cruz, Enrique Vera•, Neicer Reasco - Ezequiel Gonzalez• (Walter Calderon 77), Luis Bolanos (William Araujo 68) - Hernan Barcos (Patricio Urrutia 87). Tr: Edgardo Bauza

---

Centenario, Montevideo
12-04-2011, 19:15, 51 989, Arias PAR

Peñarol   **0**

Sebastian Sosa - Alejandro Gonzalez, Carlos Valdez, Dario Rodriguez - Matias Corujo, Luis Aguiar, Nicolas Domingo, Jonathan Urreta (Fabian Estoyanoff 59) - Matias Mier (Diego Alonso 58) - Juan Olivera♦84, Antonio Pacheco (Alejandro Martinuccio 58). Tr: Diego Aguirre

Independiente   **1**
Parra [33]

Fabian Assmann♦84 - Maximiliano Velazquez, Julian Velazquez, Carlos Matheu•, Ivan Velez - Federico Mancuello (Hernan Fredes• 76), Roberto Battion, Fernando Godoy (Jorge Ivan Perez 76) - Leandro Gracian - Jairo Castillo• (Patricio Rodriguez 46), Facundo Parra. Tr: Antonio Mohamed

---

Casa Blanca, Quito
12-04-2011, 17:15, 15 516, Oliveira BRA

LDU Quito   **2**
Bolanos.L [47], Barcos [58]

Alexander Dominguez - Neicer Reasco, Diego Calderon, Banner Caicedo, Jorge Guagua• - Luis Bolanos• (Fernando Hidalgo 76), Paul Ambrossi, Ezequiel Gonzalez, Enrique Vera• (William Araujo 71), Ulises de la Cruz (Patricio Urrutia 83) - Hernan Barcos. Tr: Edgardo Bauza

Godoy Cruz   **0**

Sebastian Torrico - Zelmar Garcia, Nicolas Sanchez, Leonardo Sigali•, Roberto Russo• - Carlos Sanchez♦62, Israel Damonte, Juan Falcon, Ariel Rojas (Fabricio Nunez• 64), Diego Villar• (Mariano Donda 71) - Alvaro Navarro (Rodrigo Salinas 65). Tr: Jorge da Silva

ROUND OF SIXTEEN

Vila Belmiro, Santos
27-04-2011, 21:50, 11 417, Larrionda URU

Santos	1
	Ganso [38]

Rafael - Jonathan, Edu Dracena, Durval, Leo - Arouca, Danilo•, Elano (Adriano• 90), Ganso - Ze Eduardo (Alan Patrick 82), Neymar. Tr: Muricy Ramalho

CF América	0

Guillermo Ochoa - Oscar Rojas•, Aquivaldo Mosquera•, Juan Carlos Valenzuela, Diego Cervantes (Miguel Layun 45••♦90) - Andres Nicolas Olivera (Vicente Sanchez 65), Rosinei, Diego Reyes, Joaquin Martinez - Vicente Matias Vuoso (Angel Reyna 52), Daniel Marquez. Tr: Carlos Reinoso

---

Arena do Jacaré, Sete Lagoas
4-05-2011, 21:50, 14 972, Arias PAR

Cruzeiro	0

Fabio - Pablo, Gil•, Mauricio Victorino - Marquinhos Parana, Gilberto, Roger••♦31, Walter Montillo, Henrique (Andres Dias 76) - Ernesto Farias• (Everton 37), Jose Ortigoza (Dudu 68). Tr: Cuca

Once Caldas	2
	Amaya [66], Moreno [71]

Luis Martinez - Elkin Calle, Diego Amaya, Alexis Henriquez•, Luis Nunez - Harrison Henao (Jhon Pajoy• 55), Alexander Mejia, Carlos Carbonero♦56, Matias Mirabaje (Jefferson Cuero 65) - Dayro Moreno (Felix Micolta 86), Wason Renteria•. Tr: Juan Carlos Osorio

---

Unico, La Plata
27-04-2011, 19:30, 15 815, Fagundes BRA

Estudiantes LP	0

Agustin Orion - Facundo Roncaglia, Leandro Desabato, German Re, Federico Fernandez• - Enzo Perez, Rodrigo Brana•, Juan Sebastian Veron• (Leandro Benitez 84), Pablo Barrientos (Leandro Gonzalez 90) - Gaston Fernandez, Rodrigo Lopez. Tr: Manolo Eduardo Berizzo

Cerro Porteño	0

Diego Barreto - Ivan Piris, Pedro Benitez•, Luis Cardozo, Cesar Benitez• - Rodrigo Burgos••♦86, Jorge Nunez, Javier Villarreal, Ivan Torres• (Luis Caceres 77) - Jonathan Fabbro (Mariano Uglessich 89), Roberto Nanni•. Tr: Leonardo Ruben Astrada

---

Casa Blanca, Quito
5-05-2011, 20:45, 19 158, Roldan COL

LDU Quito	0

Alexander Dominguez - Jorge Guagua••♦88, Norberto Araujo, Diego Calderon - Fernando Hidalgo, Enrique Vera (Patricio Urrutia 67), Ulises de la Cruz, Marlon Ganchozo (Jose Cevallos 46), Luis Bolanos - Walter Calderon (Jose Valencia 60), Hernan Barcos. Tr: Edgardo Bauza

Vélez Sarsfield	2
	Alvarez [45], Bella [80]

Marcelo Barovero• - Fabian Cubero•, Sebastian Dominguez, Fernando Ortiz, Emiliano Papa - Augusto Fernandez, Franco Razzotti, Ricardo Alvarez (Ivan Bella 69), Hector Canteros, Maximiliano Moralez (David Ramirez 44) - Juan Manuel Martinez (Agustin Vuletich 79). Tr: Ricardo Gareca

---

Corregidora, Querétaro
3-05-2011, 20:45, 32 673, Vera ECU

CF América	0

Guillermo Ochoa - Oscar Rojas, Juan Carlos Valenzuela•, Patricio Trevino, Aquivaldo Mosquera - Diego Reyes•, Rosinei, Pavel Pardo (Angel Reyna• 51) - Daniel Montenegro (Lugiani Gallardo 74) - Vicente Matias Vuoso, Vicente Sanchez• (Enrique Esqueda 55). Tr: Carlos Reinoso

Santos	0

Rafael - Jonathan, Edu Dracena (Alex Sandro 86), Durval, Leo• - Arouca (Rodrigo Possebon 58), Adriano, Danilo - Ganso - Ze Eduardo (Bruno Aguiar 63), Neymar. Tr: Muricy Ramalho

---

Victor Reyna, Tuxtla Gutierrez
27-04-2011, 17:30, 5071, Ponce ECU

Jaguares	1
	Martinez [57]

Jorge Villalpando - Miguel Angel Martinez, Ismael Fuentes, Oscar Razo, Christian Valdez - Marvin Cabrera (Alan Zamora 23), Ricardo Esqueda (Jorge Rodriguez 76), Jorge Hernandez, Damian Manso (Edgar Andrade 53) - Antonio Salazar, Jackson Martinez. Tr: Jose Guadalupe Cruz

Atlético Junior	1
	Paez [6]

Sebastian Viera - Cesar Fawcett, Juan Valencia, Harold Macias•, Braynner Garcia - Jossymar Gomez, Jhon Viafara•, Giovanni Hernandez (Wainer Caneda 89) - Luis Carlos Ruiz (Victor Cortes 64), Luis Paez (Julian Barahona 46), Carlos Bacca. Tr: Oscar Hector Quintabani

---

General Pablo Rojas, Asunción
5-05-2011, 19:15, 20 408, Ruiz COL

Cerro Porteño	0 5p

Diego Barreto - Ivan Piris, Pedro Benitez, Luis Cardozo, Cesar Benitez - Luis Caceres, Jorge Nunez• (Juan Iturbe 66), Javier Villarreal•, Ivan Torres• (Julio dos Santos 85) - Jonathan Fabbro, Roberto Nanni•. Tr: Leonardo Ruben Astrada

Estudiantes LP	0 3p

Agustin Orion• - Facundo Roncaglia•, Leandro Desabato, German Re, Federico Fernandez - Enzo Perez, Rodrigo Brana, Leandro Benitez•, Raul Iberbia - Gaston Fernandez• (Juan Pereyra 74), Rodrigo Lopez•. Tr: Manolo Eduardo Berizzo

---

Olimpico, Rio de Janeiro
28-04-2011, 22:55, 25 378, Pezzotta ARG

Fluminense	3
	Rafael Moura [3], Marquinho [71], Conca [74]

Ricardo Berna - Mariano, Gum, Edinho, Julio Cesar• (Fernando Bob 43) (Araujo 72) - Edwin Valencia, Marquinho•, Diguinho, Dario Conca• - Fred, Rafael Moura (Digao 80). Tr: Enderson Moreira

Libertad	1
	Gamarra [59]

Tobias Vargas - Carlos Bonet, Pedro Portocarrero, Ignacio Canuto, Miguel Samudio - Victor Ayala•, Rodolfo Gamarra•, Victor Caceres• - Rodrigo Rojas (Jorge Moreira 83) - Jose Nunez (Manuel Maciel 59), Nicolas Pavlovich (Angel Orue 65). Tr: Gregorio Perez

---

Palogrande, Manizales
27-04-2011, 19:50, 13 286, Carrillo PER

Once Caldas	1
	Nunez [88]

Luis Martinez - Elkin Calle (Jhon Pajoy 78), Diego Amaya, Alexis Henriquez, Luis Nunez - Harrison Henao (Mario Gonzalez 69), Alexander Mejia, Carlos Carbonero, Matias Mirabaje (Matias Mirabje 54) - Dayro Moreno, Wason Renteria. Tr: Juan Carlos Osorio

Cruzeiro	2
	Wallyson [72], Ortigoza [83]

Fabio - Marquinhos Parana, Gil, Mauricio Victorino, Gilberto (Vitor 83) - Leandro Guerreiro, Henrique, Roger (Everton 46) - Walter Montillo - Brandao (Jose Ortigoza 67), Wallyson. Tr: Cuca

---

Metropolitano, Barranquilla
5-05-2011, 20:45, 17 371, Lopes BRA

Atlético Junior	3
	Juan Valencia [35], Paez [50p], Bacca [72]

Sebastian Viera - Cesar Fawcett♦79, Jhon Valencia, Juan Valencia (Victor Cortes 69), Anselmo de Almeida, Braynner Garcia• - Jhon Viafara, Jossymar Gomez (Jose Amaya 82), Giovanni Hernandez - Luis Paez, Carlos Bacca. Tr: Oscar Hector Quintabani

Jaguares	3
	Martinez 2 [39 63], Andrade [86]

Jorge Villalpando (Fabian Villasenor 75) - Miguel Angel Martinez, Ismael Fuentes•, Oscar Razo• (Julio Frias 81), Christian Valdez - Alan Zamora (Ricardo Esqueda 69), Edgar Andrade, Jorge Hernandez, Jorge Rodriguez - Antonio Salazar, Jackson Martinez♦79. Tr: Jose Guadalupe Cruz

---

José Amalfitani, Buenos Aires
26-04-2011, 21:50, 7134, Amarilla PAR

Vélez Sarsfield	3
	Fernandez 2 [7 10], Dominguez [54]

Marcelo Barovero - Fabian Cubero, Sebastian Dominguez•, Fernando Ortiz, Emiliano Papa• - Augusto Fernandez•, Franco Razzotti (David Ramirez 72), Victor Zapata (Ricardo Alvarez 45) - Maximiliano Moralez - Juan Manuel Martinez (Agustin Vuletich 88), Tanque Silva•. Tr: Ricardo Gareca

LDU Quito	0

Alexander Dominguez - Jorge Guagua•, Norberto Araujo, Neicer Reasco♦69 - Diego Calderon, Ulises de la Cruz (Patricio Urrutia 82), Enrique Vera, Fernando Hidalgo, Jose Valencia - Luis Bolanos••♦54 - Hernan Barcos (Walter Calderon 78). Tr: Edgardo Bauza

---

Defensores del Chaco, Asunción
4-05-2011, 20:50, 2699, Silvera URU

Libertad	3
	Rojas [57], Samudio [85], Nunez [90]

Tobias Vargas - Carlos Bonet, Pedro Portocarrero, Ignacio Canuto, Miguel Samudio• - Victor Caceres, Sergio Aquino, Victor Ayala• (Rodrigo Rojas 54), Manuel Maciel (Angel Orue 82), Rodolfo Gamarra (Jose Nunez 74) - Nicolas Pavlovich•. Tr: Gregorio Perez

Fluminense	0

Ricardo Berna• - Mariano♦40, Gum, Edinho, Julio Cesar - Edwin Valencia (Digao 63), Marquinho•, Diguinho• (Rodriguinho 89), Dario Conca• - Fred•, Rafael Moura (Araujo 68). Tr: Enderson Moreira

Olímpico, Porto Alegre
26-04-2011, 19:30, 31 559, Pitana ARG

Grêmio 1
Douglas [58]

Marcelo Grohe - Rafael Marques, Neuton, Gabriel - Willian Magrao• (Lins 46), Douglas, Fabio Rochemback, Adilson•, Gilson (Damian Escudero 90) - Borges♦35, Leandro (Carlos Alberto 78). Tr: Renato Gaucho

Universidad Católica 2
Pratto 2 [28 73]

Paulo Garces - David Henriquez, Hans Martinez•, Rodrigo Valenzuela•, Juan Eluchans• - Marcelo Canete (Jose Villanueva 76), Tomas Costa• (Gonzalo Sepulveda 83), Fernando Meneses, Francisco Silva• (Felipe Gutierrez 63), Jorge Ormeno - Lucas Pratto. Tr: Juan Antonio Pizzi

San Carlos, Santiago
4-05-2011, 21:50, 13 502, Amarilla PAR

Universidad Católica 1
Mirosevic [85]

Paulo Garces - David Henriquez, Hans Martinez, Rodrigo Valenzuela, Juan Eluchans• - Marcelo Canete (Felipe Gutierrez• 72), Tomas Costa• (Milovan Mirosevic 53), Fernando Meneses, Francisco Silva, Jorge Ormeno• - Lucas Pratto (Roberto Gutierrez 90). Tr: Juan Antonio Pizzi

Grêmio 0

Marcelo Grohe - Mario Fernandes (Vinicius Pacheco 84), Rafael Marques (Leandro 63), Rodolfo, Gilson, Vilson• - Adilson, Fernando, Douglas - Lins (Damian Escudero 79), Junior Vicosa. Tr: Renato Gaucho

Centenario, Montevideo
28-04-2011, 19:30, 43 472, Torres PAR

Peñarol 1
Corujo [36]

Sebastian Sosa - Alejandro Gonzalez, Carlos Valdez•, Guillermo Rodriguez, Dario Rodriguez• - Matias Corujo, Nicolas Freitas•, Luis Aguiar, Matias Mier (Fabian Estoyanoff 71) - Alejandro Martinuccio•, Antonio Pacheco (Diego Alonso 79). Tr: Diego Aguirre

Internacional 1
Leandro Damiao [64]

Renan - Nei, Bolivar, Rodrigo, Kleber - Mario Bolatti, Pablo Guinazu, Andrezinho (Tinga• 79), Andres D'Alessandro - Leandro Damiao, Rafael Sobis (Oscar 46). Tr: Falcao

Beira-Rio, Porto Alegre
4-05-2011, 19:30, 42 863, Osses CHI

Internacional 1
Oscar [1]

Renan - Nei• (Rafael Sobis 74), Bolivar, Rodrigo, Kleber - Oscar (Tinga 62), Pablo Guinazu, Mario Bolatti, Andrezinho (Ricardo Goulart 62) - Andres D'Alessandro• - Leandro Damiao. Tr: Falcao

Peñarol 2
Martinuccio [46], Olivera [50]

Sebastian Sosa - Alejandro Gonzalez, Carlos Valdez (Emiliano Albin 72), Guillermo Rodriguez, Dario Rodriguez - Matias Corujo, Nicolas Freitas•, Luis Aguiar•, Matias Mier (Nicolas Domingo• 80) - Alejandro Martinuccio (Edison Torres 90), Juan Olivera. Tr: Diego Aguirre

QUARTER-FINALS

Palogrande, Manizales
11-05-2011, 19:50, 23 984, Soto VEN

Once Caldas 0

Luis Martinez - Alexis Henriquez, Diego Amaya, Elkin Calle••♦59 - Matias Mirabaje (Yedinson Palacios• 62), Alexander Mejia, Harrison Henao, Luis Nunez - Dayro Moreno, Wason Renteria, Jhon Pajoy (Mario Gonzalez 53). Tr: Juan Carlos Osorio

Santos 1
Alan Patrick [42]

Rafael - Jonathan, Edu Dracena•, Durval, Leo (Alex Sandro 58) - Adriano, Danilo, Elano (Bruno Aguiar 90), Alan Patrick (Felipe Anderson 74) - Ze Eduardo•, Neymar. Tr: Muricy Ramalho

Pacaembu, São Paulo
18-05-2011, 22:00, 35 135, Osses CHI

Santos 1
Neymar [11]

Rafael• - Danilo, Durval, Edu Dracena, Leo (Alex Sandro 83) - Adriano, Arouca•, Elano, Alan Patrick (Para 24) - Ze Eduardo (Keirrison 69), Neymar. Tr: Muricy Ramalho

Once Caldas 1
Renteria [29]

Luis Martinez - Yedinson Palacios, Diego Amaya, Alexis Henriquez•, Luis Nunez - Jefferson Cuero (Jhon Pajoy 77), Alexander Mejia, Matias Mirabaje (Harrison Henao 65), Carlos Carbonero, Dayro Moreno• - Wason Renteria. Tr: Juan Carlos Osorio

Victor Reyna, Tuxtla Gutierrez
12-05-2011, 20:45, 14 022, Pezzotta ARG

Jaguares 1
Pedroza [90]

Israel Villasenor - Miguel Angel Martinez•, Ismael Fuentes, Christian Valdez - Jorge Hernandez, Jorge Rodriguez (Guillermo Rojas 67), Edgar Andrade, Oscar Razo, Alan Zamora (Antonio Pedroza• 46), Ricardo Esqueda - Antonio Salazar (Julio Frias 80). Tr: Jose Guadalupe Cruz

Cerro Porteño 1
Fabbro [72]

Diego Barreto - Ivan Piris, Pedro Benitez•, Mariano Uglessich, Cesar Benitez - Luis Caceres, Javier Villarreal, Ivan Torres, Jonathan Fabbro• (Rodrigo Burgos 80) - Juan Manuel Lucero (Juan Iturbe• 62), Roberto Nanni (Freddy Bareiro 71). Tr: Leonardo Astrada

General Pablo Rojas, Asuncion
19-05-2011, 21:30, 24 178, Ubriaco URU

Cerro Porteño 1
Pedro Benitez [72]

Diego Barreto - Ivan Piris, Pedro Benitez, Mariano Uglessich•, Cesar Benitez - Luis Caceres (Jorge Nunez 69), Javier Villarreal, Ivan Torres - Jonathan Fabbro - Juan Manuel Lucero (Julio dos Santos 73), Roberto Nanni• (Freddy Bareiro 65). Tr: Leonardo Astrada

Jaguares 0

Israel Villasenor - Miguel Angel Martinez•, Ismael Fuentes•♦82, Edgar Andrade (Alan Zamora 57), Oscar Razo - Christian Valdez•, Ricardo Esqueda, Jorge Hernandez (Guillermo Rojas 80), Jorge Rodriguez - Jackson Martinez, Antonio Pedroza (Antonio Salazar 64). Tr: Jose Guadalupe Cruz

José Amalfitani, Buenos Aires
12-05-2011, 20:15, 9086, Seneme BRA

Vélez Sarsfield 3

Moralez [20], Martinez 2 [75p 80]

Marcelo **Barovero** - Fabian **Cubero**, Sebastian **Dominguez**, Fernando **Ortiz**, Emiliano **Papa** - Augusto **Fernandez** Ivan **Bella** 72), Franco **Razzotti**, Victor **Zapata** - Maximiliano **Moralez**• (Gaston Diaz 84) - David **Ramirez** (Ricardo **Alvarez** 62), Juan Manuel **Martinez**•. Tr: Ricardo **Gareca**

Libertad 0

Tobias **Vargas**• - Carlos **Bonet**, Pedro **Portocarrero**, Ignacio **Canuto**, Miguel **Samudio**• - Rodolfo **Gamarra**, Victor **Caceres**, Victor **Ayala** (Rodrigo Rojas 46), Sergio **Aquino** - Nicolas **Pavlovich** (Angel Orue 84), Manuel **Maciel** (Ariel **Nunez** 68). Tr: Gregorio **Perez**

Defensores del Chaco, Asunción
18-05-2011, 18:30, 2300, Fagundes BRA

Libertad 2

Rojas [44], Maciel [50]

Tobias **Vargas** - Carlos **Bonet** (Victor Ayala 51), Arnaldo **Vera**, Ignacio **Canuto**, Miguel **Samudio** - Rodolfo **Gamarra**, Rodrigo **Rojas**, Victor **Caceres**, Sergio **Aquino**• - Nicolas **Pavlovich** (Angel Orue 46), Manuel **Maciel**• (Ariel Nunez 71). Tr: Gregorio **Perez**

Vélez Sarsfield 4

Moralez 2 [44 66], Franco [86p], Fernandez [87]

Marcelo **Barovero** - Fabian **Cubero**, Sebastian **Dominguez**, Fernando **Ortiz**, Emiliano **Papa** - Augusto **Fernandez**, Franco **Razzotti**, Victor **Zapata**•, Ricardo **Alvarez** (Ivan **Bella** 84) - Maximiliano **Moralez** (David Ramirez 76) - Tanque **Silva**• (Guillermo **Franco** 64). Tr: Ricardo **Gareca**

Centenario, Montevideo
11-05-2011, 19:30, 46 550, Baldassi ARG

Peñarol 2

Olivera [36], Martinuccio [93+]

Sebastian **Sosa** - Alejandro **Gonzalez**, Guillermo **Rodriguez**•, Dario **Rodriguez** - Matias **Corujo**, Jonathan **Urreta** (Fabian **Estoyanoff** 79), Nicolas **Freitas**•, Luis **Aguiar**, Matias **Mier** (Emiliano **Albin** 62) - Alejandro **Martinuccio**, Juan **Olivera** (Diego Alonso 87). Tr: Diego **Aguirre**

Universidad Católica 0

Paulo **Garces** - Rodrigo **Valenzuela**, Hans **Martinez**, Alfonso **Parot**•, Juan **Eluchans**• - Tomas **Costa**, Jorge **Ormeno**, Francisco **Silva** (Felipe **Gutierrez** 58), Fernando **Meneses** (Francisco Pizarro 85), Marcelo **Canete** (Pablo Calandria 75) - Lucas **Pratto**. Tr: Juan Antonio **Pizzi**

San Carlos, Santiago
19-05-2011, 19:00, 12 942, Lopes BRA

Universidad Católica 2

Meneses [18], Gutierrez [69]

Paulo **Garces** - Rodrigo **Valenzuela**, Hans **Martinez**, Alfonso **Parot**, Juan **Eluchans** - Tomas **Costa** (Francisco Silva 51), Jorge **Ormeno**•, Milovan **Mirosevic**, Fernando **Meneses** (Marcelo **Canete** 78) - Jose **Villanueva** (Roberto Gutierrez 62), Lucas **Pratto**. Tr: Juan Antonio **Pizzi**

Peñarol 1

Estoyanoff [85]

Sebastian **Sosa** - Alejandro **Gonzalez**, Carlos **Valdez**, Guillermo **Rodriguez**, Dario **Rodriguez** - Matias **Corujo**•, Nicolas **Freitas**•, Luis **Aguiar**, Matias **Mier** (Fabian **Estoyanoff** 67) - Alejandro **Martinuccio**, Juan **Olivera** (Diego Alonso 89). Tr: Diego **Aguirre**

SEMI-FINALS

Pacaembu, São Paulo
25-05-2011, 21:50, 31 434, Larrionda URU

Santos 1

Edu Dracena [43]

Rafael - **Leo** (Alex Sandro 80), **Durval**, Edu **Dracena**, **Para** - **Elano** (Alan Patrick 89), **Danilo**, **Arouca**•, **Adriano** - Ze **Eduardo** (Maikon Leite 80), **Neymar**•. Tr: Muricy **Ramalho**

Cerro Porteno 0

Diego **Barreto** - Ivan **Piris**, Mariano **Uglessich**, Pedro **Benitez**, Cesar **Benitez** - Luis **Caceres**•, Julio dos Santos, Javier **Villarreal**• (Rodrigo Burgos 86), Ivan **Torres**• (Jorge Nunez 66), Jonathan **Fabbro** - Fredy **Bareiro** (Roberto Nanni• 74). Tr: Leonardo **Astrada**

General Pablo Rojas, Asuncion
1-06-2011, 20:50, 32 000, Roldan COL

Cerro Porteno 3

Cesar Benitez [31], Lucero [60], Fabbro [81]

Diego **Barreto** - Ivan **Piris**, Mariano **Uglessich**•, Cesar **Benitez**, Pedro **Benitez** - Rodrigo **Burgos** (Juan Lucero 40), Jonathan **Fabbro**, Ivan **Torres** (Juan Iturbe• 10), Julio dos **Santos**, Luis **Caceres** - Fredy **Bareiro** (Roberto Nanni 66). Tr: Leonardo **Astrada**

Santos 3

Ze Eduardo [2], OG [28], Neymar [45]

Rafael• - Jonathan (Para 25), **Durval**, Edu **Dracena**••♦90, Alex Sandro• - **Adriano**, **Arouca**, **Danilo**, **Elano**• (Rodrigo Possebon 70) - Ze **Eduardo** (Maikon Leite 72), **Neymar**. Tr: Muricy **Ramalho**

Centenario, Montevideo
26-05-2011, 21:50, 52 904, Amarilla PAR

Peñarol 1

Dario Rodriguez [44]

Sebastian **Sosa** - Alejandro **Gonzalez**•, Carlos **Valdez**, Guillermo **Rodriguez**, Dario **Rodriguez** - Matias **Corujo** (Fabian **Estoyanoff** 58), Nicolas **Freitas**, Luis **Aguiar**•, Matias **Mier** (Emiliano **Albin** 77) - Alejandro **Martinuccio**, Juan **Olivera** (Diego Alonso 83). Tr: Diego **Aguirre**

Vélez Sarsfield 0

Marcelo **Barovero** - Fabian **Cubero**•, Sebastian **Dominguez**, Fernando **Ortiz**, Emiliano **Papa** - Augusto **Fernandez** (Ivan **Bella** 82), Franco **Razzotti**, Victor **Zapata**•, Ricardo **Alvarez** - Tanque **Silva** (Guillermo **Franco** 87), Juan Manuel **Martinez**• (David Ramirez 76). Tr: Ricardo **Gareca**

José Amalfitani, Buenos Aires
2-06-2011, 21:50, 45 000, Osses CHI

Vélez Sarsfield 2

Tobio [45], Silva [66]

Marcelo **Barovero** - Fabian **Cubero** (Fernando Tobio 14), Sebastian **Dominguez**, Fernando **Urtz**••♦68, Emiliano **Papa** - Augusto **Fernandez**, Hector **Canteros**, Victor **Zapata** (David Ramirez 88), Maximiliano **Moralez** (Ricardo Alvarez 60) - Tanque **Silva**•, Juan Manuel **Martinez**. Tr: Ricardo **Gareca**

Peñarol 1

Mier [33]

Sebastian **Sosa** - Alejandro **Gonzalez**, Carlos **Valdez**, Guillermo **Rodriguez**, Dario **Rodriguez** - Matias **Corujo**, Nicolas **Freitas**, Luis **Aguiar**, Matias **Mier** (Fabian **Estoyanoff** 70) - Alejandro **Martinuccio** (Emiliano Albin 82), Juan **Olivera**. Tr: Diego **Aguirre**

Copa Libertadores Final 1st Leg	Estadio Centenario Montevideo	Wednesday 15-06-2011
Kick-off: 21:45		Attendance: 60 000

PENAROL   0 0   SANTOS

PENAROL

Yellow and black striped shirts, Black shorts, Yellow socks

Tr: Diego Aguirre

Sebastian Sosa

Alejandro Gonzalez 76   Carlos Valdez   Guillermo Rodriguez   Dario Rodriguez(c)

67 Matias Corujo 66   Nicolas Freitas   Luis Aguiar   Matias Mier 56
Antonio Pacheco   Fabian Estoyanoff

Alejandro Martinuccio 30   82 Juan Manuel Olivera
Diego Alonso

89 Ze Eduardo   Neymar 19
Bruno Aguiar

79 Elano(c)   Danilo   Arouca 60   Adriano
Alan Patrick

Alex Sandro   Durval †   Bruno Rodrigo   Para

Rafael

Tr: Muricy Ramalho

White shirts, White shorts, White socks

SANTOS

MATCH STATS

Peñarol		Santos
11	Shots	8
5	Shots on goal	5
16	Fouls committed	19
6	Corner kicks	3
2	Caught offside	1

MATCH OFFICIALS

REFEREE
Carlos Amarilla PAR

ASSISTANTS
Nicolas Yegros PAR
Rodney Aquino PAR

4TH OFFICIAL
Antonio Arias PAR

(C) Captain † Man of the Match

The pitch was horrible. The stadium is beautiful but the pitch is always poor. The players suffer technically.
Muricy Ramalho

We wanted the victory, but this draw was very good. Now we have 90 minutes to decide the title. We're going to play at home. If we were already competitive away, imagine us [at the Pacembu]. At home it will be different. Our supporters will create a beautiful atmosphere.
Neymar

Santos are favourites to win because they drew at our place and now they're at home in front of their fans. The odds may be with Santos, but there is a long way to go before we know the winners of this tie.
Diego Aguirre

Copa Libertadores Final 2nd Leg	Pacaembu São Paulo	Wednesday 22-06-2011
Kick-off: 21:50		Attendance: 37 952

SANTOS   2 1   PENAROL

Neymar 46, Danilo 69   **Durval OG 79**

SANTOS

White shirts, White shorts, White socks
Tr: Muricy Ramalho

MATCH STATS

Santos		Peñarol
16	Shots	2
6	Shots on goal	1
5	Fouls committed	16
8	Corner kicks	5
1	Caught offside	0

Rafael

Danilo   Edu Dracena(c)   Durval   **68** Leo / Alex Sandro

Adriano   Arouca   Elano   **86** Ganso / Para

Neymar † **35**   Ze Eduardo **58**

MATCH OFFICIALS

REFEREE
Sergio Pezzotta ARG

ASSISTANTS
Ricardo Casas ARG
Hernan Maidana ARG

4TH OFFICIAL
Juan Pompei ARG

(C) Captain † Man of the Match

Juan Manuel Olivera   Alejandro Martinuccio

63 Matias Mier / Jonathan Urretataviscaya   Nicolas Freitas **52**   Luis Aguiar   Matias Corujo **52**

Dario Rodriguez(c)   Guillermo Rodriguez   Carlos Valdez   **38** Alejandro Gonzalez **31** / Emiliano Albin / **79** Fabian Estoyanoff

Sebastian Sosa

Tr: Diego Aguirre
Yellow and black striped shirts, Black shorts, Yellow socks

PENAROL

They were a worthy opponent, but they don't know how to lose.
Leo

It's an important title for the club and players. We have been trying to win this third title for a long time now (the first since 1963) and we've made history.
Edu Dracena

We have to thank these young guys for giving us this title.
Pele

Allowing the goal so early in the second half is what killed us.

(Of the fight between the two sets of players after the final whistle...) A Santos fan entered the field and provoked us. They have to learn how to celebrate, we had accepted the loss.
Alejandro Martinuccio

COPA BRIDGESTONE SUDAMERICANA 2011

First Round

Univ. de Chile *	CHI	1	0
Fénix	URU	0	0
Olimpia *	PAR	2	1
The Strongest	BOL	0	2
Deportivo Quito *	ECU	1	0
Dep. Anzoátegui	VEN	0	2
San José *	BOL	1	0
Nacional Asuncion	PAR	0	1
Bella Vista *	URU	1	0
Univ'dad Católica	CHI	1	3
Un. César Vallejo *	PER	1	2
Santa Fe	COL	1	0
Juan Aurich	PER	0	1
La Equidad *	COL	2	2
Yaracuyanos *	VEN	1	0
LDU Quito	ECU	1	1

Second Round

Univ. de Chile *	CHI	1	2
Nacional Mont'deo	URU	0	0
At. Paranaense	BRA	0	0
Flamengo *	BRA	1	1
Olimpia *	PAR	2	2
Emelec	ECU	1	1
Estudiantes LP	ARG	0	1
Arsenal *	ARG	2	0
Universitario	PER	2	2
Dep. Anzoátegui *	VEN	1	0
Lanús *	ARG	2	0
Godoy Cruz	ARG	2	0
Aurora	BOL	1	5
Nacional Asuncion *	PAR	1	2
Palmeiras	BRA	0	3
Vasco da Gama *	BRA	2	1
Vélez Sarsfield	ARG	0	4
Argentinos Juniors *	ARG	0	0
Deportes Iquique	CHI	1	0
Univ'dad Católica *	CHI	2	0
Botafogo	BRA	2	1
Atlético Mineiro *	BRA	1	0
Deportivo Cali	COL	1	1 5p
Santa Fe *	COL	1	1 6p
Libertad	PAR	1	1
La Equidad *	COL	0	0
Ceará *	BRA	2	0
São Paulo FC	BRA	1	3
Independiente	ARG	Bye	
Trujillanos *	VEN	1	0
LDU Quito *	ECU	4	1

Round of 16

Univ. de Chile	4	1
Flamengo *	0	0
Olimpia *	0	2
Arsenal	0	3
Universitario	1	1 3p
Godoy Cruz *	1	1 2p
Aurora *	3	3
Vasco da Gama	1	8
Vélez Sarsfield	2	1
Univ'dad Católica *	0	1
Botafogo *	1	1
Santa Fe	1	4
Libertad	0	2
São Paulo FC *	1	0
Independiente	0	1
LDU Quito *	2	0

Quarter-finals

Univ. de Chile	2	3
Arsenal *	1	0
Universitario *	2	2
Vasco da Gama	0	5
Vélez Sarsfield	1	3
Santa Fe *	1	2
Libertad	0	1 4p
LDU Quito *	1	0 5p

Semi-finals

Univ. de Chile	1	2
Vasco da Gama *	1	0
Vélez Sarsfield	0	0
LDU Quito *	2	1

Final

Universidad de Chile	1	3
LDU Quito *	0	0

FINAL 1ST LEG

Casa Blanca, Quito, 8-12-2011, 19:15
Att: 41 000, Ref: Diego Abal ARG
Scorer - Vargas 43

LDU - Alexander Dominguez - Jorge Guagua, Norberto Araujo, Diego Calderon●, Neicer Reasco (Enrique Gamez 81), Paul Ambrosi - Fernando Hidalgo, Lucas Acosta, Ezequiel Gonzalez● - Hernan Barcos, Claudio Bieler (Luis Balonas 46). Tr: Edgardo Bauza

U de Chile - Jhonny Herrera● - Matias Rodriguez, Albert Acevedo, Osvaldo Gonzalez, Marcos Gonzalez, Jose Manuel Rojas - Marcelo Diaz, Charles Aranguiz (Guillermo MArino 88), Eugenio Mena - Eduardo Vargas● (Paulo Magalhaes 91+), Gustavo Canales● (Francisco Castro 73). Tr: Jorge Sampaoli

FINAL 2ND LEG

Estadio Nacional, Santiago, 14-12-2011
Att: 50 000, Ref: Wilson Seneme BRA
Scorers - Vargas 2 2 86, Lorenzetti 79

U de Chile - Jhonny Herrera - Osvaldo Gonzalez●, Marcos Gonzalez, Jose Manuel Rojas, Matias Rodriguez●◆85 - Charles Aranguiz, Marcelo Diaz●, Eugenio Mena - Francisco Castro (Gustavo Lorenzette 53), Eduardo Vargas, Gustavo Canales (Diego Rivarola 86). Tr: Jorge Sampaoli

LDU - Alexander Dominguez - Neicer Reasco (Enrique Gamez 53), Jorge Guagua◆67, Norberto Araujo, Diego Calderon, Paul Ambrosi, Lucas Acosta, Fernando Hidalgo●, Ezequiel Gonzalez●, Luis Bolanos (Walter Calderon 73), Hernan Barcos●. Tr: Edgardo Bauza

* Home team in the 1st leg

Top scorers: 11 - Eduardo Vargas CHI, Universidad de Chile ● 7 - Hernan Barcos ECU, LDU Quito

WOMEN'S TOURNAMENTS IN SOUTH AMERICA 2010

CAMPEONATO SUDAMERICANO FEMENINO ECUADOR 2010

First Round Group Stage

Group A	Pl	W	D	L	F	A	Pts	ARG	ECU	BOL	PER
Chile	4	3	0	1	9	4	9	1-2	2-1	3-0	3-1
Argentina	4	3	0	1	7	2	9		0-1	3-0	2-0
Ecuador	4	3	0	1	8	6	9			4-3	2-1
Bolivia	4	1	0	3	5	11	3				2-1
Peru	4	0	0	4	3	9	0				

Final Round Group

	Pl	W	D	L	F	A	Pts	COL	CHI	ARG
Brazil	3	3	0	0	12	1	9	5-0	3-1	4-0
Colombia	3	1	1	1	2	6	4		1-1	1-0
Chile	3	0	2	1	2	4	2			0-0
Argentina	3	0	1	2	0	5	1			

Group B	Pl	W	D	L	F	A	Pts	COL	PAR	VEN	URU
Brazil	4	4	0	0	13	1	12	2-1	3-0	4-0	4-0
Colombia	4	3	0	1	17	2	9		3-0	5-0	8-0
Paraguay	4	2	0	2	8	6	6			4-0	4-0
Venezuela	4	1	0	3	5	15	3				5-2
Uruguay	4	0	0	4	2	21	0				

Top scorer: **9** - Marta BRA • **5** - Yoreli Rincon COL

Brazil and Colombia qualified for the 2011 FIFA Women's World Cup Germany 2011 and the 2012 London Olympics
Tournament played in Latacunga, Ambato, Riobamba, Loja, Azogues, Cuenca and Quito, Ecuador from 4-11-2010 to 21-11-2010

CAMPEONATO SUDAMERICANO FEMENINO SUB-20 COLOMBIA 2010

First Round Group Stage

Group A	Pl	W	D	L	F	A	Pts	CHI	ECU	ARG	BOL
Colombia	4	4	0	0	8	2	12	2-1	3-1	2-0	1-0
Chile	4	3	0	1	6	2	9		1-0	1-0	3-0
Ecuador	4	2	0	2	4	4	6			1-0	2-0
Argentina	4	1	0	3	2	4	3				2-0
Bolivia	4	0	0	4	0	8	0				

Semi-finals

Brazil	3
Chile	1

Final

Brazil	2
Colombia	0

Group B	Pl	W	D	L	F	A	Pts	PAR	VEN	URU	PER
Brazil	4	4	0	0	20	2	12	3-1	4-1	7-0	6-0
Paraguay	4	3	0	1	13	3	9		3-0	5-0	4-0
Venezuela	4	2	0	2	6	8	6			2-1	3-0
Uruguay	4	1	0	3	4	15	3				3-1
Peru	4	0	0	4	1	16	0				

Semi-finals

Paraguay	1
Colombia	2

3rd place play-off

Paraguay	6
Chile	0

Brazil and Colombia qualified for the FIFA U-20 Women's World Cup Germany 2010
Tournament played in Bucaramanga, Colombia from 28-01-2010 to 11-02-2010

CAMPEONATO SUDAMERICANO FEMENINO SUB-17 BRAZIL 2010

First Round Group Stage

Group A	Pl	W	D	L	F	A	Pts	PAR	BOL	PER	ECU
Brazil	4	4	0	0	28	1	12	5-1	3-0	5-0	15-0
Paraguay	4	2	1	1	9	6	7		1-1	4-0	3-0
Bolivia	4	2	1	1	5	4	7			3-0	1-0
Peru	4	1	0	3	3	13	3				3-1
Ecuador	4	0	0	4	1	22	0				

Semi-finals

Brazil	6
Venezuela	2

Final

Brazil	7
Chile	0

Group B	Pl	W	D	L	F	A	Pts	VEN	ARG	COL	URU
Chile	4	2	2	0	9	3	8	2-2	1-1	2-0	4-0
Venezuela	4	2	1	1	7	4	7		0-1	1-0	4-1
Argentina	4	2	1	1	5	4	7			1-3	2-0
Colombia	4	2	0	2	6	5	6				3-1
Uruguay	4	0	0	4	2	13	0				

Semi-finals

Paraguay	1
Chile	4

3rd place play-off

Venezuela	1
Paraguay	0

Brazil, Chile and Venezuela qualified for the FIFA U-17 Women's World Cup Trinidad and Tobago 2010
Tournament played in São Paulo, Brazil from 28-01-2010 to 11-02-2010

YOUTH TOURNAMENTS IN SOUTH AMERICA 2011

SUDAMERICANO SUB-20 PERU 2011

First Round Group Stage

Group A	Pl	W	D	L	F	A	Pts	CHI	URU	PER	VEN
Argentina	4	3	1	0	8	4	10	3-1	2-1	2-1	1-1
Chile	4	2	0	2	6	8	6		0-4	2-0	3-1
Uruguay	4	1	1	2	6	5	4			0-2	1-1
Peru	4	1	1	2	4	5	4				1-1
Venezuela	4	0	3	1	4	6	3				

Group B	Pl	W	D	L	F	A	Pts	ECU	COL	PAR	BOL
Brazil	4	3	1	0	9	4	10	1-0	3-1	4-2	1-1
Ecuador	4	2	1	1	5	3	7		1-1	1-0	3-1
Colombia	4	1	2	1	7	8	5			3-3	2-1
Paraguay	4	1	1	2	6	8	4				1-0
Bolivia	4	0	1	3	3	7	1				

Final Round Group

	Pl	W	D	L	F	A	Pts	URU	ARG	ECU	CHI	COL
Brazil	5	4	0	1	15	3	12	6-0	1-2	1-0	5-1	2-0
Uruguay	5	3	1	1	4	7	10		1-0	1-1	1-0	1-0
Argentina	5	3	0	2	7	5	9			0-1	3-2	2-0
Ecuador	5	2	2	1	3	2	8				1-0	0-0
Chile	5	1	0	4	6	11	3					3-1
Colombia	5	0	1	4	1	8	1					

Top scorers: **9 - Neymar BRA • 4** - Facundo Ferreyra ARG; Lucas BRA; Edwin Cardona COL & Edson Montano ECU

Brazil and Uruguay qualified for the 2012 London Olympics. Brazil, Uruguay, Argentina and Ecuador qualified for the FIFA U-20 World Cup Colombia 2011 (Colombia qualified as hosts) • Tournament played in Moquegua, Tacna and Arequipa, Peru from 16-01-2011 to 12-02-2011

SUDAMERICANO SUB-17 ECUADOR 2011

First Round Group Stage

Group A	Pl	W	D	L	F	A	Pts	ECU	URU	PER	BOL
Argentina	4	3	0	1	10	4	9	2-0	1-2	4-2	3-0
Ecuador	4	2	1	1	4	4	7		1-0	1-1	2-1
Uruguay	4	2	0	2	4	5	6			0-3	2-0
Peru	4	1	1	2	8	9	4				2-4
Bolivia	4	1	0	3	5	9	3				

Group B	Pl	W	D	L	F	A	Pts	PAR	COL	CHI	VEN
Brazil	4	3	0	1	12	7	9	1-2	5-1	2-1	4-3
Paraguay	4	3	0	1	9	5	9		1-3	3-0	3-1
Colombia	4	2	1	1	7	8	7			2-2	1-0
Chile	4	1	1	2	5	8	4				2-1
Venezuela	4	0	0	4	5	10	0				

Final Round Group

	Pl	W	D	L	F	A	Pts	URU	ARG	ECU	COL	PAR
Brazil	5	4	1	0	10	4	13	0-0	3-2	3-1	1-0	3-1
Uruguay	5	2	3	0	8	5	9		1-1	1-1	3-2	3-1
Argentina	5	2	1	2	7	7	7			1-2	2-1	1-0
Ecuador	5	1	3	1	6	7	6				0-0	2-2
Colombia	5	1	1	3	5	7	4					2-1
Paraguay	5	0	1	4	5	11	1					

Top scorers: **7** - Edwin Cardona COL • **4** - Gonzala Barreto URU • **3** - Daniel Villalba ARG; Sergio Araujo; Gilbert Alvarez BOL & Philippe Coutinho BRA

Brazil, Uruguay, Argentina and Ecuador qualified for the FIFA U-17 World Cup Mexico 2011
Tournament played in Latacunga, Ambato, Rio Bamba, Ibarra and Quito, Ecuador from 12-03-2011 to 9-04-2011

OFC

OCEANIA FOOTBALL CONFEDERATION

After deciding that the football tournament of the 2011 Pacific Games in Noumea, New Caledonia would act as the first round of qualifying for the 2014 FIFA World Cup in Brazil, the OFC were forced into a change of plan due to the inclusion of non-OFC members in the line-up. With Guam a member of the Asian confederation and with Kiribati and Tuvalu only associate members, the OFC was informed by FIFA that it would have to host a separate tournament. That was good news for the players and fans in the region with a double dose of international football on the menu, even if it did cause logistical problems. The new qualifying format - which the OFC decided would double up as a preliminary round for the 2012 OFC Nations Cup - did produce one story which caught the imagination of news centres around the world when American Samoa beat Tonga 2-1 in a preliminary group in Apia. It was the Samoans first-ever victory in an international match and

THE FIFA BIG COUNT OF 2006 FOR OCEANIA

	Male	Female		Total
Number of players	486 000	56 000	Referees and Assistant Referees	3 000
Professionals	n/a		Admin, Coaches, Technical, Medical	29 000
Amateurs 18+	59 000		Number of clubs	2 000
Youth under 18	175 000		Number of teams	13 000
Unregistered	301 000		Clubs with women's teams	n/a
Total Players	573 000		Players as % of population	4.68%

footage of their heroic performance was included in news bulletins the world over. American Samoa had fared less well the previous month in the Pacific Games, a tournament won by the hosts New Caledonia. They beat the Solomon Islands 2-0 to retain their title in what is the region's longest-running event. At club level it was back to normal in the OFC Champions League with New Zealand reclaiming the title it had lost in 2010 after Auckland City beat first-time finalists Amicale from Vanuatu 6-1 on aggregate in the final. It was Auckland's third triumph in the competition and the fifth title for New Zealand in the past six years. At the 2011 FIFA Club World Cup in Japan, Auckland lost 2-0 to J.League champions Kashiwa Reysol in a preliminary round tie as they failed to match their performance in 2009 tournament when they beat hosts Al Ahli of the UAE to make it through to the quarter-finals.

Oceania Football Confederation (OFC)
Ericsson Stadium, 12 Maurice Road, Penrose, PO Box 62 586, Auckland 6, New Zealand
Tel +64 9 5258161   Fax +64 9 5258164
info@ofcfoot.org.nz   www.oceaniafootball.com
President: David Chung PNG
General Secretary: Tai Nicholas COK
Vice-President: Martin Alufurai SOL
OFC Formed: 1966

OFC EXECUTIVE COMMITTEE
President: David Chung PNG
Senior Vice-President: Martin Alufurai SOL   Vice-President: Lee Harmon COK   Treasurer: Dr MS Sahu Khan FIJ
Fred de Jong NZL
Lambert Matlock VAN   Toetu Petana SAM   Lord Ve'ehala TGA

MAP OF OFC MEMBER NATIONS

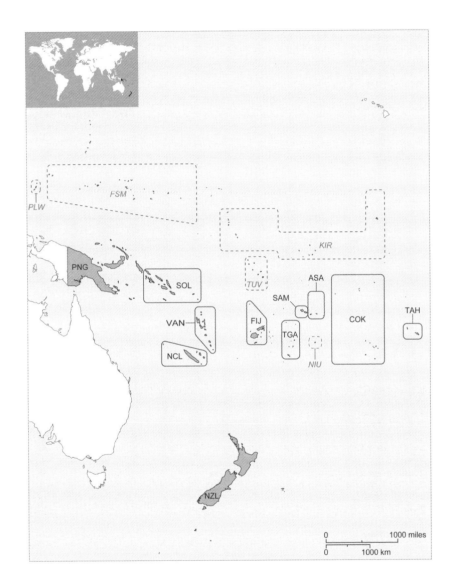

OCEANIA NATIONAL TEAM TOURNAMENTS

OCEANIA NATIONS CUP

Year	Host Country	Winners	Score	Runners-up	Venue
1973	New Zealand	New Zealand	2-0	Tahiti	Auckland
1980	New Caledonia	Australia	4-2	Tahiti	Nouméa
1996	Home & away	Australia	6-0 5-0	Tahiti	Papeete & Canberra
1998	Australia	New Zealand	1-0	Australia	Brisbane
2000	Tahiti	Australia	2-0	New Zealand	Stade de Pater, Papeete
2002	New Zealand	New Zealand	1-0	Australia	Ericsson Stadium, Auckland
2004	Home & away	Australia	5-1 6-0	Solomon Islands	Honaria & Sydney
2008	Home & away	New Zealand	3-1 3-0	New Caledonia	League system

There was no final in 2008. The results listed were between the first and second placed teams in the FIFA World Cup qualifying group for Oceania. Semi-finals were not played in 1973, 1980, 2004 and 2008

OCEANIA NATIONS CUP MEDALS TABLE

	Country	G	S	B	F	SF
1	Australia	4	2		6	4
2	New Zealand	4	1	2	4	4
3	Tahiti		3	1	3	3
4	New Caledonia		1	2		
5	Solomon Islands		1	2	1	2
6	Fiji			2		1
7	Vanuatu					2
		8	8	9	14	16

This table represents the Gold (winners), Silver (runners-up) and Bronze (semi-finalists) placings in the OFC Nations Cup, along with the number of appearances in the final and semi-finals.

FOOTBALL TOURNAMENT OF THE PACIFIC GAMES

Year	Host Country	Winners	Score	Runners-up	Venue
1963	Fiji	New Caledonia	8-2	Fiji	Suva
1966	New Caledonia	Tahiti	2-0	New Caledonia	Noumea
1969	Papua New Guinea	New Caledonia	2-1	Tahiti	Port Moresby
1971	Tahiti	New Caledonia	7-1	New Hebrides	Papeete
1975	Guam	Tahiti	2-1	New Caledonia	Guam
1979	Fiji	Tahiti	3-0	Fiji	Suva
1983	Western Samoa	Tahiti	1-0	Fiji	Apia
1987	New Caledonia	New Caledonia	1-0	Tahiti	Noumea
1991	Papua New Guinea	Fiji	1-1 ?-?p	Solomon Islands	Port Moresby
1995	Tahiti	Tahiti	2-0	Solomon Islands	Papeete
2003	Fiji	Fiji	2-0	New Caledonia	Suva
2007	Samoa	New Caledonia	1-0	Fiji	Apia
2011	New Caledonia	New Caledonia	2-0	Solomon Islands	Noumea

FOOTBALL TOURNAMENT OF THE SOUTH PACIFIC MINI GAMES

Year	Host Country	Winners	Score	Runners-up	Venue
1981	Solomon Islands	Tahiti	1-0	New Caledonia	Honiara
1985	Cook Islands	Tahiti	2-0	Fiji	Rarotonga
1989	Tonga	Papua New Guinea	0-0 4-3p	Fiji	Nuku'alofa
1993	Vanuatu	Tahiti	3-0	Fiji	Port Vila

POLYNESIAN CUP

Year	Host Country	Winners	Score	Runners-up	Venue
1994	Western Samoa	Tahiti	1-0	Tonga	Apia
1996	Tonga	Tonga	1-0	Western Samoa	Nuku'alofa
1998	Cook Islands	Tahiti	5-0	Cook Islands	Rarotonga
2000	Tahiti	Tahiti	2-0	Cook Islands	Papete

Competitions have always been organised on a league basis. The result listed is the game between the top two in the league standings

MELANESIAN CUP

Year	Host Country	Winners	Score	Runners-up	Venue
1988	Solomon Islands	Fiji	3-1	Solomon Islands	Solomon Islands
1989	Fiji	Fiji	3-0	New Caledonia	Fiji
1990	Vanuatu	Vanuatu	1-0	New Caledonia	Vanuatu
1992	Vanuatu	Fiji	2-2	New Caledonia	Vanuatu
1994	Solomon Islands	Solomon Islands	1-0	Fiji	Solomon Islands
1996	Papua New Guinea	Papua New Guinea	1-1	Solomon Islands	Papua New Guinea
1998	Vanuatu	Fiji	2-1	Vanuatu	Vanuatu
2000	Fiji	Fiji	2-2	Solomon Islands	Fiji

A final was played only in the first competition in 1988. The results listed after then are between the first two teams in the league standings

OCEANIA CLUB TOURNAMENTS

OFC CHAMPIONS LEAGUE

Year	Winners	Country	Score	Country	Runners-up
1987	Adelaide City	AUS	1-1 4-1p	NZL	Mount Wellington
1999	South Melbourne	AUS	5-1	FIJ	Nadi
2001	Wollongong City Wolves	AUS	1-0	VAN	Tafea FC
2005	Sydney FC	AUS	2-0	NCL	AS Magenta
2006	Auckland City	NZL	3-1	TAH	AS Pirae
2007	Waitakere United	NZL	1-2 1-0	FIJ	Ba
2008	Waitakere United	NZL	1-3 5-0	SOL	Kossa
2009	Auckland City	NZL	7-2 2-2	SOL	Koloale
2010	Hekari United	PNG	3-0 1-2	NZL	Waitakere United
2011	Auckland City	NZL	2-1 4-0	VAN	Amicale

OCEANIA YOUTH TOURNAMENTS

OFC U–20 CHAMPIONSHIP

Year	Host Country	Winners	Score	Runners-up	Venue
1974	Tahiti	Tahiti	2-0	New Zealand	Papeete
1978	New Zealand	Australia	5-1 †	Fiji	Auckland
1980	Fiji	New Zealand	2-0	Australia	Suva
1982	Papua New Guinea	Australia	4-3	New Zealand	Port Moresby
1985	Australia	Australia	3-2 †	Israel	Sydney
1987	New Zealand	Australia	1-1 †	Israel	Auckland
1988	Fiji	Australia	1-0	New Zealand	Suva
1990	Fiji	Australia	6-0 †	New Zealand	Suva
1992	Tahiti	New Zealand	1-0 †	Tahiti	Papeete
1994	Fiji	Australia	1-0	New Zealand	Suva
1996	Tahiti	Australia	2-1	New Zealand	Papeete

OFC U–20 CHAMPIONSHIP (CONT'D)

Year	Host Country	Winners	Score	Runners-up	Venue
1998	Samoa	Australia	2-0	Fiji	Apia
2001	New Cal/Cook Is	Australia	1-2 3-1	New Zealand	Auckland & Coffs Harbour
2003	Vanuatu/Fiji	Australia	11-0 4-0	Fiji	Melbourne & Ba
2005	Solomon Islands	Australia	3-0	Solomon Islands	Honiara
2007	New Zealand	New Zealand	3-2	Fiji	Waitakere
2009	Tahiti	Tahiti	0-0	New Caledonia	Papeete
2011	New Zealand	New Zealand	3-1	Solomon Islands	Auckland

The 1978, 1985, 1987, 1990, 1992, 2007 and 2009 tournaments were played as leagues • The results shown are those between the top two teams

OFC U–17 CHAMPIONSHIP

Year	Host Country	Winners	Score	Runners-up	Venue
1983	New Zealand	Australia	2-1	New Zealand	Mount Smart, Auckland
1986	Chinese Taipei	Australia	0-1	New Zealand	CKF Stadium, Kaohsiung
1989	Australia	Australia	5-1	New Zealand	
1991	New Zealand	Australia	1-1 1-0	New Zealand	Napier
1993	New Zealand	Australia	3-0	Soloman Islands	
1995	Vanuatu	Australia	1-0	New Zealand	
1997	New Zealand	New Zealand	1-0	Australia	
1999	Fiji	Australia	5-0	Fiji	Churchill Park, Lautoka
2001	Samoa/Cook Isl	Australia	3-0 6-0	New Zealand	Canberra & Auckland
2003	Home & away	Australia	3-1 4-0	New Caledonia	Nouméa
2005	New Caledonia	Australia	1-0	Vanuatu	Nouméa
2007	Tahiti	New Zealand	2-1	Tahiti	Papeete
2009	New Zealand	New Zealand	2-0	Tahiti	Auckland
2011	New Zealand	New Zealand	2-0	Tahiti	Auckland

From 1983 to 1991 and in 2007 and 2009 the tournaments were played as leagues • The results shown are those between the top two teams

OCEANIA WOMEN'S TOURNAMENTS

OCEANIA WOMEN'S CHAMPIONSHIP

Year	Host Country	Winners	Score	Runners-up	Venue
1983	New Caledonia	New Zealand	3-2	Australia	Nouméa
1986	New Zealand	Chinese Taipei	4-1	Australia	Christchurch
1989	Australia	Chinese Taipei	1-0	New Zealand	Brisbane
1991	Australia	New Zealand	1-0 0-1 †	Australia	Sydney
1995	Papua N. Guinea	Australia	1-2 1-0 †	New Zealand	Port Moresby
1998	New Zealand	Australia	3-1	New Zealand	Mount Smart, Auckland
2003	Australia	Australia	2-0 †	New Zealand	Belconnen, Canberra
2007	Papua N. Guinea	New Zealand	7-0	Papua New Guinea	Lae
2010	New Zealand	New Zealand	11-0	Papua New Guinea	Auckland

† The 1991, 1995, 2003 and 2007 tournaments were played as leagues • The results shown are those between the top two teams

OCEANIA WOMEN'S U-20 CHAMPIONSHIP

Year	Host Country	Winners	Score	Runners-up	Venue
2002	Tonga	Australia	6-0	New Zealand	Nuku'alofa
2004	Papua New Guinea	Australia	14-1	Papua New Guinea	Lloyd Robson Oval, Port Moresby
2006	Samoa	New Zealand	6-0	Tonga	JS Blatter Complex, Apia
2010	New Zealand	New Zealand	8-0	Cook Islands	North Harbour, Auckland

OCEANIA WOMEN'S U-17 CHAMPIONSHIP

Year	Host Country	Winners	Score	Runners-up	Venue
2010	New Zealand	New Zealand	10-0	Solomon Islands	North Harbour, Auckland

OCEANIA NATIONAL TEAM TOURNAMENTS 2011

FOOTBALL TOURNAMENT OF THE 2011 PACIFIC GAMES

First Round Group Stage — Semi-finals — Final

Group A	Pl	W	D	L	F	A	Pts	SOL	VAN	TUV	GUM	ASA
New Caledonia	5	4	0	1	31	2	12	1-2	5-0	8-0	9-0	8-0
Solomon Islands	5	4	0	1	19	3	12		0-1	6-1	7-0	4-0
Vanuatu	5	4	0	1	18	7	12			5-1	4-1	8-0
Tuvalu	5	1	1	3	7	20	4				1-1	4-0
Guam	5	1	1	3	4	21	4					2-0
American Samoa	5	0	0	5	0	26	0					

Semi-finals: New Caledonia 3 — Tahiti 1

Final: New Caledonia 2 — Solomon Islands 0

Group B	Pl	W	D	L	F	A	Pts	TAH	PNG	COK	KIR
Fiji	4	4	0	0	18	1	12	3-0	2-0	4-1	9-0
Tahiti	4	2	1	1	25	5	7		1-1	7-0	17-1
Papua New Guinea	4	2	1	1	22	4	7			4-0	17-1
Cook Islands	4	1	0	3	4	15	3				3-0
Kiribati	4	0	0	4	2	46	0				

Semi-finals: Fiji 1 — Solomon Islands 2

Third place: Tahiti 2 — Fiji 1

Top scorers: **10** - Bertrand Kai, New Caledonia • **9** - Jean Kaltak, Vanuatu • **7** - Georges Gope-Fenepej, New Caledonia

GROUP A

		PI	W	D	L	F	A	Pts	SOL	VAN	TUV	GUM	ASA
New Caledonia	NCL	5	4	0	1	31	2	12	1-2	5-0	8-0	9-0	8-0
Solomon Islands	SOL	5	4	0	1	19	3	12		0-1	6-1	7-0	4-0
Vanuatu	VAN	5	4	0	1	18	7	12			5-1	4-1	8-0
Tuvalu	TUV	5	1	1	3	7	20	4				1-1	4-0
Guam	GUM	5	1	1	3	4	21	4					2-0
American Samoa	ASA	5	0	0	5	0	26	0					

Stade Rivière Salée, Nouméa
27-08-2011, Jacques TAH

Tuvalu 4
Petoa 3 [15] [90] [92+], Tiute [30]

Jelly Selau - Kolone Pokia, Alamoana Tofuola, Etimoni Timuani, Ali Takataka, Mau Penisula(c), Vaisua Liva, Lutelu Tiute, James Lepaio•, George Panapa (Uota Ale 77), Alopua Petoa. Tr: Foppe de Haan

American Samoa 0

Nicky Salapu (Chin Fu Taase 87) - Terrence Sinapati, Tala Luvu, Natia Natia•, Ismael Herrera, Moe Kuresa, Liatama Amisone(c), Frederick Uhrle, Shalom Luani (Lemusa Alatasi 82), Uasilaa Helata (Suani Uelese 79), Pesamino Victor•. Tr: Avele Lalogafuafua

---

Stade Rivière Salée, Nouméa
27-08-2011, Varman FIJ

Solomon Islands 7
Fa'arado 2 [11] [22], Totori 3 [24] [41p] [89], Nawo [72], Paia [86]

Shadrack Ramoni - Hardies Aengari, Tome Faisi, Samson Takayama•, Nelson Sale, Benjamin Totori, Joe Lui (Jeffery Bule 71), Mostyn Beui, James Naka (Ian Paia 71), Henry Fa'arodo(c), Joses Nawo, Dida Qwaina. Tr: Jacob Moli

Guam 0

Brett Maluwelmeng - Matthew Cruz•, Scott Leon Guerrero, Edward Calvo, Shawn Spindel, Ian Mariano, Dominic Gadia(c), Elias Merfalen, Dylan Naputi, David Manibusan (Christian Schweizer 46), Mark Chargualaf. Tr: Kazua Uchida

---

Stade Rivière Salée, Nouméa
27-08-2011, Achari FIJ

New Caledonia 5
Gope-Fenepej 3 [5] [31] [63], Bako [43], Lolohea [51]

Jean Yann Dounezek - Joel Wakanumune, Cesar Lolohea (Michel Hmae 83), Dominique Wacalie, Marius Bako• (Judikael Ixoee 56), Pierre Wajoka(c)•, Georges Bearune, Emile Bearune, Georges Gope-Fenepej• (Jacques Haeko 72), Dimitri Petemou, Olivier Dokunengo, Jean Patrick Wakanumune. Tr: Christophe Coursimault

Vanuatu 0

Ernest Bong• - Alphonse Bongnaim, Selwin Sese Ala (Brian Kaltak 28), Rexley Tarivuti, Georges Tabe, Kensi Tangis, Jean Robert Yelou(c), Robert Tasso, Eddison Stephen, Chikau Mansale, Ivong Wilson, Jean Kaltak. Tr: Saby Natonga

---

Stade Rivière Salée, Nouméa
30-08-2011, Varman FIJ

Vanuatu 5
Kaltak J 4 [8] [38] [45] [80], Yelou [49p]

Chikau Mansale - Alphonse Bongnaim•, Rexley Tarivuti (Georges Tabe 87), Kensi Tangis (Daniel Michel 46), Jean Robert Yelou(c)•, Seimata Chilia, Michell Kaltak, Eddison Stephen, Filiamy Nikiau, Brian Kaltack (Daniel Natou 73), Jean Kaltak. Tr: Saby Natonga

Tuvalu 1
Ale [91+]

Jelly Selau - Kolone Pokia• (Joshua Tapasei 68), Alamoana Tofuola (Uota Ale 46), Etimoni Timuani (Okilani Tinilau 37), Ali Takataka, Mau Penisula(c), Vaisua Liva, Lutelu Tiute, James Lepaio, George Panapa, Alopua Petoa. Tr: Foppe de Haan

---

Stade Rivière Salée, Nouméa
30-08-2011, Jacques TAH

American Samoa 0

Nicky Salapu - Terrence Sinapati (Edgar Apulu 62), Tala Luvu, Natia Natia, D'Angelo Herrera, Junior Amisone(c), Charlie Uhrle•, Shalom Luani, Uasi Heleta, Pesamino Victor, Lemusa Alatasi (Jonny Saelua 62). Tr: Avele Lalogafuafua

Solomon Islands 4
Totori [8], Bule [14], Lui 2 [28] [34]

Shadrack Ramoni - Hardies Aengari (Timothy Joe 72), Nelson Sale, Michael Fifi, George Suri, Benjamin Totori (Ian Paia 62), Joe Lui, Joe Manu, Jeffery Bule•, Seni Ngava, Henry Fa'arodo(c) (Mostyn Beui 69). Tr: Jacob Moli

---

Stade Rivière Salée, Nouméa
30-08-2011, Zitouni TAH

Guam 0

Brett Maluwelmeng - Matthew Cruz, Scott Leon Guerrero, Edward Calvo, Shawn Spindel, Ian Mariano, Elias Merfalen, Dyan Naputi, David Manibusan (Dominic Gadia 75), Andre Gadia (Christian Schweizer 23), Mark Chargualaf. Tr: Kazua Uchida

New Caledonia 9
Kai 5 [12] [26] [40] [47] [91+], Boawe [70], Kaneu [73], Wakanumune [83], Hmae [85]

Jean Yann Dounezek - Joel Wakanumune, Cesar Lolohea, Patrick Qaeze, Marius Bako (Arsene Boawe 64), Iamel Kabeu (Michel Hmae 75), Pierre Wajoka(c) (Joris Gorendiawe 53), Betrand Kai, Andre Sinedo, Judikael Ixoee, Olivier Dokunengo. Tr: Christophe Coursimault

Stade Rivière Salée, Nouméa
1-09-2011, George VAN

American Samoa 0

Nicky **Salapu** - Terrence **Sinapati**, Edgar **Apulu** (Jonny **Saelua** 82), Natia **Natia**, D'Angelo **Herrera•**, Casper **Kuresa** (Leamusa **Alatasi** 45), Junior **Amisone**(c), Charlie **Uhrle**, Shalom **Luani**, Uasi **Heleta** (Daru **Taumua** 69), Pesamino **Victor**. Tr: Avele **Lalogafuafua**

Guam 2
Napitu 49, **Merfalen** 70

Brett **Maluwelmeng** (Julias **Campus** 87) - Matthew **Cruz**, Scott **Leon Guerrero**, Edward **Calvo**♦58, Shawn **Spindel**, Ian **Mariano** (Jonathan **Odell** 85), Dominic **Gadia**(c), Elias **Merfalen**, Jason **Cunliffe**, Dylan **Naputi**, Mark **Chargualaf**. Tr: Kazua **Uchida**

Stade Rivière Salée, Nouméa
1-09-2011, Kerr NZL

Tuvalu 0

Katepu **Sieni** - Alamoana **Tofuola**, Etimoni **Timuani**, Ali **Takataka** (Raj **Sogivalu** 63), Mau **Penisula**(c), Vaisua **Liva** (Joshua **Tapesei** 87), Okilani **Tinilau**, Lutelu **Tiute**, George **Panapa**, Alopua **Petoa**, Togavai **Stanley**. Tr: Foppe **de Haan**

New Caledonia 8
Gorendiawe 15, **Kabeu** 2 26 35, **Gope Fenepej** 38, **Haeko** 50, **Lolohea** 61, **Hmae** 2 67 85
Rocky **Nyikeine** - Joris **Gorendiawe**, Cesar **Lolohea•**, Dominique **Wacalie**♦90, Iamel **Kabeu** (Michel **Hmae** 61), Pierre **Wajoka**(c)•, Georges **Bearune**, Emile **Bearune**, Georges **Gope-Fenepej** (Jacques **Haeko** 46), Arsene **Boawe** (Marius **Bako•** 89), Jean Patrick **Wakanumune**. Tr: Christophe **Coursimault**

Stade Rivière Salée, Nouméa
1-09-2011, Zitouni TAH

Vanuatu 1
Kaltak.J 92+

Ernest **Bong** - Rexley **Tarivuti**, Georges **Tabe**, Kensi **Tangis**, Jean Robert **Yelou**(c), Eddison **Stephen** (Daniel **Natou** 44), Filiamy **Nikiau•**, Ivong **Wilson** (Michel **Kaltak** 78), Ricky **Tari**, Brian **Kaltack**, Jean **Kaltak**. Tr: Saby **Natonga**

Solomon Islands 0

Shadrack **Ramoni** - Hardies **Aengari**, Tome **Faisi**, Samson **Takayama**, Nelson **Sale**, Benjamin **Totori**, Joe **Lui•** (Ian **Paia** 77), Mostyn **Beui•**, James **Naka**, Henry **Fa'arodo**(c), Joses **Nawo**. Tr: Jacob **Moli**

Stade Rivière Salée, Nouméa
3-09-2011, Kerr NZL

Guam 1
Cunliffe 14

Brett **Maluwelmeng** - Matthew **Cruz**, Scott **Leon Guerrero**, Shawn **Spindel**, Ian **Mariano**, Dominic **Gadia**(c) (Joseph **Laanan** 81), Elias **Merfalen**, Jason **Cunliffe**, Christain **Schweizer•** (David **Manibusan** 84), Dylan **Naputi**, Mark **Chargualaf**. Tr: Kazua **Uchida**

Vanuatu 4
Tangis 50, **Tasso** 53, **Kaltak.J** 75, **Tari** 82

Chikau **Mansale** - Alphones **Bongnaim**, Georges **Tabe** (Rexley **Tarivuti** 64), Kensi **Tangis**, Jean Robert **Yelou**(c), Seimata **Chilia•**, Robert **Tasso•** (Michel **Kaltak** 68), Filiamy **Nikiau**, Ricky **Tari**, Brian **Kaltak**, Jean **Kaltak**. Tr: Saby **Natonga**

Stade Rivière Salée, Nouméa
3-09-2011, Jacques TAH

Solomon Islands 6
Totori 2 15 41p, **Lui** 23, **Naka** 2 37 46, **Faisi** 91+

Shadrack **Ramoni** - Timothy **Joe**, Nelson **Sale** (Tome **Faisi** 83), George **Suri**, Benjamin **Totori** (Ian **Paia** 76), Joe **Lui** (Abraham **Iniga** 67), Mostyn **Beui**, Seni **Ngava**, James **Naka**, Henry **Fa'arodo**(c)•, Joses **Nawo**. Tr: Jacob **Moli**

Tuvalu 1
Lepaio 78

Katepu **Sieni** - Ali **Takataka**, Okilani **Tinilau**, James **Lepaio**, Togavai **Stanley**, Raj **Sogivalu**, Jelly **Selau** (Alamoana **Tofuola** 46), Meauma **Petaia**, Akelei **Limaalofa** (Vaisua **Liva** 66), Lopati **Okelani**, Joshua **Tapasei**(c)• (Etimoni **Timuani** 83). Tr: Foppe **de Haan**

Stade Rivière Salée, Nouméa
3-09-2011, Varman FIJ

New Caledonia 8
Kai 4 10 38 44 66, **Haeko** 50, **Qaeze** 55, **Vendegou** 72, **Hmae** 89
Dimitri **Petemou** (Rocky **Nyikeine** 25) - Joel **Wakanumune**, Joris **Gorendiawe**, Patrick **Qaeze** (Arsene **Boawe** 70), Iamel **Kabeu**, Bertrand **Kai**, Michel **Hmae**, Andre **Sinedo**(c), Judikael **Ixoee**, Jacques **Haeko** (Kenji **Vendegou** 56), Olivier **Dokunengo**. Tr: Christophe **Coursimault**

American Samoa 0

Nicky **Salapu** - Terrence **Sinapati**, Tala **Luvu** (Jonny **Saelua** 90), Natia **Natia**, D'Angelo **Herrera**, Casper **Kuresa** (Leamusa **Alatasi** 42), Junior **Amisone**(c), Charlie **Uhrle**, Shalom **Luani**, Uasi **Heleta** (Daru **Tauma** 59), Pesamino **Victor**. Tr: Avele **Lalogafuafua**

Stade Rivière Salée, Nouméa
5-09-2011, Zitouni TAH

Guam 1
Cunliffe 18p

Brett **Maluwelmeng** - Matthew **Cruz•**, Edward **Calvo**, Shawn **Spindel**, Ian **Mariano**, Dominic **Gadia**(c), Elias **Merfalen**, Jason **Cunliffe**, Christian **Schweizer•** (David **Manibusan** 90), Dylan **Naputi**, Mark **Chargualaf**. Tr: Kazua **Uchida**

Tuvalu 1
Stanley 24

Jelly **Selau**♦17 - Etimoni **Timuani**, Mau **Penisula**(c), Vaisua **Liva•**, Lutelu **Tiute**, James **Lepaio**, George **Panapa** (Ali **Takataka** 83), Alopua **Petoa**, Togavai **Stanley**, Lopati **Okelani** (Katepu **Sieni** 17), Joshua **Tapasei**. Tr: Foppe **de Haan**

Stade Rivière Salée, Nouméa
5-09-2011, Achari FIJ

American Samoa 0

Nicky **Salapu** - Terrence **Sinapati** (Jonny **Saelua** 72), Tala **Luvu** (Daru **Taumua** 60), Natia **Natia**, D'Angelo **Herrera**, Junior **Amisone**(c), Charlie **Uhrle•**, Shalom **Luani**, Pesamino **Victor**, Lemusa **Alatasi** (Edgar **Apulu** 82), Chin Fu **Taase**. Tr: Avele **Lalogafuafua**

Vanuatu 8
Michel 2 8 22, **Garae** 43, **Kaltak.J** 3 62 70 78, **Kaltak.M** 64, **Aala** 73
Chikau **Mansale** - Alphonse **Bongnaim**, Selwin **Sese Ala**, Kensi **Tangis** (Jean **Kaltak** 46), Seimata **Chilia**(c), Richard **Garae** (Ricky **Tari** 89), Eddison **Stephen**, Andrew **Chichirua** (Michel **Kaltak•** 35), Daniel **Michel**, Lucien **Hinge**, Brian **Kaltack•**. Tr: Saby **Natonga**

Stade Rivière Salée, Nouméa
5-09-2011, Kerr NZL

Solomon Islands 2
Nawo 66, **Naka** 79

Shadrack **Ramoni** - Tome **Faisi**, Samson **Takayama**, Nelson **Sale**, Benjamin **Totori**, Mostyn **Beui** (Joe **Manu** 92+), Seni **Ngava**, James **Naka**, Abraham **Iniga**, Henry **Fa'arodo**(c), Joses **Nawo** (Joe **Lui** 74). Tr: Jacob **Moli**

New Caledonia 1
Kai 74

Rocky **Nyikeine** - Joel **Wakanumune**, Cesar **Lolohea**, Dominique **Wacalie**, Patrick **Qaeze•**, Iamel **Kabeu**, Pierre **Wajoka**(c) (Arsene **Boawe** 69), Emile **Bearune**, Georges **Gope-Fenepej** (Bertrand **Kai** 54), Olivier **Dokunengo•**, Jean Patrick **Wakanumune**. Tr: Christophe **Coursimault**

GROUP B

		Pl	W	D	L	F	A	Pts	TAH	PNG	COK	KIR
Fiji	FIJ	4	4	0	0	18	1	12	3-0	2-0	4-1	9-0
Tahiti	TAH	4	2	1	1	25	5	7		1-1	7-0	17-1
Papua New Guinea	PNG	4	2	1	1	22	4	7			4-0	17-1
Cook Islands	COK	4	1	0	3	4	15	3				3-0
Kiribati	KIR	4	0	0	4	2	46	0				

Stade Boewa, Boulari
27-08-2011, Billon NCL

Papua New Guinea   4

Hans 2 [18 50], Muta.D [55], Lepani [85]

Lesly Kalai - Valentine Nelson, Cyril Muta, Gari Moka (Nathaniel Lepani 65), Reginald Davani (Michael Foster 53), David Muta(c), Andrew Lepani, Neil Hans (Tonga Esira 74), Jeremy Yasasa, Mauri Wasi, Eric Komeng. Tr: Frank Farina

Cook Islands   0

Tony Jamieson(c) - John Pareanga•, Nathan Tisam, Roger Manuel (John Quuano 68), Joseph Ngauora, Grover Harmon (Nikorima Te Miha 58), Campbell Best (Nicholas Funnell 77), Taylor Saghabi, Mii Joseph, Tahiri Elikana, Geongsa Tisam. Tr: Maurice Tillotson

Stade Boewa, Boulari•
27-08-2011, Kerr NZL

Fiji   3

Waqa [28], OG [44], Rokotakala [86]

Simione Tamanisau(c) - Avinesh Swamy, Seveci Rokotakala, Jone Vesikula• (Esava Naqaleca 61), Alvin Singh, Malakai Tiwa•, Roy Krishna, Alvin Avinesh, Maciu Dunadamu (Pene Erenio 85), Taniela Waqa• (Lorima Dau 90), Malakai Kainihewe. Tr: Gurjit Singh

Tahiti   0

Xavier Samin(c) - Stephane Faatiarau, Tauraa Marmouyet•, Teheivarii Ludivon•, Donavan Bourebare•, Jonathan Tehau, Teaonui Tehau (Billy Mataitai 43), Lorenzo Tehau, Hiroana Poroiea (Efrain Araneda 69), Steevy Chong Hue (Taufa Neuffer 68), Temarii Tinorua. Tr: Eddy Etaeta

Stade Boewa, Boulari
30-08-2011, Assiene-Ambassa NCL

Fiji   9

Krishna 3 [17p 56 86], Suwamy [47], Avinesh [52], Dunadamu 2 [63 72], OG [91+], Manuca [92+]

Benaminio Mateinaqara - Avinesh Swamy, Seveci Rokotakala (Pene Erenio 40), Jone Vesikula•, Alvin Singh, Malakai Tiwa (Tuimasi Manuca 68), Roy Krishna(c), Alvin Avinesh, Maciu Dunadamu (Esava Naqaleca 73), Taniela Waqa, Malakai Kainihewe. Tr: Gurjit Singh

Kiribati   0

Tiaon Miika - Kaake Kamta, Kaben Ioteba, Enri Tenukai, Atanuea Eritara (Antin Nanotaake 63), Jeff Jong(c), Joseph Yan (Nabararu Batiri• 68) (Barurunteiti Kaiorake 78), Beniamina Kaintikuaba, Erene Bwakineti•, Martin Miriata, Biitamatang Keakea. Tr: Pine Iosefa

Stade Boewa, Boulari
30-08-2011, Oiaka SOL

Tahiti   7

Neuffer [48], Atani [59], OG [69], Chong Hue 2 [73 91+], Poroiae 2 [82p 89]

Xavier Samin(c) - Stephane Faatiarau, Tauraa Marmouyet, Teheivarii Ludivon, Donavan Bourebare (Hiroana Poroiea 72), Jonathan Tehau, Lorenzo Tehau (Garry Rochette 76), Stanley Atany, Efrain Araneda, Temarii Tinorua (Steevy Chong Hue 58), Sebastien Labayen. Tr: Eddy Etaeta

Cook Islands   0

Tony Jamieson - John Pareanga (Nathan Tisam 53) (Nicholas Funnel 60), Allan Boere, Joseph Ngauora, Grover Harmon, Campbell Best, Nikorima Te Miha (Paul Turepu 11), Taylor Saghabi, Mii Joseph, Tahiri Elikana•, Geongsa Tisam. Tr: Maurice Tillotson

Stade Boewa, Boulari
1-09-2011, Billon NCL

Cook Islands   3

Saghabi 2 [27 89], Pareanga [92+]

Tony Jamieson (??) - John Pareanga, Allan Boere, Joseph Ngauora, Grover Harmon, Campbell Best• (John Quijano 92+), Taylor Saghabi, Nicholas Funnell (Paul Turepu 71), Mii Joseph, Tahiri Elikana, Geongsa Tisam (Roger Manuel 64). Tr: Maurice Tillotson

Kiribati   0

Tarariki Tarotu - Kaben Ioteba, Enri Tenukai, Nabararu Batiri, Atanuea Eritara (Karotu Bakaane• 40), Antin Nanotaake, Jeff Jong(c), Joseph Yan•, Erene Bwakineti• (Antino Baraniko 58), Martin Miriata, Biitamatang Keakea. Tr: Pine Iosefa

Stade Boewa, Boulari
1-09-2011, Achari FIJ

Tahiti   1

Atani [23]

Xavier Samin(c) - Stephane Faatiarau, Tauraa Marmouyet•, Teheivarii Ludivon, Donavan Bourebare, Jonathan Tehau, Hiroana Poroiae•, Stanley Atani, Efrain Araneda (Temarii Tinorua 87), Sebastian Labayen (Billy Mataitai 78). Tr: Eddy Etaeta

Papua New Guinea   1

Muta.C [15]

Lesly Kalai - Valentine Nelson, Cyril Muta♦66, Gari Moka, Reginald Davani (Nathaniel Lepani 11) (Kelly Jampu 71), David Muta(c), Andrew Lepani, Neil Hans (Michael Foster 80), Jeremy Yasasa•, Mauri Wasi, Eric Komeng•. Tr: Frank Farina

Stade Boewa, Boulari
3-09-2011, Oiaka SOL

Kiribati   1

Bakaane [71]

Tiaon Miika (Tarariki Tarotu 46) - Kaake Kamta• (Atanuea Eritara 46), Kaben Ioteba, Enri Tenukai, Nabararu Batiri, Antin Nanotaake, Jeff Jong(c), Joseph Yan (Tongarua Akori 63), Karotu Bakaane, Martin Miriata•, Bitamatang Keakea. Tr: Pine Iosefa

Papua New Guinea   17

Kini 3 [13 79 85], Lepani 4 [15 16 54 68], Foster [16], Hans 2 [21 45p], Moka 3 [24 28 41], Yasasa 2 [73 74], Bondaluke [76], Wasi [92+]

David Aua - Valentine Nelson, Kelly Jampu, Samuel Kini, Gari Moka (Felix Bondaluke 46), Michael Foster, Nathaniel Lepani, David Muta(c) (Mauri Wasi 46), Andrew Lepani, Neil Hans (Koriak Upaiga 63), Jeremy Yasasa. Tr: Frank Farina

Stade Boewa, Boulari
3-09-2011, Assiene-Ambassa NCL

Cook Islands   1

Ngauora [41]

Tony Jamieson - John Pareanga, Roger Manuel (Geongsa Tisam 75), John Quijano, Allan Boere, Joseph Ngauora, Grover Harmon, Taylor Saghabi, Paul Turepu (Campbell Best 51), Mii Joseph, Tahiri Elikana•. Tr: Maurice Tillotson

Fiji   4

Krishna [24], Kainihewe [35], Dunadamu [57p], Suwamy [69]

Simione Tamanisau(c) - Avinesh Swamy•, Seveci Rokotakala, Pene Erenio, Alvin Singh, Roy Krishna♦85, Alvin Avinesh, Maciu Dunadamu (Archie Watkins 70), Taniela Waqa (Ilaitia Tuilau 78), Malakai Kainihewe, Esava Naqaleca. Tr: Gurjit Singh

Stade Boewa, Boulari
5-09-2011, Billon NCL

Papua New Guinea   0

Lesly Kalai - Valentine Nelson, Kelly Jampu• (Felix Bondaluke 72), Gari Moka, Nathaniel Lepani (Michael Foster 46), David Muta(c), Andrew Lepani, Neil Hans, Jeremy Yasasa, Mauri Wasi (Samuel Kini 46), Eric Komeng. Tr: Frank Farina

Fiji   2

Suwamy [37], Kainihewe [45]

Simione Tamanisau(c) - Avinesh Swamy, Seveci Rokotakala•, Pene Erenio, Pita Bolaitoga, Alvin Singh, Alvin Avinesh, Maciu Dunadamu (Yuimasi Manuca 80), Taniela Waqa• (Jone Vesikula 65), Malakai Kainihewe, Esava Naqaleca (Ilaitia Tuilau• 56). Tr: Gurjit Singh

Stade Boewa, Boulari
5-09-2011, Oiaka SOL

Kiribati   1

Bakineti [32]

Tarariki Tarotu - Tiaon Miika (Karotu Bakaane 69), Kaake Kamta•, Kaben Ioteba, Enri Tenukai (Beniamina Kaintikuaba 62), Nabararu Batiri•, Atanuea Eritara, Antin Nanotaake, Erene Bwakineti, Martin Miriata, Biitamatang Keakea(c) (Tongarua Akori 77). Tr: Pine Iosefa

Tahiti   17

Poroiae 2 [16 44p], Chong Hue 4 [19 28 33 46], Araneda [21], Mataitai [53], Ludivion [57], Tehau.T 6 [73 79 85 88 90 91+], Faatiarau [83p], Atani [86]

Mikael Roche - Stephane Faatiarau, Vetea Tepa, Tauraa Marmouyet, Teheivarii Ludivon, Taufa Neuffer(c) (Billy Mataitai 46), Hiroana Poroiae (Jonathan Tehau 72), Steevy Chong Hue, Stanley Atani, Efrain Araneda, Temarii Tinorua (Teaonui Tehau 58). Tr: Eddy Etaeta

SEMI-FINALS AND 3RD PLACE PLAY-OFF

S/F. Stade Yoshida, Koné
7-09-2011, Varman Fij

New Caledonia **3**
Gope-Fenepej 2 [89] [108], Hmae [115]

Jean Yann **Dounezek** - Joel **Wakanumune**• (Michel **Hmae** 82), Cesar **Lolohea**, Dominique **Wacalie**, Marius **Bako**, Iamel **Kabeu**(c)••♦55, Bertrand **Kai** (Arsene **Boawe** 105), Judikael **Ixoee**•, Georges **Bearune** (Georges **Gope-Fenepej**• 72), Olivier **Dokunengo**•, Jean Patrick **Wakanumune**. Tr: Christophe **Coursimault**

Tahiti **1**
Poroiae [52]

Xavier **Samin**(c) - Stephane **Faatiarau**, Vetea **Tepa** (Tauraa **Marmouyet** 65), Teheivarii **Ludivon**, Donavan **Bourebare**, Jonathan **Tehau**•, Taufa **Neuffer** (Teaonui **Tehau** 57), Hiroana **Poroiae**, Stanley **Atani**, Sebastian **Labayen**•, Billy **Mataitai** (Efrain **Araneda** 75). Tr: Eddy **Etaeta**

S/F. Stade Hnassé, Lifou
7-09-2011, Jacques TAH

Fiji **1**
Dunadamu [69]

Simione **Tamanisau**(c) - Avinesh **Swamy**, Seveci **Rokotakala**•, Pene **Erenio**•, Pita **Bolaitoga** (Archie **Watkins** 54), Alvin **Singh** (Jone **Vesikula** 51) (Lorima **Dau**• 106), Malakai **Tiwa**, Alvin **Avinesh**, Maciu **Dunadamu**•, Ilaitia **Tuilau**, Malakai **Kainihewe**. Tr: Gurjit **Singh**

Solomon Islands **2**
Nawo [77], Fa'arodo [93p]

Shadrack **Ramoni** - Tome **Faisi**, Samson **Takayama** (Timothy **Joe**• 14), Nelson **Sale**, Benjamin **Totori**•, Mostyn **Beui**, Seni **Ngava**•, James **Naka**, Abraham **Iniga** (Joe **Lui** 71), Henry **Fa'arodo**(c), Joses **Nawo**. Tr: Jacob **Moli**

3rd/P. Stade Boewa, Boulari
9-09-2011, Billon NCL

Tahiti **2**
Atani [5], Tehau.L [65]

Xavier **Samin**(c) - Stephane **Faatiarau**, Vetea **Tepa**•, Teheivarii **Ludivon**, Donavan **Bourebare**, Garry **Rochette**•, Jonathan **Tehau** (Hiroana **Poroiae** 74), Lorenzo **Tehau**, Steevy **Chong Hue**, Stanley **Atani**, Sebastian **Labayen**. Tr: Eddy **Etaeta**

Fiji **1**
Avinesh [58]

Benamino **Mateinaqara** - Avinesh **Swamy**, Seveci **Rokotakala**♦43, Pene **Erenio**, Malakai **Tiwa**•, Roy **Krishna**(c)•, Alvin **Avinesh**•, Maciu **Dunadamu**, Taniela **Waqa**•, Ilaitia **Tuilau** (Esava **Naqaleca** 73), Malakai **Kainihewe**• (Lorima **Dau** 62). Tr: Gurjit **Singh**

FINAL

Stade Rivière Salée, Nouméa
9-09-2011, 20:00, Kerr NZL

New Caledonia **2**
Gope-Fenepej [9], Bako [11]

Jean Yann **Dounezek** - Joel **Wakanumune**, Cesar **Lolohea**, Dominique **Wacalie**, Marius **Bako**•, Pierre **Wajoka**(c) (Kenji **Vendegou** 92+), Judikael **Ixoee**, Emile **Bearune**•, Georges **Gope-Fenepej** (Bertrand **Kai** 64), Olivier **Dokunengo**•, Jean Patrick **Wakanumune**. Tr: Christophe **Coursimault**

Solomon Islands **0**

Shadrack **Ramoni** - Tome **Faisi**•, Samson **Takayama** (Timothy **Joe**• 35), Nelson **Sale**, Benjamin **Totori**•, Mostyn **Beui**, Seni **Ngava** (Hardies **Afengari** 52), James **Naka**•, Abraham **Iniga** (Joe **Lui** 71), Henry **Fa'arodo**, Joses **Nawo**. Tr: Jacob **Moli**

YOUTH TOURNAMENTS IN OCEANIA 2011

OFC U-20 CHAMPIONSHIP NEW ZEALAND 2011

First Round Group Stage

Group A	Pl	W	D	L	F	A	Pts	FIJ	PNG	ASA
Vanuatu	3	3	0	0	14	2	**9**	2-0	5-2	7-0
Fiji	3	1	1	1	5	3	**4**		0-0	5-1
Papua New Guinea	3	1	1	1	7	6	**4**			5-1
American Samoa	3	0	0	3	2	17	**0**			

Semi-finals

New Zealand	6
Fiji	0

Final

New Zealand	3
Solomon Islands	1

Group B	Pl	W	D	L	F	A	Pts	SOL	NCL
New Zealand	2	2	0	0	13	0	**6**	3-0	10-0
Solomon Islands	2	1	0	1	3	4	**3**		3-1
New Caledonia	2	0	0	2	1	13	**0**		

Vanuatu	3 2p
Solomon Islands	3 3p

Third Place Play-off

Vanuatu	2
Fiji	0

Held in New Zealand from 21-04-2011 to 29-04-2011 • New Zealand qualified for the FIFA U-20 World Cup in Colombia

OFC U-17 CHAMPIONSHIP NEW ZEALAND 2011

First Round Group Stage

Group A	Pl	W	D	L	F	A	Pts	VAN	PNG	FIJ	ASA
New Zealand	4	4	0	0	13	1	12	5-1	3-0	1-0	4-0
Vanuatu	4	3	0	1	13	5	9		2-0	3-0	7-0
Papua New Guinea	4	2	0	2	4	7	6			2-1	2-1
Fiji	4	1	0	3	10	6	3				9-0
American Samoa	4	0	0	4	1	22	0				

Group B	Pl	W	D	L	F	A	Pts	SOL	NCL	COK	TGA
Tahiti	4	4	0	0	14	2	12	2-1	3-1	1-0	8-0
Solomon Islands	4	3	0	1	22	4	9		2-1	4-1	15-0
New Caledonia	4	2	0	2	27	6	6			8-1	17-0
Cook Islands	4	1	0	3	8	15	3				6-2
Tonga	4	0	0	4	2	46	0				

Held in New Zealand from 8-01-2011 to 19-01-2011 • New Zealand qualified for the FIFA U-17 World Cup in Mexico

Final

New Zealand	2
Tahiti	0

Third Place Play-off

Solomon Islands	2
Vanuatu	0

CLUB TOURNAMENTS IN OCEANIA 2010–11

OFC CHAMPIONS LEAGUE 2010-11

First Round Groups

Group A		Pl	W	D	L	F	A	Pts	VAN	SOL	FIJ	PNG
Amicale	VAN	6	3	1	2	12	7	10		2-0	5-1	3-3
Koloale	SOL	6	3	0	3	10	10	9	1-0		1-2	2-1
Lautoka	FIJ	6	2	2	2	6	13	8	1-0	1-6		0-0
Hekari United	PNG	6	1	3	2	10	8	6	1-2	4-0	1-1	

Group B		Pl	W	D	L	F	A	Pts	NZL	NZL	NCL	TAH
Auckland City	NZL	6	4	2	0	12	2	14		1-0	3-0	5-0
Waitakere United	NZL	6	2	2	2	8	8	8	1-1		2-1	3-1
AS Magenta	NCL	6	2	1	3	6	7	7	0-1	1-1		1-0
AS Tefana	TAH	6	1	1	4	5	14	4	1-1	3-1	0-3	

Top scorers: **8** - Fenedy Masauvakalo VAN, Amicale • **3** - Daniel Koprivcic CRO, Auckland City; Manuel Exposito ESP, Auckland City; Henry Fa'arodo SOL, Hekari United; Benjamin Totori SOL, Koloale & Alan Pearce NZL, Waitakere United

Final

Auckland City	2	4
Amicale	1	0

GROUP A		Pl	W	D	L	F	A	Pts	VAN	SOL	FIJ	PNG
Amicale	VAN	6	3	1	2	12	7	10		2-0	5-1	3-3
Koloale	SOL	6	3	0	3	10	10	9	1-0		1-2	2-1
Lautoka	FIJ	6	2	2	2	6	13	8	1-0	1-6		0-0
Hekari United	PNG	6	1	3	2	10	8	6	1-2	4-0	1-1	

Lawson Tama, Honiara
23-10-2010, 15:00, 16 000, Kerr NZL

Koloale	1
	Paia 35

Shadrock Ramoni - Welshman Houkarawara, Samson Takayama, Jeffrey Bule, Francis Lafai, Mostyn Beui, Steven Anisi, Benjamin Totori, Ezra Sale (Lency Saeni 59), Ian Paia (Steven Saru 76), Joses Nawo. Tr: Peter Eke

Lautoka	2
	Mayora 2 16 26

James Chronopoulos - Semesa Doidoi, Leone Vurukania, Marika Madigi• (Shameel Rao 57), Avinesh Waran Suwamy•, Nahuel Arrarte•, Valerio Nawatu, Matthew Mayora, Jone Vono, Muni Naidu, Judd Molea (Niumaia Tagi 43). Tr: Imdad Ali

PMRL, Port Moresby
23-10-2010, 15:00, 5500, Waldron NZL

Hekari United	1
	Fa'arodo 57

Gure Gabina - Gideon Omokirio, Pita Bolatoga, Koriak Upaiga, Alvin Singh•, Benjamin Mela (Niel Hans 46), David Muta, Eric Komeng (Abraham Iniga 36), Henry Fa'arodo, Tuimasi Manuca (Joachim Waroi 75), Kema Jack. Tr: Tommy Mana

Amicale	2
	Masauvakalo 23, Wetney 49

Ernest Bong - Young Paul, Selwyn Sese Ala, Richard Anisua (Alphonse Bongnaim 74), Nelson Sale•, Jean Robert Yelou•, Gibson Daudau••◆83, Alick Maemae•, Stanley Waita (Moffat Deramoa 65), Fenedy Masauvakalo, Jack Wetney (Richard Garae 67). Tr: William Malas

Govind Park, Ba
13-11-2010, 15:00, 1000, Saohu SOL

Lautoka	1
	Nawatu 19

James Chronopoulos - Samuela Kautoga, Malakai Waqa•, Ilatia Tuilau•, Avinesh Waran Suwamy, Nahuel Arrarte, Sanni Issa, Valerio Nawatu (Kamal Hassan 88), Shameel Rao, Matthew Mayora (Jone Vono 52), Muni Naidu (Leone Vurukania 77). Tr: Imdad Ali

Amicale	0

Ernest Bong - Young Paul, Selwyn Sese Ala, Richard Anisua••◆94+, Nelson Sale, Jean Robert Yelou•, Alick Maemae, Stanley Waita (Derek Malas 65), Batram Suri (Richard Garae 46), Fenedy Masauvakalo, Jack Wetney. Tr: William Malas

PMRL, Port Moresby
13-11-2010, 15:00, 6000, O'Leary NZL

Hekari United — **4**
Fa'arodo 2 [32] [64], Jack [43], Iniga [76]

Simione **Tamanisau** - Pita **Bolatoga**•, Koriak **Upaiga**•, Alvin **Singh**, David **Taro** (Andrew **Lepani** 30), Abraham **Iniga**, David **Muta**, Eric **Komeng** (Joachim **Waroi** 60), Malakai **Tiwa**• (Rex **Honu** 81), Henry **Fa'arodo**, Kema **Jack**. Tr: Tommy **Mana**

Koloale — **0**

Felix **Ray** Jr (Shadrock **Ramoni** 46) - Welshman **Houkarawara**•, Samson **Takayama**, George **Suri** (Freddie **Kini** 70), Jeffrey **Bule**, Steven **Saru**, Lency **Saeni**, Mostyn **Beui**, Benjamin **Totori**, Ian **Paia**, Joses **Nawo** (Steven **Anisi** 72). Tr: Peter **Eke**

Korman, Port Vila
4-12-2010, 15:00, 4000, Kerr NZL

Amicale — **2**
Masauvakalo 2 [15] [40]

Ernest **Bong** (Chikau **Mansale** 89) - Young **Paul**•, Selwyn Sese **Ala**, Nelson **Sale**, Alphonse **Bongnaim**, Derek **Malas**•, Alick **Maemae**, Richard **Garae** (Gibson **Daudau** 58), Stanley **Waita** (Moffat **Deramoa** 81), Fenedy **Masauvakalo**, Jack **Wetney**. Tr: William **Malas**

Koloale — **0**

Shadrock **Ramoni** - Welshman **Houkarawara** (Cecil **Buru** 43), Freddie **Kini** (Steven **Anisi** 36), Samson **Takayama**, George **Suri**, Francis **Lafai**, Lency **Saeni** (Jeffrey **Bule** 74), Mostyn **Beui**, Benjamin **Totori**, Ian **Paia**, Joses **Nawo**. Tr: Peter **Eke**

Churchill Park, Lautoka
15-01-2011, 15:00, 4000, O'Leary NZL

Lautoka — **0**

James **Chronopoulos** - Krishna **Samy**, Malakai **Waqa**, Leone **Vurukania**, Avinesh Waran **Suwamy**, Sanni **Issa**, Nahuel **Arrarte**, Kamal **Hassan** (Muni **Naidu** 81), Shameel **Rao**, Judd **Molea** (Samuela **Drudru** 63), Daniel **Severino**. Tr: Imdad **Ali**

Hekari United — **0**

Simione **Tamanisau** - Gideon **Omokirio** (David **Taro**• 69), Pita **Bolatoga**, Koriak **Upaiga**, Alvin **Singh**•, Eric **Komeng**, Malakai **Tiwa** (Tuimasi **Manuca** 83), Henry **Fa'arodo**, Osea **Vakatalesau**, Niel **Hans** (Abraham **Iniga** 46), Kema **Jack**. Tr: Tommy **Mana**

Churchill Park, Lautoka
5-02-2011, 15:00, Hester NZL

Lautoka — **1**
Nawatu [10]

Jone **Sorolo**♦[15] - Krishna **Samy**•, Semesa **Nakosia**, Malakai **Waqa**, Leone **Vurukania**, Peni **Finau** (Kamal **Hassan** 32), Avinesh Waran **Suwamy**, Sanni **Issa** (Samuela **Drudru** 71), Valerio **Nawatu**, Shameel **Rao**, Jone **Vono** (Parmesh **Prasad** 18). Tr: Imdad **Ali**

Koloale — **6**
Bule [19p], Suri [25], Totori 3 [28] [62] [77p], Sale [52]

Shadrock **Ramoni** - Cecil **Buru**, Samson **Takayama**, Jeffrey **Bule**, George **Suri** (Leonard Sale **Olea** 71), Francis **Lafai**, Mostyn **Beui**•, Steven **Anisi** (Abraham **Eke** Jr 65), Benjamin **Totori**, Ian **Paia** (Ezra **Sale** 44), Joses **Nawo**. Tr: Peter **Eke**

Korman, Port Vila
5-02-2011, 15:00, Jacques TAH

Amicale — **3**
Maemae [39p], Malas [51], Masauvakalo [74]

Ernest **Bong** - Young **Paul**, Selwyn Sese **Ala**, Nelson **Sale**, Alphonse **Bongnaim**, Jean Robert **Yelou** (Richard **Anisua** 83), Derek **Malas** (Seimata **Chilia** 62), Gibson **Daudau**, Alick **Maemae**, Fenedy **Masauvakalo**, Jack **Wetney** (Lenson **Bisili** 66). Tr: William **Malas**

Hekari United — **3**
Vaketalesau 2 [58] [87], Tiwa [94+]

Gure **Gabina** - Gideon **Omokirio**, Koriak **Upaiga**, David **Taro**, Abraham **Iniga**, David **Muta**, Malakai **Tiwa**, Henry **Fa'arodo** (Samuel **Kini** 90), Tuimasi **Manuca**•, Niel **Hans** (Osea **Vakatalesau**• 50), Kema **Jack**•. Tr: Tommy **Mana**

Lawson Tama, Honiara
26-02-2011, 15:00, Kerr NZL

Koloale — **2**
Beui 2 [20] [66]

Shadrock **Ramoni** - Samson **Takayama**, Jeffrey **Bule**, George **Suri**•[77], Francis **Lafai**•, Augustine **Samani**, Mostyn **Beui**, Steven **Anisi**•, Benjamin **Totori**•, Ian **Paia** (Ezra **Sale** 62), Joses **Nawo** (Lency **Saeni** 78). Tr: Peter **Eke**

Hekari United — **1**
Manuca [79]

Gure **Gabina** - Koriak **Upaiga**•, Alvin **Singh**•, Abraham **Iniga**, David **Muta**, Eric **Komeng** (Trevor **Ire** 77), Malakai **Tiwa**, Andrew **Setefano**, Henry **Fa'arodo**, Tuimasi **Manuca**, Niel **Hans** (Wira **Wama** 54). Tr: Tommy **Mana**

Korman, Port Vila
26-02-2011, 15:00, Benischke NZL

Amicale — **5**
Masauvakalo 3 [7] [45] [89], Maemae [29], Wetney [33]

Ernest **Bong** - Young **Paul**♦[23], Richard **Anisua**• (Lenson **Bisili** 81), Nelson **Sale**, Alphonse **Bongnaim**, Jean Robert **Yelou**, Gibson **Daudau**, Alick **Maemae**• (Richard **Garae** 74), Stanley **Waita** (Derek **Malas** 57), Fenedy **Masauvakalo**, Jack **Wetney**. Tr: William **Malas**

Lautoka — **1**
Avinesh [68p]

Ali **Cem** - Krishna **Samy**••♦[84], Leone **Vurukania**, Avinesh Waran **Suwamy**, Siga **Ali**, Sanni **Issa**, Mohammed **Mansaray** (Muni **Naidu** 15), Valerio **Nawatu**•, Adam **Belcaid** (Kamal **Hassan** 46), Yavz **Ekinci** (Samuela **Drudru** 66), Shameel **Rao**. Tr: Amdad **Ali**

Lawson Tama, Honiara
19-03-2011, 15:00, 10 000, Achari FIJ

Koloale — **1**
Nawo [83]

Shadrock **Ramoni** - Freddie **Kini**•, Samson **Takayama**, Jeffrey **Bule**, Francis **Lafai**, Leonard Sale **Olea**, Mostyn **Beui**, Steven **Anisi**, Benjamin **Totori**, Ian **Paia** (Ezra **Sale** 72), Joses **Nawo**. Tr: Peter **Eke**

Amicale — **0**

Ernest **Bong** - Selwyn Sese **Ala**, Richard **Anisua** (Moffat **Deramoa** 39), Nelson **Sale**, Alphonse **Bongnaim**, Jean Robert **Yelou**, Gibson **Daudau**•, Richard **Garae**, Stanley **Waita** (Derek **Malas** 62), Fenedy **Masauvakalo**, Jack **Wetney** (Batram **Suri** 58). Tr: William **Malas**

PMRL, Port Moresby
19-03-2011, 15:00, Saohu SOL

Hekari United — **1**
Setefano [95+]

Simione **Tamanisau** - Andrew **Lepani**, Alvin **Singh**•, David **Taro**, Abraham **Iniga** (Niel **Hans** 54), David **Muta**, Eric **Komeng**, Malakai **Tiwa**, Andrew **Setefano**, Wira **Wama**, Tuimasi **Manuca**. Tr: Tommy **Mana**

Lautoka — **1**
Finau [38]

Parmesh **Prasad** - Semesa **Nakosia**, Iskeli **Jeke**, Malakai **Waqa**, Leone **Vurukania**, Peni **Finau**•, Avinesh Waran **Suwamy**, Siga **Ali**, Kamal **Hassan**, Shameel **Rao**, Muni **Naidu**. Tr: Amdad **Ali**

GROUP B		Pl	W	D	L	F	A	Pts	NZL	NZL	NCL	TAH
Auckland City	NZL	6	4	2	0	12	2	14		1-0	3-0	5-0
Waitakere United	NZL	6	2	2	2	8	8	8	1-1		2-1	3-1
AS Magenta	NCL	6	2	1	3	6	7	7	0-1	1-1		1-0
AS Tefana	TAH	6	1	1	4	5	14	4	1-1	3-1	0-3	

Kiwitea Street, Auckland
23-10-2010, 15:00, 896, Hauata TAH

Auckland City — **3**
McGeorge [18], Mulligan [30], Koprivcic [34]

Jacob **Spooniey** - Angel **Berlanga**•, Ian **Hogg**, Sam **Campbell**, Phil **Eglinton**•, James **Pritchett**, Adam **Thomas** (Luis **Corrales** 57), David **Mulligan**, Adam **McGeorge**• (Alex **Feneridis** 62), Daniel **Koprivic**, Adam **Dickinson** (Francisco **Avendano** 80). Tr: Aaron **McFarland**

AS Magenta — **0**

Michel **Hne** - Andre **Sinedo**, Jonathan **Kakou**, Joris **Gorendiawe** (Albert **Itrema** 84), Wilson **Forest**•, Noel **Kaudre**, Marius **Bako**, Pierre **Wajoka**•, Roy **Kayara**•, Paul **Poatinda**, Francis **Watrone**• (Steeven **Longue** 84). Tr: Alain **Moizan**

Fred Taylor Park, Waitakere
24-10-2010, 14:00, 400, Achari FIJ

Waitakere United — **3**
Krishna [45], Gwyther [81], Lovemore [83]

Andrew **Ralph** - Jason **Rowley**, Aaron **Scott**, Jack **Pelter**, Ashton **Pett**, Martin **Bullock**•, Christopher **Bale**, Zane **Sole** (Sean **Lovemore** 69), Allan **Pearce** (Dakota **Lucas** 86), Roy **Krishna**, Ryan de **Vries** (Michael **Gwyther** 56). Tr: Neil **Emblen**

AS Tefana — **1**
Williams [23]

Xavier **Samin** - Pierre **Kugogne**, Jean Claude **Chang Koei Chang**, Tauraa **Marmouyet**••♦[76], Angelo **Tchen** (Stephane **Faatiarau** 84), Larry **Marmouyet**, Lorenzo **Tehau**, Sebastien **Labayen**•, Rene **Atrewe**• (Heimano **Bourebare** 64), Alvin **Tehau**• (Taufa **Neuffer** 87), Axel **Williams**. Tr: Laurent **Heinis**

Numa-Daly Magenta, Nouméa
13-11-2010, 15:00, 2000, Hester NZL

AS Magenta — **1**
Saiko [65]

Jean-Yann **Dounezek** - Benjamin **Longue**•, Judikael **Ixoee**♦[90], Steeven **Longue** (Noel **Kaudre** 55), Jonathan **Kakou**••♦[84], Joris **Gorendiawe**•, Wilson **Forest**•, Pierre **Wajoka** (Marius **Bako** 60), Roy **Kayara** (Francis **Watrone** 68), Paul **Poatinda**•, Jean-Phillipe **Saiko**. Tr: Alain **Moizan**

AS Tefana — **0**

Xavier **Samin** - Stephane **Faatiarau** (Rene **Atrewe** 66), Pierre **Kugogne**, Jean Claude **Chang Koei Chang**, Angelo **Tchen**, Heimano **Bourebare**, Larry **Marmouyet**•, Lorenzo **Tehau**, Sebastien **Labayen**, Taufa **Neuffer** (Roihau **Degage**• 74), Alvin **Tehau**. Tr: Laurent **Heinis**

Fred Taylor Park, Waitakere
14-11-2010, 14:00, Jacques TAH

Waitakere United **1**
Krishna [82]

Danny Robinson - Jason Rowley, Aaron Scott, Tim Myers, Jack Pelter•, Martin Bullock (Michael Gwyther 63), Christopher Bale, Jake Butler, Allan Pearce (Neil Emblen 87), Roy Krishna, Ryan de Vries• (Sean Lovemore 71). Tr: Neil Emblen

Auckland City **1**
Feneridis [92+]

Jacob Spoonley - Angel Berlanga, Ian Hogg, Sam Campbell•, James Pritchett, Stuart Kelly, Alex Feneridis•, Adam McGeorge•, Daniel Morgan (Adam Thomas 76), David Koprivic (Takayuki Omi 85), Adam Dickinson. Tr: Aaron McFarland

Numa-Daly Magenta, Nouméa
4-12-2010, 15:00, Saohu SOL

AS Magenta **1**
Watrone [77]

Jean-Yann Dounezek - Benjamin Longue, Steeven Longue, Andre Sinedo, Joris Gorendiawe (Andre Wahnawe 80), Noel Kaudre, Marius Bako•, Pierre Wajoka•, Roy Kayara, Paul Poatinda•, Jean-Phillipe Saiko (Francis Watrone 46). Tr: Alain Moizan

Waitakere United **1**
Pearce [70]

Danny Robinson - Jason Rowley, Aaron Scott, Tim Myers•, Jack Pelter•, Christopher Bale• (Neil Emblen 88), Jake Butler•, Zane Sole, Allan Pearce, Roy Krishna, Michael Gwyther (Ryan de Vries 80). Tr: Neil Emblen

Louis Ganivet, Faa'a
3-12-2010, 19:15, Varman FIJ

AS Tefana **1**
Marmouyet [52]

Xavier Samin - Pierre Kugogne, Jean Claude Chang Koei Chang, Tauraa Marmouyet•, Angelo Tchen, Heimano Bourebare, Larry Marmouyet, Lorenzo Tehau (James Leou 87), Sebastien Labayen, Taufa Neuffer (Roihau Degage 62), Alvin Tehau (Stephane Faatiarau 80). Tr: Laurent Heinis

Auckland City **1**
Berlanga [90]

Jacob Spoonley - Angel Berlanga•, Ian Hogg, Sam Campbell, Phil Edginton• (Luis Corrales 56), James Pritchett, Adam Thomas (Rory Kelly 87), Stuart Kelly, David Mulligan (Daniel Morgan 46), Alex Feneridis, Adam Dickinson. Tr: Aaron McFarland

Louis Ganivet, Faa'a
4-12-2011, 19:15, Billon NCL

AS Tefana **3**
Tehau.L [20], Tehau.A [30], Williams [91+]

Xavier Samin - Stephane Faatiarau, Pierre Kugogne• (Hiva Kamoise 87), Tauraa Marmouyet, Heimano Bourebare, Larry Marmouyet, Lorenzo Tehau (Roihau Degage 90), Sebastien Labayen•, Taufa Neuffer (Axel Williams 81), Kenny Nui•, Alvin Tehau. Tr: Laurent Heinis

Waitakere United **1**
Pearce [45p]

Danny Robinson - Jason Rowley•, Aaron Scott, Tim Myers, Ashton Pett (Neil Emblen 80), Christopher Bale, Jake Butler, Zane Sole• (Sean Lovemore• 39), Allan Pearce, Roy Krishna (Michael Gwyther 80), Dakota Lucas. Tr: Neil Emblen

Numa-Daly Magenta, Nouméa
21-02-2011, 19:00, Saohu SOL

AS Magenta **0**

Jean-Yann Dounezek - Jean Paul Read, Andre Sinedo•, Jonathan Kakou (Judikael Ixoee 86), Jean Claude Jewine•, Joris Gorendiawe, Wilson Forest, Noel Kaudre (Francis Watrone 88), Georges Gope-Fenepej, Cesar Lolohea, Jules Wea. Tr: Alain Moizan

Auckland City **1**
Exposito [83]

Jacob Spoonley - Ian Hogg, Sam Campbell, James Pritchett (Albert Riera 73), Ivan Vicelich, David Mulligan, Alex Feneridis, Adam McGeorge (Stuart Kelly 55), Manel Exposito•, Daniel Koprivic, Adam Dickinson• (Luis Corrales 90). Tr: Aaron McFarland

Louis Ganivet, Faa'a
25-02-2011, 19:30, Waldron NZL

AS Tefana **0**

Xavier Samin - Stephane Faatiarau, Jean Claude Chang Koei Chang, Tauraa Marmouyet, Heimano Bourebare, Larry Marmouyet (James Leou• 9) (Roihau Degage 60), Arnaud Sicot, Lorenzo Tohau, Taufa Nouffer, Kenny Nui, Axel Williams. Tr: Laurent Heinis

AS Magenta **3**
Lolohea [22], Gope-Fenepej 2 [78 81]

Jean-Yann Dounezek - Jean Paul Read•, Andre Sinedo, Joris Gorendiawe 62), Georges Gope-Fenepej, Cesar Lolohea, Jules Wea, Andre Naxue, Paul Poatinda (Jean Claude Jewine 88). Tr: Alain Moizan

Kiwitea Street, Auckland
27-02-2011, 15:00, 2500, O'Leary NZL

Auckland City **1**
Kelly [12]

Jacob Spoonley• - Angel Berlanga, Ian Hogg, Ivan Vicelich, Adam Thomas, Stuart Kelly, David Mulligan (Albert Riera 70), Alex Feneridis, Manel Exposito• (Luis Corrales 81), Daniel Koprivic (Adam McGeorge 66), Adam Dickinson. Tr: Aaron McFarland

Waitakere United **0**

Andrew Ralph - Jason Rowley•, Aaron Scott (Michael Gwyther 63), Tim Myers, Luke Adams, Martin Bullock•, Christopher Bale•, Jake Butler•, Allan Pearce•, Dakota Lucas (Luiz Del Monte 81), Ryan de Vries (Tim Payne 75). Tr: Neil Emblen

Fred Taylor Park, Waitakere
19-03-2011, 1000, Hauata TAH

Waitakere United **2**
De Vries [31], Pearce [87]

Danny Robinson - Aaron Scott, Jack Pelter•, Anthony Hobbs, Ashton Pett, Luiz Del Monte (Rory Turner 62), Neil Emblen, Zane Sole, Allan Pearce•, Michael Gwyther, Ryan de Vries (Dakota Lucas 84). Tr: Neil Emblen

AS Magenta **1**
Longue [30p]

Leopold Makalu - Jean-Yann Dounezek, Benjamin Longue, Jean Paul Read, Andre Sinedo•, Joris Gorendiawe (Alexis Duval 90), Wilson Forest♦90, Georges Gope-Fenepej•, Cesar Lolohea, Jules Wea (Jean Claude Jewine 66), Andre Naxue. Tr: Alain Moizan

Kiwitea Street, Auckland
19-03-2011, 15:00, 1500, Waugh NZL

Auckland City **5**
Vicelich [28], Kop31rivcic [44], Milne [59], Hogg [90p], Vidal [91+]

Liam Little - Angel Berlanga, Ian Hogg, James Pritchett (Adam Thomas 59), Ivan Vicelich (Sam Campbell 53), Riki van Steeden, Stuart Kelly (Aaron Bawdekar 69), Albert Riera, Andrew Milne, Luis Corrales, Daniel Koprivic. Tr: Aaron McFarland

AS Tefana **0**

Xavier Samin - Pierre Kugogne (Stephane Faatiarau• 63), Jean Claude Chang Koei Chang•, Angelo Tchen, Heimano Bourebare•, Lorenzo Tehau (Hiva Kamoise 63), Sebastien Labayen, Taufa Neuffer•, Kenny Nui, James Leou, Axel Williams (Roihau Degage• 68). Tr: Laurent Heinis

FINAL

1st leg. Korman, Port Vila
2-04-2011, 15:00, 7925, Billon NCL

Amicale **1**
Masauvakalo [67]

Ernest Bong• - Young Paul (Jerry Shem 82), Selwyn Sese Ala, Nelson Sale, Alphonse Bongnaim• - Jean Robert Yelou•, Gibson Daudau, Richard Garae• (Moffat Deramoa 53), Stanley Waita (Derek Malas 61) - Fenedy Masauvakalo, Jack Wetney. Tr: William Malas

Auckland City **2**
Exposito [22p], Corrales [82]

Jacob Spoonley - Angel Berlanga, Ian Hogg, James Pritchett, Ivan Vicelich - Stuart Kelly, David Mulligan (Luis Corrales•, 63) Alex Feneridis - Manel Exposito (Andrew Milne• 84), Daniel Koprivic (Adam Thomas 52), Adam Dickinson. Tr: Aaron McFarland

2nd leg. Kiwitea Street, Auckland
17-04-2011, 14:00, 3000, Hauata TAH

Auckland City **4**
Feneridis [26], Koprivcic [62p], Exposito [72], McGeorge [82]

Jacob Spoonley - Angel Berlanga, Ian Hogg, James Pritchett, Ivan Vicelich - David Mulligan (Luis Corrales 85), Alex Feneridis, Albert Riera - Manel Exposito, Daniel Koprivic (Adam McGeorge 81), Adam Dickinson (Andrew Milne 73). Tr: Aaron McFarland

Amicale **0**

Chikau Mansale - Young Paul, Selwyn Sese Ala (Derek Malas 74), Nelson Sale, Alphonse Bongnaim - Jean Robert Yelou (Seimata Chilia 85), Gibson Daudau, Stanley Waita (Richard Anisua 80) - Fenedy Masauvakalo•, Moffat Deramoa, Jack Wetney•. Tr: William Malas

UEFA

UNION DES ASSOCIATIONS EUROPEENNES DE FOOTBALL

By the end of 2011 there was talk of the current Barcelona side as being the greatest of all-time. Greater even than the Real Madrid team of the 1950s, the Milan team of the late 1980s and early 1990s and better even than the Brazil national team at the 1970 World Cup - widely regarded as previously topping the list. In many ways comparisons are odious with each a team of its own era, but there can be little doubt that Barcelona have set new standards and they enhanced that reputation with a majestic march to the 2011 UEFA Champions League title, thrashing Manchester United 3-1 at Wembley in the final but also beating Real Madrid 2-0 in the Bernabeu along the way. Lionel Messi scored an extraordinary 12 goals in the 13 games that Barcelona played, leading inevitably to comparisons with both Pele and Maradona. It wasn't just Messi's goals that caught the eye - he

THE FIFA BIG COUNT OF 2006 FOR EUROPE

	Male	Female		Total
Number of players	55 283 000	6 364 000	Referees and Assistant Referees	322 000
Professionals	60 000		Admin, Coaches, Technical, Medical	2 100 000
Amateurs 18+	11 101 000		Number of clubs	202 000
Youth under 18	9 386 000		Number of teams	872 000
Unregistered	40 622 000		Clubs with women's teams	13 000
Total Players	64 069 000		Players as % of population	7.59%

scored 53 in all competitions in the 2010-11 season - but the genuine air of expectation that gripped his audience when he had the ball at his feet, the sign of a truly exceptional footballer. FC Porto were the other UEFA club winners in 2011 as Portuguese clubs dominated the Europa League. In the final Porto beat Braga 1-0 in Dublin's new Aviva Arena. At national team level, 2011 was a very busy year with qualifying for the finals of Euro 2012 in Poland and Ukraine. In the event there were few surprises with Turkey the biggest name absent from the finals. Remarkably, both Germany and Spain won all of their qualifiers whilst the Netherlands won the first nine of theirs before losing to Sweden. At youth level Spain continued to lead the way winning the Under-21, Under-19 and the women's Under-17 titles - while the Netherlands beat Germany in the final of the Under-17 event. Germany were winners of the women's Under-19 tournament.

Union des associations européennes de football (UEFA)
Route de Genève 46, 1260 Nyon, Switzerland
Tel +41 22 9944444   Fax +41 22 9944488
info@uefa.com   www.uefa.com
President: Michel Platini FRA   Secretary General: Gianni Infantino ITA
UEFA Formed: 1954

UEFA EXECUTIVE COMMITTEE

President: Michel Platini FRA	1st Vice-President: Senes Erzik TUR	2nd Vice-President: Geoffrey Thompson ENG
3rd Vice-President: Angel María Villar Llona ESP	4th Vice-President: Marios Lefkaritis CYP	5th Vice-President: Joseph Mifsud MLT

ORDINARY MEMBERS OF THE EXECUTIVE COMMITTEE

Giancarlo Abete ITA	Frantisek Laurinec SVK	Dr Gilberto Madail POR
Grigory Surkis UKR	Liutauras Varanavicius LTU	Allan Hansen DEN
Avraham Luzon ISR	Mircea Sandu ROU	Michael van Praag NED
Dr Theo Zwanziger GER		Hon President: Lennart Johansson SWE
FIFA Exco member: Michel D'Hooghe BEL	Secretary General: Gianni Infantino ITA	FIFA Exco member: Franz Beckenbauer GER

MAP OF UEFA MEMBER NATIONS

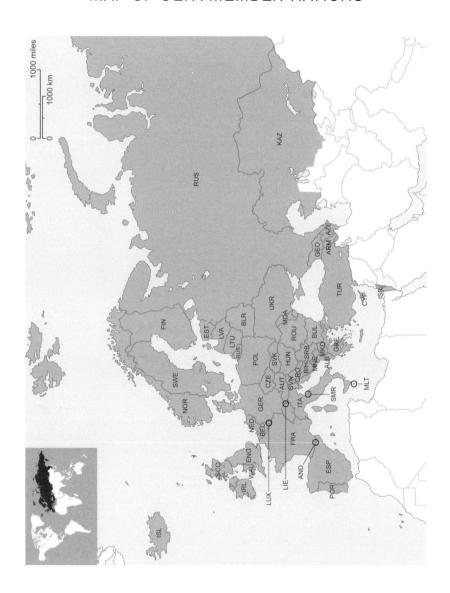

UEFA MEMBER ASSOCIATIONS (53)

ALB - **Albania** • AND - **Andorra** • ARM - **Armenia** • AUS - **Austria** • AZE - **Azerbaijan** • BLR - **Belarus** • BEL - **Belgium**
BIH - **Bosnia-Herzegovina** • BUL - **Bulgaria** • CRO - **Croatia** • CYP - **Cyprus** • CZE - **Czech Republic** • DEN - **Denmark** • ENG - **England**
EST - **Estonia** • FRO - **Faroe Islands** • FIN - **Finland** • FRA - **France** • GEO - **Georgia** • GER - **Germany** • GRE - **Greece** • HUN - **Hungary**
ISL - **Iceland** • IRL - **Republic of Ireland** • ISR - **Israel** • ITA - **Italy** • KAZ - **Kazakhstan** • LVA - **Latvia** • LIE - **Liechtenstein** • LTU - **Lithuania**
LUX - **Luxembourg** • MKD - **Macedonia FYR** • MLT - **Malta** • MDA - **Moldova** • MNE - **Montenegro** • NED - **Netherlands** • NIR - **Northern Ireland**
NOR - **Norway** • POL - **Poland** • POR - **Portugal** • ROU - **Romania** • RUS - **Russia** • SMR - **San Marino** • SCO - **Scotland** • SRB - **Serbia**
SVK - **Slovakia** • SVN - **Slovenia** • ESP - **Spain** • SWE - **Sweden** • SUI - **Switzerland** • TUR - **Turkey** • UKR - **Ukraine** • WAL - **Wales**

EUROPEAN NATIONAL TEAM TOURNAMENTS

UEFA EUROPEAN CHAMPIONSHIP

Year	Host Country	Winners	Score	Runners-up	Venue
1960	France	Soviet Union	2-1	Yugoslavia	Parc des Princes, Paris
1964	Spain	Spain	2-1	Soviet Union	Bernabeu, Madrid
1968	Italy	Italy	1-1 2-0	Yugoslavia	Stadio Olimpico, Roma
1972	Belgium	Germany FR	3-0	Soviet Union	Heysel, Brussels
1976	Yugoslavia	Czechoslovakia	2-2 5-4p	Germany FR	Crvena Zvezda, Belgrade
1980	Italy	Germany FR	2-1	Belgium	Stadio Olimpico, Rome
1984	France	France	2-0	Spain	Parc des Princes, Paris
1988	Germany FR	Netherlands	2-0	Soviet Union	Olympiastadion, Munich
1992	Sweden	Denmark	2-0	Germany	Nya Ullevi, Gothenburg
1996	England	Germany	2-1	Czech Republic	Wembley, London
2000	Belgium/Netherlands	France	2-1	Italy	Feijenoord Stadion, Rotterdam
2004	Portugal	Greece	1-0	Portugal	Estadio da Luz, Lisbon
2008	Austria/Switzerland	Spain	1-0	Germany	Ernst Happel, Vienna
2012	Poland/Ukraine				Olympic Stadium, Kyiv

UEFA EUROPEAN CHAMPIONSHIP MEDALS TABLE

	Country	G	S	B	F	SF
1	Germany	3	3	1	6	7
2	Spain	2	1		3	3
3	France	2		1	2	4
4	Soviet Union	1	3		4	5
5	Czechoslovakia	1	1	2	2	3
6	Italy	1	1	1	2	3
7	Netherlands	1		4	1	5
8	Denmark	1		1	1	3
9	Greece	1			1	1
10	Yugoslavia		2		2	3
11	Portugal		1	2	1	3
12	Belgium		1	1	1	2
13	England			2		2
14	Hungary			1		2
15	Czech Republic			1		1
	Sweden			1		1
	Russia			1		1
	Turkey			1		1
		13	13	20	26	50

This table represents the Gold (winners), Silver (runners-up) and
Bronze (semi-finalists) placings in the UEFA European
Championship, along with the number of appearances in the final
and semi-finals

EUROPEAN CLUB TOURNAMENTS

UEFA CHAMPIONS LEAGUE

Year	Winners	Country	Score	Country	Runners-up
1956	Real Madrid	ESP	4-3	FRA	Stade de Reims
1957	Real Madrid	ESP	2-0	ITA	Fiorentina
1958	Real Madrid	ESP	3-2	ITA	Milan
1959	Real Madrid	ESP	2-0	FRA	Stade de Reims
1960	Real Madrid	ESP	7-3	FRG	Eintracht Frankfurt

UEFA CHAMPIONS LEAGUE (CONT'D)

Year	Winners	Country	Score	Country	Runners-up
1961	Benfica	POR	3-2	ESP	Barcelona
1962	Benfica	POR	5-3	ESP	Real Madrid
1963	Milan	ITA	2-1	POR	Benfica
1964	Internazionale	ITA	3-1	ESP	Real Madrid
1965	Internazionale	ITA	1-0	POR	Benfica
1966	Real Madrid	ESP	2-1	YUG	Partizan Beograd
1967	Celtic	SCO	2-1	ITA	Internazionale
1968	Manchester United	ENG	4-1	POR	Benfica
1969	Milan	ITA	4-1	NED	Ajax
1970	Feyenoord	NED	2-1	SCO	Celtic
1971	Ajax	NED	2-0	GRE	Panathinaikos
1972	Ajax	NED	2-0	ITA	Internazionale
1973	Ajax	NED	1-0	ITA	Juventus
1974	Bayern München	FRG	1-1 4-0	ESP	Atlético Madrid
1975	Bayern München	FRG	2-0	ENG	Leeds United
1976	Bayern München	FRG	1-0	FRA	AS Saint-Étienne
1977	Liverpool	ENG	3-1	FRG	Borussia Mönchengladbach
1978	Liverpool	ENG	1-0	BEL	Club Brugge
1979	Nottingham Forest	ENG	1-0	SWE	Malmö FF
1980	Nottingham Forest	ENG	1-0	FRG	Hamburger SV
1981	Liverpool	ENG	1-0	ESP	Real Madrid
1982	Aston Villa	ENG	1-0	FRG	Bayern München
1983	Hamburger SV	FRG	1-0	ITA	Juventus
1984	Liverpool	ENG	1-1 4-2p	ITA	Roma
1985	Juventus	ITA	1-0	ENG	Liverpool
1986	Steaua Bucuresti	ROU	0-0 2-0p	ESP	Barcelona
1987	FC Porto	POR	2-1	FRG	Bayern München
1988	PSV Eindhoven	NED	0-0 6-5p	POR	Benfica
1989	Milan	ITA	4-0	ROU	Steaua Bucuresti
1990	Milan	ITA	1-0	POR	Benfica
1991	Crvena Zvezda Beograd	YUG	0-0 5-3p	FRA	Olympique Marseille
1992	Barcelona	ESP	1-0	ITA	Sampdoria
1993	Olympique Marseille	FRA	1-0	ITA	Milan
1994	Milan	ITA	4-0	ESP	Barcelona
1995	Ajax	NED	1-0	ITA	Milan
1996	Juventus	ITA	1-1 4-2p	NED	Ajax
1997	Borussia Dortmund	GER	3-1	ITA	Juventus
1998	Real Madrid	ESP	1-0	ITA	Juventus
1999	Manchester United	ENG	2-1	GER	Bayern München
2000	Real Madrid	ESP	3-0	ESP	Valencia
2001	Bayern München	GER	1-1 5-4p	ESP	Valencia
2002	Real Madrid	ESP	2-1	GER	Bayer Leverkusen
2003	Milan	ITA	0-0 3-2p	ITA	Juventus
2004	FC Porto	POR	3-0	FRA	Monaco
2005	Liverpool	ENG	3-3 3-2p	ITA	Milan
2006	Barcelona	ESP	2-1	ENG	Arsenal
2007	Milan	ITA	2-1	ENG	Liverpool
2008	Manchester United	ENG	1-1 6-5p	ENG	Chelsea
2009	Barcelona	ESP	2-0	ENG	Manchester United
2010	Internazionale	ITA	2-0	GER	Bayern München
2011	Barcelona	ESP	3-1	ENG	Manchester United

UEFA CHAMPIONS LEAGUE MEDALS TABLE

	Country	G	S	B	F	SF
1	Spain	13	9	21	22	43
2	Italy	12	14	8	26	34
3	England	11	7	18	18	36
4	Germany	6	8	11	14	25
5	Netherlands	6	2	5	8	13
6	Portugal	4	5	2	9	11
7	France	1	5	8	6	14
8	Scotland	1	1	6	2	8
9	Romania	1	1	2	2	4
	Serbia	1	1	2	2	4
11	Belgium		1	3	1	4
12	Greece		1	2	1	3
13	Sweden		1	1	1	2
14	Hungary			3		3
	Switzerland			3		3
	Ukraine			3		3
17	Austria			2		2
	Bulgaria			2		2
	Poland			2		2
20	Czech Republic			1		1
	Russia			1		1
	Slovakia			1		1
	Turkey			1		1
		56	56	108	112	220

This table represents the Gold (winners), Silver (runners-up) and Bronze (semi-finalists) placings of clubs representing the above countries in the UEFA Champions League, along with the number of appearances in the final and semi-finals

UEFA CHAMPIONS LEAGUE MEDALS TABLE

	Club		G	S	B
1	Real Madrid	ESP	9	3	10
2	Milan	ITA	7	4	2
3	Liverpool	ENG	5	2	3
4	Bayern München	GER	4	4	5
5	Barcelona	ESP	4	3	6
6	Ajax	NED	4	2	2
7	Manchester United	ENG	3	2	7
8	Internazionale	ITA	3	2	3
9	Juventus	ITA	2	5	3
10	Benfica	POR	2	5	1
11	FC Porto	POR	2		1
12	Nottingham Forest	ENG	2		
13	Glasgow Celtic	SCO	1	1	2
14	Hamburger SV	GER	1	1	1
	Olympique Marseille	FRA	1	1	1
	Steaua Bucuresti	ROU	1	1	1
17	Borussia Dortmund	GER	1		2
	Crvena Zvezda Beograd	SER	1		2

UEFA CHAMPIONS LEAGUE MEDALS TABLE (CONT'D)

	Club		G	S	B
	PSV Eindhoven	NED	1		2
20	Feyenoord	NED	1		1
21	Aston Villa	ENG	1		
22	Stade de Reims	FRA		2	
	Valencia	ESP		2	
24	Chelsea	ENG		1	4
25	Atlético Madrid	ESP		1	2
	Leeds United	ENG		1	2
	AS Monaco	FRA		1	2
	Panathinaikos	GRE		1	2
29	Arsenal	ENG		1	1
	Borussia Mönchengladbach	GER		1	1
	AS Saint-Étienne	FRA		1	1
32	Bayer Leverkusen	GER		1	
	Club Brugge	BEL		1	
	Eintracht Frankfurt	GER		1	
	Fiorentina	ITA		1	
	Malmö FF	SWE		1	
	Partizan Beograd	SRB		1	
	Roma	ITA		1	
	Sampdoria	ITA		1	
40	Dynamo Kyiv	UKR			3
41	RSC Anderlecht	BEL			2
	CSKA Sofia	BUL			2
	FC Zürich	SUI			2
44	FK Austria	AUT			1
	Girondins Bordeaux	FRA			1
	Deportivo La Coruna	ESP			1
	Derby County	ENG			1
	Dinamo Bucuresti	ROU			1
	Dukla Praha	CZE			1
	Dundee	SCO			1
	Dundee United	SCO			1
	Galatasaray	TUR			1
	IFK Göteborg	SWE			1
	Hibernian Edinburgh	SCO			1
	1.FC Köln	GER			1
	Legia Warszawa	POL			1
	FC Nantes	FRA			1
	Olympique Lyonnais	FRA			1
	Paris Saint-Germain	FRA			1
	Rába ETO Györ	HUN			1
	Glasgow Rangers	SCO			1
	SK Rapid Wien	AUT			1
	Real Sociedad	ESP			1
	Schalke 04	GER			1
	Spartak Moskva	RUS			1
	Spartak Trnava	SVK			1
	Standard CL	BEL			1
	Tottenham Hotspur	ENG			1
	Ujpesti TE	HUN			1
	Vasas Budapest	HUN			1
	Villarreal	ESP			1
	Widzew Lódz	POL			1
	Young Boys Berne	SUI			1
			56	56	108

EUROPEAN CUP WINNERS' CUP

Year	Winners	Country	Score	Country	Runners-up
1961	Fiorentina	ITA	2-0 2-1	SCO	Rangers
1962	Atlético Madrid	ESP	1-1 3-0	ITA	Fiorentina
1963	Tottenham Hotspur	ENG	5-1	ESP	Atlético Madrid
1964	Sporting CP	POR	3-3 1-0	HUN	MTK Budapest
1965	West Ham United	ENG	2-0	FRG	TSV München 1860
1966	Borussia Dortmund	FRG	2-1	ENG	Liverpool
1967	Bayern München	FRG	1-0	SCO	Rangers
1968	Milan	ITA	2-0	FRG	Hamburger SV
1969	Slovan Bratislava	CZE	3-2	ESP	Barcelona
1970	Manchester City	ENG	2-1	POL	Gornik Zabrze
1971	Chelsea	ENG	1-1 2-1	ESP	Real Madrid
1972	Rangers	SCO	3-2	URS	Dynamo Moskva
1973	Milan	ITA	1-0	ENG	Leeds United
1974	1.FC Magdeburg	GDR	2-0	ITA	Milan
1975	Dynamo Kyiv	URS	3-0	HUN	Ferencváros
1976	RSC Anderlecht	BEL	4-2	ENG	West Ham United
1977	Hamburger SV	FRG	2-0	BEL	RSC Anderlecht
1978	RSC Anderlecht	BEL	4-0	AUT	FK Austria
1979	Barcelona	ESP	4-3	FRG	Fortuna Düsseldorf
1980	Valencia	ESP	0-0 5-4p	ENG	Arsenal
1981	Dynamo Tbilisi	URS	2-1	GDR	Carl Zeiss Jena
1982	Barcelona	ESP	2-1	BEL	Standard CL
1983	Aberdeen	SCO	2-1	ESP	Real Madrid
1984	Juventus	ITA	2-1	POR	FC Porto
1985	Everton	ENG	3-1	AUT	SK Rapid Wien
1986	Dynamo Kyiv	URS	3-0	ESP	Atlético Madrid
1987	Ajax	NED	1-0	GDR	Lokomotive Leipzig
1988	KV Mechelen	BEL	1-0	NED	Ajax
1989	Barcelona	ESP	2-0	ITA	Sampdoria
1990	Sampdoria	ITA	2-0	BEL	RSC Anderlecht
1991	Manchester United	ENG	2-1	ESP	Barcelona
1992	Werder Bremen	GER	2-0	FRA	Monaco
1993	Parma	ITA	3-1	BEL	Royal Antwerp FC
1994	Arsenal	ENG	1-0	ITA	Parma
1995	Real Zaragoza	ESP	2-1	ENG	Arsenal
1996	Paris Saint-Germain	FRA	1-0	AUT	SK Rapid Wien
1997	Barcelona	ESP	1-0	FRA	Paris Saint-Germain
1998	Chelsea	ENG	1-0	GER	VfB Stuttgart
1999	Lazio	ITA	2-1	ESP	Real Mallorca

CUP WINNERS' CUP MEDALS TABLE

	Country	G	S	B	F	SF
1	England	8	5	8	13	21
2	Spain	7	7	5	14	19
3	Italy	7	4	9	11	20
4	Germany	4	4	9	8	17
5	Belgium	3	4	5	7	12
6	Scotland	2	2	4	4	8
7	Ukraine	2	-	-	2	2
8	France	1	2	6	3	9
9	German DR	1	2	3	3	6
10	Netherlands	1	1	6	2	8
11	Portugal	1	1	3	2	5
12	Georgia	1		1	1	2
13	Czechoslovakia	1			1	1

CUP WINNERS' CUP MEDALS TABLE (CONT'D)

	Country	G	S	B	F	SF
14	Austria		3	1	3	4
15	Hungary		2	1	2	3
16	Russia		1	5	1	6
17	Poland		1	1	1	2
18	Czech Republic			3		3
19	Croatia			2		2
	Serbia			2		2
	Bulgaria			2		2
22	Romania			1		1
	Wales			1		1
		39	39	78	78	156

This table represents the Gold (winners), Silver (runners-up) and Bronze (semi-finalists) placings of clubs representing the above countries in the European Cup Winners' Cup, along with the number of appearances in the final and semi-finals

CUP WINNERS' CUP MEDALS TABLE

	Club		G	S	B
1	Barcelona	ESP	4	2	
2	RSC Anderlecht	BEL	2	2	
3	Milan	ITA	2	1	
4	Chelsea	ENG	2		2
5	Dynamo Kyiv	UKR	2		
6	Atlético Madrid	ESP	1	2	2
	Arsenal	ENG	1	2	
8	Glasgow Rangers	SCO	1	2	
9	Sampdoria	ITA	1	1	1
	West Ham United	ENG	1	1	1
	Fiorentina	ITA	1	1	1
	Paris Saint-Germain	FRA	1	1	1
13	Ajax	NED	1	1	
	Hamburger SV	GER	1	1	
	Parma	ITA	1	1	
16	Bayern München	GER	1		3
17	Juventus	ITA	1		2
	Real Zaragoza	ESP	1		2
19	Aberdeen	SCO	1		1
	Dinamo Tbilisi	GEO	1		1
	Manchester City	ENG	1		1
	Manchester United	ENG	1		1
	KV Mechelen	BEL	1		1
	Sporting CP	POR	1		1
	Tottenham Hotspur	ENG	1		1
26	Borussia Dortmund	GER	1		
	Everton	ENG	1		
	Lazio	ITA	1		
	1.FC Magdeburg	GDR	1		
	Slovan Bratislava	SVK	1		
	Valencia	ESP	1		
	Werder Bremen	GER	1		
33	Real Madrid	ESP		2	
	SK Rapid Wien	AUT		2	
35	Dinamo Moskva	RUS		1	2
36	FK Austria	AUT		1	1
	Carl Ziess Jena	GDR		1	1
	AS Monaco	FRA		1	1
	Standard CL	BEL		1	1
	Liverpool	ENG		1	1
41	Ferencváros	HUN		1	
	Fortuna Düsseldorf	GER		1	
	Górnik Zabrze	POL		1	
	Leeds United	ENG		1	
	VfB Leipzig	GDR		1	
	Real Mallorca	ESP		1	
	MTK-VM Budapest	HUN		1	

CUP WINNERS' CUP MEDALS TABLE (CONT'D)

	Club		G	S	B
	TSV München 1860	GER		1	
	FC Porto	POR		1	
	Royal Antwerp FC	BEL		1	
	VfB Stuttgart	GER		1	
52	Feyenoord	NED			3
53	Benfica	POR			2
	Glasgow Celtic	SCO			2
	Lokomotiv Moskva	RUS			2
	PSV Eindhoven	NED			2
57	Atalanta	ITA			1
	Baník Ostrava	CZE			1
	Bayer Uerdingen	GER			1
	SK Beveren	BEL			1
	Girondins Bordeaux	FRA			1
	Borussia Mönchengladbach	GER			1
	Cardiff City	WAL			1
	Club Brugge	BEL			1
	CSKA Sofia	BUL			1
	Deportivo La Coruña	ESP			1
	1.FC Köln	GER			1
	Dukla Praha	CZE			1
	Dunfermline Athletic	SCO			1
	Berliner FC	GDR			1
	Dinamo Bucuresti	ROU			1
	Dinamo Zagreb	CRO			1
	Eintracht Frankfurt	GER			1
	Hajduk Split	CRO			1
	Legia Warszawa	POL			1
	Olympique Lyonnais	FRA			1
	Olympique Marseille	FRA			1
	FC Nantes	FRA			1
	Napoli	ITA			1
	1.FC Nürnberg	GER			1
	OFK Beograd	SER			1
	Crvena Zvezda Beograd	SER			1
	Roma	ITA			1
	FSV Zwickau	GDR			1
	FC Schalke 04	GER			1
	Slavia Sofia	BUL			1
	Sparta Praha	CZE			1
	Spartak Moskva	RUS			1
	Torino	ITA			1
	FC Twente Enschede	NED			1
	Ujpesti TE	HUN			1
	Racing Club Genk	BEL			1
	Vicenza	ITA			1
	Wolverhampton Wanderers	ENG			1
			39	39	78

FAIRS CUP

Year	Winners	Country	Score	Country	Runners-up
1958	Barcelona	ESP	2-2 6-0	ENG	London Select XI
1960	Barcelona	ESP	0-0 4-1	ENG	Birmingham City
1961	Roma	ITA	2-2 2-0	ENG	Birmingham City
1962	Valencia	ESP	6-2 1-1	ESP	Barcelona
1963	Valencia	ESP	2-1 2-0	YUG	Dinamo Zagreb

FAIRS CUP (CONT'D)

Year	Winners	Country	Score	Country	Runners-up
1964	Real Zaragoza	ESP	2-1	ESP	Valencia
1965	Ferencváros	HUN	1-0	ITA	Juventus
1966	Barcelona	ESP	0-1 4-2	ESP	Real Zaragoza
1967	Dinamo Zagreb	YUG	2-0 0-0	ENG	Leeds United
1968	Leeds United	ENG	1-0 0-0	HUN	Ferencváros
1969	Newcastle United	ENG	3-0 3-2	HUN	Ujpesti Dózsa
1970	Arsenal	ENG	1-3 3-0	BEL	RSC Anderlecht
1971	Leeds United	ENG	2-2 1-1	ITA	Juventus

FAIRS CUP MEDALS TABLE

	Country	G	S	B	F	SF
1	Spain	6	3	1	9	10
2	England	4	4	5	8	13
3	Italy	1	2	4	3	7
4	Hungary	1	2	2	3	5
5	Croatia	1	1		2	2
6	Belgium		1	2	1	3
7	Scotland			4		4
8	Germany			3		3
9	Serbia			2		2
10	Netherlands			1		1
11	Switzerland			1		1
12	Turkey			1		1
		13	13	26	26	52

This table represents the Gold (winners), Silver (runners-up) and Bronze (semi-finalists) placings of clubs representing the above countries in the Fairs Cup, along with the number of appearances in the final and semi-finals

FAIRS CUP MEDALS TABLE

	Club		G	S	B
1	Barcelona	ESP	3	1	
2	Leeds United	ENG	2	1	1
3	Valencia	ESP	2	1	
4	Ferencvaros	HUN	1	1	1
5	Dinamo Zagreb	CRO	1	1	
	Real Zaragoza	ESP	1	1	
7	Roma	ITA	1		1
8	Arsenal	ENG	1		
	Newcastle United	ENG	1		

FAIRS CUP MEDALS TABLE (CONT'D)

	Club		G	S	B
10	Birmingham City	ENG		2	1
11	Juventus	ITA		2	
12	RSC Anderlecht	BEL		1	
	London Select XI	ENG		1	
	Ujpesti TE	HUN		1	
15	Internazionale	ITA			2
	1.FC Köln	GER			2
17	Ajax	NED			1
	Atlético Madrid	ESP			1
	Belgrade Select XI	SRB			1
	Bologna	ITA			1
	Chelsea	ENG			1
	Crvena Zvezda	SRB			1
	Dundee	SCO			1
	Eintracht Frankfurt	GER			1
	Göztepe Izmir	TUR			1
	Hibernian	SCO			1
	Lausanne-Sports	SUI			1
	RFC Liège	BEL			1
	Liverpool	ENG			1
	Kilmarnock	SCO			1
	Manchester United	ENG			1
	MTK-VM Budapest	HUN			1
	Rangers	SCO			1
	Union St Gilloise	BEL			1
			13	13	26

UEFA CUP

Year	Winners	Country	Score	Country	Runners-up
1972	Tottenham Hotspur	ENG	2-1 1-1	ENG	Wolverhampton Wanderers
1973	Liverpool	ENG	3-0 0-2	FRG	Borussia Mönchengladbach
1974	Feyenoord	NED	2-2 2-0	ENG	Tottenham Hotspur
1975	Borussia Mönchengladbach	FRG	0-0 5-1	NED	FC Twente Enschede
1976	Liverpool	ENG	3-2 1-1	BEL	Club Brugge
1977	Juventus	ITA	1-0 1-2	ESP	Athletic Bilbao
1978	PSV Eindhoven	NED	0-0 3-0	FRA	SEC Bastia
1979	Borussia Mönchengladbach	FRG	1-1 1-0	YUG	Crvena Zvezda Beograd
1980	Eintracht Frankfurt	FRG	2-3 1-0	FRG	Borussia Mönchengladbach
1981	Ipswich Town	ENG	3-0 2-4	NED	AZ 67 Alkmaar
1982	IFK Göteborg	SWE	1-0 3-0	FRG	Hamburger SV
1983	RSC Anderlecht	BEL	1-0 1-1	POR	Benfica

UEFA CUP (CONT'D)

Year	Winners	Country	Score	Country	Runners-up
1984	Tottenham Hotspur	ENG	1-1 1-1 4-3p	BEL	RSC Anderlecht
1985	Real Madrid	ESP	3-0 0-1	HUN	Videoton SC
1986	Real Madrid	ESP	5-1 0-2	FRG	1.FC Köln
1987	IFK Göteborg	SWE	1-0 1-1	SCO	Dundee United
1988	Bayer Leverkusen	FRG	0-3 3-0 3-2p	ESP	Español
1989	Napoli	ITA	2-1 3-3	FRG	VfB Stuttgart
1990	Juventus	ITA	3-1 0-0	ITA	Fiorentina
1991	Internazionale	ITA	2-0 0-1	ITA	Roma
1992	Ajax	NED	2-2 0-0	ITA	Torino
1993	Juventus	ITA	3-1 3-0	GER	Borussia Dortmund
1994	Internazionale	ITA	1-0 1-0	AUT	Austria Salzburg
1995	Parma	ITA	1-0 1-1	ITA	Juventus
1996	Bayern München	GER	2-0 3-1	FRA	Bordeaux
1997	Schalke 04	GER	1-0 0-1 4-1p	ITA	Internazionale
1998	Internazionale	ITA	3-0	ITA	Lazio
1999	Parma	ITA	3-0	FRA	Olympique Marseille
2000	Galatasaray	TUR	0-0 4-1p	ENG	Arsenal
2001	Liverpool	ENG	5-4	ESP	CD Alavés
2002	Feyenoord	NED	3-2	GER	Borussia Dortmund
2003	FC Porto	POR	3-2	SCO	Glasgow Celtic
2004	Valencia	ESP	2-0	FRA	Olympique Marseille
2005	CSKA Moskva	RUS	3-1	POR	Sporting CP
2006	Sevilla	ESP	4-0	ENG	Middlesbrough
2007	Sevilla	ESP	2-2 3-1p	ESP	Espanyol
2008	Zenit St Petersburg	RUS	2-0	SCO	Rangers
2009	Shakhtar Donetsk	UKR	2-1	GER	Werder Bremen

UEFA CUP MEDALS TABLE

	Country	G	S	B	F	SF
1	Italy	9	6	12	15	27
2	Germany	6	8	22	14	36
3	England	6	4	4	10	14
4	Spain	5	4	10	9	19
5	Netherlands	4	2	2	6	8
6	Russia	2		1	2	3
7	Sweden	2			2	2
8	Belgium	1	2	3	3	6
9	Portugal	1	2	2	3	5
10	Ukraine	1		1	1	2
11	Turkey	1			1	1
12	France		4	5	4	9
13	Scotland		3		3	3
14	Austria		1	1	1	2
	Hungary		1	1	1	2
	Serbia		1	1	1	2
17	Czech Republic			2		2
	German DR			2		2
	Romania			2		2
20	Bosnia-Herzegovina			1		1
	Croatia			1		1
	Denmark			1		1
	Greece			1		1
	Switzerland			1		1
		38	38	76	76	152

This table represents the Gold (winners), Silver (runners-up) and Bronze (semi-finalists) placings of clubs representing the above countries in the UEFA Cup, along with the number of appearances in the final and semi-finals

UEFA CUP MEDALS TABLE

	Club		G	S	B
1	Internazionale	ITA	3	1	3
2	Juventus	ITA	3	1	1
3	Liverpool	ENG	3		
4	Borussia Mönchengladbach	GER	2	2	1
5	Tottenham Hotspur	ENG	2	1	1
6	Parma	ITA	2		1
	Real Madrid	ESP	2		1
8	Feyenoord	NED	2		
	IFK Göteborg	SWE	2		
	Sevilla	ESP	2		
11	RSC Anderlecht	BEL	1	1	
12	Bayern München	GER	1		3
13	Bayer Leverkusen	GER	1		1
	FC Schalke 04	GER	1		1
15	Ajax	NED	1		
	CSKA Moskva	RUS	1		
	Eintracht Frankfurt	GER	1		
	Galatasaray	TUR	1		
	Ipswich Town	ENG	1		
	Napoli	ITA	1		
	FC Porto	POR	1		
	PSV Eindhoven	NED	1		
	Shakhtar Donetsk	UKR	1		
	Valencia	ESP	1		
	Zenit St Petersburg	RUS	1		
26	Borussia Dortmund	GER		2	1
27	RCD Espanyol	ESP		2	

UEFA CUP MEDALS TABLE (CONT'D)

	Club		G	S	B
	Olympique Marseille	FRA		2	
29	1.FC Köln	GER		1	3
	Werder Bremen	GER		1	3
31	Hamburger SV	GER		1	2
	VfB Stuttgart	GER		1	2
33	AZ Alkmaar	NED		1	1
	Club Brugge	BEL		1	1
	Fiorentina	ITA		1	1
	Lazio	ITA		1	1
	Sporting CP	POR		1	1
	Twente Enschede	NED		1	1
39	Arsenal	ENG		1	
	Austria Salzburg	AUT		1	
	CD Alavés	ESP		1	
	Athletic Bilbao	ESP		1	
	SEC Bastia	FRA		1	
	Benfica	POR		1	
	Girondins Bordeaux	FRA		1	
	Glasgow Celtic	SCO		1	
	Crvena Zvezda Beograd	SRB		1	
	Dundee United	SCO		1	
	Middlesbrough	ENG		1	
	Glasgow Rangers	SCO		1	
	Roma	ITA		1	
	Torino	ITA		1	
	Videoton SC	HUN		1	
	Wolverhampton Wanderers	ENG		1	
55	Barcelona	ESP			4
56	Atlético Madrid	ESP			2
	1.FC Kaiserslautern	GER			2
	Milan	ITA			2
59	AEK Athens	GRE			1
	AJ Auxerre	FRA			1
	Boavista	POR			1

UEFA CUP MEDALS TABLE (CONT'D)

Club		G	S	B
Bohemians Praha	CZE			1
Bologna	ITA			1
Brøndbyernes IF	DEN			1
Cagliari	ITA			1
MSV Duisburg	GER			1
1.FC Dynamo Dresden	GDR			1
Dynamo Kyiv	UKR			1
Ferencváros	HUN			1
Genoa 1893	ITA			1
Grasshopper-Club	SUI			1
Hajduk Split	CRO			1
Hertha BSC Berlin	GER			1
Karlsruher SC	GER			1
Leeds United	ENG			1
VfB Leipzig	GDR			1
Racing Club Lens	FRA			1
AS Monaco	FRA			1
RWD Molenbeek	BEL			1
Newcastle United	ENG			1
Nottingham Forest	ENG			1
Osasuna	ESP			1
Paris Saint-Germain	FRA			1
Radnicki Nis	SRB			1
Slavia Praha	CZE			1
FC Sochaux	FRA			1
Spartak Moskva	RUS			1
Steaua Bucureşti	ROU			1
Tenerife	ESP			1
FC Tirol	AUT			1
Universitatea Craiova	ROU			1
Villarreal	ESP			1
KSV Waregem	BEL			1
Zeljeznicar Sarajevo	BIH			1
		38	38	76

UEFA EUROPA LEAGUE

Year	Winners	Country	Score	Country	Runners-up
2010	Atlético Madrid	ESP	2-1	ENG	Fulham
2011	FC Porto	POR	1-0	POR	SC Braga

UEFA EUROPA LEAGUE MEDALS TABLE

	Country	G	S	B	F	SF
1	Portugal	1	1	1	2	3
2	Spain	1		1	1	2
3	England		1	1	1	2
4	Germany			1		1
		1	2	4	4	8

This table represents the Gold (winners), Silver (runners-up) and Bronze (semi-finalists) placings of clubs representing the above countries in the UEFA Cup, along with the number of appearances in the final and semi-finals

UEFA EUROPA LEAGUE MEDALS TABLE

	Club		G	S	B
1	Atlético Madrid	ESP	1		
	FC Porto	POR	1		
3	SC Braga	POR		1	
	Fulham	ENG		1	
5	Benfica	POR			1
	Hamburger SV	GER			1
	Liverpool	ENG			1
	Villarreal	ESP			1
			2	2	4

EUROPEAN YOUTH TOURNAMENTS

UEFA EUROPEAN UNDER-21 CHAMPIONSHIP

Year	Host Country	Winners	Score	Runners-up	Venue
1978		Yugoslavia	1-0 4-1	German DR	Halle & Mostar
1980		Soviet Union	0-0 1-0	German DR	Rostock & Moscow
1982		England	3-1 2-3	Germany FR	Sheffield & Bremen
1984		England	1-0 2-0	Spain	Seville & Sheffield
1986		Spain	1-2 2-1 3-0p	Italy	Rome & Valladolid
1988		France	0-0 3-0	Greece	Athens & Besançon
1990		Soviet Union	4-2 3-1	Yugoslavia	Sarajevo & Simferopol
1992		Italy	2-0 0-1	Sweden	Ferrara & Växjö
1994	France	Italy	1-0	Portugal	Montpellier
1996	Spain	Italy	1-1 4-2p	Spain	Barcelona
1998	Romania	Spain	1-0	Greece	Bucharest
2000	Slovakia	Italy	2-1	Czech Republic	Bratislava
2002	Switzerland	Czech Republic	0-0 3-1p	France	St Jakob Park, Basel
2004	Germany	Italy	3-0	Serbia & Montenegro	Ruhrstadion, Bochum
2006	Portugal	Netherlands	3-0	Ukraine	Bessa, Oporto
2007	Netherlands	Netherlands	4-1	Serbia	Euroborg, Groningen
2009	Sweden	Germany	4-0	England	Swedbank Stadion, Malmö
2011	Denmark	Spain	2-0	Switzerland	Aarhus Stadion, Aarhus

UEFA EUROPEAN UNDER-19 CHAMPIONSHIP

Year	Host Country	Winners	Score	Runners-up	Venue
1981	West Germany	Germany FR	1-0	Poland	Düsseldorf
1982	Finland	Scotland	3-1	Czechoslovakia	Helsinki
1983	England	France	1-0	Czechoslovakia	White Hart Lane, London
1984	Soviet Union	Hungary	0-0 3-2p	Soviet Union	Zentralny, Moscow
1986	Yugoslavia	German DR	3-1	Italy	Subotica
1988	Czechoslovakia	Soviet Union	3-1	Portugal	Frydek-Mistek
1990	Hungary	Soviet Union	0-0 4-2p	Portugal	Bekescsaba
1992	Germany	Turkey	2-1	Portugal	Bayreuth
1993	England	England	1-0	Turkey	City Ground, Nottingham
1994	Spain	Portugal	1-1 4-1p	Germany	Merida
1995	Greece	Spain	4-1	Italy	Katerini
1996	France/Luxemb	France	1-0	Spain	Besançon
1997	Iceland	France	1-0	Portugal	Reykjavík
1998	Cyprus	Republic of Ireland	1-1 4-3p	Germany	Larnaca
1999	Sweden	Portugal	1-0	Italy	Norrköping
2000	Germany	France	1-0	Ukraine	Nürnberg
2001	Finland	Poland	3-1	Czech Republic	Helsinki
2002	Norway	Spain	1-0	Germany	Ullevaal, Oslo
2003	Liechtenstein	Italy	2-0	Portugal	Rheinpark Stadion, Vaduz
2004	Switzerland	Spain	1-0	Turkey	Colovray, Nyon
2005	Nth. Ireland	France	3-1	England	Windsor Park, Belfast
2006	Poland	Spain	2-1	Scotland	Miejski, Poznan
2007	Austria	Spain	1-0	Greece	Linzer, Linz
2008	Czech Republic	Germany	3-1	Italy	Strelnice, Jablonec nad Nisou
2009	Ukraine	Ukraine	2-0	England	Olympiyskiy, Donetsk
2010	France	France	2-1	Spain	Michel d'Ornano, Caen
2011	Romania	Spain	3-2	Czech Republic	Concordia, Chiajna

Played as an U-18 tournament from 1981 to 2001

UEFA EUROPEAN UNDER-17 CHAMPIONSHIP

Year	Host Country	Winners	Score	Runners-up	Venue
1982	Italy	Italy	1-0	Germany FR	Falconara
1984	Germany FR	Germany FR	2-0	Soviet Union	Ulm

UEFA EUROPEAN UNDER–17 CHAMPIONSHIP

Year	Host Country	Winners	Score	Runners-up	Venue
1985	Hungary	Soviet Union	4-0	Greece	Budapest
1986	Greece	Spain	2-1	Italy	Athens
1987	France	Italy	1-0	Soviet Union	Paris
1988	Spain	Spain	0-0 4-2p	Portugal	Teresa Rivero, Madrid
1989	Denmark	Portugal	4-1	German DR	Vejle
1990	East Germany	Czechoslovakia	3-2	Yugoslavia	Erfurt
1991	Swtzerland	Spain	2-0	Germany	Wankdorf, Berne
1992	Cyprus	Germany	2-1	Spain	Ammokostos, Larnaca
1993	Turkey	Poland	1-0	Italy	Inönü, Istanbul
1994	Rep. Ireland	Turkey	1-0	Denmark	Tolka Park, Dublin
1995	Belgium	Portugal	2-0	Spain	Brussels
1996	Austria	Portugal	1-0	France	Wien
1997	Germany	Spain	0-0 5-4p	Austria	Celle
1998	Scotland	Republic of Ireland	2-1	Italy	McDiarmid Park, Perth
1999	Czech Republic	Spain	4-1	Poland	Olomouc
2000	Israel	Portugal	2-1	Czech Republic	Ramat Gan
2001	England	Spain	1-0	France	Stadium of Light, Sunderland
2002	Denmark	Switzerland	0-0 4-2p	France	Farum Park, Farum
2003	Portugal	Portugal	2-1	Spain	Fontelo Municipal, Viseu
2004	France	France	2-1	Spain	Gaston Petit, Chateauroux
2005	Italy	Turkey	2-0	Netherlands	E. Mannucci, Pontedera
2006	Luxembourg	Russia	2-2 5-3p	Czech Republic	Josy Barthel, Luxembourg
2007	Belgium	Spain	1-0	England	RFC Tournai, Tournai
2008	Turkey	Spain	4-0	France	Mardan Sports Complex, Antalya
2009	Germany	Germany	2-1	Netherlands	Magdeburg Stadium, Magdeburg
2010	Liechtenstein	England	2-1	Spain	Rheinpark, Vaduz
2011	Serbia	Netherlands	5-2	Germany	Karadorde, Novi Sad

Played as an U-16 tournament prior to 2002

EUROPEAN WOMEN'S TOURNAMENTS

UEFA EUROPEAN WOMEN'S CHAMPIONSHIP

Year	Host Country	Winners	Score	Runners-up	Venue
1984		Sweden	1-0 0-1 4-3p	England	Gothenburg & Luton
1987	Norway	Norway	2-1	Sweden	Ullevål, Oslo
1989	Germany FR	Germany FR	4-1	Norway	Osnabrück
1991	Denmark	Germany	3-1	Norway	Aalborg Stadion
1993	Italy	Norway	1-0	Italy	Dino Manuzzi, Cesena
1995	Germany	Germany	3-2	Sweden	Fritz Walter Stadion, Kaiserslautern
1997	Norway/Sweden	Germany	2-0	Italy	Ullevål, Oslo
2001	Germany	Germany	1-0	Sweden	Donaustadion, Ulm
2005	England	Germany	3-1	Norway	Ewood Park, Blackburn
2009	Finland	Germany	6-2	England	Olympiastadion, Helsinki

UEFA WOMEN'S CHAMPIONS LEAGUE

Year	Winners	Country	Score	Country	Runners-up
2002	1.FFC Frankfurt	GER	2-0	SWE	Umeå IK
2003	Umeå IK	SWE	4-1 3-0	DEN	Fortuna Hjørring
2004	Umeå IK	SWE	3-0 5-0	GER	1.FFC Frankfurt
2005	1.FFC Turbine Potsdam	GER	2-0 3-1	SWE	Djurgården/Alvsjö
2006	1.FFC Frankfurt	GER	4-0 3-2	GER	1.FFC Turbine Potsdam
2007	Arsenal	ENG	1-0 0-0	SWE	Umeå IK
2008	1.FFC Frankfurt	GER	1-1 3-2	SWE	Umeå IK
2009	FCR 2001 Duisburg	GER	6-0 1-1	RUS	Zvezda-2005
2010	1.FFC Turbine Potsdam	GER	0-0 7-6p	FRA	Olympique Lyonnais
2011	Olympique Lyonnais	FRA	2-0	GER	1.FFC Turbine Potsdam

UEFA EUROPEAN WOMEN'S UNDER–19 CHAMPIONSHIP

Year	Host Country	Winners	Score	Runners-up	Venue
1998		Denmark	2-0 2-3	France	Aabenraa & Niederbronn-les-Bains
1999	Sweden	Sweden	1-0	Germany	Bromölla
2000	France	Germany	4-2	Spain	La Libération, Boulogne
2001	Norway	Germany	3-2	Norway	Aråsen, Lillestrom
2002	Sweden	Germany	3-1	France	Olympia, Helsingborg
2003	Germany	France	2-0	Norway	Alfred Kunze Sportpark, Leipzig
2004	Finland	Spain	2-1	Germany	Pohjola Stadion, Vantaa
2005	Hungary	Russia	2-2 6-5p	France	ZTE, Zalaegerszeg
2006	Switzerland	Germany	3-0	France	Neufeld, Berne
2007	Iceland	Germany	2-0	England	Laugardalsvöllur, Reykjavík
2008	France	Italy	1-0	Norway	Vallée du Cher, Tours
2009	Belarus	England	2-0	Sweden	Gorodskoi, Borisov
2010	Macedonia	France	2-1	England	Gradski, Skopje
2011	Italy	Germany	8-1	Norway	Romeo Galli, Imola

The first three tournaments were played as U-18 championships

UEFA EUROPEAN WOMEN'S UNDER–17 CHAMPIONSHIP

Year	Host Country	Winners	Score	Runners-up	Venue
2008	Switzerland	Germany	3-0	France	Colovray, Nyon
2009	Switzerland	Germany	7-0	Spain	Colovray, Nyon
2010	Switzerland	Spain	0-0 4-1p	Republic of Ireland	Colovray, Nyon
2011	Switzerland	Spain	1-0	France	Colovray, Nyon

NATIONAL TEAM TOURNAMENTS IN 2010–11

UEFA EURO 2012 POLAND/UKRAINE QUALIFYING TOURNAMENT

GROUP A	PL	W	D	L	F	A	PTS	GER	TUR	BEL	AUT	AZE	KAZ
1 Germany	10	10	0	0	34	7	30		3-0	3-1	6-2	6-1	4-0
2 Turkey	10	5	2	3	13	11	17	1-3		3-2	2-0	1-0	2-1
3 Belgium	10	4	3	3	21	15	15	0-1	1-1		4-4	4-1	4-1
4 Austria	10	3	3	4	16	17	12	1-2	0-0	0-2		3-0	2-0
5 Azerbaijan	10	2	1	7	10	26	7	1-3	1-0	1-1	1-4		3-2
6 Kazakhstan	10	1	1	8	6	24	4	0-3	0-3	0-2	0-0	2-1	

Germany qualified directly for the finals • Turkey qualified for a play-off v Croatia • Turkey 0-3 0-0 **Croatia**

GROUP B	PL	W	D	L	F	A	PTS	RUS	IRL	ARM	SVK	MKD	AND
1 Russia	10	7	2	1	17	4	23		0-0	3-1	0-1	1-0	6-0
2 Republic of Ireland	10	6	3	1	15	7	21	2-3		2-1	0-0	2-1	3-1
3 Armenia	10	5	2	3	22	10	17	0-0	0-1		3-1	4-1	4-0
4 Slovakia	10	4	3	3	7	10	15	0-1	1-1	0-4		1-0	1-0
5 Macedonia FYR	10	2	2	6	8	14	8	0-1	0-2	2-2	1-1		1-0
6 Andorra	10	0	0	10	1	25	0	0-2	0-2	0-3	0-1	0-2	

Russia qualified directly for the finals • Rep. Ireland qualified for a play-off v Estonia • Estonia 0-4 1-1 **Rep. Ireland**

GROUP C	PL	W	D	L	F	A	PTS	ITA	EST	SRB	SVN	NIR	FRO
1 Italy	10	8	2	0	20	2	26		3-0	3-0	1-0	3-0	5-0
2 Estonia	10	5	1	4	15	14	16	1-2		1-1	0-1	4-1	2-1
3 Serbia	10	4	3	3	13	12	15	1-1	1-3		1-1	2-1	3-1
4 Slovenia	10	4	2	4	11	7	14	0-1	1-2	1-0		0-1	5-1
5 Northern Ireland	10	2	3	5	9	13	9	0-0	1-2	0-1	0-0		4-0
6 Faroe Islands	10	1	1	8	6	26	4	0-1	2-0	0-3	0-2	1-1	

Italy qualified directly for the finals • Estonia qualified for a play-off v Rep. Ireland • Estonia 0-4 1-1 **Rep. Ireland**

GROUP D	PL	W	D	L	F	A	PTS	FRA	BIH	ROU	BLR	ALB	LUX
1 France	10	6	3	1	15	4	21		1-1	2-0	0-1	3-0	2-0
2 Bosnia-Herzegovina	10	6	2	2	17	8	20	0-2		2-1	1-0	2-0	5-0
3 Romania	10	3	5	2	13	9	14	0-0	3-0		2-2	1-1	3-1
4 Belarus	10	3	4	3	8	7	13	1-1	0-2	0-0		2-0	2-0
5 Albania	10	2	3	5	7	14	9	1-2	1-1	1-1	1-0		1-0
6 Luxembourg	10	1	1	8	3	21	4	0-2	0-3	0-2	0-0	2-1	

France qualified directly for the finals • Bosnia qualified for a play-off v Portugal • Bosnia 0-2 2-6 **Portugal**

GROUP E	PL	W	D	L	F	A	PTS	NED	SWE	HUN	FIN	MDV	SMR
1 Netherlands	10	9	0	1	37	8	27		4-1	5-3	2-1	1-0	11-0
2 Sweden	10	8	0	2	31	11	24	3-2		2-0	5-0	2-1	6-0
3 Hungary	10	6	1	3	22	14	19	0-4	2-1		0-0	2-1	8-0
4 Finland	10	3	1	6	16	16	10	0-2	1-2	1-2		4-1	8-0
5 Moldova	10	3	0	7	12	16	9	0-1	1-4	0-2	2-0		4-0
6 San Marino	10	0	0	10	0	53	0	0-5	0-5	0-3	0-1	0-2	

Netherlands qualified directly for the finals • Sweden qualified also as the second-placed team with the best record

GROUP F	PL	W	D	L	F	A	PTS	GRE	CRO	ISR	LVA	GEO	MLT
1 Greece	10	7	3	0	14	5	24		2-0	2-1	1-0	1-1	3-1
2 Croatia	10	7	1	2	18	5	22	0-0		3-1	2-0	2-1	3-0
3 Israel	10	5	1	4	13	11	16	0-1	1-2		2-1	1-0	3-1
4 Latvia	10	3	2	5	9	12	11	1-1	0-3	1-2		1-1	2-0
5 Georgia	10	2	4	4	7	9	10	1-2	1-0	0-0	0-1		1-0
6 Malta	10	0	1	9	4	21	1	0-1	1-3	0-2	0-2	1-1	

Greece qualified directly for the finals • Croatia qualified for a play-off v Turkey • Turkey 0-3 0-0 **Croatia**

GROUP G	PL	W	D	L	F	A	PTS	ENG	MNE	SUI	WAL	BUL
1 England	8	5	3	0	17	5	18		0-0	2-2	1-0	4-0
2 Montenegro	8	3	3	2	7	7	12	2-2		1-0	1-0	1-1
3 Switzerland	8	3	2	3	12	10	11	1-3	2-0		4-1	3-1
4 Wales	8	3	0	5	6	10	9	0-2	2-1	2-0		0-1
5 Bulgaria	8	1	2	5	3	13	5	0-3	0-1	0-0	0-1	

England qualified directly for the finals • Montenegro qualified for a play-off v Czech Republic
Czech Republic 2-0 1-0 Montenegro

GROUP H	PL	W	D	L	F	A	PTS	DEN	POR	NOR	ISL	CYP
1 Denmark	8	6	1	1	15	6	19		2-1	2-0	1-0	2-0
2 Portugal	8	5	1	2	21	12	16	3-1		1-0	5-3	4-4
3 Norway	8	5	1	2	10	7	16	1-1	1-0		1-0	3-1
4 Iceland	8	1	1	6	6	14	4	0-2	1-3	1-2		1-0
5 Cyprus	8	0	2	6	7	20	2	1-4	0-4	1-2	0-0	

Denmark qualified directly for the finals • Portugal qualified for a play-off v Bosnia • Bosnia 0-2 2-6 **Portugal**

GROUP I	PL	W	D	L	F	A	PTS	ESP	CZE	SCO	LTU	LIE
1 Spain	8	8	0	0	26	6	24		2-1	3-1	3-1	6-0
2 Czech Republic	8	4	1	3	12	8	13	0-2		1-0	0-1	2-0
3 Scotland	8	3	2	3	9	10	11	2-3	2-2		1-0	2-1
4 Lithuania	8	1	2	5	4	13	5	1-3	1-4	0-0		0-0
5 Liechtenstein	8	1	1	6	3	17	4	0-4	0-2	0-1	2-0	

Spain qualified directly for the finals • Czech Republic qualified for a play-off v Montenegro
Czech Republic 2-0 1-0 Montenegro

UEFA EURO 2012 POLAND/UKRAINE GROUP STAGE

GROUP A

Friday	8-06-2012	18:00	Poland	v	Greece	National Stadium	Warsaw
Friday	8-06-2012	20:45	Russia	v	Czech Republic	Municipal Stadium	Wroclaw
Tuesday	12-06-2012	18:00	Greece	v	Czech Republic	Municipal Stadium	Wroclaw
Tuesday	12-06-2012	20:45	Poland	v	Russia	National Stadium	Warsaw
Saturday	16-06-2012	20:45	Czech Republic	v	Poland	Municipal Stadium	Wroclaw
Saturday	16-06-2012	20:45	Greece	v	Russia	National Stadium	Warsaw

GROUP B

Saturday	9-06-2012	19:00	Netherlands	v	Denmark	Metalist Stadium	Karkiv
Saturday	9-06-2012	21:45	Germany	v	Portugal	Arena Lviv	Lviv
Wednesday	13-06-2012	19:00	Denmark	v	Portugal	Arena Lviv	Lviv
Wednesday	13-06-2012	21:45	Netherlands	v	Germany	Metalist Stadium	Karkiv
Sunday	17-06-2012	21:45	Portugal	v	Netherlands	Metalist Stadium	Karkiv
Sunday	17-06-2012	21:45	Denmark	v	Germany	Arena Lviv	Lviv

GROUP C

Sunday	10-06-2012	18:00	Spain	v	Italy	PGE Arena	Gdansk
Sunday	10-06-2012	20:45	Republic of Ireland	v	Croatia	Municipal Stadium	Poznan
Thursday	14-06-2012	18:00	Italy	v	Croatia	Municipal Stadium	Poznan
Thursday	14-06-2012	20:45	Spain	v	Republic of Ireland	PGE Arena	Gdansk
Monday	18-06-2012	20:45	Croatia	v	Spain	PGE Arena	Gdansk
Monday	18-06-2012	20:45	Italy	v	Republic of Ireland	Municipal Stadium	Poznan

GROUP D

Monday	11-06-2012	19:00	France	v	England	Donbass Arena	Donetsk
Monday	11-06-2012	21:45	Ukraine	v	Sweden	Olympic Stadium	Kyiv
Friday	15-06-2012	19:00	Ukraine	v	France	Donbass Arena	Donetsk
Friday	15-06-2012	21:45	Sweden	v	England	Olympic Stadium	Kyiv
Tuesday	19-06-2012	21:45	England	v	Ukraine	Donbass Arena	Donetsk
Tuesday	19-06-2012	21:45	Sweden	v	France	Olympic Stadium	Kyiv

UEFA EURO 2012 POLAND/UKRAINE KNOCKOUT ROUNDS

First round groups

Group A
Poland	A1
Greece	A2
Russia	
Czech Republic	

Group B
Netherlands	B1
Denmark	B2
Germany	
Portugal	

Group C
Spain	C1
Italy	C2
Republic of Ireland	
Croatia	

Group D
Ukraine	D1
Sweden	D2
France	
England	

Quarter-finals

Thursday 21st June, 20:45
National Stadium, Warsaw

Match Number

| A1 | |
| B2 | 1 |

Saturday 23rd June, 21:45
Donbass Arena, Donetsk

| C1 | |
| D2 | 3 |

Friday 22nd June, 20:45
PGE Arena, Gdansk

| B1 | |
| A2 | 2 |

Sunday 24th June, 21:45
Olympic Stadium, Kyiv

| D1 | |
| C2 | 4 |

Semi-finals

Wed'day 27th June, 21:45
Donbass Arena, Donetsk

Match Number

| 1 | |
| 3 | I |

Thursday 28th June, 20:45
National Stadium, Warsaw

| 2 | |
| 4 | II |

Final

Sunday 1st July, 21:45
Olympic Stadium, Kyiv

| I | |
| II | |

UEFA CHAMPIONS LEAGUE 2010-11

Second Qualifying Round | Third Qualifying Round | Play-off Round | Group Stage

Third Qualifying Round
BSC Young Boys SUI 2 1
Fenerbahçe TUR 2 0

Play-off Round
BSC Young Boys SUI 3 0
Tottenham Hotspur ENG 2 4

Group A		Pts
Tottenham Hotspur	ENG	11
Internazionale	ITA	10
FC Twente Enschede	NED	6
Werder Bremen	GER	6

Play-off Round
Werder Bremen GER 3 2
Sampdoria ITA 1 3

Second Qualifying Round
Omonia Nicosia	CYP	3	2
Renova Cepciste	MKD	0	0
RB Austria Salzburg	AUT	5	0
HB Tórshavn	FRO	0	1
FK Aktobe	KAZ	2	1
Olimpi Rustavi	GEO	0	1
Hapoel Tel Aviv	ISR	5	1
Zeljeznicar Sarajevo	BIH	0	0
AIK Stockholm	SWE	1	0
Jeunesse d'Esch	LUX	0	0
Linfield	NIR	0	0
Rosenborg BK	NOR	0	2
BATE Borisov	BLR	5	1
FH Hafnarfjördur	ISL	1	0

Third Qualifying Round
Omonia Nicosia CYP 1 0
RB Austria Salzburg AUT 1 1

FK Aktobe KAZ 1 1
Hapoel Tel Aviv ISR 0 3

AIK Stockholm SWE 0 0
Rosenborg BK NOR 1 3

BATE Borisov BLR 0 2
FC København DEN 0 3

Play-off Round
RB Austria Salzburg AUT 2 1
Hapoel Tel Aviv ISR 3 1

Rosenborg BK NOR 2 0
FC København DEN 1 1

Group B		Pts
Schalke 04	GER	13
Olympique Lyonnais	FRA	10
Benfica	POR	6
Hapoel Tel Aviv	ISR	5

Group C		Pts
Manchester United	ENG	14
Valencia	ESP	11
Rangers	SCO	6
Bursaspor	TUR	1

Second Qualifying Round
Levadia Tallinn	EST	1	2
Debreceni VSC	HUN	1	3
Sheriff Tiraspol	MDA	3	0
Dinamo Tiranë	ALB	1	1
Dinamo Zagreb	CRO	5	0
FC Koper	SVN	1	3
Liepajas Metalurgs	LVA	0	0
Sparta Praha	CZE	3	2
Inter Baku	AZE	0 1 9p	
Lech Poznan	POL	1 0 9p	
Litex Lovech	BUL	1	4
Rudar Pljevlja	MNE	0	0
Birkirkara	MLT	1	0
MSK Zilina	SVK	0	3

Third Qualifying Round
Debreceni VSC HUN 0 1
FC Basel SUI 2 3

Sheriff Tiraspol MDA 1 1 6p
Dinamo Zagreb CRO 1 1 5p

Sparta Praha CZE 1 1
Lech Poznan POL 0 0

Litex Lovech BUL 1 1
MSK Zilina SVK 1 3

Play-off Round
FC Basel SUI 1 3
Sheriff Tiraspol MDA 0 0

Sparta Praha CZE 0 0
MSK Zilina SVK 2 1

Group D		Pts
Barcelona	ESP	14
FC København	DEN	10
Rubin Kazan	RUS	6
Panathinaikos	GRE	2

Group E		Pts
Bayern München	GER	15
Roma	ITA	10
FC Basel	SUI	6
CFR Cluj-Napoca	ROU	4

Third Qualifying Round
Dynamo Kyiv UKR 3 3
KAA Gent BEL 0 1

Ajax NED 1 3
POAK Thessaloniki GRE 1 3

Play-off Round
Dynamo Kyiv UKR 1 1
Ajax NED 1 2

Group F		Pts
Chelsea	ENG	15
Olympique Marseille	FRA	12
Spartak Moskva	RUS	9
MSK Zilina	SVK	0

Third Qualifying Round
Unirea Urziceni ROU 0 0
Zenit St Petersburg RUS 0 1

Play-off Round
Zenit St Petersburg RUS 1 0
AJ Auxerre FRA 0 2

Group G		Pts
Real Madrid	ESP	16
Milan	ITA	8
Ajax	NED	7
AJ Auxerre	FRA	3

Third Qualifying Round
Sporting Braga POR 3 1
Celtic SCO 0 2

Play-off Round
Sporting Braga POR 1 4
Sevilla ESP 0 3

Group H		Pts
Shakhtar Donetsk	UKR	15
Arsenal	ENG	12
Sporting Braga	POR	9
Partizan Beograd	SRB	0

Second Qualifying Round
Partizan Beograd	SRB	3	1
Pyunik Yerevan	ARM	1	0
Ekranas Panevezys	LTU	1	0
HJK Helsinki	FIN	0	2
Bohemians	IRL	1	0
TNS Llansantffraid	WAL	0	4

Third Qualifying Round
Partizan Beograd SRB 3 2
HJK Helsinki FIN 0 1

TNS Llansantffraid WAL 1 0
RSC Anderlecht BEL 3 3

Play-off Round
Partizan Beograd SRB 2 2 3p
RSC Anderlecht BEL 2 2 2p

The home team in the first leg
of pre-group stage matches
is list above their opponents

First qualifying round: Santa Coloma AND 0-3 3-4 **Birkirkara** MLT • Tre Fiori SMR 0-3 1-4 **Rudar Pljevlja** MNE

CLUB TOURNAMENTS IN EUROPE 2010–11

UEFA CHAMPIONS LEAGUE 2010–11

Round of 16			Quarter-finals			Semi-finals			Final		
Barcelona	1	3									
Arsenal *	2	1									
			Barcelona *	5	1						
			Shakhtar Donetsk	1	0						
Roma *	2	0									
Shakhtar Donetsk	3	3									
						Barcelona	2	1			
						Real Madrid *	0	1			
Tottenham Hotspur	1	0									
Milan *	0	0									
			Tottenham Hotspur	0	0						
			Real Madrid *	4	1						
Olymp. Lyonnais *	1	0									
Real Madrid	1	3									
									Barcelona		3
									Manchester United		1
Schalke 04	1	3									
Valencia *	1	1									
			Schalke 04	5	2						
			Internazionale *	2	1						
Bayern München	1	2									
Internazionale *	0	3									
						Schalke 04 *	0	1			
						Manchester United	2	4			
Chelsea	2	0									
FC Kobenhavn *	0	0									
			Chelsea *	0	1						
			Manchester United	1	2						
Olymp. Marseille *	0	1									
Manchester United	0	2									

* Home team in the first leg

Top scorers: **12** - Lionel Messi ARG, Barcelona • **8** - Mario Gomez GER, Bayern München & Samuel Eto'o CMR, Internazionale • **7** - Nicolas Anelka FRA, Chelsea • **6** - Karim Benzema FRA, Real Madrid; Roberto Soldado ESP, Valencia & Cristiano Ronaldo POR, Real Madrid • **5** - Pedro Rodriguez ESP, Barcelona & Raul Gonzalez ESP, Schalke • **4** - Eduardo CRO, Shakhtar Donetsk; Marco Borriello ITA, Roma; Javier Hernandez MEX, Manchester United; Peter Crouch ENG, Tottenham; Zlatan Ibrahimovic SWE, Milan; Gareth Bale WAL, Tottenham; Luiz Adriano BRA, Shakhtar Donetsk; Wayne Rooney ENG, Manchester United; Jefferson Farfan PER, Schalke & David Villa ESP, Barcelona

See **Oliver's Almanack of World Football 2011** for details of matches played in the preliminary rounds and group stage

Europa League Qualifiers
Play-off round losers qualify for the Europa League group stage. Losers in the third qualifying round qualify for the play-off round while the third placed teams in the group stage qualify for the first knockout round

ROUND OF SIXTEEN

Emirates Stadium, London
16-02-2011, 19:45, 59 927, Rizzoli ITA

Arsenal 2
Van Persie [78], Arshavin [83]

Wojciech Szczesny - Emmanuel Eboue, Johan Djourou, Laurent Koscielny, Gael Clichy - Theo Walcott (Nicklas Bendtner 77), Alexandre Song• (Andrey Arshavin 68), Jack Wilshere, Samir Nasri• - Cesc Fabregas - Robin van Persie•. Tr: Arsene Wenger

Barcelona 1
Villa [26]

Victor Valdes - Dani Alves, Gerard Pique•, Eric Abidal, Maxwell - Sergio Busquets - Xavi, Andres Iniesta• (Adriano 89) - Pedro, Lionel Messi, David Villa (Seydou Keita 68). Tr: Josep Guardiola

Camp Nou, Barcelona
8-03-2011, 20:45, 95 486, Busacca SUI

Barcelona 3
Messi 2 [45 71p], Xavi [69]

Victor Valdes - Dani Alves, Sergio Busquets, Eric Abidal, Adriano (Maxwell 91+) - Javier Mascherano (Seydou Keita 88) - Xavi, Andres Iniesta - Pedro, Lionel Messi, David Villa (Ibrahim Afellay 82). Tr: Josep Guardiola

Arsenal 1
OG [53]

Wojciech Szczesny (Manuel Almunia 19) - Bacary Sagna•, Johan Djourou, Laurent Koscielny•, Gael Clichy - Abou Diaby, Jack Wilshere• - Tomas Rosicky (Andrey Arshavin 74), Cesc Fabregas (Nicklas Bendtner 78), Samir Nasri - Robin van Persie••♦56. Tr: Arsene Wenger

Olimpico, Rome
16-02-2011, 20:45, 35 873, Benquerenca POR

Roma 2
OG [28], Menez [61]

Doni - Marco Cassetti•, Nicolas Burdisso, Philippe Mexes, John Arne Riise (Paolo Castellini 46) - Taddei, Daniele De Rossi, Simone Perrotta• - Jeremy Menez•, Francesco Totti, Mirko Vucinic (Marco Borriello 68). Tr: Claudio Ranieri

Shakhtar Donetsk 3
Jadson [29], Douglas Costa [36], Luiz Adriano [41]

Andriy Pyatov• - Darijo Srna, Dmitro Chigrinskiy•, Yaroslav Rakitskiy•, Razvan Rat - Henrikh Mkhitaryan (Vitaliy Vitsenets 78), Tomas Hubschman - Douglas Costa (Eduardo 66), Jadson (Alex Teixeira 85), Willian - Luiz Adriano•. Tr: Mircea Lucescu

Donbass Arena, Donetsk
8-03-2011, 21:45, 46 543, Webb ENG

Shakhtar Donetsk 3
Willian 2 [18 48], Eduardo [87]

Andriy Pyatov - Darijo Srna•, Dmitro Chigrinskiy, Yaroslav Rakitskiy, Razvan Rat - Henrikh Mkhitaryan• (Alex Teixeira 67), Tomas Hubschman - Douglas Costa (Eduardo 59), Jadson, Willian - Luiz Adriano (Marcelo Moreno 75). Tr: Mircea Lucescu

Roma 0

Doni - Nicolas Burdisso, Philippe Mexes••♦41, Juan, John Arne Riise• - David Pizarro•, Daniele De Rossi - Taddei (Aleandro Rosi 46), Simone Perrotta• (Gianluca Caprari 85), Mirko Vucinic (Matteo Brighi 66) - Marco Borriello. Tr: Vicenzo Montella

San Siro, Milan
15-02-2011, 20:45, 75 652, Lannoy FRA

Milan 0

Christian Abbiati (Marco Amelia 18) - Ignazio Abate, Alessandro Nesta, Mario Yepes•, Luca Antonini - Gennaro Gattuso•, Thiago Silva, Mathieu Flamini• - Clarence Seedorf (Alexandre Pato 46) - Robinho, Zlatan Ibrahimovic. Tr: Massimiliano Allegri

Tottenham Hotspur 1
Crouch [80]

Heurelho Gomes - Vedran Corluka (Jonathan Woodgate 59), William Gallas, Michael Dawson, Benoit Assou-Ekotto - Aaron Lennon, Wilson Palacios, Sandro, Steve Pienaar (Niko Kranjcar 77) - Rafael van der Vaart (Luka Modric 62) - Peter Crouch. Tr: Harry Redknapp

White Hart Lane, London
9-03-2011, 19:45, 34 320, De Bleeckere BEL

Tottenham Hotspur 0

Heurelho Gomes - Vedran Corluka, William Gallas, Michael Dawson, Benoit Assou-Ekotto - Aaron Lennon, Sandro, Luka Modric, Steve Pienaar (Jermaine Jenas 71) - Rafael van der Vaart (Gareth Bale 66) - Peter Crouch (Roman Pavlyuchenko 66). Tr: Harry Redknapp

Milan 0

Christian Abbiati - Ignazio Abate, Alessandro Nesta, Thiago Silva, Marek Jankulovski• (Luca Antonini 70) - Mathieu Flamini• (Rodney Strasser 87), Clarence Seedorf, Kevin Prince Boateng (Alexander Merkel 76) - Zlatan Ibrahimovic, Robinho, Alexandre Pato•. Tr: Massimiliano Allegri

Stade de Gerland, Lyon
22-02-2011, 20:45, 40 299, Stark GER

Olympique Lyonnais 1
Gomis [83]

Hugo Lloris - Anthony Reveillere, Cris•, Dejan Lovren, Aly Cissokho - Jeremy Toulalan, Kim Kallstrom (Miralem Pjanic 77) - Cesar Delgado (Jeremy Pied• 70), Yoann Gourcuff, Michel Bastos• (Jimmy Briand 70) - Bafetimbi Gomis. Tr: Claude Puel

Real Madrid 1
Benzema [65]

Iker Casillas• - Sergio Ramos•, Pepe, Ricardo Carvalho, Alvaro Arbeloa - Sami Khedira (Lassana Diarra 68), Xabi Alonso - Angel Di Maria•, Mesut Ozil (Marcelo 75), Cristiano Ronaldo - Emmanuel Adebayor (Karim Benzema 65). Tr: Jose Mourinho

Bernabeu, Madrid
16-03-2011, 20:45, 70 034, Skomina SVN

Real Madrid 3
Marcelo [37], Benzema [66], Di Maria [76]

Iker Casillas - Sergio Ramos, Pepe•, Ricardo Carvalho•, Marcelo - Sami Khedira, Xabi Alonso - Angel Di Maria (Esteban Granero 78), Mesut Ozil, Cristiano Ronaldo (Emmanuel Adebayor 74) - Karim Benzema (Lassana Diarra 84). Tr: Jose Mourinho

Olympique Lyonnais 0

Hugo Lloris - Anthony Reveillere, Cris, Dejan Lovren, Aly Cissokho• - Jeremy Toulalan - Yoann Gourcuff• (Jeremy Pied 69), Kim Kallstrom - Jimmy Briand (Bafetimbi Gomis 46), Lisandro Lopez, Cesar Delgado (Miralem Pjanic 80). Tr: Claude Puel

Mestalla, Valencia
15-02-2011, 20:45, 42 703, Nikolaev RUS

Valencia 1
Soldado [17]

Guaita - Miguel, David Navarro, Ricardo Costa•, Jeremy Mathieu (Jordi Alba 78) - Ever Banega (Vicente 68), Mehmet Topal, Tino Costa - Alejandro Dominguez (Joaquin 68), Roberto Soldado, Artiz Aduriz. Tr: Unai Emery

Schalke 04 1
Raul [64]

Manuel Neuer• - Atsuto Uchida, Benedikt Howedes, Christoph Metzelder, Lukas Schmitz••♦90 - Jefferson Farfan (Julian Draxler 78), Peer Kluge, Joel Matip•, Jurado• (Edu 83) - Raul, Klaas-Jan Huntelaar (Hao Junmin 90). Tr: Felix Magath

Veltins-Arena, Gelsenkirchen
9-03-2011, 20:45, 53 517, Eriksson SWE

Schalke 04 3
Farfan 2 [40 94+], Gavranovic [52]

Manuel Neuer - Atsuto Uchida, Benedikt Howedes, Christoph Metzelder, Sergio Escudero• - Jefferson Farfan•, Peer Kluge• (Hans Sarpei 81), Joel Matip (Kyriakos Papadopoulos 60), Jurado (Julian Draxler 78) - Raul, Mario Gavranovic. Tr: Felix Magath

Valencia 1
Ricardo Costa [17]

Guaita - Bruno, David Navarro, Ricardo Costa•, Jeremy Mathieu - Ever Banega (Tino Costa 70), Mehmet Topal - Joaquin, Pablo Hernandez (Roberto Soldado 64), Juan Mata - Roberto Soldado, Artiz Aduriz (Jonas 75). Tr: Unai Emery

San Siro, Milan
23-02-2011, 20:45, 75 925, Kassai HUN

Internazionale 0

Julio Cesar - Maicon, Andrea Ranocchia (Houssine Kharja 73), Lucio, Cristian Chivu - Javier Zanetti•, Esteban Cambiasso, Thiago Motta• - Wesley Sneijder•, Dejan Stankovic - Samuel Eto'o. Tr: Leonardo

Bayern München 1
Gomez [90]

Thomas Kraft - Philipp Lahm, Anatoliy Tymoshchuk, Holger Badstuber, Danijel Pranji (Breno 38) - Bastian Schweinsteiger, Luiz Gustavo•- Arjen Robben, Thomas Muller, Franck Ribery•- Mario Gomez. Tr: Louis van Gaal

Allianz Arena, Munich
15-03-2011, 20:45, 66 000, Proenca POR

Bayern München 2
Gomez [21], Muller [31]

Thomas Kraft - Philipp Lahm, Daniel Van Buyten, (Holger Badstuber 70), Breno• (Toni Kroos 90), Danijel Pranji - Bastian Schweinsteiger, Luiz Gustavo• - Arjen Robben (Hamit Altintop 68), Thomas Muller, Franck Ribery - Mario Gomez. Tr: Louis van Gaal

Internazionale 3
Eto'o [4], Sneijder [63], Pandev [88]

Julio Cesar - Maicon, Andrea Ranocchia, Lucio•, Cristian Chivu (Yuto Nagatomo 87) - Esteban Cambiasso, Thiago Motta•- Goran Pandev• (Houssine Kharja• 90), Dejan Stankovic (Philippe Coutinho 51), Wesley Sneijder - Samuel Eto'o. Tr: Leonardo

---

Parken, Copenhagen
22-02-2011, 20:45, 36 713, Kuipers NED

FC København	0

Johan **Wiland** - Zdenek **Pospech•**, Mathias **Jorgensen•**, Mikael **Antonsson**, Oscar **Wendt** (Pierre **Bengtsson** 75) - Christian **Bolanos**, **Claudemir**, William **Kvist**, Jesper **Gronkjær** (Kenneth **Zohore** 87) - Dame **N'Doye**, Cesar **Santin** (Martin **Vingaard** 46). Tr: Stale **Solbakken**

Chelsea	2
	Anelka 2 [17 54]

Petr **Cech** - Jose **Bosingwa**, Branislav **Ivanovic**, John **Terry•**, Ashley **Cole** - **Ramires**, Michael **Essien**, Frank **Lampard**, Florent **Malouda•** (Yuriy **Zhirkov** 85) - Fernando **Torres•** (Salomon **Kalou** 92+), Nicolas **Anelka** (Didier **Drogba** 73). Tr: Carlo **Ancelotti**

Stamford Bridge, London
16-03-2011, 19:45, 36 454, Moen NOR

Chelsea	0

Petr **Cech** - Jose **Bosingwa**, Branislav **Ivanovic**, John **Terry**, Ashley **Cole** - **Ramires**, John **Mikel** (Michael **Essien** 84), Frank **Lampard**, Yuriy **Zhirkov** (Florent **Malouda** 75) - Nicolas **Anelka** (Fernando **Torres** 68), Didier **Drogba•**. Tr: Carlo **Ancelotti**

FC København	0

Johan **Wiland** - Oscar **Wendt**, Mathias **Jorgensen**, Mikael **Antonsson**, Pierre **Bengtsson** (Kenneth **Zohore** 61) - Christian **Bolanos•** (Thomas **Kristensen** 90), **Claudemir•**, William **Kvist**, Martin **Vingaard** (Cesar **Santin** 74) - Jesper **Gronkjær** - Dame **N'Doye**. Tr: Stale **Solbakken**

Velodrome, Marseille
23-02-2011, 20:45, 57 957, Brych GER

Olympique Marseille	0

Steve **Mandanda** - Rod **Fanni**, Stephane **Mbia**, Souleymane **Diawara**, Gabriel **Heinze** - Edouard **Cisse** (Benoit **Cheyrou** 70), Charles **Kabore** - Loic **Remy** (Matthieu **Valbuena** 79), Lucho **Gonzalez**, Andre **Ayew** - **Brandao**.Tr: Didier **Deschamps**

Manchester United	0

Edwin **van der Sar** - John **O'Shea**, Chris **Smalling**, Nemanja **Vidic**, Patrice **Evra** - Darren **Fletcher**, Michael **Carrick**, Darron **Gibson•** (Paul **Scholes** 73) - **Nani**, Dimitar **Berbatov**, Wayne **Rooney**. Tr: Alex **Ferguson**

Old Trafford, Manchester
15-03-2011, 19:45, 73 996, Velasco ESP

Manchester United	2
	Hernandez 2 [5 75]

Edwin **van der Sar** - John **O'Shea** (Rafael 36) (Fabio 70), Chris **Smalling**, Wes **Brown**, Patrice **Evra** - **Nani** (Luis **Valencia** 62), Michael **Carrick**, Paul **Scholes**, Ryan **Giggs** - Wayne **Rooney** - Javier **Hernandez•**. Tr: Alex **Ferguson**

Olympique Marseille	1
	OG [82]

Steve **Mandanda** - Rod **Fanni**, Souleymane **Diawara**, Gabriel **Heinze**, Taye **Taiwo** - Stephane **Mbia** (Jordan **Ayew** 80) - Loic **Remy•**, Lucho **Gonzalez**, Benoit **Cheyrou**, Andre **Ayew** - Andre-Pierre **Gignac** (Matthieu **Valbuena•** 69). Tr: Didier **Deschamps**

QUARTER-FINALS

Camp Nou, Barcelona
6-04-2011, 20:45, 86 518, Thomson SCO

Barcelona	5
Iniesta [2], Dani Alves [34], Pique [53], Keita [61], Xavi [86]	

Victor **Valdes** - Dani **Alves**, Gerard **Pique**, Sergio **Busquets**, **Adriano** (Maxwell 77) - Javier **Mascherano** - **Xavi**, Seydou **Keita** - David **Villa** (Pedro 70), Lionel **Messi**, Andres **Iniesta•** (Ibrahim **Afellai** 91+). Tr: Josep **Guardiola**

Shakhtar Donetsk	1
	Rakitskiy [60]

Andriy **Pyatov** - Darijo **Srna**, Mikola **Ishchenko**, Yaroslav **Rakitskiy•**, Razvan **Rat•** - Henrikh **Mkhitaryan**, Tomas **Hubschman** (Eduardo 83) - Douglas **Costa**, Jadson (Fernandinho• 70), **Willian** (Alex **Teixeira** 75) - Luiz **Adriano**. Tr: Mircea **Lucescu**

Donbass Arena, Donetsk
12-04-2011, 21:45, 51 759, Meyer GER

Shakhtar Donetsk	0

Andriy **Pyatov** - Vasiliy **Kobin**, Mikola **Ishchenko•**, Yaroslav **Rakitskiy**, Vyacheslav **Shevchuk** - Henrikh **Mkhitaryan•**, Tomas **Hubschman** (Fernandinho 75) - Douglas **Costa** (Eduardo 58), **Jadson**, **Willian** - Luiz **Adriano** (Marcelo **Moreno** 67). Tr: Mircea **Lucescu**

Barcelona	1
	Messi [43]

Victor **Valdes** - Dani **Alves**, Javier **Mascherano**, Gerard **Pique** (Gabriel **Milito•** 69), **Adriano** - Sergio **Busquets** - **Xavi** (Pedro 66), Seydou **Keita** - David **Villa** (Jeffren 75), Lionel **Messi**, Ibrahim **Afellai**. Tr: Josep **Guardiola**

Bernabeu, Madrid
5-04-2011, 20:45, 71 657, Brych GER

Real Madrid	4
Adebayor 2 [4 57], Di Maria [72], Ronaldo [87]	

Iker **Casillas** - Sergio **Ramos**, **Pepe•**, Ricardo **Carvalho**, **Marcelo** - Sami **Khedira** (Lassana **Diarra** 60), Xabi **Alonso** - Angel **Di Maria** (Kaka 77), Mesut **Ozil**, Cristiano **Ronaldo** - Emmanuel **Adebayor•** (Gonzalo **Higuain** 74). Tr: Jose **Mourinho**

Tottenham Hotspur	0

Heurelho **Gomes** - Vedran **Corluka** (Sebastian **Bassong** 79), William **Gallas**, Michael **Dawson**, Benoit **Assou-Ekotto** - Gareth **Bale**, Jermaine **Jenas**, **Sandro**, Luka **Modric** - Rafael **van der Vaart•** (Jermain **Defoe•** 46) - Peter **Crouch•• ♦16**. Tr: Harry **Redknapp**

White Hart Lane, London
13-04-2011, 19:45, 34 311, Rizzoli ITA

Tottenham Hotspur	0

Heurelho **Gomes** - Vedran **Corluka**, William **Gallas**, Michael **Dawson**, Benoit **Assou-Ekotto** - Aaron **Lennon** (Jermain **Defoe** 60), Tom **Huddlestone** (Sandro 71), Luka **Modric** (Niko **Kranjcar** 83), Gareth **Bale** - Rafael **van der Vaart** - Roman **Pavlyuchenko**. Tr: Harry **Redknapp**

Real Madrid	1
	Ronaldo [50]

Iker **Casillas** - Sergio **Ramos** (Esteban **Granero•** 56), Ricardo **Carvalho•**, Raul **Albiol**, Alvaro **Arbeloa** - Sami **Khedira**, Xabi **Alonso** (Karim **Benzema** 75) - Cristiano **Ronaldo** (Kaka 65), Mesut **Ozil**, **Marcelo** - Emmanuel **Adebayor**. Tr: Jose **Mourinho**

San Siro, Milan
5-04-2011, 20:45, 72 770, Atkinson ENG

Internazionale 2
Stankovic [1], Milito [34]

Julio Cesar - Maicon, Andrea Ranocchia, Cristian Chivu•♦62, Javier Zanetti - Dejan Stankovic• (Houssine Kharja 24) (Ivan Cordoba 63), Thiago Motta (Yuto Nagatomo 76), Esteban Cambiasso - Wesley Sneijder - Samuel Eto'o, Diego Milito. Tr: Leonardo

Schalke 04 5
Matip [17], Edu 2 [40 75], Raul [53], OG [57]

Manuel Neuer - Atsuto Uchida, Benedikt Howedes, Joel Matip, Hans Sarpei• - Jefferson Farfan•, Kyriakos Papadopoulos•, Jurado (Julian Draxler 83), Alexander Baumjohann (Lukas Schmitz 76) - Raul• (Ali Karimi 87), Edu. Tr: Ralf Rangnick

---

Veltins-Arena, Gelsenkirchen
13-04-2011, 20:45, 54 142, Skomina SVN

Schalke 04 2
Raul [45], Howedes [81]

Manuel Neuer - Atsuto Uchida, Christoph Metzelder, Benedikt Howedes, Hans Sarpei - Alexander Baumjohann (Julian Draxler 73), Joel Matip, Kyriakos Papadopoulos•, Jurado (Lukas Schmitz• 86) - Raul•, Edu (Angelos Charisteas 77). Tr: Ralf Rangnick

Internazionale 1
Motta [49]

Julio Cesar - Maicon, Lucio•, Andrea Ranocchia•, Yuto Nagatomo - Javier Zanetti, Thiago Motta•, Dejan Stankovic• (Goran Pandev 46) - Wesley Sneijder (Coutinho 80) - Samuel Eto'o, Diego Milito. Tr: Leonardo

---

Stamford Bridge, London
6-04-2011, 19:45, 37 915, Undiano ESP

Chelsea 0

Petr Cech - Jose Bosingwa (John Mikel 78), Branislav Ivanovic, John Terry, Ashley Cole - Ramires•, Michael Essien•, Frank Lampard, Yuriy Zhirkov• (Florent Malouda 70) - Didier Drogba (Nicolas Anelka 70), Fernando Torres•. Tr: Carlo Ancelotti

Manchester United 1
Rooney [24]

Edwin van der Sar• - Rafael (Nani 51), Rio Ferdinand, Nemanja Vidic•, Patrice Evra - Luis Valencia, Michael Carrick, Ryan Giggs, Park Ji Sung (Chris Smalling 94+) - Wayne Rooney - Javier Hernandez (Dimitar Berbatov 78). Tr: Alex Ferguson

---

Old Trafford, Manchester
12-04-2011, 19:45, 74 672, Benquerenca POR

Manchester United 2
Hernandez [43], Park Ji Sung [77]

Edwin van der Sar - John O'Shea•, Rio Ferdinand, Nemanja Vidic, Patrice Evra• - Park Ji Sung, Michael Carrick, Ryan Giggs, Nani (Luis Valencia 75) - Wayne Rooney - Javier Hernandez. Tr: Alex Ferguson

Chelsea 1
Drogba [76]

Petr Cech - Branislav Ivanovic, Alex (Paulo Ferreira 82), John Terry•, Ashley Cole - Ramires•♦♦70, Michael Essien•, Frank Lampard - Nicolas Anelka (Salomon Kalou 61), Florent Malouda• - Fernando Torres (Didier Drogba 46). Tr: Carlo Ancelotti

---

SEMI-FINALS

Bernabeu, Madrid
27-04-2011, 20:45, 71 657, Stark GER

Real Madrid 0

Iker Casillas - Alvaro Arbeloa•, Sergio Ramos•, Raul Albiol, Marcelo - Xabi Alonso - Mesut Ozil (Emmanuel Adebayor• 46), Lassana Diarra, Pepe♦61, Angel Di Maria - Cristiano Ronaldo. Tr: Jose Mourinho

Barcelona 2
Messi 2 [76 87]

Victor Valdes - Dani Alves•, Javier Mascherano•, Gerard Pique, Carles Puyol - Sergio Busquets - Xavi, Seydou Keita - David Villa (Sergi Roberto 90), Lionel Messi, Pedro (Ibrahim Afellay 71). Tr: Josep Guardiola

---

Camp Nou, Barcelona
3-05-2011, 20:45, 95 701, De Bleeckere BEL

Barcelona 1
Pedro [54]

Victor Valdes - Dani Alves, Javier Mascherano, Gerard Pique, Carles Puyol (Eric Abidal 90) - Sergio Busquets - Xavi, Andres Iniesta - Pedro• (Ibrahim Afellay 90), Lionel Messi, David Villa (Seydou Keita 74). Tr: Josep Guardiola

Real Madrid 1
Marcelo [64]

Iker Casillas - Alvaro Arbeloa•, Raul Albiol, Ricardo Carvalho•, Marcelo• - Lassana Diarra•, Xabi Alonso• - Angel Di Maria, Kaka (Mesut Ozil 60), Cristiano Ronaldo - Gonzalo Higuain (Emmanuel Adebayor• 55). Tr: Jose Mourinho

---

Veltins-Arena, Gelsenkirchen
26-04-2011, 20:45, 54 142, Velasco ESP

Schalke 04 0

Manuel Neuer - Atsuto Uchida, Joel Matip, Christoph Metzelder•, Hans Sarpei• (Sergio Escudero 73) - Jefferson Farfan, Kyriakos Papadopoulos, Jurado (Julian Draxler 83), Alexander Baumjohann (Peer Kluge 53) - Raul, Edu. Tr: Ralf Rangnick

Manchester United 2
Giggs [67], Rooney [69]

Edwin van der Sar - Fabio•, Rio Ferdinand, Nemanja Vidic, Patrice Evra - Luis Valencia, Michael Carrick, Ryan Giggs, Park Ji Sung (Paul Scholes 73) - Wayne Rooney (Nani 83) - Javier Hernandez (Anderson 73). Tr: Alex Ferguson

---

Old Trafford, Manchester
4-05-2011, 19:45, 74 687, Proenca POR

Manchester United 4
Valencia [26], Gibson [31], Anderson 2 [72 76]

Edwin van der Sar - Rafael (Patrice Evra 60), Chris Smalling, Jonny Evans, John O'Shea - Darron Gibson•, Paul Scholes• (Darren Fletcher 73), Anderson• - Luis Valencia, Dimitar Berbatov (Michael Owen 77), Nani. Tr: Alex Ferguson

Schalke 04 1
Jurado [35]

Manuel Neuer - Atsuto Uchida, Benedikt Howedes (Klass-Jan Huntelaar 70), Christoph Metzelder, Sergio Escudero• - Kyriakos Papadopoulos, Jurado - Jefferson Farfan (Joel Matip 75), Alexander Baumjohann (Edu 46), Julian Draxler - Raul. Tr: Ralf Rangnick

UEFA Champions League Final	Wembley Stadium London	Saturday 28-05-2011
Kick-off: 19:45		Attendance: 87 695

BARCELONA 3 1 MANCHESTER UTD

Pedro Rodriguez [27], Lionel Messi [54], David Villa [69]   Wayne Rooney [34]

BARCELONA

Red and blue striped shirts, red shorts, Blue socks

Tr: Josep Guardiola

MATCH STATS

Barcelona		Man Utd
19	Shots	4
12	Shots on goal	1
5	Fouls committed	16
6	Corner kicks	0
1	Caught offside	5
63%	Possession	37%

Victor Valdes [85]

Dani Alves [60]
[88] Carles Puyol   Javier Mascherano   Gerard Pique   Eric Abidal

Sergio Busquets

Xavi Hernandez(c)   Andres Iniesta

Lionel Messi†

[86] David Villa   Pedro Rodriguez [92+]
Seydou Keita   Ibrahim Afellay

MATCH OFFICIALS

REFEREE
Viktor Kassai HUN

ASSISTANTS
Gabor Eros HUN
Gyorgy Ring HUN

4TH OFFICIAL
Istvan Vad HUN

(C)Captain †Man of the Match

Javier Hernandez

Wayne Rooney

Park Ji Sung   Ryan Giggs   Michael Carrick [61]   Antonio Valencia [79]
[77] Paul Scholes

Patrice Evra   Nemanja Vidic(c)   Rio Ferdinand   [69] Fabio / Nani

Edwin vander Sar

Tr: Sir Alex Ferguson

White shirts, Black shorts, White socks

MANCHESTER UNITED

I feel very privileged to have these players. In 10 or 15 years' time I would like people to remember this team and remember having enjoyed our football. Messi is one of the best players I've ever seen - probably the best. He is unique, a one-off, so I hope he will continue being at his ease in Barcelona and enjoy having the right players around him. When he doesn't play well it's because there's something wrong with what's going on around him.

Pep Guardiola

We knew we were up against a good team before the game and we planned as best as we could. They do mesmerise you with their passing and we never really controlled Messi - but many people have said that. I think when we got the lifeline of Wayne Rooney's goal, I expected us to do better in the second half but it wasn't to be. It's alien to us to man mark players so we tried to play our normal way. It wasn't good enough on the night and we acknowledge that.

Alex Ferguson

UEFA EUROPA LEAGUE 2010-11
EARLY ROUNDS FOR TEAMS IN GROUPS A TO C

First Qualifying Round

Team		L1	L2
Trans Narva	EST	0	0
MyPa-47	FIN	2	5
NSI Runavik	FRO	0	1
Gefle IF	SWE	2	2
Dinamo Tbilisi	GEO	2	0
Flora Tallinn	EST	1	0
Ulysses Yerevan	ARM	0	0
Bnei Yehuda	ISR	0	1
Shakhter Karagandy	KAZ	1	0
Ruch Chorzow	POL	2	1
Olimpia Ljubljana	SVN	0	0
Siroki Brijeg	BIH	2	3
Kalmar FF	SWE	1	3
EB/Streymur	FRO	0	0
Zeta Golubovci	MNE	1	0
Dacia Chisinau	MDA	1	0
CS Grevenmacher	LUX	3	1
Dundalk	IRL	3	2

Second Qualifying Round

Team		L1	L2
MyPa-47	FIN	3	5
Sant Julia	AND	0	0
Differdange	LUX	3	0
Spartak Subotica	SRB	3	2
Gefle IF	SWE	1	1
Dinamo Tbilisi	GEO	2	2
Shamrock Rovers	IRL	1	1
Bnei Yehuda	ISR	1	0
Valletta	MLT	1	0
Ruch Chorzow	POL	1	0
FK Austria Wien	AUT	2	1
Siroki Brijeg	BIH	2	0
FK Baku	AZE	0	2
Buducnost P'gorica	MNE	3	1
Brøndby IF	DEN	3	0
FC Vaduz	LIE	0	0
Kalmar FF	SWE	0	2
Dacia Chisinau	MDA	0	0
Levski Sofia	BUL	6	2
Dundalk	IRL	0	0

Third Qualifying Round

Team		L1	L2
MyPa-47	FIN	1	3
FC Timisoara	ROU	2	3
Spartak Subotica	SRB	2	0
Dnipro D'petrovsk	UKR	1	2
SK Sturm Graz	AUT	2	1
Dinamo Tbilisi	GEO	0	1
Shamrock Rovers	IRL	0	0
Juventus	ITA	2	1
Jagiellonia B'stok	POL	1	2
Aris Thessaloniki	GRE	2	2
Ruch Chorzow	POL	1	0
FK Austria Wien	AUT	3	3
Nordsjælland	DEN	0	1
Sporting CP	POR	1	2
Buducnost P'gorica	MNE	1	0
Brøndby IF	DEN	2	1
Kalmar FF	SWE	1	2
Levski Sofia	BUL	1	5

Play-off Round

Team		L1	L2
FC Timisoara	ROU	0	0
Manchester City	ENG	1	2
Dnipro D'petrovsk	UKR	0	0
Lech Poznan †	POL	1	0
SK Sturm Graz	AUT	1	0
Juventus	ITA	2	1
RB Austria Salzburg	AUT	Bye	
Bayer Leverkusen	GER	3	3
Tavriya Simferopol	UKR	0	1
Aris Thessaloniki	GRE	1	1
FK Austria Wien	AUT	0	1
Atlético Madrid	ESP	Bye	
Rosenborg BK	NOR	Bye	
Sporting CP	POR	0	3
Brøndby IF	DEN	2	0
FC Vaslui	ROU	0	0
Lille OSC	FRA	0	2
Feyenoord	NED	1	0
KAA Gent †	BEL	0	2
AIK Stockholm †	SWE	0	1
Levski Sofia	BUL	0	2

† Champions League 3rd qualifying round loser • Champions League play-off round losers qualified directly for the Europa League group stage

The home teams in the first leg are listed above their opponents

UEFA EUROPA LEAGUE 2010–11
EARLY ROUNDS FOR TEAMS IN GROUPS D TO F

First Qualifying Round			Second Qualifying Round			Third Qualifying Round			Play-off Round		
Laçi	ALB	1 1									
Dnepr Mogilev	BLR	1 7	Stabæk Fotball	NOR	2 1				Villarreal	ESP	5 2
			Dnepr Mogilev	BLR	2 1	Dnepr Mogilev	BLR	1 2	Dnepr Mogilev	BLR	0 1
			WIT Georgia	GEO	0 0	Banik Ostrava	CZE	0 1			
			Banik Ostrava	CZE	6 0						
									PAOK Thessaloniki†	GRE	1 1
									Fenerbahçe †	TUR	1 0
			FK Atyrau	KAZ	0 0						
FC Nitra	SVK	2 1	Györi ETO	HUN	3 2						
Györi ETO	HUN	2 3				Györi ETO	HUN	0 1 4p			
						Montpellier	FRA	1 0 3p	Györi ETO	HUN	0 1
									Dinamo Zagreb †	CRO	2 2
									Club Brugge	BEL	2 3
						Maccabi Haifa	ISR	1 1	Dinamo Minsk	BLR	1 2
			Dinamo Minsk	BLR	5 5	Dinamo Minsk	BLR	0 3			
			Kalev Sillamäe	EST	1 0						
									Dynamo Kyiv	UKR	Bye
			Maritimo	POR	3 3				BATE Borisov †	BLR	3 2
			Sporting Fingal	IRL	2 2	Maritimo	POR	8 2	Maritimo	POR	0 1
			Honka Espoo	FIN	1 1	Bangor City	WAL	2 1			
			Bangor City	WAL	1 2	AZ Alkmaar	NED	2 0			
									AZ Alkmaar	NED	2 1
						IFK Göteborg	SWE	0 1			
									FK Aktobe †	KAZ	0 2
									Sheriff Tiraspol	MDA	Bye
TPS Turku	FIN	3 4									
Port Talbot Town	WAL	1 0	Cercle Brugge	BEL	0 2				CSKA Moskva	RUS	4 2
Anorthosis F'gusta	CYR	3 1	TPS Turku	FIN	1 1	Cercle Brugge	BEL	1 1	Anorthosis F'gusta	CYR	0 1
Banants Yerevan	ARM	0 0	Anorthosis F'gusta	CYR	0 3	Anorthosis F'gusta	CYR	0 3			
Sibenik	CRO	0 3	Sibenik	CRO	2 0						
Sliema Wanderers	MLT	0 0							Sparta Praha	CZE	Bye
			Videoton	HUN	1 0				Città di Palermo	ITA	3 2
			NK Maribor	SVN	1 2	NK Maribor	SVN	3 3	NK Maribor	SVN	0 3
			ND Gorica	SVN	0 1	Hibernian	SCO	0 2			
Randers	DEN	6 1	Randers	DEN	3 1	Randers	DEN	2 1			
F91 Dudelange	LUX	1 2	Lausanne-Sport	SUI	1 1	Lausanne-Sport	SUI	3 1	Lausanne-Sport	SUI	1 1 4p
			Borac Banja Luka	BIH	0 1				Lokomotiv Moskva	RUS	1 1 3p

† Champions League 3rd qualifying round loser • Champions League play-off round losers qualified directly for the Europa League group stage
The home teams in the first leg are listed above their opponents

UEFA EUROPA LEAGUE 2010–11
EARLY ROUNDS FOR TEAMS IN GROUPS G TO I

First Qualifying Round	Second Qualifying Round	Third Qualifying Round	Play-off Round
			Zenit St Petersburg RUS Bye
			RSC Anderlecht BEL Bye
			Dundee United SCO 0 1
Olimpia Balti MDA 0 1			AEK Athens GRE 1 1
Khazar Lenkoran AZE 0 1	Olimpia Balti MDA 0 1		
	Dinamo Bucuresti ROU 2 5	Dinamo Bucuresti ROU 3 0	
		Hajduk Split CRO 1 3	Hajduk Split CRO 4 1
			Unirea Urziceni † ROU 1 1
		Crvena Zvezda SRB 1 1	
	Molde FK NOR 1 1	Slovan Bratislava SVK 2 1	Slovan Bratislava SVK 0 2
	FK Jelgava LVA 0 2	Molde FK NOR 2 2	VfB Stuttgart GER 1 2
		VfB Stuttgart GER 3 2	
			BSC Young Boys SUI Bye
Llanelli WAL 2 2			
Tauras Taurage LTU 2 3	Tauras Taurage LTU 0 1		Getafe ESP 1 1
	APOEL Nicosia CYP 3 3	APOEL Nicosia CYP 1 3	APOEL Nicosia CYP 0 1
		FK Jablonec CZE 0 1	
Tobol Kostanay KAZ 1 1		Odense BK DEN 5 0	
Zrinjski Mostar BIH 2 2	Zrinjski Mostar BIH 4 9	Zrinjski Mostar BIH 3 0	Odense BK DEN 2 1
	Tre Penne SMR 1 2	Aalesunds SK NOR 1 0	Motherwell SCO 1 0
	Motherwell SCO 1 1	Motherwell SCO 1 3	
	Breidablik ISL 0 0	SIBIR Novosibirsk RUS 1 1	
		Apollon Limassol CYP 0 2	SIBIR Novosibirsk RUS 1 0
			PSV Eindhoven NED 0 5
			Omonia Nicosia † CYP 0 2
			Metalist Kharkiv UKR 1 2
			Sampdoria ITA Bye
			Debreceni VSC † HUN 2 2
			Litex Lovech † BUL 0 1

† Champions League 3rd qualifying round loser • Champions League play-off round losers qualified directly for the Europa League group stage
The home teams in the first leg are listed above their opponents

UEFA EUROPA LEAGUE 2010-11
EARLY ROUNDS FOR TEAMS IN GROUPS J TO L

First Qualifying Round

UE Santa Coloma	AND	0	0
Mogren Budva	MNE	3	2
Portadown	NIR	1	1
Skonto Riga	LVA	1	0
Karabakh Agdam	AZE	4	1
Metalurg Skopje	MKD	1	1
Torpedo Zhodino	BLR	3	3
Fylkir Reykjavík	ISL	0	1
KR Reykjavík	ISL	3	2
Glentoran	NIR	0	2
FC Zestafoni	GEO	5	0
Faetano	SMR	0	0
Rabotnicki Skopje	MKD	5	6
Lusitanos	AND	0	0
KF Tirana	ALB	0	1
Zalaegerszegi TE	HUN	0	0
Besiktas	TUR	3	4
Vikingur	FRO	0	0
Suduva Marijampole	LTU	0	2
SK Rapid Wien	AUT	2	4
Cliftonville	NIR	1	0
Cibalia Vinkovci	CRO	0	0

Second Qualifying Round

Besa Kavajë	ALB	0	1
Olympiacos	GRE	5	6
Maccabi Tel Aviv	ISR	2	1
Mogren Budva	MNE	0	2
Siauliai	LTU	0	0
Wisla Krakow	POL	2	5
Portadown	NIR	1	1
Karabakh Agdam	AZE	2	1
OFK Beograd	SRB	2	1
Torpedo Zhodino	BLR	2	0
KR Reykjavík	ISL	0	2
Karpaty Lviv	UKR	3	3
FC Zestafoni	GEO	3	0
Dukla B. Bystrica	SVK	0	1
Rabotnicki Skopje	MKD	1	0
Mika Ashtarak	ARM	0	0
Elfsborg IF	SWE	2	1
Iscra-Stali Ribnita	MDA	1	0
Ventspils	LVA	0	1
Teteks	MKD	0	3
FC Utrecht	NED	4	1
KF Tirana	ALB	0	1
Besiktas	TUR	3	4
Vikingur	FRO	0	0
Suduva Marijampole	LTU	0	2
SK Rapid Wien	AUT	2	4
Cliftonville	NIR	1	0
Cibalia Vinkovci	CRO	0	0

Third Qualifying Round

Olympiacos	GRE	2	0
Maccabi Tel Aviv	ISR	1	1
Wisla Krakow	POL	0	2
Karabakh Agdam	AZE	1	3
Galatasaray	TUR	2	5
OFK Beograd	SRB	2	1
Karpaty Lviv	UKR	1	1
FC Zestafoni	GEO	0	0
Rabotnicki Skopje	MKD	0	0
Liverpool	ENG	2	2
Elfsborg IF	SWE	5	2
Teteks	MKD	0	1
FC Utrecht	NED	1	3
FC Luzern	SUI	0	1
Inter Turku	FIN	1	2
KRC Genk	BEL	5	3
Viktoria Plzen	CZE	1	0
Besiktas	TUR	1	3
Beroe S. Zagora	BUL	1	0
SK Rapid Wien	AUT	1	3
CSKA Sofia	BUL	3	2
Cliftonville	NIR	0	1

Play-off Round

Paris St-Germain	FRA	2	3
Maccabi Tel Aviv	ISR	0	4
Sevilla	ESP	Bye	
Borussia Dortmund	GER	4	1
Karabakh Agdam	AZE	0	0
Galatasaray	TUR	2	1
Karpaty Lviv	UKR	2	1
Liverpool	ENG	1	2
Trabzonspor	TUR	0	1
Napoli	ITA	1	2
Elfsborg IF	SWE	0	0
Steaua Bucuresti	ROU	1 0	4p
Grasshopper-Club	SUI	0 1	3p
Celtic †	SCO	2	0
FC Utrecht	NED	0	4
KRC Genk	BEL	0	2
FC Porto	POR	3	4
Besiktas	TUR	2	4
HJK Helsinki †	FIN	0	0
SK Rapid Wien	AUT	1	3
Aston Villa	ENG	1	2
CSKA Sofia	BUL	3	2
The New Saints †	WAL	0	2

† Champions League 3rd qualifying round loser • Champions League play-off round losers qualified directly for the Europa League group stage
The home teams in the first leg are listed above their opponents

UEFA EUROPA LEAGUE 2010–11

Group Stage

Group A

		Pl	W	D	L	F	A	Pts	ENG	POL	ITA	AUT
Manchester City	ENG	6	3	2	1	11	6	11		3-1	1-1	3-0
Lech Poznan	POL	6	3	2	1	11	8	11	3-1		1-1	2-0
Juventus	ITA	6	0	6	0	7	7	6	1-1	3-3		0-0
RB Austria Salzburg ‡	AUT	6	0	2	4	1	9	2	0-2	0-1	1-1	

Group B

		Pl	W	D	L	F	A	Pts	GER	GRE	ESP	NOR
Bayer Leverkusen	GER	6	3	3	0	8	2	12		1-0	1-1	4-0
Aris Thessaloniki	GRE	6	3	1	2	7	5	10	0-0		1-0	2-0
Atlético Madrid	ESP	6	2	2	2	9	7	8	1-1	2-3		3-0
Rosenborg BK ‡	NOR	6	1	0	5	3	13	3	0-1	2-1	1-2	

Group C

		Pl	W	D	L	F	A	Pts	POR	FRA	BEL	BUL
Sporting CP	POR	6	4	0	2	14	6	12		1-0	5-1	5-0
Lille OSC	FRA	6	2	2	2	8	6	8	1-2		3-0	1-0
KAA Gent	BEL	6	2	1	3	8	13	7	3-1	1-1		1-0
Levski Sofia	BUL	6	2	1	3	6	11	7	1-0	2-2	3-2	

Group D

		Pl	W	D	L	F	A	Pts	ESP	GRE	CRO	BEL
Villarreal	ESP	6	4	0	2	8	5	12		1-0	3-0	2-1
PAOK Thessaloniki	GRE	6	3	2	1	5	3	11	1-0		1-0	1-1
Dinamo Zagreb	CRO	6	2	1	3	4	5	7	2-0	0-1		0-0
Club Brugge	BEL	6	0	3	3	4	8	3	1-2	1-1	0-2	

Group E

		Pl	W	D	L	F	A	Pts	UKR	BLR	NED	MDA
Dynamo Kyiv ‡	UKR	6	3	2	1	10	6	11		2-2	2-0	0-0
BATE Borisov	BLR	6	3	1	2	11	11	10	1-4		4-1	3-1
AZ Alkmaar	NED	6	2	1	3	8	10	7	1-2	3-0		2-1
Sheriff Tiraspol ‡	MDA	6	1	2	3	5	7	5	2-0	0-1	1-1	

Group F

		Pl	W	D	L	F	A	Pts	RUS	CZE	ITA	SUI
CSKA Moskva	RUS	6	5	1	0	18	3	16		3-0	3-1	5-1
Sparta Praha ‡	CZE	6	2	3	1	12	12	9	1-1		3-2	3-3
Città di Palermo	ITA	6	2	1	3	7	11	7	0-3	2-2		1-0
Lausanne-Sport	SUI	6	0	1	5	5	16	1	0-3	1-3	0-1	

Group G

		Pl	W	D	L	F	A	Pts	RUS	BEL	GRE	CRO
Zenit St Petersburg ‡	RUS	6	6	0	0	18	6	18		3-1	4-2	2-0
RSC Anderlecht ‡	BEL	6	2	1	3	8	8	7	1-3		3-0	2-0
AEK Athens	GRE	6	2	1	3	9	13	7	0-3	1-1		3-1
Hajduk Split	CRO	6	1	0	5	5	13	3	2-3	1-0	1-3	

Group H

		Pl	W	D	L	F	A	Pts	GER	SUI	ESP	DEN
VfB Stuttgart	GER	6	5	0	1	16	6	15		3-0	1-0	5-1
BSC Young Boys ‡	SUI	6	3	0	3	10	10	9	4-2		2-0	4-2
Getafe	ESP	6	2	1	3	4	8	7	0-3	1-0		2-1
Odense BK	DEN	6	1	1	4	8	14	4	1-2	2-0	1-1	

Group I

		Pl	W	D	L	F	A	Pts	NED	UKR	ITA	HUN
PSV Eindhoven	NED	6	4	2	0	10	3	14		0-0	1-1	3-0
Metalist Kharkiv	UKR	6	3	2	1	9	4	11	0-2		2-1	2-1
Sampdoria ‡	ITA	6	1	2	3	4	7	5	1-2	0-0		1-0
Debreceni VSC	HUN	6	1	0	5	4	13	3	1-2	0-5	2-0	

Group J

		Pl	W	D	L	F	A	Pts	FRA	ESP	GER	UKR
Paris Saint-Germain	FRA	6	3	3	0	9	4	12		4-2	0-0	2-0
Sevilla ‡	ESP	6	3	1	2	10	7	10	0-1		2-2	4-0
Borussia Dortmund	GER	6	2	3	1	10	7	9	1-1	0-1		3-0
Karpaty Lviv	UKR	6	0	1	5	4	15	1	1-1	0-1	3-4	

Group K

		Pl	W	D	L	F	A	Pts	ENG	ITA	ROU	NED
Liverpool	ENG	6	2	4	0	8	3	10		3-1	4-1	0-0
Napoli	ITA	6	1	4	1	8	9	7	0-0		1-0	0-0
Steaua Bucuresti	ROU	6	1	3	2	9	11	6	1-1	3-3		3-1
FC Utrecht	NED	6	0	5	1	5	7	5	0-0	3-3	1-1	

Group L

		Pl	W	D	L	F	A	Pts	POR	TUR	AUT	BUL
FC Porto	POR	6	5	1	0	14	4	16		1-1	3-0	3-1
Besiktas	TUR	6	4	1	1	9	6	13	1-3		2-0	1-0
SK Rapid Wien	AUT	6	1	0	5	5	12	3	1-3	1-2		1-2
CSKA Sofia	BUL	6	1	0	5	4	10	3	0-1	1-2	0-2	

Round of 32

FC Porto	2	0
Sevilla *	1	1
PAOK Thessaloníki *	0	1
CSKA Moskva	1	1
Ajax †	3	2
RSC Anderlecht *	0	0
FC Basel * †	2	1
Spartak Moskva †	3	1
FC Twente †	2	2
Rubin Kazan * †	0	2
BSC Young Boys *	2	1
Zenit St Petersburg	1	3
Bayer Leverkusen	4	2
Metalist Kharkiv *	0	0
Napoli *	0	1
Villarreal	0	2
Benfica * †	2	2
VfB Stuttgart	1	0
BATE Borisov *	2	0
Paris Saint-Germain	2	0
Rangers * †	1	2
Sporting CP	1	2
Lille OSC *	2	1
PSV Eindhoven	2	3
Dynamo Kyiv	4	4
Besiktas *	1	0
Aris Thessaloníki *	0	0
Manchester City	0	3
Liverpool	0	1
Sparta Praha *	0	0
Lech Poznan *	1	0
Sporting Braga †	0	2

UEFA EUROPA LEAGUE 2010-11

Round of 16	Quarter-Final	Semi-Final	Final

FC Porto 1 2
CSKA Moskva * 0 1

FC Porto * 5 5
Spartak Moskva 1 2

Ajax * 0 0
Spartak Moskva 1 3

FC Porto * 5 2
Villarreal 1 3

FC Twente * 3 0
Zenit St Petersburg 0 2

FC Twente 1 1
Villarreal * 5 3

Bayer Leverkusen * 2 1
Villarreal 3 2

FC Porto 1
Sporting Braga 0

Benfica * 2 1
Paris Saint-Germain 1 1

Benfica * 4 2
PSV Eindhovem 1 2

Rangers 0 0
PSV Eindhoven * 0 1

Benfica * 2 0
Sporting Braga 1 1

Dynamo Kyiv * 2 0
Manchester City 0 1

Dynamo Kyiv * 1 0
Sporting Braga 1 0

Liverpool 0 0
Sporting Braga * 1 0

* Home team in the first leg

‡ Qualified as a Champions League play-off round loser • † Qualified
as a third placed team from the Champions League group stage

UEFA EUROPA LEAGUE FINAL 2011

Aviva Stadium, Dublin, 18 05 2011, 20:45, 45 391, Carlos Velasco ESP

FC Porto 1 Falcao [44]
Sporting Braga 0

Porto - Helton• - Cristian Sapunaru•, Rolando•, Nicolas Otamendi,
Alvaro Pereira - Fernando - Freddy Guarin (Fernando Belluschi 73), Joao
Moutinho - Hulk, Radamel Falcao, Silvestre Varela (James Rodriguez
79). Tr: Andre Villas-Boas

Braga - Artur - Alberto Rodriguez (Kaka• 46), Paulao, Miguel Garcia•,
Silvio•, Custodio, Hugo Viana• (Marcio Mossoro• 46), Vandinho, Paulo
Cesar, Lima (Albert Meyong 66), Alan. Tr: Domingos Paciencia

YOUTH TOURNAMENTS IN EUROPE 2011

UEFA EUROPEAN UNDER-17 CHAMPIONSHIP 2011

Qualifying Round Group 1

	Pl	W	D	L	F	A	Pts	CRO	ISR	BUL
Greece	3	2	1	0	5	1	7	0-0	4-1	1-0
Croatia	3	1	2	0	4	3	5		2-2	2-1
Israel	3	1	1	1	4	6	4			1-0
Bulgaria	3	0	0	3	1	4	0	Played in CRO		

Qualifying Round Group 2

	Pl	W	D	L	F	A	Pts	AUT	BIH	EST
Germany	3	3	0	0	13	2	9	2-1	6-1	5-0
Austria	3	1	1	1	5	3	4		3-0	1-1
Bosnia-Herzegovina	3	1	0	2	5	10	3			4-1
Estonia	3	0	1	2	2	10	1	Played in EST		

Qualifying Round Group 3

	Pl	W	D	L	F	A	Pts	GEO	POL	SWE
England	3	2	1	0	5	1	7	1-1	1-0	3-0
Georgia	3	2	1	0	4	2	7		2-1	1-0
Poland	3	0	1	2	1	3	1			0-0
Sweden	3	0	1	2	0	4	1	Played in GEO		

Qualifying Round Group 4

	Pl	W	D	L	F	A	Pts	IRL	ALB	MLT
Norway	3	3	0	0	6	0	9	1-0	2-0	3-0
Republic of Ireland	3	2	0	1	5	2	6		2-0	3-1
Albania	3	0	1	2	1	5	1			1-1
Malta	3	0	1	2	2	7	1	Played in MLT		

Qualifying Round Group 5

	Pl	W	D	L	F	A	Pts	NIR	MNE	AZE
Portugal	3	3	0	0	8	1	9	3-1	3-0	2-0
Northern Ireland	3	1	1	1	7	3	4		0-0	6-0
Montenegro	3	1	1	1	2	4	4			2-1
Azerbaijan	3	0	0	3	1	10	0	Played in POR		

Qualifying Round Group 6

	Pl	W	D	L	F	A	Pts	BLR	KAZ	LIE
Romania	3	3	0	0	12	0	9	2-0	1-0	9-0
Belarus	3	2	0	1	18	4	6		6-2	12-0
Kazakhstan	3	1	0	2	4	7	3			2-0
Liechtenstein	3	0	0	3	0	23	0	Played in BLR		

Qualifying Round Group 7

	Pl	W	D	L	F	A	Pts	TUR	CZE	ARM
Iceland	3	2	0	1	6	5	6	2-0	2-4	2-1
Turkey	3	2	0	1	9	3	6		6-1	3-0
Czech Republic	3	1	1	1	6	9	4			1-1
Armenia	3	0	1	2	2	6	1	Played in ISL		

Qualifying Round Group 8

	Pl	W	D	L	F	A	Pts	BEL	LTU	WAL
Denmark	3	3	0	0	10	0	9	2-0	7-0	1-0
Belgium	3	2	0	1	9	4	6		5-2	4-0
Lithuania	3	1	0	2	3	12	3			1-0
Wales	3	0	0	3	0	6	0	Played in LTU		

Qualifying Round Group 9

	Pl	W	D	L	F	A	Pts	FRA	SVN	CYP
Italy	3	3	0	0	6	3	9	2-1	3-2	1-0
France	3	1	1	1	3	3	4		1-0	1-1
Slovenia	3	1	0	2	4	4	3			2-0
Cyprus	3	0	1	2	1	4	1	Played in CYP		

Qualifying Round Group 10

	Pl	W	D	L	F	A	Pts	HUN	FRO	AND
Slovakia	3	2	1	0	9	1	7	1-1	3-0	5-0
Hungary	3	2	1	0	8	1	7		2-0	5-0
Faroe Islands	3	0	1	2	0	5	1			0-0
Andorra	3	0	1	2	0	10	1	Played in HUN		

Qualifying Round Group 11

	Pl	W	D	L	F	A	Pts	UKR	LVA	SMR
Netherlands	3	2	1	0	8	1	7	1-1	1-0	6-0
Ukraine	3	1	2	0	2	1	5		0-0	1-0
Latvia	3	1	1	1	2	1	4			2-0
San Marino	3	0	0	3	0	9	0	Played in SMR		

Qualifying Round Group 12

	Pl	W	D	L	F	A	Pts	SCO	LUX	MKD
Switzerland	3	2	1	0	4	1	7	0-0	1-0	3-1
Scotland	3	2	1	0	3	1	7		2-1	1-0
Luxembourg	3	1	0	2	4	3	3			3-0
Macedonia FYR	3	0	0	3	1	7	0	Played in LUX		

Qualifying Round Group 13

	Pl	W	D	L	F	A	Pts	RUS	FIN	MDA
Spain	3	3	0	0	9	2	9	2-1	3-0	4-1
Russia	3	1	1	1	7	4	4		1-1	5-1
Finland	3	1	1	1	3	4	4			2-0
Moldova	3	0	0	3	2	11	0	Played in ESP		

Elite Round Group 1

	Pl	W	D	L	F	A	Pts	SCO	ITA	SVK
Czech Republic	3	2	1	0	4	2	7	1-1	2-1	1-0
Scotland	3	1	2	0	3	1	5		0-0	2-0
Italy	3	0	2	1	2	3	2			1-1
Slovakia	3	0	1	2	1	4	1	Played in ITA		

Elite Round Group 2

	Pl	W	D	L	F	A	Pts	CRO	AUT	POR
Netherlands	3	2	1	0	3	1	7	0-0	2-1	1-0
Croatia	3	1	2	0	2	0	5		2-0	0-0
Austria	3	1	0	2	3	4	3			2-0
Portugal	3	0	1	2	0	3	1	Played in NED		

Elite Round Group 3

	Pl	W	D	L	F	A	Pts	IRL	GRE	LVA
Denmark	3	2	1	0	4	2	7	2-2	1-0	2-0
Republic of Ireland	3	1	2	0	7	4	5		1-1	4-1
Greece	3	1	1	1	3	2	4			2-0
Latvia	3	0	0	3	1	7	0	Played in GRE		

Elite Round Group 4

	Pl	W	D	L	F	A	Pts	TUR	SUI	UKR
Germany	3	3	0	0	6	0	9	2-0	2-0	2-0
Turkey	3	1	1	1	4	5	4		2-1	2-2
Switzerland	3	1	0	2	2	4	3			1-0
Ukraine	3	0	1	2	2	5	1	Played in GER		

Elite Round Group 5

	Pl	W	D	L	F	A	Pts	ESP	NIR	BEL
England	3	3	0	0	7	4	9	2-1	3-2	2-1
Spain	3	2	0	1	9	4	6		5-1	3-1
Northern Ireland	3	1	0	2	5	9	3			2-1
Belgium	3	0	0	3	3	7	0	Played in BEL		

Elite Round Group 6

	Pl	W	D	L	F	A	Pts	NOR	BLR	GEO
France	3	2	1	0	13	2	7	2-2	9-0	2-0
Norway	3	2	1	0	12	3	7		5-1	5-0
Belarus	3	1	0	2	2	14	3			1-0
Georgia	3	0	0	3	0	8	0	Played in FRA		

Elite Round Group 7

	Pl	W	D	L	F	A	Pts	RUS	HUN	ISL
Romania	3	2	1	0	4	2	7	2-1	2-1	0-0
Russia	3	2	0	1	5	3	6		2-1	2-0
Hungary	3	1	0	2	4	4	3			2-0
Iceland	3	0	1	2	0	4	1	Played in HUN		

UEFA EUROPEAN UNDER-17 CHAMPIONSHIP SERBIA 2011

First Round Group Stage

Group A	Pl	W	D	L	F	A	Pts	ENG	FRA	SRB
Denmark	3	3	0	0	6	2	9	2-0	1-0	3-2
England	3	1	1	1	5	4	4		2-2	3-0
France	3	0	2	1	3	4	2			1-1
Serbia	3	0	1	2	3	7	1			

Group B	Pl	W	D	L	F	A	Pts	GER	CZE	ROU
Netherlands	3	2	1	0	3	0	7	2-0	0-0	1-0
Germany	3	1	1	1	2	3	4		1-1	1-0
Czech Republic	3	0	3	0	2	2	3			1-1
Romania	3	0	1	2	1	3	1			

Semi-finals

Netherlands	1
England	0

Denmark	0
Germany	2

Final

Netherlands	5
Germany	2

Finals held in Serbia from 3-05-2011 to 15-05-2011

UEFA EUROPEAN UNDER-19 CHAMPIONSHIP 2011

Qualifying Round Group 1

	Pl	W	D	L	F	A	Pts	WAL	ISL	KAZ
Turkey	3	2	1	0	10	5	7	3-3	2-1	5-1
Wales	3	1	2	0	6	5	5		2-1	1-1
Iceland	3	1	0	2	6	4	3			4-0
Kazakhstan	3	0	1	2	2	10	1	Played in WAL		

Qualifying Round Group 2

	Pl	W	D	L	F	A	Pts	NOR	SCO	LIE
Estonia	3	2	0	1	6	2	6	2-0	1-2	3-0
Norway	3	2	0	1	9	4	6		4-2	5-0
Scotland	3	2	0	1	11	5	6			7-0
Liechtenstein	3	0	0	3	0	15	0	Played in EST		

Qualifying Round Group 3

	Pl	W	D	L	F	A	Pts	GRE	AZE	GEO
Portugal	3	1	2	0	6	3	5	1-1	2-2	3-0
Greece	3	1	1	1	2	2	4		1-0	0-1
Azerbaijan	3	1	1	1	5	3	4			3-0
Georgia	3	1	0	2	1	6	3	Played in POR		

Qualifying Round Group 4

	Pl	W	D	L	F	A	Pts	RUS	DEN	SWE
Ukraine	3	2	0	1	4	2	6	1-2	2-0	1-0
Russia	3	2	0	1	7	5	6		1-2	4-2
Denmark	3	2	0	1	5	3	6			3-0
Sweden	3	0	0	3	2	8	0	Played in SWE		

Qualifying Round Group 5

	Pl	W	D	L	F	A	Pts	MKD	CZE	BIH
Belarus	3	2	0	1	5	4	8	3-0	0-3	2-1
Macedonia FYR	3	1	1	1	2	4	4		1-0	1-1
Czech Republic	3	1	1	1	3	1	4			0-0
Bosnia-Herzegovina	3	0	2	1	3	2	2	Played in BIH		

Qualifying Round Group 6

	Pl	W	D	L	F	A	Pts	POL	MDA	FIN
Hungary	3	2	0	1	3	1	6	2-0	0-1	1-0
Poland	3	1	1	1	2	2	4		0-0	2-0
Moldova	3	1	1	1	3	6	4			2-6
Finland	3	1	0	2	6	5	3	Played in HUN		

Qualifying Round Group 7

	Pl	W	D	L	F	A	Pts	CRO	LVA	FRO
Italy	3	3	0	0	8	2	9	3-1	2-1	3-0
Croatia	3	1	1	1	5	6	4		2-1	2-2
Latvia	3	1	0	2	4	5	3			2-1
Faroe Islands	3	0	1	2	3	7	1	Played in LVA		

Qualifying Round Group 8

	Pl	W	D	L	F	A	Pts	ENG	CYP	ALB
Belgium	3	3	0	0	8	2	9	2-1	4-1	2-0
England	3	2	0	1	11	3	6		4-0	6-1
Cyprus	3	0	1	2	1	8	1			0-0
Albania	3	0	1	2	1	8	1	Played in BEL		

Qualifying Round Group 9

	Pl	W	D	L	F	A	Pts	SVK	SVN	MLT
Netherlands	3	3	0	0	7	0	9	2-0	2-0	3-0
Slovakia	3	2	0	1	5	2	6		1-0	4-0
Slovenia	3	1	0	2	4	3	3			5-0
Malta	3	0	0	3	0	11	0	Played in SVN		

Qualifying Round Group 10

	Pl	W	D	L	F	A	Pts	IRL	BUL	LUX
Serbia	3	3	0	0	7	0	9	1-0	3-0	3-0
Republic of Ireland	3	2	0	1	7	2	6		2-1	5-0
Bulgaria	3	1	0	2	4	5	3			3-0
Luxembourg	3	0	0	3	0	11	0	Played in BUL		

Qualifying Round Group 11

	Pl	W	D	L	F	A	Pts	ISR	ARM	LTU
Spain	3	3	0	0	12	0	9	3-0	3-0	6-0
Israel	3	2	0	1	4	3	6		3-0	1-0
Armenia	3	1	0	2	1	6	3			1-0
Lithuania	3	0	0	3	0	8	0	Played in LTU		

Qualifying Round Group 12

	Pl	W	D	L	F	A	Pts	MNE	AUT	SMR
France	3	3	0	0	6	0	9	2-0	1-0	3-0
Montenegro	3	1	1	1	6	3	4		1-1	5-0
Austria	3	1	1	1	5	2	4			4-0
San Marino	3	0	0	3	0	12	0	Played in AUT		

Qualifying Round Group 13

	Pl	W	D	L	F	A	Pts	SUI	NIR	AND
Germany	3	2	1	0	14	3	7	2-2	2-1	10-0
Switzerland	3	1	2	0	8	2	5		0-0	6-0
Northern Ireland	3	1	1	1	3	3	4			2-1
Andorra	3	0	0	3	1	18	0	Played in GER		

Elite Round Group 1

	Pl	W	D	L	F	A	Pts	POR	CRO	EST
Belgium	3	2	1	0	4	2	7	1-0	3-2	0-0
Portugal	3	2	0	1	4	1	6		1-0	3-0
Croatia	3	1	0	2	3	4	3			1-0
Estonia	3	0	1	2	0	4	1	Played in CRO		

Elite Round Group 2

	Pl	W	D	L	F	A	Pts	ENG	SUI	MNE
Spain	3	2	1	0	6	2	7	1-1	2-1	3-0
England	3	2	1	0	5	3	7		3-2	1-0
Switzerland	3	1	0	2	6	7	3			3-2
Montenegro	3	0	0	3	2	7	0	Played in SUI		

Elite Round Group 3

	Pl	W	D	L	F	A	Pts	FRA	SVK	BLR
Greece	3	3	0	0	5	2	9	2-1	2-1	1-0
France	3	2	0	1	5	2	6		2-0	2-0
Slovakia	3	1	0	2	6	4	3			5-0
Belarus	3	0	0	3	0	8	0	Played in SVK		

Elite Round Group 4

	Pl	W	D	L	F	A	Pts	ITA	UKR	POL
Republic of Ireland	3	2	1	0	4	0	7	3-0	0-0	1-0
Italy	3	2	0	1	4	4	6		1-0	3-1
Ukraine	3	0	2	1	1	2	2			1-1
Poland	3	0	1	2	2	5	1	Played in POL		

Elite Round Group 5

	Pl	W	D	L	F	A	Pts	RUS	NED	ISR
Czech Republic	3	2	1	0	3	1	7	0-0	1-0	2-1
Russia	3	1	2	0	4	2	5		1-1	3-1
Netherlands	3	0	2	1	2	3	2			1-1
Israel	3	0	1	2	3	6	1	Played in CZE		

Elite Round Group 6

	Pl	W	D	L	F	A	Pts	WAL	NOR	MDA
Serbia	3	2	0	1	10	3	6	2-3	3-0	5-0
Wales	3	2	0	1	6	5	6		1-3	2-0
Norway	3	2	0	1	7	4	6			4-0
Moldova	3	0	0	3	0	11	0	Played in NOR		

Elite Round Group 7

	Pl	W	D	L	F	A	Pts	GER	HUN	MKD
Turkey	3	3	0	0	10	2	9	1-0	6-1	3-1
Germany	3	2	0	1	8	1	6		3-0	5-0
Hungary	3	1	0	2	5	11	3			4-2
Macedonia FYR	3	0	0	3	3	12	0	Played in TUR		

UEFA EUROPEAN UNDER-19 CHAMPIONSHIP ROMANIA 2011

First Round Group Stage

Group A	Pl	W	D	L	F	A	Pts	IRL	GRE	ROU
Czech Republic	3	3	0	0	6	2	9	2-1	1-0	3-1
Rep. of Ireland	3	1	1	1	3	3	4		2-1	0-0
Greece	3	1	0	2	2	3	3			1-0
Romania	3	0	1	2	1	4	1			

Group B	Pl	W	D	L	F	A	Pts	SRB	TUR	BEL
Spain	3	2	0	1	8	4	6	4-0	0-3	4-1
Serbia	3	1	1	1	3	5	4		2-0	1-1
Turkey	3	1	1	1	4	3	4			1-1
Belgium	3	0	2	1	3	6	2			

Semi-finals

Spain	5
Rep. of Ireland	0
Serbia	2
Czech Republic	4

Final

Spain	3
Czech Republic	2

Finals held in Romania from 20-07-2011 to 1-08-2011

UEFA EUROPEAN UNDER-21 CHAMPIONSHIP 2010-11

Qualifying Round Group 1

	Pl	W	D	L	F	A	Pts	ROU	RUS	MDA	LVA	FRO	AND
Romania	10	8	1	1	23	6	**25**		3-0	3-0	4-1	3-0	2-0
Russia	10	7	1	2	22	6	**22**	0-0		3-1	2-1	2-0	4-0
Moldova	10	4	2	4	9	13	**14**	0-1	0-3		1-0	1-0	1-0
Latvia	10	4	1	5	16	15	**13**	5-1	0-4	1-1		0-1	4-0
Faroe Islands	10	3	2	5	8	16	**11**	0-4	1-0	1-1	1-3		3-1
Andorra	10	0	1	9	3	25	**1**	0-2	0-4	1-3	0-1	1-1	

Qualifying Round Group 3

	Pl	W	D	L	F	A	Pts	ITA	WAL	HUN	BIH	LUX
Italy	8	5	1	2	12	5	**16**		1-0	2-0	1-1	2-0
Wales	8	5	1	2	15	6	**16**	2-1		4-1	2-0	5-1
Hungary	8	4	1	3	9	7	**13**	2-0	0-1		0-0	3-0
Bosnia-H'govina	8	2	2	4	4	8	**8**	0-1	2-1	0-2		0-1
Luxembourg	8	1	1	6	2	16	**4**	0-4	0-0	0-1	0-1	

Qualifying Round Group 2

	Pl	W	D	L	F	A	Pts	SUI	TUR	GEO	ARM	EST	IRL
Switzerland	10	6	2	2	15	8	**20**		0-2	1-0	2-1	0-1	1-0
Turkey	10	5	1	4	13	11	**16**	1-3		0-1	1-0	0-0	1-0
Georgia	10	4	3	3	12	9	**15**	0-0	4-0		0-2	2-0	1-1
Armenia	10	4	1	5	18	19	**13**	1-3	2-5	2-3		1-1	4-1
Estonia	10	3	3	4	9	16	**12**	1-4	1-0	2-0	2-3		1-1
Rep. of Ireland	10	1	4	5	11	15	**7**	1-1	0-3	1-1	1-2	5-0	

Qualifying Round Group 4

	Pl	W	D	L	F	A	Pts	NED	ESP	FIN	POL	LIE
Netherlands	8	7	0	1	19	5	**21**		2-1	2-1	3-2	3-0
Spain	8	6	1	1	15	5	**19**	2-1		1-0		3-1
Finland	8	3	1	4	11	7	**10**	0-1	1-1		2-0	3-0
Poland	8	3	0	5	11	13	**9**	0-4	0-1	2-1		2-0
Liechtenstein	8	0	0	8	1	27	**0**	0-3	0-4	0-4	0-5	

Qualifying Round Group 5

	Pl	W	D	L	F	A	Pts	CZE	ISL	GER	NIR	SMR
Czech Republic	8	7	1	0	25	4	**22**		3-1	1-1	2-0	5-0
Iceland	8	5	1	2	29	11	**16**	0-2		4-1	2-1	8-0
Germany	8	3	3	2	26	10	**12**	1-2	2-2		3-0	6-0
Northern Ireland	8	2	1	5	12	16	**7**	1-2	2-6	1-1		4-0
San Marino	8	0	0	8	0	51	**0**	0-8	0-6	0-11	0-3	

Qualifying Round Group 6

	Pl	W	D	L	F	A	Pts	SWE	ISR	MNE	KAZ	BUL
Sweden	8	6	1	1	15	5	**19**		1-2	2-0	5-1	2-1
Israel	8	5	1	2	18	8	**16**	0-1		5-0	1-1	4-0
Montenegro	8	4	1	3	9	11	**13**	0-2	1-0		3-1	2-0
Kazakhstan	8	1	2	5	7	17	**5**	1-1	1-2	0-2		2-0
Bulgaria	8	1	1	6	8	16	**4**	0-1	3-4	1-1	3-0	

Qualifying Round Group 7

	Pl	W	D	L	F	A	Pts	CRO	SVK	SRB	NOR	CYP
Croatia	8	5	2	1	17	10	**17**		1-1	3-1	4-1	0-2
Slovakia	8	4	2	2	11	11	**14**	1-2		2-1	1-4	1-0
Serbia	8	4	1	3	14	12	**13**	2-2	1-2		3-2	2-0
Norway	8	2	1	5	14	18	**7**	1-3	2-2	0-1		1-3
Cyprus	8	2	0	6	8	13	**6**	1-2	0-1	1-3	1-3	

Qualifying Round Group 8

	Pl	W	D	L	F	A	Pts	UKR	BEL	FRA	SVN	MLT
Ukraine	8	4	4	0	13	5	**16**		1-1	2-2	0-0	1-0
Belgium	8	4	3	1	8	5	**15**	0-2		0-0	2-0	1-0
France	8	4	3	1	12	6	**15**	2-2	0-1		1-0	2-0
Slovenia	8	2	2	4	6	10	**8**	0-2	2-2	1-3		1-0
Malta	8	0	0	8	0	13	**0**	0-3	0-1	0-2	0-2	

Qualifying Round Group 9

	Pl	W	D	L	F	A	Pts	GRE	ENG	POR	LTU	MKD
Greece	8	6	1	1	13	7	**19**		1-1	2-1	1-0	3-1
England	8	5	2	1	15	7	**17**	1-2		1-0	3-0	6-3
Portugal	8	4	1	3	12	8	**13**	2-1	0-1		4-1	3-1
Lithuania	8	1	2	5	3	11	**5**	0-1	0-0	0-1		1-0
Macedonia FYR	8	0	2	6	9	19	**2**	1-2	1-2	1-1	1-1	

Qualifying Round Group 10

	Pl	W	D	L	F	A	Pts	SCO	BLR	AUT	ALB	AZE
Scotland	8	5	2	1	16	7	**17**		1-0	3-1	5-2	2-2
Belarus	8	5	2	1	16	11	**17**	1-1		2-1	4-2	1-0
Austria	8	4	2	2	17	11	**14**	1-0	3-3		3-1	4-0
Albania	8	1	1	6	11	20	**4**	0-1	1-2	2-2		1-0
Azerbaijan	8	1	1	6	8	19	**4**	0-4	2-3	1-2	3-2	

Play-offs

Home team first leg	Score	Home team second leg
England	2-1 0-0	Romania
Netherlands	1-3 2-0	**Ukraine**
Spain	2-1 3-0	Croatia
Switzerland	4-1 1-1	Sweden
Iceland	2-1 2-1	Scotland
Czech Republic	3-0 2-0	Greece
Italy	2-0 0-3	**Belarus**

UEFA EUROPEAN UNDER-21 CHAMPIONSHIP DENMARK 2011

First Round Group Stage

Group A

	Pl	W	D	L	F	A	Pts	BLR	ISL	DEN
Switzerland	3	3	0	0	6	0	**9**	3-0	2-0	1-0
Belarus *	3	1	0	2	3	5	**3**		2-0	1-2
Iceland	3	1	0	2	3	5	**3**			3-1
Denmark	3	1	0	2	3	5	**3**			

* Belarus qualified on goal difference in the matches between the tied nations

Group B

	Pl	W	D	L	F	A	Pts	CZE	ENG	UKR
Spain	3	2	1	0	6	1	**7**	2-0	1-1	3-0
Czech Republic	3	2	0	1	4	4	**6**		2-1	2-1
England	3	0	2	1	2	3	**2**			0-0
Ukraine	3	0	1	2	1	5	**1**			

Semi-finals

Spain	3
Belarus	1

Czech Republic	0
Switzerland	

Final

Spain	2
Switzerland	0

3rd place: Belarus 1-0 Czech Republic. The top three teams qualified for the 2012 Olympic football tournament

Finals held in Denmark from 11-06-2011 to 25-06-2011

WOMEN'S TOURNAMENTS IN EUROPE 2011

UEFA WOMEN'S UNDER-17 CHAMPIONSHIP 2011

First Qualifying Round Group 1

	Pl	W	D	L	F	A	Pts	NOR	SRB	KAZ
Finland	3	2	1	0	9	0	7	0-0	1-0	8-0
Norway	3	1	2	0	11	3	5		3-3	8-0
Serbia	3	0	2	1	4	5	2			1-1
Kazakhstan	3	0	1	2	1	17	1		Played in FIN	

First Qualifying Round Group 2

	Pl	W	D	L	F	A	Pts	IRL	NIR	MKD
Czech Republic	3	3	0	0	13	0	9	2-0	3-0	8-0
Republic of Ireland	3	2	0	1	5	2	6		1-0	4-0
Northern Ireland	3	1	0	2	4	4	3			4-0
Macedonia FYR	3	0	0	3	0	16	0		Played in NIR	

First Qualifying Round Group 3

	Pl	W	D	L	F	A	Pts	SVN	HUN	MDA
Denmark	3	3	0	0	11	1	9	3-0	2-1	6-0
Slovenia	3	2	0	1	3	4	6		2-1	1-0
Hungary	3	1	0	2	8	5	3			6-1
Moldova	3	0	0	3	1	13	0		Played in HUN	

First Qualifying Round Group 4

	Pl	W	D	L	F	A	Pts	NED	BLR	GEO
Spain	3	3	0	0	16	0	9	1-0	2-0	13-0
Netherlands	3	2	0	1	17	1	6		3-0	14-0
Belarus	3	1	0	2	2	5	3			2-0
Georgia	3	0	0	3	0	29	0		Played in NED	

First Qualifying Round Group 5

	Pl	W	D	L	F	A	Pts	ITA	LTU	BUL
Iceland	3	3	0	0	29	1	9	5-1	14-0	10-0
Italy	3	2	0	1	12	5	6		7-0	4-0
Lithuania	3	1	0	2	1	21	3			1-0
Bulgaria	3	0	0	3	0	15	0		Played in BUL	

First Qualifying Round Group 6

	Pl	W	D	L	F	A	Pts	ENG	TUR	ARM
Belgium	3	2	1	0	10	0	7	0-0	3-0	7-0
England	3	2	1	0	9	0	7		2-0	7-0
Turkey	3	1	0	2	7	5	3			7-0
Armenia	3	0	0	3	0	21	0		Played in BEL	

First Qualifying Round Group 7

	Pl	W	D	L	F	A	Pts	ROU	AUT	UKR
Scotland	3	3	0	0	6	1	9	1-0	3-1	2-0
Romania	3	1	1	1	2	1	4		0-0	2-0
Austria	3	1	1	1	2	3	4			1-0
Ukraine	3	0	0	3	0	5	0		Played in AUT	

First Qualifying Round Group 8

	Pl	W	D	L	F	A	Pts	FRA	CRO	ISR
Sweden	3	3	0	0	8	2	9	3-2	3-0	2-0
France	3	2	0	1	15	3	6		4-0	9-0
Croatia	3	0	1	2	2	9	1			2-2
Israel	3	0	1	2	2	13	1		Played in FRA	

First Qualifying Round Group 9

	Pl	W	D	L	F	A	Pts	POL	EST	LVA
Switzerland	3	3	0	0	13	0	9	1-0	6-0	6-0
Poland	3	2	0	1	20	1	6		9-0	11-0
Estonia	3	1	0	2	5	16	3			5-1
Latvia	3	0	0	3	1	22	0		Played in LVA	

First Qualifying Round Group 10

	Pl	W	D	L	F	A	Pts	RUS	GRE	FRO
Wales	3	2	1	0	10	3	7	2-2	4-1	4-0
Russia	3	2	1	0	7	4	7		3-2	2-0
Greece	3	1	0	2	8	8	3			5-1
Faroe Islands	3	0	0	3	1	11	0		Played in RUS	

UEFA EUROPEAN WOMEN'S UNDER-17 CHAMPIONSHIP 2011

Second Qualifying Round

Group 1

	Pl	W	D	L	F	A	Pts	POL	ENG	SWE
Iceland	3	3	0	0	8	1	9	2-0	2-0	4-1
Poland	3	2	0	1	5	4	6		2-1	3-1
England	3	1	0	2	2	4	3			1-0
Sweden	3	0	0	3	2	8	0			

Group 2

	Pl	W	D	L	F	A	Pts	BEL	CZE	ITA
Spain	3	2	0	1	9	4	6	2-0	1-3	6-1
Belgium	3	2	0	1	2	2	6		1-0	1-0
Czech Republic	3	1	1	1	4	3	4			1-1
Italy	3	0	1	2	2	8	1			

Group 3

	Pl	W	D	L	F	A	Pts	DEN	FIN	RUS
Germany	3	3	0	0	17	0	9	3-0	5-0	9-0
Denmark	3	2	0	1	8	4	6		3-1	5-0
Finland	3	1	0	2	3	8	3			2-0
Russia	3	0	0	3	0	16	0			

Group 4

	Pl	W	D	L	F	A	Pts	SCO	WAL	SUI
France	3	3	0	0	8	1	9	4-1	2-0	2-0
Scotland	3	1	1	1	5	5	4		1-1	3-0
Wales	3	0	2	1	2	4	2			1-1
Switzerland	3	0	1	2	1	6	1			

Semi-finals

Spain	4
Iceland	0

Germany	2 5p
France	2 6p

Final

Spain	1
France	0

Third Place Play-off

Germany	8
Iceland	2

Finals in Nyon, Switzerland, 28-07-2011 to 31-07-2011
Group 1 in Poland; Group 2 in Czech Rep; Group 3 in Denmark; Group 4 in Switzerland

UEFA WOMEN'S UNDER-19 CHAMPIONSHIP 2011

First Qualifying Round Group 1

	Pl	W	D	L	F	A	Pts	FIN	MDA	ARM
England	3	3	0	0	15	0	9	2-0	4-0	9-0
Finland	3	2	0	1	9	2	6		4-0	5-0
Moldova	3	1	0	2	2	8	3			2-0
Armenia	3	0	0	3	0	16	0	Played in MDA		

First Qualifying Round Group 2

	Pl	W	D	L	F	A	Pts	LTU	EST	AZE
Belgium	3	2	0	0	10	0	6	4-0	6-0	n/p
Lithuania	3	1	0	1	1	4	3		1-0	n/p
Estonia	3	0	0	2	0	7	0			n/p
Azerbaijan	3	0	0	0	0	0	0	Played in LTU		

First Qualifying Round Group 3

	Pl	W	D	L	F	A	Pts	DEN	GRE	BIH
Spain	3	2	1	0	12	1	7	1-1	6-0	5-0
Denmark	3	2	1	0	7	1	7		4-0	2-0
Greece	3	1	0	2	3	10	3			3-0
Bosnia-Herzegovina	3	0	0	3	0	9	0	Played in BIH		

First Qualifying Round Group 4

	Pl	W	D	L	F	A	Pts	POR	HUN	LVA
Austria	3	3	0	0	21	0	9	4-0	7-0	10-0
Portugal	3	2	0	1	8	4	6		3-0	5-0
Hungary	3	1	0	2	7	10	3			7-0
Latvia	3	0	0	3	0	22	0	Played in HUN		

First Qualifying Round Group 5

	Pl	W	D	L	F	A	Pts	POL	MKD	KAZ
Switzerland	3	3	0	0	11	2	9	4-0	3-2	4-0
Poland	3	2	0	1	8	5	6		3-1	5-0
Macedonia FYR	3	1	0	2	5	7	3			2-1
Kazakhstan	3	0	0	3	1	11	0	Played in MKD		

First Qualifying Round Group 6

	Pl	W	D	L	F	A	Pts	WAL	SVN	GEO
France	3	3	0	0	17	1	9	5-1	1-0	11-0
Wales	3	2	0	1	26	7	6		4-2	15-0
Slovenia	3	1	0	2	17	5	3			15-0
Georgia	3	0	0	3	0	47	0	Played in SVN		

First Qualifying Round Group 7

	Pl	W	D	L	F	A	Pts	NOR	FRO	BLR
Netherlands	3	2	1	0	19	2	7	1-1	9-1	9-0
Norway	3	2	1	0	13	1	7		4-0	8-0
Faroe Islands	3	0	1	2	1	13	1			0-0
Belarus	3	0	1	2	0	17	1	Played in NOR		

First Qualifying Round Group 8

	Pl	W	D	L	F	A	Pts	SWE	SRB	SVK
Scotland	3	2	1	0	8	3	7	1-0	3-3	4-0
Sweden	3	2	0	1	6	1	6		2-0	4-0
Serbia	3	1	1	1	7	8	4			4-3
Slovakia	3	0	0	3	3	12	0	Played in SWE		

First Qualifying Round Group 9

	Pl	W	D	L	F	A	Pts	TUR	NIR	ROU
Czech Republic	3	2	1	0	9	3	7	1-1	4-2	4-0
Turkey	3	1	1	1	4	4	4		1-0	2-3
Northern Ireland	3	1	0	2	4	6	3			2-1
Romania	3	1	0	2	4	8	3	Played in CZE		

First Qualifying Round Group 10

	Pl	W	D	L	F	A	Pts	UKR	ISR	BUL
Iceland	3	3	0	0	8	0	9	4-0	2-0	2-0
Ukraine	3	2	0	1	3	5	6		2-1	1-0
Israel	3	1	0	2	5	5	3			4-1
Bulgaria	3	0	0	3	1	7	0	Played in BUL		

Second Qualifying Round Group 1

	Pl	W	D	L	F	A	Pts	DEN	FRA	LTU
Netherlands	3	2	0	1	14	1	6	3-0	0-1	11-0
Denmark	3	2	0	1	12	3	6		3-0	9-0
France	3	2	0	1	8	3	6			7-0
Lithuania	3	0	0	3	0	27	0	Played in DEN		

Second Qualifying Round Group 2

	Pl	W	D	L	F	A	Pts	BEL	FIN	SRB
Russia	3	2	0	1	3	2	6	0-1	1-2	2-1
Belgium	3	1	2	0	6	5	5		3-3	2-2
Finland	3	1	1	1	9	8	4			6-4
Serbia	3	0	1	2	7	10	1	Played in RUS		

Second Qualifying Round Group 3

	Pl	W	D	L	F	A	Pts	WAL	TUR	ISL
Germany	3	2	1	0	6	1	7	1-1	2-0	3-0
Wales	3	1	1	1	2	3	4		1-0	0-2
Turkey	3	1	0	2	3	4	3			3-1
Iceland	3	1	0	2	3	6	3	Played in WAL		

Second Qualifying Round Group 4

	Pl	W	D	L	F	A	Pts	ENG	POR	CRO
Norway	3	3	0	0	5	0	9	1-0	2-0	2-0
England	3	2	0	1	6	1	6		3-0	3-0
Portugal	3	1	0	2	2	6	3			2-1
Croatia	3	0	0	3	1	7	0	Played in CRO		

Second Qualifying Round Group 5

	Pl	W	D	L	F	A	Pts	SWE	CZE	UKR
Switzerland	3	2	1	0	6	2	7	1-1	4-1	1-0
Sweden	3	1	2	0	8	2	5		0-0	7-1
Czech Republic	3	1	1	1	5	5	4			4-1
Ukraine	3	0	0	3	2	12	0	Played in UKR		

Second Qualifying Round Group 6

	Pl	W	D	L	F	A	Pts	AUT	SCO	POL
Spain	3	3	0	0	9	1	9	4-0	2-1	3-0
Austria	3	1	1	1	8	7	4		3-3	5-0
Scotland	3	0	2	1	6	7	2			2-2
Poland	3	0	1	2	2	10	1	Played in AUT		

UEFA EUROPEAN WOMEN'S UNDER-19 CHAMPIONSHIP ITALY 2011

First Round Group Stage

Group A	Pl	W	D	L	F	A	Pts	SUI	RUS	BEL
Italy	3	3	0	0	6	2	9	1-0	2-1	3-1
Switzerland	3	1	1	1	4	2	4		0-0	4-1
Russia	3	1	1	1	4	3	4			3-1
Belgium	3	0	0	3	3	10	0			

Group B	Pl	W	D	L	F	A	Pts	NOR	NED	ESP
Germany	3	3	0	0	6	2	9	3-1	2-1	1-0
Norway	3	2	0	1	9	4	6		3-0	5-1
Netherlands	3	0	1	2	2	6	1			1-1
Spain	3	0	1	2	2	7	1			

Semi-finals

Germany	3
Switzerland	1

Italy	2
Norway	3

Final

Germany	8
Norway	1

Finals held in Italy from 30-05-2011 to 11-06-2011

See page 1069 for details of group 11 of the first qualifying round

UEFA WOMEN'S CHAMPIONS LEAGUE 2010–11

First Qualifying Round

Group 1

		Pl	W	D	L	F	A	Pts	BUL	MDA	TUR
Brøndby IF	DEN	3	3	0	0	21	0	9	3-0	6-0	12-0
NSA Sofia	BUL	3	2	0	1	11	3	6		4-0	7-0
Roma Calfa	MDA	3	0	1	2	3	13	1			3-3
Gazi Universitesi	TUR	3	0	1	2	3	22	1		Played in DEN	

Group 2

		Pl	W	D	L	F	A	Pts	LTU	FRO	MKD
Everton	ENG	3	3	0	0	23	0	9	7-0	6-0	10-0
Gintra Universitetas	LTU	3	1	1	1	4	7	4		0-0	4-0
KI Klaksvík	FRO	3	1	1	1	2	6	4			2-0
Borec Veles	MKD	3	0	0	3	0	16	0		Played in LTU	

Group 3

		Pl	W	D	L	F	A	Pts	SWE	ISR	BIH
Apollon Limassol	CYP	3	3	0	0	13	2	9	4-1	3-0	6-1
Umeå IK	SWE	3	2	0	1	5	4	6		3-0	1-0
ASA Tel Aviv Univ.	ISR	3	1	0	2	3	7	3			3-1
SFK 2000 Sarajevo	BIH	3	0	0	3	2	10	0		Played in CYP	

Group 4

		Pl	W	D	L	F	A	Pts	ISL	ROU	EST
Juvisy	FRA	3	2	1	0	20	4	7	3-3	5-1	12-0
Breidablik	ISL	3	2	1	0	18	4	7		7-0	8-1
FCM Târgu Mures	ROU	3	1	0	2	3	13	3			2-1
Levadia Tallinn	EST	3	0	0	3	2	22	0		Played in ISL	

Group 5

		Pl	W	D	L	F	A	Pts	SVN	WAL	GEO
Bardolino	ITA	3	3	0	0	14	1	9	4-1	7-0	3-0
Krka	SVN	3	2	0	1	9	4	6		4-0	4-0
Swansea City	WAL	3	1	0	2	2	12	3			2-1
Baia Zugdidi	GEO	3	0	0	3	1	9	0		Played in SVN	

Group 6

		Pl	W	D	L	F	A	Pts	IRL	POR	CRO
Rossiyanka	RUS	3	3	0	0	18	1	9	9-0	4-1	5-0
St Francis	IRL	3	2	0	1	9	13	6		4-1	5-3
1° Dezembro	POR	3	1	0	2	6	9	3			4-1
Osijek	CRO	3	0	0	3	4	14	0		Played in CRO	

Group 7

		Pl	W	D	L	F	A	Pts	SCO	SVK	NIR
FCR Duisburg	GER	3	3	0	0	13	1	9	4-0	3-0	6-1
Glasgow City	SCO	3	2	0	1	12	4	6		4-0	8-0
Slovan Bratislava	SVK	3	1	0	2	1	7	3			1-0
Crusaders NAS	NIR	3	0	0	3	1	15	0		Played in NIR	

Round of 32

Olymp. Lyonnais	FRA	2	8
AZ Alkmaar *	NED	1	0
Lehenda ShVSM *	UKR	1	0
Rossiyanka	RUS	3	4
Røa IL	NOR	2	0
FK Zorka-BDU *	BLR	1	0
Apollon Limassol *	CYP	1	1
Zvezda Perm	RUS	2	2
Linköping	SWE	7	5
Krka *	SVN	0	0
Sint-Truiden *	BEL	0	0
Sparta Praha	CZE	3	7
Rayo Vallecano *	ESP	3	1
Valur Reykjavík	ISL	0	1
Masinac Nis *	SRB	1	0
Arsenal	ENG	3	9
FCR Duisburg	GER	5	6
SSHVSM *	KAZ	0	0
Bardolino	ITA	0	1
Fortuna Hjørring *	DEN	8	6
Brøndby IF	DEN	2	0
Unia Racibórz *	POL	1	1
MTK Budapest *	HUN	0	1
Everton	ENG	0	7
Juvisy	FRA	3	6
Breidablik *	ISL	0	0
FC Zürich *	SUI	2	1
Torres	ESP	3	4
SV Neulengbach	AUT	0	3
PAOK *	GRE	1	0
Aland United *	FIN	0	0
Turbine Potsdam	GER	9	6

Round of 16

Olymp. Lyonnais	6	5
Rossiyanka *	1	0
Røa IL *	1	0
Zvezda Perm	1	4
Linköping *	2	1
Sparta Praha	0	0
Rayo Vallecano *	2	1
Arsenal	0	4
FCR Duisburg *	4	3
Fortuna Hjørring	2	0
Brøndby IF *	1	1
Everton	4	1
Juvisy	2	2
Torres *	1	2
SV Neulengbach	0	0
Turbine Potsdam *	7	9

UEFA WOMEN'S CHAMPIONS LEAGUE 2010-11

Quarter-finals	Semi-finals	Final

Olympique Lyonnais	0	1
Zvezda 2005 Perm *	0	0

Olympique Lyonnais *	2	3
Arsenal	0	2

Linköping	1	2
Arsenal *	1	2

Olympique Lyonnais	2
1.FFC Turbine Potsdam	0

FCR 2001 Duisburg	3	2
Everton *	1	1

FCR 2001 Duisburg *	2	0
1.FFC Turbine Potsdam	2	1

Juvisy *	0	2
1.FFC Turbine Potsdam	3	6

* Home team in the first leg

UEFA WOMEN'S CHAMPIONS LEAGUE FINAL 2011

Craven Cottage, London, 26-05-2011, 20:00, Att: 14 303, Ref: Dagmar Damkova CZE

Olympique Lyonnais	2	Renard [27], Dickenmann [85]
1.FFC Turbine Potsdam	0	

Lyon - Sarah Bouhaddi - Wendie Renard, Laura Georges, Sabrina Viguier - Amandine Henry, Louisa Necib (Lara Dickenmann 55), Shirley Cruz Trana, Sonia Bompastor (c), Camille Abily• - Lotta Schelin, Elodie Thomis (Eugenie Le Sommer 73). Tr: Patrice Lair

Potsdam - Anna Felicitas Sarholz - Babett Peter, Josephine Henning, Inka Wesely, Bianca Schmidt - Isabel Kerschowski, Fatmire Bajramaj, Jennifer Zietz (c), Viola Odebrecht - Tabea Kemme, Anja Mittag. Tr: Bernd Schroder

PART FOUR

CHAMPIONS
AND
CUP WINNERS

AFG – AFGHANISTAN

Year	Champions
2006	Ordu
2007	Ordu
2008	Hakim Sanayi
2009	
2010	
2011	

AIA – ANGUILLA

Year	Champions	Cup Winners
1998	Spartans	
1999	Attackers	
2000		
2001	Roaring Lions	
2002	Roaring Lions	
2003	Roaring Lions	
2004	Spartans	
2005		
2006	Roaring Lions	
2007	Kicks United	
2008	Attackers	Attackers
2009	Attackers	Attackers
2010	Roaring Lions	Roaring Lions
2011	Kicks United	Kicks United

ALB – ALBANIA

Year	Champions	Cup Winners
1930	SK Tiranë	
1931	SK Tiranë	
1932	SK Tiranë	
1933	Skënderbeu Korçë	
1934	SK Tiranë	
1936	SK Tiranë	
1937	SK Tiranë	
1945	Vllaznia Shkodër	
1946	Vllaznia Shkodër	
1947	Partizani Tiranë	
1948	Partizani Tiranë	Partizani Tiranë
1949	Partizani Tiranë	Partizani Tiranë
1950	Dinamo Tiranë	Dinamo Tiranë
1951	Dinamo Tiranë	Dinamo Tiranë
1952	Dinamo Tiranë	Dinamo Tiranë
1953	Dinamo Tiranë	Dinamo Tiranë
1954	Partizani Tiranë	Dinamo Tiranë
1955	Dinamo Tiranë	
1956	Dinamo Tiranë	
1957	Partizani Tiranë	Partizani Tiranë
1958	Partizani Tiranë	Partizani Tiranë
1959	Partizani Tiranë	
1960	Dinamo Tiranë	Dinamo Tiranë
1961	Partizani Tiranë	Partizani Tiranë
1963	Partizani Tiranë	17 Nëntori Tiranë
1964	Partizani Tiranë	Partizani Tiranë
1965	17 Nëntori Tiranë	Vllaznia Shkodër
1966	17 Nëntori Tiranë	Partizani Tiranë
1967	Dinamo Tiranë	
1968	17 Nëntori Tiranë	Partizani Tiranë
1970	17 Nëntori Tiranë	Partizani Tiranë
1971	Partizani Tiranë	Dinamo Tiranë
1972	Vllaznia Shkodër	Vllaznia Shkodër
1973	Dinamo Tiranë	Partizani Tiranë
1974	Vllaznia Shkodër	Dinamo Tiranë
1975	Dinamo Tiranë	Labinoti Elbasan
1976	Dinamo Tiranë	17 Nëntori Tiranë
1977	Dinamo Tiranë	17 Nëntori Tiranë
1978	Vllaznia Shkodër	Dinamo Tiranë
1979	Partizani Tiranë	Vllaznia Shkodër
1980	Dinamo Tiranë	Partizani Tiranë
1981	Partizani Tiranë	Vllaznia Shkodër
1982	17 Nëntori Tiranë	Dinamo Tiranë
1983	Vllaznia Shkodër	17 Nëntori Tiranë
1984	Labinoti Elbasan	17 Nëntori Tiranë
1985	17 Nëntori Tiranë	Flamurtari Vlorë
1986	Dinamo Tiranë	17 Nëntori Tiranë
1987	Partizani Tiranë	Vllaznia Shkodër
1988	17 Nëntori Tiranë	Flamurtari Vlorë
1989	17 Nëntori Tiranë	Dinamo Tiranë
1990	Dinamo Tiranë	Dinamo Tiranë
1991	Flamurtari Vlorë	Partizani Tiranë
1992	Vllaznia Shkodër	SK Elbasani
1993	Partizani Tiranë	Partizani Tiranë
1994	Teuta Durrës	SK Tirana
1995	SK Tirana	Teuta Durrës
1996	SK Tirana	SK Tirana
1997	SK Tirana	Partizani Tiranë
1998	Vllaznia Shkodër	Apolonia Fier
1999	SK Tirana	SK Tirana
2000	SK Tirana	Teuta Durrës
2001	Vllaznia Shkodër	SK Tirana
2002	Dinamo Tiranë	SK Tirana
2003	SK Tirana	Dinamo Tiranë
2004	SK Tirana	Partizani Tiranë
2005	SK Tirana	Teuta Durrës
2006	KF Elbasani	SK Tirana
2007	SK Tirana	Besa Kavajë
2008	Dinamo Tiranë	Vllaznia Shkodër
2009	KF Tirana	Flamurtari Vlorë
2010	Dinamo Tiranë	Besa Kavajë
2011	Skënderbeu Korçë	KF Tirana

ALG – ALGERIA

Year	Champions	Cup Winners
1963	USM Alger	Entente Setif
1964	Hamra Annaba	Entente Setif
1965	CR Belcourt	MC Saida
1966	CR Belcourt	CR Belcourt
1967	NA Hussein-Dey	Entente Setif
1968	Entente Setif	Entente Setif
1969	CR Belcourt	CR Belcourt
1970	CR Belcourt	CR Belcourt
1971	Mouloudia d'Oran	Mouloudia d'Alger
1972	Mouloudia d'Alger	Hamra Annaba
1973	JS Kabylie	Mouloudia d'Alger
1974	JS Kabylie	USM Maison Carrée
1975	Mouloudia d'Alger	Mouloudia d'Oran
1976	Mouloudia d'Alger	Mouloudia d'Oran
1977	JS Kawkabi	JS Kawkabi
1978	Mouloudia d'Alger	CM Belcourt
1979	Mouloudia d'Alger	MA Hussein Dey
1980	JE Tizi-Ouzou	Entente Setif
1981	RS Kouba	USK Alger
1982	JE Tizi-Ouzou	DNC Alger
1983	JE Tizi-Ouzou	Mouloudia d'Alger
1984	GCR Mascara	Mouloudia d'Oran
1985	JE Tizi-Ouzou	Mouloudia d'Oran
1986	JE Tizi-Ouzou	JE Tizi-Ouzou
1987	Entente Sétif	USM El-Harrach
1988	Mouloudia d'Oran	USM Alger
1989	JE Tizi-Ouzou	Entente Setif
1990	JS Kabylie	
1991	Mouloudia Con'tine	USM Bel Abbés
1992	Mouloudia d'Oran	JS Kabylie
1993	Mouloudia d'Oran	
1994	US Chaouia	JS Kabylie
1995	JS Kabylie	CR Belouizdad
1996	USM Alger	Mouloudia d'Oran
1997	CS Constantine	USM Alger
1998	USM El Harrach	WA Tlemcen
1999	Mouloudia d'Alger	USM Alger
2000	CR Belouizdad	MC Ouargla
2001	CR Belouizdad	USM Alger
2002	USM Alger	WA Tlemcen
2003	USM Alger	USM Alger
2004	JS Kabylie	USM Alger
2005	USM Alger	ASO Chlef
2006	JS Kabylie	Mouloudia d'Alger
2007	Entente Sétif	Mouloudia d'Alger
2008	JS Kabylie	JSM Béjaïa
2009	Entente Sétif	CR Belouizdad
2010	Mouloudia d'Alger	Entente Sétif
2011	ASO Chlef	JS Kabylie

AND – ANDORRA

Year	Champions	Cup Winners
1994		Principat
1995		Principat
1996	Encamp	Principat
1997	Principat	Principat
1998	Principat	Principat
1999	Principat	Principat
2000	Constelació	Constelació
2001	Santa Coloma	Santa Coloma
2002	Encamp	Lusitans
2003	Santa Coloma	Santa Coloma
2004	Santa Coloma	Santa Coloma
2005	Sant Julià	Santa Coloma
2006	Ranger's	Santa Coloma
2007	Ranger's	Santa Coloma
2008	Santa Coloma	Sant Julià
2009	Sant Julià	Santa Coloma
2010	Santa Coloma	Sant Julià
2011	Santa Coloma	Sant Julià

ANG – ANGOLA

Year	Champions	Cup Winners
1979	Primeiro de Agosto	
1980	Primeiro de Agosto	
1981	Primeiro de Agosto	
1982	Petro Atlético	Primeiro de Maio
1983	Primeiro de Maio	Primeiro de Maio
1984	Petro Atlético	Primeiro de Agosto
1985	Primeiro de Maio	Ferroviário Huila
1986	Petro Atlético	Inter Clube
1987	Petro Atlético	Petro Atlético
1988	Petro Atlético	Sagrada Esperança
1989	Petro Atlético	Ferroviário Huila
1990	Petro Atlético	Primeiro de Agosto
1991	Primeiro de Agosto	Primeiro de Agosto
1992	Primeiro de Agosto	Petro Atlético
1993	Petro Atlético	Petro Atlético
1994	Petro Atlético	Petro Atlético
1995	Petro Atlético	Atlético Aviação

Year	Champions	
1996	Primeiro de Agosto	Prog. Sambizanga
1997	Petro Atlético	Petro Atlético
1998	Primeiro de Agosto	Petro Atlético
1999	Primeiro de Agosto	Sagrada Esperança
2000	Petro Atlético	Petro Atlético
2001	Petro Atlético	Sonangol
2002	Atlético Aviação	Petro Atlético
2003	Atlético Aviação	Inter Clube
2004	Atlético Aviação	Sonangol
2005	Sagrada Esperança	Atlético Aviação
2006	Primeiro de Agosto	Primeiro de Agosto
2007	Inter Clube	Primeiro de Maio
2008	Petro Atlético	Santos
2009	Petro Atlético	Primeiro de Agosto
2010	Inter Clube	Atlético Aviação
2011	Recreativo Libolo	Inter Clube

ANT – NETHERLANDS ANTILLES

Year	Champions
1959	Jong Holland
1960	Sithoc
1961	Sithoc
1962	Sithoc
1963	
1964	RCA
1965	RCA
1966	Jong Colombia
1967	Didi
1968	Jong Colombia
1969	SUBT
1970	SV Estrella
1971	Jong Colombia
1972	Jong Colombia
1973	Jong Colombia
1974	Jong Colombia
1975	Jong Colombia
1976	Jong Holland
1977	Jong Holland
1978	Jong Colombia
1979	SUBT
1980	SUBT
1981	Jong Holland
1982	SUBT
1983	SUBT
1984	SUBT
1985	UB Banda Abou
1986	Victory Boys
1987	UD Banda Abou
1988	Jong Colombia
1989	UD Banda Abou
1990	Sithoc
1991	Sithoc
1992	Sithoc
1993	Sithoc
1994	Jong Colombia
1995	Sithoc
1996	UD Banda Abou
1997	Jong Colombia
1998	
1999	Sithoc
2000	
2001	Jong Colombia
2002	Centro Barber
2003	Centro Barber
2004	Centro Barber
2005	Centro Barber
2006	Centro Barber
2007	Centro Barber
2008	Centro Barber
2009	Hubentut Fortuna
2010	Hubentut Fortuna
2011	Hubentut Fortuna

ARG – ARGENTINA

Year	Champions	Rival League
1891	Saint Andrew's	
1893	Lomas Athletic	
1894	Lomas Athletic	
1895	Lomas Athletic	
1896	Lomas Academy	
1897	Lomas Athletic	
1898	Lomas Athletic	
1899	Belgrano Athletic	
1900	English High School	
1901	Alumni	
1902	Alumni	
1903	Alumni	
1904	Belgrano Athletic	
1905	Alumni	
1906	Alumni	
1907	Alumni	
1908	Belgrano Athletic	
1909	Alumni	
1910	Alumni	
1911	Alumni	**Rival League**
1912	Quilmes	CA Porteño
1913	Racing Club	Estudiantes LP
1914	Racing Club	CA Porteño
1915	Racing Club	
1916	Racing Club	
1917	Racing Club	
1918	Racing Club	
1919	Racing Club	Boca Juniors
1920	River Plate	Boca Juniors
1921	Racing Club	Huracán
1922	Independiente	Huracán
1923	San Lorenzo	Boca Juniors
1924	San Lorenzo	Boca Juniors
1925	Racing Club	Huracán
1926	Independiente	Boca Juniors
1927	San Lorenzo	
1928	Huracán	
1929	Gimnasia y Esgrima	
1930	Boca Juniors	
1931	Boca Juniors	Estudiantil Porteño
1932	River Plate	Sportivo Barracas
1933	San Lorenzo	Sportivo Dock Sud
1934	Boca Juniors	Estudiantil Porteño
1935	Boca Juniors	
1936	River Plate	
1937	River Plate	
1938	Independiente	
1939	Independiente	
1940	Boca Juniors	
1941	River Plate	
1942	River Plate	
1943	Boca Juniors	
1944	Boca Juniors	
1945	River Plate	
1946	San Lorenzo	
1947	River Plate	
1948	Independiente	
1949	Racing Club	
1950	Racing Club	
1951	Racing Club	
1952	River Plate	
1953	River Plate	
1954	Boca Juniors	
1955	River Plate	
1956	River Plate	
1957	River Plate	
1958	Racing Club	
1959	San Lorenzo	
1960	Independiente	
1961	Racing Club	
1962	Boca Juniors	
1963	Independiente	
1964	Boca Juniors	

Year		National Championship
1965	Boca Juniors	
1966	Racing Club	
1967	Estudiantes LP	Independiente
1968	San Lorenzo	Velez Sarsfield
1969	Chacarita Juniors	Boca Juniors
1970	Independiente	Boca Juniors
1971	Independiente	Rosario Central
1972	San Lorenzo	San Lorenzo
1973	Huracán	Rosario Central
1974	Newell's Old Boys	San Lorenzo
1975	River Plate	River Plate
1976	Boca Juniors	Boca Juniors
1977	River Plate	Independiente
1978	Quilmes	Independiente
1979	River Plate	River Plate
1980	River Plate	Rosario Central
1981	Boca Juniors	River Plate
1982	Estudiantes LP	Ferrocarril Oeste
1983	Independiente	Estudiantes LP
1984	Argentinos Juniors	Ferrocarril Oeste
1985		Argentinos Juniors
1986	River Plate	
1987	Rosario Central	
1988	Newell's Old Boys	
1989	Independiente	

Year		Apertura
1990	River Plate	
1991	Newell's Old Boys	River Plate
1992	Newell's Old Boys	Boca Juniors
1993	Vélez Sarsfield	River Plate
1994	Independiente	River Plate
1995	San Lorenzo	Vélez Sarsfield
1996	Vélez Sarsfield	River Plate
1997	River Plate	River Plate
1998	Vélez Sarsfield	Boca Juniors
1999	Boca Juniors	River Plate
2000	River Plate	Boca Juniors
2001	San Lorenzo	Racing Club
2002	River Plate	Independiente
2003	River Plate	Boca Juniors
2004	River Plate	Newell's Old Boys
2005	Vélez Sarsfield	Boca Juniors
2006	Boca Juniors	Estudiantes LP
2007	San Lorenzo	Lanús
2008	River Plate	Boca Juniors
2009	Vélez Sarsfield	Banfield
2010	Argentinos Juniors	Estudiantes LP
2011	Vélez Sarsfield	Boca Juniors

ARM – ARMENIA

Year	Champions	Cup Winners
1992	Kumajri/Homenetmen	Banants Aboyan
1993	Ararat Yerevan	Ararat Yerevan
1994	Shirak Gyumri	Ararat Yerevan
1995		Ararat Yerevan
1996	Pyunik Yerevan	Pyunik Yerevan
1997	Pyunik Yerevan	Ararat Yerevan
1998	Tsement Ararat	Tsement Ararat
1999	Shirak Gyumri	Tsement Ararat
2000	Araks Ararat	Mika Ashtarak
2001	Pyunik Yerevan	Mika Ashtarak
2002	Pyunik Yerevan	Pyunik Yerevan
2003	Pyunik Yerevan	Mika Ashtarak
2004	Pyunik Yerevan	Pyunik Yerevan
2005	Pyunik Yerevan	Mika Ashtarak
2006	Pyunik Yerevan	Mika Ashtarak
2007	Pyunik Yerevan	Banants Yerevan
2008	Pyunik Yerevan	Ararat Yerevan
2009	Pyunik Yerevan	Pyunik Yerevan
2010	Pyunik Yerevan	Pyunik Yerevan
2011	Ulysses Yerevan	Mika Ashtarak

ARU – ARUBA

Year	Champions	Cup Winners
1960	Racing Club Aruba	
1961	Dakota	
1962	Dakota	
1963	Dakota	
1964	Racing Club Aruba	
1965	Dakota	
1966	Dakota	
1967	Racing Club Aruba	
1968	Estrella	
1969	Dakota	
1970	Dakota	
1971	Dakota	
1972		
1973	Estrella	
1974	Dakota	
1975	Bubali	
1976	Dakota	
1977	Estrella	
1978	Racing Club Aruba	
1979	Racing Club Aruba	
1980	Dakota	
1981	Dakota	
1982	Dakota	
1983	Dakota	
1984	San Luis	
1985	Estrella	
1986	Racing Club Aruba	
1987	Racing Club Aruba	
1988	Estrella	
1989	Estrella	
1990	Estrella	
1991	Racing Club Aruba	
1992	Estrella	
1993	Riverplate	
1994	Racing Club Aruba	
1995	Dakota	
1996	Estrella	
1997	Riverplate	
1998	Estrella	
1999	Estrella	

Year	Nacional/Champions	
2000	Nacional	
2001	Nacional	
2002	Racing Club Aruba	
2003	Nacional	
2004		
2005	Britannia	Sportboys
2006	Estrella	Estudiantes
2007	Nacional	Dakota
2008	Racing Club Aruba	Britannia
2009	Britannia	Britannia
2010	Britannia	Britannia
2011	Racing Club Aruba	Britannia

ASA – AMERICAN SAMOA

Year	Champions
1997	Pago Eagles
1998	
1999	Konica Machine
2000	PanSa & Wild West
2001	PanSa
2002	PanSa
2003	Manumea
2004	
2005	PanSa
2006	
2007	Konica
2008	Pago Youth
2009	Black Roses
2010	Pago Youth
2011	Pago Youth

ATG – ANTIGUA & BARBUDA

Year	Champions	Cup Winners
1969	Empire	
1970	Empire	
1971	Empire	
1972	Empire	
1973	Empire	
1974	Empire	
1979	Empire	
1984	Villa Lions	
1985	Liberta	
1986	Villa Lions	
1987	Liberta	
1988	Empire	
1990	J & J Construction	
1992	Empire	
1994	Lions Hill Spliff	
1995	English Harbour	
1996	English Harbour	
1997	English Harbour	
1998	Empire	
1999	Empire	
2000	Empire	
2001	Empire	
2002	Parham	
2003	Parham	
2004	Bassa	
2005	Bassa	
2006	SAP	
2007	Bassa	
2008	Bassa	
2009	SAP	
2010	Bassa	
2011	Parham	

AUS – AUSTRALIA

Year	Champions	Cup Winners
1977	Sydney City	Brisbane City
1978	West Adelaide	Brisbane City
1979	Marconi Fairfield	Adelaide City
1980	Sydney City	Marconi-Fairfield
1981	Sydney City	Brisbane Lions
1982	Sydney City	APIA-Leichhardt
1983	St George	Sydney Olympic
1984	South Melbourne	Newcastle
1985	Brunswick	Sydney Olympic
1986	Adelaide City	Sydney City
1987	APIA Leichhardt	Sydney Croatia
1988	Marconi Fairfield	APIA Leichhardt
1989	Marconi Fairfield	Adelaide City
1990	Sydney Olympic	South Melbourne
1991	South Melbourne	Parramatta Eagles
1992	Adelaide City	Adelaide City
1993	Marconi Fairfield	Heidelberg United
1994	Adelaide City	Parramatta Eagles
1995	Melbourne Knights	Melbourne Knights
1996	Melbourne Knights	South Melbourne
1997	Brisbane Strikers	Collingwood
1998	South Melbourne	
1999	South Melbourne	
2000	Wollongong Wolves	
2001	Wollongong Wolves	
2002	Sydney Olympic	
2003	Perth Glory	
2004	Perth Glory	
2005		
2006	Sydney FC	
2007	Melbourne Victory	
2008	Newcastle Jets	
2009	Melbourne Victory	
2010	Sydney FC	
2011	Brisbane Roar	

AUS – AUSTRIA

Year	Champions	Cup Winners
1897		Cricketers
1898		First Vienna FC
1899		Not played
1900		First Vienna FC
1901		Wiener AC
1902		Cricketers
1903		Wiener AC
1904		Wiener AC
1905		Wiener Sport-Club
1906		Nor played
1907		
1908		
1909		Ferencváros
1910		Budapester TC
1911		Wiener Sport-Club
1912	SK Rapid Wien	
1913	SK Rapid Wien	
1914	Wiener AF	
1915	Wiener AC	
1916	SK Rapid Wien	
1917	SK Rapid Wien	
1918	Floridsdorfer AC	
1919	SK Rapid Wien	SK Rapid Wien
1920	SK Rapid Wien	SK Rapid Wien
1921	SK Rapid Wien	Amateure

Year		
1922	Wiener Sport-Club	Wiener AF
1923	SK Rapid Wien	Wiener Sport-Club
1924	Amateure	Amateure
1925	Hakoah Wien	Amateure
1926	Amateure	Amateure
1927	Admira Wien	SK Rapid Wien
1928	Admira Wien	Admira Wien
1929	SK Rapid Wien	First Vienna FC
1930	SK Rapid Wien	First Vienna FC
1931	First Vienna FC	Wiener AC
1932	Admira Wien	Admira Wien
1933	First Vienna FC	FK Austria
1934	Admira Wien	Admira Wien
1935	SK Rapid Wien	FK Austria
1936	Admira Wien	FK Austria
1937	Admira Wien	First Vienna FC
1938	SK Rapid Wien	Wiener AC
1939	Admira Wien	
1940	FK Austria	
1941	SK Rapid Wien	
1942	First Vienna FC	
1943	First Vienna FC	
1944	First Vienna FC	
1945		
1946	SK Rapid Wien	SK Rapid Wien
1947	Wacker Wien	Wacker Wien
1948	SK Rapid Wien	FK Austria
1949	FK Austria	FK Austria
1950	FK Austria	
1951	SK Rapid Wien	
1952	SK Rapid Wien	
1953	FK Austria	
1954	SK Rapid Wien	
1955	First Vienna FC	
1956	SK Rapid Wien	
1957	SK Rapid Wien	
1958	Wiener Sport-Club	
1959	Wiener Sport-Club	Wiener AC
1960	SK Rapid Wien	FK Austria
1961	FK Austria	SK Rapid Wien
1962	FK Austria	FK Austria
1963	FK Austria	FK Austria
1964	SK Rapid Wien	Admira Wien
1965	Linzer ASK	Linzer ASK
1966	Admira Wien	Admira Wien
1967	SK Rapid Wien	FK Austria
1968	SK Rapid Wien	SK Rapid Wien
1969	FK Austria	SK Rapid Wien
1970	FK Austria	Wacker Innsbruck
1971	Wacker Innsbruck	FK Austria
1972	Wacker Innsbruck	SK Rapid Wien
1973	Wacker Innsbruck	Wacker Innsbruck
1974	SK VÖEST Linz	FK Austria
1975	Wacker Innsbruck	Wacker Innsbruck
1976	FK Austria	SK Rapid Wien
1977	Wacker Innsbruck	FK Austria
1978	FK Austria	Wacker Innsbruck
1979	FK Austria	Wacker Innsbruck
1980	FK Austria	FK Austria
1981	FK Austria	Grazer AK
1982	SK Rapid Wien	FK Austria
1983	SK Rapid Wien	SK Rapid Wien
1984	FK Austria	SK Rapid Wien
1985	FK Austria	SK Rapid Wien
1986	FK Austria	FK Austria
1987	SK Rapid Wien	SK Rapid Wien
1988	SK Rapid Wien	Kremser SC
1989	FC Tirol	FC Tirol
1990	FC Tirol	FK Austria
1991	FK Austria	SV Stockerau
1992	FK Austria	FK Austria
1993	FK Austria	Wacker Innsbruck
1994	SV Salzburg	FK Austria
1995	SV Salzburg	SK Rapid Wien
1996	SK Rapid Wien	SK Sturm Graz
1997	SV Salzburg	SK Sturm Graz
1998	SK Sturm Graz	SV Ried
1999	SK Sturm Graz	SK Sturm Graz
2000	FC Tirol Innsbruck	Grazer AK
2001	FC Tirol Innsbruck	FC Kärnten
2002	FC Tirol Innsbruck	Grazer AK
2003	FK Austria Wien	FK Austria Wien
2004	Grazer AK	Grazer AK
2005	SK Rapid Wien	FK Austria Wien
2006	FK Austria Wien	FK Austria Wien
2007	FC RB Salzburg	FK Austria Wien
2008	SK Rapid Wien	
2009	FC RB Salzburg	FK Austria Wien
2010	FC RB Salzburg	SK Sturm Graz
2011	SK Sturm Graz	SV Ried

AZE – AZERBAIJAN

Year	Champions	Cup Winners
1992	Neftchi Baku	Inshaatchi Baku
1993	Karabakh Agdam	Karabakh Agdam
1994	Turan Tovuz	Kapaz Gança
1995	Kapaz Gança	Neftchi Baku
1996	Neftchi Baku	Neftchi Baku
1997	Neftchi Baku	Kapaz Gança
1998	Kapaz Gança	Kapaz Gança
1999	Kapaz Gança	Neftchi Baku
2000	Shamkir	Kapaz Gança
2001	Shamkir	Shafa Baku
2002		Neftchi Baku
2003		
2004	Neftchi Baku	Neftchi Baku
2005	Neftchi Baku	FK Baku
2006	FK Baku	Karabakh Agdam
2007	Khazar Lenkoran	Khazar Lenkoran
2008	Inter Baku	Khazar Lenkoran
2009	FK Baku	Karabakh Agdam
2010	Inter Baku	FK Baku
2011	Neftchi Baku	Khazar Lenkoran

BAH – BAHAMAS

Year	Champions	Cup Winners
1992	Britam United	
1993	Britam United	
1994	Britam United	
1995	Britam United	
1996	Freeport	
1997	Cavalier	
1998	Cavalier	
1999	Cavalier	
2000	Abacom United	Cavalier
2001	Cavalier	Cavalier
2002	Bears	JJ Johnson
2003	Bears	Bears
2004	Bears	Bears
2005	Caledonia Celtic	
2006	Caledonia Celtic	
2007	Bears	Bears
2008		
2009	Bears	Caledonia Celtic
2010	Bears	
2011	Bears	

BAN – BANGLADESH

Year	Champions
2000	Abahani
2001	
2002	Mohammedan
2003	Muktijoddha
2004	Brothers Union
2005	
2006	Mohammedan
2007	Abahani
2008	
2009	Abahani
2010	Abahani
2011	Sheikh Jamal

Dhaka League

Year		
1948	Victoria	
1949	E Pakistan Gymkhana	
1950	Dhaka Wanderers	
1951	Dhaka Wanderers	
1952	Bengal Govt Press	
1953	Dhaka Wanderers	
1954	Dhaka Wanderers	
1955	Dhaka Wanderers	
1956	Dhaka Wanderers	
1957	Mohammedan	
1958	Azad Sporting	
1959	Mohammedan	
1960	Dhaka Wanderers	
1961	Mohammedan	
1962	Victoria	
1963	Mohammedan	
1964	Victoria	
1965	Mohammedan	
1966	Mohammedan	
1967	East Pakistan IDC	
1968	East Pakistan IDC	
1969	Mohammedan	
1970	East Pakistan IDC	
1971		
1972		
1973	Bangladesh IDC	
1974	Abahani	
1975	Mohammedan	
1976	Mohammedan	
1977	Abahani	
1978	Mohammedan	
1979	BJMC	**Fed Cup**
1980	Mohammedan	Moh'dan & Br Union
1981	Abahani	Mohammedan
1982	Abahani	Moh'dan & Abahani
1983	Abahani	Mohammedan
1984	Abahani	
1985	Abahani	Abahani
1986	Mohammedan	Abahani
1987	Mohammedan	Mohammedan
1988		Abahani
1989	Mohammedan	Mohammedan
1990	Abahani	

Year	Champions	Cup Winners
1991		Brothers Union
1992	Abahani	
1993	Mohammedan	
1994	Abahani	Muktijoddha
1995	Abahani	Mohammedan
1996	Mohammedan	
1997		Abahani
1998	Muktijoddha	
1999	Mohammedan	Abahani
2000	Muktijoddha	Abahani
2001	Abahani	Muktijoddha
2002	Mohammedan	Mohammedan
2003		Muktijoddha
2004	Brothers Union	
2005	Brothers Union	Brothers Union
2006	*No longer the*	
2007	*senior league in*	
2008	*Bangladesh*	Mohammedan
2009		Mohammedan
2010		Abahani
2011		Sheikh Jamal

BDI – BURUNDI

Year	Champions	Cup Winners
1972	Sports Dynamic	
1973	Sports Dynamic	
1974	Inter	
1978	Inter	
1979	Vital'O	
1980	Prince Louis	
1981	Prince Louis	
1982	Vital'O	Vital'O
1983	Fantastique	Inter
1984	Vital'O	Inter
1985	Vital'O	Vital'O
1986	Vital'O	Vital'O
1987	Inter	Muzinga
1988	Inter	Vital'O
1989	Inter	Vital'O
1990	Vital'O	Inter Star
1991	Inter Star	Vital'O
1992	Vital'O	Prince Louis
1993	Vital'O	Vital'O
1994	Vital'O	Vital'O
1995	Fantastique	Vital'O
1996	Fantastique	Vital'O
1997	Maniema	Vital'O
1998	Vital'O	Elite
1999	Vital'O	Vital'O
2000	Vital'O	At. Olympique
2001	Prince Louis	
2002	Muzinga	
2003		
2004	At. Olympique	
2005	Inter Star	
2006	Vital'O	
2007	Vital'O	
2008	Inter Star	
2009	Vital'O	
2010	Vital'O	
2011	At. Olympique	

BEL – BELGIUM

Year	Champions	Cup Winners
1896	FC Liègeois	
1897	Racing CB	
1898	FC Liègeois	
1899	FC Liègeois	
1900	Racing CB	
1901	Racing CB	
1902	Racing CB	
1903	Racing CB	
1904	Union St. Gilloise	
1905	Union St. Gilloise	
1906	Union St. Gilloise	
1907	Union St. Gilloise	
1908	Racing CB	
1909	Union St. Gilloise	
1910	Union St. Gilloise	
1911	Cercle Brugge	
1912	Daring CB	Racing CB
1913	Union St. Gilloise	Union St. Gilloise
1914	Daring CB	Union St. Gilloise
1920	Club Brugge	
1921	Daring CB	
1922	Beerschot	
1923	Union St. Gilloise	
1924	Beerschot	
1925	Beerschot	
1926	Beerschot	
1927	Cercle Brugge	Cercle Brugge
1928	Beerschot	
1929	Royal Antwerp FC	
1930	Cercle Brugge	
1931	Royal Antwerp FC	
1932	Lierse SK	
1933	Union St. Gilloise	
1934	Union St. Gilloise	
1935	Union St. Gilloise	
1936	Daring CB	
1937	Daring CB	
1938	Beerschot	
1939	Beerschot	
1940		
1941		
1942	Lierse SK	
1943	KV Mechelen	
1944	Royal Antwerp FC	
1945		
1946	KV Mechelen	
1947	RSC Anderlecht	
1948	KV Mechelen	
1949	RSC Anderlecht	
1950	RSC Anderlecht	
1951	RSC Anderlecht	
1952	RFC Liègeois	
1953	RFC Liègeois	
1954	RSC Anderlecht	Standard CL
1955	RSC Anderlecht	Royal Antwerp FC
1956	RSC Anderlecht	Racing Tournai
1957	Royal Antwerp FC	
1958	Standard CL	
1959	RSC Anderlecht	
1960	Lierse SK	
1961	Standard CL	
1962	RSC Anderlecht	
1963	Standard CL	
1964	RSC Anderlecht	AA Gent
1965	RSC Anderlecht	RSC Anderlecht
1966	RSC Anderlecht	Standard CL
1967	RSC Anderlecht	Standard CL
1968	RSC Anderlecht	Club Brugge
1969	Standard CL	Lierse SK
1970	Standard CL	Club Brugge
1971	Standard CL	Beerschot
1972	RSC Anderlecht	RSC Anderlecht
1973	Club Brugge	RSC Anderlecht
1974	RSC Anderlecht	KSV Waregem
1975	RWD Molenbeek	RSC Anderlecht
1976	Club Brugge	RSC Anderlecht
1977	Club Brugge	Club Brugge
1978	Club Brugge	SK Beveren
1979	SK Beveren	Beerschot
1980	Club Brugge	Waterschei THOR
1981	RSC Anderlecht	Standard CL
1982	Standard CL	Waterschei THOR
1983	Standard CL	SK Beveren
1984	SK Beveren	AA Gent
1985	RSC Anderlecht	Cercle Brugge
1986	RSC Anderlecht	Club Brugge
1987	RSC Anderlecht	KV Mechelen
1988	Club Brugge	RSC Anderlecht
1989	KV Mechelen	RSC Anderlecht
1990	Club Brugge	RFC Liège
1991	RSC Anderlecht	Club Brugge
1992	Club Brugge	Royal Antwerp FC
1993	RSC Anderlecht	Standard CL
1994	RSC Anderlecht	RSC Anderlecht
1995	RSC Anderlecht	Club Brugge
1996	Club Brugge	Club Brugge
1997	Lierse SK	Germinal Ekeren
1998	Club Brugge	KRC Genk
1999	KRC Genk	Lierse SK
2000	RSC Anderlecht	KRC Genk
2001	RSC Anderlecht	KVC Westerlo
2002	KRC Genk	Club Brugge
2003	Club Brugge	La Louvière
2004	RSC Anderlecht	Club Brugge
2005	Club Brugge	Germinal Beerschot
2006	RSC Anderlecht	Zulte Waregem
2007	RSC Anderlecht	Club Brugge
2008	Standard CL	RSC Anderlecht
2009	Standard CL	KRC Genk
2010	RSC Anderlecht	KAA Gent
2011	KRC Genk	Standard CL

BEN – BENIN

Year	Champions	Cup Winners
1969	FAD Cotonou	
1970	AS Porto-Novo	
1971	AS Cotonou	
1972	AS Porto-Novo	
1973	AS Porto-Novo	
1974	Etoile Sportive	Etoile Sportive
1978	Dragons de l'Ouémé	Requins
1979	Dragons de l'Ouémé	Buffles de Borgou
1980	Buffles de Borgou	
1981	Ajijas Cotonou	Requins
1982	Dragons de l'Ouémé	Buffles de Borgou
1983	Dragons de l'Ouémé	Requins
1984	Lions de l'Atakory	Dragons de l'Ouémé
1985	Requins	Dragons de l'Ouémé
1986	Dragons de l'Ouémé	Dragons de l'Ouémé

Year	Champions	Cup Winners
1987	Requins	
1988		Requins
1989	Dragons de l'Ouémé	Requins
1990	Requins	Dragons de l'Ouémé
1991	Postel Sport	Mogas 90
1992	Buffles de Borgou	Mogas 90
1993	Dragons de l'Ouémé	Locomotive Cotonou
1994	Dragons de l'Ouémé	Mogas 90
1995	Toffa Cotonou	Mogas 90
1996	Mogas 90	UNB Porto-Novo
1997	Mogas 90	Energie Sport
1998	Dragons de l'Ouémé	Mogas 90
1999	Dragons de l'Ouémé	Mogas 90
2000		Mogas 90
2001		Buffles du Borgou
2002	Dragons de l'Ouémé	Jeunesse Pobe
2003	Dragons de l'Ouémé	Mogas 90
2004		Mogas 90
2005		
2006	Mogas 90	Dragons de l'Ouémé
2007	Tonnerre d'Abomey	UNB Porto Novo
2008		ASPAC
2009		
2010	ASPAC	
2011	Tonerre	Dragons de l'Ouémé

BER – BERMUDA

Year	Champions	Cup Winners
1956		Bermuda AA
1957		PHC Zebras
1958		Wellington Rovers
1959		Dock Hill Rangers
1960		PHC Zebras
1961		PHC Zebras
1962		PHC Zebras
1963		Young Men's SC
1964	Young Men's SC	Young Men's SC
1965	Young Men's SC	Young Men's SC
1966	Young Men's SC	Casuals
1967	Somerset Trojans	PHC Zebras
1968	Somerset Trojans	Somerset Trojans
1969	Somerset Trojans	Somerset Trojans
1970	Somerset Trojans	Somerset Trojans
1971	PHC Zebras	PHC Zebras
1972	Devonshire Colts	Somerset Trojans
1973	Devonshire Colts	Devonshire Colts
1974	North Village CC	Devonshire Colts
1975	Hotels International	PHC Zebras
1976	North Village CC	Somerset Trojans
1977	PHC Zebras	Somerset Trojans
1978	North Village CC	North Village
1979	North Village CC	Somerset Trojans
1980	Hotels International	PHC Zebras
1981	Southampton Rang.	Vasco da Gama
1982	Somerset Trojans	Vasco da Gama
1983	Somerset Trojans	North Village
1984	Somerset Trojans	Southampton Rang.
1985	PHC Zebras	Hotels International
1986	PHC Zebras	North Village
1987	Somerset Trojans	Dandy Town
1988	Dandy Town	Somerset Trojans
1989	PHC Zebras	North Village
1990	PHC Zebras	Somerset Trojans
1991	Boulevard Blazers	Boulevard Blazers
1992	PHC Zebras	PHC Zebras
1993	Somerset Trojans	Boulevard Blazers
1994	Dandy Town	Vasco da Gama
1995	Boulevard Blazers	Vasco da Gama
1996	Vasco da Gama	Boulevard Blazers
1997	Devonshire Colts	Boulevard Blazers
1998	Vasco da Gama	Vasco da Gama
1999	Vasco da Gama	Devonshire Colts
2000	PHC Zebras	North Village
2001	Dandy Town	Devonshire Colts
2002	North Village CC	North Village
2003	North Village CC	North Village
2004	Dandy Town	North Village
2005	Devonshire Cougars	North Village
2006	North Village CC	North Village
2007	Devonshire Cougars	Devonshire Colts
2008	PHC Zebras	PHC Zebras
2009	Devonshire Cougars	Boulevard Blazers
2010	Dandy Town	Devonshire Cougars
2011	North Village CC	Devonshire Cougars

BFA – BURKINA FASO

Year	Champions	Cup Winners
1961	ASFB	Racing Club Bobo
1962	Etoile Filante	Racing Club Bobo
1963	USFRAN	Etoile Filante
1964	USFRAN	Etoile Filante
1965	Etoile Filante	Etoile Filante
1966	ASFB	USFRAN
1967	USO	USFRAN
1968	USFRAN	ASFAV
1969	ASFAN	USFRAN
1970	ASFAN	Etoile Filante
1971	ASFAN	USFRAN
1972	Racing Club Bobo	Etoile Filante
1973	Jeanne d'Arc	
1974	Silures	USFRAN
1975	Silures	Etoile Filante
1976	Silures	Etoile Filante
1977	Silures	
1978	Silures	
1979	Silures	
1980	Silures	
1981		Silures
1982		
1983	USO	
1984	ASFAN	Racing Club Bobo
1985	Etoile Filante	Etoile Filante
1986	Etoile Filante	ASFB
1987	USFAN	Racing Club Bobo
1988	Etoile Filante	Etoile Filante
1989	ASFA-Yennenga	ASFB
1990	Etoile Filante	Etoile Filante
1991	Etoile Filante	ASFA-Yennenga
1992	Etoile Filante	Etoile Filante
1993	Etoile Filante	Etoile Filante
1994	Etoile Filante	Rail Club Kadiogo
1995	ASFA-Yennenga	ASFA-Yennenga
1996	Racing Club Bobo	Etoile Filante
1997	Racing Club Bobo	ASFB
1998	USFAN	ASFB
1999	ASFA-Yennenga	Etoile Filante
2000	USFA	Etoile Filante
2001	Etoile Filante	Etoile Filante
2002	ASFA-Yennenga	USFA
2003	ASFA-Yennenga	Etoile Filante
2004	ASFA-Yennenga	ASFB
2005	Rail Club Kadiogo	USO
2006	ASFA-Yennenga	Etoile Filante
2007	Commune FC	Racing Club Bobo
2008	Etoile Filante	Etoile Filante
2009	ASFA-Yennenga	ASFA-Yennenga
2010	ASFA-Yennenga	USFA
2011	ASFA-Yennenga	Etoile Filante

BHR – BAHRAIN

Year	Champions	Cup Winners
1952		Muharraq
1953		Muharraq
1954		Muharraq
1957	Muharraq	
1958	Muharraq	Muharraq
1959	Al Nasr	Muharraq
1960	Muharraq	Al Nusoor
1961	Muharraq	Muharraq
1962	Muharraq	Muharraq
1963	Muharraq	Muharraq
1964	Muharraq	Muharraq
1965	Muharraq	
1966	Muharraq	Muharraq
1967	Muharraq	Muharraq
1968	Bahrain Club	Al Nusoor
1969	Al Ahli	Al Arabi
1970	Muharraq	Bahrain Club
1971	Muharraq	Bahrain Club
1972	Al Ahli	Muharraq
1973	Muharraq	West Riffa
1974	Muharraq	Muharraq
1975	Al Arabi	Muharraq
1976	Muharraq	Al Hala
1977	Al Ahli	Al Nusoor
1978	Bahrain Club	Muharraq
1979	Al Hala	Muharraq
1980	Muharraq	Al Hala
1981	Bahrain Club	Al Hala
1982	West Riffa	Al Ahli
1983	Muharraq	Muharraq
1984	Muharraq	Muharraq
1985	Bahrain Club	West Riffa
1986	Muharraq	West Riffa
1987	West Riffa	Al Ahly
1988	Muharraq	Al Wahda
1989	Bahrain Club	Muharraq
1990	West Riffa	Muharraq
1991	Muharraq	Al Ahli
1992	Muharraq	Al Wahda
1993	West Riffa	Muharraq
1994	East Riffa	Al Wahda
1995	Muharraq	Muharraq
1996	Al Ahli	Muharraq
1997	West Riffa	Muharraq
1998	West Riffa	West Riffa
1999	Muharraq	East Riffa
2000	West Riffa	East Riffa
2001	Muharraq	Al Ahly
2002	Muharraq	Muharraq
2003	Riffa	Al Ahly
2004	Muharraq	Al Shabab
2005	Riffa	Muharraq
2006	Muharraq	Al Najma
2007	Muharraq	Al Najma

Year	Champions	Cup Winners
2008	Muharraq	Muharraq
2009	Muharraq	Muharraq
2010	Al Ahli	Riffa
2011	Muharraq	Muharraq

BHU – BHUTAN

Year	Champions
1996	Druk Pol
1997	Druk Pol
1998	Druk Pol
1999	Druk Pol
2000	Druk Pol
2001	Druk Star
2002	Druk Pol
2003	Druk Pol
2004	Transport United
2005	Transport United
2006	Transport United
2007	Transport United
2008	Yeedzin
2009	Druk Star
2010	Yeedzin
2011	

BIH – BOSNIA-HERZEGOVINA

Year	Champions	Cup Winners
1995	Celik Zenica	Celik Zenica
1996	Celik Zenica	Celik Zenica
1997	Celik Zenica	Sarajevo
1998	Zeljeznicar	Sarajevo
1999	No overall winner	Bosna Visoko
2000	Brotnjo Citluk	Zeljeznicar
2001	Zeljeznicar	Zeljeznicar
2002	Zeljeznicar	Sarajevo
2003	Leotar Trebinje	Zeljeznicar
2004	Siroki Brijeg	Modrica Maksima
2005	Zrinjski Mostar	Sarajevo
2006	Siroki Brijeg	Orasje
2007	Sarajevo	Siroki Brijeg
2008	Modrica Maksima	Zrinjski Mostar
2009	Zrinjski Mostar	Slavija Sarajevo
2010	Zeljeznicar	Borac Banja Luka
2011	Borac Banja Luka	Zeljeznicar

BLR – BELARUS

Year	Champions	Cup Winners
1992	Dinamo Minsk	Dinamo Minsk
1993	Dinamo Minsk	Neman Grodno
1994	Dinamo Minsk	Dinamo Minsk
1995	Dinamo Minsk	Dinamo-93 Minsk
1995	Dinamo Minsk	
1996	MPKC Mozyr	MPKC Mozyr
1997	Dinamo Minsk	Belshina Bobruisk
1998	Dnepr-Transmash	Lokomotiv Vitebsk
1999	BATE Borisov	Belshina Bobruisk
2000	Slavija Mozyr	Slavija Mozyr
2001	Belshina Bobruisk	Belshina Bobruisk
2002	BATE Borisov	FC Gomel
2003	FC Gomel	Dinamo Minsk
2004	Dinamo Minsk	Shakhtyor Soligorsk
2005	Shakhtyor Soligorsk	MTZ-RIPO Minsk
2006	BATE Borisov	BATE Borisov
2007	BATE Borisov	Dinamo Brest
2008	BATE Borisov	MTZ-RIPO Minsk
2009	BATE Borisov	Naftan Novopolotsk
2010	BATE Borisov	BATE Borisov
2011	BATE Borisov	FC Gomel

BLZ – BELIZE

Year	Champions
1992	La Victoria
1993	Acros Carib
1994	La Victoria
1995	Acros Crystal
1996	Juventus
1997	Juventus
1998	Juventus
1999	Juventus
2000	Sagitún
2001	Kulture Yabra
2002	Kulture Yabra
2003	New Erei
2004	Boca Juniors
2005	Juventus
2006	New Site Erei
2006	New Site Erei
2006	FC Belize
2007	FC Belize
2008	Hankook Verdes
2008	Ilagulei
2009	Nizhee Corozal
2009	Belize Defence Force
2010	Belize Defence Force
2011	

BOL – BOLIVIA

Year	La Paz League	
1914	The Strongest	
1915	Colegio Militar	
1916	The Strongest	
1916	The Strongest	
1917	The Strongest	
1922	The Strongest	
1923	The Strongest	
1924	The Strongest	
1925	The Strongest	
1927	Nimbles	
1928	Deportivo Militar	
1929	Universitario	
1930	The Strongest	
1931	Nimbles Railway	
1932	Bolívar	
1935	The Strongest	
1936	Ayacucho	
1937	Bolívar	
1938	The Strongest	
1939	Bolívar	
1940	Bolívar	
1941	Bolívar	
1942	Bolívar	
1943	The Strongest	
1944	Ferroviario	
1946	The Strongest	
1947	Litoral	
1948	Litoral	
1949	Litoral	
1950	Bolívar	
1951	Always Ready	
1952	The Strongest	
1953	Bolívar	
Torneo Integrado		
1954	Litoral	
1955	San José	
1956	Bolívar	
1957	Always Ready	
National		
1958	Jorge Wilstermann	
1959	Jorge Wilstermann	
1960	Deportivo Municipal	
1961	Deportivo Municipal	
1962	Deportivo Chaco	
1963	The Strongest	
1964	The Strongest	
1965	Deportivo Municipal	Deportivo Municipal
1966	Bolívar	Bolívar
1967	Jorge Wilstermann	Bolívar
1968	Bolívar	Always Ready
1969	Universitario	Bolívar
1970	Chaco Petrolero	The Strongest
1971	Oriente Petrolero	
1972	Jorge Wilstermann	Litoral
1973	Jorge Wilstermann	Deportivo Municipal
1974	The Strongest	The Strongest
1975	Guabirá	31 de Octubre
1976	Bolívar	Bolívar
Pro League		
1977	The Strongest	
1978	Bolívar	
1979	Oriente Petrolero	
1980	Jorge Wilstermann	
1981	Jorge Wilstermann	
1982	Bolívar	
1983	Bolívar	
1984	Blooming	
1985	Bolívar	
1986	The Strongest	
1987	Bolívar	
1988	Bolívar	
1989	The Strongest	
1990	Oriente Petrolero	
1991	Bolívar	
1992	Bolívar	
1993	The Strongest	
1994	Bolívar	
1995	San José	
1996	Bolívar	
1997	Bolívar	
1998	Blooming	
1999	Blooming	
2000	Jorge Wilstermann	
2001	Oriente Petrolero	
		Clausura
2002	Bolívar	
2003	The Strongest	The Strongest
2004	Bolívar	The Strongest
2005	Bolívar	Blooming
2006	Bolívar	Jorge Wilstermann
2007	Real Potosí	San José
2008	Universitario Sucre	Aurora
2009	Bolívar	Blooming
2010	Jorge Wilstermann	Oriente Petrolero
2011	Bolívar	The Strongest

BOT – BOTSWANA

Year	Champions	Cup Winners
1966		
1967	Gaborone United	
1968		Gaborone United
1969	Gaborone United	
1970	Gaborone United	Gaborone United
1971		
1972		
1973		
1974		
1975		
1976		
1977		
1978	Notwane	Gaborone United
1979	Township Rollers	Township Rollers
1980	Township Rollers	
1981	Bot. Defence Force	
1982	Township Rollers	
1983	Township Rollers	Police
1984	Township Rollers	Gaborone United
1985	Township Rollers	Gaborone United
1986	Gaborone United	Nico United
1987	Township Rollers	Nico United
1988	Bot. Defence Force	Extension Gunners
1989	Bot. Defence Force	Bot. Defence Force
1990	Gaborone United	Gaborone United
1991	Bot. Defence Force	TASC/Centre Chiefs
1992	Extension Gunners	Extension Gunners
1993	Extension Gunners	Township Rollers
1994	Extension Gunners	Township Rollers
1995	Township Rollers	Notwane
1996	Notwane	Township Rollers
1997	Bot. Defence Force	Notwane
1998	Notwane	Bot. Defence Force
1999	Mog'shane Fighters	Mog'shane Fighters
2000	Mog'shane Fighters	Mog'shane Fighters
2001	Mog'shane Fighters	TASC
2002	Bot. Defence Force	TAFIC
2003	Mog'shane Fighters	Mog'shane Fighters
2004	Bot. Defence Force	Bot. Defence Force
2005	Township Rollers	Township Rollers
2006	Police XI	Notwane
2007	ECCO City Green	Meat Commission
2008	Centre Chiefs	Centre Chiefs
2009	Gaborone United	UF Santos
2010	Township Rollers	Township Rollers
2011	Township Rollers	Extension Gunners

BRA – BRAZIL

Year	Champions	Cup Winners
1959		Bahia
1960		Palmeiras
1961		Santos
1962		Santos
1963		Santos
1964		Santos
1965		Santos
1966		Cruzeiro
1967		Palmeiras
1968		Botafogo

Year	Champions	Cup Winners
1969		
1970		
1971	Atlético Mineiro	
1972	Palmeiras	
1973	Palmeiras	
1974	Vasco da Gama	
1975	Internacional	
1976	Internacional	
1977	São Paulo FC	
1978	Guarani Campinas	
1979	Internacional	
1980	Flamengo	
1981	Grêmio	
1982	Flamengo	
1983	Flamengo	
1984	Fluminense	
1985	Coritiba	
1986	São Paulo FC	
1987	Flamengo	
1987	Sport Recife	
1988	Bahia	
1989	Vasco da Gama	Grêmio
1990	Corinthians	Flamengo
1991	São Paulo FC	Criciúma
1992	Flamengo	Internacional
1993	Palmeiras	Cruzeiro
1994	Palmeiras	Grêmio
1995	Botafogo	Corinthians
1996	Grêmio	Cruzeiro
1997	Vasco da Gama	Grêmio
1998	Corinthians	Palmeiras
1999	Corinthians	Juventude
2000	Vasco da Gama	Cruzeiro
2001	Atletico Paranaense	Gremio
2002	Santos	Corinthians
2003	Cruzeiro	Cruzeiro
2004	Santos	Santo André
2005	Corinthians	Paulista
2006	São Paulo FC	Flamengo
2007	São Paulo FC	Fluminense
2008	São Paulo FC	Sport Recife
2009	Flamengo	Corinthians
2010	Fluminense	Santos
2011	Corinthians	Vasco da Gama

BRA – BRAZIL

Year	Torneio Rio/São Paulo
1933	Palestra Itália
1950	Corinthians
1951	Palmeiras
1952	Portuguesa
1953	Corinthians
1954	Corinthians
1955	Portuguesa
1956	
1957	Fluminense
1958	Vasco da Gama
1959	Santos
1960	Fluminense
1961	Flamengo
1962	Botafogo
1963	Santos

Year	Winner	
1964	Santos & Botafogo	
1965	Palmeiras	
	Corinthians,	Taca Roberto Gomes Pedrosa
1966	Santos, Vasco da Gama & Botafogo	
1967	Palmeiras	
1968	Santos	
1969	Palmeiras	
1970	Fluminense	
1993	Palmeiras	
1997	Santos	
1998	Botafogo	
1999	Vasco da Gama	
2000	Palmeiras	
2001	São Paulo FC	
2002	Corinthians	

BRA – BRAZIL

Year	São Paulo	Rio de Janeiro
1902	São Paulo Athletic	
1903	São Paulo Athletic	
1904	São Paulo Athletic	
1905	Paulistano	
1906	Germânia	Fluminense
1907	SC Internacional	Fluminense/Botafogo
1908	Paulistano	Fluminense
1909	AA das Palmeiras	Fluminense
1910	AA das Palmeiras	Botafogo
1911	São Paulo Athletic	Fluminense
1912	Américano	Payssandu
1913	Américano	América
1913	Paulistano	
1914	Corinthians	Flamengo
1914	São Bento	
1915	Germânia	Flamengo
1915	AA das Palmeiras	
1916	Corinthians	América
1916	Paulistano	
1917	Paulistano	Fluminense
1918	Paulistano	Fluminense
1919	Paulistano	Fluminense
1920	Palestra Italia	Flamengo
1921	Paulistano	Flamengo
1922	Corinthians	América
1923	Corinthians	Vasco da Gama
1924	Corinthians	Vasco da Gama
1924		Fluminense
1925	São Bento	Flamengo
1926	Palestra Italia	São Cristovão
1926	Paulistano	
1927	Palestra Italia	Flamengo
1927	Paulistano	
1928	Corinthians	América
1928	SC Internacional	
1929	Corinthians	Vasco da Gama
1929	Paulistano	
1930	Corinthians	Botafogo
1931	São Paulo	América
1932	Palestra Italia	Botafogo
1933	Palestra Italia	Bangu
1933		Botafogo
1934	Palestra Italia	Vasco da Gama
1934		Botafogo
1935	Portuguesa	América
1935	Santos	Botafogo

Year	São Paulo	Rio de Janeiro
1936	Portuguesa	Fluminense
1936	Palestra Italia	Vasco da Gama
1937	Corinthians	Fluminense
1938	Corinthians	Fluminense
1939	Corinthians	Flamengo
1940	Palestra Italia	Fluminense
1941	Corinthians	Fluminense
1942	Palmeiras	Flamengo
1943	São Paulo FC	Flamengo
1944	Palmeiras	Flamengo
1945	São Paulo FC	Vasco da Gama
1946	São Paulo FC	Fluminense
1947	Palmeiras	Vasco da Gama
1948	São Paulo FC	Botafogo
1949	São Paulo FC	Vasco da Gama
1950	Palmeiras	Vasco da Gama
1951	Corinthians	Fluminense
1952	Corinthians	Vasco da Gama
1953	São Paulo FC	Flamengo
1954	Corinthians	Flamengo
1955	Santos	Flamengo
1956	Santos	Vasco da Gama
1957	São Paulo FC	Botafogo
1958	Santos	Vasco da Gama
1959	Palmeiras	Fluminense
1960	Santos	América
1961	Santos	Botafogo
1962	Santos	Botafogo
1963	Palmeiras	Flamengo
1964	Santos	Fluminense
1965	Santos	Flamengo
1966	Palmeiras	Bangu
1967	Santos	Botafogo
1968	Santos	Botafogo
1969	Santos	Fluminense
1970	São Paulo FC	Vasco da Gama
1971	São Paulo FC	Fluminense
1972	Palmeiras	Flamengo
1973	Santos/Portuguesa	Fluminense
1974	Palmeiras	Flamengo
1975	São Paulo FC	Fluminense
1976	Palmeiras	Fluminense
1977	Corinthians	Vasco da Gama
1978	Santos	Flamengo
1979	Corinthians	Flamengo (x2)
1980	São Paulo FC	Fluminense
1981	São Paulo FC	Flamengo
1982	Corinthians	Vasco da Gama
1983	Corinthians	Fluminense
1984	Santos	Fluminense
1985	São Paulo FC	Fluminense
1986	Internacional Limeira	Flamengo
1987	São Paulo FC	Vasco da Gama
1988	Corinthians	Vasco da Gama
1989	São Paulo FC	Botafogo
1990	Bragantino	Botafogo
1991	São Paulo FC	Flamengo
1992	São Paulo FC	Vasco da Gama
1993	Palmeiras	Vasco da Gama
1994	Palmeiras	Vasco da Gama
1995	Corinthians	Fluminense
1996	Palmeiras	Flamengo
1997	Corinthians	Botafogo
1998	São Paulo FC	Vasco da Gama
1999	Corinthians	Flamengo
2000	São Paulo FC	Flamengo
2001	Corinthians	Flamengo
2002	São Paulo FC	Fluminense
2003	Corinthians	Vasco da Gama
2004	São Caetano	Flamengo
2005	São Paulo FC	Fluminense
2006	Santos	Botafogo
2007	Santos	Flamengo
2008	Palmeiras	Flamengo
2009	Corinthians	Flamengo
2010	Santos	Botafogo
2011	Santos	Flamengo

BRB – BARBADOS

Year	Champions	Cup Winners
1960	Everton	Everton
1961		
1962	New South Wales	Everton
1963	Everton	
1964	New South Wales	
1965	Everton	
1966	Everton	
1967	New South Wales	New South Wales
1968		
1969	New South Wales	New South Wales
1970	New South Wales	New South Wales
1971	New South Wales	
1972	New South Wales	New South Wales
1973	Pan-Am Wales	
1974	Pan-Am Wales	
1975	Pan-Am Wales	New South Wales
1976	Pan-Am Wales	
1977		
1978	Weymouth Wales	
1979		
1980		
1981	Weymouth Wales	
1982	Pinelands	Notre Dame
1983		
1984	Weymouth Wales	Weymouth Wales
1985	Pinelands	
1986	Weymouth Wales	Everton
1987	Everton	Weymouth Wales
1988	Pride of Gall Hill	
1989	Paradise	Pinelands
1990	Brittons Hill	Everton
1991		
1992	Pinelands	
1993	Pride of Gall Hill	Pride of Gall Hill
1994		BDF
1995	BDF	Pride of Gall Hill
1996	Paradise	Paradise
1997	Notre Dame	Notre Dame
1998	Notre Dame	Pride of Gall Hill
1999	Notre Dame	Paradise
2000	Notre Dame	Paradise
2001	Paradise	Notre Dame
2002	Notre Dame	Youth Milan
2003	Paradise	Paradise
2004	Notre Dame	Notre Dame
2005	Notre Dame	Paradise
2006	Youth Milan	Pride of Gall Hill
2007	BDF	Brittons Hill
2008	Notre Dame	Notre Dame
2009	Brittons Hill	Youth Milan
2010	Notre Dame	Notre Dame
2011	Youth Milan	Weymouth Wales

BRU – BRUNEI DARUSSALAM

Year	Champions	Cup Winners
2002	DPMM	Wujaya
2003	Wijaya	ABDB
2004	DPMM	DPMM
2005		
2006	QAF	AH United
2007		
2008	QAF	ABDB
2009		
2010	QAF	ABDB
2011		

BUL – BULGARIA

Year	Champions	Cup Winners
1925	Vladislav Varna	
1926	Vladislav Varna	
1927	Not played	
1928	Slavia Sofia	
1929	Botev Plovdiv	
1930	Slavia Sofia	
1931	AC 23 Sofia	
1932	Shipenski Sokol	
1933	Levski Sofia	
1934	Vladislav Varna	
1935	SC Sofia	
1936	Slavia Sofia	
1937	Levski Sofia	
1938	Ticha Varna	FK 13 Sofia
1939	Slavia Sofia	Shipka Sofia
1940	JSK Sofia	FK 13 Sofia
1941	Slavia Sofia	AC 23 Sofia
1942	Levski Sofia	Levski Sofia
1943	Slavia Sofia	
1944	-	
1945	Lokomotiv Sofia	
1946	Levski Sofia	
1947	Levski Sofia	
1948	Septemvri CDW	
1949	Levski Sofia	
1950	Dinamo Sofia	
1951	CDNA Sofia	
1952	CDNA Sofia	
1953	Dinamo Sofia	
1954	CDNA Sofia	
1955	CDNA Sofia	
1956	CDNA Sofia	
1957	CDNA Sofia	
1958	CDNA Sofia	
1959	CDNA Sofia	
1960	CDNA Sofia	
1961	CDNA Sofia	
1962	CDNA Sofia	
1963	Spartak Plovdiv	
1964	Lokomotiv Sofia	
1965	Levski Sofia	
1966	CSKA-CZ Sofia	
1967	Botev Plovdiv	
1968	Levski Sofia	
1969	CSKA Sofia	
1970	Levski-Spartak	
1971	CSKA Sofia	

Year	Champions	Cup
1972	CSKA Sofia	
1973	CSKA Sofia	
1974	Levski-Spartak	
1975	CSKA Sofia	
1976	CSKA Sofia	
1977	Levski-Spartak	
1978	Lokomotiv Sofia	
1979	Levski-Spartak	
1980	CSKA Sofia	
1981	CSKA Sofia	CSKA Sofia
1982	CSKA Sofia	Levski-Spartak
1983	CSKA Sofia	CSKA Sofia
1984	Levski-Spartak	Levski-Spartak
1985	Trakia Plovdiv	CSKA Sofia
1986	Beroe Stara Zagora	Vitosha Sofia
1987	CFKA Sredets	CFKA Sredets
1988	Vitosha Sofia	CFKA Sredets
1989	CFKA Sredets	CFKA Sredets
1990	CSKA Sofia	Sliven
1991	Etar Veliko Tarnovo	Levski Sofia
1992	CSKA Sofia	Levski Sofia
1993	Levski Sofia	CSKA Sofia
1994	Levski Sofia	Levski Sofia
1995	Levski Sofia	Lokomotiv Sofia
1996	Slavia Sofia	Slavia Sofia
1997	CSKA Sofia	CSKA Sofia
1998	Liteks Lovech	Levski Sofia
1999	Liteks Lovech	CSKA Sofia
2000	Levski Sofia	Levski Sofia
2001	Levski Sofia	Litex Lovech
2002	Levski Sofia	Levski Sofia
2003	CSKA Sofia	Levski Sofia
2004	Lokomotiv Plovdiv	Litex Lovech
2005	CSKA Sofia	Levski Sofia
2006	Levski Sofia	CSKA Sofia
2007	Levski Sofia	Levski Sofia
2008	CSKA Sofia	Litex Lovech
2009	Levski Sofia	Litex Lovech
2010	Litex Lovech	Beroe Stara Zagora
2011	Litex Lovech	CSKA Sofia

BUL – BULGARIA

Year	Soviet Army Cup
1946	Levski Sofia
1947	Levski Sofia
1948	Lokomotiv Sofia
1949	Dinamo Sofia
1950	Dinamo Sofia
1951	CDNA Sofia
1952	Udarnik Sofia
1953	Lokomotiv Sofia
1954	CDNA Sofia
1955	CDNA Sofia
1956	Dinamo Sofia
1957	Levski Sofia
1958	Spartak Plovdiv
1959	Lovski Sofia
1960	Septemvri CDW Sofia
1961	CDNA Sofia
1962	Botev Plovdiv
1963	Slavia Sofia
1964	Slavia Sofia
1965	CSKA-CZ Sofia
1966	Slavia Sofia
1967	Levski Sofia
1968	Spartak Sofia
1969	CSKA Sofia
1970	Levski-Spartak
1971	Levski-Spartak
1972	CSKA Sofia
1973	CSKA Sofia
1974	CSKA Sofia
1975	Slavia Sofia
1976	Levski-Spartak
1977	Levski-Spartak
1978	Marek St. Dimitrov
1979	Levski-Spartak
1980	Slavia Sofia
1981	Trakia Plovdiv
1982	Lokomotiv Sofia
1983	Lokomotiv Plovdiv
1984	Levski-Spartak
1985	CSKA Sofia
1986	CFKA Sredets
1987	Vitosha Sofia
1988	Vitosha Sofia
1989	CFKA Sredets
1990	CSKA Sofia

CAM – CAMBODIA

Year	Champions	Cup Winners
1982	Ministry of Commerce	
1983	Ministry of Commerce	
1984	Ministry of Commerce	
1985	Defence Ministry	
1986	Defence Ministry	
1987	Ministry of Health	
1988	Kampong Cham	
1989	Ministry of Transport	
1990	Ministry of Transport	
1991	Dept of Municipal Constructions	
1992	Dept of Municipal Constructions	
1993	Defence Ministry	
1994	Civil Aviation	
1995	Civil Aviation	
1996	Body Guards Club	
1997	Body Guards Club	
1998	Royal Dolphins	
1999	Royal Dolphins	
2000	Nokorbal Cheat	
2001		
2002	Samart United	
2003		
2004		
2005	Khemera	
2006	Khemera	
2007	Nagacorp	Khemera
2008	Phnom Penh Crown	Phnom Penh Crown
2009	Nagacorp	Phnom Penh Crown
2010	Phnom Penh Crown	Defence Ministry
2011	Phnom Penh Crown	Preah Khan Reach

CAN – CANADA

Year	Voyager's Cup
2002	Montreal Impact
2003	Montreal Impact
2004	Montreal Impact
2005	Montreal Impact
2006	Montreal Impact
2007	Montreal Impact
2008	Montreal Impact
2009	Toronto FC
2010	Toronto FC
2011	Toronto FC

CAY – CAYMAN ISLANDS

Year	Champions	Cup Winners
1997	George Town	
1998	Scholars Internat'al	George Town
1999	George Town	
2000	Western Union	
2001	Scholars Internat'al	Bodden Town
2002	George Town	George Town
2003	Scholars Internat'al	Scholars Internat'al
2004	Latinos	Latinos
2005	Western Union	Western Union
2006	Scholars Internat'al	Scholars Internat'al
2007	Scholars Internat'al	Latinos
2008	Scholars Internat'al	Scholars Internat'al
2009	Elite	Bodden Town
2010	Scholars Internat'al	George Town
2011	Elite	George Town

CGO – CONGO

Year	Champions	Cup Winners
1961	Diables Noirs	
1966	Diables Noires	
1967	Abeilles FC	
1968	Etoile du Congo	
1969	Patronage St Anne	
1970	CARA Brazzaville	
1971	V. Club Mokanda	
1972	CARA Brazzaville	
1973	CARA Brazzaville	
1974	CARA Brazzaville	VC Mokanda
1975	CARA Brazzaville	
1976	CARA Brazzaville	
1977	Diables Noires	VC Mokanda
1978	Etoile du Congo	Inter Club
1979	Etoile du Congo	
1980	Etoile du Congo	
1981	CARA Brazzaville	CARA Brazzaville
1982	Kotoko Mfoa	AS Cheminots
1983	Etoile du Congo	Etoile du Congo
1984	CARA Brazzaville	AS Cheminots
1985	Etoile du Congo	Inter Club
1986	Patronage St Anne	CARA Brazzaville
1987	Etoile du Congo	Inter Club
1988	Inter Club	Patronage St Anne
1989	Etoile du Congo	Diables Noirs
1990	Inter Club	Diables Noirs
1991		Elecsport Bouansa
1992	Diables Noires	CARA Brazzaville
1993	Etoile du Congo	
1994	Etoile du Congo	Enterprise Peinture
1995	AS Cheminots	Etoile du Congo
1996	Munisport	V. Club Mokanda
1997	Munisport	
1998	Vita Club Mokanda	
1999	Vita Club Mokanda	
2000	Etoile du Congo	Etoile du Congo
2001	Etoile du Congo	AS Police

2002	AS Police	Etoile du Congo
2003	St Michel Ouenzé	Diables Noirs
2004	Diables Noirs	Munisport
2005	AS Police	Diables Noirs
2006	Etoile du Congo	Etoile du Congo
2007	Diables Noirs	JS Talangaï
2008	CARA Brazzaville	Club 57
2009	Diables Noirs	AC Léopard Dolisie
2010	St Michel Ouenzé	
2011	Diables Noirs	AC Léopard Dolisie

CHA – CHAD

Year	Champions	Cup Winners
1988	TP Elect Sports	
1989	Renaissance	Tourbillon
1990	TP Elect Sports	Renaissance
1991	Tourbillon	Postel 2000
1992	TP Elect Sports	Massinya
1993	Postel 2000	Renaissance Abeche
1994	Renaissance Abeche	
1995	Postel 2000	AS Coton Chad
1996	AS Coton Chad	Renaissance
1997	Tourbillon	Gazelle
1998	AS Coton Chad	
1999	Renaissance	AS Coton Chad
2000	Tourbillon	Gazelle
2001	Tourbillon	Gazelle
2002		
2003		
2004	Renaissance	
2005	Renaissance	
2006	Renaissance	
2007	Renaissance	
2008	TP Elect Sport	Tourbillon
2009	Gazelle	AS Coton Chad
2010	Tourbillon	Foullah Edifice
2011	Foullah Edifice	Renaissance

CHI – CHILE

Year	Champions	Cup Winners
1933	Magallanes	
1934	Magallanes	
1935	Magallanes	
1936	Audax Italiano	
1937	Colo Colo	
1938	Magallanes	
1939	Colo Colo	
1940	Univ. de Chile	
1941	Colo Colo	
1942	Santiago Morning	
1943	Union Española	
1944	Colo Colo	
1945	Green Cross Temuco	
1946	Audax Italiano	
1947	Colo Colo	
1948	Audax Italiano	
1949	Univ'dad Catolica	
1950	Everton	
1951	Union Española	
1952	Everton	
1953	Colo Colo	
1954	Univ'dad Catolica	
1955	Palestino	
1956	Colo Colo	

1957	Audax Italiano	**Cup Winners**
1958	Santiago Wanderers	Colo Colo
1959	Univ. de Chile	Santiago Wanderers
1960	Colo Colo	Deportes La Serena
1961	Univ'dad Catolica	Santiago Wanderers
1962	Univ. de Chile	Luis Cruz Martinez
1963	Colo Colo	
1964	Univ. de Chile	
1965	Univ. de Chile	
1966	Univ'dad Catolica	
1967	Univ. de Chile	
1968	Santiago Wanderers	
1969	Univ. de Chile	
1970	Colo Colo	
1971	Union San Felipe	
1972	Colo Colo	
1973	Union Española	
1974	Huachipato	Colo Colo
1975	Union Española	Palestino
1976	Everton	
1977	Union Española	
1978	Palestino	Palestino
1979	Colo Colo	Univ. de Chile
1980	Cobreloa	Deportivo Iquique
1981	Colo Colo	Colo Colo
1982	Cobreloa	Colo Colo
1983	Colo Colo	Univ'dad Catolica
1984	Univ'dad Catolica	Everton
1985	Cobreloa	Colo Colo
1986	Colo Colo	Cobreloa
1987	Univ'dad Catolica	Cobresal
1988	Cobreloa	Colo Colo
1989	Colo Colo	Colo Colo
1990	Colo Colo	Colo Colo
1991	Colo Colo	Univ'dad Catolica
1992	Cobreloa	Union Española
1993	Colo Colo	Union Española
1994	Univ. de Chile	Colo Colo
1995	Univ. de Chile	Univ'dad Catolica
1996	Colo Colo	Colo Colo
1997	Univ'dad Catolica	
1997	Colo Colo	
1998	Colo Colo	Univ. de Chile
1999	Univ. de Chile	
2000	Univ. de Chile	Univ. de Chile
2001	Santiago Wanderers	
2002	Univ'dad Catolica	
	Colo Colo	
2003	Cobreloa	
	Cobreloa	
2004	Univ de Chile	
	Cobreloa	
2005	Union Española	
	Univ'dad Catolica	
2006	Colo Colo	
	Colo Colo	
2007	Colo Colo	
	Colo Colo	
2008	Everton	
	Colo Colo	
2009	Univ. de Chile	Univ Concepción
	Colo Colo	Unión San Felipe
2010	Univ'dad Catolica	Municipal Iquique
2011	Univ. de Chile	Univ'dad Catolica
	Univ. de Chile	

CHN – CHINA PR

Year	Championship	National Games
1910		South China
1914		East China
1924		East China
1926	South China	
1927	South China	
1928	East China	
1929	East China	
1930	South China	Shanghai
1931	East China	
1933	East China	Shanghai
1935		Hong Kong
1948		Hong Hong, Police & August 1st
1951	North East China	
1953	August 1st	
1954	North East China	
1955	Central Sports Institute	
1956	Beijing Youth B	
1957	Beijing	
1958	Beijing	
1959		August 1st
1960	Tianjin	
1961	Shanghai	
1962	Shanghai	
1963	Beijing Youth	
1964	Beijing Sports Institute	
1965	Jilin	Hebei
1973	Beijing	
1974	August 1st	
1975		Guangdong & Liaoning
1977	August 1st	
1978	Liaoning	
1979	Guangdong	Shandong
1980	Tianjin	
1981	August 1st	
1982	Beijing	
1983		Shanghai
1984	Beijing	Liaoning (Cup)
1985	Liaoning	Beijing (Cup)
1986	August 1st	Liaoning (Cup)
1987	Liaoning	Guangdong
1988	Liaoning	
1989	China B	**Cup Winners**
1990	Liaoning	August 1st
1991	Liaoning	Shanghai
1992	Liaoning	Dalian
1993	Liaoning	
	Pro League	
1994	Dalian	
1995	Shanghai	Jinan
1996	Dalian	Beijing
1997	Dalian	Beijing
1998	Dalian	Shanghai
1999	Shandong	Shandong
2000	Dalian	Chongqing
2001	Dalian	Dalian
2002	Dalian	Qingdao
2003	Shanghai	Beijing
2004	Shenzhen	Shandong
2005	Dalian	Dalian
2006	Shandong	Shandong
2007	Changchun	
2008	Shandong	
2009	Beijing	
2010	Shandong	
2011	Guangzhou	Tianjin

CIV – COTE D'IVOIRE

Year	Champions	Cup Winners
1960	Onze Freres	Espoir de Man
1961	Onze Freres	Africa Sports
1962	Stade Abidjan	ASEC Mimosas
1963	ASEC Mimosas	Jeunesse
1964	Stade Abidjan	Africa Sports
1965	Stade Abidjan	
1966	Stade Abidjan	
1967	Africa Sports	ASEC Mimosas
1968	Africa Sports	ASEC Mimosas
1969	Stade Abidjan	ASEC Mimosas
1970	ASEC Mimosas	ASEC Mimosas
1971	Africa Sports	Stade Abidjan
1972	ASEC Mimosas	ASEC Mimosas
1973	ASEC Mimosas	ASEC Mimosas
1974	ASEC Mimosas	Stella Club
1975	ASEC Mimosas	Stella Club
1976	SC Gagnoa	Stade Abidjan
1977	Africa Sports	Africa Sports
1978	Africa Sports	Africa Sports
1979	Stella Club	Africa Sports
1980	ASEC Mimosas	Reveil Daloa
1981	Stella Club	Africa Sports
1982	Africa Sports	Africa Sports
1983	Africa Sports	ASEC Mimosas
1984	Stella Club	Stade Abidjan
1985	Africa Sports	Africa Sports
1986	Africa Sports	Africa Sports
1987	Africa Sports	ASC Bouake
1988	Africa Sports	ASI Abengouron
1989	Africa Sports	Africa Sports
1990	ASEC Mimosas	ASEC Mimosas
1991	ASEC Mimosas	
1992	ASEC Mimosas	
1993	ASEC Mimosas	Africa Sports
1994	ASEC Mimosas	Stade Abidjan
1995	ASEC Mimosas	ASEC Mimosas
1996	Africa Sports	SO Armée
1997	ASEC Mimosas	ASEC Mimosas
1998	ASEC Mimosas	Africa Sports
1999	Africa Sports	ASEC Mimosas
2000	ASEC Mimosas	Stade Abidjan
2001	ASEC Mimosas	Alliance Bouaké
2002	ASEC Mimosas	Africa Sports
2003	ASEC Mimosas	ASEC Mimosas
2004	ASEC Mimosas	CO Bouaflé
2005	ASEC Mimosas	ASEC Mimosas
2006	ASEC Mimosas	Issia Wazi
2007	Africa Sports	ASEC Mimosas
2008	Africa Sports	ASEC Mimosas
2009	ASEC Mimosas	Africa Sports
2010	ASEC Mimosas	Africa Sports
2011	Africa Sports	ASEC Mimosas

CMR – CAMEROON

Year	Champions	Cup Winners
1956		Oryx Douala
1957		Canon Yaoundé
1958		Tonnerre Yaoundé
1960		Lion Yaoundé
1961	Oryx Douala	Union Douala
1962	Caiman Douala	Lion Yaoundé
1963	Oryx Douala	Oryx Douala
1964	Oryx Douala	Diamant Yaoundé
1965	Oryx Douala	Lion Yaoundé
1966	Diamant Yaoundé	Lion Yaoundé
1967	Oryx Douala	Canon Yaoundé
1968	Caiman Douala	Oryx Yaoundé
1969	Union Douala	Union Douala
1970	Canon Yaoundé	Oryx Douala
1971	Aigle N'kongsamba	Diamant Yaoundé
1972	Leopard Douala	Diamant Yaoundé
1973	Leopard Douala	Canon Yaoundé
1974	Canon Yaoundé	Tonnerre Yaoundé
1975	Caiman Douala	Canon Yaoundé
1976	Union Douala	Canon Yaoundé
1977	Canon Yaoundé	Canon Yaoundé
1978	Union Douala	Canon Yaoundé
1979	Canon Yaoundé	Dynamo Douala
1980	Canon Yaoundé	Union Douala
1981	Tonnerre Yaoundé	Dynamo Douala
1982	Canon Yaoundé	Dragons Douala
1983	Tonnerre Yoaunde	Canon Yaoundé
1984	Tonnerre Yaoundé	Dihep N'kam
1985	Canon Yaoundé	Union Douala
1986	Canon Yaoundé	Canon Yaoundé
1987	Tonnerre Yaoundé	Tonnerre Yaoundé
1988	Tonnerre Yaoundé	Panthère Bangangte
1989	Racing Bafoussam	Tonnerre Yaoundé
1990	Union Douala	Prevoyance Yaoundé
1991	Canon Yaoundé	Tonnerre Yaoundé
1992	Racing Bafoussam	Olympique Mvolye
1993	Racing Bafoussam	Canon Yaoundé
1994	Aigle N'kongsamba	Olympique Mvolye
1995	Racing Bafoussam	Canon Yaoundé
1996	Unisport Bafang	Racing Bafoussam
1997	Cotonsport Garoua	Union Douala
1998	Cotonsport Garoua	Dynamo Douala
1999	Sable Batié	Canon Yaoundé
2000	Fovu Baham	Kumbo Strikers
2001	Cotonsport Garoua	Fovu Baham
2002	Canon Yaoundé	Mount Cameroon
2003	Cotonsport Garoua	Cotonsport Garoua
2004	Cotonsport Garoua	Cotonsport Garoua
2005	Cotonsport Garoua	Impôts Yaoundé
2006	Cotonsport Garoua	Union Douala
2007	Cotonsport Garoua	Cotonsport Garoua
2008	Cotonsport Garoua	Cotonsport Garoua
2009	Tiko United	Panthère Bangangte
2010	Cotonsport Garoua	Fovu Baham
2011	Cotonsport Garoua	Cotonsport Garoua

COD – CONGO DR

Year	Champions	Cup Winners
1958	St Eloi Lupopo	
1961		St Eloi Lupopo
1963	CS Imana	
1964	CS Imana	CS Imana
1965	AS Dragons	AS Dragons
1966	TP Englebert	TP Englebert
1967	TP Englebert	TP Englebert
1968	St Eloi Lupopo	St Eloi Lupopo
1969	TP Englebert	
1970	AS Vita Club	
1971	AS Vita Club	AS Vita Club
1972	AS Vita Club	AS Vita Club
1973	AS Vita Club	AS Vita Club
1974	CS Imana	CS Imana
1975	AS Vita Club	AS Vita Club
1976	TP Mazembe	TP Mazembe
1977	AS Vita Club	AS Vita Club
1978	CS Imana	CS Imana
1979	AS Bilima	TP Mazembe
1980	AS Vita Club	Lubumbashi Sports
1981	St Eloi Lupopo	AS Vita Club
1982	AS Bilima	AS Vita Club
1983	Sanga Balende	AS Vita Club
1984	AS Bilima	CS Imana
1985	US Tshinkunku	DC Motema Pembe
1986	St Eloi Lupopo	Kalamu Kinshasa
1987	TP Mazembe	Kalamu Kinshasa
1988	AS Vita Club	Kalamu Kinshasa
1989	DC Motema Pembe	Kalamu Kinshasa
1990	St Eloi Lupopo	DC Motema Pembe
1991	Mikishi	DC Motema Pembe
1992	US Bilombe	US Bilombe
1993	AS Vita Club	DC Motema Pembe
1994	DC Motema Pembe	DC Motema Pembe
1995	AS Bantous	AC Sodigraf
1996	DC Motema Pembe	AS Dragons
1997	AS Vita Club	AS Dragons
1998	DC Motema Pembe	AS Dragons
1999	DC Motema Pembe	AS Dragons
2000	TP Mazembe	TP Mazembe
2001	TP Mazembe	AS Vita Club
2002	St Eloi Lupopo	US Kenya
2003	AS Vita Club	DC Motema Pembe
2004	DC Motema Pembe	CS Cilu Lukala
2005	DC Motema Pembe	AS Vita Kabasha
2006	TP Mazembe	DC Motema Pembe
2007	TP Mazembe	Maneima Union
2008	DC Motema Pembe	OC Bukavu Dawa
2009	TP Mazembe	DC Motema Pembe
2010	AS Vita Club	DC Motema Pembe
2011	TP Mazembe	US Tshinkunku

COK – COOK ISLANDS

Year	Champions	Cup Winners
1996	Avatiu	Avatiu
1997	Avatiu	Avatiu
1998	No Tournament	Teau-o-Tonga
1999	Tupapa	Tupapa
1999	Avatiu	Avatiu
2000	Nikao Sokattacck	Avatiu
2001	Tupapa	Tupapa
2002	Tupapa	Nikao Sokattack
2003	Tupapa	Nikao Sokattack
2004	Nikao Sokattack	Tupapa
2005	Nikao Sokattack	Nikao Sokattack
2006	Nikao Sokattack	Takuvaine
2007	Tupapa	Nikao Sokattack
2008	Nikao Sokattack	
2009	Nikao Sokattack	Tupapa
2010	Tupapa	Nikao Sokattack
2011	Tupapa	Nikao Sokattack

COL – COLOMBIA

Year	Champions	Cup Winners
1948	Indep Santa Fe	
1949	Millonarios	
1950	Deportes Caldas	
1951	Millonarios	
1952	Millonarios	
1953	Millonarios	
1954	At. Nacional	
1955	Indep'te Medellin	
1956	Atlético Quindio	
1957	Indep'te Medellin	
1958	Indep Santa Fe	
1959	Millonarios	
1960	Indep Santa Fe	
1961	Millonarios	
1962	Millonarios	
1963	Millonarios	
1964	Millonarios	
1965	Deportivo Cali	
1966	Indep Santa Fe	
1967	Deportivo Cali	
1968	Union Magdalena	
1969	Deportivo Cali	
1970	Deportivo Cali	
1971	Indep Santa Fe	
1972	Millonarios	
1973	At. Nacional	
1974	Deportivo Cali	
1975	Indep Santa Fe	
1976	At. Nacional	
1977	Atlético Junior	
1978	Millonarios	
1979	América Cali	
1980	Atlético Junior	
1981	At. Nacional	
1982	América Cali	
1983	América Cali	
1984	América Cali	
1985	América Cali	
1986	América Cali	
1987	Millonarios	
1988	Millonarios	
1989	-	
1990	América Cali	
1991	At. Nacional	
1992	América Cali	
1993	Atlético Junior	
1994	At. Nacional	
1995	Atlético Junior	
1996	Deportivo Cali	
1997	América Cali	
1998	Deportivo Cali	
1999	At. Nacional	
2000	América Cali	
2001	América Cali	
2002	América Cali	
2002	Indep'te Medellin	
2003	Once Caldas	
2003	Deportes Tolima	
2004	Indep'te Medellin	
2004	Atlético Junior	
2005	At. Nacional	
2005	Deportivo Cali	
2006	Deportivo Pasto	
2006	Cúcuta	
2007	At. Nacional	
2007	At. Nacional	
2008	Boyacá Chico	
2008	América Cali	
2009	Once Caldas	
2009	Indep'te Medellin	
2010	Atlético Junior	
2010	Once Caldas	
2011	At. Nacional	
2011	Atlético Junior	

COM – COMOROS

Year	Champions	Cup Winners
2003		Coin Nord
2004		Papillon Blue
2005	Coin Nord	Elan Club
2006	AJSM Mutsamudu	Volcan Club
2007	Coin Nord	Chirazienne
2008	Etoile d'Or	Jassem
2009	Apache Club	Apache Club
2010	Elan Club	
2011	Coin Nord	Coin Nord

CPV – CAPE VERDE ISLANDS

Year	Champions
1953	Académica Mindelo
1956	CS Mindelense
1960	CS Mindelense
1961	Sporting da Praia
1962	CS Mindelense
1963	Boavista Praia
1965	Académica Praia
1966	CS Mindelense
1967	Académica Mindelo
1968	CS Mindelense
1969	Sporting da Praia
1971	CS Mindelense
1972	Travadores Praia
1973	Castilho Mindelo
1974	Sporting da Praia
1976	CS Mindelense
1977	CS Mindelense
1980	Botafogo São Filipe
1981	CS Mindelense
1983	Académico do Sal
1984	Derby São Vicente
1985	Sporting da Praia
1987	Boavista Praia
1988	CS Mindelense
1989	Académica Mindelo
1990	CS Mindelense
1991	Sporting da Praia
1992	CS Mindelense
1993	Académica Espargos
1994	Travadores Praia
1995	Boavista Praia
1996	Travadores Praia
1997	Sporting da Praia
1998	CS Mindelense
1999	GD Amarante
2000	Derby São Vicente
2001	Onze Unidos
2002	Sporting da Praia
2003	Académico do Sal
2004	Sal-Rei SC
2005	Derby São Vicente
2006	Sporting da Praia
2007	Sporting da Praia
2008	Sporting da Praia
2009	Sporting da Praia
2010	Boavista Praia
2011	CS Mindelense

CRC – COSTA RICA

Year	Champions	Cup Winners
1921	CS Herediano	
1922	CS Herediano	
1923	CS Cartagines	
1924	CS Herediano	
1925	CS La Libertad	
1926	CS La Libertad	
1927	CS Herediano	
1928	LD Alajuelense	
1929	CS LA Libertad	
1930	CS Herediano	
1931	CS Herediano	
1932	CS Herediano	
1933	CS Herediano	
1934	CS La Libertad	
1935	CS Herediano	
1936	CS Cartagines	
1937	CS Herediano	
1938	Orion FC	
1939	LD Alajeulense	
1940	CS Cartagines	
1941	LD Alajeulense	
1942	CS La Libertad	
1943	Univ'dad Nacional	
1944	Orion FC	
1945	LD Alajeulense	
1946	CS La Libertad	
1947	CS Herediano	
1948	CS Herediano	
1949	LD Alajeulense	
1950	LD Alajeulense	
1951	CS Herediano	
1952	Deportivo Saprissa	
1953	Deportivo Saprissa	
1955	CS Herediano	
1957	CS Herediano	
1958	LD Alajeulense	
1959	LD Alajeulense	
1960	LD Alajeulense	
1961	CS Herediano	
1962	Deportivo Saprissa	
1963	CS Uruguay	
1964	Deportivo Saprissa	
1965	Deportivo Saprissa	
1966	LD Alajeulense	
1967	Deportivo Saprissa	
1968	Deportivo Saprissa	
1969	Deportivo Saprissa	
1970	LD Alajeulense	
1971	LD Alajeulense	
1972	Deportivo Saprissa	
1973	Deportivo Saprissa	
1974	Deportivo Saprissa	
1975	Deportivo Saprissa	
1976	Deportivo Saprissa	
1977	Deportivo Saprissa	
1978	CS Herediano	

Year	Champions
1979	CS Herediano
1980	LD Alajeulense
1981	CS Herediano
1982	Deportivo Saprissa
1983	LD Alajeulense
1984	LD Alajeulense
1985	CS Herediano
1986	ML Puntarenas
1987	CS Herediano
1988	Deportivo Saprissa
1989	Deportivo Saprissa
1991	LD Alajeulense
1992	LD Alajeulense
1993	CS Herediano
1994	
1995	Deportivo Saprissa
1996	LD Alajeulense
1997	LD Alajeulense
1998	Deportivo Saprissa
1999	Deportivo Saprissa
2000	LD Alajeulense
2001	LD Alajeulense
2002	LD Alajeulense
2003	LD Alajeulense
2004	Deportivo Saprissa
2005	LD Alajeulense
2006	Deportivo Saprissa
2007	Deportivo Saprissa
2008	Deportivo Saprissa
2008	Deportivo Saprissa
2009	Liberia
2009	Brujas FC
2010	Deportivo Saprissa
2010	LD Alajeulense
2011	LD Alajeulense
2011	LD Alajeulense

CRO - CROATIA

Year	Champions	Cup Winners
1992	Hajduk Split	Inter Zapresic
1993	Croatia Zagreb	Hajduk Split
1994	Hajduk Split	Croatia Zagreb
1995	Hajduk Split	Hajduk Split
1996	Croatia Zagreb	Croatia Zagreb
1997	Croatia Zagreb	Croatia Zagreb
1998	Croatia Zagreb	Croatia Zagreb
1999	Croatia Zagreb	NK Osijek
2000	Dinamo Zagreb	Hajduk Split
2001	Hajduk Split	Dinamo Zagreb
2002	NK Zagreb	Dinamo Zagreb
2003	Dinamo Zagreb	Hajduk Split
2004	Hajduk Split	Dinamo Zagreb
2005	Hajduk Split	Rijeka
2006	Dinamo Zagreb	Rijeka
2007	Dinamo Zagreb	Dinamo Zagreb
2008	Dinamo Zagreb	Dinamo Zagreb
2009	Dinamo Zagreb	Dinamo Zagreb
2010	Dinamo Zagreb	Hajduk Split
2011	Dinamo Zagreb	Dinamo Zagreb

CTA - CENTRAL AFRICAN REPUBLIC

Year	Champions	Cup Winners
1968	US Cattin	
1971	Real Olympique	
1973	Réal Olympique	
1974	ASDR Fatima	Tempete Mocaf
1975	Réal Olympique	
1976	Tempete Mocaf	Red Star
1977	Stade Centrafricaine	Sodiam
1978	ASDR Fatima	Union Sport CA
1979	Real Olympique	Sodiam
1980	Union Sport CA	ASDR Fatima
1981	Sportive Mouara	ASDR Fatima
1982	Real Olympique	Tempete Mocaf
1983	ASDR Fatima	Avia Sports
1984	Tempete Mocaf	Stade Centrafricaine
1985	Stade Centrafricaine	Tempete Mocaf
1986	Sportive Mouara	
1988	ASDR Fatima	Union Sport CA
1989	Stade Centrafricaine	Réal Olympique
1990	Tempete Mocaf	Forces Armées CA
1991	Forces Armées CA	ASDR Fatima
1992	Union Sport CA	Tempete Mocaf
1993	Tempete Mocaf	ASDR Fatima
1994	Tempete Mocaf	Forces Armées CA
1995	Forces Armées CA	
1996	Tempete Mocaf	
1997	Tempete Mocaf	Union Sport CA
1998		ASDR Fatima
1999	Tempete Mocaf	Réal Olympique
2000	Olympic Réal	ASDR Fatima
2001	Olympic Réal	Stade Centrafricaine
2002		
2003	Tempete Mocaf	Tempete Mocaf
2004	Olympic Réal	Tempete Mocaf
2005	ASDR Fatima	Union Sport CA
2006		
2007		
2008	Stade Centrafricaine	ASDR Fatima
2009	DFC8	ASDR Fatima
2010	Olympique Réal	DFC8
2011	DFC8	Tempete Mocaf

CUB - CUBA

Year	Champions
1912	Rovers AC
1913	CD Hatüey
1914	Rovers AC
1915	Hispano América
1916	La Habana FC
1917	Iberia
1918	Iberia
1919	Hispano América
1920	Hispano América
1921	Hispano América
1922	Iberia
1923	Iberia
1924	Olimpia
1925	Fortuna
1926	Real Iberia
1927	Juventud Asturiana
1928	Real Iberia
1929	Real Iberia
1930	Deportivo Español
1931	DC Gallego
1932	DC Gallego
1933	Juventud Asturiana
1934	Real Iberia
1935	Juventud Asturiana
1936	Juventud Asturiana
1937	DC Gallego
1938	DC Gallego
1939	DC Gallego
1940	DC Gallego
1941	Juventud Asturiana
1942	Dep. Puentes Grandes
1943	Dep. Puentes Grandes
1944	Juventud Asturiana
1945	DC Gallego
1947	DC Gallego
1948	Juventud Asturiana
1949	Diablos Rojos
1950	Hispano América
1951	Dep. San Francisco
1952	Dep. San Francisco
1953	Dep. San Francisco
1954	Dep. San Francisco
1955	Dep. San Francisco
1956	Casino Español
1957	Dep. San Francisco
1958	Deportivo Mordazo
1959	Deportivo Mordazo
1960	Cerro
1961	Deportivo Mordazo
1963	Industriales
1964	Industriales
1965	La Habana
1966	La Habana
1967	La Habana
1968	Granjeros
1969	Granjeros
1970	Granjeros
1972	Industriales
1973	Industriales
1974	Azucareros
1975	Granjeros
1976	Azucareros
1977	Granjeros
1979	Ciudad de La Habana
1979	Ciudad de La Habana
1980	Villa Clara
1981	Villa Clara
1982	Villa Clara
1983	Villa Clara
1984	Ciudad de La Habana
1985	Cienfuegos
1986	Villa Clara
1987	Pinar del Río
1989	Pinar del Río
1990	Pinar del Río
1991	Cienfuegos
1992	Pinar del Rio
1992	Villa Clara
1993	Ciego de Avila
1994	Ciudad de La Habana
1995	Pinar del Río
1996	Villa Clara
1997	Villa Clara
1998	Ciudad de La Habana
2000	Pinar del Río
2001	Ciudad de La Habana
2002	Ciego de Avila
2003	Villa Clara
2003	Ciego de Avila
2005	Villa Clara
2006	Holguín

Year	Champions	Cup Winners
2006	Pinar del Río	
2008	Cienfuegos	
2009	Cienfuegos	
2010	Ciego de Avila	
2011	Villa Clara	

CYP – CYPRUS

Year	Champions	Cup Winners
1935	Trust AC	Trust AC
1936	APOEL Nicosia	Trust AC
1937	APOEL Nicosia	APOEL Nicosia
1938	AEL Limassol	Trust AC
1939	APOEL Nicosia	AEL Limassol
1940	APOEL Nicosia	AEL Limassol
1941	AEL Limassol	APOEL Nicosia
1945	APOEL Nicosia	EPA Larnaca
1946	EPA Larnaca	EPA Larnaca
1947	APOEL Nicosia	APOEL Nicosia
1948	APOEL Nicosia	AEL Limassol
1949	APOEL Nicosia	Anorthosis F'gusta
1950	Anorthosis F'gusta	EPA Larnaca
1951	LTSK Nicosia	APOEL Nicosia
1952	APOEL Nicosia	Chetin Kaya
1953	AEL Limassol	EPA Larnaca
1954	Pezoporikos Larnaca	Chetin Kaya
1955	AEL Limassol	EPA Larnaca
1956	AEL Limassol	
1957	Anorthosis F'gusta	
1958	Anorthosis F'gusta	
1959		
1960	Anorthosis F'gusta	
1961	Omonia Nicosia	
1962	Anorthosis F'gusta	Olympiakos Nicosia
1963	Anorthosis F'gusta	Anorthosis F'gusta
1964		
1965	APOEL Nicosia	Omonia Nicosia
1966	Omonia Nicosia	Apollon Limassol
1967	Olympiakos Nicosia	Apollon Limassol
1968	AEL Limassol	APOEL Nicosia
1969	Olympiakos Nicosia	APOEL Nicosia
1970	EPA Larnaca	Pezoporikos Larnaca
1971	Olympiakos Nicosia	Anorthosis F'gusta
1972	Omonia Nicosia	Omonia Nicosia
1973	APOEL Nicosia	APOEL Nicosia
1974	Omonia Nicosia	Omonia Nicosia
1975	Omonia Nicosia	Anorthosis F'gusta
1976	Omonia Nicosia	APOEL Nicosia
1977	Omonia Nicosia	Olympiakos Nicosia
1978	Omonia Nicosia	APOEL Nicosia
1979	Omonia Nicosia	APOEL Nicosia
1980	APOEL Nicosia	Omonia Nicosia
1981	Omonia Nicosia	Omonia Nicosia
1982	Omonia Nicosia	Omonia Nicosia
1983	Omonia Nicosia	Omonia Nicosia
1984	Omonia Nicosia	APOEL Nicosia
1985	Omonia Nicosia	AEL Limassol
1986	APOEL Nicosia	Apollon Limassol
1987	Omonia Nicosia	AEL Limassol
1988	Pezoporikos Larnaca	Omonia Nicosia
1989	Omonia Nicosia	AEL Limassol
1990	APOEL Nicosia	NEA Salamina
1991	Apollon Limassol	Omonia Nicosia
1992	APOEL Nicosia	Apollon Limassol
1993	Omonia Nicosia	APOEL Nicosia
1994	Apollon Limassol	Omonia Nicosia
1995	Anorthosis F'gusta	APOEL Nicosia
1996	APOEL Nicosia	APOEL Nicosia
1997	Anorthosis F'gusta	APOEL Nicosia
1998	Anorthosis F'gusta	Anorthosis F'gusta
1999	Anorthosis F'gusta	APOEL Nicosia
2000	Anorthosis F'gusta	Omonia Nicosia
2001	Omonia Nicosia	Apollon Limassol
2002	APOEL Nicosia	Anorthosis F'gusta
2003	Omonia Nicosia	Anorthosis F'gusta
2004	APOEL Nicosia	AEK Larnaca
2005	Anorthosis F'gusta	Omonia Nicosia
2006	Apollon Limassol	APOEL Nicosia
2007	APOEL Nicosia	Anorthosis F'gusta
2008	Anorthosis F'gusta	APOEL Nicosia
2009	APOEL Nicosia	APOP/Kinyras
2010	Omonia Nicosia	Apollon Limassol
2011	APOEL Nicosia	Omonia Nicosia

CZE – CZECH REPUBLIC

Year	Champions	Cup Winners
1896	Kickers Praha	
1896	DFC Praha	
1897	Slavia	
1897	Slavia	
1898	Slavia	
1899	Slavia	
1900	Slavia	
1901	Slavia	
1902	CAFC Vinohrady	
1903		
1904		
1905		
1906		Smichov
1907		Smichov
1908		Slavia B
1909	Starometsky	Sparta
1910		Slavia
1911		Slavia
1912	Sparta	Slavia
1913	Slavia	Viktoria Zizkov
1914		Viktoria Zizkov
1915	Slavia	Sparta
1916		Viktoria Zizkov
1917	DFC Praha	
1939	Sparta	
1940	Slavia	ASO Olomouc
1941	Slavia	Slavia
1942	Slavia	Slavia
1943	Slavia	Sparta
1944	Sparta	Sparta
1945		Slavia
1946		Sparta
1994	Sparta	Viktoria Zizkov
1995	Sparta	Hradec Králové
1996	Slavia	Sparta
1997	Sparta	Slavia
1998	Sparta	FK Jablonec
1999	Sparta	Slavia
2000	Sparta	Slovan Liberec
2001	Sparta	Viktoria Zizkov
2002	Slovan Liberec	Slavia
2003	Sparta	FK Teplice
2004	Banik Ostrava	Sparta
2005	Sparta	Banik Ostrava
2006	Slovan Liberec	Sparta
2007	Sparta	Sparta
2008	Slavia	Sparta
2009	Slavia	FK Teplice
2010	Sparta	Viktoria Plzen
2011	Viktoria Plzen	Mladá Boleslav

CZE – CZECHOSLOVAKIA

Year	Champions	Cup Winners
1918	Slavia	Sparta
1919	Sparta	Sparta
1920	Sparta	Sparta
1921	Sparta	Viktoria Zizkov
1922	Sparta	Slavia
1923	Sparta	Sparta
1924	Slavia	Sparta
1925	Slavia	Sparta
1926	Sparta	Slavia
1927	Sparta	Slavia
1928	Viktoria Zizkov	Slavia
1929	Slavia	Viktoria Zizkov
1930	Slavia	Slavia
1931	Slavia	Sparta
1932	Sparta	Slavia
1933	Slavia	Viktoria Zizkov
1934	Slavia	Sparta
1935	Slavia	Sparta
1936	Sparta	Sparta
1937	Slavia	Sparta
1938	Sparta	
1946	Sparta Praha	
1947	Slavia Praha	
1948	Sparta Praha	
1948	Dynamo Slavia	
1949	NV Bratislava	
1950	NV Bratislava	
1951	NV Bratislava	Kovosmalt Trnava
1952	Sparta Sokolovo	ATK Praha
1953	UDA Praha	
1954	Spartak Sokolovo	
1955	Slovan Bratislava	
1956	Dukla Praha	
1957		
1958	Dukla Praha	
1959	CH Bratislava	
1960	Sp. Hradec Králové	
1961	Dukla Praha	Dukla Praha
1962	Dukla Praha	Slovan Bratislava
1963	Dukla Praha	Slovan Bratislava
1964	Dukla Praha	Sparta Sokolovo
1965	Sparta Praha	Dukla Praha
1966	Dukla Praha	Dukla Praha
1967	Sparta Praha	Spartak Trnava
1968	Spartak Trnava	Slovan Bratislava
1969	Spartak Trnava	Dukla Praha
1970	Slovan Bratislava	TJ Gottwaldov
1971	Spartak Trnava	Spartak Trnava
1972	Spartak Trnava	Sparta Praha
1973	Spartak Trnava	Baník Ostrava
1974	Slovan Bratislava	Slovan Bratislava
1975	Slovan Bratislava	Spartak Trnava
1976	Baník Ostrava	Sparta Praha

1977	Dukla Praha	Lokomotiva Kosice
1978	Zbrojovka Brno	Banik Ostrava
1979	Dukla Praha	Lokomotiva Kosice
1980	Banik Ostrava	Sparta Praha
1981	Banik Ostrava	Dukla Praha
1982	Dukla Praha	Slovan Bratislava
1983	Bohemians Praha	Dukla Praha
1984	Sparta Praha	Sparta Praha
1985	Sparta Praha	Dukla Praha
1986	TJ Vitkovice	Spartak Trnava
1987	Sparta Praha	DAC D'ská Streda
1988	Sparta Praha	Sparta Praha
1989	Sparta Praha	Sparta Praha
1990	Sparta Praha	Dukla Praha
1991	Sparta Praha	Banik Ostrava
1992	Slovan Bratislava	Sparta Praha
1993	Sparta Praha	1.FC Kosice

DEN – DENMARK

Year	Champions	Cup Winners
1913	KB København	
1914	KB København	
1915		
1916	B 93 København	
1917	KB København	
1918	KB København	
1919	Akademisk	
1920	B 1903 København	
1921	Akademisk	
1922	KB København	
1923	Frem København	
1924	B 1903 København	
1925	KB København	
1926	B 1903 København	
1927	B 93 København	
1928	B 93 København	
1929	B 93 København	
1930	B 93 København	
1931	Frem København	
1932	KB København	
1933	Frem København	
1934	B 93 København	
1935	B 93 København	
1936	Frem København	
1937	Akademisk	
1938	B 1903 København	
1939	B 93 København	
1940	KB København	
1941	Frem København	
1942	B 93 København	
1943	Akademisk	
1944	Frem København	
1945	Akademisk	
1946	B 93 København	
1947	Akademisk	
1948	KR København	
1949	KB København	
1950	KB København	
1951	Akademisk	
1952	Akademisk	
1953	KB København	
1954	Koge BK	
1955	AGF Aarhus	AGF Aarhus
1956	AGF Aarhus	Frem København
1957	AGF Aarhus	AGF Aarhus
1958	Vejle BK	Vejle BK
1959	B 1909 Odense	Vejle BK
1960	AGF Aarhus	AGF Aarhus
1961	Esbjerg FB	AGF Aarhus
1962	Esbjerg FB	B 1909 Odense
1963	Esbjerg FB	B 1913 Odense
1964	B 1909 Odense	Esbjerg FB
1965	Esbjerg FB	AGF Aarhus
1966	Hvidovre BK	AAB Aalborg
1967	Akademisk	Randers Freja
1968	KB København	Randers Freja
1969	B 1903 København	KB København
1970	B 1903 København	AAB Aalborg
1971	Vejle BK	B 1909 Odense
1972	Vejle BK	Vejle BK
1973	Hvidovre BK	Randers Freja
1974	KB København	Vanlose BK
1975	Koge BK	Vejle BK
1976	B 1903 København	Esbjerg FB
1977	OB Odense	Vejle BK
1978	Vejle BK	Frem København
1979	Esbjerg FB	B 1903 København
1980	KB København	Hvidovre BK
1981	Hvidovre BK	Vejle BK
1982	OB Odense	B 93 København
1983	Lyngby BK	OB Odense
1984	Vejle BK	Lyngby BK
1985	Brøndby IF	Lyngby BK
1986	AGF Aarhus	B 1903 København
1987	Brøndby IF	AGF Aarhus
1988	Brøndby IF	AGF Aarhus
1989	OB Odense	Brøndby IF
1990	Brøndby IF	Lyngby BK
1991	Brøndby IF	OB Odense
1992	Lyngby BK	AGF Aarhus
1993	FC København	OB Odense
1994	Silkeborg IF	Brøndby IF
1995	AaB Aalborg	FC København
1996	Brøndby IF	AGF Aarhus
1997	Brøndby IF	FC København
1998	Brøndby IF	Brøndby IF
1999	AaB Aalborg	Akademisk
2000	Herfølge BK	Viborg FF
2001	FC København	Silkeborg IF
2002	Brøndby IF	OB Odense
2003	FC København	Brøndby IF
2004	FC København	FC København
2005	Brøndby IF	Brøndby IF
2006	FC København	Randers FC
2007	FC København	OB Odense
2008	AaB Aalborg	Brøndby IF
2009	FC København	FC København
2010	FC København	FC Nordsjælland
2011	FC København	FC Nordsjælland

DJI – DJIBOUTI

Year	Champions	Cup Winners
1987	ASE Merill	
1988	ASCDE	AS Port
1989		AS Port
1990		
1991	Aéroport	Aéroport
1992		ASCDE
1993		FN Police
1994		Balbala
1995		Balbala
1996	FN Police	Balbala
1997	FN Police	FN Police
1998	FN Police	FN Police
1999	FN Police	Balbala
2000	CDE Djibouti	ASCDE
2001	FN Police	Chemin de Fer
2002	AS Borreh	Jeunesse Espoir
2003	Gendarmerie	AS Borreh
2004	Gendarmerie	Chemin de Fer
2005	CDE Djibouti	Poste de Djibouti
2006	Sociéte Immobiliére	AS Ali Sabieh
2007	CDE Djibouti	Société Immobiliére
2008	Sociéte Immobiliére	CDE Djibouti
2009	AS Ali Sabieh	Guelleh Batal
2010	AS Port	AS Port
2011	AS Port	AS Port

DMA – DOMINICA

Year	Champions	Cup Winners
1965	Spartans	
1966	Domfruit Rovers	
1967	Domfruit Rovers	
1969	Spartans	
1970	Harlem United	
1972	Harlem United	
1973	Harlem United	
1974	Harlem United	
1977	Kensborough United	
1978	Kensborough United	
1979	Spartans	
1981	Harlem United	
1983	Harlem United	
1985	Antilles Kensborough/Harlem United	
1989	Harlem United	
1991	C&M Motors Potters	
1992	Harlem United	
1993	Harlem United	
1994	Harlem United	
1995	Harlem United	
1996	Black Rocks	
1997	Harlem United	
1998	ACS Zebbians	
1999	Harlem United	
2000	Harlem United	
2001	Harlem United	
2002	St Joseph	South East
2003	Harlem United	Harlem United
2004	Harlem United	Harlem United
2005	Dublanc Strikers	South East
2006	Harlem United	
2007	Sagicor South East	
2008	Centre Bath Estate	
2009	Centre Bath Estate	
2010		
2011		

DOM – DOMINICAN REPUBLIC

Year	Champions
1970	
1971	
1972	UCMM
1973	UCMM
1974	UCMM

Year			
1975			
1976	Moca		
1977			
1978	Don Bosco		
1979			
1980			
1981			
1982			
1983			
1984			
1985			
1986			
1987			
1988			
1989			
1990			
1991	Bancredicard		
1992			
1993			
1994	Bancredicard		
1995			
1996			
1997	Santos		
1998	Domingo Savio		
1999	Don Bosco		
2000			
2001	Deportivo Pantoja	Liga Mayor	
2002		Baninter Jarabacoa	
2003	Deportivo Pantoja	Baninter Jarabacoa	
2004	Case de España		
2005	Jarabacoa	Deportivo Pantoja	
2006	La Vega		
2007		Barcelona	
2008			
2009		Deportivo Pantoja	
2010		Don Bosco	
2011			

ECU - ECUADOR

Year	Champions
1957	Emelec
1958	
1959	
1960	Barcelona
1961	Emelec
1962	Everest
1963	Barcelona
1964	Deportivo Quito
1965	Emelec
1966	Barcelona
1967	El Nacional
1968	Deportivo Quito
1969	LDU Quito
1970	Barcelona
1971	Barcelona
1972	Emelec
1973	El Nacional
1974	LDU Quito
1975	LDU Quito
1976	El Nacional
1977	El Nacional
1978	El Nacional
1979	Emelec
1980	Barcelona
1981	Barcelona
1982	El Nacional
1983	El Nacional
1984	El Nacional
1985	Barcelona
1986	El Nacional
1987	Barcelona
1988	Emelec
1989	Barcelona
1990	LDU Quito
1991	Barcelona
1992	El Nacional
1993	Emelec
1994	Emelec
1995	Barcelona
1996	El Nacional
1997	Barcelona
1998	LDU Quito
1999	LDU Quito
2000	Olmedo
2001	Emelec
2002	Emelec
2003	LDU Quito
2004	Deportivo Cuenca
2005	LDU Quito
2005	El Nacional
2006	El Nacional
2007	LDU Quito
2008	Deportivo Quito
2009	Deportivo Quito
2010	LDU Quito
2011	Deportivo Quito

EGY - EGYPT

Year	Champions	Cup Winners
1922		Zamalek
1923		Al Tersana
1924		Al Ahly
1925		Al Ahly
1926		Al Ittihad
1927		Al Ahly
1928		Al Ahly
1929		Al Tersana
1930		Al Ahly
1931		Al Ahly
1932		Zamalek
1933		Olympic
1934		Olympic
1935		Zamalek
1936		Al Ittihad
1937		Al Ahly
1938		Zamalek
1939		Al Teram
1940		Al Ahly
1941		Zamalek
1942		Al Ahly
1943		Al Ahly
1944		Zamalek
1945		Al Ahly
1946		Al Ahly
1947		Al Ahly
1948		Al Ittihad
1949	Al Ahly	Al Ahly
1950	Al Ahly	Al Ahly
1951	Al Ahly	Al Ahly
1952		Zamalek
1953	Al Ahly	Al Ahly
1954	Al Ahly	Al Tersana
1955		Zamalek
1956	Al Ahly	Al Ahly
1957	Al Ahly	Zamalek
1958	Al Ahly	Zamalek
1959	Al Ahly	Zamalek
1960	Zamalek	Zamalek
1961	Al Ahly	Al Ahly
1962	Al Ahly	Zamalek
1963	Al Tersana	Al Ittihad
1964	Zamalek	Suez
1965	Zamalek	Al Tersana
1966	Olympic	Al Ahly
1967	Ismaily	Al Tersana
1968		
1969		
1970		
1971		
1972		
1973	Ghazl Al Mehalla	Al Ittihad
1974		
1975	Al Ahly	Zamalek
1976	Al Ahly	Al Ittihad
1977	Al Ahly	Zamalek
1978	Zamalek	Al Ahly
1979	Al Ahly	Zamalek
1980	Al Ahly	
1981	Al Ahly	Al Ahly
1982	Al Ahly	
1983	Mokawloon	Al Ahly
1984	Zamalek	Al Ahly
1985	Al Ahly	Al Ahly
1986	Al Ahly	Al Tersana
1987	Al Ahly	
1988	Zamalek	Zamalek
1989	Al Ahly	Al Ahly
1990		Mokawloon
1991	Ismaily	Al Ahly
1992	Zamalek	Al Ahly
1993	Zamalek	Al Ahly
1994	Al Ahly	
1995	Al Ahly	Mokawloon
1996	Al Ahly	Al Ahly
1997	Al Ahly	Ismaily
1998	Al Ahly	Al Masry
1999	Al Ahly	Zamalek
2000	Al Ahly	Ismaily
2001	Zamalek	Al Ahly
2002	Ismaily	Zamalek
2003	Zamalek	Al Ahly
2004	Zamalek	Mokawloon
2005	Al Ahly	ENPPI
2006	Al Ahly	Al Ahly
2007	Al Ahly	Al Ahly
2008	Al Ahly	Zamalek
2009	Al Ahly	Haras Al Hedod
2010	Al Ahly	Haras Al Hedod
2011	Al Ahly	ENPPI

ENG – ENGLAND

Year	Champions	Cup Winners
1872		Wanderers
1873		Wanderers
1874		Oxford University
1875		Royal Engineers
1876		Wanderers
1877		Wanderers
1878		Wanderers
1879		Old Etonians
1880		Clapham Rovers
1881		Old Carthusians
1882		Old Etonians
1883		Blackburn Olympic
1884		Blackburn Rovers
1885		Blackburn Rovers
1886		Blackburn Rovers
1887		Aston Villa
1888		West Bromwich Alb.
1889	Preston North End	Preston North End
1890	Preston North End	Blackburn Rovers
1891	Everton	Blackburn Rovers
1892	Sunderland	West Bromwich Alb.
1893	Sunderland	Wolverhampton W.
1894	Aston Villa	Notts County
1895	Sunderland	Aston Villa
1896	Aston Villa	Sheffield Wed'day
1897	Aston Villa	Aston Villa
1898	Sheffield United	Nottingham Forest
1899	Aston Villa	Sheffield United
1900	Aston Villa	Bury
1901	Liverpool	Tottenham Hotspur
1902	Sunderland	Sheffield United
1903	Sheffield Wed'day	Bury
1904	Sheffield Wed'day	Manchester City
1905	Newcastle United	Aston Villa
1906	Liverpool	Everton
1907	Newcastle United	Sheffield Wed'day
1908	Manchester United	Wolverhampton W.
1909	Newcastle United	Manchester United
1910	Aston Villa	Newcastle United
1911	Manchester United	Bradford City
1912	Blackburn Rovers	Barnsley
1913	Sunderland	Aston Villa
1914	Blackburn Rovers	Burnley
1915	Everton	Sheffield United
1916		
1917		
1918		
1919		
1920	West Bromwich Alb.	Aston Villa
1921	Burnley	Tottenham Hotspur
1922	Liverpool	Huddersfield Town
1923	Liverpool	Bolton Wanderers
1924	Huddersfield Town	Newcastle United
1925	Huddersfield Town	Sheffield United
1926	Huddersfield Town	Bolton Wanderers
1927	Newcastle United	Cardiff City
1928	Everton	Blackburn Rovers
1929	Sheffield Wed'day	Bolton Wanderers
1930	Sheffield Wed'day	Arsenal
1931	Arsenal	West Bromwich Alb.
1932	Everton	Newcastle United
1933	Arsenal	Everton
1934	Arsenal	Manchester City
1935	Arsenal	Sheffield Wed'day
1936	Sunderland	Arsenal
1937	Manchester City	Sunderland
1938	Arsenal	Preston North End
1939	Everton	Portsmouth
1940		
1941		
1942		
1943		
1944		
1945		
1946		Derby County
1947	Liverpool	Charlton Athletic
1948	Arsenal	Manchester United
1949	Portsmouth	Wolverhampton W.
1950	Portsmouth	Arsenal
1951	Tottenham Hotspur	Newcastle United
1952	Manchester United	Newcastle United
1953	Arsenal	Blackpool
1954	Wolverhampton W.	West Bromwich Alb.
1955	Chelsea	Newcastle United
1956	Manchester United	Manchester City
1957	Manchester United	Aston Villa
1958	Wolverhampton W.	Bolton Wanderers
1959	Wolverhampton W.	Nottingham Forest
1960	Burnley	Wolverhampton W.
1961	Tottenham Hotspur	Tottenham Hotspur
1962	Ipswich Town	Tottenham Hotspur
1963	Everton	Manchester United
1964	Liverpool	West Ham United
1965	Manchester United	Liverpool
1966	Liverpool	Everton
1967	Manchester United	Tottenham Hotspur
1968	Manchester City	West Bromwich Alb.
1969	Leeds Utd	Manchester City
1970	Everton	Chelsea
1971	Arsenal	Arsenal
1972	Derby County	Leeds United
1973	Liverpool	Sunderland
1974	Leeds United	Liverpool
1975	Derby County	West Ham United
1976	Liverpool	Southampton
1977	Liverpool	Manchester United
1978	Nottingham Forest	Ipswich Town
1979	Liverpool	Arsenal
1980	Liverpool	West Ham United
1981	Aston Villa	Tottenham Hotspur
1982	Liverpool	Tottenham Hotspur
1983	Liverpool	Manchester United
1984	Liverpool	Everton
1985	Everton	Manchester United
1986	Liverpool	Liverpool
1987	Everton	Coventry City
1988	Liverpool	Wimbledon
1989	Arsenal	Liverpool
1990	Liverpool	Manchester United
1991	Arsenal	Tottenham Hotspur
1992	Leeds United	Liverpool
1993	Manchester United	Arsenal
1994	Manchester United	Manchester United
1995	Blackburn Rovers	Everton
1996	Manchester United	Manchester United
1997	Manchester United	Chelsea
1998	Arsenal	Arsenal
1999	Manchester United	Manchester United
2000	Manchester United	Chelsea
2001	Manchester United	Liverpool
2002	Arsenal	Arsenal
2003	Manchester United	Arsenal
2004	Arsenal	Manchester United
2005	Chelsea	Arsenal
2006	Chelsea	Liverpool
2007	Manchester United	Chelsea
2008	Manchester United	Portsmouth
2009	Manchester United	Chelsea
2010	Chelsea	Chelsea
2011	Manchester United	Manchester City

ENG – ENGLAND

Year	League Cup Winners
1961	Aston Villa
1962	Norwich City
1963	Birmingham City
1964	Leicester City
1965	Chelsea
1966	West Bromwich Alb.
1967	Queens Park Rang.
1968	Leeds United
1969	Swindon Town
1970	Manchester City
1971	Tottenham Hotspur
1972	Stoke City
1973	Tottenham Hotspur
1974	Wolverhampton W.
1975	Aston Villa
1976	Manchester City
1977	Aston Villa
1978	Nottingahm Forest
1979	Nottingham Forest
1980	Wolverhampton W.
1981	Liverpool
1982	Liverpool
1983	Liverpool
1984	Liverpool
1985	Norwich City
1986	Oxford United
1987	Arsenal
1988	Luton Town
1989	Nottingham Forest
1990	Nottingham Forest
1991	Sheffield Wed'day
1992	Manchester United
1993	Arsenal
1994	Aston Villa
1995	Liverpool
1996	Aston Villa
1997	Leicester City
1998	Chelsea
1999	Tottenham Hotspur
2000	Leicester City
2001	Liverpool
2002	Blackburn Rovers
2003	Liverpool
2004	Middlesbrough
2005	Chelsea
2006	Manchester United
2007	Chelsea
2008	Tottenham Hotspur
2009	Manchester United
2010	Manchester United
2011	Birmingham City

EQG – EQUATORIAL GUINEA

Year	Champions	Cup Winners
1978		Union Mongomo
1979	Real Rebola	FC Akonangui
1980	Deportivo Mongomo	CD Ela Nguema
1981	Atlético Malabo	CD Ela Nguema
1982	Atlético Malabo	CD Ela Nguema
1983	Dragon FC Bata	CD Ela Nguema
1984	CD Ela Nguema	GD Lage Malabo
1985	CD Ela Nguema	Atlético Malabo
1986	CD Ela Nguema	Juvenil Reyes Bata
1987	CD Ela Nguema	Atlético Malabo
1988	CD Ela Nguema	Atlético Malabo
1989	CD Ela Nguema	Union Vesper
1990	CD Ela Nguema	Atlético Malabo
1991	CD Ela Nguema	Atlético Malabo
1992	FC Akonangui	CD Ela Nguema
1993		
1994		
1995		
1996	Cafe Bank Sportif	FC Akonangui
1997	Deportivo Mongomo	CD Ela Nguema
1998	CD Ela Nguema	Union Vesper
1999	FC Akonangui	CD Unidad
2000	CD Ela Nguema	CD Unidad
2001	FC Akonangui	Atlético Malabo
2002	CD Ela Nguema	FC Akonangui
2003	Atlético Malabo	Deportivo Mongomo
2004	Renacimiento	CD Ela Nguema
2005	Renacimiento	
2006	Renacimiento	
2007	Renacimiento	FC Akonangui
2008	Akonangui	
2009	CD Ela Nguema	Dragon FC Bata
2010	Deportivo Mongomo	
2011		

ERI – ERITREA

Year	Champions	Cup Winners
1994		
1995	Red Sea FC Asmara	
1996	Adulis Club Asmara	
1997	Al Tahir	
1998	Red Sea FC Asmara	Hintsa Asmara
1999	Red Sea FC Asmara	
2000	Red Sea FC Asmara	
2001	Hintsa Asmara	
2002	Red Sea FC Asmara	
2003	Anseba SC Keren	
2004	Adulis Club Asmara	
2005	Red Sea FC Asmara	
2006	Adulis Club Asmara	
2007	Al Tahir	
2008	Asmara Berra	
2009	Rea Sea FC Asmara	Denden
2010		
2011		

ESP – SPAIN

Year	Champions	Cup Winners
1902		Vizcaya Bilbao
1903		Athletic Bilbao
1904		Athletic Bilbao
1904		Real Madrid
1905		Real Madrid
1906		Real Madrid
1907		Real Madrid
1908		Ciclista San Sebastian
1909		Athletic Bilbao
1910		Barcelona
1910		Athletic Bilbao
1911		Barcelona
1912		Barcelona
1913		Racing Irún
1914		Athletic Bilbao
1915		Athletic Bilbao
1916		Athletic Bilbao
1917		Real Madrid
1918		Real Union Irún
1919		Arenas Guecho Bilbao
1920		Barcelona
1921		Athletic Bilbao
1922		Barcelona
1923		Athletic Bilbao
1924		Real Union Irún
1925		Barcelona
1926		Barcelona
1927		Real Union Irún
1928		Barcelona
1929	Barcelona	RCD Español
1930	Athletic Bilbao	Athletic Bilbao
1931	Athletic Bilbao	Athletic Bilbao
1932	Real Madrid	Athletic Bilbao
1933	Real Madrid	Athletic Bilbao
1934	Athletic Bilbao	Real Madrid
1935	Real Betis	Sevilla
1936	Athletic Bilbao	Real Madrid
1937		
1938		
1939		Sevilla
1940	Atlético Aviación	RCD Español
1941	Atlético Aviación	Valencia
1942	Valencia	Barcelona
1943	Athletic Bilbao	Athletic Bilbao
1944	Valencia	Athletic Bilbao
1945	Barcelona	Athletic Bilbao
1946	Sevilla	Real Madrid
1947	Valencia	Real Madrid
1948	Barcelona	Sevilla
1949	Barcelona	Valencia
1950	Atlético Madrid	Athletic Bilbao
1951	Atlético Madrid	Barcelona
1952	Barcelona	Barcelona
1953	Barcelona	Barcelona
1954	Real Madrid	Valencia
1955	Real Madrid	Athletic Bilbao
1956	Athletic Bilbao	Athletic Bilbao
1957	Real Madrid	Barcelona
1958	Real Madrid	Athletic Bilbao
1959	Barcelona	Barcelona
1960	Barcelona	Atlético Madrid
1961	Real Madrid	Atlético Madrid
1962	Real Madrid	Real Madrid
1963	Real Madrid	Barcelona
1964	Real Madrid	Real Zaragoza
1965	Real Madrid	Atlético Madrid
1966	Atlético Madrid	Real Zaragoza
1967	Real Madrid	Valencia
1968	Real Madrid	Barcelona
1969	Real Madrid	Athletic Bilbao
1970	Atlético Madrid	Real Madrid
1971	Valencia	Barcelona
1972	Real Madrid	Atlético Madrid
1973	Atlético Madrid	Athletic Bilbao
1974	Barcelona	Real Madrid
1975	Real Madrid	Real Madrid
1976	Real Madrid	Atlético Madrid
1977	Atlético Madrid	Real Betis
1978	Real Madrid	Barcelona
1979	Real Madrid	Valencia
1980	Real Madrid	Real Madrid
1981	Real Sociedad	Barcelona
1982	Real Sociedad	Real Madrid
1983	Athletic Bilbao	Barcelona
1984	Athletic Bilbao	Athletic Bilbao
1985	Barcelona	Atlético Madrid
1986	Real Madrid	Real Zaragoza
1987	Real Madrid	Real Sociedad
1988	Real Madrid	Barcelona
1989	Real Madrid	Real Madrid
1990	Real Madrid	Barcelona
1991	Barcelona	Atlético Madrid
1992	Barcelona	Atlético Madrid
1993	Barcelona	Real Madrid
1994	Barcelona	Real Zaragoza
1995	Real Madrid	Deportivo La Coruña
1996	Atlético Madrid	Atlético Madrid
1997	Real Madrid	Barcelona
1998	Barcelona	Barcelona
1999	Barcelona	Valencia
2000	Deportivo La Coruña	Espanyol
2001	Real Madrid	Real Zaragoza
2002	Valencia	Deportivo La Coruña
2003	Real Madrid	Mallorca
2004	Valencia	Real Zaragoza
2005	Barcelona	Real Betis
2006	Barcelona	Espanyol
2007	Real Madrid	Sevilla
2008	Real Madrid	Valencia
2009	Barcelona	Barcelona
2010	Barcelona	Sevilla
2011	Barcelona	Real Madrid

EST – ESTONIA

Year	Champions	Cup Winners
1992	Norma Tallinn	
1993	Norma Tallinn	Nikol Tallinn
1994	Flora Tallinn	Norma Tallinn
1995	Flora Tallinn	Flora Tallinn
1996	Lantana Tallinn	Tallinna Sadam
1997	Lantana Tallinn	Tallinna Sadam
1998	Flora Tallinn	Flora Tallinn
1998	Flora Tallinn	
1999	Levadia Maardu	Levadia Maardu
2000	Levadia Maardu	Levadia Maardu
2001	Flora Tallinn	Trans Narva
2002	Flora Tallinn	Levadia II Tallinn
2003	Flora Tallinn	TVMK Tallinn
2004	Levadia Tallinn	Levadia Tallinn
2005	TVMK Tallinn	Levadia Tallinn

Year	Champions	Cup Winners
2006	Levadia Tallinn	TVMK Tallinn
2007	Levadia Tallinn	Levadia Tallinn
2008	Levadia Tallinn	Flora Tallinn
2009	Levadia Tallinn	Flora Tallinn
2010	Flora Tallinn	Levadia Tallinn
2011	Flora Tallinn	Flora Tallinn

ETH – ETHIOPIA

Year	Champions	Cup Winners
1944	BMME	
1945		BMME
1946		Army
1947		Polisportiva
1948	Key Baher	Body Guard
1949	Army	Army
1950	Saint George	Army
1951	Army	Army
1952	Army	
1953	Army	
1954	Army	Army
1955	Hamassien Asmara	Mechal
1956	Mechal	Mechal
1957	Hamassien Asmara	Saint George
1958	Akale Guzay Eritrea	Mekuria
1959	Tele SC Asmara	Omedla
1960	Cotton Dire Dawa	Nib Debre Zeit
1961	Ethio-Cement	
1962	Cotton Dire Dawa	
1963	Cotton Dire Dawa	
1964	Ethio-Cement	
1965	Cotton Dire Dawa	
1966	Saint George	
1967	Saint George	
1968	Saint George	
1969	Tele SC Asmara	
1970	Tele SC Asmara	Asmara
1971	Saint George	EEPCO Mebrat Hail
1972	Asmara	EEPCO Mebrat Hail
1973	Asmara	Saint George
1974	Embassoyra Eritrea	Saint George
1975	Saint George	Mechal
1976	Mechal	EEPCO Mebrat Hail
1977	Railway Dire Dawa	Saint George
1978	Ogaden Anbassa	Omedla
1979	Omedla	
1980	Tegl Fre	Ermejachen
1981	Ermejachen	Red Sea Eritrea
1982	Mechal	Mechal
1983	Cotton Dire Dawa	Red Sea Eritrea
1984	Mechal	Eritrea Shoes
1985	Addis Brewery	Eritrea Shoes
1986	Addis Brewery	Construction Addis
1987	Saint George	Eritrea Shoes
1988	Mechal	Gebeya Coffee
1989	Mechal	
1990	Addis Brewery	Mechal
1991	Saint George	
1992	Saint George	
1993	EEPCO Mebrat Hail	Saint George
1994	Saint George	Muger Cement
1995	Saint George	Insurance
1996	Saint George	Awassa Flour
1997	Ethiopian Coffee	Wolaita Tussa
1998	EEPCO Mebrat Hail	Ethiopian Coffee
1999	Saint George	Saint George
2000	Saint George	Ethiopian Coffee
2001	EEPCO Mebrat Hail	EEPCO Mebrat Hail
2002	Saint George	Insurance
2003	Saint George	Ethiopian Coffee
2004	Awassa City	Banks
2005	Saint George	Awassa City
2006	Saint George	Defence
2007	Awassa City	Harar Beer
2008	Saint George	Ethiopian Coffee
2009	Saint George	
2010	Saint George	Dedebit
2011	Ethiopian Coffee	Saint George

FIJ – FIJI

Year	Champions	Inter-District
1938		Rewa
1939		Rewa
1940		Suva
1941		Lautoka
1942		Lautoka
1943		Rewa
1944		Rewa
1945		Suva
1946		Suva
1947		Rewa
1948		Suva
1949		Lautoka
1950		Lautoka
1951		Suva
1952		Suva
1953		Lautoka
1954		Suva
1955		Rewa
1956		Suva
1957		Lautoka
1958		Lautoka
1959		Lautoka
1960		Suva
1961		Ba
1962		Lautoka
1963		Ba
1964		Lautoka
1965		Lautoka
1966		Ba
1967		Ba
1968		Ba
1969		Nadi
1970		Ba
1971		Nadi
1972		Rewa
1973		Lautoka
1974		Nadi
1975		Ba
1976		Ba
1977	Ba	Ba
1978	Nadi	Ba
1979	Ba	Ba
1980	Nadi	Ba
1981	Nadi	Suva
1982	Nadi	Ba
1983	Nadi	Suva
1984	Lautoka	Lautoka
1985	Nadi	Lautoka
1986	Ba	Ba
1987	Ba	
1988	Lautoka	Nadroga
1989	Nadroga	Nadroga
1990	Nadroga	Nasinu
1991	Labasa	Ba
1992	Ba	Labasa
1993	Nadroga	Nadroga
1994	Ba	Labassa
1995	Ba	Tavua
1996	Suva	Ba
1997	Suva	Ba
1998	Nadi	Nadi
1999	Ba	Nadi
2000	Nadi	Ba
2001	Ba	Rewa
2002	Ba	Nadi
2003	Ba	Ba
2004	Ba	Ba
2005	Ba	Lautoka
2006	Ba	Ba
2007	Labasa	Ba
2008	Ba	Lautoka
2009	Lautoka	Navua
2010	Lautoka	Rewa
2011	Ba	Labasa

FIJ – FIJI

Year	B. of Giants	FA Cup
1978	Nadi	
1979	Ba	
1980	Nadi	
1981	Ba	
1982	Suva	
1983	Nadi	
1984	Ba	
1985	Lautoka	
1986	Nadi	
1987		
1988	Suva	
1989	Nadroga	
1990	Ba	
1991	Nadroga	Ba
1992	Ba	Labasa
1993	Ba	Nadroga
1994	Rewa	Tavua
1995	Suva	Suva
1996	Nadi	Nadi
1997	Labassa	Labasa
1998	Ba	Ba
1999	Ba	Labasa
2000	Ba	Lautoka
2001	Ba	Nadroga
2002	Nadroga	Lautoka
2003	Rewa	Navua
2004	Rewa	Ba
2005	Navua	Ba
2006	Ba	Ba
2007	Ba	Ba
2008	Ba	Navua
2009	Ba	Navua
2010	Rewa	Ba
2011	Rewa	Rewa

FIN – FINLAND

Year	Champions	Cup Winners
1908	Unitas Helsinki	
1909	PUS Helsinki	
1910	Abo IFK Turku	
1911	HJK Helsinki	
1912	HJK Helsinki	
1913	KIF Helsinki	
1914	Not played	
1915	KIF Helsinki	
1916	KIF Helsinki	
1917	HJK Helsinki	
1918	HJK Helsinki	
1919	HJK Helsinki	
1920	Abo IFK Turku	
1921	HPS Helsinki	
1922	HPS Helsinki	
1923	HJK Helsinki	
1924	Abo IFK Turku	
1925	HJK Helsinki	
1926	HPS Helsinki	
1927	HPS Helsinki	
1928	TPS Turku	
1929	HPS Helsinki	
1930	HIFK Helsinki	
1931	HIFK Helsinki	
1932	HPS Helsinki	
1933	HIFK Helsinki	
1934	HPS Helsinki	
1935	HPS Helsinki	
1936	HJK Helsinki	
1937	HIFK Helsinki	
1938	HJK Helsinki	
1939	TPS Turku	
1940	Sudet Kouvola	
1941	TPS Turku	
1942	Helsinki Toverit	
1943	Not played	
1944	IFK Vaasa	
1945	VPS Vaasa	
1946	IFK Vaasa	
1947	HIFK Helsinki	
1948	VPS Vaasa	
1949	TPS Turku	
1950	Ilves Kissat	
1951	KTP Kotka	
1952	KTP Kotka	
1953	IFK Vaasa	
1954	Pyrkiva Turku	
1955	KIF Helsinki	Haka Valkeakoski
1956	KuPS Kuopio	PP Voikka
1957	HPS Helsinki	Drott
1958	KuPS Kuopio	KTP Kotka
1959	HIFK Helsinki	Haka Valkeakoski
1960	Haka Valkeakoski	Haka Valkeakoski
1961	HIFK Helsinki	KTP Kotka
1962	Haka Valkeakoski	HPS Helsinki
1963	Reipas Lahti	Haka Valkeakoski
1964	HJK Helsinki	Reipas Lahti
1965	Haka Valkeakoski	Abo IFK Turku
1966	KuPS Kuopio	HJK Helsinki
1967	Reipas Lahti	KTP Kotka
1968	TPS Turku	KuPS Kuopio
1969	KPV Kokkola	Haka Valkeakoski
1970	Reipas Lahti	MP Mikkeli
1971	TPS Turku	MP Mikkeli
1972	TPS Turku	Reipas Lahti
1973	HJK Helsinki	Reipas Lahti
1974	KuPS Kuopio	Reipas Lahti
1975	TPS Turku	Reipas Lahti
1976	KuPS Kuopio	Reipas Lahti
1977	Haka Valkeakoski	Haka Valkeakoski
1978	HJK Helsinki	Reipas Lahti
1979	OPS Oulu	Ilves Tampere
1980	OPS Oulu	KTP Kotka
1981	HJK Helsinki	HJK Helsinki
1982	Kuusysi Lahti	Haka Valkeakoski
1983	Ilves Tampere	Kuusysi Lahti
1984	Kuusysi Lahti	HJK Helsinki
1985	HJK Helsinki	Haka Valkeakoski
1986	Kuusysi Lahti	RoPS Rovaniemi
1987	HJK Helsinki	Kuusysi Lahti
1988	HJK Helsinki	Haka Valkeakoski
1989	Kuusysi Lahti	KuPS Kuopio
1990	HJK Helsinki	Ilves Tampere
1991	Kuusysi Lahti	TPS Turku
1992	HJK Helsinki	MyPa-47
1993	Jazz Pori	HJK Helsinki
1994	TVP Tampere	TPS Turku
1995	Haka Valkeakoski	MyPa-47
1996	FC Jazz Pori	HJK Helsinki
1997	HJK Helsinki	Haka Valkeakoski
1998	Haka Valkeakoski	HJK Helsinki
1999	Haka Valkeakoski	Jokerit Helsinki
2000	Haka Valkeakoski	HJK Helsinki
2001	Tampere United	Atlantis Helsinki
2002	HJK Helsinki	Haka Valkeakoski
2003	HJK Helsinki	HJK Helsinki
2004	Haka Valkeakoski	MyPa-47
2005	MyPa-47	Haka Valkeakoski
2006	Tampere United	HJK Helsinki
2007	Tampere United	Tampere United
2008	Inter Turku	HJK Helsinki
2009	HJK Helsinki	Inter Turku
2010	HJK Helsinki	TPS Turku
2011	HJK Helsinki	HJK Helsinki

FIN – FINLAND

Year	League Cup Winners
1994	HJK Helsinki
1995	Haka Valkeakoski
1996	HJK Helsinki
1997	HJK Helsinki
1998	HJK Helsinki
1999	VPS Vaasa
2000	VPS Vaasa
2001	
2002	
2003	
2004	Allianssi Vantaa
2005	Allianssi Vantaa
2006	KuPS Kuopio
2007	FC Lahti
2008	Inter Turku
2009	Tampere United
2010	Honka Espoo
2011	Honka Espoo

FRA – FRANCE

Year	USFSA League	USFSA Cup
1894	Standard AC Paris	Standard AC Paris
1895	Standard AC Paris	Standard AC Paris
1896	Club Français Paris	
1897	Standard AC Paris	
1898	Standard AC Paris	
1899	Le Havre AC	
1900	Le Havre AC	
1901	Standard AC Paris	
1902	RC Roubaix	
1903	RC Roubaix	
1904	RC Roubaix	
1905	Gallia Club Paris	
1906	RC Roubaix	
1907	RC de France	
1908	RC Roubaix	
1909	Stade Helvétique	
1910	US Tourcoing	LFA League
1911	Stade Helvétique	CA Paris
1912	Stade Raphaélois	Red Star Paris
1913	Stade Helvétique	CA Paris
1914	Olympique Lillois	Etoile Levallois Paris
1915	Société Général Paris	Olympique de Pantin
1916	Stade Rennais	Olympique de Pantin
1917	Société Général Paris	Olympique de Pantin
1918	Le Havre AC	Club Français Paris
1919	Le Havre AC	Red Star Paris

Year	FCAF League	FGSPF League
1905		Etoile des Deux Lacs
1906	SM Puteaux	Etoile des Deux Lacs
1907	SM Puteaux	Etoile des Deux Lacs
1908	SM Puteaux	Patronage Olier Paris
1909	JA Saint Ouen	Bon Gars Bordeaux
1910	CA Vitry	Patronage Olier Paris
1911	CA Vitry	Etoile des Deux Lacs
1912	Vie au Grand Air	Etoile des Deux Lacs
1913	Vie au Grand Air	Etoile des Deux Lacs
1914	Vie au Grand Air	Patronage Olier Paris
1915		Jeanne d'Arc Paris
1916	UA du 20e Paris	Etoile des Deux Lacs
1917		Bousbotte Besançon
1918		Etoile Bienfaisance
1919		Etoile Bienfaisance

FRA – FRANCE

Year	League Cup Winners
1995	Paris St-Germain
1996	FC Metz
1997	RC Strasbourg
1998	Paris St-Germain
1999	RC Lens
2000	Gueugnon
2001	Olympique Lyonnais
2002	Girondins Bordeaux
2003	AS Monaco
2004	FC Sochaux
2005	RC Strasbourg
2006	AS Nancy-Lorraine
2007	Girondins Bordeaux
2008	Paris St-Germain
2009	Girondins Bordeaux
2010	Olympique Marseille
2011	Olympique Marseille

FRA – FRANCE

Year	Champions	Cup Winners
1918		Olympique de Pantin
1919		CAS Generaux
1920		CA Paris
1921		Red Star Paris
1922		Red Star Paris
1923		Red Star Paris
1924		Olympique Marseille
1925		CAS Generaux
1926		Olympique Marseille
1927		Olympique Marseille
1928		Red Star Paris
1929		SO Montpellier
1930		FC Sete
1931		Club Francais
1932		AS Cannes
1933	Olympique Lille	Excelsior Roubaix
1934	FC Sete	FC Sete
1935	FC Sochaux	Olympique Marseille
1936	Racing Club Paris	Racing Club Paris
1937	Olympique Marseille	FC Sochaux
1938	FC Sochaux	Olympique Marseille
1939	FC Sete	Racing Club Paris
1940		Racing Club Paris
1941		Girondins Bordeaux
1942		Red Star Paris
1943		Olympique Marseille
1944		Nancy-Lorraine XI
1945		Racing Club Paris
1946	Lille OSC	Lille OSC
1947	CO Roubaix	Lille OSC
1948	Olympique Marseille	Lille OSC
1949	Stade de Reims	Racing Club Paris
1950	Girondins Bordeaux	Stade de Reims
1951	OGC Nice	RC Strasbourg
1952	OGC Nice	OGC Nice
1953	Stade de Reims	Lille OSC
1954	Lille OSC	OGC Nice
1955	Stade de Reims	Lille OSC
1956	OGC Nice	FC Sedan
1957	AS Saint-Étienne	FC Toulouse
1958	Stade de Reims	Stade de Reims
1959	OGC Nice	Le Havre AC
1960	Stade de Reims	AS Monaco
1961	AS Monaco	FC Sedan
1962	Stade de Reims	AS Saint-Étienne
1963	AS Monaco	AS Monaco
1964	AS Saint-Étienne	Olympique Lyon
1965	FC Nantes	Stade de Rennes
1966	FC Nantes	RC Strasbourg
1967	AS Saint-Étienne	Olympique Lyon
1968	AS Saint-Étienne	AS Saint-Étienne
1969	AS Saint-Étienne	Olympique Marseille
1970	AS Saint-Étienne	AS Saint-Étienne
1971	Olympique Marseille	Stade de Rennes
1972	Olympique Marseille	Olympique Marseille
1973	FC Nantes	Olympique Lyon
1974	AS Saint-Étienne	AS Saint-Étienne
1975	AS Saint-Étienne	AS Saint-Étienne
1976	AS Saint-Étienne	Olympique Marseille
1977	FC Nantes	AS Saint-Étienne
1978	AS Monaco	AS Nancy
1979	RC Strasbourg	FC Nantes
1980	FC Nantes	AS Monaco
1981	AS Saint-Étienne	SEC Bastia
1982	AS Monaco	Paris St-Germain
1983	FC Nantes	Paris St-Germain
1984	Girondins Bordeaux	FC Metz
1985	Girondins Bordeaux	AS Monaco
1986	Paris St-Germain	Girondins Bordeaux
1987	Girondins Bordeaux	Girondins Bordeaux
1988	AS Monaco	FC Metz
1989	Olympique Marseille	Olympique Marseille
1990	Olympique Marseille	SCP Montpellier
1991	Olympique Marseille	AS Monaco
1992	Olympique Marseille	Olympique Marseille
1993	Olympique Marseille	Paris St-Germain
1994	Paris St-Germain	AJ Auxerre
1995	FC Nantes	Paris St-Germain
1996	AJ Auxerre	AJ Auxerre
1997	AS Monaco	OGC Nice
1998	Racing Club Lens	Paris St-Germain
1999	Girondins Bordeaux	FC Nantes
2000	AS Monaco	FC Nantes
2001	FC Nantes	RC Strasbourg
2002	Olympique Lyonnais	FC Lorient
2003	Olympique Lyonnais	AJ Auxerre
2004	Olympique Lyonnais	Paris St-Germain
2005	Olympique Lyonnais	AJ Auxerre
2006	Olympique Lyonnais	Paris St-Germain
2007	Olympique Lyonnais	Sochaux
2008	Olympique Lyonnais	Olympique Lyonnais
2009	Girondins Bordeaux	En Avant Guingamp
2010	Olympique Marseille	Paris St-Germain
2011	Lille OSC	Lille OSC

FRO – FAROE ISLANDS

Year	Champions	Cup Winners
1942	KI Klaksvík	
1943	TB Tvøroyri	
1944		
1945	KI Klaksvík	
1946	B'36 Tórshavn	
1947	SI Sørvag	
1948	B'36 Tórshavn	
1949	TB Tvøroyri	
1950	B'36 Tórshavn	
1951	TB Tvøroyri	
1952	KI Klaksvík	
1953	KI Klaksvík	
1954	KI Klaksvík	
1955	HB Tórshavn	HB Tórshavn
1956	KI Klaksvík	TB Tvøroyri
1957	KI Klaksvík	HB Tórshavn
1958	KI Klaksvík	TB Tvøroyri
1959	B'36 Tórshavn	HB Tórshavn
1960	HB Tórshavn	TB Tvøroyri
1961	KI Klaksvík	TB Tvøroyri
1962	B'36 Tórshavn	HB Tórshavn
1963	HB Tórshavn	HB Tórshavn
1964	HB Tórshavn	HB Tórshavn
1965	HB Tórshavn	B'36 Tórshavn
1966	KI Klaksvík	KI Klaksvík
1967	KI Klaksvík	KI Klaksvík
1968	KI Klaksvík	HB Tórshavn
1969	KI Klaksvík	HB Tórshavn
1970	KI Klaksvík	HB Tórshavn
1971	HB Tórshavn	HB Tórshavn
1972	KI Klaksvík	HB Tórshavn
1973	HB Tórshavn	HB Tórshavn
1974	HB Tórshavn	VB Vagur
1975	HB Tórshavn	HB Tórshavn
1976	TB Tvøroyri	HB Tórshavn
1977	TB Tvøroyri	TB Tvøroyri
1978	HB Tórshavn	HB Tórshavn
1979	IF Fuglafjørdur	HB Tórshavn
1980	TB Tvøroyri	HB Tórshavn
1981	HB Tórshavn	HB Tórshavn
1982	HB Tórshavn	HB Tórshavn
1983	GI Gøtu	GI Gøtu
1984	B'68 Toftir	HB Tórshavn
1985	B'68 Toftir	GI Gøtu
1986	GI Gøtu	NSI Runavík
1987	TB Tvøroyri	HB Tórshavn
1988	HB Tórshavn	HB Tórshavn
1989	B'71 Sandur	HB Tórshavn
1990	HB Tórshavn	KI Klaksvík
1991	KI Klaksvík	B'36 Tórshavn
1992	B'68 Toftir	HB Tórshavn
1993	GI Gøtu	B'71 Sandur
1994	GI Gøtu	KI Klaksvík
1995	GI Gøtu	HB Tórshavn
1996	GI Gøtu	GI Gøtu
1997	B'36 Tórshavn	GI Gøtu
1998	HB Tórshavn	HB Tórshavn
1999	KI Klaksvík	KI Klaksvík
2000	VB Vágur	GI Gøtu
2001	B'36 Tórshavn	B'36 Tórshavn
2002	HB Tórshavn	NSI Runavík
2003	HB Tórshavn	B'36 Tórshavn
2004	HB Tórshavn	HB Tórshavn
2005	B'36 Tórshavn	GI Gøtu
2006	HB Tórshavn	B'36 Tórshavn
2007	NSI Runavík	EB Streymur
2008	EB Streymur	EB Streymur
2009	HB Tórshavn	Vikingur
2010	HB Tórshavn	EB Streymur
2011	B'36 Tórshavn	EB Streymur

GAB – GABON

Year	Champions	Cup Winners
1964		
1965		
1966		
1967		
1968	Olympique Sportif	
1969	Aigle Royal	
1970	Aigle Royal	
1971	AS Solidarite	
1972	Olympique Sportif	
1973	AS Police	
1974	Zalang COC	
1975	Petrosport	
1976	Vautour	
1977	Vautour	
1978	FC 105	Stade Mandji
1979	Anges ABC	Stade Mandji
1980	US Mbilianzambi	
1981	US Mbilianzambi	
1982	FC 105	
1983	FC 105	

Year	Champions	Cup Winners
1984	AS Sogara	FC 105
1985	FC 105	AS Sogara
1986	FC 105	FC 105
1987	FC 105	US Mbilianzambi
1988	US Mbilianzambi	Vautour
1989	US Mbilianzambi	Petrosport
1990	JAC	Mbilinga
1991	AS Sogara	US Mbilianzambi
1992	AS Sogara	Delta Sports
1993	AS Sogara	Mbilinga
1994	AS Sogara	Mangasport
1995	Mangasport	Mbilinga
1996	Mbilinga	FC 105
1997		Mbilinga
1998	FC 105	Mbilinga
1999	Petrosport †	US Bitam
2000	Mangasport	AO Evizo
2001	FC 105	Mangasport
2002	US Mbilianzambi	US Mbilianzambi
2003	US Bitam	US Bitam
2004	Mangasport	FC 105
2005	Mangasport	Mangasport
2006	Mangasport	Delta Télestar
2007	FC 105	Mangasport
2008	Mangasport	US Mbilianzambi
2009	Stade Mandji	FC 105
2010	US Bitam	US Bitam
2011	Missile	Mangasport

GAM – GAMBIA

Year	Champions	Cup Winners
1953		Gambia United
1954		Police
1955		UAC
1956		White Phantoms
1957		Rainbow
1958		White Phantoms
1959		Black Diamonds
1960		White Phantoms
1961		White Phantoms
1962		Augustinians
1963		White Phantoms
1964		White Phantoms
1965		
1966	Augustinians	Arrance
1967	Augustinians	Arrance
1968		Augustinians
1969		Real Banjul
1970	Wallidan	Real Banjul
1971	Wallidan	Wallidan
1972		Wallidan
1973	Ports Authority	Wallidan
1974	Wallidan	Wallidan
1975	Real Banjul	GAMTEL
1976	Wallidan	Wallidan
1977	Wallidan	Wallidan
1978	Real Banjul	Wallidan
1979	Wallidan	Dingareh
1980	Starlight	GAMTEL
1981	Starlight	Wallidan
1982	Ports Authority	Starlight
1983	Real Banjul	Hawks
1984	Ports Authority	Wallidan
1985	Wallidan	Starlight
1986		Wallidan
1987		Wallidan
1988	Wallidan	Wallidan
1989		
1990		
1991		
1992	Wallidan	Wallidan
1993	Hawks	Wallidan
1994	Real Banjul	Wallidan
1995	Wallidan	Mass Sosseh
1996	Hawks	Hawks
1997	Real Banjul	Real Banjul
1998	Real Banjul	Wallidan
1999	Ports Authority	Wallidan
2000	Real Banjul	Steve Biko
2001	Wallidan	Wallidan
2002	Wallidan	Wallidan
2003	Armed Forces	Wallidan
2004	Wallidan	Wallidan
2005	Wallidan	Bakau United
2006	Ports Authority	Hawks
2007	Real Banjul	Ports Authority
2008	Wallidan	Wallidan
2009	Armed Forces	Young Africans
2010	Ports Authority	GAMTEL
2011	Brikama United	GAMTEL

GEO – GEORGIA

Year	Champions	Cup Winners
1990	Iberia Tbilisi	Guria Lanchkhuti
1991	Iberia Tbilisi	
1992	Dinamo Tbilisi	Dinamo Tbilisi
1993	Dinamo Tbilisi	Dinamo Tbilisi
1994	Dinamo Tbilisi	Dinamo Tbilisi
1995	Dinamo Tbilisi	Dinamo Tbilisi
1996	Dinamo Tbilisi	Dinamo Tbilisi
1997	Dinamo Tbilisi	Dinamo Tbilisi
1998	Dinamo Tbilisi	Dinamo Batumi
1999	Dinamo Tbilisi	Torpedo Kutaisi
2000	Torpedo Kutaisi	Lokomotivi Tbilisi
2001	Torpedo Kutaisi	Torpedo Kutaisi
2002	Torpedo Kutaisi	Lokomotivi Tbilisi
2003	Dinamo Tbilisi	Dinamo Tbilisi
2004	WIT Georgia Tbilisi	Dinamo Tbilisi
2005	Dinamo Tbilisi	Lokomotivi Tbilisi
2006	Sioni Bolnisi	Ameri Tbilisi
2007	Olimpi Rustavi	Ameri Tbilisi
2008	Dinamo Tbilisi	FC Zestafoni
2009	WIT Georgia Tbilisi	Dinamo Tbilisi
2010	Olimpi Rustavi	WIT Georgia Tbilisi
2011	FC Zestafoni	FC Gagra

GER – GERMANY

Year	Champions	Cup Winners
1903	VfB Leipzig	
1904	No final in 1904	
1905	Union 1892 Berlin	
1906	VfB Leipzig	
1907	Freiburger FC	
1908	Viktoria 89 Berlin	
1909	Phönix Karlsruhe	
1910	Karlsruher FV	
1911	Viktoria 89 Berlin	
1912	Holstein Kiel	
1913	VfB Leipzig	
1914	SpVgg Fürth	
1915		
1916		
1917		
1918		
1919		
1920	1.FC Nürnberg	
1921	1.FC Nürnberg	
1922		
1923	Hamburger SV	
1924	1.FC Nürnberg	
1925	1.FC Nürnberg	
1926	SpVgg Fürth	
1927	1.FC Nürnberg	
1928	Hamburger SV	
1929	SpVgg Fürth	
1930	Hertha BSC Berlin	
1931	Hertha BSC Berlin	
1932	Bayern München	
1933	Fortuna Düsseldorf	
1934	Schalke 04	
1935	Schalke 04	1.FC Nürnberg
1936	1.FC Nürnberg	VFB Leipzig
1937	Schalke 04	FC Schalke 04
1938	Hannover 96	SK Rapid Wien
1939	Schalke 04	1.FC Nürnberg
1940	Schalke 04	Dresdner SC
1941	SK Rapid Wien	Dresdner SC
1942	FC Schalke 04	TSV München 1860
1943	Dresdner SC	First Vienna FC
1944	Dresdner SC	
1945		
1946		
1947		
1948	1.FC Nürnberg	
1949	VfR Mannheim	
1950	VfB Stuttgart	
1951	1.FC Kaiserslautern	
1952	VfB Stuttgart	
1953	1.FC Kaiserslautern	Rot-Weiss Essen
1954	Hannover 96	VfB Stuttgart
1955	Rot-Weiss Essen	Karlsruher SC
1956	Borussia Dortmund	Karlsruher SC
1957	Borussia Dortmund	Bayern München
1958	Schalke 04	VfB Stuttgart
1959	Eintracht Frankfurt	Schwarz-Weiss Essen
1960	Hamburger SV	B. Mönchengladbach
1961	1.FC Nürnberg	Werder Bremen
1962	1.FC Köln	1.FC Nürnberg
1963	Borussia Dortmund	Hamburger SV
1964	1.FC Köln	TSV München 1860
1965	Werder Bremen	Borussia Dortmund
1966	TSV München 1860	Bayern München
1967	Eint. Braunschweig	Bayern München
1968	1.FC Nürnberg	1.FC Köln

Year	Champions	Cup Winners
1969	Bayern München	Bayern München
1970	B. Mönchengladbach	Kickers Offenbach
1971	B. Mönchengladbach	Bayern München
1972	Bayern München	Schalke 04
1973	Bayern München	B. Mönchengladbach
1974	Bayern München	Eintracht Frankfurt
1975	B. Mönchengladbach	Eintracht Frankfurt
1976	B. Mönchengladbach	Hamburger SV
1977	B. Mönchengladbach	1.FC Köln
1978	1.FC Köln	1.FC Köln
1979	Hamburger SV	Fortuna Düsseldorf
1980	Bayern München	Fortuna Düsseldorf
1981	Bayern München	Eintracht Frankfurt
1982	Hamburger SV	Bayern München
1983	Hamburger SV	1.FC Köln
1984	VfB Stuttgart	Bayern München
1985	Bayern München	Bayer Uerdingen
1986	Bayern München	Bayern München
1987	Bayern München	Hamburger SV
1988	Werder Bremen	Eintracht Frankfurt
1989	Bayern München	Borussia Dortmund
1990	Bayern München	1.FC Kaiserslautern
1991	1.FC Kaiserslautern	Werder Bremen
1992	VfB Stuttgart	Hannover 96
1993	Werder Bremen	Bayer Leverkusen
1994	Bayern München	Werder Bremen
1995	Borussia Dortmund	B. Mönchengladbach
1996	Borussia Dortmund	1.FC Kaiserslautern
1997	Bayern München	VfB Stuttgart
1998	1.FC Kaiserslautern	Bayern München
1999	Bayern München	Werder Bremen
2000	Bayern München	Bayern München
2001	Bayern München	Schalke 04
2002	Borussia Dortmund	Schalke 04
2003	Bayern München	Bayern München
2004	Werder Bremen	Werder Bremen
2005	Bayern München	Bayern München
2006	Bayern München	Bayern München
2007	VfB Stuttgart	1.FC Nürnberg
2008	Bayern München	Bayern München
2009	VfL Wolfsburg	Werder Bremen
2010	Bayern München	Bayern München
2011	Borussia Dortmund	Schalke 04

GHA – GHANA

Year	Champions	Cup
		GFA Cup
1958	Hearts of Oak	Asante Kotoko
1959	Asante Kotoko	Cornerstones
1960	Eleven Wise	Asante Kotoko
1961		
1962	Hearts of Oak	Real Republicans
1963	Real Republicans	Real Republicans
1964	Asante Kotoko	Real Republicans
1965	Asante Kotoko	Real Republicans
1966	Mysterious Dwarfs	
1967	Asante Kotoko	
1968	Asante Kotoko	Mysterious Dwarfs
1969	Asante Kotoko	
1970	Great Olympics	
1971	Hearts of Oak	
1972	Asante Kotoko	
1973	Hearts of Oak	Hearts of Oak
1974	Great Olympics	Hearts of Oak
1975	Asante Kotoko	Great Olympics
1976	Hearts of Oak	Asante Kotoko
1977	Sekondi Hasaacas	
1978	Hearts of Oak	Asante Kotoko
1979	Hearts of Oak	Hearts of Oak
1980	Asante Kotoko	
1981	Asante Kotoko	Hearts of Oak
1982	Asante Kotoko	Eleven Wise
1983	Asante Kotoko	Great Olympics
1984	Hearts of Oak	Asante Kotoko
1985	Hearts of Oak	Sekondi Hasaacas
1986	Asante Kotoko	Okwahu United
1987	Asante Kotoko	
1988	Asante Kotoko	
1989		Hearts of Oak
1990	Hearts of Oak	Asante Kotoko
1991	Asante Kotoko	
1992	Asante Kotoko	Voradep Ho
1993	Asante Kotoko	Goldfields Obuasi
1994	Goldfields Obuasi	Hearts of Oak
1995	Goldfields Obuasi	Great Olympics
1996	Goldfields Obuasi	Hearts of Oak
1997	Hearts of Oak	Ghapoha Tema
1998	Hearts of Oak	Asante Kotoko
1999	Hearts of Oak	Hearts of Oak
2000	Hearts of Oak	Hearts of Oak
2001	Hearts of Oak	Asante Kotoko
2002	Hearts of Oak	
		GHALCA Cup
2003	Asante Kotoko	
2004	Hearts of Oak	Real Tamale United
		SWAG Cup
2005	Asante Kotoko	Asante Kotoko
2006		AshantiGold
2007	Hearts of Oak	Liberty Pros
2008	Asante Kotoko	Asante Kotoko
2009	Hearts of Oak	Heart of Lions
		GFA Cup
2010	Aduana Stars	
2011	Berekum Chelsea	Nania

GNB – GUINEA-BISSAU

Year	Champions	Cup Winners
1975	Os Balantas Mansôa	
1976	UDIB Bissau	
1977	SB Benfica	UDIB Bissau
1978	SB Benfica	Bula FC
1979		Estrela Negra
1980	SB Benfica	SB Benfica
1981	SB Benfica	Ajuda Sport
1982	SB Benfica	Sporting CB
1983	Sporting CB	UDIB Bissau
1984	Sporting CB	UDIB Bissau
1985	UDIB Bissau	UDIB Bissau
1986	Sporting CB	Sporting CB
1987	Sporting Bafatá	Sporting CB
1988	SB Benfica	UDIB Bissau
1989	SB Benfica	SB Benfica
1990	SB Benfica	Desportivo Farim
1991	Sporting CB	Sporting CB
1992	Sporting CB	SB Benfica
1993	Sport Portos	Sport Portos
1994	Sporting CB	Ténis Bissau
1995		
1996	ADR Mansabá	UDIB Bissau
1997	Sporting CB	
1998	Sporting CB	Sport Portos
1999		
2000	Sporting CB	
2001		ADR Mansabá
2002	Sporting CB	Mavegro FC
2003	UDIB Bissau	
2004	Sporting CB	Mavegro FC
2005	Sporting CB	Sporting CB
2006	Os Balantas Mansôa	Sport Portos
2007	Sporting CB	
2008	Sporting Bafatá	SB Benfica
2009	Os Balantas Mansôa	SB Benfica
2010	SB Benfica	SB Benfica
2011	Atlético Bissorã	ADR Mansabá

GRE – GREECE

Year	Champions	Cup Winners
1928	Aris	
1929		
1930	Panathinaikos	
1931	Olympiacos	
1932	Aris	AEK
1933	Olympiacos	Ethnikos Piraeus
1934	Olympiacos	
1935		
1936	Olympiacos	
1937	Olympiacos	
1938	Olympiacos	
1939	AEK	AEK
1940	AEK	Panathinaikos
1941		
1942		
1943		
1944		
1945		
1946	Aris	
1947	Olympiacos	Olympiacos
1948	Olympiacos	Panathinaikos
1949	Panathinaikos	AEK
1950		AEK
1951	Olympiacos	Olympiacos
1952		Olympiacos
1953	Panathinaikos	Olympiacos
1954	Olympiacos	Olympiacos
1955	Olympiacos	Panathinaikos
1956	Olympiacos	AEK
1957	Olympiacos	Olympiacos
1958	Olympiacos	Olympiacos
1959	Olympiacos	Olympiacos
1960	Panathinaikos	Olympiacos
1961	Panathinaikos	Olympiacos
1962	Panathinaikos	Olympiacos
1963	AEK	
1964	Panathinaikos	Olympiacos
1965	Panathinaikos	Olympiacos
1966	Olympiacos	AEK
1967	Olympiacos	Panathinaikos
1968	AEK	Olympiacos
1969	Panathinaikos	Panathinaikos *
1970	Panathinaikos	Aris
1971	AEK	Olympiacos
1972	Panathinaikos	PAOK

Year	Champions	Cup Winners
1973	Olympiacos	Olympiacos
1974	Olympiacos	PAOK
1975	Olympiacos	Olympiacos
1976	PAOK	Iraklis
1977	Panathinaikos	Panathinaikos
1978	AEK	AEK
1979	AEK	Panionios
1980	Olympiacos	Kastoria
1981	Olympiacos	Olympiacos
1982	Olympiacos	Panathinaikos
1983	Olympiacos	AEK
1984	Panathinaikos	Panathinaikos
1985	PAOK	Larissa
1986	Panathinaikos	Panathinaikos
1987	Olympiacos	OFI Crete
1988	Larissa	Panathinaikos
1989	AEK	Panathinaikos
1990	Panathinaikos	Olympiacos
1991	Panathinaikos	Panathinaikos
1992	AEK	Olympiacos
1993	AEK	Panathinaikos
1994	AEK	Panathinaikos
1995	Panathinaikos	Panathinaikos
1996	Panathinaikos	AEK
1997	Olympiacos	AEK
1998	Olympiacos	Panionios
1999	Olympiacos	Olympiacos
2000	Olympiacos	AEK
2001	Olympiacos	PAOK
2002	Olympiacos	AEK
2003	Olympiacos	PAOK
2004	Panathinaikos	Panathinaikos
2005	Olympiacos	Olympiacos
2006	Olympiacos	Olympiacos
2007	Olympiacos	Larissa
2008	Olympiacos	Olympiacos
2009	Olympiacos	Olympiacos
2010	Panathinaikos	Panathinaikos
2011	Olympiacos	AEK

GRN – GRENADA

Year	Champions	Cup Winners
1996	Barba Super Stars	
1997	Seven Seas Rock City	
1998	Fontenoy United	
1999	St Andrews	
2000	Grenada Boys SS	
2001	Grenada Boys SS	
2002	QPR	
2003	Carib Hurricane	
2004		Police SC
2005	ASOMS Paradise	
2006	Carib Hurricane	
2007	ASOMS Paradise	
2008	Carib Hurricane	
2009		
2010	ASOMS Paradise	Eagles Super Strikers
2011	Hard Rock	Carib Hurricane

GUA – GUATEMALA

Year	Champions	Apertura
1943	Municipal	
1943	Tip Nac	
1945	Tip Nac	
1947	Municipal	
1951	Municipal	
1953	Tip Nac	
1954	Municipal	
1956	Comunicaciones	
1958	Comunicaciones	
1960	Comunicaciones	
1962	Xelajú	
1964	Municipal	
1964	Aurora	
1966	Municipal	
1966	Aurora	
1968	Aurora	
1969	Comunicaciones	
1970	Municipal	
1971	Comunicaciones	
1971	Comunicaciones	
1972	Comunicaciones	
1973	Municipal	
1974	Municipal	
1975	Aurora	
1976	Municipal	
1977	Comunicaciones	
1978	Aurora	
1979	Comunicaciones	
1980	Xelajú	
1981	Comunicaciones	
1982	Comunicaciones	
1983	Suchitepéquez	
1984	Aurora	
1985	Comunicaciones	
1986	Aurora	
1987	Municipal	
1988		
1989	Municipal	
1990	Municipal	
1991	Municipal	
1992	Municipal	
1993	Aurora	
1994	Municipal	
1995	Comunicaciones	
1996	Xelajú	
1997	Comunicaciones	
1998	Comunicaciones	Comunicaciones
1999	Comunicaciones	Comunicaciones
2000	Municipal	Municipal
2001	Comunicaciones	Municipal
2002	Municipal	Comunicaciones
2003	Comunicaciones	Municipal
2004	Cobán Imperial	Municipal
2005	Municipal	Municipal
2006	Municipal	Municipal
2007	Xelajú	Deportivo Jalapa
2008	Municipal	Comunicaciones
2009	Deportivo Jalapa	Municipal
2010	Municipal	Comunicaciones
2011	Comunicaciones	Municipal

GUI – GUINEA

Year	Champions	Cup Winners
1965	Conakry I	
1966	Conakry II	
1967	Conakry II	
1968	Conakry II	
1969	Conakry I	
1970	Conakry I	
1971	Hafia	
1972	Hafia	
1973	Hafia	
1974	Hafia	
1975	Hafia	
1976	Hafia	
1977	Hafia	
1978	Hafia	
1979	Hafia	
1980	Kaloum Stars	
1981	Kaloum Stars	
1982	Hafia	
1983	Hafia	
1984	Kaloum Stars	
1985	Hafia	Kaloum Stars
1986	Horoya	Olympique Kakande
1987	Kaloum Stars	ASFAG
1988	Horoya	Olympique Kakande
1989	Horoya	Horoya
1990	Horoya	Mankona
1991	Horoya	ASFAG
1992	Horoya	Hafia
1993	Kaloum Stars	Hafia
1994	Horoya	Horoya
1995	Kaloum Stars	Horoya
1996	Kaloum Stars	ASFAG
1997		Kaloum Stars
1998	Kaloum Stars	Kaloum Stars
1999		Horoya
2000	Horoya	Fello Star
2001	Horoya	Kaloum Stars
2002	Satellite	Hafia
2003	ASFAG	Etoile de Guinée
2004		Fello Star
2005	Satellite	Kaloum Stars
2006	Fello Star	Satellite
2007	Kaloum Stars	Kaloum Stars
2008	Fello Star	Satellite
2009	Fello Star	Baraka Djoma
2010	Fello Star	Séquence
2011	Horoya	Séquence

GUM – GUAM

Year	Champions	Cup Winners
1990	Univ'ty of Guam	
1991	Univ'ty of Guam	
1992	Univ'ty of Guam	
1993	Univ'ty of Guam	
1994	Tumon	
1995	CM G-Force	
1996	CM G-Force	
1997	Tumon	
1998	Anderson	
1999	Silver Bullets	
2000	Silver Bullets	
2001	Silver Bullets	
2002	Guam Shipyard	
2003	Guam Shipyard	
2004	Guam U-18	
2005	Guam Shipyard	
2006	Guam Shipyard	

Year	Champions	K&S Winners
2007	Quality Distributors	
2008	Quality Distributors	Quality Distributors
2009	Quality Distributors	Quality Distributors
2010	Quality Distributors	Guam Shipyard
2011	Cars Plus	Quality Distributors

GUY - GUYANA

Year	Champions	K&S Winners
1990	Santos	
1991	Santos	Milerock
1992		Eagles United
1993		Botafogo
1994	Western Tigers	Camptown
1995	Milerock	Topp XX
1996	Omai Gold Seekers	Beacon's
1997	Topp XX	Topp XX
1998	Santos	Milerock
1999		Doc's Khelwalaas
2000		Topp XX
2001	Conquerors	Topp XX
2002		Victoria Kings
2003		Conquerors
2004		Camptown
2005		Conquerors
2006		Topp XX
2007		Joe Public TRI
2008		Alpha United
2009	Alpha United	Pele
2010	Alpha United	Western Tigers
2011		Alpha United
2012		Caledonia AIA TRI

HAI - HAITI

Year	Champions
1938	Racing CH
1939	Violette
1940	Hatüey Bacardi
1941	Racing CH
1943	Etoile Haïtien
1943	Arsenal
1944	Etoile Haïtien
1945	Hatüey Bacardi
1946	Racing CH
1947	Racing CH
1948	Excelsior
1949	
1950	Excelsior
1951	Excelsior
1952	
1953	Aigle-Noir
1954	Racing CH
1955	Aigle-Noir
1956	Jeûnesse
1957	Violette
1958	Racing CH
1959	
1960	
1961	Etoile Haïtien
1962	Racing CH

Year	Champions	
1968	Violette	
1969	Racing CH	
1970	Aigle Noir	
1971	Don Bosco	
1983	Violette	
1988	Aigle Rouge	
1989	FICA	
1990	FICA	
1991	FICA	
1992		
1993	Tempête	
1994	FICA	
1995	Violette	
1996	Aigle Noir	
1997	AS Capoise	
1998	Aigle Noir	
1999	Violette	
2000	Racing CH	
2001	FICA	Cloture
2002	Roulado	Racing CH
2003	Don Bosco	Roulado
2004		
2005	Mirebalais	Baltimore
2006	Baltimore	
2007	Baltimore	Cavaly
2008	Tempête	Racing Gônaïves
2009	Tempête	Racing CH
2010	Tempête	Victory
2011	Baltimore	Tempête

HKG - HONG KONG

Year	Champions	Shield Winners
1897		HMS Centurion
1898		1st Batallion Rifles
1899		Hong Kong FC
1900		Welsh Fusiliers
1901		Royal Garrison
1902		Welsh Fusiliers
1903		HMS Glory
1904		HMS Albion
1905		The Queen's Own
1906		HMS Diadem
1907		Royal Garrison
1908		Hong Kong FC
1909	The Buffs	HMS Bedford
1910	Royal Garrison	The Buffs
1911	The Buffs	Navy Dockyard
1912	King's Own Rifles	King's Own Rifles
1913	Royal Garrison	Royal Engineers
1914	Duke of Cornwall	Royal Garrison
1915	Royal Garrison	Royal Engineers
1916	Royal Garrison	Hong Kong FC
1917	Royal Engineers	
1918	Royal Garrison	
1919	Royal Navy	Hong Kong FC
1920	Hong Kong FC	Police
1921	Wiltshire Regiment	HMS Titania
1922	HMS Curlew	Hong Kong FC
1923	King's Liverpool	Kowloon
1924	South China	East Surrey
1925	East Surrey	Kowloon

HKG - HONG KONG

Year	Champions	Shield Winners
1926	Kowloon	Kowloon
1927	South China	Scottish Borderers
1928	Chinese AA	Kowloon
1929	Chinese AA	South China
1930	Chinese AA	Somerset Light
1931	South China	South China
1932	Royal Navy	S. Welsh Borderers
1933	South China	South China
1934	S. Welsh Borderers	S. Welsh Borderers
1935	South China	South China B
1936	South China	South China
1937	Royal Ulster Rifles	South China
1938	South China B	South China
1939	South China	South China
1940	South China	Eastern
1941	South China	South China
1942		
1943		
1944		
1945		
1946	Royal Air Force	Royal Navy B
1947	Sing Tao	Sing Tao
1948	Kitchee	Sing Tao
1949	South China	South China
1950	Kitchee	Kitchee
1951	South China	Kowloon Motor Bus
1952	South China	Sing Tao
1953	South China	Eastern
1954	Kowloon Motor Bus	Kitchee
1955	South China	South China
1956	Eastern	Eastern
1957	South China	South China
1958	South China	South China
1959	South China	South China
1960	South China	Kitchee
1961	South China	South China
1962	South China	South China
1963	Yuen Long	Kwong Wah
1964	Kitchee	Kitchee
1965	Happy Valley	South China
1966	South China	Rangers
1967	Kowloon Motor Bus	Sing Tao
1968	South China	Yuen Long
1969	South China	Jardines
1970	Jardines	Sing Tao
1971	Rangers	Rangers
1972	South China	South China
1973	Seiko	Seiko
1974	South China	Seiko
1975	Seiko	Rangers
1976	South China	Seiko
1977	South China	Seiko
1978	South China	Happy Valley
1979	Seiko	Seiko
1980	Seiko	Seiko
1981	Seiko	Seiko
1982	Seiko	Eastern
1983	Seiko	Happy Valley
1984	Seiko	Bulova
1985	Seiko	Seiko
1986	South China	South China
1987	South China	Eastern
1988	South China	South China
1989	Happy Valley	South China

Year		
1990	South China	Happy Valley
1991	South China	South China
1992	South China	Sing Tao
1993	Eastern	Eastern
1994	Eastern	Eastern
1995	Eastern	Rangers
1996	Instant-Dict	South China
1997	South China	South China
1998	Instant-Dict	Happey Valley
1999	Happy Valley	South China
2000	South China	South China
2001	Happy Valley	O & YH Union
2002	Sun Hei	South China
2003	Happy Valley	South China
2004	Sun Hei	Happy Valley
2005	Sun Hei	Sun Hei
2006	Happy Valley	Kitchee
2007	South China	South China
2008	South China	Eastern
2009	South China	TSW Pegasus
2010	South China	South China
2011	Kitchee	Citizen

HKG – HONG KONG

Year	FA Cup Winners	Viceroy Winners
1970		Jardines
1971		Eastern
1972		South China
1973		Seiko
1974		Rangers
1975	Seiko	Rangers
1976	Seiko	Happy Valley
1977	Rangers	Caroline Hill
1978	Seiko	Seiko
1979	Yuen Long	Seiko
1980	Seiko	South China
1981	Seiko	Eastern
1982	Bulova	Bulova
1983	Bulova	Bulova
1984	Eastern	Seiko
1985	South China	Seiko
1986	Seiko	Seiko
1987	South China	South China
1988	South China	South China
1989	Lai Sun	Lai Sun
1990	South China	Lai Sun
1991	South China	South China
1992	Ernest Borel	Ernest Borel
1993	Eastern	South China
1994	Eastern	South China
1995	Rangers	Sing Tao
1996	South China	Instant-Dict
1997	Instant-Dict	Sing Tao
1998	Instant-Dict	South China
1999	South China	

Year		Lge Cup Winners
2000	Happy Valley	
2001	Instant-Dict	Happy Valley
2002	South China	South China
2003	Sun Hei	Sun Hei
2004	Happy Valley	Sun Hei
2005	Sun Hei	Sun Hei
2006	Sun Hei	Kitchee
2007	South China	Kitchee
2008	Citizen	South China
2009	Wofoo Tai Po	Sun Hei
2010	TSW Pegasus	
2011	South China	South China

HON – HONDURAS

Year	Champions	Apertura	
1966	Platense		
1967	Olimpia		
1968	Olimpia		
1969	Motagua		
1970	Olimpia		
1971	Motagua		
1972	Olimpia		
1973			
1974	Motagua		
1975	Real España		
1976	Real España		
1977	Real España		
1978	Olimpia		
1979	Motagua		
1980	Marathón		
1981	Real España		
1982	Vida		
1983	Olimpia		
1984	Vida		
1985	Olimpia		
1986	Marathón		
1987	Olimpia		
1988	Olimpia		
1989	Real España		
1990	Olimpia		
1991	Real España		
1992	Motagua		
1993	Olimpia		
1994	Real España		
1995	Victoria		
1996	Olimpia		
1997	Olimpia	Motagua	
1998	Motagua	Olimpia	
1999		Motagua	
2000	Motagua	Olimpia	
2001	Platense	Motagua	
2002	Marathón	Olimpia	
2003	Marathón	Real España	
2004	Olimpia	Marathón	
2005	Olimpia	Olimpia	
2006	Olimpia	Motagua	
2007	Real España	Marathón	
2008	Olimpia	Marathón	
2009	Olimpia	Marathón	
2010	Olimpia	Real España	
2011	Motagua	Olimpia	

HUN – HUNGARY

Year	Champions	Cup Winners
1901	Budapest TC	
1902	Budapest TC	
1903	Ferencváros	
1904	MTK Budapest	
1905	Ferencváros	
1906		
1907	Ferencváros	
1908	MTK Budapest	
1909	Ferencváros	
1910	Ferencváros	MTK Budapest
1911	Ferencváros	MTK Budapest
1912	Ferencváros	MTK Budapest
1913	Ferencváros	Ferencváros
1914	MTK Budapest	MTK Budapest
1915		
1916		
1917	MTK Budapest	
1918	MTK Budapest	
1919	MTK Budapest	
1920	MTK Budapest	
1921	MTK Budapest	
1922	MTK Budapest	Ferencváros
1923	MTK Budapest	MTK Budapest
1924	MTK Budapest	
1925	MTK Budapest	MTK Budapest
1926	Ferencváros	Kispest AC
1927	Ferencváros	Ferencváros
1928	Ferencváros	Ferencváros
1929	Hungária	
1930	Ujpesti TE	Bocskai Debrecen
1931	Ujpesti TE	111 Kerület TVE
1932	Ferencváros	Hungária
1933	Ujpesti TE	Ferencváros
1934	Ferencváros	Soroksár
1935	Ujpesti TE	Ferencváros
1936	Hungária	
1937	Hungária	
1938	Ferencváros	
1939	Ujpesti TE	
1940	Ferencváros	
1941	Ferencváros	Szolnoki MAV
1942	Csepel SC	Ferencváros
1943	Csepel SC	Ferencváros
1944	Nagyváradi AC	Ferencváros
1945	Ujpesti TE	
1946	Ujpesti TE	
1947	Ujpesti TE	
1948	Csepel SC	
1949	Ferencváros	
1950	Honvéd	
1950	Honvéd	
1951	Bástya Budapest	
1952	Honvéd	Bástya Budapest
1953	Vörös Lobogó	
1954	Honvéd	
1955	Honvéd	Vasas Budapest
1956		Ferencváros
1957	Vasas Budapest	
1958	MTK Budapest	
1959	Csepel SC	
1960	Ujpesti Dózsa	
1961	Vasas Budapest	
1962	Vasas Budapest	
1963	Ferencváros	
1963	Györ Vasas ETO	
1964	Ferencváros	Honvéd
1965	Vasas Budapest	Vasas ETO Györ
1966	Vasas Budapest	Vasas ETO Györ
1967	Ferencváros	Vasas ETO Györ
1968	Ferencváros	MTK Budapest
1969	Ujpesti Dózsa	Ujpesti Dózsa

Year	Champions	Cup Winners
1970	Ujpesti Dózsa	Ujpesti Dózsa
1971	Ujpesti Dózsa	Ujpesti Dózsa
1972	Ujpesti Dózsa	Ferencváros
1973	Ujpesti Dózsa	Vasas Budapest
1974	Ujpesti Dózsa	Ferencváros
1975	Ujpesti Dózsa	Ujpesti Dózsa
1976	Ferencváros	Ferencváros
1977	Vasas Budapest	Diósgyöri VTK
1978	Ujpesti Dózsa	Ferencváros
1979	Ujpesti Dózsa	Rába ETO Györ
1980	Honvéd	Diósgyöri VTK
1981	Ferencváros	Vasas Budapest
1982	Rába ETO Györ	Ujpesti Dózsa
1983	Rába ETO Györ	Ujpesti Dózsa
1984	Honvéd	Siófoki Bányász
1985	Honvéd	Honvéd
1986	Honvéd	Vasas Budapest
1987	MTK-VM Budapest	Ujpesti Dózsa
1988	Honvéd	Békéscsaba ESSC
1989	Honvéd	Honvéd
1990	Ujpesti Dózsa	Pécsi MSC
1991	Honvéd	Ferencváros
1992	Ferencváros	Ujpesti TE
1993	Kispest-Honvéd	Ferencvárosi TC
1994	Vac FC	Ferencváros
1995	Ferencváros	Ferencváros
1996	Ferencváros	Kispest-Honvéd
1997	MTK-Hungária	MTK-Hungária
1998	Ujpesti TE	MTK-Hungária
1999	MTK-Hungária	Debreceni VSC
2000	Dunaferr FC	MTK-Hungária
2001	Ferencváros	Debreceni VSC
2002	Zalaegerszegi TE	Ujpesti TE
2003	MTK-Hungária	Ferencváros
2004	Ferencváros	Ferencváros
2005	Debreceni VSC	Mátav FC Sopron
2006	Debreceni VSC	Fehérvár
2007	Debreceni VSC	Honvéd
2008	MTK-Hungária	Debreceni VSC
2009	Debreceni VSC	Honvéd
2010	Debreceni VSC	Debreceni VSC
2011	Videoton	Kecskemet

IDN - INDONESIA

Year	Champions	Cup Winners
1931	VIJ Jakarta	
1932	PSIM Yogyakarta	
1933	VIJ Jakarta	
1934	VIJ Jakarta	
1935	Persis Solo	
1936	Persis Solo	
1937	Persib Bandung	
1938	VIJ Jakarta	
1939	Persis Solo	
1940	Persis Solo	
1941	Persis Solo	
1942	Persis Solo	
1943	Persis Solo	
1948	Persis Solo	
1950	Persebaya Surabaya	
1951	Persebaya Surabaya	
1952	Persebaya Surabaya	
1954	Persija Jakarta	
1957	PSM Makasar	
1959	PSM Makasar	
1961	Persib Bandung	
1964	Persija Jakarta	
1965	PSM Makassar	
1966	PSM Makassar	
1967	PSMS Medan	
1969	PSMS Medan	
1971	PSMS Medan	
1973	Persija Jakarta	
1975	Persija Jakarta/PSMS Medan	
1977	Persija Jakarta	
1978	Persebaya Surabaya	
1979	Persija Jakarta	
1980	Persipura Jayapura	
1981	Persiraja Banda Aceh	
1982		
1983	PSMS Medan	
1984		
1985	PSMS Medan	Arseto
1986	Persib Bandung	Makasar Utama
1987	PSIS Semarang	Tiga Berlian
1988	Persebaya Surabaya	Tiga Berlian
1989		Tiga Berlian
1990	Persib Bandung	
1991		
1992	PSM Makasar	Semen Padang
1993		
1994	Persib Bandung	Gelora Dewata
1995	Persib Bandung	
1996	Bandung Raya	
1997	Persebaya Surabaya	
1998		
1999	PSIS Semarang	
2000	PSM Makasar	
2001	Persija Jakarta	
2002	Petrokimia Putra	
2003	Persik Kediri	
2004	Persebaya Surabaya	
2005	Persipura Jayapura	Arema Malang
2006	Persik Kediri	Arema Malang
2007	Sriwijaya Pal'bang	Sriwijaya Pal'bang
2008		
2009	Persipura Jayapura	Sriwijaya Pal'bang
2010	Arema Malang	Sriwijaya Pal'bang
2011	Persipura Jayapura	

IND - INDIA

Year	Champions	Federation Cup
1977		Indian Telephone Ind.
1978		East Bengal
1979		Border Security
1980		Mohun Bagan
1981		Mohun Bagan
1982		Mohun Bagan
1983		Mohammedan SC
1984		Mohammedan SC
1985		East Bengal
1986		Mohun Bagan
1987		Mohun Bagan
1988		Salgaocar
1989		Salgaocar
1990		Kerala Police
1991		Kerala Police
1992		Mohun Bagan
1993		Mohun Bagan
1994		Mohun Bagan
1995		JCT Mills
1996		JCT Mills
1996		East Bengal
1997	JCT Mills	Salgaocar
1998	Mohun Bagan	Mohun Bagan
1999	Salgaocar	
2000	Mohun Bagan	
2001	East Bengal	Mohun Bagan
2002	Mohun Bagan	
2003	East Bengal	Mahindra United
2004	East Bengal	Dempo
2005	Dempo	Mahindra United
2006	Mahindra United	Mohun Bagan
2007	Dempo	East Bengal
2008	Dempo	Mohun Bagan
2009	Churchill Brothers	East Bengal
2010	Dempo	East Bengal
2011	Salgaocar	Salgaocar

IND - INDIA

Year	Durand Cup Winners
1888	Royal Scots Fusiliers
1889	Highland LI
1890	Highland LI
1891	Scottish Borderers
1892	Scottish Borderers
1893	Highland LI
1894	Highland LI
1895	Highland LI
1896	Somerset LI
1897	Black Watch
1898	Black Watch
1899	Black Watch
1900	S. Wales Borderers
1901	S. Wales Borderers
1902	Hampshire Regiment
1903	Royal Irish Rifles
1904	North Staffordshire
1905	Royal Dragoons
1906	Cameronians
1907	Cameronians
1908	Lancashire Fusiliers
1909	Lancashire Fusiliers
1910	Royal Scots
1911	Black Watch
1912	Royal Scots
1913	Lancashire Fusiliers
1920	Black Watch
1921	Worcestershire Regiment
1922	Lancashire Fusiliers
1923	Cheshire Regiment
1924	Worcestershire Regiment
1925	Sherwood Foresters
1926	Durham LI
1927	York & Lancaster Regiment
1928	Sherwood Foresters
1929	York & Lancaster Regiment
1930	York & Lancaster Regiment
1931	Devonshire Regiment

Year	Team
1932	King's Shropshire LI
1933	King's Shropshire LI
1934	B Corps Signals
1935	Border Regiment
1936	A & S Highlanders
1937	Border Regiment
1938	S Wales Borderers
1939	
1940	Mohammedan SC
1950	Hyderabad Police
1951	East Bengal
1952	East Bengal
1953	Mohun Bagan
1954	Hyderabad Police
1955	Madras RC
1956	East Bengal
1957	Hyderabad Police
1958	Madras RC
1959	Mohun Bagan
1960	Mohun Bagan & East Bengal
1961	Andhra Pradesh Police
1962	
1963	Mohun Bagan
1964	Mohun Bagan
1965	Mohun Bagan
1966	Gorkha Brigade
1967	East Bengal
1968	Border Security
1969	Gorkha Brigade
1970	East Bengal
1971	Border Security
1972	East Bengal
1973	Border Security
1974	Mohun Bagan
1975	Border Security
1976	Border Security & JCT Mills
1977	Mohun Bagan
1978	East Bengal
1979	Mohun Bagan
1980	Mohun Bagan
1981	Border Security
1982	Mohun Bagan & East Bengal
1983	JCT Mills
1984	Mohun Bagan
1985	Mohun Bagan
1986	Mohun Bagan
1987	JCT Mills
1988	Border Security
1989	East Bengal
1990	East Bengal
1991	East Bengal
1992	JCT Mills
1993	East Bengal
1994	Mohun Bagan
1995	East Bengal
1996	JCT Mills
1997	FC Kochin
1998	Mahindra
1999	Salgoacar SC
2000	Mohun Bagan
2001	
2002	Mahindra United
2003	East Bengal
2004	Salgoacar SC
2005	Army XI
2006	Dempo SC
2007	Churchill Brothers
2008	Mahindra United
2009	Churchill Brothers
2010	Prayag United
2011	Churchill Brothers

IND – INDIA

Year	Calcutta League Champions
1898	Gloucestershire Regiment
1899	Calcutta FC
1900	Royal Irish Rifles
1901	Royal Irish Rifles
1902	Scottish Borderers
1903	93rd Highlanders
1904	King's Own Regiment
1905	King's Own Regiment
1906	Highlander LI
1907	Calcutta FC
1908	Gordon LI
1909	Gordon LI
1910	Dalhousie
1911	70th Company RGA
1912	Black Watch
1913	Black Watch
1914	91st Highlanders
1915	10th Middlesex
1916	Calcutta FC
1917	Lincolnshire Regiment
1918	Calcutta FC
1919	12th Special Service Battalion
1920	Calcutta FC
1921	Dalhousie
1922	Calcutta FC
1923	Calcutta FC
1924	Cameron Highlanders
1925	Calcutta FC
1926	North Staffordshire
1927	Calcutta FC
1928	Dalhousie
1929	Dalhousie
1930	
1931	Durham Light Rifles
1932	Durham Light Rifles
1933	Durham Light Rifles
1934	Mohammedan SC
1935	Mohammedan SC
1936	Mohammedan SC
1937	Mohammedan SC
1938	Mohammedan SC
1939	Mohun Bagan
1940	Mohammedan SC
1941	Mohammedan SC
1942	East Bengal
1943	Mohun Bagan
1944	Mohun Bagan
1945	East Bengal
1946	East Bengal
1947	
1948	Mohammedan SC
1949	East Bengal
1950	East Bengal
1951	Mohun Bagan
1952	East Bengal
1953	
1954	Mohun Bagan
1955	Mohun Bagan
1956	Mohun Bagan
1957	Mohammedan SC
1958	Eastern Railway
1959	Mohun Bagan
1960	Mohun Bagan
1961	East Bengal
1962	Mohun Bagan
1963	Mohun Bagan
1964	Mohun Bagan
1965	Mohun Bagan
1966	East Bengal
1967	Mohammedan SC
1968	
1969	Mohun Bagan
1970	East Bengal
1971	East Bengal
1972	East Bengal
1973	East Bengal
1974	East Bengal
1975	East Bengal
1976	Mohun Bagan
1977	East Bengal
1978	Mohun Bagan
1979	Mohun Bagan
1980	
1981	Mohammedan SC
1982	East Bengal
1983	Mohun Bagan
1984	Mohun Bagan
1985	East Bengal
1986	Mohun Bagan
1987	East Bengal
1988	East Bengal
1989	East Bengal
1990	Mohun Bagan
1991	East Bengal
1992	Mohun Bagan
1993	East Bengal
1994	Mohun Bagan
1995	East Bengal
1996	East Bengal
1997	Mohun Bagan
1998	East Bengal
1999	East Bengal
2000	East Bengal
2001	Mohun Bagan
2002	East Bengal
2003	East Bengal
2004	East Bengal
2005	Mohun Bagan
2006	East Bengal
2007	Mohun Bagan
2008	Mohun Bagan

IRL – REPUBLIC OF IRELAND

Year	Champions	Cup Winners
1922	St. James' Gate	St. James's Gate
1923	Shamrock Rovers	Alton United
1924	Bohemians	Athlone Town
1925	Shamrock Rovers	Shamrock Rovers
1926	Shelbourne	Fordsons

Year		
1927	Shamrock Rovers	Drumcondra
1928	Bohemians	Bohemians
1929	Shelbourne	Shamrock Rovers
1930	Bohemians	Shamrock Rovers
1931	Shelbourne	Shamrock Rovers
1932	Shamrock Rovers	Shamrock Rovers
1933	Dundalk	Shamrock Rovers
1934	Bohemians	Cork FC
1935	Dolphin	Bohemians
1936	Bohemians	Shamrock Rovers
1937	Sligo Rovers	Waterford
1938	Shamrock Rovers	St. James's Gate
1939	Shamrock Rovers	Shelbourne
1940	St. James' Gate	Shamrock Rovers
1941	Cork United	Cork United
1942	Cork United	Dundalk
1943	Cork United	Drumcondra
1944	Shelbourne	Shamrock Rovers
1945	Cork United	Shamrock Rovers
1946	Cork United	Drumcondra
1947	Shelbourne	Cork United
1948	Drumcondra	Shamrock Rovers
1949	Drumcondra	Dundalk
1950	Cork Athletic	Transport
1951	Cork Athletic	Cork Athletic
1952	St Patrick's Athletic	Dundalk
1953	Shelbourne	Cork Athletic
1954	Shamrock Rovers	Drumcondra
1955	St Patrick's Athletic	Shamrock Rovers
1956	St Patrick's Athletic	Shamrock Rovers
1957	Shamrock Rovers	Drumcondra
1958	Drumcondra	Dundalk
1959	Shamrock Rovers	St Patrick's Athletic
1960	Limerick United	Shelbourne
1961	Drumcondra	St Patrick's Athletic
1962	Shelbourne	Shamrock Rovers
1963	Dundalk	Shelbourne
1964	Shamrock Rovers	Shamrock Rovers
1965	Drumcondra	Shamrock Rovers
1966	Waterford	Shamrock Rovers
1967	Dundalk	Shamrock Rovers
1968	Waterford	Shamrock Rovers
1969	Waterford	Shamrock Rovers
1970	Waterford	Bohemians
1971	Cork Hibernians	Limerick
1972	Waterford	Cork Hibernians
1973	Waterford	Cork Hibernians
1974	Cork Celtic	Finn Harps
1975	Bohemians	Home Farm
1976	Dundalk	Bohemians
1977	Sligo Rovers	Dundalk
1978	Bohemians	Shamrock Rovers
1979	Dundalk	Dundalk
1980	Limerick United	Waterford
1981	Athlone Town	Dundalk
1982	Dundalk	Limerick United
1983	Athlone Town	Sligo Rovers
1984	Shamrock Rovers	University College
1985	Shamrock Rovers	Shamrock Rovers
1986	Shamrock Rovers	Shamrock Rovers
1987	Shamrock Rovers	Shamrock Rovers
1988	Dundalk	Dundalk
1989	Derry City	Derry City
1990	St Patrick's Athletic	Bray Wanderers
1991	Dundalk	Galway United
1992	Shelbourne	Bohemians
1993	Cork City	Shelbourne
1994	Shamrock Rovers	Sligo Rovers
1995	Dundalk	Derry City
1996	St Patrick's Athletic	Shelbourne
1997	Derry City	Shelbourne
1998	St Patrick's Athletic	Cork City
1999	St Patrick's Athletic	Bray Wanderers
2000	Shelbourne	Shelbourne
2001	Bohemians	Bohemians
2002	Shelbourne	Dundalk
2003	Bohemians	Derry City
2003	Shelbourne	Longford Town
2004	Shelbourne	Longford Town
2005	Cork City	Drogheda United
2006	Shelbourne	Derry City
2007	Drogheda United	Cork City
2008	Bohemians	Bohemians
2009	Bohemians	Sporting Fingal
2010	Shamrock Rovers	Sligo Rovers
2011	Shamrock Rovers	Sligo Rovers

IRL – REPUBLIC OF IRELAND

Year	Lge Cup Winners
1974	Waterford
1975	Bohemians
1976	Limerick
1977	Shamrock Rovers
1978	Dundalk
1979	Bohemians
1980	Athlone Town
1981	Dundalk
1982	Athlone Town
1983	Athlone Town
1984	Drogheda United
1985	Waterford United
1986	Galway United
1987	Dundalk
1988	Cork City
1989	Derry City
1990	Dundalk
1991	Derry City
1992	Derry City
1993	Limerick
1994	Derry City
1995	Cork City
1996	Shelbourne
1997	Galway United
1998	Sligo Rovers
1999	Cork City
2000	Derry City
2001	St Patrick's Athletic
2002	Limerick
2003	St Patrick's Athletic
2004	Longford Town
2005	Derry City
2006	Derry City
2007	Derry City
2008	Derry City
2009	Bohemians
2010	Sligo Rovers
2011	Derry City

IRN – IRAN

Year	Champions	Cup Winners
1971	Taj	
1972	Persepolis	
1973		
1974	Persepolis	
1975	Taj	
1976	Persepolis	Malavan
1977	Pas	Esteghlal
1978	Pas	
1987		Malavan
1988	Persepolis	Persepolis
1989	Shahin	Shahin
1990	Esteghlal	Malavan
1991		Persepolis
1992	Pas	
1993	Pas	
1994	Saipa	Saipa
1995	Saipa	Bahman
1996	Persepolis	Esteghlal
1997	Persepolis	Bargh
1998	Esteghlal	
1999	Persepolis	Persepolis
2000	Persepolis	Esteghlal
2001	Esteghlal	Fajr Sepasi
2002	Persepolis	Esteghlal
2003	Sepahan	Zob Ahan
2004	Pas	Sepahan
2005	Foolad	Saba Battery
2006	Esteghlal	Sepahan
2007	Saipa	Sepahan
2008	Persepolis	Esteghlal
2009	Esteghlal	Zob Ahan
2010	Sepahan	Persepolis
2011	Sepahan	Persepolis

IRQ – IRAQ

Year	Champions	Cup Winners
1974	Al Tayaran	Al Tayaran
1975	Al Tayaran	Al Tayaran
1976	Al Zawra'a	Al Zawra'a
1977	Al Zawra'a	
1978	Al Mina'a	Al Tayaran
1979	Al Zawra'a	Al Zawra'a
1980	Al Shurta	Al Jaish
1981	Al Talaba	Al Zawra'a
1982	Al Talaba	Al Zawra'a
1983	Saladaldeen	Al Jaish
1984	Al Jaish	Al Sina'a
1985		
1986	Al Talaba	
1987	Al Rasheed	Al Rashood
1988	Al Rasheed	Al Rasheed
1989	Al Rasheed	Al Zawra'a
1990	Al Tayaran	Al Zawra'a
1991	Al Zawra'a	Al Zawra'a
1992	Al Quwa Al Jawia	Al Quwa Al Jawia
1993	Al Talaba	Al Zawra'a
1994	Al Zawra'a	Al Zawra'a
1995	Al Zawra'a	Al Zawra'a
1996	Al Zawra'a	Al Zawra'a
1997	Al Quwa Al Jawia	Al Quwa Al Jawia

Year	Champions	Cup Winners
1998	Al Shurta	Al Zawra'a
1999	Al Zawra'a	Al Zawra'a
2000	Al Zawra'a	Al Zawra'a
2001	Al Zawra'a	
2002	Al Talaba	Al Talaba
2003		Al Talaba
2004		
2005	Al Quwa Al Jawia	
2006	Al Zawra'a	
2007	Arbil	
2008	Arbil	
2009	Arbil	
2010	Duhok	
2011	Al Zawra'a	

ISL – ICELAND

Year	Champions	Cup Winners
1912	KR Reykjavik	
1913	Fram Reykjavík	
1914	Fram Reykjavík	
1915	Fram Reykjavík	
1916	Fram Reykjavík	
1917	Fram Reykjavík	
1918	Fram Reykjavík	
1919	KR Reykjavík	
1920	Vikingur Reykjavík	
1921	Fram Reykjavík	
1922	Fram Reykjavík	
1923	Fram Reykjavík	
1924	Vikingur Reykjavík	
1925	Fram Reykjavík	
1926	KR Reykjavík	
1927	KR Reykjavík	
1928	KR Reykjavík	
1929	KR Reykjavík	
1930	Valur Reykjavík	
1931	KR Reykjavík	
1932	KR Reykjavík	
1933	Valur Reykjavík	
1934	KR Reykjavík	
1935	Valur Reykjavík	
1936	Valur Reykjavík	
1937	Valur Reykjavík	
1938	Valur Reykjavík	
1939	Fram Reykjavík	
1940	Valur Reykjavík	
1941	KR Reykjavík	
1942	Valur Reykjavík	
1943	Valur Reykjavík	
1944	Valur Reykjavík	
1945	Valur Reykjavík	
1946	Fram Reykjavík	
1947	Fram Reykjavík	
1948	KR Reykjavík	
1949	KR Reykjavík	
1950	KR Reykjavík	
1951	IA Akranes	
1952	KR Reykjavík	
1953	IA Akranes	
1954	IA Akranes	
1955	KR Reykjavík	
1956	Valur Reykjavík	
1957	IA Akranes	
1958	IA Akranes	
1959	KR Reykjavík	
1960	IA Akranes	KR Reykjavík
1961	KR Reykjavík	KR Reykjavík
1962	Fram Reykjavík	KR Reykjavík
1963	KR Reykjavík	KR Reykjavík
1964	IBK Keflavík	KR Reykjavík
1965	KR Reykjavík	Valur Reykjavík
1966	Valur Reykjavík	KR Reykjavík
1967	Valur Reykjavík	KR Reykjavík
1968	KR Reykjavík	IBV Vestmannaeyjar
1969	IBK Keflavík	IBA Akureyri
1970	IA Akranes	Fram Reykjavík
1971	IBK Keflavík	Vikingur Reykjavík
1972	Fram Reykjavík	IBV Vestmannaeyjar
1973	IBK Keflavík	Fram Reykjavík
1974	IA Akranes	Valur Reykjavík
1975	IA Akranes	IBK Keflavík
1976	Valur Reykjavík	Valur Reykjavík
1977	IA Akranes	Valur Reykjavík
1978	Valur Reykjavík	IA Akranes
1979	IBV Vestmannaeyjar	Fram Reykjavík
1980	Valur Reykjavík	Fram Reykjavík
1981	Vikingur Reykjavík	IBV Vestmannaeyjar
1982	Vikingur Reykjavík	IA Akranes
1983	IA Akranes	IA Akranes
1984	IA Akranes	IA Akranes
1985	Valur Reykjavík	Fram Reykjavík
1986	Fram Reykjavík	IA Akranes
1987	Valur Reykjavík	Fram Reykjavík
1988	Fram Reykjavík	Valur Reykjavík
1989	KA Akureyri	Fram Reykjavík
1990	Fram Reykjavík	Valur Reykjavík
1991	Vikingur Reykjavík	Valur Reykjavík
1992	IA Akranes	Valur Reykjavík
1993	IA Akranes	IA Akranes
1994	IA Akranes	KR Reykjavík
1995	IA Akranes	KR Reykjavík
1996	IA Akranes	IA Akranes
1997	IBV Vestmannæyjar	Keflavík
1998	IBV Vestmannæyjar	IBV Vestmannæyjar
1999	KR Reykjavík	KR Reykjavík
2000	KR Reykjavík	IA Akranes
2001	IA Akranes	Fylkir Reykjavík
2002	KR Reykjavik	Fylkir Reykjavík
2003	KR Reykjavík	IA Akranes
2004	FH Hafnarfjördur	Keflavík
2005	FH Hafnarfjördur	Valur Reykjavík
2006	FH Hafnarfjördur	Keflavík
2007	Valur Reykjavík	FH Hafnarfjördur
2008	FH Hafnarfjördur	KR Reykjavík
2009	FH Hafnarfjördur	Breidablik
2010	Breidablik	FH Hafnarfjördur
2011	KR Reykjavík	KR Reykjavík

ISR – ISRAEL

Year	Champions	Cup Winners
1928		Hapoel Tel Aviv
1929		Maccabi Tel Aviv
1930		Maccabi Tel Aviv
1931		
1932	British Police	British Police
1933		Maccabi Tel Aviv
1934	Hapoel Tel Aviv	Hapoel Tel Aviv
1935	Hapoel Tel Aviv	Maccabi Petah Tikva
1936	Maccabi Tel Aviv	
1937	Maccabi Tel Aviv	Hapoel Tel Aviv
1938		Hapoel Tel Aviv
1939		Hapoel Tel Aviv
1940	Hapoel Tel Aviv	Beitar Tel Aviv
1941	Maccabi Tel Aviv	Maccabi Tel Aviv
1942		Beitar Tel Aviv
1943	Hapoel Tel Aviv	
1944		
1945		
1946		Maccabi Tel Aviv
1947	Maccabi Tel Aviv	Maccabi Tel Aviv
1948		
1949		
1950	Maccabi Tel Aviv	
1951		
1952	Maccabi Tel Aviv	Maccabi Petah Tikva
1953		
1954	Maccabi Tel Aviv	Maccabi Tel Aviv
1955	Hapoel Petah Tikva	Maccabi Tel Aviv
1956	Maccabi Tel Aviv	
1957	Hapoel Tel Aviv	Hapoel Petah Tikva
1958	Maccabi Tel Aviv	Maccabi Tel Aviv
1959	Hapoel Petah Tikva	Maccabi Tel Aviv
1960	Hapoel Petah Tikva	Hapoel Tel Aviv
1961	Hapoel Petah Tikva	
1962	Hapoel Petah Tikva	Maccabi Haifa
1963	Hapoel Petah Tikva	Hapoel Haifa
1964	Hapoel Ramat Gan	Maccabi Tel Aviv
1965	Hakoah Ramat Gan	Maccabi Tel Aviv
1966	Hapoel Tel Aviv	Hapoel Haifa
1967		Maccabi Tel Aviv
1968	Maccabi Tel Aviv	Bnei Yehuda
1969	Hapoel Tel Aviv	Hakoah Ramat Gan
1970	Maccabi Tel Aviv	Maccabi Tel Aviv
1971	Maccabi Netanya	Hakoah Ramat Gan
1972	Maccabi Tel Aviv	Hapoel Tel Aviv
1973	Hakoah Ramat Gan	Hapoel Jerusalem
1974	Maccabi Netanya	Hapoel Haifa
1975	Hapoel Beer Sheva	Hapoel Kfar Sava
1976	Hapoel Beer Sheva	Beitar Jeusalem
1977	Maccabi Tel Aviv	Maccabi Tel Aviv
1978	Maccabi Netanya	Maccabi Netanya
1979	Maccabi Tel Aviv	Beitar Jerusalem
1980	Maccabi Netanya	Hapoel Kfar Sava
1981	Hapoel Tel Aviv	Bnei Yehuda
1982	Hapoel Kfar Sava	Hapoel Yehud
1983	Maccabi Netanya	Hapoel Tel Aviv
1984	Maccabi Haifa	Hapoel Lod
1985	Maccabi Haifa	Beitar Jerusalem
1986	Hapoel Tel Aviv	Beitar Jerusalem
1987	Beitar Jerusalem	Maccabi Tel Aviv
1988	Hapoel Tel Aviv	Maccabi Tel Aviv
1989	Maccabi Haifa	Beitar Jerusalem
1990	Bnei Yehuda	Hapoel Kfar Saba
1991	Maccabi Haifa	Maccabi Haifa
1992	Maccabi Tel Aviv	Hapoel Petah Tikva
1993	Beitar Jerusalem	Maccabi Haifa
1994	Maccabi Haifa	Maccabi Haifa
1995	Maccabi Tel Aviv	Maccabi Haifa
1996	Maccabi Tel Aviv	Maccabi Tel Aviv
1997	Beitar Jerusalem	Hapoel Beer Sheva
1998	Beitar Jerusalem	Maccabi Haifa
1999	Hapoel Haifa	Hapoel Tel Aviv

Year	Champions	Cup Winners
2000	Hapoel Tel Aviv	Hapoel Tel Aviv
2001	Maccabi Haifa	Maccabi Tel Aviv
2002	Maccabi Haifa	Maccabi Tel Aviv
2003	Maccabi Tel Aviv	Hapoel Ramat Gan
2004	Maccabi Haifa	Hapoel Bnei Sakhnin
2005	Maccabi Haifa	Maccabi Tel Aviv
2006	Maccabi Haifa	Hapoel Tel Aviv
2007	Beitar Jerusalem	Hapoel Tel Aviv
2008	Beitar Jerusalem	Beitar Jerusalem
2009	Maccabi Haifa	Beitar Jerusalem
2010	Hapoel Tel Aviv	Hapoel Tel Aviv
2011	Maccabi Haifa	Hapoel Tel Aviv

ITA – ITALY

Year	Champions	Cup Winners
1898	Genoa	
1899	Genoa	
1900	Genoa	
1901	Milan	
1902	Genoa	
1903	Genoa	
1904	Genoa	
1905	Juventus	
1906	Milan	
1907	Milan	
1908	Pro Vercelli	
1909	Pro Vercelli	
1910	Internazionale	
1911	Pro Vercelli	
1912	Pro Vercelli	
1913	Pro Vercelli	
1914	Casale	
1915	Genoa	
1916		
1917		
1918		
1919		
1920	Internazionale	
1921	Pro Vercelli	
1922	Novese	
1922	Pro Vercelli	
1923	Genoa	
1924	Genoa	
1925	Bologna	
1926	Juventus	
1927	Torino	
1928	Torino	
1929	Bologna	
1930	Ambrosiana-Inter	
1931	Juventus	
1932	Juventus	
1933	Juventus	
1934	Juventus	
1935	Juventus	
1936	Bologna	Torino
1937	Bologna	Genoa
1938	Ambrosiana-Inter	Juventus
1939	Bologna	Ambrosiana-Inter
1940	Ambrosiana-Inter	Fiorentina
1941	Bologna	Venezia
1942	Roma	Juventus
1943	Torino	Torino
1944		
1945		
1946	Torino	
1947	Torino	
1948	Torino	
1949	Torino	
1950	Juventus	
1951	Milan	
1952	Juventus	
1953	Internazionale	
1954	Internazionale	
1955	Milan	
1956	Fiorentina	
1957	Milan	
1958	Juventus	Lazio
1959	Milan	Juventus
1960	Juventus	Juventus
1961	Juventus	Fiorentina
1962	Milan	Napoli
1963	Internazionale	Atalanta
1964	Bologna	Roma
1965	Internazionale	Juventus
1966	Internazionale	Fiorentina
1967	Juventus	Milan
1968	Milan	Torino
1969	Fiorentina	Roma
1970	Cagliari	Bologna
1971	Internazionale	Torino
1972	Juventus	Milan
1973	Juventus	Milan
1974	Lazio	Bologna
1975	Juventus	Fiorentina
1976	Torino	Napoli
1977	Juventus	Milan
1978	Juventus	Internazionale
1979	Milan	Juventus
1980	Internazionale	Roma
1981	Juventus	Roma
1982	Juventus	Internazionale
1983	Roma	Juventus
1984	Juventus	Roma
1985	Hellas-Verona	Sampdoria
1986	Juventus	Roma
1987	Napoli	Napoli
1988	Milan	Sampdoria
1989	Internazionale	Sampdoria
1990	Napoli	Juventus
1991	Sampdoria	Roma
1992	Milan	Parma
1993	Milan	Torino
1994	Milan	Sampdoria
1995	Juventus	Juventus
1996	Milan	Fiorentina
1997	Juventus	Vicenza
1998	Juventus	Lazio
1999	Milan	Parma
2000	Lazio	Lazio
2001	Roma	Fiorentina
2002	Juventus	Parma
2003	Juventus	Milan
2004	Milan	Lazio
2005	Juventus	Internazionale
2006	Internazionale	Internazionale
2007	Internazionale	Roma
2008	Internazionale	Roma
2009	Internazionale	Lazio
2010	Internazionale	Internazionale
2011	Milan	Internazionale

JAM – JAMAICA

Year	Champions	Cup Winners
1974	Santos	
1975	Santos	
1976	Santos	
1977	Santos	
1978	Arnett Gardens	
1979		
1980	Santos	
1981	Cavaliers	
1982		
1983	Tivoli Gardens	
1984	Boys' Town	
1985	Defence Force	
1986	Boys' Town	
1987	Seba United	
1988	Wadadah	
1989	Boys' Town	
1990	Reno	
1991	Reno	Olympic Gardens
1992	Wadadah	Seba United
1993	Hazard United	Olympic Gardens
1994	Violet Kickers	Harbour View
1995	Reno	Reno
1996	Violet Kickers	Reno
1997	Seba United	Naggo Head
1998	Waterhouse	Harbour View
1999	Tivoli Gardens	Tivoli Gardens
2000	Harbour View	Hazard United
2001	Arnett Gardens	Harbour View
2002	Arnett Gardens	Harbour View
2003	Hazard United	Hazard United
2004	Tivoli Gardens	Waterhouse
2005	Portmore United	Portmore United
2006	Waterhouse	Tivoli Gardens
2007	Harbour View	Portmore United
2008	Portmore United	Waterhouse
2009	Tivoli Gardens	Boys' Town
2010	Harbour View	Boys' Town
2011	Tivoli Gardens	Tivoli Gardens

JOR – JORDAN

Year	Champions	Cup Winners
1944	Al Faysali	
1945	Al Faysali	
1946	Jordan	
1947	Al Ahli	
1948		
1949	Al Ahli	
1950	Al Ahli	
1951	Al Ahli	
1952	Al Jazeera	
1953		
1954	Al Ahli	
1955	Al Jazeera	
1956	Al Jazeera	
1957		
1958		
1959	Al Faysali	
1960	Al Faysali	
1961	Al Faysali	
1962	Al Faysali	
1963	Al Faysali	

Year		
1964	Al Faysali	
1965	Al Faysali	
1966	Al Faysali	
1967		
1968		
1969		
1970	Al Faysali	
1971	Al Faysali	
1972	Al Faysali	
1973	Al Faysali	
1974	Al Faysali	
1975	Al Ahli	
1976	Al Faysali	
1977	Al Faysali	
1978	Al Ahli	
1979	Al Ahli	
1980	Al Wihdat	Al Faysali
1981	Al Ramtha	Al Faysali
1982	Al Ramtha	Al Wihdat
1983	Al Faysali	Al Faysali
1984	Amman	Al Jazeera
1985	Al Faysali	Al Wihdat
1986	Al Faysali	Al Arabi
1987	Al Deffatain	
1988	Al Faysali	Al Faysali
1989	Al Faysali	Al Deffatain
1990	Al Faysali	Al Faysali
1991		Al Ramtha
1992		Al Ramtha
1992	Al Wihdat	Al Faysali
1993	Al Faysali	Al Faysali
1994	Al Faysali	Al Faysali
1995	Al Wihdat	Al Faysali
1996	Al Wihdat	Al Wihdat
1997	Al Wihdat	Al Wihdat
1997	Al Wihdat	
1998		Al Faysali
1999	Al Faysali	Al Faysali
2000	Al Faysali	Al Wihdat
2001	Al Faysali	Al Faysali
2002		Al Faysali
2003	Al Faysali	Al Faysali
2004	Al Faysali	Al Faysali
2005	Al Wihdat	Al Faysali
2006	Shabab Al Ordon	Shabab Al Ordon
2007	Al Wihdat	Shabab Al Ordon
2008	Al Wihdat	Al Faysali
2009	Al Wihdat	Al Wihdat
2010	Al Faysali	Al Wihdat
2011	Al Wihdat	Al Wihdat

JPN – JAPAN

Year	Cup Winners
1921	Tokyo Shukyu-dan
1922	Nagoya Shukyu-dan
1923	Astra Club
1924	Koijo Club
1925	Koijo Shukyu-dan
1926	
1927	Kobe-Ichi High School
1928	Waseda University
1929	Kwangaku Club
1930	Kwangaku Club
1931	Tokyo University
1932	Keio Club
1933	Tokyo OB
1934	
1935	Seoul Shukyu-dan
1936	Keio University BRB
1937	Keio University BRB
1938	Waseda University
1939	Keio University BRB
1940	Keio University BRB
1941	
1942	
1943	
1944	
1945	
1946	Tokyo University
1947	
1948	
1949	Tokyo University
1950	All Kwangaku
1951	Keio University BRB
1952	All Keio
1953	All Kwangaku
1954	Keio University BRB
1955	All Kwangaku
1956	Keio University BRB
1957	Chuo University
1958	Kwangaku Club
1959	Kwangaku Club
1960	Furukawa Electric
1961	Furukawa Electric
1962	Chuo University
1963	Waseda University
1964	Yahata Steel & Furukawa Electric

JSL

Year		
1965	Toyo Kogyo	Toyo Kogyo
1966	Toyo Kogyo	Waseda University
1967	Toyo Kogyo	Toyo Kogyo
1968	Toyo Kogyo	Yanmar Diesel
1969	Mitsubishi Motors	Toyo Kogyo
1970	Toyo Kogyo	Yanmar Diesel
1971	Yanmar Diesel	Mitsubishi Motors
1972	Hitachi	Hitachi
1973	Mitsubishi Motors	Mitsubishi Motors
1974	Yanmar Diesel	Yanmar Diesel
1975	Yanmar Diesel	Hitachi
1976	East Furukawa	East Furukawa
1977	Fujita Industries	Fujita Industries
1978	Mitsubishi Motors	Mitsubishi Motors
1979	Fujita Industries	Fujita Industries
1980	Yanmar Diesel	Mitsubishi Motors
1981	Fujita Industries	Nippon Kokan
1982	Mitsubishi Motors	Yamaha
1983	Yomiuri	Nissan
1984	Yomiuri	Yomiuri
1985		Nissan
1986	East Furukawa	Yomiuri
1987	Yomiuri	Yomiuri
1988	Yamaha	Nissan
1989	Nissan	Nissan
1990	Nissan	Matsushita
1991	Yomiuri	Nissan
1992	Yomiuri	Yokohama Marinos

J.League

Year		
1993	Verdy Kawasaki	Yokohama Flugels
1994	Verdy Kawasaki	Bellmare Hiratsuka
1995	Yokohama Marinos	Nagoya Grampus
1996	Kashima Antlers	Verdy Kawasaki
1997	Jubilo Iwata	Kashima Antlers
1998	Kashima Antlers	Yokohama Flugels
1999	Jubilo Iwata	Nagoya Grampus
2000	Kashima Antlers	Kashima Antlers
2001	Kashima Antlers	Shimizu S-Pulse
2002	Jubilo Iwata	Kyoto Purple Sanga
2003	Yokohama F.Marinos	Jubilo Iwata
2004	Yokohama F.Marinos	Tokyo Verdy 1969
2005	Gamba Osaka	Urawa Reds
2006	Urawa Reds	Urawa Reds
2007	Kashima Antlers	Kashima Antlers
2008	Kashima Antlers	Gamba Osaka
2009	Kashima Antlers	Gamba Osaka
2010	Nagoya Grampus	Kashima Antlers
2011	Kashiwa Reysol	FC Tokyo

JPN – JAPAN

Year	Lge Cup Winners
1992	Verdy Kawasaki
1993	Verdy Kawasaki
1994	Verdy Kawasaki
1995	
1996	Shimizu S-Pulse
1997	Kashima Antlers
1998	Jubilo Iwata
1999	Kashiwa Reysol
2000	Kashima Antlers
2001	Yokohama F.Marinos
2002	Kashima Antlers
2003	Urawa Reds
2004	FC Tokyo
2005	JEF United
2006	JEF United
2007	Gamba Osaka
2008	Oita Trinita
2009	FC Tokyo
2010	Jubilo Iwata
2011	Kashima Antlers

KAZ – KAZAKHSTAN

Year	Champions	Cup Winners
1992	Kairat Almaty	Kairat Almaty
1993	Ansat Pavlodar	Dostyk Almaty
1994	Yelimay Semey	Vostock Oskemen
1995	Yelimay Semey	Yelimay Semipal'sk
1996	Taraz Zhambul	Kairat Almaty
1997	Irtysh Pavlodar	
1998	Yelimay Semey	Irtysk Pavlodar
1999	Irtysh Pavlodar	Kaysar Kyzl-Orda
2000	Zhenis Astana	Kairat Almaty
2001		Zhenis Astana
2001	Zhenis Astana	Kairat Almaty
2002	Irtysh Pavlodar	Zhenis Astana
2003	Irtysh Pavlodar	Kairat Almaty
2004	Kairat Almaty	FC Taraz
2005	Aktobe Lento	Zhenis Astana
2006	FK Astana	FK Almaty
2007	FK Aktobe	Tobol Kostanay
2008	FK Aktobe	FK Aktobe
2009	FK Aktobe	FK Atyrau
2010	Tobol Kostanay	Lokomotiv Astana
2011	Shakhter Karagandy	Ordabasy Shymkent

KEN – KENYA

Year	Champions	Cup Winners
1963	Nakuru All Stars	
1964	Luo Union	Luo Union
1965	Feisal	Luo Union
1966	Abaluhya United	Luo Union
1967	Abaluhya United	Abaluhya United
1968	Gor Mahia	Abaluhya United
1969	Nakuru All Stars	
1970	Abaluhya United	
1971		
1972	Kenya Breweries	
1973	Abaluhya United	
1974	Gor Mahia	
1975	Luo Union	Kenya Breweries
1976	Gor Mahia	Gor Mahia
1977	Kenya Breweries	
1978	Kenya Breweries	
1979	Gor Mahia	
1980	Leopards	
1981	Leopards	Gor Mahia
1982	Leopards	
1983	Gor Mahia	Gor Mahia
1984	Gor Mahia	Leopards
1985	Gor Mahia	Leopards
1986	Leopards	Gor Mahia
1987	Gor Mahia	Gor Mahia
1988	Leopards	Gor Mahia
1989	Leopards	Kenya Breweries
1990	Gor Mahia	Rivatex
1991	Gor Mahia	Leopards
1992	Leopards	Gor Mahia
1993	Gor Mahia	Kenya Breweries
1994	Kenya Breweries	Leopards
1995	Gor Mahia	Rivatex
1996	Kenya Breweries	Mumias Sugar
1997	Utalii	Eldoret KCC
1998	AFC Leopards	Mathare United
1999	Tusker	Mumias Sugar
2000	Tusker	Mathare United
2001	Oserian Fastac	Leopards
2002	Oserian Fastac	Pipeline
2003	Ulinzi Stars	Utalii & Chemelil
2004	Ulinzi Stars	KCB
2005	Ulinzi Stars	World Hope
2006	Sony Sugar	
2007	Tusker	Sofapaka
2008	Mathare United	Gor Mahia
2009	Sofapaka	Leopards
2010	Ulinzi Stars	Sofapaka
2011	Tusker	Gor Mahia

KGZ – KYRGYZSTAN

Year	Champions	Cup Winners
1992	Alga Bishkek	Alga Bishkek
1993	Alga-RIFF Bishkek	Alga-RIFF Bishkek
1994	Kant-Oil Kant	Ak-Maral Tokmak
1995	Kant-Oil Kant	Semetey Kyzyl-Kiya
1996	Metallurg Kadamjay	AiK Bishkek
1997	Dinamo Bishkek	Alga-PVO Bishkek
1998	Dinamo Bishkek	SKA-PVO Bishkek
1999	Dinamo Bishkek	SKA-PVO Bishkek
2000	SKA-PVO Bishkek	SKA-PVO Bishkek
2001	SKA-PVO Bishkek	SKA-PVO Bishkek
2002	SKA-PVO Bishkek	SKA-PVO Bishkek
2003	Zhashtyk Kara-Su	SKA-PVO Bishkek
2004	Dordoi-Dynamo	Dordoi-Dynamo
2005	Dordoi-Dynamo	Dordoi-Dynamo
2006	Dordoi-Dynamo	Dordoi-Dynamo
2007	Dordoi-Dynamo	Abdish-Ata Kant
2008	Dordoi-Dynamo	Dordoi-Dynamo
2009	Dordoi-Dynamo	Abdish-Ata Kant
2010	Neftchi Kochkorata	Dordoi-Dynamo
2011	Dordoi-Dynamo	Abdish-Ata Kant

KSA – SAUDI ARABIA

Year	Champions	Cup Winners
1957		Al Wahda
1958		Al Ittihad
1959		Al Ittihad
1960		Al Ittihad
1961		Al Hilal
1962		Al Ahli
1963		Al Ittihad
1964		Al Hilal
1965		Al Ahli
1966		Al Wahda
1967		Al Ittihad
1968		Al Ittifaq
1969		Al Ahli
1970		Al Ahli
1971		Al Ahli
1972		Al Ahli
1973		Al Nasr
1974		Al Nasr
1975		
1976	Al Nasr	Al Nasr
1977	Al Hilal	Al Ahli
1978	Al Ahli	Al Ahli
1979	Al Hilal	Al Ahli
1980	Al Nasr	Al Hilal
1981	Al Nasr	Al Nasr
1982	Al Ittihad	Al Hilal
1983	Al Ittifaq	Al Ahli
1984	Al Ahli	Al Hilal
1985	Al Hilal	Al Ittifaq
1986	Al Hilal	Al Nasr
1987	Al Ittifaq	Al Nasr
1988	Al Hilal	Al Ittihad
1989	Al Nasr	Al Hilal
1990	Al Hilal	Al Nasr
1991	Al Shabab	Al Ittihad
1992	Al Shabab	Al Qadisiya
1993	Al Shabab	Al Shabab
1994	Al Nasr	Al Riyadh
1995	Al Nasr	Al Hilal
1996	Al Hilal	Al Shabab
1997	Al Ittihad	Al Ittihad
1998	Al Hilal	Al Ahli
1999	Al Ittihad	Al Shabab
2000	Al Ittihad	Al Ittihad
2001	Al Ittihad	Al Ittihad
2002	Al Hilal	Al Ahli
2003	Al Ittihad	Al Hilal
2004	Al Shabab	Al Ittihad
2005	Al Hilal	Al Hilal
2006	Al Shabab	Al Hilal
2007	Al Ittihad	Al Ahli
2008	Al Hilal	Al Hilal
2009	Al Ittihad	Al Hilal
2010	Al Hilal	Al Hilal
2011	Al Hilal	Al Hilal

KSA – SAUDI ARABIA

Year	Champions Cup
2008	Al Shabab
2009	Al Shabab
2010	Al Ittihad
2011	Al Ahli

KUW – KUWAIT

Year	Champions	Emir Winners
1962	Al Arabi	Al Arabi
1963	Al Arabi	Al Arabi
1964	Al Arabi	Al Arabi
1965	Al Kuwait	Al Qadisiya
1966	Al Arabi	Al Arabi
1967	Al Arabi	Al Qadisiya
1968	Al Kuwait	Al Qadisiya
1969	Al Qadisiya	Al Arabi
1970	Al Arabi	Al Yarmouk
1971	Al Qadisiya	Al Arabi
1972	Al Kuwait	Al Qadisiya
1973	Al Qadisiya	Al Yarmouk
1974	Al Kuwait	Al Qadisiya
1975	Al Qadisiya	Al Qadisiya
1976	Al Qadisiya	Al Kuwait
1977	Al Kuwait	Al Kuwait
1978	Al Qadisiya	Al Kuwait
1979	Al Kuwait	Al Qadisiya
1980	Al Arabi	Al Kuwait
1981	Salmiya	Al Arabi
1982	Al Arabi	Kazma
1983	Al Arabi	Al Arabi
1984	Al Arabi	Kazma
1985	Al Arabi	Al Kuwait
1986	Kazma	Al Fhayheel
1987	Kazma	Al Kuwait
1988	Al Arabi	Al Kuwait
1989	Al Arabi	Al Qadisiya
1990	Al Jahra	Kazma
1991		
1992	Al Qadisiya	Al Arabi
1993	Al Arabi	Salmiya
1994	Kazma	Al Qadisiya
1995	Salmiya	Kazma
1996	Kazma	Al Arabi
1997	Al Arabi	Kazma
1998	Salmiya	Kazma
1999	Al Qadisiya	Al Arabi
2000	Salmiya	Al Arabi
2001	Al Kuwait	Salmiya
2002	Al Arabi	Al Kuwait
2003	Al Qadisiya	Al Qadisiya
2004	Al Qadisiya	Al Qadisiya
2005	Al Qadisiya	Al Arabi
2006	Al Kuwait	Al Arabi
2007	Al Kuwait	Al Qadisiya
2008	Al Kuwait	Al Arabi
2009	Al Qadisiya	Al Kuwait
2010	Al Qadisiya	Al Qadisiya
2011	Al Qadisiya	Kazma

KUW – KUWAIT

Year	Crown Prince	Federation Cup
1994	Al Kuwait	
1995	Kazma	
1996	Al Arabi	
1997	Al Arabi	
1998	Al Qadisiya	
1999	Al Arabi	
2000	Al Arabi	
2001	Salmiya	
2002	Al Qadisiya	
2003	Al Kuwait	
2004	Al Qadisiya	
2005	Al Qadisiya	
2006	Al Qadisiya	
2007	Al Arabi	
2008	Al Kuwait	Al Qadisiya
2009	Al Qadisiya	Al Qadisiya
2010	Al Kuwait	Al Kuwait
2011	Al Kuwait	Al Qadisiya

LAO – LAOS

Year	Champions	Cup Winners
1990	Lao Army	
1991	Lao Army	
1992	Lao Army	
1993	Savannakhet & Lao Army	
1994	Lao Army	
1995	Pakse & Education Team	
1996	Lao Army	
1997	Sayaboury & Lao Army	
1998	Khammouan	
1999		
2000	Vientiane Municipality	
2001	Banks	
2002	Telecom and Transport	
2003	Telecom and Transport	MCTPC
2004	Telecom and Transport	Vientiane FC
2005	Vientiane FC	
2006	Vientiane FC	Lao American College
2007	Lao-American College	MPWT
2008	Lao Army	
2009		
2010	Banks	Banks
2011	Public Works and Transport	Banks

LBR – LIBERIA

Year	Champions	Cup Winners
1963	Invincible Eleven	
1964	Invincible Eleven	
1965	Invincible Eleven	
1966	Invincible Eleven	
1967	Mighty Barolle	
1968		
1969		
1970		
1971		
1972	Mighty Barolle	
1973	Mighty Barolle	
1974	Mighty Barolle	Mighty Barolle
1975		
1976	St Joseph Warriors	Cedar United
1977		Cedar United
1978	St Joseph Warriors	Mighty Barolle
1979	St Joseph Warriors	
1980	Invincible Eleven	
1981	Invincible Eleven	Mighty Barolle
1982		St Joseph Warriors
1983	Invincible Eleven	Mighty Barolle
1984	Invincible Eleven	Mighty Barolle
1985	Invincible Eleven	Mighty Barolle
1986	Mighty Barolle	Mighty Barolle
1987	Invincible Eleven	Invincible Eleven
1988	Mighty Barolle	LPRC Oilers
1989	Mighty Barolle	LPRC Oilers
1990		
1991	LPRC Oilers	Invincible Eleven
1992	LPRC Oilers	NPA Anchors
1993	Mighty Barolle	LPRC Oilers
1994	NPA Anchors	NPA Anchors
1995	Mighty Barolle	Mighty Barolle
1996	Junior Professionals	Junior Professionals
1997	LPRC Oilers	Invincible Eleven
1998	Invincible Eleven	Invincible Eleven
1999	Invincible Eleven	LPRC Oilers
2000		LPRC Oilers
2001	Mighty Barolle	
2002	LPRC Oilers	Mighty Blue Angles
2003		
2004	Mighty Barolle	LISCR FC
2005	LPRC Oilers	LPRC Oilers
2006	Mighty Barolle	NPA Anchors
2007	Invincible Eleven	St Joseph Warriors
2008	Black Star	Black Star
2009	Mighty Barolle	Young Controllers
2010		
2011	LISCR FC	Invincible Eleven

LBY – LIBYA

Year	Champions	Cup Winners
1964	Al Ahly Tripoli	
1965	Al Ittihad Tripoli	
1966	Al Ittihad Tripoli	
1967	Al Tahaddi Benghazi	
1968		
1969	Al Ittihad Tripoli	
1970	Al Ahly Benghazi	
1971	Al Ahly Tripoli	
1972	Al Ahly Benghazi	
1973	Al Ahly Tripoli	
1974	Al Ahly Tripoli	
1975	Al Ahly Benghazi	
1976	Al Medina Tripoli	
1977	Al Tahaddi Benghazi	
1978	Al Ahly Tripoli	
1979		
1980		
1981		
1982		
1983	Al Medina Tripoli	
1984	Al Ahly Tripoli	
1985	Al Dahra Tripoli	
1986	Al Ittihad Tripoli	
1987	Al Nasr Benghazi	
1988	Al Ittihad Tripoli	
1989	Al Ittihad Tripoli	
1990	Al Ittihad Tripoli	
1991	Al Ittihad Tripoli	
1992	Al Ahly Benghazi	
1993	Al Ahly Tripoli	
1994	Al Ahly Tripoli	
1995	Al Ahly Tripoli	
1996	Al Shaat Tripoli	
1997	Al Tahaddi Benghazi	Al Nasr Benghazi
1998	Al Mahalah Tripoli	Al Shaat Tripoli
1999	Al Mahalah Tripoli	Al Ittihad Ytipoli
2000	Al Ahly Tripoli	Al Ahly Tripoli
2001	Al Madina Tripoli	
2002	Al Ittihad Tripoli	
2003	Al Ittihad Tripoli	
2004	Olympique Az-Zwiyah	Al Ittihad Tripoli
2005	Al Ittihad Tripoli	Al Ittihad Tripoli
2006	Al Ittihad Tripoli	Al Ahly Tripoli
2007	Al Ittihad Tripoli	Al Ittihad Tripoli
2008	Al Ittihad Tripoli	Khaleej Sart
2009	Al Ittihad Tripoli	Al Ittihad Tripoli
2010	Al Ittihad Tripoli	Al Nasr
2011	Al Ittihad Tripoli	

LES – LESOTHO

Year	Champions	Cup Winners
1970	Maseru United	
1971	Majantja	
1972	Police	
1973	Linare	
1974	Matlama	
1975	Maseru FC	
1976	Maseru United	Matlama
1977	Matlama	
1978	Matlama	Maseru United
1979	Linare	Matlama
1980	Linare	Matlama
1981	Maseru Brothers	Maseru Rovers
1982	Matlama	Maseru Rovers
1983	LPF Maseru	Linare
1984	LPF Maseru	Lioli
1985	Lioli	LPF Maseru
1986	Matlama	LDF Maseru
1987	LDF Maseru	Matlama
1988	Matlama	LDF Maseru
1989	Arsenal	Arsenal
1990	LDF Maseru	LDF Maseru
1991	Arsenal	Arsenal
1992	Matlama	Matlama
1993	Arsenal	Bantu
1994	LDF Maseru	Matlama
1995	Majantja	Maseru Rovers
1996	Roma Rovers	Lerotholi Poly
1997	LDF Maseru	Bantu
1998	LDF Maseru	Arsenal
1999	LDF Maseru	Linare
2000	Prisons	LDF Maseru
2001	LDF Maseru	
2002	Prisons	
2003	Matlama	
2004	LDF Maseru	
2005	Likhopo	
2006	Likhopo	
2007	LCS Maseru	

Year		
2008	LCS Maseru	LCS Maseru
2009	Lioli	Matlama
2010	Matlama	
2011	LCS Maseru	

LIB - LEBANON

Year	Champions	Cup Winners
1934	Al Nahda	
1935	American University	
1936	Sika	
1937	American University	
1938	American University	Al Nahda
1939	Sika	Helmi Sport
1940		Helmi Sport
1941	Sika	Al Nahda
1942	Al Nahda	
1943	Al Nahda	Homenetmen
1944	Homenetmen	
1945	Homenmen	Al Nahda
1946	Homenetmen	
1947	Al Nahda	Al Nahda
1948	Homenetmen	Homenetmen
1949	Al Nahda	
1950		
1951	Homenetmen	Shabiba Al Mazra
1952		Shabiba Al Mazra
1953		
1954	Homenmen	
1955	Homenetmen	
1956	Racing Club	
1957	Homenmen	
1958		
1959		
1960		
1961	Homenmen	
1962		Homenetmen
1963	Homenetmen	
1964		Safa
1965	Racing Club	
1966		
1967	Shabiba Al Mazra	
1968		
1969	Homenetmen	
1970	Racing Club	
1971		Nijmeh
1972		
1973	Al Nijmeh *	
1974		
1975	Al Nijmeh *	
1986		Safa
1987	Salam Zgharta	Salam Zgharta
1988	Al Ansar	Al Ansar
1989	Al Ansar	Nijmeh
1990	Al Ansar	Al Ansar
1991	Al Ansar	Al Ansar
1992	Al Ansar	Al Ansar
1993	Al Ansar	Al Bourj
1994	Al Ansar	Al Ansar
1995	Al Ansar	Al Ansar
1996	Al Ansar	Al Ansar
1997	Al Ansar	Nijmeh
1998	Al Ansar	Nijmeh
1999	Al Ansar	Al Ansar
2000	Al Nijmeh	Shabab Al Sahel
2001		Al Tadamon Sur
2002	Al Nijmeh	Al Ansar
2003	Olympic Beirut	Olympic Beirut
2004	Al Nijmeh	Al Ahed
2005	Al Nijmeh	Al Ahed
2006	Al Ansar	Al Ansar
2007	Al Ansar	Al Ansar
2008	Al Ahed	Al Mabarra
2009	Al Nijmeh	Al Ahed
2010	Al Ahed	Al Ansar
2011	Al Ahed	Al Ahed

LIE - LIECHTENSTEIN

Year	Cup Winners
1946	FC Triesen
1947	FC Triesen
1948	FC Triesen
1949	FC Vaduz
1950	FC Triesen
1951	FC Triesen
1952	FC Vaduz
1953	FC Vaduz
1954	FC Vaduz
1955	FC Schaan
1956	FC Vaduz
1957	FC Vaduz
1958	FC Vaduz
1959	FC Vaduz
1960	FC Vaduz
1961	FC Vaduz
1962	FC Vaduz
1963	FC Schaan
1964	FC Balzers
1965	FC Triesen
1966	FC Vaduz
1967	FC Vaduz
1968	FC Vaduz
1969	FC Vaduz
1970	FC Vaduz
1971	FC Vaduz
1972	FC Triesen
1973	FC Balzers
1974	FC Vaduz
1975	FC Triesen
1976	USV Eschen/Mauren
1977	USV Eschen/Mauren
1978	USV Eschen/Mauren
1979	FC Balzers
1980	FC Vaduz
1981	FC Balzers
1982	FC Balzers
1983	FC Balzers
1984	FC Balzers
1985	FC Vaduz
1986	FC Vaduz
1987	USV Eschen/Mauren
1988	FC Vaduz
1989	FC Balzers
1990	FC Vaduz
1991	FC Balzers
1992	FC Vaduz
1993	FC Balzers
1994	FC Schaan
1995	FC Vaduz
1996	FC Vaduz
1997	FC Balzers
1998	FC Vaduz
1999	FC Vaduz
2000	FC Vaduz
2001	FC Vaduz
2002	FC Vaduz
2003	FC Vaduz
2004	FC Vaduz
2005	FC Vaduz
2006	FC Vaduz
2007	FC Vaduz
2008	FC Vaduz
2009	FC Vaduz
2010	FC Vaduz
2011	FC Vaduz

LTU - LITHUANIA

Year	Champions	Cup Winners
1990	Sirijus Klaipeda	Sirijus Klaipeda
1991	Zalgiris Vilnius	Zalgiris Vilnius
1992	Zalgiris Vilnius	Makabi Vilnius
1993	Ekranas Panevezys	Zalgiris Vilnius
1994	ROMAR Mazeikiai	Zalgiris Vilnius
1995	Inkaras Kaunas	Inkaras Kaunas
1996	Inkaras Kaunas	Kareda Siauliai
1997	Kareda Siauliai	Zalgiris Vilnius
1998	Kareda Siauliai	Ekranas Panevezys
1999	Zalgiris Vilnius	Kareda Siauliai
1999	FBK Kaunas	
2000	FBK Kaunas	Ekranas Panevezys
2001	FBK Kaunas	Atlantas Klaipeda
2002	FBK Kaunas	FBK Kaunas
2003		Atlantas Klaipeda
2003	FBK Kaunas	Zalgiris Vilnius
2004	FBK Kaunas	FBK Kaunas
2005	Ekranas Panevezys	FBK Kaunas
2006	FBK Kaunas	Suduva Marijampole
2007	FBK Kaunas	
2008	Ekranas Panevezys	FBK Kaunas
2009	Ekranas Panevezys	Suduva Marijampole
2010	Ekranas Panevezys	Ekranas Panevezys
2011	Ekranas Panevezys	Ekranas Panevezys

LUX - LUXEMBOURG

Year	Champions	Cup Winners
1910	Racing Club	
1911	Sporting Club	
1912	US Hollerich	
1913	-	
1914	US Hollerich	
1915	US Hollerich	
1916	US Hollerich	
1917	US Hollerich	
1918	Fola Esch	
1919	Sporting Club	
1920	Fola Esch	
1921	Jeunesse Esch	
1922	Fola Esch	Racing Club
1923	Red Boys	Fola Esch

Year	Champions	Cup Winners
1924	Fola Esch	Fola Esch
1925	AC Spora	Red Boys
1926	Red Boys	Red Boys
1927	Union Luxembourg	Red Boys
1928	AC Spora	AC Spora
1929	AC Spora	Red Boys
1930	Fola Esch	Red Boys
1931	Red Boys	Red Boys
1932	Red Boys	AC Spora
1933	Red Boys	Progres Niedercorn
1934	AC Spora	Red Boys
1935	AC Spora	Jeunesse Esch
1936	AC Spora	Red Boys
1937	Jeunesse Esch	Jeunesse Esch
1938	AC Spora	Stade Dudelange
1939	Stade Dudelange	US Dudelange
1940	Stade Dudelange	AC Spora
1941		
1942		
1943		
1944		
1945	Stade Dudelange	Progres Niedercorn
1946	Stade Dudelange	Jeunesse Esch
1947	Stade Dudelange	Union Luxembourg
1948	Stade Dudelange	Stade Dudelange
1949	AC Spora	Stade Dudelange
1950	Stade Dudelange	AC Spora
1951	Jeunesse Esch	SC Tetange
1952	National Schifflange	Red Boys
1953	Progres Niedercorn	Red Boys
1954	Jeunesse Esch	Jeunesse Esch
1955	Stade Dudelange	Fola Esch
1956	AC Spora	Stade Dudelange
1957	Stade Dudelange	AC Spora
1958	Jeunesse Esch	Red Boys
1959	Jeunesse Esch	Union Luxembourg
1960	Jeunesse Esch	National Schifflange
1961	AC Spora	Alliance Dudelange
1962	Union Luxembourg	Alliance Dudelange
1963	Jeunesse Esch	Union Luxembourg
1964	Aris Bonnevoie	Union Luxembourg
1965	Stade Dudelange	AC Spora
1966	Aris Bonnevoie	AC Spora
1967	Jeunesse Esch	Aris Bonnevoie
1968	Jeunesse Esch	US Rumelange
1969	Avenir Beggen	Union Luxembourg
1970	Jeunesse Esch	Union Luxembourg
1971	Union Luxembourg	Jeunesse Hautcharage
1972	Aris Bonnevoie	Red Boys
1973	Jeunesse Esch	Jeunesse Esch
1974	Jeunesse Esch	Jeunesse Esch
1975	Jeunesse Esch	US Rumelange
1976	Jeunesse Esch	Jeunesse Esch
1977	Jeunesse Esch	Progres Niedercorn
1978	Progres Niedercorn	Progres Niedercorn
1979	Red Boys	Red Boys
1980	Jeunesse Esch	AC Spora
1981	Progres Niedercorn	Jeunesse Esch
1982	Avenir Beggen	Red Boys
1983	Jeunesse Esch	Avenir Beggen
1984	Avenir Beggen	Avenir Beggen
1985	Jeunesse Esch	Red Boys
1986	Avenir Beggen	Union Luxembourg
1987	Jeunesse Esch	Avenir Beggen
1988	Jeunesse Esch	Jeunesse Esch
1989	AC Spora	Union Luxembourg
1990	Union Luxembourg	Swift Hesperange
1991	Union Luxembourg	Union Luxembourg
1992	Union Luxembourg	Avenir Beggen
1993	Avenir Beggen	Avenir Beggen
1994	Avenir Beggen	Avenir Beggen
1995	Jeunesse d'Esch	CS Grevenmacher
1996	Jeunesse d'Esch	Union Luxembourg
1997	Jeunesse d'Esch	Jeunesse d'Esch
1998	Jeunesse d'Esch	CS Grevenmacher
1999	Jeunesse d'Esch	Jeunesse d'Esch
2000	F'91 Dudelange	Jeunesse d'Esch
2001	F'91 Dudelange	Etzella Ettelbruck
2002	F'91 Dudelange	Avenir Beggen
2003	CS Grevenmacher	CS Grevenmacher
2004	Jeunesse d'Esch	F'91 Dudelange
2005	F'91 Dudelange	CS Petange
2006	F'91 Dudelange	F'91 Dudelange
2007	F'91 Dudelange	F'91 Dudelange
2008	F'91 Dudelange	CS Grevenmacher
2009	F'91 Dudelange	F'91 Dudelange
2010	Jeunesse d'Esch	FC Differdange 03
2011	F'91 Dudelange	FC Differdange 03

LVA – LATVIA

Year	Champions	Cup Winners
1991	Skonto Riga	Celtnieks
1992	Skonto Riga	Skonto Riga
1993	Skonto Riga	RAF Jelgava
1994	Skonto Riga	Olimpija Riga
1995	Skonto Riga	Skonto Riga
1996	Skonto Riga	RAF Jelgava
1997	Skonto Riga	Skonto Riga
1998	Skonto Riga	Skonto Riga
1999	Skonto Riga	FK Riga
2000	Skonto Riga	Skonto Riga
2001	Skonto Riga	Skonto Riga
2002	Skonto Riga	Skonto Riga
2003	Skonto Riga	FK Ventspils
2004	Skonto Riga	FK Ventspils
2005	Liepajas Metalurgs	FK Ventspils
2006	FK Ventspils	Liepajas Metalurgs
2007	FK Ventspils	FK Ventspils
2008	FK Ventspils	Daugava D'gavpils
2009	Liepajas Metalurgs	
2010	Skonto Riga	FK Jelgava
2011	FK Ventspils	FK Ventspils

MAC – MACAU

Year	Champions
1973	Polícia
1984	Wa Seng
1985	
1986	Hap Kuan
1987	Hap Kuan
1988	Wa Seng
1989	Hap Kuan
1990	
1991	Sporting CM
1992	Lam Pak
1993	Leng Ngan
1994	Lam Pak
1995	Artilheiros
1996	Artilheiros
1997	Lam Pak
1998	Lam Pak
1999	Lam Pak
2000	Polícia
2001	Lam Pak
2002	Monte Carlo
2003	Monte Carlo
2004	Monte Carlo
2005	Polícia
2006	Lam Pak
2007	Lam Pak
2008	Monte Carlo
2009	Lam Pak
2010	Windsor Arch
2011	Windsor Arch

MAD – MADAGASCAR

Year	Champions	Cup Winners
1956	Ambatondrazaka	
1962	AS Fortior	
1963	AS Fortior	
1968	Fitarikandro	
1969	US Fonctionnaires	
1970	MMM Toamasina	
1971	AS St. Michel	
1972	Fortior Mahajanga	
1973	JS Antalaha	
1974	Corps Enseignement	Fortior Mahajanga
1975	Corps Enseignement	Fortior Mahajanga
1976		Fortior Mahajanga
1977	Corps Enseignement	Fortior Mahajanga
1978	AS St. Michel	AS Sotema
1979	Fortior Mahajanga	AS Sotema
1980	MMM Toamasina	AS St. Michel
1981	AS Somasud	Dinamo Fima
1982	Dinamo Fima	AS Sotema
1983	Dinamo Fima	Dinamo Fima
1984		
1985	AS Sotema	Fortior Mahajanga
1986	BTM Antananarivo	HTMF Mahajanga
1987	JOS Nosy-Bé	BTM Antananarivo
1988	COSFAP	BFV Mahajanga
1989	AS Sotema	BTM Antananarivo
1990	ASF Fianarantsoa	BFV Mahajanga
1991	AS Sotema	BTM Antananarivo
1992	AS Sotema	COSFAP
1993	BTM Antananarivo	AS Cimelta
1994	FC Rainizafy	
1995	FC Fobar	
1996	BFV Mahajanga	Club S Namakia
1997	DSA Antananarivo	
1998	DSA Antananarivo	FC Djivan
1999	AS Fortior	FC Djivan
2000	AS Fortior	FC Djivan
2001	SOE Antananarivo	US Transfoot
2002	AS Adema	AS Fortior
2003	Ecoredipharm	Léopards
2004	USJF/Ravinala	USJF/Ravinala
2005	USCA Foot	USCA Foot

Year	Champions	Cup Winners
2006	AS Adema	Ajesaia
2007	Ajesaia	AS Adema
2008	Académie Ny Antsika	AS Adema
2009	Ajesaia	AS Adema
2010	CNaPS Sport	AS Adema
2011	Japan Actuel's	CNaPS

MAR – MOROCCO

Year	Champions	Cup Winners
1957	Wydad Casablanca	Mouloudia Oujda
1958	Kawkab Marrakech	Mouloudia Oujda
1959	Etoile Casablanca	FAR Rabat
1960	KAC Kénitra	Mouloudia Oujda
1961	FAR Rabat	KAC Kénitra
1962	FAR Rabat	Mouloudia Oujda
1963	FAR Rabat	Kawkab Marrakech
1964	FAR Rabat	Kawkab Marrakech
1965	Maghreb Fès	Kawkab Marrakech
1966	Wydad Casablanca	COD Meknès
1967	FAR Rabat	FUS Rabat
1968	FAR Rabat	Racing Casablanca
1969	Wydad Casablanca	Renaissance Settat
1970	FAR Rabat	Wydad Casablanca
1971	Renaissance Settat	FAR Rabat
1972	Douane Casablanca	
1973	KAC Kénitra	FUS Rabat
1974	Raja Béni Mellal	Raja Casablanca
1975	Mouloudia Oujda	Chabab Mohammedia
1976	Wydad Casablanca	FUS Rabat
1977	Wydad Casablanca	Raja Casablanca
1978	Wydad Casablanca	Wydad Casablanca
1979	Maghreb Fès	Wydad Casablanca
1980	Chabab Mohammedia	Maghreb Fès
1981	KAC Kénitra	Wydad Casablanca
1982	KAC Kénitra	Raja Casablanca
1983	Maghreb Fès	CLAS Casablanca
1984	FAR Rabat	FAR Rabat
1985	Maghreb Fès	FAR Rabat
1986	Wydad Casablanca	FAR Rabat
1987	FAR Rabat	Kawkab Marrakech
1988	Raja Casablanca	Maghreb Fès
1989	FAR Rabat	Wydad Casablanca
1990	Wydad Casablanca	Olympic Casablanca
1991	Wydad Casablanca	Kawkab Marrakech
1992	Kawkab Marrakech	Olympic Casablanca
1993	Wydad Casablanca	Kawkab Marrakech
1994	Olympic Casablanca	Wydad Casablanca
1995	COD Meknès	FUS Rabat
1996	Raja Casablanca	Raja Casablanca
1997	Raja Casablanca	Wydad Casablanca
1998	Raja Casablanca	Wydad Casablanca
1999	Raja Casablanca	FAR Rabat
2000	Raja Casablanca	Majd Casablanca
2001	Raja Casablanca	Wydad Casablanca
2002	Hassania Agadir	Raja Casablanca
2003	Hassania Agadir	FAR Rabat
2004	Raja Casablanca	FAR Rabat
2005	FAR Rabat	Raja Casablanca
2006	Wydad Casablanca	Olympic Khouribga
2007	Olympic Khouribga	FAR Rabat
2008	FAR Rabat	FAR Rabat
2009	Raja Casablanca	FAR Rabat
2010	Wydad Casablanca	FUS Rabat
2011	Raja Casablanca	Maghreb Fès

MAS – MALAYSIA

Year	Champions	Cup Winners
1982	Penang	
1983	Melaka	
1984	Selangor	
1985	Singapore	
1986	Kuala Lumpur	
1987	Pahang	
1988	Kuala Lumpur	
1989	Selangor	
1990	Selangor	Perak
1991	Johor	Selangor
1992	Pahang	Sarawak
1993	Kedah	Kuala Lumpur
1994	Singapore	Kuala Lumpur
1995	Pahang	Sabah
1996	Sabah	Kedah
1997	Sarawak	Selangor
1998	Penang	Johor
1999	Pahang	Kuala Lumpur
2000	Selangor	Terengganu
2001	Penang	Selangor
2002	Perak	Penang
2003	Perak	Negeri Sembilan
2004	Pahang	Perak
2005	Perlis	Selangor
2006	Negeri Sembilan	Pahang
2007	Kedah	Kedah
2008	Kedah	Kedah
2009	Selangor	Selangor
2010	Selangor	Negeri Sembilan
2011	Kelantan	Terengganu

MAS – MALAYSIA

Year	Malaysia Cup Winners
1921	Singapore
1922	Selangor
1923	Singapore
1924	Singapore
1925	Singapore
1926	Perak
1927	Selangor
1928	Singapore
1929	Singapore
1930	Singapore
1931	Perak
1932	Singapore
1933	Singapore
1934	Singapore
1935	Selangor
1936	Selangor
1937	Singapore
1938	Selangor
1939	Singapore
1940	Singapore
1941	Singapore
1948	Negeri Sembilan
1949	Selangor
1950	Singapore
1951	Singapore
1952	Singapore
1953	Penang
1954	Penang
1955	Singapore
1956	Selangor
1957	Perak
1958	Penang
1959	Selangor
1960	Singapore
1961	Selangor
1962	Selangor
1963	Selangor
1964	Singapore
1965	Singapore
1966	Selangor
1967	Perak
1968	Selangor
1969	Selangor
1970	Perak
1971	Selangor
1972	Selangor
1973	Selangor
1974	Penang
1975	Selangor
1976	Selangor
1977	Singapore
1978	Selangor
1979	Selangor
1980	Singapore
1981	Selangor
1982	Selangor
1983	Pahang
1984	Selangor
1985	Johor
1986	Selangor
1987	Kuala Lumpur
1988	Kuala Lumpur
1989	Kuala Lumpur
1990	Kedah
1991	Johor
1992	Pahang
1993	Kedah
1994	Singapore
1995	Selangor
1996	Selangor
1997	Selangor
1998	Perak
1999	Brunei
2000	Perak
2001	Terengganu
2002	Selangor
2003	Selangor MPPJ
2004	Perlis
2005	Selangor
2006	Perlis
2007	Kedah
2008	Kedah
2009	Negeri Sembilan
2010	Kelantan
2011	Negeri Sembilan

MDA – MOLDOVA

Year	Champions	Cup Winners
1992	Zimbru Chisinau	Bugeac Comrat
1993	Zimbru Chisinau	Tiligul Tiraspol
1994	Zimbru Chisinau	Tiligul Tiraspol
1995	Zimbru Chisinau	Tiligul Tiraspol
1996	Zimbru Chisinau	Constructorul

Year	Champions	Cup Winners
1997	Constructorul	Zimbru Chisinau
1998	Zimbru Chisinau	Zimbru Chisinau
1999	Zimbru Chisinau	Sheriff Tiraspol
2000	Zimbru Chisinau	Constructorul
2001	Sheriff Tiraspol	Sheriff Tiraspol
2002	Sheriff Tiraspol	Sheriff Tiraspol
2003	Sheriff Tiraspol	Zimbru Chisinau
2004	Sheriff Tiraspol	Zimbru Chisinau
2005	Sheriff Tiraspol	Nistru Otaci
2006	Sheriff Tiraspol	Sheriff Tiraspol
2007	Sheriff Tiraspol	Zimbru Chisinau
2008	Sheriff Tiraspol	Sheriff Tiraspol
2009	Sheriff Tiraspol	Sheriff Tiraspol
2010	Sheriff Tiraspol	Sheriff Tiraspol
2011	Dacia Chisinau	Iskra-Stal Rîbnita

MDV – MALDIVES

Year	Champions	Cup Winners
1985	Victory	
1986	Victory	
1987	New Radiant	
1988	Victory	Valencia
1989	Club Lagoons	New Radiant
1990	New Radiant	Club Lagoons
1991	New Radiant	New Radiant
1992	Victory	Club Lagoons
1993	Valencia	Victory
1994	Valencia	New Radiant
1995	New Radiant	Valencia
1996	Club Lagoons	New Radiant
1997	New Radiant	New Radiant
1998	Valencia	New Radiant
1999	Valencia	Valencia
2000	Victory	Victory
2001	Victory	New Radiant
2002	Victory	IFC
2003	Victory	IFC
2004	New Radiant	Valencia
2005	Victory	New Radiant
2006	Victory	New Radiant
2007	New Radiant	New Radiant
2008	Valencia	VB Sports (IFC)
2009	Victory	Victory
2010	Victory	Victory
2011	Victory	VB Sports

MDV – MALDIVES

Year	Dhivehi League	Cup Winners Cup
1996		Valencia
1997		Valencia
1998		Valencia
1999		New Radiant
2000	Victory	New Radiant
2001	Valencia	Victory
2002	Valencia	Victory
2003	Valencia	New Radiant
2004	Valencia	Valencia
2005	Hurriyya	Valencia
2006	New Radiant	Victory
2007	Victory	Valencia
2008	Valencia	New Radiant
2009	VB Sports	
2010	VB Sports	
2011	VB Sports	

MEX – MEXICO

Year	Champions	Cup Winners
1903	Orizaba	
1904	Mexico Cricket Club	
1905	Pachuca	
1906	Reforma	
1907	Reforma	
1908	British Club	Pachuca
1909	Reforma	Reforma
1910	Reforma	Reforma
1911	Reforma	British Club
1912	Reforma	Pachuca
1913	Club Mexico	
1914	España	Club Mexico
1915	España	España Club
1916	España	Rovers
1917	España	España Club
1918	Pachuca	España Club
1919	España	España Club
1920	España	
1921	España	Club Mexico
1922	España	Asturias
1923	Asturias	Asturias
1924	España	Asturias
1925	América	Necaxa
1926	América	Necaxa
1927	América	
1928	América	
1929	Marte	
1930	España	
1931		
1932	Atlante	
1933	Necaxa	Necaxa
1934	España	Asturias
1935	Necaxa	
1936	España	Necaxa
1937	Necaxa	Asturias
1938	Necaxa	América
1939	Asturias	Asturias
1940	España	Asturias
1941	Atlante	Asturias
1942	España	Atlante
1943	Marte	Moctezuma
1944	Asturias	España
1945	España	Puebla
1946	Veracruz	Atlas
1947	Atlante	Moctezuma
1948	León	Veracruz
1949	León	León
1950	Veracruz	Atlas
1951	Atlas	Atlante
1952	León	Atlante
1953	Tampico	Puebla
1954	Marte	América
1955	Zacatepec	América
1956	León	Toluca
1957	Guadalajara	Zacatepec
1958	Zacatepec	León
1959	Guadalajara	Zacatepec
1960	Guadalajara	Necaxa
1961	Guadalajara	Tampico
1962	Guadalajara	Atlas
1963	Oro Jalisco	Guadalajara
1964	Guadalajara	América
1965	Guadalajara	América
1966	América	Necaxa
1967	Toluca	León
1968	Toluca	Atlas
1969	Cruz Azul	Cruz Azul
1970	Guadalajara	Guadalajara
1970	Cruz Azul	
1971	América	León
1972	Cruz Azul	León
1973	Cruz Azul	
1974	Cruz Azul	América
1975	Toluca	UNAM Pumas
1976	América	Tigres UANL
1977	UNAM Pumas	
1978	Tigres UANL	
1979	Cruz Azul	
1980	Cruz Azul	
1981	UNAM Pumas	
1982	Tigres UANL	
1983	Puebla	
1984	América	
1985	América	
1985	América	
1986	Monterrey	
1987	Guadalajara	
1988	América	Puebla
1989	América	Toluca
1990	Puebla	Puebla
1991	UNAM Pumas	UAG Tecos
1992	León	Monterrey
1993	Atlante	
1994	UAG Tecos	
1995	Necaxa	Necaxa
1996	Necaxa	Tigres UANL
1997		Cruz Azul

	Verano	Invierno
1996		Santos Laguna
1997	Guadalajara	Cruz Azul
1998	Toluca	Necaxa
1999	Toluca	Pachuca
2000	Toluca	Monarcas Morelia
2001	Santos Laguna	Pachuca
2002	América	Toluca
2003	Monterrey	Pachuca
2004	UNAM Pumas	UNAM Pumas
2005	América	Toluca
2006	Pachuca	Guadalajara
2007	Pachuca	Atlante
2008	Santos	Toluca
2009	UNAM Pumas	Monterrey
2010	Toluca	Monterrey
2011	UNAM Pumas	Tigres UANL

MKD – FYR MACEDONIA

Year	Champions	Cup Winners
1993	Vardar Skopje	Vardar Skopje
1994	Vardar Skopje	Sileks Kratovo
1995	Vardar Skopje	Vardar Skopje
1996	Sileks Kratovo	Sloga Jugomagnat
1997	Sileks Kratovo	Sileks Kratovo
1998	Sileks Kratovo	Vardar Skopje
1999	Sloga Jugomagnat	Vardar Skopje
2000	Sloga Jugomagnat	Sloga Jugomagnat
2001	Sloga Jugomagnat	Pelister Bitola
2002	Vardar Skopje	Pobeda Prilep

2003	Vardar Skopje	Cementarnica
2004	Pobeda Prilep	Sloga Jugomagnat
2005	Rabotnicki Skopje	Baskimi Kumanovo
2006	Rabotnicki Skopje	Makedonije Skopje
2007	Pobeda Prilep	Vardar Skopje
2008	Rabotnicki Skopje	Rabotnicki Skopje
2009	Makedonija Skopje	Rabotnicki Skopje
2010	Renova Cepciste	Teteks
2011	Shkendija Tetovo	Metalurg Skopje

MLI – MALI

Year	Champions	Cup Winners
1961		Stade Malien
1962		Real Bamako
1963		Stade Malien
1964		Real Bamako
1965		Djoliba
1966	Djoliba	Real Bamako
1967	Djoliba	Real Bamako
1968	Djoliba	Real Bamako
1969	Real Bamako	Real Bamako
1970	Stade Malien	Stade Malien
1971	Djoliba	Djoliba
1972	Stade Malien	Stade Malien
1973	Djoliba	Djoliba
1974	Djoliba	Djoliba
1975	Djoliba	Djoliba
1976	Djoliba	Djoliba
1977		Djoliba
1978		Djoliba
1979	Djoliba	Djoliba
1980	Real Bamako	Real Bamako
1981	Real Bamako	Djoliba
1982	Djoliba	Stade Malien
1983	Real Bamako	Djoliba
1984	Stade Malien	Stade Malien
1985	Djoliba	Stade Malien
1986	Real Bamako	Stade Malien
1987	Stade Malien	Sigui Kayes
1988	Djoliba	Stade Malien
1989	Stade Malien	Real Bamako
1990	Djoliba	Stade Malien
1991		Stade Malien
1992	Djoliba	Stade Malien
1993	Stade Malien	Djoliba
1994		Stade Malien
1995	Stade Malien	Stade Malien
1996	Djoliba	Djoliba
1997	Djoliba	Stade Malien
1998	Djoliba	Djoliba
1999	Djoliba	Stade Malien
2000	Stade Malien	Cercle Olympique
2001	Stade Malien	Stade Malien
2002	Stade Malien	Cercle Olympique
2003	Stade Malien	Djoliba
2004	Djoliba	Djoliba
2005	Stade Malien	AS Bamako
2006	Stade Malien	Stade Malien
2007	Stade Malien	Djoliba
2008	Djoliba	Djoliba
2009	Djoliba	Djoliba
2010	Stade Malien	Réal Bamako
2011	Stade Malien	Cercle Olympique

MLT – MALTA

Year	Champions	Cup Winners
1910	Floriana	
1911		
1912	Floriana	
1913	Floriana	
1914	Hamrun Spartans	
1915	Valletta United	
1916		
1917	St. George's	
1918	Hamrun Spartans	
1919	KOMR Militia	
1920	Sliema Wanderers	
1921	Floriana	
1922	Floriana	
1923	Sliema Wanderers	
1924	Sliema Wanderers	
1925	Floriana	
1926	Sliema Wanderers	
1927	Floriana	
1928	Floriana	
1929	Floriana	
1930	Sliema Wanderers	
1931	Floriana	
1932	Valletta United	
1933	Sliema Wanderers	
1934	Sliema Wanderers	
1935	Floriana	Sliema Wanderers
1936	Sliema Wanderers	Sliema Wanderers
1937	Floriana	Sliema Wanderers
1938	Sliema Wanderers	Floriana
1939	Sliema Wanderers	Melita St. Julians
1940	Sliema Wanderers	Sliema Wanderers
1941		
1942		
1943		
1944		
1945	Valletta	Floriana
1946	Valletta	Sliema Wanderers
1947	Hamrun Spartans	Floriana
1948	Valletta	Sliema Wanderers
1949	Sliema Wanderers	Floriana
1950	Floriana	Floriana
1951	Floriana	Sliema Wanderers
1952	Floriana	Sliema Wanderers
1953	Floriana	Floriana
1954	Sliema Wanderers	Floriana
1955	Floriana	Floriana
1956	Sliema Wanderers	Sliema Wanderers
1957	Sliema Wanderers	Floriana
1958	Floriana	Floriana
1959	Valletta	Sliema Wanderers
1960	Valletta	Valletta
1961	Hibernians	Floriana
1962	Floriana	Hibernians
1963	Valletta	Sliema Wanderers
1964	Sliema Wanderers	Valletta
1965	Sliema Wanderers	Sliema Wanderers
1966	Sliema Wanderers	Floriana
1967	Hibernians	Floriana
1968	Floriana	Sliema Wanderers
1969	Hibernians	Sliema Wanderers
1970	Floriana	Hibernians
1971	Sliema Wanderers	Hibernians
1972	Sliema Wanderers	Floriana
1973	Floriana	Gzira United
1974	Valletta	Sliema Wanderers
1975	Floriana	Valletta
1976	Sliema Wanderers	Floriana
1977	Floriana	Valletta
1978	Valletta	Valletta
1979	Hibernians	Sliema Wanderers
1980	Valletta	Hibernians
1981	Hibernians	Floriana
1982	Hibernians	Hibernians
1983	Hamrun Spartans	Hamrun Spartans
1984	Valletta	Hamrun Spartans
1985	Rabat Ajax	Zurrieq
1986	Rabat Ajax	Rabat Ajax
1987	Hamrun Spartans	Hamrun Spartans
1988	Hamrun Spartans	Hamrun Spartans
1989	Sliema Wanderers	Hamrun Spartans
1990	Valletta	Sliema Wanderers
1991	Hamrun Spartans	Valletta
1992	Valletta	Hamrun Spartans
1993	Floriana	Floriana
1994	Hibernians	Floriana
1995	Hibernians	Valletta
1996	Sliema Wanderers	Valletta
1997	Valletta	Valletta
1998	Valletta	Hibernians
1999	Valletta	Valletta
2000	Birkirkara	Sliema Wanderers
2001	Valletta	Valletta
2002	Hibernians	Birkirkara
2003	Sliema Wanderers	Birkirkara
2004	Sliema Wanderers	Sliema Wanderers
2005	Sliema Wanderers	Birkirkara
2006	Birkirkara	Hibernians
2007	Marsaxlokk	Hibernians
2008	Valletta	Birkirkara
2009	Hibernians	Sliema Wanderers
2010	Birkirkara	Valletta
2011	Valletta	Floriana

MNE – MONTENEGRO

Year	Champions	Cup Winners
2007	Zeta Golubovci	Rudar Pljevlja
2008	Buducnost Podg'ica	Mogren Budva
2009	Mogren Budva	OFK Petrovac
2010	Rudar Pljevlja	Rudar Pljevlja
2011	Mogren Budva	Rudar Pljevlja

MGL – MONGOLIA

Year	Champions
1996	Erchim
1997	Delger
1998	Erchim
1999	ITI Bank-Bars
2000	Erchim
2001	Khangarid
2002	Erchim
2003	Khangarid
2004	Khangarid
2005	Khoromkhom
2006	
2007	Erchim
2008	Erchim
2009	Ulaanbaatar University
2010	Khangarid
2011	FC Ulaanbaatar

MOZ – MOZAMBIQUE

Year	Champions	Cup Winners
1956	Ferroviário LM	
1957	Desportivo LM	
1958	Ferroviário Beira	
1959	Sporting Nampula	
1960	Sporting LM	
1961	Ferroviário LM	
1962	Sporting LM	
1963	Ferroviário LM	
1964	Desportivo LM	
1965		
1966	Ferroviário LM	
1967	Ferroviário LM	
1968	Ferroviário LM	
1969	Textáfrica VP	
1970	Ferroviário LM	
1971	Textáfrica VP	
1972	Ferroviário LM	
1973	Textáfrica VP	
1974	Ferroviário Beira	
1975		
1976	Textáfrica Chimoio	
1977	Desportivo Maputo	
1978	Desportivo Maputo	Maxaquene
1979	Costa do Sol	Palmeiras Beira
1980	Costa do Sol	Costa do Sol
1981	Têxtil Púnguè	Desportivo Maputo
1982	Ferroviário Maputo	Maxaquene
1983	Desportivo Maputo	Costa do Sol
1984	Maxaquene	Ferroviário Maputo
1985	Maxaquene	
1986	Maxaquene	Maxaquene
1987	Matchedje	Maxaquene
1988	Desportivo Maputo	Costa do Sol
1989	Ferroviário Maputo	Ferroviário Maputo
1990	Matchedje	Matchedje
1991	Costa do Sol	Clube de Gaza
1992	Costa do Sol	Costa do Sol
1993	Costa do Sol	Costa do Sol
1994	Costa do Sol	Maxaquene
1995	Desportivo Maputo	Costa do Sol
1996	Ferroviário Maputo	Maxaquene
1997	Ferroviário Maputo	Costa do Sol
1998		Maxaquene
1999	Ferroviário Maputo	Costa do Sol
2000	Costa do Sol	Costa do Sol
2001	Costa do Sol	Maxaquene
2002	Ferroviário Maputo	Costa do Sol
2003	Maxaquene	Ferroviário Nampula
2004	Ferroviário Nampula	Ferroviário Maputo
2005	Ferroviário Maputo	Ferroviário Beira
2006	Desportivo Maputo	Desportivo Maputo
2007	Costa do Sol	Costa do Sol
2008	Ferroviário Maputo	Atlético Muçulmano
2009	Ferroviário Maputo	Ferroviário Maputo
2010	Liga Muçulmana	Maxaquene
2011	Liga Muçulmana	Ferroviário Maputo

MRI – MAURITIUS

Year	Champions	Cup Winners
1935	Curepipe SC	
1936	Garrison	
1937	Garrison	
1938	FC Dodo	
1939	FC Dodo	
1942	Fire Brigade	
1944	FC Dodo	
1945	FC Dodo	
1946	FC Dodo	
1947	College St Espirit	
1948	FC Dodo	
1949	Faucons	
1950	Fire Brigade	
1951	FC Dodo	
1952		
1953	FC Dodo	
1954	Faucons	
1955	Faucons	
1956		
1957	FC Dodo & Faucons	FC Dodo
1958	Faucons	
1959	FC Dodo	Faucons
1960		FC Dodo
1961	Fire Brigade	FC Dodo
1962	Police Club	Police Club
1963	Racing Club	Police Club
1964	FC Dodo	
1965	Police Club	Police Club
1966	FC Dodo	FC Dodo
1967	Police Club	Faucons
1968	FC Dodo	Police Club
1969		Hindu Scouts
1970		
1971	Police Club	
1972	Police Club	
1973	Fire Brigade	
1974	Fire Brigade	
1975	Hindu Cadets	
1976	Muslim Scouts	
1977	Hindu Cadets	Hindu Scouts
1978	Racing Club	
1979	Hindu Cadets	
1980	Fire Brigade	Fire Brigade
1981	Police Club	Fire Brigade
1982	Police Club	Fire Brigade
1983	Fire Brigade	Fire Brigade
1984	Fire Brigade	Police Club
1985	Fire Brigade	Sunrise
1986	Cadets Club	Fire Brigade
1987	Sunrise	Sunrise
1988	Fire Brigade	Cadets Club
1989	Sunrise	Fire Brigade
1990	Sunrise	Fire Brigade
1991	Sunrise	Fire Brigade
1992	Sunrise	Sunrise
1993	Fire Brigade	Sunrise
1994	Fire Brigade	Fire Brigade
1995	Sunrise	Fire Brigade
1996	Sunrise	Sunrise
1997	Sunrise	Fire Brigade
1998	Scouts Club	Fire Brigade
1999	Fire Brigade	
2000		
2001	Olympique Moka	US Beau-Basin/RH
2002	AS Port Louis 2000	AS Port Louis 2000
2003	AS Port Louis 2000	Savanne SC
2004	AS Port Louis 2000	Savanne SC
2005	AS Port Louis 2000	AS Port Louis 2000
2006	Pamplemousses SC	Curepipe Starlight
2007	Curepipe Starlight	Petite Rivière Noire
2008	Curepipe Starlight	Curepipe Starlight
2009	Curepipe Starlight	Pamplemousses SC
2010	Pamplemousses SC	AS Vacoas-Phoenix
2011	AS Port Louis 2000	

MRI – MAURITIUS

Year	Independence/Republic Cup
1982	Muslim Scouts
1983	Police
1984	Fire Brigade
1985	Cadets Club
1986	Fire Brigade
1987	Fire Brigade
1988	Fire Brigade
1989	Sunrise
1990	Sunrise
1991	Fire Brigade
1992	Sunrise
1993	Sunrise
1994	Sunrise
1995	Fire Brigade
1996	Sunrise
1997	Sunrise
1998	Sunrise
1999	Fire Brigade
2000	
2001	AS Port Louis 2000
2002	US Beau-Basin/RH
2003	Faucon Flacq
2004	AS Port Louis 2000
2005	AS Port Louis 2000
2006	AS Vacoas-Phoenix
2007	Curepipe Starlight
2008	Curepipe Starlight
2009	Savanne SC
2010	Pamplemousses SC
2011	Pamplemousses SC

MSR – MONTSERRAT

Year	Champions
1996	Royal Monterrsat Police Force
1997	
1998	
1999	
2000	Royal Monterrsat Police Force
2001	Royal Monterrsat Police Force
2002	
2003	Royal Monterrsat Police Force
2004	Ideal SC

MTN – MAURITANIA

Year	Champions	Cup Winners
1976	Garde Nationale	Equipe Espoir
1977	Garde Nationale	Espoirs
1978	Garde Nationale	Espoirs
1979	Garde Nationale	ASC Sonader Ksar
1980		
1981	ASC Police	Garde Nationale
1982	ASC Police	ASC Trarza Rosso
1983	ACS Ksar	Espoirs
1984	Garde Nationale	ASC Trarza Rosso

1985	ACS Ksar	ASC Police
1986	ASC Police	Garde Nationale
1987	ASC Police	AS Amicale Douane
1988	ASC Police	ASC Air Mauritanie
1989		Garde Nationale
1990	ASC Police	Air Mauritanie
1991	ASC Police	AS Amicale Douane
1992	ASC Sonader Ksar	SNIM Nouadhibou
1993	ASC Sonader Ksar	ASC Sonader Ksar
1994	Garde Nationale	ASC Sonader
1995	ASC Sonalec	ASC Air Mauritanie
1996		ASC Imraguens
1997		ASC Sonalec
1998	Garde Nationale	ASC Sonalec
1999	SDPA Rosso	ASC Police
2000	ASC Mauritel	Air Mauritanie
2001	FC Nouadhibou	Garde Nationale
2002	FC Nouadhibou	
2003	NASR Sebkha	Entente Sebkha
2004	ACS Ksar	FC Nouadhibou
2005	NASR Sebkha	Entente Sebkha
2006	ASC Mauritel	NASR Sebkha
2007	NASR Sebkha	ASC Mauritel
2008	ASAC Concorde	FC Nouadhibou
2009	SNIM Nouadhibou	ASAC Concorde
2010	CF Cansado	Tevragh Zeina
2011	FC Nouadhibou	Tevragh Zeina

MWI - MALAWI

Year	Champions	Chibuku Cup
1969	Wanderers	Wanderers
1970	Bullets	Bullets
1971	Bullets	Bullets
1972	Wanderers	Wanderers
1973	Wanderers	Wanderers
1974	Bullets	Bullets
1975	Bullets	Bullets
1976	Wanderers	Wanderers
1977	Hardware Stars	Bullets
1978	Bullets	Bullets
1979	Bullets	Wanderers
1980	Wanderers	Berec Power
1981	Bullets	CIVO United
1982	Tigers	CIVO United
1983	Berec Power	Sucoma
1984	Bullets	Red Lions
1985	Silver Strikers	Tigers
1986	Bullets	Bullets
1987	CIVO United	Silver Strikers
1988	MDC United	Tigers
1989	Tigers	MITCO
1990	Wanderers	Sucoma
1991	Bullets	Bullets
1992	Bullets	Silver Strikers
1993	Bullets	MDC United
1994		
1995		Super ESCOM
1996	Silver Strikers	
1997	Wanderers	
1998	Wanderers	
1999	Bullets	Moyale Barracks
2000	Bullets	
2001	Bullets	MDC United
2002	Bullets	

2003	Bullets	
2004	Bullets	FAM Cup
2005	Bullets	Wanderers
2006	Wanderers	
2007	ESCOM United	Silver Strikers
2008	Silver Strikers	Moyale Barracks
2009		Tigers
2010	Silver Strikers	
2011	ESCOM United	

MWI - MALAWI

Year	Castle/Press Cup	Kamuzu Cup
1967	Chichiri Athletics	
1968	Malawi University	
1969	Bullets	
1970	Bullets	
1971	Wanderers	
1972	Wanderers	
1973	Bullets	Kamuzu Cup
1974	Wanderers	Bullets
1975	Bullets	Bullets
1976		Wanderers
1977	Hardware Stars	Sucoma
1978	Bullets	Hardware Stars
1979	Bullets	Bullets
1980	Bullets	Bullets
1981	Bullets	Bullets
1982	Sucoma	Wanderers
1983	Civo United	Bullets
1984	Berec Power	Berec Power
1985	Bullets	Wanderers
1986	MDC United	Bullets
1987	Silver Strikers	Silver Strikers
1988	Silver Strikers	Tigers
1989	Wanderers	MITCO
1990	Silver Strikers	Tigers
1991	Silver Strikers	Silver Strikers
1992		
1993	Bullets	
1994	MDC United	
1995		Hardware Stars
1996		Wanderers
1997	Silver Strikers	Chomba/C'berg
1998	Silver Strikers	Bullets
1999	Bullets	Bullets
2000	MDC United	Wanderers
2001		Moyale Barracks
2002		Bullets

Kings Cup

1999	Bullets	
2000	Red Lions	
2001	Bullets	Top 8 Cup
2002	Bullets	Silver Strikers
2003	Bullets	Wanderers

President's Cup

2009	Wanderers
2010	CIVO United

MYA - MYANMAR

Year	Champions
1996	Finance & Revenue Yangon
1997	Finance & Revenue Yangon
1998	YCDC
1999	Finance & Revenue Yangon
2000	Finance & Revenue Yangon
2001	Commerce
2002	Finance & Revenue Yangon
2003	Finance & Revenue Yangon
2004	Finance & Revenue Yangon
2005	Finance & Revenue Yangon
2006	Finance & Revenue Yangon
2007	Kanbawza

		Cup Winners
2009	Yadanarbon	
2009	Yadanarbon	Yadanarbon
2010	Yadanarbon	Yadanarbon
2011	Yangon United	Yangon United

NAM - NAMIBIA

Year	Champions	Cup Winners
1990		Black Africa
1991	Eleven Arrows	Chief Santos
1992	Ramblers	Liverpool
1993	Chief Santos	Black Africa
1994	Black Africa	Blue Waters
1995	Black Africa	United Africa Tigers
1996	Blue Waters	United Africa Tigers
1997		
1998	Black Africa	Chief Santos
1999	Black Africa	Chief Santos
2000	Blue Waters	Chief Santos
2001		
2002	Liverpool	Orlando Pirates
2003	Chief Santos	Civics
2004	Blue Waters	Black Africans
2005	Civics	Ramblers
2006	Civics	Orlando Pirates
2007	Civics	African Stars
2008	Orlando Pirates	Civics
2009	African Stars	Orlando Pirates
2010	African Stars	African Stars
2011	Black Africa	Eleven Arrows

NCA - NICARAGUA

Year	Champions
1933	Alas
1934	Club Atlético
1935	
1936	
1937	
1938	
1939	Lido
1940	Diriangén
1941	Diriangén
1942	Diriangén
1943	Diriangén
1944	Diriangén
1945	Diriangén
1946	Ferrocarril
1947	Colegio C-A
1948	Ferrocarril
1949	Diriangén
1950	Aduana
1951	Aduana
1952	
1953	Diriangén
1954	La Salle
1955	Aduana

Year	Champions
1956	Diriangén
1957	
1958	Club Atlético
1959	Diriangén
1960	La Nica
1961	Santa Cecilia
1962	
1963	
1964	
1965	Santa Cecilia
1966	Flor de Caña
1967	Flor de Caña
1968	UCA Managua
1969	Diriangén
1970	Diriangén
1971	Santa Cecilia
1972	Santa Cecilia
1973	Santa Cecilia
1974	Diriangén
1975	UCA Managua
1976	UCA Managua
1977	UCA Managua
1978	
1979	
1980	Bufalos
1981	Diriangén
1982	Diriangén
1983	Diriangén
1984	Masaya
1985	América
1986	Masaya
1987	Diriangén
1988	América
1989	Diriangén
1990	América
1991	Real Estelí
1992	Diriangén
1993	Juventus
1994	Juventus
1995	Diriangén
1996	Diriangén
1997	Diriangén
1998	Walter Ferreti
1999	Real Estelí
2000	Diriangén
2001	Walter Ferreti
2002	Deportivo Jalapa
2003	Real Estelí
2003	Real Estelí
2004	Real Estelí
2005	Diriangén
2006	Diriangén
2007	Real Estelí
2008	Real Estelí
2009	Real Estelí
2010	Real Estelí
2011	Real Estelí

NCL – NEW CALEDONIA

Year	Nat Champions	Cup Winners
1950	Impassible	
1951	Impassible	
1952	Indépendante	
1953	Impassible	
1954	Indépendante	Indépendante

Year	Champions	Cup Winners
1955		
1956	Impassible	PLGC
1957	PLGC	Impassible
1958	PLGC	PLGC
1959	PLGC	Wé
1960	Impassible	Uniforme Fayaoué
1961		Ile des Pins
1962	USC Nouméa	Olympique Nouméa
1963	USC Nouméa	Olympique Nouméa
1964		JS Vallée du Tir
1965		JS Vallée du Tir
1966		JS Vallée du Tir
1967		JS Vallée du Tir
1968		JS Vallée du Tir
1969		ASLN Nouméa
1970		ASLN Nouméa
1971		ASLN Nouméa
1972		ASLN Nouméa
1973		UAC Yaté
1974		UAC Yaté
1975		ASLN Nouméa
1976		Kehdek Koumac
1977		USL Gélima
1978	Gélima Canala	USL Gélima
1979		USL Gélima
1980		JS Baco
1981		CA Saint-Louis
1982		USL Gélima
1983		AS Païta
1984	AS Fregate	JS Baco
1985	AS Kunié	CA Saint-Louis
1986		CA Saint-Louis
1987		JS Baco
1988		Wé-Luécilla
1989		AS Fregate
1990		CA Saint-Louis
1991		JS Baco
1992		Wé-Luécilla
1993	Wé-Luécilla	ASLN Thio
1994	JS Baco	CA Saint-Louis
1995	JS Baco	JS Baco
1996	JS Traput	AS Magenta
1997	JS Baco	CA Saint-Louis
1998	AS Poum	JS Traput
1999	FC Gaïcha	JS Traput
2000	JS Baco	AS Magenta
2001	JS Baco	AS Magenta
2002	AS Mont-Dore	AS Magenta
2003	AS Magenta	AS Magenta
2004	AS Magenta	AS Magenta
2005	AS Magenta	AS Magenta
2006		AS Mont-Dore
2007	JS Baco	AS Lössi
2008	AS Magenta	AS Mont-Dore
2009	AS Magenta	AS Mont-Dore
2010	AS Mont-Dore	AS Magenta
2011	AS Mont-Dore	FC Gaïcha

NCL – NEW CALEDONIA

Year	Division d'Honneur
2002	JS Baco
2003	AS Magenta
2004	AS Magenta
2005	AS Magenta
2006	AS Mont-Doré
2007	AS Lossi
2008	AS Magenta
2009	AS Magenta
2010	AS Magenta
2011	AS Mont-Doré

NED – NETHERLANDS

Year	Champions	Cup Winners
1898	RAP Amsterdam	
1899	RAP Amsterdam	RAP Amsterdam
1900	HVV Den Haag	Velocitas Breda
1901	HVV Den Haag	HBS Den Haag
1902	HVV Den Haag	Haarlem
1903	HVV Den Haag	HVV Den Haag
1904	HBS Den Haag	HFC Haarlem
1905	HVV Den Haag	VOC Rotterdam
1906	HBS Den Haag	Concordia
1907	HVV Den Haag	VOC Rotterdam
1908	Quick Den Haag	HBS Den Haag
1909	Sparta Rotterdam	Quick Den Haag
1910	HVV Den Haag	Quick Den Haag
1911	Sparta Rotterdam	Quick Den Haag
1912	Sparta Rotterdam	Haarlem
1913	Sparta Rotterdam	HFC Haarlem
1914	HVV Den Haag	DFC Dordrecht
1915	Sparta Rotterdam	HFC Haarlem
1916	Willem II Tilburg	Quick Den Haag
1917	Go Ahead Deventer	Ajax
1918	Ajax	RCH Haarlem
1919	Ajax	
1920	Be Quick Groningen	CVV
1921	NAC Breda	Schoten
1922	Go Ahead Eagles	
1923	RCH Haarlem	
1924	Feyenoord	
1925	HBS Den Haag	ZFC
1926	SC Enschede	LONGA Lichtenvoorde
1927	Heracles Almelo	VUC Den Haag
1928	Feyenoord	RCH Haarlem
1929	PSV Eindhoven	
1930	Go Ahead Deventer	Feyenoord
1931	Ajax	
1932	Ajax	DFC Dordrecht
1933	Go Ahead Deventer	
1934	Ajax	Velocitas Groningen
1935	PSV Eindhoven	Feyenoord
1936	Feyenoord	Roermond
1937	Ajax	Eindhoven VV
1938	Feyenoord	VSV Velsen
1939	Ajax	Wageningen
1940	Feyenoord	
1941	Heracles Almelo	
1942	ADO Den Haag	Ajax
1943	ADO Den Haag	Willem II Tilburg
1944	De Volewijckers	
1945		
1946	Haarlem	
1947	Ajax	
1948	BVV Hertogenbosch	Wageningen
1949	SVV Schiedam	Quick Nijmegen
1950	Limburg Brunssue	PSV Eindhoven
1951	PSV Eindhoven	
1952	Willem II Tilburg	
1953	RCH Haarlem	

Year	Champions	Cup Winners
1954	Eindhoven VV	
1955	Willem II Tilburg	
1956	Rapid JC Heerlen	
1957	Ajax	Fortuna '54 Geleen
1958	DOS Utrecht	Sparta Rotterdam
1959	Sparta Rotterdam	VVV Venlo
1960	Ajax	
1961	Feyenoord	Ajax
1962	Feyenoord	Sparta Rotterdam
1963	PSV Eindhoven	Willem II Tilburg
1964	DWS Amsterdam	Fortuna '54 Geleen
1965	Feyenoord	Feyenoord
1966	Ajax	Sparta Rotterdam
1967	Ajax	Ajax
1968	Ajax	ADO Den Haag
1969	Feyenoord	Feyenoord
1970	Ajax	Ajax
1971	Feyenoord	Ajax
1972	Ajax	Ajax
1973	Ajax	NAC Breda
1974	Feyenoord	PSV Eindhoven
1975	PSV Eindhoven	FC Den Haag
1976	PSV Eindhoven	PSV Eindhoven
1977	Ajax	Twente Enschede
1978	PSV Eindhoven	AZ 67 Alkmaar
1979	Ajax	Ajax
1980	Ajax	Feyenoord
1981	AZ 67 Alkmaar	AZ 67 Alkmaar
1982	Ajax	AZ 67 Alkmaar
1983	Ajax	Ajax
1984	Feyenoord	Feyenoord
1985	Ajax	FC Utrecht
1986	PSV Eindhoven	Ajax
1987	PSV Eindhoven	Ajax
1988	PSV Eindhoven	PSV Eindhoven
1989	PSV Eindhoven	PSV Eindhoven
1990	Ajax	PSV Eindhoven
1991	PSV Eindhoven	Feyenoord
1992	PSV Eindhoven	Feyenoord
1993	Feyenoord	Ajax
1994	Ajax	Feyenoord
1995	Ajax	Feyenoord
1996	Ajax	PSV Eindhoven
1997	PSV Eindhoven	Roda JC Kerkrade
1998	Ajax	
1999	Feyenoord	Ajax
2000	PSV Eindhoven	Roda JC Kerkrade
2001	PSV Eindhoven	Twente Enschede
2002	Ajax	Ajax
2003	PSV Eindhoven	FC Utrecht
2004	Ajax	FC Utrecht
2005	PSV Eindhoven	PSV Eindhoven
2006	PSV Eindhoven	Ajax
2007	PSV Eindhoven	Ajax
2008	PSV Eindhoven	Feyenoord
2009	AZ Alkmaar	SC Heerenveen
2010	Twente Enschede	Ajax
2011	Ajax	Twente Enschede

NEP – NEPAL

Year	Champions
1955	Mahabir Club
1956	Police Force
1957	Police Force
1958	Army
1959	
1960	
1961	New Road Team
1962	
1963	New Road Team
1964	Bidya Byama
1965	
1966	
1967	Mahabir Club
1968	Friends Union
1969	Deurali Club
1970	Mahabir Club
1971	Deurali Club
1972	Rani Pokhari Corner Team
1973	Rani Pokhari Corner Team
1974	Rani Pokhari Corner Team
1975	Boys Union Club
1976	Sunakhari Athletic Club
1977	Annapurna Club
1978	New Road Team
1979	Rani Pokhari Corner Team
1980	Sankata Boys Club
1982	Rani Pokhari Corner Team
1982	Annapurna Club
1983	Sankata Boys Club
1984	Rani Pokhari Corner Team
1985	Sankata Boys Club
1986	Manang Marsyangdi Club
1987	Manang Marsyangdi Club
1988	
1989	Manang Marsyangdi Club
1990	
1991	
1992	
1993	
1994	
1995	New Road Team
1996	
1997	Three Star Club
1998	Three Star Club
1999	
2000	Manang Marsyangdi Club
2001	
2002	
2003	Manang Marsyangdi Club
2004	Three Star Club
2005	
2006	Manang Marsyangdi Club
2007	Mahendra Police Club
2008	
2009	
2010	Nepal Police Club
2011	Nepal Police Club

NGA NIGERIA

Year	Champions	Cup Winners
1945		Marine
1946		Lagos Railways
1947		Marine
1948		Lagos Railways
1949		Lagos Railways
1950		Lagos UAC
1951		Lagos Railways
1952		Lagos PAN Bank
1953		Kano Pillars
1954		Calabar
1955		Port Harcourt FC
1956		Lagos Railways
1957		Lagos Railways
1958		Port Harcourt FC
1959		Ibadan Lions
1960		Lagos ECN
1961		Ibadan Lions
1962		Police
1963		Port Harcourt FC
1964		Lagos Railways
1965		Lagos ECN
1966		Ibadan Lions
1967		Stationery Stores
1968		Stationery Stores
1969		Ibadan Lions
1970		Lagos ECN
1971		WNDC Ibadan
1972	Mighty Jets	Bendel Insurance
1973	Bendel Insurance	No tournament held
1974	Enugu Rangers	Enugu Rangers
1975	Enugu Rangers	Enugu Rangers
1976	Shooting Stars	Enugu Rangers
1977		Shooting Stars
1978	Racca Rovers	Bendel Insurance
1979	Bendel Insurance	Shooting Stars
1980	Shooting Stars	Bendel Insurance
1981	Enugu Rangers	Enugu Rangers
1982	Enugu Rangers	Stationery Stores
1983	Shooting Stars	Enugu Rangers
1984	Enugu Rangers	Leventis United
1985	New Nigeria Bank	Abiola Babes
1986	Leventis United	Leventis United
1987	Iwuanyanwu Nat.	Abiola Babes
1988	Iwuanyanwu Nat.	Iwuanyanwu Nat.
1989	Iwuanyanwu Nat.	BCC Lions
1990	Iwuanyanwu Nat.	Stationery Stores
1991	Julius Berger	El Kanemi Warriors
1992	Stationery Stores	El Kanemi Warriors
1993	Iwuanyanwu Nat.	BCC Lions
1994	BCC Lions	BCC Lions
1995	Shooting Stars	Shooting Stars
1996	Udoji United	Julius Berger
1997	Eagle Cement	BCC Lions
1998	Shooting Stars	Wikki Tourists
1999	Lobi Stars	Plateau United
2000	Julius Berger	Niger Tornados
2001	Enyimba	Dolphin
2002	Enyimba	Julius Berger
2003	Enyimba	Lobi Stars
2004	Enyimba	Dolphin
2005	Enyimba	Enyimba
2006	Ocean Boys	Dolphin
2007	Enyimba	Dolphin
2008	Kano Pillars	Ocean Boys
2009	Bayelsa United	Enyimba
2010	Enyimba	Kaduna United
2011	Dolphin	Heartland

NIG – NIGER

Year	Champions	Cup Winners
1962		Amicale de Niamey
1963		
1964		
1965		Secteur 6
1966	Secteur 6	
1967	Secteur 6	
1968	Secteur 6	
1969	Secteur 6	
1970	Secteur 6	
1971	ASFAN	
1972		
1973	Secteur 7	
1974	Sahel	Sahel
1975	ASFAN	Olympic
1976	Olympic	Liberté FC Niamey
1977	Olympic	Olympic
1978	Olympic	Sahel
1979		AS Niamey
1980	AS Niamey	AS Niamey
1981	AS Niamey	AS Niamey
1982	AS Niamey	Zindourma
1983	Jangorzo	Jangorzo
1984	Espoir	Espoir
1985	Zumunta	Espoir
1986	Sahel	Sahel
1987	Sahel	Liberté
1988	Zumunta	Liberté
1989	Olympic	Liberté
1990	Sahel	Olympic
1991	Sahel	Olympic
1992	Sahel	Sahel
1993	Zumunta	Sahel
1994	Sahel	Zumunta
1995		ASFAN
1996	Sahel	Sahel
1997		JS Ténéré
1998	Olympic	JS Ténéré
1999	Olympic	JS Ténéré
2000	JS Ténéré	JS Ténéré
2001	JS Ténéré	Akokana
2002		
2003	Sahel	Olympic
2004	Sahel	Sahel
2005	AS FNIS	
2006	AS FNIS	Sahel
2007	Sahel	AS FNIS
2008	AS Police	AS Police
2009	Sahel	ASFAN
2010	ASFAN	ASFAN
2011	AS Garde Nationale	Sahel

NIR – NORTHERN IRELAND

Year	Champions	Cup Winners
1881		Moyola Park
1882		Queen's Island
1883		Cliftonville
1884		Distillery
1885		Distillery
1886		Distillery
1887		Ulster
1888		Cliftonville
1889		Distillery
1890		Gordon Highlanders
1891	Linfield	Linfield
1892	Linfield	Linfield
1893	Linfield	Linfield
1894	Glentoran	Distillery
1895	Linfield	Linfield
1896	Distillery	Distillery
1897	Glentoran	Cliftonville
1898	Linfield	Linfield
1899	Distillery	Linfield
1900	Celtic	Cliftonville
1901	Distillery	Cliftonville
1902	Linfield	Linfield
1903	Distillery	Distillery
1904	Linfield	Linfield
1905	Glentoran	Distillery
1906	Cliftonville/Distillery	Shelbourne
1907	Linfield	Cliftonville
1908	Linfield	Bohemians
1909	Linfield	Cliftonville
1910	Cliftonville	Distillery
1911	Linfield	Shelbourne
1912	Glentoran	Linfield
1913	Glentoran	Linfield
1914	Linfield	Glentoran
1915	Celtic	Linfield
1916		Linfield
1917		Glentoran
1918		Celtic
1919		Linfield
1920	Celtic	Shelbourne
1921	Glentoran	Glentoran
1922	Linfield	Linfield
1923	Linfield	Linfield
1924	Queen's Island	Queen's Island
1925	Glentoran	Distillery
1926	Celtic	Celtic
1927	Celtic	Ards
1928	Celtic	Willowfield
1929	Celtic	Ballymena United
1930	Linfield	Linfield
1931	Glentoran	Linfield
1932	Linfield	Glentoran
1933	Celtic	Glentoran
1934	Linfield	Linfield
1935	Linfield	Glentoran
1936	Celtic	Linfield
1937	Celtic	Celtic
1938	Celtic	Celtic
1939	Celtic	Linfield
1940	Celtic	Ballymena United
1941		Celtic
1942		Linfield
1943		Celtic
1944		Celtic
1945		Linfield
1946		Linfield
1947		Celtic
1948	Celtic	Linfield
1949	Linfield	Derry City
1950	Linfield	Linfield
1951	Glentoran	Glentoran
1952	Glenavon	Ards
1953	Glentoran	Linfield
1954	Linfield	Derry City
1955	Linfield	Dundela
1956	Linfield	Distillery
1957	Glenavon	Glenavon
1958	Ards	Ballymena United
1959	Linfield	Glenavon
1960	Glenavon	Linfield
1961	Linfield	Glenavon
1962	Linfield	Linfield
1963	Distillery	Linfield
1964	Glentoran	Derry City
1965	Derry City	Coleraine
1966	Linfield	Glentoran
1967	Glentoran	Crusaders
1968	Glentoran	Crusaders
1969	Linfield	Ards
1970	Glentoran	Linfield
1971	Linfield	Distillery
1972	Glentoran	Coleraine
1973	Crusaders	Glentoran
1974	Coleraine	Ards
1975	Linfield	Coleraine
1976	Crusaders	Carrick Rangers
1977	Glentoran	Coleraine
1978	Linfield	Linfield
1979	Linfield	Cliftonville
1980	Linfield	Linfield
1981	Glentoran	Ballymena United
1982	Linfield	Linfield
1983	Linfield	Glentoran
1984	Linfield	Ballymena United
1985	Linfield	Glentoran
1986	Linfield	Glentoran
1987	Linfield	Glentoran
1988	Glentoran	Glentoran
1989	Linfield	Ballymena United
1990	Portadown	Glentoran
1991	Portadown	Portadown
1992	Glentoran	Glenavon
1993	Linfield	Bangor
1994	Linfield	Linfield
1995	Crusaders	Linfield
1996	Portadown	Glentoran
1997	Crusaders	Glenavon
1998	Cliftonville	Glentoran
1999	Glentoran	Portadown
2000	Linfield	Glentoran
2001	Linfield	Glentoran
2002	Portadown	Linfield
2003	Glentoran	Coleraine
2004	Linfield	Glentoran
2005	Glentoran	Portadown
2006	Linfield	Linfield
2007	Linfield	Linfield
2008	Linfield	Linfield
2009	Glentoran	Crusaders
2010	Linfield	Linfield
2011	Linfield	Linfield

NIR – NORTHERN IRELAND

Year	League Cup Winners
1987	Linfield
1988	Coleraine
1989	Glentoran
1990	Glenavon
1991	Glentoran
1992	Linfield
1993	Bangor

NIG (continued)

Year	Champions
1994	Linfield
1995	Ards
1996	Portadown
1997	Crusaders
1998	Linfield
1999	Linfield
2000	Linfield
2001	Glentoran
2002	Linfield
2003	Glentoran
2004	Cliftonville
2005	Glentoran
2006	Linfield
2007	Glentoran
2008	Linfield
2009	Portadown
2010	Glentoran
2011	Lisburn Distillery

NOR – NORWAY

Year	Champions	Cup Winners
1902		Grane Nordstrand
1903		Odd SK Skien
1904		Odd SK Skien
1905		Odd SK Skien
1906		Odd SK Skien
1907		Mercantile
1908		SOFK Lyn Oslo
1909		SOFK Lyn Oslo
1910		SOFK Lyn Oslo
1911		SOFK Lyn Oslo
1912		Mercantile
1913		Odd SK Skien
1914		Frigg SK Oslo
1915		Odd SK Skien
1916		Frigg SK Oslo
1917		FK Sarpsborg
1918		Kvik Halden
1919		Odd SK Skien
1920		Örn FK Horten
1921		Frigg SK Oslo
1922		Odd SK Skien
1923		SK Brann Bergen
1924		Odd SK Skien
1925		SK Brann Bergen
1926		Odd SK Skien
1927		Örn FK Horten
1928		Örn FK Horten
1929		FK Sarpsborg
1930		Örn FK Horten
1931		Odd SK Skien
1932		Fredrikstad FK
1933		Mjöndalen IF
1934		Mjöndalen IF
1935		Fredrikstad FK
1936		Fredrikstad FK
1937		Mjöndalen IF
1938	Fredrikstad FK	Fredrikstad FK
1939	Fredrikstad FK	FK Sarpsborg
1940		Fredrikstad FK
1941		
1942		
1943		
1944		
1945		SOFK Lyn Oslo
1946		SOFK Lyn Oslo
1947		FK Skeid Oslo
1948	Freidig SK	FK Sarpsborg
1949	Fredrikstad FK	FK Sarpsborg
1950	Fram Larvik	Fredrikstad FK
1951	Fredrikstad FK	FK Sarpsborg
1952	Fredrikstad FK	Sparta Sarpsborg
1953	Larvik Turn IF	Viking FK Stavanger
1954	Fredrikstad FK	FK Skeid Oslo
1955	Larvik Turn IF	FK Skeid Oslo
1956	Larvik Turn IF	FK Skeid Oslo
1957	Fredrikstad FK	Fredrikstad FK
1958	Viking FK Stavanger	FK Skeid Oslo
1959	Lilleström SK	Viking FK Stavanger
1960	Fredrikstad FK	Rosenborg BK
1961	Fredrikstad FK	Fredrikstad FK
1962	SK Brann Bergen	Gjövik Lyn
1963	SK Brann Bergen	FK Skeid Oslo
1964	SOFK Lyn Oslo	Rosenborg BK
1965	Vålerengens IF Oslo	FK Skeid Oslo
1966	FK Skeid Oslo	Fredrikstad FK
1967	Rosenborg BK	SOFK Lyn Oslo
1968	SOFK Lyn Oslo	SOFK Lyn Oslo
1969	Rosenborg BK	IF Stromsgodset
1970	IF Stromsgodset	IF Stromsgodset
1971	Rosenborg BK	Rosenborg BK
1972	Viking FK Stavanger	SK Brann Bergen
1973	Viking FK Stavanger	IF Stromsgodset
1974	Viking FK Stavanger	FK Skeid Oslo
1975	Viking FK Stavanger	SOFK Bodö-Glimt
1976	Lilleström SK	SK Brann Bergen
1977	Lilleström SK	Lilleström SK
1978	Start Kristiansand	Lilleström SK
1979	Viking FK Stavanger	Viking FK Stavanger
1980	Start Kristiansand	Vålerengens IF Oslo
1981	Vålerengens IF Oslo	Lilleström SK
1982	Viking FK Stavanger	SK Brann Bergen
1983	Vålerengens IF Oslo	Moss FK
1984	Vålerengens IF Oslo	Fredrikstad FK
1985	Rosenberg BK	Lilleström SK
1986	Lilleström SK	Tromsö IL
1987	Moss FK	Bryne IL Stavanger
1988	Rosenborg BK	Rosenberg BK
1989	Lilleström SK	Viking FK Stavanger
1990	Rosenborg BK	Rosenborg BK
1991	Viking SK	Strömsgodset
1992	Rosenborg BK	Rosenborg BK
1993	Rosenborg BK	FK Bodø/Glimt
1994	Rosenborg BK	Molde FK
1995	Rosenborg BK	Rosenborg BK
1996	Rosenborg BK	Tromsø IL
1997	Rosenborg BK	Vålerenga IF
1998	Rosenborg BK	Stabæk
1999	Rosenborg BK	Rosenborg BK
2000	Rosenborg BK	Odd Grenland
2001	Rosenborg BK	Viking SK
2002	Rosenborg BK	Vålerenga
2003	Rosenborg BK	Rosenborg BK
2004	Rosenborg BK	SK Brann
2005	Vålerenga IF	Molde FK
2006	Rosenborg BK	Fredrikstad FK
2007	SK Brann	Lillestrøm SK
2008	Stabæk	Vålerenga
2009	Rosenborg BK	Aalesunds SK
2010	Rosenborg BK	Strømsgodset
2011	Molde FK	Aalesunds SK

NZL – NEW ZEALAND

Year		Cup Winners
1923		Seacliff
1924		Habour Board
1925		YMCA
1926		Sunnyside
1927		Ponsonby
1928		Petone
1929		Tramways
1930		Petone
1931		Tramurewa
1932		Marist
1933		Ponsonby
1934		Thistle
1935		Hospital
1936		Western
1937		
1938		Waterside
1939		Waterside
1940		Waterside
1941		
1942		
1943		
1944		
1945		Western
1946		Marist
1947		Waterside
1948		Tech Old Boys
1949		Petone
1950		Eden
1951		Eastern Suburbs
1952		North Shore Utd
1953		Eastern Suburbs
1954		Onehunga
1955		Western
1956		Stop Out
1957		Seatoun
1958		Seatoun
1959		Northern
1960		North Shore Utd
1961		Northern
1962		Tech Old Boys
1963		North Shore Utd
1964		Mt Roskill
1965		Eastern Suburbs
1966		Miramar Rangers
1967		North Shore Utd
1968		Eastern Suburbs
1969		Eastern Suburbs
1970	Blockhouse Bay	Blockhouse Bay
1971	Eastern Suburbs	Western Suburbs
1972	Mt Wellington	Christchurch Utd
1973	Christchurch Utd	Mt Wellington
1974	Christchurch Utd	Mt Wellington
1975	Christchurch Utd	Christchurch Utd
1976	Wellington D'mond	Christchurch Utd
1977	North Shore Utd	Nelson Utd
1978	Christchurch Utd	Manurewa
1979	Mt Wellington	North Shore United
1980	Mt Wellington	Mt Wellington
1981	Wellington D'mond	Dunedin City
1982	Mt Wellington	Mt Wellington
1983	Manurewa	Mt Wellington
1984	Gisborne City	Manurewa
1985	Wellington Utd	Napier City Rovers
1986	Mt Wellington	North Shore Utd

Year	Champions	Cup Winners
1987	Christchurch Utd	Gisborne City
1988	Christchurch Utd	Waikato Utd
1989	Napier City Rovers	Christchurch Utd
1990	Waitakere City	Mt Wellington
1991	Christchurch Utd	Christchurch Utd
1992	Waitakere City	Miramar Rangers
1993	Napier City Rovers	Napier City Rovers
1994	North Shore Utd	Waitakere City
1995	Waitakere City	Waitakere City
1996	Waitakere City	Waitakere City
1997	Waitakere City	Central Utd
1998	Napier City Rovers	Central Utd
1999	Central United	Dunedin Technical
2000	Napier City Rovers	Napier City Rovers
2001	Central United	Univ Mt Wellington
2002	Miramar Rangers	Napier City Rovers
2003	Miramar Rangers	Univ Mt Wellington
2004		Miramar Rangers
2005	Auckland City	Central Utd
2006	Auckland City	Western Suburbs
2007	Auckland City	Central United
2008	Waitakere United	East Coast Bays
2009	Auckland City	Wellington Olympic
2010	Waitakere United	Miramar Rangers
2011	Waitakere United	Wairarapa United

OMA – OMAN

Year	Champions	Cup Winners
1972		Al Ahli
1973		Sur
1974		Al Talia'a
1975		Fanja
1976		Fanja
1977	Fanja	Dhofar
1978	Rowi	Fanja
1979	Fanja	Oman Club
1980	Al Nasr	Dhofar
1981	Al Nasr	Dhofar
1982	Al Ahli	Al Ahli
1983	Dhofar	Al Ahli
1984	Fanja	Al Ahli
1985	Dhofar	Fanja
1986	Dhofar	Fanja
1987	Dhofar	Fanja
1988	Dhofar	Al Ahli
1989	Al Nasr	Fanja
1990	Dhofar	Dhofar
1991	Fanja	Fanja
1992	Dhofar	Sur
1993	Dhofar	Al Urooba
1994	Dhofar	Oman Club
1995	Sur	Al Nasr
1996	Sur	Seeb
1997	Oman Club	Seeb
1998	Al Nasr	Seeb
1999	Dhofar	Dhofar
2000	Al Urooba	Al Nasr
2001	Dhofar	Al Urooba
2002	Al Urooba	Al Nasr
2003	Rowi	Rowi
2004	Al Nasr	Dhofar
2005	Dhofar	Al Nasr
2006	Muscat	Dhofar
2007	Al Nahda	Sur
2008	Al Urooba	Al Suwaiq
2009	Al Nahda	Saham
2010	Al Suwaiq	Al Urooba
2011	Al Suwaiq	Dhofar

PAK – PAKISTAN

Year	Champions	Cup Winners
1948	Sindh Red	
1949		
1950	Balochistan Red	
1951		
1952	Punjab	
1953	Punjab	
1954	Punjab Blue	
1955	Punjab	
1956	Balochistan	
1957	Punjab	
1958	Punjab Blue	
1959	Balochistan	
1960	East Pakistan	
1962	Dacca	
1962	Dacca	
1963	Karachi	
1964		
1965	Karachi	
1966	Karachi	
1967		
1968	Peshawar	
1969	Pakistan Railways	
1970	Chiitagong	
1971	Pakistan Int Airlines	
1972	Pakistan Int Airlines	
1973	Karachi Yellow	
1975	Pakistan Int Airlines	
1975	Sindh Red	
1976	Pakistan Int Airlines	
1977		
1978	Pakistan Int Airlines	
1979	Karachi Red	Sindh Govt Press
1980	Karachi Red	
1981	Pakistan Int Airlines	
1982	Habib Bank Ltd	
1983	WAPDA	
1984	Pakistan Railways	Pakistan Int Airlines
1985	Quetta	Habib Bank Ltd
1986	Pakistan Air Force	
1987	Crescent Textile Mills	Crescent Textile Mills
1989	Punjub Red	
1989	Pakistan Int Airlines	
1990	Punjub Red	Karachi Port Trust
1991	WAPDA	Marker Club
1992	Pakistan Int Airlines	Crescent Textile Mills
1993	Pakistan Army	Nat. Bank Pakistan
1994	Crescent Textile Mills	Frontier Constab'ry
1995	Pakistan Army	
1996		Allied Bank
1997	Allied Bank	
1998	Pakistan Int Airlines	Allied Bank
1999	Allied Bank	Allied Bank
2000	Allied Bank	Pakistan Army
2001	WAPDA	Pakistan Army
2002		Allied Bank
2003	WAPDA	Pakistan Telecoms
2004	WAPDA	
2005	Pakistan Army	Pakistan Telecoms
2007	Pakistan Army	
2007	WAPDA	
2008	WAPDA	Pakistan Navy
2009	Khan Research Labs	Khan Research Labs
2010	WAPDA	Khan Research Labs
2011	Khan Research Labs	Khan Research Labs

PAN – PANAMA

Year	Champions		
1988	Plaza Amador		
1989	Tauro		
1990	Plaza Amador		
1991	Tauro		
1992	Plaza Amador		
1993	Euro Kickers		
1994			
1995	San Francisco		
1996	San Francisco		
1997	Tauro		
1998	Tauro		
1999	Arabe Unido		
2000	Tauro		
2001	Panama Viejo		
2001	Deportivo Arabe Un.		
2002	Plaza Amador		
2003	Tauro		
2004	Deportivo Arabe Un.		
2005	Plaza Amador		
2006	San Francisco	**Apertura**	
2007	Tauro	San Francisco	
2008	San Francisco	Arabe Unido	
2009	San Francisco	Arabe Unido	
2010	Arabe Unido	Tauro	
2011	San Francisco	Chorrillo	

PAR – PARAGUAY

Year	Champions	Cup Winners
1906	Guaraní	
1907	Guaraní	
1908		
1909	Nacional	
1910	Libertad	
1911	Nacional	
1912	Olimpia	
1913	Cerro Porteño	
1914	Olimpia	
1915	Cerro Porteño	
1916	Olimpia	
1917	Libertad	
1918	Cerro Porteño	
1919	Cerro Porteño	
1920	Libertad	
1921	Guaraní	
1922		
1923	Guaraní	
1924	Nacional	
1925	Olimpia	
1926	Nacional	
1927	Olimpia	
1928	Olimpia	
1929	Olimpia	
1930	Libertad	

Year	Champion
1931	Olimpia
1932	
1933	
1934	
1935	Cerro Porteño
1936	Olimpia
1937	Olimpia
1938	Olimpia
1939	Cerro Porteño
1940	Cerro Porteño
1941	Cerro Porteño
1942	Nacional
1943	Libertad
1944	Cerro Porteño
1945	Libertad
1946	Nacional
1947	Olimpia
1948	Olimpia
1949	Guaraní
1950	Cerro Porteño
1951	Sportivo Luqueño
1952	Presidente Hayes
1953	Sportivo Luqueño
1954	Cerro Porteño
1955	Libertad
1956	Olimpia
1957	Olimpia
1958	Olimpia
1959	Olimpia
1960	Olimpia
1961	Cerro Porteño
1962	Olimpia
1963	Cerro Porteño
1964	Guaraní
1965	Olimpia
1966	Cerro Porteño
1967	Guaraní
1968	Olimpia
1969	Guaraní
1970	Cerro Porteño
1971	Olimpia
1972	Cerro Porteño
1973	Cerro Porteño
1974	Cerro Porteño
1975	Olimpia
1976	Libertad
1977	Cerro Porteño
1978	Olimpia
1979	Olimpia
1980	Olimpia
1981	Olimpia
1982	Olimpia
1983	Olimpia
1984	Guaraní
1985	Olimpia
1986	Sol de América
1987	Cerro Porteño
1988	Olimpia
1989	Olimpia
1990	Cerro Porteño
1991	Sol de América
1992	Cerro Porteño
1993	Olimpia
1994	Cerro Porteño
1995	Olimpia
1996	Cerro Porteño

Year	Champion		
1997	Olimpia		
1998	Olimpia		
1999	Olimpia		
2000	Olimpia		
2001	Cerro Porteño		
2002	Libertad		
2003	Libertad		
2004	Cerro Porteño		
2005	Cerro Porteño		
2006	Libertad		
2007	Libertad	**Clausura**	
2008	Libertad	Libertad	
2009	Cerro Porteño	Nacional	
2010	Guaraní	Libertad	
2011	Nacional	Olimpia	

PER – PERU

Year Champions

Year	Champions
1926	Sport Progreso
1927	Alianza
1928	Alianza
1929	Universitario
1930	Atlético Chalaco
1931	Alianza
1932	Alianza
1933	Alianza
1934	Universitario
1935	Sport Boys
1936	
1937	Sport Boys
1938	Deportivo Municipal
1939	Universitario
1940	Deportivo Municipal
1941	Universitario
1942	Sport Boys
1943	Deportivo Municipal
1944	Mariscal Sucre
1945	Universitario
1946	Universitario
1947	Atlético Chalaco
1948	Alianza
1949	Universitario
1950	Deportivo Municipal
1951	Sport Boys
1952	Alianza
1953	Mariscal Sucre
1954	Alianza
1955	Alianza
1956	Sporting Cristal
1957	Centro Iqueño
1958	Sport Boys
1959	Universitario
1960	Universitario
1961	Sporting Cristal
1962	Alianza
1963	Alianza
1964	Universitario
1965	Alianza
1966	Universitario
1967	Universitario
1968	Sporting Cristal
1969	Universitario
1970	Sporting Cristal
1971	Universitario

Year	Champion
1972	Sporting Cristal
1973	Defensor Lima
1974	Universitario
1975	Alianza
1976	Unión Huaral
1977	Alianza
1978	Alianza
1979	Sporting Cristal
1980	Sporting Cristal
1981	Mariano Melgar
1982	Universitario
1983	Sporting Cristal
1984	Sport Boys
1985	Universitario
1986	Colegio San Agustín
1987	Universitario
1988	Sporting Cristal
1989	Union Huaral
1990	Universitario
1991	Sporting Cristal
1992	Universitario
1993	Universitario
1994	Sporting Cristal
1995	Sporting Cristal
1996	Sporting Cristal
1997	Alianza Lima
1998	Universitario
1999	Universitario
2000	Universitario
2001	Alianza Lima
2002	Sporting Cristal
2003	Alianza Lima
2004	Alianza Lima
2005	Sporting Cristal
2006	Alianza Lima
2007	Uni'dad San Martín
2008	Uni'dad San Martín
2009	Universitario
2010	Uni'dad San Martín
2011	Juan Aurich

PHI – PHILIPPINES

Year Champions

Year	Champions
1911	All Manila
1912	Bohemian Club
1913	Bohemian Club
1914	Nomads SC
1915	Bohemian Club
1916	Bohemian Club
1917	Bohemian Club
1918	Bohemian Club
1919	
1920	Bohemian Club
1921	Bohemian Club
1922	Bohemian Club
1923	Ferencváros
1924	Cantabria
1925	International
1926	Ateneo
1927	Bohemian Club
1928	San Beda College
1929	Peña Iberica

Year		
1930	San Beda AC	
1931	San Beda AC	
1932	San Beda AC	
1933	San Beda AC	
1934	University of Santo Tomas	
1935	Malaya Command	
1981	CDCP Manila	
1982	Navy	
1983	Air Force	
1984	San Miguel Corp	
1985	Air Force	
1986		
1987	Dumaguete	
1988	Lhuillier Jewellers	
1989	Air Force	
1990	Bacalod FC	
1991	Navy	
1992		
1993		
1994	Pasay City	
1995	Makati	
1996		
1997	Air Force	
1998	NCR South	
1999	NCR B	
2000		
2001		
2002		
2003		
2004	NCR	
2005	NCR	
2006	Negros Occidental	
2007	NCR	
		Cup Winners
2008	Army	
2009		Air Force
2010	Air Force	Global
2011	Air Force	Air Force

PLE – PALESTINE

Year	Championship	FA Cup
1996	Rafah Services	
1997	Shabab Al-Am'ari	Rafah Services
1998	Khadamat Rafah	
1999		
2000		
2001		
2002	Al Aqsa	
2003		
2004		
2005		
2006	West Bank	
2007	Taraji Wadi Al Neiss	Al Bireh
2008		Thagafi Tulkarm
2009	Taraji Wadi Al Neiss	
2010	Jabal Mukabar	Taraji Wadi Al Neiss
2011	Shabab Al-Am'ari	

PNG – PAPUA NEW GUINEA

Year	National
1976	Mopi
1977	Germania
1978	Tarangau
1979	Tarangau
1980	
1981	Mopi
1982	Buresong
1983	
1984	Buresong
1985	
1986	Guria
1987	
1988	
1989	
1990	
1991	
1992	
1993	
1994	
1995	ICF University
1996	ICF University
1997	ICF University
1998	ICF University
1999	Guria
2000	Unitech
2001	Sobou
2002	Sobou
2003	Sobou
2004	Sobou
2005	NSL — Sobou
2006	Hekari United — University PM
2007	
2008	Hekari United — Sunammad
2009	Hekari United
2010	Hekari United
2011	Hekari United

POL – POLAND

Year	Champions	Cup Winners
1921	Cracovia	
1922	Pogon Lwow	
1923	Pogon Lwow	
1924	-	
1925	Pogon Lwow	
1926	Pogon Lwow	Wisla Kraków
1927	Wisla Kraków	
1928	Wisla Kraków	
1929	Warta Poznan	
1930	Cracovia	
1931	Garbarnia Krakow	
1932	Cracovia	
1933	Ruch Chorzów	
1934	Ruch Chorzów	
1935	Ruch Chorzów	
1936	Ruch Chorzów	
1937	Cracovia	
1938	Ruch Chorzów	
1939		
1940		
1941		
1942		
1943		
1944		
1945		
1946	Polonia Warszawa	
1947	Warta Poznan	
1948	Cracovia	
1949	Gwardia Kraków	
1950	Gwardia Kraków	
1951	Gwardia Kraków	Unia Chorzów
1952	Unia Chorzów	Kolejarz Warszawa
1953	Unia Chorzów	
1954	Ogniwo Bytom	Gwardia Warszawa
1955	CWKS Warszawa	CWKS Warszawa
1956	CWKS Warszawa	CWKS Warszawa
1957	Górnik Zabrze	LKS Lódz
1958	LKS Lódz	
1959	Górnik Zabrze	
1960	Ruch Chorzów	
1961	Górnik Zabrze	
1962	Polonia Bytom	Zaglebie Sosnowiec
1963	Górnik Zabrze	Zaglebie Sosnowiec
1964	Górnik Zabrze	Legia Warszawa
1965	Górnik Zabrze	Górnik Zabrze
1966	Górnik Zabrze	Legia Warszawa
1967	Górnik Zabrze	Wisla Kraków
1968	Ruch Chorzów	Górnik Zabrze
1969	Legia Warszawa	Górnik Zabrze
1970	Legia Warszawa	Górnik Zabrze
1971	Górnik Zabrze	Górnik Zabrze
1972	Górnik Zabrze	Górnik Zabrze
1973	Stal Mielec	Legia Warszawa
1974	Ruch Chorzów	Ruch Chorzów
1975	Ruch Chorzów	Stal Rzeszów
1976	Stal Mielec	Slask Wroclaw
1977	Slask Wroclaw	Zaglebie Sosnowiec
1978	Wisla Kraków	Zaglebie Sosnowiec
1979	Ruch Chorzów	Arka Gdynia
1980	Szombierki Bytom	Legia Warszawa
1981	Widzew Lódz	Legia Warszawa
1982	Widzew Lódz	Lech Poznan
1983	Lech Poznan	Lechia Gdansk
1984	Lech Poznan	Lech Poznan
1985	Górnik Zabrze	Widzew Lódz
1986	Górnik Zabrze	GKS Katowice
1987	Górnik Zabrze	Slask Wroclaw
1988	Górnik Zabrze	Lech Poznan
1989	Ruch Chorzów	Legia Warszawa
1990	Lech Poznan	Legia Warszawa
1991	Zaglebie Lubin	GKS Katowice
1992	Lech Poznan	Miedz Legnica
1993	Legia Warszawa	GKS Katowice
1994	Legia Warszawa	Legia Warszawa
1995	Legia Warszawa	Legia Warszawa
1996	Widzew Lódz	Ruch Chorzów
1997	Widzew Lódz	Legia Warszawa
1998	LKS Lódz	Amica Wronki
1999	Wisla Kraków	Amica Wronki
2000	Polonia Warszawa	Amica Wronki
2001	Wisla Kraków	Polonia Warszawa
2002	Legia Warszawa	Wisla Kraków
2003	Wisla Kraków	Wisla Kraków
2004	Wisla Kraków	Lech Poznan
2005	Wisla Kraków	Groclin Grodzisk
2006	Legia Warszawa	Wisla Plock
2007	Zagliebie Lubin	Groclin Grodzisk
2008	Wisla Kraków	Legia Warszawa
2009	Wisla Kraków	Lech Poznan
2010	Lech Poznan	Jagellonia Bialystok
2011	Wisla Kraków	Legia Warszawa

POR – PORTUGAL

Year	Champions	Cup Winners
1922	FC Porto	
1923	Sporting CP	
1924	SC Olhanense	
1925	FC Porto	
1926	CS Marítimo	
1927	OS Belenenses	
1928	Carcavelinhos	
1929	OS Belenenses	
1930	Benfica	
1931	Benfica	
1932	FC Porto	
1933	OS Belenenses	
1934	Sporting CP	
1935	FC Porto	Benfica
1936	Benfica	Sporting CP
1937	Benfica	FC Porto
1938	Benfica	Sporting CP
1939	FC Porto	Académica Coimbra
1940	FC Porto	Benfica
1941	Sporting CP	Sporting CP
1942	Benfica	OS Belenenses
1943	Benfica	Benfica
1944	Sporting CP	Benfica
1945	Benfica	Sporting CP
1946	OS Belenenses	Sporting CP
1947	Sporting CP	
1948	Sporting CP	Sporting CP
1949	Sporting CP	Benfica
1950	Benfica	
1951	Sporting CP	Benfica
1952	Sporting CP	Benfica
1953	Sporting CP	Benfica
1954	Sporting CP	Sporting CP
1955	Benfica	Benfica
1956	FC Porto	FC Porto
1957	Benfica	Benfica
1958	Sporting CP	FC Porto
1959	FC Porto	Benfica
1960	Benfica	OS Belenenses
1961	Benfica	Leixoes SC
1962	Sporting CP	Benfica
1963	Benfica	Sporting CP
1964	Benfica	Benfica
1965	Benfica	Vitória Setúbal
1966	Sporting CP	Sporting Braga
1967	Benfica	Vitória Setúbal
1968	Benfica	FC Porto
1969	Benfica	Benfica
1970	Sporting CP	Benfica
1971	Benfica	Sporting CP
1972	Benfica	Benfica
1973	Benfica	Sporting CP
1974	Sporting CP	Sporting CP
1975	Benfica	Boavista FC
1976	Benfica	Boavista FC
1977	Benfica	FC Porto
1978	FC Porto	Sporting CP
1979	FC Porto	Boavista FC
1980	Sporting CP	Benfica
1981	Benfica	Benfica
1982	Sporting CP	Sporting CP
1983	Benfica	Benfica
1984	Benfica	FC Porto
1985	FC Porto	Benfica

POR – PORTUGAL

Year	Champions	Cup Winners
1986	FC Porto	Benfica
1987	Benfica	Benfica
1988	FC Porto	FC Porto
1989	Benfica	OS Belenenses
1990	FC Porto	Estrela Amadora
1991	Benfica	FC Porto
1992	FC Porto	Boavista
1993	FC Porto	Benfica
1994	Benfica	FC Porto
1995	FC Porto	Sporting CP
1996	FC Porto	Benfica
1997	FC Porto	Boavista
1998	FC Porto	FC Porto
1999	FC Porto	Beira-Mar
2000	Sporting CP	FC Porto
2001	Boavista	FC Porto
2002	Sporting CP	Sporting CP
2003	FC Porto	FC Porto
2004	FC Porto	Benfica
2005	Benfica	Vitória FC Setúbal
2006	FC Porto	FC Porto
2007	FC Porto	Sporting CP
2008	FC Porto	Sporting CP
2009	FC Porto	FC Porto
2010	Benfica	FC Porto
2011	FC Porto	FC Porto

POR – PORTUGAL

Year	League Cup
2008	Vitória FC Setúbal
2009	Benfica
2010	Benfica
2011	Benfica

PRK – KOREA DPR

Year	Champions	Cup Winners
1985	April 25	
1986	April 25	
1987	April 25	
1988	April 25	
1989	Chadongcha	
1990	April 25	
1991	Pyongyang Club	
1992	April 25	
1993	April 25	
1994	April 25	
1995	April 25	
1996	Kihwancha	
1997	Kihwancha	
1998	Kihwancha	
1999	Kihwancha	
2000	Kihwancha	
2001	Amrokgang SC	
2002	April 25	
2003	April 25	
2004	Pyongyang City SC	
2005	Pyongyang City SC	
2006	Amrokgang SC	
2007	Pyongyang City SC	
2008	Amrokgang SC	
2009	Pyongyang City SC	
2010		
2011		

PUR – PUERTO RICO

Year	Tourn' Nacional	
1996	Liga Mayor	Acad. Quintana
1997	Maunabo Leones	Acad. Quintana
1998		Acad. Quintana
1999	Puerto Rico Islanders	Nacional Carolina
2000	Vaqueros Bayamón	Acad. Quintana
2001	Puerto Rico Islanders	Acad. Quintana
2002	Vaqueros Bayamón	Acad. Quintana
2003	Sporting Carolina	
2004	Sp. San Lorenzo	Camp' Nacional
2005	Real Quintana	Fraigcomar
2006		Fraigcomar
2007	PRSL	Fraigcomar
2008	Sevilla	
2009	Bayamón	
2010	River Plate	
2011	Leones de Ponce	

QAT – QATAR

Year	Champions	Emir Cup
1964	Al Maref	
1965	Al Maref	
1966	Al Maref	
1967	Al Oruba	
1968	Al Oruba	
1969	Al Oruba	
1970	Al Oruba	
1971	Al Oruba	
1972	Al Sadd	
1973	Al Esteqlal	Al Ahli
1974	Al Sadd	Al Esteqlal
1975		Al Sadd
1976	Al Rayyan	Al Esteqlal
1977	Al Esteqlal	Al Sadd
1978	Al Rayyan	Al Arabi
1979	Al Sadd	Al Arabi
1980	Al Sadd	Al Arabi
1981	Al Sadd	Al Ahli
1982	Al Rayyan	Al Sadd
1983	Al Arabi	Al Arabi
1984	Al Rayyan	Al Arabi
1985	Al Arabi	Al Sadd
1986	Al Rayyan	Al Sadd
1987	Al Sadd	Al Ahli
1988	Al Sadd	Al Sadd
1989	Al Sadd	Al Arabi
1990	Al Rayyan	Al Arabi
1991	Al Arabi	Al Sadd
1992	Al Ittihad	Al Ahli
1993	Al Arabi	Al Arabi
1994	Al Arabi	Al Sadd
1995	Al Rayyan	Al Ittihad
1996	Al Arabi	Al Ittihad
1997	Al Ittihad	Al Ittihad
1998	Al Ittihad	Al Ittihad
1999	Al Wakra	Al Rayyan
2000	Al Sadd	Al Sadd
2001	Al Wakra	Qatar SC
2002	Al Ittihad	Al Ittihad
2003	Qatar SC	Al Sadd
2004	Al Sadd	Al Rayyan
2005	Al Gharafa	Al Sadd
2006	Al Sadd	Al Rayyan

Year		
2007	Al Sadd	Al Sadd
2008	Al Gharafa	Umm Salal
2009	Al Gharafa	Al Gharafa
2010	Al Gharafa	Al Rayyan
2011	Lekwiya	Al Rayyan

QAT – QATAR

Year	Sheikh Jassim	Crown Prince
1978	Al Sadd	
1979	Al Sadd	
1980	Al Sadd	
1981	Al Arabi	
1982	Al Sadd	
1983	Al Sadd	
1984	Qatar SC	
1985	Qatar SC	
1986	Al Sadd	
1987	Al Sadd	
1988	Qatar SC	
1989	Al Sadd	
1990	Al Wakra	
1991	Al Sadd	
1992	Al Wakra	
1993	Al Rayyan	
1994		
1995	Al Arabi	Al Rayyan
1996	Qatar SC	Al Rayyan
1997	Al Shamal	Al Arabi
1998	Al Sadd	Al Sadd
1999	Al Wakra	Al Wakra
2000	Al Sadd	Al Ittihad
2001	Al Rayyan	Al Rayyan
2002	Al Sadd	Qatar SC
2003	Khor	Al Sadd
2004	Al Shabab	Qatar SC
2005	Al Wakra	Khor
2006	Al Gharafa	Al Sadd
2007	Al Sadd	Al Sadd
2008	Al Gharafa	Al Sadd
2009	Al Arabi	Qatar SC
2010	Umm Salal	Al Gharafa
2011	Al Arabi	Al Gharafa
2012	Al Arabi	

ROU – ROMANIA

Year	Champions	Cup Winners
1921	Chinezul Timisoara	
1922	Chinezul Timisoara	
1923	Chinezul Timisoara	
1924	Chinezul Timisoara	
1925	Chinezul Timisoara	
1926	Chinezul Timisoara	
1927	Coltea Brasov	
1928	Venus Bucuresti	
1929	Juventus Bucuresti	
1930	UDR Resita	
1931	Venus Bucuresti	
1932	Ripensia Timisoara	
1933	Venus Bucuresti	
1934		Ripensia Timisoara
1935	Ripensia Timisoara	CFR Bucuresti
1936	Ripensia Timisoara	Ripensia Timisoara
1937	Venus Bucuresti	Rapid Bucuresti
1938	Ripensia Timisoara	Rapid Bucuresti
1939	Venus Bucuresti	Rapid Bucuresti
1940	Venus Bucuresti	Rapid Bucuresti
1941	Unirea Tricolor	Rapid Bucuresti
1942		Rapid Bucuresti
1943		Tirnu Severin
1944		
1945		
1946		
1947	IT Arad	
1948	IT Arad	IT Arad
1949	ICO Oradea	CSCA Bucuresti
1950	Flamura Rosie	CCA Bucuresti
1951	CCA Bucuresti	CCA Bucuresti
1952	CCA Bucuresti	CCA Bucuresti
1953	CCA Bucuresti	Flamura Rosie
1954	Flamura Rosie	Metalul Resita
1955	Dinamo Bucuresti	CCA Bucuresti
1956	CCA Bucuresti	Progresul Oradea
1957	-	-
1958	Petrolul Ploiesti	Stiinta Timisoara
1959	Petrolul Ploiesti	Dinamo Bucuresti
1960	CCA Bucuresti	Ariesul Turda
1961	CCA Bucuresti	Progresul Bucuresti
1962	Dinamo Bucuresti	Steaua Bucuresti
1963	Dinamo Bucuresti	Petrolul Ploiesti
1964	Dinamo Bucuresti	Dinamo Bucuresti
1965	Dinamo Bucuresti	Stiinta Cluj
1966	Petrolul Ploiesti	Steaua Bucuresti
1967	Rapid Bucuresti	Steaua Bucuresti
1968	Steaua Bucuresti	Dinamo Bucuresti
1969	UT Arad	Steaua Bucuresti
1970	UT Arad	Steaua Bucuresti
1971	Dinamo Bucuresti	Steaua Bucuresti
1972	FC Arges Pitesti	Rapid Bucuresti
1973	Dinamo Bucuresti	Chimia Vilcea
1974	Universit. Craiova	Jiul Petrosani
1975	Dinamo Bucuresti	Rapid Bucuresti
1976	Steaua Bucuresti	Steaua Bucuresti
1977	Dinamo Bucuresti	Universit. Craiova
1978	Steaua Bucuresti	Universit. Craiova
1979	FC Arges Pitesti	Steaua Bucuresti
1980	Universit. Craiova	Politehn. Timisoara
1981	Universit. Craiova	Universit. Craiova
1982	Dinamo Bucuresti	Dinamo Bucuresti
1983	Dinamo Bucuresti	Universit. Craiova
1984	Dinamo Bucuresti	Dinamo Bucuresti
1985	Steaua Bucuresti	Steaua Bucuresti
1986	Steaua Bucuresti	Dinamo Bucuresti
1987	Steaua Bucuresti	Steaua Bucuresti
1988	Steaua Bucuresti	Steaua Bucuresti
1989	Steaua Bucuresti	Steaua Bucuresti
1990	Dinamo Bucuresti	Dinamo Bucuresti
1991	Universit. Craiova	Universit. Craiova
1992	Dinamo Bucuresti	Steaua Bucuresti
1993	Steaua Bucuresti	Universit. Craiova
1994	Steaua Bucuresti	Gloria Bistrita
1995	Steaua Bucuresti	Petrolul Ploiesti
1996	Steaua Bucuresti	Steaua Bucuresti
1997	Steaua Bucuresti	Steaua Bucuresti
1998	Steaua Bucuresti	Rapid Bucuresti
1999	Rapid Bucuresti	Steaua Bucuresti
2000	Dinamo Bucuresti	Dinamo Bucuresti
2001	Steaua Bucuresti	Dinamo Bucuresti
2002	Dinamo Bucuresti	Rapid Bucuresti
2003	Rapid Bucuresti	Dinamo Bucuresti
2004	Dinamo Bucuresti	Dinamo Bucuresti
2005	Steaua Bucuresti	Dinamo Bucuresti
2006	Steaua Bucuresti	Rapid Bucuresti
2007	Dinamo Bucuresti	Rapid Bucuresti
2008	CFR 1907 Cluj	CFR 1907 Cluj
2009	Unirea Urziceni	CFR 1907 Cluj
2010	CFR 1907 Cluj	CFR 1907 Cluj
2011	Otelul Galati	Steaua Bucuresti

RSA – SOUTH AFRICA

Year	Champions	Cup Winners
1971	Orlando Pirates	Kaiser Chiefs
1972	AmaZulu	Kaiser Chiefs
1973	Orlando Pirates	Orlando Pirates
1974	Kaizer Chiefs	Orlando Pirates
1975	Orlando Pirates	Orlando Pirates
1976	Orlando Pirates	Kaiser Chiefs
1977	Kaizer Chiefs	Kaizer Chiefs
1978	Lusitano	Wits University
1979	Kaizer Chiefs	Kaizer Chiefs
1980	Highlands Park	Orlando Pirates
1981	Kaizer Chiefs	Kaizer Chiefs
1982	Durban City	Kaizer Chiefs
1983	Durban City	Moroka Swallows
1984	Kaizer Chiefs	Kaizer Chiefs
1985	Bush Bucks	Bloemfontein Celtic
1986	Rangers	Mamelodi Sundowns
1987	Jomo Cosmos	Kaizer Chiefs
1988	Mamelodi Sundowns	Orlando Pirates
1989	Kaizer Chiefs	Moroka Swallows
1990	Mamelodi Sundowns	Jomo Cosmos
1991	Kaizer Chiefs	Moroka Swallows
1992	Kaizer Chiefs	Kaizer Chiefs
1993	Mamelodi Sundowns	Witbank Aces
1994	Orlando Pirates	Vaal Professionals
1995	Cape Town Spurs	Cape Town Spurs
1996		
1997	Manning Rangers	Orlando Pirates
1998	Mamelodi Sundowns	Mamelodi Sundowns
1999	Mamelodi Sundowns	SuperSport United
2000	Mamelodi Sundowns	Kaiser Chiefs
2001	Orlando Pirates	Santos Cape Town
2002	Santos Cape Town	
2003	Orlando Pirates	Santos Cape Town
2004	Kaizer Chiefs	Moroka Swallows
2005	Kaizer Chiefs	SuperSport United
2006	Mamelodi Sundowns	Kaiser Chiefs
2007	Mamelodi Sundowns	Ajax Cape Town
2008	SuperSport United	Mamelodi Sundowns
2009	SuperSport United	Moroka Swallows
2010	SuperSport United	Wits University
2011	Orlando Pirates	Orlando Pirates

RSA – SOUTH AFRICA

Year	Super 8
1972	Orlando Pirates
1973	Orlando Pirates
1974	Kaizer Chiefs
1975	Moroka Swallows
1976	Kaizer Chiefs
1977	Kaizer Chiefs
1978	Orlando Pirates
1979	Moroka Swallows

Year		
1980	Witbank Black Aces	
1981	Kaizer Chiefs	League Cup
1982	Kaizer Chiefs	Arcadia
1983	Orlando Pirates	Kaizer Chiefs
1984	Wits University	Kaizer Chiefs
1985	Kaizer Chiefs	Wits University
1986	Arcadia	Kaizer Chiefs
1987	Kaizer Chiefs	Bush Bucks
1988	Mamelodi Sundowns	Kaizer Chiefs
1989	Kaizer Chiefs	Kaizer Chiefs
1990	Mamelodi Sundowns	Mamelodi Sundowns
1991	Kaizer Chiefs	Dynamos
1992	Kaizer Chiefs	Amazulu
1993	Orlando Pirates	Bush Bucks
1994	Kaizer Chiefs	Qwa Qwa Stars
1995	Wits University	Wits University
1996	Orlando Pirates	Bush Bucks
1997		Kaizer Chiefs
1998		Kaizer Chiefs
1999		Mamelodi Sundowns
2000	Orlando Pirates	Ajax Cape Town
2001	Kaizer Chiefs	Kaizer Chiefs
2002	Santos	Jomo Cosmos
2003	Jomo Cosmos	Kaizer Chiefs
2004	SuperSport United	Kaizer Chiefs
2005	Bloemfontein Celtic	Jomo Cosmos
2006	Kaizer Chiefs	Silver Stars
2007	Mamelodi Sundowns	Kaizer Chiefs
2008	Kaizer Chiefs	Ajax Cape Town
2009	Golden Arrows	
2010	Orlando Pirates	Kaizer Chiefs
2011		

RSA - SOUTH AFRICA

Year	SASL	SASL/FPL Cup
1961	Transvaal United	Cape Ramblers
1962	Avalon Athletic	Avalon Athletic
1963	Avalon Athletic	Avalon Athletic
1964	Black Swallows	
1965	Moroka Swallows	
1966	Maritzburg City	
1967	Verulam Suburbs	
1968		
1969		Aces United
1970	FPL	Verulam Suburbs
1971	Cape Town Spurs	Maritzburg City
1972	Glenville	Glenville
1973	Cape Town Spurs	Verulam Suburbs
1974	Cape Town Spurs	Berea
1975	Berea	Cape Town Spurs
1976	Cape Town Spurs	Berea
1977	Swaraj United	Manning Rangers
1978	Durban City	Durban City
1979	Cape Town Spurs	Glenville
1980	Glenville	Cape Town Spurs
1981	Cape Town Spurs	Vereeniging UB
1982	Glendene	Bosmont Chelsea
1983	Lightbody's Santos	Martitzburg United
1984	Lightbody's Santos	Tongaat Crusaders
1985	Swaraj United	Lightbody's Santos
1986	Lightbody's Santos	Real Taj
1987	Lightbody's Santos	Jakes Autolot
1988	Lightbody's Santos	Lightbody's Santos
1989	Battswood	Battswood
1990	Lightbody's Santos	Lightbody's Santos

RSA - SOUTH AFRICA

Year	NFL	NFL Cup
1959	Durban City	Rangers
1960	Highlands Park	Durban City
1961	Durban City	Highlands Park
1962	Highlands Park	Durban City
1963	Addington	Addington
1964	Highlands Park	Durban City
1965	Highlands Park	Highlands Park
1966	Highlands Park	Highlands Park
1967	Port Elizabeth City	Highlands Park
1968	Highlands Park	Durban City
1969	Durban Spurs	Maritzburg
1970	Durban City	Cape Town City
1971	Hellenic	Cape Town City
1972	Durban City	Durban United
1973	Cape Town City	Highlands Park
1974	Arcadia Shepherds	Arcadia Shepherds
1975	Highlands Park	Highlands Park
1976	Cape Town City	Cape Town City
1977	Highlands Park	Lusitano

RUS - RUSSIA

Year	Champions	Cup Winners
1992	Spartak Moskva	
1993	Spartak Moskva	Torpedo Moskva
1994	Spartak Moskva	Spartak Moskva
1995	Spartak Vladikavkaz	Dinamo Moskva
1996	Spartak Moskva	Lokomotiv Moskva
1997	Spartak Moskva	Lokomotiv Moskva
1998	Spartak Moskva	Spartak Moskva
1999	Spartak Moskva	Zenit St Petersburg
2000	Spartak Moskva	Lokomotiv Moskva
2001	Spartak Moskva	Lokomotiv Moskva
2002	Lokomotiv Moskva	CSKA Moskva
2003	CSKA Moskva	Spartak Moskva
2004	Lokomotiv Moskva	Terek Groznyi
2005	CSKA Moskva	CSKA Moskva
2006	CSKA Moskva	CSKA Moskva
2007	Zenit St Petersburg	Lokomotiv Moskva
2008	Rubin Kazan	CSKA Moskva
2009	Rubin Kazan	CSKA Moskva
2010	Zenit St Petersburg	Zenit St Petersburg
2011		CSKA Moskva

SOVIET UNION

Year	Champions	Cup Winners
1936	Dynamo Moskva	Lokomotiv Moskva
1936	Spartak Moskva	
1937	Dynamo Moskva	Dynamo Moskva
1938	Spartak Moskva	Spartak Moskva
1939	Spartak Moskva	Spartak Moskva
1940	Dynamo Moskva	
1941		
1942		
1943		
1944		Zenit Leningrad
1945	Dynamo Moskva	CDKA Moskva
1946	CDKA Moskva	Spartak Moskva
1947	CDKA Moskva	Spartak Moskva
1948	CDKA Moskva	CDKA Moskva
1949	Dynamo Moskva	Torpedo Moskva
1950	CDKA Moskva	Spartak Moskva
1951	CDSA Moskva	CDSA Moskva
1952	Spartak Moskva	Torpedo Moskva
1953	Spartak Moskva	Dynamo Moskva
1954	Dynamo Moskva	Dynamo Kiev
1955	Dynamo Moskva	CDSA Moskva
1956	Spartak Moskva	
1957	Dynamo Moskva	Lokomotiv Moskva
1958	Spartak Moskva	Spartak Moskva
1959	Dynamo Moskva	
1960	Torpedo Moskva	Torpedo Moskva
1961	Dynamo Kiev	Shachter Donetsk
1962	Spartak Moskva	Shachter Donetsk
1963	Dynamo Moskva	Spartak Moskva
1964	Dynamo Tbilisi	Dynamo Kiev
1965	Torpedo Moskva	Spartak Moskva
1966	Dynamo Kiev	Dynamo Kiev
1967	Dynamo Kiev	Dynamo Moskva
1968	Dynamo Kiev	Torpedo Moskva
1969	Spartak Moskva	SKA Karpati Lvov
1970	CSKA Moskva	Dynamo Moskva
1971	Dynamo Kiev	Spartak Moskva
1972	Zarja Vorosch'grad	Torpedo Moskva
1973	Ararat Yerevan	Ararat Yerevan
1974	Dynamo Kiev	Dynamo Kiev
1975	Dynamo Kiev	Ararat Yerevan
1976	Dynamo Moskva	Dynamo Tbilisi
1976	Torpedo Moskva	Dynamo Moskva
1977	Dynamo Kiev	Dynamo Kiev
1978	Dynamo Tbilisi	Dynamo Tbilisi
1979	Spartak Moskva	Shachter Donetsk
1980	Dynamo Kiev	SKA Rostov-na-Donu
1981	Dynamo Kiev	Dynamo Kiev
1982	Dynamo Minsk	Shachter Donetsk
1983	Dnepr D'propetrovsk	Dynamo Moskva
1984	Zenit Leningrad	Dynamo Kiev
1985	Dynamo Kiev	Torpedo Moskva
1986	Dynamo Kiev	Dynamo Kiev
1987	Spartak Moskva	Metalist Kharkov
1988	Dnepr D'propetrovsk	Dnepr D'propetrovsk
1989	Spartak Moskva	Dynamo Kiev
1990	Dynamo Kiev	CSKA Moskva
1991	CSKA Moskva	Spartak Moskva

RWA - RWANDA

Year	Champions	Cup Winners
1975	Rayon Sport	Kiyovu Sports
1976		Rayon Sport
1977		
1978		Mukura Victory
1979		Rayon Sport
1980	Panthères Noires	Rayon Sport
1981	Rayon Sport	Panthères Noires
1982		Rayon Sport
1983	Kiyovu Sports	Panthères Noires
1984	Panthères Noires	Panthères Noires
1985	Panthères Noires	Kiyovu Sports
1986	Panthères Noires	Mukura Victory
1987	Panthères Noires	Panthères Noires
1988	Mukungwa	Etincelles
1989	Mukungwa	Rayon Sport
1990		Mukura Victory
1991		
1992	Kiyovu Sports	Mukura Victory
1993	Kiyovu Sports	Rayon Sport
1994		

Year	Champions	Cup Winners
1995	APR FC	APR FC
1996	APR FC	APR FC
1997	Rayon Sport	Rwanda FC
1998	Rayon Sport	Rayon Sport
1999	APR FC	APR FC
2000	APR FC	APR FC
2001	APR FC	Les Citadins
2002	Rayon Sport	APR FC
2003	APR FC	Rayon Sport
2004	Rayon Sport	
2005	APR FC	Rayon Sport
2006	APR FC	APR FC
2007	APR FC	APR FC
2008	ATRACO	APR FC
2009	APR FC	ATRACO
2010	APR FC	APR FC
2011	APR FC	APR FC

SAM – SAMOA

Year	Champions	Cup Winners
1979	Vaivase-Tai	
1980	Vaivase-Tai	
1981	Vaivase-Tai & SCOPA	
1982	Alafua	
1983	Vaivase-Tai	
1984	Kiwi	
1985	Kiwi	
1986		
1987		
1988		
1989		
1990		
1991		
1992		
1993		
1994		
1995		
1996		
1997	Kiwi	
1998	Vaivase-Tai	
1999	Moataa	
2000	Titavi	
2001	Goldstar Sogi	
2002	Strickland Brothers	
2003	Strickland Brothers	
2004	Strickland Brothers	
2005	Tuanaimoto Breeze	
2006	Vaivase-Tai	
2007	Cruz Azul	
2008	Sinamoga	
2009		
2010	Moaula United	Kiwi
2011	Kiwi	Moaula United

SCO – SCOTLAND

Year	Champions	Cup Winners
1874		Queen's Park
1875		Queen's Park
1876		Queen's Park
1877		Vale of Levan
1878		Vale of Levan
1879		Vale of Levan
1880		Queen's Park
1881		Queen's Park
1882		Queen's Park
1883		Dumbarton
1884		Queen's Park
1885		Renton
1886		Queen's Park
1887		Hibernian
1888		Renton
1889		Third Lanark
1890		Queen's Park
1891	Dumbarton/Rangers	Heart of Midlothian
1892	Dumbarton	Celtic
1893	Celtic	Queen's Park
1894	Celtic	Rangers
1895	Heart of Midlothian	St. Bernard's
1896	Celtic	Heart of Midlothian
1897	Heart of Midlothian	Rangers
1898	Celtic	Rangers
1899	Rangers	Celtic
1900	Rangers	Celtic
1901	Rangers	Heart of Midlothian
1902	Rangers	Hibernian
1903	Hibernian	Rangers
1904	Third Lanark	Celtic
1905	Celtic	Third Lanark
1906	Celtic	Heart of Midlothian
1907	Celtic	Celtic
1908	Celtic	Celtic
1909	Celtic	Cup witheld. Celtic
1910	Celtic	Dundee
1911	Rangers	Celtic
1912	Rangers	Celtic
1913	Rangers	Falkirk
1914	Celtic	Celtic
1915	Celtic	
1916	Celtic	
1917	Celtic	
1918	Rangers	
1919	Celtic	
1920	Rangers	Kilmarnock
1921	Rangers	Partick Thistle
1922	Celtic	Morton
1923	Rangers	Celtic
1924	Rangers	Airdrieonians
1925	Rangers	Celtic
1926	Celtic	St. Mirren
1927	Rangers	Celtic
1928	Rangers	Rangers
1929	Rangers	Kilmarnock
1930	Rangers	Rangers
1931	Rangers	Celtic
1932	Motherwell	Rangers
1933	Rangers	Celtic
1934	Rangers	Rangers
1935	Rangers	Rangers
1936	Celtic	Rangers
1937	Rangers	Celtic
1938	Celtic	East Fife
1939	Rangers	Clyde
1940		
1941		
1942		
1943		
1944		
1945		
1946		
1947	Rangers	Aberdeen
1948	Hibernian	Rangers
1949	Rangers	Rangers
1950	Rangers	Rangers
1951	Hibernian	Celtic
1952	Hibernian	Motherwell
1953	Rangers	Rangers
1954	Celtic	Celtic
1955	Aberdeen	Clyde
1956	Rangers	Heart of Midlothian
1957	Rangers	Falkirk
1958	Heart of Midlothian	Clyde
1959	Rangers	St. Mirren
1960	Heart of Midlothian	Rangers
1961	Rangers	Dunfermline Ath.
1962	Dundee	Rangers
1963	Rangers	Rangers
1964	Rangers	Rangers
1965	Kilmarnock	Celtic
1966	Celtic	Rangers
1967	Celtic	Celtic
1968	Celtic	Dunfermline Ath.
1969	Celtic	Celtic
1970	Celtic	Aberdeen
1971	Celtic	Celtic
1972	Celtic	Celtic
1973	Celtic	Rangers
1974	Celtic	Celtic
1975	Rangers	Celtic
1976	Rangers	Rangers
1977	Celtic	Celtic
1978	Rangers	Rangers
1979	Celtic	Rangers
1980	Aberdeen	Celtic
1981	Celtic	Rangers
1982	Celtic	Aberdeen
1983	Dundee United	Aberdeen
1984	Aberdeen	Aberdeen
1985	Aberdeen	Celtic
1986	Celtic	Aberdeen
1987	Rangers	St. Mirren
1988	Celtic	Celtic
1989	Rangers	Celtic
1990	Rangers	Aberdeen
1991	Rangers	Motherwell
1992	Rangers	Rangers
1993	Rangers	Rangers
1994	Rangers	Dundee United
1995	Rangers	Celtic
1996	Rangers	Rangers
1997	Rangers	Kilmarnock
1998	Celtic	Heart of Midlothian
1999	Rangers	Rangers
2000	Rangers	Rangers
2001	Celtic	Celtic
2002	Celtic	Rangers
2003	Rangers	Rangers
2004	Celtic	Celtic
2005	Rangers	Celtic
2006	Celtic	Heart of Midlothian
2007	Celtic	Celtic
2008	Celtic	Rangers
2009	Rangers	Rangers
2010	Rangers	Dundee United
2011	Rangers	Celtic

SCO – SCOTLAND

Year	League Cup
1947	Rangers
1948	East Fife
1949	Rangers
1950	East Fife
1951	Motherwell
1952	Dundee
1953	Dundee
1954	East Fife
1955	Heart of Midlothian
1956	Aberdeen
1957	Celtic
1958	Celtic
1959	Heart of Midlothian
1960	Heart of Midlothian
1961	Rangers
1962	Rangers
1963	Heart of Midlothian
1964	Rangers
1965	Rangers
1966	Celtic
1967	Celtic
1968	Celtic
1969	Celtic
1970	Celtic
1971	Rangers
1972	Partick Thistle
1973	Hibernian
1974	Dundee
1975	Celtic
1976	Rangers
1977	Aberdeen
1978	Rangers
1979	Rangers
1980	Dundee United
1981	Dundee United
1982	Rangers
1983	Celtic
1984	Rangers
1985	Rangers
1986	Aberdeen
1987	Rangers
1988	Rangers
1989	Rangers
1990	Aberdeen
1991	Rangers
1992	Hibernian
1993	Rangers
1994	Rangers
1995	Raith Rovers
1996	Aberdeen
1997	Rangers
1998	Celtic
1999	Rangers
2000	Celtic
2001	Celtic
2002	Rangers
2003	Rangers
2004	Livingston
2005	Rangers
2006	Celtic
2007	Hibernian
2008	Rangers
2009	Celtic
2010	Rangers
2011	Rangers

SEN – SENEGAL

Year	Champions	Cup Winners
1960	Jeanne d'Arc	
1961		Espoir St Louis
1962		Jeanne d'Arc
1963		US Rail Thiès
1964	Olympique Thiès	US Ouakam
1965		US Gorée
1966	Olympique Thiès	AS St Louisienne
1967	Espoir St.Louis	Foyer France
1968	Foyer France	Foyer France
1969	Jeanne d'Arc	Jeanne d'Arc
1970	ASC Diaraf	ASC Diaraf
1971	ASFA Dakar	ASC La Linguère
1972	ASFA Dakar	US Gorée
1973	Jeanne d'Arc	ASC Diaraf
1974	ASFA Dakar	Jeanne d'Arc
1975	ASC Diaraf	ASC Diaraf
1976	ASC Diaraf	AS Police
1977	ASC Diaraf	Saltigues Rufisque
1978	US Gorée	AS Police
1979	ASF Police	Casa Sports
1980	SEIB Diourbel	Jeanne d'Arc
1981	US Gorée	AS Police
1982	ASC Diaraf	ASC Diaraf
1983	SEIB Diourbel	ASC Diaraf
1984	US Gorée	Jeanne d'Arc
1985	Jeanne d'Arc	ASC Diaraf
1986	Jeanne d'Arc	AS Douanes
1987	SEIB Diourbel	Jeanne d'Arc
1988	Jeanne d'Arc	ASC La Linguère
1989	ASC Diaraf	US Ouakam
1990	Port Autonome	ASC La Linguère
1991	Port Autonome	ASC Diaraf
1992	ASC Ndiambour	US Gorée
1993	AS Douanes	ASC Diaraf
1994	ASC Ndiambour	ASC Diaraf
1995	ASC Diaraf	ASC Diaraf
1996	Sonacos	US Gorée
1997	ASC Douanes	AS Douanes
1998	ASC Ndiambour	ASC Yeggo
1999	Jeanne d'Arc	ASC Ndiambour
2000	ASC Diaraf	Port Autonome
2001	Jeanne d'Arc	Sonacos
2002	Jeanne d'Arc	AS Douanes
2003	Jeanne d'Arc	AS Douanes
2004	ASC Diaraf	AS Douanes
2005	Port Autonome	AS Douanes
2006	AS Douanes	US Ouakam
2007	AS Douanes	ASC La Linguère
2008	AS Douanes	ASC Diaraf
2009	ASC La Linguère	ASC Diaraf
2010	ASC Diaraf	Touré Kounda
2011	US Ouakam	Casa Sport

SEY – SEYCHELLES

Year	Champions	Cup Winners
1995	Sunshine	Red Star
1996	St Michel United	Red Star
1997	St Michel United	St Michel United
1998	Red Star	St Michel United
1999	St Michel United	Red Star
2000	St Michel United	Sunshine
2001	Red Star	St Michel United
2002	La Passe †	Anse Reunion
2003	St Michel United	St Louis
2004	La Passe	Red Star
2005	La Passe	Seychelles MB
2006	Anse Réunion	St Michel United
2007	St Michel United	St Michel United
2008	St Michel United	St Michel United
2009	La Passe	St Michel United
2010	St Michel United	St Louis Suns
2011	St Michel United	St Michel United

SEY – SEYCHELLES

Year	League Cup
2003	La Passe
2004	St Michel United
2005	Red Star
2006	Red Star
2007	Anse Reunion
2008	St Michel United
2009	St Michel United
2010	St Michel United
2011	St Michel United

SIN – SINGAPORE

Year	Champions	Cup Winners
1975	Geylang Internat'al	Sing. Armed Forces
1976	Geylang Internat'al	Geylang Internat'al
1977	Geylang Internat'al	Toa Payoh United
1978	Sing. Armed Forces	Geylang Internat'al
1979	Tampines Rovers	Toa Payoh United
1980	Tampines Rovers	Police SA
1981	Sing. Armed Forces	Farrer Park United
1982	Farrer Park United	Tiong Bahru
1983	Tiong Bahru	Farrer Park United
1984	Tampines Rovers	Sing. Armed Forces
1985	Police SA	Tiong Bahru
1986	Sing. Armed Forces	Sing. Armed Forces
1987	Tiong Bahru	Tiong Bahru
1988	Geylang Internat'al	Tiong Bahru
1989	Geylang Internat'al	Jurong Town
1990	Geylang Internat'al	Geylang Internat'al
1991	Geylang Internat'al	Geylang Internat'al
1992	Geylang Internat'al	Balestier United
1993	Geylang Internat'al	
1994	Perth Kangaroos	Tiong Bahru
1995	S-League	Geylang Internat'al
1996	Geyland United	Geylang Internat'al
1997	Sing. Armed Forces	Sing. Armed Forces
1997		Sing. Armed Forces
1998	Sing. Armed Forces	Tanjong Pagar Utd
1998		Tanjong Pagar Utd
1999	Home United	Sing. Armed Forces
2000	Sing. Armed Forces	Home United
2001	Geylang United	Home United
2002	Sing. Armed Forces	Tampines Rovers
2003	Home United	Home United
2004	Tampines Rovers	Tampines Rovers
2005	Tampines Rovers	Home United
2006	Sing. Armed Forces	Tampines Rovers
2007	Sing. Armed Forces	Sing. Armed Forces

Year	Champions	Cup Winners
2008	Sing. Armed Forces	Sing. Armed Forces
2009	Sing. Armed Forces	Geylang United
2010	Etoile FC	Bangkok Glass
2011	Tampines Rovers	Home United

SIN – SINGAPORE

Year	League Cup
2007	Woodlands Wellington
2008	Gombak United
2009	DPMM
2010	Etoile
2011	Albirex Niigata

SKN – ST KITTS AND NEVIS

Year	Champions	Cup Winners
1980	Village Superstars	
1981	Newtown United	
1982		
1983		
1984	Newtown United	
1985		
1986	Garden Hotspurs	
1987	Newtown United	
1988	Newtown United	
1989	Newtown United	
1990	Garden Hotspurs	
1991	Village Superstars	
1992	Newtown United	
1993	Newtown United	
1994	Garden Hotspurs	
1995	Newtown United	
1996	Newtown United	
1997	Newtown United	
1998	Newtown United	
1999	St Paul's United	
2000		
2001	Garden Hotspurs	
2002	Cayon Rockets	Cayon Rockets
2003	Village Superstars	Village Superstars
2004	Newtown United	Village Superstars
2005	Village Superstars	
2006	Village Superstars	
2007	Newtown United	Newtown United
2008	Newtown United	
2009	St Pauls United	
2010	Newtown United	Newtown United
2011	Village Superstars	Village Superstars

SLE – SIERRA LEONE

Year	Champions	Cup Winners
1967		
1968	Mighty Blackpool	
1969		
1970	Ports Authority	
1971	Ports Authority	
1972	Ports Authority	
1973	Ports Authority	East End Lions
1974	Mighty Blackpool	
1975		
1976		
1977	East End Lions	
1978	Mighty Blackpool	Bai Bureh Warriors
1979	Mighty Blackpool	Wusum Stars
1980	East End Lions	East End Lions
1981	Real Republicans	Kamboi Eagles
1982	Sierra Fisheries	Bai Bureh Warriors
1983	Real Republicans	Mighty Blackpool
1984	Real Republicans	Old Edwardians
1985	East End Lions	Kamboi Eagles
1986	Sierra Fisheries	Real Republicans
1987	Sierra Fisheries	
1988	Mighty Blackpool	Mighty Blackpool
1989	Freetown United	East End Lions
1990	Old Edwardians	Ports Authority
1991	Mighty Blackpool	Ports Authority
1992	East End Lions	Diamond Stars
1993	East End Lions	
1994	East End Lions	Mighty Blackpool
1995	Ports Authority	
1996	Mighty Blackpool	
1997	East End Lions	
1998	Mighty Blackpool	
1999	East End Lions	
2000	Mighty Blackpool	Mighty Blackpool
2001	Mighty Blackpool	Old Edwardians
2002		
2003		
2004		
2005	East End Lions	
2006	Kallon FC	
2007		Kallon FC
2008	Ports Authority	
2009	East End Lions	
2010	East End Lions	
2011	Ports Authority	

SLV – EL SALVADOR

Year	Champions	Apertura
1926	Chinameca SC	
1927	Hércules	
1928	Hércules	
1930	Hércules	
1937	CD 33	
1938	CD 33	
1942	Quequeisque	
1943	Quequeisque	
1946	Libertad	
1949	Once Municipal	
1951	Dragón	
1952	Deportivo FAS	
1953	Dragón	
1954	Deportivo FAS	
1955	Atlético Marte	
1956	Atlético Marte	
1957	Atlético Marte	
1958	Deportivo FAS	
1959	CD Aguila	
1961	CD Aguila	
1962	Deportivo FAS	
1962	Deportivo FAS	
1964	CD Aguila	
1964	CD Aguila	
1966	Alianza	
1967	Alianza	
1968	CD Aguila	
1969	Atlético Marte	
1970	Atlético Marte	
1971	Juventud Olímpica	
1972	CD Aguila	
1973	Juventud Olímpica	
1975	Platense	
1976	CD Aguila	
1977	CD Aguila	
1978	Deportivo FAS	
1979	Deportivo FAS	
1980	Santiagueño	
1981	Atlético Marte	
1981	Deportivo FAS	
1982	Atlético Marte	
1983	CD Aguila	
1984	Deportivo FAS	
1985	Atlético Marte	
1987	Alianza	
1988	CD Aguila	
1989	Luis Angel Firpo	
1990	Alianza	
1991	Luis Angel Firpo	
1992	Luis Angel Firpo	
1993	Luis Angel Firpo	
1994	Alianza	
1995	Deportivo FAS	
1996	Deportivo FAS	
1997	Alianza	
1998	Luis Angel Firpo	Aguila
1999	Luis Angel Firpo	Aguila
2000	Luis Angel Firpo	Aguila
2001	Aguila	Alianza
2002	Deportivo FAS	Deportivo FAS
2003	San Salvador	Deportivo FAS
2004	Alianza	Deportivo FAS
2005	Deportivo FAS	Vista Hermosa
2006	Aguila	Once Municipal
2007	Isidro-Metapán	Luis Angel Firpo
2008	Luis Angel Firpo	Isidro-Metapán
2009	Isidro-Metapán	Deportivo FAS
2010	Isidro-Metapán	Isidro-Metapán
2011	Alianza	Isidro-Metapán

SMR – SAN MARINO

Year	Champions	Cup Winners
1986	Faetano	La Fiorita
1987	La Fiorita	Libertas
1988	Tre Fiori	Domagnano
1989	Domagnano	Libertas
1990	La Fiorita	Domagnano
1991	Faetano	Libertas
1992	Montevito	Domagnano
1993	Tre Fiori	Faetano
1994	Tre Fiori	Faetano
1995	Tre Fiori	Cosmos
1996	Libertas	Domagnano
1997	Folgore Falciano	Murata
1998	Folgore Falciano	Faetano
1999	Faetano	Cosmos
2000	Folgore Falciano	Tre Penne
2001	Cosmos	Domagnano
2002	Domagnano	Domagnano
2003	Domagnano	Domagnano
2004	Pennarossa	Pennarossa

Year	Champions	Cup Winners
2005	Domagnano	Pennarossa
2006	Murata	Libertas
2007	Murata	Murata
2008	Murata	Murata
2009	Tre Fiori	Juvenes/Dogana
2010	Tre Fiori	Tre Fiori
2011	Tre Fiori	Juvenes/Dogana

SOL - SOLOMON ISLANDS

Year	Champions	Cup Winners
2003	Koloale	
2004	Central Realas	
2005		
2006	Marist	
2007	Kossa	
2008	Koloale	
2009	Marist	
2010	Koloale	
2011	Koloale	Solomon Warriors

SOM - SOMALIA

Year	Champions	Cup Winners
1967	Somali Police	
1968	Hoga	
1969	Lavori Publici	
1970	Lavori Publici	
1971	Lavori Publici	
1972	Horseed	
1973	Horseed	
1974		
1975	Municipality	
1976		
1977	Horseed	Lavori Publici
1978	Horseed	
1979	Horseed	Marine Club
1980	Horseed	Lavori Publici
1981	Lavori Publici	Printing Agency
1982	Wagad	Horseed
1983	Printing Agency	Horseed
1984	Marine Club	Waxcol
1985	Wagad	Petroleum
1986	Municipality	Marine Club
1987	Wagad	Horseed
1988	Wagad	
1989	Municipality	
1990	Jadidka	
1991		
1992		
1993		
1994	Morris Supplies	
1995	Alba	
1996		
1997		
1998	Ports Authority	
1999	Banaadir Telecom	
2000	Elman	
2001	Elman	
2002	Elman	Dakadaha
2003	Elman	
2004		
2005		
2006	Banaadir Telecom	
2007		SITT Daallo
2008		
2009	Banaadir Telecom	
2010	Banaadir Telecom	
2011	Elman	Fenyuus

SRB - SERBIA

Year	Champions	Cup Winners
1992	Crvena Zvezda	Partizan Beograd
1993	Partizan Beograd	Crvena Zvezda
1994	Partizan Beograd	Partizan Beograd
1995	Crvena Zvezda	Crvena Zvezda
1996	Partizan Beograd	Crvena Zvezda
1997	Partizan Beograd	Crvena Zvezda
1998	FK Obilic	Partizan Beograd
1999	Partizan Beograd	Crvena Zvezda
2000	Crvena Zvezda	Crvena Zvezda
2001	Crvena Zvezda	Partizan Beograd
2002	Partizan Beograd	Crvena Zvezda
2003	Partizan Beograd	Sartid Smederevo
2004	Crvena Zvezda	Crvena Zvezda
2005	Partizan Beograd	Zeleznik Beograd
2006	Crvena Zvezda	Crvena Zvezda
2007	Crvena Zvezda	Crvena Zvezda
2008	Partizan Beograd	Partizan Beograd
2009	Partizan Beograd	Partizan Beograd
2010	Partizan Beograd	Crvena Zvezda
2011	Partizan Beograd	Partizan Beograd

SRI - SRI LANKA

Year	Champions	Cup Winners
1948		Sunrise
1949		Saunders
1950		
1951		Sunrise
1952		Saunders
1953		
1954		Saunders
1955		Saunders
1956		
1957		
1958		
1959		
1960		Saunders
1961		Army
1962		
1963		Saunders
1964		Saunders
1965		
1966		
1967		Sunrise
1968		Victory
1969		Army
1969		Colombo MCSC
1971		Colombo MCSC
1972		Colombo MCSC
1973		Police
1974		
1975		
1976		
1977		
1978		
1979		
1980		
1981		
1982		Saunders
1983		
1984		Saunders
1985	Saunders	Saunders
1986	Saunders	Air Force
1987	Saunders	Renown
1988	Old Bens	Saunders
1989	Saunders	Renown
1990	Renown	Renown
1991	Saunders	York
1992	Saunders	Saunders
1993	Renown	Saunders
1994	Renown	Renown
1995	Pettah United	Renown
1996	Saunders	Old Benedictians
1997	Saunders	Saunders
1998	Ratnam	
1999	Saunders	Saunders
2000	Ratnam	Ratnam
2001	Saunders	Saunders
2001		Ratnam
2002	Saunders	
2003	Negombo Youth	Renown
2003	Blue Stars	Ratnam
2005	Saunders	Ratnam
2006	Negombo Youth	Ratnam
2007	Ratnam	Negombo Youth
2008	Ratnam	Police
2009	Army	Ratnam
2010	Renown	Navy
2011	Don Bosco	Army

STP - SAO TOME E PRINCIPE

Year	Champions	Cup Winners
1977	Vitória Riboque	
1978	Vitória Riboque	
1979	Vitória Riboque	
1980	Desp. Guadalupe	
1981	Desp. Guadalupe	Desp. Guadalupe
1982	Sporting Praia Cruz	Sporting Praia Cruz
1983		
1984	Andorinha	Vitória Riboque
1985	Sporting Praia Cruz	Vitória Riboque
1986	Vitória Riboque	Vitória Riboque
1987		
1988	6 de Setembro	6 de Setembro
1989	Vitória Riboque	Vitória Riboque
1990	Os Operários	Vitória Riboque
1991	Santana	Santana
1992		Os Operários
1993	Os Operários	Sporting Praia Cruz
1994	Sporting Praia Cruz	Sporting Praia Cruz
1995	Inter Bom-Bom	Caixão Grande
1996	Caixão Grande	Aliança Nacional
1997		
1998	Os Operários	Sporting Praia Cruz
1999	Sporting Praia Cruz	Vitória Riboque
2000	Inter Bom-Bom	Sporting Praia Cruz
2001	Bairros Unidos	Sundy
2002		
2003	Inter Bom-Bom	Os Operários
2004	Os Operários	
2005		

Year	Champions	Cup Winners
2006		
2007	Sporting Praia Cruz	Vítoria Riboque
2008		
2009		
2010	Sundy	6 de Setembro
2011	Sporting Príncipe	Vítoria Riboque

SUD – SUDAN

Year	Champions	Cup Winners
1962	Al Hilal	
1963		Al Merreikh
1964	Al Hilal	
1965	Al Hilal	
1966	Al Hilal	
1967	Al Hilal	
1968	Al Mawrada	
1969	Burri	
1970	Al Merreikh	Al Merreikh
1971	Al Merreikh	Al Merreikh
1972	Al Merreikh	Al Merreikh
1973	Al Merreikh	
1974	Al Hilal	Al Merreikh
1974	Al Merreikh	
1975	Al Merreikh	
1976		
1977	Al Merreikh	Al Hilal
1978	Al Merreikh	Al Nil
1979		
1980		
1981	Al Hilal	Hay Al Arab
1982	Al Merreikh	Al Ahly Wad Medani
1983	Al Hilal	Al Merreikh
1984	Al Hilal	Al Merreikh
1985	Al Merreikh	Al Merreikh
1986	Al Hilal	Al Merreikh
1987	Al Hilal	Al Mawrada
1988	Al Hilal	Al Merreikh
1989	Al Hilal	Al Mawrada
1990	Al Merreikh	Al Ittihad
1991	Al Hilal	Al Merreikh
1992	Al Hilal	Al Merreikh
1993	Al Merreikh	Al Hilal
1994	Al Hilal	Al Merreikh
1995	Al Hilal	Al Mawrada
1996	Al Hilal	Al Merreikh
1997	Al Merreikh	Al Mawrada
1998	Al Hilal	Al Hilal
1999	Al Hilal	Al Mawrada
2000	Al Merreikh	Al Hilal
2001	Al Merreikh	Al Merreikh
2002	Al Merreikh	Al Hilal
2003	Al Hilal	
2004	Al Hilal	Al Hilal
2005	Al Hilal	Al Merreikh
2006	Al Hilal	Al Merreikh
2007	Al Hilal	Al Merreikh
2008	Al Merreikh	Al Merreikh
2009	Al Hilal	Al Hilal
2010	Al Hilal	Al Merreikh
2011	Al Merreikh	Al Hilal

SUI – SWITZERLAND

Year	Champions	Cup Winners
1898	Grasshopper-Club	
1899	Anglo-American	
1900	Grasshopper-Club	
1901	Grasshopper-Club	
1902	FC Zürich	
1903	BSC Young Boys	
1904	FC St. Gallen	
1905	Grasshopper-Club	
1906	FC Winterthur	
1907	Servette FC	
1908	FC Winterthur	
1909	BSC Young Boys	
1910	BSC Young Boys	
1911	BSC Young Boys	
1912	FC Aarau	
1913	Montriond Lausanne	
1914	FC Aarau	
1915	Brühl St. Gallen	
1916	Cantonal Neuchâtel	
1917	FC Winterthur	
1918	Servette FC	
1919	Et. Chaux-de-Fonds	
1920	BSC Young Boys	
1921	Grasshopper-Club	
1922	Servette FC	
1923	FC Bern	
1924	FC Zürich	
1925	Servette FC	
1926	Servette FC	Grasshopper-Club
1927	Grasshopper-Club	Grasshopper-Club
1928	Grasshopper-Club	Servette FC
1929	BSC Young Boys	Urania Genève
1930	Servette FC	BSC Young Boys
1931	Grasshopper-Club	FC Lugano
1932	Lausanne-Sports	Grasshopper-Club
1933	Servette FC	FC Basel
1934	Servette FC	Grasshopper-Club
1935	Lausanne-Sports	Lausanne-Sports
1936	Lausanne-Sports	Young Fellows
1937	Grasshopper-Club	Grasshopper-Club
1938	FC Lugano	Grasshopper-Club
1939	Grasshopper-Club	Lausanne-Sport
1940	Servette FC	Grasshopper-Club
1941	FC Lugano	Grasshopper-Club
1942	Grasshopper-Club	Grasshopper-Club
1943	Grasshopper-Club	Grasshopper-Club
1944	Lausanne-Sports	Lausanne-Sport
1945	Grasshopper-Club	BSC Young Boys
1946	Servette FC	Grasshopper-Club
1947	FC Biel	FC Basel
1948	AC Bellinzona	La Chaux-de-Fonds
1949	FC Lugano	Servette FC
1950	Servette FC	Lausanne-Sports
1951	Lausanne-Sports	La Chaux-de-Fonds
1952	Grasshopper-Club	Grasshopper-Club
1953	FC Basel	BSC Young Boys
1954	La Chaux-de-Fonds	La Chaux-de-Fonds
1955	La Chaux-de-Fonds	La Chaux-de-Fonds
1956	Grasshopper-Club	Grasshopper-Club
1957	BSC Young Boys	La Chaux-de-Fonds
1958	BSC Young Boys	BSC Young Boys
1959	BSC Young Boys	FC Grenchen
1960	BSC Young Boys	FC Lucern
1961	Servette FC	La Chaux-de-Fonds
1962	Servette FC	Lausanne-Sports
1963	FC Zürich	FC Basei
1964	La Chaux-de-Fonds	Lausanne-Sports
1965	Lausanne-Sports	FC Sion
1966	FC Zürich	FC Zürich
1967	FC Basel	FC Basel
1968	FC Zürich	FC Lugano
1969	FC Basel	FC St. Gallen
1970	FC Basel	FC Zürich
1971	Grasshopper-Club	Servette FC
1972	FC Basel	FC Zürich
1973	FC Basel	FC Zürich
1974	FC Zürich	FC Sion
1975	FC Zürich	FC Basel
1976	FC Zürich	FC Zürich
1977	FC Basel	BSC Young Boys
1978	Grasshopper-Club	Servette FC
1979	Servette FC	Servette FC
1980	FC Basel	FC Sion
1981	FC Zürich	Lausanne-Sports
1982	Grasshopper-Club	FC Sion
1983	Grasshopper-Club	Grasshopper-Club
1984	Grasshopper-Club	Servette FC
1985	Servette FC	FC Aarau
1986	BSC Young Boys	FC Sion
1987	Neuchâtel Xamax	BSC Young Boys
1988	Neuchâtel Xamax	Grasshopper-Club
1989	FC Luzern	Grasshopper-Club
1990	Grasshopper-Club	Grasshopper-Club
1991	Grasshopper-Club	FC Sion
1992	FC Sion	FC Luzern
1993	FC Aarau	FC Lugano
1994	Servette FC	Grasshopper-Club
1995	Grasshopper-Club	FC Sion
1996	Grasshopper-Club	FC Sion
1997	FC Sion	FC Sion
1998	Grasshopper-Club	Lausanne-Sports
1999	Servette FC	Lausanne-Sports
2000	FC St. Gallen	FC Zürich
2001	Grasshopper-Club	Servette FC
2002	FC Basel	FC Basel
2003	FC Basel	FC Basel
2004	FC Basel	FC Wil
2005	FC Basel	FC Zürich
2006	FC Zürich	FC Sion
2007	FC Zürich	FC Basel
2008	FC Basel	FC Basel
2009	FC Zürich	FC Sion
2010	FC Basel	FC Basel
2011	FC Basel	FC Sion

SUR – SURINAME

Year	Champions	Cup Winners
1923	Olympia	
1924		
1925	Transvaal	
1926		
1927	Ajax	
1928	Ajax	
1929		
1930		
1931	Excelsior Blauw Wit	
1932	Cicerone	
1933	Cicerone	
1934	Cicerone	

Year	Champions
1935	Cicerone
1936	Voorwaarts
1937	Transvaal
1938	Transvaal
1939	Arsenal
1940	Arsenal
1941	Voorwaarts
1942	
1943	
1944	
1945	
1946	
1947	
1948	MVV
1949	MVV
1950	Transvaal
1951	Transvaal
1952	Voorwaarts
1953	Robinhood
1954	Robinhood
1955	Robinhood
1956	Robinhood
1957	
1958	Voorwaarts
1959	Robinhood
1960	
1961	Leo Victor
1962	Transvaal
1964	Leo Victor
1964	Robinhood
1966	Transvaal
1966	Transvaal
1967	Transvaal
1968	Transvaal
1969	Transvaal
1970	Transvaal
1971	Robinhood
1972	
1973	Transvaal
1974	Transvaal
1976	Robinhood
1976	Robinhood
1977	Voorwaarts
1978	Leo Victor
1979	Robinhood
1980	Robinhood
1981	Robinhood
1982	Leo Victor
1983	Robinhood
1985	Robinhood
1986	Robinhood
1986	Robinhood
1987	Robinhood
1988	Robinhood
1989	Robinhood
1990	
1991	Transvaal
1992	Transvaal
1993	Leo Victor
1994	Robinhood
1995	Robinhood
1996	Transvaal
1997	Transvaal
1998	
1999	SNL
2000	Transvaal

Year	Champions	Cup Winners
2001		Robinhood
2002	Voorwaarts	Transvaal
2003	FCS Nacional	Leo Victor
2004	Walking Bout Co	Super Red Eagles
2005	Robinhood	FCS Nacional
2006	Walking Bout Co	Robinhood
2007	Inter Moengotapoe	Robinhood
2008	Inter Moengotapoe	Transvaal
2009	Walking Bout Co	Walking Bout Co
2010	Inter Moengotapoe	Excelsior
2011	Inter Moengotapoe	Notch

SVK - SLOVAKIA

Year	Champions	Cup Winners
1994	Slovan Bratislava	Slovan Bratislava
1995	Slovan Bratislava	Inter Bratislava
1996	Slovan Bratislava	Chemlon Humenné
1997	1.FC Kosice	Slovan Bratislava
1998	1.FC Kosice	Spartak Trnava
1999	Slovan Bratislava	Slovan Bratislava
2000	Inter Bratislava	Inter Bratislava
2001	Inter Bratislava	Inter Bratislava
2002	MSK Zilina	Koba Senec
2003	MSK Zilina	Matador Púchov
2004	MSK Zilina	Artmedia Bratislava
2005	Artmedia Bratislava	Dukla B. Bystrica
2006	MFK Ruzomberok	MFK Ruzomberok
2007	MSK Zilina	ViOn Zlaté Moravce
2008	Artmedia Petrzalka	Artmedia Petrzalka
2009	Slovan Bratislava	MFK Kosice
2010	MSK Zilina	Slovan Bratislava
2011	Slovan Bratislava	Slovan Bratislava

SVN - SLOVENIA

Year	Champions	Cup Winners
1992	Olimpija Ljubljana	Maribor
1993	Olimpija Ljubljana	Olimpija Ljubljana
1994	Olimpija Ljubljana	Maribor
1995	Olimpija Ljubljana	Mura Murska Sobota
1996	Gorica	Olimpija Ljubljana
1997	Maribor	Maribor
1998	Maribor	Rudar Velenje
1999	Maribor	Maribor
2000	Maribor	Olimpija Ljubljana
2001	Maribor	Gorica
2002	Maribor	Gorica
2003	Maribor	Olimpija Ljubljana
2004	Gorica	Maribor
2005	Gorica	Publikum Celje
2006	Gorica	Koper
2007	Domzale	Koper
2008	Domzale	Interblock Ljubljana
2009	Maribor	Interblock Ljubljana
2010	Koper	Maribor
2011	Maribor	Domzale

PVV

SWE - SWEDEN

Year	Champions	Cup Winners
Transvaal 1896		Örgryte IS
Robinhood 1897		Örgryte IS
1898		Örgryte IS
Robinhood 1899		Örgryte IS
1900		AIK Stockholm
1901	AIK Stockholm	
1902	Örgryte IS	
1903	Göteborg IF	
1904	Örgryte IS	
1905	Örgryte IS	
1906	Örgryte IS	
1907	Örgryte IS	
1908	IFK Göteborg	
1909	Örgryte IS	
1910	IFK Göteborg	
1911	AIK Stockholm	
1912	Djurgårdens IF	
1913	Örgryte IS	
1914	AIK Stockholm	
1915	Djurgårdens IF	
1916	AIK Stockholm	
1917	Djurgårdens IF	
1918	IFK Göteborg	
1919	GAIS Göteborg	
1920	Djurgårdens IF	
1921	IFK Eskilstuna	
1922	GAIS Göteborg	
1923	AIK Stockholm	
1924	Fassbergs IF	
1925	GAIS Göteborg	Brynäs IF Gävle
1926	Örgryte IS	
1927	GAIS Göteborg	
1928	Örgryte IS	
1929	Helsingborg IF	
1930	Helsingborg IF	
1931	GAIS Göteborg	
1932	AIK Stockholm	
1933	Helsingborg IF	
1934	Helsingborg IF	
1935	IFK Göteborg	
1936	IF Elfsborg	
1937	AIK Stockholm	
1938	IK Sleipner	
1939	IF Elfsborg	
1940	IF Elfsborg	
1941	Helsingborg IF	Helsingborg IF
1942	IFK Göteborg	GAIS Göteborg
1943	IFK Norrköping	IFK Norrköping
1944	Malmö FF	Malmö FF
1945	IFK Norrköping	IFK Norrköping
1946	IFK Norrköping	Malmö FF
1947	IFK Norrköping	Malmö FF
1948	IFK Norrköping	Råå IF Helsingborg
1949	Malmö FF	AIK Stockholm
1950	Malmö FF	AIK Stockholm
1951	Malmö FF	Malmö FF
1952	IFK Norrköping	
1953	Malmö FF	Malmö FF
1954	GAIS Göteborg	
1955	Djurgårdens IF	
1956	IFK Norrköping	
1957	IFK Norrköping	
1958	IFK Göteborg	
1959	Djurgårdens IF	
1960	IFK Norrköping	
1961	IF Elfsborg	
1962	IFK Norrköping	
1963	IFK Norrköping	
1964	Djurgårdens IF	
1965	Malmö FF	
1966	Djurgårdens IF	

Year	Champions	Cup Winners
1966	Djurgårdens IF	
1967	Malmö FF	Malmö FF
1968	Östers IF Växjö	
1969	IFK Göteborg	IFK Norrköping
1970	Malmö FF	Åtvidabergs FF
1971	Malmö FF	Åtvidabergs FF
1972	Åtvidabergs FF	Landskrona BoIS
1973	Åtvidabergs FF	Malmö FF
1974	Malmö FF	Malmö FF
1975	Malmö FF	Malmö FF
1976	Halmstad BK	AIK Stockholm
1977	Malmö FF	Östers IF Växjö
1978	Östers IF Växjö	Malmö FF
1979	Halmstad BK	IFK Göteborg
1980	Östers IF Växjö	Malmö FF
1981	Östers IF Växjö	Kalmar FF
1982	IFK Göteborg	IFK Göteborg
1983	IFK Göteborg	IFK Göteborg
1984	IFK Göteborg	Malmö FF
1985	Örgryte IS	AIK Stockholm
1986	Malmö FF	Malmö FF
1987	IFK Göteborg	Kalmar FF
1988	Malmö FF	IFK Norrköping
1989	IFK Norrköping	Malmö FF
1990	IFK Göteborg	Djurgårdens IF
1991	IFK Göteborg	IFK Norrköping
1992	AIK Stockholm	IFK Göteborg
1993	IFK Göteborg	Degerfors IF
1994	IFK Göteborg	IFK Norrköping
1995	IFK Göteborg	Halmstads BK
1996	IFK Göteborg	AIK Stockholm
1997	Halmstads BK	AIK Stockholm
1998	AIK Stockholm	Helsingborgs IF
1999	Helsingborgs IF	AIK Stockholm
2000	Halmstads BK	Orgryte IS
2001	Hammarby IF	IF Elfsborg
2002	Djurgårdens IF	Djurgårdens IF
2003	Djurgårdens IF	IF Elfsborg
2004	Malmö FF	Djurgårdens IF
2005	Djurgårdens IF	Djurgårdens IF
2006	Elfsborg IF	Helsingborgs IF
2007	IFK Göteborg	Kalmar FF
2008	Kalmar FF	IFK Göteborg
2009	AIK Stockholm	AIK Stockholm
2010	Malmö FF	Helsingborgs IF
2011	Helsingborgs IF	Helsingborgs IF

SWZ – SWAZILAND

Year	Champions	Cup Winners
1976	Mbabane High'ders	
1977		
1978		
1979		
1980	Mbabane High'ders	Bulembu Young Aces
1981	Peacemakers	
1982	Mbabane High'ders	Bulembu Young Aces
1983	Manzini Wanderers	Mbabane High'ders
1984	Mbabane High'ders	Manzini Wanderers
1985	Manzini Wanderers	Mbabane High'ders
1986	Mbabane High'ders	Mbabane Swallows
1987	Manzini Wanderers	Moneni Pirates
1988	Mbabane High'ders	Moneni Pirates
1989	Denver Sundowns	Denver Sundowns
1990	Denver Sundowns	Mbabane High'ders
	Mbabane High'ders	Denver Sundowns
1992	Mbabane High'ders	Denver Sundowns
1993	Mbabane Swallows	XI Men in Flight
1994	XI Men in Flight	
1995	Mbabane High'ders	Mhlam'yatsi Rovers
1996	XI Men in Flight	XI Men in Flight
1997	Mbabane High'ders	Mbabane High'ders
1998		
1999	Manzini Wanderers	Mbabane High'ders
2000	Mbabane High'ders	Mhlume United
2001	Mbabane High'ders	XI Men in Flight
2002	Manzini Wanderers	
2003	Manzini Wanderers	
2004	Mhlam'yatsi Rovers	Green Mamba
2005	Mbabane Swallows	Hub Sundowns
2006	Royal Leopards	Mbabane Swallows
2007	Royal Leopards	Royal Leopards
2008	Royal Leopards	Malanti Chiefs
2009	Mbabane Swallows	Mbabane High'ders
2010	Young Buffaloes	Mbabane High'ders
2011	Green Mamba	Royal Leopards

SYR – SYRIA

Year	Champions	Cup Winners
1962		Rmeilan
1963		
1964		Soori
1965		
1966		Al Ahly Aleppo
1967	Al Ahly Aleppo	Al Shorta
1968	Al Ahly Aleppo	Al Shorta
1969	Barada	Rmeilan
1970	Barada	Maghazel
1971		
1972		
1973	Al Jaish	Al Ittihad
1974		
1975	Al Karama	
1976	Al Jaish	
1977	Al Ittihad	
1978		Majd
1979	Al Jaish	
1980	Al Shorta	Al Shorta
1981		Al Shorta
1982	Teshrine	Al Ittihad
1983	Al Karama	Al Karama
1984	Al Karama	Al Ittihad
1985	Al Jaish	Al Ittihad
1986	Al Jaish	Al Jaish
1987	Jabala	Al Karama
1988	Jabala	Al Foutoua
1989	Jabala	Al Foutoua
1990	Al Foutoua	Al Foutoua
1991	Al Foutoua	Al Foutoua
1992	Al Horriya	Al Horriya
1993	Al Ittihad	Al Wahda
1994	Al Horriya	Al Ittihad
1995	Al Ittihad	Al Karama
1996	Al Karama	Al Karama
1997	Teshrine	Al Jaish
1998	Al Jaish	Al Jaish
1999	Al Jaish	Jabala
2000	Jabala	Al Jaish
2001	Al Jaish	Hottin
2002	Al Jaish	Al Jaish
2003	Al Jaish	Al Wahda
2004	Al Wahda	Al Jaish
2005	Al Ittihad	Al Ittihad
2006	Al Karama	Al Ittihad
2007	Al Karama	Al Karama
2008	Al Karama	Al Karama
2009	Al Karama	Al Karama
2010	Al Jaish	Al Karama
2011	Al Ittihad	

TAH – TAHITI

Year	Champions	Cup Winners
1945		CAICT
1946		Fei Pi
1947		Fei Pi
1948	Fei Pi	Fei Pi
1949	Fei Pi	Fei Pi
1950	Fei Pi	Central Sport
1951	Fei Pi	Jeunes Tahitiens
1952	Excelsior	Vénus
1953	Vénus	Central Sport
1954	Jeunes Tahitiens	Central Sport
1955	Central Sport	Fei Pi
1956	Excelsior	Fei Pi
1957	Excelsior	Central Sport
1958	Central Sport	Fei Pi
1959	Excelsior	Fei Pi
1960	Excelsior	Excelsior
1961	Jeunes Tahitiens	Central Sport
1962	Central Sport	Excelsior
1963	Central Sport	Central Sport
1964	Central Sport	Excelsior
1965	Central Sport	Excelsior
1966	Central Sport	Central Sport
1967	Central Sport	Central Sport
1968	Fei Pi	Punaruu
1969	Punaruu	Punaruu
1970	Fei Pi	Arue
1971	Fei Pi	Jeunes Tahitiens
1972	Central Sport	Central Sport
1973	Central Sport	Central Sport
1974	Central Sport	Vaiete
1975	Central Sport	Central Sport
1976	Central Sport	Central Sport
1977	Central Sport	Central Sport
1978	Central Sport	Pirae
1979	Central Sport	Pirae
1980	Arue	Pirae
1981	Central Sport	Central Sport
1982	Central Sport	Jeunes Tahitiens
1983	Central Sport	Central Sport
1984	PTT	Pirae
1985	Central Sport	PTT
1986	Excelsior	PTT
1987	Jeunes Tahitiens	Jeunes Tahitiens
1988	Excelsior	Central Sport
1989	Pirae	Jeunes Tahitiens
1990	Vénus	Vénus
1991	Pirae	Vénus
1992	Vénus	Vénus
1993	Pirae	
1994	Pirae	Pirae
1995	Vénus	Central Sport
1996	Manu Ura	Vénus
1997	Vénus	Dragon

Year	Champions	Winner
1998	Vénus	Vénus
1999	Vénus	Vénus
2000	Vénus	Pirae
2001	Pirae	Dragon
2002	Vénus	Pirae
2003	Pirae	Manu Ura
2004	Manu Ura	Dragon
2005	AS Tefana	Pirae
2006	Pirae	Temanava
2007	Manu Ura	Tefana
2008	Manu Ura	Tefana
2009	Manu Ura	Manu Ura
2010	AS Tefana	Tefana
2011	AS Tefana	

TAN – TANZANIA

Year	Champions	Cup Winners
1965	Sunderland	
1966	Sunderland	
1967	Cosmopolitans	
1968	Young Africans	
1969	Young Africans	
1970	Young Africans	
1971	Young Africans	
1972	Young Africans	
1973	Simba	
1974	Young Africans	JKU
1975	Mseto Sports	Young Africans
1976	Simba	Rangers
1977	Simba	KMKM
1978	Simba	Pan African
1979	Simba	Pan African
1980	Simba	Coastal Union
1981	Young Africans	Pan African
1982	Pan African	KMKM
1983	Young Africans	KMKM
1984	Simba	Simba
1985	Young Africans	Miembeni
1986	Tukuyu Stars	Miembeni
1987	Young Africans	Miembeni
1988	Coastal Union	Coastal Union
1989	Young Africans	Pamba
1990	Simba	Small Simba
1991	Young Africans	Railways
1992	Young Africans	Pamba
1993	Young Africans	Malindi
1994	Simba	Young Africans
1995	Simba	Simba
1996	Young Africans	Sigara
1997	Young Africans	Tanzania Stars
1998	Young Africans	Tanzania Stars
1999	Mtibwa	Young Africans
2000	Mtibwa	Simba
2001	Simba	Polisi
2002	Young Africans	JKT Ruvu Stars
2003	Simbo	
2004	Simba	
2005	Young Africans	
2006	Young Africans	
2007	Simba	
2008	Young Africans	
2009	Young Africans	
2010	Simba	
2011	Young Africans	

TAN – TANZANIA

Year Union League (Tanzania & Zanzibar)

Year	Union League
1982	Pan African
1983	Young Africans
1984	KMKM
1985	Maji Maji
1986	Maji Maji
1987	Young Africans
1988	Pan African
1989	Malindi
1990	Pamba
1991	Young Africans
1992	Malindi
1993	Simba
1994	Simba
1995	Simba
1996	Young Africans
1997	Young Africans
1998	Maji Maji
1999	Prisons
2000	Young Africans
2001	Simba
2002	Simba

TCA – TURKS AND CAICOS ISLANDS

Year	Champions	Cup Winners
1999	Tropic All Stars	
2000	Masters	Masters
2001	SWA Sharks	
2002	Beaches	
2003	Caribbean All Stars	Caribbean All Stars
2004	KPMG United	Police
2005	KPMG United	
2006	Beaches	Beaches
2007	Beaches	
2008	PWC Athletic	
2009	Digi FC	OHS Express
2010	AFC Academy	Provopool
2011	Provopool	AFC National

TGA – TONGA

Year	Champions	Cup Winners
1970		
1971		
1972		
1973		
1974		
1975		
1976		
1977		
1978		
1979		
1980		
1981		Ngele'ia
1982	Ngele'ia	Ngele'ia
1983	Ngele'ia	Ngele'ia
1984	Ngele'ia	Veitongo
1985	Ngele'ia	Ngele'ia
1986		Ngele'ia
1987		Ngele'ia
1988		Ngele'ia
1989		
1990		
1991		
1992		
1993		
1994		Navutoka
1995		
1996		
1997		
1998	SC Lotoha'apai	Veitongo
1999	SC Lotoha'apai	
2000	SC Lotoha'apai	
2001	SC Lotoha'apai	
2002	SC Lotoha'apai	Ngele'ia
2003	SC Lotoha'apai	Ngele'ia
2004	SC Lotoha'apai	
2005	SC Lotoha'apai	
2006	SC Lotoha'apai	
2007	SC Lotoha'apai	
2008	SC Lotoha'apai	
2009	Marist FC	
2010		
2011	SC Lotoha'apai	Marist

THA – THAILAND

Year Yai Cup

Year	Yai Cup
1916	Dept of Performing Arts
1917	Vajiravudh College
1918	Vajiravudh College
1919	Vajiravudh College
1920	Chulalongkorn University
1921	Royal Military Academy
1922	Royal Military Academy
1923	Royal Thai Naval Academy
1924	Royal Thai Naval Academy
1925	
1926	Kong Dem Rot
1927	Kong Dem Rot
1928	Suankularb Wittayalai School
1929	Suankularb Wittayalai School
1930	Assumption Academy
1931	Thailand Post
1932	
1933	
1934	
1935	
1936	
1937	
1938	
1939	
1940	
1941	
1942	
1943	
1944	
1945	
1946	
1947	
1948	Bang Rak Academy
1949	Assumption Academy
1950	
1951	Chai Sod
1952	Royal Thai Air Force
1953	Royal Thai Air Force
1954	Hakka Association
1955	Chula-Alumni Association
1956	Hainan Association

Year	Champions	Cup
1957	Royal Thai Air Force	
1958	Royal Thai Air Force	
1959	Royal Thai Air Force	
1960	Royal Thai Air Force	
1961	Royal Thai Air Force	
1962	Royal Thai Air Force	
1963	Royal Thai Air Force	
	Kor Royal Cup	
1964	Bangkok Bank	
1965	Royal Thai Police	
1966	Bangkok Bank	
1967	Bangkok Bank & Royal Thai Air Force	
1968	Port Authority	
1969	Raj Vithi	
1970	Raj Pracha	
1971	Raj Pracha	
1972	Port Authority	
1973	Raj Vithi	

Year	Champions	FA Cup
1974	Port Authority	
1975	Raj Vithi	Raj Pracha
1976	Port Authority	Raj Pracha
1977	Raj Vithi	
1978	Port Authority	
1979	Port Authority	
1980	Raj Pracha	Bangkok Bank
1981	Bangkok Bank	Bangkok Bank
1982	Raj Pracha	
1983	Royal Thai Army	
1984	Bangkok Bank	Lopburi
1985	Port Authority	Raj Pracha
1986	Bangkok Bank	
1987	Royal Thai Air Force	
1988	Krung Thai Bank	
1989	Krung Thai Bank	
1990	Port Authority	
1991	Thai Farmers Bank	
1992	Thai Farmers Bank	Raj Pracha
1993	Thai Farmers Bank	TOT
1994	Bangkok Bank	Raj Pracha
1995	Thai Farmers Bank	Royal Thai Air Force
1996		Royal Thai Air Force
	Premier League	
1997	Bangkok Bank	Sinthana
1997	Royal Thai Air Force	
1998	Sinthana	Bangkok Bank
1999	Royal Thai Air Force	Thai Farmers Bank
2000	BEC Tero Sasana	
2001		Royal Thai Air Force
2002	BEC Tero Sasana	
2003	Krung Thai Bank	
2004	Krung Thai Bank	
2005	Thailand Tobacco	
2006	Bangkok University	
2006	TOT	
2007	Chonburi	
2008	PEA	
2009	Muangthong United	Thai Port
2010	Muangthong United	Chonburi
2011	Buriram PEA	Buriram PEA

THA – THAILAND

Year	League	Cup
'10	Thai Port	
?uriram PEA		

TJK – TAJIKISTAN

Year	Champions	Cup Winners
1992	Pamir Dushanbe	Pamir Dushanbe
1993	Sitora Dushanbe	Sitora Dushanbe
1994	Sitora Dushanbe	Ravshan Kulob
1995	Pamir Dushanbe	Pakhtakor Dzh'lovsk
1996	Dinamo Dushanbe	
1997	Vakhsh Qurgonteppa	Vakhsh Qurgonteppa
1998	Varzob Dushanbe	FK Hujand
1998		Varzob Dushanbe
1999	Varzob Dushanbe	Varzob Dushanbe
2000	Varzob Dushanbe	
2001	Regar TadAZ	Regar TadAZ
2002	Regar TadAZ	Regar TadAZ
2002		FK Hujand
2003	Regar TadAZ	Vakhsh Qurgonteppa
2004	Regar TadAZ	Aviator B. Gafurov
2005	Vakhsh Qurgonteppa	Regar TadAZ
2006	Regar TadAZ	Regar TadAZ
2007	Regar TadAZ	Parvoz B. Gafurov
2008	Regar TadAZ	FK Hujand
2009	Vakhsh Qurgonteppa	Esteghlal Dushanbe
2010	Esteghlal Dushanbe	Esteghlal Dushanbe
2011	Esteghlal Dushanbe	Regar TadAZ

TKM – TURKMENISTAN

Year	Champions	Cup Winners
1992	Köpetdag Ashgabat	
1993	Köpetdag Ashgabat	Köpetdag Ashgabat
1994	Köpetdag Ashgabat	Köpetdag Ashgabat
1995	Köpetdag Ashgabat	Turan Dasoguz
1996	Nisa Ashgabat	
1997		Köpetdag Ashgabat
1998	Köpetdag Ashgabat	Nisa Ashgabat
1999	Nisa Ashgabat	Köpetdag Ashgabat
2000	Köpetdag Ashgabat	Köpetdag Ashgabat
2001	Nisa Ashgabat	Köpetdag Ashgabat
2002	Sagadam Turk'basy	Garagam Turk'abat
2003	Nisa Ashgabat	Nebitchi Balkanabat
2004	Nebitchi Balkanabat	Nebitchi Balkanabat
2005	HTTU Ashgabat	Merv Mary
2006	HTTU Ashgabat	HTTU Ashgabat
2007	FK Ashgabat	Sagadam Turk'basy
2008	FK Ashgabat	Merv Mary
2009	HTTU Ashgabat	Altyn Asyr
2010	Balkan Balkanabat	Balkan Balkanabat
2011	Balkan Balkanabat	HTTU Ashgabat

TOG – TOGO

Year	Champions	Cup Winners
1961	Etoile Filante	Etoile Filante
1962	Etoile Filante	
1963		
1964	Etoile Filante	
1965	Etoile Filante	
1966		
1967	Etoile Filante	
1968	Etoile Filante	
1969	Modèle	
1970	Dynamic Togolais	
1971	Dynamic Togolais	
1972	Modèle	
1973	Modèle	
1974	Lomé 1	Omnisports
1975	Lomé 1	ASKO Kara
1976	Lomé 1	ASKO Kara
1977		Edan Lomé
1978	Semassi Sokodé	
1979	Semassi Sokodé	Agaza Lomé
1980	Agaza Lomé	Semassi Sokodé
1981	Semassi Sokodé	Agaza Lomé
1982	Semassi Sokodé	Semassi Sokodé
1983	Semassi Sokodé	
1984	Agaza Lomé	Agaza Lomé
1985	ASFOSA Lomé	Foadan Dapaong
1986	ASFOSA Lomé	Entente II
1987	Doumbé	ASKO Kara
1988	ASKO Kara	Agaza Lomé
1989	ASKO Kara	Entente II
1990	Ifodjé Atakpamé	Semassi Sokodé
1991		
1992	Etoile Filante	
1993	Semassi Sokodé	
1994	Semassi Sokodé	Etoile Filante
1995	Semassi Sokodé	ASKO Kara
1996	ASKO Kara	Doumbé
1997	Dynamic Togolais	
1998		
1999	Semassi Sokodé	Agaza Lomé
2000		
2001	Dynamic Togolais	Dynamic Togolais
2002	AS Douanes	Dynamic Togolais
2003		Maranatha Fiokpo
2004	Dynamic Togolais	AS Douanes
2005	AS Douanes	Dynamic Togolais
2006	Maranatha Fiokpo	AS Togo-Port
2007	ASKO Kara	
2008		
2009	Maranatha Fiokpo	
2010		
2011		

TPE – CHINESE TAIPEI

Year	Champions
1983	Flying Camel
1984	Flying Camel
1985	Flying Camel
1986	Taipei City Bank
1987	Taipower
1988	Taipower
1989	Taipei City Bank
1990	Taipower
1991	Taipei City Bank
1992	Taipower
1993	Flying Camel
1994	Taipower
1995	Taipower
1996	Taipower
1997	Taipower
1998	Taipower
1999	Taipower
2000	
2001	Taipower

Year		
2002	Taipower	
2003	Taipower	
2004	Taipower	
2005	Ta Tung	
2006	Ta Tung	
2007	Taipower	
2008	Taipower	
2009	Kaohsiung Yaoti	
2010	Taipower	
2011	Taipower	

TRI – TRINIDAD AND TOBAGO

Year	Champions	Cup Winners
1908	Clydesdale	
1909	Casuals	
1910	Shamrock	
1911	Shamrock	
1912	Casuals	
1913	Casuals	
1914	Clydesdale	
1915	Clydesdale	
1916		
1917		
1918		
1919	Queen's Park	
1920	Royal Sussex	
1921	Casuals	
1922	Shamrock	
1923	Shamrock	
1924	Shamrock	
1925	Shamrock	
1926	Sporting Club	
1927	Maple	Shamrock
1928	Maple	Southern Casuals
1929	Casuals	Everton
1930	Everton	Everton
1931	Everton	Everton
1932	Everton	Everton
1933	Queen's Royal C'ge	
1934	Casuals	Casuals
1935	Casuals	Sporting Club
1936	Sporting Club	Shamrock
1937	Sporting Club	UBOT
1938	Casuals	West Ham
1939	Notre Dame	Casuals
1940	Casuals	Maple
1941	Casuals	UBOT
1942	Colts	Spitfire
1943	Fleet Air Arm	UBOT
1944	Shamrock	Colts
1945	Colts	Colts
1946	Notre Dame	Maple
1947	Colts	Notre Dame
1948	Malvern	Colts
1949	Malvern	Maple & Carlton
1950	Maple	UBOT
1951	Maple	UBOT & Providence
1952	Maple	Malvern
1953	Maple	Maple
1954	Sporting Club	UBOT
1955	Sporting Club	Malvern
1956	Notre Dame	TPD
1957	Colts	Shell & Shamrock
1958	Shamrock	Casuals

Year	Champions	Cup Winners
1959	Shamrock	Shamrock
1960	Maple	Malvern
1961	Maple	Malvern & Apex
1962	Maple	Dynamos
1963	Maple	Maple
1964	Paragon	Paragon
1965	Regiment	Malvern & Palo Seco
1966	Regiment	Regiment & Juniors
1967	Maple	Regiment
1968	Maple	Malvern
1969	Maple	Point Fortin
1970	Regiment	Maple
1971		
1972	Defence Force	Maple
1973	Defence Force	
1974	Defence Force	Defence Force
1975	Defence Force	Police
1976	Defence Force	FalconsMalvern
1977	Defence Force	Falcons
1978	Defence Force	
1979	Police	
1980	Defence Force	
1981	Defence Force	Defence Force
1982	ASL Sports	ASL Sports
1983	ASL Sports	ASL Sports
1984	Defence Force	Motown United
1985	Defence Force	Defence Force
1986	Trintoc	Trintoc
1987	Defence Force	La Brea Angels
1988	Trintoc	Trintoc
1989	Defence Force	Defence Force
1990	Defence Force	Police
1991	Police	Defence Force
1992	Defence Force	Motown United
1993	Defence Force	Trintoc
1994	Police	Police
1995	Defence Force	United Petrotin
1996	Defence Force	Defence Force
1997	Defence Force	United Petrotin
1998	Joe Public	San Juan Jabloteh
1999	Defence Force	W Connection
2000	W Connection	W Connection
2001	W Connection	Joe Public
2002	San Juan Jabloteh	W Connection
2003	San Juan Jabloteh	North East Stars
2004	North East Stars	
2005	W Connection	San Juan Jabloteh
2006	Joe Public	WASA
2007	San Juan Jabloteh	Joe Public
2008	San Juan Jabloteh	Caledonia AIA
2009	Joe Public	Joe Public
2010	Defence Force	San Juan Jabloteh
2011		

TRI – TRINIDAD AND TOBAGO

Year	Toyota Classic
2005	W Connection
2006	United Petrotin
2007	Joe Public
2008	San Juan Jabloteh
2009	Joe Public
2010	
2011	W Connection

TRI – TRINIDAD AND TOBAGO

Year	FCB League Cup	Pro Bowl
2000	San Juan Jabloteh	
2001	W Connection	
2002	Defence Force	
2003	San Juan Jabloteh	
2004	W Connection	
2005	W Connection	San Juan Jabloteh
2006	W Connection	San Juan Jabloteh
2007	W Connection	W Connection
2008	W Connection	Caledonia AIA
2009	Defence Force	Joe Public
2010	Joe Public	
2011	Caledonia AIA	Joe Public

TUN – TUNISIA

Year	Champions	Cup Winners
1956	CS Hammam-Lif	Stade Tunisien
1957	Stade Tunisien	Espérance Tunis
1958	Etoile du Sahel	Stade Tunisien
1959	Espérance Tunis	Etoile du Sahel
1960	Espérance Tunis	Stade Tunisien
1961	Stade Tunisien	AS Marsa
1962	Stade Tunisien	Stade Tunisien
1963	Etoile du Sahel	Etoile du Sahel
1964	Club Africain	Espérance Tunis
1965	Stade Tunisien	Club Africain
1966	Etoile du Sahel	Stade Tunisien
1967	Club Africain	Club Africain
1968	Sfax Railway	Club Africain
1969	CS Sfaxien	Club Africain
1970	Espérance Tunis	Club Africain
1971	CS Sfaxien	CS Sfaxien
1972	Etoile du Sahel	Club Africain
1973	Club Africain	Club Africain
1974	Club Africain	Etoile du Sahel
1975	Espérance Tunis	Etoile du Sahel
1976	Espérance Tunis	Club Africain
1977	JS Kairouan	AS Marsa
1978	CS Sfaxien	Espérance Tunis
1979	Club Africain	Espérance Tunis
1980	Club Africain	Espérance Tunis
1981	CS Sfaxien	Etoile du Sahel
1982	Espérance Tunis	CA Bizertin
1983	CS Sfaxien	Etoile du Sahel
1984	CA Bizertin	AS Marsa
1985	Espérance Tunis	CS Hammam-Lif
1986	Etoile du Sahel	Espérance Tunis
1987	Etoile du Sahel	CA Bizertin
1988	Espérance Tunis	CO Transports
1989	Espérance Tunis	Espérance Tunis
1990	Club Africain	AS Marsa
1991	Espérance Tunis	Espérance Tunis
1992	Club Africain	Club Africain
1993	Espérance Tunis	Olympique Béja
1994	Espérance Tunis	AS Marsa
1995	CS Sfaxien	CS Sfaxien
1996	Club Africain	Etoile du Sahel
1997	Etoile du Sahel	Espérance Tunis
1998	Espérance Tunis	Club Africain
1999	Espérance Tunis	Espérance Tunis
2000	Espérance Tunis	Club Africain
2001	Espérance Tunis	CS Hammam-Lif
2002	Espérance Tunis	Stade Tunisien

Year	Champions	Cup Winners
2003	Espérance Tunis	Stade Tunisien
2004	Espérance Tunis	CS Sfaxien
2005	CS Sfaxien	ES Zarzis
2006	Espérance Tunis	Espérance Tunis
2007	Etoile du Sahel	Espérance Tunis
2008	Club Africain	Espérance Tunis
2009	Espérance Tunis	CS Sfaxien
2010	Espérance Tunis	Olympique Béja
2011	Espérance Tunis	Espérance Tunis

TUR – TURKEY

Year	Champions	Cup Winners
1959	Fenerbahçe	
1960	Besiktas	
1961	Fenerbahçe	
1962	Galatasaray	
1963	Galatasaray	Galatasaray
1964	Fenerbahçe	Galatasaray
1965	Fenerbahçe	Galatasaray
1966	Besiktas	Galatasaray
1967	Besiktas	Altay Izmir
1968	Fenerbahçe	Fenerbahçe
1969	Galatasaray	Göztepe Izmir
1970	Fenerbahçe	Göztepe Izmir
1971	Galatasaray	Eskisehirspor
1972	Galatasaray	MKE Ankaragücü
1973	Galatasaray	Galatasaray
1974	Fenerbahçe	Fenerbahçe
1975	Fenerbahçe	Besiktas
1976	Trabzonspor	Galatasaray
1977	Trabzonspor	Trabzonspor
1978	Fenerbahçe	Trabzonspor
1979	Trabzonspor	Fenerbahçe
1980	Trabzonspor	Altay Izmir
1981	Trabzonspor	MKE Ankaragücü
1982	Besiktas	Galatasaray
1983	Fenerbahçe	Fenerbahçe
1984	Trabzonspor	Trabzonspor
1985	Fenerbahçe	Galatasaray
1986	Besiktas	Bursaspor
1987	Galatasaray	Gençlerbirligi
1988	Galatasaray	Sakaryaspor
1989	Fenerbahçe	Besiktas
1990	Besiktas	Besiktas
1991	Besiktas	Galatasaray
1992	Besiktas	Trabzonspor
1993	Galatasaray	Galatasaray
1994	Galatasaray	Besiktas
1995	Besiktas	Trabzonspor
1996	Fenerbahçe	Galatasaray
1997	Galatasaray	Kocaelispor
1998	Galatasaray	Besiktas
1999	Galatasaray	Galatasaray
2000	Galatasaray	Galatasaray
2001	Fenerbahçe	Gençlerbirligi
2002	Galatasaray	Kocaelispor
2003	Besiktas	Trabzonspor
2004	Fenerbahçe	Trabzonspor
2005	Fenerbahçe	Galatasaray
2006	Galatasaray	Besiktas
2007	Fenerbahçe	Besiktas
2008	Galatasaray	Kayserispor
2009	Besiktas	Besiktas
	Bursaspor	Trabzonspor
	.enerbahçe	Besiktas

UAE – UNITED ARAB EMIRATES

Year	Champions	Cup Winners
1974	Al Oroba	
1975	Al Ahli	Al Ahli
1976	Al Ahli	
1977	Al Ain	Al Ahli
1978	Al Nasr	
1979	Al Nasr	Sharjah
1980	Al Ahli	Sharjah
1981	Al Ain	Al Shabab
1982	Al Wasl	Sharjah
1983	Al Wasl	Sharjah
1984	Al Ain	Ajman
1985	Al Wasl	Al Nasr
1986	Al Nasr	Al Nasr
1987	Sharjah	Al Wasl
1988	Al Wasl	Al Ahli
1989	Sharjah	Al Nasr
1990	Al Shabab	Al Shabab
1991		Sharjah
1992	Al Wasl	Bani Yas
1993	Al Ain	Al Sha'ab
1994	Sharjah	Al Shabab
1995	Al Shabab	Sharjah
1996	Sharjah	Al Ahli
1997	Al Wasl	Al Shabab
1998	Al Ain	Sharjah
1999	Al Wahda	Al Ain
2000	Al Ain	Al Wahda
2001	Al Wahda	Al Ain
2002	Al Ain	Al Ahli
2003	Al Ain	Sharjah
2004	Al Ain	Al Ahli
2005	Al Wahda	Al Ain
2006	Al Ahli	Al Ain
2007	Al Wasl	Al Wasl
2008	Al Shabab	Al Ahli
2009	Al Ahli	Al Ain
2010	Al Wahda	Emirates Club
2011	Al Jazeera	Al Jazeera

UGA – UGANDA

Year	Champions	Cup Winners
1968	Prisons	
1969	Prisons	
1970	Coffee Utd Kakira	
1971	Simba	Coffee SC
1972		
1973		
1974	Express	
1975	Express	
1976	Kampala CC	Gangama United
1977	Kampala CC	Simba
1978	Simba	Nsambaya Kampala
1979	UCB Kampala	Kampala CC
1980	Nile Breweries	Kampala CC
1981	Kampala CC	Coffee SC
1982	SC Villa	Kampala CC
1983	Kampala CC	SC Villa
1984	SC Villa	Kampala CC
1985	Kampala CC	Express
1986	SC Villa	SC Villa
1987	SC Villa	Kampala CC
1988	SC Villa	SC Villa
1989	SC Villa	SC Villa
1990	SC Villa	Kampala CC
1991	Kampala CC	Express
1992	SC Villa	Express
1993	Express	Kampala CC
1994	SC Villa	Express
1995	Express	Express
1996	Express	Umeme
1997	Kampala CC	Express
1998	SC Villa	SC Villa
1999	SC Villa	Dairy Heroes
2000	SC Villa	SC Villa
2001	SC Villa	Express
2002	SC Villa	SC Villa
2003	SC Villa	Express
2004	SC Villa	Kampala CC
2005	Police Jinja	URA Kampala
2006	URA Kampala	Express
2007	URA Kampala	Express
2008	Kampala CC	Victor FC
2009	URA Kampala	SC Villa
2010	Bunamwaya Wakiso	Victor FC
2011	URA Kampala	Simba

UKR – UKRAINE

Year	Champions	Cup Winners
1992	Tavriya Simferopol	Ch'morets Odesa
1993	Dynamo Kyiv	Dynamo Kyiv
1994	Dynamo Kyiv	Ch'morets Odesa
1995	Dynamo Kyiv	Shakhtar Donetsk
1996	Dynamo Kyiv	Dynamo Kyiv
1997	Dynamo Kyiv	Shakhtar Donetsk
1998	Dynamo Kyiv	Dynamo Kyiv
1999	Dynamo Kyiv	Dynamo Kyiv
2000	Dynamo Kyiv	Dynamo Kyiv
2001	Dynamo Kyiv	Shakhtar Donetsk
2002	Shakhtar Donetsk	Shakhtar Donetsk
2003	Dynamo Kyiv	Dynamo Kyiv
2004	Dynamo Kyiv	Shakhtar Donetsk
2005	Shakhtar Donetsk	Dynamo Kyiv
2006	Shakhtar Donetsk	Dynamo Kyiv
2007	Dynamo Kyiv	Dynamo Kyiv
2008	Shakhtar Donetsk	Shakhtar Donetsk
2009	Dynamo Kyiv	Vorskla Poltava
2010	Shakhtar Donetsk	Tavriya Simferopol
2011	Shakhtar Donetsk	Shakhtar Donetsk

URU – URUGUAY

Year	Champions
1900	Peñarol
1901	Peñarol
1902	Nacional
1903	Nacional
1905	Peñarol
1906	Wanderers
1907	Peñarol
1908	River Plate
1909	Wanderers
1910	River Plate
1911	Peñarol
1912	Nacional
1913	River Plate
1914	River Plate

Year	Team
1915	Nacional
1916	Nacional
1917	Nacional
1918	Peñarol
1919	Nacional
1920	Nacional
1921	Peñarol
1922	Nacional
1923	Nacional
1923	Wanderers
1924	Nacional
1924	Peñarol
1926	Peñarol
1927	Rampla Juniors
1928	Peñarol
1929	Peñarol
1931	Wanderers
1932	Peñarol
1933	Nacional
1934	Nacional
1935	Peñarol
1936	Peñarol
1937	Peñarol
1938	Peñarol
1939	Nacional
1940	Nacional
1941	Nacional
1942	Nacional
1943	Nacional
1944	Peñarol
1945	Peñarol
1946	Nacional
1947	Nacional
1949	Peñarol
1950	Nacional
1951	Peñarol
1952	Nacional
1953	Peñarol
1954	Peñarol
1955	Nacional
1956	Nacional
1957	Nacional
1958	Peñarol
1959	Peñarol
1960	Peñarol
1961	Peñarol
1962	Peñarol
1963	Nacional
1964	Peñarol
1965	Peñarol
1966	Nacional
1967	Peñarol
1968	Peñarol
1969	Nacional
1970	Nacional
1971	Nacional
1972	Nacional
1973	Poñarol
1974	Peñarol
1975	Peñarol
1976	Defensor Sporting
1977	Nacional
1978	Peñarol
1979	Peñarol
1980	Nacional
1981	Peñarol
1982	Peñarol
1983	Nacional
1984	Central Español
1985	Peñarol
1986	Nacional
1987	Defensor Sporting
1988	Danubio
1989	Progreso
1990	Bella Vista
1991	Defensor Sporting
1992	Nacional
1993	Peñarol
1994	Peñarol
1995	Peñarol
1996	Peñarol
1997	Peñarol
1998	Nacional
1999	Peñarol
2000	Nacional
2001	Nacional
2002	Nacional
2003	Peñarol
2004	Danubio
2005	Nacional
2006	Nacional
2007	Danubio
2008	Defensor Sporting
2009	Nacional
2010	Peñarol
2011	Nacional

USA – UNITED STATES OF AMERICA

Year		Cup Winners	
1914		Brooklyn Field Club	
1915		Bethlehem Steel	
1916		Bethlehem Steel	
1917		Fall River Rovers	
1918		Bethlehem Steel	
1919		Bethlehem Steel	
1920		Ben Millers	
1921	**ASL**	Robins Dry Dock	
1922	Philadelphia FC	Scullin Steel	
1923	J & P Coats	Paterson & Scullin Steel	
1924	Fall River Marksmen	Fall River Marksmen	
1925	Fall River Marksmen	Shawsheen	
1926	Fall River Marksmen	Bethlehem Steel	
1927	Bethlehem Steel	Fall River Marksmen	
1928	Boston Wonder	New York Nationals	
1929	Fall River Marksmen	New York Hakoah	
1929	Fall River Marksmen		
1930	Fall River Marksmen	Fall River Marksmen	
1930	Fall River Marksmen		
1931	New York Giants	Fall River FC	
1932	New Bedford	New Bedford	
1933	Fall River	Stix, Baer & Fuller	
1934	Kearney Irish	Stix, Baer & Fuller	
1935	Philadelphia G-A	Central Breweries	
1936	New York Americans	Philadelphia G-A	
1937	Kearney Scots	New York Americans	
1938	Kearney Scots	Sparta	
1939	Kearney Scots	St. Mary's Celtic	
1940	Kearney Scots	Sparta & Baltimore	
1941	Kearney Scots	Pawtucket	
1942	Philadelphia Am's	Pittsburgh Gallatin	
1943	Brooklyn Hispano	Brooklyn Hispano	
1944	Philadelphia Am's	Brooklyn Hispano	
1945	Brookhattan	Brookhattan	
1946	Baltimore Am's	Chicago Vikings	
1947	Philadelphia Am's	Ponta Delgada	
1948	Philadelphia Am's	Simpkins-Ford	
1949	Philadelphia Nats	Pittsburgh Morgan	
1950	Philadelphia Nats	Simpkins-Ford	
1951	Philadelphia Nats	German-Hungarian	
1952	Philadelphia Am's	Harmarville	
1953	Philadelphia Nats	Chicago Falcons	
1954	New York Americans	New York Americans	
1955	Uhrik Truckers	Eintracht SC	
1956	Uhrik Truckers	Harmarville	
1957	New York Hakoah	Kutis SC	
1958	New York Hakoah	Los Angeles Kickers	
1959	New York Hakoah	Canvasbacks	
1960	Colombo	Ukrainian Nationals	
1961	Ukrainian Nationals	Ukrainian Nationals	
1962	Ukrainian Nationals	New York Hungaria	
1963	Ukrainian Nationals	Ukrainian Nationals	
1964	Ukrainian Nationals	Los Angeles Kickers	
1965	Hartford	New York Ukranians	
1966	Roma SC	Ukrainian Nationals	
	NASL		
1967	Los Angeles Wolves	Greek-Americans	
1967	Oakland Clippers		
1968	Atlanta Chiefs	Greek-Americans	
1969	Kansas City Spurs	Greek-Americans	
1970	Rochester Lancers	Elizabeth	
1971	Dallas Tornado	New York Hota	
1972	New York Cosmos	Elizabeth	
1973	Philadelphia Atoms	Maccabee LA	
1974	Los Angeles Aztecs	Greek-Americans	
1975	Tampa Bay Rowdies	Maccabee LA	
1976	Toronto Metros	San Francisco AC	
1977	New York Cosmos	Maccabee LA	
1978	New York Cosmos	Maccabee LA	
1979	Vancouver Wh'caps	Brooklyn Dodgers	
1980	New York Cosmos	New York Freedoms	
1981	Chicago Sting	Maccabee LA	
1982	New York Cosmos	New York Freedoms	
1983	Tulsa Roughnecks	New York Freedoms	
1984	Chicago Sting	AO Krete	
1985		Greek-Americans	
1986		Kutis SC	
1987		España Washington	
1988		Busch SC	
1989		Kickers St Pet'sburg	
1990		Chicago Eagles	
1991		Brooklyn Italians	
1992		San Jose Oaks	
1993		CD Mexico	
1994		Greek-Americans	
1995	**MLS**	Richmond Kickers	
1996	DC United	DC United	
1997	DC United	Dallas Burn	
1998	Chicago Fire	Chicago Fire	
1999	DC United	Rochester Rhinos	
2000	Kansas City Wizards	Chicago Fire	
2001	San Jose E'quakes	Los Angeles Galaxy	
2002	Los Angeles Galaxy	Columbus Crew	
2003	San Jose E'quakes	Chicago Fire	
2004	DC United	Kansas City Wizards	
2005	Los Angeles Galaxy	Los Angeles Galaxy	
2006	Houston Dynamo	Chicago Fire	

2007 Houston Dynamo	New England Revs
2008 Columbus Crew	DC United
2009 Real Salt Lake	Seattle Sounders
2010 Colorado Rapids	Seattle Sounders
2011 Los Angeles Galaxy	Seattle Sounders

UZB – UZBEKISTAN

Year Champions	Cup Winners
1992 Pakhtakor/Neftchi	Navbahor
1993 Neftchi	Pakhtakor
1994 Neftchi	Neftchi
1995 Neftchi	Navbahor
1996 Navbahor	Neftchi
1997 MHSK	Pakhtakor
1998 Pakhtakor	Navbahor
1999 Dustlik	
2000 Dustlik	Dustlik
2001 Neftchi	Pakhtakor
2002 Pakhtakor	Pakhtakor
2003 Pakhtakor	Pakhtakor
2004 Pakhtakor	Pakhtakor
2005 Pakhtakor	Pakhtakor
2006 Pakhtakor	Pakhtakor
2007 Pakhtakor	Pakhtakor
2008 Bunyodkor	Bunyodkor
2009 Bunyodkor	Pakhtakor
2010 Bunyodkor	Bunyodkor
2011 Bunyodkor	Pakhtakor

VAN – VANUATU

Year Champions
1984 Pango Green Bird
1985
1986
1987
1988
1989
1990
1991
1992
1993
1994 Tafea
1995 Tafea
1996 Tafea
1997 Tafea
1998 Tafea
1999 Tafea
2000 Tafea
2001 Tafea
2002 Tafea
2003 Tafea
2004 Tafea
2005 Tafea
2006 Tafea
2007 Tafea
2008
2009 Tafea
'10 Amicale
'micale

VEN – VENEZUELA

Year Champions	Cup Winners
1921 América	
1922 Centro Atlético	
1923 América	
1924 Centro Atlético	
1925 Loyola SC	
1926 Centro Atlético	
1927 Venzóleo	
1928 Deportivo Venezuela	
1929 Deportivo Venezuela	
1930 Centro Atlético	
1931 Deportivo Venezuela	
1932 Unión SC	
1933 Deportivo Venezuela	
1934 Unión SC	
1935 Unión SC	
1936 Dos Caminos SC	
1937 Dos Caminos SC	
1938 Dos Caminos SC	
1939 Unión SC	
1940 Unión SC	
1941 Litoral FC	
1942 Dos Caminos SC	
1943 Loyola SC	
1944 Loyola SC	
1945 Dos Caminos SC	
1946 Deportivo Espanol	
1947 Unión SC	
1948 Loyola SC	
1949 Dos Caminos SC	
1950 Unión SC	
1951 Universidad Central	
1952 Le Salle	
1953 Universidad Central	
1954 Deportivo Vasco	
1955 Le Salle	
1956 Banco Obrero	
1957 Universidad Central	
1958 Deportivo Portugués	
1959 Deportivo Español	Deportivo Portugués
1960 Deportivo Portugués	Banco Agricola
1961 Deportivo Italia	Deportivo Italia
1962 Deportivo Portugués	Deportivo Italia
1963 Deportivo Italia	Union Dep. Canarias
1964 Deportivo Galicia	Tiquire Flores
1965 Deportivo Lara	Valencia
1966 Deportivo Italia	Deportivo Galicia
1967 Deportivo Portugués	Deportivo Galicia
1968 Union Dep. Canarias	Union Dep. Canarias
1969 Deportivo Galicia	Deportivo Galicia
1970 Deportivo Galicia	Deportivo Italia
1971 Valencia	Estudiantes Merida
1972 Deportivo Italia	Deportivo Portugués
1973 Portuguesa	Portuguesa
1974 Deportivo Galicia	
1975 Portuguesa	Estudiantes Merida
1976 Portuguesa	Portuguesa
1977 Portuguesa	Portuguesa
1978 Portuguesa	Valencia
1979 Deportivo Tachira	Deportivo Galicia
1980 Estudiantes Merida	Atlético Zamora
1981 Deportivo Tachira	Deportivo Galicia
1982 At. San Cristobal	Atlético Zamora
1983 Univ. de Los Andes	
1984 Deportivo Tachira	Mineros de Guyana
1985 Estudiantes Merida	Estudiantes Merida
1986 Deportivo Tachira	Deportivo Tachira
1987 CS Maritimo	CS Maritimo
1988 CS Maritimo	Caracas FC
1989 Mineros de Guyana	CS Maritimo
1990 CS Maritimo	Dep Anzoátegui
1991 Univ. de Los Andes	Internacional PLC
1992 Caracas FC	Trujillanos
1993 CS Maritimo	
1994 Caracas FC	Caracas FC
1995 Caracas FC	Caracas FC
1996 Minervén	Univ. de Los Andes
1997 Caracas FC	Atlético Zulia
1998 Atlético Zulia	
1999 ItalChalcao	
2000 Deportivo Táchira	Caracas FC
2001 Caracas FC	
2002 Nacional Táchira	
2003 Caracas FC	
2004 Caracas FC	
2005 Unión At. Maracaibo	
2006 Caracas FC	
2007 Caracas FC	Aragua
2008 Deportivo Táchira	Dep Anzoátegui
2009 Caracas FC	Caracas FC
2010 Caracas FC	Trujillanos
2011	

VGB – BRITISH VIRGIN ISLANDS

Year Tortola	Virgin Gorda
1970 The Bronze	
1971	
1972	
1973	
1974	
1975	
1976	
1977	
1978	
1979 SKB Budweiser	
1980 Queen City Strikers	
1981 SKB Budweiser	
1982 Internat'nal Motors	
1983 Internat'nal Motors	
1984 SKB Budweiser	
1985 SKB Budweiser	
1986 SKB Budweiser	
1987 SKB Budweiser	
1988	
1989 Popeye Bombers	
1990 Jolly Rogers Strikers	
1991 Hairoun	
1992 Hairoun	
1993 Interfada	
1994 Interfada	
1995 Interfada	
1996 Black Lions	Spice United
1997 Interfada	Beverly Hills
1998 BDO BinderStingers	United Kickers
1999 Veterans	
2000 HBA Panthers	Rangers
2001 HBA Panthers	Rangers
2001 Future Stars United	

Year	Champions	Cup Winners
2002	HBA Panthers	
2003	Old Madrid	Rangers
2004	Valencia I	Rangers
2005		Rangers
2005		Hairoun
2006		Rangers
2007		Rangers
2008		Hairoun Stars
2009	National	
2010	Islanders	
2011	Islanders	

VIE - VIETNAM

Year	Champions	Cup Winners
1980	Hanoi ACB	
1981		
1982	The Cong Hanoi	
1983	The Cong Hanoi	
1984	Cong An Hanoi	
1985	Cong Nghiep	
1986	Cang Saigon	
1987	The Cong Hanoi	
1988		
1989	Dong Thap	
1990	The Cong Hanoi	
1991	Hai Quan	
1992	QuangNamDaNang	Cang Saigon
1993		QuangNamDaNang
1994	Cang Saigon	Binh Duong
1995	Cong An Thanh Pho	Hai Phong
1996	Dong Thap	Hai Quan
1997	Cang Saigon	Hai Quan
1998	The Cong Saigon	Cong An Thanh Pho
1999		
2000	Song Lam Nghe An	Cang Saigon
2001	Song Lam Nghe An	Cong An Thanh Pho
2002	Cang Saigon	Song Lam Nghe An
2003	Hoang Anh Gia Lai	Binh Dinh
2004	Hoang Anh Gia Lai	Binh Dinh
2005	Dong Tam Long An	Dong Tam Long An
2006	Dong Tam Long An	Hoa Phat Hanoi
2007	Binh Duong	Nam Dinh
2008	Binh Duong	Hanoi ACB
2009	Da Nang	Da Nang
2010	Hanoi T&T	Song Lam Nghe An
2011	Song Lam Nghe An	NaviBank Saigon

VIN - ST VINCENT/GRENADINES

Year	Champions	Cup Winners
1999	Camdonia Chelsea	
2000		
2001		
2002		
2003		
2004	Hope International	
2005	Universal Mufflers	
2006	Hope International	
2007		
2008		
2009		
2010	Avenues United	
2011	Avenues United	

VIR - US VIRGIN ISLANDS

Year	National Champions
1998	MI Roc Masters
1999	
2000	UWS Upsetters
2001	
2002	Haitian Stars
2003	
2004	
2005	Positive Vibes
2006	New Vibes
2007	Helenites
2008	Positive Vibes
2009	New Vibes
2010	
2011	

VIR - US VIRGIN ISLANDS

Year	St Croix	St Thomas
1996		MI Roc Masters
1997		St John United
1998	Helenites	MI Roc Masters
1999	Unique FC	MI Roc Masters
2000	Helenites	UWS Upsetters
2001	Helenites	UWS Upsetters
2002	Helenites	Waitikubuli United
2003	Helenites	Waitikubuli United
2004	Helenites	
2005	Helenites	Positive Vibes
2006	Helenites	Positive Vibes
2007	Helenites	Positive Vibes
2008	Helenites	Positive Vibes
2009	Helenites	New Vibes
2010	Unique FC	Positive Vibes
2011	Helenites	

WAL - WALES

Year	Cup Winners
1878	Wrexham
1879	Newtown
1880	Druids
1881	Druids
1882	Druids
1883	Wrexham
1884	Oswestry
1885	Druids
1886	Druids
1887	Chirk
1888	Chirk
1889	Bangor City
1890	Chirk
1891	Shrewsbury Town
1892	Chirk
1893	Wrexham
1894	Chirk
1895	Newtown
1896	Bangor City
1897	Wrexham
1898	Druids
1899	Druids
1900	Aberystwyth Town
1901	Oswestry
1902	Wellington
1903	Wrexham
1904	Druids
1905	Wrexham
1906	Wellington
1907	Oswestry
1908	Chester
1909	Wrexham
1910	Wrexham
1911	Wrexham
1912	Cardiff City
1913	Swansea Town
1914	Wrexham
1915	Wrexham
1916	
1917	
1918	
1919	
1920	Cardiff City
1921	Wrexham
1922	Cardiff City
1923	Cardiff City
1924	Wrexham
1925	Wrexham
1926	Ebbw Vale
1927	Cardiff City
1928	Cardiff City
1929	Connah's Quay
1930	Cardiff City
1931	Wrexham
1932	Swansea Town
1933	Chester
1934	Bristol City
1935	Tranmere Rovers
1936	Crewe Alexandra
1937	Crewe Alexandra
1938	Shrewsbury Town
1939	South Liverpool
1940	Wellington Town
1941	
1942	
1943	
1944	
1945	
1946	
1947	Chester
1948	Lovell's Athletic
1949	Merthyr Tydfil
1950	Swansea Town
1951	Merthyr Tydfil
1952	Rhyl
1953	Rhyl
1954	Flint
1955	Barry Town
1956	Cardiff City
1957	Wrexham
1958	Wrexham
1959	Cardiff City
1960	Wrexham
1961	Swansea Town
1962	Bangor City
1963	Borough United
1964	Cardiff City
1965	Cardiff City
1966	Swansea Town
1967	Cardiff City
1968	Cardiff City

Year		
1969		Cardiff City
1970		Cardiff City
1971		Cardiff City
1972		Wrexham
1973		Cardiff City
1974		Cardiff City
1975		Wrexham
1976		Cardiff City
1977		Shrewsbury Town
1978		Wrexham
1979		Shrewsbury Town
1980		Newport County
1981		Swansea City
1982		Swansea City
1983		Swansea City
1984		Shrewsbury Town
1985		Shrewsbury Town
1986		Wrexham
1987		Merthyr Tydfil
1988		Cardiff City
1989		Swansea City
1990		Hereford United
1991		Swansea City
1992		Cardiff City
1993	Cwmbran Town	Cardiff City
1994	Bangor City	Barry Town
1995	Bangor City	Wrexham
1996	Barry Town	TNS Llansantffraid
1997	Barry Town	Barry Town
1998	Barry Town	Bangor City
1999	Barry Town	Inter Cardiff
2000	TNS Llansantffraid	Bangor City
2001	Barry Town	Barry Town
2002	Barry Town	Barry Town
2003	Barry Town	Barry Town
2004	Rhyl	Rhyl
2005	TNS Llansantffraid	TNS Llansantffraid
2006	TNS Llansantffraid	Rhyl
2007	TNS Llansantffraid	Carmarthen Town
2008	Llanelli	Bangor City
2009	Rhyl	Bangor City
2010	TNS Llansantffraid	Bangor City
2011	Bangor City	Llanelli

WAL – WALES

Year	League Cup	FAW Premier
1993	Afan Lido	
1994	Afan Lido	
1995	TNS Llansantffraid	
1996	Connah's Quay	
1997	Barry Town	Wrexham
1998	Barry Town	Wrexham
1999	Barry Town	Barry Town
2000	Barry Town	Wrexham
2001	Caersws	Wrexham
2002	Caersws	Cardiff City
2003	Rhyl	Wrexham
2004	Rhyl	Wrexham
2005	Carmarthen Town	Swansea City
2006	TNS Llansantffraid	Swansea City
2007	Caersws	TNS Llansantffraid
2008	Llanelli	Newport County
2009	TNS Llansantffraid	
	TNS Llansantffraid	
	Llansantffraid	

YEM – NORTH YEMEN

Year	Champions	Cup Winners
1978		Al Wahda Sana'a
1979	Al Wahda Sana'a	Al Zuhra Sana'a
1980	Al Zuhra Sana'a	Al Ahly Sana'a
1981	Al Ahly Sana'a	Al Sha'ab Sana'a
1982	Al Sha'ab Sana'a	Al Ahly Sana'a
1983	Al Ahly Sana'a	Al Ahly Sana'a
1984	Al Ahly Sana'a	Al Ahly Sana'a
1985		
1986	Al Shorta Sana'a	
1987		
1988	Al Ahly Sana'a	
1989	Al Yarmouk Sana'a	
1990	Al Yarmouk Sana'a	

YEM – YEMEN

Year	Champions	Cup Winners
1991	Al Tilal Aden	
1992	Al Ahly Sana'a	
1993		
1994	Al Ahly Sana'a	
1995	Al Wahda Sana'a	
1996		Al Ahli Hudayda
1997	Al Wahda Sana'a	
1998	Al Wahda Sana'a	Al Ittihad Ibb
1999	Al Ahly Sana'a	
2000	Al Ahly Sana'a	Al Sha'ab Had'maut
2001	Al Ahly Sana'a	Al Ahly Sana'a
2002	Al Wahda Sana'a	Al Sha'ab Ibb
2003	Al Sha'ab Ibb	Al Sha'ab Ibb
2004	Al Sha'ab Ibb	Al Ahly Sana'a
2005	Al Tilal Aden	Al Hilal Hudaida
2006	Al Saqr Taizz	Al Sha'ab Had'maut
2007	Al Ahly Sana'a	Al Tilal Aden
2008	Al Hilal Hudayda	Al Hilal Hudaida
2009	Al Hilal Hudayda	Al Ahly Sana'a
2010	Al Saqr Taizz	Al Tilal Aden
2011	Al Urooba Zabid	

ZAM – ZAMBIA

Year	Champions	Castle Cup
1961		City of Lusaka
1962	Roan United	Roan United
1963	Mufulira Wanderers	Mufulira Blackpool
1964	City of Lusaka	City of Lusaka
1965	Mufulira Wanderers	Mufulira Wanderers
1966	Mufulira Wanderers	Mufulira Wanderers
1967	Mufulira Wanderers	Kabwe Warriors
1968	Kabwe Warriors	Mufulira Wanderers
1969	Mufulira Wanderers	Kabwe Warriors
1970	Kabwe Warriors	Ndola United
1971	Kabwe Warriors	Mufulira Wanderers
1972	Kabwe Warriors	Kabwe Warriors
1973	Zambia Army	Mufulira Wanderers
1974	Zambia Army	Mufulira Wanderers
		Independence Cup
1975	Green Buffaloes	Mufulira Wanderers
1976	Mufulira Wanderers	Mufulira Blackpool
1977	Green Buffaloes	Roan United
1978	Mufulira Wanderers	Nchanga Rangers
1979	Green Buffaloes	Power Dynamos
1980	Nchanga Rangers	Power Dynamos
1981	Green Buffaloes	Vitafoam United
1982	Nkana	Power Dynamos
1983	Nkana	Konkola Blades
1984	Power Dynamos	Kabwe Warriors
1985	Nkana	Strike Rovers
1986	Nkana	Nkana
1987	Kabwe Warriors	Kabwe Warriors
1988	Nkana	Mufulira Wanderers
1989	Nkana	Nkana
1990	Nkana	Power Dynamos
1991	Power Dynamos	Nkana
1992	Nkana	Nkana
		Mosi Cup
1993	Nkana	Nkana
1994	Power Dynamos	Roan United
1995	Mufulira Wanderers	Mufulira Wanderers
1996	Mufulira Wanderers	Roan United
1997	Power Dynamos	Power Dynamos
1998	Nchanga Rangers	Konkola Blades
1999	Nkana	Zamsure
2000	Power Dynamos	Nkana
2001	Nkana	Power Dynamos
2002	Zanaco	Zanaco
2003	Zanaco	Power Dynamos
2004	Red Arrows	Lusaka Celtic
2005	Zanaco	Green Buffaloes
2006	Zanaco	Zesco United
2007	Zesco United	Red Arrows
		Barclays Cup
2007		Zesco United
2008	Zesco United	Zesco United
2009	Zanaco	Power Dynamos
2010	Zesco United	Zesco United
2011	Power Dynamos	Power Dynamos

ZAM – ZAMBIA

Year	Top 8
1962	City of Lusaka
1963	City of Lusaka
1964	Rhokana United
1965	Nchanga Rangers
1966	Rhokana United
1967	Mufulira Wanderers
1968	Mufulira Wanderers
1969	Mufulira Wanderers
1970	Kabwe Warriors
1971	Kitwe United
1972	Kabwe Warriors
1973	Nchanga Rangers
1974	Roan United
1975	Green Buffaloes
1976	Nchanga Rangers
1977	Green Buffaloes
1978	Mufulira Wanderers
1979	Green Buffaloes
1980	Ndola United
1981	Green Buffaloes
1982	Red Arrows
1983	Roan United
1984	Mufulira Wanderers
1985	Green Buffaloes
1986	Mufulira Wanderers
1987	Zanaco
1988	Zanaco
1989	Kabwe Warriors

1990	Power Dynamos	
1991	Kabwe Warriors	
1992	Nkana	
1993	Nkana	
1994	Mufulira Wanderers	
1995	Roan United	
1996	Mufulira Wanderers	
1997	Mufulira Wanderers	
1998	Nkana	
1999	Nkana	
2000	Nkana	**League Cup**
2001	Power Dynamos	Zanaco
2002	Kabwe Warriors	Chambishi
2003	Kabwe Warriors	Power Dynamos
2004	Kitwe United	Zanaco
2005	Kabwe Warriors	Forest Rangers
2006	Zanaco	Kabwe Warriors
2007	Kabwe Warriors	Zesco United
2008	Lusaka Dynamos	

ZIM – ZIMBABWE

Year	Champions	Castle Cup
1962	Bulawayo Rovers	Bulawayo Rovers
1963	Dynamos	Salisbury Callies
1964	Bulawayo Rovers	
1965	Dynamos	Salisbury City
1966	St Pauls	Mangula
1967	Tornados	Salisbury Callies
1968	Bulawayo Sables	Arcadia United
1969	Bulawayo Sables	Arcadia United
1970	Dynamos	Wankie
1971	Arcadia United	Chibuku
1972	Salisbury Sables	Mangula
1973	Metal Box	Wankie
1974	Salisbury Sables	Chibuku
1975	Chibuku	Salisbury Callies
1976	Dynamos	Dynamos
1977	Zimbabwe Saints	Zimbabwe Saints
1978	Dynamos	Zisco Steel
1979	Caps United	Zimbabwe Saints
1980	Dynamos	Caps United
1981	Dynamos	Caps United
1982	Dynamos	Caps United
1983	Dynamos	Caps United
1984	Black Rhinos	Black Rhinos
1985	Dynamos	Dynamos
1986	Dynamos	Dynamos
1987	Black Rhinos	Zimbabwe Saints
1988	Zimbabwe Saints	Dynamos
1989	Dynamos	Dynamos
1990	Highlanders	Highlanders
1991	Dynamos	Wankie
1992	Black Aces	CAPS United
1993	Highlanders	Tanganda
1994	Dynamos	Blackpool
1995	Dynamos	Chapungu United
1996	CAPS United	Dynamos
1997	Dynamos	CAPS United
1998		CAPS United
1999	Highlanders	Amazulu
2000	Highlanders	**ZIFA Unity Cup**
2001	Highlanders	Highlanders
2002	Highlanders	Masvingo United
2003	AmaZulu	Dynamos

2004	CAPS United	CAPS United
2005	CAPS United	Masvingo United
		CBZ FA Cup
2006	Highlanders	Mwana Africa
2007	Dynamos	Dynamos
2008	Monomotapa United	CAPS United
2009	Gunners	
2010	Motor Action	**Mbada Diamonds Cup**
2011	Dynamos	Dynamos

ZIM – ZIMBABWE

Year	Independence Cup	
1983	Dynamos	
1984		
1985		
1986	Highlanders	
1987	Black Rhinos	
1988	Highlanders	
1989	Zimbabwe Saints	
1990	Dynamos	
1991	Highlanders	
1992	CAPS United	
1993	CAPS United	**League Cup**
1994	Chapungu United	Highlanders
1995	Dynamos	Dynamos
1996	CAPS United	CAPS United
1997	CAPS United	CAPS United
1998	Dynamos	CAPS United
1999	Amazulu	Black Aces
2000		Dynamos
2001	Highlanders	Shabanie Mine
2002	Highlanders	CAPS United
2003	Black Rhinos	
2004	Dynamos	CAPS United
2005	Motor Action	
2006	Masvingo United	
2007	Masvingo United	**Super 8**
2008	Shooting Stars	CAPS United
2009	Njube Sundowns	Lengthens
2010	Dynamos	Dynamos
2011	Highlanders	Motor Action

MISCELLANEOUS

BALTIC LEAGUE 2008

First round groups | **Quarter–finals** | **Semi–finals** | **Final**

Group A		Pl	W	D	L	F	A	Pts	LVA	LTU	EST
FK Riga	LVA	4	3	0	1	8	4	9		4-1	2-1
Ekranas Panevezys	LTU	4	3	0	1	7	6	9	2-1		1-0
TVMK Tallinn	EST	4	0	0	4	2	7	0	0-1	1-3	

Group B		Pl	W	D	L	F	A	Pts	LVA	LTU	EST
Skonto Riga	LVA	4	4	0	0	16	4	12		3-0	4-2
Suduva Marijampole	LTU	4	1	1	2	4	10	4	1-6		2-0
Levadia Tallin	EST	4	0	1	3	4	10	1	1-3	1-1	

Group C		Pl	W	D	L	F	A	Pts	LVA	LTU	EST
Liepajas Metalurgs	LVA	4	2	1	1	7	2	7		1-1	4-0
FBK Kaunas	LTU	4	2	1	1	6	4	7	1-0		3-1
Trans Narva	EST	4	1	0	3	3	10	3	0-2	2-1	

Group D		Pl	W	D	L	F	A	Pts	LVA	LTU	EST
FK Ventspils	LVA	4	3	0	1	5	1	9		2-0	2-0
Zalgiris Vilnius	LTU	4	3	0	1	3	2	9	1-0		1-0
Flora Tallinn	EST	4	0	0	4	0	5	0	0-1	0-1	

Quarter–finals

FBK Kaunas 4 4
Ekranas P. * 2 1

Suduva M. 0 0
FK Ventspils * 3 1

FK Riga 3 2
L. Metalurgs * 2 1

Zalgiris V. * 2 1
Skonto Riga 4 2

Semi–finals

FBK Kaunas * 1 1
FK Ventspils 1 0

FK Riga 2 0
Skonto Riga * 3 5

Final

FBK Kaunas 2
Skonto Riga 1

FINAL
Skonto, Riga
25-10-2008, 7 000
Kaasik EST
Scorers - Ancic 24,
Miklinevicius 27 for
FBK; Dvalisvili 84p for
Skonto

* Home team in the first leg

BALTIC LEAGUE 2009-10

Eighth-finals | **Quarter-finals** | **Semi-finals** | **Final**

Eighth-finals			Quarter-finals		Semi-finals		Final	
FK Ventspils	LVA	0 2						
Banga Gargzdai *	LTU	0 1	FK Ventspils	2 1				
Dinaburg *	LVA	0	Vetra Vilnius *	1 0				
Vetra Vilnius	LTU	0			FK Ventspils *	2 0		
Ekranas Panevezys	LTU	3 0			Flora Tallinn	0 0		
FK Jurmala *	LVA	1 1	Ekranas Panevezys	0 1				
KFK Siauliai *	LTU	1 1	Flora Tallinn *	0 2				
Flora Tallinn	EST	1 3					FK Ventspils	3 5p
Liepajas Metalurgs	LVA	1 5					Suduva Marijampole	3 3p
Nomme Kalju *	EST	0 2	Liepajas Metalurgs *	1 1				
Kalev Sillamäe *	EST	1 0	Skonto Riga	0 0				
Skonto Riga	LVA	3 1			Liepajas Metalurgs	0 2		
Levadia Tallinn	EST	0 3			Suduva Marij'pole *	3 1		
Tauras Taurage *	LTU	1 0	Levadia Tallinn	0 0				
Trans Narva	EST	0 1	Suduva Marij'pole *	0 1				
Suduva Marij'pole *	LTU	2 1						

CUP FINAL
Suduva, Marijampole
4-07-2011, 3000, Kaldma EST
Scorers - Dedov 82, Zigajevs 99p,
Tukura 105 for Ventspils;
Beniusis 2 93+ 114, Urbsys 121+ for
Suduva

* Home team in the first leg

BALTIC LEAGUE 2010-11

Eighth-finals				Quarter-finals			Semi-finals			Final
Skonto Riga	LVA	3	0							
Tauras Taurage *	LTU	2	0	Skonto Riga *	1	3				
Olimps RFS Riga *	LVA	0	0	Ekranas Panevezys	1	1				
Ekranas Panevezys	LTU	1	3				Skonto Riga *	5	1	
FK Jurmala *	LVA	1	2				Liepajas Metalurgs	0	0	
Kalev Sillamaë	EST	2	0	FK Jurmala *	1	1				
Banga Gargzdai *	LTU	1	1	Liepajas Metalurgs	1	5				
Liepajas Metalurgs	LVA	0	4							Skonto Riga 1 5p
KFK Siauliai	LTU	1	5							FK Ventspils 1 4p
Trans Narva *	EST	5	0	KFK Siauliai *	0	1				
Blazma Rezekne *	LVA	0	3	Levadia Tallinn	0	0				CUP FINAL
Levadia Tallinn	EST	1	5				KFK Siauliai *	0	2	Olimpiska, Ventspils
Flora Tallinn *	EST	2	2				FK Ventspils	2	2	18-06-2011, 2000
Suduva Marijampole	LTU	1	3	Flora Tallinn *	0	0				Dunauskas LTU
Nomme Kalju *	EST	2	1	FK Ventspils	1	4				Scorers - Sabala [100] for Skonto;
FK Ventspils	LVA	1	4				* Home team in the first leg			Shibamura [109] for Ventspils

The first Baltic League, Played in 2007 was covered in *Oliver's Almanack of World Football 2009*. These are the three tournaments played since.

First Qualifying Round Group 11

	Pl	W	D	L	F	A	Pts	CRO	IRL	CYP
Russia	3	3	0	0	11	0	9	1-0	3-0	7-0
Croatia	3	2	0	1	9	1	6		1-0	8-0
Republic of Ireland	3	1	0	2	5	4	3			5-0
Cyprus	3	0	0	3	0	20	0		Played in CRO	

This is group 11 from the first qualifying round of the UEFA European Women's Under-19 Championship covered on page 995

THE (VERY) UNOFFICIAL WORLD CHAMPIONSHIP

This unofficial world championship is based on the system that boxing uses to decide its world champions - if you beat the world champions then the mantle passes to you. The series starts in 1908 when the England amateur team won the first official Olympic title - then the world championship of football. In many cases the sequence leads naturally to the FIFA World Cup final, but where it doesn't the title is vacated and the final is used to restart the sequence.

THE (VERY) UNOFFICIAL WORLD CHAMPIONSHIP

Champions	Opponents	Score	Venue	Date
England	Denmark	2-0	London	24-10-1908
Denmark	England	2-1	Copenhagen	5-05-1910
England	Denmark	3-0	London	21-10-1911
Netherlands	England	2-1	The Hague	24-03-1913
England	Netherlands	2-1	Hull	15-11-1913
Denmark	England	3-0	Copenhagen	5-06-1914
Sweden	Denmark	4-0	Stockholm	8-10-1916
Denmark	Sweden	2-1	Stockholm	14-10-1917
Norway	Denmark	3-1	Oslo	16-06-1918
Denmark	Norway	4-0	Copenhagen	6-10-1918
Norway	Denmark	3-2	Oslo	21-09-1919
Sweden	Norway	3-0	Oslo	27-06-1920
Netherlands	Sweden	5-4	Antwerp	29-08-1920
Belgium	Netherlands	3-0	Antwerp	31-08-1920
Italy	Belgium	3-2	Antwerp	5-05-1921
Czechoslovakia	Italy	5-1	Prague	27-05-1923
Switzerland	Czechoslovakia	1-0	Paris	30-05-1924
Uruguay	Switzerland	3-0	Paris	9-06-1924
Argentina	Uruguay	3-2	Montevideo	31-08-1924
Uruguay	Argentina	1-0	Montevideo	16-11-1924
Argentina	Uruguay	1-0	Buenos Aires	5-01-1925
Uruguay	Argentina	2-0	Santiago	24-10-1926
Argentina	Uruguay	1-0	Montevideo	14-07-1927
Uruguay	Argentina	1-0	Buenos Aires	30-08-1927
Argentina	Uruguay	3-2	Lima	20-11-1927
Uruguay	Argentina	2-1	Amsterdam	13-06-1928
Paraguay	Uruguay	3-1	Asuncion	15-08-1928
Argentina	Paraguay	4-1	Buenos Aires	10-11-1929
Uruguay	Argentina	4-2	Montevideo	30-07-1930
Brazil	Uruguay	2-0	Rio de Janeiro	6-09-1931
Spain	Brazil	3-1	Genoa	27-05-1934
Italy	Spain	1-0	Florence	1-06-1934
England	Italy	3-2	London	14-11-1934
Scotland	England	2-0	Glasgow	6-04-1935
Wales	Scotland	2-1	Dundee	2-12-1936
England	Wales	2-1	Middlesbrough	17-11-1937
Scotland	England	1-0	London	9-04-1938
Vacated				
Italy	Hungary	4-2	Paris	19-06-1938
Switzerland	Italy	3-1	Zurich	12-11-1939
Hungary	Switzerland	3-0	Budapest	31-03-1940
Germany	Hungary	7-0	Cologne	6-04-1941
Switzerland	Germany	2-1	Berne	20-04-1941
Hungary	Switzerland	2-1	Zurich	16-11-1941
Germany	Hungary	5-3	Budapest	3-05-1942
Sweden	Germany	3-2	Berlin	20-09-1942
Switzerland	Sweden	3-1	Zurich	15-11-1942
Hungary	Switzerland	3-1	Geneva	16-05-1943
Sweden	Hungary	7-2	Budapest	7-11-1943
*zerland	Sweden	3-0	Geneva	25-11-1945

THE (VERY) UNOFFICIAL WORLD CHAMPIONSHIP

Champions	Opponents	Score	Venue	Date
England	Switzerland	4-1	London	11-05-1946
France	England	2-1	Paris	19-05-1946
England	France	3-0	London	3-05-1947
Switzerland	England	1-0	Zurich	18-05-1947
France	Switzerland	2-1	Lausanne	8-06-1947
Italy	France	3-1	Paris	4-04-1948
England	Italy	4-0	Turin	16-05-1948
Scotland	England	3-1	London	9-04-1949
England	Scotland	1-0	Glasgow	15-04-1950
USA	England	1-0	Belo Horizonte	29-06-1950
Chile	USA	5-2	Recife	2-07-1950
Vacated				
Uruguay	Brazil	2-1	Rio de Janeiro	16-07-1950
Chile	Uruguay	2-0	Santiago	13-04-1952
Brazil	Chile	3-0	Santiago	20-04-1952
Peru	Brazil	1-0	Lima	19-03-1953
Uruguay	Peru	3-0	Lima	28-03-1953
Paraguay	Uruguay	4-1	Montevideo	10-04-1954
Vacated				
West Germany	Hungary	3-2	Berne	4-07-1954
Belgium	West Germany	2-0	Brussels	26-09-1954
Italy	Belgium	1-0	Bari	16-01-1955
Yugoslavia	Italy	4-0	Turin	29-05-1955
Austria	Yugoslavia	2-1	Vienna	30-10-1955
France	Austria	3-1	Paris	25-03-1956
Hungary	France	2-1	Paris	7-10-1956
Norway	Hungary	2-1	Oslo	12-06-1957
Denmark	Norway	2-0	Tammerfors	19-06-1957
Sweden	Denmark	2-1	Copenhagen	30-06-1957
West Germany	Sweden	1-0	Hamburg	20-11-1957
Czechoslovakia	West Germany	3-2	Prague	2-04-1958
Nth. Ireland	Czechoslovakia	1-0	Halmstad	8-06-1958
Argentina	Nth. Ireland	3-1	Halmstad	11-06-1958
Czechoslovakia	Argentina	6-1	Helsingborg	15-06-1958
Nth. Ireland	Czechoslovakia	2-1	Malmö	17-06-1958
France	Nth. Ireland	4-0	Norrkoping	19-06-1958
Brazil	France	5-2	Stockholm	24-06-1958
Uruguay	Brazil	3-0	Guayaquil	12-12-1959
Argentina	Uruguay	4-0	Buenos Aires	17-08-1960
Spain	Argentina	2-0	Seville	11-06-1961
Czechoslovakia	Spain	1-0	Viña del Mar	31-05-1962
Mexico	Czechoslovakia	3-1	Viña del Mar	7-06-1962
Vacated				
Brazil	Czechoslovakia	3-1	Santiago	17-06-1962
Paraguay	Brazil	2-0	La Paz	17-03-1963
Bolivia	Paraguay	2-0	Cochabamba	24-03-1963
Paraguay	Bolivia	2-0	Asuncion	25-07-1965
Argentina	Paraguay	3-0	Buenos Aires	1-08-1965
Italy	Argentina	3-0	Turin	22-06-1966
Soviet Union	Italy	1-0	Sunderland	16-07-1966

THE (VERY) UNOFFICIAL WORLD CHAMPIONSHIP

Champions	Opponents	Score	Venue	Date
West Germany	Soviet Union	2-1	Liverpool	25-07-1966
England	West Germany	4-2	London	30-07-1966
Scotland	England	3-2	London	15-04-1967
Soviet Union	Scotland	2-0	Glasgow	10-05-1967
Austria	Soviet Union	1-0	Vienna	15-10-1967
Soviet Union	Austria	3-1	Leningrad	16-06-1968
Sweden	Soviet Union	1-0	Moscow	6-08-1969
France	Sweden	3-0	Paris	1-11-1969
Switzerland	France	2-1	Basle	3-05-1970
Vacated				
Brazil	Italy	4-1	Mexico City	21-06-1970
Italy	Brazil	2-0	Rome	9-06-1973
Poland	Italy	2-1	Stuttgart	23-06-1974
West Germany	Poland	1-0	Frankfurt	3-07-1974
England	West Germany	2-0	London	12-03-1975
Czechoslovakia	England	2-1	Bratislava	30-10-1975
West Germany	Czechoslovakia	2-0	Hanover	17-11-1976
France	West Germany	1-0	Paris	23-02-1977
Rep. Ireland	France	1-0	Dublin	30-03-1977
Bulgaria	Rep. Ireland	2-0	Sofia	1-06-1977
France	Bulgaria	3-1	Paris	16-11-1977
Italy	France	2-1	Mar del Plata	2-06-1978
Netherlands	Italy	2-1	Buenos Aires	21-06-1978
Argentina	Netherlands	3-1	Buenos Aires	25-06-1978
Bolivia	Argentina	2-1	La Paz	18-07-1979
Paraguay	Bolivia	2-0	Asuncion	1-08-1979
Chile	Paraguay	1-0	Santiago	5-12-1979
Brazil	Chile	2-1	Belo Horizonte	24-06-1980
Uruguay	Brazil	2-1	Montevideo	10-01-1981
Peru	Uruguay	2-1	Montevideo	23-08-1981
Chile	Peru	2-1	Santiago	23-03-1982
Peru	Chile	1-0	Lima	30-03-1982
Poland	Peru	5-1	La Coruna	22-06-1982
Italy	Poland	2-0	Barcelona	8-07-1982
Switzerland	Italy	1-0	Rome	27-10-1982
Soviet Union	Switzerland	1-0	Lausanne	13-04-1983
Portugal	Soviet Union	1-0	Lisbon	13-11-1983
Yugoslavia	Portugal	3-2	Lisbon	2-06-1984
Belgium	Yugoslavia	2-0	Lens	13-06-1984
France	Belgium	5-0	Nantes	16-06-1984
Bulgaria	France	2-0	Sofia	2-05-1985
Netherlands	Bulgaria	1-0	Heerenveen	4-09-1985
Belgium	Netherlands	1-0	Brussels	16-10-1985
Netherlands	Belgium	2-1	Rotterdam	20-11-1985
West Germany	Netherlands	3-1	Dortmund	14-05-1986
Denmark	West Germany	2-0	Queretaro	13-06-1986
Spain	Denmark	5-1	Queretaro	18-06-1986
Belgium	Spain	1-1 5-4p	Puebla	22-06-1986
Argentina	Belgium	2-0	Mexico City	25-06-1986
Italy	Argentina	3-1	Zurich	10-06-1987
Wales	Italy	1-0	Brescia	4-06-1988
Netherlands	Wales	1-0	Amsterdam	14-09-1988
Italy	Netherlands	1-0	Rome	16-11-1988
Romania	Italy	1-0	Sibiu	29-03-1989
Poland	Romania	2-1	Warsaw	12-04-1989
England	Poland	3-0	London	3-06-1989
Uruguay	England	2-1	London	22-05-1990
Belgium	Uruguay	3-1	Verona	17-06-1990
Spain	Belgium	2-1	Verona	21-06-1990
Yugoslavia	Spain	2-1	Verona	26-06-1990
Argentina	Yugoslavia	0-0 3-2p	Florence	30-06-1990
West Germany	Argentina	1-0	Rome	8-07-1990
Wales	Germany	1-0	Cardiff	5-06-1991
Germany	Wales	4-1	Nuremberg	16-10-1991
Italy	Germany	1-0	Turin	25-03-1992
Switzerland	Italy	1-0	Berne	1-05-1993
Portugal	Switzerland	1-0	Oporto	13-10-1993
Italy	Portugal	1-0	Milan	17-11-1993
France	Italy	1-0	Naples	6-02-1994
Vacated				
Brazil	Italy	0-0 3-2p	Los Angeles	17-07-1994
Norway	Brazil	4-2	Oslo	30-05-1997
Italy	Norway	1-0	Marseille	27-06-1998
France	Italy	0-0 4-3p	Paris	3-07-1998
Russia	France	3-2	Paris	5-06-1999
Israel	Russia	4-1	Haifa	23-02-2000
Czech Republic	Israel	4-1	Prague	26-04-2000
Germany	Czech Republic	3-2	Nuremberg	3-06-2000
England	Germany	1-0	Charleroi	17-06-2000
Romania	England	3-2	Charleroi	20-06-2000
Italy	Romania	2-0	Brussels	24-06-2000
France	Italy	2-1	Rotterdam	2-07-2000
Spain	France	2-1	Valencia	28-03-2001
Netherlands	Spain	1-0	Rotterdam	27-03-2002
Vacated				
Brazil	Germany	2-0	Yokohama	30-06-2002
Paraguay	Brazil	1-0	Fortaleza	21-08-2002
Costa Rica	Paraguay	2-1	Alajuela	29-03-2003
Chile	Costa Rica	1-0	Santiago	30-04-2003
Costa Rica	Chile	1-0	San José	8-06-2003
Canada	Costa Rica	1-0	Foxboro	12-07-2003
Cuba	Canada	2-0	Foxboro	14-07-2003
Costa Rica	Cuba	3-0	Foxboro	16-07-2003
Mexico	Costa Rica	1-0	Mexico City	24-07-2003
Peru	Mexico	3-1	New Jersey	20-08-2003
Chile	Peru	2-1	Santiago	9-09-2003
Uruguay	Chile	2-1	Montevideo	15-11-2003
Jamaica	Uruguay	2-0	Kingston	18-02-2004
Nigeria	Jamaica	2-0	London	31-05-2004
Angola	Nigeria	1-0	Luanda	20-06-2004
Zimbabwe	Angola	2-0	Harare	27-03-2005
Nigeria	Zimbabwe	5-1	Abuja	8-10-2005
Romania	Nigeria	3-0	Bucharest	16-11-2005
Uruguay	Romania	2-0	Los Angeles	23-05-2006
Vacated				
Italy	France	1-1 5-3p	Berlin	9-07-2006
Croatia	Italy	2-0	Livorno	16-08-2006
Macedonia	Croatia	2-0	Skopje	17-11-2007
Israel	Macedonia	1-0	Tel Aviv	21-11-2007
Finland	Israel	2-0	Tampere	20-08-2008
Russia	Finland	3-0	Moscow	15-10-2008
Argentina	Russia	3-2	Moscow	12-08-2009
Brazil	Argentina	3-1	Rosario	5-09-2009
Bolivia	Brazil	2-1	La Paz	11-10-2009
Peru	Bolivia	1-0	Lima	14-10-2009
Vacated				
Spain	Netherlands	1-0	Johannesburg	11-07-2010
Argentina	Spain	4-1	Buenos Aires	7-09-2010
Japan	Argentina	1-0	Saitama	8-10-2010
Korea DPR	Japan	1-0	Pyongyang	15-11-2011

CALENDAR OF EVENTS

Fixed dates for friendly internationals
29-02-2012, 15-08-2012, 14-11-2012, 6-02-2013, 14-08-2013, 5-03-2014, 13-08-2014, 19-11-2014

Fixed dates for official competitions
8/12-09-2012, 13/17-10-2012, 23/27-03-2013, 8/12-06-2013, 7/11-09-2013,
12/16-10-2013, 16/20-11-2013, 6/10-09-2014, 11/15-11-2014

Men's and Women's Olympic Football Tournaments London 2012
25th July to 11th August 2012

FIFA U-20 Women's World Cup Japan 2012
19th August to 8th September 2012

FIFA U-17 Women's World Cup Azerbaijan 2012
22nd September to 13th October 2012

FIFA Club World Cup Japan 2012
6th to 16th December 2012

FIFA Confederations Cup Brazil 2013
15th to 30th June 2013

FIFA U-20 World Cup Turkey 2013
21st June to 13th July 2013

FIFA U-17 World Cup UAE 2013
14th November to 6th December 2013

FIFA Club World Cup Morocco 2013
11th to 21st December 2013

2014 FIFA World Cup Brazil
12th June to 13th July 2014

FIFA Club World Cup Morocco 2014
10th to 20st December 2014

2018 FIFA World Cup Russia
2018

2022 FIFA World Cup Qatar
2022

AFC Asian Cup Australia 2015
4th to 26th January 2011

CAF Africa Cup of Nations South Africa 2013
19th January to 10th February 2013

CAF Africa Cup of Nations Morocco 2015
2015

CAF Africa Cup of Nations Libya 2017
2017

CONCACAF Gold Cup USA 2013
2013

Copa America Brazil 2015
2015

Copa America Chile 2019
2019

Euro 2012 Poland/Ukraine
8th June to 1st July 2012

Euro 2016 France
2016